UNIVERSITY CASEBOOK SERIES

CASES AND MATERIALS

CONSTITUTIONAL LAW

TENTH EDITION

by

WILLIAM COHEN
C. Wendell and Edith M. Carlsmith
Professor of Law, Stanford University

JONATHAN D. VARAT
Professor of Law
University of California, Los Angeles

WESTBURY, NEW YORK

THE FOUNDATION PRESS, INC.

1997

Library of Congress Cataloging-in-Publication Data

Cohen, William, 1933–
      Constitutional law : cases and materials / by William Cohen,
Jonathan D. Varat. — 10th ed.
            p.   cm. — (University casebook series)
      Includes index.
      ISBN 1–56662–529–7 (hardcover)
      1. Constitutional law—United States—Cases.   I. Varat, Jonathan
D., 1945–   .   II. Title.   III. Series.
KF4549.B3   1997
342.73—dc21   97–5442

*TEXT IS PRINTED ON 10% POST
CONSUMER RECYCLED PAPER*

For Nancy, Barbara, Becky, and Margaret
WC

For Barbara, Adam, Diana, and Jennifer
JDV

*

PREFACE

Developments of great moment may change a subject so dramatically that new editions should be reworked comprehensively. In our judgment, that kind of change has not occurred since the publication of the last edition four years ago. Justices Ginsburg and Breyer have joined the Court, replacing Justices White and Blackmun, with the result that four new Justices have been appointed since 1990 and a majority of five in the last decade. The Court has taken some steps in new and potentially significant directions, which the new edition reflects. Yet none of these developments seemed to us to call for major reorganization of the book. Indeed, the twenty new principal cases either replace earlier decisions on the same topic or add dimensions to subjects already reflected in the book's internal outlining. Because we also continue to find that the vast bulk of the organizational changes made in earlier editions have been effective pedagogically, the overall shape and blueprint of the text essentially has not changed.

Making room for the new material required us to eliminate some principal cases from the last edition and treat others in abbreviated fashion. In each instance, we attempted, without editorial comment, to highlight new refinements and to improve the clarity of presentation of materials published earlier. New developments include: increased receptiveness to equality and federalism-based limits on congressional authority; recent attention to the political question doctrine, the dormant commerce clause, and equal protection analysis of economic regulation; possibly changing standards scrutinizing sex-based classifications and addressing issues of free expression raised by new technologies for communication; new limits on unequal treatment of non-heterosexuals; new causes of action for challenging racial gerrymanders; and a variety of first amendment controversies, including new disputes about how to evaluate the validity of speech-restricting injunctions and ongoing divisions about the scope of the prohibition on establishment of religion. These and other developments contained in this edition render it current to July 1996, with the usual accompanying Supplement to be published in the summer of 1997.

Our primary goal remains, as we have emphasized in the last three editions, to provide a book that is "at the same time intellectually challenging and flexible enough to be used by law teachers with widely varying approaches to the material." As much as possible we provide "the raw materials—cases, constitutional provisions, and statutes—allowing teachers maximum freedom to pursue their own teaching strategies and requiring students to create their own generalizations from the materials." The book's organization, too, is intended "to maximize the ability of users to structure their own courses in their own ways without inhibiting their efforts at reorganization by the nature of our editing."

We also continue to seek to use historical or descriptive notes "to fill in background, developments, and illuminating detail in succinct and straightforward fashion in order to highlight and supplement the primary cases and permit teachers to assign the essential materials in effective and manageable doses." And, as we previously have indicated, "by and large we have resisted the temptation to be encyclopedic through the use of multiple short descriptions of cases, because overuse of that approach seems to us ineffective."

WILLIAM COHEN
JONATHAN D. VARAT

Stanford, California
Los Angeles, California
November 1996

SUMMARY OF CONTENTS

*

TABLE OF CONTENTS

*

TABLE OF CASES

CONSTITUTIONAL LAW

*

CONSTITUTIONAL LAW
CASES AND MATERIALS

Part I

THE CONSTITUTION AND THE COURTS: THE JUDICIAL FUNCTION IN CONSTITUTIONAL CASES

PREFATORY NOTE

A written constitution interpreted and applied by the courts as the supreme law of the nation is the hallmark of our constitutional system. A vital part of this system is the institution of judicial review, the power and duty of the courts to declare legislative or executive acts invalid insofar as they may conflict with the Constitution. How this judicial power, not explicitly provided for in the Constitution, came to be established, and how it is exercised by courts are the subjects of Part I of this book. The Constitution, along with a brief history of its adoption, is set forth in Chapter 1. Chapter 2 deals with the institution of judicial review, its historic origins, and begins exploration of the institution's purpose. Chapter 2 also discusses Congressional control of judicial review through control of federal court jurisdiction. Chapter 3 presents an introduction to the rules that govern the handling of constitutional litigation.

CHAPTER 1

THE CONSTITUTION

SECTION 1. THE CONSTITUTION OF THE UNITED STATES OF AMERICA

We the People of the United States, in Order to form a more perfect Union, establish Justice, insure domestic Tranquility, provide for the common defence, promote the general Welfare, and secure the Blessings of Liberty to ourselves and our Posterity, do ordain and establish this Constitution for the United States of America.

ARTICLE I

Section 1. All legislative Powers herein granted shall be vested in a Congress of the United States, which shall consist of a Senate and House of Representatives.

Section 2. [1] The House of Representatives shall be composed of Members chosen every second Year by the People of the several States, and the Electors in each State shall have the Qualifications requisite for Electors of the most numerous Branch of the State Legislature.

[2] No Person shall be a Representative who shall not have attained to the Age of twenty five Years, and been seven Years a Citizen of the United States, and who shall not, when elected, be an Inhabitant of that State in which he shall be chosen.

[3] Representatives and direct Taxes shall be apportioned among the several States which may be included within this Union, according to their respective Numbers, which shall be determined by adding to the whole Number of free Persons, including those bound to Service for a Term of Years, and excluding Indians not taxed, three fifths of all other Persons. The actual Enumeration shall be made within three Years after the first Meeting of the Congress of the United States, and within every subsequent Term of ten Years, in such Manner as they shall by Law direct. The Number of Representatives shall not exceed one for every thirty Thousand, but each State shall have at Least one Representative; and until such enumeration shall be made, the State of New Hampshire shall be entitled to chuse three, Massachusetts eight, Rhode Island and Providence Plantations one, Connecticut five, New York six, New Jersey four, Pennsylvania eight, Delaware one, Maryland six, Virginia ten, North Carolina five, South Carolina five, and Georgia three.

[4] When vacancies happen in the Representation from any State, the Executive Authority thereof shall issue Writs of Election to fill such Vacancies.

[5] The House of Representatives shall chuse their Speaker and other Officers; and shall have the sole Power of Impeachment.

Section 3. [1] The Senate of the United States shall be composed of two Senators from each State, chosen by the Legislature thereof, for six Years; and each Senator shall have one Vote.

[2] Immediately after they shall be assembled in Consequence of the first Election, they shall be divided as equally as may be into three Classes. The Seats of the Senators of the first Class shall be vacated at the Expiration of the Second Year, of the second Class at the Expiration of the fourth Year, and of the third Class at the Expiration of the sixth Year, so that one third may be chosen every second Year; and if Vacancies happen by Resignation, or otherwise, during the Recess of the Legislature of any State, the Executive thereof may make temporary Appointments until the next Meeting of the Legislature, which shall then fill such Vacancies.

[3] No Person shall be a Senator who shall not have attained to the Age of thirty Years, and been nine Years a Citizen of the United States, and who shall not, when elected, be an Inhabitant of that State for which he shall be chosen.

[4] The Vice President of the United States shall be President of the Senate, but shall have no Vote, unless they be equally divided.

[5] The Senate shall chuse their other Officers, and also a President pro tempore, in the Absence of the Vice President, or when he shall exercise the Office of President of the United States.

[6] The Senate shall have the sole Power to try all Impeachments. When sitting for that Purpose, they shall be on Oath or Affirmation. When the President of the United States is tried, the Chief Justice shall preside: And no Person shall be convicted without the Concurrence of two thirds of the Members present.

[7] Judgment in Cases of Impeachment shall not extend further than to removal from Office, and disqualification to hold and enjoy any Office of honor, Trust, or Profit under the United States: but the Party convicted shall nevertheless be liable and subject to Indictment, Trial, Judgment, and Punishment, according to Law.

Section 4. [1] The Times, Places and Manner of holding Elections for Senators and Representatives, shall be prescribed in each State by the Legislature thereof; but the Congress may at any time by Law make or alter such Regulations, except as to the Places of chusing Senators.

[2] The Congress shall assemble at least once in every Year, and such Meeting shall be on the first Monday in December, unless they shall by Law appoint a different Day.

Section 5. [1] Each House shall be the Judge of the Elections, Returns, and Qualifications of its own Members, and a Majority of each shall constitute a Quorum to do Business; but a smaller Number may adjourn from day to day, and may be authorized to compel the Attendance of absent Members, in such Manner, and under such Penalties as each House may provide.

[2] Each House may determine the Rules of its Proceedings, punish its Members for disorderly Behavior, and, with the Concurrence of two thirds, expel a Member.

[3] Each House shall keep a Journal of its Proceedings, and from time to time publish the same, excepting such Parts as may in their Judgment require Secrecy; and the Yeas and Nays of the Members of either House on any question shall, at the Desire of one fifth of those Present, be entered on the Journal.

[4] Neither House, during the Session of Congress, shall, without the Consent of the other, adjourn for more than three days, nor to any other Place than that in which the two Houses shall be sitting.

Section 6.   [1] The Senators and Representatives shall receive a Compensation for their Services, to be ascertained by Law, and paid out of the Treasury of the United States. They shall in all Cases, except Treason, Felony and Breach of the Peace, be privileged from Arrest during their Attendance at the Session of their respective Houses, and in going to and returning from the same; and for any Speech or Debate in either House, they shall not be questioned in any other Place.

[2]   No Senator or Representative shall, during the Time for which he was elected, be appointed to any civil Office under the Authority of the United States, which shall have been created, or the Emoluments whereof shall have been encreased during such time; and no Person holding any Office under the United States, shall be a Member of either House during his Continuance in Office.

Section 7.   [1] All Bills for raising Revenue shall originate in the House of Representatives; but the Senate may propose or concur with Amendments as on other Bills.

[2]   Every Bill which shall have passed the House of Representatives and the Senate, shall, before it become a Law, be presented to the President of the United States; If he approve he shall sign it, but if not he shall return it, with his Objections to the House in which it shall have originated, who shall enter the Objections at large on their Journal, and proceed to reconsider it. If after such Reconsideration two thirds of that House shall agree to pass the Bill, it shall be sent together with the Objections, to the other House, by which it shall likewise be reconsidered, and if approved by two thirds of that House, it shall become a Law. But in all such Cases the Votes of both Houses shall be determined by yeas and Nays, and the Names of the Persons voting for and against the Bill shall be entered on the Journal of each House respectively. If any Bill shall not be returned by the President within ten Days (Sundays excepted) after it shall have been presented to him, the Same shall be a Law, in like Manner as if he had signed it, unless the Congress by their Adjournment prevent its Return in which Case it shall not be a Law.

[3]   Every Order, Resolution, or Vote, to Which the Concurrence of the Senate and House of Representatives may be necessary (except on a question of Adjournment) shall be presented to the President of the United States; and before the Same shall take Effect, shall be approved by him, or being disapproved by him, shall be repassed by two thirds of the Senate and House of Representatives, according to the Rules and Limitations prescribed in the Case of a Bill.

Section 8.   [1] The Congress shall have Power To lay and collect Taxes, Duties, Imposts and Excises, to pay the Debts and provide for the common Defence and general Welfare of the United States; but all Duties, Imposts and Excises shall be uniform throughout the United States;

[2]   To borrow money on the credit of the United States;

[3]   To regulate Commerce with foreign Nations, and among the several States, and with the Indian Tribes;

[4]   To establish an uniform Rule of Naturalization, and uniform Laws on the subject of Bankruptcies throughout the United States;

[5]   To coin Money, regulate the Value thereof, and of foreign Coin, and fix the Standard of Weights and Measures;

[6]   To provide for the Punishment of counterfeiting the Securities and current Coin of the United States;

[7]   To Establish Post Offices and Post Roads;

[8]   To promote the Progress of Science and useful Arts, by securing for limited Times to Authors and Inventors the exclusive Right to their respective Writings and Discoveries;

[9]   To constitute Tribunals inferior to the supreme Court;

[10]   To define and punish Piracies and Felonies committed on the high Seas, and Offenses against the Law of Nations;

[11]   To declare War, grant Letters of Marque and Reprisal, and make Rules concerning Captures on Land and Water;

[12]   To raise and support Armies, but no Appropriation of Money to that Use shall be for a longer Term than two Years;

[13]   To provide and maintain a Navy;

[14]   To make Rules for the Government and Regulation of the land and naval Forces;

[15]   To provide for calling forth the Militia to execute the Laws of the Union, suppress Insurrections and repel Invasions;

[16]   To provide for organizing, arming, and disciplining, the Militia, and for governing such Part of them as may be employed in the Service of the United States, reserving to the States respectively, the Appointment of the Officers, and the Authority of training the Militia according to the discipline prescribed by Congress;

[17]   To exercise exclusive Legislation in all Cases whatsoever, over such District (not exceeding ten Miles square) as may, by Cession of particular States, and the Acceptance of Congress, become the Seat of the Government of the United States, and to exercise like Authority over all Places purchased by the Consent of the Legislature of the State in which the Same shall be, for the Erection of Forts, Magazines, Arsenals, dock-Yards, and other needful Buildings;—And

[18]   To make all Laws which shall be necessary and proper for carrying into Execution the foregoing Powers, and all other Powers vested by this Constitution in the Government of the United States, or in any Department or Officer thereof.

Section 9.   [1] The Migration or Importation of Such Persons as any of the States now existing shall think proper to admit, shall not be prohibited by the Congress prior to the Year one thousand eight hundred and eight, but a Tax or duty may be imposed on such Importation, not exceeding ten dollars for each Person.

[2]   The privilege of the Writ of Habeas Corpus shall not be suspended, unless when in Cases of Rebellion or Invasion the public Safety may require it.

[3]   No Bill of Attainder or ex post facto Law shall be passed.

[4]   No Capitation, or other direct, Tax shall be laid, unless in Proportion to the Census or Enumeration herein before directed to be taken.

[5]   No Tax or Duty shall be laid on Articles exported from any State.

[6]   No Preference shall be given by any Regulation of Commerce or Revenue to the Ports of one State over those of another: nor shall Vessels bound to, or from, one State be obliged to enter, clear, or pay Duties in another.

[7]   No money shall be drawn from the Treasury, but in Consequence of Appropriations made by Law; and a regular Statement and Account of the

Receipts and Expenditures of all public Money shall be published from time to time.

[8]   No Title of Nobility shall be granted by the United States: And no Person holding any Office of Profit or Trust under them, shall, without the Consent of the Congress, accept of any present, Emolument, Office or Title, of any kind whatever, from any King, Prince, or foreign State.

Section 10.   [1] No State shall enter into any Treaty, Alliance, or Confederation; grant Letters of Marque and Reprisal; coin Money; emit Bills of Credit; make any Thing but gold and silver Coin a Tender in Payment of Debts; pass any Bill of Attainder, ex post facto Law, or Law impairing the Obligation of Contracts, or grant any Title of Nobility.

[2]   No State shall, without the Consent of the Congress, lay any Imposts or Duties on Imports or Exports, except what may be absolutely necessary for executing its inspection Laws: and the net Produce of all Duties and Imposts, laid by any State on Imports or Exports, shall be for the Use of the Treasury of the United States; and all such Laws shall be subject to the Revision and Controul of the Congress.

[3]   No State shall, without the Consent of Congress, lay any Duty of Tonnage, keep Troops, or Ships of War in time of Peace, enter into any Agreement or Compact with another State, or with a foreign Power, or engage in War, unless actually invaded, or in such imminent Danger as will not admit of delay.

ARTICLE II

Section 1.   [1] The executive Power shall be vested in a President of the United States of America. He shall hold his Office during the Term of four Years, and, together with the Vice President, chosen for the same Term, be elected, as follows:

[2]   Each State shall appoint, in such Manner as the Legislature thereof may direct, a Number of Electors, equal to the whole Number of Senators and Representatives to which the State may be entitled in the Congress; but no Senator or Representative, or Person holding an Office of Trust or Profit under the United States, shall be appointed an Elector.

[3]   The Electors shall meet in their respective States, and vote by Ballot for two Persons, of whom one at least shall not be an Inhabitant of the same State with themselves. And they shall make a List of all the Persons voted for, and of the Number of Votes for each; which List they shall sign and certify, and transmit sealed to the Seat of the Government of the United States, directed to the President of the Senate. The President of the Senate shall, in the Presence of the Senate and House of Representatives, open all the Certificates, and the Votes shall then be counted. The Person having the greatest Number of Votes shall be the President, if such Number be a Majority of the whole Number of Electors appointed; and if there be more than one who have such Majority, and have an equal Number of Votes, then the House of Representatives shall immediately chuse by Ballot one of them for President; and if no Person have a Majority, then from the five highest on the List the said House shall in like Manner chuse the President. But in chusing the President, the Votes shall be taken by States, the Representation from each State having one Vote; A quorum for this Purpose shall consist of a Member or Members from two thirds of the States, and a Majority of all the States shall be necessary to a Choice. In every Case, after the Choice of the President, the Person having the greater Number of Votes of the Electors shall be the Vice President. But if there should

remain two or more who have equal Votes, the Senate shall chuse from them by Ballot the Vice President.

[4]   The Congress may determine the Time of chusing the Electors, and the Day on which they shall give their Votes; which Day shall be the same throughout the United States.

[5]   No person except a natural born Citizen, or a Citizen of the United States, at the time of the Adoption of this Constitution, shall be eligible to the Office of President; neither shall any Person be eligible to that Office who shall not have attained to the Age of thirty five Years, and been fourteen Years a Resident within the United States.

[6]   In case of the removal of the President from Office, or of his Death, Resignation or Inability to discharge the Powers and Duties of the said Office, the Same shall devolve on the Vice President, and the Congress may by Law provide for the Case of Removal, Death, Resignation or Inability, both of the President and Vice President, declaring what Officer shall then act as President, and such Officer shall act accordingly, until the Disability be removed, or a President shall be elected.

[7]   The President shall, at stated Times, receive for his Services, a Compensation, which shall neither be encreased nor diminished during the Period for which he shall have been elected, and he shall not receive within that Period any other Emolument from the United States, or any of them.

[8]   Before he enter on the Execution of his Office, he shall take the following Oath or Affirmation: "I do solemnly swear (or affirm) that I will faithfully execute the Office of President of the United States, and will to the best of my Ability, preserve, protect and defend the Constitution of the United States."

Section 2.   [1] The President shall be Commander in Chief of the Army and Navy of the United States, and of the militia of the several States, when called into the actual Service of the United States; he may require the Opinion, in writing, of the principal Officer in each of the executive Departments, upon any Subject relating to the Duties of their respective Offices, and he shall have Power to grant Reprieves and Pardons for Offenses against the United States, except in Cases of Impeachment.

[2]   He shall have Power, by and with the Advice and Consent of the Senate, to make Treaties, provided two thirds of the Senators present concur; and he shall nominate, and by and with the Advice and Consent of the Senate, shall appoint Ambassadors, other public Ministers and Consuls, Judges of the supreme Court, and all other Officers of the United States, whose Appointments are not herein otherwise provided for, and which shall be established by Law; but the Congress may by Law vest the Appointment of such inferior Officers, as they think proper, in the President alone, in the Courts of Law, or in the Heads of Departments.

[3]   The President shall have Power to fill up all Vacancies that may happen during the Recess of the Senate, by granting Commissions which shall expire at the End of their next Session.

Section 3.   He shall from time to time give to the Congress Information of the State of the Union, and recommend to their Consideration such Measures as he shall judge necessary and expedient; he may, on extraordinary Occasions, convene both Houses, or either of them, and in Case of Disagreement between them, with Respect to the Time of Adjournment, he may adjourn them to such Time as he shall think proper; he shall receive Ambassadors and other public

Ministers; he shall take Care that the Laws be faithfully executed, and shall Commission all the Officers of the United States.

Section 4.   The President, Vice President and all civil Officers of the United States, shall be removed from Office on Impeachment for, and Conviction of, Treason, Bribery, or other high Crimes and Misdemeanors.

ARTICLE III

Section 1.   The judicial Power of the United States, shall be vested in one supreme Court, and in such inferior Courts as the Congress may from time to time ordain and establish. The Judges, both of the supreme and inferior Courts, shall hold their Offices during good Behaviour, and shall, at stated Times, receive for their Services a Compensation, which shall not be diminished during their Continuance in Office.

Section 2.   [1] The judicial Power shall extend to all Cases, in Law and Equity, arising under this Constitution, the Laws of the United States, and Treaties made, or which shall be made, under their Authority;—to all Cases affecting Ambassadors, other public Ministers and Consuls;—to all Cases of admiralty and maritime Jurisdiction,—to Controversies to which the United States shall be a Party;—to Controversies between two or more States;—between a State and Citizens of another State;—between Citizens of different States;—between Citizens of the same State claiming Lands under the Grants of different States, and between a State, or the Citizens thereof, and foreign States, Citizens or Subjects.

[2]   In all Cases affecting Ambassadors, other public Ministers and Consuls, and those in which a State shall be a Party, the supreme Court shall have original Jurisdiction. In all the other Cases before mentioned, the supreme Court shall have appellate Jurisdiction, both as to Law and Fact, with such Exceptions and under such Regulations as the Congress shall make.

[3]   The trial of all Crimes, except in Cases of Impeachment, shall be by Jury; and such Trial shall be held in the State where the said Crimes shall have been committed; but when not committed within any State, the Trial shall be at such Place or Places as the Congress may by Law have directed.

Section 3.   [1] Treason against the United States, shall consist only in levying War against them, or, in adhering to their Enemies, giving them Aid and Comfort. No Person shall be convicted of Treason unless on the Testimony of two Witnesses to the same overt Act, or on Confession in open Court.

[2]   The Congress shall have Power to declare the Punishment of Treason, but no Attainder of Treason shall work Corruption of Blood, or Forfeiture except during the Life of the Person attainted.

ARTICLE IV

Section 1.   Full Faith and Credit shall be given in each State to the public Acts, Records, and judicial Proceedings of every other State. And the Congress may by general Laws prescribe the Manner in which such Acts, Records and Proceedings shall be proved, and the Effect thereof.

Section 2.   [1] The Citizens of each State shall be entitled to all Privileges and Immunities of Citizens in the several States.

[2]   A Person charged in any State with Treason, Felony, or other Crime, who shall flee from Justice, and be found in another State, shall on demand of the executive Authority of the State from which he fled, be delivered up, to be removed to the State having Jurisdiction of the Crime.

[3] No Person held to Service or Labour in one State, under the Laws thereof, escaping into another, shall, in Consequence of any Law or Regulation therein, be discharged from such Service or Labour, but shall be delivered up on Claim of the Party to whom such Service or Labour may be due.

Section 3. [1] New States may be admitted by the Congress into this Union; but no new State shall be formed or erected within the Jurisdiction of any other State; nor any State be formed by the Junction of two or more States, or Parts of States, without the Consent of the Legislatures of the States concerned as well as of the Congress.

[2] The Congress shall have Power to dispose of and make all needful Rules and Regulations respecting the Territory or other Property belonging to the United States; and nothing in this Constitution shall be so construed as to Prejudice any Claims of the United States, or of any particular State.

Section 4. The United States shall guarantee to every State in this Union a Republican Form of Government, and shall protect each of them against Invasion; and on Application of the Legislature, or of the Executive (when the Legislature cannot be convened) against domestic Violence.

ARTICLE V

The Congress, whenever two thirds of both Houses shall deem it necessary, shall propose Amendments to this Constitution, or, on the Application of the Legislatures of two thirds of the several States, shall call a Convention for proposing Amendments, which, in either Case, shall be valid to all Intents and Purposes, as part of this Constitution, when ratified by the Legislatures of three fourths of the several States, or by Conventions in three fourths thereof, as the one or the other Mode of Ratification may be proposed by the Congress; Provided that no Amendment which may be made prior to the Year One thousand eight hundred and eight shall in any Manner affect the first and fourth Clauses in the Ninth Section of the first Article; and that no State, without its Consent, shall be deprived of its equal Suffrage in the Senate.

ARTICLE VI

[1] All Debts contracted and Engagements entered into, before the Adoption of this Constitution shall be as valid against the United States under this Constitution, as under the Confederation.

[2] This Constitution, and the Laws of the United States which shall be made in Pursuance thereof; and all Treaties made, or which shall be made, under the Authority of the United States, shall be the supreme Law of the Land; and the Judges in every State shall be bound thereby, any Thing in the Constitution or Laws of any State to the Contrary notwithstanding.

[3] The Senators and Representatives before mentioned, and the Members of the several State Legislatures, and all executive and judicial Officers, both of the United States and of the several States, shall be bound by Oath or Affirmation, to support this Constitution; but no religious Test shall ever be required as a Qualification to any Office or public Trust under the United States.

ARTICLE VII

The Ratification of the Conventions of nine States shall be sufficient for the Establishment of this Constitution between the States so ratifying the Same.

ARTICLES IN ADDITION TO, AND AMENDMENT OF, THE CONSTITU-
TION OF THE UNITED STATES OF AMERICA, PROPOSED BY CON-
GRESS, AND RATIFIED BY THE LEGISLATURES OF THE SEVERAL
STATES PURSUANT TO THE FIFTH ARTICLE OF THE ORIGINAL
CONSTITUTION.

AMENDMENT I [1791]

Congress shall make no law respecting an establishment of religion, or
prohibiting the free exercise thereof; or abridging the freedom of speech, or of
the press; or the right of the people peaceably to assemble, and to petition the
Government for a redress of grievances.

AMENDMENT II [1791]

A well regulated Militia, being necessary to the security of a free State, the
right of the people to keep and bear Arms, shall not be infringed.

AMENDMENT III [1791]

No Soldier shall, in time of peace be quartered in any house, without the
consent of the Owner, nor in time of war, but in a manner to be prescribed by
law.

AMENDMENT IV [1791]

The right of the people to be secure in their persons, houses, papers, and
effects, against unreasonable searches and seizures, shall not be violated, and
no Warrants shall issue, but upon probable cause, supported by Oath or
affirmation, and particularly describing the place to be searched, and the
persons or things to be seized.

AMENDMENT V [1791]

No person shall be held to answer for a capital, or otherwise infamous
crime, unless on a presentment or indictment of a Grand Jury, except in cases
arising in the land or naval forces, or in the Militia, when in actual service in
time of War or public danger; nor shall any person be subject for the same
offense to be twice put in jeopardy of life or limb; nor shall be compelled in any
criminal case to be a witness against himself, nor be deprived of life, liberty, or
property, without due process of law; nor shall private property be taken for
public use, without just compensation.

AMENDMENT VI [1791]

In all criminal prosecutions, the accused shall enjoy the right to a speedy
and public trial, by an impartial jury of the State and district wherein the crime
shall have been committed, which district shall have been previously ascertained by law, and to be informed of the nature and cause of the accusation; to
be confronted with the witnesses against him; to have compulsory process for
obtaining witnesses in his favor, and to have the Assistance of Counsel for his
defence.

AMENDMENT VII [1791]

In Suits at common law, where the value in controversy shall exceed
twenty dollars, the right of trial by jury shall be preserved, and no fact tried by
jury, shall be otherwise re-examined in any Court of the United States, than
according to the rules of the common law.

AMENDMENT VIII [1791]

Excessive bail shall not be required, nor excessive fines imposed, nor cruel and unusual punishments inflicted.

AMENDMENT IX [1791]

The enumeration in the Constitution, of certain rights, shall not be construed to deny or disparage others retained by the people.

AMENDMENT X [1791]

The powers not delegated to the United States by the Constitution, nor prohibited by it to the States, are reserved to the States respectively, or to the people.

AMENDMENT XI [1798]

The Judicial power of the United States shall not be construed to extend to any suit in law or equity, commenced or prosecuted against one of the United States by Citizens of another State, or by Citizens or Subjects of any Foreign State.

AMENDMENT XII [1804]

The Electors shall meet in their respective states and vote by ballot for President and Vice–President, one of whom, at least, shall not be an inhabitant of the same state with themselves; they shall name in their ballots the person voted for as President, and in distinct ballots the person voted for as Vice–President, and they shall make distinct lists of all persons voted for as President, and of all persons voted for as Vice–President, and of the number of votes for each, which lists they shall sign and certify, and transmit sealed to the seat of the government of the United States, directed to the President of the Senate;—The President of the Senate shall, in the presence of the Senate and House of Representatives, open all the certificates and the votes shall then be counted;—The person having the greatest number of votes for President, shall be the President, if such number be a majority of the whole number of Electors appointed; and if no person have such majority, then from the persons having the highest numbers not exceeding three on the list of those voted for as President, the House of Representatives shall choose immediately, by ballot, the President. But in choosing the President, the votes shall be taken by states, the representation from each state having one vote; a quorum for this purpose shall consist of a member or members from two-thirds of the states, and a majority of all the states shall be necessary to a choice. And if the House of Representatives shall not choose a President whenever the right of choice shall devolve upon them before the fourth day of March next following, then the Vice–President shall act as President, as in the case of the death or other constitutional disability of the President.—The person having the greatest number of votes as Vice–President, shall be the Vice–President, if such number be a majority of the whole number of Electors appointed, and if no person have a majority, then from the two highest numbers on the list, the Senate shall choose the Vice–President; a quorum for the purpose shall consist of two-thirds of the whole number of Senators, and a majority of the whole number shall be necessary to a choice. But no person constitutionally ineligible to the office of President shall be eligible to that of Vice–President of the United States.

AMENDMENT XIII [1865]

Section 1.   Neither slavery nor involuntary servitude, except as a punishment for crime whereof the party shall have been duly convicted, shall exist within the United States, or any place subject to their jurisdiction.

Section 2.   Congress shall have power to enforce this article by appropriate legislation.

AMENDMENT XIV [1868]

Section 1.   All persons born or naturalized in the United States, and subject to the jurisdiction thereof, are citizens of the United States and of the State wherein they reside. No State shall make or enforce any law which shall abridge the privileges or immunities of citizens of the United States; nor shall any State deprive any person of life, liberty, or property, without due process of law; nor deny to any person within its jurisdiction the equal protection of the laws.

Section 2.   Representatives shall be apportioned among the several States according to their respective numbers, counting the whole number of persons in each State, excluding Indians not taxed. But when the right to vote at any election for the choice of electors for President and Vice President of the United States, Representatives in Congress, the Executive and Judicial officers of a State, or the members of the Legislature thereof, is denied to any of the male inhabitants of such State, being twenty-one years of age, and citizens of the United States, or in any way abridged, except for participation in rebellion, or other crime, the basis of representation therein shall be reduced in the proportion which the number of such male citizens shall bear to the whole number of male citizens twenty-one years of age in such State.

Section 3.   No person shall be a Senator or Representative in Congress, or elector of President and Vice President, or hold any office, civil or military, under the United States, or under any State, who having previously taken an oath, as a member of Congress, or as an officer of the United States, or as a member of any State legislature, or as an executive or judicial officer of any State, to support the Constitution of the United States, shall have engaged in insurrection or rebellion against the same, or given aid or comfort to the enemies thereof. But Congress may by a vote of two-thirds of each House, remove such disability.

Section 4.   The validity of the public debt of the United States, authorized by law, including debts incurred for payment of pensions and bounties for services in suppressing insurrection or rebellion, shall not be questioned. But neither the United States nor any State shall assume or pay any debt or obligation incurred in aid of insurrection or rebellion against the United States, or any claim for the loss or emancipation of any slave; but all such debts, obligations and claims shall be held illegal and void.

Section 5.   The Congress shall have power to enforce, by appropriate legislation, the provisions of this article.

AMENDMENT XV [1870]

Section 1.   The right of citizens of the United States to vote shall not be denied or abridged by the United States or by any State on account of race, color, or previous condition of servitude.

Section 2.   The Congress shall have power to enforce this article by appropriate legislation.

AMENDMENT XVI [1913]

The Congress shall have power to lay and collect taxes on incomes, from whatever source derived, without apportionment among the several States, and without regard to any census or enumeration.

AMENDMENT XVII [1913]

[1]   The Senate of the United States shall be composed of two Senators from each State, elected by the people thereof, for six years; and each Senator shall have one vote. The electors in each State shall have the qualifications requisite for electors of the most numerous branch of the State legislatures.

[2]   When vacancies happen in the representation of any State in the Senate, the executive authority of such State shall issue writs of election to fill such vacancies: *Provided*, That the legislature of any State may empower the executive thereof to make temporary appointments until the people fill the vacancies by election as the legislature may direct.

[3]   This amendment shall not be so construed as to affect the election or term of any Senator chosen before it becomes valid as part of the Constitution.

AMENDMENT XVIII [1919]

Section 1.   After one year from the ratification of this article the manufacture, sale, or transportation of intoxicating liquors within, the importation thereof into, or the exportation thereof from the United States and all territory subject to the jurisdiction thereof for beverage purposes is hereby prohibited.

Section 2.   The Congress and the several States shall have concurrent power to enforce this article by appropriate legislation.

Section 3.   This article shall be inoperative unless it shall have been ratified as an amendment to the Constitution by the legislatures of the several States, as provided in the Constitution, within seven years from the date of the submission hereof to the States by the Congress.

AMENDMENT XIX [1920]

[1]   The right of citizens of the United States to vote shall not be denied or abridged by the United States or by any State on account of sex.

[2]   Congress shall have power to enforce this article by appropriate legislation.

AMENDMENT XX [1933]

Section 1.   The terms of the President and Vice President shall end at noon on the 20th day of January, and the terms of Senators and Representatives at noon on the 3d day of January, of the years in which such terms would have ended if this article had not been ratified; and the terms of their successors shall then begin.

Section 2.   The Congress shall assemble at least once in every year, and such meeting shall begin at noon on the 3d day of January, unless they shall by law appoint a different day.

Section 3.   If, at the time fixed for the beginning of the term of the President, the President elect shall have died, the Vice President elect shall become President. If the President shall not have been chosen before the time fixed for the beginning of his term, or if the President elect shall have failed to qualify, then the Vice President elect shall act as President until a President shall have qualified; and the Congress may by law provide for the case wherein neither a President elect nor a Vice President elect shall have qualified, declaring who shall then act as President, or the manner in which one who is to act shall be selected, and such person shall act accordingly until a President or Vice President shall have qualified.

Section 4.   The Congress may by law provide for the case of the death of any of the persons from whom the House of Representatives may choose a President whenever the right of choice shall have devolved upon them, and for the case of the death of any of the persons from whom the Senate may choose a Vice President whenever the right of choice shall have devolved upon them.

Section 5.   Sections 1 and 2 shall take effect on the 15th day of October following the ratification of this article.

Section 6.   This article shall be inoperative unless it shall have been ratified as an amendment to the Constitution by the legislatures of three-fourths of the several States within seven years from the date of its submission.

AMENDMENT XXI [1933]

Section 1.   The eighteenth article of amendment to the Constitution of the United States is hereby repealed.

Section 2.   The transportation or importation into any State, Territory, or possession of the United States for delivery or use therein of intoxicating liquors, in violation of the laws thereof, is hereby prohibited.

Section 3.   This article shall be inoperative unless it shall have been ratified as an amendment to the Constitution by conventions in the several States, as provided in the Constitution, within seven years from the date of the submission hereof to the States by the Congress.

AMENDMENT XXII [1951]

Section 1.   No person shall be elected to the office of the President more than twice, and no person who has held the office of President, or acted as President, for more than two years of a term to which some other person was elected President shall be elected to the office of President more than once. But this Article shall not apply to any person holding the office of President when this Article was proposed by the Congress, and shall not prevent any person who may be holding the office of President, or acting as President, during the term within which this Article becomes operative from holding the office of President or acting as President during the remainder of such term.

Section 2.   This article shall be inoperative unless it shall have been ratified as an amendment to the Constitution by the legislatures of three-fourths of the several States within seven years from the date of its submission to the States by the Congress.

AMENDMENT XXIII [1961]

Section 1.   The District constituting the seat of Government of the United States shall appoint in such manner as the Congress may direct:

A number of electors of President and Vice President equal to the whole number of Senators and Representatives in Congress to which the District would be entitled if it were a State, but in no event more than the least populous state; they shall be in addition to those appointed by the states, but they shall be considered, for the purposes of the election of President and Vice President, to be electors appointed by a state; and they shall meet in the District and perform such duties as provided by the twelfth article of amendment.

Section 2.   The Congress shall have power to enforce this article by appropriate legislation.

AMENDMENT XXIV [1964]

Section 1. The right of citizens of the United States to vote in any primary or other election for President or Vice President, for electors for President or Vice President, or for Senator or Representative in Congress, shall not be denied or abridged by the United States or any State by reason of failure to pay any poll tax or other tax.

Section 2. The Congress shall have power to enforce this article by appropriate legislation.

AMENDMENT XXV [1967]

Section 1. In case of the removal of the President from office or of his death or resignation, the Vice President shall become President.

Section 2. Whenever there is a vacancy in the office of the Vice President, the President shall nominate a Vice President who shall take office upon confirmation by a majority vote of both Houses of Congress.

Section 3. Whenever the President transmits to the President pro tempore of the Senate and the Speaker of the House of Representatives his written declaration that he is unable to discharge the powers and duties of his office, and until he transmits to them a written declaration to the contrary, such powers and duties shall be discharged by the Vice President as Acting President.

Section 4. Whenever the Vice President and a majority of either the principal officers of the executive departments or of such other body as Congress may by law provide, transmit to the President pro tempore of the Senate and the Speaker of the House of Representatives their written declaration that the President is unable to discharge the powers and duties of his office, the Vice President shall immediately assume the powers and duties of the office as Acting President.

Thereafter, when the President transmits to the President pro tempore of the Senate and the Speaker of the House of Representatives his written declaration that no inability exists, he shall resume the powers and duties of his office unless the Vice President and a majority of either the principal officers of the executive departments or of such other body as Congress may by law provide, transmit within four days to the President pro tempore of the Senate and the Speaker of the House of Representatives their written declaration that the President is unable to discharge the powers and duties of his office. Thereupon Congress shall decide the issue, assembling within forty-eight hours for that purpose if not in session. If the Congress, within twenty-one days after receipt of the latter written declaration, or, if Congress is not in session, within twenty-one days after Congress is required to assemble, determines by two-thirds vote of both Houses that the President is unable to discharge the powers and duties of his office, the Vice President shall continue to discharge the same as Acting President; otherwise, the President shall resume the powers and duties of his office.

AMENDMENT XXVI [1971]

Section 1. The right of citizens of the United States, who are eighteen years of age or older, to vote shall not be denied or abridged by the United States or by any State on account of age.

Section 2. The Congress shall have power to enforce this article by appropriate legislation.

AMENDMENT XXVII [1992][1]

No law, varying the compensation for the services of Senators and Representatives, shall take effect, until an election for Representatives shall have intervened.

SECTION 2.   HISTORY OF THE ADOPTION OF THE CONSTITUTION AND ITS MOST SIGNIFICANT AMENDMENTS

A.   THE ARTICLES OF CONFEDERATION AND THE ORIGINAL CONSTITUTION

The Constitutional Convention, which met in Philadelphia in May, 1787, resulted from a growing belief that the federal government set up by the Articles of Confederation was inadequate. Under the Confederation, the United States were governed by Congress, a unicameral body in which each state had one vote. Nine votes were required for any significant action, and, more restrictively, "alteration" of the Articles required unanimity. There was no national executive, and no significant federal judiciary. Congress lacked the power to tax and, since states were often delinquent in responding to Congress' requisitions, Congress was perpetually hampered by lack of funds. Congress lacked the power to regulate interstate commerce, leading to commercial wars between the states.[2]

Agreement at the Constitutional Convention that a new federal government should be established, with power to act directly on individuals and not just upon the member states, masked considerable disagreement as to the extent of the powers of that new government. It took four months of debate and compromise before the final draft of the Constitution was approved on September 17, 1787. To protect free debate, the Convention adopted a secrecy rule, and no contemporary accounts were available of the debates and decisions at the Convention. A sketchy journal was kept by William Jackson, secretary of the Convention. The journal remained in the archives of the Department of State until published in 1818 under the editorship of John Quincy Adams. More comprehensive information about the Convention's deliberations is contained in James Madison's account. Madison's notes, however, were not published until 1840, four years after his death, and more than half a century after ratification.

Ratification of the Constitution by the necessary nine states was completed in 1788. The ratification controversy was intense. The Federalist Papers, produced in the debate over ratification, are an important source of information

---

[1] The twenty seventh amendment was one of twelve amendments proposed by Congress in 1789. Ten of those twelve amendments were ratified by 1791 and became the first ten amendments to the Constitution. After more than two centuries, interest in the amendment was revived and the 38th State ratified it in 1992. In the intervening years it had never been resubmitted for ratification by Congress. For discussion of the controversy concerning whether the twenty seventh amendment is part of the Constitution, see note, infra p. 144.

[2] While a number of the features of the Constitution that emerged from the Convention can be traced to perceived inadequacies in the Articles of Confederation, other provisions reflect provisions contained in the Articles. Under the Articles, Congress controlled war, peace and foreign policy; a number of lesser powers described in Art. I, § 8, of the Constitution appeared in the Articles; the concepts of privileges and immunities of state citizens, extradition of fugitives, and full faith and credit were contained in Article IV of the Articles of Confederation.

as to contemporary views of the meaning of the Constitution. They are a series of 85 letters published in the New York papers from October, 1787 to April, 1788, under the pseudonym "Publius." The Federalist Papers were, in fact, written by Alexander Hamilton, James Madison and John Jay. One should keep in mind that the Federalist Papers, despite their high quality and the prominence of their authors, were intended as partisan debate on the side of ratification and not as dispassionate analysis of the meaning of the Constitution. Historical treatments of the Confederation period and of the drafting and ratification of the Constitution include: G. Bancroft, *History of the Formation of the Constitution of the United States of America* (1893); J. Fiske, *The Critical Period of American History* (1888); M. Jensen, *The Articles of Confederation: An Interpretation of the Social–Constitutional History of the American Revolution, 1774–1781* (1940); _____, *The New Nation: A History of the United States during the Confederation, 1781–1789* (1950): _____, *The Making of the American Constitution* (1964); A. McLaughlin, *The Confederation and the Constitution: 1783–1789* (1905); C. Rossiter, *1787: The Grand Convention* (1966); C. Van Doren, *The Great Rehearsal: The Story of the Making and Ratification of the Constitution of the United States* (1948); C. Warren, *The Making of the Constitution* (1928); B. Wright, *Consensus and Continuity, 1776–1787* (1958). The Federalist is available in a number of editions. Documentary collections include: H. Commager (ed.), *Documents of American History* (9th ed. 1973); J. Elliott (ed.), *The Debates of the Several State Conventions on the Adoption of the Federal Constitution* (1836); M. Farrand (ed.), *The Records of the Federal Convention of 1787* (1911, 1937).

B. THE BILL OF RIGHTS

PROTECTION OF FREEDOM IN THE CONSTITUTION OF 1787

The emphasis that must be placed upon the Bill of Rights and other amendments to the Constitution, Professor Chafee reminds us, should not lead one to ignore the protections for individual liberty which were built into the original document; perhaps the most important of these is the limitation on suspension by the national government of the writ of *habeas corpus*.[1] Professor Chafee adds:

"Among the affirmative rights in Article I are the immunity of debates in Congress; the Interstate Commerce Clause which, without expressly mentioning any human right, has in fact been invoked to protect freedom of movement across state lines; ... and the prohibition of bills of attainder and *ex post facto* laws in the nation or the states. ... Article III on the judiciary obliges criminal cases to be tried by a jury of the neighborhood. It also contains the definition of treason.... Finally, the miscellaneous provisions found in Article IV entitle citizens of one state to enjoy in another state 'all the Privileges and Immunities' of its own citizens, and empower the United States to preserve in every state a 'Republican Form of Government' and to protect the right to life 'against domestic violence.' "[2]

Professor Chafee's brief summary does not purport to be complete. For example, the protection of economic (and even intellectual) liberty was possible under the prohibition in Article I, Section 10, against state laws impairing the obligation of contracts. But in spite of the importance of these and other

[1] Art. I, § 9. Chafee, *How Human Rights Got Into the Constitution* (1952) 51. *Commentaries on the Constitution of the United States* (4th ed. 1873) § 1859.

[2] Id. at 5–6 (Footnotes omitted.) See also: *The Federalist No. 84* (Hamilton); Story,

guaranties established by the original document, federal constitutional protection for individual liberty must be derived, for the most part, from two groups of amendments separated in time by almost eighty years: the Bill of Rights and the three post-Civil War amendments. The objectives of these two groups of amendments and the relationship between them raise questions that are as important as they are difficult.

THE BILL OF RIGHTS

The importance of a written declaration of the rights of the individual loomed large in the minds of early Americans. This tradition had grown out of struggles against royal prerogative, and was reflected in written guaranties of Magna Carta (1215),[3] the Petition of Right (1628)[4] and the Bill of Rights (1689).[5]

This tradition was carried to the New World. Many of the early Colonial Charters offered important assurances to the settlers of "all Liberties and Immunities of free and natural Subjects."[6] But the most direct antecedents of modern guarantees of individual rights appeared in the constitutions that the colonists framed for themselves at the outbreak of the Revolution. In eight state constitutions, these guarantees were gathered into separate provisions called a Bill of Rights or Declaration of Rights; three states wove them into the fabric of the document.[7] Probably the most influential of these early bills of rights was that of Virginia.

Since the Articles of Confederation (1777) did not grant significant legislative power to the central government, the absence of a bill of rights is understandable. It is more surprising that proposals for a Bill of Rights made in the Constitutional Convention of 1787 were rejected. No single explanation is compelling. There is some evidence of concern lest prohibiting Congress from intruding into enumerated areas of individual rights might suggest that Congress possessed power to invade other rights not specifically protected. Another deterrent appears to have been the fear that disagreement over the definition of individual rights might jeopardize the Convention's completion of the Constitu-

[3] Magna Carta exacted from King John numerous limitations on his prerogative. Chapter 39 read: "No freeman shall be seized or imprisoned or disseised or outlawed or in any way destroyed nor will we go against him or send against him except by the lawful judgment of his peers, or by the law of the land."

[4] The Petition of Right directed to Charles I contained the prayer that further military commissions for proceedings by martial law should not issue "lest by colour of them any of your majesty's subjects be destroyed or put to death, contrary to the laws and franchise of the land...."

[5] The Bill of Rights was designed to limit the power of William of Orange. It proclaimed "... that it is the right of the subjects to petition the king and all commitments and prosecutions for such petitioning are illegal ... that the subjects which are Protestants may have arms for their defense suitable for their conditions and as allowed by law; that election of members of parliament ought to be free; that the freedom of speech and debates or proceedings in parliament ought not to be impeached or questioned in any court or place out of parliament; that excessive bail ought not to be required, nor excessive fines imposed, nor cruel and unusual punishment inflicted; that jurors ought to be duly impanelled and returned, and jurors which pass upon men in trials for high treason ought to be freeholders...."

[6] Charter of Connecticut, 1662, in 1 Thorpe, *American Charters, Constitutions and Organic Laws*, 529, 533 (1909). Similar provisions occur in other colonial charters. See Chafee, *How Human Rights Got into the Constitution* 36 (1952). Several of the charters also had guarantees of religious freedom. Id. at 40–42. Cf. Rutland, *The Birth of the Bill of Rights* (1955).

[7] Connecticut and Rhode Island retained their colonial charters. Chafee, op. cit. supra, pp. 18–19.

tion and the launching of the new government.[8] Finally, there is evidence that the delegates were persuaded to avoid the problem by the supposition that the limited powers of Congress made a Bill of Rights unnecessary.[9]

One of the few records of the debates on this question in the constitutional convention is as follows:[10]

"Mr. Pinkney & Mr. Gerry, moved to insert a declaration 'that the liberty of the Press should be inviolably observed—'

"Mr. Sherman—It is unnecessary—The power of Congress does not extend to the Press. On the question, (it passed in the negative)."

The reasons that impelled the Constitutional Convention to omit a federal bill of rights proved unsatisfactory in crucial state ratification conventions. After relatively smooth sailing in Delaware, Pennsylvania, New Jersey, Georgia and Connecticut, the storm broke in Massachusetts. Opposition was quieted in part by the proposal that ratification be coupled with suggestions for amendments to the Constitution that would protect individual liberty; the Federalists tendered a gentleman's agreement to give them favorable consideration. Many of the subsequent state conventions suggested amendments[11] that included proposals for a bill of rights.[12]

To keep faith with these states, James Madison compiled a set of proposed amendments based on the state bills of rights and the amendments proposed by the state conventions. His conception of the role of a bill of rights is summarized in a letter to Jefferson dated October 17, 1788:[13]

"My own opinion has always been in favor of a bill of rights; providing it be so framed as not to imply powers not meant to be included in the enumeration. At the same time I have never thought the omission a material defect, nor been anxious to supply it even by *subsequent* amendment, for any other reason than that it is anxiously desired by others. I favored it because I have supposed it might be of use, and if properly executed could not be of disservice. I have not viewed it in an important light 1. because I conceive that in a certain degree, though not in the extent argued by Mr. Wilson, the rights in question are reserved by the manner in which the federal powers are granted, 2. because there is great reason to fear that a positive declaration of some of the most essential

---

[8] On September 12 a motion for a committee to prepare a bill of rights was defeated by a vote of 10–0; the only recorded objection to the motion was in connection with a proposed guaranty of jury trial in civil cases. "Mr. Gorham. It is not possible to discriminate equity cases from those in which juries are proper. The Representatives of the people may be safely trusted in this matter," 2 Farrand, *Records of the Federal Convention* (1911) 587, 588.

Speaking in the South Carolina House of Representatives, C.C. Pinckney summarized the reasons listed above and added the further point that bills of rights "generally begin with declaring that all men are by nature born free. Now, we should make that declaration with a very bad grace, when a large part of our property consists in men who are actually born slaves." 3 Id. at 256.

[9] This and other arguments against the adoption of a Bill of Rights were reviewed and answered at length by Madison in his proposals to the House of Representatives. 1 *Annals of Congress* 438–439 (1834).

[10] 2 Farrand, op. cit. supra 617–618 (Madison's notes for September 14).

[11] Bloom, *History of the Formation of the Union under the Constitution* (1941) 24–27, 280 et seq.; Hart, *Formation of the Union* (1892) 130–31; 1 Nichols & Nichols, *The Republic of the United States* (1942) 262.

[12] Madison believed that the chief basis of popular opposition to ratification of the Constitution to be its omission of such guarantees, 1 *Annals of Congress* 433 (1834).

[13] *Writings of James Madison* 269, 271–274 (Hunt ed. 1904); see further 1 *Annals of Congress* 436–44 (1834). For Jefferson's prodding of Madison see Bowers, *Jefferson and the Bill of Rights,* 41 Va.L.Rev. 709, 712–714 (1955).

rights could not be obtained in the requisite latitude ... 3. because the limited powers of the federal Government and the jealousy of the subordinate Governments, afford a security which has not existed in the case of the State Governments, and exists in no other, 4. because experience proves the inefficacy of a bill of rights on those occasions when its control is most needed. ... What use then it may be asked can a bill of rights serve in popular Governments? ... 1. The political truths declared in that solemn manner acquire by degrees the character of fundamental maxims of free Government, and as they become incorporated with the national sentiment, counteract the impulses of interest and passion. 2. Altho it be generally true ... that the danger of oppression lies in the interested majorities of the people rather than in usurped acts of the Government, yet there may be occasions on which the evil may spring from the latter source; and on such, a bill of rights will be a good ground for an appeal to the sense of the community. ... *absolute* restrictions in cases that are doubtful, or where emergencies may overrule them, ought to be avoided."

In the First Congress, Madison proposed detailed amendments to the text of the Constitution which, after material modification, led to the Bill of Rights.[14]

The original Constitution contained relatively few express limitations on state power. (The most important of these are in Section 10 of Article I, and Sections 1 and 2 of Article IV.) The addition of the Bill of Rights left state power unchanged. Forty-two years after their ratification, Chief Justice Marshall confirmed that the provisions of the Bill of Rights were limitations only on the power of the federal government. Barron v. Baltimore, 32 U.S. (7 Pet.) 243 (1833). Until after the Civil War, state constitutions—interpreted by state courts—were the source of most constitutional limitations on state government.

C. THE ADOPTION OF THE CIVIL WAR AMENDMENTS

Appomattox marked the end of the struggle over the constitutional issue of secession but it precipitated the country's most serious social problem: the future status of the four million individuals who had been held in slavery. This transition to freedom posed an acute problem of assimilation reflected in grave problems of constitutional law.

Slavery and the Thirteenth Amendment. By language only thinly veiled, the Constitution of 1787 recognized and sanctioned slavery.[1] Thus, although Lincoln's Emancipation Proclamation[2] declared an end to slavery in the Confederacy, firm legal support for the eradication of slavery required constitutional change. This support was provided in 1865 by the Thirteenth

---

[14] Madison's initial proposals called for amendments that were to be worked into the body of the Constitution, rather than supplements added to the original text. Thus, Madison's proposals included ten new provisions to be added to Article I, Section 9. 1 *Annals of Congress* 434–35 (1834). These correspond, for the most part, to the first ten amendments which finally received approval. Madison's proposals also included the following addition to Article I, Section 10: "No state shall violate the equal rights of conscience, or the freedom of the press, or the trial by jury in criminal cases." 1 *Id.* at 435. He further

proposed to rewrite Article III, Section 2 to require, inter alia, that "in all crimes punishable with loss of life or member, presentment or indictment by a grand jury shall be an essential preliminary ..." and that "In suits at common law, between man and man, the trial by jury, as one of the best securities to the rights of the people, ought to remain inviolate" Ibid.

[1] Art. I, § 2, ¶ 3; Art. I, § 9, ¶ 1; Art. IV, § 2, ¶ 3.

[2] 12 Stat. 1268 (1863).

Amendment.[3] The original proposition for the Amendment was introduced in Congress in December, 1863, achieving final passage in January, 1865. It was declared ratified and in force on December 18, 1865.

The 1866 Civil Rights Acts and the Fourteenth and Fifteenth Amendments. The Civil Rights Act of 1866 was before Congress at the same time as the Fourteenth Amendment. In large part, the Amendment was designed to assure the constitutionality of the Act.

The Act was Congress's response to the so-called "Black Codes" enacted in several states. Mississippi enactments of 1865, for example, provided:

"... Every civil officer shall, and every person may, arrest and carry back to his or her legal employer any freedman, free negro, or mulatto who shall have quit the service of his or her employer before the expiration of his or her term of service without good cause....

"... If any freedman, free negro or mulatto, convicted of any of the misdemeanors provided against in this act, shall fail or refuse for the space of five days after conviction, to pay the fine and costs imposed, such person shall be hired out by the sheriff or other officer, at the public outcry, to any white person who will pay said fine and all costs, and take the convict for the shortest time."[4]

Other provisions of some of the Black Codes barred Blacks from any business except "husbandry" without obtaining a special license, or forbade them from renting or leasing land except in towns and cities.[5]

The Civil Rights Act,[6] which was introduced in January 1866, passed in March, vetoed by President Johnson, and passed over his veto in early April, was designed to put an end to these laws. The two opening sections provided:

"Sec. 1. ... all persons born in the United States and not subject to any foreign power, excluding Indians not taxed, are hereby declared to be citizens of the United States; and such citizens, of every race and color, without regard to any previous condition of slavery or involuntary servitude, except as a punishment for crime whereof the party shall have been duly convicted, shall have the same right, in every State and Territory in the United States, to make and enforce contracts, to sue, be parties, and give evidence, to inherit, purchase, lease, sell, hold, and convey real and personal property, and to full and equal benefit of all laws and proceedings for the security of person and property, as is enjoyed by white citizens, and shall be subject to like punishment, pains, and penalties, and to none other, any law, statute, ordinance, regulation, or custom, to the contrary notwithstanding.

"Sec. 2. *And be it further enacted,* That any person who, under color of any law, statute, ordinance, regulation, or custom, shall subject, or cause to be subjected, any inhabitant of any State or Territory to the deprivation of any right secured or protected by this act, or to different punishment, pains, or penalties on account of such person having at any time been held in a condition of slavery or involuntary servitude, except as a punishment for crime whereof

---

[3] See tenBroek, *Thirteenth Amendment to the Constitution of the United States—Consummation to Abolition and Key to the Fourteenth Amendment,* 39 Calif.L.Rev. 171 (1951).

[4] Laws of Mississippi, 1865, 82, 84, 166–167. See also Laws of Mississippi, 1865, 86–96; Acts of the General Assembly of Louisiana Regulating Labor. Extra Session, 1865, 3

et seq.; 2 Commager, *Documents of American History,* 2–7 (5th ed. 1949).

[5] Stephenson, *Race Distinctions in American Law* 41–43 (1910); Maslow and Robison, *Civil Rights Legislation and the Fight for Equality,* 20 U.Chi.L.Rev. 363, 367 (1953).

[6] Act of April 9, 1866, 14 Stat. 27.

the party shall have been duly convicted, or by reason of his color or race, than is prescribed for the punishment of white persons, shall be deemed guilty of a misdemeanor, and, on conviction, shall be punished by fine not exceeding one thousand dollars, or imprisonment not exceeding one year, or both, in the discretion of the court."

The question arose: was there constitutional support for this Act? Did the racial discrimination in question reach the level of "involuntary servitude" encompassed by the Thirteenth Amendment? If not, where else could constitutional support be found? This difficulty was one of President Johnson's grounds for vetoing the bill. He said:[7]

"Hitherto every subject embraced in the enumeration of rights contained in this bill has been considered as exclusively belonging to the States. They all relate to the internal police and economy of the States. They are matters which in each State concern the domestic condition of its people, varying in each according to its own peculiar circumstances, and the safety and well-being of its own citizens. I do not mean to say that upon all these subjects there are not Federal restraints, as for instance, in the State power of legislation over contracts, there is a Federal limitation that no State shall pass a law impairing the obligations of contracts; and, as to crimes, that no State shall pass an *ex post facto* law; and, as to money that no State shall make anything but gold and silver a legal tender. But where can we find a Federal prohibition against the power of any state to discriminate, as do most of them, between aliens and citizens, between artificial persons called corporations, and natural persons, in the right to hold real estate?

"If it be granted that Congress can repeal all State laws discriminating between whites and blacks in the subjects covered by this bill, why, it may be asked, may not Congress repeal in the same way all State laws discriminating between the two races on the subjects of suffrage and office? If Congress can declare by law who shall hold lands, who shall testify, who shall have capacity to make a contract in a State, then Congress can by law also declare who, without regard to color or race, shall have the right to sit as a juror or as a judge, to hold any office, and, finally, to vote 'in every State and Territory of the United States.'"

Concurrently with the early debates on the Civil Rights Bill Congress was also considering drafts of a constitutional amendment. The Joint Committee on Reconstruction referred to Congress on February 10, 1866 a draft of an amendment designed to grant Congress general power to legislate for the protection of civil rights.[8] The draft was promptly tabled in the Senate. On February 26–28 it was debated in the House but action was postponed and it was never taken up.

Although Congress had overridden the President's veto of the Civil Rights Act, the challenge to the constitutionality was not resolved. So in April the Joint Committee on Reconstruction returned to the problem of constitutional

---

[7] Cong.Globe, 39th Cong., 1st Sess., 1680 (1866).

[8] Unlike Section 1 of the final draft, these earlier versions of the Fourteenth Amendment were, in form, grants to Congress of a general power to legislate for the protection of civil rights. The first draft reported by the committee considering the amendment read: "Congress shall have power to make all laws necessary and proper to secure to all citizens of the United States, in every State, the same political rights and privileges; and to all persons in every State equal protection in the enjoyment of life, liberty and property." See Fairman, *Does the Fourteenth Amendment Incorporate the Bill of Rights: The Original Understanding*, 2 Stanf.L.Rev. 5, 20–21 (1949); Flack, *The Adoption of the Fourteenth Amendment* (1908).

amendment, reporting a new version to Congress on April 28. This version was debated in May and June and finally adopted with amendments on June 13. By March, 1867, the Amendment had been ratified by 20 states and rejected by 11. Also in March Congress passed over the President's veto a bill setting the conditions under which the Rebel States would be entitled to representation in Congress. One of those conditions for readmission was that the state should have ratified the Fourteenth Amendment and that the Amendment should have become part of the Constitution. By July, 1868, 9 more states had ratified, including 7 of the southern states seeking readmission pursuant to the 1867 statute, and the Amendment was declared adopted on July 28.

One of the conditions imposed for the readmission of the Rebel States was that their constitutions guarantee the continuance of the suffrage provisions adopted during the period of federal control through the Reconstruction Acts. These constitutions guaranteed Negro suffrage and disenfranchised large elements of the white population. Texas, Mississippi, and Virginia were delayed in readmission because of opposition to the franchise provisions. In 1869 a bargain was struck under which these states were not required to accept the rigor of the original franchise provisions but were required to ratify a constitutional amendment then being proposed to guarantee the franchise to Negroes. The three states complied, were readmitted in early 1870, and the Fifteenth Amendment was finally ratified in March, 1870.

CHAPTER 2

JUDICIAL REVIEW

SECTION 1. THE LEGITIMACY OF JUDICIAL REVIEW

THE CONSTITUTIONAL CONVENTION

In the Constitutional Convention of 1787 the Virginia Plan proposed to the Convention by Mr. Randolph (Va.) on May 29 served as the basis for the ensuing discussion and action of the delegates.

The sixth resolution in the Virginia Plan contained the provision that the national legislature be empowered "to negative all laws passed by the several States, contravening in the opinion of the National Legislature the articles of Union...." This provision was ultimately rejected, in part because of the adoption of the Supremacy Clause, Art. VI, cl. 2.

The eighth resolution provided "that the Executive and a convenient number of the National Judiciary, ought to compose a council of revision with authority to examine every act of the National Legislature before it shall operate, & every act of a particular Legislature before a Negative thereon shall be final; and that the dissent of the said Council shall amount to a rejection, unless the Act of the National Legislature be again passed, or that of a particular Legislature be again negatived by _____ª of the members of each branch." The Convention ultimately rejected the participation of the judiciary in the veto process and adopted the executive veto. Art. I, § 7, cl. 2.

The following excerpts from the debate on the eighth resolution will give a little of the flavor of the discussion that led to its rejection. They are taken from Madison's Notes of the proceedings on July 21, 1787, 2 Farrand, *The Records of the Federal Convention of 1787* (1911) 74, 76, 78:

"Mr. [Madison]—considered the object of the motion as of great importance to the meditated Constitution. It would be useful to the Judiciary departmt. by giving it an additional opportunity of defending itself agst: Legislative encroachments; It would be useful to the Executive, by inspiring additional confidence & firmness in exerting the revisionary power: It would be useful to the Legislature by the valuable assistance it would give in preserving a consistency, conciseness, perspicuity & technical propriety in the laws, qualities peculiarly necessary; & yet shamefully wanting in our republican Codes. It would moreover be useful to the Community at large as an additional check agst. a pursuit of those unwise & unjust measures which constituted so great a portion of our calamities. If any solid objection could be urged agst. the motion, it must be on the supposition that it tended to give too much strength either to the Executive or Judiciary. He did not think there was the least ground for this apprehension. It was much more to be apprehended that notwithstanding this cooperation of the two departments, the Legislature would still be an overmatch for them. Experience in all the States had evinced a powerful tendency in the Legislature to absorb all power into its vortex. This

---

ª Blank left in original.

was the real source of danger to the American Constitutions; & suggested the necessity of giving every defensive authority to the other departments that was consistent with republican principles....

"Mr. L. Martin. considered the association of the Judges with the Executive as a dangerous innovation; as well as one which, could not produce the particular advantage expected from it. A knowledge of mankind, and of Legislative affairs cannot be presumed to belong in a higher degree to the Judges than to the Legislature. And as to the Constitutionality of laws, that point will come before the Judges in their proper official character. In this character they have a negative on the laws. Join them with the Executive in the Revision and they will have a double negative. It is necessary that the Supreme Judiciary should have the confidence of the people. This will soon be lost, if they are employed in the task of remonstrating agst. popular measures of the Legislature. Besides in what mode & proportion are they to vote in the Council of Revision? ...

"Col Mason Observed that the defence of the Executive was not the sole object of the Revisionary power. He expected even greater advantages from it. Notwithstanding the precautions taken in the Constitution of the Legislature, it would so much resemble that of the individual States, that it must be expected frequently to pass unjust and pernicious laws. This restraining power was therefore essentially necessary. It would have the effect not only of hindering the final passage of such laws; but would discourage demagogues from attempting to get them passed. It had been said (by Mr. L. Martin) that if the Judges were joined in this check on the laws, they would have a double negative, since in their expository capacity of Judges they would have one negative. He would reply that in this capacity they could impede in one case only, the operation of laws. They could declare an unconstitutional law void. But with regard to every law however unjust oppressive or pernicious, which did not come plainly under this description, they would be under the necessity as Judges to give it a free course. He wished the further use to be made of the Judges, of giving aid in preventing every improper law. Their aid will be the more valuable as they are in the habit and practice of considering laws in their true principles, and in all their consequences."

Marbury v. Madison

5 U.S. (1 Cranch) 137, 2 L.Ed. 60 (1803).

[John Marshall was Secretary of State in the Adams administration when he took office as Chief Justice on January 31, 1801. He continued as Acting Secretary of State until the last day of the Adams administration, March 3, 1801. William Marbury was one of a number of persons who were appointed justices of the peace in the District of Columbia and who were confirmed by the Senate on March 3. His commission remained in Marshall's office undelivered when the new administration took over. President Jefferson directed his Secretary of State, James Madison, to withhold several commissions, including that of Marbury. Marbury then brought this suit against Madison, taking the unusual step of starting the action in the Supreme Court, invoking its original jurisdiction.[a]]

---

[a] For accounts of the background of the case, see Burton, *The Cornerstone of Constitutional Law: The Extraordinary Case of Marbury v. Madison,* 36 A.B.A.J. 805 (1950); Van Alstyne, *A Critical Guide to Marbury v. Madison,* 1969 Duke L.J. 1.

For an interesting discussion of the last minute appointment of judges by President Adams, see Turner, *The Midnight Judges,* 109 U.Pa.L.Rev. 494 (1961).

Mr. Chief Justice Marshall delivered the opinion of the Court.

At the last term on the affidavits then read and filed with the clerk, a rule was granted in this case, requiring the secretary of state to shew cause why a mandamus should not issue, directing him to deliver to William Marbury his commission as a justice of the peace for the county of Washington, in the district of Columbia.

No cause has been shewn, and the present motion is for a mandamus. The peculiar delicacy of this case, the novelty of some of its circumstances, and the real difficulty attending the points which occur in it, require a complete exposition of the principles, on which the opinion to be given by the court, is founded.

These principles have been, on the side of the applicant, very ably argued at the bar. In rendering the opinion of the court, there will be some departure in form, though not in substance, from the points stated in that argument.

In the order in which the court has viewed this subject, the following questions have been considered and decided.

1st. Has the applicant a right to the commission he demands?

2dly. If he has a right, and that right has been violated, do the laws of his country afford him a remedy?

3dly. If they do afford him a remedy, is it a *mandamus* issuing from this court?

The first object of enquiry is,

1st. Has the applicant a right to the commission he demands?

His right originates in an act of congress passed in February 1801, concerning the district of Columbia.

After dividing the district into two counties, the 11th section of this law enacts, "that there shall be appointed in and for each of the said counties, such number of discreet persons to be justices of the peace as the president of the United States shall, from time to time, think expedient, to continue in office for five years."

It appears, from the affidavits, that in compliance with this law, a commission for William Marbury as a justice of peace for the county of Washington, was signed by John Adams, then president of the United States; after which the seal of the United States was affixed to it; but the commission has never reached the person for whom it was made out.

In order to determine whether he is entitled to this commission, it becomes necessary to enquire whether he has been appointed to the office. For if he has been appointed, the law continues him in office for five years, and he is entitled to the possession of those evidences of office, which, being completed, became his property.

The 2d section of the 2d article of the constitution, declares, that, "the president shall nominate, and, by and with the advice and consent of the senate, shall appoint ambassadors, other public ministers and consuls, and all other officers of the United States, whose appointments are not otherwise provided for."

The third section declares, that "he shall commission all the officers of the United States." . . .

It is therefore decidedly the opinion of the court, that when a commission has been signed by the President, the appointment is made; and that the commission is complete, when the seal of the United States has been affixed to it by the secretary of state....

To withhold his commission, therefore, is an act deemed by the court not warranted by law, but violative of a vested legal right.

This brings us to the second enquiry; which is,

2dly. If he has a right, and that right has been violated, do the laws of his country afford him a remedy?

The very essence of civil liberty certainly consists in the right of every individual to claim the protection of the laws, whenever he receives an injury. One of the first duties of government is to afford that protection. In Great Britain the king himself is sued in the respectful form of a petition, and he never fails to comply with the judgment of his court....

The government of the United States has been emphatically termed a government of laws, and not of men. It will certainly cease to deserve this high appellation, if the laws furnish no remedy for the violation of a vested legal right.

If this obloquy is to be cast on the jurisprudence of our country, it must arise from the peculiar character of the case....

It follows then that the question, whether the legality of an act of the head of a department be examinable in a court of justice or not, must always depend on the nature of that act....

By the constitution of the United States, the President is invested with certain important political powers, in the exercise of which he is to use his own discretion, and is accountable only to his country in his political character, and to his own conscience. To aid him in the performance of these duties, he is authorized to appoint certain officers, who act by his authority and in conformity with his orders.

In such cases, their acts are his acts; and whatever opinion may be entertained of the manner in which executive discretion may be used, still there exists, and can exist, no power to control that discretion. The subjects are political. They respect the nation, not individual rights, and being entrusted to the executive, the decision of the executive is conclusive. The application of this remark will be perceived by adverting to the act of congress for establishing the department of foreign affairs. This officer, as his duties were prescribed by that act, is to conform precisely to the will of the President. He is the mere organ by whom that will is communicated. The acts of such an officer, as an officer, can never be examinable by the courts.

But when the legislature proceeds to impose on that officer other duties; when he is directed peremptorily to perform certain acts; when the rights of individuals are dependent on the performance of those acts; he is so far the officer of the law; is amenable to the laws for his conduct; and cannot at his discretion sport away the vested rights of others.

The conclusion from this reasoning is, that where the heads of departments are the political or confidential agents of the executive, merely to execute the will of the President, or rather to act in cases in which the executive possesses a constitutional or legal discretion nothing can be more perfectly clear than that their acts are only politically examinable. But where a specific duty is assigned by law, and individual rights depend upon the performance of that duty, it seems equally clear that the individual who considers himself injured, has a right to resort to the laws of his country for a remedy....

It remains to be enquired whether,

3dly. He is entitled to the remedy for which he applies. This depends on,

1st. The nature of the writ applied for, and,

2dly. The power of this court.

1st. The nature of the writ. . . .

This writ, if awarded, would be directed to an officer of government, and its mandate to him would be, to use the words of Blackstone, "to do a particular thing therein specified, which appertains to his office and duty and which the court has previously determined, or at least supposes, to be consonant to right and justice." Or, in the words of Lord Mansfield, the applicant, in this case, has a right to execute an office of public concern, and is kept out of possession of that right.

These circumstances certainly concur in this case.

Still, to render the mandamus a proper remedy, the officer to whom it is to be directed, must be one to whom, on legal principles, such writ may be directed; and the person applying for it must be without any other specific and legal remedy.

1st. With respect to the officer to whom it would be directed. The intimate political relation, subsisting between the president of the United States and the heads of departments, necessarily renders any legal investigation of the acts of one of those high officers peculiarly irksome, as well as delicate; and excites some hesitation with respect to the propriety of entering into such investigation. Impressions are often received without much reflection or examination, and it is not wonderful that in such a case as this, the assertion, by an individual, of his legal claims in a court of justice, to which claims it is the duty of that court to attend; should at first view be considered by some, as an attempt to intrude into the cabinet, and to intermeddle with the prerogatives of the executive.

It is scarcely necessary for the court to disclaim all pretensions to such a jurisdiction. An extravagance, so absurd and excessive, could not have been entertained for a moment. The province of the court is, solely, to decide on the rights of individuals, not to enquire how the executive, or executive officers, perform duties in which they have a discretion. Questions, in their nature political, or which are, by the constitution and laws, submitted to the executive, can never be made in this court.

But, if this be not such a question; if so far from being an intrusion into the secrets of the cabinet, it respects a paper, which according to law, is upon record, and to a copy of which the law gives a right, on the payment of ten cents; if it be no intermeddling with a subject, over which the executive can be considered as having exercised any control; what is there in the exalted station of the officer, which shall bar a citizen from asserting, in a court of justice, his legal rights, or shall forbid a court to listen to the claim; or to issue a mandamus, directing the performance of a duty, not depending on executive discretion, but on particular acts of congress and the general principles of law?
. . .

This, then, is a plain case for a mandamus, either to deliver the commission, or a copy of it from the record; and it only remains to be enquired,

Whether it can issue from this court.

The act to establish the judicial courts of the United States authorizes the supreme court "to issue writs of mandamus, in cases warranted by the principles and usages of law, to any courts appointed, or persons holding office, under the authority of the United States."[b]

The secretary of the state, being a person holding an office under the authority of the United States, is precisely within the letter of the description; and if this court is not authorized to issue a writ of mandamus to such an officer, it must be because the law is unconstitutional, and therefore absolutely incapable of conferring the authority, and assigning the duties which its words purport to confer and assign.

The constitution vests the whole judicial power of the United States in one supreme court, and such inferior courts as congress shall, from time to time, ordain and establish. This power is expressly extended to all cases arising under the laws of the United States; and consequently, in some form, may be exercised over the present case; because the right claimed is given by a law of the United States.

In the distribution of this power it is declared that "the supreme court shall have original jurisdiction in all cases affecting ambassadors, other public ministers and consuls, and those in which a state shall be a party. In all other cases, the supreme court shall have appellate jurisdiction."

It has been insisted, at the bar, that as the original grant of jurisdiction to the supreme and inferior courts, is general, and the clause, assigning original jurisdiction to the supreme court, contains no negative or restrictive words; the power remains to the legislature, to assign original jurisdiction to that court in other cases than those specified in the article which has been recited; provided those cases belong to the judicial power of the United States.

If it had been intended to leave it in the discretion of the legislature to apportion the judicial power between the supreme and inferior courts according to the will of that body, it would certainly have been useless to have proceeded further than to have defined the judicial power, and the tribunals in which it should be vested. The subsequent part of the section is mere surplusage, is entirely without meaning, if such is to be the construction. If congress remains at liberty to give this court appellate jurisdiction, where the constitution has declared their jurisdiction shall be original; and original jurisdiction where the constitution has declared it shall be appellate; the distribution of jurisdiction, made in the constitution, is form without substance.

Affirmative words are often, in their operation, negative of other objects than those affirmed; and in this case a negative or exclusive sense must be given to them or they have no operation at all.

It cannot be presumed that any clause in the constitution is intended to be without effect; and therefore such a construction is inadmissible, unless the words require it.

If the solicitude of the convention, respecting our peace with foreign powers, induced a provision that the supreme court should take original jurisdiction in cases which might be supposed to affect them; yet the clause would have proceeded no further than to provide for such cases, if no further restriction on the powers of congress had been intended. That they should have

---

[b] The full sentence, a part of Section 13 of the Judiciary Act of 1789, read: "The Supreme Court shall also have appellate jurisdiction from the circuit courts and courts of the several states, in the cases herein after specially provided for; and shall have power to issue writs of prohibition to the district courts, when proceeding as courts of admiralty and maritime jurisdiction, and writs of mandamus, in cases warranted by the principles and usages of law, to any courts appointed, or persons holding office, under the authority of the United States."

appellate jurisdiction in all other cases, with such exceptions as congress might make, is no restriction; unless the words be deemed exclusive of original jurisdiction....

To enable this court then to issue a mandamus, it must be shewn to be an exercise of appellate jurisdiction, or to be necessary to enable them to exercise appellate jurisdiction.

It has been stated at the bar that the appellate jurisdiction may be exercised in a variety of forms, and that if it be the will of the legislature that a mandamus, should be used for that purpose, that will must be obeyed. This is true, yet the jurisdiction must be appellate, not original.

It is the essential criterion of appellate jurisdiction, that it revises and corrects the proceedings in a cause already instituted, and does not create that cause. Although, therefore, a mandamus may be directed to courts, yet to issue such a writ to an officer for the delivery of a paper, is in effect the same as to sustain an original action for that paper, and therefore seems not to belong to appellate, but to original jurisdiction. Neither is it necessary in such a case as this, to enable the court to exercise its appellate jurisdiction.

The authority, therefore, given to the supreme court by the act establishing the judicial courts of the United States, to issue writs of mandamus to public officers, appears not to be warranted by the constitution; and it becomes necessary to enquire whether a jurisdiction, so conferred, can be exercised.

The question, whether an act, repugnant to the constitution, can become the law of the land, is a question deeply interesting to the United States; but, happily, not of an intricacy proportioned to its interest. It seems only necessary to recognize certain principles, supposed to have been long and well established, to decide it.

That the people have an original right to establish, for their future government, such principles as, in their opinion, shall most conduce to their own happiness, is the basis, on which the whole American fabric has been erected. The exercise of this original right is a very great exertion; nor can it, nor ought it to be frequently repeated. The principles, therefore, so established, are deemed fundamental. And as the authority, from which they proceed, is supreme, and can seldom act, they are designed to be permanent.

This original and supreme will organizes the government, and assigns, to different departments, their respective powers. It may either stop here; or establish certain limits not to be transcended by those departments.

The government of the United States is of the latter description. The powers of the legislature are defined, and limited; and that those limits may not be mistaken, or forgotten, the constitution is written. To what purpose are powers limited, and to what purpose is that limitation committed to writing, if these limits may, at any time, be passed by those intended to be restrained? The distinction, between a government with limited and unlimited powers, is abolished, if those limits do not confine the persons on whom they are imposed, and if acts prohibited and acts allowed, are of equal obligation. It is a proposition too plain to be contested, that the constitution controls any legislative act repugnant to it; or, that the legislature may alter the constitution by an ordinary act.

Between these alternatives there is no middle ground. The constitution is either a superior, paramount law, unchangeable by ordinary means, or it is on a level with ordinary legislative acts, and like other acts, is alterable when the legislature shall please to alter it.

If the former part of the alternative be true, then a legislative act contrary to the constitution is not law: if the latter part be true, then written constitutions are absurd attempts, on the part of the people, to limit a power, in its own nature illimitable.

Certainly all those who have framed written constitutions contemplate them as forming the fundamental and paramount law of the nation, and consequently the theory of every such government must be, that an act of the legislature, repugnant to the constitution, is void.

This theory is essentially attached to a written constitution, and is consequently to be considered, by this court, as one of the fundamental principles of our society. It is not therefore to be lost sight of in the further consideration of this subject.

If an act of the legislature, repugnant to the constitution, is void, does it, notwithstanding its invalidity, bind the courts, and oblige them to give it effect? Or, in other words, though it be not law, does it constitute a rule as operative as if it was a law? This would be to overthrow in fact what was established in theory; and would seem, at first view, an absurdity too gross to be insisted on. It shall, however, receive a more attentive consideration.

It is emphatically the province and duty of the judicial department to say what the law is. Those who apply the rule to particular cases, must of necessity expound and interpret that rule. If two laws conflict with each other, the courts must decide on the operation of each.

So if a law be in opposition to the constitution; if both the law and the constitution apply to a particular case, so that the court must either decide that case conformably to the law disregarding the constitution, or conformably to the constitution disregarding the law; the court must determine which of these conflicting rules governs the case. This is of the very essence of judicial duty.

If then the courts are to regard the constitution, and the constitution is superior to any ordinary act of the legislature, the constitution, and not such ordinary act, must govern the case to which they both apply.

Those then who controvert the principle that the constitution is to be considered, in court, as a paramount law, are reduced to the necessity of maintaining that courts must close their eyes on the constitution, and see only the law.

This doctrine would subvert the very foundation of all written constitutions. It would declare that an act, which, according to the principles and theory of our government, is entirely void, is yet, in practice, completely obligatory. It would declare, that if the legislature shall do what is expressly forbidden, such act, notwithstanding the express prohibition, is in reality effectual. It would be giving to the legislature a practical and real omnipotence, with the same breath which professes to restrict their powers within narrow limits. It is prescribing limits, and declaring that those limits may be passed at pleasure.

That it thus reduces to nothing what we have deemed the greatest improvement on political institutions—a written constitution—would of itself be sufficient, in America, where written constitutions have been viewed with so much reverence, for rejecting the construction. But the peculiar expressions of the constitution of the United States furnish additional arguments in favour of its rejection.

The judicial power of the United States is extended to all cases arising under the constitution.

Could it be the intention of those who gave this power, to say that, in using it, the constitution should not be looked into? That a case arising under the constitution should be decided without examining the instrument under which it arises?

This is too extravagant to be maintained.

In some cases then, the constitution must be looked into by the judges. And if they can open it at all, what part of it are they forbidden to read, or to obey?

There are many other parts of the constitution which serve to illustrate this subject.

It is declared that "no tax or duty shall be laid on articles exported from any state." Suppose a duty on the export of cotton, of tobacco or of flour; and a suit instituted to recover it. Ought judgment to be rendered in such a case? ought the judges to close their eyes on the constitution, and only see the law?

The constitution declares that "no bill of attainder or *ex post facto* law shall be passed."

If, however such a bill should be passed and a person should be prosecuted under it; must the court condemn to death those victims whom the constitution endeavours to preserve?

"No person," says the constitution, "shall be convicted of treason unless on the testimony of two witnesses to the same overt act, or on confession in open court."

Here the language of the constitution is addressed especially to the courts. It prescribes, directly for them, a rule of evidence not to be departed from. If the legislature should change that rule, and declare one witness, or a confession out of court, sufficient for conviction, must the constitutional principle yield to the legislative act?

From these, and many other selections which might be made, it is apparent, that the framers of the constitution contemplated that instrument, as a rule for the government of courts, as well as of the legislature.

Why otherwise does it direct the judges to take an oath to support it? This oath certainly applies, in an especial manner, to their conduct in their official character. How immoral to impose it on them, if they were to be used as the instruments, and the knowing instruments, for violating what they swear to support.

The oath of office, too, imposed by the legislature, is completely demonstrative of the legislative opinion on this subject. It is in these words, "I do solemnly swear, that I will administer justice without respect to persons, and do equal right to the poor and to the rich; and that I will faithfully and impartially discharge all the duties incumbent on me as _____ according to the best of my abilities and understanding, agreeably to the constitution, and laws of the United States."

Why does a judge swear to discharge his duties agreeably to the constitution of the United States, if that constitution forms no rule for his government? if it is closed upon him, and cannot be inspected by him?

If such be the real state of things, this is worse than solemn mockery. To prescribe, or to take this oath, becomes equally a crime.

It is also not entirely unworthy of observation, that in declaring what shall be the supreme law of the land, the constitution itself is first mentioned; and not the laws of the United States generally, but those only which shall be made in pursuance of the constitution, have that rank.

Thus, the particular phraseology of the constitution of the United States confirms and strengthens the principle, supposed to be essential to all written constitutions, that a law repugnant to the constitution is void; and that courts, as well as other departments, are bound by that instrument.

The rule must be discharged.[c]

LEGITIMACY OF JUDICIAL REVIEW: SOME COMMENTS

(1) Gibson, J., dissenting, in Eakin v. Raub, 12 S. & R. 330, 344–358 (Pa.1825) considered the question of the legitimacy of judicial review of the constitutionality of legislation. The following excerpts will illustrate the course of his argument:

"The constitution and the *right* of the legislature to pass the act, may be in collision; but is that a legitimate subject for judicial determination? If it be, the judiciary must be a peculiar organ, to revise the proceedings of the legislature, and to correct its mistakes; and in what part of the constitution are we to look for this proud preeminence? Viewing the matter in the opposite direction, what would be thought of an act of assembly in which it should be declared that the supreme court had in a particular case, put a wrong construction on the constitution of the *United States,* and that the judgment should therefore be reversed? It would, doubtless, be thought a usurpation of judicial power. But it is by no means clear, that to declare a law void, which has been enacted according to the forms prescribed in the constitution, is not a usurpation of legislative power. It is an act of sovereignty; and sovereignty and legislative power are said by Sir William *Blackstone* to be convertible terms. It is the business of the judiciary, to interpret the laws, not scan the authority of the lawgiver; and without the latter, it cannot take cognisance of a collision between a law and the constitution. So that, to affirm that the judiciary has a right to judge of the existence of such collision, is to take for granted the very thing to be proved; and that a very cogent argument may be made in this way, I am not disposed to deny; for no conclusions are so strong as those that are drawn from the *petitio principii*. . . .

"But the judges are sworn to support the constitution, and are they not bound by it as the law of the land? In some respects they are. In the very few cases in which the judiciary, and not the legislature, is the immediate organ to execute its provisions, they are bound by it, in preference to any act of assembly to the contrary; in such cases, the constitution is a rule to the courts. But what I have in view in this inquiry, is, the supposed right of the judiciary, to interfere, in cases where the constitution is to be carried into effect through the instrumentality of the legislature, and where that organ must necessarily first decide on the constitutionality of its own act. The oath to support the constitution is not peculiar to the judges, but is taken indiscriminately by every officer of the government, and is designed rather as a test of the political

---

[c] During the tenure of Marshall as Chief Justice, the only other case holding an Act of Congress unconstitutional was the obscure decision in Hodgson v. Bowerbank, 9 U.S. (5 Cranch) 303 (1809). In a brief opinion, Marshall held a provision of the Judiciary Act of 1789 unconstitutional in conferring jurisdiction on federal courts to try suits between aliens. (For a strong argument that Marshall interpreted the statute and did not declare it to be unconstitutional, see Mahoney, *A Historical Note on Hodgson v. Bowerbank,* 49 U.Chi.L.Rev. 725 (1982)). The next Act of Congress to be declared unconstitutional was the Missouri Compromise in Dred Scott v. Sandford, 60 U.S. (19 How.) 393 (1857), overruled by the Civil War. The first Act of Congress of general applicability to be declared unconstitutional was the Legal Tender Act in Hepburn v. Griswold, 75 U.S. (8 Wall.) 603 (1870). This decision was promptly overruled by the Court itself in Knox v. Lee, 79 U.S. (12 Wall.) 457 (1871).

principles of the man, than to bind the officer in the discharge of his duty: otherwise, it were difficult to determine, what operation it is to have in the case of a recorder of deeds, for instance, who in the execution of his office, has nothing to do with the constitution. But granting it to relate to the official conduct of the judge, as well as every other officer, and not to his political principles, still, it must be understood in reference to supporting the constitution, *only as far as that may be involved in his official duty;* and consequently, if his official duty does not comprehend an inquiry into the authority of the legislature, neither does his oath.

"It is worthy of remark here, that the foundation of every argument in favor of the right of the judiciary, is found, at last, to be an assumption of the whole ground in dispute. Granting that the object of the oath is to secure a support of the constitution in the discharge of official duty, its terms may be satisfied by restraining it to official duty in the exercise of the *ordinary* judicial powers. Thus, the constitution may furnish a rule of construction, where a particular interpretation of a law would conflict with some constitutional principle; and such interpretation, where it may, is always to be avoided. But the oath was more probably designed to secure the powers of each of the different branches from being usurped by any of the rest; for instance, to prevent the house of representatives from erecting itself into a court of judicature, or the supreme court from attempting to control the legislature; and in this view, the oath furnishes an argument equally plausible *against* the right of the judiciary. But if it require a support of the constitution in anything beside official duty, it is, in fact, an oath of allegiance to a particular form of government; and considered as such, it is not easy to see, why it should not be taken by the citizens at large, as well as by the officers of the government. It has never been thought, that an officer is under greater restraint as to measures which have for their avowed end a total change of the constitution, than a citizen who has taken no oath at all. The official oath, then, relates only to the official conduct of the officer, and does not prove that he ought to stray from the path of his ordinary business, to search for violations of duty in the business of others; nor does it, as supposed, define the powers of the officer.

"But do not the judges do a *positive* act in violation of the constitution, when they give effect to an unconstitutional law? Not if the law has been passed according to the forms established in the constitution. The fallacy of the question is, in supposing that the judiciary adopts the acts of the legislature as its own; whereas, the enactment of a law and the interpretation of it are not concurrent acts, and as the judiciary is not required to concur in the enactment, neither is it in the breach of the constitution which may be the consequence of the enactment; the fault is imputable to the legislature, and on it the responsibility exclusively rests. . . . "

For a modern assessment see Murray, *Chief Justice Gibson of the Pennsylvania Supreme Court and Judicial Review,* 32 U.Pitt.L.R. 127 (1970).

(2) Abraham Lincoln, First Inaugural Address, March 4, 1861, in 4 Basler, *The Collected Works of Abraham Lincoln* 262, 268 (1953): "I do not forget the position assumed by some, that constitutional questions are to be decided by the Supreme Court; nor do I deny that such decisions must be binding in any case, upon the parties to a suit, as to the object of that suit, while they are also entitled to very high respect and consideration, in all parallel cases by all other departments of the government. And while it is obviously possible that such decision may be erroneous in any given case, still the evil effect following it, being limited to that particular case, with the chance that it may be overruled and never become a precedent for other cases, can better be borne than could

the evils of a different practice. At the same time the candid citizen must confess that if the policy of the government upon vital questions affecting the whole people, is to be irrevocably fixed by decisions of the Supreme Court, the instant they are made, in ordinary litigation between parties in personal actions, the people will have ceased, to be their own rulers, having, to that extent, practically resigned their government, into the hands of that eminent tribunal. Nor is there, in this view, any assault upon the court, or the judges. It is a duty, from which they may not shrink, to decide cases properly brought before them; and it is no fault of theirs if others seek to turn their decisions to political purposes.''

(3) In Cooper v. Aaron, 358 U.S. 1, 17 (1958) the Court made the following statements in answer to an argument that the Governor and the Legislature of Arkansas were not bound by the holding of the Court in the case of Brown v. Board of Educ., 347 U.S. 483 (1954):

"It is necessary only to recall some basic constitutional propositions which are settled doctrine.

"Article VI of the Constitution makes the Constitution the 'supreme Law of the Land'. In 1803, Chief Justice Marshall, speaking for a unanimous Court, referring to the Constitution as 'the fundamental and paramount law of the nation,' declared in the notable case of Marbury v. Madison, 1 Cranch 137, 177, that 'It is emphatically the province and duty of the judicial department to say what the law is.' This decision declared the basic principle that the federal judiciary is supreme in the exposition of the law of the Constitution, and that principle has ever since been respected by this Court and the Country as a permanent and indispensable feature of our constitutional system. It follows that the interpretation of the Fourteenth Amendment enunciated by this Court in the *Brown* case is the supreme law of the land, and Art. VI of the Constitution makes it of binding effect on the States 'any Thing in the Constitution or Laws of any State to the Contrary notwithstanding.' ''

(4) For more than a century after *Marbury v. Madison,* judicial review of legislation was largely an American phenomenon. The Twentieth Century, particularly the years following World War II, has seen an explosion of the concept both on the national and international levels. A comparison of judicial review in the United States and in Western Europe is particularly instructive. Austria, Italy and Germany have specialized constitutional courts to determine the constitutional validity of legislation. Ordinary courts cannot decide whether laws are constitutional or not, although they can refer those questions for decision to the constitutional courts. This system of "centralized" judicial review is often contrasted with the "decentralized" system represented by *Marbury v. Madison.* Nearly all of the decisions in this volume are by the Supreme Court of the United States, and most attention centers on the function of judicial review as performed by that court. The theory of *Marbury,* however, requires every court, even the most inferior, to decide whether laws are constitutional. Does it also require that executive officials determine whether their official actions are consistent with the Constitution? Compare the view of President Lincoln, in note 2 above, with that of the Court in *Cooper v. Aaron,* note 3. For an analysis and description of judicial review systems outside the United States, see Cappelletti and Cohen, *Comparative Constitutional Law: Cases and Materials* 1–196 (1979).

(5) The dispute over the legitimacy of judicial review of legislation has long raged among legal scholars. However, Bator, Meltzer, Mishkin and Shapiro, *Hart and Wechsler's The Federal Courts and the Federal System* 9 (3d ed. 1988) [hereinafter cited as Hart and Wechsler, *Federal Courts* (3d ed. 1988)], after a

modern reappraisal of the dispute conclude: "The grant of judicial power was to include the power, where necessary in the decision of cases, to disregard state or federal statutes found to be unconstitutional. Despite the curiously persisting myth of usurpation, the Convention's understanding on this point emerged from its records with singular clarity." See also Wechsler, *Principles, Politics, and Fundamental Law* 4 (1961): "Let me begin by saying that I have not the slightest doubt respecting the legitimacy of judicial review, whether the action called in question in a case which otherwise is proper for adjudication is legislative or executive, federal or state."

(6) For discussions of the role of the Supreme Court in judicial review, consult Bickel, *The Least Dangerous Branch—The Supreme Court at the Bar of Politics* (1962); Bickel, *The Supreme Court and the Idea of Progress* (1970); Gunther, *The Subtle Vices of the "Passive Virtues"—A Comment on Principle and Expediency in Judicial Review*, 64 Colum.L.Rev. 1 (1964); Tribe, *American Constitutional Law* (2d ed. 1988); Ely, *Democracy and Distrust: A Theory of Judicial Review* (1980); Choper, *Judicial Review and the National Political Process* (1980); Tushnet, *Red, White, and Blue: A Critical Analysis of Constitutional Law* (1988).

Students interested in the general historical background of judicial review should examine, in addition to the works cited above, 1 *Selected Essays on Constitutional Law* 1–173 (1938), hereinafter cited as *Selected Essays* (1938).

PROSPECTIVE AND RETROACTIVE CONSTITUTIONAL DECISIONS

The theory of judicial review expounded in *Marbury v. Madison,* coupled with the orthodox theory of the declaratory nature of judicial decision making, requires that new constitutional decisions be applied to govern conduct that preceded the decisions. In a significant number of cases beginning in 1965, however, the Supreme Court applied newly announced constitutional rules governing criminal procedure prospectively only, to avoid wholesale release of prisoners whose convictions violated the new rule. Linkletter v. Walker, 381 U.S. 618 (1965) (rule requiring exclusion of illegally seized evidence, established by Mapp v. Ohio, 367 U.S. 643 (1961), is inapplicable to convictions challenged on collateral review). The standards for measuring prospective and retroactive application became increasingly controversial, as the court declined to apply new constitutional criminal procedure rules, even in cases on direct appeal, to events that preceded the decision. E.g., Desist v. United States, 394 U.S. 244 (1969) (new interpretation of fourth amendment applicable only to police activity that occurred after the date of the decision). In a dissenting opinion, Justice Harlan argued that increasing use of the technique of prospective constitutional adjudication was inconsistent with the premises of judicial review.

"If we do not resolve all cases before us on direct review in light of our best understanding of constitutional principles, it is difficult to see why we should adjudicate any case at all. . . . In truth, the Court's assertion of power to disregard current law in adjudicating cases before us that have not already run the full course of appellate review, is quite simply an assertion that our constitutional function is not one of adjudication but in effect of legislation." Mackey v. United States, 401 U.S. 667, 675, 691 (1971) (Harlan, J., dissenting).

In Griffith v. Kentucky, 479 U.S. 314 (1987), citing Justice Harlan, the Court decided that all new rules for the conduct of criminal prosecutions would be applied to all cases pending on direct review, with no exceptions.[1]

> "Unlike a legislature, we do not promulgate new rules of constitutional criminal procedure on a broad basis. Rather, the nature of judicial review requires that we adjudicate specific cases, and each case usually becomes the vehicle for announcement of a new rule. But after we have decided a new rule in the cases selected, the integrity of judicial review requires that we apply that rule to all similar cases pending on direct review."

In Harper v. Virginia Department of Taxation, 509 U.S. 86 (1993), the Court held that the *Griffith* principle was fully applicable to civil cases.

SECTION 2.   CONGRESSIONAL CONTROL OF JUDICIAL REVIEW BY THE FEDERAL COURTS

THE SCOPE OF CONGRESSIONAL POWER OVER THE JURISDICTION OF LOWER FEDERAL COURTS

While Article III of the Constitution created the Supreme Court, it deliberately gave Congress the option to create "such inferior Courts as the Congress may from time to time ordain and establish." Since inferior federal courts, in theory, exist at the pleasure of Congress, it has always been clear that Article III does not require that any single lower federal court exercise all, or any particular part, of the judicial power described by that Article. Indeed, the current general jurisdiction of the inferior federal courts in civil cases arising under federal law was not conferred until after the Civil War. What has been an issue, however, is whether all of the judicial power must be lodged somewhere in the federal judicial system—either originally in a lower federal court, or on appeal of state court decisions to the Supreme Court.

Justice Story, in dicta in Martin v. Hunter's Lessee, 14 U.S. (1 Wheat.) 304 (1816), stressed the mandatory language of Article III ("The judicial power of the United States shall be vested...." "The judicial power shall extend....") He concluded that Congress had an obligation to vest the entire judicial power somewhere within the federal judicial system. Later, in his writings, he argued that any contrary conclusion would mean that "the judiciary, as a co-ordinate department of the government, may, at the will of Congress, be annihilated, or stripped of all its important jurisdiction." 2 *Commentaries on the Constitution of the United States* 395 (4th ed. 1873). Story's position was authoritatively rejected in Sheldon v. Sill, 49 U.S. (8 How.) 441 (1850). In upholding a restriction on the diversity jurisdiction, the Court concluded that since Congress had the option to create inferior federal courts it also had the power to create them as courts of limited jurisdiction. "[H]aving a right to prescribe, Congress may withhold from any court of its creation jurisdiction of any of the enumerated controversies. Courts created by statute can have no jurisdiction but such as the statute confers." Id. at 449. Notice that the Supreme Court,

---

[1] The Court in *Griffith* did not resolve the question whether new constitutional decisions would be applied to state criminal convictions that had become final, but were challenged collaterally through the federal writ of habeas corpus. Teague v. Lane, 489 U.S. 288 (1989), held that new rules would not be applied in cases on collateral review. For cases dealing with the issue of what is a "new" rule for this purpose, see Penry v. Lynaugh, 492 U.S. 302 (1989); Butler v. McKellar, 494 U.S. 407 (1990); Graham v. Collins, 506 U.S. 461 (1993).

which was created by the Constitution, has never had power to review state court decisions on the basis that the parties are of diverse citizenship. The result in Sheldon v. Sill was thus to deny all federal courts a portion of the judicial power. If Congress must create a supreme court, must Congress vest in that Court the judicial power not lodged somewhere else in the federal judicial system?

Ex Parte McCardle

74 U.S. (7 Wall.) 506, 19 L.Ed. 264 (1868).

Appeal from the Circuit Court for the Southern District of Mississippi.

The case was this:

The Constitution of the United States ordains as follows:

"§ 1. The judicial power of the United States shall be vested *in one Supreme Court,* and in such inferior courts as the Congress may from time to time ordain and establish."

"§ 2. The judicial power shall extend to all cases in law or equity arising *under this Constitution, the laws of the United States,* " & c.

And in these last cases the Constitution ordains that,

"The Supreme Court shall have appellate jurisdiction, both as to law and fact, *with such exceptions, and under such regulations, as the Congress shall make.*"

With these constitutional provisions in existence, Congress, on the 5th February, 1867, by "An act to amend an act to establish the judicial courts of the United States, approved September 24, 1789," provided that the several courts of the United States, and the several justices and judges of such courts, within their respective jurisdiction, in addition to the authority already conferred by law, should have power to grant writs of *habeas corpus* in all cases where any person may be restrained of his or her liberty in violation of the Constitution, or of any treaty or law of the United States. And that, from the final decision of any judge, justice, or court inferior to the Circuit Court, appeal might be taken to the Circuit Court of the United States for the district in which the cause was heard, and *from the judgment of the said Circuit Court to the Supreme Court of the United States.*

This statute being in force, one McCardle, alleging unlawful restraint by military force, preferred a petition in the court below, for the writ of *habeas corpus.*

The writ was issued, and a return was made by the military commander, admitting the restraint, but denying that it was unlawful.

It appeared that the petitioner was not in the military service of the United States, but was held in custody by military authority for trial before a military commission, upon charges founded upon the publication of articles alleged to be incendiary and libellous, in a newspaper of which he was editor. The custody was alleged to be under the authority of certain acts of Congress.

Upon the hearing, the petitioner was remanded to the military custody; but, upon his prayer, an appeal was allowed him to this court, and upon filing the usual appeal-bond, for costs, he was admitted to bail upon recognizance, with sureties, conditioned for his future appearance in the Circuit Court, to abide by and perform the final judgment of this court. The appeal was taken under the above-mentioned act of February 5, 1867.

A motion to dismiss this appeal was made at the last term, and, after argument, was denied.

Subsequently, on the 2d, 3d, 4th, and 9th March, the case was argued very thoroughly and ably upon the merits, and was taken under advisement. While it was thus held, and before conference in regard to the decision proper to be made, an act was passed by Congress, returned with objections by the President, and, on the 27th March, repassed by the constitutional majority, the second section of which was as follows:

"*And be it further enacted,* That so much of the act approved February 5, 1867, entitled 'An act to amend an act to establish the judicial courts of the United States, approved September 24, 1789', as authorized an appeal from the judgment of the Circuit Court to the Supreme Court of the United States, or the exercise of any such jurisdiction by said Supreme Court, on appeals which have been, or may hereafter be taken, be, and the same is hereby repealed."

The attention of the court was directed to this statute at the last term, but counsel having expressed a desire to be heard in argument upon its effect, and the Chief Justice being detained from his place here, by his duties in the Court of Impeachment, the cause was continued under advisement. Argument was now heard upon the effect of the repealing act. . . .

The Chief Justice delivered the opinion of the Court.

The first question necessarily is that of jurisdiction; for, if the act of March, 1868, takes away the jurisdiction defined by the act of February, 1867, it is useless, if not improper, to enter into any discussion of other questions.

It is quite true, as was argued by the counsel for the petitioner, that the appellate jurisdiction of this court is not derived from acts of Congress. It is strictly speaking, conferred by the Constitution. But it is conferred "with such exceptions and under such regulations as Congress shall make."

It is unnecessary to consider whether, if Congress had made no exceptions and no regulations, this court might not have exercised general appellate jurisdiction under rules prescribed by itself. For among the earliest acts of the first Congress, at its first session, was the act of September 24th, 1789, to establish the judicial courts of the United States. That act provided for the organization of this court, and prescribed regulations for the exercise of its jurisdiction.

The source of that jurisdiction, and the limitations of it by the Constitution and by statute, have been on several occasions subjects of consideration here. In the case of Durousseau v. The United States [6 Cranch 307 (1810)], particularly, the whole matter was carefully examined, and the court held, that while "the appellate powers of this court are not given by the judicial act, but are given by the Constitution," they are, nevertheless, "limited and regulated by that act, and by such other acts as have been passed on the subject." The court said, further, that the judicial act was an exercise of the power given by the Constitution to Congress "of making exceptions to the appellate jurisdiction of the Supreme Court." "They have described affirmatively," said the court, "its jurisdiction, and this affirmative description has been understood to imply a negation of the exercise of such appellate power as is not comprehended within it."

The principle that the affirmation of appellate jurisdiction implies the negation of all such jurisdiction not affirmed having been thus established, it was an almost necessary consequence that acts of Congress, providing for the exercise of jurisdiction, should come to be spoken of as acts granting jurisdiction, and not as acts making exceptions to the constitutional grant of it.

The exception to appellate jurisdiction in the case before us, however, is not an inference from the affirmation of other appellate jurisdiction. It is made in terms. The provision of the act of 1867, affirming the appellate jurisdiction of this court in cases of *habeas corpus* is expressly repealed. It is hardly possible to imagine a plainer instance of positive exception.

We are not at liberty to inquire into the motives of the legislature. We can only examine into its power under the Constitution; and the power to make exceptions to the appellate jurisdiction of this court is given by express words.

What, then, is the effect of the repealing act upon the case before us? We cannot doubt as to this. Without jurisdiction the court cannot proceed at all in any cause. Jurisdiction is power to declare the law, and when it ceases to exist, the only function remaining to the court is that of announcing the fact and dismissing the cause. And this is not less clear upon authority than upon principle.

. . .

It is quite clear, therefore, that this court cannot proceed to pronounce judgment in this case, for it has no longer jurisdiction of the appeal; and judicial duty is not less fitly performed by declining ungranted jurisdiction than in exercising firmly that which the Constitution and the laws confer.

Counsel seem to have supposed, if effect be given to the repealing act in question, that the whole appellate power of the court, in cases of *habeas corpus,* is denied. But this is an error. The act of 1868 does not except from that jurisdiction any cases but appeals from Circuit Courts under the act of 1867. It does not affect the jurisdiction which was previously exercised.

The appeal of the petitioner in this case must be dismissed for want of jurisdiction.

UNITED STATES v. KLEIN, 80 U.S. (13 Wall.) 128 (1872). An 1863 statute provided for seizure and sale of captured or abandoned property in areas of rebellion, and for payment of the proceeds into the United States treasury. The statute further provided that loyal owners, upon proof that they had not given aid or comfort to the rebellion, could recover those proceeds by suit in the court of claims. In United States v. Padelford, 76 U.S. (9 Wall.) 531 (1870), the statute was construed to permit recovery by a claimant who had not been loyal in fact, but who had been given a Presidential pardon. Radical Republicans in Congress were outraged with the Court's decision permitting recovery by participants in the rebellion. Congress promptly passed a statute providing that a claimant under the 1863 Act could not prove loyalty through a presidential pardon. Indeed, a pardon was proof that the claimant had given aid to the rebellion. This 1870 statute provided further that, upon proof of a pardon in either the court of claims or the Supreme Court, "the court shall forthwith dismiss the suit of such claimant." Klein's case was similar to Padelford's. At the time the 1870 Act was passed, the court of claims had given judgment for the claimant, and the government's appeal was pending in the United States Supreme Court. The government moved in the Supreme Court that Klein's suit be dismissed under the Act. The Supreme Court denied the motion, and affirmed the judgment of the court of claims.

Chief Justice Chase's opinion concluded that the 1870 statute was unconstitutional in two respects—in prescribing how a court should decide an issue of fact, and in denying effect to a Presidential pardon. Since the law was unconstitutional, the Court could not constitutionally be required to dismiss Klein's case. "We must think that Congress has inadvertently passed the limit which separates the legislative from the judicial power.... Congress has already provided that the Supreme Court shall have jurisdiction of the judgments of the Court of Claims on appeal. Can it prescribe a rule in conformity with which the court must deny to itself its jurisdiction thus conferred, because and only because the decision, in accordance with settled law, must be adverse to the government and favorable to the suitor?''

THE SCOPE OF CONGRESSIONAL POWER OVER SUPREME COURT JURISDICTION UNDER THE EXCEPTIONS CLAUSE

(1) For full accounts of the background of the *McCardle* case see Fairman, 433–514, and 2 Warren, *Supreme Court in United States History* 464–484 (Rev. ed. 1926).

(2) In his plurality opinion in Glidden v. Zdanok, 370 U.S. 530, 567–568 (1962), Justice Harlan suggested this distinction between the *McCardle* and *Klein* cases: *McCardle* sustained Congressional power to withdraw jurisdiction to proceed with a case then *sub judice; Klein* was an unconstitutional restriction of judicial power because it prescribed an unconstitutional rule of decision in a pending case. (In dissent, Justice Douglas implied that the two cases were inconsistent, and doubted whether the principle of *McCardle* could command a modern majority. Id. at 605, n. 11.) Is it significant that McCardle had lost his case below and Congress directed dismissing his *appeal,* while Klein had won in the court below and Congress directed dismissing his suit? (The Congressional direction to the Supreme Court to dismiss claimants' suits, rather than simply dismiss appeals, was not "inadvertent." Sponsors of the legislation wanted to overturn the results in the cases of claimants who had obtained judgment in the court of claims where the government's appeal was pending in the Supreme Court.)

(3) The *McCardle* case is the only example of a result-oriented restriction on the Supreme Court's appellate jurisdiction sustained by the Supreme Court. Is it significant that it *was* sustained, even as applied to a case which had been argued and submitted for decision? Less than a year after *McCardle,* another newspaper editor in military custody, who had been denied habeas corpus by a lower federal court, successfully invoked the Supreme Court's jurisdiction to issue an "original" writ of habeas corpus under Section 14 of the Judiciary Act of 1789. Ex parte Yerger, 75 U.S. (8 Wall.) 85 (1869). (The government avoided a constitutional test of the powers of military reconstruction governments by releasing Yerger from military custody, mooting the case.) Can the *McCardle* case then be explained as a narrow decision that one route of Supreme Court review can always be closed so long as another remains open? See Van Alstyne, *A Critical Guide to Ex Parte McCardle,* 15 Ariz.L.Rev. 229, 244–254 (1973).

(4) Some proposals to restrict the jurisdiction of inferior federal courts in constitutional cases would leave undisturbed the appellate jurisdiction of the Supreme Court. Does that kind of legislation present lesser constitutional problems than legislation that closes the door to the Supreme Court? Consider, for example, the "Human Life Statute," introduced in 1981 in both the Senate and House of Representatives.[1] Section 2[2] provided:

"Notwithstanding any other provision of law, no inferior Federal court ordained and established by Congress under article III of the Constitution of the United States shall have jurisdiction to issue any restraining order,

---

[1] 97th Cong., 1st Sess., H.R. 900 (Hyde and Mazzoli) and S. 158 (Helms and D'Amato).

[2] Section 1 of the Human Life Statute was a substantive provision attempting to change the result in the Supreme Court's abortion decisions by ordinary legislation. See p. 1185, infra.

temporary or permanent injunction, or declaratory judgment in any case involving or arising from any State law or municipal ordinance that (1) protects the rights of human persons between conception and birth, or (2) prohibits, limits, or regulates (a) the performance of abortions, or (b) the provision at public expense of funds, facilities, personnel, or other assistance for the performance of abortions.''

Notice that the proposed statute would leave intact the authority of the Supreme Court to review state court decisions, including both abortion convictions and state court actions for injunctions and declaratory judgments. Also undisturbed would be the lower courts' jurisdiction in habeas corpus to review state abortion convictions.

Most troublesome of all are proposals that both deny the lower federal courts' jurisdiction to entertain actions, and the Supreme Court's jurisdiction to review state court decisions, concerning particular constitutional issues. Consider the examples in the next two notes.

(5) The Omnibus Crime Control and Safe Streets Act of 1968 as it was reported to the Senate by the Senate Judiciary Committee contained the following provision which was eliminated on the floor prior to final passage of the bill: "Neither the Supreme Court nor any inferior court ordained and established by Congress under article III of the Constitution of the United States shall have jurisdiction to review or to reverse, vacate, modify, or disturb in any way, a ruling of any trial court of any State in any criminal prosecution admitting in evidence as voluntarily made an admission or confession of an accused if such ruling has been affirmed or otherwise upheld by the highest court of the State having appellate jurisdiction of the cause." See U.S.Code Cong. and Adm.News, 90th Cong.Sec.Sess.1968, p. 2138. This provision was designed to "revise" the holding in Miranda v. Arizona, 384 U.S. 436 (1966). Would it have been constitutional?

(6) In 1962 and 1963, the Court held that prayers and Bible readings in public schools were unconstitutional, whether or not objecting pupils were excused. Engel v. Vitale, 370 U.S. 421 (1962); Abington School Dist. v. Schempp and Murray v. Curlett, 374 U.S. 203 (1963). Public furor created by the decisions led to proposals for constitutional amendments, on which the House Judiciary Committee held hearings in 1964.

On April 9, 1979, the Senate passed, as a rider to a bill on Supreme Court jurisdiction, an amendment originally proposed by Senator Jesse Helms, which would have added the following two new sections to 28 U.S.C.:

§ 1259. Notwithstanding the provisions of sections 1253, 1254 and 1257 of this chapter the Supreme Court shall not have jurisdiction to review, by appeal, writ or certiorari, or otherwise, any case arising out of any State statute ... which relates to voluntary prayers in public school and public buildings.

§ 1364. Notwithstanding any other provision of law, the district courts shall not have jurisdiction of any case or question which the Supreme Court does not have jurisdiction to review under Section 1259....

If the Helms Amendment were to be enacted, and were to be sustained by the federal courts, what would be the impact of the Supreme Court's earlier decisions concerning school prayers when cases were litigated in state courts?

(7) For discussion of the limits of Congressional power to control jurisdiction of the lower federal courts, and a summary of the enormous literature on that question, see Gunther, *Congressional Power to Curtail Federal Court Jurisdiction: An Opinionated Guide to an Ongoing Debate*, 36 Stan.L.Rev. 201 (1984).

CHAPTER 3

THE JURISDICTION OF FEDERAL COURTS IN CONSTITUTIONAL CASES

Introduction. Judicial review can be understood only in the context of constitutional litigation. Minimum familiarity with jurisdictional boundaries and the special rules devised for constitutional cases is necessary to understanding the substantive doctrines. This chapter is designed to present a brief introduction to a very complicated set of doctrines.

The first two sections deal with the complexities introduced into constitutional litigation by the existence of independent state and federal court systems, each with ultimate responsibility for final interpretation of the law originating in its own level of government and with concurrent jurisdiction to adjudicate disputes in which constitutional questions arise. Section 1 covers Supreme Court jurisdiction to review decisions of state courts. Section 2 deals with constitutional litigation originating in the federal courts. Section 3 considers a variety of related doctrines that govern both Supreme Court review and the conduct of the lower federal courts. Those doctrines concern the definition of "cases" and "controversies" and the extent to which issues of constitutional interpretation are justiciable.

SECTION 1. SUPREME COURT REVIEW OF STATE COURT DECISIONS

A. HISTORY AND STRUCTURE

ARTICLE III OF THE CONSTITUTION AND SECTION 25 OF THE JUDICIARY ACT OF 1789

At the Constitutional Convention, there was general agreement that one major weakness of the central government under the Articles of Confederation was the absence of a central court system. Accordingly, there was little discussion of the question whether there should be a federal judicial system with power to act directly on individuals and member states. Article III extends the federal judicial power to cases, among others, "arising under this Constitution, the Laws of the United States, and Treaties made, or which shall be made, under their Authority."

The major dispute at the Convention concerned the nature of the tribunals that would exercise the federal judicial power. Nationalist proposals provided for mandatory establishment of both a supreme court and inferior trial courts. Competing plans provided only for a supreme court. Notice that both sides of the debate conceded the propriety of appellate review over state court decisions, and that a supreme court should be established by the Constitution itself. The controversy concerned whether appeal of state court decisions to a national supreme court was a sufficient mechanism for insuring national authority and the uniformity of application of federal laws. The resulting compromise gave Congress the option to provide for lower federal courts.

The First Congress, in 1789, exercised its option to create lower federal courts. Those courts were given exclusive jurisdiction to try federal crimes and concurrent jurisdiction with the state courts in cases in which the United States was the plaintiff. The lower federal courts were not given general jurisdiction in civil cases arising under federal law. (The most important civil jurisdiction of the lower federal courts was in diversity of citizenship and admiralty cases.) For the most part, enforcement of private federal law rights (then quite few) was entrusted to the state courts, which were required to apply federal law over inconsistent state law by the Supremacy Clause of Article VI of the Constitution.

Appellate review of state court decisions was the primary method for enforcing the Supremacy Clause. Section 25 of the Judiciary Act of 1789 provided that "a final judgment or decree in any suit, in the highest court of law or equity of a State in which a decision in the suit could be had" could be "re-examined and reversed or affirmed in the Supreme Court of the United States upon a writ of error," in three classes of cases: (1) "where is drawn in question the validity of a treaty or statute of, or an authority exercised under the United States, and the decision is against their validity"; (2) "where is drawn in question the validity of a statute of, or an authority exercised under any State, on the ground of their being repugnant to the constitution, treaties or laws of the United States, and the decision is in favour of such of their validity"; (3) "where is drawn in question the construction of any clause of the constitution, or of a treaty, or statute of, or commission held under the United States, and the decision is against the title, right, privilege or exemption ... claimed by either party, under such clause of the said Constitution, treaty, statute or commission." Notice that all three provisions limited review to those cases where state courts had rejected claims made under the federal Constitution and laws. State court decisions sustaining those claims were not reviewable. (That remained true until 1914. See p. 54, infra.)

For an extensive review of the history of Article III and the Judiciary Act of 1789, and citation to other authority, see Hart and Wechsler, Federal Courts 1–33 (4th ed. 1996).

Martin v. Hunter's Lessee

14 U.S. (1 Wheat.) 304, 4 L.Ed. 97 (1816).

[In 1816 the jurisdiction of the Supreme Court under Section 25 of the Judiciary Act of 1789 was denied by the highest court of Virginia. The Virginia estates of Lord Fairfax (who died in England in 1781) had descended to a relative, Thomas Martin. Virginia claimed to have acquired the estates in 1777 under state legislation confiscating the property of loyalist British subjects and in 1789 had made a conveyance to David Hunter. Hunter's lessee, claiming under this conveyance, brought an action of ejectment. The Fairfax heirs contended that their rights were supported by the treaties of 1783 and 1794 giving protection to British owned property. After years of negotiation and litigation, the Virginia Court of Appeals sustained Hunter's claim. The Supreme Court of the United States reversed and remanded the case, holding that the treaty of 1794 confirmed the title remaining in the Fairfax heirs. Fairfax's Devisee v. Hunter's Lessee, 11 U.S. (7 Cranch) 603 (1813). The Virginia Court of Appeals, presided over by Judge Spencer Roane,[1] refused to comply with the decision.]

See Warren, *Legislative and Judicial Attacks on the Supreme Court of the United States—A History of the Twenty–Fifth Section of the Judiciary Act,* 47 Am.L.Rev. 1, 3 (1913).

Story, J., delivered the opinion of the court:

This is a writ of error from the Court of Appeals of Virginia, founded upon the refusal of that court to obey the mandate of this court, requiring the judgment rendered in this very cause, at February term, 1813, to be carried into due execution. . . .

The government . . . can claim no powers which are not granted to it by the constitution, and the powers actually granted, must be such as are expressly given, or given by necessary implication. On the other hand, this instrument, like every other grant, is to have a reasonable construction, according to the import of its terms; and where a power is expressly given in general terms, it is not to be restrained to particular cases, unless that construction grow out of the context expressly, or by necessary implication. The words are to be taken in their natural and obvious sense, and not in a sense unreasonably restricted or enlarged. . . .

But, even admitting that the language of the constitution is not mandatory, and that Congress may constitutionally omit to vest the judicial power in courts of the United States, it cannot be denied that when it is vested it may be exercised to the utmost constitutional extent.

This leads us to the consideration of the great question as to the nature and extent of the appellate jurisdiction of the United States. We have already seen that appellate jurisdiction is given by the constitution to the Supreme Court in all cases, where it has not original jurisdiction; subject, however, to such exceptions and regulations as Congress may prescribe. It is, therefore, capable of embracing every case enumerated in the constitution, which is not exclusively to be decided by way of original jurisdiction. But the exercise of appellate jurisdiction is far from being limited by the terms of the constitution to the Supreme Court. There can be no doubt that Congress may create a succession of inferior tribunals, in each of which it may vest appellate as well as original jurisdiction. The judicial power is delegated by the constitution in the most general terms, and may, therefore, be exercised by Congress under every variety of form, of appellate or original jurisdiction. And as there is nothing in the constitution which restrains or limits this power, it must, therefore, in all other cases, subsist in the utmost latitude of which, in its own nature, it is susceptible. . . .

It must, therefore, be conceded that the constitution not only contemplated, but meant to provide for cases within the scope of the judicial power of the United States, which might yet depend before state tribunals. It was foreseen that in the exercise of their ordinary jurisdiction, state courts would incidentally take cognizance of cases arising under the constitution, the laws and treaties of the United States. Yet to all these cases the judicial power, by the very terms of the constitution, is to extend. It cannot extend by original jurisdiction if that was already rightfully and exclusively attached in the state courts, which (as has been already shown) may occur; it must, therefore, extend by appellate

---

[1] Judge Roane was the chief judicial opponent of Chief Justice Marshall's federalist views. It is commonly thought that if the Office of Chief Justice had been vacant when Thomas Jefferson became President, he would have nominated Roane for the position.

jurisdiction, or not at all. It would seem to follow that the appellate power of the United States must, in such cases, extend to state tribunals; and if in such cases, there is no reason why it should not equally attach upon all others within the purview of the constitution.

It has been argued that such an appellate jurisdiction over state courts is inconsistent with the genius of our governments, and the spirit of the constitution. That the latter was never designed to act upon state sovereignties, but only upon the people, and that if the power exists, it will materially impair the sovereignty of the states, and the independence of their courts. We cannot yield to the force of this reasoning; it assumes principles which we cannot admit, and draws conclusions to which we do not yield our assent.

It is a mistake that the constitution was not designed to operate upon states, in their corporate capacities. It is crowded with provisions which restrain or annul the sovereignty of the states in some of the highest branches of their prerogatives. The tenth section of the first article contains a long list of disabilities and prohibitions imposed upon the states. Surely, when such essential portions of state sovereignty are taken away, or prohibited to be exercised, it cannot be correctly asserted that the constitution does not act upon the states. The language of the constitution is also imperative upon the states as to the performance of many duties. It is imperative upon the state legislatures to make laws prescribing the time, places, and manner of holding elections for senators and representatives, and for electors of President and Vice–President. And in these, as well as some other cases, Congress have a right to revise, amend, or supersede the laws which may be passed by state legislatures. When, therefore, the states are stripped of some of the highest attributes of sovereignty, and the same are given to the United States; when the legislatures of the states are, in some respects, under the control of Congress, and in every case are, under the constitution, bound by the paramount authority of the United States; it is certainly difficult to support the argument that the appellate power over the decisions of state courts is contrary to the genius of our institutions. The courts of the United States can, without question, revise the proceedings of the executive and legislative authorities of the states, and if they are found to be contrary to the constitution, may declare them to be of no legal validity. Surely the exercise of the same right over judicial tribunals is not a higher or more dangerous act of sovereign power.

Nor can such a right be deemed to impair the independence of state judges. . . .

The argument urged from the possibility of the abuse of the revising power is equally unsatisfactory. It is always a doubtful course to argue against the use or existence of a power, from the possibility of its abuse. It is still more difficult, by such an argument, to ingraft upon a general power a restriction which is not to be found in the terms in which it is given. From the very nature of things, the absolute right of decision, in the last resort, must rest somewhere—wherever it may be vested it is susceptible of abuse. In all questions of jurisdiction the inferior, or appellate court, must pronounce the final judgment; and common sense, as well as legal reasoning, has conferred it upon the latter. . . .

This is not all. A motive of another kind, perfectly compatible with the most sincere respect for state tribunals, might induce the grant of appellate power over their decisions. That motive is the importance, and even necessity of uniformity of decisions throughout the whole United States, upon all subjects within the purview of the constitution. Judges of equal learning and integrity, in different states, might differently interpret a statute, or a treaty of the United States, or even the constitution itself. If there were no revising authority to control these jarring and discordant judgments, and harmonize them into uniformity, the laws, the treaties and the constitution of the United States would be different in different states, and might, perhaps, never have precisely the same construction, obligation, or efficacy, in any two states. The public mischiefs that would attend such a state of things would be truly deplorable; and it cannot be believed that they could have escaped the enlightened convention which formed the constitution. What, indeed, might then have been only prophecy, has now become fact; and the appellate jurisdiction must continue to be the only adequate remedy for such evils....

On the whole, the court are of opinion that the appellate power of the United States does extend to cases pending in the state courts; and that the 25th section of the judiciary act, which authorizes the exercise of this jurisdiction in the specified cases, by a writ of error, is supported by the letter and spirit of the constitution. We find no clause in that instrument which limits this power; and we dare not interpose a limitation where the people have not been disposed to create one....

We have thus gone over all the principal questions in the cause, and we deliver our judgment with entire confidence, that it is consistent with the constitution and laws of the land.

We have not thought it incumbent on us to give any opinion upon the question, whether this court have authority to issue a writ of mandamus to the Court of Appeals to enforce the former judgments, as we do not think it necessarily involved in the decision of this cause.

It is the opinion of the whole court that the judgment of the Court of Appeals of Virginia, rendered on the mandate in this cause, be reversed, and the judgment of the District Court, held at Winchester, be, and the same is hereby affirmed.

Johnson, J. It will be observed in this case, that the court disavows all intention to decide on the right to issue compulsory process to the state courts; thus leaving us, in my opinion, where the constitution and laws place us—supreme over persons and cases as far as our judicial powers extend, but not asserting any compulsory control over the state tribunals.

In this view, I acquiesce in their opinion, but not altogether in the reasoning, or opinion, of my brother who delivered it. Few minds are accustomed to the same habit of thinking, and our conclusions are most satisfactory to ourselves when arrived at in our own way....

STATE COURT RESISTANCE TO SUPREME COURT ORDERS

Since Martin v. Hunter's Lessee there have been many instances of state court resistance to Supreme Court orders. For a discussion of some of the episodes and of the varying techniques used to attempt to compel compliance, see Murphy, *Lower Court Checks on Supreme Court Power,* 53 Am.Pol.Sci.Rev. 1017 (1959); Note, *State Court Evasion of United States Supreme Court Mandates,* 56 Yale L.J. 574 (1947); Note, *Evasion of Supreme Court Mandates in Cases Remanded to State Courts Since 1941,* 67 Harv.L.Rev. 1251 (1954); Beatty, *State Court Evasion of United States Supreme Court Mandates During the Last Decade of the Warren Court,* 6 Valparaiso L.Rev. 260 (1972).

THE CURRENT JURISDICTION OF THE SUPREME COURT TO REVIEW STATE COURT DECISIONS

In 1916 and 1925, Congress had provided that the Supreme Court would have discretion, on writ of certiorari, whether or not to review the majority of state cases deciding federal questions. (The practice of the Supreme Court, disclosed to Congress when the 1925 statute was enacted, is that granting certiorari—scheduling a case for oral argument prior to decision on the merits—requires only the vote of four Justices.)

Between 1925 and 1988, (when most of the cases in this book were decided), two categories of state court decisions were subject to obligatory review on appeal—if a state statute was held constitutional, or if a federal statute or treaty was held unconstitutional. In 1988, Congress eliminated these appeals, as well as most appeals from decisions of lower federal courts. The current statute, 28 U.S.C. § 1257, provides in substance for discretionary Supreme Court review of all state court decisions turning on issues of federal law:

> "Final judgments or decrees rendered by the highest court of a State in which a decision could be had may be reviewed by the Supreme Court by writ of certiorari where the validity of a treaty or statute of the United States is drawn in question or where the validity of a statute of any State is drawn in question on the ground of its being repugnant to the Constitution, treaties or laws of the United States, or where any title, right, privilege, or immunity is specially set up or claimed under the Constitution or the treaties or statutes of, or any commission held or authority exercised under, the United States."

The requirement that the state court's decision be "final" has been carried forward from the Judiciary Act of 1789. The Court's current flexible definition of that requirement is discussed in Cox Broadcasting Corp. v. Cohn, 420 U.S. 469, 476–487 (1975). The requirement that the decision be of the highest state court "in which a decision could be had" also stems from the 1789 Judiciary Act. This provision can permit review of the decision of inferior state courts, if further appeals within the state system are not possible. For example, Thompson v. Louisville, 362 U.S. 199 (1960), reviewed the decision of a police court.

B. ISSUES OF STATE LAW IN THE SUPREME COURT: THE ADEQUATE AND INDEPENDENT STATE GROUND

REVIEW OF ISSUES OF STATE LAW IN CASES INVOLVING FEDERAL QUESTIONS: THE ADEQUATE AND INDEPENDENT STATE GROUND

The Judiciary Act of 1789 contained a proviso expressly limiting Supreme Court review of state court decisions to the federal questions that provided the basis for its jurisdiction. That proviso was repealed in 1867, and does not now appear in 28 U.S.C. § 1257. In a landmark case, the Supreme Court held that repeal of the proviso did not change the basic principle that state court decisions on issues of state law cannot be reviewed by the Supreme Court. Murdock v. Memphis, 87 U.S. (20 Wall.) 590 (1875). State courts are thus the final expositors of the meaning of state law.

Corollary to the finality of state court interpretations of state law is the principle that issues of federal law resolved by state courts will not be reviewed by the Supreme Court if the state court's judgment rests upon an "adequate and independent" state ground. Thus, if a state court rules against a party on two alternative grounds, one federal and one state, the Supreme Court lacks jurisdiction to inquire into the correctness of the federal law ruling. The rationale of the adequate and independent state ground rule has been explained as follows. "Our only power over state judgments is to correct them to the extent that they incorrectly adjudge federal rights. And our power is to correct wrong judgments, not to revise opinions. We are not permitted to render an advisory opinion, and if the same judgment would be rendered by the state court after we corrected its views of Federal laws, our review could amount to nothing more than an advisory opinion." Jackson, J., for the Court in Herb v. Pitcairn, 324 U.S. 117, 125–26 (1945).

The adequate and independent state ground rule has two branches. The first is procedural. It arises when the state court has refused or simply failed to rule on the merits of the federal issues because they were not presented to the state court in the manner required by state procedure. On the one hand, the procedure for raising issues in the state courts—even issues of federal law—is governed by state rules of practice and not by federal law standards. On the other hand, from the beginning the state courts have been important forums for vindication of federal rights and defenses. Complete deference to state court rulings refusing to honor federal claims because of state procedure creates possibilities that federal claims will be difficult to enforce, or that state courts will evade the supremacy of federal law. Justice Holmes said, in a famous dictum: "Whatever springes the State may set for those who are endeavoring to assert rights that the State confers, the assertion of Federal rights, when plainly and reasonably made, is not to be defeated in the name of local practice." Davis v. Wechsler, 263 U.S. 22, 24 (1923).

It is clear that a state court's failure or refusal to decide on federal law issues will not block Supreme Court review if the procedural decision is not "adequate." What is less than clear is the standard for judging the "adequacy" of state procedural grounds. Suppose, for example, that the defendant has been convicted for violating a state criminal statute claimed to violate the United States Constitution. The highest state court has affirmed the conviction, but has refused to decide whether or not the state statute is constitutional because that issue was not raised at the trial, because it was raised too late, because it was raised in improper form, or the like. Can the Supreme Court now review the question whether the statute is constitutional? The Supreme Court's last full-scale discussion of the problem was in Henry v. Mississippi, 379 U.S. 443 (1965). The Court stated that "in every case" it was necessary to inquire whether "enforcement of a procedural forfeiture" served "a legitimate state interest." The *Henry* opinion, however, failed to clarify the standard for judging the adequacy of state procedures. For different assessments of the law prior to *Henry*, and the impact of that decision, see Sandalow, *Henry v. Mississippi and the Adequate State Ground: Proposals for a Revised Doctrine*, 1965 Sup.Ct.Rev. 187 and Hill, *The Inadequate State Ground*, 65 Colum.L.Rev. 943 (1965); Matasar & Bruch, *Procedural Common Law, Federal Jurisdiction Policy, and Abandonment of the Adequate and Independent State Ground Doctrine*, 86 Colum.L.Rev. 1291 (1986). A novel and technical ruling on an issue of state procedure may still be judged inadequate either because it is suspected that the state court is evading decision of the federal issue, or because the rule throws unreasonable obstacles in the way of enforcement of federal rights. Williams v. Georgia, 349 U.S. 375, 399 (1955) (Clark, J., dissenting).

There is more certainty, and more deference to state court decisions, in the second branch of the doctrine—where the state ground is substantive. A common situation is one where the state court has held a state statute to be invalid under both the United States and state constitutions. If the state court is one of stature, its disposition of the federal question may have considerable impact in other courts. The application of the independent and adequate state ground rule in that situation is, nevertheless, clear. There is no realistic inquiry into the adequacy of the state ground. The sole issue is whether the state substantive ground is independent—that is, whether, no matter how the federal issue is resolved, the state ground will be dispositive.[1] Thus a state court decision invalidating a state law on both state and federal constitutional grounds cannot be reviewed by the Supreme Court, even if the bulk of the state court's discussion concerned the United States Constitution.

SUPREME COURT REVIEW OF STATE COURT DECISIONS UPHOLDING CLAIMS OF FEDERAL CONSTITUTIONAL RIGHT

Until 1914, the Supreme Court's authority to review state court decisions was limited to cases that denied claims of federal right. Thus, a state court decision that erroneously decided that a state law violated the United States Constitution could not be reviewed in the United States Supreme Court. The 1914 amendment permitting review of state decisions that sustained federal claims and defenses can be traced to a single case. The New York Court of Appeals held that New York's pioneer workers' compensation law was unconstitutional under the fourteenth amendment, on the ground that the employer's liability without fault was a taking of property without due process of law. Ives v. South Buffalo Ry. Co., 201 N.Y. 271, 94 N.E. 431 (1911). The decision could not be reviewed by the United States Supreme Court, because the state court had upheld the claim of federal constitutional right asserted. The decision, which has been described as "the most famous and most bitterly attacked holding of any American court regarding workmen's compensation," (Dodd, *Administration of Workmen's Compensation* 30 [1936]), led to the enactment of a provision permitting Supreme Court review of state court decisions upholding claims of federal right.

It is both ironic and instructive to note that the 1914 amendment would not, in fact, have permitted the United States Supreme Court to review the *Ives* decision. The New York Court of Appeals had also struck down the workers' compensation law as a violation of the New York Constitution—an independent state ground. New York could—and did—amend its State Constitution to authorize enactment of a workers' compensation law. The New York law was sustained by the Supreme Court in New York Central R. Co. v. White, 243 U.S. 188 (1916). For five years, however, proponents of workers' compensation laws throughout the country were confronted with a decision of the most prestigious state court that the basic principle of those laws violated the United States Constitution.

Recent years have seen an increase in the number of state court decisions that have relied on parallel state constitutional provisions, precluding Supreme Court review of decisions that state laws violate the United States Constitution. Falk, *The State Constitution: A More Than "Adequate" Non-federal Ground,* 61 Calif.L.Rev. 273 (1973); Howard, *State Courts and Constitutional Rights in the Day of the Burger Court,* 62 Va.L.Rev. 873 (1976). See also Brennan, *State Constitutions and the Protection of Individual Rights,* 90 Harv.L.Rev. 489 (1977). Where state courts have not relied on state grounds, there has been a significant increase in the number of cases reviewed, and reversed, by the Supreme Court because state courts have read the United States Constitution too expansively. Sager, *Fair Measure: The Legal Status of Underenforced Constitutional Norms,* 91 Harv.L.Rev. 1212, 1243–1247 (1978).

---

[1] Reliance on the state constitution will not preclude Supreme Court review, for example, if the state's constitution has been construed to adopt the United States Supreme Court's construction of the United States Constitution. In that case, if the state court strikes down the state law, the result is compelled by the state court's interpretation of federal law. See Delaware v. Prouse, 440 U.S. 648 (1979).

Should the Supreme Court be able to review state decisions holding state laws invalid under the United States Constitution, even when the decision is also based on the state constitution? For an argument that an interest in uniformity of interpretation of the Constitution should permit that review in appropriate cases, see Sandalow, *Henry v. Mississippi and the Adequate State Ground: Proposals for a Revised Doctrine,* 1965 Sup.Ct.Rev. 187, 199–203. On the other hand, should the Supreme Court refuse to review state court decisions holding state laws invalid under the United States Constitution, even when the decision is based entirely on the federal ground? For arguments that the state courts should have some leeway to interpret the United States Constitution more expansively than does the Supreme Court, and that review of those decisions is inappropriate or unwise, see Sager, supra, at 1247–1263, and Tribe, *American Constitutional Law,* 31–33 (1978). For a rebuttal to those arguments, see Tribe, *American Constitutional Law* 40–41 (2d ed. 1988).

Michigan v. Long

463 U.S. 1032, 103 S.Ct. 3469, 77 L.Ed.2d 1201 (1983).

Justice O'Connor delivered the opinion of the Court.

In Terry v. Ohio, 392 U.S. 1 (1968), we upheld the validity of a protective search for weapons in the absence of probable cause to arrest because it is unreasonable to deny a police officer the right "to neutralize the threat of physical harm," id., at 24, when he possesses an articulable suspicion that an individual is armed and dangerous. We did not, however, expressly address whether such a protective search for weapons could extend to an area beyond the person in the absence of probable cause to arrest. In the present case, respondent David Long was convicted for possession of marijuana found by police in the passenger compartment and trunk of the automobile that he was driving. The police searched the passenger compartment because they had reason to believe that the vehicle contained weapons potentially dangerous to the officers. We hold that the protective search of the passenger compartment was reasonable under the principles articulated in *Terry* and other decisions of this Court. We also examine Long's argument that the decision below rests upon an adequate and independent state ground, and we decide in favor of our jurisdiction.

I

The Barry County Circuit Court denied Long's motion to suppress the marijuana taken from both the interior of the car and its trunk. He was subsequently convicted of possession of marijuana. . . . The Michigan Supreme Court reversed. The court held that "the sole justification of the *Terry* search, protection of the police officers and others nearby, cannot justify the search in this case." 413 Mich., at 472, 320 N.W.2d, at 869. The marijuana found in Long's trunk was considered by the court below to be the "fruit" of the illegal search of the interior, and was also suppressed.

. . .

II

Before reaching the merits, we must consider Long's argument that we are without jurisdiction to decide this case because the decision below rests on an adequate and independent state ground. The court below referred twice to the state constitution in its opinion, but otherwise relied exclusively on federal law.

Long argues that the Michigan courts have provided greater protection from searches and seizures under the state constitution than is afforded under the Fourth Amendment, and the references to the state constitution therefore establish an adequate and independent ground for the decision below.

It is, of course, "incumbent upon this Court ... to ascertain for itself ... whether the asserted non-federal ground independently and adequately supports the judgment." Abie State Bank v. Bryan, 282 U.S. 765, 773 (1931). Although we have announced a number of principles in order to help us determine whether various forms of references to state law constitute adequate and independent state grounds,[4] we openly admit that we have thus far not developed a satisfying and consistent approach for resolving this vexing issue. In some instances, we have taken the strict view that if the ground of decision was at all unclear, we would dismiss the case.... In other instances, we have vacated, ..., or continued a case, ..., in order to obtain clarification about the nature of a state court decision.... In more recent cases, we have ourselves examined state law to determine whether state courts have used federal law to guide their application of state law or to provide the actual basis for the decision that was reached....

This *ad hoc* method of dealing with cases that involve possible adequate and independent state grounds is antithetical to the doctrinal consistency that is required when sensitive issues of federal-state relations are involved. Moreover, none of the various methods of disposition that we have employed thus far recommends itself as the preferred method that we should apply to the exclusion of others, and we therefore determine that it is appropriate to reexamine our treatment of this jurisdictional issue in order to achieve the consistency that is necessary.

The process of examining state law is unsatisfactory because it requires us to interpret state laws with which we are generally unfamiliar, and which often, as in this case, have not been discussed at length by the parties. Vacation and continuance for clarification have also been unsatisfactory both because of the delay and decrease in efficiency of judicial administration, ... and, more important, because these methods of disposition place significant burdens on state courts to demonstrate the presence or absence of our jurisdiction.... Finally, outright dismissal of cases is clearly not a panacea because it cannot be doubted that there is an important need for uniformity in federal law, and that this need goes unsatisfied when we fail to review an opinion that rests primarily upon federal grounds and where the *independence* of an alleged state ground is not apparent from the four corners of the opinion....

---

[4] For example, we have long recognized that "where the judgment of a state court rests upon two grounds one of which is federal and the other non-federal in character, our jurisdiction fails if the non-federal ground is independent of the federal ground and adequate to support the judgment." Fox Film Corp. v. Muller, 296 U.S. 207, 210 (1935). We may review a state case decided on a federal ground even if it is clear that there was an available state ground for decision on which the state court could properly have relied. Beecher v. Alabama, 389 U.S. 35, 37, n. 3 (1967). Also, if, in our view, the state court "felt compelled by what it understood to be federal constitutional considerations to construe ... its own law in the manner that it did," then we will not treat a normally adequate state ground as independent, and there will be no question about our jurisdiction. Delaware v. Prouse, 440 U.S. 648, 653 (1979) (quoting Zacchini v. Scripps–Howard Broadcasting Co., 433 U.S. 562, 568 (1977)). See also South Dakota v. Neville, 459 U.S. 553, 556, n. 5 (1983). Finally, "where the non-federal ground is so interwoven with the [federal ground] as not to be an independent matter, or is not of sufficient breadth to sustain the judgment without any decision of the other, our jurisdiction is plain." Enterprise Irrigation District v. Farmers' Mutual Canal Company, 243 U.S. 157, 164 (1917).

Respect for the independence of state courts, as well as avoidance of rendering advisory opinions, have been the cornerstones of this Court's refusal to decide cases where there is an adequate and independent state ground. It is precisely because of this respect for state courts, and this desire to avoid advisory opinions, that we do not wish to continue to decide issues of state law that go beyond the opinion that we review, or to require state courts to reconsider cases to clarify the grounds of their decisions. Accordingly, when, as in this case, a state court decision fairly appears to rest primarily on federal law, or to be interwoven with the federal law, and when the adequacy and independence of any possible state law ground is not clear from the face of the opinion, we will accept as the most reasonable explanation that the state court decided the case the way it did because it believed that federal law required it to do so. If a state court chooses merely to rely on federal precedents as it would on the precedents of all other jurisdictions, then it need only make clear by a plain statement in its judgment or opinion that the federal cases are being used only for the purpose of guidance, and do not themselves compel the result that the court has reached. In this way, both justice and judicial administration will be greatly improved. If the state court decision indicates clearly and expressly that it is alternatively based on bona fide separate, adequate, and independent grounds, we of course, will not undertake to review the decision.

This approach obviates in most instances the need to examine state law in order to decide the nature of the state court decision, and will at the same time avoid the danger of our rendering advisory opinions. It also avoids the unsatisfactory and intrusive practice of requiring state courts to clarify their decisions to the satisfaction of this Court. We believe that such an approach will provide state judges with a clearer opportunity to develop state jurisprudence unimpeded by federal interference, and yet will preserve the integrity of federal law....

The principle that we will not review judgments of state courts that rest on adequate and independent state grounds is based, in part, on "the limitations of our own jurisdiction." Herb v. Pitcairn, 324 U.S. 117, 125 (1945). The jurisdictional concern is that we not "render an advisory opinion, and if the same judgment would be rendered by the state court after we corrected its views of federal laws, our review could amount to nothing more than an advisory opinion." Id., at 126. Our requirement of a "plain statement" that a decision rests upon adequate and independent state grounds does not in any way authorize the rendering of advisory opinions. Rather, in determining, as we must, whether we have jurisdiction to review a case that is alleged to rest on adequate and independent state grounds, ... we merely assume that there are no such grounds when it is not clear from the opinion itself that the state court relied upon an adequate and independent state ground and when it fairly appears that the state court rested its decision primarily on federal law.[8]

---

8 ...

In dissent, Justice Stevens proposes the novel view that this Court should never review a state court decision unless the Court wishes to vindicate a federal right that has been endangered. The rationale of the dissent is not restricted to cases where the decision is arguably supported by adequate and independent state grounds. Rather, Justice Stevens appears to believe that even if the decision below rests exclusively on federal grounds, this Court should not review the decision as long as there is no federal right that is endangered.

The state courts handle the vast bulk of all criminal litigation in this country.... The state courts are required to apply federal constitutional standards, and they necessarily create a considerable body of "federal law" in the process. It is not surprising that this Court has become more interested in the application and development of federal law by state courts in the light of the recent significant expansion of federally created standards that we have imposed on the States.

Our review of the decision below under this framework leaves us unconvinced that it rests upon an independent state ground. Apart from its two citations to the state constitution, the court below relied *exclusively* on its understanding of *Terry* and other federal cases. Not a single state case was cited to support the state court's holding that the search of the passenger compartment was unconstitutional....

Rather than dismissing the case, or requiring that the state court reconsider its decision on our behalf solely because of a mere possibility that an adequate and independent ground supports the judgment, we find that we have jurisdiction in the absence of a plain statement that the decision below rested on an adequate and independent state ground....

IV

. . .

V

The decision of the Michigan Supreme Court is reversed, and the case is remanded for further proceedings not inconsistent with this opinion.

It is so ordered.

Justice Blackmun, concurring in part and concurring in the judgment.

Justice Stevens, dissenting.

The jurisprudential questions presented in this case are far more important than the question whether the Michigan police officer's search of respondent's car violated the Fourth Amendment. The case raises profoundly significant questions concerning the relationship between two sovereigns—the State of Michigan and the United States of America.

. . .

The nature of the case before us hardly compels a departure from tradition. These are not cases in which an American citizen has been deprived of a right secured by the United States Constitution or a federal statute. Rather, they are cases in which a state court has upheld a citizen's assertion of a right, finding the citizen to be protected under both federal and state law. The complaining party is an officer of the state itself, who asks us to rule that the state court interpreted federal rights too broadly and "overprotected" the citizen.

Such cases should not be of inherent concern to this Court. The reason may be illuminated by assuming that the events underlying this case had arisen in another country, perhaps the Republic of Finland. If the Finnish police had arrested a Finnish citizen for possession of marijuana, and the Finnish courts had turned him loose, no American would have standing to object. If instead they had arrested an American citizen and acquitted him, we might have been concerned about the arrest but we surely could not have complained about the acquittal, even if the Finnish Court had based its decision on its understanding of the United States Constitution. That would be true even if we had a treaty with Finland requiring it to respect the rights of American citizens under the United States Constitution. We would only be motivated to intervene if an American citizen were unfairly arrested, tried, and convicted by the foreign tribunal.

In this case the State of Michigan has arrested one of its citizens and the Michigan Supreme Court has decided to turn him loose. The respondent is a United States citizen as well as a Michigan citizen, but since there is no claim that he has been mistreated by the State of Michigan, the final outcome of the state processes offended no federal interest whatever. Michigan simply provided greater protection to one of its citizens than some other State might provide or, indeed, than this Court might require throughout the country.

I believe that in reviewing the decisions of state courts, the primary role of this Court is to make sure that persons who seek to *vindicate* federal rights have been fairly heard. . . .

Until recently we had virtually no interest in cases of this type. Thirty years ago, this Court reviewed only one. Nevada v. Stacher, 346 U.S. 906 (1953). Indeed, that appears to have been the only case during the entire 1952 Term in which a state even sought review of a decision by its own judiciary. Fifteen years ago, we did not review any such cases, although the total number of requests had mounted to three. Some time during the past decade, perhaps about the time of the 5-to-4 decision in Zacchini v. Scripps–Howard Broadcasting Co., 433 U.S. 562 (1977), our priorities shifted. The result is a docket swollen with requests by states to reverse judgments that their courts have rendered in favor of their citizens. I am confident that a future Court will recognize the error of this allocation of resources. When that day comes, I think it likely that the Court will also reconsider the propriety of today's expansion of our jurisdiction.

The Court offers only one reason for asserting authority over cases such as the one presented today: "an important need for uniformity in federal law [that] goes unsatisfied when we fail to review an opinion that rests primarily upon federal grounds and where the independence of an alleged state ground is not apparent from the four corners of the opinion." Of course, the supposed need to "review an opinion" clashes directly with our oft-repeated reminder that "our power is to correct wrong judgments, not to revise opinions." Herb v. Pitcairn, 324 U.S. 117, 126 (1945). The clash is not merely one of form: the "need for uniformity in federal law" is truly an ungovernable engine. That same need is no less present when it is perfectly clear that a state ground is both independent and adequate. In fact, it is equally present if a state prosecutor announces that he believes a certain policy of nonenforcement is commanded by federal law. Yet we have never claimed jurisdiction to correct such errors, no matter how egregious they may be, and no matter how much they may thwart the desires of the state electorate. We do not sit to expound our understanding of the Constitution to interested listeners in the legal community; we sit to resolve disputes. If it is not apparent that our views would affect the outcome of a particular case, we cannot presume to interfere.

. . .

I respectfully dissent.

. . .[a]

SECTION 2. CONSTITUTIONAL LITIGATION INITIATED IN THE FEDERAL COURTS

Introduction. Justice Black for the Court in Atlantic Coast Line R. Co. v. Brotherhood of Locomotive Engineers, 398 U.S. 281, 285 (1970):

". . . When this Nation was established by the Constitution, each State surrendered only a part of its sovereign power to the national government. But

---

[a] A dissent by Justices Brennan and Marshall was not addressed to the adequate and independent state ground issue.

those powers that were not surrendered were retained by the States and unless a State was restrained by 'the supreme Law of the Land' as expressed in the Constitution, laws, or treaties of the United States, it was free to exercise those retained powers as it saw fit. One of the reserved powers was the maintenance of state judicial systems for the decision of legal controversies. Many of the Framers of the Constitution felt that separate federal courts were unnecessary and that the state courts could be entrusted to protect both state and federal rights. Others felt that a complete system of federal courts to take care of federal legal problems should be provided for in the Constitution itself. This dispute resulted in compromise. One 'supreme Court' was created by the Constitution, and Congress was given the power to create other federal courts. In the first Congress this power was exercised and a system of federal trial and appellate courts with limited jurisdiction was created by the Judiciary Act of 1789, 1 Stat. 73.

"While the lower federal courts were given certain powers in the 1789 Act, they were not given any power to review directly cases from state courts, and they have not been given such powers since that time. Only the Supreme Court was authorized to review on direct appeal the decisions of state courts. Thus from the beginning we have had in this country two essentially separate legal systems. Each system proceeds independently of the other with ultimate review in this Court of the federal questions raised in either system. Understandably this dual court system was bound to lead to conflicts and frictions. Litigants who foresaw the possibility of more favorable treatment in one or the other system would predictably hasten to invoke the powers of whichever court it was believed would present the best chance of success. Obviously this dual system could not function if state and federal courts were free to fight each other for control of a particular case. Thus, in order to make the dual system work and 'to prevent needless friction between state and federal courts,' Oklahoma Packing Co. v. Gas Co., 309 U.S. 4, 9 (1940), it was necessary to work out lines of demarcation between the two systems. Some of these limits were spelled out in the 1789 Act. Others have been added by later statutes as well as judicial decisions."

A. JURISDICTION OF THE FEDERAL COURTS IN CASES INVOLVING FEDERAL LAW ISSUES

JURISDICTION OF LOWER FEDERAL COURTS TO ENFORCE FEDERAL RIGHTS

Until after the end of the Civil War, state courts, subject to review by the Supreme Court, were entrusted with litigation to enforce the limited number of private federal rights. The immediate post-Civil War period saw not only an explosion in the creation of federal rights against state governments, but a Congressional decision to use the lower federal courts as the primary mechanism for enforcing those rights.

Section 1 of the Civil Rights Act of 1866 created rights for freed slaves, while Section 2 made it a federal crime for persons to deny those rights under color of state law. After ratification of the Fourteenth Amendment, the Civil Rights Acts of 1870 and 1871 created private rights of action for those who were denied federal rights, and provided for jurisdiction in the lower federal courts to enforce those rights. Section 1 of the 1871 Act is the source of two provisions which are central to modern constitutional litigation. Section 1983 of 42 U.S.C. provides a cause of action for deprivations of federal rights:

> Every person who, under color of any statute, ordinance, regulation, custom, or usage, of any State or Territory or the District of Columbia, subjects, or causes to be subjected, any citizen of the United States or other person within the jurisdiction thereof to the deprivation of any rights, privileges, or immunities secured by the Constitution and laws, shall be liable to the party injured in an action at law, suit in equity, or other proper proceeding for redress.

The corresponding jurisdictional provision is 28 U.S.C. § 1343(a)(3):

> The district courts shall have original jurisdiction of any civil action authorized by law to be commenced by any person:....
>
> (3) to redress the deprivation, under color of any State law, statute, ordinance, regulation, custom or usage, of any right, privilege or immunity secured by the Constitution of the United States or by any Act of Congress providing for equal rights of citizens or of all persons within the jurisdiction of the United States;....

A common form of litigation concerning the constitutionality of state laws is a suit to enjoin the enforcement of those laws, or to obtain a declaratory judgment of their invalidity. Those suits are premised on 42 U.S.C. § 1983. The federal district courts are given jurisdiction over those suits, concurrent with the state courts, by 28 U.S.C. § 1343(3).[1]

No statutory provision, equivalent to 42 U.S.C. § 1983, exists for the denial of constitutional rights by federal officers. The Court has held, however, that those officers may be sued under the Constitution itself. Bivens v. Six Unknown Named Agents of the Fed. Bureau of Narcotics, 403 U.S. 388 (1971). The jurisdictional basis for those suits is 28 U.S.C. § 1331, the general federal question statute, which provides jurisdiction in all cases "arising under the Constitution or laws of the United States." The predecessor of that statute was not enacted until 1875.[2]

Questions of constitutional dimension can, of course, also arise in the course of other cases within the district courts' jurisdiction, such as federal criminal cases and civil cases within the diversity of citizenship jurisdiction, or in the course of review by the courts of appeals of formal orders of federal regulatory agencies. The full complexities surrounding the jurisdiction of federal courts are, of course, beyond the competence of a general course in constitu-

---

[1] In 1910, Congress required that a special three judge court be convened in cases seeking to enjoin the enforcement of state laws on federal constitutional grounds. Direct, and nondiscretionary, review of the decision of those courts was by the Supreme Court. Because of the heavy burdens imposed on the lower federal judiciary, and upon the Supreme Court, the three-judge court requirement was substantially repealed in 1975. (Three-judge courts are still required in cases involving apportionment of congressional districts or state legislatures. 28 U.S.C. § 2284.) Prior to its repeal, the three-judge court was a primary source of United States Supreme Court cases concerning the constitutional validity of state laws. A significant number of the cases in this book reached the Court through that route.

[2] A variety of provisions of the Judicial Code (Title 28 of the United States Code) provide for jurisdiction in other cases arising under federal law. Among the more important are, those involving: actions under federal laws regulating commerce (§ 1337); admiralty and maritime cases (§ 1333); bankruptcy cases (§ 1334); internal revenue (§ 1340); patents, copyrights, and trademarks (§ 1338); and actions in which the United States is a party (§§ 1345, 1346). Numerous substantive federal statutes contain their own provisions for federal court jurisdiction. Unlike § 1331, the jurisdiction of the federal district court is exclusive under some of these provisions, and not concurrent with the state courts.

tional law. Students interested in particular federal jurisdictional issues should consult, among other sources, Wright, *Federal Courts* (4th ed. 1983); Hart and Wechsler, *Federal Courts* (4th ed. 1996).

Review of decisions of the federal district courts is by the United States Court of Appeals. 18 U.S.C. § 3731; 28 U.S.C. §§ 1291–1292. Appeals to the courts of appeals are a matter of right. Decisions of the courts of appeals are reviewable in the Supreme Court by certiorari. 28 U.S.C. § 1254(1). The Supreme Court is empowered to review cases filed "in" a court of appeals prior to that court's judgment, and in rare important cases has done so in the interest of expedition. E.g., Youngstown Sheet & Tube Co. v. Sawyer, 343 U.S. 579 (1952), infra p. 408; United States v. Nixon, 418 U.S. 683 (1974), infra p. 448.

B.   Enforcement of Federal Rights in Suits Against State Officers: the Eleventh Amendment

Pennhurst State School & Hospital v. Halderman

465 U.S. 89, 104 S.Ct. 900, 79 L.Ed.2d 67 (1984).

Justice Powell delivered the opinion of the Court.

This case presents the question whether a federal court may award injunctive relief against state officials on the basis of state law.

I

This litigation, here for the second time, concerns the conditions of care at petitioner Pennhurst State School and Hospital, a Pennsylvania institution for the care of the mentally retarded. See Pennhurst State School & Hospital v. Halderman, 451 U.S. 1 (1981)....

This suit originally was brought in 1974 by respondent Terri Lee Halderman, a resident of Pennhurst, in the District Court for the Eastern District of Pennsylvania. Ultimately, plaintiffs included a class consisting of all persons who were or might become residents of Pennhurst; the Pennsylvania Association for Retarded Citizens (PARC); and the United States. Defendants were Pennhurst and various Pennhurst officials; the Pennsylvania Department of Public Welfare and several of its officials; and various county commissioners, county mental retardation administrators, and other officials of five Pennsylvania counties surrounding Pennhurst. Respondents' amended complaint charged that conditions at Pennhurst violated the class members' rights under the Eighth and Fourteenth Amendments; § 504 of the Rehabilitation Act of 1973, 87 Stat. 394, as amended, 29 U.S.C. § 794 (1976 ed. and Supp. V); the Developmentally Disabled Assistance and Bill of Rights Act, 42 U.S.C. §§ 6001–6081 (1976 ed. and Supp. V); and the Pennsylvania Mental Health and Mental Retardation Act of 1966 (the "MH–MR Act"), Pa.Stat.Ann., Tit. 50, §§ 4101–4704 (Purdon 1969 and Supp.1982). Both damages and injunctive relief were sought.

. . .

The Court of Appeals for the Third Circuit [decided] that respondents had a right to habilitation in the least restrictive environment, but it grounded this right solely on the "bill of rights" provision in the Developmentally Disabled Assistance and Bill of Rights Act, 42 U.S.C. § 6010. The court did not consider the constitutional issues or § 504 of the Rehabilitation Act, and while it affirmed the District Court's holding that the MH/MR Act provides a right to adequate habilitation, the court did not decide whether that state right encompassed a right to treatment in the least restrictive setting.

This Court reversed the judgment of the Court of Appeals, finding that 42 U.S.C. § 6010 did not create any substantive rights. 451 U.S. 1 (1981). We remanded the case to the Court of Appeals to determine if the remedial order could be supported on the basis of state law, the Constitution, or § 504 of the Rehabilitation Act. We also remanded for consideration of whether any relief was available under other provisions of the Developmentally Disabled Assistance and Bill of Rights Act....

On remand the Court of Appeals affirmed its prior judgment in its entirety. It determined that in a recent decision the Supreme Court of Pennsylvania had "spoken definitively" in holding that the MH/MR Act required the State to adopt the "least restrictive environment" approach for the care of the mentally retarded. The Court of Appeals concluded that this state statute fully supported its prior judgment, and therefore did not reach the remaining issues of federal law. It also rejected petitioners' argument that the Eleventh Amendment barred a federal court from considering this pendent state-law claim....

We ... reverse and remand.

II

Petitioners [contend that] the Eleventh Amendment prohibited the District Court from ordering state officials to conform their conduct to state law.... We ... find the Eleventh Amendment challenge dispositive.

A

Article III, § 2 of the Constitution provides that the federal judicial power extends, *inter alia,* to controversies "between a State and Citizens of another State." Relying on this language, this Court in 1793 assumed original jurisdiction over a suit brought by a citizen of South Carolina against the State of Georgia. Chisholm v. Georgia, 2 Dall. 419 (1793). The decision "created such a shock of surprise that the Eleventh Amendment was at once proposed and adopted." Monaco v. Mississippi, 292 U.S. 313, 325 (1934). The Amendment provides:

> "The Judicial power of the United States shall not be construed to extend to any suit in law or equity, commenced or prosecuted against one of the United States by Citizens of another State, or by Citizens or Subjects of any Foreign State."

The Amendment's language overruled the particular result in *Chisholm,* but this Court has recognized that its greater significance lies in its affirmation that the fundamental principle of sovereign immunity limits the grant of judicial authority in Art. III. Thus, in Hans v. Louisiana, 134 U.S. 1 (1890), the Court held that, despite the limited terms of the Eleventh Amendment, a federal court could not entertain a suit brought by a citizen against his own State. After reviewing the constitutional debates concerning the scope of Art. III, the Court determined that federal jurisdiction over suits against unconsenting States "was not contemplated by the Constitution when establishing the judicial power of the United States." Id., at 15. See Monaco v. Mississippi, supra, 292 U.S., at 322–323 (1934). In short, the principle of sovereign immunity is a constitutional limitation on the federal judicial power established in Art. III:

"That a State may not be sued without its consent is a fundamental rule of jurisprudence having so important a bearing upon the construction of the Constitution of the United States that it has become established by repeated decisions of this court that *the entire judicial power granted by the Constitution does not embrace authority to entertain a suit brought by private parties against a State without consent given:* not one brought by citizens of another State, or by citizens or subjects of a foreign State, because of the Eleventh Amendment; and not even one brought by its own citizens, because of the fundamental rule of which the Amendment is but an exemplification." Ex parte State of New York No. 1, 256 U.S. 490, 497 (1921) (emphasis added).

A sovereign's immunity may be waived, and the Court consistently has held that a State may consent to suit against it in federal court. See, e.g., Clark v. Barnard, 108 U.S. 436, 447 (1883). We have insisted, however, that the State's consent be unequivocally expressed. See, e.g., Edelman v. Jordan, 415 U.S. 651, 673 (1974). Similarly, although Congress has power with respect to the rights protected by the Fourteenth Amendment to abrogate the Eleventh Amendment immunity, see Fitzpatrick v. Bitzer, 427 U.S. 445 (1976), we have required an unequivocal expression of congressional intent to "overturn the constitutionally guaranteed immunity of the several States." Quern v. Jordan, 440 U.S. 332, 342 (1979) (holding that 42 U.S.C. § 1983 does not override States' Eleventh Amendment immunity). Our reluctance to infer that a State's immunity from suit in the federal courts has been negated stems from recognition of the vital role of the doctrine of sovereign immunity in our federal system. A State's constitutional interest in immunity encompasses not merely *whether* it may be sued, but *where* it may be sued. As Justice Marshall well has noted, "[b]ecause of the problems of federalism inherent in making one sovereign appear against its will in the courts of the other, a restriction upon the exercise of the federal judicial power has long been considered to be appropriate in a case such as this." Employees v. Missouri Public Health & Welfare Dep't, 411 U.S. 279, 294 (1973) (Marshall, J., concurring in result). Accordingly, in deciding this case we must be guided by "[t]he principles of federalism that inform Eleventh Amendment doctrine." Hutto v. Finney, 437 U.S. 678, 691 (1978).

B

This Court's decisions thus establish that "an unconsenting State is immune from suits brought in federal courts by her own citizens as well as by citizens of another state." *Employees,* supra, 411 U.S., at 280. There may be a question, however, whether a particular suit in fact is a suit against a State. It is clear, of course, that in the absence of consent a suit in which the State or one of its agencies or departments is named as the defendant is proscribed by the Eleventh Amendment. See, e.g., Florida Department of Health v. Florida Nursing Home Assn., 450 U.S. 147 (1981) (per curiam); Alabama v. Pugh, 438 U.S. 781 (1978) (per curiam). This jurisdictional bar applies regardless of the nature of the relief sought. See, e.g., Missouri v. Fiske, 290 U.S. 18, 27 (1933) ("Expressly applying to suits in equity as well as at law, the Amendment necessarily embraces demands for the enforcement of equitable rights and the prosecution of equitable remedies when these are asserted and prosecuted by an individual against a State").

When the suit is brought only against state officials, a question arises as to whether that suit is a suit against the State itself. Although prior decisions of this Court have not been entirely consistent on this issue, certain principles are well established. The Eleventh Amendment bars a suit against state officials when "the state is the real, substantial party in interest." Ford Motor Co. v. Department of Treasury, 323 U.S. 459, 464 (1945). See, e.g., In re Ayers, 123 U.S. 443, 487–492 (1887); Louisiana v. Jumel, 107 U.S. 711, 720–723, 727–728 (1882). Thus, "[t]he general rule is that relief sought nominally against an officer is in fact against the sovereign if the decree would operate against the latter." Hawaii v. Gordon, 373 U.S. 57, 58 (1963) (per curiam). And, as when the State itself is named as the defendant, a suit against state officials that is in fact a suit against a State is barred regardless of whether it seeks damages or injunctive relief. See Cory v. White, 457 U.S. 85, 91 (1982).

The Court has recognized an important exception to this general rule: a suit challenging the constitutionality of a state official's action is not one against the State. This was the holding in Ex parte Young, 209 U.S. 123 (1908), in which a federal court enjoined the Attorney General of the State of Minnesota from bringing suit to enforce a state statute that allegedly violated the Fourteenth Amendment. This Court held that the Eleventh Amendment did not prohibit issuance of this injunction. The theory of the case was that an unconstitutional enactment is "void" and therefore does not "impart to [the officer] any immunity from responsibility to the supreme authority of the United States." Id., at 160. Since the State could not authorize the action, the officer was "stripped of his official or representative character and [was] subjected to the consequences of his official conduct." Ibid.

While the rule permitting suits alleging conduct contrary to "the supreme authority of the United States" has survived, the theory of Young has not been provided an expansive interpretation. Thus, in Edelman v. Jordan, 415 U.S. 651 (1974), the Court emphasized that the Eleventh Amendment bars some forms of injunctive relief against state officials for violation of federal law. Id., at 666–667. In particular, Edelman held that when a plaintiff sues a state official alleging a violation of federal law, the federal court may award an injunction that governs the official's future conduct, but not one that awards retroactive monetary relief. Under the theory of Young, such a suit would not be one against the State since the federal-law allegation would strip the state officer of his official authority. Nevertheless, retroactive relief was barred by the Eleventh Amendment.

III

With these principles in mind, we now turn to the question whether the claim that petitioners violated *state law* in carrying out their official duties at Pennhurst is one against the State and therefore barred by the Eleventh Amendment. Respondents advance two principal arguments in support of the judgment below. First, they contend that under the doctrine of Edelman v. Jordan, supra, the suit is not against the State because the courts below ordered only prospective injunctive relief. Second, they assert that the state-law claim properly was decided under the doctrine of pendent jurisdiction. Respondents rely on decisions of this Court awarding relief against state officials on the basis of a pendent state-law claim. See, e.g., Siler v. Louisville & Nashville R. Co., 213 U.S. 175, 193 (1909).

A

We first address the contention that respondents' state-law claim is not barred by the Eleventh Amendment because it seeks only prospective relief as defined in Edelman v. Jordan, supra. The Court of Appeals held that if the judgment below rested on federal law, it could be entered against petitioner state officials under the doctrine established in *Edelman* and *Young* even though the prospective financial burden was substantial and ongoing. See 673

F.2d, at 656. The court assumed, and respondents assert, that this reasoning applies as well when the official acts in violation of state law. This argument misconstrues the basis of the doctrine established in *Young* and *Edelman.*

As discussed above, the injunction in *Young* was justified, notwithstanding the obvious impact on the State itself, on the view that sovereign immunity does not apply because an official who acts unconstitutionally is "stripped of his official or representative character," *Young,* 209 U.S., at 160. This rationale, of course, created the "well-recognized irony" that an official's unconstitutional conduct constitutes state action under the Fourteenth Amendment but not the Eleventh Amendment. Florida Department of State v. Treasure Salvors, Inc., 458 U.S. 670, 685 (1982) (opinion of Stevens, J.). Nonetheless, the *Young* doctrine has been accepted as necessary to permit the federal courts to vindicate federal rights and hold state officials responsible to "the supreme authority of the United States." *Young,* 209 U.S., at 160. As Justice Brennan has observed, "Ex parte Young was the culmination of efforts by this Court to harmonize the principles of the Eleventh Amendment with the effective supremacy of rights and powers secured elsewhere in the Constitution." Perez v. Ledesma, 401 U.S. 82, 106 (1971) (Brennan, J., concurring in part and dissenting in part). Our decisions repeatedly have emphasized that the *Young* doctrine rests on the need to promote the vindication of federal rights. See, e.g., Quern v. Jordan, 440 U.S. 332, 337 (1979); Scheuer v. Rhodes, 416 U.S. 232, 237 (1974); Georgia R. & Banking Co. v. Redwine, 342 U.S. 299, 304 (1952).

The Court also has recognized, however, that the need to promote the supremacy of federal law must be accommodated to the constitutional immunity of the States. This is the significance of Edelman v. Jordan, supra.... [W]e declined to extend the fiction of *Young* to encompass retroactive relief, for to do so would effectively eliminate the constitutional immunity of the States. Accordingly, we concluded that ... an award of retroactive relief necessarily "fall[s] afoul of the Eleventh Amendment if that basic constitutional provision is to be conceived of as having any present force." .... In sum *Edelman's* distinction between prospective and retroactive relief fulfills the underlying purpose of Ex parte Young while at the same time preserving to an important degree the constitutional immunity of the States.

This need to reconcile competing interests is wholly absent, however, when a plaintiff alleges that a state official has violated *state* law. In such a case the entire basis for the doctrine of *Young* and *Edelman* disappears. A federal court's grant of relief against state officials on the basis of state law, whether prospective or retroactive, does not vindicate the supreme authority of federal law. On the contrary, it is difficult to think of a greater intrusion on state sovereignty than when a federal court instructs state officials on how to conform their conduct to state law. Such a result conflicts directly with the principles of federalism that underlie the Eleventh Amendment. We conclude that *Young* and *Edelman* are inapplicable in a suit against state officials on the basis of state law.

B

The contrary view of Justice Stevens' dissent rests on fiction, is wrong on the law, and, most important, would emasculate the Eleventh Amendment. Under his view, an allegation that official conduct is contrary to a state statute would suffice to override the State's protection under that Amendment. The theory is that such conduct is contrary to the official's "instructions," and thus *ultra vires* his authority. Accordingly, official action based on a reasonable interpretation of any statute might, if the interpretation turned out to be erroneous, provide the basis for injunctive relief against the actors in their official capacities. In this case, where officials of a major state department, clearly acting within the scope of their authority, were found not to have improved conditions in a state institution adequately under state law, the dissent's result would be that the State itself has forfeited its constitutionally provided immunity.

The theory is out of touch with reality.... To the extent there was a violation of state law in this case, it is a case of the State itself not fulfilling its legislative promises.

. . .

... Under the dissent's view of the *ultra vires* doctrine, the Eleventh Amendment would have force only in the rare case in which a plaintiff foolishly attempts to sue the State in its own name, or where he cannot produce some state statute that has been violated to his asserted injury. Thus, the *ultra vires* doctrine, a narrow and questionable exception, would swallow the general rule that a suit is against the State if the relief will run against it. That result gives the dissent no pause presumably because of its view that the Eleventh Amendment and sovereign immunity "undoubtedly ru[n] counter to modern democratic notions of the moral responsibility of the State." ... The dissent totally rejects the Eleventh Amendment's basis in federalism.

C

The reasoning of our recent decisions on sovereign immunity thus leads to the conclusion that a federal suit against state officials on the basis of state law contravenes the Eleventh Amendment when—as here—the relief sought and ordered has an impact directly on the State itself. In reaching a contrary conclusion, the Court of Appeals relied principally on a separate line of cases dealing with pendent jurisdiction. The crucial point for the Court of Appeals was that this Court has granted relief against state officials on the basis of a pendent state-law claim. We therefore must consider the relationship between pendent jurisdiction and the Eleventh Amendment.

This Court long has held generally that when a federal court obtains jurisdiction over a federal claim, it may adjudicate other related claims over which the court otherwise would not have jurisdiction. See, e.g., Mine Workers v. Gibbs, 383 U.S. 715, 726 (1966); Osborn v. Bank of the United States, 9 Wheat. 738, 819–823 (1824). The Court also has held that a federal court may resolve a case solely on the basis of a pendent state-law claim, see Siler [v. Louisville & Nashville R. Co., 213 U.S. 175, at 192–193 (1909)], and that in fact the court usually should do so in order to avoid federal constitutional questions, see id., at 193; Ashwander v. TVA, 297 U.S. 288, 347 (1936) (Brandeis, J., concurring) ("[I]f a case can be decided on either of two grounds, one involving a constitutional question, the other a question of statutory construction or general law, the Court will decide only the latter"). But pendent jurisdiction is a judge-made doctrine inferred from the general language of Art. III. The question presented is whether this doctrine may be viewed as displacing the explicit limitation on federal jurisdiction contained in the Eleventh Amendment.

As the Court of Appeals noted, in *Siler* and subsequent cases concerning pendent jurisdiction, relief was granted against state officials on the basis of state-law claims that were pendent to federal constitutional claims. In none of these cases, however, did the Court so much as mention the Eleventh Amendment in connection with the state-law claim....

These cases thus did not directly confront the question before us. "[W]hen questions of jurisdiction have been passed on in prior decisions *sub silentio,* this Court has never considered itself bound when a subsequent case finally brings the jurisdictional issue before us." Hagans v. Lavine, 415 U.S. 528, 533, n. 5 (1974). We therefore view the question as an open one.

As noted, the implicit view of these cases seems to have been that once jurisdiction is established on the basis of a federal question, no further Eleventh Amendment inquiry is necessary with respect to other claims raised in the case. This is an erroneous view and contrary to the principles established in our Eleventh Amendment decisions. . . .

. . . The Eleventh Amendment should not be construed to apply with less force to this implied form of jurisdiction than it does to the explicitly granted power to hear federal claims. The history of the adoption and development of the Amendment, confirms that it is an independent limitation on all exercises of Art. III power: "the entire judicial power granted by the Constitution does not embrace authority to entertain suit brought by private parties against a State without consent given," Ex parte State of New York No. 1, 256 U.S. 490, 497 (1921). . . .

. . .

D

Respondents urge that application of the Eleventh Amendment to pendent state-law claims will have a disruptive effect on litigation against state officials. They argue that the "considerations of judicial economy, convenience, and fairness to litigants" that underlie pendent jurisdiction, see *Gibbs,* supra, 383 U.S., at 726, counsel against a result that may cause litigants to split causes of action between state and federal courts. They also contend that the policy of avoiding unnecessary constitutional decisions will be contravened if plaintiffs choose to forgo their state-law claims and sue only in federal court or, alternatively, that the policy of Ex parte Young will be hindered if plaintiffs choose to forgo their right to a federal forum and bring all of their claims in state court.

It may be that applying the Eleventh Amendment to pendent claims results in federal claims being brought in state court, or in bifurcation of claims. That is not uncommon in this area. Under Edelman v. Jordan, supra, a suit against state officials for retroactive monetary relief, whether based on federal or state law, must be brought in state court. Challenges to the validity of state tax systems under 42 U.S.C. § 1983 also must be brought in state court. Fair Assessment in Real Estate Ass'n v. McNary, 454 U.S. 100 (1981). Under the abstention doctrine, unclear issues of state law commonly are split off and referred to the state courts.

In any case, the answer to respondents' assertions is that such consider- ations of policy cannot override the constitutional limitation on the authority of the federal judiciary to adjudicate suits against a State. See Missouri v. Fiske, 290 U.S., at 25–26 ("Considerations of convenience open no avenue of escape from the [Amendment's] restriction"). That a litigant's choice of forum is reduced "has long been understood to be a part of the tension inherent in our system of federalism." Employees v. Missouri Public Health & Welfare Dept., 411 U.S. 279, 298 (1973) (Marshall, J., concurring in result).

. . .

V

The Court of Appeals upheld the judgment of the District Court solely on the basis of Pennsylvania's MH/MR Act. We hold that these federal courts lacked jurisdiction to enjoin petitioner state institutions and state officials on the basis of this state law. The District Court also rested its decision on the Eighth and Fourteenth Amendments and § 504 of the Rehabilitation Act of 1973. On remand the Court of Appeals may consider to what extent, if any, the judgment may be sustained on these bases. The court also may consider whether relief may be granted to respondents under the Developmentally Disabled Assistance and Bill of Rights Act, 42 U.S.C. §§ 6011, 6063. The judgment of the Court of Appeals is reversed, and the case remanded for further proceedings consistent with this opinion.

It is so ordered.

Justice Brennan, dissenting.

I fully agree with Justice Stevens' dissent. Nevertheless, I write separately to explain that in view of my continued belief that the Eleventh Amendment "bars federal court suits against States only by citizens of other States," ... I would hold that petitioners are not entitled to invoke the protections of that Amendment in this federal court suit by citizens of Pennsylvania.... To the extent that such nonconstitutional sovereign immunity may apply to petitioners, I agree with Justice Stevens that since petitioners' conduct was prohibited by state law, the protections of sovereign immunity do not extend to them.

Justice Stevens, with whom Justice Brennan, Justice Marshall, and Justice Blackmun join, dissenting.

... In a completely unprecedented holding, today the Court concludes that Pennsylvania's sovereign immunity prevents a federal court from enjoining the conduct that Pennsylvania itself has prohibited. No rational view of the sovereign immunity of the States supports this result. To the contrary, the question whether a federal court may award injunctive relief on the basis of state law has been answered affirmatively by this Court many times in the past. Yet the Court repudiates at least 28 cases, spanning well over a century of this Court's jurisprudence, proclaiming instead that federal courts have no power to enforce the will of the States by enjoining conduct because it violates state law. This new pronouncement will require the federal courts to decide federal constitutional questions despite the availability of state-law grounds for decision, a result inimical to sound principles of judicial restraint. Nothing in the Eleventh Amendment, the conception of state sovereignty it embodies, or the history of this institution, requires or justifies such a perverse result.

. . .

II

The majority proceeds as if this Court has not had previous occasion to consider the Eleventh Amendment argument made by petitioners, and contends that Ex parte Young, 209 U.S. 123 (1908) has no application to a suit seeking injunctive relief on the basis of state law. That is simply not the case....

. . .

... Until today the rule has been simple: conduct that exceeds the scope of an official's lawful discretion is not conduct the sovereign has authorized and hence is subject to injunction. Whether that conduct also gives rise to damage liability is an entirely separate question.

III

. . .

The pivotal consideration in *Young* was that it was not conduct of the sovereign that was at issue. The rule that unlawful acts of an officer should not be attributed to the sovereign has deep roots in the history of sovereign immunity and makes *Young* reconcilable with the principles of sovereign immunity found in the Eleventh Amendment, rather than merely an unprincipled accommodation between federal and state interests that ignores the principles contained in the Eleventh Amendment.

. . .

It follows that the basis for the *Young* rule is present when the officer sued has violated the law of the sovereign; in all such cases the conduct is of a type that would not be permitted by the sovereign and hence is not attributable to the sovereign under traditional sovereign immunity principles. In such a case, the sovereign's interest lies with those who seek to enforce its laws, rather than those who have violated them. . . . The majority's position that the Eleventh Amendment does not permit federal courts to enjoin conduct that the sovereign State itself seeks to prohibit thus is inconsistent with both the doctrine of sovereign immunity and the underlying respect for the integrity of State policy which the Eleventh Amendment protects. The issuance of injunctive relief which enforces state laws and policies, if anything, enhances federal courts' respect for the sovereign prerogatives of the States. The majority's approach, which requires federal courts to ignore questions of state law and to rest their decisions on federal bases, will create more rather than less friction between the States and the federal judiciary.

Moreover, the majority's rule has nothing to do with the basic reason the Eleventh Amendment was added to the Constitution. There is general agreement that the Amendment was passed because the States were fearful that federal courts would force them to pay their Revolutionary War debts, leading to their financial ruin. Entertaining a suit for injunctive relief based on state law implicates none of the concerns of the Framers. . . .

. . .

IV

The majority's decision in this case is especially unwise in that it overrules a long line of cases in order to reach a result that is at odds with the usual practices of this Court. In one of the most respected opinions ever written by a Member of this Court, Justice Brandeis wrote:

"The Court [has] developed, for its own governance in the cases confessedly within its jurisdiction, a series of rules under which it has avoided passing upon a large part of all the constitutional questions pressed upon it for decision. They are:

. . .

"The Court will not pass upon a constitutional question although properly presented by the record, if there is also present some other ground upon which the case may be disposed of. This rule has found most varied application. Thus, if a case can be decided on either of two grounds, one involving a constitutional question, the other a question of statutory construction or general law, the Court will decide only the latter. *Siler v.*

Louisville & Nashville R. Co., 213 U.S. 175, 191." Ashwander v. Tennessee Valley Authority, 297 U.S. 288, 346–347 (1936) (Brandeis, J., concurring).

The *Siler* case, cited with approval by Justice Brandeis in *Ashwander,* employed a remarkably similar approach to that used by the Court of Appeals in this case. A privately owned railroad corporation brought suit against the members of the railroad commission of Kentucky to enjoin the enforcement of a rate schedule promulgated by the commission. The federal circuit court found that the schedule violated the plaintiff's federal constitutional rights and granted relief. This Court affirmed, but it refused to decide the constitutional question because injunctive relief against the state officials was adequately supported by state law. The Court held that the plaintiff's claim that the schedule violated the Federal Constitution was sufficient to justify the assertion of federal jurisdiction over the case, but then declined to reach the federal question, deciding the case on the basis of state law instead:

> "Where a case in this court can be decided without reference to questions arising under the Federal Constitution, that course is usually pursued and is not departed from without important reasons. In this case we think it much better to decide it with regard to the question of a local nature, involving the construction of the state statute and the authority therein given to the commission to make the order in question, rather than to unnecessarily decide the various constitutional questions appearing in the record." Siler v. Louisville & Nashville R. Co., 213 U.S. 175, 193 (1909).

. . .

Not only does the *Siler* rule have an impressive historical pedigree, but it is also strongly supported by the interest in avoiding duplicative litigation and the unnecessary decision of federal constitutional questions. . . .

In addition, application of the *Siler* rule enhances the decisionmaking autonomy of the States. *Siler* directs the federal court to turn first to state law, which the State is free to modify or repeal. By leaving the policy determinations underlying injunctive relief in the hands of the State, the Court of Appeals' approach gives appropriate deference to established state policies.

In contrast, the rule the majority creates today serves none of the interests of the State. The majority prevents federal courts from implementing State policies through equitable enforcement of State law. Instead, federal courts are required to resolve cases on federal grounds that no State authority can undo. Leaving violations of state law unredressed and ensuring that the decisions of federal courts may never be reexamined by the States hardly comports with the respect for States as sovereign entities commanded by the Eleventh Amendment.

. . .

APPLICATION OF THE ELEVENTH AMENDMENT IN SUITS FOR "RETROACTIVE RELIEF"

Given prior law that the Eleventh Amendment applied to suits by a state's own citizens, and that it applied although only state officers were named parties if the state was the real party in interest, the "stripping doctrine" of Ex parte Young was crucial in permitting private federal court litigation to compel state compliance with the Constitution and federal laws.[1]

---

[1] The Eleventh Amendment is inapplicable to suits by the federal government against states. United States v. Texas, 143 U.S. 621 (1892). Local political subdivisions, such as

The stripping doctrine is not broad enough, however, to permit actions for "retroactive relief" that must be paid from public funds. While a judgment for damages that must be paid only from the state official's personal assets presents no Eleventh Amendment problem, Scheuer v. Rhodes, 416 U.S. 232 (1974), the Eleventh Amendment is still a serious obstacle if a private plaintiff's suit seeks the payment of state funds for past violations of federal law. That was the situation in Edelman v. Jordan, 415 U.S. 651 (1974), where welfare recipients were seeking reimbursement for past welfare payments withheld by state officials in violation of federal law. The Court held that, while the principle of Ex Parte Young supported the lower federal courts' judgment ordering state welfare officials to pay future benefits, the Eleventh Amendment barred any retroactive relief for benefits withheld in the past.

A second fiction—of state "consent" or "waiver" of sovereign immunity—had been applied to permit federal court damage actions against states for violation of federal statutes. Edelman v. Jordan, however, considerably limited that theory—concluding that a state could not be sued in federal court for retroactive relief unless Congress, "by the most express language or by such overwhelming implications from the text," demonstrated its intent to abrogate the state's immunity under the Eleventh Amendment.

In Atascadero State Hospital v. Scanlon, 473 U.S. 234 (1985), Justice Brennan's lengthy dissent reiterated his position that the Eleventh Amendment does not establish a constitutional rule of sovereign immunity. For the first time, that position gained the endorsement of three other Justices (Marshall, Blackmun and Stevens), who joined the dissent. The majority in *Scanlon* disagreed, concluding that the Eleventh Amendment creates a constitutional rule of sovereign immunity. The precise basis of the decision, however, was that Congress had not "unequivocally" expressed its intention to abrogate state sovereign immunity. When that intention has been "unequivocally" expressed, are there limits to Congress' power to permit federal court suits against unconsenting states? The following case deals with that question.

Seminole Tribe of Florida v. Florida

— U.S. —, 116 S.Ct. 1114, 134 L.Ed.2d 252 (1996).

Chief Justice Rehnquist delivered the opinion of the Court.

The Indian Gaming Regulatory Act provides that an Indian tribe may conduct certain gaming activities only in conformance with a valid compact

cities and counties are not "states" within the meaning of the Eleventh Amendment, and are fully subject to private party suits in the federal courts. Mt. Healthy City Sch. Dist. v. Doyle, 429 U.S. 274 (1977). The Eleventh Amendment is inapplicable, finally, to suits brought in state courts, Nevada v. Hall, 440 U.S. 410 (1979), although state law conceptions of sovereign immunity may bar action in the state courts.

While the Eleventh Amendment has no application to suits against the United States, Indian tribes, or foreign countries, independent conceptions of sovereign immunity do apply. In private actions against federal officials, the stripping doctrine has been applied to determine the extent of federal sovereign immunity. Larson v. Domestic & Foreign Commerce Corp., 337 U.S. 682 (1949); Dugan v. Rank, 372 U.S. 609 (1963); Note, *The Sovereign Immunity Doctrine and Judicial Review of Federal Administrative Action*, 2 U.C.L.A.L.Rev. 382 (1955). In 1976, Public Law 94–574, § 1, 90 Stat. 2721, amended the Administrative Procedure Act (5 U.S.C. §§ 702, 703) to eliminate the defense of sovereign immunity in private suits seeking relief other than money damages against the United States. (Congress had long before consented to suit for money damages for tort and contract claims against the United States.) On the immunity of Indian tribes, see Santa Clara Pueblo v. Martinez, 436 U.S. 49, 58 (1978).

between the tribe and the State in which the gaming activities are located.
...25 U.S.C. § 2710(d)(1)(C). The Act, passed by Congress under the Indian
Commerce Clause, U.S. Const., Art. I, § 10, cl. 3, imposes upon the States a
duty to negotiate in good faith with an Indian tribe toward the formation of a
compact, § 2710(d)(3)(A), and authorizes a tribe to bring suit in federal court
against a State in order to compel performance of that duty, § 2710(d)(7). We
hold that notwithstanding Congress' clear intent to abrogate the States' sovereign immunity, the Indian Commerce Clause does not grant Congress that
power, and therefore § 2710(d)(7) cannot grant jurisdiction over a State that
does not consent to be sued. We further hold that the doctrine of Ex parte
Young, 209 U.S. 123 (1908), may not be used to enforce § 2710(d)(3) against a
state official.

I

. . .

In September 1991, the Seminole Tribe of Indians, petitioner, sued the
State of Florida and its Governor, Lawton Chiles, respondents. Invoking
jurisdiction under 25 U.S.C. § 2710(d)(7)(A), as well as 28 U.S.C. §§ 1331 and
1362, petitioner alleged that respondents had "refused to enter into any
negotiation for inclusion of [certain gaming activities] in a tribal-state compact," thereby violating the "requirement of good faith negotiation" contained
in § 2710(d)(3). Respondents moved to dismiss the complaint, arguing that the
suit violated the State's sovereign immunity from suit in federal court. The
District Court denied respondents' motion. . . .

The Court of Appeals for the Eleventh Circuit reversed the decision of the
District Court, holding that the Eleventh Amendment barred petitioner's suit
against respondents. . . .

. . . [W]e granted certiorari . . . in order to consider two questions: (1) Does
the Eleventh Amendment prevent Congress from authorizing suits by Indian
tribes against States for prospective injunctive relief to enforce legislation
enacted pursuant to the Indian Commerce Clause?; and (2) Does the doctrine of
Ex parte Young permit suits against a State's governor for prospective injunctive relief to enforce the good faith bargaining requirement of the Act? We
answer the first question in the affirmative, the second in the negative, and we
therefore affirm the Eleventh Circuit's dismissal of petitioner's suit.

The Eleventh Amendment provides: "The Judicial power of the United
States shall not be construed to extend to any suit in law or equity, commenced
or prosecuted against one of the United States by Citizens of another State, or
by Citizens or Subjects of any Foreign State." Although the text of the
Amendment would appear to restrict only the Article III diversity jurisdiction
of the federal courts, "we have understood the Eleventh Amendment to stand
not so much for what it says, but for the presupposition . . . which it confirms."
. . . That presupposition, first observed over a century ago in Hans v. Louisiana, 134 U.S. 1 (1890), has two parts: first, that each State is a sovereign entity
in our federal system; and second, that "'[i]t is inherent in the nature of
sovereignty not to be amenable to the suit of an individual without its
consent.'" Id., at 13 . . . , quoting The Federalist No. 81 . . . (A.Hamilton).
. . . For over a century we have reaffirmed that federal jurisdiction over suits
against unconsenting States "was not contemplated by the Constitution when
establishing the judicial power of the United States." Hans, supra, at 15.

Here, petitioner has sued the State of Florida and it is undisputed that
Florida has not consented to the suit. . . . Petitioner nevertheless contends that

its suit is not barred by state sovereign immunity. First, it argues that Congress through the Act abrogated the States' sovereign immunity. Alternatively, petitioner maintains that its suit against the Governor may go forward under Ex parte Young, supra. We consider each of those arguments in turn.

II

... In order to determine whether Congress has abrogated the States' sovereign immunity, we ask two questions: first, whether Congress has "unequivocally expresse[d] its intent to abrogate the immunity," ... and second, whether Congress has acted "pursuant to a valid exercise of power." ...

A

Congress' intent to abrogate the States' immunity from suit must be obvious from "a clear legislative statement." ... This rule arises from a recognition of the important role played by the Eleventh Amendment and the broader principles that it reflects. ... In *Atascadero*, we held that "[a] general authorization for suit in federal court is not the kind of unequivocal statutory language sufficient to abrogate the Eleventh Amendment." ...

Here, ... Congress has in § 2710(d)(7) provided an "unmistakably clear" statement of its intent to abrogate. Section 2710(d)(7)(A)(i) vests jurisdiction in "[t]he United States district courts ... over any cause of action ... arising from the failure of a State to enter into negotiations ... or to conduct such negotiations in good faith." ... [T]he numerous references to the "State" in the text of § 2710(d)(7)(B) make it indubitable that Congress intended through the Act to abrogate the States' sovereign immunity from suit.

B

... [W]e turn now to consider whether the Act was passed "pursuant to a valid exercise of power." ...

Petitioner suggests that one consideration weighing in favor of finding the power to abrogate here is that the Act authorizes only prospective injunctive relief rather than retroactive monetary relief. But we have often made it clear that the relief sought by a plaintiff suing a State is irrelevant to the question whether the suit is barred by the Eleventh Amendment. ...

Similarly, petitioner argues that the abrogation power is validly exercised here because the Act grants the States a power that they would not otherwise have, viz., some measure of authority over gaming on Indian lands. It is true enough that the Act extends to the States a power withheld from them by the Constitution. ...Nevertheless, we do not see how that consideration is relevant to the question whether Congress may abrogate state sovereign immunity. The Eleventh Amendment immunity may not be lifted by Congress unilaterally deciding that it will be replaced by grant of some other authority. ...

Thus our inquiry into whether Congress has the power to abrogate unilaterally the States' immunity from suit is narrowly focused on one question: Was the Act in question passed pursuant to a constitutional provision granting Congress the power to abrogate? See, e.g., Fitzpatrick v. Bitzer, 427 U.S. 445, 452–456 (1976). Previously, in conducting that inquiry, we have found authority to abrogate under only two provisions of the Constitution. In *Fitzpatrick*, we recognized that the Fourteenth Amendment, by expanding federal power at the expense of state autonomy, had fundamentally altered the balance of state and federal power struck by the Constitution. ... We noted that § 1 of the Fourteenth Amendment contained prohibitions expressly directed at the States and that § 5 of the Amendment expressly provided that "The Congress shall have the power to enforce, by appropriate legislation, the provisions of this article." . . . We held that through the Fourteenth Amendment, federal power extended to intrude upon the province of the Eleventh Amendment and therefore that § 5 of the Fourteenth Amendment allowed Congress to abrogate the immunity from suit guaranteed by that Amendment.

In only one other case has congressional abrogation of the States' Eleventh Amendment immunity been upheld. In Pennsylvania v. Union Gas Co., 491 U.S. 1 (1989), a plurality of the Court found that the Interstate Commerce Clause, Art. I, § 8, cl. 3, granted Congress the power to abrogate state sovereign immunity, stating that the power to regulate interstate commerce would be "incomplete without the authority to render States liable in damages." . . . Justice White added the fifth vote necessary to the result in that case, but wrote separately in order to express that he "[did] not agree with much of [the plurality's] reasoning." . . .

. . . .

. . . [T]he plurality opinion in *Union Gas* allows no principled distinction in favor of the States to be drawn between the Indian Commerce Clause and the Interstate Commerce Clause.

. . . Generally, the principle of stare decisis, and the interests that it serves, . . . counsel strongly against reconsideration of our precedent. Nevertheless, we always have treated stare decisis as a "principle of policy," . . . and not as an "inexorable command," . . . "[W]hen governing decisions are unworkable or are badly reasoned, 'this Court has never felt constrained to follow precedent.'" . . . Our willingness to reconsider our earlier decisions has been "particularly true in constitutional cases, because in such cases 'correction through legislative action is practically impossible.'" . . .

The Court in *Union Gas* reached a result without an expressed rationale agreed upon by a majority of the Court. . . .

The plurality's rationale also deviated sharply from our established federalism jurisprudence and essentially eviscerated our decision in *Hans*. . . . It was well established in 1989 when *Union Gas* was decided that the Eleventh Amendment stood for the constitutional principle that state sovereign immunity limited the federal courts' jurisdiction under Article III. . . .

Never before the decision in *Union Gas* had we suggested that the bounds of Article III could be expanded by Congress operating pursuant to any constitutional provision other than the Fourteenth Amendment. Indeed, it had seemed fundamental that Congress could not expand the jurisdiction of the federal courts beyond the bounds of Article III. Marbury v. Madison, 1 Cranch 137 (1803). . . .

The plurality's extended reliance upon our decision in Fitzpatrick v. Bitzer, 427 U.S. 445 (1976), that Congress could under the Fourteenth Amendment abrogate the States' sovereign immunity was also, we believe, misplaced. *Fitzpatrick* was based upon a rationale wholly inapplicable to the Interstate Commerce Clause, viz., that the Fourteenth Amendment, adopted well after the adoption of the Eleventh Amendment and the ratification of the Constitution, operated to alter the pre-existing balance between state and federal power achieved by Article III and the Eleventh Amendment. . . . *Fitzpatrick* cannot be read to justify "limitation of the principle embodied in the Eleventh Amendment through appeal to antecedent provisions of the Constitution." . . .

. . . Reconsidering the decision in *Union Gas*, we conclude that none of the policies underlying stare decisis require our continuing adherence to its holding. . . . The case involved the interpretation of the Constitution and therefore may be altered only by constitutional amendment or revision by this Court. . . .

. . .

In overruling *Union Gas* today, we reconfirm that the background principle of state sovereign immunity embodied in the Eleventh Amendment is not so ephemeral as to dissipate when the subject of the suit is an area, like the regulation of Indian commerce, that is under the exclusive control of the Federal Government. Even when the Constitution vests in Congress complete law-making authority over a particular area, the Eleventh Amendment prevents congressional authorization of suits by private parties against unconsenting States. The Eleventh Amendment restricts the judicial power under Article III, and Article I cannot be used to circumvent the constitutional limitations placed upon federal jurisdiction. Petitioner 's suit against the State of Florida must be dismissed for a lack of jurisdiction.

III

Petitioner argues that we may exercise jurisdiction over its suit to enforce § 2710(d)(3) against the Governor notwithstanding the jurisdictional bar of the Eleventh Amendment. Petitioner notes that since our decision in Ex parte Young, 209 U.S. 123 (1908), we often have found federal jurisdiction over a suit against a state official when that suit seeks only prospective injunctive relief in order to "end a continuing violation of federal law." . . . The situation presented here, however, is sufficiently different from that giving rise to the traditional Ex parte Young action so as to preclude the availability of that doctrine.

Here, the "continuing violation of federal law" alleged by petitioner is the Governor's failure to bring the State into compliance with § 2710(d)(3). But the duty to negotiate imposed upon the State by that statutory provision does not stand alone. Rather, . . . Congress passed § 2710(d)(3) in conjunction with the carefully crafted and intricate remedial scheme set forth in § 2710(d)(7).

Where Congress has created a remedial scheme for the enforcement of a particular federal right, we have, in suits against federal officers, refused to supplement that scheme with one created by the judiciary. . . .

Here, Congress intended § 2710(d)(3) to be enforced against the State in an action brought under § 2710(d)(7); the intricate procedures set forth in that provision show that Congress intended therein not only to define, but also significantly to limit, the duty imposed by § 2710(d)(3). For example, where the court finds that the State has failed to negotiate in good faith, the only remedy prescribed is an order directing the State and the Indian tribe to conclude a compact within 60 days. And if the parties disregard the court's order and fail to conclude a compact within the 60–day period, the only sanction is that each party then must submit a proposed compact to a mediator who selects the one which best embodies the terms of the Act. Finally, if the State fails to accept the compact selected by the mediator, the only sanction against it is that the mediator shall notify the Secretary of the Interior who then must prescribe regulations governing Class III gaming on the tribal lands at issue. By contrast with this quite modest set of sanctions, an action brought against a state official under Ex parte Young would expose that official to the full remedial powers of a federal court, including, presumably, contempt sanctions. If § 2710(d)(3) could be enforced in a suit under Ex parte Young, § 2710(d)(7) would have been superfluous; it is difficult to see why an Indian tribe would suffer through the intricate scheme of § 2710(d)(7) when more complete and more immediate relief would be available under Ex parte Young.

Here, of course, we have found that Congress does not have authority under the Constitution to make the State suable in federal court under § 2710(d)(7). Nevertheless, the fact that Congress chose to impose upon the State a liability which is significantly more limited than would be the liability imposed upon the state officer under Ex parte Young strongly indicates that Congress had no wish to create the latter under § 2710(d)(3). Nor are we free to rewrite the statutory scheme in order to approximate what we think Congress might have wanted had it known that § 2710(d)(7) was beyond its authority. If that effort is to be made, it should be made by Congress, and not by the federal courts. We hold that Ex parte Young is inapplicable to petitioner's suit against the Governor of Florida, and therefore that suit is barred by the Eleventh Amendment and must be dismissed for a lack of jurisdiction.

IV

The Eleventh Amendment prohibits Congress from making the State of Florida capable of being sued in federal court. The narrow exception to the Eleventh Amendment provided by the Ex parte Young doctrine cannot be used to enforce § 2710(d)(3) because Congress enacted a remedial scheme, § 2710(d)(7), specifically designed for the enforcement of that right. The Eleventh Circuit's dismissal of petitioner's suit is hereby affirmed.

It is so ordered.

Justice Stevens, dissenting.

This case is about power—the power of the Congress of the United States to create a private federal cause of action against a State, or its Governor, for the violation of a federal right. ... [I]n a sharp break with the past, today the Court holds that with the narrow and illogical exception of statutes enacted pursuant to the Enforcement Clause of the Fourteenth Amendment, Congress has no such power.

The importance of the majority's decision to overrule the Court's holding in Pennsylvania v. Union Gas Co. cannot be overstated. The majority's opinion does not simply preclude Congress from establishing the rather curious statutory scheme under which Indian tribes may seek the aid of a federal court to secure a State's good faith negotiations over gaming regulations. Rather, it prevents Congress from providing a federal forum for a broad range of actions against States, from those sounding in copyright and patent law, to those concerning bankruptcy, environmental law, and the regulation of our vast national economy.

There may be room for debate over whether, in light of the Eleventh Amendment, Congress has the power to ensure that such a cause of action may be enforced in federal court by a citizen of another State or a foreign citizen. There can be no serious debate, however, over whether Congress has the power to ensure that such a cause of action may be brought by a citizen of the State being sued. Congress' authority in that regard is clear.

. . .

For these reasons, as well as those set forth in Justice Souter's opinion, I respectfully dissent.

Justice Souter, with whom Justice Ginsburg and Justice Breyer join, dissenting.

. . .

The fault I find with the majority today is not in its decision to reexamine *Union Gas*, for the Court in that case produced no majority for a single rationale supporting congressional authority. Instead, I part company from the Court because I am convinced that its decision is fundamentally mistaken, and for that reason I respectfully dissent.

. . .

It is useful to separate three questions: (1) whether the States enjoyed sovereign immunity if sued in their own courts in the period prior to ratification of the National Constitution; (2) if so, whether after ratification the States were entitled to claim some such immunity when sued in a federal court exercising jurisdiction either because the suit was between a State and a non-state litigant who was not its citizen, or because the issue in the case raised a federal question; and (3) whether any state sovereign immunity recognized in federal court may be abrogated by Congress.

The answer to the first question is not clear, although some of the Framers assumed that States did enjoy immunity in their own courts. The second question was not debated at the time of ratification, except as to citizen-state diversity jurisdiction; there was no unanimity, but in due course the Court in Chisholm v. Georgia, 2 Dall. 419 (1793), answered that a state defendant enjoyed no such immunity. As to federal question jurisdiction, state sovereign immunity seems not to have been debated prior to ratification, the silence probably showing a general understanding at the time that the States would have no immunity in such cases.

The adoption of the Eleventh Amendment soon changed the result in *Chisholm*, not by mentioning sovereign immunity, but by eliminating citizen-state diversity jurisdiction over cases with state defendants. ... The *Hans* Court erroneously assumed that a State could plead sovereign immunity against a noncitizen suing under federal question jurisdiction, and for that reason held that a State must enjoy the same protection in a suit by one of its citizens. ...

The Court's answer today to the third question is likewise at odds with the Founders' view that common law, when it was received into the new American legal systems, was always subject to legislative amendment. ...

. . .

The *Hans* doctrine was erroneous, but it has not previously proven to be unworkable. ... I would therefore treat *Hans* as it has always been treated in fact until today, as a doctrine of federal common law. For, as so understood, it has formed one of the strands of the federal relationship for over a century now, and the stability of that relationship is itself a value that stare decisis aims to respect.

In being ready to hold that the relationship may still be altered, not by the Court but by Congress, I would tread the course laid out elsewhere in our cases. ... The plain statement rule, which "assures that the legislature has in fact faced, and intended to bring into issue, the critical matters involved in the judicial decision," ... is particularly appropriate in light of our primary reliance on "[t]he effectiveness of the federal political process in preserving the States' interests." Garcia v. San Antonio Metropolitan Transit Authority, 469 U.S. 528, 552 (1985). ...

When judging legislation passed under unmistakable Article I powers, no further restriction could be required. Nor does the Court explain why more could be demanded. In the past, we have assumed that a plain statement requirement is sufficient to protect the States from undue federal encroachments upon their traditional immunity from suit. ... It is hard to contend that this rule has set the bar too low, for (except in *Union Gas*) we have never found the requirement to be met outside the context of laws passed under § 5 of the Fourteenth Amendment. The exception I would recognize today proves the rule, moreover, because the federal abrogation of state immunity comes as part of a regulatory scheme which is itself designed to invest the States with regulatory powers that Congress need not extend to them. This fact suggests to me that the political safeguards of federalism are working, that a plain statement rule is an adequate check on congressional overreaching, and that today's abandonment of that approach is wholly unwarranted.

. . .

C.   NON-CONSTITUTIONAL RESTRICTIONS ON FEDERAL COURT INJUNCTIONS AGAINST UNCONSTITUTIONAL STATE LAWS

Introduction. As the previous subsection demonstrates, the "stripping" doctrine of Ex parte Young has eliminated the possible Eleventh Amendment bar to federal court injunctions against enforcement of state laws violating federal law, or to declaratory judgments of their invalidity. A complex set of statutory restrictions on federal court jurisdiction, combined with judge-made rules of equitable restraint, still serve to control decisions by federal courts that state laws are unconstitutional. A complete assessment of those restrictions and restraints is usually undertaken in specialized courses in federal jurisdiction, and they can only be introduced briefly here. Topics examined include: the problems that arise when the challenged state law is ambiguous, and the ambiguity can only be resolved authoritatively by a state court; and whether litigants are required to exhaust state administrative and judicial remedies before going to federal court to enjoin enforcement of a state law.

ABSTENTION TO ALLOW STATE COURTS TO CONSTRUE AMBIGUOUS STATE LAW

A complication that arises when a federal court suit is brought to determine the constitutional validity of a state law is that there may be serious questions concerning the proper interpretation of that law—particularly if it was recently enacted.

When the Supreme Court reviews a state court decision concerning the constitutional validity of a state law, the Court can consider only issues of federal law. There has been, however, a decision by a state court, and an opportunity for it to address questions of state law interpretation.

When suit challenging a state law is brought in a federal court, it must determine, as a court of first instance, the entire controversy under all relevant law. If the constitutionality of the challenged law depends upon its meaning, the federal court must supply an interpretation. If the relevant issues of state law have been decided by a state's highest court, that decision is as binding on the lower federal court as it is in the Supreme Court on appeal. When there is no relevant state court decision, as is often true when the challenged statute was newly enacted, the federal court must predict the resolution of the issue by the state courts.

Until recently, federal courts were required to consider other issues of state law in suits to enjoin state laws alleged to violate the United States Constitution. Siler v. Louisville & Nashville R. Co., 213 U.S. 175 (1908), held that the federal court must first decide if the challenged state action violated state law. Even if the constitutional issue could be decided without resolving the ambiguities in state law, a policy of avoiding unnecessary federal constitutional decisions dictated that the court decide first whether the plaintiff could prevail on other issues. The 1984 decision in Pennhurst State School & Hosp. v. Halderman, page 59 supra, holding that relief based on state law is barred by the Eleventh Amendment, now bars relief against state officers under state law. *Pennhurst* requires that a federal court limit injunctive relief to claims based on federal law.

While the *Siler* doctrine required the federal court to resolve relevant state law issues, state courts were still the authoritative voice on issues of state law. If the issue of state law were important, obvious practical problems arose. The federal court's interpretation of state law might conflict with later state court decisions, or the federal court's injunction might practically foreclose later state court resolution of those issues.

The *"Pullman* doctrine" responded to the problems by allowing or requiring the federal court to withhold action, pending commencement of a state court action to resolve the issues of state law. The doctrine takes its name from Railroad Commission of Texas v. Pullman Co., 312 U.S. 496 (1941). A group of Pullman porters, all of whom were black, challenged an order of the state regulatory commission assigning work exclusively to conductors, all of whom were white. The Court concluded that the lower federal courts should not have addressed the merits of the federal constitutional attack on the commission's order. There was a question whether the commission had the authority to adopt the order under state law. The Court directed the district court to retain jurisdiction pending a suit brought in state court to resolve the state law issues.

Because of the *Pennhurst* decision, it is not clear how the *Pullman* doctrine applies when the only unresolved state law issues concern whether the challenged official action violates state law, as in *Pullman* itself. The *Pullman* doctrine is still clearly relevant, however, when the constitutionality of a challenged state law depends upon its meaning.

Bringing a second action in a state court may seriously delay decision by the federal court, however, and maintaining two lawsuits is expensive. The expense and delay may be so serious that the plaintiff will be practically forced to abandon litigating constitutional issues in the federal courts. The opposing advantages and disadvantages of *Pullman* abstention have produced a complex body of decisions. Whether abstention is appropriate in a particular case may depend on arguable conclusions concerning the degree of uncertainty in the state law issues, on the one hand, and the degree of delay and expense involved in seeking guidance from the state courts, on the other. For example, abstention may be inappropriate if there are multiple unsettled questions that cannot be easily resolved in a separate state court proceeding. Baggett v. Bullitt, 377 U.S. 360, 378 (1964).

For a detailed discussion of the *Pullman* doctrine, see Field, *Abstention in Constitutional Cases: The Scope of the Pullman Abstention Doctrine,* 122 U.Pa.L.Rev. 1071 (1974). The special problems posed by the doctrine in free speech cases are discussed below in Chapter 13, at page 1239.

EXHAUSTION OF STATE ADMINISTRATIVE REMEDIES

It used to be the unquestioned rule that a plaintiff seeking a federal court injunction against application of a state law must first exhaust reasonable and available state administrative remedies. Two cases in the 1960's developed an exception to the rule of exhaustion that was so large it virtually swallowed the rule. In McNeese v. Board of Education, 373 U.S. 668 (1963), the Court rejected an argument that plaintiffs challenging a segregated school system should first have used local procedures for reassignment of individual pupils to new schools. In Damico v. California, 389 U.S. 416 (1967), the Court decided that federal court challenges to state denials of welfare benefits did not have to await the resolution of individual administrative proceedings to determine whether benefits were properly denied.

It was possible to argue in both *McNeese* and *Damico* that a requirement of exhaustion of administrative remedies was not practically relevant to decision of the constitutional issues involved. The rationale for decision in both cases, however, was much broader. The Court concluded that cases brought under 42 U.S.C. § 1983 were a categorical exception to the rule requiring exhaustion of administrative remedies. The problem is that 42 U.S.C. § 1983 covers *all* suits against state officials to invalidate state action on the ground that it is in conflict with the United States Constitution. Some Justices have argued that the categorical exception should be pared down, and that individual challengers to state action as unconstitutional should be required to exhaust reasonable available state administrative remedies before bringing suit in a federal court. E.g., Runyon v. McCrary, 427 U.S. 160, 186 n. * (1976) (Powell, J., concurring). In Patsy v. Florida Board of Regents, 457 U.S. 496 (1982), however, a divided Court reaffirmed its previous rulings that exhaustion of administrative remedies is not required in any § 1983 actions. Thus, barring Congressional action, most constitutional challenges to state legislative or administrative action are not subject to the general rule requiring exhaustion of administrative remedies prior to federal court action.[1]

EXHAUSTION OF STATE JUDICIAL REMEDIES

The exhaustion requirement was never generally applied to require a litigant to exhaust state "judicial" as opposed to "administrative" remedies. Bacon v. Rutland R. Co., 232 U.S. 134 (1914); City Bank Farmers' Trust Co. v. Schnader, 291 U.S. 24 (1934). Thus, a federal court injunction was not precluded by the existence of an adequate remedy within the state judicial system. Two statutes enacted in the 1930s, however, preclude federal court jurisdiction where "plain, speedy and efficient" remedies are available in state courts.

The Johnson Act, enacted in 1934, and now found in 28 U.S.C. § 1342, reads as follows:

"The district courts shall not enjoin, suspend or restrain the operation of, or compliance with, any order affecting rates chargeable by a public utility and made by a State administrative agency or a rate-making body of a State political subdivision, where:

"(1) Jurisdiction is based solely on diversity of citizenship or repugnance of the order to the Federal Constitution; and,

"(2) The order does not interfere with interstate commerce; and,

"(3) The order has been made after reasonable notice and hearing; and,

"(4) A plain, speedy and efficient remedy may be had in the courts of such State."

[1] In the Civil Rights of Institutionalized Persons Act, 42 U.S.C. § 1997(e), Congress imposed a limited exhaustion requirement for adult prisoners bringing action under § 1983.

In cases not technically within the terms of the Johnson Act, the Court has relied upon principles of equitable discretion in requiring state court review of state public utility regulatory orders not affecting rates. Burford v. Sun Oil Co., 319 U.S. 315 (1943) (order permitting drilling of new oil well); Alabama Public Service Comm'n v. Southern Ry. Co., 341 U.S. 341 (1951) (order refusing to permit discontinuation of train service).

The Tax Injunction Act, passed in 1937, is now found in 28 U.S.C. § 1341 and reads as follows:

> "The district courts shall not enjoin, suspend or restrain the assessment, levy or collection of any tax under State law where a plain, speedy and efficient remedy may be had in the courts of such State."

ENJOINING STATE JUDICIAL PROCEEDINGS: THE ANTI–INJUNCTION ACT

The Anti–Injunction Act, 28 U.S.C. § 2283, provides that a federal court "may not grant an injunction to stay proceedings in a State Court except as expressly authorized by Act of Congress, or where necessary in aid of its jurisdiction, or to protect or effectuate its judgments." At one time, the statute was significant in precluding federal court action to enjoin enforcement of allegedly unconstitutional state laws if a proceeding to enforce that law was pending against the federal plaintiff in state court. While the statute was inapplicable if the federal suit was brought before the state enforcement proceeding began, the statute was a complete ban on issuing a federal injunction against a pending state proceeding unless one of the exceptions in the statute was applicable. In Mitchum v. Foster, 407 U.S. 225 (1972), the Court held that suits under 42 U.S.C. § 1983 fell within one of those exceptions, as a case where Congress had "expressly authorized" enjoining pending state actions. Since most suits to enjoin enforcement of unconstitutional state action are based on § 1983, the Anti–Injunction Act is no longer a bar to enjoining pending state proceedings in such cases.

ENJOINING STATE ENFORCEMENT PROCEEDINGS: YOUNGER V. HARRIS AND "OUR FEDERALISM"

As previous notes demonstrate, the older judicial doctrine requiring exhaustion of administrative remedies, and the statutory prohibition against enjoining pending state judicial proceedings, are inapplicable to federal court suits to enjoin state officials from enforcing unconstitutional state laws. However, as the Court noted in *Mitchum v. Foster,* supra, other "principles of equity, comity, and federalism" may still restrain federal courts when there is a pending state criminal action, civil judicial enforcement proceeding, or administrative enforcement proceeding, pending against the plaintiff in the federal court action.

The rules applicable to pending state criminal proceedings have been elaborated in some detail. The seminal decision was Younger v. Harris, 401 U.S. 37 (1971), where the Court held that—in the absence of a clear demonstration that the prosecution was in bad faith—a federal court could not entertain an action by a defendant in a state criminal case alleging that the statute under which he was prosecuted was unconstitutional.[1] Justice Black's opinion for the Court referred to a

---

[1] The Court also held that a federal court action by persons not threatened with prose- cution under the statute was premature.

"notion of 'comity,' that is, a proper respect for state functions, a recognition of the fact that the entire country is made up of a Union of separate state governments, and a continuance of the belief that the National Government will fare best if the States and their institutions are left free to perform their separate functions in their separate ways. This, perhaps for lack of a better and clearer way to describe it, is referred to by many as 'Our Federalism.' "

Justice Black described the pragmatic concerns of "Our Federalism" as the avoidance of unnecessary delay in trying state criminal cases, and preventing what amounted to review of state court decisions by lower federal courts instead of the traditional review by the Supreme Court.

If no prosecution is pending, a person threatened with prosecution is entitled to maintain a suit for declaratory judgment of unconstitutionality (as opposed to an injunction). Steffel v. Thompson, 415 U.S. 452 (1974). The *Younger* doctrine, however, bars an injunction against a later state criminal action, or a declaratory judgment, if the prosecution was begun before "proceedings of substance on the merits" have occurred in the federal action. Hicks v. Miranda, 422 U.S. 332 (1975). (As indicated in the previous note, the Anti–Injunction Act did not apply to bar an injunction against a state criminal enforcement action if the federal court action was begun first.) The federal plaintiff can avoid abatement of the action by later state prosecution (under the rule of *Hicks v. Miranda*), by obtaining a temporary injunction against prosecution on a sufficient showing of irreparable harm and likely success on the merits. Doran v. Salem Inn, Inc., 422 U.S. 922 (1975). There is some uncertainty whether, if the state statute is declared unconstitutional in the federal action, later state prosecutions under the statute can be enjoined. See Shapiro, *State Courts and Federal Declaratory Judgments,* 80 N.W.U.L.Rev. 759 (1979). The Court has held that a person convicted of violating a statute in the past can sue to enjoin future prosecutions, if the convictions have become final and the requested relief is limited to preventing prosecution in the future. Wooley v. Maynard, 430 U.S. 705 (1977).[2]

The Court has been divided on the question of the application of *Younger* rules to state enforcement of its laws through civil and administrative proceedings. The issue is whether many of the restraints previously imposed by the doctrine of exhaustion of administrative remedies, and the Anti–Injunction Act, will be reintroduced by *Younger* and "Our Federalism."

SECTION 3. CASES AND CONTROVERSIES AND JUSTICIABILITY

A. IN GENERAL

Introduction. The limitations explored below arose initially from the Court's early rejection of an advisory opinion role for the federal courts and from the theory of *Marbury v. Madison* that judicial review is simply a function of deciding ordinary litigation between adverse parties in which it becomes necessary to determine the constitutional validity of legislation to resolve the disputes.

That aspect of the decision is discussed infra, p. 1240.

[2] The application of these rules to free speech cases is discussed in Chapter 13, infra, at p. 1239.

The doctrines involved in this section are characteristically "soft" in the sense that it is difficult to define the rules with precision and in the sense that they do not appear to be consistent in their application. The imprecision and inconsistency result in part from the fact that these doctrines are used by the Court to regulate the extent of its impact. See e.g., the discussion in Rescue Army v. Municipal Court, 331 U.S. 549 (1947). An "activist" Court seeking to expand the application of certain constitutional doctrines is more likely to construe justiciability limitations narrowly in order to reach the merits of cases; a Court interested in "retrenchment and consolidation" is more likely to construe justiciability limitations broadly in order to avoid reaching the merits of cases. For varying points of view concerning the usefulness of these doctrines in regulating the impact of judicial review, see Bickel, *The Least Dangerous Branch*, Ch. 4 (1962); Gunther, *The Subtle Vices of the "Passive Virtues"—A Comment on Principle and Expediency in Judicial Review*, 64 Colum.L.Rev. 1 (1964); Brilmayer, *The Jurisprudence of Article III: Perspectives on the "Case or Controversy" Requirement*, 93 Harv.L.Rev. 297 (1979).

ADVISORY OPINIONS

In 1793 President Washington over the objection of Hamilton, who thought the matter was not within the province of the judiciary, submitted to the Justices 29 questions relating to international law, neutrality, and the construction of the French and British treaties. Secretary of State Jefferson wrote as follows to Chief Justice Jay:

"The war which has taken place among the powers of Europe produces frequent transactions within our ports and limits, on which questions arise of considerable difficulty, and of greater importance to the peace of the United States. These questions depend for their solution on the construction of our treaties, on the laws of nature and nations, and on the law of the land, and are often presented under circumstances which do not give a cognizance of them to the tribunals of the country. Yet their decision is so little analogous to the ordinary functions of the Executive as to occasion much embarrassment and difficulty to them. The President would, therefore, be much relieved if he found himself free to refer questions of this description to the opinions of the Judges of the Supreme Court of the United States, whose knowledge of the subject would secure us as against errors dangerous to the peace of the United States, and their authority ensure the respect of all parties. He has therefore asked the attendance of such of the Judges as could be collected in time for the occasion, to know, in the first place, their opinion, whether the public may, with propriety, be availed of their advice on these questions. And if they may, to present, for their advice, the abstract questions which have already occurred, or may soon occur, from which they will themselves strike out such as any circumstances might, in their opinion, forbid them to pronounce on."

After considering the matter for a few weeks the Justices replied as follows:

"We have considered the previous question stated in a letter written by your direction to us by the Secretary of State, on the 18th of last month regarding the lines of separation, drawn by the Constitution between the three departments of the government. These being in certain respects checks upon each other, and our being Judges of a Court in the last resort, are considerations which afford strong arguments against the propriety of our extra-judicially deciding the questions alluded to, especially as the power given by the Constitution to the President, of calling on the heads of departments for opinions, seems to have been *purposely* as well as express-ly united to the *Executive* departments. We exceedingly regret every event that may cause embarrassment to your Administration, but we derive consolation from the reflection that your judgment will discern what is right, and that your usual prudence, decision and firmness will surmount every obstacle to the preservation of the rights, peace, and dignity of the United States."

The Flast v. Cohen Summary

Warren, C.J., for the Court in Flast v. Cohen, 392 U.S. 83, 94–97 (1968):

"The jurisdiction of federal courts is defined and limited by Article III of the Constitution. In terms relevant to the question for decision in this case, the judicial power of federal courts is constitutionally restricted to 'cases' and 'controversies.' As is so often the situation in constitutional adjudication, those two words have an iceberg quality, containing beneath their surface simplicity submerged complexities which go to the very heart of our constitutional form of government. Embodied in the words 'cases' and 'controversies' are two comple-mentary but somewhat different limitations. In part those words limit the business of federal courts to questions presented in an adversary context and in a form historically viewed as capable of resolution through the judicial process. And in part those words define the role assigned to the judiciary in a tripartite allocation of power to assure that the federal courts will not intrude into areas committed to the other branches of government. Justiciability is the term of art employed to give expression to this dual limitation placed upon federal courts by the case and controversy doctrine.

"Justiciability is itself a concept of uncertain meaning and scope. Its reach is illustrated by the various grounds upon which questions sought to be adjudicated in federal courts have been held not to be justiciable. Thus, no justiciable controversy is presented when the parties seek adjudication of only a political question, when the parties are asking for an advisory opinion, when the question sought to be adjudicated has been mooted by subsequent develop-ments, and when there is no standing to maintain the action. Yet it remains true that '[j]usticiability is ... not a legal concept with a fixed content of susceptible or scientific verification. Its utilization is the resultant of many subtle pressures....' Poe v. Ullman, 367 U.S. 497, 508 (1961).

"Part of the difficulty in giving precise meaning and form to the concept of justiciability stems from the uncertain historical antecedents of the case and controversy doctrine.... [I]t is quite clear that 'the oldest and most consistent thread in the federal law of justiciability is that federal courts will not give advisory opinions.' Wright, Federal Courts 34 (1963). Thus, the implicit policies embodied in Article III, and not history alone, impose the rule against advisory opinions on federal courts. When the federal judicial power is invoked to pass upon the validity of actions by the Legislative and Executive Branches of the Government, the rule against advisory opinions implements the separation of powers prescribed by the Constitution and confines federal courts to the role assigned them by Article III.... However, the rule against advisory opinions also recognizes that such suits often 'are not pressed before the Court with that clear concreteness provided when a question emerges precisely framed and necessary for decision from a clash of adversary argument exploring every aspect of a multifaced situation embracing conflicting and demanding inter-ests.' United States v. Fruehauf, 365 U.S. 146, 157 (1961). Consequently, the Article III prohibition against advisory opinions reflects the complementary constitutional considerations expressed by the justiciability doctrine: Federal judicial power is limited to those disputes which confine federal courts to a role consistent with a system of separated powers and which are traditionally thought to be capable of resolution through the judicial process.

"Additional uncertainty exists in the doctrine of justiciability because that doctrine has become a blend of constitutional requirements and policy considerations. And a policy limitation is 'not always clearly distinguished from the constitutional limitation.' Barrows v. Jackson, 346 U.S. 249, 255 (1953). For example, in his concurring opinion in Ashwander v. Tennessee Valley Authority, 297 U.S. 288, 345–348 (1936), Mr. Justice Brandeis listed seven rules developed by this Court 'for its own governance' to avoid passing prematurely on constitutional questions. Because the rules operate in 'cases confessedly within [the Court's] jurisdiction,' id., at 346, they find their source in policy, rather than purely constitutional, considerations. However, several of the cases cited by Mr. Justice Brandeis in illustrating the rules of self-governance articulated purely constitutional grounds for decision. See, e.g., Massachusetts v. Mellon, 262 U.S. 447 (1923); Fairchild v. Hughes, 258 U.S. 126 (1922); Chicago & Grand Trunk R. Co. v. Wellman, 143 U.S. 339 (1892). The 'many subtle pressures' which cause policy considerations to blend into the constitutional limitations of Article III make the justiciability doctrine one of uncertain and shifting contours."

JUSTICIABILITY AND THE FORM OF THE LITIGATION— RAISING CONSTITUTIONAL ISSUES

(1) **Raising Constitutional Issues.** How do persons go about getting an adjudication concerning the constitutionality of statutes (or other governmental actions) which affect them? In any individual case one or more of the following methods may be available:

(1) If the statute is made the basis of claim or defense in a suit between private individuals, the constitutional issue can be litigated. For an important constitutional law case which arose in this manner, see Gibbons v. Ogden, 22 U.S. (9 Wheat.) 1 (1824), set out infra p. 167.

(2) If the government (federal or state) brings a civil suit based on the statute, the claim of unconstitutionality can be raised in defense. For a leading constitutional case which arose in this matter, see McCulloch v. Maryland, 17 U.S. (4 Wheat.) 316 (1819), set out infra p. 157.

(3) If the government institutes criminal proceedings based on the statute, unconstitutionality of the statute is a defense. For cases in which important issues of state and federal taxing power were raised in this fashion, see Brown v. Maryland, 25 U.S. (12 Wheat.) 419 (1827); United States v. Kahriger, 345 U.S. 22 (1953).

(4) One damaged by governmental action claimed to be unconstitutional may be able to raise the issue in a suit for damages. For a case where a plaintiff succeeded in such a suit see United States v. Causby, 328 U.S. 256 (1946).

(5) Persons held in official custody may challenge the constitutionality of their detention by writ of habeas corpus (or a statutory substitute for the writ such as 28 U.S.C. § 2255). See, e.g., Fay v. Noia, 372 U.S. 391 (1963).

(6) One may bring a suit seeking an injunction or a declaratory judgment as to the constitutionality of a statute. Frequently such an action

is brought in order to challenge constitutionality without taking the risk of civil or criminal liability involved in acting in disregard of the statute. A large portion of constitutional litigation takes this form.

(2) **Relevance of Form of Litigation to Justiciability.** Few issues of justiciability arise where constitutional issues are determined in suits taking the first five forms described above. The litigation involves adverse parties in traditional forms. The constitutional issue is posed in a way quite compatible with the theory of Marbury v. Madison. However, when suits are brought seeking to enjoin the enforcement of statutes on the ground of unconstitutionality or seeking judgments declaring statutes unconstitutional, problems of case and controversy and justiciability frequently arise. The student will notice that most of the cases in this section involve such suits.

B.   STANDING

1.   "CONVENTIONAL" STANDING

Warth v. Seldin

422 U.S. 490, 95 S.Ct. 2197, 45 L.Ed.2d 343 (1975).

Mr. Justice Powell delivered the opinion of the Court.

Petitioners, various organizations and individuals resident in the Rochester, New York, metropolitan area, brought this action in the District Court for the Western District of New York against the Town of Penfield, an incorporated municipality adjacent to Rochester, and against members of Penfield's Zoning, Planning, and Town Boards. Petitioners claimed that the town's zoning ordinance, by its terms and as enforced by the defendant board members, respondents here, effectively excluded persons of low and moderate income from living in the town, in contravention of petitioners' First, Ninth, and Fourteenth Amendment rights and in violation of 42 U.S.C. §§ 1981, 1982, and 1983. The District Court dismissed the complaint and denied a motion by petitioner Rochester Home Builders Association, Inc., for leave to intervene as party-plaintiff. The Court of Appeals for the Second Circuit affirmed, holding that none of the plaintiffs, nor Home Builders Association, had standing to prosecute the action. 495 F.2d 1187 (1974)....

. . .

II

We address first the principles of standing relevant to the claims asserted by the several categories of petitioners in this case. In essence the question of standing is whether the litigant is entitled to have the court decide the merits of the dispute or of particular issues. This inquiry involves both constitutional limitations on federal court jurisdiction and prudential limitations on its exercise. E.g., Barrows v. Jackson, 346 U.S. 249, 255–256 (1953). In both dimensions it is founded in concern about the proper—and properly limited—role of the courts in a democratic society....

In its constitutional dimension, standing imports justiciability: whether the plaintiff has made out a "case or controversy" between himself and the defendant within the meaning of Art. III. This is the threshold question in every federal case, determining the power of the court to entertain the suit. As an aspect of justiciability, the standing question is whether the plaintiff has "alleged such a personal stake in the outcome of the controversy" as to warrant *his* invocation of federal-court jurisdiction and to justify exercise of the court's remedial powers on his behalf.... The Art. III judicial power exists only to redress or otherwise to protect against injury to the complaining party, even though the court's judgment may benefit others collaterally. A federal court's jurisdiction therefore can be invoked only when the plaintiff himself has suffered "some threatened or actual injury resulting from the putatively illegal action...." Linda R.S. v. Richard D., 410 U.S. 614, 617 (1973). See Data Processing Service v. Camp, 397 U.S. 150, 151–154 (1970).

Apart from this minimum constitutional mandate, this Court has recognized other limits on the class of persons who may invoke the courts' decisional and remedial powers. First, the Court has held that when the asserted harm is a "generalized grievance" shared in substantially equal measure by all or a large class of citizens, that harm alone normally does not warrant exercise of jurisdiction.... Second, even when the plaintiff has alleged injury sufficient to meet the "case or controversy" requirement, this Court has held that the plaintiff generally must assert his own legal rights and interests, and cannot rest his claim to relief on the legal rights or interests of third parties.... Without such limitations—closely related to Art. III concerns but essentially matters of judicial self-governance—the courts would be called upon to decide abstract questions of wide public significance even though other governmental institutions may be more competent to address the questions and even though judicial intervention may be unnecessary to protect individual rights....

Although standing in no way depends on the merits of the plaintiff's contention that particular conduct is illegal, ... it often turns on the nature and source of the claim asserted. The actual or threatened injury required by Art. III may exist solely by virtue of "statutes creating legal rights, the invasion of which creates standing...." ... Moreover, the source of the plaintiff's claim to relief assumes critical importance with respect to the prudential rules of standing that, apart from Art. III's minimum requirements, serve to limit the role of the courts in resolving public disputes. Essentially, the standing question in such cases is whether the constitutional or statutory provision on which the claim rests properly can be understood as granting persons in the plaintiff's position a right to judicial relief. In some circumstances, countervailing considerations may outweigh the concerns underlying the usual reluctance to exert judicial power when the plaintiff's claim to relief rests on the legal rights of third parties.... In such instances, the Court has found, in effect, that the constitutional or statutory provision in question implies a right of action in the plaintiff.... See generally Part IV, *infra.* Moreover, Congress may grant an express right of action to persons who otherwise would be barred by prudential standing rules. Of course, Art. III's requirement remains: the plaintiff still must allege a distinct and palpable injury to himself, even if it is an injury shared by a large class of other possible litigants.... But so long as this requirement is satisfied, persons to whom Congress has granted a right of action, either expressly or by clear implication, may have standing to seek relief on the basis of the legal rights and interests of others, and, indeed, may invoke the general public interest in support of their claim....

One further preliminary matter requires discussion. For purposes of ruling on a motion to dismiss for want of standing, both the trial and reviewing courts must accept as true all material allegations of the complaint, and must construe the complaint in favor of the complaining party.... At the same time, it is within the trial court's power to allow or to require the plaintiff to supply, by amendment to the complaint or by affidavits, further particularized allegations of fact deemed supportive of plaintiff's standing. If, after this opportunity, the plaintiff's standing does not adequately appear from all materials of record, the complaint must be dismissed.

III

With these general considerations in mind, we turn first to the claims of petitioners Ortiz, Reyes, Sinkler, and Broadnax, each of whom asserts standing as a person of low or moderate income and, coincidentally, as a member of a minority racial or ethnic group. We must assume, taking the allegations of the complaint as true, that Penfield's zoning ordinance and the pattern of enforcement by respondent officials have had the purpose and effect of excluding persons of low and moderate income, many of whom are members of racial or ethnic minority groups. We also assume, for purposes here, that such intentional exclusionary practices, if proved in a proper case, would be adjudged violative of the constitutional and statutory rights of the persons excluded.

But the fact that these petitioners share attributes common to persons who may have been excluded from residence in the town is an insufficient predicate for the conclusion that petitioners themselves have been excluded, or that the respondents' assertedly illegal actions have violated their rights. Petitioners must allege and show that they personally have been injured, not that injury has been suffered by other, unidentified members of the class to which they belong and which they purport to represent. Unless these petitioners can thus demonstrate the requisite case or controversy between themselves personally and respondents, "none may seek relief on behalf of himself or any other member of the class."

In their complaint, petitioners Ortiz, Reyes, Sinkler, and Broadnax alleged in conclusory terms that they are among the persons excluded by respondents' actions. None of them has ever resided in Penfield; each claims at least implicitly that he desires, or has desired, to do so. Each asserts, moreover, that he made some effort, at some time, to locate housing in Penfield that was at once within his means and adequate for his family's needs. Each claims that his efforts proved fruitless. We may assume, as petitioners allege, that respondents' actions have contributed, perhaps substantially, to the cost of housing in Penfield. But there remains the question whether petitioners' inability to locate suitable housing in Penfield reasonably can be said to have resulted, in any concretely demonstrable way, from respondents' alleged constitutional and statutory infractions. Petitioners must allege facts from which it reasonably could be inferred that, absent the respondents' restrictive zoning practices, there is a substantial probability that they would have been able to purchase or lease in Penfield and that, if the court affords the relief requested, the asserted inability of petitioners will be removed. . . .

We find the record devoid of the necessary allegations. As the Court of Appeals noted, none of these petitioners has a present interest in any Penfield property; none is himself subject to the ordinance's strictures; and none has ever been denied a variance or permit by respondent officials. Instead, petitioners claim that respondents' enforcement of the ordinance against third parties—developers, builders, and the like—has had the consequence of precluding the construction of housing suitable to their needs at prices they might be able to afford. The fact that the harm to petitioners may have resulted indirectly does not in itself preclude standing. When a governmental prohibition or restriction imposed on one party causes specific harm to a third party, harm that a constitutional provision or statute was intended to prevent, the indirectness of the injury does not necessarily deprive the person harmed of standing to vindicate his rights. E.g., Roe v. Wade, 410 U.S. 113, 124, 147 (1973). But it may make it substantially more difficult to meet the minimum requirement of Art. III: to establish that, in fact, the asserted injury was the consequence of the defendants' actions, or that prospective relief will remove the harm.

Here, by their own admission, realization of petitioners' desire to live in Penfield always has depended on the efforts and willingness of third parties to build low-and moderate-cost housing. The record specifically refers to only two such efforts: that of Penfield Better Homes Corp., in late 1969, to obtain the rezoning of certain land in Penfield to allow the construction of subsidized cooperative townhouses that could be purchased by persons of moderate income; and a similar effort by O'Brien Homes, Inc., in late 1971. But the record is devoid of any indication that these projects, or other like projects, would have satisfied petitioners' needs at prices they could afford, or that, were the court to remove the obstructions attributable to respondents, such relief would benefit petitioners. Indeed, petitioners' descriptions of their individual financial situations and housing needs suggest precisely the contrary—that their inability to reside in Penfield is the consequence of the economics of the area housing market, rather than of respondents' assertedly illegal acts.[16] In short, the facts alleged fail to support an actionable causal relationship between Penfield's zoning practices and petitioners' asserted injury.

In support of their position, petitioners refer to several decisions in the District Courts and Courts of Appeals, acknowledging standing in low-income, minority-group plaintiffs to challenge exclusionary zoning practices. In those cases, however, the plaintiffs challenged zoning restrictions as applied to particular projects that would supply housing within their means, and of which they were intended residents. The plaintiffs thus were able to demonstrate that unless relief from assertedly illegal actions was forthcoming, their immediate and personal interests would be harmed. Petitioners here assert no like circumstances. Instead, they rely on little more than the remote possibility, unsubstantiated by allegations of fact, that their situation might have been better had respondents acted otherwise, and might improve were the court to afford relief.

We hold only that a plaintiff who seeks to challenge exclusionary zoning practices must allege specific, concrete facts demonstrating that the challenged practices harm *him,* and that he personally would benefit in a tangible way

---

[16] Ortiz states in his affidavit that he is now purchasing and resides in a six-bedroom dwelling in Wayland, N.Y.; and that he owns and receives rental income from a house in Rochester. He is concerned with finding a house or apartment large enough for himself, his wife, and seven children, but states that he can afford to spend a maximum of $120 per month for housing. Broadnax seeks a four-bedroom house or apartment for herself and six children, and can spend a maximum of about $120 per month for housing. Sinkler also states that she can spend $120 per month for housing for herself and two children. Thus, at least in the cases of Ortiz and Broadnax, it is doubtful that their stated needs could have been satisfied by the small housing units contemplated in the only moderate-cost projects specifically described in the record. Moreover, there is no indication that any of the petitioners had the resources necessary to acquire the housing available in the projects. The matter is left entirely ob-

scure. The income and housing budget figures supplied in petitioners' affidavits are presumably for the year 1972. The vague description of the proposed O'Brien development strongly suggests that the units, even if adequate for their needs, would have been beyond the means at least of Sinkler and Broadnax.... Petitioner Reyes presents a special case: she states that her family has an income of over $14,000 per year, that she can afford $231 per month for housing, and that, in the past and apparently now, she wants to purchase a residence.... Penfield Better Homes defined the term ["low and moderate income"] as between $5,000 and $8,000 per year. Since that project was to be subsidized, presumably petitioner Reyes would have been ineligible. There is no indication that in non-subsidized projects, removal of the challenged zoning restrictions—in 1972—would have reduced the price on new single-family residences to a level that petitioner Reyes thought she could afford.

from the court's intervention.[18] ... Schlesinger v. Reservists to Stop the War, 418 U.S., at 221–222.

IV

The petitioners who assert standing on the basis of their status as taxpayers of the city of Rochester present a different set of problems. These "taxpayer-petitioners" claim that they are suffering economic injury consequent to Penfield's allegedly discriminatory and exclusionary zoning practices. Their argument, in brief, is that Penfield's persistent refusal to allow or to facilitate construction of low-and moderate-cost housing forces the city of Rochester to provide more such housing than it otherwise would do; that to provide such housing, Rochester must allow certain tax abatements; and that as the amount of tax-abated property increases, Rochester taxpayers are forced to assume an increased tax burden in order to finance essential public services.

. . .

... In short the claim of these petitioners falls squarely within the prudential standing rule that normally bars litigants from asserting the rights or legal interests of others in order to obtain relief from injury to themselves. As we have observed above, this rule of judicial self-governance is subject to exceptions, the most prominent of which is that Congress may remove it by statute. Here, however, no statute expressly or by clear implication grants a right of action, and thus standing to seek relief, to persons in petitioners' position. In several cases, this Court has allowed standing to litigate the rights of third parties when enforcement of the challenged restriction against the litigant would result indirectly in the violation of third parties' rights.... But the taxpayer-petitioners are not themselves subject to Penfield's zoning practices. Nor do they allege that the challenged zoning ordinance and practices preclude or otherwise adversely affect a relationship existing between them and the persons whose rights assertedly are violated.... No relationship, other than an incidental congruity of interest, is alleged to exist between the Rochester taxpayers and persons who have been precluded from living in Penfield. Nor do the taxpayer-petitioners show that their prosecution of the suit is necessary to insure protection of the rights asserted, as there is no indication that persons who in fact have been excluded from Penfield are disabled from asserting their own right in a proper case. In sum, we discern no justification for recognizing in the Rochester taxpayers a right of action on the asserted claim.

V

We turn next to the standing problems presented by the petitioner associations—Metro–Act of Rochester, Inc., one of the original plaintiffs; Housing Council in the Monroe County Area, Inc., which the original plaintiffs sought to join as a party-plaintiff; and Rochester Home Builders Association, Inc., which moved in the District Court for leave to intervene as plaintiff. There is no question that an association may have standing in its own right to seek judicial

---

[18] This is not to say that the plaintiff who challenges a zoning ordinance or zoning practices must have a present contractual interest in a particular project. A particularized personal interest may be shown in various ways, which we need not undertake to identify in the abstract. But usually the initial focus should be on a particular project. See, e.g., cases cited in n. 17, supra. We also note that zoning laws and their provisions, long considered essential to effective urban planning, are peculiarly within the province of state and local legislative authorities. They are, of course, subject to judicial review in a proper case. But citizens dissatisfied with provisions of such laws need not overlook the availability of the normal democratic process.

relief from injury to itself and to vindicate whatever rights and immunities the association itself may enjoy. Moreover, in attempting to secure relief from injury to itself the association may assert the rights of its members, at least so long as the challenged infractions adversely affect its members' associational ties. . . . With the limited exception of Metro–Act, however, none of the associational petitioners here has asserted injury to itself.

Even in the absence of injury to itself, an association may have standing solely as the representative of its members. . . . The possibility of such representational standing, however, does not eliminate or attenuate the constitutional requirement of a case or controversy. . . . The association must allege that its members, or any one of them, are suffering immediate or threatened injury as a result of the challenged action of the sort that would make out a justiciable case had the members themselves brought suit. . . . So long as this can be established, and so long as the nature of the claim and of the relief sought does not make the individual participation of each injured party indispensable to proper resolution of the cause, the association may be an appropriate representative of its members, entitled to invoke the court's jurisdiction.

A

Petitioner Metro–Act's claims to standing on its own behalf as a Rochester taxpayer, and on behalf of its members who are Rochester taxpayers or persons of low or moderate income, are precluded by our holdings in Parts III and IV, supra, as to the individual petitioners, and require no further discussion. Metro–Act . . . alleges . . . that 9% of its membership is composed of present residents of Penfield. It claims that, as a result of the persistent pattern of exclusionary zoning practiced by respondents and the consequent exclusion of persons of low and moderate income, those of its members who are Penfield residents are deprived of the benefits of living in a racially and ethnically integrated community. Referring to our decision in Trafficante v. Metropolitan Life Ins. Co., 409 U.S. 205 (1972), Metro–Act argues that such deprivation is a sufficiently palpable injury to satisfy the Art. III case-or-controversy requirement, and that it has standing as the representative of its members to seek redress.

We agree with the Court of Appeals that *Trafficante* is not controlling here. In that case, two residents of an apartment complex alleged that the owner had discriminated against rental applicants on the basis of race, in violation of § 804 of the Civil Rights Act of 1968, 82 Stat. 83, 42 U.S.C. § 3604. . . . In light of the clear congressional purpose in enacting the 1968 Act, and the broad definition of "person aggrieved" in § 810(a), 42 U.S.C. § 3610(a), we held that petitioners, as "person[s] who claim[ed] to have been injured by a discriminatory housing practice," had standing to litigate violations of the Act. We concluded that Congress had given residents of housing facilities covered by the statute an actionable right to be free from the adverse consequences to them of racially discriminatory practices directed at and immediately harmful to others. 409 U.S., at 212.

Metro–Act does not assert on behalf of its members any right of action under the 1968 Civil Rights Act, nor can the complaint fairly be read to make out any such claim. In this, we think, lies the critical distinction between *Trafficante* and the situation here. As we have observed above, Congress may create a statutory right or entitlement the alleged deprivation of which can confer standing to sue even where the plaintiff would have suffered no judicially cognizable injury in the absence of statute. . . .

Even if we assume, *arguendo,* that apart from any statutorily created right the asserted harm to Metro–Act's Penfield members is sufficiently direct and personal to satisfy the case-or-controversy requirement of Art. III, prudential considerations strongly counsel against according them or Metro–Act standing to prosecute this action. We do not understand Metro–Act to argue that Penfield residents themselves have been denied any constitutional rights, affording them a cause of action under 42 U.S.C. § 1983. Instead, their complaint is that they have been harmed indirectly by the exclusion of others. This is an attempt to raise putative rights of third parties, and none of the exceptions that allow such claims is present here. In these circumstances, we conclude that it is inappropriate to allow Metro–Act to invoke the judicial process.

B

Petitioner Home Builders, in its intervenor-complaint, asserted standing to represent its member firms engaged in the development and construction of residential housing in the Rochester area, including Penfield. Home Builders alleged that the Penfield zoning restrictions, together with refusals by the town officials to grant variances and permits for the construction of low-and moderate-cost housing, had deprived some of its members of "substantial business opportunities and profits." Home Builders claimed damages of $750,000 and also joined in the original plaintiffs' prayer for declaratory and injunctive relief.

As noted above, to justify any relief the association must show that it has suffered harm, or that one or more of its members are injured. . . .

Home Builders alleges no monetary injury to itself, nor any assignment of the damages claims of its members. No award therefore can be made to the association as such. Moreover, in the circumstances of this case, the damages claims are not common to the entire membership, nor shared by all in equal degree. To the contrary, whatever injury may have been suffered is peculiar to the individual member concerned, and both the fact and extent of injury would require individualized proof. Thus, to obtain relief in damages, each member of Home Builders who claims injury as a result of respondents' practices must be a party to the suit, and Home Builders has no standing to claim damages on his behalf.

Home Builders' prayer for prospective relief fails for a different reason. It can have standing as the representative of its members only if it has alleged facts sufficient to make out a case or controversy had the members themselves brought suit. No such allegations were made. The complaint refers to no specific project of any of its members that is currently precluded either by the ordinance or by respondents' action in enforcing it. There is no averment that any member has applied to respondents for a building permit or a variance with respect to any current project. Indeed, there is no indication that respondents have delayed or thwarted any project currently proposed by Home Builders' members, or that any of its members has taken advantage of the remedial processes available under the ordinance. In short, insofar as the complaint seeks prospective relief, Home Builders has failed to show the existence of any injury to its members of sufficient immediacy and ripeness to warrant judicial intervention.

A like problem is presented with respect to petitioner Housing Council. The affidavit accompanying the motion to join it as plaintiff states that the Council includes in its membership "at least seventeen" groups that have been, are, or will be involved in the development of low and moderate-cost housing. But, with one exception, the complaint does not suggest that any of these groups has focused its efforts on Penfield or has any specific plan to do so. Again with the same exception, neither the complaint nor any materials of record indicate that any member of Housing Council has taken any step toward building housing in Penfield, or has had dealings of any nature with respondents. The exception is the Penfield Better Homes Corp. As we have observed above, it applied to respondents in late 1969 for a zoning variance to allow construction of a housing project designed for persons of moderate income.... It is therefore possible that in 1969, or within a reasonable time thereafter, Better Homes itself and possibly Housing Council as its representative would have had standing to seek review of respondents' action. The complaint, however, does not allege that the Penfield Better Homes project remained viable in 1972 when this complaint was filed, or that respondents' actions continued to block a then-current construction project. In short, neither the complaint nor the record supplies any basis from which to infer that the controversy between respondents and Better Homes, however vigorous it may once have been, remained a live, concrete dispute when this complaint was filed.

VI

The rules of standing, whether as aspects of the Art. III case-or-controversy requirement or as reflections of prudential considerations defining and limiting the role of the courts, are threshold determinants of the propriety of judicial intervention. It is the responsibility of the complainant clearly to allege facts demonstrating that he is a proper party to invoke judicial resolution of the dispute and the exercise of the court's remedial powers. We agree with the District Court and the Court of Appeals that none of the petitioners here has met this threshold requirement. Accordingly, the judgment of the Court of Appeals is

Affirmed.

Mr. Justice Douglas, dissenting.

. . .

Standing has become a barrier to access to the federal courts, just as "the political question" was in earlier decades. The mounting caseload of federal courts is well known. But cases such as this one reflect festering sores in our society; and the American dream teaches that if one reaches high enough and persists there is a forum where justice is dispensed. I would lower the technical barriers and let the courts serve that ancient need....

. . .

... I would let the case go to trial and have all the facts brought out. Indeed, it would be better practice to decide the question of standing only when the merits have been developed.

I would reverse the Court of Appeals.

Mr. Justice Brennan, with whom Mr. Justice White and Mr. Justice Marshall join, dissenting.

In this case, a wide range of plaintiffs, alleging various kinds of injuries, claimed to have been affected by the Penfield zoning ordinance, on its face and as applied, and by other practices of the defendant officials of Penfield. Alleging that as a result of these laws and practices low-and moderate-income and minority people have been excluded from Penfield, and that this exclusion is unconstitutional, plaintiffs sought injunctive, declaratory, and monetary relief. The Court today, in an opinion that purports to be a "standing" opinion but that actually, I believe, has overtones of outmoded notions of pleading and of justiciability, refuses to find that any of the variously situated plaintiffs can clear numerous hurdles, some constructed here for the first time, necessary to establish "standing." While the Court gives lip service to the principle, oft repeated in recent years, that "standing in no way depends on the merits of the plaintiff's contention that particular conduct is illegal," in fact the opinion, which tosses out of court almost every conceivable kind of plaintiff who could be injured by the activity claimed to be unconstitutional, can be explained only by an indefensible hostility to the claim on the merits. I can appreciate the Court's reluctance to adjudicate the complex and difficult legal questions involved in determining the constitutionality of practices which assertedly limit residence in a particular municipality to those who are white and relatively well off, and I also understand that the merits of this case could involve grave sociological and political ramifications. But courts cannot refuse to hear a case on the merits merely because they would prefer not to, and it is quite clear, when the record is viewed with dispassion, that at least three of the groups of plaintiffs have made allegations, and supported them with affidavits and documentary evidence, sufficient to survive a motion to dismiss for lack of standing.

. . .

II

Low–Income and Minority Plaintiffs

. . .

... [T]he Court's real holding is not that these petitioners have not *alleged* an injury resulting from respondents' action, but that they are not to be allowed to prove one, because "realization of petitioners' desire to live in Penfield always has depended on the efforts and willingness of third parties to build low and moderate-cost housing," and "the record is devoid of any indication that ... [any] projects, would have satisfied petitioners' needs at prices they could afford."

Certainly, this is not the sort of demonstration that can or should be required of petitioners at this preliminary stage. . . .

Here, the very fact that, as the Court stresses, these petitioners' claim rests in part upon proving the intentions and capabilities of third parties to build in Penfield suitable housing which they can afford, coupled with the exclusionary character of the claim on the merits, makes it particularly inappropriate to assume that these petitioners' lack of specificity reflects a fatal weakness in their theory of causation. Obviously they cannot be expected, prior to discovery and trial, to know the future plans of building companies, the precise details of the housing market in Penfield, or everything which has transpired in 15 years of application of the Penfield zoning ordinance, including every housing plan suggested and refused. To require them to allege such facts is to require them to prove their case on paper in order to get into court at all. . . .

III

Associations Including Building Concerns

. . .

Again, the Court ignores the thrust of the complaints and asks petitioners to allege the impossible. According to the allegations, the building concerns' experience in the past with Penfield officials has shown any plans for low- and moderate-income housing to be futile for, again according to the allegations, the respondents are engaged in a purposeful, conscious scheme to exclude such housing. Particularly with regard to a low- or moderate-income project, the cost of litigating, with respect to any particular project, the legality of a refusal to approve it may well be prohibitive. And the merits of the exclusion of this or that project is not at the heart of the complaint; the claim is that respondents will not approve *any* project which will provide residences for low and moderate-income people.

When this sort of pattern-and-practice claim is at the heart of the controversy, allegations of past injury, which members of both of these organizations have clearly made, and of a future intent, if the barriers are cleared, again to develop suitable housing for Penfield, should be more than sufficient. The past experiences, if proved at trial, will give credibility and substance to the claim of interest in future building activity in Penfield. These parties, if their allegations are proved, certainly have the requisite personal stake in the outcome of *this* controversy, and the Court's conclusion otherwise is only a conclusion that *this* controversy may not be litigated in a federal court.

I would reverse the judgment of the Court of Appeals.

VILLAGE OF ARLINGTON HEIGHTS v. METROPOLITAN HOUSING DEVELOPMENT CORP., 429 U.S. 252 (1977). Metropolitan Housing Development Corporation (MHDC), a builder of low and moderate income housing in the Chicago area, contracted to purchase a 15–acre site in the Village of Arlington Heights. The contract was contingent upon MHDC securing zoning clearances from the Village and federal approval to build a 190–unit project with subsidies under § 236 of the National Housing Act. MHDC submitted detailed plans for the project to the Village which refused to rezone the property to permit the construction of multiple-family housing. MHDC and three Black individuals brought suit in the federal district court seeking an injunction and declaratory relief, alleging that the denial was racially discriminatory. The district court held that the plaintiffs had standing but ruled for the defendants on the merits. The court of appeals reversed on the merits and the defendants petitioned for certiorari. The Supreme Court, in an opinion by Justice Powell (and with no apparent dissent on this point) held that the plaintiffs had standing, saying, in part:

"A.

"Here there can be little doubt that MHDC meets the constitutional standing requirements. The challenged action of the petitioners stands as an absolute barrier to constructing the housing MHDC had contracted to place on the Viatorian site. If MHDC secures the injunctive relief it seeks, that barrier will be removed. An injunction would not, of course, guarantee that Lincoln Green will be built. MHDC would still have to secure financing, qualify for federal subsidies, and carry through with construction. But all housing developments are subject to some extent to similar uncertainties. When a project is as detailed and specific as Lincoln Green, a court is not required to engage in undue speculation as a predicate for finding that the plaintiff has the requisite personal stake in the controversy. MHDC has shown an injury to itself that is 'likely to be redressed by a favorable decision.' . . .

"Petitioners nonetheless appear to argue that MHDC lacks standing because it has suffered no economic injury. MHDC, they point out, is not the owner of the property in question. Its contract of purchase is contingent upon securing rezoning.[8] MHDC owes the owners nothing if rezoning is denied.

"We cannot accept petitioners' argument. In the first place, it is inaccurate to say that MHDC suffers no economic injury from a refusal to rezone, despite the contingency provisions in its contract. MHDC has expended thousands of dollars on the plans for Lincoln Green and on the studies submitted to the Village in support of the petition for rezoning. Unless rezoning is granted, many of these plans and studies will be worthless even if MHDC finds another site at an equally attractive price.

"Petitioners' argument also misconceives our standing requirements. It has long been clear that economic injury is not the only kind of injury that can support a plaintiff's standing.... MHDC is a nonprofit corporation. Its interest in building Lincoln Green stems not from a desire for economic gain, but rather from an interest in making suitable low-cost housing available in areas where such housing is scarce. This is not mere abstract concern about a problem of general interest.... The specific project MHDC intends to build, whether or not it will generate profits, provides that 'essential dimension of specificity' that informs judicial decisionmaking....

"B.

"Clearly MHDC has met the constitutional requirements and it therefore has standing to assert its own rights. Foremost among them is MHDC's right to be free of arbitrary or irrational zoning actions.... [T]he heart of this litigation ... has been the claim that the Village's refusal to rezone discriminates against racial minorities in violation of the Fourteenth Amendment. As a corporation, MHDC has no racial identity and cannot be the direct target of the petitioners' alleged discrimination. In the ordinary case, a party is denied standing to assert the rights of third persons. Warth v. Seldin, 422 U.S., at 499. But we need not decide whether the circumstances of this case would justify departure from that prudential limitation and permit MHDC to assert the constitutional rights of its prospective minority tenants.... For we have at least one individual plaintiff who has demonstrated standing to assert these rights as his own.

"Respondent Ransom, a Negro, works at the Honeywell factory in Arlington Heights and lives approximately 20 miles away in Evanston in a 5–room house with his mother and his son. The complaint alleged that he seeks and would qualify for the housing MHDC wants to build in Arlington Heights. Ransom testified at trial that if Lincoln Green were built he would probably move there, since it is closer to his job.

"The injury Ransom asserts is that his quest for housing nearer his employment has been thwarted by official action that is racially discriminatory. If a court grants the relief he seeks, there is at least a 'substantial probability,' that the Lincoln Green project will materialize, affording Ransom the housing opportunity he desires in Arlington Heights. His is not a generalized grievance.

---

[8] Petitioners contend that MHDC lacks standing to pursue its claim here because a contract purchaser whose contract is contingent upon rezoning cannot contest a zoning decision in the Illinois courts. Under the law of Illinois, only the owner of the property has standing to pursue such an action....

State law of standing, however, does not govern such determinations in the federal courts. The constitutional and prudential considerations canvassed at length in Warth v. Seldin, 422 U.S. 490 (1975), respond to concerns that are peculiarly federal in nature. Illinois may choose to close its courts to applicants for rezoning unless they have an interest more direct than MHDC's, but this choice does not necessarily disqualify MHDC from seeking relief in federal courts for an asserted injury to its federal rights.

Instead, as we suggested in *Warth,* id., at 507, 508 n. 18, it focuses on a particular project and is not dependent on speculation about the possible actions of third parties not before the court.... Unlike the individual plaintiffs in *Warth,* Ransom has adequately averred an 'actionable causal relationship' between Arlington Heights' zoning practices and his asserted injury. Warth v. Seldin, 422 U.S., at 507. We therefore proceed to the merits."[a]

STANDING AND THE REQUIREMENT OF "INJURY IN FACT"

Dicta in Flast v. Cohen, 392 U.S. 83, 102 (1968), stated that to establish standing, plaintiffs must demonstrate not only that they were injured by the challenged legislation but must also show a nexus between that injury and the constitutional violation claimed. The supposed requirement of "nexus" was at issue in Duke Power Co. v. Carolina Environmental Study Group, 438 U.S. 59 (1978). People living near a nuclear power plant under construction brought suit for a declaratory judgment that the Price–Anderson Act was unconstitutional in limiting liability for nuclear accidents in federally licensed private nuclear power plants. The federal district court reached the merits, and held the statute unconstitutional as a violation of the due process clause of the fifth amendment. On direct appeal, the Supreme Court reversed, on the merits.

The Court raised on its own motion, and rejected, the argument that plaintiffs lacked standing to challenge the limitation of liability. The "injury in fact" relied upon by the Court to establish standing, however, was not the possibility that the plaintiffs would be denied adequate compensation in the event of a future nuclear accident. Instead, the relevant injury stemmed from the environmental and esthetic harm that would occur to the plaintiffs by the building of the plant. The statute "caused" the injury only because, without the limitation-of-liability provision, nuclear plants would not be built.

The Court concluded that it was not necessary, to establish standing, that plaintiffs' injuries be caused directly by the alleged unconstitutional feature of the statute—the denial of full compensation in the event of nuclear accident. It was enough to show that without the limitation-of-liability provision the proposed plant would not be built and the environmental injury would not occur. The requirement of nexus was limited to standing in taxpayers' suits.[1] In conventional lawsuits, a plaintiff need only demonstrate "injury in fact and a substantial likelihood that the judicial relief requested will prevent or redress the claimed injury" in order to establish standing.[2] Plaintiffs had met that standard.[3]

Consider the following cases dealing with the issue whether plaintiffs had shown the requisite injury in fact to establish standing. Are they consistent?[4]

Linda R.S. v. Richard D., 410 U.S. 614 (1973). The mother of a child born out of wedlock brought suit to compel a state prosecutor to prosecute the child's father for non-support. Plaintiff challenged the constitutionality of a state statute making failure to support children a crime because the state

---

[a] For the decision on the merits, see infra p. 792.

[1] The problem of standing in taxpayers' suits is examined below in subsection 3.

[2] As in *Warth v. Seldin,* the Court stated that even when the requisite injury in fact was established, other limits stemming from prudential concerns might apply.

[3] For an argument that *Duke Power* was a departure from traditional standards of standing and ripeness, see Varat, *Variable Justiciability and the Duke Power Case,* 58 Tex.L.Rev. 273 (1980).

[4] For an argument that they are not, unless many other factors beyond the issue of "injury in fact" are considered, see Nichol, *Rethinking Standing,* 72 Cal.L.Rev. 68 (1984).

courts had construed it to apply only to the parents of children born in marriage. The Supreme Court concluded plaintiff had no standing. Plaintiff had shown injury from the father's failure to pay support, but it was speculative that the relief requested—jailing the father—would remedy the injury by providing support payments from him.

Sierra Club v. Morton, 405 U.S. 727 (1972). The Court held that an environmental group lacked standing to challenge the construction of a recreation area in a national forest. The fact that the Sierra Club—which did not allege that any of its members were affected by the proposed development—had an interest in the problem of maintaining the environment did not confer standing.

United States v. SCRAP, 412 U.S. 669 (1973). An environmental group had standing to challenge a railroad rate structure of the Interstate Commerce Commission claimed to discourage the shipment, and use, of recycled materials and promote the use of raw materials. Plaintiff alleged that its members (five law students): were caused to pay more for finished products; used the forests, rivers, mountains and other natural resources in the vicinity of Washington, D.C. and those recreational uses had been affected by increased littering; breathed the air in the Washington metropolitan area, which had suffered increased air pollution. All of these effects were alleged to be caused by the ICC rate structure which caused the increased use of raw materials and decreased recycling. (In *Sierra Club* the plaintiff had alleged only a "public interest" and not the injury to its members.)

SCRAP, like *Sierra Club,* was an action based on a provision of the Administrative Procedure Act, conferring standing to sue on persons "adversely affected" or "aggrieved" by an agency's decision. The Court concluded that standing, under that provision, was neither confined to those who suffer economic harm nor denied to many people who suffer the same injury. Otherwise, the most injurious and widespread government actions could be questioned by nobody. (On the merits, the Court reversed the lower court's decision enjoining the Commission's rate structure.)

Lujan v. National Wildlife Federation, 497 U.S. 871 (1990). Members of an environmental group were not "adversely affected" or "aggrieved" by Bureau of Land Management policy decisions concerning mining on public lands. Affidavits alleged only that they used unspecified lands "in the vicinity of" large tracts, on some undetermined portions of which mining might occur because of the challenged actions.

Simon v. Eastern Kentucky Welfare Rights Organization, 426 U.S. 26 (1976). Indigent persons lacked standing to challenge Internal Revenue Service rulings granting favorable tax treatment to nonprofit hospitals providing inadequate hospital services to indigents. Allegations that the rulings "encouraged" hospitals to deny services were speculative. It was just as plausible that the relevant hospitals would forego favorable tax treatment rather than expend substantial funds for increased hospital services to indigents. Thus, plaintiffs' complaint did not demonstrate a substantial likelihood that declaring the rulings invalid would result in their receiving the hospital services they desire.

Allen v. Wright, 468 U.S. 737 (1984). Parents of black children attending public schools did not have standing to challenge IRS practices concerning denial of tax exemptions to racially discriminatory private schools. Plaintiffs' allegations that the IRS practices inhibited the process of desegregation in their children's public schools did not show injury traceable to the challenged government policy. It was speculative whether denial of tax exemption to any private school would induce it to change its policies and whether children would be transferred to public schools if their private schools were threatened with loss of tax exemption.

Lujan v. Defenders of Wildlife, 504 U.S. 555 (1992). The Endangered Species Act of 1973 requires the Secretary of Interior to promulgate a list of endangered species, and requires all federal agencies to insure that any action by them is not likely to threaten their continued existence. The Interior Department issued a regulation interpreting the Act to be inapplicable to projects undertaken outside the United States. Two scientists claimed they would be affected by overseas projects: one had observed in the past, and intended to observe in the future, crocodiles that would be endangered by rehabilitation of the Aswan Dam in Egypt; another had observed in the past, and intended to observe in the future, elephants and leopards endangered by a project in Sri Lanka. Plaintiffs lacked standing because their injury was speculative, since they alleged only that they intended to return to the overseas sites "some day," without specifying a definite date.

Associated General Contractors v. City of Jacksonville,508 U.S. 656 (1993). Non-minority contractors who alleged that they would have bid on construction work set aside for minority contractors had standing to challenge the requirement that 10% of city contracts be awarded to minority-owned businesses. It was not necessary that plaintiffs allege or prove that they would have been awarded contracts but for the challenged program. In equal protection cases, the injury in fact is not the denial of the benefit itself but the denial of equal treatment imposed by a barrier to obtaining a benefit—here the inability to compete on an equal footing in the bidding process.

United States v. Hays, __ U.S. __, 115 S.Ct. 2431 (1995). Voters attacking an alleged racial gerrymander lack standing unless they show that they, personally, have been subject to racial discrimination. White voters who neither resided in the challenged predominantly-Black district, nor were excluded from that district because they were White, had only a "generalized grievance" and had not suffered "individualized harm."

2. STANDING TO ASSERT THE RIGHTS OF THIRD PARTIES

Craig v. Boren

429 U.S. 190, 97 S.Ct. 451, 50 L.Ed.2d 397 (1976).

Mr. Justice Brennan delivered the opinion of the Court.

This action was brought in the District Court for the Western District of Oklahoma on December 20, 1972, by appellant Craig, a male then between 18 and 21 years of age, and by appellant Whitener, a licensed vendor of 3.2% beer. The complaint sought declaratory and injunctive relief against enforcement of [statutes prohibiting the sale of 3.2% beer to males under age 21 and females under age 18] on the ground that it constituted invidious discrimination against males 18–20 years of age. A three-judge court convened under 28 U.S.C. § 2281 sustained the constitutionality of the statutory differential and dismissed the action. 399 F.Supp. 1304 (1975).... We reverse.

I

We first address a preliminary question of standing. Appellant Craig attained the age of 21 after we noted probable jurisdiction. Therefore, since only declaratory and injunctive relief against enforcement of the gender-based differential is sought, the controversy has been rendered moot as to Craig. See, e.g., DeFunis v. Odegaard, 416 U.S. 312 (1974).[2] The question thus arises whether appellant Whitener, the licensed vendor of 3.2% beer, who has a live controversy against enforcement of the statute, may rely upon the equal protection objections of males 18–20 years of age to establish her claim of unconstitutionality of the age-sex differential. We conclude that she may.

Initially, it should be noted that, despite having had the opportunity to do so, appellees never raised before the District Court any objection to Whitener's reliance upon the claimed unequal treatment of 18–20–year–old males as the premise of her equal protection challenge to Oklahoma's 3.2% beer law. Indeed, at oral argument Oklahoma acknowledged that appellees always "presumed" that the vendor, subject to sanctions and loss of license for violation of the statute, was a proper party in interest to object to the enforcement of the sex-based regulatory provision. While such a concession certainly would not be controlling upon the reach of this Court's constitutional authority to exercise jurisdiction under Art. III, ... our decisions have settled that limitations on a litigant's assertion of *jus tertii* are not constitutionally mandated, but rather stem from a salutary "rule of self-restraint" designed to minimize unwarranted intervention into controversies where the applicable constitutional questions are ill-defined and speculative. See, e.g., Barrows v. Jackson, 346 U.S. 249 (1953); see also Singleton v. Wulff, 428 U.S. 106, 123–124 (1976) (Powell, J., dissenting). These prudential objectives, thought to be enhanced by restrictions on third-party standing, cannot be furthered here, where the lower court already has entertained the relevant constitutional challenge and the parties have sought—or at least have never resisted—an authoritative constitutional determination. In such circumstances, a decision by us to forgo consideration of the constitutional merits in order to await the initiation of a new challenge to the statute by injured third parties would be impermissibly to foster repetitive and time-consuming litigation under the guise of caution and prudence. More-over, insofar as the applicable constitutional questions have been and continue to be presented vigorously and "cogently," ... the denial of *jus tertii* standing in deference to a direct class suit can serve no functional purpose. Our Brother Blackmun's comment is pertinent: "[I]t may be that a class could be assembled, whose fluid membership always included some [males] with live claims. But if the assertion of the right is to be 'representative' to such an extent anyway, there seems little loss in terms of effective advocacy from allowing its assertion by" the present *jus tertii* champion. Singleton v. Wulff, supra, at 117–118.

In any event, we conclude that appellant Whitener has established inde-pendently her claim to assert *jus tertii* standing. The operation of §§ 241 and 245 plainly has inflicted "injury in fact" upon appellant sufficient to guarantee her "concrete adverseness," ... and to satisfy the constitutionally based standing requirements imposed by Art. III. The legal duties created by the statutory sections under challenge are addressed directly to vendors such as appellant. She is obliged either to heed the statutory discrimination, thereby incurring a direct economic injury through the constriction of her buyers' market, or to disobey the statutory command and suffer, in the words of Oklahoma's Assistant Attorney General, "sanctions and perhaps loss of li-cense." This Court repeatedly has recognized that such injuries establish the threshold requirements of a "case or controversy" mandated by Art. III. See, e.g., Singleton v. Wulff, supra, at 113, (doctors who receive payments for their abortion services are "classically adverse" to government as payer); Sullivan v.

---

[2] Appellants did not seek class certifica-tion of Craig as representative of other simi-larly situated males 18–20 years of age. See, e.g., Sosna v. Iowa, 419 U.S. 393, 401 (1975).

Little Hunting Park, 396 U.S. 229, 237 (1969); Barrows v. Jackson, supra, 346 U.S., at 255–256.

As a vendor with standing to challenge the lawfulness of §§ 241 and 245, appellant Whitener is entitled to assert those concomitant rights of third parties that would be "diluted or adversely affected" should her constitutional challenge fail and the statutes remain in force. Griswold v. Connecticut, 381 U.S. 479, 481; see Note, Standing to Assert Constitutional Jus Tertii, 88 Harv.L.Rev. 423, 432 (1974). Otherwise, the threatened imposition of governmental sanctions might deter appellant Whitener and other similarly situated vendors from selling 3.2% beer to young males, thereby ensuring that "enforcement of the challenged restriction against the [vendor] would result indirectly in the violation of third parties' rights." Warth v. Seldin, 422 U.S. 490, 510 (1975). Accordingly, vendors and those in like positions have been uniformly permitted to resist efforts at restricting their operations by acting as advocates of the rights of third parties who seek access to their market or function. See, e.g., Eisenstadt v. Baird, 405 U.S. 438 (1972); *Sullivan v. Little Hunting Park,* supra; *Barrows v. Jackson,* supra.[4]

Indeed, the *jus tertii* question raised here is answered by our disposition of a like argument in Eisenstadt v. Baird, supra. There, as here, a state statute imposed legal duties and disabilities upon the claimant, who was convicted of distributing a package of contraceptive foam to a third party.[5] Since the statute was directed at Baird and penalized his conduct, the Court did not hesitate—again as here—to conclude that the "case or controversy" requirement of Art. III was satisfied. 405 U.S., at 443. In considering Baird's constitutional objections, the Court fully recognized his standing to defend the privacy interests of third parties. Deemed crucial to the decision to permit *jus tertii* standing was the recognition of "the impact of the litigation on the third-party interests." Id., at 445. Just as the defeat of Baird's suit and the "[e]nforcement of the Massachusetts statute will materially impair the ability of single persons to obtain contraceptives," id., at 446, so too the failure of Whitener to prevail in this suit and the continued enforcement of §§ 241 and 245 will "materially impair the ability of" males 18–20 years of age to purchase 3.2% beer despite their classification by an overt gender-based criterion. Similarly, just as the

---

[4] The standing question presented here is not answered by the principle stated in United States v. Raines, 362 U.S. 17, 21 (1960), that "one to whom application of a statute is constitutional will not be heard to attack the statute on the ground that impliedly it might also be taken as applying to other persons or other situations in which its application might be unconstitutional." In *Raines,* the Court refused to permit certain public officials of Georgia to defend against application of the Civil Rights Act to their official conduct on the ground that the statute also might be construed to encompass the "purely private actions" of others. The *Raines* rule remains germane in such a setting, where the interests of the litigant and the rights of the proposed third parties are in no way mutually interdependent. Thus, a successful suit against Raines did not threaten to impair or diminish the independent private rights of others, and consequently, consideration of those third-party rights properly was deferred until another day.

Of course, the *Raines* principle has also been relaxed where legal action against the claimant threatens to "chill" the First Amendment rights of third parties. See, e.g., Lewis v. New Orleans, 415 U.S. 130 (1974).

[5] The fact that Baird chose to disobey the legal duty imposed upon him by the Massachusetts anticontraception statute, resulting in his criminal conviction, 405 U.S. at 440, does not distinguish the standing inquiry from that pertaining to the anticipatory attack in this case. In both *Eisenstadt* and here, the challenged statutes compel *jus tertii* claimants either to cease their proscribed activities or to suffer appropriate sanctions. The existence of Art. III "injury in fact" and the structure of the claimant's relationship to the third parties are not altered by the litigative posture of the suit. And, certainly, no suggestion will be heard that Whitener's anticipatory challenge offends the normal requirements governing such actions....

Massachusetts law in *Eisenstadt* "prohibit[ed], not use, but distribution," 405 U.S., at 446, and consequently the least awkward challenger was one in Baird's position who was subject to that proscription, the law challenged here explicitly regulates the sale rather than use of 3.2% beer, thus leaving a vendor as the obvious claimant.

We therefore hold that Whitener has standing to raise relevant equal protection challenges to Oklahoma's gender-based law. We now consider those arguments.

. . .

Mr. Chief Justice Burger, dissenting.

. . .

At the outset I cannot agree that appellant Whitener has standing arising from her status as a saloonkeeper to assert the constitutional rights of her customers. In this Court, "a litigant may only assert his own constitutional rights or immunities." United States v. Raines, 362 U.S. 17, 22 (1960). There are a few, but strictly limited exceptions to that rule; despite the most creative efforts, this case fits within none of them.

This is not Sullivan v. Little Hunting Park, 396 U.S. 229 (1969), or Barrows v. Jackson, 346 U.S. 249 (1953), for there is here no barrier whatever to Oklahoma males 18–20 years of age asserting, in an appropriate forum, any constitutional rights they may claim to purchase 3.2% beer. Craig's successful litigation of this very issue was prevented only by the advent of his 21st birthday. There is thus no danger of interminable dilution of those rights if appellant Whitener is not permitted to litigate them here . . . .

Nor is this controlled by Griswold v. Connecticut, 381 U.S. 479 (1965). It borders on the ludicrous to draw a parallel between a vendor of beer and the intimate professional physician-patient relationship which undergirded relaxation of standing rules in that case.

Even in *Eisenstadt*, the Court carefully limited its recognition of third-party standing to cases in which the relationship between the claimant and the relevant third party "was not simply the fortuitous connection between a vendor and potential vendees, but the relationship between one who acted to protect the rights of a minority and the minority itself." 405 U.S., at 445. This is plainly not the case here . . . .

In sum, permitting a vendor to assert the constitutional rights of vendees whenever those rights are arguably infringed introduces a new concept of constitutional standing to which I cannot subscribe.[a]

. . .

3. TAXPAYER AND CITIZEN STANDING

TAXPAYER STANDING

In Frothingham v. Mellon, 262 U.S. 447 (1923), a federal taxpayer brought suit challenging the constitutionality of the Maternity Act of 1921, which

---

[a] For the opinions on the merits, see page 748, infra. For critiques of the Court's doctrines, and thoughtful discussion, see Rohr, *Fighting for the Rights of Others: The Troubled Law of Third–Party Standing and Mootness in the Federal Courts*, 35 Univ. of Miami L.Rev. 393 (1981); Sedler, *The Assertion of Constitutional Jus Tertii: A Substantive Approach*, 70 Calif.L.Rev. 1308 (1982); Monaghan, *Third Party Standing*, 84 Colum.L.Rev. 277 (1984).

provided federal funding to states for maternal and infant health care. The Court held that federal taxpayers lacked standing to challenge unconstitutional federal expenditures, because any injury was "remote, fluctuating and uncertain." In Flast v. Cohen, 392 U.S. 83 (1968), the Court upheld taxpayer standing to challenge the expenditure of federal funds in violation of the establishment clause, which was a "specific constitutional limitation" on the taxing and spending powers.

The Court has reaffirmed the principle that federal taxpayers have standing to challenge federal statutes authorizing expenditures alleged to violate the establishment clause. Bowen v. Kendrick, 487 U.S. 589 (1988). However, the Court has consistently denied federal taxpayers standing to raise other constitutional challenges to federal expenditures. In United States v. Richardson, 418 U.S. 166 (1974), taxpayers lacked standing to challenge the statute appropriating funds for the Central Intelligence Agency on the ground that it violated Art. I, § 9, cl. 7 of the Constitution, which requires "a regular statement and account of the receipts and expenditures of all public money." Schlesinger v. Reservists Committee to Stop the War, 418 U.S. 208 (1974), held that taxpayers had no standing to challenge membership of Members of Congress in the military reserve, which was claimed to violate the prohibition of Art. I, § 6, cl. 2, prohibiting Members of Congress to hold "any office under the United States."

The holding in *Flast v. Cohen* was narrowed further in Valley Forge Christian College v. Americans United for Separation of Church and State, Inc., 454 U.S. 464 (1982). Federal taxpayers challenged the constitutionality of a grant of federal land to a religious college, claiming a violation of the establishment clause. The Court noted "the rigor with which the *Flast* exception to the *Frothingham* principle ought to be applied." It held that there was no taxpayer standing, because the legislation authorizing the donation was not an exercise of the taxing and spending power, but of the power under Art. IV, § 3, cl. 2, to make "rules and regulations respecting the ... property belonging to the United States."

Lujan v. Defenders of Wildlife

504 U.S. 555, 112 S.Ct. 2130, 119 L.Ed.2d 351 (1992).

Justice Scalia delivered the opinion of the Court with respect to Parts I, II, III–A, and IV, and an opinion with respect to Part III–B in which The Chief Justice, Justice White, and Justice Thomas join.

This case involves a challenge to a rule promulgated by the Secretary of the Interior interpreting § 7 of the Endangered Species Act of 1973 (ESA), 87 Stat. 892, as amended, 16 U.S.C. § 1536, in such fashion as to render it applicable only to actions within the United States or on the high seas. The preliminary issue, and the only one we reach, is whether the respondents here, plaintiffs below, have standing to seek judicial review of the rule.

I

The ESA ... seeks to protect species of animals against threats to their continuing existence caused by man.... The ESA instructs the Secretary of the Interior to promulgate by regulation a list of those species which are either endangered or threatened under enumerated criteria, and to define the critical habitat of these species.... Section 7(a)(2) of the Act then provides, in pertinent part: "Each Federal agency shall, in consultation with and with the assistance of the Secretary [of the Interior], insure that any action authorized, funded, or carried out by such agency ... is not likely to jeopardize the continued existence of any endangered species or threatened species or result in the destruction or adverse modification of habitat of such species which is determined by the Secretary, after consultation as appropriate with affected States, to be critical." ...

In 1978, the Fish and Wildlife Service (FWS) and the National Marine Fisheries Service (NMFS), on behalf of the Secretary of the Interior and the Secretary of Commerce respectively, promulgated a joint regulation stating that the obligations imposed by § 7(a)(2) extend to actions taken in foreign nations.... The next year, however, the Interior Department began to reexamine its position.... A revised joint regulation, reinterpreting § 7(a)(2) to require consultation only for actions taken in the United States or on the high seas, was proposed in 1983....

Shortly thereafter, respondents, organizations dedicated to wildlife conservation and other environmental causes, filed this action against the Secretary of the Interior, seeking a declaratory judgment that the new regulation is in error as to the geographic scope of § 7(a)(2), and an injunction requiring the Secretary to promulgate a new regulation restoring the initial interpretation.... [T]he Secretary moved for summary judgment on the standing issue, and respondents moved for summary judgment on the merits. The District Court denied the Secretary's motion, ... and ordered the Secretary to publish a revised regulation. The Eighth Circuit affirmed....

. . . .

[The court held that two members of the organization who alleged they intended to observe animals endangered by specific projects had not suffered an "injury in fact."]

IV

The Court of Appeals found that respondents had standing for an additional reason: because they had suffered a "procedural injury." The so-called "citizen-suit" provision of the ESA provides, in pertinent part, that "any person may commence a civil suit on his own behalf (A) to enjoin any person, including the United States and any other governmental instrumentality or agency ... who is alleged to be in violation of any provision of this chapter." 16 U.S.C. § 1540(g). The court held that, because § 7(a)(2) requires interagency consultation, the citizen-suit provision creates a "procedural righ[t]" to consultation in all "persons"—so that anyone can file suit in federal court to challenge the Secretary's (or presumably any other official's) failure to follow the assertedly correct consultative procedure, notwithstanding their inability to allege any discrete injury flowing from that failure. To understand the remarkable nature of this holding one must be clear about what it does not rest upon: This is not a case where plaintiffs are seeking to enforce a procedural requirement the disregard of which could impair a separate concrete interest of theirs (e.g., the procedural requirement for a hearing prior to denial of their license application, or the procedural requirement for an environmental impact statement before a federal facility is constructed next door to them). Nor is it simply a case where concrete injury has been suffered by many persons, as in mass fraud or mass tort situations. Nor, finally, is it the unusual case in which Congress has created a concrete private interest in the outcome of a suit against a private party for the government's benefit, by providing a cash bounty for the victorious plaintiff. Rather, the court held that the injury-in-fact requirement had been satisfied by congressional conferral upon all persons of an abstract, self-contained, noninstrumental "right" to have the Executive observe the procedures required by law. We reject this view.

We have consistently held that a plaintiff raising only a generally available grievance about government—claiming only harm to his and every citizen's interest in proper application of the Constitution and laws, and seeking relief that no more directly and tangibly benefits him than it does the public at large—does not state an Article III case or controversy....

. . .

... In United States v. Richardson, 418 U.S. 166 (1974), we dismissed for lack of standing a taxpayer suit challenging the Government's failure to disclose the expenditures of the Central Intelligence Agency, in alleged violation of the constitutional requirement, Art. I, § 9, cl. 7, that "a regular Statement and Account of the Receipts and Expenditures of all public Money shall be published from time to time." We held that such a suit rested upon an impermissible "generalized grievance," and was inconsistent with "the framework of Article III" because "the impact on [plaintiff] is plainly undifferentiated and common to all members of the public." ... And in Schlesinger v. Reservists Committee to Stop the War, 418 U.S. 208 (1974), we dismissed for the same reasons a citizen-taxpayer suit contending that it was a violation of the Incompatibility Clause, Art. I, § 6, cl. 2, for Members of Congress to hold commissions in the military Reserves. We said that the challenged action, "standing alone, would adversely affect only the generalized interest of all citizens in constitutional governance...." ... Since *Schlesinger* we have on two occasions held that an injury amounting only to the alleged violation of a right to have the Government act in accordance with law was not judicially cognizable because "assertion of a right to a particular kind of Government conduct, which the Government has violated by acting differently, cannot alone satisfy the requirements of Art. III without draining those requirements of meaning." *Allen,* 468 U.S., at 754; Valley Forge Christian College v. Americans United for Separation of Church and State, Inc., 454 U.S. 464, 483 (1982). And only two Terms ago, we rejected the notion that Article III permits a citizen-suit to prevent a condemned criminal's execution on the basis of "the ... Eighth Amendment;" once again, "[t]his allegation raise[d] only the generalized interest of all citizens in constitutional governance ... and [was] an inadequate basis on which to grant ... standing." *Whitmore,* 495 U.S., at 160.

To be sure, our generalized-grievance cases have typically involved Government violation of procedures assertedly ordained by the Constitution rather than the Congress. But there is absolutely no basis for making the Article III inquiry turn on the source of the asserted right. Whether the courts were to act on their own, or at the invitation of Congress, in ignoring the concrete injury requirement described in our cases, they would be discarding a principle fundamental to the separate and distinct constitutional role of the Third Branch—one of the essential elements that identifies those "Cases" and "Controversies" that are the business of the courts rather than of the political branches. "The province of the court," as Chief Justice Marshall said in Marbury v. Madison, 1 Cranch 137, 170 (1803) "is, solely, to decide on the rights of individuals." Vindicating the public interest (including the public interest in government observance of the Constitution and laws) is the function of Congress and the Chief Executive. The question presented here is whether the public interest in proper administration of the laws (specifically, in agencies' observance of a particular, statutorily prescribed procedure) can be converted into an individual right by a statute that denominates it as such, and that permits all citizens (or, for that matter, a subclass of citizens who suffer no distinctive concrete harm) to sue. If the concrete injury requirement has the separation-of-powers significance we have always said, the answer must be obvious: To permit Congress to convert the undifferentiated public interest in executive officers' compliance with the law into an "individual right" vindicable in the courts is to permit Congress to transfer from the President to the courts the Chief Executive's most important constitutional duty, to "take Care that the Laws be faithfully executed," Art. II, § 3. It would enable the courts, with the permission of Congress, "to assume a position of authority over the governmental acts of another and co-equal department," Frothingham v. Mellon, 262 U.S., at 489 ... We have always rejected that vision of our role....

Nothing in this contradicts the principle that "[t]he ... injury required by Art. III may exist solely by virtue of 'statutes creating legal rights, the invasion of which creates standing.'" *Warth,* 422 U.S., at 500 (quoting Linda R.S. v. Richard D., 410 U.S. 614, 617, n. 3 (1973)). Both of the cases used by Linda R.S. as an illustration of that principle involved Congress's elevating to the status of legally cognizable injuries concrete, de facto injuries that were previously inadequate in law (namely, injury to an individual's personal interest in living in a racially integrated community, see Trafficante v. Metropolitan Life Ins. Co., 409 U.S. 205, 208–212 (1972), and injury to a company's interest in marketing its product free from competition, see Hardin v. Kentucky Utilities Co., 390 U.S. 1, 6 (1968)). As we said in *Sierra Club,* "[Statutory] broadening [of] the categories of injury that may be alleged in support of standing is a different matter from abandoning the requirement that the party seeking review must himself have suffered an injury." 405 U.S., at 738. Whether or not the principle set forth in *Warth* can be extended beyond that distinction, it is clear that in suits against the government, at least, the concrete injury requirement must remain.

. . .

We hold that respondents lack standing to bring this action and that the Court of Appeals erred in denying the summary judgment motion filed by the United States. The opinion of the Court of Appeals is hereby reversed, and the cause remanded for proceedings consistent with this opinion.

It is so ordered.[a]

Justice Kennedy, with whom Justice Souter joins, concurring in part and concurring in the judgment.

. . .

I ... join Part IV of the Court's opinion with the following observations. As government programs and policies become more complex and far-reaching, we must be sensitive to the articulation of new rights of action that do not have clear analogs in our common-law tradition. Modern litigation has progressed far from the paradigm of Marbury suing Madison to get his commission, Marbury v. Madison, 1 Cranch 137 (1803), or Ogden seeking an injunction to halt Gibbons' steamboat operations. Gibbons v. Ogden, 9 Wheat. 1 (1824). In my view, Congress has the power to define injuries and articulate chains of causation that will give rise to a case or controversy where none existed before, and I do not read the Court's opinion to suggest a contrary view.... In exercising this power, however, Congress must at the very least identify the

---

[a] Justice Scalia's position in *Lujan* was originally propounded in Scalia, *The Doctrine of Standing as an Essential Element of the Separation of Powers,* 17 SUFFOLK U. L. REV. 831 (1983). For a critique, see Sunstein, *What's Standing After Lujan? Of Citizen Suits, "Injuries," and Article III,* 91 MICH. L. REV. 163 (1992).

injury it seeks to vindicate and relate the injury to the class of persons entitled to bring suit. The citizen-suit provision of the Endangered Species Act does not meet these minimal requirements, because while the statute purports to confer a right on "any person ... to enjoin ... the United States and any other governmental instrumentality or agency ... who is alleged to be in violation of any provision of this chapter," it does not of its own force establish that there is an injury in "any person" by virtue of any "violation." 16 U.S.C. § 1540(g)(1)(A).

The Court's holding that there is an outer limit to the power of Congress to confer rights of action is a direct and necessary consequence of the case and controversy limitations found in Article III. I agree that it would exceed those limitations if, at the behest of Congress and in the absence of any showing of concrete injury, we were to entertain citizen-suits to vindicate the public's nonconcrete interest in the proper administration of the laws. While it does not matter how many persons have been injured by the challenged action, the party bringing suit must show that the action injures him in a concrete and personal way. This requirement is not just an empty formality. It preserves the vitality of the adversarial process by assuring both that the parties before the court have an actual, as opposed to professed, stake in the outcome, and that "the legal questions presented ... will be resolved, not in the rarefied atmosphere of a debating society, but in a concrete factual context conducive to a realistic appreciation of the consequences of judicial action." Valley Forge Christian College v. Americans United for Separation of Church and State, Inc., 454 U.S. 464, 472 (1982). In addition, the requirement of concrete injury confines the Judicial Branch to its proper, limited role in the constitutional framework of government.

An independent judiciary is held to account through its open proceedings and its reasoned judgments. In this process it is essential for the public to know what persons or groups are invoking the judicial power, the reasons that they have brought suit, and whether their claims are vindicated or denied. The concrete injury requirement helps assure that there can be an answer to these questions; and, as the Court's opinion is careful to show, that is part of the constitutional design.

. . .

Justice Stevens, concurring in the judgment.

Because I am not persuaded that Congress intended the consultation requirement in § 7(a)(2) of the Endangered Species Act of 1973 (ESA), 16 U.S.C. § 1536(a)(2), to apply to activities in foreign countries, I concur in the judgment of reversal. I do not, however, agree with the Court's conclusion that respondents lack standing because the threatened injury to their interest in protecting the environment and studying endangered species is not "imminent." ...

. . .

Justice Blackmun, with whom Justice O'Connor joins, dissenting.

... I question the Court's breadth of language in rejecting standing for "procedural" injuries. I fear the Court seeks to impose fresh limitations on the constitutional authority of Congress to allow citizen-suits in the federal courts for injuries deemed "procedural" in nature. I dissent.

. . .

II

The Court concludes that any "procedural injury" suffered by respondents is insufficient to confer standing. It rejects the view that the "injury-in-fact requirement ... [is] satisfied by congressional conferral upon all persons of an abstract, self-contained, noninstrumental 'right' to have the Executive observe the procedures required by law." ...

Congress legislates in procedural shades of gray not to aggrandize its own power but to allow maximum Executive discretion in the attainment of Congress' legislative goals. Congress could simply impose a substantive prohibition on executive conduct; it could say that no agency action shall result in the loss of more than 5% of any listed species. Instead, Congress sets forth substantive guidelines and allows the Executive, within certain procedural constraints, to decide how best to effectuate the ultimate goal.... The Court never has questioned Congress' authority to impose such procedural constraints on executive power. Just as Congress does not violate separation of powers by structuring the procedural manner in which the Executive shall carry out the laws, surely the federal courts do not violate separation of powers when, at the very instruction and command of Congress, they enforce these procedures.

To prevent Congress from conferring standing for "procedural injuries" is another way of saying that Congress may not delegate to the courts authority deemed "executive" in nature. Here Congress seeks not to delegate "executive" power but only to strengthen the procedures it has legislatively mandated....

Ironically, this Court has previously justified a relaxed review of congressional delegation to the Executive on grounds that Congress, in turn, has subjected the exercise of that power to judicial review. INS v. Chadha, 462 U.S. 919, 953–954, n. 16 (1983); American Power & Light Co. v. SEC, 329 U.S., at 105–106. The Court's intimation today that procedural injuries are not constitutionally cognizable threatens this understanding upon which Congress has undoubtedly relied. In no sense is the Court's suggestion compelled by our "common understanding of what activities are appropriate to legislatures, to executives, and to courts." In my view, it reflects an unseemly solicitude for an expansion of power of the Executive Branch.

. . .

C. MOOTNESS

"The usual rule in federal cases is that an actual controversy must exist at stages of appellate or certiorari review, and not simply at the date the action is initiated." Roe v. Wade, 410 U.S. 113, 125 (1973).

DeFunis v. Odegaard

416 U.S. 312, 94 S.Ct. 1704, 40 L.Ed.2d 164 (1974).

Per Curiam.

In 1971 the petitioner, Marco DeFunis, Jr., applied for admission as a first-year student at the University of Washington Law School, a state-operated institution. The size of the incoming first-year class was to be limited to 150 persons, and the Law School received some 1,600 applications for these 150 places. DeFunis was eventually notified that he had been denied admission. He thereupon commenced this suit in a Washington trial court, contending that the procedures and criteria employed by the Law School Admissions Committee invidiously discriminated against him on account of his race in violation of the

Equal Protection Clause of the Fourteenth Amendment to the United States Constitution.

DeFunis brought the suit on behalf of himself alone, and not as the representative of any class, against the various respondents, who are officers, faculty members, and members of the Board of Regents of the University of Washington. He asked the trial court to issue a mandatory injunction commanding the respondents to admit him as a member of the first-year class entering in September of 1971, on the ground that the Law School admissions policy had resulted in the unconstitutional denial of his application for admission. The trial court agreed with his claim and granted the requested relief. DeFunis was, accordingly, admitted to the Law School and began his legal studies there in the fall of 1971. On appeal, the Washington Supreme Court reversed the judgment of the trial court and held that the Law School admissions policy did not violate the Constitution. By this time DeFunis was in his second year at the Law School.

He then petitioned this Court for a writ of certiorari, and Mr. Justice Douglas, as Circuit Justice, stayed the judgment of the Washington Supreme Court pending the "final disposition of the case by this Court." By virtue of this stay, DeFunis has remained in law school, and was in the first term of his third and final year when this Court first considered his certiorari petition in the fall of 1973. Because of our concern that DeFunis' third-year standing in the Law School might have rendered this case moot, we requested the parties to brief the question of mootness before we acted on the petition. In response, both sides contended that the case was not moot. The respondents indicated that, if the decision of the Washington Supreme Court were permitted to stand, the petitioner could complete the term for which he was then enrolled but would have to apply to the faculty for permission to continue in the school before he could register for another term.

We granted the petition for certiorari on November 19, 1973, 414 U.S. 1038. The case was in due course orally argued on February 26, 1974.

In response to questions raised from the bench during the oral argument, counsel for the petitioner has informed the Court that DeFunis has now registered "for his final quarter in law school." Counsel for the respondents have made clear that the Law School will not in any way seek to abrogate this registration. In light of DeFunis' recent registration for the last quarter of his final law school year, and the Law School's assurance that his registration is fully effective, the insistent question again arises whether this case is not moot, and to that question we now turn.

The starting point for analysis is the familiar proposition that "federal courts are without power to decide questions that cannot affect the rights of litigants in this case before them." North Carolina v. Rice, 404 U.S. 244, 246 (1971). The inability of the federal judiciary "to review moot cases derives from the requirement of Article III of the Constitution under which the exercise of judicial power depends upon the existence of a case or controversy." Liner v. Jafco, Inc., 375 U.S. 301, 306 n. 3 (1964); see also Powell v. McCormack, 395 U.S. 486, 496 n. 7 (1969); Sibron v. New York, 392 U.S. 40, 50 n. 8 (1968). Although as a matter of Washington state law it appears that this case would be saved from mootness by "the great public interest in the continuing issues raised by this appeal," 82 Wash.2d 11, 23 n. 6, 507 P.2d 1169, 1177 n. 6 (1973), the fact remains that under Art. III "[e]ven in cases arising in the state courts, the question of mootness is a federal one which a federal court must resolve before it assumes jurisdiction." North Carolina v. Rice, supra, at 246.

The respondents have represented that, without regard to the ultimate resolution of the issues in this case, DeFunis will remain a student in the law school for the duration of any term in which he has already enrolled. Since he has now registered for his final term, it is evident that he will be given an opportunity to complete all academic and other requirements for graduation, and, if he does so, will receive his diploma regardless of any decision this Court might reach on the merits of this case. In short, all parties agree that DeFunis is now entitled to complete his legal studies at the University of Washington and to receive his degree from that institution. A determination by this Court of the legal issues tendered by the parties is no longer necessary to compel that result, and could not serve to prevent it. DeFunis did not cast his suit as a class action, and the only remedy he requested was an injunction commanding his admission to the Law School. He was not only accorded that remedy, but he now has also been irrevocably admitted to the final term of the final year of the law school course. The controversy between the parties has thus clearly ceased to be "definite and concrete" and no longer "touch[es] the legal relations of parties having adverse legal interests." Aetna Life Ins. Co. v. Haworth, 300 U.S. 227, 240–241 (1937).

It matters not that these circumstances partially stem from a policy decision on the part of the respondent Law School authorities. The respondents, through their counsel, the Attorney General of the State, have professionally represented that in no event will the status of DeFunis now be affected by any view this Court might express on the merits of this controversy. And it has been the settled practice of the Court in contexts no less significant, fully to accept representations such as these as parameters for decision. . . .

It might also be suggested that this case presents a question that is "capable of repetition, yet evading review," Southern Pacific Terminal Co. v. ICC, 219 U.S. 498, 515 (1911); Roe v. Wade, 410 U.S. 113, 125 (1973), and is thus amenable to federal adjudication even though it might otherwise be considered moot. But DeFunis will never again be required to run the gantlet of the Law School's admission process, and so the question is certainly not "capable of repetition" so far as he is concerned. Moreover, just because this particular case did not reach the Court until the eve of the petitioner's graduation from law school, it hardly follows that the issue he raises will in future evade review. If the admissions procedures of the Law School remain unchanged, there is no reason to suppose that a subsequent case attacking those procedures will not come with relative speed to this Court, now that the Supreme Court of Washington has spoken. This case, therefore, in no way presents the exceptional situation in which the *Southern Pacific Terminal* doctrine might permit a departure from "[t]he usual rule in federal cases . . . that an actual controversy must exist at stages of appellate or certiorari review, and not simply at the date the action is initiated." Roe v. Wade, supra, at 125; United States v. Munsingwear, Inc., 340 U.S. 36 (1950).

Because the petitioner will complete his law school studies at the end of the term for which he has now registered regardless of any decision this Court might reach on the merits of this litigation, we conclude that the Court cannot, consistently with the limitations of Art. III of the Constitution, consider the substantive constitutional issues tendered by the parties. Accordingly, the judgment of the Supreme Court of Washington is vacated, and the cause is remanded for such proceedings as by that Court may be deemed appropriate.

It is so ordered.

Mr. Justice Douglas, dissenting.

I agree with Mr. Justice Brennan that this case is not moot, and because of the significance of the issues raised I think it is important to reach the merits....

. . .

Mr. Justice Brennan, with whom Mr. Justice Douglas, Mr. Justice White, and Mr. Justice Marshall concur, dissenting.

. . .

... [I]n endeavoring to dispose of this case as moot, the Court clearly disserves the public interest. The constitutional issues which are avoided today concern vast numbers of people, organizations and colleges and universities, as evidenced by the filing of twenty-six *amici curiae* briefs. Few constitutional questions in recent history have stirred as much debate, and they will not disappear. They must inevitably return to the federal courts and ultimately again to this Court. Cf. Richardson v. Wright, 405 U.S. 208, 212 (1972) (dissenting opinion). Because avoidance of repetitious litigation serves the public interest, that inevitability counsels against mootness determinations, as here, not compelled by the record.... Although the Court should, of course, avoid unnecessary decisions of constitutional questions, we should not transform principles of avoidance of constitutional decisions into devices for sidestepping resolution of difficult cases....

On what appears in this case, I would find that there is an extant controversy and decide the merits of the very important constitutional questions presented.

CAPABLE OF REPETITION YET EVADING REVIEW

An exception to the requirement that there be a live controversy at the time of decision exists for those controversies "capable of repetition yet evading review." In its *DeFunis* opinion, the Court concludes that the exception is inapplicable because DeFunis would not be affected by the challenged admission policy in the future and other challengers to the admission procedures could litigate the issues before their claims became moot.[1]

The simplest cases involving the exception are those where the litigated issue will always be mooted by the passage of time in litigation, and the plaintiff will be subject to the challenged action in the future. That was the situation in United States v. New York Tel. Co., 434 U.S. 159 (1977), where a telephone company challenged a federal district court order requiring it to install and use "pen registers" and furnish the Federal Bureau of Investigation with information concerning the use of two telephones. Such orders were issued only for brief periods, and even if an order was stayed pending judicial review, the showing of probable cause that supported the order would become stale before review was completed. Given the telephone company's policy of refusing to comply voluntarily with such orders, it was clear that it would be subjected to similar orders in the future.

More complex are those cases where the plaintiff will not face the litigated issue in the future, but others similarly situated will. That was the situation in Dunn v. Blumstein, 405 U.S. 330 (1972), where plaintiff challenged a state

---

[1] The issue mooted in *DeFunis* was decided by the Court four years later in Regents of the University of California v. Bakke, 438 U.S. 265 (1978), infra p. 821. Bakke had been denied admission to medical school, and was not attending the school when his case reached the Supreme Court.

requirement that voters live in the state for one year and the county for three months prior to an election. Plaintiff became eligible to vote long before termination of the litigation. Other new residents would, however, be subject to the durational residency requirement. That was also the situation in Roe v. Wade, 410 U.S. 113 (1973), where a pregnant woman challenged a state abortion statute, asserting her inability to obtain a legal abortion in the state. Plaintiff's 1970 pregnancy had obviously terminated prior to the Court's 1973 decision, and she did not allege that she was affected by the abortion statute with reference to future pregnancies. In both cases, the Court determined that the controversy was capable of repetition, yet evading review. In *Roe,* the Court said:

> "[W]hen ... pregnancy is a significant fact in the litigation, the normal 266–day gestation period is so short that the pregnancy will come to term before the usual appellate procedure is complete. If that termination makes a case moot, pregnancy litigation seldom will survive much beyond the trial stage, and appellate review will be effectively denied. Our law should not be that rigid."

Both *Dunn* and *Roe* were class actions. Where litigation is not capable of repetition as to the named plaintiff, later cases have combined concerns about whether the plaintiff's claim is "capable of repetition yet evading review" with questions whether the action to enjoin enforcement of the challenged law has been certified as a class action. In Sosna v. Iowa, 419 U.S. 393 (1975), plaintiffs challenged a state law imposing a durational residency requirement for obtaining a divorce. Sosna had satisfied the residency requirement before the completion of litigation. The Court explained that the case had not become moot because: (1) the case had been certified as a class action, with a class whose members were still subject to the durational residency requirement, *and;* (2) the problem was one capable of repetition yet evading review as to the class.[2] Since *Sosna,* complications have arisen when the claims of the named plaintiff have become moot prior to class certification.[3]

CASE AND CONTROVERSY REQUIREMENTS AS APPLIED TO CONSTITUTIONAL LITIGATION ARISING IN STATE AND FEDERAL COURTS

The *DeFunis* case is the first principal case in this section where the Supreme Court is reviewing the decision of a state court. Standing, mootness and ripeness rules apply both to constitutional litigation arising in the federal courts, and to Supreme Court review of constitutional decisions of state courts. The rules are sometimes different, however, depending on whether the Supreme Court is reviewing a state or federal court decision. One traditional explanation for the difference is that case or controversy limitations represent, in part, rules of self-limitation for the federal courts and as such are irrelevant to Supreme Court review of state decisions. Article III case or controversy

---

[2] Greenstein, *Bridging the Mootness Gap in Federal Court Class Actions,* 35 Stan. L.Rev. 897, 903 (1983), points out that the combination of two reasons is confusing. "If certification conferred legal status upon the claims of the class and if there were always class members with *current* claims, what did it matter ... that the claims were 'capable of repetition?' And in what sense were they 'evading review'?"

[3] See Deposit Guar. Nat'l Bank v. Roper, 445 U.S. 326 (1980), and United States Parole Commission v. Geraghty, 445 U.S. 388 (1980). In both cases, the trial court had denied class certification, and the individual plaintiff's claim became moot while the case was on appeal. The Court held that a justiciable controversy remained concerning whether the class should have been certified. For discussion of these cases, see Greenstein, supra note 2.

requirements, however, bind the Supreme Court, even when it is reviewing the decision of a state court. Under this view, doctrines of standing, ripeness and mootness will not block Supreme Court review of state court decisions unless there is no case or controversy in the sense of Article III. An illustrative case is Doremus v. Board of Educ., 342 U.S. 429 (1952). State taxpayers had attacked the practice of Bible reading in the public schools on federal constitutional grounds. The state court decision ruled against plaintiffs on the merits. The Court's opinion conceded that state courts were not bound by case or controversy limitations, and could even give advisory opinions on constitutional questions. Supreme Court review, however, was bound by the limitations of Article III, making an advisory opinion of a state court unreviewable. The Supreme Court had considered state taxpayers' challenges to state laws in reviewing decisions of state courts, even when the plaintiffs would have been denied standing in a federal court action. Those actions were cases or controversies within Article III. Here, however, the state taxpayers were litigating a "religious difference" rather than a "good-faith pocketbook action." Since there was no case or controversy within the meaning of Article III, plaintiffs' appeal was dismissed. Three Justices dissented from the conclusion that there was no Article III case or controversy.[1]

There are two difficulties with the explanation given in *Doremus*. First, it is dubious that the litigation in that case failed to meet the requirements of Article III. (It is likewise dubious that the issue in *DeFunis* was moot "in a constitutional sense.") Moreover, even in apparently mandatory appeals, there is a discretionary element in Supreme Court review of state court decisions.[2] A more complete explanation, then, is that the discretionary, nonconstitutional aspects of standing, mootness and ripeness doctrines apply, but are different for federal court litigation and Supreme Court review of state court decisions. A major reason for the difference may be that a decision by the Supreme Court that there is no case or controversy has a different impact, depending upon whether the case originated in federal or state court. In a federal court case, a decision that a case is not ripe for decision, or that plaintiffs lack standing, requires that the case be sent back to the lower court with directions to dismiss the litigation. The dismissal of the suit removes any formal value of the lower court decisions as precedent. In a case coming from a state court, lack of standing or ripeness requires that the appeal to the Supreme Court be dismissed, leaving the lower court decision in effect. The situation with reference to mootness is similar, but a little more complex.[3]

---

[1] The constitutionality of Bible reading in the public schools, the substantive issue involved in the *Doremus* case, was not resolved for more than a decade. In School Dist. of Abington Twp. v. Schempp, 374 U.S. 203 (1963), the practice was held unconstitutional. One of the two companion cases was a suit for an injunction brought in a federal court; the other was a suit for mandamus in a state court. School children and their parents were held to have standing in both cases. 374 U.S. at 224 n. 9. In *Doremus,* one of the plaintiffs had been the parent of a school child, but the child had graduated from public schools before appeal had been taken to the Supreme Court, mooting that aspect of the plaintiff's standing. 342 U.S. at 432–433.

[2] See Naim v. Naim, 350 U.S. 891 (1955), motion to recall mandate denied 350 U.S. 985

(1956) and Rescue Army v. Municipal Court, 331 U.S. 549 (1947). See also Poe v. Ullman, 367 U.S. 497 (1961), infra p. 114, an avowedly discretionary dismissal of an appeal from a state court on ripeness grounds.

[3] If a federal court decision becomes moot pending Supreme Court review, the decision being reviewed will be "vacated," and the case will be remanded to the trial court with directions that the action be dismissed as moot. If a state court decision becomes moot pending Supreme Court review, standard practice is not to dismiss the appeal, but to vacate and remand to the state's highest court for such proceedings as that court may deem appropriate. Stern and Gressman, *Supreme Court Practice* 722–724 (6th ed. 1986). Arguably, the difference between moot cases and cases that are not ripe or where parties

While cases concerning the requirements of standing and ripeness are often distinguished, according to whether the case arose in a federal or state court,[4] none of the cases involving mootness have drawn that distinction. In other words, if a claim is made that subsequent events have mooted a case pending Supreme Court review, there appears to be a single standard that draws no distinction between federal and state case appeals. Should it have made a difference in *DeFunis* that the Supreme Court was reviewing a state court decision, and not the decision of a federal court?

D. RIPENESS

Criminal prosecutions and suits for damages in tort or contract relate to past conduct. If it is necessary to decide a constitutional issue in order to determine the legal consequences of that conduct, no issues of ripeness or concreteness arise. Such cases present the question of judicial review in the classic *Marbury v. Madison* form.

Suits for injunctions and declaratory judgments, however, present different problems. Characteristically, they relate to the future. It may not be clear what either the plaintiff or the defendant actually will do. It may not be certain that the conduct alleged to give rise to the constitutional issue will ever take place. The declaratory judgment action, in particular, takes a form suspiciously like that of an advisory opinion. It is in such cases that the Court articulates the doctrines relating to the concreteness of the factual situation and the ripeness of the controversy.

The cases set out below constitute a sample of the Court's approach to the problem. Because of the amorphous nature of the rules being applied, the cases do not fit neatly into rational categories.

For discussions of the problems in this section from differing points of view see Bickel, *The Least Dangerous Branch* 71, 111–98 (1962); Scharpf, *Judicial Review and the Political Question: A Functional Analysis,* 75 Yale L.J. 517, 528–533 (1966).

UNITED PUBLIC WORKERS v. MITCHELL, 330 U.S. 75 (1947). The Hatch Act forbade certain classes of federal government employees from taking "any active part in political management or in political campaigns." A group of employees sought an injunction forbidding the Civil Service Commission from enforcing against them this aspect of the Hatch Act as a violation of the Constitution. One group of plaintiffs alleged that they desired to engage in specified acts of political management and political campaigning. One plaintiff (Poole) alleged that he had engaged in forbidden political activity and that proceedings leading to his discharge were under way. The Court held that the first group of plaintiffs could not have their arguments heard in a federal court but that Poole could do so. In discussing its reasons for refusing to hear the first group, the Court said, in part:

---

lack standing (where the appeal is dismissed) is that the mootness problem has arisen after the state court decision. Significantly, even though the state court's decision is "vacated" on mootness grounds, the state court remains free to reinstate its opinion if it concludes that the case is not moot by state law standards. On the *DeFunis* remand, the Washington Supreme Court's decision was inconclusive, although a plurality would have reinstated the prior opinion, in part because

the issue was of major public importance. DeFunis v. Odegaard, 84 Wn.2d 617, 529 P.2d 438 (1974). The Washington Supreme Court's opinion contains an exhaustive treatment of the United States Supreme Court's practice of disposing of moot federal and state appeals.

[4] In addition to the *Doremus* case, supra, see United Public Workers v. Mitchell, 330 U.S. 75 (1947) and Adler v. Board of Educ. 342 U.S. 485 (1952), infra at pp. 112–114.

"As is well known the federal courts established pursuant to Article III of the Constitution do not render advisory opinions. For adjudication of constitutional issues, 'concrete legal issues, presented in actual cases, not abstractions,' are requisite. This is as true of declaratory judgments as any other field. These appellants seem clearly to seek advisory opinions upon broad claims of rights protected by the First, Fifth, Ninth and Tenth Amendments to the Constitution. As these appellants are classified employees, they have a right superior to the generality of citizens, compare Fairchild v. Hughes, 258 U.S. 126, but the facts of their personal interest in their civil rights, of the general threat of possible interference with those rights by the Civil Service Commission under its rules, if specified things are done by appellants, does not make a justiciable case or controversy. Appellants want to engage in 'political management and political campaigns,' to persuade others to follow appellants' views by discussion, speeches, articles and other acts reasonably designed to secure the selection of appellants' political choices. Such generality of objection is really an attack on the political expediency of the Hatch Act, not the presentation of legal issues. It is beyond the competence of courts to render such a decision. Texas v. Interstate Commerce Commission, 258 U.S. 158, 162.

"The power of courts, and ultimately of this Court to pass upon the constitutionality of acts of Congress arises only when the interests of litigants require the use of this judicial authority for their protection against actual interference. A hypothetical threat is not enough. We can only speculate as to the kinds of political activity the appellants desire to engage in or as to the contents of their proposed public statements or the circumstances of their publication. It would not accord with judicial responsibility to adjudge, in a matter involving constitutionality, between the freedom of the individual and the requirements of public order except when definite rights appear upon the one side and definite prejudicial interferences upon the other.

"The Constitution allots the nation's judicial power to the federal courts. Unless these courts respect the limits of that unique authority, they intrude upon powers vested in the legislative or executive branches. Judicial adherence to the doctrine of the separation of powers preserves the courts for the decision of issues, between litigants, capable of effective determination. Judicial exposition upon political proposals is permissible only when necessary to decide definite issues between litigants. When the courts act continually within these constitutionally imposed boundaries of their power, their ability to perform their function as a balance for the people's protection against abuse of power by other branches of government remains unimpaired. Should the courts seek to expand their power so as to bring under their jurisdiction ill defined controversies over constitutional issues, they would become the organ of political theories. Such abuse of judicial power would properly meet rebuke and restriction from other branches. By these mutual checks and balances by and between the branches of government, democracy undertakes to preserve the liberties of the people from excessive concentrations of authority. No threat of interference by the Commission with rights of these appellants appears beyond that implied by the existence of the law and the regulations. Watson v. Buck, supra, 313 U.S. at page 400. We should not take judicial cognizance of the situation presented on the part of the appellants considered in this subdivision of the opinion. These reasons lead us to conclude that the determination of the trial court, that the individual appellants, other than Poole, could maintain this action, was erroneous."

ADLER v. BOARD OF EDUCATION, 342 U.S. 485 (1952). Plaintiffs brought suit in the New York courts seeking a judgment declaring unconstitutional the Feinberg Law, which required the discharge of teachers who belonged to allegedly subversive groups. The plaintiffs moved for a judgment on the pleadings in the trial court, which was granted. The New York Court of Appeals reversed the trial court judgment and the case came to the Supreme Court by appeal. That Court affirmed on the merits without considering issues of ripeness or concreteness. Justice Frankfurter, dissenting, said:

"The allegations in the present action fall short of these found insufficient in the *Mitchell* Case. These teachers do not allege that they have engaged in proscribed conduct or . . . that they have been, or are, deterred from supporting causes or from joining organizations for fear of the Feinberg Law's interdict, except to say generally that the system complained of will have this effect on teachers as a group. They do not assert that they are threatened with action under law, or that steps are imminent whereby they would incur the hazard of punishment for conduct innocent at the time, or under standards too vague to satisfy due process of law. They merely allege that the statutes and Rules permit such action against some teachers. Since we rightly refused in the *Mitchell* Case to hear government employees whose conduct was much more intimately affected by the law there attacked than are the claims of the plaintiffs here, this suit is wanting in the necessary basis for our review."

NOTES ON MITCHELL AND ADLER

1. *Mitchell* and *Adler* suggest that the degree of concreteness required may vary with the nature of the constitutional issue presented. By moving for a judgment on the pleadings the plaintiffs in *Adler* presented the question whether there could be any constitutional applications of the statute—a question that could be decided without reference to the particular conduct of the plaintiffs. See Scharpf, *Judicial Review and the Political Question: A Functional Analysis,* 75 Yale L.J. 517, 531–533 (1966). In United States Civil Service Comm'n. v. Letter Carriers, 413 U.S. 548 (1973) the Court upheld the Hatch Act a second time in a suit brought by plaintiffs who did no more than allege their desire to engage in various political activities—allegations essentially similar to those held inadequate in *Mitchell.* The Court did not discuss the ripeness and concreteness issues. However, this time the Court was considering contentions that the Act was unconstitutional on its face as vague and overbroad—constitutional contentions that do not depend upon the facts of the particular case for resolution.

2. Are *Adler* and *Mitchell* distinguishable on another basis? *Mitchell* arose in a federal court action, and the ripeness issue concerned the standards for granting federal declaratory judgments. In *Adler,* the Court was reviewing a state court decision holding that the challenged statute did not violate the United States Constitution, and the issue of ripeness concerned the appropriate standard for reviewing a state court decision. See Note, *Case and Controversy Requirements as Applied to Constitutional Litigation Arising in State and Federal Courts,* supra, p. 110. Contrast Poe v. Ullman, which follows, another case seeking review of a state court declaratory judgment.

POE v. ULLMAN, 367 U.S. 497 (1961). A doctor and his patients brought declaratory judgment actions in the Connecticut courts seeking a determination that a Connecticut statute making it a crime to use birth control devices was unconstitutional. The state courts upheld the validity of the statute. The Supreme Court dismissed the appeals on the ground that there was no real controversy since the Connecticut statute was not enforced and hence there was no real fear of personal liability. In discussing the declaratory judgment problem in the plurality opinion, Mr. Justice Frankfurter said: "For just as the declaratory judgment device does not 'purport to alter the character of the controversies which are the subject of the judicial power under the Constitution,' United States v. State of West Virginia, 295 U.S. 463, 475, ... it does not permit litigants to invoke the power of this Court to obtain constitutional rulings in advance of necessity. Electric Bond & Share Co. v. Securities and Exchange Comm., 303 U.S. 419, 443. The Court has been on the alert against use of the declaratory judgment device for avoiding the rigorous insistence on exigent adversity as a condition for evoking Court adjudication. This is as true of state court suits for declaratory judgments as of federal. By exercising their jurisdiction, state courts cannot determine the jurisdiction to be exercised by this Court. Tyler v. Judges of the Court of Registration, 179 U.S. 405; Doremus v. Board of Education, 342 U.S. 429. Although we have held that a state declaratory-judgment suit may constitute a case or controversy within our appellate jurisdiction, it is to be reviewed here only 'so long as the case retains the essentials of an adversary proceeding, involving a real, not a hypothetical, controversy, which is finally determined by the judgment below.' Nashville, C. & St. L.R. Co. v. Wallace, 288 U.S. 249, 264. It was with respect to a state-originating declaratory judgment proceeding that we said, in Alabama State Federation of Labor, etc. v. McAdory, 325 U.S. 450, 471, that 'The extent to which the declaratory judgment procedure may be used in the federal courts to control state action lies in the sound discretion of the Court....' Indeed, we have recognized, in such cases, that '... the discretionary element characteristic of declaratory jurisdiction, and imported perhaps from equity jurisdiction and practice without the remedial phase, offers a convenient instrument for making ... effective ...' the policy against premature constitutional decision. Rescue Army v. Municipal Court, 331 U.S. 549, 573, note 41."

EPPERSON v. ARKANSAS, 393 U.S. 97 (1968). A teacher in a public school brought suit for a declaratory judgment that a state statute prohibiting teaching the theory of evolution in public schools was unconstitutional. Her school adopted a biology textbook containing a chapter on Darwin. The Arkansas Supreme Court upheld the validity of the law. The Supreme Court reversed on the merits. The Court did not raise any question whether the decision below was reviewable. A concurring opinion by Justice Black, however, expressed doubts whether "there was a genuinely justiciable case or controversy." Justice Black pointed out that the statute had been enacted forty years before, there was no indication it had ever been enforced, and "the pallid, unenthusiastic, even apologetic defense of the Act presented by the State in this Court indicates that the State would make no attempt to enforce the law."

YOUNGER v. HARRIS, 401 U.S. 37 (1971). A suit was brought in the federal district court to enjoin the District Attorney of Los Angeles County from prosecuting the plaintiffs under the California Criminal Syndicalism Act. On the question of the concreteness of the controversy the Court said:

"Appellee Harris has been indicted, and was actually being prosecuted by California for a violation of its Criminal Syndicalism Act at the time this suit was filed. He thus has an acute, live controversy with the State and its prosecutor. But none of the other parties plaintiff in the District Court, Dan, Hirsch, or Broslawsky, has such a controversy. None has been indicted, arrested, or even threatened by the prosecutor. About these three the three-judge court said:

" 'Plaintiffs Dan and Hirsch allege that they are members of the Progressive Labor Party, which advocates change in industrial ownership and political change, and that they feel inhibited in advocating the program of their political party through peaceful, nonviolent means, because of the presence of the Act "on the books", and because of the pending criminal prosecution against

Harris. Plaintiff Broslawsky is a history instructor, and he alleges that he is uncertain as to whether his normal practice of teaching his students about the doctrines of Karl Marx and reading from the Communist Manifesto and other revolutionary works may subject him to prosecution for violation of the Act.' 281 F.Supp., at 509.

"... Whatever right Harris, who is being prosecuted under the State Syndicalism law may have, Dan, Hirsch, and Broslawsky cannot share it with him. If these three had alleged that they would be prosecuted for the conduct they planned to engage in, and if the District Court had found this allegation to be true—either on the admission of the State's district attorney or on any other evidence—then a genuine controversy might be said to exist. But here appellees Dan, Hirsch, and Broslawsky do not claim that they have ever been threatened with prosecution, that a prosecution is likely, or even that a prosecution is remotely possible. They claim the right to bring this suit solely because, in the language of their complaint, they 'feel inhibited.' We do not think this allegation even if true, is sufficient to bring the equitable jurisdiction of the federal courts into play to enjoin a pending state prosecution. A federal lawsuit to stop a prosecution in a state court is a serious matter. And persons having no fears of state prosecution except those that are imaginary or speculative, are not to be accepted as appropriate plaintiffs in such cases. See Golden v. Zwickler, 394 U.S. 103 (1969). Since Harris is actually being prosecuted under the challenged laws, however, we proceed with him as a proper party."

RIPENESS AND CRIMINAL PROSECUTIONS

In Regional Rail Reorganization Act Cases, 419 U.S. 102, 143, n. 29 (1974) the Court said: "... Because the decision to instigate a criminal prosecution is usually discretionary with the prosecuting authorities, even a person with a settled intention to disobey the law can never be sure that the sanctions of the law will be invoked against him. Further, whether or not the injury will occur is to some extent within the control of the complaining party himself, since he can decide to abandon his intention to disobey the law. For these reasons, the maturity of such disputes for resolution before a prosecution begins is decided on a case-by-case basis, by considering the likelihood that the complainant will disobey the law, the certainty that such disobedience will take a particular form, any present injury occasioned by the threat of prosecution, and the likelihood that a prosecution will actually ensue."

City of Los Angeles v. Lyons

461 U.S. 95, 103 S.Ct. 1660, 75 L.Ed.2d 675 (1983).

Justice White delivered the opinion of the Court.

The issue here is whether respondent Lyons satisfied the prerequisites for seeking injunctive relief in the federal district court.

I

This case began on February 7, 1977, when respondent, Adolph Lyons, filed a complaint for damages, injunction, and declaratory relief in the United States District Court for the Central District of California. The defendants were the City of Los Angeles and four of its police officers. The complaint alleged that on October 6, 1976, at 2 a.m., Lyons was stopped by the defendant officers for a traffic or vehicle code violation and that although Lyons offered no resistance or threat whatsoever, the officers, without provocation or justification, seized Lyons and applied a "chokehold"—either the "bar arm control" hold or the "carotid-artery control" hold or both—rendering him unconscious and causing damage to his larynx. Counts I through IV of the complaint sought damages against the officers and the City. Count V, with which we are principally concerned here, sought a preliminary and permanent injunction against the City barring the use of the control holds. That count alleged that the city's police officers, "pursuant to the authorization, instruction and encouragement of defendant City of Los Angeles, regularly and routinely apply these choke holds in innumerable situations where they are not threatened by the use of any deadly force whatsoever," that numerous persons have been injured as the result of the application of the chokeholds, that Lyons and others similarly situated are threatened with irreparable injury in the form of bodily injury and loss of life, and that Lyons "justifiably fears that any contact he has with Los Angeles police officers may result in his being choked and strangled to death without provocation, justification or other legal excuse." Lyons alleged the threatened impairment of rights protected by the First, Fourth, Eighth and Fourteenth Amendments. Injunctive relief was sought against the use of the control holds "except in situations where the proposed victim of said control reasonably appears to be threatening the immediate use of deadly force." Count VI sought declaratory relief against the City, i.e., a judgment that use of the chokeholds absent the threat of immediate use of deadly force is a *per se* violation of various constitutional rights.

The District Court, by order, granted the City's motion for partial judgment on the pleadings and entered judgment for the City on Count V and VI. The Court of Appeals reversed the judgment for the City on Count V and VI, holding over the City's objection that despite our decisions in O'Shea v. Littleton, 414 U.S. 488 (1974), and Rizzo v. Goode, 423 U.S. 362 (1976), Lyons had standing to seek relief against the application of the chokeholds. 615 F.2d 1243. The Court of Appeals held that there was a sufficient likelihood that Lyons would again be stopped and subjected to the unlawful use of force to constitute a case or controversy and to warrant the issuance of an injunction, if the injunction was otherwise authorized. We denied certiorari. 449 U.S. 934.

On remand ... [a] preliminary injunction was entered enjoining "the use of both the carotid-artery and bar arm holds under circumstances which do not threaten death or serious bodily injury." An improved training program and regular reporting and record keeping were also ordered.[3] The Court of Appeals affirmed in a brief *per curiam* opinion ... We ... reverse.

. . .

III

It goes without saying that those who seek to invoke the jurisdiction of the federal courts must satisfy the threshold requirement imposed by Article III of the Constitution by alleging an actual case or controversy....

In O'Shea v. Littleton, 414 U.S. 488 (1974), we dealt with a case brought by a class of plaintiffs claiming that they had been subjected to discriminatory enforcement of the criminal law. Among other things, a county magistrate and judge were accused of discriminatory conduct in various respects, such as

---

[3] But its terms, the injunction was to continue in force until the court approved the training program to be presented to it. It is fair to assume that such approval would not be given if the program did not confine the use of the strangleholds to those situations in which their use, in the view of the District Court, would be constitutional. Because of successive stays entered by the Court of Appeals and by this court, the injunction has not gone into effect.

sentencing members of plaintiff's class more harshly than other defendants. The Court of Appeals reversed the dismissal of the suit by the District Court, ruling that if the allegations were proved, an appropriate injunction could be entered.

We reversed for failure of the complaint to allege a case or controversy.... Although it was claimed in that case that particular members of the plaintiff class had actually suffered from the alleged unconstitutional practices, we observed that "[p]ast exposure to illegal conduct does not in itself show a present case or controversy regarding injunctive relief ... if unaccompanied by any continuing, present adverse effects." ... Past wrongs were evidence bearing on "whether there is a real and immediate threat of repeated injury." ... But the prospect of future injury rested "on the likelihood that [plaintiffs] will again be arrested for and charged with violations of the criminal law and will again be subjected to bond proceedings, trial, or sentencing before petitioners." ... The most that could be said for plaintiffs' standing was "that *if* [plaintiffs] proceed to violate an unchallenged law and *if* they are charged, held to answer, and tried in any proceedings before petitioners, they will be subjected to the discriminatory practices that petitioners are alleged to have followed." ... We could not find a case or controversy in those circumstances: the threat to the plaintiffs was not "sufficiently real and immediate to show an existing controversy simply because they anticipate violating lawful criminal statutes and being tried for their offenses...." ... It was to be assumed "that [plaintiffs] will conduct their activities within the law and so avoid prosecution and conviction as well as exposure to the challenged course of conduct said to be followed by petitioners." ...

We ... went on to hold that even if the complaint presented an existing case or controversy, an adequate basis for equitable relief against petitioners had not been demonstrated:

> "[Plaintiffs] have failed, moreover, to establish the basic requisites of the issuance of equitable relief in these circumstances—the likelihood of substantial and immediate irreparable injury, and the inadequacy of remedies at law. We have already canvassed the necessarily conjectural nature of the threatened injury to which [plaintiffs] are allegedly subjected.... [I]f any of the [plaintiffs] are ever prosecuted and face trial, or if they are illegally sentenced, there are available state and federal procedures which could provide relief from the wrongful conduct alleged." ...

Another relevant decision for present purposes is Rizzo v. Goode, 423 U.S. 362 (1976), a case in which plaintiffs alleged widespread illegal and unconstitutional police conduct aimed at minority citizens and against City residents in general.... The claim of injury rested upon "what one or a small, unnamed minority of policemen might do to them in the future because of that unknown policeman's perception" of departmental procedures.... This hypothesis was "even more attenuated than those allegations of future injury found insufficient in O'Shea to warrant [the] invocation of federal jurisdiction." ... The Court also held that plaintiffs' showing at trial of a relatively few instances of violations by individual police officers, without any showing of a deliberate policy on behalf of the named defendants, did not provide a basis for equitable relief.

Golden v. Zwickler, 394 U.S. 103 (1969), a case arising in an analogous situation, is directly apposite. Congressman Zwickler sought a declaratory judgment that a New York statute prohibiting anonymous handbills directly pertaining to election campaigns was unconstitutional. Although Zwickler had once been convicted under the statute, he was no longer a Congressman apt to run for reelection. A unanimous Court held that because it was "most unlikely" that Zwickler would again be subject to the statute, no case or controversy of "sufficient immediacy and reality" was present to allow a declaratory judgment....

. . .

IV

No extension of *O'Shea* and *Rizzo* is necessary to hold that respondent Lyons has failed to demonstrate a case or controversy with the City that would justify the equitable relief sought. Lyons' standing to seek the injunction requested depended on whether he was likely to suffer future injury from the use of the chokeholds by police officers. Count V of the complaint alleged the traffic stop and choking incident five months before. That Lyons may have been illegally choked by the police on October 6, 1976, while presumably affording Lyons standing to claim damages against the individual officers and perhaps against the City, does nothing to establish a real and immediate threat that he would again be stopped for a traffic violation, or for any other offense, by an officer or officers who would illegally choke him into unconsciousness without any provocation or resistance on his part. The additional allegation in the complaint that the police in Los Angeles routinely apply chokeholds in situations where they are not threatened by the use of deadly force falls far short of the allegations that would be necessary to establish a case or controversy between these parties.

In order to establish an actual controversy in this case, Lyons would have had not only to allege that he would have another encounter with the police but also to make the incredible assertion either, (1) that *all* police officers in Los Angeles *always* choke any citizen with whom they happen to have an encounter, whether for the purpose of arrest, issuing a citation or for questioning or, (2) that the City ordered or authorized police officers to act in such manner. Although Count V alleged that the City authorized the use of the control holds in situations where deadly force was not threatened, it did not indicate why Lyons might be realistically threatened by police officers who acted within the strictures of the City's policy. If, for example, chokeholds were authorized to be used only to counter resistance to an arrest by a suspect, or to thwart an effort to escape, any future threat to Lyons from the City's policy or from the conduct of police officers would be no more real than the possibility that he would again have an encounter with the police and that either he would illegally resist arrest or detention or the officers would disobey their instructions and again render him unconscious without any provocation.[7]

---

[7] The centerpiece of Justice Marshall's dissent is that Lyons had standing to challenge the City's policy because to recover damages he would have to prove that what allegedly occurred on October 6, 1976, was pursuant to City authorization. We agree completely that for Lyons to succeed in his damages action, it would be necessary to prove that what happened to him—that is, as alleged, he was choked without any provocation or legal excuse whatsoever—was pursuant to a City policy....

... [E]ven if the complaint must be read as containing an allegation that officers are authorized to apply the chokeholds where there is no resistance or other provocation, it does not follow that Lyons has standing to seek an injunction against the application of the restraint holds in situations that he has not experienced, as for example, where the suspect resists arrest or tries to escape but does not threaten the use of deadly force. Yet that is precisely the scope of the injunction that Lyons prayed for in Count B.

... [I]n any event, to have a case or controversy with the City that could sustain Count V, Lyons would have to credibly allege that he faced a realistic threat from the future application of the City's policy. Justice Marshall nowhere confronts this requirement—the necessity that Lyons demonstrate that he, himself, will not only again be

Under *O'Shea* and *Rizzo*, these allegations were an insufficient basis to provide a federal court with jurisdiction to entertain Count V of the complaint.... For several reasons—each of them infirm, in our view—the Court of Appeals thought reliance on *O'Shea* and *Rizzo* was misplaced and reversed the District Court.

First, the Court of Appeals thought that Lyons was more immediately threatened than the plaintiffs in those cases since, according to the Court of Appeals, Lyons need only be stopped for a minor traffic violation to be subject to the strangleholds. But even assuming that Lyons would again be stopped for a traffic or other violation in the reasonably near future, it is untenable to assert, and the complaint made no such allegation, that strangleholds are applied by the Los Angeles police to every citizen who is stopped or arrested regardless of the conduct of the person stopped. We cannot agree that the "odds" that Lyons would not only again be stopped for a traffic violation but would also be subjected to a chokehold without any provocation whatsoever are sufficient to make out a federal case for equitable relief....

... [I]t is surely no more than speculation to assert either that Lyons himself will again be involved in one of those unfortunate instances, or that he will be arrested in the future and provoke the use of a chokehold by resisting arrest, attempting to escape, or threatening deadly force or serious bodily injury.

Second, the Court of Appeals viewed *O'Shea* and *Rizzo* as cases in which the plaintiffs sought "massive structural" relief against the local law enforcement systems and therefore that the holdings in those cases were inapposite to cases such as this where the plaintiff, according to the Court of Appeals, seeks to enjoin only an "established," "sanctioned" police practice assertedly violative of constitutional rights. *O'Shea* and *Rizzo*, however, cannot be so easily confined to their facts. If Lyons has made no showing that he is realistically threatened by a repetition of his experience of October, 1976, then he has not met the requirements for seeking an injunction in a federal court, whether the injunction contemplates intrusive structural relief or the cessation of a discrete practice.

The Court of Appeals also asserted that Lyons "had a live and active claim" against the City "if only for a period of a few seconds" while the stranglehold was being applied to him and that for two reasons the claim had not become moot so as to disentitle Lyons to injunctive relief: First, because under normal rules of equity, a case does not become moot merely because the complained of conduct has ceased; and second, because Lyons' claim is "capable of repetition but evading review" and therefore should be heard. We agree that Lyons had a live controversy with the City. Indeed, he still has a claim for damages against the City that appears to meet all Article III requirements. Nevertheless, the issue here is not whether that claim has become moot but whether Lyons meets the preconditions for asserting an injunctive claim in a federal forum. The equitable doctrine that cessation of the challenged conduct does not bar an injunction is of little help in this respect, for Lyons' lack of standing does not rest on the termination of the police practice but on the speculative nature of his claim that he will again experience injury as the result of that practice even if continued.

. . .

stopped by the police but will be choked without any provocation or legal excuse. Justice Marshall plainly does not agree with that requirement, and he was in dissent in O'Shea v. Littleton. We are at issue in that respect.

V

Lyons fares no better if it be assumed that his pending damages suit affords him Article III standing to seek an injunction as a remedy for the claim arising out of the October 1976 events. . . .

. . .

Absent a sufficient likelihood that he will again be wronged in a similar way, Lyons is no more entitled to an injunction than any other citizen of Los Angeles; and a federal court may not entertain a claim by any or all citizens who no more than assert that certain practices of law enforcement officers are unconstitutional. . . .

We decline the invitation to slight the preconditions for equitable relief; for as we have held, recognition of the need for a proper balance between state and federal authority counsels restraint in the issuance of injunctions against state officers engaged in the administration of the states' criminal laws in the absence of irreparable injury which is both great and immediate. . . .

. . .

. . . [T]he state courts need not impose the same standing or remedial requirements that govern federal court proceedings. The individual states may permit their courts to use injunctions to oversee the conduct of law enforcement authorities on a continuing basis. But this is not the role of a federal court absent far more justification than Lyons has proffered in this case.

The judgment of the Court of Appeals is accordingly

Reversed.

Justice Marshall, with whom Justice Brennan, Justice Blackmun and Justice Stevens join, dissenting.

The District Court found that the City of Los Angeles authorizes its police officers to apply life-threatening chokeholds to citizens who pose no threat of violence, and that respondent, Adolph Lyons, was subjected to such a chokehold. The Court today holds that a federal court is without power to enjoin the enforcement of the City's policy, no matter how flagrantly unconstitutional it may be. Since no one can show that he will be choked in the future, no one—not even a person who, like Lyons, has almost been choked to death—has standing to challenge the continuation of the policy. The City is free to continue the policy indefinitely as long as it is willing to pay damages for the injuries and deaths that result. I dissent from this unprecedented and unwarranted approach to standing.

II

At the outset it is important to emphasize that Lyons' entitlement to injunctive relief and his entitlement to an award of damages both depend upon whether he can show that the City's chokehold policy violates the Constitution. . . .

III

Since Lyons' claim for damages plainly gives him standing, and since the success of that claim depends upon a demonstration that the City's chokehold policy is unconstitutional, it is beyond dispute that Lyons has properly invoked the District Court's authority to adjudicate the constitutionality of the City's chokehold policy. The dispute concerning the constitutionality of that policy plainly presents a "case or controversy" under Article III. The Court nevertheless holds that a federal court has no power under Article III to adjudicate Lyons' request, in the same lawsuit, for injunctive relief with respect to that very policy. . . .

A

It is simply disingenuous for the Court to assert that its decision requires "[n]o extension" of O'Shea v. Littleton, 414 U.S. 488 (1974), and Rizzo v. Goode, 423 U.S. 362 (1976). In contrast to this case O'Shea and Rizzo involved disputes focusing solely on the threat of future injury which the plaintiffs did not allege past injury and did not seek compensatory relief. In Rizzo, the plaintiffs sought only declaratory and injunctive relief and alleged past instances of police misconduct only in an attempt to establish the substantiality of the threat of future injury . . . was similarly no claim for damages based on past injuries in Ashcroft v. Mattis, 431 U.S. 171 (1977), or Golden v. Zwickler, 394 U.S. 103 (1969), on which the Court also relies.

. . . As the Court recognized in O'Shea, standing under Article III is established by an allegation of "threatened or actual injury." Id., 414 U.S., at 493, quoting Linda R.S. v. Richard D., 410 U.S. 614, 617 (1973) (emphasis added). See also 414 U.S., at 493, n. 2. Because the plaintiffs in O'Shea, Rizzo, Mattis, and Zwickler did not seek to redress past injury, their standing to sue depended entirely on the risk of future injury they faced. Apart from the desire to eliminate the possibility of future injury, the plaintiffs in those cases had no other personal stake in the outcome of the controversies.

By contrast, Lyons' request for prospective relief is coupled with his claim for damages. . . . In addition to the risk that he will be subjected to a chokehold in the future, Lyons has suffered past injury. Because he has a live claim for damages, he need not rely solely on the threat of future injury to establish his personal stake in the outcome of the controversy. In the cases relied on by the majority, the Court simply had no occasion to decide whether a plaintiff who has standing to litigate a dispute must clear a separate standing hurdle with respect to each form of relief sought.

. . .

C

By fragmenting the standing inquiry and imposing a separate standing hurdle with respect to each form of relief sought, the decision today departs significantly from this Court's traditional conception of the standing requirement and of the remedial powers of the federal courts. We have never required more than that a plaintiff have standing to litigate a claim. Whether he will be entitled to obtain particular forms of relief should he prevail has never been understood to be an issue of standing.

. . .

IV

Apart from the question of standing, the only remaining question presented in the petition for certiorari is whether the preliminary injunction issued by the District Court must be set aside because it "constitute[s] a substantial interference in the operation of a municipal police department." In my view it does not.

. . .

The principles of federalism simply do not preclude the limited preliminary injunction issued in this case. Unlike the permanent injunction at issue in *Rizzo,* the preliminary injunction involved here entails no federal supervision of the LAPD's activities. The preliminary injunction merely forbids the use of chokeholds absent the threat of deadly force, permitting their continued use where such a threat does exist. This limited ban takes the form of a preventive injunction, which has traditionally been regarded as the least intrusive form of equitable relief. Moreover, the City can remove the ban by obtaining approval of a training plan. Although the preliminary injunction also requires the City to provide records of the uses of chokeholds to respondent and to allow the court access to such records, this requirement is hardly onerous, since the LAPD already maintains records concerning the use of chokeholds.

V

Apparently because it is unwilling to rely solely on its unprecedented rule of standing, the Court goes on to conclude that, even if Lyons has standing, "[t]he equitable remedy is unavailable." . . .

. . .

The District Court concluded, on the basis of the facts before it, that Lyons was choked without provocation pursuant to an unconstitutional City policy. Given the necessarily preliminary nature of its inquiry, there was no way for the District Court to know the precise contours of the City's policy or to ascertain the risk that Lyons, who had alleged that the policy was being applied in a discriminatory manner, might again be subjected to a chokehold. But in view of the Court's conclusion that the unprovoked choking of Lyons was pursuant to a City policy, Lyons has satisfied "the usual basis for injunctive relief, 'that there exists some cognizable danger of recurrent violation'" . . . The risk of serious injuries and deaths to other citizens also supported the decision to grant a preliminary injunction. Courts of equity have much greater latitude in granting injunctive relief "in furtherance of the public interest . . . than when only private interests are involved." . . . In this case we know that the District Court would have been amply justified in considering the risk to the public, for after the preliminary injunction was stayed, five additional deaths occurred prior to the adoption of a moratorium. Under these circumstances, I do not believe that the District Court abused its discretion.

VI

The Court's decision removes an entire class of constitutional violations from the equitable powers of a federal court. It immunizes from prospective equitable relief any policy that authorizes persistent deprivations of constitutional rights as long as no individual can establish with substantial certainty that he will be injured, or injured again, in the future. . . . Under the view expressed by the majority today, if the police adopt a policy of "shoot to kill," or a policy of shooting one out of ten suspects, the federal courts will be powerless to enjoin its continuation. . . . The federal judicial power is now limited to levying a toll for such a systematic constitutional violation.

E.   POLITICAL QUESTIONS

John Marshall on Political Questions

"Even before he became a judge, Marshall was aware of a solution to the problem of the political usurpation of judges as evidenced by a speech he made in the House of Representatives.

" 'By extending the judicial power to all *cases in law and equity,* the constitution had never been understood to confer on that department any political power whatever. To come within this department a question must assume a legal form for forensic litigation and judicial decision. There must be parties to come into court, who can be reached by its process, and bound by its power; whose rights admit of ultimate decision by a tribunal to which they are bound to submit.'[38]

"Marshall knew that the court handled political issues; anyone who would deny this is foolish. But Marshall also realized that the handling of such issues by the court is not a political one but a legal one. The question must take on a legal form; it must be argued by real parties; and they are bound by the decision in the case before the bar. The court has no political power at all. What Marshall meant by this was that the court cannot act in a political way. The court can and must handle questions of public policy, political questions; but it cannot handle the question in the way of politics, but in the way of law. The entire question must be changed into a legal question, and the decision on the issue is not a policy decision but a judgment concerning the merits of the two opposing parties who have taken sides on the issue. Granted that the result of this legal decision may have grave effects for public policy and that the judge neither should nor can take his eye off these effects, the judge must always begin and end with the case before him. No matter how far afield his reasoning may take him, he is always forced to return to the case and the parties at bar. Marshall makes here an important distinction which cannot be overlooked by the modern commentators who profess to study the court as if it were an *ad hoc* legislature." Umbanhowar, *Marshall on Judging,* 7 Am.J.Leg.Hist. 210, 224 (1963).

BAKER v. CARR, 369 U.S. 186 (1962). The Court held that a suit by voters alleging that the apportionment of a state legislature denied to them the equal protection of the laws and seeking reapportionment of that legislature did not involve a nonjusticiable political question. The following discussion of the political questions doctrine in the opinion of the Court by Justice Brennan is significant:

"We have said that 'in determining whether a question falls within [the political question] category, the appropriateness under our system of government of attributing finality to the action of the political departments and also the lack of satisfactory criteria for a judicial determination are dominant considerations.' Coleman v. Miller, 307 U.S. 433, 454–455. The nonjusticiability of a political question is primarily a function of the separation of powers. Much confusion results from the capacity of the 'political question' label to obscure the need for case-by-case inquiry. Deciding whether a matter has in any measure been committed by the Constitution to another branch of government, or whether the action of that branch exceeds whatever authority has been committed, is itself a delicate exercise in constitutional interpretation, and is a responsibility of this Court as ultimate interpreter of the Constitution. To demonstrate this requires no less than to analyze representative cases and to infer from them analytical threads that make up the political question doctrine. We shall then show that none of those threads catches this case.

"*Foreign Relations.* There are sweeping statements to the effect that all questions touching foreign relations are political questions. Not only does resolution of such issues frequently turn on standards that defy judicial

---

[38] Addresses by John Marshall, U.S. House of Representatives, 1794 (on the Resolution of the Honorable Edward Livingston, relative to Thomas Nash, alias Jonathan Robbins) 13 (1848).

application, or involve the exercise of a discretion demonstrably committed to the executive or legislature; but many such questions uniquely demand single-voiced statement of the Government's views. Yet it is error to suppose that every case or controversy which touches foreign relations lies beyond judicial cognizance. Our cases in this field seem invariably to show a discriminating analysis of the particular question posed, in terms of the history of its management by the political branches, of its susceptibility to judicial handling in the light of its nature and posture in the specific case, and of the possible consequences of judicial action. For example, though a court will not ordinarily inquire whether a treaty has been terminated, since on that question 'governmental action ... must be regarded as of controlling importance,' if there has been no conclusive 'governmental action' then a court can construe a treaty and may find it provides the answer. Compare Terlinden v. Ames, 184 U.S. 270, 285, with Society for the Propagation of the Gospel in Foreign Parts v. New Haven, 8 Wheat. 464, 492–495. Though a court will not undertake to construe a treaty in a manner inconsistent with a subsequent federal statute, no similar hesitancy obtains if the asserted clash is with state law. Compare Whitney v. Robertson, 124 U.S. 190, with Kolovrat v. Oregon, 366 U.S. 187. . . .

"*Dates of Duration of Hostilities.* Though it has been stated broadly that 'the power which declared the necessity is the power to declare its cessation, and what the cessation requires,' Commercial Trust Co. v. Miller, 262 U.S. 51, 57, here too analysis reveals isolable reasons for the presence of political questions, underlying this Court's refusal to review the political departments' determination of when or whether a war has ended. Dominant is the need for finality in the political determination, for emergency's nature demands 'a prompt and unhesitating obedience,' Martin v. Mott, 12 Wheat. 19, 30 (calling up of militia). . . .

"*Validity of Enactments.* In *Coleman v. Miller,* supra, this Court held that the questions of how long a proposed amendment to the Federal Constitution remained open to ratification and what effect a prior rejection had on a subsequent ratification, were committed to congressional resolution and involved criteria of decision that necessarily escaped the judicial grasp. Similar considerations apply to the enacting process: 'the respect due to coequal and independent departments,' and the need for finality and certainty about the status of a statute contribute to judicial reluctance to inquire whether, as passed, it complied with all requisite formalities. Field v. Clark, 143 U.S. 649, 672, 676–677; see Leser v. Garnett, 258 U.S. 130, 137. But it is not true that courts will never delve into a legislature's records upon such a quest: If the enrolled statute lacks an effective date, a court will not hesitate to seek it in the legislative journals in order to preserve the enactment. Gardner v. Collector, 6 Wall. 499. The political question doctrine, a tool for maintenance of governmental order, will not be so applied as to promote only disorder. . . .

"It is apparent that several formulations which vary slightly according to the settings in which the questions arise may describe a political question, although each has one or more elements which identifies it as essentially a function of the separation of powers. Prominent on the surface of any case held to involve a political question is found a textually demonstrable constitutional commitment of the issue to a coordinate political department; or a lack of judicially discoverable and manageable standards for resolving it; or the impossibility of deciding without an initial policy determination of a kind clearly for nonjudicial discretion; or the impossibility of a court's undertaking independent resolution without expressing lack of the respect due coordinate branches of government; or an unusual need for unquestioning adherence to a political decision already made; or the potentiality of embarrassment from multifarious pronouncements by various departments on one question.

"Unless one of these formulations is inextricable from the case at bar, there should be no dismissal for non-justiciability on the ground of a political question's presence. The doctrine of which we treat is one of 'political questions,' not one of 'political cases.' The courts cannot reject as 'no law suit' a bona fide controversy as to whether some action denominated 'political' exceeds constitutional authority. The cases we have reviewed show the necessity for discriminating inquiry into the precise facts and posture of the particular case, and the impossibility of resolution by any semantic cataloguing.

"But it is argued that this case shares the characteristics of decisions that constitute a category not yet considered, cases concerning the Constitution's guaranty, in Art. IV, § 4, of a republican form of government. A conclusion as to whether the case at bar does present a political question cannot be confidently reached until we have considered those cases with special care. We shall discover that Guaranty Clause claims involve those elements which define a 'political question,' and for that reason and no other, they are nonjusticiable. In particular, we shall discover that the nonjusticiability of such claims has nothing to do with their touching upon matters of state governmental organization.

"*Republican Form of Government.* Luther v. Borden, 7 How. 1, 48 U.S. 1, though in form simply an action for damages for trespass was, as Daniel Webster said in opening the argument for the defense, 'an unusual case.' The defendants, admitting an otherwise tortious breaking and entering, sought to justify their action on the ground that they were agents of the established lawful government of Rhode Island, which State was then under martial law to defend itself from active insurrection; that the plaintiff was engaged in that insurrection; and that they entered under orders to arrest the plaintiff. The case arose 'out of the unfortunate political differences which agitated the people of Rhode Island in 1841 and 1842,' 7 How. at 34, which had resulted in a situation wherein two groups laid competing claims to recognition as the lawful government. The plaintiff's right to recover depended upon which of the two groups was entitled to such recognition; but the lower court's refusal to receive evidence or hear argument on that issue, its charge to the jury that the earlier established or 'charter' government was lawful, and the verdict for the defendants, were affirmed upon appeal to this Court....

"Clearly, several factors were thought by the Court in Luther to make the question there 'political': the commitment to the other branches of the decision as to which is the lawful state government; the unambiguous action by the President, in recognizing the charter government as the lawful authority; the need for finality in the executive's decision; and the lack of criteria by which a court could determine which form of government was republican."

Powell v. McCormack

395 U.S. 486, 89 S.Ct. 1944, 23 L.Ed.2d 491 (1969).

Mr. Chief Justice Warren delivered the opinion of the Court.

In November 1966, Petitioner Adam Clayton Powell, Jr., was duly elected from the 18th Congressional District of New York to serve in the United States House of Representatives for the 90th Congress. However, pursuant to a House resolution, he was not permitted to take his seat. Powell (and some of the voters of his district) then filed suit in Federal District Court claiming that the

House could exclude him only if it found he failed to meet the standing requirements of age, citizenship, and residence contained in Art. I, § 2, of the Constitution—requirements the House specifically found Powell met—and thus had excluded him unconstitutionally. The District Court dismissed petitioners' complaint "for want of jurisdiction of the subject matter." The Court of Appeals affirmed the dismissal, although on somewhat different grounds, each judge filing a separate opinion. We have determined that it was error to dismiss the complaint and that Petitioner Powell is entitled to a declaratory judgment that he was unlawfully excluded from the 90th Congress.

. . .

[At the organization of the 90th Congress in January, 1967, Powell was asked to step aside while the oath was administered to the other members. A Select Committee was then appointed which reported that Powell met the standing qualifications but that he had asserted an unwarranted privilege and immunity from the processes of the courts of New York; that he had wrongfully diverted House funds for the use of others and himself; and that he had made false reports on expenditures of foreign currency to a House committee. After a ruling by the Speaker that only a majority vote would be needed to exclude Powell and declare the seat vacant, the House adopted such a resolution of exclusion. By the time the case got to the Supreme Court Powell had been elected again and was seated in the 91st Congress. The Court held that the case was not moot because Powell had asked for damages. The Court also held that the vote by the House could not be treated as a vote to expel even though the actual vote exceeded a two-thirds majority. The Court's discussion of the political question objection to ruling on the validity of the action of the House follows.]

. . .

F. POLITICAL QUESTION DOCTRINE

1. TEXTUALLY DEMONSTRABLE CONSTITUTIONAL COMMITMENT

Respondents maintain that even if this case is otherwise justiciable, it presents only a political question. . . .

Respondents' first contention is that this case presents a political question because under Art. I, § 5, there has been a "textually demonstrable constitutional commitment" to the House of the "adjudicatory power" to determine Powell's qualifications. Thus it is argued that the House, and the House alone, has power to determine who is qualified to be a member.

In order to determine whether there has been a textual commitment to a co-ordinate department of the Government, we must interpret the Constitution. In other words, we must first determine what power the Constitution confers upon the House through Art. I, § 5, before we can determine to what extent, if any, the exercise of that power is subject to judicial review. Respondents maintain that the House has broad power under § 5, and, they argue, the House may determine which are the qualifications necessary for membership. On the other hand, petitioners allege that the Constitution provides that an elected representative may be denied his seat only if the House finds he does not meet one of the standing qualifications expressly prescribed by the Constitution.

If examination of § 5 disclosed that the Constitution gives the House judicially unreviewable power to set qualifications for membership and to judge whether prospective members meet those qualifications, further review of the

House determination might well be barred by the political question doctrine. On the other hand, if the Constitution gives the House power to judge only whether elected members possess the three standing qualifications set forth in the Constitution; further consideration would be necessary to determine whether any of the other formulations of the political question doctrine are "inextricable from the case at bar."[42] Baker v. Carr, supra, at 217.

. . .

In order to determine the scope of any "textual commitment" under Art. I, § 5, we necessarily must determine the meaning of the phrase "be the judge of the qualifications of its own members." ... Our examination of the relevant historical materials leads us to the conclusion that petitioners are correct and that the Constitution leaves the House without authority to *exclude* any person, duly elected by his constituents, who meets all the requirements for membership expressly prescribed in the Constitution.

[A long review of the historical precedents is omitted.]

Had the intent of the Framers emerged from these materials with less clarity, we would nevertheless have been compelled to resolve any ambiguity in favor of a narrow construction of the scope of Congress' power to exclude members-elect. A fundamental principle of our representative democracy is, in Hamilton's words, "that the people should choose whom they please to govern them." 2 Elliot's Debates 257.... Moreover, it would effectively nullify the Convention's decision to require a two-third vote for expulsion. Unquestionably, Congress has an interest in preserving its institutional integrity, but in most cases that interest can be sufficiently safeguarded by the exercise of its power to punish its members for disorderly behavior and, in extreme cases, to expel a member with the concurrence of two-thirds. In short, both the intention of the Framers, to the extent it can be determined, and an examination of the basic principles of our democratic system persuade us that the Constitution does not vest in the Congress a discretionary power to deny membership by a majority vote.

For these reasons, we have concluded that Art. I, § 5, is at most a "textually demonstrable commitment" to Congress to judge only the qualifications expressly set forth in the Constitution. Therefore, the "textual commitment" formulation of the political question doctrine does not bar federal courts from adjudicating petitioners' claims.

2.   *OTHER CONSIDERATIONS*

Respondents' alternate contention is that the case presents a political question because judicial resolution of petitioners' claim would produce a "potentially embarrassing confrontation between coordinate branches" of the Federal Government. But, as our interpretation of Art. I, § 5, discloses, a determination of Petitioner Powell's right to sit would require no more than an interpretation of the Constitution. Such a determination falls within the traditional role accorded courts to interpret the law, and does not involve a "lack of respect due [a] coordinate [branch] of government," nor does it involve an "initial policy determination of a kind clearly for nonjudicial discretion." Baker v. Carr, supra, at 217. Our system of government requires that federal courts on occasion interpret the Constitution in a manner at variance with the

---

[42] Consistent with this interpretation, federal courts might still be barred by the political question doctrine from reviewing the House's factual determination that a member did not meet one of the standing qualifications. This is an issue not presented in this case and we express no view as to its resolution.

construction given the document by another branch. The alleged conflict that such an adjudication may cause cannot justify the courts' avoiding their constitutional responsibility....

Nor are any of the other formulations of a political question "inextricable from the case at bar." Baker v. Carr, supra, at 217. Petitioners seek a determination that the House was without power to exclude Powell from the 90th Congress, which, we have seen, requires an interpretation of the Constitution—a determination for which clearly there are "judicially ... manageable standards." Finally, a judicial resolution of petitioners' claim will not result in "multifarious pronouncements by various departments on one question." For, as we noted in Baker v. Carr, supra, at 211, it is the responsibility of this Court to act as the ultimate interpreter of the Constitution. Marbury v. Madison, 5 U.S. (1 Cranch) 137 (1803). Thus, we conclude that petitioners' claim is not barred by the political question doctrine, and having determined that the claim is otherwise generally justiciable, we hold that the case is justiciable.

. . . .

Nixon v. United States

506 U.S. 224, 113 S.Ct. 732, 122 L.Ed.2d 1 (1993).

Chief Justice Rehnquist delivered the opinion of the Court.

Petitioner Walter L. Nixon, Jr., asks this court to decide whether Senate Rule XI, which allows a committee of Senators to hear evidence against an individual who has been impeached and to report that evidence to the full Senate, violates the Impeachment Trial Clause, Art. I, § 3, cl. 6. That Clause provides that the "Senate shall have the sole Power to try all Impeachments." But before we reach the merits of such a claim, we must decide whether it is "justiciable," that is, whether it is a claim that may be resolved by the courts. We conclude that it is not.

Nixon, a former Chief Judge of the United States District Court for the Southern District of Mississippi, was convicted by a jury of two counts of making false statements before a federal grand jury and sentenced to prison. . . .

On May 10, 1989, the House of Representatives adopted three articles of impeachment for high crimes and misdemeanors. . . .

After the House presented the articles to the Senate, the Senate voted to invoke its own Impeachment Rule XI, under which the presiding officer appoints a committee of Senators to "receive evidence and take testimony." . . . The Senate committee held four days of hearings ... Pursuant to Rule XI, the committee presented the full Senate with a complete transcript of the proceeding and a report stating the uncontested facts and summarizing the evidence on the contested facts. Nixon and the House impeachment managers submitted extensive final briefs to the full Senate and delivered arguments from the Senate floor during the three hours set aside for oral argument in front of that body. Nixon himself gave a personal appeal, and several Senators posed questions directly to both parties. ... The Senate voted by more than the constitutionally required two-thirds majority to convict Nixon on the first two articles. ... The presiding officer then entered judgment removing Nixon from his office as United States District Judge.

Nixon thereafter commenced the present suit, arguing that Senate Rule XI violates the constitutional grant of authority to the Senate to "try" all impeachments because it prohibits the whole Senate from taking part in the evidentiary hearings. . . . The District Court held that his claim was nonjusticiable, and the Court of Appeals for the District of Columbia Circuit agreed.

A controversy is nonjusticiable—i.e., involves a political question—where there is "a textually demonstrable constitutional commitment of the issue to a coordinate political department; or a lack of judicially discoverable and manageable standards for resolving it. . . ." Baker v. Carr, 369 U.S. 186, 217 (1962). But the courts must, in the first instance, interpret the text in question and determine whether and to what extent the issue is textually committed. . . . As the discussion that follows makes clear, the concept of a textual commitment to a coordinate political department is not completely separate from the concept of a lack of judicially discoverable and manageable standards for resolving it; the lack of judicially manageable standards may strengthen the conclusion that there is a textually demonstrable commitment to a coordinate branch.

In this case, we must examine Art. I, § 3, cl. 6, to determine the scope of authority conferred upon the Senate by the Framers regarding impeachment. It provides:

> "The Senate shall have the sole Power to try all Impeachments. When sitting for that Purpose, they shall be on Oath or Affirmation. When the President of the United States is tried, the Chief Justice shall preside: And no Person shall be convicted without the Concurrence of two thirds of the Members present."

The language and structure of this Clause are revealing. The first sentence is a grant of authority to the Senate, and the word "sole" indicates that this authority is reposed in the Senate and nowhere else. The next two sentences specify requirements to which the Senate proceedings shall conform: the Senate shall be on oath or affirmation, a two-thirds vote is required to convict, and when the President is tried the Chief Justice shall preside.

Petitioner argues that the word "try" in the first sentence imposes by implication an additional requirement on the Senate in that the proceedings must be in the nature of a judicial trial. From there petitioner goes on to argue that this limitation precludes the Senate from delegating to a select committee the task of hearing the testimony of witnesses, as was done pursuant to Senate Rule XI. . . .

There are several difficulties with this position which lead us ultimately to reject it. The word "try," both in 1787 and later, has considerably broader meanings than those to which petitioner would limit it. . . . [W]e cannot say that the Framers used the word "try" as an implied limitation on the method by which the Senate might proceed in trying impeachments. "As a rule the Constitution speaks in general terms, leaving Congress to deal with subsidiary matters of detail as the public interests and changing conditions may require. . . ." Dillon v. Gloss, 256 U.S. 368, 376 (1921).

The conclusion that the use of the word "try" in the first sentence of the Impeachment Trial Clause lacks sufficient precision to afford any judicially manageable standard of review of the Senate's actions is fortified by the existence of the three very specific requirements that the Constitution does impose on the Senate when trying impeachments: the members must be under oath, a two-thirds vote is required to convict, and the Chief Justice presides when the President is tried. These limitations are quite precise, and their nature suggests that the Framers did not intend to impose additional limitations on the form of the Senate proceedings by the use of the word "try" in the first sentence.

... [The first sentence of Clause 6] provides that "[t]he Senate shall have the sole Power to try all Impeachments." We think that the word "sole" is of considerable significance. Indeed, the word "sole" appears only one other time in the Constitution—with respect to the House of Representatives' "*sole* Power of Impeachment." Art. I, § 2, cl. 5 (emphasis added). The common sense meaning of the word "sole" is that the Senate alone shall have authority to determine whether an individual should be acquitted or convicted. ...

. . .

Petitioner ... argues that even if significance be attributed to the word "sole" in the first sentence of the clause, the authority granted is to the Senate, and this means that "the Senate—not the courts, not a lay jury, not a Senate Committee—shall try impeachments." It would be possible to read the first sentence of the Clause this way, but it is not a natural reading. Petitioner's interpretation would bring into judicial purview not merely the sort of claim made by petitioner, but other similar claims based on the conclusion that the word "Senate" has imposed by implication limitations on procedures which the Senate might adopt. Such limitations would be inconsistent with the construction of the Clause as a whole, which, as we have noted, sets out three express limitations in separate sentences.

The history and contemporary understanding of the impeachment provisions support our reading of the constitutional language. The parties do not offer evidence of a single word in the history of the Constitutional Convention or in contemporary commentary that even alludes to the possibility of judicial review in the context of the impeachment powers. R. Berger, Impeachment: The Constitutional Problems 116 (1973). This silence is quite meaningful in light of the several explicit references to the availability of judicial review as a check on the Legislature's power with respect to bills of attainder, ex post facto laws, and statutes. ...

The Framers labored over the question of where the impeachment power should lie. Significantly, in at least two considered scenarios the power was placed with the Federal Judiciary. See 1 Farrand 21–22 (Virginia Plan); id., at 244 (New Jersey Plan). Indeed, Madison and the Committee of Detail proposed that the Supreme Court should have the power to determine impeachments. See 2 id., at 551 (Madison); id., at 178–179, 186 (Committee of Detail). Despite these proposals, the Convention ultimately decided that the Senate would have "the sole Power to Try all Impeachments." Art. I, § 3, cl. 6. According to Alexander Hamilton, the Senate was the "most fit depositary of this important trust" because its members are representatives of the people. See The Federalist No. 65, p. 440 (J. Cooke ed. 1961). The Supreme Court was not the proper body because the Framers "doubted whether the members of that tribunal would, at all times, be endowed with so eminent a portion of fortitude as would be called for in the execution of so difficult a task" or whether the Court "would possess the degree of credit and authority" to carry out its judgment if it conflicted with the accusation brought by the Legislature—the people's representative. See id., at 441. In addition, the Framers believed the Court was too small in number: "The awful discretion, which a court of impeachments must necessarily have, to doom to honor or to infamy the most confidential and the most distinguished characters of the community, forbids the commitment of the trust to a small number of persons." Id., at 441–442.

There are two additional reasons why the Judiciary, and the Supreme Court in particular, were not chosen to have any role in impeachments. First, the Framers recognized that most likely there would be two sets of proceedings for individuals who commit impeachable offenses—the impeachment trial and a separate criminal trial. In fact, the Constitution explicitly provides for two separate proceedings. See Art. I, § 3, cl. 7. The Framers deliberately separated the two forums to avoid raising the specter of bias and to ensure independent judgments ... Certainly judicial review of the Senate's "trial" would introduce the same risk of bias as would participation in the trial itself.

Second, judicial review would be inconsistent with the Framers' insistence that our system be one of checks and balances. In our constitutional system, impeachment was designed to be the only check on the Judicial Branch by the Legislature. ... Judicial involvement in impeachment proceedings, even if only for purposes of judicial review, is counterintuitive because it would eviscerate the "important constitutional check" placed on the Judiciary by the Framers. ... Nixon's argument would place final reviewing authority with respect to impeachments in the hands of the same body that the impeachment process is meant to regulate.

Nevertheless, Nixon argues that judicial review is necessary in order to place a check on the Legislature. Nixon fears that if the Senate is given unreviewable authority to interpret the Impeachment Trial Clause, there is a grave risk that the Senate will usurp judicial power. The Framers anticipated this objection and created two constitutional safeguards to keep the Senate in check. The first safeguard is that the whole of the impeachment power is divided between the two legislative bodies, with the House given the right to accuse and the Senate given the right to judge. ... This split of authority "avoids the inconvenience of making the same persons both accusers and judges; and guards against the danger of persecution from the prevalency of a factious spirit in either of those branches." The second safeguard is the two-thirds supermajority vote requirement. ...

In addition to the textual commitment argument, we are persuaded that the lack of finality and the difficulty of fashioning relief counsel against justiciability. See Baker v. Carr, 369 U.S., at 210. ... This lack of finality would manifest itself most dramatically if the President were impeached. The legitimacy of any successor, and hence his effectiveness, would be impaired severely, not merely while the judicial process was running its course, but during any retrial that a differently constituted Senate might conduct if its first judgment of conviction were invalidated. Equally uncertain is the question of what relief a court may give other than simply setting aside the judgment of conviction. Could it order the reinstatement of a convicted federal judge, or order Congress to create an additional judgeship if the seat had been filled in the interim?

Petitioner finally contends that a holding of nonjusticiability cannot be reconciled with our opinion in Powell v. McCormack, 395 U.S. 486 (1969). ...

Our conclusion in *Powell* was based on the fixed meaning of "[q]ualifications" set forth in Art. I, § 2. ... The decision as to whether a member satisfied these qualifications was placed with the House, but the decision as to what these qualifications consisted of was not.

In the case before us, there is no separate provision of the Constitution which could be defeated by allowing the Senate final authority to determine the meaning of the word "try" in the Impeachment Trial Clause. We agree with Nixon that courts possess power to review either legislative or executive action that transgresses identifiable textual limits. ... But we conclude ... that the word "try" in the Impeachment Clause does not provide an identifiable textual limit on the authority which is committed to the Senate.

For the foregoing reasons, the judgment of the Court of Appeals is

Affirmed.

Justice Stevens, concurring.

For me, the debate about the strength of the inferences to be drawn from the use of the words "sole" and "try" is far less significant than the central fact that the Framers decided to assign the impeachment power to the Legislative Branch. . . . Respect for a coordinate Branch of the Government forecloses any assumption that improbable hypotheticals like those mentioned by Justice . . . Souter will ever occur. . . .

Justice White, with whom Justice Blackmun joins, concurring in the judgment.

Petitioner contends that the method by which the Senate convicted him on two articles of impeachment violates Art. I, § 3, cl. 6 of the Constitution . . . The Court is of the view that the Constitution forbids us even to consider his contention. I find no such prohibition and would therefore reach the merits of the claim. I concur in the judgment because the Senate fulfilled its constitutional obligation to "try" petitioner.

I

It should be said at the outset that, as a practical matter, it will likely make little difference whether the Court's or my view controls this case. This is so because the Senate has very wide discretion in specifying impeachment trial procedures and because it is extremely unlikely that the Senate would abuse its discretion and insist on a procedure that could not be deemed a trial by reasonable judges. Even taking a wholly practical approach, I would prefer not to announce an unreviewable discretion in the Senate to ignore completely the constitutional direction to "try" impeachment cases. . . .

II

. . .

Of course the issue in the political question doctrine is not whether the Constitutional text commits exclusive responsibility for a particular governmental function to one of the political branches. There are numerous instances of this sort of textual commitment, e.g., Art. I, § 8, and it is not thought that disputes implicating these provisions are nonjusticiable. Rather, the issue is whether the Constitution has given one of the political branches final responsibility for interpreting the scope and nature of such a power.

. . .

The historical evidence reveals above all else that the Framers were deeply concerned about placing in any branch the "awful discretion, which a court of impeachments must necessarily have." . . . Viewed against this history, the discord between the majority's position and the basic principles of checks and balances underlying the Constitution's separation of powers is clear. In essence, the majority suggests that the Framers' conferred upon Congress a potential tool of legislative dominance yet at the same time rendered Congress' exercise of that power one of the very few areas of legislative authority immune from any judicial review. . . . In a truly balanced system, impeachments tried by the Senate would serve as a means of controlling the largely unaccountable judiciary, even as judicial review would ensure that the Senate adhered to a minimal set of procedural standards in conducting impeachment trials.

. . .

III

. . .

In short, textual and historical evidence reveals that the Impeachment Trial Clause was not meant to bind the hands of the Senate beyond establishing a set of minimal procedures. Without identifying the exact contours of these procedures, it is sufficient to say that the Senate's use of a factfinding committee under Rule XI is entirely compatible with the Constitution's command that the Senate "try all impeachments." Petitioner's challenge to his conviction must therefore fail.

. . .

Justice Souter, concurring in the judgment.

I agree with the Court that this case presents a nonjusticiable political question. Because my analysis differs somewhat from the Court's, however, I concur in its judgment by this separate opinion.

. . .

Whatever considerations feature most prominently in a particular case, the political question doctrine is "essentially a function of the separation of powers," . . . existing to restrain courts "from inappropriate interference in the business of the other branches of Government," United States v. Munoz–Flores, 495 U.S. 385, 394 (1990), and deriving in large part from prudential concerns about the respect we owe the political departments. . . . Not all interference is inappropriate or disrespectful, however, and application of the doctrine ultimately turns, as Learned Hand put it, on "how importunately the occasion demands an answer." L. Hand, The Bill of Rights 15 (1958).

This occasion does not demand an answer. It seems fair to conclude that the [Impeachment Trial] Clause contemplates that the Senate may determine, within broad boundaries, such subsidiary issues as the procedures for receipt and consideration of evidence necessary to satisfy its duty to "try" impeachments. Other significant considerations confirm a conclusion that this case presents a nonjusticiable political question . . . As the Court observes, judicial review of an impeachment trial would under the best of circumstances entail significant disruption of government.

One can, nevertheless, envision different and unusual circumstances that might justify a more searching review of impeachment proceedings. If the Senate were to act in a manner seriously threatening the integrity of its results, convicting, say, upon a coin-toss, or upon a summary determination that an officer of the United States was simply "a bad guy," . . . judicial interference might well be appropriate. In such circumstances, the Senate's action might be so far beyond the scope of its constitutional authority, and the consequent impact on the Republic so great, as to merit a judicial response despite the prudential concerns that would ordinarily counsel silence. . . .

Goldwater v. Carter

444 U.S. 996, 100 S.Ct. 533, 62 L.Ed.2d 428 (1979).

ORDER

The petition for a writ of certiorari is granted. The judgment of the Court of Appeals is vacated and the case is remanded to the District Court with directions to dismiss the complaint.

Mr. Justice Marshall concurs in the result.

Mr. Justice Powell concurs in the judgment and has filed a statement.

Mr. Justice Rehnquist concurs in the judgment and has filed a statement in which Mr. Chief Justice Burger, Mr. Justice Stewart, and Mr. Justice Stevens join.

Mr. Justice White and Mr. Justice Blackmun join in the grant of the petition for a writ of certiorari but would set the case for argument and give it plenary consideration. Mr. Justice Blackmun has filed a statement in which Mr. Justice White joins.

Mr. Justice Brennan would grant the petition for certiorari and affirm the judgment of the Court of Appeals and has filed a statement.

Mr. Justice Powell, concurring.

Although I agree with the result reached by the Court, I would dismiss the complaint as not ripe for judicial review.

I.

This Court has recognized that an issue should not be decided if it is not ripe for judicial review. Buckley v. Valeo, 424 U.S. 1, 113–114 (1976) (per curiam). Prudential considerations persuade me that a dispute between Congress and the President is not ready for judicial review unless and until each branch has taken action asserting its constitutional authority. Differences between the President and the Congress are commonplace under our system. The differences should, and almost invariably do, turn on political rather than legal considerations. The Judicial Branch should not decide issues affecting the allocation of power between the President and Congress until the political branches reach a constitutional impasse. Otherwise, we would encourage small groups or even individual Members of Congress to seek judicial resolution of issues before the normal political process has the opportunity to resolve the conflict.

In this case, a few Members of Congress claim that the President's action in terminating the treaty with Taiwan has deprived them of their constitutional role with respect to a change in the supreme law of the land. Congress has taken no official action. In the present posture of this case, we do not know whether there ever will be an actual confrontation between the Legislative and Executive Branches. Although the Senate has considered a resolution declaring that Senate approval is necessary for the termination of any mutual defense treaty, no final vote has been taken on the resolution. Moreover, it is unclear whether the resolution would have retroactive effect. It cannot be said that either the Senate or the House has rejected the President's claim. If the Congress chooses not to confront the President, it is not our task to do so. I therefore concur in the dismissal of this case.

II.

Mr. Justice Rehnquist suggests, however, that the issue presented by this case is a nonjusticiable political question which can never be considered by this Court. I cannot agree. In my view, reliance upon the political-question doctrine is inconsistent with our precedents. As set forth in the seminal case of Baker v. Carr, 369 U.S. 186, 217 (1962), the doctrine incorporates three inquiries: (i) Does the issue involve resolution of questions committed by the text of the Constitution to a coordinate branch of government? (ii) Would resolution of the question demand that a court move beyond areas of judicial expertise? (iii) Do prudential considerations counsel against judicial intervention? In my opinion the answer to each of these inquiries would require us to decide this case if it were ready for review.

First, the existence of "a textually demonstrable constitutional commitment of the issue to a coordinate political branch," ibid., turns on an examination of the constitutional provisions governing the exercise of the power in question. Powell v. McCormack, 395 U.S. 486, 519 (1969). No constitutional provision explicitly confers upon the President the power to terminate treaties. Further, Art. II, § 2 of the Constitution authorizes the President to make treaties with the advice and consent of the Senate. Article VI provides that treaties shall be a part of the supreme law of the land. These provisions add support to the view that the text of the Constitution does not unquestionably commit the power to terminate treaties to the President alone....

Second, there is no "lack of judicially discoverable and manageable standards for resolving" this case; nor is a decision impossible "without an initial policy determination of a kind clearly for nonjudicial discretion." Baker v. Carr, 369 U.S., at 217. We are asked to decide whether the President may terminate a treaty under the Constitution without congressional approval. Resolution of the question may not be easy, but it only requires us to apply normal principles of interpretation to the constitutional provisions at issue. See Powell v. McCormack, 395 U.S., at 548–549. The present case involves neither review of the President's activities as Commander-in-Chief nor impermissible interference in the field of foreign affairs. Such a case would arise if we were asked to decide, for example, whether a treaty required the President to order troops into a foreign country. But "it is error to suppose that every case or controversy which touches foreign relations lies beyond judicial cognizance." Baker v. Carr, supra, 369 U.S., at 211. This case "touches" foreign relations, but the question presented to us concerns only the constitutional division of power between Congress and the President.

A simple hypothetical demonstrates the confusion that I find inherent in Mr. Justice Rehnquist's concurring opinion. Assume that the President signed a mutual defense treaty with a foreign country and announced that it would go into effect despite its rejection by the Senate. Under Mr. Justice Rehnquist's analysis that situation would present a political question even though Art. II, § 2, clearly would resolve the dispute. Although the answer to the hypothetical case seems self-evident because it demands textual rather than interstitial analysis, the nature of the legal issue presented is no different from the issue presented in the case before us. In both cases, the Court would interpret the Constitution to decide whether congressional approval is necessary to give a Presidential decision on the validity of a treaty the force of law. Such an inquiry demands no special competence or information beyond the reach of the judiciary.

Finally, the political-question doctrine rests in part on prudential concerns calling for mutual respect among the three branches of government. Thus, the Judicial Branch should avoid "the potentiality of embarrassment [that would result] from multifarious pronouncements by various departments on one question." Similarly, the doctrine restrains judicial action where there is an "unusual need for unquestioning adherence to a political decision already made." Baker v. Carr, supra, 369 U.S., at 217.

If this case were ripe for judicial review, see Part I supra, none of these prudential considerations would be present. Interpretation of the Constitution does not imply lack of respect for a coordinate branch. Powell v. McCormack, 395 U.S., at 548. If the President and the Congress had reached irreconcilable positions, final disposition of the question presented by this case would eliminate, rather than create, multiple constitutional interpretations. The spectre of the Federal Government brought to a halt because of the mutual intransigence of the President and the Congress would require this Court to provide a resolution pursuant to our duty "to say what the law is." United States v. Nixon, 418 U.S. 683, 703, quoting Marbury v. Madison, 1 Cranch 137, 177 (1803).

III.

In my view, the suggestion that this case presents a political question is incompatible with this Court's willingness on previous occasions to decide whether one branch of our government has impinged upon the power of another. See Buckley v. Valeo, 424 U.S. 1, 138 (1976); United States v. Nixon, 418 U.S. 683, 707 (1974); The Pocket Veto Case, 279 U.S. 655, 676–678 (1929); Myers v. United States, 272 U.S. 52 (1926).[2] Under the criteria enunciated in Baker v. Carr, we have the responsibility to decide whether both the Executive and Legislative Branches have constitutional roles to play in termination of a treaty. If the Congress, by appropriate formal action, had challenged the President's authority to terminate the treaty with Taiwan, the resulting uncertainty could have serious consequences for our country. In that situation, it would be the duty of this Court to resolve the issue.

Mr. Justice Rehnquist, with whom The Chief Justice, Mr. Justice Stewart, and Mr. Justice Stevens join, concurring.

I am of the view that the basic question presented by the petitioners in this case is "political" and therefore nonjusticiable because it involves the authority of the President in the conduct of our country's foreign relations and the extent to which the Senate or the Congress is authorized to negate the action of the President. In Coleman v. Miller, 307 U.S. 433 (1939), a case in which members of the Kansas Legislature brought an action attacking a vote of the State Senate in favor of the ratification of the Child Labor Amendment, Mr. Chief Justice Hughes wrote in what is referred to as the "Opinion of the Court":

"We think that ... the question of the efficacy of ratifications by state legislatures, in the light of previous rejection or attempted withdrawal, should be regarded as a political question pertaining to the political departments, with the ultimate authority in the Congress in the exercise of its control over the promulgation of the adoption of the Amendment.... The precise question as now raised is whether, when the legislature of the State, as we have found, has actually ratified the proposed Amendment, the Court should restrain the State officers from certifying the ratification to the Secretary of State, because of an earlier rejection, and thus prevent

---

[2] Coleman v. Miller, 307 U.S. 433 (1939), is not relevant here. In that case, the Court was asked to review the legitimacy of a State's ratification of a constitutional amendment. Four Members of the Court stated that Congress has exclusive power over the ratification process. Id., at 456–460 (Black, J., concurring, with whom Roberts, Frankfurter, and Douglas, JJ., joined). Three Members of the Court concluded more narrowly that the Court could not pass upon the efficacy of state ratification. They also found no standards by which the Court could fix a reasonable time for the ratification of a proposed amendment. Id., at 452–454.

The proposed constitutional amendment at issue in *Coleman* would have overruled decisions of this Court.... Thus, judicial review of the legitimacy of a State's ratification would have compelled this Court to oversee the very constitutional process used to reverse Supreme Court decisions. In such circumstances it may be entirely appropriate for the Judicial Branch of government to step aside. See Scharpf, Judicial Review and The Political Question: A Functional Analysis, 75 Yale L.J. 517, 589 (1966). The present case involves no similar principle of judicial nonintervention.

the question from coming before the political departments. We find no basis in either Constitution or statute for such judicial action. Article V, speaking solely of ratification, contains no provision as to rejection...." Id., at 450.

Thus, Mr. Chief Justice Hughes' opinion concluded that "Congress in controlling the promulgation of the adoption of a constitutional amendment has the final determination of the question whether by lapse of time its proposal of the amendment had lost its vitality prior to the required ratifications." Id., at 456.

I believe it follows *a fortiori* from *Coleman* that the controversy in the instant case is a nonjusticiable political dispute that should be left for resolution by the Executive and Legislative Branches of the Government. Here, while the Constitution is express as to the manner in which the Senate shall participate in the ratification of a Treaty, it is silent as to that body's participation in the abrogation of a Treaty. In this respect the case is directly analogous to *Coleman,* supra. As stated in Dyer v. Blair, 390 F.Supp. 1291, 1302 (N.D.Ill.1975) (three-judge court):

> "A question that might be answered in different ways for different amendments must surely be controlled by political standards rather than standards easily characterized as judicially manageable."

In light of the absence of any constitutional provision governing the termination of a Treaty, and the fact that different termination procedures may be appropriate for different treaties, the instant case in my view also "must surely be controlled by political standards."

I think that the justifications for concluding that the question here is political in nature are even more compelling than in *Coleman* because it involves foreign relations—specifically a treaty commitment to use military force in the defense of a foreign government if attacked....

The present case differs in several important respects from Youngstown Sheet & Tube Co. v. Sawyer, 343 U.S. 579 (1952), cited by petitioners as authority both for reaching the merits of this dispute and for reversing the Court of Appeals. In *Youngstown* private litigants brought a suit contesting the President's authority under his war powers to seize the Nation's steel industry, an action of profound and demonstrable domestic impact. Here, by contrast, we are asked to settle a dispute between coequal branches of our government, each of which has resources available to protect and assert its interests, resources not available to private litigants outside the judicial forum.[1] Moreover, as in *Curtiss–Wright,* the effect of this action, as far as we can tell, is "entirely external to the United States, and [falls] within the category of foreign affairs."

---

[1] As observed by Judge Wright in his concurring opinion below:

"Congress has initiated the termination of treaties by directing or requiring the President to give notice of termination, without any prior presidential request. Congress has annulled treaties without any presidential notice. It has conferred on the President the power to terminate a particular treaty, and it has enacted statutes practically nullifying the domestic effects of a treaty and thus caused the President to carry out termination.... Moreover, Congress has a variety of powerful tools for influencing foreign policy decisions that bear on treaty matters. Under Article I, Section 8 of the Constitution, it can regulate commerce with foreign nations, raise and support armies, and declare war. It has power over the appointment of ambassadors and the funding of embassies and consulates. Congress thus retains a strong influence over the President's conduct in treaty matters. As our political history demonstrates, treaty creation and termination are complex phenomena rooted in the dynamic relationship between the two political branches of our government. We thus should decline the invitation to set in concrete a particular constitutionally acceptable arrangement by which the President and Congress are to share treaty termination."

Finally, as already noted, the situation presented here is closely akin to that presented in *Coleman,* where the Constitution spoke only to the procedure for ratification of an amendment, not to its rejection.

Having decided that the question presented in this action is nonjusticiable, I believe that the appropriate disposition is for this Court to vacate the decision of the Court of Appeals and remand with instructions for the District Court to dismiss the complaint. . . .

Mr. Justice Blackmun, with whom Mr. Justice White joins, dissenting in part.

In my view, the time factor and its importance are illusory; if the President does not have the power to terminate the Treaty (a substantial issue that we should address only after briefing and oral argument), the notice of intention to terminate surely has no legal effect. It is also indefensible, without further study, to pass on the issue of justiciability or on the issues of standing or ripeness. While I therefore join in the grant of the petition for certiorari, I would set the case for oral argument and give it the plenary consideration it so obviously deserves.

Mr. Justice Brennan, dissenting.

I respectfully dissent from the order directing the District Court to dismiss this case, and would affirm the judgment of the Court of Appeals insofar as it rests upon the President's well-established authority to recognize, and withdraw recognition from, foreign governments.

In stating that this case presents a non-justiciable "political question," the plurality, in my view, profoundly misapprehends the political question principle as it applies to matters of foreign relations. Properly understood, the political question doctrine restrains courts from reviewing an exercise of foreign policy judgment by the coordinate political branch to which authority to make that judgment has been "constitutional[ly] commit[ted]." Baker v. Carr, 369 U.S. 186, 211–213, 217 (1962). But the doctrine does not pertain when a court is faced with the *antecedent* question whether a particular branch has been constitutionally designated as the repository of political decisionmaking power. Cf. Powell v. McCormack, 395 U.S. 486, 519–521 (1969). The issue of decisionmaking authority must be resolved as a matter of constitutional law, not political discretion; accordingly, it falls within the competence of the courts.

The constitutional question raised here is prudently answered in narrow terms. Abrogation of the defense treaty with Taiwan was a necessary incident to Executive recognition of the Peking government, because the defense treaty was predicated upon the now-abandoned view that the Taiwan government was the only legitimate political authority in China. Our cases firmly establish that the Constitution commits to the President alone the power to recognize, and withdraw recognition from, foreign regimes. . . . That mandate being clear, our judicial inquiry into the treaty rupture can go no further. . . .

POLITICAL QUESTIONS

(1) That aspect of the political question doctrine relying on "a textually demonstrable commitment of the issue to a coordinate political department" is, as the Court noted in Baker v. Carr, "primarily a function of the separation of powers." The issue will be raised again in Chapter 7—see especially United States v. Nixon, infra p. 448.

(2) In Baker v. Carr, the Court noted that a case might be held to involve a political question because of "a lack of judicially discoverable and manageable

standards for resolving it." The Court held that reapportionment cases did not require "the Court to enter upon policy determinations for which judicially manageable standards are lacking. Judicial standards under the Equal Protection Clause are well developed and familiar, and it has been open to courts since the enactment of the Fourteenth Amendment to determine, if on the particular facts they must, that a discrimination reflects *no* policy, but simply arbitrary and capricious action." When studying the subsequent reapportionment cases infra Chapter 10, the student should ask whether the Court's prediction as to the manageability of the standards proved to be true.

(3) Professor Henkin suggests that there is no separate political question doctrine:

> "The thesis I offer for discussion is that there may be no doctrine requiring abstention from judicial review of 'political questions.' The cases which are supposed to have established the political question doctrine required no such extra-ordinary abstention from judicial review; they called only for the ordinary respect by the courts for the political domain. Having reviewed, the Court refused to invalidate the challenged actions because they were within the constitutional authority of President or Congress. In no case did the Court have to use the phrase 'political question' . . . ."

Henkin, *Is There a "Political Question" Doctrine?*, 85 Yale L.J. 597, 600 (1976).

In connection with Professor Henkin's thesis, consider U.S. Department of Commerce v. Montana, 503 U.S. 442 (1992). Following the apportionment method dictated by a 1941 federal statute, Congressional reapportionment pursuant to the 1990 census reduced Montana's delegation from two representatives to one. Montana claimed that the federal statute was unconstitutional insofar as it caused Montana to be represented by a single district 231,189 persons larger than an average district. The Court rejected the argument that Congressional selection of an apportionment method was a political question not subject to judicial review. Article I, § 2, places substantive limitations on Congress' apportionment power, including a requirement that representatives be apportioned to the states "according to their respective numbers." Violation of that limitation would present a justiciable controversy. The Court concluded, however, that the apportionment method mandated by the 1941 statute was not unconstitutional. Since Congressional districts cannot cross State lines, it is impossible for all districts to be the same size.

> "The constitutional framework . . . must . . . delegate to Congress a measure of discretion that is broader than that accorded to the States in the much easier task of determining district sizes within State borders. . . . Its apparently good-faith choice of a method of apportionment of Representatives among the several States 'according to their respective numbers' commands far more deference than a state districting decision that is capable of being reviewed under a relatively rigid mathematical standard."

THE AMENDMENT PROCESS—A DIGRESSION

The amendment process as set out in Article V has given rise to a number of questions. Since the Court has indicated that some of these questions are non-justiciable political questions, a general look at the problems relating to Article V seems appropriate at this point.

Proposal of Amendments

Amendments may be proposed either by a two-thirds majority in both Houses of Congress or by a convention called by Congress upon the application of the legislatures of two-thirds of the states. Every proposal made thus far has come from Congress. The process has been generally uncontroversial.

While Article V's alternative mode of proposing amendments by convention has yet to be exercised, it is by no means a dead letter. Well over 300 applications calling for conventions have been sent to Congress by state legislatures to date. Every state has submitted at least one such petition. The applications have ranged from those calling for a general constitutional convention to those calling for conventions to consider such specific topics as slavery, anti-polygamy, and integration of public schools. During the 1960's, in the aftermath of the Supreme Court's decision mandating reapportionment of state legislatures to conform with population distribution, nearly two-thirds of the states submitted applications calling for a convention on the subject of apportionment. Most recently, more than thirty states have requested a convention on the issue of a balanced federal budget.

It is generally agreed that the framers made provision for the proposal of amendments by convention at least in part because they feared that the excesses of the federal government could be most difficult to curtail through amendment if only Congress could initiate constitutional change. While resort to the convention process has not been required to subdue an oppressive Congress, its prospect has operated to prod a reluctant one to action. The raft of applications for a convention to propose popular election of U.S. Senators inspired Congress to propose the Seventeenth Amendment, post haste. Recent applications, such as those addressed to reapportionment and bussing, suggest that the device may be used to apprise Congress of serious dissatisfaction with decisions of the Supreme Court and possibly to directly institute curative amendments.

The treatment in Article V of the convention method of proposing amendments is cryptic indeed, and uncertainty regarding it is the rule rather than the exception. Issues as to the meaning of Article V were widely debated in the aftermath of calls for a convention on apportionment issues in the 1960's,[1] and most recently in the context of calls for a convention on the issue of a balanced budget.[2] Among the more important questions are these:

1.   What constitutes a valid application which Congress must count? Is an application valid if it calls for an unlimited convention? If it calls for a convention applicable to a particular subject? If it calls for a convention to vote up or down the text of a particular amendment?

2.   How is it to be determined whether two-thirds of the states have applied for a convention? What is the length of time for which applications

---

[1] E.g., American Bar Association Special Constitutional Convention Study Committee, Amendment of the Constitution by the Convention Method under Article V (1974); Bonfield, *The Dirksen Amendment and the Article V Convention Process,* 66 Mich.L.Rev. 949 (1968); Ervin, *Proposed Legislation to Implement the Convention Method of Amending the Constitution,* 66 Mich.L.Rev. 875 (1968); Black, *Amending The Constitution: A Letter to a Congressman,* 82 Yale L.J. 189 (1972).

[2] E.g., Bator et al., *A Constitutional Convention: How Well Would it Work?* (American Enterprise Institute 1979); Dellinger, *The Recurring Question of the "Limited" Constitutional Convention,* 88 Yale L.J. 1623 (1979); Gunther, *The Convention Method of Amending the United States Constitution,* 14 Ga. L.Rev. 1 (1979); Van Alstyne, *Does Article V Restrict the States to Calling Unlimited Conventions Only?—A Letter to a Colleague,* 1978 Duke L.J. 1295 (1979).

will be counted? Should applications be counted if they differ with reference to the subject of the proposed convention?

3.   If it is decided that there are valid calls for a convention from two-thirds of the states, what are the powers of Congress in calling such a convention? Does Congress have discretion not to call the convention? Can Congress specify the manner of selection of delegates and their numbers? Can Congress specify the procedures to be followed by the Convention? Can Congress limit the subject matter to be considered by the convention?

4.   If a convention is called, are Congressional limitations on procedure and subject matter binding on the convention?

5.   What is the power of Congress concerning the product of a convention? Can Congress refuse to submit proposed amendments to the states for ratification if the convention ignores Congressional directions on voting requirements or limitations on subject matter?

The lack of answers to most of the preceding questions has raised the spectre of a "runaway convention," called for a limited purpose but proposing far-reaching amendments to the Constitution and the Bill of Rights.

Ratification of Amendments

Just as Article V offers two methods for proposal of amendments, it also sets forth alternative modes of ratification: "by the Legislatures of three fourths of the several states, or by Conventions in three fourths thereof, as one or the other Mode of Ratification may be proposed by the Congress...." Congress has generally preferred ratification by the state legislatures, invoking the state convention device in only one instance—the Twenty–First Amendment's repeal of national prohibition.

Since amendments to the Constitution have been ratified on eighteen occasions, questions concerning the ratification process are fewer than the untested questions concerning amendments proposed by a constitutional convention. There are questions whose answers are not obvious, however. These concern, among others, the time during which ratification may take place, the extent to which state law controls ratification by state legislatures, and the legal effect of ratification by states that previously, or subsequently, reject an amendment. Two questions that arose in the context of the unsuccessful attempt to ratify the Equal Rights Amendment are instructive.

One question concerns the time limit for ratification. The Eighteenth, Twentieth, Twenty-first and Twenty-second Amendments contain seven year time limits for ratification in their texts. (No time limit for ratification was set in connection with the Nineteenth Amendment.) Time limits for ratification of subsequent amendments were not placed in the amendment text, but in the proposing clause of the resolution submitting the amendment for ratification. The change in practice, designed to avoid "cluttering up" the text of the Constitution with obsolete provisions concerning time limits for ratification, created no legal issues prior to the proposed Equal Rights Amendment, since ratifications occurred well within the seven year limit. The requisite number of states had not ratified the ERA when the time limitation expired on March 22, 1979. In October 1978, Congress extended the time limit to June, 1982. Among the questions raised were whether it was necessary to resubmit the ERA anew, whether the extension measure required a two-thirds vote (it received substantial majorities in both houses, but less than two-thirds), and whether the

President's signature was necessary (the President in fact signed the extension measure).[3]

Extension of the time for ratification of ERA exacerbated a second issue. A number of states that had originally ratified acted to rescind their ratifications, and rescission campaigns were pending in other states. One view is that ratification is a final act that can not be withdrawn. The contrary view is that the requisite number of states must agree on ratification at the same time.[4] In approving extension of the time for ratification, Congress did not resolve this issue.

Congressional Resolution of Constitutional Issues Concerning the Amendment Process

Congress can attempt to determine whether a particular amendment has been ratified by the requisite number of states. In July of 1868, Congress passed a joint resolution declaring that the Fourteenth Amendment had been ratified by the requisite number of states—resolving the question whether states that had previously rejected the Amendment, and states that had rescinded their ratification, should be counted. The Secretary of State's proclamation that the Amendment had been ratified accordingly included both states which had earlier rejected the Amendment, and those that had purported to withdraw their ratifications.[5]

Congress can also attempt to resolve legal issues concerning the amendment process by a general statute not applicable to any particular amendment. Senator Ervin introduced legislation in 1971 and 1973 concerning proposal of amendments by constitutional conventions.[6] An identical "Federal Constitutional Procedures Act" was introduced in 1979 by Senator Helms.[7] Its controversial provisions include requiring state calls for a convention to state the nature of the amendments proposed, requiring a Congressional call for a convention to specify the subject, and authorizing Congress to block submission of amendments on other subjects.

Justiciability

In the absence of a Congressional decision, can any of the questions previously put be answered in litigation? If Congress resolves any of these questions, either in the context of a particular amendment or by general

---

[3] On the issue of time for ratification of the ERA see: *Equal Rights Amendment Extension: Hearings on H.J. Res. 638 Before the Subcomm. on Civil and Constitutional Rights of the House Comm. on the Judiciary,* 95th Cong., 1st and 2d Sess. (1977–78); *Equal Rights Amendment Extension: Hearings on S.J.Res. 134 Before the Subcomm. on the Constitution of the Senate Comm. on the Judiciary,* 95th Cong., 2d Sess. (1978); Ginsburg, *Ratification of the Equal Rights Amendment: A Question of Time,* 57 Tex. L.Rev. 919 (1979).

The proposed District of Columbia Representation in Congress Amendment, submitted by Congress for ratification on August 22, 1978, returns to the earlier pattern. The seven year time limit for ratification is contained in the amendment text.

[4] Considerable law review commentary discusses the issue of rescission. E.g., Heckman, *Ratification of a Constitutional Amend-*ment: Can a State Change Its Mind? 6 Conn. L.Rev. 28 (1973); Elder, *Article V, Justiciability and the Equal Rights Amendment,* 31 Okla.L.Rev. 63 (1978); Ginsburg, supra note 3; Comment, *The Equal Rights Amendment and Article V: A Framework for Analysis of the Extension and Recission Issues,* 127 U.Pa. L.Rev. 494 (1978); Note, *Reversals in the Federal Constitutional Amendment Process: Efficacy of State Ratifications of the Equal Rights Amendment,* 49 Ind.L.J. 147 (1973).

[5] The history of the ratification of the Fourteenth Amendment is contained in Coleman v. Miller, 307 U.S. 433, 448–449 (1939).

[6] S. 215, 92d Cong., 1st Sess., 117 Cong. Rec. 36804–38806 (1971); S. 1272, 93d Cong., 1st Sess., 119 Cong.Rec. 22731–37 (1973).

[7] S. 520, 96th Cong., 1st Sess., 125 Cong. Rec.S. 1935 (1979).

legislation, would those answers be binding on a court? Issues of justiciability are nearly as uncertain as the substantive answers to the constitutional questions.[8]

Prior to 1939, the Supreme Court adjudicated a number of issues concerning the ratification process. (Notice that none of the decisions rejected a contrary resolution of an issue by Congress.) In United States v. Sprague, 282 U.S. 716 (1931), the Supreme Court held that the choice between modes of ratification lies in the sole discretion of Congress. In an earlier Eighteenth Amendment case, Dillon v. Gloss, 256 U.S. 368 (1921), the Court held that Article V implicitly required that ratification be completed within some reasonable time after the proposal of an amendment, and that Congress could fix a definite period for the ratification. Hawke v. Smith, No. 1, 253 U.S. 221 (1920), held that the efficacy of a resolution of Ohio's legislature ratifying the Eighteenth Amendment could not be made subject by the state's constitution to the requirement of approval in a popular referendum. Leser v. Garnett, 258 U.S. 130 (1922), rejected a claim that by virtue of state constitutional constraints, certain state legislatures were without power to ratify the Nineteenth Amendment. The Court stated that the federal ratification function "transcends any limitations sought to be imposed by the people of a State." (258 U.S. at 137)[9]

Questions have been raised whether the 27th Amendment, proposed in 1789 and ratified by a thirty eighth state in 1992, has become part of the Constitution. Michigan ratified the Amendment on May 7, 1992. The Congressional leadership, responding to election-year political concerns about appearing to question a limitation on the power to raise their own salaries, announced that Congress would accept the Amendment. On May 21, 1992, Congress by joint resolution declared the 27th Amendment to be "valid ... as part of the Constitution of the United States." In the unlikely event that Congress should enact a Congressional pay raise or pay cut taking effect before an intervening election, could a Court decide whether ratification of the Amendment was effective?

As indicated, in Dillon v. Gloss, 256 U.S. 368 (1921), the Court stated that effective ratification must occur within a reasonable time after an amendment is proposed. The Court explained that the requirement insures that approval reflects "the will of the people in all sections at relatively the same period, which of course ratification scattered through a long series of years would not do." It is hard to escape the conclusion that ratification votes scattered between 1789 and 1992 do not satisfy the "reasonable time" requirements of the Dillon dictum. Has the 27th Amendment, nevertheless, become part of the Constitution because Congress, without holding hearings, has acquiesced?

In Coleman v. Miller, 307 U.S. 433 (1939), the Court held two questions concerning ratification to be political. Most interesting, in light of the contemporary controversy concerning the 27th Amendment, the Court concluded that the issue whether the child labor amendment was open to ratification thirteen years after it was proposed was not justiciable. The Court emphasized the absence of judicial criteria to determine the length of time that was reasonable. If Congress sets a time limit for ratification of a proposed amendment, as it has

---

[8] Much of the commentary cited in the previous footnotes discusses issues of justiciability. See also, Orfield, *The Amending of the Federal Constitution* (1942); Scharpf, *Judicial Review and the Political Question: A Functional Analysis*, 75 Yale L.J. 517, 589 (1966).

[9] See also the National Prohibition Cases, 253 U.S. 350 (1920) (two-thirds vote requirement for proposing amendment means two-thirds of a quorum present and voting); Hollingsworth v. Virginia, 3 U.S. (3 Dall.) 378 (1798) (Presidential participation not required in proposing an amendment).

almost always done in the last 75 years, it is obvious that the Court will accept that Congressional decision. Was it so obvious that the judicial process was incapable of resolving the issue whether thirteen years was a reasonable time for ratifying the proposed child labor amendment when Congress set no time limit? If *Dillon*'s "reasonable time" requirement is implicit in Article V, is the question whether 203 years is unreasonable beyond judicial capacity?

Is there a larger issue here beyond the question whether there are manageable judicial criteria for resolving the reasonable time question? Significantly, four concurring Justices in Coleman v. Miller (Black, Roberts, Frankfurter and Douglas) rejected prior decisions of the Court adjudicating issues concerning the amending process, including *Dillon,* and argued that all such issues were political. Was it inappropriate for the Court in *Dillon* to adjudicate the issue whether Article V implicitly requires ratification within a reasonable time?

Part II

Allocation of Governmental Powers: The Nation and the States; The President, the Congress, and the Courts

A principal concern in the Constitutional Convention was the allocation of governmental powers. Two major issues were addressed: (1) The distribution of power among the three branches of the national government—the separation of powers. The aim here was to see that no particular branch was able to achieve an undue concentration of power. (2) The division of powers between the nation and the states. The great objective of the federal system that dominated the thinking of the Framers was a national government with adequate power to handle matters of national interest while the states retained autonomy over local affairs.

One aspect of separation of powers has been introduced in Part I in connection with the discussion of the scope of the judicial power. Other separation of powers issues will appear from time to time in this part of the book, but major discussion, particularly of the relationships between the President and Congress, will be deferred until Chapter 7 at the end of this part.

The bulk of Part II will be devoted to studying the division of powers between the nation and the states. The aim is to give the student a working sense of the principal issues of federalism and the manner in which the Supreme Court addresses them.

Fortunately for our constitutional development, the Convention did not attempt any such detailed specification of national and state powers as is contained in some modern federal constitutions.[1] The Framers were content to give us a rather general enumeration of national powers (principally in Art. I, § 8) plus the principle (made explicit in the Tenth Amendment) that all power not delegated to the national government remains with the states.[2] Thus, provisions delegating power to the national government may be construed in two different contexts: (1) as fixing the scope of national power; and (2) as determining the retained powers of the states. This interrelation of national and state power is explored in Chapters 4 and 5.

In Chapter 6 on intergovernmental relationships within the federal system, attention is returned to a dual consideration of national and state power. The questions considered arise when the nation or the states attempt to tax or regulate activities of the other, or when two or more states seek solution to common problems through interstate compacts.

Whatever the particular nature of the federalism issue raised, consider the following excerpt from Gregory v. Ashcroft, 501 U.S. 452, 457–458 (1991), describing the intended design and expected benefits of dividing power between the Nation and the States:

"The Constitution created a Federal Government of limited powers.... The States thus retain substantial sovereign authority under our constitutional system. As James Madison put it:

'The powers delegated by the proposed Constitution to the federal government are few and defined. Those which are to remain in the State governments are numerous and indefinite.... The powers reserved to the several States will extend to all the objects which, in the ordinary course of affairs, concern the lives, liberties, and properties of the people, and the internal order, improvement, and prosperity of the State.' The Federalist No. 45, pp. 292–293 (C. Rossiter ed. 1961) (J. Madison).

"This federalist structure of joint sovereigns preserves to the people numerous advantages. It assures a decentralized government that will be more sensitive to the diverse needs of a heterogenous society; it increases opportunity for citizen involvement in democratic processes; it allows for more innovation

---

[1] See, for example, the 1949 Constitution of India where the division of powers is accomplished by three detailed lists annexed to the Constitution. List I (the "Union List") itemizes the exclusive powers of the central government. List II (the "State List") itemizes the powers given exclusively to the states. List III (the concurrent list) specifies the subjects with which the states may deal in the absence of inconsistent legislation by the Parliament of India. For a general treatise, see Basu, Constitutional Law of India (6th ed. 1991).

[2] The Constitution as originally adopted contains a few explicit limitations on the powers of the states. See Art. I, § 10.

and experimentation in government; and it makes government more responsive by putting the States in competition for a mobile citizenry....

"Perhaps the principal benefit of the federalist system is a check on abuses of government power.... Just as the separation and independence of the coordinate Branches of the Federal Government serves to prevent the accumulation of excessive power in any one Branch, a healthy balance of power between the States and the Federal Government will reduce the risk of tyranny and abuse from either front...."

CHAPTER 4

THE SCOPE OF NATIONAL POWER

SECTION 1. THE CONSTITUTIONAL CONVENTION AND THE ESTABLISHMENT OF A NATIONAL GOVERNMENT

Introduction. The following excerpts from the records of the Constitutional Convention of 1787 are designed to afford an intimate glimpse into the process of deliberation and compromise that produced the Constitution and also to provide a sample of the materials available for an examination of the historical setting and meaning of provisions of the Constitution.

A thorough examination of the historical setting and "legislative history" of constitutional provisions requires the weighing of voluminous material; there is room here for only a small sample. But the excerpts that follow can provide a basis for hypotheses, to be checked against the full record, concerning: (1) The weaknesses of the Articles of Confederation that the framers sought to avoid in their new constitution; (2) The choice (or compromise) between conflicting views concerning the power to be given the national government; (3) The nature and scope of the national power over commerce contemplated by the draftsmen.

Proceedings in the Federal Convention: May 29, 1787

Madison's Notes; I Farrand, Records of the Federal Convention of 1787 (1911) 18–19 (Hereafter Cited as "Farrand").[1]

Mr. Randolph [Va.] opened the main business. He expressed his regret, that it should fall to him, rather than those, who were of longer standing in life and political experience, to open the great subject of their mission. But, as the convention had originated from Virginia, and his colleagues supposed, that some proposition was expected from them, they had imposed this task on him.

He then commented on the difficulty of the crisis, and the necessity of preventing the fulfillment of the prophecies of the American downfall.

He observed that in revising the federal system we ought to inquire (1) into the properties, which such a government ought to possess, (2) the defects of the confederation, (3) the danger of our situation and (4) the remedy.

1. The character of such a governme[nt] ought to secure (1) against foreign invasion: (2) against dissentions between members of the Union, or seditions in particular states: (3) to p[ro]cure to the several states various blessings, of which an isolated situation was i[n] capable: (4) to be able to defend itself against encroachment: and (5) to be paramount to the state constitutions.

2. In speaking of the defects of the confederation he professed a high respect for its authors, and considered them as having done all that patriots

---

[1] This and the following excerpts are copied by permission of the Yale University Press. [Bracketed references to the states from which the delegates came have been added by the editors.]

could do, in the then infancy of the science, of constitutions, and of confederacies,—when the inefficiency of requisitions was unknown—no commercial discord had arisen among any states—no rebellion had appeared as in Massachusetts—foreign debts had not become urgent—the havoc of paper money had not been foreseen—treaties had not been violated—and perhaps nothing better could be obtained from the jealousy of the states with regard to their sovereignty.

He then proceeded to enumerate the defects:[a] (1) that the confederation produced no security agai[nst] foreign invasion; congress not being permitted to prevent a war nor to support it by th[eir] own authority—of this he cited many examples; most of whi[ch] tended to show that they could not cause infractions of treaties or of the law of nations, to be punished; that particular states might by their conduct provoke war without control; and that neither militia nor draughts being fit for defense on such occasions, enlistments only could be successful, and these could not be executed without money.

(2) that the foederal government could not check the quarrels between states, nor a rebellion in any not having constitutional power Nor means to interpose according to the exigency:

(3) That there were many advantages, which the U.S. might acquire, which were not attainable under the confederation—such as a productive impost—counteraction of the commercial regulations of other nations—pushing of commerce ad libitum— & c & c.

(4) that the foederal government could not defend itself against the incroachments from the states:

(5) that it was not even paramount to the state constitutions, ratified as it was in [many] of the states.

3.   He next reviewed the danger of our situation appealed to the sense of the best friends of the U.S.—the prospect of anarchy from the laxity of government everywhere; and to other considerations.

4.   He then proceeded to the remedy; the basis of which he said, must be the republican principle.

He proposed as conformable to his ideas the following resolutions, which he explained one by one.

Note. The "resolutions" to which Randolph referred at the close of this excerpt constituted the "Virginia Plan"—probably developed by James Madison. See Warren, *The Making of the Constitution* 139–141 (1928). These resolutions formed the basis for discussion and action by the Convention in the days that followed. Thus the proposition debated in the following excerpt from the proceedings of May 31 was the second part of the sixth "resolution" which Randolph proposed.

Proceedings in the Federal Convention: May 31, 1787

Madison's Notes; I Farrand 53.

On the proposition for giving "Legislative power in all cases to which the State Legislatures were individually incompetent".

---

[a] Reasons for the failure of the Articles of Confederation and the need for a stronger national union were eloquently expounded by Alexander Hamilton in The Federalist, Nos. 15 and 22. See also Kelly & Harbison, *The American Constitution* 108–110 (1970). On the influence of Hamilton, *see:* Morris, *Alexander Hamilton and the Founding of the Nation* (1957); Dietze, *Hamilton's Federalist, Treatise for Free Government,* 42 Corn.L.Q. 307, 501 (1957).

Mr. Pinkney [S.Car.] & Mr. Rutledge [S.Car.] objected to the vagueness of the term *incompetent,* and said they could not well decide how to vote until they should see an exact enumeration of the powers comprehended by this definition.

Mr. Butler [S.Car.] repeated his fears that we were running into an extreme in taking away the powers of the States, and called on Mr. Randolph for the extent of his meaning.

Mr. Randolph [Va.] disclaimed any intention to give indefinite powers to the national Legislature, declaring that he was entirely opposed to such an inroad of the State jurisdictions, and that he did not think any considerations whatever could ever change his determination. His opinion was fixed on this point.

Mr. Madison [Va.] said that he had brought with him into the Convention a strong bias in favor of an enumeration and definition of the powers necessary to be exercised by the national Legislature; but had also brought doubts concerning its practicability. His wishes remained unaltered; but his doubts had become stronger. What his opinion might ultimately be he could not yet tell. But he should shrink from nothing which should be found essential to such a form of Govt. as would provide for the safety, liberty and happiness of the Community. This being the end of all our deliberations, all the necessary means for attaining it must, however reluctantly be submitted to.

On the question for giving powers, in cases to which the States are not competent,

Massts. ay. Cont. divd. (Sherman no Ellsworth ay) N.Y. ay. N.J. ay. Pa. ay. Del. ay. Va. ay. N.C. ay. S.Carolina ay. Georgia. ay. [Ayes—9; noes—0; divided—1].

Proceedings in the Federal Convention: July 17, 1787

(a) Journal; II Farrand 21

It was moved and seconded to postpone the considn of the second clause of the Sixth resolution[b] reported from the Committee of the whole House in order to take up the following:

"To make laws binding on the People of the United States in all cases which may concern the common interests of the Union: but not to interfere with the government of the individual States in any matters of internal police, which respect the government of such States only, and wherein the general welfare of the United States is not concerned."

which passed in the negative [Ayes–2; noes–8.]

It was moved and seconded to alter the second clause of the 6th resolution so as to read as follows, namely

"and moreover to legislate in all cases for the general interests of the Union, and also in those to which the States are separately incompetent, or in which the harmony of the United States may be interrupted by the exercise of individual legislation."

[b] The Sixth Resolution, based on Randolph's propositions, as adopted by the Committee of the Whole House on May 31, 1787 (see the excerpt from Madison's notes quoted supra), provided in part: "That the national legislature ought to be empowered to enjoy the legislative rights vested in Congress by the Confederation; and moreover To legislate in all cases, to which the separate States are incompetent or in which the harmony of the United States may be interrupted by the exercise of individual legislation." See 1 Farrand 47 (Journal, May 31, 1787).

which passed in the affirmative [Ayes–6; noes–4.]

[To agree to the second clause of the 6. resolution as amended. Ayes–8; noes–2.]

(b) The same proceedings are reported more fully in Madison's Notes;

II FARRAND 25–27

The 6th Resoln. in the Report of the Comm. of the whole relating to the powers, which had been postponed in order to consider the 7 & 8th, relating to the Constitution of the Natl. Legislature, was now resumed—

Mr. Sherman [Conn.] observed that it would be difficult to draw the line between the powers of the Genl. Legislatures, and those to be left with the States; that he did not like the definition contained in the Resolution, and proposed in place of the words "of individual legislation" line 4 inclusive, to insert "to make laws binding on the people of the (United) States in all cases (which may concern the common interests of the Union); but not to interfere with (the Government of the individual States in any matters of internal police which respect the Govt. of such States only, and wherein the General) welfare of the U. States is not concerned."

Mr. Wilson [Pa.] 2ded. the amendment as better expressing the general principle.

Mr. Govr. Morris [Pa.] opposed it. The internal police, as it would be called & understood by the States ought to be infringed in many cases, as in the case of paper money & other tricks by which Citizens of other states may be affected.

Mr. Sherman, in explanation of his ideas read an enumeration of powers, including the power of levying taxes on trade, but not the power of *direct taxation.*

Mr. Govr. Morris remarked the omission, and inferred that for the deficiencies of taxes on consumption, it must have been the meaning of Mr. Sherman, that the Genl. Govt. should recur to quotas & requisitions, which are subversive of the idea of Govt.

Mr. Sherman acknowledged that his enumeration did not include direct taxation. Some provision he supposed must be made for supplying the deficiency of other taxation, but he had not formed any.

On Question on Mr. Sherman's motion, (it passed in the negative)

Mas. no. Cont. ay. N.J. no. Pa. no. Del. no. Md. ay. Va. no. N.C. no. S.C. no. Geo. no. [Ayes–2; noes–8].

Mr. Bedford [Del.] moved that the (2d. number of Resolution 6.) be so altered as to read "(and moreover) to legislate in all cases for the general interests of the Union, and also in those to which the States are 'separately incompetent,' (or in which the harmony of the U. States may be interrupted by the exercise of individual Legislation".)

Mr. Govr. Morris 2ds. (the motion.)

Mr. Randolph. This is a formidable idea indeed. It involves the power of violating all the laws and constitutions of the States, and of intermeddling with their police. The last member of the sentence is (also) superfluous, being included in the first.

Mr. Bedford. It is not more extensive or formidable than the clause as it stands: *no State* being *separately* competent to legislate for the *general interest* of the Union.

On question for agreeing to Mr. Bedford's motion (it passed in the affirmative).

Mas. ay. Cont. no. N.J. ay. Pa. ay. Del. ay. Md. ay. Va. no. N.C. ay. S.C. no. Geo. no. [Ayes–6; noes–4].

On the sentence as amended (it passed in the affirmative).

Mas. ay. Cont. ay. N.J. ay. Pa. ay. Del. ay. Md. ay. Va. ay. N.C. ay. S.C. no. Geo. no. [Ayes–8; noes–2].

Report of the Committee of Detail: August 6, 1787

II Farrand 181–182.

[On July 24, 1787, the Convention appointed a Committee of Detail[c] "to report a Constitution conformable to the Resolutions passed by the Convention" (II Farrand 106). The Report of the Committee on August 6, 1787 defined as follows the powers of the National Government:]

Art. VII, [erroneously numbered as VI by printer's error].

Sect. I. The Legislature of the United States shall have the power to lay and collect taxes, duties, imposts and excises;

To regulate commerce with foreign nations, and among the several States;

To establish an uniform rule of naturalization throughout the United States;

To coin money;

To regulate the value of foreign coin;

To fix the standard of weights and measures;

To establish Post-offices;

To borrow money, and emit bills on the credit of the United States;

To appoint a Treasurer by ballot;

To constitute tribunals inferior to the Supreme Court;

To make rules concerning captures on land and water;

To declare the law and punishment of piracies and felonies committed on the high seas, and the punishment of counterfeiting the coin of the United States, and of offences against the law of nations;

To subdue a rebellion in any State, on the application of its legislature;

To make war;

To raise armies;

To build and equip fleets;

To call forth the aid of the militia, in order to execute the laws of the Union, enforce treaties, suppress insurrections, and repel invasions;

And to make all laws that shall be necessary and proper for carrying into execution the foregoing powers, and all other powers vested, by this Constitu-

[c] The members of the Committee of Detail were John Rutledge (So.Car.), Edmund Randolph (Va.), Nathaniel Gorham (Mass.), Oliver Ellsworth (Conn.), and James Wilson (Pa.).

tion, in the government of the United States, or in any department or officer thereof.

NOTE

It is evident from the foregoing excerpts that questions of large import are presented by the shift from a general and loosely-phrased grant of power to the national government, which the Convention initially approved on May 31 and July 17, to the itemized list of national powers embodied in the August 6 report of the Committee of Detail. Consideration should be given to two conflicting interpretations: (a) The enumeration by the Committee of Detail, which the Convention employed as a basis for final action, should be construed to reach towards the same generalized grant of power to the national government which the Convention had earlier approved; (b) The decision to enumerate the powers of Congress reflects a decision sharply to circumscribe national power.[1]

With respect to the commerce clause in particular, the proposal submitted on August 6 by the Committee of Detail was unanimously approved on August 16, 1787. (II Farrand 308). After this vote, however, strong Southern opposition to this commercial power developed out of fear that commercial regulations in the interest of Northern shipping might restrict free access for Southern staples to foreign shipping and foreign markets. This opposition was in part placated by an agreement by Northern delegates to prohibit the taxation of exports (Art. I, Sec. 9, cl. 1). See II Farrand 305–308 (Aug. 16), 359–363 (Aug. 21), 414–417 (Aug. 25); Warren, *The Making of the Constitution* 567–589 (1928); 2 Curtis, *History of the United States Constitution* 279–308 (1858).

On August 29, 1787, Charles Pinckney of South Carolina proposed requiring a ⅔ vote of each House for federal regulation of commerce. The deliberation preceding the Convention's rejection of this proposal (II Farrand 449–53) included these remarks of James Madison:

"Mr. Madison [Va.] went into a pretty full view of the subject. He observed that the disadvantage to the S. States from a navigation act, lay chiefly in a temporary rise of freight, attended however with an increase of Southn. as well as Northern Shipping—with the emigration of Northern seamen & merchants to the Southern States— & with a removal of the existing & injurious retaliations among the States (on each other). The power of foreign nations to obstruct our retaliating measures on them by a corrupt influence would also be less if a majority shd be made competent than if ⅔ of each House shd. be required to legislative acts in this case. An abuse of the power would be qualified with all these good effects. But he thought an abuse was rendered improbable by the provision of 2 branches—by the independence of the Senate, by the negative of the Executive, by the interest of Connecticut & N. Jersey which were agricultural, not commercial States; by the interior interest which was also agricultural in the most commercial States—by the accession of Western States which wd. be altogether agricultural. He added that the Southern States would derive an essential advantage in the general security afforded by the increase of our maritime strength. He stated the vulnerable situation of them all, and of Virginia in particular. The increase of the Coasting trade, and of seamen, would also be favorable to the S. States, by increasing, the consumption of their produce. If the Wealth of the Eastern should in a still

---

[1] See Abel, *The Commerce Clause in the Constitutional Convention and in Contemporary Comment,* 25 Minn.L.Rev. 432 (1941). For general studies, see Warren, *The Making* of the Constitution (1928); Farrand, *The Framing of the Constitution of the United States* (1913). Cf. Brown, *Charles Beard and the Constitution* (1956).

greater proportion be augmented, that wealth wd. contribute the more to the public wants, and be otherwise a national benefit.''

SECTION 2.   SOURCES OF NATIONAL POWER: EARLY DEVELOPMENTS

A.   THE MARSHALL COURT'S VIEW

Introduction. The allocation of powers between the nation and the states in the Constitution has given rise to three major sets of issues:

(1) What is the scope of the power of the federal government to regulate? Are the specifically granted powers to be construed narrowly or broadly? What is the significance of the clause conferring on Congress the power to make all laws which shall be "necessary and proper" for executing the granted powers?

(2) What are the limits imposed on the powers of the states to regulate and to tax? Does the grant of a power to the federal government imply exclusion of the states from exercising the same power? Does the exercise of a granted power by the federal government imply exclusion of the states from exercising the same power?

(3) Does the Constitution impose any special limitations when the regulations or taxes of the national government impinge on the state governments? To what extent may the states impose regulations or collect taxes from the federal government? In short, what intergovernmental immunities are created by the Constitution?

All three of these issues came before the Court in a set of great cases between 1819 and 1851. The major cases—*McCulloch v. Maryland, Gibbons v. Ogden,* and *Cooley v. Board of Port Wardens*—are set out in this section. They provide a useful introduction to the various doctrinal threads pursued in this chapter and in Chapters 5 and 6. They are also relevant to modern concerns since they are often discussed and applied in current Supreme Court cases.

THE BANK OF THE UNITED STATES

The Bank of the United States moved into the legal arena only after a quarter-century of political controversy. The plan for the Bank was developed by Alexander Hamilton promptly upon the establishment of the new government and led to a bill enacted by Congress in 1791. This First Bank, like the Second Bank involved in *McCulloch*, was operated primarily on the basis of privately invested capital and through private control. The national government subscribed to seven millions of the Second Bank's total capitalization of thirty-five millions; the President appointed five of the twenty-five directors. The Act that established the Bank, however, imposed upon it certain public obligations such as providing for free transfer of government deposits and making frequent statements to the Secretary of the Treasury.

Disputes in President Washington's cabinet over the constitutionality of the First Bank shed some light on the issues at stake in *McCulloch*. When in 1791 the bill to establish the bank reached the President, he called upon three members of his cabinet for their opinions. Attorney General Edmund Randolph submitted two opinions, one negative and the other noncommittal. Secretary of the Treasury Alexander Hamilton prepared an opinion that Daniel Webster closely followed in his argument for the bank and which in turn was reflected in Marshall's opinion. The opinion of the Secretary of State, Thomas Jefferson, presented a sharply narrower view of the basic powers of the national government.

Washington followed the advice of Hamilton rather than of Jefferson, and signed the bill. During the next twenty years the Bank became unpopular; attempts in 1811 to renew the charter failed. However, the disorganization of the nation's business and fiscal structure during and following the War of 1812 led to support, even among Jefferson's Republican party which then was in power, for a central banking institution to stabilize the economy; in 1816 Congress adopted a plan for a second Bank of the United States that President Madison approved. This new Bank soon encountered hostility from those who believed that its policies were contributing to the financial distress of the state banks. Several states passed legislation to curb the Bank;[1] one of these laws led to the following case.

McCulloch v. Maryland

17 U.S. (4 Wheat.) 316, 4 L.Ed. 579 (1819).

[The State of Maryland brought an action for debt against McCulloch, cashier of the Baltimore branch of the Bank of the United States. It was admitted that the Bank had issued bank notes which were not on stamped paper as required by the following statute:

"An act to impose a tax on all banks or branches thereof in the state of Maryland, not chartered by the legislature.

"Be it enacted by the General Assembly of Maryland. That if any bank has established, or shall without authority from the State first had and obtained, establish any branch, office of discount and deposit, or office of pay and receipt, in any part of this state, it shall not be lawful for the said branch, office of discount and deposit, or office of pay and receipt, to issue notes in any manner, of any other denomination than five, ten, twenty, fifty, one hundred, five hundred and one thousand dollars, and no note shall be issued except upon stamped paper of the following denominations; that is to say, every five dollar note shall be upon a stamp of ten cents; every ten dollar note upon a stamp of twenty cents; every twenty dollar note, upon a stamp of thirty cents; every fifty dollar note, upon a stamp of fifty cents; every one hundred dollar note, upon a stamp of one dollar; every five hundred dollar note, upon a stamp of ten dollars; and every thousand dollar note, upon a stamp of twenty dollars; which paper shall be furnished by the Treasurer of the Western Shore, under the direction of the Governor and Council, to be paid for upon delivery. Provided always, That any institution of the above description may relieve itself from the operation of the provisions aforesaid, by paying annually, in advance, to the Treasurer of the Western Shore, for the use of the State, the sum of fifteen thousand dollars.

"And be it enacted, That the President, Cashier, each of the Directors and officers of every institution established, or to be established as aforesaid,

---

[1] See Warren, *The Supreme Court in United States History* (Rev. ed. 1932) 505–06. The Constitutions of Indiana and Illinois prohibited establishment of banks chartered outside the state. Five states, other than Maryland, resorted to taxation to accomplish the same result; Tennessee and Ohio, $50,000 per branch, North Carolina, $5,000 per branch, and Kentucky, $60,000 per branch. Georgia laid a tax of 31¼% on bank stock employed within the state which on its face appeared nondiscriminatory; the following year the legislature declared that the intent was to tax the Bank of the United States only.

offending against the provisions aforesaid, shall forfeit a sum of five hundred dollars for each and every offence ..."

The Court of Appeals of the State of Maryland affirmed a judgment for the plaintiff.]

Mr. Chief Justice Marshall delivered the opinion of the Court:

In the case now to be determined, the defendant [in error], a sovereign state, denies the obligation of a law enacted by the legislature of the Union, and the plaintiff [in error], on his part, contests the validity of an act which has been passed by the legislature of that state. The constitution of our country, in its most interesting and vital parts, is to be considered; the conflicting powers of the government of the Union and of its members, as marked in that constitution, are to be discussed; and an opinion given, which may essentially influence the great operations of the government. No tribunal can approach such a question without a deep sense of its importance, and of the awful responsibility involved in its decision. But it must be decided peacefully, or remain a source of hostile legislation, perhaps of hostility of a still more serious nature; and if it is to be so decided, by this tribunal alone can the decision be made. On the Supreme Court of the United States has the constitution of our country devolved this important duty.

The first question made in the cause is, has Congress power to incorporate a bank?[a]

. . .

The power now contested was exercised by the first Congress elected under the present constitution. The bill for incorporating the bank of the United States did not steal upon an unsuspecting legislature, and pass unobserved. Its principle was completely understood, and was opposed with equal zeal and ability. After being resisted, first in the fair and open field of debate, and afterwards in the executive cabinet, with as much persevering talent as any measure has ever experienced, and being supported by arguments which convinced minds as pure and as intelligent as this country can boast, it became a law. The original act was permitted to expire; but a short experience of the embarrassments to which the refusal to revive it exposed the government, convinced those who were most prejudiced against the measure of its necessity and induced the passage of the present law. It would require no ordinary share of intrepidity to assert that a measure adopted under these circumstances was a bold and plain usurpation, to which the constitution gave no countenance.

These observations belong to the cause; but they are not made under the impression that, were the question entirely new, the law would be found irreconcilable with the constitution.

In discussing this question, the counsel for the state of Maryland have deemed it of some importance, in the construction of the constitution, to consider that instrument not as emanating from the people, but as the act of sovereign and independent states. The powers of the general government, it has been said, are delegated by the states, who alone are truly sovereign; and must be exercised in subordination to the states who alone possess supreme dominion....

The government of the Union, ... (whatever may be the influence of this fact on the case), is, emphatically, and truly, a government of the people. In

---

[a] What is the relationship between the constitutionality of the act of Congress creating the bank and the constitutionality of the Maryland tax?

form and in substance it emanates from them. Its powers are granted by them, and are to be exercised directly on them, and for their benefit.

This government is acknowledged by all to be one of enumerated powers. The principle, that it can exercise only the powers granted to it, would seem too apparent to have required to be enforced by all those arguments which its enlightened friends, while it was depending before the people, found it necessary to urge. That principle is now universally admitted. But the question respecting the extent of the powers actually granted, is perpetually arising, and will probably continue to arise, as long as our system shall exist.

In discussing these questions, the conflicting powers of the general and state governments must be brought into view, and the supremacy of their respective laws, when they are in opposition, must be settled.

If any one proposition could command the universal assent of mankind, we might expect it would be this—that the government of the Union, though limited in its powers, is supreme within its sphere of action. This would seem to result necessarily from its nature. It is the government of all; its powers are delegated by all; it represents all, and acts for all. Though any one state may be willing to control its operations, no state is willing to allow others to control them. The nation, on those subjects on which it can act, must necessarily bind its component parts. But this question is not left to mere reason; the people have, in express terms, decided it by saying, "this constitution, and the laws of the United States, which shall be made in pursuance thereof," "shall be the supreme law of the land," and by requiring that the members of the state legislatures, and the officers of the executive and judicial departments of the states shall take the oath of fidelity to it.

The government of the United States, then, though limited in its powers, is supreme; and its laws, when made in pursuance of the constitution, form the supreme law of the land, "anything in the constitution or laws of any state to the contrary notwithstanding."

Among the enumerated powers, we do not find that of establishing a bank or creating a corporation. But there is no phrase in the instrument which, like the articles of confederation, excludes incidental or implied powers,[b] and which requires that everything granted shall be expressly and minutely described. Even the 10th amendment, which was framed for the purpose of quieting the excessive jealousies which had been excited, omits the word "expressly," and declares only that the powers "not delegated to the United States, nor prohibited to the states, are reserved to the states or to the people;" thus leaving the question, whether the particular power which may become the subject of contest has been delegated to the one government, or prohibited to the other, to depend on a fair construction of the whole instrument. The men who drew and adopted this amendment had experienced the embarrassments resulting from the insertion of this word in the articles of confederation, and probably omitted it to avoid those embarrassments. A constitution, to contain an accurate detail of all the subdivisions of which its great powers will admit, and of all the means by which they may be carried into execution, would partake of a prolixity of a legal code, and could scarcely be embraced by the human mind. It would probably never be understood by the public. Its nature, therefore, requires, that only its great outlines should be marked, its important objects designated, and the minor ingredients which compose those objects be deduced from the nature

[b] The Articles of Confederation (1777) provided in Article II: "Each State retains its sovereignty, freedom and independence, and every power, jurisdiction and right, which is not by this confederation expressly delegated to the United States, in Congress assembled."

of the objects themselves. That this idea was entertained by the framers of the American constitution, is not only to be inferred from the nature of the instrument but from the language. Why else were some of the limitations, found in the ninth section of the 1st article, introduced? It is also, in some degree, warranted by their having omitted to use any restrictive term which might prevent its receiving a fair and just interpretation. In considering this question, then, we must never forget that it is a constitution we are expounding.

Although, among the enumerated powers of government, we do not find the word "bank" or "incorporation," we find the great powers to lay and collect taxes; to borrow money; to regulate commerce; to declare and conduct a war; and to raise and support armies and navies. The sword and the purse, all the external relations, and no inconsiderable portion of the industry of the nation, are entrusted to its government. It can never be pretended that these vast powers draw after them others of inferior importance, merely because they are inferior. Such an idea can never be advanced. But it may with great reason be contended, that a government, entrusted with such ample powers, on the due execution of which the happiness and prosperity of the nation so vitally depends, must also be entrusted with ample means for their execution. The power being given, it is the interest of the nation to facilitate its execution. It can never be their interest, and cannot be presumed to have been their intention, to clog and embarrass its execution by withholding the most appropriate means. Throughout this vast republic, from the St. Croix to the Gulf of Mexico, from the Atlantic to the Pacific, revenue is to be collected and expended, armies are to be marched and supported. The exigencies of the nation may require that the treasure raised in the north should be transported to the south, that raised in the east conveyed to the west, or that this order should be reversed. Is that construction of the constitution to be preferred which would render these operations difficult, hazardous, and expensive? Can we adopt that construction (unless the words, imperiously require it) which would impute to the framers of that instrument, when granting these powers for the public good, the intention of impeding their exercise by withholding a choice of means? If, indeed, such be the mandate of the constitution, we have only to obey; but that instrument does not profess to enumerate the means by which the powers it confers may be executed; nor does it prohibit the creation of a corporation, if the existence of such a being be essential to the beneficial exercise of those powers. It is, then, the subject of fair inquiry, how far such means may be employed. . . .

But the constitution of the United States has not left the right of Congress to employ the necessary means for the execution of the powers conferred on the government to general reasoning. To its enumeration of powers is added that of making "all laws which shall be necessary and proper, for carrying into execution the foregoing powers, and all other powers vested by this constitution, in the government of the United States, or in any department thereof."

The counsel for the State of Maryland have urged various arguments, to prove that this clause, though in terms a grant of power, is not so in effect; but is really restrictive of the general right, which might otherwise be implied, of selecting means for executing the enumerated powers. . . .

But the argument on which most reliance is placed, is drawn from the peculiar language of this clause. Congress is not empowered by it to make all laws, which may have relation to the powers conferred on the government, but such only as may be "necessary and proper" for carrying them into execution. The word "necessary" is considered as controlling the whole sentence, and as limiting the right to pass laws for the execution of the granted powers, to such as are indispensable, and without which the power would be nugatory. That it excludes the choice of means, and leaves to Congress, in each case, that only which is most direct and simple.

Is it true that this is the sense in which the word "necessary" is always used? Does it always import an absolute physical necessity, so strong that one thing, to which another may be termed necessary, cannot exist without that other? We think it does not. If reference be had to its use, in the common affairs of the world, or in approved authors, we find that it frequently imports no more than that one thing is convenient, or useful, or essential to another. To employ the means necessary to an end, is generally understood as employing any means calculated to produce the end, and not as being confined to those single means, without which the end would be entirely unattainable. Such is the character of human language, that no word conveys to the mind, in all situations, one single definite idea; ... This word, then, like others, is used in various senses; and, in its construction, the subject, the context, the intention of the person using them, are all to be taken into view.

Let this be done in the case under consideration. The subject is the execution of those great powers on which the welfare of a nation essentially depends. It must have been the intention of those who gave these powers, to insure, as far as human prudence could insure, their beneficial execution. This could not be done by confining the choice of means to such narrow limits as not to leave it in the power of Congress to adopt any which might be appropriate, and which were conducive to the end. This provision is made in a constitution intended to endure for ages to come, and, consequently, to be adapted to the various crises of human affairs. To have prescribed the means by which government should, in all future time, execute its powers, would have been to change, entirely, the character of the instrument, and give it the properties of a legal code. . . .

. . .

The result of the most careful and attentive consideration bestowed upon this clause is, that if it does not enlarge, it cannot be construed to restrain the powers of Congress, or to impair the right of the legislature to exercise its best judgment in the selection of measures to carry into execution the constitutional powers of the government. If no other motive for its insertion can be suggested, a sufficient one is found in the desire to remove all doubts respecting the right to legislate on that vast mass of incidental powers which must be involved in the constitution, if that instrument be not a splendid bauble.

We admit, as all must admit, that the powers of the government are limited, and that its limits are not to be transcended. But we think the sound construction of the constitution must allow to the national legislature that discretion, with respect to the means by which the powers it confers are to be carried into execution, which will enable that body to perform the high duties assigned to it, in the manner most beneficial to the people. Let the end be legitimate, let it be within the scope of the constitution, and all means which are appropriate, which are plainly adapted to that end, which are not prohibited, but consist with the letter and spirit of the constitution, are constitutional. . . .

If a corporation may be employed indiscriminately with other means to carry into execution the powers of the government, no particular reason can be assigned for excluding the use of a bank, if required for its fiscal operations. . . .

But, were its necessity less apparent, none can deny its being an appropriate measure; and if it is, the degree of its necessity, as has been very justly observed, is to be discussed in another place. Should Congress, in the execution of its powers, adopt measures which are prohibited by the constitution; or should Congress, under the pretext of executing its powers, pass laws for the accomplishment of objects not entrusted to the government, it would become the painful duty of this tribunal, should a case requiring such a decision come before it, to say that such an act was not the law of the land. But where the law is not prohibited, and is really calculated to effect any of the objects entrusted to the government, to undertake here to inquire into the degree of its necessity, would be to pass the line which circumscribes the judicial department, and to tread on legislative ground. This court disclaims all pretensions to such a power....

After the most deliberate consideration, it is the unanimous and decided opinion of this court that the act to incorporate the bank of the United States is a law made in pursuance of the constitution, and is a part of the supreme law of the land....

It being the opinion of the court that the act incorporating the bank is constitutional, and that the power of establishing a branch in the state of Maryland might be properly exercised by the bank itself, we proceed to inquire:

2.　Whether the state of Maryland may, without violating the constitution, tax that branch?

That the power of taxation is one of vital importance; that it is retained by the states; that it is not abridged by the grant of a similar power to the government of the Union; that it is to be concurrently exercised by the two governments: are truths which have never been denied. But, such is the paramount character of the constitution that its capacity to withdraw any subject from the action of even this power, is admitted. The states are expressly forbidden to lay any duties on imports or exports, except what may be absolutely necessary for executing their inspection laws. If the obligation of this prohibition must be conceded—if it may restrain a state from the exercise of its taxing power on imports and exports—the same paramount character would seem to restrain, as it certainly may restrain, a state from such other exercise of this power, as is in its nature incompatible with, and repugnant to, the constitutional laws of the Union. A law, absolutely repugnant to another, as entirely repeals that other as if express terms of repeal were used.

On this ground the counsel for the bank place its claim to be exempted from the power of a state to tax its operations. There is no express provision for the case, but the claim has been sustained on a principle which so entirely pervades the constitution, is so intermixed with the materials which compose it, so interwoven with its web, so blended with its texture, as to be incapable of being separated from it without rending it into shreds.

This great principle is, that the constitution and the laws made in pursuance thereof are supreme; that they control the constitution and laws of the respective states, and cannot be controlled by them....

. . .

That the power to tax involves the power to destroy; that the power to destroy may defeat and render useless the power to create; that there is a plain repugnance, in conferring on one government a power to control the constitutional measures of another, which other, with respect to those very measures, is declared to be supreme over that which exerts the control, are propositions not to be denied. But all inconsistencies are to be reconciled by the magic of the word CONFIDENCE. Taxation, it is said, does not necessarily and unavoidably destroy. To carry it to the excess of destruction would be an abuse, to presume which, would banish that confidence which is essential to all government.

But is this a case of confidence? Would the people of any one state trust those of another with a power to control the most insignificant operations of their state government? We know they would not. Why, then, should we suppose that the people of any one state should be willing to trust those of another with a power to control the operations of a government to which they have confided the most important and most valuable interests? In the legislature of the Union alone, are all represented. The legislature of the Union alone, therefore, can be trusted by the people with the power of controlling measures which concern all, in the confidence that it will not be abused. This, then, is not a case of confidence, and we must consider it as it really is . . . .

If the states may tax one instrument, employed by the government in the execution of its powers, they may tax any and every other instrument. They may tax the mail; they may tax the mint; they may tax patent-rights; they may tax the papers of the custom-house; they may tax judicial process; they may tax all the means employed by the government, to an excess which would defeat all the ends of government. This was not intended by the American people. They did not design to make their government dependent on the states . . . .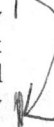

It has also been insisted, that, as the power of taxation in the general and state governments is acknowledged to be concurrent, every argument which would sustain the right of the general government to tax banks chartered by the states, will equally sustain the right of the states to tax banks chartered by the general government.

But the two cases are not on the same reason. The people of all the states have created the general government, and have conferred upon it the general power of taxation. The people of all the states, and the states themselves, are represented in Congress, and, by their representatives, exercise this power. When they tax the chartered institutions of the states, they tax their constituents; and these taxes must be uniform. But, when a state taxes the operations of the government of the United States, it acts upon institutions created, not by their own constituents, but by people over whom they claim no control. It acts upon the measures of a government created by others as well as themselves, for the benefit of others in common with themselves. The difference is that which always exists, and always must exist, between the action of the whole on a part, and the action of a part on the whole—between the laws of a government declared to be supreme, and those of a government which, when in opposition to those laws, is not supreme.

But if the full application of this argument could be admitted, it might bring into question the right of Congress to tax the state banks, and could not prove the right of the states to tax the Bank of the United States.

The court has bestowed on this subject its most deliberate consideration. The result is a conviction that the states have no power, by taxation or otherwise, to retard, impede, burden, or in any manner control the operations of the constitutional laws enacted by Congress to carry into execution the powers vested in the general government. This is, we think, the unavoidable consequence of that supremacy which the constitution has declared.

We are unanimously of opinion that the law passed by the legislature of Maryland, imposing a tax on the Bank of the United States, is unconstitutional and void.

This opinion does not deprive the states of any resources which they originally possessed. It does not extend to a tax paid by the real property of the bank, in common with the other real property within the state, nor to a tax imposed on the interest which the citizens of Maryland may hold in this institution, in common with other property of the same description throughout the state. But this is a tax on the operations of the bank, and is, consequently, a tax on the operation of an instrument employed by the government of the Union to carry its powers into execution. Such a tax must be unconstitutional.

... It is, therefore, adjudged and ordered, that the said judgment of the said Court of Appeals of the state of Maryland in this case, be, and the same hereby is, reversed and annulled. And this court, proceeding to render such judgment as the said Court of Appeals should have rendered; it is further adjudged and ordered, that the judgment of the said Baltimore County Court be reversed and annulled, and that judgment be entered in the said Baltimore County Court for the said James W. M'Culloch.

McCULLOCH AND THE SCOPE OF FEDERAL POWER

(1) Marshall rejected the argument that the powers of the federal government were delegated to it by the sovereign states. The government of the Union, he said, is a government of the people, it "emanates from them. Its powers are granted by them, and are to be exercised directly on them, and for their benefit." What is the significance of this reasoning by Marshall? If powers were granted by the states, could the states insist upon their own interpretation of the powers granted? Could a state legally secede from the Union? These questions assumed importance from the beginning of the country. Examples include the Kentucky–Virginia Resolutions of 1798, the New England resistance to the War of 1812, Calhoun's doctrine of nullification as reflected in the South Carolina Exposition of 1828 and the Statute of Nullification of 1832. The ultimate test took place in the Civil War where the right of secession was rejected on the battlefield. For an account of these early episodes and others, see Reference Note, *Interposition vs. Judicial Power,* 1 Race Rel.L.Rep. 465 (1956). The issue recurred in the middle 1950s when state legislatures passed resolutions seeking to nullify the enforcement of Brown v. Board of Educ., 347 U.S. 483 (1954). The Alabama Resolution, e.g., commenced as follows:

"WHEREAS the Constitution of the United States was formed by the sanction of the several states, given by each in its sovereign capacity; and

"WHEREAS the States, being the parties to the constitutional compact, it follows of necessity that there can be no tribunal above their authority to decide, in the last resort, whether the compact made by them be violated; and, consequently, they must decide themselves, in the last resort, such questions as may be of sufficient magnitude to require their interposition; ..." Act No. 42, Spec.Sess., 1956, Feb. 2, 1956, set out 1 Race Rel.L.Rptr. 437 (1956). Other resolutions of the time are set out id. 438–447.

The Supreme Court gave its answer to these latter-day nullifiers in Cooper v. Aaron, 358 U.S. 1 (1958).

(2) The Constitution did not contain an express power to create banks. Did Marshall rely primarily upon the "necessary and proper" clause as the basis for inferring such a power from other powers expressly granted? Or is Professor Black correct in suggesting that Marshall "does not place principal reliance on this clause as a ground of decision; that before he reaches it he has already decided, on the basis of far more general implications ...; that he addresses

himself to the ... clause only in response to counsel's arguing its *restrictive* force; and that he never really commits himself to the proposition that the necessary and proper clause enlarges governmental power...." Black, *Structure and Relationship in Constitutional Law* 14 (1969). For an elaborate exegesis of the necessary and proper clause, see Engdahl, *Constitutional Federalism* 16–73 (2d ed. 1987).

(3) Near the end of the Constitutional Convention, Benjamin Franklin moved that Congress be given "a power to provide for cutting canals where deemed necessary." Madison then suggested enlarging Franklin's motion to add the power "to grant charters of incorporation where the interest of the U.S. might require & the legislative provisions of individual States may be incompetent." The Convention rejected these proposals. II Farrand, 615–616. Consider the possible relevance of that rejection to the preceding question of federal power to charter the Bank of the United States and the following question of federal power to build roads and canals.

FEDERAL POWER TO BUILD ROADS AND CANALS

The second great issue on the scope of national legislative power grew out of proposals for the building of national roads and canals. A bill appropriating funds for such "internal improvements" was passed in 1817, but was vetoed by President Madison as not "among the enumerated powers; or ..., by any just interpretation, within the power to make laws necessary and proper for carrying into execution those or other powers vested by the Constitution in the Government of the United States." II Messages and Papers of the Presidents 569, 570 (1897). The commerce power did not reach that far "without a latitude of construction departing from the ordinary import of the terms," and to construe the power "to provide for the common defence and general welfare" to do so "would be contrary to the established and consistent rules of interpretation, as rendering the special and careful enumeration of powers, which follow the clause, nugatory and improper. Such a view of the Constitution would have the effect of giving to Congress a general power of legislation, instead of the defined and limited one hitherto understood to belong to them...." Id.

On similar strict construction grounds, President Monroe vetoed "with great regret" an appropriation passed in 1822 for the preservation and repair of the Cumberland Road. He suggested that Congress propose a constitutional amendment authorizing the necessary federal power.

McCULLOCH AND STATE POWER TO CONTROL THE SELECTION OF MEMBERS OF CONGRESS

McCulloch concluded "that the states have no power, by taxation or otherwise, to retard, impede, burden, or in any manner control the operations of the constitutional laws enacted by Congress...." Powell v. McCormack, 395 U.S. 486 (1969), held that Congress could not alter the qualifications set forth in the Constitution for election to Congress. Where Congress lacks power to act and the Constitution is silent regarding state power, does *McCulloch* bear on state power to control who may be elected to Congress to exercise federal power?

In U.S. Term Limits, Inc. v. Thornton, ___ U.S. ___, 115 S.Ct. 1842 (1995), the Court concluded that the States, like Congress, lack the power to add to the "exclusive qualifications" of age, citizenship and residency the Constitution prescribes for members of Congress. It invalidated a voter-adopted Arkansas constitutional amendment that prohibited the name of an otherwise-eligible candidate for Congress from appearing on the general election ballot if that candidate had already served three terms in the House or two terms in the Senate.

Justice Stevens' opinion for the Court relied on *McCulloch* in two respects to reject the argument that the State's voters had "reserved power" to impose term limit qualifications on candidates for Congress from their State. First, "the power to add qualifications is not within the 'original power' of the States, and thus is not reserved to the States by the Tenth Amendment." *McCulloch* "rejected the argument that the Constitution's silence on the subject of state power to tax corporations chartered by Congress implies that the States have 'reserved' power to tax such federal instrumentalities." Just as in *McCulloch* "an 'original right to tax' . . . federal entities 'never existed, and the question whether it has been surrendered, cannot arise[,]' . . . electing representatives to the National Legislature was a new right, arising from the Constitution itself[,] . . . [and] any state power to set the qualifications for membership in Congress must derive not from the reserved powers of state sovereignty, but rather from the delegated powers of national sovereignty."

Second, even if the States' original power embraced some control over congressional qualifications, "the Qualifications Clauses were intended to preclude the States from exercising any such power." Recognizing state power to add qualifications would violate the "fundamental principle of our representative democracy" that "the people should choose whom they please to govern them." That right "belongs not to the States, but to the people"—a proposition supported by *McCulloch*:

> "Permitting individual States to formulate diverse qualifications for their representatives would result in a patchwork of state qualifications, undermining the uniformity and the national character that the Framers envisioned and sought to ensure. Cf. McCulloch v. Maryland, 4 Wheat., at 428–429 (1819) ('Those means are not given by the people of a particular State, not given by the constituents of the legislature, . . . but by the people of all the States. They are given by all, for the benefit of all—and upon theory should be subjected to that government only which belongs to all'). Such a patchwork would also sever the direct link that the Framers found so critical between the National Government and the people of the United States."

Concurring separately, Justice Kennedy also emphasized *McCulloch* in support of his view that "the National Government . . . owes its existence to the act of the whole people who created it" and that there "can be no doubt, if we are to respect the republican origins of the Nation and preserve its federal character, that there exists a federal right of citizenship, a relationship between the people of the Nation and their National Government, with which the States may not interfere." Insisting "that the people of the United States . . . have a political identity . . . independent of, though consistent with, their identity as citizens of the State of their residence[,]" Justice Kennedy stated:

> "It might be objected that because the States ratified the Constitution, the people can delegate power only through the States or by acting in their capacities as citizens of particular States. But in *McCulloch v. Maryland*, the Court set forth its authoritative rejection of this idea: 'The . . . constitution . . . was submitted to the people. . . . It is true, they . . . act in their States. But the measures they adopt do not, on that account, cease to be the measures of the people themselves, or become the measures of the State governments.' . . .
>
> "The political identity of the entire people of the Union is reinforced by the proposition . . . that, though limited as to its objects, the National Government

is and must be controlled by the people without collateral interference by the States. *McCulloch* affirmed this proposition as well, when the Court rejected the suggestion that States could interfere with federal powers.... The States have no power, reserved or otherwise, over the exercise of federal authority within its proper sphere...."

Justice Thomas, joined by Chief Justice Rehnquist and Justices O'Connor and Scalia, dissented. Stressing that the "ultimate source of the Constitution's authority is the consent of the people of each individual State, not the consent of the undifferentiated people of the Nation as a whole[,]" he found nothing in *McCulloch* that denied *"the people* of the States" a reserved power under the Tenth Amendment to prescribe eligibility requirements for the candidates who seek to represent them in Congress, given the Constitution's silence on the question. The majority misunderstood *McCulloch*, he argued:

"... *McCulloch* did make clear that a power need not be 'expressly' delegated to the United States or prohibited to the States in order to fall outside the Tenth Amendment's reservation; delegations and prohibitions can also arise by necessary implication. [But] *McCulloch* indicated that all powers as to which the Constitution does not speak (whether expressly or by necessary implication) are 'reserved' to the state level ... [without] turn[ing] on whether the States had enjoyed the power before the framing.... *McCulloch* seemed to assume that the people had 'conferred on the general government the power contained in the constitution, and on the States the whole residuum of power.' ...

"The structure of *McCulloch*'s analysis also refutes the majority's position....

"For the past 175 years, *McCulloch* has been understood to rest on the proposition that the Constitution affirmatively barred Maryland from imposing its tax on the Bank's operations.... For the majority, however, *McCulloch* apparently turned on the fact that before the Constitution was adopted, the States had possessed no power to tax the instrumentalities of the governmental institutions that the Constitution created. This understanding of *McCulloch* makes most of Chief Justice Marshall's opinion irrelevant; according to the majority, there was no need to inquire into whether federal law deprived Maryland of the power in question, because the power could not fall into the category of 'reserved' powers anyway."

Justice Thomas also found "perfectly consistent with my position" *McCulloch*'s argument "that the people of a single State may not tax the instrumentalities employed by the people of all the States through the National Government, because such taxation would effectively subject the people of the several States to the taxing power of a single State":

"This sort of argument proves that the people of a single State may not prescribe qualifications for the President of the United States; the selection of the President, like the operation of the Bank of the United States, is not up to the people of any single State.... It does not follow, however, that the people of a single State may not prescribe qualifications for their own representatives in Congress."

Gibbons v. Ogden

22 U.S. (9 Wheat.) 1, 6 L.Ed. 23 (1824).

[Ogden obtained an injunction from the Court of Chancery of New York ordering Gibbons to stop operating his ferry-boats in the waters of the State of

New York. In 1803 the New York legislature had granted to Robert Livingston and Robert Fulton the exclusive right for twenty years to operate ships powered by fire or steam in New York waters; in 1808, on proof that Livingston and Fulton had built a steamboat that could operate at more than four miles per hour, the grant was extended until 1838. Ogden alleged that he held an assignment from these grantees of the exclusive right to run a steamboat between Elizabethtown, New Jersey, and New York City, and that the defendant, Gibbons, was running two boats between these points. Gibbons alleged that his boats, the *Stoudinger* and *Bellana,* had been duly enrolled and licensed under the laws of the United States for carrying on the coasting trade.

Chancellor Kent sustained the injunction prohibiting the operation of Gibbons' boats. 4 Johns. Ch. 150 (1819). The Chancellor rejected the defendant's contention that plaintiff's monopoly was inconsistent with the United States coasting license; Chancellor Kent concluded that the coasting license was designed merely to relieve American ships of the burdens imposed upon foreign shipping. In an earlier case involving the steamboat monopoly the Chancellor had further rejected the contention that this state law, in regulating interstate commerce, fell within an area exclusively reserved to Congress. On the contrary, Chancellor Kent held that the states could regulate interstate commerce unless Congress had enacted inconsistent legislation. Livingston v. Van Ingen, 9 Johns. 507 (1812).

The New York Court for the Correction of Errors affirmed the order sustaining Ogden's injunction. 17 Johns. 488 (1820).]

Mr. Chief Justice Marshall delivered the opinion of the Court, . . .

The appellant contends that this decree is erroneous, because the laws which purport to give the exclusive privilege it sustains, are repugnant to the constitution and laws of the United States.

They are said to be repugnant:

1st. To that clause in the constitution which authorizes Congress to regulate commerce. . . .

The words are: "Congress shall have power to regulate commerce with foreign nations, and among the several states, and with the Indian tribes."

The subject to be regulated is commerce; and our constitution being, as was aptly said at the bar, one of enumeration, and not of definition, to ascertain the extent of the power it becomes necessary to settle the meaning of the word. The counsel for the appellee would limit it to traffic, to buying and selling, or the interchange of commodities, and do not admit that it comprehends navigation. This would restrict a general term, applicable to many objects, to one of its significations. Commerce, undoubtedly is traffic, but it is something more; it is intercourse. It describes the commercial intercourse between nations, and parts of nations, in all its branches, and is regulated by prescribing rules for carrying on that intercourse. The mind can scarcely conceive a system for regulating commerce between nations, which shall exclude all laws concerning navigation, which shall be silent on the admission of the vessels of the one nation into the ports of the other, and be confined to prescribing rules for the conduct of individuals, in the actual employment of buying and selling, or of barter.

If commerce does not include navigation, the government of the Union has no direct power over that subject, and can make no law prescribing what shall constitute American vessels, or requiring that they shall be navigated by American seamen. Yet this power has been exercised from the commencement of the government, has been exercised with the consent of all, and has been

understood by all to be a commercial regulation. All America understands, and
has uniformly understood, the word "commerce" to comprehend navigation. It
was so understood, and must have been so understood, when the constitution
was framed. The power over commerce, including navigation, was one of the
primary objects for which the people of America adopted their government, and
must have been contemplated in forming it. The convention must have used the
word in that sense; because all have understood it in that sense, and the
attempt to restrict it comes too late. . . .

The word used in the constitution, then, comprehends, and has been
always understood to comprehend, navigation within its meaning; and a power
to regulate navigation is as expressly granted as if that term had been added to
the word "commerce."

To what commerce does this power extend? The constitution informs us, to
commerce "with foreign nations, and among the several states, and with the
Indian tribes."

It has, we believe, been universally admitted that these words comprehend
every species of commercial intercourse between the United States and foreign
nations. No sort of trade can be carried on between this country and any other,
to which this power does not extend. It has been truly said, that commerce, as
the word is used in the constitution, is a unit, every part of which is indicated
by the term.

If this be the admitted meaning of the word, in its application to foreign
nations, it must carry the same meaning throughout the sentence, and remain
a unit, unless there be some plain intelligible cause which alters it.

The subject to which the power is next applied, is to commerce "among the
several states." The word "among" means intermingled with. A thing which is
among others, is intermingled with them. Commerce among the states cannot
stop at the external boundary line of each state, but may be introduced into the
interior.

It is not intended to say that these words comprehend that commerce
which is completely internal, which is carried on between man and man in a
state, or between different parts of the same state, and which does not extend
to or affect other states. Such a power would be inconvenient, and is certainly
unnecessary.

Comprehensive as the word "among" is, it may very properly be restricted
to that commerce which concerns more states than one. The phrase is not one
which would probably have been selected to indicate the completely interior
traffic of a state, because it is not an apt phrase for that purpose; and the
enumeration of the particular classes of commerce to which the power was to
be extended, would not have been made had the intention been to extend the
power to every description. The enumeration presupposes something not enumerated; and that something, if we regard the language or the subject of the
sentence, must be the exclusively internal commerce of a state. The genius and
character of the whole government seem to be, that its action is to be applied to
all the external concerns of the nation, and to those internal concerns which
affect the states generally; but not to those which are completely within a
particular state, which do not affect other states, and with which it is not
necessary to interfere, for the purpose of executing some of the general powers
of the government. The completely internal commerce of a state, then, may be
considered as reserved for the state itself.

But, in regulating commerce with foreign nations, the power of Congress
does not stop at the jurisdictional lines of the several states. It would be a very

useless power if it could not pass those lines. The commerce of the United States with foreign nations, is that of the whole United States. Every district has a right to participate in it. The deep streams which penetrate our country in every direction, pass through the interior of almost every state in the Union, and furnish the means of exercising this right. If Congress has the power to regulate it, that power must be exercised whenever the subject exists. If it exists within the states, if a foreign voyage may commence or terminate at a port within a state, then the power of Congress may be exercised within a state.

This principle is, if possible, still more clear, when applied to commerce "among the several states." They either join each other, in which case they are separated by a mathematical line, or they are remote from each other, in which case other states lie between them. What is commerce "among" them; and how is it to be conducted? Can a trading expedition between two adjoining states commence and terminate outside of each? And if the trading intercourse be between two states remote from each other, must it not commence in one, terminate in the other, and probably pass through a third? Commerce among the states must, of necessity, be commerce with the states. In the regulation of trade with the Indian tribes, the action of the law, especially when the constitution was made, was chiefly within a state. The power of Congress, then, whatever it may be, must be exercised within the territorial jurisdiction of the several states. The sense of the nation, on this subject, is unequivocally manifested by the provisions made in the laws for transporting goods, by land, between Baltimore and Providence, between New York and Philadelphia, and between Philadelphia and Baltimore.

We are now arrived at the inquiry, What is this power?

It is the power to regulate; that is, to prescribe the rule by which commerce is to be governed. This power, like all others vested in Congress, is complete in itself, may be exercised to its utmost extent, and acknowledges no limitations, other than are prescribed in the constitution. These are expressed in plain terms, and do not affect the questions which arise in this case, or which have been discussed at the bar. If, as has always been understood, the sovereignty of Congress, though limited to specified objects, is plenary as to those objects, the power over commerce with foreign nations, and among the several States, is vested in Congress as absolutely as it would be in a single government, having in its constitution the same restrictions on the exercise of the power as are found in the constitution of the United States. The wisdom and the discretion of Congress, their identity with the people, and the influence which their constituents possess at elections, are, in this, as in many other instances, as that, for example, of declaring war, the sole restraints on which they have relied, to secure them from its abuse. They are the restraints on which the people must often rely solely, in all representative governments....

But it has been urged, with great earnestness, that although the power of Congress to regulate commerce with foreign nations, and among the several states, be co-extensive with the subject itself, and have no other limits than are prescribed in the constitution, yet the states may severally exercise the same power within their respective jurisdictions. In support of this argument, it is said that they possessed it as an inseparable attribute of sovereignty, before the formation of the constitution, and still retain it, except so far as they have surrendered it by that instrument; that this principle results from the nature of the government, and is secured by the tenth amendment; that an affirmative grant of power is not exclusive, unless in its own nature it be such that the continued exercise of it by the former possessor is inconsistent with the grant, and that this is not of that description.

The appellant, conceding these postulates, except the last, contends that full power to regulate a particular subject, implies the whole power, and leaves no residuum; that a grant of the whole is incompatible with the existence of a right in another to any part of it.

Both parties have appealed to the constitution, to legislative acts, and judicial decisions; and have drawn arguments from all these sources to support and illustrate the propositions they respectively maintain.

The grant of the power to lay and collect taxes is, like the power to regulate commerce, made in general terms, and has never been understood to interfere with the exercise of the same power by the states; and hence has been drawn an argument which has been applied to the question under consideration. But the two grants are not, it is conceived, similar in their terms or their nature. Although many of the powers formerly exercised by the states, are transferred to the government of the Union, yet the state governments remain, and constitute a most important part of our system. The power of taxation is indispensable to their existence, and is a power which, in its own nature, is capable of residing in, and being exercised by, different authorities at the same time. We are accustomed to see it placed, for different purposes, in different hands. Taxation is the simple operation of taking small portions from a perpetually accumulating mass, susceptible of almost infinite division; and a power in one to take what is necessary for certain purposes, is not, in its nature, incompatible with a power in another to take what is necessary for other purposes. Congress is authorized to lay and collect taxes, & c., to pay the debts, and provide for the common defence and general welfare of the United States. This does not interfere with the power of the States to tax for the support of their own governments; nor is the exercise of that power by the States, an exercise of any portion of the power that is granted to the United States. In imposing taxes for State purposes, they are not doing what Congress is empowered to do. Congress is not empowered to tax for those purposes which are within the exclusive province of the States. When, then, each government exercises the power of taxation, neither is exercising the power of the other. But, when a State proceeds to regulate commerce with foreign nations, or among the several States, it is exercising the very power that is granted to Congress, and is doing the very thing which Congress is authorized to do. There is no analogy, then, between the power of taxation and the power of regulating commerce....

But, the inspection laws are said to be regulations of commerce, and are certainly recognized in the constitution, as being passed in the exercise of a power remaining with the States.

That inspection laws may have a remote and considerable influence on commerce, will not be denied; but that a power to regulate commerce is the source from which the right to pass them is derived, cannot be admitted. The object of inspection laws, is to improve the quality of articles produced by the labour of a country; to fit them for exportation; or, it may be, for domestic use. They act upon the subject before it becomes an article of foreign commerce, or of commerce among the States, and prepare it for that purpose. They form a portion of that immense mass of legislation, which embraces everything within the territory of a State, not surrendered to the general government: all which can be most advantageously exercised by the States themselves. Inspection laws, quarantine laws, health laws of every description, as well as laws for regulating the internal commerce of a State, and those which respect turnpike roads, ferries, & c., are component parts of this mass.

No direct general power over these objects is granted to Congress; and, consequently, they remain subject to State legislation. If the legislative power of the Union can reach them, it must be for national purposes; it must be where the power is expressly given for a special purpose, or is clearly incidental to some power which is expressly given. It is obvious, that the government of the Union, in the exercise of its express powers, that, for example, of regulating commerce with foreign nations and among the States, may use means that may also be employed by a State, in the exercise of its acknowledged powers; that, for example, of regulating commerce within the State. If Congress license vessels to sail from one port to another, in the same State, the act is supposed to be, necessarily, incidental to the power expressly granted to Congress, and implies no claim of a direct power to regulate the purely internal commerce of a State, or to act directly on its system of police. So, if a State, in passing laws on subjects acknowledged to be within its control, and with a view to those subjects, shall adopt a measure of the same character with one which Congress may adopt, it does not derive its authority from the particular power which has been granted, but from some other, which remains with the State, and may be executed by the same means. All experience shows, that the same measures, or measures scarcely distinguishable from each other, may flow from distinct powers; but this does not prove that the powers themselves are identical. Although the means used in their execution may sometimes approach each other so nearly as to be confounded, there are other situations in which they are sufficiently distinct to establish their individuality. . . .

It has been contended by the counsel for the appellant, that, as the word "to regulate" implies in its nature full power over the thing to be regulated, it excludes, necessarily, the action of all others that would perform the same operation on the same thing. That regulation is designed for the entire result, applying to those parts which remain as they were, as well as to those which are altered. It produces a uniform whole, which is as much disturbed and deranged by changing what the regulating power designs to leave untouched, as that on which it has operated.

There is great force in this argument, and the Court is not satisfied that it has been refuted.

Since, however, in exercising the power or regulating their own purely internal affairs, whether of trading or police, the States may sometimes enact laws, the validity of which depends on their interfering with, and being contrary to, an act of Congress passed in pursuance of the constitution, the Court will enter upon the inquiry, whether the laws of New York, as expounded by the highest tribunal of that State, have, in their application to this case, come into collision with an act of Congress, and deprived a citizen of a right to which that act entitles him. Should this collision exist, it will be immaterial whether those laws were passed in virtue of a concurrent power "to regulate commerce with foreign nations and among the several States," or in virtue of a power to regulate their domestic trade and police. In one case and the other, the acts of New York must yield to the law of Congress; and the decision sustaining the privilege they confer, against a right given by a law of the Union, must be erroneous. . . .

But we will proceed briefly to notice those sections which bear more directly on the subject.

The first section declares, that vessels enrolled by virtue of a previous law, and certain other vessels, enrolled as described in that act, and having a license in force, as is by the act required, "and no others, shall be deemed ships or vessels of the United States, entitled to the privileges of ships or vessels employed in the coasting trade."

This section seems to the Court to contain a positive enactment, that the vessels it describes shall be entitled to the privileges of ships or vessels employed in the coasting trade. These privileges cannot be separated from the trade, and cannot be enjoyed, unless the trade may be prosecuted. The grant of the privilege is an idle, empty form, conveying nothing, unless it convey the right to which the privilege is attached, and in the exercise of which its whole value consists. To construe these words otherwise than as entitling the ships or vessels described, to carry on the coasting trade, would be, we think to disregard the apparent intent of the act.

. . .

But if the license be a permit to carry on the coasting trade, the respondent denies that these boats were engaged in that trade, or that the decree under consideration has restrained them from prosecuting it. The boats of the appellant were, we are told, employed in the transportation of passengers; and this is no part of that commerce which Congress may regulate.

If, as our whole course of legislation on this subject shows, the power of Congress has been universally understood in America, to comprehend navigation, it is a very persuasive, if not a conclusive argument, to prove that the construction is correct; and, if it be correct, no clear distinction is perceived between the power to regulate vessels employed in transporting men for hire, and property for hire. . . .

Powerful and ingenious minds, taking, as postulates, that the powers expressly granted to the government of the Union, are to be contracted by construction, into the narrowest possible compass, and that the original powers of the States are retained, if any possible construction will retain them, may, by a course of well digested, but refined and metaphysical reasoning, founded on these premises, explain away the constitution of our country, and leave it, a magnificent structure, indeed, to look at, but totally unfit for use. They may so entangle and perplex the understanding, as to obscure principles, which were before thought quite plain, and induce doubts where, if the mind were to pursue its own course, none would be perceived. In such a case, it is peculiarly necessary to recur to safe and fundamental principles to sustain those principles, and, when sustained, to make them the tests of the arguments to be examined.

Mr. Justice Johnson.[a] The judgment entered by the Court in this cause, has my entire approbation; but having adopted my conclusions on views of the subject materially different from those of my brethren, I feel it incumbent on me to exhibit those views. I have, also, another inducement: in questions of great importance and great delicacy, I feel my duty to the public best discharged, by an effort to maintain my opinions in my own way.

In attempts to construe the constitution, I have never found much benefit resulting from the inquiry, whether the whole, or any part of it, is to be construed strictly, or liberally. The simple, classical, precise, yet comprehensive language, in which it is couched, leaves, at most, but very little latitude for construction; and when its intent and meaning is discovered, nothing remains

[a] Justice William Johnson, of South Carolina, was appointed to the Supreme Court in 1804 by Jefferson with the hope that the new justice would provide an antidote to Marshall and his Federalism. See Morgan, Justice William Johnson, The First Dissenter (1954). Was this hope realized in the *Gibbons* case?

but to execute the will of those who made it, in the best manner to effect the purposes intended....

. . .

The power of a sovereign state over commerce, ... amounts to nothing more than a power to limit and restrain it at pleasure. And since the power to prescribe the limits to its freedom, necessarily implies the power to determine what shall remain unrestrained, it follows, that the power must be exclusive; it can reside but in one potentate; hence, the grant of this power carries with it the whole subject, leaving nothing for the State to act upon....

Commerce, in its simplest signification, means an exchange of goods; but in the advancement of society, labour, transportation, intelligence, care, and various mediums of exchange, become commodities, and enter into commerce; the subject, the vehicle, the agent, and their various operations, become the objects of commercial regulation. Ship building, the carrying trade, and propagation of seamen, are such vital agents of commercial prosperity, that the nation which could not legislate over these subjects, would not possess power to regulate commerce.

That such was the understanding of the framers of the constitution is conspicuous from provisions contained in that instrument....

It is impossible, with the views which I entertain of the principle on which the commercial privileges of the people of the United States, among themselves, rests, to concur in the view which this Court takes of the effect of the coasting license in this cause. I do not regard it as the foundation of the right set up in behalf of the appellant. If there was any one object riding over every other in the adoption of the constitution, it was to keep the commercial intercourse among the States free from all invidious and partial restraints. And I cannot overcome the conviction, that if the licensing act was repealed to-morrow, the rights of the appellant to a reversal of the decision complained of, would be as strong as it is under this license. One half the doubts in life arise from the defects of language, and if this instrument had been called an exemption instead of a license, it would have given a better idea of its character....

Decree.... [T]his Court is of opinion, that the several licenses to the steam boats, the Stoudinger and the Bellona, to carry on the coasting trade ... which were granted under an act of congress, passed in pursuance of the constitution of the United States, gave full authority to those vessels to navigate the waters of the United States, by steam or otherwise, for the purpose of carrying on the coasting trade, any law of the State of New York to the contrary notwithstanding; and that so much of the several laws of the State of New York, as prohibits vessels, licensed according to the laws of the United States, from navigating the waters of the State of New York, by means of fire or steam, is repugnant to the said constitution, and void [Reversed.][b]

[b] The arguments to the Court drove home the fact that the *Gibbons* case involved more than the run between Elizabethtown and New York. In the preceding decade, navigation by steam had developed at a rapid pace. Monopolies for the development of this modern means of travel, similar to that conferred on Fulton by New York, had been granted by New Jersey, Connecticut, Ohio, Massachusetts, New Hampshire, Vermont and Georgia; a particularly significant monopoly by Louisiana covered the mouth of the Mississippi. The legislation of New Jersey and Connecticut was designed to retaliate against New York. William Wirt's peroration enlarged on the theme that these "three states are almost on the verge of war". 9 Wheat. 184. For popular response to the *Gibbons* decision see: 1 Warren, *The Supreme Court in United States History* 615.

NOTE

The Chief Justice regarded "inspection laws, quarantine laws, health laws of every description, as well as laws for regulating the internal commerce of a State, and those which respect turnpike roads, ferries, etc." as component parts of "that immense mass of legislation, which embraces everything within the territory of a State, not surrendered to the general government." According to Justice Story, such laws "are not so much regulations of commerce as of police" and the powers exercised in their enactment "are entirely distinct in their nature from that to regulate commerce". Story on the Constitution (1833), § 1066. In what sense these powers, when applied to interstate or foreign commerce, are entirely distinct from the power to regulate such commerce was not made clear, but doctrinal foundations were thus laid which could enable the Court to sustain certain state laws affecting commerce while asserting that the power to regulate such commerce was vested exclusively in the national government. Marshall actually applied the "police power" view in only one case, which follows.

WILLSON v. BLACK-BIRD CREEK MARSH CO., 27 U.S. (2 Pet.) 245 (1829). The legislature of Delaware authorized a company owning marshy lands along Black Bird Creek to dam and bank the creek with a view to improving their lands. The creek, which was navigable, flowed into the Delaware, but was described by counsel for the company as "one of those sluggish, reptile streams, that do not run but creep, and which wherever it passes, spreads its venom, and destroys the health of all those who inhabit its marshes." The owners of a sloop, licensed and enrolled under the navigation laws of the United States, broke the dam in order to secure passage for their vessel. The company sued for the resulting damage and defendants claimed that since the dam obstructed navigation, the state law authorizing it was in violation of the commerce clause.

Chief Justice Marshall wrote a brief unanimous opinion for the Court containing the following observations: "The act of assembly by which the plaintiffs were authorized to construct their dam, shows plainly that this is one of those many creeks, passing through a deep, level marsh adjoining the Delaware, up which the tide flows for some distance. The value of the property on its banks must be enhanced by excluding the water from the marsh, and the health of the inhabitants probably improved. Measures calculated to produce these objects, provided they do not come into collision with the powers of the general government, are undoubtedly within those which are reserved to the States. . . . If congress had passed any act which bore upon the case; any act in execution of the power to regulate commerce, the object of which was to control State legislation over those small navigable creeks into which the tide flows, and which abound throughout the lower country of the middle and southern States; we should feel not much difficulty in saying that a state law coming in conflict with such act would be void. But congress has passed no such act. The repugnancy of the law of Delaware to the Constitution is placed entirely on its repugnancy to the power to regulate commerce with foreign nations and among the several States; a power which has not been so exercised as to affect the question. We do not think that the act [authorizing the dam] can, under all the circumstances of the case, be considered as repugnant to the power to regulate commerce in its dormant state, or as being in conflict with any law passed on the subject."

B.   Power of Congress to Regulate Interstate Commerce— Exclusive or Concurrent

For more than half a century after *Gibbons v. Ogden*, nearly all of the litigation under the commerce clause was concerned with the constitutionality of state rather than national laws. Crucial to the decision of challenges to state legislation was resolution of the issue that Marshall raised but did not decide in *Gibbons:* Was the grant of power to Congress exclusive? If so, a sharp line had to be drawn between the commerce that could be regulated by Congress and that the states could regulate because a determination that one had the power was also a determination that the other did not.

In order to understand the dispute over this issue—that had a substantial impact on early determinations by the Court with respect to the scope of national power—it is necessary at this point to examine some early cases involving the scope of state power to regulate and to tax—subjects that will be pursued in detail in Chapter 5.

THE LICENSE CASES, 46 U.S. (5 How.) 504 (1847). Roger Taney, appointed Chief Justice by President Jackson in 1836, attacked the view Marshall appeared to support, that the grant of power to Congress was exclusive. These cases sharply posed the issue. State laws requiring licenses to sell intoxicating liquor were challenged by sellers who brought liquor from outside the state. A unanimous Court sustained these laws but produced six opinions (covering sixty pages) giving differing reasons for the result. Chief Justice Taney summarized his view as follows:

"It is well known that upon this subject a difference of opinion has existed, and still exists, among the members of this court. But with every respect for the opinion of my brethren with whom I do not agree, it appears to me to be very clear, that the mere grant of power to the general government cannot, upon any just principles of construction, be construed to be an absolute prohibition to exercise of any power over the same subject by the States. The controlling and supreme power over commerce with foreign nations and the several States is undoubtedly conferred upon Congress. Yet, in my judgment, the State may nevertheless, for the safety or convenience of trade, or for the protection of the health of its citizens, make regulations of commerce for its own ports and harbours, and for its own territory; and such regulations are valid unless they come in conflict with a law of Congress."

Taney's opinion was vigorously seconded by Mr. Justice Catron, who wrote:

"... So minute and complicated are the wants of commerce when it reaches its port of destination, that even the State legislatures have been incapable of providing suitable means for its regulation between ship and shore, and therefore charters, granted by the State legislatures, have conferred the power on city corporations. Owing to situation and climate, every port and place where commerce enters a State must have peculiarity in its regulations; and these it would be exceedingly difficult for Congress to make; nor could it depute the power to corporations, as the States do. The difficulties standing in the way of Congress are fast increasing with the increase of commerce and the places where it is carried on. And where it enters States through their inland borders, by land and water, the complication is not less, and especially on the large rivers. There, too, Congress has the undisputed power to regulate commerce coming from State to State; but as every village would require special legislation, and constant additions as it grew and its commerce increased, to deal with the subject on the part of Congress would be next to impossible in practice. I admit that this condition of things does not settle the question of contested power; but it satisfactorily shows that Congress cannot do what the States have done, are doing, and must continue to do, from a controlling necessity, even should the exclusive power in Congress be maintained by our decision. And this state of things was too prominently manifest for the convention to overlook it.

"... Congress has stood by for nearly sixty years, and seen the States regulate the commerce of the whole country, more or less, at the ports of entry and at their borders, without objection, and for this court now to decide that the power did not exist in the States, and that all they had done in this respect was void from the beginning, would overthrow and annul entire codes of State legislation on the particular subject. We would by our decision expunge more State laws and city corporate regulations than Congress is likely to make in a century on the same subject, and on no better assumption than that Congress and the State legislatures had been altogether mistaken as to their respective powers for fifty years and more. If long usage, general acquiescence, and the absence of complaint can settle the interpretation of the clause in question, then it should be deemed as settled in conformity to the usage by the courts."

Mr. Justice McLean apparently felt that he avoided any question of collision with the national commercial power by concluding: "The license acts ... do not purport to be a regulation of commerce. They are essentially police laws." Mr. Justice Grier similarly disposed of the problem: "I do not consider the question of the exclusiveness of the power of Congress to regulate commerce as necessarily connected with the decision of this point;" and quoted with approval the view that "the powers which relate to merely municipal regulations, or what may more properly be called internal police, are not surrendered by the States...."

The divisions of the Court revealed in the License Cases were continued in the Passenger Cases, 48 U.S. (7 How.) 283 (1849). These cases (*Smith v. Turner, Health Commissioner of the Port of New York* and *Norris v. The City of Boston*) involved New York and Massachusetts laws imposing taxes on alien passengers arriving from foreign countries, the proceeds to be used to support a marine hospital (New York) and alien paupers (Massachusetts). It was argued that the laws were police power measures passed for protection against disease and pauperism from abroad. The Court held (5 to 4) that the laws were unconstitutional regulations of foreign commerce, but again there was no opinion subscribed to by a majority of the Justices. Of the dissenters, Taney, C.J., Daniel, J. and Nelson, J., reasserted the general view that the national commerce power is not exclusive. The fourth dissenter, Woodbury, J., argued that the commerce power was partly exclusive and partly concurrent but he based his vote largely on the ground of state police power.

Cooley v. Board of Wardens of the Port of Philadelphia

53 U.S. (12 How.) 299, 13 L.Ed. 996 (1851).

[A Pennsylvania statute of 1803 required vessels coming into or leaving the Port of Philadelphia to accept local pilots for pilotage through the Delaware River and upon failure to do so the master, owner or consignee of the vessel was made liable to pay half the pilotage fees as a penalty. Cooley was sued as the consignee of two vessels that sailed from Philadelphia without taking on a local pilot as required by the statute. The court below sustained judgment against Cooley.]

Mr. Justice Curtis[a] delivered the opinion of the court: ...

That the power to regulate commerce includes the regulation of navigation, we consider settled. And when we look to the nature of the service performed

---

[a] Justice Curtis had just been appointed to the Court by President Fillmore; he suc-   ceeded Justice Woodbury, who died in 1851.

by pilots, to the relations which that service and its compensations bear to navigation between the several States, and between the ports of the United States and foreign countries, we are brought to the conclusion, that the regulation of the qualifications of pilots, of the modes and times of offering and rendering their services, of the responsibilities which shall rest upon them, of the powers they shall possess, of the compensation they may demand, and of the penalties by which their rights and duties may be enforced, do constitute regulations of navigation, and consequently of commerce, within the just meaning of this clause of the Constitution.

The power to regulate navigation is the power to prescribe rules in conformity with which navigation must be carried on. It extends to the persons who conduct it, as well as to the instruments used. Accordingly, the first Congress assembled under the Constitution passed laws, requiring the masters of ships and vessels of the United States to be citizens of the United States, and established many rules for the government and regulation of officers and seamen. 1 Stat. at Large, 55, 131. These have been from time to time added to and changed, and we are not aware that their validity has been questioned. . . .

The act of 1789, (1 Stat. at Large, 54,) already referred to, contains a clear legislative exposition of the Constitution by the first Congress, to the effect that the power to regulate pilots was conferred on Congress by the Constitution; . . . . And a majority of the court are of opinion, that a regulation of pilots is a regulation of commerce, within the grant to Congress of the commercial power, contained in the third clause of the eighth section of the first article of the Constitution.

It becomes necessary, therefore, to consider whether this law of Pennsylvania, being a regulation of commerce, is valid.

The act of Congress of the 7th of August, 1789, sect. 4, is as follows:

"That all pilots in the bays, inlets, rivers, harbors, and ports of the United States shall continue to be regulated in conformity with the existing laws of the States, respectively, wherein such pilots may be, or with such laws as the States may respectively hereafter enact for the purpose, until further legislative provision shall be made by Congress."

If the law of Pennsylvania, now in question, had been in existence at the date of this act of Congress, we might hold it to have been adopted by Congress, and thus made a law of the United States, and so valid. Because this act does, in effect, give the force of an act of Congress, to the then existing State laws on this subject, so long as they should continue unrepealed by the State which enacted them.

But the law on which these actions are founded was not enacted till 1803. What effect then can be attributed to so much of the act of 1789, as declares, that pilots shall continue to be regulated in conformity, "with such laws as the States may respectively hereafter enact for the purpose, until further legislative provision shall be made by Congress"?

If the States were divested of the power to legislate on this subject by the grant of the commercial power to Congress, it is plain this act could not confer upon them power thus to legislate. If the Constitution excluded the States from making any law regulating commerce, certainly Congress cannot regrant, or in any manner reconvey to the States that power. And yet this act of 1789 gives its sanction only to laws enacted by the States. This necessarily implies a constitutional power to legislate; for only a rule created by the sovereign power of a State acting in its legislative capacity, can be deemed a law, enacted by a State; and if the State has so limited its sovereign power that it no longer extends to a particular subject, manifestly it cannot, in any proper sense, be said to enact laws thereon. Entertaining these views we are brought directly and unavoidably to the consideration of the question, whether the grant of the commercial power to Congress, did per se deprive the States of all power to regulate pilots. This question has never been decided by this court, nor, in our judgment, has any case depending upon all the considerations which must govern this one, come before this court. The grant of commercial power to Congress does not contain any terms which expressly exclude the States from exercising an authority over its subject-matter. If they are excluded it must be because the nature of the power, thus granted to Congress, requires that a similar authority should not exist in the States. If it were conceded on the one side, that the nature of this power, like that to legislate for the District of Columbia, is absolutely and totally repugnant to the existence of similar power in the States, probably no one would deny that the grant of the power to Congress, as effectually and perfectly excludes the States from all future legislation on the subject, as if express words had been used to exclude them. And on the other hand, if it were admitted that the existence of this power in Congress, like the power of taxation, is compatible with the existence of a similar power in the States, then it would be in conformity with the contemporary exposition of the Constitution, (Federalist, No. 32,) and with the judicial construction, given from time to time by this court, after the most deliberate consideration, to hold that the mere grant of such a power to Congress, did not imply a prohibition on the States to exercise the same power; that it is not the mere existence of such a power, but its exercise by Congress, which may be incompatible with the exercise of the same power by the States, and that the States may legislate in the absence of congressional regulations. Sturges v. Crowninshield, 4 Wheat. 122; Houston v. Moore, 5 Wheat. 1; Willson v. Black–Bird Creek Marsh Co., 2 Peters 245.

The diversities of opinion, therefore, which have existed on this subject, have arisen from the different views taken of the nature of this power. But when the nature of a power like this is spoken of, when it is said that the nature of the power requires that it should be exercised exclusively by Congress, it must be intended to refer to the subjects of that power, and to say they are of such a nature as to require exclusive legislation by Congress. Now the power to regulate commerce embraces a vast field, containing not only many, but exceedingly various subjects, quite unlike in their nature; some imperatively demanding a single uniform rule, operating equally on the commerce of the United States in every port; and some, like the subject now in question, as imperatively demanding that diversity, which alone can meet the local necessities of navigation.

Either absolutely to affirm, or deny that the nature of this power requires exclusive legislation by Congress, is to lose sight of the nature of the subjects of this power, and to assert concerning all of them, what is really applicable but to a part. Whatever subjects of this power are in their nature national, or admit only of one uniform system, or plan of regulation, may justly be said to be of such a nature as to require exclusive legislation by Congress. That this cannot be affirmed of laws for the regulation of pilots and pilotage is plain. The act of 1789 contains a clear and authoritative declaration by the first Congress, that the nature of this subject is such, that until Congress should find it necessary to exert its power, it should be left to the legislation of the States; that it is local and not national; that it is likely to be the best provided for, not by one system, or plan of regulations, but by as many as the legislative discretion of the several States should deem applicable to the local peculiarities of the ports within their limits.

Viewed in this light, so much of this act of 1789 as declares that pilots shall continue to be regulated "by such laws as the States may respectively hereafter enact for that purpose," instead of being held to be inoperative, as an attempt to confer on the States a power to legislate, of which the Constitution had deprived them, is allowed an appropriate and important signification. It manifests the understanding of Congress, at the outset of the government, that the nature of this subject is not such as to require its exclusive legislation. The practice of the States, and of the national government, has been in conformity with this declaration, from the origin of the national government to this time; and the nature of the subject when examined is such as to leave no doubt of the superior fitness and propriety, not to say the absolute necessity, of different systems of regulation, drawn from local knowledge and experience, and conformed to local wants. How then can we say, that by the mere grant of power to regulate commerce, the States are deprived of all the power to legislate on this subject, because from the nature of the power the legislation of Congress must be exclusive. This would be to affirm that the nature of the power is in any case, something different from the nature of the subject to which, in such case, the power extends, and that the nature of the power necessarily demands, in all cases, exclusive legislation by Congress, while the nature of one of the subjects of that power, not only does not require such exclusive legislation, but may be best provided for by many different systems enacted by the States, in conformity with the circumstances of the ports within their limits. In construing an instrument designed for the formation of a government, and in determining the extent of one of its important grants of power to legislate, we can make no such distinction between the nature of the power and the nature of the subject on which that power was intended practically to operate, nor consider the grant more extensive by affirming of the power, what is not true of its subject now in question.

It is the opinion of a majority of the court that the mere grant to Congress of the power to regulate commerce, did not deprive the States of power to regulate pilots, and that although Congress had legislated on this subject, its legislation manifests an intention, with a single exception, not to regulate this subject, but to leave its regulation to the several States. To these precise questions, which are all we are called on to decide, this opinion must be understood to be confined. It does not extend to the question what other subjects, under the commercial power, are within the exclusive control of Congress, or may be regulated by the States in the absence of all congressional legislation; nor to the general question how far any regulation of a subject by Congress may be deemed to operate as an exclusion of all legislation by the States upon the same subject. We decide the precise questions before us, upon what we deem sound principles, applicable to this particular subject in the state in which the legislation of Congress has left it. We go no further. . . .

Judgment affirmed.

[McLean and Wayne, JJ., dissented; Daniel, J., concurred for other reasons.]

QUESTIONS

(1) The *Cooley* "rule" has become famous in constitutional law; we shall meet it repeatedly in subsequent cases. What solution did it offer to the controversy over whether or not the commerce power was exclusive?

(2) The majority of the Court concluded that the pilot regulations did not deal with one of those "*subjects*" of the commerce power which "*are in their nature national, or admit only of one uniform system, or plan of regulation.*" Do

you see any reason for this conclusion other than the fact that Congress had expressly left the matter to the states? Would the result apparently have been different if Congress had said nothing on the subject?

(3) For an excellent discussion of early commerce clause theory, see Ribble, *State and National Power Over Commerce* (1937).

SUSTAINING STATE POWER TO REGULATE BY DEFINING COMMERCE AS INTRASTATE

Despite the compromise position enunciated in *Cooley,* the Court was still most comfortable with the proposition that the states could regulate and tax commerce which was intrastate and the Congress could regulate that commerce which was interstate. Full acceptance of such a position was made difficult, if not impossible, by the fact that except for water transportation Congress did not attempt to regulate much of either transportation or production and trade prior to the adoption of the Interstate Commerce Act in 1887 and the Sherman Anti–Trust Act in 1890. Railroads spread across the country. Industrialization led to increased commerce and increased concentration of industrial power in a few monopolies. Often the alternative to state regulation was no regulation. Hence, the constant pressure was to find a basis for sustaining the regulations of the states. In the process the Court wrote opinions sustaining state regulations that at the turn of the century were to be used to invalidate federal regulations as Congress began the long trend toward federal regulation of the economy.

A major portion of the Court's attention was given to marking out the boundaries between intrastate and interstate commerce. The easiest way to sustain a state regulation or tax without having to face the doctrinal battles only partially put to rest in *Cooley* was to define the underlying activity either as not constituting commerce or as not being interstate.

The Court early appeared to equate commerce with movement. In Hannibal & St. Joseph R.R. Co. v. Husen, 95 U.S. 465, 470 (1878), the Court, in holding invalid a state regulation forbidding the driving into or through the state of cattle from certain places during several months of the year, said: "Transportation is essential to commerce, or rather it is commerce itself: and every obstacle to it, or burden laid upon it by legislative authority, is regulation."

The determination that movement was essential to interstate commerce led the Court to take a generous view of the power of Congress over water transportation. In The Daniel Ball, 77 U.S. (10 Wall.) 557 (1871), e.g., the Court upheld the power of Congress to license a vessel operating, and capable of operating, only on a river wholly within the state of Michigan because the ship carried goods destined to and brought from points outside the state. But it also led naturally to the conclusion that the insurance business and such activities as farming, manufacturing, and mining were purely local, did not constitute interstate commerce, and hence were subject to state regulation and taxation. The following three cases illustrate the Court's approach during this period.

PAUL v. VIRGINIA, 75 U.S. (8 Wall.) 168 (1868). An agent of New York insurance companies was convicted of soliciting business in Virginia without complying with a Virginia statute requiring the agents of out-of-state insurance companies to obtain a license and deposit bonds with the state treasurer. The Court unanimously sustained the statute. Mr. Justice Field's opinion disposed of the commerce clause as follows:

"Issuing a policy of insurance is not a transaction of commerce. The policies are simple contracts of indemnity against loss by fire, entered into between the corporations and the assured, for a consideration paid by the latter. These contracts are not articles of commerce in any proper meaning of the word. They are not subjects of trade and barter offered in the market as something having an existence and value independent of the parties to them. They are not commodities to be shipped or forwarded from one State to another, and then put up for sale. They are like other personal contracts between parties which are completed by their signature and the transfer of the consideration. Such contracts are not interstate transactions, though the parties may be domiciled in different States. The policies do not take effect—are not executed contracts—until delivered by the agent in Virginia. They are, then, local transactions, and are governed by the local law. They do not constitute a part of the commerce between the States any more than a contract for the purchase and sale of goods in Virginia by a citizen of New York whilst in Virginia would constitute a portion of such commerce...."

COE v. TOWN OF ERROL, 116 U.S. 517 (1886). Coe cut logs in the forests of New Hampshire and, in preparation for floating them to Maine by way of the Androscoggin River, placed them on the banks of a stream in the New Hampshire town of Errol. While the logs were in Errol, they were assessed under the town's general property tax. The Court unanimously rejected an attack upon the tax; Justice Bradley wrote:

"... It seems to us untenable to hold that a crop or a herd is exempt from taxation merely because it is, by its owner, intended for exportation. If such were the rule in many States there would be nothing but the lands and real estate to bear the taxes. Some of the Western States produce very little except wheat and corn, most of which is intended for export; and so of cotton in the Southern States. Certainly, as long as these products are on the lands which produce them, they are part of the general property of the State. And so we think they continue to be until they have entered upon their final journey for leaving the State and going into another State. It is true, it was said in the case of The Daniel Ball, 10 Wall. 557, 565: 'Whenever a commodity has begun to move as an article of trade from one State to another, commerce in that commodity between the States has commenced.' But this movement does not begin until the articles have been shipped or started for transportation from the one State to the other. The carrying of them in carts or other vehicles, or even floating them, to the depot where the journey is to commence, is no part of that journey. That is all preliminary work, performed for the purpose of putting the property in a state of preparation and readiness for transportation. Until actually launched on its way to another State, or committed to a common carrier for transportation to such State, its destination is not fixed and certain. It may be sold or otherwise disposed of within the State, and never put in course of transportation out of the State. Carrying it from the farm, or the forest, to the depot, is only an interior movement of the property, entirely within the State, for the purpose, it is true, but only for the purpose, of putting it into a course of exportation; it is no part of the exportation itself. Until shipped or started on its final journey out of the State its exportation is a matter altogether in fieri, and not at all a fixed and certain thing...."

KIDD v. PEARSON, 128 U.S. 1 (1888). An Iowa distillery which sold all of its output in other states was confronted with an Iowa statute prohibiting the manufacture of intoxicating beverages. The Court unanimously sustained the law. In answering the contention that this application of the Iowa statute violated the commerce clause, Justice Lamar wrote:

"No distinction is more popular to the common mind, or more clearly expressed in economic and political literature, than that between manufactures and commerce. Manufacture is transformation—the fashioning of raw materials into a change of form for use. The functions of commerce are different. The buying and selling and the transportation incidental thereto constitute commerce; and the regulation of commerce in the constitutional sense embraces the regulation at least of such transportation. The legal definition of the term, as given by this court in County of Mobile v. Kimball, 102 U.S. 691, 702, is as follows: 'Commerce with foreign countries, and among the States, strictly considered, consists in intercourse and traffic, including in these terms navigation, and the transportation and transit of persons and property, as well as the purchase, sale, and exchange of commodities.' If it be held that the term includes the regulation of all such manufactures as are intended to be the subject of commercial transactions in the future, it is impossible to deny that it would also include all productive industries that contemplate the same thing. The result would be that Congress would be invested, to the exclusion of the States, with the power to regulate, not only manufactures, but also agriculture, horticulture, stock raising, domestic fisheries, mining—in short, every branch of human industry. For is there one of them that does not contemplate, more or less clearly, an interstate or foreign market? Does not the wheat grower of the Northwest, and the cotton planter of the South, plant, cultivate, and harvest his crop with an eye on the prices at Liverpool, New York, and Chicago? The power being vested in Congress and denied to the States, it would follow as an inevitable result that the duty would devolve on Congress to regulate all of these delicate, multiform, and vital interests—interests which in their nature are and must be, local in all the details of their successful management."

POWER OF CONGRESS TO CONSENT TO STATE REGULATION OF INTERSTATE COMMERCE

In *Cooley,* it will be remembered, the Court said: "If the Constitution excluded the States from making any law regulating commerce, certainly Congress cannot regrant, or in any manner reconvey to the States that power." By the 1890s, however, the Court had hit upon a theory that would permit Congress to redefine the distribution of power as marked out by the courts. In Leisy v. Hardin, 135 U.S. 100 (1890), the Court in holding that the state could not forbid the sale of liquor brought from another state while in the original package, said:

"Whenever ... a particular power of the general government is one which must necessarily be exercised by it, and Congress remains silent, this is not only not a concession that the powers reserved by the States may be exerted as if the specific power had not been elsewhere reposed, but, on the contrary, the only legitimate conclusion is that the general government intended that power should not be affirmatively exercised, and the action of the States cannot be permitted to effect that which would be incompatible with such intention. Hence, inasmuch as interstate commerce, consisting in the transportation, purchase, sale and exchange of commodities, is national in its character, and must be governed by a uniform system, so long as Congress does not pass any law to regulate it, or allowing the States so to do, it thereby indicates its will that such commerce shall be free and untrammelled.... Brown v. Houston, 114 U.S. 622, 631; Wabash, St. Louis & c. Railway v. Illinois, 118 U.S. 557...."

Congress took the hint and enacted the Wilson Act (26 Stat. 313) of 1890, providing that all intoxicating liquo s transported into any state or remaining therein for use, sale or storage, should "upon arrival in such state" be subject to the state's laws "enacted in the exercise of its police powers," to the same extent as though such liquor had been produced in the state and should "not be exempt therefrom by reason of being introduced therein in original packages or otherwise." The constitutionality of this statute was sustained in Wilkerson v. Rahrer, 140 U.S. 545 (1891), over the objection that as applied to liquor imported and remaining in the original packages it attempted an invalid delegation of the national commerce power to the states. The Court (per Fuller, C.J.) said: "Congress can neither delegate its own powers nor enlarge those of a state," but "Congress has not attempted to delegate the power to regulate commerce, or to exercise any power reserved to the states, or to grant a power not possessed by the states, or to adopt state laws. It has taken its own course and made its own regulation, applying to these subjects of interstate commerce one common rule, whose uniformity is not affected by variations in state laws in dealing with such property." Since the Wilson Act did not authorize state prohibition of importation, but only prohibition of sales after importation, Congress passed the Webb–Kenyon Act (37 Stat. 699) of 1913 forbidding the transportation in interstate commerce of liquor intended to be used contrary to any law of the state of destination. This Act was sustained in Clark Distilling Co. v. Western Maryland R. Co., 242 U.S. 311 (1917).

See W. Cohen, *Congressional Power to Validate Unconstitutional State Laws: A Forgotten Solution to an Old Enigma*, 35 Stan.L.Rev. 387 (1983); Bikle, *The Silence of Congress*, 41 Harv.L.Rev. 200 (1927).

SECTION 3.   THE SCOPE OF NATIONAL POWER TODAY

A.   THE COMMERCE POWER

Introduction. An evil genius choosing a time for a new constitution that would tax its capacity for adaptability could hardly have selected a more trying time than 1789. Though some foresaw that the coastal settlements might expand across the continent, the framers had no inkling of the impact of the industrial revolution. The power of steam was soon harnessed for steamships and for railroads, which by 1869 spanned the continent. This new source of power also led to undreamed expansion of industrial production. The new Constitution thus was established on the eve of the great transition from an economy based on agriculture and handicraft to an economy based on power, machines and factories. The new forms of production were accompanied by the development of legal devices to organize and concentrate wealth: the business corporation and their combination through "trusts."

Correlated with this account, Congress did not often exercise its commerce power during most of the nineteenth century, but began to do so in significant ways starting with railroad regulation in the 1887 Interstate Commerce Act, followed closely by the Sherman Antitrust Act in 1890. The quantity of congressional commerce regulation jumped sharply beginning with Franklin Roosevelt's New Deal responses to the Great Depression and has continued at high levels. In response, the Supreme Court's commerce clause decisions after Gibbons v. Ogden, supra p. 167, have fallen into three roughly 50-year periods. Until the late 1800's the Court primarily addressed, not Congress' power to legislate, but state power to regulate where Congress might have. Then, from the beginning of significant congressional regulation of the incidents of nation-wide transportation systems and industrial production until 1936, the Court adopted a variety of approaches simultaneously to limit perceived excesses of the commerce power and approve perceived needful uses. Finally, from 1937 until at least the 1995 decision in United States v. Lopez presented as a principal case hereafter, the Court largely abandoned the attempt to restrain congressional power to regulate the economy.

In lieu of more extensive treatment of these developments, the following summary tracing the Court's precedents is drawn from a portion of Justice Kennedy's concurring opinion in *United States v. Lopez*, ___ U.S. ___, ___–___, 115 S.Ct. 1624, 1634–37, augmented with footnote annotations by the editors:

"Chief Justice Marshall announced that the national authority reaches 'that commerce which concerns more States than one' and that the commerce power 'is complete in itself, may be exercised to its utmost extent, and acknowledges no limitations, other than are prescribed in the constitution.' Gibbons v. Ogden, 22 U.S. (9 Wheat.) 1, 194, 196, 6 L.Ed. 23 (1824). His statements can be understood now as an early and authoritative recognition that the Commerce Clause grants Congress extensive power and ample discretion to determine its appropriate exercise. The progression of our Commerce Clause cases from *Gibbons* to the present was not marked, however, by a coherent or consistent course of interpretation; for neither the course of technological advance nor the foundational principles for the jurisprudence itself were self-evident to the courts that sought to resolve contemporary disputes by enduring principles.

"Furthermore, for almost a century after the adoption of the Constitution, the Court's Commerce Clause decisions did not concern the authority of Congress to legislate. Rather, the Court faced the related but quite distinct question of the authority of the States to regulate matters that would be within the commerce power had Congress chosen to act. The simple fact was that in the early years of the Republic, Congress seldom perceived the necessity to exercise its power in circumstances where its authority would be called into question....

. . .

"One approach the Court used to inquire into the lawfulness of state authority was to draw content-based or subject-matter distinctions, thus defining by semantic or formalistic categories those activities that were commerce and those that were not. For instance, in deciding that a State could prohibit the in-state manufacture of liquor intended for out-of-state shipment, it distinguished between manufacture and commerce.... Kidd v. Pearson, 128 U.S. 1, 20 (1888). Though that approach likely would not have survived even if confined to the question of a State's authority to enact legislation, it was not at all propitious when applied to the quite different question of what subjects were within the reach of the national power when Congress chose to exercise it.

"This became evident when the Court began to confront federal economic regulation enacted in response to the rapid industrial development in the late 19th century. Thus, it relied upon the manufacture-commerce dichotomy in United States v. E.C. Knight Co., 156 U.S. 1 (1895), where a manufacturers' combination controlling some 98% of the Nation's domestic sugar refining capacity was held to be outside the reach of the Sherman Act. Conspiracies to control manufacture, agriculture, mining, production, wages, or prices, the Court explained, had too "indirect" an effect on interstate commerce.[a] Id., at

[a] The Court worried "that, if the national power extends to all contracts and combinations in manufacture, agriculture, mining, and other productive industries, whose ultimate result may affect external commerce, comparatively little of business operations

16. And in Adair v. United States, 208 U.S. 161 (1908), the Court rejected the view that the commerce power might extend to activities that, although local in the sense of having originated within a single state, nevertheless had a practical effect on interstate commercial activity. The Court concluded that there was not a "legal or logical connection . . . between an employe's membership in a labor organization and the carrying on of interstate commerce," id., at 178, and struck down a federal statute forbidding the discharge of an employee because of his membership in a labor organization. . . .

"Even before the Court committed itself to sustaining federal legislation on broad principles of economic practicality, it found it necessary to depart from these decisions. The Court disavowed E.C. Knight's reliance on the manufacturing-commerce distinction in Standard Oil Co. of New Jersey v. United States, 221 U.S. 1 (1911), declaring that approach 'unsound.' The Court likewise rejected the rationale of Adair when it decided, in Texas & New Orleans R. Co. v. Railway Clerks, 281 U.S. 548, 570–571 (1930), that Congress had the power to regulate matters pertaining to the organization of railroad workers.

"In another line of cases, the Court addressed Congress' efforts to impede local activities it considered undesirable by prohibiting the interstate movement of some essential element. In the Lottery Case, 188 U.S. 321 (1903), the Court rejected the argument that Congress lacked power to prohibit the interstate movement of lottery tickets because it had power only to regulate, not to prohibit. See also Hipolite Egg Co. v. United States, 220 U.S. 45 (1911); Hoke v. United States, 227 U.S. 308 (1913). In Hammer v. Dagenhart, 247 U.S. 251 (1918), however, the Court insisted that the power to regulate commerce 'is directly the contrary of the assumed right to forbid commerce from moving,' id., at 269–270, and struck down a prohibition on the interstate transportation of goods manufactured in violation of child labor laws.[b]

and affairs would be left for state control." In Addyston Pipe & Steel Co. v. United States, 175 U.S. 211 (1899), however, the Court held that the Sherman Act could apply to a conspiracy among companies engaged in the manufacture, sale, and transportation of iron pipe to divide sales territory and arrange for noncompetitive bidding, because, unlike Knight, the agreement directly restrained not only the manufacture but also the purchase, sale or exchange of the manufactured commodity among the states. And in Northern Securities Co. v. United States, 193 U.S. 197 (1904), the Court held that the Act could be applied to break up joint control of competing railroads by a holding company, because this directly embraced interstate commerce.

 [b] The Court distinguished the cases involving interstate transport of lottery tickets, impure food and drugs (Hipolite Egg), women for purposes of prostitution and debauchery (Hoke), and liquor (Clark Distilling Co. v. Western Maryland R. Co., 242 U.S. 311 (1917)), as "instances . . . of interstate transportation . . . necessary to the accomplishment of harmful results[,]" whereas in Hammer "[t]he act in its effect does not regulate transportation among the states, but aims to standardize the ages at which children may be employed in mining and manufacturing

within the states. The goods shipped are of themselves harmless. . . ." The Court also rejected the argument that the act was a valid attempt to protect business in states with high labor standards from unfair interstate competition resulting from production in those states permitting child labor conditions:

"The commerce clause was not intended to give to Congress a general authority to equalize such conditions. In some of the states laws have been passed fixing minimum wages for women, in others the local law regulates the hours of labor of women in various employments. Business done in such states may be at an economic disadvantage when compared with states which have no such regulations; surely this fact does not give Congress the power to deny transportation in interstate commerce to those who carry on business where the hours of labor and the rate of compensation for women have not been fixed by a standard in use in other states and approved by Congress. . . ."

The act was held unconstitutional as invading the reserved powers of the states.

Justice Holmes (with McKenna, Brandeis and Clarke, JJ.) dissented, saying:

"Even while it was experiencing difficulties in finding satisfactory principles in these cases, the Court was pursuing a more sustainable and practical approach in other lines of decisions, particularly those involving the regulation of railroad rates. In the Minnesota Rate Cases, 230 U.S. 352 (1913), the Court upheld a state rate order, but observed that Congress might be empowered to regulate in this area if 'by reason of the interblending of the interstate and intrastate operations of interstate carriers' the regulation of interstate rates could not be maintained without restrictions on 'intrastate rates which substantially affect the former.' Id., at 432–433. And in the Shreveport Rate Cases, 234 U.S. 342 (1914), the Court upheld an ICC order fixing railroad rates with the explanation that congressional authority, 'extending to these interstate carriers as instruments of interstate commerce, necessarily embraces the right to control their operations in all matters having such a close and substantial relation to interstate traffic that the control is essential or appropriate to the security of that traffic, to the efficiency of the interstate service, and to the maintenance of conditions under which interstate commerce may be conducted upon fair terms and without molestation or hindrance.' "c Id., at 351.

"Even the most confined interpretation of 'commerce' would embrace transportation between the States, so the rate cases posed much less difficulty for the Court than cases involving manufacture or production. Nevertheless, the Court's recognition of the importance of a practical conception of the commerce power was not altogether confined to the rate cases. In Swift & Co. v. United States, 196 U.S. 375 (1905), the Court upheld the application of federal antitrust law to a combination of meat dealers that occurred in one State but that restrained trade in cattle 'sent for sale from a place in one State, with the expectation that they will end their transit . . . in another.' Id., at 398. The Court explained that 'commerce among the States is not a technical legal conception, but a practical one, drawn from the course of business.' Id., at 398. Chief Justice Taft followed the same approach in upholding federal regulation of stockyards in Stafford v. Wallace, 258 U.S. 495 (1922). Speaking for the

"The notion that prohibition is any less prohibition when applied to things now thought evil I do not understand. But if there is any matter upon which civilized countries have agreed—far more unanimously than they have with reference to intoxicants . . .— it is the evil of premature and excessive child labor. . . .

"But I had thought that the propriety of the exercise of a power admitted to exist in some cases was for the consideration of Congress alone and that this Court always had disavowed the right to intrude its judgment upon questions of policy or morals. It is not for this Court to pronounce when prohibition is necessary to regulation if it ever may be necessary—to say that it is permissible as against strong drink but not as against the product of ruined lives.

"The Act does not meddle with anything belonging to the States. They may regulate their internal affairs and their domestic commerce as they like. But when they seek to send their products across the State line they are no longer within their rights. If there were no Constitution and no Congress their power to cross the line would depend upon their neighbors. Under the Constitution such commerce belongs not to the States but to Congress to regulate. It may carry out its views of public policy whatever indirect effect they may have upon the activities of the States. . . ."

After *Hammer*, Congress imposed a 10% tax on net profits of factories employing child labor, which the Court invalidated as being palpably prohibitory and regulatory in a manner indistinguishable from *Hammer*, rather than being a valid tax. The Child Labor Tax Case, 259 U.S. 20 (1922).

c In order to end rate discrimination, the ICC order effectively required railroads engaged in both interstate and intrastate traffic to raise rates on intrastate hauls because proportionately higher rates it had approved were in effect for interstate hauls. The Court also said: "Wherever the interstate and intrastate transactions of carriers are so related that the government of the one involves the control of the other, it is Congress, and not the state, that is entitled to prescribe the final and dominant rule, for otherwise Congress would be denied the exercise of its constitutional authority, and the state, and not the nation, would be supreme within the national field."

Court, he rejected a 'nice and technical inquiry,' id., at 519, when the local transactions at issue could not 'be separated from the movement to which they contribute,' id., at 516.

"Reluctance of the Court to adopt that approach in all of its cases caused inconsistencies in doctrine to persist, however. In addressing New Deal legislation the Court resuscitated the abandoned abstract distinction between direct and indirect effects on interstate commerce. See Carter v. Carter Coal Co., 298 U.S. 238, 309 (1936) (Act regulating price of coal and wages and hours for miners held to have only 'secondary and indirect' effect on interstate commerce);[d] Railroad Retirement Bd. v. Alton R. Co., 295 U.S. 330 (1935) (compulsory retirement and pension plan for railroad carrier employees too 'remote from any regulation of commerce as such'); A.L.A. Schechter Poultry Corp. v. United States, 295 U.S. 495 (1935) (wage and hour law provision of National Industrial Recovery Act had 'no direct relation to interstate commerce')[e].

[d] The *Carter* case arose in the middle of the Depression at the end of the Court's most active period of assault on congressional control of the economy. It held unconstitutional the Guffey Coal Act, which sought to regulate minimum coal prices and minimum wages and maximum hours for mine workers, and in which Congress declared "that the production and distribution by producers of such coal bear upon and directly affect interstate commerce, and render regulation of production and distribution imperative for the protection of such commerce...." Justice Sutherland, for the majority, said in part:

"The proposition, often advanced and as often discredited, that the power of the federal government inherently extends to purposes affecting the nation as a whole with which the states severally cannot deal or cannot adequately deal, and the related notion that Congress, entirely apart from those powers delegated by the Constitution, may enact laws to promote the general welfare, have never been accepted but always definitely rejected by this court....

. . .

"A consideration of [many cases, including *Knight*] renders inescapable the conclusion that the effect of the labor provisions of the act, including those in respect of minimum wages, wage agreements, collective bargaining, and the Labor Board and its powers, primarily falls upon production and not upon commerce; and confirms the further resulting conclusion that production is a purely local activity. It follows that none of these essential antecedents of production constitutes a transaction in or forms any part of interstate commerce . . .

. . .

"Whether the effect of a given activity or condition is direct or indirect is not always easy to determine.... And the extent of the effect bears no logical relation to its character. The distinction between a direct and an indirect effect turns, not upon the magnitude of either the cause or the effect, but entirely upon the manner in which the effect has been brought about.... It is quite true that rules of law are sometimes qualified by considerations of degree, as the government argues. But the matter of degree has no bearing upon the question here, since that question is not—What is the *extent* of the local activity or condition, or the *extent* of the effect produced upon interstate commerce? but—What is the *relation* between the activity or condition and the effect? ...."

[e] The NIRA was perhaps the most widely heralded New Deal measure designed to stimulate recovery from the Great Depression. Schechter Poultry, a Brooklyn business that bought poultry at markets or railroad terminals within New York City and slaughtered and distributed poultry wholesale to New York dealers who resold to New York consumers, was convicted of code violations "in any transaction in or affecting foreign or interstate commerce." The evidence indicated that ninety-six per cent of the live poultry marketed in New York came from other states. The Supreme Court reversed the conviction, first, because the act had attempted an unconstitutional delegation of power to the President, and second, because as applied it exceeded the commerce power. For a unanimous Court, Chief Justice Hughes concluded that the poultry transactions involved were not "in" interstate commerce: "The poultry had come to a permanent rest within the State. It was not held, used, or sold by defendants in relation to any further transactions in interstate commerce and was not destined for transportation to other states. Hence, decisions which deal with a stream of interstate commerce—where goods come to rest within a state temporarily and are later to go forward in interstate commerce—and with the regulations of transactions involved in that practical continuity of movement, are not applicable here. See Swift & Co. v. United States, 196 U.S. 375, 387, 388; ... Stafford

"The case that seems to mark the Court's definitive commitment to the practical conception of the commerce power is NLRB v. Jones & Laughlin Steel Corp., 301 U.S. 1 (1937), where the Court sustained labor laws that applied to manufacturing facilities, making no real attempt to distinguish *Carter* . . . and *Schechter*. . . . 301 U.S., at 40–41.[f] The deference given to Congress has since been confirmed. United States v. Darby, 312 U.S. 100, 116–117 (1941), overruled Hammer v. Dagenhart, supra. And in Wickard v. Filburn, 317 U.S. 111 (1942), the Court disapproved *E.C. Knight* and the entire line of direct-indirect and manufacture-production cases, explaining that 'broader interpretations of the Commerce Clause [were] destined to supersede the earlier ones,' id., at 122,

v. Wallace, 258 U.S. 495, 519. . . ." Defendant's transactions did not "directly 'affect' interstate commerce so as to be subject to federal regulation. . . . In determining how far the federal government may go in controlling intrastate transactions upon the ground that they 'affect' interstate commerce, there is a necessary and well-established distinction between direct and indirect effects. The precise line can be drawn only as individual cases arise, but the distinction is clear in principle. . . . If the commerce clause were construed to reach all enterprises and transactions which could be said to have an indirect effect upon interstate commerce, the federal authority would embrace practically all the activities of the people and the authority of the state over its domestic concerns would exist only by sufferance of the federal government. . . ." Concurring, Justice Cardozo stated: "The law is not indifferent to considerations of degree. Activities local in their immediacy do not become interstate and national because of distant repercussions. What is near and what is distant may at times be uncertain. . . . There is no penumbra of uncertainty obscuring judgment here. To find immediacy or directness here is to find it almost everywhere. If centrifugal forces are to be isolated to the exclusion of the forces that oppose and counteract them, there will be an end to our federal system."

[f] Under the National Labor Relations Act, enacted in 1935, the newly created National Labor Relations Board ordered Jones & Laughlin to cease and desist from interfering with the right of its employees at a steel and iron manufacturing plant to organize and bargain collectively. The Court upheld the NLRB's order under the commerce power, relying in part on the notion of the Shreveport Rate Case, supra, that "intrastate activities, by reason of close and intimate relation to interstate commerce, may fall within federal control. . . ." The Court now said that the "question is necessarily one of degree" and "the fact that the employees here concerned were engaged in production is not determinative. The question remains as to the effect upon interstate commerce of the labor practice involved." As to that, the Court said:

"[T]he stoppage of [respondent's manufacturing] operations by industrial strife would have a most serious effect upon interstate commerce. In view of respondent's far-flung activities, it is idle to say that the effect would be indirect or remote. It is obvious that it would be immediate and might be catastrophic. We are asked to shut our eyes to the plainest facts of our national life and to deal with the question of direct and indirect effects in an intellectual vacuum. Because there may be but indirect and remote effects upon interstate commerce in connection with a host of local enterprises throughout the country, it does not follow that other industrial activities do not have such a close and intimate relation to interstate commerce as to make the presence of industrial strife a matter of the most urgent national concern. When industries organize themselves on a national scale making their relation to interstate commerce the dominant factor in their activities, how can it be maintained that their industrial labor relations constitute a forbidden field into which Congress may not enter when it is necessary to protect interstate commerce from the paralyzing consequences of industrial war?"

After *Jones & Laughlin* the Court sustained the application of the NLRA to a variety of smaller industrial enterprises. In National Labor Relations Board v. Fainblatt, 306 U.S. 601 (1939), involving a manufacturer who processed materials into about a thousand dozen garments a month shipped in interstate commerce, the Court said that it was not important "that the volume of the commerce here involved though substantial, was relatively small as compared with that in the cases arising under the National Labor Relations Act which have hitherto engaged our attention. The power of Congress to regulate interstate commerce is plenary and extends to all such commerce be it great or small." The Court went on to note that the garment industry was one in which relatively small units contributed in the aggregate to a vast volume of commerce and that strikes in the industry would have a substantial effect on interstate commerce.

and 'whatever terminology is used, the criterion is necessarily one of degree and must be so defined. . . .', id., at 123, n. 24. . . .''

THE ROOSEVELT COURT PLAN

The initial New Deal program had been shattered by the series of major judicial defeats suffered in the Supreme Court. Stricken down in succession were the Railroad Retirement Act of 1934, the National Industrial Recovery Act of 1933, the Agricultural Adjustment Act of 1933, and the Bituminous Coal Conservation Act of 1935. By the time of the *Carter Coal* decision of May 18, 1936, a feeling was growing within the administration that something had to be done about the Supreme Court. Actual steps awaited the election of November 1936, which returned Roosevelt to the presidency by an overwhelming majority. On February 7, 1937, the President sent to Congress a message calling for legislation to "reorganize the judicial branch"—a proposal commonly known as the court-packing plan. After dealing at some length with other less controversial problems of judicial organization, the message turned to "the question of aged or infirm judges—a subject of delicacy and yet one which requires frank discussion." The message stressed the difficulty for older men to keep up with the work of the courts, and also stated: "A lowered mental or physical vigor leads men to avoid an examination of complicated and changed conditions. Little by little, new facts become blurred through old glasses fitted, as it were, for the needs of another generation; older men, assuming that the scene is the same as it was in the past, cease to explore or inquire into the present or the future." The message then recommended that legislation provide for "the appointment of additional judges, in all Federal Courts, without exception, where there are incumbent judges of retirement age who do not choose to retire or resign." At that time six members of the Supreme Court had passed the voluntary retirement age of 70: Hughes (75), Sutherland (75), Butler (71), Brandeis (81), McReynolds (75), and Van Devanter (78).

The proposal produced a hurricane of controversy which lasted for months.[a] Opposition mounted as it became increasingly clear that the President's object was to change the judicial philosophy of the Supreme Court; on June 14, 1937, the Senate Judiciary Committee recommended rejection of the proposed legislation "as a needless, futile, and utterly dangerous abandonment of constitutional principle," Report No. 711, 75th Cong., 1st Sess. (1937). On July 22, the bill was killed by recommitment to the Judiciary Committee. During this interval, there were before the Supreme Court cases involving the constitutionality of the National Labor Relations Act and the Social Security Act, which had been enacted along with the Bituminous Coal Act in the summer of 1935; National Labor Relations Board v. Jones & Laughlin Steel Corp., supra, was argued February 10, 11, 1937, and decided April 12; Chas. C. Steward Machine Co. v. Davis, 301 U.S. 548, was argued April 8, 9, 1937, and decided May 24.

[a] For subsequent developments, and especially the generalship of Chief Justice Hughes in meeting this challenge, see Pusey, *Charles Evans Hughes* (1951). Cf. Robert H. Jackson, *The Struggle for Judicial Supremacy*, 176 et seq. (1941); Leuchtenburg, *The Origins of Franklin D. Roosevelt's "Court-Packing" Plan*, 1966 Supreme Court Review 347 (1966). In answer to the charge that this proposal produced a "switch in time that saved nine", Justice Roberts left a paper with Justice Frankfurter for posthumous publication, which shows that Justice Roberts's vote to sustain state minimum wage legislation in West Coast Hotel Co. v. Parrish, 300 U.S. 379 (1937), although announced on March 29, 1937, reflected a vote taken in conference on December 19, 1936. See Frankfurter, Mr. Justice Roberts, 104 U.Pa.L.Rev. 311, 314, 315 (1955). This memorandum does not deal with the relationship between the *Carter* case, supra, and the *Jones & Laughlin* case, supra.

In both cases the legislation was held valid by votes of 5 to 4.

President Roosevelt lost the battle but won the war. Within four years he was given the opportunity to replace seven members of the Court. In 1937 Justice Van Devanter retired and was succeeded by Senator Hugo Black. The following year Justice Sutherland retired, to be succeeded by Solicitor General Stanley Reed. In 1939, Justice Cardozo was succeeded by Professor Felix Frankfurter, Justice Brandeis by William O. Douglas, Chairman of the Securities and Exchange Commission, and Justice Butler by Attorney General Frank Murphy. In 1941, Justice McReynolds resigned and was succeeded by Senator James Byrnes. Later in 1941, Chief Justice Hughes resigned, Justice Stone was made Chief Justice, and Attorney General Robert H. Jackson was added to the Court.

By 1942 the Court had dramatically reversed itself, sustaining in their broadest applications the National Labor Relations Act, the Fair Labor Standards Act, and the Agricultural Adjustment Act. As we will see in later chapters, the Court also changed its interpretation of the due process and equal protection clauses so as to increase substantially governmental regulatory powers over economic matters.

THE POST–DEPRESSION COMMERCE POWER

As Justice Kennedy hints in his survey, United States v. Darby, 312 U.S. 100 (1941), and Wickard v. Filburn, 317 U.S. 111 (1942), confirmed a sweepingly deferential approach to Congress' exercise of its commerce power. The way these twin pillars of modern commerce clause doctrine did so is noteworthy.

Darby sustained application of the Fair Labor Standards Act of 1938, first, in § 15(a)(1), to prohibit the shipment in interstate commerce of lumber manufactured by employees whose wages were less than a prescribed minimum or whose weekly hours of labor at that wage were greater than a prescribed maximum, and, second, in § 15(a)(2), to prohibit employment in the production of goods "for interstate commerce" at other than the prescribed wages and hours. As to § 15(a)(1), the Court rejected the contention "that while the prohibition is nominally a regulation of [interstate] commerce its motive or purpose is regulation of wages and hours of persons engaged in manufacture, the control of which has been reserved to the states"—that "under the guise of a regulation of interstate commerce, it undertakes to regulate wages and hours within the state contrary to the policy of the state which has elected to leave them unregulated." Justice Stone's opinion for the Court responded:

> "The motive and purpose of the present regulation are plainly to make effective the Congressional conception of public policy that interstate commerce should not be made the instrument of competition in the distribution of goods produced under substandard labor conditions, which competition is injurious to the commerce and to the states from and to which the commerce flows. The motive and purpose of a regulation of interstate commerce are matters for the legislative judgment upon the exercise of which the Constitution places no restriction and over which the courts are given no control. McCray v. United States, 195 U.S. 27; Sonzinsky v. United States, 300 U.S. 506, 513, and cases cited...."

Since the "reasoning and conclusion of the Court's opinion [in Hammer v. Dagenhart] cannot be reconciled with the conclusion which we have reached, that the power of Congress under the Commerce Clause is plenary to exclude any article from interstate commerce subject only to the specific prohibitions of the Constitution[,] ... it should be and now is overruled."

As to § 15(a)(2), "the validity of the prohibition turns on ... whether the employment, under other than the prescribed labor standards, of employees engaged in the production of goods for interstate commerce is so related to the commerce and so affects it as to be within the reach of the power of Congress to regulate it." Justice Stone gave two answers. First, "Congress, having by the present Act adopted the policy of excluding from interstate commerce all goods produced for the commerce which do not conform to the specified labor standards, it may choose the means reasonably adapted to the attainment of the permitted end, even though they involve control of intrastate activities." Second,

"... § 15(a)(2) ... is sustainable independently of § 15(a)(1).... [T]he evils aimed at by the Act are the spread of substandard labor conditions through the use of the facilities of interstate commerce for competition by the goods so produced with those produced under the prescribed or better labor conditions; and the consequent dislocation of the commerce itself caused by the impairment or destruction of local businesses by competition made effective through interstate commerce. The Act is thus directed at the suppression of a method or kind of competition in interstate commerce which it has in effect condemned as 'unfair'....

"The means adopted by § 15(a)(2) ... is so related to the commerce and so affects it as to be within the reach of the commerce power.... Congress ... has made no distinction as to the volume or amount of shipments in the commerce or of production for commerce by any particular shipper or producer. It recognized that in present day industry, competition by a small part may affect the whole and that the total effect of the competition of many small producers may be great. See H.Rept. No. 2182, 75th Cong. 1st Sess., p. 7. The legislation aimed at a whole embraces all its parts....

. . .

"Our conclusion is unaffected by the Tenth Amendment which provides: 'The powers not delegated to the United States by the Constitution, nor prohibited by it to the States, are reserved to the States respectively, or to the people'. The amendment states but a truism that all is retained which has not been surrendered...."

The decision in Wickard v. Filburn, a suit to enjoin the marketing penalty imposed by the Agricultural Adjustment Act of 1938 upon that part of Filburn's 1941 wheat crop that was available for marketing in excess of the marketing quota established for his farm, went further. As Justice Jackson's opinion for the Court said, the commerce power challenge raised "would merit little consideration since our decision in United States v. Darby, 312 U.S. 100, sustaining the federal power to regulate production of goods for commerce except for the fact that this Act extends federal regulation to production not intended in any part for commerce but wholly for consumption on the farm." The opinion contained these observations:

"The Court's recognition of the relevance of the economic effects in the application of the Commerce Clause ... has made the mechanical application of legal formulas no longer feasible. Once an economic measure of the reach of the power granted to Congress in the Commerce Clause is accepted, questions of federal power cannot be decided simply by finding the activity in question to be 'production' nor can consideration of its economic effects be foreclosed by calling them 'indirect.' ...

"... [E]ven if appellee's activity be local and though it may not be regarded as commerce, it may still, whatever its nature, be reached by Congress if it exerts a substantial economic effect on interstate commerce and this irrespective of whether such effect is what might at some earlier time have been defined as 'direct' or 'indirect.' "

The Court noted that "[c]ommerce among the states in wheat is large and important[,]" that the "wheat industry has been a problem industry for some years[,]" and that "[t]he effect of consumption of homegrown wheat on interstate commerce is due to the fact that it constitutes the most variable factor in the disappearance of the wheat crop." The Court continued:

". . . The effect of the statute before us is to restrict the amount which may be produced for market and the extent as well to which one may forestall resort to the market by producing to meet his own needs. That appellee's own contribution to the demand for wheat may be trivial by itself is not enough to remove him from the scope of federal regulation where, as here, his contribution, taken together with that of many others similarly situated, is far from trivial. . . .

". . . One of the primary purposes of the Act . . . was to increase the market price of wheat and to that end to limit the volume thereof that could affect the market. It can hardly be denied that a factor of such volume and variability as home-consumed wheat would have a substantial influence on price and market conditions. This may arise because being in marketable condition such wheat overhangs the market and if induced by rising prices tends to flow into the market and check price increases. But if we assume that it is never marketed, it supplies a need of the man who grew it which would otherwise be reflected by purchases in the open market. Home-grown wheat in this sense competes with wheat in commerce. The stimulation of commerce is a use of the regulatory function quite as definitely as prohibitions or restrictions thereon. This record leaves us in no doubt that Congress may properly have considered that wheat consumed on the farm where grown if wholly outside the scheme of regulation would have a substantial effect in defeating and obstructing its purpose to stimulate trade therein at increased prices."[a]

Heart of Atlanta Motel, Inc. v. United States

379 U.S. 241, 85 S.Ct. 348, 13 L.Ed.2d 258 (1964).

[The owner of the Motel brought a declaratory judgment action, attacking the constitutionality of Title II of the Civil Rights Act of 1964. A three-judge

[a] United States v. South–Eastern Underwriters Ass'n, 322 U.S. 533 (1944), sustained the applicability of the Sherman Anti–Trust Act to the insurance business, overturning a district court decision based on Paul v. Virginia, 8 Wall. 168 (1868), that "a policy of insurance is not a transaction of commerce" and insurance contracts "are not interstate transactions, although the parties are domiciled in different states". The opinion, by Justice Black, emphasized the size of the insurance business and the extent to which companies located in one part of the country write insurance contracts for persons in other states. The opinion also stated:

"We may grant that a contract of insurance, considered as a thing apart from negoti-ation and execution, does not itself constitute interstate commerce. . . . But . . . a nation-wide business is not deprived of its interstate character merely because it is built upon sales contracts which are local in nature. Were the rule otherwise, few businesses could be said to be engaged in interstate commerce. . . .

"The power granted Congress . . . is the power to legislate concerning transactions which, reaching across state boundaries, affect the people of more states than one;—to govern affairs which the individual states, with their limited territorial jurisdictions, are not fully capable of governing."

court sustained the Act and enjoined its further violation by the Motel. An appeal was taken to the Supreme Court.]

Mr. Justice Clark delivered the opinion of the Court.

. . .

1.   THE FACTUAL BACKGROUND AND CONTENTIONS OF THE PARTIES

. . . Appellant owns and operates the Heart of Atlanta Motel which has 216 rooms available to transient guests. The motel is located on Courtland Street, two blocks from downtown Peachtree Street. It is readily accessible to interstate highways 75 and 85 and state highways 23 and 41. Appellant solicits patronage from outside the State of Georgia through various national advertising media, including magazines of national circulation; it maintains over 50 billboards and highway signs within the State, soliciting patronage for the motel; it accepts convention trade from outside Georgia and approximately 75% of its registered guests are from out of State. Prior to passage of the Act the motel had followed a practice of refusing to rent rooms to Negroes, and it alleged that it intended to continue to do so. In an effort to perpetuate that policy this suit was filed.

. . .

Since Title II is the only portion under attack here, we confine our consideration to those public accommodation provisions.

3.   TITLE II OF THE ACT

This Title is divided into seven sections beginning with § 201(a) which provides that:

> "All persons shall be entitled to the full and equal enjoyment of the goods, services, facilities, privileges, advantages, and accommodations of any place of public accommodation, as defined in this section, without discrimination or segregation on the ground of race, color, religion, or national origin."

There are listed in § 201(b) four classes of business establishments, each of which "serves the public" and "is a place of public accommodation" within the meaning of § 201(a) "if its operations affect commerce, or if discrimination or segregation by it is supported by State action." The covered establishments are:

> "(1) any inn, hotel, motel, or other establishment which provides lodging to transient guests, other than an establishment located within a building which contains not more than five rooms for rent or hire and which is actually occupied by the proprietor of such establishment as his residence; . . . ."

Section 201(c) defines the phrase "affect commerce" as applied to the above establishments. It first declares that "any inn, hotel, motel, or other establishment which provides lodging to transient guests" affects commerce *per se*. . . .

4.   APPLICATION OF TITLE II TO HEART OF ATLANTA MOTEL

It is admitted that the operation of the motel brings it within the provisions of § 201(a) of the Act and that appellant refused to provide lodging for transient Negroes because of their race or color and that it intends to continue that policy unless restrained.

The sole question posed is, therefore, the constitutionality of the Civil Rights Act of 1964 as applied to these facts. The legislative history of the Act indicates that Congress based the Act on § 5 and the Equal Protection Clause of the Fourteenth Amendment as well as its power to regulate interstate commerce. . . .

The Senate Commerce Committee made it quite clear that the fundamental object of Title II was to vindicate "the deprivation of personal dignity that surely accompanies denials of equal access to public establishments." At the same time, however, it noted that such an objective has been and could be readily achieved "by congressional action based on the commerce power of the Constitution." S.Rep. No. 872, supra, at 16–17. Our study of the legislative record, made in the light of prior cases, has brought us to the conclusion that Congress possessed ample power in this regard, and we have therefore not considered the other grounds relied upon. . . .

. . .

6. THE BASIS OF CONGRESSIONAL ACTION

While the Act as adopted carried no congressional findings the record of its passage through each house is replete with evidence of the burdens that discrimination by race or color places upon interstate commerce. . . . This testimony included the fact that our people have become increasingly mobile with millions of people of all races traveling from State to State; that Negroes in particular have been the subject of discrimination in transient accommodations, having to travel great distances to secure the same; that often they have been unable to obtain accommodations and have had to call upon friends to put them up overnight, . . .; and that these conditions had become so acute as to require the listing of available lodging for Negroes in a special guidebook which was itself "dramatic testimony to the difficulties" Negroes encounter in travel. . . . We shall not burden this opinion with further details since the voluminous testimony presents overwhelming evidence that discrimination by hotels and motels impedes interstate travel.

7. THE POWER OF CONGRESS OVER INTERSTATE TRAVEL

. . .

[T]he determinative test of the exercise of power by the Congress under the Commerce Clause is simply whether the activity sought to be regulated is "commerce which concerns more States than one" and has a real and substantial relation to the national interest. Let us now turn to this facet of the problem.

That the "intercourse" of which the Chief Justice [Marshall] spoke [in Gibbons v. Ogden] included the movement of persons through more States than one was settled as early as 1849. . . . Nor does it make any difference whether the transportation is commercial in character. . . .

The same interest in protecting interstate commerce which led Congress to deal with segregation in interstate carriers and the white-slave traffic has prompted it to extend the exercise of its power to gambling, Lottery Case, 188 U.S. 321 (1903) . . . and to racial discrimination by owners and managers of terminal restaurants, Boynton v. Virginia, 364 U.S. 454 (1960).

That Congress was legislating against moral wrongs in many of these areas rendered its enactments no less valid. In framing Title II of this Act Congress was also dealing with what it considered a moral problem. But that fact does not detract from the overwhelming evidence of the disruptive effect that racial discrimination has had on commercial intercourse. It was this burden which empowered Congress to enact appropriate legislation, and, given this basis for the exercise of its power, Congress was not restricted by the fact that the particular obstruction to interstate commerce with which it was dealing was also deemed a moral and social wrong.

It is said that the operation of the motel here is of a purely local character. But, assuming this to be true, "[i]f it is interstate commerce that feels the pinch, it does not matter how local the operation which applies the squeeze." United States v. Women's Sportswear Mfrs. Assn., 336 U.S. 460, 464 (1949)....

. . .

We, therefore, conclude that the action of the Congress in the adoption of the Act as applied here to a motel which concededly serves interstate travelers is within the power granted it by the Commerce Clause of the Constitution, as interpreted by this Court for 140 years....

Affirmed.

[Justice Douglas's opinion stated that although he agreed with the Court's opinion, he was reluctant to rest solely on the commerce clause because of his belief that the right of people to be free of state action that discriminates against them because of race "occupies a more protected position in our constitutional system than does the movement of cattle, fruit, steel and coal across state lines." Black and Goldberg, JJ., filed concurring opinions. All of these opinions also applied to the following case.]

Katzenbach v. McClung

379 U.S. 294, 85 S.Ct. 377, 13 L.Ed.2d 290 (1964).

[This case was argued and decided with Heart of Atlanta Motel v. United States. McClung, as an owner of Ollie's Barbecue restaurant, sued to contest the constitutionality of Title II of the Civil Rights Act of 1964. A three-judge court enjoined Attorney General Katzenbach from enforcing the Act against the restaurant and an appeal was taken.]

Mr. Justice Clark delivered the opinion of the Court.

. . .

2. THE FACTS

Ollie's Barbecue is a family-owned restaurant in Birmingham, Alabama, specializing in barbecued meats and homemade pies, with a seating capacity of 220 customers. It is located on a state highway 11 blocks from an interstate one and a somewhat greater distance from railroad and bus stations. The restaurant caters to a family and white-collar trade with a take-out service for Negroes. It employs 36 persons, two-thirds of whom are Negroes.

In the 12 months preceding the passage of the Act, the restaurant purchased locally approximately $150,000 worth of food, $69,783 or 46% of which was meat that it bought from a local supplier who had procured it from outside the State. The District Court expressly found that a substantial portion of the food served in the restaurant had moved in interstate commerce. The restaurant has refused to serve Negroes in its dining accommodations since its original opening in 1927, and since July 2, 1964, it has been operating in violation of the Act. The court below concluded that if it were required to serve Negroes it would lose a substantial amount of business.

. . .

3. THE ACT AS APPLIED

... Sections 201(b)(2) and (c) place any "restaurant ... principally engaged in selling food for consumption on the premises" under the Act "if ... it serves or offers to serve interstate travelers or a substantial portion of the food which it serves ... has moved in commerce."

Ollie's Barbecue admits that it is covered by these provisions of the Act. The Government makes no contention that the discrimination at the restaurant was supported by the State of Alabama. There is no claim that interstate travelers frequented the restaurant. The sole question, therefore, narrows down to whether Title II, as applied to a restaurant receiving about $70,000 worth of food which has moved in commerce, is a valid exercise of the power of Congress. The Government has contended that Congress had ample basis upon which to find that racial discrimination at restaurants which receive from out of state a substantial portion of the food served does, in fact, impose commercial burdens of national magnitude upon interstate commerce. The appellees' major argument is directed to this premise. They urge that no such basis existed. It is to that question that we now turn.

4. THE CONGRESSIONAL HEARINGS

As we noted in *Heart of Atlanta Motel* both Houses of Congress conducted prolonged hearings on the Act.... The record is replete with testimony of the burdens placed on interstate commerce by racial discrimination in restaurants....

Moreover there was an impressive array of testimony that discrimination in restaurants had a direct and highly restrictive effect upon interstate travel by Negroes....

We believe that this testimony afforded ample basis for the conclusion that established restaurants in such areas sold less interstate goods because of the discrimination, that interstate travel was obstructed directly by it, that business in general suffered and that many new businesses refrained from establishing there as a result of it. Hence the District Court was in error in concluding that there was no connection between discrimination and the movement of interstate commerce. The court's conclusion that such a connection is outside "common experience" flies in the face of stubborn fact.

It goes without saying that, viewed in isolation, the volume of food purchased by Ollie's Barbecue from sources supplied from out of state was insignificant when compared with the total foodstuffs moving in commerce. But, as our late Brother Jackson said for the Court in Wickard v. Filburn, 317 U.S. 111 (1942): "That appellee's own contribution to the demand for wheat may be trivial by itself is not enough to remove him from the scope of federal regulation where, as here, his contribution, taken together with that of many others similarly situated, is far from trivial." ...

. . .

With this situation spreading as the record shows, Congress was not required to await the total dislocation of commerce....

5. THE POWER OF CONGRESS TO REGULATE LOCAL ACTIVITIES

... Much is said about a restaurant business being local but "even if appellee's activity be local and though it may not be regarded as commerce, it may still, whatever its nature, be reached by Congress if it exerts a substantial economic effect on interstate commerce...." ...

This Court has held time and again that this power extends to activities of retail establishments, including restaurants, which directly or indirectly burden or obstruct interstate commerce....

Nor are the cases holding that interstate commerce ends when goods come to rest in the state of destination apposite here. That line of cases has been applied with reference to state taxation or regulation but not in the field of federal regulation.

The appellees contend that Congress has arbitrarily created a conclusive presumption that all restaurants meeting the criteria set out in the Act "affect commerce." Stated another way, they object to the omission of a provision for a case-by-case determination—judicial or administrative—that racial discrimination in a particular restaurant affects commerce.

But Congress' action in framing this Act was not unprecedented. In United States v. Darby, 312 U.S. 100 (1941), this Court held constitutional the Fair Labor Standards Act....

Here, as there, Congress has determined for itself that refusals of service to Negroes have imposed burdens both upon the interstate flow of food and upon the movement of products generally. Of course, the mere fact that Congress has said when particular activity shall be deemed to affect commerce does not preclude further examination by this Court. But where we find that the legislators, in light of the facts and testimony before them, have a rational basis for finding a chosen regulatory scheme necessary to the protection of commerce, our investigation is at an end. The only remaining question—one answered in the affirmative by the court below—is whether the particular restaurant either serves or offers to serve interstate travelers or serves food a substantial portion of which has moved in interstate commerce.

. . .

Confronted as we are with the facts laid before Congress, we must conclude that it had a rational basis for finding that racial discrimination in restaurants had a direct and adverse effect on the free flow of interstate commerce.... We think in so doing that Congress acted well within its power to protect and foster commerce in extending the coverage of Title II only to those restaurants offering to serve interstate travelers or serving food, a substantial portion of which has moved in interstate commerce.

The absence of direct evidence connecting discriminatory restaurant service with the flow of interstate food, a factor on which the appellees place much reliance, is not, given the evidence as to the effect of such practices on other aspects of commerce, a crucial matter.

... The Civil Rights Act of 1964, as here applied, we find to be plainly appropriate in the resolution of what the Congress found to be a national commercial problem of the first magnitude. We find it in no violation of any express limitations of the Constitution and we therefore declare it valid.

The judgment is therefore reversed.

Reversed.

[Justices Black, Douglas, and Goldberg concurred.]

United States v. Lopez

__ U.S. __, 115 S.Ct. 1624, 131 L.Ed.2d 626 (1995).

Chief Justice Rehnquist delivered the opinion of the Court.

In the Gun–Free School Zones Act of 1990, Congress made it a federal offense "for any individual knowingly to possess a firearm at a place that the individual knows, or has reasonable cause to believe, is a school zone." 18 U.S.C. § 922(q)(1)(A).... The Act neither regulates a commercial activity nor contains a requirement that the possession be connected in any way to interstate commerce. We hold that the Act exceeds the authority of Congress "[t]o regulate Commerce ... among the several States...." U.S. Const., Art. I, § 8, cl. 3.

[Lopez, a 12th grade student, was convicted in federal district court of violating the Act for knowingly possessing a concealed handgun and bullets at his high school in San Antonio. (The Act defines "school zone" as "in, or on the grounds of, a public, parochial or private school" or "within a distance of 1,000 feet from the grounds of a public, parochial or private school." § 921(a)(25).) The Fifth Circuit reversed, holding the Act beyond the power of Congress under the Commerce Clause "in light of what it characterized as insufficient congressional findings and legislative history."] [W]e now affirm.

We start with first principles. The Constitution creates a Federal Government of enumerated powers. See U.S. Const., Art. I, § 8. As James Madison wrote, "[t]he powers delegated by the proposed Constitution to the federal government are few and defined. Those which are to remain in the State governments are numerous and indefinite." The Federalist No. 45, pp. 292–293 (C. Rossiter ed. 1961). This constitutionally mandated division of authority "was adopted by the Framers to ensure protection of our fundamental liberties." Gregory v. Ashcroft, 501 U.S. 452, 458 ... (1991).... "Just as the separation and independence of the coordinate branches of the Federal Government serves to prevent the accumulation of excessive power in any one branch, a healthy balance of power between the States and the Federal Government will reduce the risk of tyranny and abuse from either front." Ibid.

[The Chief Justice reviewed the Court's major commerce power precedents from Gibbons v. Ogden through Wickard v. Filburn and continued as follows:]

Jones & Laughlin Steel, Darby, and Wickard ushered in an era of Commerce Clause jurisprudence that greatly expanded the previously defined authority of Congress under that Clause. In part, this was a recognition of the great changes that had occurred in the way business was carried on in this country. Enterprises that had once been local or at most regional in nature had become national in scope. But the doctrinal change also reflected a view that earlier Commerce Clause cases artificially had constrained the authority of Congress to regulate interstate commerce.

But even these modern-era precedents which have expanded congressional power under the Commerce Clause confirm that this power is subject to outer limits. In Jones & Laughlin Steel, the Court warned that the scope of the interstate commerce power "must be considered in the light of our dual system of government and may not be extended so as to embrace effects upon interstate commerce so indirect and remote that to embrace them, in view of our complex society, would effectually obliterate the distinction between what is national and what is local and create a completely centralized government." 301 U.S., at 37; see also Darby, 312 U.S., at 119–120 (Congress may regulate intrastate activity that has a "substantial effect" on interstate commerce); Wickard, at 125 (Congress may regulate activity that "exerts a substantial economic effect on interstate commerce"). Since that time, the Court has heeded that warning and undertaken to decide whether a rational basis existed for concluding that a regulated activity sufficiently affected interstate commerce. See, e.g., Hodel v. Virginia Surface Mining & Reclamation Assn., Inc.,

452 U.S. 264, 276–280 (1981); Perez v. United States, 402 U.S. 146, 155–156 (1971); Katzenbach v. McClung, 379 U.S. 294, 299–301 (1964); Heart of Atlanta Motel, Inc. v. United States, 379 U.S. 241, 252–253 (1964).

Similarly, in Maryland v. Wirtz, 392 U.S. 183 (1968), the Court reaffirmed that "the power to regulate commerce, though broad indeed, has limits" that "[t]he Court has ample power" to enforce.... In response to the dissent's warnings that the Court was powerless to enforce the limitations on Congress' commerce powers because "[a]ll activities affecting commerce, even in the minutest degree, [*Wickard*], may be regulated and controlled by Congress," 392 U.S., at 204 (Douglas, J., dissenting), the *Wirtz* Court replied that the dissent had misread precedent as "[n]either here nor in *Wickard* has the Court declared that Congress may use a relatively trivial impact on commerce as an excuse for broad general regulation of state or private activities," id., at 197, n. 27. Rather, "[t]he Court has said only that where *a general regulatory statute bears a substantial relation to commerce*, the *de minimis* character of individual instances arising under that statute is of no consequence." Ibid. (first emphasis added).

Consistent with this structure, we have identified three broad categories of activity that Congress may regulate under its commerce power.... First, Congress may regulate the use of the channels of interstate commerce.... Second, Congress is empowered to regulate and protect the instrumentalities of interstate commerce, or persons or things in interstate commerce, even though the threat may come only from intrastate activities.... Finally, Congress' commerce authority includes the power to regulate those activities having a substantial relation to interstate commerce, ... i.e., those activities that substantially affect interstate commerce....

Within this final category, admittedly, our case law has not been clear whether an activity must "affect" or "substantially affect" interstate commerce in order to be within Congress' power to regulate it under the Commerce Clause.... We conclude, consistent with the great weight of our case law, that the proper test requires an analysis of whether the regulated activity "substantially affects" interstate commerce.

We now turn to consider the power of Congress, in the light of this framework, to enact § 922(q). The first two categories of authority may be quickly disposed of: § 922(q) is not a regulation of the use of the channels of interstate commerce, nor is it an attempt to prohibit the interstate transportation of a commodity through the channels of commerce; nor can § 922(q) be justified as a regulation by which Congress has sought to protect an instrumentality of interstate commerce or a thing in interstate commerce. Thus, if § 922(q) is to be sustained, it must be under the third category as a regulation of an activity that substantially affects interstate commerce.

First, we have upheld a wide variety of congressional Acts regulating intrastate economic activity where we have concluded that the activity substantially affected interstate commerce. Examples include the regulation of intrastate coal mining; ... intrastate extortionate credit transactions, ... restaurants utilizing substantial interstate supplies, ... inns and hotels catering to interstate guests, ... and production and consumption of home-grown wheat, Wickard v. Filburn, 317 U.S. 111 (1942).... Where economic activity substantially affects interstate commerce, legislation regulating that activity will be sustained.

Even *Wickard*, which is perhaps the most far reaching example of Commerce Clause authority over intrastate activity, involved economic activity in a way that the possession of a gun in a school zone does not....

Section 922(q) is a criminal statute that by its terms has nothing to do with "commerce" or any sort of economic enterprise, however broadly one might define those terms.[3] Section 922(q) is not an essential part of a larger regulation of economic activity, in which the regulatory scheme could be undercut unless the intrastate activity were regulated. It cannot, therefore, be sustained under our cases upholding regulations of activities that arise out of or are connected with a commercial transaction, which viewed in the aggregate, substantially affects interstate commerce.

Second, § 922(q) contains no jurisdictional element which would ensure, through case-by-case inquiry, that the firearm possession in question affects interstate commerce. For example, in United States v. Bass, 404 U.S. 336 (1971), the Court interpreted [the possession component of] former 18 U.S.C. § 1202(a), which made it a crime for a felon to "receiv[e], posses[s], or transpor[t] in commerce or affecting commerce . . . any firearm[]" to require an additional nexus to interstate commerce both because the statute was ambiguous and because "unless Congress conveys its purpose clearly, it will not be deemed to have significantly changed the federal-state balance." . . . The Court thus interpreted the statute to reserve the constitutional question whether Congress could regulate, without more, the "mere possession" of firearms. . . . Unlike the statute in *Bass*, § 922(q) has no express jurisdictional element which might limit its reach to a discrete set of firearm possessions that additionally have an explicit connection with or effect on interstate commerce.

Although as part of our independent evaluation of constitutionality under the Commerce Clause we of course consider legislative findings, and indeed even congressional committee findings, regarding effect on interstate commerce, . . . the Government concedes that "[n]either the statute nor its legislative history contain[s] express congressional findings regarding the effects upon interstate commerce of gun possession in a school zone." . . . We agree with the Government that Congress normally is not required to make formal findings as to the substantial burdens that an activity has on interstate commerce. . . . But to the extent that congressional findings would enable us to evaluate the legislative judgment that the activity in question substantially affected interstate commerce, even though no such substantial effect was visible to the naked eye, they are lacking here.[4]

The Government argues that Congress has accumulated institutional expertise regarding the regulation of firearms through previous enactments. . . . We agree, however, with the Fifth Circuit that importation of previous findings to justify § 922(q) is especially inappropriate here because the "prior federal enactments or Congressional findings [do not] speak to the subject matter of section 922(q) or its relationship to interstate commerce. Indeed, section 922(q)

---

[3] Under our federal system, the "'States possess primary authority for defining and enforcing the criminal law.'" . . . When Congress criminalizes conduct already denounced as criminal by the States, it effects a "change in the sensitive relation between federal and state criminal jurisdiction." . . . [S]ee also Statement of President George Bush on Signing the Crime Control Act of 1990, 26 Weekly Comp. of Pres. Doc. 1944, 1945 (Nov. 29, 1990) ("Most egregiously, section [922(q)] inappropriately overrides legitimate state firearms laws with a new and unnecessary Federal law. The policies reflected in these

provisions could legitimately be adopted by the States, but they should not be imposed upon the States by Congress").

[4] . . . [T]he Violent Crime Control and Law Enforcement Act of 1994 . . . amends § 922(q) to include congressional findings regarding the effects of firearm possession in and around schools upon interstate and foreign commerce. The Government does not rely upon these subsequent findings as a substitute for the absence of findings in the first instance. . . .

plows thoroughly new ground and represents a sharp break with the long-standing pattern of federal firearms legislation." . . .

The Government's essential contention, *in fine*, is that we may determine here that § 922(q) is valid because possession of a firearm in a local school zone does indeed substantially affect interstate commerce. . . . The Government argues that possession of a firearm in a school zone may result in violent crime and that violent crime can be expected to affect the functioning of the national economy in two ways. First, the costs of violent crime are substantial, and, through the mechanism of insurance, those costs are spread throughout the population. . . . Second, violent crime reduces the willingness of individuals to travel to areas within the country that are perceived to be unsafe. Cf. Heart of Atlanta Motel. . . . The Government also argues that the presence of guns in schools poses a substantial threat to the educational process by threatening the learning environment. A handicapped educational process, in turn, will result in a less productive citizenry. That, in turn, would have an adverse effect on the Nation's economic well-being. As a result, the Government argues that Congress could rationally have concluded that § 922(q) substantially affects interstate commerce.

We pause to consider the implications of the Government's arguments. The Government admits, under its "costs of crime" reasoning, that Congress could regulate not only all violent crime, but all activities that might lead to violent crime, regardless of how tenuously they relate to interstate commerce. . . . Similarly, under the Government's "national productivity" reasoning, Congress could regulate any activity that it found was related to the economic productivity of individual citizens: family law (including marriage, divorce, and child custody), for example. Under the theories that the Government presents in support of § 922(q), it is difficult to perceive any limitation on federal power, even in areas such as criminal law enforcement or education where States historically have been sovereign. Thus, if we were to accept the Government's arguments, we are hard-pressed to posit any activity by an individual that Congress is without power to regulate.

Although Justice Breyer argues that acceptance of the Government's rationales would not authorize a general federal police power, he is unable to identify any activity that the States may regulate but Congress may not. Justice Breyer posits that there might be some limitations on Congress' commerce power such as family law or certain aspects of education. These suggested limitations, when viewed in light of the dissent's expansive analysis, are devoid of substance.

Justice Breyer focuses, for the most part, on the threat that firearm possession in and near schools poses to the educational process and the potential economic consequences flowing from that threat. Specifically, the dissent reasons that (1) gun-related violence is a serious problem; (2) that problem, in turn, has an adverse effect on classroom learning; and (3) that adverse effect on classroom learning, in turn, represents a substantial threat to trade and commerce. This analysis would be equally applicable, if not more so, to subjects such as family law and direct regulation of education.

[I]f Congress can . . . regulate activities that adversely affect the learning environment, then, *a fortiori*, it also can regulate the educational process directly. Congress could determine that a school's curriculum has a "significant" effect on the extent of classroom learning [and] mandate a federal curriculum for local elementary and secondary schools because what is taught in local schools has a significant "effect on classroom learning," and that, in turn, has a substantial effect on interstate commerce.

Justice Breyer rejects our reading of precedent and argues that "Congress ... could rationally conclude that schools fall on the commercial side of the line." Again, Justice Breyer's rationale lacks any real limits because, depending on the level of generality, any activity can be looked upon as commercial. Under the dissent's rationale, Congress could just as easily look at child rearing as "fall[ing] on the commercial side of the line" because it provides a "valuable service—namely, to equip [children] with the skills they need to survive in life and, more specifically, in the workplace." ... We do not doubt that Congress has authority under the Commerce Clause to regulate numerous commercial activities that substantially affect interstate commerce and also affect the educational process. That authority, though broad, does not include the authority to regulate each and every aspect of local schools.

Admittedly, a determination whether an intrastate activity is commercial or noncommercial may in some cases result in legal uncertainty. But, so long as Congress' authority is limited to those powers enumerated in the Constitution, and so long as those enumerated powers are interpreted as having judicially enforceable outer limits, congressional legislation under the Commerce Clause always will engender "legal uncertainty." ...

. . .

... The possession of a gun in a local school zone is in no sense an economic activity that might, through repetition elsewhere, substantially affect any sort of interstate commerce. Respondent was a local student at a local school; there is no indication that he had recently moved in interstate commerce, and there is no requirement that his possession of the firearm have any concrete tie to interstate commerce.

To uphold the Government's contentions here, we would have to pile inference upon inference in a manner that would bid fair to convert congressional authority under the Commerce Clause to a general police power of the sort retained by the States. Admittedly, some of our prior cases have taken long steps down that road, giving great deference to congressional action.... The broad language in these opinions has suggested the possibility of additional expansion, but we decline here to proceed any further. To do so would require us to conclude that the Constitution's enumeration of powers does not presuppose something not enumerated ... and that there never will be a distinction between what is truly national and what is truly local.... This we are unwilling to do.

. . .

Justice Kennedy, with whom Justice O'Connor joins, concurring.

The history of the judicial struggle to interpret the Commerce Clause during the transition from the economic system the Founders knew to the single, national market still emergent in our own era counsels great restraint before the Court determines that the Clause is insufficient to support an exercise of the national power. That history gives me some pause about today's decision, but I join the Court's opinion with these observations on what I conceive to be its necessary though limited holding.

[Justice Kennedy also reviewed the Court's major commerce power decisions, respectively ending his summary and continuing as follows:]

... Later examples of the exercise of federal power where commercial transactions were the subject of regulation include Heart of Atlanta Motel, Inc. v. United States, 379 U.S. 241 (1964), Katzenbach v. McClung, 379 U.S. 294 (1964), and Perez v. United States, 402 U.S. 146 (1971). These and like authorities are within the fair ambit of the Court's practical conception of commercial regulation and are not called in question by our decision today.

The history of our Commerce Clause decisions contains at least two lessons of relevance to this case. The first ... is the imprecision of content-based boundaries used without more to define the limits of the Commerce Clause. The second ... is that the Court as an institution and the legal system as a whole have an immense stake in the stability of our Commerce Clause jurisprudence as it has evolved to this point. *Stare decisis* operates with great force in counseling us not to call in question the essential principles now in place respecting the congressional power to regulate transactions of a commercial nature. . . . Congress can regulate in the commercial sphere on the assumption that we have a single market and a unified purpose to build a stable national economy.

... This case requires us to consider our place in the design of the Government and to appreciate the significance of federalism in the whole structure of the Constitution.

Of the various structural elements in the Constitution, separation of powers, checks and balances, judicial review, and federalism, only concerning the last does there seem to be much uncertainty respecting the existence, and the content, of standards that allow the judiciary to play a significant role in maintaining the design contemplated by the Framers. . . .

There is irony in this, because of the four structural elements in the Constitution just mentioned, federalism was the unique contribution of the Framers to political science and political theory. . . . Though on the surface the idea may seem counterintuitive, it was the insight of the Framers that freedom was enhanced by the creation of two governments, not one. . . .

The theory that two governments accord more liberty than one requires for its realization two distinct and discernable lines of political accountability: one between the citizens and the Federal Government; the second between the citizens and the States. If, as Madison expected, the federal and state governments are to control each other, see The Federalist No. 51, and hold each other in check by competing for the affections of the people, see The Federalist No. 46, those citizens must have some means of knowing which of the two governments to hold accountable for the failure to perform a given function. . . . Were the Federal Government to take over the regulation of entire areas of traditional state concern, areas having nothing to do with the regulation of commercial activities, the boundaries between the spheres of federal and state authority would blur and political responsibility would become illusory. See New York v. United States. . . . The resultant inability to hold either branch of the government answerable to the citizens is more dangerous even than devolving too much authority to the remote central power.

. . .

[I]t would be mistaken and mischievous for the political branches to forget that the sworn obligation to preserve and protect the Constitution in maintaining the federal balance is their own in the first and primary instance. . . .

At the same time, the absence of structural mechanisms to require those officials to undertake this principled task, and the momentary political convenience often attendant upon their failure to do so, argue against a complete renunciation of the judicial role. . . .

... The substantial element of political judgment in Commerce Clause matters leaves our institutional capacity to intervene more in doubt than when we decide cases, for instance, under the Bill of Rights even though clear and bright lines are often absent in the latter class of disputes.... But our cases do not teach that we have no role at all in determining the meaning of the Commerce Clause.

Our position in enforcing the dormant Commerce Clause is instructive.... [I]n contrast to the prevailing skepticism that surrounds our ability to give meaning to the explicit text of the Commerce Clause, there is widespread acceptance of our authority to enforce the dormant Commerce Clause, which we have but inferred from the constitutional structure as a limitation on the power of the States.... True, if we invalidate a state law, Congress can in effect overturn our judgment, whereas in a case announcing that Congress has transgressed its authority, the decision is more consequential, for it stands unless Congress can revise its law to demonstrate its commercial character. This difference no doubt informs the circumspection with which we invalidate an Act of Congress, but it does not mitigate our duty to recognize meaningful limits on the commerce power of Congress.

The statute before us upsets the federal balance to a degree that renders it an unconstitutional assertion of the commerce power, and our intervention is required.... In a sense any conduct in this interdependent world of ours has an ultimate commercial origin or consequence, but we have not yet said the commerce power may reach so far. If Congress attempts that extension, then at the least we must inquire whether the exercise of national power seeks to intrude upon an area of traditional state concern.

An interference of these dimensions occurs here, for it is well established that education is a traditional concern of the States.... The proximity to schools, including of course schools owned and operated by the States or their subdivisions, is the very premise for making the conduct criminal. In these circumstances, we have a particular duty to insure that the federal-state balance is not destroyed....

The statute now before us forecloses the States from experimenting and exercising their own judgment in an area to which States lay claim by right of history and expertise, and it does so by regulating an activity beyond the realm of commerce in the ordinary and usual sense of that term.... [S]chool officials would find their own programs for the prohibition of guns in danger of displacement by the federal authority unless the State chooses to enact a parallel rule.

... While the intrusion on state sovereignty may not be as severe in this instance as in some of our recent Tenth Amendment cases, the intrusion is nonetheless significant. Absent a stronger connection or identification with commercial concerns that are central to the Commerce Clause, that interference contradicts the federal balance the Framers designed and that this Court is obliged to enforce.

For these reasons, I join in the opinion and judgment of the Court.

Justice Thomas, concurring.

... I write separately to observe that our case law has drifted far from the original understanding of the Commerce Clause....

. . . .

In an appropriate case, I believe that we must further reconsider our "substantial effects" test with an eye toward constructing a standard that reflects the text and history of the Commerce Clause without totally rejecting our more recent Commerce Clause jurisprudence.

. . .

I

At the time the original Constitution was ratified, "commerce" consisted of selling, buying, and bartering, as well as transporting for these purposes. . . .

[T]he term "commerce" was used in contradistinction to productive activities such as manufacturing and agriculture. . . .

. . .

The Constitution not only uses the word "commerce" in a narrower sense than our case law might suggest, it also does not support the proposition that Congress has authority over all activities that "substantially affect" interstate commerce. . . .

In addition to its powers under the Commerce Clause, Congress has the authority to enact such laws as are "necessary and proper" to carry into execution its power to regulate commerce among the several States. U.S. Const., Art. I, § 8, cl. 18. But on this Court's understanding of congressional power under these two Clauses, many of Congress' other enumerated powers under Art. I, § 8 are wholly superfluous. After all, if Congress may regulate all matters that substantially affect commerce, there is no need for the Constitution to specify that Congress may enact bankruptcy laws, cl. 4, or coin money and fix the standard of weights and measures, cl. 5, or punish counterfeiters of United States coin and securities, cl. 6. Likewise, Congress would not need the separate authority to establish post offices and post roads, cl. 7, or to grant patents and copyrights, cl. 8, or to "punish Piracies and Felonies committed on the high Seas," cl. 10. . . . Indeed, if Congress could regulate matters that substantially affect interstate commerce, there would have been no need to specify that Congress can regulate international trade and commerce with the Indians. As the Framers surely understood, these other branches of trade substantially affect interstate commerce.

Put simply, much if not all of Art. I, § 8 (including portions of the Commerce Clause itself) would be surplusage if Congress had been given authority over matters that substantially affect interstate commerce. . . . [T]he power we have accorded Congress has swallowed Art. I, § 8.

. . .

. . . [F]undamental textual problems should, at the very least, convince us that the "substantial effects" test should be reexamined.

II

The exchanges during the ratification campaign reveal the relatively limited reach of the Commerce Clause and of federal power generally. The Founding Fathers confirmed that most areas of life (even many matters that would have substantial effects on commerce) would remain outside the reach of the Federal Government [and] under the exclusive control of the States.

. . .

[D]espite being well aware that agriculture, manufacturing, and other matters substantially affected commerce, the founding generation did not cede authority over all these activities to Congress. . . .

Where the Constitution was meant to grant federal authority over an activity substantially affecting interstate commerce, the Constitution contains an enumerated power over that particular activity. Indeed, the Framers knew that many of the other enumerated powers in § 8 dealt with matters that substantially affected interstate commerce. Madison, for instance, spoke of the bankruptcy power as being "intimately connected with the regulation of commerce." The Federalist No. 42, at 287. . . .

. . . Even though the boundary between commerce and other matters may ignore "economic reality" and thus seem arbitrary or artificial to some, we must nevertheless respect a constitutional line that does not grant Congress power over all that substantially affects interstate commerce.

III

. . .

In my view, the dissent is wrong about the holding and reasoning of *Gibbons* . . . .

A

. . .

[In *Gibbons*,] the Court took great pains to make clear that Congress could not regulate commerce "which is completely internal, which is carried on between man and man in a State, or between different parts of the same State, and which does not extend to or affect other States." . . .

. . .

. . . From this statement, the principal dissent infers that whenever an activity affects interstate commerce, it necessarily follows that Congress can regulate such activities. Of course, Chief Justice Marshall said no such thing and the inference the dissent makes cannot be drawn.

There is a much better interpretation of the "affect[s]" language: because the Court had earlier noted that the commerce power did not extend to wholly intrastate commerce, the Court was acknowledging that although the line between intrastate and interstate/foreign commerce would be difficult to draw, federal authority could not be construed to cover purely intrastate commerce. Commerce that did not affect another State could *never* be said to be commerce "among the several States."

But even if one were to adopt the dissent's reading, the "affect[s]" language, at most, permits Congress to regulate only intrastate *commerce* that substantially affects interstate and foreign commerce. There is no reason to believe that Chief Justice Marshall was asserting that Congress could regulate all activities that affect interstate commerce. . . .

. . .

B

I am aware of no cases prior to the New Deal that characterized the power flowing from the Commerce Clause as sweepingly as does our substantial effects test. . . .

. . .

As recently as 1936, the Court continued to insist that the Commerce Clause did not reach the wholly internal business of the States. . . .

[F]rom the time of the ratification of the Constitution to the mid–1930's, it was widely understood that the Constitution granted Congress only limited powers, notwithstanding the Commerce Clause. Moreover, there was no question that activities wholly separated from business, such as gun possession, were beyond the reach of the commerce power. If anything, the "wrong turn" was the Court's dramatic departure in the 1930's from a century and a half of precedent.

IV

Apart from its recent vintage and its corresponding lack of any grounding in the original understanding of the Constitution, the substantial effects test suffers from the further flaw that it appears to grant Congress a police power over the Nation. . . . The one advantage of the dissent's standard is certainty: it is certain that under its analysis everything may be regulated under the guise of the Commerce Clause.

The substantial effects test suffers from this flaw, in part, because of its "aggregation principle." Under so-called "class of activities" statutes, Congress can regulate whole categories of activities that are not themselves either "interstate" or "commerce." In applying the effects test, we ask whether the class of activities as a whole substantially affects interstate commerce, not whether any specific activity within the class has such effects when considered in isolation. . . .

The aggregation principle is clever, but has no stopping point. . . . [O]ne always can draw the circle broadly enough to cover an activity that, when taken in isolation, would not have substantial effects on commerce. Under our jurisprudence, if Congress passed an omnibus "substantially affects interstate commerce" statute, purporting to regulate every aspect of human existence, the Act apparently would be constitutional. Even though particular sections may govern only trivial activities, the statute in the aggregate regulates matters that substantially affect commerce.

V

This extended discussion of the original understanding and our first century and a half of case law does not necessarily require a wholesale abandonment of our more recent opinions.[8] It simply reveals that our substantial effects test is far removed from both the Constitution and from our early case law and that the Court's opinion should not be viewed as "radical" or another "wrong turn" that must be corrected in the future. The analysis also suggests that we ought to temper our Commerce Clause jurisprudence.

Unless the dissenting Justices are willing to repudiate our long-held understanding of the limited nature of federal power, I would think that they too must be willing to reconsider the substantial effects test in a future case. . . .

. . .

Justice Stevens, dissenting.

The welfare of our future "Commerce with foreign Nations, and among the several States," U.S. Const., Art. I, § 8, cl. 3, is vitally dependent on the

---

[8] Although I might be willing to return to the original understanding, I recognize that many believe that it is too late in the day to undertake a fundamental reexamination of the past 60 years. Consideration of *stare decisis* and reliance interests may convince us that we cannot wipe the slate clean.

character of the education of our children. I therefore agree entirely with Justice Breyer's explanation of why Congress has ample power to prohibit the possession of firearms in or near schools—just as it may protect the school environment from harms posed by controlled substances such as asbestos or alcohol. I also agree with Justice Souter's exposition of the radical character of the Court's holding and its kinship with the discredited, pre-Depression version of substantive due process....

Guns are both articles of commerce and articles that can be used to restrain commerce. Their possession is the consequence, either directly or indirectly, of commercial activity. In my judgment, Congress' power to regulate commerce in firearms includes the power to prohibit possession of guns at any location because of their potentially harmful use; it necessarily follows that Congress may also prohibit their possession in particular markets. The market for the possession of handguns by school-age children is, distressingly, substantial. Whether or not the national interest in eliminating that market would have justified federal legislation in 1789, it surely does today.

Justice Souter, dissenting.

In reviewing congressional legislation under the Commerce Clause, we defer to what is often a merely implicit congressional judgment that its regulation addresses a subject substantially affecting interstate commerce "if there is any rational basis for such a finding." Hodel v. Virginia Surface Mining & Reclamation Assn., Inc., 452 U.S. 264, 276 (1981)....

The practice of deferring to rationally based legislative judgments "is a paradigm of judicial restraint." FCC v. Beach Communications, Inc., 508 U.S.–,–(1993). In judicial review under the Commerce Clause, it reflects our respect for the institutional competence of the Congress on a subject expressly assigned to it by the Constitution and our appreciation of the legitimacy that comes from Congress's political accountability in dealing with matters open to a wide range of possible choices....

... The modern respect for the competence and primacy of Congress in matters affecting commerce developed only after one of this Court's most chastening experiences, when it perforce repudiated an earlier and untenably expansive conception of judicial review in derogation of congressional commerce power. A look at history's sequence will serve to show how today's decision tugs the Court off course, leading it to suggest opportunities for further developments that would be at odds with the rule of restraint to which the Court still wisely states adherence.

I

... [T]he period from the turn of the century to 1937 is ... noted for a series of cases applying highly formalistic notions of "commerce" to invalidate federal social and economic legislation....

... [D]uring this same period the Court routinely invalidated state social and economic legislation under an expansive conception of Fourteenth Amendment substantive due process....

... [S]ea changes in the Court's conceptions of its authority under the Due Process and Commerce Clauses occurred virtually together, in 1937, with West Coast Hotel Co. v. Parrish, 300 U.S. 379 and NLRB v. Jones & Laughlin Steel Corp., 301 U.S. 1....

In the years following these decisions, deference to legislative policy judgments on commercial regulation became the powerful theme under both the Due Process and Commerce Clauses.... Thus, under commerce, as under due process, adoption of rational basis review expressed the recognition that the Court had no sustainable basis for subjecting economic regulation as such to judicial policy judgments, and for the past half-century the Court has no more turned back in the direction of formalistic Commerce Clause review (as in deciding whether regulation of commerce was sufficiently direct) than it has inclined toward reasserting the substantive authority of *Lochner* due process (as in the inflated protection of contractual autonomy)....

II

There is today, however, a backward glance at both the old pitfalls, as the Court treats deference under the rationality rule as subject to gradation according to the commercial or noncommercial nature of the immediate subject of the challenged regulation.... Thus, it seems fair to ask whether the step taken by the Court today does anything but portend a return to the untenable jurisprudence from which the Court extricated itself almost 60 years ago. The answer is not reassuring.... [I]f it seems anomalous that the Congress of the United States has taken to regulating school yards, the act in question is still probably no more remarkable than state regulation of bake shops 90 years ago. In any event, there is no reason to hope that the Court's qualification of rational basis review will be any more successful than the efforts at substantive economic review made by our predecessors as the century began....

Further glosses on rationality review, moreover, may be in the offing. Although this case turns on commercial character, the Court gestures toward two other considerations that it might sometime entertain in applying rational basis scrutiny (apart from a statutory obligation to supply independent proof of a jurisdictional element): does the congressional statute deal with subjects of traditional state regulation, and does the statute contain explicit factual findings supporting the otherwise implicit determination that the regulated activity substantially affects interstate commerce? Once again, any appeal these considerations may have depends on ignoring the painful lesson learned in 1937, for neither of the Court's suggestions would square with rational basis scrutiny.

A

... [A]s for the notion that the commerce power diminishes the closer it gets to customary state concerns, that idea has been flatly rejected, and not long ago....

Nor is there any contrary authority in the reasoning of our cases imposing clear statement rules in some instances of legislation that would significantly alter the state-national balance....

These clear statement rules ... are merely rules of statutory interpretation, to be relied upon only when the terms of a statute allow, ... and in cases implicating Congress's historical reluctance to trench on state legislative prerogatives or to enter into spheres already occupied by the States.... But our hesitance to presume that Congress has acted to alter the state-federal status quo (when presented with a plausible alternative) has no relevance whatever to the enquiry whether it has the commerce power to do so or to the standard of judicial review when Congress has definitely meant to exercise that power....

B

There remain questions about legislative findings. The Court of Appeals expressed the view ... that the result in this case might well have been different if Congress had made explicit findings that guns in schools have a substantial effect on interstate commerce, and the Court today does not repudiate that position. Might a court aided by such findings have subjected this legislation to less exacting scrutiny (or, put another way, should a court have deferred to such findings if Congress had made them)? The answer to either question must be no, although as a general matter findings are important and to be hoped for in the difficult cases.

The question for the courts, as all agree, is not whether as a predicate to legislation Congress in fact found that a particular activity substantially affects interstate commerce. The legislation implies such a finding.... Nor is the question whether Congress was correct in so finding. The only question is whether the legislative judgment is within the realm of reason.... If ... the Court were to make the existence of explicit congressional findings dispositive in some close or difficult cases something other than rationality review would be afoot. The resulting congressional obligation to justify its policy choices on the merits would imply either a judicial authority to review the justification (and, hence, the wisdom) of those choices, or authority to require Congress to act with some high degree of deliberateness, of which express findings would be evidence. But review for congressional wisdom would just be the old judicial pretension discredited and abandoned in 1937, and review for deliberateness would be as patently unconstitutional as an Act of Congress mandating long opinions from this Court.... [T]he rationality standard of review would be a thing of the past.

... I would not allow for the possibility, as the Court's opinion may, that the addition of congressional findings could in principle have affected the fate of the statute here.

III

Because Justice Breyer's opinion demonstrates beyond any doubt that the Act in question passes the rationality review that the Court continues to espouse, today's decision may be seen as only a misstep, its reasoning and its suggestions not quite in gear with the prevailing standard, but hardly an epochal case. I would not argue otherwise, but I would raise a caveat. Not every epochal case has come in epochal trappings. *Jones & Laughlin* did not reject the direct-indirect standard in so many words; it just said the relation of the regulated subject matter to commerce was direct enough.... But we know what happened.

I respectfully dissent.

Justice Breyer, with whom Justice Stevens, Justice Souter, and Justice Ginsburg join, dissenting.

... In my view, the statute falls well within the scope of the commerce power as this Court has understood that power over the last half-century.

I

In reaching this conclusion, I apply three basic principles of Commerce Clause interpretation. First, the power to "regulate Commerce ... among the several States," U.S. Const., Art. I, § 8, cl. 3, encompasses the power to regulate local activities insofar as they significantly affect interstate commerce....

Second, in determining whether a local activity will likely have a significant effect upon interstate commerce, a court must consider, not the effect of an individual act (a single instance of gun possession), but rather the cumulative effect of all similar instances (i.e., the effect of all guns possessed in or near schools)....

Third, the Constitution requires us to judge the connection between a regulated activity and interstate commerce, not directly, but at one remove. Courts must give Congress a degree of leeway in determining the existence of a significant factual connection between the regulated activity and interstate commerce—both because the Constitution delegates the commerce power directly to Congress and because the determination requires an empirical judgment of a kind that a legislature is more likely than a court to make with accuracy. The traditional words "rational basis" capture this leeway.... Thus, the specific question before us, as the Court recognizes, is not whether the "regulated activity sufficiently affected interstate commerce," but, rather, whether Congress could have had "a rational basis" for so concluding.

I recognize that we must judge this matter independently.... I also recognize that Congress did not write specific "interstate commerce" findings into the law under which Lopez was convicted. Nonetheless, ... the matter that we review independently (i.e., whether there is a "rational basis") already has considerable leeway built into it. And, the absence of findings, at most, deprives a statute of the benefit of some *extra* leeway....

II

Applying these principles to the case at hand, we must ask whether Congress could have had a *rational basis* for finding a significant (or substantial) connection between gun-related school violence and interstate commerce. Or, to put the question in the language of the explicit finding that Congress made when it amended this law in 1994: Could Congress rationally have found that "violent crime in school zones," through its effect on the "quality of education," significantly (or substantially) affects "interstate" or "foreign commerce"? ... As long as one views the commerce connection, not as a "technical legal conception," but as "a practical one," Swift & Co. v. United States, 196 U.S. 375, 398 (1905) (Holmes, J.), the answer to this question must be yes. Numerous reports and studies—generated both inside and outside government—make clear that Congress could reasonably have found the empirical connection that its law, implicitly or explicitly, asserts....

For one thing, reports, hearings, and other readily available literature make clear that the problem of guns in and around schools is widespread and extremely serious.... And, they report that this widespread violence in schools throughout the Nation significantly interferes with the quality of education in those schools. See, e.g., House Judiciary Committee Hearing 44 (1990) (linking school violence to dropout rate); U.S. Dept. of Health 118–119 (1978) (school-violence victims suffer academically); compare U.S. Dept. of Justice 1 (1991) (gun violence worst in inner city schools), with National Center 47 (dropout rates highest in inner cities).... Congress could therefore have found a substantial educational problem—teachers unable to teach, students unable to learn—and concluded that guns near schools contribute substantially to the size and scope of that problem.

Having found that guns in schools significantly undermine the quality of education in our Nation's classrooms, Congress could also have found, given the effect of education upon interstate and foreign commerce, that gun-related violence in and around schools is a commercial, as well as a human, problem. Education, although far more than a matter of economics, has long been inextricably intertwined with the Nation's economy....

In recent years the link between secondary education and business has strengthened, becoming both more direct and more important. Scholars on the subject report that technological changes and innovations in management techniques have altered the nature of the workplace so that more jobs now demand greater educational skills. . . .

Increasing global competition also has made primary and secondary education economically more important. . . .

Finally, there is evidence that, today more than ever, many firms base their location decisions upon the presence, or absence, of a work force with a basic education. . . . In light of this increased importance of education to individual firms, it is no surprise that half of the Nation's manufacturers have become involved with setting standards and shaping curricula for local schools, . . . that 88 percent think this kind of involvement is important, . . . that more than 20 States have recently passed educational reforms to attract new business, . . . and that business magazines have begun to rank cities according to the quality of their schools. . . .

The economic links I have just sketched seem fairly obvious. Why then is it not equally obvious, in light of those links, that a widespread, serious, and substantial physical threat to teaching and learning *also* substantially threatens the commerce to which that teaching and learning is inextricably tied? That is to say, guns in the hands of six percent of inner-city high school students and gun-related violence throughout a city's schools must threaten the trade and commerce that those schools support. The only question, then, is whether the latter threat is (to use the majority's terminology) "substantial." And, the evidence of (1) the *extent* of the gun-related violence problem, (2) the *extent* of the resulting negative effect on classroom learning, and (3) the *extent* of the consequent negative commercial effects, when taken together, indicate a threat to trade and commerce that is "substantial." At the very least, Congress could rationally have concluded that the links are "substantial."

Specifically, Congress could have found that gun-related violence near the classroom poses a serious economic threat (1) to consequently inadequately educated workers who must endure low paying jobs . . . and (2) to communities and businesses that might (in today's "information society") otherwise gain, from a well-educated work force, an important commercial advantage . . . of a kind that location near a railhead or harbor provided in the past. Congress might also have found these threats to be no different in kind from other threats that this Court has found within the commerce power, such as the threat that loan sharking poses to the "funds" of "numerous localities," Perez v. United States. . . .

To hold this statute constitutional is not to "obliterate" the "distinction of what is national and what is local"; nor is it to hold that the Commerce Clause permits the Federal Government to "regulate any activity that it found was related to the economic productivity of individual citizens," to regulate "marriage, divorce, and child custody," or to regulate any and all aspects of education. For one thing, this statute is aimed at curbing a particularly acute threat to the educational process—the possession (and use) of life-threatening firearms in, or near, the classroom. . . . For another thing, the immediacy of the connection between education and the national economic well-being is documented by scholars and accepted by society at large in a way and to a degree that may not hold true for other social institutions. It must surely be the rare case, then, that a statute strikes at conduct that (when considered in the abstract) seems so removed from commerce, but which (practically speaking) has so significant an impact upon commerce.

In sum, a holding that the particular statute before us falls within the commerce power would not expand the scope of that Clause. Rather, it simply would apply preexisting law to changing economic circumstances. . . .

III

The majority's holding ... creates three serious legal problems. First, [it] runs contrary to modern Supreme Court cases that have upheld congressional actions despite connections to interstate or foreign commerce that are less significant than the effect of school violence. In Perez v. United States, [402 U.S. 146 (1971)], the Court held that the Commerce Clause authorized a federal statute that makes it a crime to engage in loan sharking ("[e]xtortionate credit transactions") at a local level. The Court said that Congress may judge that such transactions, "though purely intrastate, ... affect interstate commerce." ... Presumably, Congress reasoned that threatening or using force, say with a gun on a street corner, to collect a debt occurs sufficiently often so that the activity (by helping organized crime) affects commerce among the States. But, why then cannot Congress also reason that the threat or use of force—the frequent consequence of possessing a gun—in or near a school occurs sufficiently often so that such activity (by inhibiting basic education) affects commerce among the States? The negative impact upon the national economy of an inability to teach basic skills seems no smaller (nor less significant) than that of organized crime.

. . . .

The second legal problem the Court creates comes from its apparent belief that it can reconcile its holding with earlier cases by making a critical distinction between "commercial" and noncommercial "transaction[s]." That is to say, the Court believes the Constitution would distinguish between two local activities, each of which has an identical effect upon interstate commerce, if one, but not the other, is "commercial" in nature.... Although the majority today attempts to categorize Perez, McClung, and Wickard as involving intrastate "economic activity," the Courts that decided each of those cases did not focus upon the economic nature of the activity regulated. Rather, they focused upon whether that activity affected interstate or foreign commerce. In fact, the Wickard Court expressly held that Wickard's consumption of home grown wheat, "though it may not be regarded as commerce," could nevertheless be regulated—"whatever its nature"—so long as "it exerts a substantial economic effect on interstate commerce." ...

More importantly, if a distinction between commercial and noncommercial activities is to be made, this is not the case in which to make it.... Schools that teach reading, writing, mathematics, and related basic skills serve both social and commercial purposes, and one cannot easily separate the one from the other....

[I]f there is a principled distinction that could work both here and in future cases, Congress (even in the absence of vocational classes, industry involvement, and private management) could rationally conclude that schools fall on the commercial side of the line. In 1990, the year Congress enacted the statute before us, primary and secondary schools spent $230 billion.... Why could Congress, for Commerce Clause purposes, not consider schools as roughly analogous to commercial investments from which the Nation derives the benefit of an educated work force?

The third legal problem created by the Court's holding is that it threatens legal uncertainty in an area of law that, until this case, seemed reasonably well settled.... [T]he legal uncertainty now created will restrict Congress' ability to enact criminal laws aimed at criminal behavior that, considered problem by problem rather than instance by instance, seriously threatens the economic, as well as social, well-being of Americans.

IV

In sum, to find this legislation within the scope of the Commerce Clause would permit "Congress ... to act in terms of economic ... realities." ... It would interpret the Clause as this Court has traditionally interpreted it, with the exception of one wrong turn subsequently corrected. See Gibbons v. Ogden, 9 Wheat., at 195 (holding that the commerce power extends "to all the external concerns of the nation, and to those internal concerns which affect the States generally"); United States v. Darby, 312 U.S., at 116–117 ("The conclusion is inescapable that Hammer v. Dagenhart [the child labor case], was a departure from the principles which have prevailed in the interpretation of the Commerce Clause both before and since the decision.... It should be and now is overruled"). Upholding this legislation would do no more than simply recognize that Congress had a "rational basis" for finding a significant connection between guns in or near schools and (through their effect on education) the interstate and foreign commerce they threaten.... [a]

B. THE TAXING POWER

Sonzinsky v. United States

300 U.S. 506, 57 S.Ct. 554, 81 L.Ed. 772 (1937).

Mr. Justice Stone delivered the opinion of the Court.

The question for decision is whether § 2 of the National Firearms Act of June 26, 1934, c. 757, 48 Stat. 1236, 26 U.S.C. §§ 1132–1132q, which imposes a $200 annual license tax on dealers in firearms, is a constitutional exercise of the legislative power of Congress.

Petitioner was convicted ... [of] violati[ng] § 2, by dealing in firearms without payment of the tax. ...

Section 2 of the National Firearms Act requires every dealer in firearms to register with the Collector of Internal Revenue in the district where he carries on business, and to pay a special excise tax of $200 a year. Importers or manufacturers are taxed $500 a year. Section 3 imposes a tax of $200 on each transfer of a firearm, payable by the transferor, and § 4 prescribes regulations for the identification of purchasers. The term "firearm" is defined by § 1 as meaning a shotgun or a rifle having a barrel less than eighteen inches in length, or any other weapon, except a pistol or revolver, from which a shot is discharged by an explosive, if capable of being concealed on the person, or a machine gun, and includes a muffler or silencer for any firearm.... Petitioner does not deny that Congress may tax his business as a dealer in firearms. He insists that the present levy is not a true tax, but a penalty imposed for the purpose of suppressing traffic in a certain noxious type of firearms, the local regulation of which is reserved to the states because not granted to the national government. To establish its penal and prohibitive character, he relies on the amounts of the tax imposed by § 2 on dealers, manufacturers and importers, and of the tax imposed by § 3 on each transfer of a "firearm," payable by the transferor. The cumulative effect on the distribution of a limited class of firearms, of relatively small value, by the successive imposition of different taxes, one on the business of the importer or manufacturer, another on that of the dealer, and a third on the transfer to a buyer, is said to be prohibitive in

---

[a] For commentary, see the contributions to Symposium, *Reflections on United States v.* *Lopez*, 94 Michigan Law Review 533–831 (1995).

effect and to disclose unmistakably the legislative purpose to regulate rather than to tax.

The case is not one where the statute contains regulatory provisions related to a purported tax in such a way as has enabled this Court to say in other cases that the latter is a penalty resorted to as a means of enforcing the regulations. See Child Labor Tax Case, 259 U.S. 20, 35; Hill v. Wallace, 259 U.S. 44; Carter v. Carter Coal Co., 298 U.S. 238. Nor is the subject of the tax described or treated as criminal by the taxing statute. Compare United States v. Constantine,[a] 296 U.S. 287. Here § 2 contains no regulation other than the mere registration provisions, which are obviously supportable as in aid of a revenue purpose. On its face it is only a taxing measure, and we are asked to say that the tax, by virtue of its deterrent effect on the activities taxed, operates as a regulation which is beyond the congressional power.

Every tax is in some measure regulatory. To some extent it interposes an economic impediment to the activity taxed as compared with others not taxed. But a tax is not any the less a tax because it has a regulatory effect, ...; and it has long been established that an Act of Congress which on its face purports to be an exercise of the taxing power is not any the less so because the tax is burdensome or tends to restrict or suppress the thing taxed. Veazie Bank v. Fenno, 8 Wall. 533, 548; McCray v. United States, 195 U.S. 27, 60–61....

Inquiry into the hidden motives which may move Congress to exercise a power constitutionally conferred upon it is beyond the competency of courts. Veazie Bank v. Fenno, supra; McCray v. United States, supra, 56–59; United States v. Doremus, supra, 93–94. They will not undertake, by collateral inquiry as to the measure of the regulatory effect of a tax, to ascribe to Congress an attempt, under the guise of taxation, to exercise another power denied by the Federal Constitution. McCray v. United States, supra; cf. Magnano Co. v. Hamilton, supra, 45.

Here the annual tax of $200 is productive of some revenue.[1] We are not free to speculate as to the motives which moved Congress to impose it, or as to the extent to which it may operate to restrict the activities taxed. As it is not attended by an offensive regulation, and since it operates as a tax, it is within the national taxing power....

Affirmed.[b]

---

[a] In the *Constantine* case (1935) the Court held invalid a federal excise tax of $1000 on liquor dealers "carrying on business ... contrary to the laws of a State ... or municipality". The tax was 10 to 50 times greater than the federal tax on dealers operating legally. The Court concluded: "The condition of the imposition is the commission of a crime. This, together with the amount of the tax, is ... significant of penal and prohibitory intent rather than the gathering of revenue." Cardozo, J., (joined by Brandeis and Stone, JJ.) dissented, saying: "Congress may reasonably have believed in view of the attendant risks, a business carried on illegally and furtively is likely to yield larger profits than one transacted openly by law-abiding men. Not repression, but payment commensurate with the gains is thus the animating motive.... Congress may also have believed that the furtive character of the business would increase the difficulty and expense of the process of tax collection."

[1] The $200 tax was paid by 27 dealers in 1934, and by 22 dealers in 1935. Annual Report of the Commissioner of Internal Revenue, Fiscal Year Ended June 30, 1935, pp. 129–131; id., Fiscal Year Ended June 30, 1936, pp. 139–141.

[b] The *McCray–Doremus–Sonzinsky* line of cases was followed in United States v. Sanchez, 340 U.S. 42 (1950), sustaining a federal tax on persons importing or dealing in marijuana.

United States v. Kahriger, 345 U.S. 22 (1953), presented the following situation: As a result of the widely publicized investigations by the Kefauver Crime Committee of the Senate, Congress included in the 1951 Revenue Act provisions requiring persons engaged in the business of accepting wagers to

UNITED STATES v. PTASYNSKI, 462 U.S. 74 (1983). The Crude Oil Windfall Profit Tax of 1980 imposed a federal tax on oil produced, but contained an exception for "exempt Alaskan oil." The exemption covered about 20% of current Alaskan oil and some oil from offshore northern waters outside of state boundaries. A suit was brought challenging the exemption as a violation of the Uniformity Clause which provides that federal taxes "shall be uniform throughout the United States." The Court, in an opinion by Justice Powell, unanimously upheld the validity of the exemption, saying:

"We do not think that the language of the Clause or this Court's decisions prohibit all geographically defined classifications.... [T]he Uniformity Clause requires that an excise tax apply, at the same rate, in all portions of the United States where the subject of the tax is found. Where Congress defines the subject of a tax in nongeographic terms, the Uniformity Clause is satisfied.... We cannot say that when Congress uses geographic terms to identify the same subject, the classification is invalidated. The Uniformity Clause gives Congress wide latitude in deciding what to tax and does not prohibit it from considering geographically isolated problems.... But where Congress does choose to frame a tax in geographic terms, we will examine the classification closely to see if there is actual geographic discrimination.

"In this case, we hold that the classification is constitutional. As discussed above, Congress considered the windfall profit tax a necessary component of its program to encourage the exploration and production of oil. It perceived that the decontrol legislation would result—in certain circumstances—in profits essentially unrelated to the objective of the program, and concluded that these profits should be taxed. Accordingly, Congress divided oil into various classes and gave more favorable treatment to those classes that would be responsive to increased prices.

pay an annual tax of $50 plus 10% of the wagers placed. Each person liable for the tax was also required to file a registration statement with the Internal Revenue Service giving his name, residence, place of business and the name and address of each person accepting wagers for him. The lower court held the tax unconstitutional under United States v. Constantine, 296 U.S. 287 (1935). The Supreme Court reversed, pointing out: "The wagering tax with which we are here concerned applies to all persons engaged in the business of receiving wagers regardless of whether such activity violates state law.... Appellee would have us say that because there is legislative history indicating a Congressional motive to suppress wagering, this tax is not a proper exercise of such taxing power.... It is conceded that a federal excise tax does not cease to be valid merely because it discourages or deters the activities taxed. Nor is the tax invalid because the revenue obtained is negligible.... Unless there are provisions extraneous to any tax need, courts are without authority to limit the exercise of the taxing power. All the provisions of this excise are adapted to the collection of a valid tax." Frankfurter, J. (joined by Douglas, J.) dissented, saying: "[W]hen oblique use is made of the taxing power as to matters which substantively are not within the powers delegated to Congress, the Court cannot shut its eyes to what is obviously, because designedly, an attempt to control conduct which the Constitution left to the responsibility of the States, merely because Congress wrapped the legislation in the verbal cellophane of a revenue measure." He believed that "the context of the circumstances which brought forth this enactment—sensationally exploited disclosures regarding gambling in big cities and small, the relation of this gambling to corrupt politics, the impatient public response to these disclosures, the feeling of ineptitude or paralysis on the part of local law-enforcing agencies—emphatically supports ... that what was formally a means of raising revenue ... was essentially an effort to check if not to stamp out professional gambling." Black and Douglas, JJ., also dissented on the ground that the reporting provisions of the act required taxpayers to incriminate themselves in violation of the Fifth Amendment. This position was later sustained in Marchetti v. United States, 390 U.S. 39 (1968), which overruled Kahriger on the self-incrimination point. For comment on the *Kahriger* case, see: 67 Harv.L.Rev. 164–7 (1953); 52 Mich. L.Rev. 150 (1953); 101 U.Pa.L.Rev. 877 (1953).

"Congress clearly viewed 'exempt Alaskan oil' as a unique class of oil that, consistent with the scheme of the Act, merited favorable treatment. It had before it ample evidence of the disproportionate costs and difficulties—the fragile ecology, the harsh environment, and the remote location—associated with extracting oil from this region. We cannot fault its determination, based on neutral factors, that this oil required separate treatment. Nor is there any indication that Congress sought to benefit Alaska for reasons that would offend the purpose of the Clause. Nothing in the Act's legislative history suggests that Congress intended to grant Alaska an undue preference at the expense of other oil-producing States. This is especially clear because the windfall profit tax itself falls heavily on the State of Alaska."

C.   THE SPENDING POWER

UNITED STATES v. BUTLER, 297 U.S. 1 (1936). One of the major measures of the "New Deal", in combating the Great Depression, was the Agriculture Adjustment Act of 1933. It was designed to raise farm prices and reduce the farm surplus of certain crops through curtailment of production and a tax upon the first processing of these crops. The Secretary of Agriculture was authorized to enter into agreements with individual farmers to reduce acreage in exchange for benefit payments computed on the basis of the reduction. Funds for the payments were derived from a tax levied upon the processor of the commodity involved, the total revenue from the tax being devoted to crop control and no part of it available for general governmental use. The Secretary entered into agreements for the reduction of acreage devoted to cotton (as well as certain other crops) and a processing tax was imposed upon the processors, including Hoosac Mills for which Butler was receiver. Suit was brought to recover the tax on the ground that it was invalid as an integral part of an unconstitutional program to control agricultural production.

The act did not purport to be a regulation of interstate or foreign commerce and the government did not attempt to uphold it on the basis of the commerce clause. The court of appeals held the tax unconstitutional and the Supreme Court affirmed.

Justice Roberts, speaking for the Court, said:

"The clause thought to authorize the legislation ... confers upon the Congress power 'to lay and collect taxes, duties, imposts and excises to pay the debts and provide for the common defence and general welfare of the United States'.... It is not contended that this provision grants power to regulate agricultural production upon the theory that such legislation would promote the general welfare.... The true construction undoubtedly is that the only thing granted is the power to tax for the purpose of providing funds for payment of the nation's debts and making provision for the general welfare....

"Since the foundation of the nation, sharp differences of opinion have persisted as to the true interpretation of the phrase [to provide for the general welfare]. Madison asserted it amounted to no more than a reference to the other powers enumerated in the subsequent clauses of the same section; that, as the United States is a government of limited and enumerated powers, the grant of power to tax and spend for the general national welfare must be confined to the enumerated legislative fields committed to the Congress. In this view the phrase is mere tautology, for taxation and appropriation are or may be necessary incidents of the exercise of any of the enumerated legislative powers. Hamilton, on the other hand, maintained the clause confers a power separate and distinct from those later enumerated, is not restricted in meaning by the grant of them, and Congress consequently has a substantive power to tax and to appropriate, limited only by the requirement that it shall be exercised to provide for the general welfare of the United States. Each contention has had the support of those whose views are entitled to weight. This court has noticed the question, but has never found it necessary to decide which is the true construction. Mr. Justice Story, in his Commentaries, espouses the Hamiltonian position. We shall not review the writings of public men and commentators or discuss the legislative practice. Study of all these leads us to conclude that the reading advocated by Mr. Justice Story is the correct one. While, therefore, the power to tax is not unlimited, its confines are set in the clause which confers it, and not in those of section 8 which bestow and define the legislative powers of the Congress. It results that the power of Congress to authorize expenditure of public moneys for public purposes is not limited by the direct grants of legislative power found in the Constitution.

"But the adoption of the broader construction leaves the power to spend subject to limitations. . . .

"We are not now required to ascertain the scope of the phrase 'general welfare of the United States' or to determine whether an appropriation in aid of agriculture falls within it. Wholly apart from that question, another principle embedded in our Constitution prohibits the enforcement of the Agricultural Adjustment Act. The act invades the reserved rights of the states. It is a statutory plan to regulate and control agricultural production, a matter beyond the powers delegated to the federal government. The tax, the appropriation of the funds raised, and the direction for their disbursement, are but parts of the plan. They are but means to an unconstitutional end.

"From the accepted doctrine that the United States is a government of delegated powers, it follows that those not expressly granted, or reasonably to be implied from such as are conferred, are reserved to the states or to the people. To forestall any suggestion to the contrary, the Tenth Amendment was adopted. The same proposition, otherwise stated, is that powers not granted are prohibited. None to regulate agricultural production is given, and therefore legislation by Congress for that purpose is forbidden.

"It is an established principle that the attainment of a prohibited end may not be accomplished under the pretext of the exertion of powers which are granted. . . .

"The power of taxation, which is expressly granted, may, of course, be adopted as a means to carry into operation another power also expressly granted. But resort to the taxing power to effectuate an end which is not legitimate, not within the scope of the Constitution, is obviously inadmissible. . . . *sub. du process!*

"In the Child Labor Tax Case, 259 U.S. 20, and in Hill v. Wallace, 259 U.S. 44, this court had before it statutes which purported to be taxing measures. But their purpose was found to be to regulate the conduct of manufacturing and trading, not in interstate commerce, but in the states—matters not within any power conferred upon Congress by the Constitution—and the levy of the tax a means to force compliance. The court held this was not a constitutional use, but an unconstitutional abuse of the power to tax. . . . These decisions demonstrate that Congress could not, under the pretext of raising revenue, lay a tax on processors who refuse to pay a certain price for cotton, and exempt those who agree so to do, with the purpose of benefiting producers.

"If the taxing power may not be used as the instrument to enforce a regulation of matters of state concern with respect to which the Congress has no authority to interfere, may it, as in the present case, be employed to raise the money necessary to purchase a compliance which the Congress is powerless to command? The government asserts that whatever might be said against the validity of the plan if compulsory, it is constitutionally sound because the end is accomplished by voluntary co-operation. There are two sufficient answers to the contention. The regulation is not in fact voluntary. The farmer, of course, may refuse to comply, but the price of such refusal is the loss of benefits. The amount offered is intended to be sufficient to exert pressure on him to agree to the proposed regulation. The power to confer or withhold unlimited benefits is the power to coerce or destroy. . . .

"But if the plan were one for purely voluntary co-operation it would stand no better so far as federal power is concerned. At best, it is a scheme for purchasing with federal funds submission to federal regulation of a subject reserved to the states. . . .

"We are not here concerned with a conditional appropriation of money, nor with a provision that if certain conditions are not complied with the appropriation shall no longer be available. . . . There is an obvious difference between a statute stating the conditions upon which moneys shall be expended and one effective only upon assumption of a contractual obligation to submit to a regulation which otherwise could not be enforced. . . .

"Congress has no power to enforce its commands on the farmer to the ends sought by the Agricultural Adjustment Act. It must follow that it may not indirectly accomplish those ends by taxing and spending to purchase compliance. . . ."

Stone, J. (joined by Brandeis and Cardozo, JJ.) dissented, stating in part:

"The Constitution requires that public funds shall be spent for a defined purpose, the promotion of the general welfare. Their expenditure usually involves payment on terms which will insure use by the selected recipients within the limits of the constitutional purpose. Expenditures would fail of their purpose and thus lose their constitutional sanction if the terms of payment were not such that by their influence on the action of the recipients the permitted end would be attained. The power of Congress to spend is inseparable from persuasion to action over which Congress has no legislative control. Congress may not command that the science of agriculture be taught in state universities. But if it would aid the teaching of that science by grants to state institutions, it is appropriate, if not necessary, that the grant be on the condition, incorporated in the Morrill Act [July 2, 1862], 12 Stat. at L. 503, chap. 130, U.S.C. title 7, § 301, August 30, 1890, 26 Stat. at L. 417, chap. 841, U.S.C. title 7, § 322, that it be used for the intended purpose. Similarly it would seem to be compliance with the Constitution, not violation of it, for the government to take and the university to give a contract that the grant would be so used. It makes no difference that there is a promise to do an act which the condition is calculated to induce. Condition and promise are alike valid since both are in furtherance of the national purpose for which the money is appropriated."

He added: "It is a contradiction in terms to say that there is power to spend for the national welfare, while rejecting the power to impose conditions reasonably adapted to the attainment of the end which alone would justify the expenditure."

CHAS. C. STEWARD MACHINE CO. v. DAVIS, 301 U.S. 548 (1937), presented a challenge to Title IX of the Social Security Act of 1935 relating to unemployment compensation. A tax was imposed on employers of eight or more persons; the proceeds were not earmarked, but went into the general funds of the Treasury. If the taxpayer made contributions to a state unemployment compensation fund created by state law certified by the Social Security Board as meeting certain minimum standards, he was entitled to credit such contributions against his federal tax up to 90% of the tax. In order to assure proper administration of the state compensation system, it was required that contributions to the state fund be paid over to the Secretary of the Treasury to the credit of the Unemployment Trust Fund, the Secretary then being required to pay back to the authorized state agency the sums requisitioned by it. Federal machinery for the administration of the Social Security Act was quickly provided and most states immediately enacted legislation making possible their participation in the program. Steward Machine Company sued Davis, a Collector of Internal Revenue, to recover payroll taxes paid, claiming that the law, particularly the 90% credit provisions, resulted in "coercion of the states" in violation of the Tenth Amendment or of restrictions implicit in our federal system.

In a 5–4 decision the Court sustained the statute. In rejecting the coercion argument, the Court referred to the widespread unemployment during the Great Depression and continued:

"... The fact developed quickly that the states were unable to give the requisite relief. The problem had become national in area and dimensions. There was need of help from the nation if the people were not to starve. It is too late today for the argument to be heard with tolerance that in a crisis so extreme the use of the moneys of the nation to relieve the unemployed and their dependents is a use for any purpose narrower than the promotion of the general welfare. Cf. United States v. Butler, 297 U.S. 1, 65, 66.... The Social Security Act is an attempt to find a method by which all these public agencies may work together to a common end. Every dollar of the new taxes will continue in all likelihood to be used and needed by the nation as long as states are unwilling, whether through timidity or for other motives, to do what can be done at home. At least the inference is permissible that Congress so believed, though retaining undiminished freedom to spend the money as it pleased. On the other hand, fulfillment of the home duty will be lightened and encouraged by crediting the taxpayer upon his account with the Treasury of the nation to the extent that his contributions under the laws of the locality have simplified or diminished the problem of relief and the probable demand upon the resources of the fisc.... The difficulty with the petitioner's contention is that it confuses motive with coercion. 'Every tax is in some measure regulatory. To some extent it interposes an economic impediment to the activity taxed as compared with others not taxed.' Sonzinsky v. United States, 300 U.S. 506. In like manner every rebate from a tax when conditioned upon conduct is in some measure a temptation. But to hold that motive or temptation is equivalent to coercion is to plunge the law in endless difficulties....

"In ruling as we do, we leave many questions open. We do not say that a tax is valid, when imposed by act of Congress, if it is laid upon the condition that a state may escape its operation through the adoption of a statute unrelated in subject-matter to activities fairly within the scope of national policy and power. No such question is before us. In the tender of this credit Congress does not intrude upon fields foreign to its function. The purpose of its intervention, as we have shown, is to safeguard its own treasury and as an incident to that protection to place the states upon a footing of equal opportunity. Drains upon its own resources are to be checked; obstructions to the freedom of the states are to be leveled. It is one thing to impose a tax dependent upon the conduct of the taxpayers, or of the state in which they live, where the conduct to be stimulated or discouraged is unrelated to the fiscal need subserved by the tax in its normal operation, or to any other end legitimately national. The Child Labor Tax Case, 259 U.S. 20, and Hill v. Wallace, 259 U.S. 44, were decided in the belief that the statutes there condemned were exposed to that reproach. Cf. United States v. Constantine, 296 U.S. 287. It is quite another thing to say that a tax will be abated upon the doing of an act that will satisfy the fiscal need, the tax and the alternative being approximate equivalents. In such circumstances, if in no others, inducement or persuasion does not go beyond the bounds of power. We do not fix the outermost line. Enough for present purposes that wherever the line may be, this statute is within it. Definition more precise must abide the wisdom of the future. . . .

"United States v. Butler, supra, is cited by petitioner as a decision to the contrary. . . . The decision was by a divided court, a minority taking the view that the objections were untenable. None of them is applicable to the situation here developed.

"(a) The proceeds of the tax in controversy are not earmarked for a special group.

"(b) The unemployment compensation law which is a condition of the credit has had the approval of the state and could not be a law without it.

"(c) The condition is not linked to an irrevocable agreement, for the state at its pleasure may repeal its unemployment law, § 903(a)(6), terminate the credit, and place itself where it was before the credit was accepted.

"(d) The condition is not directed to the attainment of an unlawful end, but to an end, the relief of unemployment, for which nation and state may lawfully cooperate. . . ."

The Court also concluded that the statute did not call "for a surrender by the states of powers essential to their quasi-sovereign existence."

". . . A credit to taxpayers for payments made to a state under a state unemployment law will be manifestly futile in the absence of some assurance that the law leading to the credit is in truth what it professes to be. An unemployment law framed in such a way that the unemployed who look to it will be deprived of reasonable protection is one in name and nothing more. What is basic and essential may be assured by suitable conditions. The terms embodied in these sections are directed to that end. A wide range of judgment is given to the several states as to the particular type of statute to be spread upon their books. . . . What they may not do if they would earn the credit, is to depart from those standards which in the judgment of Congress are to be ranked as fundamental. Even if opinion may differ as to the fundamental quality of one or more of the conditions, the difference will not avail to vitiate the statute. In determining essentials, Congress must have the benefit of a fair margin of discretion. . . ."

Justices McReynolds, Sutherland, Van Devanter and Butler dissented.

HELVERING v. DAVIS, 301 U.S. 619 (1937). This case involved the old age benefit provisions (Titles II and VIII) of the Social Security Act. In meeting the contention that the program for paying old age benefits was not authorized by the general welfare clause, the Court reviewed evidence of the widespread economic plight of the aged and added:

"The problem is plainly national in area and dimensions. Moreover, laws of the separate states cannot deal with it effectively. Congress, at least, had a basis for that belief. States and local governments are often lacking in the resources that are necessary to finance an adequate program of security for the aged. This is brought out with a wealth of illustration in recent studies of the problem. Apart from the failure of resources, states and local governments are at times reluctant to increase so heavily the burden of taxation to be borne by their residents for fear of placing themselves in a position of economic disadvantage as compared with neighbors or competitors.

"We have seen this in our study of the problem of unemployment compensation. Steward Machine Co. v. Davis, supra. A system of old age pensions has special dangers of its own, if put in force in one state and rejected in another. The existence of such a system is a bait to the needy and dependent elsewhere, encouraging them to migrate and seek a haven of repose. Only a power that is national can serve the interests of all.

"Whether wisdom or unwisdom resides in the scheme of benefits set forth in Title II, it is not for us to say. The answer to such inquiries must come from Congress, not the courts. Our concern here, as often, is with power, not with wisdom. Counsel for respondent has recalled to us the virtues of self-reliance and frugality. There is a possibility, he says, that aid from a paternal government may sap those sturdy virtues and breed a race of weaklings. If Massachusetts so believes and shapes her laws in that conviction, must her breed of sons be changed, he asks, because some other philosophy of government finds favor in the halls of Congress? But the answer is not doubtful. One might ask with equal reason whether the system of protective tariffs is to be set aside at will in one state or another whenever local policy prefers the rule of laissez faire. The issue is a closed one. It was fought out long ago. When money is spent to promote the general welfare, the concept of welfare or the opposite is shaped by Congress, not the states. So the concept be not arbitrary, the locality must yield. Constitution, Art. VI, Par. 2. . . . "

THE IMPACT OF FEDERAL GRANTS TO THE STATES

Federal grants to the states and local governments have increased rapidly in recent years. Total federal grants-in-aid and shared revenue increased from just under 11 billion dollars in 1965 to an estimated total of 228 billion in 1995. *Statistical Abstract* 1995, p. 302. The percentage of state and local government budgets received from the federal government was 23% in 1994, id.

BUCKLEY v. VALEO, 424 U.S. 1 (1976). Subtitle H of the Federal Election Campaign Act, as amended in 1974, establishes a Presidential Election Campaign Fund, financed from general revenues in the aggregate amount designated by individual taxpayers who on their income tax returns may authorize payment to the Fund of one dollar of their tax liability in case of an individual return or two dollars in case of a joint return. The Fund consists of separate accounts to finance party nominating conventions, general election campaigns, and primary campaigns. To the contention that Subtitle H is invalid as contrary to the general welfare clause of Article I, § 8, the Court responded as follows:

"Appellants' 'general welfare' contention erroneously treats the General Welfare Clause as a limitation upon congressional power. It is rather a grant of power, the scope of which is quite expansive, particularly in view of the enlargement of power by the Necessary and Proper Clause. McCulloch v. Maryland, 4 Wheat. 316, 420 (1819). Congress has power to regulate Presidential elections and primaries, United States v. Classic, 313 U.S. 299 (1941);

Burroughs v. United States, 290 U.S. 534 (1934); and public financing of Presidential elections as a means to reform the electoral process was clearly a choice within the granted power. It is for Congress to decide which expenditures will promote the general welfare: '[T]he power of Congress to authorize expenditure of public moneys for public purposes is not limited by the direct grants of legislative power found in the Constitution.' United States v. Butler, 297 U.S. 1, 66 (1936). See Helvering v. Davis, 301 U.S. 619, 640–641 (1937). Any limitations upon the exercise of that granted power must be found elsewhere in the Constitution. In this case, Congress was legislating for the 'general welfare'—to reduce the deleterious influence of large contributions on our political process, to facilitate communication by candidates with the electorate, and to free candidates from the rigors of fundraising. See S.Rep. No. 93–689, pp. 1–10 (1974). Whether the chosen means appear 'bad,' 'unwise,' or 'unworkable' to us is irrelevant; Congress has concluded that the means are 'necessary and proper' to promote the general welfare and we thus decline to find this legislation without the grant of power in Art. I, § 8.

"Appellants' challenge to the dollar check-off provision (§ 6096) fails for the same reason. They maintain that Congress is required to permit taxpayers to designate particular candidates or parties as recipients of their money. But the appropriation to the Fund in § 9006 is like any other appropriation from the general revenue except that its amount is determined by reference to the aggregate of the one- and two-dollar authorization on taxpayers' income tax returns. This detail does not constitute the appropriation any less an appropriation by Congress. The fallacy of appellants' argument is therefore apparent; every appropriation made by Congress uses public money in a manner to which some taxpayers object."[a]

D. WAR AND TREATY POWERS

THE SOURCES OF NATIONAL POWER

Since the primary purpose of the Founding Fathers was "to form a more perfect Union" with a stronger national government, one might suppose that the national powers over foreign affairs would have been quite fully and explicitly stated. But such was not the case. The constitutional provisions dealing expressly with foreign relations, or matters particularly related thereto, are rather sparse and uncorrelated. Most of them appear in the enumeration of executive powers: the President is made "Commander-in-Chief" of the armed forces; he is given the power, with the approval of two-thirds of the Senate, "to make Treaties"; and, with the "advice and consent" of the Senate, he "shall appoint Ambassadors, other public Ministers and Consuls," i.e., our representatives abroad (Art. II, § 2). Also, "he shall receive Ambassadors and other public Ministers" (Art. II, § 3). There are two additional provisions (not referring particularly to foreign affairs) under which the President has extensive undefined power. They provide "the executive power shall be vested in" him (Art. II, § 1) and "he shall take care that the Laws be faithfully executed" (Art. II, § 3).

Aside from Senate participation in the making of treaties, the powers of Congress explicitly relating to foreign affairs or national defense are: the power to regulate commerce with foreign nations; to establish "a uniform rule of naturalization"; to define and punish piracies and felonies committed on the

---

[a] For further discussion of conditional spending issues, see New York v. United States, infra p. 387. See generally Rosenthal, *Conditional Federal Spending and the Constitution*, 39 Stanford Law Review 1103 (1987).

high seas and offenses against the law of nations; to declare war; to maintain an army and navy; and to make rules for the regulation of the armed forces (Art. I, § 8).

To make clear that some of these powers are exclusively national, a few explicit limitations are imposed on the states: no State shall enter into any treaty, alliance, or confederation; nor, without the consent of Congress, lay any imposts or duties on imports or exports, except what may be necessary for executing state inspection laws; nor, without the consent of Congress, keep "troops or ships of war" in time of peace, or engage in war unless actually invaded or in imminent danger thereof (Art. I, § 10).

UNITED STATES v. CURTISS–WRIGHT EXPORT CORP., 299 U.S. 304 (1936). By a Joint Resolution of May 28, 1934, Congress purported to authorize the President to embargo the sale of arms to countries engaged in armed conflict in the Chaco. (Bolivia and Paraguay were so engaged.) The President, by proclamation, immediately imposed an embargo in accordance with the Joint Resolution. Curtiss–Wright contested the validity of the embargo on the ground that the Joint Resolution attempted an unconstitutional delegation of legislative power to the Executive. In rejecting this contention, the Court (per Sutherland, J.) expressed the view that there are fundamental differences between "the powers of the federal government in respect of foreign or external affairs and those in respect of domestic or internal affairs." The opinion continued:

"The two classes of powers are different, both in respect of their origin and their nature. The broad statement that the federal government can exercise no powers except those specifically enumerated in the Constitution, and such implied powers as are necessary and proper to carry into effect the enumerated powers, is categorically true only in respect of our internal affairs. In that field, the primary purpose of the Constitution was to carve from the general mass of legislative powers *then possessed by the states* such portions as it was thought desirable to vest in the federal government, leaving those not included in the enumeration still in the states. Carter v. Carter Coal Co., 298 U.S. 238, 294. That this doctrine applies only to powers which the states had, is self evident. And since the states severally never possessed international powers, such powers could not have been carved from the mass of state powers but obviously were transmitted to the United States from some other source....

"It results that the investment of the federal government with the powers of external sovereignty did not depend upon the affirmative grants of the Constitution. The powers to declare and wage war, to conclude peace, to make treaties, to maintain diplomatic relations with other sovereignties, if they had never been mentioned in the Constitution, would have vested in the federal government as necessary concomitants of nationality.... As a member of the family of nations, the right and power of the United States in that field are equal to the right and power of the other members of the international family. Otherwise, the United States is not completely sovereign. The power to acquire territory by discovery and occupation (Jones v. United States, 137 U.S. 202, 212), the power to expel undesirable aliens (Fong Yue Ting v. United States, 149 U.S. 698, 705 et seq.), the power to make such international agreements as do not constitute treaties in the constitutional sense (Altman & Co. v. United States, 224 U.S. 583, 600–601; Crandall, Treaties, Their Making and Enforcement, 2d ed., p. 102 and note 1), none of which is expressly affirmed by the Constitution, nevertheless exist as inherently inseparable from the conception of nationality. This the court recognized, and in each of the cases cited found the warrant for its conclusions not in the provisions of the Constitution, but in the law of nations."[1]

Woods v. Cloyd W. Miller Co.

333 U.S. 138, 68 S.Ct. 421, 92 L.Ed. 596 (1948).

Mr. Justice Douglas delivered the opinion of the Court.

The case is here on a direct appeal from a judgment of the District Court holding unconstitutional Title II of the Housing and Rent Act of 1947. 61 Stat. 193, 196.

The Act became effective on July 1, 1947, and the following day the appellee demanded of its tenants increases of 40% and 60% for rental accommodations in the Cleveland Defense–Rental Area, an admitted violation of the Act and regulations adopted pursuant thereto. Appellant thereupon instituted this proceeding under § 206(b) of the Act to enjoin the violations. A preliminary injunction issued. After a hearing it was dissolved and a permanent injunction denied.

The District Court was of the view that the authority of Congress to regulate rents by virtue of the war power (see Bowles v. Willingham, 321 U.S. 503) ended with the Presidential Proclamation terminating hostilities on December 31, 1946, since that proclamation inaugurated "peace-in-fact" though it did not mark termination of the war. . . .

We conclude, in the first place, that the war power sustains this legislation. The Court said in Hamilton v. Kentucky Distilleries Co., 251 U.S. 146, 161, that the war power includes the power "to remedy the evils which have arisen from its rise and progress" and continues for the duration of that emergency. Whatever may be the consequences when war is officially terminated, the war power does not necessarily end with the cessation of hostilities. We recently held that it is adequate to support the preservation of rights created by wartime legislation, Fleming v. Mohawk Wrecking & Lumber Co., 331 U.S. 111. But it has a broader sweep. In *Hamilton v. Kentucky Distilleries Co., supra*, and Ruppert v. Caffey, 251 U.S. 264, prohibition laws which were enacted after the Armistice in World War I were sustained as exercises of the war power because they conserved manpower and increased efficiency of production in the critical days during the period of demobilization, and helped to husband the supply of grains and cereals depleted by the war effort. Those cases followed the reasoning of Stewart v. Kahn, 11 Wall. 493, which held that Congress had the power to toll the statute of limitations of the States during the period when the process of their courts was not available to litigants due to the conditions obtaining in the Civil War.

The constitutional validity of the present legislation follows *a fortiori* from those cases. The legislative history of the present Act makes abundantly clear that there has not yet been eliminated the deficit in housing which in consider-

---

[1] Justice Sutherland's theory of extra-constitutional powers over foreign affairs has been frequently discussed but never resolved. See Henkin, *Foreign Affairs and the United States Constitution* (2d ed. 1996), Ch. I; Dodd, *Implied Powers and Implied Limitations in Constitutional Law*, 29 Yale L.J. 137 (1919), 1 Selected Essays (1938) 330; Riesenfeld, *The Power of Congress and the President in Inter-* *national Relations*, 25 Calif.L.Rev. 643 (1937). See also Henkin, *The Treaty Makers and the Law Makers*, 107 U.Pa.L.Rev. 903, 922–936 (1959); Perez v. Brownell, 356 U.S. 44, 57 (1958). *Perez* was overruled in Afroyim v. Rusk, 387 U.S. 253 (1967), but not the statement about the extra-constitutional foundations of the power over foreign relations.

able measure was caused by the heavy demobilization of veterans and by the cessation or reduction in residential construction during the period of hostilities due to the allocation of building materials to military projects. Since the war effort contributed heavily to that deficit, Congress has the power even after the cessation of hostilities to act to control the forces that a short supply of the needed article created. If that were not true, the Necessary and Proper Clause, Art. I, § 8, cl. 18, would be drastically limited in its application to the several war powers. The Court has declined to follow that course in the past. Hamilton v. Kentucky Distilleries Co., supra, pp. 155, 156; Ruppert v. Caffey, supra, pp. 299, 300. We decline to take it today. The result would be paralyzing. It would render Congress powerless to remedy conditions the creation of which necessarily followed from the mobilization of men and materials for successful prosecution of the war. So to read the Constitution would be to make it self-defeating.

We recognize the force of the argument that the effects of war under modern conditions may be felt in the economy for years and years, and that if the war power can be used in days of peace to treat all the wounds which war inflicts on our society, it may not only swallow up all other powers of Congress but largely obliterate the Ninth and the Tenth Amendments as well. There are no such implications in today's decision. We deal here with the consequences of a housing deficit greatly intensified during the period of hostilities by the war effort. Any power, of course, can be abused. But we cannot assume that Congress is not alert to its constitutional responsibilities. And the question whether the war power has been properly employed in cases such as this is open to judicial inquiry. Hamilton v. Kentucky Distilleries Co., supra; Ruppert v. Caffey, supra. . . .

Reversed.

Mr. Justice Frankfurter concurs in this opinion because it decides no more than was decided in Hamilton v. Kentucky Distilleries Co., 251 U.S. 146, and Jacob Ruppert v. Caffey, 251 U.S. 264, and merely applies those decisions to the situation now before the Court.

Mr. Justice Jackson, concurring.

I agree with the result in this case, but the arguments that have been addressed to us lead me to utter more explicit misgivings about war powers than the Court has done. The Government asserts no constitutional basis for this legislation other than this vague, undefined and undefinable "war power."

No one will question that this power is the most dangerous one to free government in the whole catalogue of powers. It usually is invoked in haste and excitement when calm legislative consideration of constitutional limitation is difficult. It is executed in a time of patriotic fervor that makes moderation unpopular. And, worst of all, it is interpreted by judges under the influence of the same passions and pressures. Always, as in this case, the Government urges hasty decision to forestall some emergency or serve some purpose and pleads that paralysis will result if its claims to power are denied or their confirmation delayed.

Particularly when the war power is invoked to do things to the liberties of people, or to their property or economy that only indirectly affect conduct of the war and do not relate to the management of the war itself, the constitutional basis should be scrutinized with care.

I think we can hardly deny that the war power is as valid a ground for federal rent control now as it has been at any time. We still are technically in a state of war. I would not be willing to hold that war powers may be indefinitely prolonged merely by keeping legally alive a state of war that had in fact ended.

I cannot accept the argument that war powers last as long as the effects and consequences of war, for if so they are permanent—as permanent as the war debts. But I find no reason to conclude that we could find fairly that the present state of war is merely technical. We have armies abroad exercising our war power and have made no peace terms with our allies, not to mention our principal enemies. I think the conclusion that the war power has been applicable during the lifetime of this legislation is unavoidable.

INTERNATIONAL AGREEMENTS

To what extent may the national government provide the law governing local affairs through entering into international agreements in areas where it is otherwise incompetent to act? This question poses the central issue to be pursued at this point in the materials. The division of authority between the President and Congress with respect to the making of international agreements will be discussed briefly in Chapter 7, Separation of Powers. The international aspects of treaties and executive agreements—the way in which they regulate relationships with other countries and international organizations—is a separate subject reserved for courses in international law and international transactions. For a general study of the problems of federal states in the field of international agreements, see Hendry, *Treaties and Federal Constitutions* (1955). For a penetrating discussion of all of the issues involved here see Henkin, *Foreign Affairs and the United States Constitution* (2d ed. 1996).

HAUENSTEIN v. LYNHAM, 100 U.S. 483 (1880). Hauenstein died intestate a resident of Richmond, Virginia, where he owned considerable real estate. The proceeds from the sale of this property were claimed by his heirs who were citizens of Switzerland. Their claim was resisted on the ground that the property had escheated to the state because Virginia law provided that aliens were not qualified to inherit property in the state. An 1850 treaty between the United States and Switzerland provided that in this situation the alien-heirs should be permitted to sell the property and withdraw the proceeds. The Virginia courts decided against the heirs.

The Supreme Court reversed and remanded the case, saying:

"That the laws of the State, irrespective of the treaty, would put the fund into her coffers, is no objection to the right or the remedy claimed by the plaintiffs in error. The efficacy of the treaty is declared and guaranteed by the Constitution of the United States. . . . If doubts could exist before the adoption of the present national government, they must be entirely removed by the sixth article of the Constitution, which provides that 'all treaties made or which shall be made under the authority of the United States, shall be *the supreme law of the land,* and the judges in every State shall be bound thereby, any thing in the Constitution or laws of any State to the contrary notwithstanding.' . . . A treaty cannot be *the supreme law of the land,* that is, of all the United States, if any act of a State legislature can stand in its way. . . . It must always be borne in mind that the Constitution, laws, and treaties of the United States are as much a part of the law of every State as its own local laws and Constitution. This is a fundamental principle in our system of complex national policy. . . . We have no doubt that this treaty is within the treaty-making power conferred by the Constitution. And it is our duty to give it full effect. We forbear to pursue the topic further. . . ."

CONGRESSIONAL LEGISLATION INCONSISTENT WITH A TREATY

A treaty that manifests an intention to become effective as domestic law of the United States supersedes inconsistent provisions of earlier acts of Congress as well as inconsistent state laws, ALI, *Restatement, Third, (The Foreign Relations Law of the United States)* §§ 111, 115 (1987).[1] However, subsequent Congressional legislation will be given effect even though inconsistent with a prior treaty. See the Chinese Exclusion Cases, 130 U.S. 581 (1889), which sustained legislation excluding the entry of Chinese even though such exclusion was in violation of a treaty with China. The Court said: "The last expression of sovereign will must control." In such a situation, enforcement of the international obligation, if any, must be found in diplomatic negotiations or an international tribunal.

Missouri v. Holland

252 U.S. 416, 40 S.Ct. 382, 64 L.Ed. 641 (1920).

Mr. Justice Holmes delivered the opinion of the Court.

This is a bill in equity brought by the State of Missouri to prevent a game warden of the United States from attempting to enforce the Migratory Bird Treaty Act of July 3, 1918, c. 128, 40 Stat. 755, and the regulations made by the Secretary of Agriculture in pursuance of the same. The ground of the bill is that the statute is an unconstitutional interference with the rights reserved to the States by the Tenth Amendment, and that the acts of the defendant done and threatened under that authority invade the sovereign right of the State and contravene its will manifested in statutes. The State also alleges a pecuniary interest, as owner of the wild birds within its borders and otherwise, admitted by the Government to be sufficient, but it is enough that the bill is a reasonable and proper means to assert the alleged quasi sovereign rights of a State. Kansas v. Colorado, 185 U.S. 125, 142 ... A motion to dismiss was sustained by the District Court on the ground that the Act of Congress is constitutional.... The State appeals.

On December 8, 1916, a treaty between the United States and Great Britain was proclaimed by the President. It recited that many species of birds in their annual migrations traversed many parts of the United States and of Canada, that they were of great value as a source of food and in destroying insects injurious to vegetation, but were in danger of extermination through lack of adequate protection. It therefore provided for specified closed seasons and protection in other forms, and agreed that the two powers would take or propose to their lawmaking bodies the necessary measures for carrying the treaty out. 39 Stat. 1702. The above mentioned act of July 3, 1918, ... prohibited the killing, capturing or selling any of the migratory birds included in the terms of the treaty except as permitted by regulations compatible with those terms to be made by the Secretary of Agriculture.... It is unnecessary to go into any details, because, as we have said, the question raised is the general one whether the treaty and statute are void as an interference with the rights reserved to the States.

To answer this question it is not enough to refer to the Tenth Amendment, reserving the powers not delegated to the United States, because by Article 2, Section 2, the power to make treaties is delegated expressly, and by Article 6 treaties made under the authority of the United States, along with the Constitution and laws of the United States made in pursuance thereof, are declared the supreme law of the land. If the treaty is valid there can be no

---

[1] There is a distinction between "self-executing" and "non-self-executing" treaties. In general, a non-self-executing treaty is one that, by its terms, requires implementation by legislative or executive action in order to be effective.

dispute about the validity of the statute under Article 1, Section 8, as a necessary and proper means to execute the powers of the Government. The language of the Constitution as to the supremacy of treaties being general, the question before us is narrowed to an inquiry into the ground upon which the present supposed exception is placed.

It is said that a treaty cannot be valid if it infringes the Constitution, that there are limits, therefore, to the treaty-making power, and that one such limit is that what an act of Congress could not do unaided, in derogation of the powers reserved to the States, a treaty cannot do. An earlier act of Congress that attempted by itself and not in pursuance of a treaty to regulate the killing of migratory birds within the States had been held bad in the District Court. United States v. Shauver, 214 Fed. 154. United States v. McCullagh, 221 Fed. 288. Those decisions were supported by arguments that migratory birds were owned by the States in their sovereign capacity for the benefit of their people, and that under cases like Geer v. Connecticut, 161 U.S. 519, this control was one that Congress had no power to displace. The same argument is supposed to apply now with equal force.

Whether the two cases cited were decided rightly or not they cannot be accepted as a test of the treaty power. Acts of Congress are the supreme law of the land only when made in pursuance of the Constitution, while treaties are declared to be so when made under the authority of the United States. It is open to question whether the authority of the United States means more than the formal acts prescribed to make the convention. We do not mean to imply that there are no qualifications to the treaty-making power; but they must be ascertained in a different way. It is obvious that there may be matters of the sharpest exigency for the national well being that an act of Congress could not deal with but that a treaty followed by such an act could, and it is not lightly to be assumed that, in matters requiring national action, "a power which must belong to and somewhere reside in every civilized government" is not to be found.... We are not yet discussing the particular case before us but only are considering the validity of the test proposed. With regard to that we may add that when we are dealing with words that also are a constituent act, like the Constitution of the United States, we must realize that they have called into life a being the development of which could not have been foreseen completely by the most gifted of its begetters. It was enough for them to realize or to hope that they had created an organism; it has taken a century and has cost their successors much sweat and blood to prove that they created a nation. The case before us must be considered in the light of our whole experience and not merely in that of what was said a hundred years ago. The treaty in question does not contravene any prohibitory words to be found in the Constitution. The only question is whether it is forbidden by some invisible radiation from the general terms of the Tenth Amendment. We must consider what this country has become in deciding what that amendment has reserved.

The State as we have intimated founds its claim of exclusive authority upon an assertion of title to migratory birds, an assertion that is embodied in statute. No doubt it is true that as between a State and its inhabitants the State may regulate the killing and sale of such birds, but it does not follow that its authority is exclusive of paramount powers. To put the claim of the State upon title is to lean upon a slender reed. Wild birds are not in the possession of anyone; and possession is the beginning of ownership. The whole foundation of the State's rights is the presence within their jurisdiction of birds that yesterday had not arrived, tomorrow may be in another State and in a week a thousand miles away. If we are to be accurate we cannot put the case of the State upon higher ground than that the treaty deals with creatures that for the moment are within the state borders, that it must be carried out by officers of the United States within the same territory, and that but for the treaty the State would be free to regulate this subject itself.

As most of the laws of the United States are carried out within the States and as many of them deal with matters which in the silence of such laws the State might regulate, such general grounds are not enough to support Missouri's claim. Valid treaties of course "are as binding within the territorial limits of the States as they are elsewhere throughout the dominion of the United States." Baldwin v. Franks, 120 U.S. 678, 683. No doubt the great body of private relations usually fall within the control of the State, but a treaty may override its power. . . .

Here a national interest of very nearly the first magnitude is involved. It can be protected only by national action in concert with that of another power. The subject matter is only transitorily within the State and has no permanent habitat therein. But for the treaty and the statute there soon might be no birds for any powers to deal with. We see nothing in the Constitution that compels the Government to sit by while a food supply is cut off and the protectors of our forests and our crops are destroyed. It is not sufficient to rely upon the States. The reliance is vain, and were it otherwise, the question is whether the United States is forbidden to act. We are of opinion that the treaty and statute must be upheld.

Decree affirmed.

Mr. Justice Van Devanter and Mr. Justice Pitney dissent.

UNITED STATES v. BELMONT, 301 U.S. 324 (1937). On November 16, 1933 President Roosevelt and Maxim Litvinov executed an agreement whereby the United States first gave recognition to the U.S.S.R. In addition, by this agreement the U.S.S.R. assigned to the United States its claims against Americans who held funds of Russian companies whose assets were confiscated by the Soviets after the revolution.

The United States brought an action based on this agreement to recover money which the Petrograd Metal Works, a Russian corporation, had deposited with the New York banker, August Belmont. The lower federal courts dismissed this action on the ground that recovery of these claims would be contrary to the policy and law of the State of New York which denied effect to decrees of foreign governments purporting to confiscate property in the state. The United States Supreme Court reversed. The opinion by Justice Sutherland included the following:

"We do not pause to inquire whether in fact there was any policy of the State of New York to be infringed, since we are of opinion that no state policy can prevail against the international compact here involved. . . .

"A treaty signifies 'a compact made between two or more independent nations with a view to the public welfare.' Altman & Co. v. United States, 224 U.S. 583, 600. But an international compact, as this was, is not always a treaty which requires the participation of the Senate. There are many such compacts, of which a protocol, a *modus vivendi*, a postal convention, and agreements like that now under consideration are illustrations. See 5 Moore, *Int.Law Digest*, 210–221. . . .

"Plainly, the external powers of the United States are to be exercised without regard to state laws or policies. The supremacy of a treaty in this respect has been recognized from the beginning. . . . And while this rule in respect of treaties is established by the express language of cl. 2, Art. VI, of the Constitution, the same rule would result in the case of all international compacts and agreements from the very fact that complete power over international affairs is in the national government and is not and cannot be subject to any curtailment or interference on the part of the several states. Compare United States v. Curtiss–Wright Export Corp., 299 U.S. 304, 316, et seq."

UNITED STATES V. PINK, 315 U.S. 203 (1942). The United States brought a further action on the Roosevelt–Litvinov agreement to recover the funds of the New York branch of a Russian Insurance Company. The New York court dismissed the action because of its rule, mentioned above, barring effect to foreign expropriation decrees. The Supreme Court again reversed. The opinion by Justice Douglas relied upon the above language of the Belmont case, and added:

"A treaty is a 'Law of the Land' under the supremacy clause (Art. 6, Cl. 2) of the Constitution. Such international compacts and agreements as the Litvinov Assignment have a similar dignity. . . .

". . . the action of New York tends to restore some of the precise irritants which had long affected the relations between these two great nations and which the policy of recognition was designed to eliminate.

". . . If state action could defeat or alter our foreign policy, serious consequences might ensue. The nation as a whole would be held to answer if a State created difficulties with a foreign power . . . Certainly, the conditions for 'enduring friendship' between the nations, which the policy of recognition in this instance was designed to effectuate, are not likely to flourish where, contrary to national policy, a lingering atmosphere of hostility is created by state action."

REID v. COVERT, 354 U.S. 1 (1957). Mrs. Covert, a civilian, killed her husband, a sergeant at a U.S. air base in England where she was residing with him. Her conviction by court-martial was challenged on the ground that it violated the guaranties of indictment and trial by jury as provided by Article III and the Fifth Amendment. A companion case involved a similar conviction of Mrs. Smith for the murder of her husband in Japan. The convictions were reversed and an opinion by Black, J. (joined by Warren, C.J., Douglas and Brennan, JJ.) contained the following discussion regarding the constitutional status of international agreements:

"At the time of Mrs. Covert's alleged offense, an executive agreement was in effect between the United States and Great Britain which permitted United States' military courts to exercise exclusive jurisdiction over offenses committed in Great Britain by American servicemen or their dependents. For its part, the United States agreed that these military courts would be willing and able to try and to punish all offenses against the laws of Great Britain by such persons. In all material respects, the same situation existed in Japan when Mrs. Smith killed her husband. Even though a court-martial does not give an accused trial by jury and other Bill of Rights protections, the Government contends that Art. 2(11) of the UCMJ, insofar as it provides for the military trial of dependents accompanying the armed forces in Great Britain and Japan, can be sustained as legislation which is necessary and proper to carry out the United States' obligations under the international agreements made with those countries. The obvious and decisive answer to this, of course, is that no agreement with a foreign nation can confer power on the Congress, or on any other branch of Government, which is free from the restraints of the Constitution.

"Article VI, the Supremacy Clause of the Constitution, declares:

" 'This Constitution, and the Laws of the United States which shall be made in Pursuance thereof; and all Treaties made, or which shall be made, under the Authority of the United States, shall be the supreme Law of the Land;. . . .'

"There is nothing in this language which intimates that treaties and laws enacted pursuant to them do not have to comply with the provisions of the Constitution. Nor is there anything in the debates which accompanied the drafting and ratification of the Constitution which even suggests such a result. These debates as well as the history that surrounds the adoption of the treaty provision in Article VI make it clear that the reason treaties were not limited to those made in 'pursuance' of the Constitution was so that the agreements made by the United States under the Articles of Confederation, including the important peace treaties which concluded the Revolutionary War, would remain in effect. It would be manifestly contrary to the objectives of those who created the Constitution, as well as those who were responsible for the Bill of Rights—let alone alien to our entire constitutional history and tradition—to construe Article VI as permitting the United States to exercise power under an international agreement without observing constitutional prohibitions. In effect, such construction would permit amendment of that document in a manner not sanctioned by Article V. The prohibitions of the Constitution were designed to apply to all branches of the National Government and they cannot be nullified by the Executive or by the Executive and the Senate combined. . . .

"There is nothing in Missouri v. Holland, 252 U.S. 416, which is contrary to the position taken here. There the Court carefully noted that the treaty involved was not inconsistent with any specific provision of the Constitution. The Court was concerned with the Tenth Amendment which reserves to the States or the people all power not delegated to the National Government. To the extent that the United States can validly make treaties, the people and the States have delegated their power to the National Government and the Tenth Amendment is no barrier. . . ."

THE UNITED NATIONS AND THE TREATY POWER

The UN Charter, Art. 55, states that "The United Nations shall promote . . . universal respect for, and observance of, human rights and fundamental freedoms for all without distinction as to race, sex, language, or religion." By Article 56, all members "pledge themselves to take joint and separate action in cooperation with the Organization for the achievement of the purposes set forth in Article 55." In Fujii v. State, 217 P.2d 481 (1950), an intermediate court of appeal in California held the state's discriminatory land law invalid on the ground that the UN Charter was self-executing. The California Supreme Court affirmed the judgment, but on the ground that the state law violated the Fourteenth Amendment, 38 Cal.2d 718, 242 P.2d 617 (1952).

Work in the United Nations toward the drafting of a Covenant on Human Rights[1] and Genocide Convention, and some of the implications of the *Belmont* and *Pink* cases, generated alarm in some quarters over the scope of the power to make treaties and other international agreements. As a result, various proposals were made to amend the Constitution. On March 5, 1956, the Senate

---

[1] Chafee, *Federal and State Powers and the U.N. Covenant on Human Rights,* 1951 Wis.L.Rev. 389, 623 (1951); Schwelb, *International Conventions on Human Rights,* 9 Int. & Comp.L.Q. 654 (1960). A striking example of the impact on internal law of the European Convention on Human Rights is reported in Golsong, *The European Convention in a German Court,* 33 Brit.Yearb. of Int.L. 317 (1957) (deportation of person convicted of crime (homosexuality) who had recently married would violate his right under the Convention "to respect for his private and family life").

Judiciary Committee favorably reported the following proposed constitutional amendment:

"Sec. 1. A provision of a treaty or other international agreement which conflicts with any provision of this Constitution shall not be of any force or effect.

"Sec. 2. On the question of advising and consenting to the ratification of a treaty, the vote shall be determined by yeas and nays, and the names of the persons voting for and against shall be entered on the journal of the Senate."

The next year Senator Bricker proposed a more detailed amendment which included a provision that, "A treaty or other international agreement shall have legislative effect within the United States as a law thereof only through legislation, except to the extent that the Senate shall provide affirmatively, in its resolution advising and consenting to a treaty, that a treaty shall have legislative effect."

None of the proposed amendments received the requisite two-thirds majority vote.[2]

Does the language in *Reid v. Covert,* supra, show that no amendment was necessary?

E.   THE PROPERTY POWER

Kleppe v. New Mexico

426 U.S. 529, 96 S.Ct. 2285, 49 L.Ed.2d 34 (1976).

Mr. Justice Marshall delivered the opinion of the Court.

At issue in this case is whether Congress exceeded its powers under the Constitution in enacting the Wild Free–Roaming Horses and Burros Act.

I.

The Wild Free–Roaming Horses and Burros Act (the Act), 85 Stat. 649–651, 16 U.S.C. (Supp. IV) §§ 1331–1340, was enacted in 1971 to protect "all unbranded and unclaimed horses and burros on public lands of the United States," § 2(b) of the Act, 16 U.S.C. § 1332(b), from "capture, branding, harassment, or death." § 1 of the Act, 16 U.S.C. § 1331. The Act provides that all such horses and burros on the public lands administered by the Secretary of the Interior through the Bureau of Land Management (BLM) or by the Secretary of Agriculture through the Forest Service are committed to the jurisdiction of the respective Secretaries, who are "directed to protect and manage [the animals] as components of the public lands . . . in a manner that is

---

[2] The debate over the proper scope of the treaty power produced voluminous and heated discussion. See e.g. Holman, *Treaty Law–Making; A Blank Check for Writing a New Constitution,* 36 A.B.A.J. 707 (1950). Finch, *The Treaty Clause Amendment: The Case for the Association,* 38 A.B.A.J. 467 (1952); Hatch, *The Treaty Power and the Constitution; The Case for Amendment,* 40 A.B.A.J. 207 (1954); Chafee, *Amending the Constitution to Cripple Treaties,* 12 La.L.Rev. 345 (1952); Sutherland, *Restricting the Treaty Power,* 65 Harv.L.Rev. 1305 (1952); Dean, *Amending the Treaty Power,* 6 Stanford L.Rev. 589 (1954); Nelson, *Subject–Matter Limitation upon the Treaty–Making Power,* 11 J.Pub.L. 122 (1962); Henkin, *Treaty Makers and the Law Makers: The Law of the Land and Foreign Relations,* 107 U. of Pa. L.Rev. 903 (1959); McLaughlin, *Scope of the Treaty Power in the United States,* 43 Minn. L.Rev. 651 (1959). See also Henkin, *Foreign Affairs and the United States Constitution* (2d ed. 1996) 185–214.

designed to achieve and maintain a thriving natural ecological balance on the public lands." § 3(a) of the Act, 16 U.S.C. § 1333(a). If protected horses or burros "stray from public lands onto privately owned land, the owners of such land may inform the nearest federal marshall or agent of the Secretary, who shall arrange to have the animals removed." § 4 of the Act, 16 U.S.C. § 1334....

The differences between the [New Mexico] Livestock Board and the Secretaries came to a head in February 1974. On February 1, 1974, a New Mexico rancher, Kelley Stephenson, was informed by BLM that several unbranded burros had been seen near Taylor Well, where Stephenson watered his cattle. Taylor Well is on federal property, and Stephenson had access to it and some 8,000 surrounding acres only through a grazing permit issued pursuant to the Taylor Grazing Act, 48 Stat. 1270, as amended, 43 U.S.C. § 315b. After BLM made it clear to Stephenson that it would not remove the burros and after he personally inspected the Taylor Well area, Stephenson complained to the Livestock Board that the burros were interfering with his livestock operation by molesting his cattle and eating their feed.

Thereupon the Board rounded up and removed 19 unbranded and unclaimed burros pursuant to the New Mexico Estray Law. Each burro was seized on the public lands of the United States and, as the director of the Board conceded, each burro fit the definition of a wild free-roaming burro under § 2(b) of the Act. App. 43. On February 18, 1974, the Livestock Board, pursuant to its usual practice, sold the burros at a public auction. After the sale, BLM asserted jurisdiction under the Act and demanded that the Board recover the animals and return them to the public lands.

On March 4, 1974, appellees filed a complaint in the United States District Court for the District of New Mexico seeking a declaratory judgment that the Wild Free–Roaming Horses and Burros Act is unconstitutional and an injunction against its enforcement. A three-judge court was convened pursuant to 28 U.S.C. § 2282.

Following an evidentiary hearing, the District Court held the Act unconstitutional and permanently enjoined the Secretary of the Interior (the Secretary) from enforcing its provisions.... We ... now reverse.

II.

The Property Clause of the Constitution provides that "Congress shall have Power to dispose of and make all needful Rules and Regulations respecting the Territory or other Property belonging to the United States." U.S. Const., Art. IV, § 3, cl. 2....

For these reasons, Congress determined to preserve and protect the wild free-roaming horses and burros on the public lands of the United States. The question under the Property Clause is whether this determination can be sustained as a "needful" regulation "respecting" the public lands. In answering this question, we must remain mindful that, while courts must eventually pass upon them, determinations under the Property Clause are entrusted primarily to the judgment of Congress.

Appellees argue that the Act cannot be supported by the Property Clause. They contend that the Clause grants Congress essentially two kinds of power: (1) the power to dispose of and make incidental rules regarding the use of federal property; and (2) the power to protect federal property. According to appellees, the first power is not broad enough to support legislation protecting wild animals that live on federal property; and the second power is not implicated since the Act is designed to protect the animals, which are not themselves federal property, and not the public lands. As an initial matter, it is far from clear that the Act was not passed in part to protect the public lands of the United States or that Congress cannot assert a property interest in the regulated horses and burros superior to that of the State. But we need not consider whether the Act can be upheld on either of these grounds, for we reject appellees' narrow reading of the Property Clause. . . .

In brief, beyond the dicta [in two cases], appellees have presented no support for their position that the Clause grants Congress only the power to dispose of, to make incidental rules regarding the use of, and to protect federal property. This failure is hardly surprising, for the Clause, in broad terms, gives Congress the power to determine what are "needful" rules "respecting" the public lands. And while the furthest reaches of the power granted by the Property Clause have not yet been definitively resolved, we have repeatedly observed that "[t]he power over the public lands thus entrusted to Congress is without limitations."

The decided cases have supported this expansive reading. It is the Property Clause, for instance, that provides the basis for governing the territories of the United States. Hooven & Allison Co. v. Evatt, 324 U.S. 652, 673–674 (1945). And even over public land within the States, "[t]he general Government doubtless has a power over its own property analogous to the police power of the several States, and the extent to which it may go in the exercise of such power is measured by the exigencies of the particular case." Camfield v. United States, 167 U.S. 518, 525 (1897). We have noted, for example, that the Property Clause gives Congress the power over the public lands "to control their occupancy and use, to protect them from trespass and injury and to prescribe the conditions upon which others may obtain rights in them. . . ." Utah Power & Light Co. v. United States, 243 U.S. 389, 405 (1917). And we have approved legislation respecting the public lands "[i]f it be found necessary for the protection of the public, or of intending settlers [on the public lands]." Camfield v. United States, 167 U.S., at 525. In short, Congress exercises the powers both of a proprietor and of a legislature over the public domain. Alabama v. Texas, 347 U.S., at 273; Sinclair v. United States, 279 U.S. 263, 297 (1929); United States v. Midwest Oil Co., 236 U.S. 459, 474 (1915). Although the Property Clause does not authorize "an exercise of a general control over public policy in a State," it does permit "an exercise of the complete power which Congress has over particular public property entrusted to it." United States v. San Francisco, 310 U.S., at 30 (footnote omitted). In our view, the "complete power" that Congress has over public lands necessarily includes the power to regulate and protect the wildlife living there. . . .

F.   OTHER FEDERAL POWERS

1.   FISCAL POWERS

NORMAN v. BALTIMORE & OHIO RAILROAD CO., 294 U.S. 240 (1935). By the Joint Resolution of June 5, 1933, Congress attempted to nullify the effect of "gold clauses"[a] in contracts for the payment of money. The Resolution (one of a series of measures relating to the currency) provided that such contracts "shall be discharged, dollar for dollar, in any coin or currency

---

[a] A "gold clause" is a provision in a contract entitling the creditor to payment in currency of equivalent value, in terms of gold, to the currency in circulation at the time the contract was made. The purpose is to protect the creditor against devaluation of the currency.

which at the time of payment is legal tender for public and private debts". The Court sustained this measure as applied to contracts previously entered into between private parties. On the question of the power of Congress to establish a monetary system, the Court observed:

"... It is unnecessary to review the historic controversy as to the extent of this power, or again to go over the ground traversed by the Court in reaching the conclusion that the Congress may make treasury notes legal tender in payment of debts previously contracted, as well as of those subsequently contracted, whether that authority be exercised in course of war or in time of peace.[b] Knox v. Lee, 12 Wall. 457; Juilliard v. Greenman, 110 U.S. 421. We need only consider certain postulates upon which that conclusion rested.

"The Constitution grants to the Congress power 'To coin money, regulate the value thereof, and of foreign coin.' Art. I, § 8, par. 5. But the Court in the legal tender cases did not derive from that express grant alone the full authority of the Congress in relation to the currency. The Court found the source of that authority in all the related powers conferred upon the Congress and appropriate to achieve 'the great objects for which the government was framed,'—'a national government, with sovereign powers.' McCulloch v. Maryland, 4 Wheat. 316, 404–407; Knox v. Lee, supra, pp. 532, 536; Juilliard v. Greenman, supra, p. 438. The broad and comprehensive national authority over the subjects of revenue, finance and currency is derived from the aggregate of the powers granted to the Congress, embracing the powers to lay and collect taxes, to borrow money, to regulate commerce with foreign nations and among the several States, to coin money, regulate the value thereof, and of foreign coin, and fix the standards of weights and measures, and the added express power 'to make all laws which shall be necessary and proper for carrying into execution' the other enumerated powers. Juilliard v. Greenman, supra, pp. 439, 440.

"The Constitution 'was designed to provide the same currency, having a uniform legal value in all the States.' It was for that reason that the power to regulate the value of money was conferred upon the Federal government, while the same power, as well as the power to emit bills of credit, was withdrawn from the States. The States cannot declare what shall be money, or regulate its value. Whatever power there is over the currency is vested in the Congress. Knox v. Lee, supra, p. 545. Another postulate of the decision in that case is that the Congress has power 'to enact that the government's promises to pay money shall be, for the time being, equivalent in value to the representative of value determined by the coinage acts, or to multiples thereof.' Id., p. 553. Or, as was stated in the *Juilliard* case, supra, p. 447, the Congress is empowered 'to issue the obligations of the United States in such form, and to impress upon them such qualities as currency for the purchase of merchandise and the payment of debts, as accord with the usage of sovereign governments.' The authority to impose requirements of uniformity and parity is an essential feature of this control of the currency. The Congress is authorized to provide 'a sound and

---

[b] The Legal Tender Acts, passed during the Civil War, made United States notes (greenbacks) legal tender for debts, with certain exceptions. The acts were held invalid as applied to antecedent debts in Hepburn v. Griswold, 8 Wall. 603 (1869). The Court (then composed of eight justices) rendered the decision by a 5 to 3 vote. The Hepburn decision was overruled (5 to 4) in Legal Tender Cases, 12 Wall. 457 (1871), President

Grant having appointed two new members of the Court, one of whom (Strong, J.) wrote the opinion. The struggles in the Court over the legal tender issue are described in Fairman, *Mr. Justice Miller and the Supreme Court*, Chap. 7 (1939) and the same author's Reconstruction and Reunion 1864–88, Part I, 677–775 (1971). See also Ratner, *Was the Supreme Court Packed by President Grant?*, 50 Pol. Sci.Q. 343 (1935).

uniform currency for the country,' and to 'secure the benefit of it to the people by appropriate legislation.' Veazie Bank v. Fenno, 8 Wall. 533, 549. . . .

"Dealing with the specific question as to the effect of the legal tender acts upon contracts made before their passage, that is, those for the payment of money generally, the Court, in the legal tender cases, recognized the possible consequences of such enactments in frustrating the expected performance of contracts,—in rendering them 'fruitless or partially fruitless.' The Court pointed out that the exercise of the powers of Congress may affect 'apparent obligations' of contracts in many ways. The Congress may pass bankruptcy acts. The Congress may declare war, or, even in peace, pass non-intercourse acts, or direct an embargo, which may operate seriously upon existing contracts. And the Court reasoned that if the legal tender acts 'were justly chargeable with impairing contract obligations, they would not, for that reason, be forbidden, unless a different rule is to be applied to them from that which has hitherto prevailed in the construction of other powers granted by the fundamental law.' The conclusion was that contracts must be understood as having been made in reference to the possible exercise of the rightful authority of the Government, and that no obligation of a contract 'can extend to the defeat' of that authority. Knox v. Lee, supra, pp. 549–551. . . ."

2.   NATURALIZATION

Article I, § 8, Clause 4, provides that Congress shall have power to "establish a uniform Rule of Naturalization." From the beginning the Court said that the power of Naturalization is vested exclusively in Congress to the exclusion of the states. Chirac v. Chirac's Lessee, 15 U.S. (2 Wheat.) 259, 269 (1817). The Court has also said that "Naturalization is a privilege, to be given, qualified or withheld as Congress may determine, and which the alien may claim as of right only upon compliance with the terms which Congress imposes." United States v. McIntosh, 283 U.S. 605, 615 (1931).

The problems of defining citizenship and of expatriation and denaturalization will be considered in Chapter 8, infra.

3.   REGULATION OF ALIENS

KLEINDIENST v. MANDEL, 408 U.S. 753 (1972). The Court upheld the Attorney General's refusal to waive a statutory provision excluding aliens who advocate world communism and grant a visa to a person invited to speak to an academic meeting in the United States. The Court noted that "Mandel personally, as an unadmitted and nonresident alien, had no constitutional right of entry to this country as a nonimmigrant or otherwise." In response to the argument that the first amendment rights of persons in this country who wished to hear Mandel were involved, the Court said, in part:

"Recognition that First Amendment rights are implicated, however, is not dispositive of our inquiry here. In accord with ancient principles of the international law of nation-states, the Court in The Chinese Exclusion Case, 130 U.S. 581, 609 (1889), and in Fong Yue Ting v. United States, 149 U.S. 698 (1893), held broadly . . . that the power to exclude aliens is 'inherent in sovereignty, necessary for maintaining normal international relations and defending the country against foreign encroachments and dangers—a power to be exercised exclusively by the political branches of government. . . .' Since that time, the Court's general reaffirmations of this principle have been legion. The Court without exception has sustained Congress' 'plenary power to make rules for the admission of aliens and to exclude those who possess those characteristics which Congress has forbidden.' Boutilier v. Immigration and Naturalization Service, 387 U.S. 118, 123 (1967). '[O]ver no conceivable subject is the legislative power of Congress more complete than it is over' the admission of aliens. Oceanic Navigation Co. v. Stranahan, 214 U.S. 320, 339 (1909). In Lem Moon Sing v. United States, 158 U.S. 538, 547 (1895), the first Mr. Justice Harlan said: 'The power of Congress to exclude aliens altogether from the United States, or to prescribe the terms and conditions upon which they may come to this country, and to have its declared policy in that regard enforced exclusively through executive officers, without judicial intervention, is settled by our previous adjudications.' Mr. Justice Frankfurter ably articulated this history in Galvan v. Press, 347 U.S. 522 (1954), a deportation case, and we can do no better. After suggesting, that 'much could be said for the view' that due process places some limitations on congressional power in this area 'were we writing on a clean slate,' he continued:

" 'But the slate is not clean. As to the extent of the power of Congress under review, there is not merely "a page of history" … but a whole volume. Policies pertaining to the entry of aliens and their right to remain here are peculiarly concerned with the political conduct of government. In the enforcement of these policies, the Executive Branch of the Government must respect the procedural safeguards of due process…. But that the formulation of these policies is entrusted exclusively to Congress has become about as firmly embedded in the legislative and judicial tissues of our body politic as any aspect of our government….'

" 'We are not prepared to deem ourselves wiser or more sensitive to human rights than our predecessors, especially those who have been most zealous in protecting civil liberties under the Constitution, and must therefore under our constitutional system recognize congressional power in dealing with aliens….'

"We are not inclined in the present context to reconsider this line of cases…."[a]

4.   THE ADMIRALTY POWER

Article III, § 2 provides that "the judicial power shall extend … to all cases of admiralty and maritime jurisdiction…." Although in form only a grant of jurisdiction to the courts, the admiralty clause early became recognized as a basis for national legislation. "The framers of the Constitution did not contemplate that the maritime law should remain unalterable. The purpose was to place the entire subject, including its substantive as well as its procedural features, under national control. From the beginning the grant was regarded as implicitly investing legislative power for that purpose in the United States. When the Constitution was adopted, the existing maritime law became the law of the United States subject to power in Congress to modify or supplement it as experience or changing conditions might require. But in amending and revising the maritime law, the Congress necessarily acts within a sphere restricted by the concept of the admiralty and maritime jurisdiction." Detroit Trust Co. v. Barlum S.S. Co. (The Thomas Barlum), 293 U.S. 21, 43–44 (1934).

This interpretation of the admiralty clause sustained the power of Congress to legislate with respect to events or transactions occurring on navigable waters of the United States (defined as including only those capable in fact of being used for interstate or foreign commerce) whether or not the particular

[a] The constitutional limitations upon the power of Congress to classify aliens who have been admitted to the country and impose special burdens on them is considered in Chapter 10, infra.

event or transaction occurred in interstate commerce. Thus in In re Garnett, 141 U.S. 1, 12 (1891), the Court upheld the Limited Liability Act as applied to all vessels on inland waters, saying:

> "It is unnecessary to invoke the power given to Congress to regulate commerce with foreign nations, and among the several States, in order to find authority to pass the law in question. The Act of Congress which limits the liability of ship owners was passed in amendment of the maritime law of the country, and the power to make such amendments is co-extensive with that law. It is not confined to the boundaries or class of subjects which limit and characterize the power to regulate commerce; but, in maritime matters, it extends to all matters and places to which the maritime law extends."

For a discussion of the early development, see Note, *From Judicial Grant to Legislative Power: The Admiralty Clause in the Nineteenth Century,* 67 Harv. L.Rev. 1214 (1954).

It may be that this is all ancient history of minimal modern relevance to federal power. It has been suggested that "the conception of the commerce power that now prevails would probably suffice, without reference to any inference from the admiralty judicial power, to validate every statutory enactment in question." Gilmore & Black, *The Law of Admiralty* 47 (2d ed. 1975). This suggestion is reinforced by Kaiser Aetna v. United States, 444 U.S. 164, 170–174 (1979), in which the Court said: "Reference to the navigability of a waterway adds little if anything to the breadth of Congress' regulatory power over interstate commerce. It has long been settled that Congress has extensive authority over this Nation's waters under the Commerce Clause." The Court added: "[A] wide spectrum of economic activities 'affect' interstate commerce and thus are susceptible of congressional regulation under the Commerce Clause irrespective of whether navigation, or, indeed, water, is involved. The cases that discuss Congress' paramount authority to regulate waters used in interstate commerce are consequently best understood when viewed in terms of more traditional Commerce Clause analysis than by reference to whether the stream in fact is capable of supporting navigation or may be characterized as 'navigable water of the United States.' "[1]

---

[1] Congress also has extensive power over American Indians based on its power to regulate commerce "with the Indian Tribes." No attempt is made to look at the work of the Supreme Court in this area. See generally F. Cohen, *Handbook of Federal Indian Law* (1982 ed.)

CHAPTER 5

THE SCOPE OF STATE POWER

SECTION 1. INTRODUCTION

A. REGULATION

In Chapter 4 we explored the early Nineteenth Century dispute in the Supreme Court between those who read the commerce clause as granting to Congress exclusive power to regulate interstate commerce and those who contended that the grant was merely concurrent, leaving full power in the states to regulate in the absence of conflicting federal regulation. In Cooley v. Board of Wardens, 53 U.S. (12 How.) 299 (1851), set out supra p. 177, the Court reached a compromise position under which the commerce clause would permit some state regulations of interstate commerce but forbid others even in the absence of federal regulation. Ever since *Cooley* the Court has been struggling to find a formula to determine when state regulations of commerce are permissible.

In *Cooley* the Court attempted to resolve the problem by looking at the subjects being regulated. "Whatever subjects of this power are in their nature national, or admit only of one uniform system, or plan of regulation may justly be said to be of such a nature as to require exclusive legislation by Congress." Other subjects (such as harbor pilots, in that case) are of such a nature "as to leave no doubt of the superior fitness and propriety, not to say the absolute necessity, of different systems of regulation, drawn from local knowledge and experience, and conformed to local wants."

Later cases were more likely to speak in terms of "direct" burdens on commerce being forbidden, "indirect" burdens permitted. Thus in Erb v. Morasch, 177 U.S. 584 (1900) the Court said that a city ordinance regulating the speed of trains was "even as to interstate trains, one only indirectly affecting interstate commerce, and is within the power of the state until at least Congress shall take action in the matter." On the other hand, in Shafer v. Farmers' Grain Co. of Embden, 268 U.S. 189 (1925), the Court held invalid a state regulation of the purchase of wheat for interstate shipment because it constituted a "direct burden" on interstate commerce.

More recently the Court has addressed the problem in substantive rather than formal terms. In Brown–Forman Distillers Corporation v. New York State Liquor Authority, 476 U.S. 573, 578 (1986), for example, the Court said:

> "This Court has adopted what amounts to a two-tiered approach to analyzing state economic regulation under the Commerce Clause. When a state statute directly regulates or discriminates against interstate commerce, or when its effect is to favor in-state economic interests over out-of-state interests, we have generally struck down the statute without further inquiry.... When, however, a statute has only indirect effects on interstate commerce and regulates evenhandedly, we have examined whether the State's interest is legitimate and whether the burden on interstate commerce clearly exceeds the local benefits. Pike v. Bruce Church, Inc., 397

U.S. 137, 142 (1970). We have also recognized that there is no clear line separating the category of state regulation that is virtually *per se* invalid under the Commerce Clause, and the category subject to the Pike v. Bruce Church balancing approach. In either situation the critical consideration is the overall effect of the statute on both local and interstate activity."

B.   TAXATION

Ever since its first case dealing with state taxation of commerce—Brown v. Maryland, 25 U.S. (12 Wheat.) 419, decided in 1827—the Court has been struggling with the question whether the Constitution intended that property moving in interstate and foreign commerce or businesses engaged in such commerce should be to some extent, at least, immune from state taxation. With respect to interstate commerce the question arises under the general grant of power to Congress to regulate commerce among the states. With respect to foreign commerce the question arises under the general power of Congress to regulate commerce with foreign nations and under the provision in Art. I, § 10: "No State shall, without the Consent of the Congress, lay any Imposts or Duties on Imports or Exports, except what may be absolutely necessary for executing its inspection Laws...."

The cases have been clear from the earliest times that taxes that formally discriminate against interstate or foreign commerce are forbidden. The import-export clause obviously was intended at least to preclude states from erecting tariff barriers on goods from abroad. In Welton v. Missouri, 91 U.S. 275 (1876), the Court firmly stated the rule against discrimination, invalidating a statute that imposed a special license tax on peddlers who sold goods "which are not the growth, produce, or manufacture of the state."

But the question which has given enormous difficulty is whether there is an immunity beyond that against discrimination. Are the states precluded from imposing nondiscriminatory taxes on goods or instrumentalities of commerce physically present within their borders merely because they are moving in interstate commerce? Are the states precluded from imposing nondiscriminatory taxes on either the net or the gross proceeds from interstate commerce activity which takes place within their borders?

In the major cases of the last century the Court, reflecting the early suggestions in the state regulation cases that the power given to Congress by the commerce clause was exclusive, tended to find a wide scope of immunity against any state taxes that could be said to bear directly upon interstate or foreign commerce.

However, the Court did not go so far as to hold that states never could secure revenue from interstate business. A broad immunity would have placed the states in the position of being required to provide governmental services to property and business within their borders without being able to secure any contribution from such property and business to the cost of government. Hence, the states sought to devise means to secure such revenues and the Court began to draw lines between permissible and impermissible taxes on commerce. Originally, the lines drawn were largely formal. A state could impose a tax on the net proceeds from interstate activity within its borders but not on gross proceeds because the former bore only indirectly upon commerce while the latter bore directly. United States Glue Co. v. Town of Oak Creek, 247 U.S. 321 (1918). A state could impose a tax on the privilege of doing business and measure it by net income, including net income from interstate commerce attributable to the state, if the company did some local business but not if all of its activity within the state was interstate commerce. Spector Motor Service v. O'Connor, 340 U.S. 602 (1951).

In Western Live Stock v. Bureau of Revenue, 303 U.S. 250, 254, 255 (1938), the Court began the search for a less formalistic basis upon which to decide the cases. It enunciated what has become known as the "multiple burdens" doctrine. First, the Court said "it was not the purpose of the commerce clause to relieve those engaged in interstate commerce from their just share of state tax burden even though it increases the cost of doing the business." Second, the Court indicated that the commerce clause should be construed to protect commerce against the multiple burdens which would result if more states than one could tax the same property or activity. In essence, the Court was simply restating the rule against discrimination when it attempted to rationalize prior cases: "The vice characteristic of those which have been held invalid is that they have placed on the commerce burdens of such a nature as to be capable in point of substance, of being imposed ... with equal right by every state which the commerce touches, merely because interstate commerce is being done, so that without the protection of the commerce clause it would bear cumulative burdens not imposed on local commerce."

The decision in *Western Live Stock* did not, however, mark an end to the older idea that interstate commerce itself could not be directly taxed. As recently as 1946 in Freeman v. Hewit, 329 U.S. 249, 256, the Court would say: "Nor is there any warrant in the constitutional principles heretofore applied by this Court to support the notion that a State may be allowed one single tax-worth of direct interference with the free flow of commerce. An exaction by a State from interstate commerce falls not because of a proven increase in the cost of the product. What makes the tax invalid is the fact that there is interference by a State with the freedom of interstate commerce.... Trade being a sensitive plant, a direct tax upon it to some extent at least deters trade even if its effect is not precisely calculable." For nearly three decades after *Western Live Stock* the cases continued to reflect first one and then the other of these conflicting approaches.

Finally, in 1977, in Complete Auto Transit, Inc. v. Brady, 430 U.S. 274, 277, the Court rejected the formalistic approaches. Mississippi imposed a tax on the privilege of transporting for compensation persons or property between points within the state. In upholding the tax, the Court began by saying:

"Appellant ... did *not* allege that its activity which Mississippi taxes does not have a sufficient nexus with the State; or that the tax discriminates against interstate commerce; or that the tax is unfairly apportioned; or that it is unrelated to services provided by the State. No such claims were made before the Mississippi Supreme Court, and although appellant argues here that a tax on 'the privilege of doing interstate commerce' creates an unacceptable risk of discrimination and undue burdens, it does not claim that discrimination or undue burdens exist in fact.

"Appellant's attack is based solely on decisions of this Court holding that a tax on the 'privilege' of engaging in an activity in the State may not be applied to an activity that is part of interstate commerce. See, e.g., Spector Motor Service v. O'Connor, 340 U.S. 602 (1951); Freeman v. Hewit, 329 U.S. 249 (1946). This rule looks only to the fact that the incidence of the tax is the 'privilege of doing business'; it deems irrelevant any consideration of the practical effect of the tax. The rule reflects an underlying philosophy that interstate commerce should enjoy a sort of 'free trade' immunity from state taxation.

"Appellee, in its turn, relies on decisions of this Court stating that '[i]t was not the purpose of the commerce clause to relieve those engaged in interstate commerce from their just share of state tax burden even though it increases the cost of doing the business,' Western Live Stock v. Bureau of Revenue, 303 U.S. 250, 254 (1938). These decisions have considered not the formal language of the tax statute, but rather its practical effect, and have sustained a tax against Commerce Clause challenge when the tax is applied to an activity with a substantial nexus with the taxing state, is fairly apportioned, does not discriminate against interstate commerce, and is fairly related to the services provided by the State.

"Over the years, the Court has applied this practical analysis in approving many types of tax that avoided running afoul of the prohibition against taxing the 'privilege of doing business,' but in each instance it has refused to overrule the prohibition. Under the present state of the law, the *Spector* rule, as it has come to be known, has no relationship to economic realities. Rather it stands only as a trap for the unwary draftsman."[a]

Despite *Complete Auto*, the Court later reaffirmed that portion of its 1967 ruling in National Bellas Hess, Inc. v. Department of Revenue of Ill., 386 U.S. 753, that states requiring out-of-state mail-order businesses with no in-state physical presence to collect and remit taxes on purchases for intrastate use thereby "created an unconstitutional burden on interstate commerce." Quill Corporation v. North Dakota, 504 U.S. 298 (1992). Although *Bellas Hess* was "decided ... in the middle of this latest rally between formalism and pragmatism" bounded by *Spector Motor* and *Complete Auto*, and "[w]hile contemporary Commerce Clause jurisprudence might not dictate the same result were the issue to arise for the first time today, *Bellas Hess* is not inconsistent with *Complete Auto* and our recent cases." Rather, said the majority opinion by Justice Stevens, "*Bellas Hess* concerns the first of [*Complete Auto*'s] tests and stands for the proposition that a vendor whose only contacts with the taxing State are by mail or common carrier lacks the 'substantial nexus' required by

---

[a] The Court refined the four-part analytical approach of *Complete Auto Transit* in two decisions upholding state taxes against commerce clause challenges. Both were especially instructive with respect to the requirement that a state tax not discriminate against interstate commerce.

In Goldberg v. Sweet, 488 U.S. 252 (1989), the taxpayers urged that a 5% Illinois tax on interstate phone calls charged to an Illinois service address discriminated against interstate commerce, despite a similar 5% tax on intrastate calls, because a larger share of the overall tax burden fell on interstate calls. In rejecting this contention the Court noted that in contrast to taxes burdening out-of-state taxpayers "who would have difficulty effecting legislative change, the economic burden of the Illinois telecommunications tax falls on the Illinois telecommunications consumer, the insider who presumably is able to complain about and change the tax through the Illinois political process." The Court then said: "It is not a purpose of the Commerce Clause to protect state residents from their own taxes." This statement provoked disagreement and separate concurrences from Justices Stevens and O'Connor, who took the

position that "a state may not discriminate among its own residents by placing a heavier tax on those who engage in interstate commerce than those who merely engage in local commerce."

In Amerada Hess Corp. v. Director, Division of Taxation, 490 U.S. 66 (1989), the Court summarized its current approach to the anti-discrimination requirement by saying that "a tax may violate the Commerce Clause if it is facially discriminatory, has a discriminatory intent, or has the effect of unduly burdening interstate commerce." The Court upheld a provision of an apportioned New Jersey tax on corporate profits and income that refused to allow a deduction to oil companies doing some business in-state for federal windfall profit taxes they had paid on oil production occurring entirely outside New Jersey. The companies were engaged in a unitary business, and the tax was "not facially discriminatory," did not "apply exclusively to a localized industry," did not emanate from a "discriminatory motive," and did not "exert a pressure on an interstate business to conduct more of its activities in New Jersey" (since oil-production can only occur where the oil reserves are located).

the Commerce Clause." Moreover, even though *Quill* did overrule that part of *Bellas Hess* holding that the Due Process Clause prohibited application of the use tax against a business lacking in-state physical presence, satisfaction of "the due process 'minimum contacts' test" did not meet "the Commerce Clause 'substantial nexus' test." Justice Stevens elaborated:

"... The second and third parts of [*Complete Auto's*] analysis, which require fair apportionment and non-discrimination,[b] prohibit taxes that pass an unfair share of the tax burden onto interstate commerce. The first and fourth prongs, which require a substantial nexus and a relationship between the tax and State-provided services, limit the reach of State taxing authority so as to ensure that State taxation does not unduly burden interstate commerce.[6] Thus, the 'substantial-nexus' requirement is not, like due process' 'minimum-contacts' requirement, a proxy for notice, but rather a means for limiting state burdens on interstate commerce. Accordingly, ... a corporation may have the 'minimum contacts' with a taxing State as required by the Due Process Clause, and yet lack the 'substantial nexus' with that State as required by the Commerce Clause.

. . .

"... [N]ot all formalism is alike.... [T]he bright-line rule of *Bellas Hess* furthers the ends of the dormant Commerce Clause. Undue burdens on interstate commerce may be avoided not only by a case-by-case evaluation of the actual burdens imposed by particular regulations or taxes, but also, in some situations, by the demarcation of a discrete realm of commercial activity that is free from interstate taxation. *Bellas Hess* followed the latter approach and created a safe harbor for vendors 'whose only connection with customers in the [taxing] State is by common carrier or the United States mail.' ...'"

The artificiality "at its edges" of the bright-line rule of *Bellas Hess* was "more than offset by the benefits of a clear rule[,]" encouraged "settled expectations and ... foster[ed] investment by businesses and individuals.

---

[b] Use taxes imposed on out-of-state sellers would be unconstitutionally discriminatory were there no corresponding sales tax imposed on in-state sellers (as there was in *Quill*). Under the "compensatory tax doctrine," an otherwise facially discriminatory tax imposed on interstate commerce does not violate the negative commerce clause if it is only "the equivalent of an 'identifiable and substantially similar tax on intrastate commerce ...'" Associated Industries of Missouri v. Lohman, 511 U.S. 641, ___ (1994). The doctrine, "designed simply to make interstate commerce bear a burden already borne by intrastate commerce[,]" is carefully circumscribed, however. Thus, in *Lohman*, the Court allowed Missouri to compensate for local sales taxes by imposing a uniform, statewide use tax on all goods purchased out-of-state but used in-state—but only in those local jurisdictions with sales tax rates equal to or greater than the use tax rate. That the sum of local sales taxes might exceed the total statewide use tax did not justify applying the use tax in locales with lower sales tax rates, for "strict parity is demanded by the compensatory tax doctrine."

More generally, Fulton Corp. v. Faulkner, ___ U.S. ___, ___, 116 S.Ct. 848, 854 (1996), "distilled" from earlier cases "three conditions necessary for a valid compensatory tax"—state identification of the intrastate tax burden prompting a compensatory tax, a showing that the tax on interstate commerce does not exceed that on intrastate commerce, and proof that the compensating taxes fall on "substantially equivalent events." Even if a state theoretically might prove that the actual incidence of any two taxes would allow "a finding of combined neutrality on interstate competition[,]" doubts are to be resolved against the state and "courts will ordinarily be unable to evaluate the economic equivalence of allegedly compensatory tax schemes that go beyond traditional sales/use taxes."

[6] North Dakota's use tax illustrates well how a state tax might unduly burden interstate commerce. On its face, North Dakota law imposes a collection duty on every vendor who advertises in the State three times in a single year.... What is more significant, similar obligations might be imposed by the Nation's 6,000–plus taxing jurisdictions....

Indeed, it is not unlikely that the mail-order industry's dramatic growth over the last quarter-century is due in part to the bright-line exemption from state taxation created in *Bellas Hess*." Finally, now that the due process impediment had been cleared away, Congress was "free to decide whether, when, and to what extent the States may burden interstate mail-order concerns with a duty to collect use taxes."

Dissenting from the Court's commerce clause ruling, Justice White objected that "[w]hat we disavowed in *Complete Auto* was not just the 'formal distinction between "direct" and "indirect" taxes on interstate commerce,' but also the whole notion underlying the *Bellas Hess* physical presence rule—that 'interstate commerce is immune from state taxation.' " He found

"no relationship between the physical presence-nexus rule the Court retains and Commerce Clause considerations that allegedly justify it. Perhaps long ago a seller's 'physical presence' was a sufficient part of a trade to condition imposition of a tax on such presence. But in today's economy, physical presence frequently has very little to do with a transaction a State might seek to tax. Wire transfers of money involving billions of dollars occur every day; purchasers place orders with sellers by fax, phone, and computer linkup; sellers ship goods by air, road, and sea through sundry delivery services without leaving their place of business.... [A]n out-of-state direct marketer derives numerous commercial benefits from the State in which it does business[,] includ[ing] laws establishing sound local banking institutions to support credit transactions; courts to insure collection of the purchase price from the seller's customers; means of waste disposal from garbage generated by mail order solicitations; and creation and enforcement of consumer protection laws.... To create, for the first time, a nexus requirement under the Commerce Clause independent of that established for due process purposes is one thing; to attempt to justify an anachronistic notion of physical presence in economic terms is quite another."

The taxation cases have run an elaborate course independently of the regulation cases. In part the difference results from the fact that balancing cannot be done in the same fashion in taxation cases as in regulation cases. In the former the state interest is the same in every case—the receipt of revenue to meet the costs of government. Therefore the issues have been primarily those of examining the burdens on commerce rather than those of comparing burdens with benefits. In Department of Revenue of Washington v. Association of Washington Stevedoring Companies, 435 U.S. 734, 748 (1978), the Court noted this difference:

"Although the balancing of safety interests naturally differs from the balancing of state financial needs, [we have] recognized that a State has a significant interest in exacting from interstate commerce its fair share of the cost of state government. All tax burdens do not impermissibly impede interstate commerce. The Commerce Clause balance tips against the tax only when it unfairly burdens commerce by exacting more than a just share from the interstate activity."

It is no longer possible in a basic constitutional law book to trace the intricate doctrines involved in the hundreds of taxation cases. Those materials must be left to specialized courses in state and local taxation. Here, an occasional tax case will be used where it helps illuminate issues involved in the regulation cases.

New Energy Co. of Indiana v. Limbach

486 U.S. 269, 108 S.Ct. 1803, 100 L.Ed.2d 302 (1988).

Justice Scalia delivered the opinion of the Court.

Appellant New Energy Company of Indiana has challenged the constitutionality of Ohio Rev.Code Ann. § 5735.145(B) (1986), a provision that awards a tax credit against the Ohio motor vehicle fuel sales tax for each gallon of ethanol sold (as a component of gasohol) by fuel dealers, but only if the ethanol is produced in Ohio or in a State that grants similar tax advantages to ethanol produced in Ohio. The question presented is whether § 5735.145(B) discriminates against interstate commerce in violation of the Commerce Clause, U.S. Const., Art. I, § 8, cl. 3.

I

Ethanol, or ethyl alcohol, is usually made from corn. In the last decade it has come into widespread use as an automotive fuel, mixed with gasoline in a ratio of 1:9 to produce what is called gasohol. The interest in ethanol emerged in reaction to the petroleum market dislocations of the early 1970's. The product was originally promoted as a means of achieving energy independence while providing a market for surplus corn; more recently, emphasis has shifted to its environmental advantages as a replacement for lead in enhancing fuel octane.... Ethanol was, however (and continues to be), more expensive than gasoline, and the emergence of ethanol production on a commercial scale dates from enactment of the first federal subsidy, in the form of an exemption from federal motor fuel excise taxes, in 1978.... Since then, many States, particularly those in the grain-producing areas of the country, have enacted their own ethanol subsidies.... Ohio first passed such a measure in 1981, providing Ohio gasohol dealers a credit of so many cents per gallon of ethanol used in their product against the Ohio motor vehicle fuel sales tax payable on both ethanol and gasoline. This credit was originally available without regard to the source of the ethanol.... In 1984, however, Ohio enacted § 5735.145(B), which denies the credit to ethanol coming from States that do not grant a tax credit, exemption, or refund to ethanol from Ohio, or, if a State grants a smaller tax advantage than Ohio's, granting only an equivalent credit ....

Appellant ... manufactures ethanol in South Bend, Indiana, for sale in several States, including Ohio. Indiana repealed its tax exemption for ethanol, effective July 1, 1985, ... at which time it also passed legislation providing a direct subsidy to Indiana ethanol producers (the sole one of which was appellant) ... Thus, by reason of Ohio's reciprocity provision, appellant's ethanol sold in Ohio became ineligible for the Ohio tax credit. Appellant sought declaratory and injunctive relief in [an Ohio state court,] alleging that § 5735.145(B) violated the Commerce Clause by discriminating against out-of-state ethanol producers to the advantage of in-state industry. The court denied relief, and the Ohio Court of Appeals affirmed. A divided Ohio Supreme Court initially reversed, finding that § 5735.145(B) discriminated without adequate justification against products of out-of-state origin, and shielded Ohio producers from out-of-state competition. [On] rehearing [it] reversed itself, a majority of the court finding that the provision was not protectionist or unreasonably burdensome. . . .

II

It has long been accepted that the Commerce Clause not only grants Congress the authority to regulate commerce among the States, but also directly limits the power of the States to discriminate against interstate commerce. See, e.g., Hughes v. Oklahoma, 441 U.S. 322, 326 (1979); H.P. Hood & Sons, Inc. v. Du Mond, 336 U.S. 525, 534–535 (1949); Welton v. Missouri, 91 U.S. 275 (1876). This "negative" aspect of the Commerce Clause prohibits economic protectionism—that is, regulatory measures designed to benefit in-state economic interests by burdening out-of-state competitors. See, e.g., Bacchus Imports, Ltd. v. Dias, 468 U.S. 263, 270–273 (1984); *H.P. Hood & Sons,* supra, at 532–533; Guy v. Baltimore, 100 U.S. 434, 443 (1880). Thus, state statutes that clearly discriminate against interstate commerce are routinely struck down, see, e.g., Sporhase v. Nebraska ex rel. Douglas, 458 U.S. 941 (1982); Lewis v. BT Investment Managers, Inc., 447 U.S. 27 (1980); Dean Milk Co. v. Madison, 340 U.S. 349 (1951), unless the discrimination is demonstrably justified by a valid factor unrelated to economic protectionism, see, e.g., Maine v. Taylor, 477 U.S. 131 (1986).

The Ohio provision at issue here explicitly deprives certain products of generally available beneficial tax treatment because they are made in certain other States, and thus on its face appears to violate the cardinal requirement of nondiscrimination. Appellees argue, however, that the availability of the tax credit to some out-of-state manufacturers (those in States that give tax advantages to Ohio-produced ethanol) shows that the Ohio provision, far from discriminating against interstate commerce, is likely to promote it, by encouraging other States to enact similar tax advantages that will spur the interstate sale of ethanol. We rejected a similar contention in an earlier "reciprocity" case, Great Atlantic & Pacific Tea Co. v. Cottrell, 424 U.S. 366 (1976). The regulation at issue there permitted milk from out of State to be sold in Mississippi only if the State of origin accepted Mississippi milk on a reciprocal basis. Mississippi put forward, among other arguments, the assertion that "the reciprocity requirement is in effect a free-trade provision, advancing the identical national interest that is served by the Commerce Clause." Id., at 378. In response, we said that "Mississippi may not use the threat of economic isolation as a weapon to force sister States to enter into even a desirable reciprocity agreement." Id., at 379. More recently, we characterized a Nebraska reciprocity requirement for the export of ground water from the State as "facially discriminatory legislation" which merited "'strictest scrutiny.' "Sporhase v. Nebraska ex rel. Douglas, supra, at 958, quoting Hughes v. Oklahoma, supra, at 337.

It is true that in *Cottrell* and *Sporhase* the effect of a State's refusal to accept the offered reciprocity was total elimination of all transport of the subject product into or out of the offering State; whereas in the present case the only effect of refusal is that the out-of-state product is placed at a substantial commercial disadvantage through discriminatory tax treatment. That makes no difference for purposes of Commerce Clause analysis. In the leading case of Baldwin v. G.A.F. Seelig, Inc., 294 U.S. 511 (1935), the New York law excluding out-of-state milk did not impose an absolute ban, but rather allowed importation and sale so long as the initial purchase from the dairy farmer was made at or above the New York State-mandated price. In other words, just as the appellant here, in order to sell its product in Ohio, only has to cut its profits by reducing its sales price below the market price sufficiently to compensate the Ohio purchaser-retailer for the forgone tax credit, so also the milk wholesaler-distributor in *Baldwin,* in order to sell its product in New York, only had to cut its profits by increasing its purchase price above the market price sufficiently to meet the New York-prescribed minimum. We viewed the New York law as "an economic barrier against competition" that was "equivalent to a rampart of customs duties." Id., at 527. Similarly, in Hunt v. Washington Apple Advertising Comm'n, 432 U.S. 333, 349–351 (1977), we found invalid under the Commerce Clause a North Carolina statute that did not exclude apples from other States, but merely imposed additional costs upon Washington sellers and deprived them of the commercial advantage of their distinctive grading system. The present law likewise imposes an economic disadvantage upon out-of-state sellers; and the promise to remove that if reciprocity is accepted no more justifies disparity of treatment than it would justify categorical exclusion. We have indicated that reciprocity requirements are not *per se* unlawful. See *Cottrell,* supra, at 378. But the case we cited for that proposition, Kane v. New Jersey, 242 U.S. 160, 167–168 (1916), discussed a context in which, if a State offered the reciprocity did not accept it, the consequence was, to be sure, *less favored* treatment for its citizens, but nonetheless treatment that complied with the minimum requirements of the Commerce Clause. Here, quite to the contrary, the threat used to induce Indiana's acceptance is, in effect, taxing a product made by its manufacturers at a rate higher than the same product made by Ohio manufacturers, without (as we shall see) justification for the disparity.

Appellees argue that § 5735.145(B) should not be considered discrimination against interstate commerce because its practical scope is so limited. Apparently only one Ohio ethanol manufacturer exists (appellee South Point Ethanol) and only one out-of-state manufacturer (appellant) is clearly disadvantaged by the provision. Our cases, however, indicate that where discrimination is patent, as it is here, neither a widespread advantage to in-state interests nor a widespread disadvantage to out-of-state competitors need be shown. For example, in *Bacchus Imports, Ltd. v. Dias,* supra, we held unconstitutional under the Commerce Clause a special exemption from Hawaii's liquor tax for certain locally produced alcoholic beverages (okolehao and fruit wine), even though other locally produced alcoholic beverages were subject to the tax. 468 U.S., at 265, 271. And in *Lewis v. BT Investment Managers, Inc.,* supra, we held unconstitutional a Florida statute that excluded from certain business activities in Florida not all out-of-state entities, but only out-of-state bank holding companies, banks, or trust companies. In neither of these cases did we consider the size or number of the in-state businesses favored or the out-of-state businesses disfavored relevant to our determination. Varying the strength of the bar against economic protectionism according to the size and number of in-state and out-of-state firms affected would serve no purpose except the creation of new uncertainties in an already complex field.

. . .

It has not escaped our notice that the appellant here, which is eligible to receive a cash subsidy under Indiana's program for in-state ethanol producers, is the potential beneficiary of a scheme no less discriminatory than the one that it attacks, and no less effective in conferring a commercial advantage over out-of-state competitors. To believe the Indiana scheme is valid, however, is not to believe that the Ohio scheme must be valid as well. The Commerce Clause does not prohibit all state action designed to give its residents an advantage in the marketplace, but only action of that description *in connection with the State's regulation of interstate commerce.* Direct subsidization of domestic industry does not ordinarily run afoul of that prohibition; discriminatory taxation of out-of-state manufactures does. Of course, even if the Indiana subsidy were invalid, retaliatory violation of the Commerce Clause by Ohio would not be acceptable. See *Cottrell*, 424 U.S., at 379–380.

III

Our cases leave open the possibility that a State may validate a statute that discriminates against interstate commerce by showing that it advances a legitimate local purpose that cannot be adequately served by reasonable nondiscriminatory alternatives. See, e.g., Maine v. Taylor, 477 U.S., at 138, 151; Sporhase v. Nebraska ex rel. Douglas, 458 U.S., at 958; Hughes v. Oklahoma, 441 U.S., at 336–337; Dean Milk Co. v. Madison, 340 U.S., at 354. This is perhaps just another way of saying that what may appear to be a "discriminatory" provision in the constitutionally prohibited sense—that is, a protectionist enactment—may on closer analysis not be so. However it be put, the standards for such justification are high. Cf. Philadelphia v. New Jersey, 437 U.S. 617, 624 (1978) ("[W]here simple economic protectionism is effected by state legislation, a virtually *per se* rule of invalidity has been erected"); Hughes v. Oklahoma, 441 U.S., at 337 ("[F]acial discrimination by itself may be a fatal defect" and "[a]t a minimum . . . invokes the strictest scrutiny").

Appellees advance two justifications for the clear discrimination in the present case: health and commerce. As to the first, they argue that the provision encourages use of ethanol (in replacement of lead as a gasoline octane-enhancer) to reduce harmful exhaust emissions, both in Ohio itself and in surrounding States whose polluted atmosphere may reach Ohio. Certainly the protection of health is a legitimate state goal, and we assume for purposes of this argument that use of ethanol generally furthers it. But § 5735.145(B) obviously does not, except perhaps by accident. As far as ethanol use in Ohio itself is concerned, there is no reason to suppose that ethanol produced in a State that does not offer tax advantages to ethanol produced in Ohio is less healthy, and thus should have its importation into Ohio suppressed by denial of the otherwise standard tax credit. And as far as ethanol use outside Ohio is concerned, surely that is just as effectively fostered by other States' subsidizing ethanol production or sale in some fashion other than giving a tax credit to Ohio-produced ethanol; but these helpful expedients do not qualify for the tax credit. It could not be clearer that health is not the purpose of the provision, but is merely an occasional and accidental effect of achieving what is its purpose, favorable tax treatment for Ohio-produced ethanol. Essentially the same reasoning also responds to appellees' second (and related) justification for the discrimination, that the reciprocity requirement is designed to increase commerce in ethanol by encouraging other States to enact ethanol subsidies. What is encouraged is not ethanol subsidies in general, but only favorable treatment for Ohio-produced ethanol. In sum, appellees' health and commerce justifications amount to no more than implausible speculation, which does not suffice to validate this plain discrimination against products of out-of-state manufacture.

. . .

Reversed.

WYOMING v. OKLAHOMA, 502 U.S. 437 (1992). An Oklahoma statute required resident coal-fired electric generating plants serving Oklahoma customers to burn at least 10% "Oklahoma mined coal." The Court, citing *New Energy*, held the statute "invalid under the Commerce Clause." Finding "that the Act, on its face and in practical effect, discriminates against interstate commerce[,]'' the Court elaborated:

> "[T]he Act expressly reserves a segment of the Oklahoma coal market for Oklahoma-mined coal, to the exclusion of coal mined in other States. Such a preference for coal from domestic sources cannot be characterized as anything other than protectionist and discriminatory, for the Act purports to exclude coal mined in other States based solely on its origin."

The Court rebuffed Oklahoma's argument "that the Act sets aside only a 'small portion' of the Oklahoma coal market, without placing an 'overall burden' on out-of-state coal producers doing business in Oklahoma." In the Court's view, "[t]he volume of commerce affected measures only the *extent* of the discrimination; it is of no relevance to the determination whether a State has discriminated against interstate commerce." The Court also rejected Oklahoma's proffered justifications for the discrimination and its argument that Congress had authorized the discrimination.

NOTE

New Energy presents the one doctrine on which all justices appear to agree—state statutes discriminating against interstate commerce will normally be found unconstitutional. Beyond this proposition there are wide areas of disagreement. Some commentators have argued that courts generally should not invalidate non-discriminatory state regulations on the basis that the burden on interstate commerce outweighs local benefits. For one example, see Regan, *The Supreme Court and State Protectionism: Making Sense of the Dormant Commerce Clause*, 84 Mich.L.Rev. 1091 (1986). For an article citing the attacks on the Court's use of the commerce clause and largely defending the Court, see Collins, *Economic Union as a Constitutional Value*, 63 New York U.L.Rev. 43 (1988). Justice Scalia rejects the balancing approach to negative commerce clause cases and says: "In my view, a state statute is invalid under the Commerce Clause if, and only if, it accords discriminatory treatment to interstate commerce in a respect not required to achieve a lawful state purpose. When such a validating purpose exists, it is for Congress and not us to determine it is not significant enough to justify the burden on commerce." Bendix Autolite Corp. v. Midwesco Enterprises, Inc., 486 U.S. 888, 898 (1988)(opinion concurring in judgment).

What the Court has done in this area can be seen in an examination of the cases.

SECTION 3.   IMPLIED RESTRICTIONS OF THE COMMERCE CLAUSE—TRANSPORTATION

STATE ECONOMIC REGULATION OF TRANSPORTATION BUSINESSES

The Supreme Court early took the position that since the right to carry on interstate commerce was conferred by the Constitution, the states had no power to require licenses as conditions of carrying on such commerce. Thus in Crutcher v. Kentucky, 141 U.S. 47 (1891), the Court held invalid a state statute requiring agents of foreign express companies to secure a license that could be secured on payment of a nominal fee and on showing a minimum level of assets. The state argued that the statute was necessary to protect citizens against unreliable and insolvent businesses. The Court responded: "To carry on interstate commerce is not a franchise or a privilege granted by the State; it is a right which every citizen of the United States is entitled to exercise under the Constitution and laws of the United States. ... We have repeatedly decided that a state law is unconstitutional which requires a party to take out a license for carrying on interstate commerce...." The principal application of that rule was in the case which follows:

BUCK v. KUYKENDALL, 267 U.S. 307 (1925), invalidated a statute of the state of Washington requiring all common carriers for hire using highways in the state to obtain certificates of convenience and necessity. The state denied a certificate to a motor carrier operating between Seattle, Washington, and Portland, Oregon on the ground that the route was already adequately served. (No federal regulation of motor carriers was in existence at the time.) The Supreme Court, in an opinion by Justice Brandeis, held the state had no power to require such a license from an interstate carrier:

> "It may be assumed that section 4 of the state statute is consistent with the Fourteenth Amendment; and also, that appropriate state regulations adopted primarily to promote safety upon the highways and conservation in their use are not obnoxious to the commerce clause, where the indirect burden imposed upon interstate commerce is not unreasonable.... The provision here in question is of a different character. Its primary purpose is not regulation with a view to safety or to conservation of the highways, but the prohibition of competition. It determines, not the manner of use, but the persons by whom the highways may be used. It prohibits such use to some persons, while permitting it to others for the same purpose and in the same manner. Moreover, it determines whether the prohibition shall be applied by resort, through state officials, to a test which is peculiarly within the province of the federal action—the existence of adequate facilities for conducting interstate commerce...."

However, the Court has upheld license requirements in cases where the state has not been asserting the authority to prevent the movement of traffic interstate. In California v. Thompson, 313 U.S. 109 (1941), the Court held valid a California statute requiring agents engaged in selling transportation on the public highways of the state to obtain a license and post a bond. Criminal prosecution was brought against an unlicensed agent who sold interstate transportation in cars not operated as regular carriers; federal regulation of motor carriers which began in 1935 did not apply to such persons. The Court said that the state statute "is not shown to be other than what on its face it appears to be, a measure to safeguard the members of the public desiring to secure transportation by motor vehicle, who are peculiarly unable to protect themselves from fraud and overreaching of those engaged in a business notoriously subject to those abuses.... Fraudulent or unconscionable conduct of those so engaged which is injurious to their patrons, is peculiarly a subject of local concern and the appropriate subject of local regulation".

The Court disclaimed any intent to overrule *Crutcher v. Kentucky*, supra, saying: "The present case is not one of prohibiting interstate commerce or licensing it on conditions which restrict or obstruct it. Cf. Crutcher v. Kentucky, 141 U.S. 47; Dahnke–Walker Co. v. Bondurant, 257 U.S. 282. For here the regulation is applied to one who is not himself engaged in the transportation but who acts only as broker or intermediary in negotiating a transportation contract between the passengers and the carrier. The license required of those engaged in such business is not conditioned upon any control or restriction of the movement of the traffic interstate but only on the good character and responsibility of those engaged locally as transportation brokers."

The federal government now imposes economic regulations on all forms of interstate transportation and communication. Problems such as those involved in *Buck* no longer arise. Thus in 1935 Congress enacted the Federal Motor Carrier Act, which became Part II of the Interstate Commerce Act and gave the Interstate Commerce Commission wide power to regulate common carriers and contract carriers engaged in interstate transportation by motor vehicle. 49 U.S.C. §§ 301–327. It is now the I.C.C. which determines whether licenses to carry on such transportation shall be issued.

STATE SAFETY REGULATIONS AND INTERSTATE TRANSPORTATION

A much more enduring problem has been that of determining the circumstances under which states may impose regulations on interstate carriers in the interests of safety. Congress was slow to move into the field of safety regulation and hence for a long time the obvious public interest in safety was served only by state regulation. In recent years federal safety regulations have become far more extensive, but the federal government has not purported to assert exclusive authority. As a result there is a continuing docket of litigation involving state safety regulations and the question whether the commerce clause of its own force prohibits them.

Originally, the Court upheld most state safety regulations, but it had difficulty in articulating coherent doctrinal reasons. A common reason given in the early cases for upholding the state regulation was that it only "indirectly" affected interstate commerce. In Erb v. Morasch, 177 U.S. 584 (1900), e.g., the Court held that a city ordinance regulating the speed of trains could be applied to interstate trains because it only "indirectly" affected commerce. The Court was not able, however, to explain why some regulations were direct and others indirect and it soon became apparent that other factors were at work. A principal example of the problem arose in litigation challenging a Georgia statute requiring all trains to check their speed at grade crossings so that they might stop if necessary to avoid hitting persons or vehicles crossing the tracks. Persons injured at grade crossings sued the railroads, seeking to base liability on the failure of the railroad to comply with the statute. In Southern Ry. Co. v. King, 217 U.S. 524 (1910), the Court upheld the sustaining of a demurrer to an answer by the railroad which merely alleged that the statute was in violation of the commerce clause and imposed a direct burden on interstate traffic. The Court said the averments were mere conclusions. "They set forth no facts which would make the operation of the statute unconstitutional. They do not show the number or location of the crossings at which the railway company would be required to check the speed of its trains, so as to interfere with their successful operation. For aught that appears as allegations of fact in this answer, the crossing at which this injury happened may have been so located and of such dangerous character as to make the slackening of trains at that point necessary to the safety of those using the public highway, and a statute making such requirement only a reasonable police regulation, and not an unlawful attempt to regulate or hinder interstate commerce." In a later case of the same type, Seaboard Air Line Ry. Co. v. Blackwell, 244 U.S. 310 (1917), the railroad's answer alleged that the train involved was running in interstate commerce from Atlanta, Georgia, to other points in Georgia and South Carolina; that in the 123–mile run from Atlanta to the state line there were 124 crossings at which the statute required each train to check its speed; that three minutes would be consumed at each crossing, or about six hours in all, thus increasing the running time between Atlanta and the state line from the scheduled 4 ½ to a total of 10 ½ hours. The Court stated that the facts alleged "compel the conclusion that the statute is a direct burden upon interstate commerce, and, being such, is unlawful". Judgment for the plaintiff was reversed.

The Court was even willing to sustain state licensing regulations, at least when they did not totally exclude carriers from interstate commerce, if reasonably necessary to promote safety. The following case, which should be contrasted with *Buck v. Kuykendall,* supra, is illustrative.

BRADLEY v. PUBLIC UTILITIES COMMISSION, 289 U.S. 92 (1933). The Ohio Public Utilities Commission denied Bradley's application for a certificate of public convenience and necessity to operate a motor carrier service over State Route No. 20 from Cleveland to Flint, Michigan. After a hearing, the Commission determined that Route 20 was so badly congested that adding Bradley's service "would create and maintain an excessive and undue hazard to the safety and security of the traveling public." The Supreme Court unanimously upheld the denial of the certificate. First, the Court noted that the order did not exclude Bradley from operating in interstate commerce. He had failed to apply for an alternate route and had not shown that a feasible route with less congestion was not available.

Second, the Court said:

"It is contended that an order denying to a common carrier by motor a certificate to engage in interstate transportation necessarily violates the Commerce Clause. The argument is that under the rule declared in Buck v. Kuykendall, 267 U.S. 307, ... an interstate carrier is entitled to a certificate as of right; and that hence the reason for the commission's refusal and its purpose are immaterial. In those cases, safety was doubtless promoted when the certificate was denied, because intensification of traffic was thereby prevented.... But there promotion of safety was merely an incident of the denial. Its purpose was to prevent competition deemed undesirable. The test employed was the adequacy of existing transportation facilities; and since the transportation in question was interstate, denial of the certificate invaded the province of Congress. In the case at bar, the purpose of the denial was to promote safety; and the test employed was congestion of the highway. The effect of the denial upon interstate commerce was merely an incident.

"Protection against accidents, as against crime, presents ordinarily a local problem. Regulation to ensure safety is an exercise of the police power. It is primarily a state function, whether the locus be private property or the public highways. Congress has not dealt with the subject. Hence, even where the motorcars are used exclusively in interstate commerce, a state may freely exact registration of the vehicle and an operator's license, Hendrick v. Maryland, 235 U.S. 610, 622.... The state may exclude from the public highways vehicles engaged exclusively in interstate commerce, if of a size deemed dangerous to the public safety, Morris v. Duby, 274 U.S. 135, 144; Sproles v. Binford, 286 U.S. 374, 389–390. Safety may require that no additional vehicle be admitted to the highway. The Commerce Clause is not violated by denial of the certificate to the appellant, if upon adequate evidence denial is deemed necessary to promote the public safety."[a]

---

[a] For an excellent discussion of the *Buck* and *Bradley* cases as well as state motor carrier regulation prior to the adoption of the Federal Motor Carrier Act in 1935, see Kauper, *State Regulation of Interstate Motor Carriers,* 31 Mich.L.Rev. 920, 1097 (1933). A

The balance of this section will present cases from 1938 to the present involving state safety regulations as applied to interstate transportation. The student should consider whether there is a coherent doctrine which explains the results in these cases.

SOUTH CAROLINA STATE HIGHWAY DEPARTMENT v. BARNWELL BROTHERS, 303 U.S. 177 (1938).

A South Carolina statute forbade the use on state highways of motor trucks whose width exceeded 90 inches and whose weight including load exceeded 20,000 pounds. A federal district court weighed conflicting evidence and determined that the width and weight limitations were more restrictive than needed to protect the highways of the state and the users of such highways. It also determined that the limitations imposed substantial burdens on interstate commerce since 85 to 90 percent of the trucks used in interstate commerce were 96 inches wide and of a gross weight when loaded in excess of 20,000 pounds.

The Supreme Court reversed in an opinion by Justice Stone, stating:

"While the constitutional grant to Congress of power to regulate interstate commerce has been held to operate of its own force to curtail state power in some measure,[2] it did not forestall all state action affecting interstate commerce. . . .

"The commerce clause by its own force, prohibits discrimination against interstate commerce, whatever its form or method, and the decisions of this Court have recognized that there is scope for its like operation when state legislation nominally of local concern is in point of fact aimed at interstate commerce, or by its necessary operation is a means of gaining a local benefit by throwing the attendant burdens on those without the state. . . . The commerce clause has also been thought to set its own limitation upon state control of interstate rail carriers so as to preclude the subordination of the efficiency and convenience of interstate traffic to local service requirements.

"But the present case affords no occasion for saying that the bare possession of power by Congress to regulate the interstate traffic forces the states to conform to standards which Congress might, but has not adopted, or curtails their power to take measures to insure the safety and conservation of their highways which may be applied to like traffic moving intrastate. Few subjects of state regulation are so peculiarly of local concern as is the use of state highways. There are few, local regulation of which is so inseparable from a substantial effect on interstate commerce. Unlike the railroads, local highways are built, owned, and maintained by the state or its municipal subdivisions. The state has a primary and immediate concern in their safe and economical administration. The present regulations, or any others of like purpose, if they are to accomplish their end, must be applied alike to interstate and intrastate traffic both moving in large volume over the highways. The fact that they affect

later brief discussion will be found in Swerer, *State Regulation of Interstate Transportation by Motor Carriers*, 16 Rocky Mt.L.Rev. 1 (1943).

[2] State regulations affecting interstate commerce, whose purpose or effect is to gain for those within the state an advantage at the expense of those without, or to burden those out of the state without any corresponding advantage to those within, have been thought to impinge upon the constitutional prohibition even though Congress has not acted. . . .

Underlying the stated rule has been the thought, often expressed in judicial opinion, that when the regulation is of such a character that its burden falls principally upon those without the state, legislative action is not likely to be subjected to those political restraints which are normally exerted on legislation where it affects adversely some interests within the state. . . .

alike shippers in interstate and intrastate commerce in large number within as well as without the state is a safeguard against their abuse.

. . .

"Congress, in the exercise of its plenary power to regulate interstate commerce, may determine whether the burdens imposed on it by state regulation, otherwise permissible, are too great, and may, by legislation designed to secure uniformity or in other respects to protect the national interest in the commerce, curtail to some extent the state's regulatory power. But that is a legislative, not a judicial, function, to be performed in the light of the congressional judgment of what is appropriate regulation of interstate commerce, and the extent to which, in that field, state power and local interests should be required to yield to the national authority and interest. In the absence of such legislation the judicial function, under the commerce clause, as well as the Fourteenth Amendment, stops with the inquiry whether the state Legislature in adopting regulations such as the present has acted within its province, and whether the means of regulation chosen are reasonably adapted to the end sought. . . .

"Here the first inquiry has already been resolved by our decisions that a state may impose nondiscriminatory restrictions with respect to the character of motor vehicles moving in interstate commerce as a safety measure and as a means of securing the economical use of its highways. In resolving the second, courts do not sit as Legislatures, either state or national. . . . When the action of a Legislature is within the scope of its power, fairly debatable questions as to its reasonableness, wisdom, and propriety are not for the determination of courts, but for the legislative body, on which rests the duty and responsibility of decision. . . . It is not any the less a legislative power committed to the states because it affects interstate commerce, and courts are not any the more entitled, because interstate commerce is affected, to substitute their own for the legislative judgment. . . .

"Since the adoption of one weight or width regulation, rather than another, is a legislative, not a judicial, choice, its constitutionality is not to be determined by weighing in the judicial scales the merits of the legislative choice and rejecting it if the weight of evidence presented in court appears to favor a different standard. . . . Being a legislative judgment it is presumed to be supported by facts known to the Legislature unless facts judicially known or proved preclude that possibility. Hence, in reviewing the present determination, we examine the record, not to see whether the findings of the court below are supported by evidence, but to ascertain upon the whole record whether it is possible to say that the legislative choice is without rational basis. . . . Not only does the record fail to exclude that possibility but it shows affirmatively that there is adequate support for the legislative judgment. . . ."

SOUTHERN PACIFIC CO. v. ARIZONA, 325 U.S. 761 (1945). An Arizona law forbade the operation of railroad trains of more than fourteen passenger or seventy freight cars and authorized the state to recover a monetary penalty for each violation. In 1940 the state brought suit against the railroad in an Arizona state court seeking to recover the statutory penalties for violation of the act. An extended trial was had after which the trial court made detailed findings of fact as to the extent to which the statute burdened commerce and the extent to which it benefited state interests and concluded that the statute was unconstitutional. The Arizona Supreme Court reversed, directing entry of judgment for the state. The Supreme Court in an opinion by Chief Justice Stone, reversed, stating in part:

"... [E]ver since Gibbons v. Ogden, 9 Wheat. 1, the states have not been deemed to have authority to impede substantially the free flow of commerce from state to state, or to regulate those phases of the national commerce which, because of the need of national uniformity, demand that their regulation, if any, be prescribed by a single authority.[2] *Cooley v. Board of Wardens,* supra.... Whether or not this long recognized distribution of power between the national and the state governments is predicated upon the implications of the commerce clause itself, Minnesota Rate Cases, supra, 399, 400; South Carolina Highway Dept. v. Barnwell Bros., supra, 185 ... or upon the presumed intention of Congress, where Congress has not spoken, ... the result is the same.

"In the application of these principles some enactments may be found to be plainly within and others plainly without state power. But between these extremes lies the infinite variety of cases in which regulation of local matters may also operate as a regulation of commerce, in which reconciliation of the conflicting claims of state and national power is to be attained only by some appraisal and accommodation of the competing demands of the state and national interests involved....

. . .

"Congress has undoubted power to redefine the distribution of power over interstate commerce. It may either permit the states to regulate the commerce in a manner which would otherwise not be permissible, In re Rahrer, supra, 140 U.S. 561, 562, ... or exclude state regulation even of matters of peculiarly local concern which nevertheless affect interstate commerce....

"But in general Congress has left it to the courts to formulate the rules thus interpreting the commerce clause in its application, doubtless because it has appreciated the destructive consequences to the commerce of the nation if their protection were withdrawn, Gwin, etc., Inc. v. Henneford, supra, 305 U.S. 441, and has been aware that in their application state laws will not be invalidated without the support of relevant factual material which will 'afford a sure basis' for an informed judgment....

"Hence the matters for ultimate determination here are the nature and extent of the burden which the state regulation of interstate trains, adopted as a safety measure, imposes on interstate commerce, and whether the relative weights of the state and national interests involved are such as to make inapplicable the rule, generally observed, that the free flow of interstate commerce and its freedom from local restraints in matters requiring uniformity of regulation are interests safeguarded by the commerce clause from state interference.

"While this Court is not bound by the findings of the state court, and may determine for itself the facts of a case upon which an asserted federal right depends, the facts found by the state trial court showing the nature of the interstate commerce involved, and the effect upon it of the train limit law, are not seriously questioned. Its findings with respect to the need for and effect of the statute as a safety measure, although challenged in some particulars which we do not regard as material to our decision, are likewise supported by

---

[2] In applying this rule the Court has often recognized that to the extent that the burden of state regulation falls on interests outside the state, it is unlikely to be alleviated by the operation of those political restraints normally exerted when interests within the state are affected....

evidence. Taken together the findings supply an adequate basis for decision of the constitutional issue.

. . .

"The unchallenged findings leave no doubt that the Arizona Train Limit Law imposes a serious burden on the interstate commerce conducted by appellant. It materially impedes the movement of appellant's interstate trains through that state and interposes a substantial obstruction to the national policy proclaimed by Congress, to promote adequate, economical and efficient railway transportation service.... Enforcement of the law in Arizona, while train lengths remain unregulated or are regulated by varying standards in other states, must inevitably result in an impairment of uniformity of efficient railroad operation because the railroads are subjected to regulation which is not uniform in its application. Compliance with a state statute limiting train lengths requires interstate trains of a length lawful in other states to be broken up and reconstituted as they enter each state according as it may impose varying limitations upon train lengths. The alternative is for the carrier to conform to the lowest train limit restriction of any of the states through which its trains pass, whose laws thus control the carriers' operations both within and without the regulating state.

. . .

"The trial court found that the Arizona law had no reasonable relation to safety, and made train operation more dangerous. Examination of the evidence and the detailed findings makes it clear that this conclusion was rested on facts found which indicate that such increased danger of accident and personal injury as may result from the greater length of trains is more than offset by the increase in the number of accidents resulting from the larger number of trains when train lengths are reduced. In considering the effect of the statute as a safety measure, therefore, the factor of controlling significance for present purposes is not whether there is basis for the conclusion of the Arizona Supreme Court that the increase in length of trains beyond the statutory maximum has an adverse effect upon safety of operation. The decisive question is whether in the circumstances the total effect of the law as a safety measure in reducing accidents and casualties is so slight or problematical as not to outweigh the national interest in keeping interstate commerce free from interferences which seriously impede it and subject it to local regulation which does not have a uniform effect on the interstate train journey which it interrupts.

. . .

"Here we conclude that the state does go too far. Its regulation of train lengths, admittedly obstructive to interstate train operation, and having a seriously adverse effect on transportation efficiency and economy, passes beyond what is plainly essential for safety since it does not appear that it will lessen rather than increase the danger of accident. Its attempted regulation of the operation of interstate trains cannot establish nation-wide control such as is essential to the maintenance of an efficient transportation system, which Congress alone can prescribe. The state interest cannot be preserved at the expense of the national interest by an enactment which regulates interstate train lengths without securing such control, which is a matter of national concern. To this the interest of the state here asserted is subordinate.

. . .

"*South Carolina State Highway Dept. v. Barnwell Bros.*, supra, was concerned with the power of the state to regulate the weight and width of motor cars passing interstate over its highways, a legislative field over which the state has a far more extensive control than over interstate railroads. In that case, ... we were at pains to point out that there are few subjects of state regulation affecting interstate commerce which are so peculiarly of local concern as is the use of the state's highways. ... "

Justices Black and Douglas dissented. Justice Black stated that the ruling of the Court "makes it necessary for a judge to hear all the evidence offered as to why a legislature passed a law and to make findings of fact as to the validity of those reasons. If under today's ruling a court does make findings, as to a danger contrary to the findings of the legislature, and the evidence heard 'lends support' to those findings, a court can then invalidate the law. In this respect, the Arizona County Court acted, and this Court today is acting, as a 'super-legislature.' "

Justice Douglas said: "My view has been that the courts should intervene only where the state legislation discriminated against interstate commerce or was out of harmony with laws which Congress had enacted."

BIBB v. NAVAJO FREIGHT LINES, INC., 359 U.S. 520 (1959). An Illinois statute required the use of a certain type of rear fender mudguard on trucks and trailers operating on highways in the state. The statute made illegal the use of straight mudflaps which were legal in at least 45 states and required in the state of Arkansas. A federal district court held the statute invalid as placing an undue burden on interstate commerce. The Supreme Court affirmed in an opinion by Justice Douglas.

Justice Douglas commenced his opinion by citing *Barnwell* for the proposition that regulation of highways is peculiarly local and that policy decisions are for the state legislature. "Unless we can conclude on the whole record that the 'total effect of the law as a safety measure in reducing accidents and casualties is so slight or problematic as not to outweigh the national interest in keeping interstate commerce free from interferences which seriously impede it' (*Southern Pacific v. Arizona* ...) we must uphold the statute."

Justice Douglas then reviewed the evidence as to the cost of equipping all interstate vehicles with contour mudguards and as to the relative safety of such mudguards and conventional mudflaps. He concluded that review by saying: "If we had here only a question whether the cost of adjusting an interstate operation to these new local safety regulations prescribed by Illinois unduly burdened interstate commerce, we would have to sustain the law.... The same result would obtain if we had to resolve the much discussed issues of safety presented in this case."

"This case," he said, "presents a different issue." The equipment here could not pass muster in every state; instead the question is whether one state can prescribe standards which will require shifting cargo to differently designed vehicles at the state border. Because of the practice of "interlining"—transferring loaded trailers between an originating carrier and another carrier—the statute would require carriers who do only a minor amount of their business in Illinois to equip all of their trailers with the contour mudguards.

He then rejected the argument that *Barnwell* stood for the proposition that despite "the rather massive showing of burden on interstate commerce", it was for the state legislature, not the courts, to weigh the relative merits of contour mudguards against any other kind. "The various exercises by the States of their police power stand ... on an equal footing. All are entitled to the same

presumption of validity when challenged under the Due Process Clause....
Similarly the various state regulatory statutes are of equal dignity when
measured against the Commerce Clause, ... Local regulation which would pass
muster under the Due Process Clause might nonetheless fail to survive other
challenges to constitutionality that bring the Supremacy Clause into play. Like
any local law that conflicts with federal regulatory measure ..., state regulations that run afoul of the policy of free trade reflected in the Commerce Clause
must also bow.

"This is one of those cases—few in number—where local safety measures
that are nondiscriminatory place an unconstitutional burden on interstate
commerce.... A State which insists on a design out of line with the requirements of almost all the other States may sometimes place a great burden of
delay and inconvenience on those interstate motor carriers entering or crossing
its territory. Such a new safety device—out of line with the requirements of the
other States—may be so compelling that the innovating State need not be the
one to give way. The present showing—balanced against the clear burden on
commerce—is far too inconclusive to make this mudguard meet that test."

Justice Harlan, joined by Justice Stewart, concurred in the judgment,
saying: "The opinion of the Court clearly demonstrates the heavy burden, in
terms of cost and interference with 'interlining' which the Illinois statute here
involved imposes on interstate commerce. In view of the findings of the District
Court ... to the effect that the contour mudflap 'possesses no advantages' in
terms of safety over the conventional flap permitted in all other States, and
indeed creates certain safety hazards, this heavy burden cannot be justified on
the theory that the Illinois statute is a necessary, appropriate, or helpful safety
measure."

Kassel v. Consolidated Freightways Corporation

450 U.S. 662, 101 S.Ct. 1309, 67 L.Ed.2d 580 (1981).

**Justice Powell announced the judgment of the Court and deliv-
ered an opinion in which Justice White, Justice Blackmun, and Justice Stevens joined.**

The question is whether an Iowa statute that prohibits the use of certain
large trucks within the State unconstitutionally burdens interstate commerce.

I

Respondent Consolidated Freightways Corporation of Delaware (Consolidated) is one of the largest common carriers in the country. It offers service in
48 States under a certificate of public convenience and necessity issued by the
Interstate Commerce Commission. Among other routes, Consolidated carries
commodities through Iowa on Interstate 80, the principal east-west route
linking New York, Chicago, and the west coast, and on Interstate 35, a major
north-south route.

Consolidated mainly uses two kinds of trucks. One consists of a three-axle
tractor pulling a 40–foot two-axle trailer. This unit, commonly called a single,
or "semi," is 55 feet in length overall. Such trucks have long been used on the
Nation's highways. Consolidated also uses a two-axle tractor pulling a single-
axle trailer which, in turn, pulls a single-axle dolly and a second single-axle
trailer. This combination, known as a double, or twin, is 65 feet long overall.
Many trucking companies, including Consolidated, increasingly prefer to use
doubles to ship certain kinds of commodities. Doubles have larger capacities,

and the trailers can be detached and routed separately if necessary. Consolidated would like to use 65–foot doubles on many of its trips through Iowa.

The State of Iowa, however, by statute restricts the length of vehicles that may use its highways. Unlike all other States in the West and Midwest, Iowa generally prohibits the use of 65–foot doubles within its borders. Instead, most truck combinations are restricted to 55 feet in length. Doubles, mobile homes, trucks carrying vehicles such as tractors and other farm equipment, and singles hauling livestock, are permitted to be as long as 60 feet. Notwithstanding these restrictions, Iowa's statute permits cities abutting the state line by local ordinance to adopt the length limitations of the adjoining State. Iowa Code § 321.457(7) (1979). Where a city has exercised this option, otherwise oversized trucks are permitted within the city limits and in nearby commercial zones. Ibid.

Iowa also provides for two other relevant exemptions. An Iowa truck manufacturer may obtain a permit to ship trucks that are as large as 70 feet. Iowa Code § 321E.10 (1979). Permits also are available to move oversized mobile homes, provided that the unit is to be moved from a point within Iowa or delivered for an Iowa resident. Id., § 321E.28(5).[7]

"This bill ... would make Iowa a bridge state as these oversized units are moved into Iowa after being manufactured in another state and sold in a third. None of this activity would be of particular economic benefit to Iowa."

Because of Iowa's statutory scheme, Consolidated cannot use its 65–foot doubles to move commodities through the State. Instead, the company must do one of four things: (i) use 55–foot singles; (ii) use 60–foot doubles; (iii) detach the trailers of a 65–foot double and shuttle each through the State separately; or (iv) divert 65–foot doubles around Iowa.

Dissatisfied with these options, Consolidated filed this suit in the District Court averring that Iowa's statutory scheme unconstitutionally burdens interstate commerce. Iowa defended the law as a reasonable safety measure enacted pursuant to its police power. The State asserted that 65–foot doubles are more dangerous than 55–foot singles and, in any event, that the law promotes safety and reduces road wear within the State by diverting much truck traffic to other States.

In a 14–day trial, both sides adduced evidence on safety, and on the burden on interstate commerce imposed by Iowa's law. On the question of safety, the District Court found that the "evidence clearly establishes that the twin is as safe as the semi." 475 F.Supp. 544, 549 (S.D.Iowa 1979). For that reason,

"there is no valid safety reason for barring twins from Iowa's highways because of their configuration.

"The evidence convincingly, if not overwhelmingly, establishes that the 65 foot twin is as safe as, if not safer than, the 60 foot twin and the 55 foot semi....

. . .

"Twins and semis have different characteristics. Twins are more maneuverable, are less sensitive to wind, and create less splash and spray. However,

---

[7] The parochial restrictions in the mobile home provision were enacted after Governor Ray vetoed a bill that would have permitted the interstate shipment of all mobile homes through Iowa. Governor Ray commented, in his veto message:

"This bill ... would make Iowa a bridge state as these oversized units are moved into Iowa after being manufactured in another state and sold in a third. None of this activity would be of particular economic benefit to Iowa."

they are more likely than semis to jackknife or upset. They can be backed only for a short distance. The negative characteristics are not such that they render the twin less safe than semis overall. Semis are more stable but are more likely to 'rear end' another vehicle." Id., at 548–549.

In light of these findings, the District Court applied the standard we enunciated in Raymond Motor Transportation, Inc. v. Rice, 434 U.S. 429 (1978), and concluded that the state law impermissibly burdened interstate commerce....

The ... Eighth Circuit affirmed....

... We now affirm.

II

. . .

The Commerce Clause does not, of course, invalidate all state restrictions on commerce.... The extent of permissible state regulation is not always easy to measure. It may be said with confidence, however, that a State's power to regulate commerce is never greater than in matters traditionally of local concern. *Washington Apple Advertising Comm.*, supra, at 350. For example, regulations that touch upon safety—especially highway safety—are those that "the Court has been most reluctant to invalidate." *Raymond*, supra, at 443; ... Indeed, "if safety justifications are not illusory, the court will not second-guess legislative judgment about their importance in comparison with related burdens on interstate commerce." *Raymond*, supra, at 449 (Blackmun, J., concurring). Those who would challenge such bona fide safety regulations must overcome a "strong presumption of validity." Bibb v. Navajo Freight Lines, Inc., 359 U.S. 520, 524 (1959).

But the incantation of a purpose to promote the public health or safety does not insulate a state law from Commerce Clause attack. Regulations designed for that salutary purpose nevertheless may further the purpose so marginally, and interfere with commerce so substantially, as to be invalid under the Commerce Clause. In the Court's recent unanimous decision in *Raymond,* we declined to "accept the State's contention that the inquiry under the Commerce Clause is ended without a weighing of the asserted safety purpose against the degree of interference with interstate commerce." 434 U.S., at 443. This "weighing" by a court requires—and indeed the constitutionality of the state regulation depends on—"a sensitive consideration of the weight and nature of the state regulatory concern in light of the extent of the burden imposed on the course of interstate commerce." ...

III

Applying these general principles, we conclude that the Iowa truck-length limitations unconstitutionally burden interstate commerce.

In Raymond Motor Transportation, Inc. v. Rice, the Court held that a Wisconsin statute that precluded the use of 65–foot doubles violated the Commerce Clause. This case is *Raymond* revisited. Here, as in *Raymond,* the State failed to present any persuasive evidence that 65–foot doubles are less safe than 55–foot singles. Moreover, Iowa's law is now out of step with the laws of all other Midwestern and Western States. Iowa thus substantially burdens the interstate flow of goods by truck. In the absence of congressional action to set uniform standards, some burdens associated with state safety regulations must be tolerated. But where, as here, the State's safety interest has been found to be illusory, and its regulations impair significantly the federal interest in efficient and safe interstate transportation, the state law cannot be harmonized with the Commerce Clause.

A

Iowa made a more serious effort to support the safety rationale of its law than did Wisconsin in *Raymond,* but its effort was no more persuasive. As noted above, the District Court found that the "evidence clearly establishes that the twin is as safe as the semi." The record supports this finding.

The trial focused on a comparison of the performance of the two kinds of trucks in various safety categories. The evidence showed, and the District Court found, that the 65–foot double was at least the equal of the 55–foot single in the ability to brake, turn, and maneuver. The double, because of its axle placement, produces less splash and spray in wet weather. And, because of its articulation in the middle, the double is less susceptible to dangerous "off-tracking," and to wind.

None of these findings is seriously disputed by Iowa. Indeed, the State points to only three ways in which the 55–foot single is even arguably superior: singles take less time to be passed and to clear intersections; they may back up for longer distances; and they are somewhat less likely to jackknife.

The first two of these characteristics are of limited relevance on modern interstate highways. As the District Court found, the negligible difference in the time required to pass, and to cross intersections, is insignificant on 4–lane divided highways because passing does not require crossing into oncoming traffic lanes, *Raymond,* 434 U.S., at 444, and interstates have few, if any, intersections. The concern over backing capability also is insignificant because it seldom is necessary to back up on an interstate. In any event, no evidence suggested any difference in backing capability between the 60–foot doubles that Iowa permits and the 65–foot doubles that it bans. Similarly, although doubles tend to jackknife somewhat more than singles, 65–foot doubles actually are less likely to jackknife than 60–foot doubles.

Statistical studies supported the view that 65–foot doubles are at least as safe overall as 55–foot singles and 60–foot doubles. One such study, which the District Court credited, reviewed Consolidated's comparative accident experience in 1978 with its own singles and doubles.... Iowa's expert statistician admitted that this study provided "moderately strong evidence" that singles have a higher injury rate than doubles. Another study, prepared by the Iowa Department of Transportation at the request of the State legislature, concluded that "[s]ixty-five foot twin trailer combinations have *not* been shown by experiences in other states to be less safe than 60–foot twin trailer combinations *or* conventional tractor-semitrailers" (emphasis in original). Numerous insurance company executives, and transportation officials from the Federal Government and various States, testified that 65–foot doubles were at least as safe as 55–foot singles. Iowa concedes that it can produce no study that establishes a statistically significant difference in safety between the 65–foot double and the kinds of vehicles the State permits. Nor ... did Iowa present a single witness who testified that 65–foot doubles were more dangerous overall than the vehicles permitted under Iowa law.... In sum, although Iowa introduced more evidence on the question of safety than did Wisconsin in *Raymond,* the record as a whole was not more favorable to the State.

B

Consolidated, meanwhile, demonstrated that Iowa's law substantially burdens interstate commerce. Trucking companies that wish to continue to use 65–

foot doubles must route them around Iowa or detach the trailers of the doubles and ship them through separately. Alternatively, trucking companies must use the smaller 55–foot singles or 60–foot doubles permitted under Iowa law. Each of these options engenders inefficiency and added expense. The record shows that Iowa's law added about $12.6 million each year to the costs of trucking companies. Consolidated alone incurred about $2 million per year in increased costs.

In addition to increasing the costs of the trucking companies (and, indirectly, of the service to consumers), Iowa's law may aggravate, rather than ameliorate, the problem of highway accidents. Fifty-five foot singles carry less freight than 65–foot doubles. Either more small trucks must be used to carry the same quantity of goods through Iowa, or the same number of larger trucks must drive longer distances to bypass Iowa. In either case, as the District Court noted, the restriction requires more highway miles to be driven to transport the same quantity of goods. Other things being equal, accidents are proportional to distance traveled. Thus, if 65–foot doubles are as safe as 55–foot singles, Iowa's law tends to *increase* the number of accidents, and to shift the incidence of them from Iowa to other States.

IV

Perhaps recognizing the weakness of the evidence supporting its safety argument, and the substantial burden on commerce that its regulations create, Iowa urges the Court simply to "defer" to the safety judgment of the State. It argues that the length of trucks is generally, although perhaps imprecisely, related to safety. The task of drawing a line is one that Iowa contends should be left to its legislature.

The Court normally does accord "special deference" to state highway safety regulations. *Raymond*, 434 U.S., at 444, n. 18. This traditional deference "derives in part from the assumption that where such regulations do not discriminate on their face against interstate commerce, their burden usually falls on local economic interests as well as other States' economic interests, thus insuring that a State's own political processes will serve as a check against unduly burdensome regulations." Ibid. Less deference to the legislative judgment is due, however, where the local regulation bears disproportionately on out-of-state residents and businesses. Such a disproportionate burden is apparent here. Iowa's scheme, although generally banning large doubles from the State, nevertheless has several exemptions that secure to Iowans many of the benefits of large trucks while shunting to neighboring States many of the costs associated with their use.

At the time of trial there were two particularly significant exemptions. First, singles hauling livestock or farm vehicles were permitted to be as long as 60 feet. Iowa Code §§ 321.457(5), 321.457(3) (1979). As the Court of Appeals noted, this provision undoubtedly was helpful to local interests. Cf. *Raymond*, supra, at 434 (exemption in Wisconsin for milk shippers). Second, cities abutting other States were permitted to enact local ordinances adopting the larger length limitation of the neighboring State. Iowa Code § 321.457(7) (1979). This exemption offered the benefits of longer trucks to individuals and businesses in important border cities without burdening Iowa's highways with interstate through traffic. Cf. *Raymond*, supra, at 446–447, and n. 24 (exemption in Wisconsin for shipments from local plants).

The origin of the "border cities exemption" also suggests that Iowa's statute may not have been designed to ban dangerous trucks, but rather to discourage interstate truck traffic. In 1974, the legislature passed a bill that would have permitted 65–foot doubles in the State. Governor Ray vetoed the bill. He said:

> "I find sympathy with those who are doing business in our state and whose enterprises could gain from increased cargo carrying ability by trucks. However, with this bill, the Legislature has pursued a course that would benefit only a few Iowa-based companies while providing a great advantage for out-of-state trucking firms and competitors at the expense of our Iowa citizens."

After the veto, the "border cities exemption" was immediately enacted and signed by the Governor.

It is thus far from clear that Iowa was motivated primarily by a judgment that 65–foot doubles are less safe than 55–foot singles. Rather, Iowa seems to have hoped to limit the use of its highways by deflecting some through traffic. In the District Court and Court of Appeals, the State explicitly attempted to justify the law by its claimed interest in keeping trucks out of Iowa. The Court of Appeals correctly concluded that a State cannot constitutionally promote its own parochial interests by requiring safe vehicles to detour around it. 612 F.2d, at 1070.

V

In sum, the statutory exemptions, their history, and the arguments Iowa has advanced in support of its law in this litigation, all suggest that the deference traditionally accorded a State's safety judgment is not warranted. See *Raymond,* supra, at 444, and n. 18, 446–447. The controlling factors thus are the findings of the District Court, accepted by the Court of Appeals, with respect to the relative safety of the types of trucks at issue, and the substantiality of the burden on interstate commerce.

Because Iowa has imposed this burden without any significant countervailing safety interest, its statute violates the Commerce Clause. The judgment of the Court of Appeals is affirmed.

It is so ordered.

Justice Brennan, with whom Justice Marshall joins, concurring in the judgment.

Iowa's truck-length regulation challenged in this case is nearly identical to the Wisconsin regulation struck down in Raymond Motor Transportation, Inc. v. Rice, 434 U.S. 429 (1978), as in violation of the Commerce Clause. In my view the same Commerce Clause restrictions that dictated that holding also require invalidation of Iowa's regulation insofar as its prohibits 65–foot doubles.

The reasoning bringing me to that conclusion does not require, however, that I engage in the debate between my Brothers Powell and Rehnquist over what the District Court record shows on the question whether 65–foot doubles are more dangerous than shorter trucks. With all respect, my Brothers ask and answer the wrong question.

For me, analysis of Commerce Clause challenges to state regulations must take into account three principles: (1) The courts are not empowered to second-guess the empirical judgments of lawmakers concerning the utility of legislation. (2) The burdens imposed on commerce must be balanced against the local benefits actually sought to be achieved by the State's lawmakers, and not against those suggested after the fact by counsel. (3) Protectionist legislation is unconstitutional under the Commerce Clause, even if the burdens and benefits are related to safety rather than economics.

I

Both the opinion of my Brother Powell and the opinion of my Brother Rehnquist are predicated upon the supposition that the constitutionality of a state regulation is determined by the factual record created by the State's lawyers in trial court. But that supposition cannot be correct, for it would make the constitutionality of state laws and regulations depend on the vagaries of litigation rather than on the judgments made by the State's lawmakers.

In considering a Commerce Clause challenge to a state regulation, the judicial task is to balance the burden imposed on commerce against the local benefits sought to be achieved by the State's *lawmakers*. See Pike v. Bruce Church, Inc., 397 U.S. 137, 142 (1970). In determining those benefits, a court should focus ultimately on the regulatory purposes identified by the lawmakers and on the evidence before or available to them that might have supported their judgment.... Since the court must confine its analysis to the purposes the lawmakers had for maintaining the regulation, the only relevant evidence concerns whether the lawmakers could rationally have believed that the challenged regulation would foster those purposes.... It is not the function of the court to decide whether *in fact* the regulation promotes its intended purpose, so long as an examination of the evidence before or available to the lawmaker indicates that the regulation is not wholly irrational in light of its purposes.[1]

II

My Brothers Powell and Rehnquist make the mistake of disregarding the intention of Iowa's lawmakers and assuming that resolution of the case must hinge upon the argument offered by Iowa's attorneys: that 65-foot doubles are more dangerous than shorter trucks. They then canvass the factual record and findings of the courts below and reach opposite conclusions as to whether the evidence adequately supports that empirical judgment. I repeat: my Brothers Powell and Rehnquist have asked and answered the wrong question. For although Iowa's lawyers in this litigation have defended the truck-length regulation on the basis of the safety advantages of 55-foot singles and 60-foot doubles over 65-foot doubles, Iowa's actual rationale for maintaining the regulation had nothing to do with these purported differences. Rather, Iowa sought to discourage interstate truck traffic on Iowa's highways. Thus, the safety advantages and disadvantages of the types and lengths of trucks involved in this case are irrelevant to the decision.[3]

---

[1] Moreover, I would emphasize that in the field of safety—and perhaps in other fields where the decisions of State lawmakers are deserving of a heightened degree of deference—the role of the courts is not to balance asserted burdens against intended benefits as it is in other fields. Compare Raymond Motor Transportation, Inc. v. Rice, 434 U.S. 429, 449 (1978) (Blackmun, J., concurring) (safety regulation) with Pike v. Bruce Church, Inc., 397 U.S. 137, 143 (1970) (regulation intended "to protect and enhance the reputation of growers within the State"). In the field of safety, once the court has established that the intended safety benefit is not illusory, insubstantial, or nonexistent, it must defer to the State's lawmakers on the appropriate balance to be struck against other interests. I therefore disagree with my Brother Powell when he asserts that the degree of interference with interstate commerce may in the first instance be "weighed" against the State's safety interests....

[3] My Brother Rehnquist claims that the "argument" that a Court should defer to the actual purposes of the lawmakers rather than to the *post hoc* justifications of counsel "has been consistently rejected by the Court in other contexts." ...

. . .

If, as here, the only purpose ever articulated by the State's lawmakers for maintain-

My Brother Powell concedes that "[i]t is ... far from clear that Iowa was motivated primarily by a judgment that 65–foot doubles are less safe than 55–foot singles. Rather, Iowa seems to have hoped to limit the use of its highways by deflecting some through traffic." This conclusion is more than amply supported by the record and the legislative history of the Iowa regulation. The Iowa legislature has consistently taken the position that size, weight, and speed restrictions on interstate traffic should be set in accordance with uniform national standards. The stated purpose was not to further safety but to achieve uniformity with other States. The Act setting the limitations challenged in this case, passed in 1947 and periodically amended since then, is entitled, "An Act *to promote uniformity with other states* in the matter of limitations on the size, weight and speed of motor vehicles...." 1947 Iowa Act, ch. 177 (emphasis added). Following the proposals of the American Association of State Highway and Transportation Officials, the State has gradually increased the permissible length of trucks from 45 feet in 1947 to the present limit of 60 feet.

In 1974, the Iowa legislature again voted to increase the permissible length of trucks to conform to uniform standards then in effect in most other States. This legislation, House Bill 671, would have increased the maximum length of twin trailer trucks operable in Iowa from 60 to 65 feet. But Governor Ray broke from prior state policy, and vetoed the legislation. The legislature did not override the veto, and the present regulation was thus maintained. In his veto, Governor Ray did not rest his decision on the conclusion that 55–foot singles and 60–foot doubles are any safer than 65–foot doubles, or on any other safety consideration inherent in the type or size of the trucks. Rather, his principal concern was that to allow 65–foot doubles would "basically ope[n] our state to literally thousands and thousands more trucks per year." This increase in interstate truck traffic would, in the Governor's estimation, greatly increase highway maintenance costs, which are borne by the citizens of the State, and increase the number of accidents and fatalities within the State. The legislative response was not to override the veto, but to accede to the Governor's action, and in accord with his basic premise, to enact a "border cities exemption." This permitted cities within border areas to allow 65–foot doubles while otherwise maintaining the 60–foot limit throughout the State to discourage interstate truck traffic.

Although the Court has stated that "[i]n no field has ... deference to state regulation been greater than that of highway safety," Raymond Motor Transportation, Inc. v. Rice, supra, 434 U.S., at 443, it has declined to go so far as to presume that size restrictions are inherently tied to public safety. The Court has emphasized that the "strong presumption of validity" of size restrictions "cannot justify a court in closing its eyes to uncontroverted evidence of record,"—here the obvious fact that the safety characteristics of 65–foot doubles did not provide the motivation for either legislators or Governor in maintaining the regulation.

III

Though my Brother Powell recognizes that the State's actual purpose in maintaining the truck-length regulation was "to limit the use of its highways

---

ing a regulation is illegitimate, I consider it contrary to precedent as well as to sound principles of constitutional adjudication for the courts to base their analysis on purposes never conceived by the lawmakers. This is especially true where, as the dissent's strained analysis of the relative safety of 65–foot doubles to shorter trucks amply demonstrates, the *post hoc* justifications are implau-

sible as well as imaginary. I would emphasize that, although my Brother Powell's plurality opinion does not give as much weight to the illegitimacy of Iowa's actual purpose as I do, see Part III, infra, both that opinion and this concurrence have found the actual motivation of the Iowa lawmakers in maintaining the truck-length regulation highly relevant to, if not dispositive of, the case.

by deflecting some through traffic," he fails to recognize that this purpose, being *protectionist* in nature, is *impermissible* under the Commerce Clause. The Governor admitted that he blocked legislative efforts to raise the length of trucks because the change "would benefit only a few Iowa-based companies while providing a great advantage for out-of-state trucking firms and competitors at the expense of our Iowa citizens." Appellant Raymond Kassel, Director of the Iowa Department of Transportation, while admitting that the greater 65–foot length standard would be *safer* overall, defended the more restrictive regulations because of their benefits *within Iowa* ...

Iowa may not shunt off its fair share of the burden of maintaining interstate truck routes, nor may it create increased hazards on the highways of neighboring States in order to decrease the hazards on Iowa highways. Such an attempt has all the hallmarks of the "simple ... protectionism" this Court has condemned in the economic area. Philadelphia v. New Jersey, 437 U.S. 617, 624 (1978). Just as a State's attempt to avoid interstate competition in economic goods may damage the prosperity of the Nation as a whole, so Iowa's attempt to deflect interstate truck traffic has been found to make the Nation's highways as a whole more hazardous. That attempt should therefore be subject to "a virtually *per se* rule of invalidity." Ibid.

This Court's heightened deference to the judgments of state lawmakers in the field of safety, is largely attributable to a judicial disinclination to weigh the interests of safety against other societal interests, such as the economic interest in the free flow of commerce. Thus, "if safety justifications are not illusory, the Court will not second-guess legislative judgment about their importance *in comparison with related burdens on interstate commerce*." Raymond Motor Transportation, Inc. v. Rice, supra, at 449 (Blackmun, J., concurring) (emphasis added). Here, the decision of Iowa's lawmakers to promote *Iowa's* safety and other interests at the direct expense of the safety and other interests of neighboring States merits no such deference. No special judicial acuity is demanded to perceive that this sort of parochial legislation violates the Commerce Clause. As Justice Cardozo has written, the Commerce Clause "was framed upon the theory that the peoples of the several states must sink or swim together, and that in the long run prosperity and salvation are in union and not division." Baldwin v. G.A.F. Seelig, Inc., 294 U.S. 511, 523 (1935).

I therefore concur in the judgment.

Justice Rehnquist, with whom The Chief Justice and Justice Stewart join, dissenting.

The result in this case suggests, to paraphrase Justice Jackson, that the only state truck-length limit "that is valid is one which this court has not been able to get its hands on." Jungersen v. Ostby & Barton Co., 335 U.S. 560, 572 (1949) (dissenting opinion). Although the plurality and concurring opinions strike down Iowa's law by different routes, I believe the analysis in both opinions oversteps our "limited authority to review state legislation under the commerce clause," Brotherhood of Locomotive Firemen v. Chicago, R.I. & P.R. Co., 393 U.S. 129, 136 (1968), and seriously intrudes upon the fundamental right of the States to pass laws to secure the safety of their citizens. Accordingly, I dissent.

I

It is necessary to elaborate somewhat on the facts as presented in the plurality opinion to appreciate fully what the Court does today. Iowa's action in limiting the length of trucks which may travel on its highways is in no sense unusual. Every State in the Union regulates the length of vehicles permitted to use the public roads. Nor is Iowa a renegade in having length limits which operate to exclude the 65–foot doubles favored by Consolidated. These trucks are prohibited in other areas of the country as well, some 17 States and the District of Columbia, including all of New England and most of the Southeast. While pointing out that Consolidated carries commodities through Iowa on Interstate 80, "the principal east-west route linking New York, Chicago, and the west coast," the plurality neglects to note that both Pennsylvania and New Jersey, through which Interstate 80 runs before reaching New York, also ban 65–foot doubles. In short, the persistent effort in the plurality opinion to paint Iowa as an oddity standing alone to block commerce carried in 65–foot doubles is simply not supported by the facts.

Nor does the plurality adequately convey the extent to which the lower courts permitted the 65–foot doubles to operate in Iowa. Consolidated sought to have the 60–foot length limit declared an unconstitutional burden on commerce when applied to the seven Interstate Highways in Iowa and "access routes to and from Plaintiff's terminals, and reasonable access from said Interstate Highways to facilities for food, fuel, repairs, or rest." The lower courts granted this relief, permitting the 65–foot doubles to travel *off the Interstates* as far as five miles for access to terminal and other facilities, or less if closer facilities were available. 475 F.Supp. 544, 553–554 (S.D.Iowa 1979). To the extent the plurality relies on characteristics of the Interstate Highways in rejecting Iowa's asserted safety justifications, it fails to recognize the scope of the District Court order it upholds.

With these additions to the relevant facts, we can now examine the appropriate analysis to be applied.

II

. . .

A determination that a state law is a rational safety measure does not end the Commerce Clause inquiry. A "sensitive consideration" of the safety purpose in relation to the burden on commerce is required. *Raymond*, supra, at 441. When engaging in such a consideration the Court does not directly compare safety benefits to commerce costs and strike down the legislation if the latter can be said in some vague sense to "outweigh" the former. Such an approach would make an empty gesture of the strong presumption of validity accorded state safety measures, particularly those governing highways. It would also arrogate to this Court functions of forming public policy, functions which, in the absence of congressional action, were left by the Framers of the Constitution to state legislatures. . . .

The purpose of the "sensitive consideration" referred to above is rather to determine if the asserted safety justification, although rational, is merely a pretext for discrimination against interstate commerce. We will conclude that it is if the safety benefits from the regulation are demonstrably trivial while the burden on commerce is great. Thus the Court in *Bibb* stated that the "strong presumption of validity" accorded highway safety measures could be overcome only when the safety benefits were "slight or problematical," 359 U.S., at 524. . . .

III

Iowa defends its statute as a highway safety regulation. There can be no doubt that the challenged statute is a valid highway safety regulation and thus entitled to the strongest presumption of validity against Commerce Clause challenges. As noted, all 50 States regulate the length of trucks which may use their highways.... There can also be no question that the particular limit chosen by Iowa—60 feet—is rationally related to Iowa's safety objective. Most truck limits are between 55 and 65 feet, and Iowa's choice is thus well within the widely accepted range.

Iowa adduced evidence supporting the relation between vehicle length and highway safety....

... In sum, there was sufficient evidence presented at trial to support the legislative determination that length is related to safety, and nothing in Consolidated's evidence undermines this conclusion.

The District Court approached the case as if the question were whether Consolidated's 65-foot trucks were as safe as others permitted on Iowa highways, and the Court of Appeals as if its task were to determine if the District Court's factual findings in this regard were "clearly erroneous." 612 F.2d, at 1069. The question, however, is whether the Iowa Legislature has acted rationally in regulating vehicle lengths and whether the safety benefits from this regulation are more than slight or problematical.... "Since the adoption of one weight or width regulation, rather than another, is a legislative and not a judicial choice, its constitutionality is not to be determined by weighing in the judicial scales the merits of the legislative choice and rejecting it if the weight of evidence presented in court appears to favor a different standard." Barnwell Brothers, 303 U.S., at 191.

. . .

It must be emphasized that there is nothing in the laws of nature which make 65-foot doubles an obvious norm. Consolidated operates 65-foot doubles on many of its routes simply because that is the largest size permitted in many States through which Consolidated travels. Doubles can and do come in smaller sizes; indeed, when Iowa adopted the present 60-foot limit in 1963, it was in accord with AASHTO recommendations. Striking down Iowa's law because Consolidated has made a voluntary business decision to employ 65-foot doubles, a decision based on the actions of other state legislatures, would essentially be compelling Iowa to yield to the policy choices of neighboring States. Under our constitutional scheme, however, there is only one legislative body which can pre-empt the rational policy determination of the Iowa Legislature and that is Congress. Forcing Iowa to yield to the policy choices of neighboring States perverts the primary purpose of the Commerce Clause, that of vesting power to regulate interstate commerce in Congress, where all the States are represented....

. . .

My Brother Brennan argues that the Court should consider only *the* purpose the Iowa legislators *actually* sought to achieve by the length limit, and not the purposes advanced by Iowa's lawyers in defense of the statute.... The argument has been consistently rejected by the Court in other contexts, compare, e.g., United States Railroad Retirement Board v. Fritz, 449 U.S. 166, 187–188 (1980) with id., at 187–188 (Brennan, J., dissenting) and Michael M. v. Superior Court of Sonoma County, [450 U.S.] at 469–470, (1981) (plurality opinion) with id., at 494–496 (Brennan, J., dissenting), and Justice Brennan can cite no authority for the proposition that possible legislative purposes suggested by a State's lawyers should not be considered in Commerce Clause cases. The problems with a view such as that advanced in the opinion concurring in the judgment are apparent. To name just a few, it assumes that individual legislators are motivated by one discernible "actual" purpose, and ignores the fact that different legislators may vote for a single piece of legislation for widely different reasons.... How, for example, would a court adhering to the views expressed in the opinion concurring in the judgment approach a statute, the legislative history of which indicated that 10 votes were based on safety considerations, 10 votes were based on protectionism, and the statute passed by a vote of 40–20? What would the *actual* purpose of the *legislature* have been in that case? This Court has wisely "never insisted that a legislative body articulate its reasons for enacting a statute." *Fritz*, supra, at 177.

Both the plurality and concurring opinions attach great significance to the Governor's veto of a bill passed by the Iowa Legislature permitting 65–foot doubles. Whatever views one may have about the significance of legislative motives, it must be emphasized that the law which the Court strikes down today was not passed to achieve the protectionist goals the plurality and the concurrence ascribe to the Governor. Iowa's 60–foot length limit was established in 1963, at a time when very few States permitted 65–foot doubles. Striking down legislation on the basis of asserted legislative motives is dubious enough, but the plurality and concurrence strike down the legislation involved in this case because of asserted impermissible motives for *not* enacting *other* legislation, motives which could not possibly have been present when the legislation under challenge here was considered and passed. Such action is, so far as I am aware, unprecedented in this Court's history.

Furthermore, the effort in both the plurality and concurring opinions to portray the legislation involved here as protectionist is in error. Whenever a State enacts more stringent safety measures than its neighbors, in an area which affects commerce, the safety law will have the incidental effect of deflecting interstate commerce to the neighboring States. Indeed, the safety and protectionist motives cannot be separated: The whole purpose of safety regulation of vehicles is to *protect* the State from unsafe vehicles. If a neighboring State chooses *not* to protect its citizens from the danger discerned by the enacting State, that is its business, but the enacting State should not be penalized when the vehicles it considers unsafe travel through the neighboring State.

The other States with truck-length limits that exclude Consolidated's 65–foot doubles would not at all be paranoid in assuming that they might be next on Consolidated's "hit list." The true problem with today's decision is that it gives no guidance whatsoever to these States as to whether their laws are valid or how to defend them. For that matter, the decision gives no guidance to Consolidated or other trucking firms either. Perhaps, after all is said and done, the Court today neither says nor does very much at all. We know only that Iowa's law is invalid and that the jurisprudence of the "negative side" of the Commerce Clause remains hopelessly confused.

FEDERAL REGULATION OF TRUCK SIZES

In 1983 Congress provided that states must allow twin trailer combinations with each trailer 28 feet long (approximate total length 65 feet) and 102 inches wide to use the interstate highway system and federal aided primary highways designated by the Secretary of Transportation. 49 U.S.C. §§ 2311, 2316. On April 6, 1983, the Federal Highway Administration designated about 140,000 miles of federally aided highways in addition to 42,000 miles of interstate highways upon which the larger trucks must be allowed to operate. 48 Fed.Reg. 14844 (1983). In 1984 the statute was amended to provide that the Federal Highway Administration could designate highways other than interstate highways only with the consent of the governor of the state. It also provided that the governor of a state may make findings that parts of the interstate system in the state are not safe for trucks as wide as 102 inches and request the Federal Highway Administration to make an exception from the normal rules for those parts of the system.

SECTION 4. IMPLIED RESTRICTIONS OF THE COMMERCE CLAUSE—PRODUCTION AND TRADE

A. RESTRICTING IMPORTATION AND INSULATING IN-STATE BUSINESS FROM OUT-OF-STATE COMPETITION

STATE QUARANTINE AND INSPECTION LAWS

From the days of Chief Justice Marshall, the Court repeatedly has asserted that the Commerce Clause, absent action by Congress, does not prevent the states from constitutionally enacting quarantine or inspection laws that affect interstate and foreign commerce, although the result has been rationalized in different ways at different times. In Hannibal & St. Joseph R. Co. v. Husen, 95 U.S. 465 (1877), the question was the validity of a Missouri statute providing that no Texas, Mexican, or Indian cattle should be driven or transported into, or remain in, the state between March 1 and November 1 of each year. The Court said: "While we unhesitatingly admit that a State may pass sanitary laws, and laws for the protection of life, liberty, health, or property within its borders; while it may prevent persons and animals suffering under contagious or infectious diseases, or convicts, etc., from entering the State; while for the purpose of self-protection it may establish quarantine, and reasonable inspection laws, it may not interfere with transportation into or through the State, beyond what is absolutely necessary for its self-protection. It may not, under the cover of exerting its police powers, substantially prohibit or burden either foreign or interstate commerce." The Court, not finding the statute to be a legitimate quarantine or inspection law because of the unconditional character of the prohibition on bringing cattle into the state during the specified months of the year, held it invalid.

However, in Kimmish v. Ball, 129 U.S. 217 (1889), the Court upheld an Iowa statute making liable in damages any person having possession of "Texas cattle" that had not wintered north of the southern boundary of Missouri or Kansas. Justice Field's opinion said: "the case is, therefore, reduced to this, whether the State may not provide that whoever permits diseased cattle in his possession to run at large within its limits shall be liable for any damages caused by the spread of the disease occasioned thereby; and upon that question we do not entertain the slightest doubt."

MINTZ v. BALDWIN, 289 U.S. 346 (1933). A New York regulation designed to guard against Bang's disease required cattle imported into New York for dairy and breeding purposes and the herds from which they came to be certified free from the disease by the chief sanitary official of the state of origin. A Wisconsin cattle breeder shipped 20 head of cattle from Wisconsin to a purchaser in New York. They were accompanied by a certificate that they were free of Bang's disease but there was nothing to show that the herd from which they came was free of the disease. The New York commissioner of agriculture refused to permit the cattle to be delivered. The shipper brought suit in a federal district court seeking an injunction against enforcement of the order. The court dismissed the suit. It made special findings to the effect that Bang's disease prevails throughout the United States, causing limitations on reproduction and milk yield and creating the risk of undulant fever in humans drinking raw milk. It also found that there was a body of expert opinion that cattle should be admitted to a state only when certified to have come from a clean herd because tests on individual cattle might not disclose the disease in its incubative stage.

The Supreme Court affirmed, stating: "The order is an inspection measure. Undoubtedly it was promulgated in good faith and is appropriate for the prevention of further spread of the disease among dairy cattle and to safeguard public health. It cannot be maintained therefore that the order so unnecessarily burdens interstate transportation as to contravene the commerce clause."

BALDWIN v. G.A.F. SEELIG, INC., 294 U.S. 511 (1935). The Great Depression of the 1930s had a particularly disastrous impact on dairy farmers. Prices paid to producers for milk in the New York area fell by some 61 percent and the milk supply was threatened as farmers slaughtered cattle rather than remain in a losing business. New York enacted the Milk Control Act of 1933 in an attempt to remedy the situation. A Milk Control Board was empowered to fix both the retail price of milk and the price paid to producers. The statute made it unlawful to sell milk which had been purchased from out-of-state producers at prices less than those required to be paid to farmers within the state.

Seelig was engaged in business as a milk dealer in New York City, buying milk in Vermont and transporting it to New York. Seelig purchased the milk in Vermont at prices lower than the minimum payable to New York producers under the New York law. The State Commissioner of Farms and Markets refused to grant Seelig a milk dealer's license to sell milk purchased from producers at prices below the minimum required by the law. Seelig brought suit to restrain the enforcement of the Milk Control Act. The Supreme Court held that an injunction should issue.

Justice Cardozo, speaking for a unanimous Court, said: "Such a power, if exerted, will set a barrier to traffic between one state and another as effective as if customs duties, equal to the price differential, had been laid upon the thing transported.... Nice distinctions have been made at times between direct and indirect burdens [on commerce]. They are irrelevant when the avowed purpose of the obstruction, as well as its necessary tendency, is to suppress or mitigate the consequences of competition between the states.... If New York in order to promote the economic welfare of her farmers, may guard them against competition with the cheaper prices of Vermont, the door has been opened to rivalries and reprisals that were meant to be averted by subjecting commerce between the states to the power of the nation."

The state argued that a major objective of the Milk Control Act was the maintenance of a regular and adequate supply of pure and wholesome milk. The Court replied: "This would be to eat up the rule under the guise of an exception. Economic welfare is always related to health, for there can be no health if men are starving. Let such an exception be admitted, and all that a state will have to do in times of stress and strain is to say that its farmers and merchants and workmen must be protected against competition from without, lest they go upon the poor relief lists or perish altogether. To give entrance to that excuse would be to invite a speedy end of our national solidarity. The Constitution was framed under the dominion of a political philosophy less parochial in range. It was framed upon the theory that the peoples of the several states must sink or swim together, and that in the long run prosperity and salvation are in union and not division.... The line of division between direct and indirect restraints of commerce involves in its marking a reference to considerations of degree. Even so, the borderland is wide between the restraints upheld as incidental and those attempted here. . . . None of these statutes [upheld by the Court]—inspection laws, game laws, laws intended to curb fraud or exterminate disease—approaches in drastic quality the statute here in controversy which would neutralize the economic consequences of free trade among the states."

Dean Milk Co. v. City of Madison, Wis.

340 U.S. 349, 71 S.Ct. 295, 95 L.Ed. 329 (1951).

Mr. Justice Clark delivered the opinion of the Court.

This appeal challenges the constitutional validity of two sections of an ordinance of the City of Madison, Wisconsin, regulating the sale of milk and milk products within the municipality's jurisdiction. One section in issue makes it unlawful to sell any milk as pasteurized unless it has been processed and bottled at an approved pasteurization plant within a radius of five miles from the central square of Madison. Another section, which prohibits the sale of milk, or the importation, receipt or storage of milk for sale, in Madison unless from a source of supply possessing a permit issued after inspection by Madison officials, is attacked insofar as it expressly relieves municipal authorities from any duty to inspect farms located beyond twenty-five miles from the center of the city.

Appellant is an Illinois corporation engaged in distributing milk and milk products in Illinois and Wisconsin. It contended below, as it does here, that both the five-mile limit on pasteurization plants and the twenty-five-mile limit on sources of milk violate the Commerce Clause and the Fourteenth Amendment to the Federal Constitution. The Supreme Court of Wisconsin upheld the five-mile limit on pasteurization. As to the twenty-five-mile limitation the court ordered the complaint dismissed for want of a justiciable controversy. This appeal [contests] both rulings. . . .

The City of Madison is the county seat of Dane County. Within the county are some 5,600 dairy farms with the total raw milk production . . . more than ten times the requirements of Madison. Aside from the milk supplied to Madison, fluid milk produced in the county moves in large quantities to Chicago and more distant consuming areas, and the remainder is used in making cheese, butter and other products. At the time of trial the Madison milkshed was not of "Grade A" quality by the standards recommended by the United States Public Health Service, and no milk labeled "Grade A" was distributed in Madison.

The area defined by the ordinance with respect to milk sources encompasses practically all of Dane County and includes some 500 farms which supply milk for Madison. Within the five-mile area for pasteurization are plants of five processors, only three of which are engaged in the general wholesale and retail trade in Madison. Inspection of these farms and plants is scheduled once every thirty days and is performed by two municipal inspectors, one of whom is full-time. The courts below found that the ordinance in question promotes convenient, economical and efficient plant inspection.

Appellant purchases and gathers milk from approximately 950 farms in northern Illinois and southern Wisconsin, none being within twenty-five miles of Madison. Its pasteurization plants are located at Chemung and Huntley, Illinois, about 65 and 85 miles respectively from Madison. Appellant was denied a license to sell its products within Madison solely because its pasteurization plants were more than five miles away.

It is conceded that the milk which appellant seeks to sell in Madison is supplied from farms and processed in plants licensed and inspected by public health authorities of Chicago, and is labeled "Grade A" under the Chicago ordinance which adopts the rating standards recommended by the United States Public Health Service. Both the Chicago and Madison ordinances, though not the sections of the latter here in issue, are largely patterned after the Model Milk Ordinance of the Public Health Service. However, Madison contends and we assume that in some particulars its ordinance is more rigorous than that of Chicago.

Upon these facts we find it necessary to determine only the issue raised under the Commerce Clause, for we agree with appellant that the ordinance imposes an undue burden on interstate commerce.

This is not an instance in which an enactment falls because of federal legislation which, as a proper exercise of paramount national power over commerce, excludes measures which might otherwise be within the police power of the states. There is no pertinent national regulation by the Congress. . . .

Nor can there be objection to the avowed purpose of this enactment. We assume that difficulties in sanitary regulation of milk and milk products originating in remote areas may present a situation in which "upon a consideration of all the relevant facts and circumstances it appears that the matter is one which may appropriately be regulated in the interest of the safety, health and well-being of local communities. . . ." . . . We also assume that since Congress has not spoken to the contrary, the subject matter of the ordinance lies within the sphere of state regulation even though interstate commerce may be affected. . . .

But this regulation, . . . in practical effect excludes from distribution in Madison wholesome milk produced and pasteurized in Illinois. . . . In thus erecting an economic barrier protecting a major local industry against competition from without the State, Madison plainly discriminates against interstate commerce.[4] This it cannot do, even in the exercise of its unquestioned power to protect the health and safety of its people, if reasonable nondiscriminatory alternatives, adequate to conserve legitimate local interest, are available. . . . A different view, that the ordinance is valid simply because it professes to be a health measure, would mean that the Commerce Clause of itself imposes no limitations on state action other than those laid down by the Due Process Clause, save for the rare instance where a state artlessly discloses an avowed purpose to discriminate against interstate goods. Our issue then is whether the discrimination inherent in the Madison ordinance can be justified in view of the character of the local interests and the available methods of protecting them. . . .

It appears that reasonable and adequate alternatives are available. If the City of Madison prefers to rely upon its own officials for inspection of distant milk sources, such inspection is readily open to it without hardship for it could charge the actual and reasonable cost of such inspection to the importing producers and processors. . . . Moreover, appellee Health Commissioner of Madison testified that as proponent of the local milk ordinance he had submitted the provisions here in controversy and an alternative proposal based on

---

[4] It is immaterial that Wisconsin milk from outside the Madison area is subjected to the same proscription as that moving in interstate commerce. . . .

§ 11 of the Model Milk Ordinance recommended by the United States Public Health Service. The model provision imposes no geographical limitation on location of milk sources and processing plants but excludes from the municipality milk not produced and pasteurized conformably to standards as high as those enforced by the receiving city. In implementing such an ordinance, the importing city obtains milk ratings based on uniform standards and established by health authorities in the jurisdiction where production and processing occur. The receiving city may determine the extent of enforcement of sanitary standards in the exporting area by verifying the accuracy of safety ratings of specific plants or of the milkshed in the distant jurisdiction through the United States Public Health Service, which routinely and on request spot checks the local ratings. The Commissioner testified that Madison consumers "would be safeguarded adequately" under either proposal and that he had expressed no preference. The milk sanitarium of the Wisconsin State Board of Health testified that the State Health Department recommends the adoption of a provision based on the Model Ordinance. Both officials agreed that a local health officer would be justified in relying upon the evaluation by the Public Health Service of enforcement conditions in remote producing areas.

To permit Madison to adopt a regulation not essential for the protection of local health interests and placing a discriminatory burden on interstate commerce would invite a multiplication of preferential trade areas destructive of the very purpose of the Commerce Clause. Under the circumstances here presented, the regulation must yield to the principle that "one state in its dealings with another may not place itself in a position of economic isolation."

For these reasons we conclude that the judgment below sustaining the five-mile provision as to pasteurization must be reversed.

The Supreme Court of Wisconsin thought it unnecessary to pass upon the validity of the twenty-five-mile limitation, apparently in part for the reason that this issue was made academic by its decision upholding the five-mile section. In view of our conclusion as to the latter provision, a determination of appellant's contention as to the other section is now necessary. As to this issue, therefore, we vacate the judgment below and remand for further proceedings not inconsistent with the principles announced in this opinion....

Judgment vacated and cause remanded.

Mr. Justice Black, with whom Mr. Justice Douglas and Mr. Justice Minton concur, dissenting.

Today's holding invalidates § 7.21 of the Madison, Wisconsin, ordinance on the following reasoning: (1) the section excludes wholesome milk coming from Illinois; (2) this imposes a discriminatory burden on interstate commerce; (3) such a burden cannot be imposed where, as here, there are reasonable, nondiscriminatory and adequate alternatives available. I disagree with the Court's premises, reasoning, and judgment.

(1) This ordinance does not exclude wholesome milk coming from Illinois or anywhere else. It does require that all milk sold in Madison must be pasteurized within five miles of the center of the city. But there was no finding in the state courts, nor evidence to justify a finding there or here, that appellant, Dean Milk Company, is unable to have its milk pasteurized within the defined geographical area. As a practical matter, so far as the record shows, Dean can easily comply with the ordinance whenever it wants to. Therefore, Dean's personal preference to pasteurize in Illinois, not the ordinance, keeps Dean's milk out of Madison.

(2) Characterization of § 7.21 as a "discriminatory burden" on interstate commerce is merely a statement of the Court's result, which I think incorrect. The section does prohibit the sale of milk in Madison by interstate and intrastate producers who prefer to pasteurize over five miles distant from the city. But both state courts below found that § 7.21 represents a good-faith attempt to safeguard public health by making adequate sanitation inspection possible. While we are not bound by these findings, I do not understand the Court to overturn them. Therefore, the fact that § 7.21, like all health regulations, imposes some burden on trade, does not mean that it "discriminates" against commerce.

(3) This health regulation should not be invalidated merely because the Court believes that alternative milk-inspection methods might insure the cleanliness and healthfulness of Dean's Illinois milk.... Since the days of Chief Justice Marshall, federal courts have left states and municipalities free to pass bona fide health regulations subject only "to the paramount authority of Congress if it decides to assume control...." ... No case is cited, and I have found none, in which a bona fide health law was struck down on the ground that some other method of safeguarding health would be as good as, or better than, the one the Court was called on to review. In my view, to use this ground now elevates the right to traffic in commerce for profit above the power of the people to guard the purity of their daily diet of milk.

If, however, the principle announced today is to be followed, the Court should not strike down local health regulations unless satisfied beyond a reasonable doubt that the substitutes it proposes would not lower health standards. I do not think that the Court can so satisfy itself on the basis of its judicial knowledge. And the evidence in the record leads me to the conclusion that the substitute health measures suggested by the Court do not insure milk as safe as the Madison ordinance requires....

From what this record shows, and from what it fails to show, I do not think that either of the alternatives suggested by the Court would assure the people of Madison as pure a supply of milk as they receive under their own ordinance. On this record I would uphold the Madison law. At the very least, however, I would not invalidate it without giving the parties a chance to present evidence and get findings on the ultimate issues the Court thinks crucial—namely, the relative merits of the Madison ordinance and the alternatives suggested by the Court today.

Minnesota v. Clover Leaf Creamery Co.

449 U.S. 456, 101 S.Ct. 715, 66 L.Ed.2d 659 (1981).

Justice Brennan delivered the opinion of the Court:

In 1977, the Minnesota Legislature enacted a statute banning the retail sale of milk in plastic nonreturnable, nonrefillable containers, but permitting such sale in other nonreturnable, nonrefillable containers, such as paperboard milk cartons. 1977, Minn.Laws, ch. 268, Minn.Stat., § 116F.21 (1978). Respondents[1] contend that the statute violates the Equal Protection and Commerce Clauses of the Constitution.

---

[1] Respondents, plaintiffs below, are a Minnesota dairy that owns equipment for producing plastic nonreturnable milk jugs, a Minnesota dairy that leases such equipment, a non-Minnesota company that manufactures such equipment, a Minnesota company that produces plastic nonreturnable milk jugs, a non-Minnesota dairy that sells milk products in Minnesota in plastic nonreturnable milk jugs, a Minnesota milk retailer, a non-Minne-

I

The purpose of the Minnesota statute is set out as § 1:

"The legislature finds that the use of nonreturnable, nonrefillable containers for the packaging of milk and other milk products presents a solid waste management problem for the state, promotes energy waste, and depletes natural resources. The legislature therefore, in furtherance of the policies stated in Minnesota Statutes, Section 116F.01, determines that the use of nonreturnable, nonrefillable containers for packaging milk and other milk products should be discouraged and that the use of returnable and reusable packaging for these products is preferred and should be encouraged." Minn.Laws 1977, ch. 268, § 1, codified as Minn.Stat., § 116F.21.

Section 2 of the Act forbids the retail sale of milk and fluid milk products, other than sour cream, cottage cheese, and yogurt, in nonreturnable, nonrefillable rigid or semirigid containers composed at least 50% of plastic.

The Act was introduced with the support of the state Pollution Control Agency, Department of Natural Resources, Department of Agriculture, Consumer Services Division, and Energy Agency, and debated vigorously in both houses of the state legislature. Proponents of the legislation argued that it would promote resource conservation, ease solid waste disposal problems, and conserve energy. Relying on the results of studies and other information, they stressed the need to stop introduction of the plastic nonreturnable container before it became entrenched in the market. Opponents of the Act, also presenting empirical evidence, argued that the Act would not promote the goals asserted by the proponents, but would merely increase costs of retail milk products and prolong the use of ecologically undesirable paperboard milk cartons.

After the Act was passed, respondents filed suit in Minnesota District Court, seeking to enjoin its enforcement. The Court conducted extensive evidentiary hearings into the Act's probable consequences, and found the evidence "in sharp conflict." Nevertheless, finding itself, "as factfinder . . . obliged to weigh and evaluate this evidence," the Court resolved the evidentiary conflicts in favor of respondents, and concluded that the Act "will not succeed in effecting the Legislature's published policy goals. . . ." The court further found that, contrary to the statement of purpose in § 1, the "actual basis" for the Act "was to promote the economic interests of certain segments of the local dairy and pulpwood industries at the expense of the economic interests of other segments of the dairy industry and the plastics industry." The court therefore declared the Act "null, void, and unenforceable" and enjoined its enforcement, basing the judgment on substantive due process under the Fourteenth Amendment to the United States Constitution and Art. I, § 7, of the Minnesota Constitution; equal protection under the Fourteenth Amendment; and prohibition of unreasonable burdens on interstate commerce under Art. I, § 8, of the United States Constitution.

The State appealed to the Supreme Court of Minnesota, which affirmed . . . on the federal equal protection and due process grounds, without reaching the Commerce Clause or state-law issues. . . . We . . . now reverse.

II

The parties agree that the standard of review applicable to this case under the Equal Protection Clause is the familiar "rational basis" test. . . . Moreover,

sota manufacturer of polyethylene resin that sells such resin in many States, including Minnesota, and a plastics industry trade association.

they agree that the purposes of the Act cited by the legislature—promoting resource conservation, easing solid waste disposal problems, and conserving energy—are legitimate state purposes. Thus, the controversy in this case centers on the narrow issue whether the legislative classification between plastic and nonplastic nonreturnable milk containers is rationally related to achievement of the statutory purposes.

. . .

We therefore conclude that the ban on plastic nonreturnable milk containers bears a rational relation to the State's objectives, and must be sustained under the Equal Protection Clause.

III

The District Court also held that the Minnesota statute is unconstitutional under the Commerce Clause because it imposes an unreasonable burden on interstate commerce.[14] We cannot agree.

When legislating in areas of legitimate local concern, such as environmental protection and resource conservation, States are nonetheless limited by the Commerce Clause.... If a state law purporting to promote environmental purposes is in reality "simple economic protectionism," we have applied a "virtually *per se* rule of invalidity." Philadelphia v. New Jersey, 437 U.S. 617, 624 (1978).[15] Even if a statute regulates "evenhandedly," and imposes only "incidental" burdens on interstate commerce, the courts must nevertheless strike it down if "the burden imposed on such commerce is clearly excessive in relation to the putative local benefits." Pike v. Bruce Church, Inc., 397 U.S. 137, 142 (1970). Moreover, "the extent of the burden that will be tolerated will of course depend on the nature of the local interest involved, and on whether it could be promoted as well with a lesser impact on interstate activities." Ibid.

Minnesota's statute does not effect "simple protectionism," but "regulates evenhandedly" by prohibiting all milk retailers from selling their products in plastic, nonreturnable milk containers, without regard to whether the milk, the containers, or the sellers are from outside the State. This statute is therefore unlike statutes discriminating against interstate commerce, which we have consistently struck down....

[14] The Minnesota Supreme Court did not reach the Commerce Clause issue.... The parties and *amici* have fully briefed and argued the question, and because of the obvious factual connection between the rationality analysis under the Equal Protection Clause and the balancing of interests under the Commerce Clause, we will reach and decide the question....

[15] A court may find that a state law constitutes "economic protectionism" on proof either of discriminatory effect, see *Philadelphia v. New Jersey*, or of discriminatory purpose, see Hunt v. Washington State Apple Advertising Comm'n, 432 U.S., at 352–353 (1977). Respondents advance a "discriminatory purpose" argument, relying on a finding by the District Court that the Act's "actual basis was to promote the economic interests of certain segments of the local dairy and pulpwood industries at the expense of the economic interests of other segments of the dairy industry and the plastics industry." We have already considered and rejected this argument in the equal protection context, see n. 7, supra, and do so in this context as well.

[In note 7 the Court said, in part: "Here, a review of the legislative history supports the Minnesota Supreme Court's conclusion that the principal purposes of the Act were to promote conservation and ease solid waste disposal problems. The contrary evidence cited by respondents is easily understood, in context, as economic defense of an Act genuinely proposed for environmental reasons. We will not invalidate a state statute under the Equal Protection Clause merely because some legislators sought to obtain votes for the measure on the basis of its beneficial side effects on state industry."]

Since the statute does not discriminate between interstate and intrastate commerce, the controlling question is whether the incidental burden imposed on interstate commerce by the Minnesota Act is "clearly excessive in relation to the putative local benefits." Pike v. Bruce Church, Inc., supra, at 142. We conclude that it is not.

The burden imposed on interstate commerce by the statute is relatively minor. Milk products may continue to move freely across the Minnesota border, and since most dairies package their products in more than one type of container, the inconvenience of having to conform to different packaging requirements in Minnesota and the surrounding States should be slight.... Within Minnesota, business will presumably shift from manufacturers of plastic nonreturnable containers to producers of paperboard cartons, refillable bottles, and plastic pouches, but there is no reason to suspect that the gainers will be Minnesota firms, or the losers out-of-state firms. Indeed, two of the three dairies, the sole milk retailer, and the sole milk container producer challenging the statute in this litigation are Minnesota firms.[17]

Pulpwood producers are the only Minnesota industry likely to benefit significantly from the Act at the expense of out-of-state firms. Respondents point out that plastic resin, the raw material used for making plastic nonreturnable milk jugs, is produced entirely by non-Minnesota firms, while pulpwood, used for making paperboard, is a major Minnesota product. Nevertheless, it is clear that respondents exaggerate the degree of burden on out-of-state interests, both because plastics will continue to be used in the production of plastic pouches, plastic returnable bottles, and paperboard itself, and because out-of-state pulpwood producers will presumably absorb some of the business generated by the Act.

Even granting that the out-of-state plastics industry is burdened relatively more heavily than the Minnesota pulpwood industry, we find that this burden is not "clearly excessive" in light of the substantial state interest in promoting conservation of energy and other natural resources and easing solid waste disposal problems, which we have already reviewed in the context of equal protection analysis. We find these local benefits ample to support Minnesota's decision under the Commerce Clause. Moreover, we find that no approach with "a lesser impact on interstate activities," Pike v. Bruce Church, Inc., supra, 397 U.S., at 142, is available. Respondents have suggested several alternative statutory schemes, but these alternatives are either more burdensome on commerce than the Act (as, for example, banning all nonreturnables) or less likely to be effective (as, for example, providing incentives for recycling).

In Exxon Corp. v. Governor of Maryland, 437 U.S. 117 (1978), we upheld a Maryland statute barring producers and refiners of petroleum products—all of which were out-of-state businesses—from retailing gasoline in the State. We stressed that the Commerce Clause "protects the interstate market, not particular interstate firms, from prohibitive or burdensome regulations." Id., at 127–128. A nondiscriminatory regulation serving substantial state purposes is not invalid simply because it causes some business to shift from a predominantly out-of-state industry to a predominantly in-state industry. Only if the burden on interstate commerce clearly outweighs the State's legitimate purposes does such a regulation violate the Commerce Clause.

The judgment of the Minnesota Supreme Court is

---

[17] See n. 1, supra. The existence of major in-state interests adversely affected by the Act is a powerful safeguard against legislative abuse. South Carolina State Highway Dept. v. Barnwell Bros., Inc., 303 U.S. 177, 187 (1938).

Reversed.

Justice Rehnquist took no part in the consideration or decision of this case.

Justice Powell, concurring in part and dissenting in part.

... I concur in the view that the statute survives equal protection challenge, and therefore join the judgment of reversal on this ground....

I would not, however, reach the Commerce Clause issue, but would remand it for consideration by the Supreme Court of Minnesota....

Justice Stevens, dissenting.

[Justice Stevens did not disagree with the Court's equal protection or commerce clause analysis. He claimed instead that the Court was not free to reject the factual conclusions reached by the Supreme Court of Minnesota and claimed that those conclusions justified a holding that the statute was in violation of the equal protection clause.]

West Lynn Creamery v. Healy

512 U.S. 186, 114 S.Ct. 2205, 129 L.Ed.2d 157 (1994).

Justice Stevens delivered the opinion of the Court.

A Massachusetts pricing order imposes an assessment on all fluid milk sold by dealers to Massachusetts retailers. About two-thirds of that milk is produced out of State. The entire assessment, however, is distributed to Massachusetts dairy farmers. The question presented is whether the pricing order unconstitutionally discriminates against interstate commerce. We hold that it does.

I

Petitioner ... is a milk dealer licensed to do business in Massachusetts. It purchases raw milk, which it processes, packages, and sells to wholesalers, retailers, and other milk dealers. About 97% of the raw milk it purchases is produced by out-of-state farmers....

... In the 1980's and early 1990's, Massachusetts dairy farmers began to lose market share to lower cost producers in neighboring States. In response, the Governor of Massachusetts appointed a Special Commission to study the dairy industry. The Commission found that many producers had sold their dairy farms during the past decade and that if prices paid to farmers for their milk were not significantly increased, a majority of the remaining farmers in Massachusetts would be "forced out of business within the year." App. 13. [R]elying on the Commission's Report, the Commissioner of the Massachusetts Department of Food and Agriculture (respondent) declared a State of Emergency ... [and promptly] issued the [challenged]pricing order.

The order requires every "dealer" in Massachusetts to make a monthly "premium payment" [based on the amount of its fluid milk product sales] into the "Massachusetts Dairy Equalization Fund." ... Each month the fund is distributed to Massachusetts producers[;.i.e, dairy farmers]. Each Massachusetts producer receives a share of the total fund equal to his proportionate contribution to the State's total production of raw milk.

Petitioners ... [sued unsuccessfully] in state court....

... We ... reverse.

II

. . .

... Massachusetts' pricing order is clearly unconstitutional. Its avowed purpose and its undisputed effect are to enable higher cost Massachusetts dairy farmers to compete with lower cost dairy farmers in other States. The "premium payments" are effectively a tax which makes milk produced out of State more expensive. Although the tax also applies to milk produced in Massachusetts, its effect on Massachusetts producers is entirely (indeed more than) offset by the subsidy provided exclusively to Massachusetts dairy farmers. Like an ordinary tariff, the tax is thus effectively imposed only on out-of-state products. The pricing order thus allows Massachusetts dairy farmers who produce at higher cost to sell at or below the price charged by lower cost out-of-state producers.[10] If there were no federal minimum prices for milk, out-of-state producers might still be able to retain their market share by lowering their prices. Nevertheless, out-of-staters' ability to remain competitive by lowering their prices would not immunize a discriminatory measure. New Energy Co. of Indiana v. Limbach, 486 U. S., at 275. In this case, because the Federal Government sets minimum prices, out-of-state producers may not even have the option of reducing prices in order to retain market share. The Massachusetts pricing order thus will almost certainly "cause local goods to constitute a larger share, and goods with an out-of-state source to constitute a smaller share, of the total sales in the market." Exxon Corp. v. Governor of Maryland, 437 U. S. 117, 126, n. 16 (1978). In fact, this effect was the motive behind the promulgation of the pricing order. This effect renders the program unconstitutional, because it, like a tariff, "neutralize[s] advantages belonging to the place of origin." Baldwin, 294 U. S., at 527.

In some ways, the Massachusetts pricing order is most similar to the law at issue in Bacchus Imports, Ltd. v. Dias, 468 U. S. 263 (1984). Both involve a broad-based tax on a single kind of good and special provisions for in-state producers. *Bacchus* involved a 20% excise tax on all liquor sales, coupled with an exemption for fruit wine manufactured in Hawaii and for okolehao, a brandy distilled from the root of a shrub indigenous to Hawaii. The Court held that Hawaii's law was unconstitutional because it "had both the purpose and effect of discriminating in favor of local products." ... By granting a tax exemption for local products, Hawaii in effect created a protective tariff. Goods produced out of State were taxed, but those produced in State were subject to no net tax. It is obvious that the result in *Bacchus* would have been the same if instead of exempting certain Hawaiian liquors from tax, Hawaii had rebated the amount of tax collected from the sale of those liquors. See New Energy Co. of Indiana v. Limbach, 486 U. S. 269 (1988) (discriminatory tax credit). And if a discriminatory tax rebate is unconstitutional, Massachusetts' pricing order is surely invalid; for Massachusetts not only rebates to domestic milk producers the tax paid on the sale of Massachusetts milk, but also the tax paid on the sale of milk produced elsewhere. The additional rebate of the tax paid on the sale of milk produced elsewhere in no way reduces the danger to the national market posed by tariff-like barriers, but instead exacerbates the danger by giving domestic producers an additional tool with which to shore up their competitive position.[14]

---

[10] ...The net effect of the tax and subsidy, like that of a tariff, is to raise the after-tax price paid by the dealers....

[14] One might attempt to distinguish *Bacchus* by noting that the rebate in this case goes not to the entity which pays the tax (milk dealers) but to the dairy farmers them-

III

Respondent advances four arguments against the conclusion that its pricing order imposes an unconstitutional burden on interstate commerce: (A) Because each component of the program—a local subsidy and a non-discriminatory tax—is valid, the combination of the two is equally valid; (B) The dealers who pay the order premiums (the tax) are not competitors of the farmers who receive disbursements from the Dairy Equalization Fund, so the pricing order is not discriminatory; (C) The pricing order is not protectionist, because the costs of the program are borne only by Massachusetts dealers and consumers, and the benefits are distributed exclusively to Massachusetts farmers; and (D) the order's incidental burden on commerce is justified by the local benefit of saving the dairy industry from collapse. . . .

A

Respondent's principal argument is that . . . if the State may impose a valid tax on dealers, it is free to use the proceeds of the tax as it chooses; and if it may independently subsidize its farmers, it is free to finance the subsidy by means of any legitimate tax.

Even granting respondent's assertion that both components of the pricing order would be constitutional standing alone,[15] the pricing order nevertheless must fall. A pure subsidy funded out of general revenue ordinarily imposes no burden on interstate commerce, but merely assists local business. The pricing order in this case, however, is funded principally from taxes on the sale of milk produced in other States.[16] By so funding the subsidy, respondent not only assists local farmers, but burdens interstate commerce. The pricing order thus violates the cardinal principle that a State may not "benefit in-state economic interests by burdening out-of-state competitors." New Energy Co. of Indiana v. Limbach, 486 U. S., at 273–274. . . .

More fundamentally, respondent errs in assuming that the constitutionality of the pricing order follows logically from the constitutionality of its component parts. By conjoining a tax and a subsidy, Massachusetts has created a program more dangerous to interstate commerce than either part alone. Nondiscriminatory measures, like the evenhanded tax at issue here, are generally upheld, in spite of any adverse effects on interstate commerce, in part because "[t]he existence of major in-state interests adversely affected . . . is a

selves. Rebating the taxes directly to producers rather than to the dealers, however, merely reinforces the conclusion that the pricing order will favor local producers. If the taxes were refunded only to the dealers, there might be no impact on interstate commerce, because the dealers might not use the funds to increase the price or quantity of milk purchased from Massachusetts dairy farmers. The refund to the dealers might, therefore, result in no advantage to in-state producers. On the other hand, by refunding monies directly to the dairy farmers, the pricing order ensures that Massachusetts producers will benefit.

[15] We have never squarely confronted the constitutionality of subsidies, and we need not do so now. We have, however, noted that "[d]irect subsidization of domestic industry does not ordinarily run afoul" of the negative Commerce Clause. New Energy Co.

of Indiana v. Limbach, 486 U. S., at 278; see also Hughes v. Alexandria Scrap Corp., 426 U. S. 794, 815 (1976) (Stevens, J., concurring). In addition, it is undisputed that States may try to attract business by creating an environment conducive to economic activity, as by maintaining good roads, sound public education, or low taxes. Zobel v. Williams, 457 U. S. 55, 67 (1982) (Brennan, J., concurring); Bacchus Imports, Ltd. v. Dias, 468 U. S., at 271; Metropolitan Life Ins. Co. v. Ward, 470 U. S. 869, 876–878 (1985).

[16] . . . [M]ost of the tax collected comes from taxes on milk from other States. In addition, the tax on in-state milk, unlike that imposed on out-of-state milk, does not impose any burden on in-state producers, because in-state dairy farmers can be confident that the taxes paid on their milk will be returned to them via the Dairy Stabilization Fund.

powerful safeguard against legislative abuse." Minnesota v. Clover Leaf Creamery Co., 449 U. S. 456, 473, n. 17 (1981).... However, when a nondiscriminatory tax is coupled with a subsidy to one of the groups hurt by the tax, a state's political processes can no longer be relied upon to prevent legislative abuse, because one of the in-state interests which would otherwise lobby against the tax has been mollified by the subsidy. So, in this case, one would ordinarily have expected at least three groups to lobby against the order premium, which, as a tax, raises the price (and hence lowers demand) for milk: dairy farmers, milk dealers, and consumers. But because the tax was coupled with a subsidy, one of the most powerful of these groups, Massachusetts dairy farmers, instead of exerting their influence against the tax, were in fact its primary supporters.[18]

. . . [W]e cannot divorce the premium payments from the use to which the payments are put. [T]he entire program ... simultaneously burdens interstate commerce and discriminates in favor of local producers. The choice of constitutional means--nondiscriminatory tax and local subsidy—cannot guarantee the constitutionality of the program as a whole. New York's minimum price order also used constitutional means—a State's power to regulate prices—but was held unconstitutional because of its deleterious effects. Baldwin v. G. A. F. Seelig, Inc., 294 U. S. 511 (1935). Similarly, the law held unconstitutional in *Bacchus* ... involved the exercise of Hawaii's undisputed power to tax and to grant tax exemptions.

. . .

B

Respondent['s argument] that since the Massachusetts milk dealers who pay the order premiums are not competitors of the Massachusetts farmers, the pricing order imposes no discriminatory burden on commerce ... cannot withstand scrutiny. Is it possible to doubt that if Massachusetts imposed a higher sales tax on milk produced in Maine than milk produced in Massachusetts that the tax would be struck down, in spite of the fact that the sales tax was imposed on consumers, and consumers do not compete with dairy farmers? For over 150 years, our cases have rightly concluded that the imposition of a differential burden on any part of the stream of commerce—from wholesaler to retailer to consumer—is invalid, because a burden placed at any point will result in a disadvantage to the out-of-state producer....

C

Respondent also argues that "the operation of the Order disproves any claim of protectionism," because "only in-state consumers feel the effect of any retail price increase ... [and] [t]he dealers themselves ... have a substantial in-state presence." ... This argument, if accepted, would undermine almost every discriminatory tax case. State taxes are ordinarily paid by in-state businesses and consumers, yet if they discriminate against out-of-state products, they are unconstitutional.... The cost of a tariff is also borne primarily by local consumers, yet a tariff is the paradigmatic Commerce Clause violation.

More fundamentally, ... the purpose and effect of the pricing order are to divert market share to Massachusetts dairy farmers. This diversion necessarily

[18] As the Governor's Special Commission ... realized, consumers would be unlikely to organize effectively to oppose the pricing order. The Commission's report remarked, "the estimated two cent increase per quart of milk would not be noticed by the consuming public," App. 18, because the price of milk varies so often and for so many reasons that consumers would be unlikely to feel the price increases or to attribute them to the pricing order.

injures the dairy farmers in neighboring States.... The obvious impact of the order on out-of-state production demonstrates that it is simply wrong to assume that the pricing order burdens only Massachusetts consumers and dealers.

D

Finally, respondent argues that any incidental burden on interstate commerce "is outweighed by the 'local benefits' of preserving the Massachusetts dairy industry." ... In a closely related argument, respondent urges that "the purpose of the order, to save an industry from collapse, is not protectionist." ... If we were to accept these arguments, we would make a virtue of the vice that the rule against discrimination condemns. Preservation of local industry by protecting it from the rigors of interstate competition is the hallmark of the economic protectionism that the Commerce Clause prohibits....

The judgment ... is reversed.

Justice Scalia, with whom Justice Thomas joins, concurring in the judgment.

. . .

I

... [W]e have never held, that every state law which obstructs a national market violates the Commerce Clause. Yet that is what the Court says today. It seems to have canvassed the entire corpus of negative-Commerce–Clause opinions, culled out every free-market snippet of reasoning, and melded them into the sweeping principle that the Constitution is violated by any state law or regulation that "artificially encourag[es] in-state production even when the same goods could be produced at lower cost in other States." ...

As the Court seems to appreciate by its eagerness expressly to reserve the question of the constitutionality of subsidies for in-state industry, this expansive view of the Commerce Clause calls into question a wide variety of state laws that have hitherto been thought permissible. It seems to me that a State subsidy would clearly be invalid under any formulation of the Court's guiding principle identified above.... [E]ven where the funding does not come in any part from taxes on out-of-state goods, "merely assist[ing]" in-state businesses unquestionably neutralizes advantages possessed by out-of-state enterprises. Such subsidies ... are often admitted to have as their purpose—indeed, are nationally advertised as having as their purpose—making it more profitable to conduct business in-state than elsewhere, i.e., distorting normal market incentives.

The Court's guiding principle also appears to call into question many garden-variety state laws heretofore permissible under the negative Commerce Clause. A state law, for example, which requires, contrary to the industry practice, the use of recyclable packaging materials, favors local non-exporting producers, who do not have to establish an additional, separate packaging operation for in-state sales....

II

... I will, on *stare decisis* grounds, enforce a self-executing "negative" Commerce Clause in two situations: (1) against a state law that facially discriminates against interstate commerce, and (2) against a state law ... indistinguishable from a type of law previously held unconstitutional by this Court....

[A]t least four possible devices ... would enable a State to produce the economic effect that Massachusetts has produced here: (1) a discriminatory tax upon the industry, imposing a higher liability on out-of-state members than on their in-state competitors; (2) a tax upon the industry that is nondiscriminatory in its assessment, but that has an "exemption" or "credit" for in-state members; (3) a nondiscriminatory tax upon the industry, the revenues from which are placed into a segregated fund, which fund is disbursed as "rebates" or "subsidies" to in-state members of the industry (the situation at issue in this case); and (4) with or without nondiscriminatory taxation of the industry, a subsidy for the in-state members of the industry, funded from the State's general revenues. It is long settled that the first of these methodologies is unconstitutional under the negative Commerce Clause.... The second ... is no different in principle from the first, and has likewise been held invalid.... The fourth methodology, application of a state subsidy from general revenues, is so far removed from what we have hitherto held to be unconstitutional, that prohibiting it must be regarded as an extension of our negative-Commerce–Clause jurisprudence and therefore, to me, unacceptable. See New Energy Co. of Indiana v. Limbach, 486 U. S. 269, 278 (1988). Indeed, in my view our negative-Commerce–Clause cases have already approved the use of such subsidies. See Hughes v. Alexandria Scrap Corp., 426 U. S. 794, 809–810 (1976).

The issue before us in the present case is whether the third of these methodologies must fall. Although the question is close, I conclude it would not be a principled point at which to disembark from the negative-Commerce–Clause train. The only difference between methodology (2) (discriminatory "exemption" from nondiscriminatory tax) and methodology (3) (discriminatory refund of nondiscriminatory tax) is that the money is taken and returned rather than simply left with the favored in-state taxpayer in the first place. The difference between (3) and (4), on the other hand, is the difference between assisting in-state industry through discriminatory taxation, and assisting in-state industry by other means. I would therefore allow a State to subsidize its domestic industry so long as it does so from nondiscriminatory taxes that go into the State's general revenue fund. Perhaps, as some commentators contend, that line comports with an important economic reality: a State is less likely to maintain a subsidy when its citizens perceive that the money (in the general fund) is available for any number of competing, non-protectionist, purposes.... That is not, however, the basis for my position, for as The Chief Justice explains, "[a]nalysis of interest group participation in the political process may serve many useful purposes, but serving as a basis for interpreting the dormant Commerce Clause is not one of them." Instead, I draw the line where I do because it is a clear, rational line at the limits of our extant negative-Commerce–Clause jurisprudence.

Chief Justice Rehnquist, with whom Justice Blackmun joins, dissenting.

. . .

Massachusetts has ... provid[ed] a subsidy to aid its beleaguered dairy farmers. In case after case, we have approved the validity under the Commerce Clause of such enactments.... "Direct subsidization of domestic industry does not ordinarily run afoul of the [dormant Commerce Clause]; discriminatory taxation of out-of-state manufacturers does." New Energy Co. of Indiana v. Limbach, 486 U. S. 269, 278 (1988). But today the Court relegates these well-established principles to a footnote and ... gratuitously casts doubt on the validity of state subsidies, observing that "[w]e have never squarely confronted" their constitutionality....

... The State has not acted to strong-arm sister States as in *Limbach*; rather, its motives are purely local....

... The Court [objects] that the method of imposing the tax and subsidy distorts the State's political process.... But as the Court itself points out, there are still at least two strong interest groups opposed to the milk order—consumers and milk dealers. More importantly, nothing in the dormant Commerce Clause suggests that the fate of state regulation should turn upon the particular lawful manner in which the state subsidy is enacted or promulgated. Analysis of interest group participation in the political process may serve many useful purposes, but serving as a basis for interpreting the dormant Commerce Clause is not one of them.

... [B]oth *Baldwin* and *Bacchus* are a far cry from this case.

... [Unlike the adverse effect on out-of-state milk producers from the minimum price regulation in *Baldwin*, here m]ilk dealers have the same incentives to purchase lower priced milk from out-of-state farmers; dealers of all milk are taxed equally....

... [And] the milk order does not produce the same effect on interstate commerce as the tax exemption in *Bacchus*. I agree with the Court's statement that *Bacchus* can be distinguished "by noting that the rebate in this case goes not to the entity which pays the tax (milk dealers) but to the dairy farmers themselves." This is not only a distinction, but a significant difference. No decided case supports the Court's conclusion that the negative Commerce Clause prohibits the State from using money that it has lawfully obtained through a neutral tax on milk dealers and distributing it as a subsidy to dairy farmers....

... The wisdom of a messianic insistence on a grim sink-or-swim policy of laissez-faire economics would be debatable had Congress chosen to enact it; but Congress has done nothing of the kind. It is the Court which has imposed the policy under the dormant Commerce Clause, a policy which bodes ill for the values of federalism which have long animated our constitutional jurisprudence.

B.   REQUIRING BUSINESS OPERATIONS TO BE PERFORMED IN THE HOME STATE

MINNESOTA v. BARBER, 136 U.S. 313 (1890). A Minnesota statute prohibited the sale for human food of fresh meat not taken from animals inspected in Minnesota within 24 hours before slaughter. The case involved the sale in Minnesota of fresh beef slaughtered in Illinois but not inspected in Minnesota as the statute required. Supporters of the legislation argued that inspection on the hoof, within a very short time before animals are slaughtered, was necessary to ascertain their condition with certainty.

The Court stated: "[I]f, as alleged, the inspection of fresh beef, veal, mutton, lamb or pork will not necessarily show whether the animal from which it was taken was diseased when slaughtered, it would not follow that a statute like the one before us is within the constitutional power of the State to enact. On the contrary, the enactment of a similar statute by each one of the States composing the Union would result in the destruction of commerce among the several States, so far as such commerce is involved in the transportation from one part of the country to another of animal meats designed for human food, and entirely free from disease. A careful examination of the Minnesota Act will place this construction of it beyond question.... As the inspection must take place within the twenty-four hours immediately before the slaughtering, the act, by its necessary operation, excludes from the Minnesota market practically all fresh beef, veal, mutton, lamb or pork—in whatever form, and although entirely sound, healthy and fit for human food—taken from animals slaughtered in other States; and directly tends to restrict the slaughtering of animals, whose meat is to be sold in Minnesota for human food, to those engaged in such business in that State. . . . It will not do to say—certainly no judicial tribunal can, with propriety, assume—that the people of Minnesota may not, with due regard to their health, rely upon inspections in other States of animals there slaughtered for purposes of human food. . . . [A] law providing for the inspection of animals whose meats are designed for human food cannot be regarded as a rightful exertion of the police powers of the State, if the inspection prescribed is of such a character, or is burdened with such conditions, as will prevent altogether the introduction into the State of sound meats, the product of animals slaughtered in other States.''

The statute was held invalid as applied in the case.

FOSTER–FOUNTAIN PACKING CO. v. HAYDEL, 278 U.S. 1 (1928). A Louisiana statute declared all shrimp in Louisiana waters to be the property of the state but authorized the taking of shrimp on certain conditions. Among these conditions was the provision that no shipment out of state could be made of shrimp from which the heads and hulls had not been removed or of the raw heads and hulls ''as they are required to be manufactured into fertilizer or used for an element in chicken feed.'' No restriction was placed on the shipment out of the state of fertilizer or chicken feed. The Court held the statute invalid, saying:

''As the representative of its people, the state might have retained the shrimp for consumption and use therein. But, in direct opposition to conservation for intrastate use, this enactment permits all parts of the shrimp to be shipped and sold outside the state. The purpose is not to retain the shrimp for the use of the people of Louisiana; it is to favor the canning of the meat and the manufacture of bran in Louisiana by withholding raw or unshelled shrimp from the Biloxi [Mississippi] plants. But by permitting its shrimp to be taken and all the products thereof to be shipped and sold in interstate commerce, the state necessarily releases its hold. . . . And those taking the shrimp . . . become entitled to the rights of private ownership and the protection of the commerce clause.''

PIKE v. BRUCE CHURCH, INC., 397 U.S. 137 (1970). Appellee grows cantaloupes of superior quality in Parker, Arizona. Since the company lacked packing sheds in Parker, it transported the cantaloupes to nearby facilities in California where they were packed under regulations similar to those of Arizona, but shipped in containers bearing the name of the California packer. Pike, a state official acting under the Arizona Fruit and Vegetable Standardization Act, which was designed to prevent deceptive packaging, entered an order prohibiting the company from shipping its cantaloupes outside the State unless they were packed in containers approved by him. He contended that his order was necessary to ensure that the cantaloupes be identified as of Arizona origin. The company sought injunctive relief, claiming that the order would require it to build packing facilities in or near Parker at a cost of about $200,000 and this would constitute an unconstitutional burden on interstate commerce. A three-judge court granted relief. The Court unanimously affirmed, saying:

''. . . Although the criteria for determining the validity of state statutes affecting interstate commerce have been variously stated, the general rule that emerges can be phrased as follows: Where the statute regulates even-handedly to effectuate a legitimate local public interest, and its effects on interstate commerce are only incidental, it will be upheld unless the burden imposed on such commerce is clearly excessive in relation to the putative local benefits. Huron Cement Co. v. Detroit, 362 U.S. 440, 443. If a legitimate local purpose is found, then the question becomes one of degree. And the extent of the burden that will be tolerated will of course depend on the nature of the local interest involved, and on whether it could be promoted as well with a lesser impact on interstate activities. Occasionally the Court has candidly undertaken a balancing approach in resolving these issues, Southern Pacific Co. v. Arizona, 325 U.S. 761, but more frequently it has spoken in terms of 'direct' and 'indirect' effects and burdens...."

Referring to the stipulation of the State that the primary purpose of the Arizona law was to protect the reputation of Arizona growers by prohibiting deceptive packaging, the Court continued: "We are not, then, dealing here with 'state legislation in the field of safety where the propriety of local regulation has long been recognized,' or with an Act designed to protect consumers in Arizona from contaminated or unfit goods. Its purpose and design are simply to protect and enhance the reputation of growers within the State. These are surely legitimate state interests. Sligh v. Kirkwood, 237 U.S. 52, 61. We have upheld a State's power to require that produce packaged in the State be packaged in a particular kind of receptacle, Pacific States Box & Basket Co. v. White, 296 U.S. 176. And we have recognized the legitimate interest of a State in maximizing the financial return to an industry within it. Parker v. Brown, 317 U.S. 341....

"But application of the Act through the appellant's order to the appellee company has a far different impact, and quite a different purpose.... The appellant ... is not complaining because the company is putting the good name of Arizona on an inferior or deceptively packaged product, but because it is not putting that name on a product that is superior and well packaged.... [T]he State's tenuous interest in having the company's cantaloupes identified as originating in Arizona cannot constitutionally justify the requirement that the company build and operate an unneeded $200,000 packing plant in the State. The nature of that burden is, constitutionally, more significant than its extent. For the Court has viewed with particular suspicion state statutes requiring business operations to be performed in the home State that could more efficiently be performed elsewhere. Even where the State is pursuing a clearly legitimate local interes, this particular burden on commerce has been declared to be virtually *per se* illegal. Foster–Fountain Packing Co. v. Haydel, 278 U.S. 1...."

C & A Carbone v. Town of Clarkstown

511 U.S. 383, 114 S.Ct. 1677, 128 L.Ed.2d 399 (1994).

Justice Kennedy delivered the opinion of the Court.

. . .

We consider a so-called flow control ordinance, which requires all solid waste to be processed at a designated transfer station before leaving the municipality. The avowed purpose of the ordinance is to retain the processing fees charged at the transfer station to amortize the cost of the facility. Because it attains this goal by depriving competitors, including out-of-state firms, of access to a local market, we hold that the flow control ordinance violates the Commerce Clause.

[To finance construction of a solid waste transfer station that would receive bulk solid waste and separate recyclable from nonrecyclable items for shipment and further processing, the Town engaged a private contractor to build it, operate it for five years, and then sell it to the Town for one dollar, in exchange for a guaranteed minimum waste flow and the right to charge haulers an $81 per ton "tipping fee" (a processing cost higher than charged on the private market). To meet the annual guarantee, the Town adopted a flow control ordinance requiring all nonhazardous solid waste within the town, whatever its origin, to be deposited at the new transfer station.]

. . . Carbone operates a [similar] recycling center in Clarkstown. . . . While the flow control ordinance permits recyclers like Carbone to continue receiving solid waste, . . . it requires them to bring the nonrecyclable residue from that waste to the Route 303 station. It thus forbids Carbone to ship the nonrecyclable waste itself, and it requires Carbone to pay a tipping fee on trash that Carbone has already sorted.

[When the Town discovered that Carbone had shipped nonrecyclable waste to other states, it sought an injunction to force compliance with the flow control ordinance. The state courts sustained the ordinance's constitutionality and issued the injunction.] We . . . reverse.

At the outset we confirm that the flow control ordinance does regulate interstate commerce, despite the town's position to the contrary. The town says that its ordinance reaches only waste within its jurisdiction and is in practical effect a quarantine: It prevents garbage from entering the stream of interstate commerce until it is made safe. This reasoning is premised, however, on an outdated and mistaken concept of what constitutes interstate commerce.

While the immediate effect of the ordinance is to direct local transport of solid waste to a designated site within the local jurisdiction, its economic effects are interstate in reach. The Carbone facility in Clarkstown receives and processes waste from places other than Clarkstown, including from out of State. By requiring Carbone to send the nonrecyclable portion of this waste to the Route 303 transfer station at an additional cost, the flow control ordinance drives up the cost for out-of-state interests to dispose of their solid waste. Furthermore, even as to waste originant in Clarkstown, the ordinance prevents everyone except the favored local operator from performing the initial processing step. The ordinance thus deprives out-of-state businesses of access to a local market. These economic effects are more than enough to bring the Clarkstown ordinance within the purview of the Commerce Clause. . . .

. . . As . . . the ordinance discriminates against interstate commerce, we need not resort to the *Pike* [balancing] test.

. . .

Clarkstown protests that its ordinance does not discriminate because it does not differentiate solid waste on the basis of its geographic origin. All solid waste, regardless of origin, must be processed at the designated transfer station before it leaves the town. . . .

. . . As the town itself points out, what makes garbage a profitable business is not its own worth but the fact that its possessor must pay to get rid of it. In other words, the article of commerce is not so much the solid waste itself, but rather the service of processing and disposing of it.

With respect to this stream of commerce, the flow control ordinance discriminates, for it allows only the favored operator to process waste that is within the limits of the town. The ordinance is no less discriminatory because in-state or in-town processors are also covered by the prohibition.... Dean Milk Co. v. Madison, 340 U.S. 349 (1951)....

In this light, the flow control ordinance is just one more instance of local processing requirements that we long have held invalid.... The essential vice in laws of this sort is that they bar the import of the processing service. Out-of-state meat inspectors, or shrimp hullers, or milk pasteurizers, are deprived of access to local demand for their services. Put another way, the offending local laws hoard a local resource—be it meat, shrimp, or milk—for the benefit of local businesses that treat it.

The flow control ordinance has the same design and effect. It hoards solid waste, and the demand to get rid of it, for the benefit of the preferred processing facility. The only conceivable distinction from the cases cited above is that the flow control ordinance favors a single local proprietor. But this difference just makes the protectionist effect of the ordinance more acute. In *Dean Milk*, the local processing requirement at least permitted pasteurizers within five miles of the city to compete. An out-of-state pasteurizer who wanted access to that market might have built a pasteurizing facility within the radius. The flow control ordinance at issue here squelches competition in the waste-processing service altogether, leaving no room for investment from outside.

Discrimination against interstate commerce in favor of local business or investment is *per se* invalid, save in a narrow class of cases in which the municipality can demonstrate, under rigorous scrutiny, that it has no other means to advance a legitimate local interest....

... Here Clarkstown has any number of nondiscriminatory alternatives for addressing the health and environmental problems alleged to justify the ordinance in question. The most obvious would be uniform safety regulations enacted without the object to discriminate. These regulations would ensure that competitors like Carbone do not underprice the market by cutting corners on environmental safety.

Nor may Clarkstown justify the flow control ordinance as a way to steer solid waste away from out-of-town disposal sites that it might deem harmful to the environment. To do so would extend the town's police power beyond its jurisdictional bounds. States and localities may not attach restrictions to exports or imports in order to control commerce in other states....

. . .

Clarkstown maintains that special financing is necessary to ensure the long-term survival of the designated facility. If so, the town may subsidize the facility through general taxes or municipal bonds.... But having elected to use the open market to earn revenues for its project, the town may not employ discriminatory regulation to give that project an advantage over rival businesses from out of State.

. . .

State and local governments may not use their regulatory power to favor local enterprise by prohibiting patronage of out-of-state competitors or their facilities....

Justice O'Connor, concurring in the judgment.

... In my view, ... the town's ordinance is unconstitutional not because of facial or effective discrimination against interstate commerce, but rather because it imposes an excessive burden on interstate commerce....

I

. . .

. . . [T]he majority cites previous decisions . . . striking down regulatory enactments requiring that a particular economic activity be performed within the jurisdiction. . . .

Local Law 9, however, lacks an important feature common to . . . these cases—namely, discrimination on the basis of geographic origin. In each of the cited cases, the challenged enactment gave a competitive advantage to local business *as a group* vis-a-vis their out-of-state or nonlocal competitors *as a group*. In effect, the regulating jurisdiction—be it a State (*Pike*), a county (Fort Gratiot Sanitary Landfill, Inc. v. Michigan Dept. of Natural Resources, 504 U. S. (1992)), or a city (*Dean Milk*)—drew a line around itself and treated those inside the line more favorably than those outside the line. Thus, in *Pike*, . . . the benefits of the discriminatory scheme benefited the Arizona packaging industry, at the expense of its competition in California. Similarly, in *Dean Milk*, on which the majority heavily relies, the city of Madison drew a line around its perimeter and required that all milk sold in the City be pasteurized only by dairies located inside the line. This type of geographic distinction, which confers an economic advantage on local interests in general, is common to all the local processing cases cited by the majority. And the Court has, I believe, correctly concluded that these arrangements are protectionist either in purpose or practical effect, and thus amount to virtually per se discrimination.

. . . [By contrast,] Local Law 9 does not give more favorable treatment to local interests as a group as compared to out-of-state or out-of-town economic interests. Rather, the garbage sorting monopoly is achieved at the expense of all competitors, be they local or nonlocal. That the ordinance does not discriminate on the basis of geographic origin is vividly illustrated by the identity of the plaintiff in this very action: petitioner is a local recycler, physically located in Clarkstown. . . . Because in-town processors—like petitioner—and out-of-town processors are treated equally, I cannot agree that Local Law 9 "discriminates" against interstate commerce. Rather, Local Law 9 "discriminates" evenhandedly against all potential participants in the waste processing business, while benefiting only the chosen operator of the transfer facility.

I believe this distinction has more doctrinal significance than the majority acknowledges. In considering state health and safety regulations such as Local Law 9, we have consistently recognized that the fact that interests within the regulating jurisdiction are equally affected by the challenged enactment counsels against a finding of discrimination. And for good reason. The existence of substantial in-state interests harmed by a regulation is "a powerful safeguard" against legislative discrimination. Minnesota v. Clover Leaf Creamery Co., 449 U. S. 456, 473, n. 17 (1981). . . . [W]hile . . . no bright line separat[es] those enactments which are virtually per se invalid and those which are not, the fact that in-town competitors of the transfer facility are equally burdened by Local Law 9 leads me to conclude that Local Law 9 does not discriminate against interstate commerce.

II

. . . Even a nondiscriminatory regulation may nonetheless impose an excessive burden on interstate trade when considered in relation to the local benefits conferred. . . .

The local interest in proper disposal of waste is obviously significant [b]ut . . . could be achieved by simply requiring that all waste disposed of in the town be properly processed somewhere. For example, the town could ensure proper processing by setting specific standards with which all town processors must comply.

In fact, however, the town's purpose is narrower than merely ensuring proper disposal. Local Law 9 is intended to ensure the financial viability of the transfer facility. I agree with the majority that this purpose can be achieved by other means that would have a less dramatic impact on the flow of goods....

In addition, "[t]he practical effect of [Local Law 9] must be evaluated not only by considering the consequences of the statute itself, but also by considering how the challenged statute may interact with the legitimate regulatory regimes of the other States and what effect would arise if not one, but many or every, [jurisdiction] adopted similar legislation." Wyoming v. Oklahoma, ... (quoting Healy v. Beer Institute, 491 U. S. 324, 336 (1989)).... Over 20 states have enacted statutes authorizing local governments to adopt flow control laws. If the localities in these States impose the type of restriction ... that Clarkstown has adopted, the free movement of solid waste in the stream of commerce will be severely impaired. Indeed, pervasive flow control would result in the type of balkanization the Clause is primarily intended to prevent. See H. P. Hood & Sons, 336 U. S., at 537–538.

... The increasing number of flow control regimes virtually ensures some inconsistency between jurisdictions, with the effect of eliminating the movement of waste between jurisdictions. I therefore conclude that the burden Local Law 9 imposes on interstate commerce is excessive in relation to Clarkstown's interest in ensuring a fixed supply of waste to supply its project.

. . .

Justice Souter, with whom The Chief Justice and Justice Blackmun join, dissenting.

... [T]he majority ignores ... the differences between our local processing cases and this one: the exclusion worked by Clarkstown's Local Law 9 bestows no benefit on a class of local private actors, but instead directly aids the government in satisfying a traditional governmental responsibility. The law does not differentiate between all local and all out-of-town providers of a service, but instead between the one entity responsible for ensuring that the job gets done and all other enterprises, regardless of their location. The ordinance thus falls outside that class of tariff or protectionist measures that the Commerce Clause has traditionally been thought to bar States from enacting against each other....

... There is no indication in the record that any out-of-state trash processor has been harmed, or that the interstate movement or disposition of trash will be affected one whit. To the degree Local Law 9 affects the market for trash processing services, it does so only by subjecting Clarkstown residents and businesses to burdens far different from the burdens of local favoritism that dormant Commerce Clause jurisprudence seeks to root out. The town has found a way to finance a public improvement, not by transferring its cost to out-of-state economic interests, but by spreading it among the local generators of trash, an equitable result with tendencies that should not disturb the Commerce Clause and should not be disturbed by us.

. . .

II

. . .

The majority ... discounts [the] difference between laws favoring all local actors and this law favoring a single municipal one[,] ... because outside investors cannot even build competing facilities within Clarkstown. But ... Clarkstown investors face the same prohibition[: the] exclusion of outside capital is part of a broader exclusion of private capital, not a discrimination against out-of-state investors as such.... Thus, while these differences may underscore the ordinance's anticompetitive effect, they substantially mitigate any protectionist effect, for subjecting out-of-town investors and facilities to the same constraints as local ones is not economic protectionism....

... Clarkstown's transfer station is essentially a municipal facility ... perform[ing] a municipal function that tradition as well as state and federal law recognize as the domain of local government....

The majority ignores this distinction between public and private enterprise.... But private businesses, whether local or out of State, first serve the private interests of their owners, and there is therefore only rarely a reason other than economic protectionism for favoring local businesses over their out-of-town competitors. The local government itself occupies a very different market position, however, being the one entity that enters the market to serve the public interest of local citizens quite apart from private interest in private gain. Reasons other than economic protectionism are accordingly more likely to explain the design and effect of an ordinance that favors a public facility....

. . .

... [I]n a market served by a municipal facility, a law that favors that single facility over all others is a law that favors the public sector over all private-sector processors, whether local or out of State. Because the favor does not go to local private competitors of out-of-state firms, out-of-state governments will at the least lack a motive to favor their own firms in order to equalize the positions of private competitors. While a preference in favor of the government may incidentally function as local favoritism as well, a more particularized enquiry is necessary before a court can say whether such a law does in fact smack too strongly of economic protectionism. If Local Law 9 is to be struck down, ... it must be under th[e] test [in] Pike v. Bruce Church, Inc., 397 U. S. 137 (1970).

III

... Although ... sometimes ... called a "balancing test," it is not so much an open-ended weighing of an ordinance's pros and cons, as an assessment of whether an ordinance discriminates in practice or otherwise unjustifiably operates to isolate a State's economy from the national common market.... "[T]he question becomes one of degree," and its answer depends on the nature of the burden on interstate commerce, the nature of the local interest, and the availability of alternative methods for advancing the local interest without hindering the national one. Id., at 142, 145.

. . .

While the monopolistic nature of the burden may be disregarded, any geographically discriminatory elements must be assessed with care.... There is, to be sure, an incidental local economic benefit, for the need to process Clarkstown's trash in Clarkstown will create local jobs. But this local boon is mitigated by another feature of the ordinance, in that it finances whatever benefits it confers on the town from the pockets of the very citizens who passed it into law. On the reasonable assumption that no one can avoid producing some trash, every resident of Clarkstown must bear a portion of the burden

Local Law 9 imposes to support the municipal monopoly, an uncharacteristic feature of statutes claimed to violate the Commerce Clause.

[M]ost of the local processing statutes we have previously invalidated imposed requirements that made local goods more expensive as they headed into the national market, so that out-of-state economies bore the bulk of any burden.... Here, in contrast, every voter in Clarkstown pays to fund the benefits of flow control.... Since ... the mandate to use the town facility will only make a difference when the tipping fee raises the cost ... above what the market would otherwise set, the Clarkstown voters are funding their benefit by assessing themselves and paying an economic penalty. Any whiff of economic protectionism is far from obvious.

An examination of the record ... shows that the burden falls entirely on Clarkstown residents.... [P]etitioner has presented no evidence that there are transfer stations outside Clarkstown capable of handling the town's business, and the record is devoid of evidence that such enterprises have lost business as a result of this ordinance.... There is ... no evidence of any disruption in the flow of trash from curbsides in Clarkstown to landfills in Florida and Ohio.[16] [T]he only business lost as a result of this ordinance is business lost in Clarkstown, ... but business lost in Clarkstown as a result of a Clarkstown ordinance is not a burden that offends the Constitution.

... [T]here are limits on any municipality's ability to incur debt or to finance facilities out of tax revenues. Protection of the public fisc is a legitimate local benefit directly advanced by the ordinance and quite unlike the generalized advantage to local businesses that we have condemned as protectionist in the past....

... In proportioning each resident's burden to the amount of trash generated, the ordinance has the added virtue of providing a direct and measurable deterrent to the generation of unnecessary waste in the first place. And ... it is far from clear that the alternative to flow control (i.e., subsidies from general tax revenues or municipal bonds) would be less disruptive of interstate commerce than flow control, since a subsidized competitor can effectively squelch competition by underbidding it.

. . .

The Commerce Clause was not passed to save the citizens of Clarkstown from themselves. It should not be wielded to prevent them from attacking their local garbage problems with an ordinance that does not discriminate between local and out-of-town participants in the private market for trash disposal services and that is not protectionist in its purpose or effect....

C. PRESERVING RESOURCES FOR IN-STATE CONSUMPTION

PENNSYLVANIA v. WEST VIRGINIA, 262 U.S. 553 (1923). In the early years of this century West Virginia was the major producing state for natural gas. Production exceeded local needs and the state permitted pipeline corporations to purchase natural gas and transport it to customers in Pennsylvania and Ohio. Large numbers of residential and industrial consumers in

---

[16] [T]he conflict Justice O'Connor hypothesizes between multiple flow control laws is not one that occurs in this case.... But more fundamentally, even if a nondiscriminatory ordinance conflicts with the law of some other jurisdiction, that fact would not, in itself, lead to its invalidation.... [T]he municipality's interests are substantial and ... the alternative means for advancing them are less desirable and potentially as disruptive of interstate commerce....

those states became dependent on the supply of gas from West Virginia. The time came when the demand for the gas exceeded the supply and that the only way more gas could be provided in one of the states was to reduce the amount supplied in the others.

West Virginia passed a statute requiring every pipeline company transporting gas produced in West Virginia to satisfy the needs, domestic or industrial, of all West Virginia customers, old or new, willing to pay for the gas and use it within the state. The states of Pennsylvania and Ohio brought suit to enjoin West Virginia from enforcing this statute. The Court held the statute invalid.

Justice Van Devanter, writing for the Court, said in part:

"Natural gas is a lawful article of commerce, and its transmission from one state to another for sale and consumption in the latter is interstate commerce. A state law, whether of the state where the gas is produced or that where it is to be sold, which by its necessary operation prevents, obstructs or burdens such transmission is a regulation of interstate commerce—a prohibited interference. . . .

"But it is urged that there are special considerations which take the act out of the general rule and sustain its validity, even though there be an interference. . . .

"[One such consideration] is that the gas is a natural product of the state and has become a necessity therein, that the supply is waning and no longer sufficient to satisfy local needs and be used abroad, and that the act is therefore a legitimate measure of conservation in the interest of the people of the state. If the situation be as stated, it affords no ground for the assumption by the state of power to regulate interstate commerce, which is what the act attempts to do. That power is lodged elsewhere."

In a dissenting opinion Justice Holmes said: "I see nothing in the commerce clause to prevent a State from giving a preference to its inhabitants in the enjoyment of its natural advantages."

H.P. Hood & Sons v. Du Mond

336 U.S. 525, 69 S.Ct. 657, 93 L.Ed. 865 (1949).

[Hood & Sons had long distributed milk and milk products to the Boston area which obtains about 90% of its milk from states other than Massachusetts. For some time Hood had obtained milk in New York State for shipment to Boston and for this purpose had operated three receiving depots in the state. It now proposed to open a fourth at Greenwich, New York, in an area which had been developed by Hood and a competitor as part of the Boston Milkshed. Greenwich is ten miles from Salem and twelve miles from Eagle Bridge, where two of Hood's existing New York depots are located. Hood applied for a license to open the new depot, as required by the New York law which provided that, before issuing the license, the Commission of Agriculture and Markets should be satisfied "that the issuance of a license will not tend to a destructive competition in a market already adequately served, and that the issuance of the license is in the public interest." Pursuant to this provision, the Commissioner refused to issue the license although Hood met all the other statutory requirements.]

Mr. Justice Jackson delivered the opinion of the Court. . . .

The Commissioner found that Hood, if licensed at Greenwich, would permit its present suppliers, at their option, to deliver at the new plant rather than the old ones and for a substantial number this would mean shorter hauls and savings in delivery costs. The new plant also would attract twenty to thirty producers, some of whose milk Hood anticipates will or may be diverted from other buyers. Other large milk distributors have plants within the general area and dealers serving Troy obtain milk in the locality. He found that Troy was inadequately supplied during the preceding short season.

. . .

Pennsylvania enacted a law including provisions to protect producers which were very similar to those of this New York Act. A concern which operated a receiving plant in Pennsylvania from which it shipped milk to the New York City market challenged the Act upon grounds thus defined by this Court: "The respondent contends that the act, if construed to require it to obtain a license, to file a bond for the protection of producers, and to pay the farmers the prices prescribed by the Board, unconstitutionally regulates and burdens interstate commerce." Milk Control Bd. v. Eisenberg Co., 306 U.S. 346, 350. This Court, specifically limiting its judgment to the Act's provisions with respect to license, bond and regulation of prices to be paid to producers, id. at 306 U.S. at 352, considered their effect on interstate commerce "incidental and not forbidden by the Constitution, in the absence of regulation by Congress." Id. at 306 U.S. at 353.

The present controversy begins where the *Eisenberg* decision left off. New York's regulations, designed to assure producers a fair price and a responsible purchaser, and consumers a sanitary and modernly equipped handler, are not challenged here but have been complied with. It is only additional restrictions, imposed for the avowed purpose and with the practical effect of curtailing the volume of interstate commerce to aid local economic interests, that are in question here, and no such measures were attempted or such ends sought to be served in the Act before the Court in the *Eisenberg* case.

Our decision in a milk litigation most relevant to the present controversy deals with the converse of the present situation. Baldwin v. G.A.F. Seelig, Inc., 294 U.S. 511, . . . is an explicit, impressive, recent and unanimous condemnation by this Court of economic restraints on interstate commerce for local economic advantage, but it does not stand alone. This Court consistently has rebuffed attempts of states to advance their own commercial interests by curtailing the movement of articles of commerce, either into or out of the state, while generally supporting their right to impose even burdensome regulations in the interests of local health and safety. As most states serve their own interests best by sending their produce to market, the cases in which this Court has been obligated to deal with prohibitions or limitations by states upon exports of articles of commerce are not numerous. . . .

[The] principle that our economic unit is the Nation, which alone has the gamut of powers necessary to control of the economy, including the vital power of erecting customs barriers against foreign competition, has as its corollary that the states are not separable economic units. As the Court said in Baldwin v. G.A.F. Seelig, Inc., 294 U.S. 511, 527, "What is ultimate is the principle that one state in its dealings with another may not place itself in a position of economic isolation." In so speaking it but followed the principle that the state may not use its admitted powers to protect the health and safety of its people as a basis for suppressing competition. In Buck v. Kuykendall, 267 U.S. 307, the Court struck down a state act because, in the language of Mr. Justice Brandeis, "Its primary purpose is not regulation with a view to safety or to conservation of the highways, but the prohibition of competition." The same argument here advanced, that limitation of competition would itself contribute to safety and conservation, and therefore indirectly serve an end permissible to the state, was there declared "not sound." 267 U.S. 307, 315. It is no better here. . . .

The material success that has come to inhabitants of the states which make up this federal free trade unit has been the most impressive in the history of commerce, but the established interdependence of the states only emphasizes the necessity of protecting interstate movement of goods against local burdens and repressions. . . .

Our system, fostered by the Commerce Clause, is that every farmer and every craftsman shall be encouraged to produce by the certainty that he will have free access to every market in the Nation, that no home embargoes will withhold his export, and no foreign state will by customs duties or regulations exclude them. Likewise, every consumer may look to the free competition from every producing area in the Nation to protect him from exploitation by any. Such was the vision of the Founders; such has been the doctrine of this Court which has given it reality. . . .

Since the statute as applied violates the Commerce Clause and is not authorized by federal legislation pursuant to that Clause, it cannot stand. The judgment is reversed and the cause remanded for proceedings not inconsistent with this opinion. It is so ordered.

Reversed and remanded.

Mr. Justice Frankfurter, with whom Mr. Justice Rutledge joins, dissenting.

. . .

Mr. Justice Black, dissenting.

In this case the Court sets up a new constitutional formula for invalidation of state laws regulating local phases of interstate commerce. I believe the New York law is invulnerable to constitutional attack under constitutional rules which the majority of this Court have long accepted. The new formula subjects state regulations of local business activities to greater constitutional hazards than they have ever had to meet before. The consequences of the new formula, as I understand it, will not merely leave a large area of local business activities free from state regulation. All local activities that fall within the scope of this new formula will be free from any regulatory control whatever. For it is inconceivable that Congress could pass uniform national legislation capable of adjustment and application to all the local phases of interstate activities that take place in the 48 states. It is equally inconceivable that Congress would attempt to control such diverse local activities through a "swarm of statutes only locally applicable, and utterly inconsistent." Kidd v. Pearson, 128 U.S. 1, 21. . . .

. . .

The language of this state Act is not discriminatory, the legislative history shows it was not so intended, and the commissioner has not administered it with a hostile eye. . . .

The basic question here is not the greatness of the commerce clause concept, but whether all local phases of interstate business are to be judicially immunized from state laws against destructive competitive business practices such as those prohibited by New York's law. Of course, there remains the bare possibility Congress might attempt to federalize all such local business activities in the forty-eight states. While I have doubt about the wisdom of this New

York law, I do not conceive it to be the function of this Court to revise that state's economic judgments. Any doubt I may have concerning the wisdom of New York's law is far less, however, than is my skepticism concerning the ability of the Federal Government to reach out and effectively regulate all the local business activities in the forty-eight states.

I would leave New York's law alone.

Mr. Justice Murphy joins in this opinion.

Philadelphia v. New Jersey

437 U.S. 617, 98 S.Ct. 2531, 57 L.Ed.2d 475 (1978).

Mr. Justice Stewart delivered the opinion of the Court.

A New Jersey law prohibits the importation of most "solid or liquid waste which originated or was collected outside the territorial limits of the State...." In this case we are required to decide whether this statutory prohibition violates the Commerce Clause of the United States Constitution.

. . .

[Operators of private landfills in New Jersey and several cities in other states that had agreements with these operators for waste disposal brought suit against New Jersey in state court challenging the validity of the statute and regulations issued under it. The New Jersey Supreme Court upheld the legislation. The plaintiffs appealed to the United States Supreme Court.]

III.

A.

. . .

The opinions of the Court through the years have reflected an alertness to the evils of "economic isolation" and protectionism, while at the same time recognizing that incidental burdens on interstate commerce may be unavoidable when a State legislates to safeguard the health and safety of its people. Thus, where simple economic protectionism is effected by state legislation, a virtually per se rule of invalidity has been erected. See, e.g., *Hood & Sons v. Du Mond,* supra; Toomer v. Witsell, 334 U.S. 385, 403–406; *Baldwin v. G.A.F. Seelig,* supra; Buck v. Kuykendall, 267 U.S. 307, 315–316. The clearest example of such legislation is a law that overtly blocks the flow of interstate commerce at a State's borders. Cf. Welton v. Missouri, 91 U.S. 275. But where other legislative objectives are credibly advanced and there is no patent discrimination against interstate trade, the Court has adopted a much more flexible approach, the general contours of which were outlined in Pike v. Bruce Church, Inc., 397 U.S. 137, 142:

... The crucial inquiry, therefore, must be directed to determining whether ch. 363 is basically a protectionist measure, or whether it can fairly be viewed as a law directed to legitimate local concerns, with effects upon interstate commerce that are only incidental.

B.

The purpose of ch. 363 is set out in the statute itself as follows:

"The Legislature finds and determines that ... the volume of solid and liquid waste continues to rapidly increase, that the treatment and disposal of these wastes continues to pose an even greater threat to the quality of the environment of New Jersey, that the available and appropriate land fill sites within the State are being diminished, that the environment continues to be threatened by the treatment and disposal of waste which originated or was collected outside the State and that the public health, safety and welfare require that the treatment and disposal within this State of all wastes generated outside of the State be prohibited.''

The New Jersey Supreme Court accepted this statement of the state legislature's purpose. The state court additionally found that New Jersey's existing landfill sites will be exhausted within a few years; that to go on using these sites or to develop new ones will take a heavy environmental toll, both from pollution and from loss of scarce open lands; that new techniques to divert waste from landfills to other methods of disposal and resource recovery processes are under development, but that these changes will require time; and finally, that "the extension of the lifespan of existing landfills, resulting from the exclusion of out-of-state waste, may be of crucial importance in preventing further virgin wetlands or other undeveloped lands from being devoted to landfill purposes." 68 N.J., at 460–465, 348 A.2d, at 509–512. Based on these findings, the court concluded that ch. 363 was designed to protect not the State's economy, but its environment, and that its substantial benefits outweigh its "slight" burden on interstate commerce. Id., at 471–478, 348 A.2d, at 515–519.

The appellants strenuously contend that ch. 363, "while outwardly cloaked 'in the currently fashionable garb of environmental protection,' . . . is actually no more than a legislative effort to suppress competition and stabilize the cost of solid waste disposal for New Jersey residents. . . .''

. . .

The appellees, on the other hand, deny that ch. 363 was motivated by financial concerns or economic protectionism. . . .

This dispute about ultimate legislative purpose need not be resolved, because its resolution would not be relevant to the constitutional issue to be decided in this case. Contrary to the evident assumption of the state court and the parties, the evil of protectionism can reside in legislative means as well as legislative ends. Thus, it does not matter whether the ultimate aim of ch. 363 is to reduce the waste disposal costs of New Jersey residents or to save remaining open lands from pollution, for we assume New Jersey has every right to protect its residents' pocketbooks as well as their environment. And it may be assumed as well that New Jersey may pursue those ends by slowing the flow of all waste into the State's remaining landfills, even though interstate commerce may incidentally be affected. But whatever New Jersey's ultimate purpose, it may not be accomplished by discriminating against articles of commerce coming from outside the State unless there is some reason, apart from their origin, to treat them differently. Both on its face and in its plain effect, ch. 363 violates this principle of nondiscrimination.

The Court has consistently found parochial legislation of this kind to be constitutionally invalid, whether the ultimate aim of the legislation was to assure a steady supply of milk by erecting barriers to allegedly ruinous outside competition, Baldwin v. G.A.F. Seelig, supra, at 522–524; or to create jobs by keeping industry within the State, Foster Packing Co. v. Haydel, 278 U.S. 1, 10; Johnson v. Haydel, 278 U.S. 16; Toomer v. Witsell, supra, at 403–404; or to preserve the State's financial resources from depletion by fencing out indigent immigrants, Edwards v. California, 314 U.S. 160, 173–174. In each of these cases, a presumably legitimate goal was sought to be achieved by the illegitimate means of isolating the State from the national economy.

Also relevant here are the Court's decisions holding that a State may not accord its own inhabitants a preferred right of access over consumers in other States to natural resources located within its borders. West v. Kansas Natural Gas Co., 221 U.S. 229; Pennsylvania v. West Virginia, 262 U.S. 553. These cases stand for the basic principle that a "State is without power to prevent privately owned articles of trade from being shipped and sold in interstate commerce on the ground that they are required to satisfy local demands or because they are needed by the people of the State." Foster Packing Co. v. Haydel, supra, at 10.

The New Jersey law at issue in this case falls squarely within the area that the Commerce Clause puts off-limits to state regulation. On its face, it imposes on out-of-state commercial interests the full burden of conserving the State's remaining landfill space. It is true that in our previous cases the scarce natural resource was itself the article of commerce, whereas here the scarce resource and the article of commerce are distinct. But that difference is without consequence. In both instances, the State has overtly moved to slow or freeze the flow of commerce for protectionist reasons. It does not matter that the State has shut the article of commerce inside the State in one case and outside the State in the other. What is crucial is the attempt by one State to isolate itself from a problem common to many by erecting a barrier against the movement of interstate trade.

The appellees argue that not all laws which facially discriminate against out-of-state commerce are forbidden protectionist regulations. In particular, they point to quarantine laws, which this Court has repeatedly upheld even though they appear to single out interstate commerce for special treatment. See Baldwin v. G.A.F. Seelig, supra, at 525; Bowman v. Chicago & Northwestern R. Co., supra, at 489. In the appellees' view, ch. 363 is analogous to such health-protective measures, since it reduces the exposure of New Jersey residents to the allegedly harmful effects of landfill sites.

It is true that certain quarantine laws have not been considered forbidden protectionist measures, even though they were directed against out-of-state commerce.... But those quarantine laws banned the importation of articles such as diseased livestock that required destruction as soon as possible because their very movement risked contagion and other evils. Those laws thus did not discriminate against interstate commerce as such, but simply prevented traffic in noxious articles, whatever their origin.

The New Jersey statute is not such a quarantine law. There has been no claim here that the very movement of waste into or through New Jersey endangers health, or that waste must be disposed of as soon and as close to its point of generation as possible. The harms caused by waste are said to arise after its disposal in landfill sites, and at that point, as New Jersey concedes, there is no basis to distinguish out-of-state waste from domestic waste. If one is inherently harmful, so is the other. Yet New Jersey has banned the former while leaving its landfill sites open to the latter. The New Jersey law blocks the importation of waste in an obvious effort to saddle those outside the State with the entire burden of slowing the flow of refuse into New Jersey's remaining landfill sites. That legislative effort is clearly impermissible under the Commerce Clause of the Constitution.

Today, cities in Pennsylvania and New York find it expedient or necessary to send their waste to New Jersey for disposal, and New Jersey claims the right to close its borders to such traffic. Tomorrow, cities in New Jersey may find it expedient or necessary to send their waste into Pennsylvania or New York for disposal, and those States might then claim the right to close their borders. The Commerce Clause will protect New Jersey in the future, just as it protects her neighbors now, from efforts by one State to isolate itself in the stream of interstate commerce from a problem shared by all.

The judgment is reversed.

Mr. Justice Rehnquist, with whom The Chief Justice joins, dissenting.

. . .

[T]he Court implies that the challenged laws must be invalidated because New Jersey has left its landfills open to domestic waste. But, as the Court notes ... this Court has repeatedly upheld quarantine laws "even though they appear to single out interstate commerce for special treatment." The fact that New Jersey has left its landfill sites open for domestic waste does not, of course, mean that solid waste is not innately harmful. Nor does it mean that New Jersey prohibits importation of solid waste for reasons other than the health and safety of its population. New Jersey must out of sheer necessity treat and dispose of its solid waste in some fashion, just as it must treat New Jersey cattle suffering from hoof-and-mouth disease. It does not follow that New Jersey must, under the Commerce Clause, accept solid waste or diseased cattle from outside its borders and thereby exacerbate its problems.

The Supreme Court of New Jersey expressly found that ch. 363 was passed "to preserve the health of New Jersey residents by keeping their exposure to solid waste and landfill areas to a minimum." ... The Court points to absolutely no evidence that would contradict this finding by the New Jersey Supreme Court. Because I find no basis for distinguishing the laws under challenge here from our past cases upholding state laws that prohibit the importation of items that could endanger the population of the State, I dissent.

NOTE

The Court reaffirmed and applied *Philadelphia v. New Jersey* in two 1992 companion cases. In Chemical Waste Management, Inc. v. Hunt, 504 U.S. 334 (1992), the Court struck down an Alabama statute imposing an additional fee for disposal of hazardous wastes generated outside the State at commercial facilities in Alabama. Alabama's legitimate health, safety, and environmental interests had to be served through less discriminatory alternatives, such as "a generally applicable per-ton additional fee on *all* hazardous waste disposed of within Alabama, ... or a per-mile tax on *all* vehicles transporting hazardous waste across Alabama roads, ... or an evenhanded cap on the total tonnage landfilled ..., which would curtail volume from all sources." Moreover, because "every concern related to quarantine applies perforce to local hazardous waste, which pays no additional fee[,]" the discrimination against interstate commerce was unjustified.

The other decision, Fort Gratiot Sanitary Landfill, Inc. v. Michigan Department of Natural Resources, 504 U.S. 353 (1992), declared invalid under the Commerce Clause a state law prohibiting private landfill operators from accepting solid waste that originated outside the *county* encompassing the landfill facilities, unless the county authorized the importation. The Court rejected an argument that the Michigan Waste Import Restrictions did not discriminate against interstate commerce "because they treat waste from other Michigan counties no differently than waste from other States." The Court said that "prior cases teach that a State (or one of its political subdivisions) may not avoid the strictures of the Commerce Clause by curtailing the movement of articles of commerce through subdivisions of the State, rather than through the State itself." Furthermore, "the fact that several Michigan counties accept out-of-state waste" may have "reduced the scope of the discrimination[,]" but it did not "qualify" the statute's "discriminatory character." *Philadelphia v. New Jersey* thus applied with full force.

In dissent, Chief Justice Rehnquist, joined by Justice Blackmun, argued in part that "this facially neutral restriction (i.e., it applies equally to both interstate and intrastate waste)" should be understood as part of a comprehensive solid waste disposal scheme that legitimately "required counties within the State to be responsible for the waste created within the county." He noted that the regulation was likely to increase disposal costs for Michigan consumers and "require some Michigan counties—those that until now have been exporting their waste to other locations in the State—to confront environmental and other risks that they previously have avoided." He then continued:

> "Commerce Clause concerns are at their nadir when a state act works in this fashion—raising prices for all the State's consumers, and working to the substantial disadvantage of other segments of the State's population— because in these circumstances 'a State's own political processes will serve as a check against unduly burdensome regulations.' . . . In sum, the law simply incorporates the commonsense notion that those responsible for a problem should be responsible for its solution *to the degree they are responsible for the problem but not further.*"

Hughes v. Oklahoma

441 U.S. 322, 99 S.Ct. 1727, 60 L.Ed.2d 250 (1979).

Mr. Justice Brennan delivered the opinion of the Court.

The question presented for decision is whether Okla.Stat., Tit. 29, § 4–115(B) (Supp.1978) violates the Commerce Clause, Art. I, § 8, cl. 3, of the United States Constitution, insofar as it provides that "No person may transport or ship minnows for sale outside the state which were seined or procured within the waters of this state. . . ."[1]

Appellant William Hughes holds a Texas license to operate a commercial minnow business near Wichita Falls, Tex. An Oklahoma Game Ranger arrested him on a charge of violating § 4–115(B) by transporting from Oklahoma to Wichita Falls a load of natural minnows purchased from a minnow dealer licensed to do business in Oklahoma. Hughes' defense that § 4–115(B) was unconstitutional because it was repugnant to the Commerce Clause was rejected, and he was convicted and fined. The Oklahoma Court of Criminal Appeals affirmed. . . . We reverse. Geer v. Connecticut, [161 U.S. 519 (1896),] on which the Court of Criminal Appeals relied, is overruled. In that circumstance, § 4–115(B) cannot survive appellant's Commerce Clause attack.

I.

. . . The cases defining the scope of permissible state regulation in areas of congressional silence reflect an often controversial evolution of rules to accommodate federal and state interests. *Geer v. Connecticut* was decided relatively

---

[1] . . . The prohibition against transportation out of State for sale thus does not apply to hatchery-bred minnows, but only to "natural" minnows seined or procured from waters within the State.

early in that evolutionary process. We hold that time has revealed the error of the early resolution reached in that case, and accordingly *Geer* is today overruled.

A.

Geer sustained against a Commerce Clause challenge a statute forbidding the transportation beyond the State of game birds that had been lawfully killed within the State. The decision rested on the holding that no interstate commerce was involved. This conclusion followed in turn from the view that the State had the power, as representative for its citizens, who "owned" in common all wild animals within the State, to control not only the *taking* of game but the *ownership* of game that had been lawfully reduced to possession. By virtue of this power, Connecticut could qualify the ownership of wild game taken within the State by, for example, prohibiting its removal from the State: "The common ownership imports the right to keep the property, if the sovereign so chooses, always within its jurisdiction for every purpose." Accordingly, the State's power to qualify ownership raised serious doubts whether the sale or exchange of wild game constituted "commerce" at all; in any event the Court held that the qualification imposed by the challenged statute removed any transactions involving wild game killed in Connecticut from *interstate* commerce.

Mr. Justice Field and the first Mr. Justice Harlan dissented, rejecting as artificial and formalistic the Court's analysis of "ownership" and "commerce" in wild game. They would have affirmed the State's power to provide for the protection of wild game, but only "so far as such protection ... does not contravene the power of Congress in the regulation of interstate commerce." Their view was that "[w]hen an animal ... is lawfully killed for the purposes of food or other uses of man, it becomes an article of commerce, and its use cannot be limited to the citizens of one state to the exclusion of citizens of another state."

B.

The view of the *Geer* dissenters increasingly prevailed in subsequent cases. Indeed, not only has the *Geer* analysis been rejected when natural resources other than wild game were involved, but even state regulations of wild game have been held subject to the strictures of the Commerce Clause under the pretext of distinctions from *Geer*.

. . .

C.

The case before us is the first in modern times to present facts essentially on all fours with *Geer*. We now conclude that challenges under the Commerce Clause to state regulations of wild animals should be considered according to the same general rule applied to state regulations of other natural resources, and therefore expressly overrule *Geer*. We thus bring our analytical framework into conformity with practical realities. Overruling *Geer* also eliminates the anomaly, created by the decisions distinguishing *Geer*, that statutes imposing the most extreme burdens on interstate commerce (essentially total embargoes) were the most immune from challenge. At the same time, the general rule we adopt in this case makes ample allowance for preserving, in ways not inconsistent with the Commerce Clause, the legitimate state concerns for conservation and protection of wild animals underlying the 19th century legal fiction of state ownership.

II.

We turn then to the question whether the burden imposed on interstate commerce in wild game by § 4–115(B) is permissible under the general rule articulated in our precedents governing other types of commerce. See, e.g., Pike v. Bruce Church, supra, 397 U.S., at 142. . . .

Section 4–115(B) on its face discriminates against interstate commerce. It forbids the transportation of natural minnows out of the State for purposes of sale, and thus "overtly blocks the flow of interstate commerce at [the] State's border." Philadelphia v. New Jersey, supra, 437 U.S., at 624. Such facial discrimination by itself may be a fatal defect, regardless of the State's purpose, because "the evil of protectionism can reside in legislative means as well as legislative ends." Id., at 626. At a minimum such facial discrimination invokes the strictest scrutiny of any purported legitimate local purpose and of the absence of nondiscriminatory alternatives.

Oklahoma argues that § 4–115(B) serves a legitimate local purpose in that it is "readily apparent as a conservation measure." The State's interest in maintaining the ecological balance in state waters by avoiding the removal of inordinate numbers of minnows may well qualify as a legitimate local purpose. . . . But the scope of legitimate state interests in "conservation" is narrower under this analysis than it was under *Geer*. A State may no longer "keep the property, if the sovereign so chooses, always within its jurisdiction for every purpose." Geer v. Connecticut, supra, 161 U.S., at 530. The fiction of state ownership may no longer be used to force those outside the State to bear the full costs of "conserving" the wild animals within its borders when equally effective nondiscriminatory conservation measures are available.

Far from choosing the least discriminatory alternative, Oklahoma has chosen to "conserve" its minnows in the way that most overtly discriminates against interstate commerce. The State places no limits on the numbers of minnows that can be taken by licensed minnow dealers; nor does it limit in any way how these minnows may be disposed of within the State. Yet it forbids the transportation of any commercially significant number of natural minnows out of the State for sale. Section 4–115(B) is certainly not a "last ditch" attempt at conservation after nondiscriminatory alternatives have proven unfeasible. It is rather a choice of the most discriminatory means even though nondiscriminatory alternatives would seem likely to fulfill the State's purported legitimate local purpose more effectively.

We therefore hold that § 4–115(B) is repugnant to the Commerce Clause.

III.

The overruling of *Geer* does not leave the States powerless to protect and conserve wild animal life within their borders. Today's decision makes clear, however, that States may promote this legitimate purpose only in ways consistent with the basic principle that "our economic unit is the Nation," H.P. Hood & Sons, Inc. v. Du Mond, supra, 336 U.S., at 537, and that when a wild animal "becomes an article of commerce . . . its use cannot be limited to the citizens of one State to the exclusion of citizens of another State." Geer v. Connecticut, supra, 161 U.S., at 538 (Field, J., dissenting).

Reversed.[a]

---

[a] Apparently Oklahoma did not argue nor did the Court consider the relevance of 16 U.S.C. § 852 making it unlawful for any person knowingly "to transport . . . in interstate or foreign commerce, any black bass and other fish, if such . . . transportation is

Mr. Justice Rehnquist, with whom the Chief Justice joins, dissenting. . . .

Contrary to the view of the Court, I do not think that Oklahoma's regulation of the commercial exploitation of natural minnows either discriminates against out-of-state enterprises in favor of local businesses or that it burdens the interstate commerce in minnows. At least, no such showing has been made on the record before us. . . . This is not a case where a State's regulation permits residents to export naturally seined minnows but prohibits nonresidents from so doing. No person is allowed to export natural minnows for sale outside of Oklahoma; the statute is evenhanded in its application. See Okla.Stat., Tit. 29, § 4–115(B). The State has not used its power to protect its own citizens from outside competition. . . . Nor is this a case where a State requires a nonresident business, as a condition to exporting minnows, to move a significant portion of its operations to the State or to use certain State resources in pursuit of its business for the benefit of the local economy. . . . And, notwithstanding the Court's protestations to the contrary, Oklahoma has not blocked the flow of interstate commerce in minnows at the State's borders. . . . Petitioner, or anyone else, may freely export as many minnows as he wishes, so long as the minnows so transported are hatchery minnows and not naturally seined minnows. On this record, I simply fail to see how interstate commerce in minnows, the commodity at issue here, is impeded in the least by Oklahoma's regulatory scheme.

Oklahoma does regulate the manner in which both residents and nonresidents procure minnows to be sold outside the State. But there is no showing in this record that requiring petitioner to purchase his minnows from hatcheries instead of from persons licensed to seine minnows from the State's waters in any way increases petitioner's costs of doing business. There also is nothing in the record to indicate that naturally seined minnows are any more desirable as items of commerce than hatchery minnows. So far as the record before us indicates, hatchery minnows and naturally seined minnows are fungible. Accordingly, any minimal burden that may result from requiring petitioner to purchase minnows destined for sale out of state from hatcheries instead of from those licensed to seine minnows is, in my view, more than outweighed by Oklahoma's substantial interest in conserving and regulating exploitation of its natural minnow population. I therefore would affirm the judgment of the Oklahoma Court of Criminal Appeals.

NEW ENGLAND POWER CO. v. NEW HAMPSHIRE, 455 U.S. 331 (1982). A power company generated large amounts of power in New Hampshire and sold most of it in other states. The state attempted to apply to this utility a statute that required corporations engaged in power production by water to obtain a commission order permitting them to do so and empowering the commission to deny a permit when it determines that the energy "is reasonably required for use within this state and that the public good requires that it be delivered for such use." The Supreme Court held the statute invalid. "Our cases consistently have held that the Commerce Clause . . . precludes a State from mandating that its residents be given a preferred right of access, over out-of-state consumers, to natural resources located within its borders or to the products derived therefrom. . . .

contrary to the law of the State . . . from which such black bass is transported." See Hellerstein, Hughes v. Oklahoma: The Court, The Commerce Clause, and State Control of Natural Resources, 1979 Sup.Ct.Rev. 51, 54. For an application of that Act to enforce a state ban on the export of fish, see United States v. Howard, 352 U.S. 212 (1957).

"The order of the New Hampshire Commission, prohibiting New England Power from selling its hydroelectric energy outside the State of New Hampshire is precisely the sort of protectionist regulation that the Commerce Clause declares off-limits to the States. The Commission has made it clear that its order is designed to gain an economic advantage for New Hampshire citizens at the expense of New England Power's customers in neighboring States. Moreover, it cannot be disputed that the Commission's 'exportation ban' places direct and substantial burdens on transactions in interstate commerce.... Such state-imposed burdens cannot be squared with the Commerce Clause when they serve only to advance 'simple economic protectionism.' "

The Court then went on to hold that the Federal Power Act did not permit the state to impose such a ban.

SPORHASE v. NEBRASKA, 458 U.S. 941 (1982). Appellants jointly own contiguous tracts of land in Nebraska and Colorado. A well physically located on the Nebraska tract pumps ground water used for irrigation in both the Nebraska and Colorado tracts. Appellants did not seek a permit pursuant to a Nebraska statute which requires a permit to transport ground water taken in the state for use in another state and specifies that the permit should be granted only if the withdrawal of ground water "is reasonable, is not contrary to the conservation and use of ground water, and is not otherwise detrimental to the public welfare" and if the state in which the water is used grants reciprocal rights to withdraw water for use in Nebraska. Nebraska brought suit in the state court to enjoin appellants from transferring the water across the border without a permit. The Nebraska trial court granted the injunction and the Nebraska Supreme Court affirmed.

The Supreme Court invalidated the statutory reciprocity requirement. In the first part of Justice Stevens' opinion, the Court concluded that ground water is an article of commerce and that "[g]round water overdraft is a national problem and Congress has the power to deal with it on that scale." In a third part of the opinion the Court held that Congress had not affirmatively authorized the state to impose otherwise impermissible burdens on interstate commerce in ground water.

In the opinion's middle section the Court appeared to say that only the reciprocity requirement was invalid and the remainder would survive if the state court found the invalid provision separable. Opening its discussion with the standard quotation from *Pike v. Bruce Church, Inc.,* the Court then said:

"The only purpose that appellee advances ... is to conserve and preserve diminishing sources of ground water. The purpose is unquestionably legitimate and highly important, and the other aspects of Nebraska's ground water regulation demonstrate that it is genuine.... [S]pecial rules and regulations governing ground water withdrawal and use [apply in] 'critical' ... townships, [and] appellants' Nebraska tract is located within a critical township.... They ... strictly limit the intrastate transfer of ground water: transfers are only permitted between lands controlled by the same ground water user, and all transfers must be approved by the district board of directors.

"The State's interest in conservation and preservation of ground water is advanced by the first three conditions ... for the withdrawal of water for an interstate transfer.... Although Commerce Clause concerns are implicated by the fact that [the statute] applies to interstate transfers but not to intrastate transfers, there are legitimate reasons for the special treatment accorded requests to transport ground water across state lines. Obviously, a State that imposes severe withdrawal and use restrictions on its own citizens is not discriminating against interstate commerce when it seeks to prevent the uncontrolled transfer of water out of the State. An exemption for interstate transfers would be inconsistent with the ideal of evenhandedness in regulation. At least in the area in which appellants' Nebraska tract is located, the first three standards ... may well be no more strict in application than the limitations upon intrastate transfers. ...

"Moreover, in the absence of a contrary view expressed by Congress, we are reluctant to condemn as unreasonable measures taken by a State to conserve and preserve for its own citizens this vital resource in times of severe shortage. Our reluctance stems from the 'confluence of [several] realities.' Hicklin v. Orbeck, 437 U.S. 518, 534 (1978). First, a State's power to regulate the use of water in times and places of shortage for the purpose of protecting the health of its citizens—and not simply the health of its economy—is at the core of its police power. For Commerce Clause purposes, we have long recognized a difference between economic protectionism, on the one hand, and health and safety regulation, on the other. See H.P. Hood & Sons v. Du Mond, 336 U.S. 525, 533 (1949). Second, the legal expectation that under certain circumstances each State may restrict water within its borders has been fostered over the years not only by our equitable apportionment decrees, see, e.g., Wyoming v. Colorado, 353 U.S. 953 (1957), but also by the negotiation and enforcement of interstate compacts. Our law therefore has recognized the relevance of state boundaries in the allocation of scarce water resources. Third, although appellee's claim to public ownership of Nebraska ground water cannot justify a total denial of federal regulatory power, it may support a limited preference for its own citizens in the utilization of the resource. See Hicklin v. Orbeck, supra, at 533–534. In this regard, it is relevant that appellee's claim is logically more substantial than claims to public ownership of other natural resources. Finally, given appellee's conservation efforts, the continuing availability of ground water in Nebraska is not simply happenstance; the natural resource has some indicia of a good publicly produced and owned in which a State may favor its own citizens in times of shortage. See Reeves, Inc. v. Stake, 447 U.S. 429 (1980). ... A facial examination of the [statute's] first three conditions ... does not, therefore, indicate that they impermissibly burden interstate commerce. Appellants, indeed, seem to concede their reasonableness.

"Appellants, however, do challenge the [reciprocity] requirement. ... Because Colorado forbids the exportation of its ground water, the reciprocity provision operates as an explicit barrier to commerce between the two States. The State therefore bears the initial burden of demonstrating a close fit between the reciprocity requirement and its asserted local purpose.

"The reciprocity requirement fails to clear this initial hurdle. For there is no evidence that this restriction is narrowly tailored to the conservation and preservation rationale. Even though the supply of water in a particular well may be abundant, or perhaps even excessive, and even though the most beneficial use of that water might be in another State, such water may not be shipped into a neighboring State that does not permit its water to be used in Nebraska. If it could be shown that the State as a whole suffers a water shortage, that the intrastate transportation of water from areas of abundance to areas of shortage is feasible regardless of distance, and that the importation of water from adjoining States would roughly compensate for any exportation to those States, then the conservation and preservation purpose might be credibly advanced for the reciprocity provision. A demonstrably arid state conceivably might be able to marshall evidence to establish a close means-end relationship between even a total ban on the exportation of water and a purpose to conserve and preserve water. Appellee, however, does not claim that such evidence exists. We therefore are not persuaded that the reciprocity requirement—when superimposed on the first three restrictions in the statute—significantly advances the State's legitimate conservation and preservation interest; it surely is not narrowly tailored to serve that purpose. The reciprocity requirement does not survive the 'strictest scrutiny' reserved for facially discriminatory legislation.''

Justices Rehnquist and O'Connor dissented.

MAINE v. TAYLOR, 477 U.S. 131 (1986). The Supreme Court sustained the constitutionality of a Maine statute prohibiting the importation of live baitfish, despite insisting that the ban "is constitutional only if it satisfies the requirements ordinarily applied under *Hughes v. Oklahoma* to local regulation that discriminates against interstate trade: the statute must serve a legitimate local purpose, and the purpose must be one that cannot be served as well by available nondiscriminatory means." For the Court, Justice Blackmun said in part:

III

"The District Court found after an evidentiary hearing that both parts of the *Hughes* test were satisfied, but the Court of Appeals disagreed. We conclude that the Court of Appeals erred in setting aside the findings of the District Court....

A

"The evidentiary hearing on which the District Court based its conclusions was one before a magistrate.... [Maine's] experts testified that live baitfish imported into the State posed two significant threats to Maine's unique and fragile fisheries. First, Maine's population of wild fish—including its own indigenous golden shiners—would be placed at risk by three types of parasites prevalent in out-of-state baitfish, but not common to wild fish in Maine. Second, non-native species inadvertently included in shipments of live baitfish could disturb Maine's aquatic ecology to an unpredictable extent by competing with native fish for food or habitat, by preying on native species, or by disrupting the environment in more subtle ways.

"The[se] experts further testified that there was no satisfactory way to inspect shipments of live baitfish for parasites or commingled species....

"Appellee's expert denied that any scientific justification supported Maine's total ban on the importation of baitfish....

"Weighing all the testimony, the magistrate concluded that both prongs of the *Hughes* test were satisfied.... [T]he District Court, after an independent review of the evidence, reached the same conclusions. First, the court found that Maine 'clearly has a legitimate and substantial purpose in prohibiting the importation of live bait fish,' because 'substantial uncertainties' surrounded the effects that baitfish parasites would have on the State's unique population of wild fish, and the consequences of introducing non-native species were similarly unpredictable.... Second, the court concluded that less discriminatory means of protecting against these threats were currently unavailable, and that, in particular, testing procedures for baitfish parasites had not yet been devised....

"Although the Court of Appeals did not expressly set aside the District Court's finding of a legitimate local purpose, it noted that several factors 'cast doubt' on that finding.... First, Maine was apparently the only State to bar all importation of live baitfish. Second, Maine accepted interstate shipments of other freshwater fish, subject to an inspection requirement. Third, 'an aura of economic protectionism' surrounded statements made in 1981 by the Maine Department of Inland Fisheries and Wildlife in opposition to a proposal by appellee himself to repeal the ban.... Finally, the court noted that parasites and non-native species could be transported into Maine in shipments of non-baitfish, and that nothing prevented fish from simply swimming into the State from New Hampshire.

"Despite these indications of protectionist intent, the Court of Appeals rested its invalidation of Maine's import ban on a different basis, concluding that Maine had not demonstrated that any legitimate local purpose served by the ban could not be promoted equally well without discriminating so heavily against interstate commerce. Specifically, the court found it 'difficult to reconcile' Maine's claim that it could not rely on sampling and inspection with the State's reliance on similar procedures in the case of other freshwater fish.

. . .

B

"Although the proffered justification for any local discrimination against interstate commerce must be subjected to 'the strictest scrutiny,' Hughes v. Oklahoma, 441 U.S., at 337, the empirical component of that scrutiny, like any other form of factfinding, 'is the basic responsibility of district courts, rather than appellate courts,' Pullman–Standard v. Swint, 456 U.S. 273, 291 (1982).... [A]ppellate courts are not to decide factual questions *de novo*, reversing any findings they would have made differently.... [N]o broader review is authorized here simply because this is a constitutional case, or because the factual findings at issue may determine the outcome of the case....

"No matter how one describes the abstract issue whether 'alternative means could promote this local purpose as well without discriminating against interstate commerce,' Hughes v. Oklahoma, 441 U.S., at 336, the more specific question whether scientifically accepted techniques exist for the sampling and inspection of live baitfish is one of fact, and the District Court's finding that such techniques have not been devised cannot be characterized as clearly erroneous. Indeed, the record probably could not support a contrary finding....

. . .

"More importantly, we agree with the District Court that the 'abstract possibility,' of developing acceptable testing procedures, particularly when there is no assurance as to their effectiveness, does not make those procedures an '[a]vailable ... nondiscriminatory alternativ[e],' *Hunt*, 432 U.S., at 353, for purposes of the Commerce Clause. A State must make reasonable efforts to avoid restraining the free flow of commerce across its borders, but it is not required to develop new and unproven means of protection at an uncertain cost. Appellee, of course, is free to work on his own or in conjunction with other bait dealers to develop scientifically acceptable sampling and inspection procedures for golden shiners; if and when such procedures are developed, Maine no longer may be able to justify its import ban. The State need not join in those efforts, however, and it need not pretend they already have succeeded.

C

"Although the Court of Appeals did not expressly overturn the District Court's finding that Maine's import ban serves a legitimate local purpose, appellee argues as an alternative ground for affirmance that this finding should be rejected. After reviewing the expert testimony presented to the magistrate, however, we cannot say that the District Court clearly erred in finding that substantial scientific uncertainty surrounds the effect that baitfish parasites and non-native species could have on Maine's fisheries. Moreover, we agree with the District Court that Maine has a legitimate interest in guarding against imperfectly understood environmental risks, despite the possibility that they may ultimately prove to be negligible....

"Nor do we think that much doubt is cast on the legitimacy of Maine's purposes by what the Court of Appeals took to be signs of protectionist intent. Shielding in-state industries from out-of-state competition is almost never a legitimate local purpose, and state laws that amount to 'simple economic protectionism' consequently have been subject to a 'virtually *per se* rule of invalidity.' Philadelphia v. New Jersey, 437 U.S. 617, 624 (1978); accord, e.g., Minnesota v. Clover Leaf Creamery Co., 449 U.S. 456, 471 (1981).[19] But there is little reason in this case to believe that the legitimate justifications the State has put forward for its statute are merely a sham or a '*post hoc* rationalization.' *Hughes*, 441 U.S., at 338, n. 20. [T]he Court of Appeals relied heavily on a 3–sentence passage near the end of a 2000–word statement submitted in 1981 by the Maine Department of Inland Fisheries and Wildlife in opposition to appellee's proposed repeal of the State's ban on the importation of live baitfish.... As the magistrate pointed out, the context of the statements ... 'reveals [they] are advanced not in direct support of the statute, but to counter the argument that inadequate bait supplies in Maine requires acceptance of the environmental risks of imports. Instead, the Department argues, Maine's own bait supplies can be increased.' Furthermore, the comments were made by a state administrative agency long after the statute's enactment, and thus constitute weak evidence of legislative intent in any event.

"The other evidence of protectionism identified by the Court of Appeals is no more persuasive. The fact that Maine allows importation of salmonids, for which standardized sampling and inspection procedures are available, hardly demonstrates that Maine has no legitimate interest in prohibiting the importation of baitfish, for which such procedures have not yet been devised. Nor is this demonstrated by the fact that other States may not have enacted similar bans, especially given the testimony that Maine's fisheries are unique and unusually fragile. Finally, it is of little relevance that fish can swim directly into Maine from New Hampshire. As the magistrate explained: 'The impediments to complete success ... cannot be a ground for preventing a state from using its best efforts to limit [an environmental] risk.'

IV

"The Commerce Clause ... does not elevate free trade above all other values.... The evidence in this case amply supports the District Court's findings that Maine's ban on the importation of live baitfish serves legitimate local purposes that could not adequately be served by available nondiscriminatory alternatives."

In dissent, Justice Stevens said:

[19] ...[However,] even overt discrimination against interstate trade may be justified where, as in this case, out-of-state goods or services are particularly likely for some reason to threaten the health and safety of a State's citizens or the integrity of its natural resources, and where 'outright prohibition of entry, rather than some intermediate form of regulation, is the only effective method of protecti[on].' Lewis v. BT Investment Managers, Inc., 447 U.S. 27, 43 (1980).

"There is something fishy about this case. Maine is the only State in the Union that blatantly discriminates against out-of-state baitfish by flatly prohibiting their importation. Although golden shiners are already present and thriving in Maine (and, perhaps not coincidentally, the subject of a flourishing domestic industry), Maine excludes golden shiners grown and harvested (and, perhaps not coincidentally, sold) in other States. This kind of stark discrimination against out-of-state articles of commerce requires rigorous justification by the discriminating State....

"... Since the State engages in obvious discrimination against out-of-state commerce, it should be put to its proof. Ambiguity about dangers and alternatives should actually defeat, rather than sustain, the discriminatory measure.

"This is not to derogate the State's interest in ecological purity. But the invocation of environmental protection or public health has never been thought to confer some kind of special dispensation from the general principle of nondiscrimination in interstate commerce.... If Maine wishes to rely on its interest in ecological preservation, it must show that interest, and the infeasibility of other alternatives, with far greater specificity. Otherwise, it must further that asserted interest in a manner far less offensive to the notions of comity and cooperation that underlie the Commerce Clause.

"... Maine's unquestionable natural splendor notwithstanding, the State has not carried its substantial burden of proving why it cannot meet its environmental concerns in the same manner as other States with the same interest in the health of their fish and ecology...."

D. PRESERVING STATE–OWNED RESOURCES FOR IN–STATE USE

Reeves, Inc. v. Stake

447 U.S. 429, 100 S.Ct. 2271, 65 L.Ed.2d 244 (1980).

Mr. Justice Blackmun delivered the opinion of the Court.

The issue in this case is whether, consistent with the Commerce Clause, U.S. Const., Art. I, § 8, ch. 3, the State of South Dakota, in a time of shortage, may confine the sale of the cement it produces solely to its residents.

I.

In 1919, South Dakota undertook plans to build a cement plant. The project, a product of the State's then prevailing Progressive political movement, was initiated in response to recent regional cement shortages that "interfered with and delayed both public and private enterprises," and that were "threatening the people of this state." Eakin v. South Dakota State Cement Comm'n, 44 S.D. 268, 272, 183 N.W. 651, 652 (1921). In 1920, the South Dakota Cement Commission anticipated "[t]hat there would be a ready market for the entire output of the plant within the state." Report of State Cement Commission 9 (1920). The plant, however, located at Rapid City, soon produced more cement than South Dakotans could use. Over the years, buyers in no less than nine nearby States purchased cement from the State's plant. Between 1970 and 1977, some 40% of the plant's output went outside the State.

The plant's list of out-of-state cement buyers included petitioner Reeves, Inc. Reeves is a ready-mix concrete distributor organized under Wyoming law and with facilities in Buffalo, Gillette, and Sheridan, Wyo. From the beginning of its operations in 1958, and until 1978, Reeves purchased about 95% of its cement from the South Dakota plant. In 1977, its purchases were $1,172,000. In turn, Reeves has supplied three northwestern Wyoming counties with more than half their ready-mix concrete needs. For 20 years the relationship between Reeves and the South Dakota cement plant was amicable, uninterrupted, and mutually profitable.

As the 1978 construction season approached, difficulties at the plant slowed production. Meanwhile, a booming construction industry spurred demand for cement both regionally and nationally. The plant found itself unable to meet all orders. Faced with the same type of "serious cement shortage" that inspired the plant's construction, the Commission "reaffirmed its policy of supplying all South Dakota customers first and to honor all contract commitments, with the remaining volume allocated on a first come, first served basis."

Reeves, which had no pre-existing long-term supply contract, was hit hard and quickly by this development. On June 30, 1978, the plant informed Reeves that it could not continue to fill Reeves' orders, and on July 5, it turned away a Reeves truck. Unable to find another supplier, Reeves was forced to cut production by 76% in mid-July.

On July 19, Reeves brought this suit against the Commission, challenging the plant's policy of preferring South Dakota buyers, and seeking injunctive relief. After conducting a hearing and receiving briefs and affidavits, the District Court found no substantial issue of material fact and permanently enjoined the Commission's practice. The court reasoned that South Dakota's "hoarding" was inimical to the national free market envisioned by the Commerce Clause.

The United States Court of Appeals for the Eighth Circuit reversed. . . . We granted Reeves' petition for certiorari to consider once again the impact of the Commerce Clause on state proprietary activity. 444 U.S. 1031 (1980).

II.

A.

[Hughes v.] Alexandria Scrap [Corp., 426 U.S. 794 (1976)] concerned a Maryland program designed to remove abandoned automobiles from the State's roadways and junkyards. To encourage recycling, a "bounty" was offered for every Maryland-titled junk car converted into scrap. Processors located both in and outside Maryland were eligible to collect these subsidies. The legislation, as initially enacted in 1969, required a processor seeking a bounty to present documentation evidencing ownership of the wrecked car. This requirement however, did not apply to "hulks," inoperable automobiles over eight years old. In 1974, the statute was amended to extend documentation requirements to hulks, which comprised a large majority of the junk cars being processed. Departing from prior practice, the new law imposed more exacting documentation requirements on out-of-state than in-state processors. By making it less remunerative for suppliers to transfer vehicles outside Maryland, the reform triggered a "precipitate decline in the number of bounty-eligible hulks supplied to appellee's [Virginia] plant from Maryland sources." 426 U.S., at 801. Indeed, "[t]he practical effect was substantially the same as if Maryland had withdrawn altogether the availability of bounties on hulks delivered by unlicensed suppliers to licensed non-Maryland processors." Id., at 803, n. 13; see id., at 819 (dissenting opinion).

Invoking the Commerce Clause, a three-judge District Court struck down the legislation. 391 F.Supp. 46 (Md.1975). It observed that the amendment imposed "substantial burdens upon the free flow of interstate commerce," id., at 62, and reasoned that the discriminatory program was not the least disruptive means of achieving the State's articulated objective. Id., at 63. See generally Pike v. Bruce Church, Inc., 397 U.S. 137, 142 (1970).

This Court reversed. It recognized the persuasiveness of the lower court's analysis if the inherent restrictions of the Commerce Clause were deemed applicable. In the Court's view, however, *Alexandria Scrap* did not involve "the kind of action with which the Commerce Clause is concerned." 426 U.S., at 805. Unlike prior cases voiding state laws inhibiting interstate trade, "Maryland has not sought to prohibit the flow of hulks, or to regulate the conditions under which it may occur. Instead, it has entered into the market itself to bid up their price," id., at 806, "as a purchaser, in effect, of a potential article of interstate commerce," and has restricted "its trade to its own citizens or businesses within the State." Id., at 808.

Having characterized Maryland as a market participant, rather than as a market regulator, the Court found no reason to "believe the Commerce Clause was intended to require independent justification for [the State's] action." Id., at 809. The Court couched its holding in unmistakably broad terms. "Nothing in the purposes animating the Commerce Clause prohibits a State, in the absence of congressional action, from participating in the market and exercising the right to favor its own citizens over others." Id., at 810 (footnote omitted).

B.

The basic distinction drawn in *Alexandria Scrap* between States as market participants and States as market regulators makes good sense and sound law. As that case explains, the Commerce Clause responds principally to state taxes and regulatory measures impeding free private trade in the national marketplace. 426 U.S., at 807–808, citing H.P. Hood & Sons v. Du Mond, 336 U.S. 525, 539 (1949) (referring to "home embargoes," "customs duties," and "regulations" excluding imports). There is no indication of a constitutional plan to limit the ability of the States themselves to operate freely in the free market. See L. Tribe, American Constitutional Law 336 (1978) ("the commerce clause was directed, as an historical matter, only at regulatory and taxing actions taken by states in their sovereign capacity"). The precedents comport with this distinction.

Restraint in this area is also counseled by considerations of state sovereignty,[10] the role of each State " 'as guardian and trustee for its people,' " Heim v. McCall, 239 U.S. 175, 191 (1915), quoting Atkin v. Kansas, 191 U.S. 207, 222–223 (1903), and "the long recognized right of trader or manufacturer, engaged in an entirely private business, freely to exercise his own independent discretion as to parties with whom he will deal." United States v. Colgate & Co., 250 U.S. 300, 307 (1919). Moreover, state proprietary activities may be, and often are, burdened with the same restrictions imposed on private market participants. Evenhandedness suggests that, when acting as proprietors, States should similarly share existing freedoms from federal constraints, including the inherent limits of the Commerce Clause.... Finally, as this case illustrates, the

---

[10] ...Considerations of sovereignty independently dictate that marketplace actions involving "integral operations in areas of traditional governmental functions"—such as the employment of certain state workers—may not be subject even to congressional regulation pursuant to the commerce power. National League of Cities v. Usery, 426 U.S. 833, 852 (1976). It follows easily that the intrinsic limits of the Commerce Clause do not prohibit state marketplace conduct that falls within this sphere. Even where "integral operations" are not implicated, States may fairly claim some measure of a sovereign interest in retaining freedom to decide how, with whom, and for whose benefit to deal. The Supreme Court, 1975 Term, 90 Harv. L.Rev. 56, 63 (1976).

competing considerations in cases involving state proprietary action often will be subtle, complex, politically charged, and difficult to assess under traditional Commerce Clause analysis. Given these factors, *Alexandria Scrap* wisely recognizes that, as a rule, the adjustment of interests in this context is a task better suited for Congress than this Court.

III.

South Dakota, as a seller of cement, unquestionably fits the "market participant" label more comfortably than a State acting to subsidize local scrap processors. Thus, the general rule of *Alexandria Scrap* plainly applies here. Petitioner argues, however, that the exemption for marketplace participation necessarily admits of exceptions. While conceding that possibility, we perceive in this case no sufficient reason to depart from the general rule.

A.

In finding a Commerce Clause violation, the District Court emphasized "that the Commission ... made an election to become part of the interstate commerce system." The gist of this reasoning, repeated by petitioner here, is that one good turn deserves another. Having long exploited the interstate market, South Dakota should not be permitted to withdraw from it when a shortage arises. This argument is not persuasive. It is somewhat self-serving to say that South Dakota has "exploited" the interstate market. An equally fair characterization is that neighboring States long have benefited from South Dakota's foresight and industry. Viewed in this light, it is not surprising that *Alexandria Scrap* rejected an argument that the 1974 Maryland legislation challenged there was invalid because cars abandoned in Maryland had been processed in neighboring States for five years. As in *Alexandria Scrap,* we must conclude that "this chronology does not distinguish the case, for Commerce Clause purposes, from one in which a State offered [cement] only to domestic [buyers] from the start." 426 U.S., at 809.

Our rejection of petitioner's market-exploitation theory fundamentally refocuses analysis. It means that to reverse we would have to void a South Dakota "residents only" policy even if it had been enforced from the plant's very first days. Such a holding, however, would interfere significantly with a State's ability to structure relations exclusively with its own citizens. It would also threaten the future fashioning of effective and creative programs for solving local problems and distributing government largesse. A healthy regard for federalism and good government renders us reluctant to risk these results....

B.

Undaunted by these considerations, petitioner advances four more arguments for reversal:

First, petitioner protests that South Dakota's preference for its residents responds solely to the "non-governmental objective[ ]"of protectionism. Therefore, petitioner argues, the policy is *per se* invalid. See Philadelphia v. New Jersey, 437 U.S. 617, 624 (1978).

We find the label "protectionism" of little help in this context. The State's refusal to sell to buyers other than South Dakotans is "protectionist" only in the sense that it limits benefits generated by a state program to those who fund the state treasury and whom the State was created to serve. Petitioner's argument apparently also would characterize as "protectionist" rules restricting to state residents the enjoyment of state educational institutions, energy generated by a state-run plant, police and fire protection, and agricultural improvement and business development programs. Such policies, while perhaps "protectionist" in a loose sense, reflect the essential and patently unobjectionable purpose of state government—to serve the citizens of the State.

Second, petitioner echoes the District Court's warning:

> "If a state in this union, were allowed to hoard its commodities or resources for the use of their own residents only, a drastic situation might evolve. For example, Pennsylvania or Wyoming might keep their coal, the northwest its timber, and the mining states their minerals. The result being that embargo may be retaliated by embargo and commerce would be halted at state lines."

See, e.g., Baldwin v. Montana Fish & Game Comm'n, 436 U.S. 371, 385–386 (1978). This argument, although rooted in the core purpose of the Commerce Clause, does not fit the present facts. Cement is not a natural resource, like coal, timber, wild game, or minerals. Cf. Hughes v. Oklahoma, 441 U.S. 322 (1979) (minnows); Philadelphia v. New Jersey, supra (landfill sites); Pennsylvania v. West Virginia, 262 U.S. 553 (1923) (natural gas); West v. Kansas Natural Gas Co., 221 U.S. 229 (1911) (same); Note, 32 Rutgers L.Rev. 741 (1979). It is the end-product of a complex process whereby a costly physical plant and human labor act on raw materials. South Dakota has not sought to limit access to the State's limestone or other materials used to make cement. Nor has it restricted the ability of private firms or sister States to set up plants within its borders. Moreover, petitioner has not suggested that South Dakota possesses unique access to the materials needed to produce cement. Whatever limits might exist on a State's ability to invoke the *Alexandria Scrap* exemption to hoard resources which by happenstance are found there, those limits do not apply here.

Third, it is suggested that the South Dakota program is infirm because it places South Dakota suppliers of ready-mix concrete at a competitive advantage in the out-of-state market; Wyoming suppliers, such as petitioner, have little chance against South Dakota suppliers who can purchase cement from the State's plant and freely sell beyond South Dakota's borders.

The force of this argument is seriously diminished, if not eliminated, by several considerations. The argument necessarily implies that the South Dakota scheme would be unobjectionable if sales in other States were totally barred. It therefore proves too much, for it would tolerate even a greater measure of protectionism and stifling of interstate commerce than the challenged system allows.... Nor is it to be forgotten that *Alexandria Scrap* approved a state program that "not only ... effectively protect[ed] scrap processors with existing plants in Maryland from the pressures of competitors with nearby out-of-state plants, but [that] implicitly offer[ed] to extend similar protection to any competitor ... willing to erect a scrap processing facility within Maryland's boundaries." 391 F.Supp., at 63. Finally, the competitive plight of out-of-state ready-mix suppliers cannot be laid solely at the feet of South Dakota. It is attributable as well to their own States' not providing or attracting alternative sources of supply and to the suppliers' own failure to guard against shortages by executing long-term supply contracts with the South Dakota plant.

In its last argument, petitioner urges that, had South Dakota not acted, free market forces would have generated an appropriate level of supply at free market prices for all buyers in the region. Having replaced free market forces, South Dakota should be forced to replicate how the free market would have operated under prevailing conditions.

This argument appears to us to be simplistic and speculative. The very reason South Dakota built its plant was because the free market had failed adequately to supply the region with cement. There is no indication, and no way to know, that private industry would have moved into petitioner's market area, and would have ensured a supply of cement to petitioner either prior to or during the 1978 construction season. Indeed, it is quite possible that petitioner would never have existed—far less operated successfully for 20 years—had it not been for South Dakota cement.

C.

We conclude, then, that the arguments for invalidating South Dakota's resident-preference program are weak at best. Whatever residual force inheres in them is more than offset by countervailing considerations of policy and fairness. Reversal would discourage similar state projects, even though this project demonstrably has served the needs of state residents and has helped the entire region for more than a half century. Reversal also would rob South Dakota of the intended benefit of its foresight, risk, and industry. Under these circumstances, there is no reason to depart from the general rule of *Alexandria Scrap.*

The judgment of the United States Court of Appeals is affirmed.

It is so ordered.

Mr. Justice Powell, with whom Mr. Justice Brennan, Mr. Justice White, and Mr. Justice Stevens join, dissenting.

The South Dakota Cement Commission has ordered that in times of shortage the state cement plant must turn away out-of-state customers until all orders from South Dakotans are filled. This policy represents precisely the kind of economic protectionism that the Commerce Clause was intended to prevent. The Court, however, finds no violation of the Commerce Clause, solely because the State produces the cement. I agree with the Court that the State of South Dakota may provide cement for its public needs without violating the Commerce Clause. But I cannot agree that South Dakota may withhold its cement from interstate commerce in order to benefit private citizens and businesses within the State.

. . .

I share the Court's desire to preserve state sovereignty. But the Commerce Clause long has been recognized as a limitation on that sovereignty, consciously designed to maintain a national market and defeat economic provincialism. The Court today approves protectionist state policies. In the absence of contrary congressional action, those policies now can be implemented as long as the State itself directly participates in the market.

By enforcing the Commerce Clause in this case, the Court would work no unfairness on the people of South Dakota. They still could reserve cement for public projects and share in whatever return the plant generated. They could not, however, use the power of the State to furnish themselves with cement forbidden to the people of neighboring States.

The creation of a free national economy was a major goal of the States when they resolved to unite under the Federal Constitution. The decision today cannot be reconciled with that purpose.

White v. Massachusetts Council of Construction Employers, Inc.

460 U.S. 204, 103 S.Ct. 1042, 75 L.Ed.2d 1 (1983).

Justice Rehnquist delivered the opinion of the Court.

In 1979 the mayor of Boston, Massachusetts, issued an executive order which required that all construction projects funded in whole or in part by city funds, or funds which the city had the authority to administer, should be performed by a work force consisting of at least half *bona fide* residents of Boston. The Supreme Judicial Court of Massachusetts decided that the order was unconstitutional, observing that the Commerce Clause "presents a clear obstacle to the city's order." 384 Mass. 466, 425 N.E.2d 346 (1981). We granted certiorari to decide whether the Commerce Clause of the United States Constitution, Art. I, § 8, cl. 3, prevents the city from giving effect to the mayor's order. 455 U.S. 919 (1982). We now conclude that it does not and reverse.

I

. . .

Alexandria Scrap and *Reeves* . . . stand for the proposition that when a state or local government enters the market as a participant it is not subject to the restraints of the Commerce Clause. As we said in *Reeves,* in this kind of case there is "a single inquiry: whether the challenged 'program constituted direct state participation in the market.'" Id., at 436, n. 7. We reaffirm that principle now.

The Supreme Judicial Court of Massachusetts concluded that the City of Boston is not participating in the market in the sense described in *Alexandria Scrap Corp.* and *Reeves* because the order applies where the city is acting in a nonproprietary capacity, has a significant impact on interstate commerce, is more sweeping than necessary to achieve its objectives, and applies to funds the city receives from federal grants. 384 Mass., at 479–480, 425 N.E.2d, at 354–355. For the same reasons the court found that the city is not a market participant, it concluded that the executive order violated the substantive restraints of the Commerce Clause. Ibid.

II

. . . The only issues before us . . . are the propriety of applying the mayor's executive order to projects funded wholly with city funds and projects funded in part with federal funds. We address first the application of the order to city funded projects.

The Supreme Judicial Court of Massachusetts expressed reservations as to the application of the "market participation" principle to the city here, reasoning that "the implementation of the mayor's order will have a significant impact on those firms which engage in specialized areas of construction and employ permanent works crews composed of out-of-State residents." 384 Mass., at 479, 425 N.E.2d, at 354. Even if this conclusion is factually correct it is not relevant to the inquiry of whether the city is participating in the marketplace when it provides city funds for building construction. If the city is a market participant, then the Commerce Clause establishes no barrier to conditions such as these which the city demands for its participation. Impact on out-of-state residents figures in the equation only after it is decided that the city is regulating the market rather than participating in it, for only in the former case need it be determined whether any burden on interstate commerce is permitted by the Commerce Clause.

. . .

The Supreme Judicial Court of Massachusetts also observed that "a significant percentage of the funds affected by the order are received from Federal sources." 384 Mass., at 479, 425 N.E.2d, at 354. The record does indicate that of approximately $54 million expended on projects affected by the mayor's executive order, some $34 million represented projects being funded in part through Urban Development Action Grants (UDAGs). While the record assigns specific dollar amounts only for UDAGs, the parties also have stipulated that the executive order applies to Community Development Block Grants (CDBGs) and Economic Development Administration Grants (EDAGs).

But all of this proves too much. The Commerce Clause is a grant of authority to Congress, and not a restriction on the authority of that body. See American Power & Light Co. v. SEC, 329 U.S. 90 (1946); Gibbons v. Ogden, 9 Wheat. 1 (1824). Congress, unlike a state legislature authorizing similar expenditures, is not limited by any negative implications of the Commerce Clause in the exercise of its spending power. Where state or local government action is specifically authorized by Congress, it is not subject to the Commerce Clause even if it interferes with interstate commerce. Southern Pacific Co. v. Arizona, 325 U.S. 761, 769 (1945). Thus, if the restrictions imposed by the city on construction projects financed in part by federal funds are directed by Congress then no dormant Commerce Clause issue is presented.

An examination of the applicable statutes reveals that these federal programs were intended to encourage economic revitalization, including improved opportunities for the poor, minorities, and unemployed. Examination of the regulations . . . indicates that the mayor's executive order sounds a harmonious note; the federal regulations for each program affirmatively permit the type of parochial favoritism expressed in the order.

III

We hold that on the record before us the application of the mayor's executive order to the contracts in question did not violate the Commerce Clause of the United States Constitution.[12] Insofar as the city expended only its own funds in entering into construction contracts for public projects, it was a market participant and entitled to be treated as such under the rule of *Hughes v. Alexandria Scrap Corp.*, supra. Insofar as the mayor's executive order was applied to projects funded in part with funds obtained from the federal programs described above, the order was affirmatively sanctioned by the pertinent regulations of those programs. The judgment of the Supreme Judicial Court of Massachusetts is therefore reversed, and the case is remanded to that court for proceedings not inconsistent with this opinion.

It is so ordered.

---

[12] Respondents ask us to decide whether the executive order offends the Privileges and Immunities Clause of Art. IV, § 2, cl. 1, which provides: "The Citizens of each State shall be entitled to all Privileges and Immunities of Citizens in several States." . . .

This question has not been, to any great extent, briefed or argued in this Court. We did not grant certiorari on the issue and remand without passing on its merits. . . . [On the Privileges and Immunities issue, see United Building and Construction Trades Council v. City of Camden, infra p. 341].

Justice Blackmun, with whom Justice White joins, concurring in part and dissenting in part.

. . .

SOUTH-CENTRAL TIMBER DEVELOPMENT v. WUNNICKE, 467 U.S. 82 (1984). Alaska announced that it would sell a large amount of timber owned by the state. A special provision in all of its contracts of sale was a requirement that the purchaser would partially process the timber (primarily by slabbing the logs on at least one side) prior to shipping it outside the state. South–Central Timber was a company which purchased logs and shipped them outside the state without any processing. It brought this action alleging, inter alia, that the processing requirement violated the commerce clause. The state argued that its restrictions on export of unprocessed timber from state-owned lands were exempt from the commerce clause under the market participation doctrine.

A plurality of the Court (Justices White, Brennan, Blackmun, and Stevens) held that the market-participation doctrine did not apply here, saying, in part:

"The limit of the market-participant doctrine must be that it allows a State to impose burdens on commerce within the market in which it is a participant, but allows it to go no further. The State may not impose conditions, whether by statute, regulation, or contract, that have a substantial regulatory effect outside of that particular market.[10] Unless the 'market' is relatively narrowly defined, the doctrine has the potential of swallowing up the rule that States may not impose substantial burdens on interstate commerce even if they act with the permissible state purpose of fostering local industry.

"At the heart of the dispute in this case is disagreement over the definition of the market. Alaska contends that it is participating in the processed timber market, although it acknowledges that it participates in no way in the actual processing. South–Central argues, on the other hand, that although the State may be a participant in the timber market, it is using its leverage in that market to exert a regulatory effect in the processing market, in which it is not a participant. We agree with the latter position.

"There are sound reasons for distinguishing between a State's preferring its own residents in the initial disposition of goods when it is a market participant and a State's attachment of restrictions on dispositions subsequent to the goods coming to rest in private hands. First, simply as a matter of intuition a State market participant has a greater interest as a 'private trader' in the immediate transaction than it has in what its purchaser does with the goods after the State no longer has an interest in them. The common law recognized such a notion in the doctrine of restraints on alienation. . . . Similarly, the antitrust laws place limits on vertical restraints. It is no defense in an action charging vertical trade restraints that the same end could be achieved through vertical integration; if it were, there would be virtually no antitrust scrutiny of vertical arrangements. We reject the contention that a State's action as a market regulator may be upheld against Commerce Clause challenge on

---

[10] The view of the market-participant doctrine expressed by Justice Rehnquist would validate under the Commerce Clause any contractual condition that the State had the economic power to impose, without regard to the relationship of the subject matter of the contract and the condition imposed. If that were the law, it would have been irrelevant that the employees in White v. Massa- chusetts Council of Construction Employers, Inc., 460 U.S. 204 (1983), were in effect "working for the city." If the only question were whether the condition is imposed by contract, a residency requirement could have been imposed with respect to the work force on all projects of any employer doing business with the city.

the ground that the State could achieve the same end as a market participant. We therefore find it unimportant for present purposes that the State could support its processing industry by selling only to Alaska processors, by vertical integration, or by direct subsidy.

"Second, downstream restrictions have a greater regulatory effect than do limitations on the immediate transaction. Instead of merely choosing its own trading partners, the State is attempting to govern the private, separate economic relationships of its trading partners; that is, it restricts the post-purchase activity of the purchaser, rather than merely the purchasing activity. In contrast to the situation in *White*, this restriction on private economic activity takes place after the completion of the parties' direct commercial obligations, rather than during the course of an ongoing commercial relationship in which the city retained a continuing proprietary interest in the subject of the contract. In sum, the State may not avail itself of the market-participant doctrine to immunize its downstream regulation of the timber-processing market in which it is not a participant."

Three justices did not reach this issue. Justice Rehnquist joined by Justice O'Connor dissented, saying:

"The contractual term at issue here no more transforms Alaska's sale of timber into 'regulation' of the processing industry than the resident-hiring preference imposed by the city of Boston in White v. Massachusetts Council of Const. Employers, 460 U.S. 204 (1983), constituted regulation of the construction industry. Alaska is merely paying the buyer of the timber indirectly, by means of a reduced price, to hire Alaska residents to process the timber. Under existing precedent, the State could accomplish that same result in any number of ways. For example, the State could choose to sell its timber only to those companies that maintain active primary-processing plants in Alaska. Reeves, Inc. v. Stake, 447 U.S. 429 (1980). Or the State could directly subsidize the primary-processing industry within the State. Hughes v. Alexandria Scrap Corp., 426 U.S. 794 (1976). The State could even pay to have the logs processed and then enter the market only to sell processed logs. It seems to me unduly formalistic to conclude that the one path chosen by the State as best suited to promote its concerns is the path forbidden it by the Commerce Clause."

NEW ENERGY CO. OF INDIANA v. LIMBACH, 486 U.S. 269 (1988). An Ohio taxing statute awarded a tax credit against the Ohio motor vehicle fuel sales tax for each gallon of ethanol sold (as a component of gasohol) by fuel dealers, but only if the ethanol was produced in Ohio or in a state that granted similar tax advantages to ethanol produced in Ohio. New Energy produced ethanol in Indiana, a state which gave a direct subsidy to local ethanol producers but no tax exemption. New Energy challenged the constitutionality of Ohio imposing a tax on the ethanol it sold in Ohio on grounds that the Ohio tax scheme discriminated against interstate commerce, a contention upheld by the Court. Ohio contended that in any event its tax scheme was valid under the market participant doctrine. The Court responded as follows:

"Appellees contend that even if § 5735.145(B) is discriminatory, the discrimination is not covered by the Commerce Clause because of the so-called market participant doctrine. That doctrine differentiates between a State's acting in its distinctive governmental capacity, and a State's acting in the more general capacity of a market participant; only the former is subject to the limitations of the negative Commerce Clause. See Hughes v. Alexandria Scrap Corp., 426 U.S. 794, 806–810 (1976). Thus, for example, when a State chooses to manufacture and sell cement, its business methods, including those that favor its residents, are of no greater constitutional concern than those of a private business. See Reeves, Inc. v. Stake, 447 U.S. 429, 438–439 (1980).

"The market participant doctrine has no application here. The Ohio action ultimately at issue is neither its purchase nor its sale of ethanol, but its assessment and computation of taxes—a primeval governmental activity. To be sure, the tax credit scheme has the purpose and effect of subsidizing a particular industry, as do many dispositions of the tax laws. That does not transform it into a form of state participation in the free market. Our opinion in *Alexandria Scrap,* supra, a case on which appellees place great reliance, does not remotely establish such a proposition. There we examined, and upheld against Commerce Clause attack on the basis of the market-participant doctrine, a Maryland cash subsidy program that discriminated in favor of in-state auto-hulk processors. The purpose of the program was to achieve the removal of unsightly abandoned autos from the State, 426 U.S., at 796–797, and the Court characterized it as proprietary rather than regulatory activity, based on the analogy of the State to a private purchaser of the auto hulks, id., at 808–810. We have subsequently observed that subsidy programs unlike that of *Alexandria Scrap* might not be characterized as proprietary. See *Reeves, Inc.,* supra, at 440, n. 14. We think it clear that Ohio's assessment and computation of its fuel sales tax, regardless of whether it produces a subsidy, cannot plausibly be analogized to the activity of a private purchaser."

E. LIMITS ON BUSINESS ENTRY

Lewis v. BT Investment Managers, Inc.

447 U.S. 27, 100 S.Ct. 2009, 64 L.Ed.2d 702 (1980).

Mr. Justice Blackmun delivered the opinion of the Court.

. . .

I.

Appellee Bankers Trust New York Corporation (Bankers Trust) is a corporation organized under the laws of the State of New York. It maintains its principal place of business in that State. It is a bank holding company within the meaning of § 2(a) of the Bank Holding Company Act of 1956, 70 Stat. 133, as amended, 12 U.S.C. § 1841(a) (1976 ed. and Supp. II) (the Act). Accordingly, it is subject to federal restrictions on the kinds of subsidiaries it may own or control. . . .

In 1972, the management of Bankers Trust decided to seek the Board [of Governors of the Federal Reserve System's] approval for an investment management subsidiary to operate in Florida. On October 3 of that year, Bankers Trust filed a formal proposal for such a subsidiary, which it planned to operate from offices in Palm Beach. Appellee BT Investment Managers, Inc. (BTIM), was Bankers Trust's intended vehicle for entry into the Florida market. It was incorporated under the laws of the State of Delaware as a wholly owned subsidiary on November 24, 1972. Three days later it qualified to do business in Florida. The application to the Board proposed that BTIM would provide "portfolio investment advice," as well as "general economic information and advice, general economic statistical forecasting services and industry studies" to persons other than banks. . . .

When Bankers Trust filed its application with the Board, certain Florida statutes restricted the ability of out-of-state bank holding companies to compete in the State's financial market. At that time Fla.Stat. § 659.141(1), added by 1972 Fla.Laws, ch. 72–96, § 1, and effective March 28, 1972, prohibited Bankers Trust from owning or controlling a bank or trust company located within the State; the same statute also prohibited it from owning businesses furnishing investment advisory services to local banks or trust companies. In addition, Fla.Stat. § 660.10 prohibited any corporation, other than a state-chartered bank and trust company or a national banking association located in Florida, from performing certain trust and fiduciary functions. Neither statute, however, directly prohibited an out-of-state bank holding company from owning or controlling a business furnishing investment advisory services to the general public. Thus, at the time Bankers Trust filed its application with the Board, it appeared that ownership of BTIM would not violate Florida law, although BTIM would be restricted in the types of financial services it could perform and the customers it could serve.

The reaction of the Florida financial community to Bankers Trust's proposed investment subsidiary was decidedly negative. The State Comptroller, the Florida Bankers Association, and the Palm Beach County Bankers Association, Inc., all filed comments with the Board objecting to the Bankers Trust proposal. More importantly for present purposes, the state legislature was persuaded to take action. On November 30, 1972, shortly after BTIM had qualified to do business in the State, a special session of the legislature amended Fla.Stat. § 659.141(1). That statute, which had been on the books only since March 28 of that year, was expanded to prohibit an out-of-state bank holding company from owning or controlling a business within the State that sells investment advisory services to any customer, rather than just to "trust companies or banks" in Florida, as the statute theretofore had read. This amendment took effect, without the Governor's approval, on December 21, 1972. There is evidence that the amendment was a direct response to Bankers Trust's pending application, and that it had the strong backing of the local financial community.

On April 26, 1973, the Board rejected Bankers Trust's proposal on the ground that it would conflict with state law. 59 Fed.Res.Bull. 364. The Board observed that the proposal contemplated *de novo* entry into the Florida investment management market rather than acquisition of an existing concern, and it noted that *de novo* entry ordinarily has a desirable procompetitive impact. Absent evidence of a contrary effect in this case, the Board intimated that it would have been favorably inclined toward the proposal. But it found that the December amendment to Fla.Stat. § 659.141(1) "was intended to, and does, prohibit the performance of investment advisory services in Florida by non-Florida bank holding companies." 59 Fed.Res.Bull. 365. In view of its obligation to respect the dictates of state law, the Board found itself constrained to reject the proposal. . . .

Within six months of the Board's decision, the two appellees [sued] seeking declaratory and injunctive relief. Count I of their complaint alleged that Fla.Stat. § 659.141(1) "is not designed to promote lawful regulatory objectives, but is intended to shelter those organizations presently conducting an investment advisory business in Florida from competition by [BTIM]." The complaint alleged violations of the due process and equal protection guarantees of the Fourteenth Amendment, as well as violation of the Commerce Clause. Count II alleged similar constitutional defects as the result of the joint operation of §§ 659.141(1), and 660.10. Appellees alleged that "[b]ut for the existence of the challenged statutes," Bankers Trust would seek authority from the Board to establish "a subsidiary trust company having a national bank charter or a Florida state charter" that would engage exclusively in one or more of the functions regulated by § 660.10. . . .

[T]he [three-judge] District Court held [on summary judgment] that the challenged portions of the two statutes violate the Commerce Clause. 461 F.Supp. 1187 (1978)....

. . .

The court issued an order granting declaratory relief against both statutes....

. . .

III.

[W]e first turn to § 659.141(1). This statute has been the chief object of controversy, since it is the statute that prevents appellees from setting up their projected investment advisory business within Florida. The statute prohibits ownership of local investment or trust businesses by firms possessing two characteristics: a certain kind of business organization and purpose, whether it be as a bank, trust company, or a bank holding company; and location of principal operations outside Florida.

Appellant and the *amici* supporting his position argue that the District Court's analysis of § 659.141(1) is flawed in three respects: First, the statute assertedly affects only matters of local character that have insufficient interstate attributes to bring federal constitutional limitations into play. Second, the District Court erroneously labeled the statute protectionist legislation and thus incorrectly relied upon the *"per se* rule of invalidity" identified in Philadelphia v. New Jersey, 437 U.S., at 624. Appellant argues that the statute should be treated as neutral legislation subject to the less stringent standards of Pike v. Bruce Church, Inc., supra, and he argues that it meets this test. Third, the District Court failed to accord proper significance, in appellant's view, to the Bank Holding Company Act of 1956. Appellant argues that the Act grants authority to the States to prohibit out-of-state bank holding companies from owning local subsidiaries that provide bank-related services.

A.

The first of these arguments needs only brief mention. We readily accept the submission that, both as a matter of history and as a matter of present commercial reality, banking and related financial activities are of profound local concern. As appellees freely concede, sound financial institutions and honest financial practices are essential to the health of any State's economy and to the well-being of its people. Thus, it is not surprising that ever since the early days of our Republic, the States have chartered banks and have actively regulated their activities.

Nonetheless, it does not follow that these same activities lack important interstate attributes....

B.

The contentions that the District Court erred by applying too stringent a standard in defining the limits of Florida's regulatory authority, and that § 659.141(1) is evenhanded local regulation, are more substantial. We nonetheless agree with the District Court's conclusion that this statute is "parochial" in the sense that it overtly prevents foreign enterprises from competing in local markets.

The statute makes the out-of-state location of a bank holding company's principal operations an explicit barrier to the presence of an investment subsidiary within the State. As Bankers Trust's application before the Board itself indicates, it thus prevents competition in local markets by out-of-state firms with the kinds of resources and business interests that make them likely to attempt *de novo* entry. Appellant virtually concedes this effect, and the circumstances of enactment suggest that it was the legislature's principal objective.

Appellant argues, however, that the statute ought not to be declared *per se* invalid because it does not prevent all out-of-state investment enterprises from entering local markets. Investment enterprises that are *not* bank holding companies, banks, or trust companies either may own investment subsidiaries in Florida or may enter the state investment market directly by obtaining a license to do business. Furthermore, locally incorporated bank holding companies are subject to the same restrictions as their foreign counterparts if they maintain their principal operations elsewhere. Appellant thus analogizes § 659.141(1) to the Maryland statute prohibiting local retail operations by vertically integrated petroleum companies that the Court upheld in Exxon Corp. v. Governor of Maryland, 437 U.S. 117 (1978). The statute, it is said, discriminates against a particular kind of corporate organizational structure more than it does against the origin or citizenship of a particular business enterprise.

The statute involved in *Exxon* flatly prohibited producers and refiners of petroleum products from opening or operating retail services within Maryland under a variety of corporate or contractual arrangements. It was enacted in response to perceived inequities in the allocation of petroleum products to retail outlets during the fuel shortage of 1973. Various oil companies, all of which engaged in production and refining as well as in sale of petroleum products, challenged the statute on a number of grounds. Among other arguments, they claimed that the statute violated the Commerce Clause because it discriminated against producers and refiners, all of which were interstate concerns, in favor of independent retailers, most of which were local businesses.

The Court rejected this contention. After holding that the statute served the legitimate state purpose of "controlling the gasoline retail market," the Court separately analyzed its effect on interstate commerce in the producing-refining and retailing ends of the petroleum industry. The Court concluded that the statute could not discriminate against interstate petroleum producers and refiners in favor of locally based competitors because, as a matter of fact, there were no such local producers or refiners to be favored. For the same reason, it concluded that the flow of petroleum products in interstate commerce would not be reduced. It also rejected a claim of discrimination at the retail level because the statute placed "no barriers whatsoever" on competition in local markets by "interstate independent dealers" that did not own production or refining facilities. Despite the fact that the number of stations operated by independent dealers was small relative to the number operated by producer-refiners, the Court concluded that neither the placing of a disparate burden on some interstate competitors nor the shifting of business from one part of the interstate market to another was enough, under the circumstances, to establish a Commerce Clause violation.

There are some points of similarity between *Exxon* and the present case. In the former, the statute in issue discriminated against vertical organization in the petroleum industry. Section 659.141(1) similarly discriminates against a particular kind of conglomerate organization in the investment and financial industries. And the Maryland statute permitted some kinds of interstate competitors free entry into the local market, as does the Florida statute at issue here.

We disagree, however, with the suggestion that *Exxon* should be treated as controlling precedent for this case. Section 659.141(1) engages in an additional form of discrimination that is highly significant for purposes of Commerce Clause analysis. Under the Florida statute, discrimination against affected business organizations is *not* evenhanded because only banks, bank holding companies, and trust companies with principal operations *outside* Florida are prohibited from operating investment subsidiaries or giving investment advice within the State. It follows that § 659.141(1) discriminates *among* affected business entities according to the extent of their contacts with the local economy. The absence of a similar discrimination between interstate and local producer-refiners was a most critical factor in *Exxon*. Both on its face and in actual effect, § 659.141(1) thus displays a local favoritism or protectionism that significantly alters its Commerce Clause status. See Philadelphia v. New Jersey, 437 U.S., at 626–627; Baldwin v. G.A.F. Seelig, Inc., 294 U.S., at 527.

We need not decide whether this difference is sufficient to render the Florida legislation *per se* invalid, for we are convinced that the disparate treatment of out-of-state bank holding companies cannot be justified as an incidental burden necessitated by legitimate local concerns. In the District Court and to some extent on this appeal, appellant and supporting *amici* have argued that the Florida legislation advances several important state policies. Among those that have been specifically identified are an interest in discouraging undue economic concentration in the arena of high finance; an interest in regulating financial practices, presumably to protect local residents from fraud; and an interest in maximizing local control over locally based financial activities. We think that these alleged purposes fail to justify the extent of the burden placed upon out-of-state bank holding companies.

Discouraging economic concentration and protecting the citizenry against fraud are undoubtedly legitimate state interests. But we are not persuaded that these interests justify the heavily disproportionate burden this statute places on bank holding companies that operate principally outside the State. Appellant has demonstrated no basis for an inference that all out-of-state bank holding companies are likely to possess the evils of monopoly power, that they are more likely to do so than their home-grown counterparts, or that they are any more inclined to engage in sharp practices than bank holding companies that are locally based. Nor is there any reason to conclude that outright prohibition of entry, rather than some intermediate form of regulation, is the only effective method of protecting against the presumed evils, particularly when other out-of-state businesses that may be just as large or far-flung are permitted to compete in the local market. We conclude that these asserted state interests simply do not suffice to eliminate § 659.141(1)'s apparent constitutional defect. . . .

With regard to the asserted interest in promoting local control over financial institutions, we doubt that the interest itself is entirely clear of any tinge of local parochialism. In almost any Commerce Clause case it would be possible for a State to argue that it has an interest in bolstering local ownership, or wealth, or control of business enterprise. Yet these arguments are at odds with the general principle that the Commerce Clause prohibits a State from using its regulatory power to protect its own citizens from outside competition. See H.P. Hood & Sons, Inc. v. Du Mond, 336 U.S., at 538; Buck v. Kuykendall, 267 U.S. 307, 315–316 (1925); cf. Toomer v. Witsell, 334 U.S. 385, 403–404 (1948). In any event, the interest is not well-served by the present legislation. The statute, for example, does not restrict out-of-state ownership of local bank holding companies. Nor, as appellant concedes does it prevent entry by out-of-state entities other than those having the prohibited organizational forms. There is thus no reason to believe that the State's interest in local control, to the extent it legitimately exists, has been significantly or evenhandedly advanced by the statutory means that have been employed.

For these reasons, we conclude that the District Court did not err in holding that § 659.141(1) directly burdens interstate commerce in a manner that contravenes the Commerce Clause's implicit limitation on state power.

. . .

V.

In summary, we affirm the judgment of the District Court insofar as it declares unconstitutional the challenged portions of § 659.141(1) and enjoins their enforcement. . . .

It is so ordered.

EDGAR v. MITE CORP., 457 U.S. 624 (1982). The Illinois Business Takeover Act requires takeover offers for acquisition of shares in Illinois-affiliated target companies[1] to be registered with the Illinois Secretary of State twenty days before the offer becomes effective. During the twenty-day period, the offeror may not communicate with shareholders, but the target company is free to disseminate information to its shareholders. The Secretary can refuse registration, after hearing, if the offer is not accompanied by full and fair disclosure, or the offer is inequitable or fraudulent. The Court held that the Illinois statute imposed an unconstitutional burden on interstate commerce.

Justice White's opinion offered two distinct rationales, only one of which commanded the votes of five Justices.[2] Those five joined Part V.B. of the opinion, which rested squarely on the "balancing approach" articulated in Pike v. Bruce Church (pp. 241–2, supra). On this point, Justice White's opinion said in part:

"The effects of allowing the Illinois Secretary of State to block a nationwide tender offer are substantial. Shareholders are deprived of the opportunity to sell their shares at a premium. The reallocation of economic resources to their highest-valued use, a process which can improve efficiency and competition, is hindered. The incentive the tender offer mechanism provides incumbent management to perform well so that stock prices remain high is reduced.

---

[1] The Act applies where Illinois residents own 10% of the securities subject to the offer. It also applies where two of three conditions are met: (1) the target company's principal executive office is in Illinois; (2) the target company is organized under Illinois law; (3) 10% of the target company's stated capital and surplus is represented within Illinois.

[2] Part V.A. of Justice White's opinion concluded that the Illinois statute placed an impermissible burden on interstate commerce because of its extraterritorial effect, regulating transactions across state lines with out-of-state shareholders. Justice Powell, one of the five Justices to join part V.B. of the opinion, did not join part V.A., which

thus received the votes of only four Justices. Justice Powell explained that he joined part V.B. (and not V.A.) because its rationale "leaves some room for state regulation of tender offers." Justice White's opinion also took the position that the Illinois Act was preempted by the Williams Act, a 1968 amendment to the Federal Securities and Exchange Act. Only Chief Justice Burger and Justice Blackmun concurred in this portion of the opinion. Justice Blackmun took no position on the commerce clause issue. Justices Brennan, Marshall and Rehnquist argued that the case was moot and did not express a position on the merits of either the commerce clause or preemption issues.

"Appellant claims the Illinois Act ... seeks to protect resident security holders.... We agree with the Court of Appeals that [this interest is] insufficient to outweigh the burdens Illinois imposes on interstate commerce.

"While protecting local investors is plainly a legitimate state objective, the state has no legitimate interest in protecting non-resident shareholders. Insofar as the Illinois law burdens out-of-state transactions, there is nothing to be weighed in the balance to sustain the law. We note, furthermore, that the Act completely exempts from coverage a corporation's acquisition of its own shares.... Thus Chicago Rivet was able to make a competing tender offer for its own stock without complying with the Illinois Act, leaving Chicago Rivet's shareholders to depend only on the protections afforded them by federal securities law, protections which Illinois views as inadequate to protect investors in other contexts. This distinction is at variance with Illinois' asserted legislative purpose, and tends to undermine appellant's justification for the burdens the statute imposes on interstate commerce.

"We are also unconvinced that the Illinois Act substantially enhances the shareholders' position. The Illinois Act seeks to protect shareholders of a company subject to a tender offer by requiring disclosures regarding the offer, assuring that shareholders have adequate time to decide whether to tender their shares, and according shareholders withdrawal, proration and equal consideration rights.... As the Court of Appeals noted, the disclosures required by the Illinois Act which go beyond those mandated by the Williams Act and the regulations pursuant to it may not substantially enhance the shareholders' ability to make informed decisions. It also was of the view that the possible benefits of the potential delays required by the Act may be outweighed by the increased risk that the tender offer will fail due to defensive tactics employed by incumbent management. We are unprepared to disagree with the Court of Appeals in these respects, and conclude that the protections the Illinois Act affords resident security holders are, for the most part, speculative."

CTS Corp. v. Dynamics Corp. of America

481 U.S. 69, 107 S.Ct. 1637, 95 L.Ed.2d 67 (1987).

Justice Powell delivered the opinion of the Court.

This case presents the questions whether the Control Share Acquisitions Chapter of the Indiana Business Corporation Law, Ind.Code § 23–1–42–1 et seq. (Supp.1986), is preempted by the Williams Act, 82 Stat. 454, as amended, 15 U.S.C. §§ 78m(d)–(e) and 78n(d)–(f) (1982 ed. and Supp. III), or violates the Commerce Clause of the Federal Constitution, Art. I, § 8, cl. 3.

I

[The Control Share Acquisitions Chapter applies only to an Indiana "issuing public corporation,"] defined as:

"a corporation that has:

"(1) one hundred (100) or more shareholders;

"(2) its principal place of business, its principal office, or substantial assets within Indiana; and

"(3) either:

"(A) more than ten percent (10%) of its shareholders resident in Indiana;

"(B) more than ten percent (10%) of its shares owned by Indiana residents; or

"(C) ten thousand (10,000) shareholders resident in Indiana." § 23–1–42–4(a).

The Act focuses on the acquisition of "control shares" in an issuing public corporation. Under the Act, an entity acquires "control shares" whenever it acquires shares that, but for the operation of the Act, would bring its voting power in the corporation to or above any of three thresholds: 20%, 33 ⅓%, or 50%. § 23–1–42–1. An entity that acquires control shares does not necessarily acquire voting rights. Rather, it gains those rights only "to the extent granted by resolution approved by the shareholders of the issuing public corporation." § 23–1–42–9(a). Section 9 requires a majority vote of all disinterested shareholders holding each class of stock for passage of such a resolution. § 23–1–42–9(b). The practical effect of this requirement is to condition acquisition of control of a corporation on approval of a majority of the pre-existing disinterested shareholders.

. . .

[Dynamics, after announcing a tender offer for a million shares in CTS, an Indiana Corporation, sought declaratory and injunctive relief in federal court against CTS's use of the Act. The District Court first held that the Williams Act pre-empted the Indiana Act and later held that it violated the Commerce Clause. The Seventh Circuit affirmed, but the Supreme Court reversed.]

II

. . .

In our view, the possibility that the Indiana Act will delay some tender offers is insufficient to require a conclusion that the Williams Act pre-empts the Act. The longstanding prevalence of state regulation in this area suggests that, if Congress had intended to pre-empt all state laws that delay the acquisition of voting control following a tender offer, it would have said so explicitly. The regulatory conditions that the Act places on tender offers are consistent with the text and the purposes of the Williams Act. Accordingly, we hold that the Williams Act does not pre-empt the Indiana Act.

III

As an alternative basis for its decision, the Court of Appeals held that the Act violates the Commerce Clause of the Federal Constitution. . . .

A

The principal objects of dormant Commerce Clause scrutiny are statutes that discriminate against interstate commerce. See, e.g., Lewis v. BT Investment Managers, Inc., 447 U.S. 27, 36–37 (1980); Philadelphia v. New Jersey, 437 U.S. 617, 624 (1978). See generally Regan, The Supreme Court and State Protectionism: Making Sense of the Dormant Commerce Clause, 84 Mich. L.Rev. 1091 (1986). The Indiana Act is not such a statute. It has the same effects on tender offers whether or not the offeror is a domiciliary or resident of Indiana. Thus, it "visits its effects equally upon both interstate and local business," Lewis v. BT Investment Managers, Inc., supra, at 36.

Dynamics nevertheless contends that the statute is discriminatory because it will apply most often to out-of-state entities. This argument rests on the contention that, as a practical matter, most hostile tender offers are launched by offerors outside Indiana. But this argument avails Dynamics little. "The fact that the burden of a state regulation falls on some interstate companies does not, by itself, establish a claim of discrimination against interstate commerce." Exxon Corp. v. Governor of Maryland, 437 U.S. 117, 126 (1978). See Minnesota v. Clover Leaf Creamery Co., 449 U.S. 456, 471–472 (1981) (rejecting a claim of discrimination because the challenged statute "regulate[d] evenhandedly ... without regard to whether the [commerce came] from outside the State"); Commonwealth Edison Co. v. Montana, 453 U.S. 609, 619 (1981) (rejecting a claim of discrimination because the "tax burden [was] borne according to the amount ... consumed and not according to any distinction between in-state and out-of-state consumers"). Because nothing in the Indiana Act imposes a greater burden on out-of-state offerors than it does on similarly situated Indiana offerors, we reject the contention that the Act discriminates against interstate commerce.

B

This Court's recent Commerce Clause cases also have invalidated statutes that adversely may affect interstate commerce by subjecting activities to inconsistent regulations. E.g., Brown–Forman Distillers Corp. v. New York State Liquor Authority, 476 U.S. 573, 583 (1986); Edgar v. MITE Corp., 457 U.S., at 642 (plurality opinion of White, J.); Kassel v. Consolidated Freightways Corp., 450 U.S. 662, 671 (1981) (plurality opinion of Powell, J.). See Southern Pacific Co. v. Arizona, 325 U.S. 761, 774 (1945) (noting the "confusion and difficulty" that would attend the "unsatisfied need for uniformity" in setting maximum limits on train lengths); Cooley v. Board of Wardens, supra, at * 319 (stating that the Commerce Clause prohibits States from regulating subjects that "are in their nature national, or admit only of one uniform system, or plan of regulation"). The Indiana Act poses no such problem. So long as each State regulates voting rights only in the corporations it has created, each corporation will be subject to the law of only one State. No principle of corporation law and practice is more firmly established than a State's authority to regulate domestic corporations, including the authority to define the voting rights of shareholders. See Restatement (Second) of Conflict of Laws § 304 (1971) (concluding that the law of the incorporating State generally should "determine the right of a shareholder to participate in the administration of the affairs of the corporation"). Accordingly, we conclude that the Indiana Act does not create an impermissible risk of inconsistent regulation by different States.

C

The Court of Appeals did not find the Act unconstitutional for either of these threshold reasons. Rather, its decision rested on its view of the Act's potential to hinder tender offers. We think the Court of Appeals failed to appreciate the significance for Commerce Clause analysis of the fact that state regulation of corporate governance is regulation of entities whose very existence and attributes are a product of state law.... Every State in this country has enacted laws regulating corporate governance. By prohibiting certain transactions, and regulating others, such laws necessarily affect certain aspects of interstate commerce. This necessarily is true with respect to corporations with shareholders in States other than the State of incorporation. Large corporations that are listed on national exchanges, or even regional exchanges, will have shareholders in many States and shares that are traded frequently. The markets that facilitate this national and international participation in ownership of corporations are essential for providing capital not only for new enterprises but also for established companies that need to expand their businesses. This beneficial free market system depends at its core upon the fact that a corporation—except in the rarest situations—is organized under, and governed by, the law of a single jurisdiction, traditionally the corporate law of the State of its incorporation.

These regulatory laws may affect directly a variety of corporate transactions. Mergers are a typical example. In view of the substantial effect that a merger may have on the shareholder's interests in a corporation, many States require supermajority votes to approve mergers.... By requiring a greater vote for mergers than is required for other transactions, these laws make it more difficult for corporations to merge. State laws also may provide for "dissenters' rights" under which minority shareholders who disagree with corporate decisions to take particular actions are entitled to sell their shares to the corporation at fair market value.... By requiring the corporation to purchase the shares of dissenting shareholders, these laws may inhibit a corporation from engaging in the specified transactions.

It thus is an accepted part of the business landscape in this country for States to create corporations, to prescribe their powers, and to define the rights that are acquired by purchasing their shares. A State has an interest in promoting stable relationships among parties involved in the corporations it charters, as well as in ensuring that investors in such corporations have an effective voice in corporate affairs.

There can be no doubt that the Act reflects these concerns. The primary purpose of the Act is to protect the shareholders of Indiana corporations. It does this by affording shareholders, when a takeover offer is made, an opportunity to decide collectively whether the resulting change in voting control of the corporation, as they perceive it, would be desirable. A change of management may have important effects on the shareholders' interests; it is well within the State's role as overseer of corporate governance to offer this opportunity. The autonomy provided by allowing shareholders collectively to determine whether the takeover is advantageous to their interests may be especially beneficial where a hostile tender offer may coerce shareholders into tendering their shares.

Appellee Dynamics responds to this concern by arguing that the prospect of coercive tender offers is illusory, and that tender offers generally should be favored because they reallocate corporate assets into the hands of management who can use them most effectively. See generally Easterbrook and Fischel, The Proper Role of a Target's Management in Responding to a Tender Offer, 94 Harv.L.Rev. 1161 (1981). As indicated, Indiana's concern with tender offers is not groundless. Indeed, the potentially coercive aspects of tender offers have been recognized by the Securities and Exchange Commission, see SEC Release No. 21079, p. 86,916, and by a number of scholarly commentators, see, e.g., Bradley & Rosenzweig, Defensive Stock Repurchases, 99 Harv.L.Rev. 1377, 1412–1413 (1986); Macey & McChesney, A Theoretical Analysis of Corporate Greenmail, 95 Yale L.J. 13, 20–22 (1985); Lowenstein, 83 Colum.L.Rev., at 307–309. The Constitution does not require the States to subscribe to any particular economic theory. We are not inclined "to second-guess the empirical judgments of lawmakers concerning the utility of legislation," Kassel v. Consolidated Freightways Corp., 450 U.S., at 679 (Brennan, J., concurring in judgment). In our view, the possibility of coercion in some takeover bids offers additional justification for Indiana's decision to promote the autonomy of independent shareholders.

Dynamics argues in any event that the State has "no legitimate interest in protecting the nonresident shareholders." Brief for Appellee Dynamics Corp. of

America 21 (quoting Edgar v. MITE Corp., 457 U.S., at 644). Dynamics relies heavily on the statement by the *MITE* Court that "[i]nsofar as the ... law burdens out-of-state transactions, there is nothing to be weighed in the balance to sustain the law." 457 U.S., at 644. But that comment was made in reference to an Illinois law that applied as well to out-of-state corporations as to in-state corporations. We agree that Indiana has no interest in protecting nonresident shareholders *of nonresident corporations.* But this Act applies only to corporations incorporated in Indiana. We reject the contention that Indiana has no interest in providing for the shareholders of its corporations the voting autonomy granted by the Act. Indiana has a substantial interest in preventing the corporate form from becoming a shield for unfair business dealing. Moreover, unlike the Illinois statute invalidated in *MITE,* the Indiana Act applies only to corporations that have a substantial number of shareholders in Indiana. See Ind.Code § 23–1–42–4(a)(3) (Supp.1986). Thus, every application of the Indiana Act will affect a substantial number of Indiana residents, whom Indiana indisputably has an interest in protecting.

D

Dynamics' argument that the Act is unconstitutional ultimately rests on its contention that the Act will limit the number of successful tender offers. There is little evidence that this will occur. But even if true, this result would not substantially affect our Commerce Clause analysis. We reiterate that this Act does not prohibit any entity—resident or nonresident—from offering to purchase, or from purchasing, shares in Indiana corporations, or from attempting thereby to gain control. It only provides regulatory procedures designed for the better protection of the corporations' shareholders. We have rejected the "notion that the Commerce Clause protects the particular structure or methods of operation in a ... market." Exxon Corp. v. Governor of Maryland, 437 U.S., at 127. The very commodity that is traded in the securities market is one whose characteristics are defined by state law. Similarly, the very commodity that is traded in the "market for corporate control"—the corporation—is one that owes its existence and attributes to state law. Indiana need not define these commodities as other States do; it need only provide that residents and nonresidents have equal access to them. . . .

IV

On its face, the Indiana Control Share Acquisitions Chapter even-handedly determines the voting rights of shares of Indiana corporations. The Act does not conflict with the provisions or purposes of the Williams Act. To the limited extent that the Act affects interstate commerce, this is justified by the State's interest in defining the attributes of shares in its corporations and in protecting shareholders. Congress has never questioned the need for state regulation of these matters. Nor do we think such regulation offends the Constitution. Accordingly, we reverse the judgment of the Court of Appeals.

It is so ordered.

Justice Scalia, concurring in part and concurring in the judgment.

I join Parts I, III–A, and III–B of the Court's opinion. However, having found, as those Parts do, that the Indiana Control Share Acquisitions Chapter neither "discriminates against interstate commerce," nor "create[s] an impermissible risk of inconsistent regulation by different States," I would conclude without further analysis that it is not invalid under the dormant Commerce Clause. While it has become standard practice at least since Pike v. Bruce Church, Inc., 397 U.S. 137 (1970), to consider, in addition to these factors, whether the burden on commerce imposed by a state statute "is clearly excessive in relation to the putative local benefits," id., at 142, such an inquiry is ill suited to the judicial function and should be undertaken rarely if at all. This case is a good illustration of the point. Whether the control shares statute "protects shareholders of Indiana corporations," or protects incumbent management seems to me a highly debatable question, but it is extraordinary to think that the constitutionality of the Act should depend on the answer. Nothing in the Constitution says that the protection of entrenched management is any less important a "putative local benefit" than the protection of entrenched shareholders, and I do not know what qualifies us to make that judgment—or the related judgment as to how effective the present statute is in achieving one or the other objective—or the ultimate (and most ineffable) judgment as to whether, given importance-level x, and effectiveness-level y, the worth of the statute is "outweighed" by impact-on-commerce z.

One commentator has suggested that, at least much of the time, we do not in fact mean what we say when we declare that statutes which neither discriminate against commerce nor present a threat of multiple and inconsistent burdens might nonetheless be unconstitutional under a "balancing" test. See Regan, The Supreme Court and State Protectionism: Making Sense of the Dormant Commerce Clause, 84 Mich.L.Rev. 1091 (1986). If he is not correct, he ought to be. As long as a State's corporation law governs only its own corporations and does not discriminate against out-of-state interests, it should survive this Court's scrutiny under the Commerce Clause, whether it promotes shareholder welfare or industrial stagnation. Beyond that, it is for Congress to prescribe its invalidity.

I also agree with the Court that the Indiana Control Shares Act is not pre-empted by the Williams Act. . . .

I do not share the Court's apparent high estimation of the beneficence of the state statute at issue here. But a law can be both economic folly and constitutional. The Indiana Control Shares Acquisition Chapter is at least the latter. I therefore concur in the judgment of the Court.

Justice White, with whom Justice Blackmun and Justice Stevens join as to Part II, dissenting.

The majority today upholds . . . a statute which will predictably foreclose completely some tender offers for stock in Indiana corporations. I disagree . . . that the Chapter is neither pre-empted by the Williams Act nor in conflict with the Commerce Clause. The Chapter undermines the policy of the Williams Act by effectively preventing minority shareholders, in some circumstances, from acting in their own best interests by selling their stock. In addition, the Chapter will substantially burden the interstate market in corporate ownership, particularly if other States follow Indiana's lead as many already have done. The Chapter, therefore, directly inhibits interstate commerce, the very economic consequences the Commerce Clause was intended to prevent. . . .

. . .

The Commerce Clause was included in our Constitution by the Framers to prevent the very type of economic protectionism Indiana's Control Share Chapter represents:

. . .

The State of Indiana, in its brief, admits that at least one of the Chapter's goals is to protect Indiana Corporations. . . . A state law which permits a majority of an Indiana corporation's stockholders to prevent individual investors, including out-of-state stockholders, from selling their stock to an out-of-state tender offeror and thereby frustrate any transfer of corporate control, is the archetype of the kind of state law that the Commerce Clause forbids.

Unlike state blue sky laws, Indiana's Control Share Acquisitions Chapter regulates the purchase and sale of stock of Indiana corporations in interstate commerce. Indeed, as noted above, the Chapter will inevitably be used to block interstate transactions in such stock. Because the Commerce Clause protects the "interstate market" in such securities, Exxon Corp. v. Governor of Maryland, 437 U.S. 117, 127 (1978), and because the Control Share Chapter substantially interferes with this interstate market, the Chapter clearly conflicts with the Commerce Clause.

With all due respect, I dissent.

Bendix Autolite Corp. v. Midwesco Enterprises, Inc.

486 U.S. 888, 108 S.Ct. 2218, 100 L.Ed.2d 896 (1988).

Justice Kennedy delivered the opinion of the Court.

Ohio recognizes a four-year statute of limitations in actions for breach of contract or fraud. The statute is tolled, however, for any period that a person or corporation is not "present" in the state. To be present in Ohio, a foreign corporation must appoint an agent for service of process, which operates as consent to the general jurisdiction of the Ohio courts. Applying well-settled constitutional principles, we find the Ohio statute that suspends limitations protection for out-of-state entities is a violation of the Commerce Clause.

I

Underlying the constitutional question presented by the Ohio statute of limitations rules is a rather ordinary contract dispute. In 1974, Midwesco Enterprises, Inc., agreed with Bendix Autolite Corporation to deliver and install a boiler system at a Bendix facility in Fostoria, Ohio. Dissatisfied with the work, Bendix claimed that the boiler system had been installed improperly and that it was insufficient to produce the quantity of steam specified in the contract. This diversity action was filed against Midwesco in the United States District Court for the Northern District of Ohio in 1980. Bendix is a Delaware corporation with its principal place of business in Ohio; Midwesco is an Illinois corporation with its principal place of business in Illinois.

When Midwesco asserted the Ohio statute of limitations as a defense, Bendix responded that the statutory period had not elapsed because under Ohio law running of the time is suspended, or tolled, for claims against entities that are not within the State and have not designated an agent for service of process. Midwesco replied that this tolling provision violated both the Commerce Clause and the Due Process Clause of the Fourteenth Amendment.

The District Court dismissed the action, finding that the Ohio tolling statute constituted an impermissible burden on interstate commerce. The Court of Appeals for the Sixth Circuit affirmed.... We now affirm.

II

Where the burden of a state regulation falls on interstate commerce, restricting its flow in a manner not applicable to local business and trade, there may be either a discrimination that renders the regulation invalid without more, or cause to weigh and assess the State's putative interests against the interstate restraints to determine if the burden imposed is an unreasonable one. See Brown–Forman Distillers Corp. v. New York State Liquor Authority, 476 U.S. 573, 578–579 (1986). The Ohio statute before us might have been held to be a discrimination that invalidates without extended inquiry. We choose, however, to assess the interests of the State, to demonstrate that its legitimate sphere of regulation is not much advanced by the statute while interstate commerce is subject to substantial restraints. We find that the burden imposed on interstate commerce by the tolling statute exceeds any local interest that the State might advance.

The burden the tolling statute places on interstate commerce is significant. Midwesco has no corporate office in Ohio, is not registered to do business there, and has not appointed an agent for service of process in the State. To gain the protection of the limitations period, Midwesco would have had to appoint a resident agent for service of process in Ohio and subject itself to the general jurisdiction of the Ohio courts. This jurisdiction would extend to any suit against Midwesco, whether or not the transaction in question had any connection with Ohio. The designation of an agent subjects the foreign corporation to the general jurisdiction of the Ohio courts in matters to which Ohio's tenuous relation would not otherwise extend. . . . The Ohio statutory scheme thus forces a foreign corporation to choose between exposure to the general jurisdiction of Ohio courts or forfeiture of the limitations defense, remaining subject to suit in Ohio in perpetuity. Requiring a foreign corporation to appoint an agent for service in all cases and to defend itself with reference to all transactions, including those in which it did not have the minimum contacts necessary for supporting personal jurisdiction, is a significant burden. . . .

Although statute of limitations defenses are not a fundamental right, . . . it is obvious that they are an integral part of the legal system and are relied upon to project the liabilities of persons and corporations active in the commercial sphere. The State may not withdraw such defenses on conditions repugnant to the Commerce Clause. Where a State denies ordinary legal defenses or like privileges to out-of-state persons or corporations engaged in commerce, the State law will be reviewed under the Commerce Clause to determine whether the denial is discriminatory on its face or an impermissible burden on commerce. The State may not condition the exercise of the defense on the waiver or relinquishment of rights that the foreign corporation would otherwise retain. . . .

The ability to execute service of process on foreign corporations and entities is an important factor to consider in assessing the local interest in subjecting out-of-state entities to requirements more onerous than those imposed on domestic parties. It is true that serving foreign corporate defendants may be more arduous than serving domestic corporations or foreign corporations with a designated agent for service, and we have held for Equal Protection purposes that a State rationally may make adjustments for this difference by curtailing limitations protection for absent foreign corporations. G.D. Searle & Co. v. Cohn, 455 U.S. 404 (1982). Nevertheless, State interests that are legitimate for equal protection or due process purposes may be insufficient to withstand Commerce Clause scrutiny.

In the particular case before us, the Ohio tolling statute must fall under the Commerce Clause. Ohio cannot justify its statute as a means of protecting its residents from corporations who become liable for acts done within the State but later withdraw from the jurisdiction, for it is conceded by all parties that the Ohio long arm statute would have permitted service on Midwesco throughout the period of limitations. The Ohio statute of limitations is tolled only for those foreign corporations that do not subject themselves to the general jurisdiction of Ohio courts. In this manner the Ohio statute imposes a greater burden on out-of-state companies than it does on Ohio companies, subjecting the activities of foreign and domestic corporations to inconsistent regulations. CTS Corp. v. Dynamics Corp. of America, 481 U.S. 69, ___ (1987).

The suggestion that Midwesco had the simple alternatives of designating an agent for service of process in its contract with Bendix or tendering an agency appointment to the Ohio Secretary of State is not persuasive. Initially, there is no statutory support for either option, and it is speculative that either device would have satisfied the Ohio requirements for the continued running of the limitations period. In any event, a designation with the Ohio Secretary of State of an agent for the service of process likely would have subjected Midwesco to the general jurisdiction of Ohio courts over transactions in which Ohio had no interest. As we have already concluded, this exaction is an unreasonable burden on commerce.

. . .

Affirmed.

Justice Scalia, concurring in judgment.

I cannot confidently assess whether the Court's evaluation and balancing of interests in this case is right or wrong. Although the Court labels the effect of exposure to the general jurisdiction of Ohio's courts "a significant burden" on commerce, I am not sure why that is. In precise terms, it is the burden of defending in Ohio (rather than some other forum) any lawsuit having all of the following features: (1) the plaintiff desires to bring it in Ohio, (2) it has so little connection to Ohio that service could not otherwise be made under Ohio's long-arm statute, and (3) it has a great enough connection to Ohio it is not subject to dismissal on *forum non conveniens* grounds. The record before us supplies no indication as to how many suits fit this description (even the present suit is not an example since appellee was subject to long-arm service), and frankly I have no idea how one would go about estimating the number. It may well be "significant," but for all we know it is "negligible."

A person or firm that takes the other alternative, by declining to appoint a general agent for service, will remain theoretically subject to suit in Ohio (as the Court says) "in perpetuity"—at least as far as the statute of limitations is concerned. But again, I do not know how we assess how significant a burden this is, unless anything that is theoretically perpetual must be significant. . . . Moreover, whatever the likelihood is, it does not seem terribly plausible that any real-world deterrent effect on interstate transactions will be produced by the incremental cost of having to defend a *delayed* suit rather than a *timely* suit. But the point is, it seems to me we can do no more than speculate.

On the other side of the scale, the Court considers the benefit of the Ohio scheme to local interests. These are, presumably, to enable the preservation of claims against defendants who have placed themselves beyond the personal jurisdiction of Ohio Courts, and (by encouraging appointment of an agent) to facilitate service upon out-of-state defendants who might otherwise be difficult to locate. . . . We have no way of knowing how often these ends are in fact achieved, and the Court thus says little about them except to call them "an important factor to consider."

Having evaluated the interests on both sides as roughly as this, the Court then proceeds to judge which is more important. This process is ordinarily called "balancing," Pike v. Bruce Church, Inc., 397 U.S. 137, 142 (1970), but the scale analogy is not really appropriate, since the interests on both sides are incommensurate. It is more like judging whether a particular line is longer than a particular rock is heavy. All I am really persuaded of by the Court's opinion is that the burdens the Court labels "significant" are more determinative of its decision than the benefits it labels "important." Were it not for the brief implication that there is here a discrimination unjustified by *any* state interest I suggest an opinion could as persuasively have been written coming out the opposite way. We sometimes make similar "balancing" judgments in determining how far the needs of the State can intrude upon the liberties of the individual, see, e.g., Boos v. Barry, 485 U.S.312, ___ (1988), but that is of the essence of the courts' function as the nonpolitical branch. Weighing the governmental interests of a State against the needs of interstate commerce is, by contrast, a task squarely within the responsibility of Congress, see U.S. Const., Art. I, § 8, cl. 3, and "ill suited to the judicial function." CTS Corp. v. Dynamics Corp. of America, 481 U.S. 69, ___ (1987) (Scalia, J., concurring in part and concurring in judgment).

I would therefore abandon the "balancing" approach to these negative commerce clause cases, first explicitly adopted 18 years ago in Pike v. Bruce Church, Inc., supra, and leave essentially legislative judgments to the Congress. Issues already decided I would leave untouched, but would adopt for the future an analysis more appropriate to our role and our abilities. This does no damage to the interests protected by the doctrine of *stare decisis*. Since the outcome of any particular still-undecided issue under the current methodology is in my view not predictable ... no expectations can possibly be upset. To the contrary, the ultimate objective of the rule of *stare decisis* will be furthered. Because the outcome of the test I would apply is considerably more clear, confident expectations will more readily be able to be entertained.

In my view, a state statute is invalid under the Commerce Clause if, and only if, it accords discriminatory treatment to interstate commerce in a respect not required to achieve a lawful state purpose. When such a validating purpose exists, it is for Congress and not us to determine it is not significant enough to justify the burden on commerce. The Ohio tolling statute, Ohio Rev.Code Ann. § 2305.15 (Supp.1987), is on its face discriminatory because it applies only to out-of-state corporations. That facial discrimination cannot be justified on the basis that "it advances a legitimate local purpose that cannot be adequately served by reasonable nondiscriminatory alternatives," New Energy Co. of Indiana v. Limbach, 486 U.S. 269, ___ (1988). A tolling statute that operated only against persons beyond the reach of Ohio's long-arm statute, or against all persons that could not be found for mail service, would be narrowly tailored to advance the legitimate purpose of preserving claims; but the present statute extends the time for suit even against corporations which (like appellee) are fully suable within Ohio, and readily reachable through the mails.

Because the present statute discriminates against interstate commerce by applying a disadvantageous rule against nonresidents for no valid state purpose that requires such a rule, I concur in the judgment that the Ohio statute violates the Commerce Clause.[a]

F. INTERSTATE MOBILITY OF PERSONS

Shortly after the Civil War the Court was called upon to consider the constitutional freedom of persons to move from state to state. Nevada had enacted a statute levying a capitation tax of one dollar upon every person leaving the state by railroad, stage coach or other vehicle employed in the

---

[a] A dissenting opinion by Chief Justice Rehnquist is omitted.

business of transporting persons for hire. The carrier was required to report the persons so transported and pay the tax. In Crandall v. Nevada, 73 U.S. (6 Wall.) (1868), the Court held this act invalid. The majority of the Court did not place the decision on the commerce clause, but stated:

"The people of these United States constitute one nation. They have a government in which all of them are deeply interested. This government has necessarily a capital established by law, where its principal operations are conducted. Here sits its legislature, composed of senators and representatives, from the States and from the people of the States. Here resides the President directing through thousands of agents, the execution of the laws over all this vast country. Here is the seat of the supreme judicial power of the nation, to which all its citizens have a right to resort to claim justice at its hands. Here are the great executive departments, administering the offices of the mails, or the public lands, of the collection and distribution of the public revenues, and of our foreign relations. These are all established and conducted under the admitted powers of the Federal government. That government has a right to call to this point any or all of its citizens to aid in its service, as members of the Congress, of the courts, of the executive departments, and to fill all its other offices; and this right cannot be made to depend upon the pleasure of a State over whose territory they must pass to reach the point where these services must be rendered. The government, also, has its offices of secondary importance in all other parts of the country. On the sea-coasts and on the rivers it has its ports of entry. In the interior it has its land offices, its revenue offices, and its sub-treasuries. In all these it demands the services of its citizens, and is entitled to bring them to those points from all quarters of the nation, and no power can exist in a State to obstruct this right that would not enable it to defeat the purposes for which the government was established....

"But if the government has these rights on her own account, the citizen also has correlative rights. He has the right to come to the seat of government to assert any claim he may have upon that government, or to transact any business he may have with it. To seek its protection, to share its offices, to engage in administering its functions. He has a right to free access to its sea-ports, through which all the operations of foreign trade and commerce are conducted, to the sub-treasuries, the land offices, the revenue offices, and the courts of justice in the several States, and this right is in its nature independent of the will of any State over whose soil he must pass in the exercise of it...."

The question of interstate mobility arose again in Edwards v. California, 314 U.S. 160 (1941), where the Court struck down a law making it a misdemeanor to bring into California "any indigent person who is not a resident of the State, knowing him to be an indigent person." Resting the decision on the commerce clause the majority of the Court quoted the *Baldwin v. Seelig* statement that the Constitution "was framed upon the theory that the peoples of the several states must sink or swim together." Referring to the language in *New York v. Miln* regarding the "moral pestilence of paupers," the Court said: "Whatever may have been the notion then prevailing, we do not think that it will now be seriously contended that because a person is without employment and without funds he constitutes a 'moral pestilence'."

But four of the Justices (Douglas, Black, Murphy and Jackson) were not willing to place their concurrence on the commerce clause. They believed that the right of persons "to move freely from state to state is an incident of national citizenship protected by the privileges and immunities clause of the Fourteenth Amendment" and added Justice Jackson: "[T]he migrations of a human being do not fit easily into my notions as to what is commerce. To hold that the measure of his rights is the commerce clause is likely to result eventually in distorting the commercial law or in denaturing human rights."

The constitutional freedom of interstate migration will be met again later. See Chapter 10.

SECTION 5. EFFECT OF OTHER CONSTITUTIONAL PROVISIONS ON STATE REGULATORY POWER

A. THE PRIVILEGES AND IMMUNITIES CLAUSE OF ARTICLE IV, SECTION 2

Article IV, Section 2 provides: "The Citizens of each State shall be entitled to all Privileges and Immunities of Citizens in the several States." The progenitor of this provision was the Fourth of the Articles of Confederation which read as follows:

"The better to secure and perpetuate mutual friendship and intercourse among the people of the different States in this Union, the free inhabitants of each of these states, paupers, vagabonds and fugitives from justice excepted, shall be entitled to all privileges and immunities of free citizens in the several States; and the people of each State shall have free ingress and regress to and from any other State, and shall enjoy therein all the privileges of trade and commerce, subject to the same duties, impositions and restrictions as the inhabitants thereof respectively . . .".

These provisions were prompted by a fundamental problem of the federal system of government—how to reconcile the advantages of a common citizenship with a dispersed sovereignty in a number of independent, or largely independent, states. The basic character of the problem is illustrated by the fact that the Constitution of Australia contains a similar provision (Sec. 117) which reads: "A subject of the Queen, resident in any State, shall not be subject in any other State, to any disability or discrimination which would not be equally applicable to him if he were a subject of the Queen resident in such other State."

The first opinion on Article IV, Section 2, was given in Corfield v. Coryell, 4 Wash.C.C. 371, 6 Fed.Cas. 546 (E.D.Pa.1823), by Justice Washington of the Supreme Court when on circuit. A New Jersey statute of 1820 made it unlawful for any person who was not "an actual inhabitant and resident" of the state to rake or gather clams, oysters, or shells in any of the rivers, bays, or waters of the state. The question was the validity of this statute as applied to a Pennsylvania citizen who was gathering oysters in New Jersey waters. Justice Washington declared that the phrase "privileges and immunities of citizens in the several states" should be confined to "those privileges and immunities which are, in their nature, *fundamental* "and "which belong, of right, to the citizens of all free governments." Among these, he said, were the "right of a citizen of one State to pass through, or to reside in any other State, for the purposes of trade, agriculture, professional pursuits, or otherwise;" the right "to take, hold and dispose of property, either real or personal; and an exemption from higher taxes or impositions than are paid by the other citizens of the State."

"But," he continued, "We cannot accede to the proposition which was insisted on by the counsel, that, under this provision of the Constitution, the citizens of the several States are permitted to participate in all *the rights* which belong exclusively to the citizens of any other particular State, merely upon the ground that they are enjoyed by those citizens; much less, that in regulating the use of the common property of the citizens of such State, the legislature is bound to extend to the citizens of all the other States the same advantages as are secured to their own citizens." The right to fish in the waters of the state for running fish or stationary shell fish, when not ceded by the state, he regarded as the common property of all the citizens of the state. "[I]t would, in our opinion, be going quite too far to construe the grant of privileges and immunities of citizens, as amounting to a grant of a co-tenancy in the common property of the State, to the citizens of all the other states."

The statute was sustained.

Justice Washington's reasoning was followed in McCready v. Virginia, 94 U.S. 391 (1877), which upheld the power of a state to limit to its own citizens the right to plant oysters in public waters.

The statute challenged in the *Corfield* case drew the line on the basis of "residence" rather than citizenship, but no point was made of this in the opinion. After the adoption of the Fourteenth Amendment it became even more difficult to distinguish between residence and state citizenship, for that Amendment provides that "All persons born or naturalized in the United States, and subject to the jurisdiction thereof, are citizens of the United States *and of the State wherein they reside.*" (Emphasis added.)

It was early held that the clause protected only individuals who are citizens and that a corporation could not claim the protection of the clause even though all of its incorporators were citizens of the state of incorporation. Bank of Augusta v. Earle, 38 U.S. (13 Pet.) 519 (1839).

United Building and Construction Trades Council of Camden County and Vicinity v. Mayor and Council of the City of Camden

465 U.S. 208, 104 S.Ct. 1020, 79 L.Ed.2d 249 (1984).

Justice Rehnquist delivered the opinion of the Court.

A municipal ordinance of the city of Camden, New Jersey requires that at least 40% of the employees of contractors and subcontractors working on city construction projects be Camden residents. Appellant, the United Building and Construction Trades Council of Camden and Vicinity (the Council), challenges that ordinance as a violation of the Privileges and Immunities Clause, Article IV, § 2, of the United States Constitution. The Supreme Court of New Jersey rejected appellant's privileges and immunities attack on the ground that the ordinance discriminates on the basis of *municipal*, not state, residency. The court "decline[d] to apply the Privileges and Immunities Clause in the context of a municipal ordinance that has identical effects upon out-of-state citizens and New Jersey citizens not residing in the locality." 88 N.J. 317, 342, 443 A.2d 148, 160 (1982). We conclude that the challenged ordinance is properly subject to the strictures of the Clause. We therefore reverse the judgment of the Supreme Court of New Jersey and remand the case for a determination of the validity of the ordinance under the appropriate constitutional standard.

On August 28, 1980, the Camden City Council, acting pursuant to a state-wide affirmative action program, adopted an ordinance setting minority hiring "goals" on all public works contracts. The ordinance also created a hiring preference for Camden residents.... As subsequently amended, the ordinance requires that on all construction projects funded by the city:

> "The developer–contractor, in hiring for jobs, shall make every effort to employ persons residing within the City of Camden but, in no event, shall less than forty percent (40%) of the entire labor force be residents of the City of Camden."

The contractor is also obliged to ensure that any subcontractors working on such projects adhere to the same requirement.

. . .

... We first address the argument, accepted by the Supreme Court of New Jersey, that the Clause does not even apply to a *municipal* ordinance such as this. Two separate contentions are advanced in support of this position: first, that the Clause only applies to laws passed by a *State* and, second, that the Clause only applies to laws that discriminate on the basis of *state* citizenship.

The first argument can be quickly rejected. The fact that the ordinance in question is a municipal, rather than a state, law does not somehow place it outside the scope of the Privileges and Immunities Clause. First of all, one cannot easily distinguish municipal from state action in this case: the municipal ordinance would not have gone into effect without express approval by the State Treasurer.... The constitutional challenge to the resident hiring preference, therefore, must also "be interpreted as a challenge to the State Treasurer's general power" to adopt such a preference....

More fundamentally, a municipality is merely a political subdivision of the State from which its authority derives. City of Trenton v. New Jersey, 262 U.S. 182, 187 (1923). It is as true of the Privileges and Immunities Clause as of the Equal Protection Clause that what would be unconstitutional if done directly by the State can no more readily be accomplished by a city deriving its authority from the State.... Thus, even if the ordinance had been adopted solely by Camden, and not pursuant to a state program or with state approval, the hiring preference would still have to comport with the Privileges and Immunities Clause.

The second argument merits more consideration. The New Jersey Supreme Court concluded that the Privileges and Immunities Clause does not apply to an ordinance that discriminates solely on the basis of *municipal* residency. The Clause is phrased in terms of *state* citizenship and was designed "to place the citizens of each State upon the same footing with citizens of other States, so far as the advantages resulting from citizenship in those States are concerned." Paul v. Virginia, 8 Wall. 168, 180 (1869)....

> "The primary purpose of this clause, like the clauses between which it is located—those relating to full faith and credit and to interstate extradition of fugitives from justice—was to help fuse into one Nation a collection of independent, sovereign States. It was designed to insure to a citizen of State A who ventures into State B the same privileges which the citizens of State B enjoy. For protection of such equality the citizen of State A was not to be restricted to the uncertain remedies afforded by diplomatic processes and official retaliation." Toomer v. Witsell, 334 U.S. 385, 395 (1948).

Municipal residency classifications, it is argued, simply do not give rise to the same concerns.

We cannot accept this argument. We have never read the Clause so literally as to apply it only to distinctions based on state citizenship. For example, in Mullaney v. Anderson, 342 U.S. 415, 419–420 (1952), the Court held that the

Alaska Territory had no more freedom to discriminate against those not residing in the Territory than did any State to favor its own citizens. And despite some initial uncertainty, ..., it is now established that the terms "citizen" and "resident" are "essentially interchangeable," Austin v. New Hampshire, 420 U.S. 656, 662, n. 8 (1975), for purposes of analysis of most cases under the Privileges and Immunities Clause. See Hicklin v. Orbeck, 437 U.S. 518, 524, n. 8 (1978); Toomer v. Witsell, 334 U.S. 385, 397 (1948). A person who is not residing in a given State is *ipso facto* not residing in a city within that State. Thus, whether the exercise of a privilege is conditioned on state residency or on municipal residency he will just as surely be excluded.

Given the Camden ordinance, an out-of-state citizen who ventures into New Jersey will not enjoy the same privileges as the New Jersey citizen residing in Camden. It is true that New Jersey citizens not residing in Camden will be affected by the ordinance as well as out-of-state citizens. And it is true that the disadvantaged New Jersey residents have no claim under the Privileges and Immunities Clause. The Slaughter–House Cases, 16 Wall. 36, 77 (1872). But New Jersey residents at least have a chance to remedy at the polls any discrimination against them. Out-of-state citizens have no similar opportunity, Austin v. New Hampshire, 420 U.S. 656, 662 (1975), and they must "not be restricted to the uncertain remedies afforded by diplomatic processes and official retaliation." Toomer v. Witsell, 334 U.S. 385, 395 (1948).[9] We conclude that Camden's ordinance is not immune from constitutional review at the behest of out-of-state residents merely because some in-state residents are similarly disadvantaged.

Application of the Privileges and Immunities Clause to a particular instance of discrimination against out-of-state residents entails a two-step inquiry. As an initial matter, the court must decide whether the ordinance burdens one of those privileges and immunities protected by the Clause. Baldwin v. Montana Fish and Game Comm'n, 436 U.S. 371, 383 (1978). Not all forms of discrimination against citizens of other States are constitutionally suspect.

> "Some distinctions between residents and nonresidents merely reflect the fact that this is a Nation composed of individual States, and are permitted; other distinctions are prohibited because they hinder the formation, the purpose, or the development of a single Union of those States. Only with respect to those 'privileges' and 'immunities' bearing upon the vitality of the Nation as a single entity must the State treat all citizens, resident and nonresident, equally."

As a threshold matter, then, we must determine whether an out-of-state resident's interest in employment on public works contracts in another State is sufficiently "fundamental" to the promotion of interstate harmony so as to "fall within the purview of the Privileges and Immunities Clause." Id., at 388. . . .

Certainly, the pursuit of a common calling is one of the most fundamental of those privileges protected by the Clause. Baldwin v. Montana Fish and Game

---

[9] The dissent suggests that New Jersey citizens not residing in Camden will adequately protect the interests of out-of-state residents and that the scope of the Privileges and Immunities Clause should be measured in light of this political reality. . . . What the dissent fails to appreciate is that the Camden ordinance at issue in this case was adopted pursuant to a comprehensive, state-wide program applicable in all New Jersey cities. The Camden resident-preference ordinance has already received state sanction and approval, and every New Jersey city is free to adopt a similar protectionist measure. Some have already done so. Thus, it is hard to see how New Jersey residents living outside Camden will protect the interests of out-of-state citizens.

. . .

Comm'n, 436 U.S. 371, 387 (1978). Many, if not most, of our cases expounding the Privileges and Immunities Clause have dealt with this basic and essential activity. See, e.g., Hicklin v. Orbeck, 437 U.S. 518 (1978); Austin v. New Hampshire, 420 U.S. 656 (1975); Mullaney v. Anderson, 342 U.S. 415 (1952); Toomer v. Witsell, 334 U.S. 385 (1948); Ward v. Maryland, 79 U.S. 418 (1871). Public employment, however, is qualitatively different from employment in the private sector; it is a subspecies of the broader opportunity to pursue a common calling. We have held that there is no fundamental right to government employment for purposes of the Equal Protection Clause. Massachusetts v. Murgia, 427 U.S. 307, 313 (1976) (per curiam). Cf. McCarthy v. Philadelphia Civil Service Comm'n, 424 U.S. 645 (1976) (per curiam) (rejecting equal protection challenge to municipal residency requirement for municipal workers). And in *White,* 103 S.Ct., at 1046, n. 7, we held that for purposes of the Commerce Clause everyone employed on a city public works project is, "in a substantial if informal sense, 'working for the city.'"

It can certainly be argued that for purposes of the Privileges and Immunities Clause everyone affected by the Camden ordinance is also "working for the city" and, therefore, has no grounds for complaint when the city favors its own residents. But we decline to transfer mechanically into this context an analysis fashioned to fit the Commerce Clause. Our decision in *White* turned on a distinction between the city acting as a market participant and the city acting as a market regulator. The question whether employees of contractors and subcontractors on public works projects were or were not, in some sense, working for the city was crucial to that analysis. The question had to be answered in order to chart the boundaries of the distinction. But the distinction between market participant and market regulator relied upon in *White* to dispose of the Commerce Clause challenge is not dispositive in this context. The two Clauses have different aims and set different standards for state conduct.

The Commerce Clause acts as an implied restraint upon state regulatory powers. Such powers must give way before the superior authority of Congress to legislate on (or leave unregulated) matters involving interstate commerce. When the State acts solely as a market participant, no conflict between state *regulation* and federal regulatory authority can arise. *White,* 103 S.Ct., at 1044; Reeves, Inc. v. Stake, 447 U.S. 429, 436–437 (1980); Hughes v. Alexandria Scrap Corp., 426 U.S. 794, 810 (1976). The Privileges and Immunities Clause, on the other hand, imposes a direct restraint on state action in the interests of interstate harmony. Hicklin v. Orbeck, 437 U.S. 518, 523–524 (1978); Ward v. Maryland, 79 U.S. 418, 430 (1871); Paul v. Virginia, 8 Wall. 168, 180 (1869). This concern with comity cuts across the market regulator-market participant distinction that is crucial under the Commerce Clause. It is discrimination against out-of-state residents on matters of fundamental concern which triggers the Clause, not regulation affecting interstate commerce. Thus, the fact that Camden is merely setting conditions on its expenditures for goods and services in the marketplace does not preclude the possibility that those conditions violate the Privileges and Immunities Clause.

In Hicklin v. Orbeck, 437 U.S. 518 (1978), we struck down as a violation of the Privileges and Immunities Clause an "Alaska Hire" statute containing a resident hiring preference for all employment related to the development of the State's oil and gas resources. Alaska argued in that case "that because the oil and gas that are the subject of Alaska Hire are *owned* by the State, this ownership, of itself, is sufficient justification for the Act's discrimination against nonresidents, and takes the Act totally without the scope of the Privileges and Immunities Clause." We concluded, however, that the State's interest in controlling those things it claims to own is not absolute. "Rather than placing a statute completely beyond the Clause, a State's ownership of the property with which the statute is concerned is a factor—although often the crucial factor—to be considered in evaluating whether the statute's discrimination against noncitizens violates the Clause." ... Much the same analysis, we think, is appropriate to a city's efforts to bias private employment decisions in favor of its residents on construction projects funded with public monies. The fact that Camden is expending its own funds or funds it administers in accordance with the terms of a grant is certainly a factor—perhaps the crucial factor—to be considered in evaluating whether the statute's discrimination violates the Privileges and Immunities Clause. But it does not remove the Camden ordinance completely from the purview of the Clause.

In sum, Camden may, without fear of violating the Commerce Clause, pressure private employers engaged in public works projects funded in whole or in part by the city to hire city residents. But that same exercise of power to bias the employment decisions of private contractors and subcontractors against out-of-state residents may be called to account under the Privileges and Immunities Clause. A determination of whether a privilege is "fundamental" for purposes of that Clause does not depend on whether the employees of private contractors and subcontractors engaged in public works projects can or cannot be said to be "working for the city." The opportunity to seek employment with such private employers is "sufficiently basic to the livelihood of the Nation," Baldwin v. Montana Fish and Game Comm'n, 436 U.S. 371, 388 (1978), as to fall within the purview of the Privileges and Immunities Clause even though the contractors and subcontractors are themselves engaged in projects funded in whole or part by the city.

The conclusion that Camden's ordinance discriminates against a protected privilege does not, of course, end the inquiry. We have stressed in prior cases that "[l]ike many other constitutional provisions, the privileges and immunities clause is not an absolute." Toomer v. Witsell, 334 U.S. 385, 396 (1948). It does not preclude discrimination against citizens of other States where there is a "substantial reason" for the difference in treatment. "[T]he inquiry in each case must be concerned with whether such reasons do exist and whether the degree of discrimination bears a close relation to them." As part of any justification offered for the discriminatory law, nonresidents must somehow be shown to "constitute a peculiar source of the evil at which the statute is aimed."

The city of Camden contends that its ordinance is necessary to counteract grave economic and social ills. Spiralling unemployment, a sharp decline in population, and a dramatic reduction in the number of businesses located in the city have eroded property values and depleted the city's tax base. The resident hiring preference is designed, the city contends, to increase the number of employed persons living in Camden and to arrest the "middle class flight" currently plaguing the city. The city also argues that all nonCamden residents employed on city public works projects, whether they reside in New Jersey or Pennsylvania, constitute a "source of the evil at which the statute is aimed." That is, they "live off" Camden without "living in" Camden. Camden contends that the scope of the discrimination practiced in the ordinance, with its municipal residency requirement, is carefully tailored to alleviate this evil without unreasonably harming nonresidents, who still have access to 60% of the available positions.

Every inquiry under the Privileges and Immunities Clause "must ... be conducted with due regard for the principle that the states should have considerable leeway in analyzing local evils and in prescribing appropriate cures." Toomer v. Witsell, 334 U.S. 385, 396 (1948). This caution is particularly appropriate when a government body is merely setting conditions on the expenditure of funds it controls. The Alaska Hire statute at issue in Hicklin v. Orbeck, 437 U.S. 518 (1978), swept within its strictures not only contractors and subcontractors dealing directly with the State's oil and gas; it also covered suppliers who provided goods and services to those contractors and subcontractors. We invalidated the Act as "an attempt to force virtually all businesses that benefit in some way from the economic ripple effect of Alaska's decision to develop its oil and gas resources to bias their employment practices in favor of the State's residents." No similar "ripple effect" appears to infect the Camden ordinance. It is limited in scope to employees working directly on city public works projects.

Nonetheless, we find it impossible to evaluate Camden's justification on the record as it now stands. No trial has ever been held in the case. No findings of fact have been made. The Supreme Court of New Jersey certified the case for direct appeal after the brief administrative proceedings that led to approval of the ordinance by the State Treasurer. It would not be appropriate for this Court either to make factual determinations as an initial matter or to take judicial notice of Camden's decay. We, therefore, deem it wise to remand the case to the New Jersey Supreme Court. That court may decide, consistent with state procedures, on the best method for making the necessary findings.

The judgment of the Supreme Court of New Jersey is reversed, and the case is remanded for proceedings not inconsistent with this opinion.

Reversed and Remanded.

Justice Blackmun, dissenting.

For over a century the underlying meaning of the Privileges and Immunities Clause of the Constitution's Article IV has been regarded as settled: at least absent some substantial, noninvidious justification, a State may not discriminate between its own residents and residents of other States on the basis of state citizenship . . .

Today, however, the Court casually extends the scope of the Clause by holding that it applies to laws that discriminate *among* state residents on the basis of *municipal* residence, simply because discrimination on the basis of municipal residence disadvantages citizens of other States "*ipso facto.*" This novel interpretation arrives accompanied by little practical justification and no historical or textual support whatsoever. Because I believe that the Privileges and Immunities Clause was not intended to apply to the kind of municipal discrimination presented by this case, I would affirm the judgment of the Supreme Court of New Jersey.

. . .

Contrary to the Court's tacit assumption, discrimination on the basis of municipal residence is substantially different in this regard from discrimination on the basis of state citizenship. The distinction is simple but fundamental: discrimination on the basis of municipal residence penalizes persons within the State's political community as well as those without. The Court itself points out that while New Jersey citizens who reside outside Camden are not protected by the Privileges and Immunities Clause, they may resort to the State's political processes to protect themselves. What the Court fails to appreciate is that this avenue of relief for New Jersey residents works to protect residents of other States as well; disadvantaged state residents who turn to the state legislature to displace ordinances like Camden's further the interests of nonresidents as well as their own. Nor is this mechanism for relief merely a theoretical one; in the past decade several States, including California and Georgia, have repealed or forbidden protectionist ordinances like the one at issue here. In short, discrimination on the basis of municipal residence simply does not consign residents of other States, in the words of *Toomer,* supra, to "the uncertain remedies afforded by diplomatic processes and official retaliation." The Court thus has applied the Privileges and Immunities Clause without regard for the political ills that it was designed to cure.

. . .

Supreme Court of Virginia v. Friedman

487 U.S. 59, 108 S.Ct. 2260, 101 L.Ed.2d 56 (1988).

Justice Kennedy delivered the opinion of the Court.

Qualified lawyers admitted to practice in other States may be admitted to the Virginia bar "on motion," that is, without taking the bar examination which Virginia otherwise requires. The State conditions such admission on a showing, among other matters, that the applicant is a permanent resident of Virginia. The question for decision is whether this residency requirement violates the Privileges and Immunities Clause of the United States Constitution, Art. IV, § 2. We hold that it does.

I

Myrna E. Friedman was admitted to the Illinois bar by examination in 1977 and to the District of Columbia bar by reciprocity in 1980. From 1977 to 1981, she was employed by the Department of the Navy in Arlington, Virginia, as a civilian attorney, and from 1982 until 1986, she was an attorney in private practice in Washington, D.C. In January 1986, she became associate general counsel for ERC International, Inc., a Delaware corporation. Friedman practices and maintains her offices at the company's principal place of business in Vienna, Virginia. Her duties at ERC International include drafting contracts and advising her employer and its subsidiaries on matters of Virginia law.

From 1977 to early 1986, Friedman lived in Virginia. In February 1986, however, she married and moved to her husband's home in Cheverly, Maryland. In June 1986, Friedman applied for admission to the Virginia bar on motion.

The applicable rule, promulgated by the Supreme Court of Virginia pursuant to statute, is Rule 1A:1. The Rule permits admission on motion of attorneys who are licensed to practice in another jurisdiction, provided the other jurisdiction admits Virginia attorneys without examination. The applicant must have been licensed for at least five years and the Virginia Supreme Court must determine that the applicant:

"(a) Is a proper person to practice law.

"(b) Has made such progress in the practice of law that it would be unreasonable to require him to take an examination.

"(c) Has become a permanent resident of the Commonwealth.

"(d) Intends to practice full time as a member of the Virginia bar."

In a letter accompanying her application, Friedman alerted the Clerk of the Virginia Supreme Court to her change of residence, but argued that her application should nevertheless be granted. Friedman gave assurance that she would be engaged full-time in the practice of law in Virginia, that she would be available for service of process and court appearances, and that she would keep informed of local rules. She also asserted "that there appears to be no reason to discriminate against my petition as a nonresident for admission to the Bar on motion," that her circumstances fit within the purview of this Court's decision in Supreme Court of New Hampshire v. Piper, 470 U.S. 274 (1985), and that accordingly she was entitled to admission under the Privileges and Immunities Clause of the Constitution Art. IV, § 2.

The Clerk wrote Friedman that her request had been denied. He explained that because Friedman was no longer a permanent resident of the Commonwealth of Virginia, she was not eligible for admission to the Virginia bar pursuant to Rule 1A:1. He added that the court had concluded that our decision in *Piper,* which invalidated a residency requirement imposed on lawyers who had passed a State's bar examination, was "not applicable" to the "discretionary requirement in Rule 1A:1 of residence as a condition of admission by reciprocity."

Friedman then commenced this action, against the Supreme Court of Virginia and its Clerk, in the United States District Court for the Eastern District of Virginia. She alleged that the residency requirement of Rule 1A:1 violated the Privileges and Immunities Clause. The District Court entered summary judgment in Friedman's favor, holding that the requirement of residency for admission without examination violates the Clause.*

The Court of Appeals for the Fourth Circuit unanimously affirmed. 822 F.2d 423 (1987)....

... We ... affirm.

II

Article IV, § 2, of the Constitution provides that the "Citizens of each State shall be entitled to all Privileges and Immunities of Citizens in the several States." The provision was designed "to place the citizens of each State upon the same footing with citizens of other States, so far as the advantages resulting from citizenship in those States are concerned." Paul v. Virginia, 8 Wall. 168, 180 (1869). See also Toomer v. Witsell, 334 U.S. 385, 395 (1948) (the Privileges and Immunities Clause "was designed to insure to a citizen of State A who ventures into State B the same privileges which the citizens of State B enjoy"). The Clause "thus establishes a norm of comity without specifying the particular subjects as to which citizens of one State coming within the jurisdiction of another are guaranteed equality of treatment." Austin v. New Hampshire, 420 U.S. 656, 660 (1975).

While the Privileges and Immunities Clause cites the term "Citizens," for analytic purposes citizenship and residency are essentially interchangeable. See United Building & Construction Trades Council v. Mayor of Camden, 465 U.S. 208, 216 (1984). When examining claims that a citizenship or residency classification offends privileges and immunities protections, we undertake a two-step inquiry. First, the activity in question must be "sufficiently basic to the livelihood of the Nation' ... as to fall within the purview of the Privileges and Immunities Clause...." Id., at 221–222, quoting Baldwin v. Montana Fish & Game Comm'n, 436 U.S. 371, 388 (1978). For it is "[o]nly with respect to those 'privileges' and 'immunities bearing on the vitality of the Nation as a single

---

* The District Court did not address Friedman's claims that the residency requirement of Rule 1A:1 also violates the Commerce Clause and the Equal Protection Clause of the Fourteenth Amendment. The Court of Appeals did not pass on these contentions either, and our resolution of Friedman's claim that the residency requirement violates the Privileges and Immunities Clause makes it unnecessary for us to reach them.

entity' that a State must accord residents and nonresidents equal treatment." Supreme Court of New Hampshire v. Piper, 470 U.S., at 279, quoting *Baldwin, supra,* at 383. Second, if the challenged restriction deprives nonresidents of a protected privilege, we will invalidate it only if we conclude that the restriction is not closely related to the advancement of a substantial State interest. *Piper, supra,* at 284. Appellants assert that the residency requirement offends neither part of this test. We disagree.

A

Appellants concede, as they must, that our decision in *Piper* establishes that a nonresident who takes and passes an examination prescribed by the State, and who otherwise is qualified for the practice of law, has an interest in practicing law that is protected by the Privileges and Immunities Clause. Appellants contend, however, that the discretionary admission provided for by Rule 1A:1 is not a privilege protected by the Clause for two reasons. First, appellants argue that the bar examination "serves as an adequate, alternative means of gaining admission to the bar." In appellants' view, "[s]o long as any applicant may gain admission to a State's bar, without regard to residence, by passing the bar examination," the State cannot be said to have discriminated against nonresidents "as a matter of fundamental concern." Second, appellants argue that the right to admission on motion is not within the purview of the Clause because, without offense to the Constitution, the State could require all bar applicants to pass an examination. Neither argument is persuasive.

We cannot accept appellants' first theory because it is quite inconsistent with our precedents. We reaffirmed in *Piper* the well-settled principle that "one of the privileges which the Clause guarantees to citizens of State A is that of doing business in State B on terms of substantial equality with the citizens of that State." *Piper, supra,* at 280, quoting Toomer v. Witsell, supra, at 396. See also *United Building & Construction Trades Council, supra,* at 219 ("Certainly, the pursuit of a common calling is one of the most fundamental of those privileges protected by the Clause"). After reviewing our precedents, we explicitly held that the practice of law, like other occupations considered in those cases, is sufficiently basic to the national economy to be deemed a privilege protected by the Clause. See *Piper, supra,* at 280–281. The clear import of *Piper* is that the Clause is implicated whenever, as is the case here, a State does not permit qualified nonresidents to practice law within its borders on terms of substantial equality with its own residents.

Nothing in our precedents, moreover, supports the contention that the Privileges and Immunities Clause does not reach a State's discrimination against nonresidents when such discrimination does not result in their total exclusion from the State. In Ward v. Maryland, 12 Wall. 418 (1871), for example, the Court invalidated a statute under which residents paid an annual fee of $12 to $150 for a license to trade foreign goods, while nonresidents were required to pay $300. Similarly, in *Toomer, supra,* the Court held that nonresident fishermen could not be required to pay a license fee one hundred times the fee charged to residents. In Hicklin v. Orbeck, 437 U.S. 518 (1978), the Court invalidated a statute requiring that residents be hired in preference to nonresidents for all positions related to the development of the State's oil and gas resources. Indeed, as the Court of Appeals correctly noted, the New Hampshire rule struck down in *Piper* did not result in the total exclusion of nonresidents from the practice of law in that State. 822 F.2d, at 427 (citing *Piper, supra,* at 277 n. 2).

Further, we find appellants' second theory—that Virginia could constitutionally require that all applicants to its bar take and pass an examination—quite irrelevant to the question whether the Clause is applicable in the circumstances of this case. A State's abstract authority to require from resident and nonresident alike that which it has chosen to demand from the nonresident alone has never been held to shield the discriminatory distinction from the reach of the Privileges and Immunities Clause. Thus, the applicability of the Clause to the present case no more turns on the legality *vel non* of an examination requirement than it turned on the inherent reasonableness of the fees charged to nonresidents in *Toomer* and *Ward*. The issue instead is whether the State has burdened the right to practice law, a privilege protected by the Privileges and Immunities Clause, by discriminating among otherwise equally qualified applicants solely on the basis of citizenship or residency. We conclude it has.

B

Our conclusion that the residents requirement burdens a privilege protected by the Privileges and Immunities Clause does not conclude the matter, of course; for we repeatedly have recognized that the Clause, like other constitutional provisions, is not an absolute. See, e.g., *Piper,* supra, at 284; *United Building & Construction Trades Council,* 465 U.S., at 222; *Toomer,* 334 U.S., at 396. The Clause does not preclude disparity in treatment where substantial reasons exist for the discrimination and the degree of discrimination bears a close relation to such reasons. See *United Building & Construction Trades Council,* supra, at 222. In deciding whether the degree of discrimination bears a sufficiently close relation to the reasons proffered by the State, the Court has considered whether, within the full panoply of legislative choices otherwise available to the State, there exist alternative means of furthering the State's purpose without implicating constitutional concerns. See *Piper,* 470 U.S., at 284.

Appellants offer two principal justifications for the Rule's requirement that applicants seeking admission on motion reside within the Commonwealth of Virginia. First, they contend that the residence requirement assures, in tandem with the full-time practice requirement, that attorneys admitted on motion will have the same commitment to service and familiarity with Virginia law that is possessed by applicants securing admission upon examination. Attorneys admitted on motion, appellants argue, have "no personal investment" in the jurisdiction; consequently, they "are entitled to no presumption that they will willingly and actively participate in bar activities and obligations, or fulfill their public service responsibilities to the State's client community." Second, appellants argue that the residency requirement facilitates enforcement of the full-time practice requirement of Rule 1A:1. We find each of these justifications insufficient to meet the State's burden of showing that the discrimination is warranted by a substantial State objective and closely drawn to its achievement.

We acknowledge that a bar examination is one method of assuring that the admitted attorney has a stake in her professional licensure and a concomitant interest in the integrity and standards of the bar. A bar examination, as we know judicially and from our own experience, is not a casual or lighthearted exercise. The question, however, is whether lawyers who are admitted in other States and seek admission in Virginia are less likely to respect the bar and further its interests solely because they are nonresidents. We cannot say this is the case. While *Piper* relied on an examination requirement as an indicium of the nonresident's commitment to the bar and to the State's legal profession, see

Piper, supra, at 285, it does not follow that when the State waives the examination it may make a distinction between residents and nonresidents.

Friedman's case proves the point. She earns her living working as an attorney in Virginia, and it is of scant relevance that her residence is located in the neighboring State of Maryland. It is indisputable that she has a substantial stake in the practice of law in Virginia. Indeed, despite appellants' suggestion at oral argument that Friedman's case is "atypical," the same will likely be true of all nonresident attorneys who are admitted on motion to the Virginia bar, in light of the State's requirement that attorneys so admitted show their intention to maintain an office and a regular practice in the State. See Application of Brown, 213 Va. 282, 286, n. 3, 191 S.E.2d 812, 815, n. 3 (1972) (interpreting full-time practice requirement of Rule 1A:1). This requirement goes a long way toward ensuring that such attorneys will have an interest in the practice of law in Virginia that is at least comparable to the interest we ascribed in *Piper* to applicants admitted upon examination. Accordingly, we see no reason to assume that nonresident attorneys who, like Friedman, seek admission to the Virginia bar on motion will lack adequate incentives to remain abreast of changes in the law or to fulfill their civic duties.

Further, to the extent that the State is justifiably concerned with ensuring that its attorneys keep abreast of legal developments, it can protect these interests through other equally or more effective means that do not themselves infringe constitutional protections. While this Court is not well-positioned to dictate specific legislative choices to the State, it is sufficient to note that such alternatives exist and that the State, in the exercise of its legislative prerogatives, is free to implement them. The Supreme Court of Virginia could, for example, require mandatory attendance at periodic continuing legal education courses. See *Piper,* supra, at 285, n. 19. The same is true with respect to the State's interest that the nonresident bar member does her share of volunteer and *pro bono* work. A "nonresident bar member, like the resident member, could be required to represent indigents and perhaps to participate in formal legal-aid work." *Piper,* supra, at 287 (footnote omitted).

We also reject appellants' attempt to justify the residency restriction as a necessary aid to the enforcement of the full-time practice requirement of Rule 1A:1. Virginia already requires, pursuant to the full-time practice restriction of Rule 1A:1, that attorneys admitted on motion maintain an office for the practice of law in Virginia. As the Court of Appeals noted, the requirement that applicants maintain an office in Virginia facilitates compliance with the full-time practice requirement in nearly the identical manner that the residency restriction does, rendering the latter restriction largely redundant. 822 F.2d, at 429. The office requirement furnishes an alternative to the residency requirement that is not only less restrictive, but also is fully adequate to protect whatever interest the State might have in the full-time practice restriction.

III

We hold that Virginia's residency requirement for admission to the State's bar without examination violates the Privileges and Immunities Clause. The nonresident's interest in practicing law on terms of substantial equality with those enjoyed by residents is a privilege protected by the Clause. A State may not discriminate against nonresidents unless it shows that such discrimination bears a close relation to the achievement of substantial State objectives. Virginia has failed to make this showing. Accordingly, the judgment of the Court of Appeals is affirmed.

It is so ordered.

Chief Justice Rehnquist, with whom Justice Scalia joins, dissenting.

Three Terms ago the Court invalidated a New Hampshire Bar rule which denied admission to an applicant who had passed the state bar examination because she was not, and would not become, a resident of the State. Supreme Court of New Hampshire v. Piper, 470 U.S. 274 (1985). In the present case the Court extends the reasoning of *Piper* to invalidate a Virginia Bar rule allowing admission on motion without examination to qualified applicants, but restricting the privilege to those applicants who have become residents of the State.

For the reasons stated in my dissent in *Piper,* I also disagree with the Court's decision in this case. I continue to believe that the Privileges and Immunities Clause of Article IV, § 2, does not require States to ignore residency when admitting lawyers to practice in the way that they must ignore residency when licensing traders in foreign goods, Ward v. Maryland, 12 Wall. 418 (1871), or when licensing commercial shrimp fishermen, Toomer v. Witsell, 334 U.S. 385 (1948).

I think the effect of today's decision is unfortunate even apart from what I believe is its mistaken view of the Privileges and Immunities Clause. Virginia's rule allowing admission on motion is an ameliorative provision, recognizing the fact that previous practice in another State may qualify a new resident of Virginia to practice there without the necessity of taking another bar examination. The Court's ruling penalizes Virginia, which has at least gone part way towards accommodating the present mobility of our population, but of course leaves untouched the rules of those States which allow no reciprocal admission on motion. Virginia may of course retain the privilege of admission on motion without enforcing a residency requirement even after today's decision, but it might also decide to eliminate admission on motion altogether.[a]

BARNARD v. THORSTENN, 489 U.S. 546 (1989). Two attorneys practicing law in New York City sought admission to practice law in the Virgin Islands without becoming residents. They challenged a rule requiring that a bar applicant demonstrate residence in the Virgin Islands for at least one year before admission and intent to continue to reside and practice law there. By statute Congress has made the Privileges and Immunities Clause of Article IV applicable to the territory of the Virgin Islands. Relying on Supreme Court of New Hampshire v. Piper, 470 U.S. 274 (1985), and Supreme Court of Virginia v. Friedman, 487 U.S. 59 (1988), the Court invalidated the rule's residency requirements. Despite the distance and geographic isolation of the Virgin Islands, the Court held that associating local counsel was an adequate alternative to serve the "interest in assuring that counsel will be available on short notice for unscheduled proceedings" and the interest in managing congested court dockets without having to accommodate delays due to attorney travel. Excluding nonresidents as a class was also not justified to solve the problems of conflicting court appearances, keeping attorneys current in their knowledge of local law, or supervising the ethics of a nationwide bar membership. Finally, with respect to the requirement that active members of the bar be available to accept appointments to appear on behalf of indigent criminal defendants, the Court found that nonresident attorneys could be required to share this burden but that making arrangements for substitute counsel when necessary, as an alternative to personal appearances, undercut the need for a "blanket exclusion of nonresidents." The Court concluded by saying:

[a] See, generally, Varat, *State "Citizenship" and Interstate Equality,* 48 U.Chi. L.Rev. 487 (1981).

"When the Privileges and Immunities Clause was made part of our Constitution, commercial and legal exchange between the distant States of the Union was at least as unsophisticated as that which exists today between the Virgin Islands and the mainland United States. Nevertheless, our Founders, in their wisdom, thought it important to our sense of nationhood that each State be required to make a genuine effort to treat nonresidents on an equal basis with residents. By extending the Privileges and Immunities Clause to the Virgin Islands, Congress has made the same decision with respect to that Territory."

Chief Justice Rehnquist, joined by Justices White and O'Connor, dissented, in the belief that "the unique circumstances of legal practice in the Virgin Islands, as compared to the mainland States, could justify upholding [the] simple residency requirement even under [*Piper*'s view of the Privileges and Immunities Clause]."

B.   THE TWENTY–FIRST AMENDMENT

Introduction. The relation of the Twenty–First Amendment to the commerce clause is quite different from that of Article IV, Section 2. Does the Amendment nullify the commerce clause as applied to the liquor trade?

Bacchus Imports, Ltd. v. Dias

468 U.S. 263, 104 S.Ct. 3049, 82 L.Ed.2d 200 (1984).

Justice White delivered the opinion of the Court.

Appellants challenge the constitutionality of the Hawaii Liquor Tax, which is a 20% excise tax imposed on sales of liquor at wholesale. Specifically at issue are exemptions from the tax for certain locally produced alcoholic beverages. The Supreme Court of Hawaii upheld the tax against challenges based upon the Equal Protection Clause, the Import–Export Clause, and the Commerce Clause.... We ... reverse.

I

The Hawaii Liquor Tax was originally enacted in 1939 to defray the costs of police and other governmental services that the Hawaii legislature concluded had been increased due to the consumption of liquor. At its inception the statute contained no exemptions. However, because the legislature sought to encourage development of the Hawaiian liquor industry, it enacted an exemption for *okolehao* from May 17, 1971, until June 20, 1981, and an exemption for fruit wine from May 17, 1976, until June 30, 1981....

Appellants—Bacchus Imports, Ltd., and Eagle Distributors, Inc.—are liquor wholesalers who sell to licensed retailers. They sell the liquor at their wholesale price plus the 20% excise tax imposed by § 244–4, plus a one-half percent tax imposed by Hawaii Rev.Stat. § 237–13. Pursuant to Hawaii Rev. Stat. § 40–35, which authorizes a taxpayer to pay taxes under protest and to commence an action in the Tax Appeal Court for the recovery of disputed sums, the wholesalers initiated protest proceedings and sought refunds of all taxes paid. Their complaint alleged that the Hawaii liquor tax was unconstitutional because it violates both the Import–Export Clause and the Commerce Clause of the United States Constitution. The wholesalers sought a refund of approximately $45 million, representing all of the liquor tax paid by them for the years in question.

The Tax Appeal Court rejected both constitutional claims. On appeal, the Supreme Court of Hawaii affirmed the decision of the Tax Appeal Court and rejected an equal protection challenge as well....

. . .

III

A cardinal rule of Commerce Clause jurisprudence is that "[n]o State, consistent with the Commerce Clause, may 'impose a tax which discriminates against interstate commerce ... by providing a direct commercial advantage to local business.' " Boston Stock Exchange v. State Tax Commission, 429 U.S. 318, 329 (1977) (quoting Northwestern States Portland Cement Co. v. Minnesota, 358 U.S. 450, 457 (1959). Despite the fact that the tax exemption here at issue seems clearly to discriminate on its face against interstate commerce by bestowing a commercial advantage on okolehao and pineapple wine, the State argues—and the Hawaii Supreme Court held—that there is no improper discrimination.

A

Much of the State's argument centers on its contention that okolehao and pineapple wine do not compete with the other products sold by the wholesalers....

... On the stipulated facts in this case, we are unwilling to conclude that no competition exists between the exempted and the nonexempted liquors.

B

. . .

... [W]e need not guess at the legislature's motivation, for it is undisputed that the purpose of the exemption was to aid Hawaiian industry. Likewise, the effect of the exemption is clearly discriminatory, in that it applies only to locally produced beverages, even though it does not apply to all such products. Consequently, as long as there is some competition between the locally produced exempt products and nonexempt products from outside the State, there is a discriminatory effect.

. . .

We therefore conclude that the Hawaii Liquor Tax exemption for okolehao and pineapple wine violated the Commerce Clause because it had both the purpose and effect of discriminating in favor of local products.

IV

The State argues in this Court that even if the tax exemption violates ordinary Commerce Clause principles, it is saved by the Twenty-first Amendment to the Constitution....

Despite broad language in some of the opinions of this Court written shortly after enactment of the Amendment,[13] more recently we have recognized

---

[13] For example, in State Board of Equalization v. Young's Market Co., 299 U.S. 59, 62 (1936), the Court stated:

"The plaintiffs ask us to limit this broad command. They request us to construe the Amendment as saying, in effect: The State may prohibit the importation of intoxicating liquors provided it prohibits the manufacture and sale within its borders; but if it permits such manufacture and sale, it must let imported liquors compete with the domestic on equal terms. To say that, would involve not a construction of the Amendment, but a rewriting of it."

the obscurity of the legislative history of § 2. See California Retail Liquor Dealers Assn. v. Midcal Aluminum, Inc., 445 U.S. 97, 107 n. 10 (1980). No clear consensus concerning the meaning of the provision is apparent. Indeed, Senator Blaine, the Senate sponsor of the Amendment resolution, appears to have espoused varying interpretations. In reporting the view of the Senate Judiciary Committee, he said that the purpose of § 2 was "to restore to the States ... absolute control over interstate commerce affecting intoxicating liquors...." 76 Cong.Rec. 4143 (1933). On the other hand, he also expressed a narrower view: "So to assure the so-called dry States against the importation of intoxicating liquor into those States, it is proposed to write permanently into the Constitution a prohibition along that line." Id., at 4141.

It is by now clear that the Amendment did not entirely remove state regulation of alcoholic beverages from the ambit of the Commerce Clause....

Approaching the case in this light, we are convinced that Hawaii's discriminatory tax cannot stand. Doubts about the scope of the Amendment's authorization notwithstanding, one thing is certain: The central purpose of the provision was not to empower States to favor local liquor industries by erecting barriers to competition. It is also beyond doubt that the Commerce Clause itself furthers strong federal interests in preventing economic Balkanization.... State laws that constitute mere economic protectionism are therefore not entitled to the same deference as laws enacted to combat the perceived evils of an unrestricted traffic in liquor. Here, the State does not seek to justify its tax on the ground that it was designed to promote temperance or to carry out any other purpose of the Twenty-first Amendment, but instead acknowledges that the purpose was "to promote a local industry." Consequently, because the tax violates a central tenet of the Commerce Clause but is not supported by any clear concern of the Twenty-first Amendment, we reject the State's belated claim based on the Amendment.

V

. . .

These refund issues, which are essentially issues of remedy for the imposition of a tax that unconstitutionally discriminated against interstate commerce, were not addressed by the state courts. Also, the Federal constitutional issues involved may well be intertwined with, or their consideration obviated by, issues of state law. Also, resolution of those issues, if required at all, may necessitate more of a record than so far has been made in this case. We are reluctant, therefore, to address them in the first instance. Accordingly, we reverse the judgment of the Supreme Court of Hawaii and remand for further proceedings not inconsistent with this opinion.

So ordered.

Justice Brennan took no part in the consideration or decision of this case.

Justice Stevens, with whom Justice Rehnquist and Justice O'Connor join, dissenting.

The Court went on to observe, however, that a high license fee for importation may "serve as an aid in policing the liquor traffic." Id., at 63.

See also Mahoney v. Joseph Triner Corp., 304 U.S. 401, 403 (1938) ("since the adoption of the Twenty-first Amendment, the equal protection clause is not applicable to imported intoxicating liquor"). Cf. Craig v. Boren, 429 U.S. 190 (1976).

... I would affirm the judgment of the Supreme Court of Hawaii because the wholesalers' Commerce Clause claim is squarely foreclosed by the Twenty-first Amendment to the United States Constitution.

. . .

III

Today the Court, in essence, holds that the Hawaii tax is unconstitutional because it places a burden on intoxicating liquors that have been imported into Hawaii for use therein that is not imposed on liquors that are produced locally. As I read the text of the Amendment, it expressly authorizes this sort of burden. Moreover, as I read Justice Brandeis' opinion for the Court in the seminal case of State Board of Equalization v. Young's Market Co., 299 U.S. 59 (1936), the Court has squarely so decided.

In *Young's Market,* the Court upheld a California statute that imposed a license fee on the privilege of importing beer to any place in California. After noting that the statute would have been obviously unconstitutional prior to the Twenty-first Amendment, the Court explained that the Amendment enables a State to establish a local monopoly and to prevent or discourage competition from imported liquors....

. . .

As a matter of pure constitutional power, Hawaii may surely prohibit the importation of all intoxicating liquors. It seems clear to me that it may do so without prohibiting the local sale of liquors that are produced within the State. In other words, even though it seems unlikely that the okolehao lobby could persuade it to do so, the Hawaii Legislature surely has the power to create a local monopoly by prohibiting the sale of any other alcoholic beverage. If the State has the constitutional power to create a total local monopoly—thereby imposing the most severe form of discrimination on competing products originating elsewhere—I believe it may also engage in a less extreme form of discrimination that merely provides a special benefit, perhaps in the form of a subsidy or a tax exemption, for locally produced alcoholic beverages.

The Court's contrary conclusion is based on the "obscurity of the legislative history" of § 2. What the Court ignores is that it was argued in *Young's Market* that a "limitation of the broad language" of § 2 was "sanctioned by its history," but the Court, observing that the language of the Amendment was "clear," determined that it was unnecessary to consider the history, 299 U.S., at 63–64—the history which the Court today considers unclear. But now, according to the Court, the force of the Twenty-first Amendment contention in this case is diminished because the "central purpose of the provision was not to empower States to favor local liquor industries by erecting barriers to competition." It follows, according to the Court, that "state laws that constitute mere economic protectionism are not entitled to the same deference as laws enacted to combat the perceived evils of an unrestricted traffic in liquor." This is a totally novel approach to the Twenty-first Amendment. The question is not one of "deference," nor one of "central purposes;" the question is whether the provision in this case is an exercise of a power expressly conferred upon the States by the Constitution. It plainly is.

Accordingly, I respectfully dissent.

BROWN-FORMAN DISTILLERS CORP. v. NEW YORK STATE LIQUOR AUTHORITY, 476 U.S. 573 (1986). This case involved an attack on a New York law requiring liquor distillers to sell liquor in the state at a price no higher than the lowest price charged for similar sales in other states. The Court first held the law in violation of the commerce clause and then rejected New York's twenty-first amendment defense, saying:

"New York finally contends that the Twenty-first Amendment, which bans the importation or possession of intoxicating liquors into a State 'in violation of the laws thereof,' saves the ABC Law from invalidation under the Commerce Clause. That Amendment gives the States wide latitude to regulate the importation and distribution of liquor within their territories, California Liquor Dealers Assn. v. Midcal Aluminum, Inc., 445 U.S. 97, 107 (1980). Therefore, New York argues, its ABC Law, which regulates the sale of alcoholic beverages within the State, is a valid exercise of the State's authority.

"It is well settled that the Twenty-first Amendment did not entirely remove state regulation of alcohol from the reach of the Commerce Clause. See Bacchus Imports, Ltd. v. Dias, 468 U.S. 263 (1984). Rather, the Twenty-first Amendment and the Commerce Clause 'each must be considered in light of the other and in the context of the issues and interests at stake in any concrete case.' Hostetter v. Idlewild Bon Voyage Liquor Corp., 377 U.S. 324, 332 (1964). Our task, then, is to reconcile the interests protected by the two constitutional provisions.

"New York has a valid constitutional interest in regulating sales of liquor within the territory of New York. Section 2 of the Twenty-first Amendment, however, speaks only to state regulation of the 'transportation or importation into any State ... for delivery or use therein' of alcoholic beverages. That Amendment, therefore, gives New York only the authority to control sales of liquor in New York, and confers no authority to control sales in other states. The Commerce Clause operates with full force whenever one State attempts to regulate the transportation and sale of alcoholic beverages destined for distribution and consumption in a foreign country, *Idlewild Bon Voyage Liquor Corp.,* supra, or another State. Our conclusion that New York has attempted to regulate sales in other States of liquor that will be consumed in other States therefore disposes of the Twenty-first Amendment issue.

"Moreover, New York's affirmation law may interfere with the ability of other States to exercise their own authority under the Twenty-first Amendment. Once a distiller has posted prices in New York, it is not free to lower them in another State, even in response to a regulatory directive by that State, without risking forfeiture of its license in New York. New York law, therefore, may force other States either to abandon regulatory goals or to deprive their citizens of the opportunity to purchase brands of liquor that are sold in New York. New York's reliance on the Twenty-first Amendment is therefore misplaced. . . ."

Capital Cities Cable, Inc. v. Crisp

467 U.S. 691, 104 S.Ct. 2694, 81 L.Ed.2d 580 (1984).

Justice Brennan delivered the opinion of the Court.

The question presented in this case is whether Oklahoma may require cable television operators in that State to delete all advertisements for alcoholic beverages contained in the out-of-state signals that they retransmit by cable to their subscribers. Petitioners contend that Oklahoma's requirement abridges their rights under the First and Fourteenth Amendments and is pre-empted by federal law. Because we conclude that this state regulation is pre-empted, we reverse the judgment of the Court of Appeals for the Tenth Circuit and do not reach the First Amendment question.

. . .

II

Petitioners and the FCC contend that the federal regulatory scheme for cable television systems administered by the Commission is intended to pre-empt any state regulation of the signals carried by cable system operators. Respondent apparently concedes that enforcement of the Oklahoma statute in this case conflicts with federal law, but argues that because the State's advertising ban was adopted pursuant to the broad powers to regulate the transportation and importation of intoxicating liquor reserved to the States by the Twenty-first Amendment, the statute should prevail notwithstanding the conflict with federal law. As in California Retail Liquor Dealers Assn. v. Midcal Aluminum, Inc., 445 U.S. 97 (1980), where we held that a California wine pricing program violated the Sherman Act notwithstanding the State's reliance upon the Twenty-first Amendment in establishing that system, we turn first before assessing the impact of the Twenty-first Amendment to consider whether the Oklahoma statute does in fact conflict with federal law.

. . .

III

Respondent contends that even if the Oklahoma advertising ban is invalid under normal pre-emption analysis, the fact that the ban was adopted pursuant to the Twenty-first Amendment rescues the statute from pre-emption. A similar claim was advanced in California Retail Liquor Dealers Assn. v. Midcal Aluminum, Inc., 445 U.S. 97 (1980). In that case, after finding that a California wine pricing program violated the Sherman Act, we considered whether § 2 of the Twenty-first Amendment, which reserves to the States certain power to regulate traffic in liquor, "permits California to countermand the congressional policy—adopted under the commerce power—in favor of competition." 445 U.S., at 106. Here, we must likewise consider whether § 2 permits Oklahoma to override the federal policy, as expressed in FCC rulings and regulations, in favor of promoting the widespread development of cable communication.

The States enjoy broad power under § 2 of the Twenty-first Amendment to regulate the importation and use of intoxicating liquor within their borders. Ziffrin, Inc. v. Reeves, 308 U.S. 132 (1939). At the same time, our prior cases have made clear that the Amendment does not license the States to ignore their obligations under other provisions of the Constitution. See, e.g., Larkin v. Grendel's Den, 459 U.S. 116, 122 n. 5 (1982); California v. LaRue, 409 U.S. 109, 115 (1972); Wisconsin v. Constantineau, 400 U.S. 433, 436 (1971); Department of Revenue v. James B. Beam Distilling Co., 377 U.S. 341, 345–346 (1964). Indeed, "[t]his Court's decisions . . . have confirmed that the Amendment primarily created an exception to the normal operation of the Commerce Clause." Craig v. Boren, 429 U.S. 190, 206 (1976). Thus, as the Court explained in Hostetter v. Idlewild Bon Voyage Liquor Corp., 377 U.S. 324 (1964), § 2 reserves to the States power to impose burdens on interstate commerce in intoxicating liquor that, absent the Amendment, would clearly be invalid under the Commerce Clause. Id., at 330; State Board of Equalization v. Young's Market Co., 299 U.S. 59, 62–63 (1936). We have cautioned, however, that "[t]o draw a conclusion . . . that the Twenty-first Amendment has somehow operated to 'repeal' the Commerce Clause wherever regulation of intoxicating liquors is concerned would . . . be an absurd oversimplification." Hostetter, supra, at 331–

332. Notwithstanding the Amendment's broad grant of power to the States, therefore, the Federal Government plainly retains authority under the Commerce Clause to regulate even interstate commerce in liquor. . . .

In rejecting the claim that the Twenty-first Amendment ousted the Federal Government of all jurisdiction over interstate traffic in liquor, we have held that when a State has not attempted directly to regulate the sale or use of liquor within its borders—the core § 2 power—a conflicting exercise of federal authority may prevail. In *Hostetter,* for example, the Court found that in-state sales of intoxicating liquor intended to be used only in foreign countries could be made under the supervision of the federal Bureau of Customs, despite contrary state law, because the state regulation was not aimed at preventing unlawful use of alcoholic beverages within the state, but rather was designed "totally to prevent transactions carried on under the aegis of a law passed by Congress in the exercise of its explicit power under the Constitution to regulate commerce with foreign nations." Similarly, in *Midcal Aluminum,* supra, we found that "the Twenty-first Amendment provides no shelter for the violation of the Sherman Act caused by the State's wine pricing program," because the State's interest in promoting temperance through the program was not substantial and was therefore clearly outweighed by the important federal objectives of the Sherman Act.

Of course, our decisions in *Hostetter* and *Midcal Aluminum* were concerned only with conflicting state and federal efforts to regulate transactions involving liquor. In this case, by contrast, we must resolve a clash between an express federal decision to pre-empt all state regulation of cable signal carriage and a state effort to apply its ban on alcoholic beverage advertisements to wine commercials contained in out-of-state signals carried by cable systems. Nonetheless, the central question presented in those cases is essentially the same as the one before us here: whether the interests implicated by a state regulation are so closely related to the powers reserved by the Twenty-first Amendment that the regulation may prevail, notwithstanding that its requirements directly conflict with express federal policies. As in *Hostetter* and *Midcal Aluminum,* resolution of this question requires a "pragmatic effort to harmonize state and federal powers" within the context of the issues and interests at stake in each case. 445 U.S., at 109.

There can be little doubt that the comprehensive regulations developed over the past twenty years by the FCC to govern signal carriage by cable television systems reflect an important and substantial federal interest. . . .

On the other hand, application of Oklahoma's advertising ban to out-of-state signals carried by cable operators in that State is designed principally to further the State's interest in discouraging consumption of intoxicating liquor. Although the District Court found that "consumption of alcoholic beverages in Oklahoma has increased substantially in the last 20 years despite the ban on advertising of such beverages," we may nevertheless accept Oklahoma's judgment that restrictions on liquor advertising represent at least a reasonable, albeit limited, means of furthering the goal of promoting temperance in the State. The modest nature of Oklahoma's interests may be further illustrated by noting that Oklahoma has chosen not to press its campaign against alcoholic beverage advertising on all fronts. For example, the State permits both print and broadcast commercials for beer, as well as advertisements for all alcoholic beverages contained in newspapers, magazines and other publications printed outside of the State. The ban at issue in this case is directed only at wine commercials that occasionally appear on out-of-state signals carried by cable operators. By their own terms, therefore, the State's regulatory aims in this area are narrow. Although a state regulatory scheme obviously need not amount to a comprehensive attack on the problems of alcohol consumption in order to constitute a valid exercise of state power under the Twenty-first Amendment, the selective approach Oklahoma has taken toward liquor advertising suggests limits on the substantiality of the interests it asserts here. In contrast to state regulations governing the conditions under which liquor may be imported or sold within the state, therefore, the application of Oklahoma's advertising ban to the importation of distant signals by cable television operators engages only indirectly the central power reserved by § 2 of the Twenty-first Amendment—that of exercising "control over whether to permit importation or sale of liquor and how to structure the liquor distribution system." *Midcal Aluminum,* 445 U.S., at 110.

When this limited interest is measured against the significant interference with the federal objective of ensuring widespread availability of diverse cable services throughout the United States—an objective that will unquestionably be frustrated by strict enforcement of the Oklahoma statute—it is clear that the state's interest is not of the same stature as the goals identified in the FCC's rulings and regulations. As in *Midcal Aluminum,* therefore, we hold that when, as here, a state regulation squarely conflicts with the accomplishment and execution of the full purposes of federal law, and the state's central power under the Twenty-first Amendment of regulating the times, places, and manner under which liquor may be imported and sold is not directly implicated, the balance between state and federal power tips decisively in favor of the federal law, and enforcement of the state statute is barred by the Supremacy Clause.[16]

IV

We conclude that the application of Oklahoma's alcoholic beverage advertising ban to out-of-state signals carried by cable operators in that State is pre-empted by federal law and that the Twenty-first Amendment does not save the regulation from pre-emption. The judgment of the Court of Appeals is

Reversed.

324 LIQUOR CORP. v. DUFFY, 479 U.S. 335 (1987). The Court held that a New York statute requiring retailers to charge at least 112 percent of the posted wholesale price for liquor, but permitting wholesalers to sell to retailers at less than the posted price, violated the Sherman Act. It then addressed the question whether the twenty-first amendment immunized the state law from the Sherman Act, saying:

"The States' Twenty-first Amendment powers, though broad, are circumscribed by other provisions of the Constitution. See Larkin v. Grendel's Den, Inc., 459 U.S. 116, 122, n. 5 (1982) (Establishment Clause); Craig v. Boren, 429 U.S. 190, 204–209 (1976) (Equal Protection Clause); Wisconsin v. Constantineau, 400 U.S. 433, 436 (1971) (procedural due process); Department of Revenue v. James Beam Co., 377 U.S. 341, 345–346 (1964) (Export–Import Clause). Although § 2 directly qualifies the federal commerce power, the Court has rejected the view that 'the Twenty-first Amendment has somehow operated to "repeal" the Commerce Clause wherever regulation of intoxicating liquors is concerned.' Hostetter v. Idlewild Liquor Corp., 377 U.S. 324 331–332 (1964). Instead the Court has engaged in a 'pragmatic effort to harmonize state and federal powers.'

---

[16] Because we have resolved the pre-emption and Twenty-first Amendment issues in petitioners' favor, we need not consider the additional question whether Oklahoma's advertising ban constitutes an invalid restriction on protected commercial speech, and we therefore express no view on that issue.

Midcal, supra, 445 U.S., at 109. The question in each case is whether the interests implicated by a state regulation are so closely related to the powers reserved by the Twenty-first Amendment that the regulation may prevail, notwithstanding that its requirements directly conflict with express federal policies. Capital Cities Cable, Inc. v. Crisp, 467 U.S. 691, 714 (1984)."

The Court then went on to find that there were no adequate state interests protected here to override the federal statute. Two justices dissented.

NORTH DAKOTA v. UNITED STATES, 495 U.S. 423 (1990). North Dakota requires all persons bringing liquor into the state to report all shipments and returns. It allows out-of-state distillers, who normally may sell only to licensed North Dakota wholesalers but not retailers, to sell liquor directly to federal enclaves within the state. When they do so, however, the distillers must label each item, indicating that the liquor is for domestic consumption only within the federal enclave. With no majority opinion, the Court upheld both the reporting and the labeling regulations over the objections of the United States that, as applied to sales of liquor destined for federal enclaves—in this case military bases over which the United States and North Dakota exercise concurrent jurisdiction—the regulations violate the federal government's constitutional immunity from state regulation and in any event are preempted by a 1986 federal procurement statute directing that liquor be obtained from the most competitive source.

Justice Stevens, for a plurality of four, acknowledged that prior cases involving state power to pass liquor control regulations burdening the Federal Government had "concluded that [a] State had no authority to regulate in an area or over a transaction that fell outside of its jurisdiction." Still, other cases "made clear that the States have the power to control shipments of liquor during their passage through their territory and to take appropriate steps to prevent the unlawful diversion of liquor into its regulated intrastate market."

"The two North Dakota regulations fall within the core of the State's power under the Twenty-first Amendment. In the interest of promoting temperance, ensuring orderly market conditions, and raising revenue, the State has established a comprehensive system for the distribution of liquor within its borders. That system is unquestionably legitimate.... [The reporting and labeling requirements] are necessary components of the regulatory regime.... The risk of diversion into the retail market and disruption of the liquor distribution system is ... both substantial and real.... Given the special protection afforded to state liquor control policies by the Twenty-first Amendment, [the regulations] are supported by a strong presumption of validity and should not be set aside lightly."

Armed with that presumption, Justice Stevens found no intergovernmental immunity violation, because neither regulation regulated the United States directly or discriminated against it or those with whom it deals. As for the preemption claim, although "Congress has the power to confer immunity from state regulation on government suppliers beyond that conferred by the Constitution alone, ... even when the state regulation is enacted pursuant to the State's powers under the Twenty-first Amendment[,] when the Court is asked to set aside a regulation at the core of [those] powers ... it must proceed with particular care." He then concluded that "Congress has not here spoken with sufficient clarity to pre-empt North Dakota's attempt to protect its liquor distribution system."

Justice Scalia concurred in the judgment, taking the position that the Twenty–First Amendment abolished the Federal Government's immunity from state liquor import regulation. Hence the State could have required that *all* liquor sold in-state be purchased from a licensed in-state wholesaler, and the fact that North Dakota gave the "Federal Government a choice between purchasing label-free bottles from in-state wholesalers or purchasing labelled bottles from out-of-state distillers, ... an option that no other retailer in the State enjoys[,]" negated any viable claim of discrimination against the Federal Government.

Four Justices agreed that the nondiscriminatory reporting requirement was lawful but would have held the labelling regulation invalid because it "substantially obstructs federal operations, and it discriminates against the Federal Government and its chosen business partners." These four also disagreed with Justice Scalia, arguing that the Twenty–First Amendment did not empower the States to regulate liquor shipments to military bases over which the Federal Government and a State share concurrent jurisdiction.

SECTION 6. PREEMPTION OF STATE LEGISLATION BY FEDERAL LEGISLATION—THE IMPACT OF THE SUPREMACY CLAUSE

Introduction. We first met the preemption problem in Gibbons v. Ogden, supra p. 167, where the Court held the New York grant of a monopoly on a steamboat route to be inconsistent with the grant of a federal license to another steamboat to operate on the route. Marshall stated the ultimate principle—should there be a "collision" between an Act of Congress passed pursuant to the Constitution and a state statute, the state law "must yield to the law of Congress."

While simple to state, the principle is difficult to apply. The Supreme Court has applied a variety of verbal formulas over the years in seeking to determine when there is such a "collision" that the state law must fall. In many early cases it took a broad view of the subject, suggesting that merely by regulating in an area Congress should be taken as having "occupied the field" and determined that the states should not regulate in that field. See, e.g., Napier v. Atlantic Coast Line R. Co., 272 U.S. 605 (1926), in which the Court held that by granting power to the Interstate Commerce Commission to prescribe rules governing the safety of locomotives, Congress "intended to occupy the field" and state statutes requiring cab curtains and particular types of firebox doors were invalid even though the Commission had not issued any rules relating to cab curtains and firebox doors.

More recently the Court has been less likely to imply Congressional intent to supersede state laws in the absence of fairly direct conflict. In Rice v. Santa Fe Elevator Corp., 331 U.S. 218, 230 (1947), e.g., the Court said that when Congress has legislated "in a field which the States have traditionally occupied," we "start with the assumption that the historic police powers of the States were not to be superseded by the Federal Act unless that was the clear and manifest purpose of Congress.... Such a purpose may be evidenced in several ways. The scheme of federal regulation may be so pervasive as to make reasonable the inference that Congress left no room for the States to supplement it.... Or the Act of Congress may touch a field in which the federal interest is so dominant that the federal system will be assumed to preclude enforcement of state laws on the same subject. Likewise, the object sought to be obtained by the federal law and the character of obligations imposed by it may reveal the same purpose.... Or the state policy may produce a result inconsistent with the objective of the federal statute.... It is often a perplexing question whether Congress has precluded state action or by the choice of selective regulatory measures has left the police power of the States undisturbed except as the state and federal regulations collide."

A useful law review note—*Pre-emption as a Preferential Ground: A New Canon of Construction*, 12 Stan.L.Rev. 308 (1959), Selected Essays on Constitutional Law, 1938–1962 (1963), 310—contains the following paragraph:

> "[T]he Court has adopted the same weighing of interests approach in pre-emption cases that it uses to determine whether a state law unjustifiably burdens interstate commerce. In a number of situations the Court has invalidated statutes on the pre-emption ground when it appeared that the state laws sought to favor local economic interests at the expense of the interstate market. On the other hand, when the Court has been satisfied that valid local interests, such as those in safety or in the reputable operation of local business, outweigh the restrictive effect on interstate commerce, the Court has rejected the pre-emption argument and allowed state regulation to stand...."

The case that follows illustrates the Court's approach to pre-emption cases. It is relevant to note that federal regulation may present pre-emption problems whether or not state law regulates interstate commerce. See, e.g., De Canas v. Bica, 424 U.S. 351 (1976), involving an alleged conflict between a California statute regulating employment of illegal aliens and the federal immigration laws.

Gade v. National Solid Wastes Management Association

505 U.S. 88, 112 S.Ct. 2374, 120 L.Ed.2d 73 (1992).

Justice O'Connor announced the judgment of the Court and delivered an opinion, Parts I, III, and IV of which represent the views of the Court, and Part II of which is joined by The Chief Justice, Justice White, and Justice Scalia.

In 1988, the Illinois General Assembly enacted the Hazardous Waste Crane and Hoisting Equipment Operators Licensing Act ... and the Hazardous Waste Laborers Licensing Act.... The stated purpose of the acts is both "to promote job safety" and "to protect life, limb and property." ... [W]e consider whether these "dual impact" statutes, which protect both workers and the general public, are pre-empted by the federal Occupational Safety and Health Act of 1970 ... (OSH Act), and the standards promulgated ... by the Occupational Safety and Health Administration (OSHA).

I

. . .

... OSHA ... promulgated regulations on "Hazardous Waste Operations and Emergency Response," including detailed regulations on worker training requirements.... The OSHA regulations require ... that workers engaged in an activity that may expose them to hazardous wastes receive a minimum of 40 hours of instruction off the site, and a minimum of three days actual field experience under the supervision of a trained supervisor.... On-site managers and supervisors directly responsible for hazardous waste operations must receive the same initial training as general employees, plus at least eight additional hours of specialized training on various health and safety programs.... Employees and supervisors are required to receive eight hours of refresher training annually....

In 1988 ... Illinois enacted the licensing acts at issue here. The laws are designated as acts "in relation to environmental protection," and their stated aim is to protect both employees and the general public by licensing hazardous waste equipment operators and laborers working at certain facilities. Both acts require a license applicant to provide a certified record of at least 40 hours of training under an approved program conducted within Illinois, to pass a written examination, and to complete an annual refresher course of at least eight hours of instruction.... In addition, applicants for a hazardous waste crane operator's license must submit "a certified record showing operation of equipment used in hazardous waste handling for a minimum of 4,000 hours."
...

   . . .

   ... [T]he Association [sued] ... to enjoin ... enforc[ement of] the Illinois licensing acts, claiming [they] were pre-empted by the OSH Act and OSHA regulations and that they violated the Commerce Clause of the United States Constitution.... [T]he District Court held [the state] acts ... not pre-empted because each protected public safety in addition to promoting job safety.... [It] invalidated the requirement that applicants for a hazardous waste license be trained "within Illinois" on the ground that the provision did not contribute to Illinois's stated purpose of protecting public safety [and] declined to consider the Association's Commerce Clause challenge for lack of ripeness....

   ... [The] Court of Appeals ... affirmed in part and reversed in part....

II

Before addressing the scope of the OSH Act's pre-emption of dual impact state regulations, we consider petitioner's threshold argument ... that the Act does not pre-empt nonconflicting state regulations at all. "[T]he question whether a certain state action is pre-empted by federal law is one of congressional intent. 'The purpose of Congress is the ultimate touchstone.' " ... "To discern Congress' intent we examine the explicit statutory language and the structure and purpose of the statute." ...

In the OSH Act, Congress endeavored "to assure so far as possible every working man and woman in the Nation safe and healthful working conditions." ... To that end, Congress authorized ... mandatory occupational safety and health standards applicable to all businesses affecting interstate commerce, ... and thereby brought the Federal Government into a field that traditionally had been occupied by the States. Federal regulation of the workplace was not intended to be all-encompassing, however. First, Congress expressly saved two areas from federal pre-emption. [One is state worker compensation laws. In addition,] Section 18(a) provides that the Act does not "prevent any State agency or court from asserting jurisdiction under State law over any occupational safety or health issue with respect to which no [federal] standard is in effect." ...

Congress ... also, in § 18(b) of the Act, gave the States the option of pre-empting federal regulation entirely. That section provides: ...

"Any State which, at any time, desires to assume responsibility for development and enforcement therein of occupational safety and health standards relating to any occupational safety or health issue with respect to which a Federal standard has been promulgated [by the Secretary under the OSH Act] shall submit a State plan for the development of such standards and their enforcement." . . .

About half the States have received the Secretary's approval for their own state plans as described in this provision. . . . Illinois is not among them.

[We agree with] the Court of Appeals . . . that § 18(b) "unquestionably" pre-empts any state law or regulation that establishes an occupational health and safety standard on an issue for which OSHA has already promulgated a standard, unless the State has obtained the Secretary's approval for its own plan. . . .

Pre-emption may be either expressed or implied, and "is compelled whether Congress' command is explicitly stated in the statute's language or implicitly contained in its structure and purpose." Jones v. Rath Packing Co., 430 U.S. 519, 525 . . . (1977); . . . . Absent explicit pre-emptive language, we have recognized at least two types of implied pre-emption: field pre-emption, where the scheme of federal regulation is "so pervasive as to make reasonable the inference that Congress left no room for the States to supplement it," . . . (quoting Rice v. Santa Fe Elevator Corp., 331 U.S. 218, 230 . . . (1947)), and conflict pre-emption, where "compliance with both federal and state regulations is a physical impossibility," Florida Lime & Avocado Growers, Inc. v. Paul, 373 U.S. 132, 142–143 . . . (1963), or where state law "stands as an obstacle to the accomplishment and execution of the full purposes and objectives of Congress." Hines v. Davidowitz, 312 U.S. 52, 67 . . . (1941); . . . .

Our ultimate task in any pre-emption case is to determine whether state regulation is consistent with the structure and purpose of the statute as a whole. Looking to "the provisions of the whole law, and to its object and policy," . . . we hold that nonapproved state regulation of occupational safety and health issues for which a federal standard is in effect is impliedly pre-empted as in conflict with the full purposes and objectives of the OSH Act. Hines v. Davidowitz, supra. The design of the statute persuades us that Congress intended to subject employers and employees to only one set of regulations, be it federal or state, and that the only way a State may regulate an OSHA-regulated occupational safety and health issue is pursuant to an approved state plan that displaces the federal standards.

The principal indication that Congress intended to pre-empt state law is § 18(b)'s statement that a State "shall" submit a plan if it wishes to "assume responsibility" for "development and enforcement . . . of occupational safety and health standards relating to any occupational safety or health issue with respect to which a Federal standard has been promulgated." The unavoidable implication of this provision is that a State may not enforce its own occupational safety and health standards without obtaining the Secretary's approval, and petitioner concedes that § 18(b) would require an approved plan if Illinois wanted to "assume responsibility" for the regulation of occupational safety and health within the State. Petitioner contends, however, that an approved plan is necessary only if the State wishes completely to replace the federal regulations, not merely to supplement them. . . .

Petitioner's interpretation . . . is not tenable in light of the OSH Act's surrounding provisions. . . . The OSH Act as a whole evidences Congress' intent to avoid subjecting workers and employers to duplicative regulation; a State may develop an occupational safety and health program tailored to its own needs, but only if it is willing completely to displace the applicable federal regulations.

Cutting against petitioner's interpretation of § 18(b) is the language of § 18(a), which saves from pre-emption any state law regulating an occupational safety and health issue with respect to which no federal standard is in effect.... [P]reservation of state authority in the absence of a federal standard presupposes a background pre-emption of all state occupational safety and health standards whenever a federal standard governing the same issue is in effect.

Our understanding of the implications of § 18(b) is likewise bolstered by § 18(c) of the Act, ... which sets forth the conditions that must be satisfied before the Secretary can approve a plan submitted by a State under subsection (b). State standards that affect interstate commerce will be approved only if they "are required by compelling local conditions" and "do not unduly burden interstate commerce." ... If a State could supplement federal regulations without undergoing the § 18(b) approval process, then the protections that § 18(c) offers to interstate commerce would easily be undercut. It would make little sense to impose such a condition on state programs intended to supplant federal regulation and not those that merely supplement it: the burden on interstate commerce remains the same.

Section 18(f) also confirms our view.... That provision gives the Secretary the authority to withdraw her approval of a state plan.... Once approval is withdrawn, the plan "cease[s] to be in effect".... Under petitioner's reading of § 18(b), § 18(f) should permit the continued exercise of state jurisdiction over purely "supplemental" and nonconflicting standards. Instead, § 18(f) assumes that the State loses the power to enforce all of its occupational safety and health standards once approval is withdrawn.

The same assumption of exclusive federal jurisdiction in the absence of an approved state plan is apparent in the transitional provisions contained in § 18(h) of the Act.... Section 18(h) authorized the Secretary of Labor, during the first two years after passage of the Act, to enter into an agreement with a State by which the State would be permitted to continue to enforce its own occupational health and safety standards for two years or until final action was taken by the Secretary pursuant to § 18(b), whichever was earlier. Significantly, § 18(h) does not say that such an agreement is only necessary when the State wishes fully to supplant federal standards. Indeed, the original Senate version of the provision would have allowed a State to enter into such an agreement only when it wished to enforce standards "not in conflict with Federal occupational health and safety standards," a category which included "any State occupational health and safety standard which provides for more stringent health and safety regulations than do the Federal standards." ... Although that provision was eliminated from the final draft of the bill, thereby allowing agreements for the temporary enforcement of less stringent state standards, it is indicative of the congressional understanding that a State was required to enter into a transitional agreement even when its standards were stricter than federal standards. The Secretary's contemporaneous interpretation of § 18(h) also expresses that understanding....

... Our review of the Act persuades us that Congress sought to promote occupational safety and health while at the same time avoiding duplicative, and possibly counterproductive, regulation. It thus established a system of uniform federal occupational health and safety standards, but gave States the option of pre-empting federal regulations by developing their own occupational safety and health programs. In addition, Congress offered the States substantial federal grant monies to assist them in developing their own programs.... To allow a State selectively to "supplement" certain federal regulations with ostensibly nonconflicting standards would be inconsistent with this federal scheme of establishing uniform federal standards, on the one hand, and encouraging States to assume full responsibility for development and enforcement of their own OSH programs, on the other.

We cannot accept petitioner's argument that the OSH Act does not preempt nonconflicting state laws because those laws, like the Act, are designed to promote worker safety. In determining whether state law "stands as an obstacle" to the full implementation of a federal law, . . . "it is not enough to say that the ultimate goal of both federal and state law" is the same. . . . "A state law also is pre-empted if it interferes with the methods by which the federal statute was designed to reach th[at] goal." . . . The OSH Act does not foreclose a State from enacting its own laws to advance the goal of worker safety, but it does restrict the ways in which it can do so. If a State wishes to regulate an issue of worker safety for which a federal standard is in effect, its only option is to obtain the prior approval of the Secretary of Labor, as described in § 18 of the Act.[2]

III

. . . We now consider whether a dual impact law can be an "occupational safety and health standard" subject to pre-emption under the Act.

. . . [P]etitioner asserts that if the state legislature articulates a purpose other than (or in addition to) workplace health and safety, then the OSH Act loses its pre-emptive force. We disagree.

Although "part of the pre-empted field is defined by reference to the purpose of the state law in question, . . . another part of the field is defined by the state law's actual effect." . . . In assessing the impact of a state law on the federal scheme, we have refused to rely solely on the legislature's professed purpose and have looked as well to the effects of the law. As we explained over two decades ago:

> "We can no longer adhere to the aberrational doctrine . . . that state law may frustrate the operation of federal law as long as the state legislature in passing its law had some purpose in mind other than one of frustration. Apart from the fact that it is at odds with the approach taken in nearly all our Supremacy Clause cases, such a doctrine would enable state legislatures to nullify nearly all unwanted federal legislation by simply publishing a legislative committee report articulating some state interest or policy—other than frustration of the federal objective—that would be tangentially

---

[2] Justice Kennedy, while agreeing on the pre-emptive scope of the OSH Act, finds that its pre-emption is express rather than implied. . . . In the end, even Justice Kennedy finds express pre-emption by relying on the negative "inference" of § 18(b), which governs when *state* law will pre-empt *federal* law. We cannot agree that the negative implications of the text, although ultimately dispositive to our own analysis, *expressly* address the issue of federal pre-emption of state law. We therefore prefer to place this case in the category of implied pre-emption. Although we have chosen to use the term "conflict" pre-emption, we could as easily have stated that the promulgation of a federal safety and health standard "pre-empts the field" for any nonapproved state law regulating the same safety and health issue. . . . ("[F]ield pre-emption may be understood as a species of conflict pre-emption: A state law that falls within a pre-empted field conflicts with Congress' intent (either express or plainly implied) to exclude state regulation"). . . . Frequently, the pre-emptive "label" we choose will carry with it substantive implications for the scope of pre-emption. In this case, however, it does not. Our disagreement with Justice Kennedy as to whether the OSH Act's pre-emptive effect is labelled "express" or "implied" is less important than our agreement that the implications of the text of the statute evince a congressional intent to pre-empt nonapproved state regulations when a federal standard is in effect.

furthered by the proposed state law.... [A]ny state legislation which frustrates the full effectiveness of federal law is rendered invalid by the Supremacy Clause." Perez v. Campbell, 402 U.S., at 651–652 ...

[A] dual impact state regulation cannot avoid OSH Act pre-emption simply because the regulation serves several objectives rather than one.... The key question is thus at what point the state regulation sufficiently interferes with federal regulation that it should be deemed pre-empted under the Act.

... [T]he Court of Appeals ... [held] that, in the absence of the approval of the Secretary, the OSH Act pre-empts all state law that "constitutes, in a direct, clear and substantial way, regulation of worker health and safety." ... We agree that this is the appropriate standard.... On the other hand, state laws of general applicability (such as laws regarding traffic safety or fire safety) that do not conflict with OSHA standards and that regulate the conduct of workers and non-workers alike would generally not be pre-empted. Although some laws of general applicability may have a "direct and substantial" effect on worker safety, they cannot fairly be characterized as "occupational" standards, because they regulate workers simply as members of the general public.... [Here,] a law directed at workplace safety is not saved from pre-emption simply because the State can demonstrate some additional effect outside of the workplace.

In sum, a state law requirement that directly, substantially, and specifically regulates occupational safety and health is an occupational safety and health standard within the meaning of the Act. That such a law may also have a nonoccupational impact does not render it any less of an occupational standard for purposes of pre-emption analysis....

IV

We recognize that "the States have a compelling interest in the practice of professions within their boundaries, and that as part of their power to protect the public health, safety, and other valid interests they have broad power to establish standards for licensing practitioners and regulating the practice of professions." ... But under the Supremacy Clause ... "any state law, however clearly within a State's acknowledged power, which interferes with or is contrary to federal law, must yield." ... We therefore reject petitioner's argument that the State's interest in licensing various occupations can save from OSH Act pre-emption those provisions that directly and substantially affect workplace safety.

... Because neither of the OSH Act's saving provisions are implicated, and because Illinois does not have an approved state plan under § 18(b), the state licensing acts are pre-empted by the OSH Act to the extent they establish occupational safety and health standards for training those who work with hazardous wastes....

Justice Kennedy, concurring in part and concurring in the judgment.

Though I concur in the Court's judgment and with the ultimate conclusion that the state law is pre-empted, I would find express pre-emption from the terms of the federal statute. I cannot agree that we should denominate this case as one of implied pre-emption. The contrary view of the plurality is based on an undue expansion of our implied pre-emption jurisprudence....

. . . .

Our decisions establish that a high threshold must be met if a state law is to be pre-empted for conflicting with the purposes of a federal Act.... In my view, this type of pre-emption should be limited to state laws which impose prohibitions or obligations which are in direct contradiction to Congress' primary objectives, as conveyed with clarity in the federal legislation.

... Any potential tension between a scheme of federal regulation of the workplace and a concurrent, supplementary state scheme would not ... rise to the level of "actual conflict" described in our pre-emption cases. Absent the express provisions of § 18 ..., I would not say that state supplementary regulation conflicts with the purposes of the OSH Act, or that it "interferes with the methods by which the federal statute was designed to reach [its] goal."

The plurality's broad view of actual conflict pre-emption is contrary to two basic principles of our pre-emption jurisprudence. First, we begin "with the assumption that the historic police powers of the States [are] not to be superseded ... unless that was the clear and manifest purpose of Congress," Rice v. Santa Fe Elevator Corp., ... (1947). Second, "the purpose of Congress is the ultimate touchstone" in all pre-emption cases.... A free-wheeling judicial inquiry into whether a state statute is in tension with federal objectives would undercut the principle that it is Congress rather than the courts that pre-empts state law.

Nonetheless, I agree with the Court ... [, because its] result is mandated by the express terms of § 18(b) of the OSH Act. It follows ... that the pre-emptive scope of the Act is also limited to the language of the statute. When the existence of pre-emption is evident from the statutory text, our inquiry must begin and end with the statutory framework itself.

... Though most statutes creating express pre-emption contain an explicit statement to that effect, a statement admittedly lacking in § 18(b), we have never required any particular magic words in our express pre-emption cases. Our task in all pre-emption cases is to enforce the "clear and manifest purpose of Congress." ... We have held, in express pre-emption cases, that Congress' intent must be divined from the language, structure, and purposes of the statute as a whole.... The language of the OSH statute sets forth a scheme in light of which the provisions of § 18 must be interpreted, and from which the express pre-emption that displaces state law follows.

As the plurality's analysis amply demonstrates, Congress has addressed the issue of pre-emption in the OSH Act.... The most reasonable inference from th[e] language [of § 18(b)]is that when a State does not submit and secure approval of a state plan, it may not enforce occupational safety and health standards in that area. Any doubt that this is what Congress intended disappears when subsection (b) is considered in conjunction with subsections (a), (c), and (f).... Unartful though the language of § 18(b) may be, the structure and language of § 18 leave little doubt that ... Congress intended to pre-empt supplementary state regulation of an occupational safety and health issue with respect to which a federal standard exists.

... The dissent would give the States, rather than the Federal Government, the power to decide whether as to any particular occupational safety and health issue there will exist a single or dual regulatory scheme. Under this theory the State may choose exclusive federal jurisdiction by not regulating; or exclusive state jurisdiction by submitting a state plan; or dual regulation by adopting supplementary rules, as Illinois did here. That position undermines the authority of OSHA in many respects. For example, § 18(c)(2) of the OSH Act allows OSHA to disapprove state plans which "unduly burden interstate commerce." The dissent would eviscerate this important administrative mechanism by allowing the States to sidestep OSHA's authority through the mechanism of supplementary regulation. Furthermore, concurrent state and federal jurisdiction might interfere with the enforcement of the federal regulations without creating a situation where compliance with both schemes is a physical impossibility, which the dissent would require for pre-emption. I would not attribute to Congress the intent to create such a hodge-podge scheme of authority. My views in this regard are confirmed by the fact that OSHA has [consistently] ... viewed § 18 as providing it with exclusive jurisdiction in areas where it issues a standard.... [W]hile the dissent may be correct that as a theoretical matter the separate provisions of § 18 may be reconciled with allowing concurrent jurisdiction, it is neither a natural nor a sound reading of the statutory scheme.

The necessary implication of finding express pre-emption in this case is that the pre-emptive scope of the OSH Act is defined by the language of § 18(b). Because this provision requires federal approval of state occupational safety and health standards alone, only state laws fitting within the description are pre-empted. For that reason I agree with the Court that state laws of general applicability are not pre-empted. I also agree that "a state law requirement that directly, substantially, and specifically regulates occupational safety and health is an occupational safety and health standard within the meaning of the Act," and therefore falls within the scope of pre-emption. So-called "dual impact" state regulations which meet this standard are pre-empted by the OSH Act, regardless of any additional purpose the law may serve, or effect the law may have, outside the workplace. As a final matter, I agree that the Illinois Acts are not saved because they operate through a licensing mechanism rather than through direct regulation of the workplace. I therefore join all but Part II of the Court's opinion, and concur in the judgment of the Court.

Justice Souter, with whom Justice Blackmun, Justice Stevens, and Justice Thomas join, dissenting.

... In light of our rule that federal pre-emption of state law is only to be found in a clear congressional purpose to supplant exercises of the States' traditional police powers, the text of the Act fails to support the Court's conclusion.

I

. . .

... [W]hether the pre-emption at issue is described as occupation of each narrow field in which a federal standard has been promulgated, as pre-emption of those regulations that conflict with the federal objective of single regulation, or, as Justice Kennedy describes it, as express pre-emption, the key is congressional intent, and I find the language of the statute insufficient to demonstrate an intent to pre-empt state law in this way.

II

Analysis begins with the presumption that "Congress did not intend to displace state law." Maryland v. Louisiana, 451 U.S. 725, 746 ... (1981).... " ... This assumption provides assurance that the 'federal-state balance,' ... will not be disturbed unintentionally by Congress or unnecessarily by the courts...." Jones, ... If the statute's terms can be read sensibly not to have a pre-emptive effect, the presumption controls and no pre-emption may be inferred.

III

At first blush, respondent's strongest argument might seem to rest on § 18(a) of the Act. . . .

. . . The plurality reasons that there must be pre-emption . . . when there is a federal standard in effect, else § 18(a) would be rendered superfluous because "there is no possibility of conflict where there is no federal regulation."

. . . The plurality ignores the possibility that the provision simply rules out field pre-emption and is otherwise entirely compatible with the possibility that pre-emption will occur only when actual conflict between a federal regulation and a state rule renders compliance with both impossible. . . . Unlike the case where field pre-emption occurs, the provision tells us, absence of a federal standard leaves a State free to do as it will on the issue. . . . [T]he provision is perfectly consistent with the conclusion that as long as compliance with both a federal standard and a state regulation is not physically impossible, . . . each standard shall be enforceable. If, indeed, the presumption against pre-emption means anything, § 18(a) must be read in just this way.

Respondent also relies on § 18(b). . . .

. . . [I]n actually providing a mechanism for a State to "assume responsibility" for an issue with respect to which a federal standard has been promulgated (that is, to pre-empt federal law), § 18(b) is far from pre-emptive of anything adopted by the States. Its heading . . . speaks expressly of the "development and enforcement of State standards to preempt applicable Federal standards." The provision does not in any way provide that absent such state pre-emption of federal rules, the State may not even supplement the federal standards with consistent regulations of its own. . . . The provision . . . makes perfect sense on the assumption that a dual regulatory scheme is permissible but subject to state pre-emption if the State wishes to shoulder enough of the federal mandate to gain approval of a plan.

Nor does the provision setting out conditions for the Secretary's approval of a plan indicate that a state regulation on an issue federally addressed is never enforceable unless incorporated in a plan so approved. . . . Respondent argues, and the plurality concludes, that if state regulations were not pre-empted, . . . States acting independently could enforce regulations that did burden interstate commerce unduly. . . . But this simply does not follow. The subsection puts a limit on the Secretary's authority to approve a plan that burdens interstate commerce, thus capping the discretion that might otherwise have been read into the congressional delegation of authority to the Secretary to approve state plans. From this restriction applying only to the Secretary's federal authority it is clearly a non sequitur to conclude that pre-emption must have been intended to avoid the equally objectionable undue burden that independent state regulation might otherwise impose. Quite the contrary; the dormant Commerce Clause can take care of that, without any need to assume pre-emption.

The final provision that arguably suggests pre-emption merely by promulgation of a federal standard is § 18(h). . . .

. . . All it necessarily means is that the Secretary could agree to permit the State for a limited time to enforce whatever State regulations would otherwise have been pre-empted, as would have been true when they actually so conflicted with the federal standard that an employer could not comply with them and still comply with federal law as well. Thus, in the case of a State wishing to submit a plan, the provision as I read it would have allowed for the possibility of just one transition, from the pre-Act state law to the post-Act state plan.

Read as the Court reads it, however, employers and employees in such a State would have been subjected first to state law on a given issue; then, after promulgation of a federal standard, to that standard; and then, after approval of the plan, to a new state regime. One enforced readjustment would have been better than two, and the statute is better read accordingly.[1]

IV

... The Act does not, in so many words, pre-empt all state regulation of issues on which federal standards have been promulgated, and respondent's contention at oral argument that reading subsections (a), (b), and (h) could leave no other "logical" conclusion but one of pre-emption is wrong. Each provision can be read consistently with the others without any implication of pre-emptive intent.... They are in fact just as consistent with a purpose and objective to permit overlapping state and federal regulation as with one to guarantee that employers and employees would be subjected to only one regulatory regime.... I can only conclude that, as long as compliance with federally promulgated standards does not render obedience to Illinois' regulations impossible, the enforcement of the state law is not prohibited by the Supremacy Clause....

---

[1] The plurality also relies on § 18(f), ... which deals with withdrawal of approval of a state plan.... At most [that subsection] assumes that the State loses its capacity to enforce the plan.... It says nothing about state law that may remain on the books exclusive of the plan's authority, or about new law enacted after withdrawal of the Secretary's approval.

CHAPTER 6

INTERGOVERNMENTAL RELATIONSHIPS WITHIN THE FEDERAL SYSTEM

SECTION 1. FEDERAL REGULATORY IMMUNITY

Leslie Miller, Inc. v. Arkansas

352 U.S. 187, 77 S.Ct. 257, 1 L.Ed.2d 231 (1956).

Per Curiam.

Appellant submitted a bid in May 1954 for construction of facilities at an Air Force Base in Arkansas over which the United States had not acquired jurisdiction pursuant to 54 Stat. 19, 40 U.S.C. § 255. The United States accepted appellant's bid, and in June appellant began work on the project. In September, the State of Arkansas filed an information accusing appellant of violation of Ark.Stat., 1947, §§ 71–701 through 71–721, for submitting a bid, executing a contract, and commencing work as a contractor in the State of Arkansas without having obtained a license under Arkansas law for such activity from its Contractors Licensing Board. The case was tried on stipulated facts. Appellant was found guilty and fined. The trial court's judgment was affirmed by the Arkansas Supreme Court, 225 Ark. 285, 281 S.W.2d 946, and the case came here on appeal. 351 U.S. 948. Appellant and the United States as *amicus curiae* contend that the application of the Arkansas statute to this contractor interferes with the Federal Government's power to select contractors and schedule construction and is in conflict with the federal law regulating procurement.

Congress provided in § 3 of the Armed Services Procurement Act of 1947, 62 Stat. 21, 23, 41 U.S.C. § 152, that awards on advertised bids "shall be made ... to that responsible bidder whose bid, conforming to the invitation for bids, will be most advantageous to the Government, price and other factors considered...." The report from the Committee on Armed Services of the House of Representatives indicated some of the factors to be considered: "The question whether a particular bidder is a 'responsible bidder' requires some business judgment, and involves an evaluation of the bidder's experience, facilities, technical organization, reputation, financial resources, and other factors." H.R.Rep. No. 109, 80th Cong., 1st Sess. 18; see S.Rep. No. 571, 80th Cong., 1st Sess. 16. The Armed Services Procurement Regulations, promulgated under the Act, set forth a list of guiding considerations, defining a responsible contractor as one who

"(a) Is a manufacturer, construction contractor, or regular dealer....

"(b) Has adequate financial resources, or ability to secure such resources;

"(c) Has the necessary experience, organization, and technical qualifications, and has or can acquire the necessary facilities (including probable subcontractor arrangements) to perform the proposed contract;

"(d) Is able to comply with the required delivery or performance schedule (taking into consideration all existing business commitments);

"(e) Has a satisfactory record of performance, integrity, judgment, and skills; and

"(f) Is otherwise qualified and eligible to receive an award under applicable laws and regulations." 32 CFR § 1.307; see also 32 CFR § 2.406–3. Under the Arkansas licensing law similar factors are set forth to guide the Contractors Licensing Board:

> "The Board, in determining the qualifications of any applicant for original license . . . shall, among other things, consider the following: (a) experience, (b) ability, © character, (d) the manner of performance of previous contracts, (e) financial condition, (f) equipment, (g) any other fact tending to show ability and willingness to conserve the public health and safety, and (h) default in complying with the provisions of this act . . . or any other law of the State. . . ." Ark.Stat., 1947, § 71–709.

Mere enumeration of the similar grounds for licensing under the state statute and for finding "responsibility" under the federal statute and regulations is sufficient to indicate conflict between this license requirement which Arkansas places on a federal contractor and the action which Congress and the Department of Defense have taken to insure the reliability of persons and companies contracting with the Federal Government. Subjecting a federal contractor to the Arkansas contractor license requirements would give the State's licensing board a virtual power of review over the federal determination of "responsibility" and would thus frustrate the expressed federal policy of selecting the lowest responsible bidder. In view of the federal statute and regulations, the rationale of Johnson v. Maryland, 254 U.S. 51, 57, is applicable:

"It seems to us that the immunity of the instruments of the United States from state control in the performance of their duties extends to a requirement that they desist from performance until they satisfy a state officer upon examination that they are competent for a necessary part of them and pay a fee for permission to go on. Such a requirement does not merely touch the Government servants remotely by a general rule of conduct; it lays hold of them in their specific attempt to obey orders and requires qualifications in addition to those that the Government has pronounced sufficient. It is the duty of the Department to employ persons competent for their work and that duty it must be presumed has been performed. . . ."

The judgment of the Supreme Court of Arkansas is reversed and the cause is remanded for further proceedings not inconsistent with this opinion.

Reversed and remanded.

HANCOCK v. TRAIN, 426 U.S. 167 (1976). The question before the Court was whether a state whose federally approved implementation plan forbids an air contaminant source to operate without a state permit may require existing federally owned or operated installations to secure such a permit. The specific question was whether obtaining a permit to operate is among those "requirements respecting control and abatement of air pollution" with which existing federal facilities must comply under § 118 of the federal Clean Air Act. The Court held that federal installations did not have to acquire state permits, prefacing its statutory construction discussion as follows:

"It is a seminal principle of our law 'that the constitution and the laws made in pursuance thereof are supreme; that they control the constitution and laws of the respective states and cannot be controlled by them.' McCulloch v. Maryland, 4 Wheat., 316, 426 (1819). From this principle is deduced the corollary that

'[i]t is the very essence of supremacy to remove all obstacles to its action within its own sphere, and so to modify every power vested in subordinate governments, as to exempt its own operation from their own influence.' Id., at 427.

"The effect of this corollary, which derives from the Supremacy Clause and is exemplified in the Plenary Powers Clause giving Congress exclusive legislative authority over federal enclaves purchased with the consent of a State, is 'that the activities of the Federal Government are free from regulation by any State.' As Mr. Justice Holmes put it in Johnson v. Maryland, 254 U.S. 51, 57 (1920),

'the immunity of the instruments of the United States from state control in the performance of their duties extends to a requirement that they desist from performance until they satisfy a state officer upon examination that they are competent for a necessary part of them....'

"Taken with the 'old and well-known rule that statutes which in general terms divest pre-existing rights or privileges will not be applied to the sovereign' 'without a clear expression or implication to that effect,' this immunity means that where 'Congress does not affirmatively declare its instrumentalities or property subject to regulation,' 'the federal function must be left free' of regulation. Particular deference should be accorded that 'old and well-known rule' where, as here, the rights and privileges of the Federal Government at stake not only find their origin in the Constitution, but are to be divested in favor of and subjected to regulation by a subordinate sovereign. Because of the fundamental importance of the principles shielding federal installations and activities from regulation by the States, an authorization of state regulation is found only when and to the extent there is 'a clear congressional mandate,' 'specific congressional action' that makes this authorization of state regulation 'clear and unambiguous.'

"... [I]t is clear from the record that prohibiting operation of the air contaminant sources for which the State seeks to require permits, is tantamount to prohibiting operation of the federal installations on which they are located.

"... We are unable to find in § 118, on its face or in relation to the Clean Air Act as a whole, or to derive from the legislative history of the Amendments any clear and unambiguous declaration by the Congress that federal installations may not perform their activities unless a state official issues a permit. Nor can congressional intention to submit federal activity to state control be implied from the claim that under Kentucky's EPA–approved implementation plan it is only through the permit system that compliance schedules and other requirements may be administratively enforced against federal installations."

SECTION 2.   STATE REGULATORY IMMUNITY

STATE IMMUNITY FROM FEDERAL REGULATION—1936–1985

United States v. California, 297 U.S. 175 (1936), sustained a penalty imposed on a state-owned railroad for violation of the Federal Safety Appliance

Act. It was not necessary to address California's argument that the non-profit operation of the railroad was performance of "a public function in its sovereign capacity." It was irrelevant whether operation of the railroad was in a sovereign or private capacity. "The sovereign power of the states is necessarily diminished to the extent of the grants of power to the federal government in the Constitution." Chief Justice Stone's opinion for the Court also rejected any analogy to a state's constitutional immunity from federal taxation. "[W]e look to the activities in which the states have traditionally engaged as marking the boundary of the restriction upon the federal taxing power. But there is no such limitation upon the plenary power to regulate commerce. The state can no more deny the power if its exercise has been authorized by Congress than can an individual."

Until 1976, constitutional attacks on application of federal regulatory statutes to state activities were uniformly rejected. Case v. Bowles, 327 U.S. 92 (1946), upheld application of a maximum price under the Emergency Price Control Act as applied to a timber sale by the State of Washington. State of California v. Taylor, 353 U.S. 553 (1957), rejected a challenge to application of the Railway Labor Act to a state owned railroad. (The Act made wages and working conditions subject to a collective bargaining agreement rather than state civil service laws.) Parden v. Terminal Ry. of Alabama State Docks Dept., 377 U.S. 184 (1964), held that a state owned railroad was subject to liability to an injured employee under the Federal Employers' Liability Act. Maryland v. Wirtz, 392 U.S. 183 (1968), sustained application of the wage and hour provisions of the Fair Labor Standards Act to employees of public schools and hospitals. Fry v. United States, 421 U.S. 542 (1975) sustained application of the Economic Stabilization Act to limit wage increases of public employees.

Significantly, however, Justices Douglas and Stewart dissented in Maryland v. Wirtz, arguing that the commerce power could not be exercised in a way that unreasonably interfered with a state's sovereign power. Justice Rehnquist's dissent in Fry v. United States argued that Maryland v. Wirtz should be overruled. Finally, a footnote to Justice Marshall's opinion for the Court in *Fry* contained this statement: "While the Tenth Amendment has been characterized as 'a truism,' ... United States v. Darby, 312 U.S. 100, 124 (1941), it is not without significance. The Amendment expressly declares the constitutional policy that Congress may not exercise power in a fashion that impairs the States' integrity or their ability to function effectively in a federal system...." 427 U.S. at 547, n. 7.

Maryland v. Wirtz was overruled in the five to four decision of the Court in National League of Cities v. Usery, 426 U.S. 833 (1976). 1974 amendments to the Fair Labor Standards Act extended the Act's maximum hour and minimum wage provisions to employees of the states and their political subdivisions. The Court held that the Act could not constitutionally be applied to state employees performing traditional governmental functions. Justice Rehnquist's opinion for the Court relied on the statement in the footnote to the *Fry* opinion that Congress could not "exercise power in a fashion that impairs the States' integrity or their ability to function effectively in a federal system." Applying the Fair Labor Standards Act to state employees would impose costs and limit flexibility. The Court concluded that "insofar as the challenged amendments operate to directly displace the States' freedom to structure integral operations in areas of traditional government functions, they are not within the authority granted Congress by" the Commerce Clause. Justice Blackmun joined the Court's opinion, but admitted in a concurrence that he was "not untroubled by certain possible implications of the Court's opinion." He explained that he joined the Court's opinion because he read it to adopt "a balancing approach" that permitted federal regulation "where the federal interest is demonstrably greater and where state ... compliance with imposed federal standards would be essential." Justice Brennan's dissent, joined by Justices White and Marshall, argued that "restraints upon exercise by Congress of its plenary commerce power lies in the political process and not in the judicial process.... [T]he political branches of our Government are structured to protect the interests of the States, as well as the Nation as a whole, and ... the States are fully able to protect their own interests...." Justice Stevens' dissent emphasized the absence of standards distinguishing invalid federal regulation and "federal regulation of state activities that I consider unquestionably permissible."

In Hodel v. Virginia Surface Mining and Reclamation Association, Inc., 452 U.S. 264 (1981), the Court summarized three requirements that *National League of Cities* challenges to federal legislation must meet in order to succeed. "First, there must be a showing that the challenged statute regulates the 'states as states.' ... Second, the federal regulation must address matters that are indisputably 'attribute[s] of state sovereignty.' ... And, third, it must be apparent that the States' compliance with the federal law would directly impair their ability 'to structure integral operations in areas of traditional governmental functions.' " (The Court also mentioned in a footnote the possibility that a challenged federal law would be valid, even if all three requirements were satisfied, under the balancing test suggested by Justice Blackmun's concurrence in *National League of Cities*.)

In United Transportation Union v. Long Island Railroad Co., 455 U.S. 678 (1982), the Court was unanimous, concluding that a state-owned railroad was not immune from application of the labor provisions of the Railway Labor Act, because operation of a railroad was not a "traditional" state function. In Equal Employment Opportunity Commission v. Wyoming, 460 U.S. 226 (1983), however, the Court divided five to four with Justice Blackmun joining the four *National League of Cities* dissenters to form the majority. The Court upheld a 1974 amendment to the Age Discrimination in Employment Act extending the Act to state employees. The case arose out of the involuntary retirement of a state game warden at age 55, which violated provisions of the Act forbidding involuntary retirement prior to age 70. Justice Brennan's opinion for the Court concluded that state compliance with the Act would be less costly than, and would not impair flexibility to the same degree as, the minimum wage and maximum hour provisions at issue in *National League of Cities*. The prohibitions of the Age Discrimination Act thus involved federal intrusion that was "sufficiently less serious" and did not impair states' ability to structure their integral operations—a question that "must depend ... on considerations of degree."

Garcia v. San Antonio Metropolitan Transit Authority

469 U.S. 528, 105 S.Ct. 1005, 83 L.Ed.2d 1016 (1985).

Justice Blackmun delivered the opinion of the Court.

We revisit in these cases an issue raised in National League of Cities v. Usery, 426 U.S. 833 (1976). In that litigation, this Court, by a sharply divided vote, ruled that the Commerce Clause does not empower Congress to enforce the minimum-wage and overtime provisions of the Fair Labor Standards Act (FLSA) against the States "in areas of traditional governmental functions." Id., at 852. Although National League of Cities supplied some examples of "traditional governmental functions," it did not offer a general explanation of how a "traditional" function is to be distinguished from a "nontraditional" one. Since then, federal and state courts have struggled with the task, thus imposed, of identifying a traditional function for purposes of state immunity under the Commerce Clause.

In the present cases, a Federal District Court concluded that municipal ownership and operation of a mass-transit system is a traditional governmental function and thus, under *National League of Cities,* is exempt from the obligations imposed by the FLSA. Faced with the identical question, three Federal Courts of Appeals and one state appellate court have reached the opposite conclusion.

Our examination of this "function" standard applied in these and other cases over the last eight years now persuades us that the attempt to draw the boundaries of state regulatory immunity in terms of "traditional governmental function" is not only unworkable but is inconsistent with established principles of federalism and, indeed, with those very federalism principles on which *National League of Cities* purported to rest. That case, accordingly, is overruled.

I

. . .

The FLSA obligations of public mass-transit systems like SATS were expanded in 1974 when Congress provided for the progressive repeal of the surviving overtime exemption for mass-transit employees. Fair Labor Standards Amendments of 1974, § 21(b), 88 Stat. 68. Congress simultaneously brought the States and their subdivisions further within the ambit of the FLSA by extending FLSA coverage to virtually all state and local-government employees. §§ 6(a)(1) and (6), 88 Stat. 58, 60, 29 U.S.C. §§ 203(d) and (x). SATS complied with the FLSA's overtime requirements until 1976, when this Court, in *National League of Cities,* supra, overruled *Maryland v. Wirtz,* and held that the FLSA could not be applied constitutionally to the "traditional governmental functions" of state and local governments. Four months after *National League of Cities* was handed down, SATS informed its employees that the decision relieved SATS of its overtime obligations under the FLSA.

. . .

 . . . After initial argument, the cases were restored to our calendar for reargument, and the parties were requested to brief and argue the following additional question:

> "Whether or not the principles of the Tenth Amendment as set forth in National League of Cities v. Usery, 426 U.S. 833 (1976), should be reconsidered?" . . .

II

The controversy in the present cases has focused on the third *Hodel* requirement—that the challenged federal statute trench on "traditional governmental functions." . . .

Thus far, this Court itself has made little headway in defining the scope of the governmental functions deemed *protected* under *National League of Cities.* In that case the Court set forth examples of protected and unprotected functions, see 426 U.S., at 851, 854, n. 18, but provided no explanation of how those examples were identified. The only other case in which the Court has had occasion to address the problem is *Long Island.* We there observed: "The determination of whether a federal law impairs a state's authority with respect

to 'areas of traditional [state] functions' may at times be a difficult one." 455 U.S., at 684, quoting National League of Cities, 426 U.S., at 852. The accuracy of that statement is demonstrated by this Court's own difficulties in *Long Island* in developing a workable standard for "traditional governmental functions." We relied in large part there on "the *historical reality* that the operation of railroads is not among the functions *traditionally* performed by state and local governments," but we simultaneously disavowed "a static historical view of state functions generally immune from federal regulation." 455 U.S., at 686 (first emphasis added; second emphasis in original)....
Finally, having disclaimed a rigid reliance on the historical pedigree of state involvement in a particular area, we nonetheless found it appropriate to emphasize the extended historical record of federal involvement in the field of rail transportation. Id., at 687–689.

Many constitutional standards involve "undoubte[d] ... gray areas," Fry v. United States, 421 U.S. 542, 558 (1975) (dissenting opinion), and, despite the difficulties that this Court and other courts have encountered so far, it normally might be fair to venture the assumption that case-by-case development would lead to a workable standard for determining whether a particular governmental function should be immune from federal regulation under the Commerce Clause....

. . .

The distinction the Court discarded as unworkable in the field of tax immunity has proved no more fruitful in the field of regulatory immunity under the Commerce Clause. Neither do any of the alternative standards that might be employed to distinguish between protected and unprotected governmental functions appear manageable. We rejected the possibility of making immunity turn on a purely historical standard of "tradition" in *Long Island,* and properly so. The most obvious defect of a historical approach to state immunity is that it prevents a court from accommodating changes in the historical functions of States, changes that have resulted in a number of once-private functions like education being assumed by the States and their subdivisions. At the same time, the only apparent virtue of a rigorous historical standard, namely, its promise of a reasonably objective measure for state immunity, is illusory. Reliance on history as an organizing principle results in linedrawing of the most arbitrary sort; the genesis of state governmental functions stretches over a historical continuum from before the Revolution to the present, and courts would have to decide by fiat precisely how longstanding a pattern of state involvement had to be for federal regulatory authority to be defeated.

A nonhistorical standard for selecting immune governmental functions is likely to be just as unworkable as is a historical standard. The goal of identifying "uniquely" governmental functions, for example, has been rejected by the Court in the field of government tort liability in part because the notion of a "uniquely" governmental function is unmanageable. See Indian Towing Co. v. United States, 350 U.S. 61, 64–68 (1955); see also Lafayette v. Louisiana Power & Light Co., 435 U.S. 389, 433 (1978) (dissenting opinion). Another possibility would be to confine immunity to "necessary" governmental services, that is, services that would be provided inadequately or not at all unless the government provided them. Cf. Flint v. Stone Tracy Co., 220 U.S., at 172. The set of services that fits into this category, however, may well be negligible. The fact that an unregulated market produces less of some service than a State deems desirable does not mean that the State itself must provide the service; in most if not all cases, the State can "contract out" by hiring private firms to provide the service or simply by providing subsidies to existing suppliers. It also is open to question how well equipped courts are to make this kind of determination about the workings of economic markets.

We believe, however, that there is a more fundamental problem at work here, a problem that explains why the Court was never able to provide a basis for the governmental-proprietary distinction in the inter-governmental tax immunity cases and why an attempt to draw similar distinctions with respect to federal regulatory authority under *National League of Cities* is unlikely to succeed regardless of how the distinctions are phrased. The problem is that neither the governmental-proprietary distinction nor any other that purports to separate out important governmental functions can be faithful to the role of federalism in a democratic society. The essence of our federal system is that within the realm of authority left open to them under the Constitution, the States must be equally free to engage in any activity that their citizens choose for the common weal, no matter how unorthodox or unnecessary anyone else— including the judiciary—deems state involvement to be. Any rule of state immunity that looks to the "traditional," "integral," or "necessary" nature of governmental functions inevitably invites an unelected federal judiciary to make decisions about which state policies it favors and which ones it dislikes. . . .

We therefore now reject, as unsound in principle and unworkable in practice, a rule of state immunity from federal regulation that turns on a judicial appraisal of whether a particular governmental function is "integral" or "traditional." Any such rule leads to inconsistent results at the same time that it disserves principles of democratic self-governance, and it breeds inconsistency precisely because it is divorced from those principles. If there are to be limits on the Federal Government's power to interfere with state functions—as undoubtedly there are—we must look elsewhere to find them. We accordingly return to the underlying issue that confronted this Court in *National League of Cities*—the manner in which the Constitution insulates States from the reach of Congress' power under the Commerce Clause.

III

The central theme of *National League of Cities* was that the States occupy a special position in our constitutional system and that the scope of Congress' authority under the Commerce Clause must reflect that position. Of course, the Commerce Clause by its specific language does not provide any special limitation on Congress' actions with respect to the States. See EEOC v. Wyoming, 460 U.S. 226, 248 (1983) (concurring opinion). It is equally true, however, that the text of the Constitution provides the beginning rather than the final answer to every inquiry into questions of federalism. . . .

What has proved problematic is not the perception that the Constitution's federal structure imposes limitations on the Commerce Clause, but rather the nature and content of those limitations. One approach to defining the limits on Congress' authority to regulate the States under the Commerce Clause is to identify certain underlying elements of political sovereignty that are deemed essential to the States' "separate and independent existence." Lane County v. Oregon, 7 Wall. 71, 76 (1869). This approach obviously underlay the Court's use of the "traditional governmental function" concept in *National League of Cities*. It also has led to the separate requirement that the challenged federal statute "address matters that are indisputably 'attribute[s] of state sovereignty.' " Hodel, 452 U.S., at 288, quoting National League of Cities, 426 U.S., at 845. In *National League of Cities* itself, for example, the Court concluded that decisions by a State concerning the wages and hours of its employees are an "undoubted attribute of state sovereignty." 426 U.S., at 845. The opinion did not explain what aspects of such decisions made them such an "undoubted attribute," and the Court since then has remarked on the uncertain scope of the concept. See EEOC v. Wyoming, 460 U.S., at 238, n. 11. The point of the inquiry, however, has remained to single out particular features of a State's internal governance that are deemed to be intrinsic parts of state sovereignty.

We doubt that courts ultimately can identify principled constitutional limitations on the scope of Congress' Commerce Clause powers over the States merely by relying on *a priori* definitions of state sovereignty. In part, this is because of the elusiveness of objective criteria for "fundamental" elements of state sovereignty, a problem we have witnessed in the search for "traditional governmental functions." There is, however, a more fundamental reason: the sovereignty of the States is limited by the Constitution itself. A variety of sovereign powers, for example, are withdrawn from the States by Article I, § 10. Section 8 of the same Article works an equally sharp contraction of state sovereignty by authorizing Congress to exercise a wide range of legislative powers and (in conjunction with the Supremacy Clause of Article VI) to displace contrary state legislation. See *Hodel,* 452 U.S., at 290–292. By providing for final review of questions of federal law in this Court, Article III curtails the sovereign power of the States' judiciaries to make authoritative determinations of law. See Martin v. Hunter's Lessee, 1 Wheat. 304 (1816). Finally, the developed application, through the Fourteenth Amendment, of the greater part of the Bill of Rights to the States limits the sovereign authority that States otherwise would possess to legislate with respect to their citizens and to conduct their own affairs.

The States unquestionably do "retai[n] a significant measure of sovereign authority." EEOC v. Wyoming, 460 U.S., at 269 (Powell, J., dissenting). They do so, however, only to the extent that the Constitution has not divested them of their original powers and transferred those powers to the Federal Government. . . .

. . .

When we look for the States' "residuary and inviolable sovereignty," The Federalist No. 39, p. 285 (B. Wright ed. 1961) (J. Madison), in the shape of the constitutional scheme rather than in predetermined notions of sovereign power, a different measure of state sovereignty emerges. Apart from the limitation on federal authority inherent in the delegated nature of Congress' Article I powers, the principal means chosen by the Framers to ensure the role of the States in the federal system lies in the structure of the Federal Government itself. It is no novelty to observe that the composition of the Federal Government was designed in large part to protect the States from overreaching by Congress.[11] The Framers thus gave the States a role in the selection both of the Executive and the Legislative Branches of the Federal Government. The States were vested with indirect influence over the House of Representatives and the Presidency by their control of electoral qualifications and their role in presidential elections. U.S. Const., Art. I, § 2, and Art. II, § 1. They were given more direct influence in the Senate, where each State received equal representation and each Senator was to be selected by the legislature of his State. Art. I, § 3.

[11] See, e.g., J. Choper, Judicial Review and the National Political Process 175–184 (1980); Wechsler, The Political Safeguards of Federalism: The Role of the States in the Composition and Selection of the National Government, 54 Colum.L.Rev. 543 (1954); La Pierre, The Political Safeguards of Federalism Redux: Intergovernmental Immunity and the States as Agents of the Nation, 60 Wash. U.L.Q. 779 (1982).

The significance attached to the States' equal representation in the Senate is underscored by the prohibition of any constitutional amendment divesting a State of equal representation without the State's consent. Art. V.

The extent to which the structure of the Federal Government itself was relied on to insulate the interests of the States is evident in the views of the Framers. James Madison explained that the Federal Government "will partake sufficiently of the spirit [of the States], to be disinclined to invade the rights of the individual States, or the prerogatives of their governments." The Federalist No. 46, p. 332 (B. Wright ed. 1961). Similarly, James Wilson observed that "it was a favorite object in the Convention" to provide for the security of the States against federal encroachment and that the structure of the Federal Government itself served that end. 2 Elliott, at 438–439. Madison placed particular reliance on the equal representation of the States in the Senate, which he saw as "at once a constitutional recognition of the portion of sovereignty remaining in the individual States, and an instrument for preserving that residuary sovereignty." The Federalist No. 62, p. 408 (B. Wright ed. 1961). He further noted that "the residuary sovereignty of the States [is] implied *and secured* by that principle of representation in one branch of the [federal] legislature" (emphasis added). The Federalist No. 43, p. 315 (B. Wright ed. 1961). See also McCulloch v. Maryland, 4 Wheat. 316, 435 (1819). In short, the Framers chose to rely on a federal system in which special restraints on federal power over the States inhered principally in the workings of the National Government itself, rather than in discrete limitations on the objects of federal authority. State sovereign interests, then, are more properly protected by procedural safeguards inherent in the structure of the federal system than by judicially created limitations on federal power.

The effectiveness of the federal political process in preserving the States' interests is apparent even today in the course of federal legislation. On the one hand, the States have been able to direct a substantial proportion of federal revenues into their own treasuries in the form of general and program-specific grants in aid. The federal role in assisting state and local governments is a longstanding one; Congress provided federal land grants to finance state governments from the beginning of the Republic, and direct cash grants were awarded as early as 1887 under the Hatch Act. In the past quarter-century alone, federal grants to States and localities have grown from $7 billion to $96 billion. As a result, federal grants now account for about one-fifth of state and local government expenditures. The States have obtained federal funding for such services as police and fire protection, education, public health and hospitals, parks and recreation, and sanitation. Moreover, at the same time that the States have exercised their influence to obtain federal support, they have been able to exempt themselves from a wide variety of obligations imposed by Congress under the Commerce Clause. For example, the Federal Power Act, the National Labor Relations Act, the Labor–Management Reporting and Disclosure Act, the Occupational Safety and Health Act, the Employee Retirement Insurance Security Act, and the Sherman Act all contain express or implied exemptions for States and their subdivisions. The fact that some federal statutes such as the FLSA extend general obligations to the States cannot obscure the extent to which the political position of the States in the federal system has served to minimize the burdens that the States bear under the Commerce Clause.

We realize that changes in the structure of the Federal Government have taken place since 1789, not the least of which has been the substitution of popular election of Senators by the adoption of the Seventeenth Amendment in 1913, and that these changes may work to alter the influence of the States in the federal political process. Nonetheless, against this background, we are convinced that the fundamental limitation that the constitutional scheme imposes on the Commerce Clause to protect the "States as States" is one of process rather than one of result. Any substantive restraint on the exercise of Commerce Clause powers must find its justification in the procedural nature of this basic limitation, and it must be tailored to compensate for possible failings in the national political process rather than to dictate a "sacred province of state autonomy." EEOC v. Wyoming, 460 U.S., at 236.

Insofar as the present cases are concerned, then, we need go no further than to state that we perceive nothing in the overtime and minimum-wage requirements of the FLSA, as applied to SAMTA, that is destructive of state sovereignty or violative of any constitutional provision. SAMTA faces nothing more than the same minimum-wage and overtime obligations that hundreds of thousands of other employers, public as well as private, have to meet.

. . .

IV

This analysis makes clear that Congress' action in affording SAMTA employees the protections of the wage and hour provisions of the FLSA contravened no affirmative limit on Congress' power under the Commerce Clause. The judgment of the District Court therefore must be reversed.

Of course, we continue to recognize that the States occupy a special and specific position in our constitutional system and that the scope of Congress' authority under the Commerce Clause must reflect that position. But the principal and basic limit on the federal commerce power is that inherent in all congressional action—the built-in restraints that our system provides through state participation in federal governmental action. The political process ensures that laws that unduly burden the States will not be promulgated. In the factual setting of these cases the internal safeguards of the political process have performed as intended.

These cases do not require us to identify or define what affirmative limits the constitutional structure might impose on federal action affecting the States under the Commerce Clause. See Coyle v. Smith, 221 U.S. 559 (1911). We note and accept Justice Frankfurter's observation in New York v. United States, 326 U.S. 572, 583 (1946):

> "The process of Constitutional adjudication does not thrive on conjuring up horrible possibilities that never happen in the real world and devising doctrines sufficiently comprehensive in detail to cover the remotest contingency. Nor need we go beyond what is required for a reasoned disposition of the kind of controversy now before the Court."

Though the separate concurrence providing the fifth vote in *National League of Cities* was "not untroubled by certain possible implications" of the decision, 426 U.S., at 856, the Court in that case attempted to articulate affirmative limits on the Commerce Clause power in terms of core governmental functions and fundamental attributes of state sovereignty. But the model of democratic decisionmaking the Court there identified underestimated, in our view, the solicitude of the national political process for the continued vitality of the States. Attempts by other courts since then to draw guidance from this model have proved it both impracticable and doctrinally barren. In sum, in *National League of Cities* the Court tried to repair what did not need repair.

We do not lightly overrule recent precedent. We have not hesitated, however, when it has become apparent that a prior decision has departed from a proper understanding of congressional power under the Commerce Clause. See United States v. Darby, 312 U.S. 100, 116–117 (1941). Due respect for the reach of congressional power within the federal system mandates that we do so now.

National League of Cities v. Usery, 426 U.S. 833 (1976), is overruled. The judgment of the District Court is reversed, and these cases are remanded to that court for further proceedings consistent with this opinion.

It is so ordered.

Justice Powell, with whom The Chief Justice, Justice Rehnquist, and Justice O'Connor join, dissenting.

The Court today, in its 5–4 decision, overrules National League of Cities v. Usery, 426 U.S. 833 (1976), a case in which we held that Congress lacked authority to impose the requirements of the Fair Labor Standards Act on state and local governments. Because I believe this decision substantially alters the federal system embodied in the Constitution, I dissent.

I

There are, of course, numerous examples over the history of this Court in which prior decisions have been reconsidered and overruled. There have been few cases, however, in which the principle of *stare decisis* and the rationale of recent decisions were ignored as abruptly as we now witness.[1] The reasoning of the Court in *National League of Cities,* and the principle applied there, have been reiterated consistently over the past eight years. Since its decision in 1976, *National League of Cities* has been cited and quoted in opinions joined by every member of the present Court. Hodel v. Virginia Surface Mining & Recl. Assn., 452 U.S. 264, 287–293 (1981); United Transportation Union v. Long Island R. Co., 455 U.S. 678, 684–686 (1982); FERC v. Mississippi, 456 U.S. 742, 764–767 (1982)....

. . .

Whatever effect the Court's decision may have in weakening the application of *stare decisis,* it is likely to be less important than what the Court has done to the Constitution itself. A unique feature of the United States is the *federal* system of government guaranteed by the Constitution and implicit in the very name of our country. Despite some genuflecting in Court's opinion to the concept of federalism, today's decision effectively reduces the Tenth Amendment to meaningless rhetoric when Congress acts pursuant to the Commerce Clause....

II

. . .

B

Today's opinion does not explain how the States' role in the electoral process guarantees that particular exercises of the Commerce Clause power will not infringe on residual State sovereignty. Members of Congress are elected from the various States, but once in office they are members of the federal government. Although the States participate in the Electoral College, this is hardly a reason to view the President as a representative of the States' interest

---

[1] *National League of Cities,* following some changes in the composition of the Court, had overruled Maryland v. Wirtz, 392 U.S. 183 (1968). Unlike *National League of Cities,* the rationale of *Wirtz* had not been repeatedly accepted by our subsequent decisions.

against federal encroachment. We noted recently "the hydraulic pressure inherent within each of the separate Branches to exceed the outer limits of its power...." Immigration and Naturalization Service v. Chadha, 462 U.S. 919, ___ (1983). The Court offers no reason to think that this pressure will not operate when Congress seeks to invoke its powers under the Commerce Clause, notwithstanding the electoral role of the States.[9]

... The fact that Congress generally does not transgress constitutional limits on its power to reach State activities does not make judicial review any less necessary to rectify the cases in which it does do so. The States' role in our system of government is a matter of constitutional law, not of legislative grace. "The powers not delegated to the United States by the Constitution, nor prohibited by it to the States, are reserved to the States, respectively, or to the people." U.S. Const., Amend. 10.

More troubling than the logical infirmities in the Court's reasoning is the result of its holding, i.e., that federal political officials, invoking the Commerce Clause, are the sole judges of the limits of their own power. This result is inconsistent with the fundamental principles of our constitutional system. See, e.g., The Federalist No. 78 (Hamilton). At least since *Marbury v. Madison* it has been the settled province of the federal judiciary "to say what the law is" with respect to the constitutionality of acts of Congress. 1 Cranch 137, 177 (1803). In rejecting the role of the judiciary in protecting the States from federal overreaching, the Court's opinion offers no explanation for ignoring the teaching of the most famous case in our history.

III

A

. . .

[9] At one time in our history, the view that the structure of the federal government sufficed to protect the States might have had a somewhat more practical, although not a more logical, basis. Professor Wechsler, whose seminal article in 1954 proposed the view adopted by the Court today, predicated his argument on assumptions that simply do not accord with current reality. Professor Wechsler wrote: "National action has ... always been regarded as exceptional in our polity, an intrusion to be justified by some necessity, the special rather than the ordinary case." Wechsler, The Political Safeguards of Federalism: The Role of the States in the Composition and Selection of the National Government, 54 Colum.L.Rev. 543, 544 (1954). Not only is the premise of this view clearly at odds with the proliferation of national legislation over the past 30 years, but "a variety of structural and political changes in this century have combined to make Congress particularly *insensitive* to state and local values." Advisory Comm'n on Intergovernmental Relations [ACIR], Regulatory Federalism: Policy, Process, Impact and Reform 50 (1984). The adoption of the Seventeenth Amendment (providing for direct election of senators), the weakening of political parties on the local level, and the rise of national media, among other things, have made Congress increasingly less representa-tive of State and local interests, and more likely to be responsive to the demands of various national constituencies. Id., at 50–51. As one observer explained, "As Senators and members of the House develop independent constituencies among groups such as farmers, businessmen, laborers, environmentalists, and the poor, each of which generally supports certain national initiatives, their tendency to identify with state interests and the positions of state officials is reduced." Kaden, "Federalism in the Courts: Agenda for the 1980s," in ACIR, The Future of Federalism in the '80s, at 97 (1981).

See also Kaden, Politics, Money, and State Sovereignty: The Judicial Role, 79 Colum.L.Rev. 847 (1979) (changes in political practices and the breadth of national initiatives mean that the political branches "may no longer be as well suited as they once were to the task of safeguarding the role of the states in the federal system and protecting the fundamental value of federalism") and ACIR, Regulatory Federalism, supra, at 1–24 (detailing the "dramatic shift" in kind of federal regulation applicable to the States over the past two decades). Thus, even if one were to ignore the numerous problems with the Court's position in terms of constitutional theory, there would remain serious questions as to its factual premises.

. . . Far from being "unsound in principle," judicial enforcement of the Tenth Amendment is essential to maintaining the federal system so carefully designed by the Framers and adopted in the Constitution.

B

. . .

The Framers believed that the separate sphere of sovereignty reserved to the States would ensure that the States would serve as an effective "counterpoise" to the power of the federal government. The States would serve this essential role because they would attract and retain the loyalty of their citizens. The roots of such loyalty, the Founders thought, were found in the objects peculiar to state government. For example, Hamilton argued that the States "regulat[e] all those personal interests and familiar concerns to which the sensibility of individuals is more immediately awake. . . ." The Federalist No. 17, p. 107. Thus, he maintained that the people would perceive the States as "the immediate and most visible guardian of life and property," a fact which "contributes more than any other circumstance to impressing upon the minds of the people affection, esteem and reverence towards the government." Ibid. Madison took the same position, explaining that "the people will be more familiarly and minutely conversant" with the business of state governments, and "with the members of these, will a greater proportion of the people have the ties of personal acquaintance and friendship, and of family and party attachments. . . ." The Federalist No. 46, p. 316. Like Hamilton, Madison saw the States' involvement in the everyday concerns of the people as the source of their citizens' loyalty. Ibid. See also Nagel, Federalism as a Fundamental Value: National League of Cities in Perspective, 1981 Sup.Ct.Rev. 81 (1981).

Thus, the harm to the States that results from federal overreaching under the Commerce Clause is not simply a matter of dollars and cents. National League of Cities, 426 U.S., at 846–851. Nor is it a matter of the wisdom or folly of certain policy choices. Rather, by usurping functions traditionally performed by the States, federal overreaching under the Commerce Clause undermines the constitutionally mandated balance of power between the States and the federal government, a balance designed to protect our fundamental liberties.

. . .

IV

The question presented in this case is whether the extension of the FLSA to the wages and hours of employees of a city-owned transit system unconstitutionally impinges on fundamental state sovereignty. . . .

I return now to the balancing test approved in National League of Cities and accepted in Hodel, Long Island R. Co., and FERC v. Mississippi. The Court does not find in this case that the "federal interest is demonstrably greater." 426 U.S., at 856 (Blackmun, J., concurring). No such finding could have been made, for the state interest is compelling. The financial impact on States and localities of displacing their control over wages, hours, overtime regulations, pensions, and labor relations with their employees could have serious, as well as unanticipated, effects on state and local planning, budgeting, and the levying of taxes. As we said in National League of Cities, federal control of the terms and conditions of employment of State employees also inevitably "displaces state policies regarding the manner in which [States] will structure delivery of those governmental services that citizens require." Id., at 847.

The Court emphasizes that municipal operation of an intracity mass transit system is relatively new in the life of our country. It nevertheless is a classic example of the type of service traditionally provided by local government. It is *local* by definition. It is indistinguishable in principle from the traditional services of providing and maintaining streets, public lighting, traffic control, water, and sewerage systems. Services of this kind are precisely those "with which citizens are more 'familiarly and minutely conversant.'" The Federalist, No. 46, p. 316. State and local officials of course must be intimately familiar with these services and sensitive to their quality as well as cost. Such officials also know that their constituents and the press respond to the adequacy, fair distribution, and cost of these services. It is this kind of state and local control and accountability that the Framers understood would insure the vitality and preservation of the federal system that the Constitution explicitly requires. See *National League of Cities,* supra, at 847–852.

V

. . .

As I view the Court's decision today as rejecting the basic precepts of our federal system and limiting the constitutional role of judicial review, I dissent.

Justice Rehnquist, dissenting.

I join both Justice Powell's and Justice O'Connor's thoughtful dissents. Justice Powell's reference to the "balancing test" approved in *National League of Cities* is not identical with the language in that case, which recognized that Congress could not act under its commerce power to infringe on certain fundamental aspects of state sovereignty that are essential to "the States' separate and independent existence." Nor is either test, or Justice O'Connor's suggested approach, precisely congruent with Justice Blackmun's views in 1976, when he spoke of a balancing approach which did not outlaw federal power in areas "where the federal interest is demonstrably greater." But under any one of these approaches the judgment in this case should be affirmed, and I do not think it incumbent on those of us in dissent to spell out further the fine points of a principle that will, I am confident, in time again command the support of a majority of this Court.

Justice O'Connor, with whom Justice Powell and Justice Rehnquist join, dissenting.

The Court today surveys the battle scene of federalism and sounds a retreat. Like Justice Powell, I would prefer to hold the field and, at the very least, render a little aid to the wounded. I join Justice Powell's opinion. I also write separately to note my fundamental disagreement with the majority's views of federalism and the duty of this Court.

. . .

... [M]any of this Court's decisions acknowledge that the means by which national power is exercised must take into account concerns for state autonomy.... The operative language of these cases varies, but the underlying principle is consistent: state autonomy is a relevant factor in assessing the means by which Congress exercises its powers.

This principle requires the Court to enforce affirmative limits on federal regulation of the States to complement the judicially crafted expansion of the interstate commerce power. *National League of Cities v. Usery* represented an attempt to define such limits. The Court today rejects *National League of Cities* and washes its hands of all efforts to protect the States. In the process, the

Court opines that unwarranted federal encroachments on state authority are and will remain "'horrible possibilities that never happen in the real world.'" There is ample reason to believe to the contrary.

. . .

The problems of federalism in an integrated national economy are capable of more responsible resolution than holding that the States as States retain no status apart from that which Congress chooses to let them retain. The proper resolution, I suggest, lies in weighing state autonomy as a factor in the balance when interpreting the means by which Congress can exercise its authority on the States as States. It is insufficient, in assessing the validity of congressional regulation of a State pursuant to the commerce power, to ask only whether the same regulation would be valid if enforced against a private party. That reasoning, embodied in the majority opinion, is inconsistent with the spirit of our Constitution. . . .

It has been difficult for this Court to craft bright lines defining the scope of the state autonomy protected by *National League of Cities*. Such difficulty is to be expected whenever constitutional concerns as important as federalism and the effectiveness of the commerce power come into conflict. Regardless of the difficulty, it is and will remain the duty of this Court to reconcile these concerns in the final instance. That the Court shuns the task today by appealing to the "essence of federalism" can provide scant comfort to those who believe our federal system requires something more than a unitary, centralized government. I would not shirk the duty acknowledged by *National League of Cities* and its progeny, and I share Justice Rehnquist's belief that this Court will in time again assume its constitutional responsibility.

I respectfully dissent.

. . .

New York v. United States

505 U.S. 144, 112 S.Ct. 2408, 120 L.Ed.2d 120 (1992).

Justice O'Connor delivered the opinion of the Court.

This case implicates one of our Nation's newest problems of public policy and perhaps our oldest question of constitutional law. The public policy issue involves the disposal of radioactive waste: In this case, we address the constitutionality of three provisions of the Low–Level Radioactive Waste Policy Amendments Act of 1985, Pub.L. 99–240, 99 Stat. 1842, 42 U.S.C. § 2021b et seq. The constitutional question is as old as the Constitution: It consists of discerning the proper division of authority between the Federal Government and the States. We conclude that while Congress has substantial power under the Constitution to encourage the States to provide for the disposal of the radioactive waste generated within their borders, the Constitution does not confer upon Congress the ability simply to compel the States to do so. We therefore find that only two of the Act's three provisions at issue are consistent with the Constitution's allocation of power to the Federal Government.

I

We live in a world full of low level radioactive waste. Radioactive material is present in luminous watch dials, smoke alarms, measurement devices, medical fluids, research materials, and the protective gear and construction materials used by workers at nuclear power plants. Low level radioactive waste is generated by the Government, by hospitals, by research institutions, and by various industries. The waste must be isolated from humans for long periods of time, often for hundreds of years. Millions of cubic feet of low level radioactive waste must be disposed of each year....

... [S]ince 1979 only three disposal sites—those in Nevada, Washington, and South Carolina—have been in operation. Waste generated in the rest of the country must be shipped to one of these three sites for disposal.... In 1979, both the Washington and Nevada sites were forced to shut down temporarily, leaving South Carolina to shoulder the responsibility of storing low level radioactive waste produced in every part of the country. The Governor of South Carolina, understandably perturbed, ordered a 50% reduction in the quantity of waste accepted at the Barnwell site. The Governors of Washington and Nevada announced plans to shut their sites permanently.

Faced with the possibility that the Nation would be left with no disposal sites for low level radioactive waste, Congress responded by enacting the Low–Level Radioactive Waste Policy Act, ... Relying largely on a report submitted by the National Governors' Association, Congress declared a federal policy of holding each State "responsible for providing for the availability of capacity either within or outside the State for the disposal of low-level radioactive waste generated within its borders," and found that such waste could be disposed of "most safely and efficiently ... on a regional basis." § 4(a)(1) ... The 1980 Act authorized States to enter into regional compacts that, once ratified by Congress, would have the authority beginning in 1986 to restrict the use of their disposal facilities to waste generated within member States. § 4(a)(2)(B) ... The 1980 Act included no penalties for States that failed to participate in this plan.

By 1985, only three approved regional compacts had operational disposal facilities; not surprisingly, these were the compacts formed around South Carolina, Nevada, and Washington, the three sited States. The following year, the 1980 Act would have given these three compacts the ability to exclude waste from nonmembers, and the remaining 31 States would have had no assured outlet for their low level radioactive waste. With this prospect looming, Congress once again took up the issue of waste disposal. The result was the legislation challenged here, the Low–Level Radioactive Waste Policy Amendments Act of 1985.

The 1985 Act was again based largely on a proposal submitted by the National Governors' Association. In broad outline, the Act embodies a compromise among the sited and unsited States. The sited States agreed to extend for seven years the period in which they would accept low level radioactive waste from other States. In exchange, the unsited States agreed to end their reliance on the sited States by 1992.

The mechanics of this compromise are intricate. The Act directs: "Each State shall be responsible for providing, either by itself or in cooperation with other States, for the disposal of ... low-level radioactive waste generated within the State," 42 U.S.C. § 2021c(a)(1)(A), with the exception of certain waste generated by the Federal Government, §§ 2021c(a)(1)(B), 2021c(b). The Act authorizes States to "enter into such [interstate] compacts as may be necessary to provide for the establishment and operation of regional disposal facilities for low-level radioactive waste." § 2021d(a)(2). For an additional seven years beyond the period contemplated by the 1980 Act, from the beginning of 1986 through the end of 1992, the three existing disposal sites "shall make disposal capacity available for low-level radioactive waste generated by any source," with certain exceptions not relevant here. § 2021e(a)(2). But the three States in which the disposal sites are located are permitted to exact a graduated surcharge for waste arriving from outside the regional compact ... § 2021e(d)(1). After the seven-year transition period expires, approved regional compacts may exclude radioactive waste generated outside the region. § 2021d(c). The Act provides three types of incentives to encourage the States to comply with their statutory obligation to provide for the disposal of waste generated within their borders.

1. *Monetary incentives.* One quarter of the surcharges collected by the sited States must be transferred to an escrow account held by the Secretary of Energy. § 2021e(d)(2)(A). The Secretary then makes payments from this account to each State that has complied with a series of deadlines. By July 1, 1986, each State was to have ratified legislation either joining a regional compact or indicating an intent to develop a disposal facility within the State. §§ 2021e(e)(1)(A), 2021e(d)(2)(B)(I). By January 1, 1988, each unsited compact was to have identified the State in which its facility would be located, and each compact or stand-alone State was to have developed a siting plan and taken other identified steps. §§ 2021e(e)(1)(B), 2021e(d)(2)(B)(ii). By January 1, 1990, each State or compact was to have filed a complete application for a license to operate a disposal facility, or the Governor of any State that had not filed an application was to have certified that the State would be capable of disposing of all waste generated in the State after 1992. §§ 2021e(e)(1)(C), 2021e(d)(2)(B)(iii). The rest of the account is to be paid out to those States or compacts able to dispose of all low level radioactive waste generated within their borders by January 1, 1993. § 2021e(d)(2)(B)(iv). Each State that has not met the 1993 deadline must either take title to the waste generated within its borders or forfeit to the waste generators the incentive payments it has received. § 2021e(d)(2)(C).

2. *Access incentives.* The second type of incentive involves the denial of access to disposal sites. States that fail to meet the July 1986 deadline may be charged twice the ordinary surcharge for the remainder of 1986 and may be denied access to disposal facilities thereafter. § 2021e(e)(2)(A). States that fail to meet the 1988 deadline may be charged double surcharges for the first half of 1988 and quadruple surcharges for the second half of 1988, and may be denied access thereafter. § 2021e(e)(2)(B). States that fail to meet the 1990 deadline may be denied access. § 2021e(e)(2)(C). Finally, States that have not filed complete applications by January 1, 1992, for a license to operate a disposal facility, or States belonging to compacts that have not filed such applications, may be charged triple surcharges. §§ 2021e(e)(1)(D), 2021e(e)(2)(D).

3. *The take title provision.* The third type of incentive is the most severe. The Act provides: "If a State (or, where applicable, a compact region) in which low-level radioactive waste is generated is unable to provide for the disposal of all such waste generated within such State or compact region by January 1, 1996, each State in which such waste is generated, upon the request of the generator or owner of the waste, shall take title to the waste, be obligated to take possession of the waste, and shall be liable for all damages directly or indirectly incurred by such generator or owner as a consequence of the failure of the State to take possession of the waste as soon after January 1, 1996, as the generator or owner notifies the State that the waste is available for shipment." § 2021e(d)(2)(C). These three incentives are the focus of petitioners' constitutional challenge.

In the seven years since the Act took effect, Congress has approved nine regional compacts, encompassing 42 of the States. All six unsited compacts and four of the unaffiliated States have met the first three statutory milestones.

New York, a State whose residents generate a relatively large share of the Nation's low level radioactive waste, did not join a regional compact. Instead, the State complied with the Act's requirements by enacting legislation providing for the siting and financing of a disposal facility in New York. The State has identified five potential sites, three in Allegany County and two in Cortland County. Residents of the two counties oppose the State's choice of location.

Petitioners—the State of New York and the two counties—filed this suit against the United States in 1990. They sought a declaratory judgment that the Act is inconsistent with the Tenth ... Amendment to the Constitution, ... and with the Guarantee Clause of Article IV of the Constitution. The States of Washington, Nevada, and South Carolina intervened as defendants. The District Court dismissed the complaint. The Court of Appeals affirmed....

II

A

In 1788, in the course of explaining to the citizens of New York why the recently drafted Constitution provided for federal courts, Alexander Hamilton observed: "The erection of a new government, whatever care or wisdom may distinguish the work, cannot fail to originate questions of intricacy and nicety; and these may, in a particular manner, be expected to flow from the establishment of a constitution founded upon the total or partial incorporation of a number of distinct sovereignties." The Federalist No. 82, p. 491 (C. Rossiter ed. 1961)....

These questions can be viewed in either of two ways. In some cases the Court has inquired whether an Act of Congress is authorized by one of the powers delegated to Congress in Article I of the Constitution. See, e.g., Perez v. United States, 402 U.S. 146 (1971); McCulloch v. Maryland, 4 Wheat. 316 (1819). In other cases the Court has sought to determine whether an Act of Congress invades the province of state sovereignty reserved by the Tenth Amendment. See, e.g., Garcia v. San Antonio Metropolitan Transit Authority, 469 U.S. 528 (1985) ... In a case like this one, involving the division of authority between federal and state governments, the two inquiries are mirror images of each other. If a power is delegated to Congress in the Constitution, the Tenth Amendment expressly disclaims any reservation of that power to the States; if a power is an attribute of state sovereignty reserved by the Tenth Amendment, it is necessarily a power the Constitution has not conferred on Congress....

It is in this sense that the Tenth Amendment "states but a truism that all is retained which has not been surrendered." United States v. Darby, 312 U.S. 100, 124 (1941). As Justice Story put it, "[t]his amendment is a mere affirmation of what, upon any just reasoning, is a necessary rule of interpreting the constitution. Being an instrument of limited and enumerated powers, it follows irresistibly, that what is not conferred, is withheld, and belongs to the state authorities." 3 J. Story, Commentaries on the Constitution of the United States 752 (1833). This has been the Court's consistent understanding: "The States unquestionably do retai[n] a significant measure of sovereign authority ... to the extent that the Constitution has not divested them of their original powers and transferred those powers to the Federal Government." Garcia v. San Antonio Metropolitan Transit Authority, supra, at 549 ...

Congress exercises its conferred powers subject to the limitations contained in the Constitution. Thus, for example, under the Commerce Clause Congress may regulate publishers engaged in interstate commerce, but Congress is constrained in the exercise of that power by the First Amendment. The Tenth Amendment likewise restrains the power of Congress, but this limit is not derived from the text of the Tenth Amendment itself, which, as we have discussed, is essentially a tautology. Instead, the Tenth Amendment confirms that the power of the Federal Government is subject to limits that may, in a given instance, reserve power to the States. The Tenth Amendment thus directs us to determine, as in this case, whether an incident of state sovereignty is protected by a limitation on an Article I power.

The benefits of this federal structure have been extensively catalogued ... Our task ... consists not of devising our preferred system of government, but of understanding and applying the framework set forth in the Constitution....

This framework has been sufficiently flexible over the past two centuries to allow for enormous changes in the nature of government. The Federal Government undertakes activities today that would have been unimaginable to the Framers in two senses; first, because the Framers would not have conceived that any government would conduct such activities; and second, because the Framers would not have believed that the Federal Government, rather than the States, would assume such responsibilities. Yet the powers conferred upon the Federal Government by the Constitution were phrased in language broad enough to allow for the expansion of the Federal Government's role. Among the provisions of the Constitution that have been particularly important in this regard, three concern us here.

First, the Constitution allocates to Congress the power "[t]o regulate Commerce ... among the several States." ... As interstate commerce has become ubiquitous, activities once considered purely local have come to have effects on the national economy, and have accordingly come within the scope of Congress' commerce power....

Second, the Constitution authorizes Congress "to pay the Debts and provide for the ... general Welfare of the United States." ... As conventional notions of the proper objects of government spending have changed over the years, so has the ability of Congress to "fix the terms on which it shall disburse federal money to the States." Pennhurst State School and Hospital v. Halderman, 451 U.S. 1, 17 (1981). Compare, e.g., United States v. Butler, supra, at 72–75 (spending power does not authorize Congress to subsidize farmers), with South Dakota v. Dole, 483 U.S. 203 (1987) (spending power permits Congress to condition highway funds on States' adoption of minimum drinking age). While the spending power is "subject to several general restrictions articulated in our cases," id., at 207, these restrictions have not been so severe as to prevent the regulatory authority of Congress from generally keeping up with the growth of the federal budget.

. . .

Finally, the Constitution provides that "the Laws of the United States ... shall be the supreme Law of the Land ... any Thing in the Constitution or Laws of any State to the Contrary notwithstanding." ... As the Federal Government's willingness to exercise power within the confines of the Constitution has grown, the authority of the States has correspondingly diminished to the extent that federal and state policies have conflicted....

. . .

B

Petitioners do not contend that Congress lacks the power to regulate the disposal of low level radioactive waste. Space in radioactive waste disposal sites is frequently sold by residents of one State to residents of another. Regulation of the resulting interstate market in waste disposal is therefore well within Congress' authority under the Commerce Clause.... Petitioners likewise do not dispute that under the Supremacy Clause Congress could, if it wished, pre-empt state radioactive waste regulation. Petitioners contend only that the Tenth Amendment limits the power of Congress to regulate in the way it has chosen. Rather than addressing the problem of waste disposal by directly regulating the generators and disposers of waste, petitioners argue, Congress has impermissibly directed the States to regulate in this field.

Most of our recent cases interpreting the Tenth Amendment have concerned the authority of Congress to subject state governments to generally applicable laws. The Court's jurisprudence in this area has traveled an unsteady path. See Maryland v. Wirtz, 392 U.S. 183 (1968) (state schools and hospitals are subject to Fair Labor Standards Act); National League of Cities v. Usery, 426 U.S. 833 (1976) (overruling *Wirtz*) (state employers are not subject to Fair Labor Standards Act); Garcia v. San Antonio Metropolitan Transit Authority, 469 U.S. 528 (1985) (overruling *National League of Cities*) (state employers are once again subject to Fair Labor Standards Act). See also ... Gregory v. Ashcroft, 501 U.S. 452 (1991). This case presents no occasion to apply or revisit the holdings of any of these cases, as this is not a case in which Congress has subjected a State to the same legislation applicable to private parties. Cf. FERC v. Mississippi, 456 U.S. 742, 758–759 (1982).

This case instead concerns the circumstances under which Congress may use the States as implements of regulation; that is, whether Congress may direct or otherwise motivate the States to regulate in a particular field or a particular way. Our cases have established a few principles that guide our resolution of the issue.

1

As an initial matter, Congress may not simply "commandee[r] the legislative processes of the States by directly compelling them to enact and enforce a federal regulatory program." Hodel v. Virginia Surface Mining & Reclamation Assn., Inc., 452 U.S. 264, 288 (1981). In *Hodel*, the Court upheld the Surface Mining Control and Reclamation Act of 1977 precisely because it did not "commandeer" the States into regulating mining. The Court found that "the States are not compelled to enforce the steep-slope standards, to expend any state funds, or to participate in the federal regulatory program in any manner whatsoever. If a State does not wish to submit a proposed permanent program that complies with the Act and implementing regulations, the full regulatory burden will be borne by the Federal Government." ...

The Court reached the same conclusion the following year in *FERC v. Mississippi*, supra. At issue in *FERC* was the Public Utility Regulatory Policies Act of 1978, a federal statute encouraging the States in various ways to develop programs to combat the Nation's energy crisis. We observed that "this Court never has sanctioned explicitly a federal command to the States to promulgate and enforce laws and regulations." ... As in *Hodel*, the Court upheld the statute at issue because it did not view the statute as such a command. The Court emphasized: "Titles I and III of [the Public Utility Regulatory Policies Act of 1978 (PURPA)]require only consideration of federal standards. And if a State has no utilities commission, or simply stops regulating in the field, it need not even entertain the federal proposals." ... Because "[t]here [wa]s nothing in PURPA 'directly compelling' the States to enact a legislative program," the statute was not inconsistent with the Constitution's division of authority between the Federal Government and the States....

These statements in *FERC* and *Hodel* were not innovations. While Congress has substantial powers to govern the Nation directly, including in areas of intimate concern to the States, the Constitution has never been understood to confer upon Congress the ability to require the States to govern according to Congress' instructions....

Indeed, the question whether the Constitution should permit Congress to employ state governments as regulatory agencies was a topic of lively debate among the Framers. Under the Articles of Confederation, Congress lacked the authority in most respects to govern the people directly. In practice, Congress "could not directly tax or legislate upon individuals; it had no explicit 'legislative' or 'governmental' power to make binding 'law' enforceable as such." Amar, Of Sovereignty and Federalism, 96 Yale L.J. 1425, 1447 (1987).

The inadequacy of this governmental structure was responsible in part for the Constitutional Convention. Alexander Hamilton observed: "The great and radical vice in the construction of the existing Confederation is in the principle of LEGISLATION for STATES or GOVERNMENTS, in their CORPORATE or COLLECTIVE CAPACITIES, and as contradistinguished from the INDIVIDUALS of whom they consist." The Federalist No. 15, p. 108 (C. Rossiter ed. 1961). As Hamilton saw it, "we must resolve to incorporate into our plan those ingredients which may be considered as forming the characteristic difference between a league and a government; we must extend the authority of the Union to the persons of the citizens—the only proper objects of government." Id., at 109. The new National Government "must carry its agency to the persons of the citizens. It must stand in need of no intermediate legislations.... The government of the Union, like that of each State, must be able to address itself immediately to the hopes and fears of individuals." Id., No. 16, p. 116.

The Convention generated a great number of proposals for the structure of the new Government, but two quickly took center stage. Under the Virginia Plan, as first introduced by Edmund Randolph, Congress would exercise legislative authority directly upon individuals, without employing the States as intermediaries.... Under the New Jersey Plan, as first introduced by William Paterson, Congress would continue to require the approval of the States before legislating, as it has under the Articles of Confederation.... These two plans underwent various revisions as the Convention progressed, but they remained the two primary options discussed by the delegates. One frequently expressed objection to the New Jersey Plan was that it might require the Federal Government to coerce the States into implementing legislation. As Randolph explained the distinction, "[t]he true question is whether we shall adhere to the federal plan [i.e., the New Jersey Plan], or introduce the national plan. The insufficiency of the former has been fully displayed.... There are but two modes, by which the end of a Gen[eral] Gov[ernment] can be attained: the 1st is by coercion as proposed by Mr. P[aterson's] plan[, the 2nd] by real legislation as prop[osed] by the other plan. Coercion [is] impracticable, expensive, cruel to individuals.... We must resort therefore to a national Legislation over individuals." ... Madison echoed this view: "The practicability of making laws, with coercive sanctions, for the States as political bodies, had been exploded on all hands." ...

Under one preliminary draft of what would become the New Jersey Plan, state governments would occupy a position relative to Congress similar to that contemplated by the Act at issue in this case: "[T]he laws of the United States ought, as far as may be consistent with the common interests of the Union, to be carried into execution by the judiciary and executive officers of the respective states, wherein the execution thereof is required." ... This idea apparently never even progressed so far as to be debated by the delegates, as contemporary accounts of the Convention do not mention any such discussion. The delegates' many descriptions of the Virginia and New Jersey Plans speak only in general terms about whether Congress was to derive its authority from the people or from the States, and whether it was to issue directives to individuals or to States....

In the end, the Convention opted for a Constitution in which Congress would exercise its legislative authority directly over individuals rather than over States; for a variety of reasons, it rejected the New Jersey Plan in favor of the Virginia Plan.... This choice was made clear to the subsequent state ratifying conventions. Oliver Ellsworth, a member of the Connecticut delegation in Philadelphia, explained the distinction to his State's convention: "This Constitution does not attempt to coerce sovereign bodies, states, in their political capacity.... But this legal coercion singles out the ... individual." ... Charles Pinckney, another delegate at the Constitutional Convention, emphasized to the South Carolina House of Representatives that in Philadelphia "the necessity of having a government which should at once operate upon the people, and not upon the states, was conceived to be indispensable by every delegation present." 4 id., at 256. Rufus King, one of Massachusetts' delegates, returned home to support ratification by recalling the Commonwealth's unhappy experience under the Articles of Confederation and arguing: "Laws, to be effective, therefore, must not be laid on states, but upon individuals." ... At New York's convention, Hamilton (another delegate in Philadelphia) exclaimed: "But can we believe that one state will ever suffer itself to be used as an instrument of coercion? The thing is a dream; it is impossible. Then we are brought to this dilemma—either a federal standing army is to enforce the requisitions, or the federal treasury is left without supplies, and the government without support. What, sir, is the cure for this great evil? Nothing, but to enable the national laws to operate on individuals, in the same manner as those of the states do." ... At North Carolina's convention, Samuel Spencer recognized that "all the laws of the Confederation were binding on the states in their political capacities, ... but now the thing is entirely different. The laws of Congress will be binding on individuals." ...

In providing for a stronger central government, therefore, the Framers explicitly chose a Constitution that confers upon Congress the power to regulate individuals, not States. As we have seen, the Court has consistently respected this choice. We have always understood that even where Congress has the authority under the Constitution to pass laws requiring or prohibiting certain acts, it lacks the power directly to compel the States to require or prohibit those acts. E.g., FERC v. Mississippi, 456 U.S., at 762–766; Hodel v. Virginia Surface Mining & Reclamation Assn., Inc., 452 U.S., at 288–289 ... The allocation of power contained in the Commerce Clause, for example, authorizes Congress to regulate interstate commerce directly; it does not authorize Congress to regulate state governments' regulation of interstate commerce.

2

This is not to say that Congress lacks the ability to encourage a State to regulate in a particular way, or that Congress may not hold out incentives to the States as a method of influencing a State's policy choices. Our cases have identified a variety of methods, short of outright coercion, by which Congress may urge a State to adopt a legislative program consistent with federal interests. Two of these methods are of particular relevance here.

First, under Congress' spending power, "Congress may attach conditions on the receipt of federal funds." South Dakota v. Dole, 483 U.S., at 206. Such conditions must (among other requirements) bear some relationship to the purpose of the federal spending, . . .; otherwise, of course, the spending power could render academic the Constitution's other grants and limits of federal authority. Where the recipient of federal funds is a State, as is not unusual today, the conditions attached to the funds by Congress may influence a State's legislative choices. . . . *Dole* was one such case: The Court found no constitutional flaw in a federal statute directing the Secretary of Transportation to withhold federal highway funds from States failing to adopt Congress' choice of a minimum drinking age. . . .

Second, where Congress has the authority to regulate private activity under the Commerce Clause, we have recognized Congress' power to offer States the choice of regulating that activity according to federal standards or having state law pre-empted by federal regulation. Hodel v. Virginia Surface Mining & Reclamation Assn., Inc., supra, at 288. See also FERC v. Mississippi, supra, at 764–765. This arrangement, which has been termed "a program of cooperative federalism," *Hodel*, supra, at 289, is replicated in numerous federal statutory schemes. These include the Clean Water Act, . . . 33 U.S.C. § 1251 et seq. . . .; the Occupational Safety and Health Act of 1970, . . . 29 U.S.C. § 651 et seq. . . .; the Resource Conservation and Recovery Act of 1976, . . . 42 U.S.C. § 6901 et seq. . . .; and the Alaska National Interest Lands Conservation Act, . . . 16 U.S.C. § 3101 et seq. . . .

By either of these two methods, as by any other permissible method of encouraging a State to conform to federal policy choices, the residents of the State retain the ultimate decision as to whether or not the State will comply. If a State's citizens view federal policy as sufficiently contrary to local interests, they may elect to decline a federal grant. If state residents would prefer their government to devote its attention and resources to problems other than those deemed important by Congress, they may choose to have the Federal Government rather than the State bear the expense of a federally mandated regulatory program, and they may continue to supplement that program to the extent state law is not pre-empted. Where Congress encourages state regulation rather than compelling it, state governments remain responsive to the local electorate's preferences; state officials remain accountable to the people.

By contrast, where the Federal Government compels States to regulate, the accountability of both state and federal officials is diminished. If the citizens of New York, for example, do not consider that making provision for the disposal of radioactive waste is in their best interest, they may elect state officials who share their view. That view can always be pre-empted under the Supremacy Clause if it is contrary to the national view, but in such a case it is the Federal Government that makes the decision in full view of the public, and it will be federal officials that suffer the consequences if the decision turns out to be detrimental or unpopular. But where the Federal Government directs the States to regulate, it may be state officials who will bear the brunt of public disapproval, while the federal officials who devised the regulatory program may remain insulated from the electoral ramifications of their decision. Accountability is thus diminished when, due to federal coercion, elected state officials cannot regulate in accordance with the views of the local electorate in matters not pre-empted by federal regulation. . . .

With these principles in mind, we turn to the three challenged provisions of the Low–Level Radioactive Waste Policy Amendments Act of 1985.

III

The parties in this case advance two quite different views of the Act. As petitioners see it, the Act imposes a requirement directly upon the States that they regulate in the field of radioactive waste disposal in order to meet Congress' mandate that "[e]ach State shall be responsible for providing . . . for the disposal of . . . low-level radioactive waste." . . . Petitioners understand this provision as a direct command from Congress, enforceable independent of the three sets of incentives provided by the Act. Respondents, on the other hand, read this provision together with the incentives, and see the Act as affording the States three sets of choices. According to respondents, the Act permits a State to choose first between regulating pursuant to federal standards and losing the right to a share of the Secretary of Energy's escrow account; to choose second between regulating pursuant to federal standards and progressively losing access to disposal sites in other States; and to choose third between regulating pursuant to federal standards and taking title to the waste generated within the State. Respondents thus interpret § 2021c(a)(1)(A), despite the statute's use of the word "shall," to provide no more than an option which a State may elect or eschew.

The Act could plausibly be understood either as a mandate to regulate or as a series of incentives. Under petitioners' view, however, § 2021c(a)(1)(A) of the Act would clearly "commandee[r] the legislative processes of the States by directly compelling them to enact and enforce a federal regulatory program." Hodel v. Virginia Surface Mining & Reclamation Assn., Inc., 452 U.S., at 288. We must reject this interpretation of the provision for two reasons. First, such an outcome would, to say the least, "upset the usual constitutional balance of federal and state powers." Gregory v. Ashcroft, 501 U.S., at ____. . . . Second, "where an otherwise acceptable construction of a statute would raise serious constitutional problems, the Court will construe the statute to avoid such problems unless such construction is plainly contrary to the intent of Congress." . . .

 We therefore decline petitioners' invitation to construe § 2021c(a)(1)(A), alone and in isolation, as a command to the States independent of the remainder of the Act. Construed as a whole, the Act comprises three sets of "incentives" for the States to provide for the disposal of low level radioactive waste generated within their borders. We consider each in turn.

A

The first set of incentives works in three steps. First, Congress has authorized States with disposal sites to impose a surcharge on radioactive waste received from other States. Second, the Secretary of Energy collects a portion of this surcharge and places the money in an escrow account. Third, States achieving a series of milestones receive portions of this fund.

The first of these steps is an unexceptionable exercise of Congress' power to authorize the States to burden interstate commerce. While the Commerce Clause has long been understood to limit the States' ability to discriminate against interstate commerce, . . . that limit may be lifted, as it has been here, by an expression of the "unambiguous intent" of Congress. *Wyoming,* supra, at ___; Prudential Ins. Co. v. Benjamin, 328 U.S. 408, 427–431 (1946). Whether or not the States would be permitted to burden the interstate transport of low level radioactive waste in the absence of Congress' approval, the States can clearly do so with Congress' approval, which is what the Act gives them.

The second step, the Secretary's collection of a percentage of the surcharge, is no more than a federal tax on interstate commerce, which petitioners do not claim to be an invalid exercise of either Congress' commerce or taxing power. . . .

The third step is a conditional exercise of Congress' authority under the Spending Clause: Congress has placed conditions—the achievement of the milestones—on the receipt of federal funds. Petitioners do not contend that Congress has exceeded its authority in any of the four respects our cases have identified. See generally South Dakota v. Dole, 483 U.S., at 207–208. The expenditure is for the general welfare . . .; the States are required to use the money they receive for the purpose of assuring the safe disposal of radioactive waste. . . . The conditions imposed are unambiguous . . .; the Act informs the States exactly what they must do and by when they must do it in order to obtain a share of the escrow account. The conditions imposed are reasonably related to the purpose of the expenditure, . . .; both the conditions and the payments embody Congress' efforts to address the pressing problem of radioactive waste disposal. Finally, petitioners do not claim that the conditions imposed by the Act violate any independent constitutional prohibition. . . .

The Act's first set of incentives, in which Congress has conditioned grants to the States upon the States' attainment of a series of milestones, is thus well within the authority of Congress under the Commerce and Spending Clauses. Because the first set of incentives is supported by affirmative constitutional grants of power to Congress, it is not inconsistent with the Tenth Amendment.

B

In the second set of incentives, Congress has authorized States and regional compacts with disposal sites gradually to increase the cost of access to the sites, and then to deny access altogether, to radioactive waste generated in States that do not meet federal deadlines. As a simple regulation, this provision would be within the power of Congress to authorize the States to discriminate against interstate commerce. See Northeast Bancorp, Inc. v. Board of Governors, Fed. Reserve System, 472 U.S. 159, 174–175 (1985). Where federal regulation of private activity is within the scope of the Commerce Clause, we have recognized the ability of Congress to offer states the choice of regulating that activity according to federal standards or having state law pre-empted by federal regulation. See Hodel v. Virginia Surface Mining & Reclamation Association, 452 U.S., at 288; FERC v. Mississippi, 456 U.S., at 764–765.

This is the choice presented to nonsited States by the Act's second set of incentives: States may either regulate the disposal of radioactive waste according to federal standards by attaining local or regional self-sufficiency, or their residents who produce radioactive waste will be subject to federal regulation authorizing sited States and regions to deny access to their disposal sites. The affected States are not compelled by Congress to regulate, because any burden caused by a State's refusal to regulate will fall on those who generate waste and find no outlet for its disposal, rather than on the State as a sovereign. A State whose citizens do not wish it to attain the Act's milestones may devote its attention and its resources to issues its citizens deem more worthy; the choice remains at all times with the residents of the State, not with Congress. The State need not expend any funds, or participate in any federal program, if local residents do not view such expenditures or participation as worthwhile. . . . Nor must the State abandon the field if it does not accede to federal direction; the State may continue to regulate the generation and disposal of radioactive waste in any manner its citizens see fit.

The Act's second set of incentives thus represents a conditional exercise of Congress' commerce power, along the lines of those we have held to be within Congress' authority. As a result, the second set of incentives does not intrude on the sovereignty reserved to the States by the Tenth Amendment.

C

The take title provision is of a different character. This third so-called "incentive" offers States, as an alternative to regulating pursuant to Congress' direction, the option of taking title to and possession of the low level radioactive waste generated within their borders and becoming liable for all damages waste generators suffer as a result of the States' failure to do so promptly. In this provision, Congress has crossed the line distinguishing encouragement from coercion.

The take title provision offers state governments a "choice" of either accepting ownership of waste or regulating according to the instructions of Congress. Respondents do not claim that the Constitution would authorize Congress to impose either option as a freestanding requirement. On one hand, the Constitution would not permit Congress simply to transfer radioactive waste from generators to state governments. Such a forced transfer, standing alone, would in principle be no different than a congressionally compelled subsidy from state governments to radioactive waste producers. The same is true of the provision requiring the States to become liable for the generators' damages. Standing alone, this provision would be indistinguishable from an Act of Congress directing the States to assume the liabilities of certain state residents. Either type of federal action would "commandeer" state governments into the service of federal regulatory purposes, and would for this reason be inconsistent with the Constitution's division of authority between federal and state governments. On the other hand, the second alternative held out to state governments—regulating pursuant to Congress' direction—would, standing alone, present a simple command to state governments to implement legislation enacted by Congress. As we have seen, the Constitution does not empower Congress to subject state governments to this type of instruction.

Because an instruction to state governments to take title to waste, standing alone, would be beyond the authority of Congress, and because a direct order to regulate, standing alone, would also be beyond the authority of Congress, it follows that Congress lacks the power to offer the States a choice between the two. Unlike the first two sets of incentives, the take title incentive does not represent the conditional exercise of any congressional power enumerated in the Constitution. In this provision, Congress has not held out the threat of exercising its spending power or its commerce power; it has instead held out the threat, should the States not regulate according to one federal instruction, of simply forcing the States to submit to another federal instruction. A choice between two unconstitutionally coercive regulatory techniques is no choice at all. Either way, "the Act commandeers the legislative processes of the States by directly compelling them to enact and enforce a federal regulatory program," Hodel v. Virginia Surface Mining & Reclamation Assn., Inc., supra, at 288, an outcome that has never been understood to lie within the authority conferred upon Congress by the Constitution.

Respondents emphasize the latitude given to the States to implement Congress' plan. The Act enables the States to regulate pursuant to Congress' instructions in any number of different ways. States may avoid taking title by contracting with sited regional compacts, by building a disposal site alone or as part of a compact, or by permitting private parties to build a disposal site. States that host sites may employ a wide range of designs and disposal methods, subject only to broad federal regulatory limits. This line of reasoning, however, only underscores the critical alternative a State lacks: A State may not decline to administer the federal program. No matter which path the State chooses, it must follow the direction of Congress.

The take title provision appears to be unique. No other federal statute has been cited which offers a state government no option other than that of implementing legislation enacted by Congress. Whether one views the take title provision as lying outside Congress' enumerated powers, or as infringing upon the core of state sovereignty reserved by the Tenth Amendment, the provision is inconsistent with the federal structure of our Government established by the Constitution.

IV

Respondents raise a number of objections to this understanding of the limits of Congress' power.

A

The United States proposes three alternative views of the constitutional line separating state and federal authority. While each view concedes that Congress generally may not compel state governments to regulate pursuant to federal direction, each purports to find a limited domain in which such coercion is permitted by the Constitution.

First, the United States argues that the Constitution's prohibition of congressional directives to state governments can be overcome where the federal interest is sufficiently important to justify state submission. This argument contains a kernel of truth: In determining whether the Tenth Amendment limits the ability of Congress to subject state governments to generally applicable laws, the Court has in some cases stated that it will evaluate the strength of federal interests in light of the degree to which such laws would prevent the State from functioning as a sovereign; that is, the extent to which such generally applicable laws would impede a state government's responsibility to represent and be accountable to the citizens of the State. See, e.g., EEOC v. Wyoming, 460 U.S., at 242, n. 17; Transportation Union v. Long Island R. Co., 455 U.S., at 684, n. 9; National League of Cities v. Usery, 426 U.S., at 853. The Court has more recently departed from this approach. See, e.g., South Carolina v. Baker, 485 U.S., at 512–513; Garcia v. San Antonio Metropolitan Transit Authority, 469 U.S., at 556–557. But whether or not a particularly strong federal interest enables Congress to bring state governments within the orbit of generally applicable federal regulation, no Member of the Court has ever suggested that such a federal interest would enable Congress to command a state government to enact state regulation. No matter how powerful the federal interest involved, the Constitution simply does not give Congress the authority to require the States to regulate. The Constitution instead gives Congress the authority to regulate matters directly and to pre-empt contrary state regulation. Where a federal interest is sufficiently strong to cause Congress to legislate, it must do so directly; it may not conscript state governments as its agents.

Second, the United States argues that the Constitution does, in some circumstances, permit federal directives to state governments. Various cases are cited for this proposition, but none support it. Some of these cases discuss the well established power of Congress to pass laws enforceable in state courts. See Testa v. Katt, 330 U.S. 386 (1947) ... These cases involve no more than an application of the Supremacy Clause's provision that federal law "shall be the supreme Law of the Land," enforceable in every State. More to the point, all involve congressional regulation of individuals, not congressional requirements that States regulate. Federal statutes enforceable in state courts do, in a sense, direct state judges to enforce them, but this sort of federal "direction" of state judges is mandated by the text of the Supremacy Clause. No comparable constitutional provision authorizes Congress to command state legislatures to legislate.

Additional cases cited by the United States discuss the power of federal courts to order state officials to comply with federal law.... Again, however, the text of the Constitution plainly confers this authority on the federal courts, the "judicial Power" of which "shall extend to all Cases, in Law and Equity, arising under this Constitution, [and] the Laws of the United States ...; [and] to Controversies between two or more States; [and] between a State and Citizens of another State." U.S. Const., Art. III, § 2. The Constitution contains no analogous grant of authority to Congress. Moreover, the Supremacy Clause makes federal law paramount over the contrary positions of state officials; the power of federal courts to enforce federal law thus presupposes some authority to order state officials to comply. See Puerto Rico v. Branstad, supra, at 227–228 (overruling Kentucky v. Dennison, 24 How. 66 (1861)).

In sum, the cases relied upon by the United States hold only that federal law is enforceable in state courts and that federal courts may in proper circumstances order state officials to comply with federal law, propositions that by no means imply any authority on the part of Congress to mandate state regulation.

Third, the United States, supported by the three sited regional compacts as amici, argues that the Constitution envisions a role for Congress as an arbiter of interstate disputes. The United States observes that federal courts, and this Court in particular, have frequently resolved conflicts among States.... Many of these disputes have involved the allocation of shared resources among the States, a category perhaps broad enough to encompass the allocation of scarce disposal space for radioactive waste.... The United States suggests that if the Court may resolve such interstate disputes, Congress can surely do the same under the Commerce Clause. The regional compacts support this argument with a series of quotations from The Federalist and other contemporaneous documents, which the compacts contend demonstrate that the Framers established a strong national legislature for the purpose of resolving trade disputes among the States.

While the Framers no doubt endowed Congress with the power to regulate interstate commerce in order to avoid further instances of the interstate trade disputes that were common under the Articles of Confederation, the Framers did not intend that Congress should exercise that power through the mechanism of mandating state regulation. The Constitution established Congress as "a superintending authority over the reciprocal trade" among the States, The Federalist No. 42, p. 268 (C. Rossiter ed. 1961), by empowering Congress to regulate that trade directly, not by authorizing Congress to issue trade-related orders to state governments. As Madison and Hamilton explained, "a sovereignty over sovereigns, a government over governments, a legislation for communities, as contradistinguished from individuals, as it is a solecism in theory, so in practice it is subversive of the order and ends of civil polity." Id., No. 20, p. 138.

B

The sited State respondents focus their attention on the process by which the Act was formulated. They correctly observe that public officials representing the State of New York lent their support to the Act's enactment. . . . Respondents note that the Act embodies a bargain among the sited and unsited States, a compromise to which New York was a willing participant and from which New York has reaped much benefit. Respondents then pose what appears at first to be a troubling question: How can a federal statute be found an unconstitutional infringement of State sovereignty when state officials consented to the statute's enactment?

The answer follows from an understanding of the fundamental purpose served by our Government's federal structure. The Constitution does not protect the sovereignty of States for the benefit of the States or state governments as abstract political entities, or even for the benefit of the public officials governing the States. To the contrary, the Constitution divides authority between federal and state governments for the protection of individuals. . . .

Where Congress exceeds its authority relative to the States, therefore, the departure from the constitutional plan cannot be ratified by the "consent" of state officials. An analogy to the separation of powers among the Branches of the Federal Government clarifies this point. The Constitution's division of power among the three Branches is violated where one Branch invades the territory of another, whether or not the encroached-upon Branch approves the encroachment. . . . The constitutional authority of Congress cannot be expanded by the "consent" of the governmental unit whose domain is thereby narrowed, whether that unit is the Executive Branch or the States.

State officials thus cannot consent to the enlargement of the powers of Congress beyond those enumerated in the Constitution. Indeed, the facts of this case raise the possibility that powerful incentives might lead both federal and state officials to view departures from the federal structure to be in their personal interests. Most citizens recognize the need for radioactive waste disposal sites, but few want sites near their homes. As a result, while it would be well within the authority of either federal or state officials to choose where the disposal sites will be, it is likely to be in the political interest of each individual official to avoid being held accountable to the voters for the choice of location. If a federal official is faced with the alternatives of choosing a location or directing the States to do it, the official may well prefer the latter, as a means of shifting responsibility for the eventual decision. If a state official is faced with the same set of alternatives—choosing a location or having Congress direct the choice of a location—the state official may also prefer the latter, as it may permit the avoidance of personal responsibility. The interests of public officials thus may not coincide with the Constitution's intergovernmental allocation of authority. Where state officials purport to submit to the direction of Congress in this manner, federalism is hardly being advanced.

Nor does the State's prior support for the Act estop it from asserting the Act's unconstitutionality. While New York has received the benefit of the Act in the form of a few more years of access to disposal sites in other States, New York has never joined a regional radioactive waste compact. Any estoppel implications that might flow from membership in a compact, . . . thus do not concern us here. The fact that the Act, like much federal legislation, embodies a compromise among the States does not elevate the Act . . . to the status of an interstate agreement requiring Congress' approval under the Compact Clause. . . . That a party collaborated with others in seeking legislation has never been understood to estop the party from challenging that legislation in subsequent litigation.

V

Petitioners also contend that the Act is inconsistent with the Constitution's Guarantee Clause, which directs the United States to "guarantee to every State in this Union a Republican Form of Government." Because we have found the take title provision of the Act irreconcilable with the powers delegated to Congress by the Constitution and hence with the Tenth Amendment's reservation to the States of those powers not delegated to the Federal Government, we need only address the applicability of the Guarantee Clause to the Act's other two challenged provisions.

We approach the issue with some trepidation, because the Guarantee Clause has been an infrequent basis for litigation throughout our history. In most of the cases in which the Court has been asked to apply the Clause, the Court has found the claims presented to be nonjusticiable under the "political question" doctrine. See, e.g., City of Rome v. United States, 446 U.S. 156, 182, n. 17 (1980) (challenge to the preclearance requirements of the Voting Rights Act); Baker v. Carr, 369 U.S. 186, 218–229 (1962) (challenge to apportionment of state legislative districts); Pacific States Tel. & Tel. Co. v. Oregon, 223 U.S. 118, 140–151 (1912) (challenge to initiative and referendum provisions of state constitution).

The view that the Guarantee Clause implicates only nonjusticiable political questions has its origin in Luther v. Borden, 7 How. 1 (1849), in which the Court was asked to decide, in the wake of Dorr's Rebellion, which of two rival governments was the legitimate government of Rhode Island. The Court held that "it rests with Congress," not the judiciary, "to decide what government is the established one in a State." Id., at 42. Over the following century, this limited holding metamorphosed into the sweeping assertion that "[v]iolation of the great guaranty of a republican form of government in States cannot be challenged in the courts." Colegrove v. Green, 328 U.S. 549, 556 (1946) (plurality opinion).

. . .

More recently, the Court has suggested that perhaps not all claims under the Guarantee Clause present nonjusticiable political questions. See Reynolds v. Sims, 377 U.S. 533, 582 (1964) ("some questions raised under the Guarantee Clause are nonjusticiable"). . . .

We need not resolve this difficult question today. Even if we assume that petitioners' claim is justiciable, neither the monetary incentives provided by the Act nor the possibility that a State's waste producers may find themselves excluded from the disposal sites of another State can reasonably be said to deny any State a republican form of government. As we have seen, these two incentives represent permissible conditional exercises of Congress' authority under the Spending and Commerce Clauses respectively, in forms that have now grown commonplace. Under each, Congress offers the States a legitimate choice rather than issuing an unavoidable command. The States thereby retain the ability to set their legislative agendas; state government officials remain accountable to the local electorate. The twin threats imposed by the first two challenged provisions of the Act—that New York may miss out on a share of federal spending or that those generating radioactive waste within New York may lose out-of-state disposal outlets—do not pose any realistic risk of altering the form or the method of functioning of New York's government. Thus even indulging the assumption that the Guarantee Clause provides a basis upon which a State or its subdivisions may sue to enjoin the enforcement of a federal statute, petitioners have not made out such a claim in this case.

VI

Having determined that the take title provision exceeds the powers of Congress, we must consider whether it is severable from the rest of the Act.

. . .

... [T]he take title provision may be severed without doing violence to the rest of the Act. The Act is still operative and it still serves Congress' objective of encouraging the States to attain local or regional self-sufficiency in the disposal of low level radioactive waste. It still includes two incentives that coax the States along this road. A State whose radioactive waste generators are unable to gain access to disposal sites in other States may encounter considerable internal pressure to provide for the disposal of waste, even without the prospect of taking title. The sited regional compacts need not accept New York's waste after the seven-year transition period expires, so any burden caused by New York's failure to secure a disposal site will not be borne by the residents of other States. The purpose of the Act is not defeated by the invalidation of the take title provision, so we may leave the remainder of the Act in force.

VII

. . .

States are not mere political subdivisions of the United States. State governments are neither regional offices nor administrative agencies of the Federal Government. The positions occupied by state officials appear nowhere on the Federal Government's most detailed organizational chart. The Constitution instead "leaves to the several States a residuary and inviolable sovereignty," The Federalist No. 39, p. 245 (C. Rossiter ed. 1961), reserved explicitly to the States by the Tenth Amendment.

Whatever the outer limits of that sovereignty may be, one thing is clear: The Federal Government may not compel the States to enact or administer a federal regulatory program. The Constitution permits both the Federal Government and the States to enact legislation regarding the disposal of low level radioactive waste. The Constitution enables the Federal Government to preempt state regulation contrary to federal interests, and it permits the Federal Government to hold out incentives to the States as a means of encouraging them to adopt suggested regulatory schemes. It does not, however, authorize Congress simply to direct the States to provide for the disposal of the radioactive waste generated within their borders. While there may be many constitutional methods of achieving regional self-sufficiency in radioactive waste disposal, the method Congress has chosen is not one of them. The judgment of the Court of Appeals is accordingly

Affirmed in part and reversed in part.

Justice White, with whom Justice Blackmun and Justice Stevens join, concurring in part and dissenting in part.

. . .

I

My disagreement with the Court's analysis begins at the basic descriptive level of how the legislation at issue in this case came to be enacted.... The Low–Level Radioactive Waste Policy Act of 1980 ..., and its amendatory Act of 1985, resulted from the efforts of state leaders to achieve a state-based set of remedies to the waste problem. They sought not federal pre-emption or intervention, but rather congressional sanction of interstate compromises they had reached.

. . .

... Unlike legislation that directs action from the Federal Government to the States, the 1980 and 1985 Acts reflected hard-fought agreements among States as refereed by Congress. The distinction is key, and the Court's failure properly to characterize this legislation ultimately affects its analysis of the take title provision's constitutionality.

II

. . .

... I am unmoved by the Court's vehemence in taking away Congress' authority to sanction a recalcitrant unsited State now that New York has reaped the benefits of the sited States' concessions.

A

In my view, New York's actions subsequent to enactment of the 1980 and 1985 Acts fairly indicate its approval of the interstate agreement process embodied in those laws within the meaning of Art. I, § 10, cl. 3....

. . .

Although unlike the 42 States that compose the nine existing and approved regional compacts, New York has never formalized its assent to the 1980 and 1985 statutes, our cases support the view that New York's actions signify assent to a constitutional interstate "agreement" for purposes of Art. I, § 10, cl. 3 ... In my view, New York acted in a manner to signify its assent to the 1985 Act's take title provision as part of the elaborate compromise reached among the States.

The State should be estopped from asserting the unconstitutionality of a provision that seeks merely to ensure that, after deriving substantial advantages from the 1985 Act, New York in fact must live up to its bargain by establishing an in-state low-level radioactive waste facility or assuming liability for its failure to act....

. . .

III

The Court announces that it has no occasion to revisit such decisions as Gregory v. Ashcroft, 501 U.S. 452 (1991); South Carolina v. Baker, 485 U.S. 505 (1988); Garcia v. San Antonio Metropolitan Transit Authority, 469 U.S. 528 (1985); EEOC v. Wyoming, 460 U.S. 226 (1983); and National League of Cities v. Usery, 426 U.S. 833 (1976) ... Although this statement sends the welcome signal that the Court does not intend to cut a wide swath through our recent Tenth Amendment precedents, it nevertheless is unpersuasive. I have several difficulties with the Court's analysis in this respect: it builds its rule around an insupportable and illogical distinction in the types of alleged incursions on state sovereignty; it derives its rule from cases that do not support its analysis; it fails to apply the appropriate tests from the cases on which it purports to base its rule; and it omits any discussion of the most recent and pertinent test for determining the take title provision's constitutionality.

The Court's distinction between a federal statute's regulation of States and private parties for general purposes, as opposed to a regulation solely on the activities of States, is unsupported by our recent Tenth Amendment cases. In no case has the Court rested its holding on such a distinction.... An incursion on state sovereignty hardly seems more constitutionally acceptable if the federal statute that "commands" specific action also applies to private parties. The alleged diminution in state authority over its own affairs is not any less because the federal mandate restricts the activities of private parties.

. . .

... In *Garcia,* we stated the proper inquiry: "[W]e are convinced that the fundamental limitation that the constitutional scheme imposes on the Commerce Clause to protect the 'States as States' is one of process rather than one of result. Any substantive restraint on the exercise of Commerce Clause powers must find its justification in the procedural nature of this basic limitation, and it must be tailored to compensate for possible failings in the national political process rather than to dictate a 'sacred province of state autonomy.' " ... [T]he Court tacitly concedes that a failing of the political process cannot be shown in this case because it refuses to rebut the unassailable arguments that the States were well able to look after themselves in the legislative process that culminated in the 1985 Act's passage.

Ultimately, I suppose, the entire structure of our federal constitutional government can be traced to an interest in establishing checks and balances to prevent the exercise of tyranny against individuals. But these fears seem extremely far distant to me in a situation such as this. We face a crisis of national proportions in the disposal of low-level radioactive waste, and Congress has acceded to the wishes of the States by permitting local decisionmaking rather than imposing a solution from Washington. New York itself participated and supported passage of this legislation at both the gubernatorial and federal representative levels, and then enacted state laws specifically to comply with the deadlines and timetables agreed upon by the States in the 1985 Act. For me, the Court's civics lecture has a decidedly hollow ring at a time when action, rather than rhetoric, is needed to solve a national problem.

IV

Though I disagree with the Court's conclusion that the take title provision is unconstitutional, I do not read its opinion to preclude Congress from adopting a similar measure through its powers under the Spending or Commerce Clauses.... Congress could ... condition the payment of funds on the State's willingness to take title if it has not already provided a waste disposal facility.... Similarly, should a State fail to establish a waste disposal facility by the appointed deadline ..., Congress has the power pursuant to the Commerce Clause to regulate directly the producers of the waste. Thus, ... Congress could amend the statute to say that if a State fails to meet the January 1, 1996 deadline for achieving a means of waste disposal, and has not taken title to the waste, no low-level radioactive waste may be shipped out of the State of New York.... [T]he threat of federal pre-emption may suffice to induce States to accept responsibility for failing to meet critical time deadlines for solving their low-level radioactive waste disposal problems, especially if that federal intervention also would strip state and local authorities of any input in locating sites for low-level radioactive waste disposal facilities. And of course, should Congress amend the statute to meet the Court's objection and a State refuse to act, the National Legislature will have ensured at least a federal solution to the waste management problem.

Finally, our precedents leave open the possibility that Congress may create federal rights of action in the generators of low-level radioactive waste against persons acting under color of state law for their failure to meet certain functions designated in federal-state programs.... In addition to compensating injured parties for the State's failure to act, the exposure to liability established by such suits also potentially serves as an inducement to compliance with the program mandate.

V

The ultimate irony of the decision today is that in its formalistically rigid obeisance to "federalism," the Court gives Congress fewer incentives to defer to the wishes of state officials in achieving local solutions to local problems. This legislation was a classic example of Congress acting as arbiter among the States in their attempts to accept responsibility for managing a problem of grave import.... By invalidating the measure designed to ensure compliance for recalcitrant States, such as New York, the Court upsets the delicate compromise achieved among the States and forces Congress to erect several additional formalistic hurdles to clear before achieving exactly the same objective. Because the Court's justifications for undertaking this step are unpersuasive to me, I respectfully dissent.

Justice Stevens, concurring in part and dissenting in part.

Under the Articles of Confederation, the Federal Government had the power to issue commands to the States.... Because that indirect exercise of federal power proved ineffective, the Framers of the Constitution empowered the Federal Government to exercise legislative authority directly over individuals within the States, even though that direct authority constituted a greater intrusion on State sovereignty. Nothing in that history suggests that the Federal Government may not also impose its will upon the several States as it did under the Articles. The Constitution enhanced, rather than diminished, the power of the Federal Government.

The notion that Congress does not have the power to issue "a simple command to state governments to implement legislation enacted by Congress," is incorrect and unsound. There is no such limitation in the Constitution. The Tenth Amendment surely does not impose any limit on Congress' exercise of the powers delegated to it by Article I. Nor does the structure of the constitutional order or the values of federalism mandate such a formal rule. To the contrary, the Federal Government directs state governments in many realms. The Government regulates state-operated railroads, state school systems, state prisons, state elections, and a host of other state functions. Similarly, there can be no doubt that, in time of war, Congress could either draft soldiers itself or command the States to supply their quotas of troops. I see no reason why Congress may not also command the States to enforce federal water and air quality standards or federal standards for the disposition of low-level radioactive wastes.

. . .

CHAPTER 7

SEPARATION OF POWERS

Introduction. James Madison, writing in the Federalist No. 47, asserted that the Constitution was true to Montesquieu's well-known maxim that the legislative, executive, and judicial departments ought to be separate and distinct:

> "The reasons on which Montesquieu grounds his maxim are a further demonstration of his meaning. 'When the legislative and executive powers are united in the same person or body,' says he, 'there can be no liberty, because apprehensions may arise lest *the same* monarch or senate should *enact* tyrannical laws to execute them in a tyrannical manner.' Again: 'Were the power of judging joined with the legislative, the life and liberty of the subject would be exposed to arbitrary control, for *the judge* would then be *the legislator*. Were it joined to the executive power, *the judge* might behave with all the violence of *an oppressor*.' Some of these reasons are more fully explained in other passages; but briefly stated as they are here, they sufficiently establish the meaning which we have put on this celebrated maxim of this celebrated author."

Chief Justice Taft, writing for the Court in J.W. Hampton, Jr., & Co. v. United States, 276 U.S. 394, 406 (1928), said:

> "The Federal Constitution and state Constitutions of this country divide the governmental power into three branches. . . . This is not to say that the three branches are not co-ordinate parts of one government and that each in the field of its duties may not invoke the action of the two other branches in so far as the action invoked shall not be an assumption of the constitutional field of action of another branch. In determining what it may do in seeking assistance from another branch, the extent and character of that assistance must be fixed according to common sense and the inherent necessities of the governmental co-ordination."

This chapter focuses on issues of division of power between the President and Congress. The coverage is, of necessity, both introductory and very selective, since the topic could easily be the sole concern of many volumes.[1] Section 1 raises the question of the extent to which the President has the power to determine national policies, with particular attention to the President's power over international relations, and the President's power to commit the nation to a war. Section 2 deals with the other side of the coin, examining some instances where it is claimed that Congress has interfered with recognized Presidential powers. The specific topics included are Congressional avoidance of the Presidential veto and usurpation of the President's power to appoint "officers of the United States." Section 3 is concerned primarily with Presidential immunity from Congressional and judicial process.

---

[1] For an overview of many of the issues discussed in this chapter, see Strauss, *The Place of Agencies in Government: Separation of Powers and the Fourth Branch,* 84 Colum.L.Rev. 573 (1984).

SECTION 1. THE PRESIDENT'S POWER TO DETERMINE NATIONAL POLICY

A. IN GENERAL

Introduction. As shown in the quote from the Federalist with which this chapter begins, a simplistic description of the division of powers between the legislature and the executive is that a nation's policies are set by the legislature in the laws, and carried into force by the executive. Even the casual student of American history knows that the reality of the division of authority between the President and Congress has been much more complex.

Youngstown Sheet & Tube Co. v. Sawyer (The Steel Seizure Case)

343 U.S. 579, 72 S.Ct. 863, 96 L.Ed. 1153 (1952).

[This important decision emerged from a tangled background of labor legislation, price and wage negotiation in the steel industry, unhappiness between Congress and President Truman and the frustrating inability of the government to find an end for the war in Korea, then in its third year. The opinions of the justices run to 130 pages; nevertheless, additional facts are needed to help us see the controversy in the round.[a]

[Part of the setting was disagreement between Congress and President Truman over the means of resolving major labor disputes. In 1947 Congress, over President Truman's veto, had passed the Taft–Hartley Act subjecting union practices to national control; one part of the Act provided that if a strike would endanger national health and safety the President was authorized to seek an injunction against the strike during a cooling-off period of eighty days during which a secret ballot of the workers could be held. These various provisions were bitterly resisted by labor. While this law was under consideration in Congress an amendment was offered for government seizure of industries to avoid serious shut-downs; Congress rejected the proposal. In his hard-hitting and astonishingly successful 1948 campaign for reelection, Truman slashed at the "do-nothing" record of this session of Congress, and called for repeal of the "oppressive" Taft–Hartley Act.

[Another dimension to the problem was the Administration's controversy with the steel industry. Wage negotiations between the United Steel Workers and the industry had been opened in November 1951, five months before the final crisis. The negotiations were deadlocked, and in December the President referred this controversy to the Wage Stabilization Board—which was part of the program of controls over wages and prices that had been established during the Korean War. The Board did not have authority to dictate a settlement; its chief sanction was to decide the extent to which labor cost increases could be

---

[a] The setting was known to the Court— and to all concerned Americans. The fullest account of the case in context is Westin, The Anatomy of a Constitutional Law Case (1958). Other accounts on which this discussion draws are Kauper, The Steel Seizure Case, 51 Mich.L.Rev. 141 (1952), Selected Essays, 129 (1963), cited as Kauper. See also: Freund, Foreword: The Year of the Steel Case, 66 Harv.L.Rev. 89 (1952); McConnell, The Steel Seizure of 1952 (1958); The Steel Seizure Case, 82d Cong., 2d Sess., H.Doc.No. 534.

taken into account by the Office of Price Stabilization in acting on requests for increases in ceiling prices. The Wage Stabilization Board recommended certain wage increases; the steel industry rejected this recommendation unless it received a $12 per ton increase in the ceiling price. The stabilization officials refused to approve this increase on the ground that high earnings of the steel industry permitted the absorption of at least a part of the increase in labor costs.

[On April 3, Philip Murray, President of the United Steelworkers, called a general steel strike for 12:01 a.m., April 9. On the night of April 8, following a radio address to the nation, President Truman issued Executive Order 10340 directing the Secretary of Commerce "to take possession" and "to operate or arrange for the operation" of the production facilities of the steel industry. The Order outlined the vital part of steel in the war effort, and concluded that "a work stoppage would immediately jeopardize and imperil our national defense." The Secretary of Commerce was instructed to leave control, insofar as possible, in the hands of the present management, but the Order included a pointed authorization to "determine and prescribe terms and conditions of employment."[b] The next morning, President Truman sent Congress a message reporting on this action and stating that if Congress preferred a different course of action, "That is a matter for the Congress to determine."

[Just before midnight on April 8, within an hour after the President's Order, attorneys for the steel companies arrived at the home of a United States District Judge with a motion for immediate relief; a hearing was set for 11:30 the next morning. The relief initially requested by the companies was the prevention of a change in wage rates during government management—a move designed to block the government's plan to force a settlement by establishing a new wage level that, as a practical matter, would be irreversible; but the case quickly reached larger dimensions and on April 29 District Judge David Pine held the seizure illegal and enjoined government officials from remaining in control of the industry. The case was rapidly carried to the Supreme Court.]

Mr. Justice Black delivered the opinion of the Court.

We are asked to decide whether the President was acting within his constitutional power when he issued an order directing the Secretary of Commerce to take possession of and operate most of the Nation's steel mills. The mill owners argue that the President's order amounts to lawmaking, a legislative function which the Constitution has expressly confided to the Congress and not to the President. The Government's position is that the order was made on findings of the President that his action was necessary to avert a national catastrophe which would inevitably result from a stoppage of steel production, and that in meeting this grave emergency the President was acting within the aggregate of his constitutional powers as the Nation's Chief Executive and the Commander–in–Chief of the Armed Forces of the United States. The issue emerges here from the following series of events:

[b] 17 Fed.Reg. 3139 (April 8, 1952); 343 U.S. 589–592. President Truman, in his radio address to the nation the evening of the seizure, emphasized the vital part played by steel in supplying the fighting forces. After discussing the above-mentioned wage recommendation of the Wage Stabilization Board, which the industry had rejected, the President added: "I think [the companies] realize that the board's recommendations on wages are reasonable, and that they are raising all this hullabaloo in an attempt to force the Government to give them a big boost in prices." The profits being made by the industry were described; after noting that the companies insisted on a price increase of $12 per ton, the President exclaimed: "That's about the most outrageous thing I ever heard of ... they want to double their money on the deal".

In the latter part of 1951, a dispute arose between the steel companies and their employees over terms and conditions that should be included in new collective bargaining agreements. Long-continued conferences failed to resolve the dispute. On December 18, 1951, the employees' representative, United Steelworkers of America, C.I.O., gave notice of an intention to strike when the existing bargaining agreements expired on December 31. The Federal Mediation and Conciliation Service then intervened in an effort to get labor and management to agree. This failing, the President on December 22, 1951, referred the dispute to the Federal Wage Stabilization Board to investigate and make recommendations for fair and equitable terms of settlement. This Board's report resulted in no settlement. On April 4, 1952, the Union gave notice of a nation-wide strike called to begin at 12:01 a.m. April 9. The indispensability of steel as a component of substantially all weapons and other war materials led the President to believe that the proposed work stoppage would immediately jeopardize our national defense and that governmental seizure of the steel mills was necessary in order to assure the continued availability of steel. Reciting these considerations for his action, the President, a few hours before the strike was to begin, issued Executive Order 10340,.... The order directed the Secretary of Commerce to take possession of most of the steel mills and keep them running. The Secretary immediately issued his own possessory orders, calling upon the presidents of the various seized companies to serve as operating managers for the United States. They were directed to carry on their activities in accordance with regulations and directions of the Secretary. The next morning the President sent a message to Congress reporting his action.... Twelve days later he sent a second message.... Congress has taken no action.

Obeying the Secretary's orders under protest, the companies brought proceedings against him in the District Court. Their complaints charged that the seizure was not authorized by an act of Congress or by any constitutional provisions. The District Court was asked to declare the orders of the President and the Secretary invalid and to issue preliminary and permanent injunctions restraining their enforcement.... [T]he United States asserted that a strike disrupting steel production for even a brief period would so endanger the well-being and safety of the Nation that the President had "inherent power" to do what he had done—power "supported by the Constitution, by historical precedent, and by court decisions." ... [T]he District Court on April 30 issued a preliminary injunction restraining the Secretary from "continuing the seizure and possession of the plants ... and from acting under the purported authority of Executive Order No. 10340." On the same day the Court of Appeals stayed the District Court's injunction. Deeming it best that the issues raised be promptly decided by this Court, we granted certiorari on May 3 and set the cause for argument on May 12.[c] ...

The President's power, if any, to issue the order must stem either from an act of Congress or from the Constitution itself. There is no statute that expressly authorizes the President to take possession of property as he did here. Nor is there any act of Congress to which our attention has been directed from which such a power can fairly be implied....

Moreover, the use of the seizure technique to solve labor disputes in order to prevent work stoppages was not only unauthorized by any congressional enactment; prior to this controversy, Congress had refused to adopt that

[c] The decision of the Supreme Court came on June 2, only 34 days after the trial court issued its injunction!

method of settling labor disputes. When the Taft–Hartley Act was under consideration in 1947, Congress rejected an amendment which would have authorized such governmental seizures in cases of emergency.... Instead, the plan sought to bring about settlements by use of the customary devices of mediation, conciliation, investigation by boards of inquiry, and public reports. In some instances temporary injunctions were authorized to provide cooling-off periods. All this failing, unions were left free to strike after a secret vote by employees as to whether they wished to accept their employers' final settlement offer.

It is clear that if the President had authority to issue the order he did, it must be found in some provision of the Constitution. And it is not claimed that express constitutional language grants this power to the President. The contention is that presidential power should be implied from the aggregate of his powers under the Constitution. Particular reliance is placed on provisions in Article II which say that "the executive Power shall be vested in a President ...."; that "he shall take Care that the Laws be faithfully executed"; and that he "shall be Commander in Chief of the Army and Navy of the United States."

The order cannot properly be sustained as an exercise of the President's military power as Commander in Chief of the Armed Forces. The Government attempts to do so by citing a number of cases upholding broad powers in military commanders engaged in day-to-day fighting in a theater of war. Such cases need not concern us here. Even though "theater of war" be an expanding concept, we cannot with faithfulness to our constitutional system hold that the Commander in Chief of the Armed Forces has the ultimate power as such to take possession of private property in order to keep labor disputes from stopping production. This is a job for the Nation's lawmakers, not for its military authorities.

Nor can the seizure order be sustained because of the several constitutional provisions that grant executive power to the President. In the framework of our Constitution, the President's power to see that the laws are faithfully executed refutes the idea that he is to be a lawmaker. The Constitution limits his functions in the lawmaking process to the recommending of laws he thinks wise and the vetoing of laws he thinks bad. And the Constitution is neither silent nor equivocal about who shall make laws which the President is to execute. The first section of the first article says that "All legislative Powers herein granted shall be vested in a Congress of the United States...." After granting many powers to the Congress, Article I goes on to provide that Congress may "make all Laws which shall be necessary and proper for carrying into Execution the foregoing Powers and all other Powers vested by this Constitution in the Government of the United States, or in any Department or Officer thereof."

The President's order does not direct that a congressional policy be executed in a manner prescribed by Congress—it directs that a presidential policy be executed in a manner prescribed by the President. The preamble of the order itself, like that of many statutes, sets out reasons why the President believes certain policies should be adopted, proclaims these policies as rules of conduct to be followed, and again, like a statute, authorizes a government official to promulgate additional rules and regulations consistent with the policy proclaimed and needed to carry that policy into execution. The power of Congress to adopt such public policies as those proclaimed by the order is beyond question. It can authorize the taking of private property for public use. It can make laws regulating the relationships between employers and employees, prescribing rules designed to settle labor disputes, and fixing wages and working conditions in certain fields of our economy. The Constitution does not subject this lawmaking power of Congress to presidential or military supervision or control.

It is said that other Presidents without congressional authority have taken possession of private business enterprises in order to settle labor disputes. But even if this be true, Congress has not thereby lost its exclusive constitutional authority to make laws necessary and proper to carry out the powers vested by the Constitution "in the Government of the United States, or in any Department or Officer thereof."

The Founders of this Nation entrusted the lawmaking power to the Congress alone in both good and bad times. It would do no good to recall the historical events, the fears of power and the hopes for freedom that lay behind their choice. Such a review would but confirm our holding that this seizure order cannot stand.

The judgment of the District Court is affirmed.

Affirmed.

[All of the Justices who joined Justice Black's opinion for the Court also wrote individual concurring opinions. Justice Frankfurter stated that questions concerning the extent of Presidential power in the absence of legislation were not before the Court. The Labor Management Relations Act of 1947 was equivalent to an explicit Congressional negation of the authority asserted by the seizure. Justice Burton stated that the "controlling fact" was that Congress had prescribed specific procedures, which did not include seizure, for the present type of emergency. Justice Douglas emphasized the fifth amendment's requirement of compensation for takings of property, arguing that Congress, as the only branch with power to appropriate money to compensate for seizures, was the only branch with power to authorize or ratify them. A few often-quoted passages from Justice Jackson's lengthy concurring opinion follow.]

Mr. Justice Jackson, concurring in the judgment and opinion of the Court.

. . .

The actual art of governing under our Constitution does not and cannot conform to judicial definitions of the power of any of its branches based on isolated clauses or even single Articles torn from context. While the Constitution diffuses power the better to secure liberty, it also contemplates that practice will integrate the dispersed powers into a workable government. It enjoins upon its branches separateness but interdependence, autonomy but reciprocity. Presidential powers are not fixed but fluctuate, depending upon their disjunction or conjunction with those of Congress. We may well begin by a somewhat over-simplified grouping of practical situations in which a President may doubt, or others may challenge, his powers, and by distinguishing roughly the legal consequences of this factor of relativity.

1. When the President acts pursuant to an express or implied authorization of Congress, his authority is at its maximum, for it includes all that he possesses in his own right plus all that Congress can delegate. In these circumstances, and in these only, may he be said (for what it may be worth), to personify the federal sovereignty. If his act is held unconstitutional under these circumstances, it usually means that the Federal Government as an undivided whole lacks power. A seizure executed by the President pursuant to an Act of Congress would be supported by the strongest of presumptions and the widest latitude of judicial interpretation, and the burden of persuasion would rest heavily upon any who might attack it.

2.   When the President acts in absence of either a congressional grant or denial of authority, he can only rely upon his own independent powers, but there is a zone of twilight in which he and Congress may have concurrent authority, or in which its distribution is uncertain. Therefore, congressional inertia, indifference or quiescence may sometimes, at least as a practical matter, enable, if not invite, measures on independent presidential responsibility. In this area, any actual test of power is likely to depend on the imperatives of events and contemporary imponderables rather than on abstract theories of law.

3.   When the President takes measures incompatible with the expressed or implied will of Congress, his power is at its lowest ebb, for then he can rely only upon his own constitutional powers minus any constitutional powers of Congress over the matter. Courts can sustain exclusive Presidential control in such a case only by disabling the Congress from acting upon the subject. Presidential claim to a power at once so conclusive and preclusive must be scrutinized with caution, for what is at stake is the equilibrium established by our constitutional system.

Into which of these classifications does this executive seizure of the steel industry fit? It is eliminated from the first by admission, for it is conceded that no congressional authorization exists for this seizure. That takes away also the support of the many precedents and declarations which were made in relation, and must be confined, to this category.

Can it then be defended under flexible tests available to the second category? It seems clearly eliminated from that class because Congress has not left seizure of private property an open field but has covered it by three statutory policies inconsistent with this seizure....

This leaves the current seizure to be justified only by the severe tests under the third grouping, where it can be supported only by any remainder of executive power after subtraction of such powers as Congress may have over the subject. In short, we can sustain the President only by holding that seizure of such strike-bound industries is within his domain and beyond control by Congress. Thus, this Court's first review of such seizures occurs under circumstances which leave Presidential power most vulnerable to attack and in the least favorable of possible constitutional postures.

. . .

But I have no illusion that any decision by this Court can keep power in the hands of Congress if it is not wise and timely in meeting its problems. A crisis that challenges the President equally, or perhaps primarily, challenges Congress. If not good law, there was worldly wisdom in the maxim attributed to Napoleon that "The tools belong to the man who can use them." We may say that power to legislate for emergencies belongs in the hands of Congress, but only Congress itself can prevent power from slipping through its fingers.

. . .

Mr. Justice Clark, concurring in the judgment of the Court ...

I conclude that where Congress has laid down specific procedures to deal with the type of crisis confronting the President, he must follow those procedures in meeting the crisis; but that in the absence of such action by Congress, the President's independent power to act depends upon the gravity of the situation confronting the nation. I cannot sustain the seizure in question because here, as in Little v. Barreme, 2 Cranch 170, Congress had prescribed methods to be followed by the President in meeting the emergency at hand....

Mr. Chief Justice Vinson, with whom Mr. Justice Reed and Mr. Justice Minton join, dissenting. . . .

[The dissenting opinion described legislation authorizing the supplying of the forces then engaged in the Korean War and other procurement and foreign aid legislation.]

The President has the duty to execute the foregoing legislative programs. Their successful execution depends upon continued production of steel and stabilized prices for steel. . . .

Secretary of Defense Lovett swore that "a work stoppage in the steel industry will result immediately in serious curtailment of production of essential weapons and munitions of all kinds." He illustrated by showing that 84% of the national production of certain alloy steel is currently used for production of military-end items and that 35% of total production of another form of steel goes into ammunition, 80% of such ammunition now going to Korea. The Secretary of Defense stated that: "We are holding the line [in Korea] with ammunition and not with the lives of our troops." . . .

One is not here called upon even to consider the possibility of executive seizure of a farm, a corner grocery store or even a single industrial plant. Such considerations arise only when one ignores the central fact of this case—that the Nation's entire basic steel production would have shut down completely if there had been no Government seizure. . . .

[W]e are not called upon today to expand the Constitution to meet a new situation. For, in this case, we need only look to history and time-honored principles of constitutional law—principles that have been applied consistently by all branches of the Government throughout our history. . . .

A review of executive action demonstrates that our Presidents have on many occasions exhibited the leadership contemplated by the Framers when they made the President Commander in Chief, and imposed upon him the trust to "take Care that the Laws be faithfully executed." With or without explicit statutory authorization, Presidents have at such times dealt with national emergencies by acting promptly and resolutely to enforce legislative programs, at least to save those programs until Congress could act. Congress and the courts have responded to such executive initiative with consistent approval. . . .

[A summary of episodes from Presidents Washington to Roosevelt is omitted.]

. . .

This is but a cursory summary of executive leadership. But it amply demonstrates that Presidents have taken prompt action to enforce the laws and protect the country whether or not Congress happened to provide in advance for the particular method of execution. . . .

Focusing now on the situation confronting the President on the night of April 8, 1952, we cannot but conclude that the President was performing his duty under the Constitution to "take Care that the Laws be faithfully executed"—a duty described by President Benjamin Harrison as "the central idea of the office." . . .

. . . Faced with the duty of executing the defense programs which Congress had enacted and the disastrous effects that any stoppage in steel production would have on those programs, the President acted to preserve those programs by seizing the steel mills. There is no question that the possession was other than temporary in character and subject to congressional direction—either approving, disapproving or regulating the manner in which the mills were to be administered and returned to the owners. The President immediately informed Congress of his action and clearly stated his intention to abide by the legislative will. No basis for claims of arbitrary action, unlimited powers or dictatorial usurpation of congressional power appears from the facts of this case. On the contrary, judicial, legislative and executive precedents throughout our history demonstrate that in this case the President acted in full conformity with his duties under the Constitution. Accordingly, we would reverse the order of the District Court.

B.   INTERNATIONAL RELATIONS

Introduction. Most of the constitutional grants of power to the federal government relating to foreign affairs appear in the enumeration of executive powers: the President is made "Commander–in–Chief" of the armed forces; he is given the power, with the approval of two-thirds of the Senate, "to make Treaties"; and, with the "advice and consent" of the Senate, he "shall appoint Ambassadors, other public Ministers and Consuls," i.e., our representatives abroad (Art. II, § 2). Also, "he shall receive Ambassadors and other public Ministers" (Art. II, § 3). Those spare provisions, however, hardly begin to capture the scope of "the executive power" to conduct the nation's foreign affairs.

United States v. Curtiss–Wright Export Corp., 299 U.S. 304, 320 (1936), concerned the validity of a delegation of power from Congress to the President. In the course of upholding the delegation the Court noted that the legislative power was combined with "the very delicate, plenary and exclusive power of the President as the sole organ of the Federal government in the field of international relations—a power which does not require as a basis for its exercise an act of Congress, but which, of course, like every other governmental power, must be exercised in subordination to the applicable provisions of the Constitution. It is quite apparent that if, in the maintenance of our international relations, embarrassment—perhaps serious embarrassment—is to be avoided and success for our aims achieved, congressional legislation which is to be made effective through negotiation and inquiry within the international field must often accord to the President a degree of discretion and freedom from statutory restriction which would not be admissible were domestic affairs alone involved. Moreover, he, not Congress, has the better opportunity of knowing the conditions which prevail in foreign countries, and especially is this true in time of war. He has his confidential sources of information. He has his agents in the form of diplomatic, consular and other officials. Secrecy in respect of information gathered by them may be highly necessary, and the premature disclosure of it productive of harmful results. Indeed, so clearly is this true that the first President refused to accede to a request to lay before the House of Representatives the instructions, correspondence and documents relating to the negotiation of the Jay Treaty—a refusal the wisdom of which was recognized by the House itself and has never since been doubted."

For an excellent and full discussion of the powers of the President in the conduct of foreign affairs, see Henkin, *Foreign Affairs and the Constitution* 37–65 (1972).

INTERNATIONAL AGREEMENTS

The scope of national power to override state law and policy through the use of international agreements was discussed in Chapter 4. In that connection we looked at United States v. Belmont, supra p. 231, and United States v. Pink, supra p. 232, relating to the power of the President to consummate international agreements without going through the process of having formal treaties ratified by the Senate and the effect of such agreements on state law.

Belmont and Pink raised a separate issue which has proved highly controversial—the extent to which executive agreements can be employed to circumvent the role of the Senate embodied in Article 2 of the Constitution. Some commentators were critical. Borchard, *Shall the Executive Agreement Replace the Treaty?*, 53 Yale L.J. 664 (1944), 54 Yale L.J. 616 (1945). Others supported the use of executive agreements (buttressed in some cases by joint action by the two houses of Congress) as a well-established means to provide flexibility in dealing with international relations. McDougal & Lans, *Treaties and Congressional–Executive or Presidential Agreements: Interchangeable Instruments of National Policy,* 54 Yale L.J. 181, 534 (1945). This dispute does not concern the propriety of the bulk of agreements made between the heads of governments in their day-to-day handling of routine arrangements (like an agreement for the exchange of visits by naval vessels) or military arrangements like the line in conquered territory where allied armies will meet. Some such arrangements may fall within the independent power of the President as "commander-in-chief", others within "the executive power" of the President to conduct the day-to-day business of foreign relations. But one of the questions stirred by the Belmont and Pink cases is whether the President might use executive agreements for basic long-range commitments of the nation—possibly because of the fear that it might be impossible to obtain the two-thirds vote of the Senate which the Constitution requires for treaty ratification.

DAMES & MOORE v. REGAN, 453 U.S. 654 (1981). On January 20, 1981, Iran released hostages captured in the seizure of the American Embassy, in Teheran, pursuant to an agreement with the United States. One provision of the agreement provided for termination of litigation in American courts against Iran, with the arbitration of those claims before an international claims tribunal. On January 19, 1981, President Carter issued Executive Orders providing for transfer of blocked Iranian funds in the United States, and nullifying attachments issued against those funds. On February 24, 1981, President Reagan ratified the January 19th Executive Orders, and suspended all claims filed in United States courts that could be presented to the claims tribunal.

Petitioner was a company that had procured a judgment against Iran in a federal trial court for breach of its contract to conduct studies for a proposed nuclear plant in Iran. This case was an action against the Secretary of the Treasury, seeking to prevent enforcement of the Executive Orders. Reserving questions whether the Executive Orders' suspension of claims constituted an uncompensated taking of property, the Court held that the Executive Orders did not exceed Presidential powers.

The provisions of the Executive Orders suspending attachments against persons holding blocked Iranian funds, and directing the transfer of those funds to Iran, were held to be authorized by provisions of the International Emergency Economic Powers Act (IEEPA). The Court concluded, however, that neither IEEPA, nor the Hostage Act of 1868,[1] specifically authorized the President to suspend claims pending in United States Courts. In upholding the

---

[1] The Act provides that, in securing release of American citizens unjustly held by foreign governments, "the President shall use such means, not amounting to acts of war, as he may think necessary and proper to obtain or effectuate the release."

validity of this aspect of the Executive Orders, Justice Rehnquist's opinion for the Court said, in part:

"Concluding that neither the IEEPA nor the Hostage Act constitutes specific authorization of the President's action suspending claims, however, is not to say that these statutory provisions are entirely irrelevant to the question of the validity of the President's action. We think both statutes highly relevant in the looser sense of indicating congressional acceptance of a broad scope for executive action in circumstances such as those presented in this case.... [T]he IEEPA delegates broad authority to the President to act in times of national emergency with respect to property of a foreign country. The Hostage Act similarly indicates congressional willingness that the President have broad discretion when responding to the hostile acts of foreign sovereigns....

"Although we have declined to conclude that the IEEPA or the Hostage Act directly authorizes the President's suspension of claims for the reasons noted, we cannot ignore the general tenor of Congress' legislation in this area in trying to determine whether the President is acting alone or at least with the acceptance of Congress. As we have noted, Congress cannot anticipate and legislate with regard to every possible action the President may find it necessary to take or every possible situation in which he might act. Such failure of Congress specifically to delegate authority does not, 'especially . . . in the areas of foreign policy and national security,' imply 'congressional disapproval' of action taken by the Executive. Haig v. Agee, 453 U.S. 280, 288 (1981). On the contrary, the enactment of legislation closely related to the question of the President's authority in a particular case which evinces legislative intent to accord the President broad discretion may be considered to 'invite' 'measures on independent presidential responsibility.' *Youngstown,* 343 U.S., at 637 (Jackson, J., concurring). At least this is so where there is no contrary indication of legislative intent and when, as here, there is a history of congressional acquiescence in conduct of the sort engaged in by the President...."

C.   WAR AND NATIONAL DEFENSE

Introduction. The Constitution is not silent about Congressional participation in one aspect of foreign affairs. Article I, Section 8, Clause 11, of the Constitution specifies that it is a Congressional prerogative "to declare war."

The Prize Cases

67 U.S. (2 Black) 635, 17 L.Ed. 459 (1863).

[In April, 1861, President Lincoln declared a blockade of southern ports. Pursuant to this blockade, in May and July, 1861, Union ships seized merchant vessels and cargoes of foreign neutrals and residents of the southern states. The ships were condemned by federal court order. The owners of the ships and cargo appealed. The Supreme Court regarded the first question to be: Had the President authority to institute a blockade of southern ports which neutrals were bound to respect? The following excerpts are addressed to that question.]

Mr. Justice Grier

. . .

By the Constitution, Congress alone has the power to declare a national or foreign war. It cannot declare war against a State or any number of States, by virtue of any clause in the Constitution. The Constitution confers on the President the whole executive power. He is bound to take care that the laws be faithfully executed. He is Commander-in-Chief of the Army and Navy of the United States, and of the militia of the several States when called into the actual service of the United States. He has no power to initiate or declare a war either against a foreign nation or a domestic State. But by the Acts of Congress of Feb. 28th, 1795 and 3d of March, 1807, he is authorized to call out the militia and use the military and naval forces of the United States in case of invasion by foreign nations, and to suppress insurrection against the government of a State or of the United States.

If a war be made by invasion of a foreign nation, the President is not only authorized but bound to resist force, by force. He does not initiate the war, but is bound to accept the challenge without waiting for any special legislative authority. And whether the hostile party be a foreign invader, or States organized in rebellion, it is none the less a war, although the declaration of it be *"unilateral."* Lord Stowell (*The Eliza Ann,* 1 Dod., 247) observes, "It is not the less a war on that account, for war may exist without declaration on either side. It is so laid down by the best writers on the law of nations. A declaration of war by one country only, is not a mere challenge to be accepted or refused at pleasure by the other."

The battles of Palo Alto and Resaca de la Palma had been fought before the passage of the Act of Congress of May 13th, 1846, ch. 16 (9 Stat. at L., 9), which recognized "a state of war as existing by the Act of the Republic of Mexico." This Act not only provided for the future prosecution of the war, but was itself a vindication and ratification of the Act of the President in accepting the challenge without a previous formal declaration of war by Congress.

This greatest of civil wars was not gradually developed by popular commotion, tumultuous assemblies, or local unorganized insurrections. However long may have been its previous conception, it nevertheless sprung forth suddenly from the parent brain, a Minerva in the full panoply of war. The President was bound to meet it in the shape it presented itself, without waiting for Congress to baptize it with a name; and no name given to it by him or them could change the fact. . . .

Whether the President in fulfilling his duties, as Commander-in-Chief, in suppressing an insurrection, has met with such armed hostile resistance, and a civil war of such alarming proportions as will compel him to accord to them the character of belligerents, is a question to be decided by him, and this court must be governed by the decisions and acts of the Political Department of the government to which this power was intrusted. "He must determine what degree of force the crisis demands." The proclamation of blockade is, itself, official and conclusive evidence to the court that a state of war existed which demanded and authorized a recourse to such a measure, under the circumstances peculiar to the case.

. . .

If it were necessary to the technical existence of a war, that it should have a legislative sanction, we find it in almost every Act passed at the extraordinary session of the Legislature of 1861, which was wholly employed in enacting laws to enable the government to prosecute the war with vigor and efficiency. And finally, in 1861, we find Congress *"ex majore cautela"* and in anticipation of such astute objections, passing an Act "approving, legalizing and making valid all the acts, proclamations, and orders of the President, & c., as if they had been issued and done under the previous express authority and direction of the Congress of the United States."

Without admitting that such an Act was necessary under the circumstances, it is plain that if the President had in any manner assumed powers which it was necessary should have the authority or sanction of Congress, that on the well known principle of law, "*omnis ratihabitio retrotrahitur et mandato equiparatur*," this ratification has operated to perfectly cure the defect....

[The decrees of condemnation were affirmed except for certain cargoes which were bought and paid for in the South before the war broke out and which were being removed shortly thereafter.]

Mr. Justice Nelson [joined by Chief Justice Taney and Justices Catron and Clifford, dissenting]. ...

The Acts of 1795 and 1807 did not, and could not, under the Constitution, confer on the President the power of declaring war against a State of this Union, or of deciding that war existed, and upon that ground authorize the capture and confiscation of the property of every citizen of the State whenever it was found on the waters. The laws of war, whether the war be civil or *inter gentes,* as we have seen, convert every citizen of the hostile State into a public enemy, and treat him accordingly, whatever may have been his previous conduct. This great power over the business and property of the citizen is reserved to the Legislative Department by the express words of the Constitution. It cannot be delegated or surrendered to the Executive. Congress alone can determine whether war exists or should be declared, and until they have acted, no citizen of the State can be punished in his person or property, unless he has committed some offense against a law of Congress passed before the act was committed, which made it a crime, and defined the punishment. The penalty of confiscation for the acts of others with which he had no concern cannot lawfully be inflicted....

[This dissenting opinion also came to the conclusion that congressional ratification of the seizures was an *ex post facto* law and hence invalid.]

Mora v. McNamara

389 U.S. 934, 88 S.Ct. 282, 19 L.Ed.2d 287 (1967).

Petition for writ of certiorari to the United States Court of Appeals for the District of Columbia Circuit.

Nov. 6, 1967. Denied.

Mr. Justice Marshall took no part in the consideration or decision of this petition.

Mr. Justice Stewart, with whom Mr. Justice Douglas joins, dissenting.

The petitioners were drafted into the United States Army in late 1965, and six months later were ordered to a West Coast replacement station for shipment to Vietnam. They brought this suit to prevent the Secretary of Defense and the Secretary of the Army from carrying out those orders, and requested a declaratory judgment that the present United States military activity in Vietnam is "illegal." The District Court dismissed the suit, and the Court of Appeals affirmed.

There exist in this case questions of great magnitude. Some are akin to those referred to by Mr. Justice Douglas in Mitchell v. United States, 386 U.S. 972. But there are others:

I.   Is the present United States military activity in Vietnam a "war" within the meaning of Article I, Section 8, Clause 11 of the Constitution?

II.   If so, may the Executive constitutionally order the petitioners to participate in that military activity, when no war has been declared by the Congress?

III.   Of what relevance to Question II are the present treaty obligations of the United States?

IV.   Of what relevance to Question II is the Joint Congressional ("Tonkin Gulf") Resolution of August 10, 1964?[a]

(a) Do present United States military operations fall within the terms of the Joint Resolution?

(b) If the Joint Resolution purports to give the Chief Executive authority to commit United States forces to armed conflict limited in scope only by his own absolute discretion, is the Resolution a constitutionally impermissible delegation of all or part of Congress' power to declare war?

These are large and deeply troubling questions. Whether the Court would ultimately reach them depends, of course, upon the resolution of serious preliminary issues of justiciability. We cannot make these problems go away simply by refusing to hear the case of three obscure Army privates. I intimate not even tentative views upon any of these matters, but I think the Court should squarely face them by granting certiorari and setting this case for oral argument.

Mr. Justice Douglas, with whom Mr. Justice Stewart concurs, dissenting.

The questions posed by Mr. Justice Stewart cover the wide range of problems which the Senate Committee on Foreign Relations recently explored, in connection with the SEATO treaty of February 19, 1955, and the Tonkin Gulf Resolution.

Mr. Katzenbach, representing the Administration, testified that he did not regard the Tonkin Gulf Resolution to be "a declaration of war" and that while the Resolution was not "constitutionally necessary" it was "politically, from an international viewpoint and from a domestic viewpoint, extremely important." He added:

"The use of the phrase 'to declare war' as it was used in the Constitution of the United States had a particular meaning in terms of the events and the practices which existed at the time it was adopted. . . .

"[I]t was recognized by the Founding Fathers that the President might have to take emergency action to protect the security of the United States, but that if there was going to be another use of the armed forces of the United States, that was a decision which Congress should check the Executive on, which Congress should support. It was for that reason that the phrase was inserted in the Constitution.

---

[a] The Tonkin Gulf Resolution was enacted at the request of President Johnson as a result of specific naval incidents in the Gulf of Tonkin. It stated that "Congress approves and supports the determination of the President, as Commander-in-Chief, to take all necessary measures to repel any armed attack against the forces of the United States and to prevent further aggression." H.R.J.Res. 1145, 88th Cong., 2d Sess., 78 Stat. 384 (1964). It was repealed December 31, 1970. Did the repeal have any effect on the President's powers to continue operations in Vietnam?

"Now, over a long period of time, ... there have been many uses of the military forces of the United States for a variety of purposes without a congressional declaration of war. But it would be fair to say that most of these were relatively minor uses of force. . . .

"A declaration of war would not, I think, correctly reflect the very limited objectives of the United States with respect to Vietnam. It would not correctly reflect our efforts there, what we are trying to do, the reasons why we are there, to use an outmoded phraseology, to declare war."

The view that Congress was intended to play a more active role in the initiation and conduct of war than the above statements might suggest has been espoused by Senator Fulbright (Cong.Rec. Oct. 11, 1967, 14683–14690), quoting Thomas Jefferson who said:

"We have already given in example one effectual check to the Dog of war by transferring the power of letting him loose from the Executive to the Legislative body, from those who are to spend to those who are to pay."

These opposed views are reflected in the Prize Cases, 2 Black 635, a five-to-four decision rendered in 1863. Mr. Justice Grier, writing for the majority, emphasized the arguments for strong presidential powers. Justice Nelson, writing for the minority of four, read the Constitution more strictly, emphasizing that what is war in actuality may not constitute war in the constitutional sense. During all subsequent periods in our history—through the Spanish–American War, the Boxer Rebellion, two World Wars, Korea, and now Vietnam—the two points of view urged in the *Prize Cases* have continued to be voiced. . . .

THE COURT AND THE VIETNAM CONTROVERSY

After the *Mora* decision, efforts to obtain a Supreme Court ruling on whether or not American military operations in Vietnam amounted to an "unconstitutional" war continued, but without success. The lower courts generally ruled that the issue was not justiciable.

Orlando v. Laird, 443 F.2d 1039 (2d Cir.1971), cert. denied 404 U.S. 869 (1971), is a notable instance in which a challenge to United States military activity in Vietnam was held to present a justiciable question. Reaching the merits of the case, the court concluded that some mutual participation of Congress in a war of this kind was required but that Congress had sufficiently authorized our South–East Asian commitments.

Dissenting again from denial of certiorari in Da Costa v. Laird, 405 U.S. 979 (1972) Justice Douglas said: "[I]t is argued that the Constitution gives to Congress the *exclusive* power to determine when it has declared war. But if there is such a 'textually demonstrable constitutional commitment,' ... it is for this Court to determine its scope."

Professor Henkin argues that the "courts, despite sometimes-misguided efforts to compel them to do so (as on Vietnam), are not likely to step into intense confrontations between President and Congress, or inhibit either when the other does not object. Whether from the sense that the boundary between Congress and President ..., cannot be defined by law, whether from realization of the inherent limitations of judicial power or from prudence, whether under a doctrine of 'political questions' or by other judicial devices and formulae for abstention, courts will not make certain what was left uncertain, will not curtail the power of the political branches, will not arbitrate their differences. Then, in time, the issues will recede, stirring neither controversy nor case." *Foreign Affairs and the Constitution*, 274–275 (1972).

See, generally, John Hart Ely, *War and Responsibility* (1993).

SECTION 2.   CONGRESSIONAL INTERFERENCE WITH PRESIDENTIAL PREROGATIVES

DELEGATION OF LEGISLATIVE POWER TO THE EXECUTIVE

[Justice O'Connor for the Court in Touby v. United States, 500 U.S. 160, 163–65 (1991).]

"The Constitution provides that '[a]ll legislative Powers herein granted shall be vested in a Congress of the United States.' U.S. Const., Art. I, § 1. From this language the Court has derived the nondelegation doctrine: that Congress may not constitutionally delegate its legislative power to another Branch of government. . . .

" . . . [T]he nondelegation doctrine does not prevent Congress from seeking assistance, within proper limits, from its coordinate Branches. . . . Thus, Congress does not violate the Constitution merely because it legislates in broad terms, leaving a certain degree of discretion to executive or judicial actors. So long as Congress 'lay[s] down by legislative act an intelligible principle to which the person or body authorized to [act] is directed to conform, such legislative action is not a forbidden delegation of legislative power.' J.W. Hampton, Jr., & Co. v. United States, 276 U.S. 394, 409 (1928).

" . . . [The Court has] upheld as providing sufficient guidance statutes authorizing the War Department to recover 'excessive profits' earned on military contracts, see Lichter v. United States, 334 U.S. 742, 778–786 (1948); authorizing the Price Administrator to fix 'fair and equitable' commodities prices, see Yakus v. United States, 321 U.S. 414, 426–427 (1944); and authorizing the Federal Communications Commission to regulate broadcast licensing in the 'public interest,' see National Broadcasting Co. v. United States, 319 U.S. 190, 225–226 (1943)."

A.   THE LEGISLATIVE VETO

Immigration and Naturalization Service v. Chadha

462 U.S. 919, 103 S.Ct. 2764, 77 L.Ed.2d 317 (1983).

Chief Justice Burger delivered the opinion of the Court.

. . . [These cases present] a challenge to the constitutionality of the provision in § 244(c)(2) of the Immigration and Nationality Act, 8 U.S.C. § 1254(c)(2), authorizing one House of Congress, by resolution, to invalidate the decision of the Executive Branch, pursuant to authority delegated by Congress to the Attorney General of the United States, to allow a particular deportable alien to remain in the United States.

I

Chadha is an East Indian who was born in Kenya and holds a British passport. He was lawfully admitted to the United States in 1966 on a non-immigrant student visa. His visa expired on June 30, 1972. On October 11, 1973, the District Director of the Immigration and Naturalization Service ordered Chadha to show cause why he should not be deported for having "remained in the United States for a longer time than permitted." App. 6. Pursuant to § 242(b) of the Immigration and Nationality Act (Act), 8 U.S.C. § 1254(b), a deportation hearing was held before an immigration judge on January 11, 1974. Chadha conceded that he was deportable for overstaying his visa and the hearing was adjourned to enable him to file an application for suspension of deportation under § 244(a)(1) of the Act, 8 U.S.C. § 1254(a)(1). Section 244(a)(1) provides:

"(a) As hereinafter prescribed in this section, the Attorney General may, in his discretion, suspend deportation and adjust the status to that of an alien lawfully admitted for permanent residence, in the case of an alien who applies to the Attorney General for suspension of deportation and—

"(1) is deportable under any law of the United States except the provisions specified in paragraph (2) of this subsection; has been physically present in the United States for a continuous period of not less than seven years immediately preceding the date of such application, and proves that during all of such period he was and is a person of good moral character; and is a person whose deportation would, in the opinion of the Attorney General, result in extreme hardship to the alien or to his spouse, parent, or child, who is a citizen of the United States or an alien lawfully admitted for permanent residence."

After Chadha submitted his application for suspension of deportation, the deportation hearing was resumed on February 7, 1974. On the basis of evidence adduced at the hearing, affidavits submitted with the application, and the results of a character investigation conducted by the INS, the immigration judge, on June 25, 1974, ordered that Chadha's deportation be suspended. The immigration judge found that Chadha met the requirements of § 244(a)(1): he had resided continuously in the United States for over seven years, was of good moral character, and would suffer "extreme hardship" if deported.

Pursuant to § 244(c)(1) of the Act, 8 U.S.C. § 1254(c)(1), the immigration judge suspended Chadha's deportation and a report of the suspension was transmitted to Congress. Section 244(c)(1) provides:

"Upon application by any alien who is found by the Attorney General to meet the requirements of subsection (a) of this section the Attorney General may in his discretion suspend deportation of such alien. If the deportation of any alien is suspended under the provisions of this subsection, a complete and detailed statement of the facts and pertinent provisions of law in the case shall be reported to the Congress with the reasons for such suspension. Such reports shall be submitted on the first day of each calendar month in which Congress is in session."

Once the Attorney General's recommendation for suspension of Chadha's deportation was conveyed to Congress, Congress had the power under § 244(c)(2) of the Act, 8 U.S.C. § 1254(c)(2), to veto the Attorney General's determination that Chadha should not be deported. Section 244(c)(2) provides:

"(2) In the case of an alien specified in paragraph (1) of subsection (a) of this subsection—

if during the session of the Congress at which a case is reported, or prior to the close of the session of the Congress next following the session at which a case is reported, either the Senate or the House of Representatives passes a resolution stating in substance that it does not favor the suspension of such deportation, the Attorney General shall thereupon deport such alien or authorize the alien's voluntary departure at his own expense under the order of deportation in the manner provided by law. If, within the time above specified, neither the Senate nor the House of Representatives shall pass such a resolution, the Attorney General shall cancel deportation proceedings."

The June 25, 1974 order of the immigration judge suspending Chadha's deportation remained outstanding as a valid order for a year and a half. For reasons not disclosed by the record, Congress did not exercise the veto authority reserved to it under § 244(c)(2) until the first session of the 94th Congress. This was the final session in which Congress, pursuant to § 244(c)(2), could act to veto the Attorney General's determination that Chadha should not be deported....

On December 12, 1975, Representative Eilberg, Chairman of the Judiciary Subcommittee on Immigration, Citizenship, and International Law, introduced a resolution opposing "the granting of permanent residence in the United States to [six] aliens", including Chadha. H.R.Res. 926, 94th Cong., 1st Sess.; 121 Cong.Rec. 40247 (1975). The resolution was referred to the House Committee on the Judiciary. On December 16, 1975, the resolution was discharged from further consideration by the House Committee on the Judiciary and submitted to the House of Representatives for a vote. 121 Cong.Rec. 40800. The resolution had not been printed and was not made available to other Members of the House prior to or at the time it was voted on. Ibid. So far as the record before us shows, the House consideration of the resolution was based on Representative Eilberg's statement from the floor that

"[i]t was the feeling of the committee, after reviewing 340 cases, that the aliens contained in the resolution [Chadha and five others] did not meet these statutory requirements, particularly as it relates to hardship; and it is the opinion of the committee that their deportation should not be suspended." Ibid.

The resolution was passed without debate or recorded vote. Since the House action was pursuant to § 244(c)(2), the resolution was not treated as an Article I legislative act; it was not submitted to the Senate or presented to the President for his action.

After the House veto of the Attorney General's decision to allow Chadha to remain in the United States, the immigration judge reopened the deportation proceedings to implement the House order deporting Chadha. Chadha moved to terminate the proceedings on the ground that § 244(c)(2) is unconstitutional. The immigration judge held that he had no authority to rule on the constitutional validity of § 244(c)(2). On November 8, 1976, Chadha was ordered deported pursuant to the House action.

Chadha appealed the deportation order to the Board of Immigration Appeals again contending that § 244(c)(2) is unconstitutional. The Board held that it had "no power to declare unconstitutional an act of Congress" and Chadha's appeal was dismissed.

Pursuant to § 106(a) of the Act, 8 U.S.C. § 1105a(a), Chadha filed a petition for review of the deportation order in the United States Court of Appeals for the Ninth Circuit. The Immigration and Naturalization Service agreed with Chadha's position before the Court of Appeals and joined him in arguing that § 244(c)(2) is unconstitutional. In light of the importance of the question, the Court of Appeals invited both the Senate and the House of Representatives to file briefs *amici curiae*.

... [T]he Court of Appeals held that the House was without constitutional authority to order Chadha's deportation ...

... [W]e now affirm.

II

Before we address the important question of the constitutionality of the one-House veto provision of § 244(c)(2), we first consider several challenges to the authority of this Court to resolve the issue raised.

. . .

B

Severability

Congress . . . contends that the provision for the one-House veto in § 244(c)(2) cannot be severed from § 244. Congress argues that if the provision for the one-House veto is held unconstitutional, all of § 244 must fall. If § 244 in its entirety is violative of the Constitution, it follows that the Attorney General has no authority to suspend Chadha's deportation under § 244(a)(1) and Chadha would be deported. From this, Congress argues that Chadha lacks standing to challenge the constitutionality of the one-House veto provision because he could receive no relief even if his constitutional challenge proves successful.

. . . Congress itself has provided the answer to the question of severability in § 406 of the Immigration and Nationality Act, 8 U.S.C. § 1101, which provides:

> "If *any* particular provision of this Act, or the application thereof to *any* person or circumstance, is held invalid, *the remainder of the Act and the application of such proposition to other persons or circumstances shall not be affected thereby.*" (Emphasis added.)

. . .

. . . Plainly, Congress' desire to retain a veto in this area cannot be considered in isolation but must be viewed in the context of Congress' irritation with the burden of private immigration bills. This legislative history is not sufficient to rebut the presumption of severability raised by § 406 because there is insufficient evidence that Congress would have continued to subject itself to the onerous burdens of private bills had it known that § 244(c)(2) would be held unconstitutional.

. . .

F

Case or Controversy

It is also contended that this is not a genuine controversy but "a friendly, non-adversary, proceeding," Ashwander v. Tennessee Valley Authority, supra, 297 U.S., at 346 (Brandeis, J., concurring), upon which the Court should not pass. This argument rests on the fact that Chadha and the INS take the same position on the constitutionality of the one-House veto. But it would be a curious result if, in the administration of justice, a person could be denied access to the courts because the Attorney General of the United States agreed with the legal arguments asserted by the individual.

III

A

We turn now to the question whether action of one House of Congress under § 244(c)(2) violates strictures of the Constitution. We begin, of course, with the presumption that the challenged statute is valid. . . .

By the same token, the fact that a given law or procedure is efficient, convenient, and useful in facilitating functions of government, standing alone, will not save it if it is contrary to the Constitution. Convenience and efficiency are not the primary objectives—or the hallmarks—of democratic government and our inquiry is sharpened rather than blunted by the fact that Congressional veto provisions are appearing with increasing frequency in statutes which delegate authority to executive and independent agencies:

"Since 1932, when the first veto provision was enacted into law, 295 congressional veto-type procedures have been inserted in 196 different statutes as follows: from 1932 to 1939, five statutes were affected; from 1940–49, nineteen statutes; between 1950–59, thirty-four statutes; and from 1960–69, forty-nine. From the year 1970 through 1975, at least one hundred sixty-three such provisions were included in eighty-nine laws." *Abourezk, The Congressional Veto: A Contemporary Response to Executive Encroachment on Legislative Prerogatives,* 52 Ind.L.Rev. 323, 324 (1977).

Justice White undertakes to make a case for the proposition that the one-House veto is a useful "political invention," and we need not challenge that assertion. We can even concede this utilitarian argument although the long range political wisdom of this "invention" is arguable. It has been vigorously debated and it is instructive to compare the views of the protagonists. See, e.g., *Javits & Klein, Congressional Oversight and the Legislative Veto: A Constitutional Analysis,* 52 N.Y.U.L.Rev. 455 (1977), and *Martin, The Legislative Veto and the Responsible Exercise of Congressional Power,* 68 Va.L.Rev. 253 (1982). But policy arguments supporting even useful "political inventions" are subject to the demands of the Constitution which defines powers and, with respect to this subject, sets out just how those powers are to be exercised.

Explicit and unambiguous provisions of the Constitution prescribe and define the respective functions of the Congress and of the Executive in the legislative process. Since the precise terms of those familiar provisions are critical to the resolution of this case, we set them out verbatim. Art. I provides:

"All legislative Powers herein granted shall be vested in a Congress of the United States, which shall consist of a Senate *and* a House of Representatives." Art. I, § 1. (Emphasis added).

"Every Bill which shall have passed the House of Representatives *and* the Senate, *shall,* before it become a Law, be presented to the President of the United States; ..." Art. I, § 7, cl. 2. (Emphasis added).

"*Every* Order, Resolution, or Vote to which the Concurrence of the Senate and House of Representatives may be necessary (except on a question of Adjournment) *shall be* presented to the President of the United States; and before the Same shall take Effect, *shall be* approved by him, or being disapproved by him, *shall be* repassed by two thirds of the Senate and House of Representatives, according to the Rules and Limitations prescribed in the Case of a Bill." Art. I, § 7, cl. 3. (Emphasis added).

... [T]he purposes underlying the Presentment Clauses, Art. I, § 7, cls. 2, 3, and the bicameral requirement of Art. I, § 1 and § 7, cl. 2, guide our resolution of the important question presented in this case. The very structure of the articles delegating and separating powers under Arts. I, II, and III exemplify the concept of separation of powers and we now turn to Art. I.

B

The Presentment Clauses

The records of the Constitutional Convention reveal that the requirement that all legislation be presented to the President before becoming law was uniformly accepted by the Framers. Presentment to the President and the Presidential veto were considered so imperative that the draftsmen took special pains to assure that these requirements could not be circumvented. During the final debate on Art. I, § 7, cl. 2, James Madison expressed concern that it might easily be evaded by the simple expedient of calling a proposed law a "resolution" or "vote" rather than a "bill." 2 M. Farrand, The Records of the Federal Convention of 1787, 301–302. As a consequence, Art. I, § 7, cl. 3, was added. Id., at 304–305.

The decision to provide the President with a limited and qualified power to nullify proposed legislation by veto was based on the profound conviction of the Framers that the powers conferred on Congress were the powers to be most carefully circumscribed. It is beyond doubt that lawmaking was a power to be shared by both Houses and the President. . . .

The President's role in the lawmaking process also reflects the Framers' careful efforts to check whatever propensity a particular Congress might have to enact oppressive, improvident, or ill-considered measures. . . . Presentment Clauses serve the important purpose of assuring that a "national" perspective is grafted on the legislative process. . . .

C

Bicameralism

The bicameral requirement of Art. I, §§ 1, 7 was of scarcely less concern to the Framers than was the Presidential veto and indeed the two concepts are interdependent. By providing that no law could take effect without the concurrence of the prescribed majority of the Members of both Houses, the Framers reemphasized their belief, already remarked upon in connection with the Presentment Clauses, that legislation should not be enacted unless it has been carefully and fully considered by the Nation's elected officials. . . .

. . .

However familiar, it is useful to recall that apart from their fear that special interests could be favored at the expense of public needs, the Framers were also concerned, although not of one mind, over the apprehensions of the smaller states. Those states feared a commonality of interest among the larger states would work to their disadvantage; representatives of the larger states, on the other hand, were skeptical of a legislature that could pass laws favoring a minority of the people. See 1 M. Farrand, supra, 176–177, 484–491. It need hardly be repeated here that the Great Compromise, under which one House was viewed as representing the people and the other the states, allayed the fears of both the large and small states.

We see therefore that the Framers were acutely conscious that the bicameral requirement and the Presentment Clauses would serve essential constitutional functions. The President's participation in the legislative process was to protect the Executive Branch from Congress and to protect the whole people from improvident laws. The division of the Congress into two distinctive bodies assures that the legislative power would be exercised only after opportunity for full study and debate in separate settings. The President's unilateral veto power, in turn, was limited by the power of two thirds of both Houses of Congress to overrule a veto thereby precluding final arbitrary action of one person. See 1 M. Farrand, supra, at 99–104. It emerges clearly that the prescription for legislative action in Art. I, §§ 1, 7 represents the Framers' decision that the legislative power of the Federal government be exercised in accord with a single, finely wrought and exhaustively considered, procedure.

IV

... [W]e must ... establish that the challenged action under § 244(c)(2) is of the kind to which the procedural requirements of Art. I, § 7 apply. Not every action taken by either House is subject to the bicameralism and presentment requirements of Art. I. Whether actions taken by either House are, in law and fact, an exercise of legislative power depends not on their form but upon "whether they contain matter which is properly to be regarded as legislative in its character and effect." S.Rep. No. 1335, 54th Cong., 2d Sess., 8 (1897).

Examination of the action taken here by one House pursuant to § 244(c)(2) reveals that it was essentially legislative in purpose and effect. In purporting to exercise power defined in Art. I, § 8, cl. 4 to "establish an uniform Rule of Naturalization," the House took action that had the purpose and effect of altering the legal rights, duties and relations of persons, including the Attorney General, Executive Branch officials and Chadha, all outside the legislative branch. . . .

. . .

Since it is clear that the action by the House under § 244(c)(2) was not within any of the express constitutional exceptions authorizing one House to act alone, and equally clear that it was an exercise of legislative power, that action was subject to the standards prescribed in Article I.[21] . . .

The veto authorized by § 244(c)(2) doubtless has been in many respects a convenient shortcut; the "sharing" with the Executive by Congress of its authority over aliens in this manner is, on its face, an appealing compromise. In purely practical terms, it is obviously easier for action to be taken by one House without submission to the President; but it is crystal clear from the records of the Convention, contemporaneous writings and debates, that the Framers ranked other values higher than efficiency. The records of the Convention and debates in the States preceding ratification underscore the common desire to define and limit the exercise of the newly created federal powers affecting the states and the people. There is unmistakable expression of a determination that legislation by the national Congress be a step-by-step, deliberate and deliberative process.

. . .

V

We hold that the Congressional veto provision in § 244(c)(2) is severable from the Act and that it is unconstitutional. Accordingly, the judgment of the Court of Appeals is

Affirmed.

---

[21] Justice Powell's position is that the one-House veto in this case is a *judicial* act and therefore unconstitutional as beyond the authority vested in Congress by the Constitution. We agree that there is a sense in which one-House action pursuant to § 244(c)(2) has a judicial cast, since it purports to "review" Executive action. . . . But the attempted analogy between judicial action and the one-House veto is less than perfect. Federal courts do not enjoy a roving mandate to correct alleged excesses of administrative agencies; we are limited by Art. III to hearing cases and controversies and no justiciable case or controversy was presented by the Attorney General's decision to allow Chadha to remain in this country. We are aware of no decision, and Justice Powell has cited none, where a federal court has reviewed a decision of the Attorney General suspending deportation of an alien pursuant to the standards set out in § 244(a)(1). This is not surprising, given that no party to such action has either the motivation or the right to appeal from it. . . .

Justice Powell, concurring in the judgment.

... [O]ur holding should be no more extensive than necessary to decide this case. In my view, the case may be decided on a narrower ground. When Congress finds that a particular person does not satisfy the statutory criteria for permanent residence in this country it has assumed a judicial function in violation of the principle of separation of powers. Accordingly, I concur in the judgment.

. . .

II

. . .

On its face, the House's action appears clearly adjudicatory. The House did not enact a general rule; rather it made its own determination that six specific persons did not comply with certain statutory criteria. It thus undertook the type of decision that traditionally has been left to other branches. Even if the House did not make a *de novo* determination, but simply reviewed the Immigration and Naturalization Service's findings, it still assumed a function ordinarily entrusted to the federal courts. ...

Justice White, dissenting.

Today the Court not only invalidates § 244(c)(2) of the Immigration and Nationality Act, but also sounds the death knell for nearly 200 other statutory provisions in which Congress has reserved a "legislative veto." ...

The prominence of the legislative veto mechanism in our contemporary political system and its importance to Congress can hardly be overstated. It has become a central means by which Congress secures the accountability of executive and independent agencies. Without the legislative veto, Congress is faced with a Hobson's choice: either to refrain from delegating the necessary authority, leaving itself with a hopeless task of writing laws with the requisite specificity to cover endless special circumstances across the entire policy landscape, or in the alternative, to abdicate its lawmaking function to the executive branch and independent agencies. To choose the former leaves major national problems unresolved; to opt for the latter risks unaccountable policy-making by those not elected to fill that role. Accordingly, over the past five decades, the legislative veto has been placed in nearly 200 statutes. The device is known in every field of governmental concern: reorganization, budgets, foreign affairs, war powers, and regulation of trade, safety, energy, the environment and the economy.

I

. . .

During the 1970's the legislative veto was important in resolving a series of major constitutional disputes between the President and Congress over claims of the President to broad impoundment, war, and national emergency powers. The key provision of the War Powers Resolution, 50 U.S.C. § 1544(c), authorizes the termination by concurrent resolution of the use of armed forces in hostilities. A similar measure resolved the problem posed by Presidential claims of inherent power to impound appropriations. Congressional Budget and Impoundment Control Act of 1974, 31 U.S.C. § 1403. In conference, a compromise was achieved under which permanent impoundments, termed "rescissions," would require approval through enactment of legislation. In contrast, temporary impoundments, or "deferrals," would become effective unless disapproved by one House. This compromise provided the President with flexibility, while preserving ultimate Congressional control over the budget. Although the War Powers Resolution was enacted over President Nixon's veto, the Impoundment Control Act was enacted with the President's approval. . . .

. . .

. . . [T]he legislative veto is more than "efficient, convenient, and useful." It is an important if not indispensable political invention that allows the President and Congress to resolve major constitutional and policy differences, assures the accountability of independent regulatory agencies, and preserves Congress' control over lawmaking. Perhaps there are other means of accommodation and accountability, but the increasing reliance of Congress upon the legislative veto suggests that the alternatives to which Congress must now turn are not entirely satisfactory.

The history of the legislative veto also makes clear that it has not been a sword with which Congress has struck out to aggrandize itself at the expense of the other branches—the concerns of Madison and Hamilton. Rather, the veto has been a means of defense, a reservation of ultimate authority necessary if Congress is to fulfill its designated role under Article I as the nation's lawmaker. While the President has often objected to particular legislative vetoes, generally those left in the hands of congressional committees, the Executive has more often agreed to legislative review as the price for a broad delegation of authority. To be sure, the President may have preferred unrestricted power, but that could be precisely why Congress thought it essential to retain a check on the exercise of delegated authority.

II

For all these reasons, the apparent sweep of the Court's decision today is regrettable. The Court's Article I analysis appears to invalidate all legislative vetoes irrespective of form or subject. Because the legislative veto is commonly found as a check upon rulemaking by administrative agencies and upon broad-based policy decisions of the Executive Branch, it is particularly unfortunate that the Court reaches its decision in a case involving the exercise of a veto over deportation decisions regarding particular individuals. . . . Unfortunately, today's holding is not so limited.

. . .

III

. . .

. . . The Court's holding today that all legislative-type action must be enacted through the lawmaking process ignores that legislative authority is routinely delegated to the Executive branch, to the independent regulatory agencies, and to private individuals and groups. . . .

This Court's decisions sanctioning such delegations make clear that Article I does not require all action with the effect of legislation to be passed as a law.

The wisdom and the constitutionality of these broad delegations are matters that still have not been put to rest. . . . There is no question but that agency rulemaking is lawmaking in any functional or realistic sense of the term. . . .

If Congress may delegate lawmaking power to independent and executive agencies, it is most difficult to understand Article I as forbidding Congress from also reserving a check on legislative power for itself. Absent the veto, the agencies receiving delegations of legislative or quasi-legislative power may issue regulations having the force of law without bicameral approval and without the President's signature. It is thus not apparent why the reservation of a veto over the exercise of that legislative power must be subject to a more exacting test. In both cases, it is enough that the initial statutory authorizations comply with the Article I requirements.

. . .

. . . If the effective functioning of a complex modern government requires the delegation of vast authority which, by virtue of its breadth, is legislative or "quasi-legislative" in character, I cannot accept that Article I—which is, after all, the source of the non-delegation doctrine—should forbid Congress from qualifying that grant with a legislative veto.

. . .

IV

. . .

I do not suggest that all legislative vetoes are necessarily consistent with separation of powers principles. A legislative check on an inherently executive function, for example that of initiating prosecutions, poses an entirely different question. But the legislative veto device here—and in many other settings—is far from an instance of legislative tyranny over the Executive. It is a necessary check on the unavoidably expanding power of the agencies, both executive and independent, as they engage in exercising authority delegated by Congress.

. . .

Justice Rehnquist, with whom Justice White joins, dissenting.

. . .

By severing § 244(c)(2), the Court permits suspension of deportation in a class of cases where Congress never stated that suspension was appropriate. I do not believe we should expand the statute in this way without some clear indication that Congress intended such an expansion. . . .

. . .

MISTRETTA v. UNITED STATES, 488 U.S. 361 (1989). The Sentencing Reform Act of 1984 created the United States Sentencing Commission, consisting of seven voting members appointed by the President with the advice and consent of the Senate. At least three of its members must be Federal judges, selected after consideration of a list of six judges recommended by the Judicial Conference of the United States. The Commission, established "as an independent commission in the judicial branch of the United States," promulgates binding sentencing guidelines for federal crimes. The Court upheld the Commission's sentencing guidelines against a claim that the Act violated the principle of separation of powers. The Court stressed that a "concern of encroachment and aggrandizement . . . has animated our separation of powers jurisprudence."

> "Accordingly, we have not hesitated to strike down provisions of law that either accrete to a single branch powers more appropriately diffused among separate branches or that undermine the authority and independence of one or another coordinate branch. . . . By the same token, we have upheld statutory provisions that to some degree commingle the functions of the

Branches, but that pose no danger of either aggrandizement or encroachment."

Locating the Commission within the judicial branch did not violate the provisions of Article III, limiting the judicial power to resolution of "cases" and "controversies." Analogous to the provisions for judicial rulemaking, "Congress may delegate to the Judicial Branch nonadjudicatory functions that do not trench upon the prerogatives of another Branch and that are appropriate to the central mission of the Judiciary." Although the Commission wields rulemaking authority, it has not aggrandized the authority of the judicial branch, since judges had, as an aggregate, determined appropriate criminal sentences prior to passage of the Act.

Although the Commission does not wield "judicial power," Article III does not prohibit Article III judges from undertaking extrajudicial duties "in their individual capacities." In each case, the issue is "whether a particular extrajudicial assignment undermines the integrity of the Judicial Branch." Service on the Commission is voluntary, and participation in promulgation of the sentencing guidelines would not affect member-judges' ability to adjudicate sentencing issues.

"Judicial contribution to the enterprise of creating rules to limit the discretion of sentencing judges does not enlist the resources or reputation of the Judicial Branch in either the legislative business of determining what conduct should be criminalized or the executive business of enforcing the law. Rather, judicial participation on the Commission ensures that judicial experience and expertise will inform the promulgation of rules for the exercise of the Judicial Branch's own business—that of passing sentence on every criminal defendant."

Justice Scalia dissented, saying:

"Today's decision follows the regrettable tendency of our recent separation-of-powers jurisprudence ... to treat the Constitution as though it were no more than a generalized prescription that the functions of the Branches should not be commingled too much—how much is too much to be determined, case-by-case, by this Court. The Constitution is not that. Rather, as its name suggests, it is a prescribed structure, a framework, for the conduct of government.... Consideration of the degree of commingling that a particular disposition produces may be appropriate at the margins, where the outline of the framework itself is not clear; but it seems to me far from a marginal question whether our constitutional structure allows for a body which is not the Congress, and yet exercises no governmental powers except the making of rules that have the effect of laws.

"... [T]here are many desirable dispositions that do not accord with the constitutional structure we live under. And in the long run the improvisation of a constitutional structure on the basis of currently perceived utility will be disastrous."

B. APPOINTMENT, DISCHARGE, AND SUPERVISION OF "OFFICERS OF THE UNITED STATES"

Morrison v. Olson

487 U.S. 654, 108 S.Ct. 2597, 101 L.Ed.2d 569 (1988).

Chief Justice Rehnquist delivered the opinion of the Court.

This case presents us with a challenge to the independent counsel provisions of the Ethics in Government Act of 1978, 28 U.S.C.A. §§ 49, 591 et seq.

(Supp.1988). We hold today that these provisions of the Act do not violate the Appointments Clause of the Constitution, Art. II, § 2, cl. 2, or the limitations of Article III, nor do they impermissibly interfere with the President's authority under Article II in violation of the constitutional principle of separation of powers.

I

Briefly stated, Title VI of the Ethics in Government Act (Title VI or the Act), 28 U.S.C.A. §§ 591–599 (Supp.1988), allows for the appointment of an "independent counsel" to investigate and, if appropriate, prosecute certain high ranking government officials for violations of federal criminal laws. The Act requires the Attorney General, upon receipt of information that he determines is "sufficient to constitute grounds to investigate whether any person [covered by the Act] may have violated any Federal criminal law," to conduct a preliminary investigation of the matter. When the Attorney General has completed this investigation, or 90 days has elapsed, he is required to report to a special court (the Special Division) created by the Act "for the purpose of appointing independent counsels." 28 U.S.C.A. § 49 (Supp.1988). If the Attorney General determines that "there are no reasonable grounds to believe that further investigation is warranted," then he must notify the Special Division of this result. In such a case, "the division of the court shall have no power to appoint an independent counsel." § 592(b)(1). If, however, the Attorney General has determined that there are "reasonable grounds to believe that further investigation or prosecution is warranted," then he "shall apply to the division of the court for the appointment of an independent counsel." The Attorney General's application to the court "shall contain sufficient information to assist the [court] in selecting an independent counsel and in defining that independent counsel's prosecutorial jurisdiction." § 592(d). Upon receiving this application, the Special Division "shall appoint an appropriate independent counsel and shall define that independent counsel's prosecutorial jurisdiction." § 593(b).

With respect to all matters within the independent counsel's jurisdiction, the Act grants the counsel "full power and independent authority to exercise all investigative and prosecutorial functions and powers of the Department of Justice, the Attorney General, and any other officer or employee of the Department of Justice." § 594(a). The functions of the independent counsel include conducting grand jury proceedings and other investigations, participating in civil and criminal court proceedings and litigation, and appealing any decision in any case in which the counsel participates in an official capacity. §§ 594(a)(1)–(3). Under § 594(a)(9), the counsel's powers include "initiating and conducting prosecutions in any court of competent jurisdiction, framing and signing indictments, filing informations, and handling all aspects of any case, in the name of the United States." The counsel may appoint employees, § 594(c), may request and obtain assistance from the Department of Justice, § 594(d), and may accept referral of matters from the Attorney General if the matter falls within the counsel's jurisdiction as defined by the Special Division, § 594(e). The Act also states that an independent counsel "shall, except where not possible, comply with the written or other established policies of the Department of Justice respecting enforcement of the criminal laws." § 594(f). In addition, whenever a matter has been referred to an independent counsel under the Act, the Attorney General and the Justice Department are required to suspend all investigations and proceedings regarding the matter. § 597(a).

An independent counsel has "full authority to dismiss matters within [his] prosecutorial jurisdiction without conducting an investigation or at any subsequent time before prosecution, if to do so would be consistent" with Department of Justice policy. § 594(g). Two statutory provisions govern the length of an independent counsel's tenure in office. The first defines the procedure for removing an independent counsel. Section 596(a)(1) provides:

> "An independent counsel appointed under this chapter may be removed from office, other than by impeachment and conviction, only by the personal action of the Attorney General and only for good cause, physical disability, mental incapacity, or any other condition that substantially impairs the performance of such independent counsel's duties."

If an independent counsel is removed pursuant to this section, the Attorney General is required to submit a report to both the Special Division and the Judiciary Committees of the Senate and the House "specifying the facts found and the ultimate grounds for such removal." § 596(a)(2). Under the current version of the Act, an independent counsel can obtain judicial review of the Attorney General's action by filing a civil action in the United States District Court for the District of Columbia. Members of the Special Division "may not hear or determine any such civil action or any appeal of a decision in any such civil action." The reviewing court is authorized to grant reinstatement or "other appropriate relief." § 596(a)(3).

The other provision governing the tenure of the independent counsel defines the procedures for "terminating" the counsel's office. Under § 596(b)(1), the office of an independent counsel terminates when he notifies the Attorney General that he has completed or substantially completed any investigations or prosecutions undertaken pursuant to the Act. In addition, the Special Division, acting either on its own or on the suggestion of the Attorney General, may terminate the office of an independent counsel at any time if it finds that "the investigation of all matters within the prosecutorial jurisdiction of such independent counsel ... have been completed or so substantially completed that it would be appropriate for the Department of Justice to complete such investigations and prosecutions." § 596(b)(2).

Finally, the Act provides for Congressional oversight of the activities of independent counsels. An independent counsel may from time to time send Congress statements or reports on his activities. § 595(a)(2). The "appropriate committees of the Congress" are given oversight jurisdiction in regard to the official conduct of an independent counsel, and the counsel is required by the Act to cooperate with Congress in the exercise of this jurisdiction. § 595(a)(1). The counsel is required to inform the House of Representatives of "substantial and credible information which [the counsel] receives ... that may constitute grounds for an impeachment." § 595(c). In addition, the Act gives certain Congressional Committee Members the power to "request in writing that the Attorney General apply for the appointment of an independent counsel." § 592(g)(1). The Attorney General is required to respond to this request within a specified time but is not required to accede to the request. § 592(g)(2).

The proceedings in this case provide an example of how the Act works in practice. In 1982, two subcommittees of the House of Representatives issued subpoenas directing the Environmental Protection Agency (EPA) to produce certain documents relating to the efforts of the EPA and the Land and Natural Resources Division of the Justice Department to enforce the "Superfund Law." At that time, appellee Olson was the Assistant Attorney General for the Office of Legal Counsel (OLC), appellee Schmults was Deputy Attorney General, and appellee Dinkins was the Assistant Attorney General for the Land and Natural

Resources Division. Acting on the advice of the Justice Department, the President ordered the Administrator of EPA to invoke executive privilege to withhold certain of the documents on the ground that they contained "enforcement sensitive information." The Administrator obeyed this order and withheld the documents. In response, the House voted to hold the Administrator in contempt, after which the Administrator and the United States together filed a lawsuit against the House. The conflict abated in March 1983, when the Administration agreed to give the House committees limited access to the documents.

The following year, the House Judiciary Committee began an investigation into the Justice Department's role in the controversy over the EPA documents. During this investigation, appellee Olson testified before a House subcommittee on March 10, 1983. Both before and after that testimony, the Department complied with several Committee requests to produce certain documents. Other documents were at first withheld, although these documents were eventually disclosed by the Department after the Committee learned of their existence. In 1985, the majority members of the Judiciary Committee published a lengthy report on the Committee's investigation. Report on Investigation of the Role of the Department of Justice in the Withholding of Environmental Protection Agency Documents from Congress in 1982–83, H.R.Rep. No. 99–435 (1985). The report not only criticized various officials in the Department of Justice for their role in the EPA executive privilege dispute, but it also suggested that appellee Olson had given false and misleading testimony to the subcommittee on March 10, 1983, and that appellees Schmults and Dinkins had wrongfully withheld certain documents from the Committee, thus obstructing the Committee's investigation. The Chairman of the Judiciary Committee forwarded a copy of the report to the Attorney General with a request, pursuant to 28 U.S.C. § 592(c), that he seek the appointment of an independent counsel to investigate the allegations against Olson, Schmults, and Dinkins.

The Attorney General directed the Public Integrity Section of the Criminal Division to conduct a preliminary investigation. The Section's report concluded that the appointment of an independent counsel was warranted to investigate the Committee's allegations with respect to all three appellees. After consulting with other Department officials, however, the Attorney General chose to apply to the Special Division for the appointment of an independent counsel solely with respect to appellee Olson. The Attorney General accordingly requested appointment of an independent counsel to investigate whether Olson's March 10, 1983, testimony "regarding the completeness of [OLC's] response to the Judiciary Committee's request for OLC documents, and regarding his knowledge of EPA's willingness to turn over certain disputed documents to Congress, violated 18 U.S.C. § 1505, § 1001, or any other provision of federal criminal law." Attorney General Report, at 2–3. The Attorney General also requested that the independent counsel have authority to investigate "any other matter related to that allegation." Id., at 11.

On April 23, 1986, the Special Division appointed James C. McKay as independent counsel . . .

McKay later resigned as independent counsel, and on May 29, 1986, the Division appointed appellant Morrison as his replacement . . .

. . . .

. . . [I]n May and June 1987, appellant caused a grand jury to issue and serve subpoenas ad testificandum and duces tecum on appellees. All three appellees moved to quash the subpoenas, claiming, among other things, that the independent counsel provisions of the Act were unconstitutional and that appellant accordingly had no authority to proceed. On July 20, 1987, the District Court upheld the constitutionality of the Act and denied the motions to quash . . . .

A divided Court of Appeals reversed . . . . We now reverse.

II

. . .

III

The Appointments Clause of Article II, reads as follows:

"[The President] shall nominate, and by and with the Advice and Consent of the Senate, shall appoint Ambassadors, other public Ministers and Consuls, Judges of the supreme Court, and all other Officers of the United States, whose Appointments are not herein otherwise provided for, and which shall be established by Law: but the Congress may by Law vest the Appointment of such inferior Officers, as they think proper, in the President alone, in the Courts of Law, or in the Heads of Departments." U.S. Const., Art. II, § 2, cl. 2.

The parties do not dispute that "[t]he Constitution for purposes of appointment . . . divides all its officers into two classes." United States v. Germaine, 99 U.S. 508, 509 (1879). As we stated in Buckley v. Valeo, 424 U.S. 1, 132 (1976), "[p]rincipal officers are selected by the President with the advice and consent of the Senate. Inferior officers Congress may allow to be appointed by the President alone, by the heads of departments, or by the Judiciary." The initial question is, accordingly, whether appellant is an "inferior" or a "principal" officer. If she is the latter, as the Court of Appeals concluded, then the Act is in violation of the Appointments Clause.

The line between "inferior" and "principal" officers is one that is far from clear, and the Framers provided little guidance into where it should be drawn . . . . We need not attempt here to decide exactly where the line falls between the two types of officers, because in our view appellant clearly falls on the "inferior officer" side of that line. Several factors lead to this conclusion.

First, appellant is subject to removal by a higher Executive Branch official. Although appellant may not be "subordinate" to the Attorney General (and the President) insofar as she possesses a degree of independent discretion to exercise the powers delegated to her under the Act, the fact that she can be removed by the Attorney General indicates that she is to some degree "inferior" in rank and authority. Second, appellant is empowered by the Act to perform only certain, limited duties. An independent counsel's role is restricted primarily to investigation and, if appropriate, prosecution for certain federal crimes. Admittedly, the Act delegates to appellant "full power and independent authority to exercise all investigative and prosecutorial functions and powers of the Department of Justice," § 594(a), but this grant of authority does not include any authority to formulate policy for the Government or the Executive Branch, nor does it give appellant any administrative duties outside of those necessary to operate her office. The Act specifically provides that in policy matters appellant is to comply to the extent possible with the policies of the Department. § 594(f).

Third, appellant's office is limited in jurisdiction. Not only is the Act itself restricted in applicability to certain federal officials suspected of certain serious federal crimes, but an independent counsel can only act within the scope of the jurisdiction that has been granted by the Special Division pursuant to a request by the Attorney General. Finally, appellant's office is limited in tenure. There is concededly no time limit on the appointment of a particular counsel. Nonetheless, the office of independent counsel is "temporary" in the sense that an independent counsel is appointed essentially to accomplish a single task, and when that task is over the office is terminated, either by the counsel herself or by action of the Special Division. Unlike other prosecutors, appellant has no ongoing responsibilities that extend beyond the accomplishment of the mission that she was appointed for and authorized by the Special Division to undertake. In our view, these factors relating to the "ideas of tenure, duration ... and duties" of the independent counsel, *Germaine,* supra, at 511, are sufficient to establish that appellant is an "inferior" officer in the constitutional sense.

This conclusion is consistent with our few previous decisions that considered the question of whether a particular government official is a "principal" or an "inferior" officer. In United States v. Eaton, 169 U.S. 331 (1898), for example, we approved Department of State regulations that allowed executive officials to appoint a "vice-consul" during the temporary absence of the consul, terming the "vice-consul" a "subordinate officer" notwithstanding the Appointments Clause's specific reference to "Consuls" as principal officers. As we stated, "Because the subordinate officer is charged with the performance of the duty of the superior for a limited time and under special and temporary conditions he is not thereby transformed into the superior and permanent official." Id., at 343. In Ex parte Siebold, 100 U.S. 371 (1880), the Court found that federal "supervisor[s] of elections," who were charged with various duties involving oversight of local congressional elections, see id., at 379–380, were inferior officers for purposes of the Clause. In Go–Bart Importing Co. v. United States, 282 U.S. 344, 352–353 (1931), we held that "United States commissioners are inferior officers." Id., at 352. These commissioners had various judicial and prosecutorial powers, including the power to arrest and imprison for trial, to issue warrants, and to institute prosecutions under "laws relating to the elective franchise and civil rights." Id., at 353, n. 2. All of this is consistent with our reference in United States v. Nixon, 418 U.S. 683, 694, 696 (1974), to the office of Watergate Special Prosecutor—whose authority was similar to that of appellant, see id., at 694, n. 8—as a "subordinate officer."

This does not, however, end our inquiry under the Appointments Clause. Appellees argue that even if appellant is an "inferior" officer, the Clause does not empower Congress to place the power to appoint such an officer outside the Executive Branch. They contend that the Clause does not contemplate congressional authorization of "interbranch appointments," in which an officer of one branch is appointed by officers of another branch. The relevant language of the Appointments Clause is worth repeating. It reads: "... but the Congress may by Law vest the Appointment of such inferior Officers, as they think proper, in the President alone, in the courts of Law, or in the Heads of Departments." On its face, the language of this "excepting clause" admits of no limitation on interbranch appointments. Indeed, the inclusion of "as they think proper" seems clearly to give Congress significant discretion to determine whether it is "proper" to vest the appointment of, for example, executive officials in the "courts of Law." We recognized as much in one of our few decisions in this area, *Ex parte Siebold,* supra, where we stated:

> "It is no doubt usual and proper to vest the appointment of inferior officers in that department of the government, executive or judicial, or in that particular executive department to which the duties of such officers appertain. But there is no absolute requirement to this effect in the

Constitution; and, if there were, it would be difficult in many cases to determine to which department an office properly belonged....

"..." 100 U.S., at 397–398.

Our only decision to suggest otherwise, Ex parte Hennen, 13 Pet. 230 (1839), from which the first sentence in the above quotation from Siebold was derived, was discussed in *Siebold* and distinguished as "not intended to define the constitutional power of Congress in this regard, but rather to express the law or rule by which it should be governed." 100 U.S., at 398. Outside of these two cases, there is very little, if any, express discussion of the propriety of interbranch appointments in our decisions, and we see no reason now to depart from the holding of *Siebold* that such appointments are not proscribed by the excepting clause.

We also note that the history of the Clause provides no support for appellees' position.... [T]here was little or no debate on the question of whether the Clause empowers Congress to provide for interbranch appointments, and there is nothing to suggest that the Framers intended to prevent Congress from having that power.

We do not mean to say that Congress' power to provide for interbranch appointments of "inferior officers" is unlimited. In addition to separation of powers concerns, which would arise if such provisions for appointment had the potential to impair the constitutional functions assigned to one of the branches, *Siebold* itself suggested that Congress' decision to vest the appointment power in the courts would be improper if there was some "incongruity" between the functions normally performed by the courts and the performance of their duty to appoint. 100 U.S., at 398 ("the duty to appoint inferior officers, when required thereto by law, is a constitutional duty of the courts; and in the present case there is no such incongruity in the duty required as to excuse the courts from its performance, or to render their acts void"). In this case, however, we do not think it impermissible for Congress to vest the power to appoint independent counsels in a specially created federal court.... We have recognized that courts may appoint private attorneys to act as prosecutor for judicial contempt judgments. See Young v. United States ex rel. Vuitton et Fils S.A., 481 U.S.787 (1987). In Go–Bart Importing Co. v. United States, 282 U.S. 344 (1931), we approved court appointment of United States commissioners, who exercised certain limited prosecutorial powers. Id., at 353, n. 2. In *Siebold,* as well, we indicated that judicial appointment of federal marshals, who are "executive officer[s]," would not be inappropriate. Lower courts have also upheld interim judicial appointments of United States Attorneys, see United States v. Solomon, 216 F.Supp. 835 (S.D.N.Y.1963), and Congress itself has vested the power to make these interim appointments in the district courts, see 28 U.S.C.A. § 546(d) (Supp.1988). Congress of course was concerned when it created the office of independent counsel with the conflicts of interest that could arise in situations when the Executive Branch is called upon to investigate its own high-ranking officers. If it were to remove the appointing authority from the Executive Branch, the most logical place to put it was in the Judicial Branch. In the light of the Act's provision making the judges of the Special Division ineligible to participate in any matters relating to an independent counsel they have appointed, 28 U.S.C. § 49(f), we do not think that appointment of the independent counsels by the court runs afoul of the constitutional limitation on "incongruous" interbranch appointments.

IV

Appellees next contend that the powers vested in the Special Division by the Act conflict with Article III of the Constitution. We have long recognized that by the express provision of Article III, the judicial power of the United States is limited to "Cases" and "Controversies." See Muskrat v. United States, 219 U.S. 346, 356 (1911). As a general rule, we have broadly stated that "executive or administrative duties of a nonjudicial nature may not be imposed on judges holding office under Art. III of the Constitution." Buckley, 424 U.S., at 123 (citing United States v. Ferreira, 13 How. 40 (1852); Hayburn's Case, 2 Dall. 408 (1792)). The purpose of this limitation is to help ensure the independence of the Judicial Branch and to prevent the judiciary from encroaching into areas reserved for the other branches.... With this in mind, we address in turn the various duties given to the Special Division by the Act.

Most importantly, the Act vests in the Special Division the power to choose who will serve as independent counsel and the power to define his or her jurisdiction. § 593(b). Clearly, once it is accepted that the Appointments Clause gives Congress the power to vest the appointment of officials such as the independent counsel in the "courts of Law," there can be no Article III objection to the Special Division's exercise of that power, as the power itself derives from the Appointments Clause, a source of authority for judicial action that is independent of Article III. Appellees contend, however, that the Division's Appointments Clause powers do not encompass the power to define the independent counsel's jurisdiction. We disagree. In our view, Congress' power under the Clause to vest the "Appointment" of inferior officers in the courts may, in certain circumstances, allow Congress to give the courts some discretion in defining the nature and scope of the appointed official's authority. Particularly when, as here, Congress creates a temporary "office" the nature and duties of which will by necessity vary with the factual circumstances giving rise to the need for an appointment in the first place, it may vest the power to define the scope of the office in the court as an incident to the appointment of the officer pursuant to the Appointments Clause. This said, we do not think that Congress may give the Division *unlimited* discretion to determine the independent counsel's jurisdiction. In order for the Division's definition of the counsel's jurisdiction to be truly "incidental" to its power to appoint, the jurisdiction that the court decides upon must be demonstrably related to the factual circumstances that gave rise to the Attorney General's investigation and request for the appointment of the independent counsel in the particular case.

The Act also vests in the Special Division various powers and duties in relation to the independent counsel that, because they do not involve appointing the counsel or defining her jurisdiction, cannot be said to derive from the Division's Appointments Clause authority. These duties include granting extensions for the Attorney General's preliminary investigation, § 592(a)(3); receiving the report of the Attorney General at the conclusion of his preliminary investigation, §§ 592(b)(1), 593(c)(2)(B); referring matters to the counsel upon request, § 594(e);[18] receiving reports from the counsel regarding expenses incurred, § 594(h)(1)(A); receiving a report from the Attorney General following the removal of an independent counsel, § 596(a)(2); granting attorney's fees upon request to individuals who were investigated but not indicted by an independent counsel, § 593(f); receiving a final report from the counsel, § 594(h)(1)(B); deciding whether to release the counsel's final report to Congress or the public and determining whether any protective orders should be

---

[18] In our view, this provision does not empower the court to expand the original scope of the counsel's jurisdiction; that may be done only upon request of the Attorney General pursuant to section 593(c)(2). At most, section 594(e) authorizes the court simply to refer matters that are "relate[d] to the independent counsel's prosecutorial jurisdiction" as already defined.

issued, § 594(h)(2); and terminating an independent counsel when his task is completed, § 596(b)(2).

Leaving aside for the moment the Division's power to terminate an independent counsel, we do not think that Article III absolutely prevents Congress from vesting these other miscellaneous powers in the Special Division pursuant to the Act. . . .[T]he powers granted by these provisions are themselves essentially ministerial. The Act simply does not give the Division the power to "supervise" the independent counsel in the exercise of her investigative or prosecutorial authority. And, the functions that the Special Division is empowered to perform are not inherently "executive"; indeed, they are directly analogous to functions that federal judges perform in other contexts . . .

We are more doubtful about the Special Division's power to terminate the office of the independent counsel pursuant to § 596(b)(2). As appellees suggest, the power to terminate, especially when exercised by the Division on its own motion, is "administrative" to the extent that it requires the Special Division to monitor the progress of proceedings of the independent counsel and come to a decision as to whether the counsel's job is "completed." § 596(b)(2). It also is not a power that could be considered typically "judicial," as it has few analogues among the court's more traditional powers. Nonetheless, we do not, as did the Court of Appeals, view this provision as a significant judicial encroachment upon executive power or upon the prosecutorial discretion of the independent counsel.

. . . [I]t is the duty of federal courts to construe a statute in order to save it from constitutional infirmities, . . . and to that end we think a narrow construction is appropriate here. The termination provisions of the Act do not give the Special Division anything approaching the power to remove the counsel while an investigation or court proceeding is still underway—this power is vested solely in the Attorney General. As we see it, "termination" may occur only when the duties of the counsel are truly "completed" or "so substantially completed" that there remains no need for any continuing action by the independent counsel. It is basically a device for removing from the public payroll an independent counsel who has served her purpose, but is unwilling to acknowledge the fact. So construed, the Special Division's power to terminate does not pose a sufficient threat of judicial intrusion into matters that are more properly within the Executive's authority to require that the Act be invalidated as inconsistent with Article III.

. . .

We emphasize . . . that the Special Division has no authority to take any action or undertake any duties that are not specifically authorized by the Act. The gradual expansion of the authority of the Special Division might in another context be a bureaucratic success story, but it would be one that would have serious constitutional ramifications. The record in other cases involving independent counsels indicate that the Special Division has at times given advisory opinions or issued orders that are not directly authorized by the Act. . . . The propriety of the Special Division's actions in these instances is not before us as such, but we nonetheless think it appropriate to point out not only that there is no authorization for such actions in the Act itself, but that the division's exercise of unauthorized powers risks the transgression of the constitutional limitations of Article III that we have just discussed.

V

We now turn to consider whether the Act is invalid under the constitutional principle of separation of powers. Two related issues must be addressed: The first is whether the provision of the Act restricting the Attorney General's power to remove the independent counsel to only those instances in which he can show "good cause," taken by itself, impermissibly interferes with the President's exercise of his constitutionally appointed functions. The second is whether, taken as a whole, the Act violates the separation of powers by reducing the President's ability to control the prosecutorial powers wielded by the independent counsel.

A

Two Terms ago we had occasion to consider whether it was consistent with the separation of powers for Congress to pass a statute that authorized a government official who is removable only by Congress to participate in what we found to be "executive powers." Bowsher v. Synar, 478 U.S. 714, 730 (1986). We held in *Bowsher* that "Congress cannot reserve for itself the power of removal of an officer charged with the execution of the laws except by impeachment." Id., at 726. A primary antecedent for this ruling was our 1925 decision in Myers v. United States, 272 U.S. 52 (1926). *Myers* had considered the propriety of a federal statute by which certain postmasters of the United States could be removed by the President only "by and with the advice and consent of the Senate." There too, Congress' attempt to involve itself in the removal of an executive official was found to be sufficient grounds to render the statute invalid. As we observed in *Bowsher,* the essence of the decision in *Myers* was the judgment that the Constitution prevents Congress from "draw[ing] to itself . . . the power to remove or the right to participate in the exercise of that power. To do this would be to go beyond the words and implications of the [Appointments Clause] and to infringe the constitutional principle of the separation of governmental powers." *Myers,* supra, at 161.

Unlike both *Bowsher* and *Myers,* this case does not involve an attempt by Congress itself to gain a role in the removal of executive officials other than its established powers of impeachment and conviction. The Act instead puts the removal power squarely in the hands of the Executive Branch; an independent counsel may be removed from office, "only by the personal action of the Attorney General, and only for good cause." § 596(a)(1). There is no requirement of congressional approval of the Attorney General's removal decision, though the decision is subject to judicial review. § 596(a)(3). In our view, the removal provisions of the Act make this case more analogous to Humphrey's Executor v. United States, 295 U.S. 602 (1935), and Wiener v. United States, 357 U.S. 349 (1958), than to *Myers* or *Bowsher.*

In *Humphrey's Executor,* the issue was whether a statute restricting the President's power to remove the commissioners of the Federal Trade Commission only for "inefficiency, neglect of duty, or malfeasance in office" was consistent with the Constitution. 295 U.S., at 619. We stated that whether Congress can "condition the [President's power of removal] by fixing a definite term and precluding a removal except for cause, will depend upon the character of the office." Id., at 631. Contrary to the implication of some dicta in *Myers,*[24] the President's power to remove government officials simply was not "all-inclusive in respect of civil officers with the exception of the judiciary provided for by the Constitution." 295 U.S., at 629. At least in regard to "quasi-

---

[24] The Court expressly disapproved of any statements in *Myers* that "are out of harmony" with the views expressed in *Humphrey's Executor.* 295 U.S., at 626. We recognized that the only issue actually decided in *Myers* was that "the President had power to remove a postmaster of the first class, without the advice and consent of the Senate as required by act of Congress." 295 U.S., at 626.

legislative" and "quasi-judicial" agencies such as the FTC,[25] "[t]he authority of Congress, in creating [such] agencies, to require them to act in discharge of their duties independently of executive control ... includes, as an appropriate incident, power to fix the period during which they shall continue in office, and to forbid their removal except for cause in the meantime." Ibid. In *Humphrey's Executor*, we found it "plain" that the Constitution did not give the President "illimitable power of removal" over the officers of independent agencies. Ibid. Were the President to have the power to remove FTC commissioners at will, the "coercive influence" of the removal power would "threate[n] the independence of [the] commission." Id., at 630.

Similarly, in *Wiener* we considered whether the President had unfettered discretion to remove a member of the War Claims Commission, which had been established by Congress in the War Claims Act of 1948, 62 Stat. 1240. The Commission's function was to receive and adjudicate certain claims for compensation from those who had suffered personal injury or property damage at the hands of the enemy during World War II. Commissioners were appointed by the President, with the advice and consent of the Senate, but the statute made no provision for the removal of officers, perhaps because the Commission itself was to have a limited existence. As in *Humphrey's Executor*, however, the Commissioners were entrusted by Congress with adjudicatory powers that were to be exercised free from executive control. In this context, "Congress did not wish to have hang over the Commission the Damocles' sword of removal by the President for no reason other than that he preferred to have on that Commission men of his own choosing." 357 U.S., at 356. Accordingly, we rejected the President's attempt to remove a Commissioner "merely because he wanted his own appointees on [the] Commission," stating that "no such power is given to the President directly by the Constitution, and none is impliedly conferred upon him by statute." Ibid.

Appellees contend that *Humphrey's Executor* and *Wiener* are distinguishable from this case because they did not involve officials who performed a "core executive function." They argue that our decision in *Humphrey's Executor* rests on a distinction between "purely executive" officials and officials who exercise "quasi-legislative" and "quasi-judicial" powers. In their view, when a "purely executive" official is involved, the governing precedent is *Myers*, not *Humphrey's Executor*. See *Humphrey's Executor*, 295 U.S., at 628. And, under *Myers*, the President must have absolute discretion to discharge "purely" executive officials at will. See *Myers*, 272 U.S., at 132–134.[26]

We undoubtedly did rely on the terms "quasi-legislative" and "quasi-judicial" to distinguish the officials involved in *Humphrey's Executor* and *Wiener* from those in *Myers*, but our present considered view is that the determination of whether the Constitution allows Congress to impose a "good cause"-type restriction on the President's power to remove an official cannot be made to turn on whether or not that official is classified as "purely execu-

---

[25] See id., at 627–628. We described the FTC as "an administrative body created by Congress to carry into effect legislative policies embodied in the statute in accordance with the legislative standard therein prescribed, and to perform other specified duties as a legislative or as a judicial aid." Such an agency was not "an arm or an eye of the executive," and the commissioners were intended to perform their duties "without executive leave and ... free from executive con-trol." Id., at 628. As we put it at the time, the powers of the FTC were not "purely" executive, but were "quasi-legislative or quasi-judicial." Ibid.

[26] This same argument was raised by the Solicitor General in Bowsher v. Synar, 478 U.S. 714 (1986), although as Justice White noted in dissent in that case, the argument was clearly not accepted by the Court at that time. Id., at 738–739, and nn. 1–3.

tive."[27] The analysis contained in our removal cases is designed not to define rigid categories of those officials who may or may not be removed at will by the President,[28] but to ensure that Congress does not interfere with the President's exercise of the "executive power" and his constitutionally appointed duty to "take care that the laws be faithfully executed" under Article II. *Myers* was undoubtedly correct in its holding, and in its broader suggestion that there are some "purely executive" officials who must be removable by the President at will if he is to be able to accomplish his constitutional role.[29] See 272 U.S., at 132–134. But as the Court noted in *Wiener,*

> "The assumption was short-lived that the *Myers* case recognized the President's inherent constitutional power to remove officials no matter what the relation of the executive to the discharge of their duties and no matter what restrictions Congress may have imposed regarding the nature of their tenure." 357 U.S., at 352.

At the other end of the spectrum from *Myers,* the characterization of the agencies in *Humphrey's Executor* and *Wiener* as "quasi-legislative" or "quasi-judicial" in large part reflected our judgment that it was not essential to the President's proper execution of his Article II powers that these agencies be headed up by individuals who were removable at will. We do not mean to suggest that an analysis of the functions served by the officials at issue is irrelevant. But the real question is whether the removal restrictions are of such a nature that they impede the President's ability to perform his constitutional duty, and the functions of the officials in question must be analyzed in that light.

---

[27] Indeed, this Court has never held that the Constitution prevents Congress from imposing limitations on the President's power to remove all executive officials simply because they wield "executive" power. *Myers* itself expressly distinguished cases in which Congress had chosen to vest the appointment of "inferior" executive officials in the head of a department. See 272 U.S., at 161–163, 164. In such a situation, we saw no specific constitutional impediment to congressionally imposed restrictions on the President's removal powers....

[28] The difficulty of defining such categories of "executive" or "quasi-legislative" officials is illustrated by a comparison of our decisions in cases such as *Humphrey's Executor,* Buckley v. Valeo, 424 U.S. 1, 140–141 (1976), and *Bowsher,* supra, 478 U.S. at 732–734. In *Buckley,* we indicated that the functions of the Federal Election Commission are "administrative," and "more legislative and judicial in nature," and are "of kinds usually performed by independent regulatory agencies or by some department in the Executive Branch under the direction of an Act of Congress." 424 U.S., at 140–141. In *Bowsher,* we found that the functions of the Comptroller General were "executive" in nature, in that he was required to "exercise judgment concerning facts that affect the application of the Act," and he must "interpret the provisions of the Act to determine precisely what bud-

getary calculations are required." 478 U.S., at 733. Compare this with the description of the FTC's powers in *Humphrey's Executor,* which we stated "occupie[d] no place in the executive department": "The [FTC] is an administrative body created by Congress to carry into effect legislative policies embodied in the statute in accordance with the legislative standard therein prescribed, and to perform other specified duties as a legislative or as a judicial aid." 295 U.S., at 628. As Justice White noted in his dissent in *Bowsher,* it is hard to dispute that the powers of the FTC at the time of *Humphrey's Executor* would at the present time be considered "executive," at least to some degree. See 478 U.S., at 761, n. 3.

[29] The dissent says that the language of Article II vesting the executive power of the United States in the President requires that every officer of the United States exercising any part of that power must serve at the pleasure of the President and be removable by him at will. This rigid demarcation—a demarcation incapable of being altered by law in the slightest degree, and applicable to tens of thousands of holders of offices neither known nor foreseen by the framers—depends upon an extrapolation from general constitutional language which we think is more than the text will bear. It is also contrary to our holding in United States v. Perkins, 116 U.S. 483 (1886), decided more than a century ago.

Considering for the moment the "good cause" removal provision in isolation from the other parts of the Act at issue in this case, we cannot say that the imposition of a "good cause" standard for removal by itself unduly trammels on executive authority. There is no real dispute that the functions performed by the independent counsel are "executive" in the sense that they are law enforcement functions that typically have been undertaken by officials within the Executive Branch. As we noted above, however, the independent counsel is an inferior officer under the Appointments Clause, with limited jurisdiction and tenure and lacking policymaking or significant administrative authority. Although the counsel exercises no small amount of discretion and judgment in deciding how to carry out her duties under the Act, we simply do not see how the President's need to control the exercise of that discretion is so central to the functioning of the Executive Branch as to require as a matter of constitutional law that the counsel be terminable at will by the President.

Nor do we think that the "good cause" removal provision at issue here impermissibly burdens the President's power to control or supervise the independent counsel, as an executive official, in the execution of her duties under the Act. This is not a case in which the power to remove an executive official has been completely stripped from the President, thus providing no means for the President to ensure the "faithful execution" of the laws. Rather, because the independent counsel may be terminated for "good cause," the Executive, through the Attorney General, retains ample authority to assure that the counsel is competently performing her statutory responsibilities in a manner that comports with the provisions of the Act. Although we need not decide in this case exactly what is encompassed within the term "good cause" under the Act, the legislative history of the removal provision also makes clear that the Attorney General may remove an independent counsel for "misconduct." See H.R.Conf.Rep. No. 100–452, p. 37 (1987). Here, as with the provision of the Act conferring the appointment authority of the independent counsel on the special court, the congressional determination to limit the removal power of the Attorney General was essential, in the view of Congress, to establish the necessary independence of the office. We do not think that this limitation as it presently stands sufficiently deprives the President of control over the independent counsel to interfere impermissibly with his constitutional obligation to ensure the faithful execution of the laws.

B

The final question to be addressed is whether the Act, taken as a whole, violates the principle of separation of powers by unduly interfering with the role of the Executive Branch. Time and again we have reaffirmed the importance in our constitutional scheme of the separation of governmental powers into the three coordinate branches. See, e.g., Bowsher v. Synar, 478 U.S., at 725 (citing *Humphrey's Executor*, 295 U.S., at 629–630). As we stated in Buckley v. Valeo, 424 U.S. 1 (1976), the system of separated powers and checks and balances established in the Constitution was regarded by the Framers as "a self-executing safeguard against the encroachment or aggrandizement of one branch at the expense of the other." Id., at 122. We have not hesitated to invalidate provisions of law which violate this principle. See id., at 123. On the other hand, we have never held that the Constitution requires that the three Branches of Government "operate with absolute independence." United States v. Nixon, 418 U.S., at 707; see also Nixon v. Administrator of General Services, 433 U.S. 425, 442 (1977) (citing James Madison in The Federalist No. 47, and Joseph Story in 1 Commentaries on the Constitution § 525 (M. Bigelow, 5th ed. 1905)). In the often-quoted words of Justice Jackson,

"While the Constitution diffuses power the better to secure liberty, it also contemplates that practice will integrate the dispersed powers into a workable government. It enjoins upon its branches separateness but interdependence, autonomy but reciprocity." Youngstown Sheet & Tube Co. v. Sawyer, 343 U.S. 579, 635 (1952) (concurring opinion).

We observe first that this case does not involve an attempt by Congress to increase its own powers at the expense of the Executive Branch. Cf. Commodity Futures Trading Comm'n v. Schor, 478 U.S., at 856. Unlike some of our previous cases, most recently Bowsher v. Synar, this case simply does not pose a "dange[r] of congressional usurpation of Executive Branch functions." 478 U.S., at 727; see also INS v. Chadha, 462 U.S. 919, 958 (1983). Indeed, with the exception of the power of impeachment—which applies to all officers of the United States—Congress retained for itself no powers of control or supervision over an independent counsel. The Act does empower certain members of Congress to request the Attorney General to apply for the appointment of an independent counsel, but the Attorney General has no duty to comply with the request, although he must respond within a certain time limit. § 529(g). Other than that, Congress' role under the Act is limited to receiving reports or other information and oversight of the independent counsel's activities, § 595(a), functions that we have recognized generally as being incidental to the legislative function of Congress. See McGrain v. Daugherty, 273 U.S. 135, 174 (1927).

Similarly, we do not think that the Act works any *judicial* usurpation of properly executive functions. As should be apparent from our discussion of the Appointments Clause above, the power to appoint inferior officers such as independent counsels is not in itself an "executive" function in the constitutional sense, at least when Congress has exercised its power to vest the appointment of an inferior office in the "courts of Law." We note nonetheless that under the Act the Special Division has no power to appoint an independent counsel *sua sponte;* it may only do so upon the specific request of the Attorney General, and the courts are specifically prevented from reviewing the Attorney General's decision not to seek appointment, § 592(f). In addition, once the court has appointed a counsel and defined her jurisdiction, it has no power to supervise or control the activities of the counsel. As we pointed out in our discussion of the Special Division in relation to Article III, the various powers delegated by the statute to the Division are not supervisory or administrative, nor are they functions that the Constitution requires be performed by officials within the Executive Branch. The Act does give a federal court the power to review the Attorney General's decision to remove an independent counsel, but in our view this is a function that is well within the traditional power of the judiciary.

Finally, we do not think that the Act "impermissibly undermine[s]" the powers of the Executive Branch, *Schor,* supra, at 856, or "disrupts the proper balance between the coordinate branches [by] prevent[ing] the Executive Branch from accomplishing its constitutionally assigned functions," Nixon v. Administrator of General Services, supra, at 443. It is undeniable that the Act reduces the amount of control or supervision that the Attorney General and, through him, the President exercises over the investigation and prosecution of a certain class of alleged criminal activity.... Nonetheless, the Act does give the Attorney General several means of supervising or controlling the prosecutorial powers that may be wielded by an independent counsel.... Notwithstanding the fact that the counsel is to some degree "independent" and free from Executive supervision to a greater extent than other federal prosecutors, in our view these features of the Act give the Executive Branch sufficient control over the independent counsel to ensure that the President is able to perform his constitutionally assigned duties.

VI

In sum, we conclude today that it does not violate the Appointments Clause for Congress to vest the appointment of independent counsels in the Special Division; that the powers exercised by the Special Division under the Act do not violate Article III; and that the Act does not violate the separation of powers principle by impermissibly interfering with the functions of the Executive Branch. The decision of the Court of Appeals is therefore

Reversed.

Justice Kennedy took no part in the consideration or decision of this case.

Justice Scalia, dissenting.

. . .

II

. . . [W]hile I will subsequently discuss why our appointments and removal jurisprudence does not support today's holding, I begin with a consideration of the fountainhead of that jurisprudence, the separation and equilibration of powers.

. . .

. . . It seems to me . . . that the decision of the Court of Appeals invalidating the present statute must be upheld on fundamental separation-of-powers principles if the following two questions are answered affirmatively: (1) Is the conduct of a criminal prosecution (and of an investigation to decide whether to prosecute) the exercise of purely executive power? (2) Does the statute deprive the President of the United States of exclusive control over the exercise of that power? Surprising to say, the Court appears to concede an affirmative answer to both questions, but seeks to avoid the inevitable conclusion that since the statute vests some purely executive power in a person who is not the President of the United States it is void.

. . .

. . . [I]t is ultimately irrelevant *how much* the statute reduces presidential control. The case is over when the Court acknowledges, as it must, that "[i]t is undeniable that the Act reduces the amount of control or supervision that the Attorney General and, through him, the President exercises over the investigation and prosecution of a certain class of alleged criminal activity." . . .

. . .

Is it unthinkable that the President should have such exclusive power, even when alleged crimes by him or his close associates are at issue? No more so than that Congress should have the exclusive power of legislation, even when what is at issue is its own exemption from the burdens of certain laws. . . . No more so than that this Court should have the exclusive power to pronounce the final decision on justiciable cases and controversies, even those pertaining to the constitutionality of a statute reducing the salaries of the Justices. . . . A system of separate and coordinate powers necessarily involves an acceptance of exclusive power that can theoretically be abused. . . . While the separation of powers may prevent us from righting every wrong, it does so in order to ensure that we do not lose liberty. The checks against any Branch's abuse of its exclusive powers are twofold: First, retaliation by one of the other Branch's use of *its* exclusive powers: Congress, for example, can impeach the Executive who willfully fails to enforce the laws; the Executive can decline to prosecute under unconstitutional statutes ...; and the courts can dismiss malicious prosecutions: Second, and ultimately, there is the political check that the people will replace those in the political branches ... who are guilty of abuse. Political pressures produced special prosecutors—for Teapot Dome and for Watergate, for example—long before this statute created the independent counsel....

. . .

III

Because appellant (who all parties and the Court agree is an officer of the United States) was not appointed by the President with the advice and consent of the Senate, but rather by the Special Division of the United States Court of Appeals, her appointment is constitutional only if (1) she is an "inferior" officer within the meaning of the above clause, and (2) Congress may vest her appointment in a court of law.

. . .

That "inferior" means "subordinate" is ... consistent with what little we know about the evolution of the Appointments Clause....

. . .

The independent counsel is not even subordinate to the President....

Because appellant is not subordinate to another officer, she is not an "inferior" officer and her appointment other than by the President with the advice and consent of the Senate is unconstitutional.

IV

... [T]he restrictions upon the removal of the independent counsel also violate our established precedent dealing with that specific subject....

. . .

Since our 1935 decision in Humphrey's Executor v. United States, 295 U.S. 602—which was considered by many at the time the product of an activist, anti-New Deal court bent on reducing the power of President Franklin Roosevelt—it has been established that the line of permissible restriction upon removal of principal officers lies at the point at which the powers exercised by those officers are no longer purely executive....

One can hardly grieve for the shoddy treatment given today to *Humphrey's Executor,* which, after all, accorded the same indignity (with much less justification) to Chief Justice Taft's opinion 10 years earlier in Myers v. United States, supra—gutting, in six quick pages devoid of textual or historical precedent for the novel principle it set forth ... *Humphrey's Executor* at least had the decency formally to observe the constitutional principle that the President had to be the repository of *all* executive power, see 295 U.S., at 627–628, which, as *Myers* carefully explained, necessarily means that he must be able to discharge those who do not perform executive functions according to his liking....

V

Under our system of government, the primary check against prosecutorial abuse is a political one. The prosecutors who exercise this awesome discretion are selected and can be removed by a President, whom the people have trusted enough to elect. Moreover, when crimes are not investigated and prosecuted fairly, nonselectively, with a reasonable sense of proportion, the President pays the cost in political damage to his administration. . . .

. . .

. . . [The Court] extends into the very heart of our most significant constitutional function the "totality of the circumstances" mode of analysis that this Court has in recent years become fond of. Taking all things into account, we conclude that the power taken away from the President here is not really *too* much. . . .

The ad hoc approach to constitutional adjudication has real attraction, even apart from its work-saving potential. It is guaranteed to produce a result, in every case, that will make a majority of the Court happy with the law. The law is, by definition, precisely what the majority thinks, taking all things into account, it *ought* to be. I prefer to rely upon the judgment of the wise men who constructed our system, and of the people who approved it, and of two centuries of history that have shown it to be sound. Like it or not, that judgment says, quite plainly, that "[t]he executive Power shall be vested in a President of the United States."

C.   IMPEACHMENT

Article II, Section 4, of the Constitution provides that the President, the Vice President "and all civil officers of the United States" may be removed from office on impeachment for, and conviction of "treason, bribery or other high crimes and misdemeanors." Article I, Section 2, provides that the House of Representatives "shall have the sole power of impeachment" and Article I, Section 3, vests "the sole power to try all impeachments" in the Senate. The aborted proceedings looking toward the impeachment of President Nixon in 1974 raised two major unresolved legal issues. Are only violations of the criminal law "high crimes and misdemeanors"? May a person impeached and convicted obtain judicial review? The Report of the Committee on Federal Legislation of the Association of the Bar of the City of New York, *The Law of Presidential Impeachment,* 29 The Record 154 (1974), concludes that: grounds for impeachment are not limited to or synonymous with criminal offenses, but are acts that "undermine the integrity of government"; judicial review is inappropriate both because the Constitution textually commits the issues to the House and Senate, and because those issues are not judicially manageable.[1]

SECTION 3.   PRESIDENTIAL AND CONGRESSIONAL IMMUNITIES

United States v. Nixon

418 U.S. 683, 94 S.Ct. 3090, 41 L.Ed.2d 1039 (1974).

Mr. Chief Justice Burger delivered the opinion of the Court.

This litigation presents for review the denial of a motion, filed on behalf of the President of the United States, in the case of United States v. Mitchell et

---

[1] The possible Nixon impeachment also renewed interest in the many procedural problems involved in House impeachment and Senate trial. See Firmage & Mangrum, *Removal of the President: Resignation and the Procedural Law of Impeachment,* 1974 Duke L.J. 1023.

al. (D.C.Crim. No. 74–110), to quash a third-party subpoena *duces tecum* issued by the United States District Court for the District of Columbia, pursuant to Fed.Rule Crim.Proc. 17(c). The subpoena directed the President to produce certain tape recordings and documents relating to his conversations with aides and advisers. The court rejected the President's claims of absolute executive privilege, of lack of jurisdiction, and of failure to satisfy the requirements of Rule 17(c). The President appealed to the Court of Appeals. We granted the United States' petition for certiorari before judgment, . . . because of the public importance of the issues presented and the need for their prompt resolution, 417 U.S. 927 and 960 (1974).

On March 1, 1974, a grand jury of the United States District Court for the District of Columbia returned an indictment charging seven named individuals[3] with various offenses, including conspiracy to defraud the United States and to obstruct justice. Although he was not designated as such in the indictment, the grand jury named the President, among others, as an unindicted coconspirator. On April 18, 1974, upon motion of the Special Prosecutor, a subpoena *duces tecum* was issued pursuant to Rule 17(c) to the President by the United States District Court and made returnable on May 2, 1974. This subpoena required the production, in advance of the September 9 trial date, of certain tapes, memoranda, papers, transcripts, or other writings relating to certain precisely identified meetings between the President and others. The Special Prosecutor was able to fix the time, place and persons present at these discussions because the White House daily logs and appointment records had been delivered to him. On April 30, the President publicly released edited transcripts of 43 conversations; portions of 20 conversations subject to subpoena in the present case were included. On May 1, 1974, the President's counsel, filed a "special appearance" and a motion to quash the subpoena . . .

On May 20, 1974, the District Court denied the motion to quash . . . It further ordered "the President or any subordinate officer, official or employee with custody or control of the documents or objects subpoenaed," to deliver to the District Court, on or before May 31, 1974, the originals of all subpoenaed items, as well as an index and analysis of those items, together with tape copies of those portions of the subpoenaed recordings for which transcripts had been released to the public by the President on April 30. . . .

. . .

II.   JUSTICIABILITY

. . . [T]he President's counsel argued that the court lacked jurisdiction to issue the subpoena because the matter was an intrabranch dispute between a subordinate and superior officer of the Executive Branch and hence not subject to judicial resolution. . . .

. . .

Our starting point is the nature of the proceeding for which the evidence is sought—here a pending criminal prosecution. It is a judicial proceeding in a federal court alleging violation of federal laws and is brought in the name of the

---

[3] The seven defendants were John N. Mitchell, H.R. Haldeman, John D. Ehrlichman, Charles W. Colson, Robert C. Mardian, Kenneth W. Parkinson, and Gordon Strachan. Each had occupied either a position of responsibility on the White House staff or the Committee for the Re-election of the President. Colson entered a guilty plea on another charge and is no longer a defendant.

United States as sovereign.... Under the authority of Art. II, § 2, Congress has vested in the Attorney General the power to conduct the criminal litigation of the United States Government. 28 U.S.C. § 516. It has also vested in him the power to appoint subordinate officers to assist him in the discharge of his duties. 28 U.S.C. §§ 509, 510, 515, 533. Acting pursuant to those statutes, the Attorney General has delegated the authority to represent the United States in these particular matters to a Special Prosecutor with unique authority and tenure. The regulation gives the Special Prosecutor explicit power to contest the invocation of executive privilege in the process of seeking evidence deemed relevant to the performance of these specially delegated duties....

So long as this regulation is extant it has the force of law....

... [I]t is theoretically possible for the Attorney General to amend or revoke the regulation defining the Special Prosecutor's authority. But he has not done so. So long as this regulation remains in force the Executive Branch is bound by it, and indeed the United States as the sovereign composed of the three branches is bound to respect and to enforce it. Moreover, the delegation of authority to the Special Prosecutor in this case is not an ordinary delegation by the Attorney General to a subordinate officer: with the authorization of the President, the Acting Attorney General provided in the regulation that the Special Prosecutor was not to be removed without the "consensus" of eight designated leaders of Congress.

. . .

IV. THE CLAIM OF PRIVILEGE

A.

... [W]e turn to the claim that the subpoena should be quashed because it demands "confidential conversations between a President and his close advisors that it would be inconsistent with the public interest to produce." The first contention is a broad claim that the separation of powers doctrine precludes judicial review of a President's claim of privilege. The second contention is that if he does not prevail on the claim of absolute privilege, the court should hold as a matter of constitutional law that the privilege prevails over the subpoena *duces tecum*.

In the performance of assigned constitutional duties each branch of the Government must initially interpret the Constitution, and the interpretation of its powers by any branch is due great respect from the others. The President's counsel, as we have noted, reads the Constitution as providing an absolute privilege of confidentiality for all presidential communications. Many decisions of this Court, however, have unequivocally reaffirmed the holding of Marbury v. Madison, 1 Cranch 137 (1803), that "it is emphatically the province and duty of the judicial department to say what the law is." Id., at 177.

. . .

Notwithstanding the deference each branch must accord the others, the "judicial Power of the United States" vested in the federal courts by Art. III, § 1 of the Constitution can no more be shared with the Executive Branch than the Chief Executive, for example, can share with the Judiciary the veto power, or the Congress share with the Judiciary the power to override a presidential veto. Any other conclusion would be contrary to the basic concept of separation of powers and the checks and balances that flow from the scheme of a tripartite government. The Federalist, No. 47, p. 313 (C.F. Mittel ed. 1938). We therefore reaffirm that it is "emphatically the province and the duty" of this Court "to say what the law is" with respect to the claim of privilege presented in this case. Marbury v. Madison, supra, at 177.

B.

In support of his claim of absolute privilege the President's counsel urges two grounds one of which is common to all governments and one of which is peculiar to our system of separation of powers. The first ground is the valid need for protection of communications between high Government officials and those who advise and assist them in the performance of their manifold duties; the importance of this confidentiality is too plain to require further discussion. Human experience teaches that those who expect public dissemination of their remarks may well temper candor with a concern for appearances and for their own interests to the detriment of the decisionmaking process. Whatever the nature of the privilege of confidentiality of presidential communications in the exercise of Art. II powers, the privilege can be said to derive from the supremacy of each branch within its own assigned area of constitutional duties. Certain powers and privileges flow from the nature of enumerated powers; the protection of the confidentiality of Presidential communications has similar constitutional underpinnings.

The second ground asserted by the President's counsel in support of the claim of absolute privilege rests on the doctrine of separation of powers. Here it is argued that the independence of the Executive Branch within its own sphere insulates a president from a judicial subpoena in an ongoing criminal prosecution, and thereby protects confidential Presidential communications.

However, neither the doctrine of separation of powers, nor the need for confidentiality of high level communications without more, can sustain an absolute, unqualified Presidential privilege of immunity from judicial process under all circumstances. The President's need for complete candor and objectivity from advisers calls for great deference from the courts. However, when the privilege depends solely on the broad, undifferentiated claim of public interest in the confidentiality of such conversations, a confrontation with other values arises. Absent a claim of need to protect military, diplomatic or sensitive national security secrets, we find it difficult to accept the argument that even the very important interest in confidentiality of Presidential communications is significantly diminished by production of such material for *in camera* inspection with all the protection that a district court will be obliged to provide.

The impediment that an absolute, unqualified privilege would place in the way of the primary constitutional duty of the Judicial Branch to do justice in criminal prosecutions would plainly conflict with the function of the courts under Art. III. In designing the structure of our Government and dividing and allocating the sovereign power among three coequal branches, the Framers of the Constitution sought to provide a comprehensive system, but the separate powers were not intended to operate with absolute independence. . . . To read the Art. II powers of the President as providing an absolute privilege as against a subpoena essential to enforcement of criminal statutes on no more than a generalized claim of the public interest in confidentiality of nonmilitary and nondiplomatic discussions would upset the constitutional balance of "a workable government" and gravely impair the role of the courts under Art. III.

C.

Since we conclude that the legitimate needs of the judicial process may outweigh Presidential privilege, it is necessary to resolve those competing interests in a manner that preserves the essential functions of each branch.

The right and indeed the duty to resolve that question does not free the Judiciary from according high respect to the representations made on behalf of the President....

... The privilege is fundamental to the operation of Government and inextricably rooted in the separation of powers under the Constitution. In Nixon v. Sirica, 159 U.S.App.D.C. 58, 487 F.2d 700 (1973), the Court of Appeals held that such Presidential communications are "presumptively privileged," and this position is accepted by both parties in the present litigation. We agree with Mr. Chief Justice Marshall's observation, therefore, that "in no case of this kind would a court be required to proceed against the president as against an ordinary individual." United States v. Burr, 25 F.Cas. at 192 (No. 14,694) (C.C.D.Va.1807).

But this presumptive privilege must be considered in light of our historic commitment to the rule of law.... The very integrity of the judicial system and public confidence in the system depend on full disclosure of all the facts, within the framework of the rules of evidence. To ensure that justice is done, it is imperative to the function of courts that compulsory process be available for the production of evidence needed either by the prosecution or by the defense.

. . .

In this case the President ... does not place his claim of privilege on the ground they are military or diplomatic secrets. As to these areas of Art. II duties the courts have traditionally shown the utmost deference to Presidential responsibilities....

No case of the Court, however, has extended this high degree of deference to a President's generalized interest in confidentiality. Nowhere in the Constitution, as we have noted earlier, is there any explicit reference to a privilege of confidentiality, yet to the extent this interest relates to the effective discharge of a President's powers, it is constitutionally based.

. . .

In this case we must weigh the importance of the general privilege of confidentiality of Presidential communications in performance of the President's responsibilities against the inroads of such a privilege on the fair administration of criminal justice. The interest in preserving confidentiality is weighty indeed and entitled to great respect. However we cannot conclude that advisers will be moved to temper the candor of their remarks by the infrequent occasions of disclosure because of the possibility that such conversations will be called for in the context of a criminal prosecution.

. . .

We conclude that when the ground for asserting privilege as to subpoenaed materials sought for use in a criminal trial is based only on the generalized interest in confidentiality, it cannot prevail over the fundamental demands of due process of law in the fair administration of criminal justice. The generalized assertion of privilege must yield to the demonstrated, specific need for evidence in a pending criminal trial.

. . .

Since this matter came before the Court during the pendency of a criminal prosecution, and on representations that time is of the essence, the mandate shall issue forthwith.

Affirmed.[a]

Mr. Justice Rehnquist took no part in the consideration or decision of these cases.

NIXON v. ADMINISTRATOR OF GENERAL SERVICES, 433 U.S. 425 (1977). The Presidential Recordings and Materials Preservation Act of 1974 directed the Administrator to take custody of former President Nixon's papers and tapes, to provide for their screening by archivists for the purpose of returning personal and private materials, and to determine conditions for public access. The public access regulations were to take into account seven factors, including "the need to protect any party's opportunity to assert any legally or constitutionally based right or privilege. . . ." The day after the Act was signed into law by President Ford, this suit was brought in the District Court for the District of Columbia, challenging the constitutionality of the law on numerous grounds, including separation of powers and Presidential privilege. The Court affirmed the lower court's dismissal of the complaint. On the issue of separation of powers, the Court noted that the Act entrusted the documents to the Executive Branch, and, as with other statutory requirements for disclosure of documents in possession of the Executive Branch (such as the Freedom of Information Act), regulation of material generated in the Executive Branch had never been considered an invasion of its autonomy. With respect to the claim of Presidential privilege, the Court rejected an argument that the privilege could be claimed only by the incumbent President. On the other hand, the fact that neither President Ford nor President Carter supported President Nixon's claim of Presidential privilege "detracts from the weight of his contention that the Act impermissibly intrudes into the executive function." Justice Brennan's opinion for the Court continued:

"The appellant bases his claim of Presidential privilege in this case on the assertion that the potential disclosure of communications given to the appellant in confidence would adversely affect the ability of future Presidents to obtain the candid advice necessary for effective decisionmaking. We are called upon to adjudicate that claim, however, only with respect to the process by which the materials will be screened and catalogued by professional archivists. For any eventual public access will be governed by the guidelines of § 104, ...

. . .

"In short, we conclude that the screening process contemplated by the Act will not constitute a more severe intrusion into Presidential confidentiality than the *in camera* inspection by the District Court approved in United States v. Nixon, 418 U.S., at 706. We must of course presume that the Administrator and the career archivists concerned will carry out the duties assigned to them by the Act. Thus, there is no basis for appellant's claim that the Act 'reverses' the presumption in favor of confidentiality of Presidential papers recognized in *United States v. Nixon.* Appellant's right to assert the privilege is specifically preserved by the Act. The guideline provisions on their face are as broad as the privilege itself. If the broadly written protections of the Act should nevertheless prove inadequate to safeguard appellant's rights or to prevent usurpation of executive powers, there will be time enough to consider that problem in a specific factual context. For the present, we hold, in agreement with the District Court, that the Act on its face does not violate the Presidential privilege."

---

[a] For discussions of United States v. Nixon, see *Symposium: United States v. Nixon,* 22 UCLA L.Rev. 4–140 (1974); Freund, *On Presidential Privilege,* 88 Harv.L.Rev. 13 (1974); Cox, *Executive Privilege,* 122 U.Pa. L.Rev. 1383 (1974).

Justices Powell and Blackmun concurred in the judgment. Justice Powell noted that "the difficult constitutional questions lie ahead" when regulations governing access are promulgated, since the Court's decision was limited to the facial validity of the Act. The Chief Justice and Justice Rehnquist dissented. As to the issue of confidential Presidential communications, Justice Rehnquist said, in part:

"The critical factor in all of this is not that confidential material might be disclosed, since the President himself might choose to 'go public' with it. The critical factor is that the determination as to whether to disclose is wrested by the Act from the President. When one speaks in confidence to a President, he necessarily relies upon the President's discretion not to disclose the sensitive. The President similarly relies on the discretion of a subordinate when instructing him. Thus it is no answer to suggest, as does the Court, that the expectation of confidentiality has always been limited because Presidential papers have in the past been turned over to Presidential libraries or otherwise subsequently disclosed. In those cases, ultimate reliance was upon the discretion of the President to cull the sensitive before disclosure. But when, as is the case under this Act, the decision whether to disclose no longer resides in the President, communication will inevitably be restrained."

NIXON v. FITZGERALD, 457 U.S. 731 (1982). The Court held that the President is absolutely immune from damage claims for any acts within the "outer perimeter" of his official responsibility. The Court concluded that lesser immunity would "subject the President to trial on virtually every allegation that an action was unlawful, or was taken for a forbidden purpose."

The four dissenting Justices argued that the President should enjoy only qualified immunity, in the absence of a showing "that the absence of absolute immunity will substantially impair his ability to carry out particular functions that are his Constitutional responsibility."[1]

In a footnote, the Court reserved the question whether Congress could expressly create a damage action against the President on behalf of wronged individuals. The dissent argued, however, that the Court's rationale would also invalidate Congressional efforts to create a statutory action against the President. In a separate concurrence, Chief Justice Burger argued that absolute Presidential immunity from civil claims is mandated by the "constitutional doctrine of separation of powers."

THE SPEECH OR DEBATE CLAUSE

Article I, Section 6, of the Constitution provides that "for any speech or debate in either House, [Senators and Representatives] shall not be questioned in any other place." The Court has read this provision broadly to provide immunity against civil and criminal actions, and against actions brought by individuals as well as the executive. In Eastland v. United States Servicemen's

---

[1] In a companion case, Harlow v. Fitzgerald, 457 U.S. 800 (1982), the Court held that Presidential aides were entitled to only qualified immunity absent a showing that: (1) the aide's responsibilities embraced a function so sensitive as to require absolute immunity from civil actions; and (2) the act for which liability is claimed was in discharge of that sensitive function.

In Mitchell v. Forsyth, 472 U.S. 511 (1985), four of the seven Justices participating concluded that the Attorney General did not share the President's absolute immunity in authorizing a warrantless wiretap on national security grounds. A different majority concluded that the Attorney General's qualified immunity protected him from civil liability in the absence of proof of violation of "clearly established statutory or constitutional rights." In this case, the former Attorney General was not liable, because the legality of warrantless national security wiretaps was an open question at the time he acted.

Fund, 421 U.S. 491 (1975), for example, the clause was held to bar an injunction action seeking to block enforcement of a subpoena *duces tecum* issued by a Senate subcommittee. On the other hand, the clause only immunizes Senators and members of Congress, and their aides, from judicial inquiry into and sanctions imposed on "legislative acts." Thus the clause provided no immunity for a Senator's aide from grand jury questioning concerning arrangements for private publication of the Pentagon Papers[2], for a Senator from suit for defamation arising from statements in press releases and newsletters,[3] or for a member of Congress from prosecution for accepting a bribe in exchange for a promise to perform a legislative act in the future.[4]

In Davis v. Passman, 442 U.S. 228 (1979), the Court raised, but did not decide, the question whether the clause provided a member of Congress immunity from suit for discharge of an employee, who claimed that her discharge constituted unconstitutional gender discrimination. Justice Powell (joined by Chief Justice Burger and Justice Rehnquist) argued in dissent, however, that, whether or not the defendant's conduct was immunized by the speech or debate clause, "[a] Congressman simply cannot perform his constitutional duties effectively, or serve his constituents properly, unless he is supported by a staff in which he has total confidence."

---

[2] Gravel v. United States, 408 U.S. 606 (1972).

[3] Hutchinson v. Proxmire, 443 U.S. 111 (1979).

[4] United States v. Brewster, 408 U.S. 501 (1972). The clause, however, precludes the United States from proving in the bribery prosecution that the promised legislative act was performed, because this would inquire into a past legislative act, and the motives for performing it. United States v. Helstoski, 442 U.S. 477 (1979).

*

Part III

GOVERNMENT AND THE INDIVIDUAL: THE PROTECTION OF LIBERTY AND PROPERTY UNDER THE DUE PROCESS AND EQUAL PROTECTION CLAUSES

In this Part, the emphasis shifts from exploring the constitutional relationships among different parts of the governmental structure to the protection of individual rights from interference by all levels and branches of government. The central question is definition of the proper judicial role in giving content to the vague language of the due process clauses of the fifth and fourteenth amendments, and of the equal protection clause of the fourteenth amendment.

Chapter 8 concerns the interrelationship between the bill of rights and the Civil War amendments to the Constitution. Chapter 9 deals with the application of the due process clause. Chapter 10 discusses the equal protection clause. Chapter 11 completes the analysis with an examination of constitutional norms of fair procedure. (The discrete problems of constitutional protection of speech and conscience under the first amendment are reserved for Part IV.)

Chapter 12 returns to an issue of division of national and state power. After examining the application of the Civil War amendments to private conduct, the bulk of this chapter concerns the extent of Congressional power to enforce the amendments.

CHAPTER 8

THE BILL OF RIGHTS, THE CIVIL WAR AMENDMENTS AND THEIR INTER-RELATIONSHIP

Introduction. In Chapter 1 it was noted that the original constitution included only a few limitations upon government power to regulate life, liberty and property. The principal restraints on state regulation were those forbidding the impairment of the obligation of contracts (Art. I, § 10), banning bills of attainder and ex post facto laws (Art. I, § 10), and guaranteeing citizens of one state the right to enjoy in another state "all the Privileges and Immunities" of its own citizens (Art. IV, § 2).

The Bill of Rights (Amendments 1–10) adopted in 1791 imposed a substantial series of protections for the individual against government. Almost 80 years later the Civil War Amendments (13, 14, and 15) specifically imposed restraints on the power of states to regulate the personal and property interests of their citizens.

The primary purpose of this Chapter is to give a brief historical introduction to the Court's application of these three sets of restraints on the power of government to regulate liberty and property. A major focus will be the dispute over the interrelationship between the Bill of Rights and the Civil War Amendments.

Early interpretations of the individual rights provisions contained in the text of the original Constitution, the Bill of Rights, and the Civil War Amendments should be augmented, however, by a preliminary reference to the possibility of nontextual constitutional restraints stemming from principles of natural justice invoked and elaborated by courts. This possibility was raised early in Calder v. Bull, 3 U.S. (3 Dall.) 386 (1798), where two Justices sharply disagreed, in an historically important exchange of *dicta*, over the propriety of basing a determination of unconstitutionality on principles not specified in the Constitution. Justice Chase upheld the challenged state law, but wrote:

> "I cannot subscribe to the omnipotence of a state Legislature, or that it is absolute and without control; although its authority should not be expressly restrained by the constitution, or fundamental law, of the state. The people of the United States erected their constitutions or forms of government, to establish justice, to promote the general welfare, to secure the blessings of liberty, and to protect their persons and property from violence. The purposes for which men enter into society will determine the nature and terms of the social compact; and as they are the foundation of the legislative power, they will decide what are the proper objects of it: The nature, and ends of legislative power will limit the exercise of it. This fundamental principle flows from the very nature of our free Republican governments, that no man should be compelled to do what the laws do not require; nor to refrain from acts which the laws permit. There are acts

which the federal, or state, Legislature cannot do, without exceeding their authority. There are certain vital principles in our free Republican governments, which will determine and overrule an apparent and flagrant abuse of legislative power; as to authorize manifest injustice by positive law; or to take away that security for personal liberty, or private property, for the protection whereof the government was established. An act of the Legislature (for I cannot call it a law) contrary to the great first principles of the social compact, cannot be considered a rightful exercise of legislative authority.... A few instances will suffice to explain what I mean. A law that punished a citizen for an innocent action, or, in other words, for an act, which, when done, was in violation of no existing law; a law that destroys, or impairs, the lawful private contracts of citizens; a law that makes a man a judge in his own cause; or a law that takes property from A. and gives it to B. It is against all reason and justice, for a people to entrust a Legislature with such powers; and, therefore, it cannot be presumed that they have done it. The genius, the nature, and the spirit, of our state governments, amount to a prohibition of such acts of legislation; and the general principles of law and reason forbid them.... To maintain that our federal, or state, Legislature possesses such powers, if they had not been expressly restrained, would, in my opinion, be a political heresy, altogether inadmissible in our free republican governments."

Justice Iredell responded:

"[S]ome speculative jurists have held, that a legislative act against natural justice must, in itself, be void; but I cannot think that, under such a government, any court of justice would possess a power to declare it so....

"[I]t has been the policy of all the American States, which have, individually, framed their state constitutions since the revolution, and of the people of the United States, when they framed the federal constitution, to define with precision the objects of the legislative power, and to restrain its exercise within marked and settled boundaries. If any act of Congress, or of the legislature of a state, violates those constitutional provisions, it is unquestionably void.... If on the other hand, the legislature of the union, or the legislature of any member of the union, shall pass a law, within the general scope of their constitutional power, the court cannot pronounce it to be void, merely because it is, in their judgment, contrary to the principles of natural justice. The ideas of natural justice are regulated by no fixed standard; the ablest and the purest men have differed upon the subject; and all that the court could properly say, in such an event, would be, that the legislature (possessed of an equal right of opinion) had passed an act which, in the opinion of the judges, was inconsistent with the abstract principles of natural justice."

The substance of this debate has been a continuing theme in constitutional law, whether framed as a debate about an expansive interpretation of an open-ended text or about a "noninterpretive" principle of fundamental right. For discussion of the contemporary dimensions of the debate, compare Grey, *Do We Have an Unwritten Constitution?*, 27 Stan.L.Rev. 703 (1975); Perry, *The Constitution, The Courts, and Human Rights* (1982); and Sedler, *The Legitimacy Debate in Constitutional Adjudication*, 44 Ohio St.L.J. 10 (1983); with Ely,

Foreword: On Discovering Fundamental Values, 92 Harv.L.Rev. 5 (1978); and Linde, *Judges, Critics, and the Realist Tradition,* 82 Yale L.J. 227 (1972).

SECTION 1.   THE PRE–CIVIL WAR BACKGROUND

A.   THE CONTRACT CLAUSE AND THE PRIVILEGES AND IMMUNITIES CLAUSE OF ARTICLE IV—EARLY INTERPRETATIONS

THE CONTRACT CLAUSE

The first case in which the Supreme Court held a state statute to be in conflict with the constitution involved the contract clause. In Fletcher v. Peck, 10 U.S. (6 Cranch.) 87 (1810), the Court held invalid an act of the Georgia legislature rescinding a sale of land it had previously approved. Marshall writing for the Court held that the contract clause applied to public contracts and that a grant of land constituted a contract not to reassert rights over the land granted. In invalidating the law he relied both on the contract clause and on the more general notion that "the nature of society and of government [ ]prescribe some limits to the legislative power."

The Court went on to decide a large number of cases under the contract clause.

> "During the nineteenth century no constitutional clause was so frequently the basis of decision by the Supreme Court of the United States as that forbidding the states to pass laws impairing the obligation of contracts. If we exclude the commerce clause as being primarily a grant of power to the national government, although it is significant because of its treatment as a restriction on state powers, the contract clause was the constitutional justification for more cases involving the validity of state laws than all of the other clauses of the Constitution together."

Wright, *The Contract Clause of the Constitution* xi (1938).

No attempt is made here to review the early cases. Much of the historical material is discussed in two modern cases, Allied Structural Steel Co. v. Spannaus, 438 U.S. 234 (1978), and United States Trust Co. of New York v. New Jersey, 431 U.S. 1 (1977), both set out, infra, Chapter 9.

THE PRIVILEGES AND IMMUNITIES CLAUSE OF ARTICLE IV

CORFIELD v. CORYELL, 4 Wash.C.C. 371, 6 Fed.Cas. 546 (1823). A New Jersey statute of 1820 made it unlawful for any person who was not "an actual inhabitant and resident" of the state to rake or gather clams, oysters, or shells in any of the rivers, bays, or waters of the state. The statute was challenged by a Pennsylvania citizen gathering oysters in New Jersey waters. In disposing of the claim made under Article IV, section 2, Supreme Court Justice Washington, sitting on circuit, said:

"The next question is, whether this act infringes that section of the constitution which declares that 'the citizens of each state shall be entitled to all the privileges and immunities of citizens in the several states?' The inquiry is, what are the privileges and immunities of citizens in the several states? We feel no hesitation in confining these expressions to those privileges and immunities which are, in their nature, fundamental; which belong, of right, to the citizens of all free governments; and which have, at all times, been enjoyed by the citizens of the several states which compose this Union, from the time of their becoming free, independent, and sovereign. What these fundamental principles are, it would perhaps be more tedious than difficult to enumerate. They may, however, be all comprehended under the following general heads: Protection by the government; the enjoyment of life and liberty, with the right to acquire and possess property of every kind, and to pursue and obtain happiness and safety; subject nevertheless to such restraints as the government may justly prescribe for the general good of the whole. The right of a citizen of one state to pass through, or to reside in any other state, for purposes of trade, agriculture, professional pursuits, or otherwise; to claim the benefit of the writ of habeas corpus; to institute and maintain actions of any kind in the courts of the state; to take hold and dispose of property, either real or personal; and an exemption from higher taxes or impositions than are paid by the other citizens of the state; may be mentioned as some of the particular privileges and immunities of citizens, which are clearly embraced by the general description of privileges deemed to be fundamental: to which may be added, the elective franchise, as regulated and established by the laws or constitution of the state in which it is to be exercised. These, and many others which might be mentioned, are, strictly speaking, privileges and immunities, and the enjoyment of them by the citizens of each state, in every other state, was manifestly calculated (to use the expressions of the preamble of the corresponding provision in the old articles of confederation) 'the better to secure and perpetuate mutual friendship and intercourse among the people of the different states of the Union.' But we cannot accede to the proposition which was insisted on by the counsel, that, under this provision of the constitution, the citizens of the several states are permitted to participate in all the rights which belong exclusively to the citizens of any other particular state, merely upon the ground that they are enjoyed by those citizens; much less, that in regulating the use of the common property of the citizens of such state, the legislature is bound to extend to the citizens of all the other states the same advantages as are secured to their own citizens. A several fishery, either as the right to it respects running fish, or such as are stationary, such as oysters, clams, and the like, is as much the property of the individual to whom it belongs, as dry land, or land covered by water; and is equally protected by the laws of the state against the aggressions of others, whether citizens or strangers. Where those private rights do not exist to the exclusion of the common right, that of fishing belongs to all the citizens or subjects of the state. It is the property of all; to be enjoyed by them in subordination to the laws which regulate its use. They may be considered as tenants in common of this property; and they are so exclusively entitled to the use of it, that it cannot be enjoyed by others without the tacit consent, or the express permission of the sovereign who has the power to regulate its use."

PAUL v. VIRGINIA, 75 U.S. (8 Wall.) 168, 180 (1868). The Court upheld a state law imposing special burdens on insurance companies incorporated in other states as a condition of doing business on the ground that a corporation is not a citizen protected by the privileges and immunities clause of Article IV. In construing the clause the Court said:

"It was undoubtedly the object of the clause in question to place the citizens of each State upon the same footing with citizens of other States, so far as the advantages resulting from citizenship in those States are concerned. It relieves them from the disabilities of alienage in other States; it inhibits discriminating legislation against them by other States; it gives them the right of free ingress into other States, and egress from them; it insures to them in other States the same freedom possessed by the citizens of those States in the acquisition and enjoyment of property and in the pursuit of happiness; and it secures to them in other States the equal protection of their laws. It has been justly said that no provision in the Constitution has tended so strongly to constitute the citizens of the United States one people as this. Lemmon v. People, 20 N.Y. 607.

"Indeed, without some provision of the kind removing from the citizens of each State the disabilities of alienage in the other States, and giving them equality of privilege with citizens of those States, the Republic would have constituted little more than a league of States; it would not have constituted the Union which now exists.

"But the privileges and immunities secured to citizens of each State in the several States, by the provision in question, are those privileges and immunities which are common to the citizens in the latter States under their Constitution and laws by virtue of their being citizens. Special privileges enjoyed by citizens in their own States are not secured in other States by this provision. It was not intended by the provision to give to the laws of one State any operation in other States. They can have no such operation, except by the permission, express or implied, of those States. The special privileges which they confer must, therefore, be enjoyed at home, unless the assent of other States to their enjoyment therein be given."

B.   THE BILL OF RIGHTS

Barron v. Mayor and City Council of Baltimore

32 U.S. (7 Pet.) 243, 8 L.Ed. 672 (1833).

[Barron brought an action on the case against the City of Baltimore. He presented evidence that municipal street construction diverted the flow of streams so that they deposited silt in front of his wharf, making the water so shallow that vessels could no longer reach the wharf. In the County Court Barron obtained a verdict for $45,000 that was reversed on appeal by the Maryland Circuit Court. By writ of error in the United States Supreme Court Barron contended that the state court had failed to grant his property the protection guaranteed it by the Fifth Amendment to the United States Constitution.]

Marshall, Ch. J., delivered the opinion of the court.

The judgment brought up by this writ of error having been rendered by the court of a state, this tribunal can exercise no jurisdiction over it, unless it be shown to come within the provisions of the 25th section of the judicial act. The plaintiff in error contends that it comes within that clause in the fifth amendment to the constitution, which inhibits the taking of private property for public use, without just compensation. He insists that this amendment, being in favor of the liberty of the citizen, ought to be so construed as to restrain the legislative power of a state, as well as that of the United States. If this proposition be untrue, the court can take no jurisdiction of the cause.

The question thus presented is, we think, of great importance, but not of much difficulty. The constitution was ordained and established by the people of the United States for themselves, for their own government, and not for the government of the individual states. Each state established a constitution for itself, and in that constitution, provided such limitations and restrictions on the powers of its particular government, as its judgment dictated. The people of the United States framed such a government for the United States as they supposed best adapted to their situation and best calculated to promote their interests. The powers they conferred on this government were to be exercised by itself; and the limitations on power, if expressed in general terms, are naturally, and, we think, necessarily, applicable to the government created by the instrument. They are limitations of power granted in the instrument itself; not of distinct governments, framed by different persons and for different purposes.

If these propositions be correct, the fifth amendment must be understood as restraining the power of the general government, not as applicable to the states. In their several constitutions, they have imposed such restrictions on their respective governments, as their own wisdom suggested; such as they deemed most proper for themselves. It is a subject on which they judge exclusively, and with which others interfere no further than they are supposed to have a common interest.

. . .

Had the people of the several states, or any of them, required changes in their constitutions; had they required additional safe-guards to liberty from the apprehended encroachments of their particular governments; the remedy was in their own hands, and could have been applied by themselves. A convention could have been assembled by the discontented state, and the required improvements could have been made by itself. The unwieldy and cumbrous machinery of procuring a recommendation from two-thirds of congress, and the assent of three-fourths of their sister states, could never have occurred to any human being, as a mode of doing that which might be effected by the state itself. Had the framers of these amendments intended them to be limitations on the powers of the state governments, they would have imitated the framers of the original constitution, and have expressed that intention. Had congress engaged in the extraordinary occupation of improving the constitutions of the several states, by affording the people additional protection from the exercise of power by their own governments, in matters which concerned themselves alone, they would have declared this purpose in plain and intelligible language.

But it is universally understood, it is a part of the history of the day, that the great revolution which established the constitution of the United States, was not effected without immense opposition. Serious fears were extensively entertained, that those powers which the patriot statesmen, who then watched over the interests of our country, deemed essential to union, and to the attainment of those invaluable objects for which union was sought, might be exercised in a manner dangerous to liberty. In almost every convention by which the constitution was adopted, amendments to guard against the abuse of power were recommended. These amendments demanded security against the apprehended encroachments of the general government—not against those of the local governments. In compliance with a sentiment thus generally expressed, to quiet fears thus extensively entertained, amendments were proposed by the required majority in congress, and adopted by the states. These amendments contain no expression indicating an intention to apply them to the state governments. This court cannot so apply them.

We are of opinion, that the provision in the fifth amendment to the constitution, declaring that private property shall not be taken for public use, without just compensation, is intended solely as a limitation on the exercise of power by the government of the United States, and is not applicable to the legislation of the states. We are, therefore, of opinion, that there is no repugnancy between the several acts of the general assembly of Maryland, given in evidence by the defendants at the trial of this cause, in the court of that state, and the constitution of the United States. This court, therefore, has no jurisdiction of the cause, and it is dismissed.

PRE–CIVIL WAR INTERPRETATIONS OF THE BILL OF RIGHTS

The decision in Barron v. Baltimore that the Bill of Rights was not designed to restrict actions of the states has been repeatedly affirmed by the Supreme Court. More striking is the fact that in the three-quarters of a century prior to the Civil War there were only a small handful of cases in which the Bill of Rights was invoked to challenge actions of the national government. See Wright, *The Growth of American Constitutional Law,* 77–78 (1942).

On two occasions, however, the Court did attempt to define the scope of the words "due process of law" in the fifth amendment. In Murray's Lessee v. Hoboken Land & Improvement Co., 59 U.S. (18 How.) 272 (1856), a fifth amendment challenge was made to a summary procedure used by the United States treasury to fix a lien on the property of a customs collector whose accounts were found to be short by over a million dollars. In upholding the procedure the Court said:

"The words, 'due process of law,' were undoubtedly intended to convey the same meaning as the words, 'by the law of the land,' in *Magna Charta.* Lord Coke, in his commentary on those words, (2 Inst. 50,) says they mean due process of law. The constitutions which had been adopted by the several States before the formation of the federal constitution, following the language of the great charter more closely, generally contained the words, 'but by the judgment of his peers, or the law of the land.' The ordinance of congress of July 13, 1787, for the government of the territory of the United States northwest of the River Ohio, used the same words.

"The constitution of the United States, as adopted, contained the provision, that 'the trial of all crimes, except in cases of impeachment, shall be by jury.' When the fifth article of amendment containing the words now in question was made, the trial by jury in criminal cases had thus already been provided for. By the sixth and seventh articles of amendment, further special provisions were separately made for that mode of trial in civil and criminal cases. To have followed, as in the state constitutions, and in the ordinance of 1787, the words of *Magna Charta,* and declared that no person shall be deprived of his life, liberty, or property but by the judgment of his peers or the law of the land, would have been in part superfluous and inappropriate. To have taken the clause, 'law of the land' without its immediate context, might possibly have given rise to doubts, which would be effectually dispelled by using those words which the great commentator on *Magna Charta* had declared to be the true meaning of the phrase, 'law of the land,' in that instrument, and which were undoubtedly then received as their true meaning.

"That the warrant now in question is legal process, is not denied. It was issued in conformity with an act of Congress. But is it 'due process of law?' The constitution contains no description of those processes which it was intended to allow or forbid. It does not even declare what principles are to be applied to ascertain whether it be due process. It is manifest that it was not left to the legislative power to enact any process which might be devised. The article is a restraint on the legislative as well as on the executive and judicial powers of the government, and cannot be so construed as to leave congress free to make any process 'due process of law,' by its mere will. To what principles, then, are we to resort to ascertain whether this process, enacted by congress, is due process? To this the answer must be twofold. We must examine the constitution itself, to see whether this process be in conflict with any of its provisions. If not found to be so, we must look to those settled usages and modes of proceeding existing in the common and statute law of England, before the emigration of our ancestors, and which are shown not to have been unsuited to their civil and political condition by having been acted on by them after the settlement of this country. . . .

"Tested by the common and statute law of England prior to the emigration of our ancestors, and by the laws of many of the States at the time of the adoption of this amendment, the proceedings authorized by the act of 1820 cannot be denied to be due process of law, when applied to the ascertainment and recovery of balances due to the government from a collector of customs, unless there exists in the constitution some other provision which restrains congress from authorizing such proceedings. For, though 'due process of law' generally implies and includes *actor, reus, judex,* regular allegations, opportunity to answer, and a trial according to some settled course of judicial proceedings, ... yet, this is not universally true. There may be, and we have seen that there are cases, under the law of England after *Magna Charta,* and as it was brought to this country and acted on here, in which process, in its nature final, issues against the body, lands, and goods of certain public debtors without any such trial; and this brings us to the question, whether those provisions of the constitution which relate to the judicial power are incompatible with these proceedings?"[a]

In Dred Scott v. Sandford, 60 U.S. (19 How.) 393 (1857), the Court had before it a challenge to the validity of the Act of Congress known as the Missouri Compromise which excluded slavery from specified northern portions of the United States territory. The opinion of the Court, by Chief Justice Taney, after referring to the free speech and other guaranties of the Bill of Rights, continued:

"These powers, and others in relation to rights of person, which it is not necessary here to enumerate, are, in express and positive terms, denied to the general government; and the rights of private property have been guarded with equal care. Thus the rights of property are united with the rights of person, and placed on the same ground by the fifth amendment to the Constitution, which provides that no person shall be deprived of life, liberty and property, without due process of law. And an Act of Congress which deprives a citizen of the United States of his liberty or property, merely because he came himself or brought his property into a particular Territory of the United States, and who had committed no offense against the laws, could hardly be dignified with the name of due process of law."

SECTION 2. THE INITIAL INTERPRETATION OF THE CIVIL WAR AMENDMENTS

Slaughter-House Cases

83 U.S. (16 Wall.) 36, 21 L.Ed. 394 (1872).

[The Louisiana legislature chartered a corporation and granted to it, for twenty-five years, an exclusive right to operate facilities in New Orleans for the

---

[a] During this period there were a few state court opinions applying state constitutional phrases such as "due process of law" and "the law of the land" not only to require fair procedure but also to invalidate special or "class" legislation and retroactive impairment of "vested rights". See, e.g., Wynehamer v. The People, 13 N.Y. 378, 393–395 (1856), quoting comparable approaches by the courts of Pennsylvania and North Carolina. For general discussion see: Corwin, *Liberty against Government* 75–82, 91–110 (1948); Mott, *Due Process of Law* 241–274 (1926); Howe, *The Meaning of "Due Process of Law" Prior to the Adoption of the Fourteenth Amendment,* 18 Calif.L.Rev. 583, 596–610 (1930).

landing, keeping, and slaughter of livestock. All competing plants were required to cease operation, and independent butchers were given a right to slaughter at the corporation's plant on paying maximum charges that were fixed by statute.

New Orleans butchers sued in the state courts to have the act declared invalid as a violation of both the Thirteenth and Fourteenth Amendments. The statute was upheld by the Louisiana Supreme Court.]

Mr. Justice Miller delivered the opinion of the court....

This statute is denounced not only as creating a monopoly and conferring odious and exclusive privileges upon a small number of persons at the expense of the great body of the community of New Orleans, but it is asserted that it deprives a large and meritorious class of citizens—the whole of the butchers of the city—of the right to exercise their trade, the business to which they have been trained and on which they depend for the support of themselves and their families; and that the unrestricted exercise of the business of butchering is necessary to the daily subsistence of the population of the city.

But a critical examination of the act hardly justifies these assertions....

The power here exercised by the legislature of Louisiana is, in its essential nature, one which has been, up to the present period in the constitutional history of this country, always conceded to belong to the States, however it may *now* be questioned in some of its details.... This is called the police power; and it is declared by Chief Justice Shaw that it is much easier to perceive and realize the existence and sources of it than to mark its boundaries, or prescribe limits to its exercise.

This power is, and must be from its very nature, incapable of any very exact definition or limitation. Upon it depends the security of social order, the life and health of the citizen, the comfort of an existence in a thickly populated community, the enjoyment of private and social life, and the beneficial use of property....

It may, therefore, be considered as established, that the authority of the legislature of Louisiana to pass the present statute is ample, unless some restraint in the exercise of that power be found in the constitution of that State or in the amendments to the Constitution of the United States, adopted since the date of the decisions we have already cited....

The plaintiffs in error accepting this issue, allege that the statute is a violation of the Constitution of the United States in these several particulars:

That it creates an involuntary servitude forbidden by the thirteenth article of amendment;

That it abridges the privileges and immunities of citizens of the United States;

That it denies to the plaintiffs the equal protection of the laws; and,

That it deprives them of their property without due process of law; contrary to the provisions of the first section of the fourteenth article of amendment.

This court is thus called upon for the first time to give construction to these articles.

We do not conceal from ourselves the great responsibility which this duty devolves upon us. No questions so far-reaching and pervading in their consequences, so profoundly interesting to the people of this country, and so important in their bearing upon the relations of the United States, and of the several States to each other and to the citizens of the States and of the United

States, have been before this court during the official life of any of its present members. . . .

Twelve articles of amendment were added to the Federal Constitution soon after the original organization of the government under it in 1789. Of these all but the last were adopted so soon afterwards as to justify the statement that they were practically contemporaneous with the adoption of the original; and the twelfth, adopted in eighteen hundred and three, was so nearly so as to have become, like all the others, historical and of another age. But within the last eight years three other articles of amendment of vast importance have been added by the voice of the people to that now venerable instrument.

The most cursory glance at these articles discloses a unity of purpose, when taken in connection with the history of the times, which cannot fail to have an important bearing on any question of doubt concerning their true meaning. Nor can such doubts, when any reasonably exist, be safely and rationally solved without a reference to that history; for in it is found the occasion and the necessity for recurring again to the great source of power in this country, the people of the States, for additional guarantees of human rights; additional powers to the Federal government; additional restraints upon those of the States. Fortunately that history is fresh within the memory of us all, and its leading features, as they bear upon the matter before us, free from doubt.

The institution of African slavery, as it existed in about half the States of the Union, and the contests pervading the public mind for many years, between those who desired its curtailment and ultimate extinction and those who desired additional safeguards for its security and perpetuation, culminated in the effort, on the part of most of the States in which slavery existed, to separate from the Federal government, and to resist its authority. This constituted the war of the rebellion, and whatever auxiliary causes may have contributed to bring about this war, undoubtedly the overshadowing and efficient cause was African slavery.

In that struggle slavery, as a legalized social relation, perished. It perished as a necessity of the bitterness and force of the conflict. When the armies of freedom found themselves upon the soil of slavery they could do nothing less than free the poor victims whose enforced servitude was the foundation of the quarrel. And when hard pressed in the contest these men (for they proved themselves men in that terrible crisis) offered their services and were accepted by thousands to aid in suppressing the unlawful rebellion, slavery was at an end wherever the Federal government succeeded in that purpose. The proclamation of President Lincoln expressed an accomplished fact as to a large portion of the insurrectionary districts, when he declared slavery abolished in them all. But the war being over, those who had succeeded in re-establishing the authority of the Federal government were not content to permit this great act of emancipation to rest on the actual results of the contest or the proclamation of the Executive, both of which might have been questioned in after times, and they determined to place this main and most valuable result in the Constitution of the restored Union as one of its fundamental articles. Hence the thirteenth article of amendment of that instrument. Its two short sections seem hardly to admit of construction, so vigorous is their expression and so appropriate to the purpose we have indicated.

. . .

To withdraw the mind from the contemplation of this grand yet simple declaration of the personal freedom of all the human race within the jurisdiction of this government—a declaration designed to establish the freedom of four millions of slaves—and with a microscopic search endeavor to find in it a reference to servitudes, which may have been attached to property in certain localities, requires an effort, to say the least of it.

That a personal servitude was meant is proved by the use of the word "involuntary," which can only apply to human beings. The exception of servitude as a punishment for crime gives an idea of the class of servitude that is meant. The word servitude is of larger meaning than slavery, as the latter is popularly understood in this country, and the obvious purpose was to forbid all shades and conditions of African slavery. It was very well understood that in the form of apprenticeship for long terms, as it had been practiced in the West India Islands, on the abolition of slavery by the English government, or by reducing the slaves to the condition of serfs attached to the plantation, the purpose of the article might have been evaded, if only the word slavery had been used. The case of the apprentice slave, held under a law of Maryland, liberated by Chief Justice Chase, on a writ of habeas corpus under this article, illustrates this course of observation. And it is all that we deem necessary to say on the application of that article to the statute of Louisiana, now under consideration.

The process of restoring to their proper relations with the Federal government and with the other States those which had sided with the rebellion, undertaken under the proclamation of President Johnson in 1865, and before the assembling of Congress, developed the fact that, notwithstanding the formal recognition by those States of the abolition of slavery, the condition of the slave race would, without further protection of the Federal government, be almost as bad as it was before. Among the first acts of legislation adopted by several of the States in the legislative bodies which claimed to be in their normal relations with the Federal government, were laws which imposed upon the colored race onerous disabilities and burdens, and curtailed their rights in the pursuit of life, liberty, and property to such an extent that their freedom was of little value, while they had lost the protection which they had received from their former owners from motives both of interest and humanity.

They were in some States forbidden to appear in the towns in any other character than menial servants. They were required to reside on and cultivate the soil without the right to purchase or own it. They were excluded from many occupations of gain, and were not permitted to give testimony in the courts in any case where a white man was a party. It was said that their lives were at the mercy of bad men, either because the laws for their protection were insufficient or were not enforced.

These circumstances, whatever of falsehood or misconception may have been mingled with their presentation, forced upon the statesmen who had conducted the Federal government in safety through the crisis of the rebellion, and who supposed that by the thirteenth article of amendment they had secured the result of their labors, the conviction that something more was necessary in the way of constitutional protection to the unfortunate race who had suffered so much. They accordingly passed through Congress the proposition for the fourteenth amendment, and they declined to treat as restored to their full participation in the government of the Union the States which had been in insurrection, until they ratified that article by a formal vote of their legislative bodies.

Before we proceed to examine more critically the provisions of this amendment, on which the plaintiffs in error rely, let us complete and dismiss the history of the recent amendments, as that history relates to the general purpose which pervades them all. A few years' experience satisfied the thoughtful men who had been the authors of the other two amendments that, notwithstanding the restraints of those articles on the States, and the laws passed under the additional powers granted to Congress, these were inadequate for the protection of life, liberty, and property, without which freedom to the slave was no boon. They were in all those States denied the right of suffrage. The laws were administered by the white man alone. It was urged that a race of men distinctively marked as was the negro, living in the midst of another and dominant race, could never be fully secured in their person and their property without the right of suffrage.

Hence the fifteenth amendment, which declares that "the right of a citizen of the United States to vote shall not be denied or abridged by any State on account of race, color, or previous condition of servitude." The negro having, by the fourteenth amendment, been declared to be a citizen of the United States, is thus made a voter in every State of the Union.

We repeat, then, in the light of this recapitulation of events, almost too recent to be called history, but which are familiar to us all; and on the most casual examination of the language of these amendments, no one can fail to be impressed with the one pervading purpose found in them all, lying at the foundation of each, and without which none of them would have been even suggested; we mean the freedom of the slave race, the security and firm establishment of that freedom, and the protection of the newly-made freeman and citizen from the oppressions of those who had formerly exercised unlimited dominion over him. It is true that only the fifteenth amendment, in terms, mentions the negro by speaking of his color and his slavery. But it is just as true that each of the other articles was addressed to the grievances of that race, and designed to remedy them as the fifteenth.

We do not say that no one else but the negro can share in this protection. Both the language and spirit of these articles are to have their fair and just weight in any question of construction. Undoubtedly while negro slavery alone was in the mind of the Congress which proposed the thirteenth article, it forbids any other kind of slavery, now or hereafter. If Mexican peonage or the Chinese coolie labor system shall develop slavery of the Mexican or Chinese race within our territory, this amendment may safely be trusted to make it void. And so if other rights are assailed by the States which properly and necessarily fall within the protection of these articles, that protection will apply, though the party interested may not be of African descent. But what we do say, and what we wish to be understood is, that in any fair and just construction of any section or phrase of these amendments, it is necessary to look to the purpose which we have said was the pervading spirit of them all, the evil which they were designed to remedy, and the process of continued addition to the Constitution, until that purpose was supposed to be accomplished, as far as constitutional law can accomplish it.

The first section of the fourteenth article, to which our attention is more specially invited, opens with a definition of citizenship—not only citizenship of the United States, but citizenship of the States. No such definition was previously found in the Constitution, nor had any attempt been made to define it by act of Congress. It had been the occasion of much discussion in the courts, by the executive departments, and in the public journals. It had been said by eminent judges that no man was a citizen of the United States, except as he was a citizen of one of the States composing the Union. Those, therefore, who had been born and resided always in the District of Columbia or in the Territories, though within the United States, were not citizens. Whether this proposition was sound or not had never been judicially decided. But it had been held by this court, in the celebrated Dred Scott case, only a few years before the outbreak of the civil war, that a man of African descent, whether a slave or not, was not and could not be a citizen of a State or of the United States. This decision, while it met the condemnation of some of the ablest statesmen and constitutional lawyers of the country, had never been overruled; and if it was to be accepted as a constitutional limitation of the right of citizenship, then all the negro race who had recently been made freemen, were still, not only not citizens, but were incapable of becoming so by anything short of an amendment to the Constitution.

To remove this difficulty primarily, and to establish a clear and comprehensive definition of citizenship which should declare what should constitute citizenship of the United States, and also citizenship of a State, the first clause of the first section was framed.

"All persons born or naturalized in the United States, and subject to the jurisdiction thereof, are citizens of the United States and of the State wherein they reside."

The first observation we have to make on this clause is, that it puts at rest both the questions which we stated to have been the subject of differences of opinion. It declares that persons may be citizens of the United States without regard to their citizenship, of a particular State, and it overturns the Dred Scott decision by making *all persons* born within the United States and subject to its jurisdiction citizens of the United States. That its main purpose was to establish the citizenship of the negro can admit of no doubt. The phrase, "subject to its jurisdiction" was intended to exclude from its operation children of ministers, consuls, and citizens or subjects of foreign States born within the United States.

The next observation is more important in view of the arguments of counsel in the present case. It is, that the distinction between citizenship of the United States and citizenship of a State is clearly recognized and established. Not only may a man be a citizen of the United States without being a citizen of a State, but an important element is necessary to convert the former into the latter. He must reside within the State to make him a citizen of it, but it is only necessary that he should be born or naturalized in the United States to be a citizen of the Union.

It is quite clear, then, that there is a citizenship of the United States, and a citizenship of a State, which are distinct from each other, and which depend upon different characteristics or circumstances in the individual.

We think this distinction and its explicit recognition in this amendment of great weight in this argument, because the next paragraph of this same section, which is the one mainly relied on by the plaintiffs in error, speaks only of privileges and immunities of citizens of the United States, and does not speak of those of citizens of the several States. The argument, however, in favor of the plaintiffs rests wholly on the assumption that the citizenship is the same, and the privileges and immunities guaranteed by the clause are the same.

The language is, "No State shall make or enforce any law which shall abridge the privileges or immunities of citizens of *the United States.*" It is a little remarkable, if this clause was intended as a protection to the citizen of a State against the legislative power of his own State, that the word citizen of the State should be left out when it is so carefully used, and used in contradistinction to citizens of the United States, in the very sentence which precedes it. It is too clear for argument that the change in phraseology was adopted understandingly and with a purpose.

Of the privileges and immunities of the citizen of the United States, and of the privileges and immunities of the citizen of the State, and what they respectively are, we will presently consider; but we wish to state here that it is only the former which are placed by this clause under the protection of the Federal Constitution, and that the latter, whatever they may be, are not intended to have any additional protection by this paragraph of the amendment.

If, then, there is a difference between the privileges and immunities belonging to a citizen of the United States as such, and those belonging to the citizen of the State as such, the latter must rest for their security and protection where they have heretofore rested; for they are not embraced by this paragraph of the amendment.

The first occurrence of the words "privileges and immunities" in our constitutional history, is to be found in the fourth of the articles of the old Confederation.

It declares "that the better to secure and perpetuate mutual friendship and intercourse among the people of the different States in this Union, the free inhabitants of each of these States, paupers, vagabonds, and fugitives from justice excepted, shall be entitled to all the privileges and immunities of free citizens in the several States; and the people of each State shall have free ingress and regress to and from any other State, and shall enjoy therein all the privileges of trade and commerce, subject to the same duties, impositions, and restrictions as the inhabitants thereof respectively."

In the Constitution of the United States, which superseded the Articles of Confederation, the corresponding provision is found in section two of the fourth article, in the following words: "The citizens of each State shall be entitled to all the privileges and immunities of citizens of the several States."

There can be but little question that the purpose of both these provisions is the same, and that the privileges and immunities intended are the same in each. In the article of the Confederation we have some of these specifically mentioned, and enough perhaps to give some general idea of the class of civil rights meant by the phrase.

Fortunately we are not without judicial construction of this clause of the Constitution. The first and the leading case on the subject is that of *Corfield v. Coryell,* decided by Mr. Justice Washington in the Circuit Court for the District of Pennsylvania in 1823.

"The inquiry," he says, "is, what are the privileges and immunities of citizens of the several States? We feel no hesitation in confining these expressions to those privileges and immunities which are *fundamental;* which belong of right to the citizens of all free governments, and which have at all times been enjoyed by citizens of the several States which compose this Union, from the time of their becoming free, independent, and sovereign. What these fundamental principles are, it would be more tedious than difficult to enumerate. They may all, however, be comprehended under the following general heads: protection by the government, with the right to acquire and possess property of every kind, and to pursue and obtain happiness and safety, subject, nevertheless, to such restraints as the government may prescribe for the general good of the whole."

... The description, when taken to include others not named, but which are of the same general character, embraces nearly every civil right for the establishment and protection of which organized government is instituted. They are, in the language of Judge Washington, those rights which are fundamental. Throughout his opinion, they are spoken of as rights belonging to the individual as a citizen of a State. They are so spoken of in the constitutional provision which he was construing. And they have always been held to be the class of rights which the State governments were created to establish and secure.

. . . [Article IV] did not create those rights, which it called privileges and immunities of citizens of the States. It threw around them in that clause no security for the citizen of the State in which they were claimed or exercised. Nor did it profess to control the power of the State governments over the rights of its own citizens.

Its sole purpose was to declare to the several States, that whatever those rights, as you grant or establish them to your own citizens, or as you limit or qualify, or impose restrictions on their exercise, the same, neither more nor less, shall be the measure of the rights of citizens of other States within your jurisdiction.

It would be the vainest show of learning to attempt to prove by citations of authority, that up to the adoption of the recent amendments, no claim or pretence was set up that those rights depended on the Federal government for their existence or protection, beyond the very few express limitations which the Federal Constitution imposed upon the States—such, for instance, as the prohibition against ex post facto laws, bills of attainder, and laws impairing the obligation of contracts. But with the exception of these and a few other restrictions, the entire domain of the privileges and immunities of citizens of the States, as above defined, lay within the constitutional and legislative power of the States, and without that of the Federal government. Was it the purpose of the fourteenth amendment, by the simple declaration that no State should make or enforce any law which shall abridge the privileges and immunities of *citizens of the United States,* to transfer the security and protection of all the civil rights which we have mentioned, from the States to the Federal government? And where it is declared that Congress shall have the power to enforce that article, was it intended to bring within the power of Congress the entire domain of civil rights heretofore belonging exclusively to the States?

All this and more must follow, if the proposition of the plaintiffs in error be sound. For not only are these rights subject to the control of Congress whenever in its discretion any of them are supposed to be abridged by State legislation, but that body may also pass laws in advance, limiting and restricting the exercise of legislative power by the States, in their most ordinary and usual functions, as in its judgment it may think proper on all such subjects. And still further, such a construction followed by the reversal of the judgments of the Supreme Court of Louisiana in these cases, would constitute this court a perpetual censor upon all legislation of the States, on the civil rights of their own citizens, with authority to nullify such as it did not approve as consistent with those rights, as they existed at the time of the adoption of this amendment. The argument we admit is not always the most conclusive which is drawn from the consequences urged against the adoption of a particular construction of an instrument. But when, as in the case before us, these consequences are so serious, so far-reaching and pervading, so great a departure from the structure and spirit of our institutions; when the effect is to fetter and degrade the State governments by subjecting them to the control of Congress, in the exercise of powers heretofore universally conceded to them of the most ordinary and fundamental character; when in fact it radically changes the whole theory of the relations of the State and Federal governments to each other and of both these governments to the people; the argument has a force that is irresistible, in the absence of language which expresses such a purpose too clearly to admit of doubt.

We are convinced that no such results were intended by the Congress which proposed these amendments, nor by the legislatures of the States which ratified them.

Having shown that the privileges and immunities relied on in the argument are those which belong to citizens of the States as such, and that they are left to the State governments for security and protection, and not by this article placed under the special care of the Federal government, we may hold ourselves excused from defining the privileges and immunities of citizens of the United States which no State can abridge, until some case involving those privileges may make it necessary to do so.

But lest it should be said that no such privileges and immunities are to be found if those we have been considering are excluded, we venture to suggest some which owe their existence to the Federal government, its National character, its Constitution, or its laws.

One of these is well described in the case of *Crandall v. Nevada.* It is said to be the right of the citizen of this great country, protected by implied guarantees of its Constitution, "to come to the seat of government to assert any claim he may have upon that government, to transact any business he may have with it, to seek its protection, to share its offices, to engage in administering its functions. He has the right of free access to its seaports, through which all operations of foreign commerce are conducted, to the sub-treasuries, land offices, and courts of justice in the several States." And quoting from the language of Chief Justice Taney in another case, it is said "that *for all the great purposes for which the Federal government* was established, we are one people, with one common country, *we are all citizens of the United States;*" and it is, as such citizens, that their rights are supported in this court in Crandall v. Nevada.

Another privilege of a citizen of the United States, is to demand the care and protection of the Federal government over his life, liberty, and property when on the high seas or within the jurisdiction of a foreign government. Of this there can be no doubt, nor that the right depends upon his character as a citizen of the United States. The right to peaceably assemble and petition for redress of grievances, the privilege of the writ of *habeas corpus,* are rights of the citizen guaranteed by the Federal Constitution. The right to use the navigable waters of the United States, however they may penetrate the territory of the several States, all rights secured to our citizens by treaties with foreign nations, are dependent upon citizenship of the United States, and not citizenship of a State. One of these privileges is conferred by the very article under consideration. It is that a citizen of the United States can, of his own volition, become a citizen of any State of the Union by a *bona fide* residence therein, with the same rights as other citizens of that State. To these may be added the rights secured by the thirteenth and fifteenth articles of amendment, and by the other clause of the fourteenth, next to be considered.

But it is useless to pursue this branch of the inquiry, since we are of opinion that the rights claimed by these plaintiffs in error, if they have any existence, are not privileges and immunities of citizens of the United States within the meaning of the clause of the fourteenth amendment under consideration. . . .

The argument has not been much pressed in these cases that the defendant's charter deprives the plaintiffs of their property without due process of law, or that it denies to them the equal protection of the law. The first of these paragraphs has been in the Constitution since the adoption of the fifth amendment, as a restraint upon the Federal power. It is also to be found in some form of expression in the constitutions of nearly all the States, as a restraint upon the power of the States. This law then, has practically been the same as it now is during the existence of the government, except so far as the present amendment may place the restraining power over the States in this matter in the hands of the Federal government.

We are not without judicial interpretation, therefore, both State and National, of the meaning of this clause. And it is sufficient to say that under no construction of that provision that we have ever seen, or any that we deem admissible, can the restraint imposed by the State of Louisiana upon the exercise of their trade by the butchers of New Orleans be held to be a deprivation of property within the meaning of that provision.

"Nor shall any State deny to any person within its jurisdiction the equal protection of the laws."

In the light of the history of these amendments, and the pervading purpose of them, which we have already discussed, it is not difficult to give a meaning to this clause. The existence of laws in the States where the newly emancipated negroes resided, which discriminated with gross injustice and hardship against them as a class, was the evil to be remedied by this clause, and by it such laws are forbidden.

If, however, the States did not conform their laws to its requirements, then by the fifth section of the article of amendment Congress was authorized to enforce it by suitable legislation. We doubt very much whether any action of a State not directed by way of discrimination against the negroes as a class, or on account of their race, will ever be held to come within the purview of this provision. It is so clearly a provision for that race and that emergency, that a strong case would be necessary for its application to any other. But as it is a State that is to be dealt with, and not alone the validity of its laws, we may safely leave that matter until Congress shall have exercised its power, or some case of State oppression, by denial of equal justice in its courts, shall have claimed a decision at our hands. We find no such case in the one before us, and do not deem it necessary to go over the argument again, as it may have relation to this particular clause of the amendment.

In the early history of the organization of the government, its statesmen seem to have divided on the line which should separate the powers of the National government from those of the State governments, and though this line has never been very well defined in public opinion, such a division has continued from that day to this.

The adoption of the first eleven amendments to the Constitution so soon after the original instrument was accepted, shows a prevailing sense of danger at that time from the Federal power. And it cannot be denied that such a jealousy continued to exist with many patriotic men until the breaking out of the late civil war. It was then discovered that the true danger to the perpetuity of the Union was in the capacity of the State organizations to combine and concentrate all the powers of the State, and of contiguous States, for a determined resistance to the General Government.

Unquestionably this has given great force to the argument, and added largely to the number of those who believe in the necessity of a strong National government.

But, however pervading this sentiment, and however it may have contributed to the adoption of the amendments we have been considering, we do not see in those amendments any purpose to destroy the main features of the general system. Under the pressure of all the excited feeling growing out of the war, our statesmen have still believed that the existence of the States with powers for domestic and local government, including the regulation of civil rights—the rights of person and of property—was essential to the perfect working of our complex form of government, though they have thought proper to impose additional limitations on the States, and to confer additional power on that of the Nation.

But whatever fluctuations may be seen in the history of public opinion on this subject during the period of our national existence, we think it will be found that this court, so far as its functions required, has always held with a steady and an even hand the balance between State and Federal power, and we trust that such may continue to be the history of its relation to that subject so long as it shall have duties to perform which demand of it a construction of the Constitution, or of any of its parts.

The judgments of the Supreme Court of Louisiana in these cases are

Affirmed.

Mr. Justice Field, dissenting:

. . . .

The act of Louisiana presents the naked case, unaccompanied by any public considerations, where a right to pursue a lawful and necessary calling, previously enjoyed by every citizen, and in connection with which a thousand persons were daily employed, is taken away and vested exclusively for twenty-five years, for an extensive district and a large population, in a single corporation, or its exercise is for that period restricted to the establishments of the corporation, and there allowed only upon onerous conditions. . . .

The question presented is, therefore, one of the gravest importance, not merely to the parties here, but to the whole country. It is nothing less than the question whether the recent amendments to the Federal Constitution protect the citizens of the United States against the deprivation of their common rights by State legislation. In my judgment the fourteenth amendment does afford such protection, and was so intended by the Congress which framed and the States which adopted it. . . .

The amendment does not attempt to confer any new privileges or immunities upon citizens, or to enumerate or define those already existing. It assumes that there are such privileges and immunities which belong of right to citizens as such, and ordains that they shall not be abridged by State legislation. If this inhibition has no reference to privileges and immunities of this character, but only refers, as held by the majority of the court in their opinion, to such privileges and immunities as were before its adoption specially designated in the Constitution or necessarily implied as belonging to citizens of the United States, it was a vain and idle enactment, which accomplished nothing, and most unnecessarily excited Congress and the people on its passage. With privileges and immunities thus designated or implied no State could ever have interfered by its laws, and no new constitutional provision was required to inhibit such interference. The supremacy of the Constitution and the laws of the United States always controlled any State legislation of that character. But if the amendment refers to the natural and inalienable rights which belong to all citizens, the inhibition has a profound significance and consequence.

What, then, are the privileges and immunities which are secured against abridgment by State legislation?

In the first section of the Civil Rights Act Congress has given its interpretation to these terms, or at least has stated some of the rights which, in its judgment, these terms include; it has there declared that they include the right "to make and enforce contracts, to sue, be parties and give evidence, to inherit, purchase, lease, sell, hold, and convey real and personal property, and to full and equal benefit of all laws and proceedings for the security of person and property." ...

The common law of England ... condemned all monopolies in any known trade or manufacture, and declared void all grants of special privileges whereby others could be deprived of any liberty which they previously had, or be hindered in their lawful trade. The statute of James I, to which I have referred, only embodied the law as it had been previously declared by the courts of England, although frequently disregarded by the sovereigns of that country.

The common law of England is the basis of the jurisprudence of the United States.... And when the Colonies separated from the mother country no privilege was more fully recognized or more completely incorporated into the fundamental law of the country than that every free subject in the British empire was entitled to pursue his happiness by following any of the known established trades and occupations of the country, subject only to such restraints as equally affected all others....

[The dissenting opinion discussed state court decisions in Illinois, Connecticut and New York striking down monopolies and exclusive privileges.]

. . .

This equality of right, with exemption from all disparaging and partial enactments, in the lawful pursuits of life, throughout the whole country, is the distinguishing privilege of citizens of the United States. To them, everywhere, all pursuits, all professions, all avocations are open without other restrictions than such as are imposed equally upon all others of the same age, sex, and condition. The State may prescribe such regulations for every pursuit and calling of life as will promote the public health, secure the good order and advance the general prosperity of society, but when once prescribed the pursuit or calling must be free to be followed by every citizen who is within the conditions designated, and will conform to the regulations. This is the fundamental idea upon which our institutions rest, and unless adhered to in the legislation of the country our government will be a republic only in name. The fourteenth amendment, in my judgment, makes it essential to the validity of the legislation of every State that this equality of right should be respected. How widely this equality has been departed from, how entirely rejected and trampled upon by the act of Louisiana, I have already shown. And it is to me a matter of profound regret that its validity is recognized by a majority of this court, for by it the right of free labor, one of the most sacred and imprescriptible rights of man, is violated. As stated by the Supreme Court of Connecticut, in the case cited, grants of exclusive privileges, such as is made by the act in question, are opposed to the whole theory of free government, and it requires no aid from any bill of rights to render them void. That only is a free government, in the American sense of the term, under which the inalienable right of every citizen to pursue his happiness is unrestrained, except by just, equal, and impartial laws.

I am authorized by the Chief Justice [Chase], Mr. Justice Swayne, and Mr. Justice Bradley, to state that they concur with me in this dissenting opinion.

[Justices Bradley and Swayne also filed dissenting opinions.]

THE PRIVILEGES AND IMMUNITIES CLAUSE OF THE FOURTEENTH AMENDMENT

Does the 14th amendment privileges and immunities clause have any independent significance as interpreted by the Court in the Slaughterhouse Cases? Would any case be decided differently because of the presence of that clause? How does it differ from the privileges and immunities clause in Art. IV?

The conventional interpretations of the Art. IV clause would render unconstitutional an attempt by a state to impose higher taxes on nonresidents doing business in the state than upon residents. See, e.g., Austin v. New Hampshire, 420 U.S. 656 (1975). In Madden v. Kentucky, 309 U.S. 83 (1940), overruling Colgate v. Harvey, 296 U.S. 404 (1935), the Court had before it a challenge to a state tax which required residents of that state to pay a higher tax on deposits in banks outside the state than in local banks. The argument was made that the privileges and immunities clause of the 14th amendment protected a resident of a state against this discrimination against property and activities outside the state. The Court rejected this argument: "[T]he privileges and immunities clause protects all citizens against abridgment by states of rights of national citizenship as distinct from the fundamental or natural rights inherent in state citizenship. . . . We think it quite clear that the right to carry out an incident to a trade, business or calling such as the deposit of money in banks is not a privilege of national citizenship."

DUE PROCESS AND JURISDICTION

Even before the adoption of the fourteenth amendment the Court restricted the jurisdiction of state legislatures and state courts without any clear constitutional basis for the restrictions. The Court held, e.g., in Baldwin v. Hale, 68 U.S. (1 Wall.) 223, 234 (1864), that "[i]nsolvent laws of one State cannot discharge the contracts of citizens of other States, because they have no extraterritorial operation, and consequently the tribunal sitting under them, unless in cases where a citizen of such other State voluntarily becomes a party to the proceedings, has no jurisdiction in the case. Legal notice cannot be given and, consequently, there can be no obligation to appear, and of course, there can be no legal default." The requirement of personal service of process within the jurisdiction or voluntary appearance as a basis for securing a valid judgment in personam was early brought under the due process rubric in Pennoyer v. Neff, 95 U.S. 714, 732 (1877).

Not until the turn of the century, however, did the Court apply the due process clause to limit the jurisdiction of the states to tax tangible property located outside the state. As an example, in Louisville & Jeffersonville Ferry Co. v. Kentucky, 188 U.S. 385, 396, 397 (1903), the Court, in holding that Kentucky could not tax a franchise granted a ferry by Indiana to convey passengers from Indiana to Kentucky, said that the taxing power of the states "is limited by a principle inhering in the very nature of constitutional government, namely, that the taxation imposed must have relation to a subject within the jurisdiction of the taxing government."

DUE PROCESS AND FAIR PROCEDURE

In 1856 in *Murray's Lessee,* supra p. 465, the Court started to mark out the limits imposed by the due process clause of the fifth amendment on procedures devised by Congress. But in 1864 the Court was still finding limits on state power to establish procedures for civil cases without any definite constitutional basis. Thus in Baldwin v. Hale, 68 U.S. (1 Wall.) 223, 233 (1864), the Court said: "Parties whose rights are to be affected are entitled to be heard; and in order that they may enjoy that right they must first be notified. Common justice requires that no man shall be condemned in his person or property without notice and an opportunity to make his defense."

After the fourteenth amendment was adopted, however, the Court quickly placed the guarantee of fair procedures in the states firmly on the due process clause of that amendment. In Hagar v. Reclamation District, 111 U.S. 701, 708 (1884), the Court said: "Undoubtedly, where life and liberty are involved, due process requires that there be a regular course of judicial proceedings, which imply that the party to be affected shall have notice and an opportunity to be heard; so, also, where title or possession of property is involved." And in Hurtado v. California, 110 U.S. 516, 534 (1884), the Court, in holding that a state could substitute a preliminary hearing for indictment by grand jury in criminal cases, said that the due process clause in the fourteenth amendment meant the same as it did in the fifth amendment and that any state proceeding constituted due process of law if it was "exerted within the limits of those fundamental principles of liberty and justice which lie at the base of all our civil and political institutions...."

THE FOURTEENTH AMENDMENT AND CITIZENSHIP

The distinction between alienage and citizenship is fundamental, and vitally important issues turn on it. A citizen may not be deported nor excluded from the United States. United States v. Wong Kim Ark, 169 U.S. 649 (1898), held, for example, that a person born in the United States and therefore a citizen could not be excluded from the country when he attempted to enter even though his foreign-born parents were not eligible for naturalization. An alien, on the other hand, may be deported for any of a substantial list of reasons. 8 U.S.C. § 1251. In Harisiades v. Shaughnessy, 342 U.S. 580 (1952), it was held that an alien (resident of the United States for thirty years) could be deported because of Communist Party membership even though this membership had terminated before enactment of the deportation statute. Aliens may also be excluded from the United States for an even longer list of reasons. 8 U.S.C. § 1182. An alien seeking entry into the United States has no constitutional right to a hearing, and the exercise of power by the Attorney General to deny admission without a hearing has been upheld. United States ex rel. Knauff v. Shaughnessy, 338 U.S. 537 (1950). However, an administrative hearing is provided by statute for most exclusion cases. 8 U.S.C. § 1226.

In Landon v. Plasencia, 459 U.S. 21 (1982), the Court held that a permanent resident alien returning from a brief trip abroad was not entitled to a deportation hearing but did have a due process right to a fair exclusion hearing. The Court said:

"This Court has long held that an alien seeking initial admission to the United States requests a privilege and has no constitutional rights regarding his application, for the power to admit or exclude aliens is a sovereign prerogative.... As we explained in Johnson v. Eisentrager, 339 U.S. 763, 770 (1950), however, once an alien gains admission to our country and begins to develop the ties that go with permanent residence his constitutional status changes accordingly. Our cases have frequently suggested that a continuously present resident alien is entitled to a fair hearing when threatened with deportation...."

The Court then cited cases which it described as holding that a permanent resident alien returning from a temporary trip abroad would be treated like an alien continuously residing and physically present in the United States, with the result that the former would be entitled as a matter of due process to a hearing on the charges underlying any attempt to exclude him.

In view of the importance of citizenship it is surprising that the constitution originally did not define it. However, the desire to assure citizenship to former slaves (who had been held not to be citizens in Dred Scott v. Sandford, 60 U.S. (19 How.) 393 (1857)) led to the definition contained in the opening sentence of the fourteenth amendment: "All persons born or naturalized in the United States, and subject to the jurisdiction thereof, are citizens of the United States and of the State wherein they reside." In United States v. Wong Kim Ark, 169 U.S. 649 (1898), it was stated that the phrase, "and subject to the jurisdiction thereof" excluded "by the fewest and fittest words (besides children of members of the Indian tribes, standing in a peculiar relation to the National Government, unknown to the common law) ... two classes of cases—children born of alien enemies in hostile occupation, and children of diplomatic representatives of a foreign state...."

By statute Congress has added three principal categories to the constitutional definition of citizenship: (1) persons born in the United States to members of Indian, Eskimo, Aleutian, or other aboriginal tribes; (2) persons born outside the United States of parents both of whom are citizens and one of whom has had a residence in the United States prior to birth of such person; and (3) persons born outside the United States where only one parent is a citizen and that parent has resided in the United States for a prescribed period. See generally 8 U.S.C. § 1401.

Congress has long recognized the right of citizens to renounce their United States citizenship. 8 U.S.C. § 1481(a)(6), (7). Major problems have arisen, however, as a result of statutory provisions providing for loss of nationality upon the doing of certain acts—e.g. obtaining naturalization in a foreign state, taking an oath of allegiance to a foreign state, entering and serving in the armed forces of a foreign state without official consent. 8 U.S.C. § 1481. In Vance v. Terrazas, 444 U.S. 252 (1980), the court addressed the subtle question whether Congress may presume an intent to renounce citizenship from performance of certain acts, e.g., taking an oath of allegiance to a foreign state. It first referred to the earlier case of Afroyim v. Rusk, 387 U.S. 253 (1967), in which it had rejected the idea that "Congress has any general power, express or implied, to take away an American citizen's citizenship without his assent" and stated that § 1 of the fourteenth amendment is "most reasonably ... read as defining a citizenship which a citizen keeps unless he voluntarily relinquishes it." The Court then held that in addition to proving that the plaintiff, a dual citizen of the United States and Mexico from birth, had taken an oath of allegiance to Mexico voluntarily, the government also had to prove that he did so intending to relinquish his citizenship. The Court also held, however, that it was constitutional for Congress to provide that the government's burden to establish intent to renounce could be a preponderance of the evidence.

SECTION 3. APPLICATION OF THE BILL OF RIGHTS TO THE STATES

Introduction. Early in the process of giving content to the due process clause of the fourteenth amendment the question arose as to the relationship between the Bill of Rights and the fourteenth amendment. An early example of the Court's approach was Twining v. New Jersey, 211 U.S. 78 (1908). The question posed was whether the provision in the fifth amendment that no person "shall be compelled in any criminal case to be a witness against himself" applied to restrain the states. Twining argued first that the "privileges and immunities of citizens of the United States" protected against state action by the fourteenth amendment included those fundamental personal rights which were protected against national action by the first eight Amendments; that this was the intention of the framers of the fourteenth amendment. The Court rejected this argument, relying on the interpretation of the privileges and immunities clause in the Slaughterhouse Cases. Second, Twining argued that a denial of the privilege against self-incrimination constituted a denial of due process of law. The Court rejected this argument, holding that the privilege against self-incrimination was not "an immutable principle of justice which is the inalienable possession of every citizen of a free government" and hence to deny it was not to deny due process.

Whether the first eight amendments could be utilized to make more specific the meaning of "due process of law" was not settled by *Twining*. The subsequent cases involved primarily criminal procedure, and detailed consideration of those cases is left to criminal procedure courses. Presented here are just a few of the principal cases illustrating the dispute over the incorporation problem and the nature of judicial review itself.

One aspect of the incorporation doctrine has become the foundation for most of the modern developments concerning freedom of speech, press, and religion. Almost casually, the Court in 1925 asserted in Gitlow v. New York, 268 U.S. 652, 666: "For present purposes we may and do assume that freedom of speech and of the press—which are protected by the 1st Amendment from abridgment by Congress—are among the fundamental personal rights and 'liberties' protected by the due process clause of the 14th Amendment from impairment by the states."

THE INCORPORATION DOCTRINE

In Chapter 9 we will see how the Court gave an early expansive meaning to such fourteenth amendment terms as "liberty", "property", and "due process of law" in the context of judicial review of the substance of economic regulations. We will also see the Court's withdrawal from that expansive interpretation in recent decades.

In the field of procedure (primarily procedure in criminal cases), a similar development had a different twist. In the early years the Court found in the fourteenth amendment restrictions upon state procedures that denied "immutable principles of justice" that are "the inalienable possession of every citizen of a free government" or that deprived the accused of "sufficient notice of the accusation" and "an adequate opportunity to defend himself". These expansive terms, and others, tended to limit rather than to expand (as was the case with respect to the substance of economic regulations) the scope of Court review of state procedures. More recently, through the idea that the fourteenth amendment applies to the states the more specific procedural guaranties in the Bill of Rights, the Court has expanded the scope of review of state court procedures while making somewhat more specific the applicable standards.

This section is designed to show the development of the incorporation doctrine and to underline the dispute within the Court as to the wisdom of seeking to restrain judicial review by confining it to the areas covered by the

Bill of Rights. In reading the cases the student should consider how successful the Court has been in achieving more specific standards.

Palko v. Connecticut

302 U.S. 319, 58 S.Ct. 149, 82 L.Ed. 288 (1937).

Mr. Justice Cardozo delivered the opinion of the Court.

A statute of Connecticut permitting appeals in criminal cases to be taken by the state is challenged by appellant as an infringement of the Fourteenth Amendment of the Constitution of the United States....

Appellant was indicted in Fairfield County, Conn., for the crime of murder in the first degree. A jury found him guilty of murder in the second degree, and he was sentenced to confinement in the state prison for life. Thereafter the State of Connecticut, with the permission of the judge presiding at the trial, gave notice of appeal to the Supreme Court of Errors. This it did pursuant to an act adopted in 1886.... Upon such appeal, the Supreme Court of Errors reversed the judgment and ordered a new trial....

Pursuant to the mandate of the Supreme Court of Errors, defendant was brought to trial again. Before a jury was impaneled, and also at later stages of the case, he made the objection that the effect of the new trial was to place him twice in jeopardy for the same offense, and in so doing to violate the Fourteenth Amendment of the Constitution of the United States. Upon the overruling of the objection the trial proceeded. The jury returned a verdict of murder in the first degree, and the court sentenced the defendant to ... death. The Supreme Court of Errors affirmed the judgment of conviction....

1. The execution of the sentence will not deprive appellant of his life without the process of law assured to him by the Fourteenth Amendment of the Federal Constitution.

The argument for appellant is that whatever is forbidden by the Fifth Amendment is forbidden by the Fourteenth also. The Fifth Amendment, which is not directed to the States, but solely to the federal government, creates immunity from double jeopardy. No person shall be "subject for the same offense to be twice put in jeopardy of life or limb." The Fourteenth Amendment ordains, "nor shall any State deprive any person of life, liberty, or property, without due process of law." To retry a defendant, though under one indictment and only one, subjects him, it is said, to double jeopardy in violation of the Fifth Amendment, if the prosecution is one on behalf of the United States. From this the consequence is said to follow that there is a denial of life or liberty without due process of law, if the prosecution is one on behalf of the people of a state....

We have said that in appellant's view the Fourteenth Amendment is to be taken as embodying the prohibitions of the Fifth. His thesis is even broader. Whatever would be a violation of the original bill of rights (Amendments 1 to 8) if done by the federal government is now equally unlawful by force of the Fourteenth Amendment if done by a state. There is no such general rule.

The Fifth Amendment provides, among other things, that no person shall be held to answer for a capital or otherwise infamous crime unless on presentment or indictment of a grand jury. This court has held that, in prosecutions by a state, presentment or indictment by a grand jury may give way to informations at the instance of a public officer. Hurtado v. California, 110 U.S. 516.... The Fifth Amendment provides also that no person shall be compelled in any criminal case to be a witness against himself. This court has said that, in prosecutions by a state, the exemption will fail if the state elects to end it. Twining v. New Jersey, 211 U.S. 78, 106, 111, 112.... The Sixth Amendment calls for a jury trial in criminal cases and the Seventh for a jury trial in civil cases at common law where the value in controversy shall exceed $20. This court has ruled that consistently with those amendments trial by jury may be modified by a state or abolished altogether. Walker v. Sauvinet, 92 U.S. 90; Maxwell v. Dow, 176 U.S. 581....

On the other hand, the due process clause of the Fourteenth Amendment may make it unlawful for a state to abridge by its statutes the freedom of speech which the First Amendment safeguards against encroachment by the Congress ... or the like freedom of the press, ... or the free exercise of religion, ... or the right of peaceable assembly, without which speech would be unduly trammeled, ... or the right of one accused of crime to the benefit of counsel (Powell v. Alabama, 287 U.S. 45). In these and other situations immunities that are valid as against the federal government by force of the specific pledges of particular amendments have been found to be implicit in the concept of ordered liberty, and thus, through the Fourteenth Amendment, become valid as against the states.

The line of division may seem to be wavering and broken if there is a hasty catalogue of the cases on the one side and the other. Reflection and analysis will induce a different view. There emerges the perception of a rationalizing principle which gives to discrete instances a proper order and coherence. The right to trial by jury and the immunity from prosecution except as the result of an indictment may have value and importance. Even so, they are not of the very essence of a scheme of ordered liberty. To abolish them is not to violate a "principle of justice so rooted in the traditions and conscience of our people as to be ranked as fundamental." Snyder v. Massachusetts, supra, 291 U.S. 97, at page 105; Brown v. Mississippi, 297 U.S. 278, at page 285; Hebert v. Louisiana, 272 U.S. 312, 316. Few would be so narrow or provincial as to maintain that a fair and enlightened system of justice would be impossible without them. What is true of jury trials and indictments is true also, as the cases show, of the immunity from compulsory self-incrimination. *Twining v. New Jersey, supra.* This too might be lost, and justice still be done. Indeed, today as in the past there are students of our penal system who look upon the immunity as a mischief rather than a benefit, and who would limit its scope, or destroy it altogether.[3] No doubt there would remain the need to give protection against torture, physical or mental. *Brown v. Mississippi, supra.* Justice, however, would not perish if the accused were subject to a duty to respond to orderly inquiry. The exclusion of these immunities and privileges from the privileges and immunities protected against the action of the States has not been arbitrary or casual. It has been dictated by a study and appreciation of the meaning, the essential implications, of liberty itself.

We reach a different plane of social and moral values when we pass to the privileges and immunities that have been taken over from the earlier articles of the Federal Bill of Rights and brought within the Fourteenth Amendment by a process of absorption. These in their origin were effective against the federal

[3] See, e.g., Bentham, Rationale of Judicial Evidence, Book IX, Pt. 4, c. III; Glueck, Crime and Justice, p. 94. Cf. Wigmore, Evidence, vol. 4, § 2251.

Compulsory self-incrimination is part of the established procedure in the law of Continental Europe. Wigmore, supra, p. 824; Gardner, Criminal Procedure in France, 25 Yale L.J. 255, 260; Sherman, Roman Law in the Modern World, vol. 2, pp. 493, 494; Stumberg, Guide to the Law and Legal Literature of France, p. 184. Double jeopardy too is not everywhere forbidden. Radin, Anglo American Legal History, p. 228.

government alone. If the Fourteenth Amendment has absorbed them, the process of absorption has had its source in the belief that neither liberty nor justice would exist if they were sacrificed.... This is true, for illustration, of freedom of thought and speech. Of that freedom one may say that it is the matrix, the indispensable condition, of nearly every other form of freedom. With rare aberrations a pervasive recognition of that truth can be traced in our history, political and legal. So it has come about that the domain of liberty, withdrawn by the Fourteenth Amendment from encroachment by the states, has been enlarged by latter-day judgments to include liberty of the mind as well as liberty of action. The extension became, indeed, a logical imperative when once it was recognized, as long ago it was, that liberty is something more than exemption from physical restraint, and that even in the field of substantive rights and duties the legislative judgment, if oppressive and arbitrary, may be overridden by the courts.... Fundamental too in the concept of due process and so in that of liberty, is the thought that condemnation shall be rendered only after trial.... The hearing, moreover, must be a real one, not a sham, or a pretense. Moore v. Dempsey, 261 U.S. 86; Mooney v. Holohan, 294 U.S. 103. For that reason, ignorant defendants in a capital case were held to have been condemned unlawfully when in truth, though not in form, they were refused the aid of counsel. Powell v. Alabama, supra, 287 U.S. 45, at pages 67, 68. The decision did not turn upon the fact that the benefit of counsel would have been guaranteed to the defendants by the provisions of the Sixth Amendment if they had been prosecuted in a federal court. The decision turned upon the fact that in the particular situation laid before us in the evidence the benefit of counsel was essential to the substance of a hearing.

Our survey of the cases serves, we think, to justify the statement that the dividing line between them, if not unfaltering throughout its course, has been true for the most part to a unifying principle. On which side of the line the case made out by the appellant has appropriate location must be the next inquiry and the final one. Is that kind of double jeopardy to which the statute has subjected him a hardship so acute and shocking that our policy will not endure it? Does it violate those "fundamental principles of liberty and justice which lie at the base of all our civil and political institutions"? ... The answer surely must be "no." What the answer would have to be if the state were permitted after a trial free from error to try the accused over again or to bring another case against him, we have no occasion to consider. We deal with the statute before us and no other. The state is not attempting to wear the accused out by a multitude of cases with accumulated trials. It asks no more than this, that the case against him shall go on until there shall be a trial free from the corrosion of substantial legal error.... This is not cruelty at all, nor even vexation in any immoderate degree. If the trial had been infected with error adverse to the accused, there might have been review at his instance, and as often as necessary to purge the vicious taint. A reciprocal privilege, subject at all times to the discretion of the presiding judge ... has now been granted to the state. There is here no seismic innovation. The edifice of justice stands, its symmetry, to many, greater than before.

2.   The conviction of appellant is not in derogation of any privileges or immunities that belong to him as a citizen of the United States.

There is argument in his behalf that the privileges and immunities clause of the Fourteenth Amendment as well as the due process clause has been flouted by the judgment.

Maxwell v. Dow, supra, 176 U.S. 581, at page 584, gives all the answer that is necessary.

The judgment is affirmed.

Mr. Justice Butler dissents.

ADAMSON v. CALIFORNIA, 332 U.S. 46 (1947). Defendant was convicted of murder in the first degree. As permitted by California law the judge and the prosecutor commented on the failure of the defendant to explain or deny evidence against him. Under California law the jury could have been made aware on cross-examination of prior convictions of the defendant if he had taken the stand. In the Supreme Court the defendant argued both that his conviction under this procedure was a denial of the Fifth Amendment privilege against self-incrimination and that it denied him a fair trial in contravention of the due process clause of the Fourteenth Amendment. The Court affirmed the conviction. Speaking for the Court, Justice Reed stated the holding as follows:

(1) The privilege against self-incrimination is not a privilege of national citizenship protected by the Fourteenth Amendment. "The Slaughter–House Cases decided ... that these rights, as privileges and immunities of state citizenship, remained under the sole protection of the state governments.... This construction has become embedded in our federal system as a functioning element in preserving the balance between national and state power."

(2) The privilege against self-incrimination does not to its full scope inhere in the right to a fair trial protected by the due process clause of the Fourteenth Amendment. "Nothing has been called to our attention that either the framers of the Fourteenth Amendment or the states that adopted intended its due process clause to draw within its scope the earlier amendments to the Constitution."

(3) The particular state procedure involved here did not violate "the protection against state action that the due process clause does grant to an accused. The due process clause forbids compulsion to testify by fear of hurt, torture or exhaustion. It forbids any other type of coercion that falls within the scope of due process."

Justice Frankfurter, concurring, said, in part:

"The short answer to the suggestion that the provision of the Fourteenth Amendment, which ordains 'nor shall any State deprive any person of life, liberty, or property, without due process of law,' was a way of saying that every State must thereafter initiate prosecutions through indictment by a grand jury, must have a trial by a jury of 12 in criminal cases, and must have trial by such a jury in common law suits where the amount in controversy exceeds \$20, is that it is a strange way of saying it. It would be extraordinarily strange for a Constitution to convey such specific commands in such a roundabout and inexplicit way. After all, an amendment to the Constitution should be read in a ' "sense most obvious to the common understanding at the time of its adoption." ... For it was for public adoption that it was proposed.' ... Those reading the English language with the meaning which it ordinarily conveys, those conversant with the political and legal history of the concept of due process, those sensitive to the relations of the States to the central government as well as the relation of some of the provisions of the Bill of Rights to the process of justice, would hardly recognize the Fourteenth Amendment as a cover for the various explicit provisions of the first eight Amendments. Some of these are enduring reflections of experience with human nature, while some express the restricted views of Eighteenth–Century England regarding the best methods for the ascertainment of facts. The notion that the Fourteenth Amendment was a covert way of imposing upon the States all the rules which it seemed important to Eighteenth Century statesmen to write into the Federal

Amendments, was rejected by judges who were themselves witnesses of the process by which the Fourteenth Amendment became part of the Constitution. Arguments that may now be adduced to prove that the first eight Amendments were concealed within the historic phrasing of the Fourteenth Amendment were not unknown at the time of its adoption. A surer estimate of their bearing was possible for judges at the time than distorting distance is likely to vouchsafe. Any evidence of design or purpose not contemporaneously known could hardly have influenced those who ratified the Amendment. Remarks of a particular proponent of the Amendment, no matter how influential, are not to be deemed part of the Amendment. What was submitted for ratification was his proposal, not his speech. Thus, at the time of the ratification of the Fourteenth Amendment the constitutions of nearly half of the ratifying States did not have the rigorous requirements of the Fifth Amendment for instituting criminal proceedings through a grand jury. It could hardly have occurred to these States that by ratifying the Amendment they uprooted their established methods for prosecuting crime and fastened upon themselves a new prosecutorial system.

"Indeed, the suggestion that the Fourteenth Amendment incorporates the first eight Amendments as such is not unambiguously urged. Even the boldest innovator would shrink from suggesting to more than half the States that they may no longer initiate prosecutions without indictment by grand jury, or that thereafter all the States of the Union must furnish a jury of 12 for every case involving a claim above $20. There is suggested merely a selective incorporation of the first eight Amendments into the Fourteenth Amendment. Some are in and some are out, but we are left in the dark as to which are in and which are out. Nor are we given the calculus for determining which go in and which stay out. If the basis of selection is merely that those provisions of the first eight Amendments are incorporated which commend themselves to individual justices as indispensable to the dignity and happiness of a free man, we are thrown back to a merely subjective test. The protection against unreasonable search and seizure might have primacy for one judge, while trial by a jury of 12 for every claim above $20 might appear to another as an ultimate need in a free society. In the history of thought 'natural law' has a much longer and much better founded meaning and justification than such subjective selection of the first eight Amendments for incorporation into the Fourteenth. If all that is meant is that due process contains within itself certain minimal standards which are 'of the very essence of a scheme of ordered liberty,' Palko v. Connecticut, 302 U.S. 319, 325, putting upon this Court the duty of applying these standards from time to time, then we have merely arrived at the insight which our predecessors long ago expressed. We are called upon to apply to the difficult issues of our own day the wisdom afforded by the great opinions in this field.... This guidance bids us to be duly mindful of the heritage of the past, with its great lessons of how liberties are won and how they are lost. As judges charged with the delicate task of subjecting the government of a continent to the Rule of Law, we must be particularly mindful that it is 'a *constitution* we are expounding,' so that it should not be imprisoned in what are merely legal forms even though they have the sanction of the Eighteenth Century....

"And so, when, as in a case like the present, a conviction in a State court is here for review under a claim that a right protected by the Due Process Clause of the Fourteenth Amendment has been denied, the issue is not whether an infraction of one of the specific provisions of the first eight Amendments is disclosed by the record. The relevant question is whether the criminal proceedings which resulted in conviction deprived the accused of the due process of law to which the United States Constitution entitled him. Judicial review of that guaranty of the Fourteenth Amendment inescapably imposes upon this Court an exercise of judgment upon the whole course of the proceedings in order to ascertain whether they offend those canons of decency and fairness which express the notions of justice of English-speaking peoples even toward those charged with the most heinous offenses. These standards of justice are not authoritatively formulated anywhere as though they were prescriptions in a pharmacopoeia. But neither does the application of the Due Process Clause imply that judges are wholly at large. The judicial judgment in applying the Due Process Clause must move within the limits of accepted notions of justice and is not to be based upon the idiosyncrasies of a merely personal judgment. The fact that judges among themselves may differ whether in a particular case a trial offends accepted notions of justice is not disproof that general rather than idiosyncratic standards are applied. An important safeguard against such merely individual judgment is an alert deference to the judgment of the State court under review."

Justices Murphy and Rutledge, dissenting, noted:

"While in substantial agreement with the views of Mr. Justice Black, I have one reservation and one addition to make.

"I agree that the specific guarantees of the Bill of Rights should be carried over intact into the first section of the Fourteenth Amendment. But I am not prepared to say that the latter is entirely and necessarily limited by the Bill of Rights. Occasions may arise where a proceeding falls so far short of conforming to fundamental standards of procedure as to warrant constitutional condemnation in terms of a lack of due process despite the absence of a specific provision in the Bill of Rights." . . .

Justice Black joined by Justice Douglas delivered a long dissenting opinion. The following paragraphs illustrate his thesis:

"This decision reasserts a constitutional theory spelled out in Twining v. New Jersey, 211 U.S. 78, that this Court is endowed by the Constitution with boundless power under 'natural law' periodically to expand and contract constitutional standards to conform to the Court's conception of what at a particular time constitutes 'civilized decency' and 'fundamental principles of liberty and justice.' Invoking this Twining rule, the Court concludes that although comment upon testimony in a federal court would violate the Fifth Amendment, identical comment in a state court does not violate today's fashion in civilized decency and fundamentals and is therefore not prohibited by the Federal Constitution as amended.

"The Twining case was the first, as it is the only decision of this Court, which has squarely held that states were free, notwithstanding the Fifth and Fourteenth Amendments, to extort evidence from one accused of crime. I agree that if Twining be reaffirmed, the result reached might appropriately follow. But I would not reaffirm the Twining decision. I think that decision and the 'natural law' theory of the Constitution upon which it relies, degrade the constitutional safeguards of the Bill of Rights and simultaneously appropriate for this Court a broad power which we are not authorized by the Constitution to exercise. . . . My reasons for believing that the Twining decision should not be revitalized can best be understood by reference to the constitutional, judicial, and general history that preceded and followed the case. . . .

"My study of the historical events that culminated in the Fourteenth Amendment, and the expressions of those who sponsored and favored, as well as those who opposed its submission and passage, persuades me that one of the chief objects that the provisions of the Amendment's first section, separately, and as a whole, were intended to accomplish was to make the Bill of Rights applicable to the states. With full knowledge of the import of the Barron decision, the framers and backers of the Fourteenth Amendment proclaimed its purpose to be to overturn the constitutional rule that case had announced. This historical purpose has never received full consideration or exposition in any opinion of this Court interpreting the Amendment....

"For this reason, I am attaching to this dissent, an appendix which contains a résumé, by no means complete, of the Amendment's history. In my judgment that history conclusively demonstrates that the language of the first section of the Fourteenth Amendment, taken as a whole, was thought by those responsible for its submission to the people, and by those who opposed its submission, sufficiently explicit to guarantee that thereafter no state could deprive its citizens of the privileges and protections of the Bill of Rights. Whether this Court ever will, or whether it now should, in the light of past decisions, give full effect to what the Amendment was intended to accomplish is not necessarily essential to a decision here. However that may be, our prior decisions, including Twining, do not prevent our carrying out that purpose, at least to the extent of making applicable to the states, not a mere part, as the Court has, but the full protection of the Fifth Amendment's provision against compelling evidence from an accused to convict him of crime. And I further contend that the 'natural law' formula which the Court uses to reach its conclusion in this case should be abandoned as an incongruous excrescence on our Constitution. I believe that formula to be itself a violation of our Constitution, in that it subtly conveys to courts, at the expense of legislatures, ultimate power over public policies in fields where no specific provision of the Constitution limits legislative power....

"I cannot consider the Bill of Rights to be an outworn 18th Century 'strait jacket' as the Twining opinion did. Its provisions may be thought outdated abstractions by some. And it is true that they were designed to meet ancient evils. But they are the same kind of human evils that have emerged from century to century wherever excessive power is sought by the few at the expense of the many. In my judgment the people of no nation can lose their liberty so long as a Bill of Rights like ours survives and its basic purposes are conscientiously interpreted, enforced and respected so as to afford continuous protection against old, as well as new, devices and practices which might thwart those purposes. I fear to see the consequences of the Court's practice of substituting its own concepts of decency and fundamental justice for the language of the Bill of Rights as its point of departure in interpreting and enforcing that Bill of Rights. If the choice must be between the selective process of the Palko decision applying some of the Bill of Rights to the States, or the Twining rule applying none of them, I would choose the Palko selective process. But rather than accept either of these choices, I would follow what I believe was the original purpose of the Fourteenth Amendment—to extend to all the people of the nation the complete protection of the Bill of Rights. To hold that this Court can determine what, if any, provisions of the Bill of Rights will be enforced, and if so to what degree, is to frustrate the great design of a written Constitution....

"It is an illusory apprehension that literal application of some or all of the provisions of the Bill of Rights to the States would unwisely increase the sum total of the powers of this Court to invalidate state legislation. The Federal Government has not been harmfully burdened by the requirement that enforcement of federal laws affecting civil liberty conform literally to the Bill of Rights. Who would advocate its repeal? It must be conceded, of course, that the natural-law-due-process formula, which the Court today reaffirms, has been interpreted to limit substantially this Court's power to prevent state violations of the individual civil liberties guaranteed by the Bill of Rights. But this formula also has been used in the past and can be used in the future, to license this Court, in considering regulatory legislation, to roam at large in the broad expanses of policy and morals and to trespass, all too freely, on the legislative domain of the States as well as the Federal Government.

"Since Marbury v. Madison, 1 Cranch 137, was decided, the practice has been firmly established for better or worse, that courts can strike down legislative enactments which violate the Constitution. This process, of course, involves interpretation, and since words can have many meanings, interpretation obviously may result in contraction or extension of the original purpose of a constitutional provision thereby affecting policy. But to pass upon the constitutionality of statutes by looking to the particular standards enumerated in the Bill of Rights and other parts of the Constitution is one thing; to invalidate statutes because of application of 'natural law' deemed to be above and undefined by the Constitution is another. 'In the one instance, courts proceeding within clearly marked constitutional boundaries seek to execute policies written into the Constitution; in the other they roam at will in the limitless area of their own beliefs as to reasonableness and actually select policies, a responsibility which the Constitution entrusts to the legislative representatives of the people.' Federal Power Commission v. Natural Gas Pipeline Co., 315 U.S. 575, 599, 601, n. 4.''

THE HISTORICAL DEBATE

Justice Black's historical thesis is more fully set out in an Appendix in *Adamson* found at 332 U.S. at 92. See also the discussion in the opinions of Justices Black and Harlan in Duncan v. Louisiana, set out *infra*. Scholars attempting to discover the true intent of the framers of the fourteenth amendment have consulted many sources, including: The pre-Civil War literature and party platforms of abolitionist groups. Judicial and legislative pronouncements in the foreground when the amendment was drafted: Barron v. Mayor and City Council Baltimore, 32 U.S. (7 Pet.) 243 (1833), Murray's Lessee v. Hoboken Land & Improvement Co., 59 U.S. (18 How.) 272 (1856), and Dred Scott v. Sandford, 60 U.S. (19 How.) 393 (1857), and the provisions of the Freedman's Bureau bill and the Civil Rights Act. Debates in the Congress and the state ratification bodies. Newspaper and magazine comment of the time. Post-ratification statements purporting to explain the meaning of the amendment by two of the draftsmen, John A. Bingham and Roscoe Conkling.

Out of this vast body of material, diverse conclusions have been drawn as to the import of almost every clause of the amendment. On the specific issue of the amendment's incorporation of the first eight amendments to the federal constitution, historical support can be mustered both for the majority and the dissenting opinions in *Adamson*. The argument for incorporation rests on the known aversion of some of the framers to Barron v. Baltimore, and focuses on the 1871 speech of Bingham stating this as the meaning of the privileges and immunities clause. This position is documented in the works of Guthrie, *The Fourteenth Article of Amendment to the Constitution of the United States* (1898); Flack, *The Adoption of the Fourteenth Amendment* (1908); 2 Crosskey, *Politics and the Constitution* chs. XXXI, XXXII (1953); Boudin, *Truth and Fiction about the Fourteenth Amendment,* 16 N.Y.U.L.Q.Rev. 19 (1938) (with additional support from the due process clause). Equally assiduous work by other researchers has led them to conclude that no such specific content was contemplated for the fourteenth amendment. The writers who argue from abolitionist history point to a greater concern for substantive protection of rights vaguely categorized as principles of natural law than to any particular set of rules for the conduct of trials. Ten Broek, *The Antislavery Origins of the Fourteenth Amendment* (1951); Graham, *The "Conspiracy Theory" of the Fourteenth Amendment,* 47 Yale L.J. 371 (1938) and Graham, *The Early Antislavery Background of the Fourteenth Amendment,* 1950 Wis.L.Rev. 479, 610. Other authors have pointed to the lack of specific debate on this point as indicative of absence of intent to achieve incorporation. They maintain that such a revolutionary change of state procedures, already then divergent from the federal model, would certainly not have been accepted *sub silentio* by the state conventions, if they had so understood the amendment. Fairman and Morrison, *Does the Fourteenth Amendment Incorporate the Bill of Rights?,* 2 Stan.L.Rev. 5, 140 (1949); and see Meyer, *The Blaine Amendment and the Bill of Rights,* 64 Harv.L.Rev. 939 (1951).

For a recent debate of the historical materials, see Curtis, *The Bill of Rights as a Limitation on State Authority: A Reply to Professor Berger,* 16 Wake Forest L.Rev. 45 (1980); Berger, *Incorporation of the Bill of Rights in the Fourteenth Amendment: A Nine–Lived Cat,* 42 Ohio St.L.J. 435 (1981); Curtis, *Further Adventures of the Nine Lived Cat: A Response to Mr. Berger on Incorporation of the Bill of Rights,* 43 Ohio St.L.J. 89 (1982); Berger, *Incorporation of the Bill of Rights: A Reply to Michael Curtis' Response,* 44 Ohio St.L.J. 1 (1983).

In appraising these historical analyses of the fourteenth amendment, you should ask yourself what the utility and relevance of conclusions derived from ambiguous historical records are for present day constitutional law. How can we validly infer the intent of Congress and the ratifying states from the speeches of individual supporters and opponents of the amendment? How can the enactment of the first section of the amendment be separated from the furor and passion accompanying the other sections, then perhaps deemed more important, and now dead letters?

Duncan v. Louisiana

391 U.S. 145, 88 S.Ct. 1444, 20 L.Ed.2d 491 (1968).

Mr. Justice White delivered the opinion of the Court.

Appellant, Gary Duncan, was convicted of simple battery[,] a misdemeanor, punishable by two years' imprisonment and a $300 fine. Appellant sought trial by jury, but because the Louisiana Constitution grants jury trials only in cases in which capital punishment or imprisonment at hard labor may be imposed, the trial judge denied the request. Appellant was convicted and sentenced to serve 60 days in the parish prison and pay a fine of $150. Appellant sought review in the Supreme Court of Louisiana, asserting that the denial of jury trial violated rights guaranteed to him by the United States Constitution. The Supreme Court, finding "no error of law in the ruling complained of," denied appellant a writ of certiorari. [A]ppellant sought review in this Court, alleging that the Sixth and Fourteenth Amendments to the United States Constitution secure the right to jury trial in state criminal prosecutions where a sentence as long as two years may be imposed. . . .

I.

The Fourteenth Amendment denies the States the power to "deprive any person of life, liberty, or property, without due process of law." In resolving conflicting claims concerning the meaning of this spacious language, the Court has looked increasingly to the Bill of Rights for guidance; many of the rights guaranteed by the first eight Amendments to the Constitution have been held to be protected against state action by the Due Process Clause of the Fourteenth Amendment. That clause now protects the right to compensation for property taken by the State; the rights of speech, press, and religion covered by the First Amendment; the Fourth Amendment rights to be free from unreasonable searches and seizures and to have excluded from criminal trials any evidence illegally seized; the right guaranteed by the Fifth Amendment to be free of compelled self-incrimination; and the Sixth Amendment rights to counsel, to a speedy and public trial, to confrontation of opposing witnesses, and to compulsory process for obtaining witnesses.

The test for determining whether a right extended by the Fifth and Sixth Amendments with respect to federal criminal proceedings is also protected against state action by the Fourteenth Amendment has been phrased in a variety of ways in the opinions of this Court. The question has been asked whether a right is among those "fundamental principles of liberty and justice which lie at the base of all our civil and political institutions," Powell v. Alabama, 287 U.S. 45, 67 (1932); whether it is "basic in our system of jurisprudence," In re Oliver, 333 U.S. 257, 273 (1948); and whether it is "a fundamental right, essential to a fair trial," Gideon v. Wainwright, 372 U.S. 335, 343–344 (1963); Malloy v. Hogan, 378 U.S. 1, 6 (1964); Pointer v. Texas, 380 U.S. 400, 403 (1965). The claim before us is that the right to trial by jury guaranteed by the Sixth Amendment meets these tests. The position of Louisiana, on the other hand, is that the Constitution imposes upon the States no duty to give a jury trial in any criminal case, regardless of the seriousness of the crime or the size of the punishment which may be imposed. Because we believe that trial by jury in criminal cases is fundamental to the American scheme of justice, we hold that the Fourteenth Amendment guarantees a right of jury trial in all criminal cases which—were they to be tried in a federal court—would come within the Sixth Amendment's guarantee.[14] Since we con-

---

[14] In one sense recent cases applying provisions of the first eight amendments to the States represent a new approach to the "incorporation" debate. Earlier the Court can be seen as having asked, when inquiring into whether some particular procedural safeguard was required of a State, if a civilized system could be imagined that would not accord the particular protection. For example, Palko v. Connecticut, 302 U.S. 319, 325 (1937), stated: "The right to trial by jury and the immunity from prosecution except as the result of an indictment may have value and importance. Even so, they are not of the very essence of a scheme of ordered liberty.... Few would be so narrow or provincial as to maintain that a fair and enlightened system of justice would be impossible without them." The recent cases, on the other hand, have proceeded upon the valid assumption that state criminal processes are not imaginary and theoretical schemes but actual systems bearing virtually every characteristic of the common-law system that has been developing contemporaneously in England and in this country. The question thus is whether given this kind of system a particular procedure is fundamental—whether, that is, a procedure is necessary to an Anglo–American regime of ordered liberty. It is this sort of inquiry that can justify the conclusions that state courts must exclude evidence seized in violation of the Fourth Amendment, Mapp v. Ohio, 367 U.S. 643 (1961); that state prosecutors may not comment on a defendant's failure to testify, Griffin v. California, 380 U.S. 609 (1965); and that criminal punishment may not be imposed for the status of narcotics addiction, Robinson v. California, 370 U.S. 660 (1962). Of immediate relevance for this case are the Court's holdings that the States must comply with certain provisions of the Sixth Amendment, specifically that the States may not refuse a speedy trial, confrontation of witnesses, and the assistance, at state expense if necessary, of counsel.... Of each of these determinations that a constitutional provision originally written to bind the Federal Government should bind the States as well it might be said that the limitation in question is not necessarily fundamental to fairness in every criminal system that might be imagined but is fundamental in the context of the criminal processes maintained by the American States.

sider the appeal before us to be such a case, we hold that the Constitution was violated when appellant's demand for jury trial was refused.

The history of trial by jury in criminal cases has been frequently told....

. . .

Even such skeletal history is impressive support for considering the right to jury trial in criminal cases to be fundamental to our system of justice, an importance frequently recognized in the opinions of this Court....

Jury trial continues to receive strong support. The laws of every State guarantee a right to jury trial in serious criminal cases; no State has dispensed with it; nor are there significant movements underway to do so....

We are aware of prior cases in this Court in which the prevailing opinion contains statements contrary to our holding today that the right to jury trial in serious criminal cases is a fundamental right and hence must be recognized by the States as part of their obligation to extend due process of law to all persons within their jurisdiction.... None of these cases, however, dealt with a State which had purported to dispense entirely with a jury trial in serious criminal cases.... Respectfully, we reject the prior dicta regarding jury trial in criminal cases.

The guarantees of jury trial in the Federal and State Constitutions reflect a profound judgment about the way in which law should be enforced and justice administered. A right to jury trial is granted to criminal defendants in order to prevent oppression by the Government.... The deep commitment of the Nation to the right of jury trial in serious criminal cases as a defense against arbitrary law enforcement qualifies for protection under the Due Process Clause of the Fourteenth Amendment, and must therefore be respected by the States.

Of course jury trial has "its weaknesses and the potential for misuse," Singer v. United States, 380 U.S. 24, 35 (1965). We are aware of the long debate, especially in this century, among those who write about the administration of justice, as to the wisdom of permitting untrained laymen to determine the facts in civil and criminal proceedings. Although the debate has been intense, with powerful voices on either side, most of the controversy has centered on the jury in civil cases. Indeed, some of the severest critics of civil juries acknowledge that the arguments for criminal juries are much stronger....

The State of Louisiana urges that holding that the Fourteenth Amendment assures a right to jury trial will cast doubt on the integrity of every trial conducted without a jury. Plainly, this is not the import of our holding. Our conclusion is that in the American States, as in the federal judicial system, a general grant of jury trial for serious offenses is a fundamental right, essential

When the inquiry is approached in this way the question whether the States can impose criminal punishment without granting a jury trial appears quite different from the way it appeared in the older cases opining that States might abolish jury trial. See, e.g., Maxwell v. Dow, 176 U.S. 581 (1900). A criminal process which was fair and equitable but used no juries is easy to imagine. It would make use of alternative guarantees and protections which would serve the purposes that the jury serves in the English and American systems. Yet no American State has undertaken to construct such a system. Instead, every American State, including Louisiana, uses the jury extensively, and imposes very serious punishments only after a trial at which the defendant has a right to a jury's verdict. In every State, including Louisiana, the structure and style of the criminal process—the supporting framework and the subsidiary procedures—are of the sort that naturally complement jury trial, and have developed in connection with and in reliance upon jury trial.

for preventing miscarriages of justice and for assuring that fair trials are provided for all defendants. We would not assert, however, that every criminal trial—or any particular trial—held before a judge alone is unfair or that a defendant may never be as fairly treated by a judge as he would be by a jury. Thus we hold no constitutional doubts about the practices, common in both federal and state courts, of accepting waivers of jury trial and prosecuting petty crimes without extending a right to jury trial. However, the fact is that in most places more trials for serious crimes are to juries than to a court alone; a great many defendants prefer the judgment of a jury to that of a court. Even where defendants are satisfied with bench trials, the right to a jury trial very likely serves its intended purpose of making judicial or prosecutorial unfairness less likely.[30]

II.

Louisiana's final contention is that even if it must grant jury trials in serious criminal cases, the conviction before us is valid and constitutional because here the petitioner was tried for simple battery and was sentenced to only 60 days in the parish prison. We are not persuaded. It is doubtless true that there is a category of petty crimes or offenses which is not subject to the Sixth Amendment jury trial provision and should not be subject to the Fourteenth Amendment jury trial requirement here applied to the States. Crimes carrying possible penalties up to six months do not require a jury trial if they otherwise qualify as petty offenses, Cheff v. Schnackenberg, 384 U.S. 373 (1966). But the penalty authorized for a particular crime is of major relevance in determining whether it is serious or not and may in itself, if severe enough, subject the trial to the mandates of the Sixth Amendment. District of Columbia v. Clawans, 300 U.S. 617 (1937). The penalty authorized by the law of the locality may be taken "as a gauge of its social and ethical judgments," 300 U.S., at 628 of the crime in question. In *Clawans* the defendant was jailed for 60 days, but it was the 90–day authorized punishment on which the Court focused in determining that the offense was not one for which the Constitution assured trial by jury. In the case before us the Legislature of Louisiana has made simple battery a criminal offense punishable by imprisonment for two years and a fine. The question, then is whether a crime carrying such a penalty is an offense which Louisiana may insist on trying without a jury.

---

[30] Louisiana also asserts that if due process is deemed to include the right to jury trial, States will be obligated to comply with all past interpretations of the Sixth Amendment, an amendment which in its inception was designed to control only the federal courts and which throughout its history has operated in this limited environment where uniformity is a more obvious and immediate consideration. In particular, Louisiana objects to application of the decisions of this Court interpreting the Sixth Amendment as guaranteeing a 12–man jury in serious criminal cases, Thompson v. Utah, 170 U.S. 343 (1898); as requiring a unanimous verdict before guilt can be found, Maxwell v. Dow, 176 U.S. 581, 586 (1900); and as barring procedures by which crimes subject to the Sixth Amendment jury trial provision are tried in the first instance without a jury but at the first appellate stage by *de novo* trial with a jury, Callan v. Wilson, 127 U.S. 540, 557 (1888). It seems very unlikely to us that our decision today will require widespread changes in state criminal processes. First, our decisions interpreting the Sixth Amendment are always subject to reconsideration, a fact amply demonstrated by the instant decision. In addition, most of the States have provisions for jury trials equal in breadth to the Sixth Amendment, if that amendment is construed, as it has been, to permit the trial of petty crimes and offenses without a jury. Indeed, there appear to be only four States in which juries of fewer than 12 can be used without the defendant's consent for offenses carrying a maximum penalty of greater than one year. Only in Oregon and Louisiana can a less-than-unanimous jury convict for an offense with a maximum penalty greater than one year....

We think not. . . .

. . .

The judgment below is reversed and the case is remanded for proceedings not inconsistent with this opinion.

Mr. Justice Black, with whom Mr. Justice Douglas joins, concurring.

. . . The dissent in this case . . . makes a spirited and forceful defense of [the] now discredited [*Twining*]doctrine. I do not believe that it is necessary for me to repeat the historical and logical reasons for my challenge to the *Twining* holding contained in my *Adamson* dissent and Appendix to it. My Brother Harlan's objections to my *Adamson* dissent history, like that of most of the objectors, relies most heavily on a criticism written by Professor Charles Fairman[,] . . . 2 Stan.L.Rev. 5 (1949) . . . [, which] in my view . . . has completely failed to refute the inferences and arguments that I suggested in my *Adamson* dissent. Professor Fairman's "history" relies very heavily on what was *not* said in the state legislatures that passed on the Fourteenth Amendment. Instead of relying on this kind of negative pregnant, my legislative experience has convinced me that it is far wiser to rely on what *was* said, and most importantly, said by the men who actually sponsored the Amendment in the Congress. . . . [B]oth its sponsors and those who opposed it believed the Fourteenth Amendment made the first eight Amendments of the Constitution (The Bill of Rights) applicable to the States.

. . . [Contrary to the dissent's view,] the words "No State shall make or enforce any law which shall abridge the privileges or immunities of citizens of the United States" seem to me an eminently reasonable way of expressing the idea that henceforth the Bill of Rights shall apply to the States.[1] What more precious "privilege" of American citizenship could there be than that privilege to claim the protections of our great Bill of Rights? I suggest that any reading of "privileges or immunities of citizens of the United States" which excludes the Bill of Rights' safeguards renders the words of this section of the Fourteenth Amendment meaningless. . . .

. . . Brother Harlan's . . . view, as was indeed the view of *Twining,* is that "due process is an evolving concept" and therefore that it entails a "gradual process of judicial inclusion and exclusion" to ascertain those "immutable principles of free government which no member of the Union may disregard." Thus the Due Process Clause is treated as prescribing no specific and clearly ascertainable constitutional command that judges must obey in interpreting the Constitution, but rather as leaving judges free to decide at any particular time whether a particular rule or judicial formulation embodies an "immutable principl[e] of free government" or "is implicit in the concept of ordered liberty," or whether certain conduct "shocks the judge's conscience" or runs counter to some other similar, undefined and undefinable standard. Thus due process, according to my Brother Harlan, is to be a word with no permanent meaning, but one which is found to shift from time to time in accordance with judges' predilections and understandings of what is best for the country. If due process means this, the Fourteenth Amendment, in my opinion, might as well have been written that "no person shall be deprived of life, liberty or property except by laws that the judges of the United States Supreme Court shall find to be consistent with the immutable principles of free government." It is impossi-

---

[1] My view has been and is that the Fourteenth Amendment, *as a whole,* makes the Bill of Rights applicable to the States. This would certainly include the language of the Privileges and Immunities Clause, as well as the Due Process Clause.

ble for me to believe that such unconfined power is given to judges in our Constitution that is a written one in order to limit governmental power.

... [Moreover,] the "fundamental fairness" test is one on a par with that of shocking the conscience of the Court. Each ... depends entirely on the particular judge's idea of ethics and morals instead of requiring him to depend on the boundaries fixed by the written words of the Constitution. Nothing in the history of the phrase "due process of law" suggests that constitutional controls are to depend on any particular judge's sense of values....

Finally ... I am not bothered by the argument that applying the Bill of Rights to the States, "according to the same standards that protect those rights against federal encroachment," interferes with our concept of federalism in that it may prevent States from trying novel social and economic experiments. I have never believed that under the guise of federalism the States should be able to experiment with the protections afforded our citizens through the Bill of Rights.... It seems to me totally inconsistent to advocate on the one hand, the power of this Court to strike down any state law or practice which it finds "unreasonable" or "unfair," and on the other hand urge that the States be given maximum power to develop their own laws and procedures. Yet the due process approach of my Brothers Harlan and Fortas ... does just that since in effect it restricts the States to practices which a majority of this Court is willing to approve on a case-by-case basis. No one is more concerned than I that the States be allowed to use the full scope of their powers as their citizens see fit. And that is why I have continually fought against the expansion of this Court's authority over the States through the use of a broad, general interpretation of due process that permits judges to strike down state laws they do not like.

... I believe as strongly as ever that the Fourteenth Amendment was intended to make the Bill of Rights applicable to the States. I have been willing to support the selective incorporation doctrine, however, as an alternative, although perhaps less historically supportable than complete incorporation. The selective incorporation process, if used properly, does limit the Supreme Court in the Fourteenth Amendment field to specific Bill of Rights' protections only and keeps judges from roaming at will in their own notions of what policies outside the Bill of Rights are desirable and what are not. And, most importantly for me, the selective incorporation process has the virtue of having already worked to make most of the Bill of Rights' protections applicable to the States.

Mr. Justice Fortas, concurring.

I join the judgments and opinions of the Court in these cases because I agree that the Due Process Clause of the Fourteenth Amendment requires that the States accord the right to jury trial in prosecutions for offenses that are not petty....

. . .

Mr. Justice Harlan, whom Mr. Justice Stewart joins, dissenting.

Every American jurisdiction provides for trial by jury in criminal cases. The question before us is not whether jury trial is an ancient institution, which it is; nor whether it plays a significant role in the administration of criminal justice, which it does; nor whether it will endure, which it shall. The question in this case is whether the State of Louisiana, which provides trial by jury for all felonies, is prohibited by the Constitution from trying charges of simple battery to the court alone. In my view, the answer to that question, mandated alike by our constitutional history and by the longer history of trial by jury, is clearly "no."

. . .

I.

I believe I am correct in saying that every member of the Court for at least the last 135 years has agreed that our Founders did not consider the requirements of the Bill of Rights so fundamental that they should operate directly against the States. They were wont to believe rather that the security of liberty in America rested primarily upon the dispersion of governmental power across a federal system. . . .

. . .

A few members of the Court have taken the position that the intention of those who drafted the first section of the Fourteenth Amendment was simply, and exclusively, to make the provisions of the first eight amendments applicable to state action. This view has never been accepted by this Court. In my view, . . . the first section of the Fourteenth Amendment was meant neither to incorporate, nor to be limited to, the specific guarantees of the first eight amendments. The overwhelming historical evidence marshalled by Professor Fairman demonstrates, to me conclusively, that the Congressmen and state legislators who wrote, debated, and ratified the Fourteenth Amendment did not think they were "incorporating" the Bill of Rights[9] and the very breadth and generality of the Amendment's provisions suggests that its authors did not suppose that the Nation would always be limited to mid–19th century conceptions of "liberty" and "due process of law" . . . [N]either history, nor sense, supports using the Fourteenth Amendment to put the States in a constitutional straitjacket with respect to their own development in the administration of criminal or civil law.

Although I therefore fundamentally disagree with the total incorporation view of the Fourteenth Amendment, it seems to me that such a position does at

---

[9] Fairman, Does the Fourteenth Amendment Incorporate the Bill of Rights? The Original Understanding, 2 Stan.L.Rev. 5 (1949). Professor Fairman was not content to rest upon the overwhelming fact that the great words of the four clauses of the first section of the Fourteenth Amendment would have been an exceedingly peculiar way to say that "The rights heretofore guaranteed against federal intrusion by the first eight Amendments are henceforth guaranteed against state intrusion as well." He therefore sifted the mountain of material comprising the debates and committee reports relating to the Amendment in both Houses of Congress and in the state legislatures that passed upon it. He found that in the immense corpus of comments on the purpose and effects of the proposed amendment, and on its virtues and defects, there is almost no evidence whatever for "incorporation." The first eight amendments are so much as mentioned by only two members of Congress, one of whom effectively demonstrated (a) that he did not understand Barron v. Baltimore, 7 Pet. 243, and therefore did not understand the question of incorporation, and (b) that he was not himself understood by his colleagues. One state legislative committee report, rejected by the legislature as a whole, found § I of the Fourteenth Amendment superfluous because it duplicated the Bill of Rights: the committee obviously did not understand Barron v. Baltimore either. That is all Professor Fairman could find, in hundreds of pages of legislative discussion prior to passage of the Amendment, that even suggests incorporation.

To this negative evidence the judicial history of the Amendment could be added. For example, it proved possible for a court whose members had lived through Reconstruction to reiterate the doctrine of Barron v. Baltimore, that the Bill of Rights did not apply to the States, without so much as questioning whether the Fourteenth Amendment had any effect on the continued validity of that principle. E.g., Walker v. Sauvinet, 92 U.S. 90; see generally Morrison, Does the Fourteenth Amendment Incorporate the Bill of Rights? The Judicial Interpretation, 2 Stan.L.Rev. 140 (1949).

least have the virtue, lacking in the Court's selective incorporation approach, of internal consistency: we look to the Bill of Rights, word for word, clause for clause, precedent for precedent because, it is said, the men who wrote the Amendment wanted it that way....

Apart from the ... absolute incorporationists, I can see only one method of analysis that has any internal logic. That is to start with the words "liberty" and "due process of law" and attempt to define them in a way that accords with American traditions and our system of government. This approach, involving a much more discriminating process of adjudication than does "incorporation," is, albeit difficult, the one that was followed throughout the Nineteenth and most of the present century. It entails a "gradual process of judicial inclusion and exclusion," seeking, with due recognition of constitutional tolerance for state experimentation and disparity, to ascertain those "immutable principles of free government which no member of the Union may disregard." ...

. . .

Today's Court still remains unwilling to accept the total incorporationists' view.... The Court is also, apparently, unwilling to face the task of determining whether denial of trial by jury in the situation before us, or in other situations, is fundamentally unfair. Consequently, the Court has compromised on the ease of the incorporationist position, without its internal logic. It has simply assumed that the question before us is whether the Jury Trial Clause of the Sixth Amendment should be incorporated into the Fourteenth, jot-for-jot and case-for-case, or ignored. Then the Court merely declares that the clause in question is "in" rather than "out."

. . .

The Court has justified neither its starting place nor its conclusion....

II.

... When a criminal defendant contends that his state conviction lacked "due process of law," the question before this Court, in my view, is whether he was denied any element of fundamental procedural fairness. Believing, as I do, that due process is an evolving concept and that old principles are subject to reevaluation in light of later experience, I think it appropriate to deal on its merits with the question whether Louisiana denied appellant due process of law when it tried him for simple assault without a jury....

In sum, there is a wide range of views on the desirability of trial by jury, and on the ways to make it most effective when it is used; there is also considerable variation from State to State in local conditions such as the size of the criminal caseload, the ease or difficulty of summoning jurors, and other trial conditions bearing on fairness.... [This situation should invoke] the celebrated dictum of Mr. Justice Brandeis [that it is]

"one of the happy incidents of the federal system that a single courageous State may, if its citizens choose, serve as a laboratory...." New State Ice Co. v. Liebmann, 285 U.S. 262, 280, 311 (dissenting opinion).

This Court, other courts, and the political process are available to correct any experiments in criminal procedure that prove fundamentally unfair to defendants.... [I]nstead, and quite without reason, the Court has chosen to impose upon every State one means of trying criminal cases; it is a good means, but it is not the only fair means, and it is not demonstrably better than the alternatives States might devise.

I would affirm the judgment of the Supreme Court of Louisiana.

INCORPORATION AND THE JURY TRIAL CASES

Prior to *Duncan* it had been assumed that the jury trial guaranteed in the sixth and seventh amendments was the traditional unanimous jury of twelve. Footnote 30 in *Duncan* opened the door to reconsideration of that assumption. The results are worth reporting.

In Williams v. Florida, 399 U.S. 78 (1970), the Court upheld as consistent with the sixth amendment, as made applicable to the states through the fourteenth, a state law permitting conviction by a unanimous jury of six in all non-capital criminal cases. Justice Harlan, concurring, accused the Court of diluting "a federal guarantee in order to reconcile the logic of 'incorporation,' the 'jot-for-jot and case-for-case' application of the federal right to the States, with the reality of federalism. Can one doubt that had Congress tried to undermine the common law right to trial by jury before *Duncan* came on the books the history today recited would have barred such action? Can we expect repeat performances when this Court is called upon to give definition and meaning to other federal guarantees that have been 'incorporated'?" Justice Black, concurring, responded: "Today's decision is in no way attributable to any desire to dilute the Sixth Amendment in order more easily to apply it to the States, but follows solely as a necessary consequence of our duty to re-examine prior decisions to reach the correct constitutional meaning in each case." In Colgrove v. Battin, 413 U.S. 149 (1973), the Court applied the logic of *Williams* in holding that a jury of six persons in a civil case in the federal courts was not in violation of the seventh amendment. However, in Ballew v. Georgia, 435 U.S. 223 (1978), the Court held that the constitutional minimum size for a jury in non-petty criminal offenses was six, invalidating a state statute providing for conviction by unanimous vote of a jury of five.

In Apodaca v. Oregon, 406 U.S. 404 (1972), the Court upheld an Oregon statute providing for conviction in criminal cases by a vote of 10 persons out of a jury of twelve. Justice Powell repeated Justice Harlan's objection in *Williams* that the Court was diluting the scope of sixth amendment rights in the federal courts in order to avoid imposing "unnecessarily rigid" requirements on the states. Most recently in Burch v. Louisiana, 441 U.S. 130 (1979), the Court held invalid a statute providing for trial "before a jury of six persons, five of whom must concur to render a verdict." The Court recognized that "having already departed from the strictly historical requirements of jury trial, it is inevitable that lines must be drawn somewhere if the substance of jury trial right is to be preserved." The Court left open the question whether it would be consistent with the sixth amendment to provide for a nonunanimous vote by any jury of less than twelve but more than six.

DUE PROCESS AS A LIMITATION ON PROCEDURES NOT FORBIDDEN BY THE BILL OF RIGHTS

Justice Black substantially won his argument that the fourteenth amendment should be construed to make the Bill of Rights applicable to the states. As the following case indicates, however, he lost his battle to confine Court review of state procedures to the "specific" provisions of the Bill of Rights.

IN RE WINSHIP, 397 U.S. 358 (1970). In a case addressing what process must be accorded in juvenile proceedings, the Court examined the requirement that proof of criminal charges be beyond a reasonable doubt, concluding that it "plays a vital role in the American scheme of criminal procedure" and that its use "is indispensable to command the respect and confidence of the community in applications of the criminal law." Based on such judgments as to the importance of the standard, the Court said:

"Lest there remain any doubt about the constitutional stature of the reasonable-doubt standard, we explicitly hold that the Due Process Clause protects the accused against conviction except upon proof beyond a reasonable doubt of every fact necessary to constitute the crime with which he is charged."

Justice Harlan concurred in the opinion and judgment. Justice Black dissented at length, opening his opinion with the following:

"... The Court has never clearly held ... that proof beyond a reasonable doubt is either expressly or impliedly commanded by any provision of the Constitution. The Bill of Rights, which in my view is made fully applicable to the States by the Fourteenth Amendment, see Adamson v. California, 332 U.S. 46, 71–75 (1947) (dissenting opinion), does by express language provide for, among other things, a right to counsel in criminal trials, a right to indictment, and the right of a defendant to be informed of the nature of the charges against him. And in two places the Constitution provides for trial by jury, but nowhere in that document is there any statement that conviction of crime requires proof of guilt beyond a reasonable doubt. The Constitution thus goes into some detail to spell out what kind of trial a defendant charged with crime should have, and I believe the Court has no power to add to or subtract from the procedures set forth by the Founders. I realize that it is far easier to substitute individual judges' ideas of 'fairness' for the fairness prescribed by the Constitution, but I shall not at any time surrender my belief that that document itself should be our guide, not our own concept of what is fair, decent, and right. That this old 'shock-the-conscience' test is what the Court is relying on, rather than the words of the Constitution, is clearly enough revealed by the reference of the majority to 'fair treatment' and to the statement by the dissenting judges in the New York Court of Appeals that failure to require proof beyond a reasonable doubt amounts to a 'lack of fundamental fairness.' As I have said time and time again, I prefer to put my faith in the words of the written Constitution itself rather than to rely on the shifting, day-to-day standards of fairness of individual judges."

More recently, disagreement within the Court has not centered around whether fourteenth amendment due process prohibits state procedures the Bill of Rights does not forbid, but around what methodology the Court should employ in defining the additional prohibitions. For example, having previously held in Browning–Ferris Industries v. Kelco Disposal, Inc., 492 U.S. 257 (1989), that the Eighth Amendment ban on excessive fines does not apply to punitive damage awards in cases between private parties, the Court decided that the Due Process Clause does circumscribe state procedures for awarding punitive damages. Pacific Mutual Life Insurance Co. v. Haslip, 499 U.S. 1 (1991).

Justice Blackmun's majority opinion upheld Alabama's traditional common-law method of assessing punitive damages, under which the decisions of court-instructed juries were subject to trial and appellate review, but only after inquiring whether that method was "inherently unfair." Furthermore, even though "well established before the Fourteenth Amendment was enacted" and with "[n]othing in that Amendment's text or history indicat[ing] an intention on the part of its drafters to overturn the prevailing method[,]" "general concerns of reasonableness and adequate guidance from the court when the case is tried to a jury properly enter into the constitutional calculus."

Justice Scalia's concurrence objected to the Court's "fairness" or "reasonableness" inquiry. In his view, "jury-assessed punitive damages" are "categorically" valid, because no Bill of Rights provision is implicated and the Due Process Clause itself is not violated so long as a particular procedure is "a traditional one." Asserting that "it is not for the Members of this Court to decide from time to time whether a process approved by the legal traditions of our people is 'due process' ...," he concluded that "traditional practice (unless contrary to the Bill of Rights) is conclusive of 'fundamental fairness.' "

Justice Kennedy concurred separately, agreeing "that the judgment of history should govern the outcome" in this case, but disagreeing with Justice Scalia "that widespread adherence to a historical practice always forecloses further inquiry when a party challenges an ancient institution or procedure as violative of due process." Justice O'Connor's even more emphatic dissent said that "[i]t does not matter that the system has been around for a long time, or that the result in this particular case may not seem glaringly unfair." She responded to Justice Scalia as follows:

"Circumstances are different than they were 200 years ago, and nothing in the Fourteenth Amendment requires us to blind ourselves to this fact.... Just the opposite is true. Due process demands that we possess some degree of confidence that the procedures employed to deprive persons of life, liberty, and property are capable of producing fair and reasonable results. When we lose that confidence, a change must be made."[a]

The separate opinions in Medina v. California, 505 U.S. 437 (1992), reflect a similar divergence of viewpoints. There the Court rejected a criminal defendant's due process claim that the State could not require him to carry the burden of proving his incompetence by a preponderance of evidence. Justice Kennedy's majority opinion said in part:

"In the field of criminal law, we 'have defined the category of infractions that violate "fundamental fairness" very narrowly' based on the recognition that, '[b]eyond the specific guarantees enumerated in the Bill of Rights, the Due Process Clause has limited operation.' Dowling v. United States, 493 U.S. 342 ... (1990);.... The Bill of Rights speaks in explicit terms to many aspects of criminal procedure, and the expansion of those constitutional guarantees under the open-ended rubric of the Due Process Clause invites undue interference with both considered legislative judgments and the careful balance that the Constitution strikes between liberty and order...."

. . .

"... [B]ecause the States have considerable expertise in matters of criminal procedure and the criminal process is grounded in centuries of com-

---

[a] Compare with *Haslip* the Court's subsequent decision in Honda Motor Co. v. Oberg, 512 U.S. 415 (1994), invalidating under due process Oregon's denial of judicial review of the size of punitive damage awards. Noting that "[o]ur recent cases have recognized a substantive limit on the size of punitive damage awards" and that judicial review as a safeguard against excessive verdicts was a well-established common law tradition from which Oregon alone had deviated (and had done so without providing a substitute procedure), Justice Stevens observed for the majority in pertinent part:

"Oregon's abrogation of a well-established common law protection against arbitrary deprivations of property raises a presumption that its procedures violate the Due Process Clause.... [T]raditional practice provides a touchstone for constitutional analysis.... Because the basic procedural protections of the common law have been regarded as so fundamental, very few cases have arisen in which a party has complained of their denial. In fact, most of our Due Process decisions involve arguments that traditional protections provide too little protection and that additional safeguards are necessary to ensure compliance with the Constitution.... Pacific Mut. Life Ins. v. Haslip...."

mon-law tradition, it is appropriate to exercise substantial deference to legislative judgments in this area. . . .

"Based on our review of the historical treatment of the burden of proof in competency proceedings, the operation of the challenged rule, and our precedents, we cannot say that the allocation of the burden of proof to a criminal defendant to prove incompetence 'offends some principle of justice so rooted in the traditions and conscience of our people as to be ranked as fundamental.' "

In particular, that review examined "[h]istorical practice"—deemed "probative of whether a procedural rule can be characterized as fundamental"; "[c]ontemporary practice"—regarded as "of limited relevance to the due process inquiry"; and "whether the rule transgresses any recognized principle of 'fundamental fairness' in operation."

Justice O'Connor concurred, joined by Justice Souter, rejecting any "intimation that the balancing of equities is inappropriate in evaluating whether state criminal procedures amount to due process." Though she "agree[d] with the Court that historical pedigree can give a procedural practice a presumption of constitutionality," she thought "the presumption must surely be rebuttable." She also said:

"... Against the historical status quo, I read the Court's opinion to allow some weight to be given countervailing considerations of fairness in operation. . . . Any less charitable reading of the Court's opinion would put it at odds with many of our criminal due process cases, in which we have required States to institute procedures that were neither required at common law nor explicitly commanded by the text of the Constitution. . . ."

Justice Blackmun's dissent, joined by Justice Stevens, also "read" the majority "to acknowledge that ... the Court [is not relieved] from evaluating the underlying fairness of imposing the burden of proof of incompetency upon the defendant." In his view, "[b]ecause the *Due* Process Clause is not the *Some* Process Clause, ... it requires careful balancing of the individual and governmental interests at stake to determine what process is due."

"INCORPORATION"—ITS CURRENT SCOPE

Which portions of the Bill of Rights have been "incorporated" by the fourteenth amendment so as to be applicable against the states? The current situation is outlined below.

(1) **The First Amendment.** The Court has long applied to the states under the fourteenth amendment the same restrictions upon regulations relating to speech, religion, and association as it applies to the federal government under the first amendment. See, e.g., West Virginia State Board of Education v. Barnette, 319 U.S. 624 (1943); Everson v. Board of Education, 330 U.S. 1 (1947); Edwards v. South Carolina, 372 U.S. 229 (1963). For a case in which there was a dissent from the application of identical standards to the states as to the federal government, see Roth v. United States, 354 U.S. 476 (1957).

(2) **The Fourth Amendment.** *Arrest and Search.* That the fourth amendment applies to the states with the same coverage as it has with respect to the federal government was decided in Mapp v. Ohio, 367 U.S. 643 (1961), and Ker v. California, 374 U.S. 23 (1963).

(3) **The Fifth Amendment**

Indictment. The Court held in Hurtado v. California, 110 U.S. 516 (1884), that states could permit prosecutions on the basis of information filed by district attorneys rather than indictments by grand juries. In Alexander v. Louisiana, 405 U.S. 625 (1972), the Court in refusing to permit a male defendant to challenge an exemption of women from the grand jury, said: "Although the Due Process Clause guarantees petitioner a fair trial, it does not require the States to observe the Fifth Amendment's provision for presentment or indictment by a grand jury.... the Court has never held that federal concepts of a 'grand jury', binding on the federal courts under the Fifth Amendment, are obligatory for the States. Hurtado v. California...."

Double Jeopardy. In Benton v. Maryland, 395 U.S. 784 (1969), the Court held that charges of double jeopardy in state proceedings "must be judged not by the watered-down standard enunciated in Palko, but under this Court's interpretations of the Fifth Amendment double jeopardy provision." In Ashe v. Swenson, 397 U.S. 436 (1970), the Court held that the doctrine of collateral estoppel is included in the fifth amendment guaranty and made applicable to the states.

Privilege Against Self-incrimination. "[T]he Fifth Amendment's exception from compulsory self-incrimination is also protected by the Fourteenth Amendment against abridgment by the States." Malloy v. Hogan, 378 U.S. 1 (1964). See also Griffin v. California, 380 U.S. 609 (1965); Williams v. Florida, 399 U.S. 78 (1970); California v. Byers, 402 U.S. 424 (1971).

Taking of Property Without Just Compensation. The "taking" clause has long been held applicable to the states. In Penn Central Transportation Co. v. New York City, 438 U.S. 104 (1978), the Court said that "of course" the taking clause "is made applicable to the States through the Fourteenth Amendment," citing Chicago, B. & Q.R. Co. v. Chicago, 166 U.S. 226 (1897).

(4) The Sixth Amendment

Speedy Trial. Klopfer v. North Carolina, 386 U.S. 213, 223 (1967): "We hold here that the right to a speedy trial is as fundamental as any of the rights secured by the Sixth Amendment." The Court reversed an order under a state procedure which permitted the prosecutor to bring a case to trial at any time on his own motion.

Public Trial. The Court first held that the fourteenth amendment guaranteed to defendants a public trial in In re Oliver, 333 U.S. 257 (1948). In Estes v. Texas, 381 U.S. 532, 538 (1965), dealing with a state prosecution the Court said: "We start with the proposition that it is a 'public trial' that the Sixth Amendment guarantees to the 'accused.'"

Jury Trial. See Duncan v. Louisiana, 391 U.S. 145 (1968), supra.

Notice of Charge. "No principle of procedural due process is more clearly established than that notice of the specific charge, and a chance to be heard in a trial of the issues raised by that charge, if desired, are among the constitutional rights of every accused in a criminal proceeding in all courts, state or federal." Cole v. Arkansas, 333 U.S. 196, 201 (1948). See also In re Oliver, 333 U.S. 257 (1948); In re Gault, 387 U.S. 1, 31 (1967).

Confrontation of Witnesses. In Pointer v. Texas, 380 U.S. 400 (1965) the Court reversed a conviction where the transcript of the testimony of a witness whom the defendant had not had a fair opportunity to cross-examine was used at the trial. "We hold today that the Sixth Amendment's right of an accused to confront the witnesses against him is likewise a fundamental right and is made obligatory on the States by the Fourteenth Amendment." See also Parker v. Gladden, 385 U.S. 363 (1966).

Compulsory Process for Obtaining Witnesses. In Washington v. Texas, 388 U.S. 14 (1967), the Court reversed a conviction where the application of a state statute forbidding persons charged as principals, accomplices, or accessories in the same crime to be witnesses for each other deprived defendant of the testimony of the only other witness to the crime. "The right of an accused to have compulsory process for obtaining witnesses in his favor stands on no lesser footing than the other Sixth Amendment rights that we have previously held applicable to the States."

Right to Counsel. The Court first held that the sixth amendment guaranty of the right to counsel applied as such to the states through the Fourteenth Amendment in Gideon v. Wainwright, 372 U.S. 335 (1963).

(5) **The Seventh Amendment.** The Court held in Walker v. Sauvinet, 92 U.S. 90 (1876), that the fourteenth amendment did not require the states to provide a jury in civil cases. In Palko v. Connecticut, 302 U.S. 319, 324 (1937), the Court said that trial by jury in civil cases can be abolished altogether. This interpretation has not been modified and the states have been left free to construct their own systems for providing jury trial in civil cases.

(6) **The Eighth Amendment**

Bail. The Court has not decided whether the states are under federal constitutional constraints with reference to bail, but in Schilb v. Kuebel, 404 U.S. 357 (1971), it noted that "the Eighth Amendment's proscription of excessive bail has been assumed to have application to the states through the Fourteenth Amendment."

Excessive Fines. In Browning–Ferris Industries v. Kelco Disposal, Inc., 492 U.S. 257, 276 n. 22 (1989), the Court expressly declined to "decide whether the Eighth Amendment's prohibition on excessive fines applies to the several States through the Fourteenth Amendment...."

Cruel and Unusual Punishment. In Robinson v. California, 370 U.S. 660, 667 (1962), the Court held that "a state law which imprisons a person (afflicted with the illness of narcotic addiction) as a criminal, even though he has never touched any narcotic drug within the State or been guilty of any irregular behavior there, inflicts a cruel and unusual punishment in violation of the Fourteenth Amendment." In Furman v. Georgia, 408 U.S. 238 (1972), the court held "that the imposition and carrying out of the death penalty in these cases constitutes cruel and unusual punishment in violation of the Eighth and Fourteenth Amendments."

CHAPTER 9

THE DUE PROCESS, CONTRACT, AND JUST COMPENSATION CLAUSES AND THE REVIEW OF THE REASONABLENESS OF LEGISLATION

SECTION 1. ECONOMIC REGULATORY LEGISLATION

A. THE RISE AND FALL OF DUE PROCESS

DUE PROCESS AS A RESTRAINT ON THE SUBSTANCE OF LEGISLATION

The due process clauses of the Fifth and Fourteenth Amendments presented two major initial problems of interpretation: (1) Were the clauses, like Magna Carta, intended only as a restraint upon the executive? Did they operate only to provide that the executive branch of the government shall operate in accordance with the common or statutory law in force? Or were they intended in the context of the United States to function as limitations upon the powers of Congress and of the state legislatures? (2) If they were intended to limit the legislatures, did they serve to restrain only the enactment of procedures which are not "due" or "fair"? Or did they serve to impose restraints on the substance of legislation?

In two cases arising under the fifth amendment prior to the Civil War the Court almost casually gave answers to these questions. In 1856 in Murray's Lessee v. Hoboken Land & Improvement Co., 59 U.S. (18 How.) 272, 276 (1855), the Court answered the first question: "It is manifest that it was not left to the legislative power to enact any process which might be devised. The article is a restraint on the legislative as well as on the executive and judicial powers of government, and cannot be so constructed as to leave congress free to make any process 'due process of law' by its mere will." In 1857 in Dred Scott v. Sandford, 60 U.S. (19 How.) 393, 450 (1857), the Court with equal casualness gave a substantive content to the clause: "And an Act of Congress which deprives a citizen of the United States of his liberty or property, merely because he came himself or brought his property into a particular Territory of the United States, and who had committed no offense against the laws, could hardly be dignified with the name of due process of law."

In the *Slaughter–House Cases* in 1872, set out supra p. 466, the Court summarily rejected a challenge to a law granting a monopoly based on due process, in the face of a dissent by Justice Bradley arguing that "a law which prohibits a large class of citizens from adopting a lawful employment, or from following a lawful employment previously adopted, does deprive them of liberty as well as property, without due process of law. Their right of choice is a portion of their liberty; their occupation is their property."

The Court addressed the issues again in 1878 in Davidson v. New Orleans, 96 U.S. 97. The Court upheld an application of a Louisiana statute providing for a special assessment against property for drainage purposes. In discussing the meaning of the due process clause the Court said: "It is easy to see that when the great Barons of England wrung from King John, at the point of the sword, the concession that neither their lives nor their property should be disposed of by the Crown, except as provided by the law of the land, they meant by 'law of the land' the ancient and customary laws of the English people, or laws enacted by the Parliament of which those Barons were a controlling element. It was not in their minds, therefore, to protect themselves against the enactment of laws by the Parliament of England. But when, in the year of grace 1866, there is placed in the Constitution of the United States a declaration that 'No State shall deprive any person of life, liberty, or property without due process of law,' can a State make anything due process of law which, by its own legislation, it chooses to declare such? To affirm this is to hold that the prohibition to the States is of no avail, or has no application where the invasion of private rights is affected under the forms of state legislation. It seems to us that a statute which declared in terms, and without more, that the full and exclusive title of a described piece of land, which is now in A, shall be and is hereby vested in B, would, if effectual, deprive A of his property without due process of law, within the meaning of the constitutional provision...."

THE FLOWERING OF ECONOMIC DUE PROCESS

In the first few economic regulation cases to come before it under the fourteenth amendment the Court indicated a very limited scope for due process review. A challenge to a statutory monopoly was rejected in the *Slaughter-House Cases,* supra. In Munn v. Illinois, 94 U.S. 113 (1877), the Court upheld an Illinois statute fixing maximum charges for the storage of grain in warehouses. The Court concluded that such warehouses were sufficiently related to the public interest that they would be governed by the common law rule requiring charges to be reasonable. Hence, whatever might be the case with respect to merely private contracts this type could be regulated and the determination as to reasonableness of the price could be made legislatively rather than judicially. "Rights of property which have been created by the common law cannot be taken away without due process; but the law itself, as a rule of conduct, may be changed at the will, or even at the whim, of the legislature, unless prevented by constitutional limitations. Indeed, the great office of statutes is to remedy defects in the common law as they are developed, and to adapt it to the changes of time and circumstances.... We know that this is a power which may be abused; but that is no argument against its existence. For protection against abuses by Legislatures the people must resort to the polls, not the courts." Justices Field and Strong dissented.

Between 1877 and 1900, the Court gradually broadened its interpretation of the meaning of the due process clause with reference to economic regulations. During this period the membership of the Court changed completely—by 1898 not a single judge remained who had sat at the time of *Munn v. Illinois.* The expressed opinions of the leaders of the bar helped create a favorable climate for this broadened interpretation. See Twiss, *Lawyers and the Constitution* (1942).

A major step was the decision that corporations were "persons" within the meaning of the fourteenth amendment and hence able to claim under the due process and equal protection clauses. The point was first argued to the Court, but not decided, in San Mateo County v. Southern Pacific R. Co., 116 U.S. 138

(1885). It was decided without argument or opinion in Santa Clara County v. Southern Pacific R. Co., 118 U.S. 394 (1886) when Chief Justice Waite announced: "The Court does not wish to hear argument on the question whether the provision in the Fourteenth Amendment to the Constitution, which forbids a State to deny to any person within its jurisdiction the equal protection of the laws, applies to these Corporations. We are all of the opinion that it does." For the story behind this decision, see Graham, *The "Conspiracy Theory" of the Fourteenth Amendment*, 47 Yale L.J. 371 (1938), 48 id. 171 (1938).

The Court's more expansive view was signaled in Mugler v. Kansas, 123 U.S. 623 (1887). While it upheld a state law prohibiting the manufacture and sale of alcoholic beverages, it stated that not every regulatory statute "is to be accepted as a legitimate exertion of the police powers of the State. There are, of necessity, limits beyond which legislation cannot rightfully go.... The courts are not bound by mere forms, nor are they to be misled by mere pretenses. They are at liberty—indeed, are under a solemn duty—to look at the substance of things, whenever they enter upon the inquiry whether the Legislature has transcended the limits of its authority. If therefore, a statute purporting to have been enacted to protect the public health, the public morals, or the public safety, has no real or substantial relations to those objects, or is a palpable invasion of rights secured by the fundamental law, it is the duty of the courts to so adjudge, and thereby give effect to the Constitution."

The first major use of the due process clause to invalidate state economic regulations arose in the context of state regulation of railroad rates. In Chicago, M. & St. P.R. Co. v. Minnesota, 134 U.S. 418 (1890), the Court held unconstitutional a Minnesota statute authorizing a state commission to fix rates to be charged by railroads and forbidding any judicial review of the rates set. The Court said that under the due process clause the railroad companies were entitled to a judicial hearing on the question whether the rates set were reasonable. "The question of the reasonableness of a rate of charge for transportation by a railroad company, involving as it does the element of reasonableness both as regards the company and as regards the public, is eminently a question for judicial investigation, requiring due process of law for its determination. If the company is deprived of the power of charging reasonable rates for the use of its property, and such deprivation takes place in the absence of an investigation by judicial machinery, it is deprived of the lawful use of its property, and thus, in substance and effect, of the property itself, without due process of law and in violation of the Constitution of the United States...."

In Smyth v. Ames, 169 U.S. 466, 546 (1898) the Court established a constitutional standard to be applied in reviewing rate regulations: "We hold ... that the basis of all calculations as to the reasonableness of rates to be charged by a corporation maintaining a highway under legislative sanction must be the fair value of the property being used by it for the convenience of the public."[1]

ALLGEYER v. LOUISIANA, 165 U.S. 578 (1897). The Court held that under the due process clause Louisiana could not make it a misdemeanor for a resident to use the mails to enter into a contract in New York with an insurance company not licensed to do business in Louisiana to insure goods

---

[1] The long and complicated history of the attempt by the courts to apply this doctrine is summarized in Cook, *History of Rate–Determination Under Due Process Clauses*, 11 U.Chi.L.Rev. 297 (1944); Jourolmon, *The Life and Death of Smyth v. Ames*, 18 Tenn.L.Rev. 347, 663, 756 (1944–45); Dakin, *The Changing Nature of Public Utility Rate Regulation: Just Compensation, Due Process, and Equal Protection*, 36 Tulane L.Rev. 401, 711 (1962).

shipped from Louisiana to Europe. The Court said: "The Supreme Court of Louisiana says that the act of writing within that State the letter of notification, was an act therein done to effect an insurance on property then in the State, in a marine insurance company which had not complied with its laws, and such act was, therefore, prohibited by the statute. As so construed we think the statute is a violation of the Fourteenth Amendment of the Federal Constitution, in that it deprives the defendants of their liberty without due process of law. The statute which forbids such act does not become due process of law, because it is inconsistent with the provisions of the Constitution of the Union. The liberty mentioned in that amendment means not only the right of the citizen to be free from the mere physical restraint of his person, as by incarceration, but the term is deemed to embrace the right of the citizen to be free in the enjoyment of all his faculties; to be free to use them in all lawful ways; to live and work where he will; to earn his livelihood by any lawful calling; to pursue any livelihood or avocation, and for that purpose to enter into all contracts which may be proper, necessary and essential to his carrying out to a successful conclusion the purposes above mentioned."

Lochner v. New York

198 U.S. 45, 25 S.Ct. 539, 49 L.Ed. 937 (1905).

Mr. Justice Peckham delivered the opinion of the Court. . . .

The indictment, it will be seen, charges that the plaintiff in error violated the 110th section of article 8, chapter 415, of the Laws of 1897, known as the labor law of the state of New York, in that he wrongfully and unlawfully required and permitted an employee working for him to work more than sixty hours in one week. . . .

It is not an act merely fixing the number of hours which shall constitute a legal day's work, but an absolute prohibition upon the employer permitting, under any circumstances, more than ten hours' work to be done in his establishment. The employee may desire to earn the extra money which would arise from his working more than the prescribed time, but this statute forbids the employer from permitting the employee to earn it.

The statute necessarily interferes with the right of contract between the employer and employees, concerning the number of hours in which the latter may labor in the bakery of the employer. The general right to make a contract in relation to his business is part of the liberty of the individual protected by the 14th Amendment of the Federal Constitution. Allgeyer v. Louisiana, 165 U.S. 578. Under that provision no state can deprive any person of life, liberty, or property without due process of law. The right to purchase or to sell labor is part of the liberty protected by this amendment, unless there are circumstances which exclude the right. There are, however, certain powers, existing in the sovereignty of each state in the Union, somewhat vaguely termed police powers, the exact description and limitation of which have not been attempted by the courts. Those powers, broadly stated, and without, at present, any attempt at a more specific limitation, relate to the safety, health, morals, and general welfare of the public. Both property and liberty are held on such reasonable conditions as may be imposed by the governing power of the state in the exercise of those powers, and with such conditions the 14th Amendment was not designed to interfere. Mugler v. Kansas, 123 U.S. 623. . . .

Therefore, when the state, by its legislature, in the assumed exercise of its police powers, has passed an act which seriously limits the right to labor or the

Issue

right of contract in regard to their means of livelihood between persons who are *sui juris* (both employer and employee), it becomes of great importance to determine which shall prevail,—the right of the individual to labor for such time as he may choose, or the right of the state to prevent the individual from laboring, or from entering into any contract to labor, beyond a certain time prescribed by the state.

This court has recognized the existence and upheld the exercise of the police powers of the states in many cases which might fairly be considered as border ones, and it has, in the course of its determination of questions regarding the asserted invalidity of such statutes, on the ground of their violation of the rights secured by the Federal Constitution, been guided by rules of a very liberal nature, the application of which has resulted, in numerous instances, in upholding the validity of state statutes thus assailed. Among the later cases where the state law has been upheld by this court is that of Holden v. Hardy, 169 U.S. 366. A provision in the act of the legislature of Utah was there under consideration, the act limiting the employment of workmen in all underground mines or workings, to eight hours per day, "except in cases of emergency, where life or property is in imminent danger." It also limited the hours of labor in smelting and other institutions for the reduction or refining of ores or metals to eight hours per day, except in like cases of emergency. The act was held to be a valid exercise of the police powers of the state....

It must, of course, be conceded that there is a limit to the valid exercise of the police power by the state.... In every case that comes before this court, therefore, where legislation of this character is concerned, and where the protection of the Federal Constitution is sought, the question necessarily arises: Is this a fair, reasonable, and appropriate exercise of the police power of the state, or is it an unreasonable, unnecessary, and arbitrary interference with the right of the individual to his personal liberty, or to enter into those contracts in relation to labor which may seem to him appropriate or necessary for the support of himself and his family? Of course the liberty of contract relating to labor includes both parties to it. The one has as much right to purchase as the other to sell labor.

This is not a question of substituting the judgment of the court for that of the legislature. If the act be within the power of the state it is valid, although the judgment of the court might be totally opposed to the enactment of such a law. But the question would still remain: Is it within the police power of the state? and that question must be answered by the court.

The question whether this act is valid as a labor law, pure and simple, may be dismissed in a few words. There is no reasonable ground for interfering with the liberty of persons or the right of free contract, by determining the hours of labor, in the occupation of a baker.... Viewed in the light of a purely labor law with no reference whatever to the question of health, we think that a law like the one before us involves neither the safety, the morals, nor the welfare of the public, and that the interest of the public is not in the slightest degree affected by such an act. The law must be upheld, if at all, as a law pertaining to the health of the individual engaged in the occupation of a baker....

We think the limit of the police power has been reached and passed in this case. There is, in our judgment, no reasonable foundation for holding this to be necessary or appropriate as a health law to safeguard the public health, or the health of the individuals who are following the trade of a baker....

It is also urged, pursuing the same line of argument, that it is to the interest of the state that its population should be strong and robust, and therefore any legislation which may be said to tend to make people healthy must be valid as health laws, enacted under the police power. If this be a valid argument and a justification for this kind of legislation, it follows that the protection of the Federal Constitution from undue interference with liberty of person and freedom of contract is visionary, wherever the law is sought to be justified as a valid exercise of the police power. Scarcely any law but might find shelter under such assumptions, and conduct, properly so called, as well as contract, would come under the restrictive sway of the legislature. Not only the hours of employees, but the hours of employers, could be regulated, and doctors, lawyers, scientists, all professional men, as well as athletes and artisans, could be forbidden to fatigue their brains and bodies by prolonged hours of exercise, lest the fighting strength of the state be impaired. We mention these extreme cases because the contention is extreme. We do not believe in the soundness of the views which uphold this law.... Statutes of the nature of that under review, limiting the hours in which grown and intelligent men may labor to earn their living, are mere meddlesome interferences with the rights of the individual, and they are not saved from condemnation by the claim that they are passed in the exercise of the police power and upon the subject of the health of the individual whose rights are interfered with, unless there be some fair ground, reasonable in and of itself, to say that there is material danger to the public health, or to the health of the employees, if the hours of labor are not curtailed....

It is impossible for us to shut our eyes to the fact that many of the laws of this character, while passed under what is claimed to be the police power for the purpose of protecting the public health or welfare, are, in reality, passed from other motives. We are justified in saying so when, from the character of the law and the subject upon which it legislates, it is apparent that the public health or welfare bears but the most remote relation to the law. The purpose of a statute must be determined from the natural and legal effect of the language employed; and whether it is or is not repugnant to the Constitution of the United States must be determined from the natural effect of such statutes when put into operation, and not from their proclaimed purpose....

It is manifest to us that the limitation of the hours of labor as provided for in this section of the statute under which the indictment was found, and the plaintiff in error convicted, has no such direct relation to, and no such substantial effect upon, the health of the employee, as to justify us in regarding the section as really a health law. It seems to us that the real object and purpose were simply to regulate the hours of labor between the master and his employees (all being men, *sui juris*), in a private business, not dangerous in any degree to morals, or in any real and substantial degree to the health of the employees. Under such circumstances the freedom of master and employee to contract with each other in relation to their employment, and in defining the same, cannot be prohibited or interfered with, without violating the Federal Constitution.

The judgment of the Court of Appeals of New York, as well as that of the Supreme Court and of the County Court of Oneida County, must be reversed and the case remanded to the County Court for further proceedings not inconsistent with this opinion.

Reversed.

Mr. Justice Harlan (with whom Mr. Justice White and Mr. Justice Day concurred) dissenting:

. . .

I take it to be firmly established that what is called the liberty of contract may, within certain limits, be subjected to regulations designed and calculated to promote the general welfare, or to guard the public health, the public morals, or the public safety. "The liberty secured by the Constitution of the United States to every person within its jurisdiction does not import," this court has recently said, "an absolute right in each person to be at all times and in all circumstances wholly freed from restraint. There are manifold restraints to which every person is necessarily subject for the common good." . . .

Granting, then, that there is a liberty of contract which cannot be violated even under the sanction of direct legislative enactment, but assuming, as according to settled law we may assume, that such liberty of contract is subject to such regulations as the state may reasonably prescribe for the common good and the well-being of society, what are the conditions under which the judiciary may declare such regulations to be in excess of legislative authority and void? Upon this point there is no room for dispute; for the rule is universal that a legislative enactment, Federal or state, is never to be disregarded or held invalid unless it be, beyond question, plainly and palpably in excess of legislative power. . . . If there be doubt as to the validity of the statute, that doubt must therefore be resolved in favor of its validity and the courts must keep their hands off leaving the legislature to meet the responsibility for unwise legislation. If the end which the legislature seeks to accomplish be one to which its power extends, and if the means employed to that end, although not the wisest or best, are yet not plainly and palpably unauthorized by law, then the court cannot interfere. In other words, when the validity of a statute is questioned, the burden of proof, so to speak, is upon those who assert it to be unconstitutional. McCulloch v. Maryland, 4 Wheat. 316, 421.

Let these principles be applied to the present case. By the statute in question it is provided that "no employee shall be required, or permitted, to work in a biscuit, bread, or cake bakery, or confectionery establishment, more than sixty hours in any one week, or more than ten hours in any one day, unless for the purpose of making a shorter work day on the last day of the week; nor more hours in any one week than will make an average of ten hours per day for the number of days during such week in which such employee shall work."

It is plain that this statute was enacted in order to protect the physical well-being of those who work in bakery and confectionery establishments. It may be that the statute had its origin, in part, in the belief that employers and employees in such establishments were not upon an equal footing, and that the necessities of the latter often compelled them to submit to such exactions as unduly taxed their strength. Be this as it may, the statute must be taken as expressing the belief of the people of New York that, as a general rule, and in the case of the average man, labor in excess of sixty hours during a week in such establishments may endanger the health of those who thus labor. Whether or not this be wise legislation it is not the province of the court to inquire. Under our systems of government the courts are not concerned with the wisdom or policy of legislation. So that, in determining the question of power to interfere with liberty of contract, the court may inquire whether the means devised by the state are germane to an end which may be lawfully accomplished and have a real or substantial relation to the protection of health, as involved in the daily work of the persons, male and female, engaged in bakery and confectionery establishments. But when this inquiry is entered upon I find it impossible, in view of common experience, to say that there is here no real or substantial relation between the means employed by the state and the end sought to be accomplished by its legislation. Mugler v. Kansas, 123 U.S. 623,

661. Nor can I say that the statute has no appropriate or direct connection with that protection to health which each state owes to her citizens ... or that it is not promotive of the health of the employees in question ... or that the regulation prescribed by the state is utterly unreasonable and extravagant or wholly arbitrary.... Still less can I say that the statute, is, beyond question, a plain, palpable invasion of rights, secured by the fundamental law.... Therefore I submit that this court will transcend its functions if it assumes to annul the statute of New York. It must be remembered that this statute does not apply to all kinds of business. It applies only to work in bakery and confectionery establishments, in which, as all know, the air constantly breathed by workmen is not as pure and healthful as that to be found in some other establishments or out of doors.

. . .

Mr. Justice Holmes dissenting:

I regret sincerely that I am unable to agree with the judgment in this case, and that I think it my duty to express my dissent.

This case is decided upon an economic theory which a large part of the country does not entertain. If it were a question whether I agreed with that theory, I should desire to study it further and long before making up my mind. But I do not conceive that to be my duty, because I strongly believe that my agreement or disagreement has nothing to do with the right of a majority to embody their opinions in law. It is settled by various decisions of this court that state constitutions and state laws may regulate life in many ways which we as legislators might think as injudicious, or if you like as tyrannical, as this, and which, equally with this, interfere with the liberty to contract. Sunday laws and usury laws are ancient examples. A more modern one is the prohibition of lotteries. The liberty of the citizen to do as he likes so long as he does not interfere with the liberty of others to do the same, which has been a shibboleth for some well-known writers, is interfered with by school laws, by the Postoffice, by every state or municipal institution which takes his money for purposes thought desirable, whether he likes it or not. The 14th Amendment does not enact Mr. Herbert Spencer's Social Statics. The other day we sustained the Massachusetts vaccination law. Jacobson v. Massachusetts, 197 U.S. 11. United States and state statutes and decisions cutting down the liberty to contract by way of combination are familiar to this court. Northern Securities Co. v. United States, 193 U.S. 197. Two years ago we upheld the prohibition of sales of stock on margins, or for future delivery, in the Constitution of California. Otis v. Parker, 187 U.S. 606. The decision sustaining an eight-hour law for miners is still recent. Holden v. Hardy, 169 U.S. 366. Some of these laws embody convictions or prejudices which judges are likely to share. Some may not. But a Constitution is not intended to embody a particular economic theory, whether of paternalism and the organic relation of the citizen to the state or of *laissez faire*. It is made for people of fundamentally differing views, and the accident of our finding certain opinions natural and familiar, or novel, and even shocking, ought not to conclude our judgment upon the question whether statutes embodying them conflict with the Constitution of the United States.

General propositions do not decide concrete cases. The decision will depend on a judgment or intuition more subtle than any articulate major premise. But I think that the proposition just stated, if it is accepted, will carry us far toward the end. Every opinion tends to become a law. I think that the word "liberty," in the 14th Amendment, is perverted when it is held to prevent the natural outcome of a dominant opinion, unless it can be said that a rational and fair man necessarily would admit that the statute proposed would infringe fundamental principles as they have been understood by the traditions of our people and our law. It does not need research to show that no such sweeping condemnation can be passed upon the statute before us. A reasonable man might think it a proper measure on the score of health. Men whom I certainly could not pronounce unreasonable would uphold it as a first instalment of a general regulation of the hours of work. Whether in the latter aspect it would be open to the charge of inequality I think it unnecessary to discuss.

THE POST–LOCHNER DEVELOPMENTS

(1) Liberty of Contract and Labor Legislation.

Maximum hours. In Muller v. Oregon, 208 U.S. 412 (1908), the Court upheld the validity of a statute forbidding the employment of women in factories or laundries more than 10 hours per day as applied to a laundry. The Court distinguished *Lochner* on the ground that the state had a stronger interest in regulating the hours of work of women than of men. The physical differences between women and men were emphasized and the Court said that "history discloses the fact that woman has always been dependent upon man." The Court, in taking judicial notice of the general belief that "woman's physical structure, and the functions she performs in consequence thereof, justify special legislation restricting or qualifying the conditions under which she should be permitted to toil," relied on a brief filed in the Court by Mr. Louis D. (later Justice) Brandeis that included a large collection of opinions from non-judicial sources.[1] It then said: "Constitutional questions ... are not settled by even a consensus of present public opinion, for it is the peculiar value of a written constitution that it places in unchanging form limitations upon legislative action, and thus gives a permanence and stability to popular government which otherwise would be lacking. At the same time, when a question of fact is debated and debatable, and the extent to which a special constitutional limitation goes is affected by the truth in respect to that fact, a widespread and long continued belief concerning it is worthy of consideration." Several years later, without mentioning *Lochner,* the Court upheld a law providing a maximum 10–hour day for factory workers of both sexes that also permitted up to three hours a day overtime at time-and-a-half rate. Bunting v. Oregon, 243 U.S. 426 (1917).

"Yellow–Dog" Contracts. In Adair v. United States, 208 U.S. 161 (1908) and Coppage v. Kansas, 236 U.S. 1 (1915), the Court held invalid federal and state legislation forbidding employers to require employees to agree not to become or remain members of any labor organizations during the period of their employment. In *Coppage* the Court said: "An interference with this liberty [to make contracts] so serious as that now under consideration, and so disturbing of equality of right, must be deemed to be arbitrary, unless it be supportable as a reasonable exercise of the police power of the State." The Court went on to reject the argument of the state that such legislation was necessary to protect the interests of employees who were not financially as able to be independent in making contracts as employers, saying: "[S]ince it is self-evident that, unless all things are held in common, some persons must have more property than others, it is from the nature of things impossible to uphold

---

[1] The famous "Brandeis Brief" has been lauded as introducing the Court "to a new technique in the weighing of constitutional issues. This occurred when Mr. Louis D. Brandeis handed the Court ... his famous brief, three pages of which were devoted to a statement of the constitutional principles in-volved and 113 pages of which were devoted to the presentation of facts and statistics, backed by scientific authorities, to show the evil effects of too long hours on women, 'the mothers of the race'." Johnson, *Social Planning Under the Constitution,* 2 Selected Essays (1938) 131, 145.

freedom of contract and the right of private property without at the same time recognizing as legitimate those inequalities of fortune that are the necessary result of the exercise of those rights."

Minimum Wages. Adkins v. Children's Hosp., 261 U.S. 525 (1923), involved an Act of Congress prescribing minimum wages for women and children in the District of Columbia. The Court held the statute invalid when challenged by a hospital that employed women at lower than the minimum rate and by a woman elevator operator who was discharged by her employer to avoid the penalties of the act. The Court prefaced its discussion by saying: "There is, of course, no such thing as absolute freedom of contract. It is subject to a great variety of restraints. But freedom of contract is, nevertheless, the general rule and restraint the exception; and the exercise of legislative authority to abridge it can be justified only by the existence of exceptional circumstances." In distinguishing Muller v. Oregon, the Court said:

"But the ancient inequality of the sexes, otherwise than physical, as suggested in the *Muller* case, has continued 'with diminishing intensity.' In view of the great—not to say revolutionary—changes which have taken place since that utterance, in the contractual, political and civil status of women, culminating in the Nineteenth Amendment, it is not unreasonable to say that these differences have now come almost, if not quite, to the vanishing point. In this aspect of the matter, while the physical differences must be recognized in appropriate cases, and legislation fixing hours or conditions of work may properly take them into account, we cannot accept the doctrine that women of mature age, sui juris, require or may be subjected to restrictions upon their liberty of contract which could not lawfully be imposed in the case of men under similar circumstances."

It then went on to say that the statute could not be justified as safeguarding the morals of women because it "cannot be shown that well paid women safeguard their morals more carefully than those who are poorly paid." It concluded that the real flaw in the statute was that "it exacts from the employer an arbitrary payment for a purpose and upon a basis having no causal connection with his business or the contract or the work the employee engages to do." This, the Court said, "is so clearly the product of a naked, arbitrary exercise of power that it cannot be allowed to stand under the Constitution of the United States."

Justice Holmes in dissent said: "It will need more than the Nineteenth Amendment to convince me that there are no differences between men and women, or that legislation cannot take those differences into account. I should not hesitate to take them into account if I thought it necessary to sustain this act.... But after Bunting v. Oregon, 243 U.S. 426, I had supposed that it was not necessary, and that Lochner v. New York, 198 U.S. 45, would be allowed a deserved repose."

(2) **Liberty of Contract and Business Regulations Relating to Prices and Other Economic Issues.**

Price Fixing. In Tyson & Bro.–United Theatre Ticket Offices v. Banton, 273 U.S. 418 (1927), the court held invalid a statute regulating the prices of theater tickets. The Court said "that the right of the owner to fix a price at which his property shall be sold or used is an inherent attribute of the property itself." Hence, the power to fix prices "does not exist in respect of merely private property or business ... but exists only where the business or the property involved has become 'affected with a public interest.' " A long line of cases developed marking out the distinction between ordinary businesses and those "affected with a public interest" and so subject to price regulations. See, e.g., Williams v. Standard Oil Co., 278 U.S. 235 (1929), holding invalid a state statute regulating the price of gasoline. For later modifications of this doctrine, see Nebbia v. New York, 291 U.S. 502 (1934), set out below.

Restrictions on Business Entry. The Court applied an approach similar to that in the price fixing cases with regard to legislation restricting entry into particular businesses. In New State Ice Co. v. Liebmann, 285 U.S. 262 (1932), it held invalid a statute requiring any person desiring to engage in the ice business to obtain a certificate of public convenience and necessity. It said that the question was "whether the business is so charged with a public use as to justify" the restriction. It also said: "Plainly, a regulation which has the effect of denying or unreasonably curtailing the common right to engage in a lawful private business, such as that under review, cannot be upheld consistent with the 14th Amendment."

(3) **Regulations of Business Designed to Protect Public Health and Safety.** Most business regulations that came before the court were upheld where the legislative objective was to protect public health and safety rather than to interfere with the free market. However, in some cases the Court held regulations invalid because they were not sufficiently related to the legislative objectives. In Weaver v. Palmer Bros. Co., 270 U.S. 402 (1926), e.g., the Court held invalid a statute completely forbidding the use of shoddy (cut up fabrics) in the manufacture of bedding and providing for the use of other second-hand materials and feathers only if sterilized. The parties conceded that shoddy could be made harmless by disinfection or sterilization and there was no evidence to show that sickness or disease had been caused by the use of shoddy. The Court recognized that state regulations designed to protect public health and to protect the public from deception were generally valid but held that this statute did not sufficiently serve those ends. The measure could not be sustained as a measure to protect health because sterilization would eliminate the danger. Nor could it be sustained as a measure to protect deception because the regulation provided for adequate notice to the public of the contents of the bedding. It then concluded: "The constitutional guarantees may not be made to yield to mere convenience ... The business here involved is legitimate and useful; and, while it is subject to all reasonable regulation, the absolute prohibition of the use of shoddy in the manufacture of comfortables is purely arbitrary and violates the due process clause of the Fourteenth Amendment."

Nebbia v. New York

291 U.S. 502, 54 S.Ct. 505, 78 L.Ed. 940 (1934).

Mr. Justice Roberts delivered the opinion of the Court.

. . .

[A New York statute provided for the fixing of maximum and minimum prices for the sale of milk. The legislature, after extensive hearings, had determined that economic conditions and destructive trade practices jeopardized an adequate milk supply at reasonable prices to consumers and producers and that price controls would help. Nebbia, owner of a grocery store, was convicted for selling milk at a price below the minimum fixed. He contended, inter alia, that the statute deprived him of due process of law. The Court upheld the law by a vote of 5 to 4. Excerpts from Justice Roberts' long opinion follow.]

The reports of our decisions abound with cases in which the citizen, individual or corporate, has vainly invoked the Fourteenth Amendment in resistance to necessary and appropriate exertion of the police power.

. . .

But we are told that because the law essays to control prices it denies due process. . . . The argument runs that the public control of rates or prices is per se unreasonable and unconstitutional save as applied to businesses affected with a public interest; that a business so affected is one in which property is devoted to an enterprise of a sort which the public itself might appropriately undertake, or one whose owner relies on a public grant or franchise for the right to conduct the business, or in which he is bound to serve all who apply; in short, such as is commonly called a public utility; or a business in its nature a monopoly. The milk industry, it is said, possesses none of these characteristics, and therefore, not being affected with a public interest, its charges may not be controlled by the state. . . .

We may as well say at once that the dairy industry is not, in the accepted sense of the phrase, a public utility. We think the appellant is also right in asserting that there is in this case no suggestion of any monopoly or monopolistic practice. It goes without saying that those engaged in the business are in no way dependent upon public grants or franchises for the privilege of conducting their activities. But if, as must be conceded, the industry is subject to regulation in the public interest, what constitutional principle bars the state from correcting existing maladjustments by legislation touching prices? We think there is no such principle. The due process clause makes no mention of sales or of prices any more than it speaks of business or contracts or buildings or other incidents of property. The thought seems nevertheless to have persisted that there is something peculiarly sacrosanct about the price one may charge for what he makes or sells, and that, however able to regulate other elements of manufacture or trade, with incidental effect upon price, the state is incapable of directly controlling the price itself. This view was negatived many years ago. Munn v. Illinois, 94 U.S. 113. . . .

It is clear that there is no closed class or category of businesses affected with a public interest, and the function of courts in the application of the Fifth and Fourteenth Amendments is to determine in each case whether circumstances vindicate the challenged regulation as a reasonable exertion of governmental authority or condemn it as arbitrary or discriminatory. . . . The phrase "affected with a public interest" can, in the nature of things, mean no more than that an industry, for adequate reason, is subject to control for the public good. In several of the decisions of this court wherein the expressions "affected with a public interest," and "clothed with a public use," have been brought forward as the criteria of the validity of price control, it has been admitted that they are not susceptible of definition and form an unsatisfactory test of the constitutionality of legislation directed at business practices or prices. These decisions must rest, finally, upon the basis that the requirements of due process were not met because the laws were found arbitrary, in their operation and effect. But there can be no doubt that upon proper occasion and by appropriate measures the state may regulate a business in any of its aspects, including the prices to be charged for the products or commodities it sells.

So far as the requirement of due process is concerned, and in the absence of other constitutional restriction, a state is free to adopt whatever economic policy may reasonably be deemed to promote public welfare, and to enforce that policy by legislation adapted to its purpose. The courts are without authority either to declare such policy, or, when it is declared by the legislature, to override it. If the laws passed are seen to have a reasonable relation to a proper legislative purpose, and are neither arbitrary nor discriminatory, the requirements of due process are satisfied, and judicial determination to that effect renders a court functus officio.... With the wisdom of the policy adopted, with the adequacy or practicability of the law enacted to forward it, the courts are both incompetent and unauthorized to deal. The course of decision in this court exhibits a firm adherence to these principles. Times without number we have said that the Legislature is primarily the judge of the necessity of such an enactment, that every possible presumption is in favor of its validity, and that though the court may hold views inconsistent with the wisdom of the law, it may not be annulled unless palpably in excess of legislative power.... Price control, like any other form of regulation, is unconstitutional only if arbitrary, discriminatory, or demonstrably irrelevant to the policy the Legislature is free to adopt, and hence an unnecessary and unwarranted interference with individual liberty.

THE OVERTURNING OF ADKINS v. CHILDREN'S HOSPITAL

In Morehead v. New York ex rel. Tipaldo, 298 U.S. 587 (1936), Justice Roberts, author of the opinion in *Nebbia,* joined with the *Nebbia* dissenters in applying *Adkins* to hold invalid a New York law providing for minimum wages for women workers. The Court noted that the petitioner had not asked the Court to reconsider the constitutional question decided in *Adkins.* Finding no sufficient basis for distinction, the Court held the statute invalid.

The next year, however, the Court, by a vote of 5 to 4 with Justice Roberts joining the majority, specifically overruled Adkins v. Children's Hospital. West Coast Hotel Co. v. Parrish, 300 U.S. 379 (1937). The Court responded to the argument based on freedom of contract by saying:

"What is freedom? The Constitution does not speak of freedom of contract. It speaks of liberty and prohibits the deprivation of liberty without due process of law.... But the liberty safeguarded is liberty in a social organization which requires the protection of law against the evils which menace the health, safety, morals and welfare of the people. Liberty under the constitution is thus necessarily subject to the restraints of due process, and regulation which is reasonable in relation to its subject and is adopted in the interests of the community is due process. This essential limitation of liberty in general governs freedom of contract in particular.

"What can be closer to the public interest than the health of women and their protection from unscrupulous and overreaching employers? And if the protection of women is a legitimate end of the exercise of state power, how can it be said that the requirement of the payment of a minimum wage fairly fixed in order to meet the very necessities of existence is not an admissible means to that end? The legislature of the State was clearly entitled to consider the situation of women in employment, the fact that they are in the class receiving the least pay, that their bargaining power is relatively weak, and that they are the ready victims of those who would take advantage of their necessitous circumstances. The legislature was entitled to adopt measures to reduce the evils of the 'sweating system,' the exploiting of workers at wages so low as to be insufficient to meet the bare cost of living, thus making their very helplessness the occasion of a most injurious competition.... The adoption of similar requirements by many States evidences a deep-seated conviction both as to the presence of the evil and as to the means adapted to check it. Legislative response to that conviction cannot be regarded as arbitrary or capricious, and that is all we have to decide. Even if the wisdom of the policy be regarded as debatable and its effects uncertain, still the legislature is entitled to its judgment."

It should be noted that the decision in *West Coast Hotel* was announced while President Roosevelt's "Court packing" proposal was pending in Congress. For a reference to the question whether this decision was intended to have an impact on that proposal, see n. a, supra p. 190.

United States v. Carolene Products Co.

304 U.S. 144, 58 S.Ct. 778, 82 L.Ed. 1234 (1938).

Mr. Justice Stone delivered the opinion of the Court.

The question for decision is whether the "Filled Milk Act" of Congress of March 4, 1923 ..., which prohibits the shipment in interstate commerce of skimmed milk compounded with any fat or oil other than milk fat, so as to resemble milk or cream, transcends the power of Congress to regulate interstate commerce or infringes the Fifth Amendment....

[On review of an indictment for shipping in interstate commerce packages of "Milnut," a compound of condensed skimmed milk and coconut oil made in imitation or semblance of condensed milk or cream, the Supreme Court first upheld the statute as being within the power of Congress to regulate commerce and then addressed the due process issue.]

... [W]e might rest decision wholly on the presumption of constitutionality. But affirmative evidence also sustains the statute. In twenty years evidence has steadily accumulated of the danger to the public health from the general consumption of foods which have been stripped of elements essential to the maintenance of health. The Filled Milk Act was adopted by Congress after committee hearings, in the course of which eminent scientists and health experts testified. An extensive investigation was made of the commerce in milk compounds in which vegetable oils have been substituted for natural milk fat, and of the effect upon the public health of the use of such compounds as a food substitute for milk. The conclusions drawn from evidence presented at the hearings were embodied in reports of the House Committee on Agriculture ... and the Senate Committee on Agriculture and Forestry.... Both committees concluded, as the statute itself declares, that the use of filled milk as a substitute for pure milk is generally injurious to health and facilitates fraud on the public.

There is nothing in the Constitution which compels a Legislature, either national or state, to ignore such evidence, nor need it disregard the other evidence which amply supports the conclusions of the Congressional committees that the danger is greatly enhanced where an inferior product, like appellee's, is indistinguishable from a valuable food of almost universal use, thus making fraudulent distribution easy and protection of the consumer difficult.

. . .

Third. We may assume for present purposes that no pronouncement of a Legislature can forestall attack upon the constitutionality of the prohibition which it enacts by applying opprobrious epithets to the prohibited act, and that a statute would deny due process which precluded the disproof in judicial proceedings of all facts which would show or tend to show that a statute depriving the suitor of life, liberty, or property had a rational basis.

But such we think is not the purpose or construction of the statutory characterization of filled milk as injurious to health and as a fraud upon the public. There is no need to consider it here as more than a declaration of the legislative findings deemed to support and justify the action taken as a constitutional exertion of the legislative power, aiding informed judicial review, as do the reports of legislative committees, by revealing the rationale of the legislation. Even in the absence of such aids, the existence of facts supporting the legislative judgment is to be presumed, for regulatory legislation affecting ordinary commercial transactions is not to be pronounced unconstitutional unless in the light of the facts made known or generally assumed it is of such a character as to preclude the assumption that it rests upon some rational basis within the knowledge and experience of the legislators.[4] . . .

Where the existence of a rational basis for legislation whose constitutionality is attacked depends upon facts beyond the sphere of judicial notice, such facts may properly be made the subject of judicial inquiry, . . . and the constitutionality of a statute predicated upon the existence of a particular state of facts may be challenged by showing to the court that those facts have ceased to exist. . . . Similarly we recognize that the constitutionality of a statute, valid on its face, may be assailed by proof of facts tending to show that the statute as applied to a particular article is without support in reason because the article, although within the prohibited class, is so different from others of the class as to be without the reason for the prohibition. . . . But by their very nature such inquiries, where the legislative judgment is drawn in question, must be restricted to the issue whether any state of facts either known or which could reasonably be assumed affords support for it. Here the demurrer challenges the validity of the statute on its face and it is evident from all the considerations presented to Congress, and those of which we may take judicial notice, that the question is at least debatable whether commerce in filled milk should be left unregulated, or in some measure restricted, or wholly prohibited. As that

---

[4] There may be narrower scope for operation of the presumption of constitutionality when legislation appears on its face to be within a specific prohibition of the Constitution, such as those of the first ten Amendments, which are deemed equally specific when held to be embraced within the Fourteenth. See Stromberg v. California, 283 U.S. 359, 369, 370; Lovell v. Griffin, 303 U.S. 444.

It is unnecessary to consider now whether legislation which restricts those political processes which can ordinarily be expected to bring about repeal of undesirable legislation, is to be subjected to more exacting judicial scrutiny under the general prohibitions of the Fourteenth Amendment than are most other types of legislation. On restrictions upon the right to vote, see Nixon v. Herndon, 273 U.S. 536; Nixon v. Condon, 286 U.S. 73; on restraints upon the dissemination of information, see Near v. Minnesota, 283 U.S. 697, 713–714, 718–720, 722; Grosjean v. American Press Co., 297 U.S. 233; Lovell v. Griffin, supra; on interferences with political organizations, see Stromberg v. California, supra,

283 U.S. 359, 369; Fiske v. Kansas, 274 U.S. 380; Whitney v. California, 274 U.S. 357, 373–378; Herndon v. Lowry, 301 U.S. 242, and see Holmes, J., in Gitlow v. New York, 268 U.S. 652, 673; as to prohibition of peaceable assembly, see De Jonge v. Oregon, 299 U.S. 353, 365.

Nor need we enquire whether similar considerations enter into the review of statutes directed at particular religious, Pierce v. Society of Sisters, 268 U.S. 510, or national, Meyer v. Nebraska, 262 U.S. 390; Bartels v. Iowa, 262 U.S. 404; Farrington v. Tokushige, 273 U.S. 284, or racial minorities. Nixon v. Herndon, supra; Nixon v. Condon, supra: whether prejudice against discrete and insular minorities may be a special condition, which tends seriously to curtail the operation of those political processes ordinarily to be relied upon to protect minorities, and which may call for a correspondingly more searching judicial inquiry. Compare McCulloch v. Maryland, 4 Wheat. 316, 428; South Carolina State Highway Department v. Barnwell Bros., 303 U.S. 177, and cases cited.

decision was for Congress, neither the finding of a court arrived at by weighing the evidence, nor the verdict of a jury can be substituted for it.[a]

. . .

Reversed.

Mr. Justice Black concurs in the result and in all of the opinion except the part marked "Third."

Mr. Justice McReynolds thinks that the judgment should be affirmed.

Mr. Justice Cardozo and Mr. Justice Reed took no part in the consideration or decision of this case.

Mr. Justice Butler.

I concur in the result. . . .

THE DEMISE OF LIBERTY OF CONTRACT

During the 1940s the Supreme Court (which received seven new members between 1937 and 1941) overturned the old precedents and rejected all challenges to legislation based on assertions of a constitutional preference for a free economic market place.

In United States v. Darby, 312 U.S. 100 (1941), the Court upheld the provisions of the Fair Labor Standards Act fixing maximum hours and minimum wages for all covered employees. The Court said that "it is no longer open to question" that it is within the legislative power to fix wages and hours for men as well as women.

In Phelps Dodge Corp. v. National Labor Relations Bd., 313 U.S. 177 (1941), the Court upheld the provision of the N.L.R.A. making it an unfair labor practice for an employer to encourage or discourage membership in any labor union, saying that "[t]he course of decisions in this Court since *Adair v. United States* . . . and *Coppage v. Kansas* . . . have completely sapped those cases of their authority."

In Olsen v. Nebraska, 313 U.S. 236 (1941), the Court upheld a state statute fixing the fees chargeable by a private employment agency and in Lincoln Fed. Labor Union v. Northwestern Iron & Metal Co., 335 U.S. 525 (1949), upheld a state law providing that no person should be denied an opportunity to obtain

[a] Thirty-four years later, after the appearance on the market of imitation milk and non-dairy creamer products that did not fall within the prohibition against interstate shipment of "filled milk," the successor company to Carolene Products Co. successfully attacked the constitutionality of this Act as applied on the ground that its enforcement against only filled milk substitutes denied equal protection—an element of the Fifth Amendment due process limitation on federal power discussed infra p. 674. Milnot Co. v. Richardson, 350 F.Supp. 221 (N.D.Ill.1972). The unappealed district court decision said that "the constitutionality of a statute predicated upon the existence of a particular state of facts may be challenged by showing to the court that those facts have ceased to exist. Chastleton Corp. v. Sinclair, 264 U.S. 543 (1924)." The Court found that "[f]rom the undisputed facts in the record here, it ap-pears crystal clear that certain imitation milk and dairy products are so similar to Milnot in composition, appearance, and use that different treatment as to interstate shipment . . . violates . . . due process. . . ." It reasoned that the "possibility of confusion, or passing off, in the marketplace, which justified the statute in 1944, can no longer be used rationally as a constitutional prop to prevent interstate shipment of Milnot" because "[t]here is at least as much danger in this regard with imitation milk as with filled milk, and actually no longer any such real danger with either." The decision was limited "to the conclusion, as a matter of law, that the Filled Milk Act, as applied to prohibit interstate shipment of Milnot, deprives the plaintiff of due process and provides no rational means for the achievement of any announced objective of the Act."

employment because he was or was not a member of a labor union. In the latter case it rejected a claim by a labor union that the "open shop" law was invalid by saying: "Just as we have held that the due process clause erects no obstacle to block legislative protection of union members, we now hold that legislative protection can be afforded non-union members."

In Daniel v. Family Sec. Life Ins. Co., 336 U.S. 220 (1949), the Court upheld a statute which prohibited life insurance companies and their agents from engaging in the undertaking business and undertakers from acting as life insurance agents. The statute was challenged by an undertaker selling "funeral insurance." His claim that the statute resulted from the activities of the "insurance lobby" was rejected by the Court: "[A] judiciary must judge by results, not by the varied factors which may have determined legislators' votes. We cannot undertake a search for motive in testing constitutionality." In rejecting the claim that the statute was arbitrary and unreasonable, the Court said: "Looking through the form of this plea to its essential basis, we cannot fail to recognize it as an argument for invalidity because this Court disagrees with the desirability of the legislation. We rehearse the obvious when we say that our function is thus misconceived. We are not equipped to decide desirability; and a court cannot eliminate measures which do not happen to suit its tastes if it seeks to maintain a democratic system. The forum for the correction of ill-considered legislation is a responsive legislature.

"We cannot say that South Carolina is not entitled to call the funeral insurance business an evil. Nor can we say that the statute has no relation to the elimination of those evils. There our inquiry must stop."

Williamson v. Lee Optical of Oklahoma, Inc.

348 U.S. 483, 75 S.Ct. 461, 99 L.Ed. 563 (1955).

Mr. Justice Douglas delivered the opinion of the Court.

This suit was instituted in the District Court to have an Oklahoma law ... declared unconstitutional and to enjoin state officials from enforcing it, ... for the reason that it allegedly violated various provisions of the Federal Constitution.

The District Court held unconstitutional portions of three sections of the Act. First, it held invalid under the Due Process Clause of the Fourteenth Amendment the portions of § 2 which make it unlawful for any person not a licensed optometrist or ophthalmologist to fit lenses to a face or to duplicate or replace into frames lenses or other optical appliances, except upon written prescriptive authority of an Oklahoma licensed ophthalmologist or optometrist.

An ophthalmologist is a duly licensed physician who specializes in the care of the eyes. An optometrist examines eyes for refractive error, recognizes (but does not treat) diseases of the eye, and fills prescriptions for eyeglasses. The optician is an artisan qualified to grind lenses, fill prescriptions, and fit frames.

The effect of § 2 is to forbid the optician from fitting or duplicating lenses without a prescription from an ophthalmologist or optometrist. In practical effect, it means that no optician can fit old glasses into new frames or supply a lens, whether it be a new lens or one to duplicate a lost or broken lens, without a prescription. The District Court conceded that it was in the competence of the police power of a State to regulate the examination of the eyes. But it rebelled at the notion that a State could require a prescription from an optometrist or ophthalmologist "to take old lenses and place them in new frames and then fit the completed spectacles to the *face* of the eyeglass wearer." ... It held that such a requirement was not "reasonably and rationally related to the health and welfare of the people." . . . The court found that through mechanical devices and ordinary skills the optician could take a broken lens or a fragment thereof, measure its power, and reduce it to prescriptive terms. The court held that "Although on this precise issue of duplication, the legislature in the instant regulation was dealing with a matter of public interest, the particular means chosen are neither reasonably necessary nor reasonably related to the end sought to be achieved." . . . It was, accordingly, the opinion of the court that this provision of the law violated the Due Process Clause by arbitrarily interfering with the optician's right to do business.

. . .

The Oklahoma law may exact a needless, wasteful requirement in many cases. But it is for the legislature, not the courts, to balance the advantages and disadvantages of the new requirement. It appears that in many cases the optician can easily supply the new frames or new lenses without reference to the old written prescription. It also appears that many written prescriptions contain no directive data in regard to fitting spectacles to the face. But in some cases the directions contained in the prescription are essential, if the glasses are to be fitted so as to correct the particular defects of vision or alleviate the eye condition. The legislature might have concluded that the frequency of occasions when a prescription is necessary was sufficient to justify this regulation of the fitting of eyeglasses. Likewise, when it is necessary to duplicate a lens, a written prescription may or may not be necessary. But the legislature might have concluded that one was needed often enough to require one in every case. Or the legislature may have concluded that eye examinations were so critical, not only for correction of vision but also for detection of latent ailments or diseases, that every change in frames and every duplication of a lens should be accompanied by a prescription from a medical expert. To be sure, the present law does not require a new examination of the eyes every time the frames are changed or the lenses duplicated. For if the old prescription is on file with the optician, he can go ahead and make the new fitting or duplicate the lenses. But the law need not be in every respect logically consistent with its aims to be constitutional. It is enough that there is an evil at hand for correction, and that it might be thought that the particular legislative measure was a rational way to correct it.

The day is gone when this Court uses the Due Process Clause of the Fourteenth Amendment to strike down state laws, regulatory of business and industrial conditions, because they may be unwise, improvident, or out of harmony with a particular school of thought. . . .

We emphasize again what Chief Justice Waite said in Munn v. State of Illinois, 94 U.S. 113, 134, "For protection against abuses by legislatures the people must resort to the polls, not to the courts."

. . .

Third, the District Court held unconstitutional, as violative of the Due Process Clause of the Fourteenth Amendment, that portion of § 3 which makes it unlawful "to solicit the sale of . . . frames, mountings . . . or any other optical appliances." The court conceded that state regulation of advertising relating to eye examinations was a matter "rationally related to the public health and welfare", 120 F.Supp. at 140, and therefore subject to regulation. . . . But regulation of the advertising of eyeglass frames was said to intrude "into a mercantile field only casually related to the visual care of the public" and restrict "an activity which in no way can detrimentally affect the people."

An eyeglass frame, considered in isolation, is only a piece of merchandise. But an eyeglass frame is not used in isolation, as Judge Murrah said in dissent below; it is used with lenses; and lenses, pertaining as they do to the human eye, enter the field of health. Therefore, the legislature might conclude that to regulate one effectively it would have to regulate the other. Or it might conclude that both the sellers of frames and the sellers of lenses were in a business where advertising should be limited or even abolished in the public interest.... The advertiser of frames may be using his ads to bring in customers who will buy lenses. If the advertisement of lenses is to be abolished or controlled, the advertising of frames must come under the same restraints; or so the legislature might think. We see no constitutional reason why a State may not treat all who deal with the human eye as members of a profession who should use no merchandising methods for obtaining customers.

Fourth, the District Court held unconstitutional, as violative of the Due Process Clause of the Fourteenth Amendment, the provision of § 4 of the Oklahoma Act which reads as follows:

> "No person, firm, or corporation engaged in the business of retailing merchandise to the general public shall rent space, sublease departments, or otherwise permit any person purporting to do eye examination or visual care to occupy space in such retail store."

It seems to us that this regulation is on the same constitutional footing as the denial to corporations of the right to practice dentistry. Semler v. Oregon State Board of Dental Examiners, supra, 294 U.S. at 611. It is an attempt to free the profession, to as great an extent as possible, from all taints of commercialism. It certainly might be easy for an optometrist with space in a retail store to be merely a front for the retail establishment. In any case, the opportunity for that nexus may be too great for safety, if the eye doctor is allowed inside the retail store. Moreover, it may be deemed important to effective regulation that the eye doctor be restricted to geographical locations that reduce the temptations of commercialism. Geographical location may be an important consideration in a legislative program which aims to raise the treatment of the human eye to a strictly professional level. We cannot say that the regulation has no rational relation to that objective and therefore is beyond constitutional bounds.

What we have said is sufficient to dispose of the appeal in No. 185 from the conclusion of the District Court that that portion of § 3 which makes it unlawful to solicit the sale of spectacles, eyeglasses, lenses, and prisms by the use of advertising media is constitutional.

. . .

Mr. Justice Harlan took no part in the consideration or decision of this case.

Ferguson v. Skrupa

372 U.S. 726, 83 S.Ct. 1028, 10 L.Ed.2d 93 (1963).

Mr. Justice Black delivered the opinion of the Court.

In this case, ... we are asked to review the judgment of a three-judge District Court enjoining, as being in violation of the Due Process Clause of the Fourteenth Amendment, a Kansas statute making it a misdemeanor for any person to engage "in the business of debt adjusting" except as an incident to "the lawful practice of law in this state." The statute defines "debt adjusting" as "the making of a contract, express, or implied with a particular debtor whereby the debtor agrees to pay a certain amount of money periodically to the person engaged in the debt adjusting business who shall for a consideration distribute the same among certain specified creditors in accordance with a plan agreed upon."

The complaint, filed by appellee Skrupa doing business as "Credit Advisors," alleged that Skrupa was engaged in the business of "debt adjusting" as defined by the statute, that his business was a "useful and desirable" one, that his business activities were not "inherently immoral or dangerous" or in any way contrary to the public welfare, and that therefore the business could not be "absolutely prohibited" by Kansas. The three-judge court heard evidence by Skrupa tending to show the usefulness and desirability of his business and evidence by the state officials tending to show that "debt adjusting" lends itself to grave abuses against distressed debtors, particularly in the lower income brackets, and that these abuses are of such gravity that a number of States have strictly regulated "debt adjusting" or prohibited it altogether. The court found that Skrupa's business did fall within the Act's proscription and concluded, one judge dissenting, that the Act was prohibitory, not regulatory, but that even if construed in part as regulatory it was an unreasonable regulation of a "lawful business," which the court held amounted to a violation of the Due Process Clause of the Fourteenth Amendment. The court accordingly enjoined enforcement of the statute.

The only case discussed by the court below as support for its invalidation of the statute was Commonwealth v. Stone, 191 Pa.Super. 117, 155 A.2d 453 (1959), in which the Superior Court of Pennsylvania struck down a statute almost identical to the Kansas act involved here.... In doing so, the Pennsylvania court relied heavily on Adams v. Tanner, 244 U.S. 590 (1917), which held that the Due Process Clause forbids a State to prohibit a business which is "useful" and not "inherently immoral or dangerous to public welfare."

Both the District Court in the present case and the Pennsylvania court in Stone adopted the philosophy of *Adams v. Tanner,* and cases like it, that it is the province of courts to draw on their own views as to the morality, legitimacy, and usefulness of a particular business in order to decide whether a statute bears too heavily upon that business and by so doing violates due process. Under the system of government created by our Constitution, it is up to legislatures, not courts, to decide on the wisdom and utility of legislation. There was a time when the Due Process Clause was used by this Court to strike down laws which were thought unreasonable, that is, unwise or incompatible with some particular economic or social philosophy. In this manner the Due Process Clause was used by this Court to strike down laws which were thought unreasonable, that is, unwise or incompatible with some particular economic or social philosophy. In this manner the Due Process Clause was used, for example, to nullify laws prescribing maximum hours for work in bakeries, Lochner v. New York, 198 U.S. 45 (1905), outlawing "yellow dog" contracts, Coppage v. Kansas, 236 U.S. 1 (1915), setting minimum wages for women, Adkins v. Children's Hospital, 261 U.S. 525 (1923), and fixing the weight of loaves of bread, Jay Burns Baking Co. v. Bryan, 264 U.S. 504 (1924). This intrusion by the judiciary into the realm of legislative value judgments was strongly objected to at the time, particularly by Mr. Justice Holmes and Mr. Justice Brandeis....

The doctrine that prevailed in *Lochner, Coppage, Adkins, Burns,* and like cases—that due process authorizes courts to hold laws unconstitutional when they believe the legislature has acted unwisely—has long since been discarded.

We have returned to the original constitutional proposition that courts do not substitute their social and economic beliefs for the judgment of legislative bodies, who are elected to pass laws....

In the face of our abandonment of the use of the "vague contours" of the Due Process Clause to nullify laws which a majority of the Court believed to be economically unwise, reliance on *Adams v. Tanner* is as mistaken as would be adherence to *Adkins v. Children's Hospital*, overruled by West Coast Hotel Co. v. Parrish, 300 U.S. 379 (1937).... We conclude that the Kansas Legislature was free to decide for itself that legislation was needed to deal with the business of debt adjusting. Unquestionably, there are arguments showing that the business of debt adjusting has social utility, but such arguments are properly addressed to the legislature, not to us. We refuse to sit as a "superlegislature to weigh the wisdom of legislation," and we emphatically refuse to go back to the time when courts used the Due Process Clause "to strike down state laws, regulatory of business and industrial conditions, because they may be unwise, inprovident, or out of harmony with a particular school of thought." Nor are we able or willing to draw lines by calling a law "prohibitory" or "regulatory." Whether the legislature takes for its textbook Adam Smith, Herbert Spencer, Lord Keynes, or some other is no concern of ours. The Kansas debt adjusting statute may be wise or unwise. But relief, if any be needed, lies not with us but with the body constituted to pass laws for the State of Kansas.

. . .

Reversed.

Mr. Justice Harlan concurs in the judgment on the ground that this state measure bears a rational relation to a constitutionally permissible objective. See Williamson v. Lee Optical Inc., 348 U.S. 483, 491.

DOES THE DUE PROCESS CLAUSE TODAY IMPOSE ANY LIMITATIONS ON THE SUBSTANCE OF ECONOMIC REGULATORY LEGISLATION?

Does the decision in *Ferguson v. Skrupa* constitute a complete abandonment by the Court of the use of due process to impose a minimum standard of rationality on legislation? Does Justice Harlan's concurring opinion indicate that he thought the Court was no longer going to insist that legislation "bear a rational relationship to a constitutionally permissible objective"?

If one looks only at the outcome of cases challenging economic regulatory legislation under due process, the answer would appear to be that no effective review is undertaken by the Court. No economic regulatory statute has been held invalid under due process since 1937. Only in cases where the Court has been able to find a "taking" of property without just compensation in violation of the taking clause of the fifth amendment or an impairment of contract within the meaning of the contract clause has it invalidated legislation in the economic area.

However, the Court continues to write opinions in which it states that it is applying a due process standard that requires legislation to bear a rational relationship to a legitimate state objective. In Exxon Corp. v. Governor of Maryland, 437 U.S. 117, 125 (1978), the Court, in upholding a statute prohibiting producers or refiners of petroleum products from operating retail service stations in the state, rejected a due process objection stating: "[W]e have no hesitancy in concluding that it bears a reasonable relation to the State's legitimate purpose in controlling the gasoline retail market." And in PruneYard

Shopping Center v. Robins, 447 U.S. 74 (1980), the Court rejected a due process challenge to a state court judgment ordering a private property owner to permit use of a portion of that property by persons soliciting signatures on petitions. It quoted from Nebbia v. New York, set out supra p. 525: "The guaranty of due process ... demands only that the law shall not be unreasonable, arbitrary or capricious, and that the means selected shall have a real and substantial relation to the objective sought to be [obtained]." The Court then added: "Appellants have failed to provide sufficient justification for concluding that this test is not satisfied by the State's asserted interest in promoting more expansive rights of free speech and petition than conferred by the Federal Constitution."

STATE COURTS AND BUSINESS REGULATIONS

Many state courts have refused to go as far as the United States Supreme Court in abandoning judicial control of economic legislation. For example, the Supreme Court in Day–Brite Lighting v. Missouri, 342 U.S. 421 (1952), held valid a Missouri statute providing that an employee could absent himself from his employment without loss of pay for up to four hours on election day for the purpose of voting. In Heimgaertner v. Benjamin Elec. Mfg. Co., 6 Ill.2d 152, 128 N.E.2d 691 (1955), however, the Supreme Court of Illinois refused to follow the Day–Brite decision and held a similar law invalid under the due process clause of the state constitution. The court rejected the Day–Brite decision with the following statement:

"Although the decision eliminates the Federal aspects of the problems surrounding such regulations, it serves to reaffirm that it is for each State to determine if its legislature is empowered to enact such a statute and to determine if the means selected to further the public welfare bear a real and substantial relation to the objects sought to be obtained. It is the duty of each State to pass upon the validity of its own legislation and, if no Federal question is involved, the United States Supreme Court will adopt and follow the decision of the State court."

For a comprehensive review of the cases, see Hetherington, *State Economic Regulation and Substantive Due Process of Law,* 53 Northwest U.L.Rev. 13, 226 (1958); Kirby, *Expansive Judicial Review of Economic Regulation Under State Constitutions,* 48 Tenn.L.Rev. 241 (1981); *Developments in the Law—The Interpretation of State Constitutional Rights,* 95 Harv.L.Rev. 1324, 1463–1493 (1982). See also Carpenter, *Our Constitutional Heritage: Economic Due Process and the State Courts,* 45 A.B.A.J. 1027 (1959); Linde, *Constitutional Law—1959 Oregon Survey,* 39 Ore.L.Rev. 138, 143–160 (1960); Paulsen, *The Persistence of Substantive Due Process in the States,* 34 Minn.L.Rev. 91 (1950); Note, 53 Col.L.Rev. 827 (1953); Note, 18 Ohio St.L.J. 384 (1957). For a discussion of state cases which advocates greater review of economic regulations by the United States Supreme Court see Struve, *The Less-Restrictive-Alternative Principle and Economic Due Process,* 80 Harv.L.Rev. 1463 (1967).

B.   THE CONTRACT CLAUSE—WHAT DOES IT ADD TO THE DUE PROCESS LIMITATION?

United States Trust Co of New York v. New Jersey

431 U.S. 1, 97 S.Ct. 1505, 52 L.Ed.2d 92 (1977).

[The New York and New Jersey Port Authority was formed by compact of the two States in 1921, as a financially independent agency. The Authority's income from bridge and tunnel tolls was pledged to the retirement of bonds it issued. In 1960, the Authority's proposed takeover of a financially troubled, privately owned commuter train led to concern that use of tolls to finance the railroad's deficits would conflict with rights of holders of the Authority's bonds. The response was the 1962 "Statutory Covenant," enacted into law in both States, which provided, as part of the legislation authorizing the takeover, that "the 2 States covenant and agree with each other and with the holders of any affected bonds" not to finance deficits of other future mass transit facilities with revenue pledged to pay bonds, except as permitted by exceptions in the 1962 statutes. In 1974, New York and New Jersey retroactively repealed the 1962 covenant, in order to permit greater use of bridge and tunnel tolls to subsidize mass transit. Appellant, trustee and holder of Authority bonds, brought suit in a New Jersey State court for a declaratory judgment that New Jersey's repeal of the 1962 covenant was prohibited by the Contract Clause. The trial court's decision, that the repeal was a reasonable exercise of New Jersey's police power and not in violation of the Contract Clause, was affirmed by the Supreme Court of New Jersey.]

Mr. Justice Blackmun delivered the opinion of the court.

. . .

II.

At the time the Constitution was adopted, and for nearly a century thereafter, the Contract Clause was one of the few express limitations on state power. The many decisions of this Court involving the Contract Clause are evidence of its important place in our constitutional jurisprudence. Over the last century, however, the Fourteenth Amendment has assumed a far larger place in constitutional adjudication concerning the States. We feel that the present role of the Contract Clause is largely illuminated by two of this Court's decisions. In each, legislation was sustained despite a claim that it had impaired the obligations of contracts.

Home Building & Loan Assn. v. Blaisdell, 290 U.S. 398 (1934), is regarded as the leading case in the modern era of Contract Clause interpretation. At issue was the Minnesota Mortgage Moratorium Law, enacted in 1933, during the depth of the Depression and when that state was under severe economic stress, and appeared to have no effective alternative. The statute was a temporary measure that allowed judicial extension of the time for redemption; a mortgagor who remained in possession during the extension period was required to pay a reasonable income or rental value to the mortgagee. A closely divided Court, in an opinion by Mr. Chief Justice Hughes, observed that "emergency may furnish the occasion for the exercise of power" and that the "constitutional question presented in the light of an emergency is whether the power possessed embraces the particular exercise of it in response to particular conditions." It noted that the debates in the Constitutional Convention were of little aid in the construction of the Contract Clause, but that the general purpose of the Clause was clear: to encourage trade and credit by promoting confidence in the stability of contractual obligations. Nevertheless, a State "continues to possess authority to safeguard the vital interests of its people. . . . This principle of harmonizing the constitutional prohibition with the necessary residuum of state power has had progressive recognition in the decisions of this Court." The great clauses of the Constitution are to be considered in the light of our whole experience, and not merely as they would be interpreted by its Framers in the conditions and with the outlook of their time.

This Court's most recent Contract Clause decision is El Paso v. Simmons, 379 U.S. 497 (1965). That case concerned a 1941 Texas statute that limited to a 5-year period the reinstatement rights of an interest-defaulting purchaser of land from the State. For many years prior to the enactment of that statute, such a defaulting purchaser, under Texas law, could have reinstated his claim to the land upon written request and payment of delinquent interest, unless rights of third parties had intervened. This Court held that "it is not every modification of a contractual promise that impairs the obligation of contract under federal law." It observed that the State "has the 'sovereign right . . . to protect the . . . general welfare of the people' " and "we must respect the 'wide discretion on the part of the legislature in determining what is and what is not necessary,' " quoting East New York Savings Bank v. Hahn, 326 U.S. 230, 232–233 (1945). The Court recognized that "the power of a State to modify or affect the obligation of contract is not without limit," but held that "the objects of the Texas statute make abundantly clear that it impairs no protected right under the Contract Clause."

Both of these cases eschewed a rigid application of the Contract Clause to invalidate state legislation. Yet neither indicated that the Contract Clause was without meaning in modern constitutional jurisprudence, or that its limitation on state power was illusory. Whether or not the protection of contract rights comports with current views of wise public policy, the Contract Clause remains a part of our written Constitution. We therefore must attempt to apply that constitutional provision to the instant case with due respect for its purpose and the prior decisions of this Court.

III.

We first examine appellant's general claim that repeal of the 1962 covenant impaired the obligation of the States' contract with the bondholders. It long has been established that the Contract Clause limits the power of the States to modify their own contracts as well as to regulate those between private parties. Fletcher v. Peck, 6 Cranch 87, 137–139 (1810); Dartmouth College v. Woodward, 4 Wheat. 518 (1819). Yet the Contract Clause does not prohibit the States from repealing or amending statutes generally, or from enacting legislation with retroactive effects.[13] Thus, as a preliminary matter, appellant's claim requires a determination that the repeal has the effect of impairing a contractual obligation.

In this case the obligation was itself created by a statute, the 1962 legislative covenant. It is unnecessary, however, to dwell on the criteria for determining whether state legislation gives rise to a contractual obligation. The trial court found, . . . and appellees do not deny, that the 1962 covenant constituted a contract between the two States and the holders of the Consolidated Bonds issued between 1962 and the 1973 prospective repeal. . . .

The trial court recognized that there was an impairment in this case: "To the extent that the repeal of the covenant authorizes the Authority to assume

---

[13] The Contract Clause is in the phrase of the Constitution which contains the prohibition against any State's enacting a bill of attainder or ex post facto law. Notwithstanding Mr. Chief Justice Marshall's reference to these two other forbidden categories in Fletcher v. Peck, 6 Cranch, at 138–139, it is clear that they limit the powers of the States only with regard to the imposition of punishment. Cummings v. Missouri, 4 Wall. 277, 322–326, 18 L.Ed. 356 (1867); Calder v. Bull, 3 Dall. 386, 390–391, 1 L.Ed. 648 (1798). The Due Process Clause of the Fourteenth Amendment generally does not prohibit retrospective civil legislation, unless the consequences are particularly "harsh and oppressive." Welch v. Henry, 305 U.S. 134, 147 (1938). See Usery v. Turner Elkhorn Mining Co., 428 U.S. 1, 14–20 (1976).

greater deficits for such purposes, it permits a diminution of the pledged revenues and reserves and may be said to constitute an impairment of the states' contract with the bondholders." . . .

Having thus established that the repeal impaired a contractual obligation of the States, we turn to the question whether that impairment violated the Contract Clause.

IV.

Although the Contract Clause appears literally to proscribe "any" impairment, this Court observed in *Blaisdell* that "the prohibition is not an absolute one and is not to be read with literal exactness like a mathematical formula." Thus, a finding that there has been a technical impairment is merely a preliminary step in resolving the more difficult question whether that impairment is permitted under the Constitution. In the instant case, as in *Blaisdell,* we must attempt to reconcile the strictures of the Contract Clause with the "essential attributes of sovereign power," necessarily reserved by the States to safeguard the welfare of their citizens.

The trial court concluded that repeal of the 1962 covenant was a valid exercise of New Jersey's police power because repeal served important public interests in mass transportation, energy conservation, and environmental protection. Yet the Contract Clause limits otherwise legitimate exercises of state legislative authority, and the existence of an important public interest is not always sufficient to overcome that limitation. "Undoubtedly, whatever is reserved of state power must be consistent with the fair intent of the constitutional limitation of that power." *Blaisdell,* 290 U.S., at 439. Moreover, the scope of the State's reserved power depends on the nature of the contractual relationship with which the challenged law conflicts.

The States must possess broad power to adopt general regulatory measures without being concerned that private contracts will be impaired, or even destroyed, as a result. Otherwise, one would be able to obtain immunity from the state regulation by making private contractual arrangements. This principle is summarized in Mr. Justice Holmes' well-known dictum: "One whose rights, such as they are, are subject to state restriction, cannot remove them from the power of the State by making a contract about them." Hudson Water Co. v. McCarter, 209 U.S. 349, 357.

Yet private contracts are not subject to unlimited modification under the police power. The Court in *Blaisdell* recognized that laws intended to regulate existing contractual relationships must serve a legitimate public purpose. A State could not "adopt as its policy the repudiation of debts or the destruction of contracts or the denial of means to enforce them." Legislation adjusting the rights and responsibilities of contracting parties must be upon reasonable conditions and of a character appropriate to the public purpose justifying its adoption. As is customary in reviewing economic and social regulation, however, courts properly defer to legislative judgment as to the necessity and reasonableness of a particular measure.

. . . .

When a State impairs the obligation of its own contract, the reserved-powers doctrine has a different basis. The initial inquiry concerns the ability of the State to enter into an agreement that limits its power to act in the future. As early as Fletcher v. Peck, the Court considered the argument that "one legislature cannot abridge the powers of a succeeding legislature." 6 Cranch, at 135. It is often stated that "the legislature cannot bargain away the police power of a State." Stone v. Mississippi, 101 U.S. 814, 817 (1880).[20] This doctrine requires a determination of the State's power to create irrevocable contract rights in the first place, rather than an inquiry into the purpose or reasonableness of the subsequent impairment. In short, the Contract Clause does not require a State to adhere to a contract that surrenders an essential attribute of its sovereignty.

In deciding whether a State's contract was invalid *ab initio* under the reserved powers doctrine, earlier decisions relied on distinctions among the various powers of the State. Thus, the police power and the power of eminent domain were among those that could not be "contracted away," but the State could bind itself in the future exercise of the taxing and spending powers.[21] Such formalistic distinctions perhaps cannot be dispositive, but they contain an important element of truth. Whatever the propriety of a State's binding itself to a future course of conduct in other contexts, the power to enter into effective financial contracts cannot be questioned. Any financial obligation could be regarded in theory as a relinquishment of the State's spending power, since money spent to repay debts is not available for other purposes. Similarly, the taxing power may have to be exercised if debts are to be repaid. Notwithstanding these effects, the Court has regularly held that the States are bound by their debt contracts.

The instant case involves a financial obligation and thus as a threshold matter may not be said automatically to fall within the reserved powers that cannot be contracted away.... [The] promise [here] is purely financial and thus not necessarily a compromise of the State's reserved powers.

Of course, to say that the financial restrictions of the 1962 covenant were valid when adopted does not finally resolve this case. The Contract Clause is not an absolute bar to subsequent modification of a State's own financial obligations. As with laws impairing the obligations of private contracts, an impairment may be constitutional if it is reasonable and necessary to serve an important public purpose. In applying this standard, however, complete deference to a legislative assessment of reasonableness and necessity is not appropriate because the State's self-interest is at stake. A governmental entity can always find a use for extra money, especially when taxes do not have to be raised. If a State could reduce its financial obligations whenever it wanted to spend the money for what it regarded as an important public purpose, the Contract Clause would provide no protection at all.

The trial court recognized to an extent the special status of a State's financial obligations when it held that *total* repudiation, presumably for even a worthwhile public purpose, would be unconstitutional. But the trial court regarded the protection of the Contract Clause as available only in such an extreme case: "The states' inherent power to protect the public welfare may be

---

[20] Stone v. Mississippi sustained the State's revocation of a 25-year charter to operate a lottery. Other cases similarly have held that a State is without power to enter into binding contracts not to exercise its police power in the future....

[21] In New Jersey v. Wilson, 7 Cranch 164 (1812), the Court held that a State could properly grant a permanent tax exemption and that the Contract Clause prohibited any impairment of such an agreement. This holding has never been repudiated, although tax exemption contracts generally have not re-

ceived a sympathetic construction. See B. Wright, The Contract Clause of the Constitution 179–194 (1938).

By contrast, the doctrine that a State cannot contract away the power of eminent domain has been established since West River Bridge Co. v. Dix, 6 How. 507 (1848). See Contributors to Pennsylvania Hospital v. Philadelphia, 245 U.S., at 23–24. The doctrine that a State cannot be bound to a contract forbidding the exercise of its police power is almost as old. See n. 20, supra.

validly exercised under the Contract Clause even if it impairs a contractual obligation so long as it does not destroy it."

The trial court's "total destruction" test is based on what we think is a misreading of W.B. Worthen Co. v. Kavanaugh, 295 U.S. 56 (1935).... The extent of impairment is certainly a relevant factor in determining its reasonableness. But we cannot sustain the repeal of the 1962 covenant simply because the bondholders' rights were not totally destroyed.

. . .

V.

Mass transportation, energy conservation, and environmental protection are goals that are important and of legitimate public concern. Appellees contend that these goals are so important that any harm to bondholders from repeal of the 1962 covenant is greatly outweighed by the public benefit. We do not accept this invitation to engage in a utilitarian comparison of public benefit and private loss. Contrary to Mr. Justice Black's fear expressed on sole dissent in El Paso v. Simmons, 379 U.S., at 517, the Court has not "balanced away" the limitation on state action imposed by the Contract Clause. Thus a State cannot refuse to meet its legitimate financial obligations simply because it would prefer to spend the money to promote the public good rather than the private welfare of its creditors. We can only sustain the repeal of the 1962 covenant if that impairment was both reasonable and necessary to serve the admittedly important purposes claimed by the State.[27]

The more specific justification offered for the repeal of the 1962 covenant was the States' plan for encouraging users of private automobiles to shift to public transportation. The States intended to discourage private automobile use by raising bridge and tunnel tolls and to use the extra revenue from those tolls to subsidize improved commuter railroad service. Appellees contend that repeal of the 1962 covenant was necessary to implement this plan because the new mass transit facilities could not possibly be self-supporting and the covenant's "permitted deficits" level had already been exceeded. We reject this justification because the repeal was neither necessary to achievement of the plan nor reasonable in light of the circumstances.

The determination of necessity can be considered on two levels. First, it cannot be said that total repeal of the covenant was essential; a less drastic modification would have permitted the contemplated plan without entirely removing the covenant's limitations on the use of Port Authority revenues and reserves to subsidize commuter railroads.[28] Second, without modifying the covenant at all, the States could have adopted alternative means of achieving their twin goals of discouraging automobile use and improving mass transit. Appellees contend, however, that choosing among these alternatives is a matter for legislative discretion. But a State is not completely free to consider impairing the obligations of its own contracts on a par with other policy alternatives. Similarly, a State is not free to impose a drastic impairment when an evident and more moderate course would serve its purposes equally well. In El Paso v. Simmons, supra, the ... Court held that adoption of a statute of limitation was

---

[27] The dissent suggests that such careful scrutiny is unwarranted in this case because the harm to bondholders is relatively small. For the same reason, however, contractual obligations of this magnitude need not impose barriers to changes in public policy. The States remain free to exercise their powers of eminent domain to abrogate such contractual rights, upon payment of just compensation.

[28] Of course, we express no opinion as to whether any of these lesser impairments would be constitutional.

a reasonable means to "restrict a party to those gains reasonably to be expected from the contract" when it was adopted.

By contrast, in the instant case the need for mass transportation in the New York metropolitan area was not a new development, and the likelihood that publicly owned commuter railroads would produce substantial deficits was well known. As early as 1922, over a half century ago, there were pressures to involve the Port Authority in mass transit. It was with full knowledge of these concerns that the 1962 covenant was adopted. Indeed, the covenant was specifically intended to protect the pledged revenues and reserves against the possibility that such concerns would lead the Port Authority into greater involvement in deficit mass transit.

During the 12–year period between adoption of the covenant and its repeal, public perception of the importance of mass transit undoubtedly grew because of increased general concern with environmental protection and energy conservation. But these concerns were not unknown in 1962, and the subsequent changes were of degree and not of kind. We cannot say that these changes caused the covenant to have a substantially different impact in 1974 than when it was adopted in 1962. And we cannot conclude that the repeal was reasonable in the light of changed circumstances.

We therefore hold that the Contract Clause of the United States Constitution prohibits the retroactive repeal of the 1962 covenant. The judgment of the Supreme Court of New Jersey is reversed.

. . .

Mr. Justice Stewart took no part in the decision of this case.

Mr. Justice Powell took no part in the consideration or decision of this case.

Mr. Chief Justice Burger, concurring.

. . .

For emphasis, I note that the Court pointedly does not hold that, on the facts of this case, any particular "less drastic modification" would pass constitutional muster, n. 28.

Mr. Justice Brennan, with whom Mr. Justice White and Mr. Justice Marshall join, dissenting.

Decisions of this Court for at least a century have construed the Contract Clause largely to be powerless in binding a State to contracts limiting the authority of successor legislatures to enact laws in furtherance of the health, safety, and similar collective interests of the polity. In short, those decisions established the principle that lawful exercises of a State's police powers stand paramount to private rights held under contract. Today's decision ... rejects this previous understanding and remolds the Contract Clause into a potent instrument for overseeing important policy determinations of the state legislature. At the same time, by creating a constitutional safe haven for property rights embodied in a contract, the decision substantially distorts modern constitutional jurisprudence governing regulation of private economic interests. I might understand, though I could not accept this revival of the Contract Clause were it in accordance with some coherent and constructive view of public policy. But elevation of the clause to the status of regulator of the municipal bond market at the heavy price of frustration of sound legislative policymaking is as demonstrably unwise as it is unnecessary....

. . .

... Given that this is the first case in some 40 years in which this Court has seen fit to invalidate purely economic and social legislation on the strength of the Contract Clause, one may only hope that it will prove a rare phenomenon, turning on the Court's particularized appraisal of the facts before it. But there also is reason for broader concern. It is worth remembering that there is nothing sacrosanct about a contract. All property rights, no less than a contract, are rooted in certain "expectations" about the sanctity of one's right of ownership. . . . And other constitutional doctrines are akin to the Contract Clause in directing their protections to the property interests of private parties. Hence the command of the Fifth Amendment that "private property [shall not] be taken for public use, without just compensation" also "remains a part of our written Constitution." And during the heyday of economic due process associated with Lochner v. New York, 198 U.S. 45 (1905), and similar cases long since discarded, . . . this Court treated "the liberty of contract" under the Due Process Clause as virtually indistinguishable from the Contract Clause. . . . In more recent times, however, the Court wisely has come to embrace a coherent, unified interpretation of all such constitutional provisions, and has granted wide latitude to "a valid exercise of [the States'] police powers," Goldblatt v. Hempstead, 369 U.S. 590, 592 (1962), even if it results in severe violations of property rights. . . . If today's case signals a return to substantive constitutional review of States' policies, and a new resolve to protect property owners whose interest or circumstances may happen to appeal to Members of this Court, then more than the citizens of New Jersey and New York will be the losers.

I would not want to be read as suggesting that the States should blithely proceed down the path of repudiating their obligations, financial or otherwise. Their credibility in the credit market obviously is highly dependent on exercising their vast lawmaking powers with self-restraint and discipline, and I, for one, have little doubt that few, if any, jurisdictions would choose to use their authority "so foolish[ly] as to kill a goose that lays golden eggs for them." But in the final analysis, there is no reason to doubt that appellant's financial welfare is being adequately policed by the political processes and the bond marketplace itself. The role to be played by the Constitution is at most a limited one. For this Court should have learned long ago that the Constitution—be it through the Contract or Due Process Clause—can actively intrude into such economic and policy matters only if my Brethren are prepared to bear enormous institutional and social costs. Because I consider the potential dangers of such judicial interference to be intolerable, I dissent.

Allied Structural Steel Co. v. Spannaus

438 U.S. 234, 98 S.Ct. 2716, 57 L.Ed.2d 727 (1978).

Mr. Justice Stewart delivered the opinion of the Court.

[Allied had its principal place of business in Illinois, but maintained an office with 30 employees in Minnesota. In 1963 it adopted a pension plan providing a vested pension, payable at 65, for employees who worked until the age of 65, employees who reached 60 and had worked for 15 years, employees who reached 55 and whose age plus work years equalled 75, and employees under 55 whose age plus work years equalled 80.]

The company not only retained a virtually unrestricted right to amend the plan in whole or in part, but was also free to terminate the plan and distribute the trust assets at any time and for any reason. . . . The plan also specifically advised employees that neither its existence nor any of its terms were to be understood as implying any assurance that employees could not be dismissed from their employment with the company at any time.

In sum, an employee who did not die, did not quit, and was not discharged before meeting one of the requirements of the plan would receive a fixed pension at age 65 if the company remained in business and elected to continue the pension plan in essentially its existing form.

[In 1974 Minnesota enacted the Private Pension Benefits Protection Act, which subjected a private employer who provided pension benefits] to a "pension funding charge" if he either terminated the plan or closed a Minnesota office. The charge was assessed if the pension funds were not sufficient to cover full pensions for all employees who had worked at least 10 years. The Act required the employer to satisfy the deficiency by purchasing deferred annuities, payable to the employees at their normal retirement age. A separate provision specified that periods of employment prior to the effective date of the Act were to be included in the 10–year employment criterion.

During the summer of 1974 the company began closing its Minnesota office. On July 31, it discharged 11 of its 30 Minnesota employees, and the following month it notified the Minnesota Commissioner of Labor and Industry, as required by the Act, that it was terminating an office in the State. At least nine of the discharged employees did not have any vested pension rights under the company's plan, but had worked for the company for 10 years or more and thus qualified as pension obligees of the company under the law that Minnesota had enacted a few months earlier. On August 18, the State notified the company that it owed a pension funding charge of approximately $185,000 under the provisions of the Private Pension Benefits Protection Act.

The company ... claimed that the Act unconstitutionally impaired its contractual obligations to its employees under its pension agreement....

II.

A.

There can be no question of the impact of the Minnesota Private Pension Benefits Protection Act upon the company's contractual relationships with its employees. The Act substantially altered those relationships by superimposing pension obligations upon the company conspicuously beyond those that it had voluntarily agreed to undertake. But it does not inexorably follow that the Act, as applied to the company, violates the Contract Clause of the Constitution.

The language of the Contract Clause appears unambiguously absolute: "No State shall ... pass any ... Law impairing the Obligation of Contracts." U.S. Const. Art. 1, § 10. The Clause is not, however, the draconian provision that its words might seem to imply. As the Court has recognized, "literalism in the construction of the contract clause ... would make it destructive of the public interest by depriving the State of its prerogative of self-protection." W.B. Worthen Co. v. Thomas, 292 U.S. 426, 433.

Although it was perhaps the strongest single constitutional check on state legislation during our early years as a Nation, the Contract Clause receded into comparative desuetude with the adoption of the Fourteenth Amendment, and particularly with the development of the large body of jurisprudence under the Due Process Clause of that Amendment in modern constitutional history. Nonetheless, the Contract Clause remains part of the Constitution. It is not a dead letter....

First of all, ... the Contract Clause does not operate to obliterate the police power of the States. "It is the settled law of this court that the interdiction of statutes impairing the obligation of contracts does not prevent the State from exercising such powers as are vested in it for the promotion of the common weal, or are necessary for the general good of the public, though contracts previously entered into between individuals may thereby be affected. This power, which in its various ramifications is known as the police power, is an exercise of the sovereign right of the Government to protect the lives, health, morals, comfort and general welfare of the people, and is paramount to any rights under contracts between individuals." Manigault v. Springs, 199 U.S. 473, 480. As Mr. Justice Holmes succinctly put the matter in his opinion for the Court in Hudson Water Co. v. McCarter, 209 U.S. 349, 357: "One whose rights, such as they are, are subject to state restriction, cannot remove them from the power of the State by making a contract about them. The contract will carry with it the infirmity of the subject matter."

B.

If the Contract Clause is to retain any meaning at all, however, it must be understood to impose some limits upon the power of a State to abridge existing contractual relationships, even in the exercise of its otherwise legitimate police power. The existence and nature of those limits were clearly indicated in a series of cases in this Court arising from the efforts of the States to deal with the unprecedented emergencies brought on by the severe economic depression of the early 1930's.

In Home Building & Loan Assn. v. Blaisdell, 290 U.S. 398, the Court upheld against a Contract Clause attack a mortgage moratorium law that Minnesota had enacted to provide relief for homeowners threatened with foreclosure. Although the legislation conflicted directly with lenders' contractual foreclosure rights, the Court there acknowledged that, despite the Contract Clause, the States retain residual authority to enact laws "to safeguard the vital interests of [their] people." . . . In upholding the state mortgage moratorium law, the Court found five factors significant. First, the state legislature had declared in the Act itself that an emergency need for the protection of homeowners existed. . . . Second, the state law was enacted to protect a basic societal interest, not a favored group. . . . Third, the relief was appropriately tailored to the emergency that it was designed to meet. . . . Fourth, the imposed conditions were reasonable. . . . And, finally, the legislation was limited to the duration of the emergency. . . .

The *Blaisdell* opinion thus clearly implied that if the Minnesota moratorium legislation had not possessed the characteristics attributed to it by the Court, it would have been invalid under the Contract Clause of the Constitution. These implications were given concrete force in three cases that followed closely in *Blaisdell's* wake.

In W.B. Worthen Co. v. Thomas, 292 U.S. 426, the Court dealt with an Arkansas law that exempted the proceeds of a life insurance policy from collection by the beneficiary's judgment creditors. Stressing the retroactive effect of the state law, the Court held that it was invalid under the Contract Clause, since it was not precisely and reasonably designed to meet a grave temporary emergency in the interest of the general welfare. In W.B. Worthen Co. v. Kavanaugh, 295 U.S. 56, the Court was confronted with another Arkansas law that diluted the rights and remedies of mortgage bondholders. The Court held the law invalid under the Contract Clause. "Even when the public welfare is invoked as an excuse," Mr. Justice Cardozo wrote for the Court, the security of a mortgage cannot be cut down "without moderation or reason or in a spirit of oppression." . . . And finally, in Treigle v. Acme

Homestead Assn., 297 U.S. 189, the Court held invalid under the Contract Clause a Louisiana law that modified the existing withdrawal rights of the members of a building and loan association. "Such an interference with the right of contract," said the Court, "cannot be justified by saying that in the public interest the operations of building associations may be controlled and regulated, or that in the same interest their charters may be amended."

. . .

III.

In applying these principles to the present case, the first inquiry must be whether the state law has, in fact, operated as a substantial impairment of a contractual relationship.[16] The severity of the impairment measures the height of the hurdle the state legislation must clear. Minimal alteration of contractual obligations may end the inquiry at its first stage. Severe impairment, on the other hand, will push the inquiry to a careful examination of the nature and purpose of the state legislation.

The severity of an impairment of contractual obligations can be measured by the factors that reflect the high value the Framers placed on the protection of private contracts. Contracts enable individuals to order their personal and business affairs according to their particular needs and interests. Once arranged, those rights and obligations are binding under the law, and the parties are entitled to rely on them.

Here, the company's contracts of employment with its employees included as a fringe benefit or additional form of compensation, the pension plan. The company's maximum obligation was to set aside each year an amount based on the plan's requirements for vesting. The plan satisfied the current federal income tax code and was subject to no other legislative requirements. And, of course, the company was free to amend or terminate the pension plan at any time. The company thus had no reason to anticipate that its employees' pension rights could become vested except in accordance with the terms of the plan. It relied heavily, and reasonably, on this legitimate contractual expectation in calculating its annual contributions to the pension fund.

The effect of Minnesota's Private Pension Benefits Protection Act on this contractual obligation was severe. The company was required in 1974 to have made its contributions throughout the pre–1974 life of its plan as if employees' pension rights had vested after 10 years, instead of vesting in accord with the terms of the plan. Thus a basic term of the pension contract—one on which the company had relied for 10 years—was substantially modified. The result was that although the company's past contributions were adequate when made, they were not adequate when computed under the 10–year statutory vesting requirement. The Act thus forced a current recalculation of the past 10 years' contributions based on the new, unanticipated 10–year vesting requirement.

[16] The novel construction of the Contract Clause expressed in the dissenting opinion is wholly contrary to the decisions of this Court. The narrow view that the Clause forbids only state laws that diminish the duties of a contractual obligor and not laws that increase them, a view arguably suggested by Satterlee v. Matthewson, 2 Pet. 380, has since been expressly repudiated.... Moreover, in any bilateral contract the diminution of duties on one side effectively increases the duties on the other.

The even narrower view that the Clause is limited in its application to state laws relieving debtors of obligations to their creditors is, as the dissent recognizes, ... completely at odds with this Court's decisions. See Dartmouth College v. Woodward, 4 Wheat. 518....

Not only did the state law thus retroactively modify the compensation that the company had agreed to pay its employees from 1963 to 1974, but it did so by changing the company's obligations in an area where the element of reliance was vital—the funding of a pension plan. . . .

Moreover, the retroactive state-imposed vesting requirement was applied only to those employers who terminated their pension plans or who, like the company, closed their Minnesota offices. The company was thus forced to make all the retroactive changes in its contractual obligations at one time. . . .

Thus, the statute . . . nullifies express terms of the company's contractual obligations and imposes a completely unexpected liability in potentially disabling amounts [without] even any provision for gradual applicability or grace periods. . . . Yet there is no showing in the record . . . that this severe disruption of contractual expectations was necessary to meet an important general social problem. The presumption favoring "legislative judgment as to the necessity and reasonableness of a particular measure," . . . simply cannot stand in this case.

. . .

This Minnesota law simply does not possess the attributes of those state laws that in the past have survived challenge under the Contract Clause. . . . The law was not even purportedly enacted to deal with a broad, generalized economic or social problem. Cf. Home Building & Loan Assn. v. Blaisdell, 290 U.S., at 445. It did not operate in an area already subject to state regulation at the time the company's contractual obligations were originally undertaken, but invaded an area never before subject to regulation by the State. . . . It did not effect simply a temporary alteration of the contractual relationships of those within its coverage, but worked a severe, permanent, and immediate change in those relationships—irrevocably and retroactively. . . . And its narrow aim was levelled not at every Minnesota employer, not even at every Minnesota employer who left the State, . . . but only at those who had in the past been sufficiently enlightened as voluntarily to agree to establish pension plans for their employees.

"Not Blaisdell's case, but Worthen's (W.B. Worthen Co. v. Thomas, [292 U.S. 426])supplies the applicable rule" here. W.B. Worthen Co. v. Kavanaugh, 295 U.S. 56, 63. It is not necessary to hold that the Minnesota law impaired the obligation of the company's employment contracts "without moderation or reason or in a spirit of oppression." . . . But we do hold that if the Contract Clause means anything at all, it means that Minnesota could not constitutionally do what it tried to do to the company in this case.

The judgment of the District Court is reversed.

. . .

Mr. Justice Blackmun took no part in the consideration or decision of this case.

Mr. Justice Brennan, with whom Mr. Justice White and Mr. Justice Marshall join, dissenting.

. . .

Today's decision greatly expands the reach of the [Contract] Clause. The . . . Act . . . does not abrogate or dilute any obligation due a party to a private contract; rather, like all positive social legislation, the Act imposes new, additional obligations on a particular class of persons. In my view, any constitutional infirmity in the law must therefore derive, not from the Contract Clause, but from the Due Process Clause of the Fourteenth Amendment. I perceive nothing in the Act that works a denial of Due Process and therefore I dissent.

. . .

II.

The primary question in this case is whether the Contract Clause is violated by state legislation enacted to protect employees covered by a pension plan by requiring an employer to make outlays ... to provide terminated employees with the equivalent of benefits reasonably to be expected under the plan. The Act does not relieve either the employer or his employees of any existing contract obligation. Rather, the Act simply creates an additional, supplemental duty of the employer, no different in kind from myriad duties created by a wide variety of legislative measures which defeat settled expectations but which have nonetheless been sustained by this Court. See, e.g., Usery v. Turner Elkhorn Mining Co., 428 U.S. 1 (1976); Hadacheck v. Sebastian, 239 U.S. 394 (1915). For this reason, the Minnesota Act ... does not implicate the Contract Clause in any way. The basic fallacy of today's decision is its mistaken view that the Contract Clause protects all contract based expectations, including that of an employer that his obligations to his employees will not be legislatively enlarged beyond those explicitly provided in his pension plan.

. . .

C.

... [I]t is no more anomalous to give effect to the term "impairment" and deny a claimant protection under the Contract Clause when new duties are created than it is to give effect to the Clause's inapplicability to acts of the National Government and deny a Contract Clause remedy when an act of Congress denies a creditor the ability to enforce a contract right to payment. Both results are simply consequences of the fact that the Clause does not protect all contract based expectations.

More fundamentally, the Court's distortion of the meaning of the Contract Clause creates anomalies of its own and threatens to undermine the jurisprudence of property rights developed over the last 40 years. The Contract Clause, of course, is but one of several clauses in the Constitution that protect existing economic values from governmental interference. The Fifth Amendment's command that "private property [shall not] be taken for public use, without just compensation" is such a clause. A second is the Due Process Clause, which during the heyday of substantive due process, see Lochner v. New York, 198 U.S. 45 (1905), largely supplanted the Contract Clause in importance and operated as a potent limitation on Government's ability to interfere with economic expectations.... Decisions over the past 50 years have developed a coherent, unified interpretation of all the constitutional provisions that may protect economic expectations and these decisions have recognized a broad latitude in States to effect even severe interference with existing economic values when reasonably necessary to promote the general welfare. See Penn Central Transp. Co. v. New York City, 438 U.S. 104.... At the same time the prohibition of the Contract Clause, consistently with its wording and historic purposes, has been limited in application to state laws that diluted, with utter indifference to the legitimate interests of the beneficiary of a contract duty, the existing contract obligation....

Today's conversion of the Contract Clause ... must inevitably produce results difficult to square with any rational conception of a constitutional order. Under the Court's opinion, any law that may be characterized as "superimposing" new obligations on those provided for by contract is to be regarded as creating "sudden, substantial, and unanticipated burdens" and then to be subjected to the most exacting scrutiny. The validity of such a law will turn upon whether judges see it as a law that deals with a generalized social problem, whether it is temporary (as few will be) or permanent, whether it operates in an area previously subject to regulation, and, finally, whether its duties apply to a broad class of persons.... The necessary consequence of the extreme malleability of these rather vague criteria is to vest judges with broad subjective discretion to protect property interests that happen to appeal to them.

To permit this level of scrutiny of laws that interfere with contract based expectations is an anomaly. There is nothing sacrosanct about expectations rooted in contract that justify according them a constitutional immunity denied other property rights. Laws that interfere with settled expectations created by state property law (and which impose severe economic burdens) are uniformly held constitutional where reasonably related to the promotion of the general welfare. Hadacheck v. Sebastian, 239 U.S. 394 (1915), is illustrative. There a property owner had established on a particular parcel of land a perfectly lawful business of a brickyard, and, in reliance on the existing law, continued to operate that business for a number of years. However, a local ordinance was passed prohibiting the operation of brickyards in the particular locale and diminishing the value of the claimant's parcel and thus of his investment by nearly 90%. Notwithstanding the effect of the ordinance on the value of the investment, the ordinance was sustained against a taking claim. See also Miller v. Schoene, 276 U.S. 272 (1928) (statute required cutting down ornamental red cedar trees because they had cedar rust which would be harmful to apple trees in the vicinity).

There is no logical or rational basis for sustaining the duties created by the laws in *Miller* and *Hadacheck,* but invalidating the duty created by the Minnesota Act. Surely, the Act effects no greater interference with reasonable reliance interests than did these other laws. Moreover, the laws operate identically: they all create duties that burden one class of persons and benefit another. The only difference between the present case and *Hadacheck* or *Miller* is that here there was a prior contractual relationship between the members of the benefited and burdened classes. I simply cannot accept that this difference should possess constitutional significance. The only means of avoiding this anomaly is to construe the Contract Clause consistently with its terms and the original understanding and hold it is inapplicable to laws which create new duties.

· · ·

ENERGY RESERVES GROUP, INC. v. KANSAS POWER & LIGHT

CO., 459 U.S. 400 (1983). In 1975 Kansas Power & Light Co. (KPL) entered into two contracts with the predecessor-in-interest of Energy Reserves Group, Inc. (ERG) to purchase natural gas from wells in Kansas. The initial price was $1.50 per thousand cubic feet (Mcf) of gas but the contracts contained a government price escalation clause under which the price would rise to any price fixed by a governmental authority.

Congress passed the Natural Gas Policy Act of 1978. Section 102 of the Act fixed a gradually increasing price for newly discovered natural gas, which in December, 1978, was $2.078 per million British thermal units. Section 109 of the Act set a price for gas not otherwise covered at $1.63 per million Btus. The Act also for the first time regulated intrastate gas sales, fixing as a maximum price that under § 102 and permitting state regulation so long as prices fixed did not exceed the § 102 price. It is agreed that the gas contracts under dispute here were intrastate and governed by this latter provision.

Kansas promptly passed a statute applicable to natural gas contracts entered before 1977 and controlling gas prices only until 1984. It specifically prohibited gas price contracts to operate so as to increase the prices of old intrastate gas beyond those set in § 109 of the federal act.

ERG took the position that under the contracts the price escalated to that of § 102 under the federal act and that the state could not change the contracts. KPL contended that the state act applied and the price should be that under § 109 of the federal act. ERG sued, but the Kansas courts held that the Kansas act applied and that the contract clause did not require otherwise. The Supreme Court, in an opinion written by Justice Blackmun, unanimously agreed with the Kansas courts.

A

"Although the language of the Contract Clause is facially absolute, its prohibition must be accommodated to the inherent police power of the State 'to safeguard the vital interests of its people.' Home Bldg. & Loan Ass'n v. Blaisdell, 290 U.S. 398, 434 (1934)....

. . .

"The threshold inquiry is 'whether the state law has, in fact, operated as a substantial impairment of a contractual relationship.' *Allied Structural Steel Co.*, 438 U.S., at 244. See *United States Trust Co.*, 431 U.S., at 17. The severity of the impairment is said to increase the level of scrutiny to which the legislation will be subjected. *Allied Structural Steel Co.*, 438 U.S., at 245. Total destruction of contractual expectations is not necessary for a finding of substantial impairment. *United States Trust Co.*, 431 U.S., at 26–27. On the other hand, state regulation that restricts a party to gains it reasonably expected from the contract does not necessarily constitute a substantial impairment. Id., at 31, citing El Paso v. Simmons, 379 U.S. 497, 515 (1965). In determining the extent of the impairment, we are to consider whether the industry the complaining party has entered has been regulated in the past. *Allied Structural Steel Co.*, 438 U.S., at 242, n. 13, citing Veix v. Sixth Ward Bldg. & Loan Ass'n, 310 U.S. 32, 38 (1940) ('When he purchased into an enterprise already regulated in the particular to which he now objects, he purchased subject to further legislation upon the same topic')....

"If the state regulation constitutes a substantial impairment, the State, in justification, must have a significant and legitimate public purpose behind the regulation, *United States Trust Co.*, 431 U.S., at 22, such as the remedying of a broad and general social or economic problem. *Allied Structural Steel Co.*, 438 U.S., at 247, 249. Furthermore, since *Blaisdell,* the Court has indicated that the public purpose need not be addressed to an emergency or temporary situation. *United States Trust Co.*, 431 U.S., at 22, n. 19; Veix v. Sixth Ward Bldg. & Loan Ass'n, 310 U.S., at 39–40. One legitimate state interest is the elimination of unforeseen windfall profits. *United States Trust Co.*, 431 U.S., at 31, n. 30. The requirement of a legitimate public purpose guarantees that the State is exercising its police power, rather than providing a benefit to special interests.

"Once a legitimate public purpose has been identified, the next inquiry is whether the adjustment of 'the rights and responsibilities of contracting parties [is based] upon reasonable conditions and [is] of a character appropriate to the public purpose justifying [the legislation's] adoption.' *United States Trust Co.,*

431 U.S., at 22. Unless the State itself is a contracting party, see id., at 23[14] '[a]s is customary in reviewing economic and social regulation, ... courts properly defer to legislative judgment as to the necessity and reasonableness of a particular measure.' Id., at 22–23.

B

"The threshold determination is whether the Kansas Act has impaired substantially ERG's contractual rights. Significant here is the fact that the parties are operating in a heavily regulated industry....

. . .

"Moreover, the contracts expressly recognize the existence of extensive regulation by providing that any contractual terms are subject to relevant present and future state and federal law. This latter provision could be interpreted to incorporate all future state price regulation, and thus dispose of the Contract Clause claim. Regardless of whether this interpretation is correct, the provision does suggest that ERG knew its contractual rights were subject to alteration by state price regulation. Price regulation existed and was foreseeable as the type of law that would alter contract obligations. Reading the Contract Clause as ERG does would mean that indefinite price escalator clauses could exempt ERG from any regulatory limitation of prices whatsoever. Such a result cannot be permitted. Hudson Water Co. v. McCarter, 209 U.S., at 357. In short, ERG's reasonable expectations have not been impaired by the Kansas Act. See El Paso v. Simmons, 379 U.S., at 515.

C

"To the extent, if any, the Kansas Act impairs ERG's contractual interests, the Kansas Act rests on, and is prompted by, significant and legitimate state interests....

"... There can be little doubt about the legitimate public purpose behind the Act.

"Nor are the means chosen to implement these purposes deficient, particularly in light of the deference to which the Kansas Legislature's judgment is entitled.

"We thus resolve the constitutional issue against ERG."

. . .

"Justice Powell, with whom The Chief Justice and Justice Rehnquist join, concurring.

"I concur in the judgment and all of the Court's opinion except Part II–C. The Court concludes in Part II–B that there has been no substantial impairment of ERG's contractual rights. The closing sentence states that 'ERG's reasonable expectations have not been impaired by the Kansas Act.' This

---

[14] See, generally, Note, A Process-Oriented Approach to the Contract Clause, 89 Yale L.J. 1623, 1647–1648 (1980) (distinguishing public from private contracts). In United States Trust Co., but not in Allied Structural Steel Co., the State was one of the contracting parties. When a State itself enters into a contract, it cannot simply walk away from its financial obligations. In almost every case, the Court has held a governmental unit to its contractual obligations when it enters financial or other markets. See United States Trust Co., 431 U.S., at 25–28. ...When the State is a party to the contract, "complete deference to a legislative assessment of reasonableness and necessity is not appropriate because the State's self-interest is at stake." United States Trust Co., 431 U.S., at 26. In the present case, of course, the stricter standard of United States Trust Co. does not apply because Kansas has not altered its own contractual obligations.

conclusion is dispositive, and it is unnecessary for the Court to address the question of whether, if there were an impairment of contractual rights, it would constitute a violation of the Contract Clause. See Allied Structural Steel Co. v. Spannaus, 438 U.S. 234, 245 (1978)."

EXXON CORP. v. EAGERTON, 462 U.S. 176 (1983). Alabama increased its severance tax on oil and gas and prohibited passing on the increase to purchasers. Some producers of oil and gas were parties to contracts made before the tax increase under which they were permitted to include in their price to customers any increase in severance taxes. The Court held unanimously that application of the pass-through prohibition to those contracts did not violate the contract clause. The Court said: "The prohibition applied to all oil and gas producers, regardless of whether they happened to be parties to sale contracts that contained a provision permitting them to pass tax increases through to their purchasers. The effect of the pass-through prohibition on existing contracts that did contain such a provision was incidental to its main effect of shielding consumers from the burden of the tax increase."[a]

C. The Just Compensation Clause of the Fifth Amendment—What Does It Add to Due Process?

Introduction. The Fifth Amendment commands that "private property [not] be taken for public use, without just compensation." The primary focus of this section (subsections 1. and 2.) is not on the explicit exercise of the power of eminent domain, but on the frequently disputed issue of what kind of government regulation affecting the use of property constitutes a "taking" of it. Some attention is also given to the issues of what constitutes "property" protected by the amendment and, in subsection 3., what government's obligation is in the event of a taking.

A fourth issue, addressed here, arises because property may not be taken, even if compensation is offered, unless the taking is for a "public use." Missouri Pacific R. Co. v. Nebraska, 164 U.S. 403 (1896). Judicial scrutiny of the "public use" requirement has been quite limited, however. In Berman v. Parker, 348 U.S. 26 (1954), for example, the Court held that taking a private, decently maintained commercial property located in an otherwise blighted area for transfer to a private redevelopment agency to build private housing as part of an area redevelopment plan satisfied the public use requirement. The Court said: "The role of the judiciary in determining whether that power [of eminent domain] is being exercised for a public purpose is an extremely narrow one." That generous approach was followed in Hawaii Housing Authority v. Midkiff, 467 U.S. 229 (1984), which allowed eminent domain to be used to force the sale of fee simple title by Hawaiian land owners to their tenants. Hawaii's historically extraordinary concentration of private land ownership in a few hands had been found by the legislature to distort the residential ownership market, and

---

[a] The contract clause is a restraint on state law only. Federal legislation impairing the obligation of contracts is subject to review under the due process clause of the Fifth Amendment, but, as the Court said in Pension Benefit Guaranty Corp. v. R.A. Gray & Co., 467 U.S. 717 (1984), the standard of review is "less searching." The Court said little more but emphasized that it had "never held ... that the principles embodied in the Fifth Amendment's Due Process Clause are coextensive with prohibitions existing against state impairments of pre-existing contracts." In National Railroad Passenger Corp. v. Atchison, Topeka and Santa Fe Railway Co., 470 U.S. 451 (1985), the Court did say that judicial scrutiny of federal legislation impairing a private contract should be "quite minimal" and added: "The party asserting a Fifth Amendment due process violation must overcome a presumption of constitutionality and 'establish that the legislature has acted in an arbitrary and irrational way.' "

reduction of the harms of oligopoly was a sufficient public purpose to justify the taking. Although the Court found the "'public use' requirement ... coterminous with the scope of a sovereign's police powers," it reiterated nonetheless that there is "a role for courts to play in reviewing a legislature's judgment of what constitutes a public use," and stated that "where the exercise of the eminent domain power is rationally related to a conceivable public purpose, the Court has never held a compensated taking to be proscribed by the Public Use Clause."

1.   RESTRICTIONS ON PROPERTY USE

Lucas v. South Carolina Coastal Council

505 U.S. 1003, 112 S.Ct. 2886, 120 L.Ed.2d 798 (1992).

Justice Scalia delivered the opinion of the Court.

In 1986, petitioner ... paid $975,000 for two residential lots on the Isle of Palms ... intend[ing] to build single-family homes. In 1988, however, the South Carolina Legislature enacted the Beachfront Management Act ... (Act), which had the direct effect of barring petitioner from erecting any permanent habitable structures on his two parcels.... A state trial court found that this prohibition rendered Lucas's parcels "valueless." ... This case requires us to decide whether the Act's dramatic effect on the economic value of Lucas's lots accomplished a taking of private property under the Fifth and Fourteenth Amendments requiring the payment of "just compensation." ...

I

A

[In 1977 South Carolina enacted a Coastal Zone Management Act requiring owners of land in "critical areas," including beaches and adjacent sand dunes, to obtain a permit from the newly created South Carolina Coastal Council before changing the land's use. Because the two lots Lucas bought in 1986 were not in a "critical area,"] he was not legally obliged to obtain a permit from the Council in advance of any development activity. His intention ... was to do what the owners of the immediately adjacent parcels had already done: erect single-family residences. He commissioned architectural drawings for this purpose.

The Beachfront Management Act ... [directed] the Council ... to establish a "baseline" connecting the landward-most "point[s] of erosion ... during the past forty years" in the region of the Isle of Palms that includes Lucas's lots.... In action not challenged here, the Council fixed this baseline landward of Lucas's parcels. That was significant, for under the Act construction of occupable improvements was flatly prohibited seaward of a line drawn 20 feet landward of, and parallel to, the baseline.... The Act provided no exceptions.

B

Lucas promptly filed suit.... [The trial court agreed with his contention] that the Act's complete extinguishment of his property's value entitled him to compensation regardless of whether the legislature had acted in furtherance of legitimate police power objectives....

The Supreme Court of South Carolina reversed....

.   .   .

I

A

Prior to Justice Holmes' exposition in Pennsylvania Coal Co. v. Mahon, 260 U.S. 393 (1922), it was generally thought that the Takings Clause reached only a "direct appropriation" of property, ... or the functional equivalent of a "practical ouster of [the owner's] possession." ... Justice Holmes recognized in *Mahon*, however, that if the protection against physical appropriations of private property was to be meaningfully enforced, the government's power to redefine the range of interests included in the ownership of property was necessarily constrained by constitutional limits.... If, instead, the uses of private property were subject to unbridled, uncompensated qualification under the police power, "the natural tendency of human nature [would be] to extend the qualification more and more until at last private property disappear[ed]." ... These considerations gave birth in that case to the oft-cited maxim that, "while property may be regulated to a certain extent, if regulation goes too far it will be recognized as a taking." ...

Nevertheless, our decision in *Mahon* offered little insight into when, and under what circumstances, a given regulation would be seen as going "too far" for purposes of the Fifth Amendment. In 70–odd years of succeeding "regulatory takings" jurisprudence, we have generally eschewed any "'set formula'" for determining how far is too far, preferring to "engag[e] in ... essentially ad hoc, factual inquiries," Penn Central Transportation Co. v. New York City, 438 U.S. 104, 124 (1978).... We have, however, described at least two discrete categories of regulatory action as compensable without case-specific inquiry into the public interest advanced in support of the restraint. The first encompasses regulations that compel the property owner to suffer a physical "invasion" of his property. In general (at least with regard to permanent invasions), no matter how minute the intrusion, and no matter how weighty the public purpose behind it, we have required compensation. For example, in Loretto v. Teleprompter Manhattan CATV Corp., 458 U.S. 419 (1982), we determined that New York's law requiring landlords to allow television cable companies to emplace cable facilities in their apartment buildings constituted a taking, ... even though the facilities occupied at most only 1 ½ cubic feet of the landlords' property.... See also United States v. Causby, 328 U.S. 256, 265, and n. 10 (1946) (physical invasions of airspace); cf. Kaiser Aetna v. United States, 444 U.S. 164 (1979) (imposition of navigational servitude upon private marina).

The second situation in which we have found categorical treatment appropriate is where regulation denies all economically beneficial or productive use of land. See Agins ...; see also Nollan v. California Coastal Comm'n, 483 U.S. 825, 834 (1987); Keystone Bituminous Coal Assn. v. DeBenedictis, 480 U.S. 470, 495 (1987); Hodel v. Virginia Surface Mining & Reclamation Assn., Inc., 452 U.S. 264, 295–296 (1981). As we have said on numerous occasions, the Fifth Amendment is violated when land-use regulation "does not substantially advance legitimate state interests *or denies an owner economically viable use of his land.*" Agins ...[7]

---

[7] Regrettably, the rhetorical force of our "deprivation of all economically feasible use" rule is greater than its precision, since the rule does not make clear the "property interest" against which the loss of value is to be measured. When, for example, a regulation requires a developer to leave 90% of a rural tract in its natural state, it is unclear whether we would analyze the situation as one in which the owner has been deprived of all economically beneficial use of the burdened portion of the tract, or as one in which the owner has suffered a mere diminution in value of the tract as a whole.... Unsurprisingly, this uncertainty regarding the composition of the denominator in our "deprivation"

We have never set forth the justification for this rule. Perhaps it is simply, as Justice Brennan suggested, that total deprivation of beneficial use is, from the landowner's point of view, the equivalent of a physical appropriation.... Surely, at least, in the extraordinary circumstance when *no* productive or economically beneficial use of land is permitted, it is less realistic to indulge our usual assumption that the legislature is simply "adjusting the benefits and burdens of economic life," Penn Central Transportation Co., ... in a manner that secures an "average reciprocity of advantage" to everyone concerned. *Pennsylvania Coal Co. v. Mahon....* And the *functional* basis for permitting the government, by regulation, to affect property values without compensation—that "Government hardly could go on if to some extent values incident to property could not be diminished without paying for every such change in the general law"—does not apply to the relatively rare situations where the government has deprived a landowner of all economically beneficial uses.

On the other side of the balance, affirmatively supporting a compensation requirement, is the fact that regulations that leave the owner of land without economically beneficial or productive options for its use—typically, as here, by requiring land to be left substantially in its natural state—carry with them a heightened risk that private property is being pressed into some form of public service under the guise of mitigating serious public harm.... The many statutes on the books, both state and federal, that provide for the use of eminent domain to impose servitudes on private scenic lands preventing developmental uses, or to acquire such lands altogether, suggest the practical equivalence in this setting of negative regulation and appropriation....

We think, in short, that there are good reasons for our frequently expressed belief that when the owner of real property has been called upon to sacrifice all economically beneficial uses in the name of the common good, that is, to leave his property economically idle, he has suffered a taking.[8]

---

fraction has produced inconsistent pronouncements by the Court. Compare Pennsylvania Coal Co. v. Mahon, 260 U.S. 393, 414 (1922) (law restricting subsurface extraction of coal held to effect a taking), with Keystone Bituminous Coal Assn. v. DeBenedictis, 480 U.S. 470, 497–502 (1987) (nearly identical law held not to effect a taking) ... The answer to this difficult question may lie in how the owner's reasonable expectations have been shaped by the State's law of property—i.e., whether and to what degree the State's law has accorded legal recognition and protection to the particular interest in land with respect to which the takings claimant alleges a diminution in (or elimination of) value. In any event, we avoid this difficulty in the present case, since the "interest in land" that Lucas has pleaded (a fee simple interest) is an estate with a rich tradition of protection at common law, and since the South Carolina Court of Common Pleas found that the Beachfront Management Act left each of Lucas's beachfront lots without economic value.

[8] Justice Stevens criticizes the "deprivation of all economically beneficial use" rule as "wholly arbitrary," in that "[the] landowner whose property is diminished in value 95% recovers nothing," while the landowner who suffers a complete elimination of value

"recovers the land's full value." This analysis errs in its assumption that the landowner whose deprivation is one step short of complete is not entitled to compensation. Such an owner might not be able to claim the benefit of our categorical formulation, but, as we have acknowledged time and again, "[t]he economic impact of the regulation on the claimant and ... the extent to which the regulation has interfered with distinct investment-backed expectations" are keenly relevant to takings analysis generally. Penn Central Transportation Co. v. New York City, 438 U.S. 104, 124 (1978). It is true that in at least some cases the landowner with 95% loss will get nothing, while the landowner with total loss will recover in full. But that occasional result is no more strange than the gross disparity between the landowner whose premises are taken for a highway (who recovers in full) and the landowner whose property is reduced to 5% of its former value by the highway (who recovers nothing). Takings law is full of these "all-or-nothing" situations. Justice Stevens similarly misinterprets our focus on "developmental" uses of property (the uses proscribed by the Beachfront Management Act) as betraying an "assumption that the only uses of property cognizable under the Constitution are developmental

B

[Because t]he trial court found Lucas's two beachfront lots to have been rendered valueless[, automatically] entitl[ing] him to compensation[, he] believed it unnecessary to take issue with either the purposes behind the Beachfront Management Act, or the means chosen by the South Carolina Legislature to effectuate those purposes. The South Carolina Supreme Court, however, thought ... the Beachfront Management Act was no ordinary enactment, but involved an exercise of South Carolina's "police powers" to mitigate the harm to the public interest that petitioner's use of his land might occasion.... By neglecting to dispute the findings enumerated in the Act or otherwise to challenge the legislature's purposes, petitioner "concede[d] that the beach-dune area of South Carolina's shores is an extremely valuable public resource; that the erection of new construction, *inter alia*, contributes to the erosion and destruction of this public resource; and that discouraging new construction in close proximity to the beach-dune area is necessary to prevent a great public harm." ... In the court's view, these concessions brought petitioner's challenge within a long line of this Court's cases sustaining against Due Process and Takings Clause challenges the State's use of its "police powers" to enjoin a property owner from activities akin to public nuisances. See Mugler v. Kansas, 123 U.S. 623 (1887) (law prohibiting manufacture of alcoholic beverages); Hadacheck v. Sebastian, 239 U.S. 394 (1915) (law barring operation of brick mill in residential area); Miller v. Schoene, 276 U.S. 272 (1928) (order to destroy diseased cedar trees to prevent infection of nearby orchards); Goldblatt v. Hempstead, 369 U.S. 590 (1962) (law effectively preventing continued operation of quarry in residential area).

It is correct that many of our prior opinions have suggested that "harmful or noxious uses" of property may be proscribed by government regulation without the requirement of compensation. For a number of reasons, however, we think the South Carolina Supreme Court was too quick to conclude that the principle decides the present case. The "harmful or noxious uses" principle was the Court's early attempt to describe in theoretical terms why government may, consistent with the Takings Clause, affect property values by regulation without incurring an obligation to compensate—a reality we nowadays acknowledge explicitly with respect to the full scope of the State's police power. See, e.g., Penn Central Transportation Co., ... (where State "reasonably conclude[s] that 'the health, safety, morals, or general welfare' would be promoted by prohibiting particular contemplated uses of land," compensation need not accompany prohibition); see also *Nollan v. California Coastal Commission,* ... ("Our cases have not elaborated on the standards for determining what constitutes a 'legitimate state interest[,]' [but] [t]hey have made clear ... that a broad range of governmental purposes and regulations satisfy these requirements"). We made this very point in *Penn Central Transportation Co.,* where, in the course of sustaining New York City's landmarks preservation program against a takings challenge, we rejected the petitioner's suggestion that *Mugler* and the cases following it were premised on, and thus limited by, some objective conception of "noxiousness": "[T]he uses in issue in *Hadacheck, Miller,* and *Goldblatt* were perfectly lawful in themselves. They involved no 'blameworthiness, ... moral wrongdoing or conscious act of dangerous risk-taking which induce[d society] to shift the cost to a pa[rt]icular individual.' Sax,

---

uses." We make no such assumption. Though our prior takings cases evince an abiding concern for the productive use of, and economic investment in, land, there are plainly a number of noneconomic interests in land whose impairment will invite exceedingly close scrutiny under the Takings Clause. See, e.g., Loretto v. Teleprompter Manhattan CATV Corp., 458 U.S. 419, 436 (1982) (interest in excluding strangers from one's land).

Takings and the Police Power, 74 Yale L.J. 36, 50 (1964). These cases are better understood as resting not on any supposed 'noxious' quality of the prohibited uses but rather on the ground that the restrictions were reasonably related to the implementation of a policy—not unlike historic preservation—expected to produce a widespread public benefit and applicable to all similarly situated property." . . . "Harmful or noxious use" analysis was, in other words, simply the progenitor of our more contemporary statements that "land-use regulation does not effect a taking if it 'substantially advance[s] legitimate state interests'. . . ." *Nollan* . . . .

The transition from our early focus on control of "noxious" uses to our contemporary understanding of the broad realm within which government may regulate without compensation was an easy one, since the distinction between "harm-preventing" and "benefit-conferring" regulation is often in the eye of the beholder. It is quite possible, for example, to describe in either fashion the ecological, economic, and aesthetic concerns that inspired the South Carolina legislature. . . . One could say that imposing a servitude on Lucas's land is necessary in order to prevent his use of it from "harming" South Carolina's ecological resources; or, instead, in order to achieve the "benefits" of an ecological preserve. . . . Whether one or the other of the competing characterizations will come to one's lips in a particular case depends primarily upon one's evaluation of the worth of competing uses of real estate. . . . Whether Lucas's construction of single-family residences on his parcels should be described as bringing "harm" to South Carolina's adjacent ecological resources thus depends principally upon whether the describer believes that the State's use interest in nurturing those resources is so important that any competing adjacent use must yield.[12]

. . . [N]oxious-use logic [thus] cannot serve as a touchstone to distinguish regulatory "takings"—which require compensation—from regulatory deprivations that do not require compensation. *A fortiori* the legislature's recitation of a noxious-use justification cannot be the basis for departing from our categorical rule that total regulatory takings must be compensated. If it were, departure would virtually always be allowed. The South Carolina Supreme Court's approach would essentially nullify *Mahon*'s affirmation of limits to the noncompensable exercise of the police power. . . . None of [our cases] that employed the logic of "harmful use" prevention to sustain a regulation involved an allegation that the regulation wholly eliminated the value of the claimant's land. . . .

Where the State seeks to sustain regulation that deprives land of all economically beneficial use, we think it may resist compensation only if the logically antecedent inquiry into the nature of the owner's estate shows that the proscribed use interests were not part of his title to begin with. This accords, we think, with our "takings" jurisprudence, which has traditionally been guided by the understandings of our citizens regarding the content of, and the State's power over, the "bundle of rights" that they acquire when they obtain title to property. It seems to us that the property owner necessarily expects the uses of his property to be restricted, from time to time, by various measures newly enacted by the State in legitimate exercise of its police powers; "[a]s long recognized, some values are enjoyed under an implied limitation and must yield to the police power." *Pennsylvania Coal Co. v. Mahon* . . . . And in

---

[12] In Justice Blackmun's view, even with respect to regulations that deprive an owner of all developmental or economically beneficial land uses, the test for required compensation is whether the legislature has recited a harm-preventing justification for its action. Since such a justification can be formulated in practically every case, this amounts to a test of whether the legislature has a stupid staff. We think the Takings Clause requires courts to do more than insist upon artful harm-preventing characterizations.

the case of personal property, by reason of the State's traditionally high degree of control over commercial dealings, he ought to be aware of the possibility that new regulation might even render his property economically worthless.... In the case of land, however, ... the notion ... that title is somehow held subject to the "implied limitation" that the State may subsequently eliminate all economically valuable use is inconsistent with the historical compact recorded in the Takings Clause that has become part of our constitutional culture.[15]

Where "permanent physical occupation" of land is concerned, we have refused to allow the government to decree it anew (without compensation), no matter how weighty the asserted "public interests" involved, *Loretto* ...— though we assuredly *would* permit the government to assert a permanent easement that was a pre-existing limitation upon the landowner's title. Compare Scranton v. Wheeler ... (1900) (interests of "riparian owner in the submerged lands ... bordering on a public navigable water" held subject to Government's navigational servitude), with *Kaiser Aetna v. United States* ... (imposition of navigational servitude on marina created and rendered navigable at private expense held to constitute a taking). We believe similar treatment must be accorded confiscatory regulations, i.e., regulations that prohibit all economically beneficial use of land: Any limitation so severe cannot be newly legislated or decreed (without compensation), but must inhere in the title itself, in the restrictions that background principles of the State's law of property and nuisance already place upon land ownership. A law or decree with such an effect must, in other words, do no more than duplicate the result that could have been achieved in the courts—by adjacent landowners (or other uniquely affected persons) under the State's law of private nuisance, or by the State under its complementary power to abate nuisances that affect the public generally, or otherwise.

On this analysis, the owner of a lake bed, for example, would not be entitled to compensation when he is denied the requisite permit to engage in a landfilling operation that would have the effect of flooding others' land. Nor the corporate owner of a nuclear generating plant, when it is directed to remove all improvements from its land upon discovery that the plant sits astride an earthquake fault. Such regulatory action may well have the effect of eliminating the land's only economically productive use, but it does not proscribe a productive use that was previously permissible under relevant property and nuisance principles. The use of these properties for what are now expressly prohibited purposes was always unlawful, and (subject to other constitutional limitations) it was open to the State at any point to make the implication of those background principles of nuisance and property law explicit.... When, however, a regulation that declares "off-limits" all economically productive or beneficial uses of land goes beyond what the relevant background principles would dictate, compensation must be paid to sustain it.[17]

---

[15] ...Justice Blackmun ... argu[es] that our description of the "understanding" of land ownership that informs the Takings Clause is not supported by early American experience. That is largely true, but entirely irrelevant. The practices of the States prior to incorporation of the Takings and Just Compensation Clauses ... were out of accord with any plausible interpretation of those provisions. Justice Blackmun is correct that early constitutional theorists did not believe the Takings Clause embraced regulations of property at all, but even he does not suggest (explicitly, at least) that we renounce the Court's contrary conclusion in *Mahon*. Since the text of the Clause can be read to encompass regulatory as well as physical deprivations ..., we decline to do so as well.

[17] Of course, the State may elect to rescind its regulation and thereby avoid having to pay compensation for a permanent deprivation. See First English Evangelical Lutheran Church.... But "where the [regulation has] already worked a taking of all use of property, no subsequent action by the government can relieve it of the duty to provide

The "total taking" inquiry we require today will ordinarily entail (as the application of state nuisance law ordinarily entails) analysis of, among other things, the degree of harm to public lands and resources, or adjacent private property, posed by the claimant's proposed activities, ... the social value of the claimant's activities and their suitability to the locality in question, ... and the relative ease with which the alleged harm can be avoided through measures taken by the claimant and the government (or adjacent private landowners) alike. . . . The fact that a particular use has long been engaged in by similarly situated owners ordinarily imports a lack of any common-law prohibition (though changed circumstances or new knowledge may make what was previously permissible no longer so ...). So also does the fact that other landowners, similarly situated, are permitted to continue the use denied to the claimant.

It seems unlikely that common-law principles would have prevented the erection of any habitable or productive improvements on petitioner's land; they rarely support prohibition of the "essential use" of land. . . . The question, however, is one of state law to be dealt with on remand. We emphasize that to win its case South Carolina must do more than proffer the legislature's declaration that the uses Lucas desires are inconsistent with the public interest, or the conclusory assertion that they violate a common-law maxim. . . . Instead, as it would be required to do if it sought to restrain Lucas in a common-law action for public nuisance, South Carolina must identify background principles of nuisance and property law that prohibit the uses he now intends in the circumstances in which the property is presently found. Only on this showing can the State fairly claim that, in proscribing all such beneficial uses, the Beachfront Management Act is taking nothing.[18]

. . .

Justice Kennedy, concurring in the judgment.

. . .

. . . I share the reservations of some of my colleagues about a finding that a beach front lot loses all value because of a development restriction. . . .

The finding of no value must be considered under the Takings Clause by reference to the owner's reasonable, investment-backed expectations. . . . Property is bought and sold, investments are made, subject to the State's power to regulate. Where a taking is alleged from regulations which deprive the property of all value, the test must be whether the deprivation is contrary to reasonable, investment-backed expectations.

There is an inherent tendency towards circularity in this synthesis, of course; for if the owner's reasonable expectations are shaped by what courts allow as a proper exercise of governmental authority, property tends to become what courts say it is. Some circularity must be tolerated in these matters, however. . . . The definition, moreover, is not circular in its entirety. The expectations protected by the Constitution are based on objective rules and customs that can be understood as reasonable by all parties involved.

compensation for the period during which the taking was effective." . . .

[18] Justice Blackmun decries our reliance on background nuisance principles at least in part because he believes those principles to be as manipulable as we find the "harm prevention"-"benefit conferral" dichotomy. There is no doubt some leeway in a court's interpretation of what existing state law permits—but not remotely as much, we think, as in a legislative crafting of the reasons for its confiscatory regulation. We stress that an affirmative decree eliminating all economically beneficial uses may be defended only if an objectively reasonable application of relevant precedents would exclude those beneficial uses in the circumstances in which the land is presently found.

[R]easonable expectations must be understood in light of the whole of our legal tradition. The common law of nuisance is too narrow a confine for the exercise of regulatory power in a complex and interdependent society.... The State should not be prevented from enacting new regulatory initiatives in response to changing conditions, and courts must consider all reasonable expectations whatever their source. The Takings Clause does not require a static body of state property law; it protects private expectations to ensure private investment. I agree with the Court that nuisance prevention accords with the most common expectations of property owners who face regulation, but I do not believe this can be the sole source of state authority to impose severe restrictions. Coastal property may present such unique concerns for a fragile land system that the State can go further in regulating its development and use than the common law of nuisance might otherwise permit.

The Supreme Court of South Carolina erred ... by reciting the general purposes for which the state regulations were enacted without a determination that they were in accord with the owner's reasonable expectations and therefore sufficient to support a severe restriction on specific parcels of property.... The promotion of tourism, for instance, ought not to suffice to deprive specific property of all value without a corresponding duty to compensate. Furthermore, the means as well as the ends of regulation must accord with the owner's reasonable expectations. Here, the State did not act until after the property had been zoned for individual lot development and most other parcels had been improved, throwing the whole burden of the regulation on the remaining lots. This too must be measured in the balance. See Pennsylvania Coal Co. v. Mahon, 260 U.S. 393, 416 (1922).

. . .

Justice Blackmun, dissenting.

. . .

The South Carolina Supreme Court ... decision rested on two premises that until today were unassailable—that the State has the power to prevent any use of property it finds to be harmful to its citizens, and that a state statute is entitled to a presumption of constitutionality.

. . .

... The Court consistently has upheld regulations imposed to arrest a significant threat to the common welfare, whatever their economic effect on the owner. See e.g., Goldblatt v. Hempstead, ... (1962); Euclid v. Ambler Realty Co., ... (1926); ... Mugler v. Kansas ... (1887).

. . .

Nothing in the record undermines the General Assembly's assessment that prohibitions on building in front of the setback line are necessary to protect people and property from storms, high tides, and beach erosion. Because that legislative determination cannot be disregarded in the absence of such evidence, ... and because its determination of harm to life and property from building is sufficient to prohibit that use under this Court's cases, the South Carolina Supreme Court correctly found no taking.

. . .

... We only recently have reaffirmed that claimants have the burden of showing a state law constitutes a taking. See *Keystone Bituminous Coal* ... See also *Goldblatt* ... (citing "the usual presumption of constitutionality" that applies to statutes attacked as takings).

Rather than invoking these traditional rules, the Court decides the State has the burden to convince the courts that its legislative judgments are correct....

IV

The Court ... create[s] a new scheme for regulations that eliminate all economic value[—]a categorical rule finding these regulations to be a taking unless the use they prohibit is a background common-law nuisance or property principle.

A

... If one fact about the Court's taking jurisprudence can be stated without contradiction, it is that "the particular circumstances of each case" determine whether a specific restriction will be rendered invalid by the government's failure to pay compensation.... This is so because although we have articulated certain factors to be considered, including the economic impact on the property owner, the ultimate conclusion "necessarily requires a weighing of private and public interests." *Agins* ... When the government regulation prevents the owner from any economically valuable use of his property, the private interest is unquestionably substantial, but we have never before held that no public interest can outweigh it....

This Court repeatedly has recognized the ability of government, in certain circumstances, to regulate property without compensation no matter how adverse the financial effect on the owner may be. More than a century ago, the Court explicitly upheld the right of States to prohibit uses of property injurious to public health, safety, or welfare without paying compensation: "A prohibition simply upon the use of property for purposes that are declared, by valid legislation, to be injurious to the health, morals, or safety of the community, cannot, in any just sense, be deemed a taking or an appropriation of property." Mugler v. Kansas ... (1887). On this basis, the Court upheld an ordinance effectively prohibiting operation of a previously lawful brewery, although the "establishments will become of no value as property." ...

Mugler was only the beginning in a long line of cases. [Justice Blackmun's discussion of several of these is omitted.]

... In First Lutheran Church v. Los Angeles County ... (1987), the owner alleged that a floodplain ordinance had deprived it of "all use" of the property.... The Court remanded the case for consideration whether, even if the ordinance denied the owner all use, it could be justified as a safety measure. And in *Keystone Bituminous Coal,* the Court summarized over 100 years of precedent: "the Court has repeatedly upheld regulations that destroy or adversely affect real property interests." ...

The Court ... claim[s] that [prior cases] never ... upheld a regulation when the owner alleged the loss of all economic value. Even if th[at] factual premise were correct, its understanding of the Court's cases is distorted. In none ... did the Court suggest that the right of a State to prohibit certain activities without paying compensation turned on the availability of some residual valuable use. Instead, the cases depended on whether the government interest was sufficient to prohibit the activity, given the significant private cost.

These cases rest on the principle that the State has full power to prohibit an owner's use of property if it is harmful to the public. "[S]ince no individual has a right to use his property so as to create a nuisance or otherwise harm others, the State has not 'taken' anything when it asserts its power to enjoin the nuisance-like activity." *Keystone Bituminous Coal* ... It would make no sense under this theory to suggest that an owner has a constitutionally protected right to harm others, if only he makes the proper showing of economic loss....

B

Ultimately even the Court ... agrees that there cannot be a categorical rule for a taking based on economic value that wholly disregards the public need asserted. Instead, ... it will permit a State to regulate all economic value only if the State prohibits uses that would not be permitted under "background principles of nuisance and property law."

Until today, the Court explicitly had rejected the contention that the government's power to act without paying compensation turns on whether the prohibited activity is a common-law nuisance.... Instead the Court has relied in the past ... on legislative judgments of what constitutes a harm.

. . .

[T]he Court's reliance on common-law principles of nuisance in its quest for a value-free taking jurisprudence [is perplexing]. In determining what is a nuisance at common law, state courts make exactly the decision that the Court finds so troubling when made by the South Carolina General Assembly today: they determine whether the use is harmful. Common-law public and private nuisance law is simply a determination whether a particular use causes harm.... There is nothing magical in the reasoning of judges long dead. They determined a harm in the same way as state judges and legislatures do today. If judges in the 18th and 19th centuries can distinguish a harm from a benefit, why not judges in the 20th century, and if judges can, why not legislators? There simply is no reason to believe that new interpretations of the hoary common law nuisance doctrine will be particularly "objective" or "value-free."
. . .

C

. . .

Although, prior to the adoption of the Bill of Rights, America was replete with land use regulations describing which activities were considered noxious and forbidden, ... the Fifth Amendment's Taking Clause originally did not extend to regulations of property, whatever the effect.[23] Most state courts agreed with this narrow interpretation of a taking....

Even when courts began to consider that regulation in some situations could constitute a taking, they continued to uphold bans on particular uses without paying compensation, notwithstanding the economic impact, under the rationale that no one can obtain a vested right to injure or endanger the public....

In addition, state courts historically have been less likely to find that a government action constitutes a taking when the affected land is undeveloped....

---

[23] James Madison, author of the Taking Clause, apparently intended it to apply only to direct, physical takings of property by the Federal Government.

With similar result, the common agrarian conception of property limited owners to "natural" uses of their land prior to and during much of the 18th century. . . .

Nor does history indicate any common-law limit on the State's power to regulate harmful uses even to the point of destroying all economic value. Nothing in the discussions in Congress concerning the Taking Clause indicates that the Clause was limited by the common-law nuisance doctrine. . . .

In short, I find no clear and accepted "historical compact" or "understanding of our citizens" justifying the Court's new taking doctrine. . . . If the Court decided that the early common law provides the background principles for interpreting the Taking Clause, then regulation, as opposed to physical confiscation, would not be compensable. If the Court decided that the law of a later period provides the background principles, then regulation might be compensable, but the Court would have to confront the fact that legislatures regularly determined which uses were prohibited, independent of the common law, and independent of whether the uses were lawful when the owner purchased. What makes the Court's analysis unworkable is its attempt to package the law of two incompatible eras and peddle it as historical fact.

. . .

Justice Stevens, dissenting.

. . .

In my opinion, the Court is doubly in error. The categorical rule the Court establishes is an unsound and unwise addition to the law and the Court's formulation of the exception to that rule is too rigid and too narrow.

The Categorical Rule

. . .

. . . We have frequently—and recently—held that, in some circumstances, a law that renders property valueless may nonetheless not constitute a taking. . . .

In addition to lacking support in past decisions, the Court's new rule is wholly arbitrary. A landowner whose property is diminished in value 95% recovers nothing, while an owner whose property is diminished 100% recovers the land's full value. . . .

Moreover, because of the elastic nature of property rights, the Court's new rule will also prove unsound in practice. In response to the rule, courts may define "property" broadly and only rarely find regulations to effect total takings. This is the approach the Court itself adopts in its revisionist reading of venerable precedents. We are told that—notwithstanding the Court's findings to the contrary in each case—the brewery in *Mugler*, the brickyard in *Hadacheck*, and the gravel pit in *Goldblatt* all could be put to "other uses" and that, therefore, those cases did not involve total regulatory takings.[3]

[3] Of course, the same could easily be said in this case: Lucas may put his land to "other uses"—fishing or camping, for example—or may sell his land to his neighbors as a buffer. In either event, his land is far from "valueless." This highlights a fundamental weakness in the Court's analysis: its failure to explain why only the impairment of "*economically* beneficial or productive use" of property is relevant in takings analysis. I should think that a regulation arbitrarily prohibiting an owner from continuing to use her property for bird-watching or sunbathing might constitute a taking under some circumstances; and, conversely, that such uses are of value to the owner. Yet the Court offers no basis for its assumption that the only uses of

On the other hand, developers and investors may market specialized estates to take advantage of the Court's new rule. The smaller the estate, the more likely that a regulatory change will effect a total taking. Thus, an investor may, for example, purchase the right to build a multi-family home on a specific lot, with the result that a zoning regulation that allows only single-family homes would render the investor's property interest "valueless." In short, the categorical rule will likely have one of two effects: Either courts will alter the definition of the "denominator" in the takings "fraction," rendering the Court's categorical rule meaningless, or investors will manipulate the relevant property interests, giving the Court's rule sweeping effect. [N]either of these results is desirable or appropriate, and both are distortions of our takings jurisprudence.

Finally, the Court's justification for its new categorical rule is remarkably thin. The Court mentions in passing three arguments in support of its rule; none is convincing. First, the Court suggests that "total deprivation of feasible use is, from the landowner's point of view, the equivalent of a physical appropriation." This argument proves too much. From the "landowner's point of view," a regulation that diminishes a lot's value by 50% is as well "the equivalent" of the condemnation of half of the lot. Yet, it is well established that a 50% diminution in value does not by itself constitute a taking. See Euclid v. Ambler Realty Co., ... (1926) (75% diminution in value). Thus, the landowner's perception of the regulation cannot justify the Court's new rule.

Second, the Court emphasizes that because total takings are "relatively rare" its new rule will not adversely affect the government's ability to "go on." This argument proves too little. Certainly ... defining a small class of regulations that are *per se* takings will not greatly hinder important governmental functions—but this is true of *any* small class of regulations. The Court's suggestion only begs the question of why regulations of *this* particular class should always be found to effect takings.

Finally, the Court suggests that "regulations that leave the owner ... without economically beneficial ... use ... carry with them a heightened risk that private property is being pressed into some form of public service." ... I agree that the risks of such singling out are of central concern in takings law. However, such risks do not justify a *per se* rule for total regulatory takings. There is no necessary correlation between "singling out" and total takings: a regulation may single out a property owner without depriving him of all of his property ...; and it may deprive him of all of his property without singling him out, see e.g., *Mugler v. Kansas* ...; *Hadachek v. Sebastian....* What matters in such cases is not the degree of diminution of value, but rather the specificity of the expropriating act. ...

In short, the Court's new rule is unsupported by prior decisions, arbitrary and unsound in practice, and theoretically unjustified....

The Nuisance Exception

Like many bright-line rules, the categorical rule established in this case is only "categorical" for a page or two in the U.S. Reports....

. . .

Under our reasoning in *Mugler,* a state's decision to prohibit or to regulate certain uses of property is not a compensable taking just because the particular uses were previously lawful. Under the Court's opinion today, however, if a state should decide to prohibit the manufacture of asbestos, cigarettes, or

property cognizable under the Constitution   are *developmental* uses.

concealable firearms, for example, it must be prepared to pay for the adverse economic consequences of its decision. One must wonder if Government will be able to "go on" effectively if it must risk compensation "for every such change in the general law." . . .

The Court's holding today effectively freezes the State's common law, denying the legislature much of its traditional power to revise the law governing the rights and uses of property. . . .

Arresting the development of the common law . . . is also profoundly unwise. The human condition is one of constant learning and evolution—both moral and practical. Legislatures implement that new learning; in doing so they must often revise the definition of property and the rights of property owners. . . . New appreciation of the significance of endangered species, . . . the importance of wetlands, . . . and the vulnerability of coastal lands . . . shapes our evolving understandings of property rights.

Of course, some legislative redefinitions of property will effect a taking and must be compensated—but it certainly cannot be the case that every movement away from common law does so. . . . The rule . . . should focus on the future, not the past.

. . .

The Court's categorical approach rule will, I fear, greatly hamper the efforts of local officials and planners who must deal with increasingly complex problems in land-use and environmental regulation. . . . Viewed more broadly, the Court's new rule and exception conflict with the very character of our takings jurisprudence. We have frequently and consistently recognized that the definition of a taking cannot be reduced to a "set formula" and that determining whether a regulation is a taking is "essentially [an] ad hoc, factual inquir[y]." *Penn Central Transportation Co.* . . . This is unavoidable, for the determination whether a law effects a taking is ultimately a matter of "fairness and justice," . . . and "necessarily requires a weighing of private and public interests." . . . The rigid rules fixed by the Court today clash with this enterprise: "fairness and justice" are often disserved by categorical rules.

III

It is well established that a takings case "entails inquiry into [several factors:] the character of the governmental action, its economic impact, and its interference with reasonable investment-backed expectations." *PruneYard* . . . The Court's analysis today focuses on the last two of these three factors: the categorical rule addresses a regulation's "economic impact," while the nuisance exception recognizes that ownership brings with it only certain "expectations." Neglected by the Court today is the first, and in some ways, the most important factor in takings analysis: the character of the regulatory action.

The Just Compensation Clause "was designed to bar Government from forcing some people alone to bear public burdens which, in all fairness and justice, should be borne by the public as a whole." . . . We have, therefore, in our takings law frequently looked to the generality of a regulation of property.

For example, in the case of so-called "developmental exactions," we have paid special attention to the risk that particular landowners might "b[e] singled out to bear the burden" of a broader problem not of his own making. *Nollan* . . . Similarly, in distinguishing between the Kohler Act (at issue in *Mahon*) and the Subsidence Act (at issue in *Keystone*), we found significant that the regulatory function of the latter was substantially broader. . . . Perhaps the most familiar application of this principle of generality arises in zoning cases. A diminution in value caused by a zoning regulation is far less likely to constitute a taking if it is part of a general and comprehensive land-use plan, see *Euclid v. Amber Realty Co.,* ...; conversely, "spot zoning" is far more likely to constitute a taking, see *Penn Central* ...

The presumption that a permanent physical occupation, no matter how slight, effects a taking is wholly consistent with this principle. A physical taking entails a certain amount of "singling out." ...

In analyzing takings claims, courts have long recognized the difference between a regulation that targets one or two parcels of land and a regulation that enforces a state-wide policy....

In considering Lucas' claim, the generality of the Beachfront Management Act is significant. The Act does not target particular landowners, but rather regulates the use of the coastline of the entire State.... Moreover, the Act did not single out owners of undeveloped land. The Act also prohibited owners of developed land from rebuilding if their structures were destroyed.... In short, the South Carolina Act imposed substantial burdens on owners of developed and undeveloped land alike. This generality indicates that the Act is not an effort to expropriate owners of undeveloped land.

. . .

The impact of the ban on developmental uses must also be viewed in light of the purposes of the Act....

In view of all of these factors, even assuming that petitioner's property was rendered valueless, the risk inherent in investments of the sort made by petitioner, the generality of the Act, and the compelling purpose motivating the South Carolina Legislature persuade me that the Act did not effect a taking of petitioner's property.

Accordingly, I respectfully dissent.[a]

2.   MANDATED ACCESS TO PROPERTY

A "taking" by regulation rather than by exercise of the power of eminent domain not only may occur when regulation excessively prohibits certain uses of property, but sometimes may occur when regulation requires that property be made physically available for public use. The Court readily acknowledges that regulation mandating access to private property affects a recognizable form of "property" interest.[1] Whether it amounts to a "taking" of the property interest, however, has been disputed in several cases.

[a] Justice Souter voted to dismiss the writ as improvidently granted, and his separate statement is omitted.

[1] A wide variety of other interests have been recognized as "property" within the meaning of the Just Compensation Clause. Interest earnings on a fund deposited in court for the benefit of creditors were held to be "incidents of ownership of the fund itself and ... property just as the fund itself is property" in Webb's Fabulous Pharmacies, Inc. v. Beckwith, 449 U.S. 155 (1980). The Court held that a state statute authorizing the court clerk to retain the fund's earnings in addition to a fee for clerk services effected a taking of "private property": "A State, by *ipse dixit,* may not transform private proper-ty into public property without compensation, even for the limited duration of the deposit in court."

In Ruckelshaus v. Monsanto Co., 467 U.S. 986 (1984), the Court held that the Fifth Amendment safeguards against uncompensated federal takings "intangible property rights protected by state law"—in that case "health, safety, and environmental data cognizable as a trade-secret property right under Missouri law." And the right to pass on very small undivided interests in land to one's heirs was protected against complete abrogation without payment in Hodel v. Irving, 481 U.S. 704 (1987), even though Congress' ban was designed to consolidate inalienable Indian allotments for the future benefit of the

In PruneYard Shopping Center v. Robins, 447 U.S. 74 (1980), for example, the Court pursued "an inquiry into such factors as the character of the governmental action, its economic impact, and its interference with reasonable investment backed expectations," and concluded that an interpretation of the California Constitution's free speech provision requiring the owner of a multi-block shopping center open to the public to allow a group of students to set up a table in a corner of the central courtyard to solicit support for a petition did not constitute an unconstitutional taking. Conceding that "one of the essential sticks in the bundle of property rights is the right to exclude others," the Court declined to find the fact that the students "physically invaded" the property "determinative." It distinguished Kaiser Aetna v. United States, 444 U.S. 164 (1979), which found a taking where the Federal Government sought to compel free public use of an exclusive private marina (open only to fee-paying members) that had been developed at great cost, along with a complete marina community, by dredging a shallow private pond to connect it with navigable water. The primary distinction drawn was the greater extent of interference with the property owner's "reasonable investment backed expectations."

In a decision the dissent thought departed from the Court's usual analysis, however, a majority found a taking by a New York law designed to facilitate tenant access to cable TV, which required property owners to permit installation of cable facilities on their properties at a one-time payment of $1. Loretto v. Teleprompter Manhattan CATV Corp., 458 U.S. 419 (1982). Stating that its holding was "very narrow" and did not "question . . . a State's broad power to impose appropriate restrictions upon an owner's *use* of his property," the Court concluded "that a permanent physical occupation authorized by government is a taking without regard to the public interests that it may serve." The dissent criticized the "strained and untenable distinction between 'temporary physical invasions,' whose constitutionality concededly 'is subject to a balancing pro-

tribe. Still, the Court did "reaffirm the continuing vitality of the long line of cases recognizing the States', and where appropriate, the United States', broad authority to adjust the rules governing the descent and devise of property without implicating the guarantees of the Just Compensation Clause."

Preseault v. Interstate Commerce Commission, 494 U.S. 1 (1990), raised the issue of the relationship between federal regulatory power and state property law in defining "property" subject to the guarantees of the Just Compensation Clause. Adjacent landowners claiming a reversionary interest in a railroad right-of-way challenged as a "taking" federal Trails Act amendments that authorized the ICC to preserve for possible future railroad use rights-of-way not currently in service and to allow interim use of the land as recreational trails. The Court found the challenge premature, holding that Congress had provided a Tucker Act remedy in the United States Claims Court for any takings claims arising from application of the amendments, a remedy the landowners had failed to pursue. In a concurring opinion, Justice O'Connor, joined by Justices Scalia and Kennedy, criticized the Court of Appeals for having concluded that "even if petition-

ers held the reversionary interest they claim, no taking occurred because 'no reversionary interest can or would vest' until the ICC determines that abandonment [not just discontinuance of the railroad right-of-way] is appropriate." Justice O'Connor said that "[t]his view conflates the scope of the ICC's power with the existence of a compensable taking and threatens to read the Just Compensation Clause out of the Constitution." She insisted that the "scope of the Commission's authority to regulate abandonments . . . is an issue quite distinct from whether the Commission's exercise of power over matters within its jurisdiction effected a taking of petitioners' property." In particular, "state law determines what property interest petitioners possess and . . . traditional [federal] takings doctrine will determine whether the Government must compensate petitioners for the burden imposed on any property interest they possess." Thus, "[t]he ICC may possess the power to postpone enjoyment of [state-created] reversionary interests, but the Fifth Amendment and well-established doctrine indicate that in certain circumstances the Government must compensate owners of those property interests when it exercises that power."

cess,' and 'permanent physical occupations,' which are 'taking[s] without regard to other factors that a court might ordinarily examine.' "

What does the following case add?

Dolan v. City of Tigard

512 U.S. 374, 114 S.Ct. 2309, 129 L.Ed.2d 304 (1994)

Chief Justice Rehnquist delivered the opinion of the Court.

Petitioner challenges the decision of the Oregon Supreme Court which held that the city of Tigard could condition the approval of her building permit on the dedication of a portion of her property for flood control and traffic improvements.... We granted certiorari to resolve a question left open by our decision in Nollan v. California Coastal Comm'n, 483 U. S. 825 (1987), of what is the required degree of connection between the exactions imposed by the city and the projected impacts of the proposed development.

I

... [The City's] Community Development Code (CDC) ... requires property owners in the area zoned Central Business District to comply with a 15% open space and landscaping requirement [and also] requires that new development facilitate [the city's plan for a pedestrian/bicycle pathway intended to encourage alternatives to automobile transportation for short trips] by dedicating land ... where provided for in the ... plan.

The city['s] ... Master Drainage Plan ... noted that flooding occurred in several areas along Fanno Creek, including areas near petitioner's property[, and] established that the increase in impervious surfaces associated with continued urbanization would exacerbate these flooding problems. To combat these risks, the Drainage Plan suggested a series of improvements to the Fanno Creek Basin, including channel excavation in the area next to petitioner's property.... Other recommendations included ensuring that the floodplain remains free of structures and that it be preserved as greenways to minimize flood damage to structures....

Petitioner Florence Dolan owns a plumbing and electric supply store ... in the Central Business District ... [on a 1.67–acre lot, through and along part of which Fanno Creek flows.] The year-round flow of the creek renders the area within the creek's 100–year floodplain virtually unusable for commercial development. The city's comprehensive plan includes the Fanno Creek floodplain as part of the city's greenway system.

Petitioner applied to the city for a permit to ... nearly doubl[e] the size of the store to 17,600 square feet, ... pav[e] a 39–space parking lot[, and in a] second phase of the project, ... to build an additional structure ... for complementary businesses, and to provide more parking. The proposed expansion and intensified use are consistent with the city's zoning scheme in the Central Business District....

The City Planning Commission granted petitioner's permit application subject to conditions imposed by the city's CDC, [including requirements] that petitioner dedicate the portion of her property lying within the 100–year floodplain for improvement of a storm drainage system along Fanno Creek and that she dedicate an additional 15–foot strip of land adjacent to the floodplain as a pedestrian/bicycle pathway. The dedication required ... encompasses approximately 7,000 square feet, or roughly 10% of the property. In accordance with city practice, petitioner could rely on the dedicated property to meet the 15% open space and landscaping requirement mandated by the city's zoning scheme....

Petitioner requested variances from the CDC standards[,] ... argu[ing] that her proposed development would not conflict with the policies of the comprehensive plan.... The Commission denied the request.

The Commission made a series of findings concerning the relationship between the dedicated conditions and the projected impacts of petitioner's project. First, the Commission noted that "[i]t is reasonable to assume that customers and employees of the future uses of this site could utilize a pedestrian/bicycle pathway adjacent to this development for their transportation and recreational needs." ... The Commission noted that the site plan has provided for bicycle parking in a rack in front of the proposed building and "[i]t is reasonable to expect that some of the users of the bicycle parking provided for by the site plan will use the pathway adjacent to Fanno Creek if it is constructed." ... In addition, the Commission found that creation of a convenient, safe pedestrian/bicycle pathway system as an alternative means of transportation "could offset some of the traffic demand on [nearby] streets and lessen the increase in traffic congestion." ...

The Commission went on to note that the required floodplain dedication would be reasonably related to petitioner's request to intensify the use of the site given the increase in the impervious surface. The Commission stated that the "anticipated increased storm water flow from the subject property to an already strained creek and drainage basin can only add to the public need to manage the stream channel and floodplain for drainage purposes." ... Based on this anticipated increased storm water flow, the Commission concluded that "the requirement of dedication of the floodplain area on the site is related to the applicant's plan to intensify development on the site." ...

[Petitioner's administrative and state court appeals were unsuccessful.]

II

The Takings Clause of the Fifth Amendment [was] made applicable to the States through the Fourteenth Amendment, Chicago, B. & Q. R. Co. v. Chicago, 166 U. S. 226, 239 (1897).... [5] One of the principal purposes of the Takings Clause is "to bar Government from forcing some people alone to bear public burdens which, in all fairness and justice, should be borne by the public as a whole." Armstrong v. United States, 364 U. S. 40, 49 (1960). Without question, had the city simply required petitioner to dedicate a strip of land along Fanno Creek for public use, rather than conditioning the grant of her permit to redevelop her property on such a dedication, a taking would have occurred. Nollan, supra, at 831. Such public access would deprive petitioner of the right to exclude others, "one of the most essential sticks in the bundle of rights that are commonly characterized as property." Kaiser Aetna v. United States, 444 U. S. 164, 176 (1979).

On the other side of the ledger, the authority of state and local governments to engage in land use planning has been sustained against constitutional

[5] Justice Stevens' dissent suggests that this case is actually grounded in "substantive" due process, rather than in the view that the Takings Clause of the Fifth Amendment was made applicable to the States by the Fourteenth Amendment. But there is no doubt that later cases have held that the Fourteenth Amendment does make the Takings Clause of the Fifth Amendment applicable to the States, see Penn Central Transp. Co. v. New York City, 438 U.S. 104, 122 (1978); Nollan v. California Coastal Comm'n, 483 U.S. 825, 827 (1987)....

challenge as long ago as our decision in Euclid v. Ambler Realty Co., 272 U. S. 365 (1926). . . . A land use regulation does not effect a taking if it "substantially advance[s] legitimate state interests" and does not "den[y] an owner economically viable use of his land." Agins v. Tiburon, 447 U. S. 255, 260 (1980).

The sort of land use regulations discussed in the cases just cited, however, differ in two relevant particulars from the present case. First, they involved essentially legislative determinations classifying entire areas of the city, whereas here the city made an adjudicative decision to condition petitioner's application for a building permit on an individual parcel. Second, the conditions imposed were not simply a limitation on the use petitioner might make of her own parcel, but a requirement that she deed portions of the property to the city. In *Nollan*, supra, we held that governmental authority to exact such a condition was circumscribed by the Fifth and Fourteenth Amendments. Under the well-settled doctrine of "unconstitutional conditions," the government may not require a person to give up a constitutional right—here the right to receive just compensation when property is taken for a public use—in exchange for a discretionary benefit conferred by the government where the property sought has little or no relationship to the benefit. See Perry v. Sindermann, 408 U. S. 593 (1972); Pickering v. Board of Ed. of Township High School Dist., 391 U. S. 563, 568 (1968).

Petitioner contends that the city has forced her to choose between the building permit and her right under the Fifth Amendment to just compensation for the public easements. Petitioner does not quarrel with the city's authority to exact some forms of dedication as a condition for the grant of a building permit, but challenges the showing made by the city to justify these exactions. She argues that the city has identified "no special benefits" conferred on her, and has not identified any "special quantifiable burdens" created by her new store that would justify the particular dedications required from her which are not required from the public at large.

III

[W]e must first determine whether the "essential nexus" exists between the "legitimate state interest" and the permit condition exacted by the city. Nollan, 483 U. S., at 837. If we find that a nexus exists, we must then decide the required degree of connection between the exactions and the projected impact of the proposed development. We were not required to reach this question in *Nollan*, because we concluded that the connection did not meet even the loosest standard. 483 U. S., at 838. Here, however, we must decide this question.

A

We addressed the essential nexus question in *Nollan*. The California Coastal Commission demanded a lateral public easement across the Nollan's beachfront lot in exchange for a permit to demolish an existing bungalow and replace it with a three-bedroom house. . . . The public easement was designed to connect two public beaches that were separated by the Nollan's property. The Coastal Commission had asserted that the public easement condition was imposed to promote the legitimate state interest of diminishing the "blockage of the view of the ocean" caused by construction of the larger house.

We agreed that the Coastal Commission's concern with protecting visual access to the ocean constituted a legitimate public interest. . . . We also agreed that the permit condition would have been constitutional "even if it consisted of the requirement that the Nollans provide a viewing spot on their property

for passersby with whose sighting of the ocean their new house would interfere." ... We resolved, however, that the Coastal Commission's regulatory
authority was set completely adrift from its constitutional moorings when it
claimed that a nexus existed between visual access to the ocean and a permit
condition requiring lateral public access along the Nollan's beachfront lot....
How enhancing the public's ability to "traverse to and along the shorefront"
served the same governmental purpose of "visual access to the ocean" from the
roadway was beyond our ability to countenance. The absence of a nexus left the
Coastal Commission in the position of simply trying to obtain an easement
through gimmickry, which converted a valid regulation of land use into "an
out-and-out plan of extortion." ...

No such gimmicks are associated with the permit conditions imposed by
the city in this case. Undoubtedly, the prevention of flooding along Fanno
Creek and the reduction of traffic congestion in the Central Business District
qualify as the type of legitimate public purposes we have upheld.... It seems
equally obvious that a nexus exists between preventing flooding along Fanno
Creek and limiting development within the creek's 100–year floodplain. Petitioner proposes to ... expand[] the impervious surface on the property and
[thus] increas[e] the amount of stormwater run-off into Fanno Creek.

The same may be said for the city's attempt to reduce traffic congestion by
providing for alternative means of transportation. In theory, a pedestrian/bicy-
cle pathway provides a useful alternative means of transportation for workers
and shoppers....

B

The second part of our analysis requires us to determine whether the
degree of the exactions demanded by the city's permit conditions bear the
required relationship to the projected impact of petitioner's proposed development. Nollan, supra, at 834, quoting Penn Central, 438 U. S. 104, 127 (1978)
("[A] use restriction may constitute a taking if not reasonably necessary to the
effectuation of a substantial government purpose"). Here the Oregon Supreme
Court deferred to what it termed the "city's unchallenged factual findings"
supporting the dedication conditions and found them to be reasonably related
to the impact of the expansion of petitioner's business....

... The city relies on the Commission's rather tentative findings that
increased stormwater flow from petitioner's property "can only add to the
public need to manage the [floodplain] for drainage purposes" to support its
conclusion that the "requirement of dedication of the floodplain area on the
site is related to the applicant's plan to intensify development on the site." ...

The city made the following specific findings relevant to the pedestrian/bi-
cycle pathway:

> "In addition, the proposed expanded use of this site is anticipated to
> generate additional vehicular traffic thereby increasing congestion on near-
> by collector and arterial streets. Creation of a convenient, safe pedestri-
> an/bicycle pathway system as an alternative means of transportation could
> offset some of the traffic demand on these nearby streets and lessen the
> increase in traffic congestion." ...

The question for us is whether these findings are constitutionally sufficient
to justify the conditions imposed by the city on petitioner's building permit.
Since state courts have been dealing with this question a good deal longer than
we have, we turn to representative decisions made by them.

In some States, very generalized statements as to the necessary connection between the required dedication and the proposed development seem to suffice.... We think this standard is too lax to adequately protect petitioner's right to just compensation if her property is taken for a public purpose.

Other state courts require a very exacting correspondence, described as the "specifi[c] and uniquely attributable" test.... Under this standard, if the local government cannot demonstrate that its exaction is directly proportional to the specifically created need, the exaction becomes "a veiled exercise of the power of eminent domain and a confiscation of private property behind the defense of police regulations." ... We do not think the Federal Constitution requires such exacting scrutiny, given the nature of the interests involved.

A number of state courts have taken an intermediate position, requiring the municipality to show a "reasonable relationship" between the required dedication and the impact of the proposed development....

. . .

We think the "reasonable relationship" test adopted by a majority of the state courts is closer to the federal constitutional norm than either of those previously discussed. But we do not adopt it as such, partly because the term "reasonable relationship" seems confusingly similar to the term "rational basis" which describes the minimal level of scrutiny under the Equal Protection Clause of the Fourteenth Amendment. We think a term such as "rough proportionality" best encapsulates what we hold to be the requirement of the Fifth Amendment. No precise mathematical calculation is required, but the city must make some sort of individualized determination that the required dedication is related both in nature and extent to the impact of the proposed development.[8]

Justice Stevens' dissent relies upon a law review article for the proposition that the city's conditional demands for part of petitioner's property are "a species of business regulation that heretofore warranted a strong presumption of constitutional validity." But simply denominating a governmental measure as a "business regulation" does not immunize it from constitutional challenge on the grounds that it violates a provision of the Bill of Rights. In Marshall v. Barlow's, Inc., 436 U. S. 307 (1978), we held that a statute authorizing a warrantless search of business premises in order to detect OSHA violations violated the Fourth Amendment.... And in Central Hudson Gas & Electric Corp. v. Public Service Comm'n of N.Y., 447 U. S. 557 (1980), we held that an order of the New York Public Service Commission, designed to cut down the use of electricity because of a fuel shortage, violated the First Amendment insofar as it prohibited advertising by a utility company to promote the use of electricity. We see no reason why the Takings Clause of the Fifth Amendment, as much a part of the Bill of Rights as the First Amendment or Fourth Amendment, should be relegated to the status of a poor relation in these comparable circumstances. We turn now to analysis of whether the findings relied upon by the city here, first with respect to the floodplain easement, and second with respect to the pedestrian/bicycle path, satisfied these requirements.

[8] Justice Stevens' dissent takes us to task for placing the burden on the city to justify the required dedication. He is correct in arguing that in evaluating most generally applicable zoning regulations, the burden properly rests on the party challenging the regulation to prove that it constitutes an arbitrary regulation of property rights. See, e.g., Euclid v. Ambler Realty Co., 272 U. S. 365 (1926). Here, by contrast, the city made an adjudicative decision to condition petitioner's application for a building permit on an individual parcel. In this situation, the burden properly rests on the city. See Nollan, 483 U. S., at 836....

... [K]eeping the floodplain open and free from development would likely confine the pressures on Fanno Creek created by petitioner's development. In fact, because petitioner's property lies within the Central Business District, the Community Development Code already required that petitioner leave 15% of it as open space and the undeveloped floodplain would have nearly satisfied that requirement.... But the city demanded more—it not only wanted petitioner not to build in the floodplain, but it also wanted petitioner's property along Fanno Creek for its Greenway system. The city has never said why a public greenway, as opposed to a private one, was required in the interest of flood control.

The difference to petitioner, of course, is the loss of her ability to exclude others. As we have noted, this right to exclude others is "one of the most essential sticks in the bundle of rights that are commonly characterized as property." Kaiser Aetna, 444 U. S., at 176. It is difficult to see why recreational visitors trampling along petitioner's floodplain easement are sufficiently related to the city's legitimate interest in reducing flooding problems along Fanno Creek, and the city has not attempted to make any individualized determination to support this part of its request.

The city contends that recreational easement along the Greenway is only ancillary to the city's chief purpose in controlling flood hazards. It further asserts that unlike the residential property at issue in *Nollan*, petitioner's property is commercial in character and therefore, her right to exclude others is compromised.... The city maintains that "[t]here is nothing to suggest that preventing [petitioner] from prohibiting [the easements] will unreasonably impair the value of [her] property as a [retail store]." PruneYard Shopping Center v. Robins, 447 U. S. 74, 83 (1980).

Admittedly, petitioner wants to build a bigger store to attract members of the public to her property. She also wants, however, to be able to control the time and manner in which they enter. The recreational easement on the Greenway is different in character from the exercise of state-protected rights of free expression and petition that we permitted in *PruneYard*. In *PruneYard*, we held that a major private shopping center that attracted more than 25,000 daily patrons had to provide access to persons exercising their state constitutional rights to distribute pamphlets and ask passersby to sign their petitions.... We based our decision, in part, on the fact that the shopping center "may restrict expressive activity by adopting time, place, and manner regulations that will minimize any interference with its commercial functions." ... By contrast, the city wants to impose a permanent recreational easement upon petitioner's property that borders Fanno Creek. Petitioner would lose all rights to regulate the time in which the public entered onto the Greenway, regardless of any interference it might pose with her retail store. Her right to exclude would not be regulated, it would be eviscerated.

If petitioner's proposed development had somehow encroached on existing greenway space in the city, it would have been reasonable to require petitioner to provide some alternative greenway space for the public either on her property or elsewhere. ...But that is not the case here. We conclude that the findings upon which the city relies do not show the required reasonable relationship between the floodplain easement and the petitioner's proposed new building.

With respect to the pedestrian/bicycle pathway, we have no doubt that the city was correct in finding that the larger retail sales facility proposed by petitioner will increase traffic on the streets of the Central Business District. The city estimates that the proposed development would generate roughly 435 additional trips per day. Dedications for streets, sidewalks, and other public ways are generally reasonable exactions to avoid excessive congestion from a proposed property use. But on the record before us, the city has not met its burden of demonstrating that the additional number of vehicle and bicycle trips generated by the petitioner's development reasonably relate to the city's requirement for a dedication of the pedestrian/bicycle pathway easement. The city simply found that the creation of the pathway "could offset some of the traffic demand . . . and lessen the increase in traffic congestion."

. . . No precise mathematical calculation is required, but the city must make some effort to quantify its findings in support of the dedication for the pedestrian/bicycle pathway beyond the conclusory statement that it could offset some of the traffic demand generated.

. . .

The judgment . . . is reversed, and the case is remanded for further proceedings consistent with this opinion.

Justice Stevens, with whom Justice Blackmun and Justice Ginsburg join, dissenting.

. . .

. . . The Court is correct in concluding that the city may not attach arbitrary conditions to a building permit or to a variance even when it can rightfully deny the application outright. . . . Yet the Court's description of the doctrinal underpinnings of its decision, the phrasing of its fledgling test of "rough proportionality," and the application of that test to this case run contrary to the traditional treatment of these cases and break considerable and unpropitious new ground.

I

. . . The state cases the Court consults . . . either fail to support or decidedly undermine the Court's conclusions in key respects.

. . .

Not one of the state cases cited by the Court announces anything akin to a "rough proportionality" requirement. . . .

In addition, the Court ignores the state courts' willingness to consider what the property owner gains from the exchange in question. . . . Dolan's acceptance of the permit, with its attached conditions, would provide her with benefits that may well go beyond any advantage she gets from expanding her business. As the United States pointed out at oral argument, the improvement that the city's drainage plan contemplates would widen the channel and reinforce the slopes to increase the carrying capacity during serious floods, "confer[ring] considerable benefits on the property owners immediately adjacent to the creek." . . .

The state court decisions also are enlightening in the extent to which they required that the *entire parcel* be given controlling importance. . . . None . . . identified the surrender of the fee owner's "power to exclude" as having any special significance. Instead, the courts uniformly examined the character of the entire economic transaction.

II

[O]ur own cases as well . . . require the analysis to focus on the impact of the city's action on the entire parcel of private property. . . . Although limitation of the right to exclude others undoubtedly constitutes a significant infringement upon property ownership, Kaiser Aetna v. United States, 444 U. S. 164, 179–180 (1979), restrictions on that right do not alone constitute a taking, and do not do so in any event unless they "unreasonably impair the value or use" of the property. PruneYard Shopping Center v. Robins, 447 U. S. 74, 82–84 (1980).

The Court's narrow focus on one strand in the property owner's bundle of rights is particularly misguided in a case involving the development of commercial property.... The exactions associated with the development of a retail business are ... a species of business regulation that heretofore warranted a strong presumption of constitutional validity.

... The city of Tigard has demonstrated that its plan is rational and impartial and that the conditions at issue are "conducive to fulfillment of authorized planning objectives." Dolan, on the other hand, has offered no evidence that her burden of compliance has any impact at all on the value or profitability of her planned development. Following the teaching of the cases on which it purports to rely, the Court should not isolate the burden associated with the loss of the power to exclude from an evaluation of the benefit to be derived from the permit to enlarge the store and the parking lot.

... Under the Court's approach, a city must not only "quantify its findings," and make "individualized determination[s]" with respect to the nature and the extent of the relationship between the conditions and the impact, but also demonstrate "proportionality." The correct inquiry should instead concentrate on whether the required nexus is present and venture beyond considerations of a condition's nature or germaneness only if the developer establishes that a concededly germane condition is so grossly disproportionate to the proposed development's adverse effects that it manifests motives other than land use regulation on the part of the city....

III

Applying its new standard, the Court finds two defects in the city's case.... Even under the Court's new rule, both defects are, at most, nothing more than harmless error.

... Given the commercial character of both the existing and the proposed use of the property as a retail store, it seems likely that potential customers "trampling along petitioner's floodplain," are more valuable than a useless parcel of vacant land. Moreover, the duty to pay taxes and the responsibility for potential tort liability may well make ownership of the fee interest in useless land a liability rather than an asset....

The Court's rejection of the bike path condition amounts to nothing more than a play on words. Everyone agrees that the bike path "could" offset some of the increased traffic flow that the larger store will generate, but the findings do not unequivocally state that it *will* do so, or tell us just how many cyclists will replace motorists. Predictions on such matters are inherently nothing more than estimates. Certainly the assumption that there will be an offsetting benefit here is entirely reasonable and should suffice whether it amounts to 100 percent, 35 percent, or only 5 percent of the increase in automobile traffic that would otherwise occur. If the Court proposes to have the federal judiciary micromanage state decisions of this kind, it is indeed extending its welcome mat to a significant new class of litigants.... [P]roperty owners have surely found a new friend today.

IV

The Court has made a serious error by abandoning the traditional presumption of constitutionality and imposing a novel burden of proof on a city implementing an admittedly valid comprehensive land use plan. Even more consequential than its incorrect disposition of this case, however, is the Court's resurrection of a species of substantive due process analysis that it firmly rejected decades ago.

... Chicago, B. & Q. R. Co. v. Chicago, 166 U. S. 226, 239 (1897), ... contains no mention of either the Takings Clause or the Fifth Amendment; it held that the protection afforded by the Due Process Clause of the Fourteenth Amendment extends to matters of substance as well as procedure, and that the substance of "the due process of law enjoined by the Fourteenth Amendment requires compensation to be made or adequately secured to the owner of private property taken for public use under the authority of a State." ... It applied the same kind of substantive due process analysis more frequently identified with a better known case that accorded similar substantive protection to a baker's liberty interest in working 60 hours a week and 10 hours a day. See Lochner v. New York, 198 U. S. 45 (1905). Later cases have interpreted the Fourteenth Amendment's substantive protection against uncompensated deprivations of private property by the States as though it incorporated the text of the Fifth Amendment's Takings Clause. See, e.g., Keystone Bituminous Coal Assn. v. DeBenedictis, 480 U. S. 470, 481, n. 10 (1987). There was nothing problematic about that interpretation in cases enforcing the Fourteenth Amendment against state action that involved the actual physical invasion of private property. See Loretto v. Teleprompter Manhattan CATV Corp., 458 U. S. 419, 427–433 (1982); Kaiser Aetna v. United States, 444 U. S. 164, 178–180 (1979). Justice Holmes charted a significant new course, however, when he opined that a state law making it "commercially impracticable to mine certain coal" had "very nearly the same effect for constitutional purposes as appropriating or destroying it." Pennsylvania Coal Co. v. Mahon, 260 U. S. 393, 414 (1922). The so-called "regulatory takings" doctrine that the Holmes dictum kindled has an obvious kinship with the line of substantive due process cases that *Lochner* exemplified. Besides having similar ancestry, both doctrines are potentially open-ended sources of judicial power to invalidate state economic regulations that Members of this Court view as unwise or unfair.

This case inaugurates an even more recent judicial innovation than the regulatory takings doctrine: the application of the "unconstitutional conditions" label to a mutually beneficial transaction between a property owner and a city.... Dolan has no right to be compensated for a taking unless the city acquires the property interests that she has refused to surrender. Since no taking has yet occurred, there has not been any infringement of her constitutional right to compensation....

Even if Dolan should accept the city's conditions in exchange for the benefit that she seeks, it would not necessarily follow that she had been denied "just compensation" since it would be appropriate to consider the receipt of that benefit in any calculation of "just compensation." ... Particularly in the absence of any evidence on the point, we should not presume that the discretionary benefit the city has offered is less valuable than the property interests that Dolan can retain or surrender at her option. But even if that discretionary benefit were so trifling that it could not be considered just compensation when it has "little or no relationship" to the property, the Court fails to explain why the same value would suffice when the required nexus is present. In this respect, the Court's reliance on the "unconstitutional conditions" doctrine is assuredly novel, and arguably incoherent. The city's conditions are by no means immune from constitutional scrutiny. The level of scrutiny, however, does not approximate the kind of review that would apply if the city had insisted on a surrender of Dolan's First Amendment rights in exchange for a building permit. One can only hope that the Court's reliance today on First Amendment cases, and its candid disavowal of the term "rational basis" to describe its new standard of review, do not signify a reassertion of the kind of superlegislative power the Court exercised during the *Lochner* era.

. . .

In our changing world one thing is certain: uncertainty will characterize predictions about the impact of new urban developments on the risks of floods, earthquakes, traffic congestion, or environmental harms. When there is doubt concerning the magnitude of those impacts, the public interest in averting them must outweigh the private interest of the commercial entrepreneur. If the government can demonstrate that the conditions it has imposed in a land-use permit are rational, impartial and conducive to fulfilling the aims of a valid land-use plan, a strong presumption of validity should attach to those conditions. The burden of demonstrating that those conditions have unreasonably impaired the economic value of the proposed improvement belongs squarely on the shoulders of the party challenging the state action's constitutionality. That allocation of burdens has served us well in the past. The Court has stumbled badly today by reversing it.

I respectfully dissent.

Justice Souter, dissenting.

. . . *Nollan* declared the need for a nexus between the nature of an exaction of an interest in land (a beach easement) and the nature of governmental interests. The Court treats this case as raising a further question, not about the nature, but about the degree, of connection required between such an exaction and the adverse effects of development. The Court's opinion announces a test to address this question, but as I read the opinion, the Court does not apply that test to these facts, which do not raise the question the Court addresses.

First, as to the floodplain and Greenway, the Court acknowledges that an easement of this land for open space (and presumably including the five feet required for needed creek channel improvements) is reasonably related to flood control, but argues that the "permanent recreational easement" for the public on the Greenway is not so related. If that is so, it is not because of any lack of proportionality between permit condition and adverse effect, but because of a lack of any rational connection at all between exaction of a public recreational area and the governmental interest in providing for the effect of increased water runoff. That is merely an application of *Nollan*'s nexus analysis. . . . But . . . the city of Tigard never sought to justify the public access portion of the dedication as related to flood control. It merely argued that whatever recreational uses were made of the bicycle path and the one foot edge on either side, were incidental to the permit condition requiring dedication of the 15–foot easement for an 8–foot-wide bicycle path and for flood control, including open space requirements and relocation of the bank of the river by some five feet. It seems to me such incidental recreational use can stand or fall with the bicycle path, which the city justified by reference to traffic congestion. As to the relationship the Court examines, between the recreational easement and a purpose never put forth as a justification by the city, the Court unsurprisingly finds a recreation area to be unrelated to flood control.

Second, as to the bicycle path, the Court ... only faults the city for saying that the bicycle path "could" rather than "would" offset the increased traffic from the store. That again ... is an application of *Nollan*, for the Court holds that the stated connection ("could offset") between traffic congestion and bicycle paths is too tenuous; only if the bicycle path "would" offset the increased traffic by some amount, could the bicycle path be said to be related to the city's legitimate interest in reducing traffic congestion.

I cannot agree that the application of *Nollan* is a sound one here, since it appears that the Court has placed the burden of producing evidence of relationship on the city, despite the usual rule in cases involving the police power that the government is presumed to have acted constitutionally. Having thus assigned the burden, the Court concludes that the City loses based on one word ("could" instead of "would"), and despite the fact that this record shows the connection the Court looks for. Dolan has put forward no evidence that the burden of granting a dedication for the bicycle path is unrelated in kind to the anticipated increase in traffic congestion, nor, if there exists a requirement that the relationship be related in degree, has Dolan shown that the exaction fails any such test. The city, by contrast, calculated the increased traffic flow that would result from Dolan's proposed development to be 435 trips per day, and its Comprehensive Plan, applied here, relied on studies showing the link between alternative modes of transportation, including bicycle paths, and reduced street traffic congestion.... *Nollan*, therefore, is satisfied, and on that assumption the city's conditions should not be held to fail a further rough proportionality test or any other that might be devised to give meaning to the constitutional limits....

In any event, on my reading, the Court's conclusions about the city's vulnerability carry the Court no further than *Nollan* has gone already, and I do not view this case as a suitable vehicle for taking the law beyond that point....

YEE v. CITY OF ESCONDIDO, 503 U.S. 519 (1992). The Court rejected a claim by owners of a mobile home park that a local rent control ordinance, taken together with a state law significantly restricting the grounds for evicting current tenants from the park and for rejecting new tenants who purchase a mobile home in the park from a current tenant with an unexpired lease, effected a *per se* physical taking of their property. The park owners argued that the laws increased the saleable value of the tenants' mobile homes in the form of a transferrable "right to occupy a pad at below-market rent indefinitely," and thus effectively transferred "from park owner to mobile home owner ... a right of physical occupation of the park owner's land." The Court concluded, however, that whatever the relevance of the owners' arguments to a *regulatory* taking claim based on use restrictions—a claim the Court decided was not properly before it—there had been no *physical* invasion of their property:

"... The government effects a physical taking only where it *requires* the landowner to submit to the physical occupation of his land....

"... Petitioners voluntarily rented their land to mobile home owners. At least on the face of the regulatory scheme, neither the City nor the State compels petitioners, once they have rented their property to tenants, to continue doing so.... [The] tenants were invited by the petitioners, not forced upon them by the government....

"... A different case would be presented were the statute, on its face or as applied, to compel a landowner over objection to rent his property or to refrain in perpetuity from terminating a tenancy.

"... When a landowner decides to rent his land to tenants, the government may place ceilings on the rents the landowner can charge ... or require the landowner to accept tenants he does not like, ... without automatically having to pay compensation.... Such forms of regulation are analyzed by engaging in the 'essentially ad hoc, factual inquiries' necessary to determine whether a regulatory taking has occurred."

3. REMEDIES FOR TAKINGS

FIRST ENGLISH EVANGELICAL LUTHERAN CHURCH OF GLENDALE v. COUNTY OF LOS ANGELES, 482 U.S. 304 (1987). Shortly after a flood destroyed the Church's creek-side buildings and campground, the County adopted an Interim Ordinance prohibiting replacement or construction of structures in a flood protection area encompassing the Church's property. The Church sued for damages for loss of all use, but the California courts held that even if all use had been denied, no damages could be recovered until the ordinance was finally declared unconstitutional, and then only for any period after that declaration for which the County continued to enforce it. The Supreme Court reversed in an opinion by Chief Justice Rehnquist that said in part:

"... The Court has recognized in more than one case that the government may elect to abandon its intrusion or discontinue regulations.... Similarly, a governmental body may acquiesce in a judicial declaration that one of its ordinances has effected an unconstitutional taking of property; the landowner has no right under the Just Compensation Clause to insist that a 'temporary' taking be deemed a permanent taking. But we have not resolved whether abandonment by the government requires payment of compensation for the period of time during which regulations deny a landowner all use of his land.

"In considering this question, we find substantial guidance in cases where the government has only temporarily exercised its right to use private property....

"These cases reflect the fact that 'temporary' takings which, as here, deny a landowner all use of his property, are not different in kind from permanent takings, for which the Constitution clearly requires compensation.... In the present case the interim ordinance was adopted by the county of Los Angeles in January 1979, and became effective immediately. Appellant filed suit within a month after the effective date of the ordinance and yet when the Supreme Court of California denied a hearing in the case on October 17, 1985, the merits of appellant's claim had yet to be determined. The United States has been required to pay compensation for leasehold interests of shorter duration than this. The value of a leasehold interest in property for a period of years may be substantial, and the burden on the property owner in extinguishing such an interest for a period of years may be great indeed.... Where this burden results from governmental action that amounted to a taking, the Just Compensation Clause of the Fifth Amendment requires that the government pay the landowner for the value of the use of the land during this period. Cf. United States v. Causby, 328 U.S., at 261 ('It is the owner's loss, not the taker's gain, which is the measure of the value of the property taken'). Invalidation of the ordinance or its successor ordinance after this period of time, though converting the taking into a 'temporary' one, is not a sufficient remedy to meet the demands of the Just Compensation Clause.

"... Once a court determines that a taking has occurred, the government retains the whole range of options already available—amendment of the regulation, withdrawal of the invalidated regulation, or exercise of eminent domain.... We merely hold that where the government's activities have already worked a taking of all use of property, no subsequent action by the government can relieve it of the duty to provide compensation for the period during which the taking was effective.

"... We ... do not deal with the quite different questions that would arise in the case of normal delays in obtaining building permits, changes in zoning ordinances, variances, and the like which are not before us. We realize that even our present holding will undoubtedly lessen to some extent the freedom and flexibility of land-use planners and governing bodies of municipal corporations when enacting land-use regulations. But such consequences necessarily flow from any decision upholding a claim of constitutional right; many of the provisions of the Constitution are designed to limit the flexibility and freedom of governmental authorities and the Just Compensation Clause of the Fifth Amendment is one of them...."

Justice Stevens dissented. He noted that a taking by regulation leaves government with a choice of abandoning the regulation or compensating the property owner, and he suggested that "repeal will, in virtually all cases, mitigate the overall effect of the regulation so substantially that the slight diminution in value that the regulation caused while in effect cannot be classified as a taking of property." He conceded that in "some situations ... even the temporary existence of a regulation has such severe consequences that invalidation or repeal will not mitigate the damage enough to remove the 'taking' label[,]" but he argued that "contrary to the Court's implications, the fact that a regulation would constitute a taking if allowed to remain in effect permanently is by no means dispositive of ... whether the effect that the regulation has already had on the property is so severe that a taking occurred during the period before the regulation was invalidated."

Justice Stevens also noted the "possibility that land-use planning, like other forms of regulation, will deprive a citizen of the right to develop his property at the time and in the manner that will best serve his economic interests[,]" but said in part:

"... In my opinion, ... it is the Due Process Clause rather than [the 'regulatory taking'] doctrine that protects the property owner from improperly motivated, unfairly conducted, or unnecessarily protracted governmental decision-making. Violation of the procedural safeguards mandated by the Due Process Clause will give rise to actions for damages under 42 U.S.C. § 1983, but I am not persuaded that delays in the development of property that are occasioned by fairly conducted administrative or judicial proceedings are compensable, except perhaps in the most unusual circumstances. On the contrary, I am convinced that the public interest in having important governmental decisions made in an orderly, fully informed way amply justifies the temporary burden on the citizen that is the inevitable by-product of democratic government."

JUST COMPENSATION

The problem of according the just compensation directed to be paid upon a taking for a public use presents great difficulties. The ground rules—that the owner's loss and not the taker's gain is the measure of compensation, United States v. Miller, 317 U.S. 369, 375 (1943); that where fair market value can be determined it is the normal measure of recovery, United States ex rel. T.V.A. v. Powelson, 319 U.S. 266, 275 (1943); and that fair market value is "what a willing buyer would pay in cash to a willing seller," *United States v. Miller,* supra—are suggestive of the varying considerations present in determining just compensation. Problems of peculiar value to the owner, of consequential damages, of enhanced value brought about by the project for which the land is condemned, of compensation for interests less than a fee, and myriads of others complicate the determination of what is just compensation. For a comprehensive study see 4 Nichols, *The Law of Eminent Domain* (rev. 4th ed. 1995).

SECTION 2.   PROTECTION OF PERSONAL LIBERTIES

A.   INTRODUCTION

In Section 1 of this chapter we saw how the Court determined that the word "liberty" in the due process clause gave special protection to the liberty to contract so that restrictions on that liberty, especially as reflected in labor legislation, were invalid unless specially justified by the state.

The liberty of contract cases have long since been overruled. But more recently the Court has derived from the word liberty a special constitutional protection for privacy, personal autonomy, and some family relationships requiring special justification for state infringements on those interests. The process by which an interest is singled out by the Court for special constitutional protection is worthy of examination as a means of understanding how general constitutional phrases become limitations on the power of legislatures.

Some issues that relate to privacy are governed by special constitutional language. The fourth amendment (incorporated by the fourteenth amendment against the states) protects persons, places, and possessions against indiscriminate searches and seizures. The fifth amendment protects against self-incrimination. But no language in the Constitution talks about privacy, family life, or personal autonomy.

In reading these cases ask yourself whether the Court adduces a principled basis for singling out these particular interests from all the other aspects of liberty that similarly might be protected.

Try also to determine what is the scope of this special protection. What kinds of regulations can be brought within the privacy rubric so as to require special state justification?

For useful general discussion, see Dixon, *The "New" Substantive Due Process and the Democratic Ethic: A Prolegomenon*, 1976 B.Y.U.L.Rev. 43; Henkin, *Privacy and Autonomy*, 74 Colum.L.Rev. 1410 (1974).

Two early cases from the *Lochner* era are frequently cited in current opinions. In Meyer v. Nebraska, 262 U.S. 390 (1923), a parochial school language teacher had been convicted of violating a law prohibiting the teaching of any subject in a language other than English in the first eight grades of public and private schools. In reversing his conviction, the Court said that the liberty protected by due process "denotes not merely freedom from bodily restraint, but also the right of the individual to contract, to engage in any of the common occupations of life, to acquire useful knowledge, to marry, establish a home and bring up children, to worship God according to the dictates of his own conscience, and, generally, to enjoy those privileges long recognized at common law as essential to the orderly pursuit of happiness by free men." The right of Meyer to teach German and the right of parents to engage him were within that zone of constitutionally-protected liberty. The Court concluded that, because no justifications for the complete abolition of the right to teach foreign languages had been shown, "the statute as applied is arbitrary, and without reasonable relation to any end within the competency of the state."

In Pierce v. Society of Sisters, 268 U.S. 510 (1925), the Court upheld a trial court injunction against the enforcement of an Oregon statute requiring parents to send children between the ages of 8 and 16 to a public school. The suit was brought by a Catholic society operating a school and a private corporation operating a military academy. The Court noted that the effect of the act would be to force private schools out of business. It then said that under the doctrine of *Meyer* "we think it entirely plain that the [statute] unreasonably interferes with the liberty of parents and guardians to direct the upbringing and education of children under their control.... The fundamental theory of liberty upon which all governments in this Union repose excludes any general power of the state to standardize its children by forcing them to accept instruction from public teachers only. The child is not the mere creature of the state; those who nurture him and direct his destiny have the right, coupled with the high duty, to recognize and prepare him for additional obligations."

Another case prior to Griswold v. Connecticut that referred to special constitutional protection for interests relating to personal autonomy and family relationships was Skinner v. Oklahoma, 316 U.S. 535 (1942). The Court held invalid under equal protection a statute providing for compulsory sterilization of criminals convicted two or more times of crimes of moral turpitude. Since the statute made grand larceny a felony of moral turpitude, while embezzlement was not, it violated the equal protection clause. The Court, in an opinion by Justice Douglas, began its discussion of the equal protection issue by saying: "We are dealing here with legislation which involves one of the basic civil rights of man. Marriage and procreation are fundamental to the very existence and survival of the race. The power to sterilize, if exercised, may have subtle, far-reaching and devastating effects.... There is no redemption for the individual whom the law touches. Any experiment which the State conducts is to his irreparable injury. He is forever deprived of a basic liberty. We mention these matters not to reexamine the scope of the police power of the States. We advert to them merely in emphasis of our view that strict scrutiny of the classification which a State makes in a sterilization law is essential...."

Griswold v. Connecticut

381 U.S. 479, 85 S.Ct. 1678, 14 L.Ed.2d 510 (1965).

Mr. Justice Douglas delivered the opinion of the Court.

Appellant Griswold is Executive Director of the Planned Parenthood League of Connecticut. Appellant Buxton is a licensed physician and a professor at the Yale Medical School who served as Medical Director for the League at its Center in New Haven—a center open and operating from November 1 to November 10, 1961, when appellants were arrested.

They gave information, instruction, and medical advice to *married persons* as to the means of preventing conception. They examined the wife and prescribed the best contraceptive device or material for her use. Fees were usually charged, although some couples were serviced free.

The statutes whose constitutionality is involved in this appeal are §§ 53–32 and 54–196 of the General Statutes of Connecticut (1938). The former provides:

"Any person who uses any drug, medicinal article or instrument for the purpose of preventing conception shall be fined not less than fifty dollars or imprisoned not less than sixty days nor more than one year or be both fined and imprisoned."

Section 54–196 provides:

"Any person who assists, abets, counsels, causes, hires or commands another to commit any offense may be prosecuted and punished as if he were the principal offender."

The appellants were found guilty as accessories and fined $100 each, against the claim that the accessory statute as so applied violated the Fourteenth Amendment. The Appellate Division of the Circuit Court affirmed. The Court of Errors affirmed that judgment. . . .

. . .

Coming to the merits, we are met with a wide range of questions that implicate the Due Process Clause of the Fourteenth Amendment. Overtones of some arguments suggest that Lochner v. State. of New York, 198 U.S. 45, should be our guide. But we decline that invitation as we did in West Coast Hotel Co. v. Parrish, 300 U.S. 379; Olsen v. State of Nebraska, 313 U.S. 236; Lincoln Federal Labor Union v. Northwestern Co., 335 U.S. 525; Williamson v. Lee Optical Co., 348 U.S. 483; Giboney v. Empire Storage Co., 336 U.S. 490. We do not sit as a super-legislature to determine the wisdom, need, and propriety of laws that touch economic problems, business affairs, or social conditions. This law, however, operates directly on an intimate relation of husband and wife and their physician's role in one aspect of that relation.

The association of people is not mentioned in the Constitution nor in the Bill of Rights. The right to educate a child in a school of the parents' choice— whether public or private or parochial—is also not mentioned. Nor is the right to study any particular subject or any foreign language. Yet the First Amendment has been construed to include certain of those rights.

By *Pierce v. Society of Sisters,* supra, the right to educate one's children as one chooses is made applicable to the States by the force of the First and Fourteenth Amendments. By *Meyer v. State of Nebraska,* supra, the same dignity is given the right to study the German language in a private school. In other words, the State may not, consistently with the spirit of the First Amendment, contract the spectrum of available knowledge. The right of freedom of speech and press includes not only the right to utter or to print, but the right to distribute, the right to receive, the right to read (Martin v. City of Struthers, 319 U.S. 141, 143) and freedom of inquiry, freedom of thought, and freedom to teach (see Wieman v. Updegraff, 344 U.S. 183, 195)—indeed the freedom of the entire university community. Sweezy v. State of New Hampshire, 354 U.S. 234, 249–250, 261–263; Barenblatt v. United States, 360 U.S. 109, 112; Baggett v. Bullitt, 377 U.S. 360, 369. Without those peripheral rights the specific rights would be less secure. And so we reaffirm the principle of the *Pierce* and the *Meyer* cases.

. . .

The foregoing cases suggest that specific guarantees in the Bill of Rights have penumbras, formed by emanations from those guarantees that help give them life and substance. See Poe v. Ullman, 367 U.S. 497, 516–522 (dissenting opinion). Various guarantees create zones of privacy. The right of association contained in the penumbra of the First Amendment is one, as we have seen. The Third Amendment in its prohibition against the quartering of soldiers "in any house" in time of peace without the consent of the owner is another facet of that privacy. The Fourth Amendment explicitly affirms the "right of the people to be secure in their persons, houses, papers, and effects, against unreasonable searches and seizures." The Fifth Amendment in its Self–Incrimination Clause enables the citizen to create a zone of privacy which government may not force him to surrender to his detriment. The Ninth Amendment provides: "The enumeration in the Constitution, of certain rights, shall not be construed to deny or disparage others retained by the people."

The Fourth and Fifth Amendments were described in Boyd v. United States, 116 U.S. 616, 630, as protection against all governmental invasions "of the sanctity of a man's home and the privacies of life." We recently referred in Mapp v. Ohio, 367 U.S. 643, 656, to the Fourth Amendment as creating a "right to privacy, no less important than any other right carefully and particularly reserved to the people." See Beaney, The Constitutional Right to Privacy, 1962 Sup.Ct.Rev. 212; Griswold, The Right to be Let Alone, 55 N.W.U.L.Rev. 216 (1960).

We have had many controversies over these penumbral rights of "privacy and repose." ... These cases bear witness that the right of privacy which presses for recognition here is a legitimate one.

The present case, then, concerns a relationship lying within the zone of privacy created by several fundamental constitutional guarantees. And it concerns a law which, in forbidding the *use* of contraceptives rather than regulating their manufacture or sale, seeks to achieve its goals by means having a maximum destructive impact upon that relationship. Such a law cannot stand in light of the familiar principle, so often applied by this Court, that a "governmental purpose to control or prevent activities constitutionally subject to state regulation may not be achieved by means which sweep unnecessarily broadly and thereby invade the area of protected freedoms." NAACP v. Alabama, 377 U.S. 288, 307. Would we allow the police to search the sacred precincts of marital bedrooms for telltale signs of the use of contraceptives? The very idea is repulsive to the notions of privacy surrounding the marriage relationship.

We deal with a right of privacy older than the Bill of Rights—older than our political parties, older than our school system. Marriage is a coming together for better or for worse, hopefully enduring, and intimate to the degree of being sacred. It is an association that promotes a way of life, not causes; a harmony in living, not political faiths; a bilateral loyalty, not commercial or social projects. Yet it is an association for as noble a purpose as any involved in our prior decisions.

Reversed.

Mr. Justice Goldberg, whom The Chief Justice and Mr. Justice Brennan join, concurring.

I agree with the Court that Connecticut's birth control law unconstitutionally intrudes upon the right of marital privacy, and I join in its opinion and judgment. Although I have not accepted the view that " 'due process' as used in the Fourteenth Amendment includes all of the first eight Amendments," id., 367 U.S. at 516 (see my concurring opinion in Pointer v. Texas, 380 U.S. 400, 410, and the dissenting opinion of Mr. Justice Brennan in Cohen v. Hurley, 366 U.S. 117), I do agree that the concept of liberty protects those personal rights that are fundamental, and is not confined to the specific terms of the Bill of Rights. My conclusion that the concept of liberty is not so restricted and that it embraces the right of marital privacy though that right is not mentioned explicitly in the Constitution is supported both by numerous decisions of this Court, referred to in the Court's opinion, and by the language and history of the Ninth Amendment. In reaching the conclusion that the right of marital privacy is protected, as being within the protected penumbra of specific guarantees of the Bill of Rights, the Court refers to the Ninth Amendment. I add these words to emphasize the relevance of that Amendment to the Court's holding.

. . .

The Ninth Amendment reads, "The enumeration in the Constitution, of certain rights, shall not be construed to deny or disparage others retained by the people." . . .

While this Court has had little occasion to interpret the Ninth Amendment,[6] "[i]t cannot be presumed that any clause in the constitution is intended to be without effect." Marbury v. Madison, 1 Cranch 137, 174. In interpreting the Constitution, "real effect should be given to all the words it uses." Myers v. United States, 272 U.S. 52, 151. The Ninth Amendment to the Constitution may be regarded by some as a recent discovery but since 1791 it has been a basic part of the Constitution which we are sworn to uphold. To hold that a right so basic and fundamental and so deep-rooted in our society as the right of privacy in marriage may be infringed because that right is not guaranteed in so many words by the first eight amendments to the Constitution is to ignore the Ninth Amendment and to give it no effect whatsoever. Moreover, a judicial construction that this fundamental right is not protected by the Constitution because it is not mentioned in explicit terms by one of the first eight amendments or elsewhere in the Constitution would violate the Ninth Amendment, which specifically states that "[t]he enumeration in the Constitution, of certain rights shall not be *construed* to deny or disparage others retained by the people." (Emphasis added.)

. . .

The entire fabric of the Constitution and the purposes that clearly underlie its specific guarantees demonstrate that the rights to marital privacy and to marry and raise a family are of similar order and magnitude as the fundamental rights specifically protected.

Although the Constitution does not speak in so many words of the right of privacy in marriage, I cannot believe that it offers these fundamental rights no protection. The fact that no particular provision of the Constitution explicitly forbids the State from disrupting the traditional relation of the family—a relation as old and as fundamental as our entire civilization—surely does not show that the Government was meant to have the power to do so. Rather, as the Ninth Amendment expressly recognizes, there are fundamental personal rights such as this one, which are protected from abridgment by the Government though not specifically mentioned in the Constitution.

. . .

The logic of the dissents would sanction federal or state legislation that seems to me even more plainly unconstitutional than the statute before us. . . .

---

[6] This Amendment has been referred to as "The Forgotten Ninth Amendment," in a book with that title by Bennet B. Patterson (1955). Other commentary on the Ninth Amendment includes Redlich, Are There "Certain Rights . . . Retained by the People"? 37 N.Y.U.L.Rev. 787 (1962), and Kelsey, The Ninth Amendment of the Federal Constitution, 11 Ind.L.J. 309 (1936). As far as I am aware, until today this Court has referred to the Ninth Amendment only in United Public Workers v. Mitchell, 330 U.S. 75, 94–95; Tennessee Electric Power Co. v. TVA, 306 U.S. 118, 143–144; and Ashwander v. TVA, 297 U.S. 288, 330–331. See also Calder v. Bull, 3 Dall. 386, 388; Loan Ass'n v. City of Topeka, 20 Wall. 655, 662–663. . . .

[I]f upon a showing of a slender basis of rationality, a law outlawing voluntary birth control by married persons is valid, then, by the same reasoning, a law requiring compulsory birth control also would seem to be valid. In my view, however, both types of law would unjustifiably intrude upon rights of marital privacy which are constitutionally protected.

. . .

In sum, I believe that the right of privacy in the marital relation is fundamental and basic—a personal right "retained by the people" within the meaning of the Ninth Amendment. Connecticut cannot constitutionally abridge this fundamental right, which is protected by the Fourteenth Amendment from infringement by the States. I agree with the Court that petitioners' convictions must therefore be reversed.

Mr. Justice Harlan, concurring in the judgment.

I fully agree with the judgment of reversal, but find myself unable to join the Court's opinion. The reason is that it seems to me to evince an approach to this case very much like that taken by my Brothers Black and Stewart in dissent, namely: the Due Process Clause of the Fourteenth Amendment does not touch this Connecticut statute unless the enactment is found to violate some right assured by the letter or penumbra of the Bill of Rights.

In other words, what I find implicit in the Court's opinion is that the "incorporation" doctrine may be used to *restrict* the reach of Fourteenth Amendment Due Process. For me this is just as unacceptable constitutional doctrine as is the use of the "incorporation" approach to *impose* upon the States all the requirements of the Bill of Rights as found in the provisions of the first eight amendments and in the decisions of this Court interpreting them. . . .

Mr. Justice White, concurring in the judgment.

In my view this Connecticut law as applied to married couples deprives them of "liberty" without due process of law, as that concept is used in the Fourteenth Amendment. I therefore concur in the judgment of the Court reversing these convictions under Connecticut's aiding and abetting statute.

. . .

Mr. Justice Black, with whom Mr. Justice Stewart joins, dissenting.

I agree with my Brother Stewart's dissenting opinion. And like him I do not to any extent whatever base my view that this Connecticut law is constitutional on a belief that the law is wise or that its policy is a good one. In order that there may be no room at all to doubt why I vote as I do, I feel constrained to add that the law is every bit as offensive to me as it is to my Brethren of the majority and my Brothers Harlan, White and Goldberg who, reciting reasons why it is offensive to them, hold it unconstitutional. There is no single one of the graphic and eloquent strictures and criticisms fired at the policy of this Connecticut law either by the Court's opinion or by those of my concurring Brethren to which I cannot subscribe—except their conclusion that the evil qualities they see in the law make it unconstitutional.

. . .

The Court talks about a constitutional "right of privacy" as though there is some constitutional provision or provisions forbidding any law ever to be passed which might abridge the "privacy" of individuals. But there is not. . . .

. . .

I realize that many good and able men have eloquently spoken and written, sometimes in rhapsodical strains, about the duty of this Court to keep the Constitution in tune with the times. The idea is that the Constitution must be changed from time to time and that this Court is charged with a duty to make those changes. For myself, I must with all deference reject that philosophy. The Constitution makers knew the need for change and provided for it. Amendments suggested by the people's elected representatives can be submitted to the people or their selected agents for ratification. That method of change was good for our Fathers, and being somewhat old-fashioned I must add it is good enough for me. And so, I cannot rely on the Due Process Clause or the Ninth Amendment or any mysterious and uncertain natural law concept as a reason for striking down this state law. The Due Process Clause with an "arbitrary and capricious" or "shocking to the conscience" formula was liberally used by this Court to strike down economic legislation in the early decades of this century, threatening, many people thought, the tranquility and stability of the nation. See, e.g., Lochner v. State. of New York, 198 U.S. 45. That formula, based on subjective considerations of "natural justice," is no less dangerous when used to enforce this Court's views about personal rights than those about economic rights. I had thought that we had laid that formula, as a means for striking down state legislation, to rest once and for all in cases like West Coast Hotel Co. v. Parrish, 300 U.S. 379; Olsen v. State of Nebraska ex rel. Western Reference & Bond Assn., 313 U.S. 236, and many other opinions....

... The late Judge Learned Hand, after emphasizing his view that judges should not use the due process formula suggested in the concurring opinions today or any other formula like it to invalidate legislation offensive to their "personal preferences,"[22] made the statement, with which I fully agree, that:

> "For myself it would be most irksome to be ruled by a bevy of Platonic Guardians, even if I knew how to choose them, which I assuredly do not."

So far as I am concerned, Connecticut's law as applied here is not forbidden by any provision of the Federal Constitution as that Constitution was written, and I would therefore affirm.

Mr. Justice Stewart, whom Mr. Justice Black joins, dissenting.

Since 1879 Connecticut has had on its books a law which forbids the use of contraceptives by anyone. I think this is an uncommonly silly law. As a practical matter, the law is obviously unenforceable, except in the oblique context of the present case. As a philosophical matter, I believe the use of contraceptives in the relationship of marriage should be left to personal and private choice, based upon each individual's moral, ethical, and religious beliefs. As a matter of social policy, I think professional counsel about methods of birth control should be available to all, so that each individual's choice can be meaningfully made. But we are not asked in this case to say whether we think this law is unwise, or even asinine. We are asked to hold that it violates the United States Constitution. And that I cannot do.

.   .   .

What provisions of the Constitution, then, does make this state law invalid? The Court says it is the right of privacy "created by several fundamental constitutional guarantees." With all deference, I can find no such general

[22] Hand, The Bill of Rights (1958) 70....

right of privacy in the Bill of Rights, in any other part of the Constitution, or in any case ever before decided by this Court.[a]

. . .

PRIVACY AS AUTONOMY VERSUS PRIVACY AS FREEDOM FROM INTRUSION AND DISCLOSURE

In *Griswold* the Court appeared to use the term "privacy" in the sense of protecting private matters from disclosure. It emphasized intrusion into "the sacred precincts of marital bedrooms." But in Roe v. Wade, infra p. 615, the Court gave the term a broader meaning protecting personal autonomy. In fact, in Carey v. Population Services Int'l., 431 U.S. 678, 687 (1977), the Court said that later decisions had "put *Griswold* in proper perspective. *Griswold* may no longer be read as holding only that a State may not prohibit a married couple's use of contraceptives. Read in the light of its progeny, the teaching of *Griswold* is that the Constitution protects individual decisions in matters of childbearing from unjustified intrusion by the State."

Since *Griswold* the Court has decided very few claims that the state had unconstitutionally invaded privacy in the sense of requiring disclosure of personal matters. Whalen v. Roe, 429 U.S. 589 (1977), presented the question whether a state could record, in a centralized computer file, the names and addresses of all persons who had obtained, pursuant to a doctor's prescription, certain drugs for which there was both a lawful and an unlawful market. In response to an argument that the state requirement invaded a constitutionally protected zone of privacy, the Court noted: "The cases sometimes characterized as protecting 'privacy' have in fact involved at least two different kinds of interests. One is the individual interest in avoiding disclosure of personal matters, and another is the interest in independence in making certain kinds of important decisions." The Court upheld the statute on the ground that the state protections against public disclosure of the data were sufficient to avoid a serious threat to either interest. It concluded its opinion with the following paragraph:

"A final word about issues we have not decided. We are not unaware of the threat to privacy implicit in the accumulation of vast amounts of personal information in computerized data banks or other massive government files. The collection of taxes, the distribution of welfare and social security benefits, the supervision of public health, the direction of our armed forces and the enforcement of the criminal laws, all require the orderly preservation of great quantities of information, much of which is personal in character and potentially embarrassing or harmful if disclosed. The right to collect and use such data for public purposes is typically accompanied by a concomitant statutory or regulatory duty to avoid unwarranted disclosures. Recognizing that in some circumstances that duty arguably has its roots in the Constitution, nevertheless New York's statutory scheme, and its implementing administrative procedures, evidence a proper concern with, and protection of, the individual's interest in privacy. We therefore need not, and do not, decide any question which might be presented by the unwarranted disclosure of accumulated private

---

[a] Helpful discussion of the Court's approach to the Griswold case may be found in: *Symposium on the Griswold Case and the Right of Privacy,* 64 Mich.L.Rev. 197 (1965); Beaney, *The Griswold Case and the Expanding Right to Privacy,* 1966 Wis.L.Rev. 979; Katin, *Griswold v. Connecticut: The Justices and Connecticut's "Uncommonly Silly Law,"* 42 Notre Dame L. 680 (1967); Franklin, *The Ninth Amendment as Civil Law Method and Its Implications for a Republican Form of Government,* 40 Tul.L.Rev. 487 (1966).

data—whether intentional or unintentional—or by a system that did not contain comparable security provisions. We simply hold that this record does not establish an invasion of any right or liberty protected by the Fourteenth Amendment."

B. FAMILY AND MARITAL RELATIONSHIPS

Moore v. City of East Cleveland, Ohio

431 U.S. 494, 97 S.Ct. 1932, 52 L.Ed.2d 531 (1977).

Mr. Justice Powell announced the judgment of the Court, and delivered an opinion in which Mr. Justice Brennan, Mr. Justice Marshall, and Mr. Justice Blackmun joined.

East Cleveland's housing ordinance, like many throughout the country, limits occupancy of a dwelling unit to members of a single family. § 1351.02. But the ordinance contains an unusual and complicated definitional section that recognizes as a "family" only a few categories of related individuals, § 1341.08.[2] Because her family, living together in her home, fits none of those categories, appellant stands convicted of a criminal offense. The question in this case is whether the ordinance violates the Due Process Clause of the Fourteenth Amendment.

I.

Appellant, Mrs. Inez Moore, lives in her East Cleveland home together with her son, Dale Moore Sr., and her two grandsons, Dale, Jr., and John Moore, Jr. The two boys are first cousins rather than brothers; we are told that John came to live with his grandmother and with the elder and younger Dale Moores after his mother's death.

In early 1973, Mrs. Moore received a notice of violation from the city, stating that John was an "illegal occupant" and directing her to comply with the ordinance. When she failed to remove him from her home, the city filed a criminal charge. Mrs. Moore moved to dismiss, claiming that the ordinance was constitutionally invalid on its face. Her motion was overruled, and upon conviction she was sentenced to five days in jail and a $25 fine. The Ohio Court of Appeals affirmed after giving full consideration to her constitutional claims, and the Ohio Supreme Court denied review. . . .

[2] Section 1341.08 (1966) provides:

" 'Family' means a number of individuals related to the nominal head of the household or to the spouse of the nominal head of the household living as a single housekeeping unit in a single dwelling unit, but limited to the following:

"(a) Husband or wife of the nominal head of the household.

"(b) Unmarried children of the nominal head of the household or of the spouse of the nominal head of the household, provided, however, that such unmarried children have no children residing with them.

"(c) Father or mother of the nominal head of the household or of the spouse of the nominal head of the household.

"(d) Notwithstanding the provisions of subsection (b) hereof, a family may include not more than one dependent married or unmarried child of the nominal head of the household or of the spouse of the nominal head of the household and the spouse and dependent children of such dependent child. For the purpose of this subsection, a dependent person is one who has more than fifty percent of his total support furnished for him by the nominal head of the household and the spouse of the nominal head of the household.

"(e) A family may consist of one individual."

II.

The city argues that our decision in Village of Belle Terre v. Boraas, 416 U.S. 1 (1974), requires us to sustain the ordinance attacked here. Belle Terre, like East Cleveland, imposed limits on the types of groups that could occupy a single dwelling unit. Applying the constitutional standard announced in this Court's leading land-use case, Euclid v. Ambler Realty Co., 272 U.S. 365 (1926), we sustained the Belle Terre ordinance on the ground that it bore a rational relationship to permissible state objectives.

But one overriding factor sets this case apart from *Belle Terre*. The ordinance there affected only *unrelated* individuals. It expressly allowed all who were related by "blood, adoption, or marriage" to live together, and in sustaining the ordinance we were careful to note that it promoted "family needs" and "family values." East Cleveland, in contrast, has chosen to regulate the occupancy of its housing by slicing deeply into the family itself. This is no mere incidental result of the ordinance. On its face it selects certain categories of relatives who may live together and declares that others may not. In particular, it makes a crime of a grandmother's choice to live with her grandson in circumstances like those presented here.

When a city undertakes such intrusive regulation of the family, neither *Belle Terre* nor *Euclid* governs; the usual judicial deference to the legislature is inappropriate. "This Court has long recognized that freedom of personal choice in matters of marriage and family life is one of the liberties protected by the Due Process Clause of the Fourteenth Amendment." ... A host of cases, tracing their lineage to Meyer v. Nebraska, 262 U.S. 390, 399–401 (1923), and Pierce v. Society of Sisters, 268 U.S. 510, 534–535 (1925), have consistently acknowledged a "private realm of family life which the state cannot enter." Prince v. Massachusetts, 321 U.S. 158, 166 (1944).... Of course, the family is not beyond regulation. See Prince v. Massachusetts. But when the government intrudes on choices concerning family living arrangements, this Court must examine carefully the importance of the governmental interests advanced and the extent to which they are served by the challenged regulation. See *Poe v. Ullman* (Harlan, J., dissenting).

When thus examined, this ordinance cannot survive. The city seeks to justify it as a means of preventing overcrowding, minimizing traffic and parking congestion, and avoiding an undue financial burden on East Cleveland's school system. Although these are legitimate goals, the ordinance before us serves them marginally, at best. For example, the ordinance permits any family consisting only of husband, wife, and unmarried children to live together, even if the family contains a half-dozen licensed drivers, each with his or her own car. At the same time it forbids an adult brother and sister to share a household, even if both faithfully use public transportation. The ordinance would permit a grandmother to live with a single dependent son and children, even if his school-age children number a dozen, yet it forces Mrs. Moore to find another dwelling for her grandson John, simply because of the presence of his uncle and cousin in the same household. We need not labor the point. Section 1341.08 has but a tenuous relation to alleviation of the conditions mentioned by the city.

III.

The city would distinguish the cases based on *Meyer* and *Pierce*. It points out that none of them "gives grandmothers any fundamental rights with respect to grandsons," and suggests that any constitutional right to live together as a family extends only to the nuclear family—essentially a couple and its dependent children.

To be sure, these cases did not expressly consider the family relationship presented here. They were immediately concerned with freedom of choice with respect to childbearing, e.g., *LaFleur, Roe v. Wade, Griswold,* supra, or with the rights of parents to the custody and companionship of their own children, Stanley v. Illinois, supra, or with traditional parental authority in matters of child rearing and education. *Yoder, Ginsberg, Pierce, Meyer,* supra. But unless we close our eyes to the basic reasons why certain rights associated with the family have been accorded shelter under the Fourteenth Amendment's Due Process Clause, we cannot avoid applying the force and rationale of these precedents to the family choice involved in this case.

. . .

Substantive due process has at times been a treacherous field for this Court. There *are* risks when the judicial branch gives enhanced protection to certain substantive liberties without the guidance of the more specific provisions of the Bill of Rights. As the history of the *Lochner* era demonstrates, there is reason for concern lest the only limits to such judicial intervention become the predilections of those who happen at the time to be Members of this Court. That history counsels caution and restraint. But it does not counsel abandonment, nor does it require what the city urges here: cutting off any protection of family rights at the first convenient, if arbitrary boundary—the boundary of the nuclear family.

Appropriate limits on substantive due process come not from drawing arbitrary lines but rather from careful "respect for the teachings of history [and] solid recognition of the basic values that underlie our society." Griswold v. Connecticut, 381 U.S., at 501 (Harlan, J., concurring).... Our decisions establish that the Constitution protects the sanctity of the family precisely because the institution of the family is deeply rooted in this Nation's history and tradition. It is through the family that we inculcate and pass down many of our most cherished values, moral and cultural.

Ours is by no means a tradition limited to respect for the bonds uniting the members of the nuclear family. The tradition of uncles, aunts, cousins, and especially grandparents sharing a household along with parents and children has roots equally venerable and equally deserving of constitutional recognition. Over the years millions of our citizens have grown up in just such an environment, and most, surely, have profited from it. Even if conditions of modern society have brought about a decline in extended family households, they have not erased the accumulated wisdom of civilization, gained over the centuries and honored throughout our history, that supports a larger conception of the family. Out of choice, necessity, or a sense of family responsibility, it has been common for close relatives to draw together and participate in the duties and the satisfactions of a common home. Decisions concerning child rearing, which *Yoder, Meyer, Pierce* and other cases have recognized as entitled to constitutional protection, long have been shared with grandparents or other relatives who occupy the same household—indeed who may take on major responsibility for the rearing of the children. Especially in times of adversity, such as the death of a spouse or economic need, the broader family has tended to come together for mutual sustenance and to maintain or rebuild a secure home life. This is apparently what happened here.

Whether or not such a household is established because of personal tragedy, the choice of relatives in this degree of kinship to live together may not lightly be denied by the State. *Pierce* struck down an Oregon law requiring all children to attend the State's public schools, holding that the Constitution "excludes any general power of the State to standardize its children by forcing them to accept instruction from public teachers only." 268 U.S., at 535. By the same token the Constitution prevents East Cleveland from standardizing its children—and its adults—by forcing all to live in certain narrowly defined family patterns.

Reversed.

Mr. Justice Brennan, with whom Mr. Justice Marshall joins, concurring.

I join the plurality's opinion. . . .

In today's America, the "nuclear family" is the pattern so often found in much of white suburbia. Sanden, Sociology: A Systematic Approach, p. 320 (1965). The Constitution cannot be interpreted, however, to tolerate the imposition by government upon the rest of us of white suburbia's preference in patterns of family living. The "extended family" that provided generations of early Americans with social services and economic and emotional support in times of hardship, and was the beachhead for successive waves of immigrants who populated our cities, remains not merely still a pervasive living pattern, but under the goad of brutal economic necessity, a prominent pattern— virtually a means of survival—for large numbers of the poor and deprived minorities of our society. For them compelled pooling of scant resources requires compelled sharing of a household.

The "extended" form is especially familiar among black families. . . .

I do not wish to be understood as implying that East Cleveland's enforcement of its ordinance is motivated by a racially discriminatory purpose: the record of this case would not support that implication. But the prominence of other than nuclear families among ethnic and racial minority groups, including our black citizens, surely demonstrates that the "extended family" pattern remains a vital tenet of our society. It suffices that in prohibiting this pattern of family living as a means of achieving its objectives, appellee city has chosen a device that deeply intrudes into family associational rights that historically have been central, and today remain central, to a large proportion of our population.

. . .

Mr. Justice Stevens, concurring in the judgment.

In my judgment the critical question presented by this case is whether East Cleveland's housing ordinance is a permissible restriction on appellant's right to use her own property as she sees fit.

. . .

Mr. Justice Stewart, with whom Mr. Justice Rehnquist joins, dissenting.

. . .

. . . The question presented, as I view it, is whether the decision in *Belle Terre* is controlling, or whether the Constitution compels a different result because East Cleveland's definition of "family" is more restrictive than that before us in the *Belle Terre* case.

. . . The *Belle Terre* decision disposes of the appellant's contentions to the extent they focus not on her blood relationships with her sons and grandsons but on more general notions about the "privacy of the home." Her suggestion that every person has a constitutional right permanently to share his residence with whomever he pleases, and that such choices are "beyond the province of legitimate governmental intrusion," amounts to the same argument that was made and found unpersuasive in *Belle Terre*.

To be sure, the ordinance involved in *Belle Terre* did not prevent blood relatives from occupying the same dwelling, and the Court's decision in that case does not, therefore, foreclose the appellant's arguments based specifically on the ties of kinship present in this case. Nonetheless, I would hold, for the reasons that follow, that the existence of those ties does not elevate either the appellant's claim of associational freedom or her claim of privacy to a level invoking constitutional protection.

. . .

The "association" in this case is not for any purpose relating to the promotion of speech, assembly, the press, or religion. And wherever the outer boundaries of constitutional protection of freedom of association may eventually turn out to be, they surely do not extend to those who assert no interest other than the gratification, convenience, and economy of sharing the same residence.

The appellant is considerably closer to the constitutional mark in asserting that the East Cleveland ordinance intrudes upon "the private realm of family life which the state cannot enter." . . .

Although the appellant's desire to share a single-dwelling unit also involves "private family life" in a sense, that desire can hardly be equated with any of the interests protected in [previous cases.] The ordinance . . . did not impede her choice to have or not to have children, and it did not dictate to her how her own children were to be nurtured and reared. The ordinance clearly does not prevent parents from living together or living with their unemancipated offspring.

. . . [7]

. . . When the Court has found that the Fourteenth Amendment placed a substantive limitation on a State's power to regulate, it has been in those rare cases in which the personal interests at issue have been deemed "implicit in the concept of ordered liberty." See Roe v. Wade, supra, at 152, quoting Palko v. Connecticut, 302 U.S. 319, 325. The interest that the appellant may have in permanently sharing a single kitchen and a suite of contiguous rooms with some of her relatives simply does not rise to that level. To equate this interest with the fundamental decisions to marry and to bear and raise children is to extend the limited substantive contours of the Due Process Clause beyond recognition.

The appellant also challenges the single-family occupancy ordinance on equal protection grounds. Her claim is that the city has drawn an arbitrary and irrational distinction between groups of people who may live together as a "family" and those who may not. . . .

---

[7] The opinion of Mr. Justice Powell and Mr. Justice Brennan's concurring opinion both emphasize the traditional importance of the extended family in American life. But I fail to understand why it follows that the residents of East Cleveland are constitutionally prevented from following what Mr. Justice Brennan calls the "pattern" of "white suburbia," even though that choice may reflect "cultural myopia." In point of fact, East Cleveland is a predominantly Negro community, with a Negro City Manager and City Commission.

Obviously, East Cleveland might have as easily and perhaps as effectively hit upon a different definition of "family." But a line could hardly be drawn that would not sooner or later become the target of a challenge like the appellant's. If "family" included all of the householder's grandchildren there would doubtless be the hard case of an orphaned niece or nephew. If, as the appellant suggests, a "family" must include all blood relatives, what of long-time friends? The point is that any definition would produce hardships in some cases without materially advancing the legislative purpose....

. . .

Mr. Justice White, dissenting.

. . .

... Realizing that the present construction of the Due Process Clause represents a major judicial gloss on its terms, as well as on the anticipation of the Framers, and that much of the underpinning for the broad, substantive application of the Clause disappeared in the conflict between the executive and the judiciary in the 1930's and 1940's, the Court should be extremely reluctant to breathe still further substantive content into the Due Process Clause so as to strike down legislation adopted by a State or city to promote its welfare. Whenever the judiciary does so, it unavoidably pre-empts for itself another part of the governance of the country without express constitutional authority.

Accepting the cases as they are and the Due Process Clause as construed by them, however, I think it evident that the threshold question in any due process attack on legislation, whether the challenge is procedural or substantive, is whether there is a deprivation of life, liberty or property....

It seems to me that Mr. Justice Douglas was closest to the mark in Poe v. Ullman, supra, at 517, when he said that the trouble with the holdings of the "old Court" was not in its definition of liberty but in its definition of the protections guaranteed to that liberty—"not in entertaining inquiries concerning the constitutionality of social legislation but in applying the standards that it did."

The term "liberty" is not, therefore, to be given a crabbed construction. I have no more difficulty than Mr. Justice Powell apparently does in concluding that petitioner in this case properly asserts a liberty interest within the meaning of the Due Process Clause. The question is not one of liberty, *vel non.* Rather, there being no procedural issue at stake, the issue is whether the precise interest involved—the interest in having more than one set of grandchildren live in her home—is entitled to such substantive protection under the Due Process Clause that this ordinance must be held invalid.

. . .

[T]he general principle [is] that "liberty may not be interfered with, under the guise of protecting the public interest, by legislative action which is arbitrary or without reasonable relation to some purpose within the competency of the state to effect." Meyer v. Nebraska, supra, at 399–400. This means-end test appears to require that any statute restrictive of liberty have an ascertainable purpose and represent a rational means to achieve that purpose, whatever the nature of the liberty interest involved....

There are various "liberties," however, which require that infringing legislation be given closer judicial scrutiny, not only with respect to existence of a purpose and the means employed, but also with respect to the importance of the purpose itself relative to the invaded interest. Some interests would appear almost impregnable to invasion, such as the freedoms of speech, press, and religion, and the freedom from cruel and unusual punishments. Other interests, for example, the right of association, the right to vote, and various claims sometimes referred to under the general rubric of the right to privacy, also weigh very heavily against state claims of authority to regulate. It is this category of interests which, as I understand it, Mr. Justice Stewart refers to as "implicit in the concept of ordered liberty." Because he would confine the reach of substantive due process protection to interests such as these and because he would not classify in this category the asserted right to share a house with the relatives involved here, he rejects the due process claim.

Given his premise, he is surely correct. Under our cases, the Due Process Clause extends substantial protection to various phases of family life, but none requires that the claim made here be sustained. I cannot believe that the interest in residing with more than one set of grandchildren is one that calls for any kind of heightened protection under the Due Process Clause. . . .

Mr. Justice Powell would apparently construe the Due Process Clause to protect from all but quite important state regulatory interests any right or privilege that in his estimate is deeply rooted in the country's traditions. For me, this suggests a far too expansive charter for this Court and a far less meaningful and less confining guiding principle than Mr. Justice Stewart would use for serious substantive due process review. . . .

. . . Had it been our task to legislate, we might have approached the problem in a different manner than did the drafters of this ordinance; but I have no trouble in concluding that the normal goals of zoning regulation are present here and that the ordinance serves these goals by limiting, in identifiable circumstances, the number of people who can occupy a single household. The ordinance does not violate the Due Process Clause.

For very similar reasons, the equal protection claim must fail, since it is not to be judged by the strict scrutiny standard employed when a fundamental interest or suspect classification is involved. . . .

[A dissenting opinion by Chief Justice Burger is omitted.][a]

Zablocki v. Redhail

434 U.S. 374, 98 S.Ct. 673, 54 L.Ed.2d 618 (1978).

Mr. Justice Marshall delivered the opinion of the Court.

[A Wisconsin statute, §§ 245.10(1), (4), (5), required any "Wisconsin resident having minor issue not in his custody and which he is under an obligation to support by any court order or judgment" to obtain court permission to marry. The marriage applicant had to demonstrate compliance with the support obligation and that the children covered by the support order "are not then and are not likely thereafter to become public charges."

In a paternity action, Redhail, an unmarried high school student, was ordered to pay $109 per month support until his child reached 18. From the date of the order in May 1972 until August 1974 he was unemployed, indigent, and consequently unable to make any support payments. His application for a marriage license the next month was denied for failure to obtain the requisite court order granting him permission to marry. It was stipulated that Redhail

---

[a] For a full discussion, see *Developments in the Law—The Constitution and the Fami-* *ly,* 93 Harv.L.Rev. 1156 (1980).

had not satisfied his support obligations (by December 1974, he was more than $3,700 in arrears), that his child had been a public charge since birth, and "that she would have been a public charge even if appellee had been current in his support payments."

Redhail brought a class action in federal district court, challenging the statute as violative of "equal protection and due process rights secured by the First, Fifth, Ninth, and Fourteenth Amendments." He alleged that he and the woman he wished to marry were expecting a child in March 1975 and wanted to be lawfully married before then. The district court held the statute invalid under the Equal Protection Clause, and the Supreme Court agreed.]

II.

In evaluating §§ 245.10(1), (4), (5) under the Equal Protection Clause, "we must first determine what burden of justification the classification created thereby must meet, by looking to the nature of the classification and the individual interests affected." ... Since our past decisions make clear that the right to marry is of fundamental importance, and since the classification at issue here significantly interferes with the exercise of that right, we believe that "critical examination" of the state interests advanced in support of the classification is required....

The leading decision of this Court on the right to marry is Loving v. Virginia, 388 U.S. 1 (1967). In that case, an interracial couple who had been convicted of violating Virginia's miscegenation laws challenged the statutory scheme on both equal protection and due process grounds. The Court's opinion could have rested solely on the ground that the statutes discriminated on the basis of race in violation of the Equal Protection Clause. But the Court went on to hold that the laws arbitrarily deprived the couple of a fundamental liberty protected by the Due Process Clause, the freedom to marry. The Court's language on the latter point bears repeating:

> "The freedom to marry has long been recognized as one of the vital personal rights essential to the orderly pursuit of happiness by free men.
>
> "Marriage is one of the 'basic civil rights of man,' fundamental to our very existence and survival." ...

Although *Loving* arose in the context of racial discrimination, prior and subsequent decisions of this Court confirm that the right to marry is of fundamental importance for all individuals....

More recent decisions have established that the right to marry is part of the fundamental "right of privacy" implicit in the Fourteenth Amendment's Due Process Clause. In Griswold v. Connecticut, 381 U.S. 479 (1965), the Court observed:

> "We deal with a right of privacy older than the Bill of Rights—older than our political parties, older than our school system. Marriage is a coming together for better or for worse, hopefully enduring, and intimate to the degree of being sacred. It is an association that promotes a way of life, not causes; a harmony in living, not political faiths; a bilateral loyalty, not commercial or social projects. Yet it is an association for as noble a purpose as any involved in our prior decisions."

. . .

Cases subsequent to *Griswold* and *Loving* have routinely categorized the decision to marry as among the personal decisions protected by the right of privacy....

It is not surprising that the decision to marry has been placed on the same level of importance as decisions relating to procreation, childbirth, child-rearing, and family relationships. As the facts of this case illustrate, it would make little sense to recognize a right of privacy with respect to other matters of family life and not with respect to the decision to enter the relationship that is the foundation of the family in our society. The woman whom appellee desired to marry had a fundamental right to seek an abortion of their expected child, see Roe v. Wade, supra, or to bring the child into life to suffer the myriad social, if not economic, disabilities that the status of illegitimacy brings. . . . Surely, a decision to marry and raise the child in a traditional family setting must receive equivalent protection. And, if appellee's right to procreate means anything at all, it must imply some right to enter the only relationship in which the State of Wisconsin allows sexual relations legally to take place.

By reaffirming the fundamental character of the right to marry, we do not mean to suggest that every state regulation which relates in any way to the incidents of or prerequisites for marriage must be subjected to rigorous scrutiny. To the contrary, reasonable regulations that do not significantly interfere with decisions to enter into the marital relationship may legitimately be imposed. See Califano v. Jobst, 434 U.S. 47 (1977). The statutory classification at issue here, however, clearly does interfere directly and substantially with the right to marry.

Under the challenged statute, no Wisconsin resident in the affected class may marry in Wisconsin or elsewhere without a court order, and marriages contracted in violation of the statute are both void and punishable as criminal offenses. Some of those in the affected class, like appellee, will never be able to obtain the necessary court order, because they either lack the financial means to meet their support obligations or cannot prove that their children will not become public charges. These persons are absolutely prevented from getting married. Many others, able in theory to satisfy the statute's requirements, will be sufficiently burdened by having to do so that they will in effect be coerced into foregoing their right to marry. And even those who can be persuaded to meet the statute's requirements suffer a serious intrusion into their freedom of choice in an area in which we have held such freedom to be fundamental.

III.

When a statutory classification significantly interferes with the exercise of a fundamental right, it cannot be upheld unless it is supported by sufficiently important state interests and is closely tailored to effectuate only those interests. . . . Appellant asserts that two interests are served by the challenged statute: the permission-to-marry proceeding furnishes an opportunity to counsel the applicant as to the necessity of fulfilling his prior support obligations; and the welfare of the out-of-custody children is protected. We may accept for present purposes that these are legitimate and substantial interests, but, since the means selected by the State for achieving these interests unnecessarily impinge on the right to marry, the statute cannot be sustained.

. . . The statute actually enacted . . . does not expressly require or provide for any counselling whatsoever, nor for any automatic granting of permission to marry by the court, and thus it can hardly be justified as a means for ensuring counselling of the persons within its coverage. Even [if] counselling does take place . . . this interest obviously cannot support the withholding of court permission to marry once counselling is completed.

With regard to safeguarding the welfare of the out-of-custody children, . . . [at oral] argument, appellant's counsel suggested that . . . the statute provides incentive for the applicant to make support payments to his children.... This "collection device" rationale cannot justify the statute's broad infringement on the right to marry.

First, with respect to individuals who are unable to meet the statutory requirements, the statute merely prevents the applicant from getting married, without delivering any money at all into the hands of the applicant's prior children. More importantly, regardless of the applicant's ability or willingness to meet the statutory requirements, the State already has numerous other means for exacting compliance with support obligations, means that are at least as effective as the instant statute's and yet do not impinge upon the right to marry. Under Wisconsin law, whether the children are from a prior marriage or were born out of wedlock, court-determined support obligations may be enforced directly via wage assignments, civil contempt proceedings, and criminal penalties. And, if the State believes that parents of children out of their custody should be responsible for ensuring that those children do not become public charges, this interest can be achieved by adjusting the criteria used for determining the amounts to be paid under their support orders.

There is also some suggestion that § 245.10 protects the ability of marriage applicants to meet support obligations to prior children by preventing the applicants from incurring new support obligations. But the challenged provisions of § 245.10 are grossly underinclusive with respect to this purpose, since they do not limit in any way new financial commitments by the applicant other than those arising out of the contemplated marriage. The statutory classification is substantially overinclusive as well: given the possibility that the new spouse will actually better the applicant's financial situation, by contributing income from a job or otherwise, the statute in many cases may prevent affected individuals from improving their ability to satisfy their prior support obligations. And, although it is true that the applicant will incur support obligations to any children born during the contemplated marriage, preventing the marriage may only result in the children being born out of wedlock, as in fact occurred in appellee's case. Since the support obligation is the same whether the child is born in or out of wedlock, the net result of preventing the marriage is simply more illegitimate children.

The statutory classification ... cannot be justified by the interests advanced in support of it. The judgment of the District Court is, accordingly, affirmed.

Mr. Chief Justice Burger, concurring.

I join Mr. Justice Marshall's opinion for the Court....

Mr. Justice Stewart, concurring in the judgment.

I cannot join the opinion of the Court. To hold, as the Court does, that the Wisconsin statute violates the Equal Protection Clause seems to me to misconceive the meaning of that constitutional guarantee. The Equal Protection Clause deals not with substantive rights or freedoms but with invidiously discriminatory classifications.... The paradigm of its violation is, of course, classification by race....

Like almost any law, the Wisconsin statute now before us affects some people and does not affect others. But to say that it thereby creates "classifications" in the equal protection sense strikes me as little short of fantasy. The problem in this case is not one of discriminatory classifications, but of unwarranted encroachment upon a constitutionally protected freedom. I think that the Wisconsin statute is unconstitutional because it exceeds the bounds of permissible state regulation of marriage, and invades the sphere of liberty protected by the Due Process Clause of the Fourteenth Amendment.

I.

I do not agree with the Court that there is a "right to marry" in the constitutional sense. That right, or more accurately, that privilege, is under our federal system peculiarly one to be defined and limited by state law. Sosna v. Iowa, 419 U.S. 393, 404. A State may not only "significantly interfere with decisions to enter into the marriage relationship," but may in many circumstances absolutely prohibit it. Surely, for example, a State may legitimately say that no one can marry his or her sibling, that no one can marry who is not at least 14 years old, that no one can marry without first passing an examination for venereal disease, or that no one can marry who has a living husband or wife. But, just as surely, in regulating the intimate human relationship of marriage, there is a limit beyond which a State may not constitutionally go.

The Constitution does not specifically mention freedom to marry, but it is settled that the "liberty" protected by the Due Process Clause of the Fourteenth Amendment embraces more than those freedoms expressly enumerated in the Bill of Rights. . . . And the decisions of this Court have made clear that freedom of personal choice in matters of marriage and family life is one of the liberties so protected. . . .

It is evident that the Wisconsin law now before us directly abridges that freedom. The question is whether the state interests that support the abridgment can overcome the substantive protections of the Constitution.

. . .

If Wisconsin had said that no one could marry who had not paid all of the fines assessed against him for traffic violations, I suppose the constitutional invalidity of the law would be apparent. For while the state interest would certainly be legitimate, that interest would be both disproportionate and unrelated to the restriction of liberty imposed by the State. But the invalidity of the law before us is hardly so clear, because its restriction of liberty seems largely to be imposed only on those who have abused the same liberty in the past.

. . .

On several occasions this Court has held that a person's inability to pay money demanded by the State does not justify the total deprivation of a constitutionally protected liberty. . . .

The principle of those cases applies here as well. The Wisconsin law makes no allowance for the truly indigent. . . .

As directed against either the indigent or the delinquent parent, the law is substantially more rational if viewed as a means of assuring the financial viability of future marriages. In this context, it reflects a plausible judgment that those who have not fulfilled their financial obligations and have not kept their children off the welfare rolls in the past are likely to encounter similar difficulties in the future. But the State's legitimate concern with the financial soundness of prospective marriages must stop short of telling people they may not marry because they are too poor or because they might persist in their financial irresponsibility. The invasion of constitutionally protected liberty and the chance of erroneous prediction are simply too great. A legislative judgment so alien to our traditions and so offensive to our shared notions of fairness offends the Due Process Clause of the Fourteenth Amendment.

II.

In an opinion of the Court half a century ago, Mr. Justice Holmes described an equal protection claim as "the usual last resort of constitutional arguments." Buck v. Bell, 274 U.S. 200, 208. Today equal protection doctrine has become the Court's chief instrument for invalidating state laws. Yet, in a case like this one, the doctrine is no more than substantive due process by another name.

Although the Court purports to examine the bases for legislative classifications and to compare the treatment of legislatively defined groups, it actually erects substantive limitations on what States may do. Thus, the effect of the Court's decision in this case is not to require Wisconsin to draw its legislative classifications with greater precision or to afford similar treatment to similarly situated persons. Rather, the message of the Court's opinion is that Wisconsin may not use its control over marriage to achieve the objectives of the state statute. Such restrictions on basic governmental power are at the heart of substantive due process.

The Court is understandably reluctant to rely on substantive due process. See Roe v. Wade, 410 U.S., at 167–168 (concurring opinion). But to embrace the essence of that doctrine under the guise of equal protection serves no purpose but obfuscation. ...

To conceal this appropriate inquiry invites mechanical or thoughtless application of misfocused doctrine. To bring it into the open forces a healthy and responsible recognition of the nature and purpose of the extreme power we wield when, in invalidating a state law in the name of the Constitution, we invalidate *pro tanto* the process of representative democracy in one of the Sovereign States of the Union.

Mr. Justice Powell, concurring in the judgment.

I concur in the judgment of the Court ... [but] write separately because the majority's rationale sweeps too broadly in an area which traditionally has been subject to pervasive state regulation. ...

I.

. . .

... Thus, *Loving* involved a denial of a "fundamental freedom" on a wholly unsupportable basis—the use of classifications "directly subversive of the principle of equality at the heart of the Fourteenth Amendment...." It does not speak to the level of judicial scrutiny of, or governmental justification for, "supportable" restrictions on the "fundamental freedom" of individuals to marry or divorce.

In my view, analysis must start from the recognition of domestic relations as "an area that has long been regarded as a virtually exclusive province of the States." Sosna v. Iowa, 419 U.S. 393, 404 (1975). The marriage relation traditionally has been subject to regulation, initially by the ecclesiastical authorities, and later by the secular state. ...State regulation has included bans on incest, bigamy, and homosexuality, as well as various preconditions to marriage, such as blood tests. Likewise, a showing of fault on the part of one of the partners traditionally has been a prerequisite to the dissolution of an unsuccessful union. A "compelling state purpose" inquiry would cast doubt on the network of restrictions that the States have fashioned to govern marriage and divorce.

II.

State power over domestic relations is not without constitutional limits. The Due Process Clause requires a showing of justification "when the government intrudes on choices concerning family living arrangements" in a manner which is contrary to deeply rooted traditions. . . .

. . .

. . . I do not agree with the suggestion in the Court's opinion that a State may never condition the right to marry on satisfaction of existing support obligations simply because the State has alternative methods of compelling such payments. To the extent this restriction applies to persons who are able to make the required support payments but simply wish to shirk their moral and legal obligation, the Constitution interposes no bar to this additional collection mechanism. The vice inheres not in the collection concept, but in the failure to make provision for those without the means to comply with child-support obligations. . . .

. . .

The marriage applicant not only is required . . . to submit proof of compliance with his support obligation, but also to demonstrate—in some unspecified way—that his children "are not then and are not likely thereafter to become public charges." . . . Apparently, no other jurisdiction has embraced this approach as a method of reducing the number of children on public assistance. Because the State has not established a justification for this unprecedented foreclosure of marriage to many of its citizens solely because of their indigency, I concur in the judgment of the Court.

Mr. Justice Stevens, concurring in the judgment.

. . .

In sum, the public charge provision is either futile or perverse insofar as it applies to childless couples, couples who will have illegitimate children if they are forbidden to marry, couples whose economic status will be improved by marriage, and couples who are so poor that the marriage will have no impact on the welfare status of their children in any event. Even assuming that the right to marry may sometimes be denied on economic grounds, this clumsy and deliberate legislative discrimination between the rich and the poor is irrational in so many ways that it cannot withstand scrutiny under the Equal Protection Clause of the Fourteenth Amendment.

Mr. Justice Rehnquist, dissenting.

. . . I would view this legislative judgment in the light of the traditional presumption of validity. I think that under the Equal Protection Clause the statute need pass only the "rational basis test," Dandridge v. Williams, 397 U.S. 471, 485 (1970), and that under the Due Process Clause it need only be shown that it bears a rational relation to a constitutionally permissible objective. Williamson v. Lee Optical Co., 348 U.S. 483, 491 (1955); Ferguson v. Skrupa, 372 U.S. 726, 733 (1963) (Harlan, J., concurring). The statute so viewed is a permissible exercise of the State's power to regulate family life and to assure the support of minor children, despite its possible imprecision in the extreme cases envisioned in the concurring opinions.

. . .

DOES EQUAL PROTECTION ANALYSIS ADD ANYTHING?

For examples of other cases where the Court has applied equal protection analysis to cases controlled by other constitutional provisions, see Carey v. Brown, 447 U.S. 455 (1980) (first amendment); Logan v. Zimmerman Brush Co., 455 U.S. 422 (1982) (procedural due process). In any of these cases, do the analysis and result differ if equal protection standards are disregarded and the case is determined under the applicable constitutional provisions? For an extended argument that they do not, see Westen, *The Empty Idea of Equality,* 95 Harv.L.Rev. 537 (1982). See also Cohen, *Is Equal Protection Like Oakland? Equality as a Surrogate for Other Rights,* 59 Tulane L.Rev. 884 (1985).

Michael H. v. Gerald D.

491 U.S. 110, 109 S.Ct. 2333, 105 L.Ed.2d 91 (1989).

Justice Scalia announced the judgment of the Court and delivered an opinion, in which The Chief Justice joins, and in all but note 6 of which Justice O'Connor and Justice Kennedy join.

Under California law, a child born to a married woman living with her husband is presumed to be a child of the marriage. Cal.Evid.Code Ann. § 621 (West Supp.1989). The presumption of legitimacy may be rebutted only by the husband or wife, and then only in limited circumstances. Ibid. The instant appeal presents the claim that this presumption infringes upon the due process rights of a man who wishes to establish his paternity of a child born to the wife of another man, and the claim that it infringes upon the constitutional right of the child to maintain a relationship with her natural father.

I

The facts of this case are, we must hope, extraordinary. . . .

[In 1978, two years after Carole D. and Gerald D. married and began living in California, Carole began "an adulterous affair with her neighbor, Michael H." Three years later she gave birth to Victoria. Blood tests "showed a 98.07% probability that Michael was Victoria's father." Victoria always lived with Carole, but during her first three years they lived intermittently with Gerald in New York, with Michael in St. Thomas or Los Angeles, and with another man in California. Whenever they were with Michael, he "held Victoria out as his daughter."]

In November 1982, [when first] rebuffed in his attempts to visit Victoria, Michael filed a filiation action in California Superior Court to establish his paternity and right to visitation. . . . [Victoria's court-appointed attorney later] filed a cross-complaint asserting that if she had more than one psychological or de facto father, she was entitled to maintain her filial relationship, with all of the attendant rights, duties, and obligations, with both. In May 1983, Carole filed a motion for summary judgment. . . . In August, however, she returned to California, became involved once again with Michael, and instructed her attorneys to remove the summary judgment motion from the calendar.

. . . In April 1984, Carole and Michael signed a stipulation that Michael was Victoria's natural father. Carole left Michael the next month, however, and instructed her attorneys not to file the stipulation. In June 1984, Carole reconciled with Gerald and joined him in New York, where they now live with Victoria and two other children since born into the marriage.

In May 1984, Michael and Victoria ... sought visitation rights for Michael pendente lite.... [Based on a court-appointed psychologist's recommendation, the court] ordered ... limited visitation privileges pendente lite.

On October 19, 1984, Gerald, who had intervened in the action, [successfully] moved for summary judgment on the ground that under Cal.Evid.Code § 621 there were no triable issues of fact as to Victoria's paternity. This law provides that "the issue of a wife cohabiting with her husband, who is not impotent or sterile, is conclusively presumed to be a child of the marriage." ... The presumption may be rebutted by blood tests, but only if a motion for such tests is made, within two years from the date of the child's birth, either by the husband or, if the natural father has filed an affidavit acknowledging paternity, by the wife....

On January 28, 1985, having found that affidavits submitted by Carole and Gerald sufficed to demonstrate that the two were cohabiting at conception and birth and that Gerald was neither sterile nor impotent, the Superior Court granted Gerald's motion for summary judgment, rejecting Michael's and Victoria's challenges to the constitutionality of § 621. The court also denied ... motions for continued visitation pending the appeal under Cal.Civ.Code § 4601, which provides that a court may, in its discretion, grant "reasonable visitation rights ... to any ... person having an interest in the welfare of the child." ...

... [T]he California Court of Appeal affirmed the judgment ... and upheld the constitutionality of the statute.... It interpreted that judgment, moreover, as having denied permanent visitation rights under § 4601....

... [T]he California Supreme Court denied discretionary review....

II

The California statute ... is, in substance, more than a century old.... In 1980, the legislature ... amended the statute to provide the husband an opportunity to introduce blood-test evidence in rebuttal of the presumption, ... and in 1981 amended it to provide the mother such an opportunity....

III

... [I]t is necessary to clarify what [Michael] sought and what he was denied. California law, like nature itself, makes no provision for dual fatherhood. Michael was seeking to be declared *the* father of Victoria. The immediate benefit he evidently sought to obtain from that status was visitation rights. See Cal.Civ.Code Ann. § 4601 (West 1983) (parent has statutory right to visitation "unless it is shown that such visitation would be detrimental to the best interests of the child"). But if Michael were successful in being declared the father, other rights would follow—most importantly, the right to be considered as the parent who should have custody, ... a status which "embrace[s] the sum of parental rights with respect to the rearing of a child, including the child's care; the right to the child's services and earnings; the right to direct the child's activities; the right to make decisions regarding the control, education, and health of the child; and the right, as well as the duty, to prepare the child for additional obligations, which includes the teaching of moral standards, religious beliefs, and elements of good citizenship." 4 California Family Law § 60.02[1][b].... All parental rights, including visitation, were automatically denied by denying Michael status as the father. While Cal.Civ.Code Ann. § 4601 places it within the discretionary power of a court to award visitation rights to a nonparent, the Superior Court here, affirmed by the Court of Appeal, held that California law denies visitation, against the wishes of the mother, to a putative father who has been prevented by § 621 from establishing his paternity.

Michael raises two related challenges to the constitutionality of § 621. First, he asserts that requirements of procedural due process prevent the State from terminating his liberty interest in his relationship with his child without affording him an opportunity to demonstrate his paternity in an evidentiary hearing. We believe this claim derives from a fundamental misconception of the nature of the California statute. While § 621 is phrased in terms of a presumption, that rule of evidence is the implementation of a substantive rule of law. California declares it to be, except in limited circumstances, *irrelevant* for paternity purposes whether a child conceived during and born into an existing marriage was begotten by someone other than the husband and had a prior relationship with him. As the Court of Appeal phrased it:

> 'The conclusive presumption is actually a substantive rule of law based upon a determination by the Legislature as a matter of overriding social policy, that given a certain relationship between the husband and wife, the husband is to be held responsible for the child, and that the integrity of the family unit should not be impugned.' . . .

Of course the conclusive presumption not only expresses the State's substantive policy but also furthers it, excluding inquiries into the child's paternity that would be destructive of family integrity and privacy.

This Court has struck down as illegitimate certain "irrebuttable presumptions." See, e.g., Stanley v. Illinois, 405 U.S. 645 (1972); Vlandis v. Kline, 412 U.S. 441 (1973); Cleveland Board of Education v. LaFleur, 414 U.S. 632 (1974). Those holdings did not, however, rest upon *procedural* due process. A conclusive presumption does, of course, foreclose the person against whom it is invoked from demonstrating, in a particularized proceeding, that applying the presumption to him will in fact not further the lawful governmental policy the presumption is designed to effectuate. But the same can be said of any legal rule that establishes general classifications, whether framed in terms of a presumption or not. In this respect there is no difference between a rule which says that the marital husband shall be irrebuttably presumed to be the father, and a rule which says that the adulterous natural father shall not be recognized as the legal father. *Both* rules deny someone in Michael's situation a hearing on whether, in the particular circumstances of his case, California's policies would best be served by giving him parental rights. Thus . . . our "irrebuttable presumption" cases must ultimately be analyzed as calling into question not the adequacy of procedures but . . . the adequacy of the "fit" between the classification and the policy that the classification serves. See LaFleur, supra, at 652 (Powell, J., concurring in result); Vlandis, supra, at 456–459 (White, J., concurring), 466–469 (Rehnquist, J., dissenting); Weinberger v. Salfi, 422 U.S. 749 (1975). We therefore reject Michael's procedural due process challenge and proceed to his substantive claim.

Michael contends as a matter of substantive due process that because he has established a parental relationship with Victoria, protection of Gerald's and Carole's marital union is an insufficient state interest to support termination of that relationship. This argument is, of course, predicated on the assertion that Michael has a constitutionally protected liberty interest in his relationship with Victoria.

It is an established part of our constitutional jurisprudence that the term "liberty" in the Due Process Clause extends beyond freedom from physical restraint. See, e.g., Pierce v. Society of Sisters, 268 U.S. 510 (1925); Meyer v. Nebraska, 262 U.S. 390 (1923). Without that core textual meaning as a limitation, defining the scope of the Due Process Clause "has at times been a treacherous field for this Court," giving "reason for concern lest the only limits to . . . judicial intervention become the predilections of those who happen at the time to be Members of this Court." Moore v. East Cleveland, 431 U.S. 494, 502 (1977). . . .

In an attempt to limit and guide interpretation of the Clause, we have insisted not merely that the interest denominated as a "liberty" be "fundamental" (a concept that, in isolation, is hard to objectify), but also that it be an interest traditionally protected by our society.[2] As we have put it, the Due Process Clause affords only those protections "so rooted in the traditions and conscience of our people as to be ranked as fundamental." Snyder v. Massachusetts, 291 U.S. 97, 105 (1934) (Cardozo, J.). Our cases reflect "continual insistence upon respect for the teachings of history [and] solid recognition of the basic values that underlie our society. . . ." Griswold v. Connecticut, 381 U.S. 479, 501 (1965) (Harlan, J., concurring in judgment).

This insistence that the asserted liberty interest be rooted in history and tradition is evident, as elsewhere, in our cases according constitutional protection to certain parental rights. Michael reads the landmark case of Stanley v. Illinois, 405 U.S. 645 (1972), and the subsequent cases of Quilloin v. Walcott, 434 U.S. 246 (1978), Caban v. Mohammed, 441 U.S. 380 (1979) and Lehr v. Robertson, 463 U.S. 248 (1983), as establishing that a liberty interest is created by biological fatherhood plus an established parental relationship—factors that exist in the present case as well. We think that distorts the rationale of those cases. As we view them, they rest not upon such isolated factors but upon the historic respect—indeed, sanctity would not be too strong a term—traditionally accorded to the relationships that develop within the unitary family. . . . In *Stanley,* for example, we forbade the destruction of such a family when, upon the death of the mother, the state had sought to remove children from the custody of a father who had lived with and supported them and their mother for 18 years. As Justice Powell stated for the plurality in *Moore v. East Cleveland,* . . .: "Our decisions establish that the Constitution protects the sanctity of the family precisely because the institution of the family is deeply rooted in this Nation's history and tradition."

Thus, the legal issue in the present case reduces to whether the relationship between persons in the situation of Michael and Victoria has been treated as a protected family unit under the historic practices of our society, or whether on any other basis it has been accorded special protection. We think it impossible to find that it has. In fact, quite to the contrary, our traditions have protected the marital family (Gerald, Carole, and the child they acknowledge to be theirs) against the sort of claim Michael asserts.[4]

---

[2] We do not understand what Justice Brennan has in mind by an interest "that society traditionally has thought important . . . without protecting it." The protection need not take the form of an explicit constitutional provision or statutory guarantee, but it must at least exclude (all that is necessary to decide the present case) a societal tradition of enacting laws *denying* the interest. . . .

[4] Justice Brennan insists that in determining whether a liberty interest exists we must look at Michael's relationship with Victoria in isolation, without reference to the circumstance that Victoria's mother was married to someone else when the child was conceived, and that that woman and her husband wish to raise the child as their own. We cannot imagine what compels this strange procedure of looking at the act which is assertedly the subject of a liberty interest in isolation from its effect upon other people—rather like inquiring whether there is a liberty interest in firing a gun where the case at hand happens to involve its discharge into another person's body. . . .

The presumption of legitimacy was a fundamental principle of the common law ... rebutt[able] only by proof that a husband was incapable of procreation or had had no access to his wife during the relevant period.... The primary policy rationale ... appears to have been an aversion to declaring children illegitimate, ... thereby depriving them of rights of inheritance and succession, 2 Kent's Commentaries 175 (1827), and likely making them wards of the state. A secondary policy concern was the interest in promoting the "peace and tranquillity of States and families," ... a goal that is obviously impaired by facilitating suits against husband and wife asserting that their children are illegitimate. Even though, as bastardy laws became less harsh, "[j]udges in both [England and the United States] gradually widened the acceptable range of evidence that could be offered by spouses, the law retained a strong bias against ruling the children of married women illegitimate." ...

We have found nothing in the older sources, nor in the older cases, addressing specifically the power of the natural father to assert parental rights over a child born into a woman's existing marriage with another man. Since it is Michael's burden to establish that such a power (at least where the natural father has established a relationship with the child) is so deeply embedded within our traditions as to be a fundamental right, the lack of evidence alone might defeat his case. But the evidence shows that even in modern times ... the ability of a person in Michael's position to claim paternity has not been generally acknowledged....

Moreover, even if it were clear that one in Michael's position generally possesses, and has generally always possessed, standing to challenge the marital child's legitimacy, that would still not establish Michael's case.... What he must establish ... is not that our society has traditionally allowed a natural father in his circumstances to establish paternity, but that it has traditionally accorded such a father parental rights, or at least has not traditionally denied them.... What counts is whether the States in fact award substantive parental rights to the natural father of a child conceived within and born into an extant marital union that wishes to embrace the child. We are not aware of a single case, old or new, that has done so. This is not the stuff of which fundamental rights qualifying as liberty interests are made.[6]

---

[6] Justice Brennan criticizes our methodology in using historical traditions specifically relating to the rights of an adulterous natural father, rather than inquiring more generally "whether parenthood is an interest that historically has received our attention and protection." There seems to us no basis for the contention that this methodology is "nove[l]." For example, in Bowers v. Hardwick, 478 U.S. 186 (1986), we noted that at the time the Fourteenth Amendment was ratified all but 5 of the 37 States had criminal sodomy laws, that all 50 of the States had such laws prior to 1961, and that 24 States and the District of Columbia continued to have them; and we concluded from that record, regarding that very specific aspect of sexual conduct, that "to claim that a right to engage in such conduct is 'deeply rooted in this Nation's history and tradition' or 'implicit in the concept of ordered liberty' is, at best, facetious." ... In Roe v. Wade, 410 U.S. 113 (1973), we spent about a fifth of our opinion negating the proposition that there was a longstanding tradition of laws proscribing abortion.... We do not understand why, having rejected our focus upon the societal tradition regarding the natural father's rights vis-a-vis a child whose mother is married to another man, Justice Brennan would choose to focus instead upon "parenthood." Why should the relevant category not be even more general—perhaps "family relationships"; or "personal relationships"; or even "emotional attachments in general"? Though the dissent has no basis for the level of generality it would select, we do: We refer to the most specific level at which a relevant tradition protecting, or denying protection to, the asserted right can be identified. If, for example, there were no societal tradition, either way, regarding the rights of the natural father of a child adulterously conceived, we would have to consult, and (if possible) reason from, the traditions regarding natural fathers in general. But there is such a more specific tradition, and it unqualifiedly denies protection to such a parent. One would think

In Lehr v. Robertson, a case involving a natural father's attempt to block his child's adoption by the unwed mother's new husband, we observed that "[t]he significance of the biological connection is that it offers the natural father an opportunity that no other male possesses to develop a relationship with his offspring," ... and we assumed that the Constitution might require some protection of that opportunity.... Where, however, the child is born into an extant marital family, the natural father's unique opportunity conflicts with the similarly unique opportunity of the husband of the marriage; and it is not unconstitutional for the State to give categorical preference to the latter. In *Lehr* we quoted approvingly from Justice Stewart's dissent in Caban v. Mohammed, 441 U.S., at 397, to the effect that although "[i]n some circumstances the actual relationship between father and child may suffice to create in the unwed father parental interests comparable to those of the married father," "the absence of a legal tie with the mother may in such circumstances appropriately place a limit on whatever substantive constitutional claims might otherwise exist." ... In accord with our traditions, a limit is also imposed by the circumstance that the mother is, at the time of the child's conception and birth, married to and cohabitating with another man, both of whom wish to raise the child as the offspring of their union.[7] It is a question of legislative policy and not constitutional law whether California will allow the presumed parenthood of a couple desiring to retain a child conceived within and born into their marriage to be rebutted.

We do not accept Justice Brennan's criticism that this result "squashes" the liberty that consists of "the freedom not to conform." It seems to us that reflects the erroneous view that there is only one side to this controversy—that one disposition can expand a "liberty" of sorts without contracting an equivalent "liberty" on the other side. Such a happy choice is rarely available. Here, to *provide* protection to an adulterous natural father is to *deny* protection to a marital father, and vice versa. If Michael has a "freedom not to conform"

that Justice Brennan would appreciate the value of consulting the most specific tradition available, since he acknowledges that "[e]ven if we can agree ... that 'family' and 'parenthood' are part of the good life, it is absurd to assume that we can agree on the content of those terms and destructive to pretend that we do." Because such general traditions provide such imprecise guidance, they permit judges to dictate rather than discern the society's views. The need, if arbitrary decision-making is to be avoided, to adopt the most specific tradition as the point of reference—or at least to announce, as Justice Brennan declines to do, some other criterion for selecting among the innumerable relevant traditions that could be consulted—is well enough exemplified by the fact that in the present case Justice Brennan's opinion and Justice O'Connor's opinion, which disapproves this footnote, *both* appeal to tradition, but on the basis of the tradition they select reach opposite results. Although assuredly having the virtue (if it be that) of leaving judges free to decide as they think best when the unanticipated occurs, a rule of law that binds neither by text nor by any particular, identifiable tradition, is no rule of law at all. Finally, we may note that this analysis is not inconsis-

tent with the result in cases such as Griswold v. Connecticut, 381 U.S. 479 (1965), or Eisenstadt v. Baird, 405 U.S. 438 (1972). None of those cases acknowledged a longstanding and still extant societal tradition withholding the very right pronounced to be the subject of a liberty interest and then rejected it. Justice Brennan must do so here. In this case, the existence of such a tradition, continuing to the present day, refutes any possible contention that the alleged right is "so rooted in the traditions and conscience of our people as to be ranked as fundamental," Snyder v. Massachusetts, 291 U.S. 97, 105 (1934), or "implicit in the concept of ordered liberty," Palko v. Connecticut, 302 U.S. 319, 325 (1937).

[7] Justice Brennan chides us for thus limiting our holding to situations in which ... the husband and wife wish to raise her child jointly.... We limit our pronouncement to the relevant facts of this case because it is at least possible that our traditions lead to a different conclusion with regard to adulterous fathering of a child whom the marital parents do not wish to raise as their own. It seems unfair for those who disagree with our holding to include among their criticisms that we have not extended the holding more broadly.

(whatever that means), Gerald must equivalently have a "freedom to conform." One of them will pay a price for asserting that "freedom"—Michael by being unable to act as father of the child he has adulterously begotten, or Gerald by being unable to preserve the integrity of the traditional family unit he and Victoria have established. Our disposition does not choose between these two "freedoms," but leaves that to the people of California. Justice Brennan's approach chooses one of them as the constitutional imperative, on no apparent basis except that the unconventional is to be preferred.

IV

We have never had occasion to decide whether a child has a liberty interest, symmetrical with that of her parent, in maintaining her filial relationship. We need not do so here because, even assuming that such a right exists, Victoria's claim must fail. Victoria's due process challenge is, if anything, weaker than Michael's.... [S]he claims a due process right to maintain filial relationships with both Michael and Gerald. This assertion merits little discussion, for, whatever the merits of the guardian ad litem's belief that such an arrangement can be of great psychological benefit to a child, the claim that a State must recognize multiple fatherhood has no support in the history or traditions of this country. Moreover, even if [her claim is only that] she has a liberty interest in maintaining a filial relationship with her natural father, Michael, we find that, at best, her claim is the obverse of Michael's and fails for the same reasons.

. . .

The judgment of the California Court of Appeal is Affirmed.

Justice O'Connor, with whom Justice Kennedy joins, concurring in part.

I concur in all but footnote 6 of Justice Scalia's opinion. This footnote sketches a mode of historical analysis to be used when identifying liberty interests protected by the Due Process Clause of the Fourteenth Amendment that may be somewhat inconsistent with our past decisions in this area. See Griswold v. Connecticut, 381 U.S. 479 (1965); Eisenstadt v. Baird, 405 U.S. 438 (1972). On occasion the Court has characterized relevant traditions protecting asserted rights at levels of generality that might not be "the most specific level" available. See Loving v. Virginia, 388 U.S. 1, 12 (1967); Turner v. Safley, 482 U.S. 78, 94 (1987).... I would not foreclose the unanticipated by the prior imposition of a single mode of historical analysis. Poe v. Ullman, 367 U.S. 497, 542, 544 (1961) (Harlan, J., dissenting).

Justice Stevens, concurring in the judgment.

As I understand this case, it raises two different questions about the validity of California's statutory scheme. First, is [§ 621] unconstitutional because it prevents Michael and Victoria from obtaining a judicial determination that he is her biological father—even if no legal rights would be affected by that determination? Second, does the California statute deny appellants a fair opportunity to prove that Victoria's best interests would be served by granting Michael visitation rights?

On the first issue I agree with Justice Scalia that the Federal Constitution imposes no obligation upon a State to "declare facts unless some legal consequence hinges upon the requested declaration." ...

On the second issue I do not agree with Justice Scalia's analysis. He seems to reject the possibility that a natural father might ever have a constitutionally protected interest in his relationship with a child whose mother was married to and cohabiting with another man at the time of the child's conception and birth. I think cases like Stanley v. Illinois, 405 U.S. 645 (1972) and Caban v. Mohammed, 441 U.S. 380 (1979), demonstrate that enduring "family" relationships may develop in unconventional settings. I therefore would not foreclose the possibility that a constitutionally protected relationship between a natural father and his child might exist in a case like this. Indeed, I am willing to assume for the purpose of deciding this case that Michael's relationship with Victoria is strong enough to give him a constitutional right to try to convince a trial judge that Victoria's best interest would be served by granting him visitation rights. I am satisfied, however, that the California statute, as applied in this case, gave him that opportunity.

Section 4601 ... plainly gave the trial judge the authority to grant Michael "reasonable visitation rights."

I recognize that my colleagues have interpreted § 621 as creating an absolute bar that would prevent a California trial judge from regarding the natural father as either a "parent" within the meaning of the first sentence of § 4601 or as "any other person" within the meaning of the second sentence. That is not only an unnatural reading of the statute's plain language, but it is also not consistent with the California courts' reading of the statute....

... [T]he trial judge ... considered the effect of § 4601 and expressly found "that, at the present time, it is not in the best interests of the child that the Plaintiff have visitation. The Court believes that the existence of two (2) 'fathers' as male authority figures will confuse the child and be counter-productive to her best interests." ...

... Because I am convinced that the trial judge had the authority under state law both to hear Michael's plea for visitation rights and to grant him such rights if Victoria's best interests so warranted, I am satisfied that the California statutory scheme is consistent with the Due Process Clause of the Fourteenth Amendment.

. . .

Justice Brennan, with whom Justice Marshall and Justice Blackmun join, dissenting.

In a case that has yielded so many opinions as has this one, it is fruitful to begin by emphasizing the common ground shared by a majority of this Court. Five Members of the Court refuse to foreclose "the possibility that a natural father might ever have a constitutionally protected interest in his relationship with a child whose mother was married to and cohabiting with another man at the time of the child's conception and birth." (Stevens, J., concurring in judgment). Five Justices agree that the flaw inhering in a conclusive presumption that terminates a constitutionally protected interest without any hearing whatsoever is a *procedural* one. See infra; (White, J., dissenting); (Stevens, J., concurring in judgment). Four Members of the Court agree that Michael H. has a liberty interest in his relationship with Victoria, see infra; (White, J., dissenting), and one assumes for purposes of this case that he does, (Stevens, J., concurring in judgment).

In contrast, only two Members of the Court fully endorse Justice Scalia's view of the proper method of analyzing questions arising under the Due Process Clause. See O'Connor, J., concurring in part....

I

. . .

... [T]he plurality pretends that tradition places a discernible border around the Constitution. The pretense is seductive; it would be comforting to believe that a search for "tradition" involves nothing more idiosyncratic or complicated than poring through dusty volumes on American history. Yet, as Justice White observed in his dissent in Moore v. East Cleveland, 431 U.S. 494, 549 (1977): "What the deeply rooted traditions of the country are is arguable." Indeed, wherever I would begin to look for an interest "deeply rooted in the country's traditions," one thing is certain: I would not stop (as does the plurality) at Bracton, or Blackstone, or Kent, or even the American Law Reports in conducting my search. Because reasonable people can disagree about the content of particular traditions, and because they can disagree even about which traditions are relevant to the definition of "liberty," the plurality has not found the objective boundary that it seeks.

Even if we could agree, moreover, on the content and significance of particular traditions, we still would be forced to identify the point at which a tradition becomes firm enough to be relevant to our definition of liberty and the moment at which it becomes too obsolete to be relevant any longer. The plurality supplies no objective means by which we might make these determinations. Indeed, as soon as the plurality sees signs that the tradition upon which it bases its decision (the laws denying putative fathers like Michael standing to assert paternity) is crumbling, it shifts ground and says that the case has nothing to do with that tradition, after all. "What is at issue here," the plurality asserts after canvassing the law on paternity suits, "is not entitlement to a state pronouncement that Victoria was begotten by Michael." But that is precisely what is at issue here, and the plurality's last-minute denial of this fact dramatically illustrates the subjectivity of its own analysis.

It is ironic that an approach so utterly dependent on tradition is so indifferent to our precedents. Citing barely a handful of this Court's numerous decisions defining the scope of the liberty protected by the Due Process Clause to support its reliance on tradition, the plurality acts as though English legal treatises and the American Law Reports always have provided the sole source for our constitutional principles. They have not. Just as common-law notions no longer define the "property" that the Constitution protects, see Goldberg v. Kelly, 397 U.S. 254 (1970), neither do they circumscribe the "liberty" that it guarantees. On the contrary, " '[l]iberty' and 'property' are broad and majestic terms. They are among the '[g]reat [constitutional] concepts ... purposely left to gather meaning from experience.... [T]hey relate to the whole domain of social and economic fact, and the statesmen who founded this Nation knew too well that only a stagnant society remains unchanged.' " Board of Regents of State Colleges v. Roth, 408 U.S. 564, 571 (1972)....

It is not that tradition has been irrelevant to our prior decisions. Throughout our decisionmaking in this important area runs the theme that certain interests and practices—freedom from physical restraint, marriage, childbearing, childrearing, and others—form the core of our definition of "liberty." Our solicitude for these interests is partly the result of the fact that the Due Process Clause would seem an empty promise if it did not protect them, and partly the result of the historical and traditional importance of these interests in our society. In deciding cases arising under the Due Process Clause, therefore, we have considered whether the concrete limitation under consideration impermissibly impinges upon one of these more generalized interests.

Today's plurality, however, does not ask whether parenthood is an interest that historically has received our attention and protection; the answer to that question is too clear for dispute. Instead, the plurality asks whether the specific variety of parenthood under consideration—a natural father's relationship with a child whose mother is married to another man—has enjoyed such protection.

If we had looked to tradition with such specificity in past cases, many a decision would have reached a different result. Surely the use of contraceptives by unmarried couples, Eisenstadt v. Baird, 405 U.S. 438 (1972), or even by married couples, Griswold v. Connecticut, 381 U.S. 479 (1965); the freedom from corporal punishment in schools, Ingraham v. Wright, 430 U.S. 651 (1977); the freedom from an arbitrary transfer from a prison to a psychiatric institution, Vitek v. Jones, 445 U.S. 480 (1980); and even the right to raise one's natural but illegitimate children, Stanley v. Illinois, 405 U.S. 645 (1972), were not "interest[s] traditionally protected by our society," at the time of their consideration by this Court. If we had asked, therefore, in *Eisenstadt, Griswold, Ingraham, Vitek,* or *Stanley* itself whether the specific interest under consideration had been traditionally protected, the answer would have been a resounding "no." That we did not ask this question in those cases highlights the novelty of the interpretive method that the plurality opinion employs today.

. . .

. . . We are not an assimilative, homogeneous society, but a facilitative, pluralistic one, in which we must be willing to abide someone else's unfamiliar or even repellant practice because the same tolerant impulse protects our own idiosyncracies. . . . "[L]iberty" must include the freedom not to conform. The plurality today squashes this freedom by requiring specific approval from history before protecting anything in the name of liberty.

. . .

II

. . .

. . . The better approach . . . is to ask whether the specific parent-child relationship under consideration is close enough to the interests that we already have protected to be deemed an aspect of "liberty" as well. [T]he question is not what "level of generality" should be used to describe the relationship between Michael and Victoria, but whether the relationship under consideration is sufficiently substantial to qualify as a liberty interest under our prior cases.

. . . [Those] cases have produced a unifying theme: although an unwed father's biological link to his child does not, in and of itself, guarantee him a constitutional stake in his relationship with that child, such a link combined with a substantial parent-child relationship will do so. . . .

. . .

The plurality's . . . language suggests that if Carole or Gerald alone wished to raise Victoria, or if both were dead and the State wished to raise her, Michael and Victoria might be found to have a liberty interest in their relationship with each other. But that would be to say that whether Michael and Victoria have a liberty interest varies with the State's interest in recognizing that interest, for it is the State's interest in protecting the marital family—and not Michael and Victoria's interest in their relationship with each other—that varies with the status of Carole and Gerald's relationship. It is a bad day for due process when the State's interest in terminating a parent-child relationship is reason to conclude that that relationship is not part of the "liberty" protected by the Fourteenth Amendment.

. . .

. . . [Also, i]n announcing that what matters is not the father's ability to claim paternity, but his ability to obtain "substantive parental rights," the plurality turns procedural due process upside down. Michael's challenge in this Court does not depend on his ability ultimately to obtain visitation rights; it would be strange indeed if, before one could be granted a hearing, one were required to prove that one would prevail on the merits. The point of procedural due process is to give the litigant a fair chance at prevailing, not to ensure a particular substantive outcome. . . .

III

Because the plurality decides that Michael and Victoria have no liberty interest in their relationship with each other, it need consider neither the effect of § 621 on their relationship nor the State's interest in bringing about that effect. It is obvious, however, that the effect of § 621 is to terminate the relationship between Michael and Victoria before affording any hearing whatsoever on the issue whether Michael is Victoria's father. This refusal to hold a hearing is properly analyzed under our procedural due process cases, which instruct us to consider the State's interest in curtailing the procedures accompanying the termination of a constitutionally protected interest. California's interest, minute in comparison with a father's interest in his relationship with his child, cannot justify its refusal to hear Michael out on his claim that he is Victoria's father.

A

. . . What Michael wants is a chance to show that he is Victoria's father. By depriving him of this opportunity, California prevents Michael from taking advantage of the best-interest standard embodied in § 4601 of California's Civil Code, which directs that *parents* be given visitation rights unless "the visitation would be detrimental to the best interests of the child." . . .

As interpreted by the California courts, . . . § 621 . . . also deprives him of any chance of maintaining his relationship with the child he claims to be his own. When, as a result of § 621, a putative father may not establish his paternity, neither may he obtain discretionary visitation rights as a "nonparent" under § 4601. . . . Justice Stevens' assertion to the contrary is mere wishful thinking. . . .

. . .

Section 621 as construed by the California courts thus cuts off the relationship between Michael and Victoria—a liberty interest protected by the Due Process Clause—without affording the least bit of process. This case, in other words, involves a conclusive presumption that is used to terminate a constitutionally protected interest—the kind of rule that our preoccupation with procedural fairness has caused us to condemn. See, e.g., Vlandis v. Kline, 412 U.S. 441 (1973); Cleveland Board of Education v. LaFleur, 414 U.S. 632 (1974); Weinberger v. Salfi, 422 U.S. 749, 770–772 (1975).

Gerald D. and the plurality . . . protest [ ]that, instead of being a conclusive presumption, it is a "substantive rule of law." . . . It may be that all conclusive presumptions are, in a sense, substantive rules of law; but § 621 then belongs in that special category of substantive rules that presumes a fact relevant to a certain class of litigation, and it is that feature that renders § 621 suspect under our prior cases. To put the point differently, a conclusive presumption takes the form of "no X's are Y's," and is typically accompanied by a rule such as, "... and only Y's may obtain a driver's license." ... Ignoring the fact that § 621 takes the form of "no X's are Y's," Gerald D. and the plurality fix upon the rule following § 621—only Y's may assert parental rights—and call § 621 a substantive rule of law....

In a further effort to show that § 621 is not a conclusive presumption, Gerald D. claims—and the plurality agrees—that whether a man is the biological father of a child whose family situation places the putative father within § 621 is simply irrelevant to the State. This is, I surmise, an attempt to avoid the implications of our cases condemning the presumption of a fact that a State has made relevant or decisive to a particular decision. See, e.g., Bell v. Burson, 402 U.S. 535 (1971). Yet the claim that California does not care about factual paternity is patently false. California cares very much about factual paternity when the husband is impotent or sterile ...; it cares very much about it when the wife and husband do not share the same home ...; and it cares very much about it when the husband himself declares that he is not the father.... Indeed, under California law as currently structured, paternity is decisive in choosing the standard that will be used in granting or denying custody or visitation. The State, though selective in its concern for factual paternity, certainly is not *indifferent* to it.[9] More fundamentally, ... [t]o say that California does not care about factual paternity in the limited circumstances of this case—where the husband is neither impotent nor sterile nor living apart from his wife—is simply another way of describing its conclusive presumption.

... [T]he plurality goes on to argue that a challenge to a conclusive presumption must rest on substantive rather than procedural due process. This is simply not so. In Weinberger v. Salfi, supra, the Court identified two lines of cases involving challenges to social-welfare legislation: those in which a legislative classification was challenged as arbitrary, and those in which a conclusive presumption was attacked. The Court fit the complaint in *Salfi* into the former category on the ground that the challenged law did not deprive anyone of a constitutionally protected interest.... Today's plurality, in contrast, classifies this case as one invoking substantive due process *before* it considers the nature of the interest at stake.... [The plurality fails] to recognize that the defect from which conclusive presumptions suffer is a *procedural* one: the State has declared a certain fact relevant, indeed controlling, yet has denied a particular class of litigants a hearing to establish that fact. This is precisely the kind of flaw that procedural due process is designed to correct.

B

. . .

[T]o say that the State must provide Michael with a hearing to prove his paternity is not to express any opinion of the ultimate state of affairs between Michael and Victoria and Carole and Gerald.... Michael first must convince a court that he is Victoria's father, and even if he is able to do this, he will be denied visitation rights if that would be in Victoria's best interests. See

---

[9] In this respect, the plurality is mistaken in suggesting that "there is no difference between a rule which says that the marital husband shall be irrebuttably presumed to be the father, and a rule which says that the adulterous natural father shall not be recognized as the legal father." In the latter case, the State has not made paternity the predominant concern in child-custody disputes and then told some putative fathers that they may not prove their paternity.

Cal.Civ.Code Ann. § 4601 (West Supp.1989). It is elementary that a determination that a State must afford procedures before it terminates a given right is not a prediction about the end result of those procedures.

. . .

Justice White, with whom Justice Brennan joins, dissenting.

California law, as the plurality describes it, tells us that, except in limited circumstances, California declares it to be *"irrelevant* for paternity purposes whether a child conceived during and born into a lawful marriage was begotten by someone other than the husband," (emphasis in original). This I do not accept, for the fact that Michael H. is the biological father of Victoria is to me highly relevant to whether he has rights, as a father or otherwise, with respect to the child. Because I believe that Michael H. has a liberty interest that cannot be denied without due process of the law, I must dissent.

I

Like Justices Brennan, Marshall, Blackmun and Stevens, I do not agree with the plurality opinion's conclusion that a natural father can never "have a constitutionally protected interest in his relationship with a child whose mother was married to and cohabiting with another man at the time of the child's conception and birth." (Stevens, J., concurring in judgment). . . . The basic principle enunciated in the Court's unwed father cases is that an unwed father who has demonstrated a sufficient commitment to his paternity by way of personal, financial, or custodial responsibilities has a protected liberty interest in a relationship with his child.

We have not before faced the question of a biological father's relationship with his child when the child was born while the mother was married to another man. On several occasions however, we have considered whether a biological father has a constitutionally cognizable interest in an opportunity to establish paternity. Stanley v. Illinois, 405 U.S. 645 (1972), recognized the biological father's right to a legal relationship with his illegitimate child, holding that the Due Process Clause of the Fourteenth Amendment entitled the biological father to a hearing on his fitness before his illegitimate children could be removed from his custody. . . .

Quilloin v. Walcott, 434 U.S. 246, 255 (1978), also expressly recognized due process rights in the biological father, even while holding that those rights were not impermissibly burdened by the State's application of a "best interests of the child" standard. Caban v. Mohammed, 441 U.S. 380 (1979), invalidated on equal protection grounds a statute under which a man's children could be adopted by their natural mother and her husband without the natural father's consent.

In Lehr v. Robertson, 463 U.S. 248, 261–262 (1983), . . . the Court said clearly that fathers who have participated in raising their illegitimate children and have developed a relationship with them have constitutionally protected parental rights. Indeed, . . . *Lehr* suggested that States must provide a biological father of an illegitimate child the means by which he may establish his paternity so that he may have the opportunity to develop a relationship with his child. The Court upheld a stepparent adoption over the natural father's objections, but acknowledged that "the existence or nonexistence of a substantial relationship between parent and child is a relevant criterion in evaluating both the rights of the parent and the best interests of the child." . . . [H]owever, the father had never established a custodial, personal or financial relationship with his child. . . .

In the case now before us, Michael H. is ... a father who has asserted his interests in raising and providing for his child since the very time of the child's birth.... Michael and Victoria lived together (albeit intermittently, given Carole's itinerant life style.) There is a personal and emotional relationship between Michael and Victoria, who grew up calling him "Daddy." Michael H. held Victoria out as his daughter and contributed to the child's financial support. The mother has never denied, and indeed has admitted that Michael H. is Victoria's father.... "When an unwed father demonstrates a full commitment to the responsibilities of parenthood by 'com[ing] forward to participate in the rearing of his child,' Caban, 441 U.S., at 392, his interest in personal contact with his child acquires substantial protection under the Due Process Clause." *Lehr,* supra, at 261. The facts in this case satisfy the *Lehr* criteria, which focused on the relationship between father and child, not on the relationship between father and mother. Under *Lehr* a "mere biological relationship" is not enough, but in light of Carole's vicissitudes, what more could Michael H. have done? It is clear enough that Michael H. ...has a liberty interest entitled to protection under the Due Process Clause of the Fourteenth Amendment.

II

California plainly denies Michael this protection.... California law not only deprives Michael H. of a legal parent-child relationship with his daughter Victoria but even denies him the opportunity to introduce blood-test evidence to rebut the demonstrable fiction that Gerald is Victoria's father.[3] Unlike *Lehr,* Michael H. has not been denied notice. He has, most definitely, however, been denied any real opportunity to be heard. The grant of summary judgment against Michael H. was based on the conclusive presumption of Cal.Evid.Code Ann. § 621 (West Supp.1989), which denied him the opportunity to prove that he is Victoria's biological father. The Court gives its blessing to § 621 by relying on the State's asserted interests in the integrity of the family (defined as Carole and Gerald) and in protecting Victoria from the stigma of illegitimacy and by balancing away Michael's interest in establishing that he is the father of the child.

The interest in protecting a child from the social stigma of illegitimacy lacks any real connection to the facts of a case where a father is seeking to establish, rather than repudiate, paternity. The "stigma of illegitimacy" argument harks back to ancient common law when there were no blood tests to ascertain that the husband could not "by the laws of nature" be the child's father. Judicial process refused to declare that a child born in wedlock was illegitimate unless the proof was positive. The only such proof was physical absence or impotency.... [W]hatever stigma remains in today's society is far less compelling in the context of a child of a married mother, especially when there is a father asserting paternity and seeking a relationship with his child. It is hardly rare in this world of divorce and remarriage for a child to live with the "father" to whom her mother is married, and still have a relationship with her biological father.

The State's professed interest in the preservation of the existing marital unit is a more significant concern. To be sure, the intrusion of an outsider asserting that he is the father of a child whom the husband believes to be his

---

[3] While the ultimate resolution of Michael's case, were he permitted to introduce such evidence, might well be visitation rights or even custody of the child, it is important to keep in mind that the question at issue here is not whether he should be granted visitation or custody but simply whether he can take the first step in any such proceeding....

own would be disruptive to say the least. On the facts of this case, however, Gerald was well aware of the liaison between Carole and Michael. The conclusive presumption of evidentiary rule § 621 virtually eliminates the putative father's chances of succeeding in his effort to establish paternity, but it by no means prevents him from asserting the claim. It may serve as a deterrent to such claims but does not eliminate the threat. Further, the argument that the conclusive presumption preserved the sanctity of the marital unit had more sway in a time when the husband was similarly prevented from challenging paternity.[4]

. . .

As the Court has said: "The significance of the biological connection is that it offers the natural father an opportunity that no other male possesses to develop a relationship with his offspring. If he grasps that opportunity and accepts some measure of responsibility for the child's future, he may enjoy the blessings of the parent-child relationship and make uniquely valuable contributions to the child's development." *Lehr*. . . . Michael H. eagerly grasped the opportunity to have a relationship with his daughter (he lived with her; he declared her to be his child; he provided financial support for her) and still, with today's opinion, his opportunity has vanished. He has been rendered a stranger to his child.

. . .

C. PERSONAL AUTONOMY

EISENSTADT v. BAIRD, 405 U.S. 438 (1972). In a prosecution of a defendant for giving a contraceptive to an unmarried person the Court had before it, among others, the question whether it was a denial of equal protection of the laws to permit the distribution of contraceptives to married persons but not to unmarried. One argument made to sustain the classification was that contraceptives were considered immoral. The counter argument was that under Griswold v. Connecticut it would be a denial of due process to prohibit the distribution of contraceptives. The Court said it did not need to decide the issue, but did make the following observation: "If the right of privacy means anything, it is the right of the *individual,* married or single, to be free from unwarranted governmental intrusion into matters so fundamentally affecting a person as the decision whether to bear or beget a child."

Roe v. Wade

410 U.S. 113, 93 S.Ct. 705, 35 L.Ed.2d 147 (1973).

Mr. Justice Blackmun delivered the opinion of the Court.

This Texas federal appeal and its Georgia companion, Doe v. Bolton, post, 410 U.S. 179, present constitutional challenges to state criminal abortion legislation. The Texas statutes under attack here are typical of those that have been in effect in many States for approximately a century. The Georgia statutes, in contrast, have a modern cast and are a legislative product that, to

---

[4] . . . In 1980, the California Legislature amended § 621 of its Evidence Code in order to permit the husband an opportunity to overcome the presumption that he is the father of his wife's child if he raises the notice of motion for blood tests not later than two years from the birth of the child. (So much for the State's interest in protecting the child from the stigma of illegitimacy!)

an extent at least, obviously reflects the influences of recent attitudinal change, of advancing medical knowledge and techniques, and of new thinking about an old issue.

We forthwith acknowledge our awareness of the sensitive and emotional nature of the abortion controversy, of the vigorous opposing views, even among physicians, and of the deep and seemingly absolute convictions that the subject inspires. One's philosophy, one's experiences, one's exposure to the raw edges of human existence, one's religious training, one's attitudes toward life and family and their values, and the moral standards one establishes and seeks to observe, are all likely to influence and to color one's thinking and conclusions about abortion.

In addition, population growth, pollution, poverty, and racial overtones tend to complicate and not to simplify the problem.

Our task, of course, is to resolve the issue by constitutional measurement free of emotion and of predilection. We seek earnestly to do this, and, because we do, we have inquired into, and in this opinion place some emphasis upon, medical and medical-legal history and what that history reveals about man's attitudes toward the abortive procedure over the centuries. We bear in mind, too, Mr. Justice Holmes' admonition in his now vindicated dissent in Lochner v. New York, 198 U.S. 45, 76 (1905):

> "It [the Constitution] is made for people of fundamentally differing views, and the accident of our finding certain opinions natural and familiar, or novel, and even shocking, ought not to conclude our judgment upon the question whether statutes embodying them conflict with the Constitution of the United States."

I.

The Texas statutes that concern us here are Arts. 1191–1194 and 1196 of the State's Penal Code, Vernon's Ann.P.C. These make it a crime to "procure an abortion," as therein defined, or to attempt one, except with respect to "an abortion procured or attempted by medical advice for the purpose of saving the life of the mother." Similar statutes are in existence in a majority of the States.

. . .

V.

The principal thrust of appellant's attack on the Texas statutes is that they improperly invade a right, said to be possessed by the pregnant woman, to choose to terminate her pregnancy. Appellant would discover this right in the concept of personal "liberty" embodied in the Fourteenth Amendment's Due Process Clause; or in personal, marital, familial, and sexual privacy said to be protected by the Bill of Rights or its penumbras, see Griswold v. Connecticut, 381 U.S. 479 (1965); Eisenstadt v. Baird, 405 U.S. 438 (1972); id., at 460 (White, J., concurring); or among those rights reserved to the people by the Ninth Amendment, Griswold v. Connecticut, 381 U.S., at 486 (Goldberg, J., concurring). Before addressing this claim, we feel it desirable briefly to survey, in several aspects, the history of abortion, for such insight as that history may afford us, and then to examine the state purposes and interests behind the criminal abortion laws.

. . .

[The Court's long historical discussion is omitted.]

VII.

Three reasons have been advanced to explain historically the enactment of criminal abortion laws in the 19th century and to justify their continued existence.

It has been argued occasionally that these laws were the product of a Victorian social concern to discourage illicit sexual conduct. Texas, however, does not advance this justification in the present case, and it appears that no court or commentator has taken the argument seriously. . . .

A second reason is concerned with abortion as a medical procedure. When most criminal abortion laws were first enacted, the procedure was a hazardous one for the woman. . . .

Modern medical techniques have altered this situation. Appellants and various *amici* refer to medical data indicating that abortion in early pregnancy, that is, prior to the end of first trimester, although not without its risk, is now relatively safe. Mortality rates for women undergoing early abortions, where the procedure is legal, appear to be as low as or lower than the rates for normal childbirth. Consequently, any interest of the State in protecting the woman from an inherently hazardous procedure, except when it would be equally dangerous for her to forgo it, has largely disappeared. Of course, important state interests in the area of health and medical standards do remain. The State has a legitimate interest in seeing to it that abortion, like any other medical procedure, is performed under circumstances that insure maximum safety for the patient. This interest obviously extends at least to the performing physician and his staff, to the facilities involved, to the availability of aftercare, and to adequate provision for any complication or emergency that might arise. The prevalence of high mortality rates at illegal "abortion mills" strengthens, rather than weakens, the State's interest in regulating the conditions under which abortions are performed. Moreover, the risk to the woman increases as her pregnancy continues. Thus the State retains a definite interest in protecting the woman's own health and safety when an abortion is proposed at a late stage of pregnancy.

The third reason is the State's interest—some phrase it in terms of duty— in protecting prenatal life. Some of the argument for this justification rests on the theory that a new human life is present from the moment of conception. The State's interest and general obligation to protect life then extends, it is argued, to prenatal life. Only when the life of the pregnant mother herself is at stake, balanced against the life she carries within her, should the interest of the embryo or fetus not prevail. Logically, of course, a legitimate state interest in this area need not stand or fall on acceptance of the belief that life begins at conception or at some other point prior to live birth. In assessing the State's interest, recognition may be given to the less rigid claim that as long as at least *potential* life is involved, the State may assert interests beyond the protection of the pregnant woman alone.

Parties challenging state abortion laws have sharply disputed in some courts the contention that a purpose of these laws, when enacted, was to protect prenatal life. Pointing to the absence of legislative history to support the contention, they claim that most state laws were designed solely to protect the woman. Because medical advances have lessened this concern, at least with respect to abortion in early pregnancy, they argue that with respect to such abortions the laws can no longer be justified by any state interest. There is some scholarly support for this view of original purpose. The few state courts called upon to interpret their laws in the late 19th and early 20th centuries did focus on the State's interest in protecting the woman's health rather than in preserving the embryo and fetus. Proponents of this view point out that in many States, including Texas, by statute or judicial interpretation, the pregnant woman herself could not be prosecuted for self-abortion or for cooperating in an abortion performed upon her by another. They claim that adoption of the "quickening" distinction through received common law and state statutes tacitly recognizes the greater health hazards inherent in late abortion and impliedly repudiates the theory that life begins at conception.

It is with these interests, and the weight to be attached to them, that this case is concerned.

VIII.

The Constitution does not explicitly mention any right of privacy. In a line of decisions, however, going back perhaps as far as Union Pacific R. Co. v. Botsford, 141 U.S. 250, 251 (1891), the Court has recognized that a right of personal privacy, or a guarantee of certain areas or zones of privacy, does exist under the Constitution. In varying contexts the Court or individual Justices have indeed found at least the roots of that right in the First Amendment, Stanley v. Georgia, 394 U.S. 557, 564 (1969); in the Fourth and Fifth Amendments, Terry v. Ohio, 392 U.S. 1, 8–9 (1968), Katz v. United States, 389 U.S. 347, 350 (1967); Boyd v. United States, 116 U.S. 616 (1886), see Olmstead v. United States, 277 U.S. 438, 478 (1928) (Brandeis, J., dissenting); in the penumbras of the Bill of Rights, Griswold v. Connecticut, 381 U.S. 479, 484–485 (1965); in the Ninth Amendment, id., at 486 (Goldberg, J., concurring); or in the concept of liberty guaranteed by the first section of the Fourteenth Amendment, see Meyer v. Nebraska, 262 U.S. 390, 399 (1923). These decisions make it clear that only personal rights that can be deemed "fundamental" or "implicit in the concept of ordered liberty," Palko v. Connecticut, 302 U.S. 319, 325 (1937), are included in this guarantee of personal privacy. They also make it clear that the right has some extension to activities relating to marriage, Loving v. Virginia, 388 U.S. 1, 12 (1967), procreation, Skinner v. Oklahoma, 316 U.S. 535 (1942), contraception, Eisenstadt v. Baird, 405 U.S. 438, 453–454 (1972); id., at 460, 463–465 (White, J., concurring), family relationships, Prince v. Massachusetts, 321 U.S. 158, 166 (1944), and child rearing and education, Pierce v. Society of Sisters, 268 U.S. 510, 535 (1925), Meyer v. Nebraska, supra.

This right of privacy, whether it be founded in the Fourteenth Amendment's concept of personal liberty and restrictions upon state action, as we feel it is, or, as the District Court determined, in the Ninth Amendment's reservation of rights to the people, is broad enough to encompass a woman's decision whether or not to terminate her pregnancy. The detriment that the State would impose upon the pregnant woman by denying this choice altogether is apparent. Specific and direct harm medically diagnosable even in early pregnancy may be involved. Maternity, or additional offspring, may force upon the woman a distressful life and future. Psychological harm may be imminent. Mental and physical health may be taxed by child care. There is also the distress, for all concerned, associated with the unwanted child, and there is the problem of bringing a child into a family already unable, psychologically and otherwise, to care for it. In other cases, as in this one, the additional difficulties and continuing stigma of unwed motherhood may be involved. All these are factors the woman and her responsible physician necessarily will consider in consultation.

On the basis of elements such as these, appellants and some *amici* argue that the woman's right is absolute and that she is entitled to terminate her pregnancy at whatever time, in whatever way, and for whatever reason she alone chooses. With this we do not agree. Appellants' arguments that Texas either has no valid interest at all in regulating the abortion decision, or no interest strong enough to support any limitation upon the woman's sole determination, is unpersuasive. The Court's decisions recognizing a right of privacy also acknowledge that some state regulation in areas protected by that right is appropriate. As noted above, a state may properly assert important interests in safeguarding health, in maintaining medical standards, and in protecting potential life. At some point in pregnancy, these respective interests become sufficiently compelling to sustain regulation of the factors that govern the abortion decision. The privacy right involved, therefore, cannot be said to be absolute. In fact, it is not clear to us that the claim asserted by some *amici* that one has an unlimited right to do with one's body as one pleases bears a close relationship to the right of privacy previously articulated in the Court's decisions. The Court has refused to recognize an unlimited right of this kind in the past. Jacobson v. Massachusetts, 197 U.S. 11 (1905) (vaccination); Buck v. Bell, 274 U.S. 200 (1927) (sterilization).

We therefore conclude that the right of personal privacy includes the abortion decision, but that this right is not unqualified and must be considered against important state interests in regulation.

We note that those federal and state courts that have recently considered abortion law challenges have reached the same conclusion. A majority, in addition to the District Court in the present case, have held state laws unconstitutional, at least in part, because of vagueness or because of over-breadth and abridgment of rights. . . .

Although the results are divided, most of these courts have agreed that the right of privacy, however based, is broad enough to cover the abortion decision; that the right, nonetheless, is not absolute and is subject to some limitations; and that at some point the state interests as to protection of health, medical standards, and prenatal life, become dominant. We agree with this approach.

Where certain "fundamental rights" are involved, the Court has held that regulation limiting these rights may be justified only by a "compelling state interest," Kramer v. Union Free School District, 395 U.S. 621, 627 (1969); Shapiro v. Thompson, 394 U.S. 618, 634 (1969); Sherbert v. Verner, 374 U.S. 398, 406 (1963), and that legislative enactments must be narrowly drawn to express only the legitimate state interests at stake. Griswold v. Connecticut, 381 U.S. 479, 485 (1965); Aptheker v. Secretary of State, 378 U.S. 500, 508 (1964); Cantwell v. Connecticut, 310 U.S. 296, 307–308 (1940); see Eisenstadt v. Baird, 405 U.S. 438, 460, 463–464 (1972) (White, J., concurring).

In the recent abortion cases . . . courts have recognized these principles. Those striking down state laws have generally scrutinized the State's interest in protecting health and potential life and have concluded that neither interest justified broad limitations on the reasons for which a physician and his pregnant patient might decide that she should have an abortion in the early stages of pregnancy. Courts sustaining state laws have held that the State's determinations to protect health or prenatal life are dominant and constitutionally justifiable.

IX.

The District Court held that the appellee failed to meet his burden of demonstrating that the Texas statute's infringement upon Roe's rights was necessary to support a compelling state interest, and that, although the defendant presented "several compelling justifications for state presence in the area of abortions," the statutes outstripped these justifications and swept "far beyond any areas of compelling state interest." 314 F.Supp., at 1222–1223. Appellant and appellee both contest that holding. Appellant ... claims an absolute right that bars any state imposition of criminal penalties in the area. Appellee argues that the State's determination to recognize and protect prenatal life from and after conception constitutes a compelling state interest. As noted above, we do not agree fully with either formulation.

A. The appellee and certain *amici* argue that the fetus is a "person" within the language and meaning of the Fourteenth Amendment. In support of this they outline at length and in detail the well-known facts of fetal development. If this suggestion of personhood is established, the appellant's case, of course, collapses, for the fetus' right to life is then guaranteed specifically by the Amendment. The appellant conceded as much on reargument. On the other hand, the appellee conceded on reargument that no case could be cited that holds that a fetus is a person within the meaning of the Fourteenth Amendment.

The Constitution does not define "person" in so many words. Section 1 of the Fourteenth Amendment contains three references to "person." The first, in defining "citizens," speaks of "persons born or naturalized in the United States." The word also appears both in the Due Process Clause and in the Equal Protection Clause. "Person" is used in other places in the Constitution: in the listing of qualifications for representatives and senators, Art. I, § 2, cl. 2, and § 3, cl. 3; in the Apportionment Clause, Art. I, § 2, cl. 3; in the Migration and Importation provision, Art. I, § 9, cl. 1; in the Emolument Clause, Art. I, § 9, cl. 8; in the Electors provisions, Art. II, § 1, cl. 2, and the superseded cl. 3; in the provision outlining qualifications for the office of President, Art. II, § 1, cl. 5; in the Extradition provisions, Art. IV, § 2, cl. 2, and the superseded Fugitive Slave cl. 3; and in the Fifth, Twelfth, and Twenty-second Amendments as well as in §§ 2 and 3 of the Fourteenth Amendment. But in nearly all these instances, the use of the word is such that it has application only postnatally. None indicates, with any assurance, that it has any possible prenatal application.[54]

All this, together with our observation, supra, that throughout the major portion of the 19th century prevailing legal abortion practices were far freer than they are today, persuades us that the word "person," as used in the Fourteenth Amendment, does not include the unborn....

This conclusion, however, does not of itself fully answer the contentions raised by Texas, and we pass on to other considerations.

B. The pregnant woman cannot be isolated in her privacy. She carries an embryo and, later, a fetus, if one accepts the medical definitions of the developing young in the human uterus. See Dorland's Illustrated Medical

---

[54] When Texas urges that a fetus is entitled to Fourteenth Amendment protection as a person, it faces a dilemma. Neither in Texas nor in any other State are all abortions prohibited. Despite broad proscription, an exception always exists. The exception contained in Art. 1196, for an abortion procured or attempted by medical advice for the purpose of saving the life of the mother, is typical. But if the fetus is a person who is not to be deprived of life without due process of law, and if the mother's condition is the sole determinant, does not the Texas exception appear to be out of line with the Amendment's command?

There are other inconsistencies between Fourteenth Amendment status and the typical abortion statute. [I]n Texas the woman is not a principal or an accomplice with respect to an abortion upon her. If the fetus is a person, why is the woman not a principal or an accomplice? Further, the penalty for criminal abortion specified by Art. 1195 is significantly less than the maximum penalty for murder prescribed by Art. 1257 of the Texas Penal Code. If the fetus is a person, may the penalties be different?

Dictionary, 478–479, 547 (24th ed. 1965). The situation therefore is inherently different from marital intimacy, or bedroom possession of obscene material, or marriage, or procreation, or education, with which *Eisenstadt, Griswold, Stanley, Loving, Skinner, Pierce,* and *Meyer* were respectively concerned. As we have intimated above, it is reasonable and appropriate for a State to decide that at some point in time another interest, that of health of the mother or that of potential human life, becomes significantly involved. The woman's privacy is no longer sole and any right of privacy she possesses must be measured accordingly.

Texas urges that, apart from the Fourteenth Amendment, life begins at conception and is present throughout pregnancy, and that, therefore, the State has a compelling interest in protecting that life from and after conception. We need not resolve the difficult question of when life begins. When those trained in the respective disciplines of medicine, philosophy, and theology are unable to arrive at any consensus, the judiciary, at this point in the development of man's knowledge, is not in a position to speculate as to the answer.

It should be sufficient to note briefly the wide divergence of thinking on this most sensitive and difficult question. There has always been strong support for the view that life does not begin until live birth. This was the belief of the Stoics. It appears to be the predominant, though not the unanimous, attitude of the Jewish faith. It may be taken to represent also the position of a large segment of the Protestant community, insofar as that can be ascertained; organized groups that have taken a formal position on the abortion issue have generally regarded abortion as a matter for the conscience of the individual and her family. [T]he common law found greater significance in quickening. Physicians and their scientific colleagues have regarded that event with less interest and have tended to focus either upon conception or upon live birth or upon the interim point at which the fetus becomes "viable," that is, potentially able to live outside the mother's womb, albeit with artificial aid.[59] Viability is usually placed at about seven months (28 weeks) but may occur earlier, even at 24 weeks.[60] The Aristotelian theory of "mediate animation," that held sway throughout the Middle Ages and the Renaissance in Europe, continued to be official Roman Catholic dogma until the 19th century, despite opposition to this "ensoulment" theory from those in the Church who would recognize the existence of life from the moment of conception. The latter is now, of course, the official belief of the Catholic Church. As one of the briefs *amicus* discloses, this is a view strongly held by many non-Catholics as well, and by many physicians. Substantial problems for precise definition of this view are posed, however, by new embryological data that purport to indicate that conception is a "process" over time, rather than an event, and by new medical techniques such as menstrual extraction, the "morning-after" pill, implantation of embryos, artificial insemination, and even artificial wombs.

In areas other than criminal abortion the law has been reluctant to endorse any theory that life, as we recognize it, begins before live birth or to accord legal rights to the unborn except in narrowly defined situations and except when the rights are contingent upon live birth. For example, the traditional rule of tort law had denied recovery for prenatal injuries even though the child was born alive. That rule has been changed in almost every jurisdiction. In most States recovery is said to be permitted only if the fetus was

[59] L. Hellman & J. Pritchard, Williams Obstetrics 493 (14th ed. 1971); Dorland's Illustrated Medical Dictionary 1689 (24th ed. 1965).

[60] Hellman & Pritchard, supra, n. 59, at 493.

viable, or at least quick, when the injuries were sustained, though few courts have squarely so held. In a recent development, generally opposed by the commentators, some States permit the parents of a stillborn child to maintain an action for wrongful death because of prenatal injuries. Such an action, however, would appear to be one to vindicate the parents' interest and is thus consistent with the view that the fetus, at most, represents only the potentiality of life. Similarly, unborn children have been recognized as acquiring rights or interests by way of inheritance or other devolution of property, and have been represented by guardians *ad litem*. Perfection of the interests involved, again, has generally been contingent upon live birth. In short, the unborn have never been recognized in the law as persons in the whole sense.

X.

In view of all this, we do not agree that, by adopting one theory of life, Texas may override the rights of the pregnant woman that are at stake. We repeat, however, that the State does have an important and legitimate interest in preserving and protecting the health of the pregnant woman, whether she be a resident of the State or a non-resident who seeks medical consultation and treatment there, and that it has still *another* important and legitimate interest in protecting the potentiality of human life. These interests are separate and distinct. Each grows in substantiality as the woman approaches term and, at a point during pregnancy, each becomes "compelling."

With respect to the State's important and legitimate interest in the health of the mother, the "compelling" point, in the light of present medical knowledge, is at approximately the end of the first trimester. This is so because of the now established medical fact, referred to above ... that until the end of the first trimester mortality in abortion is less than mortality in normal childbirth. It follows that, from and after this point, a State may regulate the abortion procedure to the extent that the regulation reasonably relates to the preservation and protection of maternal health. Examples of permissible state regulation in this area are requirements as to the qualifications of the person who is to perform the abortion; as to the licensure of that person; as to the facility in which the procedure is to be performed, that is, whether it must be a hospital or may be a clinic or some other place of less-than-hospital status; as to the licensing of the facility; and the like.

This means, on the other hand, that, for the period of pregnancy prior to this "compelling" point, the attending physician, in consultation with his patient, is free to determine, without regulation by the State, that in his medical judgment the patient's pregnancy should be terminated. If that decision is reached, the judgment may be effectuated by an abortion free of interference by the State.

With respect to the State's important and legitimate interest in potential life, the "compelling" point is at viability. This is so because the fetus then presumably has the capability of meaningful life outside the mother's womb. State regulation protective of fetal life after viability thus has both logical and biological justifications. If the State is interested in protecting fetal life after viability, it may go so far as to proscribe abortion during that period except when it is necessary to preserve the life or health of the mother.

Measured against these standards, Art. 1196 of the Texas Penal Code, in restricting legal abortions to those "procured or attempted by medical advice for the purpose of saving the life of the mother," sweeps too broadly. The statute makes no distinction between abortions performed early in pregnancy and those performed later, and it limits to a single reason, "saving" the mother's life, the legal justification for the procedure. The statute, therefore, cannot survive the constitutional attack made upon it here.

This conclusion makes it unnecessary for us to consider the additional challenge to the Texas statute asserted on grounds of vagueness. See United States v. Vuitch, 402 U.S. 62, 67–72 (1971)..

XI.

To summarize and to repeat:

1. A state criminal abortion statute of the current Texas type, that excepts from criminality only a *life saving* procedure on behalf of the mother, without regard to pregnancy stage and without recognition of the other interests involved, is violative of the Due Process Clause of the Fourteenth Amendment.

(a) For the stage prior to approximately the end of the first trimester, the abortion decision and its effectuation must be left to the medical judgment of the pregnant woman's attending physician.

(b) For the stage subsequent to approximately the end of the first trimester, the State, in promoting its interest in the health of the mother, may, if it chooses, regulate the abortion procedure in ways that are reasonably related to maternal health.

(c) For the stage subsequent to viability the State, in promoting its interest in the potentiality of human life, may, if it chooses, regulate, and even proscribe, abortion except where it is necessary, in appropriate medical judgment, for the preservation of the life or health of the mother.

2. The State may define the term "physician," as it has been employed in the preceding numbered paragraphs of this Part XI of this opinion, to mean only a physician currently licensed by the State, and may proscribe any abortion by a person who is not a physician as so defined.

In Doe v. Bolton, 410 U.S. 179, procedural requirements contained in one of the modern abortion statutes are considered. That opinion and this one, of course, are to be read together.

This holding, we feel, is consistent with the relative weights of the respective interests involved, with the lessons and example of medical and legal history, with the lenity of the common law, and with the demands of the profound problems of the present day. The decision leaves the State free to place increasing restrictions on abortion as the period of pregnancy lengthens, so long as those restrictions are tailored to the recognized state interests. The decision vindicates the right of the physician to administer medical treatment according to his professional judgment up to the points where important state interests provide compelling justifications for intervention. Up to those points the abortion decision in all its aspects is inherently, and primarily, a medical decision, and basic responsibility for it must rest with the physician. If an individual practitioner abuses the privilege of exercising proper medical judgment, the usual remedies, judicial and intra-professional, are available.

. . .

Mr. Justice Stewart, concurring.

. . .

Mr. Justice Rehnquist, dissenting.

The Court's opinion brings to the decision of this troubling question both extensive historical fact and a wealth of legal scholarship. While its opinion thus commands my respect, I find myself nonetheless in fundamental disagreement with those parts of it which invalidate the Texas statute in question, and therefore dissent.

. . .

I have difficulty in concluding, as the Court does, that the right of "privacy" is involved in this case. Texas by the statute here challenged bars the performance of a medical abortion by a licensed physician on a plaintiff such as Roe. A transaction resulting in an operation such as this is not "private" in the ordinary usage of that word. Nor is the "privacy" which the Court finds here even a distant relative of the freedom from searches and seizures protected by the Fourth Amendment to the Constitution which the Court has referred to as embodying a right to privacy. Katz v. United States, 389 U.S. 347 (1967).

. . .

The Court eschews the history of the Fourteenth Amendment in its reliance on the "compelling state interest" test. See Weber v. Aetna Cas. & Sur. Co., 406 U.S. 164, 179 (1972) (dissenting opinion). But the Court adds a new wrinkle to this test by transposing it from the legal considerations associated with the Equal Protection Clause of the Fourteenth Amendment to this case arising under the Due Process Clause of the Fourteenth Amendment. Unless I misapprehend the consequences of this transplanting of the "compelling state interest test," the Court's opinion will accomplish the seemingly impossible feat of leaving this area of the law more confused than it found it.

While the Court's opinion quotes from the dissent of Mr. Justice Holmes in Lochner v. New York, 198 U.S. 45 (1905), the result it reaches is more closely attuned to the majority opinion of Mr. Justice Peckham in that case. As in *Lochner* and similar cases, applying substantive due process standards to economic and social welfare legislation, the adoption of the compelling state interest standard will inevitably require this Court to examine the legislative policies and pass on the wisdom of these policies in the very process of deciding whether a particular state interest put forward may or may not be "compelling." The decision here to break the term of pregnancy into three distinct terms and to outline the permissible restrictions the State may impose in each one, for example, partakes more of judicial legislation than it does of a determination of the intent of the drafters of the Fourteenth Amendment.

The fact that a majority of the States, reflecting after all the majority sentiment in those States, have had restrictions on abortions for at least a century is a strong indication, it seems to me, that the asserted right to an abortion is not "so rooted in the traditions and conscience of our people as to be ranked as fundamental," Snyder v. Massachusetts, 291 U.S. 97, 105 (1934). Even today, when society's views on abortion are changing, the very existence of the debate is evidence that the "right" to an abortion is not so universally accepted as the appellants would have us believe.[a]

---

[a] For an early view criticizing the method by which the Court reached its result in the original abortion decisions, see Ely, *The Wages of Crying Wolf: A Comment on Roe v. Wade,* 82 Yale L.J. 920 (1973). For other useful commentary at the time see Epstein, *Substantive Due Process by Any Other Name: The Abortion Cases,* 1973 Sup.Ct.Rev. 159; Tribe, *Foreword: Toward a Model of Roles in the Due Process of Life and Law,* 87 Harv. L.Rev. 1 (1973).

[In the companion case of Doe v. Bolton, 410 U.S. 179 (1973), the Court held invalid a number of provisions of the Georgia statute regulating medical practice in abortion cases. The concurring and dissenting opinions which follow were addressed to both cases.]

Mr. Chief Justice Burger, concurring [in *Wade* and *Bolton*].

I agree that, under the Fourteenth Amendment to the Constitution, the abortion statutes of Georgia and Texas impermissibly limit the performance of abortions necessary to protect the health of pregnant women, using the term health in its broadest medical context. See United States v. Vuitch, 402 U.S. 62, 71–72 (1971). I am somewhat troubled that the Court has taken notice of various scientific and medical data in reaching its conclusion; however, I do not believe that the Court has exceeded the scope of judicial notice accepted in other contexts.

. . .

I do not read the Court's holding today as having the sweeping consequences attributed to it by the dissenting Justices; the dissenting views discount the reality that the vast majority of physicians observe the standards of their profession, and act only on the basis of carefully deliberated medical judgments relating to life and health. Plainly, the Court today rejects any claim that the Constitution requires abortion on demand.

Mr. Justice Douglas, concurring [in *Wade* and *Bolton*].

While I join the opinion of the Court, I add a few words.

The questions presented in the present cases go far beyond the issues of vagueness, which we considered in United States v. Vuitch, 402 U.S. 62. They involve the right of privacy, one aspect of which we considered in Griswold v. Connecticut, 381 U.S. 479, 484, when we held that various guarantees in the Bill of Rights create zones of privacy. . . .

The Ninth Amendment obviously does not create federally enforceable rights. It merely says, "The enumeration in the Constitution of certain rights, shall not be construed to deny or disparage others retained by the people." But a catalogue of these rights includes customary, traditional, and time-honored rights, amenities, privileges, and immunities that come within the sweep of "the Blessings of Liberty" mentioned in the preamble to the Constitution. Many of them in my view come within the meaning of the term "liberty" as used in the Fourteenth Amendment.

First is the autonomous control over the development and expression of one's intellect, interests, tastes, and personality.

These are rights protected by the First Amendment and in my view they are absolute, permitting of no exceptions. . . .

Second is freedom of choice in the basic decisions of one's life respecting marriage, divorce, procreation, contraception, and the education and upbringing of children.

These rights, unlike those protected by the First Amendment, are subject to some control by the police power. Thus the Fourth Amendment speaks only of "unreasonable searches and seizures" and of "probable cause." These rights are "fundamental" and we have held that in order to support legislative action the statute must be narrowly and precisely drawn and that a "compelling state interest" must be shown in support of the limitation. . . .

The liberty to marry a person of one's own choosing, Loving v. Virginia, 388 U.S. 1; the right of procreation, Skinner v. Oklahoma, 316 U.S. 535; the liberty to direct the education of one's children, Pierce v. Soc'y of Sisters, 268 U.S. 510, and the privacy of the marital relation, Griswold v. Connecticut, supra, are in this category. . . .

This right of privacy was called by Mr. Justice Brandeis the right "to be let alone." Olmstead v. United States, 277 U.S. 438, 478. That right includes the privilege of an individual to plan his own affairs, for, "outside areas of plainly harmful conduct, every American is left to shape his own life as he thinks best, do what he pleases, go where he pleases." Kent v. Dulles, 357 U.S. 116, 126.

Third is the freedom to care for one's health and person, freedom from bodily restraint or compulsion, freedom to walk, stroll, or loaf.

These rights, though fundamental, are likewise subject to regulation on a showing of "compelling state interest." . . .

The present statute has struck the balance between the woman and the State's interests wholly in favor of the latter. I am not prepared to hold that a State may equate, as Georgia has done, all phases of maturation preceding birth. . . .

In summary, the enactment is overbroad. It is not closely correlated to the aim of preserving pre-natal life. In fact, it permits its destruction in several cases, including pregnancies resulting from sex acts in which unmarried females are below the statutory age of consent. At the same time, however, the measure broadly proscribes aborting other pregnancies which may cause severe mental disorders. Additionally, the statute is overbroad because it equates the value of embryonic life immediately after conception with the worth of life immediately before birth. . . .

I also agree that the superstructure of medical supervision which Georgia has erected violates the patient's right of privacy inherent in her choice of her own physician.

Mr. Justice White, with whom Mr. Justice Rehnquist joins, dissenting [in *Wade* and *Bolton*]. . . .

With all due respect, I dissent. I find nothing in the language or history of the Constitution to support the Court's judgment. The Court simply fashions and announces a new constitutional right for pregnant mothers and, with scarcely any reason or authority for its action, invests that right with sufficient substance to override most existing state abortion statutes. The upshot is that the people and the legislatures of the 50 States are constitutionally disentitled to weigh the relative importance of the continued existence and development of the fetus on the one hand against a spectrum of possible impacts on the mother on the other hand. As an exercise of raw judicial power, the Court perhaps has authority to do what it does today; but in my view its judgment is an improvident and extravagant exercise of the power of judicial review which the Constitution extends to this Court.

The Court apparently values the convenience of the pregnant mother more than the continued existence and development of the life or potential life which she carries. Whether or not I might agree with that marshalling of values, I can in no event join the Court's judgment because I find no constitutional warrant for imposing such an order of priorities on the people and legislatures of the States. In a sensitive area such as this, involving as it does issues over which reasonable men may easily and heatedly differ, I cannot accept the Court's exercise of its clear power of choice by interposing a constitutional barrier to state efforts to protect human life and by investing mothers and doctors with the constitutionally protected right to exterminate it. This issue, for the most part, should be left with the people and to the political processes the people have devised to govern their affairs.

It is my view, therefore, that the Texas statute is not constitutionally infirm because it denies abortions to those who seek to serve only their convenience rather than to protect their life or health....

Planned Parenthood of Southeastern Pennsylvania v. Casey

505 U.S. 833, 112 S.Ct. 2791, 120 L.Ed.2d 674 (1992).

Justice O'Connor, Justice Kennedy, and Justice Souter announced the judgment of the Court and delivered the opinion of the Court with respect to Parts I, II, III, V–A, V–C, and VI, an opinion with respect to Part V–E, in which Justice Stevens joins, and an opinion with respect to Parts IV, V–B, and V–D.

I

Liberty finds no refuge in a jurisprudence of doubt. Yet 19 years after our holding that the Constitution protects a woman's right to terminate her pregnancy in its early stages, Roe v. Wade, 410 U.S. 113 (1973), that definition of liberty is still questioned. [T]he United States, as it has done in five other cases in the last decade, again asks us to overrule Roe....

[Five abortion clinics, and physicians providing abortion services, challenged each of] five provisions of the Pennsylvania Abortion Control Act [on its face].... The Act requires that a woman seeking an abortion give her informed consent prior to the abortion procedure, and specifies that she be provided with certain information at least 24 hours before the abortion is performed. § 3205. For a minor to obtain an abortion, the Act requires the informed consent of one of her parents, but provides for a judicial bypass option if the minor does not wish to or cannot obtain a parent's consent. § 3206. [T]he Act requires that, unless certain exceptions apply, a married woman seeking an abortion must sign a statement indicating that she has notified her husband of her intended abortion. § 3209. The Act exempts compliance with these three requirements in the event of a "medical emergency," which is defined in § 3203 of the Act.... [It also] imposes certain reporting requirements on facilities that provide abortion services....

... The District Court ... held all [the provisions] unconstitutional.... The Court of Appeals ... [upheld all but] the husband notification requirement....

. . .

After considering the fundamental constitutional questions resolved by Roe, principles of institutional integrity, and the rule of stare decisis, we are led to conclude this: the essential holding of Roe v. Wade should be retained and once again reaffirmed.

... Roe's essential holding, the holding we reaffirm, has three parts. First is a recognition of the right of the woman to choose to have an abortion before viability and to obtain it without undue interference from the State. Before viability, the State's interests are not strong enough to support a prohibition of abortion or the imposition of a substantial obstacle to the woman's effective right to elect the procedure. Second is a confirmation of the State's power to restrict abortions after fetal viability, if the law contains exceptions for pregnancies which endanger a woman's life or health. And third is the principle that the State has legitimate interests from the outset of the pregnancy in protecting the health of the woman and the life of the fetus that may become a child. These principles do not contradict one another; and we adhere to each.

II

. . .

Neither the Bill of Rights nor the specific practices of States at the time of the adoption of the Fourteenth Amendment marks the outer limits of the substantive sphere of liberty which the Fourteenth Amendment protects. See U.S. Const., Amend. 9. . . .

The inescapable fact is that adjudication of substantive due process claims may call upon the Court in interpreting the Constitution to exercise that same capacity which by tradition courts always have exercised: reasoned judgment. Its boundaries are not susceptible of expression as a simple rule. That does not mean we are free to invalidate state policy choices with which we disagree; yet neither does it permit us to shrink from the duties of our office. . . .

Men and women of good conscience can disagree, and we suppose some always shall disagree, about the profound moral and spiritual implications of terminating a pregnancy, even in its earliest stage. Some of us as individuals find abortion offensive to our most basic principles of morality, but that cannot control our decision. Our obligation is to define the liberty of all, not to mandate our own moral code. The underlying constitutional issue is whether the State can resolve these philosophic questions in such a definitive way that a woman lacks all choice in the matter, except perhaps in those rare circumstances in which the pregnancy is itself a danger to her own life or health, or is the result of rape or incest.

. . .

Our law affords constitutional protection to personal decisions relating to marriage, procreation, contraception, family relationships, child rearing, and education. . . . These matters, involving the most intimate and personal choices a person may make in a lifetime, choices central to personal dignity and autonomy, are central to the liberty protected by the Fourteenth Amendment. At the heart of liberty is the right to define one's own concept of existence, of meaning, of the universe, and of the mystery of human life. Beliefs about these matters could not define the attributes of personhood were they formed under compulsion of the State.

These considerations begin our analysis of the woman's interest in terminating her pregnancy but cannot end it, for this reason: though the abortion decision may originate within the zone of conscience and belief, it is more than a philosophic exercise. Abortion is a unique act. It is an act fraught with consequences for others: for the woman who must live with the implications of her decision; for the persons who perform and assist in the procedure; for the spouse, family, and society which must confront the knowledge that these procedures exist, procedures some deem nothing short of an act of violence against innocent human life; and, depending on one's beliefs, for the life or potential life that is aborted. Though abortion is conduct, it does not follow that the State is entitled to proscribe it in all instances. That is because the liberty of the woman is at stake in a sense unique to the human condition and so unique to the law. The mother who carries a child to full term is subject to anxieties, to physical constraints, to pain that only she must bear. That these sacrifices have from the beginning of the human race been endured by woman with a pride that ennobles her in the eyes of others and gives to the infant a bond of love cannot alone be grounds for the State to insist she make the sacrifice. Her suffering is too intimate and personal for the State to insist, without more, upon its own vision of the woman's role, however dominant that vision has been in the course of our history and our culture. The destiny of the woman must be shaped to a large extent on her own conception of her spiritual imperatives and her place in society.

[I]n some critical respects the abortion decision is of the same character as the decision to use contraception, to which *Griswold v. Connecticut, Eisenstadt v. Baird,* and *Carey v. Population Services International,* afford constitutional protection. We have no doubt as to the correctness of those decisions. They support the reasoning in *Roe* relating to the woman's liberty because they involve personal decisions concerning not only the meaning of procreation but also human responsibility and respect for it. . . .

. . .

While we appreciate the weight of the arguments made on behalf of the State . . ., arguments which in their ultimate formulation conclude that *Roe* should be overruled, the reservations any of us may have in reaffirming the central holding of *Roe* are outweighed by the explication of individual liberty we have given combined with the force of *stare decisis.* We turn now to that doctrine.

III

A

. . .

. . . [W]hen this Court reexamines a prior holding, its judgment is customarily informed by a series of prudential and pragmatic considerations designed to test the consistency of overruling a prior decision with the ideal of the rule of law, and to gauge the respective costs of reaffirming and overruling a prior case. . . .

. . .

1

Although *Roe* has engendered opposition, it has in no sense proven "unworkable," see Garcia v. San Antonio Metropolitan Transit Authority . . . (1985), representing as it does a simple limitation beyond which a state law is unenforceable. . . . [T]he required determinations fall within judicial competence.

2

. . .

. . . [F]or two decades of economic and social developments, people have organized intimate relationships and made choices that define their views of themselves and their places in society, in reliance on the availability of abortion in the event that contraception should fail. The ability of women to participate equally in the economic and social life of the Nation has been facilitated by their ability to control their reproductive lives. . . .

3

No evolution of legal principle has left *Roe*'s doctrinal footings weaker than they were in 1973. . . .

. . . *Roe* stands at an intersection of two lines of decisions. . . . [In the *Griswold* line,] *Roe* is clearly in no jeopardy, since subsequent constitutional developments have neither disturbed, nor do they threaten to diminish, the scope of recognized protection accorded to the liberty relating to intimate relationships, the family, and decisions about whether or not to beget or bear a child. . . .

[A]s a rule (whether or not mistaken) of personal autonomy and bodily integrity, with doctrinal affinity to cases recognizing limits on governmental power to mandate medical treatment or to bar its rejection . . . , our cases since *Roe* accord with *Roe*'s view that a State's interest in the protection of life falls short of justifying any plenary override of individual liberty claims. Cruzan v. Director, Missouri Dept. of Health . . . (1990); . . . .

Finally, [viewed] as *sui generis* . . . there clearly has been no erosion of its central determination. The original holding . . . was expressly affirmed by a majority of six in 1983, see Akron v. Akron Center for Reproductive Health, Inc., 462 U.S. 416 (1983)(*Akron I*), and by a majority of five in 1986, see Thornburgh v. American College of Obstetricians and Gynecologists, 476 U.S. 747 (1986). . . . More recently, in Webster v. Reproductive Health Services, 492 U.S. 490 (1989), although two of the present authors questioned the trimester framework in a way consistent with our judgment today, . . . a majority of the Court either decided to reaffirm or declined to address the constitutional validity of the central holding of *Roe*. . . .

. . . Even on the assumption that the central holding of *Roe* was in error, that error would go only to the strength of the state interest in fetal protection, not to the recognition afforded by the Constitution to the woman's liberty. . . .

The soundness of this prong of the *Roe* analysis is apparent from a consideration of the alternative. If indeed the woman's interest in deciding whether to bear and beget a child had not been recognized as in *Roe,* the State might as readily restrict a woman's right to choose to carry a pregnancy to term as to terminate it, to further asserted state interests in population control, or eugenics, for example. . . .

4

. . . [D]ivergences from the factual premises of 1973 have no bearing on the validity of *Roe*'s central holding, that viability marks the earliest point at which the State's interest in fetal life is constitutionally adequate to justify a legislative ban on nontherapeutic abortions. . . . Whenever it may occur, the attainment of viability may continue to serve as the critical fact. . . . [N]o change in *Roe*'s factual underpinning has left its central holding obsolete, and none supports an argument for overruling it.

5

. . . Within the bounds of normal *stare decisis* analysis, then, . . . the stronger argument is for affirming *Roe*'s central holding, with whatever degree of personal reluctance any of us may have, not for overruling it.

B

In a less significant case, *stare decisis* analysis could, and would, stop at the point we have reached. But the sustained and widespread debate *Roe* has provoked calls for some comparison between that case and others of comparable dimension.... Only two ... from the past century present themselves for examination, and in each instance the result reached by the Court accorded with the principles we apply today.

The first example is that line of cases identified with Lochner v. New York ... (1905).... West Coast Hotel Co. v. Parrish ... (1937), signalled the demise of *Lochner*.... In the meantime, the Depression had come and, with it, the lesson that seemed unmistakable to most people by 1937, that the interpretation of contractual freedom protected in *Adkins* rested on fundamentally false factual assumptions about the capacity of a relatively unregulated market to satisfy minimal levels of human welfare.... [T]he clear demonstration that the facts of economic life were different from those previously assumed warranted the repudiation of the old law.

The second comparison ... is with the cases employing the separate-but-equal rule.... They began with Plessy v. Ferguson ... (1896), ... [which] reject[ed] the argument that racial separation enforced by the legal machinery of American society treats the black race as inferior....

The Court in *Brown* ... observ[ed] that whatever may have been the understanding in *Plessy*'s time of the power of segregation to stigmatize those who were segregated with a "badge of inferiority," it was clear by 1954 that legally sanctioned segregation had just such an effect.... Society's understanding of the facts ... in 1954 was thus fundamentally different from the basis claimed for the decision in 1896. While we think *Plessy* was wrong the day it was decided, ... we must also recognize that the *Plessy* Court's explanation for its decision was so clearly at odds with the facts apparent to the Court in 1954 that the decision to reexamine *Plessy* was on this ground alone not only justified but required.

... In constitutional adjudication as elsewhere in life, changed circumstances may impose new obligations, and the thoughtful part of the Nation could accept each decision to overrule a prior case as a response to the Court's constitutional duty.

... Because neither the factual underpinnings of *Roe*'s central holding nor our understanding of it has changed (and because no other indication of weakened precedent has been shown) the Court could not pretend to be reexamining the prior law with any justification beyond a present doctrinal disposition to come out differently from the Court of 1973. To overrule prior law for no other reason than that would run counter to the view repeated in our cases, that a decision to overrule should rest on some special reason over and above the belief that a prior case was wrongly decided....

C

The examination of the conditions justifying the repudiation of *Adkins* by *West Coast Hotel* and *Plessy* by *Brown* is enough to suggest the terrible price that would have been paid if the Court had not overruled as it did. In the present case, however, ... the terrible price would be paid for overruling. [In addition,] overruling *Roe*'s central holding ... would seriously weaken the Court's capacity to exercise the judicial power and to function as the Supreme Court of a Nation dedicated to the rule of law....

... The Court's power lies ... in its legitimacy, a product of substance and perception....

... The Court must take care to speak and act in ways that allow people to accept its decisions on the terms the Court claims for them, as grounded truly in principle, not as compromises with social and political pressures having, as such, no bearing on the principled choices that the Court is obliged to make. . . .

The need for principled action to be perceived as such is implicated to some degree whenever this, or any other appellate court, overrules a prior case. . . .

. . . Where . . . the Court decides a case in such a way as to resolve the sort of intensely divisive controversy reflected in *Roe* and those rare, comparable cases, its decision has a dimension that the resolution of the normal case does not carry. It is the dimension present whenever the Court's interpretation of the Constitution calls the contending sides of a national controversy to end their national division by accepting a common mandate rooted in the Constitution.

The Court is not asked to do this very often, having thus addressed the Nation only twice in our lifetime, in the decisions of *Brown* and *Roe*. But when the Court does act in this way, its decision requires an equally rare precedential force to counter the inevitable efforts to overturn it. . . . [O]nly the most convincing justification . . . could suffice to demonstrate that a later decision overruling the first was anything but a surrender to political pressure, and an unjustified repudiation of the principle on which the Court staked its authority in the first instance. So to overrule under fire in the absence of the most compelling reason to reexamine a watershed decision would subvert the Court's legitimacy beyond any serious question. . . .

. . .

. . . A decision to overrule *Roe*'s essential holding under the existing circumstances would address error, if error there was, at the cost of both profound and unnecessary damage to the Court's legitimacy, and to the Nation's commitment to the rule of law. It is therefore imperative to adhere to the essence of *Roe*'s original decision, and we do so today.

IV

. . . [Although] much criticism has been directed at *Roe*['s line-drawing], a criticism that always inheres when the Court draws a specific rule from what in the Constitution is but a general standard[,] . . . [l]iberty must not be extinguished for want of a line that is clear. . . .

We conclude the line should be drawn at viability, so that before that time the woman has a right to choose to terminate her pregnancy. We adhere to this principle for two reasons. First, . . . *stare decisis*. . . .

[S]econd[,] the concept of viability . . . is the time at which there is a realistic possibility of maintaining and nourishing a life outside the womb, so that the independent existence of the second life can in reason and all fairness be the object of state protection that now overrides the rights of the woman. . . . The viability line also has, as a practical matter, an element of fairness. In some broad sense it might be said that a woman who fails to act before viability has consented to the State's intervention on behalf of the developing child.

The woman's right to terminate her pregnancy before viability is the most central principle of *Roe v. Wade*. It is a rule of law and a component of liberty we cannot renounce.

On the other side of the equation is the interest of the State in the protection of potential life. . . . The weight to be given this state interest, not the strength of the woman's interest, was the difficult question faced in *Roe*. We do not need to say whether each of us, . . . as an original matter, would have concluded, as the *Roe* Court did, that its weight is insufficient to justify a ban on abortions prior to viability even when it is subject to certain exceptions. The ... immediate question is not the soundness of *Roe*'s resolution of the issue, but the precedential force that must be accorded to its holding. And we have concluded that the essential holding of *Roe* should be reaffirmed.

Yet it must be remembered that *Roe v. Wade* speaks with clarity in establishing not only the woman's liberty but also the State's "important and legitimate interest in potential life." ... That portion of the decision in *Roe* has been given too little acknowledgement and implementation by the Court in its subsequent cases[, which] decided that any regulation touching upon the abortion decision must survive strict scrutiny, to be sustained only if drawn in narrow terms to further a compelling state interest.... Not all of the cases decided under that formulation can be reconciled with the holding in *Roe* itself that the State has legitimate interests in the health of the woman and in protecting the potential life within her....

. . .

The trimester framework no doubt was erected to ensure that the woman's right to choose not become so subordinate to the State's interest in promoting fetal life that her choice exists in theory but not in fact. We do not agree, however, that the trimester approach is necessary to accomplish this objective. A framework of this rigidity was unnecessary and in its later interpretation sometimes contradicted the State's permissible exercise of its powers.

Though the woman has a right to choose to terminate or continue her pregnancy before viability, it does not at all follow that the State is prohibited from taking steps to ensure that this choice is thoughtful and informed. Even in the earliest stages of pregnancy, the State may enact rules and regulations designed to encourage her to know that there are philosophic and social arguments of great weight that can be brought to bear in favor of continuing the pregnancy to full term and that there are procedures and institutions to allow adoption of unwanted children as well as a certain degree of state assistance if the mother chooses to raise the child herself....

We reject the trimester framework, which we do not consider to be part of the essential holding of *Roe*.... Measures aimed at ensuring that a woman's choice contemplates the consequences for the fetus do not necessarily interfere with the right recognized in *Roe,* although those measures have been found to be inconsistent with the rigid trimester framework announced in that case.... The trimester framework suffers from these basic flaws: in its formulation it misconceives the nature of the pregnant woman's interest; and in practice it undervalues the State's interest in potential life, as recognized in *Roe.*

. . .

... The fact that a law which serves a valid purpose, one not designed to strike at the right itself, has the incidental effect of making it more difficult or more expensive to procure an abortion cannot be enough to invalidate it. Only where state regulation imposes an undue burden on a woman's ability to make this decision does the power of the State reach into the heart of the liberty protected by the Due Process Clause....

... [T]he Court's experience applying the trimester framework has led to the striking down of some abortion regulations which in no real sense deprived women of the ultimate decision. Those decisions went too far because the right recognized by *Roe* is a right "to be free from unwarranted governmental intrusion into matters so fundamentally affecting a person as the decision whether to bear or beget a child." *Eisenstadt v. Baird*.... Not all governmental intrusion is of necessity unwarranted; and that brings us to the other basic flaw in the trimester framework: even in *Roe*'s terms, in practice it undervalues the State's interest in the potential life within the woman.

. . .

The very notion that the State has a substantial interest in potential life leads to the conclusion that not all regulations must be deemed unwarranted. Not all burdens on the right to decide whether to terminate a pregnancy will be undue. In our view, the undue burden standard is the appropriate means of reconciling the State's interest with the woman's constitutionally protected liberty.

. . .

A finding of an undue burden is a shorthand for the conclusion that a state regulation has the purpose or effect of placing a substantial obstacle in the path of a woman seeking an abortion of a nonviable fetus. A statute with this purpose is invalid because the means chosen by the State to further the interest in potential life must be calculated to inform the woman's free choice, not hinder it. And a statute which, while furthering the interest in potential life or some other valid state interest, has the effect of placing a substantial obstacle in the path of a woman's choice cannot be considered a permissible means of serving its legitimate ends.... [A]n undue burden is an unconstitutional burden.... [A] law designed to further the State's interest in fetal life which imposes an undue burden on the woman's decision before fetal viability [is un]constitutional....

Some guiding principles should emerge.... Regulations which do no more than create a structural mechanism by which the State, or the parent or guardian of a minor, may express profound respect for the life of the unborn are permitted, if they are not a substantial obstacle to the woman's exercise of the right to choose.... Unless it has that effect on her right of choice, a state measure designed to persuade her to choose childbirth over abortion will be upheld if reasonably related to that goal. Regulations designed to foster the health of a woman seeking an abortion are valid if they do not constitute an undue burden.

Even when jurists reason from shared premises, some disagreement is inevitable.... That is to be expected in the application of any legal standard which must accommodate life's complexity. We do not expect it to be otherwise with respect to the undue burden standard. We give this summary:

(a) To protect the central right recognized by *Roe v. Wade* while at the same time accommodating the State's profound interest in potential life, we will employ the undue burden analysis as explained in this opinion. An undue burden exists, and therefore a provision of law is invalid, if its purpose or effect is to place a substantial obstacle in the path of a woman seeking an abortion before the fetus attains viability.

(b) We reject the rigid trimester framework of *Roe v. Wade*. To promote the State's profound interest in potential life, throughout pregnancy the State may take measures to ensure that the woman's choice is informed, and measures designed to advance this interest will not be invalidated as long as their purpose is to persuade the woman to choose childbirth over abortion. These measures must not be an undue burden on the right.

(c) As with any medical procedure, the State may enact regulations to further the health or safety of a woman seeking an abortion. Unnecessary health regulations that have the purpose or effect of presenting a substantial obstacle to a woman seeking an abortion impose an undue burden on the right.

(d) Our adoption of the undue burden analysis does not disturb the central holding of *Roe v. Wade,* and we reaffirm that holding. Regardless of whether exceptions are made for particular circumstances, a State may not prohibit any woman from making the ultimate decision to terminate her pregnancy before viability.

(e) We also reaffirm *Roe*'s holding that "subsequent to viability, the State in promoting its interest in the potentiality of human life may, if it chooses, regulate, and even proscribe, abortion except where it is necessary, in appropriate medical judgment, for the preservation of the life or health of the mother."
. . .

These principles control our assessment of the . . . challenged provisions.

V

. . .

A

Because it is central to the operation of various other requirements, we begin with the statute's definition of medical emergency. . . .

Petitioners argue that the definition is too narrow, contending that it forecloses the possibility of an immediate abortion despite some significant health risks. If the contention were correct, we would be required to invalidate the restrictive operation of the provision, for the essential holding of *Roe* forbids a State from interfering with a woman's choice to undergo an abortion procedure if continuing her pregnancy would constitute a threat to her health. . . .

. . . While the definition could be interpreted in an unconstitutional manner, . . . [w]e . . . conclude that, as construed by the Court of Appeals, the medical emergency definition imposes no undue burden on a woman's abortion right.

B

We next consider the informed consent requirement. . . .

Our prior decisions establish that as with any medical procedure, the State may require a woman to give her written informed consent to an abortion. . . . In this respect, the statute is unexceptional. Petitioners challenge the statute's definition of informed consent because it includes the provision of specific information by the doctor and the mandatory 24–hour waiting period. The conclusions reached by a majority of the Justices in the separate opinions filed today and the undue burden standard adopted in this opinion require us to overrule in part some of the Court's past decisions. . . .

In *Akron I,* . . . we invalidated an ordinance which required that a woman seeking an abortion be provided by her physician with specific information "designed to influence the woman's informed choice between abortion or childbirth." . . .

To the extent *Akron I* and *Thornburgh* find a constitutional violation when the government requires, as it does here, the giving of truthful, nonmisleading information about the nature of the procedure, the attendant health risks and those of childbirth, and the "probable gestational age" of the fetus, those cases go too far, are inconsistent with *Roe*'s acknowledgment of an important interest in potential life, and are overruled.... [M]ost women considering an abortion would deem the impact on the fetus relevant, if not dispositive, to the decision. In attempting to ensure that a woman apprehend the full consequences of her decision, the State furthers the legitimate purpose of reducing the risk that a woman may elect an abortion, only to discover later, with devastating psychological consequences, that her decision was not fully informed. If the information the State requires to be made available to the woman is truthful and not misleading, the requirement may be permissible.

We also see no reason why the State may not require doctors to inform a woman seeking an abortion of the availability of materials relating to the consequences to the fetus, even when those consequences have no direct relation to her health.... We would think it constitutional for the State to require that in order for there to be informed consent to a kidney transplant operation the recipient must be supplied with information about risks to the donor as well as risks to himself or herself. A requirement that the physician make available information similar to that mandated by the statute here was described in *Thornburgh* as "an outright attempt to wedge the Commonwealth's message discouraging abortion into the privacy of the informed-consent dialogue between the woman and her physician." ... We conclude, however, that informed choice need not be defined in such narrow terms that all considerations of the effect on the fetus are made irrelevant.... In short, requiring that the woman be informed of the availability of information relating to fetal development and the assistance available should she decide to carry the pregnancy to full term is a reasonable measure to insure an informed choice, one which might cause the woman to choose childbirth over abortion. This requirement cannot be considered a substantial obstacle to obtaining an abortion, and, it follows, there is no undue burden.

Our prior cases also suggest that the "straitjacket," *Thornburgh* ..., of particular information which must be given in each case interferes with a constitutional right of privacy between a pregnant woman and her physician. [T]he statute now before us does not require a physician to comply with the informed consent provisions "if he or she can demonstrate by a preponderance of the evidence, that he or she reasonably believed that furnishing the information would have resulted in a severely adverse effect on the physical or mental health of the patient." ... In this respect, the statute does not prevent the physician from exercising his or her medical judgment.

Whatever constitutional status the doctor-patient relation may have as a general matter, in the present context it is derivative of the woman's position.... Thus, a requirement that a doctor give a woman certain information as part of obtaining her consent to an abortion is, for constitutional purposes, no different from a requirement that a doctor give certain specific information about any medical procedure.

. . .

The Pennsylvania statute also requires us to reconsider the holding in *Akron I* that the State may not require that a physician, as opposed to a qualified assistant, provide information relevant to a woman's informed consent.... Since there is no evidence on this record that requiring a doctor to give the information as provided by the statute would amount in practical terms to a substantial obstacle to a woman seeking an abortion, we conclude that it is not an undue burden....

Our analysis of Pennsylvania's 24–hour waiting period between the provision of the information deemed necessary to informed consent and the performance of an abortion under the undue burden standard requires us to reconsider the premise behind the decision in *Akron I* invalidating a parallel requirement. In *Akron I* we said: "Nor are we convinced that the State's legitimate concern that the woman's decision be informed is reasonably served by requiring a 24–hour delay as a matter of course." ... We consider that conclusion to be wrong. The idea that important decisions will be more informed and deliberate if they follow some period of reflection does not strike us as unreasonable, particularly where the statute directs that important information become part of the background of the decision. The statute, as construed by the Court of Appeals, permits avoidance of the waiting period in the event of a medical emergency and the record evidence shows that in the vast majority of cases, a 24–hour delay does not create any appreciable health risk. In theory, at least, the waiting period is a reasonable measure to implement the State's interest in protecting the life of the unborn, a measure that does not amount to an undue burden.

Whether the mandatory 24–hour waiting period is nonetheless invalid because in practice it is a substantial obstacle to a woman's choice to terminate her pregnancy is a closer question. The findings of fact by the District Court indicate that because of the distances many women must travel to reach an abortion provider, the practical effect will often be a delay of much more than a day because the waiting period requires that a woman seeking an abortion make at least two visits to the doctor. The District Court also found that in many instances this will increase the exposure of women seeking abortions to "the harassment and hostility of anti-abortion protestors demonstrating outside a clinic." ... As a result, the District Court found that for those women who have the fewest financial resources, those who must travel long distances, and those who have difficulty explaining their whereabouts to husbands, employers, or others, the 24–hour waiting period will be "particularly burdensome." ...

These findings are troubling in some respects, but they do not demonstrate that the waiting period constitutes an undue burden. We do not doubt that ... the waiting period has the effect of "increasing the cost and risk of delay of abortions," ... but the District Court did not conclude that the increased costs and potential delays amount to substantial obstacles. Rather, applying the trimester framework[, it] concluded that the waiting period does not further the state "interest in maternal health" and "infringes the physician's discretion to exercise sound medical judgment." ... Yet, ... under the undue burden standard a State is permitted to enact persuasive measures which favor childbirth over abortion, even if those measures do not further a health interest....

We also disagree with the District Court's conclusion that the "particularly burdensome" effects of the waiting period on some women require its invalidation. A particular burden is not of necessity a substantial obstacle. Whether a burden falls on a particular group is a distinct inquiry from whether it is a substantial obstacle even as to the women in that group. And the District Court did not conclude that the waiting period is such an obstacle even for the women who are most burdened by it. Hence, on the record before us, and in the context of this facial challenge, we are not convinced that the 24–hour waiting period constitutes an undue burden.

We are left with the argument that the various aspects of the informed consent requirement are unconstitutional because they place barriers in the way of abortion on demand. Even the broadest reading of *Roe,* however, has not suggested that there is a constitutional right to abortion on demand....

Rather, the right protected by *Roe* is a right to decide to terminate a pregnancy free of undue interference by the State. Because the informed consent requirement facilitates the wise exercise of that right it cannot be classified as an interference with the right *Roe* protects. The informed consent requirement is not an undue burden on that right.

C

Section 3209 of Pennsylvania's abortion law provides, except in cases of medical emergency, that no physician shall perform an abortion on a married woman without receiving a signed statement from the woman that she has notified her spouse that she is about to undergo an abortion. The woman has the option of providing an alternative signed statement certifying that her husband is not the man who impregnated her; that her husband could not be located; that the pregnancy is the result of spousal sexual assault which she has reported; or that the woman believes that notifying her husband will cause him or someone else to inflict bodily injury upon her. A physician who performs an abortion on a married woman without receiving the appropriate signed statement will have his or her license revoked, and is liable to the husband for damages.

[The opinion here recounted at length the district court's findings with respect to the widespread incidence and dynamics of wife-battering, marital rape, and other coerced sexual activity, as well as studies of the frequency of psychological and physical abuse of women, including homicides, by their husbands or male partners.]

... In well-functioning marriages, spouses discuss important intimate decisions such as whether to bear a child. But there are millions of women in this country who are the victims of regular physical and psychological abuse at the hands of their husbands. Should these women become pregnant, they may have very good reasons for not wishing to inform their husbands of their decision to obtain an abortion. Many may have justifiable fears of physical abuse, but may be no less fearful of the consequences of reporting prior abuse to the Commonwealth of Pennsylvania. Many may have a reasonable fear that notifying their husbands will provoke further instances of child abuse; these women are not exempt from § 3209's notification requirement. Many may fear devastating forms of psychological abuse from their husbands, including verbal harassment, threats of future violence, the destruction of possessions, physical confinement to the home, the withdrawal of financial support, or the disclosure of the abortion to family and friends. These methods of psychological abuse may act as even more of a deterrent to notification than the possibility of physical violence, but women who are the victims of the abuse are not exempt from § 3209's notification requirement. And many women who are pregnant as a result of sexual assaults by their husbands will be unable to avail themselves of the exception for spousal sexual assault, § 3209(b)(3), because the exception requires that the woman have notified law enforcement authorities within 90 days of the assault, and her husband will be notified of her report once an investigation begins. § 3128(c). If anything in this field is certain, it is that victims of spousal sexual assault are extremely reluctant to report the abuse to the government; hence, a great many spousal rape victims will not be exempt from the notification requirement imposed by § 3209.

The spousal notification requirement is thus likely to prevent a significant number of women from obtaining an abortion. It does not merely make abortions a little more difficult or expensive to obtain; for many women, it will impose a substantial obstacle. We must not blind ourselves to the fact that the significant number of women who fear for their safety and the safety of their children are likely to be deterred from procuring an abortion as surely as if the Commonwealth had outlawed abortion in all cases.

... Respondents argue that ... the statute affects fewer than one percent of women seeking abortions [and thus] the statute cannot be invalid on its face.... We disagree....

The analysis does not end with the one percent of women upon whom the statute operates; it begins there.... The proper focus of constitutional inquiry is the group for whom the law is a restriction, not the group for whom the law is irrelevant.

... [S]ection 3209's real target is narrower even than the class of women seeking abortions identified by the State: it is married women seeking abortions who do not wish to notify their husbands of their intentions and who do not qualify for one of the statutory exceptions to the notice requirement. The unfortunate yet persisting conditions we document above will mean that in a large fraction of the cases in which § 3209 is relevant, it will operate as a substantial obstacle to a woman's choice to undergo an abortion. It is an undue burden, and therefore invalid.

This conclusion is in no way inconsistent with our decisions upholding parental notification or consent requirements.... Those enactments, and our judgment that they are constitutional, are based on the quite reasonable assumption that minors will benefit from consultation with their parents and that children will often not realize that their parents have their best interests at heart. We cannot adopt a parallel assumption about adult women.

We recognize that a husband has a "deep and proper concern and interest ... in his wife's pregnancy and in the growth and development of the fetus she is carrying." ... If this case concerned a State's ability to require the mother to notify the father before taking some action with respect to a living child raised by both, therefore, it would be reasonable to conclude as a general matter that the father's interest in the welfare of the child and the mother's interest are equal.

Before birth, however, the issue takes on a very different cast. It is an inescapable biological fact that state regulation with respect to the child a woman is carrying will have a far greater impact on the mother's liberty than on the father's....

[N]ot so long ago ... a different understanding of the family and of the Constitution prevailed. In Bradwell v. Illinois, 16 Wall. 130 (1873), three Members of this Court reaffirmed the common-law principle that "a woman had no legal existence separate from her husband...." ... Only one generation has passed since this Court observed that "woman is still regarded as the center of home and family life," with attendant "special responsibilities" that precluded full and independent legal status under the Constitution.... These views, of course, are no longer consistent with our understanding of the family, the individual, or the Constitution.

... For the great many women who are victims of abuse inflicted by their husbands, or whose children are the victims of such abuse, a spousal notice requirement enables the husband to wield an effective veto over his wife's decision. Whether the prospect of notification itself deters such women from seeking abortions, or whether the husband, through physical force or psychological pressure or economic coercion, prevents his wife from obtaining an abortion until it is too late, the notice requirement will often be tantamount to the veto found unconstitutional in Danforth. The women most affected by this law—those who most reasonably fear the consequences of notifying their husbands that they are pregnant—are in the gravest danger.

The husband's interest in the life of the child his wife is carrying does not permit the State to empower him with this troubling degree of authority over his wife.... A State may not give to a man the kind of dominion over his wife that parents exercise over their children.

... Women do not lose their constitutionally protected liberty when they marry....

D

We next consider the parental consent provision. Except in a medical emergency, an unemancipated young woman under 18 may not obtain an abortion unless she and one of her parents (or guardian) provides consent.... If neither a parent nor a guardian provides consent, a court may authorize the performance of an abortion upon a determination that the young woman is mature and capable of giving informed consent and has in fact given her informed consent, or that an abortion would be in her best interests.

... Our cases establish, and we reaffirm today, that a State may require a minor seeking an abortion to obtain the consent of a parent or guardian, provided that there is an adequate judicial bypass procedure....

E

Under the recordkeeping and reporting requirements of the statute, every facility which performs abortions is required to file a report stating its name and address as well as the name and address of any related entity, such as a controlling or subsidiary organization. In the case of state-funded institutions, the information becomes public.

For each abortion performed, a report must be filed identifying: the physician (and the second physician where required); the facility; the referring physician or agency; the woman's age; the number of prior pregnancies and prior abortions she has had; gestational age; the type of abortion procedure; the date of the abortion; whether there were any pre-existing medical conditions which would complicate pregnancy; medical complications with the abortion; where applicable, the basis for the determination that the abortion was medically necessary; the weight of the aborted fetus; and whether the woman was married, and if so, whether notice was provided or the basis for the failure to give notice. Every abortion facility must also file quarterly reports showing the number of abortions performed broken down by trimester.... [T]he identity of each woman who has had an abortion remains confidential.

In *Danforth*, ... we held that recordkeeping and reporting provisions "that are reasonably directed to the preservation of maternal health and that properly respect a patient's confidentiality and privacy are permissible." [U]nder this standard, all the provisions at issue here except that relating to spousal notice are constitutional.... The collection of information with respect to actual patients is a vital element of medical research, and so it cannot be said that the requirements serve no purpose other than to make abortions more difficult. Nor do we find that the requirements impose a substantial obstacle to a woman's choice. At most they might increase the cost of some abortions by a slight amount. While at some point increased cost could become a substantial obstacle, there is no such showing on the record before us.

Subsection (12) ... requires the reporting of ... a married woman's "reason for failure to provide notice" to her husband.... This provision in effect requires women, as a condition of obtaining an abortion, to provide the Commonwealth with the precise information we have already recognized that many women have pressing reasons not to reveal. Like the spousal notice requirement itself, this provision places an undue burden on a woman's choice, and must be invalidated for that reason.

VI

Our Constitution is a covenant running from the first generation of Americans to us and then to future generations. . . . We accept our responsibility not to retreat from interpreting the full meaning of the covenant in light of all our precedents. We invoke it once again to define the freedom guaranteed by the Constitution's own promise, the promise of liberty.

. . .

Justice Stevens, concurring in part and dissenting in part.

The portions of the Court's opinion that I have joined are more important than those with which I disagree. . . .

I

. . .

I . . . accept what is implicit in the Court's analysis, namely, a reaffirmation of *Roe*'s explanation of why the State's obligation to protect the life or health of the mother must take precedence over any duty to the unborn. The Court in *Roe* carefully considered, and rejected, the State's argument "that the fetus is a 'person' within the language and meaning of the Fourteenth Amendment." . . . Thus, as a matter of federal constitutional law, a developing organism that is not yet a "person" does not have what is sometimes described as a "right to life." This has been and, by the Court's holding today, remains a fundamental premise of our constitutional law governing reproductive autonomy.

II

. . . Contrary to . . . the joint opinion, it is not a "contradiction" to recognize that the State may have a legitimate interest in potential human life and, at the same time, to conclude that that interest does not justify the regulation of abortion before viability (although other interests, such as maternal health, may). [T]hat the State's interest is legitimate does not tell us when, if ever, that interest outweighs the pregnant woman's interest in personal liberty. . . .

. . .

Identifying the State's interests . . . makes clear that the interest in protecting potential life is not grounded in the Constitution. It is, instead, an indirect interest supported by both humanitarian and pragmatic concerns. Many of our citizens believe that any abortion reflects an unacceptable disrespect for potential human life and that the performance of more than a million abortions each year is intolerable; many find third-trimester abortions performed when the fetus is approaching personhood particularly offensive. The State has a legitimate interest in minimizing such offense. The State may also have a broader interest in expanding the population. . . .

In counterpoise is the woman's constitutional interest in liberty. One aspect of this liberty is a right to bodily integrity, a right to control one's person.... This right is neutral on the question of abortion: The Constitution would be equally offended by an absolute requirement that all women undergo abortions as by an absolute prohibition on abortions....

The woman's constitutional liberty interest also involves her freedom to decide matters of the highest privacy and the most personal nature.... The authority to make such traumatic and yet empowering decisions is an element of basic human dignity. As the joint opinion so eloquently demonstrates, a woman's decision to terminate her pregnancy is nothing less than a matter of conscience.

Weighing the State's interest in potential life and the woman's liberty interest, I agree with the joint opinion that the State may "'expres[s] a preference for normal childbirth,'" that the State may take steps to ensure that a woman's choice "is thoughtful and informed," and that "States are free to enact laws to provide a reasonable framework for a woman to make a decision that has such profound and lasting meaning." Serious questions arise, however, when a State attempts to "persuade the woman to choose childbirth over abortion." Decisional autonomy must limit the State's power to inject into a woman's most personal deliberations its own views of what is best. The State may promote its preferences by funding childbirth, by creating and maintaining alternatives to abortion, and by espousing the virtues of family; but it must respect the individual's freedom to make such judgments.

. . .

... [T]he Pennsylvania statute ... require[s] a physician or counselor to provide the woman with a range of materials clearly designed to persuade her to choose not to undergo the abortion. While the State is free ... to produce and disseminate such material, the State may not inject such information into the woman's deliberations just as she is weighing such an important choice.

... [By contrast, r]equir[ing] the physician to inform a woman of the nature and risks of the abortion procedure and the medical risks of carrying to term, are neutral requirements comparable to those imposed in other medical procedures. Those sections indicate no effort by the State to influence the woman's choice in any way. If anything, such requirements enhance, rather than skew, the woman's decisionmaking.

III

The 24–hour waiting period ... raises even more serious concerns....

... [T]here is no evidence that the mandated delay benefits women or that it is necessary to enable the physician to convey any relevant information to the patient. The mandatory delay thus appears to rest on outmoded and unacceptable assumptions about the decisionmaking capacity of women. While there are well-established and consistently maintained reasons for the State to view with skepticism the ability of minors to make decisions, ... none of those reasons applies to an adult woman's decisionmaking ability. Just as we have left behind the belief that a woman must consult her husband before undertaking serious matters, so we must reject the notion that a woman is less capable of deciding matters of gravity. Cf. Reed v. Reed ... (1971).

[T]he delay requirement may be premised on the belief that the decision to terminate a pregnancy is presumptively wrong. This premise is illegitimate.... States may not presume that a woman has failed to reflect adequately merely because her conclusion differs from the State's preference....

Part of the constitutional liberty to choose is the equal dignity to which each of us is entitled. A woman who decides to terminate her pregnancy is entitled to the same respect as a woman who decides to carry the fetus to term. The mandatory waiting period denies women that equal respect.

IV

In my opinion, a correct application of the "undue burden" standard leads to the same conclusion.... A state-imposed burden on the exercise of a constitutional right is measured both by its effects and by its character: A burden may be "undue" either because the burden is too severe or because it lacks a legitimate, rational justification.

The 24–hour delay requirement fails both parts of this test. The findings of the District Court establish the severity of the burden.... [E]ven [when] the delay is not especially onerous, it is ... "undue" because there is no evidence [it] serves a useful and legitimate purpose. [T]here is no legitimate reason to require a woman who has agonized over her decision to leave the clinic or hospital and return again another day.... [A] rigid requirement that all patients wait 24 hours or (what is true in practice) much longer to evaluate the significance of information that is either common knowledge or irrelevant is an irrational and, therefore, "undue" burden.

The counseling provisions are similarly infirm.... [The mandated information must] be given to all women seeking abortions, including those for whom such information is clearly useless, such as those who are married, those who have undergone the procedure in the past and are fully aware of the options, and those who are fully convinced that abortion is their only reasonable option. Moreover, ... information [of probable gestational age] is of little decisional value in most cases, because 90% of all abortions are performed during the first trimester when fetal age has less relevance than when the fetus nears viability.... I conclude that the information requirements ... do not serve a useful purpose and thus constitute an unnecessary—and therefore undue—burden on the woman's constitutional liberty to decide to terminate her pregnancy.

Accordingly, while I disagree with Parts IV, V–B, and V–D of the joint opinion, I join the remainder of the Court's opinion.

Justice Blackmun, concurring in part, concurring in the judgment in part, and dissenting in part.

I join parts I, II, III, V–A, V–C, and VI of the joint opinion of Justices O'Connor, Kennedy, and Souter.

Three years ago, in *Webster* ... four Members of this Court appeared poised to "cas[t] into darkness the hopes and visions of every woman in this country" who had come to believe that the Constitution guaranteed her the right to reproductive choice.... But now, just when so many expected the darkness to fall, the flame has grown bright.

I do not underestimate the significance of today's joint opinion. Yet I remain steadfast in my belief that the right to reproductive choice is entitled to the full protection afforded by this Court before *Webster*. And I fear for the darkness as four Justices anxiously await the single vote necessary to extinguish the light.

I

Make no mistake, the joint opinion of Justices O'Connor, Kennedy, and Souter is an act of personal courage and constitutional principle....

... What has happened today should serve as a model for future Justices and a warning to all who have tried to turn this Court into yet another political branch.

In striking down the Pennsylvania statute's spousal notification requirement, the Court has established a framework for evaluating abortion regulations that responds to the social context of women facing issues of reproductive choice.... And in applying its test, the Court remains sensitive to the unique role of women in the decision-making process....

[W]hile ... the joint opinion errs in failing to invalidate the other regulations, I am pleased that [it] has not ruled out the possibility that these regulations may be shown to impose an unconstitutional burden. The joint opinion makes clear that its specific holdings are based on the insufficiency of the record before it.... I am confident that in the future evidence will be produced to show that "in a large fraction of the cases in which [these regulations are] relevant, [they] will operate as a substantial obstacle to a woman's choice to undergo an abortion."

II

. . .

... *Roe*'s requirement of strict scrutiny as implemented through a trimester framework should not be disturbed. No other approach has gained a majority, and no other is more protective of the woman's fundamental right. Lastly, no other approach properly accommodates the woman's constitutional right with the State's legitimate interests.

. . .

Application of the strict scrutiny standard results in the invalidation of all the challenged provisions. Indeed, as this Court has invalidated virtually identical provisions in prior cases, *stare decisis* requires that we again strike them down.

. . .

III

. . .

The Chief Justice's criticism of *Roe* follows from his stunted conception of individual liberty.... [He] construe[s] this Court's personal-liberty cases as establishing only a laundry list of particular rights, rather than a principled account of how these particular rights are grounded in a more general right of privacy. This constricted view is reinforced by The Chief Justice's exclusive reliance on tradition as a source of fundamental rights....

Even more shocking than The Chief Justice's cramped notion of individual liberty is his complete omission of any discussion of the effects that compelled childbirth and motherhood have on women's lives.... [His] view of the State's compelling interest in maternal health has less to do with health than it does with compelling women to be maternal.

. . .

But, we are reassured, there is always the protection of the democratic process. While there is much to be praised about our democracy, our country since its founding has recognized that there are certain fundamental liberties that are not to be left to the whims of an election....

IV

In one sense, the Court's approach is worlds apart from that of The Chief Justice and Justice Scalia. And yet ... the distance between the two approaches is ... but a single vote.

I am 83 years old. I cannot remain on this Court forever, and when I do step down, the confirmation process for my successor well may focus on the issue before us today. That, I regret, may be exactly where the choice between the two worlds will be made.

Chief Justice Rehnquist, with whom Justice White, Justice Scalia, and Justice Thomas join, concurring in the judgment in part and dissenting in part.

The joint opinion, following its newly-minted variation on *stare decisis*, retains the outer shell of *Roe v. Wade,* ... but beats a wholesale retreat from the substance of that case. We believe that *Roe* was wrongly decided, and that it can and should be overruled consistently with our traditional approach to *stare decisis* in constitutional cases. We would adopt the approach of the plurality in *Webster* ... and uphold the challenged provisions of the Pennsylvania statute in their entirety.

I

. . .

... Although they reject the trimester framework ..., Justices O'Connor, Kennedy, and Souter adopt a revised undue burden standard to analyze the challenged regulations. We conclude, however, that such an outcome is an unjustified constitutional compromise, one which [allows] the Court ... to closely scrutinize all types of abortion regulations despite the fact that it lacks the power to do so under the Constitution.

. . .

We have held that a liberty interest protected under the Due Process Clause of the Fourteenth Amendment will be deemed fundamental if it is "implicit in the concept of ordered liberty." Palko v. Connecticut ... (1937). Three years earlier, in Snyder v. Massachusetts ... (1934), we referred to a "principle of justice so rooted in the traditions and conscience of our people as to be ranked as fundamental." ... These expressions are admittedly not precise, but our decisions implementing this notion of "fundamental" rights do not afford any more elaborate basis on which to base such a classification.

In construing the phrase "liberty" incorporated in the Due Process Clause of the Fourteenth Amendment, we have recognized that its meaning extends beyond freedom from physical restraint.... But [our] opinions ... do not endorse any all-encompassing "right of privacy."

In *Roe v. Wade*, the Court recognized a "guarantee of personal privacy" which "is broad enough to encompass a woman's decision whether or not to terminate her pregnancy." ... We are now of the view that, in terming this right fundamental, the Court in *Roe* read the earlier opinions upon which it based its decision much too broadly. Unlike marriage, procreation and contraception, abortion "involves the purposeful termination of potential life." Harris v. McRae ... (1980). The abortion decision must therefore "be recognized as *sui generis*, different in kind from the others that the Court has protected under the rubric of personal or family privacy and autonomy." ...

Nor do the historical traditions of the American people support the view that the right to terminate one's pregnancy is "fundamental." ... At the time of the adoption of the Fourteenth Amendment, statutory prohibitions or restrictions on abortion were commonplace; in 1868, at least 28 of the then 37 States and 8 Territories had statutes banning or limiting abortion.... By the turn of the century virtually every State had a law prohibiting or restricting abortion on its books. By the middle of the present century, a liberalization trend had set in. But 21 of the restrictive abortion laws in effect in 1868 were still in effect in 1973 when *Roe* was decided, and an overwhelming majority of the States prohibited abortion unless necessary to preserve the life or health of the mother.... On this record, it can scarcely be said that any deeply rooted tradition of relatively unrestricted abortion in our history supported the classification of the right to abortion as "fundamental" under the Due Process Clause of the Fourteenth Amendment.

. . .

II

The joint opinion['s] ... discussion of the principle of *stare decisis* appears to be almost entirely dicta, because [it] does not apply that principle in dealing with *Roe*. *Roe* decided that a woman had a fundamental right to an abortion. The joint opinion rejects that view. *Roe* decided that abortion regulations were to be subjected to "strict scrutiny" and could be justified only in the light of "compelling state interests." The joint opinion rejects that view.... *Roe* analyzed abortion regulation under a rigid trimester framework, a framework which has guided this Court's decisionmaking for 19 years. The joint opinion rejects that framework.

... Decisions following *Roe,* such as *Akron* ... (1983), and *Thornburgh* ... (1986), are frankly overruled in part under the "undue burden" standard expounded in the joint opinion.

In our view, authentic principles of *stare decisis* do not require that any portion of the reasoning in *Roe* be kept intact.... Erroneous decisions in such constitutional cases are uniquely durable, because correction through legislative action, save for constitutional amendment, is impossible. It is ... our duty to reconsider constitutional interpretations that "depar[t] from a proper understanding" of the Constitution....

. . .

In the end, ... the joint opinion's argument is based solely on generalized assertions about the national psyche, on a belief that the people of this country have grown accustomed to the *Roe* decision over the last 19 years and have "ordered their thinking and living around" it. As an initial matter, one might inquire how the joint opinion can view the "central holding" of *Roe* as so deeply rooted in our constitutional culture, when it so casually uproots and disposes of that same decision's trimester framework. Furthermore, at various points in the past, the same could have been said about this Court's erroneous decisions that the Constitution allowed "separate but equal" treatment of minorities, see Plessy v. Ferguson ... (1896), or that "liberty" under the Due Process Clause protected "freedom of contract." ... The "separate but equal" doctrine lasted 58 years after *Plessy,* and *Lochner*'s protection of contractual freedom lasted 32 years. However, the simple fact that a generation or more had grown used to these major decisions did not prevent the Court from correcting its errors in those cases, nor should it prevent us from correctly interpreting the Constitution here....

Apparently realizing that conventional *stare decisis* principles do not support its position, the joint opinion advances a belief that retaining a portion of *Roe* is necessary to protect the "legitimacy" of this Court....

[T]he joint opinion goes on to state that when the Court "resolve[s] the sort of intensely divisive controversy reflected in *Roe* and those rare, comparable cases," its decision is exempt from reconsideration under established principles of *stare decisis* in constitutional cases....

[Distinguishing] cases which are "intensely divisive" ... from those that are not ... is entirely subjective....

... It [is] very odd indeed that the joint opinion chooses as benchmarks two cases in which the Court chose not to adhere to erroneous constitutional precedent, but instead enhanced its stature by acknowledging and correcting its error, apparently in violation of the joint opinion's "legitimacy" principle. See *West Coast Hotel Co. v. Parrish,* supra; *Brown v. Board of Education,* supra.... [Moreover,] ... [p]ublic protests should not alter the normal application of *stare decisis,* lest perfectly lawful protest activity be penalized by the Court itself.

Taking the joint opinion on its own terms, we doubt that its distinction between *Roe,* on the one hand, and *Plessy* and *Lochner,* on the other, withstands analysis. The joint opinion acknowledges that the Court improved its stature by overruling *Plessy* in *Brown* on a deeply divisive issue. And our decision in *West Coast Hotel,* which overruled *Adkins v. Children's Hospital,* supra, and *Lochner,* was rendered at a time when Congress was considering President Franklin Roosevelt's proposal to "reorganize" this Court and enable him to name six additional Justices in the event that any member of the Court over the age of 70 did not elect to retire. It is difficult to imagine a situation in which the Court would face more intense opposition to a prior ruling than it did at that time, and, under the general principle proclaimed in the joint opinion, the Court seemingly should have responded to this opposition by stubbornly refusing to reexamine the *Lochner* rationale, lest it lose legitimacy by appearing to "overrule under fire."

... But the [joint] opinion contends that the Court was entitled to overrule *Plessy* and *Lochner* ... only because both the Nation and the Court had learned new lessons in the interim. This is at best a feebly supported, *post hoc* rationalization for those decisions.

. . .

When the Court finally recognized its error in *West Coast Hotel,* it did not ... state that *Lochner* had been based on an economic view that had fallen into disfavor.... [T]he theme of the opinion is that the Court had been mistaken as a matter of constitutional law when it embraced "freedom of contract" 32 years previously.

... [As for *Brown,*] adherence to *Roe* today under the guise of "legitimacy" would seem to resemble more closely adherence to *Plessy* on the same ground. Fortunately, the Court did not choose that option in *Brown,* and instead frankly repudiated *Plessy....* [T]he same arguments made before the Court in *Brown* were made in *Plessy* as well. The Court in *Brown* simply recognized, as Justice Harlan had recognized beforehand, that the Fourteenth Amendment does not permit racial segregation. The rule of *Brown* is not tied to popular opinion about the evils of segregation; it is a judgment that the Equal Protection Clause does not permit racial segregation, no matter whether the public might come to believe that it is beneficial. On that ground it stands, and on that ground alone the Court was justified in properly concluding that the *Plessy* Court had erred.

There is also a suggestion in the joint opinion that the propriety of overruling a "divisive" decision depends in part on whether "most people" would now agree that it should be overruled.... [S]urely even the suggestion is totally at war with the idea of "legitimacy" in whose name it is invoked. The Judicial Branch derives its legitimacy, not from following public opinion, but from deciding by its best lights whether legislative enactments of the popular branches of Government comport with the Constitution. The doctrine of *stare decisis* is an adjunct of this duty, and should be no more subject to the vagaries of public opinion than is the basic judicial task.

... [T]he joint opinion forgets that there are two sides to any controversy.... The decision in *Roe* has engendered large demonstrations, including repeated marches on this Court and on Congress, both in opposition to and in support of that opinion. A decision either way on *Roe* can therefore be perceived as favoring one group or the other. But this perceived dilemma arises only if one assumes, as the joint opinion does, that the Court should make its decisions with a view toward speculative public perceptions. If one assumes instead, as the Court surely did in both *Brown* and *West Coast Hotel,* that the Court's legitimacy is enhanced by faithful interpretation of the Constitution irrespective of public opposition, such self-engendered difficulties may be put to one side.

... The joint opinion's message to ... protesters appears to be that they must cease their activities in order to serve their cause, because their protests will only cement in place a decision which by normal standards of *stare decisis* should be reconsidered.... Strong and often misguided criticism of a decision should not render the decision immune from reconsideration, lest a fetish for legitimacy penalize freedom of expression.

The end result of the joint opinion's paeans of praise for legitimacy is the enunciation of a brand new standard for evaluating state regulation of a woman's right to abortion—the "undue burden" standard.... *Roe*['s "fundamental right"-"strict scrutiny"] standard ... at least had a recognized basis in constitutional law.... The same cannot be said for the "undue burden" standard, which is created largely out of whole cloth by the authors of the joint opinion. It is a standard which even today does not command the support of a majority of this Court. And it will not, we believe, result in the sort of "simple limitation," easily applied, which the joint opinion anticipates. In sum, it is a standard ... not built to last.

... [T]his standard is based even more on a judge's subjective determinations than was the trimester framework.... [I]n the very matter before us now, the authors of the joint opinion would uphold Pennsylvania's 24–hour waiting period, concluding that a "particular burden" on some women is not a substantial obstacle. But the authors would at the same time strike down Pennsylvania's spousal notice provision, after finding that in a "large fraction" of cases the provision will be a substantial obstacle. And, while the authors conclude that the informed consent provisions do not constitute an "undue burden," Justice Stevens would hold that they do.

Furthermore, ... [t]he "undue burden" inquiry does not in any way supply the distinction between parental consent and spousal consent which the joint opinion adopts.... [T]he undue burden standard presents nothing more workable than the trimester framework which it discards today. Under the guise of the Constitution, this Court will still impart its own preferences on the States in the form of a complex abortion code.

. . .

... A woman's interest in having an abortion is a form of liberty protected by the Due Process Clause, but States may regulate abortion procedures in ways rationally related to a legitimate state interest....

III

A

. . .

Section 3205(a)(1) requires a physician to disclose certain information about the abortion procedure and its risks and alternatives.... [T]his information "clearly is related to maternal health and to the State's legitimate purpose in requiring informed consent." *Akron* ... An accurate description of the gestational age of the fetus and of the risks involved in carrying a child to term helps to further both those interests and the State's legitimate interest in unborn human life.... [Furthermore,] a State "may rationally decide that physicians are better qualified than counselors to impart this information and answer questions about the medical aspects of the available alternatives." ...

Section 3205(a)(2) compels the disclosure, by a physician or a counselor, of information concerning the availability of paternal child support and state-funded alternatives if the woman decides to proceed with her pregnancy.... [P]etitioners do not claim that the information required to be disclosed by statute is in any way false or inaccurate.... We conclude that this required presentation of "balanced information" is rationally related to the State's legitimate interest in ensuring that the woman's consent is truly informed, ... and in addition furthers the State's interest in preserving unborn life. That the information might create some uncertainty and persuade some women to forgo abortions does not [mean] the Constitution forbids [providing it]. Indeed, it only demonstrates that this information might very well make a difference, and that it is therefore relevant to a woman's informed choice.... We acknowledge that in *Thornburgh* this Court struck down informed consent requirements similar to the ones at issue here.... In light of our rejection of *Roe*'s "fundamental right" approach to this subject, we do not regard *Thornburgh* as controlling.

For the same reason, we do not feel bound to follow this Court's previous holding that a State's 24–hour mandatory waiting period is unconstitutional. See *Akron* ... [Though] such a provision will result in delays for some women that might not otherwise exist, therefore placing a burden on their liberty[, it] in no way prohibits abortions, and the informed consent and waiting period requirements do not apply in the case of a medical emergency.... [I]n providing time for reflection and reconsideration, the waiting period helps ensure that a woman's decision to abort is a well-considered one, and reasonably furthers the State's legitimate interest in maternal health and in the unborn life of the fetus....

B

. . .

We think it beyond dispute that a State "has a strong and legitimate interest in the welfare of its young citizens, whose immaturity, inexperience, and lack of judgment may sometimes impair their ability to exercise their rights wisely." *Hodgson v. Minnesota* ... (opinion of Stevens, J.). A requirement of parental consent to abortion ... is reasonably designed to further this important and legitimate state interest....

C

... [Petitioners] argue that the real effect of [the spousal] notice requirement is to give the power to husbands to veto a woman's abortion choice.... [I]t is not enough for petitioners to show that, in some "worst-case" circumstances, the notice provision will operate as a grant of veto power to husbands.... Because they are making a facial challenge to the provision, they must "show that no set of circumstances exists under which the [provision] would be valid." ... This they have failed to do.[2]

The question ... is therefore whether the spousal notification requirement rationally furthers any legitimate state interests. [I]t does. First, a husband's interests in procreation within marriage and in the potential life of his unborn child are certainly substantial ones.... The State itself has legitimate interests both in protecting these interests of the father and in protecting the potential life of the fetus, and the spousal notification requirement is reasonably related to advancing those state interests....

The State also has a legitimate interest in promoting "the integrity of the marital relationship." ... In our view, the spousal notice requirement is a rational attempt by the State to improve truthful communication between spouses and encourage collaborative decision-making, and thereby fosters marital integrity.... [It] will admittedly be unnecessary in some circumstances, and possibly harmful in others, but "the existence of particular cases in which a feature of a statute performs no function (or is even counter-productive) ordinarily does not render the statute unconstitutional or even constitutionally suspect." *Thornburgh* ... (White, J., dissenting). The Pennsylvania Legislature ... presumably concluded, on balance, that the provision would be beneficial. Whether this was a wise decision or not, we cannot say that it was irrational....

D

... The District Court found that the[required] reports are kept completely confidential.... We ... conclude that the[] reporting requirements rationally further the State's legitimate interests in advancing the state of medical knowledge concerning maternal health and prenatal life, in gathering statistical information with respect to patients, and in ensuring compliance with other provisions of the Act.

... Petitioners ... contend ... that the forced public disclosure of the information given by facilities receiving public funds serves no legitimate state interest. We disagree.... As the Court of Appeals observed, "[w]hen a state provides money to a private commercial enterprise, there is a legitimate public interest in informing taxpayers who the funds are benefiting and what services the funds are supporting." ... These reporting requirements rationally further this legitimate state interest.

E

Finally, petitioners challenge the medical emergency exception provided for by the Act....

. . .

---

[2] The joint opinion ... appears to ignore this point in concluding that the spousal notice provision imposes an undue burden on the abortion decision. In most instances the notification requirement operates without difficulty....

... [Under] the interpretation of the Court of Appeals in this case ... the provision ... should be upheld. When a woman is faced with any condition that poses a "significant threat to [her] life or health," she is exempted from the Act's consent and notice requirements and may proceed immediately with her abortion.

IV

[W]e would hold that each of the challenged provisions of the Pennsylvania statute is consistent with the Constitution. It bears emphasis that our conclusion in this regard does not carry with it any necessary approval of these regulations. Our task is, as always, to decide only whether the challenged provisions of a law comport with the United States Constitution. If, as we believe, these do, their wisdom as a matter of public policy is for the people of Pennsylvania to decide.

Justice Scalia, with whom The Chief Justice, Justice White, and Justice Thomas join, concurring in the judgment in part and dissenting in part.

... The States may, if they wish, permit abortion-on-demand, but the Constitution does not require them to do so. The permissibility of abortion, and the limitations upon it, are to be resolved like most important questions in our democracy: by citizens trying to persuade one another and then voting....

[T]he issue in this case [is] not whether the power of a woman to abort her unborn child is a "liberty" in the absolute sense; or even whether it is a liberty of great importance to many women. Of course it is both. The issue is whether it is a liberty protected by the Constitution of the United States. I am sure it is not. I reach that conclusion not because of anything so exalted as my views concerning the "concept of existence, of meaning, of the universe, and of the mystery of human life." Rather, I reach it ... because of two simple facts: (1) the Constitution says absolutely nothing about it, and (2) the longstanding traditions of American society have permitted it to be legally proscribed.[1] ...

. . .

... [A]pplying the rational basis test, I would uphold the Pennsylvania statute in its entirety. I must, however, respond to a few of the more outrageous arguments in today's opinion, which it is beyond human nature to leave unanswered....

. . .

... "[R]easoned judgment" does not begin by begging the question, as *Roe* and subsequent cases unquestionably did by assuming that what the State is protecting is the mere "potentiality of human life." ... The whole argument of abortion opponents is that what the Court calls the fetus and what others call

---

[1] The Court's suggestion that adherence to tradition would require us to uphold laws against interracial marriage is entirely wrong. Any tradition in that case was contradicted by a text—an Equal Protection Clause that explicitly establishes racial equality as a constitutional value.... The enterprise launched in *Roe,* by contrast, sought to establish—in the teeth of a clear, contrary tradition—a value found nowhere in the constitutional text. There is, of course, no comparable tradition barring recognition of a "liberty interest" in carrying one's child to term free from state efforts to kill it. For that reason, it does not follow that the Constitution does not protect childbirth simply because it does not protect abortion. The Court's contention that the only way to protect childbirth is to protect abortion shows the utter bankruptcy of constitutional analysis deprived of tradition as a validating factor. It drives one to say that the only way to protect the right to eat is to acknowledge the constitutional right to starve oneself to death.

the unborn child is a human life. Thus, whatever answer *Roe* came up with after conducting its "balancing" is bound to be wrong, unless it is correct that the human fetus is in some critical sense merely potentially human. There is of course no way to determine that as a legal matter; it is in fact a value judgment....

. . .

The emptiness of the "reasoned judgment" that produced *Roe* is displayed in plain view by the fact that . . . the best the Court can do to explain how it is that the word "liberty" must be thought to include the right to destroy human fetuses is to rattle off a collection of adjectives that simply decorate a value judgment and conceal a political choice.... But it is obvious to anyone applying "reasoned judgment" that the same adjectives can be applied to many forms of conduct that this Court . . . has held are not entitled to constitutional protection—because, like abortion, they are forms of conduct that have long been criminalized in American society. Those adjectives might be applied, for example, to homosexual sodomy, polygamy, adult incest, and suicide, all of which are equally "intimate" and "deep[ly] personal" decisions involving "personal autonomy and bodily integrity," and all of which can constitutionally be proscribed because it is our unquestionable constitutional tradition that they are proscribable. It is not reasoned judgment that supports the Court's decision; only personal predilection....

. . .

. . . The shortcomings of *Roe* did not include lack of clarity; Virtually all regulation of abortion before the third trimester was invalid. But . . . the joint opinion . . . calls upon federal district judges to apply an "undue burden" standard as doubtful in application as it is unprincipled in origin....

. . .

The rootless nature of the "undue burden" standard . . . is . . . reflected in the fact that the joint opinion finds it necessary expressly to repudiate the more narrow formulations used in Justice O'Connor's earlier opinions. Those opinions stated that a statute imposes an "undue burden" if it imposes "absolute obstacles or severe limitations on the abortion decision," *Akron I,* . . . (O'Connor, J., dissenting).... Those strong adjectives are conspicuously missing from the joint opinion, whose authors have for some unexplained reason now determined that a burden is "undue" if it merely imposes a "substantial" obstacle to abortion decisions. Justice O'Connor has also abandoned (again without explanation) the view she expressed in . . . *Ashcroft* . . . (1983) (dissenting opinion), that a medical regulation which imposes an "undue burden" could nevertheless be upheld if it "reasonably relate[s] to the preservation and protection of maternal health,".... In today's version, even health measures will be upheld only "if they do not constitute an undue burden." Gone too is Justice O'Connor's statement that "the State possesses compelling interests in the protection of potential human life . . . throughout pregnancy," *Akron I* . . .; instead, the State's interest in unborn human life is stealthily downgraded to a merely "substantial" or "profound" interest. (That had to be done, of course, since designating the interest as "compelling" throughout pregnancy would have been, shall we say, a "substantial obstacle" to the joint opinion's determined effort to reaffirm what it views as the "central holding" of *Roe*.) . . . And "viability" is no longer the "arbitrary" dividing line previously decried by Justice O'Connor in *Akron I* . . .; the Court now announces that "the attainment of viability may continue to serve as the critical fact." It is difficult to maintain the illusion that we are interpreting a Constitution rather than inventing one, when we amend its provisions so breezily.

. . . [O]ne must turn to the 23 pages applying that standard to the present facts for further guidance. . . . [T]he joint opinion relies extensively on the factual findings of the District Court, and repeatedly qualifies its conclusions by noting that they are contingent upon the record. . . .

. . .

To the extent I can discern any meaningful content in the "undue burden" standard as applied in the joint opinion, . . . a State may not regulate abortion in such a way as to reduce significantly its incidence. . . . [D]espite flowery rhetoric about the State's "substantial" and "profound" interest in "potential human life," and criticism of *Roe* for undervaluing that interest, the joint opinion permits the State to pursue that interest only so long as it is not too successful. . . .

. . .

The Court's reliance upon *stare decisis* can best be described as contrived. . . . I confess never to have heard of this new, keep-what-you-want-and-throw-away-the-rest version. . . .

. . . I have always thought, and I think a lot of other people have always thought, that the arbitrary trimester framework, which the Court today discards, was quite as central to *Roe* as the arbitrary viability test, which the Court today retains. . . .

. . .

The Court's description of the place of *Roe* in the social history of the United States is unrecognizable. Not only did *Roe* not . . . resolve the deeply divisive issue of abortion; it did more than anything else to nourish it, by elevating it to the national level where it is infinitely more difficult to resolve. National politics were not plagued by abortion protests, national abortion lobbying, or abortion marches on Congress, before *Roe v. Wade* was decided. Profound disagreement existed . . . but that disagreement was being worked out at the state level. As with many other issues, the division of sentiment within each State was not as closely balanced as it was among the population of the Nation as a whole, meaning not only that more people would be satisfied with the results of state-by-state resolution, but also that those results would be more stable. Pre–*Roe,* moreover, political compromise was possible.

Roe's mandate for abortion-on-demand destroyed the compromises of the past, rendered compromise impossible for the future, and required the entire issue to be resolved uniformly, at the national level. At the same time, *Roe* created a vast new class of abortion consumers and abortion proponents by eliminating the moral opprobrium that had attached to the act. . . . Many favor all of those developments, and it is not for me to say that they are wrong. But to portray *Roe* as the statesmanlike "settlement" of a divisive issue . . . is nothing less than Orwellian. *Roe* fanned into life an issue that has inflamed our national politics in general, and has obscured with its smoke the selection of Justices to this Court in particular, ever since. And by keeping us in the abortion-umpiring business, it is the perpetuation of that disruption, rather than of any *pax Roeana,* that the Court's new majority decrees.

. . .

It is particularly difficult ... to sit still for the Court's lengthy lecture upon the virtues of "constancy," of "remain[ing] steadfast," of adhering to "principle." Among the five Justices who purportedly adhere to *Roe,* at most three agree upon the principle that constitutes adherence (the joint opinion's "undue burden" standard)—and that principle is inconsistent with *Roe. . . .* To make matters worse, two of the three, in order thus to remain steadfast, had to abandon previously stated positions. . . .

I cannot agree with, indeed I am appalled by, the Court's suggestion that the decision whether to stand by an erroneous constitutional decision must be strongly influenced—against overruling, no less—by the substantial and continuing public opposition the decision has generated. . . .

[T]he notion that we would decide a case differently from the way we otherwise would have in order to show that we can stand firm against public disapproval is frightening. . . .

... Instead of engaging in the hopeless task of predicting public perception—a job not for lawyers but for political campaign managers—the Justices should do what is legally right by asking two questions: (1) Was *Roe* correctly decided? (2) Has *Roe* succeeded in producing a settled body of law? If the answer to both questions is no, *Roe* should undoubtedly be overruled.

... I am as distressed as the Court is ... about the "political pressure" directed to the Court. . . . The Court would profit, I think, from giving less attention to the fact of this distressing phenomenon, and more attention to the cause of it ...: a new mode of constitutional adjudication that relies not upon text and traditional practice to determine the law, but upon what the Court calls "reasoned judgment," which turns out to be nothing but philosophical predilection and moral intuition. . . .

... As long as this Court thought (and the people thought) that we Justices were doing essentially lawyers' work up here—reading text and discerning our society's traditional understanding of that text—the public pretty much left us alone. Texts and traditions are facts to study, not convictions to demonstrate about. But if ... our pronouncement of constitutional law rests primarily on value judgments, then a free and intelligent people's attitude towards us can be expected to be (ought to be) quite different. The people know that their value judgments are quite as good as those taught in any law school—maybe better. If, indeed, the "liberties" protected by the Constitution are, as the Court says, undefined and unbounded, then the people should demonstrate, to protest that we do not implement their values instead of ours. Not only that, but confirmation hearings for new Justices should deteriorate into question-and-answer sessions in which Senators go through a list of their constituents' most favored and most disfavored alleged constitutional rights, and seek the nominee's commitment to support or oppose them. Value judgments, after all, should be voted on, not dictated; and if our Constitution has somehow accidently committed them to the Supreme Court, at least we can have a sort of plebiscite each time a new nominee to that body is put forward. Justice Blackmun not only regards this prospect with equanimity, he solicits it.

. . .

RESTRICTIONS ON PRIVATE CONSENSUAL SEXUAL BEHAVIOR

Can the protection of privacy and personal autonomy articulated in Roe v. Wade be extended to protect private consensual sexual behavior outside the norms of the marriage relationship? In Carey v. Population Services Intern.,

431 U.S. 678 (1977), the Court said in a footnote: "Appellees argue that ... the right to privacy comprehends a right of minors as well as adults to engage in private consensual sexual behavior. We observe that the Court has not definitively answered the difficult question whether and to what extent the Constitution prohibits state statutes regulating such behavior among adults. See generally Note, On Privacy: Constitutional Protection for Personal Liberty, 48 N.Y.U.L.Rev. 670, 719–738 (1973)." Justice Powell expressed his concern that the Court "would subject all state regulation affecting adult sexual relations to the strictest standard of judicial review." Justice Rehnquist asserted that while the Court had not "ruled on every conceivable regulation affecting such conduct the facial constitutional validity of criminal statutes prohibiting certain consensual acts has been 'definitively' established." For that statement he relied on Doe v. Commonwealth's Attorney, 425 U.S. 901 (1976), in which the Court summarily affirmed a district court dismissal of a challenge by male homosexuals to Virginia's sodomy law.

Bowers v. Hardwick

478 U.S. 186, 106 S.Ct. 2841, 92 L.Ed.2d 140 (1986).

Justice White delivered the opinion of the Court.

In August 1982, respondent was charged with violating the Georgia statute criminalizing sodomy[1] by committing that act with another adult male in the bedroom of respondent's home. After a preliminary hearing, the District Attorney decided not to present the matter to the grand jury unless further evidence developed.

Respondent then brought suit in the Federal District Court, challenging the constitutionality of the statute insofar as it criminalized consensual sodomy.[2] He asserted that he was a practicing homosexual, that the Georgia sodomy statute, as administered by the defendants, placed him in imminent danger of arrest, and that the statute for several reasons violates the Federal Constitution. The District Court granted the defendants' motion to dismiss for failure to state a claim....

A divided ... Eleventh Circuit reversed. ...Relying on our decisions in Griswold v. Connecticut, 381 U.S. 479 (1965), Eisenstadt v. Baird, 405 U.S. 438 (1972), Stanley v. Georgia, 394 U.S. 557 (1969), and Roe v. Wade, 410 U.S. 113 (1973), the court went on to hold that the Georgia statute violated respondent's fundamental rights because his homosexual activity is a private and intimate

---

[1] Ga.Code Ann. § 16–6–2 (1984) provides, in pertinent part, as follows:

"(a) A person commits the offense of sodomy when he performs or submits to any sexual act involving the sex organs of one person and the mouth or anus of another....

"(b) A person convicted of the offense of sodomy shall be punished by imprisonment for not less than one nor more than 20 years...."

[2] John and Mary Doe were also plaintiffs in the action. They alleged that they wished to engage in sexual activity proscribed by § 16–6–2 in the privacy of their home, and that they had been "chilled and deterred" from engaging in such activity by both the existence of the statute and Hardwick's arrest. The District Court held, however, that because they had neither sustained, nor were in immediate danger of sustaining, any direct injury from the enforcement of the statute, they did not have proper standing to maintain the action. The Court of Appeals affirmed the District Court's judgment dismissing the Does' claim for lack of standing, 760 F.2d 1202, 1206–1207 (1985), and the Does do not challenge that holding in this Court.

The only claim properly before the Court, therefore, is Hardwick's challenge to the Georgia statute as applied to consensual homosexual sodomy. We express no opinion on the constitutionality of the Georgia statute as applied to other acts of sodomy.

association . . . beyond the reach of state regulation by reason of the Ninth Amendment and the Due Process Clause of the Fourteenth Amendment. The case was remanded for trial, at which, to prevail, the State would have to prove that the statute is supported by a compelling interest and is the most narrowly drawn means of achieving that end.

Because other Courts of Appeals have arrived at judgments contrary to that of the Eleventh Circuit in this case we granted the State's petition for certiorari questioning the holding that its sodomy statute violates the fundamental rights of homosexuals. We . . . reverse. . . .

This case does not require a judgment on whether laws against sodomy between consenting adults in general, or between homosexuals in particular, are wise or desirable. It raises no question about the right or propriety of state legislative decisions to repeal their laws that criminalize homosexual sodomy, or of state court decisions invalidating those laws on state constitutional grounds. The issue presented is whether the Federal Constitution confers a fundamental right upon homosexuals to engage in sodomy and hence invalidates the laws of the many States that still make such conduct illegal and have done so for a very long time. The case also calls for some judgment about the limits of the Court's role in carrying out its constitutional mandate.

We first register our disagreement with the Court of Appeals and with respondent that the Court's prior cases have construed the Constitution to confer a right of privacy that extends to homosexual sodomy and for all intents and purposes have decided this case. The reach of this line of cases was sketched in Carey v. Population Services International, 431 U.S. 678, 685 (1977). Pierce v. Society of Sisters, 268 U.S. 510 (1925), and Meyer v. Nebraska, 262 U.S. 390 (1923), were described as dealing with child rearing and education; Prince v. Massachusetts, 321 U.S. 158 (1944), with family relationships; Skinner v. Oklahoma ex rel. Williamson, 316 U.S. 535 (1942), with procreation; Loving v. Virginia, 388 U.S. 1 (1967), with marriage; *Griswold v. Connecticut,* supra, and *Eisenstadt v. Baird,* supra, with contraception; and Roe v. Wade, 410 U.S. 113 (1973), with abortion. The latter three cases were interpreted as construing the Due Process Clause of the Fourteenth Amendment to confer a fundamental individual right to decide whether or not to beget or bear a child. Carey v. Population Services International, supra, at 688–689.

Accepting the decisions in these cases and the above description of them, we think it evident that none of the rights announced in those cases bears any resemblance to the claimed constitutional right of homosexuals to engage in acts of sodomy that is asserted in this case. No connection between family, marriage, or procreation on the one hand and homosexual activity on the other has been demonstrated, either by the Court of Appeals or by respondent. Moreover, any claim that these cases nevertheless stand for the proposition that any kind of private sexual conduct between consenting adults is constitutionally insulated from state proscription is unsupportable. Indeed, the Court's opinion in *Carey* twice asserted that the privacy right, which the *Griswold* line of cases found to be one of the protections provided by the Due Process Clause, did not reach so far. 431 U.S., at 688, n. 5, 694, n. 17.

Precedent aside, however, respondent would have us announce, as the Court of Appeals did, a fundamental right to engage in homosexual sodomy. This we are quite unwilling to do. It is true that despite the language of the Due Process Clauses of the Fifth and Fourteenth Amendments, which appears to focus only on the processes by which life, liberty, or property is taken, the cases are legion in which those Clauses have been interpreted to have substantive content, subsuming rights that to a great extent are immune from federal or state regulation or proscription. Among such cases are those recognizing rights that have little or no textual support in the constitutional language. *Myers, Prince,* and *Pierce* fall in this category, as do the privacy cases from *Griswold* to *Carey.*

Striving to assure itself and the public that announcing rights not readily identifiable in the Constitution's text involves much more than the imposition of the Justices' own choice of values on the States and the Federal Government, the Court has sought to identify the nature of the rights qualifying for heightened judicial protection. In Palko v. Connecticut, 302 U.S. 319, 325, 326 (1937), it was said that this category includes those fundamental liberties that are "implicit in the concept of ordered liberty," such that "neither liberty nor justice would exist if [they] were sacrificed." A different description of fundamental liberties appeared in Moore v. East Cleveland, 431 U.S. 494, 503 (1977) (opinion of Powell, J.), where they are characterized as those liberties that are "deeply rooted in this Nation's history and tradition." Id., at 503 (Powell, J.). See also Griswold v. Connecticut, 381 U.S., at 506.

It is obvious to us that neither of these formulations would extend a fundamental right to homosexuals to engage in acts of consensual sodomy. Proscriptions against that conduct have ancient roots. See generally, Survey on the Constitutional Right to Privacy in the Context of Homosexual Activity, 40 Miami U.L.Rev. 521, 525 (1986). Sodomy was a criminal offense at common law and was forbidden by the laws of the original thirteen States when they ratified the Bill of Rights. In 1868, when the Fourteenth Amendment was ratified, all but 5 of the 37 States in the Union had criminal sodomy laws. In fact, until 1961, all 50 States outlawed sodomy, and today, 24 States and the District of Columbia continue to provide criminal penalties for sodomy performed in private and between consenting adults. Survey, Miami U.L.Rev., supra, at 524, n. 9. Against this background, to claim that a right to engage in such conduct is "deeply rooted in this Nation's history and tradition" or "implicit in the concept of ordered liberty" is, at best, facetious.

Nor are we inclined to take a more expansive view of our authority to discover new fundamental rights imbedded in the Due Process Clause. The Court is most vulnerable and comes nearest to illegitimacy when it deals with judge-made constitutional law having little or no cognizable roots in the language or design of the Constitution. That this is so was painfully demonstrated by the face-off between the Executive and the Court in the 1930's, which resulted in the repudiation of much of the substantive gloss that the Court had placed on the Due Process Clause of the Fifth and Fourteenth Amendments. There should be, therefore, great resistance to expand the substantive reach of those Clauses, particularly if it requires redefining the category of rights deemed to be fundamental. Otherwise, the Judiciary necessarily takes to itself further authority to govern the country without express constitutional authority. The claimed right pressed on us today falls far short of overcoming this resistance.

Respondent, however, asserts that the result should be different where the homosexual conduct occurs in the privacy of the home. He relies on Stanley v. Georgia, 394 U.S. 557 (1969), where the Court held that the First Amendment prevents conviction for possessing and reading obscene material in the privacy of his home: "If the First Amendment means anything, it means that a State has no business telling a man, sitting alone in his house, what books he may read or what films he may watch." Id., at 565.

Stanley did protect conduct that would not have been protected outside the home, and it partially prevented the enforcement of state obscenity laws; but the decision was firmly grounded in the First Amendment. The right pressed upon us here has no similar support in the text of the Constitution, and it does not qualify for recognition under the prevailing principles for construing the Fourteenth Amendment. Its limits are also difficult to discern. Plainly enough, otherwise illegal conduct is not always immunized whenever it occurs in the home. Victimless crimes, such as the possession and use of illegal drugs do not escape the law where they are committed at home. *Stanley* itself recognized that its holding offered no protection for the possession in the home of drugs, firearms, or stolen goods. Id., at 568, n. 11. And if respondent's submission is limited to the voluntary sexual conduct between consenting adults, it would be difficult, except by fiat, to limit the claimed right to homosexual conduct while leaving exposed to prosecution adultery, incest, and other sexual crimes even though they are committed in the home. We are unwilling to start down that road.

Even if the conduct at issue here is not a fundamental right, respondent asserts that there must be a rational basis for the law and that there is none in this case other than the presumed belief of a majority of the electorate in Georgia that homosexual sodomy is immoral and unacceptable. This is said to be an inadequate rationale to support the law. The law, however, is constantly based on notions of morality, and if all laws representing essentially moral choices are to be invalidated under the Due Process Clause, the courts will be very busy indeed. Even respondent makes no such claim, but insists that majority sentiments about the morality of homosexuality should be declared inadequate. We do not agree, and are unpersuaded that the sodomy laws of some 25 States should be invalidated on this basis.[8]

Accordingly, the judgment of the Court of Appeals is reversed.

Chief Justice Burger, concurring.

I join the Court's opinion, but I write separately to underscore my view that in constitutional terms there is no such thing as a fundamental right to commit homosexual sodomy.

As the Court notes, the proscriptions against sodomy have very "ancient roots." Decisions of individuals relating to homosexual conduct have been subject to state intervention throughout the history of Western Civilization. Condemnation of those practices is firmly rooted in Judeao–Christian moral and ethical standards. Homosexual sodomy was a capital crime under Roman law. See Code Theod. 9.7.6; Code Just. 9.9.31. See also D. Bailey, Homosexuality in the Western Christian Tradition 70–81 (1975). During the English Reformation when powers of the ecclesiastical courts were transferred to the King's Courts, the first English statute criminalizing sodomy was passed. 25 Hen. VIII, c. 6. Blackstone described "the infamous crime against nature" as an offense of "deeper malignity" than rape, an heinous act "the very mention of which is a disgrace to human nature," and "a crime not fit to be named." Blackstone's Commentaries *215. The common law of England, including its prohibition of sodomy, became the received law of Georgia and the other Colonies. In 1816 the Georgia Legislature passed the statute at issue here, and that statute has been continuously in force in one form or another since that time. To hold that the act of homosexual sodomy is somehow protected as a fundamental right would be to cast aside millennia of moral teaching.

---

[8] Respondent does not defend the judgment below based on the Ninth Amendment, the Equal Protection Clause or the Eighth Amendment.

This is essentially not a question of personal "preferences" but rather that of the legislative authority of the State. I find nothing in the Constitution depriving a State of the power to enact the statute challenged here.

Justice Powell, concurring.

I join the opinion of the Court. I agree with the Court that there is no fundamental right—i.e., no substantive right under the Due Process Clause—such as that claimed by respondent, and found to exist by the Court of Appeals. This is not to suggest, however, that respondent may not be protected by the Eighth Amendment of the Constitution. The Georgia statute at issue in this case, Ga.Code Ann. § 16–6–2, authorizes a court to imprison a person for up to 20 years for a single private, consensual act of sodomy. In my view, a prison sentence for such conduct—certainly a sentence of long duration—would create a serious Eighth Amendment issue. Under the Georgia statute a single act of sodomy, even in the private setting of a home, is a felony comparable in terms of the possible sentence imposed to serious felonies such as aggravated battery, § 16–5–24, first degree arson, § 16–7–60 and robbery, § 16–8–40.

In this case, however, respondent has not been tried, much less convicted and sentenced. Moreover, respondent has not raised the Eighth Amendment issue below. For these reasons this constitutional argument is not before us.

Justice Blackmun, with whom Justice Brennan, Justice Marshall, and Justice Stevens join, dissenting.

This case is no more about "a fundamental right to engage in homosexual sodomy," as the Court purports to declare than Stanley v. Georgia, 394 U.S. 557 (1969), was about a fundamental right to watch obscene movies, or Katz v. United States, 389 U.S. 347 (1967), was about a fundamental right to place interstate bets from a telephone booth. Rather, this case is about "the most comprehensive of rights and the right most valued by civilized men," namely, "the right to be let alone." Olmstead v. United States, 277 U.S. 438, 478 (1928) (Brandeis, J., dissenting).

The statute at issue ... denies individuals the right to decide for themselves whether to engage in particular forms of private, consensual sexual activity. The Court concludes that § 16–6–2 is valid essentially because "the laws of ... many States ... still make such conduct illegal and have done so for a very long time." But the fact that the moral judgments expressed by statutes like § 16–6–2 may be "natural and familiar ... ought not to conclude our judgment upon the question whether statutes embodying them conflict with the Constitution of the United States." Roe v. Wade, 410 U.S. 113, 117 (1973), quoting Lochner v. New York, 198 U.S. 45, 76 (1905) (Holmes, J., dissenting). Like Justice Holmes, I believe that "[i]t is revolting to have no better reason for a rule of law than that so it was laid down in the time of Henry IV. It is still more revolting if the grounds upon which it was laid down have vanished long since, and the rule simply persists from blind imitation of the past." Holmes, The Path of the Law, 10 Harv.L.Rev. 457, 469 (1897). I believe we must analyze respondent's claim in the light of the values that underlie the constitutional right to privacy. If that right means anything, it means that, before Georgia can prosecute its citizens for making choices about the most intimate aspects of their lives, it must do more than assert that the choice they have made is an "'abominable crime not fit to be named among Christians.' "Herring v. State, 119 Ga. 709, 721, 46 S.E. 876, 882 (1904).

I

... A fair reading of the statute and of the complaint clearly reveals that the majority has distorted the question this case presents.

First, the Court's almost obsessive focus on homosexual activity is particularly hard to justify in light of the broad language Georgia has used. Unlike the Court, the Georgia Legislature has not proceeded on the assumption that homosexuals are so different from other citizens that their lives may be controlled in a way that would not be tolerated if it limited the choices of those other citizens. Rather, Georgia has provided that "[a] person commits the offense of sodomy when he performs or submits to any sexual act involving the sex organs of one person and the mouth or anus of another." Ga.Code Ann. § 16–6–2(a). The sex or status of the persons who engage in the act is irrelevant as a matter of state law. In fact, to the extent I can discern a legislative purpose for Georgia's 1968 enactment of § 16–6–2, that purpose seems to have been to broaden the coverage of the law to reach heterosexual as well as homosexual activity. I therefore see no basis for the Court's decision to treat this case as an "as applied" challenge to § 16–6–2, or for Georgia's attempt, both in its brief and at oral argument, to defend § 16–6–2 solely on the grounds that it prohibits homosexual activity. Michael Hardwick's standing may rest in significant part on Georgia's apparent willingness to enforce against homosexuals a law it seems not to have any desire to enforce against heterosexuals.... But his claim that § 16–6–2 involves an unconstitutional intrusion into his privacy and his right of intimate association does not depend in any way on his sexual orientation.

Second, I disagree with the Court's refusal to consider whether § 16–6–2 runs afoul of the Eighth or Ninth Amendments or the Equal Protection Clause of the Fourteenth Amendment....

II

"Our cases long have recognized that the Constitution embodies a promise that a certain private sphere of individual liberty will be kept largely beyond the reach of government." Thornburgh v. American Coll. of Obst. & Gyn., 476 U.S. 747, 772 (1986). In construing the right to privacy the Court has proceeded along two somewhat distinct, albeit complementary, lines. First, it has recognized a privacy interest with reference to certain *decisions* that are properly for the individual to make. E.g., Roe v. Wade, 410 U.S. 113 (1973); Pierce v. Society of Sisters, 268 U.S. 510 (1925). Second, it has recognized a privacy interest with reference to certain *places* without regard for the particular activities in which the individuals who occupy them are engaged. E.g., United States v. Karo, 468 U.S. 705 (1984); Payton v. New York, 445 U.S. 573 (1980); Rios v. United States, 364 U.S. 253 (1960). The case before us implicates both the decisional and the spatial aspects of the right to privacy.

A

The Court concludes today that none of our prior cases dealing with various decisions that individuals are entitled to make free of governmental interference "bears any resemblance to the claimed constitutional right of homosexuals to engage in acts of sodomy that is asserted in this case." While it is true that these cases may be characterized by their connection to protection of the family, see Roberts v. United States Jaycees, 468 U.S. 609, 619 (1984), the Court's conclusion that they extend no further than this boundary ignores the warning in Moore v. East Cleveland, 431 U.S. 494, 501 (1977) (plurality opinion), against "clos[ing] our eyes to the basic reasons why certain rights associated with the family have been accorded shelter under the Fourteenth Amendment's Due Process Clause." We protect those rights not because they contribute, in some direct and material way, to the general public welfare, but because they form so central a part of an individual's life. "[T]he concept of privacy embodies the 'moral fact that a person belongs to himself and not others nor to society as a whole.' " Thornburgh v. American Coll. of Obst. & Gyn., 476 U.S. at 777, n. 5 (Stevens, J., concurring), quoting Fried, Correspondence, 6 Phil. & Pub. Affairs 288–289 (1977). And so we protect the decision whether to marry precisely because marriage "is an association that promotes a way of life, not causes; a harmony in living, not political faiths; a bilateral loyalty, not commercial or social projects." Griswold v. Connecticut, 381 U.S., at 486. We protect the decision whether to have a child because parenthood alters so dramatically an individual's self-definition, not because of demographic considerations or the Bible's command to be fruitful and multiply. Cf. Thornburgh v. American Coll. of Obst. & Gyn., supra, at 778, n. 6 (Stevens, J., concurring). And we protect the family because it contributes so powerfully to the happiness of individuals, not because of a preference for stereotypical households. Cf. Moore v. East Cleveland, 431 U.S., at 500–506 (plurality opinion). The Court recognized in *Roberts,* 468 U.S., at 619, that the "ability independently to define one's identity that is central to any concept of liberty" cannot truly be exercised in a vacuum; we all depend on the "emotional enrichment of close ties with others." Ibid.

Only the most willful blindness could obscure the fact that sexual intimacy is "a sensitive, key relationship of human existence, central to family life, community welfare, and the development of human personality," Paris Adult Theatre I v. Slaton, 413 U.S. 49, 63 (1973); see also Carey v. Population Services International, 431 U.S. 678, 685 (1977). The fact that individuals define themselves in a significant way through their intimate sexual relationships with others suggests, in a Nation as diverse as ours, that there may be many "right" ways of conducting those relationships, and that much of the richness of a relationship will come from the freedom an individual has to *choose* the form and nature of these intensely personal bonds. See Karst, The Freedom of Intimate Association, 89 Yale L.J. 624, 637 (1980); cf. Eisenstadt v. Baird, 405 U.S. 438, 453 (1972); Roe v. Wade, 410 U.S., at 153.

. . . The Court claims that its decision today merely refuses to recognize a fundamental right to engage in homosexual sodomy; what the Court really has refused to recognize is the fundamental interest all individuals have in controlling the nature of their intimate associations with others.

B

The behavior for which Hardwick faces prosecution occurred in his own home, a place to which the Fourth Amendment attaches special significance. The Court's treatment of this aspect of the case is symptomatic of its overall refusal to consider the broad principles that have informed our treatment of privacy in specific cases. Just as the right to privacy is more than the mere aggregation of a number of entitlements to engage in specific behavior, so too, protecting the physical integrity of the home is more than merely a means of protecting specific activities that often take place there. . . .

The Court's interpretation of the pivotal case of Stanley v. Georgia, 394 U.S. 557 (1969), is entirely unconvincing. . . .

. . . Indeed, the right of an individual to conduct intimate relationships in the intimacy of his or her own home seems to me to be the heart of the Constitution's protection of privacy.

III

The Court's failure to comprehend the magnitude of the liberty interests at stake in this case leads it to slight the question whether [the State] has justified

Georgia's infringement on these interests. I believe that neither of the two general justifications for § 16–6–2 that petitioner has advanced warrants dismissing respondent's challenge for failure to state a claim.

First, petitioner asserts that the acts made criminal by the statute may have serious adverse consequences for "the general public health and welfare," such as spreading communicable diseases or fostering other criminal activity. Inasmuch as this case was dismissed by the District Court on the pleadings, it is not surprising that the record before us is barren of any evidence to support petitioner's claim. In light of the state of the record, I see no justification for the Court's attempt to equate the private, consensual sexual activity at issue here with the "possession in the home of drugs, firearms, or stolen goods," to which *Stanley* refused to extend its protection....

. . .

Nor can § 16–6–2 be justified as a "morally neutral" exercise of Georgia's power to "protect the public environment," *Paris Adult Theatre I,* 413 U.S., at 68–69. Certainly, some private behavior can affect the fabric of society as a whole. Reasonable people may differ about whether particular sexual acts are moral or immoral, but "we have ample evidence for believing that people will not abandon morality, will not think any better of murder, cruelty and dishonesty, merely because some private sexual practice which they abominate is not punished by the law." H.L.A. Hart, Immorality and Treason, reprinted in The Law as Literature 220, 225 (L. Blom–Cooper ed. 1961). Petitioner and the Court fail to see the difference between laws that protect public sensibilities and those that enforce private morality. Statutes banning public sexual activity are entirely consistent with protecting the individual's liberty interest in decisions concerning sexual relations: the same recognition that those decisions are intensely private which justifies protecting them from governmental interference can justify protecting individuals from unwilling exposure to the sexual activities of others. But the mere fact that intimate behavior may be punished when it takes place in public cannot dictate how States can regulate intimate behavior that occurs in intimate places....

This case involves no real interference with the rights of others, for the mere knowledge that other individuals do not adhere to one's value system cannot be a legally cognizable interest, ... let alone an interest that can justify invading the houses, hearts, and minds of citizens who choose to live there lives differently.

IV

It took but three years for the Court to see the error in its analysis in Minersville School District v. Gobitis, 310 U.S. 586 (1940), and to recognize that the threat to national cohesion posed by a refusal to salute the flag was vastly outweighed by the threat to those same values posed by compelling such a salute. See West Virginia Board of Education v. Barnette, 319 U.S. 624 (1943). I can only hope that here, too, the Court soon will reconsider its analysis and conclude that depriving individuals of the right to choose for themselves how to conduct their intimate relationships poses a far greater threat to the values most deeply rooted in our Nation's history than tolerance of nonconformity could ever do. Because I think the Court today betrays those values, I dissent.

Justice Stevens, with whom Justice Brennan and Justice Marshall join, dissenting.

Like the statute that is challenged in this case, the rationale of the Court's opinion applies equally to the prohibited conduct regardless of whether the parties who engage in it are married or unmarried, or are of the same or different sexes. Sodomy was condemned as an odious and sinful type of behavior during the formative period of the common law. That condemnation was equally damning for heterosexual and homosexual sodomy. Moreover, it provided no special exemption for married couples. The license to cohabit and to produce legitimate offspring simply did not include any permission to engage in sexual conduct that was considered a "crime against nature."

The history of the Georgia statute before us clearly reveals this traditional prohibition of heterosexual, as well as homosexual, sodomy. Indeed, at one point in the 20th century, Georgia's law was construed to permit certain sexual conduct between homosexual women even though such conduct was prohibited between heterosexuals. The history of the statutes cited by the majority as proof for the proposition that sodomy is not constitutionally protected, similarly reveals a prohibition on heterosexual, as well as homosexual, sodomy.

Because the Georgia statute expresses the traditional view that sodomy is an immoral kind of conduct regardless of the identity of the persons who engage in it, I believe that a proper analysis of its constitutionality requires consideration of two questions: First, may a State totally prohibit the described conduct by means of a neutral law applying without exception to all persons subject to its jurisdiction? If not, may the State save the statute by announcing that it will only enforce the law against homosexuals? The two questions merit separate discussion.

I

Our prior cases make two propositions abundantly clear. First, the fact that the governing majority in a State has traditionally viewed a particular practice as immoral is not a sufficient reason for upholding a law prohibiting the practice; neither history nor tradition could save a law prohibiting miscegenation from constitutional attack. Second, individual decisions by married persons, concerning the intimacies of their physical relationship, even when not intended to produce offspring, are a form of "liberty" protected by the Due Process Clause of the Fourteenth Amendment. Griswold v. Connecticut, 381 U.S. 479 (1965). Moreover, this protection extends to intimate choices by unmarried as well as married persons. Carey v. Population Services International, 431 U.S. 678 (1977); Eisenstadt v. Baird, 405 U.S. 438 (1972).

. . .

II

If the Georgia statute cannot be enforced as it is written—if the conduct it seeks to prohibit is a protected form of liberty for the vast majority of Georgia's citizens—the State must assume the burden of justifying a selective application of its law. Either the persons to whom Georgia seeks to apply its statute do not have the same interest in "liberty" that others have, or there must be a reason why the State may be permitted to apply a generally applicable law to certain persons that it does not apply to others.

The first possibility is plainly unacceptable. Although the meaning of the principle that "all men are created equal" is not always clear, it surely must mean that every free citizen has the same interest in "liberty" that the members of the majority share. From the standpoint of the individual, the homosexual and the heterosexual have the same interest in deciding how he will live his own life, and, more narrowly, how he will conduct himself in his personal and voluntary associations with his companions. State intrusion into the private conduct of either is equally burdensome.

The second possibility is similarly unacceptable. A policy of selective application must be supported by a neutral and legitimate interest—something more substantial than a habitual dislike for, or ignorance about, the disfavored group. Neither the State not the Court has identified any such interest in this case. The Court has posited as a justification for the Georgia statute "the presumed belief of a majority of the electorate in Georgia that homosexual sodomy is immoral and unacceptable." But the Georgia electorate has expressed no such belief—instead, its representatives enacted a law that presumably reflects the belief that *all sodomy* is immoral and unacceptable. Unless the Court is prepared to conclude that such a law is constitutional, it may not rely on the work product of the Georgia Legislature to support its holding. For the Georgia statute does not single out homosexuals as a separate class meriting special disfavored treatment.

Nor, indeed, does the Georgia prosecutor even believe that all homosexuals who violate this statute should be punished. This conclusion is evident from the fact that the respondent in this very case has formally acknowledged in his complaint and in court that he has engaged, and intends to continue to engage, in the prohibited conduct, yet the State has elected not to process criminal charges against him. As Justice Powell points out, moreover, Georgia's prohibition on private, consensual sodomy has not been enforced for decades. The record of nonenforcement, in this case and in the last several decades, belies the Attorney General's representations about the importance of the State's selective application of its generally applicable law.

Both the Georgia statute and the Georgia prosecutor thus completely fail to provide the Court with any support for the conclusion that homosexual sodomy, *simpliciter,* is considered unacceptable conduct in that State, and that the burden of justifying a selective application of the generally applicable law has been met.

III

The Court orders the dismissal of respondent's complaint even though the State's statute prohibits all sodomy; even though that prohibition is concededly unconstitutional with respect to heterosexuals; and even though the State's *post hoc* explanations for selective application are belied by the State's own actions. At the very least, I think it clear at this early stage of the litigation that respondent has alleged a constitutional claim sufficient to withstand a motion to dismiss.

I respectfully dissent.

ROMER v. EVANS, ___ U.S. ___, 116 S.Ct. 1620 (1996). Without citation to *Bowers v. Hardwick,* the Court invalidated as a denial of equal protection an amendment to the Colorado Constitution precluding any level of state government from protecting the status of persons on the basis of their "homosexual, lesbian or bisexual orientation, conduct, practices, or relationships." The amendment had "the peculiar property of imposing a broad and undifferentiated disability on a single named group, an exceptional and . . . invalid form of legislation[,]" and "[s]econd, its sheer breadth is so discontinuous with the reasons offered for it that the amendment seems inexplicable by anything but animus toward the class that it affects; it lacks a rational relationship to legitimate state interests."

Justice Scalia's dissent, joined by the Chief Justice and Justice Thomas, complained that the Court had contradicted *Bowers*, which had not been challenged. He thought it obvious that, given *Bowers*, the amendment, understood as a "prohibition of special protection for homosexuals," rested on a "legitimate rational basis":

"... If it is constitutionally permissible for a State to make homosexual conduct criminal, surely it is constitutionally permissible for a State to enact other laws merely *disfavoring* homosexual conduct.... And *a fortiori* it is constitutionally permissible for a State to adopt a provision *not even* disfavoring homosexual conduct, but merely prohibiting all levels of state government from bestowing *special protections* upon homosexual conduct....

"[Even] assuming that, in Amendment 2, a person of homosexual 'orientation' is someone who does not engage in homosexual conduct but merely has a tendency or desire to do so, *Bowers* still suffices to establish a rational basis for the provision. If it is rational to criminalize the conduct, surely it is rational to deny special favor and protection to those with a self-avowed tendency or desire to engage in the conduct. Indeed, where criminal sanctions are not involved, homosexual 'orientation' is an acceptable stand-in for homosexual conduct....

. . .

"... Surely ... the only sort of 'animus' at issue here [is] moral disapproval of homosexual conduct, the same sort of moral disapproval that produced the centuries-old criminal laws that we held constitutional in *Bowers*...."

In a footnote, Justice Scalia remarked that "the Court's suggestion that ... Amendment 2 [denies] rights on account of 'status' (rather than conduct) opens up a broader debate involving the significance of *Bowers* to this case, a debate which the Court is otherwise unwilling to join." For a full report of this case, see infra p. 915.

Cruzan v. Director, Missouri Department of Health

497 U.S. 261, 110 S.Ct. 2841, 111 L.Ed.2d 224 (1990).

Chief Justice Rehnquist delivered the opinion of the Court.

Petitioner Nancy Beth Cruzan was rendered incompetent as a result of severe injuries sustained during an automobile accident. ... Nancy's parents and co-guardians, sought a court order directing the withdrawal of their daughter's artificial feeding and hydration equipment after it became apparent that she had virtually no chance of recovering her cognitive faculties. The Supreme Court of Missouri held that because there was no clear and convincing evidence of Nancy's desire to have life-sustaining treatment withdrawn under such circumstances, her parents lacked authority to effectuate such a request. We ... affirm.

... [Unconscious from the moment of the accident in 1983,] surgeons [eventually] implanted a gastrostomy feeding and hydration tube in Cruzan with the consent of her then husband. Subsequent rehabilitative efforts proved unavailing. She now lies in a Missouri state hospital in ... a persistent vegetative state: generally, a condition in which a person exhibits motor reflexes but evinces no indications of significant cognitive function. The State of Missouri is bearing the cost of her care.

After it had become apparent that Nancy Cruzan had virtually no chance of regaining her mental faculties her parents asked hospital employees to terminate the artificial nutrition and hydration procedures. All agree that such a removal would cause her death. The employees refused to honor the request without court approval. The parents then sought and received authorization from the state trial court for termination. ... The court ... found that Nancy's "expressed thoughts at age twenty-five in somewhat serious conversation with a housemate friend that if sick or injured she would not wish to continue her life unless she could live at least halfway normally suggests that given her present condition she would not wish to continue on with her nutrition and hydration." ...

The Supreme Court of Missouri reversed by a divided vote. ... It ... decided that the Missouri Living Will statute ... embodied a state policy strongly favoring the preservation of life [and] found that Cruzan's statements to her roommate regarding her desire to live or die under certain conditions were "unreliable for the purpose of determining her intent," .... It rejected the argument that Cruzan's parents were entitled to order the termination of her medical treatment, concluding that "no person can assume that choice for an incompetent in the absence of the formalities required under Missouri's Living Will statutes or the clear and convincing, inherently reliable evidence absent here." ...

We granted certiorari to consider the question of whether Cruzan has a right under the United States Constitution which would require the hospital to withdraw life-sustaining treatment from her under these circumstances.

[The Court reviewed at length relevant state court decisions.]

As these cases demonstrate, the common-law doctrine of informed consent is viewed as generally encompassing the right of a competent individual to refuse medical treatment. ... This is the first case in which we have been squarely presented with the issue of whether the United States Constitution grants what is in common parlance referred to as a "right to die." ...

... The principle that a competent person has a constitutionally protected liberty interest in refusing unwanted medical treatment may be inferred from our prior decisions. In Jacobson v. Massachusetts, 197 U.S. 11, 24–30 (1905), for instance, the Court balanced an individual's liberty interest in declining an unwanted smallpox vaccine against the State's interest in preventing disease. Decisions prior to the incorporation of the Fourth Amendment into the Fourteenth Amendment analyzed searches and seizures involving the body under the Due Process Clause and were thought to implicate substantial liberty interests....

Just this Term, in the course of holding that a State's procedures for administering antipsychotic medication to prisoners were sufficient to satisfy due process concerns, we recognized that prisoners possess "a significant liberty interest in avoiding the unwanted administration of antipsychotic drugs under the Due Process Clause of the Fourteenth Amendment." Washington v. Harper, 494 U.S. 210, ___ (1990); see also id., at ___ ("The forcible injection of medication into a nonconsenting person's body represents a substantial interference with that person's liberty"). Still other cases support the recognition of a general liberty interest in refusing medical treatment. Vitek v. Jones, 445 U.S. 480, 494 (1980) (transfer to mental hospital coupled with mandatory behavior modification treatment implicated liberty interests); Parham v. J.R., 442 U.S. 584, 600 (1979) ("a child, in common with adults, has a substantial liberty interest in not being confined unnecessarily for medical treatment").

But determining that a person has a "liberty interest" under the Due Process Clause does not end the inquiry;[7] "whether respondent's constitutional rights have been violated must be determined by balancing his liberty interests against the relevant state interests." Youngberg v. Romeo, 457 U.S. 307, 321 (1982). . . .

Petitioners insist that under the general holdings of our cases, the forced administration of life-sustaining medical treatment, and even of artificially-delivered food and water essential to life, would implicate a competent person's liberty interest. Although we think the logic of the cases discussed above would embrace such a liberty interest, the dramatic consequences involved in refusal of such treatment would inform the inquiry as to whether the deprivation of that interest is constitutionally permissible. But for purposes of this case, we assume that the United States Constitution would grant a competent person a constitutionally protected right to refuse lifesaving hydration and nutrition.

Petitioners go on to assert that an incompetent person should possess the same right in this respect as is possessed by a competent person. . . .

The difficulty with petitioners' claim is that in a sense it begs the question: an incompetent person is not able to make an informed and voluntary choice to exercise a hypothetical right to refuse treatment or any other right. Such a "right" must be exercised for her, if at all, by some sort of surrogate. Here, Missouri has in effect recognized that under certain circumstances a surrogate may act for the patient in electing to have hydration and nutrition withdrawn in such a way as to cause death, but it has established a procedural safeguard to assure that the action of the surrogate conforms as best it may to the wishes expressed by the patient while competent. Missouri requires that evidence of the incompetent's wishes as to the withdrawal of treatment be proved by clear and convincing evidence. The question, then, is whether the United States Constitution forbids the establishment of this procedural requirement by the State. We hold that it does not.

Whether or not Missouri's clear and convincing evidence requirement comports with the United States Constitution depends in part on what interests the State may properly seek to protect in this situation. Missouri relies on its interest in the protection and preservation of human life, and there can be no gainsaying this interest. As a general matter, the States—indeed, all civilized nations—demonstrate their commitment to life by treating homicide as serious crime. Moreover, the majority of States in this country have laws imposing criminal penalties on one who assists another to commit suicide. We do not think a State is required to remain neutral in the face of an informed and voluntary decision by a physically-able adult to starve to death.

But in the context presented here, a State has more particular interests at stake. The choice between life and death is a deeply personal decision of obvious and overwhelming finality. We believe Missouri may legitimately seek to safeguard the personal element of this choice through the imposition of heightened evidentiary requirements. It cannot be disputed that the Due Process Clause protects an interest in life as well as an interest in refusing life-sustaining medical treatment. Not all incompetent patients will have loved ones available to serve as surrogate decisionmakers. And even where family members are present, "[t]here will, of course, be some unfortunate situations in which family members will not act to protect a patient." In re Jobes, 108 N.J.

---

[7] Although many state courts have held that a right to refuse treatment is encompassed by a generalized constitutional right of privacy, we have never so held. We believe this issue is more properly analyzed in terms of a Fourteenth Amendment liberty interest. See Bowers v. Hardwick, 478 U.S. 186, 194–195 (1986).

394, 419, 529 A.2d 434, 447 (1987). A State is entitled to guard against potential abuses in such situations. Similarly, a State is entitled to consider that a judicial proceeding to make a determination regarding an incompetent's wishes may very well not be an adversarial one, with the added guarantee of accurate factfinding that the adversary process brings with it.[9] Finally, we think a State may properly decline to make judgments about the "quality" of life that a particular individual may enjoy, and simply assert an unqualified interest in the preservation of human life to be weighed against the constitutionally protected interests of the individual.

In our view, Missouri has permissibly sought to advance these interests through the adoption of a "clear and convincing" standard of proof to govern such proceedings. "The function of a standard of proof, as that concept is embodied in the Due Process Clause and in the realm of factfinding, is to 'instruct the factfinder concerning the degree of confidence our society thinks he should have in the correctness of factual conclusions for a particular type of adjudication.'" Addington v. Texas, 441 U.S. 418, 423 (1979) (quoting In re Winship, 397 U.S. 358, 370 (1970) (Harlan, J., concurring)). "This Court has mandated an intermediate standard of proof—'clear and convincing evidence'— when the individual interests at stake in a state proceeding are both 'particularly important' and 'more substantial than mere loss of money.'" Santosky v. Kramer, 455 U.S. 745, 756 (1982) (quoting Addington, supra, at 424). Thus, such a standard has been required in deportation proceedings, Woodby v. INS, 385 U.S. 276 (1966), in denaturalization proceedings, Schneiderman v. United States, 320 U.S. 118 (1943), in civil commitment proceedings, *Addington,* supra, and in proceedings for the termination of parental rights. *Santosky,* supra.[10] Further, this level of proof, "or an even higher one, has traditionally been imposed in cases involving allegations of civil fraud, and in a variety of other kinds of civil cases involving such issues as . . . lost wills, oral contracts to make bequests, and the like." Woodby, supra, at 285, n. 18.

We think it self-evident that the interests at stake in the instant proceedings are more substantial, both on an individual and societal level, than those involved in a run-of-the-mine civil dispute. But not only does the standard of proof reflect the importance of a particular adjudication, it also serves as "a societal judgment about how the risk of error should be distributed between the litigants." Santosky . . .; Addington, . . . The more stringent the burden of proof a party must bear, the more that party bears the risk of an erroneous

---

[9] Since Cruzan was a patient at a state hospital when this litigation commenced, the State has been involved as an adversary from the beginning. However, it can be expected that many of these types of disputes will arise in private institutions, where a guardian ad litem or similar party will have been appointed as the sole representative of the incompetent individual in the litigation. In such cases, a guardian may act in entire good faith, and yet not maintain a position truly adversarial to that of the family. Indeed, as noted by the court below, "[t]he guardian ad litem [in this case] finds himself in the predicament of believing that it is in Nancy's 'best interest to have the tube feeding discontinued,' but 'feeling that an appeal should be made because our responsibility to her as attorneys and guardians ad litem was to pursue this matter to the highest court in the

state in view of the fact that this is a case of first impression in the State of Missouri.' . . ." Cruzan's guardian ad litem has also filed a brief in this Court urging reversal of the Missouri Supreme Court's decision. None of this is intended to suggest that the guardian acted the least bit improperly in this proceeding. It is only meant to illustrate the limits which may obtain on the adversarial nature of this type of litigation.

[10] We recognize that these cases involved instances where the government sought to take action against an individual. . . . Here, by contrast, the government seeks to protect the interests of an individual, as well as its own institutional interests, in life. We do not see any reason why important individual interests should be afforded less protection simply because the government finds itself in the position of defending them. . . .

decision. We believe that Missouri may permissibly place an increased risk of an erroneous decision on those seeking to terminate an incompetent individual's life-sustaining treatment. An erroneous decision not to terminate results in a maintenance of the status quo; the possibility of subsequent developments such as advancements in medical science, the discovery of new evidence regarding the patient's intent, changes in the law, or simply the unexpected death of the patient despite the administration of life-sustaining treatment, at least create the potential that a wrong decision will eventually be corrected or its impact mitigated. An erroneous decision to withdraw life-sustaining treatment, however, is not susceptible of correction. In *Santosky*, one of the factors which led the Court to require proof by clear and convincing evidence in a proceeding to terminate parental rights was that a decision in such a case was final and irrevocable.... The same must surely be said of the decision to discontinue hydration and nutrition of a patient such as Nancy Cruzan, which all agree will result in her death.

... [M]ost, if not all, States simply forbid oral testimony entirely in determining the wishes of parties in transactions which, while important, simply do not have the consequences that a decision to terminate a person's life does. ...There is no doubt that statutes requiring wills to be in writing, and statutes of frauds which require that a contract to make a will be in writing, on occasion frustrate the effectuation of the intent of a particular decedent, just as Missouri's requirement of proof in this case may have frustrated the effectuation of the not-fully-expressed desires of Nancy Cruzan. But the Constitution does not require general rules to work faultlessly; no general rule can.

In sum, we conclude that a State may apply a clear and convincing evidence standard in proceedings where a guardian seeks to discontinue nutrition and hydration of a person diagnosed to be in a persistent vegetative state. We note that many courts which have adopted some sort of substituted judgment procedure in situations like this, whether they limit consideration of evidence to the prior expressed wishes of the incompetent individual, or whether they allow more general proof of what the individual's decision would have been, require a clear and convincing standard of proof for such evidence....

... [Trial testimony that Nancy Cruzan] would not want to live should she face life as a "vegetable," ... did not deal in terms with withdrawal of medical treatment or of hydration and nutrition. We cannot say that the Supreme Court of Missouri committed constitutional error in reaching the conclusion that [this testimony was insufficient].

Petitioners alternatively contend that Missouri must accept the "substituted judgment" of close family members even in the absence of substantial proof that their views reflect the views of the patient. They rely primarily upon our decisions in Michael H. v. Gerald D., 491 U.S. 110 (1989), and Parham v. J.R., 442 U.S. 584 (1979). But we do not think these cases support their claim. In *Michael H.*, we upheld the constitutionality of California's favored treatment of traditional family relationships; such a holding may not be turned around into a constitutional requirement that a State must recognize the primacy of those relationships in a situation like this. And in *Parham*, where the patient was a minor, we also upheld the constitutionality of a state scheme in which parents made certain decisions for mentally ill minors. Here again petitioners would seek to turn a decision which allowed a State to rely on family decisionmaking into a constitutional requirement that the State recognize such decisionmaking. But constitutional law does not work that way.

No doubt is engendered by anything in this record but that Nancy Cruzan's mother and father are loving and caring parents. If the State were required by the United States Constitution to repose a right of "substituted judgment" with anyone, the Cruzans would surely qualify. But we do not think the Due Process Clause requires the State to repose judgment on these matters with anyone but the patient herself. Close family members may have a strong feeling—a feeling not at all ignoble or unworthy, but not entirely disinterested, either—that they do not wish to witness the continuation of the life of a loved one which they regard as hopeless, meaningless, and even degrading. But there is no automatic assurance that the view of close family members will necessarily be the same as the patient's would have been had she been confronted with the prospect of her situation while competent. All of the reasons previously discussed for allowing Missouri to require clear and convincing evidence of the patient's wishes lead us to conclude that the State may choose to defer only to those wishes, rather than confide the decision to close family members.[12]

The judgment of the Supreme Court of Missouri is

Affirmed.

Justice O'Connor, concurring.

I agree that a protected liberty interest in refusing unwanted medical treatment may be inferred from our prior decisions and that the refusal of artificially delivered food and water is encompassed within that liberty interest. I write separately to clarify why I believe this to be so.

As the Court notes, the liberty interest in refusing medical treatment flows from decisions involving the State's invasions into the body. Because our notions of liberty are inextricably entwined with our idea of physical freedom and self-determination, the Court has often deemed state incursions into the body repugnant to the interests protected by the Due Process Clause. . . . Our Fourth Amendment jurisprudence has echoed this same concern. . . . The State's imposition of medical treatment on an unwilling competent adult necessarily involves some form of restraint and intrusion. A seriously ill or dying patient whose wishes are not honored may feel a captive of the machinery required for life-sustaining measures or other medical interventions. Such forced treatment may burden that individual's liberty interests as much as any state coercion. . . .

The State's artificial provision of nutrition and hydration implicates identical concerns. . . . Whether or not the techniques used to pass food and water into the patient's alimentary tract are termed "medical treatment," it is clear they all involve some degree of intrusion and restraint. . . . Requiring a competent adult to endure such procedures against her will burdens the patient's liberty, dignity, and freedom to determine the course of her own treatment. Accordingly, the liberty guaranteed by the Due Process Clause must protect, if

---

[12] We are not faced in this case with the question of whether a State might be required to defer to the decision of a surrogate if competent and probative evidence established that the patient herself had expressed a desire that the decision to terminate life-sustaining treatment be made for her by that individual. Petitioners also adumbrate in their brief a claim based on the Equal Protection Clause of the Fourteenth Amendment to the effect that Missouri has impermissibly treated incompetent patients differently from competent ones. . . . The differences between the choice made by a competent person to refuse medical treatment, and the choice made for an incompetent person by someone else to refuse medical treatment, are so obviously different that the State is warranted in establishing rigorous procedures for the latter class of cases which do not apply to the former class.

it protects anything, an individual's deeply personal decision to reject medical treatment, including the artificial delivery of food and water.

I also write separately to emphasize that the Court does not today decide the issue whether a State must also give effect to the decisions of a surrogate decisionmaker. In my view, such a duty may well be constitutionally required to protect the patient's liberty interest in refusing medical treatment. . . . [P]rocedures for surrogate decisionmaking, which appear to be rapidly gaining in acceptance, may be a valuable additional safeguard of the patient's interest in directing his medical care. Moreover, as patients are likely to select a family member as a surrogate, . . . giving effect to a proxy's decisions may also protect the "freedom of personal choice in matters of . . . family life." Cleveland Board of Education v. LaFleur, 414 U.S. 632, 639 (1974).

. . .

Justice Scalia, concurring.

. . .

While I agree with the Court's analysis today, and therefore join in its opinion, I would have preferred that we announce, clearly and promptly, that the federal courts have no business in this field; that American law has always accorded the State the power to prevent, by force if necessary, suicide—including suicide by refusing to take appropriate measures necessary to preserve one's life; that the point at which life becomes "worthless," and the point at which the means necessary to preserve it become "extraordinary" or "inappropriate," are neither set forth in the Constitution nor known to the nine Justices of this Court any better than they are known to nine people picked at random from the Kansas City telephone directory; and hence, that even when it is demonstrated by clear and convincing evidence that a patient no longer wishes certain measures to be taken to preserve her life, it is up to the citizens of Missouri to decide, through their elected representatives, whether that wish will be honored. . . .

. . . It is at least true that no "substantive due process" claim can be maintained unless the claimant demonstrates that the State has deprived him of a right historically and traditionally protected against State interference. Michael H. v. Gerald D., 491 U.S. 110, ___ (1989) (plurality opinion); Bowers v. Hardwick, 478 U.S. 186, 192 (1986); Moore, supra, at 502–503 (plurality opinion). That cannot possibly be established here.

. . . "[T]here is no significant support for the claim that a right to suicide is so rooted in our tradition that it may be deemed 'fundamental' or 'implicit in the concept of ordered liberty.' " . . .

Petitioners rely on three distinctions to separate Nancy Cruzan's case from ordinary suicide: (1) that she is permanently incapacitated and in pain; (2) that she would bring on her death not by any affirmative act but by merely declining treatment that provides nourishment; and (3) that preventing her from effectuating her presumed wish to die requires violation of her bodily integrity. None of these suffices. Suicide was not excused even when committed "to avoid those ills which [persons] had not the fortitude to endure." 4 Blackstone, supra, at *189. . . .

The second asserted distinction . . . relies on the dichotomy between action and inaction. Suicide, it is said, consists of an affirmative act to end one's life; refusing treatment is not an affirmative act "causing" death, but merely a passive acceptance of the natural process of dying. I readily acknowledge that the distinction between action and inaction has some bearing upon the legislative judgment of what ought to be prevented as suicide—though even there it would seem to me unreasonable to draw the line precisely between action and inaction, rather than between various forms of inaction. . . .

. . .

[T]he early cases considering the claimed right to refuse medical treatment dismissed as specious the nice distinction between "passively submitting to death and actively seeking it. The distinction may be merely verbal, as it would be if an adult sought death by starvation instead of a drug. If the State may interrupt one mode of self-destruction, it may with equal authority interfere with the other." . . .

The third asserted basis of distinction—that frustrating Nancy Cruzan's wish to die in the present case requires interference with her bodily integrity—is likewise inadequate, because such interference is impermissible only if one begs the question whether her refusal to undergo the treatment on her own is suicide. It has always been lawful not only for the State, but even for private citizens, to interfere with bodily integrity to prevent a felony. . . . That general rule has of course been applied to suicide. . . . It is not even reasonable, much less required by the Constitution, to maintain that although the State has the right to prevent a person from slashing his wrists it does not have the power to apply physical force to prevent him from doing so, nor the power, should he succeed, to apply, coercively if necessary, medical measures to stop the flow of blood. . . .

The dissents of Justices Brennan and Stevens make a plausible case for our intervention here only by embracing—the latter explicitly and the former by implication—a political principle that the States are free to adopt, but that is demonstrably not imposed by the Constitution. . . . [I]nsofar as balancing the relative interests of the State and the individual is concerned, there is nothing distinctive about accepting death through the refusal of "medical treatment," as opposed to accepting it through the refusal of food, or through the failure to shut off the engine and get out of the car after parking in one's garage after work. Suppose that Nancy Cruzan were in precisely the condition she is in today, except that she could be fed and digest food and water without artificial assistance. How is the State's "interest" in keeping her alive thereby increased, or her interest in deciding whether she wants to continue living reduced? It seems to me . . . that Justice Brennan's position ultimately rests upon the proposition that it is none of the State's business if a person wants to commit suicide. Justice Stevens is explicit on the point: "Choices about death touch the core of liberty. . . . [N]ot much may be said with confidence about death unless it is said from faith, and that alone is reason enough to protect the freedom to conform choices about death to individual conscience." This is a view that some societies have held, and that our States are free to adopt if they wish. But it is not a view imposed by our constitutional traditions, in which the power of the State to prohibit suicide is unquestionable.

. . . To raise up a constitutional right here we would have to create out of nothing (for it exists neither in text nor tradition) some constitutional principle whereby, although the State may insist that an individual come in out of the cold and eat food, it may not insist that he take medicine; and although it may pump his stomach empty of poison he has ingested, it may not fill his stomach with food he has failed to ingest. Are there, then, no reasonable and humane limits that ought not to be exceeded in requiring an individual to preserve his own life? There obviously are, but they are not set forth in the Due Process Clause. . . . Our salvation is the Equal Protection Clause, which requires the democratic majority to accept for themselves and their loved ones what they impose on you and me. This Court need not, and has no authority to, inject itself into every field of human activity where irrationality and oppression may theoretically occur, and if it tries to do so it will destroy itself.

Justice Brennan, with whom Justice Marshall and Justice Blackmun join, dissenting.

. . .

A

. . .

... As we said in Zablocki v. Redhail, 434 U.S. 374, 388 (1978), if a requirement imposed by a State "significantly interferes with the exercise of a fundamental right, it cannot be upheld unless it is supported by sufficiently important state interests and is closely tailored to effectuate only those interests." ... An evidentiary rule, just as a substantive prohibition, must meet these standards if it significantly burdens a fundamental liberty interest....

B

. . .

[I]f a competent person has a liberty interest to be free of unwanted medical treatment, as both the majority and Justice O'Connor concede, it must be fundamental....

The right to be free from medical attention without consent, to determine what shall be done with one's own body, is deeply rooted in this Nation's traditions, as the majority acknowledges. This right has long been "firmly entrenched in American tort law" and is securely grounded in the earliest common law.... Thus, freedom from unwanted medical attention is unquestionably among those principles "so rooted in the traditions and conscience of our people as to be ranked as fundamental." Snyder v. Massachusetts, 291 U.S. 97, 105 (1934).

That there may be serious consequences involved in refusal of the medical treatment at issue here does not vitiate the right under our common law tradition of medical self-determination....

. . .

Nor does the fact that Nancy Cruzan is now incompetent deprive her of her fundamental rights.... As the majority recognizes, the question is not whether an incompetent has constitutional rights, but how such rights may be exercised....

II

A

... For a patient like Nancy Cruzan, the sole benefit of medical treatment is being kept metabolically alive. Neither artificial nutrition nor any other form of medical treatment available today can cure or in any way ameliorate her condition....

There are also affirmative reasons why someone like Nancy might choose to forgo artificial nutrition and hydration under these circumstances. Dying is personal. And it is profound. For many, the thought of an ignoble end, steeped in decay, is abhorrent. A quiet, proud death, bodily integrity intact, is a matter of extreme consequence. . . .

. . .

Such conditions are, for many, humiliating to contemplate, as is visiting a prolonged and anguished vigil on one's parents, spouse, and children. . . . For some, the idea of being remembered in their persistent vegetative states rather than as they were before their illness or accident may be very disturbing.

B

Although the right to be free of unwanted medical intervention, like other constitutionally protected interests, may not be absolute, no State interest could outweigh the rights of an individual in Nancy Cruzan's position. Whatever a State's possible interests in mandating life-support treatment under other circumstances, there is no good to be obtained here by Missouri's insistence that Nancy Cruzan remain on life-support systems if it is indeed her wish not to do so. Missouri does not claim, nor could it, that society as a whole will be benefited by Nancy's receiving medical treatment. No third party's situation will be improved and no harm to others will be averted.

The only state interest asserted here is a general interest in the preservation of life. But the State has no legitimate general interest in someone's life, completely abstracted from the interest of the person living that life, that could outweigh the person's choice to avoid medical treatment. . . . Thus, the State's general interest in life must accede to Nancy Cruzan's particularized and intense interest in self-determination in her choice of medical treatment. There is simply nothing legitimately within the State's purview to be gained by superseding her decision.

Moreover, there may be considerable danger that Missouri's rule of decision would impair rather than serve any interest the State does have in sustaining life. . . . When the President's Commission in 1982 approved the withdrawal of life support equipment from irreversibly vegetative patients, it explained that "[a]n even more troubling wrong occurs when a treatment that might save life or improve health is not started because the health care personnel are afraid that they will find it very difficult to stop the treatment if, as is fairly likely, it proves to be of little benefit and greatly burdens the patient." . . .

III

This is not to say that the State has no legitimate interests to assert here. . . . [U]ntil Nancy's wishes have been determined, the only state interest that may be asserted is an interest in safeguarding the accuracy of that determination.

. . . Missouri may constitutionally impose only those procedural requirements that serve to enhance the accuracy of a determination of Nancy Cruzan's wishes or are at least consistent with an accurate determination. . . . Missouri's rule of decision imposes a markedly asymmetrical evidentiary burden. . . . No proof is required to support a finding that the incompetent person would wish to continue treatment.

A

The majority offers several justifications for Missouri's heightened evidentiary standard. First, the majority explains that the State may constitutionally adopt this rule to govern determinations of an incompetent's wishes in order to advance the State's substantive interests, including its unqualified interest in the preservation of human life.... [However,] Missouri has no legitimate interest in providing Nancy with treatment until it is established that this represents her choice. Just as a State may not override Nancy's choice directly, it may not do so indirectly through the imposition of a procedural rule.

Second, the majority offers two explanations for why Missouri's clear and convincing evidence standard is a means of enhancing accuracy, but neither is persuasive....

... [A]ny concern that those who come forward [to have treatment stopped] will present a one-sided view would be better addressed by appointing a guardian ad litem, who could use the State's powers of discovery to gather and present evidence regarding the patient's wishes. A guardian ad litem's task is to uncover any conflicts of interest and ensure that each party likely to have relevant evidence is consulted and brought forward.... Missouri's heightened evidentiary standard attempts to achieve balance by discounting evidence; the guardian ad litem technique achieves balance by probing for additional evidence. Where, as here, the family members, friends, doctors and guardian ad litem agree, it is not because the process has failed, as the majority suggests. It is because there is no genuine dispute as to Nancy's preference.

The majority next argues that where, as here, important individual rights are at stake, a clear and convincing evidence standard has long been held to be an appropriate means of enhancing accuracy, citing decisions concerning what process an individual is due before he can be deprived of a liberty interest.... In the cases cited by the majority, the imbalance imposed by a heightened evidentiary standard was not only acceptable but required because the standard was deployed to protect an individual's exercise of a fundamental right, as the majority admits. In contrast, the Missouri court imposed a clear and convincing standard as an obstacle to the exercise of a fundamental right.

The majority claims that the allocation of the risk of error is justified because it is more important not to terminate life-support for someone who would wish it continued than to honor the wishes of someone who would not.... But, from the point of view of the patient, an erroneous decision in either direction is irrevocable. An erroneous decision to terminate artificial nutrition and hydration, to be sure, will lead to failure of that last remnant of physiological life, the brain stem, and result in complete brain death. An erroneous decision not to terminate life-support, however, robs a patient of the very qualities protected by the right to avoid unwanted medical treatment. His own degraded existence is perpetuated; his family's suffering is protracted; the memory he leaves behind becomes more and more distorted.

. . .

B

Even more than its heightened evidentiary standard, the Missouri court's categorical exclusion of relevant evidence dispenses with any semblance of accurate factfinding....

Too few people execute living wills or equivalently formal directives for such an evidentiary rule to ensure adequately that the wishes of incompetent persons will be honored....

. . .

The testimony of close friends and family members ... may often be the best evidence available of what the patient's choice would be....

The Missouri court's disdain for Nancy's statements in serious conversations not long before her accident, for the opinions of Nancy's family and friends as to her values, beliefs and certain choice, and even for the opinion of an outside objective factfinder appointed by the State evinces a disdain for Nancy Cruzan's own right to choose. The rules by which an incompetent person's wishes are determined must represent every effort to determine those wishes. The rule that the Missouri court adopted and that this Court upholds, however, skews the result away from a determination that as accurately as possible reflects the individual's own preferences and beliefs....

. . .

C

... Missouri is virtually the only [State] to have fashioned a rule that lessens the likelihood of accurate determinations. In contrast, nothing in the Constitution prevents States from reviewing the advisability of a family decision, by requiring a court proceeding or by appointing an impartial guardian ad litem.

[The] ... various approaches to determining an incompetent patient's treatment choice in use by the several States today ..., in largest part, [are] and should be left to the States, so long as each State is seeking, in a reliable manner, to discover what the patient would want. But with such momentous interests in the balance, States must avoid procedures that will prejudice the decision....

D

Finally, I cannot agree with the majority that where it is not possible to determine what choice an incompetent patient would make, a State's role as parens patriae permits the State automatically to make that choice itself.... A State's legitimate interest in safeguarding a patient's choice cannot be furthered by simply appropriating it.

... Is there any reason to suppose that a State is more likely to make the choice that the patient would have made than someone who knew the patient intimately? ...

... A State may ensure that the person who makes the decision on the patient's behalf is the one whom the patient himself would have selected to make that choice for him. And a State may exclude from consideration anyone having improper motives. But a State generally must either repose the choice with the person whom the patient himself would most likely have chosen as proxy or leave the decision to the patient's family.

IV

. . .

... Missouri and this Court have displaced Nancy's own assessment of the processes associated with dying. They have discarded evidence of her will, ignored her values, and deprived her of the right to a decision as closely approximating her own choice as humanly possible. They have done so disingenuously in her name, and openly in Missouri's own....

Justice Stevens, dissenting.

. . .

... [I]f Nancy Cruzan has no interest in continued treatment, and if she has a liberty interest in being free from unwanted treatment, and if the cessation of treatment would have no adverse impact on third parties, and if no reason exists to doubt the good faith of Nancy's parents, then what possible basis could the State have for insisting upon continued medical treatment? ...

. . .

... Missouri's regulation is an unreasonable intrusion upon traditionally private matters encompassed within the liberty protected by the Due Process Clause.

The ... Court's opinion ... fails to respect the best interests of the patient.... The Court's decision affords no protection to children, to young people who are victims of unexpected accidents or illnesses, or to the countless thousands of elderly persons who either fail to decide, or fail to explain, how they want to be treated if they should experience a similar fate. Because Nancy Beth Cruzan did not have the foresight to preserve her constitutional right in a living will, or some comparable "clear and convincing" alternative, her right is gone forever and her fate is in the hands of the state legislature instead of in those of her family, her independent neutral guardian ad litem, and an impartial judge—all of whom agree on the course of action that is in her best interests. The Court's willingness to find a waiver of this constitutional right reveals a distressing misunderstanding of the importance of individual liberty.

. . .

... Choices about death touch the core of liberty. Our duty, and the concomitant freedom, to come to terms with the conditions of our own mortality are undoubtedly "so rooted in the traditions and conscience of our people as to be ranked as fundamental," Snyder v. Massachusetts, 291 U.S. 97, 105 (1934), and indeed are essential incidents of the unalienable rights to life and liberty endowed on us by our Creator....

. . .

... Missouri ... subordinates Nancy's body, her family, and the lasting significance of her life to the State's own interests. The decision we review ... interferes with constitutional interests of the highest order.

To be constitutionally permissible, Missouri's intrusion upon these fundamental liberties must, at a minimum, bear a reasonable relationship to a legitimate state end.... Missouri asserts that its policy is related to a state interest in the protection of life. In my view, however, it is an effort to define life, rather than to protect it, that is the heart of Missouri's policy. Missouri insists, without regard to Nancy Cruzan's own interests, upon equating her life with the biological persistence of her bodily functions....

... [F]or patients like Nancy Cruzan, who have no consciousness and no chance of recovery, there is a serious question as to whether the mere persistence of their bodies is "life" as that word is commonly understood, or as it is used in both the Constitution and the Declaration of Independence. The State's unflagging determination to perpetuate Nancy Cruzan's physical existence is comprehensible only as an effort to define life's meaning, not as an attempt to preserve its sanctity.

. . .

... [T]here is no reasonable ground for believing that Nancy Beth Cruzan has any personal interest in the perpetuation of what the State has decided is her life. . . .

My disagreement with the Court is thus unrelated to its endorsement of the clear and convincing standard of proof for cases of this kind. Indeed, I agree that the controlling facts must be established with unmistakable clarity. The critical question, however, is not how to prove the controlling facts but rather what proven facts should be controlling. In my view, the constitutional answer is clear: the best interests of the individual, especially when buttressed by the interests of all related third parties, must prevail over any general state policy that simply ignores those interests. . . .

Only because Missouri has arrogated to itself the power to define life, and only because the Court permits this usurpation, are Nancy Cruzan's life and liberty put into disquieting conflict. If Nancy Cruzan's life were defined by reference to her own interests, so that her life expired when her biological existence ceased serving any of her own interests, then her constitutionally protected interest in freedom from unwanted treatment would not come into conflict with her constitutionally protected interest in life. Conversely, if there were any evidence that Nancy Cruzan herself defined life to encompass every form of biological persistence by a human being, so that the continuation of treatment would serve Nancy's own liberty, then once again there would be no conflict between life and liberty. The opposition of life and liberty in this case are thus not the result of Nancy Cruzan's tragic accident, but are instead the artificial consequence of Missouri's effort, and this Court's willingness, to abstract Nancy Cruzan's life from Nancy Cruzan's person.

. . .

... The Court suggests that Missouri's policy "results in a maintenance of the status quo," and is subject to reversal, while a decision to terminate treatment "is not susceptible of correction" because death is irreversible. . . . Insofar as Nancy Cruzan has an interest in being remembered for how she lived rather than how she died, the damage done to those memories by the prolongation of her death is irreversible. Insofar as Nancy Cruzan has an interest in the cessation of any pain, the continuation of her pain is irreversible. Insofar as Nancy Cruzan has an interest in a closure to her life consistent with her own beliefs rather than those of the Missouri legislature, the State's imposition of its contrary view is irreversible. To deny the importance of these consequences is in effect to deny that Nancy Cruzan has interests at all, and thereby to deny her personhood in the name of preserving the sanctity of her life.

. . .

... [T]o argue that the mere possibility of error in any case suffices to allow the State's interests to override the particular interests of incompetent individuals in every case, or to argue that the interests of such individuals are unknowable and therefore may be subordinated to the State's concerns, is once again to deny Nancy Cruzan's personhood. ... [Perhaps] the best we can do is to ensure that these choices are made by those who will care enough about the patient to investigate her interests with particularity and caution. The Court seems to recognize as much when it cautions against formulating any general or inflexible rule to govern all the cases that might arise in this area of the law. The Court's deference to the legislature is, however, itself an inflexible rule, one that the Court is willing to apply in this case even though the Court's principal grounds for deferring to Missouri's legislature are hypothetical circumstances not relevant to Nancy Cruzan's interests.

. . .

... Our Constitution presupposes a respect for the personhood of every individual, and nowhere is strict adherence to that principle more essential than in the Judicial Branch....

. . .

The Cruzan family's continuing concern provides a concrete reminder that Nancy Cruzan's interests did not disappear with her vitality or her consciousness. However commendable may be the State's interest in human life, it cannot pursue that interest by appropriating Nancy Cruzan's life as a symbol for its own purposes. Lives do not exist in abstraction from persons, and to pretend otherwise is not to honor but to desecrate the State's responsibility for protecting life....

CHAPTER 10

THE EQUAL PROTECTION CLAUSE AND THE REVIEW OF THE REASONABLENESS OF LEGISLATION

SECTION 1. INTRODUCTION—THE SCOPE OF EQUAL PROTECTION

The fourteenth amendment provision that no state shall "deny to any person within its jurisdiction the equal protection of the laws," raises a host of difficult analytical problems. It can hardly be taken to be a guarantee that every law shall treat every person the same, for almost all legislation involves classifications placing special burdens on or granting special benefits to individuals or groups. But if laws may classify, what content can be given to a guarantee of "equal protection of the laws"?

THE ORIGINAL UNDERSTANDING

The Supreme Court originally took a narrow view of the scope of the equal protection clause. In the Slaughter–House Cases, 83 U.S. (16 Wall.) 36, 81 (1872), the Court said: "We doubt very much whether any action of a State not directed by way of discrimination against the negroes as a class, or on account of their race, will ever be held to come within the purview of this provision. It is so clearly a provision for that race and that emergency, that a strong case would be necessary for its application to any other." In Strauder v. West Virginia, 100 U.S. 303, 306, 307 (1880), which invalidated a statute limiting jury service to whites, the Court said: "[The fourteenth amendment] was designed to assure to the colored race the enjoyment of all the civil rights that under the law are enjoyed by white persons, and to give to that race the protection of the General Government, in that enjoyment, whenever it should be denied by the States." In referring to the equal protection clause the Court said: "What is this but declaring that the law in the States shall be the same for the black as for the white; that all persons whether colored or white, shall stand equal before the laws of the States and, in regard to the colored race, for whose protection the Amendment was primarily designed, that no discrimination shall be made against them by law because of their color."

However, the Court shortly expanded its view and brought the full range of legislative classification within the restrictions of the clause. In Barbier v. Connolly, 113 U.S. 27 (1885), the Court upheld a statute prohibiting the operation of laundries from 10 p.m. to 6 a.m., but assumed that the equal protection clause applied. The Court said that the equal protection clause guaranteed, inter alia, that "all persons should be equally entitled to pursue their happiness and acquire and enjoy property;" that "no impediment should be interposed to the pursuits of any one except as applied to the same pursuits by others under like circumstances;" and that "no greater burdens should be laid upon one than are laid upon others in the same calling or condition." The promise of *Barbier* that the equal protection clause would be applied to economic regulations was fulfilled in the following case.

GULF, COLORADO & SANTA FE RAILROAD CO. v. ELLIS, 165 U.S. 150 (1897). The Court invalidated a statute providing that successful plaintiffs in certain kinds of suits against railroad companies should receive in addition to costs reasonable attorney's fees "not to exceed $10." The following passages suggest its reasoning:

"... The act singles out a certain class of debtors and punishes them when for like delinquencies it punishes no others. They are not treated as other debtors, or equally with other debtors. They cannot appeal to the courts as other litigants under like conditions and with like protection. If litigation terminates adversely to them, they are mulcted in the attorney's fees of the successful plaintiff; if it terminates in their favor, they recover no attorney's fees. It is no sufficient answer to say that they are punished only when adjudged to be in the wrong. They do not enter the courts upon equal terms. They must pay attorney's fees if wrong; they do not recover any if right; while their adversaries recover if right and pay nothing if wrong. In the suits, therefore, to which they are parties they are discriminated against, and are not treated as others. They do not stand equal before the law. They do not receive its equal protection. All this is obvious from a mere inspection of the statute.

. . .

"While good faith and a knowledge of existing conditions on the part of a legislature is to be presumed, yet to carry that presumption to the extent of always holding that there must be some undisclosed and unknown reason for subjecting certain individuals or corporations to hostile and discriminating legislation is to make the protecting clauses of the Fourteenth Amendment a mere rope of sand, in no manner restraining state action.

. . .

"But it is said that it is not within the scope of the Fourteenth Amendment to withhold from States the power of classification, and that if the law deals alike with all of a certain class it is not obnoxious to the charge of a denial of equal protection. While, as a general proposition, this is undeniably true, . . . yet it is equally true that such classification cannot be made arbitrarily. The State may not say that all white men shall be subjected to the payment of the attorney's fees of parties successfully suing them and all black men not. It may not say that all men beyond a certain age shall be alone thus subjected, or all men possessed of a certain wealth. These are distinctions which do not furnish any proper basis for the attempted classification. That must always rest upon some difference which bears a reasonable and just relation to the act in respect to which the classification is proposed, and can never be made arbitrarily and without any such basis."

. . .

THE DOCTRINE OF REASONABLE CLASSIFICATION

In *Ellis* the Court articulated a doctrine of reasonable classification. To be valid a classification must be reasonably related to the object of the legislation and cannot be arbitrary. But what determines whether a classification is reasonable?

The following classic discussion of equal protection theory provides a framework of analysis. Tussman and tenBroek, *The Equal Protection of the Laws,* 37 Calif.L.Rev. 341 (1949):

"Here, then, is a paradox: The equal protection of the laws is a 'pledge of the protection of equal laws.' But laws may classify. And 'the very idea of classification is that of inequality.' In tackling this paradox the Court has neither abandoned the demand for equality nor denied the legislative right to classify. It has taken a middle course. It has resolved the contradictory demands of legislative specialization and constitutional generality by a doctrine of reasonable classification.

"The essence of that doctrine can be stated with deceptive simplicity. The Constitution does not require that things different in fact be treated in law as though they were the same. But it does require, in its concern for equality, that those who are similarly situated be similarly treated. The measure of the reasonableness of a classification is the degree of its success in treating similarly those similarly situated. . . .

. . .

". . . [W]here are we to look for the test of similarity of situation which determines the reasonableness of a classification? The inescapable answer is that we must look beyond the classification to the purpose of the law. A reasonable classification is one which includes all persons who are similarly situated with respect to the purpose of the law.

"The purpose of a law may be either the elimination of a public 'mischief' or the achievement of some positive public good. To simplify the discussion we shall refer to the purpose of a law in terms of the elimination of mischief, since the same argument holds in either case. We shall speak of the defining character or characteristics of the legislative classification as the trait. We can thus speak of the relation of the classification to the purpose of the law as the relation of the Trait to the Mischief.

. . .

"In other words, we are really dealing with the relation of two classes to each other. The first class consists of all individuals possessing the defining Trait; the second class consists of all individuals possessing, or rather, tainted by, the Mischief at which the law aims. The former is the legislative classification; the latter is the class of those similarly situated with respect to the purpose of the law. We shall refer to these two classes as T and M respectively.

"Now, since the reasonableness of any class T depends entirely upon its relation to a class M, it is obvious that it is impossible to pass judgment on the reasonableness of a classification without taking into consideration, or identifying, the purpose of the law. . . .

"There are five possible relationships between the class defined by the Trait and the class defined by the Mischief. These relationships can be indicated by the following diagrams:

(1)   : All *T*'s are *M*'s and all *M*'s are *T*'s

(2)   : No *T*'s are *M*'s

(3)   : All *T*'s are *M*'s but some *M*'s are not *T*'s

(4)   : All *M*'s are *T*'s but some *T*'s are not *M*'s

(5)   : Some *T*'s are *M*'s; some *T*'s are not *M*'s; and some *M*'s are not *T*'s

[C2555]

One of these five relationships holds in fact in any case of legislative classification, and we will consider each from the point of view of its "reasonableness."

"The first two situations represent respectively the ideal limits of reasonableness and unreasonableness. . . .

"Classification of the third type may be called 'under-inclusive.' All who are included in the class are tainted with the mischief, but there are others also tainted whom the classification does not include. Since the classification does not include all who are similarly situated with respect to the purpose of the law, there is a prima facie violation of the equal protection requirement of reasonable classification.

"But the Court has recognized the very real difficulties under which legislatures operate—difficulties arising out of both the nature of the legislative process and of the society which legislation attempts perennially to reshape—and it has refused to strike down indiscriminately all legislation embodying the classificatory inequality here under consideration.

"In justifying this refusal, the Court has defended under-inclusive classifications on such grounds as: the legislature may attack a general problem in a piecemeal fashion; 'some play must be allowed for the joints of the machine'; 'a statute aimed at what is deemed an evil, and hitting it presumably where experience shows it to be most felt, is not to be upset. . . .'; 'the law does all that is needed when it does all that it can. . . .'; and—perhaps with some impatience—the equal protection clause is not 'a pedagogic requirement of the impracticable.'

"These generalities, while expressive of judicial tolerance, are not, however, very helpful. They do not constitute a clear statement of the circumstances and conditions which justify such tolerance—which justify a departure from the strict requirements of the principle of equality. . . .

"The fourth type of classification imposes a burden upon a wider range of individuals than are included in the class of those tainted with the mischief at which the law aims. It can thus be called 'over-inclusive.' Herod, ordering the death of all male children born on a particular day because one of them would some day bring about his downfall, employed such a classification. It is exemplified by the quarantine and the dragnet. The wartime treatment of American citizens of Japanese ancestry is a striking recent instance of the imposition of burdens upon a large class of individuals because some of them were believed to be disloyal.

"The prima facie case against such departures from the ideal standards of reasonable classification is stronger than the case against under-inclusiveness. For in the latter case, all who are included in the class are at least tainted by the mischief at which the law aims; while over-inclusive classifications reach out to the innocent bystander, the hapless victim of circumstance or association."[a]

APPLICATION OF THE EQUAL PROTECTION LIMITATION TO THE FEDERAL GOVERNMENT THROUGH THE DUE PROCESS CLAUSE OF THE FIFTH AMENDMENT

Originally the Supreme Court took the position that "[u]nlike the Fourteenth Amendment, the Fifth contains no equal protection clause and it provides no guaranty against discriminatory legislation by Congress." Detroit Bank v. United States, 317 U.S. 329, 337 (1943). At the same time the Court indicated that discriminatory legislation "may be so arbitrary and injurious in character as to violate the due process clause of the Fifth Amendment." Id. at 338.

However, in Bolling v. Sharpe, 347 U.S. 497, 499 (1954) (a companion case to Brown v. Board of Educ. of Topeka, 347 U.S. 483 (1954)) the Court, in invalidating racial segregation in the District of Columbia schools, said:

"The Fifth Amendment which is applicable in the District of Columbia does not contain an equal protection clause as does the Fourteenth Amendment which applies only to the states. But the concepts of equal protection and due process, both stemming from our American ideal of fairness, are not mutually exclusive. The 'equal protection of the laws' is a more explicit safeguard of prohibited unfairness than 'due process of law,' and, therefore, we do not imply that the two are always interchangeable phrases. But, as this Court has recognized, discrimination may be so unjustifiable as to be violative of due process."

By 1975 the Court went so far as to say, in invalidating a gender classification in the Social Security Act: "This Court's approach to Fifth Amendment equal protection claims has always been precisely the same as to equal protection claims under the Fourteenth Amendment." Weinberger v. Wiesenfeld, 420 U.S. 636, 639, n. 2 (1975). However, the next year the Court, in holding invalid a federal regulation barring resident aliens from employment in the federal competitive civil service, distinguished decisions holding similar state laws to be a violation of equal protection by saying: "The concept of equal justice under law is served by the Fifth Amendment's guarantee of due process, as well as by the Equal Protection Clause of the Fourteenth Amendment. Although both Amendments require the same type of analysis, ... the Court of Appeals correctly stated that the two protections are not always coextensive. Not only does the language of the two Amendments differ, but more importantly, there may be overriding national interests which justify selective federal legislation that would be unacceptable for an individual State." Hampton v. Mow Sun Wong, 426 U.S. 88, 100 (1976).

In Vance v. Bradley, 440 U.S. 93, 94 (1979), the Court said regarding a federal statute that the "issue presented is whether Congress violates the equal protection component of the Fifth Amendment's Due Process Clause." In a footnote to that statement the Court said: "Concern with assuring equal protection was part of the fabric of our Constitution even before the Fourteenth Amendment expressed it most directly in applying it to the States.... Accordingly, the Court has held that the Due Process Clause of the Fifth Amendment forbids the Federal Government from denying equal protection of the laws."

Also see generally Note, *Developments in the Law—Equal Protection*, 82 Harv.L.Rev. 1065 (1969).

Yet more recently the Court asserted that benign "race-conscious classifications adopted by Congress to address racial and ethnic discrimination are subject to a different standard than such classifications prescribed by state and local governments." Metro Broadcasting, Inc. v. Federal Communications Commission, 497 U.S. 547, 565 (1990). That portion of *Metro Broadcasting* was specifically overruled in Adarand Constructors, Inc. v. Pena, ___ U.S. ___, ___, 115 S.Ct. 2097, 2115 (1995), however, where the Court declared "that the Constitution imposes upon federal, state, and local government actors the same obligation to respect the personal right to equal protection of the laws."[a]

THE STANDARD OF REVIEW

The Tussman and tenBroek excerpt does not address directly the question of the standard of review to be applied in equal protection cases. How closely must a classification be related to the purpose? How important must the purpose be? Who has the burden of proof on the issue of reasonableness of the classification?

In Lindsley v. Natural Carbonic Gas Co., 220 U.S. 61, 78 (1911), the Court stated a standard which gave substantial deference to the legislative judgment in making classifications:

> "The rules by which [the contention that a statutory classification violates the equal protection clause] must be tested, as is shown by repeated decisions of this court, are these: 1. The equal protection clause of the 14th Amendment does not take from the state the power to classify in the adoption of police laws, but admits of the exercise of a wide scope of discretion in that regard, and avoids what is done only when it is without any reasonable basis, and therefore is purely arbitrary. 2. A classification having some reasonable basis does not offend against that clause merely because it is not made with mathematical nicety, or because in practice it results in some inequality. 3. When the classification in such a law is called in question, if any state of facts reasonably can be conceived that would sustain it, the existence of that state of facts at the time the law was enacted must be assumed. 4. One who assails the classification in such a law must carry the burden of showing that it does not rest upon any reasonable basis, but is essentially arbitrary."

However, in the 1920s and early 1930s the Court invalidated a substantial number of statutes under equal protection—particularly statutes discriminating against corporations and statutes making unusual tax classifications. In many of these cases the Court, as in the due process cases of the period set out in Chapter 9, supra, appeared to be placing the burden of justifying the classifications on the state, without specifying how great that burden was. In Quaker City Cab Co. v. Pennsylvania, 277 U.S. 389, 402 (1928), e.g., the Court invalidated a law imposing a tax on corporations but not on individuals engaged in the transportation business. The Court said: "The tax is imposed merely because the owner is a corporation. The discrimination is not justified by any difference in the source of the receipts or in the situation or character of the property employed. It follows that the section fails to meet the requirement that a classification to be consistent with the equal protection clause must be based on a real and substantial difference having reasonable relation to the

---

[a] See generally Karst, *The Fifth Amendment's Guarantee of Equal Protection,* 55 N.C.L.Rev. 541 (1977).

subject of the legislation . . . In no view can [the classification] be held to have more than an arbitrary basis. . . . ''

Two cases decided on the same day in 1936 further illustrate the failure of the Court to articulate a consistent standard of review in equal protection cases. In Borden's Farm Products Co. v. Ten Eyck, 297 U.S. 251, 263 (1936), the Court upheld a provision of the New York Milk Control Law that allowed milk dealers lacking a well-advertised trade name to sell to stores at one cent per quart lower than the price fixed for those who had one: "In the light of the facts found the legislature might reasonably have thought trade conditions existed justifying the fixing of a differential. Judicial inquiry does not concern itself with the accuracy of the legislative finding, but only with the question whether it so lacks any reasonable basis as to be arbitrary." In Mayflower Farms, Inc. v. Ten Eyck, 297 U.S. 266, 274 (1936), however, the Court invalidated another provision of the New York law which limited the one cent per quart differential to milk dealers who had been continuously in business since April 10, 1933, saying:

> "The challenged provision . . . is not a regulation of a business or activity in the interest of, or for the protection of, the public, but an attempt to give an economic advantage to those engaged in a given business at an arbitrary date as against all those who enter the industry after that date. The appellees do not intimate that the classification bears any relation to the public health or welfare generally; that the provision will discourage monopoly; or that it was aimed at any abuse, cognizable by law, in the milk business. In the absence of any such showing, we have no right to conjure up possible situations which might justify the discrimination. The classification is arbitrary and unreasonable and denies the appellant the equal protection of the law."

In 1937 the Court's approach to the application of equal protection changed as did its approach to the application of due process. With respect to ordinary social and economic legislation, the standard of review is low and the cases will be reviewed in Section 2. Higher standards of review are applied to cases in which the bases of classification—race, nationality, alienage, gender, legitimacy—are held to be "suspect" and to require special justification. These cases will be reviewed in Section 3. And finally in Section 4 we will examine cases in which the Court holds that legislative classifications which burden constitutionally protected interests are invalid if not closely related to important or substantial governmental interests.

As we pursue the three strands of equal protection through this chapter, it may be helpful to have a brief overview of the analytical differences among them. Consider the implications of the following three cases.

In the first, a statute excluding resident aliens from the receipt of welfare benefits was held invalid because "classifications based on alienage, like those based on nationality or race, are inherently suspect and subject to close judicial scrutiny." Graham v. Richardson, 403 U.S. 365, 372 (1971). In the second, a statute denying welfare assistance to residents who had not resided within the state for a year was held invalid because it served "to penalize the exercise" of the constitutionally protected "right" to travel and the state had not shown that the statutory scheme was "necessary to promote a *compelling* governmental interest." Shapiro v. Thompson, 394 U.S. 618, 634 (1969). In the third, a statute providing lower welfare payments for dependent children than for the aged was upheld because it did not use a suspect classification, burden a constitutionally protected interest, or fail the general test of rationality—there was some relationship between the classification and the state objective. Jefferson v. Hackney, 406 U.S. 535, 546, 549 (1972).

SECTION 2.   SOCIAL AND ECONOMIC REGULATORY LEGISLATION

Railway Express Agency v. New York

336 U.S. 106, 69 S.Ct. 463, 93 L.Ed. 533 (1949).

Mr. Justice Douglas delivered the opinion of the Court.

Section 124 of the Traffic Regulations of the City of New York promulgated by the Police Commissioner provides:

"No person shall operate, or cause to be operated, in or upon any street an advertising vehicle; provided that nothing herein contained shall prevent the putting of business notices upon business delivery vehicles, so long as such vehicles are engaged in the usual business or regular work of the owner and not used merely or mainly for advertising."

Appellant is engaged in a nation-wide express business. It operates about 1,900 trucks in New York City and sells the space on the exterior sides of these trucks for advertising. That advertising is for the most part unconnected with its own business. It was convicted in the magistrates court and fined. The judgment of conviction was sustained in the Court of Special Sessions.... The Court of Appeals affirmed without opinion by a divided vote....

The Court of Special Sessions concluded that advertising on vehicles using the streets of New York City constitutes a distraction to vehicle drivers and to pedestrians alike and therefore affects the safety of the public in the use of the streets. We do not sit to weigh evidence on the due process issue in order to determine whether the regulation is sound or appropriate; nor is it our function to pass judgment on its wisdom. See Olsen v. State of Nebraska, 313 U.S. 236. We would be trespassing on one of the most intensely local and specialized of all municipal problems if we held that this regulation had no relation to the traffic problem of New York City. It is the judgment of the local authorities that it does have such a relation. And nothing has been advanced which shows that to be palpably false.

The question of equal protection of the laws is pressed more strenuously on us. It is pointed out that the regulation draws the line between advertisements of products sold by the owner of the truck and general advertisements. It is argued that unequal treatment on the basis of such a distinction is not justified by the aim and purpose of the regulation. It is said, for example, that one of appellant's trucks carrying the advertisement of a commercial house would not cause any greater distraction of pedestrians and vehicle drivers than if the commercial house carried the same advertisement on its own truck. Yet the regulation allows the latter to do what the former is forbidden from doing. It is therefore contended that the classification which the regulation makes has no relation to the traffic problem since a violation turns not on what kind of advertisements are carried on trucks but on whose trucks they are carried.

That, however, is a superficial way of analyzing the problem, even if we assume that it is premised on the correct construction of the regulation. The local authorities may well have concluded that those who advertised their own wares on their trucks do not present the same traffic problem in view of the nature or extent of the advertising which they use. It would take a degree of omniscience which we lack to say that such is not the case. If that judgment is correct, the advertising displays that are exempt have less incidence on traffic than those of appellants.

We cannot say that that judgment is not an allowable one. Yet if it is, the classification has relation to the purpose for which it is made and does not contain the kind of discrimination against which the Equal Protection Clause affords protection. It is by such practical considerations based on experience rather than by theoretical inconsistencies that the question of equal protection is to be answered. Patsone v. Commonwealth of Pennsylvania, 232 U.S. 138, 144.... And the fact that New York City sees fit to eliminate from traffic this kind of distraction but does not touch what may be even greater ones in a different category, such as the vivid displays on Times Square, is immaterial. It is no requirement of equal protection that all evils of the same genus be eradicated or none at all....

Affirmed.

Mr. Justice Rutledge acquiesces in the Court's opinion and judgment, dubitante on the question of equal protection of the laws.

Mr. Justice Jackson, concurring.

There are two clauses of the Fourteenth Amendment which this Court may invoke to invalidate ordinances by which municipal governments seek to solve their local problems. One says that no state shall "deprive any person of life, liberty, or property, without due process of law". The other declares that no state shall "deny to any person within its jurisdiction the equal protection of the laws."

My philosophy as to the relative readiness with which we should resort to these two clauses is almost diametrically opposed to the philosophy which prevails on this Court. While claims of denial of equal protection are frequently asserted, they are rarely sustained. But the Court frequently uses the due process clause to strike down measures taken by municipalities to deal with activities in their streets and public places which the local authorities consider to create hazards, annoyances or discomforts to their inhabitants....

The burden should rest heavily upon one who would persuade us to use the due process clause to strike down a substantive law or ordinance. Even its provident use against municipal regulations frequently disables all government—state, municipal and federal—from dealing with the conduct in question because the requirement of due process is also applicable to State and Federal Governments. Invalidation of a statute or an ordinance on due process grounds leaves ungoverned and ungovernable conduct which many people find objectionable.

Invocation of the equal protection clause, on the other hand, does not disable any governmental body from dealing with the subject at hand. It merely means that the prohibition or regulation must have a broader impact. I regard it as a salutary doctrine that cities, states and the Federal Government must exercise their powers so as not to discriminate between their inhabitants except upon some reasonable differentiation fairly related to the object of regulation. This equality is not merely abstract justice. The framers of the Constitution knew, and we should not forget today, that there is no more effective practical guaranty against arbitrary and unreasonable government than to require that the principles of law which officials would impose upon a minority must be imposed generally. Conversely, nothing opens the door to arbitrary action so effectively as to allow those officials to pick and choose only a few to whom they will apply legislation and thus to escape the political retribution that might be visited upon them if larger numbers were affected. Courts can take no better measure to assure that laws will be just than to require that laws be equal in operation. . . .

In this case, if the City of New York should assume that display of any advertising on vehicles tends and intends to distract the attention of persons using the highways and to increase the dangers of its traffic, I should think it fully within its constitutional powers to forbid it all. The same would be true if the City should undertake to eliminate or minimize the hazard by any generally applicable restraint, such as limiting the size, color, shape or perhaps to some extent the contents of vehicular advertising. Instead of such general regulation of advertising, however, the City seeks to reduce the hazard only by saying that while some may, others may not exhibit such appeals. The same display, for example, advertising cigarettes, which this appellant is forbidden to carry on its trucks, may be carried on the trucks of a cigarette dealer and might on the trucks of this appellant if it dealt in cigarettes. And almost an identical advertisement, certainly one of equal size, shape, color and appearance, may be carried by this appellant if it proclaims its own offer to transport cigarettes. But it may not be carried so long as the message is not its own but a cigarette dealer's offer to sell the same cigarettes.

. . .

The question in my mind comes to this. Where individuals contribute to an evil or danger in the same way and to the same degree, may those who do so for hire be prohibited, while those who do so for their own commercial ends but not for hire be allowed to continue? I think the answer has to be that the hireling may be put in a class by himself and may be dealt with differently than those who act on their own. But this is not merely because such a discrimination will enable the lawmaker to diminish the evil. That might be done by many classifications, which I should think wholly unsustainable. It is rather because there is a real difference between doing in self-interest and doing for hire, so that it is one thing to tolerate action from those who act on their own and it is another thing to permit the same action to be promoted for a price.

. . .

WILLIAMSON v. LEE OPTICAL OF OKLAHOMA, INC., 348 U.S. 483 (1955). The due process portions of this case are set out supra, p. 520. The Court disposed of an equal protection challenge to the portion of the law exempting sellers of ready-to-wear glasses from regulations imposed on opticians as follows:

"The problem of legislative classification is a perennial one, admitting of no doctrinaire definition. Evils in the same field may be of different dimensions and propositions, requiring different remedies. Or so the legislature may think. . . . Or the reform may take one step at a time, addressing itself to the phase of the problem which seems most acute to the legislative mind. . . . The legislature may select one phase of one field, and apply a remedy there, neglecting the others. . . . The prohibition of the Equal Protection Clause goes no further than the invidious discrimination. We cannot say that that point has been reached here. For all this record shows, the ready-to-wear branch of this business may not loom large in Oklahoma or may present problems of regulation distinct from the other branch."

SCOPE AND LEGITIMACY OF JUDICIAL REVIEW OF THE RATIONALITY OF LEGISLATION UNDER EQUAL PROTECTION

Constitutional law scholars are sharply divided on the question whether the courts should examine ordinary economic legislation under the equal protection clause to insure that such legislation is at least minimally related to some general good. Three general views are identifiable.

Some scholars assert the view that courts should examine both the means and the ends of legislation. They argue that courts cannot escape the burden of examining the outcomes of the legislative process to determine whether the regulations are reasonably related to legitimate public purposes. See, e.g. Tribe, *American Constitutional Law* 582–5, 1440, 1451 (2d ed. 1988); Tussman and tenBroek, *Equal Protection of the Laws,* 37 Calif.L.Rev. 341, 350 (1949). One such scholar, building on a Madisonian republican vision that legitimate policy must be formulated by representatives deliberating to further the public good rather than simply reflecting interest-group pressures, suggests that "[j]udicial scrutiny of the legislative process might take the form of a more serious inquiry into both process and outcome, designed to ensure that what emerges is genuinely public rather than a reflection of existing relations of private power." Sunstein, *Interest Groups in American Public Law,* 38 Stan.L.Rev. 29, 86 (1985).

Others assert that courts should not reexamine legislative choices as to the ends to be served by legislation but should engage in a real inquiry to determine whether the means selected have a real and substantial relation to the object sought to be attained. See, e.g., Gunther, *Forward: In Search of Evolving Doctrine on a Changing Court: A Model for a Newer Equal Protection,* 86 Harv.L.Rev. 1 (1972).

A third view is that the proper role of the courts is to police the structural and procedural limitations the Constitution imposes on the legislative process but not to scrutinize the outcomes for reasonableness. The proponents of this view state that, except for those constitutional provisions which place substantive limits on legislative outcomes by extending special protection to interests against the legislative process, the reach and limits of otherwise valid laws are assumed to be adequately explained by the conflicting forces within the legislative process which shaped them. See, e.g., Linde, *Due Process of Lawmaking,* 55 Neb.L.Rev. 197 (1975); Barrett, *The Rational Basis Standard for Equal Protection Review of Ordinary Legislative Classifications,* 68 Ky.L.Rev. 845 (1980).

To what extent are these views reflected in the following cases?

Federal Communications Commission v. Beach Communications, Inc.

508 U.S. 307, 113 S.Ct. 2096, 124 L.Ed.2d 211 (1993).

Justice Thomas delivered the opinion of the Court.

In providing for the regulation of cable television facilities, Congress has drawn a distinction between facilities that serve separately owned and managed buildings and those that serve one or more buildings under common ownership or management. Cable facilities in the latter category are exempt from regulation as long as they provide services without using public rights-of-way. The question before us is whether there is any conceivable rational basis justifying this distinction for purposes of the Due Process Clause of the Fifth Amendment.

I

The Cable Communications Policy Act of 1984 (Cable Act) ... provided for the franchising of cable systems by local governmental authorities.... Section 602(7) ... determines the reach of the franchise requirement by defining the operative term "cable system." A cable system means any facility designed to provide video programming to multiple subscribers through "closed transmission paths," but does not include, inter alia,

> "a facility that serves only subscribers in 1 or more multiple unit dwellings under common ownership, control, or management, unless such facility or facilities us[e] any public right-of-way." § 602(7)(B)....

In part, this provision tracks a regulatory "private cable" exemption previously promulgated by the Federal Communications Commission (FCC or Commission) pursuant to pre-existing authority under the Communications Act....

This case arises out of an FCC proceeding clarifying the agency's interpretation of the term "cable system" as it is used in the Cable Act.... In this proceeding, the Commission addressed the application of the exemption codified in § 602(7)(B) to satellite master antenna television (SMATV) facilities. Unlike a traditional cable television system, which delivers video programming to a large community of subscribers through coaxial cables laid under city streets or along utility lines, an SMATV system typically receives a signal from a satellite through a small satellite dish located on a rooftop and then retransmits the signal by wire to units within a building or complex of buildings.... The Commission ruled that an SMATV system that serves multiple buildings via a network of interconnected physical transmission lines is a cable system, unless it falls within the § 602(7)(B) exemption.... Consistent with the plain terms of the statutory exemption, the Commission concluded that such an SMATV system is subject to the franchise requirement if its transmission lines interconnect separately owned and managed buildings or if its lines use or cross any public right-of-way....

Respondents ...—SMATV operators that would be subject to franchising under the Cable Act as construed by the Commission—petitioned the Court of Appeals for review.... [A] majority of the court found merit in the claim that § 602(7) violates the implied equal protection guarantee of the Due Process Clause.... In the absence of what it termed "the predominant rationale for local franchising" (use of public rights-of-way), the court saw no rational basis "[o]n the record," and was "unable to imagine" any conceivable basis, for distinguishing between those facilities exempted by the statute and those SMATV cable systems that link separately owned and managed buildings....

Because the Court of Appeals held an Act of Congress unconstitutional, we granted certiorari.... We now reverse.

II

Whether embodied in the Fourteenth Amendment or inferred from the Fifth, equal protection is not a license for courts to judge the wisdom, fairness, or logic of legislative choices. In areas of social and economic policy, a statutory classification that neither proceeds along suspect lines nor infringes fundamental constitutional rights must be upheld against equal protection challenge if there is any reasonably conceivable state of facts that could provide a rational basis for the classification. See Sullivan v. Stroop, 496 U. S. 478, 485 (1990); Bowen v. Gilliard, 483 U. S. 587, 600–603 (1987); United States Railroad Retirement Bd. v. Fritz, 449 U. S. 166, 174–179 (1980); Dandridge v. Williams, 397 U. S. 471, 484–485 (1970). Where there are "plausible reasons" for Congress' action, "our inquiry is at an end." United States Railroad Retirement Bd. v. Fritz, supra, at 179. This standard of review is a paradigm of judicial restraint. "The Constitution presumes that, absent some reason to infer antipathy, even improvident decisions will eventually be rectified by the democratic process and that judicial intervention is generally unwarranted no matter how unwisely we may think a political branch has acted." Vance v. Bradley, 440 U. S. 93, 97 (1979) (footnote omitted).

On rational-basis review, a classification in a statute such as the Cable Act comes to us bearing a strong presumption of validity, see Lyng v. Automobile Workers, 485 U. S. 360, 370 (1988), and those attacking the rationality of the legislative classification have the burden "to negative every conceivable basis which might support it," Lehnhausen v. Lake Shore Auto Parts Co., 410 U. S. 356, 364 (1973).... Moreover, because we never require a legislature to articulate its reasons for enacting a statute, it is entirely irrelevant for constitutional purposes whether the conceived reason for the challenged distinction actually motivated the legislature. United States Railroad Retirement Bd. v. Fritz, supra, at 179. See Flemming v. Nestor, 363 U. S. 603, 612 (1960). Thus, the absence of "legislative facts" explaining the distinction "[o]n the record," ... has no significance in rational-basis analysis. See Nordlinger v. Hahn, 505 U. S., (1992) (slip op., at 13) (equal protection "does not demand for purposes of rational-basis review that a legislature or governing decisionmaker actually articulate at any time the purpose or rationale supporting its classification"). In other words, a legislative choice is not subject to courtroom fact-finding and may be based on rational speculation unsupported by evidence or empirical data. See Vance v. Bradley, supra, at 111. See also Minnesota v. Clover Leaf Creamery Co., 449 U. S. 456, 464 (1981).... Lehnhausen, supra, at 365 (quoting Carmichael v. Southern Coal & Coke Co., 301 U. S. 495, 510 (1937)).

These restraints on judicial review have added force "where the legislature must necessarily engage in a process of line-drawing." United States Railroad Retirement Bd. v. Fritz, 449 U. S., at 179. Defining the class of persons subject to a regulatory requirement—much like classifying governmental beneficiaries—"inevitably requires that some persons who have an almost equally strong claim to favored treatment be placed on different sides of the line, and the fact [that] the line might have been drawn differently at some points is a matter for legislative, rather than judicial, consideration." ... The distinction at issue here represents such a line: By excluding from the definition of "cable system" those facilities that serve commonly owned or managed buildings without using public rights-of-way, § 602(7)(B) delineates the bounds of the regulatory field. Such scope-of-coverage provisions are unavoidable components of most economic or social legislation. In establishing the franchise requirement, Congress had to draw the line somewhere; it had to choose which facilities to franchise. This necessity renders the precise coordinates of the resulting legislative judgment virtually unreviewable, since the legislature must be allowed leeway to approach a perceived problem incrementally. See, e. g., Williamson v. Lee Optical of Okla., Inc., 348 U. S. 483 (1955):

> "The problem of legislative classification is a perennial one, admitting of no doctrinaire definition. Evils in the same field may be of different dimensions and proportions, requiring different remedies. Or so the legislature may think. Or the reform may take one step at a time, addressing

itself to the phase of the problem which seems most acute to the legislative mind. The legislature may select one phase of one field and apply a remedy there, neglecting the others. The prohibition of the Equal Protection Clause goes no further than the invidious discrimination." Id., at 489 (citations omitted).

Applying these principles, we conclude that the common-ownership distinction is constitutional. There are at least two possible bases for the distinction; either one suffices. First, ... it is plausible that Congress ... adopted the FCC's earlier rationale[, under which] common ownership was thought to be indicative of those systems for which the costs of regulation would outweigh the benefits to consumers. Because the number of subscribers was a similar indicator, the Commission also exempted cable facilities that served fewer than 50 subscribers....

This regulatory-efficiency model ... provides a conceivable basis for the common-ownership exemption. A legislator might rationally assume that systems serving only commonly owned or managed buildings without crossing public rights-of-way would typically be limited in size or would share some other attribute affecting their impact on the welfare of cable viewers such that regulators could "safely ignor[e]" these systems.

Respondents argue that Congress did not intend common ownership to be a surrogate for small size, since Congress simultaneously rejected the FCC's 50-subscriber exemption by omitting it from the Cable Act.... Whether the posited reason for the challenged distinction actually motivated Congress is "constitutionally irrelevant," United States Railroad Retirement Bd. v. Fritz, supra, ... and, in any event, the FCC's explanation indicates that both common ownership and number of subscribers were considered indicia of "very small" cable systems. Respondents also contend that an SMATV operator could increase his subscription base and still qualify for the exemption simply by installing a separate satellite dish on each building served.... The additional cost of multiple dishes and associated transmission equipment, however, would impose an independent constraint on system size.

Furthermore, small size is only one plausible ownership-related factor contributing to consumer welfare. Subscriber influence is another. Where an SMATV system serves a complex of buildings under common ownership or management, individual subscribers could conceivably have greater bargaining power vis-a-vis the cable operator (even if the number of dwelling units were large), since all the subscribers could negotiate with one voice through the common owner or manager. Such an owner might have substantial leverage, because he could withhold permission to operate the SMATV system on his property. He would also have an incentive to guard the interests of his tenants. Thus, there could be less need to establish regulatory safeguards for subscribers in commonly owned complexes. Respondents acknowledge such possibilities, ... and we certainly cannot say that these assumptions would be irrational.

There is a second conceivable basis for the statutory distinction. Suppose competing SMATV operators wish to sell video programming to subscribers in a group of contiguous buildings, such as a single city block, which can be interconnected by wire without crossing a public right-of-way. If all the buildings belong to one owner or are commonly managed, that owner or manager could freely negotiate a deal for all subscribers on a competitive basis. But if the buildings are separately owned and managed, the first SMATV operator who gains a foothold by signing a contract and installing a satellite dish and associated transmission equipment on one of the buildings would enjoy a powerful cost advantage in competing for the remaining subscribers: he could connect additional buildings for the cost of a few feet of cable, whereas any competitor would have to recover the cost of his own satellite headend facility. Thus, the first operator could charge rates well above his cost and still undercut the competition. This potential for effective monopoly power might theoretically justify regulating the latter class of SMATV systems and not the former.

III

. . . [T]here are plausible rationales unrelated to the use of public rights-of-way for regulating cable facilities serving separately owned and managed buildings. The assumptions underlying these rationales may be erroneous, but the very fact that they are "arguable" is sufficient, on rational-basis review, to "immuniz[e]" the congressional choice from constitutional challenge. Vance v. Bradley, 440 U. S., at 112.

The judgment of the Court of Appeals is reversed. . . .

Justice Stevens, concurring in the judgment.

Freedom is a blessing. Regulation is sometimes necessary, but it is always burdensome. A decision not to regulate the way in which an owner chooses to enjoy the benefits of an improvement to his own property is adequately justified by a presumption in favor of freedom.

. . .

. . . In my opinion the interest in the free use of one's own property provides adequate support for an exception from burdensome regulation and franchising requirements even when the property is occupied not only by family members and guests, but by lessees and co-owners as well, and even when the property complex encompasses multiple buildings.

The master antenna serving multiple units in an apartment building is less unsightly than a forest of individual antennas, each serving a separate apartment. It was surely sensible to allow owners to make use of such an improvement without incurring the costs of franchising and economic regulation. Even though regulation might have been justified . . . a justification for nonregulation would nevertheless remain: Whenever possible, property owners should be free to use improvements to their property as they see fit.

That brings us to the "private cable" exemption as applied to Satellite Master Antenna Television (SMATV) systems. A justification for the "private cable" exemption that rests on the presumption that an owner of property should be allowed to use an improvement on his own property as he sees fit unless there is a sufficient public interest in denying him that right simply does not apply to the situation in which the improvement—here, the satellite antenna—is being used to distribute signals to subscribers on other people's property. In that situation, the property owner, or the SMATV operator, has reached out beyond the property line and is seeking to employ the satellite antenna in the broader market for television programming. While the crossing of that line need not trigger regulatory intervention, and the absence of such a crossing may not prevent such intervention, it certainly cannot be said that government is disabled, by the Constitution, from regulating in the case of the former and abstaining in the case of the latter. Such a policy is adequately justified by the presumption in favor of freedom.

Thus, while I am not fully persuaded that the "private cable" exemption is justified by the size of the market which it encompasses,[1] or by the Court's "monopoly" rationale,[2] I agree with its ultimate conclusion. In my judgment, it is reasonable to presume[3] that Congress was motivated by an interest in allowing property owners to exercise freedom in the use of their own property. Legislation so motivated surely does not violate the sovereign's duty to govern impartially. See Hampton v. Mow Sun Wong, 426 U. S. 88, 100 (1976). Accordingly, I concur in the judgment of the Court.

HELLER v. DOE, 509 U.S. 312 (1993). The Court rejected an equal protection challenge by adult mentally retarded people to Kentucky statutes (1) authorizing their involuntary civil commitment on a clear and convincing standard of proof, while requiring proof beyond a reasonable doubt for involuntary commitment of mentally ill persons, and (2) allowing close relatives and guardians of the mentally retarded, but not the mentally ill, to participate in commitment proceedings as parties entitled to present evidence and appeal. Confining itself to "rational-basis review" because that is how the case had been litigated, the Court, per Justice Kennedy, cited much of its discussion of that standard in *Beach Communications* and noted that in neither City of Cleburne v. Cleburne Living Center, infra, page 906, nor Schweiker v. Wilson, infra, page 690, "did we purport to apply a different standard of rational-basis review from that just described." Although "even the standard of rationality ... must find some footing in the realities of the subject addressed by the legislation ... Kentucky has proffered more than adequate justifications for the differences in treatment between the mentally retarded and the mentally ill."

The lower standard of proof for involuntary commitment of the mentally retarded "follows from the fact that mental retardation is easier to diagnose than is mental illness[,]" because it "tends to equalize the risks of an erroneous determination that the subject of a commitment proceeding has the condition in question." Moreover, there is a "reasonably conceivable state of facts ... from which Kentucky could conclude that the second prerequisite to commitment"—dangerousness to self or others—"is established more easily, as a general rule, in the case of the mentally retarded." That is so, because "retardation is a permanent, relatively stable condition," allowing reliance on

---

[1] Approximately 25% of all multiple dwellings units are in complexes large enough to support an SMATV system.... Furthermore, whereas the FCC had, prior to [the Cable Act], exempted from regulation cable systems of less than 50 subscribers as well as those serving commonly owned multiple unit dwellings, Congress exempted only the latter when it passed the Cable Act, leaving out the exemption based on system size. Respondent thus makes a strong argument that Congress may have rejected the very rationale upon which the FCC, and the Court, rely.

[2] The Court's theory assumes a great deal about the nature of what is essentially a hypothetical market. Moreover, the Court's analysis overlooks the competitive presence of traditional cable as a potential constraint on an SMATV operator's capacity to extract monopoly rents from landlords.

[3] The Court states that a legislative classification must be upheld "if there is any reasonably conceivable state of facts that could provide a rational basis for the classification," and that "[w]here there are 'plausible reasons' for Congress' action, 'our inquiry is at an end.' " In my view, this formulation sweeps too broadly, for it is difficult to imagine a legislative classification that could not be supported by a "reasonably conceivable state of facts." Judicial review under the "conceivable set of facts" test is tantamount to no review at all. I continue to believe that when Congress imposes a burden on one group, but leaves unaffected another that is similarly, though not identically, situated, "the Constitution requires something more than merely a 'conceivable' or 'plausible' explanation for the unequal treatment." United States Railroad Retirement Bd. v. Fritz, 449 U. S. 166, 180 (1980) (Stevens, J., concurring in judgment). In my view, when the actual rationale for the legislative classification is unclear, we should inquire whether the classification is rationally related to "a legitimate purpose that we may reasonably presume to have motivated an impartial legislature." Id., at 181 (emphasis added).

the record of previous behavior, whereas "[m]anifestations of mental illness may be sudden, and past behavior may not be an adequate predictor of future actions" and prediction is "complicated as well by the difficulties inherent in diagnosis of mental illness." Finally, a "more far-reaching rationale justifying the different burdens of proof" is that the "prevailing methods of treatment for the mentally retarded, as a general rule, are much less invasive than are those given the mentally ill." Whereas the ill typically receive psychotropic drugs and psychiatric treatment involving "intrusive inquiries into the patient's inner-most thoughts," the retarded more typically receive training for self-care and self-sufficiency. Although "the loss of liberty ... may be similar in many respects" for both groups, and "some persons committed for mental retardation are subjected to more intrusive treatments ..., it would have been plausible for the Kentucky legislature to believe that most mentally retarded individuals who are committed receive treatment which is different from, and less invasive than, that to which the mentally ill are subjected." The question being "at least debatable, ... rational-basis review permits a legislature to use just this sort of generalization." In sum, "[e]ach of these rationales, 'standing on its own, would suffice to establish a rational basis' " for the differential burden of proof.

As for the differential rights of close relatives and guardians to participate in the commitment proceeding, retardation "has its onset during a person's developmental period" and mental illness "may arise or manifest itself ... only after minority when the afflicted person's immediate family members have no knowledge of the medical condition and have long ceased to provide care and support." Moreover, adults diagnosed as mentally ill "may have a need for privacy that justifies ... confining a commitment proceeding to the smallest group compatible with due process." Hence, "Kentucky may have concluded that close relatives and guardians, both of whom likely have intimate knowledge of a mentally retarded person's abilities and experiences, have valuable insights which should be considered during the involuntary commitment process." By contrast, Kentucky also "may have concluded that participation as parties by relatives and guardians of the mentally ill would not in most cases have been of sufficient help to the trier of fact to justify the additional burden and complications of granting party status."

Justice Souter's dissent, joined in full by Justices Blackmun and Stevens, found both distinctions "not supported by any rational justification."[a] He, too, declined to address whether "heightened scrutiny" should apply, but only because it was unnecessary since the distinctions failed "rational-basis scrutiny, ... which we have previously applied to a classification on the basis of mental disability, see Cleburne v. Cleburne Living Center." He "would follow *Cleburne* here" and thought the Court's opinion left "*Cleburne*'s status ... uncertain."[b]

With respect to the burden of proof differential, Justice Souter first argued that rationality is not satisfied "if burdens of proof rise simply with difficulties of proof," because "burdens of proof are assigned and risks of error are allocated not to reflect the mere difficulty of avoiding error, but the importance

[a] Justice O'Connor also joined the dissent insofar as it found the differential standard of proof for commitment "irrational," but she agreed with the Court that "there are sufficiently plausible and legitimate reasons for the legislative determination" to differentiate regarding party status for close relatives and guardians.

[b] Justice Blackmun added a separate dissenting statement to express his "continuing adherence to the view that laws that discriminate against individuals with mental retardation," City of Cleburne v. Cleburne Living Center, Inc., 473 U.S. 432, 455 (1985) (opinion of Marshall, J., joined by Brennan and Blackmun, JJ.) ... are subject to heightened review.

of avoiding it as judged after a thorough consideration of those respective interests of the parties that will be affected by the allocation"—in this case the State's "interests of protecting society from those posing dangers and protecting the ill or helpless individual from his own incapacities" and the individual's interests in "freedom from restraint and freedom from the stigma that restraint and its justifications impose on an institutionalized person." Justice Souter could find no "differences in the respective interests of the public and the subjects of the commitment proceedings" that provided a rational basis for differentiating between the ill and the retarded:

"... Both the ill and the retarded may be dangerous, each may require care, and the State's interest is seemingly of equal strength in each category of cases. No one has or would argue that the value of liberty varies somehow depending on whether one is alleged to be ill or retarded, and a mentally retarded person has as much to lose by civil commitment to an institution as a mentally ill counterpart ... Even assuming, then, that the assertion of different degrees of difficulty of proof both of mental illness and mental retardation and of the dangerousness inherent in each condition is true (an assertion for which there is no support in the record), it lends not a shred of rational support to the decision to discriminate against the retarded in allocating the risk of erroneous curtailment of liberty."

He also disagreed with the Court that "it would have been plausible for the Kentucky legislature to believe that most mentally retarded individuals who are committed receive treatment which is ... less invasive tha[n] that to which the mentally ill are subjected." Studies conducted nationally and in neighboring states indicated widespread use—and frequent abuse—of "mind-altering medication" and "intrusive psychiatric therapy" with respect to the mentally retarded as well as the mentally ill, and "[t]here being nothing in the record to suggest that Kentucky's institutions are free from these practices, and no reason whatever to assume so, there simply is no plausible basis for the Court's assumption that the institutional response to mental retardation is in the main less intrusive ... than treatment of mental illness." Based on the "available literature ... there are no apparent differences of therapeutic regimes that would plausibly explain less rigorous commitment standards for those alleged to be mentally retarded than for those alleged to be mentally ill."

As for the involvement of family members and guardians in the commitment proceeding, Justice Souter thought that although the differences cited by the Court "might justify a scheme in which immediate relatives and guardians were automatically called as witnesses in cases seeking institutionalization on the basis of mental retardation, they are completely unrelated to ... permitting these immediate relatives and guardians to be involved 'as parties' so as to give them, among other things, the right to appeal as 'adverse' a decision not to institutionalize the individual...." Virtually all the State's involuntary commitments of the retarded are promoted by relatives or guardians, and making them parties subjects "someone ... alleged to be retarded" to "a second prosecutor." The import of this was clear to Justice Souter:

"The Court simply points to no characteristic of mental retardation that could rationally justify imposing this burden of a second prosecutor on those alleged to be mentally retarded where the State has decided not to impose it upon those alleged to be mentally ill. Even if we assumed a generally more regular connection between the relatives and guardians of those alleged to be retarded than those said to be mentally ill, it would not explain why the former should be subject to a second prosecutor when the latter are not.

"The same may be said about the Court's second suggested justification, that the mentally ill may have a need for privacy not shown by the retarded. Even assuming the ill need some additional privacy, and that participation of others in the commitment proceeding should therefore be limited 'to the smallest group compatible with due process,' why should the retarded be subject to a second prosecutor? The Court provides no answer.

"Without plausible justification, Kentucky is being allowed to draw a distinction that is difficult to see as resting on anything other than the stereotypical assumption that the retarded are 'perpetual children,' an assumption that has historically been taken to justify the disrespect and 'grotesque mistreatment' to which the retarded have been subjected. See Cleburne ... (Stevens, J., concurring)...."

ASCERTAINING LEGISLATIVE PURPOSE FOR RATIONAL BASIS REVIEW

The Court's consistent refusal to require that legislative bodies articulate the purpose of a statutory classification, or be held to an identifiable "actual" or even "reasonably presumable" purpose, in order to have the classification survive judicial review for reasonableness, has in some circumstances provoked vigorous methodological dissent. Two decisions rejecting attacks on distinctions in benefits legislation are noteworthy in this regard.

In United States Railroad Retirement Board v. Fritz, 449 U.S. 166 (1980), Congress discontinued dual railroad retirement and social security benefits for some but not all former rail employees, in part drawing a line on the basis of how recent rather than how long an employee's railroad service had been. Justice Rehnquist's majority opinion, applying the rational basis standard, stated that "the plain language of [the provision drawing the distinction] marks the beginning and end of our inquiry" into purpose. Nor was that purpose "achieved ... in a patently arbitrary or irrational way[,]" because "Congress could assume that those who had a current connection with the railroad industry when the Act was passed in 1974, or who returned to the industry before their retirement, were more likely than those who had left the industry prior to 1974, and who never returned, to be among the class of persons who pursue careers in the railroad industry, the class for whom the Railroad Retirement Act was designed." Having found "plausible reasons for Congress' action, our inquiry is at an end." Finally, the majority

"disagree[d] with the District Court's conclusion that Congress was unaware of what it accomplished or that it was misled by the groups that appeared before it. If this test were applied literally to every member of any legislature that ever voted on a law, there would be very few laws which would survive it. The language of the statute is clear, and we have historically assumed that Congress intended what it enacted."

In dissent, Justice Brennan, joined by Justice Marshall, objected to the majority's "tautological approach to statutory purpose[,]" arguing that "the 'plain language' of the statute can tell us only what the classification is; it can tell us nothing about the purpose of the classification, let alone the relationship between the classification and that purpose." He continued:

"... It may always be said that Congress intended to do what it in fact did. If that were the extent of our analysis, we would find every statute, no matter how arbitrary or irrational, perfectly tailored to achieve its purpose. But equal protection scrutiny under the rational basis test requires the courts first to deduce the independent objectives of the statute, usually from statements of purpose and other evidence in the statute and legislative history, and second to analyze whether the challenged classification rationally furthers achievement of those objectives. . . ."

Justice Brennan found in the legislative history "a 'principal purpose' . . . explicitly stated by Congress . . . to preserve the vested earned benefits of retirees who had already qualified for them." In his view, the classification, "which deprives some retirees of vested dual benefits that they had earned prior to 1974, directly conflicts with Congress' stated purpose" and, hence, is "not only rationally unrelated to the congressional purpose [but] inimical to it." In general, "[w]here Congress has expressly stated the purpose of a piece of legislation, but where the challenged classification is either irrelevant to or counter to that purpose, we must view any *post hoc* justifications proffered by Government attorneys with skepticism. A challenged classification may be sustained only if it is rationally related to achievement of an *actual* legitimate governmental purpose." Here, moreover, Congress had "asked railroad management and labor representatives to negotiate and submit a bill to restructure the Railroad Retirement system" and testimony "at congressional hearings perpetuated the inaccurate impression that all retirees with earned vested dual benefits under prior law would retain their benefits unchanged." While "a misstatement or several misstatements by witnesses before Congress would not ordinarily lead us to conclude that Congress misapprehended what it was doing . . ., where complex legislation was drafted by outside parties and Congress relied on them to explain it, where the misstatements are frequent and unrebutted, and where no Member of Congress can be found to have stated the effect of the classification correctly, we are entitled to suspect that Congress may have been misled." Accordingly, "I do not think that this classification was rationally related to an *actual* governmental purpose."

Justice Stevens, concurring in the judgment, shared Justice Brennan's concern that "judicial review [not] constitute a mere tautological recognition of the fact that Congress did what it intended to do" and urged that "[w]hen Congress deprives a small class of persons of vested rights that are protected . . . for others who are in a similar though not identical position, I believe the Constitution requires something more than merely a 'conceivable' or a 'plausible' explanation for the unequal treatment." But he did not

"share Justice Brennan's conclusion that every statutory classification must further an objective that can be confidently identified as the 'actual purpose' of the legislature. Actual purpose is sometimes unknown. Moreover, undue emphasis on actual motivation may result in identically worded statutes being held valid in one State and invalid in a neighboring State. I therefore believe that we must discover a correlation between the classification and either the actual purpose of the statute or a legitimate purpose that we may reasonably presume to have motivated an impartial legislature. If the adverse impact on the disfavored class is an apparent aim of the legislature, its impartiality would be suspect. If, however, the adverse impact may reasonably be viewed as an acceptable cost of achieving a larger goal, an impartial lawmaker could rationally decide that that cost should be incurred."

Here, though "Congress originally intended to protect *all* vested benefits, . . . it ultimately sacrificed some benefits in the interest of achieving other objectives"—ending dual benefits and "protecting the solvency of the entire railroad retirement program." As "any distinction . . . within the class of vested beneficiaries would involve a difference of degree rather than a difference in entitlement[,]" Justice Stevens was "satisfied that a distinction based upon currency of railroad employment represents an impartial method of identifying that sort of difference."

The following year the Court divided 5–4 over an equal protection challenge by residents of mental institutions denied a small welfare allowance Congress had authorized for inmates of only those public institutions receiving Medicaid payments on their behalf. Schweiker v. Wilson, 450 U.S. 221 (1981). The majority concluded that adopting the Medicaid eligibility criterion "must be considered Congress' deliberate, considered choice" and reasoned that Congress "may rationally limit the grant to Medicaid recipients, for whose care the Federal Government already has assumed the major portion of the expense" and leave it to the States, who "Congress believed . . . have a 'traditional' responsibility to care for those institutionalized in public mental institutions[,] to provide an equivalent."

Justice Powell's dissent, joined by Justices Brennan, Marshall, and Stevens, said in part:

"The deference to which legislative accommodation of conflicting interests is entitled rests in part upon the principle that the political process of our majoritarian democracy responds to the wishes of the people. Accordingly, an important touchstone for equal protection review of statutes is how readily a policy can be discerned which the legislature intended to serve. . . . [W]hether a statutory classification discriminates arbitrarily cannot be divorced from whether it was enacted to serve an identifiable purpose. When a legislative purpose can be suggested only by the ingenuity of a government lawyer litigating the constitutionality of a statute, a reviewing court may be presented not so much with a legislative policy choice as its absence.

"In my view, the Court should receive with some skepticism *post hoc* hypotheses about legislative purpose, unsupported by the legislative history.[6] When no indication of legislative purpose appears other than the current position of the Secretary, the Court should require that the classification bear a 'fair and substantial relation' to the asserted purpose. See F.S. Royster Guano Co. v. Virginia, 253 U.S. 412, 415 (1920). This marginally more demanding scrutiny indirectly would test the plausibility of the tendered purpose. . . .

"I conclude that Congress had no rational reason for refusing to pay a comfort allowance to appellees, while paying it to numerous otherwise identically situated disabled indigents. This unexplained difference in treatment must have been a legislative oversight. . . ."

MODERN RATIONAL BASIS REVIEW

Despite occasional dissenting expressions of discomfort with the "toothlessness" of rational basis review as applied in the realms of purely economic regulation and the provision of government benefits, the Court consistently has refused to invalidate any such measure, with one notable exception, for more than 50 years. In Morey v. Doud, 354 U.S. 457 (1957), the Court, with three dissenters, held that an Illinois statute imposing licensing and financial requirements on sellers and issuers of all money orders, except those of the

---

[6] Some of our cases suggest that the actual purpose of a statute is irrelevant, Flemming v. Nestor, 363 U.S. 603, 612 (1960), and that the statute must be upheld "if any state of facts reasonably may be conceived to justify" its discrimination, McGowan v. Maryland, 366 U.S. 420, 426 (1961). Although these cases preserve an important caution, they do not describe the importance of actual legislative purpose in our analysis. We recognize that a legislative body rarely acts with a single mind and that compromises blur purpose. . . . Ascertainment of actual purpose to the extent feasible, however, remains an essential step in equal protection.

"American Express Company[,]" violated equal protection. In reaching this conclusion, the Court took "all of these factors in conjunction—the remote relationship of the statutory classification to the Act's purpose or to business characteristics, and the creation of a closed class by the singling out of the money orders of a named company, with accompanying economic advantages."

Nearly twenty years later in a brief per curiam opinion, however, the Court concluded without dissent that *Morey* "was a needlessly intrusive judicial infringement on the State's legislative powers" and "so far departs from proper equal protection analysis in cases of exclusively economic regulation that it should be, and is, overruled." New Orleans v. Dukes, 427 U.S. 297 (1976). *Dukes,* which the Court found "essentially indistinguishable" from *Morey,* upheld an ordinance that exempted from a general prohibition against the selling of foodstuffs from pushcarts in New Orleans' French Quarter "vendors who have continually operated the same business [there] for eight years prior to January 1, 1972." The Court concluded that "[t]he city's classification rationally furthers the purpose . . . the city had identified as its objective . . . [;] that is, as a means 'to preserve the appearance and custom valued by the Quarter's residents and attractive to tourists.' " As for the "grandfather provision," the Court decided that "the city could rationally choose initially to eliminate vendors of more recent vintage" and gave the following rationale: "The city could reasonably decide that newer businesses were less likely to have built up substantial reliance interests in continued operations . . . and that the two vendors which qualified under the 'grandfather clause'—both of which had operated in the area for over 20 years . . .—had themselves become part of the distinctive character and charm that distinguishes the Vieux Carre."

The Court, purporting to apply the rational basis standard, has invalidated a number of legislative classifications in the modern era, but none involved solely economic regulation or distribution of government benefits. For example, the Court invoked rational basis review in striking down a gender distinction in Reed v. Reed, 404 U.S. 71 (1971), infra, page 743. Similarly, in City of Cleburne v. Cleburne Living Center, 473 U.S. 432 (1985), infra, page 906, despite Justice Marshall's dissenting criticism that it was engaging in " 'second order' rational basis review," the Court held that a city ordinance, as applied to deny a special use permit for the operation of a group home for the mentally retarded, failed rational basis scrutiny and revealed "an irrational prejudice" against that group. Of like import but without reference to *Cleburne,* the Court later invalidated an amendment to the Colorado Constitution precluding any level of state government from protecting the status of persons on the basis of their "homosexual, lesbian or bisexual orientation, conduct, practices or relationships," because "its sheer breadth is so discontinuous with the reasons offered for it that the amendment seems inexplicable by anything but animus toward the class that it affects; it lacks a rational relationship to legitimate state interests." Romer v. Evans, __ U.S. __, __, 116 S.Ct. 1620, 1627 (1996), infra page 915. Further examples include the Court's professed use of rational basis review when invalidating legislative distinctions between newly-arrived and long-term state residents, as in Zobel v. Williams, 457 U.S. 55 (1982), infra, page 1003, and classifications disadvantaging nonresidents of a State, as in Metropolitan Life Insurance Co. v. Ward, 470 U.S. 869 (1985), infra, page 1016. In these and similar cases one might ask whether and in what ways the Court may be applying a different form of rational basis review than in the opinions presented in this section, and why the Court might invoke the rational basis standard but apply it differently rather than invoke a different standard.

SECTION 3.   SUSPECT CLASSIFICATIONS

Introduction. This section presents the cases where the classifying factor rather than the burden on a fundamental interest gives rise to a heightened standard of review. Subsection A deals with the most clearly suspect classifications—those disadvantaging racial minorities. Subsection B involves a special application of the racial classification doctrine to official racial segregation of schools and other public facilities. Subsection C addresses classifications dealing with gender, where the Court uses the classifying factor to justify a heightened standard of review but one not as rigorous as that applied to racial classifications.

The cases in Subsection D typically involve legislation lacking facially suspect classifications but having a differential impact on particular groups. The question addressed is whether "suspectness" turns on the "impact" of laws or the "intent" with which they are enacted.

Subsection E discusses the most controversial and divisive issue before the Court under the equal protection clause—the validity of the use of gender and racial classifications for the purpose of aiding women or minority groups.

Subsection F deals with classifications involving aliens, and Subsection G with other classifying factors that may trigger heightened scrutiny, such as illegitimacy, mental retardation, sexual orientation, age, and poverty.

A.   CLASSIFICATIONS DISADVANTAGING RACIAL MINORITIES

Loving v. Virginia

388 U.S. 1, 87 S.Ct. 1817, 18 L.Ed.2d 1010 (1967).

Mr. Chief Justice Warren delivered the opinion of the Court.

This case presents a constitutional question never addressed by this Court: whether a statutory scheme adopted by the State of Virginia to prevent marriages between persons solely on the basis of racial classifications violates the Equal Protection and Due Process Clauses of the Fourteenth Amendment. For reasons which seem to us to reflect the central meaning of those constitutional commands, we conclude that these statutes cannot stand consistently with the Fourteenth Amendment.

In June 1958, two residents of Virginia, Mildred Jeter, a Negro woman, and Richard Loving, a white man, were married in the District of Columbia pursuant to its laws. Shortly after their marriage, the Lovings returned to Virginia and established their marital abode in Caroline County. . . . [A County] grand jury issued an indictment charging the Lovings with violating Virginia's ban on interracial marriages. On January 6, 1959, the Lovings pleaded guilty to the charge and were sentenced to one year in jail; however, the trial judge suspended the sentence for a period of 25 years on the condition that the Lovings leave the State and not return to Virginia together for 25 years, stating that:

> "Almighty God created the races white, black, yellow, malay, and red, and he placed them on separate continents. And but for the interference with his arrangement there would be no cause for such marriages. The fact

that he separated the races shows that he did not intend for the races to mix."

After their convictions the Lovings took up residence in the District of Columbia. On November 6, 1963, they filed a motion in the state trial court to vacate the judgment and set aside the sentence on the ground that the statutes which they had violated were repugnant to the Fourteenth Amendment. The motion not having been decided by October 28, 1964, the Lovings instituted a class action in the United States District Court for the Eastern District of Virginia requesting that a three-judge court be convened to declare the Virginia antimiscegenation statutes unconstitutional and to enjoin state officials from enforcing their convictions. On January 22, 1965, the state trial judge denied the motion to vacate the sentences, and the Lovings perfected an appeal to the Supreme Court of Appeals of Virginia. On February 11, 1965, the three-judge District Court continued the case to allow the Lovings to present their constitutional claims to the highest state court.

The Supreme Court of Appeals upheld the constitutionality of the antimiscegenation statutes and, after modifying the sentence, affirmed the convictions. The Lovings appealed this decision, and we noted probable jurisdiction on December 12, 1966.

The two statutes under which appellants were convicted and sentenced are part of a comprehensive statutory scheme aimed at prohibiting and punishing interracial marriages. The Lovings were convicted of violating § 20–58 of the Virginia Code:

> "*Leaving State to Evade Law.* If any white person and colored person shall go out of this State, for the purpose of being married, and with the intention of returning, and be married out of it, and afterwards return to and reside in it, cohabiting as man and wife, they shall be punished as provided in § 20–59, and the marriage shall be governed by the same law as if it had been solemnized in this State. The fact of their cohabitation here as man and wife shall be evidence of their marriage."

Section 20–59, which defines the penalty for miscegenation, provides:

> "*Punishment for Marriage.* If any white person intermarry with a colored person, or any colored person intermarry with a white person, he shall be guilty of a felony and shall be punished by confinement in the penitentiary for not less than one nor more than five years."

Other central provisions in the Virginia statutory scheme are § 20–57, which automatically voids all marriages between "a white person and a colored person" without any judicial proceeding, and §§ 20–54 and 1–14 which, respectively, define "white persons" and "colored persons and Indians" for purposes of the statutory prohibitions. The Lovings have never disputed in the course of this litigation that Mrs. Loving is a "colored person" or that Mr. Loving is a "white person" within the meanings given those terms by the Virginia statutes.

Virginia is now one of 16 States which prohibit and punish marriages on the basis of racial classifications.[5] Penalties for miscegenation arose as an incident to slavery and have been common in Virginia since the colonial period. The present statutory scheme dates from the adoption of the Racial Integrity Act of 1924, passed during the period of extreme nativism which followed the end of the First World War. The central features of this Act, and current

---

[5] . . .

Over the past 15 years, 14 States have repealed laws outlawing interracial marriage. . . .

Virginia law, are the absolute prohibition of a "white person" marrying other than another "white person," a prohibition against issuing marriage licenses until the issuing official is satisfied that the applicants' statements as to their race are correct, certificates of "racial composition" to be kept by both local and state registrars, and the carrying forward of earlier prohibitions against racial intermarriage.

I.

In upholding the constitutionality of these provisions in the decision below, the Supreme Court of Appeals of Virginia referred to its 1955 decision in Naim v. Naim, 197 Va. 80, 87 S.E.2d 749, as stating the reasons supporting the validity of these laws. In *Naim*, the state court concluded that the State's legitimate purposes were "to preserve the racial integrity of its citizens," and to prevent "the corruption of blood," "a mongrel breed of citizens," and "the obliteration of racial pride," obviously an endorsement of the doctrine of White Supremacy.... The court also reasoned that marriage has traditionally been subject to state regulation without federal intervention, and, consequently, the regulation of marriage should be left to exclusive state control by the Tenth Amendment.

While the state court is no doubt correct in asserting that marriage is a social relation subject to the State's police power, ... the State does not contend ... that its powers to regulate marriage are unlimited notwithstanding the commands of the Fourteenth Amendment. Nor could it do so in light of Meyer v. State of Nebraska, 262 U.S. 390 (1923), and Skinner v. State of Oklahoma, 316 U.S. 535 (1942). Instead, the State argues that the meaning of the Equal Protection Clause, as illuminated by the statements of the Framers, is only that state penal laws containing an interracial element as part of the definition of the offense must apply equally to whites and Negroes in the sense that members of each race are punished to the same degree. Thus, the State contends that, because its miscegenation statutes punish equally both the white and the Negro participants in an interracial marriage, these statutes, despite their reliance on racial classifications, do not constitute an invidious discrimination based upon race. The second argument advanced by the State assumes the validity of its equal application theory. The argument is that, if the Equal Protection Clause does not outlaw miscegenation statutes because of their reliance on racial classifications, the question of constitutionality would thus become whether there was any rational basis for a State to treat interracial marriages differently from other marriages. On this question, the State argues, the scientific evidence is substantially in doubt and, consequently, this Court should defer to the wisdom of the state legislature in adopting its policy of discouraging interracial marriages.

Because we reject the notion that the mere "equal application" of a statute containing racial classifications is enough to remove the classifications from the Fourteenth Amendment's proscription of all invidious racial discriminations, we do not accept the State's contention that these statutes should be upheld if there is any possible basis for concluding that they serve a rational purpose. The mere fact of equal application does not mean that our analysis of this statute should follow the approach we have taken in cases involving no racial discrimination where the Equal Protection Clause has been arrayed against a statute discriminating between the kinds of advertising which may be displayed on trucks in New York City, Railway Express Agency, Inc. v. People of State of New York, 336 U.S. 106 (1949), or an exemption in Ohio's ad valorem tax for merchandise owned by a non-resident in a storage warehouse, Allied Stores of Ohio, Inc. v. Bowers, 358 U.S. 522 (1959). In these cases, involving distinctions not drawn according to race, the Court has merely asked whether there is any rational foundation for the discriminations, and has deferred to the wisdom of the state legislatures. In the case at bar, however, we deal with statutes containing racial classifications, and the fact of equal application does not immunize the statute from the very heavy burden of justification which the Fourteenth Amendment has traditionally required of state statutes drawn according to race.

The State argues that statements in the Thirty-ninth Congress about the time of the passage of the Fourteenth Amendment indicate that the Framers did not intend the Amendment to make unconstitutional state miscegenation laws. Many of the statements alluded to by the State concern the debates over the Freedmen's Bureau Bill, which President Johnson vetoed, and the Civil Rights Act of 1866, enacted over his veto. While these statements have some relevance to the intention of Congress in submitting the Fourteenth Amendment, it must be understood that they pertained to the passage of specific statutes and not to the broader, organic purpose of a constitutional amendment. As for the various statements directly concerning the Fourteenth Amendment, we have said in connection with a related problem, that although these historical sources "cast some light" they are not sufficient to resolve the problem; "[a]t best, they are inconclusive. The most avid proponents of the post-War Amendments undoubtedly intended them to remove all legal distinctions among 'all persons born or naturalized in the United States.' Their opponents, just as certainly, were antagonistic to both the letter and the spirit of the Amendments and wished them to have the most limited effect." Brown et al. v. Board of Education of Topeka, et al., 347 U.S. 483 (1954). See also Strauder v. West Virginia, 100 U.S. 303, 310 (1880). We have rejected the proposition that the debates in the Thirty-ninth Congress or in the state legislatures which ratified the Fourteenth Amendment supported the theory advanced by the State, that the requirement of equal protection of the laws is satisfied by penal laws defining offenses based on racial classifications so long as white and Negro participants in the offense were similarly punished. McLaughlin et al. v. State of Florida, 379 U.S. 184 (1964).

The State finds support for its "equal application" theory in the decision of the Court in Pace v. Alabama, 106 U.S. 583 (1882). In that case, the Court upheld a conviction under an Alabama statute forbidding adultery or fornication between a white person and a Negro which imposed a greater penalty than that of a statute proscribing similar conduct by members of the same race. The Court reasoned that the statute could not be said to discriminate against Negroes because the punishment for each participant in the offense was the same. However, as recently as the 1964 Term, in rejecting the reasoning of that case, we stated "*Pace* represents a limited view of the Equal Protection Clause which has not withstood analysis in the subsequent decisions of this Court." *McLaughlin et al. v. Florida,* ... As we there demonstrated, the Equal Protection Clause requires the consideration of whether the classifications drawn by any statute constitute an arbitrary and invidious discrimination. The clear and central purpose of the Fourteenth Amendment was to eliminate all official state sources of invidious racial discrimination in the States. Slaughter–House Cases, 16 Wall. 36, 71 (1873); Strauder v. State of West Virginia, 100 U.S. 303, 307–308 (1880); Ex parte Virginia, 100 U.S. 339, 344–345 (1880); Shelley v. Kraemer, 334 U.S. 1 (1948); Burton v. Wilmington Parking Authority, 365 U.S. 715 (1961).

There can be no question but that Virginia's miscegenation statutes rest solely upon distinctions drawn according to race. The statutes proscribe generally accepted conduct if engaged in by members of different races. Over the years, this Court has consistently repudiated "[d]istinctions between citizens solely because of their ancestry" as being "odious to a free people whose institutions are founded upon the doctrine of equality." Hirabayashi v. United States, 320 U.S. 81, 100 (1943). At the very least, the Equal Protection Clause demands that racial classifications, especially suspect in criminal statutes, be subjected to the "most rigid scrutiny," Korematsu v. United States, 323 U.S. 214, 216 (1944), and, if they are ever to be upheld, they must be shown to be necessary to the accomplishment of some permissible state objective, independent of the racial discrimination which it was the object of the Fourteenth Amendment to eliminate. Indeed, two members of this Court have already stated that they "cannot conceive of a valid legislative purpose ... which makes the color of a person's skin the test of whether his conduct is a criminal offense." McLaughlin v. Florida, supra, 379 U.S. at 198 (Stewart, J., joined by Douglas, J., concurring).

There is patently no legitimate overriding purpose independent of invidious racial discrimination which justifies this classification. The fact that Virginia only prohibits interracial marriages involving white persons demonstrates that the racial classifications must stand on their own justification, as measures designed to maintain White Supremacy.[11] We have consistently denied the constitutionality of measures which restrict the rights of citizens on account of race. There can be no doubt that restricting the freedom to marry solely because of racial classifications violates the central meaning of the Equal Protection Clause.

. . .

These convictions must be reversed. It is so ordered.

Mr. Justice Stewart, concurring.

I have previously expressed the belief that "it is simply not possible for a state law to be valid under our Constitution which makes the criminality of an act depend upon the race of the actor." McLaughlin v. State of Florida, 379 U.S. 184, 198 (concurring opinion). Because I adhere to that belief, I concur in the judgment of the Court.

Palmore v. Sidoti

466 U.S. 429, 104 S.Ct. 1879, 80 L.Ed.2d 421 (1984).

Chief Justice Burger delivered the opinion of the Court.

We granted certiorari to review a judgment of a state court divesting a natural mother of the custody of her infant child because of her remarriage to a person of a different race.

---

[11] Appellants point out that the State's concern in these statutes, as expressed in the words of the 1924 Act's title, "An Act to Preserve Racial Integrity," extends only to the integrity of the white race. While Virginia prohibits whites from marrying any nonwhite (subject to the exception for the descendants of Pocahontas), Negroes, Orientals, and any other racial class may intermarry without statutory interference. Appellants contend that this distinction renders Virginia's miscegenation statutes arbitrary and unreasonable even assuming the constitutional validity of an official purpose to preserve "racial integrity." We need not reach this contention because we find the racial classifications in these statutes repugnant to the Fourteenth Amendment, even assuming an even-handed state purpose to protect the "integrity" of all races.

I

When petitioner Linda Sidoti Palmore and respondent Anthony J. Sidoti, both Caucasians, were divorced in May 1980 in Florida, the mother was awarded custody of their three-year-old daughter.

In September 1981 the father sought custody of the child by filing a petition to modify the prior judgment because of changed conditions. The change was that the child's mother was then cohabiting with a Negro, Clarence Palmore, Jr., whom she married two months later. Additionally, the father made several allegations of instances in which the mother had not properly cared for the child.

After hearing testimony from both parties and considering a court counselor's investigative report, the court noted that the father had made allegations about the child's care, but the court made no findings with respect to these allegations. On the contrary, the court made a finding that "there is no issue as to either party's devotion to the child, adequacy of housing facilities, or respect[a]bility of the new spouse of either parent."

The court then addressed the recommendations of the court counselor, who had made an earlier report "in [another] case coming out of this circuit also involving the social consequences of an interracial marriage. Niles v. Niles, 299 So.2d 162." From this vague reference to that earlier case, the court turned to the present case and noted the counselor's recommendation for a change in custody because "[t]he wife [petitioner] has chosen for herself and for her child, a life-style unacceptable to her father *and to society*.... The child ... is, or at school age will be, subject to environmental pressures not of choice."

The court then concluded that the best interests of the child would be served by awarding custody to the father. The court's rationale is contained in the following:

"The father's evident resentment of the mother's choice of a black partner is not sufficient to wrest custody from the mother. It is of some significance, however, that the mother did see fit to bring a man into her home and carry on a sexual relationship with him without being married to him. Such action tended to place gratification of her own desires ahead of her concern for the child's future welfare. *This Court feels that despite the strides that have been made in bettering relations between the races in this country, it is inevitable that Melanie will, if allowed to remain in her present situation and attains school age and thus more vulnerable to peer pressures, suffer from the social stigmatization that is sure to come.*"

The Second District Court of Appeal affirmed without opinion, thus denying the Florida Supreme Court jurisdiction to review the case.... We ... reverse.

II

The judgment of a state court determining or reviewing a child custody decision is not ordinarily a likely candidate for review by this Court. However, the court's opinion, after stating that the "father's evident resentment of the mother's choice of a black partner is not sufficient" to deprive her of custody, then turns to what it regarded as the damaging impact on the child from remaining in a racially-mixed household. This raises important federal concerns arising from the Constitution's commitment to eradicating discrimination based on race.

The Florida court did not focus directly on the parental qualifications of the natural mother or her present husband, or indeed on the father's qualifications to have custody of the child. The court found that "there is no issue as to either party's devotion to the child, adequacy of housing facilities, or respect[a]bility of the new spouse of either parent." This, taken with the absence of any negative finding as to the quality of the care provided by the mother, constitutes a rejection of any claim of petitioner's unfitness to continue the custody of her child.

The court correctly stated that the child's welfare was the controlling factor. But that court was entirely candid and made no effort to place its holding on any ground other than race. Taking the court's findings and rationale at face value, it is clear that the outcome would have been different had petitioner married a Caucasian male of similar respectability.

A core purpose of the Fourteenth Amendment was to do away with all governmentally-imposed discrimination based on race. See Strauder v. West Virginia, 100 U.S. 303, 307–308, 310 (1880). Classifying persons according to their race is more likely to reflect racial prejudice than legitimate public concerns; the race, not the person, dictates the category. See Personnel Administrator v. Feeney, 442 U.S. 256, 272 (1979). Such classifications are subject to the most exacting scrutiny; to pass constitutional muster, they must be justified by a compelling governmental interest and must be "necessary ... to the accomplishment" of its legitimate purpose, McLaughlin v. Florida, 379 U.S. 184, 196 (1964). See Loving v. Virginia, 388 U.S. 1, 11 (1967).

The State, of course, has a duty of the highest order to protect the interests of minor children, particularly those of tender years. In common with most states, Florida law mandates that custody determinations be made in the best interests of the children involved. Fla.Stat. § 61.13(2)(b)(1) (1983). The goal of granting custody based on the best interests of the child is indisputably a substantial governmental interest for purposes of the Equal Protection Clause.

It would ignore reality to suggest that racial and ethnic prejudices do not exist or that all manifestations of those prejudices have been eliminated. There is a risk that a child living with a step-parent of a different race may be subject to a variety of pressures and stresses not present if the child were living with parents of the same racial or ethnic origin.

The question, however, is whether the reality of private biases and the possible injury they might inflict are permissible considerations for removal of an infant child from the custody of its natural mother. We have little difficulty concluding that they are not. The Constitution cannot control such prejudices but neither can it tolerate them. Private biases may be outside the reach of the law, but the law cannot, directly or indirectly, give them effect. "Public officials sworn to uphold the Constitution may not avoid a constitutional duty by bowing to the hypothetical effects of private racial prejudice that they assume to be both widely and deeply held." Palmer v. Thompson, 403 U.S. 217, 260–261 (1971) (White, J., dissenting).

This is by no means the first time that acknowledged racial prejudice has been invoked to justify racial classifications. In Buchanan v. Warley, 245 U.S. 60 (1917), for example, this Court invalidated a Kentucky law forbidding Negroes from buying homes in white neighborhoods.

> "It is urged that this proposed segregation will promote the public peace by preventing race conflicts. Desirable as this is, and important as is the preservation of the public peace, this aim cannot be accomplished by laws or ordinances which deny rights created or protected by the Federal Constitution."

Whatever problems racially-mixed households may pose for children in 1984 can no more support a denial of constitutional rights than could the stresses that residential integration was thought to entail in 1917. The effects of racial prejudice, however real, cannot justify a racial classification removing an infant child from the custody of its natural mother found to be an appropriate person to have such custody.

The judgment of the District Court of Appeal is reversed.

It is so ordered.

THE JAPANESE CURFEW AND EVACUATION CASES

At the outset of World War II, some military authorities asserted that citizens as well as aliens of Japanese ancestry on the West Coast posed a security threat; that there was among them an actual or incipient fifth column. On February 19, 1942, President Roosevelt, acting as President and Commander-in-Chief, issued Executive Order No. 9066 authorizing such military commanders as he might designate to prescribe military areas from which any or all persons might be excluded as a security measure. Pursuant to this order he designated General DeWitt as Military Commander of the Western Defense Command. Acting under the Executive Order, the General, on March 2, 1942, established Military Area No. 1 which included the Pacific Coast states. Not willing to have these security measures entirely a matter of executive and military power, Congress, by the Act of March 21, 1942, made criminal the violation of enforcement orders issued under Executive Order 9066. Beginning on March 24, 1942, General DeWitt issued a series of orders applying to persons of Japanese ancestry residing in Military Area No. 1. One of these established a curfew for such persons between the hours of 8:00 p.m. and 6:00 a.m.; others were "exclusion orders" requiring persons of Japanese ancestry to remove from designated districts in the Military Area to "relocation centers" established further inland.

HIRABAYASHI v. UNITED STATES, 320 U.S. 81 (1943). Appellant, an American citizen of Japanese ancestry, was convicted in a federal district court of violating the curfew order and therefore the Act of March 21, 1942, by failing to remain in his residence between the hours of 8:00 p.m. and 6:00 a.m. The Court affirmed in an opinion by Chief Justice Stone, saying: "Distinctions between citizens solely because of their ancestry are by their very nature odious to a free people whose institutions are founded upon the doctrine of equality." However, the Court held that while racial discriminations are in most cases irrelevant, there was an adequate showing in this case that persons of Japanese descent presented a special danger to the community in the context of the war with Japan and that it was not feasible to determine loyalty on an individual basis.

KOREMATSU v. UNITED STATES, 323 U.S. 214 (1944). Petitioner, an American citizen of Japanese descent, was convicted in a federal district court for remaining in San Leandro, California, contrary to General DeWitt's Civilian Exclusion Order No. 34. No question was raised as to petitioner's loyalty to the United States. The Court upheld the conviction. It refused to rule on the validity of other orders which required the detention of excluded persons in relocation centers. Justice Black, speaking for the Court, said: "[A]ll legal restrictions which curtail the civil rights of a single racial group are immediately suspect. That is not to say that all such restrictions are unconstitutional. It is to say that courts must subject them to the most rigid scrutiny. Pressing public necessity may sometimes justify the existence of such restrictions; racial antagonism never can." He concluded his opinion by saying:

"To cast this case into outlines of racial prejudice, without reference to the real military dangers which were presented, merely confuses the issue. Korematsu was not excluded from the Military Area because of hostility to him or his race. He *was* excluded because we are at war with the Japanese Empire, because the properly constituted military authorities feared an invasion of our West Coast and felt constrained to take proper security measures, because they decided that the military urgency of the situation demanded that all citizens of Japanese ancestry be segregated from the West Coast temporarily, and finally, because Congress, reposing its confidence in this time of war in our military leaders—as inevitably it must—determined they should have the power to do just this. There was evidence of disloyalty on the part of some, the military authorities considered that the need for action was great, and time was short. We cannot—by availing ourselves of the calm perspective of hindsight—now say that at that time these actions were unjustified."

Justices Roberts, Murphy, and Jackson all dissented on the ground that the order constituted unjustified discrimination against loyal Japanese citizens on the basis of race. Justice Jackson noted the practical inability of the courts to interfere with military actions of this kind taken during times of war but said: "[O]nce a judicial opinion . . . rationalizes the Constitution to show that the Constitution sanctions such an order, the Court for all time has validated the principle of racial discrimination in criminal procedure and of transplanting American citizens. The principle then lies about like a loaded weapon ready for the hand of any authority that can bring forward a plausible claim of an urgent need."

EX PARTE ENDO, 323 U.S. 283 (1944). This case was decided the same day as *Korematsu* and involved a later phase of the Japanese relocation program, i.e., the continued detention of concededly loyal persons of Japanese ancestry in the relocation centers. This raised a question which had been expressly left open in *Korematsu*. Appellant, an American citizen of Japanese ancestry and unquestioned loyalty, was evacuated from Sacramento, California in 1942 and placed in an evacuation center, first in Modoc County, California, and then in Utah. In July, 1942, she filed a petition for writ of habeas corpus in the district court which denied it in July, 1943. An appeal was taken to the circuit court of appeals which certified certain questions to the Supreme Court. Justice Douglas, for the Court, said that whatever power the War Relocation Authority had to detain persons of Japanese ancestry initially, or to detain those whose loyalty was questioned, it had no authority to subject concededly loyal citizens to its "leave" procedure. The detainee seeking "indefinite leave" had to meet a number of conditions, including a showing that "public sentiment" at the detainee's "proposed destination" had been investigated and approved. The Court rested on the conclusion that the detention of a loyal citizen under these circumstances exceeded what was authorized by the Act of March 21, 1942, and the President's executive orders, but there were constitutional overtones in the opinion: ". . . We must assume that the Chief Executive and members of Congress, as well as the courts, are sensitive to and respectful of the liberties of the citizen. In interpreting a wartime measure we must assume that their purpose was to allow for the greatest possible accommodation between those liberties and the exigencies of war. . . . The purpose and objective of the Act and of these orders are plain. Their single aim was the protection of the war effort against espionage and sabotage. It is in light of that one objective that the powers conferred by the orders must be construed. . . . A citizen who is concededly loyal presents no problem of espionage or sabotage. . . . When the power to detain is derived from the power to protect the war effort against espionage and sabotage, detention which has no relationship to that objective is unauthorized.... If we assume (as we do) that the original evacuation was justified, its lawful character was derived from the fact that it was an espionage and sabotage measure, not that there was community hostility to this group of American citizens. The evacuation program rested explicitly on the former ground not on the latter as the underlying legislation shows. The authority to detain a citizen or to grant him a conditional release as protection against espionage or sabotage is exhausted at least when his loyalty is conceded...."

The district court was reversed; Roberts and Murphy, JJ., concurred but stressed their view that the entire evacuation program was unconstitutional.[a]

WHAT GROUPS ARE SPECIALLY PROTECTED AGAINST DISCRIMINATION?

In the Slaughter–House Cases, 83 U.S. (16 Wall.) 36 (1872), set out supra, p. 466, the Court said: "We doubt very much whether any action of a State not directed by way of discrimination against the negroes as a class, or on account of their race, will ever be held to come within the purview of this provision. It is so clearly a provision for that race and that emergency, that a strong case would be necessary for its application to any other." A decade and a half later, however, the Court in Yick Wo v. Hopkins, 118 U.S. 356 (1886), invalidated a classification found to discriminate against aliens of Chinese ancestry, saying:

---

[a] The Japanese evacuation cases have been subject to great criticism: Girdner & Loftis, *The Great Betrayal* (1969); Rostow, *The Japanese–American Cases—A Disaster,* in *The Sovereign Prerogative* 193 (1962); Dembitz, *Racial Discrimination and the Military Judgment,* 45 Colum.L.Rev. 175 (1945).

Cf. Chief Justice Warren, *The Bill of Rights and the Military,* in *Great Rights* 89 (Cahn ed. 1963).

For a comprehensive study of Japanese–American evacuation, see tenBroek, Barnhart & Matson, *Prejudice, War and the Constitution* (1954).

The 1980's witnessed a legal reconsideration of this historical chapter. In 1980 Congress established a Commission on Wartime Relocation and Internment of Civilians to review the evacuation episode and recommend appropriate remedies. Its report, *Personal Justice Denied* (1982), concluded that military necessity did not justify exclusion and internment and that a grave injustice had occurred. Further research published in Irons, *Justice at War* (1983), an account of the original trials and how they were prosecuted and defended, revealed internal memoranda indicating that when the government presented its arguments in these cases it deliberately misled the Court about the military judgments that actually had been made. Using these sources, Fred Korematsu and Gordon Hirabayashi successfully challenged their original convictions. Korematsu's conviction was vacated in 1984 based on a correction of "errors of fact." Korematsu v.

United States, 584 F.Supp. 1406, 1420 (N.D.Cal.1984). Hirabayashi's convictions for violating the curfew and exclusion orders were later vacated "to make the judgments of the courts conform to the judgments of history." Hirabayashi v. United States, 828 F.2d 591, 593 (9th Cir.1987). The Court of Appeals concluded that the subsequent research "demonstrate[s] that there could have been no reasonable military assessment of an emergency at the time, that the orders were based upon racial stereotypes, and that the orders caused needless suffering and shame for thousands of American citizens." Congress subsequently enacted the Civil Liberties Act of 1988, 50 U.S.C.App. §§ 1989–1989d, which declared an official apology, urged the President to pardon those convicted who had refused to accept the discriminatory treatment, and appropriated funds for restitution of $20,000. to each individual of Japanese ancestry who, during the evacuation, relocation, and internment period, was a citizen or permanent resident alien, and was confined, held in custody, relocated, or otherwise deprived of liberty or property. An equal protection challenge to the Act by a citizen of German ancestry, interned with his father during the War after his father had received an individualized hearing, was rejected in Jacobs v. Barr, 959 F.2d 313 (D.C.Cir.1992), because "Congress's finding that Japanese Americans were the victims of prejudice, while German Americans were not" was "amply supported by historical evidence" and justified compensating "interns of Japanese but not German descent."

"[The provisions of the fourteenth amendment] are universal in their application, to all persons within the territorial jurisdiction, without regard to any differences of race, or color, or of nationality." In Hernandez v. Texas, 347 U.S. 475 (1954) it was held a violation of the equal protection clause to subject a person of Mexican descent to trial before a jury from which persons of similar ancestry had been systematically excluded. In response to an argument by the state that the equal protection clause contemplated only two classes—white and Negro—the Court said:

"Throughout our history differences in race and color have defined easily identifiable groups which have at times required the aid of the courts in securing equal treatment under the laws. But community prejudices are not static, and from time to time other differences from the community norm may define other groups which need the same protection. Whether such a group exists within a community is a question of fact. When the existence of a distinct class is demonstrated, and it is further shown that the laws, as written or as applied, single out that class for different treatment not based on some reasonable classification, the guarantees of the Constitution have been violated. The Fourteenth Amendment is not directed solely against discrimination due to a 'two-class theory'—that is, based upon differences between 'white' and Negro."

ASCERTAINING THE EXISTENCE OF A RACIAL CLASSIFICATION

When a statute on its face classifies by race, as in *Loving,* no problem arises. But under what circumstances may racial discrimination be found even though a statute on its face makes no racial classification? Two distinct situations are involved.

First, a statute fair on its face may be administered in a way that results in racial discrimination. In Yick Wo v. Hopkins, supra, for example, the Court had before it an ordinance making it unlawful to operate a laundry in a wooden building without a permit from the board of supervisors. A laundryman of Chinese descent who had been denied a permit to operate his laundry in a wooden building showed that the board had denied permits to the 200 Chinese who had petitioned but granted them to 80 non-Chinese. In holding that this constituted a violation of equal protection the Court said: "Though the law itself be fair on its face, and impartial in appearance, yet, if it is applied and administered by public authority with an evil eye and an unequal hand, so as practically to make unjust and illegal discriminations between persons in similar circumstances, material to their rights, the denial of equal justice is still within the prohibition of the constitution."

Second, the contention may be that a statute which does not on its face make a racial classification in fact was designed to discriminate against a racial group. At one extreme are cases where it is apparent from the face of the statute that an ostensibly nondiscriminatory classification in fact is based on race. See, e.g., Guinn v. United States, 238 U.S. 347 (1915). The Oklahoma Constitution was amended in 1910 to provide that no person shall be registered to vote unless able to read and write a section of that Constitution, but that no person who on Jan. 1, 1866, or any time prior thereto was entitled to vote under any form of government, and no lineal descendant of such person, shall be denied the right to vote because of inability to read and write a section of the Constitution. In holding the provision invalid as a forbidden racial discrimination in voting, the Court said that the discrimination appears from the mere statement of the text. "It is true it contains no express words of an exclusion from the standard which is established of any person on account of race, color, or previous condition of servitude, prohibited by the 15th Amendment, but the standard itself inherently brings that result into existence since it is based purely upon a period of time before the enactment of the 15th Amendment, and makes that period the controlling and dominant test of the right of suffrage." At the other extreme are cases where a statute which does not make a racial classification is shown to have a disproportionate impact on a particular racial group. See, e.g., Jefferson v. Hackney, 406 U.S. 535 (1972), in which the Court upheld a state welfare statute which funded old age assistance at 100% of recognized need but aid to dependent children at 75% of such need. The Court held that a showing that 40% of the recipients of old age assistance were Negroes and Mexican–Americans while 87% of the recipients of aid to dependent children were from such groups was not sufficient to establish that the classification was based on race.

Because the problem of establishing the existence of the discrimination also arises in cases involving classifications based on gender, the cases dealing with proof of discriminatory purpose are postponed for consideration to page 786, infra.

B. RACIAL SEGREGATION IN SCHOOLS AND OTHER PUBLIC FACILITIES

Plessy v. Ferguson

163 U.S. 537, 16 S.Ct. 1138, 41 L.Ed. 256 (1896).

Mr. Justice Brown delivered the opinion of the court.

This case turns upon the constitutionality of an act of the general assembly of the state of Louisiana, passed in 1890, providing for separate railway carriages for the white and colored races....

. . .

The petition for the writ of prohibition averred that petitioner was seven-eighths Caucasian and one-eighth African blood; that the mixture of colored blood was not discernible in him; and that he was entitled to every right, privilege, and immunity secured to citizens of the United States of the white race; and that, upon such theory, he took possession of a vacant seat in a coach where passengers of the white race were accommodated, and was ordered by the conductor to vacate said coach, and take a seat in another, assigned to persons of the colored race, and, having refused to comply with such demand, he was forcibly ejected, with the aid of a police officer, and imprisoned in the parish jail to answer a charge of having violated the above act.

The constitutionality of this act is attacked upon the ground that it conflicts ... with ... the fourteenth amendment....

. . .

The object of the amendment was undoubtedly to enforce the absolute equality of the two races before the law, but, in the nature of things, it could not have been intended to abolish distinctions based upon color, or to enforce social, as distinguished from political, equality, or a commingling of the two races upon terms unsatisfactory to either. Laws permitting, and even requiring, their separation, in places where they are liable to be brought into contact, do not necessarily imply the inferiority of either race to the other, and have been generally, if not universally, recognized as within the competency of the state legislatures in the exercise of their police power. The most common instance of this is connected with the establishment of separate schools for white and colored children, which have been held to be a valid exercise of the legislative power even by courts of states where the political rights of the colored race have been longest and most earnestly enforced.

. . .

Laws forbidding the intermarriage of the two races may be said in a technical sense to interfere with the freedom of contract, and yet have been universally recognized as within the police power of the state. . . .

. . .

In this connection, it is also suggested by the learned counsel for the plaintiff in error that the same argument that will justify the state legislature in requiring railways to provide separate accommodations for the two races will also authorize them to require separate cars to be provided for people whose hair is of a certain color, or who are aliens, or who belong to certain nationalities, or to enact laws requiring colored people to walk upon one side of the street, and white people upon the other, or requiring white men's houses to be painted white, and colored men's black, or their vehicles or business signs to be of different colors, upon the theory that one side of the street is as good as the other, or that a house or vehicle of one color is as good as one of another color. The reply to all this is that every exercise of the police power must be reasonable, and extend only to such laws as are enacted in good faith for the promotion of the public good, and not for the annoyance or oppression of a particular class. . . .

So far, then, as a conflict with the fourteenth amendment is concerned, the case reduces itself to the question whether the statute of Louisiana is a reasonable regulation, and with respect to this there must necessarily be a large discretion on the part of the legislature. In determining the question of reasonableness, it is at liberty to act with reference to the established usages, customs, and traditions of the people, and with a view to the promotion of their comfort, and the preservation of the public peace and good order. Gauged by this standard, we cannot say that a law which authorizes or even requires the separation of the two races in public conveyances is unreasonable, or more obnoxious to the fourteenth amendment than the acts of congress requiring separate schools for colored children in the District of Columbia, the constitutionality of which does not seem to have been questioned or the corresponding acts of state legislatures.

We consider the underlying fallacy of the plaintiff's argument to consist in the assumption that the enforced separation of the two races stamps the colored race with a badge of inferiority. If this be so, it is not by reason of anything found in the act, but solely because the colored race chooses to put that construction upon it. The argument necessarily assumes that if, as has been more than once the case, and is not unlikely to be so again, the colored race should become the dominant power in the state legislature, and should enact a law in precisely similar terms, it would thereby relegate the white race to an inferior position. We imagine that the white race, at least, would not acquiesce in this assumption. The argument also assumes that social prejudices may be overcome by legislation, and that equal rights cannot be secured to the negro except by an enforced commingling of the two races. We cannot accept this proposition. If the two races are to meet upon terms of social equality, it must be the result of natural affinities, a mutual appreciation of each other's merits, and a voluntary consent of individuals.... Legislation is powerless to eradicate racial instincts, or to abolish distinctions based upon physical differences, and the attempt to do so can only result in accentuating the difficulties of the present situation. If the civil and political rights of both races be equal, one cannot be inferior to the other civilly or politically. If one race be inferior to the other socially, the constitution of the United States cannot put them upon the same plane....

The judgment of the court below is therefore affirmed.

Mr. Justice Brewer did not hear the argument or participate in the decision of this case.

Mr. Justice Harlan dissenting....

In respect of civil rights, common to all citizens, the constitution of the United States does not, I think, permit any public authority to know the race of those entitled to be protected in the enjoyment of such rights. Every true man has pride of race, and under appropriate circumstances, when the rights of others, his equals before the law, are not to be affected, it is his privilege to express such pride and to take such action based upon it as to him seems proper. But I deny that any legislative body or judicial tribunal may have regard to the race of citizens when the civil rights of those citizens are involved. Indeed, such legislation as that here in question is inconsistent not only with that equality of rights which pertains to citizenship, national and state, but with the personal liberty enjoyed by every one within the United States....

[The thirteenth, fourteenth, and fifteenth amendments] were welcomed by the friends of liberty throughout the world. They removed the race line from our governmental systems....

It was said in argument that the statute of Louisiana does not discriminate against either race, but prescribes a rule applicable alike to white and colored citizens. But this argument does not meet the difficulty. Everyone knows that the statute in question had its origin in the purpose, not so much to exclude white persons from railroad cars occupied by blacks; as to exclude colored people from coaches occupied by or assigned to white persons. Railroad corporations of Louisiana did not make discrimination among whites in the matter of accommodation for travelers. The thing to accomplish was, under the guise of giving equal accommodation for whites and blacks, to compel the latter to keep to themselves while traveling in railroad passenger coaches. No one would be so wanting in candor as to assert the contrary. The fundamental objection, therefore, to the statute, is that it interferes with the personal freedom of citizens.... If a white man and a black man choose to occupy the same public conveyance on a public highway, it is their right to do so; and no government, proceeding alone on grounds of race, can prevent it without infringing the personal liberty of each....

The white race deems itself to be the dominant race in this country. And so it is, in prestige, in achievements, in education, in wealth, and in power. So, I doubt not, it will continue to be for all time, if it remains true to its great heritage, and holds fast to the principles of constitutional liberty. But in view of the constitution, in the eye of the law, there is in this country no superior, dominant, ruling class of citizens. There is no caste here. Our constitution is color-blind, and neither knows nor tolerates classes among citizens. In respect of civil rights, all citizens are equal before the law. The humblest is the peer of the most powerful. The law regards man as man, and takes no account of his surroundings or of his color when his civil rights as guaranteed by the supreme law of the land are involved. It is therefore to be regretted that this high tribunal, the final expositor of the fundamental law of the land, has reached the conclusion that it is competent for a state to regulate the enjoyment by citizens of their civil rights solely upon the basis of race.

. . .

If evils will result from the commingling of the two races upon public highways established for the benefit of all, they will be infinitely less than those that will surely come from state legislation regulating the enjoyment of civil rights upon the basis of race. We boast of the freedom enjoyed by our people above all other peoples. But it is difficult to reconcile that boast with a state of the law which, practically, puts the brand of servitude and degradation upon a large class of our fellow citizens,—our equals before the law. The thin disguise of "equal" accommodations for passengers in railroad coaches will not mislead any one, nor atone for the wrong this day done. . . .

Brown v. Board of Education of Topeka

347 U.S. 483, 74 S.Ct. 686, 98 L.Ed. 873 (1954).

Mr. Chief Justice Warren delivered the opinion of the Court.

These cases come to us from the States of Kansas, South Carolina, Virginia, and Delaware. They are premised on different facts and different local conditions, but a common legal question justifies their consideration together in this consolidated opinion.

In each of the cases, minors of the Negro race, through their legal representatives, seek the aid of the courts in obtaining admission to the public schools of their community on a nonsegregated basis. In each instance, they have been denied admission to schools attended by white children under laws requiring or permitting segregation according to race. This segregation was alleged to deprive the plaintiffs of the equal protection of the laws under the Fourteenth Amendment. In each of the cases other than the Delaware case, a three-judge federal district court denied relief to the plaintiffs on the so-called "separate but equal" doctrine announced by this Court in Plessy v. Ferguson, 163 U.S. 537. Under that doctrine, equality of treatment is accorded when the races are provided substantially equal facilities, even though these facilities be separate. In the Delaware case, the Supreme Court of Delaware adhered to that doctrine, but ordered that the plaintiffs be admitted to the white schools because of their superiority to the Negro schools.

The plaintiffs contend that segregated public schools are not "equal" and cannot be made "equal," and that hence they are deprived of the equal protection of the laws. Because of the obvious importance of the question presented, the Court took jurisdiction. Argument was heard in the 1952 Term, and reargument was heard this Term on certain questions propounded by the Court.

Reargument was largely devoted to the circumstances surrounding the adoption of the Fourteenth Amendment in 1868. It covered exhaustively consideration of the Amendment in Congress, ratification by the states, then existing practices in racial segregation, and the views of proponents and opponents of the Amendment. This discussion and our own investigation convince us that, although these sources cast some light, it is not enough to resolve the problem with which we are faced. At best, they are inconclusive. The most avid proponents of the post-War Amendments undoubtedly intended them to remove all legal distinctions among "all persons born or naturalized in the United States." Their opponents, just as certainly were antagonistic to both the letter and the spirit of the Amendments and wished them to have the most limited effect. What others in Congress and the state legislatures had in mind cannot be determined with any degree of certainty.

An additional reason for the inconclusive nature of the Amendment's history, with respect to segregated schools, is the status of public education at that time. In the South, the movement toward free common schools, supported by general taxation, had not yet taken hold. Education of white children was largely in the hands of private groups. Education of Negroes was almost nonexistent, and practically all of the race were illiterate. In fact, any education of Negroes was forbidden by law in some states. Today, in contrast, many Negroes have achieved outstanding success in the arts and sciences as well as in the business and professional world. It is true that public school education at the time of the Amendment had advanced further in the North, but the effect of the Amendment on Northern States was generally ignored in the congressional debates. Even in the North, the conditions of public education did not approximate those existing today. The curriculum was usually rudimentary; ungraded schools were common in rural areas; the school term was but three months a year in many states; and compulsory school attendance was virtually unknown. As a consequence, it is not surprising that there should be so little in the history of the Fourteenth Amendment relating to its intended effect on public education.

In the first cases in this Court construing the Fourteenth Amendment, decided shortly after its adoption, the Court interpreted it as proscribing all state-imposed discriminations against the Negro race. The doctrine of "separate but equal" did not make its appearance in this Court until 1896 in the case of *Plessy v. Ferguson,* supra, involving not education but transportation. American courts have since labored with the doctrine for over half a century. In this Court, there have been six cases involving the "separate but equal" doctrine in the field of public education. In Cumming v. Board of Education of Richmond County, 175 U.S. 528, and Gong Lum v. Rice, 275 U.S. 78, the validity of the doctrine itself was not challenged. In more recent cases, all on the graduate school level, inequality was found in that specific benefits enjoyed by white students were denied to Negro students of the same educational qualifications. State of Missouri ex rel. Gaines v. Canada, 305 U.S. 337; Sipuel v. Board of Regents of University of Oklahoma, 332 U.S. 631; Sweatt v. Painter, 339 U.S. 629; McLaurin v. Oklahoma State Regents, 339 U.S. 637. In none of these cases was it necessary to reexamine the doctrine to grant relief to the Negro plaintiff. And in *Sweatt v. Painter,* supra, the Court expressly reserved decision on the question whether *Plessy v. Ferguson* should be held inapplicable to public education.

In the instant cases, that question is directly presented. Here, unlike *Sweatt v. Painter,* there are findings below that the Negro and white schools involved have been equalized, or are being equalized, with respect to buildings, curricula, qualifications and salaries of teachers, and other "tangible" factors. Our decision, therefore, cannot turn on merely a comparison of these tangible factors in the Negro and white schools involved in each of the cases. We must look instead to the effect of segregation itself on public education.

In approaching this problem, we cannot turn the clock back to 1868 when the Amendment was adopted, or even to 1896 when *Plessy v. Ferguson* was written. We must consider public education in the light of its full development and its present place in American life throughout the Nation. Only in this way can it be determined if segregation in public schools deprives these plaintiffs of the equal protection of the laws.

Today, education is perhaps the most important function of state and local governments. Compulsory school attendance laws and the great expenditures for education both demonstrate our recognition of the importance of education to our democratic society. It is required in the performance of our most basic public responsibilities, even service in the armed forces. It is the very foundation of good citizenship. Today it is a principal instrument in awakening the child to cultural values, in preparing him for later professional training, and in helping him to adjust normally to his environment. In these days, it is doubtful that any child may reasonably be expected to succeed in life if he is denied the opportunity of an education. Such an opportunity, where the state has undertaken to provide it, is a right which must be made available to all on equal terms.

We come then to the question presented: Does segregation of children in public schools solely on the basis of race, even though the physical facilities and other "tangible" factors may be equal, deprive the children of the minority group of equal educational opportunities? We believe that it does.

In *Sweatt v. Painter,* supra, in finding that a segregated law school for Negroes could not provide them equal educational opportunities, this Court relied in large part on "those qualities which are incapable of objective measurement but which make for greatness in a law school." In *McLaurin v. Oklahoma State Regents,* supra, the Court, in requiring that a Negro admitted to a white graduate school be treated like all other students, again resorted to intangible considerations: ". . . his ability to study, to engage in discussions and exchange views with other students, and, in general, to learn his profession." Such considerations apply with added force to children in grade and high schools. To separate them from others of similar age and qualifications solely because of their race generates a feeling of inferiority as to their status in the community that may affect their hearts and minds in a way unlikely ever to be undone. The effect of this separation on their educational opportunities was well stated by a finding in the Kansas case by a court which nevertheless felt compelled to rule against the Negro plaintiffs:

> "Segregation of white and colored children in public schools has a detrimental effect upon the colored children. The impact is greater when it has the sanction of the law; for the policy of separating the races is usually interpreted as denoting the inferiority of the negro group. A sense of inferiority affects the motivation of a child to learn. Segregation with the sanction of law, therefore, has a tendency to [retard] the educational and mental development of negro children and to deprive them of some of the benefits they would receive in a racial[ly] integrated school system."

Whatever may have been the extent of psychological knowledge at the time of *Plessy v. Ferguson,* this finding is amply supported by modern authority.[11] Any language in *Plessy v. Ferguson* contrary to this finding is rejected.

[11] K.B. Clark, Effect of Prejudice and Discrimination on Personality Development (Midcentury White House Conference on Children and Youth, 1950); Wittmer and Kotinsky, Personality in the Making (1952), c. VI; Deutscher and Chein, The Psychological Effects of Enforced Segregation: A Survey of Social Science Opinion, 26 J.Psychol. 259 (1948); Chein, What are the Psychological Effects of Segregation Under Conditions of Equal Facilities?, 3 Int.J.Opinion and Attitude Res. 229 (1949); Brameld, Educational Costs, in Discrimination and National Welfare (MacIver, ed., 1949), 44–48; Frazier, The Negro in the United States (1949), 674–681. And see generally Myrdal, An American Dilemma (1944).

We conclude that in the field of public education the doctrine of "separate but equal" has no place. Separate educational facilities are inherently unequal. Therefore, we hold that the plaintiffs and others similarly situated for whom the actions have been brought are, by reason of the segregation complained of, deprived of the equal protection of the laws guaranteed by the Fourteenth Amendment. This disposition makes unnecessary any discussion whether such segregation also violates the Due Process Clause of the Fourteenth Amendment.

Because these are class actions, because of the wide applicability of this decision, and because of the great variety of local conditions, the formulation of decrees in these cases presents problems of considerable complexity. On reargument, the consideration of appropriate relief was necessarily subordinated to the primary question—the constitutionality of segregation in public education. We have now announced that such segregation is a denial of the equal protection of the laws. In order that we may have the full assistance of the parties in formulating decrees, the cases will be restored to the docket, and the parties are requested to present further argument on Questions 4 and 5 previously propounded by the Court for the reargument this Term. The Attorney General of the United States is again invited to participate. The Attorneys General of the states requiring or permitting segregation in public education will also be permitted to appear as *amici curiae* upon request to do so by September 15, 1954, and submission of briefs by October 1, 1954.

It is so ordered.

Bolling v. Sharpe

347 U.S. 497, 74 S.Ct. 693, 98 L.Ed. 884 (1954).

Mr. Chief Justice Warren delivered the opinion of the Court.

This case challenges the validity of segregation in the public schools of the District of Columbia. The petitioners, minors of the Negro race, allege that such segregation deprives them of due process of law under the Fifth Amendment. They were refused admission to a public school attended by white children solely because of their race. They sought the aid of the District Court for the District of Columbia in obtaining admission. That court dismissed their complaint. The Court granted a writ of certiorari before judgment in the Court of Appeals because of the importance of the constitutional question presented. 344 U.S. 873.

We have this day held that the Equal Protection Clause of the Fourteenth Amendment prohibits the states from maintaining racially segregated public schools. The legal problem in the District of Columbia is somewhat different, however. The Fifth Amendment, which is applicable in the District of Columbia, does not contain an equal protection clause as does the Fourteenth Amendment which applies only to the states. But the concepts of equal protection and due process, both stemming from our American ideal of fairness, are not mutually exclusive. The "equal protection of the laws" is a more explicit safeguard of prohibited unfairness than "due process of law," and, therefore, we do not imply that the two are always interchangeable phrases. But, as this Court has recognized, discrimination may be so unjustifiable as to be violative of due process.

Classifications based solely upon race must be scrutinized with particular care, since they are contrary to our traditions and hence constitutionally suspect. As long ago as 1896, this Court declared the principle "that the constitution of the United States, in its present form, forbids, so far as civil and political rights are concerned, discrimination by the general government, or by the states, against any citizen because of his race." And in Buchanan v. Warley, 245 U.S. 60, the Court held that a statute which limited the right of a property owner to convey his property to a person of another race was, as an unreasonable discrimination, a denial of due process of law.

Although the Court has not assumed to define "liberty" with any great precision, that term is not confined to mere freedom from bodily restraint. Liberty under law extends to the full range of conduct which the individual is free to pursue, and it cannot be restricted except for a proper governmental objective. Segregation in public education is not reasonably related to any proper governmental objective, and thus it imposes on Negro children of the District of Columbia a burden that constitutes an arbitrary deprivation of their liberty in violation of the Due Process Clause.

In view of our decision that the Constitution prohibits the states from maintaining racially segregated public schools, it would be unthinkable that the same Constitution would impose a lesser duty on the Federal Government. We hold that racial segregation in the public schools of the District of Columbia is a denial of the due process of law guaranteed by the Fifth Amendment to the Constitution.

For the reasons set out in *Brown v. Board of Education*, this case will be restored to the docket for reargument on Questions 4 and 5 previously propounded by the Court. 345 U.S. 972.

It is so ordered.

BROWN AND THE RELEVANCE OF SOCIAL SCIENCE AND HISTORICAL MATERIALS

The Court in *Brown* relied to some extent on studies by psychologists and social scientists to support the conclusion that placing Negro children in separate schools generates feelings of inferiority unlikely to be undone. The Court's reference to this data generated immediate controversy among lawyers as to its propriety and relevance. Compare Cahn, *Science or Common Sense? A Dangerous Myth, in 1954 Annual Survey of American Law: Jurisprudence,* 30 N.Y.U.L.Rev. 150 (1955) with Honnold, *Book Review,* 33 Ind.L.J. 612, 614 (1958). More recent and elaborate consideration will be found in two symposia: *The Courts, Social Science, and School Desegregation,* 39 Law & Contemp.Prob. (No. 1, Winter, 1975, and No. 2, Spring, 1975); *School Desegregation: Lessons of the First Twenty-Five Years,* 42 Law & Contemp.Prob. (Summer 1978 and Autumn 1978).

The Court in *Brown* also directed attention to the historical background of the fourteenth amendment. For a discussion of the historical record, see Bickel, *The Original Understanding and the Segregation Decisions,* 69 Harv.L.Rev. 1 (1955), *Selected Essays on Constitutional Law,* 1938–1962 (1963) 853.

For some of the voluminous literature which followed the desegregation cases and probed their implications, see Wechsler, *Toward Neutral Principles of Constitutional Law,* 73 Harv.L.Rev. 1 (1959); Black, *The Lawfulness of the Segregation Decisions,* 69 Yale L.J. 421 (1960); Pollak, *Racial Discrimination and Judicial Integrity,* 108 U.Pa.L.Rev. 1 (1959). These articles are reprinted in *Selected Essays on Constitutional Law,* 1938–1962 (1963) at 463, 844, and 819.

SEGREGATION IN PUBLIC FACILITIES OTHER THAN SCHOOLS

In *Brown* the Court emphasized the importance of education and gave reasons why segregation in schools was inherently unequal. When presented with the question whether the same reasoning would serve to invalidate segregation in other public facilities, the Court held such segregation invalid in a series of per curiam orders without explanatory opinions. In Mayor and City Council of Baltimore City v. Dawson, 350 U.S. 877 (1955), it summarily affirmed an order enjoining racial segregation in public beaches and bathhouses. In Holmes v. Atlanta, 350 U.S. 879 (1955) the Court summarily reversed a lower court order which appeared to permit the city to allocate a municipal golf course to different races on alternate days. In Gayle v. Browder, 352 U.S. 903 (1956) it summarily affirmed a judgment enjoining enforcement of racial segregation on city buses. Similar dispositions were made in cases involving other public facilities in New Orleans City Park Improvement Ass'n v. Detiege, 358 U.S. 54 (1958) (golf course and parks); State Athletic Comm'n v. Dorsey, 359 U.S. 533 (1959) (participation in athletic contests); Schiro v. Bynum, 375 U.S. 395 (1964) (municipal auditorium).

In Johnson v. Virginia, 373 U.S. 61 (1963), the Court wrote a brief per curiam opinion reversing a conviction of a defendant for sitting in a section of a segregated courtroom reserved for whites. The Court said, without further elaboration: "Such a conviction cannot stand for it is no longer open to question that a State may not constitutionally require segregation of public facilities."[a]

Brown v. Board of Education of Topeka

349 U.S. 294, 75 S.Ct. 753, 99 L.Ed. 1083 (1955).

Mr. Chief Justice Warren delivered the opinion of the Court.

These cases were decided on May 17, 1954. The opinions of that date, declaring the fundamental principle that racial discrimination in public education is unconstitutional, are incorporated herein by reference. All provisions of federal, state, or local law requiring or permitting such discrimination must yield to this principle. There remains for consideration the manner in which relief is to be accorded.

Because these cases arose under different local conditions and their disposition will involve a variety of local problems, we requested further argument on the question of relief. In view of the nationwide importance of the decision, we invited the Attorney General of the United States and the Attorneys General of all states requiring or permitting racial discrimination in public education to present their views on that question. The parties, the United States, and the States of Florida, North Carolina, Arkansas, Oklahoma, Maryland, and Texas filed briefs and participated in the oral argument.

These presentations were informative and helpful to the Court in its consideration of the complexities arising from the transition to a system of public education freed of racial discrimination....

Full implementation of these constitutional principles may require solution of varied local school problems. School authorities have the primary responsibility for elucidating, assessing, and solving these problems; courts will have to consider whether the action of school authorities constitutes good faith imple-

---

[a] For observations on the extent to which the Court uses per curiam decisions, see Brown, *Process of Law,* 72 Harv.L.Rev. 77 (1958).

mentation of the governing constitutional principles. Because of their proximity to local conditions and the possible need for further hearings, the courts which originally heard these cases can best perform this judicial appraisal. Accordingly, we believe it appropriate to remand the cases to those courts.

In fashioning and effectuating the decrees, the courts will be guided by equitable principles. Traditionally, equity has been characterized by a practical flexibility in shaping its remedies and by a facility for adjusting and reconciling public and private needs. These cases call for the exercise of these traditional attributes of equity power. At stake is the personal interest of the plaintiffs in admission to public schools as soon as practicable on a nondiscriminatory basis. To effectuate this interest may call for elimination of a variety of obstacles in making the transition to school systems operated in accordance with the constitutional principles set forth in our May 17, 1954, decision. Courts of equity may properly take into account the public interest in the elimination of such obstacles in a systematic and effective manner. But it should go without saying that the vitality of these constitutional principles cannot be allowed to yield simply because of disagreement with them.

While giving weight to these public and private considerations, the courts will require that the defendants make a prompt and reasonable start toward full compliance with our May 17, 1954, ruling. Once such a start has been made, the courts may find that additional time is necessary to carry out the ruling in an effective manner. The burden rests upon the defendants to establish that such time is necessary in the public interest and is consistent with good faith compliance at the earliest practicable date. To that end, the courts may consider problems related to administration, arising from the physical condition of the school plant, the school transportation system, personnel, revision of school districts and attendance areas into compact units to achieve a system of determining admission to the public schools on a nonracial basis, and revision of local laws and regulations which may be necessary in solving the foregoing problems. They will also consider the adequacy of any plans the defendants may propose to meet these problems and to effectuate a transition to a racially nondiscriminatory school system. During this period of transition, the courts will retain jurisdiction of these cases.

The judgments below, except that in the Delaware case, are accordingly reversed and remanded to the District Courts to take such proceedings and enter such orders and decrees consistent with this opinion as are necessary and proper to admit to public schools on a racially nondiscriminatory basis with all deliberate speed the parties to these cases. The judgment in the Delaware case—ordering the immediate admission of the plaintiffs to schools previously attended only by white children—is affirmed on the basis of the principles stated in our May 17, 1954, opinion, but the case is remanded to the Supreme Court of Delaware for such further proceedings as that court may deem necessary in light of this opinion.

It is so ordered.

SCHOOL DESEGREGATION FROM BROWN TO SWANN

It is not possible within the limited space available in a casebook to describe the events of this period. An excellent brief account which should be consulted is Read, *Judicial Evolution of the Law of School Integration Since Brown v. Board of Education*, 39 Law & Contemp.Prob. 7 (No. 1, Winter, 1975). Some of the events are summarized in *Swann*.

Swann v. Charlotte–Mecklenburg Board of Education

402 U.S. 1, 91 S.Ct. 1267, 28 L.Ed.2d 554 (1971).

Mr. Chief Justice Burger delivered the opinion of the Court.

We granted certiorari in this case to review important issues as to the duties of school authorities and the scope of powers of federal courts under this Court's mandates to eliminate racially separate public schools established and maintained by state action. Brown v. Board of Education, 347 U.S. 483 (1954).

This case and those argued with it arose in states having a long history of maintaining two sets of schools in a single school system deliberately operated to carry out a governmental policy to separate pupils in schools solely on the basis of race. That was what *Brown v. Board of Education* was all about. These cases present us with the problem of defining in more precise terms than heretofore the scope of the duty of school authorities and district courts in implementing *Brown I* and the mandate to eliminate dual systems and establish unitary systems at once. Meanwhile district courts and courts of appeals have struggled in hundreds of cases with a multitude and variety of problems under this Court's general directive. Understandably, in an area of evolving remedies, those courts had to improvise and experiment without detailed or specific guidelines. This Court, in *Brown I*, appropriately dealt with the large constitutional principles; other federal courts had to grapple with the flinty, intractable realities of day-to-day implementation of those constitutional commands. Their efforts, of necessity, embraced a process of "trial and error," and our effort to formulate guidelines must take into account their experience.

I.

The Charlotte–Mecklenburg school system, the 43d largest in the Nation, encompasses the city of Charlotte and surrounding Mecklenburg County, North Carolina. The area is large—550 square miles—spanning roughly 22 miles east-west and 36 miles north-south. During the 1968–1969 school year the system served more than 84,000 pupils in 107 schools. Approximately 71% of the pupils were found to be white and 29% Negro. As of June 1969 there were approximately 24,000 Negro students in the system, of whom 21,000 attended schools within the city of Charlotte. Two-thirds of those 21,000—approximately 14,000 Negro students—attended 21 schools which were either totally Negro or more than 99% Negro.

[Pursuant to an order of a federal district court the school board adopted a desegregation plan for elementary schools that included grouping two or three outlying schools with one black inner city school, transporting black students from grades one through four to the outlying white schools, and transporting white students from the fifth and sixth grades to the inner city black school. Other aspects of the plan are discussed in the opinion.]

. . .

II.

Nearly 17 years ago this Court held, in explicit terms, that state-imposed segregation by race in public schools denies equal protection of the laws. At no time has the Court deviated in the slightest degree from that holding or its constitutional underpinnings....

Over the 16 years since *Brown II,* many difficulties were encountered in implementation of the basic constitutional requirement that the State not discriminate between public school children on the basis of their race. Nothing in our national experience prior to 1955 prepared anyone for dealing with changes and adjustments of the magnitude and complexity encountered since then. Deliberate resistance of some to the Court's mandates has impeded the good-faith efforts of others to bring school systems into compliance. The detail and nature of these dilatory tactics have been noted frequently by this Court and other courts.

By the time the Court considered Green v. County School Board, 391 U.S. 430, in 1968, very little progress had been made in many areas where dual school systems had historically been maintained by operation of state laws. In *Green,* the Court was confronted with a record of a freedom-of-choice program that the District Court had found to operate in fact to preserve a dual system more than a decade after *Brown II.* While acknowledging that a freedom-of-choice concept could be a valid remedial measure in some circumstances, its failure to be effective in *Green* required that:

> "The burden on a school board today is to come forward with a plan that promises realistically to work ... *now* ... until it is clear that state-imposed segregation has been completely removed."

. . .

The problems encountered by the district courts and courts of appeals make plain that we should now try to amplify guidelines, however, incomplete and imperfect, for the assistance of school authorities and courts.[5] The failure of local authorities to meet their constitutional obligations aggravated the massive problem of converting from the state-enforced discrimination of racially separate school systems. This process has been rendered more difficult by changes since 1954 in the structure and patterns of communities, the growth of student population, movement of families, and other changes, some of which had marked impact on school planning, sometimes neutralizing or negating remedial action before it was fully implemented. Rural areas accustomed for half a century to the consolidated school systems implemented by bus transportation could make adjustments more readily than metropolitan areas with dense and shifting population, numerous schools, congested and complex traffic patterns.

III.

The objective today remains to eliminate from the public schools all vestiges of state-imposed segregation. Segregation was the evil struck down by *Brown I* as contrary to the equal protection guarantees of the Constitution. That was the violation sought to be corrected by the remedial measures of *Brown II.* That was the basis for the holding in *Green* that school authorities are "clearly charged with the affirmative duty to take whatever steps might be necessary to convert to a unitary system in which racial discrimination would be eliminated root and branch." 391 U.S., at 437–438.

If school authorities fail in their affirmative obligations under these holdings, judicial authority may be invoked. Once a right and a violation have been shown, the scope of a district court's equitable powers to remedy past wrongs is broad, for breadth and flexibility are inherent in equitable remedies....

. . .

---

[5] The necessity for this is suggested by the situation in the Fifth Circuit where 166 appeals in school desegregation cases were heard between December 2, 1969, and September 24, 1970.

In seeking to define even in broad and general terms how far this remedial power extends it is important to remember that judicial powers may be exercised only on the basis of a constitutional violation. Remedial judicial authority does not put judges automatically in the shoes of school authorities whose powers are plenary. Judicial authority enters only when local authority defaults.

School authorities are traditionally charged with broad power to formulate and implement educational policy and might well conclude, for example, that in order to prepare students to live in a pluralistic society each school should have a prescribed ratio of Negro to white students reflecting the proportion for the district as a whole. To do this as an educational policy is within the broad discretionary powers of school authorities; absent a finding of a constitutional violation, however, that would not be within the authority of a federal court. As with any equity case, the nature of the violation determines the scope of the remedy. In default by the school authorities of their obligation to proffer acceptable remedies, a district court has broad power to fashion a remedy that will assure a unitary school system.

. . .

IV.

We turn now to the problem of defining with more particularity the responsibilities of school authorities in desegregating a state-enforced dual school system in light of the Equal Protection Clause. Although the several related cases before us are primarily concerned with problems of student assignment, it may be helpful to begin with a brief discussion of other aspects of the process.

In *Green,* we pointed out that existing policy and practice with regard to faculty, staff, transportation, extracurricular activities, and facilities were among the most important indicia of a segregated system. 391 U.S., at 435. Independent of student assignment, where it is possible to identify a "white school" or a "Negro school" simply by reference to the racial composition of teachers and staff, the quality of school buildings and equipment, or the organization of sports activities, a *prima facie* case of violation of substantive constitutional rights under the Equal Protection Clause is shown.

When a system has been dual in these respects, the first remedial responsibility of school authorities is to eliminate invidious racial distinctions. With respect to such matters as transportation, supporting personnel, and extracurricular activities, no more than this may be necessary. Similar corrective action must be taken with regard to the maintenance of buildings and the distribution of equipment. In these areas, normal administrative practice should produce schools of like quality, facilities, and staffs. Something more must be said, however, as to faculty assignment and new school construction.

In the companion *Davis* case, the Mobile school board has argued that the Constitution requires that teachers be assigned on a "color blind" basis. It also argues that the Constitution prohibits district courts from using their equity power to order assignment of teachers to achieve a particular degree of faculty desegregation. We reject that contention.

In United States v. Montgomery County Board of Education, 395 U.S. 225 (1969), the District Court set as a goal a plan of faculty assignment in each school with a ratio of white to Negro faculty members substantially the same throughout the system. . . .

The District Court in *Montgomery* then proceeded to set an initial ratio for the whole system of at least two Negro teachers out of each 12 in any given school. The Court of Appeals modified the order by eliminating what is regarded as "fixed mathematical ratio" of faculty and substituted an initial requirement of "substantially or approximately" a five-to-one ratio....

We reversed the Court of Appeals and restored the District Court's order in its entirety, holding that the order of the District Judge

"was adopted in the spirit of this Court's opinion in *Green* ... in that his plan 'promises realistically to work, and promises realistically to work *now*.' ..."

The principles of *Montgomery* have been properly followed by the District Court and the Court of Appeals in this case.

The construction of new schools and the closing of old ones is one of the most important functions of local school authorities and also one of the most complex. They must decide questions of location and capacity in light of population growth, finances, land values, site availability, through an almost endless list of factors to be considered. The result of this will be a decision which, when combined with one technique or another of student assignment, will determine the racial composition of the student body in each school in the system. Over the long run, the consequences of the choices will be far reaching. People gravitate toward school facilities, just as schools are located in response to the needs of people. The location of schools may thus influence the patterns of residential development of a metropolitan area and have important impact on composition of inner city neighborhoods.

In the past, choices in this respect have been used as a potent weapon for creating or maintaining a state-segregated school system....

In ascertaining the existence of legally imposed school segregation, the existence of a pattern of school construction and abandonment is thus a factor of great weight. In devising remedies where legally imposed segregation has been established, it is the responsibility of local authorities and district courts to see to it that future school construction and abandonment is not used and does not serve to perpetuate or re-establish the dual system. When necessary, district courts should retain jurisdiction to assure that these responsibilities are carried out....

V.

The central issue in this case is that of student assignment, and there are essentially four problem areas:

(1) to what extent racial balance or racial quotas may be used as an implement in a remedial order to correct a previously segregated system;

(2) whether every all-Negro and all-white school must be eliminated as an indispensable part of a remedial process of desegregation;

(3) what are the limits, if any, on the rearrangement of school districts and attendance zones, as a remedial measure; and

(4) what are the limits, if any, on the use of transportation facilities to correct state-enforced racial school segregation.

(1) *Racial Balances or Racial Quotas.* The constant theme and thrust of every holding from *Brown I* to date is that state-enforced separation of races in public schools is discrimination that violates the Equal Protection Clause. The remedy commanded was to dismantle dual school systems.

We are concerned in these cases with the elimination of the discrimination inherent in the dual school systems, not with myriad factors of human existence which can cause discrimination in a multitude of ways on racial, religious, or ethnic grounds. The target of the cases from *Brown I* to the present was the dual school system. The elimination of racial discrimination in public schools is a large task and one that should not be retarded by efforts to achieve broader purposes lying beyond the jurisdiction of school authorities. One vehicle can carry only a limited amount of baggage. It would not serve the important objective of *Brown I* to seek to use school desegregation cases for purposes beyond their scope, although desegregation of schools ultimately will have impact on other forms of discrimination. We do not reach in this case the question whether a showing that school segregation is a consequence of other types of state action, without any discriminatory action by the school authorities, is a constitutional violation requiring remedial action by a school desegregation decree. This case does not present that question and we therefore do not decide it.

Our objective in dealing with the issues presented by these cases is to see that school authorities exclude no pupil of a racial minority from any school, directly or indirectly, on account of race; it does not and cannot embrace all the problems of racial prejudice, even when those problems contribute to disproportionate racial concentrations in some schools.

In this case it is urged that the District Court has imposed a racial balance requirement of 71%–29% on individual schools. The fact that no such objective was actually achieved—and would appear to be impossible—tends to blunt that claim, yet in the opinion and order of the District Court of December 1, 1969, we find that court directing:

"that efforts should be made to reach a 71–29 ratio in the various schools so that there will be no basis for contending that one school is racially different from the others ..., that no school [should] be operated with an all-black or predominantly black student body, [and] that pupils of all grades [should] be assigned in such a way that as nearly as practicable the various schools at various grade levels have about the same proportion of black and white students."

The District Judge went on to acknowledge that variation "from that norm may be unavoidable." This contains intimations that the "norm" is a fixed mathematical racial balance reflecting the pupil constituency of the system. If we were to read the holding of the District Court to require, as a matter of substantive constitutional right, any particular degree of racial balance or mixing, that approach would be disapproved and we would be obliged to reverse. The constitutional command to desegregate schools does not mean that every school in every community must always reflect the racial composition of the school system as a whole.

. . . .

We see therefore that the use made of mathematical ratios was not more than a starting point in the process of shaping a remedy, rather than an inflexible requirement. From that starting point the District Court proceeded to frame a decree that was within its discretionary powers, an equitable remedy for the particular circumstances. As we said in *Green*, a school authority's remedial plan or a district court's remedial decree is to be judged by its effectiveness. Awareness of the racial composition of the whole school system is likely to be a useful starting point in shaping a remedy to correct past constitutional violations. In sum, the very limited use made of mathematical ratios was within the equitable remedial discretion of the District Court.

(2) *One–Race Schools.* The record in this case reveals the familiar phenomenon that in metropolitan areas minority groups are often found concentrated in one part of the city. In some circumstances certain schools may remain all or largely of one race until new schools can be provided or neighborhood patterns change. Schools all or predominantly of one race in a district of mixed population will require close scrutiny to determine that school assignments are not part of state-enforced segregation.

In light of the above, it should be clear that the existence of some small number of one-race, or virtually one-race, schools within a district is not in and of itself the mark of a system which still practices segregation by law. The district judge or school authorities should make every effort to achieve the greatest possible degree of actual desegregation and will thus necessarily be concerned with the elimination of one-race schools. No *per se* rule can adequately embrace all the difficulties of reconciling the competing interests involved; but in a system with a history of segregation the need for remedial criteria of sufficient specificity to assure a school authority's compliance with its constitutional duty warrants a presumption against schools that are substantially disproportionate in their racial composition. Where the school authority's proposed plan for conversion from a dual to a unitary system contemplates the continued existence of some schools that are all or predominately of one race, they have the burden of showing that such school assignments are genuinely nondiscriminatory. The court should scrutinize such schools, and the burden upon the school authorities will be to satisfy the court that their racial composition is not the result of present or past discriminatory action on their part.

An optional majority-to-minority transfer provision has long been recognized as a useful part of every desegregation plan. Provision for optional transfer of those in the majority racial group of a particular school to other schools where they will be in the minority is an indispensable remedy for those students willing to transfer to other schools in order to lessen the impact on them of the state-imposed stigma of segregation. In order to be effective, such a transfer arrangement must grant the transferring student free transportation and space must be made available in the school to which he desires to move. . . . The court orders in this and the companion *Davis* case now provide such an option.

(3) *Remedial Altering of Attendance Zones.* The maps submitted in these cases graphically demonstrate that one of the principal tools employed by school planners and by courts to break up the dual school system has been a frank—and sometimes drastic—gerrymandering of school districts and attendance zones. An additional step was pairing, "clustering," or "grouping" of schools with attendance assignments made deliberately to accomplish the transfer of Negro students out of formerly segregated Negro schools and transfer of white students to formerly all-Negro schools. More often than not, these zones are neither compact nor contiguous; indeed they may be on opposite ends of the city. As an interim corrective measure, this cannot be said to be beyond the broad remedial powers of a court.

Absent a constitutional violation there would be no basis for judicially ordering assignment of students on a racial basis. All things being equal, with no history of discrimination, it might well be desirable to assign pupils to schools nearest their homes. But all things are not equal in a system that has been deliberately constructed and maintained to enforce racial segregation. The remedy for such segregation may be administratively awkward, inconvenient and even bizarre in some situations and may impose burdens on some; but all awkwardness and inconvenience cannot be avoided in the interim period when remedial adjustments are being made to eliminate the dual school systems.

No fixed or even substantially fixed guidelines can be established as to how far a court can go, but it must be recognized that there are limits. The objective is to dismantle the dual school system. "Racially neutral" assignment plans proposed by school authorities to a district court may be inadequate; such plans may fail to counteract the continuing effects of past school segregation resulting from discriminatory location of school sites or distortion of school size in order to achieve or maintain an artificial racial separation. When school authorities present a district court with a "loaded game board," affirmative action in the form of remedial altering of attendance zones is proper to achieve truly nondiscriminatory assignments. In short, an assignment plan is not acceptable simply because it appears to be neutral.

In this area, we must of necessity rely to a large extent, as this Court has for more than 16 years, on the informed judgment of the district courts in the first instance and on courts of appeals.

We hold that the pairing and grouping of non-contiguous school zones is a permissible tool and such action is to be considered in light of the objectives sought. . . .

(4) *Transportation of Students.* The scope of permissible transportation of students as an implement of a remedial decree has never been defined by this Court and by the very nature of the problem it cannot be defined with precision. No rigid guidelines as to student transportation can be given for application to the infinite variety of problems presented in thousands of situations. Bus transportation has been an integral part of the public education system for years, and was perhaps the single most important factor in the transition from the one-room schoolhouse to the consolidated school. Eighteen million of the nation's public school children, approximately 39%, were transported to their schools by bus in 1969–1970 in all parts of the country.

The importance of bus transportation as a normal and accepted tool of educational policy is readily discernible in this and the companion case. The Charlotte school authorities did not purport to assign students on the basis of geographically drawn zones until 1965 and then they allowed almost unlimited transfer privileges. The District Court's conclusion that assignment of children to the school nearest their home serving their grade would not produce an effective dismantling of the dual system is supported by the record.

Thus the remedial techniques used in the District Court's order were within the court's power to provide equitable relief; implementation of the decree is well within the capacity of the school authority.

The decree provided that the buses used to implement the plan would operate on direct routes. Students would be picked up at schools near their homes and transported to the schools they were to attend. The trips for elementary school pupils average about seven miles and the District Court found that they would take "not over 35 minutes at the most." This system compares favorably with the transportation plan previously operated in Charlotte under which each day 23,600 students on all grade levels were transported an average of 15 miles one way for an average trip requiring over an hour. In these circumstances, we find no basis for holding that the local school authorities may not be required to employ bus transportation as one tool of school desegregation. Desegregation plans cannot be limited to the walk-in school.

An objection to transportation of students may have validity when the time or distance of travel is so great as to risk either the health of the children or significantly impinge on the educational process. District courts must weigh the soundness of any transportation plan in light of what is said in subdivisions (1), (2), and (3) above. It hardly needs stating that the limits on time of travel will vary with many factors, but probably with none more than the age of the students. The reconciliation of competing values in a desegregation case is, of course, a difficult task with many sensitive facets but fundamentally no more so than remedial measures courts of equity have traditionally employed.

VI.

The Court of Appeals, searching for a term to define the equitable remedial power of the district courts, used the term "reasonableness." In *Green,* supra, this Court used the term "feasible" and by implication, "workable," "effective," and "realistic" in the mandate to develop "a plan that promises realistically to work, and ... to work *now.*" On the facts of this case, we are unable to conclude that the order of the District Court is not reasonable, feasible and workable. However, in seeking to define the scope of remedial power or the limits on remedial power of courts in an area as sensitive as we deal with here, words are poor instruments to convey the sense of basic fairness inherent in equity. Substance, not semantics, must govern, and we have sought to suggest the nature of limitations without frustrating the appropriate scope of equity.

At some point, these school authorities and others like them should have achieved full compliance with this Court's decision in *Brown I.* The systems will then be "unitary" in the sense required by our decisions in *Green* and *Alexander.*

It does not follow that the communities served by such systems will remain demographically stable, for in a growing, mobile society, few will do so. Neither school authorities nor district courts are constitutionally required to make year-by-year adjustments of the racial composition of student bodies once the affirmative duty to desegregate has been accomplished and racial discrimination through official action is eliminated from the system. This does not mean that federal courts are without power to deal with future problems; but in the absence of a showing that either the school authorities or some other agency of the State has deliberately attempted to fix or alter demographic patterns to affect the racial composition of the schools, further intervention by a district court should not be necessary.

For the reasons herein set forth, the judgment of the Court of Appeals is affirmed as to those parts in which it affirmed the judgment of the District Court. The order of the District Court dated August 7, 1970, is also affirmed[a]

. . . .

---

[a] In North Carolina State Bd. of Ed. v. Swann, 402 U.S. 43 (1971), the Court held unconstitutional a state statute providing that "No student shall be assigned or compelled to attend any school on account of race, creed, color or national origin, or for the purpose of creating a balance or ratio of race, religion or national origins." The Court said that the statute would obstruct the remedies utilized in the *Swann* case and added: "Just as the race of students must be considered in determining whether a constitutional violation has occurred, so also must race be considered in formulating a remedy. To forbid, at this stage, all assignments made on the basis of race would deprive school authorities of the one tool absolutely essential to fulfillment of their constitutional obligation to eliminate existing dual school systems." See also Davis v. Board of Sch. Comm'rs, 402 U.S. 33 (1971); McDaniel v. Barresi, 402 U.S. 39 (1971).

See generally Carter, *An Evaluation of Past and Current Legal Approaches to Vindication of the Fourteenth Amendment's Guarantee of Equal Educational Opportunity,* 1972 Wash.U.L.Q. 479; Karst, *Not One Law at*

KEYES v. SCHOOL DISTRICT NO. 1, DENVER, COLO., 413 U.S. 189 (1973). This case was the first occasion for the Court to explore problems of desegregation in the north. No legally based segregation had existed in Denver—in fact, the Colorado Constitution prohibited "any classification of pupils ... on account of race or color." The complaint was, instead, that the school board had intentionally taken certain actions for the purpose of creating or maintaining segregated schools in the district. Much of the opinion of the Court, written by Justice Brennan, dealt with the questions which arise when the plaintiff proves intentional acts of segregation in one part of a school district and seeks to use them as a basis for obtaining an order desegregating the schools in another part of the district. On this issue the basic holding of the Court was that "a finding of intentionally segregative school board actions in a meaningful portion of a school system, as in this case, creates a presumption that other segregated schooling within the system is not adventitious. It establishes, in other words, a prima facie case of unlawful segregative design on the part of school authorities, and shifts to those authorities the burden of proving that other segregated schools within the system are not also the results of intentionally segregative actions."

The opinion was constructed on the assumption (not challenged by the parties) that in a school district without a history of legally imposed segregation the initial burden of a plaintiff seeking a desegregation order is to establish (1) intentional acts by the school board designed to create or maintain racially segregated schools and (2) the existence of currently segregated schools resulting from those acts. In the opinion the Court gave some indication of the kinds of proof which a plaintiff might adduce to establish intentional segregation by approving as a basis for a desegregation order findings of the district court that by the construction of a new, relatively small elementary school in the middle of the Negro community, by the gerrymandering of student attendance zones, by the use of so-called "optional zones," and by the excessive use of mobile classroom units, the school board had engaged in deliberate racial segregation.

The Court also discussed the question of how one establishes the existence of segregated schools. Does the Court's discussion—all of which follows—give adequate guidance to the district courts in determining when a plaintiff has established that schools are "segregated" in the sense that desegregation must be ordered?

"Before turning to the primary question we decide today, a word must be said about the District Court's method of defining a 'segregated' school. Denver is a tri-ethnic, as distinguished from a bi-racial, community. The over-all racial and ethnic composition of the Denver public schools is 66% Anglo, 14% Negro and 20% Hispano. The District Court in assessing the question of *de jure* segregation in the core city schools, preliminarily resolved that Negroes and Hispanos should not be placed in the same category to establish the segregated character of a school. 313 F.Supp., at 69. Later, in determining the schools that were likely to produce an inferior educational opportunity, the court concluded that a school would be considered inferior only if it had 'a concentration of either Negro or Hispano students in the general area of 70 to 75 percent.' Id., at 77. We intimate no opinion whether the District Court's 70 to 75% requirement was correct. The District Court used those figures to signify educationally inferior schools, and there is no suggestion in the record that those same figures were or would be used to define a 'segregated' school in the *de jure*

Rome and Another at Athens: The Fourteenth   Wash.U.L.Q. 383.
Amendment in Nationwide Application, 1972

context. What is or is not a segregated school will necessarily depend on the facts of each particular case. In addition to the racial and ethnic composition of a school's student body, other factors such as the racial and ethnic composition of faculty and staff and the community and administration attitudes toward the school must be taken into consideration. The District Court has recognized these specific factors as elements of the definition of a 'segregated' school, id., at 74, and we may therefore infer that the court will consider them again on remand.

"We conclude, however, that the District Court erred in separating Negroes and Hispanos for purposes of defining a 'segregated' school. We have held that Hispanos constitute an identifiable class for purposes of the Fourteenth Amendment. Hernandez v. Texas, 347 U.S. 475 (1954).... Indeed the District Court recognized this in classifying predominantly Hispano schools as 'segregated' schools in their own right. But there is also much evidence that in the Southwest Hispanos and Negroes have a great many things in common. The United States Commission on Civil Rights has recently published two Reports on Hispano education in the Southwest. Focusing on students in the States of Arizona, California, Colorado, New Mexico, and Texas, the Commission concluded that Hispanos suffer from the same educational inequities as Negroes and American Indians. In fact, the District Court itself recognized that '[o]ne of the things which the Hispano has in common with the Negro is economic and cultural deprivation and discrimination.' 313 F.Supp., at 69. This is agreement that, though of different origins Negroes and Hispanos in Denver suffer identical discrimination in treatment when compared with the treatment afforded Anglo students. In that circumstance, we think petitioners are entitled to have schools with a combined predominance of Negroes and Hispanos included in the category of 'segregated' schools."

The Court also discussed the kind of proof by a school district which might rebut the prima facie case made when the plaintiff establishes intentional acts of segregation plus the existence of segregated schools:

"... Thus, be it a statutory dual system or an allegedly unitary system where a meaningful portion of the system is found to be intentionally segregated, the existence of subsequent or other segregated schooling within the same system justifies a rule imposing on the school authorities the burden of proving that this segregated schooling is not also the result of intentionally segregative acts.

"In discharging that burden, it is not enough, of course, that the school authorities rely upon some allegedly logical, racially neutral explanation for their actions. Their burden is to adduce proof sufficient to support a finding that segregative intent was not among the factors that motivated their actions. The courts below attributed much significance to the fact that many of the Board's actions in the core city area antedated our decision in *Brown*. We reject any suggestion that remoteness in time has any relevance to the issue of intent. If the actions of school authorities were to any degree motivated by segregative intent and the segregation resulting from those actions continues to exist, the fact of remoteness in time certainly does not make those actions any less 'intentional.'

"This is not to say, however, that the prima facie case may not be met by evidence supporting a finding that a lesser degree of segregated schooling in the core city area would not have resulted even if the Board had not acted as it did. In *Swann,* we suggested that at some point in time the relationship between past segregative acts and present segregation may become so attenuated as to be incapable of supporting a finding of *de jure* segregation warranting judicial intervention.... We made it clear, however, that a connection between past segregative acts and present segregation may be present even when not apparent and that close examination is required before concluding that the connection does not exist. Intentional school segregation in the past may have been a factor in creating a natural environment for the growth of further segregation. Thus, if respondent School Board cannot disprove segregative intent, it can rebut the prima facie case only by showing that its past segregative acts did not create or contribute to the current segregated condition of the core city schools.

"The respondent School Board invoked at trial its 'neighborhood school policy' as explaining racial and ethnic concentrations within the core city schools, arguing that since the core city area population had long been Negro and Hispano, the concentrations were necessarily the result of residential patterns and not of purposefully segregative policies. We have no occasion to consider in this case whether a 'neighborhood school policy' of itself will justify racial or ethnic concentrations in the absence of a finding that school authorities have committed acts constituting *de jure* segregation. It is enough that we hold that the mere assertion of such a policy is not dispositive where, as in this case, the school authorities have been found to have practiced *de jure* segregation in a meaningful portion of the school system by techniques that indicate that the 'neighborhood school' concept has not been maintained free of manipulation."

Chief Justice Burger concurred in the result without opinion. Justice White took no part in the decision.

Justice Powell, concurring in part and dissenting in part, disagreed with the Court's assumption that northern schools should be free of any obligation to desegregate in the absence of a showing of intentional segregative acts. He said that "if our national concern is for those who attend [segregated] schools, rather than for perpetuating a legalism rooted in history rather than present reality, we must recognize that the evil of operating separate schools is no less in Denver than in Atlanta." He concluded on this point:

"... I would not, ... perpetuate the *de jure de facto* distinction nor would I leave to petitioners the initial tortuous effort of identifying 'segregative acts' and deducing 'segregatory intent.' I would hold, quite simply, that where segregated public schools exist within a school district to a substantial degree, there is a prima facie case that the duly constituted public authorities (I will usually refer to them collectively as the 'school board') are sufficiently responsible to impose upon them a nationally applicable burden to demonstrate they nevertheless are operating a genuinely integrated school system."

Justice Powell then discussed the limits he would impose upon remedial orders by the courts, North or South. Brief excerpts from his long opinion follow:

"Where school authorities have defaulted in their duty to operate an integrated school system, district courts must insure that affirmative desegregative steps ensue. Many of these can be taken effectively without damaging state and parental interests in having children attend schools within a reasonable vicinity of home. Where desegregative steps are possible within the framework of a system of 'neighborhood education' school authorities must pursue them....

"... School boards would, of course, be free to develop and initiate further plans to promote school desegregation. In a pluralistic society such as ours, it is essential that no racial minority feel demeaned or discriminated against and that students of all races learn to play, work, and cooperate with one another in their common pursuits and endeavors. Nothing in this opinion is meant to discourage school boards from exceeding minimal constitutional standards in promoting the values of an integrated school experience.

"A *constitutional requirement* of extensive student transportation solely to achieve integration presents a vastly more complex problem. It promises on the one hand a greater degree of actual desegregation, while it infringes on what may fairly be regarded as other important community aspirations and personal rights. Such a requirement is further likely to divert attention and resources from the foremost goal of any school system: the best quality education for all pupils. The Equal Protection Clause does indeed command that racial discrimination not be tolerated in the decisions of public school authorities. But it does not require that school authorities undertake widespread student transportation solely for the sake of maximizing integration.

. . .

"It is well to remember that the course we are running is a long one and the goal sought in the end—so often overlooked—is the best possible educational opportunity for all children. Communities deserve the freedom and the incentive to turn their attention and energies to this goal of quality education, free from protracted and debilitating battles over court-ordered student transportation. The single most disruptive element in education today is the widespread use of compulsory transportation, especially at elementary grade levels. This has risked distracting and diverting attention from basic educational ends, dividing and embittering communities, and exacerbating rather than ameliorating inter-racial friction and misunderstanding. It is time to return to a more balanced evaluation of the recognized interests of our society in achieving desegregation with other educational and societal interests a community may legitimately assert. This will help assure that integrated school systems will be established and maintained by rational action, will be better understood and supported by parents and children of both races, and will promote the enduring qualities of an integrated society so essential to its genuine success."

Justice Douglas, concurring in the opinion of the Court, also agreed with Justice Powell that cases from the North and the South should be treated the same. Justice Rehnquist dissented.

RACIAL BALANCE, ACHIEVING DESEGREGATION, AND MODIFYING OR DISSOLVING DESEGREGATION DECREES

In Pasadena City Bd. of Educ. v. Spangler, 427 U.S. 424 (1976), the district court had entered a desegregation order which included a provision that by 1970 there should be no school in the district "with a majority of any minority students." The school board implemented the plan in 1970, fully carrying out its terms. Over the next several years as a result of demographic changes 5 out of 32 schools in the district came to have more than 50% black students. The school board returned to the district court and sought to have the decree modified to eliminate the requirement that there be no school with a majority of minority students. The district court refused and the court of appeals affirmed. The Supreme Court reversed. It noted that there was no contention that the post–1971 changes in the racial mix of the schools resulted from any segregative acts chargeable to the school district. Instead, the changes appeared to be the result of people moving into, out of, and around the district. It concluded:

"In this case the District Court approved a plan designed to obtain racial neutrality in the attendance of students at Pasadena's public schools. No one disputes that the initial implementation of this plan accomplished *that* objective. That being the case, the District Court was not entitled to require the School District to rearrange its attendance zones each year so as to ensure that the racial mix desired by the court was maintained in perpetuity. For having once implemented a racially neutral attendance pattern in order to remedy the perceived constitutional violations on the part of the defendants, the District Court had fully performed its function of providing the appropriate remedy for previous racially discriminatory attendance patterns."

Board of Education of Oklahoma City Public Schools v. Dowell, 498 U.S. 237 (1991), addressed what a school board subject to a desegregation decree must do to have the injunctive decree dissolved. Based on findings in 1963 that over a long period Oklahoma City intentionally had segregated schools and housing, and based on subsequent findings of insufficient school board efforts to desegregate the city's schools, the district court in 1972 ordered the board to adopt a particular desegregation plan that would be more effective. In 1977 the district court granted the Board's "Motion to Close Case" based on a finding that the school system had operated the plan properly and had achieved unitary status. Although the 1977 order was not appealed, the black plaintiffs moved to reopen the case in 1985 following the Board's adoption of a neighborhood school Student Reassignment Plan (SRP) that reduced the length of bus rides of young black students but left half the 64 elementary schools in the district more than 90% black or 90% white. The district court concluded that the school district's unitary status had been maintained, that the SRP was not designed with discriminatory intent, and that the 1972 injunctive decree should be vacated. The Court of Appeals reversed, holding that by itself compliance with the injunction would not justify its dissolution.

The Supreme Court, Justice Souter not participating, unanimously agreed that the 1977 order terminating the case had not itself dissolved the desegregation decree, despite the unitariness finding. Ambiguity about whether "unitary" meant that all vestiges of past discrimination were completely remedied, or just that a school system currently was desegregated, prevented the conclusion that the 1977 order finally terminated the litigation. For a decree to be dissolved the court must provide the parties with a "rather precise statement."

The Court also unanimously agreed that the standard for whether dissolution of the decree is appropriate is whether "the purposes of the desegregation litigation [have] been fully achieved." The Court was divided, however, on what would satisfy that standard. Chief Justice Rehnquist's majority opinion held that "a finding by the District Court that the Oklahoma City School District was being operated in compliance with the commands of the Equal Protection Clause ... and that it was unlikely that the school board would return to its former ways" would meet the standard. The Court reversed the Court of Appeals, because "federal supervision of local school systems was intended as a temporary measure to remedy past discrimination" and desegregation decrees "are not intended to operate in perpetuity" or to condemn school districts that have complied in good faith for a reasonable period of time "to judicial tutelage for the indefinite future."

Rather than reinstate the district court order terminating the injunction, however, the Court remanded for that court to "decide, in accordance with this opinion, whether the Board made a sufficient showing of constitutional compliance as of 1985, when the SRP was adopted, to allow the injunction to be dissolved." In particular, the district court "should address itself to whether the Board had complied in good faith with the desegregation decree since it was entered, and whether the vestiges of past discrimination had been eliminated to the extent practicable." (As part of the latter inquiry the district court was directed to reconsider "as *res nova*" its earlier finding "that present residential segregation in Oklahoma City was the result of private decisionmaking and economics, and that it was too attenuated to be a vestige of former school segregation.") Only after the district court decided whether the decree should be terminated should it then decide the challenge to the SRP, because if released from the desegregation plan the Board no longer would require court approval for such policy changes and a successful challenge to the SRP would require new proof that its adoption was an act of *de jure* segregation.

In dissent Justice Marshall, joined by Justices Blackmun and Stevens, would have affirmed the Court of Appeals' reinstatement of the decree based on the judgment that "feasible steps could be taken to avoid one-race schools" and that it was therefore "clear that the purposes of the decree have not yet been achieved." Justice Marshall emphasized the long history of *de jure* school segregation in Oklahoma City and the Board's resistance to integration that led to the court-imposed desegregation plan in 1972. He stressed that "stigmatic injury" underlies the Court's insistence that all vestiges of *de jure* segregation be eliminated and that "[a]lthough the Court has never explicitly defined what constitutes a 'vestige' of state-enforced segregation, . . . it extends to any condition that is likely to convey the message of inferiority implicit in a policy of segregation." He was concerned that the majority had suggested a "more vague . . . and milder standard" that "ignores how the stigmatic harm . . . can persist even after the State ceases actively to enforce segregation." He continued:

"In sum, our school-desegregation jurisprudence establishes that the *effects* of past discrimination remain chargeable to the school district regardless of its lack of continued enforcement of segregation, and the remedial decree is required until those effects have been eliminated.

" . . .

"Against the background of former state-sponsorship of one-race schools, the persistence of racially identifiable schools perpetuates the message of racial inferiority associated with segregation. Therefore, such schools must be eliminated whenever feasible."

The reemergence of racially identifiable schools under the SRP meant that "lifting the decree would clearly be premature at this point." Justice Marshall faulted the majority for being too equivocal on this point, for "hint[ing] that the District Court could ignore the effect of residential segregation in perpetuating racially identifiable schools if the court finds residential segregation to be 'the result of private decisionmaking and economics[,]' "and for being too concerned with sparing "local school boards the 'Draconian' fate of 'indefinite' 'judicial tutelage' "at the "risk of not delivering a full remedy to the Afro–American children in the school system." Although "[r]etaining the decree does not require a return to active supervision" and "modification" might be "appropriate" to "improve its effectiveness and give the school district more flexibility in minimizing busing[,]" dissolving the decree would be inappropriate when the purposes of the decree had not fully been achieved.

A year later, in Freeman v. Pitts, 503 U.S. 467 (1992), the Court held that "a district court is permitted to withdraw judicial supervision with respect to discrete categories in which the school district has achieved compliance with a court-ordered desegregation plan" and "need not retain active control over every aspect of school administration until a school district has demonstrated unitary status in all facets of its system." Against a backdrop of decades of legally-mandated school segregation before *Brown v. Board of Education* and district court desegregation orders beginning in 1969, Georgia's DeKalb County School System ("DCSS") made efforts that the district court found to have "achieved maximum practical desegregation [of students] from 1969 to 1986." During that period, however, the black student population increased from 5.6% to 47%, the County experienced demographic shifts resulting in a high degree of residential segregation, and the schools, after first achieving a reasonable measure of racial balance, again became racially imbalanced. The district court "examined the interaction between DCSS policy and demographic shifts in DeKalb County" but found "no evidence that the school system's previous unconstitutional conduct may have contributed" to the pattern of residential segregation by race. Overall, the district court found DCSS "a unitary system with regard to student assignments, transportation, physical facilities, and extracurricular activities, and ruled that it would order no further relief in those areas." It also found, however, "that vestiges of the dual system remain in the areas of teacher and principal assignments, resource allocation, and quality of education" (assessed primarily on the basis of per pupil expenditures and teacher competence), and it ordered spending equalization and other remedial measures.

The Supreme Court held "that, in the course of supervising desegregation plans, federal courts have the authority to relinquish supervision and control of school districts in incremental stages, before full compliance has been achieved in every area of school operations." Justice Kennedy's majority opinion emphasized that "[p]artial relinquishment of judicial control, where justified by the facts of the case, can be an important and significant step in fulfilling the district court's duty to return the operations and control of schools to local authorities"—a duty "essential to restore their true accountability in our governmental system." The opinion also stated:

"Among the factors which must inform the sound discretion of the court in ordering partial withdrawal are the following: whether there has been full and satisfactory compliance with the decree in those aspects of the system where supervision is to be withdrawn; whether retention of judicial control is necessary or practicable to achieve compliance with the decree in other facets of the school system; and whether the school district has demonstrated ... its good faith commitment to the whole of the court's decree and to those provisions of the law and the constitution that were the predicate for judicial involvement in the first instance.

"In considering these factors a court should give particular attention to the school system's record of compliance...."

With respect to the particular issue of racial imbalance in student assignments, the Court emphasized that the "school district bears the burden of showing that any current imbalance is not traceable, in a proximate way, to the prior violation"; that "[a]s the *de jure* violation becomes more remote in time and these demographic changes intervene, it becomes less likely that a current racial imbalance in a school district is a vestige of the prior *de jure* system"; that "[t]he causal link between current conditions and the prior violation is even more attenuated if the school district has demonstrated its good faith"; and thus that given its findings "the District Court was correct to entertain the suggestion that DCSS had no duty to achieve systemwide racial balance in the student population." The Court noted that "a continuing violation in one area may need to be addressed by remedies in another" but found "no showing that racial balancing was an appropriate mechanism to cure other deficiencies in this case." The Court nonetheless suggested a remand for specific findings that student reassignments would not be a feasible or practical way to solve the faculty assignment problem and that the school district satisfied its "requirement [of] show[ing] its good faith commitment to the entirety of a desegregation plan so that parents, students and the public have assurance against further injuries or stigma[.]"

A concurring opinion by Justice Scalia suggested that the Court is close to the time when it should abandon the "extraordinary presumption" of *Green v. New Kent County School Board*, 391 U.S. 430 (1968)—"that, once state-enforced school segregation is shown to have existed in a jurisdiction in 1954, there arises a presumption, effectively irrebuttable (because the school district cannot prove a negative), that any current racial imbalance is the product of that violation, at least if that imbalance has continuously existed." The "rational basis for the extraordinary presumption of causation simply must dissipate as the *de jure* system and the school boards who produced it recede further into the past[,]" especially given the multitude of private demographic changes that occur during that time. Instead, the Court "must soon revert" to ordinary equal protection principles that require "plaintiffs alleging Equal Protection violations [to] prove intent and causation and not merely the existence of racial disparity."

Justice Souter, on the other hand, concurred separately to emphasize the obligation of district courts to make findings that "the dual school system itself [is not] a cause of the demographic shifts" leading to racial imbalance in student populations and "that there is no immediate threat of unremedied *Green*-type factors causing population or student enrollment changes that in turn may imbalance student composition.... " He also emphasized that the district court should "reassert control over student assignments if it finds that this does happen."

Justice Blackmun, joined by Justices Stevens and O'Connor, concurred in the judgment. They emphasized the district court's duty "to examine the past to determine whether the current racial imbalance in the schools is attributable in part to the former *de jure* segregated regime or any later actions by school officials." Unsatisfied, after reviewing the record, with "the District Court's finding that DCSS has met its burden of proving the racially identifiable schools are in no way the result of past segregative action[,]" they also would have remanded for further review of this issue. Justice Thomas did not participate.

FINDING DE JURE SEGREGATION IN NORTHERN SCHOOLS

In the South schools had been desegregated by law. In the North the law did not require segregation and so in each case it was necessary to show that the school district had intentionally taken acts designed to separate students on racial grounds. In two cases the Court appeared to reduce this difference substantially.

In *Columbus Bd. of Educ. v. Penick*, 443 U.S. 449 (1979), and *Dayton Bd. of Educ. v. Brinkman*, 443 U.S. 526 (1979), the Court had before it two cities where the law had not compelled segregation but it was reasonably clear that before *Brown v. Board of Education* the school boards had intentionally taken a number of acts that created virtually a segregated school system. The Court upheld the conclusion of the court of appeals that the cities since the *Brown* case had been under a duty to disestablish the dual system and had not done so. A little of the flavor of the five-Justice majority opinion is presented in the following excerpt from the *Dayton* case:

"Petitioners next contend that, even if a dual system did exist a quarter of a century ago, the Court of Appeals erred in finding any widespread violations of constitutional duty since that time.

"Given intentionally segregated schools in 1954, however, the Court of Appeals was quite right in holding that the Board was thereafter under a continuing duty to eradicate the effects of that system and that the systemwide nature of the violation furnished prima facie proof that current segregation in the Dayton schools was caused at least in part by prior intentionally segregative official acts. Thus, judgment for the plaintiffs was authorized and required absent sufficient countervailing evidence by the defendant school officials. Keyes . . .; Swann. . . . At the time of trial, Dunbar High School and the three black elementary schools, or the schools that succeeded them, remained black schools; and most of the schools in Dayton were virtually one-race schools, as were 80% of the classrooms. 'Every school which was 90 percent or more black in 1951–52 *or* 1963–64 *or* 1971–72 and which is still in use today remains 90 percent or more black. Of the 25 white schools in 1972–73, *all* opened 90 percent or more white and, if open, were 90 percent or more white in 1971–72, 1963–64 and 1951–52.' 583 F.2d, at 254 (emphasis in original), ... Against this background, the Court of Appeals held that '[t]he evidence of record demonstrates convincingly that defendants have failed to eliminate the continuing systemwide effects of their prior discrimination and have intentionally maintained a segregated school system down to the time the complaint was filed in the present case.' At the very least, defendants had failed to come forward with evidence to deny 'that the current racial composition of the school population reflects the systemwide impact' of the Board's prior discriminatory conduct.

"Part of the affirmative duty imposed by our cases . . . is the obligation not to take any action that would impede the process of disestablishing the dual system and its effects. . . . The Dayton Board, however, had engaged in many post-*Brown I* actions that had the effect of increasing or perpetuating segregation. . . . But the measure of the post-*Brown I* conduct of a school board under an unsatisfied duty to liquidate a dual system is the effectiveness, not the purpose, of the actions in decreasing or increasing the segregation caused by the dual system. . . . As was clearly established in *Keyes* and *Swann,* the Board had to do more than abandon its prior discriminatory purpose. . . . The Board has had an affirmative responsibility to see that pupil assignment policies and school construction and abandonment practices 'are not used and do not serve to perpetuate or re-establish the dual school system,' . . . and the Board has a 'heavy burden' of showing that actions that increased or continued the effects of the dual system serve important and legitimate ends."

MAY SCHOOL DESEGREGATION ORDERS EXTEND BEYOND SCHOOL DISTRICT LINES?

MILLIKEN v. BRADLEY, 418 U.S. 717 (1974). Litigation commenced in 1970 sought desegregation of the Detroit school district. At that time there were 86 school districts in the Detroit metropolitan area enrolling a million children, with about 275,000 in the Detroit district alone. The racial composition of the area school population was 81% white, 19% black. The racial composition of the Detroit district was 64% black and 34% white. Within the Detroit district most of the schools were either predominantly black or predominantly white. The trial judge found numerous actions by the Detroit School Board taken for the purpose of maintaining segregation of the schools within the district. He also found a number of actions by the State that contributed to the segregation, including a failure to provide funds for busing within Detroit while providing them in the suburbs. Eventually the judge found that it would not be possible to desegregate the schools by any remedy confined to Detroit alone, and that any remedy possible would simply create a system composed all of predominantly black schools and cause further movement of white pupils out of the public school system. The judge then determined that only an interdistrict remedy would solve the problem. Relying on the involvement of the State and requiring no showing of any segregative acts by the suburban school districts (and providing only minimal opportunity for those districts to appear and contest the ruling) the court ordered an interdistrict remedy. He designated 53 of the 85 suburban school districts plus Detroit as the "desegregation area" and appointed a panel to prepare a plan. The plan was to be based on 15 clusters containing part of the Detroit system and two or more suburban districts to "achieve the greatest degree of actual desegregation to the end that, upon implementation, no school, grade or classroom [would be] substantially disproportionate to the overall pupil racial composition." He also ordered the State to purchase or lease at least 295 buses to provide transportation under an interim plan. The court of appeals affirmed. It said that the harm to black pupils from being confined to predominantly black schools surrounded by white schools was the same whether within a single district or within a multi-district metropolitan area. It also said that the State's general responsibility for education and the acts of segregation it had committed justified the interdistrict order without showing violations by the suburban districts.

The Supreme Court reversed. Chief Justice Burger, writing for the Court, began by noting that the "target of the *Brown* holding was clear and forthright: the elimination of state mandated or deliberately maintained dual school systems with certain schools for Negro pupils and others for White pupils." He relied on language in *Swann* as showing that desegregation "in the sense of dismantling a dual school system" does not require any particular racial balance. In a footnote he added: "Disparity in the racial composition of pupils within a single district may well constitute a 'signal' to a district court at the outset, leading to inquiry into the causes accounting for a pronounced racial identifiability of schools within one school system.... However, the use of significant racial imbalance in schools within an autonomous school district as a signal which operates simply to shift the burden of proof, is a very different matter from equating racial imbalance with a constitutional violation calling for a remedy."

On the basic issue of the propriety of the interdistrict remedy, he said:

"Here the District Court's approach to what constituted 'actual desegregation' raises the fundamental question, not presented in *Swann,* as to the circumstances in which a federal court may order desegregation relief that embraces more than a single school district. The court's analytical starting point was its conclusion that school district lines are no more than arbitrary lines on a map 'drawn for political convenience.' Boundary lines may be bridged where there has been a constitutional violation calling for inter-district relief, but the notion that school district lines may be casually ignored or treated as a mere administrative convenience is contrary to the history of public education in our country. No single tradition in public education is more deeply rooted than local control over the operation of schools; local autonomy has long been thought essential both to the maintenance of community concern and support for public schools and to quality of the educational process....

"The Michigan educational structure involved in this case, in common with most States, provides for a large measure of local control, and a review of the scope and character of these local powers indicates the extent to which the

inter-district remedy approved by the two courts could disrupt and alter the structure of public education in Michigan. The metropolitan remedy would require, in effect, consolidation of 54 independent school districts historically administered as separate units into a vast new super school district.... Entirely apart from the logistical and other serious problems attending large-scale transportation of students, the consolidation would give rise to an array of other problems in financing and operating this new school system. Some of the more obvious questions would be: What would be the status and authority of the present popularly elected school boards? Would the children of Detroit be within the jurisdiction and operating control of a school board elected by the parents and residents of other districts? What board or boards would levy taxes for school operations in these 54 districts constituting the consolidated metropolitan area? What provisions could be made for assuring substantial equality in tax levies among the 54 districts, if this were deemed requisite? What provisions would be made for financing? Would the validity of long-term bonds be jeopardized unless approved by all of the component districts as well as the State? What body would determine that portion of the curricula now left to the discretion of local school boards? Who would establish attendance zones, purchase school equipment, locate and construct new schools, and indeed attend to all the myriad day-to-day decisions that are necessary to school operations affecting potentially more than three quarters of a million pupils?
. . .

. . .

"Of course, no state law is above the Constitution. School district lines and the present laws with respect to local control, are not sacrosanct and if they conflict with the Fourteenth Amendment federal courts have a duty to prescribe appropriate remedies. See, e.g., Wright v. Council of City of Emporia, 407 U.S. 451; United States v. Scotland Neck Board of Education, 407 U.S. 484 (state or local officials prevented from carving out a new school district from an existing district that was in process of dismantling a dual school system); ... But our prior holdings have been confined to violations and remedies within a single school district. We therefore turn to address, for the first time, the validity of a remedy mandating cross-district or inter-district consolidation to remedy a condition of segregation found to exist in only one district.

"The controlling principle consistently expounded in our holdings is that the scope of the remedy is determined by the nature and extent of the constitutional violation. *Swann*.... Before the boundaries of separate and autonomous school districts may be set aside by consolidating the separate units for remedial purposes or by imposing a cross-district remedy, it must first be shown that there has been a constitutional violation within one district that produces a significant segregative effect in another district. Specifically it must be shown that racially discriminatory acts of the state or local school districts, or of a single school district have been a substantial cause of inter-district segregation. Thus an inter-district remedy might be in order where the racially discriminatory acts of one or more school districts caused racial segregation in an adjacent district, or where district lines have been deliberately drawn on the basis of race. In such circumstances an inter-district remedy would be appropriate to eliminate the inter-district segregation directly caused by the constitutional violation. Conversely, without an inter-district violation and inter-district effect, there is no constitutional wrong calling for an inter-district remedy.

. . .

"In dissent Mr. Justice White and Mr. Justice Marshall undertake to demonstrate that agencies having statewide authority participated in maintaining the dual school system found to exist in Detroit. They are apparently of the view that once such participation is shown, the District Court should have a relatively free hand to reconstruct school districts outside of Detroit in fashioning relief. Our assumption, *arguendo* . . . that state agencies did participate in the maintenance of the Detroit system, should make it clear that it is not on this point that we part company. The difference between us arises instead from established doctrine laid down by our cases. *Brown,* supra, *Green,* supra, *Swann,* supra, *Scotland Neck,* supra, and *Emporia,* supra, each addressed the issue of constitutional wrong in terms of an established geographic and administrative school system populated by both Negro and White children. In such a context, terms such as 'unitary' and 'dual' systems, and 'racially identifiable schools,' have meaning, and the necessary federal authority to remedy the constitutional wrong is firmly established. But the remedy is necessarily designed, as all remedies are, to restore the victims of discriminatory conduct to the position they would have occupied in the absence of such conduct. Disparate treatment of White and Negro students occurred within the Detroit school system, and not elsewhere, and on this record the remedy must be limited to that system. *Swann,* supra, at 16.

"The constitutional right of the Negro respondents residing in Detroit is to attend a unitary school system in that district. Unless petitioners drew the district lines in a discriminatory fashion, or arranged for White students residing in the Detroit district to attend schools in Oakland and Macomb Counties, they were under no constitutional duty to make provisions for Negro students to do so. The view of the dissenters, that the existence of a dual system *in Detroit* can be made the basis for a decree requiring cross-district transportation of pupils cannot be supported on the grounds that it represents merely the devising of a suitably flexible remedy for the violation of rights already established by our prior decisions. It can be supported only by drastic expansion of the constitutional right itself, an expansion without any support in either constitutional principle or precedent."

Justice Stewart concurred in the opinion of the Court and wrote a separate opinion which included in a footnote the observation that it is the "essential fact of a predominantly Negro school population in Detroit—caused by unknown and perhaps unknowable factors such as immigration, birth rates, economic changes, or cumulative acts of private racial fears—that accounts for the 'growing core of Negro schools,' a 'core' that had grown to include virtually the entire city." He then said that the courts have no authority to attempt to change this situation in the absence of proof that it was in any significant measure caused by governmental activity.

Justices White, Douglas, Brennan, and Marshall dissented. Justice White writing for all the dissenters indicated he thought the Court was in the name of administrative convenience permitting the state to insulate itself "from its duty to provide effective desegregation remedies by vesting sufficient power over its public schools in its local school districts." Justice Marshall, also writing for all the dissenters, observed:

"After 20 years of small, often difficult steps toward that great end, the Court today takes a giant step backwards. Notwithstanding a record showing widespread and pervasive racial segregation in the educational system provided by the State of Michigan for children in Detroit, this Court holds that the District Court was powerless to require the State to remedy its constitutional violation in any meaningful fashion. Ironically purporting to base its result on the principle that the scope of the remedy in a desegregation case should be determined by the nature and the extent of the constitutional violation, the Court's answer is to provide no remedy at all for the violation proved in this case, thereby guaranteeing that Negro children in Detroit will receive the same separate and inherently unequal education in the future as they have been unconstitutionally afforded in the past.

"I cannot subscribe to this emasculation of our constitutional guarantee of equal protection of the laws and must respectfully dissent. . . .

"The rights at issue in this case are too fundamental to be abridged on grounds as superficial as those relied on by the majority today. We deal here with the right of all of our children, whatever their race, to an equal start in life and to an equal opportunity to reach their full potential as citizens. Those children who have been denied that right in the past deserve better than to see fences thrown up to deny them that right in the future. Our Nation, I fear, will be ill-served by the Court's refusal to remedy separate and unequal education for unless our children begin to learn together, there is little hope that our people will ever learn to live together. . . .

"Because of the already high and rapidly increasing percentage of Negro students in the Detroit system, as well as the prospect of white flight, a Detroit-only plan simply has no hope of achieving actual desegregation. Under such a plan white and Negro students will not go to school together. Instead, Negro children will continue to attend all-Negro schools. The very evil that *Brown I* was aimed at will not be cured, but will be perpetuated for the future. . . .

"Desegregation is not and was never expected to be an easy task. Racial attitudes ingrained in our Nation's childhood and adolescence are not quickly thrown aside in its middle years. But just as the inconvenience of some cannot be allowed to stand in the way of the rights of others, so public opposition, no matter how strident, cannot be permitted to divert this Court from the enforcement of the constitutional principles at issue in this case. Today's holding, I fear, is more a reflection of a perceived public mood that we have gone far enough in enforcing the Constitution's guarantee of equal justice than it is the product of neutral principles of law. In the short run, it may seem to be the easier course to allow our great metropolitan areas to be divided up each into two cities—one white, the other black—but it is a course, I predict, our people will ultimately regret. I dissent."[a]

MILLIKEN v. BRADLEY (MILLIKEN II), 433 U.S. 267 (1977). On remand, the district court included in its decree remedial or compensatory education programs, including in-service training for teachers and administrators, guidance and counseling programs, and revised testing procedures. The cost of these programs was to be borne equally by the Detroit Board of Education and the State of Michigan. That portion of the district court's order was affirmed by the Court of Appeals, and the State defendants appealed. They argued that, since the constitutional violation was unlawful segregation, under the principles of *Milliken I* the court's decree must be limited to redressing that violation by pupil assignments. The Supreme Court rejected that argument and affirmed. Chief Justice Burger said, for the Court:

[a] For a careful argument to the effect that the Court should extend federal remedies across school district boundaries so as to achieve maximum racial mixing in metropolitan areas, see Strickman, *School Desegregation at the Crossroads*, 70 Nw.U.L.Rev. 725 (1975). See also Sedler, *Metropolitan Desegregation in the Wake of Milliken—On Losing Big Battles and Winning Small Wars: The View Largely from Within*, 1975 Wash. U.L.Rev. 535.

"In a word, discriminatory student assignment policies can themselves manifest and breed other inequalities built into a dual system founded on racial discrimination. Federal courts need not, and cannot, close their eyes to inequalities, shown by the record, which flow from a longstanding segregated system."

NOTE

In two cases decided in 1990 the Supreme Court was asked to address the scope of the equitable and constitutional powers of federal judges to enforce compliance with court-ordered remedies for proven instances of *de jure* segregation. The first case concerned segregation of public housing, the second segregation of public schools.

SPALLONE v. UNITED STATES, 493 U.S. 265 (1990). Finding that for three decades the City of Yonkers and the Yonkers Community Development Agency had located public housing in order to perpetuate residential racial segregation, the district court entered a remedial decree requiring affirmative steps to disperse public housing throughout the City. The City failed to comply, but after the district court's liability and remedial decisions were affirmed on appeal, it agreed to a consent decree requiring the enactment of remedial legislation within 90 days. Months of further delay led the district court to threaten the City and each individual City Council member with contempt sanctions unless the legislation was enacted within several days. When the ordinance was voted down, the court imposed contempt sanctions against the City and each of the legislators on the Council who had voted no. The Court of Appeals affirmed. The Supreme Court granted a stay of the sanctions as to the individual council members, but denied a stay as to the City. (A majority of the Council finally enacted the ordinance, as the City's contempt sanction approached $1 million a day.)

Invoking the equitable doctrine that a court selecting contempt sanctions must use the "least possible power adequate to the end proposed," the Court upheld the sanctions against the City but held that the district court had abused its equitable discretion by imposing simultaneous sanctions against the individual council members. Chief Justice Rehnquist's majority opinion emphasized that the council members, unlike the City, were not parties to the action and thus had not been found liable, had not been subjected to remedial orders, and had not committed in the consent decree to enact the remedial ordinance—although if the City were to enact legislation they would have to do it. The opinion also asserted that there was a reasonable probability that sanctions against the City would have worked and that individual sanctions effect "a much greater perversion of the normal legislative process than does the imposition of sanctions on the city for the failure of these same legislators to enact an ordinance[,]" because personal fines "encourage legislators, in effect, to declare that they favor an ordinance not in order to avoid bankrupting the city for which they legislate, but in order to avoid bankrupting themselves." Consequently, "[o]nly if" proceeding with "contempt sanctions first against the city alone ... failed to produce compliance within a reasonable time should the question of imposing contempt sanctions against petitioners even have been considered." Justices Brennan, Marshall, Blackmun, and Stevens dissented.

MISSOURI v. JENKINS, 495 U.S. 33 (1990). After finding that the State of Missouri and the Kansas City, Missouri, School District (KCMSD) had operated a segregated school system within KCMSD, the district court ordered the implementation of a plan, largely offered by KCMSD, calling for a magnet school program costing over $200 million and capital improvements to the school system costing over $250 million. ("Magnet schools" are "public schools of voluntary enrollment designed to promote integration by drawing students away from their neighborhoods and private schools through distinctive curricula and high quality.") Various state law provisions effectively prevented KCMSD from raising taxes sufficient to finance the 25% portion of desegregation costs for which the district court held it liable. When KCMSD was unable to secure the funding from the voters, the city council or the state legislature, and the district court became convinced that KCMSD had exhausted its funding possibilities, the court itself ordered a significant increase in KCMSD property tax rates, notwithstanding the state law limitations. On the State's appeal, the Court of Appeals upheld the remedial orders and agreed, given the constitutional violations, that state law could not prevent KCMSD from raising funds sufficient to implement the desegregation remedy. The Court of Appeals concluded as a matter of "federal_state comity," however, that in the future the district court should not set the property tax rate itself but should authorize KCMSD to do so and should enjoin the operation of state laws hindering KCMSD from adequately funding the remedy.

The Supreme Court overturned the tax increase imposed directly by the district court but upheld the power of the district court to direct KCMSD to levy its own taxes and to enjoin state laws limiting or reducing such levies. Finding it "unnecessary to reach the difficult constitutional issues" of whether the tax increase imposed by the district court violated Article III or the Tenth Amendment, the Court agreed "with the State that the tax increase contravened the principles of comity that must govern the exercise of the District Court's equitable discretion in this area."

"... In assuming for itself the fundamental and delicate power of taxation the District Court not only intruded on local authority but circumvented it altogether. Before taking such a drastic step the District Court was obliged to assure itself that no permissible alternative would have accomplished the required task.... [O]ne of the most important considerations governing the exercise of equitable power is a proper respect for the integrity and function of local government institutions. Especially is this true where, as here, those institutions are ready, willing, and—but for the operation of state law curtailing their powers—able to remedy the deprivation of constitutional rights themselves.

"The District Court believed that it had no alternative to imposing a tax increase. But there was an alternative, the very one outlined by the Court of Appeals.... The difference between the two approaches is far more than a matter of form. Authorizing and directing local government institutions to devise and implement remedies not only protects the function of those institutions but, to the extent possible, also places the responsibility for solutions to the problems of segregation upon those who have themselves created the problems."

With respect to "financing desegregation," as with other aspects of solving desegregation problems, "local officials should at least have the opportunity to devise their own solutions."

For a majority of the Court, composed of the four dissenters in *Spallone*, supra, and himself, Justice White then affirmed that the district courts possess equitable power to apportion desegregation costs between States and local school districts and to "set aside state laws preventing local governments from raising funds sufficient to satisfy their constitutional obligations [even though] those funds could also be obtained from the States." Nor did the Constitution prohibit the exercise of that equitable power. The Tenth Amendment is no bar, because the Fourteenth Amendment, which limits state power, "permits a federal court to disestablish local government institutions that interfere with its commands." As for the State's argument that the "judicial power of Article III" does not encompass an order to increase taxes, "[w]hatever the merits of this argument when applied to the District Court's own order increasing taxes, a point we have not reached, ..., a court order directing a local government body to levy its own taxes is plainly a judicial act within the power of a federal court."

The opinion also contained the following conclusion:

"[A] local government with taxing authority may be ordered to levy taxes in excess of the limit set by state statute where there is reason based in the Constitution for not observing the statutory limitation.... To hold otherwise would fail to take account of the obligations of local governments, under the Supremacy Clause, to fulfill the requirements that the Constitution imposes on them.... Even though a particular remedy may not be required in every case to vindicate constitutional guarantees, where (as here) it has been found that a particular remedy is required, the State cannot hinder the process by preventing a local government from implementing that remedy."

Justice Kennedy, joined by Chief Justice Rehnquist and Justices O'Connor and Scalia, concurred in the judgment, but strongly disagreed with the Court's approval of the "judicial taxation" in this case. He noted the unprecedented size of the magnet school and capital renovation and new construction programs ordered by the district court and the unprecedented upholding by the Court of Appeals of a taxation order to fund a remedial decree. He urged that "[a]ny purported distinction between direct imposition of a tax by the federal court and an order commanding the school district to impose the tax is but a formalism where the court's action is predicated on elimination of state law limitations on the school district's taxing authority." That was so because "[a]bsent a change in state law, the tax is imposed by federal authority under a federal decree" and thus the "question is whether a district court possesses a power to tax under federal law, either directly or through delegation to the KCMSD."

Under Article III of the Constitution, said Justice Kennedy, "taxation is not a judicial function." The taxpayers of KCMSD were not parties before the court and received no notice of taxation or opportunity to be heard, as judicial due process requires. Unlike taxation by a legislature, moreover, "a district court order that overrides the citizens' state law protection against taxation without referendum approval can in no sense provide representational due process." Federal judges by design are "not representative or responsible to the people in a political sense" and they "may not even share the burden of taxes they attempt to impose, for they may live outside the jurisdiction their orders affect." Additionally, "operation of tax systems ... is not a function the judiciary as an institution is designed to exercise."

Previous cases relied on by the Court as support for federal judicial authority to order taxation by local governments involved either orders "to exercise *existing* authority to tax[,]" or orders to disregard limits on taxing power contained in state law "enacted in order to thwart a federal court order[,]" or state law that otherwise violates the Federal Constitution itself. As the state law limitations in this case were not themselves otherwise constitutionally objectionable, the applicable precedents should have been those holding that "where there is no state or municipal taxation authority that the federal court may by mandamus command the officials to exercise, the court is itself without authority to order taxation."

Finally, Justice Kennedy objected that the Court had no need to discuss "the important constitutional issues of judicial authority ... to decide this case." At best a taxation order should be a remedy of "last resort," and he faulted the District Court for considering it absent a finding that without it "the Constitutional violation will go unremedied" and for failing to give "due consideration to the possibility that another remedy among the 'wide range of possibilities' would have addressed the constitutional violations without giving rise to a funding crisis."

MISSOURI v. JENKINS (JENKINS III), ___ U.S. ___, 115 S.Ct. 2038 (1995). The Court had denied review of the State's challenge to the scope of the district court's remedial order when it agreed in the preceding case (*Jenkins II*) to address the validity of the district court's taxation orders for financing the remedies required. In *Jenkins III*, the Court nonetheless reached the merits of the State's claim that the district court had exceeded its constitutional remedial authority by ordering the State (1) to fund salary increases for nearly all of KCMSD's instructional and noninstructional employees and (2) to continue to fund remedial quality education programs because student achievement levels remained "at or below national norms at many grade levels." The Court ruled in the State's favor, emphasizing that the district court's "admittedly broad discretion" still had to be confined to eliminating "to the extent practicable the vestiges of prior de jure segregation within the KCMSD: a systemwide reduction in student achievement and the existence of 25 racially identifiable schools with a population of over 90% black students," and also emphasizing that the district court's additional "end purpose" is to restore state and local control of a school system operating in compliance with the Constitution.

Scrutinizing the district court's grounding of the salary orders on improving the "desegregative attractiveness" of KCMSD as a means of remedying the vestiges of segregation, Chief Justice Rehnquist noted that the district court's remedial objective was to create an entire school district equal or superior to surrounding suburban districts rather than just to address the racial identifiability of some of KCMSD's schools. The purpose of creating a "magnet district" was "not only to remedy the system-wide reduction in student achievement, but also to attract nonminority students not presently enrolled in the KCMSD." The lower courts having found no interdistrict constitutional violations, however, no interdistrict relief was warranted under *Milliken I*. The Court now ruled that those remedies designed to induce interdistrict transfer of nonminority students for redistribution within KCMSD exceeded the scope of the district court's broad remedial authority, because the district court had "devised a remedy to accomplish indirectly what it admittedly lacks the remedial authority to mandate directly." Nor, in light of the district court's record findings of no significant interdistrict effects of the de jure segregation within KCMSD and "the typical supposition ... that 'white flight' may result from desegregation, not de jure segregation," could the reliance on desegregative attractiveness be justified by claiming that de jure segregation had "led to white flight from the KCMSD to suburban districts." In short, "[a] district court seeking to remedy an intradistrict violation that has not 'directly caused' significant interdistrict effects ... exceeds its remedial authority if it orders a remedy with an interdistrict purpose." Finally, concerned that the district court's pursuit of "desegregative attractiveness" would justify remedial orders limitless in expenditure and duration, involve "many imponderables," and be "far removed from the task of eliminating the racial identifiability of the schools within the KCMSD," the Court concluded that the salary increase order "is simply too far removed from an acceptable implementation of a permissible means to remedy previous legally mandated segregation."

As for the State's challenge to "the requirement of indefinite funding of a quality education program until national norms are met," the Court noted that the district court's authority extended no further than to remedy to the extent practicable "the incremental effect that segregation has had on minority student achievement." Because not just de jure segregation, but "external factors beyond the control of the KCMSD and the State affect minority student achievement," and because all the parties agreed that "improved achievement on test scores is not necessarily required for the State to achieve partial unitary status as to the quality education programs[—a status the State had not yet requested—]the District Court [on remand] should sharply limit, if not dispense with, its reliance on" the test scores. The Court's underlying concern was that "[i]nsistence upon academic goals unrelated to the effects of legal segregation unwarrantably postpones the day when the KCMSD will be able to operate on its own."

In one concurring opinion Justice O'Connor noted that attracting whites into the school district as an "incidental" benefit of restoring KCMSD to unitary status "would be of no legal consequence[,]" but that here the district court's finding of no interdistrict violation or significant interdistrict segregative effects disallowed "remedies seeking to rectify regional demographic trends that go beyond the scope and nature of the constitutional violation." In another concurring opinion of some length, Justice Thomas questioned whether continuing high black enrollments in KCMSD schools were vestiges of pre–1954 de jure segregation and sharply criticized the district court's finding "that racial imbalances constituted an ongoing constitutional violation that continued to inflict harm on black students" as premised on "the idea that any school that is black is inferior, and that blacks cannot succeed without the benefit of the company of whites." Justice Thomas also urged that the equitable powers of the federal courts be more circumscribed by precise federalism and separation of powers restraints than they previously have been, lest "the institutional ability to set effective educational, budgetary, or administrative policy ... transform the least dangerous branch into the most dangerous one." Specifically, he argued that "absen[t] special circumstances, the remedy for de jure segregation ordinarily should not include educational programs for students who were not in school (or were even alive) during the period of segregation."

Justice Souter authored a dissenting opinion for four Justices. He argued that the Court improperly had addressed "the soundness of the magnet element of the District Court's underlying remedial scheme" in light of the history of this litigation and the State's concession that the salary and test-score questions could be answered without doing so. He contended that the salary orders were designed not only to draw students into the district's schools but to raise the level of student achievement in the KCMSD and thus that "to the extent that the District Court concludes on remand that its salary orders are justified by reference to the quality of education alone, nothing in the Court's opinion precludes those orders from remaining in effect." He understood the district court's findings of no significant interdistrict segregative effects to leave open the possibility that the de jure segregation of KCMSD "produced significant non-segregative effects outside the KCMSD that led to greater segregation within it." On that view, the Court was "rash to reverse the concurrent factual findings" of the two lower courts that the intradistrict segregation had sufficient consequences outside the district to justify the "magnet concept." Finally, Justice Souter interpreted *Milliken I* not to preclude remedial orders whose purpose is to induce interdistrict student transfers as such, but only to prevent remedies that bind "the authorities of other governmental units that are free of violations and segregative effects." Because the "District Court's remedial measures go only to the operation and quality of schools within the KCMSD, and the burden of those measures accordingly falls only on the two proven constitutional wrongdoers in this case, the KCMSD and the State," the district court had not exceeded its authority under *Milliken I.*

DISMANTLING DE JURE SEGREGATION OF STATE UNIVERSITIES

The extensive body of judicial opinions addressing state and local obligations to dismantle *de jure* segregation of public elementary and secondary schools has no counterpart when the issue is the nature and extent of the obligation to remedy de jure segregation of state institutions of higher education. The Court addressed that question in United States v. Fordice, 505 U.S. 717 (1992). Between 1848 and 1950, Mississippi created five state universities exclusively for whites and three exclusively for blacks. Despite Brown v. Board of Education, federal efforts begun in 1969, and 12 years of attempting to settle this action (filed in 1975), "[b]y the mid–1980's ... more than 99 percent of Mississippi's white students were enrolled" at the former group of campuses, whose student bodies "remained predominantly white, averaging between 80 and 91 percent white students[,]" and 71% of the State's black students attended the latter group, "where the racial composition ranged from 92 to 99 percent black." When the case finally went to trial, the state argued that it "had fulfilled its duty to disestablish its state-imposed segregative system by implementing and maintaining good-faith, nondiscriminatory race-neutral policies and practices in student admission, faculty hiring, and operations" and "that the mere continued existence of racially identifiable universities was not unlawful given the freedom of students to choose which institution to attend and the varying objectives and features of the State's universities." The district court "concluded that in the higher education context, 'the affirmative duty to desegregate does not contemplate either restricting choice or the achievement of any degree of racial balance.' " The Court of Appeals affirmed, but the Supreme Court reversed and remanded.

Writing for the Court, Justice White noted that all parties accepted that Mississippi had the constitutional duty to dismantle its formerly *de jure* dual system of higher education. He observed that prior decisions required the state to "eradicate[] policies and practices traceable to its prior *de jure* dual system that continue to foster segregation[.]" Although the Court agreed that universities differ from primary and secondary schools in student choice to seek higher education, no assignment to particular institutions, and the range of different educational missions served by different campuses, it did "not agree ... that the adoption and implementation of race-neutral policies alone suffice to demonstrate that the State has completely abandoned its prior dual system." It held that "[i]f policies traceable to the *de jure* system are still in force and have discriminatory effects, those policies too must be reformed to the extent practicable and consistent with sound educational practices."

Nor did the Court agree that Bazemore v. Friday, 478 U.S. 385 (1986), suggested otherwise:

"*Bazemore* raised the issue whether the financing and operational assistance provided by a state university's extension service to voluntary 4–H and Homemaker Clubs was inconsistent with the Equal Protection Clause because of the existence of numerous all-white and all-black clubs. Though prior to 1965 the clubs were supported on a segregated basis, the District Court had found that the policy of segregation had been completely abandoned and that no evidence existed of any lingering discrimination in either services or membership; any racial imbalance resulted from the wholly voluntary and unfettered choice of private individuals. . . . In this context, we held inapplicable the *Green* Court's judgment that a voluntary choice program was insufficient to dismantle a *de jure* dual system in public primary and secondary schools, but only after satisfying ourselves that the State had not fostered segregation by playing a part in the decision of which club an individual chose to join.

"*Bazemore* plainly does not excuse inquiry into whether Mississippi has left in place certain aspects of its prior dual system that perpetuate the racially segregated higher education system. If the State perpetuates policies and practices traceable to its prior system that continue to have segregative effects—whether by influencing student enrollment decisions or by fostering segregation in other facets of the university system—and such policies are without sound educational justification and can be practicably eliminated, the State has not satisfied its burden of proving that it has dismantled its prior system. . . ."

Without "identify[ing] an exclusive list of unconstitutional remnants of Mississippi's prior *de jure* system[,]" the Court identified "four policies" that had to be justified or eliminated: "admission standards, program duplication, institutional mission assignments, and continued operation of all eight public universities." The requirement of higher standardized test scores for automatic admission to the historically white institutions, when proportionately more blacks than whites did not achieve those scores, was "not only traceable to the *de jure* system and . . . originally adopted for a discriminatory purpose, but . . . also ha[d] present discriminatory effects." So, too, "the differential admissions requirements between universities with dissimilar programmatic missions" was "inadequately justified" given that they "are remnants of the dual system with a continuing discriminatory effect, and the mission assignments 'to some degree follow the historical racial assignments.'" And the refusal to consider high school grades in determining automatic admission when "the disparity between black and white students' high school grade averages was much narrower than the gap between their average ACT scores" was not justified by a concern "with grade inflation and the lack of comparability in grading practices and course offerings among the State's diverse high schools . . . because the ACT requirement was originally adopted for discriminatory purposes, the current requirement is traceable to that decision and seemingly continues to have segregative effects, and the State has so far failed to show that the 'ACT-only' admission standard is not susceptible to elimination without eroding sound educational policy."

Second, the "widespread duplication" of noncore programs at different campuses "was part and parcel of the prior dual system of higher education—the whole notion of 'separate but equal' required duplicative programs in two sets of schools—and . . . the present unnecessary duplication is a continuation of that practice." The district "court's holding that petitioners could not establish the constitutional defect of unnecessary duplication . . . improperly shifted the burden away from the State" and that "court failed to consider the combined effects of unnecessary program duplication with other policies, such as differential admissions standards, in evaluating whether the State had met its duty to dismantle its prior *de jure* segregated system."

Third, the "institutional mission designations adopted in 1981 ha[d] as their antecedents the policies enacted to perpetuate racial separation during the *de jure* segregated regime"—the historically white campuses being the best funded, with "the most advanced and specialized programs" and "the widest range of curricular functions." Given that background and the Court of

Appeals' finding "'that the mission designations had the effect of maintaining the more limited program scope at the historically black universities'" Justice White said:

"... We do not suggest that absent discriminatory purpose the assignment of different missions to various institutions in a State's higher education system would raise an equal protection issue where one or more of the institutions become or remain predominantly black or white. But here the issue is whether the State has sufficiently dismantled its prior dual system; and when combined with the differential admission practices and unnecessary program duplication, it is likely that the mission designations interfere with student choice and tend to perpetuate the segregated system. On remand, the court should inquire whether it would be practicable and consistent with sound educational practices to eliminate any such discriminatory effects of the State's present policy of mission assignments."

Finally, with respect to "continuing to ... operate all eight higher educational institutions[,]" although "certainly closure of one or more ... would decrease the discriminatory effects of the present system, ... based on the present record we are unable to say whether such action is constitutionally required":

"Elimination of program duplication and revision of admissions criteria may make institutional closure unnecessary. However, on remand this issue should be carefully explored by inquiring and determining whether retention of all eight institutions itself affects student choice and perpetuates the segregated higher education system, whether maintenance of each of the universities is educationally justifiable, and whether one or more of them can be practicably closed or merged with other existing institutions.

"... That an institution is predominantly white or black does not in itself make out a constitutional violation. But surely the State may not leave in place policies rooted in its prior officially-segregated system that serve to maintain the racial identifiability of its universities if those policies can practicably be eliminated without eroding sound educational policies."

At the end of his opinion, Justice White added this:

"If we understand private petitioners to press us to order the upgrading of [the three historically black institutions] solely so that they may be publicly financed, exclusively black enclaves by private choice, we reject that request. The State provides these facilities for all its citizens and it has not met its burden under *Brown* to take affirmative steps to dismantle its prior *de jure* system when it perpetuates a separate, but 'more equal' one. Whether such an increase in funding is necessary to achieve a full dismantlement under the standards we have outlined, however, is a different question, and one that must be addressed on remand."

Justice O'Connor, concurring, wrote in part:

"... [T]he circumstances in which a State may maintain a policy or practice traceable to *de jure* segregation that has segregative effects are narrow.... Where the State can accomplish legitimate educational objectives through less segregative means, the courts may infer lack of good faith.... [Also,] if the State shows that maintenance of certain remnants of its prior system is essential to accomplish its legitimate goals, then it still must prove that it has counteracted and minimized the segregative impact of such policies to the extent possible. Only by eliminating a remnant that unnecessarily continues to foster segregation or by negating insofar as possible its segregative impact can the State satisfy its constitutional obligation to dismantle the discriminatory system that should, by now, be only a distant memory."

In another concurring opinion, Justice Thomas wrote "separately to emphasize that ... because [the Court's standard] does not compel the elimination of all observed racial imbalance, it portends neither the destruction of historically black colleges nor the severing of those institutions from their distinctive histories and traditions." When a challenged policy "began during the prior *de jure* era, produces adverse impacts, and persists without sound educational justification ... we are justified in not requiring proof of a present specific intent to discriminate[,] ... both because the State has created the dispute through its own prior unlawful conduct, ... and because discriminatory intent does tend to persist through time." Yet "we do not foreclose the possibility that there exists 'sound educational justification' for maintaining historically black colleges *as such*." Rather,

"I think it undisputable that these institutions have succeeded in part because of their distinctive histories and traditions; for many, historically black colleges have become 'a symbol of the highest attainments of black culture.' ... Obviously, a State cannot maintain such traditions by closing particular institutions, historically white or historically black, to particular racial groups. Nonetheless, it hardly follows that a State cannot operate a diverse assortment of institutions—including historically black institutions—open to all on a race-neutral basis, but with established traditions and programs that might disproportionately appeal to one race or another. No one, I imagine, would argue that such institutional *diversity* is without 'sound educational justification,' or that it is even remotely akin to program *duplication*, which is designed to separate the races for the sake of separating the races ... Although I agree that a State is not constitutionally *required* to maintain its historically black institutions as such, I do not understand our opinion to hold that a State is *forbidden* from doing so. It would be ironic, to say the least, if the institutions that sustained blacks during segregation were themselves destroyed in an effort to combat its vestiges."

Justice Scalia concurred in the judgment in part, but dissented in part. In his view, only practices

"that limit access on discriminatory bases ... have the potential to generate the [stigmatic] harm *Brown I* condemned, and only they have the potential to deny students equal access to the best public education a State has to offer. Legacies of the dual system that permit (or even incidentally facilitate) free choice of racially identifiable schools—while still assuring each individual student the right to attend whatever school he wishes—do not have these consequences.

" ...

"*Bazemore's* standard for dismantling a dual system ought to control here: discontinuation of discriminatory practices and adoption of a neutral admissions policy. [M]odern racial imbalance remains a 'vestige' of past segregative practices in Mississippi's universities, in that the previously mandated racial identification continues to affect where students choose to enroll—just as it surely affected which clubs students chose to join in *Bazemore*. ... Like the club attendance in *Bazemore* (and unlike the school attendance in *Green*), attending college is voluntary, not a legal obligation, and which institution particular students attend is determined by their own choice. ...

"It is my view that the requirement of compelled integration ... does not apply to higher education. Only one aspect of an historically segregated university system need be eliminated: discriminatory admissions standards...."

Justice Scalia, although agreeing that "the Constitution does not *require* equal funding" of HBI's and HWI's, also expressed concern that the Court's test might "*prohibit*[] it." He inferred that "the Court's test is designed to achieve ... the elimination of predominantly black institutions" and objected in the following terms:

"... There is nothing unconstitutional about a 'black' school in the sense, not of a school that blacks *must* attend and that whites *cannot*, but of a school that, as a consequence of private choice in residence or in school selection, contains, and has long contained, a large black majority.... In a perverse way, in fact, the insistence, whether explicit or implicit, that such institutions not be permitted to endure perpetuates the very stigma of black inferiority that *Brown I* sought to destroy. Not only Mississippi but Congress itself seems out of step with the drum that the Court beats today, judging by its passage of an Act entitled 'Strengthening Historically Black Colleges and Universities,' which authorizes the Education Department to provide money grants to historically black colleges...."

C. CLASSIFICATIONS BASED ON GENDER

Reed v. Reed

404 U.S. 71, 92 S.Ct. 251, 30 L.Ed.2d 225 (1971).

[Section 15–314C of the Idaho Code provided that in the choice of persons to administer an intestate estate "[o]f several persons claiming and equally entitled to administer, males must be preferred to females." Solely because of this statute an Idaho court appointed the father rather than the mother of a deceased child as administrator. The mother appealed the decision.]

Mr. Chief Justice Burger delivered the opinion of the Court.

. . .

Section 15–314 is restricted in its operation to those situations where competing applications for letters of administration have been filed by both male and female members of the same entitlement class established by § 15–312. In such situations, § 15–314 provides that different treatment be accorded to the applicants on the basis of their sex; it thus establishes a classification subject to scrutiny under the Equal Protection Clause.

In applying that clause, this Court has consistently recognized that the Fourteenth Amendment does not deny to States the power to treat different classes of persons in different ways. Barbier v. Connolly, 113 U.S. 27; Lindsley v. Natural Carbonic Gas Co., 220 U.S. 61 (1911); Railway Express Agency, Inc. v. New York, 336 U.S. 106 (1949); McDonald v. Board of Election Commissioners, 394 U.S. 802 (1969). The Equal Protection Clause of that Amendment does, however, deny to States the power to legislate that different treatment be accorded to persons placed by a statute into different classes on the basis of criteria wholly unrelated to the objective of that statute. A classification "must be reasonable, not arbitrary, and must rest upon some ground of difference having a fair and substantial relation to the object of the legislation, so that all persons similarly circumstanced shall be treated alike." Royster Guano Co. v. Virginia, 253 U.S. 412, 415 (1920). The question presented by this case, then, is whether a difference in the sex of competing applicants for letters of administration bears a rational relationship to a state objective that is sought to be advanced by the operation of §§ 15–312 and 15–314.

In upholding the latter section, the Idaho Supreme Court concluded that its objective was to eliminate one area of controversy when two or more persons, equally entitled under § 15–312, seek letters of administration and thereby present the probate court "with the issue of which one should be named." The court also concluded that where such persons are not of the same sex, the elimination of females from consideration "is neither an illogical nor arbitrary method devised by the legislature to resolve an issue that would otherwise require a hearing as to the relative merits . . . of the two or more petitioning relatives. . . ." . . .

Clearly the objective of reducing the workload on probate courts by eliminating one class of contests is not without some legitimacy. The crucial question, however, is whether § 15–314 advances that objective in a manner consistent with the command of the Equal Protection Clause. We hold that it does not. To give a mandatory preference to members of either sex over members of the other, merely to accomplish the elimination of hearings on the merits, is to make the very kind of arbitrary legislative choice forbidden by the Equal Protection Clause of the Fourteenth Amendment; and whatever may be said as to the positive values of avoiding intrafamily controversy, the choice in this context may not lawfully be mandated solely on the basis of sex.

. . .

The judgment of the Idaho Supreme Court is reversed and the case remanded for further proceedings not inconsistent with this opinion.

Frontiero v. Richardson

411 U.S. 677, 93 S.Ct. 1764, 36 L.Ed.2d 583 (1973).

Mr. Justice Brennan announced the judgment of the Court in an opinion in which Mr. Justice Douglas, Mr. Justice White, and Mr. Justice Marshall join.

The question before us concerns the right of a female member of the uniformed services to claim her spouse as a "dependent" for the purposes of obtaining increased quarters allowances and medical and dental benefits under 37 U.S.C. §§ 401, 403, and 10 U.S.C. §§ 1072, 1076, on an equal footing with male members. Under these statutes, a serviceman may claim his wife as a "dependent" without regard to whether she is in fact dependent upon him for any part of her support. . . . A servicewoman, on the other hand, may not claim her husband as a "dependent" under these programs unless he is in fact dependent upon her for over one-half of his support. . . . Thus, the question for decision is whether this difference in treatment constitutes an unconstitutional discrimination against servicewomen in violation of the Due Process Clause of the Fifth Amendment. A three-judge District Court for the Middle District of Alabama, one judge dissenting, rejected this contention . . . We reverse.

I.

In an effort to attract career personnel through reenlistment, Congress established . . . fringe benefits [for] members of the uniformed services on a competitive basis with business and industry. Thus, under 37 U.S.C. § 403, a member of the uniformed services with dependents is entitled to an increased "basic allowance for quarters" and, under 10 U.S.C. § 1076, a member's dependents are provided comprehensive medical and dental care.

Appellant Sharron Frontiero, a lieutenant in the United States Air Force, sought increased quarters allowances, and housing and medical benefits for her husband ... on the ground that he was her "dependent." Although such benefits would automatically have been granted with respect to the wife of a male member of the uniformed services, appellant's application was denied because she failed to demonstrate that her husband was dependent on her for more than one-half of his support. Appellants then commenced this suit, contending that, by making this distinction, the statutes unreasonably discriminate on the basis of sex in violation of the Due Process Clause of the Fifth Amendment. In essence, appellants asserted that the discriminatory impact of the statutes is two-fold: first, as a procedural matter, a female member is required to demonstrate her spouse's dependency, while no such burden is imposed upon male members; and second, as a substantive matter, a male member who does not provide more than one-half of his wife's support receives benefits, while a similarly situated female member is denied such benefits....

Although the legislative history of these statutes sheds virtually no light on the purposes underlying the differential treatment accorded male and female members, a majority of the three-judge District Court surmised that Congress might reasonably have concluded that, since the husband in our society is generally the "breadwinner" in the family—and the wife typically the "dependent" partner—"it would be more economical to require married female members claiming husbands to prove actual dependency than to extend the presumption of dependency to such members." 341 F.Supp., at 207. Indeed, given the fact that approximately 99% of all members of the uniformed services are male, the District Court speculated that such differential treatment might conceivably lead to a "considerable saving of administrative expense and manpower." Ibid.

II.

At the outset, appellants contend that classifications based upon sex, like classifications based upon race, alienage, and national origin, are inherently suspect and must therefore be subjected to close judicial scrutiny. We agree and, indeed, find at least implicit support for such an approach in our unanimous decision only last Term in Reed v. Reed, 404 U.S. 71 (1971)....

There can be no doubt that our Nation has had a long and unfortunate history of sex discrimination. Traditionally, such discrimination was rationalized by an attitude of "romantic paternalism" which, in practical effect, put women not on a pedestal, but in a cage. Indeed, this paternalistic attitude became so firmly rooted in our national consciousness that, exactly 100 years ago, a distinguished member of this Court was able to proclaim:

"Man is, or should be, woman's protector and defender. The natural and proper timidity and delicacy which belongs to the female sex evidently unfits it for many of the occupations of civil life. The constitution of the family organization, which is founded in the divine ordinance, as well as in the nature of things, indicates the domestic sphere as that which properly belongs to the domain and functions of womanhood. The harmony, not to say identity, of interests and views which belong, or should belong, to the family institution is repugnant to the ideas of a woman adopting a distinct and independent career from that of her husband....

"... The paramount destiny and mission of women are to fulfil the noble and benign offices of wife and mother. This is the law of the

Creator." Bradwell v. Illinois, 83 U.S. [16 Wall.] 130, 141 (1873) (Bradley, J., concurring).

As a result of notions such as these, our statute books gradually became laden with gross, stereotypical distinctions between the sexes and, indeed, throughout much of the 19th century the position of women in our society was, in many respects, comparable to that of blacks under the pre-Civil War slave codes. Neither slaves nor women could hold office, serve on juries, or bring suit in their own names, and married women traditionally were denied the legal capacity to hold or convey property or to serve as legal guardians of their own children. See generally, L. Kanowitz, Women and the Law: The Unfinished Revolution 5–6 (1969); G. Mydral, An American Dilemma 1073 (2d ed. 1962). And although blacks were guaranteed the right to vote in 1870, women were denied even that right—which is itself "preservative of other basic civil and political rights"—until adoption of the Nineteenth Amendment half a century later.

It is true, of course, that the position of women in America has improved markedly in recent decades. Nevertheless, it can hardly be doubted that, in part because of the high visibility of the sex characteristic, women still face pervasive, although at times more subtle, discrimination in our educational institutions, on the job market and, perhaps most conspicuously, in the political arena.[17] See generally, K. Amundsen, The Silenced Majority: Women and American Democracy (1971); The President's Task Force on Women's Rights and Responsibilities, A Matter of Simple Justice (1970).

Moreover, since sex, like race and national origin, is an immutable characteristic determined solely by the accident of birth, the imposition of special disabilities upon the members of a particular sex because of their sex would seem to violate "the basic concept of our system that legal burdens should bear some relationship to individual responsibility...." Weber v. Aetna Casualty & Surety Co., 406 U.S. 164, 175 (1972). And what differentiates sex from such nonsuspect statuses as intelligence or physical disability, and aligns it with the recognized suspect criteria, is that the sex characteristic frequently bears no relation to ability to perform or contribute to society. As a result, statutory distinctions between the sexes often have the effect of invidiously relegating the entire class of females to inferior legal status without regard to the actual capabilities of its individual members.

We might also note that, over the past decade, Congress has itself manifested an increasing sensitivity to sex-based classifications. In Tit. VII of the Civil Rights Act of 1964, for example, Congress expressly declared that no employer, labor union, or other organization subject to the provisions of the Act shall discriminate against any individual on the basis of "race, color, religion, sex, or national origin." Similarly, the Equal Pay Act of 1963 provides that no employer covered by the Act "shall discriminate ... between employees on the basis of sex." And § 1 of the Equal Rights Amendment, passed by Congress on March 22, 1972, and submitted to the legislatures of the States for ratification, declares that "[e]quality of rights under the law shall not be denied or abridged by the United States or by any State on account of sex." Thus, Congress has itself concluded that classifications based upon sex are inherently invidious, and

---

[17] It is true, of course, that when viewed in the abstract, women do not constitute a small and powerless minority. Nevertheless, in part because of past discrimination, women are vastly underrepresented in this Nation's decisionmaking councils. There has never been a female President, nor a female member of this Court. Not a single woman presently sits in the United States Senate, and only 14 women hold seats in the House of Representatives. And, as appellants point out, this underrepresentation is present throughout all levels of our State and Federal Government.

this conclusion of a coequal branch of Government is not without significance to the question presently under consideration. . . .

With these considerations in mind, we can only conclude that classifications based upon sex, like classifications based upon race, alienage, or national origin, are inherently suspect, and must therefore be subjected to strict judicial scrutiny. Applying the analysis mandated by that stricter standard of review, it is clear that the statutory scheme now before us is constitutionally invalid.

III.

The sole basis of the classification established in the challenged statutes is the sex of the individuals involved. . . .

Moreover, the Government concedes that the differential treatment accorded men and women under these statutes serves no purpose other than mere "administrative convenience." In essence, the Government maintains that, as an empirical matter, wives in our society frequently are dependent upon their husbands, while husbands rarely are dependent upon their wives. Thus, the Government argues that Congress might reasonably have concluded that it would be both cheaper and easier simply conclusively to presume that wives of male members are financially dependent upon their husbands, while burdening female members with the task of establishing dependency in fact.[22]

The Government offers no concrete evidence, however, tending to support its view that such differential treatment in fact saves the Government any money. In order to satisfy the demands of strict judicial scrutiny, the Government must demonstrate, for example, that it is actually cheaper to grant increased benefits with respect to *all* male members, than it is to determine which male members are in fact entitled to such benefits and to grant increased benefits only to those members whose wives actually meet the dependency requirement. Here, however, there is substantial evidence that, if put to the test, many of the wives of male members would fail to qualify for benefits. And in light of the fact that the dependency determination with respect to the husbands of female members is presently made solely on the basis of affidavits rather than through the more costly hearing process, the Government's explanation of the statutory scheme is, to say the least, questionable.

In any case, our prior decisions make clear that, although efficacious administration of governmental programs is not without some importance, "the Constitution recognizes higher values than speed and efficiency." Stanley v. Illinois, 405 U.S. 645, 656 (1972). And when we enter the realm of "strict judicial scrutiny," there can be no doubt that "administrative convenience" is not a shibboleth, the mere recitation of which dictates constitutionality. See Shapiro v. Thompson, 394 U.S. 618 (1969); Carrington v. Rash, 380 U.S. 89 (1965). On the contrary, any statutory scheme which draws a sharp line between the sexes, *solely* for the purpose of achieving administrative convenience, necessarily commands "dissimilar treatment for men and women who are . . . similarly situated," and therefore involves the "very kind of arbitrary legislative choice forbidden by the [Constitution]. . . ." Reed v. Reed. . . . We therefore conclude that, by according differential treatment to male and female members of the uniformed services for the sole purpose of achieving administrative convenience, the challenged statutes violate the Due Process Clause of

---

[22] It should be noted that these statutes are not in any sense designed to rectify the effects of past discrimination against women. . . . On the contrary, these statutes seize upon a group—women—who have historical-ly suffered discrimination in employment, and rely on the effects of this past discrimination as a justification for heaping on additional economic disadvantages. . . .

the Fifth Amendment insofar as they require a female member to prove the dependency of her husband.

Reversed.

Mr. Justice Stewart concurs in the judgment, agreeing that the statutes before us work an invidious discrimination in violation of the Constitution. Reed v. Reed, 404 U.S. 71.

Mr. Justice Rehnquist dissents for the reasons stated by Judge Rives in his opinion for the District Court, Frontiero v. Laird, 341 F.Supp. 201 (1972).

Mr. Justice Powell, with whom The Chief Justice and Mr. Justice Blackmun join, concurring in the judgment.

I agree that the challenged statutes constitute an unconstitutional discrimination against service women in violation of the Due Process Clause of the Fifth Amendment, but I cannot join the opinion of Mr. Justice Brennan, which would hold that all classifications based upon sex, "like classifications based upon race, alienage, and national origin," are "inherently suspect and must therefore be subjected to close judicial scrutiny." . . . It is unnecessary for the Court in this case to characterize sex as a suspect classification, with all of the far-reaching implications of such a holding. Reed v. Reed, 404 U.S. 71 (1971), which abundantly supports our decision today, did not add sex to the narrowly limited group of classifications which are inherently suspect. In my view, we can and should decide this case on the authority of *Reed* and reserve for the future any expansion of its rationale.

There is another, and I find compelling, reason for deferring a general categorizing of sex classifications as invoking the strictest test of judicial scrutiny. The Equal Rights Amendment, which if adopted will resolve the substance of this precise question, has been approved by the Congress and submitted for ratification by the States. If this Amendment is duly adopted, it will represent the will of the people accomplished in the manner prescribed by the Constitution. By acting prematurely and unnecessarily, as I view it, the Court has assumed a decisional responsibility at the very time when state legislatures, functioning within the traditional democratic process, are debating the proposed Amendment. It seems to me that this reaching out to preempt by judicial action a major political decision which is currently in process of resolution does not reflect appropriate respect for duly prescribed legislative processes.

There are times when this Court, under our system, cannot avoid a constitutional decision on issues which normally should be resolved by the elected representatives of the people. But democratic institutions are weakened, and confidence in the restraint of the Court is impaired, when we appear unnecessarily to decide sensitive issues of broad social and political importance at the very time they are under consideration within the prescribed constitutional processes.

Craig v. Boren

429 U.S. 190, 97 S.Ct. 451, 50 L.Ed.2d 397 (1976).

Mr. Justice Brennan delivered the opinion of the Court.

The interaction of two sections of an Oklahoma statute . . . prohibits the sale of "nonintoxicating" 3.2% beer to males under the age of 21 and to females under the age of 18. The question to be decided is whether such a gender-based differential constitutes a denial to males 18–20 years of age of the Equal Protection of the Laws in violation of the Fourteenth Amendment.

This action ... by appellant Craig, a male then between 18 and 21 years of age, and by appellant Whitener, a licensed vendor of 3.2% beer ... sought declaratory and injunctive relief against enforcement of the gender-based differential on the ground that it constituted invidious discrimination against males 18–20 years of age. A three-judge court ... sustained [its] constitutionality and dismissed the action.... We reverse.

. . .

II.

A.

... To withstand constitutional challenge, previous cases establish that classifications by gender must serve important governmental objectives and must be substantially related to achievement of those objectives. Thus, in *Reed*, the objectives of "reducing the workload on probate courts," ... and "avoiding intra-family controversy," ... were deemed of insufficient importance to sustain use of an overt gender criterion in the appointment of intestate administrators. Decisions following *Reed* similarly have rejected administrative ease and convenience as sufficiently important objectives to justify gender-based classifications. See, e.g., Stanley v. Illinois, 405 U.S. 645, 656 (1972); Frontiero v. Richardson, 411 U.S. 677, 690 (1973); cf. Schlesinger v. Ballard, 419 U.S. 498, 506–507 (1975). And only two Terms ago Stanton v. Stanton, 421 U.S. 7 (1975), expressly stating that *Reed v. Reed* was "controlling," id., at 13, held that *Reed* required invalidation of a Utah differential age-of-majority statute, notwithstanding the statute's coincidence with and furtherance of the State's purpose of fostering "old notions" of role-typing and preparing boys for their expected performance in the economic and political worlds. Id., at 14–15.[6]

Reed v. Reed has also provided the underpinning for decisions that have invalidated statutes employing gender as an inaccurate proxy for other, more germane bases of classification. Hence, "archaic and overbroad" generalizations, *Schlesinger v. Ballard*, ... concerning the financial position of servicewomen, *Frontiero v. Richardson*, ... and working women, Weinberger v. Wiesenfeld, 420 U.S. 636, 643 (1975), could not justify use of a gender line in determining eligibility for certain governmental entitlements. Similarly, increasingly outdated misconceptions concerning the role of females in the home rather than in the "marketplace and world of ideas" were rejected as loose-fitting characterizations incapable of supporting state statutory schemes that were premised upon their accuracy.... In light of the weak congruence between gender and the characteristic or trait that gender purported to represent, it was necessary that the legislatures choose either to realign their substantive laws in a gender-neutral fashion, or to adopt procedures for identifying those instances where the sex-centered generalization actually com-

---

[6] Kahn v. Shevin, 416 U.S. 351 (1974) and Schlesinger v. Ballard, 419 U.S. 498 (1975), upholding the use of gender-based classifications, rested upon the Court's perception of the laudatory purposes of those laws as remedying disadvantageous conditions suffered by women in economic and military life. See 416 U.S., at 353–354; 419 U.S., at 508. Needless to say, in this case Oklahoma does not suggest that the age-sex differential was enacted to ensure the availability of 3.2% beer for women as compensation for previous deprivations.

ported to fact. See, e.g., Stanley v. Illinois, ...; cf. Cleveland Board of Educ. v. LaFleur, 414 U.S. 632, 650 (1974).

In this case, too, "*Reed* we feel, is controlling ...," *Stanton v. Stanton.* ... We turn then to the question whether, under *Reed,* the difference between males and females with respect to the purchase of 3.2% beer warrants the differential in age drawn by the Oklahoma statute. We conclude that it does not.

B.

The District Court ... found the requisite important governmental objective in the traffic-safety goal proffered by the Oklahoma Attorney General. It then concluded that the statistics introduced by the appellees established that the gender-based distinction was substantially related to achievement of that goal.

C.

We accept for purposes of discussion the District Court's identification of the objective underlying §§ 241 and 245 as the enhancement of traffic safety.[7] Clearly, the protection of public health and safety represents an important function of state and local governments. However, appellees' statistics in our view cannot support the conclusion that the gender-based distinction closely serves to achieve that objective and therefore the distinction cannot under *Reed* withstand equal protection challenge.

The appellees introduced a variety of statistical surveys. First, an analysis of arrest statistics for 1973 demonstrated that 18–20–year–old male arrests for "driving under the influence" and "drunkenness" substantially exceeded female arrests for that same age period.[8] Similarly, youths aged 17–21 were found to be overrepresented among those killed or injured in traffic accidents, with males again numerically exceeding females in this regard.[9] Third, a random roadside survey in Oklahoma City revealed that young males were more inclined to drive and drink beer than were their female counterparts.[10] Fourth, Federal Bureau of Investigation nationwide statistics exhibited a notable in-

---

[7] That this was the true purpose is not at all self-evident. The purpose is not apparent from the face of the statute and the Oklahoma Legislature does not preserve statutory history materials capable of clarifying the objectives served by its legislative enactments. The District Court acknowledged the nonexistence of materials necessary "to reveal what the actual purpose of the legislature was," but concluded that "we feel it apparent that a major purpose of the legislature was to promote the safety of the young persons affected and the public generally." 399 F.Supp., at 1311 n. 6. Similarly, the attorney for Oklahoma, while proposing traffic safety as a legitimate rationale for the 3.2% beer law, candidly acknowledged at oral argument that he is unable to assert that traffic safety is "indeed the reason" for the gender line contained in § 245. For this appeal we find adequate the appellee's representation of legislative purpose, leaving for another day consideration of whether the statement of the State's Assistant Attorney General should suffice to inform this Court of the legislature's objectives, or whether the Court must determine if the litigant simply is selecting a convenient, but false, *post-hoc* rationalization.

[8] The disparities in 18–20–year–old male-female arrests were substantial for both categories of offenses: 427 versus 24 for driving under the influence of alcohol and 966 versus 102 for drunkenness. Even if we assume that a legislature may rely on such arrest data in some situations, these figures do not offer support for a differential age line, for the disproportionate arrests of males persisted at older ages; indeed, in the case of arrests for drunkenness, the figures for all ages indicated "even more male involvement in such arrests at later ages." 399 F.Supp., at 1309. See also n. 14, infra.

[9] This survey drew no correlation between the accident figures for any age group and levels of intoxication found in those killed or injured.

[10] For an analysis of the results of this exhibit, see n. 16, infra.

crease in arrests for "driving under the influence."[11] Finally, statistical evidence gathered in other jurisdictions, particularly Minnesota and Michigan, was offered to corroborate Oklahoma's experience by indicating the pervasiveness of youthful participation in motor vehicle accidents following the imbibing of alcohol. Conceding that "the case is not free from doubt," ... the District Court nonetheless concluded that this statistical showing substantiated "a rational basis for the legislative judgment underlying the challenged classification." ...

Even were this statistical evidence accepted as accurate, it nevertheless offers only a weak answer to the equal protection question presented here. The most focused and relevant of the statistical surveys, arrests of 18–20–year–olds for alcohol-related driving offenses, exemplifies the ultimate unpersuasiveness of this evidentiary record. Viewed in terms of the correlation between sex and the actual activity that Oklahoma seeks to regulate—driving while under the influence of alcohol—the statistics broadly establish that .18% of females and 2% of males in that age group were arrested for that offense. While such a disparity is not trivial in a statistical sense, it hardly can form the basis for employment of a gender line as a classifying device. Certainly if maleness is to serve as a proxy for drinking and driving a correlation of 2% must be considered an unduly tenuous "fit." Indeed, prior cases have consistently rejected the use of sex as a decisionmaking factor even though the statutes in question certainly rested on far more predictive empirical relationships than this.[13]

Moreover, the statistics exhibit a variety of other shortcomings that seriously impugn their value to equal protection analysis. Setting aside the obvious methodological problems,[14] the surveys do not adequately justify the salient features of Oklahoma's gender-based traffic-safety law. None purports to measure the use and dangerousness of 3.2% beer as opposed to alcohol generally, a detail that is of particular importance since, in light of its low alcohol level, Oklahoma apparently considers the 3.2% beverage to be "non-intoxicating." 37 Okla.Stat. § 163.1 (1971); see State ex rel. Springer v. Bliss, 199 Okla. 198, 185 P.2d 220 (1947). Moreover, many of the studies, while graphically documenting the unfortunate increase in driving while under the influence of alcohol, make no effort to relate their findings to age-sex differentials as involved here.

[11] The FBI made no attempt to relate these arrest figures either to beer drinking or to an 18–21 age differential, but rather found that male arrests for all ages exceeded 90% of the total.

[13] For example, we can conjecture that in *Reed*, Idaho's apparent premise that women lacked experience in formal business matters (particularly compared to men) would have proved to be accurate in substantially more than 2% of all cases. And in both *Frontiero* and *Wiesenfeld*, we expressly found the government's empirical defense of mandatory dependency tests for men but not women to be unsatisfactory, even though we recognized that husbands still are far less likely to be dependent on their wives than vice versa. ...

[14] The very social stereotypes that find reflection in age differential laws, see Stanton v. Stanton, supra, 421 U.S., at 114–15, are likely substantially to distort the accuracy of these comparative statistics. Hence "reckless" young men who drink and drive are transformed into arrest statistics, whereas their female counterparts are chivalrously escorted home. See, e.g., W. Reckless & B. Kay, The Female Offender 4, 7, 13, 16–17 (Report to Pres. Comm'n on Law Enforcement & Admin. of Justice, 1967). Moreover, the Oklahoma surveys, gathered under a regime where the age-differential law in question has been in effect, are lacking in controls necessary for appraisal of the actual effectiveness of the male 3.2% beer prohibition. In this regard, the disproportionately high arrest statistics for young males—and, indeed, the growing alcohol-related arrest figures for all ages and sexes—simply may be taken to document the relative futility of controlling driving behavior by the 3.2 beer statute and like legislation, although we obviously have no means of estimating how many individuals, if any, actually were prevented from drinking by these laws.

Indeed, the only survey that explicitly centered its attention upon young drivers and their use of beer—albeit apparently not of the diluted 3.2% variety—reached results that hardly can be viewed as impressive in justifying either a gender or age classification.[16]

There is no reason to belabor this line of analysis. It is unrealistic to expect either members of the judiciary or state officials to be well versed in the rigors of experimental or statistical technique. But this merely illustrates that proving broad sociological propositions by statistics is a dubious business, and one that inevitably is in tension with the normative philosophy that underlies the Equal Protection Clause. Suffice to say that the showing offered by the appellees does not satisfy us that sex represents a legitimate, accurate proxy for the regulation of drinking and driving. In fact, when it is further recognized that Oklahoma's statute prohibits only the selling of 3.2% beer to young males and not their drinking the beverage once acquired (even after purchase by their 18–20–year-old female companions), the relationship between gender and traffic safety becomes far too tenuous to satisfy *Reed's* requirement that the gender-based difference be substantially related to achievement of the statutory objective.

We hold, therefore, that under *Reed,* Oklahoma's 3.2% beer statute invidiously discriminates against males 18–20 years of age.

D.

Appellees argue, however, that §§ 241 and 245 enforce state policies concerning the sale and distribution of alcohol and by force of the Twenty-first Amendment should therefore be held to withstand the equal protection challenge.... The Twenty-first Amendment ... primarily created an exception to the normal operation of the Commerce Clause. See, e.g., Hostetter v. Idlewild Bon Voyage Liquor Corp., 377 U.S. 324, 330 (1964);....

[Its] relevance ... to other constitutional provisions becomes increasingly doubtful....

[B]oth federal and state courts uniformly have declared the unconstitutionality of gender lines that restrain the activities of customers of state-regulated liquor establishments irrespective of the operation of the Twenty-first Amendment.... Even when state officials have posited sociological or empirical justifications for these gender-based differentiations, the courts have struck down discriminations aimed at an entire class under the guise of alcohol regulation. In fact, social science studies that have uncovered quantifiable differences in drinking tendencies dividing along both racial and ethnic lines strongly suggest the need for application of the Equal Protection Clause in preventing discriminatory treatment that almost certainly would be perceived

---

[16] The random roadside survey of drivers conducted in Oklahoma City during August of 1972 found that 78% of drivers under 20 were male. Turning to an evaluation of their drinking habits and factoring out nondrinkers, 84% of the males versus 77% of the females expressed a preference for beer. Further 16.5% of the men and 11.4% of the women had consumed some alcoholic beverage within two hours of the interview. Finally, a blood alcohol concentration greater than .1% was discovered in 14.6% of the males compared to 11.5% of the females. "The 1973 figures, although they contain some variations, reflect essentially the same pattern." 399 F.Supp., at 1309. Plainly these statistical disparities between the sexes are not substantial. Moreover, when the 18–20 age boundaries are lifted and all drivers analyzed, the 1972 roadside survey indicates that male drinking rose slightly whereas female exposure to alcohol remained relatively constant. Again, in 1973, the survey established that "compared to all drivers interviewed, ... the under–20 age group generally showed a lower involvement with alcohol in terms of having drunk within the past two hours or having a significant BAC (blood alcohol content)." Id., at 1309. In sum, this survey provides little support for a gender line among teenagers and actually runs counter to the imposition of drinking restrictions based upon age.

as invidious.[22] In sum, the principles embodied in the Equal Protection Clause are not to be rendered inapplicable by statistically measured but loose-fitting generalities concerning the drinking tendencies of aggregate groups. We thus hold that the operation of the Twenty-first Amendment does not alter the application of equal protection standards that otherwise govern this case.

We conclude that the gender-based differential contained in 37 Okla.Stat. § 245 constitutes a denial of the Equal Protection of the Laws to males aged 18–20[23] and reverse the judgment of the District Court.[24]

Mr. Justice Stewart, concurring.

. . .

Mr. Justice Blackmun, concurring.

I join the Court's opinion except Part II–D thereof. I agree, however, that the Twenty-first Amendment does not save the challenged Oklahoma statute.

Mr. Justice Powell, concurring.

I join the opinion of the Court as I am in general agreement with it. I do have reservations as to some of the discussion concerning the appropriate standard for equal protection analysis and the relevance of the statistical evidence. Accordingly, I add this concurring statement.

With respect to the equal protection standard, I agree that Reed v. Reed, 404 U.S. 71 (1971), is the most relevant precedent. But I find it unnecessary, in deciding this case, to read that decision as broadly as some of the Court's language may imply. *Reed* and subsequent cases involving gender-based classifications make clear that the Court subjects such classifications to a more critical examination than is normally applied when "fundamental" constitutional rights and "suspect classes" are not present.*

. . .

[22] Thus, if statistics were to govern the permissibility of state alcohol regulation without regard to the Equal Protection Clause as a limiting principle, it might follow that States could freely favor Jews and Italian Catholics at the expense of all other Americans, since available studies regularly demonstrate that the former two groups exhibit the lowest rates of problem drinking. . . .

In the past, some States have acted upon their notions of the drinking propensities of entire groups in fashioning their alcohol policies. The most typical recipient of this treatment has been the American Indian; indeed, several States established criminal sanctions for the sale of alcohol to an Indian or "half or quarter breed Indian." See, e.g., Fla.Stat. Ann. § 569.07 (1962) (repealed in 1972); Iowa Code Ann. § 732.5 (1950) (repealed in 1967); Minn.Stat. § 340.82 (1947) (repealed in 1969); Neb.Rev.Stat. 53–181 (1944) (repealed in 1955); Utah Code Ann. § 76–34–1 (1953) (repealed in 1955). Other statutes and constitutional provisions proscribed the introduction of alcoholic beverages onto Indian reservations. See, e.g., C. 310, § 2, 36 Stat. 558 (1910); Ariz.Ann. Const. Art. XX(3); N.M.Stat.Ann. Const. Art. XXI, § 8; Okla.

Stat.Ann. Const. Art. I, § 7. While Indian-oriented provisions were the most common, state alcohol beverage prohibitions also have been directed at other groups, notably German, Italian, and Catholic immigrants. See, e.g., J. Higham, Strangers In the Land 25, 267–268, 295 (1975). The repeal of most of these laws signals society's perception of the unfairness and questionable constitutionality of singling out groups to bear the brunt of alcohol regulation.

[23] Insofar as Goesaert v. Cleary, 335 U.S. 464 (1948), may be inconsistent, that decision is disapproved. . . .

[24] As noted in Stanton v. Stanton, supra, 421 U.S., at 17–18, the Oklahoma Legislature is free to redefine any cutoff age for the purchase and sale of 3.2 beer that it may choose, provided that the redefinition operates in a gender-neutral fashion.

* As is evident from our opinions, the Court has had difficulty in agreeing upon a standard of equal protection analysis that can be applied consistently to the wide variety of legislative classifications. There are valid reasons for dissatisfaction with the "two-tier" approach that has been prominent in the Court's decisions in the past

Mr. Justice Stevens, concurring.

There is only one Equal Protection Clause. It requires every State to govern impartially. It does not direct the courts to apply one standard of review in some cases and a different standard in other cases. Whatever criticism may be levelled at a judicial opinion implying that there are at least three such standards applies with the same force to a double standard.

I am inclined to believe that what has become known as the two-tiered analysis of equal protection claims does not describe a completely logical method of deciding cases, but rather is a method the Court has employed to explain decisions that actually apply a single standard in a reasonably consistent fashion. I also suspect that a careful explanation of the reasons motivating particular decisions may contribute more to an identification of that standard than an attempt to articulate it in all-encompassing terms. It may therefore be appropriate for me to state the principal reasons which persuaded me to join the Court's opinion.

In this case, the classification is not as obnoxious as some the Court has condemned, nor as inoffensive as some the Court has accepted. It is objectionable because it is based on an accident of birth, because it is a mere remnant of the now almost universally rejected tradition of discriminating against males in this age bracket, and because, to the extent it reflects any physical difference between males and females, it is actually perverse. The question then is whether the traffic safety justification put forward by the State is sufficient to make an otherwise offensive classification acceptable.

The classification is not totally irrational. For the evidence does indicate that there are more males than females in this age bracket who drive and also more who drink. Nevertheless, there are several reasons why I regard the justification as unacceptable. It is difficult to believe that the statute was actually intended to cope with the problem of traffic safety, since it has only a minimal effect on access to a not-very-intoxicating beverage and does not prohibit its consumption. Moreover, the empirical data submitted by the State accentuates the unfairness of treating all 18–21–year–old males as inferior to their female counterparts. The legislation imposes a restraint on one hundred percent of the males in the class allegedly because about 2% of them have probably violated one or more laws relating to the consumption of alcoholic beverages. It is unlikely that this law will have a significant deterrent effect either on that 2% or on the law-abiding 98%. But even assuming some such slight benefit, it does not seem to me that an insult to all of the young men of the State can be justified by visiting the sins of the 2% on the 98%.

Mr. Chief Justice Burger, dissenting.

I am in general agreement with Mr. Justice Rehnquist's dissent. . . .

. . .

decade. Although viewed by many as a result-oriented substitute for more critical analysis, that approach—with its narrowly limited "upper-tier"—now has substantial precedential support. As has been true of *Reed* and its progeny, our decision today will be viewed by some as a "middle-tier" approach. While I would not endorse that characterization and would not welcome a further subdividing of equal protection analysis, candor compels the recognition that the relatively deferential "rational basis" standard of review normally applied takes on a sharper focus when we address a gender-based classification. So much is clear from our recent cases. For thoughtful discussions of equal protection analysis, see, e.g., Gunther, The Supreme Court, 1971 Term—Foreword: In Search of Evolving Doctrine on a Changing Court: A Model for Newer Equal Protection, 86 Harv.L.Rev. 1 (1972); Wilkinson, The Supreme Court, the Equal Protection Clause, and the Three Faces of Constitutional Equality, 61 Va.L.Rev. 945 (1975).

Though today's decision does not go so far as to make gender-based classifications "suspect," it makes gender a disfavored classification. Without an independent constitutional basis supporting the right asserted or disfavoring the classification adopted, I can justify no substantive constitutional protection other than the normal McGowan v. Maryland, 366 U.S., at 425–426, protection afforded by the Equal Protection Clause.

. . .

Mr. Justice Rehnquist, dissenting.

The Court's disposition of this case is objectionable on two grounds. First is its conclusion that *men* challenging a gender-based statute which treats them less favorably than women may invoke a more stringent standard of judicial review than pertains to most other types of classifications. Second is the Court's enunciation of this standard, without citation to any source, as being that "classifications by gender must serve *important* governmental objectives and must be *substantially* related to achievement of those objectives." (emphasis added). The only redeeming feature of the Court's opinion, to my mind, is that it apparently signals a retreat by those who joined the plurality opinion in Frontiero v. Richardson, 411 U.S. 677 (1973), from their view that sex is a "suspect" classification for purposes of equal protection analysis. I think the Oklahoma statute challenged here need pass only the "rational basis" equal protection analysis expounded in cases such as McGowan v. Maryland, 366 U.S. 420 (1961), and Williamson v. Lee Optical Co., 348 U.S. 483 (1955), and I believe that it is constitutional under that analysis.

. . .

CLASSIFICATIONS ADVANTAGING FEMALES

The Court in Craig v. Boren (in footnote 6) refers to cases such as Kahn v. Shevin, 416 U.S. 351 (1974), upholding classifications designed to remedy past discrimination against women. That case and others will be discussed in Subsection E, infra, dealing with "benign" discrimination in cases involving gender and in cases involving race.

WHAT CONSTITUTES DISCRIMINATION BASED ON GENDER?

In Geduldig v. Aiello, 417 U.S. 484 (1974) the Court rejected a challenge to the California disability insurance program which excluded from its coverage disabilities resulting from normal pregnancy. Justice Stewart, speaking for the Court, said, in part:

"The State has a legitimate interest in maintaining the self-supporting nature of its insurance program. Similarly, it has an interest in distributing the available resources in such a way as to keep benefit payments at an adequate level for disabilities that are covered, rather than to cover all disabilities inadequately. Finally, California has a legitimate concern in maintaining the contribution rate at a level that will not unduly burden participating employees, particularly low-income employees who may be most in need of the disability insurance.

"These policies provide an objective and wholly non-invidious basis for the State's decision not to create a more comprehensive insurance program than it has. There is no evidence in the record that the selection of the risks insured by the program worked to discriminate against any definable group or class in terms of the aggregate risk protection derived by that group or class from the program.[20] There is no risk from which men are protected and women are not. Likewise, there is no risk from which women are protected and men are not.[21]

"The appellee simply contends that, although she has received insurance protection equivalent to that provided all other participating employees, she has suffered discrimination because she encountered a risk that was outside the program's protection. For the reasons we have stated, we hold that this contention is not a valid one under the Equal Protection Clause of the Fourteenth Amendment."

Justices Brennan, Douglas, and Marshall dissented on the ground that the *Reed* and *Frontiero* cases "mandate a stricter standard of scrutiny which the State's classification fails to satisfy."

In General Elec. Co. v. Gilbert, 429 U.S. 125 (1976), the Court held that a private company's disability plan which excluded disabilities arising from pregnancy did not violate Title VII of the Civil Rights Act of 1964, because, as in *Geduldig,* the classification did not involve discrimination based on sex. Justice Stevens disagreed, arguing in dissent that the classification was sex-based because "[t]he classification is between persons who face a risk of pregnancy and those who do not."

In Nashville Gas Co. v. Satty, 434 U.S. 136 (1977), the Court held that Title VII did not prohibit a private company policy providing sick leave pay for nonoccupational disabilities other than pregnancy, but did prohibit a policy that denied female employees returning to work after a pregnancy leave the accumulated seniority it granted others returning from sick leave. The Court said that the loss of seniority for pregnancy leaves differed from the failure to pay during the leave, because "petitioner has not merely refused to extend to women a benefit that men cannot and do not receive, but has imposed on women a substantial burden that men need not suffer." It also said that "[t]he distinction between burdens and benefits is more than one of semantics[,]" and that Title VII does not "permit an employer to burden female employees in such a way as to deprive them of employment opportunities because of their

[20] The dissenting opinion to the contrary, this case is thus a far cry from cases like Reed v. Reed, 404 U.S. 71, and Frontiero v. Richardson, 411 U.S. 677, involving discrimination based upon gender as such. The California insurance program does not exclude anyone from benefit eligibility because of gender but merely removes one physical condition—pregnancy—from the list of compensable disabilities. While it is true that only women can become pregnant, it does not follow that every legislative classification concerning pregnancy is a sex-based classification like those considered in *Reed,* supra, and *Frontiero,* supra. Normal pregnancy is an objectively identifiable physical condition with unique characteristics. Absent a showing that distinctions involving pregnancy are mere pretexts designed to effect an invidious discrimination against the members of one sex or the other, lawmakers are constitutionally free to include or exclude pregnancy from the coverage of legislation such as this on any reasonable basis, just as with respect to any other physical condition.

The lack of identity between the excluded disability and gender as such under this insurance program becomes clear upon the most cursory analysis. The program divides potential recipients into two groups—pregnant women and nonpregnant persons. While the first group is exclusively female, the second includes members of both sexes. The fiscal and actuarial benefits of the program thus accrue to members of both sexes.

[21] Indeed, the appellant submitted to the District Court data that indicated that both the annual claim rate and the annual claim cost are greater for women than for men. As the District Court acknowledged, "women contribute 28 per cent of the total disability insurance fund and receive back about 38 per cent of the fund in benefits." 359 F.Supp., at 800. Several *amici curiae* have represented to the Court that they have had a similar experience under private disability insurance programs.

different roles.''[a]

With these cases involving the question whether classifications based on pregnancy shall be treated as gender classifications for the purpose of determining the appropriate standard of review, compare Mathews v. Lucas, 427 U.S. 495 (1976). In that case the Social Security Act provided a presumption of dependency on a deceased father for all legitimate children and for some (but not all) illegitimate children. The Court said: "That the statutory classifications challenged here discriminate among illegitimate children does not mean, of course, that they are not also properly described as discriminating between legitimate and illegitimate children."

The cases addressing whether disparate treatment of pregnancy from other conditions constitutes gender discrimination also usefully may be compared with those where men and women receive disparate treatment based on accurate generalizations about the respective classes. In City of Los Angeles v. Manhart, 435 U.S. 702 (1978), the Court held that Title VII prohibited the Los Angeles Department of Water and Power from requiring its female employees to make larger contributions to its pension fund than its male employees, even though it assumed the truth of the generalization, based on mortality tables, that women as a class live longer than men and thus on average would receive pension benefits for a longer time. Justice Stevens wrote for the Court that the statute "precludes treatment of individuals as simply components of a racial, religious, sexual, or national class[,]" and that "[e]ven a true generalization about the class is an insufficient reason for disqualifying an individual to whom the generalization does not apply." Unlike the classification between "pregnant women and nonpregnant persons" at issue in *Gilbert* and *Geduldig*, "each of the two groups in this case is composed entirely and exclusively of members of the same sex." Consequently, "[o]n its face, this plan discriminates on the basis of sex whereas [those plans] discriminated on the basis of a special physical disability." This approach was followed in Arizona Governing Committee v. Norris, 463 U.S. 1073 (1983), which held that Arizona's pension plan providing for equal contributions from state employees of both sexes but lower pension benefits to female employees based on gender-based mortality tables violated the gender discrimination provisions of Title VII. The Court had "no hesitation in holding . . . that the classification of employees on the basis of sex is no more permissible at the pay-out stage of a retirement plan than at the pay-in stage."

A separate problem arises when a statute that on its face does not make a gender classification is challenged on the ground that it has a disparate impact on one sex. See, e.g., Personnel Adm'r of Massachusetts v. Feeney, 442 U.S. 256 (1979), in which a law providing job preferences to veterans was challenged by a showing that 98% of veterans were male. *Feeney* will be considered along with similar cases involving race in Subsection D dealing with the requirement of showing a discriminatory purpose.

[a] In 1978 Congress amended Title VII of the Civil Rights Act of 1964 to provide: "The terms 'because of sex' or 'on the basis of sex' include, but are not limited to, because of or on the basis of pregnancy, childbirth, or related medical conditions; and women affected by pregnancy, childbirth, or related medical conditions shall be treated the same for all employment-related purposes, including receipt of benefits under fringe benefit programs, as other persons not so affected but similar in their ability or inability to work, . . ." 42 U.S.C. § 2000e(k). The Court later applied this statute to hold invalid a health plan which gave lesser benefits for pregnancy-related conditions to spouses of male employees than it gave to female employees. Newport News, Shipbuilding and Dry Dock Co. v. EEOC, 462 U.S. 669 (1983).

Michael M. v. Superior Court

450 U.S. 464, 101 S.Ct. 1200, 67 L.Ed.2d 437 (1981).

Justice Rehnquist announced the judgment of the Court and delivered an opinion in which The Chief Justice, Justice Stewart, and Justice Powell joined.

The question presented ... is whether California's "statutory rape" law, § 261.5 of the Cal. Penal Code Ann. ...violates the Equal Protection Clause of the Fourteenth Amendment. Section 261.5 defines unlawful sexual intercourse as "an act of sexual intercourse accomplished with a female not the wife of the perpetrator, where the female is under the age of 18 years." The statute thus makes men alone criminally liable for the act of sexual intercourse.

In July 1978, a complaint was filed in the Municipal Court of Sonoma County, Cal., alleging that petitioner, then a 17½–year–old male, had had unlawful sexual intercourse with a female under the age of 18, in violation of § 261.5.... Prior to trial, petitioner sought to set aside the information on both state and federal constitutional grounds, asserting that § 261.5 unlawfully discriminated on the basis of gender. The trial court and the California Court of Appeal denied petitioner's request for relief and petitioner sought review in the Supreme Court of California.

The Supreme Court held that "section 261.5 discriminates on the basis of sex because only females may be victims, and only males may violate the section." The court then subjected the classification to "strict scrutiny," stating that it must be justified by a compelling state interest. It found that the classification was "supported not by mere social convention but by the immutable physiological fact that it is the female exclusively who can become pregnant." Canvassing "the tragic human cost of illegitimate teenage pregnancies," including the large number of teenage abortions, the increased medical risk associated with teenage pregnancies, and the social consequences of teenage childbearing, the court concluded that the State has a compelling interest in preventing such pregnancies. Because males alone can "physiologically cause the result which the law properly seeks to avoid," the court further held that the gender classification was readily justified as a means of identifying offender and victim. For the reasons stated below, we affirm the judgment....

As is evident from our opinions, the Court has had some difficulty in agreeing upon the proper approach and analysis in cases involving challenges to gender-based classifications. The issues posed by such challenges range from issues of standing ... to the appropriate standard of judicial review for the substantive classification. Unlike the California Supreme Court, we have not held that gender-based classifications are "inherently suspect" and thus we do not apply so-called "strict scrutiny" to those classifications.... Our cases have held, however, that the traditional minimum rationality test takes on a somewhat "sharper focus" when gender-based classifications are challenged. See Craig v. Boren, 429 U.S. 190, 210 n *(1976) (Powell, J., concurring). In Reed v. Reed, 404 U.S. 71 (1971), for example, the Court stated that a gender-based classification will be upheld if it bears a "fair and substantial relationship" to legitimate state ends, while in *Craig v. Boren,* ... the Court restated the test to require the classification to bear a "substantial relationship" to "important governmental objectives."

Underlying these decisions is the principle that a legislature may not "make overbroad generalizations based on sex which are entirely unrelated to any differences between men and women or which demean the ability or social status of the affected class." Parham v. Hughes, 441 U.S. 347, 354 (1979) (plurality opinion of Stewart, J.). But because the Equal Protection Clause does not "demand that a statute necessarily apply equally to all persons" or require "'things which are different in fact . . . to be treated in law as though they were the same,' "Rinaldi v. Yeager, 384 U.S. 305, 309 (1966), . . . this Court has consistently upheld statutes where the gender classification is not invidious, but rather realistically reflects the fact that the sexes are not similarly situated in certain circumstances. Parham v. Hughes, supra; Califano v. Webster, 430 U.S. 313 (1977); Schlesinger v. Ballard, 419 U.S. 498 (1975); Kahn v. Shevin, 416 U.S. 351 (1974). As the Court has stated, a legislature may "provide for the special problems of women." Weinberger v. Wiesenfeld, 420 U.S. 636, 653 (1975).

Applying those principles to this case, the fact that the California Legislature criminalized the act of illicit sexual intercourse with a minor female is a sure indication of its intent or purpose to discourage that conduct. Precisely why the legislature desired that result is of course somewhat less clear. This Court has long recognized that "[i]nquiries into congressional motives or purposes are a hazardous matter," United States v. O'Brien, 391 U.S. 367, 383–384 (1968); Palmer v. Thompson, 403 U.S. 217, 224 (1971), and the search for the "actual" or "primary" purpose of a statute is likely to be elusive. Arlington Heights v. Metropolitan Housing Dev. Corp., 429 U.S. 252, 265 (1977). . . . Here, for example, the individual legislators may have voted for the statute for a variety of reasons. Some legislators may have been concerned about preventing teenage pregnancies, others about protecting young females from physical injury or from the loss of "chastity," and still others about promoting various religious and moral attitudes towards premarital sex.

The justification for the statute offered by the State, and accepted by the Supreme Court of California, is that the legislature sought to prevent illegitimate teenage pregnancies. That finding, of course, is entitled to great deference. Reitman v. Mulkey, 387 U.S. 369, 373–374 (1967). And although our cases establish that the State's asserted reason for the enactment of a statute may be rejected, if it "could not have been a goal of the legislation," *Weinberger v. Wiesenfeld,* . . . this is not such a case.

We are satisfied not only that the prevention of illegitimate pregnancy is at least one of the "purposes" of the statute, but that the State has a strong interest in preventing such pregnancy. At the risk of stating the obvious, teenage pregnancies, which have increased dramatically over the last two decades, have significant social, medical and economic consequences for both the mother and her child, and the State. Of particular concern to the State is that approximately half of all teenage pregnancies end in abortion. And of those children who are born, their illegitimacy makes them likely candidates to become wards of the State.[6]

We need not be medical doctors to discern that young men and young women are not similarly situated with respect to the problems and the risks of sexual intercourse. Only women may become pregnant, and they suffer disproportionately the profound physical, emotional, and psychological consequences

---

[6] . . .

Subsequent to the decision below, the California Legislature considered and rejected proposals to render § 261.5 gender neutral, thereby ratifying the judgment of the California Supreme Court. That is enough to answer petitioner's contention that the statute was the "accidental byproduct of a traditional way of thinking about women." Califano v. Webster, 430 U.S. 313 (1977) (quoting Califano v. Goldfarb, 430 U.S. 199 (1977) (Stevens, J., concurring)). Certainly this decision of the California Legislature is as good a source as is this Court in deciding what is "current" and what is "outmoded" in the perception of women.

of sexual activity. The statute at issue here protects women from sexual intercourse at an age when those consequences are particularly severe.[7]

The question thus boils down to whether a State may attack the problem of sexual intercourse and teenage pregnancy directly by prohibiting a male from having sexual intercourse with a minor female. We hold that such a statute is sufficiently related to the State's objectives to pass constitutional muster.

Because virtually all of the significant harmful and inescapably identifiable consequences of teenage pregnancy fall on the young female, a legislature acts well within its authority when it elects to punish only the participant who, by nature, suffers few of the consequences of his conduct. It is hardly unreasonable for a legislature acting to protect minor females to exclude them from punishment. Moreover, the risk of pregnancy itself constitutes a substantial deterrence to young females. No similar natural sanctions deter males. A criminal sanction imposed solely on males thus serves to roughly "equalize" the deterrents on the sexes.

We are unable to accept petitioner's contention that the statute is impermissibly underinclusive and must, in order to pass judicial scrutiny, be *broadened* so as to hold the female as criminally liable as the male. It is argued that this statute is not *necessary* to deter teenage pregnancy because a gender-neutral statute, where both male and female would be subject to prosecution, would serve that goal equally well. The relevant inquiry, however, is not whether the statute is drawn as precisely as it might have been, but whether the line chosen by the California Legislature is within constitutional limitations. . . .

In any event, we cannot say that a gender-neutral statute would be as effective as the statute California has chosen to enact. The State persuasively contends that a gender-neutral statute would frustrate its interest in effective enforcement. Its view is that a female is surely less likely to report violations of the statute if she herself would be subject to criminal prosecution. In an area already fraught with prosecutorial difficulties, we decline to hold that the Equal Protection Clause requires a legislature to enact a statute so broad that it may well be incapable of enforcement.[10]

---

[7] Although petitioner concedes that the State has a "compelling" interest in preventing teenage pregnancy, he contends that the "true" purpose of § 261.5 is to protect the virtue and chastity of young women. As such, the statute is unjustifiable because it rests on archaic stereotypes. What we have said above is enough to dispose of that contention. The question for us—and the only question under the Federal Constitution—is whether the legislation violates the Equal Protection Clause of the Fourteenth Amendment, not whether its supporters may have endorsed it for reasons no longer generally accepted. Even if the preservation of female chastity were one of the motives of the statute, and even if that motive be impermissible, petitioner's argument must fail because "[i]t is a familiar practice of constitutional law that this court will not strike down an otherwise constitutional statute on the basis of an alleged illicit legislative motive." United States v. O'Brien, 391 U.S. 367, 383 (1968). In Orr v. Orr, 440 U.S. 268 (1979), for example, the Court rejected one asserted purpose as impermissible,

but then considered other purposes to determine if they could justify the statute. Similarly, in Washington v. Davis, 426 U.S. 229, 243 (1976) the Court distinguished Palmer v. Thompson, 403 U.S. 217 (1971), on the grounds that the purposes of the ordinance there were not open to impeachment by evidence that the legislature was actually motivated by an impermissible purpose. See also Arlington Heights v. Metropolitan Housing Dev. Corp., 429 U.S. 252, 270, n. 21 (1977); Mobile v. Bolden, 446 U.S. 55, 91 (1980) (Stevens, J., concurring in judgment).

[10] The question whether a statute is *substantially* related to its asserted goals is at best an opaque one. It can be plausibly argued that a gender-neutral statute would produce fewer prosecutions than the statute at issue here. The dissent argues, on the other hand, that "even assuming that a gender-neutral statute would be more difficult to enforce. . . . [c]ommon sense . . . suggests that a gender-neutral statutory rape law is potentially a greater deterrent of sexual ac-

We similarly reject petitioner's argument that § 261.5 is impermissibly overbroad because it makes unlawful sexual intercourse with prepubescent females, who are, by definition, incapable of becoming pregnant. Quite apart from the fact that the statute could well be justified on the grounds that very young females are particularly susceptible to physical injury from sexual intercourse, ... it is ludicrous to suggest that the Constitution requires the California Legislature to limit the scope of its rape statute to older teenagers and exclude young girls.

There remains only petitioner's contention that the statute is unconstitutional as it is applied to him because he, like Sharon, was under 18 at the time of sexual intercourse. Petitioner argues that the statute is flawed because it presumes that as between two persons under 18, the male is the culpable aggressor. We find petitioner's contentions unpersuasive. Contrary to his assertions, the statute does not rest on the assumption that males are generally the aggressors. It is instead an attempt by a legislature to prevent illegitimate teenage pregnancy by providing an additional deterrent for men. The age of the man is irrelevant since young men are as capable as older men of inflicting the harm sought to be prevented.

In upholding the California statute we also recognize that this is not a case where a statute is being challenged on the grounds that it "invidiously discriminates" against females. To the contrary, the statute places a burden on males which is not shared by females. But we find nothing to suggest that men, because of past discrimination or peculiar disadvantages, are in need of the special solicitude of the courts. Nor is this a case where the gender classification is made "solely for ... administrative convenience," as in Frontiero v. Richardson, 411 U.S. 677, 690 (1973) (emphasis omitted), or rests on "the baggage of sexual stereotypes" as in Orr v. Orr, 440 U.S., at 283. As we have held, the statute instead reasonably reflects the fact that the consequences of sexual intercourse and pregnancy fall more heavily on the female than on the male.

Accordingly the judgment of the California Supreme Court is

Affirmed.

Justice Stewart, concurring.

Section 261.5, on its face, classifies on the basis of sex. A male who engages in sexual intercourse with an underage female who is not his wife violates the statute; a female who engages in sexual intercourse with an underage male who is not her husband does not. The petitioner contends that this state law, which punishes only males for the conduct in question, violates his Fourteenth Amendment right to the equal protection of the law. The Court today correctly rejects that contention.

. . .

The Constitution is violated when government, state or federal, invidiously classifies similarly situated people on the basis of the immutable characteristics with which they were born. Thus, detrimental racial classifications by govern-

tivity than a gender-based law, for the simple reason that a gender-neutral law subjects both men and women to criminal sanctions and thus arguably has a deterrent effect on twice as many potential violators."

Where such differing speculations as to the effect of a statute are plausible, we think it appropriate to defer to the decision of the

California Supreme Court, "armed as it was with the knowledge of the facts and circumstances concerning the passage and potential impact of [the statute], and familiar with the milieu in which that provision would operate." Reitman v. Mulkey, 387 U.S. 369, 378–379 (1967).

. . .

ment always violate the Constitution, for the simple reason that, so far as the Constitution is concerned, people of different races are always similarly situated. See Fullilove v. Klutznick, 448 U.S. 448, 522 (dissenting opinion); McLaughlin v. Florida, 379 U.S. 184, 198 (concurring opinion); Brown v. Board of Ed., 347 U.S. 483; Plessy v. Ferguson, 163 U.S. 537, 552 (dissenting opinion). By contrast, while detrimental gender classifications by government often violate the Constitution, they do not always do so, for the reason that there are differences between males and females that the Constitution necessarily recognizes. In this case we deal with the most basic of these differences: females can become pregnant as the result of sexual intercourse; males cannot.

. . .

... Experienced observation confirms the common sense notion that adolescent males disregard the possibility of pregnancy far more than do adolescent females. And to the extent that § 261.5 may punish males for intercourse with prepubescent females, that punishment is justifiable because of the substantial physical risks for prepubescent females that are not shared by their male counterparts.

The petitioner argues that the California Legislature could have drafted the statute differently, so that its purpose would be accomplished more precisely. "But the issue, of course, is not whether the statute could have been drafted more wisely, but whether the lines chosen by the ... [l]egislature are within constitutional limitations." Kahn v. Shevin, 416 U.S. 351, 356, n. 10. That other States may have decided to attack the same problems more broadly, with gender-neutral statutes, does not mean that every State is constitutionally compelled to do so.

. . .

In short, the Equal Protection Clause does not mean that the physiological differences between men and women must be disregarded. While those differences must never be permitted to become a pretext for invidious discrimination, no such discrimination is presented by this case. The Constitution surely does not require a State to pretend that demonstrable differences between men and women do not really exist.

Justice Blackmun, concurring in the judgment.

It is gratifying that the plurality recognizes that "[a]t the risk of stating the obvious, teenage pregnancies ... have increased dramatically over the last two decades" and "have significant social, medical, and economic consequences for both the mother and her child, and the State." There have been times when I have wondered whether the Court was capable of this perception, particularly when it has struggled with the different but not unrelated problems that attend abortion issues. See, for example, the opinions (and the dissenting opinions) in Beal v. Doe, 432 U.S. 438 (1977); Maher v. Roe, 432 U.S. 464 (1977); Poelker v. Doe, 432 U.S. 519 (1977); Harris v. McRae, 448 U.S. 297 (1980); Williams v. Zbaraz, 448 U.S. 358 (1980); and today's opinion in *H.L. v. Matheson*, ante.

Some might conclude that the two uses of the criminal sanction—here flatly to forbid intercourse in order to forestall teenage pregnancies, and in *Matheson* to prohibit a physician's abortion procedure except upon notice to the parents of the pregnant minor—are vastly different proscriptions. But the basic social and privacy problems are much the same. Both Utah's statute in *Matheson* and California's statute in this case are legislatively created tools intended to achieve similar ends and addressed to the same societal concerns: the control and direction of young people's sexual activities. The plurality opinion impliedly concedes as much when it notes that "approximately half of all teenage pregnancies end in abortion," and that "those children who are born" are "likely candidates to become wards of the State."

I, however, cannot vote to strike down the California statutory rape law, for I think it is a sufficiently reasoned and constitutional effort to control the problem at its inception.... I am persuaded that, although a minor has substantial privacy rights in intimate affairs connected with procreation, California's efforts to prevent teenage pregnancy are to be viewed differently from Utah's efforts to inhibit a woman from dealing with pregnancy once it has become an inevitability.

Craig v. Boren, 429 U.S. 190 (1976), was an opinion which, in large part, I joined. The plurality opinion in the present case points out the Court's respective phrasings of the applicable test in Reed v. Reed, 404 U.S. 71, 76 (1971), and in Craig v. Boren, 429 U.S., at 197. I vote to affirm the judgment of the Supreme Court of California and to uphold the State's gender-based classification on that test and as exemplified by those two cases and by Schlesinger v. Ballard, 419 U.S. 498 (1975); Weinberger v. Wiesenfeld, 420 U.S. 636 (1975); and Kahn v. Shevin, 416 U.S. 351 (1974).

· · ·

Justice Brennan, with whom Justices White and Marshall join, dissenting.

I

It is disturbing to find the Court so splintered on a case that presents such a straightforward issue: whether the admittedly gender-based classification in Cal.Penal Code Ann. § 261.5 ... bears a sufficient relationship to the State's asserted goal of preventing teenage pregnancies to survive the "mid-level" constitutional scrutiny mandated by Craig v. Boren, 429 U.S. 190 (1976). Applying the analytical frame work provided by our precedents, I am convinced that there is only one proper resolution of this issue: the classification must be declared unconstitutional. I fear that the plurality and Justices Stewart and Blackmun reach the opposite result by placing too much emphasis on the desirability of achieving the State's asserted statutory goal—prevention of teenage pregnancy—and not enough emphasis on the fundamental question of whether the sex-based discrimination in the California statute is *substantially* related to the achievement of that goal.

· · ·

... [E]ven assuming that prevention of teenage pregnancy is an important governmental objective and that it is in fact an objective of § 261.5, California still has the burden of proving that there are fewer teenage pregnancies under its gender-based statutory rape law than there would be if the law were gender neutral. To meet this burden, the State must show that because its statutory rape law punishes only males, and not females, it more effectively deters minor females from having sexual intercourse.

· · ·

... [T]here are at least two serious flaws in the State's assertion that law enforcement problems created by a gender-neutral statutory rape law would make such a statute less effective than a gender-based statute in deterring sexual activity.

First, the experience of other jurisdictions, and California itself, belies the plurality's conclusion that a gender-neutral statutory rape law "may well be incapable of enforcement." ...

. . .

The second flaw ... is that even assuming that a gender-neutral statute would be more difficult to enforce, the State has still not shown that those enforcement problems would make such a statute less effective than a gender-based statute in deterring minor females from engaging in sexual intercourse. Common sense, however, suggests that a gender-neutral statutory rape law is potentially a *greater* deterrent of sexual activity than a gender-based law, for the simple reason that a gender-neutral law subjects both men and women to criminal sanctions and thus arguably has a deterrent effect on twice as many potential violators. . . .

III

Until very recently, no California court or commentator had suggested that the purpose of California's statutory rape law was to protect young women from the risk of pregnancy. Indeed, the historical development of § 261.5 demonstrates that the law was initially enacted on the premise that young women, in contrast to young men, were to be deemed legally incapable of consenting to an act of sexual intercourse. Because their chastity was considered particularly precious, those young women were felt to be uniquely in need of the State's protection. In contrast, young men were assumed to be capable of making such decisions for themselves; the law therefore did not offer them any special protection.

It is perhaps because the gender classification in California's statutory rape law was initially designed to further these outmoded sexual stereotypes, rather than to reduce the incidence of teenage pregnancies, that the State has been unable to demonstrate a substantial relationship between the classification and its newly asserted goal. . . . But whatever the reason, the State has not shown that Cal.Penal Code § 261.5 is any more effective than a gender-neutral law would be in deterring minor females from engaging in sexual intercourse. It has therefore not met its burden of proving that the statutory classification is substantially related to the achievement of its asserted goal.

I would hold that § 261.5 violates the Equal Protection Clause. . . .

Justice Stevens, dissenting.

Local custom and belief—rather than statutory laws of venerable but doubtful ancestry—will determine the volume of sexual activity among unmarried teenagers. The empirical evidence cited by the plurality demonstrates the futility of the notion that a statutory prohibition will significantly affect the volume of that activity or provide a meaningful solution to the problems created by it. Nevertheless, as a matter of constitutional power, unlike my Brother Brennan, I would have no doubt about the validity of a state law prohibiting all unmarried teenagers from engaging in sexual intercourse. The societal interests in reducing the incidence of venereal disease and teenage pregnancy are sufficient, in my judgment, to justify a prohibition of conduct that increases the risk of those harms.

My conclusion that a nondiscriminatory prohibition would be constitutional does not help me answer the question whether a prohibition applicable to only half of the joint participants in the risk-creating conduct is also valid. It cannot be true that the validity of a total ban is an adequate justification for a selective prohibition; otherwise, the constitutional objection to discriminatory rules would be meaningless. The question in this case is whether the difference between males and females justifies this statutory discrimination based entirely on sex.

... I think the plurality is quite correct in making the assumption that the joint act that this law seeks to prohibit creates a greater risk of harm for the female than for the male....

. . .

[However,] that a female confronts a greater risk of harm than a male is a reason for applying the prohibition to her—not a reason for granting her a license to use her own judgment on whether or not to assume the risk....

. . .

Finally, even if my logic is faulty and there actually is some speculative basis for treating equally guilty males and females differently, I still believe that any such speculative justification would be outweighed by the paramount interest in evenhanded enforcement of the law. A rule that authorizes punishment of only one of two equally guilty wrongdoers violates the essence of the constitutional requirement that the sovereign must govern impartially.

I respectfully dissent.

ROSTKER v. GOLDBERG, 453 U.S. 57 (1981). In 1980 President Carter recommended that Congress reactivate the draft registration process and provide for the registration of women as well as men. When Congress provided funds only for the registration of males, men subject to the draft sued as a class, claiming a violation of the Fifth Amendment's Due Process Clause. A District Court judgment in their favor was reversed by the Supreme Court. For the Court, Justice Rehnquist emphasized "[t]he customary deference accorded the judgments of Congress ... when, as here, Congress specifically considered the question of the Act's constitutionality"; an even greater "healthy deference to legislative and executive judgments in the area of military affairs"; and a judicial "lack of competence" in this area that was "marked." Finding the District Court's "efforts to divorce registration from the military and national defense context, with all the deference called for in that context, singularly unpersuasive[,]" the Court nonetheless declined to adopt the Solicitor General's argument that it should apply the "rational relation" standard "and should not examine the Act under the heightened scrutiny with which we have approached gender-based discrimination, see Michael M. v. Superior Court of Sonoma County, 450 U.S. 464 (1981); Craig v. Boren, 429 U.S. 190; *Reed v. Reed*, supra[,]" saying in part:

"We do not think that the substantive guarantee of due process or certainty in the law will be advanced by any further 'refinement' in the applicable tests as suggested by the Government. Announced degrees of 'deference' to legislative judgments, just as levels of 'scrutiny' which this Court announces that it applies to particular classifications made by a legislative body, may all too readily become facile abstractions used to justify a result.... Simply labelling the legislative decision 'military' on the one hand or 'gender-based' on the other does not automatically guide a court to the correct constitutional result."

The majority found this case to be

"quite different from several of the gender-based discrimination cases we have considered in that ... Congress did not act 'unthinkingly' or 'reflexively and not for any considered reason.' The question of registering women for the draft not only received considerable national attention and was the subject of wide-ranging public debate, but also was extensively considered by Congress in hearings, floor debate, and in committee. . . .

"The foregoing clearly establishes that the decision to exempt women from registration was not the 'accidental by-product of a traditional way of thinking about women.' Califano v. Webster, 430 U.S. 313, 320 (1977) (quoting Califano v. Goldfarb, 430 U.S. 199, 233 (1977) (Stevens, J., concurring)). In Michael M., 450 U.S., at 471, n. 6 (plurality), we rejected a similar argument because of action by the California Legislature considering and rejecting proposals to make a statute challenged on discrimination grounds gender-neutral. The cause for rejecting the argument is considerably stronger here. The issue was considered at great length, and Congress clearly expressed its purpose and intent. Contrast Califano v. Westcott, 443 U.S. 76, 87 (1979) ('The gender qualification . . . escaped virtually unnoticed in the hearings and floor debates')."

After identifying the "purpose of registration [to be] to prepare for a draft *of combat troops*[,]" the Court noted that by statute or policy women "as a group . . . are not eligible for combat" and that "Congress specifically recognized and endorsed the exclusion of women from combat in exempting women from registration." Accordingly, "[m]en and women, because of the combat restrictions on women, are simply not similarly situated for purposes of a draft or registration for a draft[,]" and "[t]he exemption of women from registration is not only sufficiently but also closely related to Congress' purpose in authorizing registration."

Finally, the Court thought the District Court had erred in "rel[ying] heavily on the President's decision to seek authority to register women and the testimony of members of the Executive Branch and the military in support of that decision[,]" including "testimony that in the event of a draft of 650,000 the military could absorb some 80,000 female inductees . . . to fill noncombat positions, freeing men to go to the front." In doing so, "the District Court palpably exceeded its authority when it ignored Congress' considered response to this line of reasoning." First, "assuming that a small number of women could be drafted for noncombat roles, Congress simply did not consider it worth the added burdens of including women in draft and registration plans." Second, "Congress also concluded that whatever the need for women for noncombat roles during mobilization, . . . it could be met by volunteers." And, "[m]ost significantly, Congress determined that staffing noncombat positions with women during a mobilization would be positively detrimental to the important goal of military flexibility." Rather than "undertaking an independent evaluation of this evidence," the District Court should have adopted "an appropriately deferential examination of *Congress'* evaluation of that evidence."

A dissent by Justice White, joined by Justice Brennan, "assume[d] what has not been challenged in this case—that excluding women from combat positions does not offend the Constitution." But "[a]s I understand the record, . . . the Government cannot rely on volunteers and must register and draft not only to fill combat positions and those noncombat positions that must be filled by combat-trained men, but also to secure the personnel needed for jobs that can be performed by persons ineligible for combat without diminishing military effectiveness." Justice White could "discern no adequate justification" for "discrimination between men and women" with respect to "the latter category of positions[.]"

In a separate dissent, also joined by Justice Brennan, Justice Marshall objected to the Court upholding a statute that "categorically excludes women from a fundamental civic obligation." He, too, emphasized that "this case does not involve a challenge to the statutes or policies that prohibit female members of the Armed Forces from serving in combat." His review of "the discussion and findings contained in the Senate Report" led him to conclude that at most the Report "demonstrates that drafting *very large numbers* of women would frustrate the achievement of a number of important [military] objectives[,] ...[b]ut ... do[es] not enable the Government to carry its burden of demonstrating that *completely* excluding women from the draft by excluding them from registration substantially furthers important governmental objectives."

MISSISSIPPI UNIVERSITY FOR WOMEN v. HOGAN, 458 U.S. 718 (1982). The Court held invalid a state statute that excluded males from enrolling in a state-supported professional nursing school. Justice O'Connor, writing for the Court, said that the "test for determining the validity of a gender-based classification is straightforward." Without citing either *Michael M.* or *Rostker* she said: "Our decisions ... establish that the party seeking to uphold a statute that classifies individuals on the basis of their gender must carry the burden of showing an 'exceedingly persuasive justification' for the classification.... The burden is met only by showing at least that the classification serves 'important governmental objectives and that the discriminatory means employed' are 'substantially related to the achievement of those objectives.'" She also noted that the "policy of excluding males from admission to the School of Nursing tends to perpetuate the stereotyped view of nursing as an exclusively women's job."

For a fuller treatment of this case, see infra p. 816. Compare with its formulation of the test for measuring the constitutionality of sex-based classifications the approach taken in each of the next two decisions.

J. E. B. v. ALABAMA EX REL. T. B., 511 U.S. 127 (1994). Beginning with Batson v. Kentucky, 476 U.S. 79 (1986), the Court had restricted the exercise of race-based peremptory challenges so that "whether the trial is criminal or civil, potential jurors, as well as litigants, have an equal protection right to jury selection procedures that are free from state-sponsored group stereotypes rooted in, and reflective of, historical prejudice." In this paternity and child support action, in which the State "used 9 of its 10 peremptory strikes to remove male jurors" (and "petitioner used all but one of his strikes to remove female jurors")—leaving the jury all-female due to a predominantly female pool—the Court extended *Batson* to "hold that gender, like race, is an unconstitutional proxy for juror competence and impartiality." It "reaffirm[ed]" that "[i]ntentional discrimination on the basis of gender by state actors violates the Equal Protection Clause, particularly where, as here, the discrimination serves to ratify and perpetuate invidious, archaic, and overbroad stereotypes about the relative abilities of men and women."

Justice Blackmun's majority opinion recounted the history of systematic discrimination against women serving on juries, from total exclusion well into the twentieth century to exemptions from mandatory jury service for women only, which the Court upheld as late as Hoyt v. Florida, 368 U.S. 57 (1961), on "the ground that women, unlike men, occupied a unique position 'as the center of home and family life.'" Then, noting the "heightened scrutiny afforded distinctions based on gender" that began in the 1970's, the Court rejected the argument that unlike racial discrimination, "gender discrimination in the selection of the petit jury should be permitted," because "'gender discrimination in this country ... has never reached the level of discrimination' against African–Americans":

"While the prejudicial attitudes toward women in this country have not been identical to those held toward racial minorities, the similarities between the experiences of racial minorities and women, in some contexts, 'overpower those differences.' Note, Beyond Batson: Eliminating Gender–Based Peremptory Challenges, 105 Harv. L. Rev. 1920, 1921 (1992).... Certainly, with respect to jury service, African–Americans and women share a history of total exclusion, a history which came to an end for women many years after the embarrassing chapter in our history came to an end for African–Americans."

In any event, it sufficed "to acknowledge" the history of sex discrimination,

> "a history which warrants the heightened scrutiny we afford all gender-based classifications today. Under our equal protection jurisprudence, gender-based classifications require 'an exceedingly persuasive justification' in order to survive constitutional scrutiny.... Thus, the only question is whether discrimination on the basis of gender in jury selection substantially furthers the State's legitimate interest in achieving a fair and impartial trial.[6] ...

"Far from proffering an exceptionally persuasive justification for its gender-based peremptory challenges, respondent maintains that its decision to strike virtually all the males from the jury in this case 'may reasonably have been based upon the perception, supported by history, that men otherwise totally qualified to serve upon a jury might be more sympathetic and receptive to the arguments of a man alleged in a paternity action to be the father of an out-of-wedlock child, while women equally qualified to serve upon a jury might be more sympathetic and receptive to the arguments of the complaining witness who bore the child.' ...

"We shall not accept as a defense to gender-based peremptory challenges 'the very stereotype the law condemns.' ... Respondent offers virtually no support for the conclusion that gender alone is an accurate predictor of juror's attitudes; yet it urges this Court to condone the same stereotypes that justified the wholesale exclusion of women from juries and the ballot box.[11] Respondent seems to assume that gross generalizations that would be deemed impermissible if made on the basis of race are somehow permissible when made on the basis of gender.

"Discrimination in jury selection, whether based on race or on gender, causes harm to the litigants, the community, and the individual jurors who are wrongfully excluded from participation in the judicial process. The litigants are harmed by the risk that the prejudice which motivated the discriminatory

---

[6] Because we conclude that gender-based peremptory challenges are not substantially related to an important government objective, we once again need not decide whether classifications based on gender are inherently suspect....

[11] Even if a measure of truth can be found in some of the gender stereotypes used to justify gender-based peremptory challenges, that fact alone cannot support discrimination on the basis of gender in jury selection. We have made abundantly clear in past cases that gender classifications that rest on impermissible stereotypes violate the Equal Protection Clause, even when some statistical support can be conjured up for the generalization.... The generalization advanced by Alabama in support of its asserted right to discriminate on the basis of gender

is, at the least, overbroad, and serves only to perpetuate the same "outmoded notions of the relative capabilities of men and women," Cleburne v. Cleburne Living Center, Inc., 473 U.S. 432, 441 (1985), that we have invalidated in other contexts. See Frontiero v. Richardson, 411 U.S. 677 (1973); Stanton v. Stanton, 421 U.S. 7 (1975); Craig v. Boren, 429 U.S. 190 (1976); Mississippi University for Women v. Hogan, 458 U.S. 718 (1982). The Equal Protection Clause, as interpreted by decisions of this Court, acknowledges that a shred of truth may be contained in some stereotypes, but requires that state actors look beyond the surface before making judgments about people that are likely to stigmatize as well as to perpetuate historical patterns of discrimination.

selection of the jury will infect the entire proceedings.... The community is harmed by the State's participation in the perpetuation of invidious group stereotypes and the inevitable loss of confidence in our judicial system that state-sanctioned discrimination in the courtroom engenders.

"When state actors exercise peremptory challenges in reliance on gender stereotypes, they ratify and reinforce prejudicial views of the relative abilities of men and women. Because these stereotypes have wreaked injustice in so many other spheres of our country's public life, active discrimination by litigants on the basis of gender during jury selection 'invites cynicism respecting the jury's neutrality and its obligation to adhere to the law.' ... The potential for cynicism is particularly acute in cases where gender-related issues are prominent, such as cases involving rape, sexual harassment, or paternity....

"In recent cases we have emphasized that individual jurors themselves have a right to nondiscriminatory jury selection procedures.... Striking individual jurors on the assumption that they hold particular views simply because of their gender is 'practically a brand upon them, affixed by law, an assertion of their inferiority.' Strauder v. West Virginia, 100 U.S. 303, 308 (1880). It denigrates the dignity of the excluded juror, and, for a woman, reinvokes a history of exclusion from political participation.[14] The message it sends to all those in the courtroom, and all those who may later learn of the discriminatory act, is that certain individuals, for no reason other than gender, are presumed unqualified by state actors to decide important questions upon which reasonable persons could disagree."

Justice Blackmun observed that the Court's conclusion did "not imply the elimination of all peremptory challenges." Rather, "gender simply may not serve as a proxy for bias." In fact, "[p]arties may ... exercise their peremptory challenges to remove from the venire any group or class of individuals normally subject to 'rational basis' review." He also emphasized, in conclusion, the importance of equal opportunity in this context, because jury service constitutes direct "participation in our democratic processes[.]"

In a concurring opinion, Justice O'Connor urged that "today's holding should be limited to the government's use of gender-based peremptory strikes." It gave her "pause" that the decision would "increase the possibility that biased jurors will be allowed onto the jury, because sometimes a lawyer will be unable to provide an acceptable gender-neutral explanation even though the lawyer is in fact correct that the juror is unsympathetic." She elaborated:

"... We know that like race, gender matters. A plethora of studies make clear that in rape cases, for example, female jurors are somewhat more likely to vote to convict than male jurors.... Moreover, though there have been no similarly definitive studies regarding, for example, sexual harassment, child custody, or spousal or child abuse, one need not be a sexist to share the intuition that in certain cases a person's gender and resulting life experience will be relevant to his or her view of the case....

"Today's decision severely limits a litigant's ability to act on this intuition.... But to say that gender makes no difference as a matter of law is not

---

[14] The popular refrain is that all peremptory challenges are based on stereotypes of some kind, expressing various intuitive and frequently erroneous biases. But where peremptory challenges are made on the basis of group characteristics other than race or gender (like occupation, for example), they do not reinforce the same stereotypes about the group's competence or predispositions that have been used to prevent them from voting, participating on juries, pursuing their chosen professions, or otherwise contributing to civic life. See B. Babcock, A Place in the Palladium, Women's Rights and Jury Service, 61 U. Cinn. L. Rev. 1139, 1173 (1993).

to say that gender makes no difference as a matter of fact. I previously have said with regard to *Batson*: 'That the Court will not tolerate prosecutors' racially discriminatory use of the peremptory challenge, in effect, is a special rule of relevance, a statement about what this Nation stands for, rather than a statement of fact.' Brown v. North Carolina, 479 U.S. 940, 941–942 (1986) (O'Connor, J., concurring in denial of certiorari). Today's decision is a statement that, in an effort to eliminate the potential discriminatory use of the peremptory, ... gender is now governed by the special rule of relevance formerly reserved for race. Though we gain much from this statement, we cannot ignore what we lose. In extending *Batson* to gender we have added an additional burden to the state and federal trial process, taken a step closer to eliminating the peremptory challenge, and diminished the ability of litigants to act on sometimes accurate gender-based assumptions about juror attitudes."

These concerns led Justice O'Connor to the "position that the Equal Protection Clause does not limit the exercise of peremptory challenges by private civil litigants and criminal defendants." She asked whether the Court later might preclude "the battered wife—on trial for wounding her abusive husband--... from using her peremptory challenges to ensure that the jury of her peers contains as many women members as possible?" Her own reply was: "I assume we will, but I hope we will not."

Concurring in the judgment, Justice Kennedy said in part:

"... For purposes of the Equal Protection Clause, an individual denied jury service because of a peremptory challenge exercised against her on account of her sex is no less injured than the individual denied jury service because of a law banning members of her sex from serving as jurors.... The injury is to personal dignity and to the individual's right to participate in the political process....

"...

"[I]t is important to recognize that a juror sits not as a representative of a racial or sexual group but as an individual citizen. Nothing would be more pernicious to the jury system than for society to presume that persons of different backgrounds go to the jury room to voice prejudice.... The jury pool must be representative of the community, but that is a structural mechanism for preventing bias, not enfranchising it...."

Chief Justice Rehnquist dissented, finding "sufficient differences between race and gender discrimination such that the principle of *Batson* should not be extended to peremptory challenges to potential jurors based on sex." Those differences include a "less searching standard of review" for gender classifications; that, unlike women, "[r]acial groups comprise numerical minorities in our society"; that "racial equality has proved a more challenging goal to achieve on many fronts than gender equality"; and that "*Batson* is best understood as a recognition that race lies at the core of the commands of the Fourteenth Amendment." Accordingly, "[u]nder the Equal Protection Clause, these differences mean that the balance should tilt in favor of peremptory challenges when sex, not race, is the issue." The Chief Justice also made these observations:

"... The two sexes differ, both biologically and, to a diminishing extent, in experience. It is not merely 'stereotyping' to say that these differences may produce a difference in outlook which is brought to the jury room. Accordingly, use of peremptory challenges on the basis of sex is generally not the sort of derogatory and invidious act which peremptory challenges directed at black jurors may be."

In a separate dissent, Justice Scalia, joined by the Chief Justice and Justice Thomas, argued that the Court's objection to "the use of sex as a proxy for particular views or sympathies ... seems to place the Court in opposition to its earlier Sixth Amendment 'fair cross-section' cases[.]" Furthermore, "if men and women jurors are (as the Court thinks) fungible, then the only arguable injury from the prosecutor's 'impermissible' use of male sex as the basis for his peremptories is injury to the stricken juror, not to the defendant." Justice Scalia also faulted the Court for "focusing unrealistically upon individual exercises of the peremptory challenge, and ignoring the totality of the practice." That all sides can exercise peremptories

"explains why peremptory challenges coexisted with the Equal Protection Clause for 120 years.... The situation would be different if both sides systematically struck individuals of one group, so that the strikes evinced group-based animus and served as a proxy for segregated venire lists.... The pattern here, however, displays not a systemic sex-based animus but each side's desire to get a jury favorably disposed to its case. That is why the Court's characterization of respondent's argument as 'reminiscent of the arguments advanced to justify the total exclusion of women from juries,' is patently false. Women were categorically excluded from juries because of doubt that they were competent; women are stricken from juries by peremptory challenge because of doubt that they are well disposed to the striking party's case.... There is discrimination and dishonor in the former, and not in the latter...."

United States v. Virginia

— U.S. —, 116 S.Ct. 2264 , 135 L.Ed.2d 735 (1996)

Justice Ginsburg delivered the opinion of the Court.

Virginia's public institutions of higher learning include an incomparable military college, Virginia Military Institute (VMI). The United States maintains that the Constitution's equal protection guarantee precludes Virginia from reserving exclusively to men the unique educational opportunities VMI affords. We agree.

I

Founded in 1839, VMI is today the sole single-sex school among Virginia's 15 public institutions of higher learning. VMI's distinctive mission is to produce "citizen-soldiers," men prepared for leadership in civilian life and in military service. VMI pursues this mission through pervasive training of a kind not available anywhere else in Virginia[—] ... an "adversative method" [that] constantly endeavors to instill physical and mental discipline in its cadets and impart to them a strong moral code. ...

. . .

Neither the goal of producing citizen-soldiers nor VMI's implementing methodology is inherently unsuitable to women. And the school's impressive record in producing leaders has made admission desirable to some women. ...

II

. . .

VMI today enrolls about 1,300 men as cadets. ...

VMI['s] ... "... adversative, or doubting, model of education" ... features "[p]hysical rigor, mental stress, absolute equality of treatment, absence of privacy, minute regulation of behavior, and indoctrination in desirable values."
...

VMI cadets live in spartan barracks where surveillance is constant and privacy nonexistent; they wear uniforms, eat together in the mess hall, and regularly participate in drills. ...Entering students are incessantly exposed to the rat line, "an extreme form of the adversative model," comparable in intensity to Marine Corps boot camp. ...

. . .

[The United States, prompted by a female applicant's complaint, sued Virginia and VMI in 1990. The District Court ruled in favor of VMI but the Fourth Circuit reversed and remanded,] suggest[ing] these options for the State: Admit women to VMI; establish parallel institutions or programs; or abandon state support, leaving VMI free to pursue its policies as a private institution. ...

... Virginia proposed a parallel program for women: Virginia Women's Institute for Leadership (VWIL). The 4–year, state-sponsored undergraduate program would be located at Mary Baldwin College, a private liberal arts school for women, and would be open, initially, to about 25 to 30 students. Although VWIL would share VMI's mission—to produce "citizen-soldiers"—the VWIL program would differ, as does Mary Baldwin College, from VMI in academic offerings, methods of education, and financial resources. ...

. . .

[T]he District Court ... decided the plan met the requirements of the Equal Protection Clause. ...

A divided Court of Appeals affirmed. ...

. . .

III

[T]his case present[s] two ultimate issues. First, does Virginia's exclusion of women from the educational opportunities provided by VMI—extraordinary opportunities for military training and civilian leadership development—deny to women "capable of all of the individual activities required of VMI cadets," ... the equal protection of the laws guaranteed by the Fourteenth Amendment? Second, if VMI's "unique" situation ....--as Virginia's sole single-sex public institution of higher education—offends the Constitution's equal protection principle, what is the remedial requirement?

IV

We note, once again, the core instruction of this Court's pathmarking decisions in J.E.B. v. Alabama ex rel. T. B., ... and *Mississippi Univ. for Women*, ...: Parties who seek to defend gender-based government action must demonstrate an "exceedingly persuasive justification" for that action.

. . .

... Since *Reed*, the Court has repeatedly recognized that neither federal nor state government acts compatibly with the equal protection principle when a law or official policy denies to women, simply because they are women, full citizenship stature—equal opportunity to aspire, achieve, participate in and contribute to society based on their individual talents and capacities. ...

... To summarize the Court's current directions for cases of official classification based on gender: Focusing on the differential treatment or denial of opportunity for which relief is sought, the reviewing court must determine whether the proffered justification is "exceedingly persuasive." The burden of justification is demanding and it rests entirely on the State. ... The State must show "at least that the [challenged] classification serves 'important governmental objectives and that the discriminatory means employed' are 'substantially related to the achievement of those objectives.'" ... The justification must be genuine, not hypothesized or invented *post hoc* in response to litigation. And it must not rely on overbroad generalizations about the different talents, capacities, or preferences of males and females. ...

The heightened review standard our precedent establishes does not make sex a proscribed classification. ... Physical differences between men and women ... are enduring. ...

"Inherent differences" between men and women ... remain cause for celebration, but not for denigration of the members of either sex or for artificial constraints on an individual's opportunity. Sex classifications may be used to compensate women "for particular economic disabilities [they have] suffered," ... to "promot[e] equal employment opportunity," ... to advance full development of the talent and capacities of our Nation's people. ... But such classifications may not be used, as they once were, ... to create or perpetuate the legal, social, and economic inferiority of women.

[W]e conclude that Virginia has shown no "exceedingly persuasive justification" for excluding all women from the citizen-soldier training afforded by VMI. ... Because the remedy proffered by Virginia—the Mary Baldwin VWIL program—does not cure the constitutional violation, i.e., it does not provide equal opportunity, we reverse. ...

V

... Virginia ... asserts two justifications in defense of VMI's exclusion of women. First, ... "single-sex education provides important educational benefits," ... and the option of single-sex education contributes to "diversity in educational approaches,". ... Second, ... "the unique VMI method of character development and leadership training," the school's adversative approach, would have to be modified were VMI to admit women. ...

A

Single-sex education affords pedagogical benefits to at least some students, ... and that reality is uncontested in this litigation. Similarly, it is not disputed that diversity among public educational institutions can serve the public good. But Virginia has not shown that VMI was established, or has been maintained, with a view to diversifying, by its categorical exclusion of women, educational opportunities within the State. In cases of this genre, our precedent instructs that "benign" justifications proffered in defense of categorical exclusions will not be accepted automatically; a tenable justification must describe actual state purposes, not rationalizations for actions in fact differently grounded. ...

. . .

Neither recent nor distant history bears out Virginia's alleged pursuit of diversity through single-sex educational options. ...

. . .

Virginia describes the current absence of public single-sex higher education for women as "an historical anomaly." . . . But the historical record indicates action more deliberate than anomalous: First, protection of women against higher education; next, schools for women far from equal in resources and stature to schools for men; finally, conversion of the separate schools to coeducation. . . .

Our 1982 decision in *Mississippi Univ. for Women* prompted VMI to reexamine its male-only admission policy. . . . A Mission Study Committee . . . studied the problem from October 1983 until May 1986, and in that month counseled against "change of VMI status as a single-sex college." . . . [W]e can hardly extract from that effort any state policy evenhandedly to advance diverse educational options. As the District Court observed, the Committee's analysis "primarily focuse[d] on anticipated difficulties in attracting females to VMI," and the report, overall, supplied "very little indication of how th[e] conclusion was reached."

In sum, we find no persuasive evidence in this record that VMI's male-only admission policy "is in furtherance of a state policy of 'diversity.'" . . . A purpose genuinely to advance an array of educational options . . . is not served by VMI's historic and constant plan—a plan to "affor[d] a unique educational benefit only to males." . . . However "liberally" this plan serves the State's sons, it makes no provision whatever for her daughters. That is not equal protection.

B

Virginia next argues that VMI's adversative method of training provides educational benefits that cannot be made available, unmodified, to women. Alterations to accommodate women would necessarily be . . . so "drastic," . . . as to transform, indeed "destroy," VMI's program. . . . Neither sex would be favored . . . : Men would be deprived of the unique opportunity currently available to them; women would not gain that opportunity because their participation would "eliminat[e] the very aspects of [the] program that distinguish [VMI] . . ." . . .

The District Court forecast from expert witness testimony, and the Court of Appeals accepted, that coeducation would materially affect "at least these three aspects of VMI's program--physical training, the absence of privacy, and the adversative approach." . . . And it is uncontested that women's admission would require accommodations, primarily in arranging housing assignments and physical training programs for female cadets. . . . It is also undisputed, however, that "the VMI methodology could be used to educate women." . . . The District Court even allowed that some women may prefer it to the methodology a women's college might pursue. . . . ["S]ome women," the expert testimony established, "are capable of all of the individual activities required of VMI cadets," [and t]he parties . . . agree that "some women can meet the physical standards [VMI] now impose[s] on men." . . . In sum, as the Court of Appeals stated, "neither the goal of producing citizen soldiers," VMI's *raison d'etre*, "nor VMI's implementing methodology is inherently unsuitable to women." . . .

. . . [T]he District Court made "findings" on "gender-based developmental differences[,]" [that] restate the opinions of Virginia's expert witnesses, opinions about typically male or typically female "tendencies." . . . For example, "[m]ales tend to need an atmosphere of adversativeness," while "[f]emales tend to thrive in a cooperative atmosphere." . . .

The United States does not challenge any expert witness estimation on average capacities or preferences of men and women. Instead, the United States emphasizes that ... we have cautioned reviewing courts to take a "hard look" at generalizations or "tendencies" of the kind pressed by Virginia, and relied upon by the District Court. ...State actors controlling gates to opportunity, we have instructed, may not exclude qualified individuals based on "fixed notions concerning the roles and abilities of males and females." ...

It may be assumed ... that most women would not choose VMI's adversative method. ...[H]owever, ... it is also probable that "many men would not want to be educated in such an environment." ... The issue, however, is not whether "women—or men—should be forced to attend VMI" [but] whether the State can constitutionally deny to women who have the will and capacity, the training and attendant opportunities that VMI uniquely affords. ...

The notion that admission of women would downgrade VMI's stature, destroy the adversative system and, with it, even the school, is a judgment hardly proved, a prediction hardly different from other "self-fulfilling prophec[ies]," ... once routinely used to deny rights or opportunities. When women first sought admission to the bar and access to legal education, concerns of the same order were expressed. ...

Medical faculties similarly resisted men and women as partners in the study of medicine. ...

Women's successful entry into the federal military academies, and their participation in the Nation's military forces, indicate that Virginia's fears for the future of VMI may not be solidly grounded. ...The State's justification for excluding all women from "citizen-soldier" training for which some are qualified, in any event, cannot rank as "exceedingly persuasive," as we have explained and applied that standard.

. . .

... Surely ... the State's great goal is not substantially advanced by women's categorical exclusion, in total disregard of their individual merit, from the State's premier "citizen-soldier" corps. Virginia, in sum, "has fallen far short of establishing the 'exceedingly persuasive justification,'" ... that must be the solid base for any gender-defined classification.

VI

In the second phase of the litigation, Virginia presented its remedial plan— maintain VMI as a male-only college and create VWIL as a separate program for women. The plan met District Court approval. The Fourth Circuit ... deferentially reviewed the State's proposal and decided that the two single-sex programs directly served Virginia's reasserted purposes: single-gender education, and "achieving the results of an adversative method in a military environment." ... [T]he Court of Appeals concluded that Virginia had arranged for men and women opportunities "sufficiently comparable" to survive equal protection evaluation....

A

A remedial decree ... must closely fit the constitutional violation; it must be shaped to place persons unconstitutionally denied an opportunity or advantage in "the position they would have occupied in the absence of [discrimination]." See Milliken v. Bradley, 433 U.S. 267, 280 (1977). ...The constitutional violation in this case is the categorical exclusion of women from an extraordinary educational opportunity afforded men. A proper remedy for an unconstitutional exclusion, we have explained, aims to "eliminate [so far as possible] the discriminatory effects of the past" and to "bar like discrimination in the future." ...

Virginia chose not to eliminate, but to leave untouched, VMI's exclusionary policy. For women only, however, Virginia proposed a separate program, different in kind from VMI and unequal in tangible and intangible facilities. ...

VWIL affords women no opportunity to experience the rigorous military training for which VMI is famed. ...Instead, the VWIL program "deemphasize[s]" military education, ... and uses a "cooperative method" of education "which reinforces self-esteem,". ...

VWIL students participate in ROTC and a "largely ceremonial" Virginia Corps of Cadets, ... but Virginia deliberately did not make VWIL a military institute. The VWIL House is not a military-style residence and VWIL students need not live together throughout the 4–year program, eat meals together, or wear uniforms during the school day. ...VWIL students thus do not experience the "barracks" life "crucial to the VMI experience," the spartan living arrangements designed to foster an "egalitarian ethic." ... Virginia deemed that core experience nonessential, indeed inappropriate, for training its female citizen-soldiers.

VWIL students ... [are k]ept away from the pressures, hazards, and psychological bonding characteristic of VMI's adversative training, [and thus] will not know the "feeling of tremendous accomplishment" commonly experienced by VMI's successful cadets. ...

Virginia maintains that these methodological differences are "justified pedagogically," based on "important differences between men and women in learning and developmental needs," "psychological and sociological differences" Virginia describes as "real" and "not stereotypes." ...

... [G]eneralizations about "the way women are," estimates of what is appropriate for *most women*, no longer justify denying opportunity to women whose talent and capacity place them outside the average description. Notably, Virginia never asserted that VMI's method of education suits *most men*. It is also revealing that Virginia accounted for its failure to make the VWIL experience "the entirely militaristic experience of VMI" on the ground that VWIL "is planned for women who do not necessarily expect to pursue military careers." ... By that reasoning, VMI's "entirely militaristic" program would be inappropriate for men in general or *as a group*, for "[o]nly about 15% of VMI cadets enter career military service." ...

In contrast to the generalizations about women on which Virginia rests, we note again these dispositive realities: VMI's "implementing methodology" is not "inherently unsuitable to women," ...; "some women ... do well under [the] adversative model," ...; "some women, at least, would want to attend [VMI] if they had the opportunity," ...; "some women are capable of all of the individual activities required of VMI cadets," ... and "can meet the physical standards [VMI] now impose[s] on men,". ...It is on behalf of these women that the United States has instituted this suit, and it is for them that a remedy must be crafted,[19] a remedy that will end their exclusion from a state-supplied

[19] Admitting women to VMI would undoubtedly require alterations necessary to afford members of each sex privacy from the other sex in living arrangements, and to adjust aspects of the physical training programs. ...Experience shows such adjustments are manageable. See U.S. Military Academy, ... Report of Admission of Women ... (1977–1980) (4–year longitudinal study of the admission of women to West Point). ...

educational opportunity for which they are fit, a decree that will "bar like discrimination in the future." . . .

B

In myriad respects other than military training, VWIL does not qualify as VMI's equal. VWIL's student body, faculty, course offerings, and facilities hardly match VMI's. Nor can the VWIL graduate anticipate the benefits associated with VMI's 157–year history, the school's prestige, and its influential alumni network.

. . . [T]he . . . VWIL program [is] fairly appraised as a "pale shadow" of VMI in terms of the range of curricular choices and faculty stature, funding, prestige, alumni support and influence. . . .

Virginia's VWIL solution is reminiscent of . . . Sweatt v. Painter, 339 U.S. 629 (1950). Reluctant to admit African Americans to its flagship University of Texas Law School, the State set up a separate school for Herman Sweatt and other black law students. . . .

. . . This Court contrasted resources at the new school with those at the school from which Sweatt had been excluded. . . .

More important than the tangible features, the Court emphasized, are "those qualities which are incapable of objective measurement but which make for greatness" in a school, including "reputation of the faculty, experience of the administration, position and influence of the alumni, standing in the community, traditions and prestige." . . . [T]he Court unanimously ruled that Texas had not shown "substantial equality in the [separate] educational opportunities" the State offered. . . . In line with *Sweatt*, we rule here that Virginia has not shown substantial equality in the separate educational opportunities the State supports at VWIL and VMI.

C

. . .

The Fourth Circuit plainly erred in exposing Virginia's VWIL plan to a deferential analysis, for "all gender-based classifications today" warrant "heightened scrutiny." . . . [T]he State has shown no "exceedingly persuasive justification" for withholding from women qualified for the experience premier training of the kind VMI affords.

. . .

Justice Thomas took no part in the consideration or decision of this case.

Chief Justice Rehnquist, concurring in the judgment.

. . .

I

Two decades ago in Craig v. Boren, 429 U.S. 190, 197 (1976), we announced that "[t]o withstand constitutional challenge, . . . classifications by gender must serve important governmental objectives and must be substantially related to achievement of those objectives." We have adhered to that standard of scrutiny ever since. . . . While the majority adheres to this test today, it also says that the State must demonstrate an "'exceedingly persuasive justification'" to support a gender-based classification. It is unfortunate that the Court thereby introduces an element of uncertainty respecting the appropriate test.

While terms like "important governmental objective" and "substantially related" are hardly models of precision, they have more content and specificity than does the phrase "exceedingly persuasive justification." That phrase is best confined, as it was first used, as an observation on the difficulty of meeting the applicable test, not as a formulation of the test itself. . . .

Our cases dealing with gender discrimination also require that the proffered purpose for the challenged law be the actual purpose. [O]n this ground . . . the Court rejects the first of two justifications Virginia offers[—]the goal of diversity among its public educational institutions. While I ultimately agree that the State has not carried the day with this justification, I disagree with the Court's method of analyzing the issue.

. . .

. . . [Not until the 1982 *Mississippi University for Women* decision was] Virginia [placed] on notice that VMI's men-only admissions policy was open to serious question.

. . .

. . . I agree with the Court that there is scant evidence in the record that [diversity in education with room for single-sex institutions] was the real reason that Virginia decided to maintain VMI as men only.* But, unlike the majority, I would consider only evidence that postdates . . . *Hogan*, and would draw no negative inferences from the State's actions before that time. [A]fter *Hogan*, the State was entitled to reconsider its policy with respect to VMI, and to not have earlier justifications, or lack thereof, held against it.

Even if diversity in educational opportunity were the State's actual objective, the State's position would still be problematic[, because] . . . the diversity benefited only one sex; there was single-sex public education available for men at VMI, but no corresponding single-sex public education available for women. . . .

I do not think, however, that the State's options were as limited as the majority may imply. . . . Had Virginia made a genuine effort to devote comparable public resources to a facility for women, and followed through on such a plan, it might well have avoided an equal protection violation. . . .

But . . . neither the governing board of VMI nor the State took any action after 1982. If diversity in the form of single-sex, as well as coeducational, institutions of higher learning were to be available to Virginians, that diversity had to be available to women as well as to men.

---

* The dissent equates our conclusion that VMI's "asserted interest in promoting diversity" is not "'genuine,'" with a "charge" that the diversity rationale is "a pretext for discriminating against women." Of course, those are not the same thing. I do not read the Court as saying that the diversity rationale is a pretext for discrimination, and I would not endorse such a proposition. We may find that diversity was not the State's real reason without suggesting, or having to show, that the real reason was "antifeminism." Our cases simply require that the proffered purpose . . . be the actual purpose, although not necessarily recorded. The dissent also says that the interest in diversity is so transparent that having to articulate it is "absurd on its face." Apparently, that rationale was not obvious to the Mission Study Committee which failed to list it among its reasons for maintaining VMI's all-men admission policy.

The dissent criticizes me for "disregarding the four all-women's private colleges in Virginia (generously assisted by public funds)." The private women's colleges are treated by the State exactly as all other private schools are treated, which includes the provision of tuition-assistance grants to Virginia residents. Virginia gives no special support to the women's single-sex education. But obviously, the same is not true for men's education. Had the State provided the kind of support for the private women's schools that it provides for VMI, this may have been a very different case. For in so doing, the State would have demonstrated that its interest in providing a single-sex education for men, was to some measure matched by an interest in providing the same opportunity for women.

Virginia offers a second justification for the single-sex admissions policy: maintenance of the adversative method. I agree with the Court that this justification does not serve an important governmental objective. A State does not have substantial interest in the adversative methodology unless it is pedagogically beneficial[, and] . . . there is no . . . evidence in the record that an adversative method is pedagogically beneficial or is any more likely to produce character traits than other methodologies.

II

. . . [I]t is not the "exclusion of women" that violates the Equal Protection Clause, but the maintenance of an all-men school without providing any—much less a comparable—institution for women.

Accordingly, the remedy should not necessarily require either the admission of women to VMI, or the creation of a VMI clone for women. An adequate remedy . . . might be a demonstration by Virginia that its interest in educating men in a single-sex environment is matched by its interest in educating women in a single-sex institution. . . . It would . . . suffic[e] if the two institutions offered the same quality of education and were of the same overall calibre.

If a state decides to create single-sex programs, [it] would, I expect, consider the public's interest and demand in designing curricula. And rightfully so. But the state should avoid assuming demand based on stereotypes; it must not assume *a priori*, without evidence, that there would be no interest in a women's school of civil engineering, or in a men's school of nursing.

In the end, . . . VWIL . . . fails as a remedy, because it is distinctly inferior to the existing men's institution and will continue to be for the foreseeable future. VWIL simply is not, in any sense, the institution that VMI is. In particular, VWIL is . . . appended to a private college, not a self-standing institution; and VWIL is substantially underfunded as compared to VMI. I therefore ultimately agree with the Court that Virginia has not provided an adequate remedy.

Justice Scalia, dissenting.

Today the Court shuts down an institution that has served the people of the Commonwealth of Virginia with pride and distinction for over a century and a half. To achieve that desired result, it rejects . . . the factual findings of two courts below, sweeps aside the precedents of this Court, and ignores the history of our people. As to facts: it explicitly rejects the finding that there exist "gender-based developmental differences" supporting Virginia's restriction of the "adversative" method to only a men's institution, and the finding that the all-male composition of . . . VMI is essential to [its] character. As to precedent: it drastically revises our established standards for reviewing sex-based classifications. And as to history: it counts for nothing the long tradition . . . of men's military colleges supported by both States and the Federal Government.

Much of the Court's opinion is devoted to deprecating the closed-mindedness of our forebears with regard to women's education, and even with regard to the treatment of women in areas that have nothing to do with education. Closed-minded they were—as every age is, including our own, with regard to matters it cannot guess, because it simply does not consider them debatable. The virtue of a democratic system with a First Amendment is that it readily enables the people, over time, to be persuaded that what they took for granted is not so, and to change their laws accordingly. That system is destroyed if the smug assurances of each age are removed from the democratic process and written into the Constitution. . . .

I

. . .

[The] abstract tests such as rational-basis, intermediate, and strict scrutiny . . . cannot supersede—and indeed ought to be crafted *so as to reflect*—those constant and unbroken national traditions that embody the people's understanding of ambiguous constitutional texts. . . .

. . . [T]he tradition of having government-funded military schools for men is as well rooted in the traditions of this country as the tradition of sending only men into military combat. The people may decide to change the one tradition, like the other, through democratic processes; but the assertion that either tradition has been unconstitutional through the centuries is not law, but politics-smuggled-into-law.

And the same applies, more broadly, to single-sex education in general, which . . . is threatened by today's decision with the cut-off of all state and federal support. . . .

. . .

II

To reject the Court's disposition today, however, it is not necessary to accept my view that the Court's made-up tests cannot displace longstanding national traditions as the primary determinant of what the Constitution means. It is only necessary to apply honestly the test the Court has been applying to sex-based classifications for the past two decades. . . .

. . . [T]he United States urged us to hold in this case "that strict scrutiny is the correct constitutional standard for evaluating classifications that deny opportunities to individuals based on their sex." . . . The Court, while making no reference to the Government's argument, effectively accepts it.

. . . [T]he Court . . . interpret[s] "exceedingly persuasive justification" in a fashion that contradicts the reasoning of *Hogan* and our other precedents.

That is essential to the Court's result, which can only be achieved by establishing that intermediate scrutiny is not survived if there are *some* women interested in attending VMI, capable of undertaking its activities, and able to meet its physical demands. . . .

Only the amorphous "exceedingly persuasive justification" phrase, and not the standard elaboration of intermediate scrutiny, can be made to yield th[e] conclusion that VMI's single-sex composition is unconstitutional because there exist several women (or, one would have to conclude under the Court's reasoning, a single woman) willing and able to undertake VMI's program.

Intermediate scrutiny has never required a least-restrictive-means analysis, but only a "substantial relation" between the classification and the state interests that it serves. ...There is simply no support in our cases for the notion that a sex-based classification is invalid unless it relates to characteristics that hold true in every instance.

Not content to execute a *de facto* abandonment of the intermediate scrutiny that has been our standard for sex-based classifications for some two decades, the Court purports to reserve the question whether, even in principle, a higher standard (i.e., strict scrutiny) should apply....

[I]f the question of the applicable standard of review for sex-based classifications were ... reconsider[ed], the stronger argument would be not for elevating the standard to strict scrutiny, but for reducing it to rational-basis review. The latter certainly has a firmer foundation in our past jurisprudence: Whereas no majority of the Court has ever applied strict scrutiny in a case involving sex-based classifications, we routinely applied rational-basis review until the 1970's. ...And of course normal, rational-basis review of sex-based classifications would be much more in accord with the genesis of heightened standards of judicial review, the famous footnote in United States v. Carolene Products Co., 304 U.S. 144 (1938). ...It is hard to consider women a "discrete and insular minorit[y]" unable to employ the "political processes ordinarily to be relied upon," when they constitute a majority of the electorate. And the suggestion that they are incapable of exerting that political power smacks of the same paternalism that the Court so roundly condemns. Moreover, a long list of legislation proves the proposition false. See, e.g., Equal Pay Act of 1963 ...; Title VII of the Civil Rights Act of 1964 ...; Title IX of the Education Amendments of 1972. ...; Women's Business Ownership Act of 1988. ...; Violence Against Women Act of 1994. ...

III

... [T]he question ... is whether the exclusion of women from VMI is "substantially related to an important governmental objective."

A

... Virginia has an important state interest in providing effective college education for its citizens. That single-sex instruction is an approach substantially related to that interest should be evident enough from the long and continuing history in this country of men's and women's colleges....

. . .

... [S]o too a State's decision to maintain within its system one school that provides the adversative method is "substantially related" to its goal of good education. Moreover, it was uncontested that "if the state were to establish a women's VMI-type [i.e., adversative] program, the program would attract an insufficient number of participants to make the program work," ...; and it was found by the District Court that if Virginia were to include women in VMI, the school "would eventually find it necessary to drop the adversative system altogether,". ...Thus, Virginia's options were an adversative method that excludes women or no adversative method at all.

[S]ingle-sex education and a distinctive educational method "represent legitimate contributions to diversity in the Virginia higher education system." . . .

... Substantial evidence in the District Court [also] demonstrated that the Commonwealth has long proceeded on the principle that "'[h]igher education resources should be viewed as a whole—public and private'"—because such an approach enhances diversity and because "'it is academic and economic waste to permit unwarranted duplication.'" ... (quoting 1974 Report of the General Assembly Commission on Higher Education to the General Assembly of Virginia). It is thus significant that, whereas there are "four all-female private [colleges] in Virginia," there is only "one private all-male college," which "indicates that the private sector is providing for th[e] [former] form of education to a much greater extent that it provides for all-male education." ... In these circumstances, Virginia's election to fund one public all-male institution and one on the adversative model—and to concentrate its resources in a single entity that serves both these interests in diversity—is substantially related to the State's important educational interests.

B

...

... The Court suggests that Virginia's ... asserted interest in promoting diversity of educational options ... is not "genuin[e]," but is a pretext for discriminating against women.... The relevance of the Mission Study Committee is that its very creation, its sober 3–year study, and the analysis it produced, utterly refute the claim that VMI has elected to maintain its all-male studentbody composition for some misogynistic reason.

The Court ... is wrong ... in its implication that ... an explicit statement of "actual purposes" is needed....

It is, moreover, not true that Virginia's contemporary reasons for maintaining VMI are not explicitly recorded.... As the parties stipulated, th[e 1990 Commission R]eport "notes that the hallmarks of Virginia's educational policy are 'diversity and autonomy.'" ...

...

... [T]he Court [also] finds fault with Virginia's failure to offer education based on the adversative training method to women[,] dismiss[ing] the District Court's " 'findings' on 'gender-based developmental differences' " ...

Ultimately, in fact, the Court does not deny the evidence supporting these findings ... [but] simply dispenses with the evidence submitted at trial—it never says that a single finding of the District Court is clearly erroneous—in favor of the Justices' own view of the world. ...

... But treating the evidence as irrelevant is absolutely necessary for the Court to reach its conclusion. ...

...

The Court's analysis ... [, a]pplied generally, ... means that whenever a State's ultimate objective is "great enough to accommodate women" (as it always will be), then the State will be held to have violated the Equal Protection Clause if it restricts to men even one means by which it pursues that objective—no matter how few women are interested in pursuing the objective by that means, no matter how much the single-sex program will have to be changed if both sexes are admitted, and no matter how beneficial that program has theretofore been to its participants.

... [T]hat VMI would not have to change very much if it were to admit women ... is irrelevant....

But if such a debate were relevant, the Court would certainly be on the losing side[, given] ... findings by two courts below, amply supported by the evidence, ... that VMI would be fundamentally altered if it admitted women. ...[5]

... Finally, the absence of a precise "all-women's analogue" to VMI is irrelevant. In Mississippi Univ. for Women v. Hogan, 458 U.S. 718 (1982), we attached no constitutional significance to the absence of an all-male nursing school. As Virginia notes, if a program restricted to one sex is necessarily unconstitutional unless there is a parallel program restricted to the other sex, "the opinion in *Hogan* could have ended with its first footnote, which observed that 'Mississippi maintains no other single-sex public university or college.' " ...

... VWIL [also] is, under our established test, irrelevant, so long as VMI's all-male character is "substantially related" to an important state goal. But VWIL now exists, and the Court's treatment of it shows how far-reaching today's decision is.

... Even though VWIL was carefully designed by professional educators who have tremendous experience in the area, and survived the test of adversarial litigation, the Court simply declares, with no basis in the evidence, that these professionals acted on "'overbroad' generalizations."

C

[T]he concurrence ... finds VMI unconstitutional on a basis that is more moderate than the Court's but only at the expense of being even more implausible. The concurrence offers three reasons: First, that there is "scant evidence in the record" that diversity of educational offering was the real reason for Virginia's maintaining VMI. ...I have cited the clearest statements of diversity as a goal for higher education in [several reports.] There is *no* evidence to the contrary, once one rejects (as the concurrence rightly does) the relevance of VMI's founding in days when attitudes towards the education of women were different. ...[I]t is absurd on its face even to *demand* "evidence" to prove that the Commonwealth's reason for maintaining a men's military academy is that a men's military academy provides a distinctive type of educational experience (i.e., fosters diversity). What other purpose *would* the Commonwealth have? One may argue, as the Court does, that this *type* of diversity is designed only to indulge hostility towards women—but that is a separate point, explicitly rejected by the concurrence, and amply refuted by the evidence....

Second, the ... pedagogical benefits of VMI's adversarial approach were not only proved, but were a given in this litigation. The reason the woman applicant who prompted this suit wanted to enter VMI was ... [that s]he wanted the distinctive adversarial education that VMI provided. ...

A third reason the concurrence offers ... is ... that after our decision in *Hogan* ... the Commonwealth should have known that what this Court expected of it was ... the creation of a state all-women's program. Any lawyer who gave that advice ... ought to have been either disbarred or committed....

---

[5] The Court's do-it-yourself approach to factfinding ... is exemplified by its invocation of the experience of the federal military academies to prove that not much change would occur. In fact, the District Court noted that "the West Point experience" supported the theory that a coeducational VMI would have to "adopt a [different] system," for West Point found it necessary upon becoming coeducational to "move away" from its adversative system. ...

In any event, "diversity in the form of single-sex, as well as coeducational, institutions of higher learning," *is* "available to women as well as to men" in Virginia. The concurrence is able to assert the contrary only by disregarding the four all-women's private colleges in Virginia (generously assisted by public funds) and the Commonwealth's longstanding policy of coordinating public with private educational offerings....

IV

. . .

Under the constitutional principles announced and applied today, single-sex public education is unconstitutional ... [even though] the Court creates the illusion that government officials in some future case will have a clear shot at justifying some sort of single-sex public education....

. . .

[T]he rationale of today's decision is sweeping: for sex-based classifications, a redefinition of intermediate scrutiny that makes it indistinguishable from strict scrutiny. Indeed, the Court indicates that if any program restricted to one sex is "uniqu[e]," it must be opened to members of the opposite sex "who have the will and capacity" to participate in it. [T]he single-sex program [in]capable of being characterized as "unique" is ... nonexistent.

. . .

There are few extant single-sex public educational programs. The potential of today's decision for widespread disruption of existing institutions lies in its application to private single-sex education. ...

... The Government ... contends that private colleges which are the direct or indirect beneficiaries of government funding are not thereby necessarily converted into state actors to which the Equal Protection Clause is then applicable. ... That is true. It is also virtually meaningless.

The issue will be not whether government assistance turns private colleges into state actors, but whether the government itself would be violating the Constitution by providing state support to single-sex colleges....

The only hope for state-assisted single-sex private schools is that the Court will not apply in the future the principles of law it has applied today. That is a substantial hope, I am happy and ashamed to say.... It will certainly be possible for this Court to write a future opinion that ignores the broad principles of law set forth today, and that characterizes as utterly dispositive the opinion's perceptions that VMI was a uniquely prestigious all-male institution, conceived in chauvinism, etc., etc. I will not join that opinion.

. . .

WHO ARE DISCRIMINATED AGAINST—MALES OR FEMALES?

In *Frontiero v. Richardson*, supra, it was clear that the discrimination was against females. A serviceman who was married received increased quarters allowances and medical and dental benefits whether or not his wife was dependent on him while a married servicewoman received the benefits only if her husband was dependent on her.

But what of statutes like the one in Weinberger v. Wiesenfeld, 420 U.S. 636 (1975)? Social Security Act benefits of a deceased husband and father covered by the Act were payable both to the widow and the minor children in her care.

Such benefits on the basis of the earnings of a deceased wife and mother covered by the Act however were paid only to the children and not to the father. Is this a discrimination against males because they receive no payments when the covered wife dies while the wife receives payments when the covered husband dies? Or is this a discrimination against women because women workers covered by the Act received less protection for their families than men workers? In *Wiesenfeld* the Court held that the discrimination was against women and held it unconstitutional.

The issue next arose in Califano v. Goldfarb, 430 U.S. 199 (1977). Under the Federal Old–Age, Survivors, and Disability Insurance Benefits program survivors benefits were paid to the widow of a deceased husband covered by the Act but were payable to a widower whose wife was covered only if he received one-half or more of his support from his deceased wife. The Court held the classification invalid—four Justices regarded it as discriminating against female workers and invalid, while Justice Stevens, concurring, regarded it as discriminating against male survivors but still invalid. The four dissenters analyzed the law as benefitting female survivors.

In Wengler v. Druggists Mutual Insurance Co., 446 U.S. 142 (1980), the Court held that a Missouri workers' compensation law unconstitutionally discriminated "against both men and women." The law provided death benefits to widows of men who died in work-related accidents without requiring proof of dependency on the husband's earnings, but did not provide such benefits to a widower unless he demonstrated actual dependence on his wife's earnings or mental or physical incapacity to earn wages. Justice White's opinion for seven Justices reasoned that the law discriminated against working women by devaluing the importance of their efforts as family providers and also discriminated against surviving husbands by withholding benefits unless they proved incapacity or dependency. The discrimination was unjustified as a means of providing for needy spouses, the Court said, because "the discriminatory means employed—discrimination against women wage earners and surviving male spouses" failed to substantially serve that important governmental objective. The claim that administrative convenience justified using gender as a proxy for dependency also was rejected. The case was remanded to allow the Missouri Supreme Court to determine "whether the defect should be cured by extending the presumption of dependence to widowers or by eliminating it for widows." Justice Stevens again concurred, arguing that the law discriminated only against males, although unjustifiably so. Males were disadvantaged whether the focus was on the requirement that a surviving dependent male had to prove dependency when a woman did not, on the fact that nondependent women could receive benefits whereas nondependent men could not, or on the wife's lesser need for life insurance on her husband's life. Justice Rehnquist dissented.

EQUAL RIGHTS AMENDMENT PROPOSED

On March 22, 1972, Congress passed and submitted to the legislatures of the states for ratification an amendment to the Constitution reading as follows:

"Section 1. Equality of rights under the law shall not be denied or abridged by the United States or by any State on account of sex.

"Section 2. The Congress shall have the power to enforce, by appropriate legislation, the provisions of this article.

"Section 3. This amendment shall take effect two years after the date of ratification."

The statute proposing the amendment provided that the ratifications must occur within seven years. By 1978, 35 states (3 less than the required three-fourths) had ratified, but three of them had rescinded their previous ratification. Congress then passed a statute extending the time for ratification to June 30, 1982. The necessary number of states did not ratify by that deadline.

D. THE REQUIREMENT OF A DISCRIMINATORY PURPOSE—THE RELEVANCE OF DISCRIMINATORY IMPACT

Washington v. Davis

426 U.S. 229, 96 S.Ct. 2040, 48 L.Ed.2d 597 (1976).

Mr. Justice White delivered the opinion of the Court.

This case involves the validity of a qualifying test administered to applicants for positions as police officers in the District of Columbia Metropolitan Police Department. The test was sustained by the District Court but invalidated by the Court of Appeals. We ... reverse....

I.

[Rejected applicants complained in the District Court] that the Department's recruiting procedures discriminated on the basis of race against black applicants by a series of practices including, but not limited to, a written personnel test which excluded a disproportionately high number of Negro applicants. These practices were asserted to violate respondents' rights "under the due process clause of the Fifth Amendment to the United States Constitution, under 42 U.S.C. § 1981 and under D.C.Code § 1–320." ... [On cross-motions for summary judgment, the] District Court granted petitioners' and denied respondents' motions....

According to the findings and conclusions of the District Court, to be accepted by the Department and to enter an intensive 17–week training program, the police recruit was required to satisfy certain physical and character standards, to be a high school graduate or its equivalent and to receive a grade of at least 40 on "Test 21," which is "an examination that is used generally throughout the federal service," which "was developed by the [United States] Civil Service Commission not the Police Department" and which was "designed to test verbal ability, vocabulary, reading and comprehension."

The validity of Test 21 was the sole issue before the court on the motions for summary judgment. The District Court noted that there was no claim of "an intentional discrimination or purposeful discriminatory actions" but only a claim that Test 21 bore no relationship to job performance and "has a highly discriminatory impact in screening out black candidates." Petitioners' evidence, the District Court said, warranted three conclusions: "(a) The number of black police officers, while substantial, is not proportionate to the population mix of the city. (b) A higher percentage of blacks fail the Test than whites. (c) The Test has not been validated to establish its reliability for measuring subsequent job performance." Ibid. This showing was deemed sufficient to shift the burden of proof to the defendants in the action, petitioners here; but the court nevertheless concluded that on the undisputed facts respondents were not entitled to relief. The District Court relied on several factors. Since August 1969, 44% of new police force recruits had been black; that figure also represented the proportion of blacks on the total force and was roughly equivalent to 20–29–year–old blacks in the 50–mile radius in which the recruiting efforts of the Police Department had been concentrated. It was undisputed that the Department had systematically and affirmatively sought to enroll black officers many of whom passed the test but failed to report for duty. The District Court rejected the assertion that Test 21 was culturally slanted to favor whites and was "satisfied that the undisputable facts prove the test to be reasonably and directly related to the requirements of the police recruit training program and that it is neither so designed nor operated to discriminate against otherwise qualified blacks." It was thus not necessary to show that Test 21 was not only a useful indicator of training school performance but had also been validated in terms of job performance—"the lack of job performance validation does not defeat the test, given its direct relationship to recruiting and the valid part it plays in this process." The District Court ultimately concluded that "the proof is wholly lacking that a police officer qualifies on the color of his skin rather than ability" and that the Department "should not be required on this showing to lower standards or to abandon efforts to achieve excellence."

Having lost on both constitutional and statutory issues in the District Court, respondents brought the case to the Court of Appeals claiming that their summary judgment motion, which rested on purely constitutional grounds, should have been granted. The tendered constitutional issue was whether the use of Test 21 invidiously discriminated against Negroes and hence denied them due process of law contrary to the commands of the Fifth Amendment. The Court of Appeals, addressing that issue, announced that it would be guided by Griggs v. Duke Power Co., 401 U.S. 424 (1971), a case involving the interpretation and application of Title VII of the Civil Rights Act of 1964, and held that the statutory standards elucidated in that case were to govern the due process question tendered in this one.... The court went on to declare that lack of discriminatory intent in designing and administering Test 21 was irrelevant; the critical fact was rather that a far greater proportion of blacks— four times as many—failed the test than did whites. This disproportionate impact, standing alone and without regard to whether it indicated a discriminatory purpose, was held sufficient to establish a constitutional violation, absent proof by petitioners that the test was an adequate measure of job performance in addition to being an indicator of probable success in the training program, a burden which the court ruled petitioners had failed to discharge.[a]

. . .

II.

Because the Court of Appeals erroneously applied the legal standards applicable to Title VII cases in resolving the constitutional issue before it, we reverse its judgment in respondents' favor. Although the petition for certiorari

[a] In Wards Cove Packing Co. v. Atonio, 490 U.S. 642 (1989), the Court interpreted *Griggs* narrowly by holding that once a plaintiff demonstrates that a particular employment practice caused an adverse disproportionate impact on nonwhites, the burden imposed on the employer is only a burden to "produce" a "legitimate business justification" for the practice, not a burden of "proof" of that or any higher level of justification. A plaintiff unable to persuade a trier of fact that a business necessity defense is illegitimate could only prevail by showing that the employer refused to adopt an equal-ly effective alternate employment practice with less disparate impact. In the Civil Rights Act of 1991, P.L. 102–166, 105 Stat. 1071, Congress overrode *Wards Cove*, at least partially, by making the employer, not the challenger, carry the burden of "persuasion" in disparate impact cases that "the challenged practice is job related ... and consistent with business necessity." The Act also forbids using an employer's "demonstration that an employment practice is required by business necessity ... as a defense against a claim of intentional discrimination...."

did not present this ground for reversal, our Rule 40(1)(d)(2) provides that we "may notice a plain error not presented"; and this is an appropriate occasion to invoke the rule.

As the Court of Appeals understood Title VII, employees or applicants proceeding under it need not concern themselves with the employer's possibly discriminatory purpose but instead may focus solely on the racially differential impact of the challenged hiring or promotion practices. This is not the constitutional rule. We have never held that the constitutional standard for adjudicating claims of invidious racial discrimination is identical to the standards applicable under Title VII, and we decline to do so today.

The central purpose of the Equal Protection Clause of the Fourteenth Amendment is the prevention of official conduct discriminating on the basis of race. It is also true that the Due Process Clause of the Fifth Amendment contains an equal protection component prohibiting the United States from invidiously discriminating between individuals or groups. Bolling v. Sharpe, 347 U.S. 497 (1954). But our cases have not embraced the proposition that a law or other official act, without regard to whether it reflects a racially discriminatory purpose, is unconstitutional *solely* because it has a racially disproportionate impact.

Almost 100 years ago, Strauder v. West Virginia, 100 U.S. 303 (1879), established that the exclusion of Negroes from grand and petit juries in criminal proceedings violated the Equal Protection Clause, but the fact that a particular jury or a series of juries does not statistically reflect the racial composition of the community does not in itself make out an invidious discrimination forbidden by the Clause. "A purpose to discriminate must be present which may be proven by systematic exclusion of eligible jurymen of the prescribed race or by an unequal application of the law to such an extent as to show intentional discrimination." Akins v. Texas, 325 U.S. 398, 403–404 (1945). A defendant in a criminal case is entitled "to require that the State not deliberately and systematically deny to the members of his race the right to participate as jurors in the administration of justice." See also Carter v. Jury Commission, 396 U.S. 320, 335–337, 339 (1970); Cassell v. Texas, 339 U.S. 282, 287–290 (1950); Patton v. Mississippi, 332 U.S. 463, 468–469 (1947).

The rule is the same in other contexts. Wright v. Rockefeller, 376 U.S. 52 (1964), upheld a New York congressional apportionment statute against claims that district lines had been racially gerrymandered. The challenged districts were made up predominantly of whites or of minority races, and their boundaries were irregularly drawn. The challengers did not prevail because they failed to prove that the New York legislature "was either motivated by racial considerations or in fact drew the districts on racial lines"; the plaintiffs had not shown that the statute "was the product of a state contrivance to segregate on the basis of race or place of origin." ... The dissenters were in agreement that the issue was whether the "boundaries ... were purposefully drawn on racial lines." ...

The school desegregation cases have also adhered to the basic equal protection principle that the invidious quality of a law claimed to be racially discriminatory must ultimately be traced to a racially discriminatory purpose. That there are both predominantly black and predominantly white schools in a community is not alone violative of the Equal Protection Clause. The essential element of *de jure* segregation is "a current condition of segregation resulting from intentional state action ... the differentiating factor between *de jure* segregation and so-called *de facto* segregation ... is *purpose* or *intent* to segregate." Keyes v. School District No. 1, 413 U.S. 189, 205, 208 (1973). The

Court has also recently rejected allegations of racial discrimination based solely on the statistically disproportionate racial impact of various provisions of the Social Security Act because "the acceptance of appellant's constitutional theory would render suspect each difference in treatment among the grant classes, however lacking the racial motivation and however rational the treatment might be." Jefferson v. Hackney, 406 U.S. 535, 548 (1972). And compare Hunter v. Erickson, 393 U.S. 385 (1969), with James v. Valtierra, 402 U.S. 137 (1971).

This is not to say that the necessary discriminatory racial purpose must be express or appear on the face of the statute, or that a law's disproportionate impact is irrelevant in cases involving Constitution-based claims of racial discrimination. A statute, otherwise neutral on its face, must not be applied so as invidiously to discriminate on the basis of race. Yick Wo v. Hopkins, 118 U.S. 356 (1886). It is also clear from the cases dealing with racial discrimination in the selection of juries that the systematic exclusion of Negroes is itself such an "unequal application of the law ... as to show intentional discrimination." Akins v. Texas, supra, at 404. Smith v. Texas, 311 U.S. 128 (1940); Pierre v. Louisiana, 306 U.S. 354 (1939); Neal v. Delaware, 103 U.S. 370 (1881). A prima facie case of discriminatory purpose may be proved as well by the absence of Negroes on a particular jury combined with the failure of the jury commissioners to be informed of eligible Negro jurors in a community, Hill v. Texas, 316 U.S. 400, 404 (1942), or with racially nonneutral selection procedures, Alexander v. Louisiana, 405 U.S. 625 (1972); Avery v. Georgia, 345 U.S. 559 (1953); Whitus v. Georgia, 385 U.S. 545 (1967). With a prima facie case made out, "the burden of proof shifts to the State to rebut the presumption of unconstitutional action by showing that permissible racially neutral selection criteria and procedures have produced the monochromatic result." Alexander, supra, at 632. See also Turner v. Fouche, 396 U.S. 346, 361 (1970); Eubanks v. Louisiana, 356 U.S. 584, 587 (1958).

Necessarily, an invidious discriminatory purpose may often be inferred from the totality of the relevant facts, including the fact, if it is true, that the law bears more heavily on one race than another. It is also not infrequently true that the discriminatory impact—in the jury cases for example, the total or seriously disproportionate exclusion of Negroes from jury venires—may for all practical purposes demonstrate unconstitutionality because in various circumstances the discrimination is very difficult to explain on nonracial grounds. Nevertheless, we have not held that a law, neutral on its face and serving ends otherwise within the power of government to pursue, is invalid under the Equal Protection Clause simply because it may affect a greater proportion of one race than of another. Disproportionate impact is not irrelevant, but it is not the sole touchstone of an invidious racial discrimination forbidden by the Constitution. Standing alone, it does not trigger the rule, McLaughlin v. Florida, 379 U.S. 184 (1964), that racial classifications are to be subjected to the strictest scrutiny and are justifiable only by the weightiest of considerations.

There are some indications to the contrary in our cases. In Palmer v. Thompson, 403 U.S. 217 (1971), the city of Jackson, Miss., following a court decree to this effect, desegregated all of its public facilities save five swimming pools which had been operated by the city and which, following the decree, were closed by ordinance pursuant to a determination by the city council that closure was necessary to preserve peace and order and that integrated pools could not be economically operated. Accepting the finding that the pools were closed to avoid violence and economic loss, this Court rejected the argument that the abandonment of this service was inconsistent with the outstanding desegregation decree and that the otherwise seemingly permissible ends served by the ordinance could be impeached by demonstrating that racially invidious motivations had prompted the city council's action. The holding was that the city was not overtly or covertly operating segregated pools and was extending identical treatment to both whites and Negroes. The opinion warned against grounding decision on legislative purpose or motivation, thereby lending support for the proposition that the operative effect of the law rather than its purpose is the paramount factor. But the holding of the case was that the legitimate purposes of the ordinance—to preserve peace and avoid deficits— were not open to impeachment by evidence that the councilmen were actually motivated by racial considerations. Whatever dicta the opinion may contain, the decision did not involve, much less invalidate, a statute or ordinance having neutral purposes but disproportionate racial consequences.

Wright v. Council of the City of Emporia, 407 U.S. 451 (1972), also indicates that in proper circumstances, the racial impact of a law, rather than its discriminatory purpose, is the critical factor. That case involved the division of a school district. The issue was whether the division was consistent with an outstanding order of a federal court to desegregate the dual school system found to have existed in the area. The constitutional predicate for the District Court's invalidation of the divided district was "the enforcement until 1969 of racial segregation in the public school system of which Emporia had always been a part." Id., at 459. There was thus no need to find "an independent constitutional violation." Ibid. Citing *Palmer v. Thompson,* we agreed with the District Court that the division of the district had the effect of interfering with the federal decree and should be set aside.

That neither *Palmer* nor *Wright* was understood to have changed the prevailing rule is apparent from *Keyes v. School District No. 1,* supra, where the principal issue in litigation was whether and to what extent there had been purposeful discrimination resulting in a partially or wholly segregated school system. Nor did other later cases, *Alexander v. Louisiana,* supra, and *Jefferson v. Hackney,* supra, indicate that either *Palmer* or *Wright* had worked a fundamental change in equal protection law.[11]

Both before and after *Palmer v. Thompson,* however, various Courts of Appeals have held in several contexts, including public employment, that the substantially disproportionate racial impact of a statute or official practice standing alone and without regard to discriminatory purpose, suffices to prove racial discrimination violating the Equal Protection Clause absent some justification going substantially beyond what would be necessary to validate most other legislative classifications. The cases impressively demonstrate that there is another side to the issue; but, with all due respect, to the extent that those cases rested on or expressed the view that proof of discriminatory racial purpose is unnecessary in making out an equal protection violation, we are in disagreement.

As an initial matter, we have difficulty understanding how a law establishing a racially neutral qualification for employment is nevertheless racially discriminatory and denies "any person equal protection of the laws" simply because a greater proportion of Negroes fail to qualify than members of other racial or ethnic groups. Had respondents, along with all others who had failed

---

[11] To the extent that *Palmer* suggests a generally applicable proposition that legislative purpose is irrelevant in constitutional adjudication, our prior cases—as indicated in the text—are to the contrary; and very shortly after *Palmer,* all Members of the Court majority in that case joined the Court's opin- ion in Lemon v. Kurtzman, 403 U.S. 602 (1971), which dealt with the issue of public financing for private schools and which announced, as the Court had several times before, that the validity of public aid to church- related schools includes close inquiry into the purpose of the challenged statute.

Test 21, whether white or black, brought an action claiming that the test denied each of them equal protection of the laws as compared with those who had passed with high enough scores to qualify them as police recruits, it is most unlikely that their challenge would have been sustained. Test 21, which is administered generally to prospective government employees, concededly seeks to ascertain whether those who take it have acquired a particular level of verbal skill; and it is untenable that the Constitution prevents the government from seeking modestly to upgrade the communicative abilities of its employees rather than to be satisfied with some lower level of competence, particularly where the job requires special ability to communicate orally and in writing. Respondents, as Negroes, could no more successfully claim that the test denied them equal protection than could white applicants who also failed. The conclusion would not be different in the face of proof that more Negroes than whites had been disqualified by Test 21. That other Negroes also failed to score well would, alone, not demonstrate that respondents individually were being denied equal protection of the laws by the application of an otherwise valid qualifying test being administered to prospective police recruits.

Nor on the facts of the case before us would the disproportionate impact of Test 21 warrant the conclusion that it is a purposeful device to discriminate against Negroes and hence an infringement of the constitutional rights of respondents as well as other black applicants. As we have said, the test is neutral on its face and rationally may be said to serve a purpose the government is constitutionally empowered to pursue. Even agreeing with the District Court that the differential racial effect of Test 21 called for further inquiry, we think the District Court correctly held that the affirmative efforts of the Metropolitan Police Department to recruit black officers, the changing racial composition of the recruit classes and of the force in general, and the relationship of the test to the training program negated any inference that the Department discriminated on the basis of race or that "a police officer qualifies on the color of his skin rather than ability." 348 F.Supp., at 18.

Under Title VII, Congress provided that when hiring and promotion practices disqualifying substantially disproportionate numbers of blacks are challenged, discriminatory purpose need not be proved, and that it is an insufficient response to demonstrate some rational basis for the challenged practices. It is necessary, in addition, that they be "validated" in terms of job performance in any one of several ways, perhaps by ascertaining the minimum skill, ability or potential necessary for the position at issue and determining whether the qualifying tests are appropriate for the selection of qualified applicants for the job in question. However this process proceeds, it involves a more probing judicial review of, and less deference to, the seemingly reasonable acts of administrators and executives than is appropriate under the Constitution where special racial impact, without discriminatory purpose, is claimed. We are not disposed to adopt this more rigorous standard for the purposes of applying the Fifth and the Fourteenth Amendments in cases such as this.

A rule that a statute designed to serve neutral ends is nevertheless invalid, absent compelling justification, if in practice it benefits or burdens one race more than another would be far reaching and would raise serious questions about, and perhaps invalidate, a whole range of tax, welfare, public service, regulatory, and licensing statutes that may be more burdensome to the poor and to the average black than to the more affluent white.[14]

---

[14] Goodman, De Facto School Segregation: Constitutional and Empirical Analysis, 60 Cal.L.Rev. 275, 300 (1972), suggests that disproportionate impact analysis might invalidate "tests and qualifications for voting, draft deferment, public employment, jury ser-

Given that rule, such consequences would perhaps be likely to follow. However, in our view, extension of the rule beyond those areas where it is already applicable by reason of statute, such as in the field of public employment, should await legislative prescription.

As we have indicated, it was error to direct summary judgment for respondents based on the Fifth Amendment.

III.

[The Court also rejected the statutory claims.]

. . . Based on the evidence before him, the District Judge concluded that Test 21 was directly related to the requirements of the police training program and that a positive relationship between the test and training course performance was sufficient to validate the former, wholly aside from its possible relationship to actual performance as a police officer. . . .

. . .

The judgment of the Court of Appeals accordingly is reversed.

So ordered.

Mr. Justice Stewart joins Parts I and II of the Court's opinion.

Mr. Justice Stevens, concurring.

While I agree with the Court's disposition of this case, I add these comments on the constitutional issue discussed in Part II. . . .

. . .

Frequently the most probative evidence of intent will be objective evidence of what actually happened rather than evidence describing the subjective state of mind of the actor. . . .

My point in making this observation is to suggest that the line between discriminatory purpose and discriminatory impact is not nearly as bright, and perhaps not quite as critical, as the reader of the Court's opinion might assume. I agree, of course, that a constitutional issue does not arise every time some disproportionate impact is shown. On the other hand, when the disproportion is as dramatic as in *Gomillion* or *Yick Wo,* it really does not matter whether the standard is phrased in terms of purpose or effect. Therefore, although I accept the statement of the general rule in the Court's opinion, I am not yet prepared to indicate how that standard should be applied in the many cases which have formulated the governing standard in different language.

. . .

Mr. Justice Brennan, with whom Mr. Justice Marshall joins, dissenting. . . .

[This opinion addressed only the statutory issues explored in Part III of the Court's opinion.]

VILLAGE OF ARLINGTON HEIGHTS v. METROPOLITAN HOUSING DEVELOPMENT CORP., 429 U.S. 252 (1977). Metropolitan Housing

vice and other government-conferred benefits and opportunities . . .; [s]ales taxes, bail schedules, utility rates, bridge tolls, license fees, and other state-imposed charges." It has also been argued that minimum wage and usury laws as well as professional licensing requirements would require major modifications in light of the unequal impact rule. Silverman, Equal Protection, Economic Legislation and Racial Discrimination, 25 Vand. L.Rev. 1183 (1972). See also Demsetz, Minorities in the Market Place, 43 N.C.L.Rev. 271.

submitted a request for the rezoning of a 15–acre parcel from single-family to multiple-family classification for the purpose of building apartments for low and moderate income families. The apartments were to be constructed under a federal program requiring an affirmative marketing plan to assure that the development would be racially integrated. Public hearings were held. Some persons objected to the introduction of low income racially integrated housing in the area. Many focussed on the fact that the surrounding land had always been zoned for and occupied by single-family housing and neighboring citizens built or purchased their homes relying on the classification. They also noted that the city's consistent policy had been to zone for multiple-family housing only in areas that would serve as a buffer between single-family and commercial developments, whereas the parcel involved here did not adjoin any commercial district. The zoning request was denied and a suit was brought in the federal district court seeking declaratory and injunctive relief. The trial judge ruled for the city but the court of appeals reversed, finding that the "ultimate effect" of the denial was racially discriminatory. The Supreme Court reversed the court of appeals.

Mr. Justice Powell, speaking for the Court, said, in part:

III.

"Our decision last Term in Washington v. Davis, 426 U.S. 229 (1976), made it clear that official action will not be held unconstitutional solely because it results in a racially disproportionate impact. . . .

"*Davis* does not require a plaintiff to prove that the challenged action rested solely on racially discriminatory purposes. Rarely can it be said that a legislature or administrative body operating under a broad mandate made a decision motivated solely by a single concern, or even that a particular purpose was the 'dominant' or 'primary' one. In fact, it is because legislators and administrators are properly concerned with balancing numerous competing considerations that courts refrain from reviewing the merits of their decisions, absent a showing of arbitrariness or irrationality. But racial discrimination is not just another competing consideration. When there is a proof that a discriminatory purpose has been a motivating factor in the decision, this judicial deference is no longer justified.[12]

"Determining whether invidious discriminatory purpose was a motivating factor demands a sensitive inquiry into such circumstantial and direct evidence of intent as may be available. The impact of the official action—whether it 'bears more heavily on one race than another,' Washington v. Davis, 426 U.S., at 242—may provide an important starting point. Sometimes a clear pattern, unexplainable on grounds other than race, emerges from the effect of the state action even when the governing legislation appears neutral on its face. Yick Wo v. Hopkins, 118 U.S. 356 (1886); Guinn v. United States, 238 U.S. 347 (1915); Lane v. Wilson, 307 U.S. 268 (1939); Gomillion v. Lightfoot, 364 U.S. 339 (1960). The evidentiary inquiry is then relatively easy.[13] But such cases are

---

[12] For a scholarly discussion of legislative motivation, see Brest, Palmer v. Thompson: An Approach to the Problem of Unconstitutional Legislative Motive, 1971 Sup.Ct.Rev. 95, 116–118.

[13] Several of our jury selection cases fall into this category. Because of the nature of the jury selection task, however, we have permitted a finding of constitutional violation even when the statistical pattern does not approach the extremes of *Yick Wo* or *Gomillion*. See, e.g., Turner v. Fouche, 396 U.S. 346, 359 (1970); Sims v. Georgia, 389 U.S. 404, 407 (1967).

rare. Absent a pattern as stark as that in *Gomillion* or *Yick Wo,* impact alone is not determinative,[14] and the Court must look to other evidence.[15]

"The historical background of the decision is one evidentiary source, particularly if it reveals a series of official actions taken for invidious purposes. . . . The specific sequence of events leading up to the challenged decision also may shed some light on the decisionmaker's purposes. . . . For example, if the property involved here always had been zoned R–5 but suddenly was changed to R–3 when the town learned of MHDC's plans to erect integrated housing, we would have a far different case. Departures from the normal procedural sequence also might afford evidence that improper purposes are playing a role. Substantive departures too may be relevant, particularly if the factors usually considered important by the decisionmaker strongly favor a decision contrary to the one reached.

"The legislative or administrative history may be highly relevant, especially where there are contemporary statements by members of the decision-making body, minutes of its meetings, or reports. In some extraordinary instances the members might be called to the stand at trial to testify concerning the purpose of the official action, although even then such testimony frequently will be barred by privilege. . . . [18]

"The foregoing summary identifies, without purporting to be exhaustive, subjects of proper inquiry in determining whether racially discriminatory intent existed. With these in mind, we now address the case before us.

IV.

. . .

"We also have reviewed the evidence. The impact of the Village's decision does arguably bear more heavily on racial minorities. Minorities comprise 18% of the Chicago area population, and 40% of the income groups said to be eligible for Lincoln Green. But there is little about the sequence of events leading up to the decision that would spark suspicion. The area around the Victorian property has been zoned R–3 since 1959, the year when Arlington Heights first adopted a zoning map. Single-family homes surround the 80–acre site, and the Village is undeniably committed to single-family homes as its dominant residential land use. The rezoning request progressed according to the usual procedures. The Plan Commission even scheduled two additional hearings, at least in part to accommodate MHDC and permit it to supplement its presentation with answers to questions generated at the first hearing.

---

[14] This is not to say that a consistent pattern of official racial discrimination is a necessary predicate to a violation of the equal protection clause. A single invidiously discriminatory governmental act—in the exercise of the zoning power as elsewhere—would not necessarily be immunized by the absence of such discrimination in the making of other comparable decisions. See City of Richmond v. United States, 422 U.S. 358, 378 (1975).

[15] In many instances, to recognize the limited probative value of disproportionate impact is merely to acknowledge the "heterogeneity" of the nation's population. Jefferson v. Hackney, 406 U.S. 535, 548 (1972); see also Washington v. Davis, 426 U.S., at 248.

[18] This Court has recognized, ever since Fletcher v. Peck, 6 Cranch 87, 130–131 (1810), that judicial inquiries into legislative or executive motivation represent a substantial intrusion into the workings of other branches of government. Placing a decisionmaker on the stand is therefore "usually to be avoided." Citizens to Preserve Overton Park v. Volpe, 401 U.S. 402, 420 (1971). The problems involved have prompted a good deal of scholarly commentary. See *Tussman & TenBroek, The Equal Protection of the Laws,* 37 Calif.L.Rev. 341, 356–361 (1949); A. Bickel, The Least Dangerous Branch, 208–221 (1962); Ely, Legislative and Administrative Motivation in Constitutional Law, 79 Yale L.J. 1205 (1970); Brest supra, n. 8.

"The statements by the Plan Commission and Village Board members, as reflected in the official minutes, focused almost exclusively on the zoning aspects of the MHDC petition, and the zoning factors on which they relied are not novel criteria in the Village's rezoning decisions. There is no reason to doubt that there has been reliance by some neighboring property owners on the maintenance of single-family zoning in the vicinity. The Village originally adopted its buffer policy long before MHDC entered the picture and has applied the policy too consistently for us to infer discriminatory purpose from its application in this case. Finally, MHDC called one member of the Village Board to the stand at trial. Nothing in her testimony supports an inference of invidious purpose.

"In sum, the evidence does not warrant overturning the concurrent findings of both courts below. Respondents simply failed to carry their burden of proving that discriminatory purpose was a motivating factor in the Village's decision.[21] This conclusion ends the constitutional inquiry. The Court of Appeals' further finding that the Village's decision carried a discriminatory 'ultimate effect' is without independent constitutional significance."

Justices Marshall and Brennan concurred in Part III of the opinion set out above but indicated that in their view the case should be remanded to the court of appeals for it to reassess the evidence on discriminatory purpose. Justice White also dissented, calling for a remand to the court of appeals. Justice Stevens took no part in the decision.

PERSONNEL ADMINISTRATOR OF MASSACHUSETTS v. FEENEY, 442 U.S. 256 (1979). Massachusetts' veterans' preference for state civil service positions was challenged as unconstitutional gender discrimination. Under the law, all veterans had an "absolute lifetime preference"; veterans with passing scores for classified civil service jobs were ranked above *all* other candidates. Since 98% of veterans were male, and the preference for veterans with passing scores was absolute, the impact of the law was, obviously, to disqualify female eligibles from consideration in much greater proportion than male eligibles. The Court rejected the argument that Massachusetts had discriminated against women in violation of the Equal Protection Clause. Justice Stewart's opinion for the Court said, in part:

"The cases of *Washington v. Davis,* and *Village of Arlington Heights v. Metropolitan Housing Development Corp.,* recognize that when a neutral law has a disparate impact upon a group that has historically been the victim of discrimination, an unconstitutional purpose may still be at work. But those cases signalled no departure from the settled rule that the Fourteenth Amendment guarantees equal laws, not equal results....

"When a statute gender-neutral on its face is challenged on the ground that its effects upon women are disproportionately adverse, a two-fold inquiry is thus appropriate. The first question is whether the statutory classification is indeed neutral in the sense that it is not gender-based. If the classification itself, covert or overt, is not based upon gender, the second question is whether

---

[21] Proof that the decision by the Village was motivated in part by a racially discriminatory purpose would not necessarily have required invalidation of the challenged decision. Such proof would, however, have shifted to the Village the burden of establishing that the same decision would have resulted even had the impermissible purpose not been considered. If this were established, the complaining party in a case of this kind no longer fairly could attribute the injury complained of to improper consideration of a discriminatory purpose. In such circumstances, there would be no justification for judicial interference with the challenged decision. But in this case respondents failed to make the required threshold showing. See Mt. Healthy City School Dist. Bd. of Education v. Doyle, 429 U.S. 274.

the adverse effect reflects invidious gender-based discrimination.... In this second inquiry, impact provides an 'important starting point,' but purposeful discrimination is 'the condition that offends the Constitution.' ...

. . .

"The question whether ch. 31, § 23 establishes a classification that is overtly or covertly based upon gender must first be considered. The appellee has conceded that ch. 31, § 23 is neutral on its face....

"... Apart from the fact that the definition of 'veterans' in the statute has always been neutral as to gender and that Massachusetts has consistently defined veteran status in a way that has been inclusive of women who have served in the military, this is not a law that can plausibly be explained only as a gender-based classification. Indeed, it is not a law that can rationally be explained on that ground. Veteran status is not uniquely male. Although few women benefit from the preference, the nonveteran class is not substantially all-female. To the contrary, significant numbers of nonveterans are men, and all nonveterans—male as well as female—are placed at a disadvantage. Too many men are affected to permit the inference that the statute is but a pretext for preferring men over women.

"Moreover, as the District Court implicitly found, the purposes of the statute provide the surest explanation for its impact. Just as there are cases in which impact alone can unmask an invidious classification, cf. *Yick Wo v. Hopkins,* there are others, in which—notwithstanding impact—the legitimate noninvidious purposes of a law cannot be missed. This is one. The distinction ... is, as it seems to be, quite simply between veterans and nonveterans, not between men and women.

"The dispositive question, then, is whether the appellee has shown that a gender-based discriminatory purpose has, at least in some measure, shaped the Massachusetts veterans' preference legislation....

"The contention that this veterans' preference is 'inherently non-neutral' or 'gender-based' presumes that the State, by favoring veterans, intentionally incorporated into its public employment policies the panoply of sex-based and assertedly discriminatory federal laws that have prevented all but a handful of women from becoming veterans. There are two serious difficulties with this argument. First, it is wholly at odds with the District Court's central finding that Massachusetts has not offered a preference to veterans for the purpose of discriminating against women. Second, it cannot be reconciled with the assumption made by both the appellee and the District Court that a more limited hiring preference for veterans could be sustained. Taken together, these difficulties are fatal.

. . .

"To be sure, this case is unusual in that it involves a law that by design is not neutral. The law overtly prefers veterans as such. As opposed to the written test at issue in *Davis,* it does not purport to define a job related characteristic. To the contrary, it confers upon a specifically described group—perceived to be particularly deserving—a competitive head start. But the District Court found, and the appellee has not disputed, that this legislative choice was legitimate. The basic distinction between veterans and nonveterans, having been found not gender-based, and the goals of the preference having been found worthy, ch. 31 must be analyzed as is any other neutral law that casts a greater burden upon women as a group than upon men as a group. The enlistment policies of the armed services may well have discriminated on the basis of sex. See *Frontiero*

v. Richardson, 411 U.S. 677; cf. Schlesinger v. Ballard, 419 U.S. 498. But the history of discrimination against women in the military is not on trial in this case.

"The appellee's ultimate argument rests upon the presumption, common to the criminal and civil law, that a person intends the natural and foreseeable consequences of his voluntary actions. . . .

". . . [I]t cannot seriously be argued that the legislature of Massachusetts could have been unaware that most veterans are men. It would thus be disingenuous to say that the adverse consequences of this legislation for women were unintended, in the sense that they were not volitional or in the sense that they were not foreseeable.

" 'Discriminatory purpose,' however, implies more than intent as volition or intent as awareness of consequences. . . . It implies that the decisionmaker, in this case a state legislature, selected or reaffirmed a particular course of action at least in part 'because of,' not merely 'in spite of,' its adverse effects upon an identifiable group. Yet nothing in the record demonstrates that this preference for veterans was originally devised or subsequently re-enacted because it would accomplish the collateral goal of keeping women in a stereotypic and predefined place in the Massachusetts Civil Service."

Justice Stevens' concurring opinion, joined by Justice White, said:

"While I concur in the Court's opinion, I confess that I am not at all sure that there is any difference between the two questions posed. . . . If a classification is not overtly based on gender, I am inclined to believe the question whether it is covertly gender-based is the same as the question whether its adverse effects reflect invidious gender-based discrimination. However the question is phrased, for me the answer is largely provided by the fact that the number of males disadvantaged by Massachusetts' Veterans Preference (1,867,-000) is sufficiently large—and sufficiently close to the number of disadvantaged females (2,954,000)—to refute the claim that the rule was intended to benefit males as a class over females as a class."

Justice Marshall's dissent, joined by Justice Brennan, concluded that Massachusetts' veterans' preference system constituted "intentional" gender-based discrimination. The foreseeable impact of the law had such a disproportionate impact that the State should have the burden to establish that "sex-based considerations played no part in the choice of the particular legislative scheme."

"Clearly, that burden was not sustained here. The legislative history of the statute reflects the Commonwealth's patent appreciation of the impact the preference system would have on women, and an equally evident desire to mitigate that impact only with respect to certain traditionally female occupations. Until 1971, the statute and implementing civil service regulations exempted from operation of the preference any job requisitions 'especially calling for women.' . . . In practice, this exemption, coupled with the absolute preference for veterans, has created a gender-based civil service hierarchy, with women occupying low grade clerical and secretarial jobs and men holding more responsible and remunerative positions.

"Thus, for over 70 years, the Commonwealth has maintained, as an integral part of its veteran's preference system, an exemption relegating female civil service applicants to occupations traditionally filled by women. Such a statutory scheme both reflects and perpetuates precisely the kind of archaic assumptions about women's roles which we have previously held invalid. . . ."

COLUMBUS BOARD OF EDUCATION v. PENICK, 443 U.S. 449 (1979). The Court upheld a finding that schools were intentionally segregated based in large measure on a finding that the schools had been intentionally segregated in 1954 when *Brown* was decided and that they had failed in the intervening years to disestablish the dual system. It rejected an argument that the lower courts had not found an intention to discriminate, concluding that the District Court "was amply cognizant of the controlling cases" and "recognized that under those cases disparate impact and foreseeable consequences, without more, do not establish a constitutional violation [but] are relevant evidence to prove the ultimate fact, forbidden purpose." The Court elaborated: "Adherence to a particular policy or practice, 'with full knowledge of the predictable effects of such adherence upon racial imbalance in a school system is one factor among many others which may be considered by a court in determining whether an inference of segregative intent should be drawn.'"

CASTANEDA v. PARTIDA, 430 U.S. 482 (1977). Partida sued in a federal district court challenging his state court criminal conviction on the ground that the grand jury that indicted him resulted from a state grand jury selection process that discriminated against Mexican–Americans. The district judge found that Partida had made out a bare prima facie case of invidious discrimination based on a statistical showing that Mexican–Americans made up 79% of the county population in the 1970 census but over an overlapping 11 year period made up only 39% of those summoned to be grand jurors. However, he held that this was overcome by the state's showing that Mexican–Americans constituted the governing majority in the county, and dismissed the petition. The court of appeals reversed and the Supreme Court affirmed the court of appeals.

Justice Blackmun, speaking for the Court, reviewed the statistical evidence and concluded that Partida established a prima facie case of discrimination against Mexican–Americans. He then went on to hold that the state did not dispel the presumption of purposeful discrimination by its governing majority showing, saying:

"Because of the many facets of human motivation, it would be unwise to presume as a matter of law that human beings of one definable group will not discriminate against other members of their group.... [20]

"Furthermore, the relevance of a governing majority of elected officials to the grand jury selection process is questionable. The fact that certain elected officials are Mexican–American demonstrates nothing about the motivations and methods of the grand jury commissioners who select persons for grand jury lists. The only arguably relevant fact in this record on the issue is that three of the five jury commissioners in respondent's case were Mexican–American. Knowing only this, we would be forced to rely on the reasoning that we have rejected—that human beings would not discriminate against their own kind—in order to find that the presumption of purposeful discrimination was rebutted. Without the benefit of this simple behavioral presumption, discriminatory intent can be rebutted only with evidence in the record about the way in which the commissioners operated and their reasons for doing so. It was the State's burden to supply such evidence, once respondent established his prima facie case....

[20] This is not a case where a majority is practicing benevolent discrimination in favor of a traditionally disfavored minority, although that situation illustrates that motivations not immediately obvious might enter into discrimination against "one's own kind."

"Finally, even if a 'governing majority' theory has general applicability in cases of this kind, the inadequacy of the record in this case does not permit such an approach. Among the evidentiary deficiencies are the lack of any indication of how long the Mexican–Americans have enjoyed 'governing majority' status, the absence of information about the relative power inherent in the elective offices held by Mexican–Americans, and the uncertain relevance of the general political power to the specific issue in this case. Even for the most recent time period, when presumably the political power of Mexican–Americans was at its greatest, the discrepancy between the number of Mexican–Americans in the total population and the number on the grand jury lists was substantial. Thus, under the facts presented in this case, the 'governing majority' theory is not developed fully enough to satisfy the State's burden of rebuttal."

Justice Marshall concurred "to express [his] profound disagreement with the views expressed by Mr. Justice Powell in his dissent":

"... Justice Powell's assumptions about human nature, plausible as they may sound, fly in the face of a great deal of social science theory and research. Social scientists agree that members of minority groups frequently respond to discrimination and prejudice by attempting to disassociate themselves from the group, even to the point of adopting the majority's negative attitudes towards the minority. Such behavior occurs with particular frequency among members of minority groups who have achieved some measure of economic or political success and thereby have gained some acceptability among the dominant group.

"But even if my Brother Powell's behavioral assumptions were more valid, I still could not agree to making them the foundation for a constitutional ruling. It seems to me that especially in reviewing claims of intentional discrimination, this Court has a solemn responsibility to avoid basing its decisions on broad generalizations concerning minority groups. If history has taught us anything, it is the danger of relying on such stereotypes. The question for decision here is not how Mexican–Americans treat other Mexican–Americans, but how the particular grand jury commissioners in Hidalgo County acted. The only reliable way to answer that question ... is for the State to produce testimony concerning the manner in which the selection process operated...."

Justice Powell, joined by The Chief Justice and Justice Rehnquist, dissented. With respect to the governing majority issue, he said:

"In this case, the following critical facts are beyond dispute: the judge who appointed the jury commissioners and later presided over respondent's trial was Mexican–American; three of the five jury commissioners were Mexican–American; 10 of the 20 members of the grand jury array were Mexican–American; five of the 12 grand jurors who returned the indictment, including the foreman, were Mexican–American, and seven of the 12 petit jurors who returned the verdict of guilt were Mexican–American. In the year in which respondent was indicted, 52.5% of the persons on the grand jury list were Mexican–American. In addition, a majority of the elected officials in Hidalgo County were Mexican–American, as were a majority of the judges. That these positions of power and influence were so held is not surprising in a community where 80% of the population is Mexican–American. As was emphasized by District Judge Garza, the able Mexican–American jurist who presided over the habeas proceedings in the District Court, this case is unique. Every other jury discrimination case reaching this Court has involved a situation where the governing majority, and the resulting power over the jury selection process, was held by a white electorate and white officials.[6]

"The most significant fact in this case, all but ignored in the Court's opinion, is that a majority of the jury commissioners were Mexican–American. The jury commission is the body vested by Texas law with the authority to select grand jurors. Under the Texas selection system, as noted by the Court, the jury commission has the opportunity to identify in advance those potential jurors who have Spanish surnames. In these circumstances, where Mexican–Americans control both the selection of jurors and the political process, rational inferences from the most basic facts in a democratic society render improbable respondent's claim of an intent to discriminate against him and other Mexican–Americans. As Judge Garza observed, 'If people in charge can choose whom they want, it is unlikely they will discriminate against themselves.' 384 F.Supp. 79, 90.

"That individuals are more likely to discriminate in favor of, than against, those who share their own identifiable attributes is the premise that underlies the cases recognizing that the criminal defendant has a personal right under the Fourteenth Amendment not to have members of his own class excluded from jury service. Discriminatory exclusion of members of the defendant's class has been viewed as unfairly excluding persons who may be inclined to favor the defendant. See Strauder v. West Virginia, 100 U.S., at 309. Were it not for the perceived likelihood that jurors will favor defendants of their own class, there would be no reason to suppose that a jury selection process that systematically excluded persons of a certain race would be the basis of any legitimate complaint by criminal defendants of that race. Only the individuals excluded from jury service would have a personal right to complain.

"... With all respect, I am compelled to say that the Court today has 'lightly' concluded that the grand jury commissioners of this county have disregarded not only their sworn duty but also their likely inclination to assure fairness to Mexican–Americans.[7]"

Chief Justice Burger, joined by Justice Powell and Justice Rehnquist, wrote a dissenting opinion challenging the adequacy of the statistical showing to make out a prima facie case of discrimination. Justice Stewart also dissented indicating that he was "in substantial agreement" with the other two dissenting opinions.

---

[6] I do not suggest, of course, that the mere fact that Mexican–Americans constitute a majority in Hidalgo County is dispositive. There are many communities in which, by virtue of historical or other reasons, a majority of the population may not be able at a particular time to control or significantly influence political decisions or the way the system operates. See *Turner v. Fouche,* supra. But no one can contend seriously that Hidalgo County is such a community. The classic situation in which a "minority group" may suffer discrimination in a community is where it is "relegated to ... a position of political powerlessness." San Antonio School District v. Rodriguez, 411 U.S. 1, 28 (1973). Here the Mexican–Americans are not politically "powerless"; they are the majoritarian political element of the community, with demonstrated capability to elect and protect their own.

Nor do I suggest that persons in positions of power can never be shown to have discriminated against other members of the same ethnic or racial group. I would hold only that respondent's statistical evidence, without more, is insufficient to prove a claim of discrimination in this case.

[7] I agree with Mr. Justice Marshall that stereotypes concerning identifiable classes in our society have no place in the decisions of this Court. For that reason, I consider it inappropriate to characterize the Mexican–American majority in Hidalgo County as a "minority group" and on that basis to suggest that these Mexican–Americans may have "adopt[ed] the majority's negative attitudes towards the minority." This type of speculation illustrates the lengths to which one must go to buttress a holding of purposeful discrimination that otherwise is based solely on a lack of proportional representation.

Rogers v. Lodge

458 U.S. 613, 102 S.Ct. 3272, 73 L.Ed.2d 1012 (1982).

Justice White delivered the opinion of the Court.

The issue in this case is whether the at-large system of elections in Burke County, Georgia violates the Fourteenth Amendment rights of Burke County's black citizens.

I

Burke County is a large, predominately rural county located in eastern Georgia. Eight hundred and thirty-one square miles in area, it is approximately two-thirds the size of the State of Rhode Island. According to the 1980 Census, Burke County had a total population of 19,349, of whom 10,385, or 53.6% were black. The average age of blacks living there is lower than the average age of whites and therefore whites constitute a slight majority of the voting age population. As of 1978, 6,373 persons were registered to vote in Burke County, of whom 38% were black.

The Burke County Board of Commissioners governs the county. It was created in 1911 ... and consists of five members elected at large to concurrent four-year terms by all qualified voters in the county. The county has never been divided into districts, either for the purpose of imposing a residency requirement on candidates or for the purpose of requiring candidates to be elected by voters residing in a district. In order to be nominated or elected, a candidate must receive a majority of the votes cast in the primary or general election, and a runoff must be held if no candidate receives a majority in the first primary or general election.... Each candidate must run for a specific seat on the Board, ... and a voter may vote only once for any candidate. No Negro has ever been elected to the Burke County Board of Commissioners.

Eight black citizens of Burke County filed this [federal district court] suit in 1976 ... on behalf of all black citizens in Burke County. The complaint alleged that the County's system of at-large elections violates appellees' First, Thirteenth, Fourteenth and Fifteenth Amendment rights, as well as their rights under 42 U.S.C. §§ 1971, 1973, and 1983 by diluting the voting power of black citizens. Following a bench trial at which both sides introduced extensive evidence, the court issued an order on September 29, 1978 stating that appellees were entitled to prevail and ordering that Burke County be divided into five districts for purposes of electing County Commissioners. The court later issued detailed findings of fact and conclusions of law in which it stated that while the present method of electing County Commissioners was "racially neutral when adopted, [it] is being *maintained* for invidious purposes" in violation of appellees' Fourteenth and Fifteenth Amendment rights.

The Court of Appeals affirmed.... It stated that while the proceedings in the District Court took place prior to ... Mobile v. Bolden, 446 U.S. 55 (1980), the District Court correctly anticipated *Mobile* and required appellees to prove that the at-large voting system was maintained for a discriminatory purpose. The Court of Appeals also held that the District Court's findings not only were not clearly erroneous, but its conclusion that the at-large system was maintained for invidious purposes was "virtually mandated by the overwhelming proof." We ... affirm.

II

At-large voting schemes and multimember districts tend to minimize the voting strength of minority groups by permitting the political majority to elect *all* representatives of the district. A distinct minority, whether it be a racial, ethnic, economic, or political group, may be unable to elect any representatives in an at-large election, yet may be able to elect several representatives if the political unit is divided into single-member districts. The minority's voting power in a multimember district is particularly diluted when bloc voting occurs and ballots are cast along strict majority-minority lines. While multimember districts have been challenged for "their winner-take-all aspects, their tendency to submerge minorities and to overrepresent the winning party," Whitcomb v. Chavis, 403 U.S. 124, 158–159 (1971), this Court has repeatedly held that they are not unconstitutional *per se*. Mobile v. Bolden ...; White v. Regester, 412 U.S. 755, 765 (1973); Whitcomb v. Chavis, supra, 403 U.S. at 142. The Court has recognized, however, that multimember districts violate the Fourteenth Amendment if "conceived or operated as purposeful devices to further racial ... discrimination" by minimizing, cancelling out or diluting the voting strength of racial elements in the voting population. Whitcomb v. Chavis.... Cases charging that multimember districts unconstitutionally dilute the voting strength of racial minorities are thus subject to the standard of proof generally applicable to Equal Protection Clause cases. Washington v. Davis, 426 U.S. 229 (1976), and Village of Arlington Heights v. Metropolitan Housing Development Corp., 429 U.S. 252 (1977), made it clear that in order for the Equal Protection Clause to be violated, "the invidious quality of a law claimed to be racially discriminatory must ultimately be traced to a racially discriminatory purpose." ... Neither case involved voting dilution, but in both cases the Court observed that the requirement that racially discriminatory purpose or intent be proven applies to voting cases by relying upon, among others, Wright v. Rockefeller, 376 U.S. 52 (1964), a districting case, to illustrate that a showing of discriminatory intent has long been required in *all* types of equal protection cases charging racial discrimination.... [5]

Arlington Heights and *Washington v. Davis* both rejected the notion that a law is invalid under the Equal Protection Clause simply because it may affect a greater proportion of one race than another.... However, both cases recognized that discriminatory intent need not be proven by direct evidence. "Necessarily, an invidious discriminatory purpose may often be inferred from the totality of the relevant facts, including the fact, if it is true, that the law bears more heavily on one race than another." Ibid. Thus determining the existence of a discriminatory purpose "demands a sensitive inquiry into such circumstantial and direct evidence of intent as may be available." *Arlington Heights*, supra, 429 U.S. at 266.

In *Mobile v. Bolden,* ... the Court was called upon to apply these principles to the at-large election system in Mobile, Alabama. Mobile is governed by three commissioners who exercise all legislative, executive, and administrative power in the municipality. Each candidate for the City Commission runs for one of three numbered posts in an at-large election and can only be elected by a majority vote. Plaintiffs brought a class action on behalf of all Negro citizens of Mobile alleging that the at-large scheme diluted their voting strength in violation of several statutory and constitutional provisions. The District Court concluded that the at-large system "violates the constitutional rights of the plaintiffs by improperly restricting their access to the political process," and ordered that the commission form of government be replaced by a mayor and a nine-member City Council elected from single-member districts. The Court of Appeals affirmed. This Court reversed.

---

[5] Purposeful racial discrimination invokes the strictest scrutiny of adverse differential treatment. Absent such purpose, differential impact is subject only to the test of rationality. Washington v. Davis, supra, at 247–248.

Justice Stewart, writing for himself and three other Justices, noted that to prevail in their contention that the at-large voting system violates the Equal Protection Clause of the Fourteenth Amendment, plaintiffs had to prove the system was "conceived or operated as [a] purposeful devic[e] to further racial ... discrimination." ... [6]

The plurality went on to conclude that the District Court had failed to comply with this standard. The District Court had analyzed plaintiffs' claims in light of the standard ... set forth in Zimmer v. McKeithen, 485 F.2d 1297 (C.A.5 1973), aff'd on other grounds *sub nom.* East Carroll Parish School Bd. v. Marshall, 424 U.S. 636 (1976) (*per curiam*). *Zimmer* set out a list of factors[8] gleaned from *Whitcomb v. Chavis,* supra, and *White v. Regester,* supra, that a court should consider in assessing the constitutionality of at-large and multi-member district voting schemes. Under *Zimmer,* voting dilution is established "upon proof of the existence of an aggregate of these factors."

The plurality in *Mobile* was of the view that *Zimmer* was "decided upon the misunderstanding that it is not necessary to show a discriminatory purpose in order to prove a violation of the Equal Protection Clause—that proof of a discriminatory effect is sufficient." The plurality observed that while "the presence of the indicia relied on in *Zimmer* may afford some evidence of a discriminatory purpose," the mere existence of those criteria is not a substitute for a finding of discriminatory purpose. The District Court's standard in *Mobile* was likewise flawed....

Because the District Court in the present case employed the evidentiary factors outlined in *Zimmer,* it is urged that its judgment is infirm for the same reasons that led to the reversal in *Mobile.* We do not agree. First, and fundamentally, we are unconvinced that the District Court in this case applied the wrong legal standard. Not only was the District Court's decision rendered a considerable time after *Washington v. Davis* and *Arlington Heights,* but the trial judge also had the benefit of Nevett v. Sides, 571 F.2d 209 (C.A.5 1978), where the Court of Appeals for the Fifth Circuit assessed the impact of *Washington v. Davis* and *Arlington Heights* and held that "a showing of racially motivated discrimination is a necessary element in an equal protection voting dilution claim ..." The court stated that "[t]he ultimate issue in a case alleging unconstitutional dilution of the votes of a racial group is whether the districting plan under attack exists because it was intended to diminish or dilute the political efficacy of that group." Id., at 226. The Court of Appeals also

[6] With respect to the Fifteenth Amendment, the plurality held that the Amendment prohibits only direct, purposefully discriminatory interference with the freedom of Negroes to vote. "Having found that Negroes in Mobile 'register and vote without hindrance,' the District Court and Court of Appeals were in error in believing that the appellants invaded the protection of [the Fifteenth] Amendment in the present case." Mobile v. Bolden, 446 U.S. 55, 65 (1980). Three Justices disagreed with the plurality's basis for putting aside the Fifteenth Amendment. Id., at 84, n. 3, (Stevens, J., concurring); Id., at 102 (White, J., dissenting); Id., at 125–135 (Marshall, J., dissenting). We express no view on the application of the Fifteenth Amendment to this case.

The plurality noted that plaintiffs' claim under § 2 of the Voting Rights Act, 79 Stat. 437, as amended, 42 U.S.C. § 1973, added nothing to their Fifteenth Amendment claim because the "legislative history of § 2 makes clear that it was intended to have an effect no different from that of the Fifteenth Amendment itself." Id., at 60–61.

[8] The primary factors listed in *Zimmer* include a lack of minority access to the candidate selection process, unresponsiveness of elected officials to minority interests, a tenuous state policy underlying the preference for multi-member or at-large districting, and the existence of past discrimination which precludes effective participation in the elector process.... Factors which enhance the proof of voting dilution are the existence of large districts, anti-single shot voting provisions, and the absence of any provision for at-large candidates to run from geographic subdistricts....

explained that although the evidentiary factors outlined in *Zimmer* were important considerations in arriving at the ultimate conclusion of discriminatory intent, the plaintiff is not limited to those factors. "The task before the fact finder is to determine, under all the relevant facts, in whose favor the 'aggregate' of the evidence preponderates. This determination is peculiarly dependent upon the facts of each case."

The District Court referred to *Nevett v. Sides* and demonstrated its understanding of the controlling standard by observing that a determination of discriminatory intent is "a requisite to a finding of unconstitutional vote dilution" under the Fourteenth and Fifteenth Amendments. Furthermore, while recognizing that the evidentiary factors identified in *Zimmer* were to be considered, the District Court was aware that it was "not limited in its determination only to the *Zimmer* factors" but could consider other relevant factors as well. The District Court then proceeded to deal with what it considered to be the relevant proof and concluded that the at-large scheme of electing commissioners, "although racially neutral when adopted, is being *maintained* for invidious purposes." That system "while neutral in origin ... has been subverted to invidious purposes." For the most part, the District Court dealt with the evidence in terms of the factors set out in *Zimmer* and its progeny, but as the Court of Appeals stated:

> "Judge Alaimo employed the constitutionally required standard ... [and] did not treat the *Zimmer* criteria as absolute, but rather considered them only to the extent they were relevant to the question of discriminatory intent."

Although a tenable argument can be made to the contrary, we are not inclined to disagree with the Court of Appeals' conclusion that the District Court applied the proper legal standard.

III

A

We are also unconvinced that we should disturb the District Court's finding that the at-large system in Burke County was being maintained for the invidious purpose of diluting the voting strength of the black population. In *White v. Regester,* ... we stated that we were not inclined to overturn the District Court's factual findings, "representing as they do a blend of history and an intensely local appraisal of the design and impact of the Bexar County multimember district in the light of past and present reality, political and otherwise." ... We are of the view that the same clearly-erroneous standard applies to the trial court's finding in this case that the at-large system in Burke County is being maintained for discriminatory purposes, as well as to the court's subsidiary findings of fact. The Court of Appeals did not hold any of the District Court's findings of fact to be clearly erroneous, and this Court has frequently noted its reluctance to disturb findings of fact concurred in by two lower courts.... We agree with the Court of Appeals that on the record before us, none of the factual findings are clearly erroneous.

B

The District Court found that blacks have always made up a substantial majority of the population in Burke County, but that they are a distinct minority of the registered voters. There was also overwhelming evidence of bloc voting along racial lines. Hence, although there had been black candidates, no black had ever been elected to the Burke County commission. These facts bear heavily on the issue of purposeful discrimination. Voting along racial lines allows those elected to ignore black interests without fear of political consequences, and without bloc voting the minority candidates would not lose elections solely because of their race. Because it is sensible to expect that at least some blacks would have been elected in Burke County, the fact that none have ever been elected is important evidence of purposeful exclusion. See White v. Regester, supra, at 766.

Under our cases, however, such facts are insufficient in themselves to prove purposeful discrimination absent other evidence such as proof that blacks have less opportunity to participate in the political processes and to elect candidates of their choice.... Both the District Court and the Court of Appeals thought the supporting proof in this case was sufficient to support an inference of intentional discrimination....

The District Court began by determining the impact of past discrimination on the ability of blacks to participate effectively in the political process. Past discrimination was found to contribute to low black voter registration because prior to the Voting Rights Act of 1965, blacks had been denied access to the political process by means such as literacy tests, poll taxes, and white primaries. The result was that "black suffrage in Burke County was virtually nonexistent." Black voter registration in Burke County has increased following the Voting Rights Act to the point that some 38 per cent of blacks eligible to vote are registered to do so. On that basis the District Court inferred that "past discrimination has had an adverse effect on black voter registration which lingers to this date." Past discrimination against blacks in education also had the same effect. Not only did Burke County schools discriminate against blacks as recently as 1969, but some schools still remain essentially segregated and blacks as a group have completed less formal education than whites.

The District Court found further evidence of exclusion from the political process. Past discrimination had prevented blacks from effectively participating in Democratic Party affairs and in primary elections. Until this law suit was filed, there had never been a black member of the County Executive Committee of the Democratic Party. There were also property ownership requirements that made it difficult for blacks to serve as chief registrar in the county. There had been discrimination in the selection of grand jurors, the hiring of county employees, and in the appointments to boards and committees which oversee the county government. The District Court thus concluded that historical discrimination had restricted the present opportunity of blacks effectively to participate in the political process. Evidence of historical discrimination is relevant to drawing an inference of purposeful discrimination, particularly in cases such as this one where the evidence shows that discriminatory practices were commonly utilized, that they were abandoned when enjoined by courts or made illegal by civil rights legislation, and that they were replaced by laws and practices which, though neutral on their face, serve to maintain the status quo.

Extensive evidence was cited by the District Court to support its finding that elected officials of Burke County have been unresponsive and insensitive to the needs of the black community, which increases the likelihood that the political process was not equally open to blacks....

The District Court also considered the depressed socio-economic status of Burke County blacks. It found that proportionately more blacks than whites have incomes below the poverty level....

Although finding that the state policy behind the at-large electoral system in Burke County was "neutral in origin," the District Court concluded that the policy "has been subverted to invidious purposes." As a practical matter, maintenance of the state statute providing for at-large elections in Burke

County is determined by Burke County's state representatives, for the legislature defers to their wishes on matters of purely local application. The court found that Burke County's state representatives "have retained a system which has minimized the ability of Burke County Blacks to participate in the political system."

The trial court considered, in addition, several factors which this Court has indicated enhance the tendency of multimember districts to minimize the voting strength of racial minorities. See *Whitcomb v. Chavis,* .... It found that the sheer geographic size of the county ... "has made it more difficult for Blacks to get to polling places or to campaign for office." The court concluded, as a matter of law, that the size of the county tends to impair the access of blacks to the political process. The majority vote requirement, Ga.Code § 34–1513 (1980), was found "to submerge the will of the minority" and thus "deny the minority's access to the system." The court also found the requirement that candidates run for specific seats, Ga.Code § 34–1015 (1980), enhances respondent's lack of access because it prevents a cohesive political group from concentrating on a single candidate. Because Burke County has no residency requirement, "[a]ll candidates could reside in Waynesboro, or in 'lily-white' neighborhoods. To that extent, the denial of access becomes enhanced."

None of the District Court's findings underlying its ultimate finding of intentional discrimination appears to us to be clearly erroneous; and as we have said, we decline to overturn the essential finding of the District Court, agreed to by the Court of Appeals, that the at-large system in Burke County has been maintained for the purpose of denying blacks equal access to the political processes in the county. As in *White v. Regester,* ... the District Court's findings were "sufficient to sustain [its] judgment ... and, on this record, we have no reason to disturb them."

IV

We also find no reason to overturn the relief ordered by the District Court. Neither the District Court nor the Court of Appeals discerned any special circumstances that would militate against utilizing single-member districts....

The judgment of the Court of Appeals is

Affirmed.

Justice Powell, with whom Justice Rehnquist joins, dissenting.

I

... In *Mobile* we reversed a finding of unconstitutional vote dilution because the lower courts had relied on factors insufficient as a matter of law to establish discriminatory intent. ...The District Court and Court of Appeals in this case based their findings of unconstitutional discrimination on the same factors held insufficient in *Mobile*. Yet the Court now finds their conclusion unexceptionable. The *Mobile* plurality also affirmed that the concept of "intent" was no mere fiction, and held that the District Court had erred in "its failure to identify the state officials whose intent it considered relevant." ... Although the courts below did not answer that question in this case, the Court today affirms their decision.

Whatever the wisdom of *Mobile,* the Court's opinion cannot be reconciled persuasively with that case. There are some variances in the largely sociological evidence presented in the two cases. But *Mobile* held that this *kind* of evidence was not enough. Such evidence, we found in *Mobile,* did not merely fall short, but "fell *far* short[,] of showing that [an at-large electoral scheme was] 'conceived or operated [as a] purposeful devic[e] to further racial ... discrimination.' " ... Because I believe that *Mobile* controls this case, I dissent.

II

The Court's decision today relies heavily on the capacity of the federal district courts—essentially free from any standards propounded by this Court—to determine whether at-large voting systems are "being maintained for the invidious purpose of diluting the voting strength of the black population." Federal courts thus are invited to engage in deeply subjective inquiries into the motivations of local officials in structuring local governments. Inquiries of this kind not only can be "unseemly," see Karst, The Costs of Motive–Centered Inquiry, 15 San Diego Law Rev. 1163, 1164 (1978); they intrude the federal courts—with only the vaguest constitutional direction—into an area of intensely local and political concern.

Emphasizing these considerations, Justice Stevens argues forcefully that the Court's focus of inquiry is seriously mistaken. I agree with much of what he says. As I do not share his views entirely, however, I write separately.

A

As I understand it, Justice Stevens' critique of the Court's approach rests on three principles with which I am in fundamental agreement.

First, it is appropriate to distinguish between "state action that inhibits an individual's right to vote and state action that affects the political strength of various groups." Mobile v. Bolden, 446 U.S. 55, 83 (Stevens, J., concurring). Under this distinction, this case is fundamentally different from cases involving direct barriers to voting. There is no claim here that blacks may not register freely and vote for whom they choose. This case also differs from one-man, one-vote cases, in which districting practices make a person's vote less weighty in some districts than in others.

Second, I agree with Justice Stevens that vote dilution cases of this kind are difficult if not impossible to distinguish—especially in their remedial aspect—from other actions to redress gerrymanders.

Finally, Justice Stevens clearly is correct in arguing that the standard used to identify unlawful racial discrimination in this area should be defined in terms that are judicially manageable and reviewable. In the absence of compelling reasons of both law and fact, the federal judiciary is unwarranted in undertaking to restructure state political systems. This is inherently a political area, where the identification of a seeming violation does not necessarily suggest an enforceable judicial remedy—or at least none short of a system of quotas or group representation. Any such system, of course, would be antithetical to the principles of our democracy.

B

Justice Stevens would accommodate these principles by holding that subjective intent is irrelevant to the establishment of a case of racial vote dilution under the Fourteenth Amendment. Despite sharing the concerns from which his position is developed, I would not accept this view. "The central purpose of the Equal Protection Clause of the Fourteenth Amendment is the prevention of official conduct discriminating on the basis of race." Washington v. Davis, 426 U.S. 229, 239 (1976). Because I am unwilling to abandon this central principle in cases of this kind, I cannot join Justice Stevens' opinion.

Nonetheless, I do agree with him that what he calls "objective" factors should be the focus of inquiry in vote-dilution cases. Unlike the considerations on which the lower courts relied in this case and in *Mobile,* the factors identified by Justice Stevens as "objective" in fact are direct, reliable, and unambiguous indices of discriminatory *intent.* If we held, as I think we should, that the district courts must place primary reliance on these factors to establish discriminatory intent, we would prevent federal court inquiries into the *subjective* thought processes of local officials—at least until enough objective evidence had been presented to warrant discovery into subjective motivations in this complex, politically charged area. By prescribing such a rule we would hold federal courts to a standard that was judicially manageable. And we would remain faithful to the central protective purpose of the Equal Protection Clause.

In the absence of proof of discrimination by reliance on the kind of objective factors identified by Justice Stevens, I would hold that the factors cited by the Court of Appeals are too attenuated as a matter of law to support an inference of discriminatory intent. I would reverse its judgment on that basis.

Justice Stevens, dissenting.

. . .

[Justice Stevens' long and interesting opinion is omitted.]

NOTE

On June 29, the day before the opinion was announced in *Rogers,* Congress passed the following amended version of Section 2 of the Voting Rights Act of 1965:

"Sec. 2(a) No voting qualification or prerequisite to voting or standard, practice, or procedure shall be imposed or applied by any State or political subdivision in a manner which results in a denial or abridgement of the right of any citizen of the United States to vote on account of race or color, or in contravention of the guarantes set forth in section 4(f)(2), as provided in subsection (b).

"(b) A violation of subsection (a) is established if, based on the totality of circumstances, it is shown that the political processes leading to nomination or election in the State or political subdivision are not equally open to participation by members of a class of citizens protected by subsection (a) in that its members have less opportunity than other members of the electorate to participate in the political process and to elect representatives of their choice. The extent to which members of a protected class have been elected to office in the State or political subdivision is one circumstance which may be considered: Provided, That nothing in this section establishes a right to have members of a protected class elected in numbers equal to their proportion in the population."

The report of the Senate Committee on the Judiciary accompanying the bill made clear that it was intended to restore the legal standard governing voting discrimination cases before the Supreme Court's decision in City of Mobile, Ala. v. Bolden, 446 U.S. 55 (1980). The Court applied the 1982 amendments in Thornburg v. Gingles, 478 U.S. 30 (1986), to hold a legislative redistricting plan using multimember districts invalid. Deciding no constitutional issues, the Court concluded that the amendments eliminated any requirement of establishing that the contested electoral practice was adopted or maintained with the intent to discriminate against minority voters. The opinions in the case contain elaborate discussion of the problems involved in showing that multimember districts operate to prejudice the voting rights of minorities.

HUNTER v. UNDERWOOD, 471 U.S. 222 (1985). Section 182 of the Alabama Constitution, adopted at a convention in 1901, disenfranchised persons convicted of, among other offenses, "any crime ... involving moral turpitude." Edwards, a black, and Underwood, a white, were blocked from the voter roles because they each had been convicted of presenting a worthless check. Their federal district court suit contended that § 182 had been intentionally adopted to disenfranchise blacks on account of their race. On this issue the district court treated Edwards as the representative of a class of black members and ruled for the defendants. The court of appeals reversed, holding that the evidence showed that § 182 had disenfranchised 10 times as many blacks as whites, and that it had been adopted for the purpose of preventing blacks from voting. The Supreme Court affirmed, all joining an opinion by Justice Rehnquist (Justice Powell not participating).

The Court said first that a neutral state law producing racially disproportionate effects will be invalidated only if it is shown that racially discriminatory intent or purpose was a substantial factor behind enacting the law.

"Proving the motivation behind official action is often a problematic undertaking. See Rogers v. Lodge, 458 U.S. 613 (1982). When we move from an examination of a board of county commissioners such as was involved in *Rogers* to a body the size of the Alabama Constitutional Convention of 1901, the difficulties in determining the actual motivations of the various legislators that produced a given decision increase." But no such difficulties were present here. Evidence from historians and from speeches at the Convention made it clear that zeal for white supremacy ran rampant at the convention. Indeed, the appellants did not seriously dispute that fact. What appellants did argue was that the real purpose behind § 182 was to disenfranchise both poor whites and blacks.

"Even were we to accept this explanation as correct, it hardly saves § 182 from invalidity. The explanation concedes both that discrimination against blacks, as well as against poor whites, was a motivating factor for the provision and that § 182 certainly would not have been adopted by the convention or ratified by the electorate in the absence of the racially discriminatory motivation.

"Citing Palmer v. Thompson, 403 U.S., at 224, and Michael M. v. Superior Court of Sonoma County, 450 U.S. 464, 472, n. 7 (1981) (plurality opinion), appellants make the further argument that the existence of a permissible motive for § 182, namely the disenfranchisement of poor whites, trumps any proof of a parallel impermissible motive. Whether or not intentional disenfranchisement of poor whites would qualify as a 'permissible motive' within the meaning of *Palmer* and *Michael M.*, it is clear that where both impermissible racial motivation and racially discriminatory impact are demonstrated, *Arlington Heights* and *Mt. Healthy* supply the proper analysis. Under the view that the Court of Appeals could properly take of the evidence, an additional purpose to discriminate against poor whites would not render nugatory the purpose to discriminate against all blacks, and it is beyond peradventure that the latter was a 'but-for' motivation for the enactment of § 182.

.   .   .

"At oral argument in this Court, the State suggested that, regardless of the original purpose of § 182, events occurring in the succeeding 80 years had legitimated the provision.... Without deciding whether § 182 would be valid if enacted today without any impermissible motivation, we simply observe that its original enactment was motivated by a desire to discriminate against blacks on account of race and the section continues to this day to have that effect. As such, it violates equal protection under *Arlington Heights.*

"Finally, appellants contend that the State is authorized by the Tenth Amendment and § 2 of the Fourteenth Amendment to deny the franchise to persons who commit misdemeanors involving moral turpitude. For the reasons we have stated, the enactment of § 182 violated the Fourteenth Amendment, and the Tenth Amendment cannot save legislation prohibited by the subsequently enacted Fourteenth Amendment. The single remaining question is whether § 182 is excepted from the operation of the Equal Protection Clause of § 1 of the Fourteenth Amendment by the 'other crime' provision of § 2 of that Amendment. Without again considering the implicit authorization of § 2 to deny the vote to citizens 'for participation in rebellion, or other crime,' see *Richardson v. Ramirez,* 418 U.S. 24 (1974), we are confident that § 2 was not designed to permit the purposeful racial discrimination attending the enactment and operation of § 182 which otherwise violates § 1 of the Fourteenth Amendment. Nothing in our opinion in *Richardson v. Ramirez* ... suggests the contrary."

E. "Benign" Discrimination: Affirmative Action, Quotas, Preferences Based on Gender or Race

1. CLASSIFICATIONS ADVANTAGING FEMALES

Kahn v. Shevin

416 U.S. 351, 94 S.Ct. 1734, 40 L.Ed.2d 189 (1974).

Mr. Justice Douglas delivered the opinion of the Court.

Since at least 1885, Florida has provided for some form of property tax exemption for widows. The current law granting all widows an annual $500 exemption, Fla.Stat. § 196.191(7), F.S.A., has been essentially unchanged since 1941. Appellant Kahn is a widower who lives in Florida and applied for the exemption to the Dade County Tax Assessor's Office. It was denied because the statute offers no analogous benefit for widowers. Kahn then sought a declaratory judgment in the Circuit Court for Dade County, Florida, and that court held the statute violative of the Equal Protection Clause of the Fourteenth Amendment because the classification "widow" was based upon gender. The Florida Supreme Court reversed, finding the classification valid because it has a "fair and substantial relation to the object of the legislation," that object being the reduction of "the disparity between the economic capabilities of a man and a woman." Kahn appealed here.... We affirm.

There can be no dispute that the financial difficulties confronting the lone woman in Florida or in any other State exceed those facing the man. Whether from overt discrimination or from the socialization process of a male dominated culture, the job market is inhospitable to the woman seeking any but the lowest paid jobs. There are of course efforts underway to remedy this situation. On the federal level Title VII of the Civil Rights Act of 1964 prohibits covered employers and labor unions from discrimination on the basis of sex, 42 U.S.C. § 2000e–2(a), (b), (c), as does the Equal Pay Act of 1963, 29 U.S.C. § 206(d). But firmly entrenched practices are resistant to such pressures, and indeed, data compiled by the Women's Bureau of the United States Department of Labor shows that in 1972 women working full time had a median income which was only 57.9% of the male median—a figure actually six points lower than had been achieved in 1955. Other data points in the same direction. The disparity is likely to be exacerbated for the widow. While the widower can usually continue in the occupation which preceded his spouse's death in many cases the widow will find herself suddenly forced into a job market with which she is unfamiliar, and in which, because of her former economic dependency, she will have fewer skills to offer.

There can be no doubt therefore that Florida's differing treatment of widows and widowers "rest[s] upon some ground of difference having a fair and substantial relation to the object of the legislation." Reed v. Reed, 404 U.S. 71, 76....

This is not a case like Frontiero v. Richardson, 411 U.S. 677, where the Government denied its female employees both substantive and procedural benefits granted males *"solely* for administrative convenience." Id., at 690 (emphasis in original).[8] We deal here with a state tax law reasonably designed to further the state policy of cushioning the financial impact of spousal loss upon the sex for whom that loss imposes a disproportionately heavy burden. We have long held that "[w]here taxation is concerned and no specific federal right, apart from equal protection, is imperilled, the States have large leeway in making classifications and drawing lines which in their judgment produce reasonable systems of taxation." Lehnhausen v. Lake Shore Auto Parts Co., 410 U.S. 356, 359. A state tax law is not arbitrary although it "discriminate[s] in favor of a certain class . . . if the discrimination is founded upon a reasonable distinction, or difference in state policy," not in conflict with the Federal Constitution. Allied Stores v. Bowers, 358 U.S. 522, 528. This principle has weathered nearly a century of Supreme Court adjudication, and it applies here as well. The statute before us is well within those limits.[10]

Affirmed.

Mr. Justice Brennan, with whom Mr. Justice Marshall joins, dissenting.

. . . In my view . . . a legislative classification that distinguishes potential beneficiaries solely by reference to their gender-based status as widows or widowers, like classifications based upon race, alienage, and national origin, must be subjected to close judicial scrutiny, because it focuses upon generally immutable characteristics over which individuals have little or no control, and

---

[8] And in *Frontiero* the plurality opinion also noted that the statutes there were "not in any sense designed to rectify the effects of past discrimination against women. On the contrary, these statutes seize upon a group—women—who have historically suffered discrimination in employment, and rely on the effects of this past discrimination as a justification for heaping on additional economic disadvantages." . . . 411 U.S. 677, 689 n. 22....

[10] The dissents argue that the Florida Legislature could have drafted the statute differently, so that its purpose would have been accomplished more precisely. But the issue of course is not whether the statute could have been drafted more wisely, but whether the lines chosen by the Florida Leg-

islature are within constitutional limitations. The dissent would use the Equal Protection Clause as a vehicle for reinstating notions of substantive due process that have been repudiated....

Gender has never been rejected as an impermissible classification in all instances. Congress has not so far drafted women into the Armed Services. 50 App.U.S.C. § 454. The famous Brandeis Brief in Muller v. Oregon, 208 U.S. 412, on which the court specifically relied, id., at 419–420, emphasized that the special physical organization of women has a bearing on the "conditions under which she should be permitted to toil." Id., at 420. These instances are pertinent to the problem in the tax field....

also because gender-based classifications too often have been inexcusably utilized to stereotype and stigmatize politically powerless segments of society. See *Frontiero v. Richardson,* 411 U.S. 677 (1973). The Court is not therefore free to sustain the statute on the ground that it rationally promotes legitimate governmental interests; rather, such suspect classifications can be sustained only when the State bears the burden of demonstrating that the challenged legislation serves overriding or compelling interests that cannot be achieved either by a more carefully tailored legislative classification or by the use of feasible less drastic means. While ... the statute serves a compelling governmental interest by "cushioning the financial impact of spousal loss upon the sex for whom that loss imposes a disproportionately heavy burden," I think [it] is invalid because the State's interest can be served equally well by a more narrowly drafted statute.

Gender-based classifications cannot be sustained merely because they promote legitimate governmental interests, such as efficacious administration of government. *Frontiero v. Richardson,* supra; Reed v. Reed, 404 U.S. 71 (1971).... On the contrary, any statutory scheme which draws a sharp line between the sexes, *solely* for the purpose of achieving administrative convenience, necessarily commands "dissimilar treatment for men and women who are ... similarly situated," and therefore involves the "very kind of arbitrary legislative choice forbidden by the [constitution]...." Reed v. Reed, 404 U.S., at 77, 76."*Frontiero v. Richardson,*.... But Florida's justification of § 196.191(7) is not that it serves administrative convenience or helps to preserve the public fisc. Rather, the asserted justification is that § 196.191(7) is an affirmative step toward alleviating the effects of past economic discrimination against women."

I agree that, in providing special benefits for a needy segment of society long the victim of purposeful discrimination and neglect, the statute serves the compelling state interest of achieving equality for such groups. No one familiar with this country's history of pervasive sex discrimination against women can doubt the need for remedial measures to correct the resulting economic imbalances. Indeed, the extent of the economic disparity between men and women is dramatized by the data cited by the Court. By providing a property tax exemption for widows, § 196.01(7) assists in reducing that economic disparity for a class of women particularly disadvantaged by the legacy of economic discrimination. In that circumstance, the purpose and effect of the suspect classification is ameliorative; the statute neither stigmatizes nor denigrates widowers not also benefited by the legislation. Moreover, inclusion of needy widowers within the class of beneficiaries would not further the State's overriding interest in remedying the economic effects of past sex discrimination for needy victims of that discrimination. While doubtless some widowers are in financial need, no one suggests that such need results from sex discrimination as in the case of widows.

The statute nevertheless fails to satisfy the requirements of equal protection, since the State has not borne its burden of proving that its compelling interest could not be achieved by a more precisely tailored statute or by use of feasible less drastic means. Section 196.191(7) is plainly overinclusive, for the $500 property tax exemption may be obtained by a financially independent heiress as well as by an unemployed widow with dependent children. The State has offered nothing to explain why inclusion of widows of substantial economic means was necessary to advance the State's interest in ameliorating the effects of past economic discrimination against women.

Moreover, alternative means of classification, narrowing the class of widow beneficiaries, appear readily available. The exemption is granted only to widows who complete and file with the tax assessor a form application establishing their status as widows. By merely redrafting that form to exclude widows who earn annual incomes, or possess assets, in excess of specified amounts, the State could readily narrow the class of beneficiaries to those widows for whom the effects of past economic discrimination against women have been a practical reality.

Mr. Justice White, dissenting.

The Florida tax exemption at issue here is available to all widows but not to widowers. The presumption is that all widows are financially more needy and less trained or less ready for the job market than men. It may be that most widows have been occupied as housewife, mother and homemaker and are not immediately prepared for employment. But there are many rich widows who need no largess from the State; many others are highly trained and have held lucrative positions long before the death of their husbands. At the same time, there are many widowers who are needy and who are in more desperate financial straits and have less access to the job market than many widows. Yet none of them qualifies for the exemption.

I find the discrimination invidious and violative of the Equal Protection Clause. There is merit in giving poor widows a tax break, but gender-based classifications are suspect and require more justification than the State has offered.

I perceive no purpose served by the exemption other than to alleviate current economic necessity, but the State extends the exemption to widows who do not need the help and denies it to widowers who do. It may be administratively inconvenient to make individual determinations of entitlement and to extend the exemption to needy men as well as needy women, but administrative efficiency is not an adequate justification for discriminations based purely on sex. Frontiero v. Richardson, 411 U.S. 677 (1973); Reed v. Reed, 404 U.S. 71 (1971).

It may be suggested that the State is entitled to prefer widows over widowers because their assumed need is rooted in past and present economic discrimination against women. But this is not a credible explanation of Florida's tax exemption; for if the State's purpose was to compensate for past discrimination against females, surely it would not have limited the exemption to women who are widows. Moreover, even if past discrimination is considered to be the criterion for current tax exemption, the State nevertheless ignores all those widowers who have felt the effects of economic discrimination, whether as a member of a racial group or as one of the many who cannot escape the cycle of poverty. It seems to me that the State in this case is merely conferring an economic benefit in the form of a tax exemption and has not adequately explained why women should be treated differently than men.

I dissent.

CALIFANO v. WEBSTER, 430 U.S. 313 (1977). A complex formula for computing retirement benefits under social security permitted a female wage earner to exclude from the computation of her "average monthly wage" three more lower earning years than a similarly situated male wage earner could exclude. This resulted in a higher level of monthly old-age benefits for the retired female wage earner. In a Per Curiam opinion the Court held the classification valid, saying, in part:

"To withstand scrutiny under the equal protection component of the Fifth Amendment's Due Process Clause, 'classifications by gender must serve important governmental objectives and must be substantially related to achievement of those objectives.' Craig v. Boren, 429 U.S. 190, 197 (1976). Reduction of the disparity in economic condition between men and women caused by the long history of discrimination against women has been recognized as such an important governmental objective. Schlesinger v. Ballard, 419 U.S. 498 (1975); Kahn v. Shevin, 416 U.S. 351 (1974). But 'the mere recitation of a benign, compensatory purpose is not an automatic shield which protects against any inquiry into the actual purposes underlying a statutory scheme.' Weinberger v. Wiesenfeld, 420 U.S. 636, 648 (1975). Accordingly, we have rejected attempts to justify gender classifications as compensation for past discrimination against women when the classifications in fact penalized women wage earners, Califano v. Goldfarb, 430 U.S. 199, Weinberger v. Wiesenfeld, supra, at 645, or when the statutory structure and its legislative history revealed that the classification was not enacted as compensation for past discrimination. . . .

"The statutory scheme involved here is more analogous to those upheld in *Kahn* and *Ballard* than to those struck down in *Wiesenfeld* and *Goldfarb*. The more favorable treatment of the female wage earner enacted here was not a result of 'archaic and overbroad generalizations' about women, *Schlesinger v. Ballard* . . . or of 'the role-typing society has long imposed' upon women, Stanton v. Stanton, 421 U.S. 7, 15 (1975), such as casual assumptions that women are 'the weaker sex' or are more likely to be child-rearers or dependents. Cf. Califano v. Goldfarb, supra; Weinberger v. Wiesenfeld, supra. Rather, 'the only discernible purpose of [§ 215's more favorable treatment is] the permissible one of redressing our society's longstanding disparate treatment of women.' Califano v. Goldfarb. . . .

"The challenged statute operated directly to compensate women for past economic discrimination. Retirement benefits under the Act are based on past earnings. But as we have recognized: 'Whether from overt discrimination or from the socialization process of a male-dominated culture, the job market is inhospitable to the woman seeking any but the lowest paid jobs.' Kahn v. Shevin, 416 U.S. at 353. . . . Thus, allowing women, who as such have been unfairly hindered from earning as much as men, to eliminate additional low-earning years from the calculation of their retirement benefits works directly to remedy some part of the effect of past discrimination. Cf. Schlesinger v. Ballard, supra, at 508.

"The legislative history of § 215(b)(3) also reveals that Congress directly addressed the justification for differing treatment of men and women in the former version of that section and purposely enacted the more favorable treatment for female wage earners to compensate for past employment discrimination against women. . . ."

Chief Justice Burger, joined by Justices Stewart, Blackmun, and Rehnquist concurred in the judgment.

ORR v. ORR, 440 U.S. 268 (1979). The Court held unconstitutional Alabama's statutory scheme imposing alimony obligations on husbands but not wives. It rejected the argument that the gender distinction was justified, because of the disparity between the economic condition of men and women, to provide support for needy wives of broken marriages. Justice Brennan's opinion for the Court said in part:

"Ordinarily, we would begin the analysis of the 'needy spouse' objective by considering whether sex is a sufficiently 'accurate proxy' for dependency to establish that the gender classification rests 'upon some ground of difference having a fair and substantial relation to the object of the legislation.' Similarly, we would initially approach the 'compensation' rationale by asking whether women had in fact been significantly discriminated against in the sphere to which the statute applied a sex-based classification, leaving the sexes '*not similarly situated with respect to opportunities*' in that sphere.[11]

"But in this case, even if sex were a reliable proxy for need, and even if the institution of marriage did discriminate against women, these factors still would 'not adequately justify the salient features of' Alabama's statutory scheme. Under the statute, individualized hearings at which the parties' relative financial circumstances are considered *already* occur. There is no reason, therefore, to use sex as a proxy for need. Needy males could be helped along with needy females with little if any additional burden on the State. In such circumstances, not even an administrative convenience rationale exists to justify operating by generalization or proxy. Similarly, since individualized hearings can determine which women were in fact discriminated against vis-a-vis their husbands, as well as which family units defied the stereotype and left the husband dependent on the wife, Alabama's alleged compensatory purpose may be effectuated without placing burdens solely on husbands. Progress toward fulfilling such a purpose would not be hampered, and it would cost the State nothing more, if it were to treat men and women equally by making alimony burdens independent of sex. 'Thus, the gender-based distinction is gratuitous; without it the statutory scheme would only provide benefits to those men who are in fact similarly situated to the women the statute aids,' and the effort to help those women would not in any way be compromised.

"Moreover, use of a gender classification actually produces perverse results in this case. As compared to a gender-neutral law placing alimony obligations on the spouse able to pay, the present Alabama statutes give an advantage only to the financially secure wife whose husband is in need. Although such a wife might have to pay alimony under a gender-neutral statute, the present statutes exempt her from that obligation. Thus, '[t]he [wives] who benefit from the disparate treatment are those who were ... nondependent on their husbands.' They are precisely those who are not 'needy spouses' and who are 'least likely to have been victims of ... discrimination,' by the institution of marriage. A gender-based classification which, as compared to a gender-neutral one, generates additional benefits only for those it has no reason to prefer cannot survive equal protection scrutiny.

"Legislative classifications which distribute benefits and burdens on the basis of gender carry the inherent risk of reinforcing the stereotypes about the 'proper place' of women and their need for special protection. Thus, even statutes purportedly designed to compensate for and ameliorate the effects of past discrimination must be carefully tailored. Where, as here, the State's compensatory and ameliorative purposes are as well served by a gender-neutral classification as one that gender-classifies and therefore carries with it the baggage of sexual stereotypes, the State cannot be permitted to classify on the basis of sex. And this is doubly so where the choice made by the State appears to redound—if only indirectly—to the benefit of those without need for special solicitude.

"Having found Alabama's alimony statutes unconstitutional, we reverse the judgment below and remand the cause for further proceedings not inconsistent with this opinion. That disposition, of course, leaves the state courts free

---

[11] We would also consider whether the purportedly compensatory "classifications in fact penalized women," and whether "the statutory structure and its legislative history revealed that the classification was not enacted as compensation for past discrimination."

... on remand to consider whether Mr. Orr's stipulated agreement to pay alimony, or other grounds of gender-neutral state law, bind him to continue his alimony payments."

Chief Justice Burger, Justice Powell, and Justice Rehnquist, dissenting on other issues, did not reach the equal protection question.

Mississippi University for Women v. Hogan

458 U.S. 718, 102 S.Ct. 3331, 73 L.Ed.2d 1090 (1982).

Justice O'Connor delivered the opinion of the Court.

This case presents the narrow issue of whether a state statute that excludes males from enrolling in a state-supported professional nursing school violates the Equal Protection Clause of the Fourteenth Amendment.

I

The facts are not in dispute. In 1884, the Mississippi legislature created the Mississippi Industrial Institute and College for the Education of White Girls of the State of Mississippi, now the oldest state-supported all-female college in the United States.... The school, known today as Mississippi University for Women (MUW), has from its inception limited its enrollment to women.

In 1971, MUW established a School of Nursing, initially offering a two-year associate degree. Three years later, the school instituted a four-year baccalaureate program in nursing and today also offers a graduate program. The School of Nursing has its own faculty and administrative officers and establishes its own criteria for admission.

Respondent, Joe Hogan, is a registered nurse but does not hold a baccalaureate degree in nursing. Since 1974, he has worked as a nursing supervisor in a medical center in Columbus, the city in which MUW is located. In 1979, Hogan applied for admission to the MUW School of Nursing's baccalaureate program. Although he was otherwise qualified, he was denied admission to the School of Nursing solely because of his sex. School officials informed him that he could audit the courses in which he was interested, but could not enroll for credit.

Hogan [sued in federal district], claiming the single-sex admissions policy of MUW's School of Nursing violated the Equal Protection Clause of the Fourteenth Amendment....

[T]he District Court denied preliminary injunctive relief....

The ... Fifth Circuit reversed, holding that, because the admissions policy discriminates on the basis of gender, the District Court improperly used a "rational relationship" test to judge the constitutionality of the policy....

We ... affirm.... [7]

---

[7] Although some statements in the Court of Appeals' decision refer to all schools within MUW, ... the factual underpinning of Hogan's claim for relief involved only his exclusion from the nursing program, and the Court of Appeals' holding applies only to Hogan's individual claim for relief.... Additionally, during oral argument, counsel verified that Hogan sought only admission to the School of Nursing. Because Hogan's claim is thus limited, and because we review judgments, not statements in opinions, Black v. Cutter Laboratories, 351 U.S. 292 (1956), we decline to address the question of whether MUW's admissions policy, as applied to males seeking admission to schools other than the School of Nursing, violates the Fourteenth Amendment.

II

We begin our analysis aided by several firmly-established principles. Because the challenged policy expressly discriminates among applicants on the basis of gender, it is subject to scrutiny under the Equal Protection Clause of the Fourteenth Amendment. Reed v. Reed, 404 U.S. 71, 75 (1971). That this statute discriminates against males rather than against females does not exempt it from scrutiny or reduce the standard of review.[8] Caban v. Mohammed, 441 U.S. 380, 394 (1979); Orr v. Orr, 440 U.S. 268, 279 (1979). Our decisions also establish that the party seeking to uphold a statute that classifies individuals on the basis of their gender must carry the burden of showing an "exceedingly persuasive justification" for the classification. Kirchberg v. Feenstra, 450 U.S. 455, 461 (1981); Personnel Administrator of Massachusetts v. Feeney, 442 U.S. 256, 273 (1979). The burden is met only by showing at least that the classification serves "important governmental objectives and that the discriminatory means employed" are "substantially related to the achievement of those objectives." Wengler v. Druggists Mutual Insurance Co., 446 U.S. 142, 150 (1980).

Although the test ... is straightforward, it must be applied free of fixed notions concerning the roles and abilities of males and females. Care must be taken in ascertaining whether the statutory objective itself reflects archaic and stereotypic notions. Thus, if the statutory objective is to exclude or "protect" members of one gender because they are presumed to suffer from an inherent handicap or to be innately inferior, the objective itself is illegitimate. See Frontiero v. Richardson ... (1973) (plurality opinion).

If the State's objective is legitimate and important, we next determine whether the requisite direct, substantial relationship between objective and means is present. The purpose of requiring that close relationship is to assure that the validity of a classification is determined through reasoned analysis rather than through the mechanical application of traditional, often inaccurate, assumptions about the proper roles of men and women. The need for the requirement is amply revealed by reference to the broad range of statutes already invalidated by this Court, statutes that relied upon the simplistic, outdated assumption that gender could be used as a "proxy for other, more germane bases of classification," Craig v. Boren, 429 U.S. 190, 198 (1976), to establish a link between objective and classification.

. . .

III

A

The State's primary justification for maintaining the single-sex admissions policy of MUW's School of Nursing is that it compensates for discrimination against women and, therefore, constitutes educational affirmative action. As applied to the School of Nursing, we find the State's argument unpersuasive.

---

[8] Without question, MUW's admissions policy worked to Hogan's disadvantage. Although Hogan could have attended classes and received credit in one of Mississippi's state-supported coeducational nursing programs, none of which was located in Columbus, he could attend only by driving a considerable distance from his home. A similarly situated female would not have been required to choose between foregoing credit and bearing that inconvenience. Moreover, since many students enrolled in the School of Nursing hold full-time jobs, Hogan's female colleagues had available an opportunity, not open to Hogan, to obtain credit for additional training. The policy of denying males the right to obtain credit toward a baccalaureate degree thus imposed upon Hogan "a burden he would not bear were he female." Orr v. Orr, 440 U.S. 268, 273 (1979).

In limited circumstances, a gender-based classification favoring one sex can be justified if it intentionally and directly assists members of the sex that is disproportionately burdened. See Schlesinger v. Ballard, 419 U.S. 498 (1975). However, we consistently have emphasized that "the mere recitation of a benign, compensatory purpose is not an automatic shield which protects against any inquiry into the actual purposes underlying a statutory scheme." Weinberger v. Wiesenfeld, 420 U.S. 636, 648 (1975). The same searching analysis must be made, regardless of whether the State's objective is to eliminate family controversy, Reed v. Reed, supra, to achieve administrative efficiency, Frontiero v. Richardson, supra, or to balance the burdens borne by males and females.

It is readily apparent that a State can evoke a compensatory purpose to justify an otherwise discriminatory classification only if members of the gender benefited by the classification actually suffer a disadvantage related to the classification. We considered such a situation in Califano v. Webster, 430 U.S. 313 (1977), which involved a challenge to a statutory classification that allowed women to eliminate more low-earning years than men for purposes of computing Social Security retirement benefits. Although the effect of the classification was to allow women higher monthly benefits than were available to men with the same earning history, we upheld the statutory scheme, noting that it took into account that women "as such have been unfairly hindered from earning as much as men" and "work[ed] directly to remedy" the resulting economic disparity.

A similar pattern of discrimination against women influenced our decision in Schlesinger v. Ballard, 419 U.S. 498 (1975). There, we considered a federal statute that granted female Naval officers a 13–year tenure of commissioned service before mandatory discharge, but accorded male officers only a nine-year tenure. We recognized that, because women were barred from combat duty, they had had fewer opportunities for promotion than had their male counterparts. By allowing women an additional four years to reach a particular rank before subjecting them to mandatory discharge, the statute directly compensated for other statutory barriers to advancement.

In sharp contrast, Mississippi has made no showing that women lacked opportunities to obtain training in the field of nursing or to attain positions of leadership in that field when the MUW School of Nursing opened its door or that women currently are deprived of such opportunities. In fact, in 1970, the year before the School of Nursing's first class enrolled, women earned 94 percent of the nursing baccalaureate degrees conferred in Mississippi and 98.6 percent of the degrees earned nationwide. United States Department of Health, Education, and Welfare, Earned Degrees Conferred: 1969–1970, 388 (1972).... As one would expect, the labor force reflects the same predominance of women in nursing. When MUW's School of Nursing began operation, nearly 98 percent of all employed registered nurses were female. United States Bureau of the Census, 1981 Statistical Abstract of the United States 402 (1981).

Rather than compensate for discriminatory barriers faced by women, MUW's policy of excluding males from admission to the School of Nursing tends to perpetuate the stereotyped view of nursing as an exclusively women's job. By assuring that Mississippi allots more openings in its state-supported nursing schools to women than it does to men, MUW's admissions policy lends credibility to the old view that women, not men, should become nurses, and makes the assumption that nursing is a field for women a self-fulfilling prophecy. See Stanton v. Stanton, 421 U.S. 7 (1975). Thus, we conclude that, although the State recited a "benign, compensatory purpose," it failed to establish that the alleged objective is the actual purpose underlying the discriminatory classification.

The policy is invalid also because it fails the second part of the equal protection test, for the State has made no showing that the gender-based classification is substantially and directly related to its proposed compensatory objective. To the contrary, MUW's policy of permitting men to attend classes as auditors fatally undermines its claim that women, at least those in the School of Nursing, are adversely affected by the presence of men.

MUW permits men who audit to participate fully in classes. Additionally, both men and women take part in continuing education courses offered by the School of Nursing, in which regular nursing students also can enroll. The uncontroverted record reveals that admitting men to nursing classes does not affect teaching style, that the presence of men in the classroom would not affect the performance of the female nursing students, and that men in coeducational nursing schools do not dominate the classroom. In sum, the record ... is flatly inconsistent with the claim that excluding men from the School of Nursing is necessary to reach any of MUW's educational goals.

Thus, considering both the asserted interest and the relationship between the interest and the methods used by the State, we conclude that the State has fallen far short of establishing the "exceedingly persuasive justification" needed to sustain the gender-based classification. Accordingly, we hold that MUW's policy denying males the right to enroll for credit in its School of Nursing violates the Equal Protection Clause of the Fourteenth Amendment.

. . .

Chief Justice Burger, dissenting.

I agree generally with Justice Powell's dissenting opinion. I write separately, however, to emphasize that the Court's holding today is limited to the context of a professional nursing school. Since the Court's opinion relies heavily on its finding that women have traditionally dominated the nursing profession, it suggests that a State might well be justified in maintaining, for example, the option of an all-women's business school or liberal arts program.

Justice Blackmun, dissenting.

. . .

I have come to suspect that it is easy to go too far with rigid rules in this area of claimed sex discrimination, and to lose—indeed destroy—values that mean much to some people by forbidding the State from offering them a choice while not depriving others of an alternate choice. . . .

. . .

I hope that we do not lose all values that some think are worthwhile (and are not based on differences of race or religion) and relegate ourselves to needless conformity. The ringing words of the Equal Protection Clause of the Fourteenth Amendment—what Justice Powell aptly describes as its "liberating spirit"—do not demand that price.

Justice Powell, with whom Justice Rehnquist joins, dissenting.

The Court's opinion bows deeply to conformity. Left without honor—indeed, held unconstitutional—is an element of diversity that has characterized much of American education and enriched much of American life. The Court in effect holds today that no State now may provide even a single institution of higher learning open only to women students....

. . .

II

The issue in this case is whether a State transgresses the Constitution when—within the context of a public system that offers a diverse range of campuses, curricula, and educational alternatives—it seeks to accommodate the legitimate personal preferences of those desiring the advantages of an all-women's college. In my view, the Court errs seriously by assuming—without argument or discussion—that the equal protection standard generally applicable to sex discrimination is appropriate here. That standard was designed to free women from "archaic and overbroad generalizations...." Schlesinger v. Ballard, 419 U.S. 498, 508 (1975). In no previous case have we applied it to invalidate state efforts to *expand* women's choices. Nor are there prior sex discrimination decisions by this Court in which a male plaintiff, as in this case, had the choice of an equal benefit....

By applying heightened equal protection analysis to this case, the Court frustrates the liberating spirit of the Equal Protection Clause. It forbids the States from providing women with an opportunity to choose the type of university they prefer. And yet it is these women whom the Court regards as the *victims* of an illegal, stereotyped perception of the role of women in our society. The Court reasons this way in a case in which no woman has complained, and the only complainant is a man who advances no claims on behalf of anyone else. His claim, it should be recalled, is not that he is being denied a substantive educational opportunity, or even the right to attend an all-male or a coeducational college. It is *only* that the colleges open to him are located at inconvenient distances.

. . .

IV

A distinctive feature of America's tradition has been respect for diversity. This has been characteristic of the peoples from numerous lands who have built our country. It is the essence of our democratic system. At stake in this case as I see it is the preservation of a small aspect of this diversity. But that aspect is by no means insignificant, given our heritage of available choice between single-sex and coeducational institutions of higher learning. The Court answers that there is discrimination—not just that which may be tolerable, as for example between those candidates for admission able to contribute most to an educational institution and those able to contribute less—but discrimination of constitutional dimension. But, having found "discrimination," the Court finds it difficult to identify the victims. It hardly can claim that women are discriminated against. A constitutional case is held to exist solely because one man found it inconvenient to travel to any of the other institutions made available to him by the State of Mississippi. In essence he insists that he has a right to attend a college in his home community. This simply is not a sex discrimination case. The Equal Protection Clause was never intended to be applied to this kind of case.

JOHNSON v. TRANSPORTATION AGENCY, SANTA CLARA COUNTY, 480 U.S. 616 (1987). A white male passed over for promotion in favor of a female employee with lower test scores sued under Title VII of the 1964 Civil Rights Act. He raised no constitutional issues, and the Court decided the case entirely under Title VII. After much discussion the Court held "that the Agency appropriately took into account as one factor the sex of Diane Joyce in determining that she should be promoted to the road dispatcher position. The decision to do so was made pursuant to an affirmative action plan that represents a moderate, flexible, case-by-case approach to effecting a gradual improvement in the representation of minorities and women in the Agency's work force." Three justices dissented.

2.   CLASSIFICATIONS ADVANTAGING RACIAL MINORITIES

Regents of the University of California v. Bakke

438 U.S. 265, 98 S.Ct. 2733, 57 L.Ed.2d 750 (1978).

Mr. Justice Powell announced the judgment of the Court.

This case presents a challenge to the special admissions program of the petitioner, the Medical School of the University of California at Davis, which is designed to assure the admission of a specified number of students from certain minority groups.... The Supreme Court of California affirmed those portions of the trial court's judgment declaring the special admissions program unlawful and enjoining petitioner from considering the race of any applicant. It modified that portion of the judgment denying respondent's requested injunction and directed the trial court to order his admission.

For the reasons stated in the following opinion, I believe that so much of the judgment of the California court as holds petitioner's special admissions program unlawful and directs that respondent be admitted to the Medical School must be affirmed. For the reasons expressed in a separate opinion, my Brothers The Chief Justice, Mr. Justice Stewart, Mr. Justice Rehnquist, and Mr. Justice Stevens concur in this judgment.

I also conclude for the reasons stated in the following opinion that the portion of the court's judgment enjoining petitioner from according any consideration to race in its admissions process must be reversed. For reasons expressed in separate opinions, my Brothers Mr. Justice Brennan, Mr. Justice White, Mr. Justice Marshall, and Mr. Justice Blackmun concur in this judgment.

Affirmed in part and reversed in part.

I.[†]

[Allan Bakke, a white male, applied to, and was rejected by, the Davis Medical School in 1973 and 1974. The School operated two admissions programs to fill the entering class of 100 seats, for which 2,464 applications were received in 1973 and 3,737 in 1974. The regular admissions program considered no one with an undergraduate grade point average below 2.5 on a 4.0 scale. About one in six of the remaining applicants (including Bakke in both years) were interviewed, and admissions decisions were then made to fill 84 seats. The faculty also had adopted a special admissions procedure, designed to increase the representation of "disadvantaged" students, which would fill the remaining 16 of the 100 seats.]

The special admissions program operated with a separate committee, a majority of whom were members of minority groups.... On the 1973 applica-

---

[†] Mr. Justice Brennan, Mr. Justice White, Mr. Justice Marshall, and Mr. Justice Blackmun join Parts I and V-C of this opin-

ion. Mr. Justice White also joins Part III-A of this opinion.

tion form, candidates were asked to indicate whether they wished to be considered as "economically and or educationally disadvantaged" applicants; on the 1974 form the question was whether they wished to be considered as members of a "minority group," which the medical school apparently viewed as "Blacks," "Chicanos," "Asians," and "American Indians." ... If these questions were answered affirmatively, the application was forwarded to the special admissions committee. No formal definition of "disadvantage" was ever produced, ... but the chairman of the special committee screened each application to see whether it reflected economic or educational deprivation. Having passed this initial hurdle, the applications then were rated by the special committee in a fashion similar to that used by the general admissions committee, except that special candidates did not have to meet the 2.5 grade point average cut-off applied to regular applicants. About one-fifth of the total number of special applicants were invited for interviews in 1973 and 1974. ...

From ... 1971 ... through 1974, the special program resulted in the admission of 21 black students, 30 Mexican–Americans, and 12 Asians, for a total of 63 minority students. Over the same period, the regular admissions program produced one black, six Mexican–Americans, and 37 Asians, for a total of 44 minority students. Although disadvantaged whites applied to the special program in large numbers, none received an offer of admission through that process. Indeed, in 1974, at least, the special committee explicitly considered only "disadvantaged" special applicants who were members of one of the designated minority groups. ...

. . .

... In both years, applicants were admitted under the special program with grade point averages, MCAT scores, and benchmark scores significantly lower than Bakke's.[7]

After the second rejection, Bakke [sued in state court seeking] mandatory, injunctive, and declaratory relief compelling his admission to the Medical School. He alleged that the Medical School's special admissions program

[7] The following table compares Bakke's science grade point average, overall grade point average, and MCAT Scores with the average scores of regular admittees and of special admittees in both 1973 and 1974. ...

Class Entering in 1973

| | SGPA | OGPA | MCAT (Percentiles) | | | |
			Verbal	Quantitative	Science	Gen. Infor.
Bakke	3.44	3.51	96	94	97	72
Average of Regular Admittees	3.51	3.49	81	76	83	69
Average of Special Admittees	2.62	2.88	46	24	35	33

Class Entering in 1974

| | SGPA | OGPA | MCAT (Percentiles) | | | |
			Verbal	Quantitative	Science	Gen. Infor.
Bakke	3.44	3.51	96	94	97	72
Average of Regular Admittees	3.36	3.29	69	67	82	72
Average of Special Admittees	2.42	2.62	34	30	37	18

Applicants admitted under the special program also had benchmark scores significantly lower than many students, including Bakke, rejected under the general admissions program, even though the special rating system apparently gave credit for overcoming "disadvantage." ...

operated to exclude him from the school on the basis of his race, in violation of his rights under the Equal Protection Clause of the Fourteenth Amendment, Art. I, § 21 of the California Constitution, and § 601 of Title VI of the Civil Rights Act of 1964, 42 U.S.C. § 2000d. The University cross-complained for a declaration that its special admissions program was lawful. The trial court found that the special program operated as a racial quota, because minority applicants in the special program were rated only against one another ... and 16 places in the class of 100 were reserved for them.... Declaring that the University could not take race into account in making admissions decisions, the trial court held the challenged program violative of the Federal Constitution, the state constitution and Title VI. The court refused to order Bakke's admission, however, holding that he had failed to carry his burden of proving that he would have been admitted but for the existence of the special program.

Bakke appealed from the portion of the trial court judgment denying him admission, and the University appealed from the decision that its special admissions program was unlawful and the order enjoining it from considering race in the processing of applications. The Supreme Court of California transferred the case directly from the trial court [and] accepted the findings of the trial court with respect to the University's program.[12] Because the special admissions program involved a racial classification, the supreme court held itself bound to apply strict scrutiny.... It then turned to the goals the University presented as justifying the special program. Although the court agreed that the goals of integrating the medical profession and increasing the number of physicians willing to serve members of minority groups were compelling state interests, ... it concluded that the special admissions program was not the least intrusive means of achieving those goals. Without passing on the state constitutional or the federal statutory grounds cited in the trial court's judgment, the California court held that the Equal Protection Clause of the Fourteenth Amendment required that "no applicant may be rejected because of his race, in favor of another who is less qualified, as measured by standards applied without regard to race." ...

Turning to Bakke's appeal, the court ruled that since Bakke had established that the University had discriminated against him on the basis of his race, the burden of proof shifted to the University to demonstrate that he would not have been admitted even in the absence of the special admissions program.... On this basis, the court initially ordered a remand for the purpose of determining whether, under the newly allocated burden of proof, Bakke would have been admitted to either the 1973 or the 1974 entering class in the absence of the special admissions program.... In its petition for rehearing below, however, the University conceded its inability to carry that burden.[14] ...

[12] Indeed, the University did not challenge the finding that applicants who were not members of a minority group were excluded from consideration in the special admissions process. 18 Cal.3d, at 44, 553 P.2d, at 1159.

[14] Several amici suggest that Bakke lacks standing, arguing that he never showed that his injury—exclusion from the medical school—will be redressed by a favorable decision, and that the petitioner "fabricated" jurisdiction by conceding its inability to meet its burden of proof. Petitioner does not object to Bakke's standing, but inasmuch as this charge concerns our jurisdiction under Art.

III, it must be considered and rejected. First, there appears to be no reason to question the petitioner's concession. It was not an attempt to stipulate to a conclusion of law or to disguise actual facts of record....

Second, even if Bakke had been unable to prove that he would have been admitted in the absence of the special program, it would not follow that he lacked standing. The constitutional element of standing is plaintiff's demonstration of any injury to himself that is likely to be redressed by favorable decision of his claim. Warth v. Seldin, 422 U.S. 490, 498 (1975). The trial court found such an injury, apart from failure to be admitted, in the

The California court thereupon amended its opinion to direct that the trial court enter judgment ordering Bakke's admission to the medical school.... That order was stayed pending review in this Court. We granted certiorari to consider the important constitutional issue.

II.

. . .

A.

... We assume only for the purposes of this case that respondent has a right of action under Title VI [of the Civil Rights Act of 1964].... [a]

B.

The language of § 601, like that of the Equal Protection Clause, is majestic in its sweep:

> "No person in the United States shall, on the ground of race, color, or national origin, be excluded from participation in, be denied the benefits of, or be subjected to discrimination under any program or activity receiving Federal financial assistance."

... Examination of the voluminous legislative history of Title VI reveals a congressional intent to halt federal funding of entities that violate a prohibition of racial discrimination similar to that of the Constitution. Although isolated statements of various legislators, taken out of context, can be marshalled in support of the proposition that § 601 enacted a purely color-blind scheme, without regard to the reach of the Equal Protection Clause, these comments must be read against the background of both the problem that Congress was addressing and the broader view of the statute that emerges from a full examination of the legislative debates.

... In view of the clear legislative intent, Title VI must be held to proscribe only those racial classifications that would violate the Equal Protection Clause or the Fifth Amendment.

III.

A.

... The parties ... disagree as to the level of judicial scrutiny to be applied to the special admissions program. Petitioner argues that ... strict scrutiny ... should be reserved for classifications that disadvantage "discrete and insular minorities." See United States v. Carolene Products Co., 304 U.S. 144, 152 n. 4

University's decision not to permit Bakke to compete for all 100 places in the class, simply because of his race.... Hence the constitutional requirements of Art. III were met. The question of respondent's admission *vel non* is merely one of relief.

Nor is it fatal to Bakke's standing that he was not a "disadvantaged" applicant. Despite the program's purported emphasis on disadvantage, it was a minority enrollment program with a secondary disadvantage element. White disadvantaged students were never considered under the special program, and the University acknowledges that its goal in devising the program was to increase minority enrollment.

[a] The question whether there is a private action for violations of Title VI was resolved, by implication, in Cannon v. University of Chicago, 441 U.S. 677 (1979). The Court held that Title IX of the Education Amendments of 1972 provided a private right of action. Title IX was patterned after Title VI of the 1964 Civil Rights Act. It used identical language, except that the word "sex" in Title IX replaced the words "race, color or national origin" in Title VI. Justice Stevens' opinion for the Court reasoned, in part, that Congress consciously modeled Title IX on Title VI, assuming that Title VI provided a private remedy. Justices White, Blackmun and Powell dissented.

(1938). Respondent ... contends that the California court correctly rejected the notion that the degree of judicial scrutiny accorded a particular racial or ethnic classification hinges upon membership in a discrete and insular minority and duly recognized that the "rights established [by the fourteenth amendment] are personal rights." Shelley v. Kraemer, 334 U.S. 1, 22 (1948).

En route to this crucial battle over the scope of judicial review,[25] the parties fight a sharp preliminary action over the proper characterization of the special admissions program. Petitioner prefers to view it as establishing a "goal" of minority representation in the medical school. Respondent, echoing the courts below, labels it a racial quota.[26]

This semantic distinction is beside the point: the special admissions program is undeniably a classification based on race and ethnic background. To the extent that there existed a pool of at least minimally qualified minority applicants to fill the 16 special admissions seats, white applicants could compete only for 84 seats in the entering class, rather than the 100 open to minority applicants. Whether this limitation is described as a quota or a goal, it is a line drawn on the basis of race and ethnic status.

The guarantees of the Fourteenth Amendment extend to persons. Its language is explicit: "No state shall ... deny to any person within its jurisdiction the equal protection of the laws." It is settled beyond question that the "rights created by the first section of the Fourteenth Amendment are, by its terms, guaranteed to the individual. They are personal rights," *Shelley v. Kraemer....* The guarantee of equal protection cannot mean one thing when applied to one individual and something else when applied to a person of another color. If both are not accorded the same protection, then it is not equal.

Nevertheless, petitioner argues that the court below erred in applying strict scrutiny to the special admissions programs because white males, such as respondent, are not a "discrete and insular minority" requiring extraordinary protection from the majoritarian political process. *Carolene Products Co., supra,* at 152–153, n. 4. This rationale, however, has never been invoked in our decisions as a prerequisite to subjecting racial or ethnic distinctions to strict

---

[25] That issue has generated a considerable amount of scholarly controversy. See, e.g., Ely, The Constitutionality of Reverse Racial Discrimination, 41 U.Chi.L.Rev. 723 (1974); Greenawalt, Judicial Scrutiny of "Benign" Racial Preferences in Law School Admissions, 75 Colum.L.Rev. 559 (1975); Kaplan, Equal Justice in an Unequal World: Equality for the Negro, 61 Nw.U.L.Rev. 363 (1966); Karst & Horowitz, Affirmative Action and Equal Protection, 60 Va.L.Rev. 955 (1974); O'Neil, Racial Preference and Higher Education: The Larger Context, 60 Va.L.Rev. 925 (1974); Posner, The DeFunis Case and the Constitutionality of Preferential Treatment of Racial Minorities, 1974 Sup.Ct.Rev. 1; Redish, Preferential Law School Admissions and the Equal Protection Clause: An Analysis of the Competing Arguments, 22 U.C.L.A.L.Rev. 343 (1974); Sandalow, Racial Preferences in Higher Education: Political Responsibility and the Judicial Role, 42 U.Chi.L.Rev. 653 (1975); Sedler, Racial Preference, Reality and the Constitution: Bakke v. Regents of the University of California, 17 Santa Clara L.Rev. 329 (1977); Seeburger, A Heuristic Argument Against Preferential Admissions, 39 U.Pitt.L.Rev. 285 (1977).

[26] Petitioner defines "quota" as a requirement which must be met but can never be exceeded, regardless of the quality of the minority applicants. Petitioner declares that there is no "floor" under the total number of minority students admitted; completely unqualified students will not be admitted simply to meet a "quota." Neither is there a "ceiling," since an unlimited number could be admitted through the general admissions process. On this basis the special admissions program does not meet petitioner's definition of a quota.

The court below found—and petitioner does not deny—that white applicants could not compete for the 16 places reserved solely for the special admissions program.... Both courts below characterized this as a "quota" system.

scrutiny.... Racial and ethnic distinctions of any sort are inherently suspect and thus call for the most exacting judicial examination.

B.

This perception of racial and ethnic distinctions is rooted in our Nation's constitutional and demographic history. The Court's initial view of the Fourteenth Amendment was that its "one pervading purpose" was "the freedom of the slave race, the security and firm establishment of that freedom, and the protection of the newly-made freeman and citizen from the oppressions of those who had formerly exercised dominion over him." Slaughter–House Cases, 16 Wall. 36, 71 (1873). The Equal Protection Clause, however, was ... relegated to decades of relative desuetude while the Due Process Clause of the Fourteenth Amendment ... flourished as a cornerstone in the Court's defense of property and liberty of contract.... [O]nly as the era of substantive due process came to a close, see, e.g., Nebbia v. New York, 291 U.S. 502 (1934); West Coast Hotel v. Parrish, 300 U.S. 379 (1937), [did] the Equal Protection Clause beg[i]n to attain a genuine measure of vitality....

By that time it was no longer possible to peg the guarantees of the Fourteenth Amendment to the struggle for equality of one racial minority. During the dormancy of the Equal Protection Clause, the United States had become a nation of minorities. Each had to struggle—and to some extent struggles still—to overcome the prejudices not of a monolithic majority, but of a "majority" composed of various minority groups of whom it was said—perhaps unfairly in many cases—that a shared characteristic was a willingness to disadvantage other groups. As the Nation filled with the stock of many lands, the reach of the Clause was gradually extended to all ethnic groups seeking protection from official discrimination. See Strauder v. West Virginia, 100 U.S. 303, 308 (1880) (Celtic Irishmen) (dictum); Yick Wo v. Hopkins, 118 U.S. 356 (1886) (Chinese); Truax v. Raich, 239 U.S. 33, 41 (1915) (Austrian resident aliens); *Korematsu,* supra (Japanese); Hernandez v. Texas, 347 U.S. 475 (1954) (Mexican–Americans). The guarantees of equal protection, said the Court in *Yick Wo,* "are universal in their application, to all persons within the territorial jurisdiction, without regard to any differences of race, of color, or of nationality; and the equal protection of the laws is a pledge of the protection of equal laws."

Although many of the Framers of the Fourteenth Amendment conceived of its primary function as bridging the vast distance between members of the Negro race and the white "majority," *Slaughter–House Cases,* supra, the Amendment itself was framed in universal terms, without reference to color, ethnic origin, or condition of prior servitude....

Over the past 30 years, this Court has embarked upon the crucial mission of interpreting the Equal Protection Clause with the view of assuring to all persons "the protection of equal laws," ... in a Nation confronting a legacy of slavery and racial discrimination. See, e.g., Shelley v. Kraemer, 334 U.S. 1 (1948); Brown v. Board of Education, 347 U.S. 483 (1954); Hills v. Gautreaux, 425 U.S. 284 (1976). Because the landmark decisions in this area arose in response to the continued exclusion of Negroes from the mainstream of American society, they could be characterized as involving discrimination by the "majority" white race against the Negro minority. But they need not be read as depending upon that characterization for their results. It suffices to say that "[o]ver the years, this Court consistently repudiated '[d]istinctions between citizens solely because of their ancestry' as being 'odious to a free people whose institutions are founded upon the doctrine of equality.' "Loving v. Virginia, 388 U.S. 1, 11 (1967), quoting *Hirabayashi,* 320 U.S., at 100.

Petitioner urges us to adopt for the first time a more restrictive view of the Equal Protection Clause and hold that discrimination against members of the white "majority" cannot be suspect if its purpose can be characterized as "benign."[34] The clock of our liberties, however, cannot be turned back to 1868. *Brown v. Board of Education* ...; accord, *Loving v. Virginia*.... It is far too late to argue that the guarantee of equal protection to all persons permits the recognition of special wards entitled to a degree of protection greater than that accorded others. "The Fourteenth Amendment is not directed solely against discrimination due to a 'two-class theory'—that is, based upon differences between 'white' and Negro." *Hernandez,* ....

Once the artificial line of a "two-class theory" of the Fourteenth Amendment is put aside, the difficulties entailed in varying the level of judicial review according to a perceived "preferred" status of a particular racial or ethnic minority are intractable. The concepts of "majority" and "minority" necessarily reflect temporary arrangements and political judgments. [T]he white "majority" itself is composed of various minority groups, most of which can lay claim to a history of prior discrimination at the hands of the state and private individuals. Not all of these groups can receive preferential treatment and corresponding judicial tolerance of distinctions drawn in terms of race and nationality, for then the only "majority" left would be a new minority of White Anglo–Saxon Protestants. There is no principled basis for deciding which groups would merit "heightened judicial solicitude" and which would not.[36]

---

[34] In the view of Mr. Justice Brennan, Mr. Justice White, Mr. Justice Marshall, and Mr. Justice Blackmun, the pliable notion of "stigma" is the crucial element in analyzing racial classifications.... The Equal Protection Clause is not framed in terms of "stigma." Certainly the word has no clearly defined constitutional meaning. It reflects a subjective judgment that is standardless. *All* state-imposed classifications that rearrange burdens and benefits on the basis of race are likely to be viewed with deep resentment by the individuals burdened. The denial to innocent persons of equal rights and opportunities may outrage those so deprived and therefore may be perceived as invidious. These individuals are likely to find little comfort in the notion that the deprivation they are asked to endure is merely the price of membership in the dominant majority and that its imposition is inspired by the supposedly benign purpose of aiding others. One should not lightly dismiss the inherent unfairness of, and the perception of mistreatment that accompanies, a system of allocating benefits and privileges on the basis of skin color and ethnic origin. Moreover, Mr. Justice Brennan, Mr. Justice White, Mr. Justice Marshall, and Mr. Justice Blackmun offer no principle for deciding whether preferential classifications reflect a benign remedial purpose or a malevolent stigmatic classification, since they are willing in this case to accept mere *post hoc* declarations by an isolated state entity— a medical school faculty—unadorned by particularized findings of past discrimination, to establish such a remedial purpose.

[36] As I am in agreement with the view that race may be taken into account as a factor in an admissions program, I agree with my Brothers Brennan, White, Marshall, and Blackmun that the portion of the judgment that would proscribe all consideration of race must be reversed. See Part V, infra. But I disagree with much that is said in their opinion.

They would require as a justification for a program such as petitioner's, only two findings: (i) that there has been some form of discrimination against the preferred minority groups "by society at large," (it being conceded that petitioner had no history of discrimination), and (ii) that "there is reason to believe" that the disparate impact sought to be rectified by the program is the "product" of such discrimination:

"If it was reasonable to conclude—as we hold that it was—that the failure of Negroes to qualify for admission at Davis under regular procedures was due principally to the effects of past discrimination, then there is a reasonable likelihood that, but for pervasive racial discrimination, respondent would have failed to qualify for admission even in the absence of Davis's special admission program." ...

The breadth of this hypothesis is unprecedented in our constitutional system. The first step is easily taken. No one denies the regrettable fact that there has been societal discrimination in this country against various racial and ethnic groups. The second step, however, involves a speculative leap: but for

Courts would be asked to evaluate the extent of the prejudice and consequent harm suffered by various minority groups. Those whose societal injury is thought to exceed some arbitrary level of tolerability then would be entitled to preferential classifications at the expense of individuals belonging to other groups. Those classifications would be free from exacting judicial scrutiny. As these preferences began to have their desired effect, and the consequences of past discrimination were undone, new judicial rankings would be necessary. The kind of variable sociological and political analysis necessary to produce such rankings simply does not lie within the judicial competence—even if they otherwise were politically feasible and socially desirable.

Moreover, there are serious problems of justice connected with the idea of preference itself. First, it may not always be clear that a so-called preference is in fact benign. Courts may be asked to validate burdens imposed upon individual members of particular groups in order to advance the group's general interest. See United Jewish Organizations v. Carey, 430 U.S. 144, 172–173 (Brennan, J., concurring in part). Nothing in the Constitution supports the notion that individuals may be asked to suffer otherwise impermissible burdens in order to enhance the societal standing of their ethnic groups. Second, preferential programs may only reinforce common stereotypes holding that certain groups are unable to achieve success without special protection based on a factor having no relationship to individual worth. See DeFunis v. Odegaard, 416 U.S. 312, 343 (Douglas, J., dissenting). Third, there is a measure of inequity in forcing innocent persons in respondent's position to bear the burdens of redressing grievances not of their making.

By hitching the meaning of the Equal Protection Clause to these transitory considerations, we would be holding, as a constitutional principle, that judicial scrutiny of classifications touching on racial and ethnic background may vary with the ebb and flow of political forces. Disparate constitutional tolerance of such classifications well may serve to exacerbate racial and ethnic antagonisms rather than alleviate them. *United Jewish Organizations,* supra, at 173–174 (Brennan, J., concurring). Also, the mutability of a constitutional principle, based upon shifting political and social judgments, undermines the chances for consistent application of the Constitution from one generation to the next, a critical feature of its coherent interpretation. Pollock v. Farmers' Loan & Trust Co., 157 U.S. 429, 650–651 (1895) (White, J., dissenting). In expounding the Constitution, the Court's role is to discern "principles sufficiently absolute to give them roots throughout the community and continuity over significant periods of time, and to lift them above the level of the pragmatic political judgments of a particular time and place." A. Cox, The Role of the Supreme Court in American Government 114 (1976).

If it is the individual who is entitled to judicial protection against classifications based upon his racial or ethnic background because such distinctions impinge upon personal rights, rather than the individual only because of his membership in a particular group, then constitutional standards may be applied consistently. Political judgments regarding the necessity for the particu-

---

this discrimination by society at large, Bakke "would have failed to qualify for admission" because Negro applicants—nothing is said about Asians . . .—would have made better scores. Not one word in the record supports this conclusion, and the plurality offers no standard for courts to use in applying such a presumption of causation to other racial or ethnic classifications. This failure is a grave one, since if it may be concluded *on this record* that each of the minority groups preferred by the petitioner's special program is entitled to the benefit of the presumption, it would seem difficult to determine that any of the dozens of minority groups that have suffered "societal discrimination" cannot also claim it, in any area of social intercourse. See Part IV–B, infra.

lar classification may be weighed in the constitutional balance, Korematsu v. United States, 323 U.S. 214 (1944), but the standard of justification will remain constant. This is as it should be, since those political judgments are the product of rough compromise struck by contending groups within the democratic process. When they touch upon an individual's race or ethnic background, he is entitled to a judicial determination that the burden he is asked to bear on that basis is precisely tailored to serve a compelling governmental interest....

C.

Petitioner contends that on several occasions this Court has approved preferential classifications without applying the most exacting scrutiny. Most of the cases upon which petitioner relies are drawn from three areas: school desegregation, employment discrimination, and sex discrimination. Each of the cases cited presented a situation materially different from the facts of this case.

The school desegregation cases are inapposite. Each involved remedies for clearly determined constitutional violations. E.g., Swann v. Charlotte–Mecklenburg Board of Education, 402 U.S. 1 (1971); McDaniel v. Barresi, 402 U.S. 39 (1971); Green v. County School Board, 391 U.S. 430 (1968). Racial classifications thus were designed as remedies for the vindication of constitutional entitlement. Moreover, the scope of the remedies was not permitted to exceed the extent of the violations. E.g., Dayton Board of Education v. Brinkman, 433 U.S. 406 (1977); Milliken v. Bradley, 418 U.S. 717 (1974); see Pasadena City Board of Education v. Spangler, 427 U.S. 424 (1976).... Here, there was no judicial determination of constitutional violation as a predicate for the formulation of a remedial classification.

The employment discrimination cases also do not advance petitioner's cause. For example, in Franks v. Bowman Transportation Co., 424 U.S. 747 (1976), we approved a retroactive award of seniority to a class of Negro truck drivers who had been the victims of discrimination—not just by society at large, but by the respondent in that case. While this relief imposed some burdens on other employees, it was held necessary "'to make [the victims] whole for injuries suffered on account of unlawful employment discrimination.' " ... But we have never approved preferential classifications in the absence of proven constitutional or statutory violations.

Nor is petitioner's view as to the applicable standard supported by the fact that gender-based classifications are not subjected to this level of scrutiny. E.g., Califano v. Webster, 430 U.S. 313, 316–317 (1977); e.g., Craig v. Boren, 429 U.S. 190, 211 n. * (1976) (Powell, J., concurring). Gender-based distinctions are less likely to create the analytical and practical problems present in preferential programs premised on racial or ethnic criteria. With respect to gender there are only two possible classifications. The incidence of the burdens imposed by preferential classifications is clear. There are no rival groups who can claim that they, too, are entitled to preferential treatment. Classwide questions as to the group suffering previous injury and groups which fairly can be burdened are relatively manageable for reviewing courts. See, e.g., Califano v. Goldfarb, 430 U.S. 199, 212–217 (1977); Weinberger v. Wiesenfeld, 420 U.S. 636, 645 (1975). The resolution of these same questions in the context of racial and ethnic preferences presents far more complex and intractable problems than gender-based classifications. More importantly, the perception of racial classifications as inherently odious stems from a lengthy and tragic history that gender-based classifications do not share. In sum, the Court has never viewed such classification as inherently suspect or as comparable to racial or ethnic classifications for the purpose of equal-protection analysis.

Petitioner also cites Lau v. Nichols, 414 U.S. 563 (1974), ... [where] we held that the failure of the San Francisco school system to provide remedial English instruction for some 1,800 students of oriental ancestry who spoke no English amounted to a violation of Title VI of the Civil Rights Act of 1964 ... and the regulations promulgated thereunder....

... [However,] the "preference" approved did not result in the denial of the relevant benefit—"meaningful participation in the educational program"— to anyone else. No other student was deprived by that preference of the ability to participate in San Francisco's school system, and the applicable regulations required similar assistance for all students who suffered similar linguistic deficiencies....

In a similar vein, petitioner contends that ... United Jewish Organizations v. Carey, 430 U.S. 144 (1977), indicates a willingness to approve racial classifications designed to benefit certain minorities, without denominating the classifications as "suspect." The State of New York had redrawn its reapportionment plan to meet objections of the Department of Justice under § 5 of the Voting Rights Act of 1965, 42 U.S.C. § 1973c. Specifically, voting districts were redrawn to enhance the electoral power of certain "nonwhite" voters found to have been the victims of unlawful "dilution" under the original reapportionment plan. *United Jewish Organizations,* like *Lau,* properly is viewed as a case in which the remedy for an administrative finding of discrimination encompassed measures to improve the previously disadvantaged group's ability to participate, without excluding individuals belonging to any other group from enjoyment of the relevant opportunity—meaningful participation in the electoral process.

In this case, unlike *Lau* and *United Jewish Organizations,* there has been no determination by the legislature or a responsible administrative agency that the University engaged in a discriminatory practice requiring remedial efforts. Moreover, the operation of petitioner's special admissions program is quite different from the remedial measures approved in those cases. It prefers the designated minority groups at the expense of other individuals who are totally foreclosed from competition for the 16 special admissions seats in every medical school class. Because of that foreclosure, some individuals are excluded from enjoyment of a state-provided benefit—admission to the medical school—they otherwise would receive. When a classification denies an individual opportunities or benefits enjoyed by others solely because of his race or ethnic background, it must be regarded as suspect. E.g., McLaurin v. Oklahoma State Regents, 339 U.S. 637, 641–642 (1950).

IV.

We have held that in "order to justify the use of a suspect classification, a State must show that its purpose or interest is both constitutionally permissible and substantial, and that its use of the classification is 'necessary ... to the accomplishment' of its purpose or the safeguarding of its interest." ... The special admissions program purports to serve the purposes of: (i) "reducing the historic deficit of traditionally disfavored minorities in medical schools and the medical profession;" (ii) countering the effects of societal discrimination; (iii) increasing the number of physicians who will practice in communities currently underserved; and (iv) obtaining the educational benefits that flow from an ethnically diverse student body. It is necessary to decide which, if any, of these purposes is substantial enough to support the use of a suspect classification.

A.

If petitioner's purpose is to assure within its student body some specified percentage of a particular group merely because of its race or ethnic origin, such a preferential purpose must be rejected not as insubstantial but as facially invalid. Preferring members of any one group for no reason other than race or ethnic origin is discrimination for its own sake. This the Constitution forbids. E.g., Loving v. Virginia, supra, at 11; McLaughlin v. Florida, supra, at 196; Brown v. Board of Education, 347 U.S. 483 (1954).

B.

The State certainly has a legitimate and substantial interest in ameliorating, or eliminating where feasible, the disabling effects of identified discrimination. The line of school desegregation cases, commencing with *Brown,* attests to the importance of this state goal and the commitment of the judiciary to affirm all lawful means towards its attainment. In the school cases, the States were required by court order to redress the wrongs worked by specific instances of racial discrimination. That goal was far more focused than the remedying of the effects of "societal discrimination," an amorphous concept of injury that may be ageless in its reach into the past.

We have never approved a classification that aids persons perceived as members of relatively victimized groups at the expense of other innocent individuals in the absence of judicial, legislative, or administrative findings of constitutional or statutory violations. ...After such findings have been made, the governmental interest in preferring members of the injured groups at the expense of others is substantial, since the legal rights of the victims must be vindicated. In such a case, the extent of the injury and the consequent remedy will have been judicially, legislatively, or administratively defined. Also, the remedial action usually remains subject to continuing oversight to assure that it will work the least harm possible to other innocent persons competing for the benefit. Without such findings of constitutional or statutory violations, it cannot be said that the government has any greater interest in helping one individual than in refraining from harming another. Thus, the government has no compelling justification for inflicting such harm.

Petitioner does not purport to have made, and is in no position to make, such findings. Its broad mission is education, not the formulation of any legislative policy or the adjudication of particular claims of illegality. For reasons similar to those stated in Part III of this opinion, isolated segments of our vast governmental structures are not competent to make those decisions, at least in the absence of legislative mandates and legislatively determined criteria. Cf. Hampton v. Mow Sun Wong, 426 U.S. 88 (1976). ...Before relying upon these sorts of findings in establishing a racial classification, a governmental body must have the authority and capability to establish, in the record, that the classification is responsive to identified discrimination. See, e.g., Califano v. Webster, 430 U.S. 313, 316–321 (1977); Califano v. Goldfarb, 430 U.S. 199, 212–217 (1977)....

Hence, the purpose of helping certain groups whom the faculty of the Davis Medical School perceived as victims of "societal discrimination" does not justify a classification that imposes disadvantages upon persons like respondent, who bear no responsibility for whatever harm the beneficiaries of the special admissions program are thought to have suffered. To hold otherwise would be to convert a remedy heretofore reserved for violations of legal rights into a privilege that all institutions throughout the Nation could grant at their pleasure to whatever groups are perceived as victims of societal discrimination.

That is a step we have never approved. Cf. Pasadena City Board of Education v. Spangler, 427 U.S. 424 (1976).

C.

Petitioner identifies, as another purpose of its program, improving the delivery of health care services to communities currently underserved. It may be assumed that in some situations a State's interest in facilitating the health care of its citizens is sufficiently compelling to support the use of a suspect classification. But there is virtually no evidence in the record indicating that petitioner's special admissions program is either needed or geared to promote that goal. . . .

. . .

D.

The fourth goal asserted by petitioner is the attainment of a diverse student body. This clearly is a constitutionally permissible goal for an institution of higher education. Academic freedom, though not a specifically enumerated constitutional right, long has been viewed as a special concern of the First Amendment. The freedom of a university to make its own judgments as to education includes the selection of its student body. . . .

. . . The atmosphere of "speculation, experiment and creation"—so essential to the quality of higher education—is widely believed to be promoted by a diverse student body. . . . [I]t is not too much to say that the "nation's future depends upon leaders trained through wide exposure" to the ideas and mores of students as diverse as this Nation of many peoples.

Thus, in arguing that its universities must be accorded the right to select those students who will contribute the most to the "robust exchange of ideas," petitioner invokes a countervailing constitutional interest, that of the First Amendment. In this light, petitioner must be viewed as seeking to achieve a goal that is of paramount importance in the fulfillment of its mission.

It may be argued that there is greater force to these views at the undergraduate level than in a medical school where the training is centered primarily on professional competency. But even at the graduate level, our tradition and experience lend support to the view that the contribution of diversity is substantial. . . . Physicians serve a heterogeneous population. An otherwise qualified medical student with a particular background—whether it be ethnic, geographic, culturally advantaged or disadvantaged—may bring to a professional school of medicine experiences, outlooks and ideas that enrich the training of its student body and better equip its graduates to render with understanding their vital service to humanity.

Ethnic diversity, however, is only one element in a range of factors a university properly may consider in attaining the goal of a heterogeneous student body. Although a university must have wide discretion in making the sensitive judgments as to who should be admitted, constitutional limitations protecting individual rights may not be disregarded. Respondent urges—and the courts below have held—that petitioner's dual admissions program is a racial classification that impermissibly infringes his rights under the Fourteenth Amendment. As the interest of diversity is compelling in the context of a university's admissions program, the question remains whether the program's racial classification is necessary to promote this interest. . . .

V.

A.

It may be assumed that the reservation of a specified number of seats in each class for individuals from the preferred ethnic groups would contribute to the attainment of considerable ethnic diversity in the student body. But petitioner's argument that this is the only effective means of serving the interest of diversity is seriously flawed. In a most fundamental sense the argument misconceives the nature of the state interest that would justify consideration of race or ethnic background. It is not an interest in simple ethnic diversity, in which a specified percentage of the student body is in effect guaranteed to be members of selected ethnic groups, with the remaining percentage an undifferentiated aggregation of students. The diversity that furthers a compelling state interest encompasses a far broader array of qualifications and characteristics of which racial or ethnic origin is but a single though important element. Petitioner's special admissions program, focused *solely* on ethnic diversity, would hinder rather than further attainment of genuine diversity.

Nor would the state interest in genuine diversity be served by expanding petitioner's two-track system into a multitrack program with a prescribed number of seats set aside for each identifiable category of applicants. Indeed, it is inconceivable that a university would thus pursue the logic of petitioner's two-track program to the illogical end of insulating each category of applicants with certain desired qualifications from competition with all other applicants.

The experience of other university admissions programs, which take race into account in achieving the educational diversity valued by the First Amendment, demonstrates that the assignment of a fixed number of places to a minority group is not a necessary means toward that end. An illuminating example is found in the Harvard College program:

"In recent years Harvard College has expanded the concept of diversity to include students from disadvantaged economic, racial and ethnic groups. Harvard College now recruits not only Californians or Louisianans but also blacks and Chicanos and other minority students.

. . .

"In practice, this new definition of diversity has meant that race has been a factor in some admission decisions. When the Committee on Admissions reviews the large middle group of applicants who are 'admissible' and deemed capable of doing good work in their courses, the race of an applicant may tip the balance in his favor just as geographic origin or a life spent on a farm may tip the balance in other candidates' cases. A farm boy from Idaho can bring something to Harvard College that a Bostonian cannot offer. Similarly, a black student can usually bring something that a white person cannot offer." . . .

. . .

"In Harvard college admissions the Committee has not set target-quotas for the number of blacks, or of musicians, football players, physicists or Californians to be admitted in a given year.... But that awareness [of the necessity of including more than a token number of black students] does not mean that the Committee sets the minimum number of blacks or of people from west of the Mississippi who are to be admitted. It means only that in choosing among thousands of applicants who are not only 'admissible' academically but have other strong qualities, the Committee, with a number of criteria in mind, pays some attention to distribution among many types and categories of students." Brief for Columbia University, Harvard University, Stanford University, and the University of Pennsylvania, as *Amici Curiae*, App. 2, 3.

In such an admissions program, race or ethnic background may be deemed a "plus" in a particular applicant's file, yet it does not insulate the individual from comparison with all other candidates for the available seats. The file of a particular black applicant may be examined for his potential contribution to diversity without the factor of race being decisive when compared, for example, with that of an applicant identified as an Italian–American if the latter is thought to exhibit qualities more likely to promote beneficial educational pluralism. Such qualities could include exceptional personal talents, unique work or service experience, leadership potential, maturity, demonstrated compassion, a history of overcoming disadvantage, ability to communicate with the poor, or other qualifications deemed important. In short, an admissions program operated in this way is flexible enough to consider all pertinent elements of diversity in light of the particular qualifications of each applicant, and to place them on the same footing for consideration, although not necessarily according them the same weight. Indeed, the weight attributed to a particular quality may vary from year to year depending upon the "mix" both of the student body and the applicants for the incoming class.

This kind of program treats each applicant as an individual in the admissions process. The applicant who loses out on the last available seat to another candidate receiving a "plus" on the basis of ethnic background will not have been foreclosed from all consideration for that seat simply because he was not the right color or had the wrong surname. It would mean only that his combined qualifications, which may have included similar nonobjective factors, did not outweigh those of the other applicant. His qualifications would have been weighed fairly and competitively, and he would have no basis to complain of unequal treatment under the Fourteenth Amendment.

It has been suggested that an admissions program which considers race only as one factor is simply a subtle and more sophisticated—but no less effective—means of according racial preference than the Davis program. A facial intent to discriminate, however, is evident in petitioner's preference program and not denied in this case. No such facial infirmity exists in an admissions program where race or ethnic background is simply one element—to be weighed fairly against other elements—in the selection process. "A boundary line," as Mr. Justice Frankfurter remarked in another connection, "is none the worse for being narrow." McLeod v. Dilworth, 322 U.S. 327, 329 (1944). And a Court would not assume that a university, professing to employ a facially nondiscriminatory admissions policy, would operate it as a cover for the functional equivalent of a quota system. In short, good faith would be presumed in the absence of a showing to the contrary in the manner permitted by our cases. See, e.g., Arlington Heights v. Metropolitan Housing Development Corp., 429 U.S. 252 (1977); Washington v. Davis, 426 U.S. 229 (1976); Swain v. Alabama, 380 U.S. 202 (1965).

B.

In summary, it is evident that the Davis special admission program involves the use of an explicit racial classification never before countenanced by this Court. It tells applicants who are not Negro, Asian, or "Chicano" that they are totally excluded from a specific percentage of the seats in an entering class. No matter how strong their qualifications, quantitative and extracurricular, including their own potential for contribution to educational diversity, they are never afforded the chance to compete with applicants from the preferred groups for the special admission seats. At the same time, the preferred applicants have the opportunity to compete for every seat in the class.

The fatal flaw in petitioner's preferential program is its disregard of individual rights as guaranteed by the Fourteenth Amendment. Shelley v. Kraemer, 334 U.S. 1, 22 (1948). Such rights are not absolute. But when a State's distribution of benefits or imposition of burdens hinges on the color of a person's skin or ancestry, that individual is entitled to a demonstration that the challenged classification is necessary to promote a substantial state interest. Petitioner has failed to carry this burden. For this reason, that portion of the California court's judgment holding petitioner's special admissions program invalid under the Fourteenth Amendment must be affirmed.

C.

In enjoining petitioner from ever considering the race of any applicant, however, the courts below failed to recognize that the State has a substantial interest that legitimately may be served by a properly devised admissions program involving the competitive consideration of race and ethnic origin. For this reason, so much of the California court's judgment as enjoins petitioner from any consideration of the race of any applicant must be reversed.

VI.

With respect to respondent's entitlement to an injunction directing his admission to the Medical School, petitioner has conceded that it could not carry its burden of proving that, but for the existence of its unlawful special admissions program, respondent still would not have been admitted. Hence, respondent is entitled to the injunction, and that portion of the judgment must be affirmed.

. . .

Opinion of Mr. Justice Brennan, Mr. Justice White, Mr. Justice Marshall, and Mr. Justice Blackmun, concurring in the judgment in part and dissenting.

The Court today ... affirms the constitutional power of Federal and State Government to act affirmatively to achieve equal opportunity for all. The difficulty of the issue presented—whether Government may use race-conscious programs to redress the continuing effects of past discrimination—and the mature consideration which each of our Brethren has brought to it have resulted in many opinions, no single one speaking for the Court. But this should not and must not mask the central meaning of today's opinions: Government may take race into account when it acts not to demean or insult any racial group but to remedy disadvantages cast on minorities by past racial prejudice, at least when appropriate findings have been made by judicial, legislative, or administrative bodies with competence to act in this area.

The Chief Justice and our Brothers Stewart, Rehnquist, and Stevens have concluded that Title VI of the Civil Rights Act of 1964 ... prohibits programs such as that at the Davis Medical School. On this statutory theory alone, they would hold that respondent Allan Bakke's rights have been violated and that he must, therefore, be admitted to the Medical School. Our Brother Powell, reaching the Constitution, concludes that, although race may be taken into account in university admissions, the particular special admissions program used by petitioner, which resulted in the exclusion of respondent Bakke, was not shown to be necessary to achieve petitioner's stated goals. Accordingly, these Members of the Court form a majority of five affirming the judgment of the Supreme Court of California insofar as it holds that respondent Bakke "is entitled to an order that he be admitted to the University." . . .

We agree with Mr. Justice Powell that, as applied to the case before us, Title VI goes no further in prohibiting the use of race than the Equal Protection Clause of the Fourteenth Amendment itself. We also agree that the effect of the California Supreme Court's affirmance of the judgment of the Superior Court of California would be to prohibit the University from establishing in the future affirmative action programs that take race into account. Since we conclude that the affirmative admissions program at the Davis Medical School is constitutional, we would reverse the judgment below in all respects. Mr. Justice Powell agrees that some uses of race in university admissions are permissible and, therefore, he joins with us to make five votes reversing the judgment below insofar as it prohibits the University from establishing race-conscious programs in the future.[1]

I.

Our Nation was founded on the principle that "all men are created equal." Yet candor requires acknowledgment that the Framers of our Constitution, to forge the Thirteen Colonies into one Nation, openly compromised this principle of equality with its antithesis: slavery. The consequences of this compromise are well known and have aptly been called our "American Dilemma." Still, it is well to recount how recent the time has been, if it has yet come, when the promise of our principles has flowered into the actuality of equal opportunity for all regardless of race or color.

The Fourteenth Amendment . . . Equal Protection Clause . . . was early turned against those whom it was intended to set free, condemning them to a "separate but equal" status before the law, a status always separate but seldom equal. Not until 1954—only 24 years ago—was this odious doctrine interred by our decision in Brown v. Board of Education, 347 U.S. 483 (1954) (*Brown I*), and its progeny, which proclaimed that separate schools and public facilities of all sorts were inherently unequal and forbidden under our Constitution. Even then inequality was not eliminated with "all deliberate speed." Brown v. Board of Education, 349 U.S. 294, 301 (1955). In 1968 and again in 1971, for example, we were forced to remind school boards of their obligation to eliminate racial discrimination root and branch. And a glance at our docket and at those of lower courts will show that even today officially sanctioned discrimination is not a thing of the past.

Against this background, claims that law must be "colorblind" or that the datum of race is no longer relevant to public policy must be seen as aspiration rather than as description of reality. This is not to denigrate aspiration; for reality rebukes us that race has too often been used by those who would stigmatize and oppress minorities. Yet we cannot—and as we shall demonstrate, need not under our Constitution or Title VI, which merely extends the constraints of the Fourteenth Amendment to private parties who receive federal funds—let color blindness become myopia which masks the reality that many "created equal" have been treated within our lifetimes as inferior both by the law and by their fellow citizens.

---

[1] We also agree with Mr. Justice Powell that a plan like the "Harvard" plan . . . is constitutional under our approach, at least so long as the use of race to achieve an integrated student body is necessitated by the lingering effects of past discrimination.

II.

. . .

In our view, Title VI prohibits only those uses of racial criteria that would violate the Fourteenth Amendment if employed by a State or its agencies; it does not bar the preferential treatment of racial minorities as a means of remedying past societal discrimination to the extent that such action is consistent with the Fourteenth Amendment. The legislative history of Title VI, administrative regulations interpreting the statute, subsequent congressional and executive action, and the prior decisions of this Court compel this conclusion. None of these sources lends support to the proposition that Congress intended to bar all race conscious efforts to extend the benefits of federally financed programs to minorities who have been historically excluded from the full benefits of American life.

. . .

We turn, therefore, to our analysis of the Equal Protection Clause of the Fourteenth Amendment.

III.

A.

The assertion of human equality is closely associated with the proposition that differences in color or creed, birth or status, are neither significant nor relevant to the way in which persons should be treated. Nonetheless, the position that such factors must be "[c]onstitutionally an irrelevance," Edwards v. California, 314 U.S. 160, 185 (1941) (Jackson, J., concurring), summed up by the shorthand phrase "[o]ur Constitution is color-blind," Plessy v. Ferguson, 163 U.S. 537, 559 (1896) (Harlan, J., dissenting), has never been adopted by this Court as the proper meaning of the Equal Protection Clause. Indeed, we have expressly rejected this proposition on a number of occasions.

Our cases have always implied that an "overriding statutory purpose," McLaughlin v. Florida, 379 U.S. 184, 192 (1964), could be found that would justify racial classifications. See, e.g., ibid.; Loving v. Virginia, 388 U.S. 1, 11 (1967); Korematsu v. United States, 323 U.S. 214, 216 (1944); Hirabayashi v. United States, 320 U.S. 81, 100–101 (1943). More recently, in McDaniel v. Barresi, 402 U.S. 39 (1971), this Court unanimously reversed the Georgia Supreme Court which had held that a desegregation plan voluntarily adopted by a local school board, which assigned students on the basis of race, was *per se* invalid because it was not colorblind. And in North Carolina State Board of Ed. v. Swann, 402 U.S. 43 (1971), we held, again unanimously, that a statute mandating colorblind school assignment plans could not stand "against the background of segregation," since such a limit on remedies would "render illusory the promise of *Brown* [*I, supra*]."

We conclude, therefore, that racial classifications are not *per se* invalid under the Fourteenth Amendment. Accordingly, we turn to the problem of articulating what our role should be in reviewing state action that expressly classifies by race.

B.

Respondent argues that racial classifications are always suspect and, consequently, that this Court should weigh the importance of the objectives served by Davis' special admissions program to see if they are compelling. In addition, he asserts that this Court must inquire whether, in its judgment, there are alternatives to racial classifications which would suit Davis' purposes. Petitioner, on the other hand, states that our proper role is simply to accept petitioner's determination that the racial classifications used by its program are reasonably related to what it tells us are its benign purposes. We reject petitioner's view, but, because our prior cases are in many respects inapposite to that before us now, we find it necessary to define with precision the meaning of that inexact term, "strict scrutiny."

Unquestionably we have held that a government practice or statute which restricts "fundamental rights" or which contains "suspect classifications" is to be subjected to "strict scrutiny" and can be justified only if it furthers a compelling government purpose and, even then, only if no less restrictive alternative is available. See, e.g., San Antonio Indep. School Dist. v. Rodriguez, 411 U.S. 1, 16–17 (1973); Dunn v. Blumstein, 405 U.S. 330 (1972). But no fundamental right is involved here. See *San Antonio,* supra, at 29–36. Nor do whites as a class have any of the "traditional indicia of suspectness: the class is not saddled with such disabilities, or subjected to such a history of purposeful unequal treatment, or relegated to such a position of political powerlessness as to command extraordinary protection from the majoritarian political process." Id., at 28; see United States v. Carolene Products Co., 304 U.S. 144, 152 n. 4 (1938).[31]

Moreover, if the University's representations are credited, this is not a case where racial classifications are "irrelevant and therefore prohibited." *Hirabayashi,* 320 U.S., at 100. Nor has anyone suggested that the University's purposes contravene the cardinal principle that racial classifications that stigmatize—because they are drawn on the presumption that one race is inferior to another or because they put the weight of government behind racial hatred and separatism—are invalid without more. . . .

On the other hand, the fact that this case does not fit neatly into our prior analytic framework for race cases does not mean that it should be analyzed by applying the very loose rational-basis standard of review that is the very least that is always applied in equal protection cases. " '[T]he mere recitation of a benign, compensatory purpose is not an automatic shield which protects against any inquiry into the actual purposes underlying a statutory scheme.' " Califano v. Webster, 430 U.S. 313, 317 (1977), quoting Weinberger v. Wiesenfeld, 420 U.S. 636, 648 (1975). Instead, a number of considerations—developed in gender discrimination cases but which carry even more force when applied to racial classifications—lead us to conclude that racial classifications designed to further remedial purposes " 'must serve important governmental objectives and must be substantially related to achievement of those objectives.' " Califano v. Webster, supra, at 316, quoting Craig v. Boren, 429 U.S. 190, 197 (1976).[35]

---

[31] Of course, the fact that whites constitute a political majority in our Nation does not necessarily mean that active judicial scrutiny of racial classifications that disadvantage whites is inappropriate. Cf. Castaneda v. Partida, 430 U.S. 482, 499–500 (1977); id., at 501 (Marshall, J., concurring).

[35] We disagree with our Brother Powell's suggestion . . . that the presence of "rival groups who can claim that they, too, are entitled to preferential treatment," . . . distinguishes the gender cases or is relevant to the question of scope of judicial review of race classifications. We are not asked to determine whether groups other than those fa-

vored by the Davis program should similarly be favored. All we are asked to do is to pronounce the constitutionality of what Davis has done.

But, were we asked to decide whether any given rival group—German–Americans for example—must constitutionally be accorded preferential treatment, we do have a "principled basis," . . . for deciding this question, one that is well-established in our cases: The Davis program expressly sets out four classes which receive preferred status. . . . The program clearly distinguishes whites, but one cannot reason from this to a conclusion that German–Americans, as a national

First, race, like, "gender-based classifications too often [has] been inexcusably utilized to stereotype and stigmatize politically powerless segments of society." Kahn v. Shevin, 416 U.S. 351, 357 (1974) (dissenting opinion)....

Second, race, like gender and illegitimacy, see Weber v. Aetna Cas. & Surety Co., 406 U.S. 164 (1972), is an immutable characteristic which its possessors are powerless to escape or set aside....

. . .

In sum, because of the significant risk that racial classifications established for ostensibly benign purposes can be misused, causing effects not unlike those created by invidious classifications, it is inappropriate to inquire only whether there is any conceivable basis that might sustain such a classification. Instead, to justify such a classification an important and articulated purpose for its use must be shown. In addition, any statute must be stricken that stigmatizes any group or that singles out those least well represented in the political process to bear the brunt of a benign program. Thus our review under the Fourteenth Amendment should be strict—not "'strict' in theory and fatal in fact," because it is stigma that causes fatality—but strict and searching nonetheless.

IV.

Davis' articulated purpose of remedying the effects of past societal discrimination is, under our cases, sufficiently important to justify the use of race-conscious admissions programs where there is a sound basis for concluding that minority underrepresentation is substantial and chronic, and that the handicap of past discrimination is impeding access of minorities to the medical school.

A.

At least since Green v. County School Board, 391 U.S. 430 (1968), it has been clear that a public body which has itself been adjudged to have engaged in racial discrimination cannot bring itself into compliance with the Equal Protection Clause simply by ending its unlawful acts and adopting a neutral stance. Three years later, Swann v. Charlotte–Mecklenburg Board of Ed., 402 U.S. 1 (1971), and its companion cases, Davis v. Board of School Comm'rs, 402 U.S. 33 (1971); *McDaniel v. Barresi, supra;* and *North Carolina State Board of Ed. v. Swann,* supra, reiterated that racially neutral remedies for past discrimination were inadequate where consequences of past discriminatory acts influence or control present decisions. See, e.g., *Charlotte–Mecklenburg,* supra, at 28. And the Court further held both that courts could enter desegregation orders which assigned students and faculty by reference to race, *Charlotte–Mecklenburg,* supra; *Davis,* supra; United States v. Montgomery County Board of Ed., 395 U.S. 225 (1969), and that local school boards could voluntarily adopt desegregation plans which made express reference to race if this was necessary to remedy

group, are singled out for invidious treatment. And even if the Davis program had a differential impact on German–Americans, they would have no constitutional claim unless they could prove that Davis intended invidiously to discriminate against German–Americans. See Village of Arlington Heights v. Metropolitan Housing Corp., 429 U.S. 252, 264–265 (1977); Washington v. Davis, 426 U.S. 229, 238–241 (1976). If this could not be shown, then "the principle that calls for the closest scrutiny of distinctions in laws denying fundamental rights ... is inapplicable,"

Katzenbach v. Morgan, 384 U.S. 641, 657 (1966), and the only question is whether it was rational for Davis to conclude that the groups it preferred had a greater claim to compensation than the groups it excluded. See ibid.; San Antonio Indep. School Dist. v. Rodriguez, 411 U.S. 1, 38–39 (1973) (applying *Katzenbach* test to state action intended to remove discrimination in educational opportunity). Thus, claims of rival groups, although they may create thorny political problems, create relatively simple problems for the courts.

the effects of past discrimination. *McDaniel v. Barresi, supra.* Moreover, we stated that school boards, even in the absence of a judicial finding of past discrimination, could voluntarily adopt plans which assigned students with the end of creating racial pluralism by establishing fixed ratios of black and white students in each school. *Charlotte–Mecklenburg, ...* In each instance, the creation of unitary school systems, in which the effects of past discrimination had been "eliminated root and branch," *Green, . . .* was recognized as a compelling social goal justifying the overt use of race.

Finally, the conclusion that state educational institutions may constitutionally adopt admissions programs designed to avoid exclusion of historically disadvantaged minorities, even when such programs explicitly take race into account, finds direct support in our cases construing congressional legislation designed to overcome the present effects of past discrimination. Congress can and has outlawed actions which have a disproportionately adverse and unjustified impact upon members of racial minorities and has required or authorized race-conscious action to put individuals disadvantaged by such impact in the position they otherwise might have enjoyed. See *Franks v. Bowman, supra;* International Brotherhood of Teamsters v. United States, 431 U.S. 324 (1977). Such relief does not require as a predicate proof that recipients of preferential advancement have been individually discriminated against; it is enough that each recipient is within a general class of persons likely to have been the victims of discrimination. Nor is it an objection to such relief that preference for minorities will upset the settled expectations of nonminorities. See *Franks, supra.* In addition, we have held that Congress, to remove barriers to equal opportunity, can and has required employers to use test criteria that fairly reflect the qualifications of minority applicants vis-a-vis nonminority applicants, even if this means interpreting the qualifications of an applicant in light of his race. See Albemarle v. Moody, 422 U.S. 405, 435 (1975).

These cases cannot be distinguished simply by the presence of judicial findings of discrimination, for race-conscious remedies have been approved where such findings have not been made. *McDaniel v. Barresi, supra; UJO, supra;* see *Califano v. Webster, supra; Schlesinger v. Ballard, supra; Kahn v. Shevin, supra.* See also Katzenbach v. Morgan, 384 U.S. 641 (1967). Indeed, the requirement of a judicial determination of a constitutional or statutory violation as a predicate for race-conscious remedial actions would be self-defeating. Such a requirement would severely undermine efforts to achieve voluntary compliance with the requirements of law. And, our society and jurisprudence have always stressed the value of voluntary efforts to further the objectives of the law. Judicial intervention is a last resort to achieve cessation of illegal conduct or the remedying of its effects rather than a prerequisite to action.

Nor can our cases be distinguished on the ground that the entity using explicit racial classifications had itself violated § 1 of the Fourteenth Amendment or an antidiscrimination regulation, for again race-conscious remedies have been approved where this is not the case. See *UJO . . . ;* cf. *Califano v. Webster . . . ; Kahn v. Shevin, supra.* Moreover, the presence or absence of past discrimination by universities or employers is largely irrelevant to resolving respondent's constitutional claims. The claims of those burdened by the race-conscious actions of a university or employer who has never been adjudged in violation of an antidiscrimination law are not any more or less entitled to deference than the claims of the burdened nonminority workers in Franks v. Bowman, 424 U.S. 747 (1976), in which the employer had violated Title VII, for in each case the employees are innocent of past discrimination. And, although it might be argued that, where an employer has violated an antidiscrimination law, the expectations of nonminority workers are themselves products of discrimination and hence "tainted," and therefore more easily upset, the same argument can be made with respect to respondent. If it was reasonable to conclude—as we hold that it was—that the failure of minorities to qualify for admission at Davis under regular procedures was due principally to the effects of past discrimination, then there is a reasonable likelihood that, but for pervasive racial discrimination, respondent would have failed to qualify for admission even in the absence of Davis' special admissions program.[41]

Thus, our cases under Title VII of the Civil Rights Act have held that, in order to achieve minority participation in previously segregated areas of public life, Congress may require or authorize preferential treatment for those likely disadvantaged by societal racial discrimination. Such legislation has been sustained even without a requirement of findings of intentional racial discrimination by those required or authorized to accord preferential treatment, or a case-by-case determination that those to be benefited suffered from racial discrimination. These decisions compel the conclusion that States also may adopt race-conscious programs designed to overcome substantial, chronic minority underrepresentation where there is reason to believe that the evil addressed is a product of past racial discrimination.[42]

... Nothing whatever in the legislative history of either the Fourteenth Amendment or the Civil Rights Acts even remotely suggests that the States are foreclosed from furthering the fundamental purpose of equal opportunity to which the Amendment and those Acts are addressed. Indeed, voluntary initiatives by the States to achieve the national goal of equal opportunity have been recognized to be essential to its attainment.... We therefore conclude that Davis' goal of admitting minority students disadvantaged by the effects of past

[41] Our cases cannot be distinguished by suggesting, as our Brother Powell does, that in none of them was anyone deprived of "the relevant benefit." ... Our school cases have deprived whites of the neighborhood school of their choice; our Title VII cases have deprived nondiscriminating employees of their settled seniority expectations; and *UJO* deprived the Hassidim of bloc voting strength. Each of these injuries was constitutionally cognizable as is respondent's here.

[42] We do not understand Mr. Justice Powell to disagree that providing a remedy for past racial prejudice can constitute a compelling purpose sufficient to meet strict scrutiny.... Yet, because petitioner is a university, he would not allow it to exercise such power in the absence of "judicial, legislative, or administrative findings of constitutional or statutory violations." ... While we agree that reversal in this case would follow *a fortiori* had Davis been guilty of invidious racial discrimination or if a federal statute mandated that universities refrain from applying any admissions policy that had a disparate and unjustified racial impact, ... we do not think it of constitutional significance that Davis has not been so adjudged.

Generally, the manner in which a State chooses to delegate governmental functions is for it to decide. Cf. Sweezy v. New Hampshire, 354 U.S. 234, 256 (1957) (Frankfurter, J., concurring). California, by constitutional

provision, has chosen to place authority over the operation of the University of California in the Board of Regents. See Cal. Const. Art. IX, § 9(a) (1978). Control over the University is to be found not in the legislature, but rather in the Regents who have been vested with full legislative (including policymaking), administrative, and adjudicative powers by the citizens of California.... This is certainly a permissible choice, see *Sweezy*, supra, and we, unlike our Brother Powell, find nothing in the Equal Protection Clause that requires us to depart from established principle by limiting the scope of power the Regents may exercise more narrowly than the powers that may constitutionally be wielded by the Assembly.

Because the Regents can exercise plenary legislative and administrative power, it elevates form over substance to insist that Davis could not use race-conscious remedial programs until it had been adjudged in violation of the Constitution or an antidiscrimination statute. For, if the Equal Protection Clause required such a violation as a predicate, the Regents could simply have promulgated a regulation prohibiting disparate treatment not justified by the need to admit only qualified students, and could have declared Davis to have been in violation of such a regulation on the basis of the exclusionary effect of the admissions policy applied during the first two years of its operation....

discrimination is sufficiently important to justify use of race-conscious admissions criteria.

B.

Properly construed, therefore, our prior cases unequivocally show that a state government may adopt race-conscious programs if the purpose of such programs is to remove the disparate racial impact its actions might otherwise have and if there is reason to believe that the disparate impact is itself the product of past discrimination, whether its own or that of society at large. There is no question that Davis' program is valid under this test.

Certainly, on the basis of the undisputed factual submissions before this Court, Davis had a sound basis for believing that the problem of underrepresentation of minorities was substantial and chronic and that the problem was attributable to handicaps imposed on minority applicants by past and present racial discrimination. Until at least 1973, the practice of medicine in this country was, in fact, if not in law, largely the prerogative of whites. In 1950, for example, while Negroes comprised 10% of the total population, Negro physicians constituted only 2.2% of the total number of physicians. The overwhelming majority of these, moreover, were educated in two predominantly Negro medical schools, Howard and Meharry. By 1970, the gap between the proportion of Negroes in medicine and their proportion in the population had widened: The number of Negroes employed in medicine remained frozen at 2.2% while the Negro population had increased to 11.1%. The number of Negro admittees to predominantly white medical schools, moreover, had declined in absolute numbers during the years 1955 to 1964.

Moreover, Davis had very good reason to believe that the national pattern of underrepresentation of minorities in medicine would be perpetuated if it retained a single admissions standard. For example, the entering classes in 1968 and 1969, the years in which such a standard was used, included only one Chicano and two Negroes out of 100 admittees. Nor is there any relief from this pattern of underrepresentation in the statistics for the regular admissions program in later years.

Davis clearly could conclude that the serious and persistent underrepresentation of minorities in medicine depicted by these statistics is the result of handicaps under which minority applicants labor as a consequence of a background of deliberate, purposeful discrimination against minorities in education and in society generally, as well as in the medical profession. From the inception of our national life, Negroes have been subjected to unique legal disabilities impairing access to equal educational opportunity....

... The generation of minority students applying to Davis Medical School since it opened in 1968—most of whom were born before or about the time *Brown I* was decided—clearly have been victims of this discrimination. Judicial decrees recognizing discrimination in public education in California testify to the fact of widespread discrimination suffered by California-born minority applicants; many minority group members living in California, moreover, were born and reared in school districts in southern States segregated by law. Since separation of school children by race "generates a feeling of inferiority as to their status in the community that may affect their hearts and minds in a way unlikely ever to be undone," *Brown I*, 347 U.S., at 494, the conclusion is inescapable that applicants to medical school must be few indeed who endured the effects of *de jure* segregation, the resistance to *Brown I*, or the equally debilitating pervasive private discrimination fostered by our long history of official discrimination, cf. Reitman v. Mulkey, supra, and yet come to the starting line with an education equal to whites.

. . .

C.

The second prong of our test—whether the Davis program stigmatizes any discrete group or individual and whether race is reasonably used in light of the program's objectives—is clearly satisfied by the Davis program.

It is not even claimed that Davis' program in any way operates to stigmatize or single out any discrete and insular, or even any identifiable, non-minority group. Nor will harm comparable to that imposed upon racial minorities by exclusion or separation on grounds of race be the likely result of the program. It does not, for example, establish an exclusive preserve for minority students apart from and exclusive of whites. Rather, its purpose is to overcome the effects of segregation by bringing the races together. True, whites are excluded from participation in the special admissions program, but this fact only operates to reduce the number of whites to be admitted in the regular admissions program in order to permit admission of a reasonable percentage—less than their proportion of the California population—of otherwise under-represented qualified minority applicants.[58]

Nor was Bakke in any sense stamped as inferior by the Medical School's rejection of him. Indeed, it is conceded by all that he satisfied those criteria regarded by the School as generally relevant to academic performance better than most of the minority members who were admitted. Moreover, there is absolutely no basis for concluding that Bakke's rejection as a result of Davis' use of racial preference will affect him throughout his life in the same way as the segregation of the Negro school children in *Brown I* would have affected them. Unlike discrimination against racial minorities, the use of racial preferences for remedial purposes does not inflict a pervasive injury upon individual whites in the sense that wherever they go or whatever they do there is a significant likelihood that they will be treated as second-class citizens because of their color. This distinction does not mean that the exclusion of a white resulting from the preferential use of race is not sufficiently serious to require justification; but it does mean that the injury inflicted by such a policy is not distinguishable from disadvantages caused by a wide range of government actions, none of which has ever been thought impermissible for that reason alone.

[58] The constitutionality of the special admissions program is buttressed by its restriction to only 16% of the positions in the Medical School, a percentage less than that of the minority population in California and to those minority applicants deemed qualified for admission and deemed likely to contribute to the medical school and the medical profession.... This is consistent with the goal of putting minority applicants in the position they would have been in if not for the evil of racial discrimination. Accordingly, this case does not raise the question whether even a remedial use of race would be unconstitutional if it admitted unqualified minority applicants in preference to qualified applicants or admitted, as a result of preferential consideration, racial minorities in numbers significantly in excess of their proportional representation in the relevant population. Such programs might well be inadequately justified by the legitimate remedial objectives. Our allusion to the proportional percentage of minorities in the population of the State administering the program is not intended to establish either that figure or that population universe as a constitutional benchmark. In this case, even respondent, as we understand him, does not argue that, if the special admissions program is otherwise constitutional, the allotment of 16 places in each entering class for special admittees is unconstitutionally high.

In addition, there is simply no evidence that the Davis program discriminates intentionally or unintentionally against any minority group which it purports to benefit. The program does not establish a quota in the invidious sense of a ceiling on the number of minority applicants to be admitted. Nor can the program reasonably be regarded as stigmatizing the program's beneficiaries or their race as inferior. The Davis program does not simply advance less qualified applicants; rather, it compensates applicants, whom it is uncontested are fully qualified to study medicine, for educational disadvantage which it was reasonable to conclude was a product of state-fostered discrimination. Once admitted, these students must satisfy the same degree requirements as regularly admitted students; they are taught by the same faculty in the same classes; and their performance is evaluated by the same standards by which regularly admitted students are judged. Under these circumstances, their performance and degrees must be regarded equally with the regularly admitted students with whom they compete for standing. Since minority graduates cannot justifiably be regarded as less well qualified than nonminority graduates by virtue of the special admissions program, there is no reasonable basis to conclude that minority graduates at schools using such programs would be stigmatized as inferior by the existence of such programs.

D.

We disagree with the lower courts' conclusion that the Davis program's use of race was unreasonable in light of its objectives. First, as petitioner argues, there are no practical means by which it could achieve its ends in the foreseeable future without the use of race-conscious measures. With respect to any factor (such as poverty or family educational background) that may be used as a substitute for race as an indicator of past discrimination, whites greatly outnumber racial minorities simply because whites make up a far larger percentage of the total population and therefore far outnumber minorities in absolute terms at every socio-economic level. For example, of a class of recent medical school applicants from families with less than $10,000 income, at least 71% were white. Of all 1970 families headed by a person *not* a high school graduate which included related children under 18, 80% were white and 20% were racial minorities. Moreover, while race is positively correlated with differences in GPA and MCAT scores, economic disadvantage is not. Thus, it appears that economically disadvantaged whites do not score less well than economically advantaged whites, while economically advantaged blacks score less well than do disadvantaged whites. These statistics graphically illustrate that the University's purpose to integrate its classes by compensating for past discrimination could not be achieved by a general preference for the economically disadvantaged or the children of parents of limited education unless such groups were to make up the entire class.

Second, the Davis admissions program does not simply equate minority status with disadvantage. Rather, Davis considers on an individual basis each applicant's personal history to determine whether he or she has likely been disadvantaged by racial discrimination. The record makes clear that only minority applicants likely to have been isolated from the mainstream of American life are considered in the special program; other minority applicants are eligible only through the regular admissions program. True, the procedure by which disadvantage is detected is informal, but we have never insisted that educators conduct their affairs through adjudicatory proceedings, and such insistence here is misplaced. A case-by-case inquiry into the extent to which each individual applicant has been affected, either directly or indirectly, by racial discrimination, would seem to be, as a practical matter, virtually impossible, despite the fact that there are excellent reasons for concluding that such effects generally exist. When individual measurement is impossible or extremely impractical, there is nothing to prevent a State from using categorical means to achieve its ends, at least where the category is closely related to the goal.... And it is clear from our cases that specific proof that a person has been victimized by discrimination is not a necessary predicate to offering him relief where the probability of victimization is great. ...

E.

Finally, Davis' special admissions program cannot be said to violate the Constitution simply because it has set aside a predetermined number of places for qualified minority applicants rather than using minority status as a positive factor to be considered in evaluating the applications of disadvantaged minority applicants. For purposes of constitutional adjudication, there is no difference between the two approaches. In any admissions program which accords special consideration to disadvantaged racial minorities, a determination of the degree of preference to be given is unavoidable, and any given preference that results in the exclusion of a white candidate is no more or less constitutionally acceptable than a program such as that at Davis. Furthermore, the extent of the preference inevitably depends on how many minority applicants the particular school is seeking to admit in any particular year so long as the number of qualified minority applicants exceeds that number. There is no sensible, and certainly no constitutional, distinction between, for example, adding a set number of points to the admissions rating of disadvantaged minority applicants as an expression of the preference with the expectation that this will result in the admission of an approximately determined number of qualified minority applicants and setting a fixed number of places for such applicants as was done here.[63]

The "Harvard" program, ... as those employing it readily concede, openly and successfully employs a racial criterion for the purpose of ensuring that some of the scarce places in institutions of higher education are allocated to disadvantaged minority students. That the Harvard approach does not also make public the extent of the preference and the precise workings of the system while the Davis program employs a specific, openly stated number, does not condemn the latter plan for purposes of Fourteenth Amendment adjudication. It may be that the Harvard plan is more acceptable to the public than is the Davis "quota." If it is, any State, including California, is free to adopt it in preference to a less acceptable alternative, just as it is generally free, as far as the Constitution is concerned, to abjure granting any racial preferences in its admissions program. But there is no basis for preferring a particular preference program simply because in achieving the same goals that the Davis Medical School is pursuing, it proceeds in a manner that is not immediately apparent to the public.

IV.

Accordingly, we would reverse the judgment of the Supreme Court of California holding the Medical School's special admissions program unconstitutional and directing respondent's admission, as well as that portion of the judgment enjoining the Medical School from according any consideration to race in the admissions process.

---

[63] The excluded white applicant, despite Mr. Justice Powell's contention to the contrary ... receives no more or less "individu-alized consideration" under our approach than under his.

Separate opinion of Mr. Justice White.

. . .

Mr. Justice Marshall.

I agree with the judgment of the Court only insofar as it permits a university to consider the race of an applicant in making admissions decisions. I do not agree that petitioner's admissions program violates the Constitution. . . .

. . .

. . . [I]t is more than a little ironic that, after several hundred years of class-based discrimination against Negroes, the Court is unwilling to hold that a class-based remedy for that discrimination is permissible. In declining to so hold, today's judgment ignores the fact that for several hundred years Negroes have been discriminated against, not as individuals, but rather solely because of the color of their skins. It is unnecessary in 20th century America to have individual Negroes demonstrate that they have been victims of racial discrimination; the racism of our society has been so pervasive that none, regardless of wealth or position, has managed to escape its impact. The experience of Negroes in America has been different in kind, not just in degree, from that of other ethnic groups. It is not merely the history of slavery alone but also that a whole people were marked as inferior by the law. And that mark has endured. The dream of America as the great melting pot has not been realized for the Negro; because of his skin color he never even made it into the pot.

These differences in the experience of the Negro make it difficult for me to accept that Negroes cannot be afforded greater protection under the Fourteenth Amendment where it is necessary to remedy the effects of past discrimination. . . .

. . .

I fear that we have come full circle. After the Civil War our government started several "affirmative action" programs. This Court in the *Civil Rights Cases* and *Plessy v. Ferguson* destroyed the movement toward complete equality. For almost a century no action was taken, and this nonaction was with the tacit approval of the courts. Then we had *Brown v. Board of Education* and the Civil Rights Acts of Congress, followed by numerous affirmative action programs. *Now,* we have this Court again stepping in, this time to stop affirmative action programs of the type used by the University of California.

Mr. Justice Blackmun.

I participate fully, of course, in the opinion, . . . that bears the names of my Brothers Brennan, White, Marshall, and myself. I add only some general observations that hold particular significance for me, and then a few comments on equal protection.

. . .

I suspect that it would be impossible to arrange an affirmative action program in a racially neutral way and have it successful. To ask that this be so is to demand the impossible. In order to get beyond racism, we must first take account of race. There is no other way. And in order to treat some persons equally, we must treat them differently. We cannot—we dare not—let the Equal Protection Clause perpetrate racial supremacy.

. . .

Mr. Justice Stevens, with whom The Chief Justice, Mr. Justice Stewart, and Mr. Justice Rehnquist join, concurring in the judgment in part and dissenting in part.

. . .

III.

Section 601 of the Civil Rights Act of 1964 provides:

> "No person in the United States shall, on the ground of race, color, or national origin, be excluded from participation in, be denied the benefits of, or be subjected to discrimination under any program or activity receiving Federal financial assistance."

The University, through its special admissions policy, excluded Bakke from participation in its program of medical education because of his race. The University also acknowledges that it was, and still is, receiving federal financial assistance. The plain language of the statute therefore requires affirmance of the judgment below. A different result cannot be justified unless that language misstates the actual intent of the Congress that enacted the statute or the statute is not enforceable in a private action. Neither conclusion is warranted.

. . .

Accordingly, I concur in the Court's judgment insofar as it affirms the judgment of the Supreme Court of California. To the extent that it purports to do anything else, I respectfully dissent.

City of Richmond v. J.A. Croson Company

488 U.S. 469, 109 S.Ct. 706, 102 L.Ed.2d 854 (1989).

Justice O'Connor announced the judgment of the Court and delivered the opinion of the Court with respect to Parts I, III–B, and IV, an opinion with respect to Part II, in which The Chief Justice and Justice White join, and an opinion with respect to Parts III–A and V, in which The Chief Justice, Justice White and Justice Kennedy join.

In this case, we confront once again the tension between the Fourteenth Amendment's guarantee of equal treatment to all citizens, and the use of race-based measures to ameliorate the effects of past discrimination on the opportunities enjoyed by members of minority groups in our society.... We ... consider the applicability of our decision in *Wygant* to a minority set-aside program adopted by the city of Richmond, Virginia.

I

On April 11, 1983, the Richmond City Council adopted the Minority Business Utilization Plan (the Plan). The Plan required prime contractors to whom the city awarded construction contracts to subcontract at least 30% of the dollar amount of the contract to one or more Minority Business Enterprises (MBEs).... The 30% set-aside did not apply to city contracts awarded to minority-owned prime contractors....

The Plan defined an MBE as "[a] business at least fifty-one (51) percent of which is owned and controlled ... by minority group members." ... "Minority group members" were defined as "[c]itizens of the United States who are Blacks, Spanish-speaking, Orientals, Indians, Eskimos, or Aleuts." ... There was no geographic limit to the Plan; an otherwise qualified MBE from anywhere in the United States could avail itself of the 30% set-aside. The Plan declared that it was "remedial" in nature, and enacted "for the purpose of promoting wider participation by minority business enterprises in the construction of public projects." ... The Plan expired on June 30, 1988, and was in effect for approximately five years....

The Plan authorized the Director of the Department of General Services to promulgate rules which "shall allow waivers in those individual situations where a contractor can prove to the satisfaction of the director that the requirements herein cannot be achieved." ... To this end, the Director promulgated Contract Clauses, Minority Business Utilization Plan (Contract Clauses). Section D of these rules provided:

> "No partial or complete waiver of the foregoing [30% set-aside] requirement shall be granted by the city other than in exceptional circumstances. To justify a waiver, it must be shown that every feasible attempt has been made to comply, and it must be demonstrated that sufficient, relevant, qualified Minority Business Enterprises ... are unavailable or unwilling to participate in the contract to enable meeting the 30% MBE goal." ...

... The Director ... made the final determination on compliance with the set-aside provisions or the propriety of granting a waiver.... His discretion in this regard appears to have been plenary. There was no direct administrative appeal from [his] denial of a waiver. Once a contract had been awarded to another firm a bidder denied an award for failure to comply with the MBE requirements had a general right of protest under Richmond procurement policies....

The Plan was adopted by the Richmond City Council after a public hearing. Seven members of the public spoke to the merits of the ordinance: five were in opposition, two in favor. Proponents of the set-aside provision relied on a study which indicated that, while the general population of Richmond was 50% black, only .67% of the city's prime construction contracts had been awarded to minority businesses in the 5–year period from 1978 to 1983. It was also established that a variety of contractors' associations, whose representatives appeared in opposition to the ordinance, had virtually no minority businesses within their membership. The city's legal counsel indicated his view that the ordinance was constitutional under this Court's decision in Fullilove v. Klutznick, 448 U.S. 448 (1980). Councilperson Marsh, a proponent of the ordinance, made the following statement:

> "There is some information, however, that I want to make sure that we put in the record. I have been practicing law in this community since 1961, and I am familiar with the practices in the construction industry in this area, in the State, and around the nation. And I can say without equivocation, that the general conduct of the construction industry in this area, and the State, and around the nation, is one in which race discrimination and exclusion on the basis of race is widespread."

There was no direct evidence of race discrimination on the part of the city in letting contracts or any evidence that the city's prime contractors had discriminated against minority-owned subcontractors....

Opponents of the ordinance questioned both its wisdom and its legality.... Representatives of various contractors' associations questioned whether there were enough MBEs in the Richmond area to satisfy the 30% set-aside requirement. [One] noted that only 4.7% of all construction firms in the United States were minority owned and that 41% of these were located in California, New York, Illinois, Florida and Hawaii. . . .

On September 6, 1983, the city . . . issued an invitation to bid on a project for the provision and installation of certain plumbing fixtures at the city jail. On September 30, 1983, Eugene Bonn, the regional manager of J.A. Croson Company (Croson), a mechanical plumbing and heating contractor, received the bid forms. The project involved the installation of stainless steel urinals and water closets in the city jail. Products of either of two manufacturers were specified, Acorn . . . or Bradley. . . . Bonn determined that to meet the 30% set-aside requirement, a minority contractor would have to supply the fixtures. The provision of the fixtures amounted to 75% of the total contract price.

On September 30, Bonn contacted five or six MBEs that were potential suppliers of the fixtures, after contacting three local and state agencies that maintained lists of MBEs. No MBE expressed interest in the project or tendered a quote. On October 12, 1983, the day the bids were due, Bonn again telephoned a group of MBEs. This time, Melvin Brown, president of Continental Metal Hose (Continental), a local MBE, indicated that he wished to participate in the project. . . .

On October 13, 1983, the sealed bids were opened. Croson turned out to be the only bidder, with a bid of $126,530. Brown and Bonn met personally at the bid opening, and Brown informed Bonn that his difficulty in obtaining credit approval had hindered his submission of a bid.

By October 19, 1983, Croson had still not received a bid from Continental. On that date it submitted a request for a waiver of the 30% set-aside. Croson's waiver request indicated that Continental was "unqualified" and that the other MBEs contacted had been unresponsive or unable to quote. Upon learning of Croson's waiver request, Brown [held] discussions with Acorn [and] submitted a bid on the fixtures to Croson. Continental's bid was $6,183.29 higher than the price Croson had included for the fixtures in its bid to the city. This constituted a 7% increase over the market price for the fixtures. With added bonding and insurance, using Continental would have raised the cost of the project by $7,663.16. On the same day that Brown contacted Acorn, he also called city procurement officials and told them that Continental, an MBE, could supply the fixtures specified in the city jail contract. On November 2, 1983, the city denied Croson's waiver request, indicating that Croson had 10 days to submit an MBE Utilization Commitment Form, and warned that failure to do so could result in its bid being considered unresponsive.

. . . Croson [sued in federal district court], arguing that the Richmond ordinance was unconstitutional on its face and as applied in this case.

The District Court upheld the Plan in all respects. . . . [A] divided panel of the Fourth Circuit Court of Appeals affirmed. . . . Relying on the great deference which this Court accorded Congress' findings of past discrimination in *Fullilove*, the panel majority indicated its view that the same standard should be applied to the Richmond City Council . . .

. . . We granted [review], vacated the opinion of the Court of Appeals, and remanded the case for further consideration in light of our intervening decision in Wygant v. Jackson Board of Education, 476 U.S. 267 (1986).

On remand, a divided . . . Court of Appeals struck down the Richmond set-aside program as violating both prongs of strict scrutiny under the Equal Protection Clause of the Fourteenth Amendment. . . .

. . .

... [W]e now affirm the judgment.

II

The parties and their supporting *amici* fight an initial battle over the scope of the city's power to adopt legislation designed to address the effects of past discrimination. Relying on our decision in *Wygant,* appellee argues that the city must limit any race-based remedial efforts to eradicating the effects of its own prior discrimination ... Appellant argues that ... *Fullilove* is controlling, [so] that ... Richmond enjoys sweeping legislative power to define and attack the effects of prior discrimination in its local construction industry. We find that neither of these two rather stark alternatives can withstand analysis.

. . .

Appellant and its supporting *amici* rely heavily on *Fullilove* for the proposition that a city council, like Congress, need not make specific findings of discrimination to engage in race-conscious relief. Thus, appellant argues "[i]t would be a perversion of federalism to hold that the federal government has a compelling interest in remedying the effects of racial discrimination in its own public works program, but a city government does not." ...

What appellant ignores is that Congress, unlike any State or political subdivision, has a specific constitutional mandate to enforce the dictates of the Fourteenth Amendment. The power to "enforce" may at times also include the power to define situations which *Congress* determines threaten principles of equality and to adopt prophylactic rules to deal with those situations. See Katzenbach v. Morgan, ... ("Correctly viewed, section 5 is a positive grant of legislative power authorizing Congress to exercise its discretion in determining whether and what legislation is needed to secure the guarantees of the Fourteenth Amendment"). See also South Carolina v. Katzenbach, 383 U.S. 301, 326 (1966) (similar interpretation of congressional power under section 2 of the Fifteenth Amendment). The Civil War Amendments themselves worked a dramatic change in the balance between congressional and state power over matters of race. Speaking of the Thirteenth and Fourteenth Amendments in Ex parte Virginia, 100 U.S. 339, 345 (1880), the Court stated: "They were intended to be, what they really are, limitations of the powers of the States and enlargements of the power of Congress."

That Congress may identify and redress the effects of society-wide discrimination does not mean that, *a fortiori*, the States and their political subdivisions are free to decide that such remedies are appropriate. Section 1 of the Fourteenth Amendment is an explicit *constraint* on state power, and the States must undertake any remedial efforts in accordance with that provision. To hold otherwise would be to cede control over the content of the Equal Protection Clause to the 50 state legislatures and their myriad political subdivisions. The mere recitation of a benign or compensatory purpose for the use of a racial classification would essentially entitle the States to exercise the full power of Congress under section 5 of the Fourteenth Amendment and insulate any racial classification from judicial scrutiny under section 1. We believe that such a result would be contrary to the intentions of the Framers of the Fourteenth Amendment, who desired to place clear limits on the States' use of race as a criterion for legislative action....

. . .

It would seem equally clear, however, that a state or local subdivision (if delegated the authority from the State) has the authority to eradicate the effects of private discrimination within its own legislative jurisdiction. This authority must, of course, be exercised within the constraints of section 1 of the Fourteenth Amendment. Our decision in *Wygant* is not to the contrary. *Wygant* addressed the constitutionality of the use of racial quotas by local school authorities pursuant to an agreement reached with the local teachers' union. It was in the context of addressing the school board's power to adopt a race-based layoff program affecting its own work force that the *Wygant* plurality indicated that the Equal Protection Clause required "some showing of prior discrimination by the governmental unit involved." ... As a matter of state law, the city of Richmond has legislative authority over its procurement policies, and can use its spending powers to remedy private discrimination, if it identifies the discrimination with the particularity required by the Fourteenth Amendment....

Thus, if the city could show that it had essentially become a "passive participant" in a system of racial exclusion practiced by elements of the local construction industry, we think it clear that the city could take affirmative steps to dismantle such a system. It is beyond dispute that any public entity, state or federal, has a compelling interest in assuring that public dollars, drawn from the tax contributions of all citizens, do not serve to finance the evil of private prejudice....

III

A

The Equal Protection Clause of the Fourteenth Amendment provides that "[N]o State shall ... deny to *any person* within its jurisdiction the equal protection of the laws" (emphasis added). As this Court has noted in the past, the "rights created by the first section of the Fourteenth Amendment are, by its terms, guaranteed to the individual. The rights established are personal rights." Shelley v. Kraemer, 334 U.S. 1, 22 (1948). The Richmond Plan denies certain citizens the opportunity to compete for a fixed percentage of public contracts based solely upon their race. To whatever racial group these citizens belong, their "personal rights" to be treated with equal dignity and respect are implicated by a rigid rule erecting race as the sole criterion in an aspect of public decisionmaking.

Absent searching judicial inquiry into the justification for such race-based measures, there is simply no way of determining what classifications are "benign" or "remedial" and what classifications are in fact motivated by illegitimate notions of racial inferiority or simple racial politics. Indeed, the purpose of strict scrutiny is to "smoke out" illegitimate uses of race by assuring that the legislative body is pursuing a goal important enough to warrant use of a highly suspect tool. The test also ensures that the means chosen "fit" this compelling goal so closely that there is little or no possibility that the motive for the classification was illegitimate racial prejudice or stereotype.

Classifications based on race carry a danger of stigmatic harm. Unless they are strictly reserved for remedial settings, they may in fact promote notions of racial inferiority and lead to a politics of racial hostility. See University of California Regents v. Bakke, 438 U.S., at 298 (opinion of Powell, J.) ("[P]referential programs may only reinforce common stereotypes holding that certain groups are unable to achieve success without special protection based on a factor having no relation to individual worth"). We thus reaffirm the view expressed by the plurality in *Wygant* that the standard of review under the Equal Protection Clause is not dependent on the race of those burdened or benefited by a particular classification....

. . .

Even were we to accept a reading of the guarantee of equal protection under which the level of scrutiny varies according to the ability of different groups to defend their interests in the representative process, heightened scrutiny would still be appropriate in the circumstances of this case. One of the central arguments for applying a less exacting standard to "benign" racial classifications is that such measures essentially involve a choice made by dominant racial groups to disadvantage themselves. If one aspect of the judiciary's role under the Equal Protection Clause is to protect "discrete and insular minorities" from majoritarian prejudice or indifference, see United States v. Carolene Products Co., 304 U.S. 144, 153 n. 4 (1938), some maintain that these concerns are not implicated when the "white majority" places burdens upon itself. See J. Ely, Democracy and Distrust 170 (1980).

In this case, blacks comprise approximately 50% of the population of the city of Richmond. Five of the nine seats on the City Council are held by blacks. The concern that a political majority will more easily act to the disadvantage of a minority based on unwarranted assumptions or incomplete facts would seem to militate for, not against, the application of heightened judicial scrutiny in this case. See Ely, The Constitutionality of Reverse Racial Discrimination, 41 U.Chi.L.Rev. 723, 739, n. 58 (1974) ("Of course it works both ways: a law that favors Blacks over Whites would be suspect if it were enacted by a predominantly Black legislature").

. . .

Justice Powell's opinion [in *Bakke*] . . . indicated that for the governmental interest in remedying past discrimination to be triggered "judicial, legislative, or administrative findings of constitutional or statutory violations" must be made. . . . Only then does the Government have a compelling interest in favoring one race over another.

In *Wygant*, . . . four Members of the Court applied heightened scrutiny to a race-based system of employee layoffs. Justice Powell, writing for the plurality, again drew the distinction between "societal discrimination" which is an inadequate basis for race-conscious classifications, and the type of identified discrimination that can support and define the scope of race-based relief. . . .

The role model theory . . . failed for two reasons. First, the statistical disparity between students and teachers had no probative value in demonstrating the kind of prior discrimination in hiring or promotion that would justify race-based relief. . . . Second, because the role model theory had no relation to some basis for believing a constitutional or statutory violation had occurred, it could be used to "justify" race-based decisionmaking essentially limitless in scope and duration. . . .

III

B

We think it clear that the factual predicate offered in support of the Richmond Plan suffers from the same two defects identified as fatal in *Wygant*. The District Court found the city council's "findings sufficient to ensure that, in adopting the Plan, it was remedying the present effects of past discrimination in the *construction industry*." . . . (emphasis added). Like the "role model" theory employed in *Wygant*, a generalized assertion that there has been past discrimination in an entire industry provides no guidance for a legislative body to determine the precise scope of the injury it seeks to remedy. It "has no logical stopping point." *Wygant*, ... Relief for such an ill-defined wrong could extend until the percentage of public contracts awarded to MBEs in Richmond mirrored the percentage of minorities in the population as a whole.

Appellant argues that it is attempting to remedy various forms of past discrimination that are alleged to be responsible for the small number of minority businesses in the local contracting industry. Among these the city cites the exclusion of blacks from skilled construction trade unions and training programs. This past discrimination has prevented them "from following the traditional path from laborer to entrepreneur." The city also lists a host of nonracial factors which would seem to face a member of any racial group attempting to establish a new business enterprise, such as deficiencies in working capital, inability to meet bonding requirements, unfamiliarity with bidding procedures, and disability caused by an inadequate track record.

While there is no doubt that the sorry history of both private and public discrimination in this country has contributed to a lack of opportunities for black entrepreneurs, this observation, standing alone, cannot justify a rigid racial quota in the awarding of public contracts in Richmond, Virginia. Like the claim that discrimination in primary and secondary schooling justifies a rigid racial preference in medical school admissions, an amorphous claim that there has been past discrimination in a particular industry cannot justify the use of an unyielding racial quota.

It is sheer speculation how many minority firms there would be in Richmond absent past societal discrimination, just as it was sheer speculation how many minority medical students would have been admitted to the medical school at Davis absent past discrimination in educational opportunities. Defining these sorts of injuries as "identified discrimination" would give local governments license to create a patchwork of racial preferences based on statistical generalizations about any particular field of endeavor.

These defects are readily apparent in this case. The 30% quota cannot in any realistic sense be tied to any injury suffered by anyone. The District Court relied upon five predicate "facts" in reaching its conclusion that there was an adequate basis for the 30% quota: (1) the ordinance declares itself to be remedial; (2) several proponents of the measure stated their views that there had been past discrimination in the construction industry; (3) minority businesses received .67% of prime contracts from the city while minorities constituted 50% of the city's population; (4) there were very few minority contractors in local and state contractors' associations; and (5) in 1977, Congress made a determination that the effects of past discrimination had stifled minority participation in the construction industry nationally.

None of these "findings," singly or together, provide the city of Richmond with a "strong basis in evidence for its conclusion that remedial action was necessary." *Wygant,* .... There is nothing approaching a prima facie case of a constitutional or statutory violation by *anyone* in the Richmond construction industry....

The District Court accorded great weight to the fact that the city council designated the Plan as "remedial." But the mere recitation of a "benign" or legitimate purpose for a racial classification, is entitled to little or no weight.... Racial classifications are suspect, and that means that simple legislative assurances of good intention cannot suffice.

The District Court also relied on the highly conclusionary statement of a proponent of the Plan that there was racial discrimination in the construction industry "in this area, and the State, and around the nation." It also noted that the city manager had related his view that racial discrimination still plagued the construction industry in his home city of Pittsburg. These statements are of little probative value in establishing identified discrimination in the Richmond construction industry. The factfinding process of legislative bodies is generally entitled to a presumption of regularity and deferential review by the judiciary. See Williamson v. Lee Optical of Oklahoma, Inc., 348 U.S. 483, 488–489 (1955). But when a legislative body chooses to employ a suspect classification, it cannot rest upon a generalized assertion as to the classification's relevance to its goals.... A governmental actor cannot render race a legitimate proxy for a particular condition merely by declaring that the condition exists.... The history of racial classifications in this country suggests that blind judicial deference to legislative or executive pronouncements of necessity has no place in equal protection analysis. See Korematsu v. United States, 323 U.S. 214, 235–240 (1944) (Murphy, J., dissenting).

Reliance on the disparity between the number of prime contracts awarded to minority firms and the minority population of the city of Richmond is similarly misplaced....

In the employment context, we have recognized that for certain entry level positions or positions requiring minimal training, statistical comparisons of the racial composition of an employer's workforce to the racial composition of the relevant population may be probative of a pattern of discrimination.... But where special qualifications are necessary, the relevant statistical pool for purposes of demonstrating discriminatory exclusion must be the number of minorities qualified to undertake the particular task....

In this case, the city does not even know how many MBEs in the relevant market are qualified to undertake prime or subcontracting work in public construction projects.... Nor does the city know what percentage of total city construction dollars minority firms now receive as subcontractors on prime contracts let by the city.

To a large extent, the set-aside of subcontracting dollars seems to rest on the unsupported assumption that white prime contractors simply will not hire minority firms.... Indeed, there is evidence in this record that overall minority participation in city contracts in Richmond is seven to eight percent, and that minority contractor participation in Community Block Development Grant *construction* projects is 17% to 22%. Without any information on minority participation in subcontracting, it is quite simply impossible to evaluate overall minority representation in the city's construction expenditures.

The city and the District Court also relied on evidence that MBE membership in local contractors' associations was extremely low. Again, standing alone this evidence is not probative of any discrimination in the local construction industry. There are numerous explanations for this dearth of minority participation, including past societal discrimination in education and economic opportunities as well as both black and white career and entrepreneurial choices. Blacks may be disproportionately attracted to industries other than construction.... The mere fact that black membership in these trade organizations is low, standing alone, cannot establish a prima facie case of discrimination....

For low minority membership in these associations to be relevant, the city would have to link it to the number of local MBEs eligible for membership. If the statistical disparity between eligible MBEs and MBE membership were great enough, an inference of discriminatory exclusion could arise. In such a case, the city would have a compelling interest in preventing its tax dollars from assisting these organizations in maintaining a racially segregated construction market....

Finally, the city and the District Court relied on Congress' finding in connection with the set-aside approved in *Fullilove* that there had been nationwide discrimination in the construction industry. The probative value of these findings for demonstrating the existence of discrimination in Richmond is extremely limited. By its inclusion of a waiver procedure in the national program addressed in *Fullilove,* Congress explicitly recognized that the scope of the problem would vary from market area to market area. . . .

Moreover, as noted above, Congress was exercising its powers under section 5 of the Fourteenth Amendment in making a finding that past discrimination would cause federal funds to be distributed in a manner which reinforced prior patterns of discrimination. While the States and their subdivisions may take remedial action when they possess evidence that their own spending practices are exacerbating a pattern of prior discrimination, they must identify that discrimination, public or private, with some specificity before they may use race-conscious relief. Congress has made national findings that there has been societal discrimination in a host of fields. If all a state or local government need do is find a congressional report on the subject to enact a set-aside program, the constraints of the Equal Protection Clause will, in effect, have been rendered a nullity. See Days 480–481 ("[I]t is essential that state and local agencies also establish the presence of discrimination in their own bailiwicks, based either upon their own fact-finding processes or upon determinations made by other competent institutions").

. . .

In sum, none of the evidence presented by the city points to any identified discrimination in the Richmond construction industry. We, therefore, hold that the city has failed to demonstrate a compelling interest in apportioning public contracting opportunities on the basis of race. To accept Richmond's claim that past societal discrimination alone can serve as the basis for rigid racial preferences would be to open the door to competing claims for "remedial relief" for every disadvantaged group. The dream of a Nation of equal citizens in a society where race is irrelevant to personal opportunity and achievement would be lost in a mosaic of shifting preferences based on inherently unmeasurable claims of past wrongs. . . . We think such a result would be contrary to both the letter and spirit of a constitutional provision whose central command is equality.

The foregoing analysis applies only to the inclusion of blacks within the Richmond set-aside program. There is *absolutely no evidence* of past discrimination against Spanish-speaking, Oriental, Indian, Eskimo, or Aleut persons in any aspect of the Richmond construction industry. The District Court took judicial notice of the fact that the vast majority of "minority" persons in Richmond were black. It may well be that Richmond has never had an Aleut or Eskimo citizen. The random inclusion of racial groups that, as a practical matter, may never have suffered from discrimination in the construction industry in Richmond, suggests that perhaps the city's purpose was not in fact to remedy past discrimination.

If a 30% set-aside was "narrowly tailored" to compensate black contractors for past discrimination, one may legitimately ask why they are forced to share this "remedial relief" with an Aleut citizen who moves to Richmond tomorrow? The gross overinclusiveness of Richmond's racial preference strongly impugns the city's claim of remedial motivation. . . . [S]ee . . . Days 482 ("Such programs leave one with the sense that the racial and ethnic groups favored by the set-aside were added without attention to whether their inclusion was justified by evidence of past discrimination").

IV

[I]t is almost impossible to assess whether the Richmond Plan is narrowly tailored to remedy prior discrimination since it is not linked to identified discrimination in any way. We limit ourselves to two observations in this regard.

First, there does not appear to have been any consideration of the use of race-neutral means to increase minority business participation in city contracting.... Many of the barriers to minority participation in the construction industry relied upon by the city to justify a racial classification appear to be race neutral. If MBEs disproportionately lack capital or cannot meet bonding requirements, a race-neutral program of city financing for small firms would, a fortiori, lead to greater minority participation. The principal opinion in *Fullilove* found that Congress had carefully examined and rejected race-neutral alternatives before enacting the MBE set-aside....

Second, the 30% quota cannot be said to be narrowly tailored to any goal, except perhaps outright racial balancing. It rests upon the "completely unrealistic" assumption that minorities will choose a particular trade in lockstep proportion to their representation in the local population....

Since the city must already consider bids and waivers on a case-by-case basis, it is difficult to see the need for a rigid numerical quota. As noted above, the congressional scheme upheld in *Fullilove* allowed for a waiver of the set-aside provision where an MBE's higher price was not attributable to the effects of past discrimination. Based upon proper findings, such programs are less problematic from an equal protection standpoint because they treat all candidates individually, rather than making the color of an applicant's skin the sole relevant consideration. Unlike the program upheld in *Fullilove,* the Richmond Plan's waiver system focuses solely on the availability of MBEs; there is no inquiry into whether or not the particular MBE seeking a racial preference has suffered from the effects of past discrimination by the city or prime contractors.

Given the existence of an individualized procedure, the city's only interest in maintaining a quota system rather than investigating the need for remedial action in particular cases would seem to be simple administrative convenience. But the interest in avoiding the bureaucratic effort necessary to tailor remedial relief to those who truly have suffered the effects of prior discrimination cannot justify a rigid line drawn on the basis of a suspect classification.... Under Richmond's scheme, a successful black, Hispanic, or Oriental entrepreneur from anywhere in the country enjoys an absolute preference over other citizens based solely on their race. We think it obvious that such a program is not narrowly tailored to remedy the effects of prior discrimination.

V

Nothing we say today precludes a state or local entity from taking action to rectify the effects of identified discrimination within its jurisdiction. If the City of Richmond had evidence before it that nonminority contractors were systematically excluding minority businesses from subcontracting opportunities it could take action to end the discriminatory exclusion. Where there is a significant statistical disparity between the number of qualified minority contractors willing and able to perform a particular service and the number of such contractors actually engaged by the locality or the locality's prime contractors, an inference of discriminatory exclusion could arise.... Under such circumstances, the city could act to dismantle the closed business system by taking appropriate measures against those who discriminate on the basis of race or other illegitimate criteria.... In the extreme case, some form of narrowly tailored racial preference might be necessary to break down patterns of deliberate exclusion.

Nor is local government powerless to deal with individual instances of racially motivated refusals to employ minority contractors. Where such discrimination occurs, a city would be justified in penalizing the discriminator and providing appropriate relief to the victim of such discrimination.... Moreover, evidence of a pattern of individual discriminatory acts can, if supported by appropriate statistical proof, lend support to a local government's determination that broader remedial relief is justified....

Even in the absence of evidence of discrimination, the city has at its disposal a whole array of race-neutral devices to increase the accessibility of city contracting opportunities to small entrepreneurs of all races.... The city may also act to prohibit discrimination in the provision of credit or bonding by local suppliers and banks....

In the case at hand, the city has not ascertained how many minority enterprises are present in the local construction market nor the level of their participation in city construction projects. The city points to no evidence that qualified minority contractors have been passed over for city contracts or subcontracts, either as a group or in any individual case....

Proper findings in this regard are necessary to define both the scope of the injury and the extent of the remedy necessary to cure its effects. Such findings also serve to assure all citizens that the deviation from the norm of equal treatment of all racial and ethnic groups is a temporary matter, a measure taken in the service of the goal of equality itself. Absent such findings, there is a danger that a racial classification is merely the product of unthinking stereotypes or a form of racial politics.... Because the city of Richmond has failed to identify the need for remedial action in the awarding of its public construction contracts, its treatment of its citizens on a racial basis violates the dictates of the Equal Protection Clause. Accordingly, the judgment of the Court of Appeals for the Fourth Circuit is

Affirmed.

Justice Stevens, concurring in part and concurring in the judgment.

... I ... do not agree with the premise that seems to underlie today's decision, as well as the decision in Wygant v. Jackson Board of Education, 476 U.S. 267 (1986), that a governmental decision that rests on a racial classification is never permissible except as a remedy for a past wrong. I do, however, agree with the Court's explanation of why the Richmond ordinance cannot be justified as a remedy for past discrimination, and therefore join Parts I, III–B, and IV of its opinion. I write separately to emphasize three aspects of the case that are of special importance to me.

First, the city makes no claim that the public interest in the efficient performance of its construction contracts will be served by granting a preference to minority-business enterprises. This case is therefore completely unlike *Wygant,* in which I thought it quite obvious that the School Board had reasonably concluded that an integrated faculty could provide educational benefits to the entire student body that could not be provided by an all-white, or nearly all-white faculty....

Second, this litigation involves an attempt by a legislative body, rather than a court, to fashion a remedy for a past wrong.... It is the judicial system, rather than the legislative process, that is best equipped to identify past wrongdoers and to fashion remedies that will create the conditions that presumably would have existed had no wrong been committed. Thus, in cases involving the review of judicial remedies imposed against persons who have been proved guilty of violations of law, I would allow the courts in racial discrimination cases the same discretion that chancellors enjoy in other areas of the law. . . .

Third, instead of engaging in a debate over the proper standard of review to apply in affirmative-action litigation, I believe it is more constructive to try to identify the characteristics of the advantaged and disadvantaged classes that may justify their disparate treatment. . . . In this case that approach convinces me that, instead of carefully identifying the characteristics of the two classes of contractors that are respectively favored and disfavored by its ordinance, the Richmond City Council has merely engaged in the type of stereotypical analysis that is a hallmark of violations of the Equal Protection Clause. Whether we look at the class of persons benefited by the ordinance or at the disadvantaged class, the same conclusion emerges.

The justification for the ordinance is the fact that in the past white contractors—and presumably other white citizens in Richmond—have discriminated against black contractors. The class of persons benefited by the ordinance is not, however, limited to victims of such discrimination—it encompasses persons who have never been in business in Richmond as well as minority contractors who may have been guilty of discriminating against members of other minority groups. Indeed, for all the record shows, all of the minority-business enterprises that have benefited from the ordinance may be firms that have prospered not-withstanding the discriminatory conduct that may have harmed other minority firms years ago. Ironically, minority firms that have survived in the competitive struggle, rather than those that have perished, are most likely to benefit from an ordinance of this kind. . . .

There is a special irony in the stereotypical thinking that prompts legislation of this kind. Although it stigmatizes the disadvantaged class with the unproven charge of past racial discrimination, it actually imposes a greater stigma on its supposed beneficiaries. . . .

. . .

Justice Kennedy, concurring in part and concurring in the judgment.

I join all but Part II of Justice O'Connor's opinion and give this further explanation.

Part II examines our caselaw upholding Congressional power to grant preferences based on overt and explicit classification by race. See Fullilove v. Klutznick, 448 U.S. 448 (1980). With the acknowledgment that the summary in Part II is both precise and fair, I must decline to join it. The process by which a law that is an equal protection violation when enacted by a State becomes transformed to an equal protection guarantee when enacted by Congress poses a difficult proposition for me; but as it is not before us, any reconsideration of that issue must await some further case. For purposes of the ordinance challenged here, it suffices to say that the State has the power to eradicate racial discrimination and its effects in both the public and private sectors, and the absolute duty to do so where those wrongs were caused intentionally by the State itself. The Fourteenth Amendment ought not to be interpreted to reduce a State's authority in this regard, unless, of course, there is a conflict with federal law or a state remedy is itself a violation of equal protection. The latter is the case presented here.

The moral imperative of racial neutrality is the driving force of the Equal Protection Clause. Justice Scalia's opinion underscores that proposition, quite properly in my view. The rule suggested in his opinion, which would strike down all preferences which are not necessary remedies to victims of unlawful discrimination, would serve important structural goals, as it would eliminate the necessity for courts to pass upon each racial preference that is enacted. Structural protections may be necessities if moral imperatives are to be obeyed. His opinion would make it crystal clear to the political branches, at least those of the States, that legislation must be based on criteria other than race.

Nevertheless, given that a rule of automatic invalidity for racial preferences in almost every case would be a significant break with our precedents that require a case-by-case test, I am not convinced we need adopt it at this point. On the assumption that it will vindicate the principle of race neutrality found in the Equal Protection Clause, I accept the less absolute rule contained in Justice O'Connor's opinion, a rule based on the proposition that any racial preference must face the most rigorous scrutiny by the courts. My reasons for doing so are as follows. First, I am confident that, in application, the strict scrutiny standard will operate in a manner generally consistent with the imperative of race neutrality, because it forbids the use even of narrowly drawn racial classifications except as a last resort. Second, the rule against race-conscious remedies is already less than an absolute one, for that relief may be the only adequate remedy after a judicial determination that a State or its instrumentality has violated the Equal Protection Clause. I note, in this connection, that evidence which would support a judicial finding of intentional discrimination may suffice also to justify remedial legislative action, for it diminishes the constitutional responsibilities of the political branches to say they must wait to act until ordered to do so by a court. Third, the strict scrutiny rule is consistent with our precedents, as Justice O'Connor's opinion demonstrates.

The ordinance before us falls far short of the standard we adopt. The nature and scope of the injury that existed; its historical or antecedent causes; the extent to which the City contributed to it, either by intentional acts or by passive complicity in acts of discrimination by the private sector; the necessity for the response adopted, its duration in relation to the wrong, and the precision with which it otherwise bore on whatever injury in fact was addressed, were all matters unmeasured, unexplored, unexplained by the City Council. We are left with an ordinance and a legislative record open to the fair charge that it is not a remedy but is itself a preference which will cause the same corrosive animosities that the Constitution forbids in the whole sphere of government and that our national policy condemns in the rest of society as well. This ordinance is invalid under the Fourteenth Amendment.

Justice Scalia, concurring in the judgment.

I agree with much of the Court's opinion, and, in particular, with its conclusion that strict scrutiny must be applied to all governmental classification by race, whether or not its asserted purpose is "remedial" or "benign." I do not agree, however, with the Court's dicta suggesting that, despite the Fourteenth Amendment, state and local governments may in some circumstances discriminate on the basis of race in order (in a broad sense) "to ameliorate the effects of past discrimination." The benign purpose of compensating for social disadvantages, whether they have been acquired by reason of prior discrimination or otherwise, can no more be pursued by the illegitimate means of racial discrimination than can other assertedly benign purposes we have repeatedly rejected.... The difficulty of overcoming the effects of past discrimination is as nothing compared with the difficulty of eradicating from our society the source of those effects, which is the tendency—fatal to a nation such as ours—to classify and judge men and women on the basis of their country of origin or the color of their skin. A solution to the first problem that aggravates the second is no solution at all. . . .

We have in some contexts approved the use of racial classifications by the Federal Government to remedy the effects of past discrimination. I do not believe that we must or should extend those holdings to the States. . . . [W]ithout revisiting what we held in *Fullilove* (or trying to derive a rationale from the three separate opinions supporting the judgment, none of which commanded more than three votes . . .), I do not believe our decision in that case controls the one before us here.

A sound distinction between federal and state (or local) action based on race rests not only upon the substance of the Civil War Amendments, but upon social reality and governmental theory. . . . What the record shows . . . is that racial discrimination against any group finds a more ready expression at the state and local than at the federal level. To the children of the Founding Fathers, this should come as no surprise. An acute awareness of the heightened danger of oppression from political factions in small, rather than large, political units dates to the very beginning of our national history. . . .

. . . Richmond [enacted] a set-aside clearly and directly beneficial to the dominant political group, which happens also to be the dominant racial group. The same thing has no doubt happened before in other cities (though the racial basis of the preference has rarely been made textually explicit)—and blacks have often been on the receiving end of the injustice. Where injustice is the game, however, turn-about is not fair play.

In my view there is only one circumstance in which the States may act *by race* to "undo the effects of past discrimination": where that is necessary to eliminate their own maintenance of a system of unlawful racial classification. If, for example, a state agency has a discriminatory pay scale compensating black employees in all positions at 20% less than their nonblack counterparts, it may assuredly promulgate an order raising the salaries of "all black employees" by 20%. . . . This distinction explains our school desegregation cases, in which we have made plain that States and localities sometimes have an obligation to adopt race-conscious remedies. While there is no doubt that those cases have taken into account the continuing "effects" of previously mandated racial school assignment, we have held those effects to justify a race-conscious remedy only because we have concluded, in that context, that they perpetuate a "dual school system." . . .

. . .

I agree with the Court's dictum that a fundamental distinction must be drawn between the effects of "societal" discrimination and the effects of "identified" discrimination, and that the situation would be different if Richmond's plan were "tailored" to identify those particular bidders who "suffered from the effects of past discrimination by the city or prime contractors." In my view, however, the reason that would make a difference is not, as the Court states, that it would justify race-conscious action—but rather that it would enable race-neutral remediation. Nothing prevents Richmond from according a contracting preference to identified victims of discrimination. While most of the beneficiaries might be black, neither the beneficiaries nor those disadvantaged by the preference would be identified *on the basis of their race*. In other words, far from justifying racial classification, identification of actual victims of discrimination makes it less supportable than ever, because more obviously unneeded.

. . .

It is plainly true that in our society blacks have suffered discrimination immeasurably greater than any directed at other racial groups. But those who believe that racial preferences can help to "even the score" display, and reinforce, a manner of thinking by race that was the source of the injustice and that will, if it endures within our society, be the source of more injustice still. The relevant proposition is not that it was blacks, or Jews, or Irish who were discriminated against, but that it was individual men and women, "created equal," who were discriminated against. And the relevant resolve is that that should never happen again. Racial preferences appear to "even the score" (in some small degree) only if one embraces the proposition that our society is appropriately viewed as divided into races, making it right that an injustice rendered in the past to a black man should be compensated for by discriminating against a white. Nothing is worth that embrace. Since blacks have been disproportionately disadvantaged by racial discrimination, any race-neutral remedial program aimed at the disadvantaged *as such* will have a disproportionately beneficial impact on blacks. Only such a program, and not one that operates on the basis of race, is in accord with the letter and the spirit of our Constitution.

Since I believe that the appellee here had a constitutional right to have its bid succeed or fail under a decisionmaking process uninfected with racial bias, I concur in the judgment of the Court.

Justice Marshall, with whom Justice Brennan and Justice Blackmun join, dissenting.

It is a welcome symbol of racial progress when the former capital of the Confederacy acts forthrightly to confront the effects of racial discrimination in its midst. In my view, nothing in the Constitution can be construed to prevent Richmond, Virginia, from allocating a portion of its contracting dollars for businesses owned or controlled by members of minority groups. Indeed, Richmond's set-aside program is indistinguishable in all meaningful respects from—and in fact was patterned upon—the federal set-aside plan which this Court upheld in Fullilove v. Klutznick, 448 U.S. 448 (1980).

. . .

. . . [T]oday's decision marks a deliberate and giant step backward in this Court's affirmative action jurisprudence. Cynical of one municipality's attempt to redress the effects of past racial discrimination in a particular industry, the majority launches a grapeshot attack on race-conscious remedies in general. The majority's unnecessary pronouncements will inevitably discourage or prevent governmental entities, particularly States and localities, from acting to rectify the scourge of past discrimination. This is the harsh reality of the majority's decision, but it is not the Constitution's command.

I

As an initial matter, the majority takes an exceedingly myopic view of the factual predicate on which the Richmond City Council relied when it passed the Minority Business Utilization Plan.... It is only against th[e] backdrop of documented national discrimination ... that the local evidence adduced by Richmond can be properly understood. The majority's refusal to recognize that Richmond has proven itself no exception to the dismaying pattern of national exclusion which Congress so painstakingly identified infects its entire analysis of this case.

Six years before Richmond acted, Congress passed, and the President signed, the Public Works Employment Act of 1977 ...

Th[is] congressional program upheld in *Fullilove* [in 1980] was based upon an array of congressional and agency studies which documented the powerful influence of racially exclusionary practices in the business world. [Justice Marshall here quoted from a 1975 and a 1977 report by the House Committee on Small Business.]

Thus, as of 1977, there was "abundant evidence" in the public domain "that minority businesses ha[d] been denied effective participation in public contracting opportunities by procurement practices that perpetuated the effects of prior discrimination." *Fullilove,* .... Significantly, this evidence demonstrated that discrimination had prevented existing or nascent minority-owned businesses from obtaining not only federal contracting assignments, but state and local ones as well. See *Fullilove,* supra, at 478.

The members of the Richmond City Council were well aware of these exhaustive congressional findings, a point the majority, tellingly, elides....

. . .

... So long as one views Richmond's local evidence of discrimination against the backdrop of systematic nationwide racial discrimination which Congress had so painstakingly identified in this very industry, this case is readily resolved.

II

... My view has long been that race-conscious classifications designed to further remedial goals "must serve important governmental objectives and must be substantially related to achievement of those objectives" in order to withstand constitutional scrutiny.... Analyzed in terms of this two-prong standard, Richmond's set-aside, like the federal program on which it was modeled, is "plainly constitutional." ...

A

1

... Richmond has two powerful interests in setting aside a portion of public contracting funds for minority-owned enterprises. The first is the city's interest in eradicating the effects of past racial discrimination. It is far too late in the day to doubt that remedying such discrimination is a compelling, let alone an important, interest....

Richmond has a second compelling interest in setting aside, where possible, a portion of its contracting dollars. That interest is the prospective one of preventing the city's own spending decisions from reinforcing and perpetuating the exclusionary effects of past discrimination....

. . .

... When government channels all its contracting funds to a white-dominated community of established contractors whose racial homogeneity is the product of private discrimination, it does more than place its imprimatur on the practices which forged and which continue to define that community. It also provides a measurable boost to those economic entities that have thrived within it, while denying important economic benefits to those entities which, but for prior discrimination, might well be better qualified to receive valuable government contracts. In my view, the interest in ensuring that the government does not reflect and reinforce prior private discrimination in dispensing public contracts is every bit as strong as the interest in eliminating private discrimination—an interest which this Court has repeatedly deemed compelling. . . .

2

The remaining question with respect to the "governmental interest" prong of equal protection analysis is whether Richmond has proffered satisfactory proof of past racial discrimination to support its twin interests in remediation and in governmental nonperpetuation. . . .

. . .

The varied body of evidence on which Richmond relied provides a "strong," "firm," and "unquestionably legitimate" basis upon which the City Council could determine that the effects of past racial discrimination warranted a remedial and prophylactic governmental response. As I have noted, Richmond acted against a backdrop of congressional and Executive Branch studies which demonstrated with such force the nationwide pervasiveness of prior discrimination that Congress presumed that "'present economic inequities' "in construction contracting resulted from "'past discriminatory systems.' "The city's local evidence confirmed that Richmond's construction industry did not deviate from this pernicious national pattern. The fact that just .67% of public construction expenditures over the previous five years had gone to minority-owned prime contractors, despite the city's racially mixed population, strongly suggests that construction contracting in the area was rife with "present economic inequities." To the extent this enormous disparity did not itself demonstrate that discrimination had occurred, the descriptive testimony of Richmond's elected and appointed leaders drew the necessary link between the pitifully small presence of minorities in construction contracting and past exclusionary practices. That *no one* who testified challenged this depiction of widespread racial discrimination in area construction contracting lent significant weight to these accounts. The fact that area trade associations had virtually no minority members dramatized the extent of present inequities and suggested the lasting power of past discriminatory systems. In sum, to suggest that the facts on which Richmond has relied do not provide a sound basis for its finding of past racial discrimination simply blinks credibility.

. . .

. . . [W]here the issue is not present discrimination but rather whether *past* discrimination has resulted in the *continuing exclusion* of minorities from an historically tight-knit industry, a contrast between population and work force is entirely appropriate to help gauge the degree of the exclusion. . . . This contrast is especially illuminating in cases like this, where a main avenue of introduction into the work force—here, membership in the trade associations whose members presumably train apprentices and help them procure subcontracting assignments—is itself grossly dominated by nonminorities. The majority's assertion that the city "does not even know how many MBE's in the relevant market are qualified," is thus entirely beside the point. If Richmond indeed has a monochromatic contracting community . . . this most likely reflects the lingering power of past exclusionary practices. Certainly this is the explanation Congress has found persuasive at the national level. See *Fullilove*, ... The city's requirement that prime public contractors set aside 30% of their subcontracting assignments for minority-owned enterprises, subject to the ordinance's provision for waivers where minority-owned enterprises are unavailable or unwilling to participate, is designed precisely to ease minority contractors into the industry.

. . .

Had the majority paused for a moment on the facts of the Richmond experience, it would have discovered that the city's leadership is deeply familiar with what racial discrimination is. The members of the Richmond City Council have spent long years witnessing multifarious acts of discrimination, including, but not limited to, the deliberate diminution of black residents' voting rights, resistance to school desegregation, and publicly sanctioned housing discrimination. Numerous decisions of federal courts chronicle this disgraceful recent history. . . .

. . .

When the legislatures and leaders of cities with histories of pervasive discrimination testify that past discrimination has infected one of their industries, armchair cynicism like that exercised by the majority has no place. . . .

Finally, I vehemently disagree with the majority's dismissal of the congressional and Executive Branch findings noted in *Fullilove* as having "extremely limited" probative value in this case. The majority concedes that Congress established nothing less than a "presumption" that minority contracting firms have been disadvantaged by prior discrimination. The majority, inexplicably, would forbid Richmond to "share" in this information, and permit only Congress to take note of these ample findings. In thus requiring that Richmond's local evidence be severed from the context in which it was prepared, the majority would require cities seeking to eradicate the effects of past discrimination within their borders to reinvent the evidentiary wheel and engage in unnecessarily duplicative, costly, and time-consuming factfinding.

No principle of federalism or of federal power, however, forbids a state or local government from drawing upon a nationally relevant historical record prepared by the Federal Government. . . .

B

In my judgment, Richmond's set-aside plan also comports with the second prong of the equal protection inquiry, for it is substantially related to the interests it seeks to serve in remedying past discrimination and in ensuring that municipal contract procurement does not perpetuate that discrimination. The most striking aspect of the city's ordinance is the similarity it bears to the "appropriately limited" federal set-aside provision upheld in *Fullilove*. . . . Like the federal provision, Richmond's is limited to five years in duration, ibid., and was not renewed when it came up for reconsideration in 1988. Like the federal provision, Richmond's contains a waiver provision freeing from its subcontracting requirements those nonminority firms that demonstrate that they cannot comply with its provisions. . . . Like the federal provision, Richmond's has a minimal impact on innocent third parties. While the measure affects 30% of public contracting dollars, that translates to only 3% of overall Richmond area contracting. . . .

Finally, like the federal provision, Richmond's does not interfere with any vested right of a contractor to a particular contract; instead it operates entirely prospectively. Ibid. Richmond's initiative affects only future economic arrangements and imposes only a diffuse burden on nonminority competitors—here, businesses owned or controlled by nonminorities which seek subcontracting work on public construction projects. The plurality in *Wygant* emphasized the importance of this not disrupting the settled and legitimate expectations of innocent parties....

... The majority takes issue ... with two aspects of Richmond's tailoring: the city's refusal to explore the use of race-neutral measures to increase minority business participation in contracting, and the selection of a 30% set-aside figure. The majority's first criticism is flawed in two respects. First, the majority overlooks the fact that since 1975, Richmond has barred both discrimination by the city in awarding public contracts and discrimination by public contractors[, but] this ban has not succeeded in redressing the impact of past discrimination or in preventing city contract procurement from reinforcing racial homogeneity. Second, ... race-neutral measures ..., while theoretically appealing, have been discredited by Congress as ineffectual in eradicating the effects of past discrimination in this very industry....

As for Richmond's 30% target, the majority ... ignores two important facts. First, the set-aside measure affects only 3% of overall city contracting; thus, any imprecision in tailoring has far less impact than the majority suggests. But more important, the majority ignores the fact that Richmond's 30% figure was patterned directly on the *Fullilove* precedent. Congress' 10% figure fell "roughly halfway between the present percentage of minority contractors and the percentage of minority group members in the Nation." *Fullilove,* ... (Powell, J., concurring). The Richmond City Council's 30% figure similarly falls roughly halfway between the present percentage of Richmond-based minority contractors (almost zero) and the percentage of minorities in Richmond (50%). In faulting Richmond for not presenting a different explanation for its choice of a set-aside figure, the majority honors *Fullilove* only in the breach.

III

I would ordinarily end my analysis at this point and conclude that Richmond's ordinance satisfies both the governmental interest and substantial relationship prongs of our Equal Protection Clause analysis. However, ... the majority has gone beyond the facts of this case to announce a set of principles which unnecessarily restrict the power of governmental entities to take race-conscious measures to redress the effects of prior discrimination.

A

Today, for the first time, a majority of this Court has adopted strict scrutiny as its standard of Equal Protection Clause review of race-conscious remedial measures. This is an unwelcome development. A profound difference separates governmental actions that themselves are racist, and governmental actions that seek to remedy the effects of prior racism or to prevent neutral governmental activity from perpetuating the effects of such racism ...

Racial classifications "drawn on the presumption that one race is inferior to another or because they put the weight of government behind racial hatred and separatism" warrant the strictest judicial scrutiny because of the very irrelevance of these rationales.... By contrast, racial classifications drawn for the purpose of remedying the effects of discrimination that itself was race-based have a highly pertinent basis: the tragic and indelible fact that discrimination against blacks and other racial minorities in this Nation has pervaded our Nation's history and continues to scar our society....

In concluding that remedial classifications warrant no different standard of review under the Constitution than the most brute and repugnant forms of state-sponsored racism, a majority of this Court signals that it regards racial discrimination as largely a phenomenon of the past, and that government bodies need no longer preoccupy themselves with rectifying racial injustice. I, however, do not believe this Nation is anywhere close to eradicating racial discrimination or its vestiges. In constitutionalizing its wishful thinking, the majority today does a grave disservice not only to those victims of past and present racial discrimination in this Nation whom government has sought to assist, but also to this Court's long tradition of approaching issues of race with the utmost sensitivity.

B

I am also troubled by the majority's assertion that, even if it did not believe generally in strict scrutiny of race-based remedial measures, "the circum- stances of this case" require this Court to look upon the Richmond City Council's measure with the strictest scrutiny. The sole such circumstance which the majority cites, however, is the fact that blacks in Richmond are a "dominant racial grou[p]" in the city. . . .

While I agree that the numerical and political supremacy of a given racial group is a factor bearing upon the level of scrutiny to be applied, this Court has never held that numerical inferiority, standing alone, makes a racial group "suspect" and thus entitled to strict scrutiny review. Rather, we have identified other "traditional indicia of suspectness": whether a group has been "saddled with such disabilities, or subjected to such a history of purposeful unequal treatment, or relegated to such a position of political powerlessness as to command extraordinary protection from the majoritarian political process." San Antonio Independent School District v. Rodriguez, 411 U.S. 1, 28 (1973).

It cannot seriously be suggested that nonminorities in Richmond have any "history of purposeful unequal treatment." Ibid. Nor is there any indication that they have any of the disabilities that have characteristically afflicted those groups this Court has deemed suspect. Indeed, the numerical and political dominance of nonminorities within the State of Virginia and the Nation as a whole provide an enormous political check against the "simple racial politics" at the municipal level which the majority fears. If the majority really believes that groups like Richmond's nonminorities, which comprise approximately half the population but which are outnumbered even marginally in political fora, are deserving of suspect class status for these reasons alone, this Court's decisions denying suspect status to women, . . . and to persons with below-average incomes, . . . stand on extremely shaky ground. . . .

. . . .

. . . The majority's view that remedial measures undertaken by municipali- ties with black leadership must face a stiffer test of Equal Protection Clause scrutiny than remedial measures undertaken by municipalities with white leadership implies a lack of political maturity on the part of this Nation's elected minority officials that is totally unwarranted. Such insulting judgments have no place in constitutional jurisprudence.

C

. . . .

Nothing in the Constitution or in the prior decisions of this Court supports limiting state authority to confront the effects of past discrimination to those situations in which a prima facie case of a constitutional or statutory violation can be made out....

. . .

To the degree that this parsimonious standard is grounded on a view that either section 1 or section 5 of the Fourteenth Amendment substantially disempowered States and localities from remedying past racial discrimination, the majority is seriously mistaken.... Certainly *Fullilove* did not view section 5 either as limiting the traditionally broad police powers of the States to fight discrimination, or as mandating a zero-sum game in which state power wanes as federal power waxes. On the contrary, the *Fullilove* plurality invoked section 5 only because it provided specific and certain authorization for the Federal Government's attempt to impose a race-conscious condition on the dispensation of federal funds by state and local grantees....

As for section 1, it is too late in the day to assert seriously that the Equal Protection Clause prohibits States—or for that matter, the Federal Government, to whom the equal protection guarantee has largely been applied, see Bolling v. Sharpe, 347 U.S. 497 (1954)—from enacting race-conscious remedies. Our cases in the areas of school desegregation, voting rights, and affirmative action have demonstrated time and again that race is constitutionally germane, precisely because race remains dismayingly relevant in American life.

. . .

The fact is that Congress' concern in passing the Reconstruction Amendments, and particularly their congressional authorization provisions, was that States would *not* adequately respond to racial violence or discrimination against newly freed slaves. To interpret any aspect of these Amendments as proscribing state remedial responses to these very problems turns the Amendments on their heads....

In short, there is simply no credible evidence that the Framers of the Fourteenth Amendment sought "to transfer the security and protection of all the civil rights ... from the States to the Federal government." The Slaughter-House Cases, 16 Wall. 36, 77–78 (1873)....

IV

The majority today sounds a full-scale retreat from the Court's longstanding solicitude to race-conscious remedial efforts "directed toward deliverance of the century-old promise of equality of economic opportunity." *Fullilove*.... I, however, profoundly disagree with the cramped vision of the Equal Protection Clause which the majority offers today and with its application of that vision to Richmond, Virginia's, laudable set-aside plan. The battle against pernicious racial discrimination or its effects is nowhere near won. I must dissent.[a]

Adarand Constructors, Inc. v. Pena

___ U.S. ___, 115 S.Ct. 2097, 132 L.Ed.2d 158 (1995).

Justice O'Connor announced the judgment of the Court and delivered an opinion with respect to Parts I, II, III–A, III–B, III–D, and IV, which is for the Court except insofar as it might be inconsistent with

---

[a] A separate dissenting opinion by Justice Blackmun, joined by Justice Brennan, is omitted.

the views expressed in Justice Scalia's concurrence, and an opinion with respect to Part III–C in which Justice Kennedy joins.

Petitioner Adarand Constructors, Inc., claims that the Federal Government's practice of giving general contractors on government projects a financial incentive to hire subcontractors controlled by "socially and economically disadvantaged individuals," and in particular, the Government's use of race-based presumptions in identifying such individuals, violates the equal protection component of the Fifth Amendment's Due Process Clause. The Court of Appeals rejected Adarand's claim. We conclude, however, that courts should analyze cases of this kind under a different standard of review than the one the Court of Appeals applied. We therefore vacate the Court of Appeals' judgment and remand the case for further proceedings.

I

[In 1989 an agency of the United States Department of Transportation (DOT) awarded the prime contract for a highway construction project in Colorado to Mountain Gravel & Construction Company. Mountain Gravel subcontracted the guardrail portion of the contract to Gonzales Construction Company rather than to Adarand, the low bidder, because the prime contract authorized additional compensation for hiring subcontractors certified as small businesses controlled by "socially and economically disadvantaged individuals."] Federal law requires [such] a subcontracting clause . . . in most federal agency contracts, and it also requires the clause to state that "[t]he contractor shall presume that socially and economically disadvantaged individuals include Black Americans, Hispanic Americans, Native Americans, Asian Pacific Americans, and other minorities, or any other individual found to be disadvantaged by the [Small Business] Administration [SBA] pursuant to section 8(a) of the Small Business Act." 15 U.S.C. §§ 637(d)(2), (3). Adarand claims that the presumption set forth in that statute discriminates on the basis of race in violation of the Federal Government's Fifth Amendment obligation not to deny anyone equal protection of the laws.

These fairly straightforward facts implicate a complex scheme of federal statutes and regulations. The Small Business Act . . . defines "socially disadvantaged individuals" as "those who have been subjected to racial or ethnic prejudice or cultural bias because of their identity as a member of a group without regard to their individual qualities," § 8(a)(5), . . . and it defines "economically disadvantaged individuals" as "those socially disadvantaged individuals whose ability to compete in the free enterprise system has been impaired due to diminished capital and credit opportunities as compared to others in the same business area who are not socially disadvantaged." § 8(a)(6)(A). . . .

. . .

[Two SBA programs were relevant. The "8(a) program" confers numerous benefits, including automatic eligibility for the challenged subcontractor compensation provisions, on small businesses 51% owned by individuals who qualify as "socially and economically disadvantaged." The SBA presumes that Black, Hispanic, Asian Pacific, Subcontinent Asian, and Native Americans, as well as "members of other groups designated from time to time by SBA," are "socially disadvantaged," but it allows any other individual to prove social disadvantage. Every 8(a) participant must also prove "economic disadvantage." The "8(d) subcontracting program" is limited to eligibility for such subcontracting provisions, and it operates like the 8(a) program, except that the Court felt "some uncertainty . . . whether participation in the 8(d) subcontracting program requires an individualized showing of economic disadvantage." For particular participants in both the 8(a) and 8(d) programs, third parties can rebut the presumptions of economic or social disadvantage.

[Funds for the highway project were appropriated in the Surface Transportation and Uniform Relocation Assistance Act of 1987 (STURAA), which required no less than 10% of those funds to be spent with certified disadvantaged small businesses. STURAA incorporated the Small Business Act's definitions, including the race-based presumptions, and required the Transportation Secretary to set minimum criteria for State governments to use in certifying eligible businesses. The Secretary's regulations required certifying authorities to use rebuttable race-based presumptions of both social and economic disadvantage. The record did not reveal whether Gonzales had been certified under these regulations or under either the SBA's 8(a) or 8(d) program.]

Adarand [sued] various federal officials ..., claiming that the race-based presumptions involved in the use of subcontracting compensation clauses violate Adarand's right to equal protection. The District Court granted the Government's motion for summary judgment.... The ... Tenth Circuit affirmed.... It understood our decision in Fullilove v. Klutznick, 448 U.S. 448 (1980), to have adopted "a lenient standard, resembling intermediate scrutiny, in assessing" the constitutionality of federal race-based action.... Applying that "lenient standard," as further developed in Metro Broadcasting, Inc. v. FCC, 497 U.S. 547 (1990), the Court of Appeals upheld the use of subcontractor compensation clauses....

. . .

III

The Government urges that "[t]he Subcontracting Compensation Clause program is ... a program based on disadvantage, not on race," and thus that it is subject only to "the most relaxed judicial scrutiny." ... To the extent that the statutes and regulations involved in this case are race neutral, we agree. The Government concedes, however, that "the race-based rebuttable presumption used in some certification determinations under the Subcontracting Compensation Clause" is subject to some heightened level of scrutiny....

Adarand's claim arises under the Fifth Amendment [Due Process Clause.] Although this Court has always understood that Clause to provide some measure of protection against arbitrary treatment by the Federal Government, it is not as explicit a guarantee of equal treatment as the Fourteenth Amendment [Equal Protection Clause].... Our cases have accorded varying degrees of significance to the difference in the language of those two Clauses....

A

Through the 1940s, this Court had routinely taken the view in non-race-related cases that, "[u]nlike the Fourteenth Amendment, the Fifth contains no equal protection clause and it provides no guaranty against discriminatory legislation by Congress." Detroit Bank v. United States, 317 U.S. 329, 337 (1943).... When the Court first faced a Fifth Amendment equal protection challenge to a federal racial classification, it adopted a similar approach, with most unfortunate results. In Hirabayashi v. United States, 320 U.S. 81 (1943), the Court considered a curfew applicable only to persons of Japanese ancestry. The Court observed—correctly—that "[d]istinctions between citizens solely because of their ancestry are by their very nature odious to a free people whose institutions are founded upon the doctrine of equality," and that "racial discriminations are in most circumstances irrelevant and therefore prohibited."

... But it also cited *Detroit Bank* for the proposition that the Fifth Amendment "restrains only such discriminatory legislation by Congress as amounts to a denial of due process," ... and upheld the curfew....

... Korematsu v. United States, 323 U.S. 214 (1944), ... did not address the view ... that the Federal Government's obligation to provide equal protection differs significantly from that of the States. Instead, it began by noting that "all legal restrictions which curtail the civil rights of a single racial group are immediately suspect ... [and] courts must subject them to the most rigid scrutiny." ... That promising dictum might be read to undermine the view that the Federal Government is under a lesser obligation to avoid injurious racial classifications than are the States.... But ... the Court ... inexplicably relied on "the principles we announced in the *Hirabayashi* case" ... to conclude that, although "exclusion from the area in which one's home is located is a far greater deprivation than constant confinement to the home from 8 p.m. to 6 a.m.," ... the racially discriminatory order was nonetheless within the Federal Government's power.

In Bolling v. Sharpe, 347 U.S. 497 (1954), the Court for the first time explicitly questioned the existence of any difference between the obligations of the Federal Government and the States to avoid racial classifications....

Bolling's facts concerned school desegregation, but its reasoning was not so limited....

Later cases in contexts other than school desegregation did not distinguish between the duties of the States and the Federal Government to avoid racial classifications....

... Thus, in 1975, the Court stated explicitly that "[t]his Court's approach to Fifth Amendment equal protection claims has always been precisely the same as to equal protection claims under the Fourteenth Amendment." Weinberger v. Wiesenfeld, 420 U.S. 636, 638, n. 2 (1975).... We do not understand a few contrary suggestions appearing in cases in which we found special deference to the political branches of the Federal Government to be appropriate, e.g., Hampton v. Mow Sun Wong ... (1976) (federal power over immigration), to detract from this general rule.

B

Most of the cases discussed above involved classifications burdening groups that have suffered discrimination in our society. In 1978, the Court confronted the question whether race-based governmental action designed to benefit such groups should also be subject to "the most rigid scrutiny." Regents of Univ. of California v. Bakke ... did not produce an opinion for the Court....

Two years after *Bakke*, the Court faced another challenge to remedial race-based action, this time involving action undertaken by the Federal Government. In Fullilove v. Klutznick, 448 U.S. 448 (1980), the Court upheld Congress' inclusion of a 10% set-aside for minority-owned businesses in the Public Works Employment Act of 1977. As in *Bakke*, there was no opinion for the Court. Chief Justice Burger, in an opinion joined by Justices White and Powell, observed that "[a]ny preference based on racial or ethnic criteria must necessarily receive a most searching examination to make sure that it does not conflict with constitutional guarantees." ... That opinion, however, "d[id] not adopt, either expressly or implicitly, the formulas of analysis articulated in such cases as [*Bakke*]." ... It employed instead a two-part test which asked, first, "whether the objectives of th[e] legislation are within the power of Congress," and second, "whether the limited use of racial and ethnic criteria, in the context presented, is a constitutionally permissible means for achieving the congressional objectives." ... It then upheld the program under that test, adding at the end of the opinion that the program also "would survive judicial review under either 'test' articulated in the several *Bakke* opinions." ... Justice Powell wrote separately to express his view that the plurality opinion had essentially applied "strict scrutiny" as described in his *Bakke* opinion—i. e., it had determined that the set-aside was "a necessary means of advancing a compelling governmental interest"—and had done so correctly.... Justice Stewart (joined by then-Justice Rehnquist) dissented, arguing that the Constitution required the Federal Government to meet the same strict standard as the States when enacting racial classifications, ... and that the program before the Court failed that standard. Justice Stevens also dissented, arguing that "[r]acial classifications are simply too pernicious to permit any but the most exact connection between justification and classification," ... and that the program before the Court could not be characterized "as a 'narrowly tailored' remedial measure." ... Justice Marshall (joined by Justices Brennan and Blackmun) concurred in the judgment, reiterating the view of four Justices in *Bakke* that any race-based governmental action designed to "remed[y] the present effects of past racial discrimination" should be upheld if it was "substantially related" to the achievement of an "important governmental objective"—i. e., such action should be subjected only to what we now call "intermediate scrutiny." ...

In Wygant v. Jackson Board of Ed., 476 U.S. 267 (1986), the Court considered ... whether a school board could adopt race-based preferences in determining which teachers to lay off....

The Court's failure to produce a majority opinion in *Bakke*, *Fullilove*, and *Wygant* left unresolved the proper analysis for remedial race-based governmental action....

The Court resolved the issue, at least in part, in 1989. Richmond v. J.A. Croson Co., 488 U.S. 469 (1989), concerned a city's determination that 30% of its contracting work should go to minority-owned businesses. A majority of the Court in *Croson* held that "the standard of review under the Equal Protection Clause is not dependent on the race of those burdened or benefited by a particular classification," and that the single standard of review for racial classifications should be "strict scrutiny." ...

With *Croson*, the Court finally agreed that the Fourteenth Amendment requires strict scrutiny of all race-based action by state and local governments. But *Croson* of course had no occasion to declare what standard of review the Fifth Amendment requires for such action taken by the Federal Government. *Croson* observed simply that the Court's "treatment of an exercise of congressional power in *Fullilove* cannot be dispositive here," because *Croson*'s facts did not implicate Congress' broad power under § 5 of the Fourteenth Amendment....

Despite lingering uncertainty in the details, however, the Court's cases through *Croson* had established three general propositions with respect to governmental racial classifications. First, skepticism: "'[a]ny preference based on racial or ethnic criteria must necessarily receive a most searching examination,'" ... Second, consistency: "the standard of review under the Equal Protection Clause is not dependent on the race of those burdened or benefited by a particular classification," Croson ..., i. e., all racial classifications reviewable under the Equal Protection Clause must be strictly scrutinized. And third, congruence: "[e]qual protection analysis in the Fifth Amendment area is the same as that under the Fourteenth Amendment,".... Taken together, these three propositions lead to the conclusion that any person, of whatever race, has the right to demand that any governmental actor subject to the Constitution justify any racial classification subjecting that person to unequal treatment under the strictest judicial scrutiny. . . .

A year later, however, the Court took a surprising turn. Metro Broadcasting, Inc. v. FCC, 497 U.S. 547 (1990), involved a Fifth Amendment challenge to two race-based policies of the Federal Communications Commission. In *Metro Broadcasting*, the Court repudiated the long-held notion that "it would be unthinkable that the same Constitution would impose a lesser duty on the Federal Government" than it does on a State to afford equal protection of the laws . . . by holding that "benign" federal racial classifications need only satisfy intermediate scrutiny, even though *Croson* had recently concluded that such classifications enacted by a State must satisfy strict scrutiny. "[B]enign" federal racial classifications, the Court said, "—even if those measures are not 'remedial' in the sense of being designed to compensate victims of past governmental or societal discrimination—are constitutionally permissible to the extent that they serve important governmental objectives within the power of Congress and are substantially related to achievement of those objectives." . . . The Court did not explain how to tell whether a racial classification should be deemed "benign," other than to express "confiden[ce] that an 'examination of the legislative scheme and its history' will separate benign measures from other types of racial classifications." . . .

Applying this test, the Court first noted that the FCC policies at issue did not serve as a remedy for past discrimination. . . . Proceeding on the assumption that the policies were nonetheless "benign," it concluded that they served the "important governmental objective" of "enhancing broadcast diversity," . . . and that they were "substantially related" to that objective. . . . It therefore upheld the policies.

By adopting intermediate scrutiny as the standard of review for congressionally mandated "benign" racial classifications, *Metro Broadcasting* departed from prior cases in two significant respects. First, it turned its back on *Croson*'s explanation of why strict scrutiny of all governmental racial classifications is essential:

> "Absent searching judicial inquiry into the justification for such race-based measures, there is simply no way of determining what classifications are 'benign' or 'remedial' and what classifications are in fact motivated by illegitimate notions of racial inferiority or simple racial politics. Indeed, the purpose of strict scrutiny is to 'smoke out' illegitimate uses of race by assuring that the legislative body is pursuing a goal important enough to warrant use of a highly suspect tool. The test also ensures that the means chosen 'fit' this compelling goal so closely that there is little or no possibility that the motive for the classification was illegitimate racial prejudice or stereotype." . . . We adhere to that view today, despite the surface appeal of holding "benign" racial classifications to a lower standard, because "it may not always be clear that a so-called preference is in fact benign," *Bakke* . . . (opinion of Powell, J.). . . .

Second, *Metro Broadcasting* squarely rejected one of the three propositions established by the Court's earlier equal protection cases, namely, congruence between the standards applicable to federal and state racial classifications, and in so doing also undermined the other two—skepticism of all racial classifications, and consistency of treatment irrespective of the race of the burdened or benefited group. . . . Under *Metro Broadcasting*, certain racial classifications ("benign" ones enacted by the Federal Government) should be treated less skeptically than others; and the race of the benefited group is critical to the determination of which standard of review to apply. *Metro Broadcasting* was thus a significant departure from much of what had come before it.

The three propositions undermined by *Metro Broadcasting* all derive from the basic principle that the Fifth and Fourteenth Amendments to the Constitution protect persons, not groups. It follows . . . that all governmental action based on race . . . should be subjected to detailed judicial inquiry to ensure that the personal right to equal protection of the laws has not been infringed. . . . Accordingly, we hold today that all racial classifications, imposed by whatever federal, state, or local governmental actor, must be analyzed by a reviewing court under strict scrutiny. In other words, such classifications are constitutional only if they are narrowly tailored measures that further compelling governmental interests. To the extent that *Metro Broadcasting* is inconsistent with that holding, it is overruled.

In dissent, Justice Stevens['s] . . . criticisms reflect a serious misunderstanding of our opinion.

. . . What he fails to recognize is that strict scrutiny does take "relevant differences" into account—indeed, that is its fundamental purpose. The point of carefully examining the interest asserted by the government in support of a racial classification, and the evidence offered to show that the classification is needed, is precisely to distinguish legitimate from illegitimate uses of race in governmental decisionmaking. And Justice Stevens concedes that "some cases may be difficult to classify"; all the more reason, in our view, to examine all racial classifications carefully. Strict scrutiny does not "trea[t] dissimilar race-based decisions as though they were equally objectionable"; to the contrary, it evaluates carefully all governmental race-based decisions in order to decide which are constitutionally objectionable and which are not. By requiring strict scrutiny of racial classifications, we require courts to make sure that a governmental classification based on race . . . is legitimate, before permitting unequal treatment based on race to proceed.

Justice Stevens chides us for our "supposed inability to differentiate between 'invidious' and 'benign' discrimination," because it is in his view sufficient that "people understand the difference between good intentions and bad." But . . . the point of strict scrutiny is to "differentiate between" permissible and impermissible governmental use of race. And Justice Stevens himself has already explained in his dissent in *Fullilove* why "good intentions" alone are not enough . . .: "[E]ven though it is not the actual predicate for this legislation, a statute of this kind inevitably is perceived by many as resting on an assumption that those who are granted this special preference are less qualified in some respect that is identified purely by their race. Because that perception—especially when fostered by the Congress of the United States—can only exacerbate rather than reduce racial prejudice, it will delay the time when race will become a truly irrelevant, or at least insignificant, factor. . . . ; see also id., at 537 ("Racial classifications are simply too pernicious to permit any but the most exact connection between justification and classification"); Croson, supra, at 516–517 (Stevens, J., concurring in part and concurring in judgment) ("Although [the legislation at issue] stigmatizes the disadvantaged class with the unproven charge of past racial discrimination, it actually imposes a greater stigma on its supposed beneficiaries"). . . . These passages make a persuasive case for requiring strict scrutiny of congressional racial classifications.

Perhaps it is not the standard of strict scrutiny itself, but our use of the concepts of "consistency" and "congruence" in conjunction with it, that leads Justice Stevens to dissent. According to Justice Stevens, our view of consistency "equate[s] remedial preferences with invidious discrimination," and ignores the difference between "an engine of oppression" and an effort "to foster equality in society," or, more colorfully, "between a 'No Trespassing' sign and a welcome mat." It does nothing of the kind. The principle of consistency simply means that whenever the government treats any person unequally because of his or her race, that person has suffered an injury that falls squarely within the language and spirit of the Constitution's guarantee of equal protection. It says nothing about the ultimate validity of any particular law; that determination is the job of the court applying strict scrutiny. The principle of consistency explains the circumstances in which the injury requiring strict scrutiny occurs. The application of strict scrutiny, in turn, determines whether a compelling governmental interest justifies the infliction of that injury.

Consistency does recognize that any individual suffers an injury when he or she is disadvantaged by the government because of his or her race, whatever that race may be. This Court clearly stated that principle in *Croson*.... Justice Stevens does not explain how his views square with *Croson*, or with the long line of cases understanding equal protection as a personal right.

Justice Stevens also claims that we have ignored any difference between federal and state legislatures. But requiring that Congress, like the States, enact racial classifications only when doing so is necessary to further a "compelling interest" does not contravene any principle of appropriate respect for a co-equal Branch of the Government. [T]rue[,] various Members of this Court have taken different views of the authority § 5 of the Fourteenth Amendment confers upon Congress to deal with the problem of racial discrimination, and the extent to which courts should defer to Congress' exercise of that authority.... We need not, and do not, address these differences today. For now, it is enough to observe that Justice Stevens' suggestion that any Member of this Court has repudiated in this case his or her previously expressed views on the subject is incorrect.

C

. . .

It is worth pointing out the difference between the applications of *stare decisis* in this case and in Planned Parenthood of Southeastern Pa. v. Casey, 505 U.S. 833 (1992). *Casey* explained how considerations of *stare decisis* inform the decision whether to overrule a long-established precedent that has become integrated into the fabric of the law. Overruling precedent of that kind naturally may have consequences for "the ideal of the rule of law".... In addition, such precedent is likely to have engendered substantial reliance, as was true in *Casey* itself.... But ... we do not face a precedent of that kind, because *Metro Broadcasting* itself departed from our prior cases—and did so quite recently. By refusing to follow *Metro Broadcasting*, then, we do not depart from the fabric of the law; we restore it. [A]lso[,] reliance on a case that has recently departed from precedent is likely to be minimal, particularly where, as here, the rule ... in that case is unlikely to affect primary conduct in any event....

... [W]e think that well-settled legal principles pointed toward a conclusion different from that reached in *Metro Broadcasting*, and we therefore disagree with Justice Stevens that "the law at the time of that decision was entirely open to the result the Court reached." ... There is nothing new about the notion that Congress, like the States, may treat people differently because of their race only for compelling reasons.

"The real problem ... is whether a principle shall prevail over its later misapplications." ... *Metro Broadcasting*'s untenable distinction between state and federal racial classifications lacks support in our precedent, and undermines the fundamental principle of equal protection as a personal right. In this case, as between that principle and "its later misapplications," the principle must prevail.

D

Our action today makes explicit what Justice Powell thought implicit in the *Fullilove* lead opinion: federal racial classifications, like those of a State, must serve a compelling governmental interest, and must be narrowly tailored to further that interest.... [I]t follows that to the extent (if any) that *Fullilove* held federal racial classifications to be subject to a less rigorous standard, it is no longer controlling. But we need not decide today whether the program upheld in *Fullilove* would survive strict scrutiny as our more recent cases have defined it.

Some have questioned the importance of debating the proper standard of review of race-based legislation.... But we agree with Justice Stevens that, "[b]ecause racial characteristics so seldom provide a relevant basis for disparate treatment, and because classifications based on race are potentially so harmful to the entire body politic, it is especially important that the reasons for any such classification be clearly identified and unquestionably legitimate," and that "[r]acial classifications are simply too pernicious to permit any but the most exact connection between justification and classification." *Fullilove* ... (dissenting opinion).... We think that requiring strict scrutiny is the best way to ensure that courts will consistently give racial classifications that kind of detailed examination, both as to ends and as to means. *Korematsu* demonstrates vividly that even "the most rigid scrutiny" can sometimes fail to detect an illegitimate racial classification.... Any retreat from the most searching judicial inquiry can only increase the risk of another such error occurring in the future.

Finally, we wish to dispel the notion that strict scrutiny is "strict in theory, but fatal in fact." ... The unhappy persistence of both the practice and the lingering effects of racial discrimination against minority groups in this country is an unfortunate reality, and government is not disqualified from acting in response to it. As recently as 1987, for example, every Justice of this Court agreed that the Alabama Department of Public Safety's "pervasive, systematic, and obstinate discriminatory conduct" justified a narrowly tailored race-based remedy. See United States v. Paradise, 480 U. S., at 167 (plurality opinion of Brennan, J.); id., at 190 (Stevens, J., concurring in judgment); id., at 196 (O'Connor, J., dissenting). When race-based action is necessary to further a compelling interest, such action is within constitutional constraints if it satisfies the "narrow tailoring" test this Court has set out in previous cases.

IV

Because our decision today alters the playing field in some important respects, we think it best to remand ... for further consideration in light of the principles we have announced. The Court of Appeals, following *Metro Broadcasting* and *Fullilove*, analyzed the case in terms of intermediate scrutiny. It ... did not decide ... whether the interests served by the use of subcontractor compensation clauses are properly described as "compelling." It also did not address the question of narrow tailoring in terms of our strict scrutiny cases, by asking, for example, whether there was "any consideration of the use of race-neutral means to increase minority business participation" in government contracting, *Croson* ..., or whether the program was appropriately limited such that it "will not last longer than the discriminatory effects it is designed to eliminate," *Fullilove* ... (Powell, J., concurring).

Moreover, unresolved questions remain concerning the details of the complex regulatory regimes implicated by the use of subcontractor compensation clauses. For example, the SBA's 8(a) program requires an individualized inquiry into the economic disadvantage of every participant, ... whereas the DOT's regulations implementing STURAA § 106(c) do not.... And the regulations seem unclear as to whether 8(d) subcontractors must make individualized showings, or instead whether the race-based presumption applies both to social and economic disadvantage.... We also note an apparent discrepancy between the definitions of which socially disadvantaged individuals qualify as economically disadvantaged for the 8(a) and 8(d) programs; the former requires a showing that such individuals' ability to compete has been impaired "as compared to others in the same or similar line of business who are not socially disadvantaged," ... while the latter requires that showing only "as compared to others in the same or similar line of business,".... The question whether any of the ways in which the Government uses subcontractor compensation clauses can survive strict scrutiny, and any relevance distinctions such as these may have to that question, should be addressed in the first instance by the lower courts.

. . .

Justice Scalia, concurring in part and concurring in the judgment.

I join the opinion of the Court, except Part III–C, and except insofar as it may be inconsistent with the following: In my view, government can never have a "compelling interest" in discriminating on the basis of race in order to "make up" for past racial discrimination in the opposite direction.... Individuals who have been wronged by unlawful racial discrimination should be made whole; but under our Constitution there can be no such thing as either a creditor or a debtor race. That concept is alien to the Constitution's focus upon the individual ... and its rejection of dispositions based on race, see Amdt. 15, § 1 (prohibiting abridgment of the right to vote "on account of race") or based on blood, see Art. III, § 3 ("[N]o Attainder of Treason shall work Corruption of Blood"); Art. I, § 9 ("No Title of Nobility shall be granted by the United States"). To pursue the concept of racial entitlement—even for the most admirable and benign of purposes—is to reinforce and preserve for future mischief the way of thinking that produced race slavery, race privilege and race hatred. In the eyes of government, we are just one race here. It is American.

It is unlikely, if not impossible, that the challenged program would survive under this understanding of strict scrutiny, but I am content to leave that to be decided on remand.

Justice Thomas, concurring in part and concurring in the judgment.

I agree with the majority's conclusion that strict scrutiny applies to all government classifications based on race. I write separately, however, to express my disagreement with the premise underlying Justice Stevens' and Justice Ginsburg's dissents: that there is a racial paternalism exception to the principle of equal protection. I believe that there is a "moral [and] constitutional equivalence" (Stevens, J., dissenting) between laws designed to subjugate a race and those that distribute benefits on the basis of race in order to foster some current notion of equality. Government cannot make us equal; it can only recognize, respect, and protect us as equal before the law.

That these programs may have been motivated, in part, by good intentions cannot provide refuge from the principle that under our Constitution, the government may not make distinctions on the basis of race. As far as the Constitution is concerned, it is irrelevant whether a government's racial classifications are drawn by those who wish to oppress a race or by those who have a sincere desire to help those thought to be disadvantaged. There can be no doubt that the paternalism that appears to lie at the heart of this program is at war with the principle of inherent equality that underlies and infuses our Constitution. . . .

These programs . . . also undermine the moral basis of the equal protection principle. Purchased at the price of immeasurable human suffering, the equal protection principle reflects our Nation's understanding that such classifications ultimately have a destructive impact on the individual and our society. . . . [T]here can be no doubt that racial paternalism and its unintended consequences can be as poisonous and pernicious as any other form of discrimination. So-called "benign" discrimination teaches many that because of chronic and apparently immutable handicaps, minorities cannot compete with them without their patronizing indulgence. Inevitably, such programs engender attitudes of superiority or, alternatively, provoke resentment among those who believe that they have been wronged by the government's use of race. These programs stamp minorities with a badge of inferiority and may cause them to develop dependencies or to adopt an attitude that they are "entitled" to preferences. . . .

In my mind, government-sponsored racial discrimination based on benign prejudice is just as noxious as discrimination inspired by malicious prejudice. In each instance, it is racial discrimination, plain and simple.

Justice Stevens, with whom Justice Ginsburg joins, dissenting.

Instead of deciding this case in accordance with controlling precedent, the Court today delivers a disconcerting lecture about the evils of governmental racial classifications. . . . I believe this Court has a duty to affirm. . . .

I

The Court's concept of skepticism is, at least in principle, a good statement of law and of common sense. Undoubtedly, a court should be wary of a governmental decision that relies upon a racial classification. . . . [B]ecause uniform standards are often anything but uniform, we should evaluate the Court's comments on "consistency," "congruence," and *stare decisis* with the same type of skepticism that the Court advocates for the underlying issue.

II

The Court's concept of "consistency" assumes that there is no significant difference between a decision by the majority to impose a special burden on the members of a minority race and a decision by the majority to provide a benefit to certain members of that minority notwithstanding its incidental burden on some members of the majority. [T]hat assumption is untenable. There is no moral or constitutional equivalence between a policy that is designed to perpetuate a caste system and one that seeks to eradicate racial subordination. Invidious discrimination is an engine of oppression, subjugating a disfavored group to enhance or maintain the power of the majority. Remedial race-based preferences reflect the opposite impulse: a desire to foster equality in society.

No sensible conception of the Government's constitutional obligation to "govern impartially" . . . should ignore this distinction.[1]

. . .

The consistency that the Court espouses would disregard the difference between a "No Trespassing" sign and a welcome mat. It would treat a Dixiecrat Senator's decision to vote against Thurgood Marshall's confirmation in order to keep African Americans off the Supreme Court as on a par with President Johnson's evaluation of his nominee's race as a positive factor. It would equate a law that made black citizens ineligible for military service with a program aimed at recruiting black soldiers. An attempt by the majority to exclude members of a minority race from a regulated market is fundamentally different from a subsidy that enables a relatively small group of newcomers to enter that market. An interest in "consistency" does not justify treating differences as though they were similarities.

The Court's explanation for treating dissimilar race-based decisions as though they were equally objectionable is a supposed inability to differentiate between "invidious" and "benign" discrimination. But the term "affirmative action" is common and well understood. Its presence in everyday parlance shows that people understand the difference between good intentions and bad. As with any legal concept, some cases may be difficult to classify, but our equal protection jurisprudence has identified a critical difference between state action that imposes burdens on a disfavored few and state action that benefits the few "in spite of" its adverse effects on the many. *Feeney*, 442 U. S., at 279.

Indeed, our jurisprudence has made the standard to be applied in cases of invidious discrimination turn on whether the discrimination is "intentional," or whether, by contrast, it merely has a discriminatory "effect." Washington v. Davis, 426 U.S. 229 (1976). Surely this distinction is at least as subtle, and at least as difficult to apply . . . as the usually obvious distinction between a measure intended to benefit members of a particular minority race and a measure intended to burden a minority race. A state actor inclined to subvert the Constitution might easily hide bad intentions in the guise of unintended "effects"; but I should think it far more difficult to enact a law intending to preserve the majority's hegemony while casting it plausibly in the guise of affirmative action for minorities.

Nothing is inherently wrong with applying a single standard to fundamentally different situations, as long as that standard takes relevant differences into account. For example, if the Court in all equal protection cases were to insist that differential treatment be justified by relevant characteristics of the members of the favored and disfavored classes that provide a legitimate basis for disparate treatment, such a standard would treat dissimilar cases differently while still recognizing that there is, after all, only one Equal Protection Clause. . . . Under such a standard, subsidies for disadvantaged businesses may be constitutional though special taxes on such businesses would be invalid. But

---

[1] As Justice Ginsburg observes, the majority's "flexible" approach to "strict scrutiny" may well take into account differences between benign and invidious programs. . . . Even if . . . so, . . . it is unfortunate that the majority insists on applying the label "strict scrutiny" to benign race-based programs. That label has usually been understood to spell the death of any governmental action to which a court may apply it. The Court suggests today that "strict scrutiny" means something different—something less strict— when applied to benign racial classifications. Although I agree that benign programs deserve different treatment than invidious programs, there is a danger that the fatal language of "strict scrutiny" will skew the analysis and place well-crafted benign programs at unnecessary risk.

a single standard that purports to equate remedial preferences with invidious discrimination cannot be defended in the name of "equal protection."

Moreover, the Court may find that its new "consistency" approach to race-based classifications is difficult to square with its insistence upon rigidly separate categories for discrimination against different classes of individuals. For example, as the law currently stands, the Court will apply "intermediate scrutiny" to cases of invidious gender discrimination and "strict scrutiny" to cases of invidious race discrimination, while applying the same standard for benign classifications as for invidious ones. If this remains the law, then today's lecture about "consistency" will produce the anomalous result that the Government can more easily enact affirmative-action programs to remedy discrimination against women than it can enact affirmative-action programs to remedy discrimination against African Americans—even though the primary purpose of the Equal Protection Clause was to end discrimination against the former slaves.... When a court becomes preoccupied with abstract standards, it risks sacrificing common sense at the altar of formal consistency.

As a matter of constitutional and democratic principle, a decision by representatives of the majority to discriminate against the members of a minority race is fundamentally different from those same representatives' decision to impose incidental costs on the majority of their constituents in order to provide a benefit to a disadvantaged minority.[5] Indeed, ... the former is virtually always repugnant to the principles of a free and democratic society, whereas the latter is, in some circumstances, entirely consistent with the ideal of equality....

III

The Court's concept of "congruence" assumes ... no significant difference between a decision by the Congress ... to adopt an affirmative-action program and such a decision by a State or a municipality. [T]hat assumption ... ignores important practical and legal differences between federal and state or local decisionmakers.

[5] ...Justice Thomas argues that the most significant cost associated with an affirmative-action program is its adverse stigmatic effect on its intended beneficiaries. Although I agree that this cost may be more significant than many people realize, ... I do not think it applies to the facts of this case. First, ... [n]o beneficiaries of the specific program under attack today have challenged its constitutionality—perhaps because they do not find the preferences stigmatizing, or perhaps because their ability to opt out of the program provides them all the relief they would need. Second, even if ... a minority-owned business challeng[ed] the stigmatizing effect of this program, I would not find Justice Thomas' extreme proposition—that there is a moral and constitutional equivalence between an attempt to subjugate and an attempt to redress the effects of a caste system—at all persuasive. It is one thing to question the wisdom of affirmative-action programs: there are many responsible arguments against them, including the one based upon stigma, that Congress might find persuasive when it decides whether to enact or retain race-based preferences. It is another thing altogether to equate the many well-meaning and intelligent lawmakers and their constituents—whether members of majority or minority races—who have supported affirmative action over the years, to segregationists and bigots. Finally, although Justice Thomas is more concerned about the potential effects of these programs than the intent of those who enacted them ..., I am not persuaded that the psychological damage brought on by affirmative action is as severe as that engendered by racial subordination. That, in any event, is a judgment the political branches can be trusted to make. In enacting affirmative action programs, a legislature intends to remove obstacles that have unfairly placed individuals of equal qualifications at a competitive disadvantage.... I do not believe such action, whether wise or unwise, deserves such an invidious label as "racial paternalism." If the legislature is persuaded that its program is doing more harm than good to the individuals it is designed to benefit, then we can expect the legislature to remedy the problem. Significantly, this is not true of a government action based on invidious discrimination.

These differences have been identified repeatedly and consistently both in opinions of the Court and in separate opinions authored by members of today's majority. Thus, in Metro Broadcasting, Inc. v. FCC, 497 U.S. 547 (1990), ... we identified the special "institutional competence" of our National Legislature.... We recalled the several opinions in *Fullilove* that admonished this Court to "approach our task with appropriate deference to the Congress, a co-equal branch charged by the Constitution with the power to 'provide for the ... general Welfare of the United States' and 'to enforce, by appropriate legislation,' the equal protection guarantees of the Fourteenth Amendment. ...'" ...

... In his separate opinion in Richmond v. J.A. Croson Co., 488 U.S. 469, 520–524 (1989), Justice Scalia discussed the basis for this distinction....

In her plurality opinion in *Croson*, Justice O'Connor also emphasized the importance of this distinction when she responded to the City's argument that *Fullilove* was controlling. She wrote: "What appellant ignores is that Congress, unlike any State or political subdivision, has a specific constitutional mandate to enforce the dictates of the Fourteenth Amendment. The power to 'enforce' may at times also include the power to define situations which Congress determines threaten principles of equality and to adopt prophylactic rules to deal with those situations. The Civil War Amendments themselves worked a dramatic change in the balance between congressional and state power over matters of race." ...

An additional reason for giving greater deference to the National Legislature than to a local law-making body is that federal affirmative-action programs represent the will of our entire Nation's elected representatives, whereas a state or local program may have an impact on nonresident entities who played no part in the decision to enact it. Thus, in the state or local context, individuals who were unable to vote for the local representatives who enacted a race-conscious program may nonetheless feel the effects of that program. This difference recalls the goals of the Commerce Clause, U.S. Const., Art. I, § 8, cl. 3, which permits Congress to legislate on certain matters of national importance while denying power to the States in this area for fear of undue impact upon out-of-state residents....

Ironically, after all of the time, effort, and paper this Court has expended in differentiating between federal and state affirmative action, the majority today virtually ignores the issue. It provides not a word of direct explanation for its sudden and enormous departure from the reasoning in past cases. Such silence, however, cannot erase the difference between Congress' institutional competence and constitutional authority to overcome historic racial subjugation and the States' lesser power to do so.

Presumably, the majority is now satisfied that its theory of "congruence" between the substantive rights provided by the Fifth and Fourteenth Amendments disposes of the objection based upon divided constitutional powers. But it is one thing to say (as no one seems to dispute) that the Fifth Amendment encompasses a general guarantee of equal protection as broad as that contained within the Fourteenth Amendment. It is another thing entirely to say that Congress' institutional competence and constitutional authority entitles it to no greater deference when it enacts a program designed to foster equality than the deference due a State legislature. The latter is an extraordinary proposition; ... our precedents have rejected it explicitly and repeatedly.

Our opinion in *Metro Broadcasting* relied on several constitutional provisions to justify the greater deference we owe to Congress when it acts with respect to private individuals.... In the programs challenged in this case, Congress has acted both with respect to private individuals and, as in *Fullilove*, with respect to the States themselves.[9] When Congress does this, it draws its power directly from § 5 of the Fourteenth Amendment.... The Fourteenth Amendment directly empowers Congress at the same time it expressly limits the States.[11] This is no accident. It represents our Nation's consensus, achieved after hard experience throughout our sorry history of race relations, that the Federal Government must be the primary defender of racial minorities against the States, some of which may be inclined to oppress such minorities. A rule of "congruence" that ignores a purposeful "incongruity" so fundamental to our system of government is unacceptable.

. . .

IV

The Court's concept of *stare decisis* treats some of the language we have used in explaining our decisions as though it were more important than our actual holdings....

This is the third time in the Court's entire history that it has considered the constitutionality of a federal affirmative-action program. On each of the two prior occasions, the first in 1980, Fullilove v. Klutznick, 448 U.S. 448, and the second in 1990, Metro Broadcasting, Inc. v. FCC, 497 U.S. 547, the Court upheld the program....

In the Court's view, our decision in *Metro Broadcasting* was inconsistent with the rule announced in Richmond v. J.A. Croson Co., 488 U.S. 469 (1989). But two decisive distinctions separate those two cases. First, *Metro Broadcasting* involved a federal program, whereas *Croson* involved a city ordinance. *Metro Broadcasting* thus drew primary support from *Fullilove*, which predated *Croson* and which *Croson* distinguished on the grounds of the federal-state dichotomy that the majority today discredits. Although members of today's majority trumpeted the importance of that distinction in *Croson*, they now reject it in the name of "congruence." It is therefore quite wrong for the Court to suggest today that overruling *Metro Broadcasting* merely restores the *status quo ante*, for the law at the time of that decision was entirely open to the result

---

[9] The funding for the preferences challenged in this case comes from ... STURAA ..., in which Congress has granted funds to the States in exchange for a commitment to foster subcontracting by disadvantaged business enterprises, or "DBE's." STURAA is also the source of funding for DBE preferences in federal highway contracting. Approximately 98% of STURAA's funding is allocated to the States.... Moreover, under STURAA States are empowered to certify businesses as "disadvantaged" for purposes of receiving subcontracting preferences in both state and federal contracts.... In this case, Adarand has sued only the federal officials responsible for implementing federal highway contracting policy; it has not directly challenged DBE preferences granted in state contracts funded by STURAA. It is not entirely clear, then, whether the majority's "congruence" rationale would apply to federally regulated state contracts, which may conceivably be within the majority's view of Congress' § 5 authority even if the federal contracts are not. See Metro Broadcasting, 497 U. S., at 603–604 (O'Connor, J., dissenting). As I read the majority's opinion, however, it draws no distinctions between direct federal preferences and federal preferences achieved through subsidies to States. The extent to which STURAA intertwines elements of direct federal regulations with elements of federal conditions on grants to the States would make such a distinction difficult to sustain.

[11] We have read § 5 as a positive grant of authority to Congress, not just to punish violations, but also to define and expand the scope of the Equal Protection Clause. Katzenbach v. Morgan, 384 U.S. 641 (1966). In *Katzenbach*, this meant that Congress under § 5 could require the States to allow non-English-speaking citizens to vote, even if denying such citizens a vote would not have been an independent violation of § 1.... Congress, then, can expand the coverage of § 1 by exercising its power under § 5 when it acts to foster equality. Congress has done just that here; it has decided that granting certain preferences to minorities best serves the goals of equal protection.

the Court reached. *Today's* decision is an unjustified departure from settled law.

Second, *Metro Broadcasting*'s holding rested on more than its application of "intermediate scrutiny." ... What truly distinguishes *Metro Broadcasting* from our other affirmative-action precedents is the distinctive goal of the federal program in that case. Instead of merely seeking to remedy past discrimination, the FCC program was intended to achieve future benefits in the form of broadcast diversity....

[P]rior to *Metro Broadcasting*, the interest in diversity had been mentioned in a few opinions, but it is perfectly clear that the Court had not yet decided whether that interest had sufficient magnitude to justify a racial classification. *Metro Broadcasting*, of course, answered that question in the affirmative. The majority today overrules *Metro Broadcasting* only insofar as it is "inconsistent with [the] holding" that strict scrutiny applies to "benign" racial classifications promulgated by the Federal Government. The proposition that fostering diversity may provide a sufficient interest to justify such a program is *not* inconsistent with the Court's holding today—indeed, the question is not remotely presented in this case—and I do not take the Court's opinion to diminish that aspect of our decision in *Metro Broadcasting*.

The Court's suggestion that it may be necessary in the future to overrule *Fullilove* in order to restore the fabric of the law is even more disingenuous than its treatment of *Metro Broadcasting*. For the Court endorses the "strict scrutiny" standard that Justice Powell applied in *Bakke* and acknowledges that he applied that standard in *Fullilove* as well. Moreover, Chief Justice Burger also expressly concluded that the program we considered in *Fullilove* was valid under any of the tests articulated in *Bakke*, which of course included Justice Powell's.... The Court thus adopts a standard applied in *Fullilove* at the same time it questions that case's continued vitality and accuses it of departing from prior law.... As was true of *Metro Broadcasting*, the Court in *Fullilove* decided an important, novel, and difficult question. Providing a different answer to a similar question today cannot fairly be characterized as merely "restoring" previously settled law.

V

The Court's holding in *Fullilove* surely governs the result in this case. The Public Works Employment Act of 1977 (1977 Act) ... is different in several critical respects from the portions of the Small Business Act (SBA) ... and STURAA ... challenged in this case. Each of those differences makes the current program ... significantly less objectionable than the 1977 categorical grant of $400 million in exchange for a 10% set-aside in public contracts to "a class of investors defined solely by racial characteristics." *Fullilove*, 448 U. S., at 532 (Stevens, J., dissenting). In no meaningful respect is the current scheme more objectionable than the 1977 Act. Thus, if the 1977 Act was constitutional, then so must be the SBA and STURAA. Indeed, even if my dissenting views in *Fullilove* had prevailed, this program would be valid.

Unlike the 1977 Act, the present statutory scheme does not make race the sole criterion of eligibility for participation in the program. Race does give rise to a rebuttable presumption of social disadvantage which, at least under STURAA, gives rise to a second rebuttable presumption of economic disadvantage.... But a small business may qualify as a DBE, by showing that it is both socially and economically disadvantaged, even if it receives neither of these presumptions.... Thus, the current preference is more inclusive than the 1977 Act because it does not make race a necessary qualification.

More importantly, race is not a sufficient qualification. Whereas a million-aire with a long history of financial successes ... would have qualified for a preference under the 1977 Act merely because he was an Asian American or an African American, ... neither the SBA nor STURAA creates any such anomaly. The DBE program excludes members of minority races who are not, in fact, socially or economically disadvantaged.... The presumption of social disadvan-tage reflects the unfortunate fact that irrational racial prejudice—along with its lingering effects—still survives. The presumption of economic disadvantage embodies a recognition that success in the private sector of the economy is often attributable, in part, to social skills and relationships. Unlike the 1977 set-asides, the current preference is designed to overcome the social and economic disadvantages that are often associated with racial characteristics. If, in a particular case, these disadvantages are not present, the presumptions can be rebutted.... The program is thus designed to allow race to play a part in the decisional process only when there is a meaningful basis for assuming its relevance.

[I]t is particularly significant that the current program targets the negotia-tion of subcontracts between private firms. The 1977 Act applied entirely to the award of public contracts, an area of the economy in which social relationships should be irrelevant and in which proper supervision of government contracting officers should preclude any discrimination against particular bidders on ac-count of their race. [Here], the program seeks to overcome barriers of prejudice between private parties—specifically, between general contractors and subcon-tractors. The SBA and STURAA embody Congress' recognition that such barriers may actually handicap minority firms seeking business as subcontrac-tors from established leaders in the industry that have a history of doing business with their golfing partners. Indeed, minority subcontractors may face more obstacles than direct, intentional racial prejudice: they may face particu-lar barriers simply because they are more likely to be new in the business and less likely to know others in the business. Given such difficulties, Congress could reasonably find that a minority subcontractor is less likely to receive favors from the entrenched businesspersons who award subcontracts only to people with whom—or with whose friends—they have an existing relationship. This program, then, if in part a remedy for past discrimination, is most importantly a forward-looking response to practical problems faced by minority subcontractors.

The current program contains another forward-looking component that the 1977 set-asides did not share. Section 8(a) of the SBA provides for periodic review of the status of DBE's, ... and DBE status can be challenged by a competitor at any time under any of the routes to certification.... Such review prevents ineligible firms from taking part in the program solely because of their minority ownership, even when those firms were once disadvantaged but have since become successful. The emphasis on review also indicates the Administra-tion's anticipation that after their presumed disadvantages have been over-come, firms will "graduate" into a status in which they will be able to compete for business, including prime contracts, on an equal basis.... As with other phases of the statutory policy of encouraging the formation and growth of small business enterprises, this program is intended to facilitate entry and increase competition in the free market.

Significantly, the current program, unlike the 1977 set-aside, does not establish any requirement—numerical or otherwise—that a general contractor must hire DBE subcontractors. The program we upheld in *Fullilove* required that 10% of the federal grant for every federally funded project be expended on minority business enterprises. In contrast, the current program contains no quota. Although it provides monetary incentives to general contractors to hire DBE subcontractors, it does not require them to hire DBE's, and they do not lose their contracts if they fail to do so. The importance of this incentive to general contractors (who always seek to offer the lowest bid) should not be underestimated; but the preference here is far less rigid, and thus more narrowly tailored, than the 1977 Act. Cf. *Bakke*, 438 U. S., at 319–320 (opinion of Powell, J.) (distinguishing between numerical set-asides and consideration of race as a factor).

Finally, the record shows a dramatic contrast between the sparse deliberations that preceded the 1977 Act ... and the extensive hearings conducted in several Congresses before the current program was developed.... If the 1977 program of race-based set-asides satisfied the strict scrutiny dictated by Justice Powell's vision of the Constitution—a vision the Court expressly endorses today—it must follow as night follows the day that the Court of Appeals' judgment upholding this more carefully crafted program should be affirmed.

. . .

Justice Souter, with whom Justice Ginsburg and Justice Breyer join, dissenting.

. . .

... The statutory scheme must be treated as constitutional if Fullilove v. Klutznick, 448 U.S. 448 (1980), is applied, and petitioners did not identify any of the factual premises on which *Fullilove* rested as having disappeared since that case was decided.

. . .

In these circumstances, I agree with Justice Stevens's conclusion that stare decisis compels the application of *Fullilove*.... *Fullilove* ... produced a result on shared grounds that petitioner does not attack: that discrimination in the construction industry had been subject to government acquiescence, with effects that remain and that may be addressed by some preferential treatment falling within the congressional power under § 5 of the Fourteenth Amendment.[1] ... Once *Fullilove* is applied, as Justice Stevens points out, it follows that the statutes in question here (which are substantially better tailored to the harm being remedied than the statute endorsed in *Fullilove*....) pass muster under Fifth Amendment due process and Fourteenth Amendment equal protection.

The Court ... does not reach the application of *Fullilove* ..., and on remand ... the Government and petitioner [must] address anew the facts upon which statutes like these must be judged on the Government's remedial theory of justification: facts about the current effects of past discrimination, the necessity for a preferential remedy, and the suitability of this particular preferential scheme.... [I]t seems fair to ask whether the statutes will meet a different fate from what *Fullilove* would have decreed. The answer is, quite probably not, though of course there will be some interpretive forks in the road

---

[1] If the statutes are within the § 5 power, they are just as enforceable when the national government makes a construction contract directly as when it funnels construction money through the states. In any event, as Justice Stevens has noted, it is not clear whether the current challenge implicates only Fifth Amendment due process or Fourteenth Amendment equal protection as well.

before the significance of strict scrutiny for congressional remedial statutes becomes entirely clear.

. . . Indeed, the Court's very recognition today that strict scrutiny can be compatible with the survival of a classification so reviewed demonstrates that our concepts of equal protection enjoy a greater elasticity than the standard categories might suggest. . . .

In assessing the degree to which today's holding portends a departure from past practice, it is also worth noting that nothing in today's opinion implies any view of Congress's § 5 power and the deference due its exercise that differs from the views expressed by the *Fullilove* plurality. . . . Thus, today's decision should leave § 5 exactly where it is as the source of an interest of the national government sufficiently important to satisfy the corresponding requirement of the strict scrutiny test.

Finally, . . . I do not understand that today's decision will necessarily have any effect on the . . . long accepted . . . view that constitutional authority to remedy past discrimination is not limited to the power to forbid its continuation, but extends to eliminating those effects that would otherwise persist and skew the operation of public systems even in the absence of current intent to practice any discrimination. . . . This is so whether the remedial authority is exercised by a court, . . . the Congress, . . . or some other legislature. . . . Indeed, a majority of the Court today reiterates that there are circumstances in which Government may, consistently with the Constitution, adopt programs aimed at remedying the effects of past invidious discrimination. . . .

When the extirpation of lingering discriminatory effects is thought to require a catch-up mechanism, like the racially preferential inducement under the statutes considered here, the result may be that some members of the historically favored race are hurt by that remedial mechanism, however innocent they may be of any personal responsibility for any discriminatory conduct. When this price is considered reasonable, it is in part because it is a price to be paid only temporarily; if the justification for the preference is eliminating the effects of a past practice, the assumption is that the effects will themselves recede into the past, becoming attenuated and finally disappearing. . . .

Surely the transition from the *Fullilove* plurality view (in which Justice Powell joined) to today's strict scrutiny (which will presumably be applied as Justice Powell employed it) does not signal a change in the standard by which the burden of a remedial racial preference is to be judged as reasonable or not at any given time. If in the District Court Adarand had chosen to press a challenge to the reasonableness of the burden of these statutes, more than a decade after *Fullilove* had examined such a burden, I doubt that the claim would have fared any differently from the way it will now be treated on remand from this Court.

Justice Ginsburg, with whom Justice Breyer joins, dissenting.

For the reasons stated by Justice Souter, and in view of the attention the political branches are currently giving the matter of affirmative action, I see no compelling cause for the intervention the Court has made in this case. I further agree with Justice Stevens that . . . large deference is owed by the Judiciary to "Congress' institutional competence and constitutional authority to overcome historic racial subjugation." I write separately to underscore . . . the considerable field of agreement . . . revealed in opinions that together speak for a majority of the Court.

I

. . .

The divisions in this difficult case should not obscure the Court's recognition of the persistence of racial inequality and a majority's acknowledgement of Congress' authority to act affirmatively, not only to end discrimination, but also to counteract discrimination's lingering effects. . . . Those effects, reflective of a system of racial caste only recently ended, are evident in our workplaces, markets, and neighborhoods. Job applicants with identical resumes, qualifications, and interview styles still experience different receptions, depending on their race. White and African–American consumers still encounter different deals. People of color looking for housing still face discriminatory treatment by landlords, real estate agents, and mortgage lenders. Minority entrepreneurs sometimes fail to gain contracts though they are the low bidders, and they are sometimes refused work even after winning contracts. Bias both conscious and unconscious, reflecting traditional and unexamined habits of thought, keeps up barriers that must come down if equal opportunity and nondiscrimination are ever genuinely to become this country's law and practice.

Given this history and its practical consequences, Congress surely can conclude that a carefully designed affirmative action program may help to realize, finally, the "equal protection of the laws" the Fourteenth Amendment has promised since 1868.

II

The lead opinion uses one term, "strict scrutiny," to describe the standard of judicial review for all governmental classifications by race. But that opinion's elaboration strongly suggests that the strict standard announced is indeed "fatal" for classifications burdening groups that have suffered discrimination in our society. That seems to me, and, I believe, to the Court, the enduring lesson one should draw from Korematsu v. United States, 323 U.S. 214 (1944). . . . A *Korematsu*-type classification, as I read the opinions in this case, will never again survive scrutiny. . . .

For a classification made to hasten the day when "we are just one race," (Scalia, J., concurring in part and concurring in judgment), however, the lead opinion has dispelled the notion that "strict scrutiny" is "'fatal in fact.'" . . . Properly, a majority of the Court calls for review that is searching, in order to ferret out classifications in reality malign, but masquerading as benign. The Court's once lax review of sex-based classifications demonstrates the need for such suspicion. See, e.g., Hoyt v. Florida, 368 U.S. 57, 60 (1961) (upholding women's "privilege" of automatic exemption from jury service). . . .

Close review also is in order for this further reason. . . . [S]ome members of the historically favored race can be hurt by catch-up mechanisms designed to cope with the lingering effects of entrenched racial subjugation. Court review can ensure that preferences are not so large as to trammel unduly upon the opportunities of others or interfere too harshly with legitimate expectations of persons in once-preferred groups. . . .

* * *

While I would not disturb the programs challenged in this case, and would leave their improvement to the political branches, I see today's decision as one that allows our precedent to evolve, still to be informed by and responsive to changing conditions.

Miller v. Johnson

___ U.S. ___, 115 S.Ct. 2475, 132 L.Ed.2d 762 (1995).

[The Report in This Case Appears Infra at p. 962.]

RACIAL GERRYMANDERING AND THE VOTING RIGHTS ACT

[This Note Appears Infra at p. 974.]

F. CLASSIFICATIONS DISADVANTAGING ALIENS

Graham v. Richardson

403 U.S. 365, 91 S.Ct. 1848, 29 L.Ed.2d 534 (1971).

Mr. Justice Blackmun delivered the opinion of the Court.

These are welfare cases. They provide yet another aspect of the widening litigation in this area. The issue here is whether the Equal Protection Clause of the Fourteenth Amendment prevents a State from conditioning welfare benefits either (a) upon the beneficiary's possession of United States citizenship, or (b) if the beneficiary is an alien, upon his having resided in this country for a specified number of years. . . .

I.

. . .

[Aliens denied welfare benefits challenged an Arizona law that provided welfare to citizens but not to aliens unless they had resided in the United States for 15 years and a Pennsylvania law that excluded aliens from certain state funded welfare benefits. In each case a three-judge district court ruled that the statute violated equal protection.]

II.

The appellants argue initially that the States, consistent with the Equal Protection Clause, may favor United States citizens over aliens in the distribution of welfare benefits. It is said that this distinction involves no "invidious discrimination" . . . for the State is not discriminating with respect to race or nationality.

The Fourteenth Amendment provides, "[N]or shall any State deprive any person of life, liberty, or property, without due process of law; nor deny to any person within its jurisdiction the equal protection of the laws." It has long been settled, and it is not disputed here, that the term "person" in this context encompasses lawfully admitted resident aliens as well as citizens of the United States and entitles both citizens and aliens to the equal protection of the laws of the State in which they reside. Yick Wo v. Hopkins, 118 U.S. 356, 369 (1886); Truax v. Raich, 239 U.S. 33, 39 (1915); Takahashi v. Fish & Game Commission, 334 U.S., at 420. Nor is it disputed that the Arizona and Pennsylvania statutes in question create two classes of needy persons, indistinguishable except with respect to whether they are or are not citizens of this country. Otherwise qualified United States citizens living in Arizona are entitled to federally funded categorical assistance benefits without regard to length of national residency, but aliens must have lived in this country for 15 years in order to qualify for aid. United States citizens living in Pennsylvania, unable to meet the requirements for federally funded benefits, may be eligible for state supported general assistance, but resident aliens as a class are precluded from that assistance.

Under traditional equal protection principles, a State retains broad discretion to classify as long as its classification has a reasonable basis.... This is so in "the area of economics and social welfare." Dandridge v. Williams, 397 U.S. 471, 485 (1970). But the Court's decisions have established that classifications based on alienage, like those based on nationality or race, are inherently suspect and subject to close judicial scrutiny. Aliens as a class are a prime example of a "discrete and insular" minority (see United States v. Carolene Products Co., 304 U.S. 144, 152–153 n. 4 (1938)) for whom such heightened judicial solicitude is appropriate. Accordingly, it was said in Takahashi, 334 U.S., at 420, that "... the power of a state to apply its laws exclusively to its alien inhabitants as a class is confined within narrow limits."

Arizona and Pennsylvania seek to justify their restrictions on the eligibility of aliens for public assistance solely on the basis of a State's "special public interest" in favoring its own citizens over aliens in the distribution of limited resources such as welfare benefits....

... [W]e conclude that a State's desire to preserve limited welfare benefits for its own citizens is inadequate to justify Pennsylvania's making noncitizens ineligible for public assistance, and Arizona's restricting benefits to citizens and longtime resident aliens....

. . .

We agree with the three-judge court in the Pennsylvania case that the "justification of limiting expenses is particularly inappropriate and unreasonable when the discriminated class consists of aliens...." There can be no "special public interest" in tax revenues to which aliens have contributed on an equal basis with the residents of the State.

Accordingly, we hold that a state statute that denies welfare benefits to resident aliens and one that denies them to aliens who have not resided in the United States for a specified number of years violates the Equal Protection Clause.

III.

An additional reason why the state statutes at issue in these cases do not withstand constitutional scrutiny emerges from the area of federal-state relations. The National Government has "broad constitutional powers in determining what aliens shall be admitted to the United States, the period they may remain, regulation of their conduct before naturalization, and the terms and conditions of their naturalization." Takahashi v. Fish & Game Commission, 334 U.S., at 419; Hines v. Davidowitz, 312 U.S. 52, 66 (1941); see also Chinese Exclusion Case, 130 U.S. 581 (1889); United States ex rel. Turner v. Williams, 194 U.S. 279 (1904); Fong Yue Ting v. United States, 149 U.S. 698 (1893); Harisiades v. Shaughnessy, 342 U.S. 580 (1952). Pursuant to that power, Congress has provided, as part of a comprehensive plan for the regulation of immigration and naturalization, that "[A]liens who are paupers, professional beggars, or vagrants" or aliens who "are likely at any time to become public charges" shall be excluded from admission into the United States, 8 U.S.C. §§ 1182(a)(8) and 1182(a)(15), and that any alien lawfully admitted shall be deported who "has within five years after entry become a public charge from causes not affirmatively shown to have arisen after entry...." 8 U.S.C. § 1251(a)(8). Admission of aliens likely to become public charges may be conditioned upon the posting of a bond or cash deposit. 8 U.S.C. § 1138. But Congress has not seen fit to impose any burden or restriction on aliens who become indigent after their entry into the United States. Rather, it has broadly declared that "All persons within the jurisdiction of the United States shall have the same right in every State and Territory ... to the full and equal benefit of all laws and proceedings for the security of persons and property as is enjoyed by white citizens...." 42 U.S.C. § 1981. The protection of this statute has been held to extend to aliens as well as to citizens. *Takahashi*.... Moreover, this Court has made it clear that, whatever may be the scope of the constitutional right of interstate travel, aliens lawfully within this country have a right to enter and abide in any State in the Union "on an equality of legal privileges with all citizens under nondiscriminatory laws." *Takahashi*....

State laws that restrict the eligibility of aliens for welfare benefits merely because of their alienage conflict with these overriding national policies in an area constitutionally entrusted to the Federal Government.... State alien residency requirements, that either deny welfare benefits to noncitizens or condition them on longtime residency, equate with the assertion of a right, inconsistent with federal policy, to deny entrance and abode. Since such laws encroach upon exclusive federal power, they are constitutionally impermissible.

. . .

The judgments appealed from are affirmed.

It is so ordered.

Mr. Justice Harlan joins in Parts III and IV of the Court's opinion, and in the judgment of the Court.

Bernal v. Fainter

467 U.S. 216, 104 S.Ct. 2312, 81 L.Ed.2d 175 (1984).

Justice Marshall delivered the opinion of the Court.

The question ... is whether a statute of the State of Texas violates the Equal Protection Clause of the Fourteenth Amendment ... by denying aliens the opportunity to become notaries public. The Court of Appeals for the Fifth Circuit held that the statute does not offend the Equal Protection Clause. We ... reverse.

I

Petitioner, a native of Mexico, is a resident alien who has lived in the United States since 1961. He works as a paralegal for Texas Rural Legal Aid, Inc., helping migrant farm workers on employment and civil rights matters. In order to administer oaths to these workers and to notarize their statements for use in civil litigation, petitioner applied in 1978 to become a notary public. Under Texas law, notaries public authenticate written instruments, administer oaths, and take out-of-court depositions. The Texas Secretary of State denied petitioner's application because he failed to satisfy the statutory requirement that a notary public be a citizen of the United States. Tex.Civ.Stat.Ann., Art. 5949(2).... After an unsuccessful administrative appeal, petitioner brought suit in the federal district court, claiming that the citizenship requirement mandated by Article 5942(2) violated the federal Constitution.

The District Court ruled in favor of petitioner.... A divided panel of the Court of Appeals for the Fifth Circuit reversed, concluding that the proper standard for review was the rational relationship test and that Article 5949(2) satisfied that test because it "bears a rational relationship to the state's interest in the proper and orderly handling of a countless variety of legal documents of importance to the state." Vargas v. Strake, 710 F.2d 190, 195 (C.A.5 1983).

II

As a general matter, a State law that discriminates on the basis of alienage can be sustained only if it can withstand strict judicial scrutiny. In order to withstand strict scrutiny, the law must advance a compelling State interest by the least restrictive means available. Applying this principle, we have invalidated an array of State statutes that denied aliens the right to pursue various occupations. In Sugarman v. Dougall, 413 U.S. 634 (1973), we struck down a State statute barring aliens from employment in permanent positions in the competitive class of the State civil service. In In re Griffiths, 413 U.S. 717 (1973), we nullified a State law excluding aliens from eligibility for membership in the State bar. And in Examining Board v. Flores de Otero, 426 U.S. 572 (1976), we voided a State law that excluded aliens from the practice of civil engineering.

We have, however, developed a narrow exception to the rule that discrimination based on alienage triggers strict scrutiny. This exception has been labelled the "political function" exception and applies to laws that exclude aliens from positions intimately related to the process of democratic self-government. The contours of the "political function" exception are outlined by our prior decisions. In Foley v. Connelie, 435 U.S. 291 (1978), we held that a State may require police to be citizens because, in performing a fundamental obligation of government, police "are clothed with authority to exercise an almost infinite variety of discretionary powers" often involving the most sensitive areas of daily life. In Ambach v. Norwick, 441 U.S. 68 (1979), we held that a State may bar aliens who have not declared their intent to become citizens from teaching in the public schools because teachers, like police, possess a high degree of responsibility and discretion in the fulfillment of a basic governmental obligation. They have direct, day-to-day contact with students, exercise unsupervised discretion over them, act as role models and influence their students about the government and the political process. Finally, in Cabell v. Chavez–Salido, 454 U.S. 432 (1982), we held that a State may bar aliens from positions as probation officers because they, like police and teachers, routinely exercise discretionary power, involving a basic governmental function, that places them in a position of direct authority over other individuals.

The rationale behind the political function exception is that within broad boundaries a State may establish its own form of government and limit the right to govern to those who are full-fledged members of the political community. Some public positions are so closely bound up with the formulation and implementation of self-government that the State is permitted to exclude from those positions persons outside the political community, hence persons who have not become part of the process of democratic self-determination.

> "The exclusion of aliens from basic governmental processes is not a deficiency in the democratic system but a necessary consequence of the community's process of political self-definition. Self-government, whether direct or through representatives, begins by defining the scope of the community of the governed and thus of the governors as well: Aliens are by definition those outside of this community."

We have therefore lowered our standard of review when evaluating the validity of exclusions that entrust only to citizens important elective and nonelective positions whose operations "go to the heart of representative government." Sugarman v. Dougall, supra, 413 U.S., at 647. "While not retreating from the position that restrictions on lawfully resident aliens that primarily affect economic interests are subject to heightened judicial scrutiny ... we have concluded that strict scrutiny is out of place when the restriction primarily serves a political function...." Cabell v. Chavez–Salido, supra, 454 U.S., at 439.

To determine whether a restriction based on alienage fits within the narrow political function exception, we devised in *Cabell* a two-part test.

> "First, the specificity of the classification will be examined: a classification that is substantially overinclusive or underinclusive tends to undercut the governmental claim that the classification serves legitimate political ends.... Second, even if the classification is sufficiently tailored, it may be applied in the particular case only to 'persons holding state elective or important nonelective executive, legislative, and judicial positions,' those officers who 'participate directly in the formulation, execution, or review of broad public policy' and hence 'perform functions that go right to the heart of representative government.' "[7]

III

We now turn to Article 5949(2) to determine whether it satisfies the *Cabell* test. The statute provides that "[t]o be eligible for appointment as a Notary Public, a person shall be a resident citizen of the United States and of this state ..." Unlike the statute invalidated in *Sugarman,* Article 5949(2) does not indiscriminately sweep within its ambit a wide range of offices and occupations but specifies only one particular post with respect to which the State asserts a right to exclude aliens. Clearly, then, the statute is not overinclusive; it applies narrowly to only one category of persons: those wishing to obtain appointments as notaries. Less clear is whether Article 5942(2) is fatally underinclusive. Texas does not require court reporters to be United States citizens even though they perform some of the same services as notaries. Nor does Texas require that its Secretary of State be a citizen, even though he holds the highest appointive position in the State and performs many important functions, including supervision of the licensing of all notaries public. We need not decide this issue, however, because of our decision with respect to the second prong of the *Cabell* test.

In support of the proposition that notaries public fall within that category of officials who perform functions that "go to the heart of representative government," the State emphasizes that notaries are designated as public officers by the Texas Constitution. Texas maintains that this designation indicates that the State views notaries as important officials occupying posts central to the State's definition of itself as a political community. This Court, however, has never deemed the *source* of a position—whether it derives from a State's statute or its Constitution—as the dispositive factor in determining whether a State may entrust the position only to citizens. Rather, this Court has always looked to the actual *function* of the position as the dispositive factor.

---

[7] We emphasize, as we have in the past, that the political-function exception must be narrowly construed; otherwise the exception will swallow the rule and depreciate the significance that should attach to the designa- tion of a group as a "discrete and insular" minority for whom heightened judicial solicitude is appropriate. See Nyquist v. Mauclet, 432 U.S. 1, 11 (1977).

The focus of our inquiry has been whether a position was such that the officeholder would necessarily exercise broad discretionary power over the formulation or execution of public policies importantly affecting the citizen population—power of the sort that a self-governing community could properly entrust only to full-fledged members of that community. As the Court noted in *Cabell,* in determining whether the function of a particular position brings the position within the narrow ambit of the exception, "the Court will look to the importance of the function as a factor giving substance to the concept of democratic self-government."

The State maintains that even if the actual function of a post is the touchstone of a proper analysis, Texas notaries public should still be classified among those positions from which aliens can properly be excluded because the duties of Texas notaries entail the performance of functions sufficiently consequential to be deemed "political." . . .

We recognize the critical need for a notary's duties to be carried out correctly and with integrity. But a notary's duties, important as they are, hardly implicate responsibilities that go to the heart of representative government. Rather, these duties are essentially clerical and ministerial. In contrast to state troopers, *Foley v. Connelie,* notaries do not routinely exercise the State's monopoly of legitimate coercive force. Nor do notaries routinely exercise the wide discretion typically enjoyed by public school teachers when they present materials that educate youth respecting the information and values necessary for the maintenance of a democratic political system. See Ambach v. Norwick, 441 U.S., at 77. To be sure, considerable damage could result from the negligent or dishonest performance of a notary's duties. But the same could be said for the duties performed by cashiers, building inspectors, the janitors who clean up the offices of public officials, and numerous other categories of personnel upon whom we depend for careful, honest service. What distinguishes such personnel from those to which the political function exception is properly applied is that the latter are either invested with policy-making responsibility or broad discretion in the execution of public policy that requires the routine exercise of authority over individuals. Neither of these characteristics pertain to the functions performed by Texas notaries.

The inappropriateness of applying the political function exception to Texas notaries is further underlined by our decision in *In re Griffiths* . . . in which we subjected to strict scrutiny a Connecticut statute that prohibited non-citizens from becoming members of the State bar. Along with the usual powers and privileges accorded to members of the bar, Connecticut gave to members of its bar additional authority that encompasses the very duties performed by Texas notaries—authority to "sign writs and subpoenas, take recognizances, administer oaths and take depositions and acknowledgement of deeds." In striking down Connecticut's citizenship requirement, we concluded that "[i]t in no way denigrates a lawyer's high responsibility to observe that [these duties] hardly involve matters of state policy or acts of such unique responsibility as to entrust them only to citizens." If it is improper to apply the political function exception to a citizenship requirement governing eligibility for membership in a State bar, it would be anomalous to apply the exception to the citizenship requirement that governs eligibility to become a Texas notary. We conclude, then, that the "political function" exception is inapplicable to Article 5949(2) and that the statute is therefore subject to strict judicial scrutiny.

IV

To satisfy strict scrutiny, the State must show that Article 5949(2) furthers a compelling State interest by the least restrictive means practically available.

Respondent maintains that Article 5949(2) serves its "legitimate concern that notaries be reasonably familiar with state law and institutions" and "that notaries may be called upon years later to testify to acts they have performed." However both of these asserted justifications utterly fail to meet the stringent requirements of strict scrutiny. There is nothing in the record that indicates that resident aliens, as a class, are so incapable of familiarizing themselves with Texas law as to justify the State's absolute and class-wide exclusion. The possibility that some resident aliens are unsuitable for the position cannot justify a wholesale ban against all resident aliens. Furthermore, if the State's concern with ensuring a notary's familiarity with state law were truly "compelling," one would expect the State to give some sort of test actually measuring a person's familiarity with the law. The State, however, administers no such test. To become a notary public in Texas, one is merely required to fill out an application that lists one's name and address and that answers four questions pertaining to one's age, citizenship, residency and criminal record—nothing that reflects the State's asserted interest in insuring that notaries are familiar with Texas law. Similarly inadequate is the State's purported interest in insuring the later availability of notaries' testimony. This justification fails because the State fails to advance a factual showing that the unavailability of notaries' testimony presents a real, as opposed to a merely speculative, problem to the State. Without a factual underpinning, the State's asserted interest lacks the weight we have required of interests properly denominated as compelling.

V

We conclude that Article 5949(2) violates the Fourteenth Amendment.... Accordingly the judgment . . . is reversed, and the case is remanded for further proceedings consistent with this opinion.

Justice Rehnquist, dissenting.

I dissent for the reasons stated in my dissenting opinion in Sugarman v. Dougall, 413 U.S. 634, 649 (1973).

Mathews v. Diaz

426 U.S. 67, 96 S.Ct. 1883, 48 L.Ed.2d 478 (1976).

Mr. Justice Stevens delivered the opinion of the Court.

The question presented by the Secretary's appeal is whether Congress may condition an alien's eligibility for participation in a federal medical insurance program on continuous residence in the United States for a five-year period and admission for permanent residence. The District Court held that the first condition was unconstitutional and that it could not be severed from the second. Since we conclude that both conditions are constitutional, we reverse.

Each of the appellees is a resident alien who was lawfully admitted to the United States less than five years ago. Appellees Diaz and Clara are Cuban refugees who remain in this country at the discretion of the Attorney General; appellee Espinosa has been admitted for permanent residence. All three are over 65 years old and have been denied enrollment in the Medicare Part B supplemental medical insurance program established by . . . the Social Security Act.... They brought this action to challenge the statutory basis for that denial. Specifically, they attack 42 U.S.C. § 1395o(2), which grants eligibility to resident citizens who are 65 or older but denies eligibility to such aliens unless they have been admitted for permanent residence and also have resided in the United States for at least five years. . . .

. . .

II.

There are literally millions of aliens within the jurisdiction of the United States. The Fifth Amendment, as well as the Fourteenth Amendment, protects every one of these persons from deprivation of life, liberty or property without due process of law. Wong Yang Sung v. McGrath, 339 U.S. 33, 48–51; Wong Wing v. United States, 163 U.S. 228, 238; see Russian Volunteer Fleet v. United States, 282 U.S. 481, 489. Even one whose presence in this country is unlawful, involuntary, or transitory, is entitled to that constitutional protection. *Wong Yang Sung,* supra; *Wong Wing,* supra.

The fact that all persons, aliens and citizens alike, are protected by the Due Process Clause does not lead to the further conclusion that all aliens are entitled to enjoy all the advantages of citizenship or, indeed, to the conclusion that all aliens must be placed in a single homogenous legal classification. For a host of constitutional and statutory provisions rest on the premise that a legitimate distinction between citizens and aliens may justify attributes and benefits for one class not accorded to the other;[12] and the class of aliens is itself a heterogenous multitude of persons with a wide-ranging variety of ties to this country.

In the exercise of its broad power over naturalization and immigration, Congress regularly makes rules that would be unacceptable if applied to citizens. The exclusion of aliens and the reservation of the power to deport have no permissible counterpart in the Federal Government's power to regulate the conduct of its own citizenry. The fact that an act of Congress treats aliens differently from citizens does not in itself imply that such disparate treatment is "invidious."

In particular, the fact that Congress has provided some welfare benefits for citizens does not require it to provide like benefits for *all aliens*. Neither the overnight visitor, the unfriendly agent of a hostile foreign power, the resident diplomat, nor the illegal entrant, can advance even a colorable constitutional claim to a share in the bounty that a conscientious sovereign makes available to its own citizens and *some* of its guests. The decision to share that bounty with our guests may take into account the character of the relationship between the alien and this country: Congress may decide that as the alien's tie grows stronger, so does the strength of his claim to an equal share of that munificence.

The real question presented by this case is not whether discrimination between citizens and aliens is permissible; rather, it is whether the statutory discrimination *within* the class of aliens—allowing benefits to some aliens but not to others—is permissible. We turn to that question.

---

[12] The Constitution protects the privileges and immunities only of citizens, Amend. XIV, § 1; see Art. IV, § 2, cl. 1, and the right to vote only of citizens. Amends. XV, XIX, XXIV, XXVI. It requires that Representatives have been citizens for seven years, Art. I, § 2, cl. 2, and Senators citizens for nine, Art. I, § 3, cl. 3, and that the President be a "natural born Citizen." Art. II, § 1, cl. 5.

A multitude of federal statutes distinguish between citizens and aliens. The whole of Title 8 of the United States Code, regulating aliens and nationality, is founded on the legitimacy of distinguishing citizens and aliens. A variety of other federal statutes provide for disparate treatment of aliens and citizens. . . .

III.

For reasons long recognized as valid, the responsibility for regulating the relationship between the United States and our alien visitors has been committed to the political branches of the Federal Government. Since decisions in these matters may implicate our relations with foreign powers, and since a wide variety of classifications must be defined in the light of changing political and economic circumstances, such decisions are frequently of a character more appropriate to either the legislature or the executive than to the judiciary. This very case illustrates the need for flexibility in policy choices rather than the rigidity often characteristic of constitutional adjudication. Appellees Diaz and Clara are but two of over 440,000 Cuban refugees who arrived in the United States between 1961 and 1972. And the Cuban parolees are but one of several categories of aliens who have been admitted in order to make a humane response to a natural catastrophe or an international political situation. Any rule of constitutional law that would inhibit the flexibility of the political branches of government to respond to changing world conditions should be adopted only with the greatest caution. The reasons that preclude judicial review of political questions also dictate a narrow standard of review of decisions made by the Congress or the President in the area of immigration and naturalization.

Since it is obvious that Congress has no constitutional duty to provide *all aliens* with the welfare benefits provided to citizens, the party challenging the constitutionality of the particular line Congress has drawn has the burden of advancing principled reasoning that will at once invalidate that line and yet tolerate a different line separating some aliens from others. In this case the appellees have challenged two requirements, first that the alien be admitted as a permanent resident, and second that his residence be of a duration of at least five years. But if these requirements were eliminated, surely Congress would at least require that the alien's entry be lawful; even then, unless mere transients are to be held constitutionally entitled to benefits, *some* durational requirement would certainly be appropriate. In short, it is unquestionably reasonable for Congress to make an alien's eligibility depend on both the character and the duration of his residence. Since neither requirement is wholly irrational, this case essentially involves nothing more than a claim that it would have been more reasonable for Congress to select somewhat different requirements of the same kind.

We may assume that the five-year line drawn by Congress is longer than necessary to protect the fiscal integrity of the program. We may also assume that unnecessary hardship is incurred by persons just short of qualifying. But it remains true that some line is essential, that any line must produce some harsh and apparently arbitrary consequences, and, of greatest importance, that those who qualify under the test Congress has chosen may reasonably be presumed to have a greater affinity to the United States than those who do not. In short, citizens and those who are most like citizens qualify. Those who are less like citizens do not.

The task of classifying persons for medical benefits, like the task of drawing lines for federal tax purposes, inevitably requires that some persons who have an almost equally strong claim to favored treatment be placed on different sides of the line; the differences between the eligible and the ineligible are differences in degree rather than differences in the character of their respective claims. When this kind of policy choice must be made, we are especially reluctant to question the exercise of congressional judgment. In this case, since appellees have not identified a principled basis for prescribing a different standard than the one selected by Congress, they have, in effect, merely invited us to substitute our judgment for that of Congress in deciding which aliens shall be eligible to participate in the supplementary insurance program on the same conditions as citizens. We decline the invitation.

IV.

The cases on which appellees rely are consistent with our conclusion that this statutory classification does not deprive them of liberty or property without due process of law.

Graham v. Richardson, 403 U.S. 365, provides the strongest support for appellees' position. That case holds that state statutes that deny welfare benefits to resident aliens, or to aliens not meeting a requirement of durational residence within the United States, violate the Equal Protection Clause of the Fourteenth Amendment and encroach upon the exclusive federal power over the entrance and residence of aliens. Of course, the latter ground of decision actually supports our holding today that it is the business of the political branches of the Federal Government, rather than that of either the States or the federal judiciary, to regulate the conditions of entry and residence of aliens. The equal protection analysis also involves significantly different considerations because it concerns the relationship between aliens and the States rather than between aliens and the Federal Government.

Insofar as state welfare policy is concerned, there is little, if any, basis for treating persons who are citizens of another State differently from persons who are citizens of another country. Both groups are noncitizens as far as the State's interests in administering its welfare programs are concerned. Thus, a division by a State of the category of persons who are not citizens of that State into subcategories of United States citizens and aliens has no apparent justification, whereas, a comparable classification by the Federal Government is a routine and normally legitimate part of its business. Furthermore, whereas the Constitution inhibits every State's power to restrict travel across its own borders, Congress is explicitly empowered to exercise that type of control over travel across the borders of the United States.

. . .

We hold that § 1395o(2)(B) has not deprived appellees of liberty or property without due process of law.

The judgment of the District Court is reversed.

G.   WHAT OTHER CLASSIFICATIONS WILL PROVOKE HEIGHTENED SCRUTINY?

1.   CLASSIFICATIONS DISADVANTAGING NON–MARITAL CHILDREN

THE STANDARD OF REVIEW FOR LEGITIMACY CLASSIFICATIONS

In Levy v. Louisiana, 391 U.S. 68 (1968), the Court held invalid a state statute permitting legitimate but not illegitimate children to sue for wrongful death of their mother. The Court indicated that the classification did not meet the lowest standard of review. "Legitimacy or illegitimacy of birth has no relation to the nature of the wrong allegedly inflicted on the mother." In Labine v. Vincent, 401 U.S. 532 (1971), the Court upheld a statute under which illegitimate children acknowledged but not legitimated by the father could not take by intestate succession from the father. The next year, in Weber v. Aetna Cas. and Sur. Co., 406 U.S. 164 (1972), the Court held invalid a statute that did not permit dependent, unacknowledged children of a father to recover workers' compensation benefits for death of the father, saying that the classification "is justified by no legitimate state interest, compelling or otherwise." In the next three cases to come before it the Court invalidated legitimacy classifications: Gomez v. Perez, 409 U.S. 535 (1973) (father obligated to support legitimate but not illegitimate children); New Jersey Welfare Rights Organization v. Cahill, 411 U.S. 619 (1973) (state welfare statute); Jimenez v. Weinberger, 417 U.S. 628 (1974) (federal classification that did not permit some illegitimate children to obtain benefits under parent's disability insurance).

In Mathews v. Lucas, 427 U.S. 495 (1976), the Court upheld a provision of the Social Security Act that gave a survivor's benefit to a minor dependent child of a deceased parent, but extended a presumption of dependency to all children except certain classes of illegitimate children. Justice Blackmun, speaking for the Court, said that the trial judge was wrong in treating the classification as suspect requiring strict scrutiny:

"It is true, of course, that the legal status of illegitimacy, however defined, is like race or national origin, a characteristic determined by causes not within the control of the illegitimate individual, and it bears no relation to the individual's ability to participate in and contribute to society. The Court recognized in *Weber* that visiting condemnation upon the child in order to express society's disapproval of the parents' liaisons

'is illogical and unjust. Moreover, imposing disabilities on the illegitimate child is contrary to the basic concept of our system that legal burdens should bear some relationship to individual responsibility or wrongdoing. Obviously, no child is responsible for his birth and penalizing the illegitimate child is an ineffectual—as well as an unjust—way of deterring the parent.' ...

"But where the law is arbitrary in such a way, we have had no difficulty in finding the discrimination impermissible on less demanding standards than those advocated here. New Jersey Welfare Rights Organization v. Cahill, 411 U.S. 619 (1973); Richardson v. Davis, 409 U.S. 1069 (1972); Richardson v. Griffin, 409 U.S. 1069 (1972); *Weber,* supra; Levy v. Louisiana, 391 U.S. 68 (1968). And such irrationality in some classifications does not in itself demonstrate that other, possibly rational, distinctions made in part on the basis of legitimacy are inherently untenable. Moreover, while the law has long placed the illegitimate child in an inferior position relative to the legitimate in certain circumstances, particularly in regard to obligations of support or other aspects of family law, see generally, e.g., H. Krause, *Illegitimacy: Law and Social Policy* 21–42 (1971); Gray & Rudovsky, *The Court Acknowledges the Illegitimate: Levy v. Louisiana and Glona v. American Guarantee & Liability Insurance Co.,* 118 U.Pa.L.Rev. 1, 19–38 (1969), perhaps in part because the roots of the discrimination rest in the conduct of the parents rather than the child, and perhaps in part because illegitimacy does not carry an obvious badge, as race or sex do, this discrimination against illegitimates has never approached the severity or pervasiveness of the historic legal and political discrimination against women and Negroes. See Frontiero v. Richardson, 411 U.S. 677, 684–686 (1973) (plurality opinion).

"We therefore adhere to our earlier view, see Labine v. Vincent, 401 U.S. 532 (1971), that the Act's discrimination between individuals on the basis of their legitimacy does not 'command extraordinary protection from the majoritarian political process,' San Antonio Independent School District v. Rodriguez, 411 U.S. 1, 28 (1973), which our most exacting scrutiny would entail."

Later in the opinion he referred to the showing necessary to demonstrate that the relationship between the statutory classifications and the likelihood of dependency was not sufficiently material: "[T]he scrutiny by which their showing is to be judged is not a toothless one" but "the burden remains upon the appellees to demonstrate the insubstantiality of that relation."

Lalli v. Lalli

439 U.S. 259, 99 S.Ct. 518, 58 L.Ed.2d 503 (1978).

Mr. Justice Powell announced the judgment of the Court in an opinion, in which The Chief Justice and Mr. Justice Stewart join.

This case presents a challenge to the constitutionality of § 4–1.2 of New York's Estates, Powers, and Trusts Law, which requires illegitimate children who would inherit from their fathers by intestate succession to provide a particular form of proof of paternity. Legitimate children are not subject to the same requirement.

I.

Appellant Robert Lalli claims to be the illegitimate son of Mario Lalli who died intestate on January 7, 1973, in the State of New York. Appellant's mother, who died in 1968, never was married to Mario. After Mario's widow, Rosamond Lalli, was appointed administratrix of her husband's estate, appellant petitioned the Surrogate's Court for Westchester County for a compulsory accounting, claiming that he and his sister Maureen Lalli were entitled to inherit from Mario as his children. Rosamond Lalli opposed the petition. She argued that even if Robert and Maureen were Mario's children, they were not lawful distributees of the state because they had failed to comply with § 4–1.2, which provides in part:

"An illegitimate child is the legitimate child of his father so that he and his issue inherit from his father if a court of competent jurisdiction has, during the lifetime of the father, made an order of filiation declaring paternity in a proceeding instituted during the pregnancy of the mother or within two years from the birth of the child."

Appellant conceded that he had not obtained an order of filiation during his putative father's lifetime. He contended, however, that § 4–1.2, by imposing this requirement, discriminated against him on the basis of his illegitimate birth in violation of the Equal Protection Clause of the Fourteenth Amendment. Appellant tendered certain evidence of his relationship with Mario Lalli, including a notarized document in which Lalli, in consenting to appellant's marriage, referred to him as "my son," and several affidavits by persons who stated that Lalli had acknowledged openly and often that Robert and Maureen were his children.

The Surrogate's Court ... ruled that appellant was properly excluded as a distributee of Lalli's estate and therefore lacked status to petition for a compulsory accounting.

On direct appeal the New York Court of Appeals affirmed....

Appellant appealed the Court of Appeals' decision to this Court. While that case was pending here, we decided Trimble v. Gordon, 430 U.S. 762 (1977).

Because the issues in these two cases were similar in some respects, we vacated and remanded to permit further consideration in light of *Trimble.*

On remand, the New York Court of Appeals, with one judge dissenting, adhered to its former disposition. . . .

Appellant again sought review here. . . . We now affirm.

II.

We begin our analysis with *Trimble.* At issue in that case was the constitutionality of an Illinois statute providing that a child born out of wedlock could inherit from his intestate father only if the father had "acknowledged" the child and the child had been legitimated by the intermarriage of the parents. The appellant in *Trimble* was a child born out of wedlock whose father had neither acknowledged her nor married her mother. He had, however, been found to be her father in a judicial decree ordering him to contribute to her support. When the father died intestate, the child was excluded as a distributee because the statutory requirements for inheritance had not been met.

We concluded that the Illinois statute discriminated against illegitimate children in a manner prohibited by the Equal Protection Clause. Although, as decided in Mathews v. Lucas, 427 U.S. 495 (1976), and reaffirmed in *Trimble,* classifications based on illegitimacy are not subject to "strict scrutiny," they nevertheless are invalid under the Fourteenth Amendment if they are not substantially related to permissible state interests. [W]e found that the Illinois law failed that test.

Two state interests were proposed which the statute was said to foster: the encouragement of legitimate family relationships and the maintenance of an accurate and efficient method of disposing of an intestate decedent's property. Granting that the State was appropriately concerned with the integrity of the family unit, we viewed the statute as bearing "only the most attenuated relationship to the asserted goal." We again rejected the argument that "persons will shun illicit relationships because the offspring may not one day reap the benefits" that would accrue to them were they legitimate. Weber v. Aetna Casualty & Surety Co., 406 U.S. 164 (1972). The statute therefore was not defensible as an incentive to enter legitimate family relationships.

Illinois' interest in safeguarding the orderly disposition of property at death was more relevant to the statutory classification. We recognized that devising "an appropriate legal framework" in the furtherance of that interest "is a matter particularly within the competence of the individual States." An important aspect of that framework is a response to the often difficult problem of proving the paternity of illegitimate children and the related danger of spurious claims against intestate estates. These difficulties, we said, "might justify a more demanding standard for illegitimate children claiming under their fathers' estates than that required either for illegitimate children claiming under their mothers' estates or for legitimate children generally."

The Illinois statute, however, was constitutionally flawed, because, by insisting upon not only an acknowledgment by the father, but also the marriage of the parents, it excluded "at least some significant categories of illegitimate children of intestate men [whose] inheritance rights can be recognized without jeopardizing the orderly settlement of estates or the dependability of titles of property passing under intestacy laws." We concluded that the Equal Protection Clause required that a statute placing exceptional burdens on illegitimate children in the furtherance of proper State objectives must be more "carefully tuned to alternative considerations," than was true of the broad disqualification in the Illinois law.

III.

The New York statute, enacted in 1965, was intended to soften the rigors of previous law which permitted illegitimate children to inherit only from their mothers. By lifting the absolute bar to paternal inheritance, § 4–1.2 tended to achieve its desired effect. As in *Trimble,* however, the question before us is whether the remaining statutory obstacles to inheritance by illegitimate children can be squared with the Equal Protection Clause.

A.

At the outset we observe that § 4–1.2 is different in important respects from the statutory provision overturned in *Trimble.* The Illinois statute required, in addition to the father's acknowledgment of paternity, the legitimation of the child through the intermarriage of the parents as an absolute precondition to inheritance. This combination of requirements eliminated "the possibility of a middle ground between the extremes of complete exclusion and case-by-case determination of paternity." *Trimble,* supra. As illustrated by the facts in *Trimble,* even a judicial declaration of paternity was insufficient to permit inheritance.

Under § 4–1.2, by contrast, the marital status of the parents is irrelevant. The single requirement at issue here is an evidentiary one—that the paternity of the father be declared in a judicial proceeding sometime before his death. The child need not have been legitimated in order to inherit from his father. Had the appellant in *Trimble* been governed by § 4–1.2, she would have been a distributee of her father's estate.

A related difference between the two provisions pertains to the state interests said to be served by them. The Illinois law was defended, in part, as a means of encouraging legitimate family relationships. No such justification has been offered in support of § 4–1.2. The Court of Appeals disclaimed that the purpose of the statute, "even in small part, was to discourage illegitimacy, to mold human conduct or to set societal norms." The absence in § 4–1.2 of any requirement that the parents intermarry or otherwise legitimate a child born out of wedlock and our review of the legislative history of the statute confirm this view.

Our inquiry, therefore, is focused narrowly. We are asked to decide whether the discrete procedural demands that § 4–1.2 places on illegitimate children bear an evident and substantial relation to the particular state interests this statute is designed to serve.

B.

The primary state goal underlying the challenged aspects of § 4–1.2 is to provide for the just and orderly disposition of property at death. We long have recognized that this is an area with which the States have an interest of considerable magnitude.

This interest is directly implicated in paternal inheritance by illegitimate children because of the peculiar problems of proof that are involved. Establishing maternity is seldom difficult. . . . Proof of paternity, by contrast, frequently is difficult when the father is not part of a formal family unit. . . .

Thus, a number of problems arise that counsel against treating illegitimate children identically to all other heirs of an intestate father. These were the subject of a comprehensive study by the Temporary State Commission on the Modernization, Revision and Simplification of the Law of Estates. This group, known as the Bennett Commission, consisted of individuals experienced in the practical problems of estate administration. The Commission issued its report and recommendations to the Legislature in 1965. The statute now codified as § 4–1.2 was included.

Although the overarching purpose of the proposed statute was "to alleviate the plight of the illegitimate child," the Bennett Commission considered it necessary to impose the strictures of § 4–1.2 in order to mitigate serious difficulties in the administration of the estates of both testate and intestate decedents. The Commission's perception of some of these difficulties was described by Surrogate Sobel, a member of "the busiest [surrogate's] court in the State measured by the number of intestate estates which traffic daily through this court," and a participant in some of the Commission's deliberations:

> "An illegitimate, if made an unconditional distributee in intestacy, must be served with process in the estate of his parent or if he is a distributee in the estate of the kindred of a parent. . . . And, in probating the will of his parent (though not named a beneficiary) or in probating the will of any person who makes a class disposition to 'issue' of such parent, the illegitimate must be served with process. . . . How does one cite and serve an illegitimate of whose existence neither family nor personal representative may be aware? And of greatest concern, how achieve finality of decree in *any* estate when there always exists the possibility however remote of a secret illegitimate lurking in the buried past of a parent or an ancestor of a class of beneficiaries? . . . ."

Even where an individual claiming to be the illegitimate child of a deceased man makes himself known, the difficulties facing an estate are likely to persist. Because of the particular problems of proof, spurious claims may be difficult to expose. The Bennett Commission therefore sought to protect "innocent adults and those rightfully interested in their estates from fraudulent claims of heirship and harassing litigation instituted by those seeking to establish themselves as illegitimate heirs."

C.

As the State's interests are substantial, we now consider the means adopted by New York to further these interests. In order to avoid the problems described above, the Commission recommended a requirement designed to ensure the accurate resolution of claims of paternity and to minimize the potential for disruption of estate administration. Accuracy is enhanced by placing paternity disputes in a judicial forum during the lifetime of the father. . . .

The administration of an estate will be facilitated, and the possibility of delay and uncertainty minimized, where the entitlement of an illegitimate child to notice and participation is a matter of judicial record before the administration commences. Fraudulent assertions of paternity will be much less likely to succeed, or even to arise, where the proof is put before a court of law at a time when the putative father is available to respond, rather than first brought to light when the distribution of the assets of an estate is in the offing.[8]

_____

[8] In affirming the judgment below, we do not, of course, restrict a State's freedom to require proof of paternity by means other than a judicial decree. Thus a State may prescribe any *formal* method of proof, whether it be similar to that provided by § 4–1.2 or

Appellant contends that § 4–1.2, like the statute at issue in *Trimble,* excludes "significant categories of illegitimate children" who could be allowed to inherit "without jeopardizing the orderly settlement" of their intestate fathers' estates. He urges that those in his position—"known" illegitimate children who, despite the absence of an order of filiation obtained during their fathers' lifetimes, can present convincing proof of paternity—cannot rationally be denied inheritance as they pose none of the risks § 4–1.2 was intended to minimize.

We do not question that there will be some illegitimate children who would be able to establish their relationship to their deceased fathers without serious disruption of the administration of estates and that, as applied to such individuals, § 4–1.2 appears to operate unfairly. But few statutory classifications are entirely free from the criticism that they sometimes produce inequitable results. Our inquiry under the Equal Protection Clause does not focus on the abstract "fairness" of a state law, but on whether the statute's relation to the state interests it is intended to promote is so tenuous that it lacks the rationality contemplated by the Fourteenth Amendment.

. . .

We conclude that the requirement imposed by § 4–1.2 on illegitimate children who would inherit from their fathers is substantially related to the important state interests the statute is intended to promote. We therefore find no violation of the Equal Protection Clause.

The judgment of the New York Court of Appeals is affirmed.

For the reasons stated in his dissent in Trimble v. Gordon, **Mr. Justice Rehnquist** concurs in the judgment of affirmance.

Mr. Justice Stewart, concurring.

It seems to me that Mr. Justice Powell's opinion convincingly demonstrates the significant differences between the New York law at issue here and the Illinois law at issue in *Trimble v. Gordon* . . . . Therefore, I cannot agree with the view expressed in the concurring opinion that *Trimble v. Gordon* is now "a derelict," or with the implication that in deciding the two cases the way it has this Court has failed to give authoritative guidance to the courts and legislatures of the several States.

Mr. Justice Blackmun, concurring in the judgment.

I agree with the result the Court has reached and concur in its judgment. I also agree with much that has been said in the plurality opinion. My point of departure, of course, is at the plurality's valiant struggle to distinguish, rather than overrule, *Trimble v. Gordon* . . . , decided just last Term, and involving a small probate estate (an automobile worth approximately $2,500) and a sad and appealing fact situation. Four Members of the Court . . . were in dissent.

I would overrule *Trimble,* but the Court refrains from doing so on the theory that the result in *Trimble* is justified because of the peculiarities of the Illinois Probate Act there under consideration. This, of course, is an explanation, but, for me, it is an unconvincing one. I therefore must regard *Trimble* as a derelict, explainable only because of the overtones of its appealing facts and offering little precedent for constitutional analysis of State intestate succession laws. If *Trimble* is not a derelict, the corresponding statutes of other States will

some other regularized procedure that would assure the authenticity of the acknowledgment.

be of questionable validity until this Court passes them, one by one, as being on the *Trimble* side of the line, or the *Vincent–Lalli* side.

Mr. Justice Brennan, with whom Mr. Justice White, Mr. Justice Marshall, and Mr. Justice Stevens join, dissenting.

Trimble v. Gordon . . . declares that the state interest in the accurate and efficient determination of paternity can be adequately served by requiring the illegitimate child to offer into evidence a "formal acknowledgment of paternity." The New York statute is inconsistent with this command. Under the New York scheme, an illegitimate child may inherit intestate only if there has been a judicial finding of paternity during the lifetime of the father.

. . .

I see no reason to retreat from . . . *Trimble v. Gordon.* The New York statute . . . like the Illinois statute in *Trimble,* excludes "forms of proof which do not compromise the State['s] interests." The statute thus discriminates against illegitimates through means not substantially related to the legitimate interests that the statute purports to promote. . . .

CLARK v. JETER, 486 U.S. 456 (1988). Under Pennsylvania law an illegitimate child must prove paternity before seeking support from his or her father. Although legitimate children could seek parental support at any time, illegitimate children were required to bring suits to establish paternity within six years of birth. The Court unanimously held that this six year limitation denied illegitimate children the equal protection of the laws.[a] Justice O'Connor's opinion said that "intermediate scrutiny . . . generally has been applied to discriminatory classifications based on sex or illegitimacy" and that "[t]o withstand intermediate scrutiny, a statutory classification must be substantially related to an important governmental objective." Relying on Mills v. Habluetzel, 456 U.S. 91 (1982), and Pickett v. Brown, 462 U.S. 1 (1983), which respectively invalidated a one-year and a two-year statute of limitations for such suits, the Court concluded that "[e]ven six years does not necessarily provide a reasonable opportunity to assert a claim on behalf of an illegitimate child" but indicated that even if six years might be reasonable that period was "not substantially related to Pennsylvania's interest in avoiding the litigation of stale or fraudulent claims." In concluding that the statute "does not withstand heightened scrutiny," the Court noted the fact that Pennsylvania places no limits on when paternity issues may be litigated in other kinds of cases, the new law extending the period to 18 years, and the availability of increasingly sophisticated scientific technology.

PARENTAL RIGHTS OF FATHERS OF ILLEGITIMATE CHILDREN

It is a common statutory pattern for the father of an illegitimate child to be given fewer parental rights than the child's mother, or than the father of a child born in wedlock or legitimated. That statutory pattern has raised substantive due process questions concerning state regulation of the relationship between parent and child, as well as questions of procedural due process and equal protection.

[a] While the paternity suit was pending in this case, Pennsylvania amended its law to conform to federal legislation requiring all states participating in the federal child support program to have procedures to establish the paternity of any child under 18. The Court declined to address a federal preemption claim, however, because it had not been adequately raised in the state courts, which applied the six-year statute of limitations to this case.

In Stanley v. Illinois, 405 U.S. 645 (1972), the unmarried parents of three children lived together for 18 years before the mother's death. Illinois law provided that illegitimate children become wards of the State upon the mother's death. The Court held that denying Stanley a hearing on his fitness as a parent denied him procedural due process and equal protection. As to the equal protection claim, "all Illinois parents are constitutionally entitled to a hearing on their fitness before their children are removed from their custody"; hence the distinction between unmarried fathers on the one hand, and unmarried mothers, married parents and divorced parents on the other, was contrary to the equal protection clause.

In Quilloin v. Walcott, 434 U.S. 246 (1978), the natural father had neither lived with the child's mother, nor had custody of the child. The child's mother consented to the child's adoption by her husband. State courts dismissed the father's objection to the adoption under a law requiring only the mother's consent for adoption of an illegitimate child. The Court's conclusion that the father had not been denied substantive due process was limited to the facts of the case—the father had not sought custody of the child, and the adoption recognized "a family unit already in existence." The Court also rejected an equal protection challenge based on the argument that a married father who was separated or divorced would have been permitted to veto the adoption. An argument that an unmarried father should, as matter of equal protection, be given the same rights as an unmarried mother, was not considered because it had not been properly presented.

That argument, however, proved crucial in Caban v. Mohammed, 441 U.S. 380 (1979). The father had lived with the children as their father in their early years. At the time of the petition for adoption by the children's mother and her husband, the father and mother were engaged in a legal battle for the children's custody. The Court held that New York's law, which permitted an unwed mother to block her child's adoption but gave no similar right to the father, was an unconstitutional distinction on the basis of gender. Although Justice Powell's opinion for the Court rejected the argument that the gender distinction could be justified by the difference in maternal and paternal roles, it conceded that the distinction could be applied constitutionally in cases of adoption at birth or in cases where the father had not participated in the rearing of the child. Chief Justice Burger, and Justices Stewart, Rehnquist and Stevens dissented.

On the same day the *Caban* case was decided, Justice Powell concurred with the dissenters in that case to sustain a distinction between unwed mothers and fathers. Parham v. Hughes, 441 U.S. 347 (1979), involved a Georgia law permitting the mother of an illegitimate child to sue for the wrongful death of a child, while denying that right to the child's father. The four *Caban* dissenters, in an opinion by Justice Stewart, argued that the gender based distinction was not invidious—the father's right to sue was not denied solely because of his male sex, but because he had taken no steps to legitimate the child. Justice Powell concurred in the result on the narrower ground that the gender-based distinction was justified by problems of proving paternity after an illegitimate child's death. Justice White's dissent, joined by Justices Brennan, Marshall and Blackmun, argued that Georgia's interest in rejecting spurious claims could not justify categorically eliminating all claims of fathers of illegitimate children "on the basis of sex."

The Court returned to the problem in Lehr v. Robertson, 463 U.S. 248 (1983). Lehr, an unmarried father, had lived with the mother before the child was born, visited the mother and child in the hospital, but thereafter had little contact, neither providing support nor offering to marry the mother. The mother married another man eight months after the child's birth and when the child was two years old the mother and her husband sought to adopt the child. Without notice to Lehr, the court granted the adoption after it had become aware that Lehr had filed a paternity and visitation proceeding in another county. Lehr sued to set aside the adoption proceeding as violating the due process and equal protection clauses. The New York courts denied his claim and the Supreme Court affirmed.

Justice Stevens, writing for the majority, noted that New York maintains a "putative father registry" in which a person claiming to be the father may enter his name and have the right to receive notice of any proceeding to adopt the child. The law also provides notice to men who have been adjudicated to be fathers, who have been identified as fathers on the child's birth certificate, who live openly with the child and the child's mother and hold themselves out as fathers, who have been identified as father by the mother in a sworn written statement, and who were married to the child's mother before the child was six months old. This law, the Court said, adequately protected the opportunity of the putative father to establish a relationship with the illegitimate child. Lehr had not complied with that statute and had not established any relationship with the child. Under these circumstances it was not a denial of due process to enter the order of adoption without notice to Lehr, even though the judge in the adoption proceeding had knowledge of the paternity petition filed by Lehr. "Since the New York statutes adequately protected appellant's inchoate interest in establishing a relationship with ... [the child], we find no merit in the claim that his constitutional rights were offended because the family court strictly complied with the notice provisions of the statute."

The Court also held that there was no denial of equal protection. It said that the parents here were in a different position than those in *Caban v. Mohammed.* Lehr never established any custodial, personal, or financial relations with the child. "If one parent has an established custodial relationship with the child and the other parent has either abandoned or never established a relationship, the Equal Protection Clause does not prevent a state from according the two parents different legal rights."

Justices White, Marshall and Blackmun dissented, arguing that it was a denial of due process to deny notice and an opportunity to be heard in an adoption proceeding to a putative father when the state has actual notice of his existence, whereabouts, and interest in the child.

In Michael H. v. Gerald D., 491 U.S. 110 (1989), the Court was confronted with a variety of constitutional challenges to a California law establishing a conclusive presumption, as against all but husband and wife, that a child born to a married woman cohabiting with her husband is a child of the marriage. The California courts had applied the presumption to bar a claim of paternity and visitation rights by Michael, a man who wished to offer blood tests showing to a 98% probability that he is the biological father of Victoria, whose mother was married to and cohabiting with her husband at Victoria's conception and 1981 birth, but who had then had an affair with, and later intermittently lived with, Michael. The child had always lived with her mother, which meant sometimes with Michael and sometimes (and eventually) with Gerald, the husband. The Court addressed Michael's procedural and substantive due process claims to a relationship with Victoria and Victoria's due process and equal protection claims to a relationship with her natural father.

Justice Scalia, joined by the Chief Justice and Justices O'Connor and Kennedy, rejected Michael's procedural due process claims on the view that conclusive presumption problems raise issues of substantive, not procedural, due process. After extended discussion, they concluded that Michael lacked "a constitutionally protected liberty interest in his relationship with Victoria[,]" at least in circumstances where "the husband and wife wish to raise her child jointly." As to Victoria, the plurality concluded that she had no "due process right to maintain a filial relationship with both Michael and Gerald[,]" because "the claim that a State must recognize multiple fatherhood has no support in the traditions or history of this country." Her claim of "a liberty interest in maintaining a filial relationship with her natural father" failed "for the same reasons" as Michael's claim. The plurality also rejected her claim that allowing the presumption of her legitimacy to be rebutted by her mother and presumed father, but not by her, violated equal protection. Victoria was treated as legitimate, not illegitimate, by California law and thus "the ordinary 'rational relationship' standard" applied. Preventing "the child—or, more accurately, ... a court-appointed guardian ad litem—" from rebutting the presumption of legitimacy rationally served the legitimate end of protecting the integrity of the marital union; it differed rationally from allowing husband or wife to contest the child's legitimacy, because in such cases "the stability of the marriage has already been shaken."

Justice Stevens concurred in the judgment. He "would not foreclose the possibility that a constitutionally protected relationship between a natural father and his child might exist in a case like this[,]" but concluded, based on his reading of California law and the determination of the California courts in this case, that "Michael was given a fair opportunity to show that he is Victoria's natural father, that he had developed a relationship with her, and that her interests would be served by granting him visitation rights." He found "nothing fundamentally unfair about the exercise of a judge's discretion that, in the end, allows the mother to decide whether her child's best interest would be served by allowing the natural father visitation privileges."

Justice Brennan's dissent, joined by Justices Marshall and Blackmun, dismissed Justice Stevens' reading of California law as "wishful thinking." Disagreeing sharply with the plurality's interpretive sources and method, he concluded that "unwed fathers have a constitutionally protected interest in their relationships with their children"; that the case was "properly analyzed under our procedural due process cases[,]" because the statute's "effect ... is to terminate the relationship ... before affording any hearing whatsoever on the issue whether Michael is Victoria's father"; and that California's interest in preserving family privacy could not justify terminating the parent-child relationship without a hearing.

In a separate dissent, Justice White, joined by Justice Brennan, concluded that the "basic principle enumerated in the Court's unwed father cases is that an unwed father who has demonstrated a sufficient commitment to his paternity by way of personal, financial, or custodial responsibilities has a protected liberty interest in a relationship with his child." Michael had done all he could to establish his relationship with Victoria, and he was denied procedural due process, because "he is foreclosed from establishing his paternity and is ultimately precluded, by the State, from developing a relationship with his child" without ever being allowed to present the blood test evidence of his paternity.

For the full report of this case, see supra, p. 591.

2. CLASSIFICATIONS DISADVANTAGING THE RETARDED, HOMOSEXUALS, THE ELDERLY, THE POOR, ETC.

City of Cleburne v. Cleburne Living Center
473 U.S. 432, 105 S.Ct. 3249, 87 L.Ed.2d 313 (1985).

Justice White delivered the opinion of the Court.

A Texas city denied a special use permit for the operation of a group home for the mentally retarded, acting pursuant to a municipal zoning ordinance requiring permits for such homes. The Court of Appeals for the Fifth Circuit held that mental retardation is a "quasi-suspect" classification and that the ordinance violated the Equal Protection Clause because it did not substantially further an important governmental purpose. We hold that a lesser standard of scrutiny is appropriate, but conclude that under that standard the ordinance is invalid as applied in this case.

I

... [The] anticipated [group] home would house 13 retarded men and women ... under the constant supervision of CLC staff members....

... [A] special use permit, renewable annually, was required for the construction of "[h]ospitals for the insane or feeble-minded, or alcoholic [sic] or drug addicts, or penal or correctional institutions." The city had determined that the proposed group home should be classified as a "hospital for the feeble-minded." After holding a public hearing on CLC's application, the city council voted three to one to deny a special use permit.

CLC [sued] ... alleging, *inter alia*, that the zoning ordinance was invalid on its face and as applied because it discriminated against the mentally retarded.... The [district] court deemed the ordinance, as written and applied, to be rationally related to the City's legitimate interests in "the legal responsibility of CLC and its residents, ... the safety and fears of residents in the adjoining neighborhood," and the number of people to be housed....

The ... Fifth Circuit reversed, ... [applying] intermediate-level scrutiny.... [It] held that the ordinance was invalid on its face because it did not substantially further any important governmental interests [and] that the ordinance was also invalid as applied....

II

. . .

We have declined ... to extend heightened review to differential treatment based on age:

"While the treatment of the aged in this Nation has not been wholly free of discrimination, such persons, unlike, say, those who have been discriminated against on the basis of race or national origin, have not experienced a 'history of purposeful unequal treatment' or been subjected to unique disabilities on the basis of stereotyped characteristics not truly indicative of their abilities." Massachusetts Board of Retirement v. Murgia, 427 U.S. 307, 313 (1976).[a]

[a] *Murgia* applied a rational basis standard and upheld a Massachusetts compulsory retirement law for state police officers who attained age fifty, rejecting the challenge of an officer who had passed an annual physical examination administered four months before he was retired involuntarily. The Court concluded that the objective of assuring physical fitness was rationally furthered by a maximum age limitation and that it was not necessary for the state to use individualized testing after age 50 even if that might determine fitness more precisely. The state did not have to choose the "best means" to accomplish its purpose, only a rational one.

The Court similarly has upheld a mandatory retirement age of 60 for Foreign Service officers, Vance v. Bradley, 440 U.S. 93 (1979), and a provision of the Missouri Constitution requiring nearly all state judges to retire at age 70. Gregory v. Ashcroft, 111 S.Ct. 2395 (1991). In *Gregory* the Court rejected arguments "that the mandatory retirement provision makes two irrational distinctions: between judges who have reached age 70 and younger judges, and between judges 70 and

The lesson of *Murgia* is that where individuals in the group affected by a law have distinguishing characteristics relevant to interests the state has the authority to implement, the courts have been very reluctant, as they should be in our federal system and with our respect for the separation of powers, to closely scrutinize legislative choices as to whether, how and to what extent those interests should be pursued. In such cases, the Equal Protection Clause requires only a rational means to serve a legitimate end.

III

[W]e conclude for several reasons that the Court of Appeals erred in holding mental retardation a quasi-suspect classification calling for a more exacting standard of judicial review than is normally accorded economic and social legislation. First, ... th[e] mentally retarded have a reduced ability to cope with and function in the everyday world.... They are thus different, immutably so, in relevant respects, and the states' interest in dealing with and providing for them is plainly a legitimate one.[10] How this large and diversified group is to be treated under the law is a difficult and often a technical matter, very much a task for legislators guided by qualified professionals and not by the perhaps ill-informed opinions of the judiciary. Heightened scrutiny inevitably involves substantive judgments about legislative decisions, and we doubt that the predicate for such judicial oversight is present where the classification deals with mental retardation.

Second, ... lawmakers have been addressing their difficulties in a manner that belies a continuing antipathy or prejudice and a corresponding need for more intrusive oversight by the judiciary. Thus, the federal government has not only outlawed discrimination against the mentally retarded in federally funded programs, see § 504 of the Rehabilitation Act of 1973, 29 U.S.C. § 794, but it has also provided the retarded with the right to receive "appropriate treatment, services, and habilitation" in a setting that is "least restrictive of [their] personal liberty." Developmental Disabilities Assistance and Bill of Rights Act, 42 U.S.C. §§ 6010(1), (2). In addition, the government has conditioned federal education funds on a State's assurance that retarded children will enjoy an education that, "to the maximum extent appropriate," is integrated with that of non-mentally retarded children. Education of the Handicapped Act, 20 U.S.C.

over and other state employees of the same age who are not subject to mandatory retirement." The age distinction was rationally related to Missouri's "legitimate, indeed compelling, interest in maintaining a judiciary fully capable of performing the demanding tasks that judges must perform." The alternatives of voluntary retirement, impeachment, and retention elections rationally could be perceived as inadequate checks on judges whose performance has declined with advancing age. That judges serve longer terms, often run unopposed, and are less scrutinized by the public rationally explained "the distinction between judges and other state employees, in whom a deterioration in performance is more readily discernible and who are more easily removed." Although it is "probably not true that most" judges "suffer significant deterioration in performance at age 70" and "may not be true at all[,]" the "people of Missouri rationally could conclude that the threat of deterioration at age 70 is sufficient-

ly great, and the alternatives for removal sufficiently inadequate, that they will require all judges to step aside at age 70."

10 As Dean Ely has observed:

"Surely one has to feel sorry for a person disabled by something he or she can't do anything about, but I'm not aware of any reason to suppose that elected officials are unusually unlikely to share that feeling. Moreover, classifications based on physical disability and intelligence are typically accepted as legitimate, even by judges and commentators who assert that immutability is relevant. The explanation, when one is given, is that *those* characteristics (unlike the one the commentator is trying to render suspect) are often relevant to legitimate purposes. At that point there's not much left of the immutability theory, is there?" J. Ely, Democracy and Distrust 150 (1980) (footnote omitted). See also id., at 154–155.

§ 1412(5)(B). The government has also facilitated the hiring of the mentally retarded into the federal civil service by exempting them from the requirement of competitive examination.... Texas has similarly enacted legislation that acknowledges the special status of the mentally retarded by conferring certain rights upon them, such as "the right to live in the least restrictive setting appropriate to [their] individual needs and abilities," including "the right to live ... in a group home." Mentally Retarded Persons Act of 1977....

... That a civilized and decent society expects and approves such legislation indicates that governmental consideration of those differences in the vast majority of situations is not only legitimate but desirable. It may be, as CLC contends, that legislation designed to benefit, rather than disadvantage, the retarded would generally withstand examination under a test of heightened scrutiny. The relevant inquiry, however, is whether heightened scrutiny is constitutionally mandated in the first instance. [M]erely requiring the legislature to justify its efforts in these terms may lead it to refrain from acting at all. Much recent legislation intended to benefit the retarded also assumes the need for measures that might be perceived to disadvantage them. The Education of the Handicapped Act, for example, requires an "appropriate" education, not one that is equal in all respects to the education of non-retarded children; clearly, admission to a class that exceeded the abilities of a retarded child would not be appropriate. Similarly, the Developmental Disabilities Assistance Act and the Texas act give the retarded the right to live only in the "least restrictive setting" appropriate to their abilities, implicitly assuming the need for at least some restrictions that would not be imposed on others. Especially given the wide variation in the abilities and needs of the retarded themselves, governmental bodies must have a certain amount of flexibility and freedom from judicial oversight in shaping and limiting their remedial efforts.

Third, the legislative response ... negates any claim that the mentally retarded are politically powerless in the sense that they have no ability to attract the attention of the lawmakers....

Fourth, if the large and amorphous class of the mentally retarded were deemed quasi-suspect ..., it would be difficult to find a principled way to distinguish a variety of other groups who have perhaps immutable disabilities setting them off from others, who cannot themselves mandate the desired legislative responses, and who can claim some degree of prejudice from at least part of the public at large. One need mention ... only the aging, the disabled, the mentally ill, and the infirm. We are reluctant to set out on that course....

... Because mental retardation is a characteristic that the government may legitimately take into account in a wide range of decisions, and because both state and federal governments have recently committed themselves to assisting the retarded, we will not presume that any given legislative action, even one that disadvantages retarded individuals, is rooted in considerations that the Constitution will not tolerate.

Our refusal to recognize the retarded as a quasi-suspect class does not leave them entirely unprotected from invidious discrimination[;] legislation that distinguishes between the mentally retarded and others must be rationally related to a legitimate governmental purpose....

IV

... We inquire first whether requiring a special use permit ... in the circumstances here deprives respondents of the equal protection of the laws. If it does, there will be no occasion to decide whether the special use permit provision is facially invalid where the mentally retarded are involved.... This is the preferred course of adjudication since it enables courts to avoid making unnecessarily broad constitutional judgments....

... The City does not require a special use permit in an R–3 zone for apartment houses, multiple dwellings, boarding and lodging houses, fraternity or sorority houses, dormitories, apartment hotels, hospitals, sanitariums, nursing homes for convalescents or the aged (other than for the insane or feeble-minded or alcoholics or drug addicts), private clubs or fraternal orders, and other specified uses.... May the city require the permit for this facility when other care and multiple dwelling facilities are freely permitted?

... Because in our view the record does not reveal any rational basis for believing that the ... home would pose any special threat to the city's legitimate interests, we affirm the judgment below insofar as it holds the ordinance invalid as applied....

The District Court found that the City Council's insistence on the permit rested on several factors. First, the Council was concerned with the negative attitude of the majority of property owners located within 200 feet of the Featherston facility, as well as with the fears of elderly residents of the neighborhood. But mere negative attitudes, or fear, unsubstantiated by factors which are properly cognizable in a zoning proceeding, are not permissible bases for treating a home for the mentally retarded differently from apartment houses, multiple dwellings, and the like.... [T]he City may not ... defer[] to the wishes or objections of some fraction of the body politic. "Private biases may be outside the reach of the law, but the law cannot, directly or indirectly, give them effect." Palmore v. Sidoti, 466 U.S. 429, 433 (1984).

Second, the Council had two objections to the location of the facility. [It] was across the street from a junior high school, and [the Council] feared that the students might harass the occupants.... But the school itself is attended by about 30 mentally retarded students, and denying a permit based on such vague, undifferentiated fears is again permitting some portion of the community to validate what would otherwise be an equal protection violation. The other objection to the home's location was that it was located on "a five hundred year flood plain." This concern ..., however, can hardly be based on a distinction between the Featherston home and, for example, nursing homes, homes for convalescents or the aged, or sanitariums or hospitals.... The same may be said of another concern of the Council—doubts about the legal responsibility for actions which the mentally retarded might take. If there is no concern about legal responsibility with respect to other uses ... such as boarding and fraternity houses, it is difficult to believe that ... mildly or moderately mentally retarded individuals ... would present any different or special hazard.

Fourth, ... [given that] there would be no restrictions on the number of people who could occupy this home as a boarding house, nursing home, family dwelling, fraternity house, or dormitory[,] ... this record does not clarify how ... the characteristics of the intended occupants ... rationally justify denying [them] what would be permitted to groups occupying the same site for different purposes. Th[ey] are the type of individuals who, with supporting staff, satisfy federal and state standards for group housing in the community; and there is no dispute that the home would meet the federal square-footage-per-resident requirement for facilities of this type.... In the words of the Court of Appeals, "The City never justifies its apparent view that other people can live under such 'crowded' conditions when mentally retarded persons cannot."

In the courts below the city also urged that the ordinance is aimed at avoiding concentration of population and at lessening congestion of the streets. These concerns obviously fail to explain why apartment houses, fraternity and sorority houses, hospitals and the like, may freely locate in the area without a permit. So, too, the expressed worry about fire hazards, the serenity of the neighborhood, and the avoidance of danger to other residents fail rationally to justify singling out [this] home ... for the special use permit....

The short of it is that requiring the permit in this case appears to us to rest on an irrational prejudice against the mentally retarded....

The judgment ... is affirmed insofar as it invalidates the zoning ordinance as applied to the ... home [and] is otherwise vacated.

It is so ordered.

Justice Stevens, with whom The Chief Justice joins, concurring.

... [O]ur cases reflect a continuum of judgmental responses to differing classifications ... ranging from "strict scrutiny" at one extreme to "rational basis" at the other. I have never been persuaded that these so called "standards" adequately explain the decisional process. Cases involving classifications based on alienage, illegal residency, illegitimacy, gender, age, or—as in this case—mental retardation, do not fit well into sharply defined classifications.

. . .

Every law that places the mentally retarded in a special class is not presumptively irrational. The differences between mentally retarded persons and those with greater mental capacity are obviously relevant to certain legislative decisions. An impartial lawmaker—indeed, even a member of a class of persons defined as mentally retarded—could rationally vote in favor of a law providing funds for special education and special treatment for the mentally retarded. A mentally retarded person could also recognize that he is a member of a class that might need special supervision in some situations, both to protect himself and to protect others. Restrictions on his right to drive cars or to operate hazardous equipment might well seem rational even though they deprived him of employment opportunities and the kind of freedom of travel enjoyed by other citizens....

Even so, the Court of Appeals correctly observed that through ignorance and prejudice the mentally retarded "have been subjected to a history of unfair and often grotesque mistreatment." ... The record convinces me that this permit was required because of the irrational fears of neighboring property owners, rather than for the protection of the mentally retarded persons who would reside in respondent's home.

... In this Court, the city has argued that the discrimination was really motivated by a desire to protect the mentally retarded from the hazards presented by the neighborhood. Zoning ordinances are not usually justified on any such basis, and in this case, for the reasons explained by the Court, I find that justification wholly unconvincing. I cannot believe that a rational member of this disadvantaged class could ever approve of the discriminatory application of the city's ordinance in this case.

Accordingly, I join the opinion of the Court.

Justice Marshall, with whom Justice Brennan and Justice Blackmun join, concurring in the judgment in part and dissenting in part.

. . .

I cannot agree ... with the way in which the Court reaches its result or with the narrow, as-applied remedy it provides.... The Court ... disclaims that anything special, in the form of heightened scrutiny, is taking place. Yet

Cleburne's ordinance surely would be valid under the traditional rational basis test applicable to economic and commercial regulation. In my view, it is important to articulate, as the Court does not, the facts and principles that justify subjecting this zoning ordinance to the searching review—the heightened scrutiny—that actually leads to its invalidation. Moreover, in invalidating Cleburne's exclusion of the "feebleminded" only as applied . . . , rather than on its face, the Court radically departs from our equal protection precedents. . . .

I

. . .

I share the Court's criticisms of the overly broad lines that Cleburne's zoning ordinance has drawn. But if the ordinance is to be invalidated for its imprecise classifications, it must be pursuant to more powerful scrutiny than the minimal rational-basis test used to review classifications affecting only economic and commercial matters. The same imprecision in a similar ordinance that required opticians but not optometrists to be licensed to practice, see *Williamson v. Lee Optical Co.,* supra, or that excluded new but not old businesses from parts of a community, see *New Orleans v. Dukes,* supra, would hardly be fatal to the statutory scheme.

The refusal to acknowledge that something more than minimum rationality review is at work here is . . . unfortunate in at least two respects. [It] creates precedent . . . to subject economic and commercial classifications to similar and searching "ordinary" rational basis review—a small and regrettable step back toward the days of Lochner v. New York, 198 U.S.45 (1905). Moreover, by failing to articulate the factors that justify today's "second order" rational basis review, the Court provides no principled foundation for determining when more searching inquiry is to be invoked. . . .

II

I have long believed the level of scrutiny employed in an equal protection case should vary with "the constitutional and societal importance of the interest adversely affected and the recognized invidiousness of the basis upon which the particular classification is drawn." San Antonio Independent School District v. Rodriguez, 411 U.S. 1, 99 (1973) (Marshall, J., dissenting). . . . When a zoning ordinance works to exclude the retarded from all residential districts in a community, these two considerations require that the ordinance be convincingly justified as substantially furthering legitimate and important purposes. . . .

First, the interest of the retarded in establishing group homes is substantial. The right to "establish a home" has long been cherished as one of the fundamental liberties embraced by the Due Process Clause. See Meyer v. Nebraska, 262 U.S. 390, 399 (1923). For retarded adults, this right means living together in group homes, for as deinstitutionalization has progressed, group homes have become the primary means by which retarded adults can enter life in the community. . . .

Second, the mentally retarded have been subject to a "lengthy and tragic history," University of California Regents v. Bakke, 438 U.S. 265, 303 (1978) (opinion of Powell, J.), of segregation and discrimination that can only be called grotesque. During much of the nineteenth century, mental retardation was viewed as neither curable nor dangerous and the retarded were largely left to their own devices. By the latter part of the century and during the first decades of the new one, however, social views of the retarded underwent a radical transformation. Fueled by the rising tide of Social Darwinism, the "science" of eugenics, and the extreme xenophobia of those years, leading medical authorities and others began to portray the "feeble minded" as a "menace to society and civilization ... responsible in a large degree for many, if not all, of our social problems." A regime of state-mandated segregation and degradation soon emerged that in its virulence and bigotry rivaled, and indeed paralleled, the worst excesses of Jim Crow. Massive custodial institutions were built to warehouse the retarded for life; the aim was to halt reproduction of the retarded and "nearly extinguish their race." Retarded children were categorically excluded from public schools, based on the false stereotype that all were ineducable and on the purported need to protect nonretarded children from them. State laws deemed the retarded "unfit for citizenship."

Segregation was accompanied by eugenic marriage and sterilization laws that extinguished for the retarded one of the "basic civil rights of man"—the right to marry and procreate. Skinner v. Oklahoma, 316 U.S. 535, 541 (1942). Marriages of the retarded were made, and in some states continue to be, not only voidable but also often a criminal offense. The purpose of such limitations, which frequently applied only to women of child bearing age, was unabashedly eugenic: to prevent the retarded from propagating. To assure this end, 29 states enacted compulsory eugenic sterilization laws between 1907 and 1931. J. Landman, Human Sterilization 302–303 (1932). See Buck v. Bell, 274 U.S. 200, 207 (1927) (Holmes, J.); cf. Plessy v. Ferguson, 163 U.S. 537 (1896); Bradwell v. Illinois, 16 Wall. 130, 141 (1873) (Bradley, J., concurring in judgment).

Prejudice, once let loose, is not easily cabined.... As of 1979, most states still categorically disqualified "idiots" from voting, without regard to individual capacity and with discretion to exclude left in the hands of low-level election officials. Not until Congress enacted the Education of the Handicapped Act ... were "the door[s] of public education" opened wide to handicapped children. Hendrick Hudson District Board of Education v. Rowley, 458 U.S. 176, 192 (1982). But most important, lengthy and continuing isolation of the retarded has perpetuated the ignorance, irrational fears, and stereotyping that long have plagued them.

In light of the importance of the interest at stake and the history of discrimination the retarded have suffered, the Equal Protection Clause requires us to do more than review the distinctions drawn by Cleburne's zoning ordinance as if they appeared in a taxing statute or in economic or commercial legislation.[17] The searching scrutiny I would give to restrictions on the ability of the retarded to establish community group homes leads me to conclude that Cleburne's vague generalizations for classifying the "feeble minded" with drug addicts, alcoholics, and the insane, and excluding them where the elderly, the

---

[17] This history of discrimination may well be directly relevant to the issue before the Court. Cleburne's current exclusion of the "feeble minded" in its 1965 zoning ordinance appeared as a similar exclusion of the "feeble minded" in the City's 1947 ordinance ... the latter tracked word for word a similar exclusion in the 1929 comprehensive zoning ordinance for the nearby City of Dallas.... Although we have been presented with no legislative history for Cleburne's zoning ordinances, this genealogy strongly suggests that Cleburne's current exclusion of the "feeble minded" was written in the darkest days of segregation and stigmatization of the retard-

ed and simply carried over to the current ordinance. Recently we held that extant laws originally motivated by a discriminatory purpose continue to violate the Equal Protection Clause, even if they would be permissible were they reenacted without a discriminatory motive. See Hunter v. Underwood, 471 U.S. 222, ___ (1985). But in any event, the roots of a law that by its terms excludes from a community the "feeble minded" are clear. As the examples above attest, "feeble minded" was the defining term for all retarded people in the era of overt and pervasive discrimination.

ill, the boarder, and the transient are allowed, are not substantial or important enough to overcome the suspicion that the ordinance rests on impermissible assumptions or outmoded and perhaps invidious stereotypes. . . .

III

. . .

The Court downplays the lengthy "history of purposeful unequal treatment" of the retarded, . . . by pointing to recent legislative action that is said to "beli[e] a continuing antipathy or prejudice." . . .

. . . Shifting cultural, political, and social patterns at times come to make past practices appear inconsistent with fundamental principles upon which American society rests, an inconsistency legally cognizable under the Equal Protection Clause. It is natural that evolving standards of equality come to be embodied in legislation. When that occurs, courts should look to the fact of such change as a source of guidance on evolving principles of equality. . . .

. . .

[L]egislative change . . . certainly does not eviscerate the underlying constitutional principle. The Court, for example, has never suggested that race-based classifications became any less suspect once extensive legislation had been enacted on the subject. See Palmore v. Sidoti, 466 U.S. 429 (1984).

For the retarded, just as for Negroes and women, much has changed in recent years, but much remains the same; out-dated statutes are still on the books, and irrational fears or ignorance, traceable to the prolonged social and cultural isolation of the retarded, continue to stymie recognition of the dignity and individuality of retarded people. Heightened judicial scrutiny of action appearing to impose unnecessary barriers to the retarded is required in light of increasing recognition that such barriers are inconsistent with evolving principles of equality embedded in the Fourteenth Amendment.

. . .

IV

In light of the scrutiny that should be applied here, Cleburne's ordinance sweeps too broadly to dispel the suspicion that it rests on a bare desire to treat the retarded as outsiders, pariahs who do not belong in the community. . . . [H]owever, the Court invalidates it merely as applied. . . . I must dissent from the novel proposition that "the preferred course of adjudication" is to leave standing a legislative act resting on "irrational prejudice" thereby forcing individuals in the group discriminated against to continue to run the act's gauntlet.

. . .

Invalidating on its face the ordinance's special treatment of the "feeble-minded", in contrast, would place the responsibility for tailoring and updating Cleburne's unconstitutional ordinance where it belongs: with the legislative arm of the City of Cleburne. . . . [It] might separate group homes (presently treated nowhere in the ordinance) from hospitals, and it might define a narrow sub-class of the retarded for whom even group homes could legitimately be excluded. Special treatment of the retarded might be ended altogether. But whatever the contours such an ordinance might take, the city should not be allowed to keep its ordinance on the books intact and thereby shift to the courts the responsibility to confront the complex empirical and policy questions involved in updating statutes affecting the mentally retarded. A legislative solution would yield standards and provide the sort of certainty to retarded applicants and administrative officials that case-by-case judicial rulings cannot provide. Retarded applicants should not have to continue to attempt to surmount Cleburne's vastly overbroad ordinance.

. . .

HELLER v. DOE, 509 U.S. 312 (1993). The report in this case appears supra at p. 685.

Romer v. Evans

___ U.S. ___, 116 S.Ct. 1620, 134 L.Ed.2d 855 (1996).

Justice Kennedy delivered the opinion of the Court.

One century ago, the first Justice Harlan admonished this Court that the Constitution "neither knows nor tolerates classes among citizens." Plessy v. Ferguson, 163 U.S. 537, 559 (1896) (dissenting opinion). Unheeded then, those words now are understood to state a commitment to the law's neutrality where the rights of persons are at stake. The Equal Protection Clause enforces this principle and today requires us to hold invalid a provision of Colorado's Constitution.

I

[A]n amendment to the Constitution of the State of Colorado, adopted in a 1992 statewide referendum ... as "Amendment 2," ... [stemmed] in large part from ordinances that had been passed in various Colorado municipalities[,] bann[ing] discrimination in many transactions and activities, including housing, employment, education, public accommodations, and health and welfare services.... What gave rise to the statewide controversy was the protection the ordinances afforded to persons discriminated against by reason of their sexual orientation....

Yet Amendment 2, in explicit terms, does more than repeal or rescind these provisions. It prohibits all legislative, executive or judicial action at any level of state or local government designed to protect the named class, a class we shall refer to as homosexual persons or gays and lesbians. The amendment reads:

> "No Protected Status Based on Homosexual, Lesbian, or Bisexual Orientation. Neither the State of Colorado, through any of its branches or departments, nor any of its agencies, political subdivisions, municipalities or school districts, shall enact, adopt or enforce any statute, regulation, ordinance or policy whereby homosexual, lesbian or bisexual orientation, conduct, practices or relationships shall constitute or otherwise be the basis of or entitle any person or class of persons to have or claim any minority status, quota preferences, protected status or claim of discrimination. This Section of the Constitution shall be in all respects self-executing." ...

Soon after Amendment 2 was adopted, this litigation to declare its invalidity and enjoin its enforcement was commenced in [state court by] homosexual persons, some of them government employees[, and by] governmental entities which had acted earlier to protect homosexuals from discrimination but would be prevented by Amendment 2 from continuing to do so....

The trial court granted a preliminary injunction.... [On appeal, s]ustaining the interim injunction and remanding the case for further proceedings, the

State Supreme Court held that Amendment 2 was subject to strict scrutiny under the Fourteenth Amendment because it infringed the fundamental right of gays and lesbians to participate in the political process.... To reach this conclusion, the state court relied on our voting rights cases, e.g., Reynolds v. Sims, 377 U.S. 533 (1964); Carrington v. Rash, 380 U.S. 89 (1965); Harper v. Virginia Bd. of Elections, 383 U.S. 663 (1966); Williams v. Rhodes, 393 U.S. 23 (1968), and on our precedents involving discriminatory restructuring of governmental decisionmaking, see, e.g., Hunter v. Erickson, 393 U.S. 385 (1969); Reitman v. Mulkey, 387 U.S. 369 (1967); Washington v. Seattle School Dist. No. 1, 458 U.S. 457 (1982); Gordon v. Lance, 403 U.S. 1 (1971). On remand, the State advanced various arguments in an effort to show that Amendment 2 was narrowly tailored to serve compelling interests, but the trial court found none sufficient. It enjoined enforcement of Amendment 2, and the Supreme Court of Colorado ... affirmed.... We ... affirm ..., but on a rationale different from that adopted by the State Supreme Court.

II

The State's principal argument in defense of Amendment 2 is that it puts gays and lesbians in the same position as all other persons. So, the State says, the measure does no more than deny homosexuals special rights. This reading of the amendment's language is implausible. We rely ... upon the authoritative construction of Colorado's Supreme Court[, which] ... found it invalid even on a modest reading of its implications....

> "The immediate objective of Amendment 2 is, at a minimum, to repeal existing statutes, regulations, ordinances, and policies of state and local entities that barred discrimination based on sexual orientation....

> "The 'ultimate effect' of Amendment 2 is to prohibit any governmental entity from adopting similar, or more protective statutes, regulations, ordinances, or policies in the future unless the state constitution is first amended to permit such measures." ...

Sweeping and comprehensive is the change in legal status effected by this law.... Homosexuals, by state decree, are put in a solitary class with respect to transactions and relations in both the private and governmental spheres. The amendment withdraws from homosexuals, but no others, specific legal protection from the injuries caused by discrimination, and it forbids reinstatement of these laws and policies.

The change that Amendment 2 works in the legal status of gays and lesbians in the private sphere is far-reaching, both on its own terms and when considered in light of the structure and operation of modern anti-discrimination laws.... [M]ost States have chosen to counter discrimination by enacting detailed statutory schemes....

Colorado's state and municipal laws typify this emerging tradition of statutory protection.... The laws first enumerate the persons or entities subject to a duty not to discriminate.... The Boulder ordinance, for example, has a comprehensive definition of entities deemed places of "public accommodation." ... The Denver ordinance is of similar breadth, applying, for example, to hotels, restaurants, hospitals, dental clinics, theaters, banks, common carriers, travel and insurance agencies, and "shops and stores dealing with goods or services of any kind,".…

These statutes and ordinances also depart from the common law by enumerating the groups or persons within their ambit of protection.... Colorado's state and local governments have not limited anti-discrimination laws to groups that have so far been given the protection of heightened equal protection scrutiny under our cases.... Rather, they set forth an extensive catalogue of traits which cannot be the basis for discrimination, including age, military status, marital status, pregnancy, parenthood, custody of a minor child, political affiliation, physical or mental disability of an individual or of his or her associates—and, in recent times, sexual orientation....

Amendment 2 bars homosexuals from securing protection against the injuries that these public-accommodations laws address ... [and] nullifies specific legal protections for this targeted class in all transactions in housing, sale of real estate, insurance, health and welfare services, private education, and employment....

Not confined to the private sphere, Amendment 2 also operates to repeal and forbid all laws or policies providing specific protection for gays or lesbians from discrimination by every level of Colorado government. The State Supreme Court cited two examples[—] ... Colorado Executive Order D0035 (1990), which forbids employment discrimination against "'all state employees, classified and exempt' on the basis of sexual orientation[,]" [and] "various provisions prohibiting discrimination based on sexual orientation at state colleges." ... The repeal of these measures and the prohibition against their future reenactment demonstrates that Amendment 2 has the same force and effect in Colorado's governmental sector as it does elsewhere and that it applies to policies as well as ordinary legislation.

Amendment 2's reach may not be limited to specific laws passed for the benefit of gays and lesbians. It is a fair, if not necessary, inference from the broad language of the amendment that it deprives gays and lesbians even of the protection of general laws and policies that prohibit arbitrary discrimination in governmental and private settings.... At some point in the systematic administration of these laws, an official must determine whether homosexuality is an arbitrary and thus forbidden basis for decision. Yet a decision to that effect would itself amount to a policy prohibiting discrimination on the basis of homosexuality, and so would appear to be no more valid under Amendment 2 than the specific prohibitions against discrimination the state court held invalid.

If this consequence follows from Amendment 2, as its broad language suggests, it would compound the constitutional difficulties the law creates. The state court did not decide whether the amendment has this effect, however, and neither need we. In the course of rejecting the argument that Amendment 2 is intended to conserve resources to fight discrimination against suspect classes, the Colorado Supreme Court made the limited observation that the amendment is not intended to affect many anti-discrimination laws protecting non-suspect classes.... In our view that does not resolve the issue. In any event, even if, as we doubt, homosexuals could find some safe harbor in laws of general application, we cannot accept the view that Amendment 2's prohibition on specific legal protections does no more than deprive homosexuals of special rights. To the contrary, the amendment imposes a special disability upon those persons alone. Homosexuals are forbidden the safeguards that others enjoy or may seek without constraint. They can obtain specific protection against discrimination only by enlisting the citizenry of Colorado to amend the state constitution or perhaps, on the State's view, by trying to pass helpful laws of general applicability. This is so no matter how local or discrete the harm, no matter how public and widespread the injury. We find nothing special in the protections Amendment 2 withholds. These are protections taken for granted by most people either because they already have them or do not need them; these are protections against exclusion from an almost limitless number of transactions and endeavors that constitute ordinary civic life in a free society.

III

The Fourteenth Amendment's promise that no person shall be denied the equal protection of the laws must co-exist with the practical necessity that most legislation classifies for one purpose or another, with resulting disadvantage to various groups or persons.... We have attempted to reconcile the principle with the reality by stating that, if a law neither burdens a fundamental right nor targets a suspect class, we will uphold the legislative classification so long as it bears a rational relation to some legitimate end. See, e.g., Heller v. Doe, 509 U.S. 312, ___ (1993).

Amendment 2 fails, indeed defies, even this conventional inquiry. First, the amendment has the peculiar property of imposing a broad and undifferentiated disability on a single named group, an exceptional and, as we shall explain, invalid form of legislation. Second, its sheer breadth is so discontinuous with the reasons offered for it that the amendment seems inexplicable by anything but animus toward the class that it affects; it lacks a rational relationship to legitimate state interests.

Taking the first point, even in the ordinary equal protection case calling for the most deferential of standards, we insist on knowing the relation between the classification adopted and the object to be attained. The search for the link between classification and objective gives substance to the Equal Protection Clause; it provides guidance and discipline for the legislature, which is entitled to know what sorts of laws it can pass; and it marks the limits of our own authority. In the ordinary case, a law will be sustained if it can be said to advance a legitimate government interest, even if the law seems unwise or works to the disadvantage of a particular group, or if the rationale for it seems tenuous. See New Orleans v. Dukes, 427 U.S. 297 (1976) ...; Williamson v. Lee Optical of Okla., Inc., 348 U.S. 483 (1955) ... ; Railway Express Agency, Inc. v. New York, 336 U.S. 106 (1949).... The laws challenged in the cases just cited were narrow enough in scope and grounded in a sufficient factual context for us to ascertain that there existed some relation between the classification and the purpose it served. By requiring that the classification bear a rational relationship to an independent and legitimate legislative end, we ensure that classifications are not drawn for the purpose of disadvantaging the group burdened by the law....

Amendment 2 confounds this normal process of judicial review. It is at once too narrow and too broad. It identifies persons by a single trait and then denies them protection across the board. The resulting disqualification of a class of persons from the right to seek specific protection from the law is unprecedented in our jurisprudence....

It is not within our constitutional tradition to enact laws of this sort. Central both to the idea of the rule of law and to our own Constitution's guarantee of equal protection is the principle that government and each of its parts remain open on impartial terms to all who seek its assistance.... Respect for this principle explains why laws singling out a certain class of citizens for disfavored legal status or general hardships are rare. A law declaring that in general it shall be more difficult for one group of citizens than for all others to seek aid from the government is itself a denial of equal protection of the laws in the most literal sense....

Davis v. Beason, 133 U.S. 333 (1890), not cited by the parties but relied upon by the dissent, is not evidence that Amendment 2 is within our constitutional tradition, and any reliance upon it as authority for sustaining the amendment is misplaced. In *Davis*, the Court approved an Idaho territorial statute denying Mormons, polygamists, and advocates of polygamy the right to vote and to hold office because, as the Court construed the statute, it "simply excludes from the privilege of voting, or of holding any office of honor, trust or profit, those who have been convicted of certain offences, and those who advocate a practical resistance to the laws of the Territory and justify and approve the commission of crimes forbidden by it." ... To the extent *Davis* held that persons advocating a certain practice may be denied the right to vote, it is no longer good law. Brandenburg v. Ohio, 395 U.S. 444 (1969) (per curiam). To the extent it held that the groups designated in the statute may be deprived of the right to vote because of their status, its ruling could not stand without surviving strict scrutiny, a most doubtful outcome.... To the extent *Davis* held that a convicted felon may be denied the right to vote, its holding is not implicated by our decision and is unexceptionable. See Richardson v. Ramirez, 418 U.S. 24 (1974).

A second and related point is that laws of the kind now before us raise the inevitable inference that the disadvantage imposed is born of animosity toward the class of persons affected. "[I]f the constitutional conception of 'equal protection of the laws' means anything, it must at the very least mean that a bare ... desire to harm a politically unpopular group cannot constitute a legitimate governmental interest." Department of Agriculture v. Moreno, 413 U.S. 528, 534 (1973). Even laws enacted for broad and ambitious purposes often can be explained by reference to legitimate public policies which justify the incidental disadvantages they impose on certain persons. Amendment 2, however, in making a general announcement that gays and lesbians shall not have any particular protections from the law, inflicts on them immediate, continuing, and real injuries that outrun and belie any legitimate justifications that may be claimed for it. We conclude that, in addition to the far-reaching deficiencies of Amendment 2 that we have noted, the principles it offends, in another sense, are conventional and venerable; a law must bear a rational relationship to a legitimate governmental purpose, ... and Amendment 2 does not.

The primary rationale the State offers for Amendment 2 is respect for other citizens' freedom of association, and in particular the liberties of landlords or employers who have personal or religious objections to homosexuality. Colorado also cites its interest in conserving resources to fight discrimination against other groups. The breadth of the Amendment is so far removed from these particular justifications that we find it impossible to credit them. We cannot say that Amendment 2 is directed to any identifiable legitimate purpose or discrete objective. It is a status-based enactment divorced from any factual context from which we could discern a relationship to legitimate state interests; it is a classification of persons undertaken for its own sake, something the Equal Protection Clause does not permit....

We must conclude that Amendment 2 classifies homosexuals not to further a proper legislative end but to make them unequal to everyone else. This Colorado cannot do. A State cannot so deem a class of persons a stranger to its laws. Amendment 2 violates the Equal Protection Clause, and the judgment of the Supreme Court of Colorado is affirmed.

. . .

Justice Scalia, with whom The Chief Justice and Justice Thomas join, dissenting.

The Court has mistaken a Kulturkampf for a fit of spite. The constitutional amendment before us here is not the manifestation of a "'bare ... desire to harm'" homosexuals, but is rather a modest attempt by seemingly tolerant Coloradans to preserve traditional sexual mores against the efforts of a politically powerful minority to revise those mores through use of the laws. That objective, and the means chosen to achieve it, are not only unimpeachable under any constitutional doctrine hitherto pronounced ...; they have been specifically approved by the Congress of the United States and by this Court.

In holding that homosexuality cannot be singled out for disfavorable treatment, the Court contradicts a decision, unchallenged here, pronounced only 10 years ago, see Bowers v. Hardwick, 478 U.S. 186 (1986), and places the prestige of this institution behind the proposition that opposition to homosexuality is as reprehensible as racial or religious bias. Whether it is or not is precisely the cultural debate that gave rise to the Colorado constitutional amendment (and to the preferential laws against which the amendment was directed). Since the Constitution of the United States says nothing about this subject, it is left to be resolved by normal democratic means, including the democratic adoption of provisions in state constitutions. This Court has no business imposing upon all Americans the resolution favored by the elite class from which the Members of this institution are selected, pronouncing that "animosity" toward homosexuality is evil. I vigorously dissent.

I

. . .

... The clear import of the Colorado court's [decision] is that "general laws and policies that prohibit arbitrary discrimination" would continue to prohibit discrimination on the basis of homosexual conduct as well.... The amendment prohibits *special treatment* of homosexuals, and nothing more. It would not affect, for example, a requirement of state law that pensions be paid to all retiring state employees with a certain length of service; homosexual employees, as well as others, would be entitled to that benefit. But it would prevent the State or any municipality from making death-benefit payments to the "life partner" of a homosexual when it does not make such payments to the long-time roommate of a nonhomosexual employee. Or again, it does not affect the requirement of the State's general insurance laws that customers be afforded coverage without discrimination unrelated to anticipated risk. Thus, homosexuals could not be denied coverage, or charged a greater premium, with respect to auto collision insurance; but neither the State nor any municipality could require that distinctive health insurance risks associated with homosexuality (if there are any) be ignored.

[T]he Court's opinion ultimately does not dispute all this, but assumes it to be true. The only denial of equal treatment it contends homosexuals have suffered is this: They may not obtain *preferential treatment* without amending the state constitution. That is to say, the principle underlying the Court's opinion is that one who is accorded equal treatment under the laws, but cannot as readily as others obtain *preferential treatment* under the laws, has been denied equal protection of the laws. If merely stating this alleged "equal protection" violation does not suffice to refute it, our constitutional jurisprudence has achieved terminal silliness.

The central thesis of the Court's reasoning is that any group is denied equal protection when, to obtain advantage (or, presumably, to avoid disadvantage), it must have recourse to a more general and hence more difficult level of political decisionmaking than others. The world has never heard of such a principle.... And it seems to me most unlikely that any multilevel democracy can function under such a principle. For whenever a disadvantage is imposed, or conferral of a benefit is prohibited, at one of the higher levels of democratic decisionmaking (i.e., by the state legislature rather than local government, or by the people at large in the state constitution rather than the legislature), the affected group has (under this theory) been denied equal protection. [C]onsider a state law prohibiting the award of municipal contracts to relatives of mayors or city councilmen. Once ... passed, ... relatives must, in order to get the benefit of city contracts, persuade the state legislature—unlike all other citizens, who need only persuade the municipality. It is ridiculous to consider this a denial of equal protection....

The Court might reply that the example I have given is *not* a denial of equal protection only because the same "rational basis" (avoidance of corruption) which renders constitutional the *substantive discrimination* against relatives (i.e., the fact that they alone cannot obtain city contracts) also automatically suffices to sustain what might be called the *electoral-procedural discrimination* against them (i.e., the fact that they must go to the state level to get this changed). This is of course a perfectly reasonable response, and would explain why "electoral-procedural discrimination" has not hitherto been heard of: a law that is valid in its substance is automatically valid in its level of enactment. But the Court cannot afford to make this argument, for as I shall discuss next, there is no doubt of a rational basis for the substance of the prohibition at issue here. The Court's entire novel theory rests upon the proposition that there is something *special*—something that cannot be justified by normal "rational basis" analysis—in making a disadvantaged group (or a nonpreferred group) resort to a higher decisionmaking level. That proposition finds no support in law or logic.

II

I turn next to whether there was a legitimate rational basis for the substance of the constitutional amendment—for the prohibition of special protection for homosexuals.[1] It is unsurprising that the Court avoids discussion of this question, since the answer is so obviously yes. The case most relevant to the issue before us today is not even mentioned in the Court's opinion: In Bowers v. Hardwick, 478 U.S. 186 (1986), we held that the Constitution does not prohibit what virtually all States had done from the founding of the Republic until very recent years--making homosexual conduct a crime.... If it is constitutionally permissible for a State to make homosexual conduct criminal, surely it is constitutionally permissible for a State to enact other laws merely *disfavoring* homosexual conduct.... And *a fortiori* it is constitutionally permissible for a State to adopt a provision *not even* disfavoring homosexual conduct, but merely prohibiting all levels of state government from bestowing *special protections* upon homosexual conduct. Respondents ... counter *Bowers* with the argument that a greater-includes-the-lesser rationale cannot justify Amendment 2's application to individuals who do not engage in homosexual acts, but are merely of homosexual "orientation." ...

But assuming that, in Amendment 2, a person of homosexual "orientation" is someone who does not engage in homosexual conduct but merely has a

---

[1] The Court evidently agrees that "rational basis" ... is the governing standard. The trial court rejected respondents' argument that homosexuals constitute a "suspect" or "quasi-suspect" class, and respondents elected not to appeal that ruling to the Supreme Court of Colorado.... And the Court implicitly rejects the Supreme Court of Colorado's holding ... that Amendment 2 infringes upon a "fundamental right" of "independently identifiable class[es]" to "participate equally in the political process."

tendency or desire to do so, *Bowers* still suffices to establish a rational basis for the provision. If it is rational to criminalize the conduct, surely it is rational to deny special favor and protection to those with a self-avowed tendency or desire to engage in the conduct. Indeed, where criminal sanctions are not involved, homosexual "orientation" is an acceptable stand-in for homosexual conduct. A State "does not violate the Equal Protection Clause merely because the classifications made by its laws are imperfect," Dandridge v. Williams, 397 U.S. 471, 485 (1970). Just as a policy barring the hiring of methadone users as transit employees does not violate equal protection simply because some methadone users pose no threat to passenger safety, see New York City Transit Authority v. Beazer, 440 U.S. 568 (1979), and just as a mandatory retirement age of 50 for police officers does not violate equal protection even though it prematurely ends the careers of many policemen over 50 who still have the capacity to do the job, see Massachusetts Bd. of Retirement v. Murgia, 427 U.S. 307 (1976) (per curiam), Amendment 2 is not constitutionally invalid simply because it could have been drawn more precisely so as to withdraw special antidiscrimination protections only from those of homosexual "orientation" who actually engage in homosexual conduct....

Moreover, even if the provision regarding homosexual "orientation" *were* invalid, respondents' challenge to Amendment 2—which is a facial challenge—must fail.... It would not be enough for respondents to establish (if they could) that Amendment 2 is unconstitutional as applied to those of homosexual "orientation"; since, under *Bowers*, Amendment 2 is unquestionably constitutional as applied to those who engage in homosexual conduct, the facial challenge cannot succeed....

III

... What [Colorado] has done is not only unprohibited, but eminently reasonable, with close, congressionally approved precedent in earlier constitutional practice.

First, as to its eminent reasonableness. The Court's opinion contains grim, disapproving hints that Coloradans have been guilty of "animus" or "animosity" toward homosexuality, as though that has been established as Unamerican. Of course it is our moral heritage that one should not hate any human being or class of human beings. But I had thought that one could consider certain conduct reprehensible—murder, for example, or polygamy, or cruelty to animals—and could exhibit even "animus" toward such conduct. Surely that is the only sort of "animus" at issue here: moral disapproval of homosexual conduct, the same sort of moral disapproval that produced the centuries-old criminal laws that we held constitutional in *Bowers*. The Colorado amendment does not, to speak entirely precisely, prohibit giving favored status to people who are *homosexuals*; they can be favored for many reasons—for example, because they are senior citizens or members of racial minorities. But it prohibits giving them favored status *because of their homosexual conduct*—that is, it prohibits favored status *for homosexuality*.

But though Coloradans are ... *entitled* to be hostile toward homosexual conduct, the fact is that the degree of hostility reflected by Amendment 2 is the smallest conceivable. The Court's portrayal of Coloradans as a society fallen victim to pointless, hate-filled "gay-bashing" is so false as to be comical. Colorado not only is one of the 25 States that have repealed their antisodomy laws, but was among the first to do so.... But the society that eliminates criminal punishment for homosexual acts does not necessarily abandon the view that homosexuality is morally wrong and socially harmful; often, abolition simply reflects the view that enforcement of such criminal laws involves unseemly intrusion into the intimate lives of citizens. . . .

There is a problem, however, which arises when criminal sanction of homosexuality is eliminated but moral and social disapprobation of homosexuality is meant to be retained. . . . The problem (a problem, that is, for those who wish to retain social disapprobation of homosexuality) is that, because those who engage in homosexual conduct tend to reside in disproportionate numbers in certain communities, . . . have high disposable income, . . . and of course care about homosexual-rights issues much more ardently than the public at large, they possess political power much greater than their numbers, both locally and statewide. Quite understandably, they devote this political power to achieving not merely a grudging social toleration, but full social acceptance, of homosexuality. . . .

By the time Coloradans were asked to vote on Amendment 2, . . . Aspen, Boulder, and Denver . . . had enacted ordinances that listed "sexual orientation" as an impermissible ground for discrimination, equating the moral disapproval of homosexual conduct with racial and religious bigotry. . . . The . . . Governor . . . had signed an executive order pronouncing that "in the State of Colorado we recognize the diversity in our pluralistic society and strive to bring an end to discrimination in any form," and directing state agency-heads to "ensure non-discrimination" in hiring and promotion based on, among other things, "sexual orientation." . . . I do not mean to be critical of these legislative successes; homosexuals are as entitled to use the legal system for reinforcement of their moral sentiments as are the rest of society. But they are subject to being countered by lawful, democratic countermeasures as well.

. . . Amendment 2 . . . sought to counter both the geographic concentration and the disproportionate political power of homosexuals by (1) resolving the controversy at the statewide level, and (2) making the election a single-issue contest for both sides. . . . The Court today asserts that this most democratic of procedures . . . *must* be unconstitutional, because it has never happened before. . . . [T]his is proved false every time a state law prohibiting or disfavoring certain conduct is passed, because such a law prevents the adversely affected group—whether drug addicts, or smokers, or gun owners, or motorcyclists—from changing the policy thus established in "each of [the] parts" of the State. What the Court says is even demonstrably false at the constitutional level. The Eighteenth Amendment to the Federal Constitution, for example, deprived those who drank alcohol not only of the power to alter the policy of prohibition *locally* or through *state legislation*, but even of the power to alter it through *state constitutional amendment* or *federal legislation*. The Establishment Clause of the First Amendment prevents theocrats from having their way by converting their fellow citizens at the local, state, or federal statutory level; as does the Republican Form of Government Clause prevent monarchists.

But . . . a much closer analogy . . . involves precisely the effort by the majority of citizens to preserve its view of sexual morality statewide, against the efforts of a geographically concentrated and politically powerful minority to undermine it. The constitutions of the States of Arizona, Idaho, New Mexico, Oklahoma, and Utah *to this day* contain provisions stating that polygamy is "forever prohibited." . . . Polygamists, and those who have a polygamous "orientation," have been "singled out" by these provisions for much more severe treatment than merely denial of favored status; and that treatment can only be changed by achieving amendment of the state constitutions. The Court's disposition today suggests that these provisions are unconstitutional, and that polygamy must be permitted in these States on a state-legislated, or perhaps even local-option, basis—unless, of course, polygamists for some reason have fewer constitutional rights than homosexuals.

... Congress ... *required* the inclusion of these antipolygamy provisions in the constitutions of Arizona, New Mexico, Oklahoma, and Utah, as a condition of their admission to statehood.... Thus, this "singling out" of the sexual practices of a single group for statewide, democratic vote ... has not only happened, but has received the explicit approval of ... Congress.

I cannot say that this Court has explicitly approved any of these state constitutional provisions; but it has approved a territorial statutory provision that went even further, depriving polygamists of the ability even to achieve a constitutional amendment, by depriving them of the power to vote. In Davis v. Beason, 133 U.S. 333 (1890), Justice Field wrote for a unanimous Court.... [T]he proposition that polygamy can be criminalized, and those engaging in that crime deprived of the vote, remains good law. See Richardson v. Ramirez, 418 U.S. 24, 53 (1974). *Beason* rejected the argument that "such discrimination is a denial of the equal protection of the laws." Brief for Appellant in Davis v. Beason, O.T. 1889.... [3]

This Court cited *Beason* with approval as recently as 1993, in an opinion authored by the same Justice who writes for the Court today. That opinion said: "[A]dverse impact will not always lead to a finding of impermissible targeting. For example, a social harm may have been a legitimate concern of government for reasons quite apart from discrimination.... See, e.g., ... Davis v. Beason, 133 U.S. 333 (1890)." Church of Lukumi Babalu Aye, Inc. v. Hialeah, 508 U.S. 520, 535 (1993). It remains to be explained how § 501 of the Idaho Revised Statutes was not an "impermissible targeting" of polygamists, but (the much more mild) Amendment 2 is an "impermissible targeting" of homosexuals. Has the Court concluded that the perceived social harm of polygamy is a "legitimate concern of government," and the perceived social harm of homosexuality is not?

IV

I strongly suspect that the answer to the last question is yes, which leads me to the last point I wish to make: The Court today ... employs a constitutional theory heretofore unknown to frustrate Colorado's reasonable effort to preserve traditional American moral values. The Court's stern disapproval of "animosity" towards homosexuality might be compared with what an earlier Court (including the revered Justices Harlan and Bradley) said in Murphy v. Ramsey, 114 U.S. 15 (1885), rejecting a constitutional challenge to a United States statute that denied the franchise in federal territories to those who

---

[3] The Court labors mightily to get around *Beason*, but cannot escape the central fact that this Court found the statute at issue—which went much further than Amendment 2, denying polygamists not merely special treatment but the right to vote -"not open to any constitutional or legal objection," rejecting the appellant's argument (much like the argument of respondents today) that the statute impermissibly "single[d] him out," Brief for Appellant in Davis v. Beason, O.T. 1889.... The Court ... [makes] the claim that "[t]o the extent [*Beason*]held that the groups designated in the statute may be deprived of the right to vote because of their status, its ruling could not stand without surviving strict scrutiny, a most doubtful outcome." But if that is so, it is only because we have declared the right to vote to be a "fundamental political right," see, e.g., Dunn v. Blumstein, 405 U.S. 330, 336 (1972), deprivation of which triggers strict scrutiny. Amendment 2, of course, does not deny the fundamental right to vote, and the Court rejects the Colorado court's view that there exists a fundamental right to participate in the political process. Strict scrutiny is thus not in play here. Finally, the Court's suggestion that § 501 of the Revised Statutes of Idaho, and Amendment 2, deny rights on account of "status" (rather than conduct) opens up a broader debate involving the significance of *Bowers* to this case, a debate which the Court is otherwise unwilling to join.

engaged in polygamous cohabitation: "[C]ertainly no legislation can be sup-posed more wholesome and necessary in the founding of a free, self-governing commonwealth, fit to take rank as one of the co-ordinate States of the Union, than that which seeks to establish it on the basis of the idea of the family, as consisting in and springing from the union for life of one man and one woman in the holy estate of matrimony; the sure foundation of all that is stable and noble in our civilization; the best guaranty of that reverent morality which is the source of all beneficent progress in social and political improvement." ... I would not myself indulge in such official praise for heterosexual monogamy, because I think it no business of the courts (as opposed to the political branches) to take sides in this culture war.

But the Court today has done so, not only by inventing a novel and extravagant constitutional doctrine to take the victory away from traditional forces, but even by verbally disparaging as bigotry adherence to traditional attitudes. To suggest, for example, that this constitutional amendment springs from nothing more than "'a bare ... desire to harm a politically unpopular group,'" is nothing short of insulting. (It is also nothing short of preposterous to call "politically unpopular" a group which enjoys enormous influence in American media and politics, and which, as the trial court here noted, though composing no more than 4% of the population had the support of 46% of the voters on Amendment 2....)

When the Court takes sides in the culture wars, it tends to ... reflect[] the views and values of the lawyer class from which the Court's Members are drawn. How that class feels about homosexuality will be evident to anyone who wishes to interview job applicants at virtually any of the Nation's law schools.... [I]f the interviewer should wish not to be an associate or partner of an applicant because he disapproves of the applicant's homosexuality, ... he will have violated the pledge which the Association of American Law Schools requires all its member-schools to exact from job interviewers: "assurance of the employer's willingness" to hire homosexuals.... This law-school view of what "prejudices" must be stamped out may be contrasted with the more plebeian attitudes that apparently still prevail in ... Congress, which has been unresponsive to repeated attempts to extend to homosexuals the protections of federal civil rights laws, see, e.g., Employment Non–Discrimination Act of 1994, S. 2238, 103d Cong., 2d Sess. (1994); Civil Rights Amendments of 1975, H.R. 5452, 94th Cong., 1st Sess. (1975), and which took the pains to exclude them specifically from the Americans With Disabilities Act of 1990, see 42 U.S.C. § 12211(a) (1988 ed., Supp. V).

* * *

Today's opinion has no foundation in American constitutional law, and barely pretends to. The people of Colorado have adopted an entirely reasonable provision which does not even disfavor homosexuals in any substantive sense, but merely denies them preferential treatment. Amendment 2 is designed to prevent piecemeal deterioration of the sexual morality favored by a majority of Coloradans, and is not only an appropriate means to that legitimate end, but a means that Americans have employed before. Striking it down is an act, not of judicial judgment, but of political will. I dissent.

WEALTH CLASSIFICATIONS

Legislative classifications disadvantaging the poor most frequently take the form of financial charges applied to the indigent as well as the relatively more affluent, or withholding of welfare or other assistance from some indigents but not others. As a result, the issues normally involve disproportionate impact on the poor rather than explicit disadvantaging of them. Implicitly, these issues may involve whether equal protection not only requires treating similarly situated people similarly, but differently situated people differently, and whether the Constitution imposes affirmative obligations to assist the poor. The due process and equal protection dimensions of issues of poverty and the provision of government benefits and services are more fully discussed infra in section 4. D. (p. 1025).

The Court generally states, however, that wealth classifications are not suspect. In Harper v. Virginia State Board of Elections, 383 U.S. 663 (1966) (set out fully infra p. 984), the Court did hold it a denial of equal protection to condition the right to vote in state elections on payment of a poll tax. Justice Douglas' opinion for the Court said: "Lines drawn on the basis of wealth or property, like those of race . . ., are traditionally disfavored." But subsequently, in other contexts, the Court has not followed this approach. In Ortwein v. Schwab, 410 U.S. 656 (1973), for example, the Court upheld a $25 state appellate court filing fee as applied to an indigent challenging a welfare agency determination. The Court said: "No suspect classification, such as race, nationality, or alienage, is present. . . . The applicable standard is that of rational justification." Similarly, in Harris v. McRae, 448 U.S. 297 (1980) (set out fully infra p. 1034), the Court rejected an equal protection challenge to a federal statute prohibiting the expenditure of federal funds for abortions, despite conceding that the principal impact "falls on the indigent." The Court said that "that fact does not itself render the funding restriction constitutionally invalid, for this Court has held repeatedly that poverty, standing alone, is not a suspect classification. See, e.g., James v. Valtierra, 402 U.S. 137." Most recently, in Kadrmas v. Dickinson Public Schools, 487 U.S. 450 (1988), the Court rejected an indigent's equal protection challenge to a fee for bus service from a student's home to school. The Court declined "to apply a form of strict or 'heightened' scrutiny" and said: "We have previously rejected the suggestion that statutes having different effects on the wealthy and the poor should on that account alone be subjected to strict equal protection scrutiny. See, e.g., Harris v. McRae . . .; Ortwein v. Schwab. . . ."

SECTION 4.   PROTECTION OF PERSONAL LIBERTIES

A.   EQUAL PROTECTION AND RIGHTS SECURED BY OTHER CONSTITUTIONAL PROVISIONS

Zablocki v. Redhail
434 U.S. 374, 98 S.Ct. 673, 54 L.Ed.2d 618 (1978)

The report in this case appears supra at p. 584.

DOES EQUAL PROTECTION ANALYSIS ADD ANYTHING?

This note appears supra at p. 591.

B.   VOTING AND ELECTIONS

1.   INTRODUCTION

THE CONSTITUTION AND THE FRANCHISE

(1) **The Constitution of 1789.** As originally adopted the Constitution left it to the States to determine who should have the right to vote in national as

well as state elections. Art. II, § 1 provided for the selection of the President by electors appointed in each state "in such Manner as the Legislature thereof may direct"—a provision that has remained unchanged. Art. 1, § 2, cl. 1 provided that the persons voting for members of the House of Representatives "shall have the Qualifications requisite for Electors of the most numerous Branch of the State Legislature." Art. 1, § 3, cl. 1 provided that the members of the Senate should be chosen by the legislature of each State. It was not until the adoption of the seventeenth amendment in 1913 that it was provided that members of the Senate should be elected "by the people" of the respective States. That amendment also provided that the persons voting for members of the Senate "shall have the qualifications requisite for electors of the most numerous branch of the State legislatures." Art. I, § 4, cl. 1 provided that the "Times, Places and Manner of holding Elections for Senators and Representatives shall be prescribed in each State by the Legislature thereof; but the Congress may at any time by Law make or alter such Regulations, except as to the Places of choosing Senators."

(2) The Civil War Amendments. Before the Civil War all but six States discriminated against Negroes in establishing qualifications to vote. Stephanson, *Race Distinctions in American Law* 285 (1910). The fourteenth amendment did not directly forbid discrimination in voting. Section 2 of the amendment did provide for a reduction in representation in the House of Representatives in proportion to the number of "male inhabitants" who were not permitted to vote. However, the fifteenth amendment was soon adopted providing that the "right of citizens of the United States to vote shall not be denied or abridged by the United States or by any State on account of race, color, or previous condition of servitude."

(3) The Nineteenth, Twenty–Fourth, and Twenty–Sixth Amendments. The Civil War amendments did not extend the franchise to all. Women were, of course, citizens but citizenship did not carry the right to vote. Minor v. Happersett, 88 U.S. (21 Wall.) 162 (1875). Only after a long campaign for women's suffrage was the Nineteenth Amendment ratified in 1920 providing that the right of citizens to vote "shall not be denied or abridged by the United States or by any State on account of sex." In 1964 the Twenty-Fourth Amendment was adopted providing that the right of any citizen to vote for the President, Vice–President, or members of Congress "shall not be denied or abridged by the United States or any State by reason of failure to pay any poll tax or other tax." Finally the Twenty-Sixth Amendment was adopted in 1971 providing that the right of any citizen eighteen years or older to vote "shall not be denied or abridged by the United States or by any State on account of age."

THE EQUAL PROTECTION CLAUSE AS THE SOURCE OF A RIGHT TO VOTE AND RUN FOR ELECTIVE OFFICE

In reading the cases in this section two general questions should be considered: (1) Does the court use the general language of the equal protection clause to establish a substantive right to vote and participate in elections that goes beyond the specific constitutional provisions summarized above? (2) Is there special constitutional justification for the Court to go beyond the express language of the Constitution to guarantee the broadest access to the political processes? Cf. Ely, *Democracy and Distrust* 117 (1980): "[u]nblocking stoppages in the democratic process is what judicial review ought preeminently to be about, and denial of the vote seems the quintessential stoppage."

The cases will be discussed in two groups: (1) Those relating to legislative districting; and (2) those relating to qualifications of voters.

2. LEGISLATIVE DISTRICTING

Reynolds v. Sims

377 U.S. 533, 84 S.Ct. 1362, 12 L.Ed.2d 506 (1964).

Mr. Chief Justice Warren delivered the opinion of the Court.

Involved in these cases are an appeal and two cross-appeals from a decision of the Federal District Court . . . holding invalid, under the Equal Protection Clause of the Federal Constitution, the existing and two legislatively proposed plans for the apportionment of seats in the two houses of the Alabama Legislature, and ordering into effect a temporary reapportionment plan comprised of parts of the proposed but judicially disapproved measures.

. . .

[Under the existing plan, in the Senate one county of 15,417 population had a Senate seat and another county of over 600,000 people also had only a single seat. In the House one county with a population of 13,462 had two seats while another of 314,301 had only three seats. The two proposed plans reduced these disparities somewhat but still had a House in which the population for a seat in one district was 5 times that of another district and a Senate still in the neighborhood of 59 to 1.]

Undeniably the Constitution of the United States protects the right of all qualified citizens to vote, in state as well as in federal elections. A consistent line of decisions by this Court in cases involving attempts to deny or restrict the right of suffrage has made this indelibly clear. It has been repeatedly recognized that all qualified voters have a constitutionally protected right to vote, Ex parte Yarbrough, 110 U.S. 651, and to have their votes counted, United States v. Mosley, 238 U.S. 383. In *Mosley* the Court stated that it is "as equally unquestionable that the right to have one's vote counted is as open to protection . . . as the right to put a ballot in a box." 238 U.S., at 386. The right to vote can neither be denied outright, . . . nor can it be destroyed by alteration of ballots, see United States v. Classic, 313 U.S. 299, 315, nor diluted by ballot-box stuffing. . . . As the Court stated in *Classic,* "Obviously included within the right to choose, secured by the Constitution, is the right of qualified voters within a state to cast their ballots and have them counted. . . ." 313 U.S., at 315. Racially based gerrymandering, Gomillion v. Lightfoot, 364 U.S. 339, and the conducting of white primaries, Nixon v. Herndon, 273 U.S. 536, Nixon v. Condon, 286 U.S. 73, Smith v. Allwright, 321 U.S. 649, Terry v. Adams, 345 U.S. 461, both of which result in denying to some citizens their right to vote, have been held to be constitutionally impermissible. And history has seen a continuing expansion of the scope of the right of suffrage in this country. The right to vote freely for the candidate of one's choice is of the essence of a democratic society, and any restrictions on that right strike at the heart of representative government. And the right of suffrage can be denied by a debasement or dilution of the weight of a citizen's vote just as effectively as by wholly prohibiting the free exercise of the franchise.

. . .

In Gray v. Sanders, 372 U.S. 368, we held that the Georgia county unit system, applicable in statewide primary elections, was unconstitutional since it resulted in a dilution of the weight of the votes of certain Georgia voters merely because of where they resided. . . .

In Wesberry v. Sanders, 376 U.S. 1, decided earlier this Term, we held that attacks on the constitutionality of congressional districting plans enacted by state legislatures do not present nonjusticiable questions and should not be dismissed generally for "want of equity." We determined that the constitutional test for the validity of congressional districting schemes was one of substantial equality of population among the various districts established by a state legislature for the election of members of the Federal House of Representatives.

. . .

Gray and *Wesberry* are of course not dispositive of or directly controlling on our decision in these cases involving state legislative apportionment controversies. Admittedly, those decisions, in which we held that, in statewide and in congressional elections, one person's vote must be counted equally with those of all other voters in a State, were based on different constitutional considerations and were addressed to rather distinct problems. But neither are they wholly inapposite. *Gray,* though not determinative here since involving the weighting of votes in statewide elections, established the basic principle of equality among voters within a State, and held that voters cannot be classified, constitutionally, on the basis of where they live, at least with respect to voting in statewide elections. And our decision in *Wesberry* was of course grounded on that language of the Constitution which prescribes that members of the Federal House of Representatives are to be chosen "by the People," while attacks on state legislative apportionment schemes, such as that involved in the instant cases, are principally based on the Equal Protection Clause of the Fourteenth Amendment. Nevertheless, *Wesberry* clearly established that the fundamental principle of representative government in this country is one of equal representation for equal numbers of people, without regard to race, sex, economic status, or place of residence within a State. Our problem, then, is to ascertain, in the instant cases, whether there are any constitutionally cognizable principles which would justify departures from the basic standard of equality among voters in the apportionment of seats in state legislatures.

III.

A predominant consideration in determining whether a State's legislative apportionment scheme constitutes an invidious discrimination violative of rights asserted under the Equal Protection Clause is that the rights allegedly impaired are individual and personal in nature. . . .

Legislators represent people, not trees or acres. Legislators are elected by voters, not farms or cities or economic interests. As long as ours is a representative form of government, and our legislatures are those instruments of government elected directly by and directly representative of the people, the right to elect legislators in a free and unimpaired fashion is a bedrock of our political system. It could hardly be gainsaid that a constitutional claim had been asserted by an allegation that certain otherwise qualified voters had been entirely prohibited from voting for members of their state legislature. And, if a State should provide that the votes of citizens in one part of the State should be given two times, or five times, or 10 times the weight of votes of citizens in another part of the State, it could hardly be contended that the right to vote of those residing in the disfavored areas had not been effectively diluted. It would appear extraordinary to suggest that a state could be constitutionally permitted to enact a law providing that certain of the state's voters could vote two, five, or 10 times for their legislative representatives, while voters living elsewhere could vote only once. And it is inconceivable that a state law to the effect that, in counting votes for legislators, the votes of citizens in one part of the State would be multiplied by two, five, or 10, while the votes of persons in another area would be counted only at face value, could be constitutionally sustainable. Of course, the effect of state legislative districting schemes which give the same number of representatives to unequal numbers of constituents is identical. Overweighting and overvaluation of the votes of those living here has the certain effect of dilution and undervaluation of the votes of those living there. The resulting discrimination against those individual voters living in disfavored areas is easily demonstrable mathematically. Their right to vote is simply not the same right to vote as that of those living in a favored part of the State. Two, five, or 10 of them must vote before the effect of their voting is equivalent to that of their favored neighbor. Weighting the votes of citizens differently, by any method or means, merely because of where they happen to reside, hardly seems justifiable. . . .

. . . Since the achieving of fair and effective representation for all citizens is concededly the basic aim of legislative apportionment, we conclude that the Equal Protection Clause guarantees the opportunity for equal participation by all voters in the election of state legislators. Diluting the weight of votes because of place of residence impairs basic constitutional rights under the Fourteenth Amendment just as much as invidious discriminations based upon factors such as race, Brown v. Board of Education, 347 U.S. 483, or economic status, Griffin v. People of State of Illinois, 351 U.S. 12, Douglas v. People of State of California, 372 U.S. 353. Our constitutional system amply provides for the protection of minorities by means other than giving them majority control of state legislatures. And the democratic ideals of equality and majority rule, which have served this Nation so well in the past, are hardly of any less significance for the present and the future.

We are told that the matter of apportioning representation in a state legislature is a complex and many-faceted one. We are advised that States can rationally consider factors other than population in apportioning legislative representation. We are admonished not to restrict the power of the States to impose differing views as to political philosophy on their citizens. We are cautioned about the dangers of entering into political thickets and mathematical quagmires. Our answer is this: a denial of constitutionally protected rights demands judicial protection; our oath and our office require no less of us.

. . . Population is, of necessity, the starting point for consideration and the controlling criterion for judgment in legislative apportionment controversies. A citizen, a qualified voter, is no more nor no less so because he lives in the city or on the farm. This is the clear and strong command of our Constitution's Equal Protection Clause. This is an essential part of the concept of a government of laws and not men. This is at the heart of Lincoln's vision of "government of the people, by the people, [and] for the people." The Equal Protection Clause demands no less than substantially equal state legislative representation for all citizens, of all places as well as of all races.

IV.

We hold that, as a basic constitutional standard, the Equal Protection Clause requires that the seats in both houses of a bicameral state legislature must be apportioned on a population basis. Simply stated, an individual's right to vote for state legislators is unconstitutionally impaired when its weight is in a substantial fashion diluted when compared with votes of citizens living in other parts of the State. Since, under neither the existing apportionment provisions nor under either of the proposed plans was either of the houses of the Alabama Legislature apportioned on a population basis, the District Court correctly held that all three of these schemes were constitutionally invalid.

V.

. . .

The system of representation in the two Houses of the Federal Congress is one ingrained in our Constitution, as part of the law of the land. It is one conceived out of compromise and concession indispensable to the establishment of our federal republic. Arising from unique historical circumstances, it is based on the consideration that in establishing our type of federalism a group of formerly independent States bound themselves together under one national government....

Political subdivisions of States—counties, cities, or whatever—never were and never have been considered as sovereign entities. Rather, they have been traditionally regarded as subordinate governmental instrumentalities created by the State to assist in the carrying out of state governmental functions.... The relationship of the States to the Federal Government could hardly be less analogous.

. . .

Since we find the so-called federal analogy inapposite to a consideration of the constitutional validity of state legislative apportionment schemes, we necessarily hold that the Equal Protection Clause requires both houses of a state legislature to be apportioned on a population basis....

VI.

By holding that as a federal constitutional requisite both houses of a state legislature must be apportioned on a population basis, we mean that the Equal Protection Clause requires that a State make an honest and good faith effort to construct districts, in both houses of its legislature, as nearly of equal population as is practicable. We realize that it is a practical impossibility to arrange legislative districts so that each one has an identical number of residents, or citizens, or voters. Mathematical exactness or precision is hardly a workable constitutional requirement....

. . .

A State may legitimately desire to maintain the integrity of various political subdivisions, insofar as possible, and provide for compact districts of contiguous territory in designing a legislative apportionment scheme. Valid considerations may underlie such aims. Indiscriminate districting, without any regard for political subdivision or natural or historical boundary lines, may be little more than an open invitation to partisan gerrymandering. Single-member districts may be the rule in one State, while another State might desire to achieve some flexibility by creating multimember or floterial districts. Whatever the means of accomplishment, the overriding objective must be substantial equality of population among the various districts, so that the vote of any citizen is approximately equal in weight to that of any other citizen in the State....

But neither history alone, nor economic or other sorts of group interests, are permissible factors in attempting to justify disparities from population-based representation. Citizens, not history or economic interests, cast votes. Considerations of area alone provide an insufficient justification for deviations from the equal-population principle. Again, people, not land or trees or pastures, vote. Modern developments and improvements in transportation and communications make rather hollow, in the mid–1960's, most claims that deviations from population-based representation can validly be based solely on geographical considerations. Arguments for allowing such deviations in order to insure effective representation for sparsely settled areas and to prevent legislative districts from becoming so large that the availability of access of citizens to their representatives is impaired are today, for the most part, unconvincing.

A consideration that appears to be of more substance in justifying some deviations from population-based representation in state legislatures is that of insuring some voice to political subdivisions, as political subdivisions. Several factors make more than insubstantial claims that a State can rationally consider according political subdivisions some independent representation in at least one body of the state legislature, as long as the basic standard of equality of population among districts is maintained. . . .

VIII.

That the Equal Protection Clause requires that both houses of a state legislature be apportioned on a population basis does not mean that States cannot adopt some reasonable plan for periodic revision of their apportionment schemes. Decennial reapportionment appears to be a rational approach to readjustment of legislative representation in order to take into account population shifts and growth. . . . In substance, we do not regard the Equal Protection Clause as requiring daily, monthly, annual or biennial reapportionment, so long as a State has a reasonably conceived plan for periodic readjustment of legislative representation. . . .

. . .

Affirmed and remanded.

[Justices Clark and Stewart concurred. Justice Harlan filed a lengthy dissenting opinion.]

REYNOLDS AND THE FIRST ROUND OF REAPPORTIONMENT

(1) Along with *Reynolds* the Court decided cases involving five other States. One is worth special note. In Colorado the voters in 1962 had defeated a proposed constitutional amendment providing for apportionment of both houses of the legislature on a population basis and adopted another amendment providing for a lower house based on population and an upper house based on a combination of population and other factors. In Lucas v. Forty–Fourth General Assembly of Colorado, 377 U.S. 713 (1964), the Court held this plan invalid despite the fact that it had been adopted by a majority of the voters, saying: "An individual's constitutionally protected right to cast an equally weighted vote cannot be denied even by a vote of a majority of the State's electorate, if the apportionment scheme adopted by the voters fails to measure up to the requirements of the Equal Protection Clause."

(2) *Reynolds* touched off a nation-wide effort to reapportion legislatures in accordance with its standards based on the 1960 census. In many States the political processes were incapable of achieving such a result and the federal courts found themselves faced with the duty of prescribing apportionment plans. Judicial doctrine developed rapidly towards the point that only mathematically equal districts would be approved—one-person, one-vote became a constitutional standard—and various state limitations on the construction of legislative districts were invalidated as interfering with mathematical equality. Little or no attention was paid in the cases to the realities of political

representation. Legislators discovered that with the aid of computers mathematically equal districts could be created in ways which would favor incumbents or give undue representation in the legislatures to particular parties or interest groups. For an elaborate and useful discussion of the background of *Reynolds* and its companion cases and of the litigation up to 1968, see Dixon, *Democratic Representation: Reapportionment in Law and Politics* (1968). The literature on reapportionment during this period was enormous. Aside from innumerable articles, there were, in addition to Dixon's, the following significant books:

Baker, *The Reapportionment Revolution* (1966); Cortner, *The Apportionment Cases* (1970); Lee, *One Man, One Vote: WMCA and the Struggle for Equal Representation* (1967); McKay, *The Law and Politics of Equal Representation* (1965); McKay, *Reapportionment Reappraisal: A Report on the One Man, One Vote Principle in Practice* (1968); Polsby (Ed.), *Reapportionment in the 1970s* (1971).

(3) The Court decided several more cases based on the reapportionments of the 1960s. Since they are referred to in the more recent cases set out below, no attempt will be made here to cite or discuss them.

THE 1970 CENSUS AND THE SECOND ROUND OF REAPPORTIONMENT

The 1970 census set off a second round of reapportionment struggles in the legislatures and in the courts. The legislatures faced the problem on the assumption that the Supreme Court would hold them very close to the goal of mathematical equality and would not inquire too deeply into the political and other consequences of apportionments meeting the numerical standard. A mathematical standard could be easily quantified and measured. To determine whether a particular apportionment scheme produced a fair representation of the various political groups or served to dilute the political power of particular minority groups was much more difficult.

The Supreme Court, perhaps influenced by the spate of literature and the presence of more sophisticated advocates, surprised many by shifting away from its almost exclusive reliance on equal numbers as the constitutional test when the 1970 cases began to come to it.

MAHAN v. HOWELL, 410 U.S. 315 (1973). A Virginia statute apportioned the House of Delegates so that the maximum percentage variation from the ideal was 16.4%—one district being 6.8% under the ideal and another 9.6% over. The minimum population percentage necessary to elect a majority of the House was 49.29%. The districts followed political jurisdictional lines of the counties and cities, except for Fairfax County, which was divided into two five-member districts. In a suit challenging this plan the district court held it violated constitutional standards and ordered into effect its own plan, which reduced the maximum percentage variation to 10% but extended districts across subdivision lines in 12 instances. The Supreme Court reversed and reinstated the statutory plan. Justice Rehnquist, for the Court, said that the strict standards applicable to congressional districting did not apply to state legislatures and stated the standard of review to be applied as follows:

"We are not prepared to say that the decision of the people of Virginia to grant the General Assembly the power to enact local legislation dealing with the political subdivisions is irrational. And if that be so, the decision of the General Assembly to provide representation to subdivisions *qua* subdivisions in order to implement that constitutional power is likewise valid when measured against the Equal Protection Clause of the Fourteenth Amendment. The inquiry then becomes whether it can reasonably be said that the state policy urged by Virginia to justify the divergences in the legislative reapportionment plan of the House is indeed furthered by the plan adopted by the legislature, and whether if so justified the divergences are also within tolerable limits. For a State's policy urged in justification of disparity in district population, however rational, cannot constitutionally be permitted to emasculate the goal of substantial equality."

He applied this standard as follows:

"We hold that the legislature's plan for apportionment of the House of Delegates may reasonably be said to advance the rational state policy of respecting the boundaries of political subdivisions. The remaining inquiry is whether the population disparities among the districts which have resulted from the pursuit of this plan exceed constitutional limits. We conclude that they do not.

. . .

"Neither courts nor legislatures are furnished any specialized calipers which enable them to extract from the general language of the Equal Protection Clause of the Fourteenth Amendment the mathematical formula which establishes what range of percentage deviations are permissible, and what are not. The 16–odd percent maximum deviation which the District Court found to exist in the legislative plan for the reapportionment of the House is substantially less than the percentage deviations which have been found invalid in the previous decisions of this Court. While this percentage may well approach tolerable limits, we do not believe it exceeds them. Virginia has not sacrificed substantial equality to justifiable deviations."

Justices Brennan, Douglas, and Marshall, dissenting, stated their view of the constitutional standards to be applied:

"The holdings of our prior decisions can be restated in two unequivocal propositions. First the paramount goal of reapportionment must be the drawing of district lines so as to achieve precise equality in the population of each district. . . . The Constitution does not permit a State to relegate considerations of equality to secondary status and reserve as the primary goal of apportionment the service of some other state interest.

"Second, it is open to the State, in the event that it should fail to achieve the goal of population equality, to attempt to justify its failure by demonstrating that precise equality could not be achieved without jeopardizing some critical governmental interest. The Equal Protection Clause does not exalt the principle of equal representation to the point of nullifying every competing interest of the State. But we have held firmly to the view that variations in weight accorded each vote can be approved only where the State meets its burden of presenting cogent reasons in explanation of the variations, and even then only where the variations are small."

GAFFNEY v. CUMMINGS, 412 U.S. 735 (1973). Pursuant to the Connecticut Constitution, after the state legislature, and then an eight-member bipartisan commission, could not agree on a reapportionment plan following the 1970 census, a three-member Apportionment Board, consisting of one judge chosen by the Democratic Speaker of the House of Representatives, another judge chosen by the Republican Minority Leader of the House, and a third judge chosen by the other two, filed a reapportionment plan in 1971, with one member dissenting. The plan was soon challenged in federal court as a denial of equal protection because (1) the numerical deviations from population equality (a maximum deviation of 1.81% between the largest and smallest senatorial districts and of 7.83% between the largest and smallest House districts) were too great, and (2) the Board deliberately followed "a policy of 'political fairness,' which aimed at a rough scheme of proportional representation of the two major political parties" by using "the party voting results in the preceding three statewide elections" to create "a proportionate number of Republican and Democratic legislative seats." The Supreme Court rejected both claims.

Justice White's majority opinion said that prior cases had established "that the larger variations from substantial equality are too great to be justified by any state interest so far suggested[,]" although "as *Mahan v. Howell* demonstrates, population deviations among districts may be sufficiently large to require justification but nonetheless be justifiable and legally sustainable." It was, however, "now time to recognize that minor deviations from mathematical equality among state legislative districts are insufficient to make out a prima facie case of invidious discrimination under the Fourteenth Amendment so as to require justification by the State." Because "the basic statistical materials which legislatures and courts usually have to work with are the results of the United States census taken at 10–year intervals" and "they are inherently less than absolutely accurate[,]" "it makes little sense to conclude from relatively minor 'census population' variations among legislative districts that any person's vote is being substantially diluted." Constant changes in district populations and the fact that "'census persons' are not voters" also argued against exact insistence on census population equality. The opinion went further:

"More fundamentally, *Reynolds* recognized that 'the achieving of fair and effective representation for all citizens is . . . the basic aim of legislative apportionment', and it was for that reason that the decision insisted on substantial equality of populations among districts.

" . . . Fair and effective representation may be destroyed by gross population variations among districts, but it is apparent that such representation does not depend solely on mathematical equality among district populations. There are other relevant factors to be taken into account and other important interests that States may legitimately be mindful of. . . . An unrealistic overemphasis on raw population figures, a mere nose count in the districts, may submerge these other considerations and itself furnish a ready tool for ignoring factors that in day-to-day operation are important to an acceptable representation and apportionment arrangement.

"Nor is the goal of fair and effective representation furthered by making the standards of reapportionment so difficult to satisfy that the reapportionment task is recurringly removed from legislative hands and performed by federal courts who themselves must make the political decisions necessary to formulate a plan or accept those made by reapportionment plaintiffs, who may have wholly different goals than those embodied in the official plan. . . ."

The majority also rejected the claim "that even if acceptable population-wise, the Apportionment Board's plan was invidiously discriminatory because a 'political fairness principle' was followed in making up the districts":

" . . . The very essence of districting is to produce a different—a more 'politically fair'—result than would be reached with elections at large, in which the winning party would take 100% of the legislative seats. Politics and political considerations are inseparable from districting and apportionment. . . . The reality is that districting inevitably has and is intended to have substantial political consequences.

"It may be suggested that those who redistrict and reapportion should work with census, not political, data and achieve population equality without regard for political impact. But this politically mindless approach may produce, whether intended or not, the most grossly gerrymandered results; and, in any event, it is most unlikely that the political impact of such a plan would remain undiscovered by the time it was proposed or adopted, in which event the results would be both known and, if not changed, intended.

". . . [M]ultimember districts may be vulnerable, if racial or political groups have been fenced out of the political process and their voting strength invidiously minimized. See White v. Regester, 412 U.S. 755; *Whitcomb v. Chavis,* supra. See also Gomillion v. Lightfoot, 364 U.S. 339 (1960). Beyond this, we have not ventured far or attempted the impossible task of extirpating politics from what are the essentially political processes of the sovereign States. Even more plainly, judicial interest should be at its lowest ebb when a State purports fairly to allocate political power to the parties in accordance with their voting strength and, within quite tolerable limits, succeeds in doing so.... "

[Justices Brennan, Douglas and Marshall dissented.]

Karcher v. Daggett

462 U.S. 725, 103 S.Ct. 2653, 77 L.Ed.2d 133 (1983).

Justice Brennan delivered the opinion of the Court.

The question presented ... is whether an apportionment plan for congressional districts satisfies Art. I, § 2 without need for further justification if the population of the largest district is less than one percent greater than the population of the smallest district. A three-judge District Court declared New Jersey's 1982 reapportionment plan unconstitutional on the authority of Kirkpatrick v. Preisler, 394 U.S. 526 (1969), and White v. Weiser, 412 U.S. 783 (1973), because the population deviations among districts, although small, were not the result of a good-faith effort to achieve population equality. We affirm.

I

[The New Jersey Legislature adopted] the Feldman Plan contain[ing] 14 districts, with an average population per district (as determined by the 1980 census) of 526,059.... On the average, each district differed from the "ideal" figure by 0.1384%, or about 726 people. The largest ... had a population of 527,472, and the smallest ... a population of 523,798. The difference ... was 3,674 people, or 0.6984% of the average district. The populations of the other districts also varied....

The Legislature had before it other plans with appreciably smaller population deviations between the largest and smallest districts.... [One] had a maximum population difference of 2,375, or 0.4514% of the average figure.

Almost immediately after the Feldman Plan became law, a group of individuals with varying interests, including all incumbent Republican members of Congress from New Jersey, sought a declaration that the apportionment plan violated Article I, § 2 of the Constitution and an injunction against proceeding with the primary election for United States Representatives under the plan....

. . .

II

Article I, § 2, establishes a "high standard of justice and common sense" for the apportionment of congressional districts: "equal representation for equal numbers of people." Wesberry v. Sanders, 376 U.S. 1, 18 (1964). Precise mathematical equality, however, may be impossible to achieve in an imperfect world; therefore the "equal representation" standard is enforced only to the extent of requiring that districts be apportioned to achieve population equality "as nearly as is practicable." ...

Thus two basic questions shape litigation over population deviations in state legislation apportioning congressional districts. First, the court must consider whether the population differences among districts could have been reduced or eliminated altogether by a good-faith effort to draw districts of equal population. Parties challenging apportionment legislation must bear the burden of proof on this issue, and if they fail to show that the differences could have been avoided the apportionment scheme must be upheld. If, however, the plaintiffs can establish that the population differences were not the result of a good-faith effort to achieve equality, the State must bear the burden of proving that each significant variance between districts was necessary to achieve some legitimate goal. *Kirkpatrick*....

III

Appellants' principal argument ... contend[s] that the Feldman Plan should be regarded *per se* as the product of a good-faith effort to achieve population equality because the maximum population deviation among districts is smaller than the predictable undercount in available census data.

A

Kirkpatrick squarely rejected a nearly identical argument. "The whole thrust of the 'as nearly as practicable' approach is inconsistent with adoption of fixed numerical standards which excuse population variances without regard to the circumstances of each particular case." ...; see *White v. Weiser*.... Adopting any standard other than population equality, using the best census data available, ... would subtly erode the Constitution's ideal of equal representation. If state legislators knew that a certain *de minimis* level of population differences were acceptable, they would doubtless strive to achieve that level rather than equality.... Furthermore, choosing a different standard would import a high degree of arbitrariness into the process of reviewing apportionment plans.... In this case, appellants argue that a maximum deviation of approximately 0.7% should be considered *de minimis*. If we accept that argument, how are we to regard deviations of 0.8%, 0.95%, 1%, or 1.1%?

Any standard, including absolute equality, involves a certain artificiality. As appellants point out, even the census data are not perfect, and the well-known restlessness of the American people means that population counts for particular localities are outdated long before they are completed. Yet problems with the data at hand apply equally to any population-based standard we could choose. As between two standards—equality or something-less-than equality—only the former reflects the aspirations of Art. I, § 2.

To accept the legitimacy of unjustified, though small population deviations in this case would mean to reject the basic premise of *Kirkpatrick* and *Wesberry*. We decline ... to go that far. The unusual rigor of their standard has been noted several times. Because of that rigor, we have required that absolute population equality be the paramount objective of apportionment only in the case of congressional districts, for which the command of Art. I, § 2, as regards the National Legislature outweighs the local interests that a State may deem relevant in apportioning districts for representatives to state and local legislatures, but we have not questioned the population equality standard for congressional districts. See, e.g., White v. Weiser, 412 U.S., at 793; White v. Regester, 412 U.S. 755, 763 (1973); Mahan v. Howell, 410 U.S. 315, 321–323 (1973). The principle of population equality for congressional districts has not proved unjust or socially or economically harmful in experience.... If anything, this standard should cause less difficulty now for state legislatures than it did when we adopted it in *Wesberry*. The rapid advances in computer technology and education during the last two decades make it relatively simple to draw contiguous districts of equal population and at the same time to further whatever secondary goals the State has.... We thus reaffirm that there are no *de minimis* population variations, which could practicably be avoided, but which nonetheless meet the standard of Art. I, § 2 without justification.[6]

. . .

B

The sole difference between appellants' theory and the argument we rejected in *Kirkpatrick* is that appellants have proposed a *de minimis* line that gives the illusion of rationality and predictability: the "inevitable statistical imprecision of the census." ...

. . .

The census may systematically undercount population, and the rate of undercounting may vary from place to place. Those facts, however, do not render meaningless the differences in population between congressional districts, as determined by uncorrected census counts. To the contrary, the census data provide the only reliable—albeit less than perfect—indication of the districts' "real" relative population levels.... Furthermore, because the census count represents the "best population data available," ... it is the only basis for good-faith attempts to achieve population equality. Attempts to explain population deviations on the basis of flaws in census data must be supported with a precision not achieved here....

C

Given that the census-based population deviations in the Feldman Plan reflect real differences among the districts, it is clear that they could have been avoided or significantly reduced with a good-faith effort to achieve population equality. For that reason alone, it would be inappropriate to accept the

---

[6] Justice White objects that "the rule of absolute equality is perfectly compatible with 'gerrymandering' of the worst sort," Wells v. Rockefeller, 394 U.S. 542, 551 (1969) (Harlan, J., dissenting). That may certainly be true to some extent: beyond requiring States to justify population deviations with explicit, precise reasons, which might be expected to have some inhibitory effect, *Kirkpatrick* does little to prevent what is known as gerrymandering.... *Kirkpatrick*'s object, achieving population equality, is far less ambitious than what would be required to address gerrymandering on a constitutional level.

In any event, the additional claim that *Kirkpatrick* actually promotes gerrymandering (as opposed to merely failing to stop it) is completely empty. A federal principle of population equality does not prevent any State from taking steps to inhibit gerrymandering, so long as a good-faith effort is made to achieve population equality as well. See, e.g., Colo. Const. art. V, § 47 (guidelines as to compactness, contiguity, boundaries of political subdivisions, and communities of interest); Mass. Const. art. CI, § 1 (boundaries); N.Y.Elec.Law § 4–100(b) (McKinney 1978) (compactness and boundaries).

. . .

Feldman Plan as "functionally equivalent" to a plan with districts of equal population.

. . .

IV

. . . [A]ppellees' success in proving that the Feldman Plan was not the product of a good-faith effort to achieve population equality means only that the burden shifted to the State to prove that the population deviations in its plan were necessary to achieve some legitimate state objective. *White v. Weiser* demonstrates that we are willing to defer to state legislative policies, so long as they are consistent with constitutional norms, even if they require small differences in the population of congressional districts. . . . Any number of consistently applied legislative policies might justify some variance, including, for instance, making districts compact, respecting municipal boundaries, preserving the cores of prior districts, and avoiding contests between incumbent Representatives. As long as the criteria are nondiscriminatory, see Gomillion v. Lightfoot, 364 U.S. 339 (1960), these are all legitimate objectives that on a proper showing could justify minor population deviations. . . . The State must, however, show with some specificity that a particular objective required the specific deviations in its plan, rather than simply relying on general assertions. The showing required to justify population deviations is flexible, depending on the size of the deviations, the importance of the State's interests, the consistency with which the plan as a whole reflects those interests, and the availability of alternatives that might substantially vindicate those interests yet approximate population equality more closely. By necessity, whether deviations are justified requires case-by-case attention to these factors.

. . .

The District Court properly found that appellants did not justify the population deviations in this case.

V

The District Court properly applied the two-part test of *Kirkpatrick v. Preisler.* . . . It correctly held that the population deviations in the plan were not functionally equal as a matter of law, and it found that the plan was not a good-faith effort to achieve population equality using the best available census data. It also correctly rejected appellants' attempt to justify the population deviations as not supported by the evidence. [Its] judgment . . . is affirmed.

Justice Stevens, concurring.

As an alternative ground for affirmance, the appellees contended at oral argument that the bizarre configuration of New Jersey's congressional districts is sufficient to demonstrate that the plan was not adopted in "good faith." This argument, as I understand it, is a claim that the district boundaries are unconstitutional because they are the product of political gerrymandering. Since my vote is decisive in this case, it seems appropriate to explain how this argument influences my analysis of the question that divides the Court. As I have previously pointed out, political gerrymandering is one species of "vote dilution" that is proscribed by the Equal Protection Clause. . . .

I

. . . It can be demonstrated . . . that the holding in *Wesberry,* as well as our holding today, has firmer roots in the Constitution than those provided by Article I, § 2.

. . .

The Equal Protection Clause requires every State to govern impartially. [R]ules governing its election machinery or defining electoral boundaries ... must serve the interests of the entire community. See Reynolds v. Sims, supra, 377 U.S., at 565–566. If they serve no purpose other than to favor one segment—whether racial, ethnic, religious, economic, or political—that may occupy a position of strength at a particular point in time, or to disadvantage a politically weak segment of the community, they violate the constitutional guarantee of equal protection.

... [P]rotection against vote dilution cannot be confined to racial groups. As long as [the Equal Protection Clause] proscribes gerrymandering against such groups, its proscription must provide comparable protection for other cognizable groups of voters as well. . . .

II

Like Justice White, I am convinced that judicial preoccupation with the goal of perfect population equality is an inadequate method of judging the constitutionality of an apportionment plan. I would not hold that an obvious gerrymander is wholly immune from attack simply because it comes closer to perfect population equality than every competing plan. On the other hand, I do not find any virtue in the proposal to relax the standard set forth in *Wesberry* and subsequent cases, and to ignore population disparities after some arbitrarily defined threshold has been crossed. . . .

. . .

III

In this case it is not necessary to go beyond the reasoning in the Court's opinions in Wesberry v. Sanders, 376 U.S. 1 (1964), Kirkpatrick v. Preisler, 394 U.S. 526 (1969), and White v. Weiser, 412 U.S. 783 (1973), to reach the correct result. . . . [T]he plan's shortcomings regarding shape and compactness, subdivision boundaries, and neutral decisionmaking ... strengthen my conclusion that [it] violates the Equal Protection Clause.

A glance at the map shows district configurations well deserving the kind of descriptive adjectives—"uncouth" and "bizarre"—that have traditionally been used to describe acknowledged gerrymanders. . . . [W]hile disregarding geographical compactness, the redistricting scheme wantonly disregards county boundaries. . . .

Such a map prompts an inquiry into the process that led to its adoption. . . . [T]he record indicates that [it] was far from neutral. It was designed to increase the number of Democrats, and to decrease the number of Republicans, that New Jersey's voters would send to Congress in future years. . . .

Because I have not made a comparative study of other districting plans, and because the State has not had the opportunity to offer justifications specifically directed toward the additional concerns I have discussed, I cannot conclude with absolute certainty that the New Jersey plan was an unconstitutional partisan gerrymander. But I am in full agreement with the Court's holding that, because the plan embodies deviations from population equality that have not been justified by any neutral state objective, it cannot stand. . . .

Justice White, with whom The Chief Justice, Justice Powell, and Justice Rehnquist join, dissenting.

. . .

I respectfully dissent from the Court's unreasonable insistence on an unattainable perfection in the equalizing of congressional districts. The Court's decision today is not compelled by Kirkpatrick v. Preisler, 394 U.S. 526 (1969), and White v. Weiser, 412 U.S. 783 (1973), and if the Court is convinced that our cases demand the result reached today, the time has arrived to reconsider these precedents. . . .

I

"The achieving of fair and effective representation for all citizens is concededly the basic aim of legislative apportionment." Reynolds v. Sims, 377 U.S. 533, 566 (1964). One must suspend credulity to believe that the Court's draconian response to a trifling 0.6984% maximum deviation promotes "fair and effective representation" for the people of New Jersey. The requirement that "as nearly as is practicable one man's vote in a congressional election is to be worth as much as another's," Wesberry v. Sanders, 376 U.S. 1, 7–8 (1964), must be understood in light of the malapportionment in the states at the time *Wesberry* was decided. The plaintiffs in *Wesberry* were voters in a congressional district (pop. 823,680) encompassing Atlanta that was three times larger than Georgia's smallest district (272,154) and more than double the size of an average district. Because the state had not reapportioned for 30 years, the Atlanta District possessing one-fifth of Georgia's population had only one-tenth of the Congressmen. Georgia was not atypical; congressional districts throughout the country had not been redrawn for decades and deviations of over 50% were the rule. These substantial differences in district size diminished, in a real sense, the representativeness of congressional elections. The Court's invalidation of these profoundly unequal districts should not be read as a demand for precise mathematical equality between the districts. Indeed, the Court sensibly observed that "it may not be possible [for the states] to draw Congressional districts with mathematical precision." . . .

. . . .

. . . I fear that the Court's [ruling] invites further litigation of virtually every congressional redistricting plan in the nation. At least twelve states which have completed redistricting on the basis of the 1980 census have adopted plans with a higher deviation than that presented here, and four others have deviations quite similar to New Jersey's. [U]nder the Court's rationale, even Rhode Island's plan—whose two districts have a deviation of 0.02% or about 95 people—would be subject to constitutional attack.

In all such cases, state legislatures will be hard pressed to justify their preference for the selected plan. . . . When the state fails to sustain its burden, the result will generally be that a court must select an alternative plan. . . .

The only way a legislature or bipartisan commission can hope to avoid litigation will be to dismiss all other legitimate concerns and opt automatically for the districting plan with the smallest deviation. Yet no one can seriously contend that such an inflexible insistence upon mathematical exactness will serve to promote "fair and effective representation." The more likely result of today's extension of *Kirkpatrick* is to move closer to fulfilling Justice Fortas' prophecy that "a legislature might have to ignore the boundaries of common sense, running the congressional district line down the middle of the corridor of an apartment house or even dividing the residents of a single-family house between two districts." 394 U.S., at 538. Such sterile and mechanistic application only brings the principle of "one man, one vote" into disrepute.

II

... [T]he Court offers no positive virtues that will follow from its decision....

Instead the Court is purely defensive....

. . .

Yet today the Court—with no mention of the contrary holdings in *Kirkpatrick*—opines: "Any number of consistently applied legislative policies might justify some variance, including for instance, making districts compact, respecting municipal boundaries, preserving the cores of prior districts, and avoiding contests between incumbent Representatives." I, of course, welcome the Court's overruling of these ill-considered holdings of *Kirkpatrick*. There should be no question but that state legislatures may account for political and geographic boundaries in order to preserve traditional subdivisions and achieve compact and contiguous districts. Justice Stevens recognizes that courts should "give greater weight to the importance of the State's interests and the consistency with which those interests are served than to the size of the deviations." Thus, a majority of the Court appears ready to apply this new standard "with a strong measure of deference to the legitimate concerns of the State." Post, (Powell, J., dissenting).

In order that legislatures have room to accommodate these legitimate noncensus factors, a range of *de minimis* population deviation, like that permitted in the legislative reapportionment cases, is required. The Court's insistence that every deviation, no matter how small, be justified with specificity discourages legislatures from considering these "legitimate" factors in making their plans, lest the justification be found wanting, the plan invalidated, and a judicially drawn substitute put in its place. Moreover, the requirement of precise mathematical equality continues to invite those who would bury their political opposition to employ equipopulous gerrymanders. A *de minimis* range would not preclude such gerrymanders but would at least force the political cartographer to justify his work on its own terms.

III

Our cases dealing with state legislative apportionment have taken a more sensible approach. We have recognized that certain small deviations do not, in themselves, ordinarily constitute a *prima facie* constitutional violation. Gaffney v. Cummings, 412 U.S. 735 (1973); White v. Regester, 412 U.S. 755 (1973). Moreover, we have upheld plans with reasonable variances that were necessary to account for political subdivisions, Mahan v. Howell, 410 U.S. 315 (1973), to preserve the voting strength of minority groups, and to insure political fairness, *Gaffney v. Cummings*, supra....

Bringing together our legislative and congressional cases does not imply overlooking relevant differences between the two. States normally draw a larger number of legislative districts, which accordingly require a greater margin to account for geographical and political boundaries. "[C]ongressional districts are not so intertwined and freighted with strictly local interests as are state legislative districts." *White v. Weiser*.... Furthermore, because Congressional districts are generally much larger than State Legislative districts, each percentage point of variation represents a commensurately greater number of people. But these are differences of degree. They suggest that the level at which courts should entertain challenges to districting plans, absent unusual circumstances, should be lower in the congressional cases, but not altogether nonexistent. Although I am not wedded to a precise figure, in light of the current range of population deviations, a 5% cutoff appears reasonable. I would not entertain judicial challenges, absent extraordinary circumstances, where the maximum deviation is less than 5%. Somewhat greater deviations, if rationally related to an important state interest, may also be permissible. Certainly, the maintaining of compact, contiguous districts, the respecting of political subdivisions, and efforts to assure political fairness, e.g., *Gaffney v. Cummings,* . . . constitute such interests.

I would not hold up New Jersey's plan as a model reflection of such interests. Nevertheless, the deviation involved here is *de minimis,* and, regardless of what other infirmities the plan may have, constitutional or otherwise, there is no violation of Art. I, § 2—the sole issue before us. It would, of course, be a different matter if appellees could demonstrate that New Jersey's plan invidiously discriminated against a racial or political group. See White v. Regester, 412 U.S. 755 (1973); Gaffney v. Cummings, supra, at 751–754; Whitcomb v. Chavis, 403 U.S. 124 (1971); Gomillion v. Lightfoot, 364 U.S. 339 (1960).

. . .

Justice Powell, dissenting.

I join Justice White's excellent dissenting opinion, and reaffirm my previously expressed doubt that "the Constitution—a vital and living charter after nearly two centuries because of the wise flexibility of its key provisions—could be read to require a rule of mathematical exactitude in legislative reapportionment." White v. Weiser, 412 U.S. 783, 798 (1973) (Powell, J., concurring). I write separately to express some additional thoughts on gerrymandering and its relation to apportionment factors that presumably were not thought relevant under Kirkpatrick v. Preisler, 394 U.S. 526 (1969).

. . .

I . . . am prepared to entertain constitutional challenges to partisan gerrymandering that reaches the level of discrimination described by Justice Stevens.

. . .

. . . Because this precise issue was not addressed by the District Court, however, it need not be reached here. . . .

BROWN v. THOMSON, 462 U.S. 835 (1983). The Wyoming Constitution provides that its House of Representatives shall be apportioned according to population, except that each county shall have at least one representative. In 1981 the apportionment statute provided a representative for Niobrara County even though its population was 60% below the mean. Overall the plan provided a maximum deviation of 89% and an average deviation of 16%. The statute also provided that if the allocation of a seat to Niobrara County was held invalid its population should be added to another county and the number of seats in the House reduced from 64 to 63. In a suit brought to challenge this scheme the Court upheld the statute as applied to Niobrara County. Justice Powell's majority opinion said that only its receiving a seat was challenged and hence it was not necessary to consider whether adherence to county boundaries justified the population deviations that exist throughout Wyoming districts. Looking only at the marginal effects of the grant to the one county, the Court found that "this case presents an unusually strong example of an apportionment plan the population variations of which are entirely the result of the consistent and nondiscriminatory application of a legitimate state policy." The Court found that Wyoming's interest in maintaining county representation in the legislature was not outweighed by the marginal impact giving a seat to Niobrara County had on representation in the entire House.

Justice O'Connor, joined by Justice Stevens, both of whom had voted with the majority in *Karcher v. Daggett,* added a statement noting that the Court was deciding only the additional deviation caused by the allocation of a seat to Niobrara County and saying: "I have the gravest doubts that a statewide legislative plan with an 85% maximum deviation would survive constitutional scrutiny despite the presence of the State's strong interest in preserving county boundaries. I join the Court's opinion on the understanding that nothing in it suggests that this Court would uphold such a scheme."

[Justices Brennan, White, Marshall, and Blackmun dissented.]

REYNOLDS AND LOCAL GOVERNMENTAL UNITS

In Hadley v. Junior College Dist., 397 U.S. 50 (1970), eight school districts had combined to form a junior college district governed by six trustees. The governing statute provided that if no school district had more than 33 ⅓% of the population all trustees were elected at large; if a district had between 33 ⅓% and 50% of the population it would elect two trustees with the rest elected at large from the remaining districts; if a district had between 50% and 66 ⅔% it would elect three trustees; and if over 66 ⅔% it would elect four. In a suit by residents of a school district having 60% of the population but permitted to elect only 50% of the trustees, the Court held this scheme invalid. Justice Black, for the majority, said, in part: "[In Avery v. Midland County, 390 U.S. 474 (1968), we held that] a qualified voter in a local election also has a constitutional right to have his vote counted with substantially the same weight as that of any other voter in a case where the elected officials exercised 'general governmental powers over the entire geographic area served by the body.'

"... Appellants argue that since the trustees can levy and collect taxes, issue bonds with certain restrictions, hire and fire teachers, make contracts, collect fees, supervise and discipline students, pass on petitions to annex school districts, acquire property by condemnation, and in general manage the operations of the junior college, their powers are equivalent, for apportionment purposes, to those exercised by the county commissioners in *Avery.* We feel that these powers, while not fully as broad as those of the Midland County Commissioners,[6] certainly show that the trustees perform important governmental functions within the districts, and we think these powers are general enough and have sufficient impact throughout the district ... that the principle ... applied in *Avery* should also be applied here....

. . .

"When a court is asked to decide whether a State is required by the Constitution to give each qualified voter the same power in an election open to all, there is no discernible, valid reason why constitutional distinctions should be drawn on the basis of the purpose of the election. If one person's vote is given less weight through unequal apportionment, his right to equal voting

---

[6] The Midland County Commissioners established and maintained the county jail, appointed numerous county officials, made contracts, built roads and bridges, administered the county welfare system, performed duties in connection with elections, set the county tax rate, issued bonds, adopted the county budget, built and ran hospitals, airports, and libraries, fixed school district boundaries, established a housing authority, and determined the election districts for county commissioners. *Avery,* supra, at 476–477.

participation is impaired just as much when he votes for a school board member as when he votes for a state legislator. . . .

"It has also been urged that we distinguish for apportionment purposes between elections for 'legislative' officials and those for 'administrative' officers. Such a suggestion would leave courts with an equally unmanageable principle since governmental activities 'cannot easily be classified in the neat categories favored by civics texts', *Avery*, . . . and it must also be rejected. We therefore hold today that as a general rule, whenever a state or local government decides to select persons by popular election to perform governmental functions, the Equal Protection Clause of the Fourteenth Amendment requires that each qualified voter must be given an equal opportunity to participate in that election, and when members of an elected body are chosen from separate districts, each district must be established on a basis that will insure, as far as is practicable, that equal numbers of voters can vote for proportionally equal numbers of officials. It is of course possible that there might be some case in which a State elects certain functionaries whose duties are so far removed from normal governmental activities and so disproportionately affect different groups that a popular election in compliance with *Reynolds,* . . . might not be required, but certainly we see nothing in the present case that indicates that the activities of these trustees fit in that category. Education has traditionally been a vital governmental function, and these trustees, whose election the State has opened to all qualified voters, are governmental officials in every relevant sense of that term. . . .

". . . [T]he Act necessarily results in a systematic discrimination against voters in the more populous school districts[,] . . . because whenever a large district's percentage of the total enumeration falls within a certain percentage range it is always allocated the number of trustees corresponding to the bottom of that range. . . . Such built-in discrimination against voters in large districts cannot be sustained as a sufficient compliance with the constitutional mandate that each person's vote count as much as another's, as far as practicable. . . .

"In holding that the guarantee of equal voting strength for each voter applies in all elections of governmental officials, we do not feel that the States will be inhibited in finding ways to insure that legitimate political goals of representation are achieved. We have previously upheld against constitutional challenge an election scheme that required that candidates be residents of certain districts that did not contain equal numbers of people. Dusch v. Davis, 387 U.S. 112 (1967). Since all the officials in that case were elected at large, the right of each voter was given equal treatment.[a] We have also held that where a State chooses to select members of an official body by appointment rather than election, and that choice does not itself offend the Constitution, the fact that each official does not 'represent' the same number of people does not deny those people equal protection of the laws. Sailors v. Board of Education, 387 U.S. 105 (1967); cf. Fortson v. Morris, 385 U.S. 231 (1966).[b] And a State may,

---

[a] See also Dallas County, Ala. v. Reese, 421 U.S. 477 (1975), in which the Court upheld a requirement that county commissioners be elected by countywide balloting but with a requirement that a member be elected from each of four districts having substantial population disparities. The Court said such a scheme could be overturned only on a showing that it "in fact operates impermissibly to dilute the voting strength of an identifiable element of the voting population."

[b] In *Fortson* the Court upheld a provision of the Constitution of Georgia that when no candidate for the office of Governor receives a majority of votes cast in the general election the Governor shall be elected by a majority of the members of the Georgia General Assembly from the two persons having the highest number of votes. The Court said: "There is no provision of the United States Constitution or any of its amendments which either expressly or impliedly dictates the

in certain cases, limit the right to vote to a particular group or class of people. As we said before, '[v]iable local governments may need many innovations, numerous combinations of old and new devices, great flexibility in municipal arrangements to meet changing urban conditions. We see nothing in the Constitution to prevent experimentation.' *Sailors....* But once a State has decided to use the process of popular election and 'once the class of voters is chosen and their qualifications specified, we see no constitutional way by which equality of voting power may be evaded.' Gray v. Sanders, 372 U.S. 368, 381 (1963)."

In Lockport v. Citizens for Community Action, 430 U.S. 259 (1977), a New York law provided that a new county charter would go into effect only if approved in a referendum election by separate majorities of the voters who live in the cities within the county, and of those who live outside the cities. The Court held that this arrangement did not violate the equal protection clause in a case where there were many more voters in the cities than in the county outside the cities and where the charter was rejected, despite a majority of all the voters in the entire county having voted in favor, because of its failure to secure a majority of the noncity voters. The Court noted that the interests of the city and the noncity voters were likely to be quite different with respect to the adoption of a new county charter, and concluded:

"The provisions of New York law here in question no more than recognize the realities of these substantially differing electoral interests. Granting to these provisions the presumption of constitutionality to which every duly enacted state and federal law is entitled, we are unable to conclude that they violate the Equal Protection Clause of the Fourteenth Amendment."

In Salyer Land Co. v. Tulare Lake Basin Water Storage Dist., 410 U.S. 719 (1973), the defendant water storage district was organized under a California law providing for elections for directors in which only the holders of title to land in the district were entitled to vote and in which each such voter was entitled to cast one vote for each $100 value of land and improvements in the district. 77 persons resided within the district. 189 persons owned land in amounts up to 80 acres each. Four large operators owned 85% of the land, with one corporation owning enough to give it a majority of the board of directors. A landowner, a lessee, and a resident of the district asserted that the restriction of voting to landowners and the weighting of votes according to valuation of land owned were unconstitutional. The trial court ruled for the defendant and the Supreme Court affirmed.

Justice Rehnquist, for the Court, distinguished earlier cases invalidating restricting voting to landowners on the ground that those cases involved residents of local government units exercising general governmental power, whereas the district here "by reason of its special limited purpose and of the disproportionate effect of its activities on landowners as a group" is an exception to the rule of *Reynolds* and *Hadley.*

---

method a State must use to select its Governor. A method which would be valid if initially employed is equally valid when employed as an alternative."

The Court relied on *Fortson* in Rodriguez v. Popular Democratic Party, 457 U.S. 1 (1982), sustaining a Puerto Rico statute permitting the political party of an incumbent legislator to appoint an interim replacement when the legislator vacates the position. The Court rejected an argument that the Constitution requires election of state legislators. The Constitution confers no "right to vote, *per se,* "but a right to participate on an equal basis when elections are held.

"The appellee district in this case ... has relatively limited authority. [T]he reason for its existence, is to provide for the acquisition, storage, and distribution of water for farming in the Tulare Lake Basin. It provides no other general public services such as schools, housing, transportation, utilities, roads or anything else of the type ordinarily financed by a municipal body. There are no towns, shops, hospitals or other facilities designed to improve the quality of life within the district boundaries and it does not have a fire department, police, buses, or trains.

"Not only does the district not exercise what might be thought of as 'normal governmental' authority, but its actions disproportionately affect landowners. All of the costs of district projects are assessed against land by assessors in proportion to the benefits received. Likewise, charges for services rendered are collectible from persons receiving their benefit in proportion to the services. When such persons are delinquent in payment, just as in the case of delinquency in payments of assessments, such charges become a lien on the land. Calif. Water Code §§ 47183, 46280. In short, there is no way that the economic burdens of district operations can fall on residents *qua* residents, and the operations of the districts primarily affect the land within their boundaries.

"Under these circumstances it is quite understandable that the statutory framework for election of directors of the appellee focuses on the land benefited, rather than on people as such."

As to the argument that weighting the vote according to assessed valuation denied equal protection, he noted that the benefits and burdens to each landowner in the district are in proportion to the assessed value of the land. Thus, in a recent district project a small landowner with one vote was assessed $46 as his share of the cost while the large corporate farm with 37,825 votes was assessed $817,685 as its share. "We cannot say that the California legislative decision to permit voting in the same proportion is not rationally based."

Justices Douglas, Brennan and Marshall dissented.

In Ball v. James, 451 U.S. 355 (1981), the Court applied *Salyer Land* to uphold the system under which the Salt River Project Agricultural Improvement and Power District in Arizona elects its directors, with voting limited to landowners and voting power apportioned according to the amount of land the voter owns. The Salt River District encompasses almost half the population of Arizona, including large parts of Phoenix and other cities. While all of its water is allocated according to land ownership, 25% goes for urban uses. The District generates and sells electric power, with 98% of its revenues coming from such sales. Despite these facts demonstrating that the District plays a major role in the lives of most Arizonans, Justice Stewart, writing for the majority, said:

"[T]he District simply does not exercise the sort of governmental powers that invoke the strict demands of *Reynolds*. The District cannot impose ad valorem property taxes or sales taxes. It cannot enact any laws governing the conduct of citizens, nor does it administer such normal functions of government as the maintenance of streets, the operations of schools, or sanitation, health, or welfare services."

He concluded that limiting the vote to landowners and making the weight of their vote dependent on the number of acres owned was valid because it bears "a reasonable relationship to its statutory objectives."

Justice Powell concurred in the Court's opinion and added that in this case the public was adequately protected by the fact that the Arizona legislature could control the electoral composition of the District. Justices White, Brennan, Marshall, and Blackmun dissented.

Salyer Land and *Ball v. James* were distinguished in Quinn v. Millsap, 491 U.S. 95 (1989), which held unanimously that a property ownership requirement, for membership on a "board of freeholders" responsible for proposing to the voters a plan of reorganization of the governments of the City of St. Louis and St. Louis County, violated equal protection. The Court first rejected the Missouri Supreme Court's interpretation of *Salyer* and *Ball* as having held that the equal protection clause is completely inapplicable to government units lacking general governmental powers: "On the contrary, the Court expressly applied equal protection analysis and concluded that the voting qualifications at issue passed constitutional scrutiny." Nor did the fact that the board only "recommend[ed] a plan of reorganization to the voters ... immunize [it] from equal protection scrutiny[,]" for "the Equal Protection Clause protects the 'right to be considered for public service without the burden of invidiously discriminatory disqualifications.' "Finding it unnecessary to apply any more than "rationality review[,]" the Court concluded that neither an understanding of community issues nor a stake in the community's future depended on property ownership. Finally, "the mere fact that the board of freeholders considers land-use issues cannot suffice to sustain a land-ownership requirement in this case." Unlike the water district cases, the "purpose of the board ... is not so directly linked with land ownership." Its "mandate is far more encompassing: it has the power to draft and submit a plan to reorganize the entire governmental structure of St. Louis city and county." Its "work ... thus affects all citizens of the city and county, regardless of land ownership."

In Board of Estimate v. Morris, 489 U.S. 688 (1989), the Court held that New York City's electoral scheme for the Board of Estimate violated the "one person, one vote" apportionment requirements of equal protection. The Board of Estimate is composed of eight elected officials who automatically become members of the Board upon election to their respective primary positions. Three officials—the Mayor, the comptroller, and the president of the City Council—are elected in city-wide elections and cast two votes each on matters before the Board (except that the Mayor has no vote on the acceptance or modification of his budget proposal). The remaining five—the presidents of each of the City's 5 boroughs—are elected by the voters in their respective boroughs and cast one vote each. Voters from Brooklyn, the most populous borough, challenged the method of constituting the Board, citing the substantial disparity in population among the various boroughs, which include the Bronx, Brooklyn, Manhattan, Queens, and Richmond (Staten Island).

The Court first found that the range of the Board's fiscal responsibilities and land use, franchise, and contracting powers over the City's seven million inhabitants, together with the legislative functions it shares with the City Council in approving or modifying the Mayor's proposed budget, "situate the Board comfortably within the category of governmental bodies whose 'powers are general enough and have sufficient impact throughout the district' to require that elections to the body comply with Equal Protection strictures. See *Hadley v. Junior College Dist.*" The Court then rejected the city's claim that "the Board's composition survives constitutional challenge because the city-wide members cast a 6–5 majority of board votes and hence are in a position to control the outcome of board actions." The votes of the borough presidents are sometimes determinative, and thus voters in some boroughs retain more power than voters in other boroughs, because the at-large Board members "often do not vote together" and, given that "the Mayor has no vote on budget issues, the citywide members alone cannot control budgetary decisions."

Excepting Justices Brennan and Stevens, who concurred separately on this point, the Court did fault the Court of Appeals for failing to factor the presence of at-large members on the board into the calculation of the deviation between the more and less populous boroughs, because "the voters in each borough vote for the at-large members as well as their borough president, and they are also represented by those members." The correct method of calculation only reduced the maximum percentage deviation from 132% to 78%, however, and the Court could find no justification for "such a substantial departure from the one-person, one-vote ideal."

THE EQUAL PROTECTION CLAUSE AND THE REQUIREMENT OF SUPER-MAJORITIES

In Gordon v. Lance, 403 U.S. 1 (1971), the Court upheld a state constitutional provision requiring the approval of 60% of the voters in a referendum election before political subdivisions could incur bonded indebtedness or increase tax rates. The case resulted from a school election in which a bond issue and a tax increase received 51.5% of the vote but were declared defeated. The Court said, in part:

"Although West Virginia has not denied any group access to the ballot, it has indeed made it more difficult for some kinds of governmental actions to be taken. Certainly any departure from strict majority rule gives disproportionate power to the minority. But there is nothing in the language of the Constitution, our history or our cases that requires that a majority always prevail on every issue.

. . . .

"The Federal Constitution itself provides that a simple majority vote is insufficient on some issues; the provisions on impeachment and ratification of treaties are but two examples. Moreover, the Bill of Rights removes entire areas of legislation from the concept of majoritarian supremacy. . . . "

CONGRESSIONAL APPORTIONMENT OF REPRESENTATIVES AMONG THE SEVERAL STATES

In contrast to the usual suit challenging a state's scheme of intrastate apportionment of congressional or state legislative districts, U.S. Department of Commerce v. Montana, 503 U.S. 442 (1992), concerned Montana's challenge to a 1941 Act of Congress directing the use of a particular method for apportioning among the 50 States, after each decennial census, the 435 seats in the House of Representatives. Application of that method following the 1990 census reduced Montana's congressional delegation from two representatives to one. A lower federal court "decided that the principle of equal representation for equal numbers of people that was applied to intrastate districting in Wesberry v. Sanders, 376 U.S. 1 (1964), should also be applied to the apportionment of seats among the States" and invalidated the Act for producing a "variance between the population of Montana's single district and the ideal district" that "could not be justified[.]"

A unanimous Supreme Court reversed. Justice Stevens' opinion first set forth these basic constitutional parameters:

"The general admonition in Article I, § 2, that Representatives shall be apportioned among the several States 'according to their respective numbers' is constrained by three requirements. The number of representatives shall not exceed one for every 30,000 persons; each State shall have at least one Representative; and district boundaries may not cross state lines...."

The opinion examined the nature and effects of the various apportionment methods Congress had used before 1941 and the expert studies and reports upon which Congress relied in adopting the current method. It then rejected the suggestion that Congress' choice of apportionment method is a judicially unreviewable political question. On the merits, the Court noted that, unlike reducing population variances among districts within a State, reducing absolute population differences among districts located in different States increases relative differences from the nationwide average and worsens another State's deviation from the ideal size district at the same time that it lessens the deviation of a complaining State. The Court found no "substantive principle of commanding constitutional significance" in the various "alternative measures of inequality" from among which Congress chose its preferred method of apportionment. It noted that "[t]he constitutional guarantee of one Representative for each State inexorably compels a significant departure from the ideal" and that "the need to allocate a fixed number of indivisible Representatives among 50 States of varying populations makes it virtually impossible to have the same size district in any pair of States, let alone in all 50." Invoking the "spirit of compromise that provided two Senators for every State and Representatives of the People 'according to their respective Numbers' in the House[,]" Justice Stevens explained that "some compromise between the interests of larger and smaller States must be made to achieve a fair apportionment for the entire country." Given these premises:

> "The constitutional framework that generated the need for compromise in the apportionment process must also delegate to Congress a measure of discretion that is broader than that accorded the States in the much easier task of determining district sizes within State borders.... Its apparently good-faith choice of a method of apportionment ... commands far more deference than a state districting decision that is capable of being reviewed under a relatively rigid mathematical standard."

A footnote at this point in the Court's opinion noted that "Montana does not contend that the [Act's chosen] method systematically favors a particular party, nor that its retention over a 50–year period reflects efforts to maintain partisan political advantage." The Court concluded that "Congress had ample power to enact the statutory procedure in 1941 and to apply the method ... after the 1990 census."[a]

---

a The Court subsequently held that even more deference was due decisions concerning "the Federal Government's conduct of the census—a context even further removed from intrastate districting than is congressional apportionment." Wisconsin v. City of New York, ___ U.S. ___, ___, 116 S.Ct. 1091, 1100 (1996). The Court unanimously rejected a claim that the Secretary of Commerce acted unconstitutionally when he decided not to use a particular statistical adjustment designed to correct an undercount (and the accompanying differential undercount of racial minorities) in the initial 1990 census enumeration. The Secretary had concluded that since the primary purpose of the census was to apportion political representation among the States, it was more important to achieve "distributive accuracy"—having the proportions of people in different areas most accurate—than to achieve the best "numerical accuracy." The Court found "no constitutional basis ... for preferring numerical accuracy to distributive accuracy, or for preferring gross accuracy to some particular measure of accuracy." Given "the Constitution's broad grant of authority to Congress, the Secretary's decision not to adjust need bear only a reasonable relationship to the accomplishment of an actual enumeration of the population, keeping in mind the constitutional purpose of the census"—a standard the Secretary had met by his focus on distributive accuracy.

Davis v. Bandemer

478 U.S. 109, 106 S.Ct. 2797, 92 L.Ed.2d 85 (1986).

Justice White announced the judgment of the Court and delivered the opinion of the Court as to Part II and an opinion in which Justice Brennan, Justice Marshall, and Justice Blackmun joined as to Parts I, III, and IV.

[A] three-judge District Court ... sustained an equal protection challenge to Indiana's 1981 state apportionment on the basis that the law unconstitutionally diluted the votes of Indiana Democrats. 603 F.Supp. 1479 (1984). Although we find such political gerrymandering to be justiciable, we conclude that the District Court applied an insufficiently demanding standard in finding unconstitutional vote dilution. Consequently, we reverse.

I

. . .

[Indiana's General Assembly passed the 1981 reapportionment plans for its 50 Senate seats (all single-member districts) and 100 House seats (7 triple-member, 9 double-member, and 61 single-member districts) with Republican majorities in both houses and a Republican Governor.] Although county and city lines were not consistently followed, township lines generally were. [E]ach Senate district was not divided exactly into two House districts. There appears to have been little relation between the lines drawn in the two plans.

In early 1982 ... several Indiana Democrats ... [sued] various state officials ... alleging that the ... plans constituted a political gerrymander intended to disadvantage Democrats. Specifically, they contended that the particular district lines that were drawn and the mix of single-and multi-member districts were intended to and did violate their right, as Democrats, to equal protection under the Fourteenth Amendment....

In November 1982, before ... trial, elections were held under the new districting plan. All of the House seats and half of the Senate seats were up for election. Over all the House races statewide, Democratic candidates received 51.9% of the vote. Only 43 Democrats, however, were elected to the House. Over all the Senate races statewide, Democratic candidates received 53.1% of the vote. Thirteen (of 25) Democrats were elected. In Marion and Allen Counties, both divided into multi-member House districts, Democratic candidates drew 46.6% of the vote, but only 3 of the 21 House seats were filled by Democrats.

On December 13, 1984, a divided District Court ... declar[ed] the reapportionment ... unconstitutional, enjoin[ed] the appellants from holding elections pursuant to the 1981 redistricting, order[ed] the General Assembly to prepare a new plan, and retain[ed] jurisdiction over the case....

To the District Court majority, the results of the 1982 elections seemed "to support an argument that there is a built-in bias favoring the majority party, the Republicans, which instituted the reapportionment plan." Although the court thought that these figures were unreliable predictors of future elections, it concluded that they warranted further examination of the circumstances surrounding the passage of the reapportionment statute. [T]he court noted the irregular shape of some district lines, the peculiar mix of single-and multi-member districts, and the failure of the district lines to adhere consistently to political subdivision boundaries to define communities of interest. The court also found inadequate the other explanations given for the configuration of the districts, such as adherence to the one-person, one-vote imperative and the Voting Right Act's no retrogression requirement. These factors, concluded the court, evidenced an intentional effort to favor Republican incumbents and candidates and to disadvantage Democratic voters. This was achieved by "stacking" Democrats into districts with large Democratic majorities and "splitting" them in other districts so as to give Republicans safe but not excessive majorities in those districts. Because the 1982 elections indicated that the plan also had a discriminatory effect in that the proportionate voting influence of Democratic voters had been adversely affected and because any scheme "which purposely inhibit[s] or prevent[s] proportional representation cannot be tolerated," the District Court invalidated the statute.

The defendants appealed, seeking review of the District Court's rulings that the case was justiciable and that, if justiciable, an equal protection violation had occurred....

II

We address first ... whether this case presents ... a nonjusticiable political question....

A

Since Baker v. Carr, 369 U.S. 186 (1962), we have consistently adjudicated equal protection claims in the legislative districting context regarding inequalities in population between districts. In the course of these cases, we have developed and enforced the "one person, one vote" principle. See, e.g., Reynolds v. Sims, 377 U.S. 533 (1964).

Our past decisions also make clear that even where there is no population deviation among the districts, racial gerrymandering presents a justiciable equal protection claim. In the multi-member district context, we have reviewed, and on occasion rejected, districting plans that unconstitutionally diminished the effectiveness of the votes of racial minorities. See Rogers v. Lodge, 458 U.S. 613 (1982); Mobile v. Bolden, 446 U.S. 55 (1980); White v. Regester, 412 U.S. 755 (1973); Whitcomb v. Chavis, 403 U.S. 124 (1971); Burns v. Richardson, 384 U.S. 73 (1966); Fortson v. Dorsey, 379 U.S. 433 (1965). We have also adjudicated claims that the configuration of single-member districts violated equal protection with respect to racial and ethnic minorities, although we have never struck down an apportionment plan because of such a claim. See United Jewish Organizations of Williamsburgh, Inc. v. Carey, 430 U.S. 144 (1977); Wright v. Rockefeller, 376 U.S. 52 (1964).

In the multi-member district cases, we have also repeatedly stated that districting that would "operate to minimize or cancel out the voting strength of racial *or political* elements of the voting population" would raise a constitutional question. *Fortson* ... (emphasis added). See also Gaffney v. Cummings, 412 U.S. 735, 751 (1973); *Whitcomb v. Chavis,* ... *Burns v. Richardson* ... Finally, in *Gaffney v. Cummings,* ... we upheld against an equal protection political gerrymandering challenge a state legislative single-member redistricting scheme that was formulated in a bipartisan effort to try to provide political representation on a level approximately proportional to the strength of political parties in the State. In that case, we adjudicated the type of purely political equal protection claim that is brought here, although we did not ... expressly hold such a claim to be justiciable....

In the years since *Baker v. Carr,* both before and after *Gaffney,* however, we have also affirmed a number of decisions in which the lower courts rejected the justiciability of purely political gerrymandering claims....

... The issue ... deserves further consideration.

B

The outlines of the political question doctrine were described and to a large extent defined in *Baker v. Carr*....

[*Baker* involved] an equal protection claim based on a state legislative apportionment that allowed substantial disparities in the number of voters represented by each state representative.... In holding that claim to be justiciable, the Court concluded that none of the identifying characteristics of a political question were present:

"The question here is the consistency of state action with the Federal Constitution. We have no question decided, or to be decided, by a political branch of government coequal with this Court. Nor do we risk embarrassment of our government abroad, or grave disturbance at home if we take issue with Tennessee as to the constitutionality of her action here challenged. Nor need the appellants, in order to succeed in this action, ask the Court to enter upon policy determinations for which judicially manageable standards are lacking. Judicial standards under the Equal Protection Clause are well developed and familiar, and it has been open to courts since the enactment of the Fourteenth Amendment to determine, if on the particular facts they must, that a discrimination reflects *no* policy, but simply arbitrary and capricious action." ...

This analysis applies equally to the question now before us. Disposition of this question does not involve us in a matter more properly decided by a coequal branch of our Government. There is no risk of foreign or domestic disturbance, and in light of our cases since *Baker* we are not persuaded that there are no judicially discernible and manageable standards by which political gerrymander cases are to be decided.

It is true that the type of claim ... presented in *Baker v. Carr* was subsequently resolved in this Court by the formulation of the "one person, one vote" rule. See, e.g., Reynolds v. Sims, 377 U.S., at 557–561. The mere fact, however, that we may not now similarly perceive a likely arithmetic presumption in the instant context does not compel a conclusion that the claims presented here are nonjusticiable. The one person, one vote principle had not yet been developed when *Baker* was decided.... [T]he Court contemplated simply that legislative line-drawing in the districting context would be susceptible of adjudication under the applicable constitutional criteria.

Furthermore, in formulating the one-person, one-vote formula, the Court characterized the question posed by election districts of disparate size as an issue of fair representation....

The issue here is of course different from ... *Reynolds*. ... [T]he claim is that each political group in a State should have the same chance to elect representatives of its choice as any other political group. Nevertheless, the issue is one of representation, and we decline to hold that such claims are never justiciable.

Our racial gerrymander cases such as *White v. Regester* and *Whitcomb v. Chavis* indicate as much. In those cases, there was no population variation among the districts, and no one was precluded from voting. The claim instead was that an identifiable racial or ethnic group had an insufficient chance to elect a representative of its choice and that district lines should be redrawn to remedy this alleged defect. In both cases, we adjudicated the merits.... [I]n *Gaffney v. Cummings* ... we said that "we *must* ... respond to [the] claims

... that even if acceptable populationwise, the ... plan was invidiously discriminatory because a 'political fairness principle' was followed...." ...

... As *Gaffney* demonstrates, that the claim is submitted by a political group, rather than a racial group, does not distinguish it in terms of justiciability....

In fact, Justice O'Connor's attempt to distinguish this political gerrymandering claim from the racial gerrymandering claims that we have consistently adjudicated demonstrates the futility of such an effort. Her conclusion that the claim in this case is not justiciable seems to rest on a dual concern that no judicially manageable standards exist and that adjudication of such claims requires an initial policy decision that the judiciary should not make. Yet she does not point out how the standards that we set forth here for adjudicating this political gerrymandering claim are less manageable than the standards that have been developed for racial gerrymandering claims. Nor does she demonstrate what initial policy decision—regarding, for example, the desirability of fair group representation—we have made here that we have not made in the race cases.[9] She merely asserts that because race has historically been a suspect classification individual minority voters' rights are more immediately related to a racial minority group's voting strength. This, in combination with "the greater warrant the Equal Protection Clause gives the federal courts to intervene for protection against racial discrimination, suffice to render racial gerrymandering claims justiciable."

... Justice O'Connor's analysis is flawed because it focuses on the perceived need for judicial review and on the potential practical problems with allowing such review. Validation of the consideration of such amorphous and wide-ranging factors in assessing justiciability would alter substantially the analysis the Court enunciated in *Baker v. Carr*, and we decline Justice O'Connor's implicit invitation to rethink that approach.

III

[W]e turn to ... whether the District Court erred in holding that appellees had alleged and proved a violation of the Equal Protection Clause.

A

... [T]he appellees' claim ... is that Democratic voters over the State as a whole, not Democratic voters in particular districts, have been subjected to unconstitutional discrimination. Although the statewide discrimination ... was allegedly accomplished through the manipulation of individual district lines, the focus of the equal protection inquiry is necessarily somewhat different from that involved in the review of individual districts.

We also agree with the District Court that in order to succeed the Bandemer plaintiffs were required to prove both intentional discrimination

---

[9] As to the illegitimate policy determinations that Justice O'Connor believes that we have made, she points to two. The first is a preference for nonpartisan as opposed to partisan gerrymanders, and the second is a preference for proportionality. On a group level, however, which must be our focus in this type of claim, neither of these policy determinations is "of a kind clearly for nonjudicial discretion." Baker v. Carr, 369 U.S., at 217. The first merely recognizes that nonpartisan gerrymanders in fact are aimed at guaranteeing rather than infringing fair group representation. The second, which is not a preference for proportionality *per se* but a preference for a level of parity between votes and representation sufficient to ensure that significant minority voices are heard and that majorities are not consigned to minority status, is hardly an illegitimate extrapolation from our general majoritarian ethic and the objective of fair and adequate representation recognized in Reynolds v. Sims, 377 U.S. 533 (1964).

against an identifiable political group and an actual discriminatory effect on that group. See, e.g., Mobile v. Bolden, 446 U.S., at 67–68. Further, we are confident that if the law challenged here had discriminatory effects on Democrats, this record would support a finding that the discrimination was intentional. Thus, we decline to overturn the District Court's finding of discriminatory intent as clearly erroneous.

Indeed, ... we think it most likely that whenever a legislature redistricts, those responsible for the legislation will know the likely political composition of the new districts and will have a prediction as to whether a particular district is a safe one for a Democratic or Republican candidate or is a competitive district that either candidate might win.... As long as redistricting is done by a legislature, it should not be very difficult to prove that the likely political consequences of the reapportionment were intended.

B

We do not accept, however, the District Court's legal and factual bases for concluding that the 1981 Act visited a sufficiently adverse effect on the appellees' constitutionally protected rights to make out a violation of the Equal Protection Clause. The District Court held that because any apportionment scheme that purposely prevents proportional representation is unconstitutional, Democratic voters need only show that their proportionate voting influence has been adversely affected. Our cases, however, clearly foreclose any claim that the Constitution requires proportional representation or that legislatures in reapportioning must draw district lines to come as near as possible to allocating seats to the contending parties in proportion to what their anticipated statewide vote will be. *Whitcomb v. Chavis* ...; *White v. Regester*....

The typical election for legislative seats in the United States is conducted in described geographical districts, with the candidate receiving the most votes in each district winning the seat allocated to that district. If all or most of the districts are competitive—defined by the District Court in this case as districts in which the anticipated split in the party vote is within the range of 45% to 55%—even a narrow statewide preference for either party would produce an overwhelming majority for the winning party in the state legislature. This consequence, however, is inherent in winner-take-all, district-based elections, and we cannot hold that such a reapportionment law would violate the Equal Protection Clause because the voters in the losing party do not have representation in the legislature in proportion to the statewide vote received by their party candidates.... "[W]e are unprepared to hold that district-based elections decided by plurality vote are unconstitutional in either single-or multi-member districts simply because the supporters of losing candidates have no legislative seats assigned to them." *Whitcomb v. Chavis*.... This is true of a racial as well as a political group. *White v. Regester*.... It is also true of a statewide claim as well as an individual district claim.

To draw district lines to maximize the representation of each major party would require creating as many safe seats for each party as the demographic and predicted political characteristics of the State would permit. This in turn would leave the minority in each safe district without a representative of its choice. We upheld this "political fairness" approach in *Gaffney v. Cummings,* despite its tendency to deny safe district minorities any realistic chance to elect their own representatives. But *Gaffney* in no way suggested that the Constitution requires the approach that Connecticut had adopted in that case.

In cases involving individual multi-member districts, we have required a substantially greater showing of adverse effects than a mere lack of proportional representation to support a finding of unconstitutional vote dilution. Only where there is evidence that excluded groups have "less opportunity to participate in the political processes and to elect candidates of their choice" have we refused to approve the use of multi-member districts. *Rogers v. Lodge*.... In these cases, we have also noted the lack of responsiveness by those elected to the concerns of the relevant groups. See *Rogers v. Lodge* ...; *White v. Regester*.... [12]

These holdings rest on a conviction that the mere fact that a particular apportionment scheme makes it more difficult for a particular group in a particular district to elect the representatives of its choice does not render that scheme constitutionally infirm. This conviction, in turn, stems from a perception that the power to influence the political process is not limited to winning elections. An individual or a group of individuals who votes for a losing candidate is usually deemed to be adequately represented by the winning candidate and to have as much opportunity to influence that candidate as other voters in the district. We cannot presume in such a situation, without actual proof to the contrary, that the candidate elected will entirely ignore the interests of those voters. This is true even in a safe district where the losing group loses election after election. Thus, a group's electoral power is not unconstitutionally diminished by the simple fact of an apportionment scheme that makes winning elections more difficult, and a failure of proportional representation alone does not constitute impermissible discrimination under the Equal Protection Clause. See *Mobile v. Bolden* ... (Marshall, J., dissenting).

As with individual districts, where unconstitutional vote dilution is alleged in the form of statewide political gerrymandering, the mere lack of proportional representation will not be sufficient to prove unconstitutional discrimination. Again, without specific supporting evidence, a court cannot presume in such a case that those who are elected will disregard the disproportionately underrepresented group. Rather, unconstitutional discrimination occurs only when the electoral system is arranged in a manner that will consistently degrade a voter's or a group of voters' influence on the political process as a whole.

Although this is a somewhat different formulation than we have previously used in describing unconstitutional vote dilution in an individual district, the focus ... is essentially the same. In both contexts, the question is whether a particular group has been unconstitutionally denied its chance to effectively influence the political process. In a challenge to an individual district, this inquiry focuses on the opportunity of members of the group to participate in party deliberations in the slating and nomination of candidates, their opportunity to register and vote, and hence their chance to directly influence the election returns and to secure the attention of the winning candidate. Statewide, however, the inquiry centers on the voters' direct or indirect influence on the elections of the state legislature as a whole. And, as in individual district cases, an equal protection violation may be found only where the electoral system substantially disadvantages certain voters in their opportunity to influence the political process effectively. In this context, such a finding of unconstitutionality must be supported by evidence of continued frustration of the will of

---

[12] Although these cases involved racial groups, we believe that the principles developed in these cases would apply equally to claims by political groups in individual districts. We note, however, that the elements necessary to a successful vote dilution claim may be more difficult to prove in relation to a claim by a political group. For example, historical patterns of exclusion from the political processes, evidence which would support a vote dilution claim, are in general more likely to be present for a racial group than for a political group.

a majority of the voters or effective denial to a minority of voters of a fair chance to influence the political process.

Based on these views, we would reject the District Court's apparent holding that *any* interference with an opportunity to elect a representative of one's choice would be sufficient to allege or make out an equal protection violation, unless justified by some acceptable state interest that the State would be required to demonstrate. In addition to being contrary to the above-described conception of an unconstitutional political gerrymander, such a low threshold for legal action would invite attack on all or almost all reapportionment statutes. District-based elections hardly ever produce a perfect fit between votes and representation. The one-person, one-vote imperative often mandates departure from this result as does the no-retrogression rule required by § 5 of the Voting Rights Act. Inviting attack on minor departures from some supposed norm would too much embroil the judiciary in second-guessing what has consistently been referred to as a political task for the legislature, a task that should not be monitored too closely unless the express or tacit goal is to effect its removal from legislative halls. We decline to take a major step toward that end, ... so much at odds with our history and experience.

... [I]t is ... appropriate to require allegations and proof that the challenged legislative plan has had or will have effects that are sufficiently serious to require intervention by the federal courts in state reapportionment decisions.[14]

C

The District Court's findings do not satisfy this threshold condition to stating and proving a cause of action. [That] Court relied primarily on the results of the 1982 elections.

Relying on a single election ... is unsatisfactory.... The District Court did not find that because of the 1981 Act the Democrats could not in one of the next few elections secure a sufficient vote to take control of the assembly.... The District Court did not ask by what percentage the statewide Democratic vote would have had to increase to control either the House or the Senate. The appellants argue here, without a persuasive response from appellees, that had the Democratic candidates received an additional few percentage points of the votes cast statewide, they would have obtained a majority of the seats in both houses. Nor was there any finding that the 1981 reapportionment would consign the Democrats to a minority status in the Assembly throughout the 1980's or that the Democrats would have no hope of doing any better in the reapportionment that would occur after the 1990 census. Without findings of this nature, the District Court erred....

... [Moreover, s]imply showing that there are multi-member districts in the State and that those districts are constructed so as to be safely Republican or Democratic in no way bolsters the contention that there has been *statewide* discrimination against Democratic voters....

. . .

... For constitutional purposes, the Democratic claim in this case, insofar as it challenges *vel non* the legality of the multi-member districts in certain counties, is like that of the Negroes in *Whitcomb* who failed to prove a racial

---

[14] The requirement of a threshold showing is derived from the peculiar characteristics of these political gerrymandering claims. We do not contemplate that a similar requirement would apply to our Equal Protection cases outside of this particular context.

gerrymander, for it boils down to a complaint that they failed to attract a majority of the voters in the challenged multi-member districts.

D

... Justice Powell suggests an alternative method for evaluating equal protection claims of political gerrymandering. In his view, courts should look at a number of factors in considering these claims: the nature of the legislative procedures by which the challenged redistricting was accomplished and the intent behind the redistricting; the shapes of the districts and their conformity with political subdivision boundaries; and "evidence concerning population disparities and statistics tending to show vote dilution." The District Court ... reviewed these factors ..., and Justice Powell concludes that its findings on the[m]—and on the ultimate question of vote discrimination—should be upheld....

... [T]he crux of Justice Powell's analysis seems to be that—at least in some cases—the intentional drawing of district boundaries for partisan ends and for no other reason violates the Equal Protection Clause in and of itself. We disagree.... Specifically, even if a state legislature redistricts with the specific intention of disadvantaging one political party's election prospects, we do not believe that there has been an unconstitutional discrimination against members of that party unless the redistricting does in fact disadvantage it at the polls.

Moreover, ... a mere lack of proportionate results in one election cannot suffice.... In the individual multi-member district cases, we have found equal protection violations only where a history of disproportionate results appeared in conjunction with strong indicia of lack of political power and the denial of fair representation. [R]acial minorities ... had essentially been shut out of the political process. In the statewide political gerrymandering context, these prior cases lead to the analogous conclusion that equal protection violations may be found only where a history (actual or projected) of disproportionate results appears in conjunction with similar indicia....

· · ·

... Justice Powell's view would allow a constitutional violation to be found where the only proven effect on a political party's electoral power was disproportionate results in one (or possibly two) elections. This view, however, contains no explanation of why a lack of proportionate election results should suffice in these political gerrymandering cases while it does not in the cases involving racial gerrymandering. In fact, Justice Powell's opinion is silent as to the relevance of the substantive standard developed in the multi-member district cases to these political gerrymandering cases.

In rejecting Justice Powell's approach, we do not mean to intimate that the factors he considers are entirely irrelevant ... to a showing of the effects required to prove a political gerrymandering claim[,] ... to intent, ... [or] to whether the districting plan met legitimate state interests.

· · ·

... [But] undifferentiated consideration of the various factors ... disguises the essential conclusion of [his] opinion: that disproportionate election results alone are a sufficient effect to support a finding of a constitutional violation.

... We recognize that our own view may be difficult of application.... Nevertheless, we believe that it recognizes the delicacy of intruding on this most political of legislative functions and is at the same time consistent with our prior cases regarding individual multi-member districts, which have formulated a parallel standard.

IV

In sum, we hold that political gerrymandering cases are properly justiciable under the Equal Protection Clause. We also conclude, however, that a threshold showing of discriminatory vote dilution is required for a prima facie case of an equal protection violation. In this case, the findings made by the District Court of an adverse effect on the appellees do not surmount the threshold requirement. Consequently, the judgment ... is reversed.[a]

Justice O'Connor, with whom The Chief Justice and Justice Rehnquist join, concurring in the judgment.[b]

... I would hold that the partisan gerrymandering claims of major political parties raise a nonjusticiable political question ... as the Framers of the Constitution unquestionably intended....

. . .

Of course, in one sense a requirement of proportional representation, whether loose or absolute, is judicially manageable. If this Court were to declare that the Equal Protection Clause required proportional representation within certain fixed tolerances, I have no doubt that district courts would be able to apply this edict. The flaw ... however, would be the use of the Equal Protection Clause as the vehicle for making a fundamental policy choice that is contrary to the intent of its Framers and to the traditions of this republic. The political question doctrine as articulated in *Baker v. Carr* rightly requires that we refrain from making such policy choices in order to evade what would otherwise be a lack of judicially manageable standards....

Unfortunately, a drift towards proportional representation is apparent even in the plurality opinion. Although at times the plurality seems to require that the political party be "essentially ... shut out of the political process" before a constitutional violation will be found, the plurality's ... approach focuses not on access to the political process as a whole, but entirely on statewide electoral success....

... [T]he plurality itself conclu[des] that foreseeable, disproportionate *long-term* election results suffice to prove a constitutional violation.

Thus, the plurality opinion ultimately rests on a political preference for proportionality—not an outright claim that proportional results are required, but a conviction that the greater the departure from proportionality, the more suspect an apportionment plan becomes. This preference for proportionality is in serious tension with essential features of state legislative elections. Districting itself represents a middle ground between winner-take-all statewide elections and proportional representation for political parties. If there is a constitutional preference for proportionality, the legitimacy of districting itself is called into question: the voting strength of less evenly distributed groups will invariably be diminished by districting as compared to at-large proportional systems for electing representatives. Moreover, one implication of the districting system is that voters cast votes for candidates in their districts, not for a statewide slate of legislative candidates put forward by the parties. Consequently, efforts

[a] See Lowenstein, *Bandemer's Gap: Gerrymandering and Equal Protection* in *Political Gerrymandering and the Courts* (B. Grofman ed. 1990).

[b] Chief Justice Burger's separate opinion concurring in the judgment is omitted.

to determine party voting strength presuppose a norm that does not exist—statewide elections for representatives along party lines.

The plurality's theory is also internally inconsistent. The plurality recognizes that, given a normal dispersion of party strength and winner-take-all district-based elections, it is likely that even a narrow statewide preference for one party will give that party a disproportionately large majority in the legislature. But this means that the plurality would extend greater protection to a party that can command a majority of the statewide vote than to a party that cannot. . . .

Because a statewide majority for a party's candidates will frequently result only if the "winning" party attracts independent voters and voters from the other party, under the plurality's approach a great deal will turn on whether the support of these voters is included as part of the party's voting strength. The plurality would reserve this question, but, however it is ultimately answered anomalies will result. To measure a party's voting strength by including voters who only occasionally vote for that party's candidates is arbitrary; to ignore the role these voters play will be to further discriminate against parties that do not command a permanent majority of the electorate in a given State.

I would avoid the difficulties generated by the plurality's efforts to confine the effects of a generalized group right to equal representation by not recognizing such a right in the first instance. To allow district courts to strike down apportionment plans on the basis of their prognostications as to the outcome of future elections or future apportionments invites "findings" on matters as to which neither judges nor anyone else can have any confidence. Once it is conceded that "a group's electoral power is not unconstitutionally diminished by the simple fact of an apportionment scheme that makes winning elections more difficult," the virtual impossibility of reliably predicting how difficult it will be to win an election in 2, or 4, or 10 years should, in my view, weigh in favor of holding such challenges nonjusticiable. Racial gerrymandering should remain justiciable, for the harms it engenders run counter to the central thrust of the Fourteenth Amendment. But no such justification can be given for judicial intervention on behalf of mainstream political parties, and the risks such intervention poses to our political institutions are unacceptable. "Political affiliation is the keystone of the political trade. Race, ideally, is not." United Jewish Organizations of Williamsburgh, Inc. v. Carey, 430 U.S. 144, 171 n. 1 (1977) (Brennan, J., concurring).

Justice Powell, with whom Justice Stevens joins, concurring in Part II, and dissenting.

. . .

. . . I agree, that a partisan political gerrymander violates the Equal Protection Clause only on proof of "both intentional discrimination against an identifiable political group and an actual discriminatory effect on that group." . . . The plurality argues . . . that appellees failed to establish that their voting strength was diluted statewide despite uncontradicted proof that certain key districts were grotesquely gerrymandered to enhance the election prospects of Republican candidates. . . . Since the essence of a gerrymandering claim is that the members of a political party as a group have been denied their right to "fair and effective representation," Reynolds v. Sims, 377 U.S. 533, 565 (1964), I believe that the claim cannot be tested solely by reference to "one person, one vote." Rather, a number of other relevant neutral factors must be considered. Because the plurality ignores such factors and fails to enunciate standards by which to determine whether a legislature has enacted an unconstitutional gerrymander, I dissent.

. . .

II

A

Gerrymandering is "the deliberate and arbitrary distortion of district boundaries and populations for partisan or personal political purposes." Kirkpatrick v. Preisler, 394 U.S. 526, 538 (1969) (Fortas, J., concurring). As Justice Stevens correctly observed, gerrymandering violates the Equal Protection Clause only when the redistricting plan serves "no purpose other than to favor one segment—whether racial, ethnic, religious, economic, or political—that may occupy a position of strength at a particular time, or to disadvantage a politically weak segment of the community." Karcher v. Daggett, 462 U.S. 725, 748 (1983) (Stevens, J., concurring).

The term "gerrymandering," however, is also used loosely to describe the common practice of the party in power to choose the redistricting plan that gives it an advantage at the polls. An intent to discriminate in this sense may be present whenever redistricting occurs. See Gaffney v. Cummings, 412 U.S. 735, 753 (1973).... Moreover, since legislative bodies rarely reflect accurately the popular voting strength of the principal political parties, the effect of any particular redistricting may be perceived as unfair.... Consequently, only a sensitive and searching inquiry can distinguish gerrymandering in the "loose" sense from gerrymandering that amounts to unconstitutional discrimination. Because it is difficult to develop and apply standards that will identify the unconstitutional gerrymander, courts may seek to avoid their responsibility to enforce the Equal Protection Clause by finding that a claim of gerrymandering is nonjusticiable. I agree with the plurality that such a course is mistaken....

Moreover, I am convinced that appropriate judicial standards can and should be developed. Justice Fortas' definition of unconstitutional gerrymandering properly focuses on whether the boundaries of the voting districts have been distorted deliberately and arbitrarily to achieve illegitimate ends. *Kirkpatrick v. Preisler,....* Under this definition, the merits of a gerrymandering claim must be determined by reference to the configurations of the districts, the observance of political subdivision lines, and other criteria that have independent relevance to the fairness of redistricting. See Karcher v. Daggett, 462 U.S., at 755–759 (Stevens, J., concurring). In this case, the District Court examined the redistricting in light of such factors and found, among other facts, that the boundaries of a number of districts were deliberately distorted to deprive Democratic voters of an equal opportunity to participate in the State's legislative processes. The plurality makes no reference to any of these findings of fact. It rejects the District Court's ultimate conclusion with no explanation of the respects in which appellees' proof fell short of establishing discriminatory effect....

. . .

V

... I want to make clear the limits of the standard that I believe the Equal Protection Clause imposes on legislators engaged in redistricting.... Federal courts ... should impose a heavy burden of proof on those who allege that a redistricting plan violates the Constitution. [T]his case presents a paradigm example of unconstitutional discrimination against the members of a political party that happened to be out of power. The well-grounded findings of the District Court to this effect have not been, and I believe cannot be, held clearly erroneous.

Accordingly, I would affirm the judgment.... [25]

Miller v. Johnson

___ U.S. ___, 115 S.Ct. 2475, 132 L.Ed.2d 762 (1995).

Justice Kennedy delivered the opinion of the Court.

The constitutionality of Georgia's congressional redistricting plan is at issue here. In Shaw v. Reno, 509 U.S. 630 (1993), we held that a plaintiff states a claim under the Equal Protection Clause by alleging that a state redistricting plan, on its face, has no rational explanation save as an effort to separate voters on the basis of race. The question we now decide is whether Georgia's new Eleventh District gives rise to a valid equal protection claim under the principles announced in Shaw, and, if so, whether it can be sustained nonetheless as narrowly tailored to serve a compelling governmental interest.

I

A

The Equal Protection Clause['s] ... central mandate is racial neutrality in governmental decisionmaking. See, e.g., Loving v. Virginia, 388 U.S. 1, 11 (1967); McLaughlin v. Florida, 379 U.S. 184, 191–192 (1964); see also Brown v. Board of Education, 347 U.S. 483 (1954).... Laws classifying citizens on the basis of race cannot be upheld unless they are narrowly tailored to achieving a compelling state interest. See, e.g., Adarand ...; Croson ... (plurality opinion); Wygant v. Jackson Bd. of Ed., 476 U.S. 267, 274, 280, and n. 6 (1986) (plurality opinion).

In Shaw v. Reno ... we recognized that these equal protection principles govern a State's drawing of congressional districts, though, as our cautious approach there discloses, application of these principles to electoral districting is a most delicate task.... [W]e held that "redistricting legislation that is so bizarre on its face that it is 'unexplainable on grounds other than race,' ... demands the same close scrutiny that we give other state laws that classify citizens by race." ...

. . .

B

In 1965, the Attorney General designated Georgia a covered jurisdiction under § 4(b) of the Voting Rights Act.... In consequence, § 5 of the Act requires Georgia to obtain either administrative preclearance by the Attorney General or approval by the United States District Court for the District of Columbia of any change in a "standard, practice, or procedure with respect to voting" made after November 1, 1964.... The preclearance mechanism applies to congressional redistricting plans, see, e.g., Beer v. United States, 425 U.S.

---

[25] As is evident from the several opinions filed today, there is no "Court" for a standard that properly should be applied in determining whether a challenged redistricting plan is an unconstitutional partisan political gerrymander. The standard proposed by the plurality is explicitly rejected by two Justices, and three Justices also have expressed the view that the plurality's standard will "prove unmanageable and arbitrary." Ante, ... (O'Connor, J., joined by Burger, C.J., and Rehnquist, J., concurring in the judgment).

130, 133 (1976), and requires that the proposed change "not have the purpose and will not have the effect of denying or abridging the right to vote on account of race or color." . . . "[T]he purpose of § 5 has always been to insure that no voting-procedure changes would be made that would lead to a retrogression in the position of racial minorities with respect to their effective exercise of the electoral franchise." . . .

Between 1980 and 1990, one of Georgia's 10 congressional districts was a majority-black district, that is, a majority of the district's voters were black. The 1990 Decennial Census indicated that Georgia's population of 6,478,216 persons, 27% of whom are black, entitled it to an additional eleventh congressional seat, . . . prompting Georgia's General Assembly to redraw the State's congressional districts. Both the House and the Senate adopted redistricting guidelines which, among other things, required single-member districts of equal population, contiguous geography, nondilution of minority voting strength, fidelity to precinct lines where possible, and compliance with §§ 2 and 5 of the Act. . . . Only after these requirements were met did the guidelines permit drafters to consider other ends, such as maintaining the integrity of political subdivisions, preserving the core of existing districts, and avoiding contests between incumbents. . . .

[Two successive redistricting plans submitted to the Attorney General for preclearance, each containing two majority-minority districts, were rejected because the Justice Department, "relying on alternative plans proposing three majority-minority districts"—one alternative being "the so-called 'max-black' plan . . . drafted by the American Civil Liberties Union (ACLU) for the General Assembly's black caucus"—"concluded that Georgia had 'failed to explain adequately' its failure to create a third majority-minority district."] The State did not seek a declaratory judgment from the District Court for the District of Columbia. . . .

Twice spurned, the General Assembly set out to create three majority-minority districts to gain preclearance. . . . Using the ACLU's "max-black" plan as its benchmark, . . . the General Assembly enacted a plan that "bore all the signs of [the Justice Department's] involvement. . . ." The Eleventh District lost the black population of Macon, but picked up Savannah, thereby connecting the black neighborhoods of metropolitan Atlanta and the poor black populace of coastal Chatham County, though 260 miles apart in distance and worlds apart in culture. In short, the social, political and economic makeup of the Eleventh District tells a tale of disparity, not community. . . . As the attached appendices attest,

"[t]he populations of the Eleventh are centered around four discrete, widely spaced urban centers that have absolutely nothing to do with each other, and stretch the district hundreds of miles across rural counties and narrow swamp corridors." . . .

"The dense population centers . . . were all majority-black, all at the periphery of the district, and in the case of Atlanta, Augusta and Savannah, all tied to a sparsely populated rural core by even less populated land bridges. Extending from Atlanta to the Atlantic, the Eleventh covered 6,748.2 square miles, splitting eight counties and five municipalities along the way." . . .

Georgia's plan included three majority-black districts, though, and received Justice Department preclearance. . . .

Elections were held under the new congressional redistricting plan on November 4, 1992, and black candidates were elected to Congress from all three majority-black districts.... [F]ive white voters from the Eleventh District [sued,] ... alleg[ing] that Georgia's Eleventh District was a racial gerrymander and so a violation of the Equal Protection Clause as interpreted in *Shaw v. Reno*.... A majority of the [three-judge] District Court [held] the Eleventh District ... invalid under *Shaw*, with one judge dissenting....

II

A

Finding that the "evidence of the General Assembly's intent to racially gerrymander the Eleventh District is overwhelming, and practically stipulated by the parties involved," the District Court held that race was the predominant, overriding factor in drawing the Eleventh District.... Appellants do not take issue with the court's factual finding of this racial motivation. Rather, they contend that evidence of a legislature's deliberate classification of voters on the basis of race cannot alone suffice to state a claim under *Shaw*. They argue that, regardless of the legislature's purposes, a plaintiff must demonstrate that a district's shape is so bizarre that it is unexplainable other than on the basis of race, and that appellees failed to make that showing here. Appellants' conception of the constitutional violation misapprehends our holding in *Shaw* and the Equal Protection precedent upon which *Shaw* relied.

Shaw recognized a claim "analytically distinct" from a vote dilution claim.... Whereas a vote dilution claim alleges that the State has enacted a particular voting scheme as a purposeful device "to minimize or cancel out the voting potential of racial or ethnic minorities," Mobile v. Bolden, 446 U.S. 55, 66 (1980) ..., an action disadvantaging voters of a particular race, the essence of the equal protection claim recognized in *Shaw* is that the State has used race as a basis for separating voters into districts. Just as the State may not, absent extraordinary justification, segregate citizens on the basis of race in its public parks, New Orleans City Park Improvement Assn. v. Detiege, 358 U.S. 54 (1958) (per curiam), buses, Gayle v. Browder, 352 U.S. 903 (1956) (per curiam), golf courses, Holmes v. Atlanta, 350 U.S. 879 (1955) (per curiam), beaches, Mayor and City Council of Baltimore v. Dawson, 350 U.S. 877 (1955) (per curiam), and schools, *Brown*, *supra*, so did we recognize in *Shaw* that it may not separate its citizens into different voting districts on the basis of race. The idea is a simple one: "At the heart of the Constitution's guarantee of equal protection lies the simple command that the Government must treat citizens 'as individuals', not 'as simply components of a racial, religious, sexual or national class.'" Metro Broadcasting, Inc. v. FCC, 497 U.S. 547, 602 (1990) (O'Connor, J., dissenting) ... When the State assigns voters on the basis of race, it engages in the offensive and demeaning assumption that voters of a particular race, because of their race, "think alike, share the same political interests, and will prefer the same candidates at the polls." *Shaw*.... Race-based assignments ... also cause society serious harm. As we concluded in *Shaw*: "Racial classifications with respect to voting carry particular dangers. Racial gerrymandering, even for remedial purposes, may balkanize us into competing racial factions; it threatens to carry us further from the goal of a political system in which race no longer matters—a goal that the Fourteenth and Fifteenth Amendments embody, and to which the Nation continues to aspire. It is for these reasons that race-based districting by our state legislatures demands close judicial scrutiny." ...

Our observation in *Shaw* of the consequences of racial stereotyping was not meant to suggest that a district must be bizarre on its face before there is a constitutional violation.... Shape is relevant not because bizarreness is a necessary element of the constitutional wrong or a threshold requirement of proof, but because it may be persuasive circumstantial evidence that race for its own sake, and not other districting principles, was the legislature's dominant and controlling rationale in drawing its district lines. The logical implication . . . is that parties may rely on evidence other than bizarreness to establish race-based districting. . . .

. . . We recognized in *Shaw* that, outside the districting context, statutes are subject to strict scrutiny under the Equal Protection Clause . . . when, though race neutral on their face, they are motivated by a racial purpose or object. . . . [In prior cases,] the presumed racial purpose of state action, not its stark manifestation, [was] the constitutional violation. . . .

Shaw applied these same principles to redistricting. . . .

Appellants and some of their amici argue that the Equal Protection Clause's general proscription on race-based decisionmaking does not obtain in the districting context because redistricting by definition involves racial considerations. Underlying their argument are the very stereotypical assumptions the Equal Protection Clause forbids. It is true that redistricting in most cases will implicate a political calculus in which various interests compete for recognition, but it does not follow from this that individuals of the same race share a single political interest. The view that they do is "based on the demeaning notion that members of the defined racial groups ascribe to certain 'minority views' that must be different from those of other citizens," *Metro Broadcasting* . . . (Kennedy, J., dissenting), the precise use of race as a proxy the Constitution prohibits. . . .

In sum, . . . parties alleging that a State has assigned voters on the basis of race are neither confined in their proof to evidence regarding the district's geometry and makeup nor required to make a threshold showing of bizarreness. Today's case requires us further to consider the requirements of the proof necessary to sustain this equal protection challenge.

B

. . . Redistricting legislatures will . . . almost always be aware of racial demographics; but it does not follow that race predominates in the redistricting process. . . . The distinction between being aware of racial considerations and being motivated by them may be difficult to make. This evidentiary difficulty, together with the sensitive nature of redistricting and the presumption of good faith that must be accorded legislative enactments, requires courts to exercise extraordinary caution in adjudicating claims that a state has drawn district lines on the basis of race. The plaintiff's burden is to show, either through circumstantial evidence of a district's shape and demographics or more direct evidence going to legislative purpose, that race was the predominant factor motivating the legislature's decision to place a significant number of voters within or without a particular district. To make this showing, a plaintiff must prove that the legislature subordinated traditional race-neutral districting principles, including but not limited to compactness, contiguity, respect for political subdivisions or communities defined by actual shared interests, to racial considerations. . . .

In our view, the District Court applied the correct analysis, and its finding that race was the predominant factor motivating the drawing of the Eleventh District was not clearly erroneous. The court found it was "exceedingly obvious" from the shape of the Eleventh District, together with the relevant racial demographics, that the drawing of narrow land bridges to incorporate within the District outlying appendages containing nearly 80% of the district's total black population was a deliberate attempt to bring black populations into the district.... Although by comparison with other districts the geometric shape of the Eleventh District may not seem bizarre on its face, when its shape is considered in conjunction with its racial and population densities, the story of racial gerrymandering seen by the District Court becomes much clearer.... Although this evidence is quite compelling, we need not determine whether it was, standing alone, sufficient to establish a *Shaw* claim.... The District Court had before it considerable additional evidence showing that the General Assembly was motivated by a predominant, overriding desire to assign black populations to the Eleventh District....

The court found that "it became obvious," both from the Justice Department's objection letters and the three preclearance rounds in general, "that [the Justice Department] would accept nothing less than abject surrender to its maximization agenda." ... It further found that the General Assembly acquiesced and as a consequence was driven by its overriding desire to comply with the Department's maximization demands. The court supported its conclusion ... with the State's own concessions.... [I]n its brief to this Court, the State concedes that "[i]t is undisputed that Georgia's eleventh is the product of a desire by the General Assembly to create a majority black district." ... On this record, we fail to see how the District Court could have reached any conclusion other than that race was the predominant factor in drawing Georgia's Eleventh District; and in any event we conclude the court's finding is not clearly erroneous....

In light of its well-supported finding, the District Court was justified in rejecting the various alternative explanations offered for the District. Although a legislature's compliance with "traditional districting principles such as compactness, contiguity, and respect for political subdivisions" may well suffice to refute a claim of racial gerrymandering, *Shaw* ..., appellants cannot make such a refutation where, as here, those factors were subordinated to racial objectives....

Nor can the State's districting legislation be rescued by mere recitation of purported communities of interest. The evidence was compelling "that there are no tangible 'communities of interest' spanning the hundreds of miles of the Eleventh District." ... [N]ot alleged shared interests but rather the object of maximizing the District's black population and obtaining Justice Department approval ... explained the General Assembly's actions.... A State is free to recognize communities that have a particular racial makeup, provided its action is directed toward some common thread of relevant interests. "[W]hen members of a racial group live together in one community, a reapportionment plan that concentrates members of the group in one district and excludes them from others may reflect wholly legitimate purposes." *Shaw*.... But where the State assumes from a group of voters' race that they "think alike, share the same political interests, and will prefer the same candidates at the polls," it engages in racial stereotyping at odds with equal protection mandates....

. . .

III

To satisfy strict scrutiny, the State must demonstrate that its districting legislation is narrowly tailored to achieve a compelling interest.... There is a "significant state interest in eradicating the effects of past racial discrimination." *Shaw*.... The State does not argue, however, that it created the Eleventh District to remedy past discrimination, and with good reason: there is little doubt that the State's true interest in designing the Eleventh District was creating a third majority-black district to satisfy the Justice Department's preclearance demands.... Whether or not in some cases compliance with the Voting Rights Act, standing alone, can provide a compelling interest independent of any interest in remedying past discrimination, it cannot do so here. As we suggested in *Shaw*, compliance with federal antidiscrimination laws cannot justify race-based districting where the challenged district was not reasonably necessary under a constitutional reading and application of those laws.... The congressional plan challenged here was not required by the Voting Rights Act under a correct reading of the statute.

. . .

We do not accept the contention that the State has a compelling interest in complying with whatever preclearance mandates the Justice Department issues.... Where a State relies on the Department's determination that race-based districting is necessary to comply with the Voting Rights Act, the judiciary retains an independent obligation in adjudicating consequent equal protection challenges to ensure that the State's actions are narrowly tailored to achieve a compelling interest....

... [W]e have rejected agency interpretations to which we would otherwise defer where they raise serious constitutional questions.... When the Justice Department's interpretation of the Act compels race-based districting, it by definition raises a serious constitutional question, ... and should not receive deference.

Georgia's drawing of the Eleventh District was not required under the Act because there was no reasonable basis to believe that Georgia's earlier enacted plans violated § 5. Wherever a plan is "ameliorative," a term we have used to describe plans increasing the number of majority-minority districts, it "cannot violate § 5 unless the new apportionment itself so discriminates on the basis of race or color as to violate the Constitution." *Beer*.... Georgia's first and second proposed plans increased the number of majority-black districts from 1 out of 10 (10%) to 2 out of 11 (18.18%). These plans were "ameliorative" and could not have violated § 5's non-retrogression principle.... Acknowledging as much, ... the United States [objects] that Georgia failed to proffer a nondiscriminatory purpose for its refusal in the first two submissions to take the steps necessary to create a third majority-minority district.

The Government's position is insupportable.... Although ... the State has the burden to prove a nondiscriminatory purpose under § 5, ... Georgia's Attorney General provided a detailed explanation for the State's initial decision not to enact the max-black plan.... The District Court accepted this explanation ... and found an absence of any discriminatory intent.... The State's policy of adhering to other districting principles instead of creating as many majority-minority districts as possible does not support an inference that the plan "so discriminates on the basis of race or color as to violate the Constitution," *Beer* ..., and thus cannot provide any basis under § 5 for the Justice Department's objection.

Instead of grounding its objections on evidence of a discriminatory purpose, it would appear the Government was driven by its policy of maximizing majority-black districts.... In utilizing § 5 to require States to create majority-minority districts wherever possible, the Department of Justice expanded its authority under the statute beyond what Congress intended and we have upheld.

. . .

[W]e recognized in *Beer* that "the purpose of § 5 has always been to insure that no voting-procedure changes would be made that would lead to a retrogression in the position of racial minorities with respect to their effective exercise of the electoral franchise." . . . The Justice Department's maximization policy seems quite far removed from this purpose. We are especially reluctant to conclude that § 5 justifies that policy given the serious constitutional concerns it raises. In South Carolina v. Katzenbach, 383 U.S. 301 (1966), we upheld § 5 as a necessary and constitutional response to some states' "extraordinary stratagem[s] of contriving new rules of various kinds for the sole purpose of perpetuating voting discrimination in the face of adverse federal court decrees." . . . But our belief in *Katzenbach* that the federalism costs exacted by § 5 preclearance could be justified by those extraordinary circumstances does not mean they can be justified in the circumstances of this case. And the Justice Department's implicit command that States engage in presumptively unconstitutional race-based districting brings the Voting Rights Act, once upheld as a proper exercise of Congress' authority under § 2 of the Fifteenth Amendment, *Katzenbach* . . ., into tension with the Fourteenth Amendment. . . . We need not, however, resolve these troubling and difficult constitutional questions today. There is no indication Congress intended such a far-reaching application of § 5, so we reject the Justice Department's interpretation of the statute and avoid the constitutional problems that interpretation raises. . . .

IV

The Voting Rights Act, and its grant of authority to the federal courts to uncover official efforts to abridge minorities' right to vote, has been of vital importance in eradicating invidious discrimination from the electoral process and enhancing the legitimacy of our political institutions. Only if our political system and our society cleanse themselves of that discrimination will all members of the polity share an equal opportunity to gain public office regardless of race. As a Nation we share both the obligation and the aspiration of working toward this end. The end is neither assured nor well served, however, by carving electorates into racial blocs. . . . It takes a shortsighted and unauthorized view of the Voting Rights Act to invoke that statute, which has played a decisive role in redressing some of our worst forms of discrimination, to demand the very racial stereotyping the Fourteenth Amendment forbids.

* * *

The judgment of the District Court is affirmed, and the case is remanded for further proceedings consistent with this decision.

It is so ordered.

Justice O'Connor, concurring.

I understand the threshold standard the Court adopts—"that the legislature subordinated traditional race-neutral districting principles . . . to racial considerations"—to be a demanding one. To invoke strict scrutiny, a plaintiff must show that the State has relied on race in substantial disregard of customary and traditional districting practices. Those practices provide a crucial frame of reference and therefore constitute a significant governing principle in cases of this kind. The standard would be no different if a legislature had drawn the boundaries to favor some other ethnic group; certainly the standard does not treat efforts to create majority-minority districts less favorably than similar efforts on behalf of other groups. Indeed, the driving force behind the adoption of the Fourteenth Amendment was the desire to end legal discrimination against blacks.

Application of the Court's standard does not throw into doubt the vast majority of the Nation's 435 congressional districts, where presumably the States have drawn the boundaries in accordance with their customary districting principles. That is so even though race may well have been considered in the redistricting process. See Shaw v. Reno.... But application of the Court's standard helps achieve *Shaw*'s basic objective of making extreme instances of gerrymandering subject to meaningful judicial review. I therefore join the Court's opinion.

Justice Stevens, dissenting.

... I believe the respondents ... have not suffered any legally cognizable injury.

In [*Shaw*] the Court crafted a new cause of action with two novel, troubling features. First, the Court misapplied the term "gerrymander," previously used to describe grotesque line-drawing by a dominant group to maintain or enhance its political power at a minority's expense, to condemn the efforts of a majority (whites) to share its power with a minority (African Americans). Second, the Court dispensed with its previous insistence in vote dilution cases on a showing of injury to an identifiable group of voters, but it failed to explain adequately what showing a plaintiff must make to establish standing to litigate the newly minted *Shaw* claim. Neither in *Shaw* itself nor in the cases decided today has the Court coherently articulated what injury this cause of action is designed to redress....

Even assuming the validity of *Shaw*, I cannot see how respondents ... could assert the injury the Court attributes to them.... The Court's conclusion [regarding] standing ... appears to rest on a theory that their placement in the Eleventh District caused them "'representational harms.'" ... *Shaw* ... explained the concept of "representational harms" as follows: "When a district obviously is created solely to effectuate the perceived common interests of one racial group, elected officials are more likely to believe that their primary obligation is to represent only the members of that group, rather than their constituency as a whole." ... [R]epresentational harms ... can only come about ... if all or most black voters support the same candidate, and ... if the successful candidate ignores the interests of her white constituents. Respondents' standing, in other words, ultimately depends on the very premise the Court purports to abhor: that voters of a particular race "'think alike, share the same political interests, and will prefer the same candidates at the polls.'" ... This generalization, as the Court recognizes, is "offensive and demeaning."

[A] vote dilution claim ... allows voters to allege that gerrymandered district lines have impaired their ability to elect a candidate of their own race. The Court emphasizes, however, that a so-called *Shaw* claim is "'analytically distinct' from a vote dilution claim." [But] the Court [has not] answered the question its analytic distinction raises: If the *Shaw* injury does not flow from an increased probability that white candidates will lose, then how can the increased probability that black candidates will win cause white voters, such as respondents, cognizable harm?

The Court attempts an explanation ... by equating the injury it imagines respondents have suffered with the injuries African Americans suffered under segregation.... [But o]ur desegregation cases redressed the *exclusion* of black citizens from public facilities reserved for whites. In this case, in contrast, any voter, black or white, may live in the Eleventh District. What respondents contest is the *inclusion* of too many black voters in the District as drawn. [I]f respondents allege no vote dilution, that inclusion can cause them no conceivable injury.[a]

[Also,] legal segregation frustrated the public interest in diversity and tolerance by barring African Americans from joining whites in the activities at issue. The districting plan here, in contrast, serves the interest in diversity and tolerance by increasing the likelihood that a meaningful number of black representatives will add their voices to legislative debates. . . .

. . . I do not see how a districting plan that favors a politically weak group can violate equal protection. . . .

The Court's refusal to distinguish an enactment that helps a minority group from enactments that cause it harm is especially unfortunate at the intersection of race and voting, given that African Americans and other disadvantaged groups have struggled so long and so hard for inclusion in that most central exercise of our democracy. . . . [T]reating racial groups differently from other identifiable groups of voters, as the Court does today, is itself an invidious racial classification. Racial minorities should receive neither more nor less protection than other groups against gerrymanders. *A fortiori*, racial minorities should not be less eligible than other groups to benefit from districting plans the majority designs to aid them.

I respectfully dissent.

Justice Ginsburg, with whom Justices Stevens and Breyer join, and with whom Justice Souter joins except as to Part III–B, dissenting.

. . .

. . . Because I do not endorse the Court's new standard and would not upset Georgia's plan, I dissent.

---

[a] In the companion case of United States v. Hays, ___ U.S. ___, 115 S.Ct. 2431 (1995), the Court declined to rule on the merits of a "racial gerrymander" challenge to a Louisiana congressional districting plan, because the challengers lacked standing to raise it: they did not live in the majority-minority district that was the "primary focus of their racial gerrymandering claim, and they have not otherwise demonstrated that they, personally, have been subjected to a racial classification." Justice O'Connor's opinion for the Court, rejecting the claim that "anybody in the State has a claim," observed in part:

"We discussed the harms caused by racial classifications in *Shaw*. We noted that, in general, '[t]hey threaten to stigmatize individuals by reason of their membership in a racial group and to incite racial hostility.' . . . We also noted 'representational harms'. . . . Any citizen able to demonstrate that he or she, personally, has been injured by that kind of racial classification has standing to challenge the classification in federal court.

"Demonstrating the individualized harm our standing doctrine requires may not be easy in the racial gerrymandering context. . . . Where a plaintiff resides in a racially gerrymandered district, however, the plaintiff has been denied equal treatment because of the legislature's reliance on racial criteria, and therefore has standing to challenge the legislature's action. . . . Voters in such districts may suffer the special representational harms racial classifications can cause in the voting context. On the other hand, where a plaintiff does not live in such a district, he or she does not suffer those special harms, and any inference that the plaintiff has personally been subjected to a racial classification would not be justified absent specific evidence tending to support that inference. . . ."

Justice Breyer, joined by Justice Souter "join[ed] the Court's opinion to the extent that it discusses voters . . . who do not reside within the district that they challenge." Justice Ginsburg concurred in the judgment without comment, and Justice Stevens did so in an opinion objecting to the Court's willingness to recognize that residents of racially gerrymandered districts may suffer individualized harms:

". . . What I do not understand is the majority's view that these racially diverse respondents should fare better if they resided in black-majority districts instead of white-majority districts. . . ."

I

. . .

... [T]hat the Georgia General Assembly took account of race in drawing district lines—a fact not in dispute—does not render the State's plan invalid. To offend the Equal Protection Clause, all agree, the legislature had to do more than consider race. How much more, is the issue that divides the Court today.

. . .

II

A

Before [*Shaw*], this Court invoked the Equal Protection Clause to justify intervention in the quintessentially political task of legislative districting in two circumstances: to enforce the one-person-one-vote requirement ...; and to prevent dilution of a minority group's voting strength....

In *Shaw*, the Court recognized a third basis[, but] wrote cautiously, emphasizing that judicial intervention is exceptional.... The problem in *Shaw* was ..., in the Court's estimation, ... race alone steering placement of district lines.

B

The record before us does not show that race similarly overwhelmed traditional districting practices in Georgia....

In contrast to the snake-like North Carolina district inspected in *Shaw*, Georgia's Eleventh District is hardly "bizarre," "extremely irregular," or "irrational on its face." ... Instead, [its] design reflects significant consideration of "traditional districting factors (such as keeping political subdivisions intact) and the usual political process of compromise and trades for a variety of nonracial reasons." 864 F. Supp. 1354, 1397, n. 5 (S.D.Ga.1994) (Edmondson, J., dissenting).... The District covers a core area in central and eastern Georgia, and its total land area of 6,780 square miles is about average for the State....

Nor does [it] disrespect the boundaries of political subdivisions. Of the 22 counties in the District, 14 are intact and 8 are divided[—]about the state average in divided counties.... Seventy-one percent of [its] boundaries track the borders of political subdivisions.... Of the State's 11 districts, 5 score worse than the Eleventh District on this criterion, and 5 score better.... Eighty-three percent of [its] geographic area is composed of intact counties, above average for the State's congressional districts.... And notably, the Eleventh District's boundaries largely follow precinct lines.

Evidence at trial similarly shows that considerations other than race went into determining the Eleventh District's boundaries. For a "political reason" ... the DeKalb County portion of the Eleventh District was drawn to include a particular (largely white) precinct.... The corridor through Effingham County was substantially narrowed at the request of a (white) State Representative.... In Chatham County, the District was trimmed to exclude a heavily black community in Garden City because a State Representative wanted to keep the city intact inside the neighboring First District.... The Savannah extension was configured by "the narrowest means possible" to avoid splitting the city of Port Wentworth....

Georgia's Eleventh District, in sum, is not an outlier district shaped without reference to familiar districting techniques. Tellingly, the District that the Court's decision today unsettles is not among those on a statistically calculated list of the 28 most bizarre districts in the United States, a study prepared in the wake of our decision in *Shaw* . . . .

C

The Court suggests that . . . the U.S. Department of Justice . . . effectively drew the lines . . . with nothing but race in mind. Yet the "Max–Black" plan advanced by the Attorney General was not the plan passed by the Georgia General Assembly. . . .

And . . . Georgia could have demanded relief from the Department's objections by instituting a civil action in the United States District Court for the District of Columbia, with ultimate review in this Court. Instead . . . the State chose to adopt the plan [it] forcefully defends before us. . . .

D

[T]he Court recognizes as an appropriate districting principle, "respect for . . . communities defined by actual shared interests." The Court finds no community here, however, because a report in the record showed "fractured political, social, and economic interests within the Eleventh District's black population."

But ethnicity itself can tie people together, as volumes of social science literature have documented—even people with divergent economic interests. For this reason, ethnicity is a significant force in political life. . . .

To accommodate the reality of ethnic bonds, legislatures have long drawn voting districts along ethnic lines. Our Nation's cities are full of districts identified by their ethnic character--Chinese, Irish, Italian, Jewish, Polish, Russian, for example. . . . The creation of ethnic districts reflecting felt identity is not ordinarily viewed as offensive or demeaning to those included in the delineation.

III

To separate permissible and impermissible use of race in legislative apportionment, the Court orders strict scrutiny for districting plans "predominantly motivated" by race. No longer can a State avoid judicial oversight by giving . . . genuine and measurable consideration to traditional districting practices. . . . This invitation to litigate against the State seems to me neither necessary nor proper.

A

The Court derives its test from diverse opinions on the relevance of race in contexts distinctly unlike apportionment. . . .

In adopting districting plans, however, States do not treat people as individuals. Apportionment schemes, by their very nature, assemble people in groups. States do not assign voters to districts based on merit or achievement, standards States might use in hiring employees or engaging contractors. Rather, legislators classify voters in groups—by economic, geographical, political, or social characteristics—and then "reconcile the competing claims of [these] groups." Davis v. Bandemer, 478 U.S. 109, 147 (1986) (O'Connor, J., concurring in judgment).

That ethnicity defines some of these groups is a political reality. . . . Until now, no constitutional infirmity has been seen in districting Irish or Italian voters together, for example, so long as the delineation does not abandon familiar apportionment practices.... If Chinese–Americans and Russian–Americans may seek and secure group recognition in the delineation of voting districts, then African–Americans should not be dissimilarly treated. Otherwise, in the name of equal protection, we would shut out "the very minority group whose history in the United States gave birth to the Equal Protection Clause." See *Shaw* ... (Stevens, J., dissenting).[12]

B

Under the Court's approach, judicial review of the same intensity, *i.e.*, strict scrutiny, is in order once it is determined that an apportionment is predominantly motivated by race. It matters not at all, in this new regime, whether the apportionment dilutes or enhances minority voting strength. As very recently observed, however, "[t]here is no moral or constitutional equivalence between a policy that is designed to perpetuate a caste system and one that seeks to eradicate racial subordination." Adarand Constructors, Inc. v. Pena, ... (Stevens, J., dissenting).

Special circumstances justify vigilant judicial inspection to protect minority voters—circumstances that do not apply to majority voters. A history of exclusion from state politics left racial minorities without clout to extract provisions for fair representation in the lawmaking forum.... The equal protection rights of minority voters thus could have remained unrealized absent the Judiciary's close surveillance. Cf. United States v. Carolene Products Co., 304 U.S. 144, 153, n. 4 (1938) (referring to the "more searching judicial inquiry" that may properly attend classifications adversely affecting "discrete and insular minorities"). The majority, by definition, encounters no such blockage. White voters in Georgia do not lack means to exert strong pressure on their state legislators. The force of their numbers is itself a powerful determiner of what the legislature will do that does not coincide with perceived majority interests.

State legislatures like Georgia's today operate under federal constraints imposed by the Voting Rights Act—constraints justified by history and designed by Congress to make once-subordinated people free and equal citizens. But these federal constraints do not leave majority voters in need of extraordinary judicial solicitude. The Attorney General, who administers the Voting Rights Act's preclearance requirements, is herself a political actor. She has a duty to enforce the law Congress passed, and she is no doubt aware of the political cost of venturing too far to the detriment of majority voters. Majority voters, furthermore, can press the State to seek judicial review if the Attorney General refuses to preclear a plan that the voters favor. Finally, the Act is itself a political measure, subject to modification in the political process.

C

The Court's disposition renders redistricting perilous work for state legislatures. Statutory mandates and political realities may require States to consider race when drawing district lines.... But today's decision is a counterforce; it opens the way for federal litigation if "traditional ... districting principles" arguably were accorded less weight than race.... Genuine attention to traditional districting practices and avoidance of bizarre configurations seemed,

---

[12] Race-conscious practices a State may elect to pursue, of course, are not as limited as those it may be required to pursue. See Voinovich v. Quilter, 507 U.S. 146, ___ (1993) ("[F]ederal courts may not order the creation of majority-minority districts unless necessary to remedy a violation of federal law. But that does not mean that the State's powers are similarly limited. Quite the opposite is true....").

under *Shaw*, to provide a safe harbor.... In view of today's decision, that is no longer the case.

Only after litigation—under either the Voting Rights Act, the Court's new *Miller* standard, or both—will States now be assured that plans conscious of race are safe. Federal judges in large numbers may be drawn into the fray. This enlargement of the judicial role is unwarranted. The reapportionment plan that resulted from Georgia's political process merited this Court's approbation, not its condemnation. Accordingly, I dissent.

RACIAL GERRYMANDERING AND THE VOTING RIGHTS ACT

A year after Miller v. Johnson, the Court, by the same 5–4 alignment, invalidated four more majority-minority districts—three from Texas and one from North Carolina—constructed after the 1990 census with attention to the perceived requirements of the Voting Rights Act ("VRA") and the Justice Department's ("DOJ") enforcement of it. The new companion cases again addressed issues of the nature of the cause of action first recognized in Shaw v. Reno, 509 U.S. 630 (1993)(*Shaw I*); the threshold showing required to trigger strict scrutiny of congressional districts configured in race-conscious fashion; compliance with the Voting Rights Act as a compelling state interest; and the elements of narrow tailoring necessary to satisfy strict scrutiny.

The North Carolina case, Shaw v. Hunt, ___ U.S. ___, 116 S.Ct. 1894 (1996)(*Shaw II*), reversed a decision of the District Court, on remand of *Shaw I*, that the State's two majority-minority districts, though deliberately drawn to produce a certain racial composition, were "constitutional, nonetheless, because ... narrowly tailored to further the State's compelling interests in complying with §§ 2 and 5 of the Voting Rights Act...." Refusing to address the challenge to one of the majority-minority districts, because no plaintiffs resided within it nor "provided specific evidence that they personally were assigned to their voting districts on the basis of race[,]" the Court held the other district unconstitutional as "not narrowly tailored to serve a compelling state interest."

The State's initial districting plan had included only one majority-minority district, but when DOJ refused preclearance under VRA § 5 for failure "to give effect to black and Native American voting strength" in a *southern* part of the State for reasons DOJ considered "pretextual," the State submitted, and received preclearance for, a revised plan with a second majority-black district (District 12) in a *northern* part of the State. Applying *Miller*, Chief Justice Rehnquist's majority opinion first found race to be the "predominant factor in drawing" District 12 given the bizarre shape and racial demographics of the serpentine district ("dubbed the least geographically compact district in the Nation"); the State's express acknowledgement in its preclearance submission that the "*overriding* purpose" was to comply with DOJ "dictates ... and to create two congressional districts with effective black voting majorities[;]" the principal draftsman's testimony that creating two majority-black districts was the "principal reason" for the shape of District 12; and the State's initial similar concession to the District Court. That "in shaping District 12, the State effectuated its interest in creating one rural and one urban district, and that partisan politicking was actively at work in the districting process ... does not in any way refute the fact that race was the legislature's predominant consideration. Race was the criterion ... that could not be compromised; respecting communities of interest and protecting Democratic incumbents came into play only after the race-based decision had been made." Hence, District 12 had to satisfy strict scrutiny.

The State could not rely on a compelling interest in remedying past or present racial discrimination, because the District Court had found that such an interest "did not actually precipitate the use of race in the redistricting plan." As for the claim "that the race-based redistricting was constitutionally justified by the State's duty to comply with the Voting Rights Act[,]" the Court "once again" did "not reach" the "question whether under the proper circumstances compliance with the Voting Rights Act, on its own, could be a compelling interest[,] ... because we find that creating an additional majority-black district was not required under a correct reading of § 5 and that District 12, as drawn, is not a remedy narrowly tailored to the State's professed interest in avoiding § 2 liability." Since the State's "first plan ... was ameliorative, having created the first majority-black district in recent history[,]" *Miller* made clear that the plan would not violate § 5 and its "nonretrogression" standard, unless it independently manifested unconstitutional racial discrimination. The nonracial reasons the State initially gave for declining to draw a second majority-black district precluded a finding of any such purpose to discriminate, and, as in *Miller*, the DOJ's pursuit of the "policy of maximizing the number of majority-black districts ... is not properly grounded in § 5 and the Department's authority thereunder."

The argument in favor of District 12 based on avoiding § 2 liability elicited this response:

" ... Our precedent establishes that a plaintiff may allege a § 2 violation in a single-member district if the manipulation of districting lines fragments politically cohesive minority voters among several districts or packs them into one district or a small number of districts, and thereby dilutes the voting strength of members of the minority population.... To prevail on such a claim, a plaintiff must prove that the minority group 'is sufficiently large and geographically compact to constitute a majority in a single-member district'; that the minority group 'is politically cohesive'; and that 'the white majority votes sufficiently as a bloc to enable it ... usually to defeat the minority's preferred candidate.' Thornburg v. Gingles, 478 U.S. 30, 50–51 (1986); Growe v. Emison, 507 U.S. 25 (1993) (recognizing that the three *Gingles* preconditions would apply to a § 2 challenge to a single-member district). A court must also consider all other relevant circumstances and must ultimately find based on the totality of those circumstances that members of a protected class 'have less opportunity than other members of the electorate to participate in the political process and to elect representatives of their choice.' [§ 2(b)]....

"We assume, *arguendo*, for the purpose of resolving this case, that compliance with § 2 could be a compelling interest, and we likewise assume, *arguendo*, that the General Assembly believed a second majority-minority district was needed in order not to violate § 2, and that the legislature at the time it acted had a strong basis in evidence to support that conclusion. We hold that even with the benefit of these assumptions, the North Carolina plan does not survive strict scrutiny because the remedy—the creation of District 12—is not narrowly tailored to the asserted end.

" ... [T]he legislative action [must] substantially address, if not achieve, the avowed purpose.... [H]ere, ... the legislative action must, at a minimum, remedy the anticipated [§ 2] violation or achieve compliance to be narrowly tailored.[7]

---

[7] We do not suggest that where the governmental interest is eradicating the effects of past discrimination the race-based action necessarily would have to achieve fully its task to be narrowly tailored.

"District 12 could not remedy any potential § 2 violation.... No one looking at District 12 could reasonably suggest that the district contains a 'geographically compact' population of any race.... Therefore where that district sits, 'there neither has been a wrong nor can be a remedy.' ...

"Appellees ..., however[,] ... contend, and a majority of the District Court agreed, ... that once a legislature has a strong basis in evidence for concluding that a § 2 violation exists in the State, it may draw a majority-minority district anywhere, even if the district is in no way coincident with the compact *Gingles* district, as long as racially polarized voting exists where the district is ultimately drawn....

"We find this position singularly unpersuasive.... The vote dilution injuries suffered by [people in one area of the State] are not remedied by creating a safe majority-black district somewhere else in the State. [I]f a geographically compact, cohesive minority population lives in south-central to southeastern North Carolina, as the Justice Department's objection letter suggested, District 12 ... would not address that § 2 violation. The black voters of the south-central to southeastern region would still be suffering precisely the same injury that they suffered before District 12 was drawn. District 12 would not address the professed interest of relieving the vote dilution, much less be narrowly tailored to accomplish the goal.

"[The argument] ... derives from a misconception of the vote-dilution claim. To accept that the district may be placed anywhere implies that the claim, and hence the coordinate right to an undiluted vote (to cast a ballot equal among voters), belongs to the minority as a group and not to its individual members. It does not....

"[Finally, that a portion] of the concentration of minority voters that would have given rise to a § 2 claim [may have resided in] not more than 20% of the district [was an insufficient] degree of incorporation [to] mean that District 12 substantially addresses the § 2 violation. We hold, therefore, that District 12 is not narrowly tailored to the State's asserted interest in complying with § 2 of the Voting Rights Act."

Unlike *Shaw II*, the companion Texas case, Bush v. Vera, ___ U.S. ___, 116 S.Ct. 1941 (1996), revealed important disagreements among the five majority Justices regarding the level of race-consciousness in districting that will provoke strict scrutiny and their willingness to announce that compliance with the results test of § 2 is a compelling state interest—even though they agreed that under *Shaw I* and *Miller* the District Court was correct to invalidate all three districts. A plurality opinion by Justice O'Connor, joined by Chief Justice Rehnquist and Justice Kennedy, expressly noted that "[s]trict scrutiny does not apply merely because redistricting is performed with consciousness of race ... [nor] to all cases of intentional creation of majority-minority districts[, but only where] ... legitimate districting principles were 'subordinated' to race." Justice Kennedy concurred to note:

"I join the plurality opinion, but the statements ... that strict scrutiny would not apply to all cases of intentional creation of majority-minority districts require comment. I do not consider these dicta to commit me to any position on ... whether race is predominant whenever a State ... foreordains that one race be the majority in a certain number of districts or in a certain part of the State. In my view, we would no doubt apply strict scrutiny if a State decreed that certain districts had to be at least 50 percent white, and our analysis should be no different if the State so favors minority races."

And Justice Thomas, joined by Justice Scalia, concurred only in the judgment to disagree "with Justice O'Connor's assertion that strict scrutiny is not invoked by the intentional creation of majority-minority districts":

"... [T]he intentional creation of a majority-minority district certainly means more than mere awareness that application of traditional, race-neutral districting principles will result in the creation of a district in which a majority of the district's residents are members of a particular minority group. See Personnel Administrator of Mass. v. Feeney, 442 U.S. 256, 279 (1979) (distinguishing discriminatory intent from 'intent as volition' or 'intent as awareness of consequences'). In my view, it means that the legislature affirmatively undertakes to create a majority-minority district that would not have existed but for the express use of racial classifications—in other words, that a majority-minority district is created 'because of,' and not merely 'in spite of,' racial demographics. See ibid. When that occurs, traditional race-neutral districting principles are necessarily subordinated (and race necessarily predominates), and the legislature has classified persons on the basis of race. The resulting redistricting must be viewed as a racial gerrymander.

" ...

"... Texas readily admits that it intentionally created majority-minority districts and that those districts would not have existed but for its affirmative use of racial demographics.... That is enough to require application of strict scrutiny in this case."

The plurality, "differ[ing] from Justice Thomas, who would apparently hold that it suffices that racial considerations be *a* motivation for the drawing of a majority-minority district[,]" thought further inquiry was necessary, as it found the "present case ... a mixed motive case" in that, besides the conceded goal of producing majority-minority districts, "other goals, particularly incumbency protection ... also played a role in the drawing of the district lines." Nonetheless, the combination of the District Court's "findings—that the State substantially neglected traditional districting criteria such as compactness, that it was committed from the outset to creating majority-minority districts, and that it manipulated district lines to exploit unprecedentedly detailed racial data—together weigh in favor of the application of strict scrutiny[, although w]e do not hold that any one of these factors is independently sufficient to require strict scrutiny." The District Court also had "found that incumbency protection influenced the redistricting plan to an unprecedented extent[,]" however, compelling scrutiny of "each challenged district to determine whether the District Court's conclusion that race predominated over legitimate districting considerations, including incumbency, can be sustained."

Undertaking this individualized examination, the plurality ultimately concluded that race predominated in the drawing of each of the three districts' "bizarre shapes." With respect to the majority-black District 30 in Dallas County, the plurality acknowledged that "[i]n some circumstances, incumbency protection might explain as well as, or better than, race a State's decision to depart from other traditional districting principles, such as compactness, in the drawing of bizarre district lines[,]" but it emphasized that "to the extent that race is used as a proxy for political characteristics [i.e., assuming that to include blacks is to include Democrats], a racial stereotype requiring strict scrutiny is in operation." In a disagreement with Justice Stevens' dissent that the plurality regarded as "largely factual," they concluded:

"The record discloses intensive and pervasive use of race both as a proxy to protect the political fortunes of adjacent incumbents, and for its own sake in maximizing the minority population of District 30 regardless of traditional districting principles. District 30's combination of a bizarre, noncompact shape and overwhelming evidence that that shape was essentially dictated by racial considerations of one form or another is exceptional [and] leads us to conclude that District 30 is subject to strict scrutiny."

With respect to the interlocking majority-black and majority-Hispanic districts in the Houston area—"two of the three least regular districts in the country"—the influence of incumbency protection was "overwhelmed ... by the State's efforts to maximize racial divisions"—especially since "the district lines correlate almost perfectly with race, ... while both districts are similarly solidly Democratic[,]" and given "the intricacy of the lines drawn, separating Hispanic voters from African–American voters on a block-by-block basis, betray[ing] the critical impact of the block-by-block racial data available on the [computer software] program."

As in *Shaw II*, each of the districts was "not narrowly tailored" to a compelling state interest. The plurality again assumed without deciding that compliance with the results test of § 2 "can be a compelling state interest[,]" though Justice O'Connor separately concurred in her own plurality opinion to join the dissenters in affirming for a different Court majority that "the States have a compelling interest in complying with the results test as this Court has interpreted it." The plurality "also reaffirm[ed] that the 'narrow tailoring' requirement of strict scrutiny allows the States a limited degree of leeway" and leaves the States "flexibility that federal courts enforcing § 2 lack, ... insofar as deference is due to their reasonable fears of, and to their reasonable efforts to avoid, § 2 liability." Indeed, a "§ 2 district that is reasonably compact and regular, taking into account traditional districting principles ... may pass strict scrutiny without having to defeat rival compact districts designed by plaintiffs' experts in endless 'beauty contests.' " Here, however,

"the districts are [not] narrowly tailored to serve the State's interest in avoiding liability under § 2, because § 2 does not require a State to create, on predominantly racial lines, a district that is not 'reasonably compact.' ... If, because of the dispersion of the minority population, a reasonably compact majority-minority district cannot be created, § 2 does not require a majority-minority district; if a reasonably compact district can be created, nothing in § 2 requires the race-based creation of a district that is far from compact.

"... Significant deviations from traditional districting principles, such as the bizarre shape and noncompactness demonstrated by the districts here, cause constitutional harm insofar as they convey the message that political identity is, or should be, predominantly racial. For example, the bizarre shaping of Districts 18 and 29, cutting across pre-existing precinct lines and other natural or traditional divisions, is not merely evidentially significant; it is part of the constitutional problem insofar as it disrupts nonracial bases of political identity and thus intensifies the emphasis on race.[a]

"... The districts before us exhibit a level of racial manipulation that exceeds what § 2 could justify."[b]

---

[a] Justice Kennedy's concurring opinion noted, with respect to these two districts, that "[a]lthough the State could have drawn either a majority-African–American or majority-Hispanic district in Harris County without difficulty, there is no evidence that two reasonably compact majority-minority districts could have been drawn there.... Section 2 does not require the State to create

two noncompact majority-minority districts just because a compact district could be drawn for either minority independently."

[b] Nor, for the same reasons, were the Districts narrowly tailored to serve the State's compelling interest in remedying the "effects of racially polarized voting attributable to past and present racial discrimination." And the claim that the Houston major-

The plurality concluded by rejecting the dissenters' calls for reconsidering the *Shaw I* cause of action, stating in part:

"Legislators and district courts nationwide have modified their practices— or, rather, reembraced the traditional districting practices that were almost universally followed before the 1990 census—in response to *Shaw I*. Those practices and our precedents, which acknowledge voters as more than mere racial statistics, play an important role in defining the political identity of the American voter. Our Fourteenth Amendment jurisprudence evinces a commitment to eliminate unnecessary and excessive governmental use and reinforcement of racial stereotypes.... We decline to retreat from that commitment today."

Justice O'Connor's separate opinion also addressed the dissenters:

"Although I agree with the dissenters about § 2's role as part of our national commitment to racial equality, I differ from them in my belief that that commitment can and must be reconciled with the complementary commitment of our Fourteenth Amendment jurisprudence to eliminate the unjustified use of racial stereotypes. At the same time that we combat the symptoms of racial polarization in politics, we must strive to eliminate unnecessary race-based state action that appears to endorse the disease.

"... The Voting Rights Act requires the States and the courts to take action to remedy the reality of racial inequality in our political system, sometimes necessitating race-based action, while the Fourteenth Amendment requires us to look with suspicion on the excessive use of racial considerations by the government. But I believe that the States, playing a primary role, and the courts, in their secondary role, are capable of distinguishing the appropriate and reasonably necessary uses of race from its unjustified and excessive uses."

Justice Stevens, joined by Justices Ginsburg and Breyer, filed separate, extended dissents in *Shaw II* and *Vera* that both elaborated previous objections to *Shaw I*'s " 'analytically distinct' jurisprudence of racial gerrymandering" and criticized the Court's application of that jurisprudence "even on its own terms."[c] Justice Souter's lengthy dissent, filed in *Vera* but applicable to both

---

ity-black district was justified by a compelling interest in complying with VRA § 5 was rejected because the argument sought "to justify not maintenance, but substantial augmentation, of the African–American population percentage"—a result "beyond what was reasonably necessary to avoid retrogression."

[c] Justices Ginsburg and Breyer did not join that portion of Justice Stevens' dissent in *Shaw II* elaborating his criticism in *Miller* and *Hays* that the Court's conception of "standing" and "injury" in its "emerging and misguided race-based districting jurisprudence" was fundamentally flawed. Justice Stevens wrote in part:

"[I]t appears that no individual has been burdened more than any other. The supposedly insidious messages that *Shaw I* contends will follow from extremely irregular race-based districting will presumably be received in equal measure by all State residents. For that reason, the claimed violation of a shared right to a color-blind districting process would not seem to implicate the Equal Protection Clause at all precisely because it rests

neither on a challenge to the State's decision to distribute burdens and benefits unequally, nor on a claim that the State's formally equal treatment of its citizens in fact stamps persons of one race with a badge of inferiority.

"... [T]he Court's decision to entertain the claim of these plaintiffs would seem to emanate less from the Equal Protection Clause's bar against racial discrimination than from the Court's unarticulated recognition of a new substantive due process right to 'color-blind' districting itself.... [T]he constitutional claim ... ultimately depends for its success on little more than speculative judicial suppositions about the societal message that is to be gleaned from race-based districting. I know of no workable constitutional principle, however, that can discern whether the message conveyed is a distressing endorsement of racial separatism, or an inspiring call to integrate the political process.

"The fact that our Equal Protection jurisprudence requires strict scrutiny of a claim cases, was also joined by Justices Ginsburg and Breyer. It called on the Court "to admit *Shaw*'s failure" and abandon the *Shaw* cause of action altogether.

Justice Stevens thought strict scrutiny inappropriate in both cases. He interpreted the Court's precedents to allow States to avoid strict scrutiny unless challengers proved "that the State did not respect traditional districting principles in drawing majority-minority districts." In *Shaw II* he emphasized that precisely because North Carolina had chosen "the winding contours of District 12 over the more cartographically pleasant boundaries [of the alternative majority-black district] proposed by the Attorney General[,]" its "noncompact appearance ... fails to show that North Carolina engaged in suspect race-based districting." Instead, "the record reveals that two race-neutral, traditional districting criteria determined District 12's shape: the interest in ensuring that incumbents would remain residents of the districts they have previously represented; and the interest in placing predominantly rural voters in one district and predominantly urban voters in another." In any event, insofar as the majority assumed that the State had drawn District 12 to avoid § 2 liability, "it cannot be correct to say that a racially discriminatory purpose controlled its line-drawing. A more accurate conclusion would be that the State took race into account only to the extent necessary to meet the requirements of a carefully thought out federal statute. ... The majority's implicit equation of the intentional consideration of race in order to comply with the Voting Rights Act with intentional racial discrimination reveals the inadequacy of the framework it adopts for considering the constitutionality of race-based districting."

In *Vera*, he argued that "the fair implications of the District Court's findings" were "that Texas' entire map is a political, not a racial gerrymander"—even though it was "clear that race also played a role. . . ." He noted and reinforced the Court's endorsement of the view that a State constitutionally may consider race in the deliberate creation of majority-minority districts, reasoning that "when the state action (i) has neither the intent nor effect of harming any particular group, (ii) is not designed to give effect to irrational prejudices held by its citizens but to break them down, and (iii) uses race as a classification because race is 'relevant' to the benign goal of the classification, . . . we need not view the action with the typically fatal skepticism that we have used to strike down the most pernicious forms of state behavior."

Particularly with respect to District 30, Justice Stevens objected that none of the factors relied on by the majority "either singly or in combination . . . suggests that racial considerations 'subordinated' race-neutral districting principles."[4] Instead, he found "overwhelming evidence that incumbency protection was the critical motivating factor in the creation of the bizarre Texas districts," and explained that "[a]lthough aspects of our dispute with the plurality are

that the State has used race as a criterion for imposing burdens on some persons but not others does not mean that the Constitution demands that a similar level of review obtain for a claim that the State has used race to impose equal burdens on the polity as a whole, or upon some nonracially defined portion thereof. . . .

"If under *Hays* the so-called 'stigmatic' harms which result from extreme race-based districting suffice to secure standing, then I fail to see why it matters whether the litigants live within the 'gerrymandered' district or were placed in a district as a result of their race. . . . [A]ll voters in North Carolina would seem to be equally affected by the messages

of 'balkanization' or 'racial apartheid' that racially gerrymandered maps supposedly convey. . . ."

[4] He found the two Houston districts "a closer question on the application of strict scrutiny[,]" because besides evidence of the "same race-neutral factors motivating the zigzags of District 30[,]" there was "also evidence that the interlocking shapes of the Houston districts were specifically, and almost exclusively, the result of an effort to create, out of largely integrated communities, both a majority-black and a majority-Hispanic district."

'largely factual,' they arise not out of our disagreement with the District Court's credibility assessments, but out of that court's erroneous conclusion that the state's overwhelming reliance on this race-neutral factor was illegitimate and irrelevant to its evaluation of the factors involved in the shifting of this District's lines." As to the plurality's "fall-back position ... that even if the predominant reason for the bizarre features of the majority-minority districts was incumbency protection, the State impermissibly used race as a proxy for determining the likely political affiliation of blocks of voters[,]" Justice Stevens found the "demographic calculus far more complex than simple racial stereotyping[,]" doubted its impact compared to the nonracial reasons for forcing the district lines "away from its core[,]" and thought it "neither irrational, nor invidious ... to assume that a black resident of a particular community is a Democrat if reliable statistical evidence discloses that 97% of the blacks in that community vote in Democratic primary elections."

Even assuming the applicability of strict scrutiny, Justice Stevens thought the challenged districts were narrowly tailored to the compelling interest of compliance with the VRA. In *Shaw II*, he thought it irrelevant that District 12 "did not 'remedy' any potential violation of § 2" in southern North Carolina, because a second majority-minority district anywhere in the State would have precluded § 2 liability, and "if a State's new plan successfully avoids the potential litigation entirely, there is no reason why it must also take the form of a 'remedy' for an unproven violation." He thought the "Court's analysis g[ave] rise to the unfortunate suggestion that a State which fears a § 2 lawsuit must draw the precise district that it believes a federal court would have the power to impose." As for the Texas districts in *Vera*, Justice Stevens, for similar reasons, objected to the Court's "insist[ence] that the lack of compactness in the districts prevent them from being 'narrowly tailored'....":

"... While a State can be liable for a § 2 violation only if it could have drawn a compact district and failed to do so, it does not follow that creating such a district is the only way to avoid a § 2 violation.... The plurality admits that a State retains 'a limited degree of leeway' in drawing a district to alleviate fears of § 2 liability, but if there is no independent constitutional duty to create compact districts in the first place, and the Court suggests none, there is no reason why noncompact districts should not be a permissible method of avoiding violations of law. The fact that they might be unacceptable judicial remedies does not speak to the question whether they may be acceptable when adopted by a state legislature...."

Justice Stevens also noted the

"great irony ... that by requiring the State to place the majority-minority district in a particular place and with a particular shape, the district may stand out as a stark, placid island in a sea of oddly shaped majority-white neighbors.... The Court-imposed barriers limiting the shape of the district will interfere more directly with the ability of minority voters to participate in the political process than did the oddly shaped districts that the Court has struck down in recent cases. Unaffected by the new racial jurisprudence, majority-white communities will be able to participate in the districting process by requesting that they be placed into certain districts, divided between districts in an effort to maximize representation, or grouped with more distant communities that might nonetheless match their interests better than communities next door. By contrast, none of this political maneuvering will be permissible for majority-minority districts, thereby segregating and balkanizing them far more effectively than the Districts at issue here, in which they were manipulated in the political process as easily as white voters. This result ... involves 'discrimination' in a far more concrete manner than did the odd shapes that so offended the Court's sensibilities in *Miller, Shaw II,* and *Bush.*"

He concluded with these statements:

"... Perhaps minority candidates, forced to run in majority-white districts, will be able to overcome the long history of stereotyping and discrimination that has heretofore led the vast majority of majority-white districts to reject minority candidacies. Perhaps not. I am certain only that bodies of elected federal and state officials are in a far better position than anyone on this Court to assess whether the Nation's long history of discrimination has been overcome, and that nothing in the Constitution requires this unnecessary intrusion into the ability of States to negotiate solutions to political differences while providing long-excluded groups the opportunity to participate effectively in the democratic process...."

Justice Souter's dissent complained that the Court had not yet succeeded in "describ[ing] the elements and defin[ing] the contours of the *Shaw* cause of action ... for reasons that go to the conceptual bone." Moreover, "to the extent that some clarity follows from the knowledge that race may be considered when reasonably necessary to conform to the Voting Rights Act, today's opinions raise the specter that this ostensible progress may come with a heavy constitutional price [—] ... the practical elimination of a State's discretion to apply traditional districting principles...." He urged the Court "to recognize that *Shaw*'s problems result from a basic misconception about the relation between race and districting principles ... that no amount of case-by-case tinkering can eliminate."

He emphasized that the Court, in "assum[ing] over the years that traditional districting principles widely accepted among States represent[] an informal baseline of acceptable districting practices[,] ... has recognized the basically associational character of voting rights in a representative democracy." And in a footnote he observed that the Court had "never disagreed in principle" that "to recognize that racial groups, like all other groups, play a real and legitimate role in political decisionmaking ... involves nothing more than an acknowledgement of the reality that our concepts of common interest, geography, and personal allegiances are in many places simply too bound up with race to deny some room for a theory of representative democracy allowing for the consideration of racially conceived interests."

Like Justice Stevens, he found "the logic of traditional equal protection analysis ... at odds with *Shaw*'s concept of injury": the "expressive" harm *Shaw I* is supposed to address "is not confined to any identifiable class singled out for disadvantage ... [but] would seem ... to fall on every citizen and every representative alike"; there is no objection "to segregation but to the particular racial proportions of the district"; and "this use of race ... conveys no message about the inferiority or outsider status of members of the white majority excluded from a district ... [and] implies nothing about the capacity or value of the minority to which it gives the chance of electoral success." Moreover, *Shaw* has the "further conceptual inadequacy [that w]hereas it defines injury as the reinforcement of the notion that members of a racial group will prefer the same candidates at the polls, the immediate object of the constitutional prohibition against the intentional dilution of minority voting strength is to protect the right of minority voters to make just such a preference effective":

"Indeed, if there were no correlation between race and candidate preference, it would make no sense to say that minority voters had less opportunity than others to elect whom they would.... When voting is ... racially polarized, ... majority-minority districts provide the only practical means of avoiding dilution or remedying the dilution injury that has occurred already.... So it is that the Court's definition of injury is so broad as to cover constitutionally necessary efforts to prevent or remedy a violation of the Fourteenth and Fifteenth Amendments and of § 2 of the Voting Rights Act."

Justice Souter raised special objection to the unmanageability of *Miller*'s "predominant motive" standard, "not merely" because "the very nature of districting decisions makes it difficult to identify whether any particular consideration, racial or otherwise," predominated, but "more fundamental[ly,]" because "in the political environment in which race can affect election results, many of these traditional districting principles cannot be applied without taking race into account and are thus, as a practical matter, inseparable from the supposedly illegitimate racial considerations":

"If ... a legislature may draw district lines to preserve the integrity of a given community, ... this objective is inseparable from preserving the community's racial identity when the community is characterized, or even self-defined, by the race of the majority of those who live there. This is an old truth, having been recognized every time the political process produced an Irish or Italian or Polish ward.

"Or take the traditional principle of providing protection for incumbents. The plurality seems to assume that incumbents may always be protected by drawing lines on the basis of data about political parties. But what if the incumbent has drawn support largely for racial reasons? What, indeed, if the incumbent was elected in a majority-minority district created to remedy vote dilution that resulted from racial bloc voting? It would be sheer fantasy to assume that consideration of race in these circumstances is somehow separable from application of the traditional principle of incumbency protection, and sheer incoherence to think that the consideration of race that is constitutionally required to remedy Fourteenth and Fifteenth Amendment vote dilution somehow becomes unconstitutional when aimed at protecting the incumbent the next time the census requires redistricting. Thus, it is as impossible in theory as in practice to untangle racial consideration from the application of traditional districting principles in a society plagued by racial-bloc voting with a racial minority population of political significance, or at least the unrealized potential for achieving it. And it is for just this fundamental reason that a test turning on predominant purpose is incapable of producing any answer when traditional districting principles are applied in the political environment in which *Shaw I* actions are brought."

According to Justice Souter, *Shaw*'s "basic deficiencies" entail "endemic unpredictability" and "the destruction of any clear incentive for the States with substantial minority populations to take action to avoid vote dilution." The "developments" in these cases "fall short of curing *Shaw*'s unworkability" and corrective "options ... are few." To "impos[e] a principle of colorblindness ... would be [to] submerg[e] the votes of those whom the Fourteenth and Fifteenth Amendments were adopted to protect, ... unless the attitudes that produce racial bloc voting were eliminated along with traditional districting principles[,] ... [and] the Court has repeatedly made it plain that *Shaw* was in no way intended to effect a revolution by eliminating traditional districting practice for the sake of colorblindness." Hence, the options are "to confine the cause of action by adopting a quantifiable shape test or to eliminate the cause of action entirely." Despite taking "the commands of *stare decisis* very seriously," Justice Souter urged complete withdrawal "from the presently untenable state of the law."

3.   QUALIFICATIONS OF VOTERS

Harper v. Virginia State Board of Elections

383 U.S. 663, 86 S.Ct. 1079, 16 L.Ed.2d 169 (1966).

Mr. Justice Douglas delivered the opinion of the Court.[a]

These are suits by Virginia residents to have declared unconstitutional Virginia's poll tax. The three-judge District Court, feeling bound by our decision in Breedlove v. Suttles, 302 U.S. 277, dismissed the complaint....

While the right to vote in federal elections is conferred by Art. I, § 2, of the Constitution ... the right to vote in state elections is nowhere expressly mentioned. It is argued that the right to vote in state elections is implicit, particularly by reason of the First Amendment and that it may not constitutionally be conditioned upon the payment of a tax or fee.... We do not stop to canvass the relation between voting and political expression. For it is enough to say that once the franchise is granted to the electorate, lines may not be drawn which are inconsistent with the Equal Protection Clause of the Fourteenth Amendment. That is to say, the right of suffrage "is subject to the imposition of state standards which are not discriminatory and which do not contravene any restriction that Congress, acting pursuant to its constitutional powers, has imposed." Lassiter v. Northampton County Board of Elections, 360 U.S. 45, 51. We were speaking there of a state literacy test which we sustained, warning that the result would be different if a literacy test, fair on its face, were used to discriminate against a class.... But the *Lassiter* case does not govern the result here, because, unlike a poll tax, the "ability to read and write ... has some relation to standards designed to promote intelligent use of the ballot."
. . .

We conclude that a State violates the Equal Protection Clause of the Fourteenth Amendment whenever it makes the affluence of the voter or payment of any fee an electoral standard. Voter qualifications have no relation to wealth nor to paying or not paying this or any other tax. Our cases demonstrate that the Equal Protection Clause of the Fourteenth Amendment restrains the States from fixing voter qualifications which invidiously discriminate. Thus without questioning the power of a State to impose reasonable residence restrictions on the availability of the ballot (see Pope v. Williams, 193 U.S. 621), we held in Carrington v. Rash, 380 U.S. 89, that a State may not deny the opportunity to vote to a bona fide resident merely because he is a member of the armed services. "By forbidding a soldier ever to controvert the presumption of non-residence, the Texas Constitution imposes an invidious discrimination in violation of the Fourteenth Amendment." ... Previously we had said that neither homesite nor occupation "affords a permissible basis for distinguishing between qualified voters within the State." Gray v. Sanders, 372 U.S. 368, 380. We think the same must be true of requirements of wealth or affluence or payment of a fee.

[a] In the two decades 1934–1954, five states abolished the poll tax: Louisiana, Florida, Georgia, South Carolina and Tennessee. This voluntary action then stopped—probably because of feelings stirred by the 1954 *Brown* decision. As of 1963, payment of a poll tax was a prerequisite to voting in five states: Alabama, Arkansas, Mississippi, Texas and Virginia. Burke Marshall reported: "By now the tax is a negligible, bi-racial deterrent to voting." 27 Law & Contemp.Pr. 455, 464 (1962). In 1962 Congress proposed, and by 1964 the requisite number of States had ratified, the Twenty-fourth Amendment outlawing the "poll tax or other tax" as a condition for voting in federal elections.

Long ago in Yick Wo v. Hopkins, 118 U.S. 356, 370, the Court referred to "the political franchise of voting" as a "fundamental political right, because preservative of all rights." Recently in Reynolds v. Sims, 377 U.S. 533, 561–562, we said: "Undoubtedly, the right of suffrage is a fundamental matter in a free and democratic society. Especially since the right to exercise the franchise in a free and unimpaired manner is preservative of other basic civil and political rights, any alleged infringement of the right of citizens to vote must be carefully and meticulously scrutinized." . . .

It is argued that a State may exact fees from citizens for many different kinds of licenses; that if it can demand from all an equal fee for a driver's license, it can demand from all an equal poll tax for voting. But we must remember that the interest of the State, when it comes to voting, is limited to the power to fix qualifications. Wealth, like race, creed, or color, is not germane to one's ability to participate intelligently in the electoral process. Lines drawn on the basis of wealth or property, like those of race (Korematsu v. United States, 323 U.S. 214, 216), are traditionally disfavored. See Edwards v. People of State of California, 314 U.S. 160, 184–185 (Jackson, J., concurring); Griffin v. People of State of Illinois, 351 U.S. 12; Douglas v. People of State of California, 372 U.S. 353. To introduce wealth or payment of a fee as a measure of a voter's qualifications is to introduce a capricious or irrelevant factor. The degree of the discrimination is irrelevant. In this context—that is, as a condition of obtaining a ballot—the requirement of fee paying causes an "invidious" discrimination (Skinner v. State of Oklahoma, 316 U.S. 535, 541) that runs afoul of the Equal Protection Clause. Levy "by the poll," as stated in Breedlove v. Suttles, . . . is an old familiar form of taxation; and we say nothing to impair its validity so long as it is not made a condition to the exercise of the franchise. *Breedlove v. Suttles* sanctioned its use as "a prerequisite of voting." . . . To that extent the *Breedlove* case is overruled.

We agree, of course, with Mr. Justice Holmes that the Due Process Clause of the Fourteenth Amendment "does not enact Mr. Herbert Spencer's Social Statics" (Lochner v. People of State of New York, 198 U.S. 45, 75). Likewise, the Equal Protection Clause is not shackled to the political theory of a particular era. In determining what lines are unconstitutionally discriminatory, we have never been confined to historic notions of equality, any more than we have restricted due process to a fixed catalogue of what was at a given time deemed to be the limits of fundamental rights. See Malloy v. Hogan, 378 U.S. 1, 5–6. Notions of what constitutes equal treatment for purposes of the Equal Protection Clause *do* change. This Court in 1896 held that laws providing for separate public facilities for white and Negro citizens did not deprive the latter of the equal protection and treatment that the Fourteenth Amendment commands. Plessy v. Ferguson, 163 U.S. 537. Seven of the eight Justices then sitting subscribed to the Court's opinion, thus joining in expressions of what constituted unequal and discriminatory treatment that sound strange to a contemporary ear. When, in 1954—more than a half-century later—we repudiated the "separate-but-equal" doctrine of *Plessy* as respects public education we stated: "In approaching this problem, we cannot turn the clock back to 1868 when the Amendment was adopted, or even to 1896 when Plessy v. Ferguson was written." Brown v. Board of Education, 347 U.S. 483, 492.

In a recent searching re-examination of the Equal Protection Clause, we held, as already noted, that "the opportunity for equal participation by all voters in the election of state legislators" is required. Reynolds v. Sims, supra, 377 U.S. at 566. We decline to qualify that principle by sustaining this poll tax. Our conclusion, like that in *Reynolds v. Sims,* is founded not on what we think governmental policy should be, but on what the Equal Protection Clause requires.

We have long been mindful that where fundamental rights and liberties are asserted under the Equal Protection Clause, classifications which might invade or restrain them must be closely scrutinized and carefully confined. See, e.g., Skinner v. State of Oklahoma, 316 U.S. 535, 541; Reynolds v. Sims, 377 U.S. 533, 561–562; Carrington v. Rash, supra; Baxstrom v. Herold, 383 U.S. 107; Cox v. State of Louisiana, 379 U.S. 536, 580–581 (Black, J., concurring).

Those principles apply here. For to repeat, wealth or fee paying has, in our view, no relation to voting qualifications; the right to vote is too precious, too fundamental to be so burdened or conditioned.

Reversed.

Mr. Justice Black, dissenting.

... The Court ... overrules *Breedlove* in part, but its opinion reveals that it does so not by using its limited power to interpret the original meaning of the Equal Protection Clause, but by giving that clause a new meaning which it believes represents a better governmental policy. From this action I dissent.

. . .

The Court's justification for consulting its own notions rather than following the original meaning of the Constitution, as I would, apparently is based on the belief of the majority of the Court that for this Court to be bound by the original meaning of the Constitution is an intolerable and debilitating evil; that our Constitution should not be "shackled to the political theory of a particular era," and that to save the country from the original Constitution the Court must have constant power to renew it and keep it abreast with this Court's more enlightening theories of what is best for our society. It seems to me that this is not only an attack on the great value of our Constitution itself but also on the concept of a written constitution which is to survive through the years as originally written unless changed through the amendment process which the Framers wisely provided. Moreover, when a "political theory" embodied in our Constitution becomes outdated, it seems to me that a majority of the nine members of this Court are not only without constitutional power but are far less qualified to choose a new constitutional political theory than the people of this country proceeding in the manner provided by Article V.

The people have not found it impossible to amend their Constitution to meet new conditions. The Equal Protection Clause itself is the product of the peoples' desire to use their constitutional power to amend the Constitution to meet new problems. . . .

Mr. Justice Harlan, whom Mr. Justice Stewart joins, dissenting.

The final demise of state poll taxes, already totally proscribed by the Twenty–Fourth Amendment with respect to federal elections and abolished by the States themselves in all but four States with respect to state elections, is perhaps in itself not of great moment. But the fact that the *coup de grace* has been administered by this Court instead of being left to the affected States or to the federal political process should be a matter of continuing concern to all interested in maintaining the proper role of this tribunal under our scheme of government.

. . .

DUNN v. BLUMSTEIN, 405 U.S. 330 (1972). In holding invalid a statute imposing as a condition of voting residence in the state for one year and the county for three months prior to the election, the Court said:

A.

"Durational residence requirements completely bar from voting all residents not meeting the fixed durational standards. By denying some citizens the right to vote, such laws deprive them of 'a fundamental political right, . . . preservative of all rights.' Reynolds v. Sims, 377 U.S. 533, 562 (1964). There is no need to repeat now the labors undertaken in earlier cases to analyze this right to vote and to explain in detail the judicial role in reviewing state statutes which selectively distribute the franchise. In decision after decision, this Court has made clear that a citizen has a constitutionally protected right to participate in elections on an equal basis with other citizens in the jurisdiction. See, e.g., Evans v. Cornman, 398 U.S. 419, 421–422 (1970);[a] Kramer v. Union Free School District No. 15, 395 U.S. 621, 626–628 (1969);[b] Cipriano v. City of Houma, 395 U.S. 701, 706 (1969);[c] Harper v. Virginia State Board of Elections, 383 U.S. 663, 667 (1966); Carrington v. Rash, 380 U.S. 89, 93–94 (1965);[d] Reynolds v. Sims, supra. This 'equal right to vote,' Evans v. Cornman, . . . is not absolute; the States have the power to impose voter qualifications, and to regulate access to the franchise in other ways. . . . But, as a general matter, 'before that right [to vote] can be restricted, the purpose of the restriction and the assertedly overriding interests served by it must meet close constitutional scrutiny.' Evans v. Cornman . . .; see Bullock v. Carter, 405 U.S. 134 (1972).[e]

"Tennessee urges that this case is controlled by Drueding v. Devlin, 380 U.S. 125 (1965). Drueding was a decision upholding Maryland's durational residence requirements. The District Court tested those requirements by the equal protection standard applied to ordinary state regulations: whether the

[a] Persons living on the grounds of the National Institutes of Health, a federal reservation or enclave located within the boundaries of Maryland, were denied the right to vote in Maryland elections on the ground that they were not residents of Maryland. The Court held the denial unconstitutional: "In nearly every election, federal, state, and local, for offices from the Presidency to the school board, and on the entire variety of ballot propositions, appellees have a stake equal to that of other Maryland residents. As the District Court concluded, they are entitled under the Fourteenth Amendment to protect that stake by exercising the equal right to vote."

[b] A New York law provided that residents of school districts could vote in school district elections only if they (1) own or lease taxable real property in the district, or (2) are parents or have custody of children enrolled in the local public schools. The Court noted that the statute was to be given "a close and exacting examination" because "statutes distributing the franchise constitute the foundation of our representative society." The Court then held the statute unconstitutional because the state had not demonstrated a "compelling state interest" justifying the limitation on the franchise.

[c] A state provision giving only "property taxpayers" the right to vote in elections called to approve the issuance of revenue bonds by a municipal utility was held unconstitutional. The Court found no basis for the limitation since "the benefits and burdens of the bond issue fall indiscriminately on the property owner and nonproperty owner alike."

[d] The Court held invalid a Texas constitutional provision prohibiting a member of the armed forces who moves his home to Texas from voting in any election so long as he is a member of the armed forces.

[e] A Texas law requiring candidates to pay large filing fees in order to have their names placed on the ballot in primary elections was held invalid. The Court said:

"Because the Texas filing fee scheme has a real and appreciable impact on the exercise of the franchise, and because this impact is related to the resources of the voters supporting a particular candidate, we conclude, as in Harper, that the laws must be 'closely scrutinized' and found reasonably necessary to the accomplishment of legitimate state objectives in order to pass constitutional muster."

exclusions are reasonably related to a permissible state interest. 234 F.Supp. 721, 724–725 (D.Md.1964). We summarily affirmed *per curiam* without the benefit of argument. But if it was not clear then, it is certainly clear now that a more exacting test is required for any statute which 'place[s] a condition on the exercise of the right to vote.' Bullock v. Carter. . . . This development in the law culminated in Kramer v. Union Free School District No. 15, supra, 395 U.S. 621 (1969). There we canvassed in detail the reasons for strict review of statutes distributing the franchise, . . . noting *inter alia* that such statutes 'constitute the foundation of our representative society.' We concluded that if a challenged statute grants the right to vote to some citizens and denies the franchise to others, 'the Court must determine whether the exclusions are *necessary* to promote a *compelling* state interest.' Id., at 627 (emphasis added); Cipriano v. City of Houma, 395 U.S. 701, 704 (1969); City of Phoenix v. Kolodziejski, 399 U.S. 204, 205, 209 (1970).[f] Cf. Harper v. Virginia State Board of Elections, supra, 383 U.S., at 670. This is the test we apply here."

MARSTON v. LEWIS, 410 U.S. 679 (1973). Arizona required a voter to have resided in the state for 50 days before an election and also to register at least 50 days prior. The Court held this requirement valid in light of a state showing that it would be difficult to do the necessary paper work in any shorter period before the election, stating: "In the present case, we are confronted with a recent and amply justifiable legislative judgment that 50 days rather than 30 is necessary to promote the State's important interest in accurate voter lists. The Constitution is not so rigid that that determination and others like it may not stand." A dissent argued that the Court had fixed in *Dunn* the line of 30 days as that beyond which reliance on administrative convenience is extremely questionable and "we can avoid an unprincipled numbers game only if we insist that any deviations from the line we have drawn, after mature consideration, be justified by far more substantial evidence than that produced" in this case.

HILL v. STONE, 421 U.S. 289 (1975). Issuance of bonds to finance construction of a city library was defeated in a Fort Worth election. Residents brought this federal court action challenging the provision of Texas law limiting the right to vote in city bond issue elections to persons who have "rendered" or listed real, mixed, or personal property for taxation in the election district. Under the law mere listing of the property—not the payment of any tax—was the prerequisite to voting. The Court, by a vote of five to three, held the statute invalid under the Equal Protection Clause, stating, in part:

"The basic principle . . . is that as long as the election in question is not one of special interest, any classification restricting the franchise on grounds other than residence, age, and citizenship cannot stand unless the district or State can demonstrate that the classification serves a compelling state interest. See *Kramer* . . .; *Cipriano*. . . .

"The appellant's claim that the Ft. Worth election was one of special interest and thus outside the principles of the *Kramer* case runs afoul of our decision in *City of Phoenix v. Kolodziejski,* supra. In the *Phoenix* case, we expressly stated that a general obligation bond issue—even where the debt service will be paid entirely out of property taxes as in Ft. Worth—is a matter of general interest, and that the principles of *Kramer* apply to classifications limiting eligibility among registered voters.

"In making the alternative contentions that the 'rendering requirement' creates no real 'classification,' or that the classification created should be

---

[f] The Court held that a State could not restrict to real property taxpayers the vote in elections to approve the issuance of general obligation bonds.

upheld as being reasonable, the appellant misconceives the rationale of *Kramer* and its successors. Appellant argues that since all property is required to be rendered for taxation, and since anyone can vote in a bond election if he renders any property, no matter how little, the Texas scheme does not discriminate on the basis of wealth or property. Our cases, however, have not held or intimated that only property-based classifications are suspect; in an election of general interest, restrictions on the franchise of any character must meet a stringent test of justification. The Texas scheme creates a classification based on rendering, and it in effect disfranchises those who have not rendered their property for taxation in the year of the bond election. Mere reasonableness will therefore not suffice to sustain the classification created in this case.

B.

"The appellant has sought to justify the State's rendering requirement solely on the ground that it extends some protection to property owners, who will bear the direct burden of retiring the city's bonded indebtedness. The *Phoenix* case, however, rejected this analysis of the 'direct' imposition of costs on property owners. Even under a system in which the responsibility of retiring the bonded indebtedness falls directly on property taxpayers, all members of the community share in the cost in various ways. Moreover, the construction of a library is not likely to be of special interest to a particular, well-defined portion of the electorate. . . .

"The appellee city officials argue that the rendering qualifications furthers another state interest: it encourages prospective voters to render their property and thereby helps enforce the State's tax laws. This argument is difficult to credit. The use of the franchise to compel compliance with other, independent state objectives is questionable in any context. . . .

"In sum, the Texas rendering requirement erects a classification that impermissibly disenfranchises persons otherwise qualified to vote, solely because they have not rendered some property for taxation. The *Phoenix* case establishes that Ft. Worth's election was not a 'special interest' election, and the state interests proffered by appellant and the city officials fall far short of meeting the 'compelling state interest' test consistently applied in *Kramer, Cipriano,* and *Phoenix.*"

NOTE

In Richardson v. Ramirez, 418 U.S. 24 (1974), the Court held valid California constitutional provisions and implementing statutes disenfranchising persons convicted of an "infamous crime." The Court said, in part:

"As we have seen, however, the exclusion of felons from the vote has an affirmative sanction in § 2 of the Fourteenth Amendment, a sanction which was not present in the case of the other restrictions on the franchise which were invalidated in the cases on which respondents rely. We hold that the understanding of those who adopted the Fourteenth Amendment, as reflected in the express language of § 2 and in the historical and judicial interpretation of the Amendment's applicability to state laws disenfranchising felons, is of controlling significance in distinguishing such laws from those other state limitations on the franchise which have been held invalid under the Equal Protection Clause by this Court."

THE FIRST AMENDMENT AS A LIMITATION ON STATE POWER TO FIX QUALIFICATIONS FOR VOTERS

The first amendment may also be a restriction on state power to set voter qualifications. In Kusper v. Pontikes, 414 U.S. 51 (1973), the Court held invalid a provision of the Illinois Election Code prohibiting a person from voting in the primary election of a political party if that person has voted in another party's primary within the preceding 23 months. The Court said: "There can no longer be any doubt that freedom to associate with others for the common advancement of political beliefs and ideas is a form of 'orderly group activity' protected by the First and Fourteenth Amendments.... The right to associate with the political party of one's choice is an integral part of this basic constitutional freedom.... To be sure, administration of the electoral process is a matter that the Constitution largely entrusts to the States. But, in exercising their powers of supervision over elections and in setting qualifications for voters, the States may not infringe upon basic constitutional protections." The Court went on to hold that the state had not shown that the restriction on voting in primary elections was closely related to a compelling state interest and hence it was invalid.

ACCESS TO THE BALLOT AND OTHER ELECTION LAWS

In addition to determining voter qualifications, states have extensively regulated the electoral process. Regulations relating to the following major areas exist: (1) Access of political parties and independent candidates to the ballot. (2) Political party nominating procedures. (3) Eligibility requirements for candidates. (4) Campaign regulations. See *Developments in the Law— Elections*, 88 Harv.L.Rev. 1111 (1975).

These laws have been attacked both as violations of equal protection and of the first amendment. For a discussion of the first amendment problems, see p. 1482 infra.

The following cases are among those relying principally on the equal protection clause.

BULLOCK v. CARTER, 405 U.S. 134 (1972). Texas imposed very high filing fees as a condition of becoming a candidate in a primary election. They were challenged by prospective candidates who asserted they were financially unable to pay the fees. The Court held the statute unconstitutional. In determining the standard of review to be applied, the Court said:

"The initial and direct impact of filing fees is felt by aspirants for office, rather than voters, and the Court has not heretofore attached such fundamental status to candidacy as to invoke a rigorous standard of review. However, the rights of voters and the rights of candidates do not lend themselves to neat separation; laws that affect candidates always have at least some theoretical, correlative effect on voters. Of course, not every limitation or incidental burden on the exercise of voting rights is subject to a stringent standard of review."

The Court then went on to note that the statute would exclude candidates without personal wealth or affluent backers. Not only would this limit the voters in their choice of candidates but also it would likely fall more heavily on the less affluent segments of society. Hence, because the scheme has a significant impact on the exercise of the franchise and because the impact is related to the resources of the voters, the Court concluded "that the laws must be 'closely scrutinized' and found reasonably necessary to the accomplishment of legitimate state objectives...." The Court went on to hold that the state interests, including that of regulating the number of candidates on the ballot, did not justify the regulation.

LUBIN v. PANISH, 415 U.S. 709 (1974). California imposed modest filing fees for primary elections fixed at one to two percent of the annual salary for the office. The Court upheld a challenge by a candidate who alleged that he could not afford to pay any filing fee, concluding:

"The absence of any alternative means of gaining access to the ballot inevitably renders the California system exclusionary as to some aspirants.... [T]he payment of a fee is an absolute, not an alternative, condition, and failure to meet it is a disqualification from running for office. Thus, California has chosen to achieve the important and legitimate interest of maintaining the integrity of elections by means which can operate to exclude some potentially serious candidates from the ballot without providing them with any alternative means of coming before the voters. Selection of candidates solely on the basis of ability to pay a fixed fee without providing any alternative means is not reasonably necessary to the accomplishment of the State's legitimate election interests. Accordingly, we hold that in the absence of reasonable alternative means of ballot access, a State may not ... require from an indigent candidate filing fees he cannot pay."

CLEMENTS v. FASHING, 457 U.S. 957 (1982). A Texas statute provided that judges and other office holders could not cut short their existing terms of office in order to serve in the Texas legislature. A Justice of the Peace claimed that this statute violated equal protection. The Court rejected the claim 5 to 4 but without a majority opinion. The plurality opinion by Justice Rehnquist said that the statute "need only rest on a rational predicate in order to survive challenge under the Equal Protection Clause" and that it met this challenge. Justice Stevens, concurring, objected to the plurality's discussion of levels of scrutiny. The Court also upheld the statute against a claim based on the first amendment.

C. TRAVEL AND INTERSTATE MIGRATION, LENGTH OF STATE RESIDENCE, AND DISADVANTAGING NONRESIDENTS

Introduction. Section A. addressed whether equal protection analysis is sometimes used to decide cases involving rights secured by other constitutional provisions. This section addresses a set of cases, all analyzed in the equal protection framework, that involve constitutional claims of freedom to seek opportunity through interstate movement, migration, or trade, without being disadvantaged relative to those who already live where the opportunity is sought. Moreover, these cases not only implicate constitutional values of federalism in interstate relationships, but they combine, as do many other equal protection cases, concern about highly valued personal liberty with concern about the nature of the disadvantaging classification. Thus they may usefully be compared with cases like Harper v. Virginia Board of Elections, supra p. 984, which focused on both voting as a specially protected interest and wealth as a classification; the cases in Section D. infra on poverty and welfare; and many others.

Although the cases do not divide neatly into those emphasizing the liberty of interstate opportunity and those emphasizing distinctions based on the fact or length of residency, they are divided here into three subsections. The first addresses interstate travel and migration, the second distinctions among state residents based on their length of residence, and the third distinctions between residents and nonresidents.

1. TRAVEL AND INTERSTATE MIGRATION

Shapiro v. Thompson

394 U.S. 618, 89 S.Ct. 1322, 22 L.Ed.2d 600 (1969).

Mr. Justice Brennan delivered the opinion of the Court.

These three appeals were restored to the calendar for reargument.... Each is an appeal from a decision of a three-judge District Court holding unconstitutional a State or District of Columbia statutory provision which denies welfare assistance to residents of the State or District who have not resided within their jurisdictions for at least one year immediately preceding their applications for such assistance. We affirm....

II.

There is no dispute that the effect of the waiting-period requirement in each case is to create two classes of needy resident families indistinguishable from each other except that one is composed of residents who have resided a year or more, and the second of residents who have resided less than a year, in the jurisdiction. On the basis of this sole difference the first class is granted and the second class is denied welfare aid upon which may depend the ability of the families to obtain the very means to subsist—food, shelter, and other necessities of life. In each case, the District Court found that appellees met the test for residence in their jurisdictions, as well as all other eligibility requirements except the requirement of residence for a full year prior to their applications. On reargument, appellees' central contention is that the statutory prohibition of benefits to residents of less than a year creates a classification which constitutes an invidious discrimination denying them equal protection of the laws. We agree. The interests which appellants assert are promoted by the classification either may not constitutionally be promoted by government or are not compelling governmental interests.

III.

Primarily, appellants justify the waiting-period requirement as a protective device to preserve the fiscal integrity of state public assistance programs. It is asserted that people who require welfare assistance during their first year of residence in a State are likely to become continuing burdens on state welfare programs. Therefore, the argument runs, if such people can be deterred from entering the jurisdiction by denying them welfare benefits during the first year, state programs to assist long-time residents will not be impaired by a substantial influx of indigent newcomers.

There is weighty evidence that exclusion from the jurisdiction of the poor who need or may need relief was the specific objective of these provisions....

We do not doubt that the one-year waiting period device is well suited to discourage the influx of poor families in need of assistance. An indigent who desires to migrate, resettle, find a new job, start a new life will doubtless hesitate if he knows that he must risk making the move without the possibility of falling back on state welfare assistance during his first year of residence, when his need may be most acute. But the purpose of inhibiting migration by needy persons into the State is constitutionally impermissible.

This Court long ago recognized that the nature of our Federal Union and our constitutional concepts of personal liberty unite to require that all citizens be free to travel throughout the length and breadth of our land uninhibited by statutes, rules or regulations which unreasonably burden or restrict this movement....

We have no occasion to ascribe the source of this right to travel interstate to a particular constitutional provision. It suffices that, as Mr. Justice Stewart said for the Court in United States v. Guest, 383 U.S. 745, 757–758 (1966):

"The constitutional right to travel from one State to another ... occupies a position fundamental to the concept of our Federal Union. It is a right that has been firmly established and repeatedly recognized.

"[The] right finds no explicit mention in the Constitution. The reason, it has been suggested, is that a right so elementary was conceived from the beginning to be a necessary concomitant of the stronger Union the Constitution created. In any event, freedom to travel throughout the United States has long been recognized as a basic right under the Constitution."

Thus, the purpose of deterring the in-migration of indigents cannot serve as justification for the classification created by the one-year waiting period, since that purpose is constitutionally impermissible. If a law has "no other purpose ... than to chill the assertion of constitutional rights by penalizing those who choose to exercise them, then it [is] patently unconstitutional." United States v. Jackson, 390 U.S. 570, 581 (1968).

Alternatively, appellants argue that even if it is impermissible for a State to attempt to deter the entry of all indigents, the challenged classification may be justified as a permissible state attempt to discourage those indigents who would enter the State solely to obtain larger benefits. We observe first that none of the statutes before us is tailored to serve that objective....

More fundamentally, a State may no more try to fence out those indigents who seek higher welfare benefits than it may try to fence out indigents generally. Implicit in any such distinction is the notion that indigents who enter a State with the hope of securing higher welfare benefits are somehow less deserving than indigents who do not take this consideration into account. But we do not perceive why a mother who is seeking to make a new life for herself and her children should be regarded as less deserving because she considers, among other factors, the level of a State's public assistance. Surely such a mother is no less deserving than a mother who moves into a particular State in order to take advantage of its better educational facilities.

Appellants argue further that the challenged classification may be sustained as an attempt to distinguish between new and old residents on the basis of the contribution they have made to the community through the payment of taxes. We have difficulty seeing how long-term residents who qualify for welfare are making a greater present contribution to the State in taxes than indigent residents who have recently arrived. If the argument is based on contributions made in the past by the long-term residents, there is some question, as a factual matter, whether this argument is applicable in Pennsylvania where the record suggests that some 40% of those denied public assistance because of the waiting period had lengthy prior residence in the State. But we need not rest on the particular facts of these cases. Appellants' reasoning would logically permit the State to bar new residents from schools, parks, and libraries or deprive them of police and fire protection. Indeed it would permit the State to apportion all benefits and services according to the past tax contributions of its citizens. The Equal Protection Clause prohibits such an apportionment of state services.[10]

We recognize that a State has a valid interest in preserving the fiscal integrity of its programs. It may legitimately attempt to limit its expenditures, whether for public assistance, public education, or any other program. But a State may not accomplish such a purpose by invidious distinctions between classes of its citizens. It could not, for example, reduce expenditures for

[10] We are not dealing here with state insurance programs which may legitimately tie the amount of benefits to the individual's contributions.

education by barring indigent children from its schools. Similarly, in the cases before us, appellants must do more than show that denying welfare benefits to new residents saves money. The saving of welfare costs cannot be an independent ground for an invidious classification.

In sum, neither deterrence of indigents from migrating to the State nor limitation of welfare benefits to those regarded as contributing to the State is a constitutionally permissible state objective.

IV.

Appellants next advance as justification certain administrative and related governmental objectives allegedly served by the waiting-period requirement. They argue that the requirement (1) facilitates the planning of the welfare budget; (2) provides an objective test of residency; (3) minimizes the opportunity for recipients fraudulently to receive payments from more than one jurisdiction; and (4) encourages early entry of new residents into the labor force.

At the outset, we reject appellants' argument that a mere showing of a rational relationship between the waiting period and these four admittedly permissible state objectives will suffice to justify the classification.... The waiting-period provision denies welfare benefits to otherwise eligible applicants solely because they have recently moved into the jurisdiction. But in moving from State to State or to the District of Columbia appellees were exercising a constitutional right, and any classification which serves to penalize the exercise of that right, unless shown to be necessary to promote a *compelling* governmental interest, is unconstitutional....

The argument that the waiting-period requirement facilitates budget predictability is wholly unfounded. The records in all three cases are utterly devoid of evidence that either State or the District of Columbia in fact uses the one-year requirement as a means to predict the number of people who will require assistance in the budget year....

The argument that the waiting period serves as an administratively efficient rule of thumb for determining residency similarly will not withstand scrutiny. The residence requirement and the one-year waiting-period requirement are distinct and independent prerequisites for assistance under these three statutes, and the facts relevant to the determination of each are directly examined by the welfare authorities. Before granting an application, the welfare authorities investigate the applicant's employment, housing, and family situation and in the course of the inquiry necessarily learn the facts upon which to determine whether the applicant is a resident.

Similarly, there is no need for a State to use the one-year waiting period as a safeguard against fraudulent receipt of benefits; for less drastic means are available, and are employed, to minimize that hazard. Of course, a State has a valid interest in preventing fraud by any applicant, whether a newcomer or a long-time resident. It is not denied however that the investigations now conducted entail inquiries into facts relevant to that subject. In addition, cooperation among state welfare departments is common. The District of Columbia, for example, provides interim assistance to its former residents who have moved to a State which has a waiting period. As a matter of course, District officials send a letter to the welfare authorities in the recipient's new community "to request the information needed to continue assistance." A like procedure would be an effective safeguard against the hazard of double payments. Since double payments can be prevented by a letter or a telephone call, it is unreasonable to accomplish this objective by the blunderbuss method of denying assistance to all indigent newcomers for an entire year.

Pennsylvania suggests that the one-year waiting period is justified as a means of encouraging new residents to join the labor force promptly. But this logic would also require a similar waiting period for long-term residents of the State. A state purpose to encourage employment provides no rational basis for imposing a one-year waiting-period restriction on new residents only.

We conclude therefore that appellants in these cases do not use and have no need to use the one-year requirement for the governmental purposes suggested. Thus, even under traditional equal protection tests a classification of welfare applicants according to whether they have lived in the State for one year would seem irrational and unconstitutional. But, of course, the traditional criteria do not apply in these cases. Since the classification here touches on the fundamental right of interstate movement, its constitutionality must be judged by the stricter standard of whether it promotes a *compelling* state interest. Under this standard, the waiting period requirement clearly violates the Equal Protection Clause.

V.

Connecticut and Pennsylvania argue, however, that the constitutional challenge to the waiting period requirements must fail because Congress expressly approved the imposition of the requirement by the States as part of the jointly funded AFDC program....

But even if we were to assume, *arguendo,* that Congress did approve the imposition of a one-year waiting period, it is the responsive *state* legislation which infringes constitutional rights. By itself § 402(b) has absolutely no restrictive effect. It is therefore not that statute but only the state requirements which pose the constitutional question.

Finally, even if it could be argued that the constitutionality of § 402(b) is somehow at issue here, it follows from what we have said that the provision, insofar as it permits the one-year waiting-period requirement, would be unconstitutional. Congress may not authorize the States to violate the Equal Protection Clause. Perhaps Congress could induce wider state participation in school construction if it authorized the use of joint funds for the building of segregated schools. But could it seriously be contended that Congress would be constitutionally justified in such authorization by the need to secure state cooperation? Congress is without power to enlist state cooperation in a joint federal-state program by legislation which authorizes the States to violate the Equal Protection Clause. Katzenbach v. Morgan, 384 U.S. 641, 651 (1966).

VI.

The waiting-period requirement in the District of Columbia Code ... is also unconstitutional even though it was adopted by Congress as an exercise of federal power. In terms of federal power, the discrimination created by the one-year requirement violates the Due Process Clause of the Fifth Amendment. "[W]hile the Fifth Amendment contains no equal protection clause, it does forbid discrimination that is 'so unjustifiable as to be violative of due process.' " Schneider v. Rusk, 377 U.S. 163, 168 (1964); Bolling v. Sharpe, 347 U.S. 497 (1954). For the reasons we have stated in invalidating the Pennsylvania and Connecticut provisions, the District of Columbia provision is also invalid—the Due Process Clause of the Fifth Amendment forbids Congress from denying public assistance to poor persons otherwise eligible solely on the ground that they have not been residents of the District of Columbia for one year at the time their applications are filed.

. . .

Affirmed.

Mr. Justice Stewart, concurring.

In joining the opinion of the Court, I add a word in response to the dissent of my Brother Harlan, who, I think, has quite misapprehended what the Court's opinion says.

The Court today does *not* "pick out particular human activities, characterize them as 'fundamental,' and give them added protection...." To the contrary, the Court simply recognizes, as it must, an established constitutional right, and gives to that right no less protection than the Constitution itself demands....

Mr. Chief Justice Warren, with whom Mr. Justice Black joins, dissenting.

In my opinion the issue before us can be simply stated: may Congress, acting under one of its enumerated powers, impose minimal nationwide residence requirements or authorize the States to do so? Since I believe that Congress does have this power and has constitutionally exercised it in these cases, I must dissent....

Mr. Justice Harlan, dissenting....

In upholding the equal protection argument, the Court has applied an equal protection doctrine of relatively recent vintage: the rule that statutory classifications which either are based upon certain "suspect" criteria or affect "fundamental rights" will be held to deny equal protection unless justified by a "compelling" governmental interest....

The "compelling interest" doctrine, which today is articulated more explicitly than ever before, constitutes an increasingly significant exception to the long-established rule that a statute does not deny equal protection if it is rationally related to a legitimate governmental objective. The "compelling interest" doctrine has two branches. The branch which requires that classifications based upon "suspect" criteria be supported by a compelling interest apparently had its genesis in cases involving racial classifications, which have at least since Korematsu v. United States, 323 U.S. 214, 216 (1944), been regarded as inherently "suspect." The criterion of "wealth" apparently was added to the list of "suspects" as an alternative justification for the rationale in Harper v. Virginia Bd. of Elections, 383 U.S. 663, 668 (1966), in which Virginia's poll tax was struck down. The criterion of political allegiance may have been added in Williams v. Rhodes, 393 U.S. 23 (1968). Today the list apparently has been further enlarged to include classifications based upon recent interstate movement, and perhaps those based upon the exercise of *any* constitutional right, ...

I think that this branch of the "compelling interest" doctrine is sound when applied to racial classifications, for historically the Equal Protection Clause was largely a product of the desire to eradicate legal distinctions founded upon race. However, I believe that the more recent extensions have been unwise....

The second branch of the "compelling interest" principle is even more troublesome. For it has been held that a statutory classification is subject to the "compelling interest" test if the result of the classification may be to affect a "fundamental right," regardless of the basis of the classification....

I think this branch of the "compelling interest" doctrine particularly unfortunate and unnecessary. It is unfortunate because it creates an exception which threatens to swallow the standard equal protection rule. Virtually every state statute affects important rights. This Court has repeatedly held, for example, that the traditional equal protection standard is applicable to statutory classifications affecting such fundamental matters as the right to pursue a particular occupation, the right to receive greater or smaller wages or to work more or less hours, and the right to inherit property. Rights such as these are in principle indistinguishable from those involved here, and to extend the "compelling interest" rule to all cases in which such rights are affected would go far toward making this Court a "super-legislature." This branch of the doctrine is also unnecessary. When the right affected is one assured by the federal Constitution, any infringement can be dealt with under the Due Process Clause. But when a statute affects only matters not mentioned in the federal Constitution and is not arbitrary or irrational, I must reiterate that I know of nothing which entitles this Court to pick out particular human activities, characterize them as "fundamental," and give them added protection under an unusually stringent equal protection test. . . .

DUNN v. BLUMSTEIN, 405 U.S. 330 (1972). In this case the Court upheld a challenge to a Tennessee law providing that in order to vote one must be a resident of the state for one year and of the county for three months before the election. The Court, in an opinion by Justice Marshall, held that the residence requirement had to meet the *Shapiro* compelling state interest test because (1) it burdened the right to vote, and (2) it burdened the right to travel. The aspects of the case dealing with voting were considered supra, p. 983. The Court responded to the State's argument that durational residence requirements do not abridge the right to travel because they neither seek to deter travel nor actually do deter travel as follows:

"This view represents a fundamental misunderstanding of the law. It is irrelevant whether disenfranchisement or denial of welfare is the more potent deterrent to travel. *Shapiro* did not rest upon a finding that denial of welfare actually deterred travel. Nor have other 'right to travel' cases in this Court always relied on the presence of actual deterrence. In *Shapiro* we explicitly stated that the compelling state interest test would be triggered by 'any classification which serves to *penalize* the exercise of that right [to travel]. . . .'

"Of course it is true that the two individual interests affected by Tennessee's durational residence requirements are affected in different ways. Travel is permitted, but only at a price; voting is prohibited. The right to travel is merely penalized, while the right to vote is absolutely denied. But these differences are irrelevant for present purposes. . . .

"The right to travel is 'an *unconditional* personal right,' a right whose exercise may not be conditioned. . . . Durational residence laws impermissibly condition and penalize the right to travel by imposing their prohibitions on only those persons who have recently exercised that right. In the present case, such laws force a person who wishes to travel and change residences to choose between travel and the basic right to vote. . . . Absent a compelling state interest, a State may not burden the right to travel in this way."

The Court also restated what the State must show to justify a statute burdening the right to travel or the right to vote:

"It is not sufficient for the State to show that durational residence requirements further a very substantial state interest. In pursuing that important interest, the State cannot choose means which unnecessarily burden or restrict constitutionally protected activity. Statutes affecting constitutional rights must be drawn with 'precision,' . . . and must be 'tailored' to serve their legitimate objectives. *Shapiro v. Thompson* . . . . And if there are other, reasonable ways to achieve those goals with a lesser burden on constitutionally protected activity, a State may not choose the way of greater interference. If it acts at all, it must choose 'less drastic means.' "

It then went on to hold that while the State had identified important and presumably "compelling" state interests—prevention of fraudulent voting and assuring knowledgeable voters—the durational residence requirement was not closely enough related to either of those interests.

Chief Justice Burger dissented. Justice Blackmun concurred in the result. Justices Powell and Rehnquist took no part in the decision.

MEMORIAL HOSPITAL v. MARICOPA COUNTY, 415 U.S. 250 (1974). Applying *Shapiro* and *Dunn*, the Court held invalid an Arizona statute requiring a year's residence in a county as a condition to receiving nonemergency hospitalization or medical care at the county's expense. The challenge was brought by an indigent suffering from a chronic asthmatic and bronchial illness who suffered a severe respiratory attack within a month after he moved from New Mexico to Phoenix, Arizona. Justice Marshall's majority opinion said in part:

"The right of interstate travel has repeatedly been recognized as a basic constitutional freedom. Whatever its ultimate scope, however, the right to travel was involved in only a limited sense in *Shapiro*. The Court was there concerned only with the right to '[migrate], with intent to settle and abide' or, as the Court put it, 'to migrate, resettle, find a new job and start a new life.' Even a bona fide residence requirement would burden the right to travel, if travel meant merely movement. But, in *Shapiro*, the Court explained that '[t]he residence requirement and the one-year waiting-period requirement are distinct and independent prerequisites' for assistance and only the latter was held to be unconstitutional.... Later, in invalidating a durational residency requirement for voter registration on the basis of *Shapiro*, we cautioned that our decision was not intended to 'cast doubt on the validity of appropriately defined and uniformly applied bona fide residence requirements.' Dunn v. Blumstein....

The opinion later said:

"Although any durational residence requirement impinges to some extent on the right to travel, the Court in *Shapiro* did not declare such requirements to be *per se* unconstitutional....

"...

"Thus, *Shapiro* and *Dunn* stand for the proposition that a classification which 'operates to *penalize* those persons ... who have exercised their constitutional right of interstate migration,' must be justified by a compelling state interest.... Although any durational residency requirement imposes a potential cost on migration, the Court, in *Shapiro*, cautioned that some 'waiting-periods ... may not be penalties.' 394 U.S., at 638 n. 21. In *Dunn v. Blumstein*, supra, the Court found that the denial of the franchise, 'a fundamental political right,' Reynolds v. Sims, 377 U.S. 533, 562 (1964), was a penalty requiring application of the compelling state interest test. In *Shapiro*, the Court found denial of the basic 'necessities of life' to be a penalty. Nonetheless, the Court has declined to strike down state statutes requiring one year of residence as a condition to lower tuition at state institutions of higher education. [Citing Vlandis v. Kline, 412 U.S. 441, 452–453 n. 9 (1973).]

"Whatever the ultimate parameters of the *Shapiro* penalty analysis, it is at least clear that medical care is as much 'a basic necessity of life' to an indigent as welfare assistance. And, governmental privileges or benefits necessary to basic sustenance have often been viewed as being of greater constitutional significance than less essential forms of governmental entitlements. See, e.g., *Shapiro,* supra; Goldberg v. Kelly, 397 U.S. 254, 264 (1970); Sniadach v. Family Finance Corp., 395 U.S. 337, 340–342 (1969). It would be odd, indeed, to find that the State of Arizona was required to afford Evaro welfare assistance to keep him from discomfort of inadequate housing or the pangs of hunger but could deny him the medical care necessary to relieve him from the wheezing and gasping for breath that attend his illness.

"...

"Not unlike the admonition of the Bible that, 'Ye shall have one manner of law, as well for the stranger as for one of your country.' Leviticus, 24:22, the right of interstate travel must be seen as insuring new residents the same right to vital government benefits and privileges in the States to which they migrate as are enjoyed by other residents. The State of Arizona's durational residency requirement for free medical care penalizes indigents for exercising their right to migrate to and settle in that State. Accordingly, the classification created by the residency requirement, 'unless shown to be necessary to promote a *compelling* [state] interest, is unconstitutional.' *Shapiro,* ... (Emphasis original.)"

Using an analysis like that in *Shapiro,* Justice Marshall concluded that "[a]ppellees have not met their heavy burden of justification, nor demonstrated that the State, in pursuing legitimate objectives, has chosen means which do not unnecessarily impinge on constitutionally protected interests." Chief Justice Burger and Justice Blackmun concurred in the result.

Justice Douglas wrote separately to say that "[s]o far as interstate travel *per se* is considered, I share the doubts of my Brother Rehnquist" but that "in the setting of this case the invidious discrimination against the poor, Harper v. Virginia Board of Elections, 383 U.S. 663 (1966), not the right to travel interstate is ... the critical issue."

Justice Rehnquist dissented, saying in part:

"The legal question in this case is simply whether the State of Arizona has acted arbitrarily in determining that access to local hospital facilities for nonemergency medical care should be denied to persons until they have established residency for one year. The impediment which this quite rational determination has placed on petitioner Evaro's 'right to travel' is so remote as to be negligible: so far as the record indicates Evaro moved from New Mexico to Arizona three years ago and has remained ever since. The eligibility requirement has not the slightest resemblance to the actual barriers to the right of free ingress and egress protected by the Constitution, and struck down in cases such as *Crandall* and *Edwards.* And unlike *Shapiro* it does not involve an urgent need for the necessities of life or a benefit funded from current revenues to which the claimant may well have contributed. It is a substantial broadening of, and departure from, all of these holdings, all the more remarkable for the lack of explanation which accompanies the result."

Sosna v. Iowa

419 U.S. 393, 95 S.Ct. 553, 42 L.Ed.2d 532 (1975).

Mr. Justice Rehnquist delivered the opinion of the Court.

Appellant Carol Sosna married Michael Sosna on September 5, 1964, in Michigan. They lived together in New York between October 1967 and August 1971, after which date they separated but continued to live in New York. In August 1972, appellant moved to Iowa with her three children, and the following month she petitioned the District Court of Jackson County, Iowa, for a dissolution of her marriage. . . . The Iowa court dismissed the petition for lack of jurisdiction, finding that Michael Sosna was not a resident of Iowa and appellant had not been a resident of the State of Iowa for one year preceding the filing of her petition. In so doing the Iowa court applied the provisions of Iowa Code § 598.6 requiring that the petitioner in such an action be "for the last year a resident of the state."

Instead of appealing this ruling to the Iowa appellate courts, appellant filed a complaint in [federal court] asserting that Iowa's durational residency requirement for invoking its divorce jurisdiction violated the United States Constitution. . . .

A three-judge court . . . held that the Iowa durational residency requirement was constitutional. . . . We . . . decide that this case is not moot, and hold that the Iowa durational residency requirement for divorce does not offend the United States Constitution. . . .

The durational residency requirement . . . is a part of Iowa's comprehensive statutory regulation of domestic relations, an area that has long been regarded as a virtually exclusive province of the States. . . .

The imposition of a durational residency requirement for divorce is scarcely unique to Iowa, since 48 States impose such a requirement as a condition for maintaining an action for divorce. As might be expected, the periods vary among the States and range from six weeks to two years. The one-year period selected by Iowa is the most common length of time prescribed.

Appellant contends that the Iowa requirement of one year's residence is unconstitutional . . . because it establishes two classes of persons and discriminates against those who have recently exercised their right to travel to Iowa, thereby contravening the Court's holdings in Shapiro v. Thompson, 394 U.S. 618 (1969); Dunn v. Blumstein, 405 U.S. 330 (1972), and Memorial Hospital v. Maricopa County, 415 U.S. 250 (1974); . . .

State statutes imposing durational residency requirements were of course invalidated when imposed by States as a qualification for welfare payments, *Shapiro,* supra, for voting, *Dunn,* supra, and for medical care, *Maricopa County,* supra. But none of those cases intimated that the States might never impose durational residency requirements, and such a proposition was in fact expressly disclaimed. What those cases had in common was that the durational residency requirements they struck down were justified on the basis of budgetary or record-keeping considerations which were held insufficient to outweigh the constitutional claims of the individuals. But Iowa's divorce residency requirement is of a different stripe. Appellant was not irretrievably foreclosed from obtaining some part of what she sought, as was the case with the welfare recipients in *Shapiro,* the voters in *Dunn,* or the indigent patient in *Maricopa County.* She would eventually qualify for the same sort of adjudication which she demanded virtually upon her arrival in the State. Iowa's requirement delayed her access to the courts, but, by fulfilling it, a plaintiff could ultimately obtain the same opportunity for adjudication which she asserts ought to be hers at an earlier point in time.

Iowa's residency requirement may reasonably be justified on grounds other than purely budgetary considerations or administrative convenience. Cf. Kahn v. Shevin, 416 U.S. 351 (1974). A decree of divorce is not a matter in which the only interested parties are the State as a sort of "grantor," and a plaintiff such as appellant in the role of "grantee." Both spouses are obviously interested in the proceedings, since it will affect their marital status and very likely their property rights. Where a married couple has minor children, a decree of divorce would usually include provisions for their custody and support. With consequences of such moment riding on a divorce decree issued by its courts, Iowa may insist that one seeking to initiate such a proceeding have the modicum of attachment to the State required here.

Such a requirement additionally furthers the State's parallel interests in both avoiding officious intermeddling in matters in which another State has a paramount interest, and in minimizing the susceptibility of its own divorce decrees to collateral attack. A State such as Iowa may quite reasonably decide that it does not wish to become a divorce mill for unhappy spouses who have lived there as short a time as appellant had when she commenced her action in the state court after having long resided elsewhere. Until such time as Iowa is convinced that appellant intends to remain in the State, it lacks the "nexus between person and place of such permanence as to control the creation of legal relations and responsibilities of the utmost significance." Williams v. North Carolina, 325 U.S. 226, 229 (1945). Perhaps even more importantly, Iowa's interests extend beyond its borders and include the recognition of its divorce decrees by other States under the Full Faith and Credit Clause of the Constitution, Art. IV, § 1. For that purpose, this Court has often stated that "judicial power to grant a divorce—jurisdiction, strictly speaking—is founded on domicil." *Williams,* supra; Andrews v. Andrews, 188 U.S. 14 (1903); Bell v. Bell, 181 U.S. 175 (1901). Where a divorce decree is entered after a finding of domicile in *ex parte* proceedings, this Court has held that the finding of domicile is not binding upon another State and may be disregarded in the face of "cogent evidence" to the contrary.... For that reason, the State asked to enter such a decree is entitled to insist that the putative divorce plaintiff satisfy something more than the bare minimum of constitutional requirements before a divorce may be granted. The State's decision to exact a one-year residency requirement as a matter of policy is therefore buttressed by a quite permissible inference that this requirement not only effectuates state substantive policy but likewise provides a greater safeguard against successful collateral attack than would a requirement of bona fide residence alone. This is precisely the sort of determination that a State in the exercise of its domestic relations jurisdiction is entitled to make.

We therefore hold that the state interest in requiring that those who seek a divorce from its courts be genuinely attached to the State, as well as a desire to insulate divorce decrees from the likelihood of collateral attack, requires a different resolution of the constitutional issue presented than was the case in *Shapiro,* supra, *Dunn,* supra, and *Maricopa County,* supra.

. . .

[The Court also held that the statute did not violate due process by invoking a permanent and irrebuttable presumption of non-residence.]

Affirmed.

Mr. Justice White, dissenting.

. . .

Because I find that the case before the Court has become moot, I must respectfully dissent.

Mr. Justice Marshall, with whom Mr. Justice Brennan joins, dissenting.

The Court today departs sharply from the course we have followed in analyzing durational residency requirements since Shapiro v. Thompson, 394 U.S. 618 (1969). Because I think the principles set out in that case and its progeny compel reversal here, I respectfully dissent.

As we have made clear in *Shapiro* and subsequent cases, any classification that penalizes exercise of the constitutional right to travel is invalid unless it is justified by a compelling governmental interest....

The Court's failure to address the instant case in these terms suggests a new distaste for the mode of analysis we have applied to this corner of equal protection law. In its stead, the Court has employed what appears to be an *ad hoc* balancing test, under which the State's putative interest in ensuring that its divorce plaintiffs establish some roots in Iowa is said to justify the one-year residency requirement. I am concerned not only about the disposition of this case, but also about the implications of the majority's analysis for other divorce statutes and for durational residency requirement cases in general.

JONES v. HELMS, 452 U.S. 412 (1981). A Georgia statute provided that parental abandonment of a child is a misdemeanor, but is a felony if the parent thereafter leaves the State. The lower federal court held the statute invalid because it infringed upon the right to travel, and the State's interests could be protected by less drastic means. On appeal, the Supreme Court unanimously reversed. Justice Stevens' opinion for the Court concluded that defendant's criminal conduct "necessarily qualified his right" to travel interstate. He noted, moreover, that this case did not involve, as did earlier "right to travel" cases, disparate treatment of residents and non-residents, or old and new residents. The question was the narrower one whether a state could enhance criminal punishment if the offender left the state after committing the crime. "Thus, although a simple penalty for leaving a State is plainly impermissible, if departure aggravates the consequences of conduct that is otherwise punishable, the State may treat the entire sequence of events, from the initial offense to departure from the State, as more serious than its separate components."

BONA FIDE RESIDENCE REQUIREMENTS

In McCarthy v. Philadelphia Civil Service Commission, 424 U.S. 645 (1976), the Court summarily rejected a city fire department employee's challenge to a requirement that city employees be residents of the city. The per curiam opinion distinguished *Shapiro, Dunn,* and *Memorial Hospital:*

"... Neither in those cases, nor in any others, have we questioned the validity of a condition placed upon municipal employment that a person be a resident *at the time* of his application. In this case appellant claims a constitutional right to be employed by the city of Philadelphia *while* he is living elsewhere. There is no support in our cases for such a claim.

"We have previously differentiated between a requirement of continuing residency and a requirement of prior residency of a given duration. Thus in *Shapiro,* ... we stated '[t]he residence requirement and the one-year waiting-period requirement are distinct and independent prerequisites'. And in *Memorial Hospital,* ... quoting *Dunn,* ... the Court explained that *Shapiro* and *Dunn* did not question 'the validity of appropriately defined and uniformly applied bona fide residence requirements.'

"This case involves that kind of bona fide continuing residence requirement. The judgment of the Commonwealth Court of Pennsylvania is therefore affirmed."

In Martinez v. Bynum, 461 U.S. 321 (1983), the Supreme Court upheld on its face a Texas law that permits a school district to deny tuition-free admission to a minor who lives apart from a parent or guardian, if the minor's presence in the school district is for the primary purpose of attending public schools. The durational residence cases permit "bona fide residence requirements." In Vlandis v. Kline, 412 U.S. 441, 453–454 (1973), the Court had stated that a state's interest in preserving the right of residents to attend state universities on a preferential tuition basis permits a state to "establish such reasonable criteria for in-state status as to make virtually certain that students who are not, in fact, bona fide residents of the State, but who have come there solely for educational purposes, cannot take advantage of the in-state rates." A school district would thus be justified in denying admission to all minor children whose parents did not satisfy traditional criteria of residency. The Texas statute was not invalid because it went further and allowed enrollment by children whose parents were present in the district, without intent to remain indefinitely, or children who were present in the district for some purpose other than attending school. Justice Marshall dissented. (A fuller report in this case appears infra, p. 1065.)

2. LENGTH OF STATE RESIDENCE DISTINCTIONS

Zobel v. Williams

457 U.S. 55, 102 S.Ct. 2309, 72 L.Ed.2d 672 (1982).

Chief Justice Burger, delivered the opinion of the Court.

The question ... is whether a statutory scheme by which a State distributes income derived from its natural resources to the adult citizens of the State in varying amounts, based on the length of each citizen's residence, violates the equal protection rights of newer state citizens. The Alaska Supreme Court sustained the constitutionality of the statute....

We reverse.

I

The 1967 discovery of large oil reserves on state-owned land in the Prudhoe Bay area of Alaska resulted in a windfall to the State. The State, which had a total budget of $124 million in 1969, before the oil revenues began to flow into the state coffers, received $3.7 billion in petroleum revenues during the 1981 fiscal year. This income will continue, and most likely grow for some years in the future. Recognizing that its mineral reserves, although large, are finite and that the resulting income will not continue in perpetuity, the State took steps to assure that its current good fortune will bring long range benefits. To accomplish this Alaska in 1976 adopted a constitutional amendment establishing the Permanent Fund into which the State must deposit at least 25% of its mineral income each year. Alaska Const., Art. IX, § 15. The amendment prohibits the legislature from appropriating any of the principal of the fund but permits use of the fund's earnings for general governmental purposes.

In 1980, the legislature enacted a dividend program to distribute annually a portion of the Fund's earnings directly to the State's adult residents. Under the plan, each citizen 18 years of age or older receives one dividend unit for each year of residency subsequent to 1959, the first year of statehood. The statute fixed the value of each dividend unit at $50 for the 1979 fiscal year; a one-year resident thus would receive one unit, or $50, while a resident of

Alaska since it became a State in 1959 would receive 21 units, or $1,050. The value of a dividend unit will vary each year depending on the income of the Permanent Fund and the amount of that income the State allocates for other purposes. The State now estimates that the 1985 fiscal year dividend will be nearly four times as large as that for 1979.

Appellants, residents of Alaska since 1978, brought this suit in 1980 challenging the dividend distribution plan as violative of their right to equal protection guarantees and their constitutional right to migrate to Alaska, to establish residency there and thereafter to enjoy the full rights of Alaska citizenship on the same terms as all other citizens of the State. . . .

II

The Alaska dividend distribution law is quite unlike the durational residency requirements we examined in Sosna v. Iowa, 419 U.S. 393 (1975); Memorial Hospital v. Maricopa County, 415 U.S. 250 (1974); Dunn v. Blumstein, 405 U.S. 330 (1972); and Shapiro v. Thompson, 394 U.S. 618 (1969). Those cases involved laws which required new residents to reside in the State a fixed minimum period to be eligible for certain benefits available on an equal basis to all other residents. The asserted purpose of the durational residency requirements was to assure that only persons who had established *bona fide* residence received rights and benefits provided for residents.

The Alaska statute does not impose any threshold waiting period on those seeking dividend benefits; persons with less than a full year of residency are entitled to share in the distribution. Alaska Stat. § 43.23.010. Nor does the statute purport to establish a test of the *bona fides* of state residence. Instead, the dividend statute creates fixed, permanent distinctions between an ever increasing number of perpetual classes of concededly *bona fide* residents, based on how long they have been in the State.

Appellants established residence in Alaska two years before the dividend law was passed. The distinction they complain of is not one which the State makes between those who arrived in Alaska after the enactment of the dividend distribution law and those who were residents prior to its enactment. Appellants instead challenge the distinctions made within the class of persons who were residents when the dividend scheme was enacted in 1980. The distinctions appellants attack include the preference given to persons who were residents when Alaska became a State in 1959 over all those who have arrived since then, as well as the distinctions made between all *bona fide* residents who settled in Alaska at different times during the 1959 to 1980 period.[5]

. . . Appellants claim that the distinctions made by the Alaska law should be subjected to the higher level of scrutiny applied to the durational residency requirements in Shapiro v. Thompson, supra and Memorial Hospital v. Maricopa County, supra. The State, on the other hand, asserts that the law need only meet the minimum rationality test. In any event, if the statutory scheme cannot pass even the minimal test proposed by the State, we need not decide whether any enhanced scrutiny is called for.

---

[5] . . .

The statute does not involve the kind of discrimination which the Privileges and Immunities Clause of Art. IV was designed to prevent. That Clause "was designed to insure to a citizen of State A who ventures into State B the same privileges which the citizens of State B enjoy." Toomer v. Witsell, 334 U.S. 385, 395 (1948). The Clause is thus not applicable to this case.

A

The State advanced and the Alaska Supreme Court accepted three purposes justifying the distinctions made by the dividend program: (a) creation of a financial incentive for individuals to establish and maintain residence in Alaska; (b) encouragement of prudent management of the Permanent Fund; and (c) apportionment of benefits in recognition of undefined "contributions of various kinds, both tangible and intangible, which residents have made during their years of residency."

As the Alaska Supreme Court apparently realized, the first two state objectives—creating a financial incentive for individuals to establish and maintain Alaska residence, and assuring prudent management of the Permanent Fund and the State's natural and mineral resources—are not rationally related to the distinctions Alaska seeks to make between newer residents and those who have been in the State since 1959. Assuming *arguendo* that granting increased dividend benefits for each year of continued Alaska residence might give some residents an incentive to stay in the state in order to reap increased dividend benefits in the future, the State's interest is not in any way served by granting greater dividends to persons for their residency during the 21 years prior to the enactment.

Nor does the State's purpose of furthering the prudent management of the Permanent Fund and the state's resources support retrospective application of its plan to the date of statehood. On this score the state's contention is straightforward:

"... If residents believed that twenty years from now they would be required to share permanent fund income on a per capita basis with the large population that Alaska will no doubt have by then, the temptation would be great to urge the legislature to provide immediately for the highest possible return on the investments of the permanent fund principal, which would require investments in riskier ventures."

The State similarly argues that equal per capita distribution would encourage rapacious development of natural resources. Even if we assume that the state interest is served by increasing the dividend for each year of residency beginning with the date of enactment, is it rationally served by granting greater dividends in varying amounts to those who resided in Alaska during the 21 years prior to enactment? We think not.

The last of the State's objectives—to reward citizens for past contributions—alone was relied upon by the Alaska Supreme Court to support the retrospective application of the law to 1959. However, that objective is not a legitimate state purpose. A similar "past contributions" argument was made and rejected in *Shapiro v. Thompson* ...: ... Similarly, in Vlandis v. Kline, 412 U.S. 441 (1973), we noted that "apportion[ment] of tuition rates on the basis of old and new residency ... would give rise to grave problems under the Equal Protection Clause of the Fourteenth Amendment."

If the States can make the amount of a cash dividend depend on length of residence, what would preclude varying university tuition on a sliding scale based on years of residence—or even limiting access to finite public facilities, eligibility for student loans, for civil service jobs, or for government contracts by length of domicile? Could States impose different taxes based on length of residence? Alaska's reasoning could open the door to state apportionment of other rights, benefits and services according to length of residency. It would permit the states to divide citizens into expanding numbers of permanent classes. Such a result would be clearly impermissible.

B

We need not consider whether the State could enact the dividend program prospectively only. . . .

III

. . .

We hold that the Alaska dividend distribution plan violates the . . . Equal Protection Clause. . . . [T]he judgment . . . is reversed and the case is remanded for further proceedings not inconsistent with this opinion.

Justice Brennan, with whom Justice Marshall, Justice Blackmun, and Justice Powell join, concurring.

I join the opinion of the Court, and agree with its conclusion that the retrospective aspects of Alaska's dividend-distribution law are not rationally related to a legitimate state purpose. I write separately only to emphasize that the pervasive discrimination embodied in the Alaska distribution scheme gives rise to constitutional concerns of somewhat larger proportions than may be evident on a cursory reading of the Court's opinion. In my view, these concerns might well preclude even the prospective operation of Alaska's scheme.

. . .

. . . In my view, it is difficult to escape from the recognition that underlying any scheme of classification on the basis of duration of residence, we shall almost invariably find the unstated premise that "some citizens are more equal than others." We rejected that premise and, I believe, implicitly rejected most forms of discrimination based upon length of residence, when we adopted the Equal Protection Clause.

Justice O'Connor, concurring in the judgment.

The Court strikes Alaska's distribution scheme, purporting to rely solely upon the Equal Protection Clause of the Fourteenth Amendment. The phrase "right to travel" appears only fleetingly in the Court's analysis, dismissed with an observation that "right to travel analysis refers to little more than a particular application of equal protection analysis." The Court's reluctance to rely explicitly on a right to travel is odd, because its holding depends on the assumption that Alaska's desire "to reward citizens for past contributions . . . is not a legitimate state purpose." Nothing in the Equal Protection Clause itself, however, declares this objective illegitimate. Instead, as a full reading of Shapiro v. Thompson, 394 U.S. 618 (1969) and Vlandis v. Kline, 412 U.S. 441 (1973), reveals, the Court has rejected this objective only when its implementation would abridge an interest in interstate travel or migration.

I respectfully suggest, therefore, that the Court misdirects its criticism when it labels Alaska's objective illegitimate. A desire to compensate citizens for their prior contributions is neither inherently invidious nor irrational. Under some circumstances, the objective may be wholly reasonable. . . .

Alaska's distribution plan distinguishes between long-term residents and recent arrivals. Stripped to its essentials, the plan denies non-Alaskans settling in the State the same privileges afforded longer-term residents. The Privileges and Immunities Clause of Article IV, which guarantees "[t]he Citizens of each State . . . all Privileges and Immunities of Citizens in the several States," addresses just this type of discrimination. Accordingly, I would measure Alaska's scheme against the principles implementing the Privileges and Immunities Clause. In addition to resolving the particular problems raised by Alaska's scheme, this analysis supplies a needed foundation for many of the "right to travel" claims discussed in the Court's prior opinions.

I

. . .

... Surely this scheme imposes one of the "disabilities of alienage" prohibited by Article IV's Privileges and Immunities Clause. See Paul v. Virginia, 8 Wall. 168, 180 (1869).

It could be argued that Alaska's scheme does not trigger the Privileges and Immunities Clause because it discriminates among classes of residents, rather than between residents and nonresidents. This argument, however, misinterprets the force of Alaska's distribution system.... Each group of citizens who migrated to Alaska in the past, or chooses to move there in the future, lives in the State on less favorable terms than those who arrived earlier. The circumstance that some of the disfavored citizens already live in Alaska does not negate the fact that "the citizen of State A who ventures into [Alaska]" to establish a home labors under a continuous disability.

If the Privileges and Immunities Clause applies to Alaska's distribution system, then our prior opinions describe the proper standard of review....

Once the Court ascertains that discrimination burdens an "essential activity," it will test the constitutionality of the discrimination under a two-part test. First, there must be "something to indicate that noncitizens constitute a peculiar source of the evil at which the statute is aimed." Hicklin v. Orbeck, 437 U.S. 518, 525–526 (1978) (quoting Toomer v. Witsell, 334 U.S. 385, 398 (1948)). Second, the Court must find a "substantial relationship" between the evil and the discrimination practiced against the noncitizens.

Certainly the right infringed in this case is "fundamental." Alaska's statute burdens those nonresidents who choose to settle in the State. It is difficult to imagine a right more essential to the Nation as a whole than the right to establish residence in a new State....

Alaska has not shown that its new residents are the "peculiar source" of any evil addressed by its disbursement scheme....

Even if new residents were the peculiar source of these evils, Alaska has not chosen a cure that bears a "substantial relationship" to the malady....

For these reasons, I conclude that Alaska's disbursement scheme violates Article IV's Privileges and Immunities Clause. I thus reach the same destination as the Court, but along a course that more precisely identifies the evils of the challenged statute.

. . .

Justice Rehnquist, dissenting.

Alaska's dividend distribution scheme represents one State's effort to apportion unique economic benefits among its citizens. Although the wealth received from the oil deposits of Prudhoe Bay may be quite unlike the economic resources enjoyed by most States, Alaska's distribution of that wealth is in substance no different from any other State's allocation of economic benefits. The distribution scheme being in the nature of economic regulation, I am at a loss to see the rationality behind the Court's invalidation of it as a denial of equal protection. This Court has long held that state economic regulations are presumptively valid, and violate the Fourteenth Amendment only in the rarest of circumstances: ...

... [T]he illegitimacy of a State's recognizing the past contributions of its citizens has been established by the Court only in certain cases considering an infringement of the right to travel, and the majority itself rightly declines to apply the strict scrutiny analysis of those right-to-travel cases. The distribution scheme at issue in this case impedes no person's right to travel to and settle in Alaska; if anything, the prospect of receiving annual cash dividends would encourage immigration to Alaska. The State's third justification cannot, therefore, be dismissed simply by quoting language about its legitimacy from right-to-travel cases which have no relevance to the question before us.

. . .

Attorney General of New York v. Soto–Lopez

476 U.S. 898, 106 S.Ct. 2317, 90 L.Ed.2d 899 (1986).

Justice Brennan announced the judgment of the Court and delivered an opinion in which Justice Marshall, Justice Blackmun, and Justice Powell joined.

The question ... is whether a preference in civil service employment opportunities offered by the State of New York solely to resident veterans who lived in the State at the time they entered military service violates the constitutional rights of resident veterans who lived outside the State when they entered military service.

I

The State of New York, through its Constitution, N.Y. Const., Art. V, § 6, and its Civil Service Law, N.Y.Civ.Serv.Law § 85 ... grants a civil service employment preference, in the form of points added to examination scores, to New York residents who are honorably-discharged veterans of the United States armed forces, who served during time of war, and who were residents of New York when they entered military service. This preference may be exercised only once, either for original hiring or for one promotion....

Appellees ... are veterans of the United States Army and long-time residents of New York. Both men claim to have met all the eligibility criteria for the New York State civil service preference except New York residence when they entered the Army. Both ... passed New York City civil service examinations, but were denied the veterans' preference by the New York City Civil Service Commission because they were residents of Puerto Rico at the time they joined the military. Appellees sued the City in Federal District Court, alleging that the requirement of residence when they joined the military violated the Equal Protection Clause of the Fourteenth Amendment and the constitutionally protected right to travel....

The District Court dismissed appellees' complaint.... The Court of Appeals for the Second Circuit reversed.... It ... held that the prior residence requirement of the New York civil service preference offends both the Equal Protection Clause and the right to travel.... We affirm.

"[F]reedom to travel throughout the United States has long been recognized as a basic right under the Constitution." *Dunn v. Blumstein*.... And, it is clear that the freedom to travel includes the "freedom to enter and abide in any State in the Union." *Dunn* ...

The textual source of the constitutional right to travel, or, more precisely, the right of free interstate migration, though, has proven elusive. It has been variously assigned to the Privileges and Immunities Clause of Art. IV, ... to the Commerce Clause, ... and to the Privileges and Immunities Clause of the Fourteenth Amendment,.... The right has also been inferred from the federal structure of government adopted by our Constitution.... However, in light of the unquestioned historic acceptance of the principle of free interstate migration, and of the important role that principle has played in transforming many States into a single Nation, we have not felt impelled to locate this right definitively in any particular constitutional provision.... Whatever its origin, the right to migrate is firmly established and has been repeatedly recognized by our cases. See, e.g., Hooper v. Bernalillo County Assessor, 472 U.S. 612, 618, n. 6 (1985); *Zobel,* ...

A state law implicates the right to travel when it actually deters such travel, ... when impeding travel is its primary objective, ..., or when it uses "'any classification which serves to penalize the exercise of that right.'" ... Our right to migrate cases have principally involved the latter, indirect manner of burdening the right. More particularly, our recent cases have dealt with state laws that, by classifying residents according to the time they established residence, resulted in the unequal distribution of rights and benefits among otherwise qualified bona fide residents.[3]

Because the creation of different classes of residents raises equal protection concerns, we have also relied upon the Equal Protection Clause in these cases. Whenever a state law infringes a constitutionally protected right, we undertake intensified equal protection scrutiny of that law.... Thus, in several cases, we asked expressly whether the distinction drawn by the State between older and newer residents burdens the right to migrate. Where we found such a burden, we required the State to come forward with a compelling justification.... In other cases, where we concluded that the contested classifications did not survive even rational basis scrutiny, we had no occasion to inquire whether enhanced scrutiny was appropriate. *Hooper,* supra; *Zobel,* supra. The analysis in all of these cases, however, is informed by the same guiding principle—the right to migrate protects residents of a State from being disadvantaged, or from being treated differently, simply because of the timing of their migration, from other similarly situated residents.[4] ...

New York's eligibility requirements for its civil service preference conditions a benefit on New York residence at a particular past time in an individual's life. It favors those veterans who were New York residents at a past fixed point over those who were not New York residents at the same point in their lives. Our cases have established that similar methods of favoring "prior" residents over "newer" ones, such as limiting a benefit to those who resided in the State by a fixed past date, *Hooper,* supra; granting incrementally greater benefits for each year of residence, *Zobel,* supra; and conditioning eligibility for certain benefits on completion of a fixed period of residence, see, e.g., *Memorial Hospital,* supra; Dunn v. Blumstein, 405 U.S. 330 (1972); *Shapiro,* supra, warrant careful judicial review.[5] But, our cases have also

---

[3] We have always carefully distinguished between bona fide residence requirements, which seek to differentiate between residents and nonresidents, and residence requirements, such as durational, fixed date, and fixed point residence requirements, which treat established residents differently based on the time they migrated into the State....

[4] Of course, regardless of the label we place on our analysis—right to migrate or equal protection—once we find a burden on the right to migrate the standard of review is the same. Laws which burden that right must be necessary to further a compelling state interest. See, e.g., *Memorial Hospital,* supra; *Dunn,* supra; *Shapiro,* supra.

[5] We have cautioned, however, that not all waiting periods are impermissible. See, e.g., *Memorial Hospital,* supra, at 258–259; *Shapiro,* supra, at 638, n. 21. Indeed, in

established that only where a State's law "operates to penalize those persons . . . who have exercised their constitutional right of interstate migration" is heightened scrutiny triggered. *Memorial Hospital* . . . .

Our task in this case, then, is first to determine whether New York's restriction of its civil service preference to veterans who entered the armed forces while residing in New York operates to penalize those persons who have exercised their right to migrate. If we find that it does, appellees must prevail unless New York can demonstrate that its classification is necessary to accomplish a compelling state interest.[6] . . .

III

A

In previous cases, we have held that even temporary deprivations of very important benefits and rights can operate to penalize migration. For example, in *Shapiro,* supra, and in *Memorial Hospital,* supra, we found that recently arrived indigent residents were deprived of life's necessities by durational residence requirements for welfare assistance and for free, nonemergency medical care, respectively, which were available to other poor residents. In *Dunn,* supra, we held that new residents were denied a basic right by a durational residence requirement for establishing eligibility to vote. The fact that these deprivations were temporary did not offset the Court's conclusions that they were so severe and worked such serious inequities among otherwise qualified residents that they effectively penalized new residents for the exercise of their rights to migrate.

More recently, in Hooper v. Bernalillo, 472 U.S. 612 (1985), and *Zobel v. Williams,* supra, we struck down state laws that created permanent distinctions among residents based on the length or timing of their residence in the State. At issue in *Hooper* was a New Mexico statute that granted a tax exemption to Vietnam veterans who resided in the State before May 8, 1976. *Zobel* concerned an Alaska statute granting residents one state mineral income dividend unit for each year of residence subsequent to 1959. Because we employed rational basis equal protection analysis in those cases, we did not face directly the question whether the contested laws operated to penalize interstate migration. Nonetheless, the conclusion that they did penalize migration may be inferred from our

Sosna v. Iowa, 419 U.S. 393 (1975), we upheld a 1-year residency condition for maintaining an action for divorce. We noted the State's strong, traditional interest in setting the terms of and procedures for marriage and divorce. Weighing the fact that appellant's access to the desired state procedure was only temporarily delayed, against the State's important interest, we concluded that her right to migrate was not violated.

We have also sustained domicile requirements, which incorporated 1-year waiting periods, for resident tuition at state universities. Starns v. Malkerson, 401 U.S. 985 (1971), summarily aff'g 326 F.Supp. 234 (Minn.1970) (three-judge court); Sturgis v. Washington, 414 U.S. 1057 (1973), summarily aff'g 368 F.Supp. 38 W.D. (Wash.) (three-judge court). See also Vlandis v. Kline, 412 U.S. 441, 452–454 (1973).

[6] In his concurrence, The Chief Justice takes the Court to task for asking in the first

instance what is the appropriate standard of review to employ in evaluating New York's laws. The Chief Justice argues that we should initially run the laws through a rational basis analysis and then, if they survive that level of scrutiny, ask whether a higher level is appropriate.

We disagree. The logical first question to ask when presented with an equal protection claim, and the one we usually ask first, is what level of review is appropriate. . . .

It is true, as The Chief Justice suggests, that in *Hooper,* supra, and *Zobel,* supra, the Court did not follow this same logical sequence of analysis. We think that the better approach is that which the Court has employed in other equal protection cases—to inquire first as to the proper level of scrutiny and then to apply it.

determination that "the Constitution will not tolerate a state benefit program that 'creates fixed, permanent distinctions ... between ... classes of concededly bona fide residents, based on how long they have been in the State.' " *Hooper* ... (quoting *Zobel* ...).

[Appellees] have been denied a significant benefit that is granted to all veterans similarly situated except for state of residence at the time of their entry into the military. While the benefit sought here may not rise to the same level of importance as the necessities of life and the right to vote, it is unquestionably substantial. The award of bonus points can mean the difference between winning or losing civil service employment, with its attendant job security, decent pay, and good benefits.... Furthermore, appellees have been permanently deprived of the veterans' credits that they seek. As the Court of Appeals observed, "[t]he veteran's ability to satisfy the New York residence requirement is ... fixed. He either was a New York resident at the time of his initial induction or he was not; he cannot earn a change in status." 755 F.2d, at 275. Such a permanent deprivation of a significant benefit, based only on the fact of nonresidence at a past point in time, clearly operates to penalize appellees for exercising their rights to migrate.

B

New York offers four interests in justification of its fixed point residence requirement: (1) the encouragement of New York residents to join the armed services; (2) the compensation of residents for service in time of war by helping these veterans reestablish themselves upon coming home; (3) the inducement of veterans to return to New York after wartime service; and (4) the employment of a "uniquely valuable class of public servants" who possess useful experience acquired through their military service. All four justifications fail to withstand heightened scrutiny on a common ground—each of the State's asserted interests could be promoted fully by granting bonus points to *all* otherwise qualified veterans. New York residents would still be encouraged to join the services. Veterans who served in time of war would be compensated. And, both former New Yorkers and prior residents of other States would be drawn to New York after serving the Nation, thus providing the State with an even larger pool of potentially valuable public servants.

. . .

IV

... The State has not met its heavy burden of proving that it has selected a means of pursuing a compelling state interest which does not impinge unnecessarily on constitutionally protected interests. Consequently, we conclude that New York's veterans' preference violates appellees' constitutionally protected rights to migrate and to equal protection of the law.

. . .

Affirmed.

Chief Justice Burger, concurring in the judgment.

... Both *Zobel* and *Hooper* held that the classifications used by the States to award preferences to certain citizens failed to pass a rational basis test *under the Equal Protection Clause.* As a result, we had no occasion to reach the issues whether the classifications would survive heightened scrutiny or whether the right to travel was violated....

The Court's opinion, however, instead *begins* the analysis by addressing the "right to migrate." Moreover, heightened scrutiny is employed without first determining whether the challenged New York classification would survive even rational basis analysis....

. . .

I would affirm the judgment of the Court of Appeals based on our reasoning and holdings in *Hooper* and *Zobel*, rather than adding dicta concerning the right to travel.

Justice White, concurring in the judgment.

I agree with Justice O'Connor that the right to travel is not sufficiently implicated in this case to require heightened scrutiny. Hence, I differ with Justice Brennan in this respect. But I agree with The Chief Justice that the New York statute at issue denies equal protection of the laws because the classification it employs is irrational. I therefore concur in the judgment.

Justice Stevens, dissenting.

. . .

Justice O'Connor, with whom Justice Rehnquist and Justice Stevens join, dissenting.

... Because I believe that New York's veterans' preference scheme is not constitutionally offensive under the Equal Protection Clause, does not penalize some free-floating "right to migrate," and does not violate the Privileges and Immunities Clause of Art. IV, § 2, of the Constitution, I dissent.

I

The Court's constitutional analysis runs generally as follows: because the classification imposed by New York's limited, one-time veterans' civil service preference "penalizes" appellees' constitutional "right to migrate," the preference program must be subjected to heightened scrutiny, which it does not survive because it is insufficiently narrowly tailored to serve its asserted purposes. On the strength of this reasoning, the Court concludes that the preference program violates both appellees' constitutional "right to migrate" and their right to equal protection of the law, although it does not make clear how much of its analysis is necessary or sufficient to find a violation of the "right to migrate" independently of an Equal Protection Clause violation.

In pursuing this new dual analysis, the Court simply rejects the equal protection approach the Court has previously employed in similar cases, see, e.g., Hooper v. Bernalillo County Assessor, 472 U.S. 612 (1985), without bothering to explain why its novel use of both "right to migrate" analysis and strict equal protection scrutiny is more appropriate, necessary or doctrinally coherent. Cf. Jones v. Helms, 452 U.S. 412, 426–427 (1981) (White, J., concurring). Indeed, the Court does not even feel "impelled to locate ['the right to migrate'] definitively in any particular constitutional provision," despite the fact that its ruling rests in major part on its determination that the preference scheme penalizes that right....

. . .

It is unfortunate that the Court has once again failed to articulate and justify by reference to textual sources a single constitutional principle or analysis upon which it can rely in deciding cases such as this. I adhere to my belief that the Privileges and Immunities Clause of Art. IV, § 2, of the

Constitution supplies the relevant basis for analysis in evaluating claims like appellees', where the principal allegation is that the state scheme impermissibly distinguishes between state residents, allegedly imposing a relative burden on those who have more recently exercised their right to establish residence in the State. See Zobel v. Williams ... (O'Connor, J., concurring in judgment). I also continue to believe that a State's desire to compensate its citizens for their prior contributions is "neither inherently invidious nor irrational," either under the Court's "right to migrate" or under some undefined, substantive component of the Equal Protection Clause.... This case presents one of those instances in which the recognition of state citizens' past sacrifices constitutes a valid state interest that does not infringe any constitutionally protected interest, including the fundamental right to settle in another State which is protected by the Privileges and Immunities Clause of Art. IV, § 2....

II

. . .

The New York law certainly does not directly restrict or burden appellees' freedom to move to New York and to establish residence there by imposing discriminatory fees, taxes, or other direct restraints....

Finally, the New York scheme does not effectively penalize those who exercise their fundamental right to settle in the State of their choice by requiring newcomers to accept a status inferior to that of all oldtime residents of New York upon their arrival. Cf. Zobel v. Williams, 457 U.S., at 74 (O'Connor, J., concurring in judgment). Those veterans who were not New York residents when they joined the United States Armed Forces, who subsequently move to New York, and who endeavor to secure civil service employment are treated exactly the same as the vast majority of New York citizens; they are in no sense regarded as "second-class citizens" when compared with the vast majority of New Yorkers or even the majority of the candidates against whom they must compete in obtaining civil employment. Cf. Hicklin v. Orbeck, 437 U.S. 518 (1978). To the extent that persons such as appellees labor under any practical disability, it is a disability that they share in equal measure with countless other New York residents, including New York residents who joined the Armed Forces from New York but are ineligible for the veterans' preference for other reasons.

... New York's veterans' preference scheme requires that veterans satisfy a number of preconditions, of which prior residency is only one, before they qualify for the preference. Moreover, the preference only increases the possibility of securing a civil service appointment; it does not guarantee it. Those newly arrived veterans who achieve a sufficiently high score on the exam may not be disadvantaged at all by the preference program; conversely, the chances of those who receive a very low score may not be affected by the fact that their competitors received bonus points. Finally, the bonus program is a one-time benefit. Veterans who join the service in New York, who satisfy the other statutory requirements, and who achieve a sufficiently high score on the exam to bring them within range of securing employment may only use the bonus points on one examination for appointment and in one job for promotion. Thus, persons such as appellees are not forced to labor under a "continuous disability" by comparison even to this discrete group of New York citizens. Zobel v. Williams, supra, at 75 (O'Connor, J., concurring in judgment).

. . .

In sum, finding that this scheme in theory or practical effect constitutes a "penalty" on appellees' fundamental right to settle in New York or on their "right to migrate" seems to me ephemeral, and completely unnecessary to safeguard the constitutional purpose of "maintaining a Union rather than a mere 'league of States.'" Zobel v. Williams, supra, at 73 (O'Connor, J., concurring in judgment).... Thus, heightened scrutiny, either under the "right to migrate" or the Equal Protection Clause is inappropriate.

Under rational basis review, New York's program plainly passes constitutional muster....

. . .

Whether this issue is tested under the "right to migrate," the Equal Protection Clause, or the Privileges and Immunities Clause of Art. IV, § 2, something more than the minimal effect on the right to travel or migrate that exists in this case must be required to trigger heightened scrutiny or the Court's right to travel analysis will swallow all the traditional deference shown to state economic and social regulation. The modest scheme at issue here does not penalize in a constitutional sense veterans who joined the Armed Forces in other States for choosing to eventually settle in New York, and does not deny them equal protection.... [a]

WILLIAMS v. VERMONT, 472 U.S. 14 (1985). A majority of the Court understood state law to exempt from the motor vehicle use tax imposed when cars are registered in Vermont, not only those who had already paid sales tax on cars purchased in Vermont, but those who were Vermont residents when they purchased and first registered a car in another, reciprocating State to the extent they had paid a sales or use tax there. The Court upheld an equal protection claim by new residents of Vermont denied the exemption because they had bought and registered a car in such a State before moving to Vermont. Justice White's majority opinion noted that it was still "unnecessary to reach" a question the Court previously had "expressly reserved"—"whether a State must credit a sales tax paid to another State against its own use tax"—because "[w]hatever the general rule may be, to provide a credit only to those who were residents at the time they paid the sales tax is an arbitrary distinction that violates the Equal Protection Clause." After noting that normally this kind of tax exemption "will be sustained if the legislature could reasonably have concluded that the challenged classification would promote a legitimate state purpose[,]" the opinion continued:

"We perceive no legitimate purpose, however, that is furthered by this discriminatory exemption. As we said in holding that the use tax base cannot be broader than the sales tax base, 'equal treatment for in-state and out-of-state taxpayers similarly situated is the condition precedent for a valid use tax on goods imported from out-of-state.' Halliburton Oil Well Co. v. Reily, 373 U.S. 64, 70 (1963).[7] A State may not treat those within its borders unequally solely on the basis of their different residences or States of incorporation. WHYY v. Glassboro, 393 U.S. 117, 119 (1968); Wheeling Steel Corp. v. Glander, 337 U.S. 562, 571–572 (1949). In the present case, residence at the time of purchase is a

---

[a] See generally Cohen, *Equal Treatment for Newcomers: The Core Meaning of National and State Citizenship,* 1 Const.Commentary 9 (1984).

[7] *Halliburton* was decided under the Commerce Clause and is not dispositive. We do not consider in what way, if any, the failure to give appellants a credit might burden interstate commerce. The critical point is the Court's emphasis on the need for equal treatment of taxpayers who can be distinguished only on the basis of residence. See also Henneford v. Silas Mason Co., 300 U.S. 577, 583–584 (1937).

wholly arbitrary basis on which to distinguish among present Vermont registrants—at least among those who used their cars elsewhere before coming to Vermont.[8] Having registered a car in Vermont they are similarly situated for all relevant purposes. Each is a Vermont resident, using a car in Vermont, with an equal obligation to pay for the maintenance and improvement of Vermont's roads. The purposes of the statute would be identically served, and with an identical burden, by taxing each. The distinction between them bears no relation to the statutory purpose. See Zobel v. Williams, 457 U.S. 55, 61 (1982)....

"In sum, we can see no relevant difference between motor vehicle registrants who purchased their cars out-of-state while they were Vermont residents and those who only came to Vermont after buying a car elsewhere. To free one group and not the other from the otherwise applicable tax burden violates the Equal Protection Clause."

Justice Powell took no part in the decision of the case. Justice Brennan concurred, stating:

"I join the Court's opinion for the reasons stated therein and in my concurring opinion in Zobel v. Williams, 457 U.S. 55, 65 (1982). General application of distinctions of the kind made by the Vermont statute would clearly, though indirectly, threaten the 'federal interest in free interstate migration.' Id., at 66. In addition, the statute makes distinctions among residents that are not 'supported by a valid state interest independent of the discrimination itself.' Id., at 70."

Justice Blackmun, joined by Justices Rehnquist and O'Connor, dissented. He first accused the majority of "imagin[ing] a fanciful, hypothetical discrimination" in favor of a "phantom beneficiary"—the "Vermont resident who leaves the State to purchase an automobile, pays the sales tax and registers the car in the foreign State of purchase, lives there for a while, and then returns to Vermont and registers the car there." Assuming the Court correctly had identified a real issue, however, Justice Blackmun continued:

"The reason nonresidents who purchase cars out-of-state are taxed if they subsequently relocate in Vermont, while resident out-of-state purchasers are not, is that it was presumed that people will use their cars primarily in the States in which they reside. Most people who do not reside in Vermont and do not purchase their cars in that State, will not use their cars primarily in Vermont. If at some time in the future they move to Vermont and register their automobiles there, the assumption is that they will have used their cars in two different States. On the other hand, most people who reside in Vermont and purchase their cars out-of-state will return to Vermont immediately with their cars. Thus, the out-of-state purchaser is taxed, while the Vermont purchaser is exempted to the extent that he already has paid a sales tax. This distinction is hardly irrational, and the fact that there may be a Vermont resident who both purchases and uses his car out-of-state ... surely does not render the scheme irrational. A tax classification does not violate the demands of equal protection simply because it may not perfectly identify the class of people it wishes to single out....

[8] The dissent does not disagree that such people are similarly situated, nor does it identify any justification for preferential treatment of the resident. It merely argues that the inequity is the acceptable result of the imprecision of a generally rational classification. Under rational-basis scrutiny, legislative classifications are of course allowed some play in the joints. But the choice of a proxy criterion—here, residence for State of use—cannot be so casual as this, particularly when a more precise and direct classification is easily drawn.

"... The Court ... ignores the purpose of the tax and of the classification. Vermont does not wish to 'distinguish among present Vermont registrants,' but to distinguish those who will likely use Vermont's roads immediately after they have purchased cars out-of-state from those who will not. Residency is not an irrational way to enact such a classification ..."

3.   CLASSIFICATIONS DISADVANTAGING NONRESIDENTS

Metropolitan Life Insurance Co. v. Ward

470 U.S. 869, 105 S.Ct. 1676, 84 L.Ed.2d 751 (1985).

Justice Powell delivered the opinion of the Court.

This case presents the question whether Alabama's domestic preference tax statute, Ala.Code §§ 27–4–4 and 27–4–5 (1975), that taxes out-of-state insurance companies at a higher rate than domestic insurance companies, violates the Equal Protection Clause.

I

... [F]oreign life insurance companies pay a tax on their gross premiums received from business conducted in Alabama at a rate of 3 percent, and foreign companies selling other types of insurance pay at a rate of 4 percent. Ala.Code § 27–4–4(a) (1975). All domestic insurance companies, in contrast, pay at a rate of only 1 percent on all types of insurance premiums. § 27–4–5(a)....

. . .

II

Appellants, a group of insurance companies incorporated outside of the State of Alabama, filed claims with the Alabama Department of Insurance in 1981, contending that the domestic preference tax statute, as applied to them, violated the Equal Protection Clause....

... Relying on this Court's opinion in Western & Southern Life Ins. Co. v. State Board of Equalization of California, 451 U.S. 648 (1981), the [trial] court ruled that the Alabama statute did not violate the Equal Protection Clause because it served "at least two purposes, in addition to raising revenue: (1) encouraging the formation of new insurance companies in Alabama, and (2) encouraging capital investment by foreign insurance companies in the Alabama assets and governmental securities set forth in the statute." The court also found that the distinction the statute created between foreign and domestic companies was rationally related to those two purposes and that the Alabama Legislature reasonably could have believed that the classification would have promoted those purposes.

... [T]he Court of Civil Appeals ... affirmed ... as to the existence of the two legitimate state purposes, but remanded for an evidentiary hearing on the issue of rational relationship, concluding that summary judgment was inappropriate on that question because the evidence was in conflict.... Appellants petitioned the Supreme Court of Alabama for certiorari on the affirmance of the legitimate state purpose issue, and the State and the intervenors petitioned for review of the remand order.... The Supreme Court denied certiorari on all claims. [Because appellants] waived their rights to an evidentiary hearing on the rational relationship issue ..., judgment was entered for the State and the intervenors....

III

Prior to our decision in Western & Southern Life Ins. Co. v. State Board of Equalization of California, supra, the jurisprudence of the applicability of the Equal Protection Clause to discriminatory tax statutes had a somewhat checkered history. Lincoln National Life Ins. Co. v. Read, 325 U.S. 673 (1945), held that so-called "privilege" taxes, required to be paid by a foreign corporation before it would be permitted to do business within a State, were immune from equal protection challenge. That case stood in stark contrast, however, to the Court's prior decisions in Southern R. Co. v. Greene, 216 U.S. 400, 30 S.Ct. 287 (1910), and Hanover Fire Ins. Co. v. Harding, 272 U.S. 494 (1926), as well as to later decisions, in which the Court had recognized that the Equal Protection Clause placed limits on other forms of discriminatory taxation imposed on out-of-state corporations solely because of their residence. See, e.g., WHYY, Inc. v. Glassboro, 393 U.S. 117 (1968); Allied Stores of Ohio, Inc. v. Bowers, 358 U.S. 522 (1959); Wheeling Steel Corp. v. Glander, 337 U.S. 562 (1949).

In *Western & Southern,* ... we reviewed all of these cases for the purpose of deciding whether to permit an equal protection challenge to a California statute imposing a retaliatory tax on foreign insurance companies doing business within the State, when the home States of those companies imposed a similar tax on California insurers entering their borders. We concluded that *Lincoln* was no more than "a surprising throwback" to the days before enactment of the Fourteenth Amendment and in which incorporation of a domestic corporation or entry of a foreign one had been granted only as a matter of privilege by the State in its unfettered discretion.... We therefore rejected the longstanding but "anachronis[tic]" rule of *Lincoln* and explicitly held that the Equal Protection Clause imposes limits upon a State's power to condition the right of a foreign corporation to do business within its borders.... We held that "[w]e consider it now established that, whatever the extent of a State's authority to exclude foreign corporations from doing business within its boundaries, that authority does not justify imposition of more onerous taxes or other burdens on foreign corporations than those imposed on domestic corporations, unless the discrimination between foreign and domestic corporations bears a rational relation to a legitimate state purpose." ...

Because appellants waived their right to an evidentiary hearing on the issue whether the classification in the Alabama domestic preference tax statute bears a rational relation to the two purposes upheld by the Circuit Court, the only question before us is whether those purposes are legitimate.[5]

A

(1)

The first of the purposes found by the trial court to be a legitimate reason for the statute's classification between foreign and domestic corporations is that it encourages the formation of new domestic insurance companies in Alabama. The State, agreeing with the Court of Civil Appeals, contends that this Court has long held that the promotion of domestic industry, in and of itself, is a legitimate state purpose that will survive equal protection scrutiny.

---

[5] The State and the intervenors advanced some 15 additional purposes in support of the Alabama statute. As neither the Circuit Court nor the Court of Civil Appeals ruled on the legitimacy of those purposes,

that question is not before us, and we express no view as to it. On remand, the State will be free to advance again its arguments relating to the legitimacy of those purposes.

. . .

In so contending, it relies on a series of cases, including *Western & Southern,* that are said to have upheld discriminatory taxes....

The cases cited lend little or no support to the State's contention. In *Western & Southern,* the case principally relied upon, we did not hold as a general rule that promotion of domestic industry is a legitimate state purpose under equal protection analysis.[6] Rather, we held that California's purpose in enacting the retaliatory tax—to promote the *interstate* business of domestic insurers by deterring *other States* from enacting discriminatory or excessive taxes—was a legitimate one.... In contrast, Alabama asks us to approve its purpose of promoting the business of its domestic insurers *in Alabama* by penalizing foreign insurers who also want to do business in the State. Alabama has made no attempt, as California did, to influence the policies of other States in order to enhance its domestic companies' ability to operate interstate; rather, it has erected barriers to foreign companies who wish to do interstate business in order to improve its domestic insurers' ability to compete at home.

The crucial distinction between the two cases lies in the fact that Alabama's aim to promote domestic industry is purely and completely discriminatory, designed only to favor domestic industry within the State, no matter what the cost to foreign corporations also seeking to do business there. Alabama's purpose, contrary to California's, constitutes the very sort of parochial discrimination that the Equal Protection Clause was intended to prevent.... Unlike the retaliatory tax involved in *Western & Southern,* which only burdens residents of a State that imposes its own discriminatory tax on outsiders, the domestic preference tax gives the "home team" an advantage by burdening *all* foreign corporations seeking to do business within the State, no matter what they or their States do.

The validity of the view that a State may not constitutionally favor its own residents by taxing foreign corporations at a higher rate solely because of their residence is confirmed by a long line of this Court's cases so holding. WHYY, Inc. v. Glassboro, 393 U.S., at 119–120; Wheeling Steel Corp. v. Glander, 337 U.S., at 571; Hanover Fire Ins. Co. v. Harding, 272 U.S., at 511; Southern R. Co. v. Greene, 216 U.S., at 417. See Reserve Life Ins. Co. v. Bowers, 380 U.S. 258 (1965) (per curiam). As the Court stated in *Hanover Fire Ins. Co.,* with respect to general tax burdens on business, "the foreign corporation stands equal, and is to be classified with domestic corporations of the same kind." 272 U.S., at 511. In all of these cases, the discriminatory tax was imposed by the State on foreign corporations doing business within the State solely because of their residence, presumably to promote domestic industry within the State. In relying on these cases and rejecting *Lincoln* in *Western & Southern,* we reaffirmed the continuing viability of the Equal Protection Clause as a means of challenging a statute that seeks to benefit domestic industry within the State only by grossly discriminating against foreign competitors.

. . .

---

[6] We find the other cases on which the State relies also to be inapposite to this inquiry. *Bacchus Imports, Pike,* and *Parker* discussed whether promotion of local industry is a valid state purpose under the Commerce Clause. The Commerce Clause, unlike the Equal Protection Clause, is integrally concerned with whether a state purpose implicates local or national interests. The Equal Protection Clause, in contrast, is concerned with whether a state purpose is impermissibly discriminatory; whether the discrimination involves local or other interests is not central to the inquiry to be made. Thus, the fact that promotion of local industry is a legitimate state interest in the Commerce Clause context says nothing about its validity under equal protection analysis....

. . .

(2)

The State argues nonetheless that it is impermissible to view a discriminatory tax such as the one at issue here as violative of the Equal Protection Clause. This approach, it contends, amounts to no more than "Commerce Clause rhetoric in equal protection clothing." The State maintains that because Congress, in enacting the McCarran–Ferguson Act, 15 U.S.C. §§ 1011–1015, intended to authorize States to impose taxes that burden interstate commerce in the insurance field, the tax at issue here must stand. Our concerns are much more fundamental than as characterized by the State. Although the McCarran–Ferguson Act exempts the insurance industry from Commerce Clause restrictions, it does not purport to limit in any way the applicability of the Equal Protection Clause. As noted above, our opinion in *Western & Southern* expressly reaffirmed the viability of equal protection restraints on discriminatory taxes in the insurance context.

Moreover, the State's view ignores the differences between Commerce Clause and equal protection analysis and the consequent different purposes those two constitutional provisions serve. Under Commerce Clause analysis, the State's interest, if legitimate, is weighed against the burden the state law would impose on interstate commerce. In the equal protection context, however, if the State's purpose is found to be legitimate, the state law stands as long as the burden it imposes is found to be rationally related to that purpose, a relationship that is not difficult to establish....

The two constitutional provisions perform different functions in the analysis of the permissible scope of a State's power—one protects interstate commerce, and the other protects persons from unconstitutional discrimination by the States.... The effect of the statute at issue here is to place a discriminatory tax burden on foreign insurers who desire to do business within the State, thereby also incidentally placing a burden on interstate commerce. Equal protection restraints are applicable even though the effect of the discrimination in this case is similar to the type of burden with which the Commerce Clause also would be concerned. We reaffirmed the importance of the Equal Protection Clause in the insurance context in *Western & Southern* and see no reason now for reassessing that view.

In whatever light the State's position is cast, acceptance of its contention that promotion of domestic industry is always a legitimate state purpose under equal protection analysis would eviscerate the Equal Protection Clause in this context. A State's natural inclination frequently would be to prefer domestic business over foreign. If we accept the State's view here, then any discriminatory tax would be valid if the State could show it reasonably was intended to benefit domestic business.[10] A discriminatory tax would stand or fall depending primarily on how a State framed its purpose—as benefiting one group or as harming another. This is a distinction without a difference, and one that we rejected last term in an analogous context arising under the Commerce Clause. Bacchus Imports, Ltd. v. Dias, 468 U.S., at 273. We hold that under the circumstances of this case, promotion of domestic business by discriminating against nonresident competitors is not a legitimate state purpose.

---

[10] Indeed, under the State's analysis, *any* discrimination subject to the rational relation level of scrutiny could be justified simply on the ground that it favored one group at the expense of another. This case does not involve or question, as the dissent suggests, the broad authority of a State to promote and regulate its own economy. We hold only that such regulation may not be accomplished by imposing discriminatorily higher taxes on nonresident corporations solely because they are nonresidents.

B

The second purpose found by the courts below to be legitimate was the encouragement of capital investment in the Alabama assets and governmental securities specified in the statute. We do not agree that this is a legitimate state purpose when furthered by discrimination. Domestic insurers remain entitled to the more favorable rate of tax regardless of whether they invest in Alabama assets. Moreover, the investment incentive provision of the Alabama statute does not enable foreign insurance companies to eliminate the discriminatory effect of the statute. No matter how much of their assets they invest in Alabama, foreign insurance companies are still required to pay a higher gross premiums tax than domestic companies. The State's investment incentive provision therefore does not cure, but reaffirms, the statute's impermissible classification based solely on residence. We hold that encouraging investment in Alabama assets and securities in this plainly discriminatory manner serves no legitimate state purpose.

IV

We conclude that neither of the two purposes furthered by the Alabama domestic preference tax statute and addressed by the Circuit Court for Montgomery County ... is legitimate under the Equal Protection Clause to justify the imposition of the discriminatory tax at issue here. The judgment of the Alabama Supreme Court accordingly is reversed, and the case is remanded for further proceedings not inconsistent with this opinion.

It is so ordered.

Justice O'Connor, with whom Justice Brennan, Justice Marshall and Justice Rehnquist join, dissenting.

This case presents a simple question: Is it legitimate for a state to use its taxing power to promote a domestic insurance industry and to encourage capital investment within its borders? In a holding that can only be characterized as astonishing, the Court determines that these purposes are illegitimate. This holding is unsupported by precedent and subtly distorts the constitutional balance, threatening the freedom of both state and federal legislative bodies to fashion appropriate classifications in economic legislation. Because I disagree with both the Court's method of analysis and its conclusion, I respectfully dissent.

I

... Appellants rely on the Equal Protection Clause because, as corporations, they are not "citizens" protected by the privileges and immunities clauses of the Constitution. Hemphill v. Orloff, 277 U.S. 537, 548–550 (1928). Similarly, they cannot claim Commerce Clause protection because Congress in the McCarran–Ferguson Act, 59 Stat. 33, 15 U.S.C. § 1011 et seq., explicitly suspended Commerce Clause restraints on state taxation of insurance and placed insurance regulation firmly within the purview of the several States. Western & Southern Life Ins. Co. v. State Board of Equalization, 451 U.S. 648, 655 (1981).

... [T]he Court ... meld[s] the proper two-step inquiry regarding the State's purpose and the classification's relationship to that purpose into a single unarticulated judgment. This tactic enables the Court to characterize State goals that have been legitimated by Congress itself as improper solely because it disagrees with the concededly rational means of differential taxation selected by the legislature. This unorthodox approach leads to further error.

The Court gives only the most cursory attention to the factual and legal bases supporting the State's purposes and ignores both precedent and significant evidence in the record establishing their legitimacy. Most troubling, the Court discovers in the Equal Protection Clause an implied prohibition against classifications whose purpose is to give the "home team" an advantage over interstate competitors even where Congress has authorized such advantages.

... Judicial deference is strongest where a tax classification is alleged to infringe the right to equal protection. "[I]n taxation, even more than in other fields, legislatures possess the greatest freedom in classification." Madden v. Kentucky, 309 U.S. 83, 88 (1940). "Where the public interest is served one business may be left untaxed and another taxed, in order to promote the one or to restrict or suppress the other." Carmichael v. Southern Coal & Coke Co., 301 U.S. 495, 512 (1937) (citations omitted). As the Court emphatically noted in *Allied Stores of Ohio, Inc. v. Bowers:*

> "[I]t has repeatedly been held and appears to be entirely settled that a statute which encourages the location within the State of needed and useful industries by exempting them, though not also others, from its taxes is not arbitrary and does not violate the Equal Protection Clause of the Fourteenth Amendment. Similarly, it has long been settled that a classification, though discriminatory, is not arbitrary or violative of the Equal Protection Clause of the Fourteenth Amendment if any state of facts reasonably can be conceived that would sustain it." 358 U.S. 522 (1959) (citations omitted).

See also Western & Southern Life Ins. Co. v. State Board of Equalization, supra, 451 U.S., at 674; Minnesota v. Clover Leaf Creamery Co., 449 U.S. 456, 464 (1981).

. . .

III

. . .

... Alabama does *not* tax at a higher rate solely on the basis of residence; it taxes insurers, domestic as well as foreign, who do not maintain a principal place of business or substantial assets in Alabama, based on conceded distinctions in the contributions of these insurers *as a class* to the State's insurance objectives. The majority obscures the issue by observing that a given "foreign insurance company doing the same type and volume of business in Alabama as a domestic company" will pay a higher tax.... Rational basis scrutiny does not require that the classification be mathematically precise or that *every* foreign insurer or *every* domestic company fit to perfection the general profile on which the classification is based....

IV

... The Court[,] by a remarkable evasive tactic[,] simply declares that the ends of promoting a domestic insurance industry and attracting investments to the State *when accomplished through the means of discriminatory taxation* are not legitimate state purposes.... By collapsing the two prongs of the rational basis test into one, the Court arrives at the ultimate issue—whether the *means* are constitutional—without ever engaging in the deferential inquiry we have adopted as a brake on judicial impeachment of legislative policy choices. In addition to unleashing an undisciplined form of Equal Protection Clause scrutiny, the Court's approach today has serious implications for the authority of Congress under the Commerce Clause....

. . .

... Favoring local business as an end in itself might be "rational" but would be antithetical to federalism. Accepting arguendo this interpretation, we have shown that the measure at issue here does not benefit local business as an end in itself but serves important ulterior goals. Moreover, any federalism component of equal protection is fully vindicated where Congress has explicitly validated a parochial focus. Surely the Equal Protection Clause was not intended to supplant the Commerce Clause, foiling Congress' decision under its commerce powers to "affirmatively permit [some measure of] parochial favoritism" when necessary to a healthy federation. White v. Massachusetts Council of Construction Employers, 460 U.S. 204, 212 (1983). Such a view of the Equal Protection Clause cannot be reconciled with the McCarran–Ferguson Act and our decisions in *Western & Southern* and *Benjamin.*

Western & Southern established that a state may validly tax out-of-state corporations at a higher rate if its goal is to promote the ability of its domestic businesses to compete in *interstate* markets. Nevertheless, the Court today concludes that the converse policy is forbidden, striking down legislation whose purpose is to encourage the *intrastate* activities of local business concerns by permitting them to compete effectively on their home turf. In essence, the Court declares "We will excuse an unequal burden on foreign insurers if the State's purpose is to foster its domestic insurer's activities in *other* States, but the same unequal burden will be unconstitutional when employed to further a policy that places a higher social value on the domestic insurer's *homestate* than interstate activities." This conclusion is not drawn from the Commerce Clause, the textual source of constitutional restrictions on State interference with interstate competition. Reliance on the Commerce Clause would, of course, be unavailing here in view of the McCarran–Ferguson Act. Instead the Court engrafts its own economic values on the Equal Protection Clause. Beyond guarding against arbitrary or irrational discrimination, as interpreted by the Court today this Clause now prohibits the effectuation of economic policies, even where sanctioned by Congress, that elevate local concerns over interstate competition....

... This newly unveiled power of the Equal Protection Clause would come as a surprise to the Congress that passed the McCarran–Ferguson Act and the Court that sustained the Act against constitutional attack. In the McCarran–Ferguson Act, Congress expressly sanctioned such economic parochialism in the context of state regulation and taxation of insurance.

The doctrine adopted by the majority threatens the freedom not only of the States but also of the Federal Government to formulate economic policy. The dangers in discerning in the Equal Protection Clause a prohibition against barriers to interstate business irrespective of the Commerce Clause should be self-evident. The Commerce Clause is a flexible tool of economic policy that Congress may use as it sees fit, letting it lie dormant or invoking it to limit as well as promote the free flow of commerce. Doctrines of equal protection are constitutional limits that constrain the acts of federal and state legislatures alike. See, e.g., Califano v. Webster, 430 U.S. 313 (1977); Cohen, Congressional Power to Validate Unconstitutional State Laws: A Forgotten Solution to an Old Enigma, 35 Stan.L.Rev. 387, 400–413 (1983). The Court's analysis casts a shadow over numerous congressional enactments that adopted as federal policy "the type of parochial favoritism" the Court today finds unconstitutional. White v. Massachusetts Council of Construction Employers, 460 U.S., at 213.

Contrary to the reasoning in *Benjamin,* the Court today indicates the Equal Protection Clause stands as an independent barrier if courts should determine that either Congress or a State has ventured the "wrong" direction down what has become, by judicial fiat, the one-way street of the Commerce Clause. Nothing in the Constitution or our past decisions supports forcing such an economic straight-jacket on the federal system.

V

Today's opinion charts an ominous course. I can only hope this unfortunate adventure away from the safety of our precedents will be an isolated episode.... [a]

NORTHEAST BANCORP, INC. v. BOARD OF GOVERNORS OF THE FEDERAL RESERVE SYSTEM, 472 U.S. 159 (1985). The Bank Holding Company Act, enacted by Congress in 1965, prohibits approval of an application of a bank holding company or a bank located in one state to acquire a bank or a bank holding company located in another state unless the acquisition "is specifically authorized by the statute laws of the State in which such bank is located by language to that effect and not merely by implication." In 1982 Massachusetts enacted a statute permitting an out-of-state bank holding company with its principal place of business in one of the other New England states to establish or acquire a Massachusetts based bank or bank holding company, provided that the other New England state accords equivalent reciprocal privileges to Massachusetts banking organizations. Connecticut enacted a similar statute in 1983. A Connecticut bank holding company sought permission from the Federal Reserve Board to purchase a bank holding company in Massachusetts and a Massachusetts bank holding company sought permission to acquire a Connecticut bank holding company. The Board approved the acquisitions and the court of appeals affirmed.

Justice Rehnquist, writing for the Court, said first that there was no commerce clause objection because Congress had specifically consented to the kind of state regulations involved here. He also addressed as follows the contention that under *Metropolitan Life Insurance Co. v. Ward* to permit the States to favor banks from the New England region as opposed to those outside of that region denied equal protection:

"In *Metropolitan Life* we held that encouraging the formation of new domestic insurance companies within a State and encouraging capital investment in the State's assets and governmental securities were not, standing alone, legitimate state purposes which could permissibly be furthered by discriminating against out-of-state corporations in favor of local corporations. There we said:

'This case does not involve or question, as the dissent suggests, the broad authority of a State, to promote and regulate its own economy. We hold only that such regulation may not be accomplished by imposing discriminatorily higher taxes on nonresident corporations solely because they are nonresidents.'

"Here the States in question—Massachusetts and Connecticut—are not favoring local corporations at the expense of out-of-state corporations. They are favoring out-of-state corporations domiciled within the New England region over out-of-state corporations from other parts of the country, and to this extent their laws may be said to 'discriminate' against the latter. But with

[a] See generally, Cohen, *Federalism in Equality Clothing: A Comment on Metropolitan Life Insurance Company v. Ward,* 38 Stan.L.Rev. 1 (1985).

respect to the business of banking, we do not write on a clean slate; recently in Lewis v. B.T. Investment Managers, Inc., 447 U.S., at 38, we said that 'banking and related financial activities are of profound local concern.' This statement is a recognition of the historical fact that our country traditionally has favored widely dispersed control of banking. While many other western nations are dominated by a handful of centralized banks, we have some 15,000 commercial banks attached to a greater or lesser degree to the communities in which they are located. The Connecticut legislative Commission that recommended adoption of the Connecticut statute in question considered interstate banking on a regional basis to combine the beneficial effect of increasing the number of banking competitors with the need to preserve a close relationship between those in the community who need credit and those who provide credit. The debates in the Connecticut Legislature preceding the enactment of the Connecticut law evince concern that immediate acquisition of Connecticut banks by holding companies headquartered outside the New England region would threaten the independence of local banking institutions. No doubt similar concerns motivated the Massachusetts Legislature.

"We think that the concerns which spurred Massachusetts and Connecticut to enact the statutes here challenged, different as they are from those which motivated the enactment of the Alabama statute in *Metropolitan,* meet the traditional rational basis for judging equal protection claims under the Fourteenth Amendment. Barry v. Barchi, 443 U.S. 55, 67 (1979); Vance v. Bradley, 440 U.S. 93, 97 (1979)."

Justice O'Connor, concurring, said:

"I agree that the state banking statutes at issue here do not violate the Commerce Clause, the Compact Clause, or the Equal Protection Clause. I write separately to note that I see no meaningful distinction for Equal Protection Clause purposes between the Massachusetts and Connecticut statutes we uphold today and the Alabama statute at issue in Metropolitan Life Insurance Co. v. Ward, 470 U.S. 869 (1985).

"The Court distinguishes this case from *Metropolitan Life* on the ground that Massachusetts and Connecticut favor neighboring out-of-state banks over all other out-of-state banks. It is not clear to me why completely barring the banks of 44 States from doing business is less discriminatory than Alabama's scheme of taxing the insurance companies from 49 States at a slightly higher rate. Nor is it clear why the Equal Protection Clause should tolerate a regional 'home team' when it condemns a state 'home team.'

"The Court emphasizes that here we do not write on a clean slate as the business of banking is 'of profound local concern.' The business of insurance is also of uniquely local concern. Prudential Insurance Co. v. Benjamin, 328 U.S. 408, 415–416 (1946). Both industries historically have been regulated by the States in recognition of the critical part they play in securing the financial well-being of local citizens and businesses. . . . States have regulated insurance since 1851. Like the local nature of banking, the local nature of insurance is firmly ensconced in federal law. . . .

. . .

"Especially where Congress has sanctioned the barriers to commerce that fostering of local industries might engender, this Court has no authority under the Equal Protection Clause to invalidate classifications designed to encourage local businesses because of their special contributions. Today's opinion is consistent with the longstanding doctrine that the Equal Protection Clause permits economic regulation that distinguishes between groups that *are* legitimately different—as local institutions so often are—in ways relevant to the proper goals of the State."

Justice Powell took no part in deciding the case.

D.   COURT ACCESS, WELFARE, AND THE POOR

Introduction. The Court has addressed arguments for heightened scrutiny based on both the nature of the liberty interest affected and the nature of the disadvantaged class in a number of contexts. Here the emphasis is on two sets of claims: that fees for representation in, and resolution of, legal disputes unconstitutionally have deprived the poor of access to appropriate judicial services; and that the poor unconstitutionally have been denied welfare benefits. As suggested in the Note on Wealth Classifications, supra p. 925, the issues generally arise in the context of differential impact on the poor, rather than in the context of explicit disadvantaging of them for being poor as such. Another common thread linking these two groups of cases is that the basis of the claims may be due process, equal protection, or both. The court access and welfare cases are presented together to allow for consideration of these complexities and connections.

THE RIGHTS OF THE POOR DEFENDANT IN THE CRIMINAL JUSTICE SYSTEM

During the past 40 years the Court has had before it a number of cases involving the criminal appellate process. It invalidated a series of state statutes that by requiring filing fees and transcripts barred access to appeal by a defendant who was indigent. See, e.g., Griffin v. Illinois, 351 U.S. 12 (1956); Draper v. Washington, 372 U.S. 487 (1963). In Douglas v. California, 372 U.S. 353 (1963), the Court also held that a state had a duty to furnish counsel to an indigent taking his first appeal as of right. In Ross v. Moffitt, 417 U.S. 600 (1974), however, the Court held that an indigent defendant was not entitled to have counsel provided in taking a discretionary appeal to the highest state court or in petitioning for certiorari in the United States Supreme Court.

The Court said:

"The precise rationale for the *Griffin* and *Douglas* line of cases has never been explicitly stated, some support being derived from the Equal Protection Clause of the Fourteenth Amendment, and some from the Due Process Clause of that Amendment. Neither clause by itself provides an entirely satisfactory basis for the result reached, each depending on a different inquiry which emphasizes different factors. 'Due process' emphasizes fairness between the State and the individual dealing with the State, regardless of how other individuals in the same situation may be treated. 'Equal protection,' on the other hand, emphasizes disparity in treatment by a State between classes of individuals whose situations are arguably indistinguishable."

The Court went on to hold that the denial of counsel in this case was constitutional under either clause. The Court concluded:

"[T]he fact that a particular service might be of benefit to an indigent defendant does not mean that the service is constitutionally required. The duty of the State under our cases is not to duplicate the legal arsenal that may be privately retained by a criminal defendant in a continuing effort to reverse his conviction, but only to assure the indigent defendant an adequate opportunity to present his claims fairly in the context of the State's appellate process."

Justices Douglas, Brennan, and Marshall dissented.

In Pennsylvania v. Finley, 481 U.S. 551 (1987) the Court reaffirmed *Ross v. Moffitt,* holding that the state has no constitutional duty under either the due process or equal protection clauses to provide counsel to a defendant in postconviction proceedings.

In Murray v. Giarratano, 492 U.S. 1 (1989), indigent prisoners sentenced to death argued that due process and the Eighth Amendment ban on cruel and unusual punishment required the state to provide them with counsel in postconviction proceedings. Four Justices (Rehnquist, White, O'Connor, and Scalia) rejected these claims outright, finding no greater obligation to provide counsel on collateral review in capital cases than in any others. Justice Kennedy concurred in the judgment, concluding that the due process requirement of "meaningful access" to court recognized in Bounds v. Smith, 430 U.S. 817 (1977), was satisfied in this case. He rejected a categorical requirement of appointed counsel in every case, because the meaningful court access obligation "can be satisfied in various ways[.]" He also asserted that "collateral relief proceedings are a central part of the review process for prisoners sentenced to death" and that the "complexity of our jurisprudence in this area ... makes it unlikely that capital defendants will be able to file successful petitions for collateral relief without the assistance of persons learned in the law." In this case, however, he was not prepared to find a violation of the meaningful court access right, because "no prisoner on death row in Virginia has been unable to obtain counsel to represent him in postconviction proceedings, and Virginia's prison system is staffed with institutional lawyers to assist in preparing petitions for postconviction relief."

In dissent, Justice Stevens, joined by Justices Brennan, Marshall and Blackmun, would have required the "appointment of counsel for indigent death row inmates who wish to pursue state postconviction relief."

ACCESS OF THE POOR TO THE COURTS IN CIVIL CASES

BODDIE v. CONNECTICUT, 401 U.S. 371 (1971). A welfare recipient challenged the state procedures under which a plaintiff in a divorce action was required to pay fees of about $60 in order to file the action. The Court discussed the case as one involving procedural due process, concluding "that the State's refusal to admit these appellants to its courts, the sole means in Connecticut for obtaining a divorce, must be regarded as the equivalent of denying them an opportunity to be heard upon their claimed right to a dissolution of their marriages, and, in the absence of a sufficient countervailing justification for the State's action, a denial of due process." Justices Douglas and Brennan in concurring opinions argued that the decision should have been rested on the equal protection clause because of discrimination against the poor. Justice Black dissented. For a discussion which preceded *Boddie,* see Goodpaster, *The Integration of Equal Protection, Due Process Standards, and the Indigent's Right of Free Access to the Courts,* 56 Iowa L.Rev. 223 (1970).

UNITED STATES v. KRAS, 409 U.S. 434 (1973). An indigent petitioner seeking voluntary bankruptcy sought to proceed without paying the fees (not more than $50 in this case) that were a condition of discharge. The district court found for the petitioner, relying on *Boddie.* The Supreme Court reversed. Justice Blackmun, speaking for the Court, said, in part:

"We agree with the Government that our decision in *Boddie* does not control the disposition of this case and that the District Court's reliance upon *Boddie* is misplaced.

"A. *Boddie* was based on the notion that a State cannot deny access, simply because of one's poverty, to a 'judicial proceeding [that is] the only effective means of resolving the dispute at hand.' 401 U.S., at 376. Throughout the opinion there is constant and recurring reference to Connecticut's exclusive control over the establishment, enforcement, and dissolution of the marital relationship. The Court emphasized that 'marriage involves interests of basic importance in our society' ibid., and spoke of 'state monopolization of the means for legally dissolving this relationship.' '[R]esort to the state courts [was] the only avenue to dissolution of . . . marriages,' which was 'not only the paramount dispute-settlement technique, but, in fact the only available one.'. . . . In the light of all this, we concluded that resort to the judicial process was 'no more voluntary in a realistic sense than that of the defendant called upon to defend his interests in court' and we resolved the case 'in light of the principles enunciated in our due process decisions that delimit rights of defendants compelled to litigate their differences in the judicial forum.'

"B. The appellants in *Boddie*, on the one hand, and Robert Kras, on the other stand in materially different postures. The denial of access to the judicial forum in *Boddie* touched directly, as has been noted, on the marital relationship and on the associational interests that surround the establishment and dissolution of that relationship. On many occasions we have recognized the fundamental importance of these interests under our Constitution. See, for example, Loving v. Virginia, 388 U.S. 1 (1967). . . . The *Boddie* appellants' inability to dissolve their marriages seriously impaired their freedom to pursue other protected associational activities. Kras' alleged interest in the elimination of his debt burden, and in obtaining his desired new start in life, although important and so recognized by the enactment of the Bankruptcy Act, does not rise to the same constitutional level. See Dandridge v. Williams, 397 U.S. 471 (1970); Richardson v. Belcher, 404 U.S. 78 (1971). If Kras is not discharged in bankruptcy, his position will not be materially altered in any constitutional sense. Gaining or not gaining a discharge will effect no change with respect to basic necessities. We see no fundamental interest that is gained or lost depending on the availability of a discharge in bankruptcy.

"C. Nor is the government's control over the establishment, enforcement, or dissolution of debts nearly so exclusive as Connecticut's control over the marriage relationship in *Boddie*. In contrast with divorce, bankruptcy is not the only method available to a debtor for the adjustment of his legal relationship with his creditors. The utter exclusiveness of court access and court remedy, as has been noted, was a potent factor in *Boddie*. But '[w]ithout a prior judicial imprimatur, individuals may freely enter into and rescind commercial contracts. . . .' 401 U.S., at 376.

"However unrealistic the remedy may be in a particular situation, a debtor, in theory, and often in actuality, may adjust his debts by negotiated agreement with his creditors. At times the happy passage of the applicable limitation period, or other acceptable creditor arrangement, will provide the answer. Government's role with respect to the private commercial relationship is qualitatively and quantitatively different than its role in the establishment, enforcement, and dissolution of marriage.

"Resort to the Court, therefore, is not Kras' sole path to relief. *Boddie's* emphasis on exclusivity finds no counterpart in the bankrupt's situation. . . .

"D. We are also of the opinion that the filing fee requirement does not deny Kras the equal protection of the laws. Bankruptcy is hardly akin to free speech or marriage or to those other rights, so many of which are imbedded in the First Amendment, that the Court has come to regard as fundamental and that demand the lofty requirement of a compelling governmental interest before they may be significantly regulated. See Shapiro v. Thompson, 394 U.S. 618, 638 (1969). Neither does it touch upon what has been said to be the suspect criteria of race, nationality or alienage. Graham v. Richardson, 403 U.S. 365, 375 (1971). Instead, bankruptcy legislation is in the area of economics and social welfare. See Dandridge v. Williams, 397 U.S., at 484–485; Richardson v. Belcher, 404 U.S., at 81; Lindsey v. Normet, 405 U.S. 56, 74 (1972); Jefferson v. Hackney, 406 U.S. 535, 546 (1972). This being so, the applicable standard, in measuring the propriety of Congress' classification, is that of rational justification."

Justices Stewart, Douglas, and Marshall, dissented.

ORTWEIN v. SCHWAB, 410 U.S. 656 (1973). Ortwein, a recipient of old-age assistance, had his award reduced by the county welfare agency. As provided by state law he appealed to the state public welfare agency, which held a hearing and upheld the county agency's decision. Judicial review of the state agency decision was provided by law in the state appellate court. Ortwein sought to appeal without paying the $25 filing fee required in all civil cases filed in that court, alleging that he was indigent and unable to pay the fee. The state court denied this contention and refused to hear the appeal without the fee. The Supreme Court, in a *per curiam* opinion, affirmed, indicating that *Kras* rather than *Boddie* was the controlling precedent. The Court gave three principal reasons for its decision:

(1) The interest in increased welfare benefits "has far less constitutional significance" than the inability to dissolve one's marriage except through the courts.

(2) Ortwein did receive a pre-termination evidentiary hearing (the required due process minimum) not conditioned on the payment of a fee. "This Court has long recognized that, even in criminal cases, due process does not require a State to provide an appellate system."

(3) The filing fee does not violate the Equal Protection Clause by discriminating against the poor. The litigation, which deals with welfare payments, is in the area of economics and social welfare. "No suspect classification, such as race, nationality, or alienage, is present.... The applicable standard is that of rational justification." The filing fee makes a contribution toward the cost of operating the court system, hence the "requirement of rationality is met."

Justices Stewart, Douglas, Brennan and Marshall dissented.

LITTLE v. STREATER, 452 U.S. 1 (1981). A unanimous Court concluded that refusal to furnish blood grouping tests to an indigent defendant in a civil paternity case denied that defendant "a meaningful opportunity to be heard" within the rationale of *Boddie v. Connecticut*. The Court relied on these factors: this action was not simply a civil proceeding between private parties since the child's mother was compelled to bring the action by State welfare officials and the State Attorney General was a party to the action; under State law, the defendant's testimony in a paternity action, standing alone, was insufficient to overcome the mother's testimony.

LASSITER v. DEPARTMENT OF SOCIAL SERVICES, 452 U.S. 18 (1981). A majority of the Court concluded that due process required the appointment of counsel, for an indigent parent in a proceeding brought by the state to terminate parental status, only in appropriate circumstances. The majority held that in this case, those special factors requiring the appointment of counsel were not present in that: no allegations of neglect or abuse had been made; no expert witness testified; and the presence of counsel could not have made a determinative difference in the result. The four dissenting Justices (Blackmun, Brennan, Marshall and Stevens) argued that due process should require the appointment of counsel for indigents in all proceedings brought by the State to terminate parental rights.

PROVISION OF ESSENTIAL GOVERNMENTAL BENEFITS AND SERVICES TO THE POOR

The general question raised here is whether the Constitution provides a basis for a higher level of judicial scrutiny of legislation that relates to the provision by government to the poor of basic human necessities—food, medical care, education, housing—than it does to economic regulations. Three separate constitutional arguments may be made to support an affirmative answer to that question.

(1) Does the constitution (through the due process clause or otherwise) guarantee some minimum entitlement by the poor to the basic necessities of life? Is the due process clause not only a shield against governmental deprivations of liberty and property but also a sword which imposes affirmative obligations on government? Professor Michelman, *On Protecting the Poor Through the Fourteenth Amendment*, 83 Harv.L.Rev. 7, 9 (1969), argues that the purposes of the Supreme Court decisions dealing with equal protection and wealth classifications "could be more soundly and satisfyingly understood as vindication of a state's duty to protect against certain hazards which are endemic in an unequal society, rather than vindication of a duty to avoid complicity in unequal treatment." He goes on to elaborate the proposition that the Court should be talking of "minimum protection against economic hazard" rather than "equal protection." Professor Tribe refers to "[e]merging notions that government has an affirmative obligation somehow to provide at least a minimally decent subsistence with respect to the most basic human needs, subject to all of the familiar difficulties with judicial enforcement of affirmative duties." *American Constitutional Law*, 1336 (2d ed. 1988). Professor Michelman restated his thesis in *Welfare Rights in a Constitutional Democracy*, 1979 Wash.U.L.Q. 659. In commentary on that restatement Professor Bork asserted "that the argument for welfare rights is unconnected with either the Constitution or its history" and therefore "offers inadequate guidelines and so requires political decision making by the judiciary." *The Impossibility of Finding Welfare Rights in the Constitution*, 1979 Wash.U.L.Q. 695. See also Appleton, *Professor Michelman's Quest for a Constitutional Welfare Right*, 1979 Wash. U.L.Q. 715.

(2) Should classifications in statutes providing governmental services to the poor be subject to a heightened standard of review under the equal protection clause because they involve the basic economic needs of impoverished human beings?

(3) Should classifications based on wealth be held to be constitutionally "suspect" and hence to require special justification in order to be valid? This argument was discussed supra p. 925.

WELFARE AS A FUNDAMENTAL RIGHT CALLING FOR STRICT SCRUTINY

A conscious attempt was made by lawyers involved in legal services programs to deal with what they regarded as inadequate welfare grants by persuading the Court to read a "right to life" into the equal protection clause that would guarantee an adequate minimum payment for every needy individual in society. The story of this attempt is told in Krislov, *The OEO Lawyers Fail to Constitutionalize a Right to Welfare: A Study in the Uses and Limits of the Judicial Process,* 58 Minn.L.Rev. 211 (1973); Sparer, *The Right to Welfare* in *The Rights of Americans* 65 (N. Dorsen, ed. 1971).

Dandridge v. Williams

397 U.S. 471, 90 S.Ct. 1153, 25 L.Ed.2d 491 (1970).

[Maryland participated in the federal Aid to Families with Dependent Children program (AFDC), providing grants of a certain amount for each child but imposing an upper limit of $250 per month that any family could receive. Recipients with large families that received less aid per child than smaller families not affected by the maximum challenged the regulation in federal district court. They contended that the state limit contravened the federal statute and discriminated against them merely because of the size of their families in violation of the equal protection clause. The Court upheld the state limit, rejecting both the statutory and the constitutional claims. Portions of the opinions relating to the constitutional issues are printed below.]

Mr. Justice Stewart delivered the opinion of the Court.

. . .

II.

Although a State may adopt a maximum grant system in allocating its funds available for AFDC payments without violating the Act, it may not, of course, impose a regime of invidious discrimination in violation of the Equal Protection Clause of the Fourteenth Amendment. Maryland says that its maximum grant regulation is wholly free of any invidiously discriminatory purpose or effect, and that the regulation is rationally supportable on at least four entirely valid grounds. The regulation can be clearly justified, Maryland argues, in terms of legitimate state interests in encouraging gainful employment, in maintaining an equitable balance in economic status as between welfare families and those supported by a wage-earner, in providing incentives for family planning, and in allocating available public funds in such a way as fully to meet the needs of the largest possible number of families. The District Court, while apparently recognizing the validity of at least some of these state concerns, nonetheless held that the regulation "is invalid on its face for overreaching,"—that it violates the Equal Protection Clause "[b]ecause it cuts too broad a swath on an indiscriminate basis as applied to the entire group of AFDC eligibles to which it purports to apply, ..."

If this were a case involving government action claimed to violate the First Amendment guarantee of free speech, a finding of "overreaching" would be significant and might be crucial. For when otherwise valid governmental regulation sweeps so broadly as to impinge upon activity protected by the First Amendment, its very overbreadth may make it unconstitutional. See, e.g., Shelton v. Tucker, 364 U.S. 479. But the concept of "overreaching" has no place in this case. For here we deal with state regulation in the social and economic field, not affecting freedoms guaranteed by the Bill of Rights, and claimed to violate the Fourteenth Amendment only because the regulation results in some disparity in grants of welfare payments to the largest AFDC families.[16] For this Court to approve the invalidation of state economic or social

---

[16] Cf. Shapiro v. Thompson, 394 U.S. 618, where by contrast, the Court found state interference with the constitutionally protected freedom of interstate travel.

regulation as "overreaching" would be far too reminiscent of an era when the Court thought the Fourteenth Amendment gave it power to strike down state laws "because they may be unwise, improvident, or out of harmony with a particular school of thought." Williamson v. Lee Optical of Oklahoma, Inc., 348 U.S. 483, 488. That era long ago passed into history. Ferguson v. Skrupa, 372 U.S. 726.

In the area of economics and social welfare, a State does not violate the Equal Protection Clause merely because the classifications made by its laws are imperfect. If the classification has some "reasonable basis," it does not offend the Constitution simply because the classification "is not made with mathematical nicety or because in practice it results in some inequality." Lindsley v. Natural Carbonic Gas Co., 220 U.S. 61, 78.... "A statutory discrimination will not be set aside if any state of facts reasonably may be conceived to justify it." McGowan v. Maryland, 366 U.S. 420, 426.

To be sure, the cases cited, and many others enunciating this fundamental standard under the Equal Protection Clause, have in the main involved state regulation of business or industry. The administration of public welfare assistance, by contrast, involves the most basic economic needs of impoverished human beings. We recognize the dramatically real factual difference between the cited cases and this one, but we can find no basis for applying a different constitutional standard.[17] ... It is a standard that has consistently been applied to state legislation restricting the availability of employment opportunities. Goesaert v. Cleary, 335 U.S. 464; Kotch v. Board of River Port Pilot Comm'rs, 330 U.S. 552.... And it is a standard that is true to the principle that the Fourteenth Amendment gives the federal courts no power to impose upon the States their views of what constitutes wise economic or social policy.

Under this long-established meaning of the Equal Protection Clause, it is clear that the Maryland maximum grant regulation is constitutionally valid. We need not explore all the reasons that the State advances in justification of the regulation. It is enough that a solid foundation for the regulation can be found in the State's legitimate interest in encouraging employment and in avoiding discrimination between welfare families and the families of the working poor. By combining a limit on the recipient's grant with permission to retain money earned, without reduction in the amount of the grant, Maryland provides an incentive to seek gainful employment. And by keying the maximum family AFDC grants to the minimum wage a steadily employed head of a household receives, the State maintains some semblance of an equitable balance between families on welfare and those supported by an employed breadwinner.

It is true that in some AFDC families there may be no person who is employable. It is also true that with respect to AFDC families whose determined standard of need is below the regulatory maximum, and who therefore receive grants equal to the determined standard, the employment incentive is absent. But the Equal Protection Clause does not require that a State must choose between attacking every aspect of a problem or not attacking the problem at all. Lindsley v. Natural Carbonic Gas Co., 220 U.S. 61. It is enough that the State's action be rationally based and free from invidious discrimination. The regulation before us meets that test.

---

[17] It is important to note that there is no contention that the Maryland regulation is infected with a racially discriminatory purpose or effect such as to make it inherently suspect. Cf. McLaughlin v. Florida, 379 U.S. 184.

We do not decide today that the Maryland regulation is wise, that it best fulfills the relevant social and economic objectives that Maryland might ideally espouse, or that a more just and humane system could not be devised. Conflicting claims of morality and intelligence are raised by opponents and proponents of almost every measure, certainly including the one before us. But the intractable economic, social, and even philosophical problems presented by public welfare assistance programs are not the business of this Court. The Constitution may impose certain procedural safeguards upon systems of welfare administration, Goldberg v. Kelly, 397 U.S. 254. But the Constitution does not empower this Court to second-guess state officials charged with the difficult responsibility of allocating limited public welfare funds among the myriad of potential recipients.

The judgment is reversed.

[Justice Black, joined by Chief Justice Burger, and Justice Harlan filed concurring opinions. Justice Douglas dissented on the statutory issue.]

Mr. Justice Marshall, whom Mr. Justice Brennan joins, dissenting.

. . .

This classification process effected by the maximum grant regulation produces a basic denial of equal treatment. Persons who are concededly similarly situated (dependent children and their families), are not afforded equal, or even approximately equal, treatment under the maximum grant regulation. Subsistence benefits are paid with respect to some needy dependent children; nothing is paid with respect to others. Some needy families receive full subsistence assistance as calculated by the State; the assistance paid to other families is grossly below their similarly calculated needs.

Yet, as a general principle, individuals should not be afforded different treatment by the State unless there is a relevant distinction between them and "a statutory discrimination must be based on differences that are reasonably related to the purposes of the Act in which it is found." Morey v. Doud, 354 U.S. 457, 465 (1957). See Gulf, Colorado & Santa Fe R. Co. v. Ellis, 165 U.S. 150, 155 (1897). Consequently, the State may not, in the provision of important services or the distribution of governmental payments, supply benefits to some individuals while denying them to others who are similarly situated. . . .

In the instant case, the only distinction between those children with respect to whom assistance is granted and those children who are denied such assistance is the size of the family into which the child permits himself to be born. The class of individuals with respect to whom payments are actually made (the first four or five eligible dependent children in a family), is grossly underinclusive in terms of the class that the AFDC program was designed to assist, namely, *all* needy dependent children. Such underinclusiveness manifests "a prima facie violation of the equal protection requirement of reasonable classification," compelling the State to come forward with a persuasive justification for the classification.

The Court never undertakes to inquire for such a justification; rather it avoids the task by focusing upon the abstract dichotomy between two different approaches to equal protection problems that have been utilized by this Court.

Under the so-called "traditional test," a classification is said to be permissible under the Equal Protection Clause unless it is "without any reasonable basis." Lindsley v. Natural Carbonic Gas Co., 220 U.S. 61, 78 (1911). On the other hand, if the classification affects a "fundamental right," then the state interest in perpetuating the classification must be "compelling" in order to be sustained. See, e.g., *Shapiro v. Thompson,* supra;....

This case simply defies easy characterization in terms of one or the other of these "tests." The cases relied on by the Court, in which a "mere rationality" test was actually used, e.g., Williamson v. Lee Optical of Oklahoma, Inc., 348 U.S. 483 (1955), are most accurately described as involving the application of equal protection reasoning to the regulation of business interests. The extremes to which the Court has gone in dreaming up rational bases for state regulation in that area may in many instances be ascribed to a healthy revulsion from the Court's earlier excesses in using the Constitution to protect interests that have more than enough power to protect themselves in the legislative halls. This case, involving the literally vital interests of a powerless minority—poor families without breadwinners—is far removed from the area of business regulation, as the Court concedes. Why then is the standard used in those cases imposed here? We are told no more than that this case falls in "the area of economics and social welfare," with the implication that from there the answer is obvious.

In my view, equal protection analysis of this case is not appreciably advanced by the *a priori* definition of a "right," fundamental or otherwise. Rather, concentration must be placed upon the character of the classification in question, the relative importance to individuals in the class discriminated against of the governmental benefits that they do not receive, and the asserted state interests in support of the classification....

It is the individual interests here at stake that, as the Court concedes, most clearly distinguish this case from the "business regulation" equal protection cases. AFDC support to needy dependent children provides the stuff that sustains those children's lives: food, clothing, shelter. And this Court has already recognized several times that when a benefit, even a "gratuitous" benefit, is necessary to sustain life, stricter constitutional standards, both procedural and substantive, are applied to the deprivation of that benefit.

. . .

In any event, it cannot suffice merely to invoke the spectre of the past and to recite from *Lindsley v. Natural Carbonic Gas Co.* and *Williamson v. Lee Optical of Oklahoma, Inc.* to decide the case. Appellees are not a gas company or an optical dispenser; they are needy dependent children and families who are discriminated against by the State. The basis of that discrimination—the classification of individuals into large and small families—is too arbitrary and too unconnected to the asserted rationale, the impact on those discriminated against—the denial of even a subsistence existence—too great, and the supposed interests served too contrived and attenuated to meet the requirements of the Constitution....

I would affirm the judgment of the District Court.

Harris v. McRae

448 U.S. 297, 100 S.Ct. 2671, 65 L.Ed.2d 784 (1980).

Mr. Justice Stewart delivered the opinion of the Court.

This case presents statutory and constitutional questions concerning the public funding of abortions under Title XIX of the Social Security Act, commonly known as the "Medicaid" Act, and recent annual appropriations acts containing the so-called "Hyde Amendment." The statutory question is whether Title XIX requires a State that participates in the Medicaid program to fund the cost of medically necessary abortions for which federal reimbursement is unavailable under the Hyde Amendment. The constitutional question, which arises only if Title XIX imposes no such requirement, is whether the Hyde Amendment, by denying public funding for certain medically necessary abortions, contravenes the liberty or equal protection guarantees of the Due Process Clause of the Fifth Amendment, or either of the Religion Clauses of the First Amendment.

I.

. . .

Since September 1976, Congress has prohibited . . . the use of any federal funds to reimburse the cost of abortions under the Medicaid program except under certain specified circumstances. This funding restriction is commonly known as the "Hyde Amendment," after its original congressional sponsor, Representative Hyde. The current version of the Hyde Amendment, applicable for fiscal year 1980, provides:

> "[N]one of the funds provided by this joint resolution shall be used to perform abortions except where the life of the mother would be endangered if the fetus were carried to term; or except for such medical procedures necessary for the victims of rape or incest when such rape or incest has been reported promptly to a law enforcement agency or public health service." Pub.L. No. 96–123, § 109, 93 Stat. 926. See also Pub.L. No. 96–86, § 118, 93 Stat. 662.

. . .

[T]he District Court . . . invalidat[ed] all versions of the Hyde Amendment on constitutional grounds. . . .

. . .

II.

. . .

. . . [W]e conclude that Title XIX does not require a participating State to pay for those medically necessary abortions for which federal reimbursement is unavailable under the Hyde Amendment.[16]

III.

[Hence,] we must consider the constitutional validity of the Hyde Amendment. The appellees assert that the funding restrictions of the Hyde Amendment violate several rights secured by the Constitution—(1) the right of a woman, implicit in the Due Process Clause of the Fifth Amendment, to decide whether to terminate a pregnancy, (2) the prohibition under the Establishment Clause of the First Amendment against any "law respecting an establishment of religion," and (3) the right to freedom of religion protected by the Free Exercise Clause of the First Amendment. The appellees also contend that, quite apart from substantive constitutional rights, the Hyde Amendment violates the equal protection component of the Fifth Amendment.

---

[16] A participating State is free, if it so chooses, to include in its Medicaid plan those medically necessary abortions for which federal reimbursement is unavailable. See Beal v. Doe, supra, 432 U.S., at 447; Preterm, Inc. v. Dukekis, supra, 591 F.2d at 134. We hold only that a State *need* not include such abortions in its Medicaid plan.

It is well settled that, quite apart from the guarantee of equal protection, if a law "impinges upon a fundamental right explicitly or implicitly secured by the Constitution [it] is presumptively unconstitutional." Mobile v. Bolden, 446 U.S. 55, 76 (plurality opinion). Accordingly, before turning to the equal protection issue in this case, we examine whether the Hyde Amendment violates any substantive rights secured by the Constitution.

A.

We address first the appellees' argument that the Hyde Amendment, by restricting the availability of certain medically necessary abortions under Medicaid, impinges on the "liberty" protected by the Due Process Clause as recognized in Roe v. Wade, 410 U.S. 113, and its progeny.

In the *Wade* case, this Court held unconstitutional a Texas statute making it a crime to procure or attempt an abortion except on medical advice for the purpose of saving the mother's life. The constitutional underpinning of *Wade* was a recognition that the "liberty" protected by the Due Process Clause of the Fourteenth Amendment includes not only the freedoms explicitly mentioned in the Bill of Rights, but also a freedom of personal choice in certain matters of marriage and family life. This implicit constitutional liberty, the Court in *Wade* held, includes the freedom of a woman to decide whether to terminate a pregnancy.

But the Court in *Wade* also recognized that a State has legitimate interests during a pregnancy in both ensuring the health of the mother and protecting potential human life. These state interests, which were found to be "separate and distinct" and to "grow[ ]in substantiality as the woman approaches term," pose a conflict with a woman's untrammeled freedom of choice....

In Maher v. Roe, 432 U.S. 464, the Court was presented with the question whether the scope of personal constitutional freedom recognized in *Roe v. Wade* included an entitlement to Medicaid payments for abortions that are not medically necessary. At issue in *Maher* was a Connecticut welfare regulation under which Medicaid recipients received payments for medical services incident to childbirth, but not for medical services incident to nontherapeutic abortions. The District Court held that the regulation violated the Equal Protection Clause of the Fourteenth Amendment because the unequal subsidization of childbirth and abortion impinged on the "fundamental right to abortion" recognized in *Wade* and its progeny.

It was the view of this Court that "the District Court misconceived the nature and scope of the fundamental right recognized in *Roe.* "432 U.S., at 471. The doctrine of *Roe v. Wade,* the Court held in *Maher,* "protects the woman from unduly burdensome interference with her freedom to decide whether to terminate her pregnancy," such as the severe criminal sanctions at issue in *Roe v. Wade,* supra, or the absolute requirement of spousal consent for an abortion challenged in Planned Parenthood of Central Missouri v. Danforth, 428 U.S. 52.

But the constitutional freedom recognized in *Wade* and its progeny, the *Maher* Court explained, did not prevent Connecticut from making "a value judgment favoring childbirth over abortion, and ... implement[ing] that judgment by the allocation of public funds." As the Court elaborated:

> "The Connecticut regulation before us is different in kind from the laws invalidated in our previous abortion decisions. The Connecticut regulation places no obstacles—absolute or otherwise—in the pregnant woman's path to an abortion. An indigent woman who desires an abortion suffers no disadvantage as a consequence of Connecticut's decision to fund childbirth;

she continues as before to be dependent on private sources for the service she desires. The State may have made childbirth a more attractive alternative, thereby influencing the woman's decision, but it has imposed no restriction on access to abortions that was not already there. The indigency that may make it difficult—and in some cases, perhaps, impossible—for some women to have abortions is neither created nor in any way affected by the Connecticut regulation."

The Court in *Maher* noted that its description of the doctrine recognized in *Wade* and its progeny signaled "no retreat" from those decisions. In explaining why the constitutional principle recognized in *Wade* and later cases—protecting a woman's freedom of choice—did not translate into a constitutional obligation of Connecticut to subsidize abortions, the Court cited the "basic difference between direct state interference with a protected activity and state encouragement of an alternative activity consonant with legislative policy. Constitutional concerns are greatest when the State attempts to impose its will by force of law; the State's power to encourage actions deemed to be in the public interest is necessarily far broader." Thus, even though the Connecticut regulation favored childbirth over abortion by means of subsidization of one and not the other, the Court in *Maher* concluded that the regulation did not impinge on the constitutional freedom recognized in *Wade* because it imposed no governmental restriction on access to abortions.

The Hyde Amendment, like the Connecticut welfare regulation at issue in *Maher,* places no governmental obstacle in the path of a woman who chooses to terminate her pregnancy, but rather, by means of unequal subsidization of abortion and other medical services, encourages alternative activity deemed in the public interest. The present case does differ factually from *Maher* insofar as that case involved a failure to fund nontherapeutic abortions, whereas the Hyde Amendment withholds funding of certain medically necessary abortions. Accordingly, the appellees argue that because the Hyde Amendment affects a significant interest not present or asserted in *Maher*—the interest of a woman in protecting her health during pregnancy—and because that interest lies at the core of the personal constitutional freedom recognized in *Wade;* the present case is constitutionally different from *Maher*. . . .

. . . [True,] the Court in *Wade* emphasized the fact that the woman's decision carries with it significant personal health implications—both physical and psychological. In fact, . . . the Court held that even after fetal viability a State may not prohibit abortions "necessary to preserve the life or health of the mother." Because even the compelling interest of the State in protecting potential life after fetal viability was held to be insufficient to outweigh a woman's decision to protect her life or health, it could be argued that the freedom of a woman to decide whether to terminate her pregnancy for health reasons does in fact lie at the core of the constitutional liberty identified in *Wade*.

But, . . . it simply does not follow that a woman's freedom of choice carries with it a constitutional entitlement to the financial resources to avail herself of the full range of protected choices. The reason why was explained in *Maher:* although government may not place obstacles in the path of a woman's exercise of her freedom of choice, it need not remove those not of its own creation. Indigency falls in the latter category. The financial constraints that restrict an indigent woman's ability to enjoy the full range of constitutionally protected freedom of choice are the product not of governmental restrictions on access to abortions, but rather of her indigency. Although Congress has opted to subsidize medically necessary services generally, but not certain medically necessary abortions, the fact remains that the Hyde Amendment leaves an indigent woman with at least the same range of choice in deciding whether to obtain a medically necessary abortion as she would have had if Congress had chosen to subsidize no health care costs at all. We are thus not persuaded that the Hyde Amendment impinges on the constitutionally protected freedom of choice recognized in *Wade*.[19]

Although the liberty protected by the Due Process Clause affords protection against unwarranted government interference with freedom of choice in the context of certain personal decisions, it does not confer an entitlement to such funds as may be necessary to realize all the advantages of that freedom. To hold otherwise would mark a drastic change in our understanding of the Constitution. It cannot be that because government may not prohibit the use of contraceptives, Griswold v. Connecticut, 381 U.S. 479, or prevent parents from sending their child to a private school, Pierce v. Society of Sisters, 268 U.S. 510, government, therefore, has an affirmative constitutional obligation to ensure that all persons have the financial resources to obtain contraceptives or send their children to private schools. To translate the limitation on governmental power implicit in the Due Process Clause into an affirmative funding obligation would require Congress to subsidize the medically necessary abortion of an indigent woman even if Congress had not enacted a Medicaid program to subsidize other medically necessary services. Nothing in the Due Process Clause supports such an extraordinary result. Whether freedom of choice that is constitutionally protected warrants federal subsidization is a question for Congress to answer, not a matter of constitutional entitlement. Accordingly, we conclude that the Hyde Amendment does not impinge on the due process liberty recognized in *Wade*.

B.

The appellees also argue that the Hyde Amendment contravenes rights secured by the Religion Clauses of the First Amendment....

. . .

[The Court held that the Hyde Amendment did not contravene the establishment clause of the first amendment and that the parties lacked standing to raise a challenge under the free exercise clause.]

---

[19] The appellees argue that the Hyde Amendment is unconstitutional because it "penalizes" the exercise of a woman's choice to terminate a pregnancy by abortion. See Memorial Hospital v. Maricopa County, 415 U.S. 250; Shapiro v. Thompson, 394 U.S. 618. This argument falls short of the mark. In *Maher,* the Court found only a "semantic difference" between the argument that Connecticut's refusal to subsidize nontherapeutic abortions "unduly interfere[d]" with the exercise of the constitutional liberty recognized in *Wade* and the argument that it "penalized" the exercise of that liberty. And, regardless of how the claim was characterized, the *Maher* Court rejected the argument that Connecticut's refusal to subsidize protected conduct, without more, impinged on the constitutional freedom of choice. This reasoning is equally applicable in the present case. A substantial constitutional question would arise if Congress had attempted to withhold all Medicaid benefits from an otherwise eligible candidate simply because that candidate had exercised her constitutionally protected freedom to terminate her pregnancy by abortion. This would be analogous to Sherbert v. Verner, 374 U.S. 398, where this Court held that a State may not, consistent with the First and Fourteenth Amendments, withhold *all* unemployment compensation benefits from a claimant who would otherwise be eligible for such benefits but for the fact that she is unwilling to work one day per week on her Sabbath. But the Hyde Amendment, unlike the statute at issue in *Sherbert*, does not provide for such a broad disqualification from receipt of public benefits. Rather, the Hyde Amendment, like the Connecticut welfare provision at issue in *Maher*, represents simply a refusal to subsidize certain protected conduct. A refusal to fund protected activity, without more, cannot be equated with the imposition of a "penalty" on that activity.

C.

It remains to be determined whether the Hyde Amendment violates the equal protection component of the Fifth Amendment. This challenge is premised on the fact that, although federal reimbursement is available under Medicaid for medically necessary services generally, the Hyde Amendment does not permit federal reimbursement of all medically necessary abortions. The District Court held, and the appellees argue here, that this selective subsidization violates the constitutional guarantee of equal protection.

The guarantee of equal protection under the Fifth Amendment is not a source of substantive rights or liberties,[25] but rather a right to be free from invidious discrimination in statutory classifications and other governmental activity. It is well-settled that where a statutory classification does not itself impinge on a right or liberty protected by the Constitution, the validity of classification must be sustained unless "the classification rests on grounds wholly irrelevant to the achievement of [any legitimate governmental] objective." McGowan v. Maryland, supra, 366 U.S., at 425. This presumption of constitutional validity, however, disappears if a statutory classification is predicated on criteria that are, in a constitutional sense, "suspect," the principal example of which is a classification based on race, e.g., Brown v. Board of Education, 347 U.S. 483.

1.

For the reasons stated above, we have already concluded that the Hyde Amendment violates no constitutionally protected substantive rights. We now conclude as well that it is not predicated on a constitutionally suspect classification. In reaching this conclusion, we again draw guidance from the Court's decision in *Maher v. Roe.* As to whether the Connecticut welfare regulation providing funds for childbirth but not for nontherapeutic abortions discriminated against a suspect class, the Court in *Maher* observed:

> "An indigent woman desiring an abortion does not come within the limited category of disadvantaged classes so recognized by our cases. Nor does the fact that the impact of the regulation falls upon those who cannot pay lead to a different conclusion. In a sense, every denial of welfare to an indigent creates a wealth classification as compared to nonindigents who are able to pay for the desired goods or services. But this Court has never held that financial need alone identifies a suspect class for purposes of equal protection analysis." ...

Thus, the Court in *Maher* found no basis for concluding that the Connecticut regulation was predicated on a suspect classification.

[T]he present case is indistinguishable from *Maher* in this respect. Here, as in *Maher,* the principal impact of the Hyde Amendment falls on the indigent. But that fact does not itself render the funding restriction constitutionally invalid, for this Court has held repeatedly that poverty, standing alone, is not a suspect classification. See, e.g., James v. Valtierra, 402 U.S. 137. That *Maher* involved the refusal to fund nontherapeutic abortions, whereas the present case involves the refusal to fund medically necessary abortions, has no bearing on

---

[25] An exception to this statement is to be found in Reynolds v. Sims, 377 U.S. 533, and its progeny. Although the Constitution of the United States does not confer the right to vote in state elections, see Minor v. Happersett, 21 Wall. 162, 178, *Reynolds* held that if a State adopts an electoral system, the Equal Protection Clause of the Fourteenth Amendment confers upon a qualified voter a substantive right to participate in the electoral process equally with other qualified voters. See, e.g., Dunn v. Blumstein, 405 U.S. 330, 336.

the factors that render a classification "suspect" within the meaning of the constitutional guarantee of equal protection.

2.

The remaining question then is whether the Hyde Amendment is rationally related to a legitimate governmental objective. It is the Government's position that the Hyde Amendment bears a rational relationship to its legitimate interest in protecting the potential life of the fetus. We agree.

. . .

. . . By subsidizing the medical expenses of indigent women who carry their pregnancies to term while not subsidizing the comparable expenses of women who undergo abortions (except those whose lives are threatened), Congress has established incentives that make childbirth a more attractive alternative than abortion for persons eligible for Medicaid. These incentives bear a direct relationship to the legitimate congressional interest in protecting potential life. Nor is it irrational that Congress has authorized federal reimbursement for medically necessary services generally, but not for certain medically necessary abortions. Abortion is inherently different from other medical procedures, because no other procedure involves the purposeful termination of a potential life.

After conducting an extensive evidentiary hearing into issues surrounding the public funding of abortions, the District Court concluded that "[t]he interests of . . . the federal government . . . in the fetus and in preserving it are not sufficient, weighed in the balance with the woman's threatened health, to justify withdrawing medical assistance unless the woman consents . . . to carry the fetus to term." In making an independent appraisal of the competing interests involved here, the District Court went beyond the judicial function. . . .

Where, as here, the Congress has neither invaded a substantive constitutional right or freedom, nor enacted legislation that purposefully operates to the detriment of a suspect class, the only requirement of equal protection is that congressional action be rationally related to a legitimate governmental interest. The Hyde Amendment satisfies that standard. It is not the mission of this Court or any other to decide whether the balance of competing interests reflected in the Hyde Amendment is wise social policy. If that were our mission, not every Justice who has subscribed to the judgment of the Court today could have done so. But we cannot, in the name of the Constitution, overturn duly enacted statutes simply "because they may be unwise, improvident, or out of harmony with a particular school of thought." Williamson v. Lee Optical Co., 348 U.S. 483, 488, quoted in Dandridge v. Williams, 397 U.S. 471, 484. Rather, "when an issue involves policy choices as sensitive as those implicated [here] . . ., the appropriate forum for their resolution in a democracy is the legislature." Maher v. Roe, supra, at 479.

. . .

. . . [T]he judgment . . . is reversed, and the case is remanded . . . for further proceedings consistent with this opinion.

It is so ordered.

Mr. Justice White, concurring.

. . .

Mr. Justice Brennan, with whom Mr. Justice Marshall and Mr. Justice Blackmun join, dissenting.

I agree entirely with my Brother Stevens that the State's interest in protecting the potential life of the fetus cannot justify the exclusion of financially and medically needy women from the benefits to which they would otherwise be entitled solely because the treatment that a doctor has concluded is medically necessary involves an abortion. I write separately to express my continuing disagreement with the Court's mischaracterization of the nature of the fundamental right recognized in Roe v. Wade, 410 U.S. 113 (1973), and its misconception of the manner in which that right is infringed by federal and state legislation withdrawing all funding for medically necessary abortions.

... *Roe* and its progeny established that the pregnant woman has a right to be free from state interference with her choice to have an abortion ... The proposition for which these cases stand thus is not that the State is under an affirmative obligation to ensure access to abortions for all who may desire them; it is that the State must refrain from wielding its enormous power and influence in a manner that might burden the pregnant woman's freedom to choose whether to have an abortion. The Hyde Amendment's denial of public funds for medically necessary abortions plainly intrudes upon this constitutionally protected decision, for both by design and in effect it serves to coerce indigent pregnant women to bear children that they would otherwise elect not to have.[4]

When viewed in the context of the Medicaid program to which it is appended, it is obvious that the Hyde Amendment is nothing less than an attempt by Congress to circumvent the dictates of the Constitution and achieve indirectly what *Roe v. Wade* said it could not do directly. Under Title XIX of the Social Security Act, the Federal Government reimburses participating States for virtually all medically necessary services it provides to the categorically needy. The sole limitation of any significance is the Hyde Amendment's prohibition against the use of any federal funds to pay for the costs of abortions (except where the life of the mother would be endangered if the fetus were carried to term). As my Brother Stevens persuasively demonstrates, exclusion of medically necessary abortions from Medicaid coverage cannot be justified as a cost-saving device. Rather, the Hyde Amendment is a transparent attempt by the Legislative Branch to impose the political majority's judgment of the morally acceptable and socially desirable preference on a sensitive and intimate decision that the Constitution entrusts to the individual. Worse yet, the Hyde Amendment does not foist that majoritarian viewpoint with equal measure upon everyone in our Nation, rich and poor alike; rather, it imposes that viewpoint only upon that segment of our society which, because of its position of political powerlessness, is least able to defend its privacy rights from the encroachments of state-mandated morality. The instant legislation thus calls for more exacting judicial review than in most other cases. "When elected leaders cower before public pressure, this Court, more than ever, must not shirk its duty to enforce the Constitution for the benefit of the poor and powerless." Beal v. Doe, 432 U.S. 438, 442 (1977) (Marshall, J., dissenting)....

---

[4] My focus throughout this opinion is upon the coercive impact of the congressional decision to fund one outcome of pregnancy—childbirth—while not funding the other—abortion. Because I believe this alone renders the Hyde Amendment unconstitutional, I do not dwell upon the other disparities that the Amendment produces in the treatment of rich and poor, pregnant and nonpregnant. I concur completely, however, in my Brother Stevens' discussion of those disparities....

Moreover, it is clear that the Hyde Amendment not only was designed to inhibit, but does in fact inhibit the woman's freedom to choose abortion over childbirth.... [U]nder the Hyde Amendment, the Government will fund only those procedures incidental to childbirth. By thus injecting coercive financial incentives favoring childbirth into a decision that is constitutionally guaranteed to be free from governmental intrusion, the Hyde Amendment deprives the indigent woman of her freedom to choose abortion over maternity, thereby impinging on the due process liberty right recognized in *Roe v. Wade.*

... [T]he Court fails to appreciate ... that it is not simply the woman's indigency that interferes with her freedom of choice, but the combination of her own poverty and the government's unequal subsidization of abortion and childbirth.

A poor woman in the early stages of pregnancy confronts two alternatives: she may elect either to carry the fetus to term or to have an abortion. In the abstract, of course, this choice is hers alone, and the Court rightly observes that the Hyde Amendment "places no governmental obstacle in the path of a woman who chooses to terminate her pregnancy." But the reality of the situation is that the Hyde Amendment has effectively removed this choice from the indigent woman's hands. By funding all of the expenses associated with childbirth and none of the expenses incurred in terminating pregnancy, the government literally makes an offer that the indigent woman cannot afford to refuse. It matters not that in this instance the government has used the carrot rather than the stick. What is critical is the realization that as a practical matter, many poverty-stricken women will choose to carry their pregnancy to term simply because the government provides funds for the associated medical services, even though these same women would have chosen to have an abortion if the government had also paid for that option, or indeed if the government had stayed out of the picture altogether and had defrayed the costs of neither procedure.

The fundamental flaw in the Court's due process analysis, then, is its failure to acknowledge that the discriminatory distribution of the benefits of governmental largesse can discourage the exercise of fundamental liberties just as effectively as can an outright denial of those rights through criminal and regulatory sanctions....

It would belabor the obvious to expound at any great length on the illegitimacy of a state policy that interferes with the exercise of fundamental rights through the selective bestowal of governmental favors. It suffices to note that we have heretofore never hesitated to invalidate any scheme of granting or withholding financial benefits that incidentally or intentionally burdens one manner of exercising a constitutionally protected choice....

The Medicaid program cannot be distinguished from these other statutory schemes that unconstitutionally burdened fundamental rights.[6] ...

I respectfully dissent.

---

[6] ...[I]t is no answer to assert that no "penalty" is being imposed because the State is only refusing to pay for the specific costs of the protected activity rather than withholding other Medicaid benefits to which the recipient would be entitled or taking some other action more readily characterized as "punitive." Surely the government could not provide free transportation to the polling booths only for those citizens who vote for Democratic candidates, even though the fail-ure to provide the same benefit to Republicans "represents simply a refusal to subsidize certain protected conduct," ibid., and does not involve the denial of any other governmental benefits. Whether the State withholds only the special costs of a disfavored option or penalizes the individual more broadly for the manner in which she exercises her choice, it cannot interfere with a constitutionally protected decision through the coercive use of governmental largesse.

Mr. Justice Marshall, dissenting.

. . .

. . . The Court's decision today marks a retreat from *Roe v. Wade* and represents a cruel blow to the most powerless members of our society. I dissent.

. . .

I.

The record developed below reveals that the standards set forth in the Hyde Amendment exclude the majority of cases in which the medical profession would recommend abortion as medically necessary. Indeed, in States that have adopted a standard more restrictive than the "medically necessary" test of the Medicaid Act, the number of funded abortions has decreased by over 98%.

. . .

An optimistic estimate indicates that as many as 100 excess deaths may occur each year as a result of the Hyde Amendment. The record contains no estimate of the health damage that may occur to poor women, but it shows that it will be considerable.

II.

The Court resolves the equal protection issue in this case through a relentlessly formalistic catechism. Adhering to its "two-tiered" approach to equal protection, the Court first decides that so-called strict scrutiny is not required because the Hyde Amendment does not violate the Due Process Clause and is not predicated on a constitutionally suspect classification. . . .

I continue to believe that the rigid "two-tiered" approach is inappropriate and that the Constitution requires a more exacting standard of review than mere rationality in cases such as this one. Further, in my judgment the Hyde Amendment cannot pass constitutional muster even under the rational-basis standard of review.

A.

This case is perhaps the most dramatic illustration to date of the deficiencies in the Court's obsolete "two-tiered" approach to the Equal Protection Clause. See San Antonio School Dist. v. Rodriguez, 411 U.S. 1, 98–110 (1973) (Marshall, J., dissenting); Massachusetts v. Murgia, 427 U.S. 307, 318–321 (1976) (Marshall, J., dissenting); Maher v. Roe, supra, at 457–458 (Marshall, J., dissenting); Vance v. Bradley, 440 U.S. 93, 113–115 (1979) (Marshall, J., dissenting). With all deference, I am unable to understand how the Court can afford the same level of scrutiny to the legislation involved here—whose cruel impact falls exclusively on indigent pregnant women—that it has given to legislation distinguishing opticians from ophthalmologists, or to other legislation that makes distinctions between economic interests more than able to protect themselves in the political process. . . . Heightened scrutiny of legislative classifications has always been designed to protect groups "saddled with such disabilities or subjected to such a history of purposeful unequal treatment, or relegated to such a position of political powerlessness as to command extraordinary protection from the majoritarian political process." San Antonio School District v. Rodriguez, supra, at 28 (1973).[4] And while it is now clear that

[4] For this reason the Court has on occasion suggested that classifications discriminating against the poor are subject to special scrutiny under the Fifth and Fourteenth

traditional "strict scrutiny" is unavailable to protect the poor against classifications that disfavor them, Dandridge v. Williams, 397 U.S. 471 (1970), I do not believe that legislation that imposes a crushing burden on indigent women can be treated with the same deference given to legislation distinguishing among business interests.

B.

. . .

The class burdened by the Hyde Amendment consists of indigent women, a substantial proportion of whom are members of minority races. As I observed in *Maher,* nonwhite women obtain abortions at nearly double the rate of whites. . . . In my view, the fact that the burden of the Hyde Amendment falls exclusively on financially destitute women suggests "a special condition, which tends seriously to curtail the operation of those political processes ordinarily to be relied upon to protect minorities, and which may call for a correspondingly more searching judicial inquiry." United States v. Carolene Products, 304 U.S. 144, 152–153, n. 4 (1938). For this reason, I continue to believe that "a showing that state action has a devastating impact on the lives of minority racial groups must be relevant" for purposes of equal protection analysis. Jefferson v. Hackney, 406 U.S. 535, 575–576 (1972) (Marshall, J., dissenting).

As I explained in *Maher,* the asserted state interest in protecting potential life is insufficient to "outweigh the deprivation or serious discouragement of a vital constitutional right of especial importance to poor and minority women."

. . .

C.

Although I would abandon the strict-scrutiny_rational-basis dichotomy in equal protection analysis, it is by no means necessary to reject that traditional approach to conclude, as I do, that the Hyde Amendment is a denial of equal protection. My Brother Brennan has demonstrated that the Amendment is unconstitutional because it impermissibly infringes upon the individual's constitutional right to decide whether to terminate a pregnancy. And as my Brother Stevens demonstrates the Government's interest in protecting fetal life is not a legitimate one when it is in conflict with "the preservation of the life or health of the mother," *Roe v. Wade,* . . . and when the Government's effort to make serious health damage to the mother "a more attractive alternative than abortion" does not rationally promote the governmental interest in encouraging normal childbirth.

The Court treats this case as though it were controlled by *Maher.* To the contrary, this case is the mirror image of *Maher.* The result in *Maher* turned on the fact that the legislation there under consideration discouraged only nontherapeutic, or medically unnecessary, abortions. In the Court's view, denial of Medicaid funding for nontherapeutic abortions was not a denial of equal protection because Medicaid funds were available only for medically necessary procedures. Thus the plaintiffs were seeking benefits which were not available to others similarly situated. I continue to believe that *Maher* was wrongly decided. But it is apparent that while the plaintiffs in *Maher* were seeking a benefit not available to others similarly situated, respondents are protesting their exclusion from a benefit that is available to all others similarly situated.

Amendments. See McDonald v. Board of Election, 394 U.S. 802, 807 (1969); Harper v. Virginia Bd. of Elections, 383 U.S. 663, 668 (1966).

This, it need hardly be said, is a crucial difference for equal protection purposes.

. . .

III.

. . .

Ultimately, the result reached today may be traced to the Court's unwillingness to apply the constraints of the Constitution to decisions involving the expenditure of governmental funds. . . .

More than 35 years ago, Mr. Justice Jackson observed that the "task of translating the majestic generalities of the Bill of Rights . . . into concrete restraints on officials dealing with the problems of the twentieth century, is one to disturb self-confidence." West Virginia State Bd. of Educ. v. Barnette, 319 U.S. 624, 640 (1943). These constitutional principles, he observed for the Court, "grew in soil which also produced a philosophy that the individual['s] . . . liberty was attainable through mere absence of government restraints." Ibid. Those principles must be "transplant[ed] . . . to a soil in which the *laissez-faire* concept or principle of non-interference has withered at least as to economic affairs, and social advancements are increasingly sought through closer integration of society and through expanded and strengthened governmental controls." Id., at 640.

In this case, the Federal Government has taken upon itself the burden of financing practically all medically necessary expenditures. One category of medically necessary expenditure has been singled out for exclusion, and the sole basis for the exclusion is a premise repudiated for purposes of constitutional law in *Roe v. Wade.* The consequence is a devastating impact on the lives and health of poor women. I do not believe that a Constitution committed to the equal protection of the laws can tolerate this result. I dissent.

Mr. Justice Blackmun, dissenting.

I join the dissent of Mr. Justice Brennan and agree wholeheartedly with his and Mr. Justice Stevens' respective observations and descriptions of what the Court is doing in this latest round of "abortion cases." I need add only that I find what I said in dissent in Beal v. Doe, 432 U.S. 438, 442 (1977), and its two companion cases, Maher v. Roe, 432 U.S. 464 (1977), and Poelker v. Doe, 432 U.S. 519 (1977), continues for me to be equally pertinent and equally applicable in these Hyde Amendment cases. There is "condescension" in the Court's holding "that she may go elsewhere for her abortion"; this is "disingenuous and alarming"; the Government "punitively impresses upon a needy minority its own concepts of the socially desirable, the publicly acceptable, and the morally sound"; the "financial argument, of course, is specious"; there truly is "another world 'out there,' the existence of which the Court, I suspect, either chooses to ignore or fears to recognize"; the "cancer of poverty will continue to grow"; and "the lot of the poorest among us," once again, and still, is not to be bettered.

Mr. Justice Stevens, dissenting.

. . .

This case involves a special exclusion of women who, by definition, are confronted with a choice between two serious harms: serious health damage to themselves on the one hand and abortion on the other. The competing interests are the interest in maternal health and the interest in protecting potential human life. It is now part of our law that the pregnant woman's decision as to which of these conflicting interests shall prevail is entitled to constitutional protection.

. . .

... The Hyde Amendments not only exclude financially and medically needy persons from the pool of benefits for a constitutionally insufficient reason; they also require the expenditure of millions and millions of dollars in order to thwart the exercise of a constitutional right, thereby effectively inflicting serious and long lasting harm on impoverished women who want and need abortions for valid medical reasons. In my judgment, these amendments constitute an unjustifiable, and indeed blatant, violation of the sovereign's duty to govern impartially.

I respectfully dissent.

LYNG v. CASTILLO, 477 U.S. 635. In two steps Congress amended the Federal Food Stamp Program, which determines eligibility and benefit levels on a "household" rather than an individual basis, to treat as a single household parents and children (1981), or siblings (1982), who live together, whether or not they usually eat together. Families fitting these profiles, except that they generally bought their food and prepared their meals as separate economic units, sued in federal district court to prevent the consequent loss or reduction of food stamps and to be treated as separate households, contending that "the statutory distinction between parents, children, and siblings, and all other groups of individuals violates the guarantee of equal treatment in the Due Process Clause of the Fifth Amendment." The district court, "persuaded that the statutory definition had a rational basis[,]" nonetheless applied "a stricter standard of review" based "primarily on United States Department of Agriculture v. Moreno, 413 U.S. 528, 534 (1973), ... which it construed as holding that a 'Congressional desire to harm a politically unpopular group' could not justify the exclusion of household groups which contained unrelated persons," and from which it "reasoned that 'if the Supreme Court is willing to protect unpopular political groups it should even be more willing to protect the traditional family value of living together.'" The Supreme Court reversed. For the Court, Justice Stevens said in part:

"The District Court erred in [using] 'heightened scrutiny.' The disadvantaged class [of] parents, children, and siblings [is] not a 'suspect' or 'quasi-suspect' class. As a historical matter, they have not been subjected to discrimination; they do not exhibit obvious, immutable, or distinguishing characteristics that define them as a discrete group; and they are not a minority or politically powerless. See, e.g., Massachusetts Board of Retirement v. Murgia, 427 U.S. 307, 313–314 (1976) (per curiam). In fact, quite the contrary is true.

"Nor does the statutory classification 'directly and substantially' interfere with family living arrangements and thereby burden a fundamental right. Zablocki v. Redhail, 434 U.S. 374, 386–387, and n. 12 (1978).... The 'household' definition does not order or prevent any group of persons from dining together. Indeed, in the overwhelming majority of cases it probably has no effect at all. It is exceedingly unlikely that close relatives would choose to live apart simply to increase their allotment of food stamps, for the cost of separate housing would almost certainly exceed the incremental value of the additional stamps.... Thus, just as in *United States Department of Agriculture v. Moreno*—the decision which the District Court read to require 'heightened scrutiny'—the 'legislative classification must be sustained if the classification itself is rationally related to a legitimate governmental interest.' ...[3]

For several reasons the Court was "persuaded that Congress could rationally conclude that the two categories merited differential treatment":

"... Congress could reasonably determine that close relatives sharing a home—almost by definition—tend to purchase and prepare meals together while distant relatives and unrelated individuals might not be so inclined. In that event, even though close relatives are undoubtedly as honest as other food stamp recipients, the potential for mistaken or misstated claims of separate dining would be greater in the case of close relatives than would be true for those with weaker communal ties, simply because a greater percentage of the former category in fact prepare meals jointly than the comparable percentage in the latter category. The additional fact that close relatives represent by far the largest proportion of food stamp recipients, might well have convinced Congress that limited funds would not permit the accommodation given distant relatives and unrelated persons to be stretched to embrace close relatives as well. Finally, Congress might have reasoned that it would be somewhat easier for close relatives—again, almost by definition—to accommodate their living habits to a federal policy favoring common meal preparation than it would be for more distant relatives or unrelated persons to do so...."

Three Justices each dissented, finding the classification "irrational." One, Justice Marshall, first complained that "the Court's rigid, bipolar approach, which purports to apply rational basis scrutiny unless a suspect classification is involved or the exercise of a fundamental right is impeded puts legislative classifications impinging upon sensitive issues of family structure and survival on the same plane as a refusal to let a merchant hawk his wares on a particular street corner." Since "food stamp benefits ... are necessary for the affected families' very survival, and the Federal Government denies that benefit to families who do not, by preparing their meals together, structure themselves in a manner that the Government believes will minimize unnecessary expenditures[,] ... the Government is ... directly and substantially influencing the living arrangements of families whose resources are so low that they must rely on their relatives for shelter. The Government has thus chosen to intrude into the family dining room ... where ... the right to privacy exists in its strongest form." As the "challenged classifications amount to a conclusive presumption that related families living under the same roof do all of their cooking together[,] the regulation [also] affect[s] the even more vital interest in survival[,]" because "some separate families liv[ing] in the same house ... cannot prepare meals together because of different work schedules or lack of cooking or eating utensils."

In a later portion of his opinion, with which Justice White agreed, Justice Marshall also found "Congress' undeniably legitimate desire to prevent fraud

---

[3] In United States Department of Agriculture v. Moreno, 413 U.S. 528 (1973), we held that the definition of the term "household" in the Food Stamp Act as amended in 1971, 84 Stat. 2048, was unconstitutional. That definition drew a distinction between households composed entirely of persons who are related to one another and households containing one or more members who are unrelated to the rest. Unlike the present statute, the 1971 definition completely disqualified all households in the latter category. Not only were all groups of unrelated persons ineligible for benefits, but even groups of related persons would lose their benefits if they admitted one nonrelative to their household. We concluded that this definition did not further the interest in preventing fraud, or any other legitimate purpose of the Food Stamp Program....

The 1971 definition was, therefore, "wholly without any rational basis" and "invalid under the Due Process Clause of the Fifth Amendment." 413 U.S., at 538.

and waste in the food stamp program ... related at best tenuously to the achievement of those goals." He had

"some doubt that the classification used here could pass even a rational-basis test. In United States Dept. of Agriculture v. Moreno, 413 U.S. 528 (1973), we held that a definition of 'household' that excluded any living group containing an individual unrelated to any other member of the group did not rationally further the Government's interest in preventing fraud in the food stamp program. Despite the Court's attempts to distinguish this case from *Moreno,* the critical fact in both cases is that the statute drew a distinction that bears no necessary relation to the prevention of fraud.... In the present case, the Government has provided no justification for the conclusion that related individuals living together are more likely to lie about their living arrangements than are unrelated individuals. Nor has it demonstrated that fraudulent conduct by related households is more difficult to detect than similar abuses by unrelated households.

"Congress ... cite[d] no hard evidence that related persons living together were in fact significant sources of fraud....

"... Congress ... recogniz[ed] that distinct families living together often are genuinely separate households, and that the food stamp program should permit separate families that are not related to live together but maintain separate households.... Congress nevertheless assumed that related families are less likely to be genuinely separate households than are unrelated families, and failed even to provide related families a chance to rebut the legislative presumption."

E.   EDUCATION

San Antonio Independent School Dist. v. Rodriguez

411 U.S. 1, 93 S.Ct. 1278, 36 L.Ed.2d 16 (1973).

Mr. Justice Powell delivered the opinion of the Court.

This suit attacking the Texas system of financing public education was initiated by Mexican–American parents whose children attend the elementary and secondary schools in the Edgewood Independent School District, an urban school district in San Antonio, Texas. They brought a class action on behalf of school children throughout the State who are members of minority groups or who are poor and reside in school districts having a low property tax base. Named as defendants were the State Board of Education, the Commissioner of Education, the State Attorney General, and the Bexar County (San Antonio) Board of Trustees.... In December 1971 the [three-judge] panel rendered its judgment in a *per curiam* opinion holding the Texas school finance system unconstitutional under the Equal Protection Clause of the Fourteenth Amendment.... [W]e reverse....

I.

. . .

[The Court described at length the Texas system of school financing. For present purposes it is enough to note that half of the total educational expenditures in Texas came from the Texas Minimum Foundation School Program. State revenues financed 80% of the Program, with the remaining 20% (known as the Local Fund Assignment) coming from the local districts under a formula designed to reflect each district's relative taxpaying ability. Each school district imposed a property tax to raise funds to satisfy its Local Fund Assignment and to provide the revenues needed above those received under the Foundation Program.]

The school district in which appellees reside, the Edgewood Independent School District, has been compared throughout this litigation with the Alamo Heights Independent School District. This comparison between the least and most affluent districts in the San Antonio area serves to illustrate the manner in which the dual system of finance operates and to indicate the extent to which substantial disparities exist despite the State's impressive progress in recent years. Edgewood is one of seven public school districts in the metropolitan area. Approximately 22,000 students are enrolled in its 25 elementary and secondary schools. The district is situated in the core-city sector of San Antonio in a residential neighborhood that has little commercial or industrial property. The residents are predominantly of Mexican–American descent: approximately 90% of the student population is Mexican–American and over 6% is Negro. The average assessed property value per pupil is $5,960—the lowest in the metropolitan area—and the median family income ($4,686) is also the lowest. At an equalized tax rate of $1.05 per $100 of assessed property—the highest in the metropolitan area—the district contributed $26 to the education of each child for the 1967–1968 school year above its Local Fund Assignment for the Minimum Foundation Program. The Foundation Program contributed $222 per pupil for a state-local total of $248. Federal funds added another $108 for a total of $356 per pupil.

Alamo Heights is the most affluent school district in San Antonio. Its six schools, housing approximately 5,000 students, are situated in a residential community quite unlike the Edgewood District. The school population is predominantly Anglo, having only 18% Mexican–Americans and less than 1% Negroes. The assessed property value per pupil exceeds $49,000 and the median family income is $8,001. In 1967–1968 the local tax rate of $.85 per $100 of valuation yielded $333 per pupil over and above its contribution to the Foundation Program. Coupled with the $225 provided from that Program, the district was able to supply $558 per student. Supplemented by a $36 per pupil grant from federal sources, Alamo Heights spent $594 per pupil.

... [1970–1971] figures also reveal the extent to which these two districts' allotments were funded from their own required contributions to the Local Fund Assignment. Alamo Heights, because of its relative wealth, was required to contribute out of its local property tax collections approximately $100 per pupil, or about 20% of its Foundation grant. Edgewood, on the other hand, paid only $8.46 per pupil, which is about 2.4% of its grant. It does appear then that, at least as to these two districts, the Local Fund Assignment does reflect a rough approximation of the relative taxpaying potential of each.

Despite ... recent increases, substantial interdistrict disparities in school expenditures found by the District Court to prevail in San Antonio and in varying degrees throughout the State still exist. And it was these disparities, largely attributable to differences in the amounts of money collected through local property taxation, that led the District Court to conclude that Texas' dual system of public school finance violated the Equal Protection Clause....

Texas virtually concedes that its historically rooted dual system of financing education could not withstand the strict judicial scrutiny that this Court has found appropriate in reviewing legislative judgments that interfere with fundamental constitutional rights or that involve suspect classifications. If, as previous decisions have indicated, strict scrutiny means that the State's system is not entitled to the usual presumption of validity, that the State rather than the complainants must carry a "heavy burden of justification," that the State must demonstrate that its educational system has been structured with "precision" and is "tailored" narrowly to serve legitimate objectives and that it has selected the "least drastic means" for effectuating its objectives, the Texas financing system and its counterpart in virtually every other State will not pass muster. The State candidly admits that "[n]o one familiar with the Texas system would contend that it has yet achieved perfection." Apart from its concession that educational finance in Texas has "defects" and "imperfections," the State defends the system's rationality with vigor and disputes the District Court's finding that it lacks a "reasonable basis."

This, then, establishes the framework for our analysis. We must decide, first, whether the Texas system of financing public education operates to the disadvantage of some suspect class or impinges upon a fundamental right explicitly or implicitly protected by the Constitution, thereby requiring strict judicial scrutiny. If so, the judgment of the District Court should be affirmed. If not, the Texas scheme must still be examined to determine whether it rationally furthers some legitimate, articulated state purpose and therefore does not constitute an invidious discrimination in violation of the Equal Protection Clause of the Fourteenth Amendment.

II.

. . .

A.

The wealth discrimination discovered by the District Court in this case, and by several other courts that have recently struck down school financing laws in other States,[48] is quite unlike any of the forms of wealth discrimination heretofore reviewed by this Court. Rather than focusing on the unique features of the alleged discrimination, the courts in these cases have virtually assumed their findings of a suspect classification through a simplistic process of analysis: since, under the traditional systems of financing public schools, some poorer people receive less expensive educations than other more affluent people, these systems discriminate on the basis of wealth. This approach largely ignores the hard threshold questions, including whether it makes a difference for purposes of consideration under the Constitution that the class of disadvantaged "poor" cannot be identified or defined in customary equal protection terms, and whether the relative—rather than absolute—nature of the asserted deprivation is of significant consequence. Before a State's laws and the justifications for the classifications they create are subjected to strict judicial scrutiny, we think these threshold considerations must be analyzed more closely than they were in the court below.

. . .

However described, it is clear that appellees' suit asks this Court to extend its most exacting scrutiny to review a system that allegedly discriminates against a large, diverse, and amorphous class, unified only by the common factor of residence in districts that happen to have less taxable wealth than other districts. The system of alleged discrimination and the class it defines have none of the traditional indicia of suspectness: the class is not saddled with

---

[48] Serrano v. Priest, 96 Cal.Rptr. 601, 487 P.2d 1241, 5 Cal.3d 584 (1971); Van Dusartz v. Hatfield, 334 F.Supp. 870 (D.Minn.1971); Robinson v. Cahill, 118 N.J.Super. 223, 287 A.2d 187 (1972); Milliken v. Green, No. 53, 809 (Mich. 1973).

such disabilities, or subjected to such a history of purposeful unequal treatment, or relegated to such a position of political powerlessness as to command extraordinary protection from the majoritarian political process.

We thus conclude that the Texas system does not operate to the peculiar disadvantage of any suspect class. But in recognition of the fact that this Court has never heretofore held that wealth discrimination alone provides an adequate basis for invoking strict scrutiny, appellees have not relied solely on this contention. They also assert that the State's system impermissibly interferes with the exercise of a "fundamental" right and that accordingly the prior decisions of this Court require the application of the strict standard of judicial review.... It is this question—whether education is a fundamental right, in the sense that it is among the rights and liberties protected by the Constitution—which has so consumed the attention of courts and commentators in recent years.[68]

B.

In Brown v. Board of Education, 347 U.S. 483 (1954), a unanimous Court recognized that "education is perhaps the most important function of state and local governments." Id., at 493. What was said there in the context of racial discrimination has lost none of its vitality with the passage of time: ...

Nothing this Court holds today in any way detracts from our historic dedication to public education. We are in complete agreement with the conclusion of the three-judge panel below that "the grave significance of education both to the individual and to our society" cannot be doubted. But the importance of a service performed by the State does not determine whether it must be regarded as fundamental for purposes of examination under the Equal Protection Clause. Mr. Justice Harlan, dissenting from the Court's application of strict scrutiny to a law impinging upon the right of interstate travel, admonished that "[v]irtually every state statute affects important rights." Shapiro v. Thompson, 394 U.S. 618, 655, 661 (1969). In his view, if the degree of judicial scrutiny of state legislation fluctuated depending on a majority's view of the importance of the interest affected, we would have gone "far toward making this Court a 'super-legislature.' "We would indeed then be assuming a legislative role and one for which the Court lacks both authority and competence. But Mr. Justice Stewart's response in *Shapiro* to Mr. Justice Harlan's concern correctly articulates the limits of the fundamental rights rationale employed in the Court's equal protection decisions:

"The Court today does *not* 'pick out particular human activities, characterize them as' fundamental, 'and give them added protection....' To the contrary, the Court simply recognizes, as it must, an established constitutional right, and gives to that right no less protection than the Constitution itself demands." 394 U.S., at 642. (Emphasis from original.)

. . . .

---

[68] See Serrano v. Priest, 96 Cal.Rptr. 601, 487 P.2d 1241, 5 Cal.3d 584 (1971); Van Dusartz v. Hatfield, 334 F.Supp. 870 (D.Minn.1971); Robinson v. Cahill, 118 N.J.Super. 223, 287 A.2d 187 (1972); J. Coons, W. Clune, and S. Sugarman, supra, n. 13, at 339–394; Goldstein, supra, n. 38, at 534–541; Vieira, Unequal Educational Expenditures: Some Minority Views on Serrano v. Priest, 37 Mo.L.Rev. 617, 618–624 (1972); Comment, Educational Financing, Equal Protection of the Laws, and the Supreme Court, 70 Mich.L.Rev. 1324, 1335–1342 (1972); Note, The Public School Financing Cases: Interdistrict Inequalities and Wealth Discrimination, 14 Ariz.L.Rev. 88, 120–124 (1972).

... The right to interstate travel had long been recognized as a right of constitutional significance, and the Court's decision therefore did not require an *ad hoc* determination as to the social or economic importance of that right.

. . .

The lesson of these cases in addressing the question now before the Court is plain. It is not the province of this Court to create substantive constitutional rights in the name of guaranteeing equal protection of the laws. Thus the key to discovering whether education is "fundamental" is not to be found in comparisons of the relative societal significance of education as opposed to subsistence or housing. Nor is it to be found by weighing whether education is as important as the right to travel. Rather, the answer lies in assessing whether there is a right to education explicitly or implicitly guaranteed by the Constitution. Eisenstadt v. Baird, 405 U.S. 438 (1972);[73] Dunn v. Blumstein, 405 U.S. 330 (1972);[74] Police Department of the City of Chicago v. Mosley, 408 U.S. 92 (1972);[75] Skinner v. Oklahoma, 316 U.S. 535 (1942).[76]

Education, of course, is not among the rights afforded explicit protection under our Federal Constitution. Nor do we find any basis for saying it is implicitly so protected....

We have carefully considered each of the arguments supportive of the District Court's finding that education is a fundamental right or liberty and have found those arguments unpersuasive. In one further respect we find this a particularly inappropriate case in which to subject state action to strict judicial scrutiny.... Each of our prior cases involved legislation which "deprived," "infringed," or "interfered" with the free exercise of some such fundamental personal right or liberty. See Skinner v. Oklahoma, supra, at 536; Shapiro v. Thompson, supra, at 634; Dunn v. Blumstein, supra, at 338–343. A critical distinction between those cases and the one now before us lies in what Texas is endeavoring to do with respect to education.... The Texas system of school finance ... was implemented in an effort to *extend* public education and to improve its quality. Of course, every reform that benefits some more than others may be criticized for what it fails to accomplish. But we think it plain that, in substance, the thrust of the Texas system is affirmative and reforma-

[73] In *Eisenstadt*, the Court struck down a Massachusetts statute that prohibited the distribution of contraceptive devices, finding that the law failed "to satisfy even the more lenient equal protection standard." Id., at 447 n. 7. Nevertheless, in *dictum*, the Court recited the correct form of equal protection analysis: "if we were to conclude that the Massachusetts statute impinges upon fundamental freedoms under Griswold [v. Connecticut, 381 U.S. 479 (1965)], the statutory classification would have to be not merely *rationally related* to a valid public purpose but *necessary* to the achievement of a *compelling* state interest." Ibid. (emphasis from original).

[74] *Dunn* fully canvasses this Court's voting rights cases and explains that "this Court has made clear that a citizen has a *constitutionally protected right* to participate in elections on an equal basis with other citizens in the jurisdiction." Id., at 336 (emphasis supplied). The constitutional underpinnings of the right to equal treatment in the voting process can no longer be doubted even though, as the Court noted in Harper v. Virginia Bd. of Elections, 383 U.S. 663, 665 (1966), "the right to vote in state elections is nowhere expressly mentioned." ...

[75] In *Mosley*, the Court struck down a Chicago antipicketing ordinance that exempted labor picketing from its prohibitions. The ordinance was held invalid under the Equal Protection Clause after subjecting it to careful scrutiny and finding that the ordinance was not narrowly drawn. The stricter standard of review was appropriately applied since the ordinance was one "affecting First Amendment interests." Id., at 101.

[76] *Skinner* applied the standard of close scrutiny to a state law permitting forced sterilization of "habitual criminals." Implicit in the Court's opinion is the recognition that the right of procreation is among the rights of personal privacy protected under the Constitution. See Roe v. Wade, 410 U.S. 113 (1973).

tory and, therefore, should be scrutinized under judicial principles sensitive to the nature of the State's efforts and to the rights reserved to the States under the Constitution.

C.

. . .

We need not rest our decision, however, solely on the inappropriateness of the strict scrutiny test. A century of Supreme Court adjudication under the Equal Protection Clause affirmatively supports the application of the traditional standard of review, which requires only that the State's system be shown to bear some rational relationship to legitimate state purposes. This case represents far more than a challenge to the manner in which Texas provides for the education of its children. We have here nothing less than a direct attack on the way in which Texas has chosen to raise and disburse state and local tax revenues. We are asked to condemn the State's judgment in conferring on political subdivisions the power to tax local property to supply revenues for local interests. In so doing, appellees would have the Court intrude in an area in which it has traditionally deferred to state legislatures. This Court has often admonished against such interferences with the State's fiscal policies under the Equal Protection Clause. . . .

Thus we stand on familiar ground when we continue to acknowledge that the Justices of this Court lack both the expertise and the familiarity with local problems so necessary to the making of wise decisions with respect to the raising and disposition of public revenues. . . .

In addition to matters of fiscal policy, this case also involves the most persistent and difficult questions of educational policy, another area in which this Court's lack of specialized knowledge and experience counsels against premature interference with the informed judgments made at the state and local levels. . . .

. . .

The foregoing considerations buttress our conclusion that Texas' system of public school finance is an inappropriate candidate for strict judicial scrutiny. These same considerations are relevant to the determination whether that system, with its conceded imperfections, nevertheless bears some rational relationship to a legitimate state purpose. It is to this question that we next turn our attention.

III.

. . .

In sum, to the extent that the Texas system of school finance results in unequal expenditures between children who happen to reside in different districts, we cannot say that such disparities are the product of a system that is so irrational as to be invidiously discriminatory. Texas has acknowledged its shortcomings and has persistently endeavored—not without some success—to ameliorate the differences in levels of expenditures without sacrificing the benefits of local participation. The Texas plan is not the result of hurried, ill-conceived legislation. It certainly is not the product of purposeful discrimination against any group or class. On the contrary, it is rooted in decades of experience in Texas and elsewhere, and in major part is the product of responsible studies by qualified people. In giving substance to the presumption of validity to which the Texas system is entitled, Lindsley v. Natural Carbonic

Gas Co., 220 U.S. 61, 78 (1911), it is important to remember that at every stage of its development it has constituted a "rough accommodation" of interests in an effort to arrive at practical and workable solutions.... One also must remember that the system here challenged is not peculiar to Texas or to any other State. In its essential characteristics the Texas plan for financing public education reflects what many educators for a half century have thought was an enlightened approach to a problem for which there is no perfect solution. We are unwilling to assume for ourselves a level of wisdom superior to that of legislators, scholars, and educational authorities in 49 States, especially where the alternatives proposed are only recently conceived and nowhere yet tested. The constitutional standard under the Equal Protection Clause is whether the challenged state action rationally furthers a legitimate state purpose or interest. McGinnis v. Royster, 410 U.S. 263, 270 (1973). We hold that the Texas plan abundantly satisfies this standard.

. . . .

Reversed.

Mr. Justice Stewart, concurring.

. . .

Unlike other provisions of the Constitution, the Equal Protection Clause confers no substantive rights and creates no substantive liberties.[2] The function of the Equal Protection Clause, rather, is simply to measure the validity of *classifications* created by state laws.

There is hardly a law on the books that does not affect some people differently from others. But the basic concern of the Equal Protection Clause is with state legislation whose purpose or effect is to create discrete and objectively identifiable classes. And with respect to such legislation, it has long been settled that the Equal Protection Clause is offended only by laws that are invidiously discriminatory—only by classifications that are wholly arbitrary or capricious....

. . .

Mr. Justice Brennan, dissenting.

Although I agree with my Brother White that the Texas statutory scheme is devoid of any rational basis, and for that reason is violative of the Equal Protection Clause, I also record my disagreement with the Court's rather distressing assertion that a right may be deemed "fundamental" for the purposes of equal protection analysis only if it is "explicitly or implicitly guaranteed by the Constitution." ... As my Brother Marshall convincingly demonstrates, our prior cases stand for the proposition that "fundamentality" is, in large measure, a function of the right's importance in terms of the effectuation of those rights which are in fact constitutionally guaranteed. Thus, "[a]s the nexus between the specific constitutional guarantee and the nonconstitutional interest draws closer, the nonconstitutional interest becomes more

---

[2] There is one notable exception to the above statement: It has been established in recent years that the Equal Protection Clause confers the substantive right to participate on an equal basis with other qualified voters whenever the State has adopted an electoral process for determining who will represent any segment of the State's population. See, e.g., Reynolds v. Sims, 377 U.S. 533; Kramer v. Union School District, 395 U.S. 621; Dunn v. Blumstein, 405 U.S. 330, 336. But there is no constitutional right to vote, as such. Minor v. Happersett, 88 U.S. 162. If there were such a right, both the Fifteenth Amendment and the Nineteenth Amendment would have been wholly unnecessary.

fundamental and the degree of judicial scrutiny applied when the interest is infringed on a discriminatory basis must be adjusted accordingly." ...

Here, there can be no doubt that education is inextricably linked to the right to participate in the electoral process and to the rights of free speech and association guaranteed by the First Amendment.... This being so, any classification affecting education must be subjected to strict judicial scrutiny, and since even the State concedes that the statutory scheme now before us cannot pass constitutional muster under this stricter standard of review, I can only conclude that the Texas school financing scheme is constitutionally invalid.

Mr. Justice White, with whom Mr. Justice Douglas and Mr. Justice Brennan join, dissenting.

. . .

The Equal Protection Clause permits discriminations between classes but requires that the classification bear some rational relationship to a permissible object sought to be attained by the statute. It is not enough that the Texas system before us seeks to achieve the valid, rational purpose of maximizing local initiative; the means chosen by the State must also be rationally related to the end sought to be achieved....

Neither Texas nor the majority heeds this rule. If the State aims at maximizing local initiative and local choice, by permitting school districts to resort to the real property tax if they choose to do so, it utterly fails in achieving its purpose in districts with property tax bases so low that there is little if any opportunity for interested parents, rich or poor, to augment school district revenues. Requiring the State to establish only that unequal treatment is in furtherance of a permissible goal, without also requiring the State to show that the means chosen to effectuate that goal are rationally related to its achievement, makes equal protection analysis no more than an empty gesture. In my view, the parents and children in Edgewood, and in like districts, suffer from an invidious discrimination violative of the Equal Protection Clause.

. . .

Mr. Justice Marshall, with whom Mr. Justice Douglas concurs, dissenting.

. . .

II.

... [In the majority's view,] the Texas scheme must be tested by nothing more than that lenient standard of rationality which we have traditionally applied to discriminatory state action in the context of economic and commercial matters.... By so doing the Court avoids the telling task of searching for a substantial state interest which the Texas financing scheme, with its variations in taxable district property wealth, is necessary to further. I cannot accept such an emasculation of the Equal Protection Clause in the context of this case.

A.

To begin, I must once more voice my disagreement with the Court's rigidified approach to equal protection analysis. See Dandridge v. Williams, 397 U.S. 471, 519–521 (1970) (dissenting opinion); Richardson v. Belcher, 404 U.S. 78, 90 (1971) (dissenting opinion). The Court apparently seeks to establish today that equal protection cases fall into one of two neat categories which dictate the appropriate standard of review—strict scrutiny or mere rationality. But this Court's decisions in the field of equal protection defy such easy categorization. A principled reading of what this Court has done reveals that it has applied a spectrum of standards in reviewing discrimination allegedly violative of the Equal Protection Clause. This spectrum clearly comprehends variations in the degree of care with which the Court will scrutinize particular classifications, depending, I believe, on the constitutional and societal importance of the interest adversely affected and the recognized invidiousness of the basis upon which the particular classification is drawn. I find in fact that many of the Court's recent decisions embody the very sort of reasoned approach to equal protection analysis for which I previously argued—that is, an approach in which "concentration [is] placed upon the character of the classification in question, the relative importance to the individuals in the class discriminated against of the governmental benefits they do not receive, and the asserted state interests in support of the classification." Dandridge v. Williams, 397 U.S., at 520–521 (dissenting opinion).

I therefore cannot accept the majority's labored efforts to demonstrate that fundamental interests, which call for strict scrutiny of the challenged classification, encompass only established rights which we are somehow bound to recognize from the text of the Constitution itself. To be sure, some interests which the Court has deemed to be fundamental for purposes of equal protection analysis are themselves constitutionally protected rights.... But it will not do to suggest that the "answer" to whether an interest is fundamental for purposes of equal protection analysis is *always* determined by whether that interest "is a right ... explicitly or implicitly guaranteed by the Constitution." . . .

. . . .

The majority is, of course, correct when it suggests that the process of determining which interests are fundamental is a difficult one. But I do not think the problem is insurmountable. And I certainly do not accept the view that the process need necessarily degenerate into an unprincipled, subjective "picking-and-choosing" between various interests or that it must involve this Court in creating "substantive constitutional rights in the name of guaranteeing equal protection of the laws." ... Although not all fundamental interests are constitutionally guaranteed, the determination of which interests are fundamental should be firmly rooted in the text of the Constitution. The task in every case should be to determine the extent to which constitutionally guaranteed rights are dependent on interests not mentioned in the Constitution. As the nexus between the specific constitutional guarantee and the nonconstitutional interest draws closer, the nonconstitutional interest becomes more fundamental and the degree of judicial scrutiny applied when the interest is infringed on a discriminatory basis must be adjusted accordingly. Thus, it cannot be denied that interests such as procreation, the exercise of the state franchise, and access to criminal appellate processes are not fully guaranteed to the citizen by our Constitution. But these interests have nonetheless been afforded special judicial consideration in the face of discrimination because they are, to some extent, interrelated with constitutional guarantees. Procreation is now understood to be important because of its interaction with the established constitutional right of privacy. The exercise of the state franchise is closely tied to basic civil and political rights inherent in the First Amendment. And access to criminal appellate processes enhances the integrity of the range of rights implicit in the Fourteenth Amendment guarantee of due process of law. Only if we closely protect the related interests from state discrimination do we ultimately ensure the integrity of the constitutional guarantee itself. This is the real lesson that must be taken from our previous decisions involving interests deemed to be fundamental.

. . .

In summary, it seems to me inescapably clear that this Court has consistently adjusted the care with which it will review state discrimination in light of the constitutional significance of the interests affected and the invidiousness of the particular classification.... The majority suggests, however, that a variable standard of review would give this Court the appearance of a "super-legislature." ... I cannot agree. Such an approach seems to me a part of the guarantees of our Constitution and of the historic experiences with oppression of and discrimination against discrete, powerless minorities which underlie that document. In truth, the Court itself will be open to the criticism raised by the majority so long as it continues on its present course of effectively selecting in private which cases will be afforded special consideration without acknowledging the true basis of its action.[67] ...

. . .

As the Court points out, ... no previous decision has deemed the presence of just a wealth classification to be sufficient basis to call forth "rigorous judicial scrutiny" of allegedly discriminatory state action. Compare, e.g., *Harper v. Virginia Board of Elections,* supra, with e.g., James v. Valtierra, 402 U.S. 137 (1971). That wealth classifications alone have not necessarily been considered to bear the same high degree of suspectness as have classifications based on, for instance, race or alienage may be explainable on a number of grounds. The "poor" may not be seen as politically powerless as certain discrete and insular minority groups. Personal poverty may entail much the same social stigma as historically attached to certain racial or ethnic groups. But personal poverty is not a permanent disability; its shackles may be escaped. Perhaps, most importantly, though, personal wealth may not necessarily share the general irrelevance as basis for legislative action that race or nationality is recognized to have. While the "poor" have frequently been a legally disadvantaged group, it cannot be ignored that social legislation must frequently take cognizance of the economic status of our citizens. Thus, we have generally gauged the invidiousness of wealth classifications with an awareness of the importance of the interests being affected and the relevance of personal wealth to those interests. See *Harper v. Virginia Board of Elections,* supra.

When evaluated with these considerations in mind, it seems to me that discrimination on the basis of group wealth in this case likewise calls for careful judicial scrutiny....

. . .

Plyler v. Doe

457 U.S. 202, 102 S.Ct. 2382, 72 L.Ed.2d 786 (1982).

Justice Brennan delivered the opinion of the Court.

The question presented by these cases is whether, consistent with the Equal Protection Clause of the Fourteenth Amendment, Texas may deny to

---

[67] See generally Gunther, The Supreme Court, 1971 Term: Foreword, In Search of Evolving Doctrine on a Changing Court: A Model for a Newer Equal Protection, 86 Harv.L.Rev. 1 (1972).

undocumented school-age children the free public education that it provides to children who are citizens of the United States or legally admitted aliens.

I

Since the late nineteenth century, the United States has restricted immigration into this country. Unsanctioned entry into the United States is a crime, 8 U.S.C. § 1325, and those who have entered unlawfully are subject to deportation, 8 U.S.C. §§ 1251–1252. But despite the existence of these legal restrictions, a substantial number of persons have succeeded in unlawfully entering the United States....

In May 1975, the Texas legislature revised its education laws to withhold from local school districts any state funds for the education of children who were not "legally admitted" into the United States. The 1975 revision also authorized local school districts to deny enrollment in their public schools to children not "legally admitted" to the country.... These cases involve constitutional challenges to those provisions.

. . .

II

The Fourteenth Amendment provides that "No State shall ... deprive any person of life, liberty, or property, without due process of law; nor deny to *any person within its jurisdiction* the equal protection of the laws." Appellants argue at the outset that undocumented aliens, because of their immigration status, are not "persons within the jurisdiction" of the State of Texas, and that they therefore have no right to the equal protection of Texas law. We reject this argument. Whatever his status under the immigration laws, an alien is surely a "person" in any ordinary sense of that term. Aliens, even aliens whose presence in this country is unlawful, have long been recognized as "persons" guaranteed due process of law by the Fifth and Fourteenth Amendments. Shaughnessy v. Mezei, 345 U.S. 206, 212 (1953); Wong Wing v. United States, 163 U.S. 228, 238 (1896); Yick Wo v. Hopkins, 118 U.S. 356, 369 (1886). Indeed, we have clearly held that the Fifth Amendment protects aliens whose presence in this country is unlawful from invidious discrimination by the Federal Government. Mathews v. Diaz, 426 U.S. 67, 77 (1976).

. . .

III

... In applying the Equal Protection Clause to most forms of state action, we ... seek only the assurance that the classification at issue bears some fair relationship to a legitimate public purpose.

But we would not be faithful to our obligations under the Fourteenth Amendment if we applied so deferential a standard to every classification. The Equal Protection Clause was intended as a restriction on state legislative action inconsistent with elemental constitutional premises. Thus we have treated as presumptively invidious those classifications that disadvantage a "suspect class,"[14] or that impinge upon the exercise of a "fundamental right."[15] With

---

[14] Several formulations might explain our treatment of certain classifications as "suspect." Some classifications are more likely than others to reflect deep-seated prejudice rather than legislative rationality in pursuit of some legitimate objective. Legislation predicated on such prejudice is easily recognized as incompatible with the constitutional understanding that each person is to be judged individually and is entitled to equal justice under the law. Classifications treated as suspect tend to be irrelevant to any proper legis-

[15] See note 15 on page 1058.

respect to such classifications, [we] requir[e] the State to demonstrate that its classification has been precisely tailored to serve a compelling governmental interest. In addition, we have recognized that certain forms of legislative classification, while not facially invidious, nonetheless give rise to recurring constitutional difficulties; in these limited circumstances we have sought the assurance that the classification reflects a reasoned judgment consistent with the ideal of equal protection by inquiring whether it may fairly be viewed as furthering a substantial interest of the State.[16] We turn to a consideration of the standard appropriate for the evaluation of § 21.031.

A

Sheer incapability or lax enforcement of the laws barring entry into this country, coupled with the failure to establish an effective bar to the employment of undocumented aliens, has resulted in the creation of a substantial "shadow population" of illegal migrants—numbering in the millions—within our borders. This situation raises the specter of a permanent caste of undocumented resident aliens, encouraged by some to remain here as a source of cheap labor, but nevertheless denied the benefits that our society makes available to citizens and lawful residents. The existence of such an underclass presents most difficult problems for a Nation that prides itself on adherence to principles of equality under law.[19]

lative goal. See McLaughlin v. Florida, 379 U.S. 184, 192 (1964); Hirabayashi v. United States, 320 U.S. 81, 100 (1943). Finally, certain groups, indeed largely the same groups, have historically been "relegated to such a position of political powerlessness as to command extraordinary protection from the majoritarian political process." San Antonio School District v. Rodriguez, 411 U.S. 1, 28 (1973); Graham v. Richardson, 403 U.S. 365, 372 (1971); see United States v. Carolene Products Co., 304 U.S. 144, 152–153, n. 4 (1938). The experience of our Nation has shown that prejudice may manifest itself in the treatment of some groups. Our response to that experience is reflected in the Equal Protection Clause of the Fourteenth Amendment. Legislation imposing special disabilities upon groups disfavored by virtue of circumstances beyond their control suggests the kind of "class or caste" treatment that the Fourteenth Amendment was designed to abolish.

[15] In determining whether a class-based denial of a particular right is deserving of strict scrutiny under the Equal Protection Clause, we look to the Constitution to see if the right infringed has its source, explicitly or implicitly, therein. But we have also recognized the fundamentality of participation in state "elections on an equal basis with other citizens in the jurisdiction," Dunn v. Blumstein, supra, at 336, even though "the right to both, per se, is not a constitutionally protected right." San Antonio School District, 411 U.S., at 35, n. 78. With respect to suffrage, we have explained the need for strict scrutiny as arising from the significance of the franchise as the guardian of all other rights. See Harper v. Virginia Bd. of Elections, 383 U.S. 663, 667 (1966); Reynolds v. Sims, 377 U.S. 533, 562 (1964); Yick Wo v. Hopkins, 118 U.S. 356, 370 (1886).

[16] See Craig v. Boren, 429 U.S. 190 (1976); Lalli v. Lalli, 439 U.S. 259 (1978). This technique of "intermediate" scrutiny permits us to evaluate the rationality of the legislative judgment with reference to well-settled constitutional principles. "In expounding the Constitution, the Court's role is to discern 'principles sufficiently absolute to give them roots throughout the community and continuity over significant periods of time, and to lift them above the level of the pragmatic political judgments of a particular time and place.'" University of California Regents v. Bakke, 438 U.S. 265, 299 (1978) (Opinion of Powell, J.), quoting A. Cox, The Role of the Supreme Court in American Government 114 (1976). Only when concerns sufficiently absolute and enduring can be clearly ascertained from the Constitution and our cases do we employ this standard to aid us in determining the rationality of the legislative choice.

[19] We reject the claim that "illegal aliens" are a "suspect class." No case in which we have attempted to define a suspect class, see e.g., n. 14 supra, has addressed the status of persons unlawfully in our country. Unlike most of the classifications that we have recognized as suspect, entry into this class, by virtue of entry into this country, is the product of voluntary action. Indeed, entry into the class is itself a crime. In addition, it could hardly be suggested that undocu-

The children who are plaintiffs in these cases are special members of this underclass. Persuasive arguments support the view that a State may withhold its beneficence from those whose very presence within the United States is the product of their own unlawful conduct. These arguments do not apply with the same force to classifications imposing disabilities on the minor *children* of such illegal entrants. At the least, those who elect to enter our territory by stealth and in violation of our law should be prepared to bear the consequences, including, but not limited to, deportation. But the children of those illegal entrants are not comparably situated. Their "parents have the ability to conform their conduct to societal norms," and presumably the ability to remove themselves from the State's jurisdiction; but the children who are plaintiffs in these cases "can affect neither their parents' conduct nor their own status." Trimble v. Gordon, 430 U.S. 762, 770 (1977). Even if the State found it expedient to control the conduct of adults by acting against their children, legislation directing the onus of a parent's misconduct against his children does not comport with fundamental conceptions of justice. . . .

Of course, undocumented status is not irrelevant to any proper legislative goal. Nor is undocumented status an absolutely immutable characteristic since it is the product of conscious, indeed unlawful, action. But § 21.031 is directed against children, and imposes its discriminatory burden on the basis of a legal characteristic over which children can have little control. It is thus difficult to conceive of a rational justification for penalizing these children for their presence within the United States. Yet that appears to be precisely the effect of § 21.031.

Public education is not a "right" granted to individuals by the Constitution. San Antonio School District, supra, at 35. But neither is it merely some governmental "benefit" indistinguishable from other forms of social welfare legislation. Both the importance of education in maintaining our basic institutions, and the lasting impact of its deprivation on the life of the child, mark the distinction. The "American people have always regarded education and the acquisition of knowledge as matters of supreme importance." Meyer v. Nebraska, 262 U.S. 390, 400 (1923). We have recognized "the public school as a most vital civic institution for the preservation of a democratic system of government," Abington School District v. Schempp, 374 U.S. 203, 230 (1963) (Brennan, J., concurring), and as the primary vehicle for transmitting "the values on which our society rests." Ambach v. Norwick, 441 U.S. 68, 76 (1979). . . . In addition, education provides the basic tools by which individuals might lead economically productive lives to the benefit of us all. In sum, education has a fundamental role in maintaining the fabric of our society. We cannot ignore the significant social costs borne by our Nation when select groups are denied the means to absorb the values and skills upon which our social order rests.

In addition to the pivotal role of education in sustaining our political and cultural heritage, denial of education to some isolated group of children poses an affront to one of the goals of the Equal Protection Clause: the abolition of governmental barriers presenting unreasonable obstacles to advancement on the basis of individual merit. Paradoxically, by depriving the children of any

mented status is a "constitutional irrelevancy." With respect to the actions of the federal government, alienage classifications may be intimately related to the conduct of foreign policy, to the federal prerogative to control access to the United States, and to the plenary federal power to determine who has sufficiently manifested his allegiance to become a citizen of the Nation. No State may independently exercise a like power. But if the Federal Government has by uniform rule prescribed what it believes to be appropriate standards for the treatment of an alien subclass, the States may, of course, follow the federal direction. See De Canas v. Bica, 424 U.S. 351 (1976).

disfavored group of an education, we foreclose the means by which that group might raise the level of esteem in which it is held by the majority. But more directly, "education prepares individuals to be self-reliant and self-sufficient participants in society." Wisconsin v. Yoder, supra, at 221. Illiteracy is an enduring disability. The inability to read and write will handicap the individual deprived of a basic education each and every day of his life. The inestimable toll of that deprivation on the social, economic, intellectual and psychological well-being of the individual, and the obstacle it poses to individual achievement, makes it most difficult to reconcile the cost or the principle of a status-based denial of basic education with the framework of equality embodied in the Equal Protection Clause. What we said 28 years ago in Brown v. Board of Education, 347 U.S. 483 (1954), still holds true:

> "... In these days, it is doubtful that any child may reasonably be expected to succeed in life if he is denied the opportunity of an education. Such an opportunity, where the state has undertaken to provide it, is a right which must be made available to all on equal terms."

B

These well-settled principles allow us to determine the proper level of deference to be afforded § 21.031. Undocumented aliens cannot be treated as a suspect class because their presence in this country in violation of federal law is not a "constitutional irrelevancy." Nor is education a fundamental right; a State need not justify by compelling necessity every variation in the manner in which education is provided to its population. See San Antonio School Dist. v. Rodriguez, 411 U.S. 1, 28–39 (1973). But more is involved in this case than the abstract question whether § 21.031 discriminates against a suspect class, or whether education is a fundamental right. Section 21.031 imposes a lifetime hardship on a discrete class of children not accountable for their disabling status. The stigma of illiteracy will mark them for the rest of their lives. By denying these children a basic education, we deny them the ability to live within the structure of our civic institutions, and foreclose any realistic possibility that they will contribute in even the smallest way to the progress of our Nation. In determining the rationality of § 21.031, we may appropriately take into account its costs to the Nation and to the innocent children who are its victims. In light of these countervailing costs, the discrimination contained in § 21.031 can hardly be considered rational unless it furthers some substantial goal of the State.

IV

It is the State's principal argument, and apparently the view of the dissenting Justices, that the undocumented status of these children *vel non* establishes a sufficient rational basis for denying them benefits that a State might choose to afford other residents. The State notes that while other aliens are admitted "on an equality of legal privileges with all citizens under non-discriminatory laws," Takahashi v. Fish & Game Comm'n, 334 U.S. 410, 420 (1948), the asserted right of these children to an education can claim no implicit congressional imprimatur. Indeed, on the State's view, Congress' apparent disapproval of the presence of these children within the United States, and the evasion of the federal regulatory program that is the mark of undocumented status, provides authority for its decision to impose upon them special disabilities. Faced with an equal protection challenge respecting the treatment of aliens, we agree that the courts must be attentive to congressional policy; the exercise of congressional power might well affect the State's preroga-tives to afford differential treatment to a particular class of aliens. But we are unable to find in the congressional immigration scheme any statement of policy that might weigh significantly in arriving at an equal protection balance concerning the State's authority to deprive these children of an education.

. . .

To be sure, like all persons who have entered the United States unlawfully, these children are subject to deportation. 8 U.S.C. §§ 1251–1252. But there is no assurance that a child subject to deportation will ever be deported. An illegal entrant might be granted federal permission to continue to reside in this country, or even to become a citizen. See, e.g., 8 U.S.C. §§ 1252, 1253(h), 1254. In light of the discretionary federal power to grant relief from deportation, a State cannot realistically determine that any particular undocumented child will in fact be deported until after deportation proceedings have been completed. It would of course be most difficult for the State to justify a denial of education to a child enjoying an inchoate federal permission to remain.

We are reluctant to impute to Congress the intention to withhold from these children, for so long as they are present in this country through no fault of their own, access to a basic education. In other contexts, undocumented status, coupled with some articulable federal policy, might enhance State authority with respect to the treatment of undocumented aliens. But in the area of special constitutional sensitivity presented by this case, and in the absence of any contrary indication fairly discernible in the present legislative record, we perceive no national policy that supports the State in denying these children an elementary education. The State may borrow the federal classification. But to justify its use as a criterion for its own discriminatory policy, the State must demonstrate that the classification is reasonably adapted to *"the purposes for which the state desires to use it."* Oyama v. California, 332 U.S. 633, 664–665 (1948) (Murphy, J., concurring) (emphasis added). We therefore turn to the state objectives that are said to support § 21.031.

V

Appellants argue that the classification at issue furthers an interest in the "preservation of the state's limited resources for the education of its lawful residents." Of course, a concern for the preservation of resources standing alone can hardly justify the classification used in allocating those resources. Graham v. Richardson, supra, 403 U.S., at 374–375. The State must do more than justify its classification with a concise expression of an intention to discriminate. Examining Board v. Flores de Otero, 426 U.S. 572, 605 (1976). Apart from the asserted state prerogative to act against undocumented children solely on the basis of their undocumented status—an asserted prerogative that carries only minimal force in the circumstances of this case—we discern three colorable state interests that might support § 21.031.

First, appellants appear to suggest that the State may seek to protect the State from an influx of illegal immigrants. While a State might have an interest in mitigating the potentially harsh economic effects of sudden shifts in population, § 21.031 hardly offers an effective method of dealing with an urgent demographic or economic problem. There is no evidence in the record suggesting that illegal entrants impose any significant burden on the State's economy. To the contrary, the available evidence suggests that illegal aliens underutilize public services, while contributing their labor to the local economy and tax money to the State fisc. . . .

Second, while it is apparent that a state may "not . . . reduce expenditures for education by barring [some arbitrarily chosen class of] children from its schools," Shapiro v. Thompson, 394 U.S. 618, 633 (1969), appellants suggest that undocumented children are appropriately singled out for exclusion because of the special burdens they impose on the State's ability to provide high quality public education. But the record in no way supports the claim that exclusion of undocumented children is likely to improve the overall quality of education in the State. . . .

Finally, appellants suggest that undocumented children are appropriately singled out because their unlawful presence within the United States renders them less likely than other children to remain within the boundaries of the State, and to put their education to productive social or political use within the State. Even assuming that such an interest is legitimate, it is an interest that is most difficult to quantify. The State has no assurance that any child, citizen or not, will employ the education provided by the State within the confines of the State's borders. In any event, the record is clear that many of the undocumented children disabled by this classification will remain in this country indefinitely, and that some will become lawful residents or citizens of the United States. It is difficult to understand precisely what the State hopes to achieve by promoting the creation and perpetuation of a subclass of illiterates within our boundaries, surely adding to the problems and costs of unemployment, welfare, and crime. It is thus clear that whatever savings might be achieved by denying these children an education, they are wholly insubstantial in light of the costs involved to these children, the State, and the Nation.

VI

If the State is to deny a discrete group of innocent children the free public education that it offers to other children residing within its borders, that denial must be justified by a showing that it furthers some substantial state interest. No such showing was made here. Accordingly, the judgment of the Court of Appeals in each of these cases is

Affirmed.

Justice Marshall, concurring.

While I join the Court opinion, I do so without in any way retreating from my opinion in San Antonio School District v. Rodriguez, 411 U.S. 1, 70–133 (Marshall, J., dissenting). I continue to believe that an individual's interest in education is fundamental, and that this view is amply supported "by the unique status accorded public education and some of our most basic constitutional values." Furthermore, I believe that the facts of these cases demonstrate the wisdom of rejecting a rigidified approach to equal protection analysis, and of employing an approach that allows for varying levels of scrutiny depending upon "the constitutional and societal importance of the interest adversely affected and the recognized invidiousness of the basis upon which the particular classification is drawn." . . .

Justice Blackmun, concurring.

I join the opinion and judgment of the Court.

Like Justice Powell, I believe that the children involved in this litigation "should not be left on the streets uneducated." I write separately, however, because in my view the nature of the interest at stake is crucial to the proper resolution of this case.

The "fundamental rights" aspect of the Court's equal protection analysis—the now-familiar concept that governmental classifications bearing on certain interests must be closely scrutinized—has been the subject of some controversy. . . .

. . .

I joined Justice Powell's opinion for the Court in *Rodriguez,* and I continue to believe that it provides the appropriate model for resolving most equal protection disputes. Classifications infringing substantive constitutional rights necessarily will be invalid, if not by force of the Equal Protection Clause, then through operation of other provisions of the Constitution. Conversely, classifications bearing on nonconstitutional interests—even those involving "the most basic economic needs of impoverished human beings," Dandridge v. Williams, 397 U.S. 471, 485 (1970)—generally are not subject to special treatment under the Equal Protection Clause, because they are not distinguishable in any relevant way from other regulations in "the area of economics and social welfare." Ibid.

With all this said, however, I believe the Court's experience has demonstrated that the *Rodriguez* formulation does not settle every issue of "fundamental rights" arising under the Equal Protection Clause. Only a pedant would insist that there are *no* meaningful distinctions among the multitude of social and political interests regulated by the States, and *Rodriguez* does not stand for quite so absolute a proposition. . . .

. . .

In my view, when the State provides an education to some and denies it to others, it immediately and inevitably creates class distinctions of a type fundamentally inconsistent with ... the Equal Protection Clause. Children denied an education are placed at a permanent and insurmountable competitive disadvantage, for an uneducated child is denied even the opportunity to achieve. And when those children are members of an identifiable group, that group—through the State's action—will have been converted into a discrete underclass. Other benefits provided by the State, such as housing and public assistance, are of course important; to an individual in immediate need, they may be more desirable than the right to be educated. But classifications involving the complete denial of education are in a sense unique, for they strike at the heart of equal protection values by involving the State in the creation of permanent class distinctions. Cf. *Rodriguez,* 411 U.S., at 115, n. 74 (Marshall, J., dissenting). In a sense, then, denial of an education is the analogue of denial of the right to vote: the former relegates the individual to second-class social status; the latter places him at a permanent political disadvantage.

This conclusion is fully consistent with *Rodriguez.* The Court there reserved judgment on the constitutionality of a state system that "occasioned an absolute denial of educational opportunities to any of its children," noting that "no charge fairly could be made that the system [at issue in *Rodriguez*]fails to provide each child with an opportunity to acquire ... basic minimal skills." 411 U.S., at 37. . . .

... Whatever the State's power to classify deportable aliens, ... and whatever the Federal Government's ability to draw more precise and more acceptable alienage classifications—the statute at issue here sweeps within it a substantial number of children who will in fact, and who may well be entitled to, remain in the United States. Given the extraordinary nature of the interest involved, this makes the classification here fatally imprecise. And, as the Court demonstrates, the Texas legislation is not otherwise supported by any substantial interests.

Because I believe that the Court's carefully worded analysis recognizes the importance of the equal protection and preemption interests I consider crucial, I join its opinion as well as its judgment.

Justice Powell, concurring.

I join the opinion of the Court, and write separately to emphasize the unique character of the case before us.

. . .

Although the analogy is not perfect, our holding today does find support in decisions of this Court with respect to the status of illegitimates. In Weber v. Aetna Casualty & Surety Co., 406 U.S. 164, 175 (1972) we said: "visiting . . . condemnation on the head of an infant" for the misdeeds of the parents is illogical, unjust, and "contrary to the basic concept of our system that legal burdens should bear some relationship to individual responsibility or wrongdoing."

. . .

In my view, the State's denial of education to these children bears no substantial relation to any substantial state interest. Both of the district courts found that an uncertain but significant percentage of illegal alien children will remain in Texas as residents and many eventually will become citizens....

. . . [I]t hardly can be argued rationally that anyone benefits from the creation within our borders of a subclass of illiterate persons many of whom will remain in the State, adding to the problems and costs of both State and National Governments attendant upon unemployment, welfare and crime.

Chief Justice Burger, with whom Justice White, Justice Rehnquist, and Justice O'Connor join, dissenting.

Were it our business to set the Nation's social policy, I would agree without hesitation that it is senseless for an enlightened society to deprive any children—including illegal aliens—of an elementary education. I fully agree that it would be folly—and wrong—to tolerate creation of a segment of society made up of illiterate persons, many having a limited or no command of our language. However, the Constitution does not constitute us as "Platonic Guardians" nor does it vest in this Court the authority to strike down laws because they do not meet our standards of desirable social policy, "wisdom," or "common sense." See Tennessee Valley Authority v. Hill, 437 U.S. 153, 194–195 (1978). We trespass on the assigned function of the political branches under our structure of limited and separated powers when we assume a policy making role as the court does today.

The Court makes no attempt to disguise that it is acting to make up for Congress' lack of "effective leadership" in dealing with the serious national problems caused by the influx of uncountable millions of illegal aliens across our borders. The failure of enforcement of the immigration laws over more than a decade and the inherent difficulty and expense of sealing our vast borders have combined to create a grave socio-economic dilemma. It is a dilemma that has not yet even been fully assessed, let alone addressed. However, it is not the function of the judiciary to provide "effective leadership" simply because the political branches of government fail to do so.

The Court's holding today manifests the justly criticized judicial tendency to attempt speedy and wholesale formulation of "remedies" for the failures—or simply the laggard pace—of the political processes of our system of government. The Court employs, and in my view abuses, the Fourteenth Amendment in an effort to become an omnipotent and omniscient problem solver. That the motives for doing so are noble and compassionate does not alter the fact that the Court distorts our constitutional function to make amends for the defaults of others.

. . .

Once it is conceded—as the Court does—that illegal aliens are not a suspect class, and that education is not a fundamental right, our inquiry should focus on and be limited to whether the legislative classification at issue bears a rational relationship to a legitimate state purpose. Vance v. Bradley, 440 U.S. 93, 97 (1979); Dandridge v. Williams, 397 U.S. 471, 485–487 (1970).

. . .

Denying a free education to illegal alien children is not a choice I would make were I a legislator. Apart from compassionate considerations, the long-range costs of excluding any children from the public schools may well outweigh the costs of educating them. But that is not the issue; the fact that there are sound *policy* arguments against the Texas legislature's choice does not render that choice an unconstitutional one.

. . .

Congress, "vested by the Constitution with the responsibility of protecting our borders and legislating with respect to aliens," bears primary responsibility for addressing the problems occasioned by the millions of illegal aliens flooding across our southern border. Similarly, it is for Congress, and not this Court, to assess the "social costs borne by our Nation when select groups are denied the means to absorb the values and skills upon which our social order rests." While the "specter of a permanent caste" of illegal Mexican residents of the United States is indeed a disturbing one, it is but one segment of a larger problem, which is for the political branches to solve. I find it difficult to believe that Congress would long tolerate such a self-destructive result—that it would fail to deport these illegal alien families or to provide for the education of their children. Yet instead of allowing the political processes to run their course—albeit with some delay—the Court seeks to do Congress' job for it, compensating for congressional inaction. It is not unreasonable to think that this encourages the political branches to pass their problems to the judiciary.

The solution to this seemingly intractable problem is to defer to the political processes, unpalatable as that may be to some.

MARTINEZ v. BYNUM, 461 U.S. 321 (1983). A child born in Texas (and thus a United States citizen) lived with his parents in Mexico, where they were citizens, until he returned to Texas at age 8 to live with his sister in order to attend public school there. He challenged the constitutionality on its face of a Texas law denying tuition-free admission to local public schools to minors who live apart from their parents or guardians, if the minor's presence in the school district is "for the primary purpose of attending the public free schools." The Court rejected the facial attack. Justice Powell's majority opinion said that a "bona fide residence requirement, appropriately defined and uniformly applied, furthers the substantial state interest in assuring that services provided for its residents are enjoyed only by residents." As discussed in the report of this case supra p. 1003, the Court concluded that the law "does not burden or penalize the constitutional right of interstate travel[.]" By granting "the benefits of residency to everyone who satisfies the traditional residence definition [of physical presence and an intention to remain indefinitely] and to some who legitimately could be classified as nonresidents"—those who do not intend to remain indefinitely in the district but currently reside there other than for the sole purpose of attending school—the state adopted a legitimate bona fide residence requirement. Justice Powell also found an "independent justification for local residence requirements in the public-school context" in the maintenance of school quality: "Absent residence requirements, . . . the proper planning and operation of the schools would suffer significantly."

Justice Brennan concurred separately "to stress that this case involves only a facial challenge." Justice Marshall dissented, concluding that "the statutory classification, which deprives some children of an education because of their motive for residing in Texas, is not adequately justified by the asserted state interests."

FINANCIAL INEQUALITY BETWEEN AND WITHIN SCHOOL DISTRICTS

In two decisions that distinguished *Rodriguez* and *Plyler,* respectively, the Court addressed further claims of impermissible state favoritism of some local school districts over others or of impermissible distinctions among students within school districts. Papasan v. Allain, 478 U.S. 265 (1986), involved a challenge to Mississippi's unequal distribution between the State's northern and southern counties of money derived from different assets the Federal Government had conveyed for the use of the State's schools. In the course of remanding the case to the lower courts to consider whether federal requirements or variations in local management responsibilities concerning the federal assets might provide a rational basis for the funding disparities, the Court noted that *Rodriguez* and *Plyler* had "not yet definitively settled . . . whether a minimally adequate education is a fundamental right and whether a statute alleged to discriminatorily infringe that right should be accorded heightened equal protection review." Those issues still did not have to be resolved, however, because the complaint did not allege facts supporting an assertion that the students had been denied a minimally adequate education. Nor, unlike *Rodriguez,* was "the overall organization of the Mississippi public school financing program" challenged. Instead, Justice White's majority opinion indicated that because Mississippi decided "to divide state resources unequally among school districts[,]" whereas the unequal financing in *Rodriguez* was "traceable to school district funds available from local real estate taxation," the "rationality of the disparity in *Rodriguez,*" which was based on "allowing meaningful local control over school funding, [did] not settle the constitutionality of disparities alleged in this case." A dissent by Justice Powell, joined by Chief Justice Burger and Justice Rehnquist, objected to the Court's remand. He emphasized that the federally derived funds "account for only 1 ½% of overall funds provided for schools" and argued that "[t]he Equal Protection Clause, at least in the context of state funding of schools, is concerned with *substance,* not with the *de minimis* variations of funding among the districts."

Kadrmas v. Dickinson Public Schools, 487 U.S. 450 (1988), involved a North Dakota law authorizing "nonreorganized" school districts to charge a fee for transporting students to school. A student who was refused bus service when her parents did not pay fees imposed by such a district challenged both the statute's authorization to charge a fee and its distinction between reorganized and nonreorganized districts. The Court, 5–4, rejected both challenges.

With respect to charging for bus service per se, Justice O'Connor's majority opinion declined to apply any form of "'heightened' scrutiny[,]" whether the argument was "that the busing fee unconstitutionally places a greater obstacle to education in the path of the poor than it does in the path of wealthier families[,]" or "that the Equal Protection Clause affirmatively requires government to provide free transportation to school, at least for some class of students that would include Sarita Kadrmas." The Court declined to "extend" *Plyler* and did not find it controlling, as Kadrmas "has not been penalized by the government for illegal conduct by her parents" and the user fee did not threaten to create or perpetuate a sub-class of illiterates. Precedents holding "that government may not withhold certain especially important services from those ... unable to pay for them" were also inapposite, because unlike those cases "the Kadrmas family could and did find a private alternative to the public school bus service for which Dickinson charged a fee." Because the "Constitution does not require that such service be provided at all," it sufficed that allowing "local school boards the option of charging patrons a user fee" rationally encouraged them "to provide school bus service."

The Court also upheld the rationality of the distinction between reorganized and nonreorganized school districts. Much of North Dakota being thinly populated, reorganized districts are those consolidated into larger districts and that thus entail larger distances from home to school. Under state law, reorganization plans must contain transportation provisions that only voter approval subsequently can change. The Court thought state law might allow a reorganized district to charge a transportation fee as well, so that the only "definitely established difference between reorganized and nonreorganized districts is this: in the latter, local school boards may impose a bus service user fee on their own authority, while the direct approval of the voters would be required in reorganized districts." Because "[t]hat difference ... simply reflects voluntary agreements made during the history of North Dakota's reorganization process, ... it could scarcely be thought to make the State's laws arbitrary or irrational." Even assuming reorganized districts were forbidden to charge for bus service, the Court thought it "evident that the legislature could conceivably have believed that such a policy would serve the legitimate purpose of fulfilling the reasonable expectations of those residing in districts with free busing arrangements imposed by reorganization plans"—a purpose having "no application to nonreorganized districts."

A dissent by Justice Marshall, joined by Justice Brennan, asserted that, for poor children, "imposing a fee for transportation is no different in practical effect from imposing a fee directly for education" and thus the case presented "the question whether a State may discriminate against the poor in providing access to education." In prior cases he discerned "a deep distrust of policies that specially burden the access of disadvantaged persons to the governmental institutions and processes that offer members of our society an opportunity to improve their status and better their lives." Citing *Plyler,* he noted the "intent of the Fourteenth Amendment ... to abolish caste legislation" and urged that "exacting scrutiny" be applied. He found *Plyler*'s "reasoning ... fully applicable[,]" because the State had "acted to burden the educational opportunities of a disadvantaged group of children, who need an education to become full participants in society." The State's fiscal interest in failing to exempt "indigent families from the busing fee" was "insubstantial" and could not justify the challenged discrimination.

In a separate dissent, Justice Stevens, joined by Justice Blackmun, argued that the distinction between reorganized and nonreorganized districts was irrational. Looking only to the "actual purpose of the geographic discrimination" identified by the North Dakota Supreme Court—to encourage reorganization "by alleviating parental concerns regarding the cost of student transportation in the reorganized district"—he thought it plain that "free bus transportation is an important component of public education in a sparsely populated State" and that "after the voters in a school district have had a fair opportunity to decide whether or not to reorganize, there is no longer any justification at all for allowing the nonreorganized districts to place an obstacle in the path of poor children seeking an education in some parts of the State that has been removed in other parts...."

CHAPTER 11

DEFINING THE SCOPE OF "LIBERTY" AND "PROPERTY" PROTECTED BY THE DUE PROCESS CLAUSE—THE PROCEDURAL DUE PROCESS CASES

Introduction. In Chapter 8 we examined whether the due process clause was intended to provide more than a requirement of fair procedure. In Chapter 9 we examined at length the substantive interests that are protected under the due process clause. The purpose of this chapter is to return to the issue of procedure in order to pursue the general question whether the interests protected by a requirement of fair procedure are the same as those protected by commands of fairness in substance. No attempt is made in this chapter to present a complete picture of the constitutional requirements of fair procedure in criminal, civil, and administrative proceedings. Those requirements are discussed at length in separate courses.

Section 1 deals with whether there is, or ought to be, a difference in the interests protected by "substantive" and "procedural" due process. The question arises in two contexts. First, is every interest that is given substantive protection also accorded procedural protection? Does a determination that a particular interest is "liberty" or "property" that is substantively protected (in the sense that the state must establish some reason for imposing a burden on it) carry with it a correlative right to some kind of a hearing in which it can be determined whether the particular burden is justified? Second, does the requirement of fair procedure extend beyond those interests given substantive protection by the Constitution? When government extends protection to an interest it is not constitutionally required to recognize, is there a constitutionally imposed right to a hearing in which it can be determined that the particular burden on the interest is justified? For example, if a state provides for the payment of welfare to persons meeting certain criteria, may it also provide for the removal of individual recipients from the welfare rolls without some form of a hearing in which it can be determined whether the recipients meet the statutory criteria?

A second problem is what constitutes "deprivation" of a protectible liberty or property interest, and a third relates to the nature and timing of the hearing required. To some degree decisions determining whether a hearing is required have been influenced by the timing and formality of the hearing contemplated. No attempt is made here to pursue this issue systematically, though a summary discussion is presented at the end of the cases in Section 1.

Section 2 presents the "irrebuttable presumption" cases that deal with the analytically separate question of the extent to which the due process clause limits the legislative power to classify by imposing a requirement of individualized hearings.

SECTION 1.   WHEN DOES DUE PROCESS MANDATE CONSTITUTIONAL PROCEDURES?

A.   WHAT "PROPERTY" AND "LIBERTY" IS PROTECTED?

Board of Regents of State Colleges v. Roth

408 U.S. 564, 92 S.Ct. 2701, 33 L.Ed.2d 548 (1972).

Mr. Justice Stewart delivered the opinion of the Court.

In 1968 the respondent, David Roth, was hired for his first teaching job as assistant professor of political science at Wisconsin State University–Oshkosh. He was hired for a fixed term of one academic year. The notice of his faculty appointment specified that his employment would begin on September 1, 1968, and would end on June 30, 1969. The respondent completed that term. But he was informed that he would not be rehired for the next academic year.

The respondent had no tenure rights to continued employment. Under Wisconsin statutory law a state university teacher can acquire tenure as a "permanent" employee only after four years of year-to-year employment. Having acquired tenure, a teacher is entitled to continued employment "during efficiency and good behavior." A relatively new teacher without tenure, however, is under Wisconsin law entitled to nothing beyond his one-year appointment. There are no statutory or administrative standards defining eligibility for re-employment. State law thus clearly leaves the decision whether to rehire a nontenured teacher for another year to the unfettered discretion of University officials.

The procedural protection afforded a Wisconsin State University teacher before he is separated from the University corresponds to his job security. As a matter of statutory law, a tenured teacher cannot be "discharged except for cause upon written charges" and pursuant to certain procedures. A nontenured teacher, similarly, is protected to some extent *during* his one-year term. Rules promulgated by the Board of Regents provide that a nontenured teacher "dismissed" before the end of the year may have some opportunity for review of the "dismissal." But the Rules provide no real protection for a nontenured teacher who simply is not re-employed for the next year. He must be informed by February first "concerning retention or non-retention for the ensuing year." But "no reason for non-retention need be given. No review or appeal is provided in such case."

In conformance with these Rules, the President of Wisconsin State University–Oshkosh informed the respondent before February 1, 1969, that he would not be rehired for the 1969–1970 academic year. He gave the respondent no reason for the decision and no opportunity to challenge it at any sort of hearing.

The respondent then brought this action in a federal district court alleging that the decision not to rehire him for the next year infringed his Fourteenth Amendment rights. He attacked the decision both in substance and procedure. First, he alleged that the true reason for the decision was to punish him for certain statements critical of the University administration, and that it therefore violated his right to freedom of speech. Second, he alleged that the failure of University officials to give him notice of any reason for nonretention and an opportunity for a hearing violated his right to procedural due process of law.

The District Court granted summary judgment for the respondent on the procedural issue, ordering the University officials to provide him with reasons and a hearing. The Court of Appeals, with one judge dissenting, affirmed this partial summary judgment. We granted certiorari. The only question presented to us at this stage in the case is whether the respondent had a constitutional right to a statement of reasons and a hearing on the University's decision not to rehire him for another year. We hold that he did not.

I.

The requirements of procedural due process apply only to the deprivation of interests encompassed within the Fourteenth Amendment's protection of liberty and property. When protected interests are implicated the right to some kind of prior hearing is paramount. But the range of interests protected by procedural due process is not infinite.

. . .

"Liberty" and "property" are broad and majestic terms. They are among the "[g]reat [constitutional] concepts . . . purposely left to gather meaning from experience. . . . [T]hey relate to the whole domain of social and economic fact, and the statesmen who founded this Nation knew too well that only a stagnant society remains unchanged." National Ins. Co. v. Tidewater Co., 337 U.S. 582, 646 (Frankfurter, J., dissenting). For that reason the Court has fully and finally rejected the wooden distinction between "rights" and "privileges" that once seemed to govern the applicability of procedural due process rights. The Court has also made clear that the property interests protected by procedural due process extend well beyond actual ownership of real estate, chattels, or money. By the same token, the Court has required due process protection for deprivations of liberty beyond the sort of formal constraints imposed by the criminal process.

. . .

Yet, while the Court has eschewed rigid or formalistic limitations on the protection of procedural due process, it has at the same time observed certain boundaries. For the words "liberty" and "property" in the Due Process Clause of the Fourteenth Amendment must be given some meaning.

II.

. . .

There might be cases in which a State refused to re-employ a person under such circumstances that interests in liberty would be implicated. But this is not such a case.

The State, in declining to rehire the respondent, did not make any charge against him that might seriously damage his standing and associations in his community. It did not base the nonrenewal of his contract on a charge, for example, that he had been guilty of dishonesty, or immorality. Had it done so, this would be a different case. . . . In such a case, due process would accord an opportunity to refute the charge before University officials.[12] In the present

---

[12] The purpose of such notice and hearing is to provide the person an opportunity to clear his name. Once a person has cleared his name at a hearing, his employer, of course,

case, however, there is no suggestion whatever that the respondent's interest in his "good name, reputation, honor or integrity" is at stake.

Similarly, there is no suggestion that the State, in declining to reemploy the respondent, imposed on him a stigma or other disability that foreclosed his freedom to take advantage of other employment opportunities. The State, for example, did not invoke any regulations to bar the respondent from all other public employment in State universities. Had it done so, this, again, would be a different case. . . .

To be sure, the respondent has alleged that the non-renewal of his contract was based on his exercise of his right to freedom of speech. But this allegation is not now before us. The District Court stayed proceedings on this issue, and the respondent has yet to prove that the decision not to rehire him was, in fact, based on his free speech activities.[14]

Hence, on the record before us, all that clearly appears is that the respondent was not rehired for one year at one University. It stretches the concept too far to suggest that a person is deprived of "liberty" when he simply is not rehired in one job but remains as free as before to seek another. Cafeteria Workers v. McElroy, supra, at 895–896.

III.

The Fourteenth Amendment's procedural protection of property is a safeguard of the security of interests that a person has already acquired in specific benefits. These interests—property interests—may take many forms.

. . .

Certain attributes of "property" interests protected by procedural due process emerge from these decisions. To have a property interest in a benefit, a person clearly must have more than an abstract need or desire for it. He must have more than a unilateral expectation of it. He must, instead, have a legitimate claim of entitlement to it. It is a purpose of the ancient institution of property to protect those claims upon which people rely in their daily lives, reliance that must not be arbitrarily undermined. It is a purpose of the constitutional right to a hearing to provide an opportunity for a person to vindicate those claims.

Property interests, of course, are not created by the Constitution. Rather, they are created and their dimensions are defined by existing rules or understandings that stem from an independent source such as state law—rules or

---

may remain free to deny him future employment for other reasons.

14 . . .

When a State would directly impinge upon interests in free speech or free press, this Court has on occasion held that opportunity for a fair adversary hearing must precede the action, whether or not the speech or press interest is clearly protected under substantive First Amendment standards. Thus we have required fair notice and opportunity for an adversary hearing before an injunction is issued against the holding of rallies and public meetings. Carroll v. Princess Anne, 393 U.S. 175. Similarly, we have indicated the necessity of procedural safeguards before

a State makes a large-scale seizure of a person's allegedly obscene books, magazines and so forth. A Quantity of Books v. Kansas, 378 U.S. 205; Marcus v. Search Warrant, 367 U.S. 717. See Freedman v. Maryland, 380 U.S. 51; Bantam Books v. Sullivan, 372 U.S. 58. See generally Monaghan, First Amendment "Due Process," 83 Harv.L.Rev. 518.

In the respondent's case, however, the State has not directly impinged upon interests in free speech or free press in any way comparable to a seizure of books or an injunction against meetings. Whatever may be a teacher's rights of free speech, the interest in holding a teaching job at a state university, *simpliciter,* is not itself a free speech interest.

understandings that secure certain benefits and that support claims of entitlement to those benefits. Thus the welfare recipients in *Goldberg v. Kelly,* supra, had a claim of entitlement to welfare payments that was grounded in the statute defining eligibility for them. The recipients had not yet shown that they were, in fact, within the statutory terms of eligibility. But we held that they had a right to a hearing at which they might attempt to do so.

Just as the welfare recipients' "property" interest in welfare payments was created and defined by statutory terms, so the respondent's "property" interest in employment at the Wisconsin State University–Oshkosh was created and defined by the terms of his appointment. Those terms secured his interest in employment up to June 30, 1969. But the important fact in this case is that they specifically provided that the respondent's employment was to terminate on June 30. They did not provide for contract renewal absent "sufficient cause." Indeed, they made no provision for renewal whatsoever.

Thus the terms of the respondent's appointment secured absolutely no interest in re-employment for the next year. They supported absolutely no possible claim of entitlement to re-employment. Nor, significantly, was there any state statute or University rule or policy that secured his interest in re-employment or that created any legitimate claim to it.[16] In these circumstances, the respondent surely had an abstract concern in being rehired, but he did not have a *property* interest sufficient to require the University authorities to give him a hearing when they declined to renew his contract of employment.

IV.

. . .

. . . [T]he respondent has not shown that he was deprived of liberty or property protected by the Fourteenth Amendment. The judgment of the Court of Appeals, accordingly, is reversed and the case is remanded for further proceedings consistent with this opinion.

It is so ordered.

Mr. Justice Marshall, dissenting.

. . .

In my view, every citizen who applies for a government job is entitled to it unless the government can establish some reason for denying the employment. This is the "property" right that I believe is protected by the Fourteenth Amendment and that cannot be denied "without due process of law." And it is also liberty—liberty to work—which is the "very essence of the personal freedom and opportunity" secured by the Fourteenth Amendment.

. . .

It may be argued that to provide procedural due process to all public employees or prospective employees would place an intolerable burden on the machinery of government. Cf. Goldberg v. Kelly, supra. The short answer to that argument is that it is not burdensome to give reasons when reasons exist. Whenever an application for employment is denied, an employee is discharged,

---

[16] To be sure, the respondent does suggest that most teachers hired on a year-to-year basis by the Wisconsin State University–Oshkosh are, in fact, rehired. But the District Court has not found that there is anything approaching a "common law" of re-employment, see Perry v. Sindermann, post, at 602, so strong as to require University officials to give the respondent a statement of reasons and a hearing on their decision not to rehire him.

or a decision not to rehire an employee is made, there should be some reason for the decision. It can scarcely be argued that government would be crippled by a requirement that the reason be communicated to the person most directly affected by the government's action.

Where there are numerous applicants for jobs, it is likely that few will choose to demand reasons for not being hired. But, if the demand for reasons is exceptionally great, summary procedures can be devised that would provide fair and adequate information to all persons. As long as the government has a good reason for its actions it need not fear disclosure. It is only where the government acts improperly that procedural due process is truly burdensome. And that is precisely when it is most necessary. . . . [a]

LAW THAT DEFINES SUBSTANTIVE ENTITLEMENTS TOGETHER WITH PROCEDURAL QUALIFICATIONS

Not long after *Roth* and *Sindermann*, the Court divided over the proper treatment of statutes that simultaneously appeared to create legitimate expectations of continued employment absent some kind of cause for dismissal and limited procedures for determining the existence of such cause. Should the entitlement provisions be thought to stand alone as creating a "property" interest whose deprivation required procedural protections mandated by the Due Process clauses? Or should the procedural qualification provisions be understood to define a more circumscribed "property" interest whose deprivation only required compliance with the requirements of the entitlement granting law?

In Arnett v. Kennedy, 416 U.S. 134 (1974), six Justices writing in separate concurring and dissenting opinions, seemed to take the former approach. In Bishop v. Wood, 426 U.S. 341 (1976), four of those dissented from a majority's decision that a discharged policeman was not deprived "of a property interest protected by the Fourteenth Amendment." Justice Stevens' majority opinion concluded that a "tenable" interpretation of state law by the lower federal courts was that the local ordinance, which provided that a permanent employee could be discharged for failing to perform work up to the standard of his classification, or for negligence, inefficiency or unfitness, might "be construed as granting no right to continued employment but merely conditioning an employee's removal on compliance with certain specified procedures" and thus

---

[a] Dissenting opinions by Justice Douglas and Brennan are omitted. Justice Powell took no part in the decision.

In Perry v. Sindermann, 408 U.S. 593 (1972) a teacher's employment was terminated without notice of reasons or hearing after being employed by the college for four successive years under a series of one-year contracts. In his suit he alleged that the decision not to rehire him was based on his public criticism of policies of the college administration and thus infringed his right to free speech and that the failure to give him notice and hearing violated procedural due process. The trial court granted summary judgment for the defendant college on the basis of affidavits denying that plaintiff's criticism was involved and asserting no need to provide a hearing. The Court held that this decision was in error for two reasons: (1)

Plaintiff was entitled to a full hearing on his free speech claim because "a teacher's public criticism of his superiors on matters of public concern may be constitutionally protected and may, therefore, be an impermissible basis for termination of his employment." (2) Plaintiff was also entitled to a hearing on his allegation that he had in fact some form of tenure under the practices of the college. There "may be an unwritten 'common law' in a particular university that certain employees shall have the equivalent of tenure." Plaintiff was entitled to show whether that existed in this case and, if it did, he would be entitled to an order obligating college officials to give him a hearing.

See Simon, *Liberty and Property in the Supreme Court: A Defense of Roth and Perry*, 71 Calif.L.Rev. 146 (1983).

"that petitioner 'held his position at the will and pleasure of the city.'" On that construction *Arnett* was irrelevant, the Court said, for there "the Court concluded that because the employee could only be discharged for cause, he had a property interest . . . entitled to constitutional protection."

Justice White's dissent, joined by Justices Brennan, Marshall and Blackmun, thought *Arnett* indistinguishable, for he understood the ordinance to contain "unequivocal language . . . that [petitioner] may be dismissed only for certain kinds of cause[,]" so that the majority's holding "rests . . . on the fact that state law provides no *procedures* for assuring that the City Manager dismiss him only for cause. The right to his job apparently given by the first two sentences of the ordinance is thus redefined, according to the majority, by the procedures provided for in the third sentence and as redefined is infringed only if the procedures are not followed." In a footnote, Justice White said that he did "not disagree with the majority or the courts below on the meaning of the state law"—that "as a matter of state law petitioner has no remedy no matter how arbitrarily or erroneously the City Manager has acted." Rather, "I differ . . . only with respect to the constitutional significance of an unambiguous state law. A majority of the Justices in Arnett v. Kennedy . . . stood on the proposition that the Constitution required procedures *not* required by state law when the state conditions dismissal on 'cause.'"

Nearly a decade later, the Court addressed this problem more definitively in the following case.

CLEVELAND BOARD OF EDUCATION v. LOUDERMILL, 470 U.S. 532 (1985). An Ohio statute provided that classified civil service employees were entitled to retain their positions "during good behavior and efficient service" and could not be dismissed except for "misfeasance, malfeasance, or nonfeasance in office." It also required that an employee dismissed for cause be provided with an order of removal giving the reasons therefor and allowed an appeal to a state administrative board whose judgment could be reviewed in the state trial court.

A state security guard stated on his job application that he had never been convicted of a felony. Several months after he was hired the Board of Education discovered that he had been convicted of grand larceny, discharged him, and gave him a letter stating this reason. He appealed to the Civil Service Commission, which upheld his dismissal. He then filed this case in the federal district court, arguing that the state statute was unconstitutional on its face because it did not give him a chance to respond to charges before dismissal. A bus mechanic fired by the Parma Board of Education after failing an eye examination filed a similar suit after the Civil Service Commission ordered his reinstatement but without back pay. The district court rejected both claims, but the court of appeals reversed and the Supreme Court affirmed.

Justice White's opinion for the Court said:

". . . The statute plainly supports the conclusion, reached by both lower courts, that respondents possessed property rights in continued employment. . . .

"The Parma Board argues, however, that the property right is defined by, and conditioned on, the legislature's choice of procedures for its deprivation. . . . The procedures were adhered to in these cases. According to petitioner, '[t]o require additional procedures would in effect expand the scope of the property interest itself'. . . .

"This argument . . . has its genesis in the plurality opinion in *Arnett v. Kennedy*. . . . *Arnett* involved a challenge by a former federal employee to the procedures by which he was dismissed. The plurality reasoned that where the legislation conferring the substantive right also sets out the procedural mechanism for enforcing that right, the two cannot be separated:

'The employee's statutorily defined right is not a guarantee against removal without cause in the abstract, but such a guarantee as enforced by the procedures which Congress has designated for the determination of cause.

. . .

'. . . [W]here the grant of a substantive right is inextricably intertwined with the limitations on the procedures which are to be employed in determining that right, a litigant in the position of appellee must take the bitter with the sweet.' . . .

After pointing out that six Justices in *Arnett* had specifically rejected this view and discussing subsequent cases, Justice White wrote:

"In light of these holdings, it is settled that the 'bitter with the sweet' approach misconceives the constitutional guarantee. If a clearer holding is needed, we provide it today. The point is straightforward: the Due Process Clause provides that certain substantive rights—life, liberty, and property— cannot be deprived except pursuant to constitutionally adequate procedures. The categories of substance and procedure are distinct. Were the rule otherwise, the Clause would be reduced to a mere tautology. 'Property' cannot be defined by the procedures provided for its deprivation any more than can life or liberty. The right to due process 'is conferred, not be legislative grace, but by constitutional guarantee. While the legislature may elect not to confer a property interest in [public] employment, it may not constitutionally authorize the deprivation of such an interest, once conferred, without appropriate procedural safeguards.' Arnett v. Kennedy, supra, 416 U.S., at 167 (Powell, J., concurring in part and concurring in result in part); see id., at 185 (White, J., concurring in part and dissenting in part).

"In short, once it is determined that the Due Process Clause applies, 'the question remains what process is due.' Morrissey v. Brewer, 408 U.S. 471, 481 (1972). The answer to that question is not to be found in the Ohio statute."

The Court then held that an employee must have some kind of hearing before discharge when he has a constitutionally protected property interest in his employment. But when a full administrative hearing and judicial review is available after termination, the employee does not have a right to a full adversarial evidentiary hearing before discharge. "The tenured public employee is entitled to oral or written notice of the charges against him, an explanation of the employer's evidence, and an opportunity to present his side of the story. . . . To require more than this prior to termination would intrude to an unwarranted extent on the government's interest in quickly removing an unsatisfactory employee."

Justice Marshall argued that the employee should receive a full adversarial evidentiary pre-termination hearing.

Justice Rehnquist dissented alone on the issue raised in *Arnett:*

"We ought to recognize the totality of the State's definition of the property right in question, and not merely seize upon one of several paragraphs in a unitary statute to proclaim that in that paragraph the State has inexorably conferred upon a civil service employee something which it is powerless under the United States Constitution to qualify in the next paragraph of the statute. This practice ignores our duty under *Roth* to rely on state law as the source of property interests for purposes of applying the Due Process

Clause of the Fourteenth Amendment. While it does not impose a federal definition of property, the Court departs from the full breadth of the holding in *Roth* by its selective choice from among the sentences the Ohio legislature chooses to use in establishing and qualifying a right."

THE INTERRELATIONSHIPS OF SUBSTANTIVE AND PROCEDURAL DUE PROCESS

What is the relationship between the constitutional requirements of "fair substance" and "fair procedure"? In theory, the procedural requirement is conceptually distinct from any constitutional limit on the substance of government policy.

Hearings reinforce the rule of law by insuring official regularity and minimizing the scope for arbitrary decision-making. The procedural requirement may also serve, however, as a means for forcing the state to take more seriously than it might otherwise the substantive issues at stake. In Fuentes v. Shevin, 407 U.S. 67 (1972), the Court held invalid a state law which permitted summary seizure of property under a writ of replevin without prior notice or hearing to the possessor of the property. As part of its justification for requiring a prior hearing the Court said:

"The constitutional right to be heard is a basic aspect of the duty of government to follow a fair process of decisionmaking when it acts to deprive a person of his possessions. The purpose of this requirement is not only to ensure abstract fair play to the individual. Its purpose, more particularly, is to protect his use and possession of property from arbitrary encroachment—to minimize substantively unfair or mistaken deprivations of property, a danger that is especially great when the State seizes goods simply upon the application of and for the benefit of a private party. So viewed, the prohibition against the deprivation of property without due process of law reflects the high value, embedded in our constitutional and political history, that we place on a person's right to enjoy what is his, free of governmental interference. See Lynch v. Household Finance Corp., 405 U.S. 538.

"The requirement of notice and an opportunity to be heard raises no impenetrable barrier to the taking of a person's possessions. But the fair process of decisionmaking that it guarantees works, by itself, to protect against arbitrary deprivation of property. For when a person has an opportunity to speak up in his own defense, and when the State must listen to what he has to say, substantively unfair and simply mistaken deprivations of property interests can be prevented."

The problem of distinguishing substance and procedure is most complex where the state provides benefits it is not constitutionally compelled to provide. What are the procedural requirements, if any, when the state discharges an employee or terminates welfare benefits? Three situations must be distinguished:

(1) The state in creating the benefit also creates standards to govern its termination. For example, a state provides that certain government employees can be discharged only for "good cause". Even though the government is not obligated to provide the job, is it required by procedural due process to provide a fair hearing in applying its own standards to take a job away?

(2) The state in creating the benefit provides that it may be taken away at will. For example, a state provides that particular government employees may be fired in their superiors' discretion. The question now is

whether the state may terminate a job in the unconstrained discretion of an administrative official. Is that question one of substantive due process? Or of procedural due process? If it is decided that the state can use standardless discretion to terminate the benefit, can there be any requirement of fair procedure? Or is the necessity for a hearing obviated in these situations because, as Justice Stevens observed in Codd v. Velger, 429 U.S. 624 (1977), "a hearing would [be] pointless because nothing plaintiff [can] prove [will] entitle him to keep his job"?

(3) The state creates the benefit, establishes standards to govern its termination, and provides the procedures to be used in determining whether the standards for termination have been met. If those procedures do not meet the minimum standards of fairness required by due process, will they be held invalid? *Loudermill* says yes. Can that be reconciled with the view that the state may avoid any hearing requirement when it authorizes standardless discretion for termination of employment?

Michael H. v. Gerald D.

491 U.S. 110, 109 S.Ct. 2333, 105 L.Ed.2d 91 (1989).

[The report in this case appears, supra at p. 591.]

Sandin v. Conner

___ U.S. ___, 115 S.Ct. 2293, 132 L.Ed.2d 418 (1995).

Chief Justice Rehnquist delivered the opinion of the Court.

We granted certiorari to reexamine the circumstances under which state prison regulations afford inmates a liberty interest protected by the Due Process Clause.

I

[While serving an indeterminate sentence of 30 years to life in a Hawaii prison, Conner reacted angrily to a strip-search and was charged with "high misconduct" for physical interference with a correctional function and "low moderate misconduct" for using abusive or obscene language and for harassing employees. An adjustment committee held a hearing at which Conner appeared but was not allowed to present witnesses. The committee found him guilty and sentenced him, inter alia, to 30 days disciplinary segregation for the physical obstruction charge. On appeal, months after serving this punishment, the deputy administrator found unsupported, and so expunged, the high misconduct charge. In the interim, Conner had sued in federal court, claiming that the refusal to allow him to present witnesses deprived him of procedural due process.] The District Court granted summary judgment in favor of the prison officials.

The Court of Appeals ... reversed.... It concluded that Conner had a liberty interest in remaining free from disciplinary segregation ... based ... on a prison regulation that instructs the committee to find guilt when a charge of misconduct is supported by substantial evidence.... [It] reasoned from Kentucky Department of Corrections v. Thompson, 490 U.S. 454 (1989), that the committee's duty to find guilt was nondiscretionary. From the language of the regulation, it drew a negative inference that the committee may not impose segregation if it does not find substantial evidence of misconduct.... It viewed this as a state-created liberty interest.... We ... reverse.

II

Our due process analysis begins with Wolff [v. McDonnell, 418 U.S. 539 (1974), where] Nebraska inmates challenged the decision of prison officials to revoke good time credits without adequate procedures.... Inmates earned good time credits under a state statute that bestowed mandatory sentence reductions for good behavior, ... revocable only for "flagrant or serious misconduct[.]" ... We held that the Due Process Clause itself does not create a liberty interest in credit for good behavior, but that the statutory provision created a liberty interest in a "shortened prison sentence" which resulted from good time credits, credits which were revocable only if the prisoner was guilty of serious misconduct.... The Court characterized this liberty interest as one of "real substance"....

Inmates in Meachum [v. Fano, 427 U.S. 215 (1976), challenged] transfers from a Massachusetts medium security prison to a maximum security facility with substantially less favorable conditions.... The Court began with the proposition that the Due Process Clause does not protect every change in the conditions of confinement having a substantial adverse impact on the prisoner. It then held that the Due Process Clause did not itself create a liberty interest in prisoners to be free from intrastate prison transfers.... It reasoned that transfer to a maximum security facility, albeit one with more burdensome conditions, was "within the normal limits or range of custody which the conviction has authorized the State to impose." ... The Court distinguished *Wolff* by noting that there the protected liberty interest in good time credit had been created by state law; here no comparable Massachusetts law stripped officials of the discretion to transfer prisoners to alternate facilities "for whatever reason or for no reason at all." ...

Shortly after *Meachum*, the Court embarked on a different approach to defining state-created liberty interests. Because dictum in *Meachum* distinguished *Wolff* by focusing on whether state action was mandatory or discretionary, the Court in later cases laid ever greater emphasis on this somewhat mechanical dichotomy....

[In Hewitt v. Helms, 459 U.S. 460 (1983), the Court] evaluat[ed] the claims of inmates who had been confined to administrative segregation[. I]t first rejected the inmates' claim of a right to remain in the general population.... The Due Process Clause standing alone confers no liberty interest in freedom from state action taken "'within the sentence imposed[.]'" It then concluded that the transfer to less amenable quarters for nonpunitive reasons was "ordinarily contemplated by a prison sentence." ... Examination of the possibility that the State had created a liberty interest by virtue of its prison regulations followed. Instead of looking to whether the State created an interest of "real substance" comparable to the good time credit scheme of *Wolff*, the Court asked whether the State had gone beyond issuing mere procedural guidelines and had used "language of an unmistakably mandatory character" such that the incursion on liberty would not occur "absent specified substantive predicates." ... Finding such mandatory directives in the regulations before it, the Court decided that the State had created a protected liberty interest....

As this methodology took hold, no longer did inmates need to rely on a showing that they had suffered a "'grievous loss'" of liberty retained even after sentenced to terms of imprisonment. Morrissey v. Brewer, 408 U.S. 471, 481

(1972).... For the Court had ceased to examine the "nature" of the interest with respect to interests allegedly created by the State.... In a series of cases since *Hewitt*, the Court has wrestled with the language of intricate, often rather routine prison guidelines to determine whether mandatory language and substantive predicates created an enforceable expectation that the state would produce a particular outcome with respect to the prisoner's conditions of confinement.

. . .

By shifting the focus of the liberty interest inquiry to one based on the language of a particular regulation, and not the nature of the deprivation, the Court encouraged prisoners to comb regulations in search of mandatory language on which to base entitlements to various state-conferred privileges. Courts have, in response, and not altogether illogically, drawn negative inferences from mandatory language in the text of prison regulations. The Court of Appeals' approach in this case is typical: it inferred from the mandatory directive that a finding of guilt "shall" be imposed under certain conditions the conclusion that the absence of such conditions prevents a finding of guilt.

Such a conclusion may be entirely sensible in the ordinary task of construing a statute defining rights and remedies available to the general public. It is a good deal less sensible in the case of a prison regulation primarily designed to guide correctional officials in the administration of a prison....

Hewitt has produced at least two undesirable effects. First, it creates disincentives for States to codify prison management procedures in the interest of uniform treatment.... States may avoid creation of "liberty" interests by having scarcely any regulations, or by conferring standardless discretion on correctional personnel.

Second, the *Hewitt* approach has led to the involvement of federal courts in the day-to-day management of prisons, often squandering judicial resources with little offsetting benefit to anyone....

[W]e believe that the search for a negative implication from mandatory language in prisoner regulations has strayed from the real concerns undergirding the liberty protected by the Due Process Clause. The time has come to return to the due process principles ... in *Wolff* and *Meachum*. Following *Wolff*, we recognize that States may under certain circumstances create liberty interests which are protected by the Due Process Clause. ...But these interests will be generally limited to freedom from restraint which, while not exceeding the sentence in such an unexpected manner as to give rise to protection by the Due Process Clause of its own force, see, e.g., Vitek, 445 U. S., at 493 (transfer to mental hospital), and Washington, 494 U. S., at 221–222 (involuntary administration of psychotropic drugs), nonetheless imposes atypical and significant hardship on the inmate in relation to the ordinary incidents of prison life.

Conner asserts, incorrectly, that any state action taken for a punitive reason encroaches upon a liberty interest under the Due Process Clause even in the absence of any state regulation. Neither Bell v. Wolfish, 441 U.S. 520 (1979), nor Ingraham v. Wright, 430 U.S. 651 (1977), requires such a rule. *Bell* dealt with the interests of pretrial detainees and not convicted prisoners....

... *Ingraham* ... addressed the rights of schoolchildren to remain free from arbitrary corporal punishment. The Court noted that the Due Process Clause historically encompassed the notion that the state could not "physically punish an individual except in accordance with due process of law" and so found schoolchildren sheltered....

The punishment of incarcerated prisoners, on the other hand, serves different aims than those found invalid in *Bell* and *Ingraham*. The process does not impose retribution in lieu of a valid conviction, nor does it maintain physical control over free citizens forced by law to subject themselves to state control over the educational mission. It effectuates prison management and prisoner rehabilitative goals.... Admittedly, prisoners do not shed all constitutional rights at the prison gate, ... but "'[l]awful incarceration brings about the necessary withdrawal or limitation of many privileges and rights, a retraction justified by the considerations underlying our penal system.'" ... Discipline by prison officials in response to a wide range of misconduct falls within the expected parameters of the sentence imposed by a court of law.

This case, though concededly punitive, does not present a dramatic departure from the basic conditions of Conner's indeterminate sentence. Although Conner points to dicta in cases implying that solitary confinement automatically triggers due process protection, ... this Court has not had the opportunity to address in an argued case the question whether disciplinary confinement of inmates itself implicates constitutional liberty interests. We hold that Conner's discipline in segregated confinement did not present the type of atypical, significant deprivation in which a state might conceivably create a liberty interest. The record shows that ... disciplinary segregation ... mirrored those conditions imposed upon inmates in administrative segregation and protective custody. We note also that the State expunged Conner's disciplinary record with respect to the "high misconduct" charge 9 months after Conner served time in segregation. Thus, Conner's confinement did not exceed similar, but totally discretionary confinement in either duration or degree of restriction.... Based on a comparison between inmates inside and outside disciplinary segregation, the State's actions in placing him there for 30 days did not work a major disruption in his environment.

Nor does Conner's situation present a case where the State's action will inevitably affect the duration of his sentence....

We hold, therefore, that neither the Hawaii prison regulation in question, nor the Due Process Clause itself, afforded Conner a protected liberty interest that would entitle him to the procedural protections set forth in *Wolff*. The regime to which he was subjected as a result of the misconduct hearing was within the range of confinement to be normally expected for one serving an indeterminate term of 30 years to life.

The judgment of the Court of Appeals is accordingly

Reversed.

Justice Ginsburg, with whom Justice Stevens joins, dissenting.

. . .

Unlike the Court, I conclude that Conner had a liberty interest, protected by the Fourteenth Amendment's Due Process Clause, in avoiding the disciplinary confinement he endured. As Justice Breyer details, Conner's prison punishment effected a severe alteration in the conditions of his incarceration. Disciplinary confinement as punishment for "high misconduct" not only deprives prisoners of privileges for protracted periods; unlike administrative segregation and protective custody, disciplinary confinement also stigmatizes them and diminishes parole prospects. Those immediate and lingering consequences should suffice to qualify such confinement as liberty-depriving for purposes of Due Process Clause protection.... [1]

---

[1] ... The Court notes ... that the State eventually expunged Conner's disciplinary record as a result of his successful administrative appeal. But hindsight cannot tell us

I see the Due Process Clause itself, not Hawaii's prison code, as the wellspring of the protection due Conner. Deriving protected liberty interests from mandatory language in local prison codes would make of the fundamental right something more in certain States, something less in others.... [2]

Deriving the prisoner's due process right from the code for his prison, moreover, yields this practical anomaly: a State that scarcely attempts to control the behavior of its prison guards may, for that very laxity, escape constitutional accountability; a State that tightly cabins the discretion of its prison workers may, for that attentiveness, become vulnerable to constitutional claims. An incentive for ruleless prison management disserves the State's penological goals and jeopardizes the welfare of prisoners.

. . .

Justice Breyer, with whom Justice Souter joins, dissenting.

. . . The majority, asking whether [Conner's] punishment "imposes atypical and significant hardship on the inmate in relation to the ordinary incidents of prison life" concludes that it does not do so. The majority's reasoning, however, particularly when read in light of this Court's precedents, seems to me to lead to the opposite conclusion. And, for that reason, I dissent.

. . .

II

. . . In determining whether state officials have deprived an inmate . . . of a procedurally protected "liberty," this Court traditionally has looked either (1) to the nature of the deprivation (how severe, in degree or kind) or (2) to the State's rules governing the imposition of that deprivation (whether they, in effect, give the inmate a "right" to avoid it). See, e.g., Kentucky Department of Corrections v. Thompson, 490 U.S. 454, 460–461, 464–465 (1989). Thus, this Court has said that certain changes in conditions may be so severe or so different from ordinary conditions of confinement that, whether or not state law gives state authorities broad discretionary power to impose them, the state authorities may not do so "without complying with minimum requirements of due process." Vitek v. Jones, 445 U.S. 480, 491–494 (1980) ("involuntary commitment to a mental hospital"); Washington v. Harper, 494 U.S. 210, 221–222 (1990) ("unwanted administration of antipsychotic drugs"). The Court has also said that deprivations that are less severe or more closely related to the original terms of confinement nonetheless will amount to deprivations of procedurally protected liberty, provided that state law (including prison regulations) narrowly cabins the legal power of authorities to impose the deprivation (thereby giving the inmate a kind of right to avoid it). See Hewitt v. Helms. . . .

If we apply these general pre-existing principles to the relevant facts before us, it seems fairly clear . . . that the prison punishment . . . deprived Conner of

whether a liberty interest existed at the outset. One must . . . know at the start the character of the interest at stake in order to determine then what process, if any, is constitutionally due. . . .

[2] The Court describes a category of liberty interest that is something less than the one the Due Process Clause itself shields, something more than anything a prison code provides. The State may create a liberty interest, the Court tells us, when "atypical and significant hardship [would be borne by] the inmate in relation to the ordinary incidents of prison life." What design lies beneath these key words? The Court ventures no examples, leaving consumers of the Court's work at sea, unable to fathom what would constitute an "atypical, significant deprivation" and yet not trigger protection under the Due Process Clause directly.

constitutionally protected "liberty." For one thing, the punishment worked a fairly major change in Conner's conditions. . . .

Moreover, irrespective of whether this punishment amounts to a deprivation of liberty independent of state law, here the prison's own disciplinary rules severely cabin the authority of prison officials to impose this kind of punishment. They . . . (1) impose a punishment that is substantial, (2) restrict its imposition as a punishment to instances in which an inmate has committed a defined offense, and (3) prescribe nondiscretionary standards for determining whether or not an inmate committed that offense.

Accordingly, under this Court's liberty-defining standards, imposing the punishment would "deprive" Conner of "liberty" within the meaning of the Due Process Clause. . . .

III

The majority . . . seeks to change, or to clarify, [those] "liberty" defining standards in one important respect[: by] . . . impos[ing] a minimum standard, namely that a deprivation falls within the Fourteenth Amendment's definition of "liberty" only if it "imposes atypical and significant hardship on the inmate in relation to the ordinary incidents of prison life."

I am not certain whether or not the Court means this standard to change prior law radically. . . . There is no need, however, for . . . significant change . . . to read the Constitution's Due Process Clause to protect inmates against deprivations of freedom that are important, not comparatively insignificant. Rather, . . . this concern simply requires elaborating, and explaining, the Court's present standards (without radical revision) [so as] not [to] create procedurally protected "liberty" interests where only minor matters are at stake.

Three sets of considerations, taken together, support my conclusion. . . . First, although this Court . . . continues to say, that some deprivations of an inmate's freedom are so severe in kind or degree (or so far removed from the original terms of confinement) that they amount to deprivations of liberty, irrespective of whether state law (or prison rules) "cabin discretion," . . . it is not easy to specify just when, or how much of, a loss triggers this protection. There is a broad middle category of imposed restraints or deprivations that, considered by themselves, are neither obviously so serious as to fall within, nor obviously so insignificant as to fall without, the Clause's protection.

Second, the difficult line-drawing task that this middle category implies helps to explain why this Court developed its additional liberty-defining standard, which looks to local law (examining whether that local law creates a "liberty" by significantly limiting the discretion of local authorities to impose a restraint). . . . Despite its similarity to the way in which the Court determines the existence, or nonexistence, of "property" for Due Process Clause purposes, the justification for looking at local law is not the same in the prisoner liberty context. In protecting property, the Due Process Clause often aims to protect reliance, say, reliance upon an "entitlement" that local (i.e., nonconstitutional) law itself has created or helped to define. . . . In protecting liberty, however, the Due Process Clause protects . . . an absence of government restraint, the very absence of restraint that we call freedom. . . .

Nevertheless, there are several other important reasons, in the prison context, to consider the provisions of state law. The fact that a further deprivation of an inmate's freedom takes place under local rules that cabin the authorities' discretionary power to impose the restraint suggests, other things being equal, that the matter is more likely to have played an important role in the life of the inmate. . . . It suggests, other things being equal, that the matter is more likely of a kind to which procedural protections historically have applied, and where they normally prove useful, for such rules often single out an inmate and condition a deprivation upon the existence, or nonexistence, of particular facts. . . . It suggests, other things being equal, that the matter will not involve highly judgmental administrative matters that call for the wise exercise of discretion—matters where courts reasonably should hesitate to second-guess prison administrators. . . . It suggests, other things being equal, that the inmate will have thought that he himself, through control of his own behavior, could have avoided the deprivation, and thereby have believed that (in the absence of his misbehavior) the restraint fell outside the "sentence imposed" upon him. . . . Finally, courts can identify the presence or absence of cabined discretion fairly easily and objectively, at least much of the time. . . . These characteristics of "cabined discretion" mean that courts can use it as a kind of touchstone that can help them, when they consider the broad middle category of prisoner restraints, to separate those kinds of restraints that, in general, are more likely to call for constitutionally guaranteed procedural protection, from those that more likely do not. . . . I believe courts will continue to find this touchstone helpful as they seek to apply the majority's middle category standard.

Third, there is, therefore, no need to apply the "discretion-cabining" approach—the basic purpose of which is to provide a somewhat more objective method for identifying deprivations of protected "liberty" within a broad middle-range of prisoner restraints—where a deprivation is unimportant enough (or so similar in nature to ordinary imprisonment) that it rather clearly falls outside that middle category. Prison, by design, restricts the inmates' freedom. And, one cannot properly view unimportant matters that happen to be the subject of prison regulations as substantially aggravating a loss that has already occurred. Indeed, a regulation about a minor matter . . . may amount simply to an instruction to the administrator about how to do his job, rather than a guarantee to the inmate of a "right" to the status quo. . . . Thus, this Court has never held that comparatively unimportant prisoner "deprivations" fall within the scope of the Due Process Clause even if local law limits the authority of prison administrators to impose such minor deprivations. . . . And . . . it should now simply specify that they do not.

I recognize that, as a consequence, courts must separate the unimportant from the potentially significant, without the help of the more objective "discretion-cabining" test. Yet, making that judicial judgment seems no more difficult than many other judicial tasks. . . . It seems to me possible to separate less significant matters such as television privileges . . . from more significant matters, such as the solitary confinement at issue here. Indeed, prison regulations themselves may help in this respect, such as the regulations here which separate (from more serious matters) "low moderate" and "minor" misconduct. . . .

[T]he problems that the majority identifies suggest . . . mak[ing] explicit the lower definitional limit, in the prison context, of "liberty" under the Due Process Clause—a limit . . . already implicit in this Court's precedent. . . . Th[ey] do not require abandoning that precedent. . . .

IV

The Court today reaffirms that the "liberty" protected by the Fourteenth Amendment includes interests that state law may create. It excludes relatively minor matters from that protection.... And, it does not question the vast body of case law ... recognizing that segregation can deprive an inmate of constitutionally-protected "liberty." ... That being so, it is difficult to see why the Court reverses, rather than affirms, the Court of Appeals in this case.

. . .

I agree [that the] conditions in administrative and disciplinary segregation are relatively similar in Hawaii [and that] the rules governing administrative segregation do, indeed, provide prison officials with broad leeway. But, I disagree with the majority's assertion about the relevance of the expungement. How can a later decision of prison authorities transform Conner's segregation for a violation of a specific disciplinary rule into a term of segregation under the administrative rules? How can a later expungement restore to Conner the liberty that, in fact, he had already lost? ...

In sum, expungement or no, Conner suffered a deprivation that was significant, not insignificant. And, that deprivation took place under disciplinary rules that ... do cabin official discretion sufficiently. I would therefore hold that Conner was deprived of "liberty" within the meaning of the Due Process Clause.

V

Other related legal principles ... should further alleviate the majority's fear that application of the Due Process Clause to significant prison disciplinary action ... will lead federal courts to intervene improperly.... [T]he "process" that is "due" in the context of prison discipline is not the full blown procedure that accompanies criminal trials [but is] flexible [and] must take account of the legitimate needs of prison administration....

More importantly for present purposes, ... the Due Process Clause does not require process unless, in the individual case, there is a relevant factual dispute between the parties. ...[It] does not entitle an inmate to additional disciplinary hearing procedure (such as the calling of a witness) unless there is a factual dispute (relevant to guilt) that the additional procedure might help to resolve....

... [T]he record before us indicates that ... if we were to affirm, it would pose an important obstacle to Conner's eventual success. The ... adjustment committee's report ... says that its finding of guilt rests upon Conner's own admissions. ...[and] contains no explanation ... of how the witnesses he wanted to call ... could have led to any evidence relevant to the facts at issue.

. . .

WASHINGTON v. HARPER, 494 U.S. 210 (1990). A mentally ill but not incompetent prisoner challenged, *inter alia,* the state's failure to provide him with a judicial hearing before administering antipsychotic medication against his will. The Washington Supreme Court held that due process required this and other procedural safeguards. It also held that the substance of the state's policy violated due process, because it allowed forced medication of any inmate found to be mentally ill and "gravely disabled" or dangerous to himself, others or their property, without also requiring proof that the state has a compelling interest in administering the medication and that the administration of the drugs is necessary and effective to further that interest. The Supreme Court overturned both holdings. Justice Kennedy's majority opinion said, in part:

"The Washington Supreme Court's decision ... has both substantive and procedural aspects. It is axiomatic that procedural protections must be examined in terms of the substantive rights at stake. But identifying the contours of the substantive right remains a task distinct from deciding what procedural protections are necessary to protect that right. '[T]he substantive issue involves a definition of th[e] protected constitutional interest, as well as identification of the conditions under which competing state interests might outweigh it. The procedural issue concerns the minimum procedures required by the Constitution for determining that the individual's liberty interest actually is outweighed in a particular instance.' . . .

"Restated in the terms of this case, the substantive issue is what factual circumstances must exist before the State may administer antipsychotic drugs to the prisoner against his will; the procedural issue is whether the State's nonjudicial mechanisms used to determine the facts in a particular case are sufficient. . . .

"As a matter of state law, the Policy itself undoubtedly confers . . . a right to be free from the arbitrary administration of antipsychotic drugs. . . . By permitting a psychiatrist to treat an inmate with antipsychotic drugs against his wishes only if he is found to be (1) mentally ill and (2) gravely disabled or dangerous, the Policy creates a justifiable expectation on the part of the inmate that the drugs will not be administered unless those conditions exist. . . .

"We have no doubt that, in addition to the liberty interest created by the State's Policy, respondent possesses a significant liberty interest in avoiding the unwanted administration of antipsychotic drugs under the Due Process Clause of the Fourteenth Amendment. . . . Upon full consideration of the administrative scheme, however, we find that the Due Process Clause confers upon respondent no greater right than that recognized under state law.

"Respondent contends that the State, under the mandate of the Due Process Clause, may not override his choice to refuse antipsychotic drugs unless he has been found to be incompetent, and then only if the factfinder makes a substituted judgment that he, if competent, would consent to drug treatment. We disagree. The extent of a prisoner's right . . . must be defined in the context of the inmate's confinement. The Policy . . . requires the State to establish, by a medical finding, that a mental disorder exists which is likely to cause harm if not treated. Moreover, the fact that the medication must first be prescribed by a psychiatrist, and then approved by a reviewing psychiatrist, ensures that the treatment in question will be ordered only if it is in the prisoner's medical interests, given the legitimate needs of his institutional confinement. These standards, which recognize both the prisoner's medical interests and the State's interests, meet the demands of the Due Process Clause.

". . . [T]he proper standard for determining the validity of a prison regulation claimed to infringe on an inmate's constitutional rights is to ask whether the regulation is 'reasonably related to legitimate penological interests.' . . . This is true even when the constitutional right claimed to have been infringed is fundamental, and the State under other circumstances would have been required to satisfy a more rigorous standard of review. . . . The [Washington Supreme Court] erred in refusing to apply the standard of reasonableness."

Applying the reasonableness standard, the Court held "that, given the requirements of the prison environment, the Due Process Clause permits the State to treat a prison inmate who has a serious mental illness with antipsychotic drugs against his will, if the inmate is dangerous to himself or others and the treatment is in the inmate's medical interest." Then, "[h]aving determined that state law recognizes a liberty interest, also protected by the Due Process Clause, which permits refusal of antipsychotic drugs unless certain preconditions are met," the Court addressed "what procedural protections are necessary to ensure the decision to medicate ... is neither arbitrary nor erroneous under the standards we have discussed above." Despite concluding that "[t]he forcible injection of medication into a nonconsenting person's body represents a substantial interference with that person's liberty" and that "[w]hile the therapeutic benefits of antipsychotic drugs are well documented, it is also true that the drugs can have serious, even fatal, side effects[,]" the Court held that a judicial hearing was unnecessary and that the particular administrative hearing procedures provided by the State satisfied procedural due process.

Justice Stevens dissented in an opinion joined by Justices Brennan and Marshall. He thought the majority had undervalued the liberty interest it had acknowledged:

> "[T]he several dimensions of the liberty ... are both physical and intellectual. Every violation of a person's bodily integrity is an invasion of his or her liberty. The invasion is particularly intrusive if it creates a substantial risk of permanent injury and premature death. Moreover, any such action is degrading if it overrides a competent person's choice to reject a specific form of medical treatment. And when the purpose or effect of forced drugging is to alter the will and the mind of the subject, it constitutes a deprivation of liberty in the most literal and fundamental sense."

Justice Stevens had "no doubt ... that a competent individual's right to refuse such medication is a fundamental liberty interest deserving the highest order of protection." He found the state's policy invalid, because it "sweepingly sacrifices the inmate's substantive liberty interest to refuse psychotropic drugs, regardless of his medical interests, to institutional and administrative concerns." He also criticized the Court's opinion for failing to separate sufficiently the state's interest in institutional convenience from its interest in helping the inmate's medical condition. Finally, in view of the strength of the liberty interest implicated, he found the state's procedures constitutionally deficient for failing "to have the treatment decision made or reviewed by an impartial person or tribunal."

B. WHAT CONSTITUTES A DEPRIVATION?

Daniels v. Williams

474 U.S. 327, 106 S.Ct. 662, 88 L.Ed.2d 662 (1986).

Justice Rehnquist delivered the opinion of the Court.

In Parratt v. Taylor, 451 U.S. 527 (1981), a state prisoner sued under 42 U.S.C. § 1983, claiming that prison officials had negligently deprived him of his property without due process of law. After deciding that § 1983 contains no independent state-of-mind requirement, we concluded that although petitioner had been "deprived" of property within the meaning of the Due Process Clause of the Fourteenth Amendment, the State's postdeprivation tort remedy provided the process that was due. Petitioner's claim in this case, which also rests on an alleged Fourteenth Amendment "deprivation" caused by the negligent conduct of a prison official, leads us to reconsider our statement in *Parratt* that "the alleged loss, even though negligently caused, amounted to a deprivation." ... We conclude that the Due Process Clause is simply not implicated by a *negligent* act of an official causing unintended loss of or injury to life, liberty or property.

In this § 1983 action, petitioner seeks to recover damages for back and ankle injuries allegedly sustained when he fell on a prison stairway. He claims that, while an inmate at the city jail in Richmond, Virginia, he slipped on a pillow negligently left on the stairs by respondent, a correctional deputy stationed at the jail. Respondent's negligence, the argument runs, "deprived" petitioner of his "liberty" interest in freedom from bodily injury ...; because respondent maintains that he is entitled to the defense of sovereign immunity in a state tort suit, petitioner is without an "adequate" state remedy.... Accordingly, the deprivation of liberty was without "due process of law."

. . .

In *Parratt,* before concluding that Nebraska's tort remedy provided all the process that was due, we said that the loss of the prisoner's hobby kit, "even though negligently caused, amounted to a deprivation [under the Due Process Clause]." ... Justice Powell, concurring in the result, criticized the majority for "pass[ing] over" this important question of the state of mind required to constitute a "deprivation" of property.... He argued that negligent acts by state officials, though causing loss of property, are not actionable under the Due Process Clause. To Justice Powell, mere negligence could not "wor[k] a deprivation in the *constitutional sense.*" ... Not only does the word "deprive" in the Due Process Clause connote more than a negligent act, but we should not "open the federal courts to lawsuits where there has been no affirmative abuse of power." ... Upon reflection, we agree and overrule *Parratt* to the extent that it states that mere lack of due care by a state official may "deprive" an individual of life, liberty or property under the Fourteenth Amendment.

The Due Process Clause of the Fourteenth Amendment provides: "[N]or shall any State deprive any person of life, liberty, or property, without due process of law." Historically, this guarantee of due process has been applied to *deliberate* decisions of government officials to deprive a person of life, liberty or property.... No decision of this Court before *Parratt* supported the view that negligent conduct by a state official, even though causing injury, constitutes a deprivation under the Due Process Clause. This history reflects the traditional and common-sense notion that the Due Process Clause, like its forebear in the Magna Carta, ... was "'intended to secure the individual from the arbitrary exercise of the powers of government,' "Hurtado v. California, 110 U.S. 516, 527 (1884). By requiring the government to follow appropriate procedures when its agents decide to "deprive any person of life, liberty, or property," the Due Process Clause promotes fairness in such decisions. And by barring certain government actions regardless of the fairness of the procedures used to implement them, ... it serves to prevent governmental power from being "used for purposes of oppression," Murray's Lessee v. Hoboken Land & Improvement Co., 59 U.S. (18 How.) 272, 277 (1856) (discussing Due Process Clause of Fifth Amendment).

We think that the actions of prison custodians in leaving a pillow on the prison stairs, or mislaying an inmate's property, are quite remote from the concerns just discussed. Far from an abuse of power, lack of due care suggests no more than a failure to measure up to the conduct of a reasonable person. To hold that injury caused by such conduct is a deprivation within the meaning of the Fourteenth Amendment would trivialize the centuries-old principle of due process of law.

... Our Constitution deals with the large concerns of the governors and the governed, but it does not purport to supplant traditional tort law in laying down rules of conduct to regulate liability for injuries that attend living together in society. We have previously rejected reasoning that "would make of the Fourteenth Amendment a font of tort law to be superimposed upon whatever systems may already be administered by the States," Paul v. Davis, 424 U.S. 693, 701 (1976), quoted in Parratt v. Taylor, 451 U.S., at 544.

The only tie between the facts of this case and anything governmental in nature is the fact that respondent was a sheriff's deputy at the Richmond city jail and petitioner was an inmate confined in that jail. But while the Due Process Clause of the Fourteenth Amendment obviously speaks to some facets of this relationship, see e.g., Wolff v. McDonnell, 418 U.S. 539 (1974), we do not believe its protections are triggered by lack of due care by prison officials. "Medical malpractice does not become a constitutional violation merely because the victim is a prisoner," Estelle v. Gamble, 429 U.S. 97, 106 (1976), and "false imprisonment does not become a violation of the Fourteenth Amendment merely because the defendant is a state official." Baker v. McCollan, 443 U.S. 137, 146 (1979). Where a government official's act causing injury to life, liberty or property is merely negligent, "no procedure for compensation is *constitutionally* required." *Parratt,* 451 U.S., at 548 (Powell, J., concurring in result) (emphasis added.)[1]

That injuries inflicted by governmental negligence are not addressed by the United States Constitution is not to say that they may not raise significant legal concerns and lead to the creation of protectible legal interests. The enactment of tort claim statutes, for example, reflects the view that injuries caused by such negligence should generally be redressed. It is no reflection on either the breadth of the United States Constitution or the importance of traditional tort law to say that they do not address the same concerns.

In support of his claim that negligent conduct can give rise to a due process "deprivation," petitioner makes several arguments, none of which we find persuasive.... [3]

. . .

Affirmed.

Justice Marshall concurs in the result.

Justice Blackmun, concurring in the judgment.

I concur in the result.... [a]

DAVIDSON v. CANNON, 474 U.S. 344 (1986), was a companion case to Daniels v. Williams. A prisoner sent a note to prison authorities reporting a threat from another prisoner. The note was put aside and forgotten, and the prisoner was assaulted. Justice Rehnquist's opinion for the Court treated the prisoner's § 1983 suit as involving simple negligence by prison officials, which, under *Daniels,* did not implicate due process concerns. "Respondents' lack of due care in this case led to serious injury, but that lack of care simply does not approach the sort of abusive government conduct that the Due Process Clause was designed to prevent."

---

[1] Accordingly, we need not decide whether, as petitioner contends, the possibility of a sovereign immunity defense in a Virginia tort suit would render that remedy "inadequate" under *Parratt* and Hudson v. Palmer, 468 U.S. 517 (1984).

[3] [P]etitioner concedes that respondent was at most negligent. Accordingly, this case affords us no occasion to consider whether something less than intentional conduct, such as recklessness or "gross negligence," is enough to trigger the protections of the Due Process Clause.

[a] An opinion by Justice Stevens concurring in the judgment in this case and in *Davidson v. Cannon* is omitted here but described below.

Justice Brennan dissented. He took the view "that official conduct which causes personal injury due to recklessness or deliberate indifference, does deprive the victim of liberty within the meaning of the Fourteenth Amendment[,]" and he urged a remand for review of "the District Court's holding that respondents' conduct was not reckless."

Justice Blackmun also dissented, joined by Justice Marshall. In addition to agreeing with Justice Brennan's position, he argued that "[i]n some cases ... governmental negligence is an abuse of power." In particular, "when a State assumes sole responsibility for one's physical security and then ignores his call for help," due process is implicated. "In the context of prisons, this means that once the State has taken away an inmate's means of protecting himself from attack by other inmates, a prison official's negligence in providing protection can amount to a deprivation of the inmate's liberty, at least absent extenuating circumstances."

Justice Stevens concurred in the judgments in both *Daniels* and *Davidson* on the ground that in each case the state had provided adequate procedures for the vindication of the plaintiff's claims. But he rejected the conclusion that due process was not required for official negligence. He wrote:

"... 'Deprivation,' ... identifies, not the actor's state of mind, but the victim's infringement or loss. The harm to a prisoner is the same whether a pillow is left negligently, recklessly, or intentionally; so too, the harm resulting to a prisoner from an attack is the same whether his request for protection is ignored negligently, recklessly, or deliberately. In each instance, the prisoner is losing—being 'deprived' of—an aspect of liberty as the result, in part, of a form of state action."

C.   What Process Is Due and When?

The determination that due process requires compliance with procedural safeguards before government deprives a person of a protected interest triggers a further inquiry into what the timing and nature of the constitutionally required procedures must be. Those often complex questions cannot be explored in depth here, but some flavor of the kinds of considerations that are implicated may be gathered from a brief discussion.

As the Court indicated in Parratt v. Taylor, 451 U.S. 527 (1981), "[t]he fundamental requirement of due process is the opportunity to be heard and it is an 'opportunity which must be granted at a meaningful time and in a meaningful manner.' "As to timing, this normally but not always means that the opportunity must be made available before the deprivation occurs. *Parratt* reaffirmed that due process necessitates "some kind of hearing ... at some time before a State finally deprives a person of his property interests," but it held that "either the necessity of quick action by the State or the impracticability of providing any meaningful predeprivation process can, when coupled with the availability of some meaningful means by which to assess the propriety of the State's action at some time after the initial taking, satisfy the requirements of procedural due process." As applied in *Parratt,* the impracticality of requiring a predeprivation hearing before prison officials negligently lost an inmate's property in an unauthorized random act, together with the availability of a state postdeprivation tort remedy for damages, satisfied the demands of due process. (As Daniels v. Williams, supra p. 1086, indicates, *Parratt* had assumed that negligent loss of a prisoner's hobby kit amounted to a "deprivation.")

Parratt's willingness to accept a subsequent judicial tort remedy in place of a predeprivation hearing was extended in Hudson v. Palmer, 468 U.S. 517

(1984), to random and unauthorized, but intentional, deprivations of property—in that case the intentional destruction by prison officials of a prisoner's property during a search. The Court said that the underlying rationale was the same for both negligent and intentional acts: "[W]hen deprivations of property are effected through random and unauthorized conduct of a state employee, predeprivation procedures are simply 'impracticable' since the state cannot know when such deprivations will occur." Accordingly, a subsequent intentional tort remedy against the employee satisfied due process. The Court also held, however, that the ability to obtain relief in a subsequent independent tort action does not justify omitting a predeprivation hearing when deprivation of a protected interest results from some established state procedure rather than from a state employee's random and unauthorized act. Logan v. Zimmerman Brush Co., 455 U.S. 422 (1982). See generally, Smolla, *The Displacement of Federal Due Process Claims by State Tort Remedies: Parratt v. Taylor and Logan v. Zimmerman Brush Company,* 1982 U.Ill.L.Rev. 831.

A postdeprivation damages remedy also was held insufficient to satisfy due process in Zinermon v. Burch, 494 U.S. 113 (1990), a suit by a person who, after having been found disoriented and hurt, was admitted to a mental health care facility and detained for five months, pursuant to state procedures for consenting, "voluntary" treatment of the mentally ill. He claimed that the hospital staff knew or should have known that he was incapable of voluntary, understanding informed consent and that they wilfully and recklessly deprived him of his liberty without due process by not following the state's more elaborate procedures for "involuntary" admission and treatment. The Court rejected the categorical contention that deprivations of liberty always require a predeprivation hearing, observing that "the reasoning of *Parratt* and *Hudson* emphasizes the State's inability to provide predeprivation process because of the random and unpredictable nature of the deprivation, not the fact that only property losses were at stake." But the Court also held those cases distinguishable for three reasons. First, the liberty deprivation was predictable, because "[i]t is hardly unforeseeable that a person requesting treatment for mental illness might be incapable of informed consent, and that state officials with the power to admit patients might take their apparent willingness to be admitted at face value and not initiate involuntary placement procedures." Second, predeprivation process was possible by having the State limit and guide the power to admit patients so that the established procedures for involuntary admission are afforded not only to "those who are unwilling" but also "those who are unable to give consent." Third, the staff's conduct was not "unauthorized" in the same sense as in *Parratt* and *Hudson,* because "[t]he State delegated to them the power and authority to effect the very deprivation complained of here . . . and also delegated to them the concomitant duty to initiate the procedural safeguards set up by state law to guard against unlawful confinement." Four Justices dissented, taking the view that since Burch had not attacked the state's commitment procedures, but only the staff's reckless and wanton failure to employ them, the allegations amounted to the same kind of unpredictable, wrongful departure from established state policy for which a postdeprivation tort action satisfied due process under *Parratt* and *Hudson.*

The procedural demands of due process not only raise issues of timing, but also of the nature of the hearing that must be provided in different contexts, ranging from what kind of notice is needed, to whether counsel and a judicial or less formal decisionmaker are required, to whether informal process on written submissions or more formal proceedings involving the availability of oral and evidentiary presentation and rights of confrontation and cross-examination is the minimum process due. The Court's classic general formulation of what is required in particular contexts is found in Mathews v. Eldridge, 424 U.S. 319 (1976), which said "that identification of the specific dictates of due process generally requires consideration of three distinct factors: First, the private interest that will be affected by the official action; second, the risk of an erroneous deprivation of such interest through the procedures used, and the probable value, if any, of additional or substitute procedural safeguards; and finally, the Government's interest, including the function involved and the fiscal and administrative burdens that the additional or substitute procedural requirement would entail." For a general critique, see Mashaw, *Due Process in the Administrative State* (1985).

SECTION 2.   PROCEDURAL DUE PROCESS AND IRREBUTTABLE PRESUMPTIONS

Introduction. In Vance v. Bradley, 440 U.S. 93 (1979), the Court had before it a challenge under the equal protection clause to a statute requiring all foreign service officers to retire at age 60. In upholding the age classification the Court found it rational because Congress could reasonably believe that *many* employees at age 60 would be unfit to perform some of the tasks required of foreign service officers.

The cases in this section raise a potentially separate constitutional challenge to a classification such as that in *Bradley*. Congress could not reasonably believe that *all* employees were unfit at age 60. Can the due process clause then be read to require an individual hearing for each foreign service employee on the question of that employee's fitness? Or does the resolution of the equal protection issue limit the hearing right to the issue whether the employee has attained age 60?

Would the question be different if the statute read that all foreign service officers shall be subject to compulsory retirement when they become unfit to perform the relevant tasks and that it shall be conclusively presumed that any officer 60 years of age or older is unfit? Does casting the statute in that form give each employee who is retired at age 60 a due process right to a hearing on the issue of fitness?

Vlandis v. Kline

412 U.S. 441, 93 S.Ct. 2230, 37 L.Ed.2d 63 (1973).

[Connecticut required non-residents who enrolled in the state university system to pay tuition and other fees at higher rates than residents. It defined an unmarried student as a non-resident if his or her legal address for any part of the one-year period prior to applying for admission was outside of Connecticut. It defined a married student as a non-resident if his or her legal address at the time of application for admission was outside of Connecticut. It then provided that a student's residency status at the time of admission should continue for the student's entire period of attendance.

Two students, one married and one unmarried, were classified as non-residents at the time of application to the state university, but later became residents. They brought suit in the federal district court challenging the conclusive presumption of nonresidence as applied to force them to pay higher fees than other residents of the state. The district court ruled in their favor. The state appealed.]

Mr. Justice Stewart delivered the opinion of the Court.

. . .

Statutes creating permanent irrebuttable presumptions have long been disfavored under the Due Process Clause of the Fifth and Fourteenth Amendments....

The ... case of Bell v. Burson, 402 U.S. 535 (1971), involved a Georgia statute which provided that if an uninsured motorist was involved in an accident and could not post security for the amount of damages claimed, his driver's license must be suspended without any hearing on the question of fault or responsibility. The Court held that since the State purported to be concerned with fault in suspending a driver's license, it could not, consistent with procedural due process, conclusively presume fault from the fact that the uninsured motorist was involved in an accident, and could not, therefore, suspend his driver's license without a hearing on that crucial factor.

Likewise, in Stanley v. Illinois, 405 U.S. 645 (1972), the Court struck down, as violative of the Due Process Clause, Illinois' irrebuttable statutory presumption that all unmarried fathers are unqualified to raise their children....

The same considerations obtain here. It may be that most applicants to Connecticut's university system who apply from outside the State or within a year of living out of State have no real intention of becoming Connecticut residents and will never do so. But it is clear that not all of the applicants from out of State inevitably fall in this category. Indeed, in the present case, both appellees possess many of the indicia of Connecticut residency, such as year-round Connecticut homes, Connecticut driver's licenses, car registrations, voter registrations, etc.; and both were found by the District Court to have become bona fide residents of Connecticut before the 1972 Spring semester. Yet, under the State's statutory scheme, neither was permitted any opportunity to demonstrate the bona fides of her Connecticut residency for tuition purposes, and neither will ever have such an opportunity in the future so long as she remains a student....

In sum, since Connecticut purports to be concerned with residency in allocating the rates for tuition and fees at its university system, it is forbidden by the Due Process Clause to deny an individual the resident rates on the basis of a permanent and irrebuttable presumption of nonresidence, when that presumption is not necessarily or universally true in fact, and when the State has reasonable alternative means of making the crucial determination. Rather, standards of due process require that the State allow such an individual the opportunity to present evidence showing that he is a bona fide resident entitled to the in-state rates. Since § 126 precluded the appellees from ever rebutting the presumption that they were nonresidents of Connecticut, that statute operated to deprive them of a significant amount of their money without due process of law.

We are aware, of course, of the special problems involved in determining the bona fide residence of college students who come from out of State to attend that State's public university. Our holding today should in no wise be taken to mean that Connecticut must classify the students in its university system as residents, for purposes of tuition and fees, just because they go to school there. Nor should our decision be construed to deny a State the right to impose on a student, as one element in demonstrating bona fide residence, a reasonable durational residency requirement, which can be met while in student status. We fully recognize that a State has a legitimate interest in protecting and preserving the quality of its colleges and universities and the right of its own bona fide residents to attend such institutions on a preferential tuition basis.

We hold only that a permanent irrebuttable presumption of nonresidence—the means adopted by Connecticut to preserve that legitimate interest—is violative of the Due Process Clause, because it provides no opportunity for students who applied from out of State to demonstrate that they have become bona fide Connecticut residents. The State can establish such reasonable criteria for in-state status as to make virtually certain that students who are not, in fact, bona fide residents of the State, but who have come there solely for educational purposes, cannot take advantage of the in-state rates....

Judgment affirmed.

Mr. Justice Marshall, with whom Mr. Justice Brennan joins, concurring.

I join the opinion of the Court except insofar as it suggests that a State may impose a one-year residency requirement as a prerequisite to qualifying for in-state tuition benefits.... That question is not presented by this case since here we deal with a permanent, irrebuttable presumption of nonresidency based on the fact that a student was a nonresident at the time he applied for admission to the state university system....

Mr. Justice White, concurring in the judgment....

Mr. Chief Justice Burger, with whom Mr. Justice Rehnquist joins, dissenting.

. . .

Mr. Justice Rehnquist, with whom The Chief Justice and Mr. Justice Douglas join, dissenting.

The Court's opinion relegates to the limbo of unconstitutionality a Connecticut law that requires higher tuition from those who come from out of State to attend its state universities than from those who come from within the State. The opinion accomplishes this result by a highly theoretical analysis that relies heavily on notions of substantive due process that have been authoritatively repudiated by subsequent decisions of the Court. Believing as I do that the Connecticut statutory scheme is a constitutionally permissible means of dealing with an increasingly acute problem facing state systems of higher education, I dissent....

Cleveland Board of Education v. LaFleur

414 U.S. 632, 94 S.Ct. 791, 39 L.Ed.2d 52 (1974).

Mr. Justice Stewart delivered the opinion of the Court.

[LaFleur and Nelson brought suit challenging a school board rule requiring every pregnant teacher to take maternity leave without pay at least five months before the expected birth of her child, with application filed two weeks prior to date of departure. Despite their wish to finish the school year they were forced to take leave in March. Their babies were born in late July and August. Cohen challenged the rule in another district requiring leave without pay four months before the expected birth with written notice six months before the date of expected birth. She was required to leave her job in December, and her baby was born in May. The Court found the regulations unconstitutional.]

. . .

II.

This Court has long recognized that freedom of personal choice in matters of marriage and family life is one of the liberties protected by the Due Process Clause of the Fourteenth Amendment. Roe v. Wade, 410 U.S. 113 (1973); Loving v. Virginia, 388 U.S. 1, 12 (1967); Griswold v. Connecticut, 381 U.S. 479 (1965); Pierce v. Society of Sisters, 268 U.S. 510 (1925); Meyer v. Nebraska, 262 U.S. 390 (1923). See also Prince v. Massachusetts, 321 U.S. 158 (1944); Skinner v. Oklahoma, 316 U.S. 535 (1942). As we noted in Eisenstadt v. Baird, 405 U.S. 438, 453 (1972), there is a right "to be free from unwarranted governmental intrusion into matters so fundamentally affecting a person as the decision whether to bear or beget a child."

By acting to penalize the pregnant teacher for deciding to bear a child, overly restrictive maternity leave regulations can constitute a heavy burden on the exercise of these protected freedoms. Because public school maternity leave rules directly affect "one of the basic civil rights of man," Skinner v. Oklahoma, supra, 316 U.S., at 541, the Due Process Clause of the Fourteenth Amendment requires that such rules must not needlessly, arbitrarily, or capriciously impinge upon this vital area of a teacher's constitutional liberty. The question before us in these cases is whether the interests advanced in support of the rules of the Cleveland and Chesterfield County School Boards can justify the particular procedures they have adopted.

The school boards in these cases have offered two essentially overlapping explanations for their mandatory maternity leave rules. First, they contend that the firm cut-off dates are necessary to maintain continuity of classroom instruction, since advance knowledge of when a pregnant teacher must leave facilitates the finding and hiring of a qualified substitute. Secondly, the school boards seek to justify their maternity rules by arguing that at least some teachers become physically incapable of adequately performing certain of their duties during the latter part of pregnancy. By keeping the pregnant teacher out of the classroom during these final months, the maternity leave rules are said to protect the health of the teacher and her unborn child, while at the same time assuring that students have a physically capable instructor in the classroom at all times.

It cannot be denied that continuity of instruction is a significant and legitimate educational goal. Regulations requiring pregnant teachers to provide early notice of their condition to school authorities undoubtedly facilitate administrative planning toward the important objective of continuity....

Thus, while the advance notice provisions in the Cleveland and Chesterfield County rules are wholly rational and may well be necessary to serve the objective of continuity of instruction, the absolute requirements of termination at the end of the fourth or fifth month of pregnancy are not. Were continuity the only goal, cut-off dates much later during pregnancy would serve as well or better than the challenged rules, providing that ample advance notice requirements were retained. Indeed, continuity would seem just as well attained if the teacher herself were allowed to choose the date upon which to commence her leave, at least so long as the decision were required to be made and notice given of it well in advance of the date selected.

. . .

We thus conclude that the arbitrary cut-off dates embodied in the mandatory leave rules before us have no rational relationship to the valid state interest of preserving continuity of instruction. As long as the teacher is required to give substantial advance notice of her condition, the choice of firm dates later in pregnancy would serve the boards' objectives just as well, while imposing a far lesser burden on the women's exercise of constitutionally protected freedom.

The question remains as to whether the fifth and sixth month cut-off dates can be justified on the other ground advanced by the school boards—the necessity of keeping physically unfit teachers out of the classroom. There can be no doubt that such an objective is perfectly legitimate, both on educational and safety grounds. And, despite the plethora of conflicting medical testimony in these cases, we can assume *arguendo* that at least some teachers become physically disabled from effectively performing their duties during the latter stages of pregnancy.

The mandatory termination provisions of the Cleveland and Chesterfield County rules surely operate to insulate the classroom from the presence of potentially incapacitated pregnant teachers. But the question is whether the rules sweep too broadly. See Shelton v. Tucker, 364 U.S. 479 (1960). That question must be answered in the affirmative, for the provisions amount to a conclusive presumption that every pregnant teacher who reaches the fifth or sixth month of pregnancy is physically incapable of continuing. There is no individualized determination by the teacher's doctor—or the school board's—as to any particular teacher's ability to continue at her job. The rules contain an irrebuttable presumption of physical incompetency, and that presumption applies even when the medical evidence as to an individual woman's physical status might be wholly to the contrary.

As the Court noted last Term in Vlandis v. Kline, 412 U.S. 441, 446 (1973), "permanent irrebuttable presumptions have long been disfavored under the Due Process Clause of the Fifth and Fourteenth Amendments." ...

. . .

These principles control our decision in the cases before us. While the medical experts in these cases differed on many points, they unanimously agreed on one—the ability of any particular pregnant woman to continue at work past any fixed time in her pregnancy is very much an individual matter. Even assuming *arguendo* that there are some women who would be physically unable to work past the particular cut-off dates embodied in the challenged rules, it is evident that there are large numbers of teachers who are fully capable of continuing work for longer than the Cleveland and Chesterfield County regulations will allow. Thus, the conclusive presumption embodied in these rules, like that in *Vlandis,* is neither "necessarily nor universally true," and is violative of the Due Process Clause.

The school boards have argued that the mandatory termination dates serve the interest of administrative convenience, since there are many instances of teacher pregnancy, and the rules obviate the necessity for case-by-case determinations. Certainly, the boards have an interest in devising prompt and efficient procedures to achieve their legitimate objectives in this area. . . .

While it might be easier for the school boards to conclusively presume that all pregnant women are unfit to teach past the fourth or fifth month or even the first month, of pregnancy, administrative convenience alone is insufficient to make valid what otherwise is a violation of due process of law.[13] The

---

[13] This is not to say that the only means for providing appropriate protection for the rights of pregnant teachers is an individualized determination in each case and in every circumstance. We are not dealing in these cases with maternity leave regulations requiring a termination of employment at some firm date during the last few weeks of preg-

Fourteenth Amendment requires the school boards to employ alternative administrative means, which do not so broadly infringe upon basic constitutional liberty, in support of their legitimate goals.

We conclude, therefore, that neither the necessity for continuity of instruction nor the state interest in keeping physically unfit teachers out of the classroom can justify the sweeping mandatory leave regulations that the Cleveland and Chesterfield County School Boards have adopted. While the regulations no doubt represent a good-faith attempt to achieve a laudable goal, they cannot pass muster under the Due Process Clause of the Fourteenth Amendment, because they employ irrebuttable presumptions that unduly penalize a female teacher for deciding to bear a child.

. . .

Mr. Justice Douglas concurs in the result.

Mr. Justice Powell (concurring in the result).

I concur in the Court's result, but I am unable to join its opinion. In my view these cases should not be decided on the ground that the mandatory maternity leave regulations impair any right to bear children or create an "irrebuttable presumption." It seems to me that equal protection analysis is the appropriate frame of reference. . . .

. . .

Mr. Justice Rehnquist, with whom The Chief Justice joins (dissenting).

The Court rests its invalidation of the school regulations involved in these cases on the Due Process Clause of the Fourteenth Amendment, rather than on any claim of sexual discrimination under the Equal Protection Clause of that Amendment. My Brother Stewart thereby enlists the Court in another quixotic engagement in his apparently unending war on irrebuttable presumptions. In this case we are told that although a regulation "requiring a termination of employment at some firm date during the last few weeks of pregnancy" (n. 13, opinion of the Court), might pass muster, the regulations here challenged requiring termination at the end of the fourth or fifth month of pregnancy violate due process of law. . . .

The lines drawn by the school boards in the city of Cleveland and Chesterfield County in these cases require pregnant teachers to take forced leave at a stage of their pregnancy when medical evidence seems to suggest that a majority of them might well be able to continue teaching without any significant possibility of physical impairment. But so far as I am aware, the medical evidence also suggests that in some cases there may be physical impairment at the stage of pregnancy fastened on by the regulations in question, and that the probability of physical impairment increases as the pregnancy advances. If legislative bodies are to be permitted to draw a general line anywhere short of the delivery room, I can find no judicial standard of

nancy. We therefore have no occasion to decide whether such regulations might be justified by considerations not presented in these records—for example, widespread medical consensus about the "disabling" effect of pregnancy on a teacher's job performance during these latter days, or evidence showing that such firm cutoffs were the only reason-

able method of avoiding the possibility of labor beginning while some teacher was in the classroom, or proof that adequate substitutes could not be procured without at least some minimal lead time and certainty as to the dates upon which their employment was to begin.

measurement which says the ones drawn here were invalid. I therefore dissent.[a]

Weinberger v. Salfi

422 U.S. 749, 95 S.Ct. 2457, 45 L.Ed.2d 522 (1975).

Mr. Justice Rehnquist delivered the opinion of the Court.

Appellants, the Department of Health, Education, and Welfare, its Secretary, the Social Security Administration and various of its officials, appeal from a [district court] decision ... invalidating duration-of-relationship Social Security eligibility requirements for surviving wives and stepchildren of deceased wage earners. 373 F.Supp. 961 (1974)....

I.

Appellee Salfi married the deceased wage earner, Londo L. Salfi, on May 27, 1972. Despite his alleged apparent good health at the time of the marriage, he suffered a heart attack less than a month later, and died on November 21, 1972, less than six months after the marriage. Appellee filed applications for mother's insurance benefits for herself and child's insurance benefits for her daughter by a previous marriage.... These applications were denied by the Social Security Administration, both initially and on reconsideration at the regional level, solely on the basis of the duration-of-relationship requirements of §§ 416(c)(5) and (e)(2), which define "widow" and "child." The definitions exclude surviving wives and stepchildren who had their respective relationships to a deceased wage earner for less than nine months prior to his death.

The named appellees then filed this action....

A three-judge District Court ... on cross-motions for summary judgment ... granted substantially all of the relief prayed for by appellees....

III.

The District Court relied on congressional history for the proposition that the duration-of-relationship requirement was intended to prevent the use of sham marriages to secure Social Security payments. As such, ... "the requirement constitutes a presumption that marriages like Mrs. Salfi's, which did not precede the wage earner's death by at least nine months, were entered into for the purpose of securing Social Security benefits." The presumption was moreover, conclusive, because applicants were not afforded an opportunity to disprove the presence of the illicit purpose. The court held that under our decisions in Cleveland Board of Education v. LaFleur, 414 U.S. 632 (1974), Vlandis v. Kline, 412 U.S. 441 (1973), and Stanley v. Illinois, 405 U.S. 645 (1972), the requirement was unconstitutional, because it presumed a fact which was not necessarily or universally true.

. . .

We hold that these cases are not controlling on the issue before us now. Unlike the claims involved in *Stanley* and *LaFleur,* a noncontractual claim to receive funds from the public treasury enjoys no constitutionally protected

---

[a] In Turner v. Department of Employment, 423 U.S. 44 (1975), the Court invalidated a Utah law making pregnant women ineligible for unemployment benefits for a period extending from 12 weeks before the expected date of childbirth until a date six weeks after childbirth. The Court relied on the conclusive presumption analysis in the *Cleveland Board* case.

status, *Dandridge v. Williams,* supra, though of course Congress may not invidiously discriminate among such claimants on the basis of a "bare congressional desire to harm a politically unpopular group," U.S. Dept. of Agriculture v. Moreno, 413 U.S. 528, 534 (1973), or on the basis of criteria which bear no rational relation to a legitimate legislative goal. Jimenez v. Weinberger, 417 U.S. 628, 636 (1974); U.S. Dept. of Agriculture v. Murry, 413 U.S. 508, 513–514 (1973). Unlike the statutory scheme in *Vlandis* ... the Social Security Act does not purport to speak in terms of the bona fides of the parties to a marriage, but then make plainly relevant evidence of such bona fides inadmissible. ...

We think that the District Court's extension of the holdings of *Stanley, Vlandis* and *LaFleur* to the eligibility requirement in issue here would turn the doctrine of those cases into a virtual engine of destruction of countless legislative judgments which have heretofore been thought wholly consistent with the Fifth and Fourteenth Amendments to the Constitution. ...

. . .

More recently, in Mourning v. Family Publications Service, Inc., 411 U.S. 356 (1973), the Court sustained the constitutionality of a regulation promulgated under the Truth in Lending Act which made the Act's disclosure provisions applicable whenever credit is offered to a consumer "for which either a finance charge is or may be imposed or which pursuant to an agreement, is or may be payable in more than four installments." Id., at 362. The regulation was challenged because it was said to conclusively presume that payments made under an agreement providing for more than four installments necessarily included a finance charge, when in fact that might not be the case. The Court rejected the constitutional challenge in this language:

> "The rule was intended as a prophylactic measure; it does not presume that all creditors who are within its ambit assess finance charges, but rather, imposes a disclosure requirement on all members of a defined class in order to discourage evasion by a substantial portion of that class."

If the Fifth and Fourteenth Amendments permit this latitude to legislative decisions regulating the private sector of the economy, they surely allow no less latitude in prescribing the conditions upon which funds shall be dispensed from the public treasury. Dandridge v. Williams, supra. With these principles in mind, we turn to consider the statutory provisions which the District Court held invalid.

. . .

Under those standards, the question raised is not whether a statutory provision precisely filters out those, and only those, who are in the factual position which generated the congressional concern reflected in the statute. Such a rule would ban all prophylactic provisions, and would be directly contrary to our holding in *Mourning,* supra. Nor is the question whether the provision filters out a substantial part of the class which caused congressional concern, or whether it filters out more members of the class than nonmembers. The question is whether Congress, its concern having been reasonably aroused by the possibility of an abuse which it legitimately desired to avoid, could rationally have concluded both that a particular limitation or qualification would protect against its occurrence, and that the expense and other difficulties of individual determinations justified the inherent imprecision of a prophylactic rule. We conclude that the duration-of-relationship test meets this constitutional standard.

The danger of persons entering a marriage relationship not to enjoy its traditional benefits, but instead to enable one spouse to claim benefits upon the anticipated early death of the wage earner, has been recognized from the very beginning of the Social Security program. . . .

Undoubtedly the concerns reflected in this congressional material are legitimate, involving as they do the integrity of both the Social Security Trust Fund and the marriage relationship. It is also undoubtedly true that the duration-of-relationship requirement operates to lessen the likelihood of abuse through sham relationships entered in contemplation of imminent death. We also think that Congress could rationally have concluded that any imprecision from which it might suffer was justified by its ease and certainty of operation.

. . . .

While it is possible to debate the wisdom of excluding legitimate claimants in order to discourage sham relationships, and of relying on a rule which may not exclude some obviously sham arrangements, we think it clear that Congress could rationally choose to adopt such a course. . . .

The administrative difficulties of individual eligibility determinations are without doubt matters which Congress may consider when determining whether to rely on rules which sweep more broadly than the evils with which they seek to deal. In this sense, the duration-of-relationship requirement represents not merely a substantive policy determination that benefits should be awarded only on the basis of genuine marital relationships, but also a substantive policy determination that limited resources would not be well spent in making individual determinations. It is an expression of Congress' policy choice that the Social Security system, and its millions of beneficiaries, would be best served by a prophylactic rule which bars claims arising from the bulk of sham marriages which are actually entered, which discourages such marriages from ever taking place, and which is also objective and easily administered.

The Constitution does not preclude such policy choices as a price for conducting programs for the distribution of social insurance benefits. Cf. Geduldig v. Aiello, supra, at 496. Unlike criminal prosecutions, or the custody proceedings at issue in *Stanley v. Illinois,* such programs do not involve affirmative government action which seriously curtails important liberties cognizable under the Constitution. There is thus no basis for our requiring individualized determinations when Congress can rationally conclude not only that generalized rules are appropriate to its purposes and concerns, but also that the difficulties of individual determinations outweigh the marginal increments in the precise effectuation of congressional concern which they might be expected to produce.

The judgment of the District Court is

Reversed.

Mr. Justice Douglas, dissenting.

. . . .

On the merits, I believe that the main problem with these legislatively created presumptions is that they frequently invade the right to a jury trial. See Tot v. United States, 319 U.S. 463, 473 (1943) (concurring opinion). The present law was designed to bar payment of certain Social Security benefits when the purpose of the marriage was to obtain such benefits. Whether this was the aim of a particular marriage is a question of fact, to be decided by the jury in an appropriate case. I therefore would vacate and remand the case to give Mrs. Salfi the right to show that her marriage did not offend the statutory scheme, that it was not a sham.

Mr. Justice Brennan, with whom Mr. Justice Marshall joins, dissenting.

. . .

The merits of this case can be dealt with very briefly. For it is, I believe, apparent on the face of the Court's opinion that today's holding is flatly contrary to several recent decisions, specifically Vlandis v. Kline, 412 U.S. 441 (1973); U.S. Dept. of Agriculture v. Murry, 413 U.S. 508 (1973), and Jimenez v. Weinberger, 417 U.S. 628 (1974).

. . .

USERY v. TURNER ELKHORN MINING CO., 428 U.S. 1 (1976). Section 411(c)(3) of the Federal Coal Mine Health and Safety Act provides that a miner shown by X-ray or other clinical evidence to be afflicted with complicated pneumoconiosis is "irrebuttably presumed" to be totally disabled due to pneumoconiosis; if he has died, it is irrebuttably presumed that he was totally disabled by pneumoconiosis at the time of his death, and that his death was due to pneumoconiosis. In rejecting a challenge by coal mine operators to this provision the Court said:

"... We think the District Court erred in equating this case with those in the mold of *Stanley* and *Vlandis*.

"As an operational matter, the effect of § 411(c)(3)'s 'irrebuttable presumption' of total disability is simply to establish entitlement in the case of a miner who is clinically diagnosable as extremely ill with pneumoconiosis arising out of coal mine employment. Indeed, the legislative history discloses that it was precisely this advanced and progressive stage of the disease that Congress sought most certainly to compensate. Were the Act phrased simply and directly to provide that operators were bound to provide benefits for all miners clinically demonstrating their affliction with complicated pneumoconiosis arising out of employment in the mines, we think it clear that there could be no due process objection to it. For, as we have already observed, destruction of earning capacity is not the sole legitimate basis for compulsory compensation of employees by their employers. New York Central R.R. Co. v. Bianc, 250 U.S. 596 (1919). We cannot say that it would be irrational for Congress to conclude that impairment of health alone warrants compensation. Since Congress can clearly draft a statute to accomplish precisely what it has accomplished through § 411(c)(3)'s presumption of disability, the argument is essentially that Congress has accomplished its result in an impermissible manner—by defining eligibility in terms of 'total disability' and erecting an 'irrebuttable presumption' of total disability upon a factual showing that does not necessarily satisfy the statutory definition of total disability. But in a statute such as this, regulating purely economic matters, we do not think that Congress' choice of statutory language can invalidate the enactment when its operation and effect are clearly permissible. Cf. Weinberger v. Salfi, 422 U.S. 749, 767–785 (1975); McDonald v. Board of Election, 394 U.S. 802, 809 (1969); United States v. Carolene Products Co., 304 U.S. 144, 154 (1938)."

Michael H. v. Gerald D.

491 U.S. 110, 109 S.Ct. 2333, 105 L.Ed.2d 91 (1989).

[The report in this case appears, supra at p. 591]

CHAPTER 12

APPLICATION OF THE POST CIVIL WAR AMENDMENTS TO PRIVATE CONDUCT: CONGRESSIONAL POWER TO ENFORCE THE AMENDMENTS

Introduction This chapter presents a mixture of issues that can best be described as those involved in the Civil Rights Cases with which this chapter begins. That 1883 decision took a narrow view of the reach of section 1 of the thirteenth amendment and section 1 of the fourteenth amendment in their application to private racial discrimination. The decision also adopted a correspondingly narrow view of Congressional power to enforce the amendments. After setting out the decision in the Civil Rights Cases in section 1, the remainder of this chapter explores the question whether its basic conceptions are still valid. Section 2, dealing with the "state action" concept, includes those cases concerning the application of constitutional limits of governmental action to private conduct. The subject of the rest of the chapter is Congressional power to enforce the Civil War Amendments, focusing particularly on the extent of the power to prohibit both private and state action that would be lawful in the absence of federal legislation. Section 3 presents a brief review of the surviving fragments of Reconstruction era legislation, and contemporary federal legislation protecting civil rights. Section 4 addresses the issue of Congressional power to prohibit private racial discrimination in enforcing the thirteenth amendment's prohibition of slavery and involuntary servitude. Section 5 focuses on Congressional power under the fourteenth amendment to prohibit private racial, and non-racial, discrimination. Section 6 broadens the focus beyond issues of private discrimination, examining the extent of Congressional power to prohibit state laws and practices that violate neither section 1 of the fourteenth amendment nor section 1 of the fifteenth amendment. This last section considers both the scope of Congressional power to provide broad remedies for conceded constitutional violations and, most controversial, to modify the substantive content of constitutional rights.

SECTION 1. EARLY INTERPRETATION

Civil Rights Cases

109 U.S. 3, 3 S.Ct. 18, 27 L.Ed. 835 (1883).

Bradley, J. These cases are all founded on the first and second sections of the act of congress known as the "Civil Rights Act," passed March 1, 1875, entitled "An act to protect all citizens in their civil and legal rights." 18 Stat.

335. Two of the cases, those against Stanley and Nichols, are indictments for denying to persons of color the accommodations and privileges of an inn or hotel; two of them, those against Ryan and Singleton, are, one an information, the other an indictment, for denying to individuals the privileges and accommodations of a theater, the information against Ryan being for refusing a colored person a seat in the dress circle of Maguire's theater in San Francisco; and the indictment against Singleton being for denying to another person, whose color is not stated, the full enjoyment of the accommodations of the theater known as the Grand Opera House in New York, "said denial not being made for any reasons by law applicable to citizens of every race and color, and regardless of any previous condition of servitude." The case of Robinson and wife against the Memphis & Charleston Railroad Company was an action brought in the circuit court of the United States for the western district of Tennessee, to recover the penalty of $500 given by the second section of the act; and the *gravamen* was the refusal by the conductor of the railroad company to allow the wife to ride in the ladies' car, for the reason, as stated in one of the counts, that she was a person of African descent. The jury rendered a verdict for the defendants in this case upon the merits under a charge of the court, to which a bill of exceptions was taken by the plaintiffs....

It is obvious that the primary and important question in all the cases is the constitutionality of the law; for if the law is unconstitutional none of the prosecutions can stand.

The sections of the law referred to provide as follows:

"Section 1. That all persons within the jurisdiction of the United States shall be entitled to the full and equal enjoyment of the accommodations, advantages, facilities, and privileges of inns, public conveyances on land or water, theaters, and other places of public amusement; subject only to the conditions and limitations established by law, and applicable alike to citizens of every race and color, regardless of any previous condition of servitude.

"Section 2. That any person who shall violate the foregoing section by denying to any citizen, except for reasons by law applicable to citizens of every race and color, and regardless of any previous condition of servitude, the full enjoyment of any of the accommodations, advantages, facilities, or privileges in said section enumerated, or by aiding or inciting such denial, shall, for every such offense, forfeit and pay the sum of $500 to the person aggrieved thereby, to be recovered in an action of debt, with full costs; and shall, also, for every such offense, be deemed guilty of a misdemeanor, and upon conviction thereof shall be fined not less than $500 nor more than $1,000, or shall be imprisoned not less than 30 days nor more than one year...."

Has congress constitutional power to make such a law? Of course, no one will contend that the power to pass it was contained in the constitution before the adoption of the last three amendments. The power is sought, first, in the fourteenth amendment, and the views and arguments of distinguished senators, advanced while the law was under consideration, claiming authority to pass it by virtue of that amendment, are the principal arguments adduced in favor of the power....

The first section of the fourteenth amendment,—which is the one relied on,—after declaring who shall be citizens of the United States, and of the several states, is prohibitory in its character, and prohibitory upon the states. It declares that "no state shall make or enforce any law which shall abridge the privileges or immunities of citizens of the United States; nor shall any state deprive any person of life, liberty, or property without due process of law; nor deny to any person within its jurisdiction the equal protection of the laws.'' It is state action of a particular character that is prohibited. Individual invasion of individual rights is not the subject-matter of the amendment. It has a deeper and broader scope. It nullifies and makes void all state legislation, and state action of every kind, which impairs the privileges and immunities of citizens of the United States, or which injures them in life, liberty, or property without due process of law, or which denies to any of them the equal protection of the laws. It not only does this, but, in order that the national will, thus declared, may not be a mere *brutum fulmen*, the last section of the amendment invests congress with power to enforce it by appropriate legislation. To enforce what? To enforce the prohibition. To adopt appropriate legislation for correcting the effects of such prohibited state laws and state acts, and thus to render them effectually null, void, and innocuous. This is the legislative power conferred upon congress, and this is the whole of it. It does not invest congress with power to legislate upon subjects which are within the domain of state legislation; but to provide modes of relief against state legislation, or state action, of the kind referred to. It does not authorize congress to create a code of municipal law for the regulation of private rights; but to provide modes of redress against the operation of state laws, and the action of state officers, executive or judicial, when these are subversive of the fundamental rights specified in the amendment. . . .

In this connection it is proper to state that civil rights, such as are guaranteed by the constitution against state aggression, cannot be impaired by the wrongful acts of individuals, unsupported by state authority in the shape of laws, customs, or judicial or executive proceedings. The wrongful act of an individual, unsupported by any such authority, is simply a private wrong, or a crime of that individual; an invasion of the rights of the injured party, it is true, whether they affect his person, his property, or his reputation; but if not sanctioned in some way by the state, or not done under state authority, his rights remain in full force, and may presumably be vindicated by resort to the laws of the state for redress. An individual cannot deprive a man of his right to vote, to hold property, to buy and to sell, to sue in the courts, or to be a witness or a juror; he may, by force or fraud, interfere with the enjoyment of the right in a particular case; he may commit an assault against the person, or commit murder, or use ruffian violence at the polls, or slander the good name of a fellow-citizen; but unless protected in these wrongful acts by some shield of state law or state authority, he cannot destroy or injure the right; he will only render himself amenable to satisfaction or punishment; and amenable therefor to the laws of the state where the wrongful acts are committed. . . .

Of course, these remarks do not apply to those cases in which congress is clothed with direct and plenary powers of legislation over the whole subject, accompanied with an express or implied denial of such power to the states, as in the regulation of commerce with foreign nations, among the several states, and with the Indian tribes, the coining of money, the establishment of post-offices and post-roads, the declaring of war, etc. In these cases congress has power to pass laws for regulating the subjects specified, in every detail and the conduct and transactions of individuals in respect thereof.

. . .

. . . [T]he power of congress to adopt direct and primary, as distinguished from corrective, legislation on the subject in hand, is sought, in the second place, from the thirteenth amendment, which abolishes slavery. This amendment declares ''that neither slavery, nor involuntary servitude, except as a punishment for crime, whereof the party shall have been duly convicted, shall exist within the United States, or any place subject to their jurisdiction;" and it gives congress power to enforce the amendment by appropriate legislation....

It is true that slavery cannot exist without law any more than property in lands and goods can exist without law, and therefore the thirteenth amendment may be regarded as nullifying all state laws which establish or uphold slavery. But it has a reflex character also, establishing and decreeing universal civil and political freedom throughout the United States; and it is assumed that the power vested in congress to enforce the article by appropriate legislation, clothes congress with power to pass all laws necessary and proper for abolishing all badges and incidents of slavery in the United States; and upon this assumption it is claimed that this is sufficient authority for declaring by law that all persons shall have equal accommodations and privileges in all inns, public conveyances, and places of public amusement; the argument being that the denial of such equal accommodations and privileges is in itself a subjection to a species of servitude within the meaning of the amendment....

It may be that by the black code, (as it was called), in the times when slavery prevailed, the proprietors of inns and public conveyances were forbidden to receive persons of the African race, because it might assist slaves to escape from the control of their masters. This was merely a means of preventing such escapes, and was no part of the servitude itself. A law of that kind could not have any such object now, however justly it might be deemed an invasion of the party's legal right as a citizen, and amenable to the prohibitions of the fourteenth amendment.

The long existence of African slavery in this country gave us very distinct notions of what it was, and what were its necessary incidents. Compulsory service of the slave for the benefit of the master, restraint of his movements except by the master's will, disability to hold property, to make contracts, to have a standing in court, to be a witness against a white person, and such like burdens and incapacities were the inseparable incidents of the institution. Severer punishments for crimes were imposed on the slave than on free persons guilty of the same offenses. Congress, as we have seen, by the civil rights bill of 1866, passed in view of the thirteenth amendment, before the fourteenth was adopted, undertook to wipe out these burdens and disabilities, the necessary incidents of slavery, constituting its substance and visible form; and to secure to all citizens of every race and color, and without regard to previous servitude, those fundamental rights which are the essence of civil freedom, namely, the same right to make and enforce contracts, to sue, be parties, give evidence, and to inherit, purchase, lease, sell, and convey property, as is enjoyed by white citizens. Whether this legislation was fully authorized by the thirteenth amendment alone, without the support which it afterwards received from the fourteenth amendment, after the adoption of which it was re-enacted with some additions, it is not necessary to inquire. It is referred to for the purpose of showing that at that time (in 1866) congress did not assume, under the authority given by the thirteenth amendment, to adjust what may be called the social rights of men and races in the community; but only to declare and vindicate those fundamental rights which appertain to the essence of citizenship, and the enjoyment or deprivation of which constitutes the essential distinction between freedom and slavery....

The only question under the present head, therefore, is, whether the refusal to any persons of the accommodations of an inn, or a public conveyance, or a place of public amusement, by an individual, and without any sanction or support from any state law or regulation, does inflict upon such persons any manner of servitude, or form of slavery, as those terms are understood in this country? . . .

Now, conceding, for the sake of the argument, that the admission to an inn, a public conveyance, or a place of public amusement, on equal terms with all other citizens, is the right of every man and all classes of men, is it any more than one of those rights which the states by the Fourteenth Amendment are forbidden to deny to any person? And is the Constitution violated until the denial of the right has some State sanction or authority? Can the act of a mere individual, the owner of the inn, the public conveyance, or place of amusement, refusing the accommodation, be justly regarded as imposing any badge of slavery or servitude upon the applicant, or only as inflicting an ordinary civil injury, properly cognizable by the laws of the state, and presumably subject to redress by those laws until the contrary appears?

After giving to these questions all the consideration which their importance demands, we are forced to the conclusion that such an act of refusal has nothing to do with slavery or involuntary servitude, and that if it is violative of any right of the party, his redress is to be sought under the laws of the state; or, if those laws are adverse to his rights and do not protect him, his remedy will be found in the corrective legislation which congress has adopted, or may adopt, for counteracting the effect of state laws, or state action, prohibited by the fourteenth amendment. It would be running the slavery argument into the ground to make it apply to every act of discrimination which a person may see fit to make as to the guests he will entertain, or as to the people he will take into his coach or cab or car, or admit to his concert or theater, or deal with in other matters of intercourse or business. Innkeepers and public carriers, by the laws of all the states, so far as we are aware, are bound, to the extent of their facilities, to furnish proper accommodation to all unobjectionable persons who in good faith apply for them. If the laws themselves make any unjust discrimination, amenable to the prohibitions of the fourteenth amendment, congress has full power to afford a remedy under that amendment and in accordance with it.

When a man has emerged from slavery, and by the aid of beneficent legislation has shaken off the inseparable concomitants of that state, there must be some stage in the progress of his elevation when he takes the rank of a mere citizen, and ceases to be the special favorite of the laws, and when his rights as a citizen, or a man, are to be protected in the ordinary modes by which other men's rights are protected. There were thousands of free colored people in this country before the abolition of slavery, enjoying all the essential rights of life, liberty, and property the same as white citizens; yet no one, at that time, thought that it was any invasion of their personal *status* as freemen because they were not admitted to all the privileges enjoyed by white citizens, or because they were subjected to discriminations in the enjoyment of accommodations in inns, public conveyances, and places of amusement. Mere discriminations on account of race or color were not regarded as badges of slavery. If, since that time, the enjoyment of equal rights in all these respects has become established by constitutional enactment, it is not by force of the thirteenth amendment, (which merely abolishes slavery,) but by force of the fourteenth and fifteenth amendments.

On the whole, we are of opinion that no countenance of authority for the passage of the law in question can be found in either the thirteenth or fourteenth amendment of the constitution; and no other ground of authority for its passage being suggested, it must necessarily be declared void, at least so far as its operation in the several states is concerned. . . .

Mr. Justice Harlan dissenting:

The opinion in these cases proceeds, it seems to me, upon grounds entirely too narrow and artificial. I cannot resist the conclusion that the substance and spirit of the recent Amendments of the Constitution have been sacrificed by a subtle and ingenious verbal criticism. "It is not the words of the law but the internal sense of it that makes the law; the letter of the law is the body; the sense and reason of the law is the soul." Constitutional provisions, adopted in the interest of liberty, and for the purpose of securing, through national legislation, if need be, rights inhering in a state of freedom, and belonging to American citizenship, have been so construed as to defeat the ends the people desired to accomplish, which they attempted to accomplish, and which they supposed they had accomplished by changes in their fundamental law....

[In a long opinion Justice Harlan argued that both the 13th and 14th Amendments gave Congress power to legislate directly with reference to private individuals engaged in such quasi-public businesses as those involved in this case.]

My brethren say, that when a man has emerged from slavery, and by the aid of beneficent legislation has shaken off the inseparable concomitants of that state, there must be some stage in the progress of his elevation when he takes the rank of a mere citizen, and ceases to be the special favorite of the laws, and when his rights as a citizen, or a man, are to be protected in the ordinary modes by which other men's rights are protected. It is, I submit, scarcely just to say that the colored race has been the special favorite of the laws. The Statute of 1875, now adjudged to be unconstitutional, is for the benefit of citizens of every race and color. What the Nation, through Congress, has sought to accomplish in reference to that race, is—what had already been done in every State of the Union for the white race—to secure and protect rights belonging to them as freemen and citizens; nothing more. It was not deemed enough "to help the feeble up, but to support him after." The one underlying purpose of congressional legislation has been to enable the black race to take the rank of mere citizens. The difficulty has been to compel a recognition of the legal right of the black race to take the rank of citizens, and to secure the enjoyment of privileges belonging, under the law, to them as a component part of the people for whose welfare and happiness government is ordained. At every step, in this direction, the Nation has been confronted with class tyranny, which a contemporary English historian says is, of tyrannies, the most intolerable, "For it is ubiquitous in its operation, and weighs, perhaps, most heavily on those whose obscurity or distance would withdraw them from the notice of a single despot." Today, it is the colored race which is denied, by corporations and individuals wielding public authority, rights fundamental in their freedom and citizenship. At some future time, it may be that some other race will fall under the ban of race discrimination. If the constitutional Amendments be enforced, according to the intent with which, as I conceive, they were adopted, there cannot be in this Republic, any class of human beings in practical subjection to another class, with power in the latter to dole out to the former just such privileges as they may choose to grant. The supreme law of the land has decreed that no authority shall be exercised in this country upon the basis of discrimination, in respect of civil rights, against freemen and citizens because of their race, color or previous condition of servitude. To that decree—for the due enforcement of which, by appropriate legislation, Congress has been invested with express power—every one must bow, whatever may have been, or whatever now are, his individual views as to the wisdom or policy, either of the recent changes in the fundamental law, or of the legislation which has been enacted to give them effect.

For the reasons stated I feel constrained to withhold my assent to the opinion of the court.

THE RELATIONSHIP BETWEEN CONGRESSIONAL POWER TO ENFORCE THE CONSTITUTION AND SELF–ENFORCING PROVISIONS OF THE CONSTITUTION

While the ultimate issue in the Civil Rights Cases concerned the constitutional validity of a federal statute prohibiting private discrimination, the bulk of the opinion discusses the question whether private racial discrimination would violate the Constitution had there been no federal legislation. The case was a major decision concerning the application of the Constitution to private conduct only because the Court's rationale was that Congressional power to enforce the thirteenth and fourteenth amendments necessarily tracked the self-executing provisions of those amendments. The next section of this chapter will explore the extent to which the fourteenth amendment applies of its own force to private conduct. Sections 4 through 6 will return to the issue of Congressional power. It is appropriate at this point to entertain a preliminary inquiry whether the interpretations of section one of the thirteenth amendment and section one of the fourteenth amendment should mark the outer limits of Congress' power to "enforce" those amendments.

Consider the facts of one of the cases grouped for decision in the Civil Rights Cases—the owner of a private theater enforcing a racially discriminatory policy in the selection of patrons. What are the consequences of a judicial decision that section one of the fourteenth amendment requires preferring the rights of the excluded patrons to those of the owner? What are the consequences of a judicial decision that Congress has the power under section five of the fourteenth amendment to require the theater owner to desist from racial discrimination in choice of patrons? Do those different consequences suggest that there should be differences in the reach of the self-enforcing provisions of section one and Congressional power under section five? Can major differences in the reach of section one and Congressional power under section five be recognized without giving Congress limitless power no longer tied to any limitation that it be directed to "enforcing" the fourteenth amendment?

SECTION 2. APPLICATION OF THE CONSTITUTION TO PRIVATE CONDUCT

Introduction to the State Action Concept. With the exception of the thirteenth amendment the Constitution is a restraint on governmental action and does not provide one private citizen with rights against another. The Bill of Rights restrains the action of the federal government. The fourteenth amendment provides that "no state shall" deprive any person of due process or equal protection. The fifteenth amendment prohibits denial of voting rights "by the United States or by any State...." The same verbal formula appears in the voting right protections of the nineteenth, twenty-fourth and twenty-sixth amendments.

A basic conception of the opinion in the Civil Rights Cases was that "civil rights, such as are guaranteed by the Constitution against state aggression, cannot be impaired by the wrongful acts of individuals, unsupported by state authority in the shape of laws, customs, or judicial or executive proceedings." In a general sense, however, all private action is "supported by state authority" if the state has not chosen to make that private action illegal. It has proved to be extremely difficult to determine when state involvement with private action, beyond mere failure to prohibit it, brings into play the constitutional limitations on governmental action.

It has also proved to be difficult to organize the cases that involve the problem. Subsection A deals with the argument that constitutional limits apply because a private party is performing a function normally performed by government. Subsection B collects the cases where it is claimed that government has enforced the racially discriminatory decisions of private parties. Subsection C includes, quite simply, the rest of the cases where the argument has been made that government has "supported" the conduct of private parties by approving it, regulating it, or providing financial support to it.

From the end of World War II through 1968, all Supreme Court decisions that reached the question whether unconstitutional state action was present decided that it was. Since 1970, most Supreme Court decisions considering the same issue have not found unconstitutional state action. Part of the explanation may be found in significant changes in the Court's membership. (Compare Evans v. Newton, 382 U.S. 296 [1966], infra p. 1110, with Evans v. Abney, 396 U.S. 435 [1970], infra p. 1124, Amalgamated Food Employees Union Local 590 v. Logan Valley Plaza, Inc., 391 U.S. 308 [1968], with Lloyd Corp., Ltd. v. Tanner, 407 U.S. 551 [1972], both discussed infra p. 1110.) Other explanations may stem from the fact that nearly all of the cases prior to 1968 dealt with racial discrimination. Since 1970, issues such as first amendment rights of access to private property and due process rights of fair procedure have been prominent. Is the extent of governmental action required to invoke constitutional protection less where racial discrimination is claimed than when other forms of discrimination, or other constitutional rights, are involved?

A related question concerns the impact of the growing body of federal legislation prohibiting private racial discrimination. (See sections 3, 4, 5 and 6 of this chapter.) The Civil Rights Act of 1964 prohibits private racial discrimination in places of public accommodation, employment, and activities—including private education—receiving Federal financial assistance. The 1968 Civil Rights Act prohibits racial discrimination in the private housing market, and provides criminal penalties for many forms of private racial violence. And, in 1968, the Court discovered that remaining fragments of the Civil Rights Act of 1866 reached broad areas of private racial discrimination. (See section 4 of this chapter.) There are few cases now where the issue whether federal law prohibits private racial discrimination will turn on whether sufficient indicia of state action are present to invoke the provisions of the fourteenth amendment. Does this suggest legitimate reasons for limiting state action doctrines, even as applied to racial discrimination?

A.   PRIVATE PERFORMANCE OF "GOVERNMENT" FUNCTIONS

THE WHITE PRIMARY CASES

Despite the clear terms of the fifteenth amendment, for three-quarters of a century an effective means to block voting by Blacks was their exclusion from the Democratic Party in Southern States. Initially, it was argued that primary voting was beyond constitutional protection, even if state law mandated exclusion of Black voters from participation in the Democratic primaries. In Nixon v. Herndon, 273 U.S. 536 (1927), however, a Texas statute excluding Blacks from Democratic primaries was held to be unconstitutional as racial discrimination by the state. Texas' response was to repeal the offending statute, and to provide that a party's executive committee had the power to determine the party's membership. Exclusion of Blacks from the Democratic primary was again held unconstitutional on the ground that the new Texas statute had made the committee an agent of the state. Nixon v. Condon, 286 U.S. 73 (1932). When the Texas Democratic Party once again excluded Blacks from party membership, however, the exclusion survived constitutional attack on the ground that it was not state action, but the action of a private group. Grovey v. Townsend, 295 U.S. 45 (1935). Grovey v. Townsend was overruled in Smith v. Allwright, 321 U.S. 649 (1944), because "the place of the primary in the electoral scheme makes clear that state delegation to a party of the power to fix the qualifications of primary elections is delegation of a state function that may make the party's action the action of the state." That the Constitution prohibited exclusion of Blacks from participating in elections, whatever form the election took, was dramatized in Terry v. Adams, 345 U.S. 461 (1953), where Blacks were excluded from voting in a pre-primary straw vote of a Texas county political organization called the Jaybird Democratic Organization. Because winners in the Jaybird primary ran unopposed in the formal Democratic primaries, the Court decided that exclusion of Blacks from the Jaybird primary was a violation of the fifteenth amendment, despite the absence of formal state involvement in their exclusion.

STEELE v. LOUISVILLE AND NASHVILLE RAILROAD CO., 323 U.S. 192 (1944). The Brotherhood of Locomotive Firemen and Enginemen, under the terms of the Railway Labor Act, was exclusive bargaining representative for the railway firemen. Blacks who constituted a substantial minority of the labor force, were excluded from membership in the Brotherhood. As a result of negotiations an agreement was made in 1941 between the Railroad and the Brotherhood providing for restrictions on the hiring and promotion of Blacks with the ultimate aim of their exclusion from work as firemen. Steele, a Black fireman, brought suit against the Railroad and the Brotherhood based on the foregoing facts. The Supreme Court of Alabama affirmed the dismissal of the complaint. The United States Supreme Court, speaking through Chief Justice Stone, said:

"If, as the state court has held, the Act confers this power on the bargaining representative of a craft or class of employees without any commensurate statutory duty toward its members, constitutional questions arise. For the representative is clothed with power not unlike that of a legislature which is subject to constitutional limitations on its power to deny, restrict, destroy or discriminate against the rights of those for whom it legislates and which is also under an affirmative constitutional duty equally to protect those rights. . . .

"We think that the Railway Labor Act imposes upon the statutory representatives of a craft at least as exacting a duty to protect equally the interests of the members of the craft as the Constitution imposes upon a legislature to give equal protection to the interests of those for whom it legislates. Congress has seen fit to clothe the bargaining representative with powers comparable to those possessed by a legislative body both to create and restrict the rights of those whom it represents, . . . but it has also imposed on the representative a corresponding duty. . . .

"Reversed."

Justice Murphy, concurring, stated that the case presented "a grave constitutional issue that should be squarely faced." The Railway Labor Act must be construed to bar this discrimination: "Otherwise the Act would bear the stigma of unconstitutionality under the Fifth Amendment in this respect."

ACCESS TO COMPANY TOWNS AND SHOPPING CENTERS

Marsh v. Alabama, 326 U.S. 501 (1946), was one of two pre–1970 Supreme Court decisions, that presented the state action issue in some context other than racial discrimination. A member of Jehovah's Witnesses was prosecuted for trespass when she distributed religious literature on the streets of a company-owned town and refused to leave when ordered to do so. The town involved was described by the Court as being accessible to and freely used by the public in general with nothing to distinguish it from any other town except the fact that the title to the property belonged to a private corporation. In reversing the conviction the Court talked primarily about first amendment issues. It stated that had the corporation owned the segment of the state highway that paralleled the business street of the company town and operated that segment it would "have been the performance of a public function." The opinion then continued:

> "We do not think it makes any significant constitutional difference as to the relationship between the rights of the owner and those of the public that here the State, instead of permitting the corporation to operate a highway, permitted it to use its property as a town, operate a 'business block' in the town and a street and sidewalk on that business block.... Whether a corporation or a municipality owns or possesses the town the public in either case has an identical interest in the functioning of the community in such manner that the channels of communication remain free."

The other pre–1970 case not involving racial discrimination was Amalgamated Food Employees Union Local 590 v. Logan Valley Plaza, Inc., 391 U.S. 308 (1968), which extended *Marsh* to require that picketers be given access to a large privately-owned shopping center. Justice Marshall's opinion for the majority concluded that there was no reason to draw a distinction between a privately owned business district surrounded by residential property under the same ownership, and one surrounded by property under other ownership. Justice Black, the author of the *Marsh* opinion but one of three dissenters in *Logan Valley,* argued that the company town in *Marsh* had all the attributes of a conventional municipality, but that the shopping center had only one— ownership of the business block. *Logan Valley* was criticized, but distinguished, in Lloyd Corp., Ltd. v. Tanner, 407 U.S. 551 (1972), where anti-war leafletters were held not to have a constitutional right of access to a large privately-owned shopping center. The four Justices in the *Logan Valley* majority who were still on the Court dissented in *Lloyd*. In Hudgens v. NLRB, 424 U.S. 507 (1976), the Court concluded that *Lloyd* had overruled *Logan Valley* and that speakers had no constitutional right of access to large privately-owned shopping centers.

EVANS v. NEWTON, 382 U.S. 296 (1966). In 1911, Senator Augustus O. Bacon executed a will devising land to the City of Macon, Georgia, for a park for Whites only. The city kept the park segregated for decades, but in some years prior to this suit permitted Blacks to use it on the ground that the city could not constitutionally maintain a segregated park. (See Pennsylvania v. Board of City Trusts, infra, p. 1122.) This suit sought to remove the city as trustee. Black citizens of Macon intervened, asking the state court to refuse to appoint new private trustees. The trial court accepted the resignation of the city as trustee and appointed private trustees. The Supreme Court of Georgia affirmed. The United States Supreme Court reversed, holding that the park could not be maintained on a segregated basis, despite the city's resignation as trustee. Justice Douglas' opinion for the Court gave two reasons. First, his opinion read the record below as showing that the city remained "entwined in the management or control of the park." Second, the opinion stated:

"This conclusion [that the substitution of trustees did not transfer the park to the 'private sector'] is buttressed by the nature of the service rendered the community by a park. The service rendered even by a private park of this character is municipal in nature. It is open to every white person, there being no selective element other than race. Golf clubs, social centers, luncheon clubs, schools such as Tuskegee was at least in origin, and other like organizations in the private sector are often racially oriented. A park, on the other hand, is more like a fire department or police department that traditionally serves the community. Mass recreation through the use of parks is plainly in the public domain, Watson v. Memphis, 373 U.S. 526; and state courts that aid private parties to perform that public function on a segregated basis implicate the State in conduct proscribed by the Fourteenth Amendment. Like the streets of the company town in Marsh v. Alabama, supra, the elective process of Terry v. Adams, supra, and the transit system of Public Util. Comm'n v. Pollak, supra, the predominant character and purpose of this park are municipal."

Justice White concurred in the result. Justices Black, Harlan and Stewart dissented.

Flagg Brothers, Inc. v. Brooks

436 U.S. 149, 98 S.Ct. 1729, 56 L.Ed.2d 185 (1978).

Mr. Justice Rehnquist delivered the opinion of the Court.

The question presented by this litigation is whether a warehouseman's proposed sale of goods entrusted to him for storage, as permitted by New York Uniform Commercial Code § 7–210, is an action properly attributable to the State of New York. . . .

I.

According to her complaint, the allegations of which we must accept as true, respondent Shirley Brooks and her family were evicted from their apartment in Mount Vernon, N.Y., on June 13, 1973. The City Marshal arranged for Brooks' possessions to be stored by petitioner Flagg Brothers, Inc., in its warehouse. Respondent was informed of the cost of moving and storage, and she instructed the workmen to proceed, although she found the price too high. On August 25, 1973, after a series of disputes over the validity of the charges being claimed by petitioner, Flagg Brothers, Brooks received a letter demanding that her account be brought up to date within 10 days "or your furniture will be sold." . . . A series of subsequent letters from respondent and her attorneys produced no satisfaction.

Brooks thereupon initiated this class action in the District Court under 42 U.S.C. § 1983, seeking damages, an injunction against the threatened sale of her belongings, and the declaration that such a sale pursuant to § 7–210 would violate the Due Process and Equal Protection Clauses of the Fourteenth Amendment. . . . [T]he District Court, dismissed the complaint for failure to state a claim for relief under § 1983.

A divided panel of the Court of Appeals reversed.

. . .

II.

A claim upon which relief may be granted to respondents against Flagg Brothers under § 1983 must embody at least two elements. Respondents are first bound to show that they have been deprived of a right "secured by the Constitution and the laws" of the United States. They must secondly show that Flagg Brothers deprived them of this right acting "under color of any statute" of the State of New York. It is clear that these two elements denote two separate areas of inquiry. . . .

It must be noted that respondents have named no public officials as defendants in this action. The city marshal, who supervised their evictions, was dismissed from the case by the consent of all the parties. This total absence of overt official involvement plainly distinguishes this case from earlier decisions imposing procedural restrictions on creditors' remedies. . . . While as a factual matter any person with sufficient physical power may deprive a person of his property, only a State or a private person whose action "may fairly be treated as that of the State itself," . . . may deprive him of "an interest encompassed within the Fourteenth Amendment's protection," . . . Thus, the only issue presented by this case is whether Flagg Brothers' action may fairly be attributed to the State of New York. We conclude that it may not.

III.

Respondents' primary contention is that New York has delegated to Flagg Brothers a power "traditionally exclusively reserved to the State." *Jackson.* . . . They argue that the resolution of private disputes is a traditional function of civil government, and that the State in § 7–210 has delegated this function to Flagg Brothers. Respondents, however, have read too much into the language of our previous cases. While many functions have been traditionally performed by governments, very few have been "exclusively reserved to the State."

One such area has been elections. While the Constitution protects private rights of association and advocacy with regard to the election of public officials, our cases make it clear that the conduct of the elections themselves is an exclusively public function. . . .

A second line of cases under the public function doctrine originated with Marsh v. Alabama, 326 U.S. 501 (1946). Just as the Texas Democratic Party in *Smith* and the Jaybird Democratic Association in *Terry* effectively performed the entire public function of selecting public officials, so too the Gulf Shipbuilding Corp. performed all the necessary municipal functions in the town of Chickasaw, Ala., which it owned. . . .

These two branches of the public function doctrine have in common the feature of exclusivity.[8] Although the elections held by the Democratic Party and its affiliates were the only meaningful elections in Texas, and the streets owned by the Gulf Shipbuilding Corp. were the only streets in Chickasaw, the

---

[8] Respondents also contend that Evans v. Newton, 382 U.S. 296 (1966), establishes that the operation of a park for recreational purposes is an exclusively public function. We doubt that *Newton* intended to establish any such broad doctrine in the teeth of the experience of several American entrepreneurs who amassed great fortunes by operating parks for recreational purposes. We think *Newton* rests on a finding of ordinary state action under extraordinary circumstances. The Court's opinion emphasizes that the record showed "no change in the municipal maintenance and concern over this facility," id., at 301, after the transfer of title to private trustees. That transfer had not been shown to have eliminated the actual involvement of the city in the daily maintenance and care of the park.

proposed sale by Flagg Brothers under § 7–210 is not the only means of resolving this purely private dispute. . . .

Whatever the particular remedies available under New York law, we do not consider a . . . detailed description of them necessary to our conclusion that the settlement of disputes between debtors and creditors is not traditionally an exclusive public function. . . .

Thus, even if we were inclined to extend the sovereign function doctrine outside of its present carefully confined bounds, the field of private commercial transactions would be a particularly inappropriate area into which to expand it. We conclude that our sovereign function cases do not support a finding of state action here.

. . . [T]here are a number of state and municipal functions not covered by our election cases nor governed by the reasoning of *Marsh* which have been administered with a greater degree of exclusivity by States and municipalities than has the function of so-called "dispute resolution." Among these are such functions as education, fire and police protection, and tax collection. We express no view as to the extent, if any, to which a city or State might be free to delegate to private parties the performance of such functions and thereby avoid the strictures of the Fourteenth Amendment. The mere recitation of these possible permutations and combinations of factual situations suffices to caution us that their resolution should abide the necessity of deciding them.

IV.

Respondents further urge that Flagg Brothers' proposed action is properly attributable to the State because the State has authorized and encouraged it in enacting § 7–210. Our cases state "that a State is responsible for the . . . act of a private party when the State, by its law, has compelled the act." . . . This Court, however, has never held that a State's mere acquiescence in a private action converts that action into that of the State. . . .

. . .

Here, the State of New York has not compelled the sale of a bailor's goods, but has merely announced the circumstances under which its courts will not interfere with a private sale. Indeed, the crux of respondents' complaint is not that the State *has* acted, but that it has *refused* to act. This statutory refusal to act is no different in principle from an ordinary statute of limitations whereby the State declines to provide a remedy for private deprivations of property after the passage of a given period of time.

. . .

Reversed.

Mr. Justice Brennan took no part in the consideration or decision of this case.

Mr. Justice Stevens, with whom Mr. Justice White and Mr. Justice Marshall join, dissenting.

. . . In my judgment the Court's holding is fundamentally inconsistent with, if not foreclosed by, our prior decisions which have imposed procedural restrictions on the State's authorization of certain creditors' remedies. . . .

There is no question in this case but that respondents have a property interest in the possessions that the warehouseman proposes to sell. It is also clear that, whatever power of sale the warehouseman has, it does not derive from the consent of the respondents. The claimed power derives solely from the

State, and specifically from § 7–210 of the New York Uniform Commercial Code. The question is whether a state statute which authorizes a private party to deprive a person of his property without his consent must meet the requirements of the Due Process Clause of the Fourteenth Amendment. This question must be answered in the affirmative unless the State has virtually unlimited power to transfer interests in private property without any procedural protections.

In determining that New York's statute cannot be scrutinized under the Due Process Clause, the Court reasons that the warehouseman's proposed sale is solely private action because the state statute *"permits* but does not compel" the sale, ... (emphasis added), and because the warehouseman has not been delegated a power *"exclusively* reserved to the State," ... (emphasis added). Under this approach a State could enact laws authorizing private citizens to use self-help in countless situations without any possibility of federal challenge. ... [T]he distinctions between "permission" and "compulsion" on the one hand, and "exclusive" and "non-exclusive," on the other, cannot be determinative factors in state-action, analysis. ... In this case, the State of New York, by enacting § 7–210 of the Uniform Commercial Code, has acted in the most effective and unambiguous way a State can act. This section specifically authorizes petitioner to sell respondents' possessions; it details the procedures that petitioner must follow; and it grants petitioner the power to convey good title to goods that are now owned by respondents to a third party.

While Members of this Court have suggested that statutory authorization alone may be sufficient to establish state action, it is not necessary to rely on those suggestions in this case because New York has authorized the warehouseman to perform what is clearly a state function. The test of what is a state function for purposes of the Due Process Clause has been variously phrased. Most frequently the issue is presented in terms of whether the State has delegated a function traditionally and historically associated with sovereignty. ...In this Court, petitioners have attempted to argue that the nonconsensual transfer of property rights is not a traditional function of the sovereign. The overwhelming historical evidence is to the contrary, however, and the Court wisely does not adopt this position. Instead, the Court reasons that state action cannot be found because the State has not delegated to the warehouseman an *exclusive* sovereign function. This distinction, however, is not consistent with our prior decisions on state action[9]....

. . .

Whether termed "traditional," "exclusive," or "significant," the state power to order binding, nonconsensual resolution of a conflict between debtor and creditor is exactly the sort of power with which the Due Process Clause is concerned. And the State's delegation of that power to a private party is, accordingly, subject to due process scrutiny. ...

It is important to emphasize that, contrary to the Court's apparent fears, this conclusion does not even remotely suggest that "all private deprivations of property [will] be converted into public acts whenever the State, for whatever reason, denies relief sought by the putative property owner." ... The focus is not on the private deprivation but on the state authorization. "[W]hat is always

---

[9] The Court, for instance, attempts to distinguish Evans v. Newton, 382 U.S. 296. *Newton* concededly involved a function which is not exclusively sovereign—the operation of a park, but the Court claims that *Newton* actually rested on a determination that the City was still involved in the "daily maintenance and care of the park." Ante, n. 8. This stark attempt to rewrite the rationale of the *Newton* opinion is fully answered by Mr. Justice White's opinion in that case. ...

vital to remember is that it is the *state's* conduct, whether action or inaction, not the *private* conduct, that gives rise to constitutional attack." H. Friendly, The Dartmouth College Case and The Public–Private Penumbra, p. 17 (emphasis in original). The State's conduct in this case takes the concrete form of a statutory enactment, and it is that statute that may be challenged.

My analysis in this case thus assumes that petitioner's proposed sale will conform to the procedure specified by the state legislature and that respondents' challenge therefore will be to the constitutionality of that process. It is only what the State itself has enacted that they may ask the federal court to review in a § 1983 case. If there should be a deviation from the state statute—such as a failure to give the notice required by the state law—the defect could be remedied by a state court and there would be no occasion for § 1983 relief. . . .

On the other hand, if there is compliance with the New York statute, the state legislative action which enabled the deprivation to take place must be subject to constitutional challenge in a federal court. Under this approach, the federal courts do not have jurisdiction to review every foreclosure proceeding in which the debtor claims that there has been a procedural defect constituting a denial of due process of law. Rather, the Federal District Court's jurisdiction under § 1983 is limited to challenges to the constitutionality of the state procedure itself. . . .

Finally, it is obviously true that the overwhelming majority of disputes in our society are resolved in the private sphere. But it is no longer possible, if it ever was, to believe that a sharp line can be drawn between private and public actions. The Court today holds that our examination of state delegations of power should be limited to those rare instances where the State has ceded one of its "exclusive" powers. As indicated, I believe that this limitation is neither logical nor practical. More troubling, this description of what is state action does not even attempt to reflect the concerns of the Due Process Clause, for the state action doctrine is, after all, merely one aspect of this broad constitutional protection.

In the broadest sense, we expect government "to provide a reasonable and fair framework of rules which facilitate commercial transactions. . . ." Mitchell v. W.T. Grant, . . . 416 U.S., at 624 (Powell, J., concurring). This "framework of rules" is premised on the assumption that the State will control nonconsensual deprivations of property and that the State's control will, in turn, be subject to the restrictions of the Due Process Clause. The power to order legally binding surrenders of property and the constitutional restrictions on that power are necessary correlatives in our system. In effect, today's decision allows the State to divorce these two elements by the simple expedient of transferring the implementation of its policy to private parties. Because the Fourteenth Amendment does not countenance such a division of power and responsibility, I respectfully dissent.[a]

SAN FRANCISCO ARTS & ATHLETICS, INC. v. UNITED STATES OLYMPIC COMMITTEE, 483 U.S. 522 (1987). Section 110 of the Amateur Sports Act of 1978 grants the Committee the right to prohibit commercial and promotional uses of the word "Olympic." The Court rejected an argument that the Committee violated the equal protection component of the Fifth Amendment by discriminatory enforcement of its exclusive right. The Committee was

---

[a] See Brest, *State Action and Liberal Theory: A Casenote on* Flagg Brothers v. Brooks, 130 U.Pa.L.Rev. 96 (1982).

not a governmental actor and did not perform functions that have been traditionally the exclusive prerogative of the federal government. There was no evidence of governmental involvement in the Committee's choice of how it enforced its right. Four dissenters argued that the Committee was a governmental actor because there was a "symbiotic relationship" between the Committee and the Federal Government in coordinating amateur athletics in international competition. Two of the four dissenters argued, in addition, that the Committee performed a public function in governing international amateur athletics.

B. GOVERNMENTAL ENFORCEMENT OF "PRIVATE" DECISIONS

Shelley v. Kraemer

334 U.S. 1, 68 S.Ct. 836, 92 L.Ed. 1161 (1948).

Mr. Chief Justice Vinson delivered the opinion of the Court.

These cases present for our consideration questions relating to the validity of court enforcement of private agreements, generally described as restrictive covenants, which have as their purpose the exclusion of persons of designated race or color from the ownership or occupancy of real property. Basic constitutional issues of obvious importance have been raised.

The first of these cases comes to this Court on certiorari to the Supreme Court of Missouri. On February 16, 1911, thirty out of a total of thirty-nine owners of property fronting both sides of Labadie Avenue between Taylor Avenue and Cora Avenue in the city of St. Louis, signed an agreement, which was subsequently recorded providing in part:

> "... the said property is hereby restricted to the use and occupancy for the term of Fifty (50) years from this date, so that it shall be a condition all the time and whether recited and referred to as [sic] not in subsequent conveyances and shall attach to the land, as a condition precedent to the sale of the same, that hereafter no part of said property or any portion thereof shall be, for said term of Fifty-years, occupied by any person not of the Caucasian race, it being intended hereby to restrict the use of said property for said period of time against the occupancy as owners or tenants of any portion of said property for resident or other purpose by people of the Negro or Mongolian Race."

The entire district described in the agreement included fifty-seven parcels of land. The thirty owners who signed the agreement held title to forty-seven parcels, including the particular parcel involved in this case. ...

On August 11, 1945, pursuant to a contract of sale, petitioners Shelley, who are Negroes, for valuable consideration received from one Fitzgerald a warranty deed to the parcel in question. The trial court found that petitioners had no actual knowledge of the restrictive agreement at the time of the purchase.

On October 9, 1945, respondents, as owners of other property subject to the terms of the restrictive covenant, brought suit in the Circuit Court of the city of St. Louis praying that petitioners Shelley be restrained from taking possession of the property and that judgment be entered divesting title out of petitioners Shelley and revesting title in the immediate grantor or in such other person as the court should direct. The trial court denied the requested relief on the ground that the restrictive agreement, upon which respondents based their action, had never become final and complete. . . .

The Supreme Court of Missouri sitting *en banc* reversed and directed the trial court to grant the relief for which respondents had prayed. That court held the agreement effective and concluded that enforcement of its provisions violated no rights guaranteed to petitioners by the Federal Constitution. At the time the court rendered its decision, petitioners were occupying the property in question.

The second of the cases under consideration comes to this Court from the Supreme Court of Michigan. The circumstances presented do not differ materially from the Missouri case. . . .

Petitioners have placed primary reliance on their contentions, first raised in the state courts, that judicial enforcement of the restrictive agreements in these cases has violated rights guaranteed to petitioners by the Fourteenth Amendment of the Federal Constitution and Acts of Congress passed pursuant to that Amendment. Specifically, petitioners urge that they have been denied the equal protection of the laws, deprived of property without due process of law, and have been denied privileges and immunities of citizens of the United States. We pass to a consideration of those issues.

I.

Whether the equal protection clause of the Fourteenth Amendment inhibits judicial enforcement by state courts of restrictive covenants based on race or color is a question which this Court has not heretofore been called upon to consider. . . .

. . .

It should be observed that these covenants do not seek to proscribe any particular use of the affected properties. Use of the properties for residential occupancy, as such, is not forbidden. The restrictions of these agreements, rather are directed toward a designated class of persons and seek to determine who may and who may not own or make use of the properties for residential purposes. The excluded class is defined wholly in terms of race or color; "simply that and nothing more."

It cannot be doubted that among the civil rights intended to be protected from discriminatory state action by the Fourteenth Amendment are the rights to acquire, enjoy, own and dispose of property. . . .

It is likewise clear that restrictions on the right of occupancy of the sort sought to be created by the private agreements in these cases could not be squared with the requirements of the Fourteenth Amendment if imposed by state statute or local ordinance. We do not understand respondents to urge the contrary. In the case of Buchanan v. Warley [245 U.S. 60] a unanimous Court declared unconstitutional the provisions of a city ordinance which denied to colored persons the right to occupy houses in blocks in which the greater number of houses were occupied by white persons, and imposed similar restrictions on white persons with respect to blocks in which the greater number of houses were occupied by colored persons. During the course of the opinion in that case, this Court stated: "The Fourteenth Amendment and these statutes enacted in furtherance of its purpose operate to qualify and entitle a colored man to acquire property without state legislation discriminating against him solely because of color."

In Harmon v. Tyler, 273 U.S. 668 (1927), a unanimous court, on the authority of *Buchanan v. Warley,* supra, declared invalid an ordinance which forbade any Negro to establish a home on any property in a white community or any white person to establish a home in a Negro community, "except on the written consent of a majority of the persons of the opposite race inhabiting such community or portion of the City to be affected."

But the present cases, unlike those just discussed, do not involve action by state legislatures or city councils. Here the particular patterns of discrimination and the areas in which the restrictions are to operate, are determined, in the first instance, by the terms of agreements among private individuals. Participation of the State consists in the enforcement of the restrictions so defined. The crucial issue with which we are here confronted is whether this distinction removes these cases from the operation of the prohibitory provisions of the Fourteenth Amendment.

Since the decision of this Court in the Civil Rights Cases, 109 U.S. 3 (1883), the principle has become firmly embedded in our constitutional law that the action inhibited by the first section of the Fourteenth Amendment is only such action as may fairly be said to be that of the States. That Amendment erects no shield against merely private conduct, however discriminatory or wrongful.

We conclude, therefore, that the restrictive agreements standing alone cannot be regarded as a violation of any rights guaranteed to petitioners by the Fourteenth Amendment. So long as the purposes of those agreements are effectuated by voluntary adherence to their terms, it would appear clear that there has been no action by the State and the provisions of the Amendment have not been violated. Cf. *Corrigan v. Buckley,* supra.

But here there was more. These are cases in which the purposes of the agreements were secured only by judicial enforcement by state courts of the restrictive terms of the agreements. The respondents urge that judicial enforcement of private agreements does not amount to state action; or, in any event, the participation of the State is so attenuated in character as not to amount to state action within the meaning of the Fourteenth Amendment. Finally, it is suggested, even if the States in these cases may be deemed to have acted in the constitutional sense, their action did not deprive petitioners of rights guaranteed by the Fourteenth Amendment. We move to a consideration of these matters.

II.

That the action of state courts and of judicial officers in their official capacities is to be regarded as action of the State within the meaning of the Fourteenth Amendment, is a proposition which has long been established by decisions of this Court. That principle was given expression in the earliest cases involving the construction of the terms of the Fourteenth Amendment. ...

One of the earliest applications of the prohibitions contained in the Fourteenth Amendment to action of state judicial officials occurred in cases in which Negroes had been excluded from jury service in criminal prosecutions by reason of their race or color. These cases demonstrate, also, the early recognition by this Court that state action in violation of the Amendment's provisions is equally repugnant to the constitutional commands whether directed by state statute or taken by a judicial official in the absence of statute. ...

The action of state courts in imposing penalties or depriving parties of other substantive rights without providing adequate notice and opportunity to defend, has, of course, long been regarded as a denial of the due process of law guaranteed by the Fourteenth Amendment. *Brinkerhoff–Faris Trust & Savings Co. v. Hill,* supra. Cf. Pennoyer v. Neff, 5 U.S. 714 (1878).

In numerous cases, this Court has reversed criminal convictions in state courts for failure of those courts to provide the essential ingredients of a fair hearing. . . .

But the examples of state judicial action which have been held by this Court to violate the Amendment's commands are not restricted to situations in which the judicial proceedings were found in some manner to be procedurally unfair. It has been recognized that the action of state courts in enforcing a substantive common-law rule formulated by those courts, may result in the denial of rights guaranteed by the Fourteenth Amendment, even though the judicial proceedings in such cases may have been in complete accord with the most rigorous conceptions of procedural due process. Thus in American Federation of Labor v. Swing, 1941, 312 U.S. 321, enforcement by state courts of the common-law policy of the State, which resulted in the restraining of peaceful picketing, was held to be state action of the sort prohibited by the Amendment's guaranties of freedom of discussion. . . .

The short of the matter is that from the time of the adoption of the Fourteenth Amendment until the present, it has been the consistent ruling of this Court that the action of the States to which the Amendment has reference, includes action of state courts and state judicial officials. Although, in construing the terms of the Fourteenth Amendment, differences have from time to time been expressed as to whether particular types of state action may be said to offend the Amendment's prohibitory provisions, it has never been suggested that state court action is immunized from the operation of those provisions simply because the act is that of the judicial branch of the state government.

III.

Against this background of judicial construction, extending over a period of some three-quarters of a century, we are called upon to consider whether enforcement by state courts of the restrictive agreements in these cases may be deemed to be the acts of those States; and, if so, whether that action has denied these petitioners the equal protection of the laws which the Amendment was intended to insure.

We have no doubt that there has been state action in these cases in the full and complete sense of the phrase. The undisputed facts disclose that petitioners were willing purchasers of properties upon which they desired to establish homes. The owners of the properties were willing sellers; and contracts of sale were accordingly consummated. It is clear that but for the active intervention of the state courts, supported by the full panoply of state power, petitioners would have been free to occupy the properties in question without restraint.

These are not cases, as has been suggested, in which the States have merely abstained from action, leaving private individuals free to impose such discriminations as they see fit. Rather, these are cases in which the States have made available to such individuals the full coercive power of government to deny to petitioners, on the grounds of race or color, the enjoyment of property rights in premises which petitioners are willing and financially able to acquire and which the grantors are willing to sell. The difference between judicial enforcement and nonenforcement of the restrictive covenants is the difference to petitioners between being denied rights of property available to other members of the community and being accorded full enjoyment of those rights on an equal footing.

The enforcement of the restrictive agreements by the state courts in these cases was directed pursuant to the common-law policy of the States as formulated by those courts in earlier decisions. In the Missouri case, enforcement of the covenant was directed in the first instance by the highest court of the State after the trial court had determined the agreement to be invalid for want of the requisite number of signatures. In the Michigan case, the order of enforcement by the trial court was affirmed by the highest state court. The judicial action in each case bears the clear and unmistakable imprimatur of the State. We have noted that previous decisions of this Court have established the proposition that judicial action is not immunized from the operation of the Fourteenth Amendment simply because it is taken pursuant to the state's common-law policy. Nor is the Amendment ineffective simply because the particular pattern of discrimination, which the State has enforced, was defined initially by the terms of a private agreement. State action, as that phrase is understood for the purposes of the Fourteenth Amendment, refers to exertions of state power in all forms. And when the effect of that action is to deny rights subject to the protection of the Fourteenth Amendment, it is the obligation of this Court to enforce the constitutional commands.

We hold that in granting judicial enforcement of the restrictive agreements in these cases, the States have denied petitioners the equal protection of the laws and that, therefore, the action of the state courts cannot stand. We have noted that freedom from discrimination by the States in the enjoyment of property rights was among the basic objectives sought to be effectuated by the framers of the Fourteenth Amendment. That such discrimination has occurred in these cases is clear. Because of the race or color of these petitioners they have been denied rights of ownership or occupancy enjoyed as a matter of course by other citizens of different race or color. . . .

Respondents urge, however, that since the state courts stand ready to enforce restrictive covenants excluding white persons from the ownership or occupancy of property covered by such agreements, enforcement of covenants excluding colored persons may not be deemed a denial of equal protection of the laws to the colored persons who are thereby affected. This contention does not bear scrutiny. The parties have directed our attention to no case in which a court, state or federal, has been called upon to enforce a covenant excluding members of the white majority from ownership or occupancy of real property on grounds of race or color. But there are more fundamental considerations. The rights created by the first section of the Fourteenth Amendment are, by its terms, guaranteed to the individual. The rights established are personal rights. It is, therefore, no answer to these petitioners to say that the courts may also be induced to deny white persons rights of ownership and occupancy on grounds of race or color. Equal protection of the laws is not achieved through indiscriminate imposition of inequalities. . . .

. . .

For the reasons stated, the judgment of the Supreme Court of Missouri and the judgment of the Supreme Court of Michigan must be reversed.

Reversed.

Mr. Justice Reed, Mr. Justice Jackson, and Mr. Justice Rutledge took no part in the consideration or decision of these cases.

RESTRICTIVE COVENANTS

Restrictive covenants directed against minorities were used widely prior to the *Shelley* case, particularly in large cities in the North and West. These covenants were not only against Blacks but also Armenians, Jews, Mexicans, Syrians, Japanese, Chinese and American Indians. It has been estimated that 80% of the land in Chicago was restricted. *To Secure These Rights—The Report of the President's Committee on Civil Rights 67–70* (1947).

The use of these covenants prior to *Shelley* contributed to the isolation of Blacks in congested and substandard housing. Partly as a result of limitations of Blacks' access to housing, they often were forced to pay higher rentals than Whites. Helfield & Groner, *Race Discrimination in Housing,* 57 Yale L.J. 426, 426–33 (1948). Would such evidence have been relevant to the *Shelley* decision? See Martin, *Segregation of Residences of Negroes,* 32 Mich.L.Rev. 721 (1934).[1]

BARROWS v. JACKSON, 346 U.S. 249 (1953). Plaintiff's predecessor and defendant, owners of real estate in the same neighborhood, entered into an agreement, recorded on the deeds and running against subsequent takers, that their property would be occupied only by Caucasians. Plaintiff sued defendant for damages alleging that, in violation of their agreement, defendant had sold his property without including the agreed restriction in the deed, and had permitted non-Caucasians to move in and occupy the premises. The California courts sustained a demurrer to the complaint on the authority of the *Shelley* case. Decisions in Missouri and Oklahoma had awarded damages in similar situations; the Supreme Court granted certiorari.

The United States Supreme Court affirmed California's denial of relief. Justice Minton, for the Court, wrote: "This Court will not permit or require California to coerce respondent to respond in damages for failure to observe a restrictive covenant that this Court would deny California the right to enforce in equity. . . ." The defendant, although a Caucasian, had standing to assert the constitutional question. In view of the demand for damages he had a real financial interest in the issue, and "it would be difficult if not impossible for the persons whose rights are asserted to present their grievance before any court."

Chief Justice Vinson dissented; Justices Reed and Jackson did not participate.

PROSECUTION OF "SIT–IN" DEMONSTRATORS IN THE 1960S

A significant phase of the civil rights struggle was the use of "sit-in" demonstrations at Southern restaurants or lunch counters where Blacks were segregated or refused service. Typically, Blacks would sit at a table or counter, be asked to leave, and be arrested and convicted of trespass when they refused. The Supreme Court reviewed the constitutionality of the convictions of literally hundreds of sit-in demonstrators in the early sixties. While the convictions were reversed, a majority of the Court never faced squarely the question whether enforcement of a private property owner's discrimination was unconstitutional state action under Shelley v. Kraemer. In some cases, convictions were reversed on the ground that the state trespass statute gave inadequate warning as to whether it prohibited remaining on private property after being asked to leave as well as unauthorized "entry." Bouie v. City of Columbia, 378 U.S. 347 (1964). Where convictions were reversed because of unconstitutional state action, the grounds were narrow. E.g., Robinson v. Florida, 378 U.S. 153

---

[1] See also: Karst & Van Alstyne, *State Action,* 14 Stan.L.Rev. 3 (1961); Henkin, *Shelley v. Kraemer: Notes for a Revised Opinion,* 110 U.Pa.L.Rev. 473 (1962); *Effect of State Court Interpretation of a Contract,* 55 Mich.L.Rev. 871 (1957); *Police Enforcement* of *Private Discrimination,* 52 N.W.U.L.Rev. 774 (1958); *Criminal Penalties to Enforce Private Discrimination,* 57 Mich.L.Rev. 122 (1958); *Impact of Shelley v. Kraemer on the State Action Concept,* 44 Cal.L.Rev. 718 (1956).

(1964) (city ordinance required segregation although restaurant manager stated that Blacks were excluded for business reasons); Griffin v. Maryland, 378 U.S. 130 (1964) (amusement park employee who asked Blacks to leave and arrested them was also deputized as a sheriff).

The *Griffin* case is particularly interesting. The state argued that the constitutional issues in the case were indistinguishable from those where the trespass arrest had been made by a police officer not employed by the park. The Court did not resolve the state's broad contention that no constitutional violation followed from a police arrest and state conviction for trespass of a person refusing to leave private property. The Court noted that Collins, the park employee who asked the defendants to leave, wore a sheriff's badge and "consistently identified himself as a deputy sheriff" when asking defendants to leave and placing them under arrest. Collins had a contractual obligation to enforce the park's policy. The case thus fell within the rule that a state (Collins) could not undertake an obligation to enforce a private policy of racial discrimination. The three dissenters conceded that Collins was exercising state authority, but argued that "the involvement of the State is no different from what it would have been had the arrests been made by a regular policeman dispatched from police headquarters." Suppose Collins had not worn his badge nor identified himself as a sheriff when he asked defendants to leave the amusement park. When they refused, he called a regular policeman who arrived and made the arrest. Can you think of a tenable theory that supports a conclusion that there was unconstitutional state action on the facts in *Griffin,* but that there would not be on the supposed facts?

The sit-in cases came to an end with the enactment of Title II of the Civil Rights Act of 1964 which prohibited discrimination in places of public accommodation. (The Court held that the statute abated sit-in prosecutions that had occurred prior to its enactment. Hamm v. City of Rock Hill, 379 U.S. 306 [1964].) In one of the last of the sit-in cases, five Justices did reach the broader issue of the application of Shelley v. Kraemer to the sit-in situation. Bell v. Maryland, 378 U.S. 226 (1964). Justice Douglas, joined by Justice Goldberg, argued that *Shelley* should govern when trespass convictions were used to enforce private discrimination that represented business preferences rather than personal prejudices. (Justice Goldberg, joined by Chief Justice Warren and Justice Douglas, also argued that access to public accommodations was a privilege of national citizenship). Justice Black's dissent, joined by Justices Harlan and White, argued that *Shelley* was inapplicable. A citizen who sought the law's protection of his property rights was not cast outside the law's protection because he called on law officers to enforce those rights. Shelley v. Kraemer was a case, according to Justice Black, where enforcement of a restrictive covenant operated to prohibit a willing seller from conveying to a Black purchaser and its principle did not apply to cases where the property owner was unwilling to permit occupation of his property by Blacks.

PENNSYLVANIA v. BOARD OF CITY TRUSTS

353 U.S. 230, 77 S.Ct. 806, 1 L.Ed.2d 792 (1957).

Per Curiam.

The motion to dismiss the appeal for want of jurisdiction is granted, 28 U.S.C. § 1257(2). Treating the papers whereon the appeal was taken as a petition for writ of certiorari, 28 U.S.C. § 2103, the petition is granted. 28 U.S.C. § 1257(3).

Stephen Girard, by a will probated in 1831, left a fund in trust for the erection, maintenance, and operation of a "college." The will provided that the college was to admit "as many poor white male orphans, between the ages of six and ten years, as the said income shall be adequate to maintain." The will named as trustee the City of Philadelphia. The provisions of the will were carried out by the State and City and the college was opened in 1848. Since 1869, by virtue of an act of the Pennsylvania Legislature, the trust has been administered and the college operated by the "Board of Directors of City Trusts of the City of Philadelphia." Pa.Laws 1869, No. 1258, p. 1276; Purdon's Pa.Stat.Ann., 1957, Tit. 53, § 16365.[a]

In February 1954, the petitioners Foust and Felder applied for admission to the college. They met all qualifications except that they were Negroes. For this reason the Board refused to admit them. They petitioned the Orphans' Court of Philadelphia County for an order directing the Board to admit them, alleging that their exclusion because of race violated the Fourteenth Amendment to the Constitution. The State of Pennsylvania and the City of Philadelphia joined in the suit also contending the Board's action violated the Fourteenth Amendment. The Orphans' Court rejected the constitutional contention and refused to order the applicants' admission. ... This was affirmed by the Pennsylvania Supreme Court. 386 Pa. 548, 127 A.2d 287.

The Board which operates Girard College is an agency of the State of Pennsylvania. Therefore, even though the Board was acting as a trustee, its refusal to admit Foust and Felder to the college because they were Negroes was discrimination by the State. Such discrimination is forbidden by the Fourteenth Amendment. Brown v. Board of Education, 347 U.S. 483. Accordingly, the judgment of the Supreme Court of Pennsylvania is reversed and the cause is remanded for further proceedings not inconsistent with this opinion.

It is so ordered.

STATE ENFORCEMENT OF CHARITABLE TRUSTS

After the decision in Pennsylvania v. Board of City Trusts, Pennsylvania courts substituted private trustees to effectuate Stephen Girard's "dominant purpose" to limit the College to White orphans. In re Girard College Trusteeship, 391 Pa. 434, 138 A.2d 844 (1958). The Supreme Court never reached the merits of the questions whether Girard College could be administered by private trustees and continue to exclude Blacks or whether the state court's substitution of trustees to permit continued exclusion of Blacks was itself unconstitutional state action. (The appeal was dismissed for lack of jurisdiction and certiorari was denied. 357 U.S. 570 (1958).) The grounds of decision in Evans v. Newton, supra p. 1110, made it unnecessary to decide whether state enforcement of discriminatory testamentary trusts was in all cases unconstitutional state action.

Charitable trusts do not have identifiable beneficiaries and are enforced, at least nominally, by state officials. States will not enforce such trusts unless

[a] The Board is composed of 15 persons, including the mayor, the president of the City Council and twelve other citizens appointed by the judges of the Court of Common Pleas of the County of Philadelphia. The treasurer of the city serves as treasurer of the board. Pursuant to the terms of the will the funds of the trust were held and invested by the city treasurer and an annual accounting made to the legislature. The expenses of operating the school were defrayed wholly from the trust fund. It appears that the Board of City Trusts took an active role in directing the administration of the School. See In re Girard's Estate, 386 Pa. 548, 127 A.2d 287 (1956), certiorari granted, judgment reversed 353 U.S. 230 (1957).

they serve worthy purposes. Finally, charitable trusts are exempt from taxation, and are free from otherwise applicable restrictions on indefinite accumulation of trust property. (The Girard trust grew from 2 to 98 million dollars.) Do these elements of state contact impose a constitutional obligation on all private trusts to avoid racial discrimination? See Clark, *Charitable Trusts, the Fourteenth Amendment and the Will of Stephen Girard,* 66 Yale L.J. 979 (1957). An additional issue presented in both the Girard trust litigation and Evans v. Newton was whether, under the doctrine of Shelley v. Kraemer, the action of a state court in replacing a government trustee with a private trustee, for the purpose of effectuating a testator's desire to discriminate, was in itself unconstitutional state action.

Lower federal courts have dealt with some of these issues in the context of educational testamentary trusts. The Court of Appeals for the Third Circuit held the state courts' substitution of private trustees in the *Girard College* case was unconstitutional state action. Commonwealth of Pennsylvania v. Brown, 392 F.2d 120 (3d Cir.1968), cert. denied 391 U.S. 921 (1968). Earlier, a United States District Court decided that the terms of an 1833 bequest limiting Tulane University to the education of Whites were no longer binding. Guillory v. Administrators of Tulane University of La., 212 F.Supp. 674 (E.D.La.1962). Does the Supreme Court's decision in Evans v. Abney, which follows, cast doubt on the soundness of those lower court decisions?

EVANS v. ABNEY, 396 U.S. 435 (1970). After the decision in Evans v. Newton, the Supreme Court of Georgia ruled that Senator Bacon's intention to provide a park for whites only had become impossible to fulfill and that accordingly the trust had failed and the parkland and other trust property had reverted by operation of Georgia law to the heirs of the Senator. The Supreme Court upheld this action. Justice Black, writing for the Court, said, in part:

"When a city park is destroyed because the Constitution required it to be integrated, there is reason for everyone to be disheartened. We agree with petitioners that in such a case it is not enough to find that the state court's result was reached through the application of established principles of state law.... Here, however, the action of the Georgia Supreme Court declaring the Baconsfield trust terminated presents no violation of constitutionally protected rights, and any harshness that may have resulted from the State court's decision can be attributed solely to its intention to effectuate as nearly as possible the explicit terms of Senator Bacon's will.

"Petitioners first argue that the action of the Georgia court violates the United States Constitution in that it imposes a drastic 'penalty,' the 'forfeiture' of the park, merely because of the city's compliance with the constitutional mandate expressed by this Court in Evans v. Newton. Of course, Evans v. Newton did not speak to the problem of whether Baconsfield should or could continue to operate as a park; it held only that its continued operation as a park had to be without racial discrimination. But petitioners now want to extend that holding to forbid the Georgia courts from closing Baconsfield on the ground that such a closing would penalize the city and its citizens for complying with the Constitution. We think, however, that the will of Senator Bacon and Georgia law provide all the justification necessary for imposing such a 'penalty.' The construction of wills is essentially a state-law question ... and in this case the Georgia Supreme Court, as we read its opinion, interpreted Senator Bacon's will as embodying a preference for termination of the park rather than its integration. Given this, the Georgia court had no alternative under its relevant trust laws, which are long standing and neutral with regard to race, but to end the Baconsfield trust and return the property to the Senator's heirs."

Justice Marshall took no part. Justices Brennan and Douglas dissented.

PEREMPTORY CHALLENGES TO EXCLUDE JURORS ON ACCOUNT OF RACE

In Powers v. Ohio, 499 U.S. 400 (1991), the Court held that a prosecutor's exclusion of petit jurors through race-based peremptory challenges denied the excluded jurors equal protection, and that the criminal defendant had third-party standing to raise that issue. In two subsequent cases, the principal issue was whether there was state action in juror challenges by a private litigant and a criminal defendant.

Edmonson v. Leesville Concrete Co., Inc., 500 U.S. 614 (1991), held that the Constitution prohibited juror challenges by a private litigant. The Court applied a two part test to determine the state action question. First, did a private party's exercise of a right or privilege have its "source in state authority"? Peremptory challenges are permitted only when government allows them through statute or decisional law. Second, can the private party charged with constitutional violation "be described in all fairness as a state actor"? Private parties could not exercise juror challenges "absent the overt, significant assistance of the court," and juror challenges involved the performance of a traditional public function—selecting an entity (the jury) that is a "quintessential governmental body." The Court distinguished Polk County v. Dodson, 454 U.S. 312 (1981), which had held that a public defender, although employed by government, was not a state actor in a case claiming constitutionally inadequate representation. A defense lawyer in a criminal case is ethically committed to be an adversary to the government, while there is no adversarial relationship between the private litigant and government in the jury selection process.

Dodson was harder to distinguish in Georgia v. McCollum, 505 U.S. 42 (1992), where the Court held that it is unconstitutional for a criminal defense lawyer to use race-based peremptory challenges. Whether a public defender is a state actor "depends on the nature and context of the function he is performing." The public defender's function in exercising a peremptory challenge is different from other actions taken in the accused's defense, because it involves "the power to choose a quintessential governmental body."

C. GOVERNMENT FINANCING, REGULATION AND AUTHORIZATION OF PRIVATE CONDUCT

1. PRIVATE ACTIVITY ON GOVERNMENT PROPERTY

Burton v. Wilmington Parking Authority

365 U.S. 715, 81 S.Ct. 856, 6 L.Ed.2d 45 (1961).

[The Eagle Coffee Shoppe is a restaurant located within an offstreet automobile parking building in Wilmington, Delaware. The parking building is owned and operated by the Wilmington Parking Authority, an agency of the State of Delaware, and the restaurant is the Authority's lessee. Before it began actual construction of the facility, the Authority was advised by its retained experts that the anticipated revenue from the parking of cars and proceeds from sale of its bonds would not be sufficient to finance the construction costs of the facility. Moreover, the bonds were not expected to be marketable if payable solely out of parking revenues. To secure additional capital needed for its "debt-service" requirements, and thereby to make bond financing practicable, the Authority decided it was necessary to enter long-term leases with responsible tenants for commercial use of some of the space available in the projected "garage building." The public was invited to bid for these leases.

[In April 1957 such a private lease, for 20 years and renewable for another 10 years, was made with Eagle Coffee Shoppe, Inc., for use as a "restaurant, dining room, banquet hall, cocktail lounge and bar and for no other use and purpose." Other portions of the structure were leased to other tenants, including a bookstore, a retail jeweler, and a food store. Upon completion of the building, the Authority located at appropriate places thereon official signs indicating the public character of the building, and flew from mastheads on the roof both the state and national flags.

[In August 1958 Burton parked his car in the building and walked around to enter the restaurant by its front door on Ninth Street. He was refused service. He then filed this action seeking a declaratory judgment, alleging that he was refused service solely because he was a Negro. On motions for summary judgment the trial court ruled for Burton. The Delaware Supreme Court reversed on the ground that Eagle Coffee Shoppe was under no duty to serve because of a state statute providing: "No keeper of an inn, tavern, hotel, or restaurant, or other place of public entertainment or refreshment of travelers, guests, or customers shall be obliged, by law, to furnish entertainment or refreshment to persons whose reception or entertainment by him would be offensive to the major part of his customers and would injure his business . . . ."]

Mr. Justice Clark delivered the opinion of the Court.

. . .

It is clear, as it always has been since the Civil Rights Cases (U.S.) supra, that "Individual invasion of individual rights is not the subject-matter of the amendment," and that private conduct abridging individual rights does no violence to the Equal Protection Clause unless to some significant extent the State in any of its manifestations has been found to have become involved in it. Because the virtue of the right to equal protection of the laws could lie only in the breadth of its application, its constitutional assurance was reserved in terms whose imprecision was necessary if the right were to be enjoyed in the variety of individual-state relationships which the Amendment was designed to embrace. For the same reason, to fashion and apply a precise formula for recognition of state responsibility under the Equal Protection Clause is an "impossible task" which "This Court has never attempted." Kotch v. River Port Pilot Comrs., 330 U.S. 552, 556. Only by sifting facts and weighing circumstances can the nonobvious involvement of the State in private conduct be attributed its true significance. . . .

Addition of all these activities, obligations and responsibilities of the Authority, the benefits mutually conferred, together with the obvious fact that the restaurant is operated as an integral part of a public building devoted to a public parking service, indicates that degree of state participation and involvement in discriminatory action which it was the design of the Fourteenth Amendment to condemn. It is irony amounting to grave injustice that in one part of a single building, erected and maintained with public funds by an agency of the State to serve a public purpose, all persons have equal rights, while in another portion, also serving the public, a Negro is a second-class citizen, offensive because of his race, without rights and unentitled to service, but at the same time fully enjoys equal access to nearby restaurants in wholly privately owned buildings. As the Chancellor pointed out, in its lease with Eagle the Authority could have affirmatively required Eagle to discharge the responsibilities under the Fourteenth Amendment imposed upon the private enterprise as a consequence of state participation. But no State may effectively abdicate its responsibilities by either ignoring them or by merely failing to discharge them whatever the motive may be. It is of no consolation to an individual denied the equal protection of the laws that it was done in good faith. Certainly the conclusions drawn in similar cases by the various Courts of Appeals do not depend upon such a distinction. By its inaction, the Authority, and through it the State, has not only made itself a party to the refusal of service, but has elected to place its power, property and prestige behind the admitted discrimination. The State has so far insinuated itself into a position of interdependence with Eagle that it must be recognized as a joint participant in the challenged activity, which, on that account, cannot be considered to have been so "purely private" as to fall without the scope of the Fourteenth Amendment.

Because readily applicable formulae may not be fashioned, the conclusions drawn from the facts and circumstances of this record are by no means declared as universal truths on the basis of which every state leasing agreement is to be tested.... Specifically defining the limits of our inquiry, what we hold today is that when a State leases public property in the manner and for the purpose shown to have been the case here, the proscriptions of the Fourteenth Amendment must be complied with by the lessee as certainly as though they were binding covenants written into the agreement itself.

The judgment of the Supreme Court of Delaware is reversed and the cause remanded for further proceedings consistent with this opinion.

[Justice Stewart concurred. Justices Frankfurter, Harlan, and Whittaker, dissented.]

REALITY v. APPEARANCE OF STATE ACTION

Consider the following hypothesis. In cases concerning racial discrimination, an important factor of decision is whether all of the circumstances create a public perception that the state approves the private discriminatory decision. Are appearances of state approval more important than an inquiry whether, appearances aside, racial discrimination can be traced to governmental decisions? The suggested hypothesis would support the results in the preceding cases of Pennsylvania v. Board of Trusts and Burton v. Wilmington Parking Authority. So long as the city ran the school, it appeared that the city and not the testator was making the choice to engage in a policy of racial discrimination. So long as the city operated the parking garage, it would appear that it approved racial discrimination by tenants in the parking structure. It can also be argued that the hypothesis explains the disparate results in the two cases concerning Senator Bacon's will—Evans v. Newton, supra p. 1110, and Evans v. Abney, supra p. 1124. The city had operated the park for so long as a segregated park that merely turning it over to a private trustee for continued segregated operation would not remove the appearance of a segregated city park. On the other hand, terminating the operation of the park because the city could no longer follow Senator Bacon's wish that it be segregated did not give the appearance that the city approved the testator's choice. (Consider the case of a private university refusing to accept a bequest because it *disapproves* conditions attached to it.)

Are you persuaded that *Abney* and *Newton* are both appropriately decided under the hypothesis suggested here? Do you think that the hypothesis is useful in marking the limits of state action doctrine? Is the hypothesis useful in explaining the disparate state-action and no-state-action conclusions in the cases that follow?

GILMORE v. MONTGOMERY, ALA., 417 U.S. 556 (1974). The case involved actions by a city in permitting the use of public park recreational facilities by private segregated school groups and any other non-school groups that allegedly discriminate in their membership on the basis of race. The Court held it invalid for the city to allocate use of park facilities to private segregated school groups where that action facilitated the avoidance of an outstanding school desegregation order. With respect to the use by other segregated groups the Court found the facts insufficiently developed to permit a ruling and sent the case back to the district court. In concluding its opinion the Court said:

"We close with this word of caution. It should be obvious that the exclusion of any person or group—all-Negro, all-oriental, or all-white—from public facilities infringes upon the freedom of the individual to associate as he chooses. Mr. Justice Douglas emphasized this in his dissent, joined by Mr. Justice Marshall, in *Moose Lodge*. He observed, 'The associational rights which our system honors permit all white, all black, all brown and all yellow clubs to be formed. They also permit all Catholic, all Jewish, or all agnostic clubs to be established. Government may not tell a man or woman who his or her associates must be. The individual can be as selective as he desires.' 407 U.S., at 179–180. The freedom to associate applies to the beliefs we share, and to those we consider reprehensible. It tends to produce the diversity of opinion that oils the machine of democratic government and insures peaceful, orderly change. Because its exercise is largely dependent on the right to own or use property, Healy v. James, 408 U.S. 169, 181–183 (1972), any denial of access to public facilities must withstand close scrutiny and be carefully circumscribed. Certainly, a person's mere membership in an organization which possesses a discriminatory admissions policy would not alone be ground for his exclusion from public facilities. Having said this, however, we must also be aware that the very exercise of the freedom to associate by some may serve to infringe that freedom for others. Invidious discrimination takes its own toll on the freedom to associate, and it is not subject to affirmative constitutional protection when it involves state action. Norwood v. Harrison, 413 U.S., at 470.''

2. GOVERNMENT FINANCIAL ASSISTANCE TO PRIVATE ACTIVITIES

NORWOOD v. HARRISON, 413 U.S. 455 (1973). Mississippi had a statutory program under which textbooks were purchased by the state and lent to students in both public and private schools. A suit was brought challenging the application of this statute in lending textbooks to students attending schools with racially discriminatory admission policies. The Court held the statute invalid as applied to such schools. The Court said that it did not question the right of private citizens to operate such schools nor of parents to have their children attend them. It said that the question was rather whether the state may "provide tangible assistance to students attending private schools" which are racially discriminatory. On this question, the Court said:

"This Court has consistently affirmed decisions enjoining state tuition grants to students attending racially discriminatory private schools. A textbook lending program is not legally distinguishable from the forms of state assistance foreclosed by the prior cases. Free textbooks, like tuition grants directed to private school students, are a form of financial assistance inuring to the benefit of the private schools themselves. An inescapable educational cost for students in both public and private schools is the expense of providing all necessary learning materials. When, as here, that necessary expense is borne by the State, the economic consequence is to give aid to the enterprise; if the school engages in discriminatory practices the State by tangible aid in the form of textbooks thereby gives support to such discrimination. Racial discrimination in state-operated schools is barred by the Constitution and '[i]t is also axiomatic that a state may not induce, encourage or promote private persons to accomplish what it is constitutionally forbidden to accomplish.' Lee v. Macon County Bd. of Educ., 267 F.Supp. 458, 475–476 (M.D.Ala.1967).

"We do not suggest that a State violates its constitutional duty merely because it has provided *any* form of state service that benefits private schools said to be racially discriminatory. Textbooks are a basic educational tool and, like tuition grants, they are provided only in connection with schools; they are to be distinguished from generalized services government might provide to schools in common with others. Moreover, the textbooks provided to private school students by the State in this case are a form of assistance readily available from sources entirely independent of the State—unlike, for example, 'such necessities of life as electricity, water, and police and fire protection.' Moose Lodge No. 107 v. Irvis, 407 U.S. 163, 173 (1972). The State has neither an absolute nor operating monopoly on the procurement of school textbooks; anyone can purchase them on the open market.

"The District Court laid great stress on the absence of showing by appellants that 'any child enrolled in private school, if deprived of free textbooks, would withdraw from private school and subsequently enroll in the public schools.' 340 F.Supp., at 1013. We can accept this factual assertion; we cannot and do not know, on this record at least, whether state textbook assistance is the determinative factor in the enrollment of any students in any of the private schools in Mississippi. We do not agree with the District Court in its analysis of the legal consequences of this uncertainty, for the Constitution does not permit the State to aid discrimination even when there is no precise causal relationship between state financial aid to a private school and the continued well-being of that school. A State may not grant the type of tangible financial aid here involved if that aid has a significant tendency to facilitate, reinforce, and support private discrimination."

BLUM v. YARETSKY, 457 U.S. 991 (1982). A class of Medicaid patients brought suit claiming that private nursing homes violated their rights to procedural due process in transferring them to lower levels of care, or discharging them. The nursing homes receive reimbursement from the state for their services in caring for Medicaid patients. Decisions by the nursing home result in lower Medicaid benefits. The Court held that there was no state action that would trigger the Fourteenth Amendment's requirement of procedural due process. Justice Rehnquist's opinion for the Court said, in part:

> "Respondents ... argue that the State 'affirmatively commands' the summary discharge or transfer of Medicaid patients who are thought to be inappropriately placed in their nursing facilities. Were this characterization accurate, we would have a different question before us. However, our review of the statutes and regulations identified by respondents does not support respondents' characterization of them.

. . . .

"... [R]espondents' complaint is about nursing home decisions to discharge or transfer, not to admit, Medicaid patients. But we are not satisfied that the State is responsible for those decisions.... The regulations cited by respondents require [nursing homes] 'to make all efforts possible to transfer patients to the appropriate level of care or home as indicated by the patient's medical condition or needs' ... The nursing homes are required to complete patient care assessment forms designed by the State and 'provide the receiving facility or provider with a current copy of same at the time of discharge to an alternate level of care facility or home.' ...

"These regulations do not require the nursing homes to rely on the forms in making discharge or transfer decisions, nor do they demonstrate that the State is responsible for the decision to discharge or transfer particular patients. Those decisions ultimately turn on medical judgments made by private parties according to professional standards that are not established by the State. This case, therefore, is not unlike Polk County v. Dodson, 454 U.S. 312 (1981), in which the question was whether a public defender acts 'under color of' state law within the meaning of 42 U.S.C. § 1983 when representing an indigent defendant in a state criminal proceeding. Although the public defender was employed by the State and appointed by the State to represent the respondent, we concluded that '[t]his assignment entailed functions and obligations in no way dependent on state authority.' ... The decisions made by the public defender in the course of representing his client were framed in accordance with professional canons of ethics, rather than dictated by any rule of conduct imposed by the State. The same is true of nursing home decisions to discharge or transfer particular patients because the care they are receiving is medically inappropriate."

Justices Brennan and Marshall dissented.

RENDELL–BAKER v. KOHN, 457 U.S. 830 (1982). Plaintiffs were discharged teachers, previously employed by a private school for maladjusted high school students. Most of the school's students had been referred to it by city and state agencies. Public funds account for 90 to 99% of the school's operating budget. Plaintiffs brought suit under 42 U.S.C. § 1983, claiming that their discharges were for constitutionally protected speech, in violation of the first amendment, and that they had been denied procedural due process. The Court held that the private school did not act under color of state law in dismissing the plaintiffs. Chief Justice Burger's opinion said, in part:

"The school ... is not fundamentally different from many private corporations whose business depends primarily on contracts to build roads, bridges, dams, ships, or submarines for the government. Acts of such private contractors do not become acts of the government by reason of their significant or even total engagement in performing public contracts."

Justices Marshall and Brennan dissented.

3. GOVERNMENT REGULATION OF PRIVATE ACTIVITY

Moose Lodge No. 107 v. Irvis

407 U.S. 163, 92 S.Ct. 1965, 32 L.Ed.2d 627 (1972).

Mr. Justice Rehnquist delivered the opinion of the Court.

Appellee Irvis, a Negro ..., was refused service by appellant Moose Lodge, a local branch of the national fraternal organization located in Harrisburg,

Pennsylvania. Appellee then brought this action under 42 U.S.C. § 1983 for injunctive relief in the United States District Court for the Middle District of Pennsylvania. He claimed that because the Pennsylvania liquor board had issued appellant Moose Lodge a private club license that authorized the sale of alcoholic beverages on its premises, the refusal of service to him was "state action" for the purposes of the Equal Protection Clause of the Fourteenth Amendment. He named both Moose Lodge and the Pennsylvania Liquor Authority as defendants, seeking injunctive relief that would have required the defendant liquor board to revoke Moose Lodge's license so long as it continued its discriminatory practices. Appellee sought no damages.

A three-judge district court, convened at appellee's request, upheld his contention on the merits, and entered a decree declaring invalid the liquor license issued to Moose Lodge "as long as it follows a policy of racial discrimination in its membership or operating policies or practices." Moose Lodge alone appealed from the decree, and we postponed decision as to jurisdiction until the hearing on the merits, 401 U.S. 992. Appellant urges in the alternative that we either vacate the judgment below because there is not presently a case or controversy between the parties, or that we reverse on the merits.

I.

The District Court in its opinion found that "a Caucasian member in good standing brought plaintiff, a Negro, to the Lodge's dining room and bar as his guest and requested service of food and beverages. The Lodge through its employees refused service to plaintiff solely because he is a Negro." It is undisputed that each local Moose Lodge is bound by the constitution and general by-laws of the Supreme Lodge, the latter of which contains a provision limiting membership in the lodges to white male Caucasians. The District Court in this connection found that "[t]he lodges accordingly maintain a policy and practice of restricting membership to the Caucasian race and permitting members to bring only Caucasian guests on lodge premises, particularly to the dining room and bar."

. . .

Any injury to appellee from the conduct of Moose Lodge stemmed not from the lodge's membership requirements, but from its policies with respect to the serving of guests of members. Appellee has standing to seek redress for injuries done to him, but may not seek redress for injuries done to others.... While this Court has held that in exceptional situations a concededly injured party may rely on the constitutional rights of a third party in obtaining relief, Barrows v. Jackson, 346 U.S. 249 (1953), in this case appellee was not injured by Moose Lodge's membership policy since he never sought to become a member....

Because appellee had no standing to litigate a constitutional claim arising out of Moose Lodge's membership practices, the District Court erred in reaching that issue on the merits. But it did not err in reaching the constitutional claim of appellee that Moose Lodge's guest service practices under these circumstances violated the Fourteenth Amendment. Nothing in the positions taken by the parties since the entry of the District Court decree has mooted that claim, and we therefore turn to its disposition.

II.

Moose Lodge is a private club in the ordinary meaning of that term. It is a local chapter of a national fraternal organization having well defined requirements for membership. It conducts all of its activities in a building that is owned by it. It is not publicly funded. Only members and guests are permitted in any lodge of the order; one may become a guest only by invitation of a member or upon invitation of the house committee.

Appellee, while conceding the right of private clubs to choose members upon a discriminatory basis, asserts that the licensing of Moose Lodge to serve liquor by the Pennsylvania Liquor Control Board amounts to such State involvement with the club's activities as to make its discriminatory practices forbidden by the Equal Protection Clause of the Fourteenth Amendment. The relief sought and obtained by appellee in the District Court was an injunction forbidding the licensing by the liquor authority of Moose Lodge until it ceased its discriminatory practices. We conclude that Moose Lodge's refusal to serve food and beverages to a guest by reason of the fact that he was a Negro does not, under the circumstances here presented, violate the Fourteenth Amendment.

. . .

While the principle is easily stated, the question of whether particular discriminatory conduct is private, on the one hand, or amounts to "state action," on the other hand, frequently admits of no easy answer. . . .

Our cases make clear that the impetus for the forbidden discrimination need not originate with the State if it is state action that enforces privately originated discrimination. Shelley v. Kraemer, supra. . . .

The Court has never held, of course, that discrimination by an otherwise private entity would be violative of the Equal Protection Clause if the private entity receives any sort of benefit or service at all from the State, or if it is subject to state regulation in any degree whatever. Since state-furnished services include such necessities of life as electricity, water, and police and fire protection, such a holding would utterly emasculate the distinction between private as distinguished from state conduct set forth in The Civil Rights Cases, supra, and adhered to in subsequent decisions. Our holdings indicate that where the impetus for the discrimination is private, the State must have "significantly involved itself with invidious discriminations," Reitman v. Mulkey, 387 U.S. 369, 380 (1967), in order for the discriminatory action to fall within the ambit of the constitutional prohibition.

Our prior decisions dealing with discriminatory refusal of service in public eating places are significantly different factually from the case now before us. Peterson v. City of Greenville, 373 U.S. 244 (1963), dealt with trespass prosecution of persons who "sat in" at a restaurant to protest its refusal of service to Negroes. There the Court held that although the ostensible initiative for the trespass prosecution came from the proprietor, the existence of a local ordinance requiring segregation of races in such places was tantamount to the State having "commanded a particular result," 373 U.S., at 248. . . .

Here there is nothing approaching the symbiotic relationship between lessor and lessee that was present in *Burton,* where the private lessee obtained the benefit of locating in a building owned by the state created parking authority, and the parking authority was enabled to carry out its primary public purpose of furnishing parking space by advantageously leasing portions of the building constructed for that purpose to commercial lessees such as the owner of the Eagle Restaurant. Unlike *Burton,* the Moose Lodge building is located on land owned by it, not by any public authority. Far from apparently holding itself out as a place of public accommodation, Moose Lodge quite ostentatiously proclaims the fact that it is not open to the public at large. Nor is it located and operated in such surroundings that although private in name, it discharges a function or performs a service that would otherwise in all likelihood be performed by the State. In short, while Eagle was a public restaurant in a public building, Moose Lodge is a private social club in a private building.

With the exception hereafter noted, the Pennsylvania Liquor Control Board plays absolutely no part in establishing or enforcing the membership or guest policies of the club that it licenses to serve liquor.[3] There is no suggestion in this record that the Pennsylvania law, either as written or as applied, discriminates against minority groups either in their right to apply for club licenses themselves or in their right to purchase and be served liquor in places of public accommodation. The only effect that the state licensing of Moose Lodge to serve liquor can be said to have on the right of any other Pennsylvanian to buy or be served liquor on premises other than those of Moose Lodge is that for some purposes club licenses are counted in the maximum number of licenses which may be issued in a given municipality. Basically each municipality has a quota of one retail license for each 1,500 inhabitants. Licenses issued to hotels, municipal golf courses and airport restaurants are not counted in this quota, nor are club licenses until the maximum number of retail licenses is reached. Beyond that point, neither additional retail licenses nor additional club licenses may be issued so long as the number of issued and outstanding retail licenses remains at or above the statutory maximum.

The District Court was at pains to point out in its opinion what it considered to be the "pervasive" nature of the regulation of private clubs by the Pennsylvania Liquor Control Board....

However detailed this type of regulation may be in some particulars, it cannot be said to in any way foster or encourage racial discrimination. Nor can it be said to make the State in any realistic sense a partner or even a joint venturer in the club's enterprise. The limited effect of the prohibition against obtaining additional club licenses when the maximum number of retail licenses allotted to a municipality has been issued, when considered together with the availability of liquor from hotel, restaurant, and retail licensees falls far short of conferring upon club licensees a monopoly in the dispensing of liquor in any given municipality or in the State as a whole. We therefore hold that, with the exception hereafter noted, the operation of the regulatory scheme enforced by the Pennsylvania Liquor Control Board does not sufficiently implicate the State in the discriminatory guest policies of Moose Lodge so as to make the latter "state action" within the ambit of the Equal Protection Clause of the Fourteenth Amendment.

The District Court found that the regulations of the Liquor Control Board adopted pursuant to statute affirmatively require that "every club licensee shall adhere to all the provisions of its Constitution and By–Laws." Appellant argues that the purpose of this provision "is purely and simply and plainly the prevention of subterfuge," pointing out that the *bona fides* of a private club, as opposed to a place of public accommodation masquerading as a private club, is a matter with which the State Liquor Control Board may legitimately concern itself. Appellee concedes this to be the case, and expresses disagreement with the District Court on this point. There can be no doubt that the label "private club" can and has been used to evade both regulations of state and local liquor authorities, and statutes requiring places of public accommodation to serve all

---

[3] Unlike the situation in Public Utilities Comm'n v. Pollak, 343 U.S. 451 (1952), where the regulatory agency had affirmatively approved the practice of the regulated entity after full investigation, the Pennsylvania Liquor Control Board has neither approved nor endorsed the racially discriminatory practices of Moose Lodge.

persons without regard to race, color, religion, or national origin. This Court in *Daniel v. Paul*, 395 U.S. 298 (1969), had occasion to address this issue in connection with the application of Title II of the Civil Rights Act of 1964, 78 Stat. 243, 42 U.S.C. § 2000a et seq.

. . .

Even though the Liquor Control Board regulation in question is neutral in its terms, the result of its application in a case where the constitution and by-laws of a club required racial discrimination would be to invoke the sanctions of the State to enforce a concededly discriminatory private rule. State action, for purposes of the Equal Protection Clause, may emanate from rulings of administrative and regulatory agencies as well as from legislative or judicial action. *Robinson v. Florida*, 378 U.S. 153, 156 (1964). *Shelley v. Kraemer*, 334 U.S. 1 (1948), makes it clear that the application of state sanctions to enforce such a rule would violate the Fourteenth Amendment. Although the record before us is not as clear as one would like, appellant has not persuaded us that the District Court should have denied any and all relief.

Appellee was entitled to a decree enjoining the enforcement of § 113.09 of the regulations promulgated by the Pennsylvania Liquor Control Board insofar as that regulation requires compliance by Moose Lodge with provisions of its constitution and by-laws containing racially discriminatory provisions. He was entitled to no more. The judgment of the District Court is reversed, and the cause remanded with instructions to enter a decree in conformity with this opinion.

Mr. Justice Douglas, with whom Mr. Justice Marshall joins, dissenting.

My view of the First Amendment and the related guarantees of the Bill of Rights is that they create a zone of privacy which precludes government from interfering with private clubs or groups. The associational rights which our system honors permits all white, all black, all brown, and all yellow clubs to be formed. They also permit all Catholic, all Jewish, or all agnostic clubs to be established. Government may not tell a man or woman who his or her associates must be. The individual can be as selective as he desires. So the fact that the Moose Lodge allows only Caucasians to join or come as guests is constitutionally irrelevant, as is the decision of the Black Muslims to admit to their services only members of their race.

The problem is different, however, where the public domain is concerned. I have indicated in *Garner v. Louisiana*, 368 U.S. 157, and *Lombard v. Louisiana*, 373 U.S. 267, that where restaurants or other facilities serving the public are concerned and licenses are obtained from the State for operating the business, the "public" may not be defined by the proprietor to include only people of his choice; nor may a State or municipal service be granted only to some. *Evans v. Newton*, 382 U.S. 296, 298–299.

Those cases are not precisely apposite, however, for a private club, by definition, is not in the public domain. And the fact that a private club gets some kind of permit from the State or municipality does not make it *ipso facto* a public enterprise or undertaking, any more than the grant to a householder of a permit to operate an incinerator puts the householder in the public domain. We must therefore examine whether there are special circumstances involved in the Pennsylvania scheme which differentiate the liquor license possessed by Moose Lodge from the incinerator permit.

. . .

Were this regulation [enforcing the discriminatory membership clause] the only infirmity in Pennsylvania's licensing scheme, I would perhaps agree with the majority that the appropriate relief would be a decree enjoining its enforcement. But there is another flaw in the scheme not so easily cured. Liquor licenses in Pennsylvania, unlike driver's licenses, or marriage licenses, are not freely available to those who meet racially neutral qualifications. There is a complex quota system, which the majority accurately describes. What the majority neglects to say is that the Harrisburg quota, where Moose Lodge No. 107 is located, has been full for many years. No more club licenses may be issued in that city.

This state-enforced scarcity of licenses restricts the ability of blacks to obtain liquor, for liquor is commercially available *only* at private clubs for a significant portion of each week. Access by blacks to places that serve liquor is further limited by the fact that the state quota is filled. A group desiring to form a nondiscriminatory club which would serve blacks must purchase a license held by an existing club, which can exact a monopoly price for the transfer. The availability of such a license is speculative at best, however, for, as Moose Lodge itself concedes, without a liquor license a fraternal organization would be hard-pressed to survive.

Thus, the State of Pennsylvania is putting the weight of its liquor license, concededly a valued and important adjunct to a private club, behind racial discrimination. . . .

I would affirm the judgment below.

Mr. Justice Brennan, with whom Mr. Justice Marshall joins, dissenting.

When Moose Lodge obtained its liquor license, the State of Pennsylvania became an active participant in the operation of the Lodge bar. Liquor licensing laws are only incidentally revenue measures; they are primarily pervasive regulatory schemes under which the State dictates and continually supervises virtually every detail of the operation of the licensee's business. Very few, if any, other licensed businesses experience such complete state involvement. Yet the Court holds that that involvement does not constitute "state action" making the Lodge's refusal to serve a guest liquor solely because of his race a violation of the Fourteenth Amendment. The vital flaw in the Court's reasoning is its complete disregard of the fundamental value underlying the "state action" concept. . . .

Plainly, the State of Pennsylvania's liquor regulations intertwine the State with the operation of the Lodge bar in a "significant way [and] lend [the State's] authority to the sordid business of racial discrimination." . . .

This is thus a case requiring application of the principle that until today has governed our determinations of the existence of "state action": "Our prior decisions leave no doubt that the mere existence of efforts by the State, through legislation or otherwise, to authorize, encourage, or otherwise support racial discrimination in a particular facet of life constitutes illegal state involvement in those pertinent private acts of discrimination that subsequently occur." Adickes v. Kress & Co., 398 U.S., at 202 (separate opinion of Brennan, J.). . . .

I therefore dissent and would affirm the final decree entered by the District Court.

Jackson v. Metropolitan Edison Co.

419 U.S. 345, 95 S.Ct. 449, 42 L.Ed.2d 477 (1974).

[Plaintiff brought suit against defendant, a privately owned and operated utility corporation which holds a certificate of public convenience issued by the

Pennsylvania Utilities Commission, seeking damages and injunctive relief under 42 U.S.C. § 1983 for termination of her electric service allegedly before she had been afforded notice, a hearing, and an opportunity to pay any amounts due. Plaintiff claimed that under state law she was entitled to reasonably continuous electric service and that respondent's termination for alleged nonpayment, permitted by a provision of its general tariff filed with the Commission, was state action depriving her of her property without due process of law. The Court of Appeals affirmed the District Court's dismissal of her complaint. The Supreme Court affirmed.]

Mr. Justice Rehnquist delivered the opinion of the Court.

. . .

Here the action complained of was taken by a utility company which is privately owned and operated, but which in many particulars of its business is subject to extensive state regulation. The mere fact that a business is subject to state regulation does not by itself convert its action into that of the State for purposes of the Fourteenth Amendment. Moose Lodge No. 107 v. Irvis, supra, 407 U.S. at 176–177. Nor does the fact that the regulation is extensive and detailed, as in the case of most public utilities, do so. Public Utilities Comm'n v. Pollak, 343 U.S. 451, 462 (1952). It may well be that acts of a heavily regulated utility with at least something of a governmentally protected monopoly will more readily be found to be "state" acts than will the acts of an entity lacking these characteristics. But the inquiry must be whether there is a sufficiently close nexus between the State and the challenged action of the regulated entity so that the action of the latter may be fairly treated as that of the State itself. Moose Lodge No. 107, supra, at 176. The true nature of the State's involvement may not be immediately obvious, and detailed inquiry may be required in order to determine whether the test is met. Burton v. Wilmington Parking Authority, supra.

Petitioner advances a series of contentions which, in her view, lead to the conclusion that this case should fall on the *Burton* side of the line drawn in the *Civil Rights Cases,* supra, rather than on the *Moose Lodge* side of that line. We find none of them persuasive.

Petitioner first argues that "state action" is present because of the monopoly status allegedly conferred upon Metropolitan by the State of Pennsylvania. As a factual matter, it may well be doubted that the State ever granted or guaranteed Metropolitan a monopoly. But assuming that it had, this fact is not determinative in considering whether Metropolitan's termination of service to petitioner was "state action" for purposes of the Fourteenth Amendment. In *Pollak,* supra, where the Court dealt with the activities of the District of Columbia Transit Company, a congressionally established monopoly, we expressly disclaimed reliance on the monopoly status of the transit authority. Id., 343 U.S. at 462. Similarly, although certain monopoly aspects were presented in *Moose Lodge No. 107,* supra, we found that the Lodge's action was not subject to the provisions of the Fourteenth Amendment. In each of those cases, there was insufficient relationship between the challenged actions of the entities involved and their monopoly status. There is no indication of any greater connection here.

Petitioner next urges that state action is present because respondent provides an essential public service required to be supplied on a reasonably continuous basis by 66 Pa.Stat. § 1171, and hence performs a "public function." We have of course found state action present in the exercise by a private entity of powers traditionally exclusively reserved to the State. See, e.g., Nixon

v. Condon, 286 U.S. 73 (1931) (election); Terry v. Adams, 345 U.S. 461 (1953) (election); Marsh v. Alabama, 326 U.S. 501 (1946) (company town); Evans v. Newton, 382 U.S. 296 (1966) (municipal park). If we were dealing with the exercise by Metropolitan of some power delegated to it by the State which is traditionally associated with sovereignty, such as eminent domain, our case would be quite a different one. But while the Pennsylvania statute imposes an obligation to furnish service on regulated utilities, it imposes no such obligation on the State. The Pennsylvania courts have rejected the contention that the furnishing of utility services is either a state function or a municipal duty. Girard Life Insurance Co. v. City of Philadelphia, 88 Pa. 393 (1879); Bailey v. Philadelphia, 184 Pa. 594, 39 A. 494 (1898).

Perhaps in recognition of the fact that the supplying of utility service is not traditionally the exclusive prerogative of the State, petitioner invites the expansion of the doctrine of this limited line of cases into a broad principle that all businesses "affected with the public interest" are state actors in all their actions.

We decline the invitation for reasons stated long ago in Nebbia v. New York, 291 U.S. 502 (1934), in the course of rejecting a substantive due process attack on state legislation: ...

Doctors, optometrists, lawyers, Metropolitan, and Nebbia's upstate New York grocery selling a quart of milk are all in regulated businesses, providing arguably essential goods and services, "affected with a public interest." We do not believe that such a status converts their every action, absent more, into that of the State.

We also reject the notion that Metropolitan's termination is state action because the State "has specifically authorized and approved" the termination practice. In the instant case, Metropolitan filed with the Public Utilities Commission a general tariff—a provision of which states Metropolitan's right to terminate service for nonpayment. This provision has appeared in Metropolitan's previously filed tariffs for many years and has never been the subject of a hearing or other scrutiny by the Commission.[11] Although the Commission did hold hearings on portions of Metropolitan's general tariff relating to a general rate increase, it never even considered the reinsertion of this provision in the newly filed general tariff. The provision became effective 60 days after filing when not disapproved by the Commission.

As a threshold matter, it is less than clear under state law that Metropolitan was even required to file this provision as part of its tariff or that the Commission would have had the power to disapprove it. The District Court observed that the sole connection of the Commission with this regulation was Metropolitan's simple notice filing with the Commission and the lack of any Commission action to prohibit it.

The case most heavily relied on by petitioner is Public Utilities Comm'n v. Pollak, supra. There the Court dealt with the contention that Capital Transit's installation of a piped music system on its buses violated the First Amendment rights of the bus riders. It is not entirely clear whether the Court alternatively held that Capital Transit's action was action of the "State" for First Amendment purposes, or whether it merely assumed *arguendo* that it was and went on to resolve the First Amendment question adversely to the bus riders. In either event, the nature of the state involvement there was quite different than

[11] Petitioner does not contest the fact that Metropolitan had this right at common law. . . .

it is here. The District of Columbia Public Utilities Commission, on its own motion, commenced an investigation of the effects of the piped music, and after a full hearing concluded not only that Capital Transit's practices were "not inconsistent with public convenience, comfort, and safety," 81 P.U.R.(N.S.) 122, 126 (1950), but also that the practice "in fact through the creation of better will among passengers, ... tends to improve the conditions under which the public rides." Id. Here, on the other hand, there was no such imprimatur placed on the practice of Metropolitan about which petitioner complains. The nature of governmental regulation of private utilities is such that a utility may frequently be required by the state regulatory scheme to obtain approval for practices a business regulated in less detail would be free to institute without any approval from a regulatory body. Approval by a state utility commission of such a request from a regulated utility, where the commission has not put its own weight on the side of the proposed practice by ordering it, does not transmute a practice initiated by the utility and approved by the commission into "state action." At most, the Commission's failure to overturn this practice amounted to no more than a determination that a Pennsylvania utility was authorized to employ such a practice if it so desired. Respondent's exercise of the choice allowed by state law where the initiative comes from it and not from the State, does not make its action in doing so "state action" for purposes of the Fourteenth Amendment.

We also find absent in the instant case the symbiotic relationship presented in Burton v. Wilmington Parking Authority, 365 U.S. 715 (1961)....

Metropolitan is a privately owned corporation, and it does not lease its facilities from the State of Pennsylvania. It alone is responsible for the provision of power to its customers. In common with all corporations of the State it pays taxes to the State, and it is subject to a form of extensive regulation by the State in a way that most other business enterprises are not. But this was likewise true of the appellant club in Moose Lodge No. 107 v. Irvis, ...

All of petitioner's arguments taken together show no more than that Metropolitan was a heavily regulated private utility, enjoying at least a partial monopoly in the providing of electrical service within its territory, and that it elected to terminate service to petitioner in a manner which the Pennsylvania Public Utilities Commission found permissible under state law. Under our decision this is not sufficient to connect the State of Pennsylvania with respondent's action so as to make the latter's conduct attributable to the State for purposes of the Fourteenth Amendment.

We conclude that the State of Pennsylvania is not sufficiently connected with respondent's action in terminating petitioner's service so as to make respondent's conduct in so doing attributable to the State for purposes of the Fourteenth Amendment. We therefore have no occasion to decide whether petitioner's claim to continued service was "property" for purposes of that Amendment, or whether "due process of law" would require a State taking similar action to accord petitioner the procedural rights for which she contends. The judgment of the Court of Appeals for the Third Circuit is therefore

Affirmed.

Mr. Justice Douglas, dissenting.

I reach the opposite conclusion from that reached by the majority on the state action issue....

Mr. Justice Brennan, dissenting.

I do not think that a controversy existed between petitioner and respondent entitling petitioner to be heard in this action. . . .

Mr. Justice Marshall, dissenting.

I agree with my Brother Brennan that this case is a very poor vehicle for resolving the difficult and important questions presented today. . . . Since the Court has disposed of the case by finding no state action, however, I think it appropriate to register my dissent on that point. . . .

. . .

The fact that the Metropolitan Edison Company supplies an essential public service that is in many communities supplied by the government weighs more heavily for me than for the majority. . . .

Private parties performing functions affecting the public interest can often make a persuasive claim to be free of the constitutional requirements applicable to governmental institutions because of the value of preserving a private sector in which the opportunity for individual choice is maximized. See Evans v. Newton, 382 U.S., at 298, H. Friendly, The Dartmouth College Case and the Private–Public Penumbra (1969). Maintaining the private status of parochial schools, cited by the majority, advances just this value. In the due process area, a similar value of diversity may often be furthered by allowing various private institutions the flexibility to select procedures that fit their particular needs. See Wahba v. New York University, 492 F.2d 96, 102 (2d Cir.), cert. denied, 419 U.S. 874 (1974). But it is hard to imagine any such interests that are furthered by protecting public utility companies from meeting the constitutional standards that would apply if the companies were state-owned. The values of pluralism and diversity are simply not relevant when the private company is the only electric company in town.

. . .

What is perhaps most troubling about the Court's opinion is that it would appear to apply to a broad range of claimed constitutional violations by the company. The Court has not adopted the notion, accepted elsewhere, that different standards should apply to state action analysis when different constitutional claims are presented. See Adickes v. S.H. Kress & Co., 398 U.S. 144, 190–191 (1970) (Brennan, J., concurring and dissenting); Grafton v. Brooklyn Law School, 478 F.2d 1137, 1142 (2d Cir.1973). Thus, the majority's analysis would seemingly apply as well to a company that refused to extend service to Negroes, welfare recipients, or any other group that the company preferred, for its own reasons, not to serve. I cannot believe that this Court would hold that the State's involvement with the utility company was not sufficient to impose upon the company an obligation to meet the constitutional mandate of nondiscrimination. Yet nothing in the analysis of the majority opinion suggests otherwise.

I dissent.

4. GOVERNMENT APPROVAL OF PRIVATE ACTIVITY

Reitman v. Mulkey

387 U.S. 369, 87 S.Ct. 1627, 18 L.Ed.2d 830 (1967).

Mr. Justice White delivered the opinion of the Court.

The question here is whether Art. I, § 26 of the California Constitution denies "to any person . . . the equal protection of the laws" within the meaning of the Fourteenth Amendment of the Constitution of the United States. Section 26 of Art. I, an initiated measure submitted to the people as Proposition 14 in a statewide ballot in 1964, provides in part as follows:

> "Neither the State nor any subdivision or agency thereof shall deny, limit or abridge, directly or indirectly, the right of any person, who is willing or desires to sell, lease or rent any part or all of his real property, to decline to sell, lease or rent such property to such person or persons as he, in his absolute discretion, chooses."

The real property covered by § 26 is limited to residential property and contains an exception for state-owned real estate.

... [T]he Mulkeys who are husband and wife and respondents here, sued under § 51 and § 52 of the California Civil Code alleging that petitioners had refused to rent them an apartment solely on account of their race. An injunction and damages were demanded. Petitioners moved for summary judgment on the ground that §§ 51 and 52, insofar as they were the basis for the Mulkeys' action, had been rendered null and void by the adoption of Proposition 14 after the filing of the complaint. The trial court granted the motion and respondents took the case to the California Supreme Court.

... [That court reversed, holding] that Art. I, § 26, was invalid as denying the equal protection of the laws guaranteed by the Fourteenth Amendment. 64 Cal.2d 529, 50 Cal.Rptr. 881, 413 P.2d 825....

We affirm the judgment of the California Supreme Court. We first turn to the opinion of that court ..., which quite properly undertook to examine the constitutionality of § 26 in terms of its "immediate objective," its "ultimate effect" and its "historical context and the conditions existing prior to its enactment." Judgments such as these we have frequently undertaken ourselves.... But here the California Supreme Court has addressed itself to these matters and we should give careful consideration to its views because they concern the purpose, scope, and operative effect of a provision of the California Constitution.

First, the court considered whether § 26 was concerned at all with private discriminations in residential housing. This involved a review of past efforts by the California Legislature to regulate such discriminations. The Unruh Act, Civ.Code §§ 51–52, on which respondents based their cases, was passed in 1959. The Hawkins Act, formerly Health & Saf.Code §§ 35700–35741, followed and prohibited discriminations in publicly assisted housing. In 1961, the legislature enacted proscriptions against restrictive covenants. Finally, in 1963, came the Rumford Fair Housing Act, Health & Saf.Code §§ 35700–35744, superseding the Hawkins Act and prohibiting racial discriminations in the sale or rental of any private dwelling containing more than four units. That act was enforceable by the State Fair Employment Practice Commission.

It was against this background that Proposition 14 was enacted. Its immediate design and intent, the California court said, was "to overturn state laws that bore on the right of private sellers and lessors to discriminate," the Unruh and Rumford Acts, and "to forestall future state action that might circumscribe this right." This aim was successfully achieved: the adoption of Proposition 14 "generally nullifies both the Rumford and Unruh Acts as they apply to the housing market," and establishes "a purported constitutional right to *privately* discriminate on grounds which admittedly would be unavailable under the Fourteenth Amendment *should state action* be involved."

Second, the court conceded that the State was permitted a neutral position with respect to private racial discriminations and that the State was not bound by the Federal Constitution to forbid them. But, because a significant state involvement in private discriminations could amount to unconstitutional state action, Burton v. Wilmington Parking Authority, 365 U.S. 715, the court deemed it necessary to determine whether Proposition 14 invalidly involved the State in racial discriminations in the housing market. Its conclusion was that it did.

To reach this result, the state court examined certain prior decisions in this Court in which discriminatory state action was identified. Based on these cases, . . . it concluded that a prohibited state involvement could be found "even where the state can be charged with only encouraging," rather than commanding discrimination. . . . To the California court "[t]he instant case presents an undeniably analogous situation" wherein the State had taken affirmative action designed to make private discriminations legally possible. Section 26 was said to have changed the situation from one in which discriminatory practices were restricted "to one wherein it is encouraged, within the meaning of the cited decisions"; § 26 was legislative action "which authorized private discrimination" and made the State "at least a partner in the instant act of discrimination. . . ." The court could "conceive of no other purpose for an application of section 26 aside from authorizing the perpetration of a purported private discrimination. . . ." The judgment of the California court was that § 26 unconstitutionally involves the State in racial discriminations and is therefore invalid under the Fourteenth Amendment.

There is no sound reason for rejecting this judgment. Petitioners contend that the California court has misconstrued the Fourteenth Amendment since the repeal of any statute prohibiting racial discrimination, which is constitutionally permissible, may be said to "authorize" and "encourage" discrimination because it makes legally permissible that which was formerly proscribed. But as we understand the California court, it did not posit a constitutional violation on the mere repeal of the Unruh and Rumford Acts. It did not read either our cases or the Fourteenth Amendment as establishing an automatic constitutional barrier to the repeal of an existing law prohibiting racial discriminations in housing; nor did the court rule that a State may never put in statutory form an existing policy of neutrality with respect to private discriminations. What the court below did was first to reject the notion that the State was required to have a statute prohibiting racial discriminations in housing. Second, it held the purpose and intent of § 26 was to authorize private racial discriminations in the housing market, to repeal the Unruh and Rumford Acts and to create a constitutional right to discriminate on racial grounds in the sale and leasing of real property. Hence, the court dealt with § 26 as though it expressly authorized and constitutionalized the private right to discriminate. Third, the court assessed the ultimate impact of § 26 in the California environment and concluded that the section would encourage and significantly involve the State in private racial discrimination contrary to the Fourteenth Amendment.

The California court could very reasonably conclude that § 26 would and did have wider impact than a mere repeal of existing statutes. Section 26 mentioned neither the Unruh nor Rumford Acts in so many words. Instead, it announced the constitutional right of any person to decline to sell or lease his real property to anyone to whom he did not desire to sell or lease. Unruh and Rumford were thereby *pro tanto* repealed. But the section struck more deeply and more widely. Private discriminations in housing were now not only free from Rumford and Unruh but they also enjoyed a far different status than was true before the passage of those statutes. The right to discriminate, including the right to discriminate on racial grounds, was now embodied in the State's basic charter, immune from legislative, executive, or judicial regulation at any level of the state government. Those practicing racial discriminations need no longer rely solely on their personal choice. They could now invoke express constitutional authority, free from censure or interference of any kind from official sources. All individuals, partnerships, corporations and other legal entities, as well as their agents and representatives, could now discriminate with respect to their residential real property, which is defined as any interest in real property of any kind or quality, "irrespective of how obtained or financed," and seemingly irrespective of the relationship of the State to such interests in real property. Only the State is excluded with respect to property owned by it.

... Here the California court, armed as it was with the knowledge of the facts and circumstances concerning the passage and potential impact of § 26, and familiar with the milieu in which that provision would operate, has determined that the provision would involve the State in private racial discriminations to an unconstitutional degree. We accept this holding of the California court.

The assessment of § 26 by the California court is similar to what this Court has done in appraising state statutes or other official actions in other contexts....

None of these cases squarely controls the case we now have before us. But they do illustrate the range of situations in which discriminatory state action has been identified. They do exemplify the necessity for a court to assess the potential impact of official action in determining whether the State has significantly involved itself with invidious discriminations. Here we are dealing with a provision which does not just repeal an existing law forbidding private racial discriminations. Section 26 was intended to authorize, and does authorize, racial discrimination in the housing market. The right to discriminate is now one of the basic policies of the State. The California Supreme Court believes that the section will significantly encourage and involve the State in private discriminations. We have been presented with no persuasive considerations indicating that this judgment should be overturned.

Affirmed.

Mr. Justice Douglas, concurring.

While I join the opinion of the Court, I add a word to indicate the dimensions of our problem.

This is not a case as simple as the one where a man with a bicycle or a car or a stock certificate or even a log cabin asserts the right to sell it to whomsoever he pleases, excluding all others whether they be Negro, Chinese, Japanese, Russians, Catholics, Baptists, or those with blue eyes. We deal here with a problem in the realm of zoning, similar to the one we had in Shelley v. Kraemer, 334 U.S. 1, where we struck down restrictive covenants.

. . .

Since the real estate brokerage business is one that can be and is state regulated and since it is state licensed, it must be dedicated, like the telephone companies and the carriers and the hotels and motels to the requirements of service to all without discrimination—a standard that in its modern setting is conditioned by the demands of the Equal Protection Clause of the Fourteenth Amendment.

Mr. Justice Harlan, whom Mr. Justice Black, Mr. Justice Clark, and Mr. Justice Stewart join, dissenting.

I consider that this decision, which cuts deeply into state political processes, is supported neither by anything "found" by the Supreme Court of California nor by any of our past cases decided under the Fourteenth Amendment. In my view today's holding, salutary as its result may appear at first blush, may in the long run actually serve to handicap progress in the extremely difficult field of racial concerns. I must respectfully dissent. . . .

. . .

In the case at hand California, acting through the initiative and referendum, has decided to remain "neutral" in the realm of private discrimination affecting the sale or rental of private residential property; in such transactions private owners are now free to act in a discriminatory manner previously forbidden to them. In short, all that has happened is that California has effected a *pro tanto* repeal of its prior statutes forbidding private discrimination. This runs no more afoul of the Fourteenth Amendment than would have California's failure to pass any such antidiscrimination statutes in the first instance. The fact that such repeal was also accompanied by a constitutional prohibition against future enactment of such laws by the California Legislature cannot well be thought to affect, from a federal constitutional standpoint, the validity of what California has done. The Fourteenth Amendment does not reach such state constitutional action any more than it does a simple legislative repeal of legislation forbidding private discrimination.

I.

The Court attempts to fit § 26 within the coverage of the Equal Protection Clause by characterizing it as in effect an affirmative call to residents of California to discriminate. The main difficulty with this viewpoint is that it depends upon a characterization of § 26 that cannot fairly be made. The provision is neutral on its face, and it is only by in effect asserting that this requirement of passive official neutrality is camouflage that the Court is able to reach its conclusion. In depicting the provision as tantamount to active state encouragement of discrimination the Court essentially relies on the fact that the California Supreme Court so concluded. It is said that the findings of the highest court of California as to the meaning and impact of the enactment are entitled to great weight. I agree, of course, that *findings of fact* by a state court should be given great weight, but this familiar proposition hardly aids the Court's holding in this case. . . .

. . . Put in another way, I cannot transform the California court's conclusion of law into a finding of fact that the State through the adoption of § 26 is actively promoting racial discrimination. It seems to me manifest that the state court decision rested entirely on what that court conceived to be the compulsion of the Fourteenth Amendment, not on any fact-finding by the state courts.

II.

There is no question that the adoption of § 26, repealing the former state antidiscrimination laws and prohibiting the enactment of such state laws in the future, constituted "state action" within the meaning of the Fourteenth Amendment. The only issue is whether this provision impermissibly deprives any person of equal protection of the laws. . . .

A moment of thought will reveal the far-reaching possibilities of the Court's new doctrine, which I am sure the Court does not intend. Every act of private discrimination is either forbidden by state law or permitted by it. There can be little doubt that such permissiveness—whether by express constitutional or statutory provision, or implicit in the common law—to some extent "encourages" those who wish to discriminate to do so. Under this theory "state action" in the form of laws that do nothing more than passively permit private discrimination could be said to tinge *all* private discrimination with the taint of unconstitutional state encouragement.

. . . I believe the state action required to bring the Fourteenth Amendment into operation must be affirmative and purposeful, actively fostering discrimination. Only in such a case is ostensibly "private" action more properly labeled "official." I do not believe that the mere enactment of § 26, on the showing made here, falls within this class of cases.

III.

I think that this decision is not only constitutionally unsound, but in its practical potentialities short-sighted. Opponents of state antidiscrimination statutes are now in a position to argue that such legislation should be defeated because, if enacted, it may be unrepealable. More fundamentally, the doctrine underlying this decision may hamper, if not preclude, attempts to deal with the delicate and troublesome problems of race relations through the legislative process. . . .[a]

PRECURSORS AND SUCCESSORS TO REITMAN v. MULKEY

The theory of Reitman v. Mulkey had been anticipated in two individual concurring opinions in significant state action cases. In Burton v. Wilmington Parking Auth., supra p. 1125, Justice Stewart concurred because the Delaware Supreme Court had relied on a statute which authorized restaurant proprietors to refuse to serve persons whose presence would be offensive to a majority of customers. Justice Harlan's dissent in the same case conceded that if the Delaware court had construed the statute to authorize discriminatory classification based exclusively on race, he would "certainly agree" that the statute violated the Fourteenth Amendment. In Evans v. Newton, supra p. 1110, Justice White's concurrence was premised on a Georgia statute which had been enacted in 1905, six years before Senator Bacon's will was executed. That statute explicitly authorized charitable trusts for public parks for the use of one race. While the statute did not compel trust settlors to discriminate, "if the validity of the racial condition in Senator Bacon's trust would have been in doubt but for the 1904 statute and if the statute removed such doubt only for racial restrictions, leaving the validity of nonracial restrictions still in question. . . . such a statute would depart from a policy of strict neutrality in matters of private discrimination. . . ."

Is the disagreement between the majority and dissenting opinions in Reitman v. Mulkey applicable to those cases where a statute validating private conduct uses an express racial classification? In Hunter v. Erickson, 393 U.S. 385 (1969), the Court held invalid a city charter provision which prevented the city council from implementing any ordinance dealing with racial, religious, or ancestral discrimination in housing without the approval of the majority of the city voters. Justices Harlan and Stewart concurred, noting that since the challenged provision was discriminatory on its face, it bore a far heavier burden

---

[a] For discussion of the issues in Reitman v. Mulkey, see Black, *"State Action," Equal Protection, and California's Proposition 14,* 81 Harv.L.Rev. 69 (1967); Note, *The Unconstitutionality of Proposition 14,* 19 Stan. L.Rev. 232 (1966); Comments, 14 U.C.L.A.L.Rev. 1 (1966).

of justification than was required in *Reitman*. Justice Black was the sole dissenter.

Justice Black, however, wrote the Court's opinion in James v. Valtierra, 402 U.S. 137 (1971), which upheld a provision of the California constitution requiring a referendum for publicly supported low-rent housing projects, because "California's entire history demonstrates the repeated use of referendums to give citizens a voice on questions of public policy." Three Justices dissented, arguing that the challenged provision rested on the explicit suspect classification of poverty. Without challenging the dissent's argument that explicit de jure classifications based on wealth were suspect, the Court concluded that the challenged provision could be invalidated only by extending the rationale of *Hunter* beyond cases where racial classifications were used, "and this we decline to do."[1]

The Court relied on Hunter v. Erickson in Washington v. Seattle Sch. Dist. No. 1, 458 U.S. 457 (1982). A voter initiative of the State of Washington was passed shortly after Seattle adopted a mandatory busing program to achieve desegregation. The initiative's terms prohibited local school boards from requiring students to attend schools other than those nearest the students' homes. The provision also barred seven methods of "indirect student assignment" by school boards, including the redefinition of attendance zones, pairing of schools, and the use of feeder schools. The initiative permitted assignment of pupils to distant schools for purposes of special education, because of health or safety hazards, or physical barriers or obstacles between residence and school, or if the nearest school was overcrowded or lacked physical facilities. Finally, the initiative expressly permitted busing for racial balance if ordered by a court of competent jurisdiction "adjudicating constitutional issues." Holding the initiative unconstitutional, Justice Blackmun's opinion for the Court summarized the principle of Hunter v. Erickson as follows:

> ... "As Justice Harlan noted while concurring in the Court's opinion in *Hunter,* laws structuring political institutions or allocating political power according to 'neutral principles'—such as the executive veto, or the typically burdensome requirements for amending state constitutions—are not subject to equal protection attack, though they may 'make it more difficult for minorities to achieve favorable legislation.' 393 U.S., at 394. Because such laws make it more difficult for *every* group in the community to enact comparable laws, they 'provid[e] a just framework within which the diverse political groups in our society may fairly compete.' Id., at 393. Thus, the political majority may generally restructure the political process to place obstacles in the path of everyone seeking to secure the benefits of governmental action. But a different analysis is required when the State allocates governmental power non-neutrally, by explicitly using the *racial* nature of a decision to determine the decisionmaking process. State action of this kind, the Court said, 'places *special* burdens on racial minorities within the governmental process,' id., at 391 (emphasis added), thereby 'making it *more* difficult for certain racial and religious minorities [than for other members of the community] to achieve legislation that is in their interest.' Id., at 395 (emphasis added) (Harlan, J., concurring). Such a structuring of

---

[1] In Romer v. Evans, ___ U.S. ___, 116 S.Ct. 1620 (1996), the Court dealt with an amendment to the Colorado Constitution that precluded any level of state government from protecting the status of persons based on their "homosexual, lesbian or bisexual orientation, conduct, practices or relation- ships." The Colorado Supreme Court held the measure unconstitutional, relying in part on Hunter v. Erickson. The Supreme Court affirmed, but did not rely upon or cite *Hunter,* nor did the Court advert to the issue of state action. The full report of this case appears supra, p. 915.

the political process, the Court said, was 'no more permissible than [is] denying [members of a racial minority] the vote, on an equal basis with others.' Id., at 391.''

In this case, the initiative dealt only with desegregation of public schools, which "at bottom inures primarily to the benefit of the minority." And, by placing the power over desegregation at the state level, the initiative restructured the State's political process on the basis of a classification that differentiated between "racial matters and ... other problems in the same area." Finally, the Court held that no inquiry was required into the question whether there was an "intent" to discriminate, under the doctrine of Washington v. Davis, 426 U.S. 229 (1976). When "racially conscious" political decisionmaking "is singled out for peculiar and disadvantageous treatment, the government action plainly rests on distinctions based on race." Justice Powell, joined by Chief Justice Burger, Justice Rehnquist, and Justice O'Connor, dissented. Justice Powell argued that "racial minorities are not uniquely or comparatively burdened by the State's adoption of a policy that would be lawful if adopted by any School District in the State.... The Constitution does not dictate to the States at what level of government decisions affecting the public schools must be taken."

Compare the decision in Crawford v. Los Angeles Board of Education, 458 U.S. 527 (1982). California courts had required mandatory busing in the Los Angeles school district, interpreting the California Constitution to require alleviation of de facto, as well as de jure, school segregation. An initiative amended the California Constitution to forbid California courts to order busing unless required by the United States Constitution. The Court held that the initiative was constitutional. Justice Powell's opinion for the Court explained that the initiative employed no racial classification, and no discriminatory purpose had been shown. "[T]he simple repeal or modification of desegregation or anti-discrimination laws, without more, never has been viewed as embodying a presumptively invalid racial classification." Justice Blackmun, concurring, argued that Washington v. Seattle Sch. Dist. No. 1 differed from *Crawford* because "the people of California—the same entity that put in place the State Constitution, and created the enforceable obligation to desegregate—have made the desegregation obligation judicially unenforceable." Justice Marshall dissented, stating: "I fail to see how a fundamental redefinition of the governmental decisionmaking structure with respect to the same racial issue can be unconstitutional when the State seeks to remove the authority from local school boards, yet constitutional when the State attempts to achieve the same result by limiting the power of its courts."

SECTION 3.   FEDERAL CIVIL RIGHTS LEGISLATION

A.   THE RECONSTRUCTION LEGACY

From 1866 to 1875 Congressional leaders attached great importance to national legislation in aid of civil rights. State action which violated the new constitutional rights of freedmen could be resisted in court; but this means of vindicating constitutional guaranties depended on successful litigation by ex-slaves, and carried no sanction to deter unconstitutional action in those cases where private litigation could not succeed. Hence Congress added the possibility of federal criminal prosecution, directed not only against state officials but also against private individuals who interfered with the liberty of the new freedmen.

Only the following fragments remain.

REMAINING RECONSTRUCTION—ERA FEDERAL CIVIL RIGHTS STATUTES

1. Criminal Provisions:

18 U.S.C. § 241.[1] *"Conspiracy Against Rights of Citizens.* If two or more persons conspire to injure, oppress, threaten, or intimidate any citizen in the free exercise or enjoyment of any right or privilege secured to him by the Constitution or laws of the United States, or because of his having so exercised the same; or

"If two or more persons go in disguise on the highway, or on the premises of another, with intent to prevent or hinder his free exercise or enjoyment of any right or privilege so secured—

"They shall be fined not more than $10,000 or imprisoned not more than ten years, or both; and if death results, they shall be subject to imprisonment for any term of years or for life."

18 U.S.C. § 242.[2] *"Deprivation of Rights under Color of Law.* Whoever, under color of any law, statute, ordinance, regulation, or custom, willfully subjects any inhabitant of any State, Territory, or District to the deprivation of any rights, privileges, or immunities secured or protected by the Constitution or laws of the United States, or to different punishments, pains, or penalties, on account of such inhabitant being an alien, or by reason of his color, or race, than are prescribed for the punishment of citizens, shall be fined not more than $1,000 or imprisoned not more than one year, or both; and if bodily injury results shall be fined under this title and imprisoned not more than ten years, or both; and if death results shall be subject to imprisonment for any term of years or for life."

2. Civil Provisions:

42 U.S.C. § 1981.[3] *"Equal Rights under the Law."*

"(a) All persons within the jurisdiction of the United States shall have the same right in every State and Territory to make and enforce contracts, to sue, be parties, give evidence, and to the full and equal benefit of all laws and proceedings for the security of persons and property as is enjoyed by white citizens, and shall be subject to like punishment, pains, penalties, taxes, licenses, and exactions of every kind, and to no other."

"(b) For purposes of this section, the term 'make and enforce contracts' includes the making, performance, modification, and termination of contracts, and the enjoyment of all benefits, privileges, terms, and conditions of the contractual relationship."

"(c) The rights protected by this section are protected against impairment by nongovernmental discrimination and impairment under color of State law."

42 U.S.C. § 1982.[4] *"Property Rights of Citizens.* All citizens of the United States shall have the same right, in every State and Territory, as is enjoyed by white citizens thereof to inherit, purchase, lease, sell, hold, and convey real and personal property."

[1] From § 6 of the 1870 Act.

[2] From § 2 of the 1866 Act, as amended by § 17 of the 1870 Act.

[3] From the 1866 and 1870 Acts.

[4] From the 1866 Act.

42 U.S.C. § 1983.[5] *"Civil Action for Deprivation of Rights.* Every person who, under color of any statute, ordinance, regulation, custom, or usage, of any State or Territory or the District of Columbia, subjects, or causes to be subjected, any citizen of the United States or other persons within the jurisdiction thereof to the deprivation of any rights, privileges or immunities secured by the Constitution and laws, shall be liable to the person injured in an action of law, suit in equity, or other proper proceedings for redress...."

42 U.S.C. § 1985.[6] *"Conspiracy to Interfere with Civil Rights.* (1) [conspiracies to prevent federal officers from performing duties].... (2) [obstructing justice].... (3) If two or more persons in any State or Territory conspire or go in disguise on the highway or on the premises of another, for the purpose of depriving ... any person or class of persons of the equal protection of the laws, or of equal privileges and immunities under the laws; or for the purpose of preventing or hindering the constituted authorities of any State or Territory from giving or securing to all persons within such State or Territory the equal protection of the laws ... the party so injured or deprived may have an action for the recovery of damages, occasioned by such injury or deprivation, against any one or more of the conspirators."

ENFORCING AND INTERPRETING THE CIVIL RIGHTS STATUTES

Sections 4 and 5 of this chapter will focus on issues of interpretation of these Reconstruction statutes that are relevant to issues of the scope of Congressional power to protect civil rights against the conduct of private individuals. These represent, however, only a fraction of the issues surrounding contemporary application of these statutes.

The civil rights acts were enforced vigorously during Reconstruction. In the peak year of 1873 there were 1271 prosecutions under their criminal provisions in Southern federal courts. Even before the decision in the Civil Rights Cases, the end of Reconstruction and the withdrawal of federal troops marked a significant change in enforcement. In 1878, there were 25 criminal cases. The change in national mood was reflected both in Congress and the Supreme Court. The last of the federal civil rights laws was enacted in 1875, and Congress retired from the scene for more than three quarters of a century. One year later the Court decided in United States v. Cruikshank, 92 U.S. (2 Otto) 542 (1876), that an indictment against members of a lynch mob accused of killing two Blacks failed to state an offense under the 1870 Act. Other provisions of the civil rights acts were invalidated prior to the decision in the Civil Rights Cases. United States v. Reese, 92 U.S. (2 Otto) 214 (1876), held provisions of the 1870 Act dealing with voting rights invalid because they were not limited to interference with voting on account of race, color or previous condition of servitude. United States v. Harris, 106 U.S. (16 Otto) 629 (1883), invalidated the antilynching provisions of the 1871 Act, holding that Congress lacked power to punish private persons who removed Black prisoners from state custody and abused or killed them.

The decision in the Civil Rights Cases was followed by later decisions curtailing the power of the federal government to protect Blacks from private violence. For example, Hodges v. United States, 203 U.S. 1 (1906), held that Congress lacked power to protect Blacks from private violence that interfered with their employment. From 1909 to 1939, the criminal provisions of the

[5] From § 1 of the 1871 Act.   [6] From the 1871 Act.

federal civil rights acts lay dormant until Attorney General Frank Murphy established a Civil Rights Section in the Department of Justice.

One target of prosecution was unlawful violence against prisoners and arrestees. In those prosecutions under the predecessor of 18 U.S.C. § 242, two problems arose. First, it was contended that the lawless and unauthorized conduct of the police was not "under color of ... law"; second, it was claimed that the uncertain contours of constitutional rights rendered the criminal punishment of state officials for violating those rights unconstitutionally vague. Screws v. United States, 325 U.S. 91 (1945), held that state officials who wielded state power acted under color of law whether or not their conduct was illegal under state law. The problem of vagueness was addressed by requiring that the federal constitutional rights denied by the defendant be specifically defined by prior law or court decisions, and that the defendant be proved to have acted "wilfully" with specific intent to deprive the victim of those rights.

Vigorous enforcement of the criminal provisions of the remaining fragments of Reconstruction civil rights acts also led to rediscovery of their civil provisions. 42 U.S.C. § 1983 has become the primary vehicle for litigation requiring state officials to obey the commands of federal constitutional or statutory law. (See Chapter 3, page 58.) Problems of interpretation have been numerous, particularly where the complaint under § 1983 seeks the award of damages. In Monroe v. Pape, 365 U.S. 167 (1961), the Court held that damages were available under § 1983 against police officers who engaged in an unlawful search and seizure. The Court adopted the definition of "color of law" from Screws v. United States, supra, but held the requirement of that case, that the defendant act "wilfully," inapplicable since § 1983 provided a civil remedy and was not a criminal statute. Thus, damages could be awarded although the constitutional right denied was not specifically defined and the defendant did not act with specific intent to deny that right.

The potential for damage awards against legislators who enacted laws later determined to be unconstitutional, judges who applied those laws, and state prosecutors who enforced them, has led to an elaborate body of judicially developed immunities from liability for damages under § 1983. An example of a controversial decision concerning the scope of the immunity from damage awards is Stump v. Sparkman, 435 U.S. 349 (1978), where a divided Court held that a judge was not liable for ordering the involuntary sterilization of a minor despite the "clear absence of all jurisdiction." In addition, individual defendants not entitled to absolute immunity have been allowed the defense that their action was taken in "good faith." In Wood v. Strickland, 420 U.S. 308 (1975), the Court divided 5–4 on the definition of good faith in a suit against school officials who expelled students without an adequate hearing. The potential for damage liability may also have resulted, in some cases, in a narrow definition of constitutional rights.

Section 1983 provides no basis for an action against state governments as such. Quern v. Jordan, 440 U.S. 332, 341 (1979). *Monroe v. Pape,* supra, had also held that local governments were not subject to suit under § 1983. That aspect of *Monroe* was overruled in Monell v. New York City Dept. of Social Services, 436 U.S. 658 (1978). Municipalities are not liable under *Monell,* however, on a respondeat superior theory for acts of their employees. Municipal liability for damages is limited to the denial of federal rights by "official policy." On the other hand, municipalities are not entitled to defend a § 1983 action based on the good faith of their officials. Owen v. City of Independence, Mo., 445 U.S. 622 (1980).

B.   CONTEMPORARY FEDERAL CIVIL RIGHTS LEGISLATION

The Civil Rights Act of 1964. The most comprehensive of contemporary federal civil rights laws is the Civil Rights Act of 1964 (78 Stat. 241). Title II on Discrimination in Places of Public Accommodation (42 U.S.C. § 2000a) sets forth elaborate provisions for injunctive relief against racial discrimination by hotels, restaurants, theaters and similar establishments. The scope and constitutional support for these provisions have already been examined in Chapter 4. Katzenbach v. McClung, 379 U.S. 294 (1964), page ___, supra. Title III authorizes civil actions by the Attorney General against discrimination in public facilities; Title IV (*inter alia*)authorizes similar remedial action by the Attorney General against continued discrimination in public education (42 U.S.C. §§ 2000b–2000c). Title VI prohibits "discrimination under any program or activity receiving Federal financial assistance" (42 U.S.C. § 2000d)—a provision of sweeping potential in view of the widespread dependence on federal spending.[7] Title VII on Equal Employment Opportunity broadly prohibits discrimination in employment. (42 U.S.C. § 2000e).

The Voting Rights Act of 1965. The confrontation at the bridge in Selma, Alabama crystallized support that led to the Voting Rights Act of 1965 (79 Stat. 437, 42 U.S.C. § 1973). The central theory of the Act was to move beyond the case-by-case litigation strategy of prior legislation, which had accomplished little in enforcing the command of the Fifteenth Amendment. The Act made special provision for "covered jurisdictions"—states or political subdivisions that on November 1, 1964, had used literacy tests as a qualification for voting, and where less than half of the voting-age residents voted in the 1964 presidential election. Literacy tests were suspended in covered jurisdictions and the Attorney General could appoint federal voting registrars. Any electoral changes in covered jurisdictions were made inoperative, unless precleared by the Attorney General, on a finding that the changes would not perpetuate voting discrimination. The preclearance procedures were extended by the 1970, 1975, and 1982 Acts, the 1982 Act extending them for an additional 25 years. The 1982 Act also provided for judicial challenges to existing voting legislation and voting laws of non-covered jurisdictions, that had the effect of denying voting rights to racial minorities. (As to the last-mentioned provision, see p. 808, supra.)

The only provision of the 1965 Act dealing with literacy tests beyond those in covered jurisdictions was § 4(e)—not part of the original bill, but introduced from the floor. New York excused from its literacy test for voting persons who had completed six grades of schooling in the English language. The effect of § 4(e) was to require New York to exempt also those who had successfully completed six grades in a school in Puerto Rico, even though the language of instruction was Spanish.

The 1965 provisions suspending literacy tests in covered jurisdictions, and § 4(e), were made obsolete in the 1970 Act. Congress suspended literacy tests for voting nationwide for a period of five years. The suspension was made permanent in the 1975 Act. The 1970 Act also contained a significant provision going beyond racial discrimination in voting, lowering the minimum age for voters in state and federal elections to 18. That provision was superseded by the twenty-sixth amendment in 1971.

---

[7] In Grove City College v. Bell, 465 U.S. 555 (1984), the Court held that Title VI applied only to programs receiving Federal assistance. 1987 legislation, passed over President Reagan's veto, extends coverage to substantially all activities of an institution receiving Federal assistance.

The Civil Rights Act of 1968. The assassination of Dr. Martin Luther King on April 4, 1968, released emotions and pressures that speeded the enactment on April 11, 1968, of a further Civil Rights Act (P.L. 90–284; 90th Cong., H.R. 2516). The most controversial subject reached by the 1968 Act was racial discrimination in housing. But this is only one part (Title VIII) of a complex piece of legislation embracing ten Titles.

Title I establishes heavy criminal penalties for the use of force or threats to interfere with "federally protected activities" (18 U.S.C. § 245)—generally those activities that have been blocked or deterred by racial discrimination.

Title VIII (Secs. 801–819) prohibits discrimination "because of race, color, religion or national origin" in sales or rentals of housing. 1988 amendments provide for enhanced enforcement, as well as adding to the categories of prohibited discrimination.

SECTION 4. FEDERAL POWER TO REGULATE PRIVATE CONDUCT UNDER THE THIRTEENTH AMENDMENT

Introduction. It will be recalled that the decision in the Civil Rights Cases conceded that Congressional power to enforce the thirteenth amendment extended to private racial discrimination that could be described as a badge of slavery. Its narrow construction of that concept, however, led to a narrow definition of Congressional power under the thirteenth amendment to regulate private racial discrimination. The cases discussed in this section, all decided since 1968, raise two questions. First, under the modern decisions, are there any forms of private racial discrimination that are *not* within Congressional power to prohibit? Second, to the extent that the thirteenth amendment empowers Congress to prohibit private *racial* discrimination, would the thirteenth amendment power sustain prohibition of similar *non-racial* discrimination, such as discrimination based on national origin, religion, gender, age or physical handicap?

Jones v. Alfred H. Mayer Co.

392 U.S. 409, 88 S.Ct. 2186, 20 L.Ed.2d 1189 (1968).

Mr. Justice Stewart delivered the opinion of the Court.

In this case we are called upon to determine the scope and the constitutionality of an Act of Congress, 42 U.S.C. § 1982, which provides that:

> "All citizens of the United States shall have the same right, in every State and Territory, as is enjoyed by white citizens thereof to inherit, purchase, lease, sell, hold, and convey real and personal property."

On September 2, 1965, the petitioners filed a complaint in the District Court for the Eastern District of Missouri, alleging that the respondents had refused to sell them a home in the Paddock Woods community of St. Louis County for the sole reason that petitioner Joseph Lee Jones is a Negro. Relying in part upon § 1982, the petitioners sought injunctive and other relief. The District Court sustained the respondents' motion to dismiss the complaint, and the Court of Appeals for the Eighth Circuit affirmed, concluding that § 1982 applies only to state action and does not reach private refusals to sell. We granted certiorari to consider the questions thus presented. For the reasons that follow, we reverse the judgment of the Court of Appeals. We hold that

§ 1982 bars *all* racial discrimination, private as well as public, in the sale or rental of property, and that the statute, thus construed, is a valid exercise of the power of Congress to enforce the Thirteenth Amendment.

I.

At the outset, it is important to make clear precisely what this case does *not* involve. Whatever else it may be, 42 U.S.C. § 1982 is not a comprehensive open housing law. In sharp contrast to the Fair Housing Title (Title VIII) of the Civil Rights Act of 1968, Pub.L. 90–284, 82 Stat. 73, the statute in this case deals only with racial discrimination and does not address itself to discrimination on grounds of religion or national origin. It does not deal specifically with discrimination in the provision of services or facilities in connection with the sale or rental of a dwelling. It does not prohibit advertising or other representations that indicate discriminatory preferences. It does not refer explicitly to discrimination in financing arrangements or in the provision of brokerage services. It does not empower a federal administrative agency to assist aggrieved parties. It makes no provision for intervention by the Attorney General. And, although it can be enforced by injunction, it contains no provision expressly authorizing a federal court to order the payment of damages.

Thus, although § 1982 contains none of the exemptions that Congress included in the Civil Rights Act of 1968, it would be a serious mistake to suppose that § 1982 in any way diminishes the significance of the law recently enacted by Congress. . . .

. . .

III.

We begin with the language of the statute itself. In plain and unambiguous terms, § 1982 grants to all citizens, without regard to race or color, "the same right" to purchase and lease property "as is enjoyed by white citizens." As the Court of Appeals in this case evidently recognized, that right can be impaired as effectively by "those who place property on the market" as by the State itself. For, even if the State and its agents lend no support to those who wish to exclude persons from their communities on racial grounds, the fact remains that, whenever property "is placed on the market for whites only, whites have a right denied to Negroes." So long as a Negro citizen who wants to buy or rent a home can be turned away simply because he is not white, he cannot be said to enjoy "the *same* right . . . as is enjoyed by white citizens . . . to . . . purchase [and] lease . . . real and personal property." 42 U.S.C. § 1982. (Emphasis added.)

On its face, therefore, § 1982 appears to prohibit *all* discrimination against Negroes in the sale or rental of property—discrimination by private owners as well as discrimination by public authorities. Indeed, even the respondents seem to concede that, if § 1982 "means what it says"—to use the words of the respondents' brief—then it must encompass every racially motivated refusal to sell or rent and cannot be confined to officially sanctioned segregation in housing. Stressing what they consider to be the revolutionary implications of so literal a reading of § 1982, the respondents argue that Congress cannot possibly have intended any such result. Our examination of the relevant history, however, persuades us that Congress meant exactly what it said.

. . .

V.

The remaining question is whether Congress has power under the Constitution to do what § 1982 purports to do: to prohibit all racial discrimination, private and public, in the sale and rental of property. Our starting point is the Thirteenth Amendment, for it was pursuant to that constitutional provision that Congress originally enacted what is now § 1982. . . .

As its text reveals, the Thirteenth Amendment "is not a mere prohibition of State laws establishing or upholding slavery, but an absolute declaration that slavery or involuntary servitude shall not exist in any part of the United States." Civil Rights Cases, 109 U.S. 3, 20. It has never been doubted, therefore, "that the power vested in Congress to enforce the article by appropriate legislation," ibid., includes the power to enact laws "direct and primary, operating upon the acts of individuals, whether sanctioned by State legislation or not." Id., at 23.

Thus, the fact that § 1982 operates upon the unofficial acts of private individuals, whether or not sanctioned by state law, presents no constitutional problem. If Congress has power under the Thirteenth Amendment to eradicate conditions that prevent Negroes from buying and renting property because of their race or color, then no federal statute calculated to achieve that objective can be thought to exceed the constitutional power of Congress simply because it reaches beyond state action to regulate the conduct of private individuals. The constitutional question in this case, therefore, comes to this: Does the authority of Congress to enforce the Thirteenth Amendment "by appropriate legislation" include the power to eliminate all racial barriers to the acquisition of real and personal property? We think the answer to that question is plainly yes.

"By its own unaided force and effect," the Thirteenth Amendment "abolished slavery, and established universal freedom." Civil Rights Cases, 109 U.S. 3, 20. Whether or not the Amendment *itself* did any more than that—a question not involved in this case—it is at least clear that the Enabling Clause of that Amendment empowered Congress to do much more. For that clause clothed "Congress with power to pass *all laws necessary and proper for abolishing all badges and incidents of slavery in the United States.*" Ibid. (Emphasis added.)

. . .

. . . Surely Congress has the power under the Thirteenth Amendment rationally to determine what are the badges and the incidents of slavery, and the authority to translate that determination into effective legislation. Nor can we say that the determination Congress has made is an irrational one. For this Court recognized long ago that, whatever else they may have encompassed, the badges and incidents of slavery—its "burdens and disabilities"—included restraints upon "those fundamental rights which are the essence of civil freedom, namely, the same right . . . to inherit, purchase, lease, sell and convey property, as is enjoyed by white citizens." Civil Rights Cases, 109 U.S. 3, 22. Just as the Black Codes, enacted after the Civil War to restrict the free exercise of those rights, were substitutes for the slave system, so the exclusion of Negroes from white communities became a substitute for the Black Codes. And when racial discrimination herds men into ghettos and makes their ability to buy property turn on the color of their skin, then it too is a relic of slavery.

Negro citizens North and South, who saw in the Thirteenth Amendment a promise of freedom—freedom to "go and come at pleasure" and to "buy and sell when they please"—would be left with "a mere paper guarantee" if

Congress were powerless to assure that a dollar in the hands of a Negro will purchase the same thing as a dollar in the hands of a white man. At the very least, the freedom that Congress is empowered to secure under the Thirteenth Amendment includes the freedom to buy whatever a white man can buy, the right to live wherever a white man can live. If Congress cannot say that being a free man means at least this much, then the Thirteenth Amendment made a promise the Nation cannot keep.

Representative Wilson of Iowa was the floor manager in the House for the Civil Rights Act of 1866. In urging that Congress had ample authority to pass the pending bill, he recalled the celebrated words of Chief Justice Marshall in McCulloch v. Maryland, 4 Wheat. 316, 421:

"Let the end be legitimate, let it be within the scope of the constitution, and all means which are appropriate, which are plainly adapted to that end, which are not prohibited, but consist with the letter and spirit of the constitution, are constitutional."

"The end is legitimate," the Congressman said, "because it is defined by the Constitution itself. The end is the maintenance of freedom.... A man who enjoys the civil rights mentioned in this bill cannot be reduced to slavery.... This settles the appropriateness of this measure, and that settles its constitutionality."

We agree. The judgment is reversed.[1]

Mr. Justice Harlan, whom Mr. Justice White joins, dissenting.

The decision in this case appears to me to be most ill-considered and ill-advised.

. . .

For reasons which follow, I believe that the Court's construction of § 1982 as applying to purely private action is almost surely wrong, and at the least is open to serious doubt. The issue of the constitutionality of § 1982, as construed by the Court, and of liability under the Fourteenth Amendment alone, also present formidable difficulties. Moreover, the political processes of our own era have, since the date of oral argument in this case, given birth to a civil rights statute embodying "fair housing" provisions which would at the end of this year make available to others, though apparently not to the petitioners themselves, the type of relief which the petitioners now seek. It seems to me that this latter factor so diminishes the public importance of this case that by far the wisest course would be for this Court to refrain from decision and to dismiss the writ as improvidently granted.

. . .

Like the Court, I began analysis of § 1982 by examining its language.... The Court finds it "plain and unambiguous" that this language forbids purely private as well as state-authorized discrimination. With all respect, I do not find it so. For me, there is an inherent ambiguity in the term "right," as used in § 1982. The "right" referred to may either be a right to equal status under the law, in which case the statute operates only against state-sanctioned discrimination, or it may be an "absolute" right enforceable against private individuals. To me, the words of the statute, taken alone, suggest the former interpretation,

---

[1] A concurring opinion by Justice Douglas is omitted.

not the latter.[9]

. . .

In sum, the most which can be said with assurance about the intended impact of the 1866 Civil Rights Act upon purely private discrimination is that the Act probably was envisioned by most members of Congress as prohibiting official, community-sanctioned discrimination in the South, engaged in pursuant to local "customs" which in the recent time of slavery probably were embodied in laws or regulations. Acts done under the color of such "customs" were, of course, said by the Court in the Civil Rights Cases . . . to constitute "state action" prohibited by the Fourteenth Amendment. . . . Adoption of a "state action" construction of the Civil Rights Act would therefore have the additional merit of bringing its interpretation into line with that of the Fourteenth Amendment, which this Court has consistently held to reach only "state action." This seems especially desirable in light of the wide agreement that a major purpose of the Fourteenth Amendment, at least in the minds of its congressional proponents, was to assure that the rights conferred by the then recently enacted Civil Rights Act could not be taken away by a subsequent Congress.

. . .

OTHER INTERPRETATIONS OF RECONSTRUCTION–ERA CIVIL RIGHTS LEGISLATION PREMISED ON THE THIRTEENTH AMENDMENT

Since the decision in Jones v. Alfred H. Mayer Co., the Court has interpreted or re-interpreted a number of Reconstruction-era federal civil rights laws. Consider the implications of these decisions on the issue of the scope of Congressional enforcement power under § 2 of the thirteenth amendment.

(1) Application of 42 U.S.C. §§ 1981 and 1982 to conduct of private parties. In addition to § 1982, involved in Jones v. Alfred H. Mayer Co., another fragment of § 1 of the Civil Rights Act of 1866 is § 1981, providing that "all persons within the jurisdiction of the United States" have the same right "as is enjoyed by white citizens," to "make and enforce contracts." The Court has reaffirmed that the right to purchase property under § 1982 is a prohibition of private discrimination, and has extended that rationale to the right to make and enforce contracts under § 1981. Runyon v. McCrary, 427 U.S. 160 (1976).

(2) Application of § 1982 to "property." In Sullivan v. Little Hunting Park, Inc., 396 U.S. 229 (1969), the Court held that § 1982 applied to refusal by a residents' association, running a community swimming pool, to approve assignment of a membership share from a white owner to a black tenant. Since

---

[9] . . . In the Civil Rights Cases, 109 U.S. 3, the Court said of identical language in the predecessor statute to § 1982:

"[C]ivil rights, such as are guaranteed by the constitution against state aggression, cannot be impaired by the wrongful acts of individuals, unsupported by state authority. . . . The wrongful act of an individual, unsupported by any such authority, is simply a private wrong, or a crime of that individual; an invasion of the rights of the injured party, it is true . . .; but if not sanctioned in some way by the state, or not done under State authority, his rights remain in full force, and may presumably be vindicated by resort to the laws of the State for redress. An individual cannot deprive a man of his right . . . to hold property, to buy and sell . . .; he may, by force or fraud, interfere with the enjoyment of the right in a particular case; . . . but, unless protected in these wrongful acts by some shield of state law or state authority, he cannot destroy or injure the right. . . ." 109 U.S., at 17.

the tenant paid part of his monthly rental for assignment of the membership share, refusal to approve the membership transfer was an interference with his right to "lease" the house. In City of Memphis v. Greene, 451 U.S. 100 (1981), however, the Court concluded that closing a street through a white residential community did not give rise to a cause of action, under § 1982, for black residents of a nearby predominantly black neighborhood. Plaintiffs' injury was not an impairment of their "property interests."

(3) **Application of § 1981 to discrimination in private employment and admission to private schools.** McDonald v. Santa Fe Trail Transportation Co., 427 U.S. 273 (1976), confirmed earlier decisions that the equal right to "make and enforce contracts" affords a remedy against discrimination in private employment on the basis of race. Runyon v. McCrary, supra, held that § 1981 reaches a private schools' racial discrimination in admission.

(4) **Redress of private racial violence under 42 U.S.C. § 1985(3).** This statute provides an action for damages for private conspiracies "for the purpose of depriving . . . any person or class of persons of the equal protection of the laws, or of equal privileges and immunities under the laws." Collins v. Hardyman, 341 U.S. 651 (1951), had held that this provision was applicable only to conspiracies under color of state law. Griffin v. Breckenridge, 403 U.S. 88 (1971), overruled Collins v. Hardyman on this point, holding that § 1985(3) applied to conspiratorial private violence based on "racial, or perhaps otherwise class-based, invidious discriminatory animus." The *Collins* decision had reasoned that narrow construction of the statute was necessary to avoid constitutional problems. As applied to private racial violence, the perceived constitutional problems "simply do not exist" because "Congress was wholly within its powers under § 2 of the Thirteenth Amendment in creating a statutory cause of action for Negro citizens who have been the victims of conspiratorial, racially discriminatory private action aimed at depriving them of the basic rights that the law secures to all free men."

In Bray v. Alexandria Women's Health Clinic, 506 U.S. 263 (1993), the Court held that § 1985(3) did not provide a federal cause of action against defendants who obstructed access to abortion clinics. Defendants' opposition to abortion was not "class-based invidiously discriminatory animus" because it did not focus on women "by reason of their sex." (The Court did not decide the question left open in *Griffin*—whether § 1985(3) was limited to cases involving racial animus.)

(5) **Application of §§ 1981 and 1982 to situations exempted from modern federal civil rights statutes.** The Court's expansive interpretation of §§ 1981 and 1982 has extended these fragments of the Civil Rights Act of 1866 to areas of private racial discrimination that are the subject of modern federal civil rights acts, such as housing, employment, and public accommodations. As the Court notes in its opinion in Jones v. Alfred H. Mayer Co., for example, the prohibition of housing discrimination in § 1982 "contains none of the exemptions that Congress included in the Civil Rights Act of 1968." Consider, particularly, the exemption for the "private club or other [private] establishment" in the public accommodation provisions of the Civil Rights Act of 1964. If an institution that meets the definition of a "private club" excludes racial minorities from its dining facilities, its conduct is not prohibited by the 1964 Act. Is that conduct also beyond the reach of § 1981? The Court has not yet squarely faced the question of how far exemptions in modern civil rights statutes should be read as an "implied repeal" of the unqualified provisions of §§ 1981 and 1982. In Sullivan v. Little Hunting Park, supra, the Court concluded that the defendant residents' association was not a "private club,"

since its membership was open to all residents of the geographic area without exclusiveness other than race. And, in Runyon v. McCrary, supra, the private club exemption of the 1964 Act, applicable only to discrimination in public accommodations, was irrelevant to discrimination in admission to a private school.

(6) Application of § 1981 to "private" associational or contractual relationships. The broad definition of the right to be free from discrimination in making "contracts" has raised the concern that § 1981 will be applied to a variety of "private associational relationships" where persons are excluded on the ground of race. In Runyon v. McCrary, supra, the argument was made that § 1981, as applied to a private school's admissions policy, would violate "constitutionally protected rights of free association and privacy, or a parent's right to direct the education of his children." The Court did not resolve the question whether § 1981 should be interpreted as inapplicable to certain "private" relationships. It rejected the argument on the ground that the rights of parents to send children to private schools, and the rights of parents and schools to determine the content of instruction, did not confer a right on private schools to operate "unfettered by reasonable government regulations". (The Court's opinion stated that the case did not present the question of the right of a private social organization to limit its membership on racial grounds.)

Justices White and Rehnquist, dissenting, suggested that future cases would involve the issue of private associational rights.

"Imaginative judicial construction of the word 'contract' is foreseeable; Thirteenth Amendment limitations on Congress' power to ban 'badges and incidents of slavery' may be discovered; the doctrine of the right to association may be bent to cover a specific situation. In any event, courts will be called upon to balance sensitive policy considerations against each other—which considerations have never been addressed by any Congress— all under the guise of 'construing' a statute. This is a task appropriate for the Legislature, not for the Judiciary."

Concurring, Justice Powell saw fewer difficulties in identifying contracts beyond the reach of § 1981 because they were "so personal as to have a discernible rule of exclusivity which is inoffensive to § 1981."

"§ 1981, as interpreted by our prior decisions, does reach certain acts that are 'private' in the sense that they involve no *state* action. But choices, including those involved in entering into a contract, that are 'private' in the sense that they are not part of a commercial relationship offered generally or widely, and that reflect the selectivity exercised by an individual entering into a personal relationship, certainly were not intended to be restricted by the 19th Century Civil Rights Acts."

For a discussion of the range of possible constitutional issues that might arise in the application of §§ 1981 and 1982 to "private" associations, see the majority and concurring opinions in Roberts v. United States Jaycees, infra page 1463.

(7) Application of § 1981 to discrimination against white persons. In McDonald v. Santa Fe Trail Transportation Co., supra, the Court rejected an argument that § 1981 was inapplicable to private racial discrimination against white persons. The Court conceded that the rejected argument was supported by a "mechanical reading" of the language granting all persons the same rights "as is enjoyed by white citizens." The legislative history of the 1866 Act, however, showed that it was not intended solely for the protection of nonwhites.

The Court also relied on the legislative history of the 1866 Act in Shaare Tefila Congregation v. Cobb, 481 U.S. 615 (1987) and Saint Francis College v. Al–Khazraji, 481 U.S. 604 (1987). Sections 1981 and 1982 are limited to "racial" discrimination, and do not reach discrimination on the basis of national origin or religion. The concept of "race" used by Congress in 1866, however, was not based on the modern scientific understanding of the term. Thus, the Court held that actions by an Arab under § 1981 and by Jews under § 1982 stated claims for "racial" discrimination. "Congress intended to protect from discrimination identifiable classes of persons who are subjected to intentional discrimination solely because of their ancestry or ethnic characteristics."

SECTION 5.   FEDERAL POWER TO REGULATE PRIVATE CONDUCT UNDER THE FOURTEENTH AMENDMENT

CIVIL RIGHTS LEGISLATION AND THE COMMERCE AND SPENDING POWERS

Whatever the scope of Congressional power under the thirteenth amendment to prohibit private racial discrimination, current decisions have not addressed the question of the reach of that power to other forms of discrimination. While the equal protection component of the fourteenth amendment has been extended beyond issues of racial discrimination, there are still unanswered questions about the reach of the fourteenth amendment enforcement power as applied to private conduct. It may be asked, however, whether it will ever be necessary to resolve those questions to sustain Congressional legislation prohibiting private discrimination. Modern civil rights laws have often been based upon Congress' power to regulate the economy and to control the conduct of federal grantees, and not upon the enforcement powers under the Reconstruction Amendments. The public accommodation provisions of the 1964 Civil Rights Act were based squarely upon the commerce power, for example, and were sustained by the Court in Heart of Atlanta Motel v. United States, supra p. 193, and Katzenbach v. McClung, supra p. 196, on that basis. In United Brotherhood of Carpenters v. Scott, 463 U.S. 825 (1983), the Court held that a private conspiracy to infringe first amendment rights, not motivated by racial bias, was not a violation of 42 U.S.C. § 1985(3). The four dissenters (Justice Blackmun, joined by Justices Brennan, Marshall and O'Connor) interpreted § 1985(3) to provide a cause of action for private conspiracies to interfere with first amendment rights. Both the majority and the dissent stated that if § 1985(3) were interpreted to reach private interference with first amendment rights, Congress would have power to ban such conspiracies under the commerce clause. Under those decisions, can you think of any case where it would be necessary to determine the reach of Congress' power under section 5 of the fourteenth amendment in order to define Congress' power to regulate private conduct? Consider, particularly, those cases in Section 2 of this Chapter that have found insufficient state action to subject private conduct to the provisions of section one of the fourteenth amendment. Would any of those situations be beyond Congressional regulatory power under the commerce clause?

PRIVILEGES OF NATIONAL CITIZENSHIP

Curiously, one long established source of federal power to control private conduct stems from the concept of privileges of national citizenship recognized by the Slaughter–House Cases, supra p. 466. The curiosity is that the only express constitutional recognition of privileges of national citizenship is contained in section one of the fourteenth amendment. Nevertheless, the rationale of the Civil Rights Cases—that since section one of the fourteenth amendment prohibited only state action the enforcement power under section five did not extend to private conduct—was never held applicable to Congressional legislation that protected privileges of national citizenship from private interference. That is because the Slaughter–House Cases defined privileges of national citizenship as those "which owe their existence to the Federal government, its National character, its Constitution, or its laws." Under that definition, privileges of national citizenship did not "owe their existence" to their inclusion in the fourteenth amendment, and Congressional power to protect them stemmed from implied federal power that was not limited to the enforcement power under the fourteenth amendment.

The decision in the Slaughter–House Cases doomed much of the Reconstruction legislation by its narrow interpretation of the privileges and immunities clause. But, within that narrow interpretation, portions of those laws that were directed at purely private conduct were upheld as applied, and those provisions have survived. In this connection, the provisions of 18 U.S.C. § 241, penalizing private conspiracies to injure "any citizen in the free exercise or enjoyment of any right or privilege secured to him by the Constitution or laws of the United States," and of 42 U.S.C. § 1985(3), providing a civil action for private conspiracies to deny any person "equal privileges or immunities under the law," continue to be relevant.

A list of the privileges of national citizenship is contained in Justice Moody's opinion in Twining v. New Jersey, 211 U.S. 78, 97 (1908). Dicta or holdings in prosecutions under § 241 have identified these privileges of national citizenship, with concomitant federal power to protect them from private conduct. In United States v. Cruikshank, 92 U.S. 542 (1876), the Court held that the general rights of speech and assembly were not within the privileges of national citizenship, but announced in dicta that there was a federal right to assemble to petition Congress for a redress of grievances. Ex parte Yarbrough (Ku Klux Cases), 110 U.S. 651 (1884), added the right to vote in federal elections. (A more modern case, United States v. Classic, 313 U.S. 299 [1941], extended the right to primary elections for federal officers.) Logan v. United States, 144 U.S. 263 (1892), sustained prosecution of members of a lynch mob conspiring to injure a prisoner in custody of a United States Marshal. (Compare the decision nine years earlier, United States v. Harris, 106 U.S. 629 [1883], which declared unconstitutional a provision of the 1875 Act as applied to a lynch mob killing a state prisoner.) In re Quarles, 158 U.S. 532 (1895) decided that one right of federal citizenship was the right to inform federal officials of a violation of federal law.

In more recent cases, the "right to pass freely from State to State," which appeared first in Justice Moody's list of national privileges in *Twining,* has been prominent. One aspect of the decision in United States v. Guest, 383 U.S. 745 (1966), sustained an indictment under § 241 that alleged that defendants conspired to intimidate "Negro citizens of the United States" in their right to "travel freely to and from the State of Georgia." (That case grew out of the murder of Lemuel Penn, a nationally prominent incident involving Southern violence by Whites against Blacks, in 1964. Other aspects of the *Guest* decision will be discussed in the two notes that follow this one.) The Court concluded that not only did Congress have power under the commerce clause to protect free interstate travel, but that the right was one of those privileges protected by § 241. The *Guest* holding was reaffirmed in Griffin v. Breckenridge, 403 U.S. 88 (1971), which held that a private conspiracy to prevent persons from traveling interstate was actionable under § 1985(3).

Whether § 241 is applicable to other yet undefined privileges beyond those discussed in the preceding paragraphs is doubtful. The Court's opinion in *Guest* noted that criminal prosecution under § 241 was permissible for a conspiracy to interfere with interstate travel only because the right had been specifically defined in previous cases, and a specific intent by defendants to interfere with that right must be proved. (See Screws v. United States, discussed supra, p. 1149.) Justice Brennan, in his separate opinion, noted that § 241 was not "model legislation," and that relying on courts to "determine on a case-by-case basis whether the right purportedly threatened is a federal right ... brings § 241 close to the danger line of being void for vagueness." 18 U.S.C. § 245, enacted two years later as part of the 1968 Civil Rights Act, is more specific. Among the private violence and intimidation made criminal by that statute are intended interferences with participation in programs, facilities or activities provided or administered by the United States, with federal employment, with service as a federal juror, and with participation in programs receiving federal financial assistance. Section 245 also punishes private interference with voting or campaigning in *any* election. The concept of privileges of national citizenship would sustain that statute as applied to federal elections. What theory sustains its application to elections for state and local offices? (See the note on *Private Interference With Fourteenth Amendment Rights* below, p. 1161.)

DENIAL OF FOURTEENTH AMENDMENT RIGHTS UNDER COLOR OF LAW OR CUSTOM

Even under the narrowest interpretation of the Civil Rights Cases, federal legislation can reach private conduct interfering with fourteenth amendment rights when that conduct contains sufficient indicia of state action to be prohibited by section one of the fourteenth amendment. Two important fragments of Reconstruction legislation explicitly reach denial of constitutional rights under color of law or "custom." Criminal penalties are provided by 18 U.S.C. § 242, and a civil action by 42 U.S.C. § 1983.

The two leading cases construing these statutes both involved allegations of unlawful police conduct. In Screws v. United States, 325 U.S. 91 (1945), the indictment under § 242 alleged that Screws, who held a grudge against his Black victim and had threatened to "get" him, had beaten him to death after arresting him and bringing him to the courthouse square where the jail was located. Monroe v. Pape, 365 U.S. 167 (1961), was a civil action under § 1983, alleging that the defendant police illegally invaded the plaintiff's home and searched it. In both cases, the Court rejected arguments that the police did not act "under color of law" if their conduct violated state law.

United States v. Price, 383 U.S. 787 (1966), for example, grew out of the widely publicized murder of three civil rights workers, Chaney, Goodman and Schwerner, outside Philadelphia, Mississippi in 1964. The indictment alleged a conspiracy between three law enforcement officials and fifteen private individuals to deprive the victims of their fourteenth amendment rights not to be "punished" without due process of law. The lower court had dismissed the indictments against the private defendants on the ground that they had not acted under color of law. The Court reversed and reinstated the indictments, holding that private parties jointly engaged with state officials in prohibited action are acting under color of law within the meaning of § 242. More recently, in Lugar v. Edmondson Oil Co., Inc., 457 U.S. 922 (1982), the same rationale was applied to a creditor using unconstitutional judicial procedures to collect a private debt, because he "acted in joint participation with state officials in seizure of the disputed property."

In United States v. Guest, supra, the indictment charged that defendants conspired to deprive Blacks of fourteenth amendment rights by, among other things, causing their arrest by false reports that they had committed criminal acts. The indictment was held to be a sufficient allegation of state involvement which could be proved by showing active connivance of state agents in making of the false reports "or other conduct amounting to official discrimination." (The opinion, although ambiguous, can be read to conclude by implication that there would be no state action if the proof merely showed that private individuals had made the false reports, without any involvement by public officials, and public officials had acted on those reports in good faith. The Court did state, however, that the case did not require, in order to sustain the indictment, any "determination of the threshold level that state action must attain in order to create rights under the Equal Protection Clause.")

Adickes v. Kress & Co., 398 U.S. 144 (1970), was a civil action under 42 U.S.C. § 1983 by a white woman who had been refused service in a lunch counter that she entered in the company of Blacks. Plaintiff claimed that the defendant had refused her service pursuant to a "custom of the community to segregate the races in public eating places." The majority of the Court interpreted the statute as requiring a showing of "state involvement" and "not simply a practice that reflects longstanding social habits, generally observed by the people in a locality." Hence, the plaintiff was required to show that custom "have the force of law by virtue of persistent practices of state officials." Justice Douglas, dissenting, asserted that it should be sufficient for plaintiff to show a custom in the sense of "the unwritten commitment, stronger than ordinances, statutes and regulations, by which men live and arrange their lives." Justice Brennan's dissent said it "means custom of the people of a State, not custom of state officials."

PRIVATE INTERFERENCE WITH FOURTEENTH AMENDMENT RIGHTS

It is time to return, once more, to a basic conception of the Civil Rights Cases. It will be recalled that the Court reasoned that, because section one of the fourteenth amendment prohibited only discrimination by the state, Congress lacked power under section five to prohibit private discrimination in public accommodations. Would that still be true? Could Congress have passed Title II of the 1964 Act (public accommodations), Title VII of the 1964 Act (employment), and Title VIII of the 1968 Act (housing), under its power to enforce the fourteenth amendment's guarantee of equal protection of the laws? (Note that all three statutes reach beyond racial discrimination, unlike the public accommodations law invalidated in the Civil Rights Cases.) While six Justices in United States v. Guest, supra, agreed to an important dictum that section five of the fourteenth amendment empowers Congress to enact laws punishing private interference with fourteenth amendment rights, the answers to the questions posed are still not clear.

To understand the ambiguity, it is necessary to analyze the Guest decision in some detail. The indictment alleged that the defendants, all private individuals, had conspired to deny Blacks the right to "equal utilization, without discrimination upon the basis of race" of state owned facilities. The district court had dismissed the indictment on the ground that the criminal provisions of § 241, which contain no requirement that defendants act under color of law, were limited to privileges of national citizenship and did not reach fourteenth amendment rights. In the Price case, supra, decided the same day, the Court had held that conspiracies under color of law to deprive victims of fourteenth amendment rights were punishable under § 241. In *Guest,* a majority of the Court concluded that a conspiracy to deny victims' fourteenth amendment rights could not be prosecuted under § 241 in the absence of proof of state action. (As indicated in the previous note, dismissal of the indictment was reversed on the ground that the indictment could be read to allege state action.)

Justice Brennan, Chief Justice Warren and Justice Douglas dissented from the Court's conclusion that all conspiracies to deprive persons of fourteenth amendment rights were beyond the reach of § 241 unless state involvement in the conspiracy was proved. Justice Brennan concluded that Congress had the power to enact § 241, if it were construed to reach private conspiracies to deny fourteenth amendment rights, and criticized the Court's opinion as casting doubt on that Congressional power. That, in turn, led three members of the majority (Justices Clark, Black and Fortas) to write separately, stressing that the majority had merely construed the statute, and had decided no questions concerning the scope of Congress' power to "punish private conspiracies that interfere with fourteenth amendment rights, such as the right to utilize public facilities." They concluded summarily that there was "no doubt" that Congress had that power. Justice Brennan then responded that a majority cf the Court had expressed the view that Congress could control private conduct interfering with the exercise of fourteenth amendment rights.[1]

It should be emphasized that the portion of the indictment at issue in *Guest* alleged that the private defendants had conspired to deny their victims equal access to state facilities. The focus of the constitutional discussion in Justice Brennan's dissent and Justice Clark's separate opinion was the power to reach that conduct. Justice Brennan's rationale was that, in order to protect the constitutional right to equal utilization of state facilities, it was appropriate for Congress to punish private individuals who made it impossible for their victims to exercise those rights. (Contrast that with the position of the Civil Rights Cases that individuals who made it impossible for others to exercise their rights had not deprived them of those rights, and that Congress could not reach that individual conduct.)

The rationale of the six Justices in *Guest* can easily be expanded to other cases where private individuals effectively destroy or interfere with their victims' rights against the state. Specific provisions of 18 U.S.C. § 245, enacted in 1968, provide criminal penalties for individuals who deny others "because of . . . race, color, religion or national origin" their rights to attend public schools, participate in programs provided or administered by the state, or serve as jurors in state courts. The theory would probably also support federal power, that had been denied in United States v. Harris, 106 U.S. 629 (1883), to punish members of a lynch mob who took a prisoner from state custody.

Would the theory be broad enough to reach private conduct that was unrelated to any relationship between the victim and the state? Would it permit

---

[1] Justice Brennan was required to discuss the constitutional question by his interpretation of § 241. As Justice Harlan remarked in his separate opinion, it was "extraordinary" that three members of the majority, who were not required to reach the constitutional question "cursorily pronounc[ed] themselves on the far-reaching constitutional questions deliberately not reached." An explanation is that President Johnson had, earlier in 1966, called for new legislation protecting civil rights workers and others exercising federal rights from violence and intimidation. The specific shape that legislation would take was delayed, awaiting the Court's decisions in the *Price* and *Guest* cases. A month after the decisions, the President submitted specific proposals. While those proposals died in a Senate filibuster, they were included in President Johnson's proposed 1967 civil rights bill and, with substantial amendments, were enacted as 18 U.S.C. § 245 in 1968.

Congress to punish private discrimination by owners of restaurants and hotels, employers, and landlords? Those are questions beyond the scope of the *Guest* opinions, and there are no decisions squarely in point. To answer the questions, it is necessary to consider further the Court's contemporary treatment of the enforcement powers under the Civil War Amendments. The cases in the next section of this chapter are concerned with Congressional power under the fourteenth and fifteenth amendments to protect the franchise against contrary state laws. They thus do not involve directly the question of the extent of Congressional power to control private conduct. The theories that are advanced and discussed should be considered, however, for the additional light they might throw on the questions raised in this note.

SECTION 6.   THE SCOPE OF CONGRESSIONAL POWER TO REDEFINE THE AMENDMENTS

A.   "REMEDIAL" POWER

City of Rome v. United States

446 U.S. 156, 100 S.Ct. 1548, 64 L.Ed.2d 119 (1980).

Mr. Justice Marshall delivered the opinion of the Court.

At issue in this case is the constitutionality of the Voting Rights Act of 1965 and its applicability to electoral changes and annexations made by the city of Rome, Ga.

I.

This is a declaratory judgment action brought by appellant city of Rome, a municipality in northwestern Georgia, under the Voting Rights Act of 1965, 42 U.S.C. § 1971 et seq. (1976). In 1970 the city had a population of 30,759, the racial composition of which was 76.6% white and 23.4% Negro. The voting-age population in 1970 was 79.4% white and 20.6% Negro.

The governmental structure of the city is established by a charter enacted in 1918 by the General Assembly of Georgia. Before the amendments at issue in this case, Rome's city charter provided for a nine-member city commission and a five-member board of education to be elected concurrently on an at-large basis by a plurality of the vote. The city was divided into nine wards, with one city commissioner from each ward to be chosen in the citywide election. There was no residency requirement for board of education candidates.

In 1966, the General Assembly of Georgia passed several laws of local application that extensively amended the electoral provisions of the city's charter. These enactments altered the Rome electoral scheme in the following ways:

(1) the number of wards was reduced from nine to three;

(2) each of the nine commissioners would henceforth be elected at-large to one of three numbered posts established within each ward;

(3) each commissioner would be elected by majority rather than plurality vote, and if no candidate for a particular position received a majority, a run-off election would be held between the two candidates who had received the largest number of votes;

(4) the terms of the three commissioners from each ward would be staggered;

(5) the board of education was expanded from five to six members;

(6) each board member would be elected at-large, by majority vote, for one of two numbered posts created in each of the three wards, with runoff procedures identical to those applicable to city commission elections;

(7) board members would be required to reside in the wards from which they were elected;

(8) the terms of the two members from each ward would be staggered.

Section 5 of the Voting Rights Act of 1965 requires preclearance by the Attorney General or the United States District Court for the District of Columbia of any change in a "standard, practice, or procedure with respect to voting," 42 U.S.C. § 1973c (1976), made after November 1, 1964, by jurisdictions that fall within the coverage formula set forth in § 4(b) of the Act, 42 U.S.C. § 1973b(b) (1976). In 1965, the Attorney General designated Georgia a covered jurisdiction under the Act, 30 Fed.Reg. 9897, and the municipalities of that State must therefore comply with the preclearance procedure, United States v. Board of Commissioners of Sheffield, Alabama, 435 U.S. 110 (1978).

. . .

... The Attorney General declined to preclear the provisions for majority vote, numbered posts, and staggered terms for city commission and board of education elections, as well as the residency requirement for board elections. He concluded that in a city such as Rome, in which the population is predominately white and racial bloc voting has been common, these electoral changes would deprive Negro voters of the opportunity to elect a candidate of their choice. . . .

. . .

The city and two of its officials then filed this action, seeking relief from the Act based on a variety of claims. A three-judge court, convened pursuant to 42 U.S.C. §§ 1973b(a) and 1973c (1976), rejected the city's arguments and granted summary judgment for the defendants. 472 F.Supp. 221 (D.D.C.1979). We noted probable jurisdiction, . . . and now affirm.

A.

The appellants contend that the city may exempt itself from the coverage of the Act. To evaluate this argument, we must examine the provisions of the Act in some detail.

Section 5 of the Act requires that a covered jurisdiction that wishes to enact any "standard, practice, or procedure with respect to voting different from that in force or effect on November 1, 1964," must seek preclearance from the Attorney General or the United States District Court for the District of Columbia. 42 U.S.C. § 1973c (1976). Section 4(a) of the Act, 42 U.S.C. § 1973b(a) (1976), provides that the preclearance requirement of § 5 is applicable to "any State" that the Attorney General has determined qualifies under the coverage formula of § 4(b), 42 U.S.C. § 1973b(b) (1973), and to "any political subdivision with respect to which such determinations have been made as a separate unit." As we have noted, the city of Rome comes within the preclearance requirement because it is a political unit in a covered jurisdiction, the State of Georgia. United States v. Board of Commissioners of Sheffield, Alabama, 435 U.S. 110 (1978).

Section 4(a) also provides, however, a procedure for exemption from the Act. This so-called "bail out" provision allows a covered jurisdiction to escape the preclearance requirement of § 5 by bringing a declaratory judgment action before a three-judge panel of the United States District Court for the District of Columbia and proving that no "test or device" has been used in the jurisdiction "during the seventeen years preceding the filing of the action for the purpose or with the effect of denying or abridging the right to vote on account of race or color." The District Court refused to allow the city to "bail out" of the Act's coverage, holding that the political units of a covered jurisdiction cannot independently bring a § 4(a) bailout action. We agree.

. . . Under the plain language of the statute, it appears that any bailout action to exempt the city must be filed by, and seek to exempt all of, the State of Georgia.

III.

The appellants raise five issues of law in support of their contention that the Act may not properly be applied to the electoral changes and annexations disapproved by the Attorney General.

A.

The District Court found that the disapproved electoral changes and annexations had not been made for any discriminatory purpose, but did have a discriminatory effect. The appellants argue that § 5 of the Act may not be read as prohibiting voting practices that have only a discriminatory effect. The appellants do not dispute that the plain language of § 5 commands that the Attorney General may clear a practice only if it "does not have the purpose *and* will not have the effect of denying or abridging the right to vote on account of race or color." 42 U.S.C. § 1973c (1976) (emphasis added). By describing the elements of discriminatory purpose and effect in the conjunctive, Congress plainly intended that a voting practice not be precleared unless *both* discriminatory purpose and effect are absent. . . .

The appellants urge that we abandon this settled interpretation because in their view § 5, to the extent that it prohibits voting changes that have only a discriminatory effect, is unconstitutional. Because the statutory meaning and congressional intent are plain, however, we are required to reject the appellants' suggestion that we engage in a saving construction and avoid the constitutional issues they raise. . . . Instead we now turn to their constitutional contentions.

B.

Congress passed the Act under the authority accorded it by the Fifteenth Amendment. The appellants contend that the Act is unconstitutional because it exceeds Congress' power to enforce that Amendment. They claim that § 1 of the Amendment prohibits only purposeful racial discrimination in voting, and that in enforcing that provision pursuant to § 2, Congress may not prohibit voting practices lacking discriminatory intent even if they are discriminatory in effect. We hold that, even if § 1 of the Amendment prohibits only purposeful discrimination, the prior decisions of this Court foreclose any argument that Congress may not, pursuant to § 2, outlaw voting practices that are discriminatory in effect.

The appellants are asking us to do nothing less than overrule our decision in South Carolina v. Katzenbach, 383 U.S. 301 (1966), in which we upheld the constitutionality of the Act. The Court in that case observed that, after making an extensive investigation, Congress had determined that its earlier attempts to remedy the "insidious and pervasive evil" of racial discrimination in voting had failed because of "unremitting and ingenious defiance of the Constitution" in some parts of this country. Id., at 309. Case-by-case adjudication had proved too ponderous a method to remedy voting discrimination, and, when it had produced favorable results, affected jurisdictions often "merely switched to discriminatory devices not covered by the federal decrees." Id., at 314. In response to its determination that "sterner and more elaborate measures" were necessary, id., at 309, Congress adopted the Act, a "complex scheme of stringent remedies aimed at areas where voting discrimination has been most flagrant," id., at 315.

The Court then turned to the question whether the Fifteenth Amendment empowered Congress to impose the rigors of the Act upon the covered jurisdictions. The Court examined the interplay between the judicial remedy created by § 1 of the Amendment and the legislative authority conferred by § 2:

> "By adding this authorization [in § 2], the Framers indicated that Congress was to be chiefly responsible for implementing the rights created by § 1. 'It is the power of Congress which has been enlarged. Congress is authorized to *enforce* the prohibitions by appropriate legislation. Some legislation is contemplated to make the [civil war] amendments fully effective.' Ex parte Virginia, 100 U.S. 339, 345. Accordingly, in addition to the courts, Congress has full remedial powers to effectuate the constitutional prohibition against racial discrimination in voting." Id., at 325–326 (emphasis in original).

Congress' authority under § 2 of the Fifteenth Amendment, we held, was no less broad than its authority under the Necessary and Proper Clause, see McCulloch v. Maryland, 4 Wheat. 316, 421 (1819). This authority, as applied by longstanding precedent to congressional enforcement of the Civil War Amendments, is defined in these terms:

> " 'Whatever legislation is appropriate, that is, adapted to carry out the objects the [civil war] amendments have in view, whatever tends to enforce submission to the prohibitions they contain, and to secure to all persons the enjoyment of perfect equality of civil rights and the equal protection of the laws against State denial or invasion, if not prohibited, is brought within the domain of congressional power.' Ex parte Virginia, 100 U.S. [339,] 345–346." South Carolina v. Katzenbach, supra, at 327.

Applying this standard, the Court held that the coverage formula of § 4(b), the ban on the use of literacy tests and related devices, the requirement that new voting rules must be precleared and must lack both discriminatory purpose and effect, and the use of federal examiners were all appropriate methods for Congress to use to enforce the Fifteenth Amendment. Id., at 329–337.

The Court's treatment in South Carolina v. Katzenbach of the Act's ban on literacy tests demonstrates that, under the Fifteenth Amendment, Congress may prohibit voting practices that have only a discriminatory effect. The Court had earlier held in Lassiter v. Northampton County Board of Elections, 360 U.S. 45 (1959), that the use of a literacy test that was fair on its face and was not employed in a discriminatory fashion did not violate § 1 of the Fifteenth Amendment. In upholding the Act's *per se* ban on such tests in *South Carolina v. Katzenbach,* the Court found no reason to overrule *Lassiter.* Instead, the Court recognized that the prohibition was an appropriate method of enforcing the Fifteenth Amendment because for many years most of the covered jurisdictions had imposed such tests to effect voting discrimination and the continued use of even nondiscriminatory, fairly administered literacy tests would "freeze the effect" of past discrimination by allowing white illiterates to remain on the voting rolls while excluding illiterate Negroes. South Carolina v. Katzenbach, supra, 383 U.S., at 334. This holding makes clear that Congress may, under the authority of § 2 of the Fifteenth Amendment, prohibit state action that, though in itself not violative of § 1, perpetuates the effects of past discrimination.

Other decisions of this Court also recognize Congress' broad power to enforce the Civil War Amendments. In Katzenbach v. Morgan, 384 U.S. 641 (1966), the Court held that legislation enacted under authority of § 5 of the Fourteenth Amendment would be upheld so long as the Court could find that the enactment "'is plainly adapted to [the] end' "of enforcing the Equal Protection Clause and "is not prohibited by but is consistent with 'the letter and spirit of the constitution,' "regardless of whether the practices outlawed by Congress in themselves violated the Equal Protection Clause. Id., at 651 (quoting McCulloch v. Maryland, supra, at 421). The Court stated that, "[c]orrectly viewed, § 5 is a positive grant of legislative power authorizing Congress to exercise its discretion in determining whether and what legislation is needed to secure the guarantees of the Fourteenth Amendment." Ibid. Four years later, in Oregon v. Mitchell, 400 U.S. 112 (1970), the Court unanimously upheld a provision of the Voting Rights Act Amendments of 1970, Pub.L. No. 91–285, 84 Stat. 315, imposing a five-year nationwide ban on literacy tests and similar requirements for registering to vote in state and federal elections. The Court concluded that Congress could rationally have determined that these provisions were appropriate methods of attacking the perpetuation of earlier, purposeful racial discrimination, regardless of whether the practices they prohibited were discriminatory only in effect. See id., at 132–133 (opinion of Black, J.); id., at 144–147 (opinion of Douglas, J.); id., at 216–217 (opinion of Harlan, J.); id., at 231–236 (opinion of Brennan, White, and Marshall, JJ.); id., at 282–284 (opinion of Stewart, J., joined by The Chief Justice and Blackmun, J.).

It is clear, then, that under § 2 of the Fifteenth Amendment Congress may prohibit practices that in and of themselves do not violate § 1 of the Amendment, so long as the prohibitions attacking racial discrimination in voting are "appropriate," as that term is defined in McCulloch v. Maryland and Ex parte Virginia. In the present case, we hold that the Act's ban on electoral changes that are discriminatory in effect is an appropriate method of promoting the purposes of the Fifteenth Amendment, even if it is assumed that § 1 of the Amendment prohibits only intentional discrimination in voting. Congress could rationally have concluded that, because electoral changes by jurisdictions with a demonstrable history of intentional racial discrimination in voting create the risk of purposeful discrimination, it was proper to prohibit changes that have a discriminatory impact. See South Carolina v. Katzenbach, supra, at 335; Oregon v. Mitchell, supra, at 216 (opinion of Harlan, J.). We find no reason, then, to disturb Congress' considered judgment that banning electoral changes that have a discriminatory impact is an effective method of preventing States from "'undo[ing] or defeat[ing] the rights recently won' by Negroes." Beer v. United States, 425 U.S. 130, 140 (1976) (quoting H.R.Rep. No. 91–397, 91st Cong. 1st Sess., 8 (1969)).

C.

The appellants next assert that, even if the Fifteenth Amendment authorized Congress to enact the Voting Rights Act, that legislation violates principles of federalism articulated in National League of Cities v. Usery, 426 U.S. 833 (1976). This contention necessarily supposes that *National League of Cities* signifies a retreat from our decision in *South Carolina v. Katzenbach,* supra, where we rejected the argument that the Act "exceed[s] the powers of Congress and encroach[es] on an area reserved to the States by the Constitution," 383 U.S., at 323, and determined that, "[a]s against the reserved powers of the States, Congress may use any rational means to effectuate the constitutional prohibition of racial discrimination in voting," id., at 324. To the contrary, we find no inconsistency between these decisions.

In *National League of Cities,* the Court held that federal legislation regulating minimum wages and hours could not constitutionally be extended to employees of state and local governments. The Court determined that the Commerce Clause did not provide Congress the authority to enact legislation "directly displac[ing] the States' freedom to structure integral operations in areas of traditional governmental functions," 426 U.S., at 852, which, it held, included employer-employee relationships in programs traditionally conducted by States, id., at 851–852.

The decision in *National League of Cities* was based solely on an assessment of congressional power under the Commerce Clause, and we explicitly reserved the question "whether different results might obtain if Congress seeks to affect integral operations of State governments by exercising authority granted it under other sections of the Constitution such as ... § 5 of the Fourteenth Amendment." Id., at 852, n. 17. The answer to this question came four days later in Fitzpatrick v. Bitzer, 427 U.S. 445 (1976). That case presented the issue whether, in spite of the Eleventh Amendment, Congress had the authority to bring the States as employers within the coverage of Title VII of the Civil Rights Act of 1964, 42 U.S.C. § 2000e et seq., and to provide that successful plaintiffs could recover retroactive monetary relief. The Court held that this extension of Title VII was an appropriate method of enforcing the Fourteenth Amendment....

We agree with the court below that *Fitzpatrick* stands for the proposition that principles of federalism that might otherwise be an obstacle to congressional authority are necessarily overridden by the power to enforce the Civil War Amendments "by appropriate legislation." Those Amendments were specifically designed as an expansion of federal power and an intrusion on state sovereignty. Applying this principle, we hold that Congress had the authority to regulate state and local voting through the provisions of the Voting Rights Act. *National League of Cities,* then, provides no reason to depart from our decision in South Carolina v. Katzenbach that "the Fifteenth Amendment supersedes contrary exertions of state power," 383 U.S., at 325, and that the Act is "an appropriate means for carrying out Congress' constitutional responsibilities," id., at 308.[a]

D.

The appellants contend in the alternative that even if the Act and its preclearance requirement were appropriate means of enforcing the Fifteenth Amendment in 1965, they had outlived their usefulness by 1975, when Congress extended the Act for another seven years. We decline this invitation to overrule Congress' judgment that the 1975 extension was warranted.

. . .

---

[a] A dictum in Justice O'Connor's opinion for the Court in Gregory v. Ashcroft, 501 U.S. 452, 468 (1991), conceded that *City of Rome* stood for the proposition that "principles of federalism ... are attenuated when Congress acts pursuant to its powers under the Civil War Amendments." But, Justice O'Connor also insisted that the Court "has never held that the Amendment may be applied in complete disregard for a State's constitutional powers." For example, a State's power to define the qualifications of State officers "has force even as against the proscriptions of the Fourteenth Amendment." The Fourteenth Amendment "does not override all principles of federalism."

It must not be forgotten that in 1965, *95 years* after ratification of the Fifteenth Amendment extended the right to vote to all citizens regardless of race or color, Congress found that racial discrimination in voting was an "insidious and pervasive evil which had been perpetuated in certain parts of our country through unremitting and ingenious defiance of the Constitution." South Carolina v. Katzenbach, supra, at 309. In adopting the Voting Rights Act, Congress sought to remedy this century of obstruction by shifting "the advantage of time and inertia from the perpetrators of the evil to its victims." Id., at 328. Ten years later, Congress found that a seven-year extension of the Act was necessary to preserve the "limited and fragile" achievements of the Act and to promote further amelioration of voting discrimination. When viewed in this light, Congress' considered determination that at least another seven years of statutory remedies were necessary to counter the perpetuation of 95 years of pervasive voting discrimination is both unsurprising and unassailable. The extension of the Act, then, was plainly a constitutional method of enforcing the Fifteenth Amendment.

Mr. Justice Stevens, concurring.

Although I join the Court's opinion, the dissenting opinions prompt me to emphasize two points that are crucial to my analysis of the case; both concern the statewide nature of the remedy Congress authorized when it enacted the Voting Rights Act of 1965. The critical questions are: (1) whether, as a statutory matter, Congress has prescribed a statewide remedy that denies local political units within a covered State the right to "bail out" separately; and (2) if so, whether, as a constitutional matter, such statewide relief exceeds the enforcement powers of Congress. If, as I believe, Congress could properly impose a statewide remedy and in fact did so in the Voting Rights Act, then the fact that the city of Rome has been innocent of any wrongdoing for the last 17 years is irrelevant; indeed, we may assume that there has never been any racial discrimination practiced in the city of Rome. If racially discriminatory voting practices elsewhere in the State of Georgia were sufficiently pervasive to justify the statewide remedy Congress prescribed, that remedy may be applied to each and every political unit within the State, including the city of Rome.

I.

... The political subdivisions of a covered State, while subject to § 5's preclearance requirements, are not entitled to bail out in a piecemeal fashion; rather, they can only be relieved of their preclearance obligations if the entire State meets the conditions for a bailout.

. . . .

II.

The second question is whether Congress has the power to prescribe a statewide remedy for discriminatory voting practices if it does not allow political units that can prove themselves innocent of discrimination to bail out of the statute's coverage. In Part III–B of its opinion, the Court explains why Congress, under the authority of § 2 of the Fifteenth Amendment, may prohibit voting practices that have a discriminatory effect in instances in which there is ample proof of a longstanding tradition of purposeful discrimination. I think it is equally clear that remedies for discriminatory practices that were widespread within a State may be applied to every governmental unit within the State even though some of those local units may have never engaged in purposeful discrimination themselves.[5] In short, Congress has the constitutional power to regulate voting practices in Rome, so long as it has the power to regulate such practices in the entire State of Georgia. Since there is no claim that the entire State is entitled to relief from the federal restrictions, Rome's separate claim must fail.

I therefore join the Court's opinion.

Mr. Justice Powell dissenting.

Two years ago this Court held that the term "State" in § 4(a) of the Voting Rights Act includes all political subdivisions that control election processes, and that those subdivisions are subject to the requirement in § 5 of the Act that federal authorities preclear changes in voting procedures. United States v. Board of Commissioners of Sheffield, Alabama, 435 U.S. 110 (1978) (*Sheffield*). Today the Court concludes that those subdivisions are within the term "State" when it comes to an action to "bail out" from the preclearance requirement. Because this decision not only conflicts with *Sheffield* but also raises grave questions as to the constitutionality of the Act, I dissent.

. . .

III.

There is, however, more involved here than incorrect construction of the statute. The Court's interpretation of § 4(a) renders the Voting Rights Act unconstitutional as applied to the city of Rome. The preclearance requirement both intrudes on the prerogatives of state and local governments and abridges the voting rights of all citizens in States covered under the Act. Under § 2 of the Fifteenth Amendment, Congress may impose such constitutional deprivations only if it is acting to remedy violations of voting rights. See South Carolina v. Katzenbach, 383 U.S. 301, 327–328 (1966); Katzenbach v. Morgan, 384 U.S. 641, 667 (1966) (Harlan, J., dissenting). In view of the District Court finding that Rome has not denied or abridged the voting rights of blacks, the Fifteenth Amendment provides no authority for continuing those deprivations until the entire State of Georgia satisfies the bailout standards of § 4(a).

When this Court first sustained the Voting Rights Act of 1965, it conceded that the legislation was "an uncommon exercise of congressional power." South Carolina v. Katzenbach, supra, 383 U.S., at 334. The Court recognized that preclearance under the Act implicates serious federalism concerns. Id., at 324–327. As Mr. Justice Stevens noted in *Sheffield,* the statute's "encroachment on state sovereignty is significant and undeniable." 435 U.S., at 141 (dissenting opinion). That encroachment is especially troubling because it destroys local control of the means of self-government, one of the central values of our policy. Unless the federal structure provides some protection for a community's ordering of its own democratic procedures, the right of each community to determine its own course within the boundaries marked by the Constitution is at risk. Preclearance also operates at an individual level to diminish the voting rights of residents of covered areas. Federal review of local voting practices reduces the influence that citizens have over policies directly affecting them, and strips locally elected officials of their autonomy to chart policy.

---

[5] The same principle applies to a court's exercise of its remedial powers. . . . The Court has recently applied this principle to school desegregation cases, holding that a systemwide remedy—as opposed to a remedy concentrating on specific instances of discrimination—may be justified by a prior history of pervasive, systemwide discrimination. Columbus Bd. of Educ. v. Penick, 443 U.S. 449; Dayton Bd. of Educ. v. Brinkman, 443 U.S. 526.

The Court in South Carolina v. Katzenbach, supra, did not lightly approve these intrusions on federalism and individual rights. It upheld the imposition of preclearance as a prophylactic measure based on the remedial power of Congress to enforce the Fifteenth Amendment. . . .

The Court in South Carolina v. Katzenbach emphasized, however, that a government subjected to preclearance could be relieved of federal oversight if voting discrimination in fact did not continue or materialize during the prescribed period. . . . As long as the bailout option is available, there is less cause for concern that the Voting Rights Act may overreach congressional powers by imposing preclearance on a nondiscriminating government. Without bailout, the problem of constitutional authority for preclearance becomes acute.

IV.

If there were reason to believe that today's decision would protect the voting rights of minorities in any way, perhaps this case could be viewed as one where the Court's ends justify dubious analytical means. But the District Court found, and no one denies, that for at least 17 years there has been no voting discrimination by the city of Rome. Despite this record, the Court today continues federal rule over the most local decisions made by this small city in Georgia. Such an outcome must vitiate the incentive for any local government in a State covered by the Act to meet diligently the Act's requirements. Neither the Framers of the Fifteenth Amendment nor the Congress that enacted the Voting Rights Act could have intended that result.

Mr. Justice Rehnquist, with whom Mr. Justice Stewart joins, dissenting.

We have only today held that the city of Mobile does not violate the Constitution by maintaining an at-large system of electing city officials unless voters can prove that system is a product of purposeful discrimination. City of Mobile v. Bolden, 446 U.S. 55 (1980). This result is reached even though the black residents of Mobile have demonstrated that racial "bloc" voting has prevented them from electing a black representative to the city government. The Court correctly concluded that a city has no obligation under the Constitution to structure its representative system in a manner that maximizes the black community's ability to elect a black representative. Yet in the instant case, the city of Rome is prevented from instituting precisely the type of structural changes which the Court says Mobile may maintain consistently with the Civil War Amendments, so long as their purpose be legitimate, because Congress has prohibited these changes under the Voting Rights Act as an exercise of its "enforcement" power conferred by those Amendments.

It is not necessary to hold that Congress is limited to merely providing a forum in which aggrieved plaintiffs may assert rights under the Civil War Amendments in order to disagree with the Court's decision permitting Congress to strait-jacket the city of Rome in this manner. Under § 5 of the Fourteenth Amendment and § 2 of the Fifteenth Amendment, Congress is granted only the power to "enforce" by "appropriate" legislation the limitations on state action embodied in those Amendments. While the presumption of constitutionality is due to any act of a coordinate branch of the Federal Government or of one of the States, it is this Court which is ultimately responsible for deciding challenges to the exercise of power by those entities. Marbury v. Madison, 5 U.S. (1 Cranch) 137 (1803); United States v. Nixon, 418 U.S. 683 (1974). Today's decision is nothing less than a total abdication of that authority, rather than an exercise of the deference due to a coordinate branch of the government.

. . .

II.

The Court holds today that the city of Rome can constitutionally be compelled to seek congressional approval for most of its governmental changes even though it has not engaged in any discrimination against blacks for at least 17 years. Moreover, the Court also holds that federal approval can be constitutionally denied even after the city has proven that the changes are not purposefully discriminatory. While I agree with Mr. Justice Powell's conclusion that requiring localities to *submit* to preclearance is a significant intrusion on local autonomy, it is an even greater intrusion on that autonomy to *deny* preclearance sought.

. . . Section 2 of the Fifteenth Amendment and § 5 of the Fourteenth provide that Congress shall have the power to "enforce" § 1 "by appropriate legislation." Congressional power to prohibit the electoral changes proposed by Rome is dependent upon the scope and nature of that power. There are three theories of congressional enforcement power relevant to this case. First, it is clear that if the proposed changes would violate the Constitution, Congress could certainly prohibit their implementation. It has never been seriously maintained, however, that Congress can do no more than the judiciary to enforce the Amendments' commands. Thus, if the electoral changes in issue do not violate the Constitution, as judicially interpreted, it must be determined whether Congress could nevertheless appropriately prohibit these changes under the other two theories of congressional power. Under the second theory, Congress can act remedially to enforce the judicially established substantive prohibitions of the Amendments. If not properly remedial, the exercise of this power could be sustained only if this Court accepts the premise of the third theory that Congress has the authority under its enforcement powers to determine, without more, that electoral changes with a disparate impact on race violate the Constitution, in which case Congress by a legislative Act could effectively amend the Constitution.

I think it is apparent that neither of the first two theories for sustaining the exercise of congressional power support this application of the Voting Rights Act. After our decision in *City of Mobile* there is little doubt that Rome has not engaged in *constitutionally* prohibited conduct. I also do not believe that prohibition of these changes can genuinely be characterized as a remedial exercise of congressional enforcement powers. Thus, the result of the Court's holding is that Congress effectively has the power to determine for itself that this conduct violates the Constitution. This result violates previously well-established distinctions between the Judicial Branch and the Legislative or Executive Branches of the Federal Government. See United States v. Nixon, 418 U.S. 683 (1974), Marbury v. Madison, (1 Cranch) 137 (1803).

A.

If the enforcement power is construed as a "remedial" grant of authority, it is this Court's duty to ensure that a challenged congressional act does no more than "enforce" the limitations on state power established in the Fourteenth and Fifteenth Amendments. *Marbury v. Madison.* The Court has not resolved the question of whether it is an appropriate exercise of remedial power for Congress to prohibit local governments from instituting structural changes in their government, which although not racially motivated, will have the effect of decreasing the ability of a black voting bloc to elect a black candidate.

. . .

The precedent on which the Court relies simply does not support its remedial characterization. Neither Oregon v. Mitchell, 400 U.S. 112 (1970), nor South Carolina v. Katzenbach, supra, legitimize the use of an irrebuttable presumption that "vote diluting" changes are motivated by a discriminatory animus. The principal electoral practice in issue in those cases was the use of literacy tests. . . .

The presumption that the literacy tests were either being used to purposefully discriminate, or that the disparate effects of those tests were attributable to discrimination in state-administered education was not very wide of the mark. . . .

The nationwide ban was also found necessary to effectively remedy past constitutional violations. . . .

Presumptive prohibition of vote diluting procedures is not similarly an "appropriate" means of exacting state compliance with the Civil War Amendments. First, these prohibitions are quite unlike the literacy ban, where the disparate effects were traceable to the discrimination of governmental bodies in education even if their present desire to use the tests was legitimate. Any disparate impact associated with the nondiscriminatory electoral changes in issue here results from bloc voting—private rather than governmental discrimination. . . .

It is also clear that while most States still utilizing literacy tests may have been doing so to discriminate, a similar generalization could not be made about all government structures which have some disparate impact on black voting strength. . . .

Nor does the prohibition of all practices with a disparate impact enhance congressional prevention of purposeful discrimination. The changes in issues are not, like literacy tests, though fair on their face, subject to discriminatory application by local authorities. See Yick Wo v. Hopkins, 118 U.S. 356 (1886). They are either discriminatory from the outset or not.

Finally, the advantages supporting the imposition of a nationwide ban are simply not implicated in this case. No added administrative burdens are in issue since Congress has provided the mechanism for preclearance suits in any event, and the burden of proof for this issue is on the locality. And it is certain that the only constitutional wrong implicated—purposeful dilution—can be effectively remedied by prohibiting it where it occurs. For all these reasons, I do not think that the present case is controlled by the result in Oregon. By prohibiting all electoral changes with a disparate impact, Congress has attempted to prevent disparate impacts—not purposeful discrimination.

Congress unquestionably has the power to prohibit and remedy state action which intentionally deprives citizens of Fourteenth and Fifteenth Amendment rights. But unless these powers are to be wholly uncanalized, it cannot be appropriate remedial legislation for Congress to prohibit Rome from structuring its government in the manner as its population sees fit absent a finding or unrebutted presumption that Rome has been, or is, intentionally discriminating against its black citizens. Rome has simply committed no constitutional violations, as this Court has defined them.

B.   "INTERPRETIVE" POWER

Katzenbach v. Morgan

384 U.S. 641, 86 S.Ct. 1717, 16 L.Ed.2d 828 (1966).

Mr. Justice Brennan delivered the opinion of the court.

These cases concern the constitutionality of § 4(e) of the Voting Rights Act of 1965. That law, in the respects pertinent in these cases, provides that no person who has successfully completed the sixth primary grade in a public school in, or a private school accredited by, the Commonwealth of Puerto Rico in which the language of instruction was other than English shall be denied the right to vote in any election because of his inability to read or write English. Appellees, registered voters in New York City, brought this suit to challenge the constitutionality of § 4(e) insofar as it *pro tanto* prohibits the enforcement of the election laws of New York requiring an ability to read and write English as a condition of voting. Under these laws many of the several hundred thousand New York City residents who have migrated there from the Commonwealth of Puerto Rico had previously been denied the right to vote, and appellees attack § 4(e) insofar as it would enable many of these citizens to vote. Pursuant to § 14(b) of the Voting Rights Act of 1965, appellees commenced this proceeding in the District Court for the District of Columbia seeking a declaration that § 4(e) is invalid and an injunction prohibiting appellants, the Attorney General of the United States and the New York City Board of Elections, from either enforcing or complying with § 4(e). A three-judge district court ... granted the declaratory and injunctive relief appellees sought.... We reverse. We hold that, in the application challenged in these cases, § 4(e) is a proper exercise of the powers granted to Congress by § 5 of the Fourteenth Amendment and that by force of the Supremacy Clause, Article VI, the New York English literacy requirement cannot be enforced to the extent that it is inconsistent with § 4(e).

Under the distribution of powers effected by the Constitution, the States establish qualifications for voting for state officers, and the qualifications established by the States for voting for members of the most numerous branch of the state legislature also determine who may vote for United States Representatives and Senators, Art. I, § 2; Seventeenth Amendment; Ex parte Yarbrough, 110 U.S. 651, 663. But, of course, the States have no power to grant or withhold the franchise on conditions that are forbidden by the Fourteenth Amendment, or any other provision of the Constitution. Such exercises of state power are no more immune to the limitations of the Fourteenth Amendment than any other state action. The Equal Protection Clause itself has been held to forbid some state laws that restrict the right to vote.

The Attorney General of the State of New York argues that an exercise of congressional power under § 5 of the Fourteenth Amendment that prohibits the enforcement of a state law can only be sustained if the judicial branch determines that the state law is prohibited by the provisions of the Amendment that Congress sought to enforce ... We disagree. Neither the language nor history of § 5 supports such a construction.... A construction of § 5 that would require a judicial determination that the enforcement of the state law precluded by Congress violated the Amendment, as a condition of sustaining the congressional enactment, would depreciate both congressional resourcefulness and congressional responsibility for implementing the Amendment. It would confine the legislative power in this context to the insignificant role of abrogating only those state laws that the judicial branch was prepared to adjudge unconstitutional, or of merely informing the judgment of the judiciary by particularizing the "majestic generalities" of § 1 of the Amendment. See Fay v. New York, 332 U.S. 261, 282–284.

Thus our task in this case is not to determine whether the New York English literacy requirement as applied to deny the right to vote to a person who successfully completed the sixth grade in a Puerto Rican school violates the Equal Protection Clause. Accordingly, our decision in Lassiter v. Northampton Election Bd., 360 U.S. 45, sustaining the North Carolina English literacy requirement as not in all circumstances prohibited by the first sections of the Fourteenth and Fifteenth Amendments is inapposite.... *Lassiter* did not present the question before us here: Without regard to whether the judiciary would find that the Equal Protection Clause itself nullifies New York's English literacy requirement as so applied, could Congress prohibit the enforcement of the state law by legislating under § 5 of the Fourteenth Amendment? In answering this question, our task is limited to determining whether such legislation is, as required by § 5, appropriate legislation to enforce the Equal Protection Clause.

By including § 5 the draftsmen sought to grant to Congress, by a specific provision applicable to the Fourteenth Amendment, the same broad powers expressed in the Necessary and Proper Clause, Art. I, § 8, cl. 18. The classic formulation of the reach of those two powers was established by Chief Justice Marshall in McCulloch v. Maryland, 4 Wheat. 316, 421.

"Let the end be legitimate, let it be within the scope of the constitution, and all means which are appropriate, which are plainly adapted to that end, which are not prohibited, but consist with the letter and spirit of the constitution, are constitutional."

. . .

We therefore proceed to the consideration whether § 4(e) is "appropriate legislation" to enforce the Equal Protection Clause, that is, under the McCulloch v. Maryland standard, whether § 4(e) may be regarded as an enactment to enforce the Equal Protection Clause, whether it is "plainly adapted to that end" and whether it is not prohibited by but is consistent with "the letter and spirit of the constitution."[10]

There can be no doubt that § 4(e) may be regarded as an enactment to enforce the Equal Protection Clause. Congress explicitly declared that it enacted § 4(e) "to secure the rights under the fourteenth amendment of persons educated in American-flag schools in which the predominant classroom language was other than English." The persons referred to include those who have migrated from the Commonwealth of Puerto Rico to New York and who have been denied the right to vote because of their inability to read and write English, and the Fourteenth Amendment rights referred to include those emanating from the Equal Protection Clause. More specifically, § 4(e) may be viewed as a measure to secure for the Puerto Rican community residing in New York nondiscriminatory treatment by government—both in the imposition of

---

[10] Contrary to the suggestion of the dissent, § 5 does not grant Congress power to exercise discretion in the other direction and to enact "statutes so as in effect to dilute equal protection and due process decisions of this Court." We emphasize that Congress' power under § 5 is limited to adopting measures to enforce the guarantees of the Amendment: § 5 grants Congress no power to restrict, abrogate, or dilute these guarantees. Thus, for example, an enactment authorizing the States to establish racially segregated systems of education would not be—as required by § 5—a measure "to enforce" the Equal Protection Clause since that clause of its own force prohibits such state laws.

voting qualifications and the provision or administration of governmental services, such as public schools, public housing and law enforcement.

Section 4(e) may be readily seen as "plainly adapted" to furthering these aims of the Equal Protection Clause. The practical effect of § 4(e) is to prohibit New York from denying the right to vote to large segments of its Puerto Rican community. Congress has thus prohibited the State from denying to that community the right that is "preservative of all rights." Yick Wo v. Hopkins, 118 U.S. 356, 370. This enhanced political power will be helpful in gaining nondiscriminatory treatment in public services for the entire Puerto Rican community. Section 4(e) thereby enables the Puerto Rican minority better to obtain "perfect equality of civil rights and the equal protection of the laws." It was well within congressional authority to say that this need of the Puerto Rican minority for the vote warranted federal intrusion upon any state interests served by the English literacy requirement. It was for Congress, as the branch that made this judgment, to assess and weigh the various conflicting considerations—the risk or pervasiveness of the discrimination in governmental services, the effectiveness of eliminating the state restriction on the right to vote as a means of dealing with the evil, the adequacy or availability of alternative remedies, and the nature and significance of the state interests that would be affected by the nullification of the English literacy requirement as applied to residents who have successfully completed the sixth grade in a Puerto Rican school. It is not for us to review the congressional resolution of these factors. It is enough that we be able to perceive a basis upon which the Congress might resolve the conflict as it did. There plainly was such a basis to support § 4(e) in the application in question in this case. Any contrary conclusion would require us to be blind to the realities familiar to the legislators.

The result is no different if we confine our inquiry to the question whether § 4(e) was merely legislation aimed at the elimination of an invidious discrimination in establishing voter qualifications.... Here again, it is enough that we perceive a basis upon which Congress might predicate a judgment that the application of New York's English literacy requirement to deny the right to vote to a person with a sixth grade education in Puerto Rican schools in which the language of instruction was other than English constituted an invidious discrimination in violation of the Equal Protection Clause.

There remains the question whether the congressional remedies adopted in § 4(e) constitute means which are not prohibited by, but are consistent "with the letter and spirit of the constitution." The only respect in which appellees contend that § 4(e) fails in this regard is that the section itself works an invidious discrimination in violation of the Fifth Amendment by prohibiting the enforcement of the English literacy requirement only for those educated in American-flag schools (schools located within United States jurisdiction) in which the language of instruction was other than English, and not for those educated in schools beyond the territorial limits of the United States in which the language of instruction was also other than English. This is not a complaint that Congress, in enacting § 4(e), has unconstitutionally denied or diluted anyone's right to vote but rather that Congress violated the Constitution by not extending the relief effected in § 4(e) to those educated in non-American-flag schools....

Section 4(e) does not restrict or deny the franchise but in effect extends the franchise to persons who otherwise would be denied it by state law. Thus we need not decide whether a state literacy law conditioning the right to vote on achieving a certain level of education in an American-flag school (regardless of the language of instruction) discriminates invidiously against those educated in non-American-flag schools. We need only decide whether the challenged limitation on the relief effected in § 4(e) was permissible. In deciding that question, the principle that calls for the closest scrutiny of distinctions in laws *denying* fundamental rights, is inapplicable; for the distinction challenged by appellees is presented only as a limitation on a reform measure aimed at eliminating an existing barrier to the exercise of the franchise. Rather, in deciding the constitutional propriety of the limitations in such a reform measure we are guided by the familiar principles that a "statute is not invalid under the Constitution because it might have gone farther than it did," Roschen v. Ward, 279 U.S. 337, 339, that a legislature need not "strike at all evils at the same time," Semler v. Dental Examiners, 294 U.S. 608, 610, and that "reform may take one step at a time, addressing itself to the phase of the problem which seems most acute to the legislative mind," Williamson v. Lee Optical Co., 348 U.S. 483, 489.

Guided by these principles, we are satisfied that appellees' challenge to this limitation in § 4(e) is without merit. In the context of the case before us, the congressional choice to limit the relief effected in § 4(e) may, for example, reflect Congress' greater familiarity with the quality of instruction in American-flag schools, a recognition of the unique historic relationship between the Congress and the Commonwealth of Puerto Rico, an awareness of the Federal Government's acceptance of the desirability of the use of Spanish as the language of instruction in Commonwealth schools, and the fact that Congress has fostered policies encouraging migration from the Commonwealth to the States. We have no occasion to determine in this case whether such factors would justify a similar distinction embodied in a voting-qualification law that denied the franchise to persons educated in non-American-flag schools. We hold only that the limitation on relief effected in § 4(e) does not constitute a forbidden discrimination since these factors might well have been the basis for the decision of Congress to go "no farther than it did."

We therefore conclude that § 4(e), in the application challenged in this case, is appropriate legislation to enforce the Equal Protection Clause and that the judgment of the District Court must be and hereby is

Reversed.

Mr. Justice Douglas joins the Court's opinion except for the discussion of the question whether the congressional remedies adopted in § 4(e) constitute means which are not prohibited by, but are consistent with "the letter and spirit of the constitution." On that question, he reserves judgment until such time as it is presented by a member of the class against which that particular discrimination is directed.

Mr. Justice Harlan, whom Mr. Justice Stewart joins, dissenting.

Worthy as its purposes may be thought by many, I do not see how § 4(e) of the Voting Rights Act of 1965, 79 Stat. 439, 42 U.S.C. § 1973b(e) (1964 ed. Supp. I), can be sustained except at the sacrifice of fundamentals in the American constitutional system—the separation between the legislative and judicial function and the boundaries between federal and state political authority. . . .

The pivotal question in this instance is what effect the added factor of a congressional enactment has on the straight equal protection argument dealt with above. The Court declares that since § 5 of the Fourteenth Amendment gives to the Congress power to "enforce" the prohibitions of the Amendment by "appropriate" legislation, the test for judicial review of any congressional determination in this area is simply one of rationality; that is, in effect, was Congress acting rationally in declaring that the New York statute is irrational? Although § 5 most certainly does give to the Congress wide powers in the field of devising remedial legislation to effectuate the Amendment's prohibition on arbitrary state action, Ex parte Virginia, 100 U.S. 339, I believe the Court has confused the issue of how much enforcement power Congress possesses under § 5 with the distinct issue of what questions are appropriate for congressional determination and what questions are essentially judicial in nature.

When recognized state violations of federal constitutional standards have occurred, Congress is of course empowered by § 5 to take appropriate remedial measures to redress and prevent the wrongs. See Strauder v. West Virginia, 100 U.S. 303, 310. But it is a judicial question whether the condition with which Congress has thus sought to deal is in truth an infringement of the Constitution, something that is the necessary prerequisite to bringing the § 5 power into play at all. . . .

. . . The question here is not whether the statute is appropriate remedial legislation to cure an established violation of a constitutional command, but whether there has in fact been an infringement of that constitutional command, that is, whether a particular state practice or, as here, a statute is so arbitrary or irrational as to offend the command of the Equal Protection Clause of the Fourteenth Amendment. That question is one for the judicial branch ultimately to determine. Were the rule otherwise, Congress would be able to qualify this Court's constitutional decisions under the Fourteenth and Fifteenth Amendments, let alone those under other provisions of the Constitution, by resorting to congressional power under the Necessary and Proper Clause. In view of this Court's holding in *Lassiter,* supra, that an English literacy test is a permissible exercise of state supervision over its franchise, I do not think it is open to Congress to limit the effect of that decision as it has undertaken to do by § 4(e). In effect the Court reads § 5 of the Fourteenth Amendment as giving Congress the power to define the *substantive* scope of the Amendment. If that indeed be the true reach of § 5, then I do not see why Congress should not be able as well to exercise its § 5 "discretion" by enacting statutes so as in effect to dilute equal protection and due process decisions of this Court. In all such cases there is room for reasonable men to differ as to whether or not a denial of equal protection or due process has occurred, and the final decision is one of judgment. Until today this judgment has always been one for the judiciary to resolve.

I do not mean to suggest in what has been said that a legislative judgment of the type incorporated in § 4(e) is without any force whatsoever. Decisions on questions of equal protection and due process are based not on abstract logic, but on empirical foundations. To the extent "legislative facts" are relevant to a judicial determination, Congress is well equipped to investigate them, and such determinations are of course entitled to due respect. . . .

But no such factual data provide a legislative record supporting § 4(e)[9] by way of showing that Spanish-speaking citizens are fully as capable of making informed decisions in a New York election as are English-speaking citizens. Nor was there any showing whatever to support the Court's alternative argument that § 4(e) should be viewed as but a remedial measure designed to cure or assure against unconstitutional discrimination of other varieties, e.g., in "public schools, public housing and law enforcement," to which Puerto Rican

---

[9] There were no committee hearings or reports referring to this section, which was introduced from the floor during debate on the full Voting Rights Act. See 111 Cong.Rec. 11027, 15666, 16234.

minorities might be subject in such communities as New York. There is simply no legislative record supporting such hypothesized discrimination of the sort we have hitherto insisted upon when congressional power is brought to bear on constitutionally reserved state concerns. See *Heart of Atlanta Motel,* supra; *State of South Carolina v. Katzenbach,* supra.

Thus, we have here not a matter of giving deference to a congressional estimate, based on its determination of legislative facts, bearing upon the validity *vel non* of a statute, but rather what can at most be called a legislative announcement that Congress believes a state law to entail an unconstitutional deprivation of equal protection. Although this kind of declaration is of course entitled to the most respectful consideration, coming as it does from a concurrent branch and one that is knowledgeable in matters of popular political participation, I do not believe it lessens our responsibility to decide the fundamental issue of whether in fact the state enactment violates federal constitutional rights.

In assessing the deference we should give to this kind of congressional expression of policy, it is relevant that the judiciary has always given to congressional enactments a presumption of validity. ... However, it is also a canon of judicial review that state statutes are given a similar presumption, ... Whichever way this case is decided, one statute will be rendered inoperative in whole or in part, and although it has been suggested that this Court should give somewhat more deference to Congress than to a state legislature,[10] such a simple weighing of presumptions is hardly a satisfying way of resolving a matter that touches the distribution of state and federal power in an area so sensitive as that of the regulation of the franchise. Rather it should be recognized that while the Fourteenth Amendment is a "brooding omnipresence" over all state legislation, the substantive matters which it touches are all within the primary legislative competence of the States. Federal authority, legislative no less than judicial, does not intrude unless there has been a denial by state action of Fourteenth Amendment limitations, in this instance a denial of equal protection. At least in the area of primary state concern a state statute that passes constitutional muster under the judicial standard of rationality should not be permitted to be set at naught by a mere contrary congressional pronouncement unsupported by a legislative record justifying that conclusion.

To deny the effectiveness of this congressional enactment is not of course to disparage Congress' exertion of authority in the field of civil rights; it is simply to recognize that the Legislative Branch like the other branches of federal authority is subject to the governmental boundaries set by the Constitution. To hold, on this record, that § 4(e) overrides the New York literacy requirement seems to me tantamount to allowing the Fourteenth Amendment to swallow the State's constitutionally ordained primary authority in this field. For if Congress by what, as here, amounts to mere *ipse dixit* can set that otherwise permissible requirement partially at naught I see no reason why it could not also substitute its judgment for that of the States in other fields of their exclusive primary competence as well.

I would affirm the judgments in each of these cases.

OREGON v. MITCHELL, 400 U.S. 112 (1970). The Court had before it the validity of the Voting Rights Act Amendments of 1970. It held unanimously that Congress had the power to bar the use of literacy tests for voting for a

---

[10] See Thayer, The Origin and Scope of   7 Harv.L.Rev. 129, 154–155 (1893).
the American Doctrine of Constitutional Law,

period of five years in all elections, state and national. It held with but one dissent that Congress had power to regulate residency requirements and provide for absentee balloting in national elections for presidential and vice-presidential electors. It held by a vote of 5 to 4 that Congress had power to establish a minimum age of 18 for voters in elections for national officers. It also held by a vote of 5 to 4 that Congress had no power to establish a minimum age of 18 for voters in state and local elections—a result later changed by the 26th amendment.

In the debate over the validity of the provision setting a minimum age of 18 for voters in state and local elections, several of the Justices addressed the question of the power of Congress to redefine the scope of the fourteenth amendment. Justice Black asserted that the Civil War amendments gave Congress enhanced power to deal with racial discrimination in voting. He noted that the 18 year old vote provisions were not related to disenfranchisement by race. Then, he concluded:

"Since Congress has attempted to invade an area preserved to the States by the Constitution without a foundation for enforcing the Civil War amendments' ban on racial discrimination, I would hold that Congress has exceeded its powers in attempting to lower the voting age in state and local elections. On the other hand, where Congress legislates in a domain not exclusively reserved by the Constitution to the States, its enforcement power need not be tied so closely to the goal of eliminating discrimination on account of race."

Justice Stewart, joined by Chief Justice Burger and Justice Blackmun said:

"Although it was found necessary to amend the Constitution to confer a federal right to vote upon Negroes and upon females, the Government asserts that a federal right to vote can be conferred upon people between 18 and 21 years of age simply by this Act of Congress. Our decision in Katzenbach v. Morgan, 384 U.S. 641, it is said, established the power of Congress, under § 5 of the Fourteenth Amendment, to nullify state laws requiring voters to be 21 years of age or older if Congress could rationally have concluded that such laws are not supported by a 'compelling state interest.'

"In my view, neither the Morgan case, nor any other case upon which the Government relies, establishes such congressional power, even assuming that all those cases were rightly decided. . . .

"Katzenbach v. Morgan, supra, does not hold that Congress has the power to determine what are and what are not 'compelling state interests' for equal protection purposes. . . . The Court upheld the statute on two grounds: that Congress could conclude that enhancing the political power of the Puerto Rican community by conferring the right to vote was an appropriate means of remedying discriminatory treatment in public services; and that Congress could conclude that the New York statute was tainted by the impermissible purpose of denying the right to vote to Puerto Ricans, an undoubted invidious discrimination under the Equal Protection Clause. Both of these decisional grounds were far reaching. The Court's opinion made clear that Congress could impose on the States a remedy for the denial of equal protection that elaborated upon the direct command of the Constitution, and that it could override state laws on the ground that they were in fact used as instruments of invidious discrimination even though a court in an individual lawsuit might not have reached that factual conclusion.

"But it is necessary to go much further to sustain § 302. The state laws that it invalidates do not invidiously discriminate against any discrete and insular minority. Unlike the statute considered in Morgan, § 302 is valid only if

Congress has the power not only to provide the means of eradicating situations that amount to a violation of the Equal Protection Clause, but also to determine as a matter of substantive constitutional law what situations fall within the ambit of the clause, and what state interests are 'compelling.' I concurred in Mr. Justice Harlan's dissent in Morgan. That case, as I now read it, gave congressional power under § 5 the furthest possible legitimate reach. Yet to sustain the constitutionality of § 302 would require an enormous extension of that decision's rationale. I cannot but conclude that § 302 was beyond the constitutional power of Congress to enact."

Justice Brennan, joined by Justices White and Marshall, took a broader view. Justice Douglas took a similar view in a separate opinion. Justice Brennan said, in part:

"As we have often indicated, questions of constitutional power frequently turn in the last analysis on questions of fact. This is particularly the case when an assertion of state power is challenged under the Equal Protection Clause of the Fourteenth Amendment. ...When a state legislative classification is subjected to judicial challenge as violating the Equal Protection Clause, it comes before the courts cloaked by the presumption that the legislature has, as it should, acted within constitutional limitations. Accordingly, '[a] statutory discrimination will not be set aside as the denial of equal protection of the laws if any state of facts reasonably may be conceived to justify it.' Metropolitan Cas. Ins. Co. v. Brownell, 294 U.S. 580, 584 (1935).

"But, as we have consistently held, this limitation on judicial review of state legislative classifications is a limitation stemming, not from the Fourteenth Amendment itself, but from the nature of judicial review. ...The nature of the judicial process makes it an inappropriate forum for the determination of complex factual questions of the kind so often involved in constitutional adjudication. Courts, therefore, will overturn a legislative determination of a factual question only if the legislature's finding is so clearly wrong that it may be characterized as 'arbitrary,' 'irrational,' or 'unreasonable.'

"Limitations stemming from the nature of the judicial process, however, have no application to Congress. ... Should Congress ... undertake an investigation in order to determine whether the factual basis necessary to support a state legislative discrimination actually exists, it need not stop once it determines that some reasonable men could believe the factual basis exists. Section 5 empowers Congress to make its own determination on the matter. ... It should hardly be necessary to add that if the asserted factual basis necessary to support a given state discrimination does not exist, § 5 of the Fourteenth Amendment vests Congress with power to remove the discrimination by appropriate means. ... The scope of our review in such matters has been established by a long line of consistent decisions.[31] ...

"This scheme is consistent with our prior decisions in related areas. The core of dispute over the constitutionality of Title III of the 1970 Amendments is a conflict between state and federal legislative determinations of the factual issues upon which depends decision of a federal constitutional question—the legitimacy, under the Equal Protection Clause, of state discrimination against

---

[31] As we emphasized in Katzenbach v. Morgan, supra, "§ 5 does not grant Congress power to ... enact 'statutes so as in effect to dilute equal protection and due process decisions of this Court.' "384 U.S., at 651 n. 10. As indicated above, a decision of this Court striking down a state statute expresses, among other things, our conclusion that the legislative findings upon which the statute is based are so far wrong as to be unreasonable. Unless Congress were to unearth new evidence in its investigation, its identical findings on the identical issue would be no more reasonable than those of the state legislature.

persons between the ages of 18 and 21. Our cases have repeatedly emphasized that, when state and federal claims come into conflict, the primacy of federal power requires that the federal finding of fact control.... The Supremacy Clause requires an identical result when the conflict is one of legislative, not judicial, findings.

. . .

"In sum, Congress had ample evidence upon which it could have based the conclusion that exclusion of citizens 18 to 21 years of age from the franchise is wholly unnecessary to promote any legitimate interest the States may have in assuring intelligent and responsible voting.... If discrimination is unnecessary to promote any legitimate state interest, it is plainly unconstitutional under the Equal Protection Clause, and Congress has ample power to forbid it under § 5 of the Fourteenth Amendment. We would uphold § 302 of the 1970 Amendments as a legitimate exercise of congressional power."

THE VITALITY OF KATZENBACH v. MORGAN AS PRECEDENT

In Oregon v. Mitchell, Justice Stewart's opinion characterized the portion of the Court's opinion in *Katzenbach v. Morgan* concerning Congressional power to interpret the fourteenth amendment as dicta. Whether or not that is the correct analysis, does the interpretive rationale of Katzenbach v. Morgan survive the decision in *Oregon v. Mitchell* ? Five Justices did agree that Congressional power to enforce the fourteenth amendment did not authorize Congress to establish a minimum voting age of 18 in state elections. The absence of any opinion for the Court in Oregon v. Mitchell, however, complicates the question. Consider the following portion of Justice Rehnquist's dissent in City of Rome v. United States, which argues that Oregon v. Mitchell is an authoritative rejection of Katzenbach v. Morgan.

"[T]he theory that Congress was empowered to [interpret] the Fourteenth or Fifteenth Amendments ... was rejected in the Civil Rights Cases, 109 U.S. 3 (1883). The Court emphasized that the power conferred was 'remedial' only. The Court reasoned that the structure of the Amendment made it clear that it did not 'authorize Congress to create a code of municipal law for the regulation of private rights; but to provide modes of redress against the operation of State laws, and the action of State officers ..., when these are subversive of the fundamental right specified in the Amendment.' This interpretation is consonant with the legislative history surrounding the enactment of the Amendment.

"This construction has never been refuted by a majority of the Members of this Court. Support for this construction in current years has emerged in South Carolina v. Katzenbach, and Oregon v. Mitchell.[8] In South Carolina v. Katzenbach, the Court observed that Congress could not attack evils not comprehended by the Fifteenth Amendment. 383 U.S., at 326. In Oregon v. Mitchell, 400

---

[8] Explicit support can also be derived from Mr. Justice Harlan's dissenting opinion, joined by Mr. Justice Stewart, in Katzenbach v. Morgan, 384 U.S. 641 (1966). Mr. Justice Harlan clarified the need for the remedial construction of congressional powers. It is also unnecessary, however, to read the majority opinion as establishing the Court's rejection of the remedial construction of the *Civil Rights Cases*. While Mr. Justice Brennan's majority opinion did contain language suggesting a rejection of the "remedial" con-struction of the enforcement powers, the opinion also advanced a remedial rationale which supports the determination reached by the Court. Compare the rationales forwarded at 384 U.S., at 654 with the statements, at 656. It would be particularly inappropriate to construe Katzenbach v. Morgan as a rejection of the remedial interpretation of congression-al powers in view of this Court's subsequent decision in Oregon v. Mitchell, 400 U.S. 112 (1970).

U.S. 112 (1970), five Members of the Court were unwilling to conclude that Congress had the power to determine that establishing the age limitation for voting at 21 denied equal protection to those between the ages of 18 and 20.

"The opinion of Mr. Justice Stewart in that case, joined by Chief Justice Burger and Mr. Justice Blackmun, reaffirmed that Congress only has the power under the Fourteenth Amendment to 'provide the means of eradicating situations that amount to a violation of the Equal Protection Clause' but not to 'determine as a matter of substantive constitutional law that situations fall within the ambit of the clause.' Id., at 296. Mr. Justice Harlan, in a separate opinion, reiterated his belief that it is the duty of the Court, and not the Congress, to determine when States have exceeded constitutional limitations imposed upon their powers. Id., at 204–207. Cf. Oregon v. Hass, 420 U.S. 714 (1975); Cooper v. Aaron, 358 U.S. 1, 18 (1958). Mr. Justice Black also was unwilling to accept the broad construction of enforcement powers formulated in the opinion of Mr. Justice Brennan, joined by Justices White and Marshall.[9]"

CONGRESSIONAL EXPANSION OF DUE PROCESS AND EQUAL PROTECTION

It was suggested, at the beginning of section 5 of this chapter, that the wide scope of other Congressional powers may make it unnecessary to resolve the question whether the fourteenth amendment's enforcement powers are broad enough to support federal legislation forbidding private discrimination. It is appropriate now to ask whether that legislation could be supported on the ground that Congress can define the meaning of state action, or on the less contentious ground that the prohibition is an appropriate remedy for constitutional violations by the state.[1]

Ironically, the most troublesome issues of Congressional power to expand fourteenth amendment protections may concern federal legislation directed at states, rather than private individuals. That is because the one restriction defined by modern cases on the scope of the commerce power is that Congress may not impair the essential integrity of the states. On the other hand, the Court indicated in the *City of Rome* decision that the same limitation is inapplicable to Congressional enforcement of the Civil War Amendments.

Mississippi University for Women v. Hogan

458 U.S. 718, 102 S.Ct. 3331, 73 L.Ed.2d 1090 (1982).

[The report in this case appears supra, p. 816.]

CONGRESSIONAL POWER TO DILUTE CONSTITUTIONAL RIGHTS

A major concern about conceding Congressional power to define due process and equal protection was expressed in Justice Harlan's dissent in *Katzenbach v. Morgan.* He stated that if Congress had the power to expand the

---

[9] Since Mr. Justice Black found that congressional powers were more circumscribed when not acting to counter racial discrimination under the Fourteenth Amendment, he did not have to determine the precise nature of congressional powers when they were exercised in the field of racial relations. His analysis of the nationwide ban on literacy tests, also presented in Oregon v. Mitchell, however, is consistent with a remedial interpretation of those powers.

[1] See Leeds, *State Action Limitations on Courts and Congressional Power,* 60 No.Car. L.Rev. 747 (1982).

substantive scope of the fourteenth amendment "I do not see why Congress should not be able as well to exercise its § 5 'discretion' by enacting statutes so as in effect to dilute equal protection and due process decisions of this Court." Consider Justice Brennan's contrary assertions in footnote 10 to his opinion for the Court in Katzenbach v. Morgan and footnote 31 to his opinion in Oregon v. Mitchell.[1] If Congressional power to expand due process and equal protection is based on Congress' asserted superior competence either to draw lines or to determine legislative facts, is it possible to maintain at the same time that Congress does not have equal competence to decide that a challenged state law is *constitutional?* Moreover, even if Justice Brennan is right that Congress can only expand constitutional rights, how will that theory be applied when Congress attempts to overrule a Supreme Court decision that adjusts competing constitutional rights?[2] Commentators who have approved the substantive results reached by Justice Brennan have questioned whether his theory opens the door to Congressional power to overrule unpopular constitutional decisions by ordinary legislation.[3]

It can be asked, finally, whether the possibility of Congressional veto of unpopular constitutional decisions of the Supreme Court can be avoided by a theory that limits the superior competence of Congress to defining the remedies which are appropriate for constitutional violations.[4] The obvious question arises whether Congress' power to expand judicially created remedies implies a concomitant power to restrict them. That issue has arisen in two contexts: Congressional attempts to permit the introduction of confessions in federal criminal prosecutions despite failure of federal law enforcement officials to

---

[1] Justice Brennan made a similar assertion in his opinion for the Court in Shapiro v. Thompson, 394 U.S. 618 (1969), supra p. 991. Chief Justice Warren, joined by Justice Black, argued in dissent that Congress had approved state durational residency requirements of one year or less. Justice Brennan's opinion concluded that Congress had not done so, and if it had, "Congress may not authorize the States to violate the Equal Protection Clause." He cited footnote 10 of *Katzenbach v. Morgan* for the proposition.

[2] Justice White, who joined Justice Brennan's opinions in both *Katzenbach v. Morgan* and *Oregon v. Mitchell,* made this argument for Congressional power to define constitutional rights in Welsh v. United States, 398 U.S. 333 (1970). At issue was the claim that § 6(j) of the Selective Service Act was an establishment of religion. Section 6(j) defined religious training and belief, for purposes of the conscientious objector exemption from combat service, as "belief in a relation to a Supreme Being." The Court avoided the constitutional question whether the law would be invalid if it were limited to theistic religious beliefs by interpreting the statute to allow conscientious objector classification to those whose pacifist beliefs stemmed from sincere and deeply held non-theistic beliefs. Justice White dissented from the Court's construction of the statute, and argued that his narrower construction was not a violation of the Establishment Clause. He argued that the Congressional judgment should be accept-

ed so long as the Court could "perceive a basis" for its resolution of a potential conflict between competing values of the free exercise and establishment clauses. He also asserted that his conclusion "involves no surrender of the Court's function as ultimate arbiter in disputes over interpretation of the Constitution," while citing Katzenbach v. Morgan as support. Chief Justice Burger and Justice Stewart, both of whom have denied any Congressional power to interpret the fourteenth amendment, joined Justice White's dissent. Note that the statute at issue was a federal statute, and the constitutional question thus involved solely the first amendment. Would Congress have more or less power to interpret the Bill of Rights as applied to federal laws than to interpret the Bill of Rights as incorporated into the fourteenth amendment and applied to state laws?

[3] See Burt, *Miranda and Title II: A Morganatic Marriage,* 1969 Sup.Ct.Rev. 81; Cox, *The Role of Congress in Constitutional Determinations,* 40 U.Cin.L.Rev. 199 (1971); Cohen, *Congressional Power to Interpret Due Process and Equal Protection,* 27 Stan.L.Rev. 603 (1975). Critics of the results have also stressed the potential for dilution of constitutional rights. Bickel, *The Voting Rights Cases,* 1966 Sup.Ct.Rev. 79, 85–101; Engdahl, *Constitutionality of the Voting Age Statute,* 39 Geo.Wash.L.Rev. 1 (1970).

[4] See Cohen, supra note 3, at 608–609.

comply with the requirements of Miranda v. Arizona, 384 U.S. 436 (1966); Congressional attempts to restrict the integration remedies employed by federal courts in school desegregation cases.[5]

Miranda's requirements that police give formal warnings concerning the right to remain silent and the right to counsel, and that they cease interrogation if a suspect asserts his right to remain silent, were justified as remedies to protect the suspect's privilege against self-incrimination. The Court expressly noted that "Congress and the States are free to develop their own safeguards for the privilege, so long as they are fully as effective. . . ."[6] The Congressional response, two years later, was a statute providing that in federal criminal trials, voluntary confessions were admissible in evidence.[7] Would a Congressional judgment that pre-*Miranda* law excluding involuntary confessions on a case-by-case basis was "fully effective" to protect against self-incrimination be controlling on the courts?[8]

The most controversial issue surrounding contemporary school integration cases has been the proper scope of the remedy for constitutional violations proved—including the propriety of "system-wide" remedies and court ordered school busing. President Nixon's 1972 proposals to limit federal court remedies in school integration cases were premised on the argument that the issue involved remedies and not rights.[9] In 1974, Congress enacted the Equal Education Opportunities and Transportation of Students Act. One provision forbids courts to order a plan requiring "transportation of a student to a school other than the school closest or next closest to his place of residence." Would that bind a federal court that otherwise would have concluded that busing was the only effective remedy for the defendants' constitutional violations? That issue will not need to be resolved, because another provision in the statute provides that it is "not intended to diminish the authority of the courts of the United States to enforce fully the fifth and fourteenth amendments. . . ."[10]

The proposed "Human Life Statute," introduced in both houses of Congress in 1981 (97th Cong., 1st Sess., H.R. 900 and S. 158), provided:

"The Congress finds that present-day scientific evidence indicates a significant likelihood that actual human life exists from conception.

"The Congress further finds that the fourteenth amendment to the Constitution of the United States was intended to protect all human beings.

---

[5] This legislation also raises the question of Congressional power to control the jurisdiction of federal courts. See Chapter 2, pp. 40–47, supra.

[6] 384 U.S. at 490. *Miranda* was decided the same day as Katzenbach v. Morgan.

[7] 18 U.S.C. § 3501. For extensive discussion of the enactment of this statute, its interpretation, and its constitutionality, see Burt, supra note 3.

[8] Apparently, the United States Department of Justice has followed a policy of not invoking 18 U.S.C. § 3501 to justify the admission of confessions in federal prosecutions, and no federal court has determined whether a "voluntary" confession to federal officers is admissible if *Miranda* requirements have not been met. One issue that arises in connection with statutes repealing

or restricting judicial remedies is whether the remedy was itself required by the Constitution. See Chief Justice Burger's dissent in Bivens v. Six Unknown Agents, 403 U.S. 388, 411 (1971), urging Congress to enact legislation providing a "reasonable and effective" substitute for the rule excluding illegally seized evidence.

[9] Bork, *Constitutionality of the President's Busing Proposals* (1972).

[10] Consider the decision in North Carolina State Bd. of Ed. v. Swann, 402 U.S. 43 (1971), described, supra p. 720 which held unconstitutional a state statute forbidding any school assignment on the basis of race. Would a federal statute forbidding racial assignments as a "remedy" in federal school integration litigation fare any better?

"Upon the basis of these findings, and in the exercise of the powers of the Congress, including its power under section 5 of the fourteenth amendment to the Constitution of the United States, the Congress hereby declares that for the purpose of enforcing the obligation of the States under the fourteenth amendment not to deprive persons of life without due process of law, human life shall be deemed to exist from conception, without regard to race, sex, age, health, defect, or condition of dependency; and for this purpose 'person' shall include all human life as defined herein."

If enacted, would this legislation have overruled the Supreme Court's decisions placing constitutional limits on state abortion laws? If so, would it be constitutional?[11]

FEDERALISM AND CONGRESSIONAL CONSENT TO UNCONSTITUTIONAL STATE LAWS

The examples and problems discussed in the previous note concern constitutional limits that bind Congress and the states alike. A number of constitutional limitations—the contract clause of Article I, Section 10, and the privileges and immunities clause of Article IV, Section 2, for example—apply only as limitations on the states. Other constitutional limitations that restrict both the national government and the states do so in different ways. Despite the "incorporation" of equal protection standards into the fifth amendment, Congress can adopt policies for the treatment of aliens that would be unconstitutional if contained in state legislation.[1] Limits on state territorial jurisdiction, such as the rules under the due process clause of the fourteenth amendment concerning the scope of in personam jurisdiction of state courts,[2] will not apply to a national government with nationwide territorial jurisdiction.

In one context, it is clear beyond dispute that Congress can "consent" to state laws that would otherwise violate a constitutional limit applicable to the states, but inapplicable to the national government. By ordinary legislation, Congress can validate state laws that would be unconstitutional unreasonable burdens on interstate commerce.[3] The traditional explanation for the power to consent has been two-fold: limitation on state power is not express, but an implication from Congressional power to regulate interstate commerce; the limitation stems from an assumption that, if Congress is silent, it is presumed that Congress desired an unburdened interstate market.[4] Notice that those explanations are inapplicable to other constitutional limitations on state power

---

[11] See Estreicher, *Congressional Power and Constitutional Rights: Reflections on Proposed "Human Life" Legislation*, 68 Va. L.Rev. 333 (1982).

[1] See Mathews v. Diaz, 426 U.S. 67 (1976), supra page 893; Hampton v. Mow Sun Wong, 426 U.S. 88 (1976); Plyler v. Doe, 457 U.S. 202 (1982), supra page 1086.

[2] The Court described the inability of a state court to bind an absent defendant as stemming from the due process clause of the fourteenth amendment in Pennoyer v. Neff, 95 U.S. (5 Otto) 714, 733–734 (1878). Even before the adoption of the fourteenth amendment, however, the Court enforced limitations on state judicial jurisdiction without tying them to any particular clause of the

constitution. See page 478, supra. Commerce clause limitations on state power have sometimes been concerned with the extraterritorial impact of state laws. See Baldwin v. G.A.F. Seelig, Inc., 294 U.S. 511 (1935), supra page 273; Edgar v. MITE Corp., 457 U.S. 624 (1982), supra page 335. Most recent cases limiting state power to tax interstate business have relied more on limits of territorial power imposed by the due process clause of the fourteenth amendment than on the limitations imposed by the commerce clause.

[3] These cases are discussed at pages 183–184, supra.

[4] See Dowling, *Interstate Commerce and State Power—Revised Version*, 47 Colum.L.Rev. 547 (1947).

that are express, and not merely implied from the existence of federal power. Justice Rutledge's opinion for the Court in Prudential Ins. Co. v. Benjamin, 328 U.S. 408 (1946) stated, however, that the conventional explanations "did not go to the heart of the matter," and do not explain the power of Congress to consent to state laws unreasonably burdening commerce.

Benjamin involved the McCarran–Ferguson Act of 1945, which provided that "silence on the part of the Congress shall not be construed to impose any barrier" to state regulation or taxation of insurance.[5] The Court held that the Act validated discriminatory state taxes on out-of-state insurance companies that would otherwise violate the commerce clause. Justice Rutledge's opinion explained that:

> "The power of Congress over commerce exercised without reference to coordinated action of the states is not restricted ... by any limitation which forbids it to discriminate against interstate commerce and in favor of local trade.... This broad authority Congress may exercise alone [subject to constitutional limits on Congress' power], or in conjunction with coordinated action by the states, in which case limitations imposed for the preservation of their powers become inoperative and only those designed to forbid action altogether by any power or combination of powers in our governmental system remain effective.... Clear and gross must be the evil which would nullify such an exertion, one which could arise only by exceeding ... limitation[s] imposed by a constitutional provision or provisions designed and intended to outlaw the action entirely from our constitutional framework."

Does this mean that Congress can validate any state law, so long as Congress would have had the power to enact an identical or analogous law? For an argument along those lines, see W. Cohen, *Congressional Power to Validate Unconstitutional State Laws: A Forgotten Solution to an Old Enigma,* 35 Stan.L.Rev. 387 (1983).

In Metropolitan Life Insurance Co. v. Ward, 470 U.S. 869 (1985), supra page 1016, the Court held that a discriminatory tax identical to that in *Benjamin,* was unconstitutional as a violation of the equal protection clause. The Court concluded that Congress had not intended to validate laws that violated the due process or equal protection clause. If Congress had specifically provided that discriminatory taxes on out-of-state insurance companies were valid as against an equal protection challenge, would this have changed the outcome in *Ward* ? For an argument that it would, see W. Cohen, *Federalism in Equality Clothing: A Comment on* Metropolitan Life Insurance Company v. Ward, 38 Stan.L.Rev. 1 (1985). Compare Northeast Bancorp, Inc. v. Board of Governors of the Federal Reserve System, 472 U.S. 159 (1985), supra page 1023 (state legislation excluding out-of-state banks, with Congressional permission, does not violate the equal protection clause).

---

[5] The Act was a response to the decision in United States v. South–Eastern Underwriters Ass'n, 322 U.S. 533 (1944).

*

Part IV

CONSTITUTIONAL PROTECTION OF EXPRESSION AND CONSCIENCE

The first four chapters in this part provide a detailed look at issues of freedom of expression. Chapter 13 examines the definition of constitutionally protected speech, and focuses on doctrine dealing with prohibition of expression because of its content. Chapter 14 deals with government restriction that purports to control the time, place, or manner of speaking rather than the content of expression. Chapter 15 concerns indirect government restrictions on expression and the definition of peripheral first amendment rights. (Specific topics include the control of communicative conduct, compelled affirmation and disclosure, denial of government employment because of an employee's speech or association, denial of other government benefits, and freedom of political association.) Chapter 16 pulls together cases concerning the printed and electronic media. That chapter examines whether the guarantee of freedom of the press imposes restrictions on government independent of, and in addition to, those imposed by the guarantee of freedom of speech. The protection of religious conscience and conduct is reserved for Chapter 17.

CHAPTER 13

GOVERNMENTAL CONTROL OF THE CONTENT OF EXPRESSION

Introduction. This chapter focuses on the core problem in defining the contours of freedom of expression—the extent to which speech can be punished by government because of its content. Section 1 deals at length with speech advocating the violent overthrow of government. Section 2 is a deliberate digression, examining judicial techniques for avoiding decision whether speech can be controlled because of its content. This section examines the doctrine of prior restraint, and the doctrines of vagueness and overbreadth. Section 3 returns to the problem of content control, examining the Court's efforts to draw the distinction between protected and unprotected speech in four different contexts—defamation and privacy, obscenity, fighting words and offensive speech, and commercial speech.

SECTION 1. AN INTRODUCTION TO PROBLEMS OF CONTENT CONTROL OF SPEECH

A. HISTORICAL INTRODUCTION—THE STATUS OF FREE SPEECH UP TO THE 1920's

1. THE ENGLISH BACKGROUND

Freedom of thought and expression is taken so much as a matter of course in most western societies today that we are apt to forget how recently it has come to be accepted. As the distinguished English historian, J.B. Bury, emphasized in *A History of Freedom of Thought* (1913), "human societies (there are some brilliant exceptions) have been generally opposed to freedom of thought" and "it has taken centuries to persuade the most enlightened peoples that liberty to publish one's opinions and to discuss all questions is a good and not a bad thing" (Home University Library Ed., 1952, p. 2). This is due in part to the persistent inclination of people to cling to familiar and accepted opinion, and to dislike what is new, but other reasons are not difficult to discover.

Both the society and outlook of the Middle Ages were authoritarian; truth was divinely revealed and error was sin. Consequently to extirpate erroneous views was not only permissible but a high moral obligation and the unifying structure of the medieval Church provided the central authority for determining what was true and what was false. Thus the churchmen who in 1633 condemned Galileo to live the rest of his life in seclusion because he insisted that the earth was not the stationary center of the universe were only performing their duty as determined by the standards under which they had lived.[1]

[1] This incident is told in detail in De Santillana, *The Crime of Galileo* (1955).

1190

Even after the impact of the Renaissance and Reformation, the rebirth of learning, and the development of nation-states, the modern concept of freedom of thought was slow to develop. Diversity replaced the unity of the Middle Ages and the invention of the printing press brought a new and previously unequaled medium of communication. But on the whole, the dissenters and reformers sought only to establish a new brand of truth (their own) and did not recognize the value of general freedom of thought and speech as the means of arriving at truth.

The three centuries that elapsed between the appearance of the first book printed in England, by Caxton in 1476, and the Declaration of Independence in 1776 provide the immediate background of the American constitutional system, and the struggles of this period are particularly relevant in the area of freedom of thought and expression. They concerned two issues above all others, the separation of the English Church from that of Rome and the limitation of the prerogative of the Crown. Neither of these developments assured the freedom of the individual, but supplanted one religious establishment with another and made parliament supreme in areas that theretofore had been the province of the King. Dispute and domestic turmoil fomented discussion, as they always do, but the very limited freedom permitted to thought and speech is shown by the position of the press.

The invention of printing was almost as frightening to the mind of the fifteenth century as has been the discovery of atomic fission to the mind of the twentieth. The printing press, unless rigidly controlled, gave to dissident groups a powerful medium for "dangerous doctrine." No friend of the established order could view this situation with complacency at a time when religious truth, then an all-consuming subject, was deemed a matter of prior revelation and when political controversy was entering the crisis of the life-and-death struggle between King and Parliament. Three instruments for the legal control of discussion were used: (1) the concept of constructive treason; (2) the doctrine of seditious libel; and (3) the domination of the press through state monopoly and licensing.

The law of treason was based on the Statute 25 Edward III (1351), which defined the crime to include (1) compassing or imagining the King's death, (2) levying war against the King, or (3) adhering to his enemies. These three clauses, strictly construed, did not offer complete protection for the security of the monarch and of the state, or so it was believed. Hence there arose in the seventeenth century that judicial extension of the statute known as constructive treason. Compassing or imagining the King's death, like intending to wage war against him, being a mental state, could be proved only by overt acts. During the latter part of the seventeenth century the judges ruled that printed and sometimes spoken words could constitute overt acts. Thus John Twyn was convicted of treason and hanged, drawn, and quartered in 1664 for printing a book asserting that the King was accountable to the people who were entitled to revolt and take the government into their own hands.[2]

However, prosecutions for constructive treason were rare, only two printers being executed for the crime during the seventeenth century and one during the eighteenth.[3] A more effective method of suppression was available, the law of seditious libel, under which convictions ran into the hundreds. Conviction for this crime did not bring death but the penalties were often severe, including indefinite imprisonment and heavy fines. The law of seditious

[2] This and similar cases are recounted in Siebert, *Freedom of the Press in England, 1476–1776* (1952), p. 267.

[3] Siebert, op. cit., p. 365.

libel was developed in prosecutions before the Court of Star Chamber in the late sixteenth century, and when that body was abolished in 1641, the rules were taken over by the common law courts. The original theory of the offense was that the King was the fountainhead of justice and law whose acts were beyond popular criticism and that consequently it was wrong to censure him openly.[4] This doctrine was carried to such lengths that any reflection on the government in written or printed form might be held seditious libel. In 1704 Chief Justice Holt declared: "If people should not be called to account for possessing the people with an ill opinion of the government, no government can subsist. For it is very necessary for all governments that the people should have a good opinion of it. And nothing can be worse to any government than to endeavour to procure animosities as to the management of it; this has always been looked upon as a crime, and no government can be safe without it."[5]

As the eighteenth century progressed juries became less inclined to bring in verdicts of guilty in seditious libel cases. The judges then took the position that truth was no defense and that the only issue to be submitted to the jury was whether or not the defendant had published the allegedly seditious statements. Whether or not the statements constituted a libel was a matter of law to be determined by the judge. This trend was strenuously opposed by the distinguished English barrister Thomas Erskine, among others, who contended that the jury should be asked to bring in a general verdict of guilty or not guilty and to determine the defendant's criminal intent as in other criminal cases. The final result of this struggle was the passage in 1792 of Fox's Libel Act which established Erskine's views and gave the jury the power to render a general verdict on the whole issue in a libel case rather than merely on the issue of publication.

The French revolution brought a flurry of seditious libel cases, including the prosecution of Thomas Paine in 1792 for the publication of his "Rights of Man", but these prosecutions and the enactment of Fox's Libel Act marked the end of seditious libel as an instrument for the suppression of free speech in England.[6]

The third method of controlling expression of opinion, and on the whole the most effective one, was the elaborate system of printing monopolies and licensing. The authority to regulate the printing press in England was claimed by the Crown as one of its prerogative rights until the supremacy of Parliament was established by the revolution of 1688. Beginning with Henry VIII (1509–1547) the press was held in check through royal proclamations, licenses, patents of monopoly, orders in Council, and Star Chamber decrees. The first English index of prohibited "heretical and blasphemous" books was created by royal proclamation in 1529 and a licensing system for all books was established in 1538 by a proclamation designed to stamp out "seditious opinions" as well as heretical views. Licensors were appointed and no book could lawfully be printed and distributed without their prior approval. The system was modified and extended by the charter granted the Stationers Company in 1557. Members of the Company were given extensive control over the press by the provision of the Charter prohibiting all printing within the realm except by members of the Company or by those having special license from the Crown. The Company enforced both its own licensing ordinances and those issued by the Crown; all

[4] Stephen, *History of Criminal Law in England* (1883) Vol. II, p. 299.

[5] Rex v. Tutchin, 14 *State Trials*, p. 1095, quoted in Siebert, op. cit., p. 271.

[6] The efforts of Thomas Erskine on behalf of liberalism in eighteenth century England, including his defense of Thomas Paine, are told in Lloyd Paul Stryker's biography of Erskine, *For the Defense* (1947).

member printers were required to obtain a license from the officers of the Company before printing any works and all presses were required to be registered with the Company.

The seventeenth century brought great changes to England in the form of the Puritan Revolution, the Commonwealth, and the triumph of Parliament through the revolution of 1688, but it did not bring freedom of the press, although eloquent voices, such as John Milton's,[7] were raised in its behalf. The licensing and other controls became less effective during this century, but the principal change was the shift in power from the Crown to Parliament. The objection of the Puritans to the control of the press was not so much to the control as to the fact that it was exercised by the King. With the fall of Charles I (1649) power passed to Parliament, and after the struggles of the Commonwealth (1649–1653), the Protectorate (1653–1659), and the Stuart restoration (1660–1689), the supremacy of Parliament was confirmed by the Revolution of 1688 and the Bill of Rights of 1689. However, that great document of English constitutional development did not contain any statement espousing general freedom of speech or the press. Its only provision on the subject merely stated: "That the freedom of speech and debates or proceedings in parliament ought not to be impeached or questioned in any court or place out of parliament". It was freedom of speech *in* Parliament, *not outside,* that was recognized.

The control of the press exercised by Parliament gradually relaxed during the century following the Bill of Rights. At the end of the seventeenth century the power of the Stationers Company was broken by the refusal of Parliament to continue its monopolies and special privileges. The methods of control then shifted from licensing to subsidization and taxation. The government resorted to subsidization in order to promote the opinion it desired; such literary figures as Defoe, Swift, Addison, Steele, and Fielding all engaged in political pamphleteering or journalism for which they were compensated in one form or another by the government or political leaders. In 1712, newspapers, pamphlets, advertisements, and paper were subjected to taxes which had the effect of suppressing many of the smaller ephemeral publications then sniping at the policies of the government. That this was the purpose of the taxes is suggested by the fact that books were exempted. These taxes were continued with varying degrees of effectiveness until the first half of the nineteenth century.

It was in the light of this background that Blackstone discussed freedom of thought and expression in his Commentaries, first published in 1765. It is important to note that he wrote at a time when licensing had been abandoned but the law of seditious libel was still in full vigor. His comments are as follows:

"The liberty of the press is indeed essential to the nature of a free state; but this consists in laying no *previous* restraints upon publications, and not

---

[7] Milton had difficulties with the Stationers Company and the authorities over the publication of his pamphlets on divorce. He made his reply in Areopagitica (1644) which was a plea for the abolition of the licensing system. See Siebert, op. cit., p. 195. Milton's argument for freedom of the press cannot be given here, but the following sentences deserve quotation: "Where there is much desire to learn, there of necessity will be much arguing, much writing, many opinions; for opinion in good men is but knowledge in the making.... And though all the winds of doctrine were let loose to play upon the earth, so Truth be in the field we do injuriously, by licensing and prohibiting, to misdoubt her strength. Let her and Falsehood grapple; whoever knew Truth put to the worse, in a free and open encounter? Her confuting is the best and surest suppressing...." However, apparently Milton had reservations about complete freedom of expression, for he also said he would not tolerate "popery and open superstition."—Furthermore that "which is impious or evil absolutely either against faith or manners no law can possibly permit, that intends not to unlaw itself...." *The Tradition of Freedom* (Mayer ed. 1957) pp. 26, 28, 29.

in freedom from censure for criminal matter when published. Every freeman has an undoubted right to lay what sentiments he pleases before the public: to forbid this, is to destroy the freedom of the press; but if he publishes what is improper, mischievous, or illegal, he must take the consequence of his own temerity. To subject the press to the restrictive power of a licenser, as was formerly done, both before and since the revolution, is to subject all freedom of sentiment to the prejudices of one man, and make him the arbitrary and infallible judge of all controverted points in learning, religion, and government. But to punish (as the law does at present) any dangerous or offensive writings, which, when published, shall on a fair and impartial trial be adjudged of a pernicious tendency, is necessary for the preservation of peace and good order, of government and religion, the only solid foundations of civil liberty. Thus the will of individuals is still left free; the abuse only of that free will is the object of legal punishment. Neither is any restraint hereby laid upon freedom of thought or inquiry: liberty of private sentiment is still left; the disseminating, or making public, of bad sentiments, destructive of the ends of society, is the crime which society corrects." (*Commentaries*, Book IV, pp. 151–152.)[8]

2. THE ADOPTION OF THE FIRST AMENDMENT AND THE CONTROVERSY OVER THE ALIEN AND SEDITION LAWS

(1) **The Original Intent.** Scholars have not been able to agree as to the purpose intended to be served by the first amendment. The basic question is whether it was intended as a charter of freedom or as no more than a determination that regulation of speech and press according to common law principles should be reserved to the states. The most recent scholarship supports the latter position. Leonard Levy concludes, for example, that the amendment was intended only as a restraint on Congress and not on the courts in enforcing the common law crime of seditious libel and "that the prohibition on Congress was motivated far less by a desire to give immunity to political expression than by a solicitude for states' rights and the federal principle. The primary purpose of the first amendment was to reserve to the states an exclusive authority, as far as legislation was concerned, in the field of speech and press." *Freedom of Press from Zenger v. Jefferson* lix (1966).[1] For a different view, see Brant, *The Bill of Rights* 223–236 (1965).

(2) **The Sedition Act.** The Sedition Act (part of a package known as the Alien and Sedition Laws), passed in 1798, made it a crime carrying imprisonment up to two years to write, utter, or publish "any false, scandalous and malicious writing ... against the government of the United States, or either house of the congress ... or the President ... with intent to defame [them] ... or to bring them ... into contempt or disrepute; or to excite against them ... the hatred of the good people of the United States, or to stir up sedition within

---

[8] For a general review of the English background of our Bill of Rights, see Brant, *The Bill of Rights,* 3–219 (1965). See also Chafee, *How Human Rights Got into the Constitution* (1952) and *Three Human Rights in the Constitution of 1787* (1956). For a convenient collection of the documentary sources, see Perry and Cooper, *Sources of our Liberties* (1959).

[1] Professor Levy in *Legacy of Suppression* (1960) reviews freedom of expression in early American history and concludes that in colonial America the people did not understand that freedom of thought means equal freedom for the other fellow, especially the one with hated ideas.

the United States, or to excite any unlawful combinations therein, for opposing or resisting any law of the United States, or any act of the President of the United States, done in pursuance of any such law, or of the powers vested in him by the constitution of the United States, or to resist, oppose, or defeat any such law or act. . . ." The Act also provided that truth could be offered in defense and that the jury "shall have a right to determine the law and the fact, under the direction of the court, as in other cases." 1 Stat. 596 (1798).

The Sedition Act became the center of an enormous political controversy. Much attention was paid to the question whether it violated the first amendment. Levy contends that in this controversy there was a sudden breakthrough in libertarian thought with the Jeffersonian Republicans abandoning common law notions, arguing that free government required freedom of discussion, and asserting that only injurious conduct as manifested by deeds rather than words should be subjected to criminal punishment. *Freedom of the Press from Zenger to Jefferson* lxx–lxxix (1966).[2]

The Sedition Act by its own terms was to be in force only until March 3, 1801. One of Jefferson's first acts as President was to pardon all persons convicted under the act. Jefferson's own view of the first amendment, however, seemed to be one of federalism rather than freedom—at least in his role as President subject to scurrilous attacks in opposition newspapers. In 1803 he wrote a letter to Governor McKean of Pennsylvania referring to the licentiousness and lying of the press and then asserting: "This is a dangerous state of things, and the press ought to be restored to its credibility if possible. The restraints provided by the laws of the states are sufficient for this if applied. And I have therefore long thought that a few prosecutions of the most prominent offenders would have a wholesome effect in restoring the integrity of the presses. Not a general prosecution, for that would look like persecution: but a selected one. The paper I now inclose appears to me to offer as good an instance in every respect to make an example of, as can be selected."[3]

In 1806 a common law prosecution of Connecticut editors for libel of President Jefferson and the Congress was brought in the federal courts. That avenue for controlling the press was eliminated by the Supreme Court on appeal from the conviction in that case—not because the prosecution violated the first amendment, but rather on the general proposition that federal courts had no common law criminal jurisdiction. *United States v. Hudson* and Goodwin, 11 U.S. (7 Cranch) 32 (1812).[4]

3.   FREEDOM OF SPEECH AND PRESS IN THE NINETEENTH CENTURY

(1) **Introduction.** The Supreme Court did not begin to elaborate the protection accorded by the first amendment until the time of World War I. One

---

[2] More recently another author contends that the opposition to the Sedition Act was founded primarily on notions of states' rights rather than civil liberties with a primary motivation being the preservation of slavery. Berns, *Freedom of the Press and the Alien and Sedition Laws: A Reappraisal,* 1970 Sup. Ct.Rev. 109.

[3] The letter is set out in Levy, *Freedom of the Press from Zenger to Jefferson* 364

(1966). In a letter to Abigail Adams in 1804 he also said: "While we deny that Congress have a right to control the freedom of the press, we have ever asserted the right of the States, and their exclusive right, to do so." Id. at 366, 367.

[4] For the story of the case and Jefferson's somewhat belated disapproval of the prosecution, see Levy, *Jefferson and Civil Liberties—The Darker Side* 61 (1963).

should not draw from that fact the conclusion that there were no intrusions on freedom of speech and the press during this period of time. Developments in the states were unaffected by the first amendment. It was not until 1925 that the Court indicated that the fourteenth amendment had made the first applicable to the states. But there were episodes involving federal control, particularly of the press, that were not subjected to testing by the Supreme Court.[1]

(2) **Punishment for Contempt of Court.** Under the Judiciary Act of 1789 which authorized federal courts to punish "all contempts of authority in any cause or hearing" before them, federal courts early asserted the authority to punish newspapers and others who criticized court decisions. In one early case a federal district judge, James H. Peck, had one Lawless imprisoned and disbarred for publishing a criticism of a decision by Peck which was on appeal. Lawless had powerful political friends and as a result impeachment proceedings were brought against Judge Peck. Peck was acquitted but immediately thereafter Congress amended the statute to limit the contempt power to "misbehaviour of any person or persons in the presence of the said courts, or so near thereto as to obstruct the administration of justice." The story of this episode is told in Nye v. United States, 313 U.S. 33, 45 (1941). As a result of the change in the statute the federal courts for a long time did not assert the power to punish critics. (State courts, however, began increasingly to use contempt to punish comments outside the court on the ground that they tended to interfere with the administration of justice.) In 1918 in Toledo Newspaper Co. v. United States, 247 U.S. 402 (1918), the Supreme Court interpreted the federal statute as not applying a geographical limitation on the contempt power of the federal courts and said that the test under the statute was "the character of the act done and its direct tendency to prevent and obstruct the discharge of judicial duty." The Court also rejected the claim that freedom of the press was violated when contempt was used to punish under this test. To state that proposition was to answer it, the Court said, "since it involves in its very statement the contention that the freedom of the press is the freedom to do wrong with impunity, and implies the right to frustrate and defeat the discharge of those governmental duties upon the performance of which the freedom of all, including that of the press, depends." By 1928 the judicial use of the contempt power to punish the press was widespread with most of the cases involving comments impugning the fairness, independence, or integrity of the judge.[2]

(3) **Control of Public Discussion of the Slavery Question.** Antislavery speech was regarded in the South as presenting a very real danger to the institution of slavery. While local dissenters were easily dealt with, the South also sought to exclude from the South any antislavery publications. In 1835 President Jackson asked Congress to enact a law prohibiting the circulation in the South through the mails "of incendiary publications intended to instigate the slaves to insurrection." Calhoun opposed this as a violation of freedom of the press, as being similar to the Sedition Act, but then he proposed a statute making it unlawful for a postmaster to receive and put into the mail any paper "touching the subject of slavery" and addressed to any person in a state which forbade by law the circulation of such materials. Neither of these bills passed but in practice postmasters in the South responded to local pressures and refused to deliver antislavery materials. By 1863 the Postmaster General was

---

[1] For an excellent brief general account of this period see Nelson, *Freedom of the Press from Hamilton to the Warren Court xix-xxxvii (1967).*

[2] For an account of the times, see Nelles & King, *Contempt by Publication in the United States,* 28 Colum.L.Rev. 401, 524 (1928).

asserting the power—which was not challenged for a long time—to remove from the mails or prevent delivery of anti-Union writings or material considered to be obscene. This restraint on discussion of slavery carried over into Congress in which the House by a series of gag rules refused from 1836 to 1845 to entertain or to discuss any petition relating to slavery.[3]

(4) **The Civil War.** During the war there existed both a substantial amount of freedom by the press and a substantial amount of suppression by the military and the President. In one case President Lincoln went so far as to suppress newspapers and order trials of the publishers before military tribunals. For the documents in that case see Nelson, supra note 1, at 232–247. For a fuller account of the relationships between Lincoln and the press, see Randall, *Constitutional Problems Under Lincoln* 477–510 (1951).

(5) **Obscenity, and Control of the Mails.** In 1873 Congress passed the "Comstock law" providing for punishment of those who used the mails to transport obscene materials. State and federal prosecutions for obscenity reached new highs after the turn of the century.[4]

(6) **Civil and Criminal Libel under State Law.** Even if the Sedition Act controversy were viewed as excluding federal libel laws, states remained free of federal constitutional restraint. As late as 1922, the Supreme Court maintained that "neither the Fourteenth Amendment nor any other provision of the Constitution of the United States imposes upon the States any restrictions about 'freedom of speech'. . . ." Prudential Ins. Co. v. Cheek, 259 U.S. 530, 543 (1922). While decisional law established truth as a complete defense in civil libel cases, the press was subject to practically strict liability for statements that were innocently false. Criminal libel laws often provided only a qualified defense of truth. Prosecutions for criminal libel in the state courts increased sharply in the later 1800's and stayed high through World War I. In 1918, a law review author could still assert:

"There is no such thing as an unlimited right to print whatever one may choose to print, regardless of its character and effect. Without law there can be no liberty, and freedom of the press does not mean irresponsibility for what is printed. All right-thinking men will join with Alexander Hamilton in his reprobation of 'the pestilential doctrine of an unchecked press,' and agree with him that ill-fated would be our country were this doctrine to prevail.

"It is for the state to say what publications are harmful, what use of the press is permissible. It would be an act of tyranny under normal conditions to deprive a citizen of the right to own a gun, but it is essential to public safety to prevent him from using it to the injury of others. So it is with the printing press, an instrument not less dangerous than a shot gun. It is not tyrannous nor inconsistent with the freedom of the press that its owner should be held accountable for any improper use he may make of it."[5]

---

[3] For a fuller treatment of these episodes, see Berns, *Freedom of the Press and the Alien and Sedition Laws: A Reappraisal*, 1970, Sup.Ct.Rev. 109, 142, 150; Nelson, *Freedom of the Press from Hamilton to the Warren Court* xxii-xxvi (1967).

[4] See generally on this period, Nelson, *Freedom of the Press from Hamilton to the Warren Court* xxviii-xxxii (1967). For an account of postal censorship see Deutsch, *The Freedom of the Press and of the Mails*, 36 Mich.L.Rev. 703 (1938).

[5] Long, *The Freedom of the Press*, 5 Va. L.Rev. 225, 228, 229 (1918).

B.   WORLD WAR I AND THE POST-WAR YEARS: PENALIZING THE ADVOCACY OF THE OVERTHROW OF GOVERNMENT BY FORCE OR VIOLENCE

THE CONCERN FOR RADICAL SPEECH IN THE FIRST QUARTER OF THE TWENTIETH CENTURY

In the early years, principal free speech and press disputes had involved the role of newspapers and periodicals—typically those of a different political persuasion than the party in power—in acting as critics of government. A rising concern with radicals began to surface at the turn of the century. Following President McKinley's assassination, the New York Criminal Anarchy law, which became a model for later state and federal legislation, made it a crime to belong to an organization that taught the doctrine that government should be overthrown by force of violence. The Immigration Act of 1903 provided that persons who believed in or advocated the overthrow of government by force and violence should be barred from entering the country, or deported if already here.

The fear of radicals was brought to a head, and fused with concern over enemy sympathizers, by the country's entry into the First World War.

In 1917 Congress passed the Espionage Act. This act made it a crime when the country was at war to "willfully make or convey false reports or false statements with intent to interfere" with the prosecution of the war or to promote the success of enemies, or willfully to "cause or attempt to cause" insubordination, disloyalty, mutiny, or refusal of duty, in the military or naval forces of the United States, or willfully to "obstruct the recruiting or enlistment service of the United States." Another provision of the act forbade the mailing of any material in violation of the provisions of the act or "advocating or urging treason, insurrection, or forcible resistance to any law of the United States. . . ." In 1918 the statute was amended to make criminal the utterance of language "intended to bring the form of government of the United States into contempt, scorn, contumely, or disrepute." This 1918 version of the Sedition Act was repealed in 1921. There were nearly 2,000 prosecutions under the 1917 and 1918 Acts, many publications were excluded from the mails, and a series of challenges under the first amendment came quickly to the Supreme Court.[1]

The antiradical sentiment of the war years became more intense after the war ended. The country was plagued by rumors of radical takeover of government. There was labor unrest, and the news featured incidents of riots and bombings. Radical leaders were prosecuted under state laws modeled after the 1902 New York Criminal Anarchy Law. Some of these cases, too, reached the Supreme Court and renewed the judicial debate concerning the meaning of free speech in the context of attempts to punish the advocates of radical doctrines.[2]

MASSES PUBLISHING CO. v. PATTEN, 244 Fed. 535 (S.D.N.Y.1917). The publisher of a revolutionary journal called "The Masses" brought suit to enjoin the postmaster of New York from refusing to accept the magazine in the mails. The postmaster argued that the magazine was nonmailable under the provision of the Espionage Act making nonmailable any publication that violated the other provisions of the Act. Part of the focus here was on the

---

[1] See generally Chafee, *Freedom of Speech* (1920) for an account of the period.

[2] For a review of the cases from *Schenck* to *Whitney*, see Cover, *The Left, The Right* *and the First Amendment,* 40 Md.L.Rev. 349 (1981).

provisions of the Act penalizing the willful causing of disaffection in the military services and the willful obstruction of recruitment. On these points Judge Learned Hand construed the statute[3] as follows:

"The next phrase relied upon is that which forbids any one from willfully causing insubordination, disloyalty, mutiny, or refusal of duty in the military or naval forces of the United States. The defendant's position is that to arouse discontent and disaffection among the people with the prosecution of the war and with the draft tends to promote a mutinous and insubordinate temper among the troops. This, too, is true; men who become satisfied that they are engaged in an enterprise dictated by the unconscionable selfishness of the rich, and effectuated by a tyrannous disregard for the will of those who must suffer and die, will be more prone to insubordination than those who have faith in the cause and acquiesce in the means. Yet to interpret the word 'cause' so broadly would, as before, involve necessarily as a consequence the suppression of all hostile criticism, and of all opinion except what encouraged and supported the existing policies, or which fell within the range of temperate argument. It would contradict the normal assumption of democratic government that the suppression of hostile criticism does not turn upon the justice of its substance or the decency and propriety of its temper. Assuming that the power to repress such opinion may rest in Congress in the throes of a struggle for the very existence of the state, its exercise is so contrary to the use and wont of our people that only the clearest expression of such a power justifies the conclusion that it was intended.

"The defendant's position, therefore, in so far as it involves the suppression of the free utterance of abuse and criticism of the existing law, or of the policies of the war, is not, in my judgment, supported by the language of the statute. Yet there has always been a recognized limit to such expressions, incident indeed to the existence of any compulsive power of the state itself. One may not counsel or advise others to violate the law as it stands. Words are not only the keys of persuasion, but the triggers of action, and those which have no purport but to counsel the violation of law cannot by any latitude of interpretation be a part of that public opinion which is the final source of government in a democratic state. The defendant asserts not only that the magazine indirectly through its propaganda leads to a disintegration of loyalty and a disobedience of law, but that in addition it counsels and advises resistance to existing law, especially to the draft. The consideration of this aspect of the case more properly arises under the third phrase of section 3, which forbids any willful obstruction of the recruiting or enlistment service of the United States, but, as the defendant urges that the magazine falls within each phrase, it is as well to take it up now. To counsel or advise a man to an act is to urge upon him either that it is his interest or his duty to do it. While, of course, this may be accomplished as well by indirection as expressly, since words carry the meaning that they impart, the definition is exhaustive, I think, and I shall use it. Political agitation, by the passions it arouses or the convictions it engenders, may in fact stimulate men to the violation of law. Detestation of existing policies is easily transformed into forcible resistance of the authority which puts them in execution, and it would be folly to disregard the causal relation between the two. Yet to assimilate agitation, legitimate as such, with direct incitement to violent resistance, is to disregard the tolerance of all methods of political agitation which in normal times is a safeguard of free government. The

---

[3] Hand's grant of an injunction, based on that construction, was reversed by the Court of Appeals. 246 Fed. 24 (2d Cir.1917).

distinction is not a scholastic subterfuge, but a hard-bought acquisition in the fight for freedom, and the purpose to disregard it must be evident when the power exists. If one stops short of urging upon others that it is their duty or their interest to resist the law, it seems to me one should not be held to have attempted to cause its violation. If that be not the test, I can see no escape from the conclusion that under this section every political agitation which can be shown to be apt to create a seditious temper is illegal. I am confident that by such language Congress had no such revolutionary purpose in view.

"It seems to me, however, quite plain that none of the language and none of the cartoons in this paper can be thought directly to counsel or advise insubordination or mutiny, without a violation of their meaning quite beyond any tolerable understanding. I come, therefore, to the third phrase of the section, which forbids any one from willfully obstructing the recruiting or enlistment service of the United States. I am not prepared to assent to the plaintiff's position that this only refers to acts other than words, nor that the act thus defined must be shown to have been successful. One may obstruct without preventing, and the mere obstruction is an injury to the service; for it throws impediments in its way. Here again, however, since the question is of the expression of opinion, I construe the sentence, so far as it restrains public utterance, as I have construed the other two, and as therefore limited to the direct advocacy of resistance to the recruiting and enlistment service. If so, the inquiry is narrowed to the question whether any of the challenged matter may be said to advocate resistance to the draft, taking the meaning of the words with the utmost latitude which they can bear."

SCHENCK v. UNITED STATES, 249 U.S. 47 (1919). Section 3 of Title I of the Espionage Act of 1917 established three offenses: "[1] Whoever, when the United States is at war, shall willfully make or convey false reports or false statements with intent to interfere with the operation or success of the military or naval forces of the United States or to promote the success of its enemies and [2] whoever, when the United States is at war, shall willfully cause or attempt to cause insubordination, disloyalty, mutiny, or refusal of duty, in the military or naval forces of the United States, or [3] shall willfully obstruct the recruiting or enlistment Service of the United States, to the injury of the service or of the United States, shall be punished by a fine of not more than $10,000 or imprisonment for not more than twenty years, or both."[1] Section 4 of the same Title punished persons conspiring to violate Section 3, if any one of them did any act to effect the object of the conspiracy. Schenck and the other defendants were indicted and convicted of a conspiracy to violate Section 3, by sending to drafted men, circulars calculated to cause insubordination in the armed services and to obstruct the recruiting and enlistment service of the United States. The circulars asserted that conscription violated the idea of the Thirteenth Amendment and was despotism in the interest of Wall Street's chosen few. Although the message "in form at least confined itself to peaceful measures," it urged the conscript not to "submit to intimidation" and denied the power of the government to send citizens abroad to shoot persons of other lands. Defendant did not deny that the tendency of the circulars was to influence persons to obstruct the draft, but contended that any such tendency was protected by the First Amendment.

Justice Holmes' unanimous opinion for the Supreme Court contains the following statement:

[1] 40 Stat. 219, which became 50 U.S.C. § 33, repealed June 25, 1948 when the present United States Code was enacted. The numbers have been inserted to indicate the different clauses of the provision.

"We admit that in many places and in ordinary times the defendants in saying all that was said in the circular would have been within their constitutional rights. But the character of every act depends upon the circumstances in which it is done.... The most stringent protection of free speech would not protect a man in falsely shouting fire in a theatre and causing a panic. It does not even protect a man from an injunction against uttering words that may have all the effect of force.... The question in every case is whether the words used are used in such circumstances and are of such a nature as to create a clear and present danger that they will bring about the substantive evils that Congress has a right to prevent. It is a question of proximity and degree. When a nation is at war many things that might be said in time of peace are such a hindrance to its effort that their utterance will not be endured so long as men fight and that no Court could regard them as protected by any constitutional right. It seems to be admitted that if an actual obstruction of the recruiting service were proved, liability for words that produced that effect might be enforced. The statute of 1917 in § 4 punishes conspiracies to obstruct as well as actual obstruction. If the act, (speaking, or circulating a paper,) its tendency and the intent with which it is done are the same, we perceive no ground for saying that success alone warrants making the act a crime."

The convictions were affirmed.[2]

ABRAMS v. UNITED STATES, 250 U.S. 616 (1919), involved the 1918 amendment to the Espionage Act. Offenses under the Act included uttering, printing, writing, or publishing any disloyal, profane, scurrilous or abusive language or language intended to cause contempt, scorn, contumely or disrepute as regards the form of government of the United States; any language intended to incite resistance to the United States or promote the cause of its enemies; or any language urging curtailment of production of any things necessary to the prosecution of war with intent to hinder such prosecution. Abrams and his fellow defendants were indicted and convicted of conspiring to violate these provisions of the 1918 amendment, in that they printed and distributed some 5000 circulars in New York City on about August 22, 1918, which circulars were intended to bring the form of government of the United States into contempt; to encourage resistance to the United States in World War I; and to incite curtailment of war production. In the circulars, President Wilson was denounced as a hypocrite and a coward for sending troops into Russia to support the anti-Bolshevik forces; the workers of the world were urged to awake and put down the common enemy—capitalism; the general strike was advocated as the necessary reply to the "barbaric intervention" in Russia; and the toilers of America were to pledge themselves "to create so great a disturbance that the autocrats of America shall be compelled to keep their armies at home, and not be able to spare any for Russia."

The majority concluded that any question regarding the constitutionality of the Espionage Act as a whole had been disposed of by *Schenck* and related

[2] One week later, on the authority of the *Schenck* decision, the Court sustained the conviction of a prominent socialist, *Eugene V. Debs,* under the same statute. In the course of a general address on socialism and opposition to the war, Debs praised draft resisters and stated: "You need to know that you are fit for something better than slavery and cannon fodder." Debs' 10 year sentence was affirmed because the jury could find that his remarks had a tendency to obstruct recruiting, and Debs had that intent. Justice Holmes stated that, even if the tendency of the speech and Debs' intent were incidental to Debs' main point in his speech—opposition to the war—his speech was not "protected by reason of its being part of a general program and expressions of a general and conscientious belief." Debs v. United States, 249 U.S. 211, 215 (1919).

cases, leaving, as the major issue, the sufficiency of the evidence to sustain the guilty verdict. They held that it had been proved that the defendants published their circulars with intent to encourage resistance to the war with Germany and to incite curtailment of war production.[1]

Justice Holmes, joined by Justice Brandeis, wrote a dissenting opinion in which he concluded that the circulars did not show the requisite intent to provoke resistance to the war with Germany or to curtail production in order to cripple the war effort. The opinion concludes with the following paragraphs.

"In this case sentences of twenty years imprisonment have been imposed for the publishing of two leaflets that I believe the defendants had as much right to publish as the Government has to publish the Constitution of the United States now vainly invoked by them. Even if I am technically wrong and enough can be squeezed from these poor and puny anonymities to turn the color of legal litmus paper; I will add, even if what I think the necessary intent were shown; the most nominal punishment seems to me all that possibly could be inflicted, unless the defendants are to be made to suffer not for what the indictment alleges but for the creed that they avow—a creed that I believe to be the creed of ignorance and immaturity when honestly held, as I see no reason to doubt that it was held here, but which, although made the subject of examination at the trial, no one has a right even to consider in dealing with the charges before the Court.

"Persecution for the expression of opinions seems to me perfectly logical. If you have no doubt of your premises or your power and want a certain result with all your heart you naturally express your wishes in law and sweep away all opposition. To allow opposition by speech seems to indicate that you think the speech impotent, as when a man says that he has squared the circle, or that you do not care whole-heartedly for the result, or that you doubt either your power or your premises. But when men have realized that time has upset many fighting faiths, they may come to believe even more than they believe the very foundations of their own conduct that the ultimate good desired is better reached by free trade in ideas—that the best test of truth is the power of the thought to get itself accepted in the competition of the market, and that truth is the only ground upon which their wishes safely can be carried out. That at any rate is the theory of our Constitution. It is an experiment, as all life is an experiment. Every year if not every day we have to wager our salvation upon some prophecy based upon imperfect knowledge. While that experiment is part of our system I think that we should be eternally vigilant against attempts to check the expression of opinions that we loathe and believe to be fraught with death, unless they so imminently threaten immediate interference with the lawful and pressing purposes of the law that an immediate check is required to save the country. I wholly disagree with the argument of the Government that the First Amendment left the common law as to seditious libel in force. History seems to me against the notion. I had conceived that the United States through many years had shown its repentance for the Sedition Act of 1798, by repaying fines that it imposed. Only the emergency that makes it immediately dangerous to leave the correction of evil counsels to time warrants making any exception to the sweeping command, 'Congress shall make no law ... abridging the freedom of speech.' Of course I am speaking only of expressions of opinion and exhortations, which were all that were uttered here, but I regret that I cannot put into more impressive words my belief that in their conviction upon this

---

[1] The majority found it unnecessary to review defendants' conviction on the count charging that the circulars were intended to bring the form of government of the United States into contempt.

indictment the defendants were deprived of their rights under the Constitution of the United States."[2]

HAND'S "ADVOCACY" TEST VS. HOLMES' "CLEAR AND PRESENT" TEST

Professor Corwin summarized the holdings of the *Schenck* and *Abrams* cases as follows:

"To sum up, the following propositions seem to be established with respect to constitutional freedom of speech and press: first, Congress is not limited to forbidding words which are of a nature 'to create a clear and present danger' to national interest, but it may forbid words which are intended to endanger those interests if in the exercise of a fair legislative discretion it finds it 'necessary and proper' to do so; second, the intent of the accused in uttering the alleged forbidden words may be presumed from the reasonable consequences of such words, though the presumption is a rebuttable one; third, the court will not scrutinize on appeal the findings of juries in this class of cases more strictly than in other penal cases. In short, the cause of freedom of speech and press is largely in the custody of legislative majorities and of juries, which, so far as there is evidence to show, is just where the framers of the Constitution intended it to be." Corwin, *Freedom of Speech and Press Under the First Amendment: A Resume,* 30 Yale L.J. 48, 55 (1920), reprinted in 2 Selected Essays on Constitutional Law 1060, 1067 (1938).

In an excellent article—Gunther, *Learned Hand and the Origins of Modern First Amendment Doctrine: Some Fragments of History,* 27 Stan.L.Rev. 719 (1975)—contemporary correspondence between Judge Hand and Justice Holmes is set forth making it clear that they had quite different points of view as to the appropriate limits on the punishment of radical speech. Holmes, in fact, started with the observation that "free speech stands no differently than freedom from vaccination." In a letter to Professor Chafee in 1921 Hand summarized his objections to the Holmes approach as set forth in *Schenck* and *Abrams:*

"I am not wholly in love with Holmesy's test and the reason is this. Once you admit that the matter is one of degree, while you may put it where it genuinely belongs, you so obviously make it a matter of administration, i.e. you give to Tomdickandharry, D.J., so much latitude that the jig is at once up. Besides their ineffabilities, the Nine Elder Statesmen, have not shown themselves wholly immune from the 'herd instinct' and what seems 'immediate and direct' today may seem very remote next year even though the circumstances surrounding the utterance be unchanged. I

---

[2] The Abrams case was the only one under the 1918 Act to reach the Supreme Court. That Act was repealed in 1921 (41 Stat. 1359), leaving the original 1917 Act to become what is now 18 U.S.C. § 2388. There have been intermittent prosecutions under the legislation. See Hartzel v. United States, 322 U.S. 680 (1944); United States v. Powell, 156 F.Supp. 526 (N.D.Cal.1957). The 1917 Act (by its original terms and as carried into 18 U.S.C. § 2388) applies only "when the United States is at war."

Related to the above legislation is a provision of the Universal Military Training and Service Act of 1948 which provides that one "who knowingly counsels, aids, or abets another to refuse or evade registration or service in the armed forces or any of the requirements of this title" is guilty of a crime. 50 U.S.C.App. § 462(a). Under this section, a dean of a college was convicted for telling a student who was refusing to register, "Do not let them coerce you into registering." Gara v. United States, 178 F.2d 38 (6th Cir.1949), affirmed by an equally divided vote, 340 U.S. 857 (1950).

own I should prefer a qualitative formula, hard, conventional, difficult to evade." Id. at 770.

The *Abrams* case suggested a somewhat different problem than *Schenck*. In *Schenck,* the statutory language prohibited conduct. *Abrams* involved a statute making criminal "language intended to incite resistance to the United States" and "language urging curtailment of production of any things necessary to the prosecution of war with intent to hinder such prosecution." In Gitlow v. New York, which is set out below, New York's statute penalized the advocacy of the "duty, necessity, or propriety" of overturning the government by force or violence.

Gitlow v. New York

268 U.S. 652, 45 S.Ct. 625, 69 L.Ed. 1138 (1925).

Mr. Justice Sanford delivered the opinion of the Court.

Benjamin Gitlow was indicted in the Supreme Court of New York, with three others, for the statutory crime of criminal anarchy. New York Penal Law §§ 160, 161. He was separately tried, convicted, and sentenced to imprisonment. The judgment was affirmed by the Appellate Division and by the Court of Appeals. . . .

The contention here is that the statute, by its terms and as applied in this case, is repugnant to the due process clause of the Fourteenth Amendment. Its material provisions are:

"§ 160. *Criminal anarchy defined.* Criminal anarchy is the doctrine that organized government should be overthrown by force or violence, or by assassination of the executive head or of any of the executive officials of government, or by any unlawful means. The advocacy of such doctrine either by word of mouth or writing is a felony.

"§ 161. *Advocacy of criminal anarchy.* Any person who:

"1. By word of mouth or writing advocates, advises or teaches the duty, necessity or propriety of overthrowing or overturning organized government by force or violence, or by assassination of the executive head or of any of the executive officials of government, or by any unlawful means; or,

"2. Prints, publishes, edits, issues or knowingly circulates, sells, distributes or publicly displays any book, paper, document, or written or printed matter in any form, containing or advocating, advising or teaching the doctrine that organized government should be overthrown by force, violence or any unlawful means, . . .

"Is guilty of a felony and punishable" by imprisonment or fine, or both.

The indictment was in two counts. The first charged that the defendant had advocated, advised and taught the duty, necessity and propriety of overthrowing and overturning organized government by force, violence and unlawful means, by certain writings therein set forth entitled "The Left Wing Manifesto"; the second that he had printed, published and knowingly circulated and distributed a certain paper called "The Revolutionary Age," containing the writings set forth in the first count advocating, advising and teaching the doctrine that organized government should be overthrown by force, violence and unlawful means.

The following facts were established on the trial by undisputed evidence and admissions: . . . It was admitted that the defendant signed a card subscribing to the Manifesto and Program of the Left Wing, which all applicants were required to sign before being admitted to membership; that he went to different parts of the State to speak to branches of the Socialist Party about the principles of the Left Wing and advocated their adoption; and that he was responsible for the Manifesto as it appeared, that "he knew of the publication, in a general way and he knew of its publication afterwards, and is responsible for its circulation."

There was no evidence of any effect resulting from the publication and circulation of the Manifesto.

No witnesses were offered in behalf of the defendant.

. . .

The court, among other things, charged the jury, in substance, that they must determine what was the intent, purpose and fair meaning of the Manifesto; that its words must be taken in their ordinary meaning, as they would be understood by people whom it might reach; that a mere statement or analysis of social and economic facts and historical incidents, in the nature of an essay, accompanied by prophecy as to the future course of events, but with no teaching, advice or advocacy of action, would not constitute the advocacy, advice or teaching of a doctrine for the overthrow of government within the meaning of the statute; that a mere statement that unlawful acts might accomplish such a purpose would be insufficient, unless there was a teaching, advising and advocacy of employing such unlawful acts for the purpose of overthrowing government; and that if the jury had a reasonable doubt that the Manifesto did teach, advocate or advise the duty, necessity or propriety of using unlawful means for the overthrowing of organized government, the defendant was entitled to an acquittal.

The defendant's counsel submitted two requests to charge which embodied in substance the statement that to constitute criminal anarchy within the meaning of the statute it was necessary that the language used or published should advocate, teach or advise the duty, necessity or propriety of doing "some definite or immediate act or acts" of force, violence or unlawfulness directed toward the overthrowing of organized government. These were denied further than had been charged. Two other requests to charge embodied in substance the statement that to constitute guilt the language used or published must be "reasonably and ordinarily calculated to incite certain persons" to acts of force, violence or unlawfulness, with the object of overthrowing organized government. These were also denied.

. . .

. . . The sole contention here is, essentially, that as there was no evidence of any concrete result flowing from the publication of the Manifesto or of circumstances showing the likelihood of such result, the statute as construed and applied by the trial court penalizes the mere utterance, as such, of "doctrine" having no quality of incitement, without regard either to the circumstances of its utterance or to the likelihood of unlawful sequences; and that, as the exercise of the right of free expression with relation to government is only punishable "in circumstances involving likelihood of substantive evil," the statute contravenes the due process clause of the Fourteenth Amendment. . . .

. . .

The statute does not penalize the utterance or publication of abstract "doctrine" or academic discussion having no quality of incitement to any concrete action. It is not aimed against mere historical or philosophical essays. It does not restrain the advocacy of changes in the form of government by constitutional and lawful means. What it prohibits is language advocating, advising or teaching the overthrow of organized government by unlawful means. These words imply urging to action. . . .

The Manifesto, plainly, is neither the statement of abstract doctrine nor, as suggested by counsel, mere prediction that industrial disturbances and revolutionary mass strikes will result spontaneously in an inevitable process of evolution in the economic system. It advocates and urges in fervent language mass action which shall progressively foment industrial disturbances and through political mass strikes and revolutionary mass action overthrow and destroy organized parliamentary government. It concludes with a call to action in these words:

"The proletariat revolution and the Communist reconstruction of society—*the struggle for these*—is now indispensable. . . . The Communist International calls the proletariat of the world to the final struggle!"

This is not the expression of philosophical abstraction, the mere prediction of future events; it is the language of direct incitement.

The means advocated for bringing about the destruction of organized parliamentary government, namely, mass industrial revolts usurping the functions of municipal government, political mass strikes directed against the parliamentary state, and revolutionary mass action for its final destruction, necessarily imply the use of force and violence, and in their essential nature are inherently unlawful in a constitutional government of law and order. That the jury were warranted in finding that the Manifesto advocated not merely the abstract doctrine of overthrowing organized government by force, violence and unlawful means, but action to that end, is clear.

For present purposes we may and do assume that freedom of speech and of the press—which are protected by the First Amendment from abridgment by Congress—are among the fundamental personal rights and "liberties" protected by the due process clause of the Fourteenth Amendment from impairment by the States. . . .

. . .

By enacting the present statute the State has determined, through its legislative body, that utterances advocating the overthrow of organized government by force, violence and unlawful means, are so inimical to the general welfare and involve such danger of substantive evil that they may be penalized in the exercise of its police power. That determination must be given great weight. . . . That utterances inciting to the overthrow of organized government by unlawful means, present a sufficient danger of substantive evil to bring their punishment within the range of legislative discretion, is clear. Such utterances, by their very nature, involve danger to the public peace and to the security of the State. They threaten breaches of the peace and ultimate revolution. And the immediate danger is none the less real and substantial, because the effect of a given utterance cannot be accurately foreseen. The State cannot reasonably be required to measure the danger from every such utterance in the nice balance of a jeweler's scale. A single revolutionary spark may kindle a fire that, smouldering for a time, may burst into a sweeping and destructive conflagration. It cannot be said that the State is acting arbitrarily or unreasonably when in the exercise of its judgment as to the measures necessary to protect the public peace and safety, it seeks to extinguish the spark without waiting until it has enkindled the flame or blazed into the conflagration. It cannot reasonably be required to defer the adoption of measures for its own peace and safety until the revolutionary utterances lead to actual disturbances of the public peace or imminent and immediate danger of its own destruction; but it may, in the exercise of its judgment, suppress the threatened danger in its incipiency....

We cannot hold that the present statute is an arbitrary or unreasonable exercise of the police power of the State unwarrantably infringing the freedom of speech or press; and we must and do sustain its constitutionality.

This being so it may be applied to every utterance—not too trivial to be beneath the notice of the law—which is of such a character and used with such intent and purpose as to bring it within the prohibition of the statute.... In other words, when the legislative body has determined generally, in the constitutional exercise of its discretion, that utterances of a certain kind involve such danger of substantive evil that they may be punished, the question whether any specific utterance coming within the prohibited class is likely, in and of itself, to bring about the substantive evil, is not open to consideration. It is sufficient that the statute itself be constitutional and that the use of the language comes within its prohibition.

It is clear that the question in such cases is entirely different from that involved in those cases where the statute merely prohibits certain acts involving the danger of substantive evil, without any reference to language itself, and it is sought to apply its provisions to language used by the defendant for the purpose of bringing about the prohibited results. There, if it be contended that the statute cannot be applied to the language used by the defendant because of its protection by the freedom of speech or press, it must necessarily be found, as an original question, without any previous determination by the legislative body, whether the specific language used involved such likelihood of bringing about the substantive evil as to deprive it of the constitutional protection. In such cases it has been held that the general provisions of the statute may be constitutionally applied to the specific utterance of the defendant if its natural tendency and probable effect was to bring about the substantive evil which the legislative body might prevent. Schenck v. United States [249 U.S. 47, 51]; Debs v. United States [249 U.S. 211, 215, 216]. And the general statement in the *Schenck Case,* p. 52, that the "question in every case is whether the words used are used in such circumstances and are of such a nature as to create a clear and present danger that they will bring about the substantive evils,"— upon which great reliance is placed in the defendant's argument—was manifestly intended, as shown by the context, to apply only in cases of this class, and has no application to those like the present, where the legislative body itself has previously determined the danger of substantive evil arising from utterances of a specified character....

And finding, for the reasons stated, that the statute is not in itself unconstitutional, and that it has not been applied in the present case in derogation of any constitutional right, the judgment of the Court of Appeals is

Affirmed.

Mr. Justice Holmes, dissenting. Mr. Justice Brandeis and I are of opinion that this judgment should be reversed. The general principle of free speech, it seems to me, must be taken to be included in the Fourteenth Amendment, in view of the scope that has been given to the word "liberty" as there used, although perhaps it may be accepted with a somewhat larger latitude of interpretation than is allowed to Congress by the sweeping language that governs or ought to govern the laws of the United States. If I am right then I think that the criterion sanctioned by the full Court in Schenck v. United States, 249 U.S. 47, 52, applies.... It is true that in my opinion this criterion was departed from in Abrams v. United States, 250 U.S. 616, but the convictions that I expressed in that case are too deep for it to be possible for me as yet to believe that it and Schaefer v. United States, 251 U.S. 466, have settled the law. If what I think the correct test is applied, it is manifest that there was no present danger of an attempt to overthrow the government by force on the part of the admittedly small minority who shared the defendant's views. It is said that this manifesto was more than a theory, that it was an incitement. Every idea is an incitement. It offers itself for belief and if believed it is acted on unless some other belief outweighs it or some failure of energy stifles the movement at its birth. The only difference between the expression of an opinion and an incitement in the narrower sense is the speaker's enthusiasm for the result. Eloquence may set fire to reason. But whatever may be thought of the redundant discourse before us it had no chance of starting a present conflagration. If in the long run the beliefs expressed in proletarian dictatorship are destined to be accepted by the dominant forces of the community, the only meaning of free speech is that they should be given their chance and have their way.

If the publication of this document had been laid as an attempt to induce an uprising against government at once and not at some indefinite time in the future it would have presented a different question. The object would have been one with which the law might deal, subject to the doubt whether there was any danger that the publication could produce any result, or in other words whether it was not futile and too remote from possible consequences. But the indictment alleges the publication and nothing more.

WHITNEY v. CALIFORNIA, 274 U.S. 357 (1927), arose under the California Criminal Syndicalism Act that defined "criminal syndicalism" as any doctrine advocating, teaching or abetting sabotage or other unlawful acts of violence as a means of accomplishing industrial or political change. It was a crime for any person to organize, assist in organizing, or knowingly become a member of any organization or group of persons associated to advocate, teach or abet criminal syndicalism.

Whitney was a socialist who in 1919 became a temporary member of the new Communist Labor Party and went as a delegate to a convention for organizing a California branch. There she supported a resolution which would have committed the organization to the use of peaceful and lawful methods of change, but this resolution lost and the convention adopted a program resembling Gitlow's Left Wing Manifesto. Whitney was found guilty under the act in that she assisted in organizing and knowingly became a member of a group formed to advocate criminal syndicalism.

The United States Supreme Court sustained the conviction. The majority opinion made two principal points: (a) Whether or not Miss Whitney helped organize and became a member of the Communist Labor Party with knowledge of its program of criminal syndicalism was a question of fact upon which the verdict of the jury was conclusive. (b) The California act "may not be declared unconstitutional unless it is an arbitrary or unreasonable attempt to exercise the authority vested in the state in the public interest." Because of the danger to the public peace and security from an organization advocating violent and unlawful methods of change, the act could not be regarded as an unreasonable exercise of the police power, unwarrantably infringing any right of free speech and assembly.

Justice Brandeis, although concurring in affirmance for procedural reasons, wrote a major opinion, joined by Justice Holmes, disagreeing with the Court's analysis. He said in part:

"Those who won our independence believed that the final end of the State was to make men free to develop their faculties, and that in its government the deliberative forces should prevail over the arbitrary. They valued liberty both as an end and as a means. They believed liberty to be the secret of happiness and courage to be the secret of liberty. They believed that freedom to think as you will and to speak as you think are means indispensable to the discovery and spread of political truth; that without free speech and assembly discussion would be futile; that with them, discussion affords ordinarily adequate protection against the dissemination of noxious doctrine; that the greatest menace to freedom is an inert people; that public discussion is a political duty; and that this should be a fundamental principle of the American government. They recognized the risks to which all human institutions are subject. But they knew that order cannot be secured merely through fear of punishment for its infraction; that it is hazardous to discourage thought, hope and imagination; that fear breeds repression; that repression breeds hate; that hate menaces stable government; that the path of safety lies in the opportunity to discuss freely supposed grievances and proposed remedies; and that the fitting remedy for evil counsels is good ones. Believing in the power of reason as applied through public discussion, they eschewed silence coerced by law—the argument of force in its worst form. Recognizing the occasional tyrannies of governing majorities, they amended the Constitution so that free speech and assembly should be guaranteed.

"Fear of serious injury cannot alone justify suppression of free speech and assembly. Men feared witches and burnt women. It is the function of speech to free men from the bondage of irrational fears. To justify suppression of free speech there must be reasonable ground to fear that serious evil will result if free speech is practiced. There must be reasonable ground to believe that the danger apprehended is imminent. There must be reasonable ground to believe that the evil to be prevented is a serious one. Every denunciation of existing law tends in some measure to increase the probability that there will be a violation of it. Condonation of a breach enhances the probability. Expressions of approval add to the probability. Propagation of the criminal state of mind by teaching syndicalism increases it. Advocacy of law-breaking heightens it still further. But even advocacy of violation, however reprehensible morally, is not a justification for denying free speech where the advocacy falls short of incitement and there is nothing to indicate that the advocacy would be immediately acted on. The wide difference between advocacy and incitement, between preparation and attempt, between assembling and conspiracy, must be borne in mind. In order to support a finding of clear and present danger it must be shown either that immediate serious violence was to be expected or was advocated, or that the past conduct furnished reason to believe that such advocacy was then contemplated."

"Those who won our independence by revolution were not cowards. They did not fear political change. They did not exalt order at the cost of liberty. To courageous, self-reliant men, with confidence in the power of free and fearless reasoning applied through the processes of popular government, no danger flowing from speech can be deemed clear and present, unless the incidence of the evil apprehended is so imminent that it may befall before there is opportunity for full discussion. If there be time to expose through discussion the falsehood and fallacies, to avert the evil by the processes of education, the remedy to be applied is more speech, not enforced silence. Only an emergency can justify repression. Such must be the rule if authority is to be reconciled with freedom. Such, in my opinion, is the command of the Constitution. It is therefore always open to Americans to challenge a law abridging free speech and assembly by showing that there was no emergency justifying it.

"Moreover, even imminent danger cannot justify resort to prohibition of these functions essential to effective democracy, unless the evil apprehended is relatively serious. Prohibition of free speech and assembly is a measure so stringent that it would be inappropriate as the means for averting a relatively trivial harm to society. A police measure may be unconstitutional merely because the remedy, although effective as means of protection, is unduly harsh or oppressive. Thus, a State might, in the exercise of its police power, make any trespass upon the land of another a crime, regardless of the results or of the intent or purpose of the trespasser. It might, also, punish an attempt, a conspiracy, or an incitement to commit the trespass. But it is hardly conceivable that this Court would hold constitutional a statute which punished as a felony the mere voluntary assembly with a society formed to teach that pedestrians had the moral right to cross unenclosed, unposted, waste lands and to advocate their doing so, even if there was imminent danger that advocacy would lead to a trespass. The fact that speech is likely to result in some violence or in destruction of property is not enough to justify its suppression. There must be the probability of serious injury to the State. Among free men, the deterrents ordinarily to be applied to prevent crime are education and punishment for violations of the law, not abridgement of the rights of free speech and assembly...."[a]

THE BASIS OF THE BRANDEIS CONCURRENCE IN THE WHITNEY CASE

Because Justice Brandeis' opinion in *Whitney* is both the most articulate and passionate defense of the clear and present danger test, it is often forgotten that he and Justice Holmes voted to affirm Anita Whitney's conviction. The reason for concurrence was explained as follows:

"Whether in 1919, when Miss Whitney did the things complained of, there was in California such clear and present danger of serious evil, might have been made the important issue in the case. She might have required that the issue be determined either by the court or the jury. She claimed below that the statute as applied to her violated the Federal Constitution; but she did not claim that it was void because there was no clear and present danger of serious evil, nor did she request that the existence of these conditions of a valid measure thus restricting the rights of free speech and assembly be passed upon by the court or a jury. On the other hand, there was evidence on which the court or jury might have found that such danger existed. I am unable to assent to the suggestion in the opinion of the Court that assembling with a political party, formed to advocate the desirability of a proletarian revolution by mass action at some date necessarily far in the future, is not a right within the protection of the Fourteenth Amendment. In the present case, however, there was other testimony which tended to establish the existence of a conspiracy, on the part of members of the International Workers of the World, to commit present serious crimes; and likewise to show that such a conspiracy would be furthered by the activity of the society of which Miss Whitney was a member.

[a] The Whitney case and its background are discussed in Chafee, *Free Speech in the United States* (1941), pp. 343–354. Shortly after the Supreme Court's decision, Miss Whitney was pardoned by Governor Young of California, who in giving reasons for his action made reference to the opinion of Justice Brandeis.

Under these circumstances the judgment of the state court cannot be disturbed."

Note that the defendant was not charged with illegal advocacy, but was convicted for organizing and being a member of a group engaged in unlawful advocacy. Moreover, there was no evidence that she engaged personally in the unlawful advocacy. To the contrary, she had sponsored a competing resolution at the group's organizing meeting calling for peaceful and lawful change. Suppose the clear and present danger defense had been raised at the criminal trial, but it had been found, on sufficient evidence, that the party advocated present serious crimes, and that there was a clear and present danger that those crimes would be committed. Under the position of Justices Brandeis and Holmes, would the fact that defendant disagreed with the advocacy of criminal conduct and did not personally participate in that advocacy be the basis of a viable first amendment defense? Would it be sufficient for conviction that she remained as an active party member, knowing of its illegal advocacy?

DE JONGE v. OREGON, 299 U.S. 353 (1937). De Jonge was convicted on an indictment charging violation of the Oregon Criminal Syndicalism Law which defined "criminal syndicalism" as "the doctrine which advocates crime, physical violence, sabotage or any unlawful acts or methods as a means of accomplishing or effecting industrial or political change or revolution." Among the offenses created were the teaching of criminal syndicalism, the printing or distribution of material advocating the doctrine, the organization of a society or group which advocates it, and presiding at or assisting in conducting a meeting of such an organization, society or group.

The indictment charged that the defendant had unlawfully presided at, and assisted in conducting "an assemblage of persons", to wit, the Communist Party, "which said assemblage of persons" did then and there unlawfully teach and advocate the doctrine of criminal syndicalism.

The evidence showed that De Jonge was a member of the Communist Party; that he presided over and otherwise participated in the public meeting held in Portland, Oregon, under the auspices of the Communist Party; that the meeting was held to protest against illegal raids on workers' halls and homes, and against the shooting of striking longshoremen by the Portland police; and at the meeting there were no unlawful acts done, nor any advocacy of criminal syndicalism. The Supreme Court of Oregon affirmed the conviction on the ground that in addition to the above evidence, there was evidence to show, as the indictment had charged, that the Communist Party at other times and places in Oregon, had taught and advocated criminal syndicalism.

Chief Justice Hughes, speaking for a unanimous Court, delivered an opinion containing the following paragraphs:

"Conviction upon a charge not made would be sheer denial of due process. It thus appears that, while defendant was a member of the Communist Party, he was not indicted for participating in its organization, or for joining it, or for soliciting members or for distributing its literature. He was not charged with teaching or advocating criminal syndicalism or sabotage or any unlawful acts, either at the meeting or elsewhere. He was accordingly deprived of the benefit of evidence as to the orderly and lawful conduct of the meeting and that it was not called or used for the advocacy of criminal syndicalism or sabotage or any unlawful action. His sole offense as charged, and for which he was convicted and sentenced to imprisonment for seven years, was that he had assisted in the conduct of a public meeting, albeit otherwise lawful, which was held under the auspices of the Communist Party.

"...

"Freedom of speech and of the press are fundamental rights which are safeguarded by the due process clause of the Fourteenth Amendment of the Federal Constitution.... The right of peaceable assembly is a right cognate to those of free speech and free press and is equally fundamental. As this Court said in United States v. Cruikshank, 92 U.S. 542, 552: 'The very idea of a government, republican in form, implies a right on the part of its citizens to meet peaceably for consultation in respect to public affairs and to petition for a redress of grievances.' The First Amendment of the Federal Constitution expressly guarantees that right against abridgment by Congress. But explicit mention there does not argue exclusion elsewhere. For the right is one that cannot be denied without violating those fundamental principles of liberty and justice which lie at the base of all civil and political institutions—principles which the Fourteenth Amendment embodies in the general terms of its due process clause....

"...

"It follows from these considerations that, consistently with the Federal Constitution, peaceable assembly for lawful discussion cannot be made a crime. The holding of meetings for peaceable political action cannot be proscribed. Those who assist in the conduct of such meetings cannot be branded as criminals on that score. The question, if the rights of free speech and peaceable assembly are to be preserved, is not as to the auspices under which the meeting is held but as to its purpose; not as to the relations of the speakers, but whether their utterances transcend the bounds of the freedom of speech which the Constitution protects. If the persons assembling have committed crimes elsewhere, if they have formed or are engaged in a conspiracy against the public peace and order, they may be prosecuted for their conspiracy or other violation of valid laws. But it is a different matter when the State, instead of prosecuting them for such offenses, seizes upon mere participation in a peaceable assembly and a lawful public discussion as the basis for a criminal charge.

"We are not called upon to review the findings of the state court as to the objectives of the Communist Party. Notwithstanding those objectives, the defendant still enjoyed his personal right of free speech and to take part in a peaceable assembly having a lawful purpose, although called by that Party. The defendant was none the less entitled to discuss the public issues of the day and thus in a lawful manner, without incitement to violence or crime, to seek redress of alleged grievances. That was of the essence of his guaranteed personal liberty."

C.   THE POST WORLD WAR II COLD WAR ERA: PROSECUTION OF COMMUNISTS UNDER THE SMITH ACT

THE SMITH ACT

During the years that followed the Second World War, anti-radical hysteria surpassed that of the Great Red Scare of the 1920's. The focus this time was the Russian threat, and the specific concern was espionage and subversion by the Communist Party of the United States. The output of both the national and state legislatures, passing laws dealing with loyalty and security, was enormous during this period. So too, were the number of cases, many decided by the United States Supreme Court. The cases that follow are only a small part of the story of the Supreme Court's treatment of anti-Communist legislation during the years of the cold war and after. They are, however, an important part since they continue the debate begun in *Schenck, Abrams, Gitlow* and *Whitney*.

The *Dennis* case, which follows, resulted from federal prosecution of the Communist Party's top national leaders. The *Yates* and *Scales* cases involved prosecutions of lower level Communist Party officials, that followed in the wake of the Court's affirmance of the convictions in *Dennis*. Ironically, the legislation under which the prosecutions were initiated had been enacted prior to the war. The Smith Act was passed in 1940 as a rider to other legislation and received little attention in or out of Congress until it was employed, after the war, as the vehicle for prosecution of Communist Party officials. The Smith Act was patterned on the New York Criminal Anarchy Act which had been sustained in Gitlow v. New York.

DENNIS v. UNITED STATES, 341 U.S. 494 (1951). Petitioners, leaders of the Communist Party, were prosecuted and convicted in a federal district court in New York of violating the Smith Act which provided:

"Sec. 2(a). It shall be unlawful for any person—

"(1) to knowingly or willfully advocate, abet, advise, or teach the duty, necessity, desirability, or propriety of overthrowing or destroying any government in the United States by force or violence, or by the assassination of any officer of any such government;

" . . .

"(3) to organize or help to organize any society, group, or assembly of persons who teach, advocate, or encourage the overthrow or destruction of any government in the United States by force or violence; or to be or become a member of, or affiliate with, any such society, group, or assembly of persons, knowing the purposes thereof. . . .

"Sec. 3. It shall be unlawful for any person to attempt to commit, or to conspire to commit, any of the acts prohibited by the provisions of this title."

The indictment charged petitioners with conspiring (1) to organize as the Communist Party of the United States a group of persons who teach and advocate the overthrow of the Government of the United States by force and violence, and (2) to advocate and teach the duty and necessity of overthrowing the government of the United States by force and violence. After a protracted trial, the judge gave the jury instructions which included the following:

"In further construction and interpretation of the statute I charge you that it is not the abstract doctrine of overthrowing or destroying organized government by unlawful means which is denounced by this law, but the teaching and advocacy of action for the accomplishment of that purpose, by language reasonably and ordinarily calculated to incite persons to such action. Accordingly, you cannot find the defendants or any of them guilty of the crime charged unless you are satisfied beyond a reasonable doubt that they conspired to organize a society, group and assembly of persons who teach and advocate the overthrow or destruction of the Government of the United States by force and violence and to advocate and teach the duty and necessity of overthrowing or destroying the Government of the United States by force and violence, with the intent that such teaching and advocacy be of a rule or principle of action and by language reasonably and ordinarily calculated to incite persons to such action, all with the intent to cause the overthrow or destruction of the Government of the United States by force and violence as speedily as circumstances would permit.

"...

"If you are satisfied that the evidence establishes beyond a reasonable doubt that the defendants, or any of them, are guilty of a violation of the statute, as I have interpreted it to you, I find as matter of law that there is sufficient danger of a substantive evil that the Congress has a right to prevent to justify the application of the statute under the First Amendment of the Constitution.

"This is [a] matter of law about which you have no concern. It is a finding on a matter of law which I deem essential to support my ruling that the case should be submitted to you to pass upon the guilt or innocence of the defendants."

The convictions were affirmed by the Court of Appeals and the Supreme Court granted certiorari limited to the question of the constitutionality of the Smith Act as construed and applied. Several opinions were written, none of which obtained the approval of sufficient Justices to make it the opinion of the Court.

The opinion receiving the greatest assent was by Chief Justice Vinson, joined by Justices Reed, Burton and Minton. "The obvious purpose of the statute," said the Chief Justice, "is to protect existing Government, not from change by peaceable, lawful and constitutional means, but from change by violence, revolution and terrorism." Although the statute was inapplicable to "peaceful studies and discussions or teaching and advocacy in the realm of ideas," it did limit speech. Therefore, the case "squarely presented" the Court with the application of the "clear and present danger" test and required a decision as to "what that phrase imports."[a]

"Obviously, the words cannot mean that before the Government may act, it must wait until the *putsch* is about to be executed, the plans have been laid and the signal is awaited. If Government is aware that a group aiming at its overthrow is attempting to indoctrinate its members and to commit them to a course whereby they will strike when the leaders feel the circumstances permit, action by the Government is required. The argument that there is no need for Government to concern itself, for Government is strong, it possesses ample powers to put down a rebellion, it may defeat the revolution with ease needs no answer. For that is not the question. Certainly an attempt to overthrow the Government by force, even though doomed from the outset because of inadequate numbers or power of the revolutionists, is a sufficient evil for Congress to prevent....

"The situation with which Justices Holmes and Brandeis were concerned in *Gitlow* was a comparatively isolated event, bearing little relation in their minds to any substantial threat to the safety of the community.... They were not confronted with any situation comparable to the instant one—the development of an apparatus designed and dedicated to the overthrow of the Government, in the context of world crisis after crisis.

"Chief Judge Learned Hand, writing for the majority below, interpreted the phrase as follows: 'In each case [courts] must ask whether the gravity of the "evil," discounted by its improbability, justifies such invasion of free speech as is necessary to avoid the danger.' 183 F.2d at 212. We adopt this statement of the rule. As articulated by Chief Judge Hand, it is as succinct and inclusive as

[a] The Chief Justice made it clear that he regarded the views of Holmes and Brandeis as having won the acceptance of the Court. "Although no case subsequent to *Whitney* and *Gitlow* has expressly overruled the majority opinions in those cases, there is little doubt that subsequent opinions have inclined toward the Holmes–Brandeis rationale."

any other we might devise at this time. It takes into consideration those factors which we deem relevant, and relates their significances. More we cannot expect from words.

"Likewise, we are in accord with the court below, which affirmed the trial court's finding that the requisite danger existed. The mere fact that from the period 1945 to 1948 petitioners' activities did not result in an attempt to overthrow the Government by force and violence is of course no answer to the fact that there was a group that was ready to make the attempt. The formation by petitioners of such a highly organized conspiracy, with rigidly disciplined members subject to call when the leaders, these petitioners, felt that the time had come for action, coupled with the inflammable nature of world conditions, similar uprisings in other countries, and the touch-and-go nature of our relations with countries with whom petitioners were in the very least ideologically attuned, convince us that their convictions were justified on this score. And this analysis disposes of the contention that a conspiracy to advocate, as distinguished from the advocacy itself, cannot be constitutionally restrained, because it comprises only the preparation. It is the existence of the conspiracy which creates the danger.... If the ingredients of the reaction are present, we cannot bind the Government to wait until the catalyst is added."

The Chief Justice also approved of the ruling below that withheld the issue of clear and present danger from the jury. "Bearing, as it does, the marks of a 'question of law,' the issue is properly one for the judge to decide."

He concluded that the convictions should be affirmed.

Justice Frankfurter wrote an extensive concurring opinion in which he emphasized the importance of a careful examination of the conflicting interests of national security and free speech which the Court was required to assess in order to arrive at its decision. He believed that the prior decisions resolving conflicts between speech and competing interests, when viewed as a whole, expressed an attitude toward the judicial function and a standard of values which were decisive of the case. "Free-speech cases are not an exception to the principle that we are not legislators, that direct policy-making is not our province. How best to reconcile competing interests is the business of legislatures, and the balance they strike is a judgment not to be displaced by ours, but to be respected unless outside the pale of fair judgment."

Justice Jackson's concurring opinion contended that the clear and present danger test was inapplicable since the prosecution was for conspiracy and under circumstances greatly different from those in *Gitlow, Whitney,* and earlier cases. "I would save it, unmodified, for application as a 'rule of reason' in the kind of case for which it was devised. When the issue is criminality of a hot-headed speech on a street corner, or circulation of a few incendiary pamphlets, or parading by some zealots behind a red flag, or refusal of a handful of school children to salute our flag, it is not beyond the capacity of the judicial process to gather, comprehend, and weigh the necessary materials for decision whether it is a clear and present danger of substantive evil or a harmless letting off of steam."

Justice Black's dissenting opinion emphasized that petitioners were not charged with an attempt to overthrow the Government, or with overt acts designed to overthrow the Government, or even with saying anything or writing anything designed to overthrow the Government. He argued that section 3 of the Smith Act was unconstitutional as a "virulent form of prior censorship of speech and press" in violation of the First Amendment. Justice Douglas also dissented, warning against the dangers of basing a prosecution for seditious conspiracy on speech alone. To make the criminality of the teaching of doctrine turn solely on the intent with which it is taught, made the offense similar to the old English crime of constructive treason. As to the clear and present danger rule, he observed:

"There comes a time when even speech loses its constitutional immunity. Speech innocuous one year may at another time fan such destructive flames that it must be halted in the interests of the safety of the Republic. That is the meaning of the clear and present danger test. When conditions are so critical that there will be no time to avoid the evil that the speech threatens, it is time to call a halt. Otherwise, free speech which is the strength of the Nation will be the cause of its destruction.

"Yet free speech is the rule, not the exception. The restraint to be constitutional must be based on more than fear, on more than passionate opposition against the speech, on more than a revolted dislike for its contents. There must be some immediate injury to society that is likely if speech is allowed."

Justice Clark did not participate in the disposition of the case. The convictions were affirmed by a vote of six to two.

CLEAR AND PRESENT DANGER AS A TEST FOR THE VALIDITY OF LEGISLATION

It will be recalled that the Court in Gitlow v. New York rejected the clear and present danger test, noting that it had been used in Schenck v. United States only for the purpose of deciding when a defendant's speech violated a law that punished conduct. The *Gitlow* majority held that clear and present danger was an irrelevant concept when a law criminally punished certain categories of speech. Chief Justice Vinson's plurality opinion in Dennis v. United States conceded that the *Gitlow* rationale would make the clear and present danger test inapplicable to the Smith Act convictions reviewed by the Court, but he concluded that intervening Court opinions "have inclined toward the Holmes–Brandeis rationale." Accordingly, he interpreted that rationale as requiring an inquiry as to whether a clear and present danger justified application of the Smith Act to the particular facts. (The Court did not, however, review the sufficiency of the evidence to sustain the convictions, since that question had been removed from the case by the Court's limited grant of certiorari.)

Hans Linde argues that, although the decision was wrong in its result, the *Gitlow* court was right in rejecting clear and present danger as a test for determining the validity of laws that punish speech. Linde, *"Clear and Present Danger" Reexamined: Dissonance in the Brandenburg Concerto,* 22 Stan.L.Rev. 1163 (1970). He summarizes his position as follows: "The objective conditions under which the particular expression occurs . . .—whether stated as 'clear and present danger' or some other formula—can be a factor at the time when suppression of that particular occurrence is before a court. It cannot easily be an element in the constitutionality of the decision to make a law proscribing a kind of speech or publication for the future." (Linde would reserve the clear and present danger test for cases, like *Schenck,* where the statute punished conduct and the defendant's speech was claimed to be a violation. He would invalidate the Smith Act under his standard for reviewing legislation directed against the communicative content of speech or press, arguing that the first amendment invalidates a law punishing speech if the proscribed content falls *under any circumstances* within the protection of the first amendment.)

Yates v. United States

354 U.S. 298, 77 S.Ct. 1064, 1 L.Ed.2d 1356 (1957).

Mr. Justice Harlan delivered the opinion of the Court.

We brought these cases here to consider certain questions arising under the Smith Act ... and otherwise to review the convictions of these petitioners for conspiracy to violate that Act. Among other things, the convictions are claimed to rest upon an application of the Smith Act which is hostile to the principles upon which its constitutionality was upheld in Dennis v. United States, 341 U.S. 494.

These 14 petitioners stand convicted, after a jury trial in the United States District Court for the Southern District of California, upon a single count indictment charging them with conspiring (1) to advocate and teach the duty and necessity of overthrowing the Government of the United States by force and violence, and (2) to organize, as the Communist Party of the United States, a society of persons who so advocate and teach, all with the intent of causing the overthrow of the Government by force and violence as speedily as circumstances would permit....

. . .

Petitioners contend that the instructions to the jury were fatally defective in that the trial court refused to charge that, in order to convict, the jury must find that the advocacy which the defendants conspired to promote was of a kind calculated to "incite" persons to action for the forcible overthrow of the Government. It is argued that advocacy of forcible overthrow as mere *abstract doctrine* is within the free speech protection of the First Amendment; that the Smith Act, consistently with that constitutional provision, must be taken as proscribing only the sort of advocacy which incites to illegal *action;* and that the trial court's charge, by permitting conviction for mere advocacy, unrelated to its tendency to produce forcible action, resulted in an unconstitutional application of the Smith Act. The Government, which at the trial also requested the court to charge in terms of "incitement," now takes the position, however, that the true constitutional dividing line is not between inciting and abstract advocacy of forcible overthrow, but rather between advocacy as such, irrespective of its inciting qualities, and the mere discussion or exposition of violent overthrow as an abstract theory....

There can be no doubt from the record that in so instructing the jury the court regarded as immaterial, and intended to withdraw from the jury's consideration, any issue as to the character of the advocacy in terms of its capacity to stir listeners to forcible action....

We are thus faced with the question whether the Smith Act prohibits advocacy and teaching of forcible overthrow as an abstract principle, divorced from any effort to instigate action to that end, so long as such advocacy or teaching is engaged in with evil intent. We hold that it does not.

The distinction between advocacy of abstract doctrine and advocacy directed at promoting unlawful action is one that has been consistently recognized in the opinions of this Court, beginning with Fox v. Washington, 236 U.S. 273; and Schenck v. United States, 249 U.S. 47. This distinction was heavily underscored in Gitlow v. New York, 268 U.S. 652....

We need not, however, decide the issue before us in terms of constitutional compulsion, for our first duty is to construe this statute. In doing so we should not assume that Congress chose to disregard a constitutional danger zone so clearly marked, or that it used the words "advocate" and "teach" in their ordinary dictionary meanings when they had already been construed as terms of art carrying a special and limited connotation. . . .

. . .

In failing to distinguish between advocacy of forcible overthrow as an abstract doctrine and advocacy of action to that end, the District Court appears to have been led astray by the holding in *Dennis* that advocacy of violent action to be taken at some future time was enough. It seems to have considered that, since "inciting" speech is usually thought of as something calculated to induce immediate action, and since *Dennis* held advocacy of action for future overthrow sufficient, this meant that advocacy, irrespective of its tendency to generate action, is punishable, provided only that it is uttered with a specific intent to accomplish overthrow. In other words, the District Court apparently thought that *Dennis* obliterated the traditional dividing line between advocacy of abstract doctrine and advocacy of action.

This misconceives the situation confronting the Court in *Dennis* and what was held there. Although the jury's verdict, interpreted in light of the trial court's instructions, did not justify the conclusion that the defendants' advocacy was directed at, or created any danger of, immediate overthrow, it did establish that the advocacy was aimed at building up a seditious group and maintaining it in readiness for action at a propitious time. . . . The essence of the *Dennis* holding was that indoctrination of a group in preparation for future violent action, as well as exhortation to immediate action, by advocacy found to be directed to "action for the accomplishment" of forcible overthrow, to violence as "a rule or principle of action," and employing "language of incitement," . . . is not constitutionally protected when the group is of sufficient size and cohesiveness, is sufficiently oriented towards action, and other circumstances are such as reasonably to justify apprehension that action will occur. This is quite a different thing from the view of the District Court here that mere doctrinal justification of forcible overthrow, if engaged in with the intent to accomplish overthrow, is punishable *per se* under the Smith Act. That sort of advocacy, even though uttered with the hope that it may ultimately lead to violent revolution, is too remote from concrete action to be regarded as the kind of indoctrination preparatory to action which was condemned in *Dennis*. As one of the concurring opinions in *Dennis* put it: "Throughout our decisions there has recurred a distinction between the statement of an idea which may prompt its hearers to take unlawful action, and advocacy that such action be taken." . . . There is nothing in *Dennis* which makes that historic distinction obsolete.

. . .

In light of the foregoing we are unable to regard the District Court's charge upon this aspect of the case as adequate. The jury was never told that the Smith Act does not denounce advocacy in the sense of preaching abstractly the forcible overthrow of the Government. We think that the trial court's statement that the proscribed advocacy must include the "urging," "necessity," and "duty" of forcible overthrow, and not merely its "desirability" and "propriety," may not be regarded as a sufficient substitute for charging that the Smith Act reaches only advocacy of action for the overthrow of government by force and violence. The essential distinction is that those to whom the advocacy is addressed must be urged to *do* something, now or in the future, rather than merely to *believe* in something. . . .

. . .

[The Court ordered an acquittal of five of the 14 petitioners,[a] finding "no adequate evidence in the record" to sustain their convictions on retrial.][b]

Mr. Justice Brennan and Mr. Justice Whittaker took no part in the consideration or decision of this case.

Mr. Justice Black, with whom Mr. Justice Douglas joins, concurring in part and dissenting in part.

I would reverse every one of these convictions and direct that all the defendants be acquitted. In my judgment the statutory provisions on which these prosecutions are based abridge freedom of speech, press and assembly in violation of the First Amendment to the United States Constitution. See my dissent and that of Mr. Justice Douglas in Dennis v. United States, 341 U.S. 494, 579, 581. . . .

. . .

Mr. Justice Clark, dissenting.

The petitioners, principal organizers and leaders of the Communist Party in California, have been convicted for a conspiracy covering the period 1940 to 1951. They were engaged in this conspiracy with the defendants in Dennis v. United States, 341 U.S. 494 (1951). . . .

. . .

The conspiracy includes the same group of defendants as in the *Dennis* case though petitioners here occupied a lower echelon in the party hierarchy. . . . The convictions here were based upon evidence closely paralleling that adduced in *Dennis* . . .

I would affirm the convictions. . . .

. . .

Scales v. United States

367 U.S. 203, 81 S.Ct. 1469, 6 L.Ed.2d 782 (1961).

[Petitioner, Chairman of the North and South Carolina Districts of the Communist Party, was convicted of violating the membership clause of the Smith Act (18 U.S.C. § 2385), which made it a crime to become a member of an organization advocating the overthrow of the government by force or violence, knowing the purposes of such organization.[1] The trial court had instructed the

---

[a] Upon remand of the *Yates* case, the lower court dismissed the indictments against the remaining defendants who had not been acquitted by the Supreme Court. This action was "reluctantly" requested by the Government because it could not "satisfy the evidentiary requirements laid down by the Supreme Court in its opinion reversing the conviction in this matter." New York Times, Dec. 3, 1957, p. 71.

[b] The types of evidence that led the Court to order the five acquitted, and not the remaining nine, are summarized in *Scales v. United States*, infra.

[1] Section 2385 (whose membership clause we place in italics) reads: . . .

"Whoever organizes or helps or attempts to organize any society, group, or assembly of persons who teach, advocate, or encourage the overthrow or destruction of any such government by force or violence; *or becomes or is a member of*, or affiliates with, *any such society, group, or assembly of persons, knowing the purposes thereof—*

"Shall be fined not more than $20,000 or imprisoned not more than twenty years, or both, and shall be ineligible for employment by the United States or any department or agency thereof, for the five years next following his conviction." . . .

[Court's footnote.]

jury that in order to convict it must find that (1) the Communist Party advocated the violent overthrow of the government, in the sense of present "advocacy of action" to accomplish that end as soon as circumstances were propitious; and (2) petitioner was an "active" member of the Party, and not merely "a nominal, passive, inactive, or purely technical" member with knowledge of the Party's illegal advocacy and a specific intent to bring about overthrow "as speedily as circumstances would permit." The Supreme Court affirmed the conviction.]

Mr. Justice Harlan delivered the opinion of the Court.

. . .

1.   Constitutional Challenge to the Membership Clause on Its Face. . . .

Any thought that due process puts beyond the reach of the criminal law all individual associational relationships, unless accompanied by the commission of specific acts of criminality, is dispelled by familiar concepts of the law of conspiracy and complicity. . . . In this instance it is an organization which engages in criminal activity, and we can perceive no reason why one who actively and knowingly works in the ranks of that organization, intending to contribute to the success of those specifically illegal activities, should be any more immune from prosecution than he to whom the organization has assigned the task of carrying out the substantive criminal act . . .

. . . It must indeed be recognized that a person who merely becomes a member of an illegal organization, by that "act" alone need be doing nothing more than signifying his assent to its purposes and activities on one hand, and providing, on the other, only the sort of moral encouragement which comes from the knowledge that others believe in what the organization is doing. . . .

. . . [T]hese factors have weight and must be found to be overborne in a total constitutional assessment of the statute. We think, however, they are duly met when the statute is found to reach only "active" members having also a guilty knowledge and intent, and which therefore prevents a conviction on what otherwise might be regarded as merely an expression of sympathy with the alleged criminal enterprise, unaccompanied by any significant action in its support or any commitment to undertake such action.

. . .

. . . It was settled in *Dennis* that the advocacy with which we are here concerned is not constitutionally protected speech, and it was further established that a combination to promote such advocacy, albeit under the aegis of what purports to be a political party, is not such association as is protected by the First Amendment. We can discern no reason why membership, when it constitutes a purposeful form of complicity in a group engaging in this same forbidden advocacy, should receive any greater degree of protection from the guarantees of that Amendment. . . .

2.   Evidentiary Challenge

. . .

On this phase of the case petitioner's principal contention is that the evidence was insufficient to establish that the Communist Party was engaged in present advocacy of violent overthrow of the Government in the sense required by the Smith Act, that is, in "advocacy of action" for the accomplishment of such overthrow either immediately or as soon as circumstances proved propitious, and uttered in terms reasonably calculated to "incite" to such action. . . .

This contention rests largely on the proposition that the evidence on this aspect of the case does not differ materially from that which the Court in *Yates* stated was inadequate to establish that sort of Party advocacy there.

. . .

We agree with petitioner that the evidentiary question here is controlled in large part by *Yates*. The decision in *Yates* rested on the view (not articulated in the opinion, though perhaps it should have been) that the Smith Act offenses, involving as they do subtler elements than are present in most other crimes, call for strict standards in assessing the adequacy of the proof needed to make out a case of illegal advocacy. This premise is as applicable to prosecutions under the membership clause of the Smith Act as it is to conspiracy prosecutions under that statute as we had in *Yates*.

The impact of *Yates* with respect to this petitioner's evidentiary challenge is not limited, however, to that decision's requirement of strict standards of proof. *Yates* also articulates general criteria for the evaluation of evidence in determining whether this requirement is met. The *Yates* opinion, through its characterizations of large portions of the evidence which were either described in detail or referred to by reference to the record, indicates what type of evidence is needed to permit a jury to find that (a) there was "advocacy of action" and (b) the Party was responsible for such advocacy.

First, *Yates* makes clear what type of evidence is not *in itself* sufficient to show illegal advocacy. This category includes evidence of the following: the teaching of Marxism–Leninism and the connected use of Marxist "classics" as textbooks; the official general resolutions and pronouncements of the Party at past conventions; dissemination of the Party's general literature, including the standard outlines on Marxism; the Party's history and organizational structure; the secrecy of meetings and the clandestine nature of the Party generally; statements by officials evidencing sympathy for and alliance with the U.S.S.R. It was the predominance of evidence of this type which led the Court to order the acquittal of several *Yates* defendants, with the comment that they had not themselves "made a single remark or been present when someone else made a remark which would tend to prove the charges against them." However, this kind of evidence, while insufficient in itself to sustain a conviction, is not irrelevant. Such evidence in the context of other evidence, may be of value in showing illegal advocacy.

Second, the *Yates* opinion also indicates what kind of evidence is sufficient. There the Court pointed to two series of events which justified the denial of directed acquittals as to nine of the *Yates* defendants. The Court noted that with respect to seven of the defendants, meetings in San Francisco . . . might be considered to be "the systematic teaching and advocacy of illegal action which is condemned by the statute." . . . In those meetings, a small group of members were not only taught that violent revolution was inevitable, but they were also taught techniques for achieving that end. For example, the *Yates* record reveals that members were directed to be prepared to convert a general strike into a revolution and to deal with Negroes so as to prepare them specifically for revolution. In addition to the San Francisco meetings, the Court referred to certain activities in the Los Angeles area "which might be considered to amount to 'advocacy of action' "and with which two *Yates* defendants were linked. . . . Thus, one member was "surreptitiously indoctrinated in methods . . . of moving 'masses of people in time of crisis' "; others were told to adopt such Russian prerevolutionary techniques as the development of a special communication system through a newspaper similar to Pravda. . . . Viewed together, these events described in *Yates* indicate at least two patterns of evidence sufficient to show illegal advocacy: (a) the teaching of forceful overthrow, accompanied by directions as to the type of illegal action which must be taken when the time for the revolution is reached; and (b) the teaching of forceful overthrow, accompanied by a contemporary, though legal, course of conduct clearly undertaken for the specific purpose of rendering effective the later illegal activity which is advocated. . . .

Finally, *Yates* is also relevant here in indicating, at least by implication, the type and quantum of evidence necessary to attach liability for illegal advocacy to the Party. In discussing the Government's "conspiratorial-nexus theory" the Court found that the evidence there was insufficient because the incidents of illegal advocacy were infrequent, sporadic, and not fairly related to the period covered by the indictment. In addition, the Court indicated that the illegal advocacy was not sufficiently tied to officials who spoke for the Party as such.

Thus, in short, *Yates* imposes a strict standard of proof, and indicates the kind of evidence that is insufficient to show illegal advocacy under that standard, the kind of evidence that is sufficient, and what pattern of evidence is necessary to hold the Party responsible for such advocacy. With these criteria in mind, we now proceed to an examination of the evidence in this case.

[The Court's summary of the evidence is omitted.]

We conclude that this evidence sufficed to make a case for the jury on the issue of illegal Party advocacy. *Dennis* and *Yates* have definitely laid at rest any doubt that present advocacy of *future* action for violent overthrow satisfies statutory and constitutional requirements equally with advocacy of *immediate* action to that end. . . . Hence this record cannot be considered deficient because it contains no evidence of advocacy for immediate overthrow.

Since the evidence amply showed that Party leaders were continuously preaching during the indictment period the inevitability of eventual forcible overthrow, the first and basic question is a narrow one: whether the jury could permissibly infer that such preaching, in whole or in part, "was aimed at building up a seditious group and maintaining it in readiness for action at a propitious time . . . the kind of indoctrination preparatory to action which was condemned in *Dennis*." . . . On this score, we think that the jury, under instructions which fully satisfied the requirements of *Yates*, was entitled to infer from this systematic preaching . . . that "advocacy of action" was engaged in.

. . .

Affirmed.

Mr. Justice Black, dissenting.

. . .

. . . I think it is important to point out the manner in which this case re-emphasizes the freedom-destroying nature of the "balancing test" presently in use by the Court to justify its refusal to apply specific constitutional protections of the Bill of Rights. . . . Petitioner is being sent to jail for the express reason that he has associated with people who have entertained unlawful ideas and said unlawful things, and that of course is a *direct* abridgment of his freedoms of speech and assembly—under any definition that has ever been used for that term. . . .

. . .

Mr. Justice Douglas, dissenting.

. . .

The case is not saved by showing that petitioner was an active member. None of the activity constitutes a crime . . . .

Not one single illegal act is charged to petitioner. That is why the essence of the crime covered by the indictment is merely belief—belief in the proletarian revolution, belief in Communist creed.

. . .

Mr. Justice Brennan, with whom The Chief Justice and Mr. Justice Douglas join, dissenting.

[These justices argued that in § 4(f) of the Internal Security Act Congress legislated immunity from prosecution under the membership clause of the Smith Act.][a]

AFTERMATH OF THE YATES, SCALES AND NOTO CASES

Of 141 people indicted under the Smith Act, 29 served prison terms. These included the 11 defendants in *Dennis,* 17 defendants in two cases prior to *Yates* that the Court declined to review, and the single defendant in *Scales.* Emerson, *The System of Freedom of Expression* 124 (1970). The government had turned to membership clause prosecutions after *Yates,* because it concluded that it would be unable to satisfy the Court's requirement that each defendant be proved to have personally advocated specific illegal acts or have participated in such advocacy by others. While the Court sustained the constitutionality of the membership clause in *Scales,* and also sustained the conviction, the *Scales* case marked the end of Smith Act prosecutions. Under the *Scales* and *Noto* cases, was the government required, in a membership clause case, to satisfy the same proof requirements imposed by *Yates?*

Consider, also, whether proof meeting the criteria imposed by the *Yates, Scales* and *Noto* cases would also sustain conviction under two older statutes contained in the federal criminal code, United States Code, Title 18:

§ 2383.   Rebellion or Insurrection

Whoever incites, sets on foot, assists, or engages in any rebellion or insurrection against the authority of the United States or the laws thereof, or gives aid or comfort thereto, shall be fined not more than $10,000 or imprisoned not more than ten years, or both; and shall be incapable of holding any office under the United States.

§ 2384.   Seditious Conspiracy

If two or more persons in any State or Territory, or in any place subject to the jurisdiction of the United States, conspire to overthrow, put

---

[a] Decided the same day as *Scales,* Noto v. United States, 367 U.S. 290 (1961), involved another prosecution under the membership clause of the Smith Act. The conviction was reversed because there was insufficient evidence of illegal Communist Party advocacy. Dicta stated that there must also be proof of the defendant's personal criminal purpose. "This element of the membership crime, like its others, must be judged *strictissimi juris,* for otherwise there is a danger that one in sympathy with the legitimate aims of such an organization, but not specifically intending to accomplish them by resort to violence, might be punished for his adherence to lawful and constitutionally protected purposes, because of other and unprotected purposes which he does not necessarily share." See United States v. Spock, 416 F.2d 165 (1st Cir.1969), reversing the conviction of Dr. Spock and others for conspiracy to counsel, aid, and abet registrants to resist the draft.

down, or to destroy by force the Government of the United States, or to levy war against them, or to oppose by force the authority thereof, or by force to prevent, hinder, or delay the execution of any law of the United States, or by force to seize, take, or possess any property of the United States contrary to the authority thereof, they shall each be fined not more than $20,000 or imprisoned not more than twenty years, or both.

D. THE CURRENT STATUS OF THE CLEAR AND PRESENT DANGER TEST—THE "BRANDENBURG CONCERTO"[1]

Brandenburg v. Ohio

395 U.S. 444, 89 S.Ct. 1827, 23 L.Ed.2d 430 (1969).

Per Curiam.

The appellant, a leader of a Ku Klux Klan group, was convicted under the Ohio Criminal Syndicalism statute for "advocat[ing] . . . the duty, necessity, or propriety of crime, sabotage, violence, or unlawful methods of terrorism as a means of accomplishing industrial or political reform" and for "voluntarily assembl[ing] with any society, group, or assemblage of persons formed to teach or advocate the doctrines of criminal syndicalism." Ohio Rev. Code Ann. § 2923.13. He was fined $1,000 and sentenced to one to 10 years' imprisonment. The appellant challenged the constitutionality of the criminal syndicalism statute under the First and Fourteenth Amendments to the United States Constitution, but the intermediate appellate court of Ohio affirmed his conviction without opinion. The Supreme Court of Ohio dismissed his appeal, *sua sponte,* "for the reason that no substantial constitutional question exists herein." . . . Appeal was taken to this Court, . . . We reverse.

The record shows that a man, identified at trial as the appellant, telephoned an announcer-reporter on the staff of a Cincinnati television station and invited him to come to a Ku Klux Klan "rally" to be held at a farm in Hamilton County. With the cooperation of the organizers, the reporter and a cameraman attended the meeting and filmed the events. Portions of the films were later broadcast on the local station and on a national network.

The prosecution's case rested on the films and on testimony identifying the appellant as the person who communicated with the reporter and who spoke at the rally. The State also introduced into evidence several articles appearing in the film, including a pistol, a rifle, a shotgun, ammunition, a Bible, and a red hood worn by the speaker in the films.

One film showed 12 hooded figures, some of whom carried firearms. They were gathered around a large wooden cross, which they burned. No one was present other than the participants and the newsmen who made the film. Most of the words uttered during the scene were incomprehensible when the film was projected, but scattered phrases could be understood that were derogatory of Negroes and, in one instance, of Jews.[1] Another scene on the same film

---

[1] Linde, supra, p. 1216.

[1] The significant portions that could be understood were:

"How far is the nigger going to—yeah."

"This is what we are going to do to the niggers."

"A dirty nigger."

"Send the Jews back to Israel."

"Let's give them back to the dark garden."

"Save America."

showed the appellant, in Klan regalia, making a speech. The speech, in full, was as follows:

"This is an organizers' meeting. We have had quite a few members here today which are—we have hundreds, hundreds of members throughout the State of Ohio. I can quote from a newspaper clipping from the Columbus, Ohio Dispatch, five weeks ago Sunday morning. The Klan has more members in the State of Ohio than does any other organization. We're not a revengent organization, but if our President, our Congress, our Supreme court, continues to suppress the white, Caucasian race, it's possible that there might have to be some revengeance taken.

"We are marching on Congress July the Fourth, four hundred thousand strong. From there we are dividing into two groups, one group to march on St. Augustine, Florida, the other group to march into Mississippi. Thank you."

The second film showed six hooded figures one of whom, later identified as the appellant, repeated a speech very similar to that recorded on the first film. The reference to the possibility of "revengeance" was omitted, and one sentence was added: "Personally, I believe the nigger should be returned to Africa, the Jew returned to Israel." Though some of the figures in the films carried weapons, the speaker did not.

The Ohio Criminal Syndicalism Statute was enacted in 1919. From 1917 to 1920, identical or quite similar laws were adopted by 20 States and two territories. E. Dowell, A History of Criminal Syndicalism Legislation in the United States 21 (1939). In 1927, this Court sustained the constitutionality of California's Criminal Syndicalism Act, ... the text of which is quite similar to that of the laws of Ohio. Whitney v. California, 274 U.S. 357 (1927). The Court upheld the statute on the ground that, without more, "advocating" violent means to effect political and economic change involves such danger to the security of the State that the State may outlaw it. Cf. Fiske v. Kansas, 274 U.S. 380 (1927). But *Whitney* has been thoroughly discredited by later decisions. See Dennis v. United States, 341 U.S. 494, at 507 (1951). These later decisions have fashioned the principle that the constitutional guarantees of free speech and free press do not permit a State to forbid or proscribe advocacy of the use of force or of law violation except where such advocacy is directed to inciting or producing imminent lawless action and is likely to incite or produce such action.[2] As we said in Noto v. United States, 367 U.S. 290, 297–298 (1961), "the mere abstract teaching ... of the moral propriety or even moral necessity for a resort to force and violence, is not the same as preparing a group for violent action and steeling it to such action." See also Herndon v. Lowry, 301 U.S. 242, 259–261 (1937); Bond v. Floyd, 385 U.S. 116, 134 (1966). A statute which fails to draw this distinction impermissibly intrudes upon the freedoms guaranteed by the First and Fourteenth Amendments. It sweeps within its condemnation

"Let's go back to constitutional betterment."

"Bury the niggers."

"We intend to do our part."

"Give us our state rights."

"Freedom for the whites."

"Nigger will have to fight for every inch he gets from now on."

[2] It was on the theory that the Smith Act, 54 Stat. 670, 18 U.S.C. § 2385, embodied such a principle and that it had been applied only in conformity with it that this Court sustained the Act's constitutionality. Dennis v. United States, 341 U.S. 494 (1951). That this was the basis for *Dennis* was emphasized in Yates v. United States, 354 U.S. 298, 320–324 (1957), in which the Court overturned convictions for advocacy of the forcible overthrow of the Government under the Smith Act, because the trial judge's instructions had allowed conviction for mere advocacy, unrelated to its tendency to produce forcible action.

speech which our Constitution has immunized from governmental control. Cf. Yates v. United States, 354 U.S. 298 (1957); De Jonge v. Oregon, 299 U.S. 353 (1937); Stromberg v. California, 283 U.S. 359 (1931)....

Measured by this test, Ohio's Criminal Syndicalism Act cannot be sustained. The Act punishes persons who "advocate or teach the duty necessity, or propriety" of violence "as a means of accomplishing industrial or political reform"; or who publish or circulate or display any book or paper containing such advocacy; or who "justify" the commission of violent acts "with intent to exemplify, spread or advocate the propriety of the doctrines of criminal syndicalism"; or who "voluntarily assemble" with a group formed "to teach or advocate the doctrines of criminal syndicalism." Neither the indictment nor the trial judge's instructions to the jury in any way refined the statute's bald definition of the crime in terms of mere advocacy not distinguished from incitement to imminent lawless action.[3]

Accordingly, we are here confronted with a statute which, by its own words and as applied, purports to punish mere advocacy and to forbid, on pain of criminal punishment, assembly with others merely to advocate the described type of action.[4] Such a statute falls within the condemnation of the First and Fourteenth Amendments. The contrary teaching of Whitney v. California, supra, cannot be supported, and that decision is therefore overruled.

Reversed.

Mr. Justice Black, concurring.

I agree with the views expressed by Mr. Justice Douglas in his concurring opinion in this case that the "clear and present danger" doctrine should have no place in the interpretation of the First Amendment. I join the Court's opinion, which, as I understand it, simply cites Dennis v. United States, 341 U.S. 494 (1951), but does not indicate any agreement on the Court's part with the "clear and present danger" doctrine on which *Dennis* purported to rely.

Mr. Justice Douglas, concurring.

While I join the opinion of the Court, I desire to enter a *caveat.*

. . .

... I see no place in the regime of the First Amendment for any "clear and present danger" test, whether strict and tight as some would make it, or freewheeling as the Court in *Dennis* rephrased it.

When one reads the opinions closely and sees when and how the "clear and present danger" test has been applied, great misgivings are aroused. First, the threats were often loud but always puny and made serious only by judges so wedded to the *status quo* that critical analysis made them nervous. Second, the

---

[3] The first count of the indictment charged that appellant "did unlawfully by word of mouth advocate the necessity, or propriety of crime, violence, or unlawful methods of terrorism as a means of accomplishing political reform...." The second count charged that appellant "did unlawfully voluntarily assemble with a group or assemblage of persons formed to advocate the doctrines of criminal syndicalism...." The trial judge's charge merely followed the language of the indictment. No construction of the statute by the Ohio courts has brought it within constitutionally permissible limits. The Ohio Supreme Court has considered the statute in only one previous case, State v. Kassay, 126 Ohio St. 177, 184 N.E. 521 (1932), where the constitutionality of the statute was sustained.

[4] Statutes affecting the right of assembly, like those touching on freedom of speech, must observe the established distinctions between mere advocacy and incitement to imminent lawless action, for as Chief Justice Hughes wrote in De Jonge v. Oregon, supra at 364: "The right of peaceable assembly is a right cognate to those of free speech and free press and is equally fundamental." ...

test was so twisted and perverted in *Dennis* as to make the trial of those teachers of Marxism an all-out political trial which was part and parcel of the cold war that has eroded substantial parts of the First Amendment.

. . .

The line between what is permissible and not subject to control and what may be made impermissible and subject to regulation is the line between ideas and overt acts.

The example usually given by those who would punish speech is the case of one who falsely shouts fire in a crowded theatre.

This is, however, a classic case where speech is brigaded with action. They are indeed inseparable and a prosecution can be launched for the overt acts actually caused. Apart from rare instances of that kind, speech is, I think, immune from prosecution. Certainly there is no constitutional line between advocacy of abstract ideas as in *Yates* and advocacy of political action as in *Scales*. The quality of advocacy turns on the depth of the conviction; and government has no power to invade that sanctuary of belief and conscience.[a]

THE CONSTITUTIONAL LAW IMPLICATIONS OF THE COURT'S SMITH ACT INTERPRETATION

Despite the fact that it is a *per curiam* decision[1] and despite possible arguments that much of the discussion of clear and present danger is dicta, *Brandenburg* has been read as an authoritative statement of the Court's position on the minimum protection afforded speech.[2] Subsequent cases have converted other aspects of the Court's construction of the Smith Act in the *Yates* and *Scales* cases into constitutional doctrine.

Even under the position taken by Justices Brandeis and Holmes, people could be punished for knowing membership in an organization advocating the commission of serious crimes, if there was a clear and present danger that those crimes would be committed. Justice Brandeis' *Whitney* concurrence did not require proof that the defendant participated in the advocacy or shared the organization's illegal purposes. Dicta in the *Scales* and *Noto* cases, however, required that there be proof, beyond defendant's knowledge of illegal advocacy by the organization, of the defendant's "active membership" and specific intent to accomplish the organization's illegal aims. Application of those requirements would have required the acquittal of the defendant in the *Whitney* case, even upon proof that her organization advocated specific criminal conduct and that there was a clear and present danger. Those requirements have, however, been converted from interpretations of the Smith Act to first amendment doctrine. The development occurred in a series of cases dealing with government re-

[a] For a review of the development of clear and present danger doctrine from prior to World War I through *Brandenburg,* see Rabban, *The Emergence of Modern First Amendment Doctrine*, 50 U.Chi.L.Rev. 1205 (1983).

[1] It is unusual that the Court's major expression of contemporary first amendment doctrine is contained in an unsigned opinion. The editors have been informed by a reliable source that the opinion had been written by Justice Fortas, who resigned prior to the Court's announcement of the decision. The same source states that the case was regard-

ed as easy in its result, and very little attention was paid to what the opinion said.

[2] E.g., a state conviction for disorderly conduct based on an intemperate speech at a campus anti-war demonstration was reversed, on the authority of *Brandenburg,* in Hess v. Indiana, 414 U.S. 105 (1973). Specifically, the Court held that the *Brandenburg* criteria had not been met both because the defendant's speech did not advocate specific unlawful action, and there was insufficient evidence that his words were likely to produce imminent disorder.

quests for information, qualification for government employment and loyalty oaths; none of the cases involved criminal punishment.[3]

DEFERENCE TO LEGISLATIVE JUDGMENT CONCERNING THE PRESENCE AND EXTENT OF DANGER

A major issue in the clear and present danger debate is whether courts should defer to legislative judgments concerning the danger posed by classes of speech or the defendant's speech. It will be recalled that, in *Gitlow,* the Court noted the New York legislature's implicit determination that *all* revolutionary speech was dangerous, and concluded "it must be given great weight." Justice Frankfurter's concurring opinion in *Dennis* argued that the case presented a clash of interests "[i]t is not for us to decide" since Congress had decided that the danger created by Communist Party speech justified its restriction. 341 U.S. at 550. Chief Justice Vinson's plurality opinion accepted clear and present danger as the appropriate standard, with the obligation of courts to examine whether there is a clear and present danger to justify application of the statute to the specific situation, and thus did not articulately refer to sustaining of legislative judgments. (The rejection of any requirement of imminence allowed the plurality to discover the requisite danger. The Court had, moreover, not granted certiorari to consider the sufficiency of the evidence, so the Court was not required to determine whether any particular Communist Party speech created danger.) Chief Justice Vinson's opinion can be read as implicitly deferring to contemporary legislative and executive judgments concerning the danger to internal security presented by the Communist Party.

The Court discussed the issue of deference to legislative judgment in Landmark Communications, Inc. v. Virginia, 435 U.S. 829 (1978). Chief Justice Burger's opinion for the Court said, in part:

"... Properly applied, the test requires a court to make its own inquiry into the imminence and magnitude of the danger said to flow from the particular utterance and then to balance the character of the evil, as well as its likelihood, against the need for free and unfettered expression. The possibility that other measures will serve the State's interests should also be weighed.

. . .

"A legislature appropriately inquires into and may declare the reasons impelling legislative action but the judicial function commands analysis of whether the specific conduct charged falls within the reach of the statute and if so whether the legislation is consonant with the Constitution. Were it otherwise, the scope of freedom of speech and of the press would be subject to legislative definition and the function of the First Amendment as a check on legislative power would be nullified."

THE CLEAR AND PRESENT DANGER DEBATE—SOME GENERAL CONSIDERATIONS

The earlier debate, in an extensive literature, argued whether a tightly-drawn clear and present danger test was a *necessary* condition for protection of freedom of speech.[1] The Court's current adherence to it has muted that debate,

---

[3] Elfbrandt v. Russell, 384 U.S. 11, 15–16 (1966); Keyishian v. Board of Regents, 385 U.S. 589, 606 (1967); Law Students Civil Rights Research Council, Inc. v. Wadmond, 401 U.S. 154, 165 (1971).

[1] The most articulate defense of the clear and present danger test is contained in Chafee, *Free Speech in the United States* (1941). For a contemporary defense, see Redish, *Ad-*

and brought to the fore the question whether any version of the clear and present danger test is a *sufficient* condition for protection of freedom of speech.[2] Before turning to some of the arguments made in the debate, however, it is important to note that clear and present danger is not a doctrine for all first amendment seasons. In its focus on the danger of illegal conduct, at most its literal application is limited to those cases where the only societal interest asserted for restricting speech is that danger. As will be seen in Section 3 of this chapter, and in the following two chapters, whether or not clear and present danger is the appropriate test for speech urging violation of the law, it is not helpful in other problem areas.[3] Some general themes in the debate are, however, of broader application. Some of those themes are singled out for brief mention, below.

(1) Political Speech Contrasted with Other Forms of Speech. While the clear and present danger test is by its terms directed at any speech advocating the commission of a crime, all of the Supreme Court's cases have, in fact, involved some form of political speech—whether the general platform of a radical organization or a hot-tempered street-corner protest speech. A major criticism of the clear and present danger approach is that it permits stifling of radical political speech based on problematic assessments of public danger, while it over-protects dangerous speech in a non-political context.

The application of first amendment principles to criminal defendants who incite or solicit others, or agree among themselves to commit specific, serious crimes in a non-political context has not been much explored.[4] Professor Chafee, the most ardent defender of Holmes' clear and present danger approach, argued that its source could be found in the general criminal law of attempt, which required that the defendant had made "dangerous progress toward the consummation" of the crime.[5] It will be recalled, however, that Holmes' opinions in *Schenck* and *Abrams* focused at least as much on the speakers' "intent" as on their "dangerous progress." The requirement of progress toward consummation of the criminal conduct urged by speech seems not to be clearly reflected in criminal law doctrines of solicitation and conspira-

---

vocacy of Unlawful Conduct and The First Amendment: In Defense of Clear and Present Danger, 70 Calif.L.Rev. 1159 (1982).

[2] The earliest critical scholarly attack on the test as insufficiently protective of speech is Meiklejohn, *Free Speech and Its Relation to Self–Government* (1948).

[3] Prior to the *Dennis* case, the Court had employed the clear and present danger test in the context of a state contempt of court conviction of a newspaper and a labor leader for allegedly prejudicial statements concerning pending cases. Justice Black's opinion for the Court in Bridges v. California, 314 U.S. 252 (1941), held that these publications could not constitutionally constitute contempt in the absence of a clear and present danger to the administration of justice. Later cases involving contempt prosecutions for media criticism of judicial decisions have continued to reverse the convictions using the idiom of clear and present danger. Pennekamp v. Florida, 328 U.S. 331 (1946); Craig v. Harney, 331 U.S. 367 (1947); Wood v. Georgia, 370 U.S. 375 (1962). Those cases, however, can be read as

imposing an absolute ban on contempt prosecution for media statements concerning pending cases, or criticism of judicial action. See Baltimore Radio Show, Inc. v. State, 193 Md. 300, 67 A.2d 497 (1949), cert. denied 338 U.S. 912 (1950).

Bridges, Pennekamp and *Craig* were prominent among the cases cited by Chief Justice Vinson in his opinion in the *Dennis* case for the proposition that the Court had "inclined toward the Holmes–Brandeis rationale." 341 U.S. at 507.

[4] Compare, however, State v. Robertson, 293 Or. 402, 649 P.2d 569 (1982). The Oregon Supreme Court, in an opinion by Justice Linde, invalidated a statute making "criminal coercion" a crime. The challenged statute concerned compelling or inducing a person to do something he has a legal right not to do by making a threat to inflict specific harms, including exposing a secret. For extended comment on the decision, see Greenawalt, *Criminal Coercion and Freedom of Speech,* 78 Northwestern L.Rev. 1081 (1983).

[5] Chafee, supra note 1, at 47.

cy, which also focus primarily on issues of proof of the defendant's intent. The Model Penal Code, § 5.02, provides that a person is guilty of solicitation to commit a crime "if with the purpose of facilitating its commission he commands, encourages or requests another person to engage in specific conduct which would constitute such crime." No requirement that the person solicited is likely to commit the crime has been imposed. The crime of conspiracy, whether or not it requires the commission of an overt act as well as the agreement, has similarly not required a showing that the ultimate object of the conspiracy would occur.

The argument that clear and present danger affords too little protection in the arena of political speech was first put forward by Alexander Meiklejohn.[6] He argued that the principle of freedom of speech was rooted in principles of self-government, and that there should be absolute protection for the discussion of public issues, but considerably less protection for speech that did not discuss issues of public interest.[7] Critics of the Meiklejohn approach have questioned the ability to draw the distinction between political and other forms of speech, and have objected to the low level of protection afforded non-political speech under his theory.[8] Advocates of a political speech principle have disagreed with Meiklejohn's assessment of the level of protection to be afforded political speech[9] or with his conclusion that the first amendment was inapplicable to non-political speech.[10] It is, however, a useful inquiry to consider whether the pattern of the Court's decisions reflects a distinction between speech discussing public affairs and other kinds of communication.

(2) Absolutes and Balances. Justice Black was a consistent opponent of balancing competing interests as a technique of judicial adjudication. While his early opinions spoke of clear and present danger, he indicated in his *Dennis* dissent that he believed clear and present danger did not mark the outer boundaries of protected expression. For him, clear and present danger had become simply another technique for balancing competing interests. (Justice Frankfurter's *Dennis* concurrence, by contrast, criticized clear and present danger as too wooden a standard to permit the sensitive balancing of competing interests.) The position adopted by Justices Black and Douglas was that the first amendment forbids any government restriction on "speech" but permits the government to regulate "conduct." In their opinions in a number of cases, Justices Black and Harlan debated the question whether freedom of speech was absolutely protected[11] with Justice Black consistently maintaining that "the men who drafted our Bill of Rights did all the 'balancing' that was to be done in this field."[12]

Criticisms of both the balancers and the absolutists should be obvious. Given the intractable problem of assigning values to competing interests, it is

---

[6] Meiklejohn, supra note 2.

[7] Specifically, Meiklejohn argued that "freedom of speech" protected by the first amendment was non-abridgable, but that "liberty of speech" was protected only by the concept of due process and could be regulated for sufficient reasons. Id. at 37–39.

[8] E.g., Emerson, *The System of Freedom of Expression* 541 (1970); Chafee, *Book Review of Meiklejohn's Free Speech and its Relation to Self–Government,* 62 Harv.L.Rev. 891 (1949).

[9] Bork, *Neutral Principles and Some First Amendment Problems,* 47 Ind.L.J. 1 (1971).

[10] Be Vier, *The First Amendment and Political Speech: An Inquiry into the Substance and Limits of Principle,* 30 Stan.L.Rev. 299 (1978).

[11] E.g., Barenblatt v. United States, 360 U.S. 109 (1959); Konigsberg v. State Bar, 366 U.S. 36 (1961); cf. Cohen v. California, 403 U.S. 15 (1971).

[12] 366 U.S. at 61.

claimed that balancing is not a process but simply a convenient method of rationalizing subjective conclusions. Moreover, it often has been employed with excessive deference to the interests that justify suppression of speech. Absolute protection, it is argued, over-protects intolerable speech, or requires sophistry in drawing speech-conduct distinctions, or both.[13] The clash of contentions about absolutism and balancing has abated in contemporary free speech cases, but some of the competing arguments may have re-appeared in a new form.

(3) Ad Hoc and Definitional Balancing. A major dispute in the debate surrounding clear and present danger was whether it was appropriate to focus on the danger of all revolutionary speech, or the danger of the defendant's particular speech in its context.[14] An analogous argument concerns the method for reconciling free speech values with competing governmental interests. Ad hoc balancing requires weighing the value of particular speech against the strength of competing interests in the particular case. Definitional balancing suggests that the competing interests should result not in ad hoc decisions but the framing of rules of general application.[15] For a "definitional balancer," the proper rule in a particular context may be one of absolute protection for speech, which may trigger at least part of the controversy between absolutism and balancing. Moreover, the distinction between ad hoc and definitional balancing is itself slippery, since it turns on the level of generality at which a balance is struck or whether there is predictable content in a rule. The student should be alert, in the materials that follow, to the question whether particular free speech issues have been resolved by ad hoc or definitional balancing. A final question is whether the results reached, or the reasons given, represent a single, coherent theory of freedom of expression.

[13] A sampling of the law review discussion includes Griswold, *Absolute is in the Dark—A Discussion of the Approach of the Supreme Court to Constitutional Questions,* 8 Utah L.Rev. 167 (1963); Frantz, *The First Amendment in the Balance,* 71 Yale L.J. 1424 (1962); Mendelson, *On the Meaning of the First Amendment: Absolutes in the Balance,* 50 Calif.L.Rev. 821 (1962); Frantz, *Is the First Amendment Law?—A Reply to Professor Mendelson,* 51 Calif.L.Rev. 729 (1963); Kalven, *Upon Re-reading Mr. Justice Black on the First Amendment,* 14 U.C.L.A.L.Rev. 428 (1967); Gunther, *In Search of Judicial Quality on a Changing Court: The Case of Justice Powell,* 24 Stanf.L.Rev. 1001 (1972); Powe, *Evolution to Absolutism: Justice Douglas and the First Amendment,* 74 Colum.L.Rev. 371 (1974).

It can be argued that Justice Black was forced to manipulate the boundaries separating expression and action. In Giboney v. Empire Storage and Ice Co., 336 U.S. 490 (1949), he wrote the opinion for a unanimous court sustaining a restraint of trade conviction of union picketers whose placards urged an ice distributor to stop selling ice to nonunion peddlers. His opinion stated that the placards were to effectuate an unlawful purpose, and the defendants had engaged in illegal conduct "carried out by means of language." In Co-

hen v. California, 403 U.S. 15 (1971), infra, p. 1291, the Court overturned a breach of the peace conviction of a person who wore a jacket in a courthouse bearing the words "Fuck the Draft." Justice Black joined Justice Blackmun's dissent, which stated that the defendant's "antic . . . was mainly conduct and little speech."

[14] See Linde, supra page 1216.

[15] The term "definitional balancing" first appears in Nimmer, *The Right to Speak from Times to Time: First Amendment Theory Applied to Libel and Misapplied to Privacy,* 56 Cal.L.Rev. 935 (1968), which still contains the most lucid description of the distinction between definitional and ad hoc balancing. Id. at 939–948. The most comprehensive treatment of freedom of expression issues which rejects both absolutism and ad hoc balancing is contained in Emerson, supra note 8. Another attempt to construct a general structure avoiding ad hoc balancing is contained in a series of articles by Professor C. Edwin Baker. They are cited in Shiffrin, *The First Amendment and Economic Regulation: Away from a General Theory of the First Amendment,* 78 Northwestern L.Rev. 1212, 1224 n. 83 (1983), and Baker's approach is both explained and criticized, id. at 1239–1251.

SECTION 2.   INTERMEZZO: AN INTRODUCTION TO THE CONCEPTS OF VAGUENESS, OVERBREADTH AND PRIOR RESTRAINT

Introduction. Section 3 of this chapter will continue the inquiry begun in Section 1—exploring the societal interests that justify government control of the content of expression. This section involves judicial techniques that permit courts to reverse a defendant's conviction, or invalidate a statute, without deciding whether or not the content of expression or publication is constitutionally protected. The question to be asked is whether these techniques, as they are employed, respond to legitimate constitutional concerns or whether they are devices to avoid or postpone harder decisions concerning the limits of constitutionally protected speech. This section will not exhaust the study of vagueness, overbreadth and prior restraint. Decisions included in the remainder of this chapter, and the succeeding three chapters, are often based on these concepts.

A.   VAGUENESS AND OVERBREADTH

HERNDON v. LOWRY, 301 U.S. 242 (1937). Herndon, who was Black, had gone to Alabama as a paid organizer for the Communist Party during the depression years of the 1930's. He enrolled at least five members and held some meetings. When he was arrested he had in his possession Communist literature, including a pamphlet urging self determination for Blacks and advocating strikes, boycotts and a revolutionary struggle for power. It did not appear that he had distributed the literature found in his possession nor that he had advocated anything other than relief for the needy. Herndon received a heavy sentence under a Georgia statute that had been aimed at slave insurrections in its earlier form, before the Civil War. (The statute would have permitted imposition of the death penalty in Herndon's case.) The statute defined "attempt to incite insurrection" as "any attempt, by persuasion or otherwise, to induce others to join in any combined resistance to the lawful authority of the State." Herndon appealed his conviction to the Georgia Supreme Court, arguing that the evidence was insufficient to sustain his conviction, because there was no proof that immediate serious violence was expected or advocated. The Georgia Supreme Court affirmed the conviction, ruling that such proof was unnecessary. A defendant did not have to intend that an insurrection should follow "instantly or at any given time, but it would be sufficient that he intended it to happen at any time, as a result of his influence, by those whom he sought to incite."

Herndon's major argument in the Supreme Court was that the insurrection statute as construed was unconstitutional, since no clear and present danger was required for conviction. The Court, however, reversed the conviction without overruling the holding of Gitlow v. New York, 268 U.S. 652 (1925), that a legislature could make revolutionary speech a crime without requiring proof of clear and present danger. The Court first analyzed the evidence, and concluded that Herndon had been convicted for merely talking about unemployment relief, since there was no proof he had distributed the single copies of the more inflammatory literature in his possession. Relying in part on De Jonge v. Oregon, 299 U.S. 353 (1937) (Section 1, supra), the Court held on these facts that Herndon's conviction was an "unwarranted invasion of the right of freedom of speech." The Court's second ground of decision was that the insurrection statute was unconstitutional. Portions of Justice Roberts' discussion of that ground follow:

"The statute, as construed and applied in the appellant's trial, does not furnish a sufficiently ascertainable standard of guilt. . . .

". . . To be guilty under the law, as construed, a defendant need not advocate resort to force. He need not teach any particular doctrine to come within its purview. Indeed, he need not be active in the formation of a combination or group if he agitate for a change in the frame of government, however peaceful his own intent. If, by the exercise of prophesy, he can forecast that, as a result of a chain of causation, following his proposed action a group may arise at some future date which will resort to force, he is bound to make the prophesy and abstain, under pain of punishment, possibly of execution. Every person who attacks existing conditions, who agitates for a change in the form of government, must take the risk that if a jury should be of opinion he ought to have foreseen that his utterances might contribute in any measure to some future forcible resistance to the existing government he may be convicted of the offense of inciting insurrection. Proof that the accused in fact believed that his effort would cause a violent assault upon the state would not be necessary to conviction. It would be sufficient if the jury thought he reasonably might foretell that those he persuaded to join the party might, at some time in the indefinite future, resort to forcible resistance of government. The question thus proposed to a jury involves pure speculation as to future trends of thought and action. Within what time might one reasonably expect that an attempted organization of the Communist Party in the United States would result in violent action by that party? If a jury returned a special verdict saying twenty years or even fifty years the verdict could not be shown to be wrong. The law, as thus construed, licenses the jury to create its own standard in each case. . . .

" . . .

"The statute as construed and applied, amounts merely to a dragnet which may enmesh any one who agitates for a change of government if a jury can be persuaded that he ought to have foreseen his words would have some effect in the future conduct of others. No reasonably ascertainable standard of guilt is prescribed. So vague and indeterminate are the boundaries thus set to the freedom of speech and assembly that the law necessarily violates the guarantees of liberty embodied in the Fourteenth Amendment."[a]

Coates v. Cincinnati

402 U.S. 611, 91 S.Ct. 1686, 29 L.Ed.2d 214 (1971).

Mr. Justice Stewart delivered the opinion of the Court.

A Cincinnati, Ohio, ordinance makes it a criminal offense for "three or more persons to assemble . . . on any of the sidewalks . . . and there conduct themselves in a manner annoying to persons passing by. . . ." The issue before us is whether this ordinance is unconstitutional on its face.

The appellants were convicted of violating the ordinance, and the convictions were ultimately affirmed by a closely divided vote in the Supreme Court of Ohio, upholding the constitutional validity of the ordinance. An appeal from

[a] For an interesting discussion of Herndon v. Lowry, see Chafee, *Free Speech in the* *United States* 388–398 (1941).

that judgment was brought here.... The record brought before the reviewing courts tells us no more than that the appellant Coates was a student involved in a demonstration and the other appellants were pickets involved in a labor dispute. For throughout this litigation it has been the appellants' position that the ordinance on its face violates the First and Fourteenth Amendments of the Constitution. . . .

In rejecting this claim and affirming the convictions the Ohio Supreme Court did not give the ordinance any construction at variance with the apparent plain import of its language. . . .

. . .

We are thus relegated, at best, to the words of the ordinance itself. If three or more people meet together on a sidewalk or street corner, they must conduct themselves so as not to annoy any police officer or other person who should happen to pass by. In our opinion this ordinance is unconstitutionally vague because it subjects the exercise of the right of assembly to an unascertainable standard, and unconstitutionally broad because it authorizes the punishment of constitutionally protected conduct.

Conduct that annoys some people does not annoy others. Thus, the ordinance is vague not in the sense that it requires a person to conform his conduct to an imprecise but comprehensible normative standard, but rather in the sense that no standard of conduct is specified at all. As a result, "men of common intelligence must necessarily guess at its meaning." Connally v. General Construction Co., 269 U.S. 385, 391.

It is said that the ordinance is broad enough to encompass many types of conduct clearly within the city's constitutional power to prohibit. And so, indeed, it is. The city is free to prevent people from blocking sidewalks, obstructing traffic, littering streets, committing assaults, or engaging in countless other forms of anti-social conduct. It can do so through the enactment and enforcement of ordinances directed with reasonable specificity toward the conduct to be prohibited. ...It cannot constitutionally do so through the enactment and enforcement of an ordinance whose violation may entirely depend upon whether or not a policeman is annoyed.

But the vice of the ordinance lies not alone in its violation of the due process standard of vagueness. The ordinance also violates the constitutional right of free assembly and association. Our decisions establish that mere public intolerance or animosity cannot be the basis for abridgment of these constitutional freedoms.... The First and Fourteenth Amendments do not permit a State to make criminal the exercise of the right of assembly simply because its exercise may be "annoying" to some people. If this were not the rule, the right of the people to gather in public places for social or political purposes would be continually subject to summary suspension through the good-faith enforcement of a prohibition against annoying conduct. And such a prohibition, in addition, contains an obvious invitation to discriminatory enforcement against those whose association together is "annoying" because their ideas, their lifestyle or their physical appearance is resented by the majority of their fellow citizens.

The ordinance before us makes a crime out of what under the Constitution cannot be a crime. It is aimed directly at activity protected by the Constitution. We need not lament that we do not have before us the details of the conduct found to be annoying. It is the ordinance on its face that sets the standard of conduct and warns against transgression. The details of the offense could no more serve to validate this ordinance than could the details of an offense charged under an ordinance suspending unconditionally the right of assembly and free speech.

The judgment is reversed.

Mr. Justice White, with whom The Chief Justice and Mr. Justice Blackmun join, dissenting.

The claim in this case, in part, is that the Cincinnati ordinance is so vague that it may not constitutionally be applied to any conduct. But the ordinance prohibits persons from assembling with others and "conduct[ing] themselves in a manner annoying to persons passing by...." ... Any man of average comprehension should know that some kinds of conduct, such as assault or blocking passage on the street, will annoy others and are clearly covered by the "annoying conduct" standard of the ordinance. It would be frivolous to say that these and many other kinds of conduct are not within the foreseeable reach of the law.

It is possible that a whole range of other acts, defined with unconstitutional imprecision, is forbidden by the ordinance. But as a general rule, when a criminal charge is based on conduct constitutionally subject to proscription and clearly forbidden by a statute, it is no defense that the law would be unconstitutionally vague if applied to other behavior. Such a statute is not vague on its face. It may be vague as applied in some circumstances, but ruling on such a challenge obviously requires knowledge of the conduct with which a defendant is charged.

. . .

So ... in United States v. National Dairy Corp., 372 U.S. 29 (1963), where we considered a statute forbidding sales of goods at "unreasonably" low prices to injure or eliminate a competitor, 15 U.S.C. § 13a, we thought the statute gave a seller adequate notice that sales below costs were illegal. The statute was therefore not facially vague, although it might be difficult to tell whether certain other kinds of conduct fell within this language. ... This approach is consistent with the host of cases holding that "one to whom application of a statute is constitutional will not be heard to attack the statute on the ground that impliedly it might also be taken as applying to other persons or other situations in which its application might be unconstitutional." United States v. Raines, 362 U.S. 17, 21 (1960), and cases there cited.

Our cases, however, including *National Dairy,* recognize a different approach where the statute at issue purports to regulate or proscribe rights of speech or press protected by the First Amendment. ...Although a statute may be neither vague, overbroad, nor otherwise invalid as applied to the conduct charged against a particular defendant, he is permitted to raise its vagueness or unconstitutional overbreadth as applied to others. And if the law is found deficient in one of these respects, it may not be applied to him either, until and unless a satisfactory limiting construction is placed on the statute. Dombrowski v. Pfister, 380 U.S. 479, 491–492 (1965). The statute, in effect, is stricken down on its face. This result is deemed justified since the otherwise continued existence of the statute in unnarrowed form would tend to suppress constitutionally protected rights. ...

Even accepting the overbreadth doctrine with respect to statutes clearly reaching speech, the Cincinnati ordinance does not purport to bar or regulate speech as such. It prohibits persons from assembling and "conduct[ing]" themselves in a manner annoying to other persons. Even if the assembled defendants in this case were demonstrating and picketing, we have long recognized that picketing is not solely a communicative endeavor and has aspects which the State is entitled to regulate even though there is incidental impact on speech. In Cox v. Louisiana, 379 U.S. 559 (1965), the Court held valid on its face a statute forbidding picketing and parading near a courthouse. This was deemed a valid regulation of conduct rather than pure speech. . . .

In the case before us, I would deal with the Cincinnati ordinance as we would with the ordinary criminal statute. The ordinance clearly reaches certain conduct but may be illegally vague with respect to other conduct. The statute is not infirm on its face and since we have no information from this record as to what conduct was charged against these defendants, we are in no position to judge the statute as applied. That the ordinance may confer wide discretion in a wide range of circumstances is irrelevant when we may be dealing with conduct at its core.

I would therefore affirm the judgment of the Ohio Supreme Court.

Mr. Justice Black.

. . .

. . . [T]he First Amendment which forbids the State to abridge freedom of speech, would invalidate this city ordinance if it were used to punish the making of a political speech, even if that speech were to annoy other persons. In contrast, however, the ordinance could properly be applied to prohibit the gathering of persons in the mouths of alleys to annoy passersby by throwing rocks or by some other conduct not at all connected with speech. It is a matter of no little difficulty to determine when a law can be held void on its face and when such summary action is inappropriate. This difficulty has been aggravated in this case, because the record fails to show in what conduct these defendants had engaged to annoy other people. In my view, a record showing the facts surrounding the conviction is essential to adjudicate the important constitutional issues in this case. I would therefore, vacate the judgment and remand the case to the court below to give both parties an opportunity to supplement the record so that we may determine whether the conduct actually punished is the kind of conduct which it is within the power of the State to punish.

BROADRICK v. OKLAHOMA, 413 U.S. 601 (1973). An Oklahoma statute proscribed partisan political activity by state civil servants. Plaintiffs, who had engaged in partisan political activities (including solicitation of money) among their co-workers, brought suit to enjoin enforcement of the statute. They conceded that the statute validly could prohibit the conduct they had engaged in but sought to have it declared unconstitutional because it forbade the wearing of political buttons and displaying bumper stickers—activity they had not engaged in. They argued that the statute was overbroad because buttons and stickers were protected expression.

Justice White, writing for the Court rejected this contention:

"[T]he Court has altered its traditional rules of standing to permit—in the First Amendment area—'attacks on overly broad statutes with no requirement that the person making the attack demonstrate that his own conduct could not be regulated by a statute drawn with the requisite specificity.' Dombrowski v. Pfister, 380 U.S. 479, 486 (1965). Litigants, therefore, are permitted to challenge a statute not because their own rights of free expression are violated, but because of a judicial prediction or assumption that the statute's very existence may cause others not before the court to refrain from constitutionally protected speech or expression.

"Such claims of facial overbreadth have been entertained in cases involving statutes which, by their terms, seek to regulate 'only spoken words.' Gooding v. Wilson, 405 U.S. 518, 520 (1972).... In such cases, it has been the judgment of this Court that the possible harm to society in permitting some unprotected speech to go unpunished is outweighed by the possibility that protected speech of others may be muted and perceived grievances left to fester because of the possible inhibitory effects of overly broad statutes. Overbreadth attacks have also been allowed where the Court thought rights of association were ensnared in statutes which, by their broad sweep, might result in burdening innocent associations. ...Facial overbreadth claims have also been entertained where statutes, by their terms, purport to regulate the time, place and manner of expressive or communicative conduct, ... and where such conduct has required official approval under laws that delegated standardless discretionary power to local functionaries, resulting in virtually unreviewable prior restraints on First Amendment rights. ...

"The consequence of our departure from traditional rules of standing in the First Amendment area is that any enforcement of a statute thus placed at issue is totally forbidden until and unless a limiting construction or partial invalidation so narrows it as to remove the seeming threat or deterrence to constitutionally protected expression. Application of the overbreadth doctrine in this manner is, manifestly, strong medicine. It has been employed by the Court sparingly and only as a last resort....

"It remains a 'matter of no little difficulty' to determine when a law may properly be held void on its face and when 'such summary action' is inappropriate. ... But the plain import of our cases is, at the very least, that facial overbreadth adjudication is an exception to our traditional rules of practice and that its function, a limited one at the outset, attenuates as the otherwise unprotected behavior that it forbids the State to sanction moves from 'pure speech' towards conduct and that conduct—even if expressive—falls within the scope of otherwise valid criminal laws that reflect legitimate state interests in maintaining comprehensive controls over harmful, constitutionally unprotected conduct. Although such laws, if too broadly worded, may deter protected speech to some unknown extent, there comes a point where that effect—at best a prediction—cannot, with confidence, justify invalidating a statute on its face and so prohibiting a State from enforcing the statute against conduct that is admittedly within its power to proscribe. ... To put the matter another way, particularly where conduct and not merely speech is involved, we believe that the overbreadth of a statute must not only be real, but substantial as well, judged in relation to the statute's plainly legitimate sweep. It is our view that § 818 is not substantially overbroad and that whatever overbreadth may exist should be cured through case-by-case analysis of the fact situations to which its sanctions, assertedly, may not be applied.[14]"

Justice Douglas dissented on the ground that the whole statute violated the first amendment. Justice Brennan concluded a dissenting opinion joined by Justices Stewart and Marshall as follows:

"At this stage, it is obviously difficult to estimate the probable impact of today's decision. If the requirement of 'substantial' overbreadth is construed to

[14] ... The dissent ... insists that Coates v. City of Cincinnati, 402 U.S. 611 (1971), must be taken as overruled. But we are unpersuaded that *Coates* stands as a barrier to a rule that would invalidate statutes for overbreadth only when the flaw is a substantial concern in the context of the statute as a whole. Our judgment is that the Oklahoma statute, when authoritative administrative constructions are accepted, is not invalid under such a rule.

mean only that facial review is inappropriate where the likelihood of an impermissible application of the statute is too small to generate a 'chilling effect' on protected speech or conduct, then the impact is likely to be small. On the other hand, if today's decision necessitates the drawing of artificial distinctions between protected speech and protected conduct, and if the 'chill' on protected conduct is rarely, if ever, found sufficient to require the facial invalidation of an overbroad statute, then the effect could be very grave indeed. In my view, the principles set forth in Coates v. City of Cincinnati, are essential to the preservation and enforcement of the First Amendment guarantees. Since no subsequent development has persuaded me that the principles are ill-founded or that *Coates* was incorrectly decided, I would reverse the judgment of the District Court on the strength of that decision and hold ... the Oklahoma Merit Act unconstitutional on its face."

BROCKETT v. SPOKANE ARCADES, INC., 472 U.S. 491 (1985). The Court concluded that a state obscenity statute was overbroad because it used the term "lust" in defining obscene matter. (The definition included materials that appealed to "only normal sexual appetites," and were thus constitutionally protected.) The Court decided, however, that the lower federal court had erred in declaring the statute invalid as a whole. On this issue, the Court's opinion said:

"For its holding that in First Amendment cases an overbroad statute must be stricken down on its face, the Court of Appeals relied on that line of cases exemplified by Thornhill v. Alabama, 310 U.S. 88 (1940), and more recently by Village of Schaumburg v. Citizens for a Better Environment, 444 U.S. 620 (1980). In those cases, an individual whose own speech or expressive conduct may validly be prohibited or sanctioned is permitted to challenge a statute on its face because it also threatens others not before the court—those who desire to engage in legally protected expression but who may refrain from doing so rather than risk prosecution or undertake to have the law declared partially invalid. If the overbreadth is 'substantial,'[12] the law may not be enforced against anyone, including the party before the court, until it is narrowed to reach only unprotected activity, whether by legislative action or by judicial construction or partial invalidation. Broadrick v. Oklahoma, 413 U.S. 601 (1973).

"It is otherwise where the parties challenging the statute are those who desire to engage in protected speech that the overbroad statute purports to punish, or who seek to publish both protected and unprotected material. There is then no want of a proper party to challenge the statute, no concern that an attack on the statute will be unduly delayed or protected speech discouraged. The statute may forthwith be declared invalid to the extent that it reaches too far, but otherwise left intact.

"The cases before us are ones governed by the normal rule that partial, rather than facial, invalidation is the required course. The Washington statute was faulted by the Court of Appeals only because it reached material that incited normal as well as unhealthy interest in sex, and appellees, or some of them, desiring to publish this sort of material, claimed that they faced punishment if they did so. Unless there are countervailing considerations, the Washington law should have been invalidated only insofar as the word 'lust' is to be understood as reaching protected materials.

. . .

[12] The Court of Appeals erred in holding that the substantial overbreadth requirement is inapplicable where pure speech rather than conduct is at issue. . . .

"Partial invalidation would be improper if it were contrary to legislative intent in the sense that the legislature had passed an inseverable Act or would not have passed it had it known the challenged provision was invalid. . . . It would be frivolous to suggest, and no one does, that the Washington Legislature, if it could not proscribe materials that appealed to normal as well as abnormal sexual appetites, would have refrained from passing the moral nuisance statute. And it is quite evident that the remainder of the statute retains its effectiveness as a regulation of obscenity. In these circumstances, the issue of severability is no obstacle to partial invalidation, which is the course the Court of Appeals should have pursued."

FEDERAL COURT INJUNCTIONS AGAINST VAGUE AND OVERBROAD STATUTES

It is accurate to say that laws are judged for vagueness and overbreadth on their "face" only in the sense, as Justice Stewart points out in *Coates,* that it is unnecessary to know the details of the defendant's conduct, or to determine whether it was constitutionally protected. It is a mistake to conclude that statutes are judged for vagueness and overbreadth only with reference to their literal statutory language. A statute may appear to be vague and overbroad, but those problems may disappear if judicial construction clarifies its prohibitions and limits its potentially overbroad applications. A good example is the Smith Act, considered at length in Section 1 of this chapter. Were it not for the limiting constructions given the statute in the *Yates, Scales* and *Noto* cases, its literal application would require a conclusion that it is overbroad. State courts, too, can remove potential issues of vagueness and overbreadth by a limiting construction of the statute involved. Thus, in reviewing a case that originated in a state court, the issue before the Supreme Court is whether the statute, as construed by the state courts, is vague or overbroad. (Notice that in *Herndon* the vagueness problem stemmed, in part, from the state court's construction and, in *Coates,* the state court had not construed the statute beyond its plain language.)

In any case in which issues of first amendment vagueness and overbreadth are raised there are difficult questions of degree—determining the degree of vagueness or overbreadth that will be fatal and deciding whether a party can raise the challenge that the statute is vague or overbroad as to other persons. Those problems are, however, further complicated when the challenges are raised in a federal court suit to enjoin enforcement of the law as opposed to Supreme Court review of a state criminal conviction. The first problem for the federal court is that it can only guess whether state courts would give an apparently vague or overbroad law a narrowing construction that would obviate the problem. That can be particularly troublesome when the law sought to be enjoined is newly enacted and has never been construed in the state courts. The second problem is to define standing to raise the challenges—obviously less of a problem where a defendant seeking Supreme Court review is attempting to overturn the very statutory provision under which he was convicted. Allowing a defendant in a state criminal action to enjoin a pending prosecution can create inordinate delay in the state criminal process or create a mechanism by which state court decisions on federal issues are reviewed and "reversed" by lower federal courts and not by the Supreme Court. On the other hand, permitting suit by any person who alleges a future intent to engage in behavior arguably within the statutory prohibition practically allows anyone to mount a vagueness or overbreadth challenge to a state law. Allowing anyone alleging a subjective "chill" to ask a federal court to strike down a state law on the basis that there are some hypothetical uncertainties or applications to protected speech produces litigation with many of the undesirable features of advisory opinions. The complex federal jurisdiction rules addressed to these problems were explored, in general terms, earlier in Chapter 3. They will be examined here with reference to their impact on litigation of vagueness and overbreadth challenges.

(1) Postponing Decision. A technique for addressing the possibility that state courts might narrow the statute's apparent vagueness or overbreadth is for the federal court to stay the action before it, allowing the parties to obtain an "authoritative" state court construction of the law. (See Chapter 3, Section 2, Subsection C.) In Baggett v. Bullitt, 377 U.S. 360 (1964), the Court invalidated, as impermissibly vague, a Washington loyalty oath for teachers requiring affirmation that the teacher was not a "subversive person." In Dombrowski v. Pfister, 380 U.S. 479 (1965), a Louisiana law requiring registration of "subversive organizations" was invalidated for vagueness and overbreadth. In both cases, the Court refused to postpone exercise of jurisdiction to allow state court interpretation. Portions of Justice Brennan's opinion in *Dombrowski* can be read as suggesting that abstention to clarify state law is never appropriate when the law is challenged on vagueness and overbreadth grounds. He emphasized that a major premise of vagueness and overbreadth doctrine was that such laws operated to chill constitutionally protected speech by those not "hardy enough to risk criminal prosecution." He further pointed out that the abstention process was time consuming and, in the intervening time, those affected remained subject to the statute's "chilling effect." Both opinions, however, also emphasized that the challenged laws presented a multitude of issues of interpretation that were not likely to be resolved in any single proceeding. Babbitt v. United Farm Workers Nat'l Union, 442 U.S. 289 (1979) held that abstention to allow state court interpretation is required where the uncertainty of a challenged statute concerns a single issue that can be resolved by state courts in a single proceeding.

(2) Dismissal. Justice Brennan's discussion in *Dombrowski* of the "chilling effect" of vague and overbroad statutes upon parties not before the court led lower federal courts to permit a proliferation of vagueness and overbreadth challenges to state criminal statutes. Younger v. Harris, 401 U.S. 37 (1971), substantially curbed that litigation. At issue in the case was the constitutional validity of the California criminal syndicalism law which had been upheld in Whitney v. California, 274 U.S. 357 (1927) (supra Section 1). Harris had been indicted under the act, and sued to enjoin his state prosecution. Other parties plaintiff were allowed to intervene—Progressive Labor Party members who alleged that Harris' prosecution inhibited them from advocacy of Party programs, and a college instructor who claimed he was uncertain whether he could teach about Marxism. The lower federal courts enjoined Harris' prosecution, holding the law unconstitutional. The Supreme Court reversed, concluding that the federal injunction suit should have been dismissed. The intervenors had not alleged a credible threat they would be prosecuted, and as to them there was no "live controversy." Allowing Harris to sue presented the opposite problem— undue interference with a pending state criminal proceeding. Harris could raise his constitutional defense in the pending prosecution. More broadly, Justice Black's opinion for the Court stated: "Procedures for testing the constitutionality of a statute 'on its face' in the manner apparently contemplated by *Dombrowski,* and for then enjoining all action to enforce the statute until the State can obtain court approval for a modified version, are fundamentally at odds with the function of . . . federal courts in our constitutional plan." Among the difficulties, he listed the "speculative and amorphous nature of the required line-by-line analysis of detailed statutes [which] ordinarily results in a kind of case that is wholly unsatisfactory for deciding constitutional questions."

The seed of *Younger v. Harris* has grown into a luxuriant forest of rules. (See Chapter 3, Section 2, Subsection C.) Barring suit by persons actually prosecuted and those not threatened with prosecution has left a narrow corridor for bringing federal court actions to determine the constitutionality of state criminal laws. Suit for declaratory judgment of unconstitutionality (as opposed to an injunction) is permitted where the plaintiff shows a credible threat of prosecution, but has not been prosecuted. Steffel v. Thompson, 415 U.S. 452 (1974). Further, a temporary injunction against prosecution *pendente lite* may be issued on a sufficient showing of irreparable harm and likely success on the merits. Doran v. Salem Inn, Inc., 422 U.S. 922 (1975). If a temporary injunction is not entered, and state prosecution is begun before "proceedings of substance on the merits" have occurred in the federal declaratory judgment action, the federal action must be dismissed. Hicks v. Miranda, 422 U.S. 332 (1975). If a federal declaratory judgment of unconstitutionality is issued, it is an open question whether subsequent state prosecutions can then be enjoined by the federal court. (Justices White and Rehnquist expressed polar positions on that issue in concurring opinions in Hicks v. Miranda.) The question may be particularly perplexing if the statute is declared unconstitutional for vagueness and overbreadth, but there is a possibility that state court construction of the statute in the subsequent state prosecution might narrow the statute's interpretation. Shapiro, *State Courts and Federal Declaratory Judgments*, 74 N.W.U.L.Rev. 759 (1979).

An interesting situation occurs when the defendant has been prosecuted in a state court, and the conviction has become final. The defendant wishes to continue the conduct that resulted in conviction, and, without seeking to set aside the past conviction, asks a federal court to bar future prosecution. In that situation, a federal court may enjoin future state criminal prosecutions. Since the federal plaintiff is willing to let the past criminal conviction stand, there is no interference with state criminal actions and, in form, the federal trial court is not exercising quasi-appellate review of a state court decision. Wooley v. Maynard, 430 U.S. 705 (1977), infra, p. 1456; Carey v. Brown, 447 U.S. 455 (1980). Neither *Wooley* nor *Carey* was decided on vagueness or overbreadth grounds. The implications of those cases, however, for vagueness and overbreadth challenges should be noted. The past state conviction gives some concreteness to the federal litigation. It is known what the defendant has done and intends to do in the future. The particular features of the statute at issue are defined by the previous conviction. And, most significant, a state court has had a prior opportunity to construe the statute and narrow its interpretation.

B. PRIOR RESTRAINT

Introduction. The historical introduction to this chapter referred to the English history of licensed presses and Blackstone's conclusion in 1765 that liberty of the press consisted in an absence of prior restraints upon publication, but imposed no limit on punishing the publisher after publication. (Section 1, Subsection A, 1.) As late as 1907, Justice Holmes, on first encountering the problem, repeated the Blackstone proposition that the Constitution forbade "all such *previous restraints* upon publication, as had been practiced by other governments" but not "the subsequent punishment of such as may be deemed contrary to the public welfare."[1] It is now obvious that the Constitution does

---

[1] Patterson v. Colorado, 205 U.S. 454, 462 (1907). It was not until 1919 that Holmes announced: "I wholly disagree with the argument ... that the First Amendment left the

impose serious limits on the punishment of speech and publications. The prior restraint concept is not obsolete, however. A person, whose publication or speech is not constitutionally protected from punishment, under a properly drawn criminal statute, can still complain if it is inhibited by an unconstitutional prior restraint.

The traditional system of prior restraint was an administrative licensing mechanism, with the publisher forbidden to publish without prior approval of an executive official. The Court has upheld administrative licensing systems, where official permission in advance has been required for expressive activities conducted on public property. (The problems posed by requirements for parade permits are discussed below, beginning at page 1246.) The Court has sustained an administrative licensing system in only one context not involving use of public property. In Times Film Corp. v. City of Chicago, 365 U.S. 43 (1961), the Court concluded that a motion picture licensing ordinance was not invalid "on its face." The nation's existing motion picture licensing systems, however, did not survive the decision four years later in Freedman v. Maryland, 380 U.S. 51 (1965). The Court concluded that the motion picture licensing system under review was invalid because: (1) it did not require the administrative censor to seek judicial review if a permit was refused; (2) if the exhibitor sought judicial review, exhibition of the film was not permitted pending review; (3) there was no assurance of prompt judicial determination. The Court explained that there were important differences between judicial and administrative proceedings. "Unlike a prosecution for obscenity, a censorship proceeding puts the initial burden on the exhibitor or distributor. Because the censor's business is to censor, there inheres the danger that he may well be less responsive than a court—part of an independent branch of government—to the constitutionally protected interests in free expression." The Court also said that "only a judicial determination in an adversary proceeding ensures the necessary sensitivity to freedom of expression."

The next case does not involve administrative censorship but a court injunction. *Near v. Minnesota,* the Court's seminal decision on prior restraint, equated injunctions with administrative censorship. Is an injunction any more "prior" than a criminal statute forbidding the same conduct?

Near v. Minnesota

283 U.S. 697, 51 S.Ct. 625, 75 L.Ed. 1357 (1931).

Mr. Chief Justice Hughes delivered the opinion of the Court.

Chapter 285 of the Session Laws of Minnesota for the year 1925 provides for the abatement, as a public nuisance, of a "malicious, scandalous and defamatory newspaper, magazine or other periodical." . . .

. . .

Under this statute . . . the county attorney of Hennepin county brought this action to enjoin the publication of what was described as a "malicious, scandalous and defamatory newspaper, magazine or other periodical," known as The Saturday Press, published by the defendants in the city of Minneapolis. . . .

common law as to seditious libel in force."
Abrams v. United States, 250 U.S. 616, 630
(1919) (dissenting opinion).

... [T]he articles charged, in substance, that a Jewish gangster was in control of gambling, bootlegging, and racketeering in Minneapolis, and that law enforcing officers and agencies were not energetically performing their duties.... There is no question but that the articles made serious accusations against the public officers named and others in connection with the prevalence of crimes and the failure to expose and punish them....

... The court ... found that the defendants through these publications "did engage in the business of regularly and customarily producing, publishing and circulating a malicious, scandalous and defamatory newspaper," and that "the said publication under said name of The Saturday Press, or any other name, constitutes a public nuisance under the laws of the State." Judgment was thereupon entered adjudging that "the newspaper, magazine and periodical known as The Saturday Press," as a public nuisance, "be and is hereby abated." The judgment perpetually enjoined the defendants "from producing, editing, publishing, circulating, having in their possession, selling or giving away any publication whatsoever which is a malicious, scandalous or defamatory newspaper, as defined by law," and also "from further conducting said nuisance under the name and title of said The Saturday Press or any other name or title."

[The judgment was affirmed by the State Supreme Court.]

This statute, for the suppression as a public nuisance of a newspaper or periodical, is unusual, if not unique, and raises questions of grave importance transcending the local interests involved in the particular action. It is no longer open to doubt that the liberty of the press, and of speech, is within the liberty safeguarded by the due process clause of the Fourteenth Amendment from invasion by state action....

First. The statute is not aimed at the redress of individual or private wrongs. Remedies for libel remain available and unaffected. The statute, said the state court, "is not directed at threatened libel but at an existing business which, generally speaking, involves more than libel." It is aimed at the distribution of scandalous matter as "detrimental to public morals and to the general welfare," tending "to disturb the peace of the community" and "to provoke assaults and the commission of crime." ...

Second. The statute is directed not simply at the circulation of scandalous and defamatory statements with regard to private citizens, but at the continued publication by newspapers and periodicals of charges against public officers of corruption, malfeasance in office, or serious neglect of duty. Such charges by their very nature create a public scandal. They are scandalous and defamatory within the meaning of the statute, which has its normal operation in relation to publications dealing prominently and chiefly with the alleged derelictions of public officers.

Third. The object of the statute is not punishment, in the ordinary sense, but suppression of the offending newspaper or periodical. The reason for the enactment, as the state court has said, is that prosecutions to enforce penal statutes for libel do not result in "efficient repression or suppression of the evils of scandal." ...

This suppression is accomplished by enjoining publication and that restraint is the object and effect of the statute.

Fourth. The statute not only operates to suppress the offending newspaper or periodical, but to put the publisher under an effective censorship. When a newspaper or periodical is found to be "malicious, scandalous and defamatory," and is suppressed as such, resumption of publication is punishable as a contempt of court by fine or imprisonment. Thus where a newspaper or periodical has been suppressed because of the circulation of charges against public officers of official misconduct, it would seem to be clear that the renewal of the publication of such charges would constitute a contempt, and that the judgment would lay a permanent restraint upon the publisher, to escape which he must satisfy the court as to the character of a new publication. Whether he would be permitted again to publish matter deemed to be derogatory to the same or other public officers would depend upon the court's ruling. . . .

If we cut through mere details of procedure, the operation and effect of the statute in substance is that public authorities may bring the owner or publisher of a newspaper or periodical before a judge upon a charge of conducting a business of publishing scandalous and defamatory matter—in particular that the matter consists of charges against public officers of official dereliction—and unless the owner or publisher is able and disposed to bring competent evidence to satisfy the judge that the charges are true and are published with good motives and for justifiable ends, his newspaper or periodical is suppressed and further publication is made punishable as a contempt. This is of the essence of censorship.

The question is whether a statute authorizing such proceedings in restraint of publication is consistent with the conception of the liberty of the press as historically conceived and guaranteed. In determining the extent of the constitutional protection, it has been generally, if not universally, considered that it is the chief purpose of the guaranty to prevent previous restraints upon publication. . . .

. . .

The objection has . . . been made that the principle as to immunity from previous restraint is stated too broadly, if every such restraint is deemed to be prohibited. That is undoubtedly true; the protection even as to previous restraint is not absolutely unlimited. But the limitation has been recognized only in exceptional cases: "When a nation is at war many things that might be said in time of peace are such a hindrance to its effort that their utterance will not be endured so long as men fight and that no Court could regard them as protected by any constitutional right." Schenck v. United States, 249 U.S. 47, 52. No one would question but that a government might prevent actual obstruction to its recruiting service or the publication of the sailing dates of transports or the number and location of troops. On similar grounds, the primary requirements of decency may be enforced against obscene publications. The security of the community life may be protected against incitements to acts of violence and the overthrow by force of orderly government. . . . These limitations are not applicable here. Nor are we now concerned with questions as to the extent of authority to prevent publications in order to protect private rights according to the principles governing the exercise of the jurisdiction of courts of equity.

The exceptional nature of its limitations places in a strong light the general conception that liberty of the press, historically considered and taken up by the Federal Constitution, has meant, principally although not exclusively, immunity from previous restraints or censorship. . . .

. . .

The statute in question cannot be justified by reason of the fact that the publisher is permitted to show, before injunction issues, that the matter published is true and is published with good motives and for justifiable ends. . . .

. . .

For these reasons we hold the statute, so far as it authorized the proceedings in this action under clause (b) of section one, to be an infringement of the liberty of the press guaranteed by the Fourteenth Amendment. We should add that this decision rests upon the operation and effect of the statute, without regard to the question of the truth of the charges contained in the particular periodical. The fact that the public officers named in this case, and those associated with the charges of official dereliction, may be deemed to be impeccable, cannot affect the conclusion that the statute imposes an unconstitutional restraint upon publication.

Judgement reversed.

Mr. Justice Butler, dissenting.

. . .

The Court quotes Blackstone in support of its condemnation of the statute as imposing a previous restraint upon publication. But the *previous restraints* referred to by him subjected the press to the arbitrary will of an administrative officer. . . .

. . .

The Minnesota statute does not operate as a *previous* restraint on publication within the proper meaning of that phrase. It does not authorize administrative control in advance such as was formerly exercised by the licensers and censors but prescribes a remedy to be enforced by a suit in equity. In this case there was previous publication made in the course of the business of regularly producing malicious, scandalous and defamatory periodicals. The business and publications unquestionably constitute an abuse of the right of free press. The statute denounces the things done as a nuisance on the ground, as stated by the state supreme court, that they threaten morals, peace, and good order. There is no question of the power of the state to denounce such transgressions. The restraint authorized is only in respect of continuing to do what has been duly adjudged to constitute a nuisance. . . . It is fanciful to suggest similarity between the granting or enforcement of the decree authorized by this statute to prevent *further* publication of malicious, scandalous, and defamatory articles and the *previous restraint* upon the press by licensers as referred to by Blackstone and described in the history of the times to which he alludes.

. . .

The judgment should be affirmed.

Mr. Justice Van Devanter, Mr. Justice McReynolds, and Mr. Justice Sutherland concur in this opinion.

INJUNCTIONS AND PRIOR RESTRAINT

In Pittsburgh Press Co. v. Pittsburgh Human Relations Comm'n, 413 U.S. 376, 389–390 (1973), the Court noted that not all injunctions against future publications were invalid prior restraints. "The special vice of a prior restraint is that communication will be suppressed, either directly or by inducing excessive caution in the speaker, before an adequate determination that it is protected by the First Amendment." The Court indicated that the challenged order—which required the newspaper to desist from segregating "help wanted" advertisements by gender—was not a prior restraint for two reasons: there was a continuing course of past conduct identical to that enjoined, making it unnecessary "to speculate as to the effect of publication"; the publication enjoined was clearly defined and not constitutionally protected.

A restraining order issued *ex parte,* prohibiting speech without notice or hearing, obviously can create substantial constitutional questions. E.g., Carroll v. President and Commissioners of Princess Anne, 393 U.S. 175 (1968) (*ex parte* order forbidding rally is unconstitutional where no showing that it was impossible to notify opposing parties and provide hearing); Fort Wayne Books, Inc. v. Indiana, 489 U.S. 46 (1989) (pre-trial seizure of adult bookstore under state racketeering law is unconstitutional prior restraint). If the injunction in *Near* had forbidden the defendants to publish any newspaper, the overbroad remedy might violate the first amendment.

In *Near,* does the constitutionality of the challenged injunction procedures depend on the question whether a contempt action for violation of the injunction would permit a defense that the alleged contempt was a constitutionally protected publication or exhibition? In Near v. Minnesota, Justice Butler's dissent made the point that in a contempt action the newspaper publisher would have available all defenses available in a criminal libel action. 283 U.S. at 730. Chief Justice Hughes' opinion did not challenge that assertion. If one assumes that a criminal libel law is constitutional, and that only publications that constituted criminal libel could be punished as contempt, should an injunction against future libelous publications still be characterized as a prior restraint?

See Blasi, *Toward a Theory of Prior Restraint: The Central Linkage,* 66 Minn.L.Rev. 11 (1981); Mayton, *Toward a Theory of First Amendment Process: Injunctions of Speech, Subsequent Punishment and the Costs of Prior Restraint Doctrine,* 67 Corn.L.Q. 245 (1982); Jeffries, *Rethinking Prior Restraint,* 92 Yale L.J. 409 (1983).

PARADE AND DEMONSTRATION PERMIT SYSTEMS

Despite traditional prior restraint law, systems requiring official permission in advance for parades and demonstrations have been upheld. In Cox v. New Hampshire, 312 U.S. 569 (1941), the Court sustained a licensing system for parades on public streets, designed to prevent traffic congestion and overlapping parades at the same time and place, and to give authorities notice in advance to afford opportunity for proper policing. A parade or demonstration permit ordinance is unconstitutional, however, if it allows the administrative official standardless discretion to deny permission, or if it authorizes denial on the basis of impermissible standards.[1] In Shuttlesworth v. Birmingham, 394 U.S. 147 (1969), for example, a parade ordinance was unconstitutional because it authorized denial of a permit if "the public welfare, peace, safety, health, decency, good order, morals, or convenience require that it be refused." A number of complex issues have arisen, however, with reference to the appropri-

---

[1] In Forsyth County v. Nationalist Movement, 505 U.S. 123 (1992), the Court did not resolve the question whether the first amendment limits the amount of any fee for a parade permit to a "nominal sum." The Court held invalid an ordinance that allowed the administrator to "adjust the amount to be paid [up to a maximum of $1,000 per day] in order to meet the expense incident to the administration of the ordinance and to the maintenance of public order in the matter licensed." The court concluded that the ordinance gave the administrator unbridled discretion to set fees, and that assessing the fee with reference to security costs would increase permit fees based on content, because the fee would include the projected cost of controlling hostile crowds.

ate procedures for testing the constitutional validity of parade and demonstration permit ordinances and of individual decisions denying permits.

It is clear that if the ordinance is unconstitutional because it provides inadequate standards for granting or denial of permits, the defense is available in a prosecution for parading or demonstrating without a permit. The defendant need not have sought a permit, nor, if a permit were sought, have taken steps to review the official decision denying permission. The issue of the validity of the ordinance is open, too, whether or not permission could have been denied under a properly drafted provision.[2] The rationale has been that the unconstitutional ordinance is "void" and therefore it is appropriate to contest its validity without first seeking a permit under it. Lovell v. Griffin, Ga., 303 U.S. 444 (1938).

Suppose, however, that the ordinance is valid but the licensing official denies permission for unconstitutional reasons. Poulos v. New Hampshire, 345 U.S. 395 (1953), establishes that a state can require that the applicant seek review of the invalid denial of the permit under a valid ordinance. *Poulos* reasoned that the rationale for requiring permission in advance for a parade or demonstration allowed the state to insist that the disappointed applicant not ignore the official denial of permission, and to require challenge through appropriate procedures before the parade or demonstration is held. *Poulos* presents a real dilemma to the applicant unconstitutionally denied permission.[3] The ordinance in *Poulos* required the applicant to seek judicial review of the denial and precluded him from holding his planned meeting pending those judicial proceedings. Justice Reed's opinion in that case rejected the argument that judicial review would be so time-consuming as to make it impossible to hold the planned meeting, stating that while delay was "unfortunate," it was "a price citizens must pay for life in an orderly society." In Freedman v. Maryland, 380 U.S. 51 (1965), however, a motion picture censorship ordinance was held unconstitutional because it did not require the licensing official to go to court after denying a license, and did not provide for prompt judicial review. Southeastern Promotions v. Conrad, 420 U.S. 546 (1975), required the directors of a municipal auditorium to follow the *Freedman* procedures upon denial of permission to use the auditorium. The Court has never considered whether *Freedman* requires that there be prompt judicial review or that licensing officials seek that review in denying parade and demonstration permits.

In Walker v. Birmingham, 388 U.S. 307 (1967), the Court reviewed the criminal contempt conviction of Black ministers who had been enjoined by a state court from holding a Good Friday march to protest racial discrimination. The Court's decision in Shuttlesworth v. Birmingham, note 3 supra, two years

---

[2] In Kunz v. New York, 340 U.S. 290 (1951), for example, defendant's license application was denied because he had in the past ridiculed and denounced the religious beliefs of others, and there had been disorder. His conviction for holding a public worship meeting on the streets without a permit was reversed because the ordinance lacked standards for permit denials.

[3] The dilemma is exacerbated if there is uncertainty concerning the constitutional validity of the underlying ordinance. In Cox v. New Hampshire, 312 U.S. 569 (1941), the parade permit ordinance under which the defendants were convicted was silent about the standards for granting or denying permits. The convictions were affirmed, howev-

er, because the New Hampshire Supreme Court interpreted the ordinance, on the defendants' appeal, to allow denial only upon considerations such as traffic congestion, overlapping parades, and risks of disorder. In Shuttlesworth v. Birmingham, Ala., 394 U.S. 147 (1969), the Court reversed a conviction for parading without a license despite a similar limiting construction of the ordinance under which the defendants were convicted. Given the language of the ordinance, and past administrative practice, it "would have taken extraordinary clairvoyance" for defendants to have foreseen, when they held their parade, the "remarkable job of plastic surgery" by the state court four years later.

later made clear that the parade permit ordinance on which the injunction was based was unconstitutional, and that the clearly stated position of police commissioner Eugene "Bull" Conner, that no permit would be issued, rested on unconstitutional considerations. Moreover, the grant of an *ex parte* injunction, without notice or opportunity to participate in the proceedings, probably also violated the first amendment.[4] Alabama, however, was among the states following the rule that an injunction must be obeyed, even if erroneous, until it is set aside on appellate review.[5] Accordingly, the Alabama Supreme Court refused to consider constitutional attacks on the injunction or the underlying parade ordinance. The Supreme Court affirmed, by a vote of five to four. Justice Stewart's opinion for the Court said that the "case would arise in quite a different constitutional posture if the petitioners, before disobeying the injunction, had challenged it in the Alabama courts, and had been met with delay or frustration of their constitutional claims." In United States v. Ryan, 402 U.S. 530, 532 n. 4 (1971), the Court said: "Our holding [in Walker v. Birmingham] that the claims there sought to be asserted were not open on review of petitioners' contempt convictions was based [upon] the availability of review of those claims at an earlier stage."

SECTION 3.   SPEECH CONFLICTING WITH OTHER COMMUNITY VALUES: GOVERNMENT CONTROL OF THE CONTENT OF SPEECH

Introduction. Section 1 of this chapter examined the lengthy controversy concerning speech that advocates the commission of a crime, and speech advocating the violent overthrow of existing government. This section returns to the inquiry whether there are legitimate government interests that will justify punishing the speaker because of speech content. The four areas examined here—defamation and privacy, obscenity, fighting words and offensive speech, and commercial speech—have one thing in common. In the early 1940's, the Court stated categorically that they were outside the area of constitutional protection normally afforded by the first amendment. In Chaplinsky v. New Hampshire, 315 U.S. 568, 571–572 (1942), Justice Murphy's opinion for a unanimous court said:

> "There are certain well-defined and narrowly limited classes of speech, the prevention and punishment of which has never been thought to raise any Constitutional problem. These include the lewd and obscene, the profane, the libelous, and the insulting or 'fighting' words—those which by their very utterance inflict injury or tend to incite an immediate breach of the peace. It has been well observed that such utterances are no essential part of any exposition of ideas, and are of such slight social value as a step to truth that any benefit that may be derived from them is clearly outweighed by the social interest in order and morality."

Barely more than a month later, in Valentine v. Chrestensen, 316 U.S. 52 (1942), the Court added "purely commercial advertising" to the list of subjects outside the realm of first amendment protection.

Definitional problems to one side (and definitional problems have been particularly serious in the obscenity field), the approach of *Chaplinsky* and

[4] Carroll v. President and Comm'rs of Princess Anne, 393 U.S. 175 (1968).

[5] The rule is the same in the federal courts. United States v. United Mine Workers of America, 330 U.S. 258 (1947).

Valentine has not proved enduring. Within these areas of expression, the Court has imposed significant first amendment barriers to government control of the content of expression. At the same time, the Court has recognized legitimate governmental interests in these cases that permit some control of content. The most important question to be asked is whether the Court has drawn the lines that define constitutionally protected speech content in the right places. A second question is whether the first amendment law that has crystallized in each of these four categories is consistent with that in the other three.

A. PROTECTION OF INDIVIDUAL REPUTATION AND PRIVACY

BEAUHARNAIS v. ILLINOIS, 343 U.S. 250 (1952). An Illinois statute made criminal any publication which "portrays depravity, criminality, unchastity, or lack of virtue of a class of citizens, of any race, color, creed or religion which said publication ... exposes the citizens of any race, color, creed or religion to contempt, derision, or obloquy or which is productive of breach of the peace or riots." Beauharnais was convicted under this statute for passing out leaflets in the form of a petition to the Mayor and City Council of Chicago "to halt the further encroachment, harassment and invasion of white people, their property, neighborhoods and persons, by the Negro." It also included a statement: "If persuasion and the need to prevent the white race from becoming mongrelized by the Negro will not unite us, then the aggressions ... rapes, robberies, knives, guns and marijuana of the Negro, surely will." The Supreme Court upheld his conviction with four Justices dissenting. Justice Frankfurter, speaking for the Court, examined in detail the status of libel laws in the states and referred to earlier statements to the effect that punishment for libel presents no constitutional problem. He then said: "[I]f an utterance directed at an individual may be the object of criminal sanctions, we cannot deny to a State power to punish the same utterance directed at a defined group, unless we can say this is a wilful and purposeless restriction unrelated to the peace and well-being of the State." After discussing problems in the cities he concluded that "we would deny experience to say that the Illinois legislature was without reason" in enacting the law.

At the end of his opinion he included the following paragraph: "Libelous utterances not being within the area of constitutionally protected speech, it is unnecessary, either for us or for the State courts, to consider the issues behind the phrase 'clear and present danger.' Certainly no one would contend that obscene speech, for example, may be punished only upon a showing of such circumstances. Libel, as we have seen, is in the same class."

Justice Black, in dissent, complained that the Court was degrading first amendment freedoms to the "rational basis" level. He concluded as follows: "To say that a legislative body can, with this Court's approval, make it a crime to petition for and publicly discuss proposed legislation seems as far-fetched to me as it would be to say that a valid law could be enacted to punish a candidate for President for telling the people his views. I think the First Amendment, with the Fourteenth, 'absolutely' forbids such laws without any 'ifs' or 'buts' or 'whereases.' Whatever the danger, if any, in such public discussions, it is a danger the Founders deemed outweighed by the danger incident to the stifling of thought and speech. The Court does not act on this view of the Founders. It calculates what it deems to be the danger of public discussion, holds the scales are tipped on the side of state suppression, and upholds state censorship.... If there be minority groups who hail this holding as their victory, they might consider the possible relevancy of this ancient remark: 'Another such victory and I am undone.' "

New York Times Co. v. Sullivan

376 U.S. 254, 84 S.Ct. 710, 11 L.Ed.2d 686 (1964).

Mr. Justice Brennan delivered the opinion of the Court.

We are required in this case to determine for the first time the extent to which the constitutional protections for speech and press limit a State's power to award damages in a libel action brought by a public official against critics of his official conduct.

Respondent L.B. Sullivan is one of the three elected Commissioners of the City of Montgomery, Alabama. He testified that he was "Commissioner of Public Affairs and the duties are supervision of the Police Department, Fire Department, Department of Cemetery and Department of Scales." He brought this civil libel action against the four individual petitioners, who are Negroes and Alabama clergymen, and against petitioner the New York Times Company, a New York corporation which publishes the New York Times, a daily newspaper. A jury in the Circuit Court of Montgomery County awarded him damages of $500,000, the full amount claimed, against all the petitioners, and the Supreme Court of Alabama affirmed. . . .

Respondent's complaint alleged that he had been libeled by statements in a full-page advertisement that was carried in the New York Times on March 29, 1960. Entitled "Heed Their Rising Voices," the advertisement [charged that peaceful demonstrations of Southern Negro students in behalf of their rights guaranteed by the Constitution] ". . . are being met by an unprecedented wave of terror by those who would deny and negate that document which the whole world looks upon as setting the pattern for modern freedom. . . ." Succeeding paragraphs purported to illustrate the "wave of terror" by describing certain alleged events. The text concluded with an appeal for funds for three purposes: support of the student movement, "the struggle for the right-to-vote," and the legal defense of Dr. Martin Luther King, Jr., leader of the movement, against a perjury indictment then pending in Montgomery. . . .

Of the 10 paragraphs of text in the advertisement, the third and a portion of the sixth were the basis of respondent's claim of libel. They read as follows:

> Third paragraph:
>
> "In Montgomery, Alabama, after students sang 'My Country, 'Tis of Thee' on the State Capitol steps, their leaders were expelled from school, and truckloads of police armed with shotguns and tear-gas ringed the Alabama State College Campus. When the entire student body protested to state authorities by refusing to re-register, their dining hall was padlocked in an attempt to starve them into submission."
>
> Sixth paragraph:
>
> "Again and again the Southern violators have answered Dr. King's peaceful protests with intimidation and violence. They have bombed his home almost killing his wife and child. They have assaulted his person. They have arrested him seven times—for 'speeding,' 'loitering' and similar 'offenses.' And now they have charged him with 'perjury'—a *felony* under which they could imprison him for *ten years* . . . ."

Although neither of these statements mentions respondent by name, he contended that the word "police" in the third paragraph referred to him as the Montgomery Commissioner who supervised the Police Department, so that he was being accused of "ringing" the campus with police. He further claimed that the paragraph would be read as imputing to the police, and hence to him, the padlocking of the dining hall in order to starve the students into submission. As to the sixth paragraph, he contended that since arrests are ordinarily made by the police, the statement "They have arrested [Dr. King] seven times" would be read as referring to him; he further contended that the "They" who did the arresting would be equated with the "They" who committed the other described acts and with the "Southern violators." . . .

It is uncontroverted that some of the statements contained in the two paragraphs were not accurate descriptions of events which occurred in Montgomery. Although Negro students staged a demonstration on the State Capitol steps, they sang the National Anthem and not "My Country, 'Tis of Thee." Although nine students were expelled by the State Board of Education, this was not for leading the demonstration at the Capitol, but for demanding service at a lunch counter in the Montgomery County Courthouse on another day. Not the entire student body, but most of it, had protested the expulsion, not by refusing to register, but by boycotting classes on a single day; virtually all the students did register for the ensuing semester. The campus dining hall was not padlocked on any occasion, and the only students who may have been barred from eating there were the few who had neither signed a preregistration application nor requested temporary meal tickets. Although the police were deployed near the campus in large numbers on three occasions, they did not at any time "ring" the campus, and they were not called to the campus in connection with the demonstration on the State Capitol steps, as the third paragraph implied. Dr. King had not been arrested seven times, but only four; and although he claimed to have been assaulted some years earlier in connection with his arrest for loitering outside a courtroom, one of the officers who made the arrest denied that there was such an assault.

On the premise that the charges in the sixth paragraph could be read as referring to him, respondent was allowed to prove that he had not participated in the events described. Although Dr. King's home had in fact been bombed twice when his wife and child were there, both of these occasions antedated respondent's tenure as Commissioner, and the police were not only not implicated in the bombings, but had made every effort to apprehend those who were. Three of Dr. King's four arrests took place before respondent became Commissioner. Although Dr. King had in fact been indicted (he was subsequently acquitted) on two counts of perjury, each of which carried a possible five-year sentence, respondent had nothing to do with procuring the indictment.

Respondent made no effort to prove that he suffered actual pecuniary loss as a result of the alleged libel. One of his witnesses, a former employer, testified that if he had believed the statements, he doubted whether he "would want to be associated with anybody who would be a party to such things that are stated in that ad," and that he would not re-employ respondent if he believed "that he allowed the Police Department to do the things that the paper say he did." But neither this witness nor any of the others testified that he had actually believed the statements in their supposed reference to respondent. . . .

The trial judge submitted the case to the jury under instructions that the statements in the advertisement were "libelous per se" and were not privileged, so that petitioners might be held liable if the jury found that they had published the advertisement and that the statements were made "of and concerning" respondent. . . .

. . .

We reverse the judgment. We hold that the rule of law applied by the Alabama courts is constitutionally deficient for failure to provide the safeguards for freedom of speech and of the press that are required by the First and Fourteenth Amendments in a libel action brought by a public official against critics of his official conduct. We further hold that under the proper safeguards the evidence presented in this case is constitutionally insufficient to support the judgment for respondent. . . .

Under Alabama law as applied in this case, a publication is "libelous per se" if the words "tend to injure a person . . . in his reputation" or to "bring [him] into public contempt"; the trial court stated that the standard was met if the words are such as to "injure him in his public office, or impute misconduct to him in his office, or want of official integrity, or want of fidelity to a public trust. . . ." The jury must find that the words were published "of and concerning" the plaintiff, but where the plaintiff is a public official his place in the governmental hierarchy is sufficient evidence to support a finding that his reputation has been affected by statements that reflect upon the agency of which he is in charge. Once "libel per se" has been established, the defendant has no defense as to stated facts unless he can persuade the jury that they were true in all their particulars. . . . Unless he can discharge the burden of proving truth, general damages are presumed, and may be awarded without proof of pecuniary injury. . . .

The question before us is whether this rule of liability, as applied to an action brought by a public official against critics of his official conduct, abridges the freedom of speech and of the press that is guaranteed by the First and Fourteenth Amendments.

Respondent relies heavily, as did the Alabama courts, on statements of this Court to the effect that the Constitution does not protect libelous publications. Those statements do not foreclose our inquiry here. None of the cases sustained the use of libel laws to impose sanctions upon expression critical of the official conduct of public officials. . . . Like insurrection, contempt, advocacy of unlawful acts, breach of the peace, obscenity, solicitation of legal business, and the various other formulae for the repression of expression that have been challenged in this Court, libel can claim no talismanic immunity from constitutional limitations. It must be measured by standards that satisfy the First Amendment.

The general proposition that freedom of expression upon public questions is secured by the First Amendment has long been settled by our decisions. The constitutional safeguard, we have said, "was fashioned to assure unfettered interchange of ideas for the bringing about of political and social changes desired by the people." Roth v. United States, 354 U.S. 476, 484. . . .

Thus we consider this case against the background of a profound national commitment to the principle that debate on public issues should be uninhibited, robust, and wide-open, and that it may well include vehement, caustic, and sometimes unpleasantly sharp attacks on government and public officials. See Terminiello v. Chicago, 337 U.S. 1, 4; De Jonge v. Oregon, 299 U.S. 353, 365. The present advertisement, as an expression of grievance and protest on one of the major public issues of our time, would seem clearly to qualify for the constitutional protection. The question is whether it forfeits that protection by the falsity of some of its factual statements and by its alleged defamation of respondent.

Authoritative interpretations of the First Amendment guarantees have consistently refused to recognize an exception for any test of truth—whether administered by judges, juries, or administrative officials—and especially not one that puts the burden of proving truth on the speaker. Cf. Speiser v. Randall, 357 U.S. 513, 525–526. The constitutional protection does not turn upon "the truth, popularity, or social utility of the ideas and beliefs which are offered." N.A.A.C.P. v. Button, 371 U.S. 415, 445. As Madison said, "Some degree of abuse is inseparable from the proper use of every thing; and in no instance is this more true than in that of the press." 4 Elliot's Debates on the Federal Constitution (1876), p. 571....

Injury to official reputation affords no more warrant for repressing speech that would otherwise be free than does factual error. Where judicial officers are involved, this Court has held that concern for the dignity and reputation of the courts does not justify the punishment as criminal contempt of criticism of the judge or his decision. Bridges v. California, 314 U.S. 252....

If neither factual error nor defamatory content suffices to remove the constitutional shield from criticism of official conduct, the combination of the two elements is no less inadequate. This is the lesson to be drawn from the great controversy over the Sedition Act of 1798, 1 Stat. 596, which first crystallized a national awareness of the central meaning of the First Amendment. See Levy, Legacy of Suppression (1960), at 258 et seq.; Smith, Freedom's Fetters (1956), at 426, 431 and *passim*....

Although the Sedition Act was never tested in this Court, the attack upon its validity has carried the day in the court of history.... These views reflect a broad consensus that the Act, because of the restraint it imposed upon criticism of government and public officials, was inconsistent with the First Amendment.

. . .

What a State may not constitutionally bring about by means of a criminal statute is likewise beyond the reach of its civil law of libel. The fear of damage awards under a rule such as that invoked by the Alabama courts here may be markedly more inhibiting than the fear of prosecution under a criminal statute.... The judgment awarded in this case—without the need for any proof of actual pecuniary loss—was one thousand times greater than the maximum fine provided by the Alabama criminal statute, and one hundred times greater than that provided by the Sedition Act. And since there is no double-jeopardy limitation applicable to civil lawsuits, this is not the only judgment that may be awarded against petitioners for the same publication. Whether or not a newspaper can survive a succession of such judgments, the pall of fear and timidity imposed upon those who would give voice to public criticism is an atmosphere in which the First Amendment freedoms cannot survive. Plainly the Alabama law of civil libel is "a form of regulation that creates hazards to protected freedoms markedly greater than those that attend reliance upon the criminal law." Bantam Books, Inc. v. Sullivan, 372 U.S. 58, 70.

The state rule of law is not saved by its allowance of the defense of truth.... Allowance of the defense of truth, with the burden of proving it on the defendant, does not mean that only false speech will be deterred.... Under such a rule, would-be critics of official conduct may be deterred from voicing their criticism, even though it is believed to be true and even though it is in fact true, because of doubt whether it can be proved in court or fear of the expense of having to do so. They tend to make only statements which "steer far wider of the unlawful zone." Speiser v. Randall, supra, 357 U.S., at 526. The rule thus dampens the vigor and limits the variety of public debate. It is inconsistent with the First and Fourteenth Amendments.

The constitutional guarantees require, we think, a federal rule that prohibits a public official from recovering damages for a defamatory falsehood relating to his official conduct unless he proves that the statement was made with "actual malice"—that is, with knowledge that it was false or with reckless disregard of whether it was false or not....

. . .

... We think the evidence against the Times supports at most a finding of negligence in failing to discover the misstatements, and is constitutionally insufficient to show the recklessness that is required for a finding of actual malice....

We also think the evidence was constitutionally defective in another respect: it was incapable of supporting the jury's finding that the allegedly libelous statements were made "of and concerning" respondent. Respondent relies on the words of the advertisement and the testimony of six witnesses to establish a connection between it and himself....

Reversed and remanded.

Mr. Justice Black, with whom Mr. Justice Douglas joins, concurring.

... I base my vote to reverse on the belief that the First and Fourteenth Amendments not merely "delimit" a State's power to award damages to "public officials against critics of their official conduct" but completely prohibit a State from exercising such a power. The Court goes on to hold that a State can subject such critics to damages if "actual malice" can be proved against them. "Malice," even as defined by the Court, is an elusive, abstract concept, hard to prove and hard to disprove. The requirement that malice be proved provides at best an evanescent protection for the right critically to discuss public affairs and certainly does not measure up to the sturdy safeguard embodied in the First Amendment. Unlike the Court, therefore, I vote to reverse exclusively on the ground that the Times and the individual defendants had an absolute, unconditional constitutional right to publish in the Times advertisement their criticisms of the Montgomery agencies and officials....

. . .

Mr. Justice Goldberg, with whom Mr. Justice Douglas joins (concurring in the result).

. . .

In my view, the First and Fourteenth Amendments to the Constitution afford to the citizen and to the press an absolute, unconditional privilege to criticize official conduct despite the harm which may flow from excesses and abuses....

NEW YORK TIMES AND "THE CENTRAL MEANING OF THE FIRST AMENDMENT"

The relationship of *New York Times* to the old law of seditious libel and its potential importance for the future is explored in an excellent article. Kalven, *The New York Times Case: A note on "the Central Meaning of the First Amendment,"* 1964 Sup.Ct.Rev. 191, 209. Professor Kalven contended that freedom from prosecutions for seditious libel—freedom to criticize government—is essential to the existence of a free society. After careful examination he concluded that a major purpose of the opinion was to make it clear that the "central meaning" of the first amendment was that seditious libel cannot be sanctioned: "Although the total structure of the opinion is not without its difficulties, it seems to me to convey, however imperfectly, the following crucial syllogism: The central meaning of the Amendment is that seditious libel cannot be made the subject of government sanction. The Alabama rule on fair comment is closely akin to making seditious libel an offense. The Alabama rule therefore violated the central meaning of the Amendment.''

Gertz v. Robert Welch, Inc.

418 U.S. 323, 94 S.Ct. 2997, 41 L.Ed.2d 789 (1974).

Mr. Justice Powell delivered the opinion of the Court.

This Court has struggled for nearly a decade to define the proper accommodation between the law of defamation and the freedoms of speech and press protected by the First Amendment. With this decision we return to that effort. We granted certiorari to reconsider the extent of a publisher's constitutional privilege against liability for defamation of a private citizen. 410 U.S. 925 (1973).

I.

In 1968 a Chicago policeman named Nuccio shot and killed a youth named Nelson. The state authorities prosecuted Nuccio for the homicide and ultimately obtained a conviction for murder in the second degree. The Nelson family retained petitioner Elmer Gertz, a reputable attorney, to represent them in civil litigation against Nuccio.

Respondent publishes American Opinion, a monthly outlet for the views of the John Birch Society. Early in the 1960's the magazine began to warn of a nationwide conspiracy to discredit local law enforcement agencies and create in their stead a national police force capable of supporting a Communist dictatorship. As part of the continuing effort to alert the public to this assumed danger, the managing editor of American Opinion commissioned an article on the murder trial of Officer Nuccio. For this purpose he engaged a regular contributor to the magazine. In March of 1969 respondent published the resulting article under the title "FRAME–UP: Richard Nuccio And The War On Police." The article purports to demonstrate that the testimony against Nuccio at his criminal trial was false and that his prosecution was part of the Communist campaign against the police.

In his capacity as counsel for the Nelson family in the civil litigation, petitioner attended the coroner's inquest into the boy's death and initiated actions for damages, but he neither discussed Officer Nuccio with the press nor played any part in the criminal proceeding. Notwithstanding petitioner's remote connection with the prosecution of Nuccio, respondent's magazine portrayed him as an architect of the "frame-up." According to the article, the police file on petitioner took "a big, Irish cop to lift." The article stated that petitioner had been an official of the "Marxist League for Industrial Democracy, originally known as the Intercollegiate Socialist Society, which has advocated the violent seizure of our government." It labelled Gertz a "Leninist" and a "Communist-fronter." It also stated that Gertz had been an officer of the National Lawyers Guild, described as a Communist organization that "probably did more than any other outfit to plan the Communist attack on the Chicago police during the 1968 Democratic convention."

These statements contained serious inaccuracies. The implication that petitioner had a criminal record was false. Petitioner had been a member and officer of the National Lawyers Guild some 15 years earlier, but there was no evidence that he or that organization had taken any part in planning the 1968 demonstrations in Chicago. There was also no basis for the charge that petitioner was a "Leninist" or a "Communist-fronter." And he had never been a member of the "Marxist League for Industrial Democracy" or the "Intercollegiate Socialist Society."

The managing editor of American Opinion made no effort to verify or substantiate the charges against petitioner. Instead, he appended an editorial introduction stating that the author had "conducted extensive research into the Richard Nuccio case." And he included in the article a photograph of petitioner and wrote the caption that appeared under it: "Elmer Gertz of Red Guild harasses Nuccio." Respondent placed the issue of American Opinion containing the article on sale at newsstands throughout the country and distributed reprints of the article on the streets of Chicago.

Petitioner filed a diversity action for libel in the United States District Court for the Northern District of Illinois. ...

. . .

... [T]he District Court concluded that the *New York Times* standard should govern this case even though petitioner was not a public official or public figure. ...

Petitioner appealed to contest the applicability of the *New York Times* standard to this case. ... The Court of Appeals ... affirmed. ... [W]e reverse.

II.

. . .

Three years after *New York Times,* a majority of the Court agreed to extend the constitutional privilege to defamatory criticism of "public figures." This extension was announced in Curtis Publishing Co. v. Butts and its companion Associated Press v. Walker, 388 U.S. 130, 162 (1967). The first case involved the Saturday Evening Post's charge that Coach Wally Butts of the University of Georgia had conspired with Coach Bear Bryant of the University of Alabama to fix a football game between their respective schools. *Walker* involved an erroneous Associated Press account of former Major General Edwin Walker's participation in a University of Mississippi campus riot. Because Butts was paid by a private alumni association and Walker had resigned from the Army, neither could be classified as a "public official" under *New York Times*. Although Mr. Justice Harlan announced the result in both cases, a majority of the Court agreed with Mr. Chief Justice Warren's conclusion that the *New York Times* test should apply to criticism of "public figures" as well as "public officials." The Court extended the constitutional privilege announced in that case to protect defamatory criticism of nonpublic persons who "are nevertheless intimately involved in the resolution of important public questions or, by reason of their fame, shape events in areas of concern to society at large." Id., at 164. ...

. . .

III.

We begin with the common ground. Under the First Amendment there is no such thing as a false idea. However pernicious an opinion may seem, we depend for its correction not on the conscience of judges and juries but on the competition of other ideas. But there is no constitutional value in false statements of fact. Neither the intentional lie nor the careless error materially advances society's interest in "uninhibited, robust, and wide-open" debate on public issues. New York Times Co. v. Sullivan, 376 U.S., at 270. . . .

Although the erroneous statement of fact is not worthy of constitutional protection, it is nevertheless inevitable in free debate. . . . And punishment of error runs the risk of inducing a cautious and restrictive exercise of the constitutionally guaranteed freedoms of speech and press. Our decisions recognize that a rule of strict liability that compels a publisher or broadcaster to guarantee the accuracy of his factual assertions may lead to intolerable self-censorship. Allowing the media to avoid liability only by proving the truth of all injurious statements does not accord adequate protection to First Amendment liberties. . . .

The need to avoid self-censorship by the news media is, however, not the only societal value at issue. If it were, this Court would have embraced long ago the view that publishers and broadcasters enjoy an unconditional and indefeasible immunity from liability for defamation. . . . Such a rule would indeed obviate the fear that the prospect of civil liability for injurious falsehood might dissuade a timorous press from the effective exercise of First Amendment freedoms. Yet absolute protection for the communications media requires a total sacrifice of the competing value served by the law of defamation.

The legitimate state interest underlying the law of libel is the compensation of individuals for the harm inflicted on them by defamatory falsehood. We would not lightly require the State to abandon this purpose. . . .

. . .

The *New York Times* standard defines the level of constitutional protection appropriate to the context of defamation of a public person. Those who, by reason of the notoriety of their achievements or the vigor and success with which they seek the public's attention, are properly classed as public figures and those who hold governmental office may recover for injury to reputation only on clear and convincing proof that the defamatory falsehood was made with knowledge of its falsity or with reckless disregard for the truth. This standard administers an extremely powerful antidote to the inducement to media self-censorship of the common law rule of strict liability for libel and slander. And it exacts a correspondingly high price from the victims of defamatory falsehood. . . . For the reasons stated below, we conclude that the state interest in compensating injury to the reputation of private individuals requires that a different rule should obtain with respect to them.

. . .

. . . [W]e have no difficulty in distinguishing among defamation plaintiffs. The first remedy of any victim of defamation is self-help—using available opportunities to contradict the lie or correct the error and thereby to minimize its adverse impact on reputation. Public officials and public figures usually enjoy significantly greater access to the channels of effective communication and hence have a more realistic opportunity to counteract false statements than private individuals normally enjoy. Private individuals are therefore more vulnerable to injury, and the state interest in protecting them is correspondingly greater.

More important than the likelihood that private individuals will lack effective opportunities for rebuttal, there is a compelling normative consideration underlying the distinction between public and private defamation plaintiffs. An individual who decides to seek governmental office must accept certain necessary consequences of that involvement in public affairs. He runs the risk of closer public scrutiny than might otherwise be the case. And society's interest in the officers of government is not strictly limited to the formal discharge of official duties. . . .

Those classed as public figures stand in a similar position. Hypothetically, it may be possible for someone to become a public figure through no purposeful action of his own, but the instances of truly involuntary public figures must be exceedingly rare. For the most part those who attain this status have assumed roles of especial prominence in the affairs of society. Some occupy positions of such persuasive power and influence that they are deemed public figures for all purposes. More commonly, those classed as public figures have thrust themselves to the forefront of particular public controversies in order to influence the resolution of the issues involved. In either event, they invite attention and comment.

Even if the foregoing generalities do not obtain in every instance, the communications media are entitled to act on the assumption that public officials and public figures have voluntarily exposed themselves to increased risk of injury from defamatory falsehood concerning them. No such assumption is justified with respect to a private individual. He has not accepted public office nor assumed an "influential role in ordering society." Curtis Publishing Co. v. Butts, 388 U.S., at 164 (Warren, C.J., concurring in result). He has relinquished no part of his interest in the protection of his own good name, and consequently he has a more compelling call on the courts for redress of injury inflicted by defamatory falsehood. Thus, private individuals are not only more vulnerable to injury than public officials and public figures; they are also more deserving of recovery.

For these reasons we conclude that the States should retain substantial latitude in their efforts to enforce a legal remedy for defamatory falsehood injurious to the reputation of a private individual. The extension of the *New York Times* test proposed by the *Rosenbloom* plurality would abridge this legitimate state interest to a degree that we find unacceptable. . . .

We hold that, so long as they do not impose liability without fault, the States may define for themselves the appropriate standard of liability for a publisher or broadcaster of defamatory falsehood injurious to a private individual. This approach provides a more equitable boundary between the competing concerns involved here. It recognizes the strength of the legitimate state interest in compensating private individuals for wrongful injury to reputation, yet shields the press and broadcast media from the rigors of strict liability for defamation. At least this conclusion obtains where, as here, the substance of the defamatory statement "makes substantial danger to reputation apparent." This phrase places in perspective the conclusion we announce today. Our inquiry would involve considerations somewhat different from those discussed above if a State purported to condition civil liability on a factual misstatement whose content did not warn a reasonably prudent editor or broadcaster of its defamatory potential. Cf. Time, Inc. v. Hill, 385 U.S. 374 (1967). Such a case is not now before us, and we intimate no view as to its proper resolution.

IV.

. . . For the reasons stated below, we hold that the States may not permit recovery of presumed or punitive damages, at least when liability is not based on a showing of knowledge of falsity or reckless disregard for the truth.

The common law of defamation is an oddity of tort law, for it allows recovery of purportedly compensatory damages without evidence of actual loss. Under the traditional rules pertaining to actions for libel, the existence of injury is presumed from the fact of publication. Juries may award substantial sums as compensation for supposed damage to reputation without any proof that such harm actually occurred. The largely uncontrolled discretion of juries to award damages where there is no loss unnecessarily compounds the potential of any system of liability for defamatory falsehood to inhibit the vigorous exercise of First Amendment freedoms. Additionally, the doctrine of presumed damages invites juries to punish unpopular opinion rather than to compensate individuals for injury sustained by the publication of a false fact. More to the point, the States have no substantial interest in securing for plaintiffs such as this petitioner gratuitous awards of money damages far in excess of any actual injury.

. . . It is necessary to restrict defamation plaintiffs who do not prove knowledge of falsity or reckless disregard for the truth to compensation for actual injury. We need not define "actual injury," as trial courts have wide experience in framing appropriate jury instructions in tort actions. Suffice it to say that actual injury is not limited to out-of-pocket loss. Indeed, the more customary types of actual harm inflicted by defamatory falsehood include impairment of reputation and standing in the community, personal humiliation, and mental anguish and suffering. Of course, juries must be limited by appropriate instructions, and all awards must be supported by competent evidence concerning the injury, although there need be no evidence which assigns an actual dollar value to the injury.

We also find no justification for allowing awards of punitive damages against publishers and broadcasters held liable under state-defined standards of liability for defamation. In most jurisdictions jury discretion over the amounts awarded is limited only by the gentle rule that they not be excessive. Consequently, juries assess punitive damages in wholly unpredictable amounts bearing no necessary relation to the actual harm caused. And they remain free to use their discretion selectively to punish expressions of unpopular views. Like the doctrine of presumed damages, jury discretion to award punitive damages unnecessarily exacerbates the danger of media self-censorship, but, unlike the former rule, punitive damages are wholly irrelevant to the state interest that justifies a negligence standard for private defamation actions. They are not compensation for injury. Instead, they are private fines levied by civil juries to punish reprehensible conduct and to deter its future occurrence. In short, the private defamation plaintiff who establishes liability under a less demanding standard than that stated by *New York Times* may recover only such damages as are sufficient to compensate him for actual injury.

V.

Notwithstanding our refusal to extend the *New York Times* privilege to defamation of private individuals, respondent contends that we should affirm the judgment below on the ground that petitioner is either a public official or a public figure. There is little basis for the former assertion. Several years prior to the present incident, petitioner had served briefly on housing committees appointed by the mayor of Chicago, but at the time of publication he had never held any remunerative governmental position. Respondent admits this but argues that petitioner's appearance at the coroner's inquest rendered him a "de facto public official." Our cases recognize no such concept. Respondent's suggestion would sweep all lawyers under the *New York Times* rule as officers of the court and distort the plain meaning of the "public official" category beyond all recognition. We decline to follow it.

Respondent's characterization of petitioner as a public figure raises a different question. That designation may rest on either of two alternative bases. In some instances an individual may achieve such pervasive fame or notoriety that he becomes a public figure for all purposes and in all contexts. More commonly, an individual voluntarily injects himself or is drawn into a particular public controversy and thereby becomes a public figure for a limited range of issues. In either case such persons assume special prominence in the resolution of public questions.

Petitioner has long been active in community and professional affairs. He has served as an officer of local civic groups and of various professional organizations, and he has published several books and articles on legal subjects. Although petitioner was consequently well-known in some circles, he had achieved no general fame or notoriety in the community. None of the prospective jurors called at the trial had ever heard of petitioner prior to this litigation, and respondent offered no proof that this response was atypical of the local population. We would not lightly assume that a citizen's participation in community and professional affairs rendered him a public figure for all purposes. Absent clear evidence of general fame or notoriety in the community, and pervasive involvement in the affairs of society, an individual should not be deemed a public personality for all aspects of his life. It is preferable to reduce the public figure question to a more meaningful context by looking to the nature and extent of an individual's participation in the particular controversy giving rise to the defamation.

In this context it is plain that petitioner was not a public figure. He played a minimal role at the coroner's inquest, and his participation related solely to his representation of a private client. He took no part in the criminal prosecution of Officer Nuccio. Moreover, he never discussed either the criminal or civil litigation with the press and was never quoted as having done so. He plainly did not thrust himself into the vortex of this public issue, nor did he engage the public's attention in an attempt to influence its outcome. We are persuaded that the trial court did not err in refusing to characterize petitioner as a public figure for the purpose of this litigation.

We therefore conclude that the *New York Times* standard is inapplicable to this case and that the trial court erred in entering judgment for respondent. Because the jury was allowed to impose liability without fault and was permitted to presume damages without proof of injury, a new trial is necessary. We reverse and remand for further proceedings in accord with this opinion.

It is so ordered.[a]

Mr. Justice Douglas, dissenting.

The Court describes this case as a return to the struggle of "defin[ing] the proper accommodation between the law of defamation and the freedoms of speech and press protected by the First Amendment." It is indeed a struggle, once described by Mr. Justice Black as "the same quagmire" in which the Court "is now helplessly struggling in the field of obscenity." Curtis Publishing Co. v. Butts, 388 U.S. 130, 171 (concurring opinion). I would suggest that the struggle is a quite hopeless one, for, in light of the command of the First Amendment, no "accommodation" of its freedoms can be "proper" except those made by the Framers themselves.

. . .

---

[a] A concurrence by Justice Blackmun and a dissent by Chief Justice Burger are omitted.

Mr. Justice Brennan, dissenting.

... [W]e strike the proper accommodation between avoidance of media self-censorship and protection of individual reputations only when we require States to apply the New York Times Co. v. Sullivan, 376 U.S. 254 (1964), knowing-or-reckless-falsity standard in civil libel actions concerning media reports of the involvement of private individuals in events of public or general interest.

. . .

Mr. Justice White, dissenting.

. . .

... As I see it, there are wholly insufficient grounds for scuttling the libel laws of the States in such wholesale fashion, to say nothing of deprecating the reputation interest of ordinary citizens and rendering them powerless to protect themselves. I do not suggest that the decision is illegitimate or beyond the bounds of judicial review, but it is an ill-considered exercise of the power entrusted to this Court, particularly when the Court has not had the benefit of briefs and argument addressed to most of the major issues which the Court now decides. I respectfully dissent.

. . .

Dun & Bradstreet, Inc. v. Greenmoss Builders, Inc.

472 U.S. 749, 105 S.Ct. 2939, 86 L.Ed.2d 593 (1985).

Justice Powell announced the judgment of the Court and delivered an opinion, in which Justice Rehnquist and Justice O'Connor joined.

... The question presented in this case is whether [the] rule of *Gertz* applies when the false and defamatory statements do not involve matters of public concern.

I

Petitioner Dun & Bradstreet, a credit reporting agency, provides subscribers with financial and related information about businesses. All the information is confidential; under the terms of the subscription agreement the subscribers may not reveal it to anyone else. On July 26, 1976, petitioner sent a report to five subscribers indicating that respondent, a construction contractor, had filed a voluntary petition for bankruptcy. This report was false and grossly misrepresented respondent's assets and liabilities. . . .

. . .

Respondent then brought this defamation action in Vermont state court. It alleged that the false report had injured its reputation and sought both compensatory and punitive damages. . . .

After trial, the jury returned a verdict in favor of respondent and awarded $50,000 in compensatory or presumed damages and $300,000 in punitive damages. Petitioner moved for a new trial. . . . The trial court indicated some doubt as to whether *Gertz* applied to "nonmedia cases," but granted a new trial "[b]ecause of ... dissatisfaction with its charge and ... conviction that the interests of justice require[d]" it.

The Vermont Supreme Court reversed.... [T]he court held "that as a matter of federal constitutional law, the media protections outlined in *Gertz* are inapplicable to nonmedia defamation actions."

. . .

IV

We have never considered whether the *Gertz* balance obtains when the defamatory statements involve no issue of public concern. To make this determination, we must employ the approach approved in *Gertz* and balance the State's interest in compensating private individuals for injury to their reputation against the First Amendment interest in protecting this type of expression. This state interest is identical to the one weighed in *Gertz*....

The First Amendment interest, on the other hand, is less important than the one weighed in *Gertz*. We have long recognized that not all speech is of equal First Amendment importance. It is speech on "'matters of public concern'" that is "at the heart of the First Amendment's protection." First National Bank of Boston v. Bellotti, 435 U.S. 765, 776 (1978), citing Thornhill v. Alabama, 310 U.S. 88, 101 (1940).... In contrast, speech on matters of purely private concern is of less First Amendment concern. [461 U.S.,] at 146–147. As a number of state courts, including the court below, have recognized, the role of the Constitution in regulating state libel law is far more limited when the concerns that activated *New York Times* and *Gertz* are absent....

... [C]ourts for centuries have allowed juries to presume that some damage occurred from many defamatory utterances and publications.... This rule furthers the state interest in providing remedies for defamation by ensuring that those remedies are effective. In light of the reduced constitutional value of speech involving no matters of public concern, we hold that the state interest adequately supports awards of presumed and punitive damages—even absent a showing of "actual malice."

V

The only remaining issue is whether petitioner's credit report involved a matter of public concern. In a related context, we have held that "[w]hether ... speech addresses a matter of public concern must be determined by [the expression's] content, form, and context ... as revealed by the whole record." Connick v. Myers, [461 U.S.,] at 147–148. These factors indicate that petitioner's credit report concerns no public issue. It was speech solely in the individual interest of the speaker and its specific business audience. Cf. Central Hudson Gas & Elec. v. Public Service Comm., 447 U.S. 557, 561 (1980). This particular interest warrants no special protection when—as in this case—the speech is wholly false and clearly damaging to the victim's business reputation. Cf. id., at 566; Virginia Pharmacy Board v. Virginia Consumer Council, 425 U.S. 748, 771–772 (1976). Moreover, since the credit report was made available to only five subscribers, who, under the terms of the subscription agreement, could not disseminate it further, it cannot be said that the report involves any "strong interest in the free flow of commercial information." Id., at 764. There is simply no credible argument that this type of credit reporting requires special protection to ensure that "debate on public issues [will] be uninhibited, robust, and wide-open." New York Times Co. v. Sullivan, 376 U.S., at 270.

In addition, the speech here, like advertising, is hardy and unlikely to be deterred by incidental state regulation. See Virginia Pharmacy Board v. Virginia Consumer Council, supra, at 771–772. It is solely motivated by the desire for profit, which, we have noted, is a force less likely to be deterred than others.

Ibid. Arguably, the reporting here was also more objectively verifiable than speech deserving of greater protection. See ibid. In any case, the market provides a powerful incentive to a credit reporting agency to be accurate, since false credit reporting is of no use to creditors. Thus, any incremental "chilling" effect of libel suits would be of decreased significance.

VI

We conclude that permitting recovery of presumed and punitive damages in defamation cases absent a showing of "actual malice" does not violate the First Amendment when the defamatory statements do not involve matters of public concern. Accordingly, we affirm the judgment of the Vermont Supreme Court.

It is so ordered.

Chief Justice Burger, concurring in the judgment.

. . .

I continue to believe . . . that *Gertz* was ill-conceived, and therefore agree with Justice White that *Gertz* should be overruled. . . .

Justice White, concurring in the judgment.

. . .

. . . I remain convinced that *Gertz* was erroneously decided. I have also become convinced that the Court struck an improvident balance in the *New York Times* case between the public's interest in being fully informed about public officials and public affairs and the competing interest of those who have been defamed in vindicating their reputation.

. . .

The *New York Times* rule . . . countenances two evils: first, the stream of information about public officials and public affairs is polluted and often remains polluted by false information; and second, the reputation and professional life of the defeated plaintiff may be destroyed by falsehoods that might have been avoided with a reasonable effort to investigate the facts. In terms of the First Amendment and reputational interests at stake, these seem grossly perverse results.

. . .

I still believe the common-law rules should have been retained where plaintiff is not a public official or public figure. . . .

It is interesting that Justice Powell declines to follow the *Gertz* approach in this case. I had thought that the decision in *Gertz* was intended to reach cases that involve any false statements of fact injurious to reputation, whether the statement is made privately or publicly and whether or not it implicates a matter of public importance. Justice Powell, however, distinguishes *Gertz* as a case that involved a matter of public concern, an element absent here. Wisely, in my view, Justice Powell does not rest his application of a different rule here on a distinction drawn between media and nonmedia defendants. On that issue, I agree with Justice Brennan that the First Amendment gives no more protection to the press in defamation suits than it does to others exercising their freedom of speech. None of our cases affords such a distinction; to the contrary, the Court has rejected it at every turn. It should be rejected again, particularly in this context, since it makes no sense to give the most protection to those publishers who reach the most readers and therefore pollute the channels of communication with the most misinformation and do the most damage to private reputation. If *Gertz* is to be distinguished from this case, on the ground that it applies only where the allegedly false publication deals with a matter of general or public importance, then where the false publication does not deal with such a matter, the common-law rules would apply whether the defendant is a member of the media or other public disseminator or a nonmedia individual publishing privately. Although Justice Powell speaks only of the inapplicability of the *Gertz* rule with respect to presumed and punitive damages, it must be that the *Gertz* requirement of some kind of fault on the part of the defendant is also inapplicable in cases such as this.

. . .

Justice Brennan, with whom Justice Marshall, Justice Blackmun and Justice Stevens join, dissenting.

. . .

II

The question presented here is narrow. Neither the parties nor the courts below have suggested that Respondent Greenmoss Builders should be required to show actual malice to obtain a judgment and actual compensatory damages. Nor do the parties question the requirement of *Gertz* that respondent must show fault to obtain a judgment and actual damages. The only question presented is whether a jury award of presumed and punitive damages based on less than a showing of actual malice is constitutionally permissible. *Gertz* provides a forthright negative answer. To preserve the jury verdict in this case, therefore, the opinions of Justice Powell and Justice White have cut away the protective mantle of *Gertz*.

A

Relying on the analysis of the Vermont Supreme Court, Respondent urged that this pruning be accomplished by restricting the applicability of *Gertz* to cases in which the defendant is a "media" entity. Such a distinction is irreconcilable with the fundamental First Amendment principle that "[t]he inherent worth of ... speech in terms of its capacity for informing the public does not depend upon the identity of its source, whether corporation, association, union, or individual." First National Bank of Boston v. Bellotti, 435 U.S. 765, 777 (1978). First Amendment difficulties lurk in the definitional questions such an approach would generate.... Perhaps most importantly, the argument that *Gertz* should be limited to the media misapprehends our cases. We protect the press to ensure the vitality of First Amendment guarantees. This solicitude implies no endorsement of the principle that speakers other than the press deserve lesser First Amendment protection....

... [A]t least six Members of this Court (the four who join this opinion and Justice White and The Chief Justice) agree today that, in the context of defamation law, the rights of the institutional media are no greater and no less than those enjoyed by other individuals or organizations engaged in the same activities.[10]

B

Eschewing the media-nonmedia distinction, the opinions of both Justice White and Justice Powell focus primarily on the content of the credit report as a reason for restricting the applicability of *Gertz*....

. . .

---

[10] Justice Powell's opinion does not expressly reject the media-nonmedia distinction, but does expressly decline to apply that distinction to resolve this case.

... The credit reporting at issue here surely involves a subject matter of sufficient public concern to require the comprehensive protections of *Gertz*. Were this speech appropriately characterized as a matter of only private concern, moreover, the elimination of the *Gertz* restrictions on presumed and punitive damages would still violate basic First Amendment requirements.

. . .

Even if the subject matter of credit reporting were properly considered—in the terms of Justice White and Justice Powell—as purely a matter of private discourse, this speech would fall well within the range of valuable expression for which the First Amendment demands protection. Much expression that does not directly involve public issues receives significant protection. Our cases do permit some diminution in the degree of protection afforded one category of speech about economic or commercial matters. "Commercial speech"—defined as advertisements that "[do] no more than propose a commercial transaction," Pittsburgh Press Co. v. Human Relations Comm'n, 413 U.S. 376, 385 (1973)— may be more closely regulated than other types of speech. Even commercial speech, however, receives substantial First Amendment protection....

. . .

The credit reports of Dun & Bradstreet bear few of the earmarks of commercial speech that might be entitled to somewhat less rigorous protection. In *every* case in which we have permitted more extensive state regulation on the basis of a commercial speech rationale the speech being regulated was pure advertising—an offer to buy or sell goods and services or encouraging such buying and selling. Credit reports are not commercial advertisements for a good or service or a proposal to buy or sell such a product. We have been extremely chary about extending the "commercial speech" doctrine beyond this narrowly circumscribed category of advertising because often vitally important speech will be uttered to advance economic interests and because the profit motive making such speech hardy dissipates rapidly when the speech is not advertising. Compare Central Hudson Gas & Elec. Corp. v. Public Service Comm., 447 U.S. 557 (1980) with Consolidated Edison Co. v. Public Service Comm'n, 447 U.S. 530 (1980).

. . .

Of course, the commercial context of Dun & Bradstreet's reports is relevant to the constitutional analysis.... The special harms caused by inaccurate credit reports, the lack of public sophistication about or access to such reports, and the fact that such reports by and large contain statements that are fairly readily susceptible of verification, all may justify appropriate regulation designed to prevent the social losses caused by false credit reports. And in the libel context, the States' regulatory interest in protecting reputation is served by rules permitting recovery for actual compensatory damages upon a showing of fault. Any further interest in deterring potential defamation through case-by-case judicial imposition of presumed and punitive damage awards on less than a showing of actual malice simply exacts too high a toll on First Amendment values. Accordingly, Greenmoss Builders should be permitted to recover for any actual damage it can show resulted from Dun & Bradstreet's negligently false credit report, but should be required to show actual malice to receive presumed or punitive damages. Because the jury was not instructed in accordance with these principles, we would reverse and remand for further proceedings not inconsistent with this opinion.

The Florida Star v. B.J.F.

491 U.S. 524, 109 S.Ct. 2603, 105 L.Ed.2d 443 (1989).

Justice Marshall delivered the opinion of the Court.

Florida Stat. section 794.03 (1987) makes it unlawful to "print, publish, or broadcast ... in any instrument of mass communication" the name of the victim of a sexual offense. Pursuant to this statute, appellant The Florida Star was found civilly liable for publishing the name of a rape victim which it had obtained from a publicly released police report. The issue presented here is whether this result comports with the First Amendment. We hold that it does not.

I

The Florida Star is a weekly newspaper which serves the community of Jacksonville, Florida, and which has an average circulation of approximately 18,000 copies. A regular feature of the newspaper is its "Police Reports" section. That section, typically two to three pages in length, contains brief articles describing local criminal incidents under police investigation.

On October 20, 1983, appellee B.J.F. reported to the Duval County, Florida, Sheriff's Department (the Department) that she had been robbed and sexually assaulted by an unknown assailant. The Department prepared a report on the incident which identified B.J.F., by her full name. The Department then placed the report in its press room. The Department does not restrict access either to the press room or to the reports made available therein.

A Florida Star reporter-trainee sent to the press room copied the police report verbatim, including B.J.F.'s full name, on a blank duplicate of the Department's forms. A Florida Star reporter then prepared a one-paragraph article about the crime, derived entirely from the trainee's copy of the police report. The article included B.J.F.'s full name. It appeared in the "Robberies" subsection of the "Police Reports" section on October 29, 1983, one of fifty-four police blotter stories in that day's edition. The article read:

"[B.J.F.] reported on Thursday, October 20, she was crossing Brentwood Park, which is in the 500 block of Golfair Boulevard, enroute to her bus stop, when an unknown black man ran up behind the lady and placed a knife to her neck and told her not to yell. The suspect then undressed the lady and had sexual intercourse with her before fleeing the scene with her 60 cents, Timex watch and gold necklace. Patrol efforts have been suspended concerning this incident because of a lack of evidence."

In printing B.J.F.'s full name, The Florida Star violated its internal policy of not publishing the names of sexual offense victims.

On September 26, 1984, B.J.F. filed suit in the Circuit Court of Duval County against the Department and The Florida Star, alleging that these parties negligently violated section 794.03. . . .

. . .

. . . The jury awarded B.J.F. $75,000 in compensatory damages and $25,-000 in punitive damages. . . .

The First District Court of Appeal affirmed in a three-paragraph per curiam opinion. . . . The Supreme Court of Florida denied discretionary review.

. . . We . . . reverse.

II

The tension between the right which the First Amendment accords to a free press, on the one hand, and the protections which various statutes and common-law doctrines accord to personal privacy against the publication of truthful information, on the other, is a subject we have addressed several times in recent years. Our decisions in cases involving government attempts to sanction the accurate dissemination of information as invasive of privacy, have not, however, exhaustively considered this conflict. On the contrary, although our decisions have without exception upheld the press' right to publish, we have emphasized each time that we were resolving this conflict only as it arose in a discrete factual context.

The parties to this case frame their contentions in light of a trilogy of cases which have presented, in different contexts, the conflict between truthful reporting and state-protected privacy interests. In Cox Broadcasting Corp. v. Cohn, 420 U.S. 469 (1975), we found unconstitutional a civil damages award entered against a television station for broadcasting the name of a rape-murder victim which the station had obtained from courthouse records. In Oklahoma Publishing Co. v. District Court, 430 U.S. 308 (1977), we found unconstitutional a state court's pretrial order enjoining the media from publishing the name or photograph of an 11–year–old boy in connection with a juvenile proceeding involving that child which reporters had attended. Finally, in Smith v. Daily Mail Publishing Co., 443 U.S. 97 (1979), we found unconstitutional the indictment of two newspapers for violating a state statute forbidding newspapers to publish, without written approval of the juvenile court, the name of any youth charged as a juvenile offender. The papers had learned about a shooting by monitoring a police band radio frequency, and had obtained the name of the alleged juvenile assailant from witnesses, the police, and a local prosecutor.

. . .

We conclude that imposing damages on appellant for publishing B.J.F.'s name violates the First Amendment ... Despite the strong resemblance this case bears to *Cox Broadcasting,* that case cannot fairly be read as controlling here. The name of the rape victim in that case was obtained from courthouse records that were open to public inspection, a fact which Justice White's opinion for the Court repeatedly noted.... Significantly, one of the reasons we gave in *Cox Broadcasting* for invalidating the challenged damages award was the important role the press plays in subjecting trials to public scrutiny and thereby helping guarantee their fairness.... That role is not directly compromised where, as here, the information in question comes from a police report prepared and disseminated at a time at which not only had no adversarial criminal proceedings begun, but no suspect had been identified.

Nor need we accept appellant's invitation to hold broadly that truthful publication may never be punished consistent with the First Amendment. Our cases have carefully eschewed reaching this ultimate question, mindful that the future may bring scenarios which prudence counsels our not resolving anticipatorily.... Indeed, in *Cox Broadcasting,* we pointedly refused to answer even the less sweeping question "whether truthful publications may ever be subjected to civil or criminal liability" for invading "an area of privacy" defined by the State.... Respecting the fact that press freedom and privacy rights are both "plainly rooted in the traditions and significant concerns of our society," we instead focused on the less sweeping issue of "whether the State may impose sanctions on the accurate publication of the name of a rape victim obtained from public records—more specifically, from judicial records which are maintained in connection with a public prosecution and which themselves are open to public inspection." ... We continue to believe that the sensitivity and significance of the interests presented in clashes between First Amendment and privacy rights counsel relying on limited principles that sweep no more broadly than the appropriate context of the instant case.

In our view, this case is appropriately analyzed with reference to such a limited First Amendment principle. It is the one, in fact, which we articulated in *Daily Mail* in our synthesis of prior cases involving attempts to punish truthful publication:

> "[I]f a newspaper lawfully obtains truthful information about a matter of public significance then state officials may not constitutionally punish publication of the information, absent a need to further a state interest of the highest order." 443 U.S., at 103.

According the press the ample protection provided by that principle is supported by at least three separate considerations. . . .

First, because the *Daily Mail* formulation only protects the publication of information which a newspaper has "lawfully obtain[ed]," ... the government retains ample means of safeguarding significant interests upon which publication may impinge, including protecting a rape victim's anonymity. To the extent sensitive information rests in private hands, the government may under some circumstances forbid its nonconsensual acquisition, thereby bringing outside of the *Daily Mail* principle the publication of any information so acquired. To the extent sensitive information is in the government's custody, it has even greater power to forestall or mitigate the injury caused by its release. The government may classify certain information, establish and enforce procedures ensuring its redacted release, and extend a damages remedy against the government or its officials where the government's mishandling of sensitive information leads to its dissemination. Where information is entrusted to the government, a less drastic means than punishing truthful publication almost always exists for guarding against the dissemination of private facts. . . . [8]

A second consideration undergirding the *Daily Mail* principle is the fact that punishing the press for its dissemination of information which is already publicly available is relatively unlikely to advance the interests in the service of which the State seeks to act. It is not, of course, always the case that information lawfully acquired by the press is known, or accessible, to others. But where the government has made certain information publicly available, it is highly anomalous to sanction persons other than the source of its release. . . . The *Daily Mail* formulation reflects the fact that it is a limited set of cases indeed where, despite the accessibility of the public to certain information, a meaningful public interest is served by restricting its further release by other entities, like the press. . . .

A third and final consideration is the "timidity and self-censorship" which may result from allowing the media to be punished for publishing certain truthful information. . . . *Cox Broadcasting* noted this concern with overdeterrence in the context of information made public through official court records, but the fear of excessive media self-suppression is applicable as well to other information released, without qualification, by the government. A contrary rule, depriving protection to those who rely on the government's implied representations of the lawfulness of dissemination, would force upon the media

---

[8] The *Daily Mail* principle does not settle the issue of whether, in cases where information has been acquired *unlawfully* by a newspaper or by a source, government may ever punish not only the unlawful acquisition, but the ensuing publication as well. . . . We have no occasion to address it here.

the onerous obligation of sifting through government press releases, reports, and pronouncements to prune out material arguably unlawful for publication. This situation could inhere even where the newspaper's sole object was to reproduce, with no substantial change, the government's rendition of the event in question.

Applied to the instant case, the *Daily Mail* principle clearly commands reversal. The first inquiry is whether the newspaper "lawfully obtain[ed] truthful information about a matter of public significance." . . . It is undisputed that the news article describing the assault on B.J.F. was accurate. In addition, appellant lawfully obtained B.J.F.'s name. Appellee's argument to the contrary is based on the fact that under Florida law, police reports which reveal the identity of the victim of a sexual offense are not among the matters of "public record" which the public, by law, is entitled to inspect. But the fact that state officials are not required to disclose such reports does not make it unlawful for a newspaper to receive them when furnished by the government. Nor does the fact that the Department apparently failed to fulfill its obligation under section 794.03 not to "cause or allow to be . . . published" the name of a sexual offense victim make the newspaper's ensuing receipt of this information unlawful. Even assuming the Constitution permitted a State to proscribe *receipt* of information, Florida has not taken this step. It is, clear, furthermore, that the news article concerned "a matter of public significance," . . . in the sense in which the *Daily Mail* synthesis of prior cases used that term. That is, the article generally, as opposed to the specific identity contained within it, involved a matter of paramount public import: the commission, and investigation, of a violent crime which had been reported to authorities. . . .

The second inquiry is whether imposing liability on appellant pursuant to section 794.03 serves "a need to further a state interest of the highest order." . . . Appellee argues that a rule punishing publication furthers three closely related interests: the privacy of victims of sexual offenses; the physical safety of such victims, who may be targeted for retaliation if their names become known to their assailants; and the goal of encouraging victims of such crimes to report these offenses without fear of exposure.

At a time in which we are daily reminded of the tragic reality of rape, it is undeniable that these are highly significant interests, a fact underscored by the Florida Legislature's explicit attempt to protect these interests by enacting a criminal statute prohibiting much dissemination of victim identities. We accordingly do not rule out the possibility that, in a proper case, imposing civil sanctions for publication of the name of a rape victim might be so overwhelmingly necessary to advance these interests as to satisfy the Daily Mail standard. For three independent reasons, however, imposing liability for publication under the circumstances of this case is too precipitous a means of advancing these interests to convince us that there is a "need" within the meaning of the *Daily Mail* formulation for Florida to take this extreme step.

First is the manner in which appellant obtained the identifying information in question. As we have noted, where the government itself provides information to the media, it is most appropriate to assume that the government had, but failed to utilize, far more limited means of guarding against dissemination than the extreme step of punishing truthful speech. That assumption is richly borne out in this case. B.J.F.'s identity would never have come to light were it not for the erroneous, if inadvertent, inclusion by the Department of her full name in an incident report made available in a press room open to the public. Florida's policy against disclosure of rape victims' identities, reflected in section 794.03, was undercut by the Department's failure to abide by this policy. Where, as here, the government has failed to police itself in disseminating information, it is clear under *Cox Broadcasting, Oklahoma Publishing,* and *Landmark Communications* that the imposition of damages against the press for its subsequent publication can hardly be said to be a narrowly tailored means of safeguarding anonymity. Once the government has placed such information in the public domain, ... hopes for restitution must rest upon the willingness of the government to compensate victims for their loss of privacy, and to protect them from the other consequences of its mishandling of the information which these victims provided in confidence.

That appellant gained access to the information in question through a government news release makes it especially likely that, if liability were to be imposed, self-censorship would result. Reliance on a news release is a paradigmatically "routine newspaper reporting techniqu[e]." *Daily Mail,* 443 U.S., at 103. The government's issuance of such a release, without qualification, can only convey to recipients that the government considered dissemination lawful, and indeed expected the recipients to disseminate the information further. Had appellant merely reproduced the news release prepared and released by the Department, imposing civil damages would surely violate the First Amendment. The fact that appellant converted the police report into a news story by adding the linguistic connecting tissue necessary to transform the report's facts into full sentences cannot change this result.

A second problem with Florida's imposition of liability for publication is the broad sweep of the negligence per se standard applied under the civil cause of action implied from section 794.03. Unlike claims based on the common law tort of invasion of privacy, ... civil actions based on section 794.03 require no case-by-case findings that the disclosure of a fact about a person's private life was one that a reasonable person would find highly offensive. On the contrary, under the per se theory of negligence adopted by the courts below, liability follows automatically from publication. This is so regardless of whether the identity of the victim is already known throughout the community; whether the victim has voluntarily called public attention to the offense; or whether the identity of the victim has otherwise become a reasonable subject of public concern—because, perhaps, questions have arisen whether the victim fabricated an assault by a particular person. Nor is there a scienter requirement of any kind under section 794.03, engendering the perverse result that truthful publications challenged pursuant to this cause of action are less protected by the First Amendment than even the least protected defamatory falsehoods: those involving purely private figures, where liability is evaluated under a standard, usually applied by a jury, of ordinary negligence. See Gertz v. Robert Welch, Inc., 418 U.S. 323 (1974)....

Third, and finally, the facial underinclusiveness of section 794.03 raises serious doubts about whether Florida is, in fact, serving, with this statute, the significant interests which appellee invokes ... Section 794.03 prohibits the publication of identifying information only if this information appears in an "instrument of mass communication," a term the statute does not define. Section 794.03 does not prohibit the spread by other means of the identities of victims of sexual offenses. An individual who maliciously spreads word of the identity of a rape victim is thus not covered, despite the fact that the communication of such information to persons who live near, or work with, the victim may have consequences equally devastating as the exposure of her name to large numbers of strangers....

When a State attempts the extraordinary measure of punishing truthful publication in the name of privacy, it must demonstrate its commitment to advancing this interest by applying its prohibition evenhandedly, to the small-time disseminator as well as the media giant. Where important First Amendment interests are at stake, the mass scope of disclosure is not an acceptable surrogate for injury. A ban on disclosures effected by "instrument[s] of mass communication" simply cannot be defended on the ground that partial prohibitions may effect partial relief. . . . Without more careful and inclusive precautions against alternative forms of dissemination, we cannot conclude that Florida's selective ban on publication by the mass media satisfactorily accomplishes its stated purpose.

III

Our holding today is limited. We do not hold that truthful publication is automatically constitutionally protected, or that there is no zone of personal privacy within which the State may protect the individual from intrusion by the press, or even that a State may never punish publication of the name of a victim of a sexual offense. We hold only that where a newspaper publishes truthful information which it has lawfully obtained, punishment may lawfully be imposed, if at all, only when narrowly tailored to a state interest of the highest order, and that no such interest is satisfactorily served by imposing liability under section 794.03 to appellant under the facts of this case. The decision below is therefore

Reversed.

Justice Scalia concurring in part and concurring in the judgment.

I think it sufficient to decide this case to rely upon the third ground set forth in the Court's opinion: that a law cannot [justify] . . . a restriction upon truthful speech, when it leaves appreciable damage to that supposedly vital interest unprohibited. In the present case, I would anticipate that the rape victim's discomfort at the dissemination of news of her misfortune among friends and acquaintances would be at least as great as her discomfort at its publication by the media to people to whom she is only a name. Yet the law in question does not prohibit the former in either oral or written form. Nor is it at all clear, as I think it must be to validate this statute, that Florida's general privacy law would prohibit such gossip. . . .

This law has every appearance of a prohibition that society is prepared to impose upon the press but not upon itself. . . .

Justice White, with whom the Chief Justice and Justice O'Connor join, dissenting.

. . .

I

The Court finds its result compelled, or at least supported in varying degrees, by three of our prior cases . . . None of these cases requires the harsh outcome reached today.

. . .

These facts—that the disclosure came in judicial proceedings, which were open to the public—were critical to our analysis in *Cox Broadcasting*. . . .

Cox Broadcasting stands for the proposition that the State cannot make the press its first line of defense in withholding private information from the public—it cannot ask the press to secrete private facts that the State makes no effort to safeguard in the first place. . . .

Finding *Cox Broadcasting* inadequate to support its result, the Court relies on Smith v. Daily Mail Publishing Co. as its principal authority. But the flat rule from *Daily Mail* on which the Court places so much reliance ... was introduced in *Daily Mail* with the cautious qualifier that such a rule was "suggest[ed]" by our prior cases, "[n]one of [which] ... directly control[led]"
...

More importantly, at issue in *Daily Mail* was the disclosure of the name of the perpetrator of an infamous murder of a 15–year–old student.... Surely the rights of those accused of crimes and those who are their victims must differ with respect to privacy concerns....

Consequently, I cannot agree that *Cox Broadcasting,* or *Oklahoma Publishing,* or *Daily Mail* require—or even substantially support—the result reached by the Court today.

II

We are left, then, to wonder whether the three "independent reasons" the Court cites for reversing the judgment for B.J.F. support its result.

The first of these reasons relied on by the Court is the fact "appellant gained access to [B.J.F.'s name] through a government news release." ... Here, the "release" of information provided by the government was not, as the Court says, "without qualification." As the Star's own reporter conceded at trial, the crime incident report that inadvertently included B.J.F.'s name was posted in a room that contained signs making it clear that the names of rape victims were not matters of public record, and were not to be published....

. . .

Second, the Court complains that appellant was judged here under too strict a liability standard....

... Permitting liability under a negligence per se theory does not mean that defendants will be held liable without a showing of negligence, but rather, that the standard of care has been set by the legislature, instead of the courts.... [T]he legislature—reflecting popular sentiment—has determined that disclosure of the fact that a person was raped is categorically a revelation that reasonable people find offensive. And as for the Court's suggestion that the Florida courts' theory permits liability without regard for whether the victim's identity is already known, or whether she herself has made it known—these are facts that would surely enter into the calculation of damages in such a case....

Third, the Court faults the Florida criminal statute for being underinclusive ... But our cases which have struck down laws that limit or burden the press due to their underinclusiveness have involved situations where a legislature has singled out one segment of the news media or press for adverse treatment, ... or singled out the press for adverse treatment when compared to other similarly situated enterprises.... Here, the Florida law evenhandedly covers all "instrument[s] of mass communication" no matter their form, media, content, nature or purpose.... Florida wanted to prevent the widespread distribution of rape victim's names, and therefore enacted a statute tailored almost as precisely as possible to achieving that end.

. . .

Consequently, neither the State's "dissemination" of B.J.F.'s name, nor the standard of liability imposed here, nor the underinclusiveness of Florida tort law require setting aside the verdict for B.J.F.... I turn, therefore, to the more general principles at issue here to see if they recommend the Court's result.

III

At issue in this case is whether there is any information about people, which—though true—may not be published in the press. By holding that only "a state interest of the highest order" permits the State to penalize the publication of truthful information, and by holding that protecting a rape victim's right to privacy is not among those state interests of the highest order, the Court accepts appellant's invitation to obliterate one of the most noteworthy legal inventions of the 20th–Century: the tort of the publication of private facts.... If the First Amendment prohibits wholly private persons (such as B.J.F.) from recovering for the publication of the fact that she was raped, I doubt that there remain any "private facts" which persons may assume will not be published in the newspapers, or broadcast on television.

Of course, the right to privacy is not absolute. Even the Article widely relied upon in cases vindicating privacy rights, Warren & Brandeis, The Right to Privacy, 4 Harv.L.Rev., at 193, recognized that this right inevitably conflicts with the public's right to know about matters of general concern—and that sometimes, the latter must trump the former. Id., at 214–215. Resolving this conflict is a difficult matter, and I do not fault the Court for attempting to strike an appropriate balance between the two, but rather, for according too little weight to B.J.F.'s side of equation, and too much on the other.

... a

ZACCHINI v. SCRIPPS–HOWARD BROADCASTING CO., 433 U.S. 562 (1977). Hugo Zacchini was an entertainer, whose 15 second act consisted of being shot from a cannon into a net 200 feet away. A reporter for a local television station, attending the county fair where Zacchini was performing, was asked by Zacchini not to film his act. The reporter, however, returned the next day and videotaped the entire act. The tape, which ran 15 seconds, was shown on the 11:00 o'clock news that night. In the state trial court, Zacchini was awarded summary judgment in an action for appropriation of his "professional property." The Ohio Supreme Court reversed, relying on Time Inc. v. Hill, 385 U.S. 374 (1967), for the proposition that the television station had a privilege to report the act as a newsworthy event. The Supreme Court reversed. The Court's opinion, by Justice White, concluded that the *Hill* case was inapposite:

"Time, Inc. v. Hill, which was hotly contested and decided by a divided Court, involved an entirely different tort from the 'right of publicity' recognized by the Ohio Supreme Court. As the opinion reveals in Time, Inc. v. Hill, the Court was steeped in the literature of privacy law and was aware of the developing distinctions and nuances in this branch of the law.... The Court was aware that it was adjudicating a 'false light' privacy case involving a matter of public interest, not a case involving 'intrusion,' ... 'appropriation' of a name or likeness for the purposes of trade, ... or 'private details' about a non-newsworthy person or event.... It is also abundantly clear that Time, Inc. v. Hill did not involve a performer, a person with a name having commercial value, or any claim to a 'right of publicity.' This discrete kind of 'appropriation' case was plainly identified in the literature cited by the Court and had been adjudicated in the reported cases.

---

a Chief Justice Burger concurred without opinion. Concurrences by Justice Douglas, and a dissent on jurisdictional grounds by Justice Rehnquist, are omitted.

"...

"... Wherever the line in particular situations is to be drawn between media reports that are protected and those that are not, we are quite sure that the First and Fourteenth Amendments do not immunize the media when they broadcast a performer's entire act without his consent. The Constitution no more prevents a State from requiring respondent to compensate petitioner for broadcasting his act on television than it would privilege respondent to film and broadcast a copyrighted dramatic work without liability to the copyright owner...."

Justice Powell's dissent, joined by Justices Brennan and Marshall, emphasized that the case involved a 15 second clip that was part of a routine daily news program.

"In my view the First Amendment commands a different analytical starting point from the one selected by the Court. Rather than begin with a quantitative analysis of the performer's behavior—is this or is this not his entire act?—we should direct initial attention to the actions of the news media: what use did the station make of the film footage? When a film is used, as here, for a routine portion of a regular news program, I would hold that the First Amendment protects the station from a 'right of publicity' or 'appropriation' suit, absent a strong showing by the plaintiff that the news broadcast was a subterfuge or cover for private or commercial exploitation."

Justice Stevens, dissenting, would have remanded the case to the Ohio Supreme Court for clarification as to whether its decision denying liability rested on the constitutional ground.

B. CONTROL OF OBSCENITY AND PORNOGRAPHY

Paris Adult Theatre I v. Slaton

413 U.S. 49, 93 S.Ct. 2628, 37 L.Ed.2d 446 (1973).

Mr. Chief Justice Burger delivered the opinion of the Court.

Petitioners are two Atlanta, Georgia, movie theaters and their owners and managers, operating in the style of "adult" theaters. On December 28, 1970, respondents, the local state district attorney and the solicitor for the local state trial court, filed civil complaints in that court alleging that petitioners were exhibiting to the public for paid admission two allegedly obscene films ...

Respondents' complaints, made on behalf of the State of Georgia, demanded that the two films be declared obscene and that petitioners be enjoined from exhibiting the films....

... Certain photographs, ... produced at trial, were stipulated to portray the single entrance to both Paris Adult Theatre I and Paris Adult Theatre II as it appeared at the time of the complaints. These photographs show a conventional, inoffensive theater entrance, without any pictures, but with signs indicating that the theaters exhibit "Atlanta's Finest Mature Feature Films." On the door itself is a sign saying: "Adult Theatre—You must be 21 and able to prove it. If viewing the nude body offends you, Please Do Not Enter."

... [T]he trial judge dismissed respondents' complaints.... On appeal, the Georgia Supreme Court unanimously reversed....

. . .

II

We categorically disapprove the theory, apparently adopted by the trial judge, that obscene, pornographic films acquire constitutional immunity from state regulation simply because they are exhibited for consenting adults only. This holding was properly rejected by the Georgia Supreme Court. Although we have often pointedly recognized the high importance of the state interest in regulating the exposure of obscene materials to juveniles and unconsenting adults, ... this Court has never declared these to be the only legitimate state interests permitting regulation of obscene material....

In particular, we hold that there are legitimate state interests at stake in stemming the tide of commercialized obscenity, even assuming it is feasible to enforce effective safeguards against exposure to juveniles and to passersby.... These include the interest of the public in the quality of life and the total community environment, the tone of commerce in the great city centers, and, possibly, the public safety itself.... [T]here is at least an arguable correlation between obscene material and crime. Quite apart from sex crimes, however, there remains one problem of large proportions aptly described by Professor Bickel:

> "It concerns the tone of the society, the mode, or to use terms that have perhaps greater currency, the style and quality of life, now and in the future. A man may be entitled to read an obscene book in his room, or expose himself indecently there.... We should protect his privacy. But if he demands a right to obtain the books and pictures he wants in the market, and to foregather in public places—discreet, if you will, but accessible to all—with others who share his tastes, *then to grant him his right is to affect the world about the rest of us, and to impinge on other privacies.* Even supposing that each of us can, if he wishes, effectively avert the eye and stop the ear (which, in truth, we cannot), what is commonly read and seen and heard and done intrudes upon us all, want it or not." 22 The Public Interest 25–26 (Winter 1971). (Emphasis added.) ...

But, it is argued, there are no scientific data which conclusively demonstrate that exposure to obscene material adversely affects men and women or their society.... It is not for us to resolve empirical uncertainties underlying state legislation, save in the exceptional case where that legislation plainly impinges upon rights protected by the Constitution itself.... Although there is no conclusive proof of a connection between antisocial behavior and obscene material, the legislature of Georgia could quite reasonably determine that such a connection does or might exist....

. . .

If we accept the unprovable assumption that a complete education requires the reading of certain books, ... and the well nigh universal belief that good books, plays, and art lift the spirit, improve the mind, enrich the human personality, and develop character, can we then say that a state legislature may not act on the corollary assumption that commerce in obscene books, or public exhibitions focused on obscene conduct, have a tendency to exert a corrupting and debasing impact leading to antisocial behavior? ... The sum of experience, including that of the past two decades, affords an ample basis for legislatures to conclude that a sensitive, key relationship of human existence, central to family life, community welfare, and the development of human personality, can be debased and distorted by crass commercial exploitation of sex. Nothing in the Constitution prohibits a State from reaching such a conclusion and acting on it legislatively simply because there is no conclusive evidence or empirical data.

It is argued that individual "free will" must govern, even in activities beyond the protection of the First Amendment and other constitutional guarantees of privacy, and that government cannot legitimately impede an individual's desire to see or acquire obscene plays, movies, and books. We do indeed base our society on certain assumptions that people have the capacity for free choice. Most exercises of individual free choice—those in politics, religion, and expression of ideas—are explicitly protected by the Constitution. Totally unlimited play for free will, however, is not allowed in our or any other society. . . .

. . .

It is asserted, however, that standards for evaluating state commercial regulations are inapposite in the present context, as state regulation of access by consenting adults to obscene material violates the constitutionally protected right to privacy enjoyed by petitioners' customers. . . . [I]t is unavailing to compare a theater, open to the public for a fee, with the private home of Stanley v. Georgia, [394 U.S.,] at 568, and the marital bedroom of Griswold v. Connecticut, supra, [381 U.S.,] at 485–486. . . .

. . .

It is also argued that the State has no legitimate interest in "control [of] the moral content of a person's thoughts," Stanley v. Georgia, supra, [394 U.S.,] at 565, and we need not quarrel with this. But we reject the claim that the State of Georgia is here attempting to control the minds or thoughts of those who patronize theaters. Preventing unlimited display or distribution of obscene material, . . . is distinct from a control of reason and the intellect. . . . Where communication of ideas, protected by the First Amendment, is not involved, or the particular privacy of the home protected by *Stanley,* or any of the other "areas or zones" of constitutionally protected privacy, the mere fact that, as a consequence, some human "utterances" or "thoughts" may be incidentally affected does not bar the State from acting to protect legitimate state interests. . . .

Finally, petitioners argue that conduct which directly involves "consenting adults" only has, for that sole reason, a special claim to constitutional protection. Our Constitution establishes a broad range of conditions on the exercise of power by the States, but for us to say that our Constitution incorporates the proposition that conduct involving consenting adults only is always beyond state regulation, is a step we are unable to take. . . .

. . .

Mr. Justice Brennan, with whom Mr. Justice Stewart and Mr. Justice Marshall join, dissenting.

. . . I am convinced that the approach initiated 16 years ago in Roth v. United States, 354 U.S. 476 (1957), and culminating in the Court's decision today, cannot bring stability to this area of the law without jeopardizing fundamental First Amendment values, and I have concluded that the time has come to make a significant departure from that approach.

. . .

Our experience with the *Roth* approach has certainly taught us that the outright suppression of obscenity cannot be reconciled with the fundamental principles of the First and Fourteenth Amendments. . . . [W]e have failed to formulate a standard that sharply distinguishes protected from unprotected speech . . .

... [A]fter 16 years of experimentation and debate I am reluctantly forced to the conclusion that none of the available formulas, including the one announced today, can reduce the vagueness to a tolerable level while at the same time striking an acceptable balance between the protections of the First and Fourteenth Amendments, on the one hand, and on the other the asserted state interest in regulating the dissemination of certain sexually oriented materials.... Although we have assumed that obscenity does exist and that we "know it when [we] see it," Jacobellis v. Ohio, [378 U.S.] at 197 (Stewart, J., concurring), we are manifestly unable to describe it in advance except by reference to concepts so elusive that they fail to distinguish clearly between protected and unprotected speech.

. . .

The problems of fair notice and chilling protected speech are very grave standing alone. But it does not detract from their importance to recognize that a vague statute in this area creates a third, although admittedly more subtle, set of problems. These problems concern the institutional stress that inevitably results where the line separating protected from unprotected speech is excessively vague....

... [A]lmost every case is "marginal." And since the "margin" marks the point of separation between protected and unprotected speech, we are left with a system in which almost every obscenity case presents a constitutional question of exceptional difficulty....

. . .

The Court evidently recognizes that difficulties with the *Roth* approach necessitate a significant change of direction. But the Court does not describe its understanding of those difficulties, nor does it indicate how the restatement of the *Memoirs* test is in any way responsive to the problems that have arisen. In my view, the restatement leaves unresolved the very difficulties that compel our rejection of the underlying *Roth* approach, while at the same time contributing substantial difficulties of its own. The modification of the *Memoirs* test may prove sufficient to jeopardize the analytic underpinnings of the entire scheme. And today's restatement will likely have the effect, whether or not intended, of permitting far more sweeping suppression of sexually oriented expression, including expression that would almost surely be held protected under our current formulation.

. . .

In any case, even if the Court's approach left undamaged the conceptual framework of *Roth,* and even if it clearly barred the suppression of works with at least some social value, I would nevertheless be compelled to reject it....

. . .

Ultimately, the reformulation must fail because it still leaves in this Court the responsibility of determining in each case whether the materials are protected by the First Amendment....

. . .

... I have considered the view, urged so forcefully since 1957 by our Brothers Black and Douglas, that the First Amendment bars the suppression of any sexually oriented expression. That position would effect a sharp reduction, although perhaps not a total elimination, of the uncertainty that surrounds our current approach. Nevertheless, I am convinced that it would achieve that desirable goal only by stripping the States of power to an extent that cannot be justified by the commands of the Constitution, at least so long as there is available an alternative approach that strikes a better balance between the guarantee of free expression and the States' legitimate interests.

. . .

In short, while I cannot say that the interests of the State—apart from the question of juveniles and unconsenting adults—are trivial or nonexistent, I am compelled to conclude that these interests cannot justify the substantial damage to constitutional rights and to this Nation's judicial machinery that inevitably results from state efforts to bar the distribution even of unprotected material to consenting adults.... I would hold, therefore, that at least in the absence of distribution to juveniles or obtrusive exposure to unconsenting adults, the First and Fourteenth Amendments prohibit the State and Federal Governments from attempting wholly to suppress sexually oriented materials on the basis of their allegedly "obscene" contents. Nothing in this approach precludes those governments from taking action to serve what may be strong and legitimate interests through regulation of the manner of distribution of sexually oriented material.

... Difficult questions must still be faced, notably in the areas of distribution to juveniles and offensive exposure to unconsenting adults. Whatever the extent of state power to regulate in those areas, it should be clear that the view I espouse today would introduce a large measure of clarity to this troubled area, would reduce the institutional pressure on this Court and the rest of the State and Federal Judiciary, and would guarantee fuller freedom of expression while leaving room for the protection of legitimate governmental interests....

Mr. Justice Douglas, dissenting.

My Brother Brennan is to be commended for seeking a new path through the thicket which the Court entered when it undertook to sustain the constitutionality of obscenity laws and to place limits on their application. I have expressed on numerous occasions my disagreement with the basic decision that held that "obscenity" was not protected by the First Amendment....

. . .

I applaud the effort of my Brother Brennan to forsake the low road which the Court has followed in this field. The new regime he would inaugurate is much closer than the old to the policy of abstention which the First Amendment proclaims. But since we do not have here the unique series of problems raised by government-imposed or government-approved captive audiences, cf. Public Utilities Comm'n v. Pollak, 343 U.S. 451, I see no constitutional basis for fashioning a rule that makes a publisher, producer, bookseller, librarian, or movie house operator criminally responsible, when he fails to take affirmative steps to protect the consumer against literature, books, or movies offensive to those who temporarily occupy the seats of the mighty.

. . .

Miller v. California

413 U.S. 15, 93 S.Ct. 2607, 37 L.Ed.2d 419 (1973).

Mr. Chief Justice Burger delivered the opinion of the Court.

This is one of a group of "obscenity-pornography" cases being reviewed by the Court in a re-examination of standards enunciated in earlier cases ...

Appellant conducted a mass mailing campaign to advertise the sale of illustrated books, euphemistically called "adult" material. After a jury trial, he was convicted of violating California Penal Code § 311.2(a), a misdemeanor, by knowingly distributing obscene matter,[1] and the Appellate Department, Superior Court of California, County of Orange, summarily affirmed the judgment without opinion. Appellant's conviction was specifically based on his conduct in causing five unsolicited advertising brochures to be sent through the mail in an envelope addressed to a restaurant in Newport Beach, California. The envelope was opened by the manager of the restaurant and his mother. They had not requested the brochures; they complained to the police.

The brochures advertise four books entitled "Intercourse," "Man–Woman," "Sex Orgies Illustrated," and "An Illustrated History of Pornography," and a film entitled "Marital Intercourse." While the brochures contain some descriptive printed material, primarily they consist of pictures and drawings very explicitly depicting men and women in groups of two or more engaging in a variety of sexual activities, with genitals often prominently displayed.

I

... This Court has recognized that the States have a legitimate interest in prohibiting dissemination or exhibition of obscene material when the mode of dissemination carries with it a significant danger of offending the sensibilities of unwilling recipients or of exposure to juveniles.... It is in this context that we are called on to define the standards which must be used to identify obscene material that a State may regulate without infringing on the First Amendment as applicable to the States through the Fourteenth Amendment.

... In Roth v. United States, 354 U.S. 476 (1957), the Court sustained a conviction under a federal statute punishing the mailing of "obscene, lewd, lascivious or filthy ..." materials. The key to that holding was the Court's rejection of the claim that obscene materials were protected by the First Amendment....

Nine years later, in Memoirs v. Massachusetts, 383 U.S. 413 (1966), the Court ... articulated a new test of obscenity. The plurality held that under the *Roth* definition

"as elaborated in subsequent cases, three elements must coalesce: it must be established that (a) the dominant theme of the material taken as a whole appeals to a prurient interest in sex; (b) the material is patently offensive because it affronts contemporary community standards relating to the description or representation of sexual matters; and © the material is utterly without redeeming social value." Id., at 418....

While *Roth* presumed "obscenity" to be "utterly without redeeming social importance," *Memoirs* required that to prove obscenity it must be affirmatively established that the material is "utterly without redeeming social value." Thus, ... the *Memoirs* plurality [required] the prosecution to prove a negative, i.e.,

---

[1] At the time of the commission of the alleged offense, ... § 311 of the California Penal Code read in relevant part:

. . .

"As used in this chapter:

"(a) 'Obscene' means that to the average person, applying contemporary standards, the predominant appeal of the matter, taken as a whole, is to prurient interest, i.e., a shameful or morbid interest in nudity, sex, or excretion, which goes substantially beyond customary limits of candor in description or representation of such matters and is matter which is utterly without redeeming social importance." ...

that the material was "utterly without redeeming social value"—a burden virtually impossible to discharge under our criminal standards of proof....

Apart from the initial formulation in the *Roth* case, no majority of the Court has at any given time been able to agree on a standard to determine what constitutes obscene, pornographic material subject to regulation under the States' police power.... [3] ...

The case we now review was tried on the theory that the California Penal Code § 311 approximately incorporates the three-stage *Memoirs* test, supra. But now the *Memoirs* test has been abandoned as unworkable by its author, and no Member of the Court today supports the *Memoirs* formulation.

II

... [W]e now confine the permissible scope of [obscenity] regulation to works which depict or describe sexual conduct. That conduct must be specifically defined by the applicable state law, as written or authoritatively construed. A state offense must also be limited to works which, taken as a whole, appeal to the prurient interest in sex, which portray sexual conduct in a patently offensive way, and which, taken as a whole, do not have serious literary, artistic, political, or scientific value.

The basic guidelines for the trier of fact must be: (a) whether "the average person, applying contemporary community standards" would find that the work, taken as a whole, appeals to the prurient interest; (b) whether the work depicts or describes, in a patently offensive way, sexual conduct specifically defined by the applicable state law; and © whether the work, taken as a whole, lacks serious literary, artistic, political, or scientific value. We do not adopt as a constitutional standard the "utterly without redeeming social value" test of *Memoirs v. Massachusetts;* that concept has never commanded the adherence of more than three Justices at one time. If a state law that regulates obscene material is thus limited, as written or construed, the First Amendment values applicable to the States through the Fourteenth Amendment are adequately protected by the ultimate power of appellate courts to conduct an independent review of constitutional claims when necessary....

... [A] few plain examples of what a state statute could define for regulation under part (b) of the standard announced in this opinion [are]:

(a) Patently offensive representations or descriptions of ultimate sexual acts, normal or perverted, actual or simulated.

(b) Patently offensive representations or descriptions of masturbation, excretory functions, and lewd exhibition of the genitals.

... At a minimum, prurient, patently offensive depiction or description of sexual conduct must have serious literary, artistic, political, or scientific value to merit First Amendment protection.... For example, medical books ... necessarily use graphic illustrations and descriptions of human anatomy. In resolving the inevitably sensitive questions of fact and law, we must continue to rely on the jury system ...

. . .

---

[3] In the absence of a majority view, this Court was compelled to embark on the practice of summarily reversing convictions for the dissemination of materials that at least five members of the Court, applying their separate tests, found to be protected by the First Amendment. Redrup v. New York, 386 U.S. 767 (1967). Thirty-one cases have been decided in this manner.... The *Redrup* procedure has cast us in the role of an unreviewable board of censorship for the 50 States, subjectively judging each piece of material brought before us.

Under the holdings announced today, no one will be subject to prosecution for the sale or exposure of obscene materials unless these materials depict or describe patently offensive "hard core" sexual conduct specifically defined by the regulating state law, as written or construed. We are satisfied that these specific prerequisites will provide fair notice . . .

III

Under a National Constitution, fundamental First Amendment limitations on the powers of the States do not vary from community to community, but this does not mean that there are, or should or can be, fixed, uniform national standards of precisely what appeals to the "prurient interest" or is "patently offensive." These are essentially questions of fact . . . When triers of fact are asked to decide whether "the average person, applying contemporary community standards" would consider certain materials "prurient," it would be unrealistic to require that the answer be based on some abstract formulation. . . . To require a State to structure obscenity proceedings around evidence of a national "community standard" would be an exercise in futility.

We conclude that neither the State's alleged failure to offer evidence of "national standards," nor the trial court's charge that the jury consider state community standards, were constitutional errors. . . .

. . . [T]he primary concern with requiring a jury to apply the standard of "the average person, applying contemporary community standards" is to be certain that, so far as material is not aimed at a deviant group, it will be judged by its impact on an average person, rather than a particularly susceptible or sensitive person—or indeed a totally insensitive one. . . . [T]he requirement that the jury evaluate the materials with reference to "contemporary standards of the State of California" serves this protective purpose and is constitutionally adequate.

. . .

Mr. Justice Douglas, dissenting.

. . .

My contention is that until a civil proceeding has placed a tract beyond the pale, no criminal prosecution should be sustained. . . .

. . .

If a specific book, play, paper, or motion picture has in a civil proceeding been condemned as obscene and review of that finding has been completed, and thereafter a person publishes, shows, or displays that particular book or film, then a vague law has been made specific. There would remain the underlying question whether the First Amendment allows an implied exception in the case of obscenity. I do not think it does . . . But at least a criminal prosecution brought at that juncture would not violate the time-honored void-for-vagueness test.

. . .

Mr. Justice Brennan, with whom Mr. Justice Stewart and Mr. Justice Marshall join, dissenting.

. . . [I]t is clear that under my dissent in *Paris Adult Theatre I,* the statute under which the prosecution was brought is unconstitutionally overbroad, and therefore invalid on its face. . . .

Jenkins v. Georgia

418 U.S. 153, 94 S.Ct. 2750, 41 L.Ed.2d 642 (1974).

Mr. Justice Rehnquist delivered the opinion of the Court.

Appellant was convicted in Georgia of the crime of distributing obscene material. His conviction, in March 1972, was for showing the film "Carnal Knowledge" in a movie theater in Albany, Georgia....

... We conclude here that the film "Carnal Knowledge" is not obscene under the constitutional standards announced in Miller v. California, 413 U.S. 15 (1973), and that the First and Fourteenth Amendments therefore require that the judgment of the Supreme Court of Georgia affirming appellant's conviction be reversed.

. . .

Miller states that the questions of what appeals to the "prurient interest" and what is "patently offensive" under the obscenity test which it formulates are "essentially questions of fact." ...

But all of this does not lead us to agree with the Supreme Court of Georgia's apparent conclusion that the jury's verdict against appellant virtually precluded all further appellate review of appellant's assertion that his exhibition of the film was protected by the First and Fourteenth Amendments. Even though questions of appeal to the "prurient interest" or of patent offensiveness are "essentially questions of fact," it would be a serious misreading of *Miller* to conclude that juries have unbridled discretion in determining what is "patently offensive." ... [W]e made it plain that under that holding "no one will be subject to prosecution for the sale or exposure of obscene materials unless these materials depict or describe patently offensive 'hard core' sexual conduct...." Id., at 27.

We also took pains in *Miller* to "give a few plain examples of what a state statute could define for regulation under part (b) of the standard announced," that is, the requirement of patent offensiveness. Id., at 25. These examples include "representations or descriptions of ultimate sexual acts, normal or perverted, actual or simulated," and "representations or descriptions of masturbation, excretory functions, and lewd exhibition of the genitals." Ibid. While this did not purport to be an exhaustive catalog of what juries might find patently offensive, it was certainly intended to fix substantive constitutional limitations, deriving from the First Amendment, on the type of material subject to such a determination. It would be wholly at odds with this aspect of *Miller* to uphold an obscenity conviction based upon a defendant's depiction of a woman with a bare midriff, even though a properly charged jury unanimously agreed on a verdict of guilty.

Our own viewing of the film satisfies us that "Carnal Knowledge" could not be found under the *Miller* standards to depict sexual conduct in a patently offensive way. Nothing in the movie falls within either of the two examples given in *Miller* of material which may constitutionally be found to meet the "patently offensive" element of those standards, nor is there anything sufficiently similar to such material to justify similar treatment. While the subject matter of the picture is, in a broader sense, sex, and there are scenes in which sexual conduct including "ultimate sexual acts" is to be understood to be taking place, the camera does not focus on the bodies of the actors at such times. There is no exhibition whatever of the actors' genitals, lewd or otherwise, during these scenes. There are occasional scenes of nudity, but nudity alone is not enough to make material legally obscene under the *Miller* standards.

Appellant's showing of the film "Carnal Knowledge" is simply not the "public portrayal of hard core sexual conduct for its own sake, and for the ensuing commercial gain" which we said was punishable in *Miller*. Id., at 35. We hold that the film could not, as a matter of constitutional law, be found to depict sexual conduct in a patently offensive way, and that it is therefore not outside the protection of the First and Fourteenth Amendments because it is obscene....

Mr. Justice Brennan, with whom Mr. Justice Stewart and Mr. Justice Marshall join, concurring in the result.

... Today's decision confirms my observation in Paris Adult Theatre I v. Slaton ... that the Court's new formulation does not extricate us from the mire of case-by-case determinations of obscenity....

After the Court's decision today, there can be no doubt that *Miller* requires appellate courts—including this Court—to review independently the constitutional fact of obscenity....

In order to make the review mandated by *Miller,* the Court was required to screen the film "Carnal Knowledge" and make an independent determination of obscenity *vel non*....

. . .

Mr. Justice Douglas, being of the view that any ban on obscenity is prohibited by the First Amendment, ... concurs in the reversal of this conviction....

NEW YORK v. FERBER, 458 U.S. 747 (1982). A New York statute prohibits the distribution of materials depicting sexual performances by children under the age of 16. Ferber's conviction, for selling films of young boys masturbating, was reversed by the New York Court of Appeals, which reasoned that the statute violated the first amendment because it applied to materials that were not obscene. The Court reversed, holding that "child pornography" was a category of material outside the protection of the first amendment. Advertising and selling of child pornography could be prohibited to advance the state's interest in preventing sexual exploitation of children. The harm to the children portrayed is exacerbated by distribution of the materials, and closing the channels of commercial distribution is necessary to control initial production of the material. Permitting live performances and photographic reproductions of children engaged in sexual activity had value which is "exceedingly modest, if not *de minimus*." The Court refused to apply overbreadth analysis and did not consider whether the statute could be applied outside "the hard core of child pornography." Concurring, Justice Brennan, joined by Justice Marshall, commented that, in his view, application of the statute to depictions with "serious literary, artistic, scientific or medical value" would violate the first amendment.

OSBORNE v. OHIO, 495 U.S. 103 (1990). The Court held that it is constitutional to prohibit viewing and possession of child pornography. "Given the importance of the State's interest in protecting the victims of child pornography," it was appropriate "to stamp out this vice at all levels in the distribution chain."

American Booksellers Association, Inc. v. Hudnut

771 F.2d 323 (7th Cir.1985).

Before Cudahy and Easterbrook, Circuit Judges, and Swygert, Senior Circuit Judge.

Easterbrook, Circuit Judge.

Indianapolis enacted an ordinance defining "pornography" as a practice that discriminates against women. "Pornography" is to be redressed through the administrative and judicial methods used for other discrimination. The City's definition of "pornography" is considerably different from "obscenity," which the Supreme Court has held is not protected by the First Amendment.

To be "obscene" under Miller v. California, 413 U.S. 15 (1973), "a publication must, taken as a whole, appeal to the prurient interest, must contain patently offensive depictions or descriptions of specified sexual conduct, and on the whole have no serious literary, artistic, political, or scientific value." Brockett v. Spokane Arcades, Inc., 472 U.S. 491 (1985). Offensiveness must be assessed under the standards of the community. Both offensiveness and an appeal to something other than "normal, healthy sexual desires" ... are essential elements of "obscenity."

"Pornography" under the ordinance is "the graphic sexually explicit subordination of women, whether in pictures or in words, that also includes one or more of the following:

(1) Women are presented as sexual objects who enjoy pain or humiliation; or

(2) Women are presented as sexual objects who experience sexual pleasure in being raped; or

(3) Women are presented as sexual objects tied up or cut up or mutilated or bruised or physically hurt, or as dismembered or truncated or fragmented or severed into body parts; or

(4) Women are presented as being penetrated by objects or animals; or

(5) Women are presented in scenarios of degradation, injury, abasement, torture, shown as filthy or inferior, bleeding, bruised, or hurt in a context that makes these conditions sexual; or

(6) Women are presented as sexual objects for domination, conquest, violation, exploitation, possession, or use, or through postures or positions of servility or submission or display." Indianapolis Code § 16–3(q).

The statute provides that the "use of men, children, or transsexuals in the place of women in paragraphs (1) through (6) above shall also constitute pornography under this section." The ordinance as passed in April 1984 defined "sexually explicit" to mean actual or simulated intercourse or the uncovered exhibition of the genitals, buttocks or anus. An amendment in June 1984 deleted this provision, leaving the term undefined.

The Indianapolis ordinance does not refer to the prurient interest, to offensiveness, or to the standards of the community. It demands attention to particular depictions, not to the work judged as a whole. It is irrelevant under the ordinance whether the work has literary, artistic, political, or scientific value. The City and many amici point to these omissions as virtues. They maintain that pornography influences attitudes, and the statute is a way to alter the socialization of men and women rather than to vindicate community standards of offensiveness. And as one of the principal drafters of the ordinance has asserted, "if a woman is subjected, why should it matter that the work has other value?" Catharine A. MacKinnon, Pornography, Civil Rights, and Speech, 20 Harv.Civ.Rts.—Civ.Lib.L.Rev. 1, 21 (1985).

Civil rights groups and feminists have entered this case as amici on both sides. Those supporting the ordinance say that it will play an important role in reducing the tendency of men to view women as sexual objects, a tendency that leads to both unacceptable attitudes and discrimination in the workplace and violence away from it. Those opposing the ordinance point out that much radical feminist literature is explicit and depicts women in ways forbidden by the ordinance and that the ordinance would reopen old battles. It is unclear how Indianapolis would treat works from James Joyce's *Ulysses* to Homer's *Iliad;* both depict women as submissive objects for conquest and domination.

We do not try to balance the arguments for and against an ordinance such as this. The ordinance discriminates on the ground of the content of the speech. Speech treating women in the approved way—in sexual encounters "premised on equality" (MacKinnon, supra, at 22)—is lawful no matter how sexually explicit. Speech treating women in the disapproved way—as submissive in matters sexual or as enjoying humiliation—is unlawful no matter how significant the literary, artistic, or political qualities of the work taken as a whole. The state may not ordain preferred viewpoints in this way. The Constitution forbids the state to declare one perspective right and silence opponents.

I

The ordinance contains four prohibitions. People may not "traffic" in pornography, "coerce" others into performing in pornographic works, or "force" pornography on anyone. Anyone injured by someone who has seen or read pornography has a right of action against the maker or seller.

Trafficking is defined in § 16–3(g)(4) as the "production, sale, exhibition, or distribution of pornography." The offense excludes exhibition in a public or educational library, but a "special display" in a library may be sex discrimination. Section 16–3(g)(4)(C) provides that the trafficking paragraph "shall not be construed to make isolated passages or isolated parts actionable."

"Coercion into pornographic performance" is defined in § 16–3(g)(5) as "[c]oercing, intimidating or fraudulently inducing any person ... into performing for pornography...." The ordinance specifies that proof of any of the following "shall not constitute a defense: I. That the person is a woman; ... VI. That the person has previously posed for sexually explicit pictures ... with anyone ...; ... VIII. That the person actually consented to a use of the performance that is changed into pornography; ... IX. That the person knew that the purpose of the acts or events in question was to make pornography; ... XI. That the person signed a contract, or made statements affirming a willingness to cooperate in the production of pornography; XII. That no physical force, threats, or weapons were used in the making of the pornography; or XIII. That the person was paid or otherwise compensated."

"Forcing pornography on a person," according to § 16–3(g)(5), is the "forcing of pornography on any woman, man, child, or transsexual in any place of employment, in education, in a home, or in any public place." The statute does not define forcing, but one of its authors states that the definition reaches pornography shown to medical students as part of their education or given to language students for translation. MacKinnon, supra, at 40–41.

Section 16–3(g)(7) defines as a prohibited practice the "assault, physical attack, or injury of any woman, man, child, or transsexual in a way that is directly caused by specific pornography."

For purposes of all four offenses, it is generally "not ... a defense that the respondent did not know or intend that the materials were pornography...." Section 16–3(g)(8). But the ordinance provides that damages are unavailable in trafficking cases unless the complainant proves "that the respondent knew or had reason to know that the materials were pornography." It is a complete defense to a trafficking case that all of the materials in question were pornography only by virtue of category (6) of the definition of pornography. In cases of assault caused by pornography, those who seek damages from "a seller, exhibitor or distributor" must show that the defendant knew or had reason to know of the material's status as pornography. By implication, those who seek damages from an author need not show this.

A woman aggrieved by trafficking in pornography may file a complaint "as a woman acting against the subordination of women" with the office of equal opportunity. Section 16–17(b). A man, child, or transsexual also may protest trafficking "but must prove injury in the same way that a woman is injured...." Ibid. Subsection (a) also provides, however, that "any person claiming to be aggrieved" by trafficking, coercion, forcing, or assault may complain against the "perpetrators." We need not decide whether § 16–17(b) qualifies the right of action in § 16–17(a).

. . .

The district court held the ordinance unconstitutional....

II

The plaintiffs are a congeries of distributors and readers of books, magazines, and films. The American Booksellers Association comprises about 5,200 bookstores and chains. The Association for American Publishers includes most of the country's publishers. Video Shack, Inc., sells and rents video cassettes in Indianapolis. Kelly Bentley, a resident of Indianapolis, reads books and watches films. There are many more plaintiffs. Collectively the plaintiffs (or their members, whose interest they represent) make, sell, or read just about every kind of material that could be affected by the ordinance, from hard-core films to W.B. Yeats's poem "Leda and the Swan" (from the myth of Zeus in the form of a swan impregnating an apparently subordinate Leda), to the collected works of James Joyce, D.H. Lawrence, and John Cleland.

. . .

III

"If there is any fixed star in our constitutional constellation, it is that no official, high or petty, can prescribe what shall be orthodox in politics, nationalism, religion, or other matters of opinion or force citizens to confess by word or act their faith therein." West Virginia State Board of Education v. Barnette, 319 U.S. 624, 642 (1943). Under the First Amendment the government must leave to the people the evaluation of ideas. Bald or subtle, an idea is as powerful as the audience allows it to be. A belief may be pernicious—the beliefs of Nazis led to the death of millions, those of the Klan to the repression of millions. A pernicious belief may prevail. Totalitarian governments today rule much of the planet, practicing suppression of billions and spreading dogma that may enslave others. One of the things that separates our society from theirs is our absolute right to propagate opinions that the government finds wrong or even hateful.

The ideas of the Klan may be propagated. Brandenburg v. Ohio, 395 U.S. 444 (1969). Communists may speak freely and run for office. DeJonge v. Oregon, 299 U.S. 353 (1937). The Nazi Party may march through a city with a large Jewish population. Collin v. Smith, 578 F.2d 1197 (7th Cir.), cert. denied, 439 U.S. 916 (1978).... People may teach religions that others despise. People may seek to repeal laws guaranteeing equal opportunity in employment or to revoke the constitutional amendments granting the vote to blacks and women. They may do this because "above all else, the First Amendment means that government has no power to restrict expression because of its message [or] its ideas...." Police Department v. Mosley, 408 U.S. 92, 95 (1972)....

Under the ordinance graphic sexually explicit speech is "pornography" or not depending on the perspective the author adopts. Speech that "subordinates" women and also, for example, presents women as enjoying pain, humiliation, or rape, or even simply presents women in "positions of servility or submission or display" is forbidden, no matter how great the literary or political value of the work taken as a whole. Speech that portrays women in positions of equality is lawful, no matter how graphic the sexual content. This is thought control. It establishes an "approved" view of women, of how they may react to sexual encounters, of how the sexes may relate to each other. Those who espouse the approved view may use sexual images; those who do not, may not.

Indianapolis justifies the ordinance on the ground that pornography affects thoughts. Men who see women depicted as subordinate are more likely to treat them so. Pornography is an aspect of dominance. It does not persuade people so much as change them. It works by socializing, by establishing the expected and the permissible. In this view pornography is not an idea; pornography is the injury. There is much to this perspective. Beliefs are also facts. People often act in accordance with the images and patterns they find around them. People raised in a religion tend to accept the tenets of that religion, often without independent examination. People taught from birth that black people are fit only for slavery rarely rebelled against that creed; beliefs coupled with the self-interest of the masters established a social structure that inflicted great harm while enduring for centuries. Words and images act at the level of the subconscious before they persuade at the level of the conscious. Even the truth has little chance unless a statement fits within the framework of beliefs that may never have been subjected to rational study.

Therefore we accept the premises of this legislation. Depictions of subordination tend to perpetuate subordination. The subordinate status of women in turn leads to affront and lower pay at work, insult and injury at home, battery and rape on the streets. In the language of the legislature, "[p]ornography is central in creating and maintaining sex as a basis of discrimination. Pornography is a systematic practice of exploitation and subordination based on sex which differentially harms women. The bigotry and contempt it produces, with the acts of aggression it fosters, harm women's opportunities for equality and rights [of all kinds]." Indianapolis Code § 16–1(a)(2).

Yet this simply demonstrates the power of pornography as speech. All of these unhappy effects depend on mental intermediation. Pornography affects how people see the world, their fellows, and social relations. If pornography is what pornography does, so is other speech.... The Alien and Sedition Acts passed during the administration of John Adams rested on a sincerely held belief that disrespect for the government leads to social collapse and revolution—a belief with support in the history of many nations. Most governments of the world act on this empirical regularity, suppressing critical speech. In the

United States, however, the strength of the support for this belief is irrelevant....

Racial bigotry, anti-semitism, violence on television, reporters' biases—these and many more influence the culture and shape our socialization. None is directly answerable by more speech, unless that speech too finds its place in the popular culture. Yet all is protected as speech, however insidious. Any other answer leaves the government in control of all of the institutions of culture, the great censor and director of which thoughts are good for us.

Sexual responses often are unthinking responses, and the association of sexual arousal with the subordination of women therefore may have a substantial effect. But almost all cultural stimuli provoke unconscious responses. Religious ceremonies condition their participants. Teachers convey messages by selecting what not to cover; the implicit message about what is off limits or unthinkable may be more powerful than the messages for which they present rational argument. Television scripts contain unarticulated assumptions. People may be conditioned in subtle ways. If the fact that speech plays a role in a process of conditioning were enough to permit governmental regulation, that would be the end of freedom of speech.

It is possible to interpret the claim that the pornography is the harm in a different way. Indianapolis emphasizes the injury that models in pornographic films and pictures may suffer. The record contains materials depicting sexual torture, penetration of women by red-hot irons and the like. These concerns have nothing to do with written materials subject to the statute, and physical injury can occur with or without the "subordination" of women. As we discuss in Part IV, a state may make injury in the course of producing a film unlawful independent of the viewpoint expressed in the film.

The more immediate point, however, is that the image of pain is not necessarily pain. In *Body Double,* a suspense film directed by Brian DePalma, a woman who has disrobed and presented a sexually explicit display is murdered by an intruder with a drill. The drill runs through the woman's body. The film is sexually explicit and a murder occurs—yet no one believes that the actress suffered pain or died. In *Barbarella* a character played by Jane Fonda is at times displayed in sexually explicit ways and at times shown "bleeding, bruised, [and] hurt in a context that makes these conditions sexual"—and again no one believes that Fonda was actually tortured to make the film. In *Carnal Knowledge* a woman grovels to please the sexual whims of a character played by Jack Nicholson; no one believes that there was a real sexual submission, and the Supreme Court held the film protected by the First Amendment. Jenkins v. Georgia, 418 U.S. 153 (1974). And this works both ways. The description of women's sexual domination of men in *Lysistrata* was not real dominance. Depictions may affect slavery, war, or sexual roles, but a book about slavery is not itself slavery, or a book about death by poison a murder.

Much of Indianapolis's argument rests on the belief that when speech is "unanswerable," and the metaphor that there is a "marketplace of ideas" does not apply, the First Amendment does not apply either. The metaphor is honored; Milton's *Aeropagitica* and John Stewart Mill's *On Liberty* defend freedom of speech on the ground that the truth will prevail, and many of the most important cases under the First Amendment recite this position. The Framers undoubtedly believed it. As a general matter it is true. But the Constitution does not make the dominance of truth a necessary condition of freedom of speech. To say that it does would be to confuse an outcome of free speech with a necessary condition for the application of the amendment.

A power to limit speech on the ground that truth has not yet prevailed and is not likely to prevail implies the power to declare truth. At some point the government must be able to say (as Indianapolis has said): "We know what the truth is, yet a free exchange of speech has not driven out falsity, so that we must now prohibit falsity." If the government may declare the truth, why wait for the failure of speech? Under the First Amendment, however, there is no such thing as a false idea, Gertz v. Robert Welch, Inc., 418 U.S. 323, 339 (1974), so the government may not restrict speech on the ground that in a free exchange truth is not yet dominant.

At any time, some speech is ahead in the game; the more numerous speakers prevail. Supporters of minority candidates may be forever "excluded" from the political process because their candidates never win, because few people believe their positions. This does not mean that freedom of speech has failed.

. . .

We come, finally, to the argument that pornography is "low value" speech, that it is enough like obscenity that Indianapolis may prohibit it. Some cases hold that speech far removed from politics and other subjects at the core of the Framers' concerns may be subjected to special regulation. E.g., FCC v. Pacifica Foundation, 438 U.S. 726 (1978); Young v. American Mini Theatres, Inc., 427 U.S. 50, 67–70 (1976) (plurality opinion); Chaplinsky v. New Hampshire, 315 U.S. 568, 571–72 (1942). These cases do not sustain statutes that select among viewpoints, however. In *Pacifica* the FCC sought to keep vile language off the air during certain times. The Court held that it may; but the Court would not have sustained a regulation prohibiting scatological descriptions of Republicans but not scatological descriptions of Democrats, or any other form of selection among viewpoints. . . .

At all events, "pornography" is not low value speech within the meaning of these cases. Indianapolis seeks to prohibit certain speech because it believes this speech influences social relations and politics on a grand scale, that it controls attitudes at home and in the legislature. This precludes a characterization of the speech as low value. True, pornography and obscenity have sex in common. But Indianapolis left out of its definition any reference to literary, artistic, political, or scientific value. The ordinance applies to graphic sexually explicit subordination in works great and small.[3] The Court sometimes balances the value of speech against the costs of its restriction, but it does this by category of speech and not by the content of particular works. . . . Indianapolis has created an approved point of view and so loses the support of these cases.

Any rationale we could imagine in support of this ordinance could not be limited to sex discrimination. Free speech has been on balance an ally of those seeking change. Governments that want stasis start by restricting speech. Culture is a powerful force of continuity; Indianapolis paints pornography as

---

[3] Indianapolis briefly argues that Beauharnais v. Illinois, 343 U.S. 250 (1952), which allowed a state to penalize "group libel," supports the ordinance. In Collin v. Smith, 578 F.2d at 1205, we concluded that cases such as *New York Times v. Sullivan* had so washed away the foundations of *Beauharnais* that it could not be considered authoritative. If we are wrong in this, however, the case still does not support the ordinance. It is not clear that depicting women as subordinate in sexually explicit ways, even combined with a depiction of pleasure in rape, would fit within the definition of a group libel. The well received film Swept Away used explicit sex, plus taking pleasure in rape, to make a political statement, not to defame. Work must be an insult or slur for its own sake to come within the ambit of *Beauharnais,* and a work need not be scurrilous at all to be "pornography" under the ordinance.

part of the culture of power. Change in any complex system ultimately depends on the ability of outsiders to challenge accepted views and the reigning institutions. Without a strong guarantee of freedom of speech, there is no effective right to challenge what is.

IV

The definition of "pornography" is unconstitutional. No construction or excision of particular terms could save it. The offense of trafficking in pornography necessarily falls with the definition. . . .

. . . The district court came to the same conclusion. Its judgment is therefore

Affirmed.[a]

C.   CONTROL OF "FIGHTING WORDS" AND OFFENSIVE SPEECH

CANTWELL v. CONNECTICUT, 310 U.S. 296 (1940). Cantwell, a member of the Jehovah's Witnesses, was engaged in proselyting in the streets of New Haven. He was convicted of a common law breach of the peace based on a showing that he stopped two men in the street, asked, and received, permission to play an anti-Catholic phonograph record. Both listeners were incensed by the contents of the record and were tempted to strike Cantwell unless he went away. On being told to be on his way he left their presence. The Court reversed his conviction. Justice Roberts, speaking for the Court, said, in part:

"The offense known as breach of the peace embraces a great variety of conduct destroying or menacing public order and tranquility. It includes not only violent acts but acts and words likely to produce violence in others. No one would have the hardihood to suggest that the principle of freedom of speech sanctions incitement to riot or that religious liberty connotes the privilege to exhort others to physical attack upon those belonging to another sect. When clear and present danger of riot, disorder, interference with traffic upon the public streets, or other immediate threat to public safety, peace, or order, appears, the power of the state to prevent or punish is obvious. Equally obvious is it that a state may not unduly suppress free communication of views, religious or other, under the guise of conserving desirable conditions. Here we have a situation analogous to a conviction under a statute sweeping in a great variety of conduct under a general and indefinite characterization, and leaving to the executive and judicial branches too wide a discretion in its application.

" . . .

"We find in the instant case no assault or threatening of bodily harm, no truculent bearing, no intentional discourtesy, no personal abuse. On the contrary, we find only an effort to persuade a willing listener to buy a book or to contribute money in the interest of what Cantwell, however misguided others may think him, conceived to be true religion.

" . . .

"Although the contents of the record not unnaturally aroused animosity, we think that, in the absence of a statute narrowly drawn to define and punish specific conduct as constituting a clear and present danger to a substantial

[a] A concurrence by Judge Swygert is omitted. The decision was summarily affirmed by the Supreme Court without argument or opinion. (Chief Justice Burger, and Justices Rehnquist and O'Connor dissented, stating that the case should be set for argument.) 475 U.S. 1001 (1986).

interest of the State, the petitioner's communication, considered in the light of the constitutional guarantees, raised no such clear and present menace to public peace and order as to render him liable to conviction of the common law offense in question."

CHAPLINSKY v. NEW HAMPSHIRE, 315 U.S. 568 (1942). Defendant, a Jehovah's Witness, got into an altercation on a public sidewalk with the City Marshal of Rochester, New Hampshire, and allegedly told the officer: "You are a God damned racketeer" and a "damned Fascist." Defendant was convicted under a statute forbidding a person to address "any offensive, derisive or annoying word to any other person who is lawfully in any street or other public place." The statute was construed by the state court to ban only "such words, as ordinary men know, are likely to cause a fight," thus to prohibit "the face-to-face words plainly likely to cause a breach of the peace by the addressee." Justice Murphy's opinion for the Court stated that fighting words—"those which by their very utterance inflict injury or tend to incite an immediate breach of the peace"—were not protected by the Constitution. A unanimous Court sustained the conviction.

Cohen v. California

403 U.S. 15, 91 S.Ct. 1780, 29 L.Ed.2d 284 (1971).

[Defendant was convicted of violating a California statute that prohibited "maliciously and willfully disturb[ing] the peace or quiet of any neighborhood or person" by "offensive conduct." In a Los Angeles courthouse corridor he had worn a jacket bearing the plainly visible words "Fuck the Draft." Women and children were present in the corridor. He testified that he wore the jacket as a means of informing the public of the depth of his feelings against the Vietnam war and the draft. In affirming, the California Court of Appeals held that "offensive conduct" means "behavior which has a tendency to provoke *others* to acts of violence or to in turn disturb the peace"; it was "certainly reasonably foreseeable" that defendant's conduct might cause others to commit an act of violence against defendant or attempt to forcibly remove his jacket.]

Mr. Justice Harlan delivered the opinion of the Court.

. . .

... [A]s it comes to us, this case cannot be said to fall within those relatively few categories of instances where prior decisions have established the power of government to deal more comprehensively with certain forms of individual expression simply upon a showing that such a form was employed. This is not, for example, an obscenity case. Whatever else may be necessary to give rise to the States' broader power to prohibit obscene expression, such expression must be, in some significant way, erotic. Roth v. United States, 354 U.S. 476 (1957). It cannot plausibly be maintained that this vulgar allusion to the Selective Service System would conjure up such psychic stimulation in anyone likely to be confronted with Cohen's crudely defaced jacket.

This Court has also held that the States are free to ban the simple use, without a demonstration of additional justifying circumstances, of so-called "fighting words," those personally abusive epithets which, when addressed to the ordinary citizen, are, as a matter of common knowledge, inherently likely to provoke violent reaction. Chaplinsky v. New Hampshire, 315 U.S. 568 (1942). While the four-letter word displayed by Cohen in relation to the draft is not uncommonly employed in a personally provocative fashion, in this instance it was clearly not "directed to the person of the hearer." Cantwell v. Connecticut,

310 U.S. 296, 309 (1940). No individual actually or likely to be present could reasonably have regarded the words on appellant's jacket as a direct personal insult. Nor do we have here an instance of the exercise of the State's police power to prevent a speaker from intentionally provoking a given group to hostile reaction. Cf. Feiner v. New York, 340 U.S. 315 (1951); Terminiello v. Chicago, 337 U.S. 1 (1949). There is ... no showing that anyone who saw Cohen was in fact violently aroused or that appellant intended such a result.

Finally, in arguments before this Court much has been made of the claim that Cohen's distasteful mode of expression was thrust upon unwilling or unsuspecting viewers, and that the State might therefore legitimately act as it did in order to protect the sensitive from otherwise unavoidable exposure to appellant's crude form of protest. Of course, the mere presumed presence of unwitting listeners or viewers does not serve automatically to justify curtailing all speech capable of giving offense. ...While this Court has recognized that government may properly act in many situations to prohibit intrusion into the privacy of the home of unwelcome views and ideas which cannot be totally banned from the public dialogue, e.g., Rowan v. Post Office Dept., 397 U.S. 728 (1970), we have at the same time consistently stressed that "we are often 'captives' outside the sanctuary of the home and subject to objectionable speech." Id., at 738. The ability of government, consonant with the Constitution, to shut off discourse solely to protect others from hearing it is, in other words, dependent upon a showing that substantial privacy interests are being invaded in an essentially intolerable manner. Any broader view of this authority would effectively empower a majority to silence dissidents simply as a matter of personal predilections.

In this regard, persons confronted with Cohen's jacket were in a quite different posture than, say, those subjected to the raucous emissions of sound trucks blaring outside their residences. Those in the Los Angeles courthouse could effectively avoid further bombardment of their sensibilities simply by averting their eyes. And while it may be that one has a more substantial claim to a recognizable privacy interest when walking through a courthouse corridor than, for example, strolling through Central Park, surely it is nothing like the interest in being free from unwanted expression in the confines of one's own home.... Given the subtlety and complexity of the factors involved, if Cohen's "speech" was otherwise entitled to constitutional protection, we do not think the fact that some unwilling "listeners" in a public building may have been briefly exposed to it can serve to justify this breach of the peace conviction where, as here, there was no evidence that persons powerless to avoid appellant's conduct did in fact object to it, and where that portion of the statute upon which Cohen's conviction rests evinces no concern, either on its face or as construed by the California courts, with the special plight of the captive auditor, but, instead, indiscriminately sweeps within its prohibitions all "offensive conduct" that disturbs "any neighborhood or person."

Against this background, the issue flushed by this case stands out in bold relief. It is whether California can excise, as "offensive conduct," one particular scurrilous epithet from the public discourse, either upon the theory of the court below that its use is inherently likely to cause violent reaction or upon a more general assertion that the States, acting as guardians of public morality, may properly remove this offensive word from the public vocabulary.

The rationale of the California court is plainly untenable.... We have been shown no evidence that substantial numbers of citizens are standing ready to strike out physically at whoever may assault their sensibilities with execrations like that uttered by Cohen....

Admittedly, it is not so obvious that the First and Fourteenth Amendments must be taken to disable the States from punishing public utterance of this unseemly expletive in order to maintain what they regard as a suitable level of discourse within the body politic. We think, however, that examination and reflection will reveal the shortcomings of a contrary viewpoint.

. . .

Against this perception of the constitutional policies involved, we discern certain more particularized considerations that peculiarly call for reversal of this conviction. First, the principle contended for by the State seems inherently boundless. How is one to distinguish this from any other offensive word? . . . For, while the particular four-letter word being litigated here is perhaps more distasteful than most others of its genre, it is nevertheless often true that one man's vulgarity is another's lyric. Indeed, we think it is largely because governmental officials cannot make principled distinctions in this area that the Constitution leaves matters of taste and style so largely to the individual.

Additionally, we cannot overlook the fact, because it is well illustrated by the episode involved here, that much linguistic expression serves a dual communicative function: it conveys not only ideas capable of relatively precise, detached explication, but otherwise inexpressible emotions as well. In fact, words are often chosen as much for their emotive as their cognitive force. . . .

Finally, and in the same vein, we cannot indulge the facile assumption that one can forbid particular words without also running a substantial risk of suppressing ideas in the process. Indeed, governments might soon seize upon the censorship of particular words as a convenient guise for banning the expression of unpopular views. . . .

It is, in sum, our judgment that, absent a more particularized and compelling reason for its actions, the State may not, consistently with the First and Fourteenth Amendments, make the simple public display here involved of this single four-letter expletive a criminal offense. . . .

Reversed.[a]

Mr. Justice Blackmun, with whom The Chief Justice and Mr. Justice Black join.

I dissent. . . .

Cohen's absurd and immature antic, in my view, was mainly conduct and little speech. . . .

Denver Area Educational Telecommunications Consortium, Inc. v. Federal Communications Commission

___ U.S. ___, 116 S.Ct. 2374, 135 L.Ed.2d 888 (1996).

Justice Breyer announced the judgment of the Court and delivered the opinion of the Court with respect to Part III, an opinion with respect to Parts I, II, and V, in which Justice Stevens, Justice O'Connor, and Justice Souter join, and an opinion with respect to Parts IV and VI, in which Justice Stevens and Justice Souter join.

These cases present First Amendment challenges to three statutory provisions that seek to regulate the broadcasting of "patently offensive" sex-related

---

[a] See Cohen, *A Look Back at* Cohen v. California, 34 U.C.L.A.L.Rev. 1595 (1987).

material on cable television. Cable Television Consumer Protection and Competition Act of 1992 (1992 Act or Act), 106 Stat. 1486, §§ 10(a), 10(b), and 10(c), 47 U.S.C. §§ 532(h), 532(j), and note following § 531. The provisions apply to programs broadcast over cable on what are known as "leased access channels" and "public, educational, or governmental channels." Two of the provisions essentially permit a cable system operator to prohibit the broadcasting of "programming" that the "operator reasonably believes describes or depicts sexual or excretory activities or organs in a patently offensive manner." 1992 Act, § 10(a); see § 10(c). ...The remaining provision requires cable system operators to segregate certain "patently offensive" programming, to place it on a single channel, and to block that channel from viewer access unless the viewer requests access in advance and in writing. 1992 Act, § 10(b); 47 CFR § 76.701(g) (1995).

We conclude that the first provision—that permits the operator to decide whether or not to broadcast such programs on leased access channels—is consistent with the First Amendment. The second provision, that requires leased channel operators to segregate and to block that programming, and the third provision, applicable to public, educational, and governmental channels, violate the First Amendment, for they are not appropriately tailored to achieve the basic, legitimate objective of protecting children from exposure to "patently offensive" material.

I

Cable operators typically own a physical cable network used to convey programming over several dozen cable channels into subscribers' houses. Program sources vary from channel to channel. Most channels carry programming produced by independent firms, including "many national and regional cable programming networks that have emerged in recent years," Turner Broadcasting System, Inc. v. FCC, 512 U.S. 622, ___ (1994), as well as some programming that the system operator itself (or an operator affiliate) may provide. Other channels may simply retransmit through cable the signals of over-the-air broadcast stations. Certain special channels here at issue, called "leased channels" and "public, educational, or governmental channels," carry programs provided by those to whom the law gives special cable system access rights.

A "leased channel" is a channel that federal law requires a cable system operator to reserve for commercial lease by unaffiliated third parties. About 10 to 15 percent of a cable system's channels would typically fall into this category. ...."[P]ublic, educational, or governmental channels" (which we shall call "public access" channels) are channels that, over the years, local governments have required cable system operators to set aside for public, educational, or governmental purposes as part of the consideration an operator gives in return for permission to install cables under city streets and to use public rights-of-way. ...Between 1984 and 1992 federal law (as had much pre–1984 state law, in respect to public access channels) prohibited cable system operators from exercising any editorial control over the content of any program broadcast over either leased or public access channels. ...

In 1992, in an effort to control sexually explicit programming conveyed over access channels, Congress enacted the three provisions before us. The first two provisions relate to leased channels. The first says: "This subsection shall permit a cable operator to enforce prospectively a written and published policy of prohibiting programming that the cable operator reasonably believes describes or depicts sexual or excretory activities or organs in a patently offensive manner as measured by contemporary community standards." 1992 Act, § 10(a)(2), 106 Stat. 1486.

The second provision applicable only to leased channels requires cable operators to segregate and to block similar programming if they decide to permit, rather than to prohibit, its broadcast. The provision tells the Federal Communications Commission (FCC or Commission) to promulgate regulations that will (a) require "programmers to inform cable operators if the program[ming] would be indecent as defined by Commission regulations"; (b) require "cable operators to place" such material "on a single channel"; and © require "cable operators to block such single channel unless the subscriber requests access to such channel in writing." 1992 Act, § 10(b)(1). . . .

The third provision is similar to the first provision, but applies only to public access channels. The relevant statutory section instructs the FCC to promulgate regulations that will "enable a cable operator of a cable system to prohibit the use, on such system, of any channel capacity of any public, educational, or governmental access facility for any programming which contains obscene material, sexually explicit conduct, or material soliciting or promoting unlawful conduct." 1992 Act, § 10(c), . . .

The upshot is, as we said at the beginning, that the federal law before us . . . now permits cable operators either to allow or to forbid the transmission of "patently offensive" sex-related materials over both leased and public access channels, and requires those operators, at a minimum, to segregate and to block transmission of that same material on leased channels.

Petitioners, claiming that the three statutory provisions, as implemented by the Commission regulations, violate the First Amendment, sought judicial review of [FCC orders implementing them.] A panel of [the District of Columbia] Circuit agreed with petitioners that the provisions violated the First Amendment. The entire Court of Appeals, however, heard the case en banc and reached the opposite conclusion. . . .

II

We turn initially to the provision that permits cable system operators to prohibit "patently offensive" (or "indecent") programming transmitted over leased access channels. 1992 Act, § 10(a). . . .

We recognize that the First Amendment, the terms of which apply to governmental action, ordinarily does not itself throw into constitutional doubt the decisions of private citizens to permit, or to restrict, speech—and this is so ordinarily even where those decisions take place within the framework of a regulatory regime such as broadcasting. Were that not so, courts might have to face the difficult, and potentially restrictive, practical task of deciding which, among any number of private parties involved in providing a program (for example, networks, station owners, program editors, and program producers), is the "speaker" whose rights may not be abridged, and who is the speech-restricting "censor." Furthermore, as this Court has held, the editorial function itself is an aspect of "speech," see *Turner*, 512 U. S., at ___, and a court's decision that a private party, say, the station owner, is a "censor," could itself interfere with that private "censor's" freedom to speak as an editor. Thus, not surprisingly, this Court's First Amendment broadcasting cases have dealt with governmental efforts to restrict, not governmental efforts to provide or to maintain, a broadcaster's freedom to pick and to choose programming. . . .

Nonetheless, petitioners, while conceding that this is ordinarily so, point to circumstances that, in their view, make the analogy with private broadcasters inapposite and make this case a special one, warranting a different constitutional result. As a practical matter, they say, cable system operators have considerably more power to "censor" program viewing than do broadcasters, for individual communities typically have only one cable system, linking broadcasters and other program providers with each community's many subscribers. . . . . Moreover, concern about system operators' exercise of this considerable power originally led government—local and federal—to insist that operators provide leased and public access channels free of operator editorial control. . . . To permit system operators to supervise programming on leased access channels will create the very private-censorship risk that this anticensorship effort sought to avoid. At the same time, petitioners add, cable systems have two relevant special characteristics. They are unusually involved with government, for they depend upon government permission and government facilities (streets, rights-of-way) to string the cable necessary for their services. And in respect to leased channels, their speech interests are relatively weak because they act less like editors, such as newspapers or television broadcasters, than like common carriers, such as telephone companies.

Under these circumstances, petitioners conclude, Congress' "permissive" law, in actuality, will "abridge" their free speech. And this Court should treat that law as a congressionally imposed, content-based, restriction unredeemed as a properly tailored effort to serve a "compelling interest." . . . And, finally, petitioners say that the legal standard the law contains (the "patently offensive" standard) is unconstitutionally vague. . . .

Like the petitioners, Justices Kennedy and Thomas would have us decide this case simply by transferring and applying literally categorical standards this Court has developed in other contexts. For Justice Kennedy, leased access channels are like a common carrier, cablecast is a protected medium, strict scrutiny applies, § 10(a) fails this test, and, therefore, § 10(a) is invalid. For Justice Thomas, the case is simple because the cable operator who owns the system over which access channels are broadcast, like a bookstore owner with respect to what it displays on the shelves, has a predominant First Amendment interest. Both categorical approaches suffer from the same flaws: they import law developed in very different contexts into a new and changing environment, and they lack the flexibility necessary to allow government to respond to very serious practical problems without sacrificing the free exchange of ideas the First Amendment is designed to protect.

. . .

Over the years, this Court has restated and refined . . . basic First Amendment principles, adopting them more particularly to the balance of competing interests and the special circumstances of each field of application. . . .

This tradition teaches that the First Amendment embodies an overarching commitment to protect speech from Government regulation through close judicial scrutiny, thereby enforcing the Constitution's constraints, but without imposing judicial formulae so rigid that they become a straightjacket that disables Government from responding to serious problems. . . . [N]o definitive choice among competing analogies (broadcast, common carrier, bookstore) allows us to declare a rigid single standard, good for now and for all future media and purposes. That is not to say that we reject all the more specific formulations of the standard—they appropriately cover the vast majority of cases involving Government regulation of speech. Rather, aware as we are of the changes taking place in the law, the technology, and the industrial structure, related to telecommunications, . . . we believe it unwise and unnecessary definitively to pick one analogy or one specific set of words now. . . . We therefore think it premature to answer the broad questions that Justices Kennedy and Thomas raise in their efforts to find a definitive analogy, deciding, for example, the extent to which private property can be designated a public forum . . .; whether public access channels are a public forum . . .; whether the Government's viewpoint neutral decision to limit a public forum is subject to the same scrutiny as a selective exclusion from a pre-existing public forum . . .; whether exclusion from common carriage must for all purposes be treated like exclusion from a public forum . . .; and whether the interests of the owners of communications media always subordinate the interests of all other users of a medium. . . .

Rather than decide these issues, we can decide this case more narrowly, by closely scrutinizing § 10(a) to assure that it properly addresses an extremely important problem, without imposing, in light of the relevant interests, an unnecessarily great restriction on speech. The importance of the interest at stake here—protecting children from exposure to patently offensive depictions of sex; the accommodation of the interests of programmers in maintaining access channels and of cable operators in editing the contents of their channels; the similarity of the problem and its solution to those at issue in [Federal Communications Commission v.] Pacifica [Foundation, 438 U.S. 726 (1978)]; and the flexibility inherent in an approach that permits private cable operators to make editorial decisions, lead us to conclude that § 10(a) is a sufficiently tailored response to an extraordinarily important problem.

First, the provision before us comes accompanied with an extremely important justification, one that this Court has often found compelling—the need to protect children from exposure to patently offensive sex-related material. . . .

Second, the provision arises in a very particular context—congressional permission for cable operators to regulate programming that, but for a previous Act of Congress, would have had no path of access to cable channels free of an operator's control. The First Amendment interests involved are therefore complex, and involve a balance between those interests served by the access requirements themselves . . ., and the disadvantage to the First Amendment interests of cable operators and other programmers . . .

Third, the problem Congress addressed here is remarkably similar to the problem addressed by the FCC in *Pacifica*, and the balance Congress struck is commensurate with the balance we approved there. In *Pacifica* this Court considered a governmental ban of a radio broadcast of "indecent" materials, defined in part, like the provisions before us, to include "language that describes, in terms patently offensive as measured by contemporary community standards for the broadcast medium, sexual or excretory activities and organs, at times of the day when there is a reasonable risk that children may be in the audience." . . . The Court found this ban constitutionally permissible primarily because "broadcasting is uniquely accessible to children" and children were likely listeners to the program there at issue—an afternoon radio broadcast. . . . In addition, the Court wrote, "the broadcast media have established a uniquely pervasive presence in the lives of all Americans," . . . "[p]atently offensive, indecent material . . . confronts the citizen, not only in public, but also in the privacy of the home," generally without sufficient prior warning to allow the recipient to avert his or her eyes or ears, ibid.; and "[a]dults who feel the need may purchase tapes and records or go to theaters and nightclubs" to hear similar performances. . . .

All these factors are present here. Cable television broadcasting, including access channel broadcasting, is as "accessible to children" as over-the-air broadcasting, if not more so. . . . Cable television systems, including access channels, "have established a uniquely pervasive presence in the lives of all Americans." . . . "Patently offensive" material from these stations can "confron[t] the citizen" in the "privacy of the home," . . . , with little or no prior warning. . . . There is nothing to stop "adults who feel the need" from finding similar programming elsewhere, say, on tape or in theaters. In fact, the power of cable systems to control home program viewing is not absolute. Over-the-air broadcasting and direct broadcast satellites already provide alternative ways for programmers to reach the home, and are likely to do so to a greater extent in the near future. . . .

Fourth, the permissive nature of § 10(a) means that it likely restricts speech less than, not more than, the ban at issue in *Pacifica*. The provision removes a restriction as to some speakers—namely, cable operators. Moreover, although the provision does create a risk that a program will not appear, that risk is not the same as the certainty that accompanies a governmental ban. In fact, a glance at the programming that cable operators allow on their own (nonaccess) channels suggests that this distinction is not theoretical, but real. . . . . Finally, the provision's permissive nature brings with it a flexibility that allows cable operators, for example, not to ban broadcasts, but, say, to rearrange broadcast times, better to fit the desires of adult audiences while lessening the risks of harm to children. . . .

Of course, cable system operators may not always rearrange or reschedule patently offensive programming. Sometimes, as petitioners fear, they may ban the programming instead. But the same may be said of *Pacifica*'s ban. . . .

. . .

Our basic disagreement with Justice Kennedy is narrow. . . . While we cannot agree with Justice Thomas that everything turns on the rights of the cable owner, we also cannot agree with Justice Kennedy that we must ignore the expressive interests of cable operators altogether. Second, . . . [r]ather than seeking an analogy to [the public forum cases], . . . we found that *Pacifica* provides the closest analogy and lends considerable support to our conclusion.

Petitioners and Justice Kennedy, argue that the opposite result is required by two other cases: Sable Communications of Cal., Inc. v. FCC, 492 U.S. 115 (1989), a case in which this Court found unconstitutional a statute that banned "indecent" telephone messages, and *Turner*, in which this Court stated that cable broadcast receives full First Amendment protection. The ban at issue in *Sable*, however, was not only a total governmentally imposed ban on a category of communications, but also involved a communications medium, telephone service, that was significantly less likely to expose children to the banned material, was less intrusive, and allowed for significantly more control over what comes into the home than either broadcasting or the cable transmission system before us. . . . The Court's distinction in *Turner*, furthermore, between cable and broadcast television, relied on the inapplicability of the spectrum scarcity problem to cable. . . . While that distinction was relevant in *Turner* to the justification for structural regulations at issue there (the "must carry" rules), it has little to do with a case that involves the effects of television viewing on children. Those effects are the result of how parents and children view television programming, and how pervasive and intrusive that programming is. In that respect, cable and broadcast television differ little, if at all. ...

The petitioners also rely on this Court's "public forum" cases. ...Justice Kennedy adds by analogy that the decision to exclude certain content from common carriage is similarly subject to strict scrutiny ...

For three reasons, however, it is unnecessary, indeed, unwise, for us definitively to decide whether or how to apply the public forum doctrine to leased access channels. First, while it may be that content-based exclusions from the right to use common carriers could violate the First Amendment, it is not at all clear that the public forum doctrine should be imported wholesale into the area of common carriage regulation. ...Second, it is plain from this Court's cases that a public forum "may be created for a limited purpose." ... Our cases have not yet determined, however, that the Government's decision to dedicate a public forum to one type of content or another is necessarily subject to the highest level of scrutiny. Must a local government, for example, show a compelling state interest if it builds a band shell in the park and dedicates it solely to classical music (but not to jazz)? The answer is not obvious. ....But, at a minimum, this case does not require us to answer it. Finally, and most important, the effects of Congress' decision on the interests of programmers, viewers, cable operators, and children are the same, whether we characterize Congress' decision as one that limits access to a public forum, discriminates in common carriage, or constrains speech because of its content. If we consider this particular limitation of indecent television programming acceptable as a constraint on speech, we must no less accept the limitation it places on access to the claimed public forum or on use of a common carrier.

. . . .

Finally, petitioners argue that the definition of the materials subject to the challenged provisions is too vague, thereby granting cable system operators too broad a program-screening authority. ...

The provisions, as augmented by FCC regulations, permit cable system operators to prohibit "programming that the cable operator reasonably believes describes or depicts sexual or excretory activities or organs in a patently offensive manner as measured by contemporary community standards." ... This language is similar to language adopted by this Court in Miller v. California, 413 U.S. 15, 24 (1973) as a "guidelin[e]" for identifying materials that states may constitutionally regulate as obscene. ...In § 10(a) and the FCC regulations, ... the language would seem to refer to material that would be offensive enough to [be obscene] but for the fact that the material also has "serious literary, artistic, political or scientific value" or nonprurient purposes.

This history suggests that the statute's language aims at the kind of programming to which its sponsors referred—pictures of oral sex, bestiality, and rape ...—and not at scientific or educational programs (at least unless done with a highly unusual lack of concern for viewer reaction). Moreover, as this Court pointed out in *Pacifica*, what is "patently offensive" depends on context (the kind of program on which it appears), degree (not "an occasional expletive"), and time of broadcast (a "pig" is offensive in "the parlor" but not the "barnyard"). ...

Further, the statute protects against overly broad application of its standards insofar as it permits cable system operators to screen programs only pursuant to a "written and published policy." ... A cable system operator would find it difficult to show that a leased access program prohibition reflects a rational "policy" if the operator permits similarly "offensive" programming to run elsewhere on its system at comparable times or in comparable ways. . . .

For the reasons discussed, we conclude that § 10(a) is consistent with the First Amendment.

III

The statute's second provision significantly differs from the first, for it does not simply permit, but rather requires, cable system operators to restrict speech—by segregating and blocking "patently offensive" sex-related material appearing on leased channels (but not on other channels). 1992 Act, § 10(b). . . .

These requirements have obvious restrictive effects. The several up-to–30–day delays, along with single channel segregation, mean that a subscriber cannot decide to watch a single program without considerable advance planning and without letting the "patently offensive" channel in its entirety invade his household for days, perhaps weeks, at a time. . . . Moreover, the "written notice" requirement will further restrict viewing by subscribers who fear for their reputations should the operator, advertently or inadvertently, disclose the list of those who wish to watch the "patently offensive" channel. . . . Further, the added costs and burdens that these requirements impose upon a cable system operator may encourage that operator to ban programming that the operator would otherwise permit to run, even if only late at night.

The Government argues that, despite these adverse consequences, the "segregate and block" requirements are lawful because they are "the least restrictive means of realizing" a "compelling interest," namely "protecting the physical and psychological well-being of minors." It adds that, in any event, the First Amendment, as applied in *Pacifica*, "does not require that regulations of indecency on television be subject to the strictest" First Amendment "standard of review."

We . . . do not agree that the "segregate and block" requirements properly accommodate the speech restrictions they impose and the legitimate objective they seek to attain. Nor need we here determine whether, or the extent to which, *Pacifica* does, or does not, impose some lesser standard of review where indecent speech is at issue . . . That is because once one examines this governmental restriction, it becomes apparent that, not only is it not a "least restrictive alternative," and is not "narrowly tailored" to meet its legitimate objective, it also seems considerably "more extensive than necessary." . . .

Several circumstances lead us to this conclusion. For one thing, the law, as recently amended, uses other means to protect children from similar "patently offensive" material broadcast on unleased cable channels, i.e., broadcast over any of a system's numerous ordinary, or public access, channels. The law, as recently amended, requires cable operators to "scramble or . . . block" such programming on any (unleased) channel "primarily dedicated to sexually-oriented programming." . . . In addition, cable operators must honor a subscriber's request to block any, or all, programs on any channel to which he or she does not wish to subscribe. . . . And manufacturers, in the future, will have to make television sets with a so-called "V-chip"—a device that will be able automatically to identify and block sexually explicit or violent programs. . . .

Although we cannot, and do not, decide whether the new provisions are themselves lawful (a matter not before us), we note that they are significantly less restrictive than the provision here at issue. . . . [I]f these provisions do not adequately protect children from "patently offensive" material broadcast on ordinary channels, how could one justify more severe leased channel restrictions when (given ordinary channel programming) they would yield so little additional protection for children?

. . .

... We have no empirical reason to believe, for example, that sex-dedicated channels are all (or mostly) leased channels, or that "patently offensive" programming on non-sex-dedicated channels is found only (or mostly) on leased channels. ...

. . .

The record's description and discussion of a different alternative—the "lockbox"—leads, through a different route, to a similar conclusion. The Cable Communications Policy Act of 1984 required cable operators to provide "upon the request of a subscriber, a device by which the subscriber can prohibit viewing of a particular cable service during periods selected by the subscriber." ... This device ... would help protect children by permitting their parents to "lock out" those programs or channels that they did not want their children to see. ...

. . .

No provision, we concede, short of an absolute ban, can offer certain protection against assault by a determined child. We have not, however, generally allowed this fact alone to justify "reduc[ing] the adult population ... to ... only what is fit for children." ... But, ... the ... practical difficulties would seem to call, not for "segregate and block" requirements, but, rather, for informational requirements, for a simple coding system, for readily available blocking equipment (perhaps accessible by telephone), for imposing cost burdens upon system operators (who may spread them through subscription fees); or perhaps even for a system that requires lockbox defaults to be set to block certain channels (say, sex-dedicated-channels). These kinds of requirements resemble those that Congress has recently imposed upon all but leased channels. ...

. . .

Consequently, we cannot find that the "segregate and block" restrictions on speech are a narrowly, or reasonably, tailored effort to protect children. ...

IV

The statute's third provision, as implemented by FCC regulation, is similar to its first provision, in that it too permits a cable operator to prevent transmission of "patently offensive" programming, in this case on public access channels. 1992 Act, § 10(c) ... But there are four important differences.

The first is the historical background. ... [C]able operators have traditionally agreed to reserve channel capacity for public, governmental, and educational channels as part of the consideration they give municipalities that award them cable franchises. ...Significantly, these are channels over which cable operators have not historically exercised editorial control. ...Unlike § 10(a) therefore, § 10(c) does not restore to cable operators editorial rights that they once had, and the countervailing First Amendment interest is nonexistent, or at least much diminished....

The second difference is the institutional background that has developed as a result of the historical difference. When a "leased channel" is made available by the operator to a private lessee, the lessee has total control of programming during the leased time slot. ...Public access channels, on the other hand, are normally subject to complex supervisory systems of various sorts, often with both public and private elements. ...Municipalities generally provide in their cable franchising agreements for an access channel manager, who is most commonly a nonprofit organization, but may also be the municipality, or, in some instances, the cable system owner. ...Access channel activity and management are partly financed with public funds—through franchise fees or other payments pursuant to the franchise agreement, or from general municipal funds—and are commonly subject to supervision by a local supervisory board. . . .

This system of public, private, and mixed nonprofit elements, through its supervising boards and nonprofit or governmental access managers, can set programming policy and approve or disapprove particular programming services. ...[T]here is a locally accountable body capable of addressing the problem, should it arise, of patently offensive programming broadcast to children, making it unlikely that many children will in fact be exposed to programming considered patently offensive in that community. ...

Third, the existence of a system aimed at encouraging and securing programming that the community considers valuable strongly suggests that a "cable operator's veto" is less likely necessary to achieve the statute's basic objective, protecting children, than a similar veto in the context of leased channels. ...

Finally, our examination of the legislative history and the record before us is consistent with what common sense suggests, namely that the public/nonprofit programming control systems now in place would normally avoid, minimize, or eliminate any child-related problems concerning "patently offensive" programming.

. . .

The upshot, in respect to the public access channels, is a law that could radically change present programming-related relationships among local community and nonprofit supervising boards and access managers, which relationships are established through municipal law, regulation, and contract. In doing so, it would not significantly restore editorial rights of cable operators, but would greatly increase the risk that certain categories of programming (say, borderline offensive programs) will not appear. At the same time, given present supervisory mechanisms, the need for this particular provision, aimed directly at public access channels, is not obvious. ...

V

Finally, we must ask whether § 10(a) is severable from the two other provisions. ...

... [W]e believe the valid provision is severable from the others.

VI

For these reasons, the judgment of the Court of Appeals is affirmed insofar as it upheld § 10(a); the judgment of the Court of Appeals is reversed insofar as it upheld § 10(b) and § 10(c).

It is so ordered.

Justice Stevens, concurring.

The difference between § 10(a) and § 10(c) is the difference between a permit and a prohibition. . . . While I join the Court's opinion, I add these comments to emphasize the difference between the two provisions and to endorse the analysis in Part III–B of Justice Kennedy's opinion even though I do not think it necessary to characterize the public access channels as public fora. . . .

I

. . . [Section] 10(a) constitutes a reasonable, viewpoint neutral limitation on a federally-created access right for certain cable programmers.

II

. . . [T]he public, educational and governmental access channels that are regulated by § 10(c) are not creations of the Federal Government. . . .

As their name reflects, so-called PEG channels are subject to a variety of local governmental controls and regulations. . . .

What is of critical importance to me . . . is that if left to their own devices, those authorities may choose to carry some programming that the Federal Government has decided to restrict. As I read § 10(c), the federal statute would disable local governments from making that choice. . . .

Section 10(c) operates as a direct restriction on speech that, in the absence of federal intervention, might flow freely. . . .

. . .

Justice Souter, concurring.

Justice Kennedy's separate opinion stresses the worthy point that First Amendment values generally are well-served by categorizing speech protection. . . . Reviewing speech regulations under fairly strict categorical rules keeps the starch in the standards for those moments when the daily politics cries loudest for limiting what may be said. . . . The value of the categorical approach generally to First Amendment security prompts a word to explain why I join the Court's unwillingness to announce a definitive categorical analysis in this case.

. . .

All of the relevant characteristics of cable are presently in a state of technological and regulatory flux. Recent and far-reaching legislation not only affects the technical feasibility of parental control over children's access to undesirable material, . . . but portends fundamental changes in the competitive structure of the industry and, therefore, the ability of individual entities to act as bottlenecks to the free flow of information. . . . As cable and telephone companies begin their competition for control over the single wire that will carry both their services, we can hardly settle rules for review of regulation on the assumption that cable will remain a separable and useful category of First Amendment scrutiny. And as broadcast, cable, and the cyber-technology of the Internet and the World Wide Web approach the day of using a common receiver, we can hardly assume that standards for judging the regulation of one of them will not have immense, but now unknown and unknowable, effects on the others.

Accordingly, in charting a course that will permit reasonable regulation in light of the values in competition, we have to accept the likelihood that the media of communication will become less categorical and more protean. Because we cannot be confident that for purposes of judging speech restrictions it will continue to make sense to distinguish cable from other technologies, and because we know that changes in these regulated technologies will enormously alter the structure of regulation itself, we should be shy about saying the final word today about what will be accepted as reasonable tomorrow. In my own ignorance I have to accept the real possibility that "if we had to decide today ... just what the First Amendment should mean in cyberspace, ... we would get it fundamentally wrong." Lessig, The Path of Cyberlaw, 104 Yale L.J. 1743, 1745 (1995).

The upshot of appreciating the fluidity of the subject that Congress must regulate is simply to accept the fact that not every nuance of our old standards will necessarily do for the new technology, and that a proper choice among existing doctrinal categories is not obvious. Rather than definitively settling the issue now, Justice Breyer wisely reasons by direct analogy rather than by rule. . . .

. . .

Justice O'Connor, concurring in part and dissenting in part.

I agree that § 10(a) is constitutional and that § 10(b) is unconstitutional, and I join Parts I, II, III, and V, and the judgment in part. I am not persuaded, however, that the asserted "important differences" between §§ 10(a) and 10(c) are sufficient to justify striking down § 10(c). I find the features shared by § 10(a), which covers leased access channels, and § 10(c), which covers public access channels, to be more significant than the differences. For that reason, I would find that § 10(c) too withstands constitutional scrutiny.

. . .

... I am not persuaded that the difference in the origin of the access channels is sufficient to justify upholding § 10(a) and striking down § 10(c). The interest in protecting children remains the same, whether on a leased access channel or a public access channel, and allowing the cable operator the option of prohibiting the transmission of indecent speech seems a constitutionally permissible means of addressing that interest. Nor is the fact that public access programming may be subject to supervisory systems in addition to the cable operator sufficient in my mind to render § 10(c) so ill-tailored to its goal as to be unconstitutional.

. . .

Justice Kennedy, with whom Justice Ginsburg joins, concurring in part, concurring in the judgment in part, and dissenting in part.

The plurality opinion, insofar as it upholds § 10(a) of the 1992 Cable Act, is adrift. The opinion treats concepts such as public forum, broadcaster, and common carrier as mere labels rather than as categories with settled legal significance; it applies no standard, and by this omission loses sight of existing First Amendment doctrine. When confronted with a threat to free speech in the context of an emerging technology, we ought to have the discipline to analyze the case by reference to existing elaborations of constant First Amendment principles. ... Although I join Part III of the opinion (there for the Court) striking down § 10(b) of the Act, and concur in the judgment that § 10(c) is unconstitutional, with respect I dissent from the remainder.

I

. . .

Though the two provisions differ in significant respects, [§§ 10(a) and 10(c)] have common flaws. In both instances, Congress singles out one sort of speech for vulnerability to private censorship in a context where content-based discrimination is not otherwise permitted. . . .

. . .

. . . As a general matter, a private person may exclude certain speakers from his or her property without violating the First Amendment, . . . and if §§ 10(a) and (c) were no more than affirmations of this principle they might be unremarkable. Access channels, however, are property of the cable operator dedicated or otherwise reserved for programming of other speakers or the government. A public access channel is a public forum, and laws requiring leased access channels create common carrier obligations. When the government identifies certain speech on the basis of its content as vulnerable to exclusion from a common carrier or public forum, strict scrutiny applies. These laws cannot survive this exacting review. However compelling Congress' interest in shielding children from indecent programming, the provisions in this case are not drawn with enough care to withstand scrutiny under our precedents.

II

. . .

. . . I have expressed misgivings about judicial balancing under the First Amendment, . . . but strict scrutiny at least confines the balancing process in a manner protective of speech . . .

. . . [T]he creation of standards and adherence to them, even when it means affording protection to speech unpopular or distasteful, is the central achievement of our First Amendment jurisprudence. Standards are the means by which we state in advance how to test a law's validity, rather than letting the height of the bar be determined by the apparent exigencies of the day. They also provide notice and fair warning to those who must predict how the courts will respond to attempts to suppress their speech. Yet formulations like strict scrutiny, used in a number of constitutional settings to ensure that the inequities of the moment are subordinated to commitments made for the long run, . . . mean little if they can be watered down whenever they seem too strong. They mean still less if they can be ignored altogether when considering a case not on all fours with what we have seen before.

The plurality seems distracted by the many changes in technology and competition in the cable industry. . . . The laws challenged here, however, do not retool the structure of the cable industry or (with the exception of § 10(b)) involve intricate technologies. The straightforward issue here is whether the Government can deprive certain speakers, on the basis of the content of their speech, of protections afforded all others. There is no reason to discard our existing First Amendment jurisprudence in answering this question.

While it protests against standards, the plurality does seem to favor one formulation of the question in this case: namely, whether the Act "properly addresses an extremely important problem, without imposing, in light of the relevant interests, an unnecessarily great restriction on speech." . . . This description of the question accomplishes little, save to clutter our First Amendment case law by adding an untested rule with an uncertain relationship to the others we use to evaluate laws restricting speech. . . .

... The words end up being a legalistic cover for an ad hoc balancing of interests.... [C]omparisons and analogies to other areas of our First Amendment case law ... provide discipline to the Court and guidance for others, and give clear content to our standards—all the things I find missing in the plurality's opinion. ...

Another troubling aspect of the plurality's approach is its suggestion that Congress has more leeway than usual to enact restrictions on speech where emerging technologies are concerned, because we are unsure what standard should be used to assess them. ...

I turn now to the issues presented, and explain why strict scrutiny is warranted.

III

A

. . .

My principal concern is with public access channels.... These are the channels open to programming by members of the public. ...No local governmental entity or school system has petitioned for relief in this case, and none of the petitioners who are viewers has asserted an interest in viewing educational or governmental programming or briefed the relevant issues.

B

The public access channels established by franchise agreements tend to have certain traits. They are available at low or no cost to members of the public, often on a first-come, first-served basis. ...The programmer on one of these channels most often has complete control over, as well as liability for, the content of its show. ...The entity managing the technical aspects of public access, such as scheduling and transmission, is not always the cable operator; it may be the local government or a third party that runs the access centers, which are facilities made available for the public to produce programs and transmit them on the access channels. ...

. . .

... Required by the franchise authority as a condition of the franchise and open to all comers, [public access channels] are a designated public forum of unlimited character. ...

It is important to understand that public access channels are public forums created by local or state governments in the cable franchise. Section § 10(c) does not, as the Court of Appeals thought, just return rightful First Amendment discretion to the cable operator.... The cable operator may own the cables transmitting the signal, but it is the franchise ... that allocates some channels to the full discretion of the cable operator while reserving others for public access.

In providing public access channels under their franchise agreements, cable operators therefore are not exercising their own First Amendment rights. They serve as conduits for the speech of others. ...Section 10(c) thus restores no power of editorial discretion over public access channels that the cable operator once had; the discretion never existed. ...By enacting a law in 1992 excluding indecent programming from protection but retaining the prohibition on cable operators' editorial control over all other protected speech, the Federal Government at the same time ratified the public-forum character of public access channels but discriminated against certain speech based on its content.

. . .

C

. . .

In my view, strict scrutiny also applies to § 10(a)'s authorization to cable operators to exclude indecent programming from [leased access] channels.

. . .

Before 1992, cable operators were forbidden editorial control over any video programming on leased access channels, and could not consider the content of the programming except to set the price of access. . . . Section 10(a) of the 1992 Act modifies the no-discretion rule. . . .

. . .

The constitutionality under *Turner Broadcasting* . . . of requiring a cable operator to set aside leased access channels is not before us. For purposes of this case, we should treat the cable operator's rights in these channels as extinguished, and address the issue these petitioners present: namely, whether the Government can discriminate on the basis of content in affording protection to certain programmers. I cannot agree with Justice Thomas that the cable operator's rights inform this analysis.

Laws requiring cable operators to provide leased access are the practical equivalent of making them common carriers, analogous in this respect to telephone companies: They are obliged to provide a conduit for the speech of others. . . .

. . .

Laws removing common-carriage protection from a single form of speech based on its content should be reviewed under the same standard as content-based restrictions on speech in a public forum. Making a cable operator a common carrier does not create a public forum in the sense of taking property from private control and dedicating it to public use; rather, regulations of a common carrier dictate the manner in which private control is exercised. A common-carriage mandate, nonetheless, serves the same function as a public forum. It ensures open, nondiscriminatory access to the means of communication. . . . The functional equivalence of designating a public forum and mandating common carriage suggests the same scrutiny should be applied to attempts in either setting to impose content discrimination by law. Under our precedents, the scrutiny is strict. . . .

In Police Dept. of Chicago v. Mosley, 408 U.S. 92 (1972), we made clear that selective exclusions from a public forum were unconstitutional. Invoking the First and Fourteenth Amendments to strike down a city ordinance allowing only labor picketing on any public way near schools, we held the "government may not grant the use of a forum to people whose views it finds acceptable, but deny use to those wishing to express less favored or more controversial views." . . . [T]here is no reason the kind of selective exclusion we condemned in *Mosley* should be tolerated here.

. . .

I do not foreclose the possibility that the Government could create a forum limited to certain topics or to serving the special needs of certain speakers or audiences without its actions being subject to strict scrutiny. This possibility seems to trouble the plurality, which wonders if a local government must "show a compelling state interest if it builds a band shell in the park and dedicates it solely to classical music (but not to jazz)." This is not the correct analogy. Our case is more akin to the Government's creation of a band shell in which all types of music might be performed except for rap music. The provisions here are content-based discriminations in the strong sense of suppressing a certain form of expression that the Government dislikes, or otherwise wishes to exclude on account of its effects, and there is no justification for anything but strict scrutiny here.

Giving government free rein to exclude speech it dislikes by delimiting public forums (or common carriage provisions) would have pernicious effects in the modern age. Minds are not changed in streets and parks as they once were. To an increasing degree, the more significant interchanges of ideas and shaping of public consciousness occur in mass and electronic media. . . . The extent of public entitlement to participate in those means of communication may be changed as technologies change; and in expanding those entitlements the Government has no greater right to discriminate on suspect grounds than it does when it effects a ban on speech against the backdrop of the entitlements to which we have been more accustomed. It contravenes the First Amendment to give Government a general license to single out some categories of speech for lesser protection so long as it stops short of viewpoint discrimination.

D

The Government advances a different argument for not applying strict scrutiny in this case. The nature of access channels to one side, it argues the nature of the speech in question—indecent broadcast (or cablecast)—is subject to the lower standard of review it contends was applied in FCC v. Pacifica Foundation, 438 U.S. 726, 748 (1978). . . .

Pacifica did not purport, however, to apply a special standard for indecent broadcasting. Emphasizing the narrowness of its holding, the Court in *Pacifica* conducted a context-specific analysis of the FCC's restriction on indecent programming during daytime hours. . . . It relied on the general rule that "broadcasting . . . has received the most limited First Amendment protection." . . . We already have rejected the application of this lower broadcast standard of review to infringements on the liberties of cable operators, even though they control an important communications medium. Turner Broadcasting, 512 U. S., at ___. There is even less cause for a lower standard here.

Pacifica did identify two important considerations relevant to the broadcast of objectionable material. . . .

These concerns are weighty and will be relevant to whether the law passes strict scrutiny. They do not justify, however, a blanket rule of lesser protection for indecent speech. Other than the few categories of expression which can be proscribed, . . . we have been reluctant to mark off new categories of speech for diminished constitutional protection. Our hesitancy reflects skepticism about the possibility of courts' drawing principled distinctions to use in judging governmental restrictions on speech and ideas, . . . a concern heightened here by the inextricability of indecency from expression. . . . In artistic or political settings, indecency may have strong communicative content, protesting conventional norms or giving an edge to a work by conveying "otherwise inexpressible emotions," . . . . In scientific programs, the more graphic the depiction (even if to the point of offensiveness), the more accurate and comprehensive the portrayal of the truth may be. Indecency often is inseparable from the ideas and viewpoints conveyed, or separable only with loss of truth or expressive power. Under our traditional First Amendment jurisprudence, factors perhaps justifying some restriction on indecent cable programming may all be taken into account without derogating this category of protected speech as marginal.

IV

. . .

The Government has no compelling interest in restoring a cable operator's First Amendment right of editorial discretion. As to § 10(c), Congress has no interest at all, since under most franchises operators had no rights of editorial discretion over PEG access channels in the first place. As to § 10(a), any governmental interest in restoring operator discretion over indecent programming on leased access channels is too minimal to justify the law. First, the transmission of indecent programming over leased access channels is not forced speech of the operator. . . . Second, the discretion conferred by the law is slight. The operator is not authorized to place programs of its own liking on the leased access channels, nor to remove other speech (racist or violent, for example) that might be offensive to it or to viewers. The operator is just given a veto over the one kind of lawful speech Congress disdains.

Congress does have, however, a compelling interest in protecting children from indecent speech. . . . This interest is substantial enough to justify some regulation of indecent speech even under, I will assume, the indecency standard used here.

Sections 10(a) and © nonetheless are not narrowly tailored to protect children from indecent programs on access channels. First, to the extent some operators may allow indecent programming, children in localities those operators serve will be left unprotected. Partial service of a compelling interest is not narrow tailoring. . . . Put another way, the interest in protecting children from indecency only at the caprice of the cable operator is not compelling. . . .

Second, to the extent cable operators prohibit indecent programming on access channels, not only children but adults will be deprived of it. . . . When applying strict scrutiny, we will not assume plausible alternatives will fail to protect compelling interests. . . .

Sections 10(a) and © present a classic case of discrimination against speech based on its content. There are legitimate reasons why the Government might wish to regulate or even restrict the speech at issue here, but §§ 10(a) and 10© are not drawn to address those reasons with the precision the First Amendment requires.

. . .

VI

In agreement with the plurality's analysis of § 10(b) of the Act, insofar as it applies strict scrutiny, I join Part III of its opinion. Its position there, however, cannot be reconciled with upholding § 10(a). . . .

Justice Thomas, joined by the Chief Justice and Justice Scalia, concurring in the judgment in part and dissenting in part.

I agree with the plurality's conclusion that § 10(a) is constitutionally permissible, but I disagree with its conclusion that §§ 10(b) and (c) violate the First Amendment. For many years, we have failed to articulate how and to what extent the First Amendment protects cable operators, programmers, and viewers from state and federal regulation. I think it is time we did so, and I cannot go along with the plurality's assiduous attempts to avoid addressing that issue openly.

I

The text of the First Amendment makes no distinction between print, broadcast, and cable media, but we have done so. In Red Lion Broadcasting Co. v. FCC, 395 U.S. 367 (1969), we held that, in light of the scarcity of broadcasting frequencies, the Government may require a broadcast licensee "to share his frequency with others and to conduct himself as a proxy or fiduciary with obligations to present those views and voices which are representative of his community and which would otherwise, by necessity, be barred from the airwaves." ...

In contrast, we have not permitted that level of government interference in the context of the print media. ...

Our First Amendment distinctions between media, dubious from their infancy, placed cable in a doctrinal wasteland in which regulators and cable operators alike could not be sure whether cable was entitled to the substantial First Amendment protections afforded the print media or was subject to the more onerous obligations shouldered by the broadcast media. ...Over time, however, we have drawn closer to recognizing that cable operators should enjoy the same First Amendment rights as the nonbroadcast media.

. . .

In *Turner*, by adopting much of the print paradigm, and by rejecting *Red Lion*, we adopted with it a considerable body of precedent that governs the respective First Amendment rights of competing speakers. In *Red Lion*, we had legitimized consideration of the public interest and emphasized the rights of viewers, at least in the abstract. ...After *Turner*, however, that view can no longer be given any credence in the cable context. It is the operator's right that is preeminent. ...

By recognizing the general primacy of the cable operator's editorial rights over the rights of programmers and viewers, *Turner* raises serious questions about the merits of petitioners' claims. None of the petitioners in these cases are cable operators; they are all cable viewers or access programmers or their representative organizations. ...It is not intuitively obvious that the First Amendment protects the interests petitioners assert, and neither petitioners nor the plurality have adequately explained the source or justification of those asserted rights.

. . .

... [L]eased and public access are a type of forced speech. Though the constitutionality of leased and public access channels is not directly at issue in these cases, the position adopted by the Court in *Turner* ineluctably leads to the conclusion that the federal access requirements are subject to some form of heightened scrutiny. ...

Petitioners must concede that cable access is not a constitutionally required entitlement and that the right they claim to leased and public access has, by definition, been governmentally created at the expense of cable operators' editorial discretion. Just because the Court has apparently accepted, for now, the proposition that the Constitution permits some degree of forced speech in the cable context does not mean that the beneficiaries of a government-imposed forced speech program enjoy additional First Amendment protections beyond those normally afforded to purely private speakers.

. . .

It is one thing to compel an operator to carry leased and public access speech, in apparent violation of *Tornillo*, but it is another thing altogether to say that the First Amendment forbids Congress to give back part of the operators' editorial discretion, which all recognize as fundamentally protected, in favor of a broader access right. It is no answer to say that leased and public access are content neutral and that §§ 10(a) and (c) are not, for that does not change the fundamental fact, which petitioners never address, that it is the operators' journalistic freedom that is infringed, whether the challenged restrictions be content neutral or content based.

. . .

B

. . . Labeling leased access a common carrier scheme has no real First Amendment consequences. It simply does not follow from common carrier status that cable operators may not, with Congress' blessing, decline to carry indecent speech on their leased access channels. Common carriers are private entities and may, consistent with the First Amendment, exercise editorial discretion in the absence of a specific statutory prohibition. . . .

. . . [T]he fact that the leased access provisions impose a form of common carrier obligation on cable operators does not alter my view that Congress' leased access scheme burdens the constitutionally protected speech rights of cable operators in order to expand the speaking opportunities of access programmers, but does not independently burden the First Amendment rights of programmers or viewers.

C

. . . I do not agree with petitioners' . . . assertion that public access channels are public fora.

. . .

. . . The public forum doctrine is a rule governing claims of "a right of access to public property," . . . and has never been thought to extend beyond property generally understood to belong to the government. . . .

. . .

. . . Our public forum cases have involved property in which the government has held at least some formal easement or other property interest permitting the government to treat the property as its own in designating the property as a public forum. . . .

. . .

. . . [E]ven were I inclined to view public access channels as public property, which I am not, the numerous additional obligations imposed on the cable operator in managing and operating the public access channels convince me that these channels share few, if any, of the basic characteristics of a public forum. As I have already indicated, public access requirements, in my view, are a regulatory restriction on the exercise of cable operators' editorial discretion, not a transfer of a sufficient property interest in the channels to support a designation of that property as a public forum. . . .

III

Most sexually oriented programming appears on premium or pay-per-view channels that are naturally blocked from nonpaying customers by market forces, and it is only governmental intervention in the first instance that requires access channels, on which indecent programming may appear, to be made part of the basic cable package. Section 10(b) does nothing more than adjust the nature of government-imposed leased access requirements in order to emulate the market forces that keep indecent programming primarily on premium channels (without permitting the operator to charge subscribers for that programming).

Unlike §§ 10(a) and (c), § 10(b) clearly implicates petitioners' free speech rights. Though § 10(b) by no means bans indecent speech, it clearly places content-based restrictions on the transmission of private speech by requiring cable operators to block and segregate indecent programming that the operator has agreed to carry. Consequently, § 10(b) must be subjected to strict scrutiny.... The parties agree that Congress has a "compelling interest in protecting the physical and psychological well-being of minors" and that its interest "extends to shielding minors from the influence of [indecent speech] that is not obscene by adult standards." ... Because § 10(b) is narrowly tailored to achieve that well-established compelling interest, I would uphold it. I therefore dissent from the Court's decision to the contrary.

. . .

The Court strikes down § 10(b) by pointing to alternatives, such as reverse-blocking and lockboxes, that it says are less restrictive than segregation and blocking. Though these methods attempt to place in parents' hands the ability to permit their children to watch as little, or as much, indecent programming as the parents think proper, they do not effectively support parents' authority to direct the moral upbringing of their children. ...The FCC recognized that leased-access programming comes "from a wide variety of independent sources, with no single editor controlling [its] selection and presentation." ... Thus, indecent programming on leased access channels is "especially likely to be shown randomly or intermittently between non-indecent programs." Rather than being able to simply block out certain channels at certain times, a subscriber armed with only a lockbox must carefully monitor all leased-access programming and constantly reprogram the lockbox to keep out undesired programming. Thus, even assuming that cable subscribers generally have the technical proficiency to properly operate a lockbox, by no means a given, this distinguishing characteristic of leased access channels makes lockboxes and reverse-blocking largely ineffective.

. . .

The segregation and blocking requirement was not intended to be a replacement for lockboxes, V-chips, reverse-blocking, or other subscriber-initiated measures. ...Once a subscriber requests access to blocked programming, however, the subscriber remains free to use other methods, such as lockboxes, to regulate the kind of programming shown on those channels in that home. ...Given the limited scope of § 10(b) as a default setting, I see nothing constitutionally infirm about Congress' decision to permit the cable operator 30 days to unblock or reblock the segregated channel.

. . .

In arguing that Congress could not impose a blocking requirement without also imposing that requirement on public access and nonaccess channels, petitioners fail to allege, much less argue, that doing so would further Congress' compelling interest. While it is true that indecent programming appears on nonaccess channels, that programming appears almost exclusively on "per-program or per channel services that subscribers must specifically request in advance, in the same manner as under the blocking approach mandated by section 10(b)." ... In contrast to these premium services, leased access channels are part of the basic cable package, and the segregation and blocking scheme Congress imposed does nothing more than convert sexually oriented leased access programming into a free "premium service." ...

The United States has carried its burden of demonstrating that § 10(b) and its implementing regulations are narrowly tailored to satisfy a compelling governmental interest. Accordingly, I would affirm the judgment of the Court of Appeals in its entirety. I therefore concur in the judgment upholding § 10(a) and respectfully dissent from that portion of the judgment striking down §§ 10(b) and (c).

City of Houston, Texas v. Hill

482 U.S. 451, 107 S.Ct. 2502, 96 L.Ed.2d 398 (1987).

Justice Brennan delivered the opinion of the Court.

This case presents the question whether a municipal ordinance that makes it unlawful to interrupt a police officer in the performance of his or her duties is unconstitutionally overbroad under the First Amendment.

I

Appellee Raymond Wayne Hill is a lifelong resident of Houston, Texas. At the time this lawsuit began, he worked as a paralegal and as executive director of the Houston Human Rights League. A member of the board of the Gay Political Caucus, which he helped found in 1975, Hill was also affiliated with a Houston radio station, and had carried city and county press passes since 1975. He lived in Montrose, a "diverse and eclectic neighborhood" that is the center of gay political and social life in Houston.

The incident that sparked this lawsuit occurred in the Montrose area ... Hill observed a friend, Charles Hill, intentionally stopping traffic on a busy street, evidently to enable a vehicle to enter traffic. Two Houston police officers, one of whom was named Kelley, approached Charles and began speaking with him. ... Hill began shouting at the officers "in an admitted attempt to divert Kelley's attention from Charles Hill." Hill first shouted: "Why don't you pick on somebody your own size?" After Officer Kelley responded: "Are you interrupting me in my official capacity as a Houston police officer?" Hill then shouted: "Yes, why don't you pick on somebody my size?" Hill was arrested under Houston Code of Ordinances section 34–11(a) for "wilfully or intentionally interrupting a city policeman ... by verbal challenge during an investigation." Charles Hill was not arrested. Hill was then acquitted after a nonjury trial in Municipal Court.

Code of Ordinances, City of Houston, Texas, § 34–11(a) (1984) reads:

"Sec. 34–11. Assaulting or interfering with policemen.

"(a) It shall be unlawful for any person to assault, strike or in any manner oppose, molest, abuse or interrupt any policeman in the execution of his duty, or any person summoned to aid in making an arrest."

Following his acquittal in the Charles Hill incident, Hill brought the suit in the Federal District Court for the Southern District of Texas seeking (1) a declaratory judgment that § 34–11(a) was unconstitutional both on its face and as it had been applied to him . . .

At trial, Hill introduced records provided by the City regarding both the frequency with which arrests had been made for violation of the ordinance and the type of conduct with which those arrested had been charged. He also introduced evidence and testimony concerning the arrests of several reporters under the ordinance. Finally, Hill introduced evidence regarding his own experience with the ordinance, under which he has been arrested four times since 1975, but never convicted.

The District Court held that Hill's evidence did not demonstrate that the ordinance had been unconstitutionally applied. . . .

. . . [T]he Court of Appeals, by a vote of 8–7, [reversed]. . . .

. . .

. . . We . . . affirm.

II

. . .

The City's principal argument is that the ordinance does not inhibit the exposition of ideas, and that it bans "core criminal conduct" not protected by the First Amendment. In its view, the application of the ordinance to Hill illustrates that the police employ it only to prohibit such conduct, and not "as a subterfuge to control or dissuade free expression." Since the ordinance is "content-neutral," and since there is no evidence that the City has applied the ordinance to chill particular speakers or ideas, the City concludes that the ordinance is not substantially overbroad.

We disagree with the city's characterization for several reasons. First, the enforceable portion of the ordinance deals not with core criminal conduct, but with speech. As the city has conceded, the language in the ordinance making it unlawful for any person to "assault" or "strike" a police officer is preempted by the Texas Penal Code. . . . Accordingly, the enforceable portion of the ordinance makes it "unlawful for any person to . . . in any manner oppose, molest, abuse or interrupt any policeman in the execution of his duty," and thereby prohibits verbal interruptions of police officers.

Second, contrary to the city's contention, the First Amendment protects a significant amount of verbal criticism and challenge directed at police officers. "Speech is often provocative and challenging. . . . [But it] is nevertheless protected against censorship or punishment, unless shown likely to produce a clear and present danger of a serious substantive evil that rises far above public inconvenience, annoyance, or unrest." Terminiello v. Chicago, 337 U.S. 1, 4 (1949). In Lewis v. City of New Orleans, . . . a municipal ordinance . . . made it a crime "'for any person wantonly to curse or revile or to use obscene or opprobrious language toward or with reference to any member of the city police while in the actual performance of his duty.' " . . . We . . . invalidated the ordinance as facially overbroad. . . . Moreover, in a concurring opinion in Lewis, Justice Powell suggested that even the "fighting words" exception recognized in Chaplinsky v. New Hampshire, 315 U.S. 568 (1942), might require a narrower application in cases involving words addressed to a police officer, because "a properly trained officer may reasonably be expected to 'exercise a higher degree of restraint' than the average citizen, and thus be less likely to respond belligerently to 'fighting words.' "   415 U.S., at 135 (citation omitted).

The Houston ordinance is much more sweeping than the municipal ordinance struck down in *Lewis*. It is not limited to fighting words nor even to obscene or opprobrious language, but prohibits speech that "in any manner . . . interrupt[s]" an officer. The Constitution does not allow such speech to be made a crime.[11] The freedom of individuals verbally to oppose or challenge police action without thereby risking arrest is one of the principal characteristics by which we distinguish a free nation from a police state.

The city argues, however, that even if the ordinance encompasses some protected speech, its sweeping nature is both inevitable and essential to maintain public order. The City recalls this Court's observation in Smith v. Goguen, 415 U.S. 566, 581 (1974):

> "There are areas of human conduct where, by the nature of the problems presented, legislatures simply cannot establish standards with great precision. Control of the broad range of disorderly conduct that may inhibit a policeman in the performance of his official duties may be one such area requiring as it does an on-the-spot assessment of the need to keep order."

The city further suggests that its ordinance is comparable to the disorderly conduct statute upheld against a facial challenge in Colten v. Kentucky, 407 U.S. 104 (1972).

This Houston ordinance, however, is not narrowly tailored to prohibit only disorderly conduct or fighting words, and in no way resembles the law upheld in *Colten*. Although we appreciate the difficulties of drafting precise laws, we have repeatedly invalidated laws that provide the police with unfettered discretion to arrest individuals for words or conduct that annoy or offend them. . . . In *Lewis*, Justice Powell elaborated the basis for our concern with such sweeping, dragnet laws:

> "This ordinance, as construed by the Louisiana Supreme Court, confers on police a virtually unrestrained power to arrest and charge persons with a violation. . . . The present type of ordinance tends to be invoked only where there is no other valid basis for arresting an objectionable or

---

11 . . .

. . . [T]oday's decision does not leave municipalities powerless to punish physical obstruction of police action. For example, Justice Powell states that "a municipality constitutionally may punish an individual who chooses to stand near a police officer and persistently attempt to engage the officer in conversation while the officer is directing traffic at a busy intersection." We agree, however, that such conduct might constitutionally be punished under a properly tailored statute, such as a disorderly conduct statute that makes it unlawful to fail to disperse in response to a valid police order or to create a traffic hazard. E.g., Colten v. Kentucky, 407 U.S. 104 (1972). What a municipality may not do, however, and what Houston has done in this case, is to attempt to punish such conduct by broadly criminalizing speech directed to an officer—in this case, by authorizing the police to arrest a person who in any manner verbally interrupts an officer.

Justice Powell also observes that "contentious and abusive" speech can interrupt an officer's investigation, and offers as an example a person who "run[s] beside [an officer pursuing a felon] in a public street shouting at the officer." But what is of concern in that example is not simply contentious speech, but rather the possibility that by shouting and running beside the officer the person may physically obstruct the officer's investigation. Although that person might constitutionally be punished under a tailored statute that prohibited individuals from physically obstructing an officer's investigation, he or she may not be punished under a broad statute aimed at speech.

suspicious person. The opportunity for abuse, especially where a statute has received a virtually open-ended interpretation, is self-evident."

. . .

Houston's ordinance criminalizes a substantial amount of constitutionally protected speech, and accords the police unconstitutional discretion in enforcement. The ordinance's plain language is admittedly violated scores of times daily, yet only some individuals—those chosen by the police in their unguided discretion—are arrested.... We conclude that the ordinance is substantially overbroad, and that the Court of Appeals did not err in holding it facially invalid.

. . .

IV

Today's decision reflects the constitutional requirement that, in the face of verbal challenges to police action, officers and municipalities must respond with restraint. We are mindful that the preservation of liberty depends in part upon the maintenance of social order.... But the First Amendment recognizes, wisely we think, that a certain amount of expressive disorder not only is inevitable in a society committed to individual freedom, but must itself be protected if that freedom would survive. We therefore affirm the judgment of the Court of Appeals.

It is so ordered.[a]

Justice Blackmun, concurring.

I join the Court's opinion and its judgment except that I do not agree with any implication—if one exists—that Gooding v. Wilson, 405 U.S. 518 (1972), and Lewis v. City of New Orleans, 415 U.S. 130 (1974), are good law in the context of their facts, or that they lend any real support to the judgment under review in this case....

Justice Powell, with whom Justice O'Connor joins, and with whom The Chief Justice joins as to Parts I and II, and Justice Scalia joins as to Parts II and III, concurring in the judgment in part and dissenting in part.

... In my view, the Court should not have reached the merits of the constitutional claims, but instead should have certified a question to the Texas Court of Criminal Appeals.... Finally, although I agree that the ordinance as interpreted by the Court violates the Fourteenth Amendment, I write separately because I cannot join the Court's reasoning.

. . .

III

I agree with the Court's conclusion that the ordinance violates the Fourteenth Amendment, but do not join the Court's reasoning.

A

... Lewis v. City of New Orleans, 415 U.S. 130 (1974), is clearly distinguishable.... On its face, the New Orleans ordinance criminalizes only the use of language.... By contrast, the ordinance presented in this case could be applied to activity that involves no element of speech or communication. For

[a] A concurring statement by Justice Scalia is omitted.

example, the ordinance evidently would punish individuals who—without say-ing a single word—obstructed an officer's access to the scene of an ongoing public disturbance, or indeed the scene of a crime. Accordingly, I cannot agree with the Court that this ordinance punishes only speech.

... I have no doubt that a municipality constitutionally may punish an individual who chooses to stand near a police officer and persistently attempt to engage the officer in conversation while the officer is directing traffic at a busy intersection. Similarly, an individual, by contentious and abusive speech, could interrupt an officer's investigation of possible criminal conduct. A person observing an officer pursuing a person suspected of a felony could run beside him in a public street shouting at the officer. Similar tactics could interrupt a policeman lawfully attempting to interrogate persons believed to be witnesses to a crime.

. . .

B

Despite the concerns expressed above, I nevertheless agree that the ambig-uous terms of this ordinance "confe[r] on police a virtually unrestrained power to arrest and charge persons with a violation.... The opportunity for abuse, especially where a statute has received a virtually open-ended interpretation, is self-evident." Lewis v. City of New Orleans, supra, at 135–136 (Powell, J., concurring in result). No Texas court has placed a limiting construction on the ordinance. Also, it is clear that Houston has made no effort to curtail the wide discretion of police officers under the present ordinance. The record contains a sampling of complaints filed under the ordinance in 1981 and 1982. People have been charged with such crimes as "Failure to remain silent and stationary," "Remaining," "Refusing to remain silent," and "Talking." ... Although some of these incidents may have involved unprotected conduct, the vagueness of these charges suggests that, with respect to this ordinance, Houston officials have not been acting with proper sensitivity to the constitutional rights of their citizens. When government protects society's interests in a manner that re-stricts some speech the law must be framed more precisely than the ordinance before us. Accordingly, I agree with the Court that the Houston ordinance is unconstitutional.

... In view of the difficulty of drafting precise language that never restrains speech and yet serves the public interest, the attempts of States and municipalities to draft laws of this type should be accorded some leeway. I am convinced, however, that the Houston ordinance is too vague to comport with the First and Fourteenth Amendments.... [I]t should be possible for the present ordinance to be reframed in a way that would limit the present broad discretion of officers and at the same time protect substantially the city's legitimate interests. For example, the ordinance could make clear that it applies to speech only if the purpose of the speech were to interfere with the performance by a police officer of his lawful duties. In this situation, the difficulties of drafting precisely should not justify upholding this ordinance.

. . .

Chief Justice Rehnquist, dissenting.

I join Parts I and II of Justice Powell's opinion concurring in the judgment in part and dissenting in part. I do not agree, however, that the Houston ordinance, in the absence of an authoritative construction by the Texas courts, is unconstitutional....

R.A.V. v. City of St. Paul, Minnesota

505 U.S. 377, 112 S.Ct. 2538, 120 L.Ed.2d 305 (1992).

Justice Scalia delivered the opinion of the Court.

In the predawn hours of June 21, 1990, petitioner and several other teenagers allegedly assembled a crudely-made cross by taping together broken chair legs. They then allegedly burned the cross inside the fenced yard of a black family that lived across the street from the house where petitioner was staying. Although this conduct could have been punished under any of a number of laws,[1] one of the two provisions under which respondent city of St. Paul chose to charge petitioner (then a juvenile) was the St. Paul Bias–Motivated Crime Ordinance, St. Paul, Minn.Legis.Code § 292.02 (1990), which provides: "Whoever places on public or private property a symbol, object, appellation, characterization or graffiti, including, but not limited to, a burning cross or Nazi swastika, which one knows or has reasonable grounds to know arouses anger, alarm or resentment in others on the basis of race, color, creed, religion or gender commits disorderly conduct and shall be guilty of a misdemeanor." Petitioner moved to dismiss this count on the ground that the St. Paul ordinance was substantially overbroad and impermissibly content-based and therefore facially invalid under the First Amendment.[2] The trial court granted this motion, but the Minnesota Supreme Court reversed. That court rejected petitioner's overbreadth claim because, as construed in prior Minnesota cases, ... the modifying phrase "arouses anger, alarm or resentment in others" limited the reach of the ordinance to conduct that amounts to "fighting words," i.e., "conduct that itself inflicts injury or tends to incite immediate violence ...," ...

I

... [W]e accept the Minnesota Supreme Court's authoritative statement that the ordinance reaches only those expressions that constitute "fighting words" within the meaning of *Chaplinsky*. Petitioner and his amici urge us to modify the scope of the *Chaplinsky* formulation, thereby invalidating the ordinance as "substantially overbroad," ... We find it unnecessary to consider this issue. Assuming, arguendo, that all of the expression reached by the ordinance is proscribable under the "fighting words" doctrine, we nonetheless conclude that the ordinance is facially unconstitutional in that it prohibits otherwise permitted speech solely on the basis of the subjects the speech addresses.

The First Amendment generally prevents government from proscribing speech ... because of disapproval of the ideas expressed. Content-based regulations are presumptively invalid.... From 1791 to the present, however, our society, like other free but civilized societies, has permitted restrictions upon the content of speech in a few limited areas, which are "of such slight social value as a step to truth that any benefit that may be derived from them is clearly outweighed by the social interest in order and morality." *Chaplinsky*,

---

[1] The conduct might have violated Minnesota statutes carrying significant penalties. See, e.g., Minn.Stat. § 609.713(1) (1987) (providing for up to five years in prison for terroristic threats); § 609.563 (arson) (providing for up to five years and a $10,000 fine, depending on the value of the property intended to be damaged); § 606.595 (Supp. 1992) (criminal damage to property) (provid-ing for up to one year and a $3,000 fine, depending upon the extent of the damage to the property).

[2] Petitioner has also been charged, in Count I of the delinquency petition, with a violation of Minn.Stat. § 609.2231(4) (Supp. 1990) (racially motivated assaults). Petitioner did not challenge this count.

supra, at 572. We have recognized that "the freedom of speech" referred to by the First Amendment does not include a freedom to disregard these traditional limitations.... Our decisions since the 1960's have narrowed the scope of the traditional categorical exceptions for defamation, ... but a limited categorical approach has remained an important part of our First Amendment jurisprudence.

We have sometimes said that these categories of expression are "not within the area of constitutionally protected speech," ... or that the "protection of the First Amendment does not extend" to them, ... Such statements must be taken in context, however, and are no more literally true than is the occasionally repeated shorthand characterizing obscenity "as not being speech at all," Sunstein, Pornography and the First Amendment, 1986 Duke L.J. 589, 615, n. 146. What they mean is that these areas of speech can, consistently with the First Amendment, be regulated because of their constitutionally proscribable content (obscenity, defamation, etc.)—not that they are categories of speech entirely invisible to the Constitution, so that they may be made the vehicles for content discrimination unrelated to their distinctively proscribable content. Thus, the government may proscribe libel; but it may not make the further content discrimination of proscribing only libel critical of the government....

Our cases surely do not establish the proposition that the First Amendment imposes no obstacle whatsoever to regulation of particular instances of such proscribable expression ... That would mean that a city council could enact an ordinance prohibiting only those legally obscene works that contain criticism of the city government or, indeed, that do not include endorsement of the city government. Such a simplistic, all-or-nothing-at-all approach to First Amendment protection is at odds with common sense and with our jurisprudence as well. It is not true that "fighting words" have at most a "de minimis" expressive content, ibid., or that their content is in all respects "worthless and undeserving of constitutional protection"; sometimes they are quite expressive indeed. We have not said that they constitute "no part of the expression of ideas," but only that they constitute "no essential part of any exposition of ideas." *Chaplinsky,* 315 U.S., at 572....

The proposition that a particular instance of speech can be proscribable on the basis of one feature (e.g., obscenity) but not on the basis of another (e.g., opposition to the city government) is commonplace, and has found application in many contexts. We have long held, for example, that nonverbal expressive activity can be banned because of the action it entails, but not because of the ideas it expresses—so that burning a flag in violation of an ordinance against outdoor fires could be punishable, whereas burning a flag in violation of an ordinance against dishonoring the flag is not. See *Johnson,* 491 U.S., at 406–407.... Similarly, we have upheld reasonable "time, place, or manner" restrictions, but only if they are "justified without reference to the content of the regulated speech." ... And just as the power to proscribe particular speech on the basis of a noncontent element (e.g., noise) does not entail the power to proscribe the same speech on the basis of a content element; so also, the power to proscribe it on the basis of one content element (e.g., obscenity) does not entail the power to proscribe it on the basis of other content elements.

In other words, the exclusion of "fighting words" from the scope of the First Amendment simply means that, for purposes of that Amendment, the unprotected features of the words are, despite their verbal character, essentially a "nonspeech" element of communication. Fighting words are thus analogous to a noisy sound truck: Each is ... a "mode of speech," ... but neither has, in and of itself, a claim upon the First Amendment. As with the sound truck, however, so also with fighting words: The government may not regulate use based on hostility—or favoritism—towards the underlying message expressed.

The concurrences describe us as setting forth a new First Amendment principle that prohibition of constitutionally proscribable speech cannot be "underinclusiv[e],"—a First Amendment "absolutism" whereby "within a particular 'proscribable' category of expression, . . . a government must either proscribe all speech or no speech at all." That easy target is of the concurrences' own invention. In our view, the First Amendment imposes not an "underinclusiveness" limitation but a "content discrimination" limitation upon a State's prohibition of proscribable speech. There is no problem whatever, for example, with a State's prohibiting obscenity (and other forms of proscribable expression) only in certain media or markets, for although that prohibition would be "underinclusive," it would not discriminate on the basis of content. . . .

Even the prohibition against content discrimination that we assert the First Amendment requires is not absolute. It applies differently in the context of proscribable speech than in the area of fully protected speech. The rationale of the general prohibition, after all, is that content discrimination "rais[es] the specter that the Government may effectively drive certain ideas or viewpoints from the marketplace," . . . But content discrimination among various instances of a class of proscribable speech often does not pose this threat.

When the basis for the content discrimination consists entirely of the very reason the entire class of speech at issue is proscribable, no significant danger of idea or viewpoint discrimination exists. Such a reason, having been adjudged neutral enough to support exclusion of the entire class of speech from First Amendment protection, is also neutral enough to form the basis of distinction within the class. To illustrate: A State might choose to prohibit only that obscenity which is the most patently offensive in its prurience—i.e., that which involves the most lascivious displays of sexual activity. But it may not prohibit, for example, only that obscenity which includes offensive political messages. . . . And the Federal Government can criminalize only those threats of violence that are directed against the President, see 18 U.S.C. § 871—since the reasons why threats of violence are outside the First Amendment (protecting individuals from the fear of violence, from the disruption that fear engenders, and from the possibility that the threatened violence will occur) have special force when applied to the person of the President. See Watts v. United States, 394 U.S. 705, 707 (1969) (upholding the facial validity of § 871 because of the "overwhelmin[g] interest in protecting the safety of [the] Chief Executive and in allowing him to perform his duties without interference from threats of physical violence"). But the Federal Government may not criminalize only those threats against the President that mention his policy on aid to inner cities. And to take a final example (one mentioned by Justice Stevens), a State may choose to regulate price advertising in one industry but not in others, because the risk of fraud (one of the characteristics of commercial speech that justifies depriving it of full First Amendment protection . . .) is in its view greater there. . . . But a State may not prohibit only that commercial advertising that depicts men in a demeaning fashion. . . .

Another valid basis for according differential treatment to even a content-defined subclass of proscribable speech is that the subclass happens to be associated with particular "secondary effects" of the speech, so that the regulation is "justified without reference to the content of the . . . speech," Renton v. Playtime Theatres, Inc., 475 U.S. 41, 48 (1986) . . . A State could, for example, permit all obscene live performances except those involving minors.

Moreover, since words can in some circumstances violate laws directed not against speech but against conduct (a law against treason, for example, is violated by telling the enemy the nation's defense secrets), a particular content-based subcategory of a proscribable class of speech can be swept up incidentally within the reach of a statute directed at conduct rather than speech.... Thus, for example, sexually derogatory "fighting words," among other words, may produce a violation of Title VII's general prohibition against sexual discrimination in employment practices ... Where the government does not target conduct on the basis of its expressive content, acts are not shielded from regulation merely because they express a discriminatory idea or philosophy.

These bases for distinction refute the proposition that the selectivity of the restriction is "even arguably 'conditioned upon the sovereign's agreement with what a speaker may intend to say.' " ... There may be other such bases as well. Indeed, to validate such selectivity (where totally proscribable speech is at issue) it may not even be necessary to identify any particular "neutral" basis, so long as the nature of the content discrimination is such that there is no realistic possibility that official suppression of ideas is afoot. (We cannot think of any First Amendment interest that would stand in the way of a State's prohibiting only those obscene motion pictures with blue-eyed actresses.) Save for that limitation, the regulation of "fighting words," like the regulation of noisy speech, may address some offensive instances and leave other, equally offensive, instances alone....

II

Applying these principles to the St. Paul ordinance, we conclude that, even as narrowly construed by the Minnesota Supreme Court, the ordinance is facially unconstitutional. Although the phrase in the ordinance, "arouses anger, alarm or resentment in others," has been limited by the Minnesota Supreme Court's construction to reach only those symbols or displays that amount to "fighting words," the remaining, unmodified terms make clear that the ordinance applies only to "fighting words" that insult, or provoke violence, "on the basis of race, color, creed, religion or gender." Displays containing abusive invective, no matter how vicious or severe, are permissible unless they are addressed to one of the specified disfavored topics. Those who wish to use "fighting words" in connection with other ideas—to express hostility, for example, on the basis of political affiliation, union membership, or homosexuality—are not covered. The First Amendment does not permit St. Paul to impose special prohibitions on those speakers who express views on disfavored subjects....

In its practical operation, moreover, the ordinance goes even beyond mere content discrimination, to actual viewpoint discrimination. Displays containing some words—odious racial epithets, for example—would be prohibited to proponents of all views. But "fighting words" that do not themselves invoke race, color, creed, religion, or gender—aspersions upon a person's mother, for example—would seemingly be usable *ad libitum* in the placards of those arguing *in favor* of racial, color, etc. tolerance and equality, but could not be used by that speaker's opponents. One could hold up a sign saying, for example, that all "anti-Catholic bigots" are misbegotten; but not that all "papists" are, for that would insult and provoke violence "on the basis of religion." St. Paul has no such authority to license one side of a debate to fight freestyle, while requiring the other to follow Marquis of Queensbury Rules.

What we have here, it must be emphasized, is not a prohibition of fighting words that are directed at certain persons or groups (which would be facially valid if it met the requirements of the Equal Protection Clause); but rather, a prohibition of fighting words that contain (as the Minnesota Supreme Court repeatedly emphasized) messages of "bias-motivated" hatred and in particular, as applied to this case, messages "based on virulent notions of racial supremacy." One must wholeheartedly agree with the Minnesota Supreme Court that "[i]t is the responsibility, even the obligation, of diverse communities to confront such notions in whatever form they appear," but the manner of that confrontation cannot consist of selective limitations upon speech. St. Paul's brief asserts that a general "fighting words" law would not meet the city's needs because only a content-specific measure can communicate to minority groups that the "group hatred" aspect of such speech "is not condoned by the majority." The point of the First Amendment is that majority preferences must be expressed in some fashion other than silencing speech on the basis of its content.

. . . Justice Stevens suggests that . . . the ordinance . . . is directed . . . not to speech of a particular content, but to particular "injur[ies]" that are "qualitatively different" from other injuries. This is word-play. What makes the anger, fear, sense of dishonor, etc. produced by violation of this ordinance distinct from the anger, fear, sense of dishonor, etc. produced by other fighting words is nothing other than the fact that it is caused by a distinctive idea, conveyed by a distinctive message. The First Amendment cannot be evaded that easily. It is obvious that the symbols which will arouse "anger, alarm or resentment in others on the basis of race, color, creed, religion or gender" are those symbols that communicate a message of hostility based on one of these characteristics. St. Paul concedes . . . that the ordinance applies only to "racial, religious, or gender-specific symbols" such as "a burning cross, Nazi swastika or other instrumentality of like import." . . .

The content-based discrimination reflected in the St. Paul ordinance comes within neither any of the specific exceptions to the First Amendment prohibition we discussed earlier, nor within a more general exception for content discrimination that does not threaten censorship of ideas. It assuredly does not fall within the exception for content discrimination based on the very reasons why the particular class of speech at issue (here, fighting words) is proscribable. As explained earlier, the reason why fighting words are categorically excluded from the protection of the First Amendment is not that their content communicates any particular idea, but that their content embodies a particularly intolerable (and socially unnecessary) mode of expressing whatever idea the speaker wishes to convey. St. Paul has not singled out an especially offensive mode of expression—it has not, for example, selected for prohibition only those fighting words that communicate ideas in a threatening (as opposed to a merely obnoxious) manner. Rather, it has proscribed fighting words of whatever manner that communicate messages of racial, gender, or religious intolerance. Selectivity of this sort creates the possibility that the city is seeking to handicap the expression of particular ideas. That possibility would alone be enough to render the ordinance presumptively invalid, but St. Paul's comments and concessions in this case elevate the possibility to a certainty.

St. Paul argues that the ordinance comes within another of the specific exceptions we mentioned, the one that allows content discrimination aimed only at the "secondary effects" of the speech, see Renton v. Playtime Theatres, Inc., 475 U.S. 41 (1986). According to St. Paul, the ordinance is intended, "not to impact on [sic] the right of free expression of the accused," but rather to "protect against the victimization of a person or persons who are particularly vulnerable because of their membership in a group that historically has been discriminated against." Even assuming that an ordinance that completely proscribes, rather than merely regulates, a specified category of speech can ever be considered or be directed only to the secondary effects of such speech, it is clear that the St. Paul ordinance is not directed to secondary effects within the meaning of *Renton*. As we said in Boos v. Barry, 485 U.S. 312 (1988), "[l]isteners' reactions to speech are not the type of 'secondary effects' we referred to in *Renton*." ...[7]

It hardly needs discussion that the ordinance does not fall within some more general exception permitting all selectivity that for any reason is beyond the suspicion of official suppression of ideas. The statements of St. Paul in this very case afford ample basis for, if not full confirmation of, that suspicion.

Finally, St. Paul and its amici defend the conclusion of the Minnesota Supreme Court that, even if the ordinance regulates expression based on hostility towards its protected ideological content, this discrimination is nonetheless justified because it is narrowly tailored to serve compelling state interests. Specifically, they assert that the ordinance helps to ensure the basic human rights of members of groups that have historically been subjected to discrimination, including the right of such group members to live in peace where they wish. We do not doubt that these interests are compelling, and that the ordinance can be said to promote them. But the "danger of censorship" presented by a facially content-based statute, ... requires that that weapon be employed only where it is "necessary to serve the asserted [compelling] interest," ... The existence of adequate content-neutral alternatives thus "undercut[s] significantly" any defense of such a statute ... The dispositive question in this case, therefore, is whether content discrimination is reasonably necessary to achieve St. Paul's compelling interests; it plainly is not. An ordinance not limited to the favored topics, for example, would have precisely the same beneficial effect. In fact the only interest distinctively served by the content limitation is that of displaying the city council's special hostility towards the particular biases thus singled out.[8] That is precisely what the First Amendment forbids. The politicians of St. Paul are entitled to express that hostility—but not through the means of imposing unique limitations upon speakers who (however benightedly) disagree.

. . .

Let there be no mistake about our belief that burning a cross in someone's front yard is reprehensible. But St. Paul has sufficient means at its disposal to prevent such behavior without adding the First Amendment to the fire.

The judgment of the Minnesota Supreme Court is reversed, and the case is remanded for proceedings not inconsistent with this opinion.

It is so ordered.

---

[7] St. Paul has not argued in this case that the ordinance merely regulates that subclass of fighting words which is most likely to provoke a violent response. But even if one assumes (as appears unlikely) that the categories selected may be so described, that would not justify selective regulation under a "secondary effects" theory. The only reason why such expressive conduct would be especially correlated with violence is that it conveys a particularly odious message; ... the St. Paul ordinance regulates on the basis of the "primary" effect of the speech—i.e., its persuasive (or repellant) force.

[8] A plurality of the Court reached a different conclusion with regard to the Tennessee anti-electioneering statute considered earlier this Term in Burson v. Freeman, 504 U.S. 191 (1992). In light of the "logical connection" between electioneering and the State's compelling interest in preventing voter intimidation and election fraud ... the plurality concluded that it was faced with one of those "rare case[s]" in which the use of a facially content-based restriction was justified by interests unrelated to the suppression of ideas....

Justice White, with whom Justice Blackmun and Justice O'Connor join, and with whom Justice Stevens joins except as to Part I(A), concurring in the judgment.

I agree with the majority that the judgment of the Minnesota Supreme Court should be reversed. However, our agreement ends there.

This case could easily be decided within the contours of established First Amendment law by holding, as petitioner argues, that the St. Paul ordinance is fatally overbroad because it criminalizes not only unprotected expression but expression protected by the First Amendment. Instead, "find[ing] it unnecessary" to consider the questions upon which we granted review, the Court holds the ordinance facially unconstitutional on a ground that was never presented to the Minnesota Supreme Court, a ground that has not been briefed by the parties before this Court, a ground that requires serious departures from the teaching of prior cases and is inconsistent with the plurality opinion in Burson v. Freeman, 504 U.S. 191 (1992). . . .

. . .

I

A

. . .

. . . [T]his Court has long held certain discrete categories of expression to be proscribable on the basis of their content. For instance, the Court has held that the individual who falsely shouts "fire" in a crowded theatre may not claim the protection of the First Amendment. Schenck v. United States, 249 U.S. 47, 52 (1919). The Court has concluded that neither child pornography, nor obscenity, is protected by the First Amendment. . . . And the Court has observed that, "[l]eaving aside the special considerations when public officials [and public figures] are the target, a libelous publication is not protected by the Constitution." . . .

All of these categories are content based. But the Court has held that the First Amendment does not apply to them because their expressive content is worthless or of de minimis value to society. *Chaplinsky,* supra, at 571–572. We have not departed from this principle, emphasizing repeatedly that, "within the confines of [these] given classification[s], the evil to be restricted so overwhelmingly outweighs the expressive interests, if any, at stake, that no process of case-by-case adjudication is required." . . . This categorical approach has provided a principled and narrowly focused means for distinguishing between expression that the government may regulate freely and that which it may regulate on the basis of content only upon a showing of compelling need.

. . .

. . . [T]he majority holds that the First Amendment protects those narrow categories of expression long held to be undeserving of First Amendment protection—at least to the extent that lawmakers may not regulate some fighting words more strictly than others because of their content. The Court announces that such content-based distinctions violate the First Amendment because "the government may not regulate use based on hostility—or favoritism—towards the underlying message expressed." Should the government want to criminalize certain fighting words, the Court now requires it to criminalize all fighting words.

... It is inconsistent to hold that the government may proscribe an entire category of speech because the content of that speech is evil, ... but that the government may not treat a subset of that category differently without violating the First Amendment; the content of the subset is by definition worthless and undeserving of constitutional protection.

... Fighting words are not a means of exchanging views, rallying supporters, or registering a protest; they are directed against individuals to provoke violence or to inflict injury.... Therefore, a ban on all fighting words or on a subset of the fighting words category would restrict only the social evil of hate speech, without creating the danger of driving viewpoints from the marketplace.

... The overbreadth doctrine has the redeeming virtue of attempting to avoid the chilling of protected expression, ... but the Court's new "underbreadth" creation serves no desirable function. Instead, it permits, indeed invites, the continuation of expressive conduct that in this case is evil and worthless in First Amendment terms ... until the city of St. Paul cures the underbreadth by adding to its ordinance a catch-all phrase such as "and all other fighting words that may constitutionally be subject to this ordinance."

Any contribution of this holding to First Amendment jurisprudence is surely a negative one, since it necessarily signals that expressions of violence, such as the message of intimidation and racial hatred conveyed by burning a cross on someone's lawn, are of sufficient value to outweigh the social interest in order and morality that has traditionally placed such fighting words outside the First Amendment. Indeed, by characterizing fighting words as a form of "debate," the majority legitimates hate speech as a form of public discussion.

Furthermore, the Court obscures the line between speech that could be regulated freely on the basis of content (i.e., the narrow categories of expression falling outside the First Amendment) and that which could be regulated on the basis of content only upon a showing of a compelling state interest (i.e., all remaining expression). By placing fighting words, which the Court has long held to be valueless, on at least equal constitutional footing with political discourse and other forms of speech that we have deemed to have the greatest social value, the majority devalues the latter category....

B

In a second break with precedent, the Court refuses to sustain the ordinance even though it would survive under the strict scrutiny applicable to other protected expression. Assuming, arguendo, that the St. Paul ordinance is a content-based regulation of protected expression, it nevertheless would pass First Amendment review under settled law upon a showing that the regulation "is necessary to serve a compelling state interest and is narrowly drawn to achieve that end." ... [T]he Court treats strict scrutiny analysis as irrelevant to the constitutionality of the legislation ... Under the majority's view, a narrowly drawn, content-based ordinance could never pass constitutional muster if the object of that legislation could be accomplished by banning a wider category of speech. This appears to be a general renunciation of strict scrutiny review, a fundamental tool of First Amendment analysis.

This abandonment of the doctrine is inexplicable in light of our decision in *Burson v. Freeman,* supra, which was handed down just a month ago. In *Burson,* ... the strict scrutiny standard applied in a case involving a First Amendment challenge to a content-based statute.... The statute at issue prohibited the solicitation of votes and the display or distribution of campaign materials within 100 feet of the entrance to a polling place. The plurality concluded that the legislation survived strict scrutiny because the State has asserted a compelling interest in regulating electioneering near polling places and because the statute at issue was narrowly tailored to accomplish that goal. . . .

Significantly, the statute in *Burson* did not proscribe all speech near polling places; it restricted only political speech. . . . The *Burson* plurality . . . concluded that the distinction between types of speech required application of strict scrutiny, but it squarely rejected the proposition that the legislation failed First Amendment review because it could have been drafted in broader, content-neutral terms: . . .

Had the analysis adopted by the majority in the present case been applied in *Burson,* the challenged election law would have failed constitutional review, for its content-based distinction between political and nonpolitical speech could not have been characterized as "reasonably necessary," to achieve the State's interest in regulating polling place premises.

. . . The majority appears to believe that its doctrinal revisionism is necessary to prevent our elected lawmakers from prohibiting libel against members of one political party but not another and from enacting similarly preposterous laws. The majority is misguided.

Although the First Amendment does not apply to categories of unprotected speech, such as fighting words, the Equal Protection Clause requires that the regulation of unprotected speech be rationally related to a legitimate government interest. A defamation statute that drew distinctions on the basis of political affiliation or "an ordinance prohibiting only those legally obscene works that contain criticism of the city government," would unquestionably fail rational basis review.

. . . [T]he St. Paul ordinance . . . would pass equal protection review. The ordinance proscribes a subset of "fighting words," those that injure "on the basis of race, color, creed, religion or gender." This selective regulation reflects the City's judgment that harms based on race, color, creed, religion, or gender are more pressing public concerns than the harms caused by other fighting words. In light of our Nation's long and painful experience with discrimination, this determination is plainly reasonable. . . .

C

The Court has patched up its argument with an apparently nonexhaustive list of ad hoc exceptions . . .

For instance, if the majority were to give general application to the rule on which it decides this case, today's decision would call into question the constitutionality of the statute making it illegal to threaten the life of the President. . . .

To save the statute, the majority has engrafted the following exception onto its newly announced First Amendment rule: Content-based distinctions may be drawn within an unprotected category of speech if the basis for the distinctions is "the very reason the entire class of speech at issue is proscribable." . . .

The exception swallows the majority's rule. Certainly, it should apply to the St. Paul ordinance, since "the reasons why [fighting words] are outside the First Amendment . . . have special force when applied to [groups that have historically been subjected to discrimination]."

To avoid the result of its own analysis, the Court suggests that fighting words are simply a mode of communication, rather than a content-based category, and that the St. Paul ordinance has not singled out a particularly objectionable mode of communication. Again, the majority confuses the issue. A prohibition on fighting words is not a time, place, or manner restriction; it is a ban on a class of speech that conveys an overriding message of personal injury and imminent violence, ... a message that is at its ugliest when directed against groups that have long been the targets of discrimination. Accordingly, the ordinance falls within the first exception to the majority's theory.

As its second exception, the Court posits that certain content-based regulations will survive under the new regime if the regulated subclass "happens to be associated with particular 'secondary effects' of the speech ...," which the majority treats as encompassing instances in which "words can ... violate laws directed not against speech but against conduct ..." Again, there is a simple explanation for the Court's eagerness to craft an exception to its new First Amendment rule: Under the general rule the Court applies in this case, Title VII hostile work environment claims would suddenly be unconstitutional.

Title VII makes it unlawful to discriminate "because of [an] individual's race, color, religion, sex, or national origin," ... and the regulations covering hostile workplace claims forbid "sexual harassment," which includes "[u]nwelcome sexual advances, requests for sexual favors, and other verbal or physical conduct of a sexual nature" which creates "an intimidating, hostile, or offensive working environment." ... The regulation does not prohibit workplace harassment generally; it focuses on what the majority would characterize as the "disfavored topi[c]" of sexual harassment. In this way, Title VII is similar to the St. Paul ordinance that the majority condemns because it "impose[s] special prohibitions on those speakers who express views on disfavored subjects." Under the broad principle the Court uses to decide the present case, hostile work environment claims based on sexual harassment should fail First Amendment review; because a general ban on harassment in the workplace would cover the problem of sexual harassment, any attempt to proscribe the subcategory of sexually harassing expression would violate the First Amendment.

Hence, the majority's second exception, which the Court indicates would insulate a Title VII hostile work environment claim from an underinclusiveness challenge because "sexually derogatory 'fighting words' ... may produce a violation of Title VII's general prohibition against sexual discrimination in employment practices." But application of this exception to a hostile work environment claim does not hold up under close examination.

First, the hostile work environment regulation is not keyed to the presence or absence of an economic quid pro quo, ... but to the impact of the speech on the victimized worker. Consequently, the regulation would no more fall within a secondary effects exception than does the St. Paul ordinance. Second, the majority's focus on the statute's general prohibition on discrimination glosses over the language of the specific regulation governing hostile working environment, which reaches beyond any "incidental" effect on speech.... [A]ll St. Paul need do to bring its ordinance within this exception is to add some prefatory language concerning discrimination generally.

As the third exception to the Court's theory for deciding this case, the majority concocts a catchall exclusion to protect against unforeseen problems, a concern that is heightened here given the lack of briefing on the majority's decisional theory. This final exception would apply in cases in which "there is no realistic possibility that official suppression of ideas is afoot." As I have demonstrated, this case does not concern the official suppression of ideas....

. . .

II

Although I disagree with the Court's analysis, I do agree with its conclusion: The St. Paul ordinance is unconstitutional. However, I would decide the case on overbreadth grounds.

. . .

Petitioner contends that the St. Paul ordinance is not susceptible to a narrowing construction and that the ordinance therefore should be considered as written, and not as construed by the Minnesota Supreme Court. Petitioner is wrong. Where a state court has interpreted a provision of state law, we cannot ignore that interpretation, even if it is not one that we would have reached if we were construing the statute in the first instance....

Of course, the mere presence of a state court interpretation does not insulate a statute from overbreadth review. We have stricken legislation when the construction supplied by the state court failed to cure the overbreadth problem.... But in such cases, we have looked to the statute as construed in determining whether it contravened the First Amendment. Here, the Minnesota Supreme Court has provided an authoritative construction of the St. Paul antibias ordinance. Consideration of petitioner's overbreadth claim must be based on that interpretation.

I agree with petitioner that the ordinance is invalid on its face. Although the ordinance as construed reaches categories of speech that are constitutionally unprotected, it also criminalizes a substantial amount of expression that—however repugnant—is shielded by the First Amendment.

... The Minnesota Supreme Court erred in its application of the *Chaplinsky* fighting words test and consequently interpreted the St. Paul ordinance in a fashion that rendered the ordinance facially overbroad.

In construing the St. Paul ordinance, the Minnesota Supreme Court drew upon the definition of fighting words that appears in *Chaplinsky*—words "which by their very utterance inflict injury or tend to incite an immediate breach of the peace." Id., at 572. However, the Minnesota court was far from clear in identifying the "injur[ies]" inflicted by the expression that St. Paul sought to regulate.... I ... understand the court to have ruled that St. Paul may constitutionally prohibit expression that "by its very utterance" causes "anger, alarm or resentment."

Our fighting words cases have made clear, however, that such generalized reactions are not sufficient to strip expression of its constitutional protection. The mere fact that expressive activity causes hurt feelings, offense, or resentment does not render the expression unprotected....

... Although the ordinance reaches conduct that is unprotected, it also makes criminal expressive conduct that causes only hurt feelings, offense, or resentment, and is protected by the First Amendment.... The ordinance is therefore fatally overbroad and invalid on its face.

. . .

Justice Blackmun, concurring in the judgment.

. . .

I see no First Amendment values that are compromised by a law that prohibits hoodlums from driving minorities out of their homes by burning crosses on their lawns, but I see great harm in preventing the people of Saint Paul from specifically punishing the race-based fighting words that so prejudice their community.

I concur in the judgment, however, because I agree with Justice White that this particular ordinance reaches beyond fighting words to speech protected by the First Amendment.

Justice Stevens, with whom Justice White and Justice Blackmun join as to Part I, concurring in the judgment.

Conduct that creates special risks or causes special harms may be prohibited by special rules. Lighting a fire near an ammunition dump or a gasoline storage tank is especially dangerous; such behavior may be punished more severely than burning trash in a vacant lot. Threatening someone because of her race or religious beliefs may cause particularly severe trauma or touch off a riot, and threatening a high public official may cause substantial social disruption; such threats may be punished more severely than threats against someone based on, say, his support of a particular athletic team. There are legitimate, reasonable, and neutral justifications for such special rules.

This case involves the constitutionality of one such ordinance. Because the regulated conduct has some communicative content—a message of racial, religious or gender hostility—the ordinance raises two quite different First Amendment questions. Is the ordinance "overbroad" because it prohibits too much speech? If not, is it "underbroad" because it does not prohibit enough speech?

In answering these questions, my colleagues today wrestle with two broad principles: first, that certain "categories of expression [including 'fighting words'] are 'not within the area of constitutionally protected speech,' "and second, that "[c]ontent-based regulations [of expression] are presumptively invalid." Although in past opinions the Court has repeated both of these maxims, it has—quite rightly—adhered to neither with the absolutism suggested by my colleagues. Thus, while I agree that the St. Paul ordinance is unconstitutionally overbroad for the reasons stated in Part II of Justice White's opinion, I write separately to suggest how the allure of absolute principles has skewed the analysis of both the majority and concurring opinions.

I

Fifty years ago, the Court articulated a categorical approach to First Amendment jurisprudence. . . .

The Court today revises this categorical approach. It is not, the Court rules, that certain "categories" of expression are "unprotected," but rather that certain "elements" of expression are wholly "proscribable." To the Court, an expressive act, like a chemical compound, consists of more than one element. Although the act may be regulated because it contains a proscribable element, it may not be regulated on the basis of another (nonproscribable) element it also contains. Thus, obscene antigovernment speech may be regulated because it is obscene, but not because it is antigovernment. It is this revision of the categorical approach that allows the Court to assume that the St. Paul ordinance proscribes only fighting words, while at the same time concluding that the ordinance is invalid because it imposes a content-based regulation on expressive activity.

. . .

I am ... troubled by the second step of the Court's analysis—namely, its conclusion that the St. Paul ordinance is an unconstitutional content-based regulation of speech.... [T]he Court establishes a near-absolute ban on content-based regulations of expression and holds that the First Amendment prohibits the regulation of fighting words by subject matter. Thus, while the Court rejects the "all-or-nothing-at-all" nature of the categorical approach, it promptly embraces an absolutism of its own: within a particular "proscribable" category of expression, the Court holds, a government must either proscribe all speech or no speech at all. This aspect of the Court's ruling fundamentally misunderstands the role and constitutional status of content-based regulations on speech ...

Although the Court has, on occasion, declared that content-based regulations of speech are "never permitted," ... such claims are overstated.... [C]ontent-based distinctions, far from being presumptively invalid, are an inevitable and indispensable aspect of a coherent understanding of the First Amendment.

This is true at every level of First Amendment law. In broadest terms, our entire First Amendment jurisprudence creates a regime based on the content of speech. The scope of the First Amendment is determined by the content of expressive activity: Although the First Amendment broadly protects "speech," it does not protect the right to "fix prices, breach contracts, make false warranties, place bets with bookies, threaten, [or] extort." Schauer, Categories and the First Amendment: A Play in Three Acts, 34 Vand.L.Rev. 265, 270 (1981). Whether an agreement among competitors is a violation of the Sherman Act or protected activity under the Noerr–Pennington doctrine hinges upon the content of the agreement. Similarly, "the line between permissible advocacy and impermissible incitation to crime or violence depends, not merely on the setting in which the speech occurs, but also on exactly what the speaker had to say." ...

Likewise, whether speech falls within one of the categories of "unprotected" or "proscribable" expression is determined, in part, by its content. Whether a magazine is obscene, a gesture a fighting word, or a photograph child pornography is determined, in part, by its content. Even within categories of protected expression, the First Amendment status of speech is fixed by its content.... [S]peech about public officials or matters of public concern receives greater protection than speech about other topics. It can, therefore, scarcely be said that the regulation of expressive activity cannot be predicated on its content: much of our First Amendment jurisprudence is premised on the assumption that content makes a difference.

Consistent with this general premise, we have frequently upheld content-based regulations of speech.... In FCC v. Pacifica Foundation, 438 U.S. 726 (1978) (plurality opinion), we upheld a restriction on the broadest of specific indecent words. In Lehman v. City of Shaker Heights, 418 U.S. 298 (1974) (plurality opinion), we upheld a city law that permitted commercial advertising, but prohibited political advertising, on city buses. In Broadrick v. Oklahoma, 413 U.S. 601 (1973), we upheld a state law that restricted the speech of state employees, but only as concerned partisan political matters. We have long recognized the power of the Federal Trade Commission to regulate misleading advertising and labeling, ... and the National Labor Relations Board's power to regulate an employer's election-related speech on the basis of its content.... It is also beyond question that the Government may choose to limit advertisements for cigarettes, ... but not for cigars; choose to regulate airline advertising, ... but not bus advertising; or choose to monitor solicitation by lawyers, ... but not by doctors.

All of these cases involved the selective regulation of speech based on content—precisely the sort of regulation the Court invalidates today. Such selective regulations are unavoidably content based, but they are not, in my opinion, "presumptively invalid." ...

... [T]he Court today ... applies the prohibition on content-based regulation to speech that the Court had until today considered wholly "unprotected" by the First Amendment—namely, fighting words. This new absolutism in the prohibition of content-based regulations severely contorts the fabric of settled First Amendment law.

Our First Amendment decisions have created a rough hierarchy in the constitutional protection of speech. Core political speech occupies the highest, most protected position; commercial speech and nonobscene, sexually explicit speech are regarded as a sort of second-class expression; obscenity and fighting words receive the least protection of all. Assuming that the Court is correct that this last class of speech is not wholly "unprotected," it certainly does not follow that fighting words and obscenity receive the same sort of protection afforded core political speech. Yet in ruling that proscribable speech cannot be regulated based on subject matter, the Court does just that. Perversely, this gives fighting words greater protection than is afforded commercial speech. If Congress can prohibit false advertising directed at airline passengers without also prohibiting false advertising directed at bus passengers and if a city can prohibit political advertisements in its buses while allowing other advertisements, it is ironic to hold that a city cannot regulate fighting words based on "race, color, creed, religion or gender" while leaving unregulated fighting words based on "union membership or homosexuality." ...

Perhaps because the Court recognizes these perversities, it quickly offers some ad hoc limitations on its newly extended prohibition on content-based regulations. First, the Court states that a content-based regulation is valid "[w]hen the content discrimination is based upon the very reason the entire class of speech ... is proscribable." In a pivotal passage, the Court writes "the Federal Government can criminalize only those physical threats that are directed against the President, see 18 U.S.C. § 871—since the reasons why threats of violence are outside the First Amendment ... have special force when applied to the ... President." ...

Precisely this same reasoning, however, compels the conclusion that St. Paul's ordinance is constitutional. Just as Congress may determine that threats against the President entail more severe consequences than other threats, so St. Paul's City Council may determine that threats based on the target's race, religion, or gender cause more severe harm to both the target and to society than other threats....

Next, the Court recognizes that a State may regulate advertising in one industry but not another because "the risk of fraud (one of the characteristics that justifies depriving [commercial speech] of full First Amendment protection ...)" in the regulated industry is "greater" than in other industries. Again, the same reasoning demonstrates the constitutionality of St. Paul's ordinance.... Certainly a legislature that may determine that the risk of fraud is greater in the legal trade than in the medical trade may determine that the risk of injury or breach of peace created by race-based threats is greater than that created by other threats. Similarly, it is impossible to reconcile the Court's analysis of the St. Paul ordinance with its recognition that "a prohibition of fighting words that are directed at certain persons or groups ... would be facially valid." A selective proscription of unprotected expression designed to protect "certain persons or groups" (for example, a law proscribing threats directed at the elderly) would be constitutional if it were based on a legitimate determination that the harm created by the regulated expression differs from that created by the unregulated expression (that is, if the elderly are more severely injured by threats than are the nonelderly).... St. Paul has determined—reasonably in my judgment—that fighting-word injuries "based on race, color, creed, religion or gender" are qualitatively different and more severe than fighting-word injuries based on other characteristics. Whether the selective proscription of proscribable speech is defined by the protected target ("certain persons or groups") or the basis of the harm (injuries "based on race, color, creed, religion or gender") makes no constitutional difference: what matters is whether the legislature's selection is based on a legitimate, neutral, and reasonable distinction.

. . . .

II

Although I agree with much of Justice White's analysis, I do not join Part I–A of his opinion because I have reservations about the "categorical approach" to the First Amendment....

Admittedly, the categorical approach to the First Amendment has some appeal: either expression is protected or it is not—the categories create safe harbors for governments and speakers alike. But this approach sacrifices subtlety for clarity and is, I am convinced, ultimately unsound. As an initial matter, the concept of "categories" fits poorly with the complex reality of expression. Few dividing lines in First Amendment law are straight and unwavering, and efforts at categorization inevitably give rise only to fuzzy boundaries....

Moreover, the categorical approach does not take seriously the importance of context. The meaning of any expression and the legitimacy of its regulation can only be determined in context. Whether, for example, a picture or a sentence is obscene cannot be judged in the abstract, but rather only in the context of its setting, its use, and its audience ...

Perhaps sensing the limits of such an all-or-nothing approach, the Court has applied its analysis less categorically than its doctrinal statements suggest. The Court has recognized intermediate categories of speech (for example, for indecent nonobscene speech and commercial speech) and geographic categories of speech (public fora, limited public fora, nonpublic fora) entitled to varying levels of protection. The Court has also stringently delimited the categories of unprotected speech. While we once declared that "[l]ibelous utterances [are] not ... within the area of constitutionally protected speech, ... our rulings ... have substantially qualified this broad claim. Similarly, we have consistently construed the 'fighting words' exception set forth in *Chaplinsky* narrowly.... In the case of commercial speech, our ruling that 'the Constitution imposes no ... restraint on government [regulation] as respects purely commercial advertising,' was expressly repudiated ... In short, the history of the categorical approach is largely the history of narrowing the categories of unprotected speech."

This evolution, I believe, indicates that the categorical approach is unworkable and the quest for absolute categories of "protected" and "unprotected" speech ultimately futile. My analysis of the faults and limits of this approach persuades me that the categorical approach presented in Part I–A of Justice

White's opinion is not an adequate response to the novel "underbreadth" analysis the Court sets forth today.

III

. . . I believe our decisions establish a more complex and subtle analysis, one that considers the content and context of the regulated speech, and the nature and scope of the restriction on speech. Applying this analysis and assuming arguendo (as the Court does) that the St. Paul ordinance is not overbroad, I conclude that such a selective, subject-matter regulation on proscribable speech is constitutional.

. . . [W]e have considered a number of factors in determining the validity of such regulations.

First, as suggested above, the scope of protection provided expressive activity depends in part upon its content and character. . . .

The protection afforded expression turns as well on the context of the regulated speech. . . .

Finally, in considering the validity of content-based regulations we have also looked more broadly at the scope of the restrictions. . . .

All of these factors play some role in our evaluation of content-based regulations on expression. Such a multi-faceted analysis cannot be conflated into two dimensions. Whatever the allure of absolute doctrines, it is just too simple to declare expression "protected" or "unprotected" or to proclaim a regulation "content-based" or "content-neutral."

In applying this analysis to the St. Paul ordinance, I assume arguendo—as the Court does—that the ordinance regulates only fighting words and therefore is not overbroad. Looking to the content and character of the regulated activity, two things are clear. First, by hypothesis the ordinance bars only low-value speech, namely, fighting words. . . . Second, the ordinance regulates "expressive conduct [rather] than . . . the written or spoken word." . . .

Looking to the context of the regulated activity, it is again significant that the statute (by hypothesis) regulates only fighting words. Whether words are fighting words is determined in part by their context. Fighting words are not words that merely cause offense; fighting words must be directed at individuals so as to "by their very utterance inflict injury." By hypothesis, then, the St. Paul ordinance restricts speech in confrontational and potentially violent situations. The case at hand is illustrative. The cross-burning in this case—directed as it was to a single African–American family trapped in their home—was nothing more than a crude form of physical intimidation. That this cross-burning sends a message of racial hostility does not automatically endow it with complete constitutional protection. Significantly, the St. Paul ordinance regulates speech not on the basis of its subject matter or the viewpoint expressed, but rather on the basis of the harm the speech causes. In this regard, the Court fundamentally misreads the St. Paul ordinance. The Court describes the St. Paul ordinance as regulating expression "addressed to one of [several] specified disfavored topics," as policing "disfavored subjects," and as "prohibit[ing] . . . speech solely on the basis of the subjects the speech addresses." Contrary to the Court's suggestion, the ordinance regulates only a subcategory of expression that causes injuries based on "race, color, creed, religion or gender," not a subcategory that involves discussions that concern those characteristics. . . .

Moreover, even if the St. Paul ordinance did regulate fighting words based on its subject matter, such a regulation would, in my opinion, be constitutional. As noted above, subject-matter based regulations on commercial speech are widespread and largely unproblematic. As we have long recognized, subject-matter regulations generally do not raise the same concerns of government censorship and the distortion of public discourse presented by viewpoint regulations. Thus, in upholding subject-matter regulations we have carefully noted that viewpoint-based discrimination was not implicated. . . .

. . .

The St. Paul ordinance is evenhanded. In a battle between advocates of tolerance and advocates of intolerance, the ordinance does not prevent either side from hurling fighting words at the other on the basis of their conflicting ideas, but it does bar both sides from hurling such words on the basis of the target's "race, color, creed, religion or gender." . . . Finally, it is noteworthy that the St. Paul ordinance is, as construed by the Court today, quite narrow. The St. Paul ordinance does not ban all "hate speech," nor does it ban, say, all cross-burnings or all swastika displays. Rather it only bans a subcategory of the already narrow category of fighting words. Such a limited ordinance leaves open and protected a vast range of expression on the subjects of racial, religious, and gender equality. . . .

In sum, the St. Paul ordinance (as construed by the Court) regulates expressive activity that is wholly proscribable and does so not on the basis of viewpoint, but rather in recognition of the different harms caused by such activity. Taken together, these several considerations persuade me that the St. Paul ordinance is not an unconstitutional content-based regulation of speech. Thus, were the ordinance not overbroad, I would vote to uphold it.

WISCONSIN v. MITCHELL, 508 U.S. 476 (1993). A Wisconsin statute enhances the penalty for an offense whenever the defendant "[i]ntentionally selects the person against whom the crime . . . is committed . . . because of the race, religion, color, disability, sexual orientation, national origin or ancestry of that person. . . ." Mitchell's maximum possible sentence for aggravated battery was enhanced from two to seven years because a jury found that he had selected his victim because of race. The Wisconsin Supreme Court concluded that the penalty enhancement statute violated the First Amendment, relying on R.A.V. v. St. Paul. The Supreme Court reversed.

Chief Justice Rehnquist wrote for a unanimous court. Traditionally, a defendant's motive for committing a crime has been a factor in fixing sentences. "[M]otive plays the same role under the Wisconsin statute as it does under federal and state antidiscrimination laws . . ." The Court distinguished *R.A.V.* ". . . [W]hereas the ordinance struck down in *R. A. V.* was explicitly directed at expression . . . , the statute in this case is aimed at conduct unprotected by the First Amendment." In addition, the "statute singles out for enhancement bias-inspired conduct because this conduct is thought to inflict greater individual and societal harm"—such as "provok[ing] retaliatory crimes, inflict[ing] distinct emotional harms on their victims, and incit[ing] community unrest." "The State's desire to redress these perceived harms provides an adequate explanation for its penalty-enhancement provision over and above mere disagreement with offenders' beliefs or biases."

D.   REGULATION OF COMMERCIAL SPEECH

Virginia State Board of Pharmacy v. Virginia Citizens Consumer Council, Inc.
425 U.S. 748, 96 S.Ct. 1817, 48 L.Ed.2d 346 (1976).

Mr. Justice Blackmun delivered the opinion of the Court.

The plaintiff-appellees in this case attack, as violative of the First and Fourteenth Amendments, that portion of § 54–524.35 of Va.Code Ann. (1974), which provides that a pharmacist licensed in Virginia is guilty of unprofessional conduct if he "(3) publishes, advertises or promotes, directly or indirectly, in any manner whatsoever, any amount, price, fee, premium, discount, rebate or credit terms ... for any drugs which may be dispensed only by prescription." The three-judge District Court declared the quoted portion of the statute "void and of no effect," ...

I.

. . .

Inasmuch as only a licensed pharmacist may dispense prescription drugs in Virginia, § 54–524.48, advertising or other affirmative dissemination of prescription drug price information is effectively forbidden in the State. ... The prohibition does not extend to nonprescription drugs, but neither is it confined to prescriptions that the pharmacist compounds himself. Indeed, about 95% of all prescriptions now are filled with dosage forms prepared by the pharmaceutical manufacturer.

II.

. . .

The present ... attack on the statute is one made not by one directly subject to its prohibition, that is, a pharmacist, but by prescription drug consumers who claim that they would greatly benefit if the prohibition were lifted and advertising freely allowed. The plaintiffs are an individual Virginia resident who suffers from diseases that require her to take prescription drugs on a daily basis, and two nonprofit organizations. Their claim is that the First Amendment entitles the user of prescription drugs to receive information that pharmacists wish to communicate to them through advertising and other promotional means, concerning the prices of such drugs.

Certainly that information may be of value. Drug prices in Virginia, for both prescription and nonprescription items, strikingly vary from outlet to outlet even within the same locality. ...

III.

The question first arises whether, even assuming that First Amendment protection attaches to the flow of drug price information, it is a protection enjoyed by the appellees as recipients of the information, and not solely, if at all, by the advertisers themselves who seek to disseminate that information.

Freedom of speech presupposes a willing speaker. But where a speaker exists, as is the case here, the protection afforded is to the communication, to its source and to its recipients both. This is clear from the decided cases. In Lamont v. Postmaster General, 381 U.S. 301 (1965), the Court upheld the First Amendment rights of citizens to receive political publications sent from abroad. More recently, in Kleindienst v. Mandel, 408 U.S. 753, 762–763 (1972), we acknowledged that this Court has referred to a First Amendment right to "receive information and ideas," and that freedom of speech "necessarily protects the right to receive." And in Procunier v. Martinez, 416 U.S. 396, 408–409 (1974), where censorship of prison inmates' mail was under examination, we thought it unnecessary to assess the First Amendment rights of the inmates themselves, for it was reasoned that such censorship equally infringed the rights of nominates to whom the correspondence was addressed. ... If there is a right to advertise, there is a reciprocal right to receive the advertising, and it may be asserted by these appellees.

IV.

The appellants contend that the advertisement of prescription drug prices is outside the protection of the First Amendment because it is "commercial speech." There can be no question that in past decisions the Court has given some indication that commercial speech is unprotected. In Valentine v. Chrestensen, [316 U.S. 52 (1942)], the Court upheld a New York statute that prohibited the distribution of any "handbill, circular . . . or other advertising matter whatsoever in or upon any street." The Court concluded that, although the First Amendment would forbid the banning of all communication by handbill in the public thoroughfares, it imposed "no such restraint on government as respects purely commercial advertising." 316 U.S., at 54. Further support for a "commercial speech" exception to the First Amendment may perhaps be found in Breard v. Alexandria, 341 U.S. 622 (1951), where the Court upheld a conviction for violation of an ordinance prohibiting door-to-door solicitation of magazine subscriptions. The Court reasoned: "The selling . . . brings into the transaction a commercial feature," and it distinguished *Martin v. Struthers,* supra, where it had reversed a conviction for door-to-door distribution of leaflets publicizing a religious meeting, as a case involving "no element of the commercial." 341 U.S., at 642–643. . . .

. . .

Last Term, in Bigelow v. Virginia, 421 U.S. 809 (1975), the notion of unprotected "commercial speech" all but passed from the scene. . . .

Some fragment of hope for the continuing validity of a "commercial speech" exception arguably might have persisted because of the subject matter of the advertisement in *Bigelow*. We noted that in announcing the availability of legal abortions in New York, the advertisement "did more than simply propose a commercial transaction. It contained factual material of clear 'public interest.' " . . .

Here, in contrast, the question whether there is a First Amendment exception for "commercial speech" is squarely before us. Our pharmacist does not wish to editorialize on any subject, cultural, philosophical, or political. He does not wish to report any particularly newsworthy fact, or to make generalized observations even about commercial matters. The "idea" he wishes to communicate is simply this: "I will sell you the X prescription drug at the Y price." Our question, then, is whether this communication is wholly outside the protection of the First Amendment.

V.

We begin with several propositions that already are settled or beyond serious dispute. It is clear, for example, that speech does not lose its First Amendment protection because money is spent to project it, as in a paid advertisement of one form or another. . . . Speech likewise is protected even though it is carried in a form that is "sold" for profit, . . . and even though it may involve a solicitation to purchase or otherwise pay or contribute money.
. . .

If there is a kind of commercial speech that lacks all First Amendment protection, therefore, it must be distinguished by its content. Yet the speech whose content deprives it of protection cannot simply be speech on a commercial subject. No one would contend that our pharmacist may be prevented from being heard on the subject of whether, in general, pharmaceutical prices should be regulated, or their advertisement forbidden. Nor can it be dispositive that a commercial advertisement is noneditorial, and merely reports a fact. Purely factual matter of public interest may claim protection. . . .

Our question is whether speech which does "no more than propose a commercial transaction," Pittsburgh Press Co. v. Pittsburgh Comm'n on Human Relations, 413 U.S., at 385, is so removed from any "exposition of ideas," Chaplinsky v. New Hampshire, 315 U.S. 568, 572 (1942), and from " 'truth, science, morality, and arts in general, in its diffusion of liberal sentiments on the administration of Government,' " Roth v. United States, 354 U.S. 476, 484 (1957), that it lacks all protection. Our answer is that it is not.

Focusing first on the individual parties to the transaction that is proposed in the commercial advertisement, we may assume that the advertiser's interest is a purely economic one. That hardly disqualifies him for protection under the First Amendment. . . .

As to the particular consumer's interest in the free flow of commercial information, that interest may be as keen, if not keener by far, than his interest in the day's most urgent political debate. Appellees' case in this respect is a convincing one. Those whom the suppression of prescription drug price information hits the hardest are the poor, the sick, and particularly the aged. A disproportionate amount of their income tends to be spent on prescription drugs; yet they are the least able to learn, by shopping from pharmacist to pharmacist, where their scarce dollars are best spent. When drug prices vary as strikingly as they do, information as to who is charging what becomes more than a convenience. It could mean the alleviation of physical pain or the enjoyment of basic necessities.

Generalizing, society also may have a strong interest in the free flow of commercial information. Even an individual advertisement, though entirely "commercial," may be of general public interest. . . . Obviously, not all commercial messages contain the same or even a very great public interest element. There are few to which such an element, however, could not be added. Our pharmacist, for example, could cast himself as a commentator on store-to-store disparities in drug prices, giving his own and those of a competitor as proof. We see little point in requiring him to do so, and little difference if he does not.

Moreover, there is another consideration that suggests that no line between publicly "interesting" or "important" commercial advertising and the opposite kind could ever be drawn. Advertising, however tasteless and excessive it sometimes may seem, is nonetheless dissemination of information as to who is producing and selling what product for what reason, and at what price. So long as we preserve a predominantly free enterprise economy, the allocation of our resources in large measure will be made through numerous private economic decisions. It is a matter of public interest that those decisions, in the aggregate, be intelligent and well informed. To this end, the free flow of commercial information is indispensable. . . . And if it is indispensable to the proper allocation of resources in a free enterprise system, it is also indispensable to the formation of intelligent opinions as to how that system ought to be regulated or altered. Therefore, even if the First Amendment were thought to be primarily an instrument to enlighten public decisionmaking in a democracy, we could not say that the free flow of information does not serve that goal.

Arrayed against these substantial individual and societal interests are a number of justifications for the advertising ban. These have to do principally with maintaining a high degree of professionalism on the part of licensed pharmacists. Indisputably, the State has a strong interest in maintaining that professionalism....

Price advertising, it is argued, will place in jeopardy the pharmacist's expertise and, with it, the customer's health. It is claimed that the aggressive price competition that will result from unlimited advertising will make it impossible for the pharmacist to supply professional services in the compounding, handling, and dispensing of prescription drugs.... Price advertising, it is said, will reduce the pharmacist's status to that of a mere retailer.

The strength of these proffered justifications is greatly undermined by the fact that high professional standards, to a substantial extent, are guaranteed by the close regulation to which pharmacists in Virginia are subject. And this case concerns the retail sale by the pharmacist more than it does his professional standards. Surely, any pharmacist guilty of professional dereliction that actually endangers his customer will promptly lose his license. At the same time, we cannot discount the Board's justifications entirely. The Court regarded justifications of this type sufficient to sustain the advertising bans challenged on due process and equal protection grounds in Head v. New Mexico Board, supra; Williamson v. Lee Optical Co., supra; and Semler v. Dental Examiners, supra.

The challenge now made, however, is based on the First Amendment. This casts the Board's justifications in a different light....

It appears to be feared that if the pharmacist who wishes to provide low cost, and assertedly low quality services is permitted to advertise, he will be taken up on his offer by too many unwitting customers....

There is, of course, an alternative to this highly paternalistic approach. That alternative is to assume that this information is not in itself harmful, that people will perceive their own best interests if only they are well enough informed, and that the best means to that end is to open the channels of communication rather than to close them. If they are truly open, nothing prevents the "professional" pharmacist from marketing his own assertedly superior product, and contrasting it with that of the low-cost, high-volume prescription drug retailer. But the choice among these alternative approaches is not ours to make or the Virginia General Assembly's. It is precisely this kind of choice, between the dangers of suppressing information, and the dangers of its misuse if it is freely available, that the First Amendment makes for us. Virginia is free to require whatever professional standards it wishes of its pharmacists; it may subsidize them or protect them from competition in other ways. Cf. Parker v. Brown, 317 U.S. 341 (1943). But it may not do so by keeping the public in ignorance of the entirely lawful terms that competing pharmacists are offering. In this sense, the justifications Virginia has offered for suppressing the flow of prescription drug price information, far from persuading us that the flow is not protected by the First Amendment, have reinforced our view that it is. We so hold.

VI.

In concluding that commercial speech, like other varieties, is protected, we of course do not hold that it can never be regulated in any way. Some forms of commercial speech regulation are surely permissible. We mention a few only to make clear that they are not before us and therefore are not foreclosed by this case.

There is no claim, for example, that the prohibition on prescription drug price advertising is a mere time, place, and manner restriction. We have often approved restrictions of that kind provided that they are justified without reference to the content of the regulated speech, that they serve a significant governmental interest, and that in so doing they leave open ample alternative channels for communication of the information.... Whatever may be the proper bounds of time, place, and manner restrictions on commercial speech, they are plainly exceeded by this Virginia statute, which singles out speech of a particular content and seeks to prevent its dissemination completely.

Nor is there any claim that prescription drug price advertisements are forbidden because they are false or misleading in any way. Untruthful speech, commercial or otherwise, has never been protected for its own sake. Gertz v. Robert Welch, Inc., 418 U.S. 323, 340 (1974); Konigsberg v. State Bar, 366 U.S. 36, 49 and n. 10 (1961). Obviously, much commercial speech is not provably false, or even wholly false, but only deceptive or misleading. We foresee no obstacle to a State's dealing effectively with this problem.[24] The First Amendment, as we construe it today, does not prohibit the State from insuring that the stream of commercial information flows cleanly as well as freely. See, for example, Va.Code Ann. § 18.2–216 (1975).

Also, there is no claim that the transactions proposed in the forbidden advertisements are themselves illegal in any way.... Finally, the special problems of the electronic broadcast media are likewise not in this case....

What is at issue is whether a State may completely suppress the dissemination of concededly truthful information about entirely lawful activity, fearful of that information's effect upon its disseminators and its recipients. Reserving other questions, we conclude that the answer to this one is in the negative.

The judgment of the District Court is affirmed.

It is so ordered.

Mr. Justice Stevens took no part in the consideration or decision of this case.

Mr. Chief Justice Burger, concurring.

... Our decision today ... deals largely with the State's power to prohibit pharmacists from advertising the retail price of *prepackaged* drugs.... [Q]uite different factors would govern were we faced with a law regulating or even

---

[24] In concluding that commercial speech enjoys First Amendment protection, we have not held that it is wholly undifferentiable from other forms. There are commonsense differences between speech that does "no more than propose a commercial transaction" Pittsburgh Press Co. v. Pittsburgh Comm'n on Human Relations, 413 U.S., at 385, and other varieties. Even if the differences do not justify the conclusion that commercial speech is valueless, and thus subject to complete suppression by the State, they nonetheless suggest that a different degree of protection is necessary to insure that the flow of truthful and legitimate commercial information is unimpaired. The truth of commercial speech, for example, may be more easily verifiable by its disseminator than, let us say, news reporting or political commentary, in that ordinarily the advertiser seeks to disseminate information about a specific product or service that he himself provides and presumably knows more about than anyone else. Also, commercial speech may be more durable than other kinds. Since advertising is the sine qua non of commercial profits, there is little likelihood of its being chilled by proper regulation and foregone entirely.

Attributes such as these, the greater objectivity and hardiness of commercial speech, may make it less necessary to tolerate inaccurate statements for fear of silencing the speaker. Compare New York Times Co. v. Sullivan, 376 U.S. 254 (1964), with Dun & Bradstreet, Inc. v. Grove, 404 U.S. 898 (1971). They may also make it appropriate to require that a commercial message appear in such a form, or include such additional information, warnings and disclaimers, as are necessary to prevent its being deceptive.... They may also make inapplicable the prohibition against prior restraints....

prohibiting advertising by the traditional learned professions of medicine or law. . . .

. . .

Mr. Justice Stewart, concurring.

. . .

Today the Court ends the anomalous situation created by *Chrestensen* and holds that a communication which does no more than propose a commercial transaction is not "wholly outside the protection of the First Amendment." But since it is a cardinal principle of the First Amendment that "government has no power to restrict expression because of its message, its ideas, its subject matter, or its content," the Court's decision calls into immediate question the constitutional legitimacy of every state and federal law regulating false or deceptive advertising. I write separately to explain why I think today's decision does not preclude such governmental regulation. . . .

. . .

. . . Since the factual claims contained in commercial price or product advertisements relate to tangible goods or services, they may be tested empirically and corrected to reflect the truth without in any manner jeopardizing the free dissemination of thought. Indeed, the elimination of false and deceptive claims serves to promote the one facet of commercial price and product advertising that warrants First Amendment protection—its contribution to the flow of accurate and reliable information relevant to public and private decisionmaking.

Mr. Justice Rehnquist, dissenting.

The logical consequences of the Court's decision in this case, a decision which elevates commercial intercourse between a seller hawking his wares and a buyer seeking to strike a bargain to the same plane as has been previously reserved for the free marketplace of ideas, are far reaching indeed. Under the Court's opinion the way will be open not only for dissemination of price information but for active promotion of prescription drugs, liquor, cigarettes and other products the use of which it has previously been thought desirable to discourage. Now, however, such promotion is protected by the First Amendment so long as it is not misleading or does not promote an illegal product or enterprise. In coming to this conclusion, the Court has overruled a legislative determination that such advertising should not be allowed and has done so on behalf of a consumer group which is not directly disadvantaged by the statute in question. This effort to reach a result which the Court obviously considers desirable is a troublesome one, for two reasons. It extends standing to raise First Amendment claims beyond the previous decisions of this Court. It also extends the protection of that Amendment to purely commercial endeavors which its most vigorous champions on this Court had thought to be beyond its pale.

. . .

ATTORNEY ADVERTISING

Chief Justice Burger's attempt, in his concurrence, to distinguish prohibitions on professional advertising, proved to be unavailing. In Bates v. State Bar of Arizona, 433 U.S. 350 (1977), the Court held 5–4 that lawyers could not be prohibited from advertising the price of "routine legal services." In subsequent cases, a number of other lines have been drawn. The Court has distinguished between commercial solicitation and solicitation of legal employment by advocacy organizations. Ohralik v. Ohio State Bar Ass'n, 436 U.S. 447 (1978), sustained discipline of an attorney for personal solicitation of contingent fee employment, while In re Primus, 436 U.S. 412 (1978), reversed discipline of an ACLU lawyer. The Court noted that Primus' letter (offering legal assistance to a woman who had been sterilized as a condition of receiving welfare) came within the "generous zone of First Amendment protection reserved for associational freedom." The Court has also distinguished between in-person solicitation, involved in the *Ohralik* decision, and solicitation by advertisement and letter. In Zauderer v. Office of Disciplinary Counsel, 471 U.S. 626 (1985), the Court struck down a categorical prohibition of attorney advertising containing information or advice about legal problems. In *Shapero v. Kentucky Bar Ass'n,* 486 U.S. 466 (1988), the Court held that a state rule, prohibiting attorney mailings of advertisements "precipitated by a specific event . . . involving or relating to the addressee," was invalid. Both newspaper and direct mail advertising posed less risk of "overreaching or undue influence" than in-person solicitation.

The Court distinguished *Shapero* in Florida Bar v. Went For It, Inc., ___ U.S. ___, 115 S.Ct. 2371 (1995). *Shapero* had dealt with a rule imposing a ban on direct mail solicitation "whatever the time frame and whoever the recipient." Justice O'Connor's opinion for the Court concluded that a rule forbidding solicitation of accident victims during a 30–day period after the accident was constitutional. "The Bar has substantial interest both in protecting injured Floridians from invasive conduct by lawyers and in preventing the erosion of confidence in the profession that such repeated invasions have engendered. . . . The palliative devised by the Bar to address these harms is narrow both in scope and in duration." Justice Kennedy's dissent, joined by Justices Stevens, Souter and Ginsburg, argued that the rule prejudiced accident victims "to vindicate the State's purported desire for more dignity in the legal profession."

The Court has been divided on the question whether the contents of particular lawyer-advertisements were misleading. In *Zauderer,* a majority concluded that advertising a contingent fee was misleading because there was no disclosure that clients could be liable for significant litigation costs. In *Shapero,* a plurality concluded that a letter sent to persons against whom foreclosure suits had been filed could not be prohibited merely because it liberally used underscored, uppercase letters (e.g., "Call *NOW,* don't wait. . . . Remember it is *FREE* and there is *NO* charge for calling.") or contained subjective predictions of customer satisfaction (e.g., "It may surprise you what I may be able to do for you.") In Ibanez v. Florida Department of Business and Professional Regulation, Board of Accountancy, 512 U.S. 136 (1994), a lawyer was also a state-licensed Certified Public Accountant and was authorized to use the designation "Certified Financial Planner" by the Certified Financial Planner Board of Standards, a private organization. The Court held that she could not be disciplined for referring to those two credentials in her yellow pages listing, on her business cards, and on her law offices stationery, because neither was false or misleading.

The Court distinguished CPAs from attorneys in Edenfield v. Fane, 507 U.S. 761 (1993). As noted, the Court had held in *Ohralik* that in-person solicitation by attorneys could be prohibited. In *Edenfield,* the Court concluded that a ban on in-person solicitation by accountants violated the First Amendment. While lawyers are trained in the art of persuasion, accountants are trained to emphasize independence and objectivity. Moreover, an accountant's typical potential client is an experienced business executive. Therefore, CPA solicitation is not "inherently conducive to overreaching."

OVERBREADTH AND COMMERCIAL SPEECH

Justice Blackmun, for the Court, in Bates v. State Bar, 433 U.S. 350, 379–381 (1977):

"In the usual case involving a restraint on speech, a showing that the challenged rule served unconstitutionally to suppress speech would end our analysis. In the First Amendment context, the Court has permitted attacks on overly broad statutes without requiring that the person making the attack demonstrate that in fact his specific conduct was protected.... Having shown that the disciplinary rule interferes with protected speech, appellants ordinarily could expect to benefit regardless of the nature of their acts.

"The First Amendment overbreadth doctrine, however, represents a departure from the traditional rule that a person may not challenge a statute on the ground that it might be applied unconstitutionally in circumstances other than those before the court.... The reason for the special rule in First Amendment cases is apparent: an overbroad statute might serve to chill protected speech. First Amendment interests are fragile interests, and a person who contemplates protected activity might be discouraged by the *in terrorem* effect of the statute.... Indeed, such a person might choose not to speak because of uncertainty whether his claim of privilege would prevail if challenged. The use of overbreadth analysis reflects the conclusion that the possible harm to society from allowing unprotected speech to go unpunished is outweighed by the possibility that protected speech will be muted.

"But the justification for the application of overbreadth analysis applies weakly, if at all, in the ordinary commercial context. ...Since advertising is linked to commercial well-being, it seems unlikely that such speech is particularly susceptible to being crushed by overbroad regulation.... Moreover, concerns for uncertainty in determining the scope of protection are reduced; the advertiser seeks to disseminate information about a product or service that he provides, and presumably he can determine more readily than others whether his speech is truthful and protected. Ibid. Since overbreadth has been described by this Court as 'strong medicine,' which 'has been employed ... sparingly and only as a last resort,' Broadrick v. Oklahoma, 413 U.S., at 613, we decline to apply it to professional advertising, a context where it is not necessary to further its intended objective."

Central Hudson Gas & Electric Corp. v. Public Service Commission

447 U.S. 557, 100 S.Ct. 2343, 65 L.Ed.2d 341 (1980).

Mr. Justice Powell delivered the opinion of the Court.

This case presents the question whether a regulation of the Public Service Commission of the State of New York violates the First and Fourteenth Amendments because it completely bans promotional advertising by an electrical utility.

I.

In December 1973, the Commission, appellee here, ordered electric utilities in New York State to cease all advertising that "promot[es] the use of electricity." The order was based on the Commission's finding that "the interconnected utility system in New York State does not have sufficient fuel stocks or sources of supply to continue furnishing all customer demands for the 1973–1974 winter."

Three years later, when the fuel shortage had eased, the Commission requested comments from the public on its proposal to continue the ban on promotional advertising. Central Hudson Gas & Electric Corp., the appellant in this case, opposed the ban on First Amendment grounds. After reviewing the public comments, the Commission extended the prohibition in a Policy Statement issued on February 25, 1977.

The Policy Statement divided advertising expenses "into two broad categories: promotional—advertising intended to stimulate the purchase of utility services—and institutional and informational, a broad category inclusive of all advertising not clearly intended to promote sales." The Commission declared all promotional advertising contrary to the national policy of conserving energy. It acknowledged that the ban is not a perfect vehicle for conserving energy. For example, the Commission's order prohibits promotional advertising to develop consumption during periods when demand for electricity is low. By limiting growth in "off-peak" consumption, the ban limits the "beneficial side effects" of such growth in terms of more efficient use of existing powerplants. And since oil dealers are not under the Commission's jurisdiction and thus remain free to advertise, it was recognized that the ban can achieve only "piecemeal conservationism." Still, the Commission adopted the restriction because it was deemed likely to "result in some dampening of unnecessary growth" in energy consumption.

The Commission's order explicitly permitted "informational" advertising designed to encourage "*shifts* of consumption" from peak demand times to periods of low electricity demand. Informational advertising would not seek to increase aggregate consumption, but would invite a leveling of demand throughout any given 24–hour period. The agency offered to review "specific proposals by the companies for specifically described [advertising] programs that meet these criteria."

. . .

Appellant challenged the order in state court, arguing that the Commission had restrained commercial speech in violation of the First and Fourteenth Amendments. The Commission's order was upheld by the trial court and at the intermediate appellate level. The New York Court of Appeals affirmed.... We ... reverse.

II.

The Commission's order restricts only commercial speech, that is, expression related solely to the economic interests of the speaker and its audience.... In applying the First Amendment to this area, we have rejected the "highly paternalistic" view that government has complete power to suppress or regulate commercial speech....

Nevertheless, our decisions have recognized "the 'commonsense' distinction between speech proposing a commercial transaction, which occurs in an area traditionally subject to government regulation and other varieties of speech." ...[5] The Constitution therefore accords a lesser protection to commer-

---

[5] ...[T]he concurring opinion of Mr. Justice Stevens views the Commission's order as suppressing more than commercial speech because it would outlaw, for example, advertising that promoted electricity consumption by touting the environmental benefits of such uses. Apparently the concurring opinion would accord full First Amendment

cial speech than to other constitutionally guaranteed expression.... The protection available for particular commercial expression turns on the nature both of the expression and of the governmental interests served by its regulation.

. . .

If the communication is neither misleading nor related to unlawful activity, the government's power is more circumscribed. The State must assert a substantial interest to be achieved by restrictions on commercial speech. Moreover, the regulatory technique must be in proportion to that interest. The limitation on expression must be designed carefully to achieve the State's goal. Compliance with this requirement may be measured by two criteria. First, the restriction must directly advance the state interest involved; the regulation may not be sustained if it provides only ineffective or remote support for the government's purpose. Second, if the governmental interest could be served as well by a more limited restriction on commercial speech, the excessive restrictions cannot survive.... [8]

. . .

In commercial speech cases, then, a four-part analysis has developed. At the outset, we must determine whether the expression is protected by the First Amendment. For commercial speech to come within that provision, it at least must concern lawful activity and not be misleading. Next, we ask whether the asserted governmental interest is substantial. If both inquiries yield positive answers, we must determine whether the regulation directly advances the governmental interest asserted, and whether it is not more extensive than is necessary to serve that interest.

III.

We now apply this four-step analysis for commercial speech to the Commission's arguments in support of its ban on promotional advertising.

A.

The Commission does not claim that the expression at issue either is inaccurate or relates to unlawful activity. Yet the New York Court of Appeals questioned whether Central Hudson's advertising is protected commercial speech. Because appellant holds a monopoly over the sale of electricity in its service area, the state court suggested that the Commission's order restricts no commercial speech of any worth. The court stated that advertising in a "noncompetitive market" could not improve the decisionmaking of consumers. 47 N.Y.2d, at 110; 390 N.E.2d, at 757. The court saw no constitutional problem with barring commercial speech that it viewed as conveying little useful information.

protection to all promotional advertising that includes claims "relating to ... questions frequently discussed and debated by our political leaders."

Although this approach responds to the serious issues surrounding our national energy policy as raised in this case, we think it would blur further the line the Court has sought to draw in commercial speech cases. It would grant broad constitutional protection to any advertising that links a product to a current public debate. But many, if not most, products may be tied to public concerns with the environment, energy, economic policy, or individual health and safety. ...

[8] This analysis is not an application of the "overbreadth" doctrine....

In this case, the Commission's prohibition acts directly against the promotional activities of Central Hudson, and to the extent the limitations are unnecessary to serve the State's interest, they are invalid.

This reasoning falls short of establishing that appellant's advertising is not commercial speech protected by the First Amendment. Monopoly over the supply of a product provides no protection from competition with substitutes for that product. Electric utilities compete with suppliers of fuel oil and natural gas in several markets, such as those for home heating and industrial power. . . .

. . .

B.

. . . The Commission argues, and the New York court agreed, that the State's interest in conserving energy is sufficient to support suppression of advertising designed to increase consumption of electricity. In view of our country's dependence on energy resources beyond our control, no one can doubt the importance of energy conservation. Plainly, therefore, the state interest asserted is substantial.

. . .

C.

Next, we focus on the relationship between the State's interests and the advertising ban. . . .

. . .

There is an immediate connection between advertising and demand for electricity. Central Hudson would not contest the advertising ban unless it believed that promotion would increase its sales. Thus, we find a direct link between the state interest in conservation and the Commission's order.

D.

We come finally to the critical inquiry in this case: whether the Commission's complete suppression of speech ordinarily protected by the First Amendment is no more extensive than necessary to further the State's interest in energy conservation. The Commission's order reaches all promotional advertising, regardless of the impact of the touted service on overall energy use. But the energy conservation rationale, as important as it is, cannot justify suppressing information about electric devices or services that would cause no net increase in total energy use. In addition, no showing has been made that a more limited restriction on the content of promotional advertising would not serve adequately the State's interests.

Appellant insists that but for the ban, it would advertise products and services that use energy efficiently. These include the "heat pump," which both parties acknowledge to be a major improvement in electric heating, and the use of electric heat as a "back-up" to solar and other heat sources. Although the Commission has questioned the efficiency of electric heating before this Court, neither the Commission's Policy Statement nor its order denying rehearing made findings on this issue. In the absence of authoritative findings to the contrary, we must credit as within the realm of possibility the claim that electric heat can be an efficient alternative in some circumstances.

The Commission's order prevents appellant from promoting electric services that would reduce energy use by diverting demand from less efficient sources, or that would consume roughly the same amount of energy as do alternative sources. In neither situation would the utility's advertising endanger conservation or mislead the public. To the extent that the Commission's order suppresses speech that in no way impairs the State's interest in energy conservation, the Commission's order violates the First and Fourteenth Amendments and must be invalidated. See First National Bank of Boston v. Bellotti, 435 U.S. 765 (1978).

The Commission also has not demonstrated that its interest in conservation cannot be protected adequately by more limited regulation of appellant's commercial expression. To further its policy of conservation, the Commission could attempt to restrict the format and content of Central Hudson's advertising. It might, for example, require that the advertisements include information about the relative efficiency and expense of the offered service, both under current conditions and for the foreseeable future.... In the absence of a showing that more limited speech regulation would be ineffective, we cannot approve the complete suppression of Central Hudson's advertising.

IV.

Our decision today in no way disparages the national interest in energy conservation. We accept without reservation the argument that conservation, as well as the development of alternative energy sources, is an imperative national goal. Administrative bodies empowered to regulate electric utilities have the authority—and indeed the duty—to take appropriate action to further this goal. When, however, such action involves the suppression of speech, the First and Fourteenth Amendments require that the restriction be no more extensive than is necessary to serve the state interest. In this case, the record before us fails to show that the total ban on promotional advertising meets this requirement.

Accordingly, the judgment of the New York Court of Appeals is reversed.

. . .

Mr. Justice Blackmun with whom Mr. Justice Brennan joins, concurring in the judgment.

I agree with the Court that the Public Service Commission's ban on promotional advertising of electricity by public utilities is inconsistent with the First and Fourteenth Amendments. I concur only in the Court's judgment, however, because I believe the test now evolved and applied by the Court is not consistent with our prior cases and does not provide adequate protection for truthful, nonmisleading, noncoercive commercial speech.

. . .

I seriously doubt whether suppression of information concerning the availability and price of a legally offered product is ever a permissible way for the State to "dampen" demand for or use of the product. Even though "commercial" speech is involved, such a regulatory measure strikes at the heart of the First Amendment. This is because it is a covert attempt by the State to manipulate the choices of its citizens, not by persuasion or direct regulation, but by depriving the public of the information needed to make a free choice....

. . .

It appears that the Court would permit the State to ban all direct advertising of air conditioning, assuming that a more limited restriction on such advertising would not effectively deter the public from cooling its homes. In my view, our cases do not support this type of suppression. If a governmental unit believes that use or overuse of air conditioning is a serious problem, it must attack that problem directly, by prohibiting air conditioning or regulating thermostat levels. ...

Mr. Justice Stevens, with whom Mr. Justice Brennan joins, concurring in the judgment.

Because "commercial speech" is afforded less constitutional protection than other forms of speech, it is important that the commercial speech concept not be defined too broadly lest speech deserving of greater constitutional protection be inadvertently suppressed. The issue in this case is whether New York's prohibition on the promotion of the use of electricity through advertising is a ban on nothing but commercial speech.

In my judgment one of the two definitions the Court uses in addressing that issue is too broad and the other may be somewhat too narrow. The Court first describes commercial speech as "expression related solely to the economic interests of the speaker and its audience." Although it is not entirely clear whether this definition uses the subject matter of the speech or the motivation of the speaker as the limiting factor, it seems clear to me that it encompasses speech that is entitled to the maximum protection afforded by the First Amendment. Neither a labor leader's exhortation to strike, nor an economist's dissertation on the money supply, should receive any lesser protection because the subject matter concerns only the economic interests of the audience. Nor should the economic motivation of a speaker qualify his constitutional protection; even Shakespeare may have been motivated by the prospect of pecuniary reward. Thus, the Court's first definition of commercial speech is unquestionably too broad.

The Court's second definition refers to "'speech proposing a commercial transaction.' "A salesman's solicitation, a broker's offer, and a manufacturer's publication of a price list or the terms of his standard warranty would unquestionably fit within this concept. Presumably, the definition is intended to encompass advertising that advises possible buyers of the availability of specific products at specific prices and describes the advantages of purchasing such items. Perhaps it also extends to other communications that do little more than make the name of a product or a service more familiar to the general public. Whatever the precise contours of the concept, and perhaps it is too early to enunciate an exact formulation, I am persuaded that it should not include the entire range of communication that is embraced within the term "promotional advertising."

This case involves a governmental regulation that completely bans promotional advertising by an electric utility. This ban encompasses a great deal more than mere proposals to engage in certain kinds of commercial transactions. It prohibits all advocacy of the immediate or future use of electricity. It curtails expression by an informed and interested group of persons of their point of view on questions relating to the production and consumption of electrical energy—questions frequently discussed and debated by our political leaders. For example, an electric company's advocacy of the use of electric heat for environmental reasons, as opposed to wood-burning stoves, would seem to fall squarely within New York's promotional advertising ban and also within the bounds of maximum First Amendment protection. The breadth of the ban thus exceeds the boundaries of the commercial speech concept, however that concept may be defined.

The justification for the regulation is nothing more than the expressed fear that the audience may find the utility's message persuasive. Without the aid of any coercion, deception, or misinformation, truthful communication may persuade some citizens to consume more electricity than they otherwise would. I assume that such a consequence would be undesirable and that government may therefore prohibit and punish the unnecessary or excessive use of electricity than they otherwise would. I assume that such a consequence would be undesirable and that government may therefore prohibit and punish the unnecessary or excessive use of electricity. But if the perceived harm associated with greater electrical usage is not sufficiently serious to justify direct regulation, surely it does not constitute the kind of clear and present danger that can justify the suppression of speech.

In sum I concur in the result because I do not consider this to be a "commercial speech" case. Accordingly, I see no need to decide whether the Court's four-part analysis, adequately protects commercial speech—as properly defined—in the face of a blanket ban of the sort involved in this case.

Mr. Justice Rehnquist, dissenting.

. . .

The Court's decision today fails to give due deference to [the] subordinate position of commercial speech. The Court in so doing returns to the bygone era of Lochner v. New York, 198 U.S. 45 (1905), in which it was common practice for this Court to strike down economic regulations adopted by a State based on the Court's own notions of the most appropriate means for the State to implement its considered policies.

. . . New York's order here is in my view more akin to an economic regulation to which virtually complete deference should be accorded by this Court.

I doubt there would be any question as to the constitutionality of New York's conservation effort if the Public Service Commission had chosen to raise the price of electricity, . . . to condition its sale on specified terms, . . . or to restrict its production, ... In terms of constitutional values, I think that such controls are virtually indistinguishable from the State's ban on promotional advertising.

. . .

THE DEFINITION OF COMMERCIAL SPEECH

The conventional definition of commercial speech is that it is speech "proposing a commercial transaction." Justice Powell's *Central Hudson* opinion also defines commercial speech as that "related solely to the economic interests of the speaker and its audience." Are there differences between those two definitions? In Bolger v. Youngs Drug Products Corp., 463 U.S. 60 (1983), the Court determined that "informational pamphlets" discussing the desirability of prophylactics in general and the manufacturer's products in particular were commercial speech even though they were linked to a public debate. On the other hand, the Court stated in Board of Trustees of the State University of New York v. Fox, 492 U.S. 469 (1989), that giving legal advice or medical consultation for a fee was not commercial speech—speech for a profit was not necessarily speech that proposes a commercial transaction.

Consider whether the speech involved in the following cases falls within the parameters of commercial speech doctrine. Dun & Bradstreet, Inc. v. Greenmoss Builders, Inc., 472 U.S. 749 (1985), page 1261, supra (commercial credit report); Lowe v. Securities and Exchange Commission, 472 U.S. 181 (1985) (newsletters containing investment advice and commentary); San Francisco Arts & Athletics, Inc. v. United States Olympic Committee, 483 U.S. 522 (1987) (federal statute granting Committee power to prohibit commercial and promotional uses of the word "Olympic"); City of Cincinnati v. Discovery Network, Inc., 507 U.S. 410 (1993) (free magazine, consisting primarily of promotional material relating to publisher's adult education program, also included information about current events of general interest; free magazine, consisting primarily of advertisements of real estate for sale, also included information about interest rates, market trends, and other real estate matters).

44 Liquormart, Inc. v. Rhode Island

__ U.S. __, 116 S.Ct. 1495, 134 L.Ed.2d 711 (1996).

Justice Stevens announced the judgment of the Court and delivered the opinion of the Court with respect to Parts I, II, VII, and VIII, an opinion with respect to Parts III and V, in which Justice Kennedy, Justice Souter, and Justice Ginsburg join, an opinion with respect to Part VI, in which Justice Kennedy, Justice Thomas, and Justice Ginsburg join, and an opinion with respect to Part IV, in which Justice Kennedy and Justice Ginsburg join.

Last Term we held that a federal law abridging a brewer's right to provide the public with accurate information about the alcoholic content of malt beverages is unconstitutional. Rubin v. Coors Brewing Co., 514 U.S. __, __ (1995). We now hold that Rhode Island's statutory prohibition against advertisements that provide the public with accurate information about retail prices of alcoholic beverages is also invalid. Our holding rests on the conclusion that such an advertising ban is an abridgment of speech protected by the First Amendment and that it is not shielded from constitutional scrutiny by the Twenty-first Amendment.

I

In 1956, the Rhode Island Legislature enacted two separate prohibitions against advertising the retail price of alcoholic beverages. The first applies to vendors licensed in Rhode Island as well as to out-of-state manufacturers, wholesalers, and shippers. It prohibits them from "advertising in any manner whatsoever" the price of any alcoholic beverage offered for sale in the State; the only exception is for price tags or signs displayed with the merchandise within licensed premises and not visible from the street. The second statute applies to the Rhode Island news media. It contains a categorical prohibition against the publication or broadcast of any advertisements—even those referring to sales in other States—that "make reference to the price of any alcoholic beverages."

. . .

II

Petitioners 44 Liquormart, Inc. (44 Liquormart), and Peoples Super Liquor Stores, Inc. (Peoples), are licensed retailers of alcoholic beverages. Petitioner 44 Liquormart operates a store in Rhode Island and petitioner Peoples operates several stores in Massachusetts that are patronized by Rhode Island residents. Peoples uses alcohol price advertising extensively in Massachusetts, where such advertising is permitted, but Rhode Island newspapers and other media outlets have refused to accept such ads.

Complaints from competitors about an advertisement placed by 44 Liquormart in a Rhode Island newspaper in 1991 generated enforcement proceedings that in turn led to the initiation of this litigation. The advertisement did not state the price of any alcoholic beverages. Indeed, it noted that "State law prohibits advertising liquor prices." The ad did, however, state the low prices at which peanuts, potato chips, and Schweppes mixers were being offered, identify various brands of packaged liquor, and include the word "WOW" in large letters next to pictures of vodka and rum bottles. Based on the conclusion that the implied reference to bargain prices for liquor violated the statutory ban on price advertising, the Rhode Island Liquor Control Administrator assessed a $400 fine.

After paying the fine, 44 Liquormart, joined by Peoples, filed this action ... in the Federal District Court seeking a declaratory judgment that the two statutes and the administrator's implementing regulations violate the First Amendment ...

. . .

... [The District Court] concluded that the price advertising ban was unconstitutional ...

The Court of Appeals reversed. ...

. . .

III

. . .

In Central Hudson Gas & Elec. Corp. v. Public Serv. Comm'n of N. Y., 447 U.S. 557 (1980), we took stock of our developing commercial speech jurisprudence. ...

. . .

... [T]he majority explained that although the special nature of commercial speech may require less than strict review of its regulation, special concerns arise from "regulations that entirely suppress commercial speech in order to pursue a nonspeech-related policy." Id., at 566, n. 9. In those circumstances, "a ban on speech could screen from public view the underlying governmental policy." Ibid. As a result, the Court concluded that "special care" should attend the review of such blanket bans, and it pointedly remarked that "in recent years this Court has not approved a blanket ban on commercial speech unless the speech itself was flawed in some way, either because it was deceptive or related to unlawful activity." Ibid.

IV

As our review of the case law reveals, Rhode Island errs in concluding that all commercial speech regulations are subject to a similar form of constitutional review simply because they target a similar category of expression. The mere fact that messages propose commercial transactions does not in and of itself dictate the constitutional analysis that should apply to decisions to suppress them. ...

When a State regulates commercial messages to protect consumers from misleading, deceptive, or aggressive sales practices, or requires the disclosure of beneficial consumer information, the purpose of its regulation is consistent with the reasons for according constitutional protection to commercial speech and therefore justifies less than strict review. However, when a State entirely prohibits the dissemination of truthful, nonmisleading commercial messages for reasons unrelated to the preservation of a fair bargaining process, there is far less reason to depart from the rigorous review that the First Amendment generally demands.

Sound reasons justify reviewing the latter type of commercial speech regulation more carefully. Most obviously, complete speech bans, unlike content-neutral restrictions on the time, place, or manner of expression, ... are particularly dangerous because they all but foreclose alternative means of disseminating certain information.

. . .

The special dangers that attend complete bans on truthful, nonmisleading commercial speech cannot be explained away by appeals to the "commonsense distinctions" that exist between commercial and noncommercial speech. ... Regulations that suppress the truth are no less troubling because they target objectively verifiable information, nor are they less effective because they aim at durable messages. As a result, neither the "greater objectivity" nor the "greater hardiness" of truthful, nonmisleading commercial speech justifies reviewing its complete suppression with added deference. ....

It is the State's interest in protecting consumers from "commercial harms" that provides "the typical reason why commercial speech can be subject to greater governmental regulation than noncommercial speech." ... Yet bans that target truthful, nonmisleading commercial messages rarely protect consumers from such harms. Instead, such bans often serve only to obscure an "underlying governmental policy" that could be implemented without regulating speech. ....In this way, these commercial speech bans not only hinder consumer choice, but also impede debate over central issues of public policy. ...

Precisely because bans against truthful, nonmisleading commercial speech rarely seek to protect consumers from either deception or overreaching, they usually rest solely on the offensive assumption that the public will respond "irrationally" to the truth. ... The First Amendment directs us to be especially skeptical of regulations that seek to keep people in the dark for what the government perceives to be their own good. That teaching applies equally to state attempts to deprive consumers of accurate information about their chosen products. ....

V

In this case, there is no question that Rhode Island's price advertising ban constitutes a blanket prohibition against truthful, nonmisleading speech about a lawful product. There is also no question that the ban serves an end unrelated to consumer protection. Accordingly, we must review the price advertising ban with "special care," *Central Hudson*, 447 U. S., at 566, n. 9, mindful that speech prohibitions of this type rarely survive constitutional review. Ibid.

The State argues that the price advertising prohibition should nevertheless be upheld because it directly advances the State's substantial interest in promoting temperance, and because it is no more extensive than necessary. ...Although there is some confusion as to what Rhode Island means by temperance, we assume that the State asserts an interest in reducing alcohol consumption.

In evaluating the ban's effectiveness in advancing the State's interest, we note that a commercial speech regulation "may not be sustained if it provides only ineffective or remote support for the government's purpose." *Central Hudson*, 447 U. S., at 564. For that reason, the State bears the burden of showing not merely that its regulation will advance its interest, but also that it will do so "to a material degree." ... The need for the State to make such a showing is particularly great given the drastic nature of its chosen means—the wholesale suppression of truthful, nonmisleading information. Accordingly, we must determine whether the State has shown that the price advertising ban will significantly reduce alcohol consumption.

We can agree that common sense supports the conclusion that a prohibition against price advertising, like a collusive agreement among competitors to refrain from such advertising, will tend to mitigate competition and maintain prices at a higher level than would prevail in a completely free market. Despite the absence of proof on the point, we can even agree with the State's contention that it is reasonable to assume that demand, and hence consumption throughout the market, is somewhat lower whenever a higher, noncompetitive price level prevails. However, without any findings of fact, or indeed any evidentiary support whatsoever, we cannot agree with the assertion that the price advertising ban will significantly advance the State's interest in promoting temperance.

Although the record suggests that the price advertising ban may have some impact on the purchasing patterns of temperate drinkers of modest means, the State has presented no evidence to suggest that its speech prohibition will significantly reduce market-wide consumption. Indeed, the District Court's considered and uncontradicted finding on this point is directly to the contrary. Moreover, the evidence suggests that the abusive drinker will probably not be deterred by a marginal price increase, and that the true alcoholic may simply reduce his purchases of other necessities.

In addition, as the District Court noted, the State has not identified what price level would lead to a significant reduction in alcohol consumption, nor has it identified the amount that it believes prices would decrease without the ban. Thus, the State's own showing reveals that any connection between the ban and a significant change in alcohol consumption would be purely fortuitous.

As is evident, any conclusion that elimination of the ban would significantly increase alcohol consumption would require us to engage in the sort of "speculation or conjecture" that is an unacceptable means of demonstrating that a restriction on commercial speech directly advances the State's asserted interest. ...Such speculation certainly does not suffice when the State takes aim at accurate commercial information for paternalistic ends.

The State also cannot satisfy the requirement that its restriction on speech be no more extensive than necessary. It is perfectly obvious that alternative forms of regulation that would not involve any restriction on speech would be more likely to achieve the State's goal of promoting temperance. As the State's own expert conceded, higher prices can be maintained either by direct regulation or by increased taxation. Per capita purchases could be limited as is the case with prescription drugs. Even educational campaigns focused on the problems of excessive, or even moderate, drinking might prove to be more effective.

As a result, even under the less than strict standard that generally applies in commercial speech cases, the State has failed to establish a "reasonable fit" between its abridgment of speech and its temperance goal. ...It necessarily follows that the price advertising ban cannot survive the more stringent constitutional review that *Central Hudson* itself concluded was appropriate for the complete suppression of truthful, nonmisleading commercial speech. ...

VI

The State responds by arguing that it merely exercised appropriate "legislative judgment" in determining that a price advertising ban would best promote temperance. Relying on the *Central Hudson* analysis set forth in Posadas de Puerto Rico Associates v. Tourism Co. of P. R., 478 U.S. 328 (1986), and United States v. Edge Broadcasting Co., 509 U.S. 418 (1993), Rhode Island first argues that, because expert opinions as to the effectiveness of the price advertising ban "go both ways," the Court of Appeals correctly concluded that the ban constituted a "reasonable choice" by the legislature. The State next contends that precedent requires us to give particular deference to that legislative choice because the State could, if it chose, ban the sale of alcoholic beverages outright. See *Posadas*, 478 U. S., at 345–346. Finally, the State argues that deference is appropriate because alcoholic beverages are so-called "vice" products. See *Edge*, 509 U.S. at ___; *Posadas*, 478 U. S., at 346–347. We consider each of these contentions in turn.

The State's first argument fails to justify the speech prohibition at issue. Our commercial speech cases recognize some room for the exercise of legislative judgment. . . . However, Rhode Island errs in concluding that *Edge* and *Posadas* establish the degree of deference that its decision to impose a price advertising ban warrants.

In *Edge*, we upheld a federal statute that permitted only those broadcasters located in States that had legalized lotteries to air lottery advertising. The statute was designed to regulate advertising about an activity that had been deemed illegal in the jurisdiction in which the broadcaster was located. . . . Here, by contrast, the commercial speech ban targets information about entirely lawful behavior.

Posadas is more directly relevant. There, a five-Member majority held that, under the *Central Hudson* test, it was "up to the legislature" to choose to reduce gambling by suppressing in-state casino advertising rather than engaging in educational speech. . . . Rhode Island argues that this logic demonstrates the constitutionality of its own decision to ban price advertising in lieu of raising taxes or employing some other less speech-restrictive means of promoting temperance.

The reasoning in *Posadas* does support the State's argument, but, on reflection, we are now persuaded that *Posadas* erroneously performed the First Amendment analysis. The casino advertising ban was designed to keep truthful, nonmisleading speech from members of the public for fear that they would be more likely to gamble if they received it. As a result, the advertising ban served to shield the State's antigambling policy from the public scrutiny that more direct, nonspeech regulation would draw. See *Posadas*, 478 U. S., at 351 (Brennan, J., dissenting).

Given our longstanding hostility to commercial speech regulation of this type, *Posadas* clearly erred in concluding that it was "up to the legislature" to choose suppression over a less speech-restrictive policy. The *Posadas* majority's conclusion on that point cannot be reconciled with the unbroken line of prior cases striking down similarly broad regulations on truthful, nonmisleading advertising when non-speech-related alternatives were available. . . .

Because the 5-to-4 decision in Posadas marked such a sharp break from our prior precedent, and because it concerned a constitutional question about which this Court is the final arbiter, we decline to give force to its highly deferential approach. Instead, in keeping with our prior holdings, we conclude that a state legislature does not have the broad discretion to suppress truthful, nonmisleading information for paternalistic purposes that the *Posadas* majority was willing to tolerate. . . .

We also cannot accept the State's second contention, which is premised entirely on the "greater-includes-the-lesser" reasoning endorsed toward the end of the majority's opinion in *Posadas*. There, the majority stated that "the greater power to completely ban casino gambling necessarily includes the lesser power to ban advertising of casino gambling." 478 U. S., at 345–346. It went on to state that "because the government could have enacted a wholesale prohibition of [casino gambling] it is permissible for the government to take the less intrusive step of allowing the conduct, but reducing the demand through restrictions on advertising." Id., at 346. The majority concluded that it would "surely be a strange constitutional doctrine which would concede to the legislature the authority to totally ban a product or activity, but deny to the legislature the authority to forbid the stimulation of demand for the product or activity through advertising on behalf of those who would profit from such increased demand." Ibid. On the basis of these statements, the State reasons that its undisputed authority to ban alcoholic beverages must include the power to restrict advertisements offering them for sale.

In Rubin v. Coors Brewing Co., 514 U.S. ___ (1995), the United States advanced a similar argument as a basis for supporting a statutory prohibition against revealing the alcoholic content of malt beverages on product labels. We rejected the argument, noting that the statement in the *Posadas* opinion was made only after the majority had concluded that the Puerto Rican regulation "survived the *Central Hudson* test." . . . Further consideration persuades us that the "greater-includes-the-lesser" argument should be rejected for the additional and more important reason that it is inconsistent with both logic and well-settled doctrine.

Although we do not dispute the proposition that greater powers include lesser ones, we fail to see how that syllogism requires the conclusion that the State's power to regulate commercial activity is "greater" than its power to ban truthful, nonmisleading commercial speech. Contrary to the assumption made in *Posadas*, we think it quite clear that banning speech may sometimes prove far more intrusive than banning conduct. . . . [W]e reject the assumption that words are necessarily less vital to freedom than actions, or that logic somehow proves that the power to prohibit an activity is necessarily "greater" than the power to suppress speech about it.

As a matter of First Amendment doctrine, the *Posadas* syllogism is even less defensible. The text of the First Amendment makes clear that the Constitution presumes that attempts to regulate speech are more dangerous than attempts to regulate conduct. That presumption accords with the essential role that the free flow of information plays in a democratic society. As a result, the First Amendment directs that government may not suppress speech as easily as it may suppress conduct, and that speech restrictions cannot be treated as simply another means that the government may use to achieve its ends.

These basic First Amendment principles clearly apply to commercial speech; indeed, the *Posadas* majority impliedly conceded as much by applying the *Central Hudson* test. Thus, it is no answer that commercial speech concerns products and services that the government may freely regulate. . . .

. . .

Thus, just as it is perfectly clear that Rhode Island could not ban all obscene liquor ads except those that advocated temperance, we think it equally clear that its power to ban the sale of liquor entirely does not include a power

to censor all advertisements that contain accurate and nonmisleading information about the price of the product. As the entire Court apparently now agrees,
the statements in the *Posadas* opinion on which Rhode Island relies are no
longer persuasive.

Finally, we find unpersuasive the State's contention that, under *Posadas*
and *Edge*, the price advertising ban should be upheld because it targets
commercial speech that pertains to a "vice" activity. The appellees premise
their request for a so-called "vice" exception to our commercial speech doctrine
on language in *Edge* which characterized gambling as a "vice".... The
respondents misread our precedent. Our decision last Term striking down an
alcohol-related advertising restriction effectively rejected the very contention
respondents now make. See Rubin v. Coors Brewing Co., 514 U. S., at ___, ___,
n. 2.

Moreover, the scope of any "vice" exception to the protection afforded by
the First Amendment would be difficult, if not impossible, to define. Almost any
product that poses some threat to public health or public morals might
reasonably be characterized by a state legislature as relating to "vice activity".
Such characterization, however, is anomalous when applied to products such as
alcoholic beverages, lottery tickets, or playing cards, that may be lawfully
purchased on the open market. The recognition of such an exception would also
have the unfortunate consequence of either allowing state legislatures to justify
censorship by the simple expedient of placing the "vice" label on selected
lawful activities, or requiring the federal courts to establish a federal common
law of vice. ...For these reasons, a "vice" label that is unaccompanied by a
corresponding prohibition against the commercial behavior at issue fails to
provide a principled justification for the regulation of commercial speech about
that activity.

VII

. . .

... [T]he text of the Twenty-first Amendment supports the view that,
while it grants the States authority over commerce that might otherwise be
reserved to the Federal Government, it places no limit whatsoever on other
constitutional provisions. Nevertheless, Rhode Island argues ... that in this
case the Twenty-first Amendment tilts the First Amendment analysis in the
State's favor.

In reaching its conclusion, the Court of Appeals relied on our decision in
California v. LaRue, 409 U.S. 109 (1972). In *LaRue*, five Members of the Court
relied on the Twenty-first Amendment to buttress the conclusion that the First
Amendment did not invalidate California's prohibition of certain grossly sexual
exhibitions in premises licensed to serve alcoholic beverages. Specifically, the
opinion stated that the Twenty-first Amendment required that the prohibition
be given an added presumption in favor of its validity. ...We are now
persuaded that the Court's analysis in *LaRue* would have led to precisely the
same result if it had placed no reliance on the Twenty-first Amendment.

Entirely apart from the Twenty-first Amendment, the State has ample
power to prohibit the sale of alcoholic beverages in inappropriate locations.
Moreover, in subsequent cases the Court has recognized that the States'
inherent police powers provide ample authority to restrict the kind of "baccha-
nalian revelries" described in the *LaRue* opinion regardless of whether alcoholic beverages are involved. ...As we recently noted: "*LaRue* did not involve
commercial speech about alcohol, but instead concerned the regulation of nude

dancing in places where alcohol was served." Rubin v. Coors Brewing Co., 514 U. S., at ___, n. 2.

Without questioning the holding in *LaRue*, we now disavow its reasoning insofar as it relied on the Twenty-first Amendment. As we explained in a case decided more than a decade after LaRue, although the Twenty-first Amendment limits the effect of the dormant Commerce Clause on a State's regulatory power over the delivery or use of intoxicating beverages within its borders, "the Amendment does not license the States to ignore their obligations under other provisions of the Constitution." Capital Cities Cable, Inc. v. Crisp, 467 U.S. 691, 712 (1984). ... The Twenty-first Amendment, therefore, cannot save Rhode Island's ban on liquor price advertising.

VIII

Because Rhode Island has failed to carry its heavy burden of justifying its complete ban on price advertising, we conclude that R.I. Gen. Laws §§ 3–8–7 and 3–8–8.1, as well as Regulation 32 of the Rhode Island Liquor Control Administration, abridge speech in violation of the First Amendment as made applicable to the States by the Due Process Clause of the Fourteenth Amendment. The judgment of the Court of Appeals is therefore reversed.

It is so ordered.

Justice Scalia, concurring in part and concurring in the judgment.

I share Justice Thomas's discomfort with the *Central Hudson* test, which seems to me to have nothing more than policy intuition to support it. I also share Justice Stevens' aversion towards paternalistic governmental policies that prevent men and women from hearing facts that might not be good for them. On the other hand, it would also be paternalism for us to prevent the people of the States from enacting laws that we consider paternalistic, unless we have good reason to believe that the Constitution itself forbids them. I will take my guidance as to what the Constitution forbids, with regard to a text as indeterminate as the First Amendment's preservation of "the freedom of speech," and where the core offense of suppressing particular political ideas is not at issue, from the long accepted practices of the American people. ...

The briefs and arguments of the parties in the present case provide no illumination on that point; understandably so, since both sides accepted *Central Hudson*. ... I consider ... relevant the state legislative practices prevalent at the time the First Amendment was adopted, since almost all of the States had free-speech constitutional guarantees of their own, whose meaning was not likely to have been different from the federal constitutional provision derived from them. Perhaps more relevant still are the state legislative practices at the time the Fourteenth Amendment was adopted, since it is most improbable that that adoption was meant to overturn any existing national consensus regarding free speech. ... The parties and their amici provide no evidence on these points.

Since I do not believe we have before us the wherewithal to declare *Central Hudson* wrong—or at least the wherewithal to say what ought to replace it—I must resolve this case in accord with our existing jurisprudence, which all except Justice Thomas agree would prohibit the challenged regulation. I am not disposed to develop new law, or reinforce old, on this issue, and accordingly I merely concur in the judgment of the Court. ...

Justice Thomas, concurring in Parts I, II, VI, and VII, and concurring in the judgment.

In cases such as this, in which the government's asserted interest is to keep legal users of a product or service ignorant in order to manipulate their choices in the marketplace, the balancing test adopted in Central Hudson Gas & Elec. Corp. v. Public Serv. Comm'n of N. Y., 447 U.S. 557 (1980), should not be applied, in my view. Rather, such an "interest" is per se illegitimate and can no more justify regulation of "commercial" speech than it can justify regulation of "noncommercial" speech.

. . .

II

I do not join the principal opinion's application of the *Central Hudson* balancing test because I do not believe that such a test should be applied to a restriction of "commercial" speech, at least when, as here, the asserted interest is one that is to be achieved through keeping would-be recipients of the speech in the dark. Application of the advancement-of-state-interest prong of *Central Hudson* makes little sense to me in such circumstances. Faulting the State for failing to show that its price advertising ban decreases alcohol consumption "significantly," as Justice Stevens does, seems to imply that if the State had been more successful at keeping consumers ignorant and thereby decreasing their consumption, then the restriction might have been upheld. This contradicts *Virginia Pharmacy Bd.*'s rationale for protecting "commercial" speech in the first instance.

Both Justice Stevens and Justice O'Connor appear to adopt a stricter, more categorical interpretation of the fourth prong of *Central Hudson* than that suggested in some of our other opinions, one that could, as a practical matter, go a long way toward the position I take. ...In their application of the fourth prong, both ... hold that because the State can ban the sale of lower priced alcohol altogether by instituting minimum prices or levying taxes, it cannot ban advertising regarding lower priced liquor. Although the tenor of Justice O'Connor's opinion (and, to a lesser extent, that of Justice Stevens's opinion) might suggest that this is just another routine case-by-case application of *Central Hudson*'s fourth prong, the Court's holding will in fact be quite sweeping if applied consistently in future cases. The opinions would appear to commit the courts to striking down restrictions on speech whenever a direct regulation (i.e., a regulation involving no restriction on speech regarding lawful activity at all) would be an equally effective method of dampening demand by legal users. But it would seem that directly banning a product (or rationing it, taxing it, controlling its price, or otherwise restricting its sale in specific ways) would virtually always be at least as effective in discouraging consumption as merely restricting advertising regarding the product would be, and thus virtually all restrictions with such a purpose would fail the fourth prong of the *Central Hudson* test. This would be so even if the direct regulation is, in one sense, more restrictive of conduct generally. In this case, for example, adoption of minimum prices or taxes will mean that those who, under the current legal system, would have happened across cheap liquor or would have sought it out, will be forced to pay more. Similarly, a State seeking to discourage liquor sales would have to ban sales by convenience stores rather than banning convenience store liquor advertising; it would have to ban liquor sales after midnight, rather than banning advertising by late-night liquor sellers; and so on.

The upshot of the application of the fourth prong in the opinions of Justice Stevens and of Justice O'Connor seems to be that the government may not, for the purpose of keeping would-be consumers ignorant and thus decreasing demand, restrict advertising regarding commercial transactions-or at least that it may not restrict advertising regarding commercial transactions except to the extent that it outlaws or otherwise directly restricts the same transactions within its own borders. I welcome this outcome; but, rather than "applying" the fourth prong of *Central Hudson* to reach the inevitable result that all or most such advertising restrictions must be struck down, I would [hold] that all attempts to dissuade legal choices by citizens by keeping them ignorant are impermissible.

. . .

Justice O'Connor, with whom the Chief Justice, Justice Souter, and Justice Breyer join, concurring in the judgment.

. . . I agree with the Court that Rhode Island's price-advertising ban is invalid. I would resolve this case more narrowly, however, by applying our established *Central Hudson* test to determine whether this commercial-speech regulation survives First Amendment scrutiny.

Under that test, we first determine whether the speech at issue concerns lawful activity and is not misleading, and whether the asserted governmental interest is substantial. If both these conditions are met, we must decide whether the regulation "directly advances the governmental interest asserted, and whether it is not more extensive than is necessary to serve that interest." . . .

. . .

Both parties agree that the first two prongs of the *Central Hudson* test are met. Even if we assume arguendo that Rhode Island's regulation also satisfies the requirement that it directly advance the governmental interest, Rhode Island's regulation fails the final prong; that is, its ban is more extensive than necessary to serve the State's interest.

. . .

. . . Rhode Island says that the ban is intended to keep alcohol prices high as a way to keep consumption low. . . .

The fit between Rhode Island's method and this particular goal is not reasonable. If the target is simply higher prices generally to discourage consumption, the regulation imposes too great, and unnecessary, a prohibition on speech in order to achieve it. The State has other methods at its disposal—methods that would more directly accomplish this stated goal without intruding on sellers' ability to provide truthful, nonmisleading information to customers. Indeed, Rhode Island's own expert conceded that "the objective of lowering consumption of alcohol by banning price advertising could be accomplished by establishing minimum prices and/or by increasing sales taxes on alcoholic beverages." . . . The ready availability of such alternatives—at least some of which would far more effectively achieve Rhode Island's only professed goal, at comparatively small additional administrative cost—demonstrates that the fit between ends and means is not narrowly tailored. . . .

Respondents point for support to Posadas de Puerto Rico Associates v. Tourism Co. of P. R., 478 U.S. 328 (1986), where, applying the *Central Hudson* test, we upheld the constitutionality of a Puerto Rico law that prohibited the advertising of casino gambling aimed at residents of Puerto Rico, but permitted such advertising aimed at tourists.

. . .

It is true that *Posadas* accepted as reasonable, without further inquiry, Puerto Rico's assertions that the regulations furthered the government's interest and were no more extensive than necessary to serve that interest. Since

Posadas, however, this Court has examined more searchingly the State's professed goal, and the speech restriction put into place to further it, before accepting a State's claim that the speech restriction satisfies First Amendment scrutiny. ...The closer look that we have required since *Posadas* comports better with the purpose of the analysis set out in *Central Hudson*, by requiring the State to show that the speech restriction directly advances its interest and is narrowly tailored. Under such a closer look, Rhode Island's price-advertising ban clearly fails to pass muster.

Because Rhode Island's regulation fails even the less stringent standard set out in *Central Hudson*, nothing here requires adoption of a new analysis for the evaluation of commercial speech regulation. ...I would not here undertake the question whether the test we have employed since *Central Hudson* should be displaced.

. . .

... While I agree with the Court's finding that the regulation is invalid, I would decide that issue on narrower grounds. I therefore concur in the judgment.

CHAPTER 14

RESTRICTIONS ON TIME, PLACE, OR MANNER OF EXPRESSION

Introduction. The title of this chapter signals an obvious shift in emphasis from controlling expression because of its content to restricting the time, place, or manner of expression. It is, however, a shift rather than a break in the analysis of freedom of speech. Time, place, or manner issues were prominent in some of the cases in the preceding chapter. Issues of speech content are often central to time, place, or manner restrictions. A repetitive question is whether any consistent principle can be formulated where government restrictions of expression blend considerations of time, place, or manner with considerations of content.

SECTION 1. THE TRADITIONAL PUBLIC FORUM: SPEECH ACTIVITIES IN STREETS AND PARKS

SCHNEIDER v. NEW JERSEY, TOWN OF IRVINGTON, 308 U.S. 147 (1939). The Court had before it three cases involving city ordinances forbidding the distribution of handbills in the streets (and in one case in any public place). The cases involved convictions of persons distributing handbills giving notice of meetings on public issues in two cases and as an incident to labor picketing in the third. As to the question whether cities could forbid all distribution of handbills on public streets, the Court held they could not. The Court reversed the convictions in these three cases. Justice Roberts, speaking for the Court, said, in part:

"Municipal authorities, as trustees for the public, have the duty to keep their communities' streets open and available for movement of people and property, the primary purpose to which the streets are dedicated. So long as legislation to this end does not abridge the constitutional liberty of one rightfully upon the street to impart information through speech or the distribution of literature, it may lawfully regulate the conduct of those using the streets. For example, a person could not exercise this liberty by taking his stand in the middle of a crowded street, contrary to traffic regulations, and maintain his position to the stoppage of all traffic; a group of distributors could not insist upon a constitutional right to form a cordon across the street and to allow no pedestrian to pass who did not accept a tendered leaflet; nor does the guarantee of freedom of speech or of the press deprive a municipality of power to enact regulations against throwing literature broadcast in the streets. Prohibition of such conduct would not abridge the constitutional liberty since such activity bears no necessary relationship to the freedom to speak, write, print or distribute information or opinion.

. . .

"The motive of the legislation under attack in Numbers 13, 18 and 29 is held by the courts below to be the prevention of littering of the streets and, although the alleged offenders were not charged with themselves scattering paper in the streets, their convictions were sustained upon the theory that distribution by them encouraged or resulted in such littering. We are of opinion that the purpose to keep the streets clean and of good appearance is insufficient to justify an ordinance which prohibits a person rightfully on a public street from handing literature to one willing to receive it. Any burden imposed upon the city authorities in cleaning and caring for the streets as an indirect consequence of such distribution results from the constitutional protection of the freedom of speech and press. This constitutional protection does not deprive a city of all power to prevent street littering. There are obvious methods of preventing littering. Amongst these is the punishment of those who actually throw papers on the streets."

MINIMUM ACCESS v. EQUAL ACCESS TO THE PUBLIC FORUM

There are two famous quotations expressing polar positions. While sitting on the Massachusetts Supreme Judicial Court, Justice Holmes observed: "For the Legislature absolutely or conditionally to forbid public speaking in a highway or public park is no more an infringement of the rights of a member of the public than for the owner of a private house to forbid it in his house." Commonwealth v. Davis, 162 Mass. 510, 511, 39 N.E. 113 (1895), affirmed 167 U.S. 43, 47–48 (1897). Justice Roberts' plurality opinion in Hague v. C.I.O., 307 U.S. 496, 515–516 (1939) contains this often quoted dictum: "Wherever the title of streets and parks may rest, they have immemorially been held in trust for the use of public and, time out of mind, have been used for purposes of assembly, communicating thoughts between citizens, and discussing public questions. Such use of the streets and public places has, from ancient times, been a part of the privileges, immunities, rights, and liberties of citizens."

No Supreme Court decision has confronted the constitutionality of a municipality's decision to reserve its streets entirely for traffic and its parks as facilities for quiet rest and relaxation. In that context, the issue may be more theoretical than real. The cases before the Court have either involved time, place, or manner restrictions that did not totally preclude use of parks and streets for expression, or restrictions that denied equal access to the public facilities involved. Does resolution of the debate whether all parks and streets could be closed to expression affect the results in those cases? Does Justice Roberts' opinion in *Schneider* implicitly rest on accepting his dictum in *Hague*?

For discussion of these issues see Kalven, *The Concept of the Public Forum: Cox v. Louisiana*, 1965 Sup.Ct.Rev. 1.

Frisby v. Schultz

487 U.S. 474, 108 S.Ct. 2495, 101 L.Ed.2d 420 (1988).

Justice O'Connor delivered the opinion of the Court.

Brookfield, Wisconsin, has adopted an ordinance that completely bans picketing "before or about" any residence. This case presents a facial First Amendment challenge to that ordinance.

I

Brookfield, Wisconsin, is a residential suburb of Milwaukee with a population of approximately 4,300. The appellees, Sandra C. Schultz and Robert C.

Braun, are individuals strongly opposed to abortion and wish to express their views on the subject by picketing on a public street outside the Brookfield residence of a doctor who apparently performs abortions at two clinics in neighboring towns. Appellees and others engaged in precisely that activity, assembling outside the doctor's home on at least six occasions between April 20, 1985, and May 20, 1985, for periods ranging from one to one and a half hours. The size of the group varied from 11 to more than 40. The picketing was generally orderly and peaceful; the town never had occasion to invoke any of its various ordinances prohibiting obstruction of the streets, loud and unnecessary noises, or disorderly conduct. Nonetheless, the picketing generated substantial controversy and numerous complaints.

The Town Board therefore resolved to enact an ordinance to restrict the picketing. On May 7, 1985, the town passed an ordinance that prohibited all picketing in residential neighborhoods except for labor picketing. But after reviewing this Court's decision in Carey v. Brown, 447 U.S. 455 (1980), which invalidated a similar ordinance as a violation of the Equal Protection Clause, the town attorney instructed the police not to enforce the new ordinance and advised the Town Board that the ordinance's labor picketing exception likely rendered it unconstitutional. This ordinance was repealed on May 15, 1985, and replaced with the following flat ban on all residential picketing:

> "It is unlawful for any person to engage in picketing before or about the residence or dwelling of any individual in the Town of Brookfield."

The ordinance itself recites the primary purpose of this ban: "the protection and preservation of the home" through assurance "that members of the community enjoy in their homes and dwellings a feeling of well-being, tranquility, and privacy." The Town Board believed that a ban was necessary because it determined that "the practice of picketing before or about residences and dwellings causes emotional disturbance and distress to the occupants . . . [and] has as its object the harassing of such occupants." The ordinance also evinces a concern for public safety, noting that picketing obstructs and interferes with "the free use of public sidewalks and public ways of travel."

. . . [A]ppellees ceased picketing in Brookfield and filed this lawsuit in United States District Court for the Eastern District of Wisconsin [seeking] . . . declaratory as well as preliminary and permanent injunctive relief on the grounds that the ordinance violated the First Amendment. . . .

The District Court granted appellees' motion for a preliminary injunction[, specifying] that unless the appellants requested a trial on the merits within 60 days or appealed, the preliminary injunction would become permanent. . . .

A divided panel of the United States Court of Appeals for the Seventh Circuit affirmed. . . .

. . .

II

The antipicketing ordinance operates at the core of the First Amendment by prohibiting appellees from engaging in picketing on an issue of public concern. . . .[W]e have traditionally subjected restrictions on public issue picketing to careful scrutiny. See, e.g., Boos v. Barry, 485 U.S. 312, 318 (1988); United States v. Grace, 461 U.S. 171 (1983); Carey v. Brown, 447 U.S. 455 (1980). . . .

To ascertain what limits, if any, may be placed on protected speech, we have often focused on the "place" of that speech, considering the nature of the forum the speaker seeks to employ. Our cases have recognized that the standards by which limitations on speech must be evaluated "differ depending on the character of the property at issue." Perry Education Assn. v. Perry Local Educators' Assn., 460 U.S. 37, 44 (1983). Specifically, we have identified three types of fora: "the traditional public forum, the public forum created by government designation, and the nonpublic forum." . . .

The relevant forum here may be easily identified: appellees wish to picket on the public streets of Brookfield. Ordinarily, a determination of the nature of the forum would follow automatically from this identification; we have repeatedly referred to public streets as the archetype of a traditional public forum. . . . "[T]ime out of mind" public streets and sidewalks have been used for public assembly and debate, the hallmarks of a traditional public forum. . . . Hague v. CIO, 307 U.S. 496, 515 (1939) (Roberts, J.). Appellants, however, urge us to disregard these "clichés." They argue that the streets of Brookfield should be considered a nonpublic forum. Pointing to the physical narrowness of Brookfield's streets as well as to their residential character, appellants contend that such streets have not by tradition or designation been held open for public communication.

We reject this suggestion. Our prior holdings make clear that a public street does not lose its status as a traditional public forum simply because it runs through a residential neighborhood. In *Carey v. Brown*—which considered a statute similar to the one at issue here, ultimately striking it down as a violation of the Equal Protection Clause because it included an exception for labor picketing—we expressly recognized that "public streets and sidewalks in residential neighborhoods," were "public for[a]." 447 U.S., at 460–461. This rather ready identification virtually forecloses appellants' argument. . . .

In short, our decisions identifying public streets and sidewalks as traditional public fora are not accidental invocations of a "cliché," but recognition that "[w]herever the title of streets and parks may rest, they have immemorially been held in trust for the use of the public." Hague v. CIO, supra, at 515 (Roberts, J.). No particularized inquiry into the precise nature of a specific street is necessary; all public streets are held in the public trust and are properly considered traditional public fora. Accordingly, the streets of Brookfield are traditional public fora. The residential character of those streets may well inform the application of the relevant test, but it does not lead to a different test; the antipicketing ordinance must be judged against the stringent standards we have established for restrictions on speech in traditional public fora:

> "In these quintessential public for[a], the government may not prohibit all communicative activity. For the State to enforce a content-based exclusion it must show that its regulation is necessary to serve a compelling state interest and that it is narrowly drawn to achieve that end. . . . The State may also enforce regulations of the time, place, and manner of expression which are content-neutral, are narrowly tailored to serve a significant government interest, and leave open ample alternative channels of communication." *Perry*, [460 U.S.] at 45 (citations omitted).

As *Perry* makes clear, the appropriate level of scrutiny is initially tied to whether the statute distinguishes between prohibited and permitted speech on the basis of content. . . . [W]e accept the lower courts' conclusion that the Brookfield ordinance is content neutral. Accordingly, we turn to consider whether the ordinance is "narrowly tailored to serve a significant government interest" and whether it "leave[s] open ample alternative channels of communication." *Perry*, 460 U.S., at 45.

Because the last question is so easily answered, we address it first. Of course, before we are able to assess the available alternatives, we must consider more carefully the reach of the ordinance. The precise scope of the ban is not further described within the text of the ordinance, but in our view the ordinance is readily subject to a narrowing construction that avoids constitutional difficulties.... To the extent they endorsed a broad reading of the ordinance, the lower courts ran afoul of the well-established principle that statutes will be interpreted to avoid constitutional difficulties.... Thus, ... we are unable to accept their potentially broader view of the ordinance's scope. We instead construe the ordinance more narrowly. This narrow reading is supported by the representations of counsel for the town at oral argument, which indicate that the town takes, and will enforce, a limited view of the "picketing" proscribed by the ordinance. Thus, generally speaking, "picketing would be having the picket proceed on a definite course or route in front of a home." The picket need not be carrying a sign, but in order to fall within the scope of the ordinance the picketing must be directed at a single residence. General marching through residential neighborhoods, or even walking a route in front of an entire block of houses, is not prohibited by this ordinance. Accordingly, we construe the ban to be a limited one; only focused picketing taking place solely in front of a particular residence is prohibited.

So narrowed, the ordinance permits the more general dissemination of a message. As appellants explain, the limited nature of the prohibition makes it virtually self-evident that ample alternatives remain:

> "Protestors have not been barred from the residential neighborhoods. They may enter such neighborhoods, alone or in groups, even marching.... They may go door-to-door to proselytize their views. They may distribute literature in this manner ... or through the mails. They may contact residents by telephone, short of harassment."

We readily agree that the ordinance preserves ample alternative channels of communication and thus move on to inquire whether the ordinance serves a significant government interest. We find that such an interest is identified within the text of the ordinance itself: the protection of residential privacy.

"The State's interest in protecting the well-being, tranquility, and privacy of the home is certainly of the highest order in a free and civilized society." Carey v. Brown, 447 U.S., at 471. Our prior decisions have often remarked on the unique nature of the home, "the last citadel of the tired, the weary, and the sick," Gregory v. Chicago, 394 U.S. 111, 125 (1969) (Black J., concurring), and have recognized that "[p]reserving the sanctity of the home, the one retreat to which men and women can repair to escape from the tribulations of their daily pursuits, is surely an important value." *Carey*, supra, at 471.

One important aspect of residential privacy is protection of the unwilling listener. Although in many locations, we expect individuals simply to avoid speech they do not want to hear, ... the home is different. ...[W]e have repeatedly held that individuals are not required to welcome unwanted speech into their own homes and that the government may protect this freedom. See, e.g., FCC v. Pacifica Foundation, 438 U.S. 726, 748–749 (1978) (offensive radio broadcasts); ... Kovacs v. Cooper, 336 U.S. 77, 86–87 (1949) (sound trucks).

. . .

It remains to be considered, however, whether the Brookfield ordinance is narrowly tailored to protect only unwilling recipients of the communications. A statute is narrowly tailored if it targets and eliminates no more than the exact source of the "evil" it seeks to remedy....

... The type of focused picketing prohibited by the Brookfield ordinance is fundamentally different from more generally directed means of communication that may not be completely banned in residential areas. ...In such cases "the flow of information [is not] into ... household[s], but to the public." Organization for a Better Austin v. Keefe, 402 U.S. 415, 420 (1971). Here, in contrast, the picketing is narrowly directed at the household, not the public. The type of picketers banned by the Brookfield ordinance generally do not seek to disseminate a message to the general public, but to intrude upon the targeted resident, and to do so in an especially offensive way. Moreover, even if some such picketers have a broader communicative purpose, their activity nonetheless inherently and offensively intrudes on residential privacy. The devastating effect of targeted picketing on the quiet enjoyment of the home is beyond doubt ...

In this case, for example, appellees subjected the doctor and his family to the presence of a relatively large group of protesters on their doorstep in an attempt to force the doctor to cease performing abortions. But the actual size of the group is irrelevant; even a solitary picket can invade residential privacy.... The offensive and disturbing nature of the form of the communication banned by the Brookfield ordinance thus can scarcely be questioned....

The First Amendment permits the government to prohibit offensive speech as intrusive when the "captive" audience cannot avoid the objectionable speech. ...The target of the focused picketing banned by the Brookfield ordinance is just such a "captive." The resident is figuratively, and perhaps literally, trapped within the home, and because of the unique and subtle impact of such picketing is left with no ready means of avoiding the unwanted speech. ...Accordingly, the Brookfield ordinance's complete ban of that particular medium of expression is narrowly tailored.

Of course, this case presents only a facial challenge to the ordinance. Particular hypothetical applications of the ordinance—to, for example, a particular resident's use of his or her home as a place of business or public meeting, or to picketers present at a particular home by invitation of the resident—may present somewhat different questions. Initially, the ordinance by its own terms may not apply in such circumstances, since the ordinance's goal is the protection of residential privacy, and since it speaks only of a "residence or dwelling," not a place of business. Cf. *Carey,* supra, at 457 (quoting an antipicketing ordinance expressly rendered inapplicable by use of home as a place of business or to hold a public meeting). Moreover, since our First Amendment analysis is grounded in protection of the unwilling residential listener, the constitutionality of applying the ordinance to such hypotheticals remains open to question. These are, however, questions we need not address today in order to dispose of appellees' facial challenge.

Because the picketing prohibited by the Brookfield ordinance is speech directed primarily at those who are presumptively unwilling to receive it, the State has a substantial and justifiable interest in banning it. The nature and scope of this interest make the ban narrowly tailored. The ordinance also leaves open ample alternative channels of communication and is content neutral. Thus, largely because of its narrow scope, the facial challenge to the ordinance must fail. The contrary judgment of the Court of Appeals is

Reversed.

Justice White, concurring in the judgment.

I agree with the Court that an ordinance which only forbade picketing before a single residence would not be unconstitutional on its face....

. . .

Justice Brennan, with whom Justice Marshall joins, dissenting.

The Court today sets out the appropriate legal tests and standards governing the question presented, and proceeds to apply most of them correctly. Regrettably, though, the Court errs in the final step of its analysis, and approves an ordinance banning significantly more speech than is necessary to achieve the government's substantial and legitimate goal. Accordingly, I must dissent.

. . .

Without question there are many aspects of residential picketing that, if unregulated, might easily become intrusive or unduly coercive. Indeed, some of these aspects are illustrated by this very case. As the District Court found, before the ordinance took effect up to 40 sign-carrying, slogan-shouting protesters regularly converged on Dr. Victoria's home and, in addition to protesting, warned young children not to go near the house because Dr. Victoria was a "baby killer." Further, the throng repeatedly trespassed onto the Victorias' property and at least once blocked the exits to their home. Surely it is within the government's power to enact regulations as necessary to prevent such intrusive and coercive abuses. Thus, for example, the government could constitutionally regulate the number of residential picketers, the hours during which a residential picket may take place, or the noise level of such a picket. In short, substantial regulation is permitted to neutralize the intrusive or unduly coercive aspects of picketing around the home. But to say that picketing may be substantially regulated is not to say that it may be prohibited in its entirety. Once size, time, volume, and the like have been controlled to ensure that the picket is no longer intrusive or coercive, only the speech itself remains, conveyed perhaps by a lone, silent individual, walking back and forth with a sign.... Such speech, which no longer implicates the heightened governmental interest in residential privacy, is nevertheless banned by the Brookfield law. Therefore, the ordinance is not narrowly tailored.

. . .

Justice Stevens, dissenting.

. . .

I do not believe we advance the inquiry by rejecting ... the " ... argument that residential streets are something less than public fora." ... The streets in a residential neighborhood that has no sidewalks are quite obviously a different type of forum than a stadium or a public park. Attaching the label "public forum" to the area in front of a single family dwelling does not help us decide whether the town's interest in the safe and efficient flow of traffic or its interest in protecting the privacy of its citizens justifies denying picketers the right to march up and down the streets at will.

. . .

... The scope of the ordinance gives the town officials far too much discretion in making enforcement decisions; while we sit by and await further developments, potential picketers must act at their peril. ...[I]t is a simple matter for the town to amend its ordinance and to limit the ban to conduct that unreasonably interferes with the privacy of the home and does not serve a reasonable communicative purpose. Accordingly, I respectfully dissent.

Capitol Square Review and Advisory Board v. Pinette

___ U.S. ___, 115 S.Ct. 2440, 132 L.Ed.2d 650 (1995).

[The report in this case appears infra, page 1638.]

Madsen v. Women's Health Center, Inc.

512 U.S. 753, 114 S.Ct. 2516, 129 L.Ed.2d 593 (1994).

Chief Justice Rehnquist delivered the opinion of the Court.

Petitioners challenge the constitutionality of an injunction entered by a Florida state court which prohibits antiabortion protestors from demonstrating in certain places and in various ways outside of a health clinic that performs abortions. We hold that the establishment of a 36–foot buffer zone on a public street from which demonstrators are excluded passes muster under the First Amendment, but that several other provisions of the injunction do not.

I

Respondents operate abortion clinics throughout central Florida. Petitioners and other groups and individuals are engaged in activities near the site of one such clinic in Melbourne, Florida. They picketed and demonstrated where the public street gives access to the clinic. In September 1992, a Florida state court permanently enjoined petitioners from blocking or interfering with public access to the clinic, and from physically abusing persons entering or leaving the clinic. Six months later, respondents sought to broaden the injunction, complaining that access to the clinic was still impeded by petitioners' activities and that such activities had also discouraged some potential patients from entering the clinic, and had deleterious physical effects on others. The trial court thereupon issued a broader injunction, which is challenged here.

The court found that, despite the initial injunction, protesters continued to impede access to the clinic by congregating on the paved portion of the street—Dixie Way—leading up to the clinic, and by marching in front of the clinic's driveways. It found that as vehicles heading toward the clinic slowed to allow the protesters to move out of the way, "sidewalk counselors" would approach and attempt to give the vehicle's occupants antiabortion literature. The number of people congregating varied from a handful to 400, and the noise varied from singing and chanting to the use of loudspeakers and bullhorns.

The protests, the court found, took their toll on the clinic's patients. A clinic doctor testified that, as a result of having to run such a gauntlet to enter the clinic, the patients "manifested a higher level of anxiety and hypertension causing those patients to need a higher level of sedation to undergo the surgical procedures, thereby increasing the risk associated with such procedures." The noise produced by the protesters could be heard within the clinic, causing stress in the patients both during surgical procedures and while recuperating in the recovery rooms. And those patients who turned away because of the crowd to return at a later date, the doctor testified, increased their health risks by reason of the delay.

Doctors and clinic workers, in turn, were not immune even in their homes. Petitioners picketed in front of clinic employees' residences; shouted at passersby; rang the doorbells of neighbors and provided literature identifying the particular clinic employee as a "baby killer." Occasionally, the protestors would confront minor children of clinic employees who were home alone. This and similar testimony led the state court to conclude that its original injunction had proved insufficient "to protect the health, safety and rights of women in Brevard and Seminole County, Florida, and surrounding counties seeking access to [medical and counseling] services." Id., at 5. The state court therefore amended its prior order, enjoining a broader array of activities. The amended injunction prohibits petitioners from engaging in the following acts:

"(1) At all times on all days, from entering the premises and property of the Aware Woman Center for Choice [the Melbourne clinic]....

"(2) At all times on all days, from blocking, impeding, inhibiting, or in any other manner obstructing or interfering with access to, ingress into and egress from any building or parking lot of the Clinic.

"(3) At all times on all days, from congregating, picketing, patrolling, demonstrating or entering that portion of public right-of-way or private property within [36] feet of the property line of the Clinic.... An exception to the 36 foot buffer zone is the area immediately adjacent to the Clinic on the east.... The [petitioners] ... must remain at least [5] feet from the Clinic's east line. Another exception to the 36 foot buffer zone relates to the record title owners of the property to the north and west of the Clinic. The prohibition against entry into the 36 foot buffer zones does not apply to such persons and their invitees. The other prohibitions contained herein do apply, if such owners and their invitees are acting in concert with the [petitioners]....

"(4) During the hours of 7:30 a.m. through noon, on Mondays through Saturdays, during surgical procedures and recovery periods, from singing, chanting, whistling, shouting, yelling, use of bullhorns, auto horns, sound amplification equipment or other sounds or images observable to or within earshot of the patients inside the Clinic.

"(5) At all times on all days, in an area within [300] feet of the Clinic, from physically approaching any person seeking the services of the Clinic unless such person indicates a desire to communicate by approaching or by inquiring of the [petitioners]....

"(6) At all times on all days, from approaching, congregating, picketing, patrolling, demonstrating or using bullhorns or other sound amplification equipment within [300] feet of the residence of any of the [respondents'] employees, staff, owners or agents, or blocking or attempting to block, barricade, or in any other manner, temporarily or otherwise, obstruct the entrances, exits or driveways of the residences of any of the [respondents'] employees, staff, owners or agents. The [petitioners] and those acting in concert with them are prohibited from inhibiting or impeding or attempting to impede, temporarily or otherwise, the free ingress or egress of persons to any street that provides the sole access to the street on which those residences are located.

"(7) At all times on all days, from physically abusing, grabbing, intimidating, harassing, touching, pushing, shoving, crowding or assaulting persons entering or leaving, working at or using services at the [respondents'] Clinic or trying to gain access to, or leave, any of the homes of owners, staff or patients of the Clinic.

"(8) At all times on all days, from harassing, intimidating or physically abusing, assaulting or threatening any present or former doctor, health care professional, or other staff member, employee or volunteer who assists in providing services at the [respondents'] Clinic.

"(9) At all times on all days, from encouraging, inciting, or securing other persons to commit any of the prohibited acts listed herein."

The Florida Supreme Court upheld the constitutionality of the trial court's amended injunction. ...

. . .

II

We begin by addressing petitioners' contention that the state court's order, because it is an injunction that restricts only the speech of antiabortion protesters, is necessarily content or viewpoint based. Accordingly, they argue, we should examine the entire injunction under the strictest standard of scrutiny. ...We disagree. To accept petitioners' claim would be to classify virtually every injunction as content or viewpoint based. An injunction, by its very nature, applies only to a particular group (or individuals) and regulates the activities, and perhaps the speech, of that group. It does so, however, because of the group's past actions in the context of a specific dispute between real parties. The parties seeking the injunction assert a violation of their rights; the court hearing the action is charged with fashioning a remedy for a specific deprivation, not with the drafting of a statute addressed to the general public.

The fact that the injunction in the present case did not prohibit activities of those demonstrating in favor of abortion is justly attributable to the lack of any similar demonstrations by those in favor of abortion, and of any consequent request that their demonstrations be regulated by injunction. There is no suggestion in this record that Florida law would not equally restrain similar conduct directed at a target having nothing to do with abortion; none of the restrictions imposed by the court were directed at the contents of petitioner's message.

Our principal inquiry in determining content neutrality is whether the government has adopted a regulation of speech "without reference to the content of the regulated speech." ... We thus look to the government's purpose as the threshold consideration. Here, the state court imposed restrictions on petitioners incidental to their antiabortion message because they repeatedly violated the court's original order. That petitioners all share the same viewpoint regarding abortion does not in itself demonstrate that some invidious content or viewpoint-based purpose motivated the issuance of the order. It suggests only that those in the group whose conduct violated the court's order happen to share the same opinion regarding abortions being performed at the clinic. In short, the fact that the injunction covered people with a particular viewpoint does not itself render the injunction content or viewpoint based. ...[2]Accordingly, the injunction issued in this case does not

[2] We also decline to adopt the prior restraint analysis urged by petitioners. Prior restraints do often take the form of injunctions. See, e.g., New York Times Co. v. United States, 403 U. S. 713 (1971)(refusing to enjoin publications of the "Pentagon Papers"); Vance v. Universal Amusement Co., 445 U. S. 308 (1980) (per curiam) (holding that Texas public nuisance statute which authorized state judges, on the basis of a showing that a theater had exhibited obscene films in the past, to enjoin its future exhibition of films not yet found to be obscene was unconstitutional as authorizing an invalid prior restraint.) Not all injunctions which may incidentally affect expression, however, are "prior restraints" in the sense that that term was used in *New York Times Co.*, supra, or *Vance*, supra. Here petitioners are not prevented from expressing their message in any one of several different ways; they are simply prohibited from expressing it within the 36–foot buffer zone. Moreover, the injunction

demand the level of heightened scrutiny set forth in Perry Education Assn., 460 U. S., at 45. And we proceed to discuss the standard which does govern.

III

If this were a content-neutral, generally applicable statute, instead of an injunctive order, its constitutionality would be assessed under the standard set forth in Ward v. Rock Against Racism,[491 U.S.] at 791, and similar cases. Given that the forum around the clinic is a traditional public forum ... we would determine whether the time, place, and manner regulations were "narrowly tailored to serve a significant governmental interest." ...

There are obvious differences, however, between an injunction and a generally applicable ordinance. Ordinances represent a legislative choice regarding the promotion of particular societal interests. Injunctions, by contrast, are remedies imposed for violations (or threatened violations) of a legislative or judicial decree. ...Injunctions also carry greater risks of censorship and discriminatory application than do general ordinances. Injunctions, of course, have some advantages over generally applicable statutes in that they can be tailored by a trial judge to afford more precise relief than a statute where a violation of the law has already occurred. ...

We believe that these differences require a somewhat more stringent application of general First Amendment principles in this context. In past cases evaluating injunctions restricting speech ... we have relied upon such general principles while also seeking to ensure that the injunction was no broader than necessary to achieve its desired goals. ...Our close attention to the fit between the objectives of an injunction and the restrictions it imposes on speech is consistent with the general rule, quite apart from First Amendment considerations, "that injunctive relief should be no more burdensome to the defendants than necessary to provide complete relief to the plaintiffs." ... Accordingly, when evaluating a content-neutral injunction, we think that our standard time, place, and manner analysis is not sufficiently rigorous. We must ask instead whether the challenged provisions of the injunction burden no more speech than necessary to serve a significant government interest. ...

Both Justice Stevens and Justice Scalia disagree with the standard we announce, for policy reasons. Justice Stevens believes that "injunctive relief should be judged by a more lenient standard than legislation," because injunctions are imposed on individuals or groups who have engaged in illegal activity. "Justice Scalia, by contrast, believes that content-neutral injunctions are 'at least as deserving of strict scrutiny as a statutory, content-based restriction.'" Justice Scalia bases his belief on the danger that injunctions, even though they might not "attack content as content," may be used to suppress particular ideas; that individual judges should not be trusted to impose injunctions in this context; and that an injunction is procedurally more difficult to challenge than a statute. We believe that consideration of all of the differences and similarities between statutes and injunctions supports, as a matter of policy, the standard we apply here.

Justice Scalia ... cites a number of cases in which we have struck down, with little or no elaboration, prior restraints on free expression. As we have explained, however, we do not believe that this injunction constitutes a prior

---

was issued not because of the content of petitioners' expression, as was the case in *New York Times Co.* and *Vance,* but because of their prior unlawful conduct.

restraint, and we therefore believe that the "heavy presumption" against its constitutionality does not obtain here. See n. 2, supra.

. . .

The Florida Supreme Court concluded that numerous significant government interests are protected by the injunction. It noted that the State has a strong interest in protecting a woman's freedom to seek lawful medical or counseling services in connection with her pregnancy. The State also has a strong interest in ensuring the public safety and order, in promoting the free flow of traffic on public streets and sidewalks, and in protecting the property rights of all its citizens. In addition, the court believed that the State's strong interest in residential privacy, acknowledged in Frisby v. Schultz, 487 U. S. 474 (1988), applied by analogy to medical privacy. The court observed that while targeted picketing of the home threatens the psychological well-being of the "captive" resident, targeted picketing of a hospital or clinic threatens not only the psychological, but the physical well-being of the patient held "captive" by medical circumstance. We agree with the Supreme Court of Florida that the combination of these governmental interests is quite sufficient to justify an appropriately tailored injunction to protect them. We now examine each contested provision of the injunction to see if it burdens more speech than necessary to accomplish its goal.

. . .

A

1

We begin with the 36–foot buffer zone. . . . This speech-free buffer zone requires that petitioners move to the other side of Dixie Way and away from the driveway of the clinic, where the state court found that they repeatedly had interfered with the free access of patients and staff. . . . The buffer zone also applies to private property to the north and west of the clinic property. We examine each portion of the buffer zone separately.

We have noted a distinction between the type of focused picketing banned from the buffer zone and the type of generally disseminated communication that cannot be completely banned in public places, such as handbilling and solicitation. . . . Here the picketing is directed primarily at patients and staff of the clinic.

The 36–foot buffer zone protecting the entrances to the clinic and the parking lot is a means of protecting unfettered ingress to and egress from the clinic, and ensuring that petitioners do not block traffic on Dixie Way. . . .

The need for a complete buffer zone near the clinic entrances and driveway may be debatable, but some deference must be given to the state court's familiarity with the facts and the background of the dispute between the parties even under our heightened review. . . . On balance, we hold that the 36–foot buffer zone around the clinic entrances and driveway burdens no more speech than necessary to accomplish the governmental interest at stake.

. . .

2

The inclusion of private property on the back and side of the clinic in the 36–foot buffer zone raises different concerns. The accepted purpose of the buffer zone is to protect access to the clinic and to facilitate the orderly flow of traffic on Dixie Way. Patients and staff wishing to reach the clinic do not have to cross the private property abutting the clinic property on the north and west, and nothing in the record indicates that petitioners' activities on the private property have obstructed access to the clinic. . . .We hold that on the record before us the 36–foot buffer zone as applied to the private property to the north and west of the clinic burdens more speech than necessary to protect access to the clinic.

B

In response to high noise levels outside the clinic, the state court restrained the petitioners from "singing, chanting, whistling, shouting, yelling, use of bullhorns, auto horns, sound amplification equipment or other sounds or images observable to or within earshot of the patients inside the [c]linic" during the hours of 7:30 a.m. through noon on Mondays through Saturdays. . . .Noise control is particularly important around hospitals and medical facilities during surgery and recovery periods . . .

We hold that the limited noise restrictions imposed by the state court order burden no more speech than necessary to ensure the health and well-being of the patients at the clinic. The First Amendment does not demand that patients at a medical facility undertake Herculean efforts to escape the cacophony of political protests. . . .

C

The same, however, cannot be said for the "images observable" provision of the state court's order. Clearly, threats to patients or their families, however communicated, are proscribable under the First Amendment. But rather than prohibiting the display of signs that could be interpreted as threats or veiled threats, the state court issued a blanket ban on all "images observable." This broad prohibition on all "images observable" burdens more speech than necessary to achieve the purpose of limiting threats to clinic patients or their families. Similarly, if the blanket ban on "images observable" was intended to reduce the level of anxiety and hypertension suffered by the patients inside the clinic, it would still fail. The only plausible reason a patient would be bothered by "images observable" inside the clinic would be if the patient found the expression contained in such images disagreeable. But it is much easier for the clinic to pull its curtains than for a patient to stop up her ears, and no more is required to avoid seeing placards through the windows of the clinic. This provision of the injunction violates the First Amendment.

D

The state court ordered that petitioners refrain from physically approaching any person seeking services of the clinic "unless such person indicates a desire to communicate" in an area within 300 feet of the clinic. The state court was attempting to prevent clinic patients and staff from being "stalked" or "shadowed" by the petitioners as they approached the clinic. . . .

But it is difficult, indeed, to justify a prohibition on all uninvited approaches of persons seeking the services of the clinic, regardless of how peaceful the contact may be, without burdening more speech than necessary to prevent intimidation and to ensure access to the clinic. Absent evidence that the protesters' speech is independently proscribable (i.e., "fighting words" or threats), or is so infused with violence as to be indistinguishable from a threat of physical harm, . . . this provision cannot stand. . . .The "consent" requirement alone invalidates this provision; it burdens more speech than is necessary to prevent intimidation and to ensure access to the clinic.

E

The final substantive regulation challenged by petitioners relates to a prohibition against picketing, demonstrating, or using sound amplification equipment within 300 feet of the residences of clinic staff. The prohibition also covers impeding access to streets that provide the sole access to streets on which those residences are located. The same analysis applies to the use of sound amplification equipment here as that discussed above: the government may simply demand that petitioners turn down the volume if the protests overwhelm the neighborhood. . . .

. . .

. . . [T]he 300–foot zone around the residences in this case is much larger than the zone provided for in the ordinance which we approved in *Frisby*. The ordinance at issue there . . . was limited to "focused picketing taking place solely in front of a particular residence." . . . By contrast, the 300–foot zone would ban "[g]eneral marching through residential neighborhoods, or even walking a route in front of an entire block of houses." . . . The record before us does not contain sufficient justification for this broad a ban on picketing; it appears that a limitation on the time, duration of picketing, and number of pickets outside a smaller zone could have accomplished the desired result.

IV

Petitioners also challenge the state court's order as being vague and overbroad. They object to the portion of the injunction making it applicable to those acting "in concert" with the named parties. But petitioners themselves are named parties in the order, and they therefore lack standing to challenge a portion of the order applying to persons who are not parties. Nor is that phrase subject, at the behest of petitioners, to a challenge for "overbreadth"; the phrase itself does not prohibit any conduct, but is simply directed at unnamed parties who might later be found to be acting "in concert" with the named parties. . . .

. . .

V

In sum, we uphold the noise restrictions and the 36–foot buffer zone around the clinic entrances and driveway because they burden no more speech than necessary to eliminate the unlawful conduct targeted by the state court's injunction. We strike down as unconstitutional the 36–foot buffer zone as applied to the private property to the north and west of the clinic, the "images observable" provision, the 300–foot no-approach zone around the clinic, and the 300–foot buffer zone around the residences, because these provisions sweep more broadly than necessary to accomplish the permissible goals of the injunction. Accordingly, the judgment of the Florida Supreme Court is

Affirmed in part, and reversed in part.*

Justice Stevens, concurring in part and dissenting in part.

. . . I . . . join Parts II and IV of the Court's opinion . . . I part company with the Court, however, on its . . . enunciation of the applicable standard of review.

---

* A brief concurring opinion by Justice   is omitted.
Souter, who also joined the Court's opinion,

I

I agree with the Court that a different standard governs First Amendment challenges to generally applicable legislation than the standard that measures such challenges to judicial remedies for proven wrongdoing . . . . . Unlike the Court, however, I believe that injunctive relief should be judged by a more lenient standard than legislation. As the Court notes, legislation is imposed on an entire community, regardless of individual culpability. By contrast, injunctions apply solely to an individual or a limited group of individuals who, by engaging in illegal conduct, have been judicially deprived of some liberty-the normal consequence of illegal activity. Given this distinction, a statute prohibiting demonstrations within 36 feet of an abortion clinic would probably violate the First Amendment, but an injunction directed at a limited group of persons who have engaged in unlawful conduct in a similar zone might well be constitutional.

The standard governing injunctions has two obvious dimensions. On the one hand, the injunction should be no more burdensome than necessary to provide complete relief, . . . In a First Amendment context, as in any other, the propriety of the remedy depends almost entirely on the character of the violation and the likelihood of its recurrence. For this reason, standards fashioned to determine the constitutionality of statutes should not be used to evaluate injunctions.

On the other hand, even when an injunction impinges on constitutional rights, more than "a simple proscription against the precise conduct previously pursued" may be required . . . [R]epeated violations may justify sanctions that might be invalid if applied to a first offender or if enacted by the legislature. . . .

In this case, the trial judge heard three days of testimony and found that petitioners not only had engaged in tortious conduct, but also had repeatedly violated an earlier injunction. The injunction is thus twice removed from a legislative proscription applicable to the general public and should be judged by a standard that gives appropriate deference to the judge's unique familiarity with the facts.

II

The second question presented by the certiorari petition asks whether the "consent requirement before speech is permitted" within a 300-foot buffer zone around the clinic unconstitutionally infringes on free speech. . . .[T]he Court seems to suggest that, even in a more narrowly defined zone, such a consent requirement is constitutionally impermissible. . . .

That paragraph does not purport to prohibit speech; it prohibits a species of conduct. Specifically, it prohibits petitioners "from physically approaching any person seeking the services of the Clinic unless such person indicates a desire to communicate by approaching or by inquiring" of petitioners. The meaning of the term "physically approaching" is explained by the detailed prohibition that applies when the patient refuses to converse with, or accept delivery of literature from, petitioners. . . .

Petitioners' "counseling" of the clinic's patients is a form of expression analogous to labor picketing. It is a mixture of conduct and communication. . . .Just as it protects picketing, the First Amendment protects the speaker's right to offer "sidewalk counseling" to all passersby. That protection, however, does not encompass attempts to abuse an unreceptive or captive audience, at least under the circumstances of this case. . . .

. . .

. . . I thus conclude that, under the circumstances of this case, the prohibition against "physically approaching" in the 300–foot zone around the clinic withstands petitioners' First Amendment challenge. I therefore dissent from Part III–D.

III

. . .

IV

For the reasons stated, I concur in Parts I, II, III–E, and IV of the Court's opinion, and respectfully dissent from the remaining portions.

Justice Scalia, with whom Justice Kennedy and Justice Thomas join, concurring in the judgment in part and dissenting in part.

The judgment in today's case has an appearance of moderation and Solomonic wisdom, upholding as it does some portions of the injunction while disallowing others. That appearance is deceptive. The entire injunction in this case departs so far from the established course of our jurisprudence that in any other context it would have been regarded as a candidate for summary reversal.

But the context here is abortion. . . . Today's decision . . . makes it painfully clear that no legal rule or doctrine is safe from ad hoc nullification by this Court when an occasion for its application arises in a case involving state regulation of abortion. . . . Today the ad hoc nullification machine claims its latest, greatest, and most surprising victim: the First Amendment.

Because I believe that the judicial creation of a 36–foot zone in which only a particular group, which had broken no law, cannot exercise its rights of speech, assembly, and association, and the judicial enactment of a noise prohibition, applicable to that group and that group alone, are profoundly at odds with our First Amendment precedents and traditions, I dissent.

I

. . .

The videotape and the rest of the record, including the trial court's findings, show that a great many forms of expression and conduct occurred in the vicinity of the clinic. These include singing, chanting, praying, shouting, the playing of music both from the clinic and from handheld boom boxes, speeches, peaceful picketing, communication of familiar political messages, handbilling, persuasive speech directed at opposing groups on the issue of abortion, efforts to persuade individuals not to have abortions, personal testimony, interviews with the press, and media efforts to report on the protest. What the videotape, the rest of the record, and the trial court's findings do not contain is any suggestion of violence near the clinic, nor do they establish any attempt to prevent entry or exit.

II

A

. . .

. . . The Court begins, in Part II of the opinion, by considering petitioners' contention that, since the restriction is content based, strict scrutiny should govern. It rejects the premise, and hence rejects the conclusion. It then proceeds, in Part III, to examination of respondents' contention that plain old intermediate scrutiny should apply. It says no to that, too, because of the distinctive characteristics of injunctions that it discusses, and hence decides to supplement intermediate scrutiny with intermediate-intermediate scrutiny. But this neatly staged progression overlooks an obvious option. The real question in this case is not whether intermediate scrutiny, which the Court assumes to be some kind of default standard, should be supplemented because of the distinctive characteristics of injunctions; but rather whether those distinctive characteristics are not, for reasons of both policy and precedent, fully as good a reason as "content-basis" for demanding strict scrutiny. . . .

. . . [A] restriction upon speech imposed by injunction (whether nominally content based or nominally content neutral) is at least as deserving of strict scrutiny as a statutory, content-based restriction.

That is so for several reasons: The danger of content-based statutory restrictions upon speech is that they may be designed and used precisely to suppress the ideas in question rather than to achieve any other proper governmental aim. But that same danger exists with injunctions. Although a speech-restricting injunction may not attack content as content (in the present case, as I shall discuss, even that is not true), it lends itself just as readily to the targeted suppression of particular ideas. When a judge, on the motion of an employer, enjoins picketing at the site of a labor dispute, he enjoins (and he knows he is enjoining) the expression of pro-union views. Such targeting of one or the other side of an ideological dispute cannot readily be achieved in speech-restricting general legislation except by making content the basis of the restriction; it is achieved in speech-restricting injunctions almost invariably. The proceedings before us here illustrate well enough what I mean. The injunction was sought against a single-issue advocacy group by persons and organizations with a business or social interest in suppressing that group's point of view.

The second reason speech-restricting injunctions are at least as deserving of strict scrutiny is obvious enough: they are the product of individual judges rather than of legislatures-and often of judges who have been chagrined by prior disobedience of their orders. The right to free speech should not lightly be placed within the control of a single man or woman. And the third reason is that the injunction is a much more powerful weapon than a statute, and so should be subjected to greater safeguards. Normally, when injunctions are enforced through contempt proceedings, only the defense of factual innocence is available. . . . Thus, persons subject to a speech-restricting injunction who have not the money or not the time to lodge an immediate appeal face a Hobson's choice: they must remain silent, since if they speak their First Amendment rights are no defense in subsequent contempt proceedings. This is good reason to require the strictest standard for issuance of such orders.

. . . [T]he Court errs in thinking that the vice of content-based statutes is that they necessarily have the invidious purpose of suppressing particular ideas. . . . The vice of content-based legislation—what renders it deserving of the high standard of strict scrutiny—is not that it is always used for invidious, thought-control purposes, but that it lends itself to use for those purposes. And, because of the unavoidable "targeting" discussed above, precisely the same is true of the speech-restricting injunction.

. . . .

III

. . .

B

I turn now to the Court's performance in the present case. I am content to evaluate it under the lax (intermediate-intermediate scrutiny) standard that the Court has adopted, because even by that distorted light it is inadequate.

. . .

To sum up: The interests assertedly protected by the supplementary injunction did not include any interest whose impairment was a violation of Florida law or of a Florida-court injunction. Unless the Court intends today to overturn long-settled jurisprudence, that means that the interests cannot possibly qualify as "significant interests" under the Court's new standard.

C

Finally, I turn to the Court's application of the second part of its test: whether the provisions of the injunction "burden no more speech than necessary" to serve the significant interest protected.

. . . With regard to the 36–foot speech-free zone, . . . the test which the Court sets for itself has not been met.

Assuming a "significant state interest" of the sort cognizable for injunction purposes (i.e., one protected by a law that has been or is threatened to be violated) in both (1) keeping pedestrians off the paved portion of Dixie Way, and (2) enabling cars to cross the public sidewalk at the clinic's driveways without having to slow down or come to even a "momentary" stop, there are surely a number of ways to protect those interests short of banishing the entire protest demonstration from the 36–foot zone. . . .

. . .

For these reasons, I dissent from that portion of the judgment upholding parts of the injunction.

THE HECKLER'S VETO

In Feiner v. New York, 340 U.S. 315 (1951), the Court sustained the disorderly conduct conviction of a speaker who disobeyed a police order to stop speaking. The Court relied on findings by the state courts that the officers had been motivated solely by "a proper concern for the preservation of order." The dissent argued that Feiner, who had called the mayor a bum, characterized the American Legion as a "Nazi Gestapo," and said that "Negroes . . . should rise up in arms and fight for their rights," had been sentenced to jail for expressing his unpopular views to an unsympathetic audience, given the slim evidence of a potential for violence.

In the 1960s, *Feiner* was distinguished in Southern cases arising from the civil rights movement. Despite evidence of more likelihood of disorder than in *Feiner,* Edwards v. South Carolina, 372 U.S. 229 (1963), reversed the breach of peace convictions of Black students who marched to the South Carolina State House, in view of a hostile crowd, to protest racial discrimination. The Court stated that the situation in *Edwards* was a "far cry from the situation in Feiner v. New York." The Court relied on *Edwards* in Cox v. Louisiana (Cox I), 379 U.S. 536 (1965), reversing the conviction of 23 of 2000 Black students assembled near a courthouse to protest lunch counter segregation.

SECTION 2.   THE NON-TRADITIONAL FORUM—SPEECH ACTIVITIES IN PUBLIC PROPERTY OTHER THAN PARKS AND STREETS

Adderley v. Florida
385 U.S. 39, 87 S.Ct. 242, 17 L.Ed.2d 149 (1966).

Mr. Justice Black delivered the opinion of the Court.

Petitioners ... were convicted on a charge of "trespass with a malicious and mischievous intent" upon the premises of the county jail contrary to § 821.18 of the Florida statutes.... Petitioners, apparently all students of the Florida A. & M. University in Tallahassee, had gone from the school to the jail about a mile away, along with many other students, to "demonstrate" at the jail their protests of arrests of other protesting students the day before, and perhaps to protest more generally against state and local policies and practices of racial segregation, including segregation of the jail. The county sheriff, legal custodian of the jail and jail grounds, tried to persuade the students to leave the jail grounds. When this did not work, he notified them that they must leave, that if they did not leave he would arrest them for trespassing, and that if they resisted he would charge them with that as well. Some of the students left but others, including petitioners, remained and they were arrested. On appeal the convictions were affirmed....

Petitioners have insisted from the beginning of this case that it is controlled by and must be reversed because of our prior cases of Edwards v. South Carolina, 372 U.S. 229, and Cox v. Louisiana, 379 U.S. 536, 559. We cannot agree.

... In *Edwards,* the demonstrators went to the South Carolina State Capitol grounds to protest. In this case they went to the jail. Traditionally, state capitol grounds are open to the public. Jails, built for security purposes, are not. The demonstrators at the South Carolina Capitol went in through a public driveway and as they entered they were told by state officials there that they had a right as citizens to go through the State House grounds as long as they were peaceful. Here the demonstrators entered the jail grounds through a driveway used only for jail purposes and without warning to or permission from the sheriff. More importantly, South Carolina sought to prosecute its State Capitol demonstrators by charging them with the common-law crime of breach of the peace. The South Carolina breach-of-the-peace statute was ... struck down as being so broad and all-embracing as to jeopardize speech, press, assembly and petition,.... And it was on this same ground of vagueness that in Cox v. Louisiana, supra, at 551–552, the Louisiana breach-of-the-peace law used to prosecute Cox was invalidated.

The Florida trespass statute under which these petitioners were charged cannot be challenged on this ground. It is aimed at conduct of one limited kind, that is, for one person or persons to trespass upon the property of another with a malicious and mischievous intent. There is no lack of notice in this law, nothing to entrap or fool the unwary.

Petitioners seem to argue that the Florida trespass law is void for vagueness because it requires a trespass to be "with a malicious and mischievous intent...." But these words do not broaden the scope of trespass so as to make it cover a multitude of types of conduct as does the common-law breach-of-the-peace charge. On the contrary, these words narrow the scope of the offense. . . .

. . .

. . . [T]he jury was authorized to find that the State had proven every essential element of the crime, as it was defined by the state court. That interpretation is, of course, binding on us, leaving only the question of whether conviction of the state offense, thus defined, unconstitutionally deprives petitioners of their rights to freedom of speech, press, assembly or petition. We hold it does not. The sheriff, as jail custodian, had power, as the state courts have here held, to direct that this large crowd of people get off the grounds. There is not a shred of evidence in this record that this power was exercised, or that its exercise was sanctioned by the lower courts, because the sheriff objected to what was being sung or said by the demonstrators or because he disagreed with the objectives of their protest. The record reveals that he objected only to their presence on that part of the jail grounds reserved for jail uses. There is no evidence at all that on any other occasion had similarly large groups of the public been permitted to gather on this portion of the jail grounds for any purpose. Nothing in the Constitution of the United States prevents Florida from even-handed enforcement of its general trespass statute against those refusing to obey the sheriff's order to remove themselves from what amounted to the curtilage of the jailhouse. The State, no less than a private owner of property, has power to preserve the property under its control for the use to which it is lawfully dedicated. For this reason there is no merit to the petitioners' argument that they had a constitutional right to stay on the property, over the jail custodian's objections, because this "area chosen for the peaceful civil rights demonstration was not only 'reasonable' but also particularly appropriate. . . ." Such an argument has as its major unarticulated premise the assumption that people who want to propagandize protests or views have a constitutional right to do so whenever and however and wherever they please. That concept of constitutional law was vigorously and forthrightly rejected in two of the cases petitioners rely on, Cox v. Louisiana, supra, at 554–555 and 563–564. We reject it again. The United States Constitution does not forbid a State to control the use of its own property for its own lawful nondiscriminatory purpose.

These judgments are affirmed.

Mr. Justice Douglas, with whom The Chief Justice, Mr. Justice Brennan, and Mr. Justice Fortas concur, dissenting.

. . .

The jailhouse, like an executive mansion, a legislative chamber, a courthouse, or the statehouse itself (Edwards v. South Carolina, supra) is one of the seats of government whether it be the Tower of London, the Bastille, or a small county jail. And when it houses political prisoners or those who many think are unjustly held, it is an obvious center for protest. . . .

There is no question that petitioners had as their purpose a protest against the arrest of Florida A. & M. students for trying to integrate public theatres. The sheriff's testimony indicates that he well understood the purpose of the rally. . . . There was no violence; no threats of violence; no attempted jail break; no storming of a prison; no plan or plot to do anything but protest. . . .

We do violence to the First Amendment when we permit this "petition for redress of grievances" to be turned into a trespass action. . . .

. . .

There may be some public places which are so clearly committed to other purposes that their use for the airing of grievances is anomalous. There may be some instances in which assemblies and petitions for redress of grievances are not consistent with other necessary purposes of public property. A noisy meeting may be out of keeping with the serenity of the statehouse or the quiet of the courthouse. . . . But this is quite different from saying that all public places are off limits to people with grievances. . . . And it is farther yet from saying that the "custodian" of the public property in his discretion can decide when public places shall be used for the communication of ideas, especially the constitutional right to assemble and petition for redress of grievances. . . .

VIEWPOINT–NEUTRAL RULES DENYING ACCESS TO NON–TRADITIONAL PUBLIC FORA

From the 1966 decision in *Adderley* until 1992 the Court consistently refused to classify any public property other than the parks and streets as a traditional public forum. Moreover, viewpoint-neutral rules restricting access to non-traditional public fora were nearly-consistently upheld under an approach that sustained those rules if reasonably consistent with the government's interest in preserving the property for non-speech uses. (The one extreme exception was Board of Airport Commrs. of Los Angeles v. Jews for Jesus, Inc., 482 U.S. 569 (1987), which struck down an airport rule forbidding "all First Amendment activities" in the terminal. The rule literally prohibited talking and reading.)

The cases include: Greer v. Spock, 424 U.S. 828 (1976) (regulation forbidding demonstrations and political speeches on military base); Heffron v. International Society for Krishna Consciousness, 452 U.S. 640 (1981) (state fair rule limiting sale or distribution of written materials to fixed locations); Perry Education Association v. Perry Local Educators' Association, 460 U.S. 37 (1983) (teachers' organization other than elected bargaining representative forbidden to use school mailboxes to communicate with teachers); Los Angeles v. Taxpayers for Vincent, 466 U.S. 789 (1984) (municipal ordinance forbids placing signs on public property); Cornelius v. NAACP Legal Defense and Educational Fund, 473 U.S. 788 (1985) (legal defense and advocacy organizations excluded from participating in federal employees' charity drive); Ward v. Rock Against Racism, 491 U.S. 781 (1989) (regulation of music volume at public amphitheater); United States v. Kokinda, 497 U.S. 720 (1990) (postal regulation forbids soliciting charitable contributions on postal premises).

International Society for Krishna Consciousness, Inc. v. Lee

505 U.S. 672, 112 S.Ct. 2701, 120 L.Ed.2d 541 (1992).

Chief Justice Rehnquist delivered the opinion of the Court.

In this case we consider whether an airport terminal operated by a public authority is a public forum and whether a regulation prohibiting solicitation in the interior of an airport terminal violates the First Amendment.

The relevant facts in this case are not in dispute. Petitioner International Society for Krishna Consciousness, Inc. (ISKCON) is a not-for-profit religious corporation whose members perform a ritual known as sankirtan. The ritual consists of "'going into public places, disseminating religious literature and soliciting funds to support the religion.'" The primary purpose of this ritual is raising funds for the movement.

Respondent Walter Lee ... was the police superintendent of the Port Authority of New York and New Jersey and was charged with enforcing the regulation at issue. The Port Authority owns and operates three major airports in the greater New York City area....

. . .

The Port Authority has adopted a regulation forbidding within the terminals the repetitive solicitation of money or distribution of literature. The regulation states:

"1. The following conduct is prohibited within the interior areas of buildings or structures at an air terminal if conducted by a person to or with passers-by in a continuous or repetitive manner:

"(a) The sale or distribution of any merchandise, including but not limited to jewelry, food stuffs, candles, flowers, badges and clothing.

"(b) The sale or distribution of flyers, brochures, pamphlets, books or any other printed or written material.

"(c) Solicitation and receipt of funds."

The regulation governs only the terminals; the Port Authority permits solicitation and distribution on the sidewalks outside the terminal buildings. The regulation effectively prohibits petitioner from performing sankirtan in the terminals. As a result, petitioner brought suit seeking declaratory and injunctive relief ... [T]he District Court granted petitioner summary judgment.

The Court of Appeals affirmed in part and reversed in part. 925 F.2d 576 (1991). Relying on our recent decision in United States v. Kokinda, 497 U.S. 720 (1990), a divided panel concluded that the terminals are not public fora. As a result, the restrictions were required only to satisfy a standard of reasonableness. The Court of Appeals then concluded that, presented with the issue, this Court would find that the ban on solicitation was reasonable, but the ban on distribution was not. Petitioner sought certiorari respecting the Court of Appeals' decision that the terminals are not public fora and upholding the solicitation ban. Respondent cross-petitioned respecting the court's holding striking down the distribution ban.... [3]

It is uncontested that the solicitation at issue in this case is a form of speech protected under the First Amendment. Heffron v. International Society for Krishna Consciousness, Inc., 452 U.S. 640 (1981); ... Schaumburg v. Citizens for a Better Environment, 444 U.S. 620, 629 (1980) ... But it is also well settled that the government need not permit all forms of speech on property that it owns and controls.... Where the government is acting as a proprietor, managing its internal operations, rather than acting as lawmaker with the power to regulate or license, its action will not be subjected to the heightened review to which its actions as a lawmaker may be subject.... Thus, we have upheld a ban on political advertisements in city-operated transit

---

[3] We deal here only with ISKCON's petition raising the permissibility of solicitation. Respondent's cross-petition concerning the leafletting ban is disposed of in the companion case, *Lee v. International Society for Krishna Consciousness, Inc.*

vehicles, Lehman v. City of Shaker Heights, 418 U.S. 298 (1974), even though the city permitted other types of advertising on those vehicles. Similarly, we have permitted a school district to limit access to an internal mail system used to communicate with teachers employed by the district. Perry Education Assn. v. Perry Local Educators' Ass'n, 460 U.S. 37 (1983).

These cases reflect, either implicitly or explicitly, a "forum-based" approach for assessing restrictions that the government seeks to place on the use of its property. Cornelius v. NAACP Legal Defense and Educational Fund, Inc., 473 U.S. 788, 800 (1985). Under this approach, regulation of speech on government property that has traditionally been available for public expression is subject to the highest scrutiny. Such regulations survive only if they are narrowly drawn to achieve a compelling state interest.... The second category of public property is the designated public forum, whether of a limited or unlimited character—property that the state has opened for expressive activity by part or all of the public. ...Regulation of such property is subject to the same limitations as that governing a traditional public forum. ...Finally, there is all remaining public property. Limitations on expressive activity conducted on this last category of property must survive only a much more limited review. The challenged regulation need only be reasonable, as long as the regulation is not an effort to suppress the speaker's activity due to disagreement with the speaker's view. ...

The parties do not disagree that this is the proper framework. Rather, they disagree whether the airport terminals are public fora or nonpublic fora. They also disagree whether the regulation survives the "reasonableness" review governing nonpublic fora, should that prove the appropriate category. Like the Court of Appeals, we conclude that the terminals are nonpublic fora and that the regulation reasonably limits solicitation.

The suggestion that the government has a high burden in justifying speech restrictions relating to traditional public fora made its first appearance in Hague v. Committee for Industrial Organization, 307 U.S. 496, 515, 516 (1939). Justice Roberts, concluding that individuals have a right to use "streets and parks for communication of views," reasoned that such a right flowed from the fact that "streets and parks ... have immemorially been held in trust for the use of the public and, time out of mind, have been used for purposes of assembly, communicating thoughts between citizens, and discussing public questions." We confirmed this observation in Frisby v. Schultz, 487 U.S. 474, 481 (1988), where we held that a residential street was a public forum.

Our recent cases provide additional guidance on the characteristics of a public forum. In *Cornelius* we noted that a traditional public forum is property that has as "a principal purpose ... the free exchange of ideas." ... Moreover, consistent with the notion that the government—like other property owners— "has power to preserve the property under its control for the use to which it is lawfully dedicated," ... the government does not create a public forum by inaction. Nor is a public forum created "whenever members of the public are permitted freely to visit a place owned or operated by the Government." ... The decision to create a public forum must instead be made "by intentionally opening a nontraditional forum for public discourse." ... Finally, we have recognized that the location of property also has bearing because separation from acknowledged public areas may serve to indicate that the separated property is a special enclave, subject to greater restriction. ...

These precedents foreclose the conclusion that airport terminals are public fora. Reflecting the general growth of the air travel industry, airport terminals have only recently achieved their contemporary size and character. ...But given the lateness with which the modern air terminal has made its appearance, it hardly qualifies for the description of having "immemorially ... time out of mind" been held in the public trust and used for purposes of expressive activity. ...Moreover, even within the rather short history of air transport, it is only "[i]n recent years [that] it has become a common practice for various religious and non-profit organizations to use commercial airports as a forum for the distribution of literature, the solicitation of funds, the proselytizing of new members, and other similar activities." ... Thus, the tradition of airport activity does not demonstrate that airports have historically been made available for speech activity. Nor can we say that these particular terminals, or airport terminals generally, have been intentionally opened by their operators to such activity; the frequent and continuing litigation evidencing the operators' objections belies any such claim. In short, there can be no argument that society's time-tested judgment, expressed through acquiescence in a continuing practice, has resolved the issue in petitioner's favor.

Petitioner attempts to circumvent the history and practice governing airport activity by pointing our attention to the variety of speech activity that it claims historically occurred at various "transportation nodes" such as rail stations, bus stations, wharves, and Ellis Island. Even if we were inclined to accept petitioner's historical account describing speech activity at these locations, an account respondent contests, we think that such evidence is of little import for two reasons. First, much of the evidence is irrelevant to public fora analysis, because sites such as bus and rail terminals traditionally have had private ownership. ...The development of privately owned parks that ban speech activity would not change the public fora status of publicly held parks. But the reverse is also true. The practices of privately held transportation centers do not bear on the government's regulatory authority over a publicly owned airport.

Second, the relevant unit for our inquiry is an airport, not "transportation nodes" generally. When new methods of transportation develop, new methods for accommodating that transportation are also likely to be needed. And with each new step, it therefore will be a new inquiry whether the transportation necessities are compatible with various kinds of expressive activity. To make a category of "transportation nodes," therefore, would unjustifiably elide what may prove to be critical differences of which we should rightfully take account. The "security magnet," for example, is an airport commonplace that lacks a counterpart in bus terminals and train stations. And public access to air terminals is also not infrequently restricted—just last year the Federal Aviation Administration required airports for a 4-month period to limit access to areas normally publicly accessible. ...To blithely equate airports with other transportation centers, therefore, would be a mistake.

The differences among such facilities are unsurprising since ... airports are commercial establishments funded by users fees and designed to make a regulated profit, and where nearly all who visit do so for some travel related purpose. As commercial enterprises, airports must provide services attractive to the marketplace. In light of this, it cannot fairly be said that an airport terminal has as a principal purpose "promoting the free exchange of ideas." ... To the contrary, ... Port Authority management considers the purpose of the terminals to be the facilitation of passenger air travel, not the promotion of expression. ...Even if we look beyond the intent of the Port Authority to the manner in which the terminals have been operated, the terminals have never been dedicated (except under the threat of court order) to expression in the form sought to be exercised here: i.e., the solicitation of contributions and the distribution of literature.

The terminals here are far from atypical. Airport builders and managers focus their efforts on providing terminals that will contribute to efficient air travel. . . .Although many airports have expanded their function beyond merely contributing to efficient air travel, few have included among their purposes the designation of a forum for solicitation and distribution activities. Thus, we think that neither by tradition nor purpose can the terminals be described as satisfying the standards we have previously set out for identifying a public forum.

The restrictions here challenged, therefore, need only satisfy a requirement of reasonableness. [T]he restriction "'need only be reasonable; it need not be the most reasonable or the only reasonable limitation.'" . . . We have no doubt that under this standard the prohibition on solicitation passes muster.

We have on many prior occasions noted the disruptive effect that solicitation may have on business. . . .Passengers who wish to avoid the solicitor may have to alter their path, slowing both themselves and those around them. The result is that the normal flow of traffic is impeded. . . . This is especially so in an airport . . .

In addition, face-to-face solicitation presents risks of duress that are an appropriate target of regulation. The skillful, and unprincipled, solicitor can target the most vulnerable, including those accompanying children or those suffering physical impairment and who cannot easily avoid the solicitation. . . .The unsavory solicitor can also commit fraud through concealment of his affiliation or through deliberate efforts to shortchange those who agree to purchase. . . .Compounding this problem is the fact that, in an airport, the targets of such activity frequently are on tight schedules. This in turn makes such visitors unlikely to stop and formally complain to airport authorities. As a result, the airport faces considerable difficulty in achieving its legitimate interest in monitoring solicitation activity to assure that travelers are not interfered with unduly.

The Port Authority has concluded that its interest in monitoring the activities can best be accomplished by limiting solicitation and distribution to the sidewalk areas outside the terminals. This sidewalk area is frequented by an overwhelming percentage of airport users. Thus the resulting access of those who would solicit the general public is quite complete. In turn we think it would be odd to conclude that the Port Authority's terminal regulation is unreasonable despite the Port Authority having otherwise assured access to an area universally traveled.

The inconveniences to passengers and the burdens on Port Authority officials flowing from solicitation activity may seem small, but viewed against the fact that "pedestrian congestion is one of the greatest problems facing the three terminals," the Port Authority could reasonably worry that even such incremental effects would prove quite disruptive. Moreover, "the justification for the Rule should not be measured by the disorder that would result from granting an exemption solely to ISKCON." . . . For if petitioner is given access, so too must other groups. . . . As a result, we conclude that the solicitation ban is reasonable.

For the foregoing reasons, the judgment of the Court of Appeals sustaining the ban on solicitation in Port Authority terminals is

Affirmed.

Justice O'Connor, concurring . . .

In the decision below, the Court of Appeals upheld a ban on solicitation of funds within the airport terminals operated by the Port Authority of New York and New Jersey, but struck down a ban on the repetitive distribution of printed or written material within the terminals. I would affirm both parts of that judgment.

I ... agree that publicly owned airports are not public fora. Unlike public streets and parks, both of which our First Amendment jurisprudence has identified as "traditional public fora," airports do not count among their purposes the "free exchange of ideas,".... There is little doubt that airports are among those publicly owned facilities that could be closed to all except those who have legitimate business there.... Public access to airports is thus not "inherent in the open nature of the locations," as it is for most streets and parks, but is rather a "matter of grace by government officials." ... I also agree with the Court that the Port Authority has not expressly opened its airports to the types of expression at issue here and therefore has not created a "limited" or "designated" public forum relevant to this case.

For these reasons, the Port Authority's restrictions on solicitation and leafletting within the airport terminals do not qualify for the strict scrutiny that applies to restriction of speech in public fora. That airports are not public fora, however, does not mean that the government can restrict speech in whatever way it likes.... For example, in Board of Airport Commrs. of Los Angeles v. Jews for Jesus, Inc., 482 U.S. 569 (1987), we unanimously struck down a regulation that prohibited "all First Amendment activities" in the Los Angeles International Airport (LAX) without even reaching the question whether airports were public fora.... We found it "obvious that such a ban cannot be justified even if LAX were a nonpublic forum because no conceivable governmental interest would justify such an absolute prohibition of speech." Moreover, we have consistently stated that restrictions on speech in nonpublic fora are valid only if they are "reasonable" and "not an effort to suppress expression merely because public officials oppose the speaker's view." ... The determination that airports are not public fora thus only begins our inquiry.

... In this case, the "special attributes" and "surrounding circumstances" of the airports operated by the Port Authority are determinative. Not only has the Port Authority chosen not to limit access to the airports under its control, it has created a huge complex open to travelers and nontravelers alike. The airports house restaurants, cafeterias, snack bars, coffee shops, cocktail lounges, post offices, banks, telegraph offices, clothing shops, drug stores, food stores, nurseries, barber shops, currency exchanges, art exhibits, commercial advertising displays, bookstores, newsstands, dental offices and private clubs. The International Arrivals Building at JFK Airport even has two branches of Bloomingdale's.

We have said that a restriction on speech in a nonpublic forum is "reasonable" when it is "consistent with the [government's] legitimate interest in 'preserv[ing] the property ... for the use for which it is lawfully dedicated.' " ... Ordinarily, this inquiry is relatively straightforward, because we have almost always been confronted with cases where the fora at issue were discrete, single-purpose facilities.... The Port Authority urges that this case is no different and contends that it, too, has dedicated its airports to a single purpose—facilitating air travel—and that the speech it seeks to prohibit is not consistent with that purpose. But the wide range of activities promoted by the Port Authority is no more directly related to facilitating air travel than are the types of activities in which ISKCON wishes to engage.... In my view, the Port Authority is operating a shopping mall as well as an airport. The reasonableness inquiry, therefore, is not whether the restrictions on speech are "consistent with ... preserving the property" for air travel, ... but whether they are reasonably related to maintaining the multipurpose environment that the Port Authority has deliberately created.

Applying that standard, I agree with the Court . . . that the ban on solicitation is reasonable. Face-to-face solicitation is incompatible with the airport's functioning in a way that the other, permitted activities are not. . . . [T]he problems of congestion and fraud that we have identified with solicitation in other contexts have also proved true in the airports' experience. . . .

In my view, however, the regulation banning leafletting—or, in the Port Authority's words, the "continuous or repetitive . . . distribution of . . . printed or written material"—cannot be upheld as reasonable on this record. I therefore concur in the judgment . . . striking down that prohibition. . . . With the possible exception of avoiding litter, see Schneider v. State, 308 U.S. 147, 162 (1939), it is difficult to point to any problems intrinsic to the act of leafletting that would make it naturally incompatible with a large, multipurpose forum such as those at issue here.

We have only once before considered restrictions on speech in a nonpublic forum that sustained the kind of extensive, nonforum-related activity found in the Port Authority airports, and I believe that case is instructive. In Greer v. Spock, 424 U.S. 828 (1976), the Court held that even though certain parts of a military base were open to the public, they still did not constitute a public forum in light of "'the historically unquestioned power of [a] commanding officer summarily to exclude civilians from the area of his command.'" . . . The Court then proceeded to uphold a regulation banning the distribution of literature without the prior approval of the base commander. In so doing, the Court "emphasized" that the regulation on leafletting did "not authorize the Fort Dix authorities to prohibit the distribution of conventional political campaign literature." . . . In contrast, the regulation at issue in this case effects an absolute prohibition and is not supported by any independent justification outside of the problems caused by the accompanying solicitation.

Moreover, the Port Authority has not offered any justifications or record evidence to support its ban on the distribution of pamphlets alone. Its argument is focused instead on the problems created when literature is distributed in conjunction with a solicitation plea. . . . [T]he Port Authority has provided no independent reason for prohibiting leafletting . . . Because I cannot see how peaceful pamphleteering is incompatible with the multipurpose environment of the Port Authority airports, I cannot accept that a total ban on that activity is reasonable without an explanation as to why such a restriction "preserv[es] the property" for the several uses to which it has been put. . . .

Of course, it is still open for the Port Authority to promulgate regulations of the time, place, and manner of leafletting which are "content-neutral, narrowly tailored to serve a significant government interest, and leave open ample alternative channels of communication." . . . For example, during the many years that this litigation has been in progress, the Port Authority has not banned sankirtan completely from JFK International Airport, but has restricted it to a relatively uncongested part of the airport terminals, the same part that houses the airport chapel. In my view, that regulation meets the standards we have applied to time, place, and manner restrictions of protected expression. . . .

. . .

Justice Kennedy, with whom Justice Blackmun, Justice Stevens, and Justice Souter join as to Part I, concurring in the judgment.

While I concur in the judgment affirming in this case, my analysis differs in substantial respects from that of the Court. In my view the airport corridors and shopping areas outside of the passenger security zones, areas operated by the Port Authority, are public forums, and speech in those places is entitled to protection against all government regulation inconsistent with public forum principles. The Port Authority's blanket prohibition on the distribution or sale of literature cannot meet those stringent standards, and I agree it is invalid under the First and Fourteenth Amendments. The Port Authority's rule disallowing in-person solicitation of money for immediate payment, however, is in my view a narrow and valid regulation of the time, place, and manner of protected speech in this forum, or else is a valid regulation of the nonspeech element of expressive conduct. I would sustain the Port Authority's ban on solicitation and receipt of funds.

I

An earlier opinion expressed my concern that "[i]f our public forum jurisprudence is to retain vitality, we must recognize that certain objective characteristics of Government property and its customary use by the public may control" the status of the property. United States v. Kokinda, 497 U.S. 720, 737 (1990) (Kennedy, J., concurring in judgment). The case before us does not heed that principle. Our public forum doctrine ought not to be a jurisprudence of categories rather than ideas ...

... The Court today holds that traditional public forums are limited to public property which have as "'a principal purpose ... the free exchange of ideas'"; and that this purpose must be evidenced by a long-standing historical practice of permitting speech. The Court also holds that designated forums consist of property which the government intends to open for public discourse. All other types of property are, in the Court's view, nonpublic forums (in other words, not public forums), and government-imposed restrictions of speech in these places will be upheld so long as reasonable and viewpoint-neutral. Under this categorical view the application of public-forum analysis to airport terminals seems easy. ...[A]irports must be nonpublic forums, subject to minimal First Amendment protection.

This analysis is flawed at its very beginning. It leaves the government with almost unlimited authority to restrict speech on its property by doing nothing more than articulating a non-speech-related purpose for the area, and it leaves almost no scope for the development of new public forums absent the rare approval of the government. ...

. . .

The Court's approach is contrary to the underlying purposes of the public forum doctrine. ...Public places are of necessity the locus for discussion of public issues, as well as protest against arbitrary government action. ...

. . .

The Court's analysis rests on an inaccurate view of history. The notion that traditional public forums are property which have public discourse as their principal purpose is a most doubtful fiction. The types of property that we have recognized as the quintessential public forums are streets, parks, and sidewalks. ... It would seem apparent that the principal purpose of streets and sidewalks, like airports, is to facilitate transportation, not public discourse, and we have recognized as much. ...Similarly, the purpose for the creation of public parks may be as much for beauty and open space as for discourse. Thus under the Court's analysis, even the quintessential public forums would appear to lack the necessary elements of what the Court defines as a public forum.

The effect of the Court's narrow view of the first category of public forums is compounded by its description of the second purported category, the so-called "designated" forum. The requirements for such a designation are so stringent that I cannot be certain whether the category has any content left at all. In any event, it seems evident that under the Court's analysis today few if any types of property other than those already recognized as public forums will be accorded that status.

The Court's answer to these objections appears to be a recourse to history as justifying its recognition of streets, parks, and sidewalks, but apparently no other types of government property, as traditional public forums. The Court ignores the fact that the purpose of the public forum doctrine is to give effect to the broad command of the First Amendment to protect speech from governmental interference. The jurisprudence is rooted in historic practice, but it is not tied to a narrow textual command limiting the recognition of new forums. In my view the policies underlying the doctrine cannot be given effect unless we recognize that open, public spaces and thoroughfares which are suitable for discourse may be public forums, whatever their historical pedigree and without concern for a precise classification of the property. . . . In a country where most citizens travel by automobile, and parks all too often become locales for crime rather than social intercourse, our failure to recognize the possibility that new types of government property may be appropriate forums for speech will lead to a serious curtailment of our expressive activity.

One of the places left in our mobile society that is suitable for discourse is a metropolitan airport. It is of particular importance to recognize that such spaces are public forums because in these days an airport is one of the few government-owned spaces where many persons have extensive contact with other members of the public. Given that private spaces of similar character are not subject to the dictates of the First Amendment, . . . it is critical that we preserve these areas for protected speech. In my view, our public forum doctrine must recognize this reality, and allow the creation of public forums which do not fit within the narrow tradition of streets, sidewalks, and parks. . . .

I agree with the Court that government property of a type which by history and tradition has been available for speech activity must continue to be recognized as a public forum. In my view, however, constitutional protection is not confined to these properties alone. Under the proper circumstances I would accord public forum status to other forms of property, regardless of its ancient or contemporary origins and whether or not it fits within a narrow historic tradition. . . . The most important considerations . . . are whether the property shares physical similarities with more traditional public forums, whether the government has permitted or acquiesced in broad public access to the property, and whether expressive activity would tend to interfere in a significant way with the uses to which the government has as a factual matter dedicated the property. In conducting the last inquiry, courts must consider the consistency of those uses with expressive activities in general, rather than the specific sort of speech at issue in the case before it; otherwise the analysis would be one not of classification but rather of case-by-case balancing, and would provide little guidance to the State regarding its discretion to regulate speech. Courts must also consider the availability of reasonable time, place, and manner restrictions in undertaking this compatibility analysis. The possibility of some theoretical inconsistency between expressive activities and the property's uses should not bar a finding of a public forum, if those inconsistencies can be avoided through simple and permitted regulations.

The second category of the Court's jurisprudence, the so-called designated forum, provides little, if any, additional protection for speech. Where government property does not satisfy the criteria of a public forum, the government retains the power to dedicate the property for speech, whether for all expressive activity or for limited purposes only. . . . [W]hen property has been designated for a particular expressive use, the government may choose to eliminate that designation. But this increases the need to protect speech in other places, where discourse may occur free of such restrictions. . . .

Under this analysis, it is evident that the public spaces of the Port Authority's airports are public forums. First, . . . the public spaces in the airports are broad, public thoroughfares full of people and lined with stores and other commercial activities. An airport corridor is of course not a street, but that is not the proper inquiry. The question is one of physical similarities, sufficient to suggest that the airport corridor should be a public forum for the same reasons that streets and sidewalks have been treated as public forums by the people who use them.

Second, the airport areas involved here are open to the public without restriction. Plaintiffs do not seek access to the secured areas of the airports, nor do I suggest that these areas would be public forums. And while most people who come to the Port Authority's airports do so for a reason related to air travel, either because they are passengers or because they are picking up or dropping off passengers, this does not distinguish an airport from streets or sidewalks, which most people use for travel. Further, the group visiting the airports encompasses a vast portion of the public: In 1986 the Authority's three airports served over 78 million passengers. It is the very breadth and extent of the public's use of airports that makes it imperative to protect speech rights there. Of course, airport operators retain authority to restrict public access when necessary, for instance to respond to special security concerns. But if the Port Authority allows the uses and open access to airports that is shown on this record, it cannot argue that some vestigial power to change its practices bars the conclusion that its airports are public forums, any more than the power to bulldoze a park bars a finding that a public forum exists so long as the open use does.

Third, and perhaps most important, it is apparent from the record, and from the recent history of airports, that when adequate time, place, and manner regulations are in place, expressive activity is quite compatible with the uses of major airports. The Port Authority's primary argument to the contrary is that the problem of congestion in its airports' corridors makes expressive activity inconsistent with the airports' primary purpose, which is to facilitate air travel. The First Amendment is often inconvenient. But that is beside the point. Inconvenience does not absolve the government of its obligation to tolerate speech. The Authority makes no showing that any real impediments to the smooth functioning of the airports cannot be cured with reasonable time, place, and manner regulations. . . .

The danger of allowing the government to suppress speech is shown in the case now before us. A grant of plenary power allows the government to tilt the dialogue heard by the public, to exclude many, more marginal voices. The first challenged Port Authority regulation establishes a flat prohibition on "[t]he sale or distribution of flyers, brochures, pamphlets, books or any other printed or written material," if conducted within the airport terminal, "in a continuous or repetitive manner." We have long recognized that the right to distribute flyers and literature lies at the heart of the liberties guaranteed by the Speech and Press Clauses of the First Amendment. . . . The Port Authority's rule, which prohibits almost all such activity, is among the most restrictive possible of those liberties. The regulation is in fact so broad and restrictive of speech, Justice O'Connor finds it void even under the standards applicable to government regulations in nonpublic forums. . . .

II

It is my view, however, that the Port Authority's ban on the "solicitation and receipt of funds" within its airport terminals should be upheld under the standards applicable to speech regulations in public forums. The regulation may be upheld as either a reasonable time, place, and manner restriction, or as a regulation directed at the nonspeech element of expressive conduct. The two standards have considerable overlap in a case like this one.

It is well settled that "even in a public forum the government may impose reasonable restrictions on the time, place, or manner of protected speech, provided the restrictions 'are justified without reference to the content of the regulated speech, that they are narrowly tailored to serve a significant governmental interest, and that they leave open ample alternative channels for communication of the information.' " . . . We have held further that the government in appropriate circumstances may regulate conduct, even if the conduct has an expressive component. United States v. O'Brien, 391 U.S. 367 (1968). And . . . we have recognized that the standards for assessing time, place, and manner restrictions are little, if any, different from the standards applicable to regulations of conduct with an expressive component. . . . The confluence of the two tests is well demonstrated by a case like this, where the government regulation at issue can be described with equal accuracy as a regulation of the manner of expression, or as a regulation of conduct with an expressive component.

I am in full agreement with the statement of the Court that solicitation is a form of protected speech. . . . If the Port Authority's solicitation regulation prohibited all speech which requested the contribution of funds, I would conclude that it was a direct, content-based restriction of speech in clear violation of the First Amendment. The Authority's regulation does not prohibit all solicitation, however; it prohibits the "solicitation and receipt of funds." I do not understand this regulation to prohibit all speech that solicits funds. It reaches only personal solicitations for immediate payment of money. . . . In other words, the regulation permits expression that solicits funds, but limits the manner of that expression to forms other than the immediate receipt of money.

So viewed, I believe the Port Authority's rule survives our test for speech restrictions in the public forum. In-person solicitation of funds, when combined with immediate receipt of that money, creates a risk of fraud and duress which is well recognized, and which is different in kind from other forms of expression or conduct. Travelers who are unfamiliar with the airport, perhaps even unfamiliar with this country, its customs and its language, are an easy prey for the money solicitor. . . . As the Court recounts, questionable practices associated with solicitation can include the targeting of vulnerable and easily coerced persons, misrepresentation of the solicitor's cause, and outright theft. . . .

. . .

To survive scrutiny, the regulation must be drawn in narrow terms to accomplish its end and leave open ample alternative channels for communication. Regarding the former requirement, we have held that to be narrowly tailored a regulation need not be the least restrictive or least intrusive means of achieving an end. The regulation must be reasonable, and must not burden substantially more speech than necessary. . . . Under this standard the solicitation ban survives with ease, because it prohibits only solicitation of money for immediate receipt. The regulation does not burden any broader category of speech or expressive conduct than is the source of the evil sought to be avoided. And in fact, the regulation is even more narrow because it only prohibits such behavior if conducted in a continuous or repetitive manner. The Port Authority has made a reasonable judgment that this type of conduct raises the most serious concerns, and it is entitled to deference. My conclusion is not altered by the fact that other means . . . may be available to address the problems associated with solicitation, because the existence of less intrusive means is not decisive. Our cases do not so limit the government's regulatory flexibility. . . .

I have little difficulty in deciding that the Port Authority has left open ample alternative channels for the communication of the message which is an aspect of solicitation. . . . It is only if the solicitor accepts immediate payment that a violation occurs. Thus the solicitor can continue to disseminate his message . . .

Much of what I have said about the solicitation of funds may seem to apply to the sale of literature, but the differences between the two activities are of sufficient significance to require they be distinguished for constitutional purposes. . . . For one, the government interest in regulating the sales of literature is not as powerful as in the case of solicitation. The danger of a fraud arising from such sales is much more limited than from pure solicitation, because in the case of a sale the nature of the exchange tends to be clearer to both parties. Also, the Port Authority's sale regulation is not as narrowly drawn as the solicitation rule, since it does not specify the receipt of money as a critical element of a violation. And perhaps most important, the flat ban on sales of literature leaves open fewer alternative channels of communication than the Port Authority's more limited prohibition on the solicitation and receipt of funds. Given the practicalities and ad hoc nature of much expressive activity in the public forum, sales of literature must be completed in one transaction to be workable. . . . Thus the Port Authority's regulation allows no practical means for advocates and organizations to sell literature within the public forums which are its airports.

Against all of this must be balanced the great need, recognized by our precedents, to give the sale of literature full First Amendment protection. We have long recognized that to prohibit distribution of literature for the mere reason that it is sold would leave organizations seeking to spread their message without funds to operate. . . .

For these reasons I agree that the Court of Appeals should be affirmed in full in finding the Port Authority's ban on the distribution or sale of literature unconstitutional, but upholding the prohibition on solicitation and immediate receipt of funds.

Justice Souter, with whom Justice Blackmun and Justice Stevens join, concurring . . . **and dissenting** . . .

I

I join in Part I of Justice Kennedy's opinion. . . .

. . .

I also agree with Justice Kennedy's statement of the public forum principle: we should classify as a public forum any piece of public property that is "suitable for discourse" in its physical character, where expressive activity is "compatible" with the use to which it has actually been put. . . .

II

From the Court's conclusion . . . sustaining the total ban on solicitation of money for immediate payment, I respectfully dissent. . . .

Even if I assume arguendo that the ban on the petitioners' activity at issue here is both content neutral and merely a restriction on the manner of communication, the regulation must be struck down for its failure to satisfy the requirements of narrow tailoring to further a significant state interest . . .

As Justice Kennedy's opinion indicates, the respondent comes closest to justifying the restriction as one furthering the government's interest in preventing coercion and fraud. The claim to be preventing coercion is weak to start with. While a solicitor can be insistent, a pedestrian on the street or airport concourse can simply walk away or walk on. In any event, we have held in a far more coercive context than this one, that of a black boycott of white stores in Claiborne County, Mississippi, that "Speech does not lose its protected character . . . simply because it may embarrass others or coerce them into action." NAACP v. Claiborne Hardware Co., 458 U.S. 886, 910 (1982). . . . Since there is here no evidence of any type of coercive conduct, over and above the merely importunate character of the open and public solicitation, that might justify a ban, . . . the regulation cannot be sustained to avoid coercion.

As for fraud, our cases do not provide government with plenary authority to ban solicitation just because it could be fraudulent. "Broad prophylactic rules in the area of free expression are suspect," . . . and more than a laudable intent to prevent fraud is required to sustain the present ban. . . . The evidence of fraudulent conduct here is virtually nonexistent. . . .

Even assuming a governmental interest adequate to justify some regulation, the present ban would fall when subjected to the requirement of narrow tailoring. . . .

Finally, I do not think the Port Authority's solicitation ban leaves open the "ample" channels of communication required of a valid content-neutral time, place and manner restriction. A distribution of preaddressed envelopes is unlikely to be much of an alternative. The practical reality of the regulation, which this Court can never ignore, is that it shuts off a uniquely powerful avenue of communication for organizations like the International Society for Krishna Consciousness, and may, in effect, completely prohibit unpopular and poorly funded groups from receiving funds in response to protected solicitation. . . .

. . .

LEE v. INTERNATIONAL SOCIETY FOR KRISHNA CONSCIOUSNESS, INC., 505 U.S. 830 (1992). In the companion case to International Society for Krishna Consciousness, Inc. v. Lee, the Court affirmed the judgment of the Court of Appeals that the ban on distribution of literature is invalid under the first amendment. The Court's Per Curiam opinion stated that affirmance was "[f]or the reasons expressed in the opinions of Justice O'Connor, Justice Kennedy, and Justice Souter in *International Society for Kirshna Consciousness*." Justice Rehnquist's dissent, joined by Justices White, Scalia and Thomas, also relied on his opinion in that case. He said, in addition:

"The risks and burdens posed by leafletting are quite similar to those posed by solicitation. The weary, harried, or hurried traveler may have no less desire and need to avoid the delays generated by having literature foisted upon him than he does to avoid delays from a financial solicitation. And while a busy passenger perhaps may succeed in fending off a leafletter with minimal disruption to himself by agreeing simply to take the proffered material, this does not completely ameliorate the dangers of congestion flowing from such leafletting. Others may choose not simply to accept the material but also to stop and engage the leafletter in debate, obstructing those who follow. Moreover, those who accept material may often simply drop it on the floor once out of the leafletter's range, creating an eyesore, a safety hazard, and additional clean-up work for airport staff."

SECTION 3. SPEECH ON PRIVATE PREMISES

City of Ladue v. Gilleo

512 U.S. 43, 114 S.Ct. 2038, 129 L.Ed.2d 36 (1994).

Justice Stevens delivered the opinion of the Court.

An ordinance of the City of Ladue prohibits homeowners from displaying any signs on their property except "residence identification" signs, "for sale" signs, and signs warning of safety hazards. The ordinance permits commercial establishments, churches, and nonprofit organizations to erect certain signs that are not allowed at residences. The question presented is whether the ordinance violates a Ladue resident's right to free speech.

I

Respondent Margaret P. Gilleo owns one of the 57 single-family homes in the Willow Hill subdivision of Ladue. On December 8, 1990, she placed on her front lawn a 24 by 36 inch sign printed with the words "Say No to War in the Persian Gulf, Call Congress Now." After that sign disappeared, Gilleo put up another but it was knocked to the ground. When Gilleo reported these incidents to the police, they advised her that such signs were prohibited in Ladue. The City Council denied her petition for a variance. Gilleo then filed this action under 42 U. S. C. § 1983 against the City, the Mayor, and members of the City Council, alleging that Ladue's sign ordinance violated her First Amendment right of free speech.

The District Court issued a preliminary injunction against enforcement of the ordinance. Gilleo then placed an 8.5 by 11 inch sign in the second story window of her home stating, "For Peace in the Gulf." The Ladue City Council responded to the injunction by repealing its ordinance and enacting a replacement. Like its predecessor, the new ordinance contains a general prohibition of "signs" and defines that term broadly. The ordinance prohibits all signs except those that fall within one of ten exemptions. Thus, "residential identification signs" no larger than one square foot are allowed, as are signs advertising "that the property is for sale, lease or exchange" and identifying the owner or agent. Also exempted are signs "for churches, religious institutions, and schools," "[c]ommercial signs in commercially or industrial zoned districts," and on-site signs advertising "gasoline filling stations." Unlike its predecessor, the new ordinance contains a lengthy "Declaration of Findings, Policies, Interests, and Purposes," part of which recites that the "proliferation of an unlimited number of signs in private, residential, commercial, industrial, and public areas of the City of Ladue would create ugliness, visual blight and clutter, tarnish the natural beauty of the landscape as well as the residential and commercial architecture, impair property values, substantially impinge upon the privacy and special ambience of the community, and may cause safety and traffic hazards to motorists, pedestrians, and children[.]''

Gilleo amended her complaint to challenge the new ordinance, which explicitly prohibits window signs like hers. The District Court held the ordinance unconstitutional, and the Court of Appeals affirmed. . . .

We . . . affirm.

II

While signs are a form of expression protected by the Free Speech Clause, they pose distinctive problems that are subject to municipalities' police powers. Unlike oral speech, signs take up space and may obstruct views, distract motorists, displace alternative uses for land, and pose other problems that legitimately call for regulation. It is common ground that governments may regulate the physical characteristics of signs--just as they can, within reasonable bounds and absent censorial purpose, regulate audible expression in its capacity as noise. . . .

In Linmark Associates, Inc. v. Willingboro, 431 U. S. 85 (1977), we addressed an ordinance that sought to maintain stable, integrated neighborhoods by prohibiting homeowners from placing ''For Sale'' or ''Sold'' signs on their property. Although we recognized the importance of Willingboro's objective, we held that the First Amendment prevented the township from ''achieving its goal by restricting the free flow of truthful information.'' Id., at 95. In some respects *Linmark* is the mirror image of this case. For instead of prohibiting ''For Sale'' signs without banning any other signs, Ladue has exempted such signs from an otherwise virtually complete ban. Moreover, whereas in *Linmark* we noted that the ordinance was not concerned with the promotion of aesthetic values unrelated to the content of the prohibited speech, id., at 93–94, here Ladue relies squarely on that content-neutral justification for its ordinance.

. . .

[There are] two analytically distinct grounds for challenging the constitutionality of a municipal ordinance regulating the display of signs. One is that the measure in effect restricts too little speech because its exemptions discriminate on the basis of the signs' messages. . . .Alternatively, such provisions are subject to attack on the ground that they simply prohibit too much protected speech. . . .The City of Ladue contends, first, that the Court of Appeals' reliance on the former rationale was misplaced because the City's regulatory purposes are content-neutral, and, second, that those purposes justify the comprehensiveness of the sign prohibition. A comment on the former contention will help explain why we ultimately base our decision on a rejection of the latter.

III

While surprising at first glance, the notion that a regulation of speech may be impermissibly underinclusive is firmly grounded in basic First Amendment principles. Thus, an exemption from an otherwise permissible regulation of speech may represent a governmental ''attempt to give one side of a debatable public question an advantage in expressing its views to the people.'' First Nat.

Bank of Boston v. Bellotti, 435 U. S. 765, 785–786 (1978). Alternatively, through the combined operation of a general speech restriction and its exemptions, the government might seek to select the "permissible subjects for public debate" and thereby to "control . . . the search for political truth." Consolidated Edison Co. of N.Y. v. Public Service Comm'n of N.Y. 447 U. S. 530, 538 (1980).

The City argues that its sign ordinance implicates neither of these concerns, and that the Court of Appeals therefore erred in demanding a "compelling" justification for the exemptions. The mix of prohibitions and exemptions in the ordinance, Ladue maintains, reflects legitimate differences among the side effects of various kinds of signs. These differences are only adventitiously connected with content, and supply a sufficient justification, unrelated to the City's approval or disapproval of specific messages, for carving out the specified categories from the general ban. Thus, according to the Declaration of Findings, Policies, Interests, and Purposes supporting the ordinance, the permitted signs, unlike the prohibited signs, are unlikely to contribute to the dangers of "unlimited proliferation" associated with categories of signs that are not inherently limited in number. Because only a few residents will need to display "for sale" or "for rent" signs at any given time, permitting one such sign per marketed house does not threaten visual clutter. Because the City has only a few businesses, churches, and schools, the same rationale explains the exemption for on-site commercial and organizational signs. Moreover, some of the exempted categories (e.g., danger signs) respond to unique public needs to permit certain kinds of speech. Even if we assume the validity of these arguments, the exemptions in Ladue's ordinance nevertheless shed light on the separate question of whether the ordinance prohibits too much speech.

Exemptions from an otherwise legitimate regulation of a medium of speech may be noteworthy for a reason quite apart from the risks of viewpoint and content discrimination: they may diminish the credibility of the government's rationale for restricting speech in the first place. In this case, at the very least, the exemptions from Ladue's ordinance demonstrate that Ladue has concluded that the interest in allowing certain messages to be conveyed by means of residential signs outweighs the City's aesthetic interest in eliminating outdoor signs. Ladue has not imposed a flat ban on signs because it has determined that at least some of them are too vital to be banned.

Under the Court of Appeals' content discrimination rationale, the City might theoretically remove the defects in its ordinance by simply repealing all of the exemptions. If, however, the ordinance is also vulnerable because it prohibits too much speech, that solution would not save it. Moreover, if the prohibitions in Ladue's ordinance are impermissible, resting our decision on its exemptions would afford scant relief for respondent Gilleo. She is primarily concerned not with the scope of the exemptions available in other locations, such as commercial areas and on church property. She asserts a constitutional right to display an antiwar sign at her own home. Therefore, we first ask whether Ladue may properly prohibit Gilleo from displaying her sign, and then, only if necessary, consider the separate question whether it was improper for the City simultaneously to permit certain other signs. In examining the propriety of Ladue's near-total prohibition of residential signs, we will assume, arguendo, the validity of the City's submission that the various exemptions are free of impermissible content or viewpoint discrimination.

IV

. . . Ladue's sign ordinance is supported principally by the City's interest in minimizing the visual clutter associated with signs, an interest that is concededly valid but certainly no more compelling than the interests at stake in *Linmark*. Moreover, whereas the ordinance in *Linmark* applied only to a form of commercial speech, Ladue's ordinance covers even such absolutely pivotal speech as a sign protesting an imminent governmental decision to go to war.

The impact on free communication of Ladue's broad sign prohibition, moreover, is manifestly greater than in *Linmark*. Gilleo and other residents of Ladue are forbidden to display virtually any "sign" on their property. The ordinance defines that term sweepingly. . . .

. . . Ladue has almost completely foreclosed a venerable means of communication that is both unique and important. It has totally foreclosed that medium to political, religious, or personal messages. Signs that react to a local happening or express a view on a controversial issue both reflect and animate change in the life of a community. Often placed on lawns or in windows, residential signs play an important part in political campaigns, during which they are displayed to signal the resident's support for particular candidates, parties, or causes. They may not afford the same opportunities for conveying complex ideas as do other media, but residential signs have long been an important and distinct medium of expression.

Our prior decisions have voiced particular concern with laws that foreclose an entire medium of expression. Thus, we have held invalid ordinances that completely banned the distribution of pamphlets within the municipality, Lovell v. Griffin, 303 U. S. 444, 451–452 (1938); handbills on the public streets, Jamison v. Texas, 318 U. S. 413, 416 (1943); the door-to-door distribution of literature, Martin v. Struthers, 319 U. S. 141, 145–149 (1943); Schneider v. State, 308 U. S. 147, 164–165 (1939), and live entertainment, Schad v. Mount Ephraim, 452 U. S. 61, 75–76 (1981). . . . Although prohibitions foreclosing entire media may be completely free of content or viewpoint discrimination, the danger they pose to the freedom of speech is readily apparent—by eliminating a common means of speaking, such measures can suppress too much speech.

Ladue contends, however, that its ordinance is a mere regulation of the "time, place, or manner" of speech because residents remain free to convey their desired messages by other means, such as hand-held signs, "letters, handbills, flyers, telephone calls, newspaper advertisements, bumper stickers, speeches, and neighborhood or community meetings." . However, even regulations that do not foreclose an entire medium of expression, but merely shift the time, place, or manner of its use, must "leave open ample alternative channels for communication." . . . In this case, we are not persuaded that adequate substitutes exist for the important medium of speech that Ladue has closed off.

Displaying a sign from one's own residence often carries a message quite distinct from placing the same sign someplace else, or conveying the same text or picture by other means. Precisely because of their location, such signs provide information about the identity of the "speaker." As an early and eminent student of rhetoric observed, the identity of the speaker is an important component of many attempts to persuade. A sign advocating "Peace in the Gulf" in the front lawn of a retired general or decorated war veteran may provoke a different reaction than the same sign in a 10–year-old child's bedroom window or the same message on a bumper sticker of a passing automobile. An espousal of socialism may carry different implications when displayed on the grounds of a stately mansion than when pasted on a factory wall or an ambulatory sandwich board.

Residential signs are an unusually cheap and convenient form of communication. Especially for persons of modest means or limited mobility, a yard or window sign may have no practical substitute. Even for the affluent, the added costs in money or time of taking out a newspaper advertisement, handing out leaflets on the street, or standing in front of one's house with a hand-held sign may make the difference between participating and not participating in some public debate. Furthermore, a person who puts up a sign at her residence often intends to reach neighbors, an audience that could not be reached nearly as well by other means.

A special respect for individual liberty in the home has long been part of our culture and our law ... ; that principle has special resonance when the government seeks to constrain a person's ability to speak there. ...Most Americans would be understandably dismayed, given that tradition, to learn that it was illegal to display from their window an 8 by 11 inch sign expressing their political views. ...

Our decision that Ladue's ban on almost all residential signs violates the First Amendment by no means leaves the City powerless to address the ills that may be associated with residential signs. It bears mentioning that individual residents themselves have strong incentives to keep their own property values up and to prevent "visual clutter" in their own yards and neighborhoods—incentives markedly different from those of persons who erect signs on others' land, in others' neighborhoods, or on public property. Residents' self-interest diminishes the danger of the "unlimited" proliferation of residential signs that concerns the City of Ladue. We are confident that more temperate measures could in large part satisfy Ladue's stated regulatory needs without harm to the First Amendment rights of its citizens. As currently framed, however, the ordinance abridges those rights.

Accordingly, the judgment of the Court of Appeals is Affirmed.

Justice O'Connor, concurring.

It is unusual for us, when faced with a regulation that on its face draws content distinctions, to "assume, arguendo, the validity of the City's submission that the various exemptions are free of impermissible content or viewpoint discrimination." With rare exceptions, content discrimination in regulations of the speech of private citizens on private property or in a traditional public forum is presumptively impermissible, and this presumption is a very strong one. ...The normal inquiry that our doctrine dictates is, first, to determine whether a regulation is content-based or content-neutral, and then, based on the answer to that question, to apply the proper level of scrutiny. ...

Over the years, some cogent criticisms have been leveled at our approach. See, e.g., ... Farber, Content Regulation and the First Amendment: A Revisionist View, 68 Geo. L. J. 727 (1980); Stephan, The First Amendment and Content Discrimination, 68 Va. L. Rev. 203 (1982). And it is quite true that regulations are occasionally struck down because of their content-based nature, even though common sense may suggest that they are entirely reasonable. The content distinctions present in this ordinance may, to some, be a good example of this.

But though our rule has flaws, it has substantial merit as well. It is a rule, in an area where fairly precise rules are better than more discretionary and more subjective balancing tests. ...On a theoretical level, it reflects important insights into the meaning of the free speech principle-for instance, that content-based speech restrictions are especially likely to be improper attempts to value some forms of speech over others, or are particularly susceptible to being used by the government to distort public debate. ...On a practical level, it has in application generally led to seemingly sensible results. And, perhaps most importantly, no better alternative has yet come to light.

I would have preferred to apply our normal analytical structure in this case, which may well have required us to examine this law with the scrutiny appropriate to content-based regulations. Perhaps this would have forced us to confront some of the difficulties with the existing doctrine; perhaps it would have shown weaknesses in the rule, and led us to modify it to take into account the special factors this case presents. But such reexamination is part of the process by which our rules evolve and improve.

Nonetheless, I join the Court's opinion, because I agree with its conclusion in Part IV that even if the restriction were content-neutral, it would still be invalid, and because I do not think Part III casts any doubt on the propriety of our normal content discrimination inquiry.

City of Renton v. Playtime Theatres, Inc.

475 U.S. 41, 106 S.Ct. 925, 89 L.Ed.2d 29 (1986).

Justice Rehnquist delivered the opinion of the Court.

This case involves a constitutional challenge to a zoning ordinance, enacted by appellant, city of Renton, Washington, that prohibits adult motion picture theaters from locating within 1,000 feet of any residential zone, single-or multiple-family dwelling, church, park, or school. . . .

In May 1980, the Mayor of Renton, a city of approximately 32,000 people located just south of Seattle, suggested to the Renton City Council that it consider the advisability of enacting zoning legislation dealing with adult entertainment uses. No such uses existed in the city at that time. Upon the Mayor's suggestion, the City Council referred the matter to the city's Planning and Development Committee. The committee held public hearings, reviewed the experiences of Seattle and other cities, and received a report from the City Attorney's Office advising as to developments in other cities. The City Council, meanwhile, adopted Resolution No. 2368, which imposed a moratorium on the licensing of "any business . . . which . . . has as its primary purpose the selling, renting or showing of sexually explicit materials." The resolution contained a clause explaining that such businesses "would have a severe impact upon surrounding businesses and residences."

In April 1981, acting on the basis of the Planning and Development Committee's recommendation, the City Council enacted Ordinance No. 3526. The ordinance prohibited any "adult motion picture theater" from locating within 1,000 feet of any residential zone, single-or multiple-family dwelling, church, or park, and within one mile of any school. The term "adult motion picture theater" was defined as "[a]n enclosed building used for presenting motion picture films, video cassettes, cable television, or any other such visual media, distinguished or characteri[zed] by an emphasis on matter depicting, describing or relating to 'specified sexual activities' or 'specified anatomical areas' . . . for observation by patrons therein."

In early 1982, respondents acquired two existing theaters in downtown Renton, with the intention of using them to exhibit feature-length adult films. The theaters were located within the area proscribed by Ordinance No. 3526. At about the same time, respondents filed [a] lawsuit challenging the ordinance on First and Fourteenth Amendment grounds, and seeking declaratory and injunctive relief. While the federal action was pending, the City Council amended the ordinance in several respects, adding a statement of reasons for its enactment and reducing the minimum distance from any school to 1,000 feet.

. . .

The District Court ... entered summary judgment in favor of Renton.... Relying on Young v. American Mini Theatres, Inc., 427 U.S. 50 (1976), and United States v. O'Brien, 391 U.S. 367 (1968), the court held that the Renton ordinance did not violate the First Amendment.

The Court of Appeals for the Ninth Circuit reversed....

In our view, the resolution of this case is largely dictated by our decision in Young v. American Mini Theatres, Inc., supra. There, although five Members of the Court did not agree on a single rationale for the decision, we held that the city of Detroit's zoning ordinance, which prohibited locating an adult theater within 1,000 feet of any two other "regulated uses" or within 500 feet of any residential zone, did not violate the First and Fourteenth Amendments. Id., at 72–73 (plurality opinion of Stevens, J., joined by Burger, C.J., and White and Rehnquist, JJ.); id., at 84 (Powell, J., concurring). The Renton ordinance, like the one in *American Mini Theatres,* does not ban adult theaters altogether, but merely provides that such theaters may not be located within 1,000 feet of any residential zone, single-or multiple-family dwelling, church, park, or school. The ordinance is therefore properly analyzed as a form of time, place, and manner regulation....

Describing the ordinance as a time, place, and manner regulation is, of course, only the first step in our inquiry. This Court has long held that regulations enacted for the purpose of restraining speech on the basis of its content presumptively violate the First Amendment.... On the other hand, so-called "content-neutral" time, place, and manner regulations are acceptable so long as they are designed to serve a substantial governmental interest and do not unreasonably limit alternative avenues of communication....

At first glance, the Renton ordinance, like the ordinance in *American Mini Theatres,* does not appear to fit neatly into either the "content-based" or the "content-neutral" category. To be sure, the ordinance treats theaters that specialize in adult films differently from other kinds of theaters. Nevertheless, as the District Court concluded, the Renton ordinance is aimed not at the *content* of the films shown at "adult motion picture theatres," but rather at the *secondary effects* of such theaters on the surrounding community. The District Court found that the City Council's "*predominate* concerns" were with the secondary effects of adult theaters, and not with the content of adult films themselves. But the Court of Appeals ... held that this was not enough to sustain the ordinance. According to the Court of Appeals, if "a *motivating factor* "in enacting the ordinance was to restrict respondents' exercise of First Amendment rights the ordinance would be invalid, apparently no matter how small a part this motivating factor may have played in the City Council's decision. This view of the law was rejected in United States v. O'Brien, 391 U.S. [367,] 382–386 (1968), the very case that the Court of Appeals said it was applying:

> "It is a familiar principle of constitutional law that this Court will not strike down an otherwise constitutional statute on the basis of an alleged illicit legislative motive. . . ."

. . .

The District Court's finding as to "predominate" intent, left undisturbed by the Court of Appeals, is more than adequate to establish that the city's pursuit of its zoning interests here was unrelated to the suppression of free expression. The ordinance by its terms is designed to prevent crime, protect the city's retail trade, maintain property values, and generally "protec[t] and preserv[e] the quality of [the city's] neighborhoods, commercial districts, and the quality of urban life," not to suppress the expression of unpopular views. As Justice Powell observed in *American Mini Theatres,* "[i]f [the city] had been concerned with restricting the message purveyed by adult theaters, it would have tried to close them or restrict their number rather than circumscribe their choice as to location." 427 U.S., at 82, n. 4.

... The ordinance does not contravene the fundamental principle that underlies our concern about "content-based" speech regulations: that "government may not grant the use of a forum to people whose views it finds acceptable, but deny use to those wishing to express less favored or more controversial views." ...

It was with this understanding in mind that, in *American Mini Theatres,* a majority of this Court decided that, at least with respect to businesses that purvey sexually explicit materials, zoning ordinances designed to combat the undesirable secondary effects of such businesses are to be reviewed under the standards applicable to "content-neutral" time, place, and manner regulations. ...

The appropriate inquiry in this case, then, is whether the Renton ordinance is designed to serve a substantial governmental interest and allows for reasonable alternative avenues of communication.... It is clear that the ordinance meets such a standard. As a majority of this Court recognized in *American Mini Theatres,* a city's "interest in attempting to preserve the quality of urban life is one that must be accorded high respect." ...

The Court of Appeals ruled, however, that because the Renton ordinance was enacted without the benefit of studies specifically relating to "the particular problems or needs of Renton," the city's justifications for the ordinance were "conclusory and speculative." We think the Court of Appeals imposed on the city an unnecessarily rigid burden of proof. The record in this case reveals that Renton relied heavily on the experience of, and studies produced by, the city of Seattle. In Seattle, as in Renton, the adult theater zoning ordinance was aimed at preventing the secondary effects caused by the presence of even one such theater in a given neighborhood....

... The First Amendment does not require a city, before enacting such an ordinance, to conduct new studies or produce evidence independent of that already generated by other cities, so long as whatever evidence the city relies upon is reasonably believed to be relevant to the problem that the city addresses. That was the case here. Nor is our holding affected by the fact that Seattle ultimately chose a different method of adult theater zoning than that chosen by Renton, since Seattle's choice of a different remedy to combat the secondary effects of adult theaters does not call into question either Seattle's identification of those secondary effects or the relevance of Seattle's experience to Renton.

We also find no constitutional defect in the method chosen by Renton to further its substantial interests. Cities may regulate adult theaters by dispersing them, as in Detroit, or by effectively concentrating them, as in Renton. ...Moreover, the Renton ordinance is "narrowly tailored" to affect only that category of theaters shown to produce the unwanted secondary effects, thus avoiding the flaw that proved fatal to the regulations in Schad v. Mount Ephraim, 452 U.S. 61 (1981), and Erznoznik v. City of Jacksonville, 422 U.S. 205 (1975).

Respondents contend that the Renton ordinance is "under-inclusive," in that it fails to regulate other kinds of adult businesses that are likely to produce secondary effects similar to those produced by adult theaters. On this record the contention must fail. There is no evidence that, at the time the Renton ordinance was enacted, any other adult business was located in, or was contemplating moving into, Renton. . . .

Finally, turning to the question whether the Renton ordinance allows for reasonable alternative avenues of communication, we note that the ordinance leaves some 520 acres, or more than five percent of the entire land area of Renton, open to use as adult theater sites. The District Court found, and the Court of Appeals did not dispute the finding, that the 520 acres of land consists of "[a]mple, accessible real estate," including "acreage in all stages of development from raw land to developed, industrial, warehouse, office, and shopping space that is criss-crossed by freeways, highways, and roads."

Respondents argue, however, that some of the land in question is already occupied by existing businesses, that "practically none" of the undeveloped land is currently for sale or lease, and that in general there are no "commercially viable" adult theater sites within the 520 acres left open by the Renton ordinance. The Court of Appeals accepted these arguments, concluded that the 520 acres was not truly "available" land, and therefore held that the Renton ordinance "would result in a substantial restriction" on speech.

We disagree with both the reasoning and the conclusion of the Court of Appeals. That respondents must fend for themselves in the real estate market, on an equal footing with other prospective purchasers and lessees, does not give rise to a First Amendment violation. . . . [W]e have never suggested that the First Amendment compels the Government to ensure that adult theaters, or any other kinds of speech-related businesses for that matter, will be able to obtain sites at bargain prices. . . . In our view, the First Amendment requires only that Renton refrain from effectively denying respondents a reasonable opportunity to open and operate an adult theater within the city, and the ordinance before us easily meets this requirement.

In sum, we find that the Renton ordinance represents a valid governmental response to the "admittedly serious problems" created by adult theaters. . . . The judgment of the Court of Appeals is therefore

Reversed.

Justice Blackmun concurs in the result.

Justice Brennan, with whom Justice Marshall joins, dissenting.

Renton's zoning ordinance selectively imposes limitations on the location of a movie theater based exclusively on the content of the films shown there. The constitutionality of the ordinance is therefore not correctly analyzed under standards applied to content-neutral time, place, and manner restrictions. But even assuming that the ordinance may fairly be characterized as content neutral, it is plainly unconstitutional under the standards established by the decisions of this Court. Although the Court's analysis is limited to cases involving "businesses that purvey sexually explicit materials," and thus does not affect our holdings in cases involving state regulation of other kinds of speech, I dissent.

I

. . .

The fact that adult movie theaters may cause harmful "secondary" land use effects may arguably give Renton a compelling reason to regulate such establishments; it does not mean, however, that such regulations are content neutral. Because the ordinance imposes special restrictions on certain kinds of speech on the basis of *content,* I cannot simply accept, as the Court does, Renton's claim that the ordinance was not designed to suppress the content of adult movies. ...In this case, both the language of the ordinance and its dubious legislative history belie the Court's conclusion that "the city's pursuit of its zoning interests here was unrelated to the suppression of free expression."

In sum, the circumstances here strongly suggest that the ordinance was designed to suppress expression, even that constitutionally protected, and thus was not to be analyzed as a content-neutral time, place, and manner restriction. ...Rather than speculate about Renton's motives for adopting such measures, our cases require that the ordinance, like any other content-based restriction on speech, is constitutional "only if the [city] can show that [it] is a precisely drawn means of serving a compelling [governmental] interest." ...

Applying this standard to the facts of this case, the ordinance is patently unconstitutional. Renton has not shown that locating adult movie theaters in proximity to its churches, schools, parks, and residences will necessarily result in undesirable "secondary effects," or that these problems could not be effectively addressed by less intrusive restrictions.

II

Even assuming that the ordinance should be treated like a content-neutral time, place, and manner restriction, I would still find it unconstitutional....

A

... The city made no showing as to how uses "protected" by the ordinance would be affected by the presence of an adult movie theater. Thus, the Renton ordinance is clearly distinguishable from the Detroit zoning ordinance upheld in Young v. American Mini Theatres, Inc., 427 U.S. 50 (1976). The Detroit ordinance, which was designed to disperse adult theaters throughout the city, was supported by the testimony of urban planners and real estate experts regarding the adverse effects of locating several such businesses in the same neighborhood.... Here, the Renton Council was aware only that some residents had complained about adult movie theaters, and that other localities had adopted special zoning restrictions for such establishments. These are not "facts" sufficient to justify the burdens the ordinance imposed upon constitutionally protected expression.

B

Finally, the ordinance is invalid because it does not provide for reasonable alternative avenues of communication. The District Court found that the ordinance left 520 acres in Renton available for adult theater sites, an area comprising about five percent of the city. ...

Despite the evidence in the record, the Court reasons that the fact "[t]hat respondents must fend for themselves in the real estate market, on an equal footing with other prospective purchasers and lessees, does not give rise to a First Amendment violation." However, respondents are not on equal footing with other prospective purchasers and lessees, but must conduct business under severe restrictions not imposed upon other establishments. The Court also argues that the First Amendment does not compel "the government to ensure that adult theatres, or any other kinds of speech-related businesses for that matter, will be able to obtain sites at bargain prices." However, respondents do not ask Renton to guarantee low-price sites for their businesses, but seek only a reasonable opportunity to operate adult theaters in the city. By denying them this opportunity, Renton can effectively ban a form of protected speech from its borders. . . .

Consolidated Edison Co. of New York v. Public Service Commission

447 U.S. 530, 100 S.Ct. 2326, 65 L.Ed.2d 319 (1980).

Mr. Justice Powell delivered the opinion of the Court.

The question in this case is whether the First Amendment, as incorporated by the Fourteenth Amendment, is violated by an order of the Public Service Commission of the State of New York that prohibits the inclusion in monthly electric bills of inserts discussing controversial issues of public policy.

I

The Consolidated Edison Company of New York, appellant in this case, placed written material entitled "Independence Is Still a Goal, and Nuclear Power Is Needed To Win the Battle" in its January 1976 billing envelope. The bill insert stated Consolidated Edison's views on "the benefits of nuclear power," saying that they "far outweigh any potential risk" and that nuclear power plants are safe, economical, and clean. The utility also contended that increased use of nuclear energy would further this country's independence from foreign energy sources.

In March 1976, the Natural Resources Defense Council, Inc. (NRDC) requested Consolidated Edison to enclose a rebuttal prepared by NRDC in its next billing envelope. When Consolidated Edison refused, NRDC asked the Public Service Commission of the State of New York to open Consolidated Edison's billing envelopes to contrasting views on controversial issues of public importance.

On February 17, 1977, the Commission, appellee here, denied NRDC's request, but prohibited "utilities from using bill inserts to discuss political matters, including the desirability of future development of nuclear power." The Commission explained its decision in a Statement of Policy on Advertising and Promotional Practices of Public Utilities issued on February 25, 1977. The Commission concluded that Consolidated Edison customers who receive bills containing inserts are a captive audience of diverse views who should not be subjected to the utility's beliefs. Accordingly, the Commission barred utility companies from including bill inserts that express "their opinions or viewpoints on controversial issues of public policy." The Commission did not, however, bar utilities from sending bill inserts discussing topics that are not "controversial issues of public policy." . . .

Consolidated Edison sought review of the Commission's order in the New York state courts. . . . The Court of Appeals held that the order did not violate the Constitution because it was a valid time, place and manner regulation designed to protect the privacy of Consolidated Edison's customers. . . . We reverse.

II

The restriction on bill inserts cannot be upheld on the ground that Consolidated Edison is not entitled to freedom of speech. In First National Bank of Boston v. Bellotti, 435 U.S. 765 (1978), we rejected the contention that a State may confine corporate speech to specified issues....

. . .

... [T]he Commission's prohibition of discussion of controversial issues strikes at the heart of the freedom to speak.

III

... The Commission's arguments require us to consider three theories that might justify the state action. We must determine whether the prohibition is (i) a reasonable time, place, or manner restriction, (ii) a permissible subject-matter regulation, or (iii) a narrowly tailored means of serving a compelling state interest.

A

. . .

A restriction that regulates only the time, place or manner of speech may be imposed so long as it is reasonable. But when regulation is based on the content of speech, governmental action must be scrutinized more carefully. ...Therefore, a constitutionally permissible time, place, or manner restriction may not be based upon either the content or subject matter of speech.

The Commission does not pretend that its action is unrelated to the content or subject matter of bill inserts. Indeed, it has undertaken to suppress certain bill inserts precisely because they address controversial issues of public policy. ...The Commission, with commendable candor, justifies its ban on the ground that consumers will benefit from receiving "useful" information, but not from the prohibited information. The Commission's own rationale demonstrates that its action cannot be upheld as a content-neutral time, place, or manner regulation.

B

The Commission next argues that its order is acceptable because it applies to all discussion of nuclear power, whether pro or con, in bill inserts. The prohibition, the Commission contends, is related to subject matter rather than to the views of a particular speaker. Because the regulation does not favor either side of a political controversy, the Commission asserts that it does not unconstitutionally suppress freedom of speech.

The First Amendment's hostility to content-based regulation extends not only to restrictions on particular viewpoints, but also to prohibition of public discussion of an entire topic....

. . .

C

Where a government restricts the speech of a private person, the state action may be sustained only if the government can show that the regulation is a precisely drawn means of serving a compelling state interest.... The Commission argues finally that its prohibition is necessary (i) to avoid forcing Consolidated Edison's views on a captive audience, (ii) to allocate limited resources in the public interest, and (iii) to ensure that ratepayers do not subsidize the cost of the bill inserts.

The State Court of Appeals largely based its approval of the prohibition upon its conclusion that the bill inserts intruded upon individual privacy. The court stated that the Commission could act to protect the privacy of the utility's customers because they have no choice whether to receive the insert and the views expressed in the insert may inflame their sensibilities.... But the Court of Appeals erred in its assessment of the seriousness of the intrusion.

Even if a short exposure to Consolidated Edison's views may offend the sensibilities of some consumers, the ability of government "to shut off discourse solely to protect others from hearing it [is] dependent upon a showing that substantial privacy interests are being invaded in an essentially intolerable manner." Cohen v. California, 403 U.S., at 21.... Where a single speaker communicates to many listeners, the First Amendment does not permit the government to prohibit speech as intrusive unless the "captive" audience cannot avoid objectionable speech.

. . .

The Commission contends that because a billing envelope can accommodate only a limited amount of information, political messages should not be allowed to take the place of inserts that promote energy conservation or safety, or that remind consumers of their legal rights. The Commission relies upon Red Lion Broadcasting Co. v. F.C.C., [395 U.S. 367 (1969)], in which the Court held that the regulation of radio and television broadcast frequencies permit the Federal Government to exercise unusual authority over speech. But billing envelopes differ from broadcast frequencies in two ways. First, a broadcaster communicates through use of a scarce, publicly owned resource. No person can broadcast without a license, whereas all persons are free to send correspondence to private homes through the mails. Thus, it cannot be said that billing envelopes are a limited resource comparable to the broadcast spectrum. Second, the Commission has not shown on the record before us that the presence of the bill inserts at issue would preclude the inclusion of other inserts that Consolidated Edison might be ordered lawfully to include in the billing envelope. ...

Finally, the Commission urges that its prohibition would prevent ratepayers from subsidizing the costs of policy-oriented bill inserts. But the Commission did not base its order on an inability to allocate costs between the shareholders of Consolidated Edison and the ratepayers. ...Accordingly, there is no basis on this record to assume that the Commission could not exclude the cost of these bill inserts from the utility's rate base....

IV

The Commission's suppression of bill inserts that discuss controversial issues of public policy directly infringes the freedom of speech protected by the First and Fourteenth Amendments. The state action is neither a valid time, place, or manner restriction, nor a permissible subject-matter regulation, nor a narrowly drawn prohibition justified by a compelling state interest. Accordingly, the regulation is invalid....

. . .

Mr. Justice Stevens, concurring in the judgment.

Any student of history who has been reprimanded for talking about the World Series during a class discussion of the First Amendment knows that it is incorrect to state that a "time, place, or manner restriction may not be based upon either the content or subject matter of speech." And every lawyer who has read our Rules, or our cases upholding various restrictions on speech with specific reference to subject matter must recognize the hyperbole in the dictum: "But, above all else, the First Amendment means that Government has no power to restrict expression because of its message, its ideas, its subject matter, or its content." Police Department of Chicago v. Mosley, 408 U.S. 92, 95. Indeed, if that were the law, there would be no need for the Court's detailed rejection of the justifications put forward by the State for the restriction involved in this case.

There are, in fact, many situations in which the subject matter, or, indeed, even the point of view of the speaker, may provide a justification for a time, place and manner regulation. Perhaps the most obvious example is the regulation of oral argument in this Court; the appellant's lawyer precedes his adversary solely because he seeks reversal of a judgment. As is true of many other aspects of liberty, some forms of orderly regulation actually promote freedom more than would a state of total anarchy.

Instead of trying to justify our conclusion by reasoning from honey-combed premises, I prefer to identify the basis of decision in more simple terms. . . . A regulation of speech that is motivated by nothing more than a desire to curtail expression of a particular point of view on controversial issues of general interest is the purest example of a "law . . . abridging the freedom of speech, or of the press." A regulation that denies one group of persons the right to address a selected audience on "controversial issues of public policy" is plainly such a regulation.

The only justification for the regulation relied on by the New York Court of Appeals is that the utilities' bill inserts may be "offensive" to some of their customers. But a communication may be offensive in two different ways. Independently of the message the speaker intends to convey, the form of his communication may be offensive—perhaps because it is too loud or too ugly in a particular setting. Other speeches, even though elegantly phrased in dulcet tones, are offensive simply because the listener disagrees with the speaker's message. The fact that the offensive form of some communication may subject it to appropriate regulation surely does not support the conclusion that the offensive character of an idea can justify an attempt to censor its expression. Since the Public Service Commission has candidly put forward this impermissible justification for its censorial regulation, it plainly violates the First Amendment.

Accordingly, I concur in the judgment of the Court.

Mr. Justice Blackmun, with whom Mr. Justice Rehnquist as to Parts I and II joins, dissenting.

. . .

. . . I cannot agree with the Court that the New York Public Service Commission's ban on the utility bill insert somehow deprives the utility of its First and Fourteenth Amendment rights. Because of Consolidated Edison's monopoly status and its rate structure, the use of the insert amounts to an exaction from the utility's customers by way of forced aid for the utility's speech. And, contrary to the Court's suggestion, an allocation of the insert's cost between the utility's shareholders and the ratepayers would not eliminate this coerced subsidy.

I

A public utility is a state-created monopoly.... Under the laws of New York and other States, ... a public utility cannot include in the rate base the costs of political advertising and lobbying.... These costs cannot be passed on to consumers because ratepayers derive no service-related benefits from political advertisements. The purpose of such advertising and lobbying is to benefit the utility's shareholders, and its cost must be deducted from profits otherwise available for the shareholders....

II

The Commission concluded, properly in my view, that use of the billing envelope to distribute management's pamphlets amounts to a forced subsidy of the utility's speech by the ratepayers. Consolidated Edison would counter this argument by pointing out that it is willing to allocate to shareholders the *additional* costs attributable to the inserts....

. . .

In suggesting that the State's interest in eliminating forced subsidization of the utility's speech can be achieved by allocating the expenses of the inserts to the utility's shareholders, the Court has glossed over the difficult allocation issue underlying this controversy. It is not clear to me from the Court's opinion whether it believes that charging the shareholders with the marginal costs associated with the inserts, that is, the costs of printing and putting them into the envelope, will satisfy the State's interest, or whether the Court is suggesting some division of the fixed costs of the mailing, that is, the postage, the envelope, the creation and maintenance of the mailing list, and any other overhead expense.

. . .

... The Commission's ban on bill inserts does not restrict the utility from using the shareholders' resources to finance communication of its viewpoints on any topic. Consolidated Edison is completely free to use the mails and any other medium of communication on the same basis as any other speaker. ...

. . .

SECTION 4. SPEECH IN THE PUBLIC SCHOOLS

THE GOVERNMENT AS SPEAKER

(1) The Role of Government Speech in Public Debate. No Supreme Court decision has interpreted the first amendment to require that government communications be neutral or present all sides of debate on controversial public issues, other than issues of religious doctrine. The Court's most relevant discussion was in Buckley v. Valeo, 424 U.S. 1, 92–93 (1976), where the Court rejected a first amendment challenge to provisions of the Federal Election Campaign Act of 1971 for public financing of presidential election campaigns. The Court's opinion stated:

> "Appellants next argue that 'by analogy' to the Religion Clauses of the First Amendment public financing of election campaigns, however meritorious, violates the First Amendment. We have of course held that the Religion Clauses—'Congress shall make no law respecting an establishment of religion, or prohibiting the free exercise thereof'—require Con-

gress, and the States through the Fourteenth Amendment, to remain neutral in matters of religion.... The Government may not aid one religion to the detriment of others or impose a burden on one religion that is not imposed on others, and may not even aid all religions.... But the analogy is patently inapplicable to our issue here. Although 'Congress shall make no law ... abridging the freedom of speech, or of the press,' Subtitle H is a congressional effort, not to abridge, restrict, or censor speech, but rather to use public money to facilitate and enlarge public discussion and participation in the electoral process, goals vital to a self-governing people. Thus, Subtitle H furthers, not abridges, pertinent First Amendment values.[127]"

(2) The Issue of Neutrality in Connection with the Government Forum. In the traditional public forum cases, involving communication in parks and streets, the constitutional requirement of government content neutrality was established in a context where government was playing no part in communication. Where the government operates a forum whose primary purpose is communication, government may play a variety of communicative roles—ranging from choosing the communication and communicators allowed to use the forum, to editor, to active speaker. Is it possible to reconcile a constitutional requirement of government content neutrality in the public forum with a conception of government as a partisan communicator? Consider Columbia Broadcasting System, Inc. v. National Democratic Committee, 412 U.S. 94 (1973), infra, p. 1591. The Court rejected statutory and constitutional claims that radio and television stations could not refuse to sell editorial advertising time. Justice Brennan's dissent, joined by Justice Marshall, concluded that the scheme of federal regulation of the electronic media constituted sufficient governmental action to require application of the first amendment to decisions made by owners of radio and television stations. He argued that the fact that the broadcast forum was designed specifically for communication made arguments for applying constitutional requirements of equal access to that forum even stronger than in the case of parks and streets, since a requirement of access "would in no sense divert that spectrum from its intended use." He conceded that broadcasters have a first amendment interest in exercising "journalistic supervision," which would operate in "normal programming time," but concluded that the right of broadcasters to speak was less central to decisions that deal "only with the allocation of advertising time." Contrast Justice Douglas' assertion in his opinion concurring in the result in Lehman v. City of Shaker Heights, 418 U.S. 298, 306 (1974), that "[t]he First Amendment ... draws no distinction between press privately owned, and press owned otherwise." (In the *C.B.S.* case, in polar contradiction to Justice Brennan, Justice Douglas argued that existing federal statutory requirements of broadcast impartiality and public access were unconstitutional.) Is it possible to reconcile an interpretation of the first amendment that overturns government requirements of neutrality for a privately owned communicative forum with

[127] The historical bases of the Religion and Speech Clauses are markedly different. Intolerable persecutions throughout history led to the Framers' firm determination that religious worship—both in method and belief—must be strictly protected from government intervention.... But the central purpose of the Speech and Press Clauses was to assure a society in which "uninhibited, robust, and wide-open" public debate concerning matters of public interest would thrive, for only in such a society can a healthy representative democracy flourish. New York Times Co. v. Sullivan, 376 U.S. 254, 270 (1964). Legislation to enhance these First Amendment values is the rule, not the exception. Our statute books are replete with laws providing financial assistance to the exercise of free speech, such as aid to public broadcasting and other forms of educational media, 47 U.S.C. §§ 390–399, and preferential postal rates and antitrust exemptions for newspapers, 39 CFR § 132.2 (1975); 15 U.S.C. §§ 1801–1804.

another first amendment interpretation that imposes a constitutional requirement of neutrality for a similar governmentally owned forum? See Canby, *The
First Amendment and the State as Editor: Implications for Public Broadcasting,*
52 Tex.L.Rev. 1123 (1974).

Tinker v. Des Moines Independent Community School District

393 U.S. 503, 89 S.Ct. 733, 21 L.Ed.2d 731 (1969).

[In December, 1965, petitioners, Des Moines high school and junior high
students, wore black armbands to school to publicize their objections to United
States operations in Vietnam. Anticipating such action, the school authorities
had adopted a policy that any student wearing an armband to school would be
requested to remove it, and if he refused he would be suspended until he
returned without the armband. Petitioners refused to remove their armbands
and were suspended. They sought a federal injunction restraining the school
officials from disciplining them; the lower federal courts upheld the action of
the school authorities on the ground that it was reasonable in order to prevent
disturbance of school discipline.]

Mr. Justice Fortas delivered the opinion of the Court.

. . .

. . . [T]he wearing of armbands in the circumstances of this case was
entirely divorced from actually or potentially disruptive conduct by those
participating in it. It was closely akin to "pure speech" which, we have
repeatedly held, is entitled to comprehensive protection under the First Amendment. . . .

First Amendment rights, applied in light of the special characteristics of
the school environment, are available to teachers and students. It can hardly be
argued that either students or teachers shed their constitutional rights to
freedom of speech or expression at the schoolhouse gate. This has been the
unmistakable holding of this Court for almost 50 years. In Meyer v. Nebraska,
262 U.S. 390 (1923), and Bartels v. Iowa, 262 U.S. 404 (1923), this Court, in
opinions by Mr. Justice McReynolds, held that the Due Process Clause of the
Fourteenth Amendment prevents States from forbidding the teaching of a
foreign language to young students. Statutes to this effect, the Court held,
unconstitutionally interfere with the liberty of teacher, student, and parent.[2]

. . .

. . . On the other hand, the Court has repeatedly emphasized the need for
affirming the comprehensive authority of the States and of school officials,
consistent with fundamental constitutional safeguards, to prescribe and control
conduct in the schools. See Epperson v. Arkansas, supra, [393 U.S.] at 104;

---

[2] Hamilton v. Regents of Univ. of Cal.,
293 U.S. 245 (1934) is sometimes cited for
the broad proposition that the State may
attach conditions to attendance at a state
university that require individuals to violate
their religious convictions. The case involved
dismissal of members of a religious denomination from a land grant college for refusal to
participate in military training. Narrowly
viewed, the case turns upon the Court's conclusion that merely requiring a student to
participate in school training in military "science" could not conflict with his constitutionally protected freedom of conscience. The decision cannot be taken as establishing that
the State may impose and enforce any conditions that it chooses upon attendance at public institutions of learning, however violative
they may be of fundamental constitutional
guaranties. See, e.g., West Virginia v. Barnette, 319 U.S. 624 (1943). . . .

Meyer v. Nebraska, supra, [262 U.S.] at 402. Our problem lies in the area where students in the exercise of First Amendment rights collide with the rules of the school authorities.

The problem posed by the present case does not relate to regulation of the length of skirts or the type of clothing, to hair style or deportment.... It does not concern aggressive, disruptive action or even group demonstrations. Our problem involves direct, primary First Amendment rights akin to "pure speech."

The school officials banned and sought to punish petitioners for a silent, passive, expression of opinion, unaccompanied by any disorder or disturbance on the part of petitioners. There is here no evidence whatever of petitioners' interference, actual or nascent, with the school's work or of collision with the rights of other students to be secure and to be let alone....

.   .   .

In order for the State in the person of school officials to justify prohibition of a particular expression of opinion, it must be able to show that its action was caused by something more than a mere desire to avoid the discomfort and unpleasantness that always accompany an unpopular viewpoint....

In the present case, the District Court made no such finding, and our independent examination of the record fails to yield evidence that the school authorities had reason to anticipate that the wearing of the armbands would substantially interfere with the work of the school or impinge upon the rights of other students....

On the contrary, the action of the school authorities appears to have been based upon an urgent wish to avoid the controversy which might result from the expression, even by the silent symbol of armbands, of opposition to this Nation's part in the conflagration of Vietnam....

It is also relevant that the school authorities did not purport to prohibit the wearing of all symbols of political or controversial significance. The record shows that students in some of the schools wore buttons relating to national political campaigns, and some even wore the Iron Cross, traditionally a symbol of Nazism. The order prohibiting the wearing of armbands did not extend to these. Instead, a particular symbol—black armbands worn to exhibit opposition to this Nation's involvement in Vietnam—was singled out for prohibition. Clearly, the prohibition of expression of one particular opinion, at least without evidence that it is necessary to avoid material and substantial interference with schoolwork or discipline, is not constitutionally permissible.

.   .   .

The principal use to which the schools are dedicated is to accommodate students during prescribed hours for the purpose of certain types of activities. Among those activities is personal intercommunication among the students. This is not only an inevitable part of the process of attending school; it is also an important part of the educational process. A student's rights therefore, do not embrace merely the classroom hours. When he is in the cafeteria, or on the playing field, or on the campus during the authorized hours, he may express his opinions, even on controversial subjects like the conflict in Vietnam, if he does so without "materially and substantially interfer[ing] with ... appropriate discipline in the operation of the school" and without colliding with the rights of others. Burnside v. Byars, [363 F.2d] at 749. But conduct by the student, in class or out of it, which for any reason—whether it stems from time, place, or type of behavior—materially disrupts classwork or involves substantial disorder or invasion of the rights of others is, of course, not immunized by the constitutional guarantee of freedom of speech....

. . .

As we have discussed, the record does not demonstrate any facts which might reasonably have led school authorities to forecast substantial disruption of or material interference with school activities, and no disturbances or disorders on the school premises in fact occurred. These petitioners merely went about their ordained rounds in school. Their deviation consisted only in wearing on their sleeve a band of black cloth, not more than two inches wide. They wore it to exhibit their disapproval of the Vietnam hostilities and their advocacy of a truce, to make their views known, and, by their example, to influence others to adopt them. They neither interrupted school activities nor sought to intrude in the school affairs or the lives of others. They caused discussion outside of the classrooms, but no interference with work and no disorder. In the circumstances, our Constitution does not permit officials of the State to deny their form of expression.

We express no opinion as to the form of relief which should be granted, this being a matter for the lower courts to determine. We reverse and remand for further proceedings consistent with this opinion.

Reversed and remanded.[a]

Mr. Justice Stewart, concurring.

Although I agree with much of what is said in the Court's opinion, and with its judgment in this case, I cannot share the Court's uncritical assumption that, school discipline aside, the First Amendment rights of children are co-extensive with those of adults....

Mr. Justice White, concurring.

While I join the Court's opinion, I deem it appropriate to note ... that the Court continues to recognize a distinction between communicating by words and communicating by acts or conduct which sufficiently impinge on some valid state interest....

Mr. Justice Black, dissenting.

... I think the record overwhelmingly shows that the armbands did exactly what the elected school officials and principals foresaw they would, that is, took the students' minds off their classwork and diverted them to thoughts about the highly emotional subject of the Vietnam war....

I deny ... that it has been the "unmistakable holding of this Court for almost 50 years" that "students" and "teachers" take with them into the "schoolhouse gate" constitutional rights to "freedom of speech or expression." ... The truth is that a teacher of kindergarten, grammar school, or high school pupils no more carries into a school with him a complete right to freedom of speech and expression than an anti-Catholic or anti-Semite carries with him a complete freedom of speech and religion into a Catholic church or Jewish synagogue. Nor does a person carry with him into the United States Senate or House, or into the Supreme Court, or any other court, a complete constitutional right to go into those places contrary to their rules and speak his mind on any subject he pleases. It is a myth to say that any person has a constitutional right to say what he pleases, where he pleases, and when he pleases....

. . .

---

[a] A dissent by Justice Harlan has been omitted.

Bethel School District No. 403 v. Fraser

478 U.S. 675, 106 S.Ct. 3159, 92 L.Ed.2d 549 (1986).

Chief Justice Burger delivered the opinion of the Court.

We granted certiorari to decide whether the First Amendment prevents a school district from disciplining a high school student for giving a lewd speech at a school assembly.

I

A

On April 26, 1983, respondent Matthew N. Fraser, a student at Bethel High School in Pierce County, Washington, delivered a speech nominating a fellow student for student elective office. Approximately 600 high school students, many of whom were 14–year–olds, attended the assembly. Students were required to attend the assembly or to report to the study hall. The assembly was part of a school-sponsored educational program in self-government. Students who elected not to attend the assembly were required to report to study hall. During the entire speech, Fraser referred to his candidate in terms of an elaborate, graphic, and explicit sexual metaphor.

Two of Fraser's teachers, with whom he discussed the contents of his speech in advance, informed him that the speech was "inappropriate and that he probably should not deliver it," and that his delivery of the speech might have "severe consequences."

During Fraser's delivery of the speech, a school counselor observed the reaction of students to the speech. Some students hooted and yelled; some by gestures graphically simulated the sexual activities pointedly alluded to in respondent's speech. Other students appeared to be bewildered and embarrassed by the speech. One teacher reported that on the day following the speech, she found it necessary to forgo a portion of the scheduled class lesson in order to discuss the speech with the class.

A Bethel High School disciplinary rule prohibiting the use of obscene language in the school provides:

> "Conduct which materially and substantially interferes with the educational process is prohibited, including the use of obscene, profane language or gestures."

The morning after the assembly, the Assistant Principal called Fraser into her office and notified him that the school considered his speech to have been a violation of this rule. Fraser was presented with copies of five letters submitted by teachers, describing his conduct at the assembly; he was given a chance to explain his conduct, and he admitted to having given the speech described and that he deliberately used sexual innuendo in the speech. Fraser was then informed that he would be suspended for three days, and that his name would be removed from the list of candidates for graduation speaker at the school's commencement exercises.

Fraser sought review of this disciplinary action through the School District's grievance procedures. The hearing officer determined that the speech given by respondent was "indecent, lewd, and offensive to the modesty and decency of many of the students and faculty in attendance at the assembly." The examiner determined that the speech fell within the ordinary meaning of "obscene," as used in the disruptive-conduct rule, and affirmed the discipline in its entirety. Fraser served two days of his suspension, and was allowed to return to school on the third day.

B

Respondent, by his father as guardian ad litem, then brought this action in the United States District Court for the Western District of Washington. Respondent alleged a violation of his First Amendment right to freedom of speech and sought both injunctive relief and monetary damages under 42 U.S.C. § 1983. The District Court held that the school's sanctions violated respondent's right to freedom of speech under the First Amendment to the United States Constitution. . . .

The Court of Appeals for the Ninth Circuit affirmed the judgment of the District Court. . . .

. . . We reverse.

II

. . .

The marked distinction between the political "message" of the armbands in *Tinker* and the sexual content of respondent's speech in this case seems to have been given little weight by the Court of Appeals. In upholding the students' right to engage in a nondisruptive, passive expression of a political viewpoint in *Tinker,* this Court was careful to note that the case did "not concern speech or action that intrudes upon the work of the schools or the rights of other students." Id., at 508.

It is against this background that we turn to consider the level of First Amendment protection accorded to Fraser's utterances and actions before an official high school assembly attended by 600 students.

III

The role and purpose of the American public school system were well described by two historians, who stated: "[P]ublic education must prepare pupils for citizenship in the Republic. . . . It must inculcate the habits and manners of civility as values in themselves conducive to happiness and as indispensable to the practice of self-government in the community and the nation." C. Beard & M. Beard, New Basic History of the United States 228 (1968). In Ambach v. Norwick, 441 U.S. 68, 76–77 (1979), we echoed the essence of this statement of the objectives of public education as the "inculcation of fundamental values necessary to the maintenance of a democratic political system."

These fundamental values of "habits and manners of civility" essential to a democratic society must, of course, include tolerance of divergent political and religious views, even when the views expressed may be unpopular. But these "fundamental values" must also take into account consideration of the sensibilities of others, and, in the case of a school, the sensibilities of fellow students. The undoubted freedom to advocate unpopular and controversial views in schools and classrooms must be balanced against the society's countervailing interest in teaching students the boundaries of socially appropriate behavior. Even the most heated political discourse in a democratic society requires consideration for the personal sensibilities of the other participants and audiences.

In our Nation's legislative halls, where some of the most vigorous political debates in our society are carried on, there are rules prohibiting the use of expressions offensive to other participants in the debate.... Can it be that what is proscribed in the halls of Congress is beyond the reach of school officials to regulate?

The First Amendment guarantees wide freedom in matters of adult public discourse. A sharply divided Court upheld the right to express an antidraft viewpoint in a public place, albeit in terms highly offensive to most citizens. See Cohen v. California, 403 U.S. 15 (1971). It does not follow, however, that simply because the use of an offensive form of expression may not be prohibited to adults making what the speaker considers a political point, that the same latitude must be permitted to children in a public school....

Surely it is a highly appropriate function of public school education to prohibit the use of vulgar and offensive terms in public discourse. Indeed, the "fundamental values necessary to the maintenance of a democratic political system" disfavor the use of terms of debate highly offensive or highly threatening to others. Nothing in the Constitution prohibits the states from insisting that certain modes of expression are inappropriate and subject to sanctions. The inculcation of these values is truly the "work of the schools." *Tinker,* 393 U.S., at 508 ... The determination of what manner of speech in the classroom or in school assembly is inappropriate properly rests with the school board.

The process of educating our youth for citizenship in public schools is not confined to books, the curriculum, and the civics class; schools must teach by example the shared values of a civilized social order. Consciously or otherwise, teachers—and indeed the older students—demonstrate the appropriate form of civil discourse and political expression by their conduct and deportment in and out of class. Inescapably, like parents, they are role models. The schools, as instruments of the state, may determine that the essential lessons of civil, mature conduct cannot be conveyed in a school that tolerates lewd, indecent, or offensive speech and conduct such as that indulged in by this confused boy.

The pervasive sexual innuendo in Fraser's speech was plainly offensive to both teachers and students—indeed to any mature person. By glorifying male sexuality, and in its verbal content, the speech was acutely insulting to teenage girl students. The speech could well be seriously damaging to its less mature audience, many of whom were only 14 years old and on the threshold of awareness of human sexuality. Some students were reported as bewildered by the speech and the reaction of mimicry it provoked.

. . .

We hold that petitioner School District acted entirely within its permissible authority in imposing sanctions upon Fraser in response to his offensively lewd and indecent speech. Unlike the sanctions imposed on the students wearing armbands in *Tinker,* the penalties imposed in this case were unrelated to any political viewpoint. The First Amendment does not prevent the school officials from determining that to permit a vulgar and lewd speech such as respondent's would undermine the school's basic educational mission. A high school assembly or classroom is no place for a sexually explicit monologue directed towards an unsuspecting audience of teenage students. Accordingly, it was perfectly appropriate for the school to disassociate itself to make the point to the pupils that vulgar speech and lewd conduct is wholly inconsistent with the "fundamental values" of public school education....

IV

Respondent contends that the circumstances of his suspension violated due process because he had no way of knowing that the delivery of the speech in question would subject him to disciplinary sanctions. This argument is wholly without merit.... Given the school's need to be able to impose disciplinary sanctions for a wide range of unanticipated conduct disruptive of the educational process, the school disciplinary rules need not be as detailed as a criminal code which imposes criminal sanctions....

The judgment of the Court of Appeals for the Ninth Circuit is reversed.

Justice Blackmun concurs in the result.

Justice Brennan, concurring in the judgment.

Respondent gave the following speech at a high school assembly in support of a candidate for student government office:

"I know a man who is firm—he's firm in his pants, he's firm in his shirt, his character is firm—but most ... of all, his belief in you, the students of Bethel, is firm.

"Jeff Kuhlman is a man who takes his point and pounds it in. If necessary, he'll take an issue and nail it to the wall. He doesn't attack things in spurts—he drives hard, pushing and pushing until finally—he succeeds.

"Jeff is a man who will go to the very end—even the climax, for each and every one of you.

"So vote for Jeff for A.S.B. vice-president—he'll never come between you and the best our high school can be."

The Court, referring to these remarks as "obscene," "vulgar," "lewd," and "offensively lewd," concludes that school officials properly punished respondent for uttering the speech. Having read the full text of respondent's remarks, I find it difficult to believe that it is the same speech the Court describes....

The Court today reaffirms the unimpeachable proposition that students do not "shed their constitutional rights to freedom of speech or expression at the schoolhouse gate." If respondent had given the same speech outside of the school environment, he could not have been penalized simply because government officials considered his language to be inappropriate, see Cohen v. California, 403 U.S. 15 (1971); the Court's opinion does not suggest otherwise. Moreover, despite the Court's characterizations, the language respondent used is far removed from the very narrow class of "obscene" speech which the Court has held is not protected by the First Amendment. ...It is true, however, that the State has interests in teaching high school students how to conduct civil and effective public discourse and in avoiding disruption of educational school activities. Thus, the Court holds that under certain circumstances, high school students may properly be reprimanded for giving a speech at a high school assembly which school officials conclude disrupted the school's educational mission. Respondent's speech may well have been protected had he given it in school but under different circumstances, where the school's legitimate interests in teaching and maintaining civil public discourse were less weighty.

. . .

... I believe that school officials did not violate the First Amendment in determining that respondent should be disciplined for the disruptive language he used while addressing a high school assembly. Thus, I concur in the judgment reversing the decision of the Court of Appeals.

Justice Marshall, dissenting.

I agree with the principles that Justice Brennan sets out in his opinion concurring in the judgment. I dissent from the Court's decision, however, because in my view the School District failed to demonstrate that respondent's remarks were indeed disruptive. . . .

Justice Stevens, dissenting.

· · ·

. . . [I]f a student is to be punished for using offensive speech, he is entitled to fair notice of the scope of the prohibition and the consequences of its violation. The interest in free speech protected by the First Amendment and the interest in fair procedure protected by the Due Process Clause of the Fourteenth Amendment combine to require this conclusion.

· · ·

It seems fairly obvious that respondent's speech would be inappropriate in certain classroom and formal social settings. On the other hand, in a locker room or perhaps in a school corridor the metaphor in the speech might be regarded as rather routine comment. If this be true, and if respondent's audience consisted almost entirely of young people with whom he conversed on a daily basis, can we—at this distance—confidently assert that he must have known that the school administration would punish him for delivering it?

· · ·

I would affirm the judgment of the Court of Appeals.

Board of Education v. Pico

457 U.S. 853, 102 S.Ct. 2799, 73 L.Ed.2d 435 (1982).

Justice Brennan announced the judgment of the Court and delivered an opinion in which Justice Marshall and Justice Stevens joined, and in which Justice Blackmun joined except for Part II–A–(1).

The principal question presented is whether the First Amendment imposes limitations upon the exercise by a local school board of its discretion to remove library books from high school and junior high school libraries.

I

Petitioners are the Board of Education of the Island Trees Union Free School District No. 26, in New York, and [officers and members of the Board]. . . . Respondents . . . were students at the High School, and . . . a student at the Junior High School.

In September 1975 [3 officers and members of the board] attended a conference sponsored by Parents of New York United (PONYU), a politically conservative organization of parents concerned about education legislation in the State of New York. At the conference these petitioners obtained lists of books described . . . as "objectionable," and . . . as "improper fare for school students." It was later determined that the High School library contained nine of the listed books, and that another listed book was in the Junior High School library.[2] In February 1976, at a meeting with the Superintendent of Schools

---

[2] The nine books in the High School library were: Slaughter House Five, by Kurt Vonnegut, Jr.; The Naked Ape, by Desmond Morris; Down These Mean Streets, by Piri

and the Principals of the High School and Junior High School, the Board gave an "unofficial direction" that the listed books be removed from the library shelves and delivered to the Board's offices, so that Board members could read them. When this directive was carried out, it became publicized, and the Board issued a press release justifying its action. It characterized the removed books as "anti-American, anti-Christian, anti-Semitic, and just plain filthy," and concluded that "[i]t is our duty, our moral obligation, to protect the children in our schools from this moral danger as surely as from physical and medical dangers."

A short time later, the Board appointed a "Book Review Committee," consisting of four Island Trees parents and four members of the Island Trees schools staff, to read the listed books and to recommend to the Board whether the books should be retained, taking into account the books' "educational suitability," "good taste," "relevance," and "appropriateness to age and grade level." In July, the Committee made its final report to the Board, recommending that five of the listed books be retained and that two others be removed from the school libraries. As for the remaining four books, the Committee could not agree on two, took no position on one, and recommended that the last book be made available to students only with parental approval. The Board substantially rejected the Committee's report later that month, deciding that only one book should be returned to the High School library without restriction, that another should be made available subject to parental approval, but that the remaining nine books should "be removed from elementary and secondary libraries and [from] use in the curriculum." The Board gave no reasons for rejecting the recommendations of the Committee that it had appointed.

Respondents reacted to the Board's decision by bringing the present action under 42 U.S.C. § 1983 in the United States District Court for the Eastern District of New York. They alleged that petitioners had

> "ordered the removal of the books from school libraries and proscribed their use in the curriculum because particular passages in the books offended their social, political and moral tastes and not because the books, taken as a whole, were lacking in educational value."

Respondents claimed that the Board's actions denied them their rights under the First Amendment. They asked the court for a declaration that the Board's actions were unconstitutional, and for preliminary and permanent injunctive relief ordering the Board to return the nine books to the school libraries and to refrain from interfering with the use of those books in the schools' curricula.

. . . .

II

We emphasize at the outset the limited nature of the substantive question presented by the case before us. Our precedents have long recognized certain constitutional limits upon the power of the State to control even the curriculum and classroom. For example, Meyer v. Nebraska, 262 U.S. 390 (1923), struck down a state law that forbade the teaching of modern foreign languages in public and private schools, and Epperson v. Arkansas, 393 U.S. 97 (1968),

---

Thomas; Best Short Stories of Negro Writers, edited by Langston Hughes; Go Ask Alice, of anonymous authorship; Laughing Boy, by Oliver LaFarge; Black Boy, by Richard Wright; A Hero Ain't Nothin' But A Sandwich, by Alice Childress; and Soul On Ice, by Eldridge Cleaver. The book in the Junior High School library was A Reader for Writers, edited by Jerome Archer. Still another listed book, The Fixer, by Bernard Malamud, was found to be included in the curriculum of a 12th–grade literature course.

declared unconstitutional a state law that prohibited the teaching of the Darwinian theory of evolution in any state-supported school. But the current action does not require us to re-enter this difficult terrain, which *Meyer* and *Epperson* traversed without apparent misgiving. For as this case is presented to us, it does not involve textbooks, or indeed any books that Island Trees students would be required to read. Respondents do not seek in this Court to impose limitations upon their school board's discretion to prescribe the curricula of the Island Trees schools. On the contrary, the only books at issue in this case are *library* books, books that by their nature are optional rather than required reading. Our adjudication of the present case thus does not intrude into the classroom, or into the compulsory courses taught there. Furthermore, even as to library books, the action before us does not involve the *acquisition* of books. Respondents have not sought to compel their school board to add to the school library shelves any books that students desire to read. Rather, the only action challenged in this case is the *removal* from school libraries of books originally placed there by the school authorities, or without objection from them.

The substantive question before us is still further constrained by the procedural posture of this case. Petitioners were granted summary judgment by the District Court. The Court of Appeals reversed that judgment, and remanded the action for a trial on the merits of respondents' claims. We can reverse the judgment of the Court of Appeals, and grant petitioners' request for reinstatement of the summary judgment in their favor, only if we determine that "there is no genuine issue as to any material fact," and that petitioners are "entitled to a judgment as a matter of law." Fed.Rule Civ.Proc. 56(c). In making our determination, any doubt as to the existence of a genuine issue of material fact must be resolved against petitioners as the moving party. . . .

In sum, the issue before us in this case is a narrow one, both substantively and procedurally. It may best be restated as two distinct questions. First, Does the First Amendment impose *any* limitations upon the discretion of petitioners to remove library books from the Island Trees High School and Junior High School? Second, If so, do the affidavits and other evidentiary materials before the District Court, construed most favorably to respondents, raise a genuine issue of fact whether petitioners might have exceeded those limitations? If we answer either of these questions in the negative, then we must reverse the judgment of the Court of Appeals and reinstate the District Court's summary judgment for petitioners. If we answer both questions in the affirmative, then we must affirm the judgment below. We examine these questions in turn.

A

(1)

The Court has long recognized that local school boards have broad discretion in the management of school affairs. . . . We are therefore in full agreement with petitioners that local school boards must be permitted "to establish and apply their curriculum in such a way as to transmit community values," and that "there is a legitimate and substantial community interest in promoting respect for authority and traditional values be they social, moral, or political."

At the same time, however, we have necessarily recognized that the discretion of the States and local school boards in matters of education must be exercised in a manner that comports with the transcendent imperatives of the First Amendment. In West Virginia Board of Education v. Barnette, 319 U.S. 624 (1943), we held that under the First Amendment a student in a public school could not be compelled to salute the flag. We reasoned that

"Boards of Education ... have, of course, important, delicate, and highly discretionary functions, but none that they may not perform within the limits of the Bill of Rights. That they are educating the young for citizenship is reason for scrupulous protection of Constitutional freedoms of the individual, if we are not to strangle the free mind at its source and teach youth to discount important principles of our government as mere platitudes." Id., at 637....

. . .

Of course, courts should not "intervene in the resolution of conflicts which arise in the daily operations of school systems" unless "basic constitutional values" are "directly and sharply implicate[d]" in those conflicts. Epperson v. Arkansas, 393 U.S., at 104. But we think that the First Amendment rights of students may be directly and sharply implicated by the removal of books from the shelves of a school library. Our precedents have focused "not only on the role of the First Amendment in fostering individual self-expression but also on its role in affording the public access to discussion, debate, and the dissemination of information and ideas." First National Bank of Boston v. Bellotti, 435 U.S. 765, 783 (1978). And we have recognized that "the State may not, consistently with the spirit of the First Amendment, contract the spectrum of available knowledge." Griswold v. Connecticut, 381 U.S. 479, 482 (1965). In keeping with this principle, we have held that in a variety of contexts "the Constitution protects the right to receive information and ideas." Stanley v. Georgia, 394 U.S. 557, 564 (1969); see Kleindienst v. Mandel, 408 U.S. 753, 762–763 (1972) (citing cases). This right is an inherent corollary of the rights of free speech and press that are explicitly guaranteed by the Constitution, in two senses. First, the right to receive ideas follows ineluctably from the *sender's* First Amendment right to send them: "The right of freedom of speech and press ... embraces the right to distribute literature, and necessarily protects the right to receive it." Martin v. Struthers, 319 U.S. 141, 143 (1943) (citation omitted).

. . .

... [J]ust as access to ideas makes it possible for citizens generally to exercise their rights of free speech and press in a meaningful manner, such access prepares students for active and effective participation in the pluralistic, often contentious society in which they will soon be adult members. Of course all First Amendment rights accorded to students must be construed "in light of the special characteristics of the school environment." Tinker v. Des Moines School Dist., 393 U.S., at 506. But the special characteristics of the school *library* make that environment especially appropriate for the recognition of the First Amendment rights of students.

... Petitioners emphasize the inculcative function of secondary education, and argue that they must be allowed *unfettered* discretion to "transmit community values" through the Island Trees schools. But that sweeping claim overlooks the unique role of the school library. It appears from the record that use of the Island Trees school libraries is completely voluntary on the part of students. Their selection of books from these libraries is entirely a matter of free choice; the libraries afford them an opportunity at self-education and individual enrichment that is wholly optional. Petitioners might well defend their claim of absolute discretion in matters of *curriculum* by reliance upon their duty to inculcate community values. But we think that petitioners' reliance upon that duty is misplaced where, as here, they attempt to extend their claim of absolute discretion beyond the compulsory environment of the classroom, into the school library and the regime of voluntary inquiry that there holds sway.

(2)

In rejecting petitioners' claim of absolute discretion to remove books from their school libraries, we do not deny that local school boards have a substantial legitimate role to play in the determination of school library content. We thus must turn to the question of the extent to which the First Amendment places limitations upon the discretion of petitioners to remove books from their libraries. . . .

. . . Petitioners rightly possess significant discretion to determine the content of their school libraries. But that discretion may not be exercised in a narrowly partisan or political manner. If a Democratic school board, motivated by party affiliation, ordered the removal of all books written by or in favor of Republicans, few would doubt that the order violated the constitutional rights of the students denied access to those books. The same conclusion would surely apply if an all-white school board, motivated by racial animus, decided to remove all books authored by blacks or advocating racial equality and integration. Our Constitution does not permit the official suppression of *ideas*. Thus whether petitioners' removal of books from their school libraries denied respondents their First Amendment rights depends upon the motivation behind petitioners' action. If petitioners *intended* by their removal decision to deny respondents access to ideas with which petitioners disagreed, and if this intent was the decisive factor in petitioners' decision, then petitioners have exercised their discretion in violation of the Constitution. To permit such intentions to control official actions would be to encourage the precise sort of officially prescribed orthodoxy unequivocally condemned in *Barnette*. On the other hand, respondents implicitly concede that an unconstitutional motivation would *not* be demonstrated if it were shown that petitioners had decided to remove the books at issue because those books were pervasively vulgar. And again, respondents concede that if it were demonstrated that the removal decision was based solely upon the "educational suitability" of the books in question, then their removal would be "perfectly permissible." In other words, in respondents' view such motivations, if decisive of petitioners' actions, would not carry the danger of an official suppression of ideas, and thus would not violate respondents' First Amendment rights.

As noted earlier, nothing in our decision today affects in any way the discretion of a local school board to choose books to *add* to the libraries of their schools. Because we are concerned in this case with the suppression of ideas, our holding today affects only the discretion to *remove* books. In brief, we hold that local school boards may not remove books from school library shelves simply because they dislike the ideas contained in those books and seek by their removal to "prescribe what shall be orthodox in politics, nationalism, religion, or other matters of opinion." West Virginia Board of Education v. Barnette, 319 U.S., at 642. Such purposes stand inescapably condemned by our precedents.

B

We now turn to the remaining question presented by this case: Do the evidentiary materials that were before the District Court, when construed most favorably to respondents, raise a genuine issue of material fact whether petitioners exceeded constitutional limitations in exercising their discretion to remove the books from the school libraries? We conclude that the materials do raise such a question, which forecloses summary judgment in favor of petitioners.

. . .

. . . The evidence plainly does not foreclose the possibility that petitioners' decision to remove the books rested decisively upon disagreement with constitutionally protected ideas in those books, or upon a desire on petitioners' part to impose upon the students of the Island Trees High School and Junior High School a political orthodoxy to which petitioners and their constituents adhered. Of course, some of the evidence before the District Court might lead a finder of fact to accept petitioners' claim that their removal decision was based upon constitutionally valid concerns. But that evidence at most creates a genuine issue of material fact on the critical question of the credibility of petitioners' justifications for their decision. . . .

The mandate shall issue forthwith.

Affirmed.

Justice Blackmun, concurring in part and concurring in the judgment.

While I agree with much in today's plurality opinion, and while I accept the standard laid down by the plurality to guide proceedings on remand, I write separately because I have a somewhat different perspective on the nature of the First Amendment right involved.

I

To my mind, this case presents a particularly complex problem because it involves two competing principles of constitutional stature. On the one hand, . . . [it] seems entirely appropriate that the State use "public schools [to] . . . inculcat[e] fundamental values necessary to the maintenance of a democratic political system." Ambach v. Norwick, 441 U.S., at 77.

On the other hand, as the plurality demonstrates, it is beyond dispute that schools and school boards must operate within the confines of the First Amendment. . . .

In my view, . . . the principle involved here is both narrower and more basic than the "right to receive information" identified by the plurality. I do not suggest that the State has any affirmative obligation to provide students with information or ideas, something that may well be associated with a "right to receive." And I do not believe, as the plurality suggests, that the right at issue here is somehow associated with the peculiar nature of the school library if schools may be used to inculcate ideas, surely libraries may play a role in that process. Instead, I suggest that certain forms of state discrimination between ideas are improper. In particular, our precedents command the conclusion that the State may not act to deny access to an idea simply because state officials disapprove of that idea for partisan or political reasons.

. . .

II

In my view, we strike a proper balance here by holding that school officials may not remove books for the purpose of restricting access to the political ideas or social perspectives discussed in them, when that action is motivated simply by the officials' disapproval of the ideas involved. . . .

. . .

Because I believe that the plurality has derived a standard similar to the one compelled by my analysis, I join all but Part II–A(1) of the plurality opinion.

Justice White, concurring in the judgment.

The District Court found that the books were removed from the school library because the school board believed them "to be, in essence, vulgar". Both Court of Appeals judges in the majority concluded, however, that there was a material issue of fact that precluded summary judgment sought by petitioners. The unresolved factual issue, as I understand it, is the reason or reasons underlying the school board's removal of the books. I am not inclined to disagree with the Court of Appeals on such a fact-bound issue and hence concur in the judgment of affirmance. Presumably this will result in a trial and the making of a full record and findings on the critical issues.

The plurality seems compelled to go further and issue a dissertation on the extent to which the First Amendment limits the discretion of the school board to remove books from the school library. I see no necessity for doing so at this point. When findings of fact and conclusions of law are made by the District Court, that may end the case. If, for example, the District Court concludes after a trial that the books were removed for their vulgarity, there may be no appeal. In any event, if there is an appeal, if there is dissatisfaction with the subsequent Court of Appeals' judgment, and if certiorari is sought and granted, there will be time enough to address the First Amendment issues that may then be presented.

. . .[a]

Chief Justice Burger, with whom Justice Powell, Justice Rehnquist, and Justice O'Connor join, dissenting.

. . .

Whatever role the government might play as a conduit of information, schools in particular ought not be made a slavish courier of the material of third parties. . . . [Since] schools may legitimately be used as vehicles for "inculcating fundamental values necessary to the maintenance of a democratic political system," Ambach v. Norwick, 441 U.S. 68, 77 (1979), school authorities must have broad discretion to fulfill that obligation. Presumably all activity within a primary or secondary school involves the conveyance of information and at least an implied approval of the worth of that information. How are "fundamental values" to be inculcated except by having school boards make content-based decisions about the appropriateness of retaining materials in the school library and curriculum. In order to fulfill its function, an elected school board *must* express its views on the subjects which are taught to its students. In doing so those elected officials express the views of their community; they may err, of course, and the voters may remove them. It is a startling erosion of the very idea of democratic government to have this Court arrogate to itself the power the plurality asserts today.

. . .

[a] Dissenting opinions by Justices Powell and O'Connor are omitted.

Justice Rehnquist, with whom The Chief Justice and Justice Powell join, dissenting.

Addressing only those aspects of the constitutional question which must be decided to determine whether or not the District Court was correct in granting summary judgment, I conclude that it was....

I

A

. . .

... Petitioners did not, for the reasons stated hereafter, run afoul of the First and Fourteenth Amendments by removing these particular books from the library in the manner in which they did. I would save for another day—feeling quite confident that that day will not arrive—the extreme examples posed in Justice Brennan's opinion.

B

Considerable light is shed on the correct resolution of the constitutional question in this case by examining the role played by petitioners. Had petitioners been the members of a town council, I suppose all would agree that, absent a good deal more than is present in this record, they could not have prohibited the sale of these books by private booksellers within the municipality. But we have also recognized that the government may act in other capacities than as sovereign, and when it does the First Amendment may speak with a different voice. . . .

... When it acts as an educator, at least at the elementary and secondary school level, the government is engaged in inculcating social values and knowledge in relatively impressionable young people. Obviously there are innumerable decisions to be made as to what courses should be taught, what books should be purchased, or what teachers should be employed. In every one of these areas the members of a school board will act on the basis of their own personal or moral values, will attempt to mirror those of the community, or will abdicate the making of such decisions to so-called "experts." ... In the very course of administering the many-faceted operations of a school district, the mere decision to purchase some books will necessarily preclude the possibility of purchasing others. The decision to teach a particular subject may preclude the possibility of teaching another subject. A decision to replace a teacher because of ineffectiveness may by implication be seen as a disparagement of the subject matter taught. In each of these instances, however, the book or the exposure to the subject matter may be acquired elsewhere. The managers of the school district are not proscribing it as to the citizenry in general, but are simply determining that it will not be included in the curriculum or school library. In short, actions by the government as educator do not raise the same First Amendment concerns as actions by the government as sovereign.

II

. . .

A

Despite Justice Brennan's suggestion to the contrary, this Court has never held that the First Amendment grants junior high school and high school students a right of access to certain information in school....

. . .

... Our past decisions are ... unlike this case where the removed books are readily available to students and non students alike at the corner bookstore or the public library.

B

There are even greater reasons for rejecting Justice Brennan's analysis, however, than the significant fact that we have never adopted it in the past. ...The idea that such students have a right of access, *in the school,* to information other than that thought by their educators to be necessary is contrary to the very nature of an inculcative education.

Education consists of the selective presentation and explanation of ideas. The effective acquisition of knowledge depends upon an orderly exposure to relevant information....

. . .

... The libraries of such schools serve as supplements to this inculcative role. Unlike university or public libraries, elementary and secondary school libraries are not designed for free-wheeling inquiry; they are tailored, as the public school curriculum is tailored, to the teaching of basic skills and ideas. Thus, Justice Brennan cannot rely upon the nature of school libraries to escape the fact that the First Amendment right to receive information simply has no application to the one public institution which, by its very nature, is a place for the selective conveyance of ideas.

After all else is said, however, the most obvious reason that petitioners' removal of the books did not violate respondents' right to receive information is the ready availability of the books elsewhere. ...Indeed, following the removal from the school library of the books at issue in this case, the local public library put all nine books on display for public inspection. Their contents were fully accessible to any inquisitive student.

C

Justice Brennan's own discomfort with the idea that students have a right to receive information from their elementary or secondary schools is demonstrated by the artificial limitations which he places upon the right—limitations which are supported neither by logic nor authority and which are inconsistent with the right itself. The attempt to confine the right to the library is one such limitation, the fallacies of which have already been demonstrated.

As a second limitation, Justice Brennan distinguishes the act of removing a previously acquired book from the act of refusing to acquire the book in the first place: ... The failure of a library to acquire a book denies access to its contents just as effectively as does the removal of the book from the library's shelf. As a result of either action the book cannot be found in the "principal locus" of freedom discovered by Justice Brennan.

. . .

The final limitation placed by Justice Brennan upon his newly discovered right is a motive requirement: the First Amendment is violated only "[i]f petitioners *intended* by their removal decision to deny respondents access to ideas with which petitioners disagreed." But bad motives and good motives alike deny access to the books removed. If Justice Brennan truly recognizes a constitutional right to receive information, it is difficult to see why the reason for the denial makes any difference. Of course Justice Brennan's view is that intent matters because the First Amendment does not tolerate an officially prescribed orthodoxy. But this reasoning mixes First Amendment apples and oranges. The right to receive information differs from the right to be free from an officially prescribed orthodoxy. Not every educational denial of access to information casts a pall of orthodoxy over the classroom.

. . .

Hazelwood School District v. Kuhlmeier

484 U.S. 260, 108 S.Ct. 562, 98 L.Ed.2d 592 (1988).

Justice White delivered the opinion of the Court.

This case concerns the extent to which educators may exercise editorial control over the contents of a high school newspaper produced as part of the school's journalism curriculum.

I

. . . Respondents [three former Hazelwood East High School students who were staff members of Spectrum, the school newspaper] . . . contend that school officials violated their First Amendment rights by deleting two pages of articles from the May 13, 1983, issue of Spectrum.

Spectrum was written and edited by the Journalism II class at Hazelwood East. The newspaper was published every three weeks or so during the 1982–1983 school year. More than 4,500 copies of the newspaper were distributed during that year to students, school personnel, and members of the community.

The Board of Education allocated funds from its annual budget for the printing of Spectrum. These funds were supplemented by proceeds from sales of the newspaper. The printing expenses during the 1982–1983 school year totaled $4,668.50; revenue from sales was $1,166.84. The other costs associated with the newspaper—such as supplies, textbooks, and a portion of the journalism teacher's salary—were borne entirely by the Board.

. . .

The practice at Hazelwood East during the spring 1983 semester was for the journalism teacher to submit page proofs of each Spectrum issue to Principal Reynolds for his review prior to publication. On May 10, Emerson [the faculty newspaper adviser] delivered the proofs of the May 13 edition to Reynolds, who objected to two of the articles scheduled to appear in that edition. One of the stories described three Hazelwood East students' experiences with pregnancy; the other discussed the impact of divorce on students at the school.

Reynolds was concerned that, although the pregnancy story used false names "to keep the identity of these girls a secret," the pregnant students still might be identifiable from the text. He also believed that the article's references to sexual activity and birth control were inappropriate for some of the younger students at the school. In addition, Reynolds was concerned [with] a student identified by name in the divorce story. . . .

Reynolds believed that there was no time to make the necessary changes in the stories before the scheduled press run and that the newspaper would not appear before the end of the school year if printing were delayed to any significant extent. He concluded that his only options under the circumstances were to publish a four-page newspaper instead of the planned six-page newspaper, eliminating the two pages on which the offending stories appeared, or to publish no newspaper at all. . . .

Respondents subsequently commenced this action in the United States District Court for the Eastern District of Missouri seeking a declaration that their First Amendment rights had been violated, injunctive relief, and monetary damages. After a bench trial, the District Court denied an injunction, holding that no First Amendment violation had occurred.

. . .

The Court of Appeals for the Eighth Circuit reversed. . . .

. . .

We . . . reverse.

II

. . .

A

We deal first with the question whether Spectrum may appropriately be characterized as a forum for public expression. The public schools do not possess all of the attributes of streets, parks, and other traditional public forums. . . . Hence, school facilities may be deemed to be public forums only if school authorities have "by policy or by practice" opened those facilities "for indiscriminate use by the general public," Perry Education Assn. v. Perry Local Educators' Assn., 460 U.S. 37 47 (1983), or by some segment of the public, such as student organizations. Id., at 46, n. 7 (citing Widmar v. Vincent). If the facilities have instead been reserved for other intended purposes, "communicative or otherwise," then no public forum has been created . . .

The policy of school officials toward Spectrum was reflected in Hazelwood School Board Policy . . . that "[s]chool sponsored publications are developed within the adopted curriculum and its educational implications in regular classroom activities." The Hazelwood East Curriculum Guide described the Journalism II course as a "laboratory situation in which the students publish the school newspaper applying skills they have learned in Journalism I." . . . Students received grades and academic credit for their performance in the course.

School officials did not deviate in practice from their policy that production of Spectrum was to be part of the educational curriculum and a "regular classroom activit[y]." . . .

. . . Accordingly, school officials were entitled to regulate the contents of Spectrum in any reasonable manner. . . . It is this standard, rather than our decision in *Tinker,* that governs this case.

B

The question whether the First Amendment requires a school to tolerate particular student speech—the question that we addressed in *Tinker*—is different from the question whether the First Amendment requires a school affirmatively to promote particular student speech. The former question addresses educators' ability to silence a student's personal expression that happens to occur on the school premises. The latter question concerns educators' authority over school-sponsored publications, theatrical productions, and other expressive activities that students, parents, and members of the public might reasonably perceive to bear the imprimatur of the school. These activities may fairly be characterized as part of the school curriculum, whether or not they occur in a traditional classroom setting, so long as they are supervised by faculty members and designed to impart particular knowledge or skills to student participants and audiences.[3]

Educators are entitled to exercise greater control over this second form of student expression to assure that participants learn whatever lessons the activity is designed to teach, that readers or listeners are not exposed to material that may be inappropriate for their level of maturity, and that the views of the individual speaker are not erroneously attributed to the school.... [A] school must be able to take into account the emotional maturity of the intended audience in determining whether to disseminate student speech on potentially sensitive topics, which might range from the existence of Santa Claus in an elementary school setting to the particulars of teenage sexual activity in a high school setting. A school must also retain the authority to refuse to sponsor student speech that might reasonably be perceived to advocate drug or alcohol use, irresponsible sex, ... or to associate the school with any position other than neutrality on matters of political controversy....

Accordingly, we conclude that the standard articulated in *Tinker* for determining when a school may punish student expression need not also be the standard for determining when a school may refuse to lend its name and resources to the dissemination of student expression. Instead, we hold that educators do not offend the First Amendment by exercising editorial control over the style and content of student speech in school-sponsored expressive activities so long as their actions are reasonably related to legitimate pedagogical concerns.

... It is only when the decision to censor a school-sponsored publication, theatrical production, or other vehicle of student expression has no valid educational purpose that the First Amendment ... require[s] judicial intervention to protect students' constitutional rights.

III

We also conclude that Principal Reynolds acted reasonably in requiring the deletion from the May 13 issue of Spectrum of the pregnancy article, the divorce article, and the remaining articles that were to appear on the same pages of the newspaper.

. . .

In sum, we cannot reject as unreasonable Principal Reynolds' conclusion that neither the pregnancy article nor the divorce article was suitable for publication in Spectrum. Reynolds could reasonably have concluded that the students who had written and edited these articles had not sufficiently mastered those portions of the Journalism II curriculum that pertained to the treatment of controversial issues and personal attacks, the need to protect the privacy of individuals whose most intimate concerns are to be revealed in the newspaper, and "the legal, moral, and ethical restrictions imposed upon journalists within [a] school community" that includes adolescent subjects and readers. Finally, we conclude that the principal's decision to delete two pages of

---

3 The distinction that we draw between speech that is sponsored by the school and speech that is not is fully consistent with Papish v. Board of Curators of University of Missouri, 410 U.S. 667 (1973) (per curiam), which involved an off-campus "underground" newspaper that school officials merely had allowed to be sold on a state university campus.

Spectrum, rather than to delete only the offending articles or to require that they be modified, was reasonable under the circumstances as he understood them. Accordingly, no violation of First Amendment rights occurred.

. . .

Justice Brennan, with whom Justice Marshall and Justice Blackmun join, dissenting.

. . .

I

. . .

[The Court has never] intimated a distinction between personal and school-sponsored speech in any other context. Particularly telling is this Court's heavy reliance on *Tinker* in two cases of First Amendment infringement on state college campuses. See Papish v. University of Missouri Board of Curators, 410 U.S. 667, 671, n. 6 (1973) (per curiam); Healy v. James, 408 U.S. 169, 180, 189, and n. 18, 191 (1972). One involved the expulsion of a student for lewd expression in a newspaper that she sold on campus pursuant to university authorization, see *Papish,* supra, at 667–668, and the other involved the denial of university recognition and concomitant benefits to a political student organization, see *Healy,* supra, at 174, 176, 181–182. Tracking *Tinker* 's analysis, the Court found each act of suppression unconstitutional. In neither case did this Court suggest the distinction, which the Court today finds dispositive, between school-sponsored and incidental student expression.

II

Even if we were writing on a clean slate, I would reject the Court's rationale for abandoning *Tinker* in this case. . . .

. . .

The mere fact of school sponsorship does not, as the Court suggests, license . . . thought control in the high school, whether through school suppression of disfavored viewpoints or through official assessment of topic sensitivity. The former would constitute unabashed and unconstitutional viewpoint discrimination. . . . [S]chool officials may not, out of like motivation, discriminatorily excise objectionable ideas from a student publication. The State's prerogative to dissolve the student newspaper entirely (or to limit its subject matter) no more entitles it to dictate which viewpoints students may express on its pages, than the State's prerogative to close down the schoolhouse entitles it to prohibit the nondisruptive expression of antiwar sentiment within its gates.

. . . .

SECTION 5. GOVERNMENT SUBSIDIES TO SPEECH

Rust v. Sullivan

500 U.S. 173, 111 S.Ct. 1759, 114 L.Ed.2d 233 (1991).

Chief Justice Rehnquist delivered the opinion of the Court.

These cases concern a facial challenge to Department of Health and Human Services (HHS) regulations which limit the ability of Title X fund recipients to engage in abortion-related activities. . . .

I

A

In 1970, Congress enacted Title X of the Public Health Service Act (Act), 84 stat. 1506, as amended, 42 U.S.C. §§ 300–300a–41, which provides federal funding for family-planning services. The Act authorizes the Secretary to "make grants to and enter into contracts with public or nonprofit private entities to assist in the establishment and operation of voluntary family planning projects which shall offer a broad range of acceptable and effective family planning methods and services." ... Section 1008 of the Act ... provides that "[n]one of the funds appropriated under this subchapter shall be used in programs where abortion is a method of family planning." ... That restriction was intended to ensure that Title X funds would "be used only to support preventive family planning services, population research, infertility services, and other related medical, informational, and educational activities." H.R.Conf.Rep. No. 91–1667, p. 8 (1970).

In 1988, the Secretary promulgated new regulations designed to provide "'clear and operational guidance' to grantees about how to preserve the distinction between Title X programs and abortion as a method of family planning." 53 Fed.Reg. 2923–2924 (1988). The regulations clarify, through the definition of the term "family planning," that Congress intended Title X funds "to be used only to support preventive family planning services." ...

The regulations attach three principal conditions on the grant of federal funds for Title X projects. First, the regulations specify that a "Title X project may not provide counseling concerning the use of abortion as a method of family planning or provide referral for abortion as a method of family planning." 42 CFR 59.8(a)(1) (1989). Because Title X is limited to preconceptional services, the program does not furnish services related to childbirth. Only in the context of a referral out of the Title X program is a pregnant woman given transitional information. § 59.8(a)(2). Title X projects must refer every pregnant client "for appropriate prenatal and/or social services by furnishing a list of available providers that promote the welfare of the mother and the unborn child." Ibid. The list may not be used indirectly to encourage or promote abortion, "such as by weighing the list of referrals in favor of health care providers which perform abortions, by including on the list of referral providers health care providers whose principal business is the provision of abortions, by excluding available providers who do not provide abortions, or by 'steering' clients to providers who offer abortion as a method of family planning." § 59.8(a)(3). The Title X project is expressly prohibited from referring a pregnant woman to an abortion provider, even upon specific request. One permissible response to such an inquiry is that "the project does not consider abortion an appropriate method of family planning and therefore does not counsel or refer for abortion." § 59.8(b)(5).

Second, the regulations broadly prohibit a Title X project from engaging in activities that "encourage, promote or advocate abortion as a method of family planning." § 59.10(a). Forbidden activities include lobbying for legislation that would increase the availability of abortion as a method of family planning, developing or disseminating materials advocating abortion as a method of family planning, providing speakers to promote abortion as a method of family planning, using legal action to make abortion available in any way as a method of family planning, and paying dues to any group that advocates abortion as a method of family planning as a substantial part of its activities. Ibid.

Third, the regulations require that Title X projects be organized so that they are "physically and financially separate" from prohibited abortion activities. § 59.9. To be deemed physically and financially separate, "a Title X project must have an objective integrity and independence from prohibited activities. Mere bookkeeping separation of Title X funds from other monies is not sufficient." Ibid. The regulations provide a list of nonexclusive factors for the Secretary to consider in conducting a case-by-case determination of objective integrity and independence, such as the existence of separate accounting records and separate personnel, and the degree of physical separation of the project from facilities for prohibited activities. Ibid.

B

Petitioners are Title X grantees and doctors who supervise Title X funds suing on behalf of themselves and their patients. Respondent is the Secretary of the Department of Health and Human Services. After the regulations had been promulgated, but before they had been applied, petitioners filed two separate actions, later consolidated, challenging the facial validity of the regulations and seeking declaratory and injunctive relief to prevent implementation of the regulations. Petitioners challenged the regulations on the grounds that they were not authorized by Title X and that they violate the First and Fifth Amendment rights of Title X clients and the First Amendment rights of Title X health providers. After initially granting the petitioners a preliminary injunction, the District Court rejected petitioners' statutory and constitutional challenges to the regulations and granted summary judgment in favor of the Secretary.

A panel of the Court of Appeals for the Second Circuit affirmed. . . .

. . .

II

We begin by pointing out the posture of the cases before us. Petitioners are challenging the facial validity of the regulations. Thus, we are concerned only with the question whether, on their face, the regulations are both authorized by the Act, and can be construed in such a manner that they can be applied to a set of individuals without infringing upon constitutionally protected rights. Petitioners face a heavy burden in seeking to have the regulations invalidated as facially unconstitutional. . . .

We turn first to petitioners' contention that the regulations exceed the Secretary's authority under Title X and are arbitrary and capricious. We begin with an examination of the regulations concerning abortion counseling, referral, and advocacy, which every Court of Appeals has found to be authorized by the statute, and then turn to the "program integrity requirement," with respect to which the courts below have adopted conflicting positions. We then address petitioner's claim that the regulations must be struck down because they raise a substantial constitutional question.

. . .

B

Petitioners . . . contend that the regulations must be invalidated because they raise serious questions of constitutional law. . . .

The principle ... is a categorical one: "as between two possible interpretations of a statute, by one of which it would be unconstitutional and by the other valid, our plain duty is to adopt that which will save the Act." Blodgett v. Holden, 275 U.S. 142, 148 (1927) (opinion of Holmes, J.). This principle is based at least in part on the fact that a decision to declare an act of Congress unconstitutional "is the gravest and most delicate duty that this Court is called on to perform." Id. ...[T]he corollary doctrine [is] that "[a] statute must be construed, if fairly possible, so as to avoid not only the conclusion that it is unconstitutional but also grave doubts upon that score." ... It is qualified by the proposition that "avoidance of a difficulty will not be pressed to the point of disingenuous evasion." Moore Ice Cream Co. v. Rose, 289 U.S. 373, 379 (1933).

... While we do not think that the constitutional arguments made by petitioners in this case are without some force, in Part III, infra, we hold that they do not carry the day. Applying the canon of construction under discussion as best we can, we hold that the regulations promulgated by the Secretary do not raise the sort of "grave and doubtful constitutional questions," ... that would lead us to assume Congress did not intend to authorize their issuance. Therefore, we need not invalidate the regulations in order to save the statute from unconstitutionality.

III

Petitioners contend that the regulations violate the First Amendment by impermissibly discriminating based on viewpoint because they prohibit "all discussion about abortion as a lawful option—including counseling, referral, and the provision of neutral and accurate information about ending a pregnancy—while compelling the clinic or counselor to provide information that promotes continuing a pregnancy to term." They assert that the regulations violate the "free speech rights of private health care organizations that receive Title X funds, of their staff, and of their patients" by impermissibly imposing "viewpoint-discriminatory conditions on government subsidies" and thus "penaliz[e] speech funded with non-Title X monies."... Relying on Regan v. Taxation With Representation of Wash., and Arkansas Writers Project, Inc. v. Ragland, 481 U.S. 221, 234 (1987), petitioners also assert that while the Government may place certain conditions on the receipt of federal subsidies, it may not "discriminate invidiously in its subsidies in such a way as to 'ai[m] at the suppression of dangerous ideas.'" ...

There is no question but that the statutory prohibition contained in § 1008 is constitutional. In Maher v. Roe ... we upheld a state welfare regulation under which Medicaid recipients received payments for services related to childbirth, but not for nontherapeutic abortions. ...The Government can, without violating the Constitution, selectively fund a program to encourage certain activities it believes to be in the public interest, without at the same time funding an alternate program which seeks to deal with the problem in another way. In so doing, the Government has not discriminated on the basis of viewpoint; it has merely chosen to fund one activity to the exclusion of the other. ...

The challenged regulations implement the statutory prohibition by prohibiting counseling, referral, and the provision of information regarding abortion as a method of family planning. They are designed to ensure that the limits of the federal program are observed. The Title X program is designed not for prenatal care, but to encourage family planning. A doctor who wished to offer prenatal care to a project patient who became pregnant could properly be prohibited from doing so because such service is outside the scope of the federally funded program. The regulations prohibiting abortion counseling and referral are of the same ilk; "no funds appropriated for the project may be used in programs where abortion is a method of family planning," and a doctor employed by the project may be prohibited in the course of his project duties from counseling abortion or referring for abortion. This is not a case of the Government "suppressing a dangerous idea," but of a prohibition on a project grantee or its employees from engaging in activities outside of its scope.

To hold that the Government unconstitutionally discriminates on the basis of viewpoint when it chooses to fund a program dedicated to advance certain permissible goals, because the program in advancing those goals necessarily discourages alternate goals, would render numerous government programs constitutionally suspect. When Congress established a National Endowment for Democracy to encourage other countries to adopt democratic principles, 22 U.S.C. § 4411(b), it was not constitutionally required to fund a program to encourage competing lines of political philosophy such as Communism and Fascism. . . .

We believe that petitioners' reliance upon our decision in *Arkansas Writers' Project,* supra, is misplaced. That case involved a state sales tax which discriminated between magazines on the basis of their content. Relying on this fact, and on the fact that the tax "targets a small group within the press," contrary to our decision in Minneapolis Star & Tribune Co. v. Minnesota Comm'r of Revenue, 460 U.S. 575 (1983), the Court held the tax invalid. But we have here not the case of a general law singling out a disfavored group on the basis of speech content, but a case of the Government refusing to fund activities, including speech, which are specifically excluded from the scope of the project funded.

Petitioners rely heavily on their claim that the regulations would not, in the circumstance of a medical emergency, permit a Title X project to refer a woman whose pregnancy places her life in imminent peril to a provider of abortions or abortion-related services. This case, of course, involves only a facial challenge to the regulations, and we do not have before us any application by the Secretary to a specific fact situation. On their face, we do not read the regulations to bar abortion referral or counseling in such circumstances. Abortion counseling as a "method of family planning" is prohibited, and it does not seem that a medically necessitated abortion in such circumstances would be the equivalent of its use as a "method of family planning." Neither § 1008 nor the specific restrictions of the regulations would apply. . . . [4]

Petitioners also contend that the restrictions on the subsidization of abortion-related speech contained in the regulations are impermissible because they condition the receipt of a benefit, in this case Title X funding, on the relinquishment of a constitutional right, the right to engage in abortion advocacy and counseling. Relying on Perry v. Sindermann, 408 U.S. 593, 597 (1972), and FCC v. League of Women Voters of Cal., 468 U.S. 364 (1984), petitioners argue that "even though the government may deny [a] . . . benefit

---

[4] We also find that, on their face, the regulations are narrowly tailored to fit Congress' intent in Title X that federal funds not be used to "promote or advocate" abortion as a "method of family planning." The regulations are designed to ensure compliance with the prohibition of § 1008 that none of the funds appropriated under Title X be used in a program where abortion is a method of family planning. We have recognized that Congress' power to allocate funds for public purposes includes an ancillary power to ensure that those funds are properly applied to the prescribed use. See South Dakota v. Dole, 483 U.S. 203, 207–209 (1987) (upholding against Tenth Amendment challenge requirement that States raise drinking age as condition to receipt of federal highway funds); Buckley v. Valeo, 424 U.S. 1, 99 (1976).

for any number of reasons, there are some reasons upon which the government may not rely. It may not deny a benefit to a person on a basis that infringes his constitutionally protected interests—especially his interest in freedom of speech." Perry, supra, at 597.

Petitioners' reliance on these cases is unavailing, however, because here the government is not denying a benefit to anyone, but is instead simply insisting that public funds be spent for the purposes for which they were authorized. The Secretary's regulations do not force the Title X grantee to give up abortion-related speech; they merely require that the grantee keep such activities separate and distinct from Title X activities. Title X expressly distinguishes between a Title X grantee and a Title X project. The grantee, which normally is a health care organization, may receive funds from a variety of sources for a variety of purposes. The grantee receives Title X funds, however, for the specific and limited purpose of establishing and operating a Title X project. 42 U.S.C. § 300(a). The regulations govern the scope of the Title X project's activities, and leave the grantee unfettered in its other activities. The Title X grantee can continue to perform abortions, provide abortion-related services, and engage in abortion advocacy; it simply is required to conduct those activities through programs that are separate and independent from the project that receives Title X funds. 42 CFR 59.9 (1989).

In contrast, our "unconstitutional conditions" cases involve situations in which the government has placed a condition on the recipient of the subsidy rather than on a particular program or service, thus effectively prohibiting the recipient from engaging in the protected conduct outside the scope of the federally funded program. In FCC v. League of Women Voters of Cal., we invalidated a federal law providing that noncommercial television and radio stations that receive federal grants may not "engage in editorializing." Under that law, a recipient of federal funds was "barred absolutely from all editorializing" because it "is not able to segregate its activities according to the source of its funding" and thus "has no way of limiting the use of its federal funds to all noneditorializing activities." The effect of the law was that "a noncommercial educational station that receives only 1% of its overall income from [federal] grants is barred absolutely from all editorializing" and "barred from using even wholly private funds to finance its editorial activity." 468 U.S., at 400. We expressly recognized, however, that were Congress to permit the recipient stations to "establish 'affiliate' organizations which could then use the station's facilities to editorialize with nonfederal funds, such a statutory mechanism would plainly be valid." Ibid. Such a scheme would permit the station "to make known its views on matters of public importance through its nonfederally funded, editorializing affiliate without losing federal grants for its noneditorializing broadcast activities." Ibid.

Similarly, in *Regan* we held that Congress could, in the exercise of its spending power, reasonably refuse to subsidize the lobbying activities of tax-exempt charitable organizations by prohibiting such organizations from using tax-deductible contributions to support their lobbying efforts. In so holding, we explained that such organizations remained free "to receive deductible contributions to support ... nonlobbying activit[ies]." 461 U.S., at 545. Thus, a charitable organization could create, under § 501(c)(3) of the Internal Revenue Code of 1954, 26 U.S.C. § 501(c)(3), an affiliate to conduct its nonlobbying activities using tax-deductible contributions, and at the same time establish, under § 501(c)(4), a separate affiliate to pursue its lobbying efforts without such contributions.... Given that alternative, the Court concluded that "Congress has not infringed any First Amendment rights or regulated any First Amendment activity[; it] has simply chosen not to pay for [appellee's] lobbying." . . . We also noted that appellee "would, of course, have to ensure that the § 501(c)(3) organization did not subsidize the § 501(c)(4) organization; otherwise, public funds might be spent on an activity Congress chose not to subsidize." . . . The condition that federal funds will be used only to further the purposes of a grant does not violate constitutional rights. "Congress could, for example, grant funds to an organization dedicated to combating teenage drug abuse, but condition the grant by providing that none of the money received from Congress should be used to lobby state legislatures." . . .

By requiring that the Title X grantee engage in abortion-related activity separately from activity receiving federal funding, Congress has, consistent with our teachings in *League of Women Voters* and *Regan,* not denied it the right to engage in abortion-related activities. Congress has merely refused to fund such activities out of the public fisc, and the Secretary has simply required a certain degree of separation from the Title X project in order to ensure the integrity of the federally funded program.

The same principles apply to petitioners' claim that the regulations abridge the free speech rights of the grantee's staff. Individuals who are voluntarily employed for a Title X project must perform their duties in accordance with the regulation's restrictions on abortion counseling and referral. The employees remain free, however, to pursue abortion-related activities when they are not acting under the auspices of the Title X project. The regulations, which govern solely the scope of the Title X project's activities, do not in any way restrict the activities of those persons acting as private individuals. The employees' freedom of expression is limited during the time that they actually work for the project; but this limitation is a consequence of their decision to accept employment in a project, the scope of which is permissibly restricted by the funding authority.[5]

This is not to suggest that funding by the Government, even when coupled with the freedom of the fund recipients to speak outside the scope of the Government-funded project, is invariably sufficient to justify government control over the content of expression. For example, this Court has recognized that the existence of a Government "subsidy," in the form of Government-owned property, does not justify the restriction of speech in areas that have "been traditionally open to the public for expressive activity," . . . Similarly, we have recognized that the university is a traditional sphere of free expression so fundamental to the functioning of our society that the Government's ability to

---

[5] Petitioners also contend that the regulations violate the First Amendment by penalizing speech funded with non-Title X monies. They argue that since Title X requires that grant recipients contribute to the financing of Title X projects through the use of matching funds and grant-related income, the regulation's restrictions on abortion counseling and advocacy penalize privately funded speech. We find this argument flawed for several reasons. First, Title X subsidies are just that, subsidies. The recipient is in no way compelled to operate a Title X project; to avoid the force of the regulations, it can simply decline the subsidy. See Grove City College v. Bell, 465 U.S. 555, 575 (1984) (petitioner's First Amendment rights not violated because it "may terminate its participation in the [federal] program and thus avoid the requirements of [the federal program]"). By accepting Title X funds, a recipient voluntarily consents to any restrictions placed on any matching funds or grant-related income. Potential grant recipients can choose between accepting Title X funds—subject to the Government's conditions that they provide matching funds and forgo abortion counseling and referral in the Title X project—or declining the subsidy and financing their own unsubsidized program. We have never held that the Government violates the First Amendment simply by offering that choice. Second, the Secretary's regulations apply only to Title X programs. A recipient is therefore able to "limi[t] the use of its federal funds to [Title X] activities." FCC v. League of Women Voters of Cal., 468 U.S. 364, at 400 (1984). It is in no way "barred from using even wholly private funds to finance" its pro-abortion activities outside the Title X program. Ibid. The regulations are limited to Title X funds; the recipient remains free to use private, non-Title X funds to finance abortion-related activities.

control speech within that sphere by means of conditions attached to the expenditure of Government funds is restricted by the vagueness and over-breadth doctrines of the First Amendment, Keyishian v. Board of Regents, 385 U.S. 589, 603, 605–606 (1967). It could be argued by analogy that traditional relationships such as that between doctor and patient should enjoy protection under the First Amendment from government regulation, even when subsidized by the Government. We need not resolve that question here, however, because the Title X program regulations do not significantly impinge upon the doctor-patient relationship. Nothing in them requires a doctor to represent as his own any opinion that he does not in fact hold. Nor is the doctor-patient relationship established by the Title X program sufficiently all-encompassing so as to justify an expectation on the part of the patient of comprehensive medical advice. The program does not provide post-conception medical care, and therefore a doctor's silence with regard to abortion cannot reasonably be thought to mislead a client into thinking that the doctor does not consider abortion an appropriate option for her. The doctor is always free to make clear that advice regarding abortion is simply beyond the scope of the program. In these circumstances, the general rule that the Government may choose not to subsidize speech applies with full force.

IV

We turn now to petitioners' argument that the regulations violate a woman's Fifth Amendment right to choose whether to terminate her pregnancy. . . .

That the regulations do not impermissibly burden a woman's Fifth Amendment rights is evident from the line of cases beginning with *Maher* and *McRae* and culminating in our most recent decision in *Webster*. . . .

.   .   .

The Secretary's regulations are a permissible construction of Title X and do not violate either the First or Fifth Amendments to the Constitution. Accordingly, the judgment of the Court of Appeals is

Affirmed.

Justice Blackmun, with whom Justice Marshall joins, with whom Justice Stevens joins as to Parts II and III, and with whom Justice O'Connor joins as to Part I, dissenting.

. . . [T]he Court, for the first time, upholds viewpoint-based suppression of speech solely because it is imposed on those dependent upon the Government for economic support. Under essentially the same rationale, the majority upholds direct regulation of dialogue between a pregnant woman and her physician when that regulation has both the purpose and the effect of manipulating her decision as to the continuance of her pregnancy. I conclude that the Secretary's regulation of referral, advocacy, and counseling activities exceeds his statutory authority, and, also, that the Regulations violate the First and Fifth Amendments of our Constitution. Accordingly, I dissent . . .

I

.   .   .

. . . [T]he question squarely presented by the Regulations—the extent to which the Government may attach an otherwise unconstitutional condition to the receipt of a public benefit—implicates a troubled area of our jurisprudence in which a court ought not entangle itself unnecessarily. . . .

. . .

Because I conclude that a plainly constitutional construction of § 1008 "is not only 'fairly possible' but entirely reasonable," . . . I would reverse the judgment of the Court of Appeals on this ground without deciding the constitutionality of the Secretary's Regulations.

II

I also strongly disagree with the majority's disposition of petitioners' constitutional claims . . .

A

Until today, the Court never has upheld viewpoint-based suppression of speech simply because that suppression was a condition upon the acceptance of public funds. . . .

Nothing in the Court's opinion in Regan v. Taxation With Representation of Washington, 461 U.S. 540 (1983), can be said to challenge this long-settled understanding. In *Regan,* the Court upheld a content-neutral provision of the Internal Revenue Code, 26 U.S.C. § 501(c)(3), that disallowed a particular tax-exempt status to organizations that "attempt[ed] to influence legislation," while affording such status to veterans' organizations irrespective of their lobbying activities. . . . [T]he Court explained: "The case would be different if Congress were to discriminate invidiously in its subsidies in such a way as to 'ai[m] at the suppression of dangerous ideas.' . . ." . . .

It cannot seriously be disputed that the counseling and referral provisions at issue in the present cases constitute content-based regulation of speech. Title X grantees may provide counseling and referral regarding any of a wide range of family planning and other topics, save abortion. . . .

The Regulations are also clearly viewpoint-based. While suppressing speech favorable to abortion with one hand, the Secretary compels anti-abortion speech with the other. For example, the Department of Health and Human Services' own description of the Regulations makes plain that "Title X projects are required to facilitate access to prenatal care and social services, including adoption services, that might be needed by the pregnant client to promote her well-being and that of her child, while making it abundantly clear that the project is not permitted to promote abortion by facilitating access to abortion through the referral process." 53 Fed.Reg. 2927 (1988) . . .

Moreover, the Regulations command that a project refer for prenatal care each woman diagnosed as pregnant, irrespective of the woman's expressed desire to continue or terminate her pregnancy. 42 CFR § 59.8(a)(2) (1990). If a client asks directly about abortion, a Title X physician or counselor is required to say, in essence, that the project does not consider abortion to be an appropriate method of family planning. § 59.8(b)(4). Both requirements are antithetical to the First Amendment. . . .

The Regulations pertaining to "advocacy" are even more explicitly viewpoint-based. These provide: "A Title X project may not encourage, promote or advocate abortion as a method of family planning." § 59.10 (emphasis added). They explain: "This requirement prohibits actions to assist women to obtain abortions or increase the availability or accessibility of abortion for family planning purposes." § 59.10(a) (emphasis added). The Regulations do not, however, proscribe or even regulate anti-abortion advocacy. These are clearly restrictions aimed at the suppression of "dangerous ideas."

Remarkably, the majority concludes that "the Government has not discriminated on the basis of viewpoint; it has merely chosen to fund one activity to the exclusion of another." But the majority's claim that the Regulations merely limit a Title X project's speech to preventive or preconceptional services rings hollow in light of the broad range of non-preventive services that the Regulations authorize Title X projects to provide. . . .

The majority's reliance upon *Regan* in this connection is also misplaced. That case stands for the proposition that government has no obligation to subsidize a private party's efforts to petition the legislature regarding its views. Thus, if the challenged Regulations were confined to non-ideological limitations upon the use of Title X funds for lobbying activities, there would exist no violation of the First Amendment. The advocacy Regulations at issue here, however, are not limited to lobbying but extend to all speech having the effect of encouraging, promoting, or advocating abortion as a method of family planning. § 59.10(a). . . . This type of intrusive, ideologically based regulation of speech goes far beyond the narrow lobbying limitations approved in *Regan,* and cannot be justified simply because it is a condition upon the receipt of a governmental benefit.

B

The Court concludes that the challenged Regulations do not violate the First Amendment rights of Title X staff members because any limitation of the employees' freedom of expression is simply a consequence of their decision to accept employment at a federally funded project. But it has never been sufficient to justify an otherwise unconstitutional condition upon public employment that the employee may escape the condition by relinquishing his or her job. . . .

. . . Under the majority's reasoning, the First Amendment could be read to tolerate any governmental restriction upon an employee's speech so long as that restriction is limited to the funded workplace. This is a dangerous proposition, and one the Court has rightly rejected in the past.

. . . At the least, such conditions require courts to balance the speaker's interest in the message against those of government in preventing its dissemination. . . .

. . . When a client becomes pregnant, the full range of therapeutic alternatives includes the abortion option, and Title X counselors' interest in providing this information is compelling.

The Government's articulated interest in distorting the doctor-patient dialogue—ensuring that federal funds are not spent for a purpose outside the scope of the program—falls far short of that necessary to justify the suppression of truthful information and professional medical opinion regarding constitutionally protected conduct. . . . By failing to balance or even to consider the free speech interests claimed by Title X physicians against the Government's asserted interest in suppressing the speech, the Court falters in its duty to implement the protection that the First Amendment clearly provides for this important message.

C

Finally, it is of no small significance that the speech the Secretary would suppress is truthful information regarding constitutionally protected conduct of vital importance to the listener. One can imagine no legitimate governmental interest that might be served by suppressing such information. . . .

. . .

Justice Stevens, dissenting.

. . .

The entirely new approach adopted by the Secretary in 1988 was not, in my view, authorized by the statute. The new regulations did not merely reflect a change in a policy determination that the Secretary had been authorized by Congress to make. . . . Rather, they represented an assumption of policymaking responsibility that Congress had not delegated to the Secretary. . . .

. . .

Even if I thought the statute were ambiguous, however, I would reach the same result for the reasons stated in Justice O'Connor's dissenting opinion. As she also explains, if a majority of the Court had reached this result, it would be improper to comment on the constitutional issues that the parties have debated. Because the majority has reached out to decide the constitutional questions, however, I am persuaded that Justice Blackmun is correct in concluding that the majority's arguments merit a response. . . .

Justice O'Connor, dissenting.

. . .

One may well conclude, as Justice Blackmun does . . ., that the regulations are unconstitutional. . . . The canon of construction that Justice Blackmun correctly applies here is grounded in large part upon our time-honored practice of not reaching constitutional questions unnecessarily. . . .

. . . If we rule solely on statutory grounds, Congress retains the power to force the constitutional question by legislating more explicitly. It may instead choose to do nothing. That decision should be left to Congress; we should not tell Congress what it cannot do before it has chosen to do it. It is enough in this case to conclude that neither the language nor the history of § 1008 compels the Secretary's interpretation, and that the interpretation raises serious First Amendment concerns. On this basis alone, I would reverse the judgment of the Court of Appeals and invalidate the challenged regulations.

Rosenberger v. Rector and Visitors of the University of Virginia

___ U.S. ___, 115 S.Ct. 2510, 132 L.Ed.2d 700 (1995).

[The report in this case appears infra, page 1676.]

CHAPTER 15

PROTECTION OF PENUMBRAL FIRST AMENDMENT RIGHTS

Introduction. The constitutional protection of expression, belief and association extends to "peripheral" areas beyond individual freedom to utter or print. It should be emphasized that the term "peripheral" does not suggest lesser importance. The terms "penumbras" and "peripheral rights" first appeared in Griswold v. Connecticut, 381 U.S. 479 (1965). In demonstrating that the protection of the first amendment was not confined to the right to utter or print, Justice Douglas explained that "[w]ithout those peripheral rights the specific rights would be less secure."

SECTION 1. SYMBOLIC SPEECH

United States v. O'Brien

391 U.S. 367, 88 S.Ct. 1673, 20 L.Ed.2d 672 (1968).

Mr. Chief Justice Warren delivered the opinion of the Court.

[O'Brien burned his selective service registration certificate on the steps of the South Boston Courthouse in the presence of a sizable crowd. He was convicted for violation of a federal statute that made it a crime to knowingly destroy or mutilate the certificate.]

. . .

II.

O'Brien first argues that the [statute] is unconstitutional as applied to him because his act of burning his registration certificate was protected "symbolic speech" within the First Amendment. His argument is that the freedom of expression which the First Amendment guarantees includes all modes of "communication of ideas by conduct," and that his conduct is within this definition because he did it in "demonstration against the war and against the draft."

We cannot accept the view that an apparently limitless variety of conduct can be labelled "speech" whenever the person engaging in the conduct intends thereby to express an idea. However, even on the assumption that the alleged communicative element in O'Brien's conduct is sufficient to bring into play the First Amendment, it does not necessarily follow that the destruction of a registration certificate is constitutionally protected activity. This Court has held that when "speech" and "nonspeech" elements are combined in the same course of conduct, a sufficiently important governmental interest in regulating the nonspeech element can justify incidental limitations on First Amendment freedoms. To characterize the quality of the governmental interest which must appear, the Court has employed a variety of descriptive terms: compelling; substantial; subordinating; paramount; cogent; strong. Whatever imprecision inheres in these terms, we think it clear that a government regulation is sufficiently justified if it is within the constitutional power of the Government; if it furthers an important or substantial governmental interest; if the governmental interest is unrelated to the suppression of free expression; and if the incidental restriction on alleged First Amendment freedom is no greater than is essential to the furtherance of that interest. We find that the [statute] meets all of these requirements, and consequently that O'Brien can be constitutionally convicted for violating it.

.   .   .

The many functions performed by Selective Service certificates establish beyond doubt that Congress has a legitimate and substantial interest in preventing their wanton and unrestrained destruction and assuring their continuing availability by punishing people who knowingly and wilfully destroy or mutilate them. . . .

.   .   .

. . . The governmental interest and the scope of the [statute] are limited to preventing a harm to the smooth and efficient functioning of the Selective Service System. When O'Brien deliberately rendered unavailable his registration certificate, he wilfully frustrated this governmental interest. For this noncommunicative impact of his conduct, and for nothing else, he was convicted.

The case at bar is therefore unlike one where the alleged governmental interest in regulating conduct arises in some measure because the communication allegedly integral to the conduct is itself thought to be harmful. In Stromberg v. California, 283 U.S. 359 (1931), for example, this Court struck down a statutory phrase which punished people who expressed their "opposition to organized government" by displaying "any flag, badge, banner, or device." Since the statute there was aimed at suppressing communication it could not be sustained as a regulation of noncommunicative conduct. . . .

In conclusion, we find that because of the Government's substantial interest in assuring the continuing availability of issued Selective Service certificates, because [the statute] is an appropriately narrow means of protecting this interest and condemns only the independent noncommunicative impact of conduct within its reach, and because the noncommunicative impact of O'Brien's act of burning his registration certificate frustrated the Government's interest, a sufficient governmental interest has been shown to justify O'Brien's conviction.

III.

O'Brien finally argues that the 1965 Amendment is unconstitutional as enacted because what he calls the "purpose" of Congress was "to suppress freedom of speech." We reject this argument because under settled principles the purpose of Congress, as O'Brien uses that term, is not a basis for declaring this legislation unconstitutional.

It is a familiar principle of constitutional law that this Court will not strike down an otherwise constitutional statute on the basis of an alleged illicit legislative motive. . . .

Inquiries into congressional motives or purposes are a hazardous matter. When the issue is simply the interpretation of legislation, the Court will look to statements by legislators for guidance as to the purpose of the legislature, because the benefit to sound decision-making in this circumstance is thought sufficient to risk the possibility of misreading Congress' purpose. It is entirely a different matter when we are asked to void a statute that is, under well-settled criteria, constitutional on its face, on the basis of what fewer than a handful of Congressmen said about it. What motivates one legislator to make a speech about a statute is not necessarily what motivates scores of others to enact it, and the stakes are sufficiently high for us to eschew guesswork. We decline to void essentially on the ground that it is unwise legislation which Congress had the undoubted power to enact and which could be reenacted in its exact form if the same or another legislator made a "wiser" speech about it.

. . .

We think it not amiss, in passing, to comment upon O'Brien's legislative-purpose argument. There was little floor debate on this legislation in either House. Only Senator Thurmond commented on its substantive features in the Senate.... In the House debate only two Congressmen addressed themselves to the Amendment—Congressmen Rivers and Bray.... It is principally on the basis of the statements by these three Congressmen that O'Brien makes his congressional-"purpose" argument. We note that if we were to examine legislative purpose in the instant case, we would be obliged to consider not only these statements but also the more authoritative reports of the Senate and House Armed Services Committees. The portions of those reports explaining the purpose of the Amendment are reproduced in the Appendix in their entirety. While both reports make clear a concern with the "defiant" destruction of so-called "draft cards" and with "open" encouragement to others to destroy their cards, both reports also indicate that this concern stemmed from an apprehension that unrestrained destruction of cards would disrupt the smooth functioning of the Selective Service System.

IV.

... [T]he Court of Appeals should have affirmed the judgment of conviction entered by the District Court.... [a]

Mr. Justice Marshall took no part in the consideration or decision of these cases.

Mr. Justice Harlan, concurring.

The crux of the Court's opinion, which I join, is of course its general statement, that:

> "a government regulation is sufficiently justified if it is within the constitutional power of the Government; if it furthers an important or substantial governmental interest; if the governmental interest is unrelated to the suppression of free expression; and if the incidental restriction on alleged First Amendment freedoms is no greater than is essential to the furtherance of that interest."

I wish to make explicit my understanding that this passage does not foreclose consideration of First Amendment claims in those rare instances when an "incidental" restriction upon expression, imposed by a regulation which fur-

---

[a] On the issue of legislative motivation in O'Brien, see Ely, *Legislative and Administrative Motivation in Constitutional Law*, 79 Yale L.J. 1205 (1970), and Brest, *Palmer v. Thompson: An Approach to the Problem of Unconstitutional Legislative Motive*, 1971 Sup.Ct.Rev. 95. Does the Court's treatment of the relevance of a legislative motivation to prohibit a form of expression require modification in light of the later decision in Washington v. Davis, 426 U.S. 229 (1976), supra p. 786?

thers an "important or substantial" governmental interest and satisfies the Court's other criteria, in practice has the effect of entirely preventing a "speaker" from reaching a significant audience with whom he could not otherwise lawfully communicate. This is not such a case, since O'Brien manifestly could have conveyed his message in many ways other than by burning his draft card.

Mr. Justice Douglas, dissenting.

[Justice Douglas' dissent was limited to the point that the case should be re-argued to consider the issue of the validity of peacetime conscription. Later, however, in his concurring opinion in Brandenburg v. Ohio, 395 U.S. 444, 455 (1969), he said: "O'Brien was not prosecuted for not having his draft card available when asked for by a federal agent. He was indicted, tried, and convicted for burning the card. And this Court's affirmance of that conviction was not, with all respect, consistent with the First Amendment."]

Texas v. Johnson

491 U.S. 397, 109 S.Ct. 2533, 105 L.Ed.2d 342 (1989).

Justice Brennan delivered the opinion of the Court.

After publicly burning an American flag as a means of political protest, Gregory Lee Johnson was convicted of desecrating a flag in violation of Texas law. This case presents the question whether his conviction is consistent with the First Amendment. We hold that it is not.

I

While the Republican National Convention was taking place in Dallas in 1984, respondent Johnson participated in a political demonstration dubbed the "Republican War Chest Tour." . . .

The demonstration ended in front of Dallas City Hall, where Johnson unfurled the American flag, doused it with kerosene, and set it on fire. While the flag burned, the protestors chanted, "America, the red, white, and blue, we spit on you." After the demonstrators dispersed, a witness to the flag-burning collected the flag's remains and buried them in his backyard. No one was physically injured or threatened with injury, though several witnesses testified that they had been seriously offended by the flag-burning.

Of the approximately 100 demonstrators, Johnson alone was charged with a crime. The only criminal offense with which he was charged was the desecration of a venerated object . . .[1] After a trial, he was convicted, sentenced to one year in prison, and fined $2,000. The Court of Appeals for the Fifth District of Texas at Dallas affirmed Johnson's conviction, . . . but the Texas Court of Criminal Appeals reversed . . .

. . . .

[1] Tex.Penal Code Ann. section 42.09 (1989) provides . . . :

   "Section 42.09. Desecration of Venerated Object

   "(a) A person commits an offense if he intentionally or knowingly desecrates:

      (1) a public monument;

      (2) a place of worship or burial; or

      (3) a state or national flag.

   "(b) For purposes of this section, 'desecrate' means deface, damage, or otherwise physically mistreat in a way that the actor knows will seriously offend one or more persons likely to observe or discover his action. . . . "

... We ... affirm.

II

Johnson was convicted of flag desecration for burning the flag rather than for uttering insulting words. This fact somewhat complicates our consideration of his conviction under the First Amendment. We must first determine whether Johnson's burning of the flag constituted expressive conduct, permitting him to invoke the First Amendment in challenging his conviction. See, e.g., Spence v. Washington, 418 U.S. 405, 409–411 (1974). If his conduct was expressive, we next decide whether the State's regulation is related to the suppression of free expression. See, e.g., United States v. O'Brien, 391 U.S. 367, 377 (1968); *Spence,* supra, at 414, n. 8. If the State's regulation is not related to expression, then the less stringent standard we announced in United States v. O'Brien for regulations of noncommunicative conduct controls.... If it is, then we are outside of *O'Brien* 's test, and we must ask whether this interest justifies Johnson's conviction under a more demanding standard.[3] See *Spence,* supra, at 411. A third possibility is that the State's asserted interest is simply not implicated on these facts, and in that event the interest drops out of the picture. See 418 U.S., at 414, n. 8.

The First Amendment literally forbids the abridgement only of "speech," but we have long recognized that its protection does not end at the spoken or written word....

In deciding whether particular conduct possesses sufficient communicative elements to bring the First Amendment into play, we have asked whether "[a]n intent to convey a particularized message was present, and [whether] the likelihood was great that the message would be understood by those who viewed it." 418 U.S., at 410–411. Hence, we have recognized the expressive nature of students' wearing of black armbands to protest American military involvement in Vietnam, Tinker v. Des Moines Independent Community School Dist., 393 U.S. 503, 505 (1969); of a sit-in by blacks in a "whites only" area to protest segregation, Brown v. Louisiana, 383 U.S. 131, 141–142 (1966); of the wearing of American military uniforms in a dramatic presentation criticizing American involvement in Vietnam, Schacht v. United States, 398 U.S. 58 (1970); and of picketing about a wide variety of causes, see, e.g., Food Employees v. Logan Valley Plaza, Inc., 391 U.S. 308, 313–314 (1968); United States v. Grace, 461 U.S. 171, 176 (1983).

Especially pertinent to this case are our decisions recognizing the communicative nature of conduct relating to flags. Attaching a peace sign to the flag, *Spence,* supra, at 409–410; saluting the flag, Barnette, 319 U.S., at 632; and displaying a red flag, Stromberg v. California, 283 U.S. 359, 368–369 (1931), we have held, all may find shelter under the First Amendment.... That we have had little difficulty identifying an expressive element in conduct relating to flags should not be surprising. The very purpose of a national flag is to serve as a symbol of our country ...

. . .

[3] Although Johnson has raised a facial challenge to Texas' flag-desecration statute, we choose to resolve this case on the basis of his claim that the statute as applied to him violates the First Amendment. Section 42.09 regulates only physical conduct with respect to the flag, not the written or spoken word.... Because the prosecution of a person who had not engaged in expressive conduct would pose a different case, and because we are capable of disposing of this case on narrower grounds, we address only Johnson's claim that section 42.09 as applied to political expression like his violates the First Amendment.

We have not automatically concluded, however, that any action taken with respect to our flag is expressive. Instead, in characterizing such action for First Amendment purposes, we have considered the context in which it occurred. In *Spence,* for example, we emphasized that Spence's taping of a peace sign to his flag was "roughly simultaneous with and concededly triggered by the Cambodian incursion and the Kent State tragedy." ... The State of Washington had conceded, in fact, that Spence's conduct was a form of communication ...

The State of Texas conceded for purposes of its oral argument in this case that Johnson's conduct was expressive conduct, and this concession seems to us as prudent as was Washington's in *Spence.* Johnson burned an American flag as part—indeed, as the culmination—of a political demonstration that coincided with the convening of the Republican Party and its renomination of Ronald Reagan for President. The expressive, overtly political nature of this conduct was both intentional and overwhelmingly apparent.... In these circumstances, Johnson's burning of the flag was conduct "sufficiently imbued with elements of communication," *Spence,* 418 U.S., at 409, to implicate the First Amendment.

III

The Government generally has a freer hand in restricting expressive conduct than it has in restricting the written or spoken word.... It may not, however, proscribe particular conduct *because* it has expressive elements.... It is ... not simply the verbal or nonverbal nature of the expression, but the governmental interest at stake, that helps to determine whether a restriction on that expression is valid.

... [W]e have limited the applicability of O'Brien's relatively lenient standard to those cases in which "the governmental interest is unrelated to the suppression of free expression." ...

In order to decide whether *O'Brien's* test applies here, therefore, we must decide whether Texas has asserted an interest in support of Johnson's conviction that is unrelated to the suppression of expression.... The State offers two separate interests to justify this conviction: preventing breaches of the peace, and preserving the flag as a symbol of nationhood and national unity. We hold that the first interest is not implicated on this record and that the second is related to the suppression of expression.

A

Texas claims that its interest in preventing breaches of the peace justifies Johnson's conviction for flag desecration. ...The only evidence offered by the State at trial to show the reaction to Johnson's actions was the testimony of several persons who had been seriously offended by the flag-burning.

The State's position, therefore, amounts to a claim that an audience that takes serious offense at particular expression is necessarily likely to disturb the peace and that the expression may be prohibited on this basis....

[W]e have not permitted the Government to assume that every expression of a provocative idea will incite a riot, but have instead required careful consideration of the actual circumstances surrounding such expression.... To accept Texas' arguments that it need only demonstrate "the potential for a breach of the peace," and that every flag-burning necessarily possesses that potential, would be to eviscerate our holding in *Brandenburg.* This we decline to do.

Nor does Johnson's expressive conduct fall within that small class of "fighting words" that are "likely to provoke the average person to retaliation, and thereby cause a breach of the peace." Chaplinsky v. New Hampshire, 315 U.S. 568, 574 (1942). No reasonable onlooker would have regarded Johnson's generalized expression of dissatisfaction with the policies of the Federal Government as a direct personal insult or an invitation to exchange fisticuffs....

We thus conclude that the State's interest in maintaining order is not implicated on these facts....

B

The State also asserts an interest in preserving the flag as a symbol of nationhood and national unity. In *Spence,* we acknowledged that the Government's interest in preserving the flag's special symbolic value "is directly related to expression in the context of activity" such as affixing a peace symbol to a flag.... We are equally persuaded that this interest is related to expression in the case of Johnson's burning of the flag. The State, apparently, is concerned that such conduct will lead people to believe either that the flag does not stand for nationhood and national unity, but instead reflects other, less positive concepts, or that the concepts reflected in the flag do not in fact exist, that is, we do not enjoy unity as a Nation. These concerns blossom only when a person's treatment of the flag communicates some message, and thus are related "to the suppression of free expression" within the meaning of *O'Brien.* We are thus outside of *O'Brien*'s test altogether.

IV

It remains to consider whether the State's interest in preserving the flag as a symbol of nationhood and national unity justifies Johnson's conviction.

As in *Spence,* "[w]e are confronted with a case of prosecution for the expression of an idea through activity," and "[a]ccordingly, we must examine with particular care the interests advanced by [petitioner] to support its prosecution." ... Johnson was not, we add, prosecuted for the expression of just any idea; he was prosecuted for his expression of dissatisfaction with the policies of this country, expression situated at the core of our First Amendment values....

Moreover, Johnson was prosecuted because he knew that his politically charged expression would cause "serious offense." If he had burned the flag as a means of disposing of it because it was dirty or torn, he would not have been convicted of flag desecration under this Texas law ... The Texas law is thus not aimed at protecting the physical integrity of the flag in all circumstances, but is designed instead to protect it only against impairments that would cause serious offense to others....

Whether Johnson's treatment of the flag violated Texas law thus depended on the likely communicative impact of his expressive conduct....

... Johnson's political expression was restricted because of the content of the message he conveyed. We must therefore subject the State's asserted interest in preserving the special symbolic character of the flag to "the most exacting scrutiny." Boos v. Barry, 485 U.S., at 321.[8]

[8] Our inquiry is, of course, bounded by the particular facts of this case and by the statute under which Johnson was convicted. There was no evidence that Johnson himself stole the flag he burned, nor did the prosecu-tion or the arguments urged in support of it depend on the theory that the flag was stolen.... [N]othing in our opinion should be taken to suggest that one is free to steal a flag so long as one later uses it to communi-

Texas argues that its interest in preserving the flag as a symbol of nationhood and national unity survives this close analysis.... [T]he State's claim is that it has an interest in preserving the flag as a symbol of *nationhood* and *national unity,* a symbol with a determinate range of meanings. According to Texas, if one physically treats the flag in a way that would tend to cast doubt on either the idea that nationhood and national unity are the flag's referents or that national unity actually exists, the message conveyed thereby is a harmful one and therefore may be prohibited.

If there is a bedrock principle underlying the First Amendment, it is that the Government may not prohibit the expression of an idea simply because society finds the idea itself offensive or disagreeable....

We have not recognized an exception to this principle even where our flag has been involved. In Street v. New York, 394 U.S. 576 (1969), we held that a State may not criminally punish a person for uttering words critical of the flag....

... In *Spence,* we held that the same interest asserted by Texas here was insufficient to support a criminal conviction under a flag-misuse statute for the taping of a peace sign to an American flag....

In short, nothing in our precedents suggests that a State may foster its own view of the flag by prohibiting expressive conduct relating to it.[10] To bring its argument outside our precedents, Texas attempts to convince us that even if its interest in preserving the flag's symbolic role does not allow it to prohibit words or some expressive conduct critical of the flag, it does permit it to forbid the outright destruction of the flag. The State's argument cannot depend here on the distinction between written or spoken words and nonverbal conduct. That distinction, we have shown, is of no moment where the nonverbal conduct is expressive, as it is here, and where the regulation of that conduct is related to expression, as it is here. In addition, both *Barnette* and *Spence* involved expressive conduct, not only verbal communication, and both found that conduct protected.

Texas' focus on the precise nature of Johnson's expression, moreover, misses the point of our prior decisions: their enduring lesson, that the Government may not prohibit expression simply because it disagrees with its message, is not dependent on the particular mode in which one chooses to express an idea. If we were to hold that a State may forbid flag-burning wherever it is likely to endanger the flag's symbolic role, but allow it wherever burning a flag promotes that role—as where, for example, a person ceremoniously burns a dirty flag—we would be saying that when it comes to impairing the flag's physical integrity, the flag itself may be used as a symbol ... only in one direction.

---

cate an idea. We also emphasize that Johnson was prosecuted *only* for flag desecration—not for trespass, disorderly conduct, or arson.

[10] Our decision in Halter v. Nebraska, 205 U.S. 34 (1907), addressing the validity of a state law prohibiting certain commercial uses of the flag, is not to the contrary. That case was decided "nearly 20 years before the Court concluded that the First Amendment applies to the States by virtue of the Fourteenth Amendment." Spence v. Washington, 418 U.S. 405, 413, n. 7 (1974). More important, as we continually emphasized in *Halter* itself, that case involved purely commercial rather than political speech.... Nor does San Francisco Arts & Athletics v. Olympic Committee, 483 U.S. 522, 524 (1987), addressing the validity of Congress' decision to "author-iz[e] the United States Olympic Committee to prohibit certain commercial and promotional uses of the word 'Olympic,'" ... tell us whether the Government may criminally punish physical conduct towards the flag engaged in as a means of political protest.

We never before have held that the Government may ensure that a symbol be used to express only one view of that symbol or its referents. . . .

. . .

There is, moreover, no indication—either in the text of the Constitution or in our cases interpreting it—that a separate juridical category exists for the American flag alone. . . . The First Amendment does not guarantee that other concepts virtually sacred to our Nation as a whole—such as the principle that discrimination on the basis of race is odious and destructive—will go unquestioned in the marketplace of ideas. . . . We decline, therefore, to create for the flag an exception to the joust of principles protected by the First Amendment.

. . .

We are fortified in today's conclusion by our conviction that forbidding criminal punishment for conduct such as Johnson's will not endanger the special role played by our flag or the feelings it inspires. . . .

. . .

V

Johnson was convicted for engaging in expressive conduct. The State's interest in preventing breaches of the peace does not support his conviction because Johnson's conduct did not threaten to disturb the peace. Nor does the State's interest in preserving the flag as a symbol of nationhood and national unity justify his criminal conviction for engaging in political expression. The judgment of the Texas Court of Criminal Appeals is therefore

Affirmed.[a]

Chief Justice Rehnquist, with whom Justice White and Justice O'Connor join, dissenting.

In holding this Texas statute unconstitutional, the Court ignores Justice Holmes' familiar aphorism that "a page of history is worth a volume of logic." New York Trust Co. v. Eisner, 256 U.S. 345, 349 (1921). For more than 200 years, the American flag has occupied a unique position as the symbol of our Nation, a uniqueness that justifies a governmental prohibition against flag burning in the way respondent Johnson did here.

. . .

[In Chaplinsky v. New Hampshire, 315 U.S. 568 (1942),] [t]he Court upheld Chaplinsky's conviction . . .

Here it may equally well be said that the public burning of the American flag by Johnson was no essential part of any exposition of ideas, and at the same time it had a tendency to incite a breach of the peace. Johnson was free to make any verbal denunciation of the flag that he wished; indeed, he was free to burn the flag in private. He could publicly burn other symbols of the Government or effigies of political leaders. . . .

. . .

. . . The Texas statute deprived Johnson of only one rather inarticulate symbolic form of protest—a form of protest that was profoundly offensive to many—and left him with a full panoply of other symbols and every conceivable

---

[a] A concurring opinion by Justice Kennedy, who also joined the opinion of the Court, is omitted.

form of verbal expression to express his deep disapproval of national policy. Thus, in no way can it be said that Texas is punishing him because his hearers—or any other group of people—were profoundly opposed to the message that he sought to convey. Such opposition is no proper basis for restricting speech or expression under the First Amendment. It was Johnson's use of this particular symbol, and not the idea that he sought to convey by it or by his many other expressions, for which he was punished.

Our prior cases dealing with flag desecration statutes have left open the question that the Court resolves today. In Street v. New York ... [t]he Court ... expressly reserved the question of whether a defendant could constitutionally be convicted for burning the flag....

.   .   .

In Spence v. Washington, ... there was no risk of a breach of the peace, no one other than the arresting officers saw the flag, and the defendant owned the flag in question. The Court was careful to note, however, that the defendant "was not charged under the desecration statute, nor did he permanently disfigure the flag or destroy it." ...

.   .   .

... The Court decides that the American flag is just another symbol, about which not only must opinions pro and con be tolerated, but for which the most minimal public respect may not be enjoined. The government may conscript men into the Armed Forces where they must fight and perhaps die for the flag, but the government may not prohibit the public burning of the banner under which they fight. I would uphold the Texas statute as applied in this case.

Justice Stevens, dissenting.

As the Court analyzes this case, it presents the question whether the State of Texas, or indeed the Federal Government, has the power to prohibit the public desecration of the American flag. The question is unique. In my judgment rules that apply to a host of other symbols, such as state flags, armbands, or various privately promoted emblems of political or commercial identity, are not necessarily controlling. Even if flag burning could be considered just another species of symbolic speech under the logical application of the rules that the Court has developed in its interpretation of the First Amendment in other contexts, this case has an intangible dimension that makes those rules inapplicable.

.   .   .

UNITED STATES v. EICHMAN, 496 U.S. 310 (1990). After the decision in Texas v. Johnson, Congress passed the Flag Protection Act of 1989, which provided:

"(a)(1) Whoever knowingly mutilates, defaces, physically defiles, burns, maintains on the floor or ground, or tramples upon any flag of the United States shall be fined under this title or imprisoned for not more than one year, or both.

"(2) This subsection does not prohibit any conduct consisting of the disposal of a flag when it has become worn or soiled.

"(b) As used in this section, the term 'flag of the United States' means any flag of the United States, or any part thereof, made of any substance, of any size, in a form that is commonly displayed."

Prosecuted for burning flags, defendants moved to dismiss the charges on the ground that the Act violated the first amendment. Two United States District Courts held the Act unconstitutional. The Supreme Court affirmed.

The United States argued that the federal statute differed from the Texas law challenged in *Johnson* because it proscribed mistreatment of a flag without regard to the actor's motive or the likely effect on onlookers. Justice Brennan's opinion for the Court rejected that argument. Although the Act contained no express content-based limitation, the asserted interest in protecting the "physical integrity" of a privately owned flag necessarily rested on a desire to preserve the flag as a symbol. That interest was implicated only when mistreatment of the flag communicated a message inconsistent with national ideals. Moreover, each of the specified prohibitions—"physically defiles, burns, maintains on the floor or ground, or tramples"—focused on acts likely to damage the flag's symbolic value. The Court held that the case was governed by *Johnson*, rejecting an argument that *Johnson* should be reassessed in light of Congress' recognition of a national consensus favoring a prohibition on flag-burning.

> "[A]ny suggestion that the Government's interest in suppressing speech becomes more weighty as popular opposition to that speech grows is foreign to the First Amendment."

Justice Stevens, joined by Chief Justice Rehnquist, Justice White and Justice O'Connor, dissented. Justice Stevens elaborated the argument in his *Johnson* dissent that Congress had a legitimate interest in preserving the symbolic value of the flag that outweighed "the admittedly important interest in allowing every speaker to choose the method of expressing his or her ideas that he or she deems most effective and appropriate."

Barnes v. Glen Theatre, Inc.

501 U.S. 560, 111 S.Ct. 2456, 115 L.Ed.2d 504 (1991).

Chief Justice Rehnquist announced the judgment of the Court and delivered an opinion in which Justice O'Connor and Justice Kennedy joined.

Respondents are two establishments in South Bend, Indiana, that wish to provide totally nude dancing as entertainment, and individual dancers who are employed at these establishments. They claim that the First Amendment's guarantee of freedom of expression prevents the State of Indiana from enforcing its public indecency law to prevent this form of dancing. We reject their claim.

. . .

Respondents sued in the United States District Court for the Northern District of Indiana to enjoin the enforcement of the Indiana public indecency statute, Ind.Code § 35–45–4–1 (1988), asserting that its prohibition against complete nudity in public places violated the First Amendment.... [T]he District Court concluded that "the type of dancing these plaintiffs wish to perform is not expressive activity protected by the Constitution of the United States," and rendered judgment in favor of the defendants.... The Court of Appeals ... heard the case en banc, and the court rendered a series of comprehensive and thoughtful opinions. The majority concluded that non-obscene nude dancing performed for entertainment is expression protected by the First Amendment, and that the public indecency statute was an improper infringement of that expressive activity because its purpose was to prevent the message of eroticism and sexuality conveyed by the dancers. We ... hold that the Indiana statutory requirement that the dancers in the establishments involved in this case must wear pasties and a G-string does not violate the First Amendment.

Several of our cases contain language suggesting that nude dancing of the kind involved here is expressive conduct protected by the First Amendment. ... In Schad v. Borough of Mount Ephraim, 452 U.S. 61, 66 (1981), we said that "... nude dancing is not without its First Amendment protections from official regulation" ... These statements support the conclusion of the Court of Appeals that nude dancing of the kind sought to be performed here is expressive conduct within the outer perimeters of the First Amendment, though we view it as only marginally so. This, of course, does not end our inquiry. We must determine the level of protection to be afforded to the expressive conduct at issue, and must determine whether the Indiana statute is an impermissible infringement of that protected activity.

Indiana, of course, has not banned nude dancing as such, but has proscribed public nudity across the board. The Supreme Court of Indiana has construed the Indiana statute to preclude nudity in what are essentially places of public accommodation ...

. . .

Applying the four-part *O'Brien* test ..., we find that Indiana's public indecency statute is justified despite its incidental limitations on some expressive activity. The public indecency statute is clearly within the constitutional power of the State and furthers substantial governmental interests. It is impossible to discern, other than from the text of the statute, exactly what governmental interest the Indiana legislators had in mind when they enacted this statute, for Indiana does not record legislative history, and the state's highest court has not shed additional light on the statute's purpose. Nonetheless, the statute's purpose of protecting societal order and morality is clear from its text and history. Public indecency statutes of this sort are of ancient origin, and presently exist in at least 47 States. Public indecency, including nudity, was a criminal offense at common law ... Public indecency statutes such as the one before us reflect moral disapproval of people appearing in the nude among strangers in public places.

. . .

This and other public indecency statutes were designed to protect morals and public order. The traditional police power of the States is defined as the authority to provide for the public health, safety, and morals, and we have upheld such a basis for legislation. ...

Thus, the public indecency statute furthers a substantial government interest in protecting order and morality.

This interest is unrelated to the suppression of free expression. Some may view restricting nudity on moral grounds as necessarily related to expression. We disagree. It can be argued, of course, that almost limitless types of conduct—including appearing in the nude in public—are "expressive," and in one sense of the word this is true. People who go about in the nude in public may be expressing something about themselves by so doing. But the court rejected this expansive notion of "expressive conduct" in *O'Brien*, saying:

"We cannot accept the view that an apparently limitless variety of conduct can be labelled 'speech' whenever the person engaging in the conduct intends thereby to express an idea." 391 U.S., at 376.

. . .

Respondents contend that even though prohibiting nudity in public generally may not be related to suppressing expression, prohibiting the performance of nude dancing is related to expression because the state seeks to prevent its erotic message. Therefore, they reason that the application of the Indiana statute to the nude dancing in this case violates the First Amendment, because it fails the third part of the *O'Brien* test, viz: the governmental interest must be unrelated to the suppression of free expression.

But we do not think that when Indiana applies its statute to the nude dancing in these nightclubs it is proscribing nudity because of the erotic message conveyed by the dancers. Presumably numerous other erotic performances are presented at these establishments and similar clubs without any interference from the state, so long as the performers wear a scant amount of clothing. Likewise, the requirement that the dancers don pasties and a G-string does not deprive the dance of whatever erotic message it conveys; it simply makes the message slightly less graphic. The perceived evil that Indiana seeks to address is not erotic dancing, but public nudity. The appearance of people of all shapes, sizes and ages in the nude at a beach, for example, would convey little if any erotic message, yet the state still seeks to prevent it. Public nudity is the evil the state seeks to prevent, whether or not it is combined with expressive activity.

This conclusion is buttressed by ... *O'Brien....* It was assumed that O'Brien's act in burning the certificate had a communicative element in it sufficient to bring into play the First Amendment, 391 U.S., at 376, but it was for the noncommunicative element that he was prosecuted. So here with the Indiana statute; while the dancing to which it was applied had a communicative element, it was not the dancing that was prohibited, but simply its being done in the nude.

The fourth part of the *O'Brien* test requires that the incidental restriction on First Amendment freedom be no greater than is essential to the furtherance of the governmental interest. As indicated in the discussion above, the governmental interest served by the text of the prohibition is societal disapproval of nudity in public places and among strangers. The statutory prohibition is not a means to some greater end, but an end in itself. It is without cavil that the public indecency statute is "narrowly tailored;" Indiana's requirement that the dancers wear at least pasties and a G-string is modest, and the bare minimum necessary to achieve the state's purpose.

The judgment of the Court of Appeals accordingly is

Reversed.

Justice Scalia, concurring in the judgment.

I agree that the judgment of the Court of Appeals must be reversed. In my view, however, the challenged regulation must be upheld, not because it survives some lower level of First–Amendment scrutiny, but because, as a general law regulating conduct and not specifically directed at expression, it is not subject to First–Amendment scrutiny at all.

I

The intent to convey a "message of eroticism" (or any other message) is not a necessary element of the statutory offense of public indecency; nor does one commit that statutory offense by conveying the most explicit "message of eroticism," ...

Indiana's statute is in the line of a long tradition of laws against public nudity, which have never been thought to run afoul of traditional understanding of "the freedom of speech." ...

The dissent confidently asserts, that the purpose of restricting nudity in public places in general is to protect nonconsenting parties from offense; and argues that since only consenting, admission-paying patrons see respondents dance, that purpose cannot apply and the only remaining purpose must relate to the communicative elements of the performance. ...The purpose of Indiana's nudity law would be violated, I think, if 60,000 fully consenting adults crowded into the Hoosierdome to display their genitals to one another, even if there were not an offended innocent in the crowd. Our society prohibits, and all human societies have prohibited, certain activities not because they harm others but because they are considered, in the traditional phrase, "contra bonos mores," i.e., immoral. In American society, such prohibitions have included, for example, sadomasochism, cockfighting, bestiality, suicide, drug use, prostitution, and sodomy. ...The purpose of the Indiana statute, as both its text and the manner of its enforcement demonstrate, is to enforce the traditional moral belief that people should not expose their private parts indiscriminately, regardless of whether those who see them are disedified....

II

Since the Indiana regulation is a general law not specifically targeted at expressive conduct, its application to such conduct does not in my view implicate the First Amendment.

. . .

This is not to say that the First Amendment affords no protection to expressive conduct. Where the government prohibits conduct precisely because of its communicative attributes, we hold the regulation unconstitutional. ...Where that has not been the case, however—where suppression of communicative use of the conduct was merely the incidental effect of forbidding the conduct for other reasons—we have allowed the regulation to stand. *O'Brien*, 391 U.S., at 377 ...; FTC v. Superior Court Trial Lawyers Assn., 493 U.S. 411 (1990) (Sherman Act upheld in application against restraint of trade to protest low pay); cf. United States v. Albertini, 472 U.S. 675, 687–688 (1985) (rule barring petitioner from military base upheld in application against entrance on base to protest war); Clark v. Community for Creative Non–Violence, 468 U.S. 288 (1984) (rule barring sleeping in parks upheld in application against persons engaging in such conduct to dramatize plight of homeless)....

All our holdings (though admittedly not some of our discussion) support the conclusion that "the only First Amendment analysis applicable to laws that do not directly or indirectly impede speech is the threshold inquiry of whether the purpose of the law is to suppress communication. If not, that is the end of the matter so far as First Amendment guarantees are concerned ..." ...

. . .

III

While I do not think the plurality's conclusions differ greatly from my own, I cannot entirely endorse its reasoning. . . . I think we should avoid wherever possible, moreover, a method of analysis that requires judicial assessment of the "importance" of government interests—and especially of government interests in various aspects of morality.

. . .

Justice Souter, concurring in the judgment.

. . .

. . . I agree with the plurality and the dissent that an interest in freely engaging in the nude dancing at issue here is subject to a degree of First Amendment protection.

I also agree with the plurality that the appropriate analysis to determine the actual protection required by the First Amendment is the four-part enquiry described in United States v. O'Brien . . . I nonetheless write separately to rest my concurrence in the judgment, not on the possible sufficiency of society's moral views to justify the limitations at issue, but on the State's substantial interest in combating the secondary effects of adult entertainment establishments of the sort typified by respondents' establishments.

It is, of course, true that this justification has not been articulated by Indiana's legislature or by its courts. . . .

. . .

In Renton v. Playtime Theatres, Inc., 475 U.S. 41 (1986), we upheld a city's zoning ordinance designed to prevent the occurrence of harmful secondary effects . . . Of particular importance to the present enquiry, we held that the city of Renton was not compelled to justify its restrictions by studies specifically relating to the problems that would be caused by adult theaters in that city. . . .

The type of entertainment respondents seek to provide is plainly of the same character as that at issue in *Renton* . . . It therefore is no leap to say that live nude dancing of the sort at issue here is likely to produce the same pernicious secondary effects . . . [T]he State of Indiana could reasonably conclude that forbidding nude entertainment . . . furthers its interest in preventing prostitution, sexual assault, and associated crimes. . . . The statute as applied to nudity of the sort at issue here therefore satisfies the second prong of *O'Brien.*

. . .

. . . [T]he "secondary effects" justification means that enforcement of the Indiana statute against nude dancing is "justified without reference to the content of the regulated [expression]," . . . which is sufficient, at least in the context of sexually explicit expression, to satisfy the third prong of the *O'Brien* test.

The fourth *O'Brien* condition, that the restriction be no greater than essential to further the governmental interest, requires little discussion. . . . Dropping the final stitch is prohibited, but the limitation is minor when measured against the dancer's remaining capacity and opportunity to express the erotic message. . . .

Accordingly, I find *O'Brien* satisfied and concur in the judgment.

Justice White, with whom Justice Marshall, Justice Blackmun, and Justice Stevens join, dissenting.

... [T]he Court ... concedes that "nude dancing of the kind sought to be performed here is expressive conduct within the outer perimeters of the First Amendment...." This is no more than recognizing, as the Seventh Circuit observed, that dancing is an ancient art form and "inherently embodies the expression and communication of ideas and emotions."

. . .

... [T]he simple references to the State's general interest in promoting societal order and morality is not sufficient justification for a statute which concededly reaches a significant amount of protected expressive activity. Instead, in applying the *O'Brien* test, we are obligated to carefully examine the reasons the State has chosen to regulate this expressive conduct in a less than general statute. In other words, when the State enacts a law which draws a line between expressive conduct which is regulated and nonexpressive conduct of the same type which is not regulated, *O'Brien* places the burden on the State to justify the distinctions it has made. Closer inquiry as to the purpose of the statute is surely appropriate.

... The purpose of forbidding people from appearing nude in parks, beaches, hot dog stands, and like public places is to protect others from offense. But that could not possibly be the purpose of preventing nude dancing in theaters and barrooms since the viewers are exclusively consenting adults who pay money to see these dances. The purpose of the proscription in these contexts is to protect the viewers from what the State believes is the harmful message that nude dancing communicates.... [T]he perceived harm is the communicative aspect of the erotic dance. As the State now tells us, ... the State's goal ... is "deterrence of prostitution, sexual assaults, criminal activity, degradation of women, and other activities which break down family structure." The attainment of these goals, however, depends on preventing an expressive activity.

The Court nevertheless holds that the third requirement of the *O'Brien* test, that the governmental interest be unrelated to the suppression of free expression, is satisfied because in applying the statute to nude dancing, the State is not "proscribing nudity because of the erotic message conveyed by the dancers." ... [T]he emotional or erotic impact of the dance is intensified by the nudity of the performers. As Judge Posner argued in his thoughtful concurring opinion in the Court of Appeals, the nudity of the dancer is an integral part of the emotions and thoughts that a nude dancing performance evokes.... The sight of a fully clothed, or even a partially clothed, dancer generally will have a far different impact on a spectator than that of a nude dancer, even if the same dance is performed. The nudity is itself an expressive component of the dance, not merely incidental "conduct." We have previously pointed out that " '[n]udity alone' does not place otherwise protected material outside the mantle of the First Amendment." Schad v. Mount Ephraim, 452 U.S. 61, 66 (1981).

This being the case, it cannot be that the statutory prohibition is unrelated to expressive conduct.... It is only because nude dancing performances may generate emotions and feelings of eroticism and sensuality among the spectators that the State seeks to regulate such expressive activity, apparently on the assumption that creating or emphasizing such thoughts and ideas in the minds of the spectators may lead to increased prostitution and the degradation of women. But generating thoughts, ideas, and emotions is the essence of communication. The nudity element of nude dancing performances cannot be neatly pigeonholed as mere "conduct" independent of any expressive component of the dance.

That fact dictates the level of First Amendment protection to be accorded the performance at issue here....

. . .

... [E]ven if there were compelling interests, the Indiana statute is not narrowly drawn. If the State is genuinely concerned with prostitution and associated evils, ... it can adopt restrictions that do not interfere with the expressiveness of nonobscene nude dancing performances. For instance, the State could perhaps require that, while performing, nude performers remain at all times a certain minimum distance from spectators, that nude entertainment be limited to certain hours, or even that establishments providing such entertainment be dispersed throughout the city.... Likewise, the State clearly has the authority to criminalize prostitution and obscene behavior.... Furthermore, if nude dancing in barrooms, as compared with other establishments, is the most worrisome problem, the State could invoke its Twenty-first Amendment powers and impose appropriate regulation....

As I see it, our cases require us to affirm absent a compelling state interest supporting the statute. Neither the Court nor the State suggest that the statute could withstand scrutiny under that standard.

. . .

SECTION 2. COMPELLED AFFIRMATION OF BELIEF

WEST VIRGINIA STATE BOARD OF EDUCATION v. BARNETTE, 319 U.S. 624 (1943). A resolution of the Board of Education made the flag salute a regular part of the school program and required all teachers and pupils to participate. Refusal to salute the flag was made "an act of insubordination" to "be dealt with accordingly," i.e., expulsion from school. A class action to restrain the enforcement of this regulation against Jehovah's Witnesses (who are conscientiously opposed to saluting the flag) was heard by a three-judge court. A restraining order issued; the Board of Education appealed.

Justice Jackson, in his opinion for the Court found the compulsory salute invalid on general first amendment grounds. Minersville School District v. Gobitis, 310 U.S. 586 (1940), which had sustained the validity of an identical requirement, was overruled. Justice Jackson noted that the flag salute in connection with the pledge is a form of utterance and that it requires "affirmation of a belief and an attitude of mind." His opinion included the following observations:

> "It is now a commonplace that censorship or suppression of expression of opinion is tolerated by our Constitution only when the expression presents a clear and present danger of action of a kind the State is empowered to prevent and punish. It would seem that involuntary affirmation could be commanded only on even more immediate and urgent grounds than silence. But here the power of compulsion is invoked without any allegation that remaining passive during a flag salute ritual creates a clear and present danger that would justify an effort even to muffle expression. To sustain the compulsory flag salute we are required to say that a Bill of Rights which guards the individual's right to speak his own

mind, left it open to public authorities to compel him to utter what is not in his mind.

. . .

"Nor does the issue as we see it turn on one's possession of particular religious views or the sincerity with which they are held. While religion supplies appellees' motive for enduring the discomforts of making the issue in this case, many citizens who do not share these religious views hold such a compulsory rite to infringe constitutional liberty of the individual. It is not necessary to inquire whether nonconformist beliefs will exempt from the duty to salute unless we first find power to make the salute a legal duty.

. . .

"If there is any fixed star in our constitutional constellation, it is that no official, high or petty, can prescribe what shall be orthodox in politics, nationalism, religion, or other matters of opinion or force citizens to confess by word or act their faith therein. If there are any circumstances which permit an exception, they do not now occur to us."

WOOLEY v. MAYNARD, 430 U.S. 705 (1977). George and Maxine Maynard were Jehovah's Witnesses, who had moral, religious and political objections to New Hampshire's license plate motto—"Live Free or Die." When they covered up the motto on their vehicle's license plates, Mr. Maynard was arrested and convicted under a law making it a misdemeanor to obscure the figures or letters on license plates. The federal district court enjoined the State from arresting or prosecuting the Maynards for covering the motto on the license plate. The United States Supreme Court affirmed.

Chief Justice Burger, in his opinion for the Court, decided that the case was controlled by West Virginia Board of Education v. Barnette.

"New Hampshire's statute in effect requires that appellees use their private property as a 'mobile billboard' for the State's ideological message—or suffer a penalty, as Maynard already has. As a condition to driving an automobile—a virtual necessity for most Americans—the Maynards must display 'Live Free or Die' to hundreds of people each day. The fact that most individuals agree with the thrust of New Hampshire's motto is not the test; most Americans also find the flag salute acceptable. The First Amendment protects the right of individuals to hold a point of view different from the majority and to refuse to foster, in the way New Hampshire commands, an idea they find morally objectionable.

"Identifying the Maynards' interests as implicating First Amendment protections does not end our inquiry however. We must also determine whether the State's countervailing interest is sufficiently compelling to justify requiring appellees to display the state motto on their license plates.... The two interests advanced by the state are that display of the motto (1) facilitates the identification of passenger vehicles, and (2) promotes appreciation of history, individualism and state pride.

"The State first points out that only passenger vehicles, but not commercial, trailer, or other vehicles are required to display the state motto. Thus, the argument proceeds, officers of the law are more easily able to determine whether passenger vehicles are carrying the proper plates.... Even were we to credit the State's reasons and 'even though the governmental purpose be legitimate and substantial, that purpose cannot be pursued by means that broadly stifle fundamental personal liberties when the end can be more narrowly achieved. The breadth of legislative abridgment must be viewed in the light of less drastic means for achieving the same basic purpose.'

"The State's second claimed interest is not ideologically neutral. The State is seeking to communicate to others an official view as to proper appreciation of history, state pride, and individualism. Of course, the State may legitimately pursue such interests in any number of ways. However, where the State's interest is to disseminate an ideology, no matter how acceptable to some, such interest cannot outweigh an individual's First Amendment right to avoid becoming the courier for such message."

Justice Rehnquist, joined by Justice Blackmun, in dissent, argued that the Maynards had not been forced to advocate any point of view.

"Since any implication that they affirm the motto can be so easily displaced, I cannot agree that the state statutory system for motor vehicle identification and tourist promotion may be invalidated under the fiction that appellees are unconstitutionally forced to affirm, or profess belief in, the state motto.

"The logic of the Court's opinion leads to startling, and I believe totally unacceptable, results. For example, the mottoes 'In God We Trust' and 'E Pluribus Unum' appear on the coin and currency of the United States. I cannot imagine that the statutes, see 18 U.S.C. §§ 331 and 333, proscribing defacement of U.S. currency impinge upon the First Amendment rights of an atheist. The fact that an atheist carries and uses United States currency does not, in any meaningful sense, convey any affirmation of belief on his part in the motto 'In God We Trust.'"

SECTION 3. FREEDOM OF ASSOCIATION

A. INTRODUCTION

NAACP v. Alabama

357 U.S. 449, 78 S.Ct. 1163, 2 L.Ed.2d 1488 (1958).

[The NAACP conducted activity in Alabama through unincorporated affiliates and considered itself exempt from the requirement that foreign corporations register with the Alabama Secretary of State before doing business in the State. In 1956 the State Attorney General brought suit in a state court to enjoin the Association from conducting further activities within the State. It was alleged, among other things, that the Association had recruited members, solicited contributions and opened a regional office in the State; also it had assisted Negro students seeking admission to the State University and had supported the Negro boycott of the bus lines in Montgomery to compel the seating of passengers without regard to race. The State's pre-trial motion for the production of a large number of the Association's records, including the names and addresses of all of its Alabama "members" and "agents," was granted. The Association produced a large portion of the records, but refused to supply the membership lists, and was fined for contempt.]

Mr. Justice Harlan, delivered the opinion of the Court.

. . .

Effective advocacy of both public and private points of view, particularly controversial ones, is undeniably enhanced by group association,.... It is beyond debate that freedom to engage in association for the advancement of beliefs and ideas is an inseparable aspect of the "liberty" assured by the Due Process Clause of the Fourteenth Amendment, which embraces freedom of speech.... Of course, it is immaterial whether the beliefs sought to be advanced by association pertain to political, economic, religious or cultural matters, and state action which may have the effect of curtailing the freedom to associate is subject to the closest scrutiny.

. . .

We think that the production order, in the respects here drawn in question, must be regarded as entailing the likelihood of a substantial restraint upon the exercise by petitioner's members of their right to freedom of association. Petitioner has made an uncontroverted showing that on past occasions revelation of the identity of its rank-and-file members has exposed these members to economic reprisal, loss of employment, threat of physical coercion, and other manifestations of public hostility. Under these circumstances, we think it apparent that compelled disclosure of petitioner's Alabama membership is likely to affect adversely the ability of petitioner and its members to pursue their collective effort to foster beliefs which they admittedly have the right to advocate, in that it may induce members to withdraw from the Association and dissuade others from joining it because of fear of exposure of their beliefs shown through their associations and of the consequences of this exposure.

. . .

We turn to the final question whether Alabama has demonstrated an interest in obtaining the disclosures it seeks from petitioner which is sufficient to justify the deterrent effect which we have concluded these disclosures may well have on the free exercise by petitioner's members of their constitutionally protected right of association....

. . .

Whether there was "justification" in this instance turns solely on the substantiality of Alabama's interest in obtaining the membership lists.... Without intimating the slightest view upon the merits of these issues, we are unable to perceive that the disclosure of the names of petitioner's rank-and-file members has a substantial bearing on either of them....

. . .

We hold that the immunity from state scrutiny of membership lists which the Association claims on behalf of its members is here so related to the right of the members to pursue their lawful private interest privately and to associate freely with others in so doing as to come within the protection of the Fourteenth Amendment. And we conclude that Alabama has fallen short of showing a controlling justification for the deterrent effect on the free enjoyment of the right to associate which disclosure of membership lists is likely to have. Accordingly, the judgment of civil contempt and the $100,000 fine which resulted from petitioner's refusal to comply with the production order in this respect must fall....

. . .

SPEECH AND NON–SPEECH ASSOCIATION

NAACP v. Button, 371 U.S. 415 (1963), concerned application of Virginia statutes, forbidding solicitation of legal business, to the NAACP's activities in litigating public school desegregation cases. The Court concluded that NAACP litigation was expression. It was "not a technique of resolving private differences" but a "means of achieving the lawful objectives of equality of treatment by all government." It was thus "a form of political expression." The Court held that restrictions imposed on the NAACP's litigation activities violated the first amendment.

Button emphasized that the first amendment rights involved stemmed from "[r]esort to the courts to seek vindication of constitutional rights" rather than "avaricious use of the legal process for purely private gain." In Brotherhood of R.R. Trainmen v. Virginia, 377 U.S. 1 (1964), however, the Court considered application of the Virginia prohibition of solicitation of legal business to the group legal services plan of a labor union. The plan channeled workers' personal injury suits to a group of lawyers. The Court concluded that the union's activities fell "just as clearly within the protection of the First Amendment" as those involved in *Button,* and application of the statute violated the first amendment.[a]

NAACP v. Alabama had spoken of "association for the advancement of beliefs and ideas." NAACP v. Button stressed group activity seeking "through lawful means to achieve political ends." The *R.R. Trainmen* case, however, more broadly extended first amendment association rights to group activities "for the lawful purpose of helping and advising one another in asserting . . . rights." Does the first amendment's protection of freedom of association extend to all group activities of groups with political objectives? Does it extend to association for any purpose?

B.   LIMITS ON ASSOCIATION ACTIVITIES

NAACP v. Claiborne Hardware Co.

458 U.S. 886, 102 S.Ct. 3409, 73 L.Ed.2d 1215 (1982).

Justice Stevens delivered the opinion of the Court.

The term "concerted action" encompasses unlawful conspiracies and constitutionally protected assemblies. The "looseness and pliability" of legal doctrine applicable to concerted action led Justice Jackson to note that certain joint activities have a "chameleon-like" character. The boycott of white merchants in Claiborne County, Miss., that gave rise to this litigation had such a character; it included elements of criminality and elements of majesty. Evidence that fear of reprisals caused some black citizens to withhold their patronage from respondents' businesses convinced the Supreme Court of Mississippi that the entire boycott was unlawful and that each of the 92 petitioners was liable for all of its economic consequences. Evidence that persuasive rhetoric, determination to remedy past injustices, and a host of voluntary decisions by free citizens were the critical factors in the boycott's success

---

[a] State restrictions on other labor union group legal services arrangements were held to violate the first amendment in United Mine Workers v. Illinois Bar Ass'n, 389 U.S. 217 (1967) and United Transp. Union v. State Bar, 401 U.S. 576 (1971). For an argument that restrictions on the "unauthorized practice of law" also raise first amendment concerns, see Rhode, *Policing the Professional Monopoly: A Constitutional and Empirical Analysis of Unauthorized Practice Prohibitions,* 34 Stan.L.Rev. 1 (1981).

presents us with the question whether the state court's judgment is consistent with the Constitution of the United States.

I

[The boycott, begun in 1966, led to this state court action, filed in 1969 by several merchants, for damages and injunctive relief. Named as defendants were the NAACP, MAP (a Mississippi coalition implementing the federal "head start" program), Aaron Henry (President of the Mississippi NAACP), Charles Evers (Field Secretary for the Mississippi NAACP), and 144 individuals participating in the boycott. After a lengthy trial that concluded in 1976, the trial court found the defendants liable on three theories: the tort of malicious interference with plaintiffs' business, violation of a state statutory prohibition of secondary boycotts, and violation of the state antitrust statute. A broad permanent injunction was entered, and damages in excess of one and one quarter million dollars were awarded. The Mississippi Supreme Court upheld the imposition of liability only on the common law tort theory. Judgments against MAP and 37 individuals were reversed for insufficiency of proof, and the case was remanded to the trial court for recomputation of damages. The Supreme Court granted a petition for certiorari.]

II

... We consider first whether petitioners' activities are protected in any respect by the Federal Constitution and, if they are, what effect such protection has on a lawsuit of this nature.

A

The boycott of white merchants at issue in this case took many forms. The boycott was launched at a meeting of a local branch of the NAACP attended by several hundred persons. Its acknowledged purpose was to secure compliance by both civic and business leaders with a lengthy list of demands for equality and racial justice. The boycott was supported by speeches and nonviolent picketing. Participants repeatedly encouraged others to join in its cause.

Each of these elements of the boycott is a form of speech or conduct that is ordinarily entitled to protection under the First and Fourteenth Amendments. The black citizens named as defendants in this action banded together and collectively expressed their dissatisfaction with a social structure that had denied them rights to equal treatment and respect....

. . .

Speech itself also was used to further the aims of the boycott. Nonparticipants repeatedly were urged to join the common cause, both through public address and through personal solicitation. These elements of the boycott involve speech in its most direct form. In addition, names of boycott violators were read aloud at meetings at the First Baptist Church and published in a local black newspaper. Petitioners admittedly sought to persuade others to join the boycott through social pressure and the "threat" of social ostracism. Speech does not lose its protected character, however, simply because it may embarrass others or coerce them into action....

. . .

In sum, the boycott clearly involved constitutionally protected activity.... Through exercise of these First Amendment rights, petitioners sought to bring about political, social, and economic change. Through speech, assembly, and petition—rather than through riot or revolution—petitioners sought to change a social order that had consistently treated them as second-class citizens.

The presence of protected activity, however, does not end the relevant constitutional inquiry. Governmental regulation that has an incidental effect on First Amendment freedoms may be justified in certain narrowly defined instances. See United States v. O'Brien, 391 U.S. 367. A nonviolent and totally voluntary boycott may have a disruptive effect on local economic conditions. This Court has recognized the strong governmental interest in certain forms of economic regulation, even though such regulation may have an incidental effect on rights of speech and association. See Giboney v. Empire Storage & Ice Co., 336 U.S. 490; NLRB v. Retail Store Employees, 447 U.S. 607. The right of business entities to "associate" to suppress competition may be curtailed. National Society of Professional Engineers v. United States, 435 U.S. 679. Unfair trade practices may be restricted. Secondary boycotts and picketing by labor unions may be prohibited, as part of "Congress' striking of the delicate balance between union freedom of expression and the ability of neutral employers, employees, and consumers to remain free from coerced participation in industrial strife." NLRB v. Retail Store Employees, supra, at 617–618 (Blackmun, J., concurring in part). See International Longshoremen's Assoc. v. Allied International, Inc., 456 U.S. 212, 222–223, and note 20.[a]

While States have broad power to regulate economic activity, we do not find a comparable right to prohibit peaceful political activity such as that found in the boycott in this case....

. . .

It is not disputed that a major purpose of the boycott in this case was to influence governmental action.... Petitioners sought to vindicate rights of equality and of freedom that lie at the heart of the Fourteenth Amendment itself. The right of the States to regulate economic activity could not justify a complete prohibition against a nonviolent, politically motivated boycott designed to force governmental and economic change and to effectuate rights guaranteed by the Constitution itself.

In upholding an injunction against the state supersedeas bonding requirement in this case, Judge Ainsworth of the Court of Appeals for the Fifth Circuit cogently stated:

"At the heart of the Chancery Court's opinion lies the belief that the mere organization of the boycott and every activity undertaken in support thereof could be subject to judicial prohibition under state law. This view accords insufficient weight to the First Amendment's protection of political speech and association. There is no suggestion that the NAACP, MAP or the individual defendants were in competition with the white businesses or that the boycott arose from parochial economic interests. On the contrary, the boycott grew out of a racial dispute with the white merchants and city government of Port Gibson and all of the picketing, speeches, and other communication associated with the boycott were directed to the elimination of racial discrimination in the town. This differentiates this case from

---

[a] The cited case was decided two and one-half months before *Claiborne Hardware*. A unanimous Court held that a politically motivated refusal by a longshoremen's union to unload cargo from the Soviet Union was a secondary boycott prohibited by the National Labor Relations Act. A first amendment argument by the union was rejected summarily. Secondary labor picketing was not protected by the first amendment. "It would seem even clearer that conduct designed not to communicate but to coerce merits still less consideration."

a boycott organized for economic ends, for speech to protest racial discrimination is essential political speech lying at the core of the First Amendment." Henry v. First National Bank of Clarksdale, 595 F.2d 291, 303 (1979) (footnote omitted).

We hold that the nonviolent elements of petitioners' activities are entitled to the protection of the First Amendment.

B

. . . [W]e consider here the effect of our holding that much of petitioners' conduct was constitutionally protected on the ability of the State to impose liability for elements of the boycott that were not so protected.

The First Amendment does not protect violence. . . . Although the extent and significance of the violence in this case is vigorously disputed by the parties, there is no question that acts of violence occurred. No federal rule of law restricts a State from imposing tort liability for business losses that are caused by violence and by threats of violence. When such conduct occurs in the context of constitutionally protected activity, however, "precision of regulation" is demanded. NAACP v. Button, 371 U.S. 415, 438. Specifically, the presence of activity protected by the First Amendment imposes restraints on the grounds that may give rise to damage liability and on the persons who may be held accountable for those damages.

. . .

. . . Civil liability may not be imposed merely because an individual belonged to a group, some members of which committed acts of violence. For liability to be imposed by reason of association alone, it is necessary to establish that the group itself possessed unlawful goals and that the individual held a specific intent to further those illegal aims. . . .

III

The chancellor awarded respondents damages for all business losses that were sustained during a 7 year period beginning in 1966 and ending December 31, 1972. With the exception of Aaron Henry, all defendants were held jointly and severally liable for these losses. The chancellor's findings were consistent with his view that voluntary participation in the boycott was a sufficient basis on which to impose liability. The Mississippi Supreme Court properly rejected that theory; it nevertheless held that petitioners were liable for all damages "resulting from the boycott." In light of the principles set forth above, it is evident that such a damage award may not be sustained in this case.

. . .

IV

. . .

At times the difference between lawful and unlawful collective action may be identified easily by reference to its purpose. In this case, however, petitioners' ultimate objectives were unquestionably legitimate. The charge of illegality—like the claim of constitutional protection—derives from the means employed by the participants to achieve those goals. The use of speeches, marches, and threats of social ostracism cannot provide the basis for a damages award. But violent conduct is beyond the pale of constitutional protection.

The taint of violence colored the conduct of some of the petitioners. They, of course, may be held liable for the consequences of their violent deeds. The burden of demonstrating that it colored the entire collective effort, however, is not satisfied by evidence that violence occurred or even that violence contributed to the success of the boycott. A massive and prolonged effort to change the social, political, and economic structure of a local environment cannot be characterized as a violent conspiracy simply by reference to the ephemeral consequences of relatively few violent acts. Such a characterization must be supported by findings that adequately disclose the evidentiary basis for concluding that specific parties agreed to use unlawful means, that carefully identify the impact of such unlawful conduct, and that recognize the importance of avoiding the imposition of punishment for constitutionally protected activity. The burden of demonstrating that fear rather than protected conduct was the dominant force in the movement is heavy. A court must be wary of a claim that the true color of a forest is better revealed by reptiles hidden in the weeds than by the foliage of countless freestanding trees. The findings of the chancellor, framed largely in the light of two legal theories rejected by the Mississippi Supreme Court, are constitutionally insufficient to support the judgment that all petitioners are liable for all losses resulting from the boycott.

The judgment is reversed. The case is remanded for further proceedings not inconsistent with this opinion.

It is so ordered.

Justice Rehnquist concurs in the result.

Justice Marshall took no part in the consideration or decision of this case.

C.   LIMITS ON ASSOCIATION MEMBERSHIP POLICIES

Roberts v. United States Jaycees

468 U.S. 609, 104 S.Ct. 3244, 82 L.Ed.2d 462 (1984).

Justice Brennan delivered the opinion of the Court.

This case requires us to address a conflict between a State's efforts to eliminate gender-based discrimination against its citizens and the constitutional freedom of association asserted by members of a private organization. ...

I

A

The United States Jaycees (Jaycees), founded in 1920 as the Junior Chamber of Commerce, is a nonprofit membership corporation ... The organization's bylaws establish seven classes of membership ... Regular membership is limited to young men between the ages of 18 and 35, while associate membership is available to individuals or groups ineligible for regular membership, principally women and older men. An associate member, whose dues are somewhat lower than those charged regular members, may not vote, hold local or national office, or participate in certain leadership training and awards programs.... At the time of trial in August 1981, the Jaycees had approximately 295,000 members in 7,400 local chapters affiliated with 51 state organizations. There were at that time about 11,915 associate members. The national organization's executive vice president estimated at trial that women associate members make up about two percent of the Jaycees' total membership.

New members are recruited to the Jaycees through the local chapters, although the state and national organizations are also actively involved in recruitment through a variety of promotional activities. A new regular member pays an initial fee followed by annual dues; in exchange, he is entitled to participate in all of the activities of the local, state, and national organizations. The national headquarters employs a staff to develop "program kits" for use by local chapters that are designed to enhance individual development, community development, and members' management skills. These materials include courses in public speaking and personal finances as well as community programs related to charity, sports, and public health. The national office also makes available to members a range of personal products, including travel accessories, casual wear, pins, awards, and other gifts. The programs, products, and other activities of the organization are all regularly featured in publications made available to the membership, including a magazine entitled "Future."

B

[After the Minneapolis and St. Paul chapters of the Jaycees began to admit women as regular members, the national organization imposed sanctions and, in 1978, advised the chapters that their charters would be revoked. The chapters filed charges of discrimination with the Minnesota Department of Human Rights, alleging that exclusion of women by the national organization violated the Minnesota Human Rights Act. The Act prohibits, in part, discrimination on the basis of sex by a business offering goods or services to the public. The national organization brought suit in the United States District Court to enjoin enforcement of the Act against it. The District Court's judgment in favor of the state officials was reversed by the Court of Appeals.]

II

Our decisions have referred to constitutionally protected "freedom of association" in two distinct senses. In one line of decisions, the Court has concluded that choices to enter into and maintain certain intimate human relationships must be secured against undue intrusion by the State because of the role of such relationships in safeguarding the individual freedom that is central to our constitutional scheme. In this respect, freedom of association receives protection as a fundamental element of personal liberty. In another set of decisions, the Court has recognized a right to associate for the purpose of engaging in those activities protected by the First Amendment—speech, assembly, petition for the redress of grievances, and the exercise of religion. The Constitution guarantees freedom of association of this kind as an indispensable means of preserving other individual liberties.

The intrinsic and instrumental features of constitutionally protected association may, of course, coincide. In particular, when the State interferes with individuals' selection of those with whom they wish to join in a common endeavor, freedom of association in both of its forms may be implicated. The Jaycees contend that this is such a case. Still, the nature and degree of constitutional protection afforded freedom of association may vary depending on the extent to which one or the other aspect of the constitutionally protected liberty is at stake in a given case. We therefore find it useful to consider separately the effect of applying the Minnesota statute to the Jaycees on what could be called its members' freedom of intimate association and their freedom of expressive association.

A

The Court has long recognized that, because the Bill of Rights is designed to secure individual liberty, it must afford the formation and preservation of certain kinds of highly personal relationships a substantial measure of sanctuary from unjustified interference by the State. E.g., Pierce v. Society of Sisters, 268 U.S. 510, 534–535 (1925); Meyer v. Nebraska, 262 U.S. 390, 399 (1923). Without precisely identifying every consideration that may underlie this type of constitutional protection, we have noted that certain kinds of personal bonds have played a critical role in the culture and traditions of the Nation by cultivating and transmitting shared ideals and beliefs; they thereby foster diversity and act as critical buffers between the individual and the power of the State.... Moreover, the constitutional shelter afforded such relationships reflects the realization that individuals draw much of their emotional enrichment from close ties with others. Protecting these relationships from unwarranted state interference therefore safeguards the ability independently to define one's identity that is central to any concept of liberty....

The personal affiliations that exemplify these considerations, and that therefore suggest some relevant limitations on the relationships that might be entitled to this sort of constitutional protection, are those that attend the creation and sustenance of a family—marriage, e.g., Zablocki v. Redhail, [434 U.S. 374 (1978)]; childbirth, e.g., Carey v. Population Services International, [431 U.S. 678 (1977)]; the raising and education of children, e.g., Smith v. Organization of Foster Families, [431 U.S. 816 (1977)]; and cohabitation with one's relatives, e.g., Moore v. East Cleveland, [431 U.S. 494 (1977)]. Family relationships, by their nature, involve deep attachments and commitments to the necessarily few other individuals with whom one shares not only a special community of thoughts, experiences, and beliefs but also distinctively personal aspects of one's life. Among other things, therefore, they are distinguished by such attributes as relative smallness, a high degree of selectivity in decisions to begin and maintain the affiliation, and seclusion from others in critical aspects of the relationship. As a general matter, only relationships with these sorts of qualities are likely to reflect the considerations that have led to an understanding of freedom of association as an intrinsic element of personal liberty. Conversely, an association lacking these qualities—such as a large business enterprise—seems remote from the concerns giving rise to this constitutional protection. Accordingly, the Constitution undoubtedly imposes constraints on the State's power to control the selection of one's spouse that would not apply to regulations affecting the choice of one's fellow employees....

Between these poles, of course, lies a broad range of human relationships that may make greater or lesser claims to constitutional protection from particular incursions by the State. Determining the limits of state authority over an individual's freedom to enter into a particular association therefore unavoidably entails a careful assessment of where that relationship's objective characteristics locate it on a spectrum from the most intimate to the most attenuated of personal attachments. See generally Runyon v. McCrary, 427 U.S. 160, 187–189 (1976) (Powell, J., concurring). We need not mark the potentially significant points on this terrain with any precision. We note only that factors that may be relevant include size, purpose, policies, selectivity, congeniality, and other characteristics that in a particular case may be pertinent. In this case, however, several features of the Jaycees clearly place the organization outside of the category of relationships worthy of this kind of constitutional protection.

The undisputed facts reveal that the local chapters of the Jaycees are large and basically unselective groups. At the time of the state administrative hearing, the Minneapolis chapter had approximately 430 members, while the St. Paul chapter had about 400. Apart from age and sex, neither the national organization nor the local chapters employs any criteria for judging applicants for membership, and new members are routinely recruited and admitted with no inquiry into their backgrounds.... Furthermore, despite their inability to vote, hold office, or receive certain awards, women affiliated with the Jaycees attend various meetings, participate in selected projects, and engage in many of the organization's social functions. Indeed, numerous non-members of both genders regularly participate in a substantial portion of activities central to the decision of many members to associate with one another, including many of the organization's various community programs, awards ceremonies, and recruitment meetings.

In short, the local chapters of the Jaycees are neither small nor selective. Moreover, much of the activity central to the formation and maintenance of the association involves the participation of strangers to that relationship. Accordingly, we conclude that the Jaycees chapters lack the distinctive characteristics that might afford constitutional protection to the decision of its members to exclude women. We turn therefore to consider the extent to which application of the Minnesota statute to compel the Jaycees to accept women infringes the group's freedom of expressive association.

B

An individual's freedom to speak, to worship, and to petition the government for the redress of grievances could not be vigorously protected from interference by the State unless a correlative freedom to engage in group effort toward those ends were not also guaranteed. According protection to collective effort on behalf of shared goals is especially important in preserving political and cultural diversity and in shielding dissident expression from suppression by the majority.... Consequently, we have long understood as implicit in the right to engage in activities protected by the First Amendment a corresponding right to associate with others in pursuit of a wide variety of political, social, economic, educational, religious, and cultural ends.... In view of the various protected activities in which the Jaycees engages, that right is plainly implicated in this case.

Government actions that may unconstitutionally infringe upon this freedom can take a number of forms. Among other things, government may seek to impose penalties or withhold benefits from individuals because of their membership in a disfavored group ...; it may attempt to require disclosure of the fact of membership in a group seeking anonymity ...; and it may try to interfere with the internal organization or affairs of the group ... By requiring the Jaycees to admit women as full voting members, the Minnesota Act works an infringement of the last type. There can be no clearer example of an intrusion into the internal structure or affairs of an association than a regulation that forces the group to accept members it does not desire. Such a regulation may impair the ability of the original members to express only those views that brought them together. Freedom of association therefore plainly presupposes a freedom not to associate....

The right to associate for expressive purposes is not, however, absolute. Infringements on that right may be justified by regulations adopted to serve compelling state interests, unrelated to the suppression of ideas, that cannot be achieved through means significantly less restrictive of associational freedoms.... We are persuaded that Minnesota's compelling interest in eradicating discrimination against its female citizens justifies the impact that application of the statute to the Jaycees may have on the male members' associational freedoms.

On its face, the Minnesota Act does not aim at the suppression of speech, does not distinguish between prohibited and permitted activity on the basis of viewpoint, and does not license enforcement authorities to administer the statute on the basis of such constitutionally impermissible criteria. Nor does the Jaycees contend that the Act has been applied in this case for the purpose of hampering the organization's ability to express its views. ...

By prohibiting gender discrimination in places of public accommodation, the Minnesota Act protects the State's citizenry from a number of serious social and personal harms. In the context of reviewing state actions under the Equal Protection Clause, this Court has frequently noted that discrimination based on archaic and overbroad assumptions about the relative needs and capacities of the sexes forces individuals to labor under stereotypical notions that often bear no relationship to their actual abilities. It thereby both deprives persons of their individual dignity and denies society the benefits of wide participation in political, economic, and cultural life. These concerns are strongly implicated with respect to gender discrimination in the allocation of publicly available goods and services....

. . .

In applying the Act to the Jaycees, the State has advanced those interests through the least restrictive means of achieving its ends. Indeed, the Jaycees has failed to demonstrate that the Act imposes any serious burdens on the male members' freedom of expressive association.... To be sure, as the Court of Appeals noted, a "not insubstantial part" of the Jaycees' activities constitutes protected expression on political, economic, cultural, and social affairs.... There is, however, no basis in the record for concluding that admission of women as full voting members will impede the organization's ability to engage in these protected activities or to disseminate its preferred views....

While acknowledging that "the specific content of most of the resolutions adopted over the years by the Jaycees has nothing to do with sex," the Court of Appeals nonetheless entertained the hypothesis that women members might have a different view or agenda with respect to these matters so that, if they are allowed to vote, "some change in the Jaycees' philosophical cast can reasonably be expected," ... Although such generalizations may or may not have a statistical basis in fact with respect to particular positions adopted by the Jaycees, we have repeatedly condemned legal decisionmaking that relies uncritically on such assumptions.... In the absence of a showing far more substantial than that attempted by the Jaycees, we decline to indulge in the sexual stereotyping that underlies appellee's contention that, by allowing women to vote, application of the Minnesota Act will change the content or impact of the organization's speech....

In any event, even if enforcement of the Act causes some incidental abridgement of the Jaycees' protected speech, that effect is no greater than is necessary to accomplish the State's legitimate purposes. As we have explained, acts of invidious discrimination in the distribution of publicly available goods, services, and other advantages cause unique evils that government has a compelling interest to prevent—wholly apart from the point of view such conduct may transmit. Accordingly, like violence or other types of potentially expressive activities that produce special harms distinct from their communicative impact, such practices are entitled to no constitutional protection....

III

We turn finally to appellee's contentions that the Minnesota Act, as interpreted by the State's highest court, is unconstitutionally vague and overbroad....

In deciding that the Act reaches the Jaycees, the Minnesota Supreme Court used a number of specific and objective criteria—regarding the organization's size, selectivity, commercial nature, and use of public facilities—typically employed in determining the applicability of state and federal anti discrimination statutes to the membership policies of assertedly private clubs.... The Court of Appeals seemingly acknowledged that the Minnesota court's construction of the Act by use of these familiar standards ensures that the reach of the statute is readily ascertainable. It nevertheless concluded that the Minnesota court introduced a constitutionally fatal element of uncertainty into the statute by suggesting that the Kiwanis Club might be sufficiently "private" to be outside the scope of the Act....

The contrast between the Jaycees and the Kiwanis Club drawn by the Minnesota court ... disposes of appellee's contention that the Act is unconstitutionally overbroad.... The state court's articulated willingness to adopt limiting constructions that would exclude private groups from the statute's reach, together with the commonly used and sufficiently precise standards it employed to determine that the Jaycees is not such a group, establish that the Act, as currently construed, does not create an unacceptable risk of application to a substantial amount of protected conduct....

IV

The judgment of the Court of Appeals is

Reversed.

Justice Rehnquist concurs in the judgment.

The Chief Justice and Justice Blackmun took no part in the decision of this case.

Justice O'Connor, concurring in part and concurring in the judgment.

. . .

I part company with the Court over its First Amendment analysis in Part II–B of its opinion. ...I believe the Court has adopted a test that unadvisedly casts doubt on the power of States to pursue the profoundly important goal of ensuring nondiscriminatory access to commercial opportunities in our society. At the same time, the Court has adopted an approach to the general problem presented by this case that accords insufficient protection to expressive associations and places inappropriate burdens on groups claiming the protection of the First Amendment.

I

... The Court declares that the Jaycees' right of association depends on the organization's making a "substantial" showing that the admission of unwelcome members "will change the message communicated by the group's speech." ...

Imposing such a requirement, especially in the context of the balancing-of-interests test articulated by the Court, raises the possibility that certain commercial associations, by engaging occasionally in certain kinds of expressive activities, might improperly gain protection for discrimination.... Whether an association is or is not constitutionally protected in the selection of its membership should not depend on what the association says or why its members say it.

The Court's readiness to inquire into the connection between membership and message reveals a more fundamental flaw in its analysis....

On the one hand, an association engaged exclusively in protected expression enjoys First Amendment protection of both the content of its message and the choice of its members.... Protection of the association's right to define its membership derives from the recognition that the formation of an expressive association is the creation of a voice, and the selection of members is the definition of that voice....

On the other hand, there is only minimal constitutional protection of the freedom of *commercial* association. There are, of course, some constitutional protections of commercial speech—speech intended and used to promote a commercial transaction with the speaker. But the State is free to impose any rational regulation on the commercial transaction itself. The Constitution does not guarantee a right to choose employees, customers, suppliers, or those with whom one engages in simple commercial transactions, without restraint from the State. A shopkeeper has no constitutional right to deal only with persons of one sex.

. . .

In my view, an association should be characterized as commercial, and therefore subject to rationally related state regulation of its membership and other associational activities, when, and only when, the association's activities are not predominantly of the type protected by the First Amendment. It is only when the association is predominantly engaged in protected expression that state regulation of its membership will necessarily affect, change, dilute, or silence one collective voice that would otherwise be heard. An association must choose its market. Once it enters the marketplace of commerce in any substantial degree it loses the complete control over its membership that it would otherwise enjoy if it confined its affairs to the marketplace of ideas.

. . .

II

Minnesota's attempt to regulate the membership of the Jaycees chapters operating in that State presents a relatively easy case for application of the expressive-commercial dichotomy....

... Notwithstanding its protected expressive activities, the Jaycees ... is, first and foremost, an organization that, at both the national and local levels, promotes and practices the art of solicitation and management. ...

Recruitment and selling are commercial activities, even when conducted for training rather than for profit. The "not insubstantial" volume of protected Jaycees activity found by the Court of Appeals is simply not enough to preclude state regulation of the Jaycees' commercial activities. ...The members of the Jaycees may not claim constitutional immunity from Minnesota's anti-discrimination law by seeking to exercise their First Amendment rights through this commercial organization.

. . .

BOARD OF DIRECTORS OF ROTARY INTERNATIONAL v. ROTARY CLUB OF DUARTE, 481 U.S. 537 (1987). The Court held that application of a state antidiscrimination law to require admission of women to membership in local Rotary clubs did not deny freedom of private association or freedom of expressive association. As to freedom of private association, the critical factors were the organization's "size, purpose, selectivity, and whether others are excluded from critical aspects of the relationship." As to freedom of expressive association, Rotary clubs do not take positions on "public questions" as a matter of policy. Even if the state antidiscrimination act "does work some slight infringement" on expressive association, it was justified by the "compelling interest in eliminating discrimination against women." In a footnote, the Court noted that it had not decided the extent of First Amendment protection of associational rights "in the many clubs and other entities with selective membership." Each case would require "a careful inquiry into the objective characteristics of the particular relationship at issue."

D.   COMPULSORY ASSOCIATION MEMBERSHIP

Keller v. State Bar of California

496 U.S. 1, 110 S.Ct. 2228, 110 L.Ed.2d 1 (1990).

Chief Justice Rehnquist delivered the opinion of the Court.

Petitioners, members of the State Bar of California, sued that body claiming its use of their membership dues to finance certain ideological or political activities to which they were opposed violated their rights under the First Amendment of the United States Constitution. The Supreme Court of California rejected this challenge on the grounds that respondent State Bar is a state agency, and as such may use the dues for any purpose within its broad statutory authority. We agree that lawyers admitted to practice in the State may be required to join and pay dues to the State Bar, but disagree as to the scope of permissible dues-financed activities in which respondent may engage.

Respondent State Bar is an organization created under California law to regulate the State's legal profession. It is an entity commonly referred to as an "integrated bar"—an association of attorneys in which membership and dues are required as a condition of practicing law in a State.... The association performs a variety of functions such as "examining applicants for admission, formulating rules of professional conduct, disciplining members for misconduct, preventing unlawful practice of the law, and engaging in study and recommendation of changes in procedural law and improvement of the administration of justice." Respondent also engages in a number of other activities which are the subject of the dispute in this case. "[T]he State Bar for many years has lobbied the Legislature and other governmental agencies, filed amicus curiae briefs in pending cases, held an annual conference of delegates at which issues of current interest are debated and resolutions approved, and engaged in a variety of education programs." These activities are financed principally through the use of membership dues.

Petitioners, 21 members of the State Bar, sued in state court claiming that through these activities respondent expends mandatory dues payments to advance political and ideological causes to which they do not subscribe....

. . . .

In Lathrop v. Donohue, 367 U.S. 820 (1961), a Wisconsin lawyer claimed that he could not constitutionally be compelled to join and financially support a state bar association which expressed opinions on, and attempted to influence, legislation. Six Members of this Court, relying on Railway Employees v. Hanson, 351 U.S. 225 (1956), rejected this claim.

> "In our view the case presents a claim of impingement upon freedom of association no different from that which we decided in [Hanson]. We there held that ... the Railway Labor Act ... did not on its face abridge protected rights of association in authorizing union-shop agreements between interstate railroads and unions of their employees conditioning the employees' continued employment on payment of union dues, initiation fees and assessments.... Both in purport and in practice the bulk of State Bar activities serve the function, or at least so Wisconsin might reasonably believe, of elevating the educational and ethical standards of the Bar to the end of improving the quality of the legal service available to the people of the State, without any reference to the political process. It cannot be denied that this is a legitimate end of state policy.... Wisconsin, in order to further the State's legitimate interests in raising the quality of professional services, may constitutionally require that the costs of improving the profession in this fashion should be shared by the subjects and beneficiaries of the regulatory program, the lawyers, even though the organization created to attain the objective also engages in some legislative activity...."
> ... (plurality opinion) ...

. . .

The *Lathrop* plurality emphasized, however, the limited scope of the question it was deciding ... [T]he plurality expressly reserved judgment on Lathrop's additional claim that his free speech rights were violated by the Wisconsin Bar's use of his mandatory dues to support objectionable political activities, believing that the record was not sufficiently developed to address this particular claim. Petitioners here present this very claim for decision, contending that the use of their compulsory dues to finance political and ideological activities of the State Bar with which they disagree violates their rights of free speech guaranteed by the First Amendment.

In Abood v. Detroit Board of Education, 431 U.S. 209 (1977), the Court confronted the issue of whether, consistent with the First Amendment, agency-shop dues of nonunion public employees could be used to support political and ideological causes of the union which were unrelated to collective-bargaining activities. We held that while the Constitution did not prohibit a union from spending "funds for the expression of political views ... or toward the advancement of other ideological causes not germane to its duties as collective-bargaining representative," the Constitution did require that such expenditures be "financed from charges, dues, or assessments paid by employees who [did] not object to advancing those ideas and who [were] not coerced into doing so against their will by the threat of loss of governmental employment." ... While the decision in *Abood* was also predicated on the grounds that a public employee could not be compelled to relinquish First Amendment rights as a condition of public employment, ... in the later case of Ellis v. Railway Clerks, 466 U.S. 435 (1984), the Court made it clear that the principles of *Abood* apply equally to employees in the private sector....

Although several federal and state courts have applied the *Abood* analysis in the context of First Amendment challenges to integrated bar association, ... the California Supreme Court in this case held that respondent's status as a regulated state agency exempted it from any constitutional constraints on the use of its dues.... Respondent also urges this position, invoking the so-called "government speech" doctrine [arguing that] "[t]he government must take substantive positions and decide disputed issues to govern.... So long as it bases its actions on legitimate goals, government may speak despite citizen disagreement with its message, for government is not required to be content-neutral." ...

... The State Bar of California is a good deal different from most other entities that would be regarded in common parlance as "governmental agencies." Its principal funding comes not from appropriations made to it by the legislature, but from dues levied on its members by the Board of Governors. Only lawyers admitted to practice in the State of California are members of the State Bar, and all 122,000 lawyers admitted to practice in the State must be members. Respondent undoubtedly performs important and valuable services for the State by way of governance of the profession, but those services are essentially advisory in nature. The State Bar does not admit anyone to the practice of law, it does not finally disbar or suspend anyone, nor does it ultimately establish ethical codes of conduct. All of those functions are reserved by California law to the State Supreme Court....

There is, by contrast, a substantial analogy between the relationship of the State Bar and its members, on the one hand, and the relation of the employee unions and their members, on the other. The reason behind the legislative enactment of "agency shop" laws is to prevent "free riders"—those who receive the benefit of union negotiation with their employers, but who do not choose to join the union and pay dues—from avoiding their fair share of the cost of a process from which they benefit. The members of the State Bar concededly do not benefit as directly from respondent's activities as do employees from union negotiations with management, but the position of the organized bars has generally been that they prefer a large measure of self-regulation to regulation conducted by a government body which has little or no connection with the profession. The plan established by California for the regulation of the profession is for recommendations as to admission to practice, the disciplining of lawyers, codes of conduct, and the like to be made to the courts or the legislature by the organized bar. It is entirely appropriate that all of the lawyers who derive benefit from the unique status of being among those admitted to practice before the courts should be called upon to pay a fair share of the cost of the professional involvement in this effort.

But the very specialized characteristics of the State Bar of California discussed above served to distinguish it from the role of the typical government official or agency. Government officials are expected as a part of the democratic process to represent and to espouse the views of a majority of their constituents. With countless advocates outside of the government seeking to influence its policy, it would be ironic if those charged with making governmental decisions were not free to speak for themselves in the process. If every citizen were to have a right to insist that no one paid by public funds express a view with which he disagreed, debate over issues of great concern to the public would be limited to those in the private sector, and the process of government as we know it radically transformed....

The State Bar of California was created, not to participate in the general government of the State, but to provide specialized professional advice to those with the ultimate responsibility of governing the legal profession. Its members and officers are such not because they are citizens or voters, but because they are lawyers. We think that these differences between the State Bar, on the one hand, and traditional government agencies and officials, on the other hand, render unavailing respondent's argument that it is not subject to the same constitutional rule with respect to the use of compulsory dues as are labor unions representing public and private employees.

Respondent would further distinguish the two situations on the grounds that the compelled association in the context of labor unions serves only a private economic interest in collective bargaining, while the State Bar serves more substantial public interests. But legislative recognition that the agency shop arrangements serve vital national interests in preserving industrial peace ... indicates that such arrangements serve substantial public interests as well. We are not possessed of any scales which would enable us to determine that the one outweighs the other sufficiently to produce a different result here.

Abood held that a union could not expend a dissenting individual's dues for ideological activities not "germane" to the purpose for which compelled association was justified: collective bargaining. Here the compelled association and integrated bar is justified by the State's interest in regulating the legal profession and improving the quality of legal services. The State Bar may therefore constitutionally fund activities germane to those goals out of the mandatory dues of all members. It may not, however, in such manner fund activities of an ideological nature which fall outside of those areas of activity. The difficult question, of course, is to define the latter class of activities.

Construing the Railway Labor Act in *Ellis,* supra, we held:

> "[W]hen employees such as petitioners object to being burdened with particular union expenditures, the test must be whether the challenged expenditures are necessarily or reasonably incurred for the purpose of performing the duties of an exclusive representative of the employees in dealing with the employer on labor-management issues. Under this standard, objecting employees may be compelled to pay their fair share of not only the direct costs of negotiating and administering a collective-bargaining contract and of settling grievances and disputes, but also the expenses of activities or undertakings normally or reasonably employed to implement or effectuate the duties of the union as exclusive representative of the employees in the bargaining unit." ...

We think these principles are useful guidelines for determining permissible expenditures in the present context as well. Thus, the guiding standard must be whether the challenged expenditures are necessarily or reasonably incurred for the purpose of regulating the legal profession or "improving the quality of the legal service available to the people of the State." *Lathrop,* 367 U.S., at 843 (plurality opinion).

. . .

Petitioners assert that the State Bar has engaged in, inter alia, lobbying for or against state legislation (1) prohibiting state and local agency employers from requiring employees to take polygraph tests; (2) prohibiting possession of armor-piercing handgun ammunition; (3) creating an unlimited right of action to sue anybody causing air pollution; and (4) requesting Congress to refrain from enacting a guest worker program or from permitting the importation of workers from other countries. Petitioners' complaint also alleges that the Conference of Delegates funded and sponsored by the State Bar endorsed a gun control initiative, disapproved statements of a United States senatorial candidate regarding court review of a victim's bill of rights, endorsed a nuclear weapons freeze initiative, and opposed federal legislation limiting federal court jurisdiction over abortions, public school prayer and busing.

Precisely where the line falls between those State Bar activities in which the officials and members of the Bar are acting essentially as professional advisors to those ultimately charged with the regulation of the legal profession, on the one hand, and those activities having political or ideological coloration which are not reasonably related to the advancement of such goals, on the other, will not always be easy to discern. But the extreme ends of the spectrum are clear: Compulsory dues may not be expended to endorse or advance a gun control or nuclear weapons freeze initiative; at the other end of the spectrum petitioners have no valid constitutional objection to their compulsory dues being spent for activities connected with disciplining members of the bar or proposing ethical codes for the profession.

In declining to apply our *Abood* decision to the activities of the State Bar, the Supreme Court of California noted that it would entail "an extraordinary burden...." ...

In Teachers v. Hudson, 475 U.S. 292 (1986), where we outlined a minimum set of procedures by which a union in an agency shop relationship could meet its requirement under *Abood*, we had a developed record regarding different methods fashioned by unions to deal with the "free rider" problem in the organized labor setting. We do not have any similar record here. We believe an integrated bar could certainly meet its *Abood* obligation by adopting the sort of procedures described in *Hudson*. Questions as to whether one or more alternate procedures would likewise satisfy that obligation are better left for consideration upon a more fully developed record.

In addition to their claim for relief based on respondent's use of their mandatory dues, petitioners' complaint also requested an injunction prohibiting the State Bar from using its name to advance political and ideological causes or beliefs. This request for relief appears to implicate a much broader freedom of association claim than was at issue in *Lathrop*. Petitioners challenge not only their "compelled financial support of group activities," but urge that they cannot be compelled to associate with an organization that engages in political or ideological activities beyond those for which mandatory financial support is justified under the principles of *Lathrop* and *Abood*. The California courts did not address this claim, and we decline to do so in the first instance. The state courts remain free, of course, to consider this issue on remand.

The judgment of the Supreme Court of California is reversed, and the case is remanded for further proceedings not inconsistent with this opinion.

Reversed.

E.   COMPULSORY SPEECH ACCESS FOR THIRD PARTIES

PRUNEYARD SHOPPING CENTER v. ROBINS, 447 U.S. 74 (1980). A group of high school students sought to solicit support for petitions opposing a United Nations resolution against "Zionism." They were ordered by the owner of a large privately-owned shopping center to leave the premises, and brought suit to enjoin the owner from denying them access. The California Supreme Court interpreted the California Constitution to require the owner to allow use of its shopping center for speech and petitioning. The United States Supreme Court rejected an argument that private property owners were being required to participate in disseminating ideological messages they might oppose. It was unlikely that the owner would be identified with the messages of others, and any false identification could be easily disavowed. Concurring in the result, Justices Powell and White argued that there would be serious first amendment issues if speakers using the owner's premises expressed views strongly opposed by the owner.

Pacific Gas and Electric Company v. Public Utilities Commission of California

475 U.S. 1, 106 S.Ct. 903, 89 L.Ed.2d 1 (1986).

Justice Powell announced the judgment of the Court and delivered an opinion in which the Chief Justice, Justice Brennan, and Justice O'Connor join.

The question in this case is whether the California Public Utilities Commission may require a privately owned utility company to include in its billing envelopes speech of a third party with which the utility disagrees.

I

For the past 62 years, appellant Pacific Gas and Electric Company has distributed a newsletter in its monthly billing envelope. Appellant's newsletter, called *Progress*, reaches over three million customers. It has included political editorials, feature stories on matters of public interest, tips on energy conservation, and straightforward information about utility services and bills.

In 1980, appellee Toward Utility Rate Normalization (TURN), an intervenor in a ratemaking proceeding before California's Public Utilities Commission, another appellee, urged the Commission to forbid appellant to use the billing envelopes to distribute political editorials, on the ground that the appellant's customers should not bear the expense of appellant's own political speech. The Commission decided that the envelope space that appellant had used to disseminate *Progress* is the property of the ratepayers. This "extra space" was defined as "the space remaining in the billing envelope, after inclusion of the monthly bill and any required legal notices, for inclusion of other materials up to such total envelope weight as would not result in any additional postage cost."

In an effort to apportion this "extra space" between appellant and its customers, the Commission permitted TURN to use the "extra space" four times a year for the next two years.... The Commission placed no limitations on what TURN or appellant could say in the envelope, except that TURN is required to state that its messages are not those of appellant. The Commission reserved the right to grant other groups access to the envelopes in the future.

Appellant appealed the Commission's order to the California Supreme Court, arguing that it has a First Amendment right not to help spread a message with which it disagrees, see Wooley v. Maynard, 430 U.S. 705 (1977), and that the Commission's order infringes that right. The California Supreme Court denied discretionary review. We ... now reverse.

II

The constitutional guarantee of free speech "serves significant societal interests" wholly apart from the speaker's interest in self-expression. First National Bank of Boston v. Bellotti, 435 U.S. 765, 776 (1978). By protecting those who wish to enter the marketplace of ideas from government attack, the First Amendment protects the public's interest in receiving information.... The identity of the speaker is not decisive in determining whether speech is protected. Corporations and other associations, like individuals, contribute to the "discussion, debate, and the dissemination of information and ideas" that the First Amendment seeks to foster. . . . [I]n Consolidated Edison Co. v. Public Service Comm'n of N.Y., 447 U.S. 530, 544 (1980), we invalidated a state order prohibiting a privately owned utility company from discussing controversial political issues in its billing envelopes. . . . [T]he critical considerations were that the State sought to abridge speech that the First Amendment is designed to protect, and that such prohibitions limited the range of information and ideas to which the public is exposed. . . .

There is no doubt that under these principles appellant's newsletter *Progress* receives the full protection of the First Amendment. . . . In appearance no different from a small newspaper, *Progress'* contents range from energy-saving tips to stories about wildlife conservation, and from billing information to recipes. *Progress* thus extends well beyond speech that proposes a business transaction, . . . and includes the kind of discussion of "matters of public concern" that the First Amendment both fully protects and implicitly encourages. . . .

The Commission recognized as much, but concluded that requiring appellant to disseminate TURN's views did not infringe upon First Amendment rights. It reasoned that appellant remains free to mail its own newsletter except for the four months in which TURN is given access. The Commission's conclusion necessarily rests on one of two premises: (i) compelling appellant to grant TURN access to a hitherto private forum does not infringe appellant's right to speak; or (ii) appellant has no property interest in the relevant forum and therefore has no constitutionally protected right in restricting access to it. We now examine those propositions.

III

Compelled access like that ordered in this case both penalizes the expression of particular points of view and forces speakers to alter their speech to conform with an agenda they do not set. These impermissible effects are not remedied by the Commission's definition of the relevant property rights.

A

This Court has previously considered the question whether compelling a private corporation to provide a forum for views other than its own may infringe the corporation's freedom of speech. Miami Herald Publishing Co. v. Tornillo, 418 U.S. 241 (1974) . . . *Tornillo* involved a challenge to Florida's right-of-reply statute. The Florida law provided that, if a newspaper assailed a candidate's character or record, the candidate could demand that the newspaper print a reply of equal prominence and space. . . .

We found that the right-of-reply statute directly interfered with the newspaper's right to speak in two ways. . . . First, the newspaper's expression of a particular viewpoint triggered an obligation to permit other speakers, with whom the newspaper disagreed, to use the newspaper's facilities to spread their own message. The statute purported to advance free discussion, but its effect was to deter newspapers from speaking out in the first instance: by forcing the newspaper to disseminate opponents' views, the statute penalized the newspaper's own expression. . . . [6]

---

[6] This Court has sustained a limited government-enforced right of access to broadcast media. Red Lion Broadcasting Co. v. FCC, 395 U.S. 367 (1969). Cf. Columbia Broadcasting System, Inc. v. Democratic National Committee, 412 U.S. 94 (1973). Appellant's billing envelopes do not, however, present the same constraints that justify the result in *Red Lion:* "[A] broadcaster communicates through use of a scarce, publicly owned resource. No person can broadcast without a license, whereas all persons are free to send

Second, we noted that the newspaper's "treatment of public issues and public officials—whether fair or unfair—constitute[s] the exercise of editorial control and judgment." ... Florida's statute interfered with this "editorial control and judgment" by forcing the newspaper to tailor its speech to an opponent's agenda, and to respond to candidates' arguments where the newspaper might prefer to be silent....

The concerns that caused us to invalidate the compelled access rule in *Tornillo* apply to appellant as well as to the institutional press.... Just as the State is not free to "tell a newspaper in advance what it can print and what it cannot," ... the State is not free either to restrict appellant's speech to certain topics or views or to force appellant to respond to views that others may hold.... Under *Tornillo* a forced access rule that would accomplish these purposes indirectly is similarly forbidden.

The Court's decision in PruneYard Shopping Center v. Robins, [447 U.S. 74 (1980)], is not to the contrary.... Notably absent from *PruneYard* was any concern that access to this area might affect the shopping center owner's exercise of his own right to speak: the owner did not even allege that he objected to the content of the pamphlets; nor was the access right content based. *PruneYard* thus does not undercut the proposition that forced associations that burden protected speech are impermissible.[8]

B

The Commission's order is inconsistent with these principles. The order does not simply award access to the public at large; rather, it discriminates on the basis of the viewpoints of the selected speakers. ...Access is limited to persons or groups—such as TURN—who disagree with appellant's views as expressed in *Progress* and who oppose appellant in Commission proceedings.

Such one-sidedness impermissibly burdens appellant's own expression. *Tornillo* illustrates the point. Access to the newspaper in that case was content-based in two senses: (I) it was triggered by a particular category of newspaper speech, and (ii) it was awarded only to those who disagreed with the newspaper's views. The Commission's order is not, in *Tornillo* 's words, a "content-based penalty" in the first sense, because TURN's access to appellant's envelopes is not conditioned on any particular expression by appellant.... But because access is awarded only to those who disagree with appellant's views and who are hostile to appellant's interests, appellant must contend with the fact that whenever it speaks out on a given issue, it may be forced—at TURN's discretion—to help disseminate hostile views....

Appellant does not, of course, have the right to be free from vigorous debate. But it *does* have the right to be free from government restrictions that abridge its own rights in order to "enhance the relative voice" of its opponents.... The Commission's order requires *appellant* to assist in disseminating *TURN* 's views; it does not equally constrain both sides of the debate about utility regulation.[10] ...

correspondence to private homes through the mails." Consolidated Edison Co. v. Public Service Comm'n of N.Y., 447 U.S. 530, 543 (1980).

[8] In addition, the relevant forum in *PruneYard* was the open area of the shopping center into which the general public was invited. This area was, almost by definition, peculiarly public in nature.... There is no correspondingly public aspect to appellant's billing envelopes.

[10] Justice Stevens analogizes this aspect of the Commission's order to Securities and Exchange Commission regulations that require management to transmit proposals of minority shareholders in shareholder mailings. The analogy is inappropriate. The regulations Justice Stevens cites differ from the

The Commission's access order also impermissibly requires appellant to associate with speech with which appellant may disagree. The order on its face leaves TURN free to use the billing envelopes to discuss any issues it chooses. Should TURN choose, for example, to urge appellant's customers to vote for a particular slate of legislative candidates, or to argue in favor of legislation that could seriously affect the utility business, appellant may be forced either to appear to agree with TURN's views or to respond....[12] ...

. . .

C

The Commission has emphasized that appellant's customers own the "extra space" in the billing envelopes. According to appellees, it follows that appellant cannot have a constitutionally protected interest in restricting access to the envelopes. This argument misperceives both the relevant property rights and the nature of the State's First Amendment violation.

The Commission expressly declined to hold that under California law appellant's customers own the entire billing envelopes and everything contained therein. It decided only that the ratepayers own the "extra space" in the envelope, defined as that space left over after including the bill and required notices, up to a weight of one ounce. The envelopes themselves, the bills, and *Progress* all remain appellant's property. The Commission's access order thus clearly requires appellant to use its property as a vehicle for spreading a message with which it disagrees. In Wooley v. Maynard, we held that New Hampshire could not require two citizens to display a slogan on their license plates and thereby "use their private property as a 'mobile billboard' for the State's ideological message." 430 U.S., at 715. The "private property" that was used to spread the unwelcome message was the automobile, not the license plates. Similarly, the Commission's order requires appellant to use its property—the billing envelopes—to distribute the message of another. This is so whoever is deemed to own the "extra space."

A different conclusion would necessarily imply that our decision in *Tornillo* rested on the Miami Herald's ownership of the space that would have been used to print candidate replies. Nothing in *Tornillo* suggests that the result would have been different had the Florida Supreme Court decided that the newspaper space needed to print candidates' replies was the property of the newspaper's readers, or had the court ordered the Miami Herald to distribute inserts owned and prepared by the candidates together with its newspapers. The constitutional difficulty with the right-of-reply statute was that it required the newspaper to disseminate a message with which the newspaper disagreed.

Commission's order in two important ways. First, they allocate shareholder property between management and certain groups of shareholders. Management has no interest in corporate property except such interest as derives from the shareholders; therefore, regulations that limit management's ability to exclude some shareholders' views from corporate communications do not infringe corporate First Amendment rights. Second, the regulations govern speech by a corporation *to itself*. *Bellotti* and *Consolidated Edison* establish that the Constitution protects corporations' right to speak to the public based on the informational value of corporate speech. Rules that define how corporations govern themselves do not limit the range of information that the corporation may contribute to the public debate. The Commission's order, by contrast, burdens appellant's right freely to speak to the public at large.

[12] The Commission's order is thus readily distinguishable from orders requiring appellant to carry various legal notices, such as notices of upcoming Commission proceedings or of changes in the way rates are calculated. The State, of course, has substantial leeway in determining appropriate information disclosure requirements for business corporations....

This difficulty did not depend on whether the particular paper on which the replies were printed belonged to the newspaper or to the candidate.

Appellees' argument suffers from the same constitutional defect. The Commission's order forces appellant to disseminate TURN's speech in envelopes that appellant owns and that bear appellant's return address. Such forced association with potentially hostile views burdens the expression of views different from TURN's and risks forcing appellant to speak where it would prefer to remain silent. Those effects do not depend on who "owns" the "extra space."

IV

Notwithstanding that it burdens protected speech, the Commission's order could be valid if it were a narrowly tailored means of serving a compelling state interest....

A

Appellees identify two assertedly compelling state interests that the access order is said to advance. First, appellees argue that the order furthers the State's interest in effective ratemaking proceedings. TURN has been a regular participant in those proceedings, and the Commission found that TURN has aided the Commission in performing its regulatory task. Appellees argue that the access order permits TURN to continue to help the Commission by assisting TURN in raising funds from the ratepayers whose interest TURN seeks to serve.

The State's interest in fair and effective utility regulation may be compelling. The difficulty with appellees' argument is that the State can serve that interest through means that would not violate appellant's First Amendment rights, such as awarding costs and fees....

Second, appellees argue that the order furthers the State's interest in promoting speech by making a variety of views available to appellant's customers.... We have noted above that this interest is not furthered by an order that is not content neutral. Moreover, the means chosen to advance variety tend to inhibit expression of appellant's views in order to promote TURN's. ...It follows that the Commission's order is not a narrowly tailored means of furthering this interest.

. . .

V

We conclude that the Commission's order impermissibly burdens appellant's First Amendment rights because it forces appellant to associate with the views of other speakers, and because it selects the other speakers on the basis of their viewpoints. The order is not a narrowly tailored means of furthering a compelling state interest,....

For these reasons, the decision of the California Public Utilities Commission must be vacated. The case is remanded to the California Supreme Court for further proceedings not inconsistent with this opinion.

It is so ordered.

Justice Blackmun took no part in the consideration or decision of this case.

Chief Justice Burger, concurring.

I join Justice Powell's opinion, but think we need not go beyond the authority of Wooley v. Maynard, 430 U.S. 705 (1977) to decide this case. I would not go beyond the central question presented by this case, which is the infringement of Pacific's right to be free from forced association with views with which it disagrees. I would also rely on that part of Miami Herald Publishing Co. v. Tornillo, 418 U.S. 241 (1974), holding that a forced right of reply violates a newspaper's right to be free from forced dissemination of views it would not voluntarily disseminate, just as we held that Maynard must be free from being forced by the State to disseminate views with which he disagreed. . . .

Justice Marshall, concurring in the judgment.

. . . Two significant differences between the State's grant of access in this case and the grant of access in *PruneYard* lead me to find a constitutional barrier here that I did not find in the earlier case.

The first difference is the degree of intrusiveness of the permitted access. . . .

In the present case . . . appellant has never opened up its billing envelope to the use of the public. Appellant has not abandoned its right to exclude others from its property to the degree that the shopping center owner had done in *PruneYard*. Were appellant to use its billing envelope as a sort of community billboard, regularly carrying the messages of third parties, its desire to exclude a particular speaker would be deserving of lesser solicitude . . .

The second difference between this case and *PruneYard* is that the State has chosen to give TURN a right to speak at the expense of appellant's ability to use the property in question as a forum for the exercise of its own First Amendment rights. While the shopping center owner in *PruneYard* wished to be free of unwanted expression, he nowhere alleged that his own expression was hindered in the slightest. In contrast, the present case involves a forum of inherently limited scope. . . .

. . .

Justice Rehnquist, with whom Justice White and Justice Stevens join as to Part I, dissenting.

. . . I do not believe that the right of access here will have any noticeable deterrent effect. Nor do I believe that negative free speech rights, applicable to individuals and perhaps the print media, should be extended to corporations generally. I believe that the right of access here is constitutionally indistinguishable from the right of access approved in PruneYard Shopping Center v. Robins, 447 U.S. 74 (1980), and therefore I dissent.

I

. . . Our cases cannot be squared . . . with the view that the First Amendment prohibits governmental action that only *indirectly* and *remotely* affects a speaker's contribution to the overall mix of information available to society.

. . .

. . . [T]he plurality stretches *Tornillo* to stand for the general proposition that the First Amendment prohibits any regulation that deters a corporation from engaging in some expressive behavior. But the deterrent effect of any statute is an empirical question of degree. When the potential deterrent effect of a particular state law is remote and speculative, the law simply is not subject to heightened First Amendment scrutiny. . . .

... The order does not prevent PG & E from using the billing envelopes in the future to distribute inserts whenever it wishes. Nor does its vitality depend on whether PG & E includes inserts in any future billing envelopes. Moreover, the central reason for the access order—to provide for an effective ratepayer voice—would not vary in importance if PG & E had never distributed the inserts or ceased distributing them tomorrow. The most that can be said about the connection between the inserts and the order is that the existence of the inserts quite probably brought to TURN's attention the possibility of requesting access.

Nor does the access order create any cognizable risk of deterring PG & E from expressing its views in the most candid fashion. Unlike the reply statute in *Tornillo,* which conditioned access upon discrete instances of certain expression, the right of access here bears no relationship to PG & E's future conduct. PG & E cannot prevent the access by remaining silent or avoiding discussion of controversial subjects....

II

The plurality argues, however, that the right of access also implicates PG & E's right not to speak or to associate with the speech of others, thereby triggering heightened scrutiny....

There is, however, a ... fundamental flaw in the plurality's analysis. This Court has recognized that natural persons enjoy negative free speech rights because of their interest in self-expression; an individual's right not to speak or to associate with the speech of others is a component of the broader constitutional interest of natural persons in freedom of conscience....

. . .

Extension of the individual freedom of conscience decisions to business corporations strains the rationale of those cases beyond the breaking point. To ascribe to such artificial entities an "intellect" or "mind" for freedom of conscience purposes is to confuse metaphor with reality. Corporations generally have not played the historic role of newspapers as conveyers of individual ideas and opinion....

. . .

III

PG & E is not an individual or a newspaper publisher; it is a regulated utility. The insistence on treating identically for constitutional purposes entities that are demonstrably different is as great a jurisprudential sin as treating differently those entities which are the same. Because I think this case is governed by *PruneYard,* and not by *Tornillo,* or *Wooley,* I would affirm the judgment of the Supreme Court of California.

Justice Stevens, dissenting.

... In my view, this requirement differs little from regulations applied daily to a variety of commercial communications that have rarely been challenged—and to my knowledge never invalidated—on First Amendment grounds.

. . .

I assume that the plurality would not object to a utility commission rule dictating the format of the bill, even as to required warnings and the type size of various provisos and disclaimers. Such regulation is not too different from that applicable to credit card bills, loan forms, and media advertising.... I assume also the plurality would permit the Commission to require the utility to disseminate legal notices of public hearings and ratemaking proceedings written by it. These compelled statements differ little from mandating disclosure of information in the bill itself, as the plurality recognizes.

Given that the Commission can require the utility to make certain statements and to carry the Commission's own messages to its customers, it seems but a small step to acknowledge that the Commission can also require the utility to act as the conduit for a public interest group's message that bears a close relationship to the purpose of the billing envelope. An analog to this requirement appears in securities law: the Securities and Exchange Commission requires the incumbent board of directors to transmit proposals of dissident shareholders which it opposes. Presumably the plurality does not doubt the constitutionality of the SEC's requirement under the First Amendment, and yet—although the analogy is far from perfect—it performs the same function as the Commission's rule by making accessible the relevant audience, whether it be shareholders investing in the corporation or consumers served by the utility, to individuals or groups with demonstrable interests in reaching that audience for certain limited and approved purposes.

If the California Public Utilities Commission had taken over company buildings and vehicles for propaganda purposes, or even engaged in viewpoint discrimination among speakers desirous of sending messages via the billing envelope, I would be concerned. But nothing in this case presents problems even remotely resembling or portending the ones just mentioned....

HURLEY v. IRISH–AMERICAN GAY, LESBIAN AND BISEXUAL GROUP OF BOSTON, ___ U.S. ___, 115 S.Ct. 2338 (1995). Since 1947, the South Boston Allied War Veterans Council has received a permit to conduct Boston's St. Patrick's Day parade. The parade has included as many as 20,000 marchers and drawn up to 1 million watchers. In 1993, gay, lesbian and bisexual descendants of Irish immigrants were denied permission to participate in the march by the Veterans Council. The Court reversed state court decisions holding that, under the state public accommodations law, the Gay, Lesbian and Bisexual Group was entitled to participate in the parade. Justice Souter's opinion for the Court said, in part:

"... the object of the [public accommodations] law is to ensure by statute for gays and lesbians desiring to make use of public accommodations what the old common law promised to any member of the public wanting a meal at the inn, that accepting the usual terms of service, they will not be turned away merely on the proprietor's exercise of personal preference. When the law is applied to expressive activity in the way it was done here, its apparent object is simply to require speakers to modify the content of their expression to whatever extent beneficiaries of the law choose to alter it with messages of their own. But in the absence of some further, legitimate end, this object is merely to allow exactly what the general rule of speaker's autonomy forbids."

SECTION 4.   APPLICATION OF THE FIRST AMENDMENT TO GOVERNMENT REGULATION OF ELECTIONS

A.   CHOOSING AND ELECTING CANDIDATES FOR PUBLIC OFFICE

POLITICAL ASSOCIATION AND SELECTION OF DELEGATES TO MAJOR NATIONAL PARTY CONVENTIONS

At one extreme, the activities of major political parties in candidate selection may be so influential in the election process that the activity will not be viewed as "private" political association at all. As the White Primary Cases demonstrate, a formally private political group that uniformly dictates the choice of the winning candidate performs a public function, and its freedom to bar participation in its election processes is limited by the fourteenth and fifteenth amendments. (See supra, pp. 1108–1109.) Even where political parties' candidate selection processes are not themselves "state action" for constitutional purposes, it is clear that a wide variety of state regulation of parties' delegate and candidate selection processes is justified as an indispensable part of regulation of elections.

Two cases raise the question whether there is a point where state legislation controlling the organization, delegate selection processes, and candidate selection processes, of political parties violates the rights of the party and its members to free political association. Both cases involved rules of the Democratic National Party concerning delegate selection for the Party's national convention. The Party's newly enacted rules, in both cases, conflicted with state law.

In Cousins v. Wigoda, 419 U.S. 477 (1975) the Court reviewed the decision of a state court that Illinois law governed seating of a state delegation at the 1972 Democratic National Convention. Illinois law was in conflict with party rules regarding, inter alia, inclusion of minorities, women, and young people, in the delegation. The Court decided that the Illinois law was unconstitutional. The Party's associational rights included the right to identify the people who comprised the Party and, subsidiary to that, the right to determine seating at the Convention. Illinois' interest in controlling electoral processes did not justify its insistence that the Convention seat the delegation chosen according to state law.

Primary elections, however, play an increasing role in the delegate selection process for major national party conventions. Democratic Party of United States v. Wisconsin ex rel. LaFollette, 450 U.S. 107 (1981), demonstrates that it is not easy to distinguish state interests in regulating primary elections and party interests in controlling delegate selection. Wisconsin's "open primary" law, enacted in 1903 and first applied to presidential primaries in 1906, allows voters to participate in any party's primary without regard to party affiliation and without public declaration of party preference. Delegates to party conventions are not chosen by the primary vote, but are bound to vote at national conventions in accord with the election results. In an action that was aimed at minimizing the cross-over voting in Wisconsin primaries, the National Democratic Party enacted a rule that participation in the delegate selection process for the 1980 Convention would be restricted to voters "who publicly declare their party preference." The Court held, 6–3, that Wisconsin could not compel the National Party to seat a delegation bound, under state law, to vote for candidates according to the results of the open primary.

Justice Stewart's opinion for the Court conceded that Wisconsin could conduct an open primary. He said:

> "The State has a substantial interest in the manner in which its elections are conducted, and the National Party has a substantial interest in the manner in which the delegates to its National Convention are selected. But these interests are not incompatible, and to the limited extent they clash in this case, both interests can be preserved. The National Party rules do not forbid Wisconsin to conduct an open primary. But if Wisconsin does open its primary, it cannot require that Wisconsin delegates to the National Party Convention vote there in accordance with the primary results, if to do so would violate Party rules. Since the Wisconsin Supreme

Court has declared that the National Party cannot disqualify delegates who are bound to vote in accordance with the results of the Wisconsin open primary, its judgment is reversed."

Justice Powell's dissent (joined by Justices Blackmun and Rehnquist) characterized Wisconsin's law as directed to the conduct of the presidential preference primary, and only "indirectly" to the selection of delegates. Wisconsin's interest in open participation in primary elections, compared to the Party's minimal interest in requiring voters to formally identify with the Party before voting, justified that "indirect" infringement in requiring delegates to vote according to the primary results. Because national parties are not organized around the achievement of defined ideological goals, he noted that neither major party had ever sought to exclude participation by those with differing views. Justice Powell concluded:

> "The history of state regulation of the major political parties suggests a continuing accommodation of the interests of the parties with those of the States and their citizens. In the process, 'the States have evolved comprehensive, and in many respects complex, election codes regulating in most substantial ways, with respect to both federal and state elections, the time, place, and manner of holding primary and general elections, the registration and qualifications of voters, and the selection and qualification of candidates.' Storer v. Brown, 415 U.S. 724, 730 (1974). Today, the Court departs from this process of accommodation. It does so, it seems to me, by upholding a First Amendment claim by one of the two major parties without any serious inquiry into the extent of the burden on associational freedoms and without due consideration of the countervailing state interests."

ANDERSON v. CELEBREZZE, 460 U.S. 780 (1983). The Court held that an Ohio statute—requiring independent candidates for President to file statements of candidacy and nominating petitions in March in order to appear on the general election ballot in November—violated the first amendment. An early filing date burdens independent voters and candidates, because it excludes independent candidates who appeal to voters dissatisfied with the choices within the two major parties. Moreover, State restrictions on Presidential election processes, as contrasted to elections for statewide offices, have an impact beyond State borders implicating a "uniquely important national interest." Given modern communications, the early filing deadline did not substantially serve a goal of educating voters concerning candidate qualifications. The early filing requirement did not serve the goal of treating independent candidates equally with party primary candidates, who must declare their candidacy on the same date; the names of the eventual nominees of the major parties will appear on the Ohio general election ballot in November, even if the nominees had not qualified for the Ohio primary. The requirement was not justified, finally, by an interest in political stability; even if the State had an interest in preventing factionalism in the major parties, a political party cannot invoke State powers "to assure monolithic control over its own members and supporters." Justice Rehnquist, joined by Justices White, Powell, and O'Connor, dissented. The State's interest in the stability of the political system should allow denial of ballot access to unsuccessful party candidates who seek to refight party battles by forming an independent candidacy.

Tashjian v. Republican Party of Connecticut
479 U.S. 208, 107 S.Ct. 544, 93 L.Ed.2d 514 (1986).

Justice Marshall delivered the opinion of the Court.

Appellee Republican Party of the State of Connecticut (the Party) in 1984 adopted a Party rule which permits independent voters—registered voters not affiliated with any political party—to vote in Republican primaries for federal and statewide offices.... [T]he State's election statutes ... [require] voters in any party primary to be registered members of that party. Conn.Gen.Stat. § 9–431 (1985). Appellees ... challenged this eligibility provision on the ground that it deprives the Party of its First Amendment right to enter into political association with individuals of its own choosing. The District Court granted summary judgment in favor of appellees. The Court of Appeals affirmed. We ... affirm.

I

In 1955, Connecticut adopted its present primary election system. For major parties, the process of candidate selection for federal and statewide offices requires a statewide convention of party delegates; district conventions are held to select candidates for seats in the state legislature. The party convention may certify as the party-endorsed candidate any person receiving more than 20% of the votes cast in a roll-call vote at the convention. Any candidate not endorsed by the party who received 20% of the vote may challenge the party-endorsed candidate in a primary election, in which the candidate receiving the plurality of votes becomes the party's nominee. ...Candidates selected by the major parties, whether through convention or primary, are automatically accorded a place on the ballot at the general election. ...The costs of primary elections are paid out of public funds. ...

The statute challenged in these proceedings ... has remained substantially unchanged since the adoption of the State's primary system. In 1976, the statute's constitutionality was upheld by a three-judge District Court against a challenge by an independent voter who sought a declaration of his right to vote in the Republican primary. Nader v. Schaffer, 417 F.Supp. 837 (Conn.), summarily aff'd, 429 U.S. 989 (1976). In that action, the Party opposed the plaintiff's efforts to participate in the Party primary.

Subsequent to the decision in *Nader,* however, the Party changed its views with respect to participation by independent voters in Party primaries. ...In January 1984 the state convention adopted the Party rule now at issue, which provides:

> "Any elector enrolled as a member of the Republican Party and any elector not enrolled as a member of a party shall be eligible to vote in primaries for nomination of candidates for the offices of United States Senator, United States Representative, Governor, Lieutenant Governor, Secretary of the State, Attorney General, Comptroller and Treasurer."

During the 1984 session, the Republican leadership in the state legislature ... proposed to amend the statute to allow independents to vote in primaries when permitted by Party rules. The proposed legislation was defeated, substantially along party lines, in both houses of the legislature, which at that time were controlled by the Democratic Party.

. . .

II

We begin from the recognition that "[c]onstitutional challenges to specific provisions of a State's election laws ... cannot be resolved by any 'litmus-paper test' that will separate valid from invalid restrictions." Anderson v. Celebrezze, 460 U.S. 780, 789 (1983) (quoting Storer v. Brown, 415 U.S. 724, 730 (1974)).

"Instead, a court … must first consider the character and magnitude of the asserted injury to the rights protected by the First and Fourteenth Amendments that the plaintiff seeks to vindicate. It then must identify and evaluate the precise interests put forward by the State as justifications for the burden imposed by its rule. In passing judgment, the Court must not only determine the legitimacy and strength of each of those interests, it also must consider the extent to which those interests make it necessary to burden the plaintiff's rights." 460 U.S., at 789.

The nature of appellees' First Amendment interest is evident…. "The right to associate with the political party of one's choice is an integral part of this basic constitutional freedom." Kusper v. Pontikes, 414 U.S. 51, 57 (1973).

The Party here contends that § 9–431 impermissibly burdens the right of its members to determine for themselves with whom they will associate, and whose support they will seek, in their quest for political success. The Party's attempt to broaden the base of public participation in and support for its activities is conduct undeniably central to the exercise of the right of association. As we have said, the freedom to join together in furtherance of common political beliefs "necessarily presupposes the freedom to identify the people who constitute the association." Democratic Party of United States v. Wisconsin ex rel. LaFollette, 450 U.S. 107, 122 (1981).

. . .

Were the State to restrict by statute financial support of the Party's candidates to Party members, or to provide that only Party members might be selected as the Party's chosen nominees for public office, such a prohibition of potential association with nonmembers would clearly infringe upon the rights of the Party's members under the First Amendment to organize with like-minded citizens in support of common political goals…. [6] The statute here places limits upon the group of registered voters whom the Party may invite to participate in the "basic function" of selecting the Party's candidates…. The State thus limits the Party's associational opportunities at the crucial juncture at which the appeal to common principles may be translated into concerted action, and hence to political power in the community.

It is, of course, fundamental to appellant's defense of the State's statute that this impingement upon the associational rights of the Party and its members occurs at the ballot box, for the Constitution grants to the States a broad power to prescribe the "Times, Places and Manner of holding Elections for Senators and Representatives," Art. I, § 4, cl. 1, which power is matched by state control over the election process for state offices. But this authority does not extinguish the State's responsibility to observe the limits established by the

---

[6] It is this element of potential interference with the rights of the Party's members which distinguishes the present case from others in which we have considered claims by nonmembers of a party seeking to vote in that party's primary despite the party's opposition. In this latter class of cases, the nonmember's desire to participate in the party's affairs is overborne by the countervailing and legitimate right of the party to determine its own membership qualifications. See Rosario v. Rockefeller, 410 U.S. 752 (1973); Nader v. Schaffer, 417 F.Supp. 837 (D.Conn.), summarily affd, 429 U.S. 989 (1976). Similarly, the Court has upheld the right of national political parties to refuse to seat at their conventions delegates chosen in state selection processes which did not conform to party rules. See Democratic Party of United States v. Wisconsin ex rel. LaFollette, 450 U.S. 107 (1981); Cousins v. Wigoda, 419 U.S. 477 (1975). These situations are analytically distinct from the present case, in which the Party and its members seek to provide enhanced opportunities for participation by willing nonmembers. Under these circumstances, there is no conflict between the associational interests of members and nonmembers. . . .

First Amendment rights of the State's citizens. . . . We turn then to an examination of the interests which appellant asserts to justify the burden cast by the statute upon the associational rights of the Party and its members.

III

Appellant contends that § 9–431 is a narrowly tailored regulation which advances the State's compelling interests by ensuring the administrability of the primary system, preventing raiding, avoiding voter confusion, and protecting the responsibility of party government.

A

Although it was not presented to the Court of Appeals as a basis for the defense of the statute, appellant argues here that the administrative burden imposed by the Party rule is a sufficient ground on which to uphold the constitutionality of § 9–431. Appellant contends that the Party's rule would require the purchase of additional voting machines, the training of additional poll workers, and potentially the printing of additional ballot materials specifically intended for independents voting in the Republican primary. . . .

. . . [T]he possibility of future increases in the cost of administering the election system is not a sufficient basis here for infringing appellees' First Amendment rights. . . . While the State is of course entitled to take administrative and financial considerations into account in choosing whether or not to have a primary system at all, it can no more restrain the Republican Party's freedom of association for reasons of its own administrative convenience than it could on the same ground limit the ballot access of a new major party.

B

Appellant argues that § 9–431 is justified as a measure to prevent raiding, a practice "whereby voters in sympathy with one party designate themselves as voters of another party so as to influence or determine the results of the other party's primary." Rosario v. Rockefeller, 410 U.S. 752, 760 (1973). While we have recognized that "a State may have a legitimate interest in seeking to curtail 'raiding,' since that practice may affect the integrity of the electoral process," Kusper v. Pontikes, 414 U.S., at 59–60; Rosario v. Rockefeller, supra, at 761, that interest is not implicated here. . . . [A] raid on the Republican Party primary by independent voters, a curious concept only distantly related to the type of raiding discussed in *Kusper* and *Rosario*, is not impeded by § 9–431. . . . Indeed, under Conn.Gen.Stat. § 9–56 (1985), which permits an independent to affiliate with the Party as late as noon on the business day preceding the primary, the State's election statutes actually *assist* a "raid" by independents, which could be organized and implemented at the 11th hour. The State's asserted interest in the prevention of raiding provides no justification for the statute challenged here.

C

Appellant's next argument in support of § 9–431 is that the closed primary system avoids voter confusion. Appellant contends that "[t]he legislature could properly find that it would be difficult for the general public to understand what a candidate stood for who was nominated in part by an unknown amorphous body outside the party, while nevertheless using the party name."
. . .

. . . [A]ppellant's concern that candidates selected under the Party rule will be the nominees of an "amorphous" group using the Party's name is inconsistent with the facts. The Party is not proposing that independents be allowed to choose the Party's nominee without Party participation; on the contrary, to be listed on the Party's primary ballot continues to require, under a statute not challenged here, that the primary candidate have obtained at least 20% of the vote at a Party convention, which only Party members may attend. . . .

. . . [A]ppellant also disregards the substantial benefit which the Party rule provides to the Party and its members in seeking to choose successful candidates. Given the numerical strength of independent voters in the State, one of the questions most likely to occur to Connecticut Republicans in selecting candidates for public office is, how can the Party most effectively appeal to the independent voter? By inviting independents to assist in the choice at the polls between primary candidates selected at the Party convention, the Party rule is intended to produce the candidate and platform most likely to achieve that goal. . . .

D

Finally, appellant contends that § 9–431 furthers the State's compelling interest in protecting the integrity of the two-party system and the responsibility of party government. . . .

The relative merits of closed and open primaries have been the subject of substantial debate since the beginning of this century, and no consensus has as yet emerged.[11] Appellant invokes a long and distinguished line of political scientists and public officials who have been supporters of the closed primary. But our role is not to decide whether the state legislature was acting wisely in enacting the closed primary system in 1955, or whether the Republican Party makes a mistake in seeking to depart from the practice of the past 30 years.

We have previously recognized the danger that "splintered parties and unrestrained factionalism may do significant damage to the fabric of government." Storer v. Brown, 415 U.S., at 736. We upheld a California statute which denied access to the ballot to any independent candidate who had voted in a party primary or been registered as a member of a political party within one year prior to the immediately preceding primary election. . . .

The statute in *Storer* was designed to protect the parties and the party system against the disorganizing effect of independent candidacies launched by unsuccessful putative party nominees. This protection, like that accorded to parties threatened by raiding in Rosario v. Rockefeller, 410 U.S. 752 (1973), is undertaken to prevent the disruption of the political parties from without, and not, as in this case, to prevent the parties from taking internal steps affecting their own process for the selection of candidates. The forms of regulation upheld in *Storer* and *Rosario* imposed certain burdens upon the protected First and Fourteenth Amendment interests of some individuals, both voters and potential candidates, in order to protect the interests of others. In the present case, the state statute is defended on the ground that it protects the integrity of the Party against the Party itself.

---

[11] At the present time, 21 States provide for "closed" primaries of the classic sort, in which the primary voter must be registered as a member of the party for some period of time prior to the holding of the primary election. . . . Sixteen States allow a voter previously unaffiliated with any party to vote in a party primary if he affiliates with the party at the time of, or for the purpose of, voting in the primary. . . . Four States provide for nonpartisan primaries in which all registered voters may participate, . . . while nine States have adopted classical "open" primaries, in which all registered voters may choose in which party primary to vote. . . .

Under these circumstances, the views of the State, which to some extent represent the views of the one political party transiently enjoying majority power, as to the optimum methods for preserving party integrity lose much of their force.... [13]

We conclude that the State's enforcement, under these circumstances, of its closed primary system burdens the First Amendment rights of the Party. The interests which the appellant adduces in support of the statute are insubstantial, and accordingly the statute, as applied to the Party in this case, is unconstitutional.

IV

Appellant argues here, as in the courts below, that implementation of the Party rule would violate the Qualifications Clause of the Constitution, Art. I, § 2, cl. 1, and the Seventeenth Amendment because it would establish qualifications for voting in congressional elections which differ from the voting qualifications in elections for the more numerous house of the state legislature. The Party rule as adopted permits independent voters to vote in Party primaries for the offices of United States Senator and Member of the House of Representatives, and for statewide offices, but is silent as regards primaries held to contest nominations for seats in the state legislature. Appellant contends that the Qualifications Clause and the Seventeenth Amendment require an absolute symmetry of qualifications to vote in elections for Congress and the lower house of the state legislature, and that the Party rule, if implemented according to its terms, would require lesser qualifications for voting in Party primaries for federal office than for state legislative office.

. . .

We recognize that the Federal Convention, in adopting the Qualifications Clause of Article I, § 2, was not contemplating the effects of that provision upon the modern system of party primaries.... The fundamental purpose underlying Article I, § 2, that "[t]he House of Representatives shall be composed of Members chosen ... by the People of the several States," like the parallel provision of the Seventeenth Amendment, applies to the entire process by which federal legislators are chosen. ...

Accordingly, we hold that the Qualifications Clauses of Article I, § 2, and the Seventeenth Amendment are applicable to primary elections in precisely the same fashion that they apply to general congressional elections. Our task is then to discover whether, as appellant contends, those provisions require that voter qualifications, such as party membership, in primaries for federal office must be absolutely symmetrical with those pertaining to primaries for state legislative office.

Our inquiry begins with an examination of the Framers' purpose in enacting the first Qualifications Clause. ...

... Far from being a device to limit the federal suffrage, the Qualifications Clause was intended by the Framers to prevent the mischief which would arise

---

[13] Our holding today does not establish that state regulation of primary voting qualifications may never withstand challenge by a political party or its membership. A party seeking, for example, to open its primary to all voters, including members of other parties, would raise a different combination of considerations. Under such circumstances, the effect of one party's broadening of participation would threaten other parties with the disorganization effects which the statutes in Storer v. Brown, 415 U.S. 724 (1974), and Rosario v. Rockefeller, 410 U.S. 752 (1973), were designed to prevent. We have observed on several occasions that a State may adopt a "policy of confining each voter to a single nominating act," a policy decision which is not involved in the present case....

if state voters found themselves disqualified from participation in federal elections. The achievement of this goal does not require that qualifications for exercise of the federal franchise be at all times precisely equivalent to the prevailing qualifications for the exercise of the franchise in a given State. The fundamental purpose of the Qualifications Clauses contained in Article I, § 2, and the Seventeenth Amendment is satisfied if all those qualified to participate in the selection of members of the more numerous branch of the state legislature are also qualified to participate in the election of Senators and Members of the House of Representatives.

. . .

V

We conclude that § 9–431 impermissibly burdens the rights of the Party and its members protected by the First and Fourteenth Amendments. The interests asserted by appellant in defense of the statute are insubstantial. The judgment of the Court of Appeals is

Affirmed.

Justice Stevens, with whom Justice Scalia joins, dissenting.

The threshold issue presented by this case is whether, consistently with the Constitution, a State may permit a voter to participate in elections to the Congress while preventing that same person from voting for candidates to the most numerous branch of the state legislature. If we respect the plain language of Article I, § 2, cl. 1 of the Constitution and the Seventeenth Amendment, [and] the intent of the Framers, ... we must answer that question in the negative.

. . .

Justice Scalia, with whom The Chief Justice and Justice O'Connor join, dissenting.

. . .

In my view, the Court's opinion exaggerates the importance of the associational interest at issue, if indeed it does not see one where none exists. There is no question here of restricting the Republican Party's ability to recruit and enroll Party members by offering them the ability to select Party candidates; Conn.Gen.Stat. § 9–56 (1985) permits an independent voter to join the Party as late as the day before the primary. ...Nor is there any question of restricting the ability of the Party's members to select whatever candidate they desire. Appellees' only complaint is that the Party cannot leave the selection of its candidate to persons who are *not* members of the Party, and are unwilling to become members. It seems to me fanciful to refer to this as an interest in freedom of association between the members of the Republican Party and the putative independent voters. The Connecticut voter who, while steadfastly refusing to register as a Republican, casts a vote in the Republican primary, forms no more meaningful an "association" with the Party than does the independent or the registered Democrat who responds to questions by a Republican Party pollster. If the concept of freedom of association is extended to such casual contacts, it ceases to be of any analytic use....

The ability of the members of the Republican Party to select their own candidate, on the other hand, unquestionably implicates an associational freedom—but it can hardly be thought that that freedom is unconstitutionally impaired here. The Party is entirely free to put forward, if it wishes, that candidate who has the highest degree of support among Party members and independents combined. The State is under no obligation, however, to let its party primary be used, instead of a party-funded opinion poll, as the means by which the party identifies the relative popularity of its potential candidates among independents. Nor is there any reason apparent to me why the State cannot insist that this decision to support what might be called the independents' choice be taken *by the party membership in a democratic fashion,* rather than through a process that permits the members' votes to be diluted—and perhaps even absolutely outnumbered—by the votes of outsiders.

. . .

B. POLITICAL FUNDRAISING AND EXPENDITURES

Buckley v. Valeo

424 U.S. 1, 96 S.Ct. 612, 46 L.Ed.2d 659 (1976).

Per Curiam.

These appeals present constitutional challenges to the key provisions of the Federal Election Campaign Act of 1971, . . . as amended in 1974.

. . .

[A suit was brought in the district court in the District of Columbia pursuant to a special statutory review procedure. The plaintiffs included political candidates, contributors to candidates, party organizations, and other organizations; defendants were the relevant federal officials. A declaration of unconstitutionality and an injunction against enforcement were sought.]

I. Contribution and Expenditure Limitations

The intricate statutory scheme adopted by Congress to regulate federal election campaigns includes restrictions on political contributions and expenditures that apply broadly to all phases of and all participants in the election process. The major contribution and expenditure limitations in the Act prohibit individuals from contributing more than $25,000 in a single year or more than $1,000 to any single candidate for an election campaign and from spending more than $1,000 a year "relative to a clearly identified candidate." Other provisions restrict a candidate's use of personal and family resources in his campaign and limit the overall amount that can be spent by a candidate in campaigning for federal office.

. . .

A. General Principles

The Act's contribution and expenditure limitations operate in an area of the most fundamental First Amendment activities. Discussion of public issues and debate on the qualifications of candidates are integral to the operation of the system of government established by our Constitution. . . .

The First Amendment protects political association as well as political expression. . . .

It is with these principles in mind that we consider the primary contentions of the parties with respect to the Act's limitations upon the giving and spending of money in political campaigns. Those conflicting contentions could not more sharply define the basic issues before us. Appellees contend that what the Act regulates is conduct, and that its effect on speech and association is incidental at most. Appellants respond that contributions and expenditures are at the very core of political speech, and that the Act's limitations thus constitute restraints on First Amendment liberty that are both gross and direct.

. . .

We cannot share the view that the present Act's contribution and expenditure limitations are comparable to the restrictions on conduct upheld in *O'Brien*. The expenditure of money simply cannot be equated with such conduct as destruction of a draft card. Some forms of communication made possible by the giving and spending of money involve speech alone, some involve conduct primarily, and some involve a combination of the two. Yet this Court has never suggested that the dependence of a communication on the expenditure of money operates itself to introduce a nonspeech element or to reduce the exacting scrutiny required by the First Amendment. . . .

Nor can the Act's contribution and expenditure limitations be sustained, as some of the parties suggest, by reference to the constitutional principles reflected in such decisions as Cox v. Louisiana, supra, Adderley v. Florida, 385 U.S. 39 (1966), and Kovacs v. Cooper, 336 U.S. 77 (1949). . . . The critical difference between this case and those time, place and manner cases is that the present Act's contribution and expenditure limitations impose direct quantity restrictions on political communication and association by persons, groups, candidates and political parties in addition to any reasonable time, place, and manner regulations otherwise imposed.

A restriction on the amount of money a person or group can spend on political communication during a campaign necessarily reduces the quantity of expression by restricting the number of issues discussed, the depth of their exploration, and the size of the audience reached. This is because virtually every means of communicating ideas in today's mass society requires the expenditure of money. . . .

The expenditure limitations contained in the Act represent substantial rather than merely theoretical restraints on the quantity and diversity of political speech. The $1,000 ceiling on spending "relative to a clearly identified candidate," 18 U.S.C. § 608(e)(1) . . . would appear to exclude all citizens and groups except candidates, political parties and the institutional press from any significant use of the most effective modes of communication. Although the Act's limitations on expenditures by campaign organizations and political parties provide substantially greater room for discussion and debate, they would have required restrictions in the scope of a number of past congressional and Presidential campaigns and would operate to constrain campaigning by candidates who raise sums in excess of the spending ceiling.

By contrast with a limitation upon expenditures for political expression, a limitation upon the amount that any one person or group may contribute to a candidate or political committee entails only a marginal restriction upon the contributor's ability to engage in free communication. A contribution serves as a general expression of support for the candidate and his views, but does not communicate the underlying basis for the support. . . . While contributions may result in political expression if spent by a candidate or an association to present views to the voters, the transformation of contributions into political debate involves speech by someone other than the contributor.

Given the important role of contributions in financing political campaigns, contribution restrictions could have a severe impact on political dialogue if the limitations prevented candidates and political committees from amassing the resources necessary for effective advocacy. There is no indication, however, that the contribution limitations imposed by the Act would have any dramatic adverse effect on the funding of campaigns and political associations. The overall effect of the Act's contribution ceilings is merely to require candidates and political committees to raise funds from a greater number of persons and to compel people who would otherwise contribute amounts greater than the statutory limits to expend such funds on direct political expression, rather than to reduce the total amount of money potentially available to promote political expression.

The Act's contribution and expenditure limitations also impinge on protected associational freedoms. Making a contribution, like joining a political party, serves to affiliate a person with a candidate. In addition, it enables like-minded persons to pool their resources in furtherance of common political goals. The Act's contribution ceilings thus limit one important means of associating with a candidate or committee, but leave the contributor free to become a member of any political association and to assist personally in the association's efforts on behalf of candidates. And the Act's contribution limitations permit associations and candidates to aggregate large sums of money to promote effective advocacy. By contrast, the Act's $1,000 limitation on independent expenditures "relative to a clearly identified candidate" precludes most associations from effectively amplifying the voice of their adherents, the original basis for the recognition of First Amendment protection of the freedom of association. . . .

In sum, although the Act's contribution and expenditure limitations both implicate fundamental First Amendment interests, its expenditure ceilings impose significantly more severe restrictions on protected freedoms of political expression and association than do its limitations on financial contributions.

B. Contribution Limitations

1. The $1,000 Limitation on Contributions by Individuals and Groups to Candidates and Authorized Campaign Committees . . .

(A)

As the general discussion in Part I–A, supra, indicated, the primary First Amendment problem raised by the Act's contribution limitations is their restriction of one aspect of the contributor's freedom of political association. . . .

. . .

The Act's $1,000 contribution limitation focuses precisely on the problem of large campaign contributions—the narrow aspect of political association where the actuality and potential for corruption have been identified—while leaving persons free to engage in independent political expression, to associate actively through volunteering their services, and to assist to a limited but nonetheless substantial extent in supporting candidates and committees with financial resources. Significantly, the Act's contribution limitations in themselves do not undermine to any material degree the potential for robust and effective discussion of candidates and campaign issues by individual citizens, associations, the institutional press, candidates, and political parties.

We find that, under the rigorous standard of review established by our prior decisions, the weighty interests served by restricting the size of financial contributions to political candidates are sufficient to justify the limited effect upon First Amendment freedoms caused by the $1,000 contribution ceiling.

. . .

(C)

Apart from these First Amendment concerns, appellants argue that the contribution limitations work such an invidious discrimination between incumbents and challengers that the statutory provisions must be declared unconstitutional on their face. In considering this contention, it is important at the outset to note that the Act applies the same limitations on contributions to all candidates regardless of their present occupations, ideological views, or party affiliations. Absent record evidence of invidious discrimination against challengers as a class, a court should generally be hesitant to invalidate legislation which on its face imposes evenhanded restrictions. . . .

. . .

The charge of discrimination against minor-party and independent candidates is more troubling, but the record provides no basis for concluding that the Act invidiously disadvantages such candidates. As noted above, the Act on its face treats all candidates equally with regard to contribution limitations. And the restriction would appear to benefit minor-party and independent candidates relative to their major-party opponents because major-party candidates receive far more money in large contributions. Although there is some force to appellants' response that minor-party candidates are primarily concerned with their ability to amass the resources necessary to reach the electorate rather than with their funding position relative to their major-party opponents, the record is virtually devoid of support for the claim that the $1,000 contribution limitation will have a serious effect on the initiation and scope of minor-party and independent candidacies. Moreover, any attempt to exclude minor parties and independents en masse from the Act's contribution limitations overlooks the fact that minor-party candidates may win elective office or have a substantial impact on the outcome of an election.

In view of these considerations, we conclude that the impact of the Act's $1,000 contribution limitation on major-party challengers and on minor-party candidates does not render the provision unconstitutional on its face.

[The Court also upheld the $5,000 limit on contributions by political committees, limitations on volunteers' incidental expenses, and the $25,000 limitation on total contributions during any calendar year.]

C. Expenditure Limitations

The Act's expenditure ceilings impose direct and substantial restraints on the quantity of political speech. . . . It is clear that a primary effect of these expenditure limitations is to restrict the quantity of campaign speech by individuals, groups, and candidates. The restrictions, while neutral as to the ideas expressed, limit political expression "at the core of our electoral process and of the First Amendment freedoms." Williams v. Rhodes, 393 U.S. 23, 32 (1968).

1. The $1,000 Limitation on Expenditures "Relative to a Clearly Identified Candidate"

. . .

. . . [T]he constitutionality of § 608(e)(1) turns on whether the governmental interests advanced in its support satisfy the exacting scrutiny applicable to limitations on core First Amendment rights of political expression.

We find that the governmental interest in preventing corruption and the appearance of corruption is inadequate to justify § 608(e)(1)'s ceiling on independent expenditures. . . .

. . .

It is argued, however, that the ancillary governmental interest in equalizing the relative ability of individuals and groups to influence the outcome of elections serves to justify the limitation on express advocacy of the election or defeat of candidates imposed by § 608(e)(1)'s expenditure ceiling. But the concept that government may restrict the speech of some elements of our society in order to enhance the relative voice of others is wholly foreign to the First Amendment . . . The First Amendment's protection against governmental abridgment of free expression cannot properly be made to depend on a person's financial ability to engage in public discussion. . . .

For the reasons stated, we conclude that § 608(e)(1)'s independent expenditure limitation is unconstitutional under the First Amendment.

2. Limitation on Expenditures by Candidates from Personal or Family Resources

. . .

The ceiling on personal expenditures by candidates on their own behalf, like the limitations on independent expenditures contained in § 608(e)(1), imposes a substantial restraint on the ability of persons to engage in protected First Amendment expression. . . .

. . .

The ancillary interest in equalizing the relative financial resources of candidates competing for elective office, therefore, provides the sole relevant rationale for § 608(a)'s expenditure ceiling. That interest is clearly not sufficient to justify the provision's infringement of fundamental First Amendment rights. . . .

3. Limitations on Campaign Expenditures

Section 608(c) places limitations on overall campaign expenditures by candidates seeking nomination for election and election to federal office. . . .

No governmental interest that has been suggested is sufficient to justify the restriction on the quantity of political expression imposed by § 608(c)'s campaign expenditure limitations. The major evil associated with rapidly increasing campaign expenditures is the danger of candidate dependence on large contributions. The interest in alleviating the corrupting influence of large contributions is served by the Act's contribution limitations and disclosure provisions rather than by § 608(c)'s campaign expenditure ceilings. . . .

The interest in equalizing the financial resources of candidates competing for federal office is no more convincing a justification for restricting the scope of federal election campaigns. . . .

The campaign expenditure ceilings appear to be designed primarily to serve the governmental interests in reducing the allegedly skyrocketing costs of political campaigns.... The First Amendment denies government the power to determine that spending to promote one's political views is wasteful, excessive, or unwise. In the free society ordained by our Constitution it is not the government but the people—individually as citizens and candidates and collectively as associations and political committees—who must retain control over the quantity and range of debate on public issues in a political campaign.

For these reasons we hold that § 608(c) is constitutionally invalid.

In sum, the provisions of the Act that impose a $1,000 limitation on contributions to a single candidate, § 608(b)(1), a $5,000 limitation on contributions by a political committee to a single candidate, § 608(b)(2), and a $25,000 limitation on total contributions by an individual during any calendar year, § 608(b)(3), are constitutionally valid. These limitations along with the disclosure provisions, constitute the Act's primary weapons against the reality or appearance of improper influence stemming from the dependence of candidates on large campaign contributions. The contribution ceilings thus serve the basic governmental interest in safeguarding the integrity of the electoral process without directly impinging upon the rights of individual citizens and candidates to engage in political debate and discussion. By contrast, the First Amendment requires the invalidation of the Act's independent expenditure ceiling, § 608(e)(1), its limitation on a candidate's expenditures from his own personal funds, § 608(a), and its ceilings on overall campaign expenditures, § 608(c). These provisions place substantial and direct restrictions on the ability of candidates, citizens, and associations to engage in protected political expression, restrictions that the First Amendment cannot tolerate.

[Chief Justice Burger and Justice Blackmun dissented from the ruling upholding the contribution limitations. Justice Marshall dissented from the ruling that it was unconstitutional to limit expenditures from the candidate's personal or family funds. Justice White dissented from the ruling that the expenditure limitations were invalid.]

CONTRIBUTIONS TO BALLOT MEASURE CAMPAIGNS

The rationale of Buckley v. Valeo, sustaining contribution limitations to *candidates,* was inapplicable to contribution limits in connection with *ballot measures.* In Citizens Against Rent Control/Coalition For Fair Housing v. Berkeley, 454 U.S. 290 (1981), the Court invalidated a city ordinance limiting contributions to committees supporting or opposing ballot measures. The interest in preventing corruption of officials was inapplicable, and an interest in allowing voters to identify those speaking through ballot measure committees was served by disclosure requirements.

MEYER v. GRANT, 486 U.S. 414 (1988). A Colorado statute, requiring signatures of 5% of qualified voters on petitions to put an initiative measure on the ballot, forbade paying petition circulators. A unanimous Court concluded that the prohibition on the use of paid petition circulators violated the First Amendment. The circulation of an initiative petition constitutes "core political speech." Forbidding payment burdens circulation. Asserted justifications did not survive "exacting scrutiny." An interest in requiring grass roots support for ballot initiatives was protected by the requirement that a specified number of signatures be obtained. An interest in protecting integrity of the initiative process was not served at all by the prohibition.

POLITICAL ACTION COMMITTEES

In California Medical Association v. Federal Election Commission, 453 U.S. 182 (1981), the Court upheld the $5000 political contribution limitation, as applied to a contribution by the association to its multi-candidate political action committee. The Court rejected the argument that, as applied, the restriction operated as a limit on expenditures rather than contributions. Only five Justices spoke to the merits, four dissenting on jurisdictional grounds. Four of the Justices reaching the merits stated that speech by proxy through an association's contributions to its political action committee was not "entitled to full First Amendment protection." The fifth Justice argued that the limitation should be tested by a "rigorous standard of review" but concluded that it was constitutional under that standard.

Federal Election Commission v. National Conservative Political Action Committee, 470 U.S. 480 (1985) held that section 9012(f) of the Presidential Election Campaign Fund Act was invalid. That section prohibited independent political committees from expending more than $1,000 to further the election of a presidential candidate who had opted to receive public financing. The Court rejected the argument that PAC spending presented a greater potential for corruption because the breadth of PAC organizations permitted expenditures larger than individual expenditures.

First National Bank of Boston v. Bellotti

435 U.S. 765, 98 S.Ct. 1407, 55 L.Ed.2d 707 (1978).

Mr. Justice Powell delivered the opinion of the Court.

In sustaining a state criminal statute that forbids certain expenditures by banks and business corporations for the purpose of influencing the vote on referendum proposals, the Massachusetts Supreme Judicial Court held that the First Amendment rights of a corporation are limited to issues that materially affect its business, property, or assets. The court rejected appellants' claim that the statute abridges freedom of speech in violation of the First and Fourteenth Amendments. The issue presented in this context is one of first impression in this Court. We ... reverse.

I

The statute at issue, Mass.Gen.Laws ch. 55, § 8, prohibits appellants, two national banking associations and three business corporations, from making contributions or expenditures "for the purpose of ... influencing or affecting the vote on any question submitted to the voters, other than one materially affecting any of the property, business or assets of the corporation." The statute further specifies that "[n]o question submitted to the voters solely concerning the taxation of the income, property or transactions of individuals shall be deemed materially to affect the property, business or assets of the corporation." ...

Appellants wanted to spend money to publicize their views on a proposed constitutional amendment that was to be submitted to the voters as a ballot question at a general election on November 2, 1976. The amendment would have permitted the legislature to impose a graduated tax on the income of individuals. After appellee, the Attorney General of Massachusetts, informed appellants that he intended to enforce § 8 against them, they brought this action seeking to have the statute declared unconstitutional....

. . .

III

The court below framed the principal question in this case as whether and to what extent corporations have First Amendment rights. We believe that the court posed the wrong question. The Constitution often protects interests broader than those of the party seeking their vindication. The First Amendment, in particular, serves significant societal interests. The proper question therefore is not whether corporations "have" First Amendment rights and, if so, whether they are coextensive with those of natural persons. Instead, the question must be whether § 8 abridges expression that the First Amendment was meant to protect. We hold that it does.

A

. . .

. . . The question in this case, simply put, is whether the corporate identity of the speaker deprives this proposed speech of what otherwise would be its clear entitlement to protection. We turn now to that question.

B

. . .

. . . [A]ppellee suggests that First Amendment rights generally have been afforded only to corporations engaged in the communications business or through which individuals express themselves . . .

The press cases emphasize the special and constitutionally recognized role of that institution in informing and educating the public, offering criticism, and providing a forum for discussion and debate. . . . But the press does not have a monopoly on either the First Amendment or the ability to enlighten. . . .

Nor do our recent commercial speech cases lend support to appellee's business interest theory. They illustrate that the First Amendment goes beyond protection of the press and the self-expression of individuals to prohibit government from limiting the stock of information from which members of the public may draw. A commercial advertisement is constitutionally protected not so much because it pertains to the seller's business as because it furthers the societal interest in the "free flow of commercial information . . ."

C

. . .

Section 8 permits a corporation to communicate to the public its views on certain referendum subjects—those materially affecting its business—but not others. It also singles out one kind of ballot question—individual taxation—as a subject about which corporations may never make their ideas public. The legislature has drawn the line between permissible and impermissible speech according to whether there is a sufficient nexus, as defined by the legislature, between the issue presented to the voters and the business interests of the speaker.

In the realm of protected speech, the legislature is constitutionally disqualified from dictating the subjects about which persons may speak and the speakers who may address a public issue. . . . If a legislature may direct business corporations to "stick to business," it also may limit other corporations—religious, charitable, or civic—to their respective "business" when addressing the public. Such power in government to channel the expression of views is unacceptable under the First Amendment. Especially where, as here, the legislature's suppression of speech suggests an attempt to give one side of a debatable public question an advantage in expressing its views to the people, the First Amendment is plainly offended. Yet the State contends that its action is necessitated by governmental interests of the highest order. We next consider these asserted interests.

IV

. . .

. . . Appellee . . . advances two principal justifications for the prohibition of corporate speech. The first is the State's interest in sustaining the active role of the individual citizen in the electoral process and thereby preventing diminution of the citizen's confidence in government. The second is the interest in protecting the rights of shareholders whose views differ from those expressed by management on behalf of the corporation. However weighty these interests may be in the context of partisan candidate elections, they either are not implicated in this case or are not served at all, or in other than a random manner, by the prohibition in § 8.

A

Preserving the integrity of the electoral process, preventing corruption, and "sustain[ing] the active, alert responsibility of the individual citizen in a democracy for the wise conduct of government" are interests of the highest importance. . . . Preservation of the individual citizen's confidence in government is equally important. . . .

Appellee advances a number of arguments in support of his view that these interests are endangered by corporate participation in discussion of a referendum issue. They hinge upon the assumption that such participation would exert an undue influence on the outcome of a referendum vote, and—in the end—destroy the confidence of the people in the democratic process and the integrity of government. According to appellee, corporations are wealthy and powerful and their views may drown out other points of view. If appellee's arguments were supported by record or legislative findings that corporate advocacy threatened imminently to undermine democratic processes, thereby denigrating rather than serving First Amendment interests, these arguments would merit our consideration. . . . But there has been no showing that the relative voice of corporations has been overwhelming or even significant in influencing referenda in Massachusetts, or that there has been any threat to the confidence of the citizenry in government. . . .

Nor are appellee's arguments inherently persuasive or supported by the precedents of this Court. Referenda are held on issues, not candidates for public office. The risk of corruption perceived in cases involving candidate elections, . . . simply is not present in a popular vote on a public issue. To be sure, corporate advertising may influence the outcome of the vote; this would be its purpose. But the fact that advocacy may persuade the electorate is hardly a reason to suppress it. . . .

B

Finally, the appellee argues that § 8 protects corporate shareholders, an interest that is both legitimate and traditionally within the province of state law. . . . The statute is said to serve this interest by preventing the use of corporate resources in furtherance of views with which some shareholders may disagree. This purpose is belied, however, by the provisions of the statute, which are both underinclusive and overinclusive.

The underinclusiveness of the statute is self-evident. Corporate expenditures with respect to a referendum are prohibited, while corporate activity with respect to the passage or defeat of legislation is permitted, even though corporations may engage in lobbying more often than they take positions on ballot questions submitted to the voters. Nor does § 8 prohibit a corporation from expressing its views, by the expenditure of corporate funds, on any public issue until it becomes the subject of a referendum, though the displeasure of disapproving shareholders is unlikely to be any less.

The fact that a particular kind of ballot question has been singled out for special treatment undermines the likelihood of a genuine state interest in protecting shareholders. It suggests instead that the legislature may have been concerned with silencing corporations on a particular subject. Indeed, appellee has conceded that "the legislative and judicial history of the statute indicates . . . that the second crime was 'tailor-made' to prohibit corporate campaign contributions to oppose a graduated income tax amendment."

Nor is the fact that § 8 is limited to banks and business corporations without relevance. Excluded from its provisions and criminal sanctions are entities or organized groups in which numbers of persons may hold an interest or membership, and which often have resources comparable to those of large corporations. Minorities in such groups or entities may have interests with respect to institutional speech quite comparable to those of minority shareholders in a corporation. Thus the exclusion of Massachusetts business trusts, real estate investment trusts, labor unions, and other associations undermines the plausibility of the State's purported concern for the persons who happen to be shareholders in the banks and corporations covered by § 8.

The overinclusiveness of the statute is demonstrated by the fact that § 8 would prohibit a corporation from supporting or opposing a referendum proposal even if its shareholders unanimously authorized the contribution or expenditure. Ultimately shareholders may decide, through the procedures of corporate democracy, whether their corporation should engage in debate on public issues.[34] Acting through their power to elect the board of directors or to insist upon protective provisions in the corporation's charter, shareholders normally are presumed competent to protect their own interests. In addition to intracorporate remedies, minority shareholders generally have access to the judicial remedy of a derivative suit to challenge corporate disbursements alleged to have been made for improper corporate purposes or merely to further the personal interests of management.

Assuming, *arguendo,* that protection of shareholders is a "compelling" interest under the circumstances of this case, we find "no substantially relevant correlation between the governmental interest asserted and the State's effort" to prohibit appellants from speaking. . . .

V

Because that portion of § 8 challenged by appellants prohibits protected speech in a manner unjustified by a compelling state interest, it must be

---

[34] . . .*Street* and *Abood* are irrelevant to the question presented in this case. . . .

The critical distinction here is that no shareholder has been "compelled" to contribute anything. Apart from the fact, noted by the dissent, that compulsion by the State is wholly absent, the shareholder invests in a corporation of his own volition and is free to withdraw his investment at any time and for any reason. . . .

invalidated. The judgment of the Supreme Judicial Court is reversed.[a]

Mr. Justice White, with whom Mr. Justice Brennan and Mr. Justice Marshall join, dissenting.

The Massachusetts statute challenged here forbids the use of corporate funds to publish views about referenda issues having no material effect on the business, property or assets of the corporation.... I do not suggest for a moment that the First Amendment requires a State to forbid such use of corporate funds, but I do strongly disagree that the First Amendment forbids state interference with managerial decisions of this kind.

... The Court's fundamental error is its failure to realize that the state regulatory interests in terms of which the alleged curtailment of First Amendment rights accomplished by the statute must be evaluated are themselves derived from the First Amendment. ...

I

. . .

I recognize that there may be certain communications undertaken by corporations which could not be restricted without impinging seriously upon the right to receive information. In the absence of advertising and similar promotional activities, for example, the ability of consumers to obtain information relating to products manufactured by corporations would be significantly impeded. There is also a need for employees, customers, and shareholders of corporations to be able to receive communications about matters relating to the functioning of corporations. Such communications are clearly desired by all investors and may well be viewed as an associational form of self-expression.... Moreover, it is unlikely that such information would be disseminated by sources other than corporations. It is for such reasons that the Court has extended a certain degree of First Amendment protection to activities of this kind. None of these considerations, however, are implicated by a prohibition upon corporate expenditures relating to referenda concerning questions of general public concern having no connection with corporate business affairs.

. . .

This Nation has for many years recognized the need for measures designed to prevent corporate domination of the political process. The Corrupt Practices Act, first enacted in 1907, has consistently barred corporate contributions in connection with federal elections. This Court has repeatedly recognized that one of the principal purposes of this prohibition is "to avoid the deleterious influences on federal elections resulting from the use of money by those who exercise control over large aggregations of capital." ... Although this Court has never adjudicated the constitutionality of the Act, there is no suggestion in its cases construing it ... that this purpose is in any sense illegitimate or deserving of other than the utmost respect; indeed, the thrust of its opinions, until today, has been to the contrary....

II

There is an additional overriding interest related to the prevention of corporate domination which is substantially advanced by Massachusetts' restrictions upon corporate contributions: assuring that shareholders are not

[a] A concurring opinion by Chief Justice Burger, and a dissenting opinion by Justice Rehnquist, are omitted.

compelled to support and financially further beliefs with which they disagree where, as is the case here, the issue involved does not materially affect the business, property, or other affairs of the corporation. The State has not interfered with the prerogatives of corporate management to communicate about matters that have material impact on the business affairs entrusted to them, however much individual stockholders may disagree on economic or ideological grounds. Nor has the State forbidden management from formulating and circulating its views at its own expense or at the expense of others, even where the subject at issue is irrelevant to corporate business affairs. But Massachusetts *has* chosen to forbid corporate management from spending corporate funds in referenda elections absent some demonstrable effect of the issue on the economic life of the company. In short, corporate management may not use corporate monies to promote what does not further corporate affairs but what in the last analysis are the purely personal views of the management, individually or as a group.

This is not only a policy which a State may adopt consistent with the First Amendment but one which protects the very freedoms that this Court has held to be guaranteed by the First Amendment.... Last Term, in Abood v. Detroit Board of Education, 431 U.S. 209 (1977), we confronted these constitutional questions and held that a State may not, even indirectly, require an individual to contribute to the support of an ideological cause he may oppose as a condition of employment. ...

Presumably, unlike the situations presented by *Street* and *Abood*, the use of funds invested by shareholders with opposing views by Massachusetts corporations in connection with referenda or elections would not constitute state action and, consequently, would not violate the First Amendment. Until now, however, the States have always been free to adopt measures designed to further rights protected by the Constitution even when not compelled to do so. It could hardly be plausibly contended that just because Massachusetts' regulation of corporations is less extensive than Michigan's regulation of labor-management relations, Massachusetts may not constitutionally prohibit the very evil which Michigan may not constitutionally permit. Yet this is precisely what the Court today holds.

The Court ... proposes that the aggrieved shareholder assert his interest in preventing the expenditure of funds for nonbusiness causes he finds unconscionable through the channels provided by "corporate democracy" ... It should be obvious that the alternative means upon the adequacy of which the majority is willing to predicate a constitutional adjudication is no more able to satisfy the State's interest than a ruling in *Street* and *Abood* leaving aggrieved employees to the remedies provided by union democracy would have satisfied the demands of the First Amendment....

· · ·

The necessity of prohibiting corporate political expenditures in order to prevent the use of corporate funds for purposes with which shareholders may disagree is not a unique perception of Massachusetts. This Court has repeatedly recognized that one of the purposes of the Corrupt Practices Act was to prevent the use of corporate or union funds for political purposes without the consent of the shareholders or union members and to protect minority interests from domination by corporate or union leadership....

· · ·

In my view, the interests in protecting a system of freedom of expression, set forth supra, are sufficient to justify any incremental curtailment in the volume of expression which the Massachusetts statute might produce....

. . .

FEDERAL ELECTION COMMISSION v. NATIONAL RIGHT TO WORK COMMITTEE, 459 U.S. 197 (1982). The 1971 Federal Election Campaign Act of 1971 forbids corporations and labor unions from making contributions and expenditures in connection with federal elections. An exception permits these organizations to establish "separate segregated funds" for political purposes, subject to important restrictions. The restriction at issue in this case was a provision that a corporation without capital stock may solicit contributions to a fund it has established only from "members" of the corporation. The Court interpreted this provision to prohibit the Committee, a nonprofit corporation, from soliciting contributions to a fund to receive and make contributions on behalf of federal candidates. The Court concluded that its construction of the Act did not violate the First Amendment. Pointing to the long history of federal legislation forbidding corporation and union contributions to candidates for federal office, the Court accepted Congress' judgment that the prohibition prevented "both the actual corruption threatened by large financial contributions and the eroding of public confidence in the electoral process through the appearance of corruption." The statute could be applied to solicitation by "corporations and labor unions without great financial resources, as well as those more favorably situated" because the Court would not "second guess a legislative determination as to the need for prophylactic measures where corruption is the evil feared." In a footnote, the Court distinguished First National Bank of Boston v. Bellotti, as dealing with a prohibition of corporate contributions to a referendum measure rather than a candidate.

Austin v. Michigan Chamber of Commerce

494 U.S. 652, 110 S.Ct. 1391, 108 L.Ed.2d 652 (1990).

Justice Marshall delivered the opinion of the Court.

In this appeal, we must determine whether § 54(1) of the Michigan Campaign Finance Act violates either the First or the Fourteenth Amendment to the Constitution. Section 54(1) prohibits corporations from using corporate treasury funds for independent expenditures in support of or in opposition to any candidate in elections for state office.... Corporations are allowed, however, to make such expenditures from segregated funds used solely for political purposes.... In response to a challenge brought by the Michigan State Chamber of Commerce, the Sixth Circuit held that § 54(1) could not be applied to the Chamber, a Michigan nonprofit corporation, without violating the First Amendment. Although we agree that expressive rights are implicated in this case, we hold that application of § 54(1) to the Chamber is constitutional because the provision is narrowly tailored to serve a compelling state interest. Accordingly, we reverse the judgment of the Court of Appeals.

I

Section 54(1) of the Michigan Campaign Finance Act prohibits corporations from making contributions and independent expenditures in connection with state candidate elections.[1] The issue before us is only the constitutionality of the State's ban on independent expenditures. The Act defines "expenditure" as "a payment, donation, loan, pledge, or promise of payment of money or anything of ascertainable monetary value for goods, materials, services, or facilities in assistance of, or in opposition to, the nomination or election of a candidate." ... An expenditure is considered independent if it is "not made at the direction of, or under the control of, another person and if the expenditure is not a contribution to a committee." ... The Act exempts from this general prohibition against corporate political spending any expenditure made from a segregated fund.... A corporation may solicit contributions to its political fund only from an enumerated list of persons associated with the corporation....

The Michigan State Chamber of Commerce, a nonprofit Michigan corporation, challenges the constitutionality of this statutory scheme. The Chamber comprises more than 8,000 members, three-quarters of whom are for-profit corporations. The Chamber's general treasury is funded through annual dues required of all members. Its purposes, as set out in the bylaws, are to promote economic conditions favorable to private enterprise; to analyze, compile, and disseminate information about laws of interest to the business community and to publicize to the government the views of the business community on such matters; to train and educate its members; to foster ethical business practices; to collect data on and investigate matters of social, civic, and economic importance to the State; to receive contributions and to make expenditures for political purposes and to perform any other lawful political activity; and to coordinate activities with other similar organizations.

In June 1985 Michigan scheduled a special election to fill a vacancy in the Michigan House of Representatives. Although the Chamber had established and funded a separate political fund, it sought to use its general treasury funds to place in a local newspaper an advertisement supporting a specific candidate. As the Act made such an expenditure punishable as a felony, ... the Chamber brought suit in District Court for injunctive relief against enforcement of the Act, arguing that the restriction on expenditures is unconstitutional under both the First and the Fourteenth Amendments.

. . .

II

To determine whether Michigan's restrictions on corporate political expenditures may constitutionally be applied to the Chamber, we must ascertain whether they burden the exercise of political speech and, if they do, whether they are narrowly tailored to serve a compelling state interest. Buckley v. Valeo, 424 U.S. 1, 44–45 (1976) (per curiam). Certainly, the use of funds to support a political candidate is "speech" ... The mere fact that the Chamber is a corporation does not remove its speech from the ambit of the First Amendment. See, e.g., First National Bank of Boston v. Bellotti, 435 U.S. 765, 777 (1978).

A

This Court concluded in FEC v. Massachusetts Citizens for Life, Inc., 479 U.S. 238 (1986) *(MCFL),* that a federal statute requiring corporations to make independent political expenditures only through special segregated funds, 2

---

[1] Section 54(1) is modeled on a provision of the Federal Election Campaign Act of 1971, 86 Stat. 11, as amended, 2 U.S.C. sections 431–455, that requires corporations and labor unions to use segregated funds to finance independent expenditures made in federal elections. Section 441b.

U.S.C. § 441b, burdens corporate freedom of expression.... The Court reasoned that the small nonprofit corporation in that case would face certain organizational and financial hurdles in establishing and administering a segregated political fund. For example, the statute required the corporation to appoint a treasurer for its segregated fund, keep records of all contributions, file a statement of organization containing information about the fund, and update that statement periodically.... In addition, the corporation was permitted to solicit contributions to its segregated fund only from "members," which did not include persons who merely contributed to or indicated support for the organization.... These hurdles "impose[d] administrative costs that many small entities [might] be unable to bear" and "create[d] a disincentive for such organizations to engage in political speech." ...

Despite the Chamber's success in administering its separate political fund, Michigan's segregated fund requirement still burdens the Chamber's exercise of expression because "the corporation is not free to use its general funds for campaign advocacy purposes." *MCFL,* supra, at 252 (plurality opinion). The Act imposes requirements similar to those in the federal statute involved in *MCFL:* a segregated fund must have a treasurer, ... and its administrators must keep detailed accounts of contributions, ... and file with state officials a statement of organization.... In addition, a nonprofit corporation like the Chamber may solicit contributions to its political fund only from members, stockholders of members, officers or directors of members, and the spouses of any of these persons.... Although these requirements do not stifle corporate speech entirely, they do burden expressive activity.... Thus, they must be justified by a compelling state interest.

B

The State contends that the unique legal and economic characteristics of corporations necessitate some regulation of their political expenditures to avoid corruption or the appearance of corruption. See FEC v. National Conservative Political Action Comm., 470 U.S. 480, 496–497 (1985) *(NCPAC)* ("[P]reventing corruption or the appearance of corruption are the only legitimate and compelling government interests thus far identified for restricting campaign finances"). State law grants corporations special advantages—such as limited liability, perpetual life, and favorable treatment of the accumulation and distribution of assets—that enhance their ability to attract capital and to deploy their resources in ways that maximize the return on their shareholders' investments. These state-created advantages not only allow corporations to play a dominant role in the nation's economy, but also permit them to use "resources amassed in the economic marketplace" to obtain "an unfair advantage in the political marketplace." *MCFL,* 479 U.S., at 257. As the Court explained in *MCFL,* the political advantage of corporations is unfair because

> "[t]he resources in the treasury of a business corporation ... are not an indication of popular support for the corporation's political ideas. They reflect instead the economically motivated decisions of investors and customers. The availability of these resources may make a corporation a formidable political presence, even though the power of the corporation may be no reflection of the power of its ideas." Id., at 258.

We therefore have recognized that "the compelling governmental interest in preventing corruption support[s] the restriction of the influence of political war chests funneled through the corporate form." *NCPAC,* supra, at 500–501....

The Chamber argues that this concern about corporate domination of the political process is insufficient to justify restrictions on independent expenditures. Although this Court has distinguished these expenditures from direct contributions in the context of federal laws regulating individual donors, *Buckley,* 424 U.S., at 47, it has also recognized that a legislature might demonstrate a danger of real or apparent corruption posed by such expenditures when made by corporations to influence candidate elections, *Bellotti,* 435 U.S., at 788, n. 26. Regardless of whether this danger of "financial quid pro quo" corruption ... may be sufficient to justify a restriction on independent expenditures, Michigan's regulation aims at a different type of corruption in the political arena: the corrosive and distorting effects of immense aggregations of wealth that are accumulated with the help of the corporate form and that have little or no correlation to the public's support for the corporation's political ideas. The Act ... ensures that expenditures reflect actual public support for the political ideas espoused by corporations. We emphasize that the mere fact that corporations may accumulate large amounts of wealth is not the justification for § 54; rather, the unique state-conferred corporate structure that facilitates the amassing of large treasuries warrants the limit on independent expenditures. Corporate wealth can unfairly influence elections when it is deployed in the form of independent expenditures, just as it can when it assumes the guise of political contributions. We therefore hold that the State has articulated a sufficiently compelling rationale to support its restriction on independent expenditures by corporations.

C

We next turn to the question whether the Act is sufficiently narrowly tailored to achieve its goal. We find that the Act is precisely targeted to eliminate the distortion caused by corporate spending while also allowing corporations to express their political views.... [T]he Act does not impose an *absolute* ban on all forms of corporate political spending but permits corporations to make independent political expenditures through separate segregated funds. Because persons contributing to such funds understand that their money will be used solely for political purposes, the speech generated accurately reflects contributors' support for the corporation's political views....

The Chamber argues that § 54(1) is substantially overinclusive, because it includes within its scope closely held corporations that do not possess vast reservoirs of capital. We rejected a similar argument in FEC v. National Right to Work Committee, 459 U.S. 197 (1982) (*NRWC*), in the context of federal restrictions on the persons from whom corporations could solicit contributions to their segregated funds.... Although some closely held corporations, just as some publicly held ones, may not have accumulated significant amounts of wealth, they receive from the State the special benefits conferred by the corporate structure and present the potential for distorting the political process. This potential for distortion justifies § 54(1)'s general applicability to all corporations. The section therefore is not substantially overbroad.

III

The Chamber contends that even if the Campaign Finance Act is constitutional with respect to for-profit corporations, it nonetheless cannot be applied to a nonprofit ideological corporation like a chamber of commerce. In *MCFL,* we held that the nonprofit organization there had "features more akin to voluntary political associations than business firms, and therefore should not have to bear burdens on independent spending solely because of [its] incorporated status." 479 U.S., at 263. In reaching that conclusion, we enumerated three characteristics of the corporation that were "essential" to our holding. Ibid. Because the Chamber does not share these crucial features, the Constitution does not require that it be exempted from the generally applicable provisions of § 54(1).

The first characteristic of Massachusetts Citizens for Life, Inc., that distinguished it from ordinary business corporations was that the organization "was formed for the express purpose of promoting political ideas, and cannot engage in business activities." . . .

In contrast, the Chamber's bylaws set forth more varied purposes, several of which are not inherently political. For instance, the Chamber compiles and disseminates information relating to social, civic, and economic conditions, trains and educates its members, and promotes ethical business practices. Unlike MCFL's, the Chamber's educational activities are not expressly tied to political goals; many of its seminars, conventions, and publications are politically neutral and focus on business and economic issues. . . . The Chamber's nonpolitical activities therefore suffice to distinguish it from *MCFL* in the context of this characteristic.

We described the second feature of MCFL as the absence of "shareholders or other persons affiliated so as to have a claim on its assets or earnings. This ensures that persons connected with the organization will have no economic disincentive for disassociating with it if they disagree with its political activity." 479 U.S., at 264. Although the Chamber also lacks shareholders, many of its members may be similarly reluctant to withdraw as members even if they disagree with the Chamber's political expression, because they wish to benefit from the Chamber's nonpolitical programs and to establish contacts with other members of the business community. The Chamber's political agenda is sufficiently distinct from its educational and outreach programs that members who disagree with the former may continue to pay dues to participate in the latter. . . .

The final characteristic upon which we relied in *MCFL* was the organization's independence from the influence of business corporations. On this score, the Chamber differs most greatly from the Massachusetts organization. MCFL was not established by, and had a policy of not accepting contributions from, business corporations. Thus it could not "serv[e] as [a] condui[t] for the type of direct spending that creates a threat to the political marketplace." Ibid. In striking contrast, more than three-quarters of the Chamber's members are business corporations. . . . Business corporations . . . could circumvent the Act's restrictions by funneling money through the Chamber's general treasury. Because the Chamber accepts money from for-profit corporations, it could, absent application of § 54(1), serve as a conduit for corporate political spending. . . .

IV

The Chamber also attacks § 54(1) as underinclusive because it does not regulate the independent expenditures of unincorporated labor unions.[4] Whereas unincorporated unions, and indeed individuals, may be able to amass large treasuries, they do so without the significant state-conferred advantages of the corporate structure. . . . The desire to counterbalance those advantages unique to the corporate form is the State's compelling interest in this case; thus, excluding from the statute's coverage unincorporated entities that also have the

---

[4] The Federal Election Campaign Act restricts the independent expenditures of labor organizations as well as those of corporations. 2 U.S.C. § 441b(a).

capacity to accumulate wealth "does not undermine its justification for regulating corporations." ...

Moreover, labor unions differ from corporations in that union members who disagree with a union's political activities need not give up full membership in the organization to avoid supporting its political activities. Although a union and an employer may require that all bargaining unit employees become union members, a union may not compel those employees to support financially "union activities beyond those germane to collective bargaining, contract administration, and grievance adjustment." Communications Workers of Am. v. Beck, 487 U.S. 735, 745 (1988). See also Abood v. Detroit Bd. of Educ., 431 U.S. 209 (1977).... An employee who objects to a union's political activities thus can decline to contribute to those activities, while continuing to enjoy the benefits derived from the union's performance of its duties as the exclusive representative of the bargaining unit on labor-management issues. As a result, the funds available for a union's political activities more accurately reflect members' support for the organization's political views than does a corporation's general treasury. Michigan's decision to exclude unincorporated labor unions from the scope of § 54(1) is therefore justified by the crucial differences between unions and corporations.

V

Because we hold that § 54(1) does not violate the First Amendment, we must address the Chamber's contention that the provision infringes its rights under the Fourteenth Amendment. The Chamber argues that the statute treats similarly situated entities unequally. Specifically, it contends that the State should also restrict the independent expenditures of unincorporated associations with the ability to accumulate large treasuries and of corporations engaged in the media business.

Because the right to engage in political expression is fundamental to our constitutional system, statutory classifications impinging upon that right must be narrowly tailored to serve a compelling governmental interest. Police Department of Chicago v. Mosley, 408 U.S. 92, 101 (1972). We find that, even under such strict scrutiny, the statute's classifications pass muster under the Equal Protection Clause. As we explained in the context of our discussions of whether the statute was overinclusive, or underinclusive, the State's decision to regulate only corporations is precisely tailored to serve the compelling state interest of eliminating from the political process the corrosive effect of political "war chests" amassed with the aid of the legal advantages given to corporations.

Similarly, we find that the Act's exemption of media corporations from the expenditure restrictions does not render the statute unconstitutional. The "media exception" excludes from the definition of "expenditure" any "expenditure by a broadcasting station, newspaper, magazine, or other periodical or publication for any news story, commentary, or editorial in support of or opposition to a candidate for elective office ... in the regular course of publication or broadcasting,".... [5] ... [T]he exception will undoubtedly result in the imposition of fewer restrictions on the expression of corporations that

---

[5] The Federal Election Campaign Act contains a similar exemption that excludes from the definition of expenditure "any news story, commentary, or editorial distributed through the facilities of any broadcasting sta-tion, newspaper, magazine, or other periodical publication, unless such facilities are owned or controlled by any political party, political committee, or candidate." 2 U.S.C. § 431(9)(B)(I).

are in the media business. Thus, it cannot be regarded as neutral, and the distinction must be justified by a compelling state purpose.

Although all corporations enjoy the same state-conferred benefits inherent in the corporate form, media corporations differ significantly from other corporations in that their resources are devoted to the collection of information and its dissemination to the public. . . . The Act's definition of "expenditure," . . . conceivably could be interpreted to encompass election-related news stories and editorials. The Act's restrictions on independent expenditures therefore might discourage incorporated news broadcasters or publishers from serving their crucial societal role. The media exception ensures that the Act does not hinder or prevent the institutional press from reporting on and publishing editorials about newsworthy events. . . . A valid distinction thus exists between corporations that are part of the media industry and other corporations that are not involved in the regular business of imparting news to the public. Although the press' unique societal role may not entitle the press to greater protection under the Constitution, . . . it does provide a compelling reason for the State to exempt media corporations from the scope of political expenditure limitations. We therefore hold that the Act does not violate the Equal Protection Clause.

VI

Michigan identified as a serious danger the significant possibility that corporate political expenditures will undermine the integrity of the political process, and it has implemented a narrowly tailored solution to that problem. By requiring corporations to make all independent political expenditures through a separate fund made up of money solicited expressly for political purposes, the Michigan Campaign Finance Act reduces the threat that huge corporate treasuries amassed with the aid of favorable state laws will be used to influence unfairly the outcome of elections. The Michigan Chamber of Commerce does not exhibit the characteristics identified in MCFL that would require the State to exempt it from generally applicable restrictions on independent corporate expenditures. We therefore reverse the decision of the Court of Appeals.

It is so ordered.

Justice Stevens, concurring.

In my opinion the distinction between individual expenditures and individual contributions that the Court identified in Buckley v. Valeo, 424 U.S. 1, 45–47 (1976), should have little, if any, weight in reviewing corporate participation in candidate elections. In that context, I believe the danger of either the fact, or the appearance, of quid pro quo relationships provides an adequate justification for state regulation of both expenditures and contributions. Moreover, as we recognized in First National Bank of Boston v. Bellotti, 435 U.S. 765 (1978), there is a vast difference between lobbying and debating public issues on the one hand, and political campaigns for election to public office on the other. Accordingly, I join the Court's opinion and judgment.

Justice Brennan, concurring.

I join the Court's opinion. As one of the "Orwellian" "censors" derided by the dissents, and as the author of our recent decision in FEC v. Massachusetts Citizens for Life, Inc., 479 U.S. 238 (1986) *(MCFL),* I write separately to explain my views in this case.

. . .

The PAC requirement may be unconstitutional as applied to some corporations because they do not present the dangers at which expenditure limitations are aimed. Indeed, we determined that Massachusetts Citizens for Life—the antiabortion advocacy organization at issue in *MCFL*—fell into this category. . . .

The majority today persuasively demonstrates that the situation in this case is markedly different from that in *MCFL*. . . .

. . .

Justice Scalia, dissenting.

"Attention all citizens. To assure the fairness of elections by preventing disproportionate expression of the views of any single powerful group, your Government has decided that the following associations of persons shall be prohibited from speaking or writing in support of any candidate: _____" In permitting Michigan to make private corporations the first object of this Orwellian announcement, the Court today endorses the principle that too much speech is an evil that the democratic majority can proscribe. I dissent because that principle is contrary to our case law and incompatible with the absolutely central truth of the First Amendment: that government cannot be trusted to assure, through censorship, the "fairness" of political debate.

I

A

. . .

. . . We held in Buckley v. Valeo . . . that independent expenditures to express the political views of individuals and associations do not raise a sufficient threat of corruption to justify prohibition. . . . Neither the Court's opinion nor either of the concurrences makes any effort to distinguish that case . . . The plaintiffs in the case included corporations. . . .

Buckley v. Valeo should not be overruled, because it is entirely correct. . . .

. . .

II

. . .

Perhaps the Michigan law before us here has an unqualifiedly noble objective—to "equalize" the political debate by preventing disproportionate expression of corporations' points of view. . . . The premise of our Bill of Rights, however, is that there are some things—even some seemingly *desirable* things—that government cannot be trusted to do. The very first of these is establishing the restrictions upon speech that will assure "fair" political debate. . . . Perhaps the Michigan legislature was genuinely trying to assure a "balanced" presentation of political views; on the other hand, perhaps it was trying to give unincorporated unions (a not insubstantial force in Michigan) political advantage over major employers. Or perhaps it was trying to assure a "balanced" presentation because it knows that with evenly balanced speech incumbent officeholders generally win. The fundamental approach of the First Amendment, I had always thought, was to assume the worst, and to rule the regulation of political speech "for fairness sake" simply out of bounds.

. . .

... [T]he object of the law we have approved today is not to prevent wrongdoing but to prevent speech. Since those private associations known as corporations have so much money, they will speak so much more, and their views will be given inordinate prominence in election campaigns. This is not an argument that our democratic traditions allow—neither with respect to individuals associated in corporations nor with respect to other categories of individuals whose speech may be "unduly" extensive (because they are rich) or "unduly" persuasive (because they are movie stars) or "unduly" respected (because they are clergymen). The premise of our system is that there is no such thing as too much speech—that the people are not foolish but intelligent, and will separate the wheat from the chaff. . . .

. . .

Justice Kennedy, with whom Justice O'Connor and Justice Scalia join, dissenting.

The majority opinion validates not one censorship of speech but two. One is Michigan's content-based law which decrees it a crime for a nonprofit corporate speaker to endorse or oppose candidates for Michigan public office.
. . .

The other censorship scheme, I most regret to say, is of our own creation. It is value-laden, content-based speech suppression that permits some nonprofit corporate groups but not others to engage in political speech. . . .

I

. . .

A

The State has conceded that among those communications prohibited by its statute are the publication by a nonprofit corporation of its own assessment of a candidate's voting record. With the imprimatur of this Court, it is now a felony in Michigan for the Sierra Club, or the American Civil Liberties Union, or the Michigan State Chamber of Commerce, to advise the public how a candidate voted on issues of urgent concern to their members. In both practice and theory, the prohibition aims at the heart of political debate.

. . .

First, the Act prohibits corporations from speaking on a particular subject, the subject of candidate elections. It is a basic precept that the State may not confine speech to certain subjects. Content-based restrictions are the essence of censorial power. . . .

Second, the Act discriminates on the basis of the speaker's identity. Under the Michigan law, any person or group other than a corporation may engage in political debate over candidate elections; but corporations, even nonprofit corporations that have unique views of vital importance to the electorate, must remain mute. . . .

. . .

B

The second censorship scheme validated by today's holding is the one imposed by the Court. In FEC v. Massachusetts Citizens for Life, Inc., 479 U.S. 238 (1986) (*MCFL*), a First Amendment right to use corporate treasury funds was recognized for the nonprofit corporation then before us. Those who thought that the First Amendment exists to protect all points of view in candidate elections will be disillusioned by the Court's opinion today; for that protection is given only to a preferred class of nonprofit corporate speakers: small, single issue nonprofit corporations that pass the Court's own vague test for determining who are the favored participants in the electoral process. There can be no doubt that if a State were to enact a statute empowering an administrative board to determine which corporations could place candidate advertisements in newspapers and which could not, with authority to enforce the guidelines the Court adopts today to distinguish between the Massachusetts Citizens for Life and the Michigan Chamber of Commerce, the statute would be held unconstitutional. The First Amendment does not permit courts to exercise speech suppression authority denied to legislatures.

. . .

II

The Act does not meet our standards for laws that burden fundamental rights. The State cannot demonstrate that a compelling interest supports its speech restriction, nor can it show that its law is narrowly tailored to the purported statutory end. . . .

A

. . .

The majority almost admits that, in the case of independent expenditures, the danger of a political quid pro quo is insufficient to justify a restriction of this kind. . . . [T]he majority invents a new interest: combating the "corrosive and distorting effects of immense aggregations of wealth," accumulated in corporate form without shareholder or public support. . . .

. . .

With regard to nonprofit corporations in particular, there is no reason to assume that the corporate form has an intrinsic flaw that makes it corrupt, or that all corporations possess great wealth, or that all corporations can buy more media coverage for their views than can individuals or other groups. . . .

. . .

The Court purports to distinguish *MCFL* on the ground that the nonprofit corporation permitted to speak in that case received no funds from profit-making corporations. . . . But this distinction rests on the fallacy that the source of the speaker's funds is somehow relevant to the speaker's right of expression or society's interest in hearing what the speaker has to say. . . . A wooden rule prohibiting independent expenditures by nonprofit corporations that receive funds from business corporations invites discriminatory distinctions. The principled approach is to acknowledge that where political speech is concerned, freedom to speak extends to all nonprofit corporations, not the special favorites of a majority of this Court.

B

. . .

That the censorship applies to the nonprofit corporate speaker itself and not to a PAC that it has organized, far from being a saving feature of the regulation, further condemns it. The argument that the availability of a PAC as an alternate means . . . can save a restriction on independent corporate expenditures was rejected by the Court in *MCFL,* ... as a costly and burdensome disincentive to speech. The record in this case tended to show that between 25 and 50 percent of a PAC's funds are required to establish and administer the PAC. While the corporation can direct the PAC to make expenditures on behalf of candidates, the PAC can be funded only by contributions from shareholders, directors, officers, and managerial employees, and cannot receive corporate treasury funds. . . .

. . .

The majority relies on the state interest in protecting members from the use of nonprofit corporate funds to support candidates whom they may oppose. We should reject this interest as insufficient to save the Act here, just as we rejected the argument in *Bellotti* . . . .

The Court takes refuge in the argument that some members or contributors to nonprofit corporations may find their own views distorted by the organization, and cites our holding in Abood v. Detroit Board of Education, 431 U.S. 209 (1977). *Abood* does not apply here, as the disincentives to dissociate are not comparable. . . . One need not become a member of the Michigan Chamber of Commerce or the Sierra Club in order to earn a living. To the extent that members disagree with a nonprofit corporation's policies, they can seek change from within, withhold financial support, cease to associate with the group, or form a rival group of their own. . . .

To create second-class speakers that can be stifled on the subject of candidate qualifications is to silence some of the most significant participants in the American public dialogue, as evidenced by the amici briefs filed on behalf of the Chamber of Commerce by the American Civil Liberties Union, the Center for Public Interest Law, the American Medical Association, the National Association of Realtors, the American Insurance Association, the National Organization for Women, Greenpeace Action, the National Abortion Rights Action League, the National Right to Work Committee, the Planned Parenthood Federation of America, the Fund for the Feminist Majority, the Washington Legal Foundation, and the Allied Educational Foundation. . . .

. . .

III

An independent ground for invalidating this statute is the blanket exemption for media corporations. . . .

The web of corporate ownership that links media and nonmedia corporations is difficult to untangle for the purpose of any meaningful distinction. Newspapers, television networks, and other media may be owned by parent corporations with multiple business interests. Nothing in the statutory scheme prohibits a business corporate parent from directing its newspaper to support or oppose a particular candidate. The Act not only permits that discretion or control, but makes it a crime for a public-interest nonprofit corporation to bring to light such activity if to do so infers candidate support or opposition. I can find no permissible basis under the First Amendment for the States to make this unsupported distinction among corporate speakers.

. . .

COLORADO REPUBLICAN FEDERAL CAMPAIGN COMMITTEE v. FEDERAL ELECTION COMMISSION, __ U.S. __, 116 S.Ct. 2309 (1996). The "Party Expenditure Provision" of the Federal Election Campaign Act of 1971 imposes dollar limits on "expenditure[s] in connection with the

general election campaign of a [congressional] candidate." 2 U.S.C.
§ 441a(d)(3). After the Colorado Republican Party selected its 1986 candidate
for United States Senate, it bought radio advertisements attacking the likely
Democratic Party candidate. While seven Justices agreed that the Constitution
precluded enforcement of the Act in this case, there was no opinion for the
Court. Three Justices (Breyer, O'Connor and Souter) concluded that the Party
Expenditure Provision was unconstitutional as applied to "independent" party
expenditures that were not an "indirect campaign contribution" to a candidate.
Justice Breyer's opinion took no position concerning the validity of party
expenditure limitations as applied to a party expenditure "in cooperation,
consultation, or concert with ... a candidate." Four Justices (Kennedy, Rehnquist, Scalia and Thomas) would have held the Party Expenditure Provision
unconstitutional on its face, even in the latter context. Justice Kennedy (joined
by the Chief Justice and Justice Scalia) argued that all party expenditures fell
within the rationale of Buckley v. Valeo, that forbids limitation on spending
money on one's own speech. Justice Thomas (also joined by the Chief Justice
and Justice Scalia) argued that *Buckley*'s corruption rationale was inapplicable
to contributions by a party to its own candidate.[1] Justice Stevens (joined by
Justice Ginsburg) dissented, arguing that spending limits on political parties
were constitutional, serving "an important interest in leveling the electoral
field by constraining the cost of federal campaigns."

C.   DISCLOSURE REQUIREMENTS

Buckley v. Valeo

424 U.S. 1, 96 S.Ct. 612, 46 L.Ed.2d 659 (1976).

Per Curiam.

These appeals present constitutional challenges to the key provisions of the
Federal Election Campaign Act of 1971, ... as amended in 1974.

. . .

[A suit was brought against the relevant federal officials in the district
court in the District of Columbia pursuant to a special statutory review
procedure. The plaintiffs included political candidates, contributors to candidates, party organizations and other organizations. A declaration of unconstitutionality and an injunction against enforcement were sought. Only the portion
of the opinion relating to reporting and disclosure requirements is presented
here.]

II.   REPORTING AND DISCLOSURE REQUIREMENTS

. . .

Each political committee is required to register with the Commission,
§ 433, and to keep detailed records of both contributions and expenditures,
§§ 432(c), (d). These records must include the name and address of everyone
making a contribution in excess of $10, along with the date and amount of the
contribution. If a person's contributions aggregate more than $100, his occupa-
tion and principal place of business are also to be included. § 432(c)(2). ...

---

[1] In a portion of his opinion where he
spoke only for himself, Justice Thomas argued that *Buckley*'s distinction between contribution limits and spending limits should be
rejected.

Each committee and each candidate also is required to file quarterly reports. § 434(a). The reports are to contain detailed financial information, including the full name, mailing address, occupation, and principal place of business of each person who has contributed over $100 in a calendar year, as well as the amount and date of the contributions. § 434(b). They are to be made available by the Commission "for public inspection and copying." § 438(a)(4). Every candidate for federal office is required to designate a "principal campaign committee," which is to receive reports of contributions and expenditures made on the candidate's behalf from other political committees and to compile and file these reports, together with its own statements, with the Commission. § 432(f).

Every individual or group, other than a political committee or candidate, who makes "contributions" or "expenditures" of over $100 in a calendar year "other than by contribution to a political committee or a candidate" is required to file a statement with the Commission. § 434(e). Any violation of these recordkeeping and reporting provisions is punishable by a fine of not more than $1,000 or a prison term of not more than a year, or both. § 441(a).

A.   General Principles

Unlike the overall limitations on contributions and expenditures, the disclosure requirements impose no ceiling on campaign-related activities. But we have repeatedly found that compelled disclosure, in itself, can seriously infringe on privacy of association and belief guaranteed by the First Amendment. E.g., Gibson v. Florida Legislative Comm., 372 U.S. 539 (1963); NAACP v. Button, 371 U.S. 415 (1963); Shelton v. Tucker, 364 U.S. 479 (1960); Bates v. Little Rock, 361 U.S. 516 (1960); NAACP v. Alabama, 357 U.S. 449 (1958).

We long have recognized that significant encroachments on First Amendment rights of the sort that compelled disclosure imposes cannot be justified by a mere showing of some legitimate governmental interest. Since NAACP v. Alabama we have required that the subordinating interests of the State must survive exacting scrutiny. . . .

. . .

The strict test established by NAACP v. Alabama is necessary because compelled disclosure has the potential for substantially infringing the exercise of First Amendment rights. But we have acknowledged that there are governmental interests sufficiently important to outweigh the possibility of infringement, particularly when the "free functioning of our national institutions" is involved. Communist Party v. Subversive Activities Control Bd., 367 U.S. 1, 97 (1961).

The governmental interests sought to be vindicated by the disclosure requirements are of this magnitude. They fall into three categories. First, disclosure provides the electorate with information "as to where political campaign money comes from and how it is spent by the candidate" in order to aid the voters in evaluating those who seek federal office. It allows voters to place each candidate in the political spectrum more precisely than is often possible solely on the basis of party labels and campaign speeches. The sources of a candidate's financial support also alert the voter to the interests to which a candidate is most likely to be responsive and thus facilitate predictions of future performance in office.

Second, disclosure requirements deter actual corruption and avoid the appearance of corruption by exposing large contributions and expenditures to the light of publicity. This exposure may discourage those who would use money for improper purposes either before or after the election. A public armed with information about a candidate's most generous supporters is better able to detect any post-election special favors that may be given in return. And, as we recognized in Burroughs v. United States, 290 U.S., at 548, Congress could reasonably conclude that full disclosure during an election campaign tends "to prevent the corrupt use of money to affect elections." . . .

Third, and not least significant, record keeping, reporting, and disclosure requirements are an essential means of gathering the data necessary to detect violations of the contribution limitations described above.

The disclosure requirements, as a general matter, directly serve substantial governmental interests. In determining whether these interests are sufficient to justify the requirements we must look to the extent of the burden that they place on individual rights.

It is undoubtedly true that public disclosure of contributions to candidates and political parties will deter some individuals who otherwise might contribute. In some instances, disclosure may even expose contributors to harassment or retaliation. These are not insignificant burdens on individual rights, and they must be weighed carefully against the interests which Congress has sought to promote by this legislation. In this process, we note and agree with appellants' concession that disclosure requirements—certainly in most applications—appear to be the least restrictive means of curbing the evils of campaign ignorance and corruption that Congress found to exist. Appellants argue, however, that the balance tips against disclosure when it is required of contributors to certain parties and candidates. We turn now to this contention.

B. Application to Minor Parties and Independents

Appellants contend that the Act's requirements are overbroad insofar as they apply to contributions to minor parties and independent candidates because the governmental interest in this information is minimal and the danger of significant infringement on First Amendment rights is greatly increased.

1. Requisite Factual Showing

. . .

There could well be a case, similar to those before the Court in *NAACP v. Alabama* and *Bates,* where the threat to the exercise of First Amendment rights is so serious and the state interest furthered by disclosure so insubstantial that the Act's requirements cannot be constitutionally applied. But no appellant in this case has tendered record evidence of the sort proffered in *NAACP v. Alabama.* Instead, appellants primarily rely on "the clearly articulated fears of individuals, well experienced in the political process." At best they offer the testimony of several minor-party officials that one or two persons refused to make contributions because of the possibility of disclosure. On this record, the substantial public interest in disclosure identified by the legislative history of this Act outweighs the harm generally alleged.

2. Blanket Exemption

. . .

We recognize that unduly strict requirements of proof could impose a heavy burden, but it does not follow that a blanket exemption for minor parties is necessary. Minor parties must be allowed sufficient flexibility in the proof of injury to assure a fair consideration of their claim. The evidence offered need show only a reasonable probability that the compelled disclosure of a party's contributors' names will subject them to threats, harassment or reprisals from either Government officials or private parties. The proof may include, for example, specific evidence of past or present harassment of members due to their associational ties, or of harassment directed against the organization itself. A pattern of threats or specific manifestations of public hostility may be sufficient. New parties that have no history upon which to draw may be able to offer evidence of reprisals and threats directed against individuals or organizations holding similar views.

Where it exists the type of chill and harassment identified in *NAACP v. Alabama* can be shown. We cannot assume that courts will be insensitive to similar showings when made in future cases. We therefore conclude that a blanket exemption is not required.

C.   *Section 434(e)*

Section 434(e) requires "[e]very person (other than a political committee or candidate) who makes contributions or expenditures" aggregating over $100 in a calendar year "other than by contribution to a political committee or candidate" to file a statement with the Commission. Unlike the other disclosure provisions, this section does not seek the contribution list of any association. Instead, it requires direct disclosure of what an individual or group contributes or spends.

In considering this provision we must apply the same strict standard of scrutiny, for the right of associational privacy developed in *NAACP v. Alabama* derives from the rights of the organization's members to advocate their personal points of view in the most effective way. . . .

. . .

Unlike [§ 608(e)(1)], § 434(e) as construed bears a sufficient relationship to a substantial governmental interest. As narrowed, § 434(e), like § 608(e)(1), does not reach all partisan discussion for it only requires disclosure of those expenditures that expressly advocate a particular election result. This might have been fatal if the only purpose of § 434(e) were to stem corruption or its appearance by closing a loophole in the general disclosure requirements. But the disclosure provisions, including § 434(e), serve another, informational interest, and even as construed § 434(e) increases the fund of information concerning those who support the candidates. It goes beyond the general disclosure requirements to shed the light of publicity on spending that is unambiguously campaign related but would not otherwise be reported because it takes the form of independent expenditures or of contributions to an individual or group not itself required to report the names of its contributors. By the same token, it is not fatal that § 434(e) encompasses purely independent expenditures uncoordinated with a particular candidate or his agent. The corruption potential of these expenditures may be significantly different, but the informational interest can be as strong as it is in coordinated spending, for disclosure helps voters to define more of the candidates' constituencies.

Section 434(e), as we have construed it, does not contain the infirmities of the regulations before the Court in Talley v. California, 362 U.S. 60 (1960) and Thomas v. Collins, 323 U.S. 516 (1945). The ordinance found wanting in *Talley* forbade all distribution of handbills that did not contain the name of the printer, author, or manufacturer, and the name of the distributor. . . . Here, as we have seen, the disclosure requirement is narrowly limited to those situations where the information sought has a substantial connection with the governmental interests sought to be advanced. ...

D. Thresholds

Appellants' third contention, based on alleged overbreadth, is that the monetary thresholds in the record-keeping and reporting provisions lack a substantial nexus with the claimed governmental interests, for the amounts involved are too low even to attract the attention of the candidate, much less have a corrupting influence.

. . .

The $10 and $100 thresholds are indeed low. Contributors of relatively small amounts are likely to be especially sensitive to recording or disclosure of their political preferences. These strict requirements may well discourage participation by some citizens in the political process, a result that Congress hardly could have intended. ... The line is necessarily a judgmental decision, best left in the context of this complex legislation to congressional discretion. We cannot say, on this bare record, that the limits designated are wholly without rationality.

. . .

[Chief Justice Burger dissented from the ruling upholding the "irrationally low ceilings of $10 and $100 for anonymous contributions." Justices White, Blackmun, and Rehnquist concurred in the Court's holding with reference to the reporting and disclosure requirements. Justice Stevens took no part in the decision.]

BROWN v. SOCIALIST WORKERS '74 CAMPAIGN COMMITTEE, 459 U.S. 87 (1982). Ohio requires candidates for political office to report campaign contributions and disbursements. The Court held that the first amendment prohibited enforcement of the disclosure requirements as to candidates of the Socialist Workers Party, which had been the object of harassment by government officials and private parties. Three dissenters (Justices O'Connor, Rehnquist and Stevens) argued that a stronger showing should be necessary to claim exemption from disclosure of campaign disbursements than from disclosure of campaign contributions. The purpose of requiring disclosure of expenditures was to prevent illegal expenditures. Disclosure that a person received expenditures from a minor unpopular party had less deterrent impact than disclosure that one had contributed to it.

McIntyre v. Ohio Elections Commission

__ U.S. __, 115 S.Ct. 1511, 131 L.Ed.2d 426 (1995).

Justice Stevens delivered the opinion of the Court.

The question presented is whether an Ohio statute that prohibits the distribution of anonymous campaign literature is a "law ... abridging the freedom of speech" within the meaning of the First Amendment.

I

On April 27, 1988, Margaret McIntyre distributed leaflets to persons attending a public meeting at the Blendon Middle School in Westerville, Ohio. At this meeting, the superintendent of schools planned to discuss an imminent referendum on a proposed school tax levy. The leaflets expressed Mrs. McIntyre's opposition to the levy. There is no suggestion that the text of her message was false, misleading, or libelous. She had composed and printed it on her home computer and had paid a professional printer to make additional copies. Some of the handbills identified her as the author; others merely purported to express the views of "CONCERNED PARENTS AND TAX PAYERS." Except for the help provided by her son and a friend, who placed some of the leaflets on car windshields in the school parking lot, Mrs. McIntyre acted independently.

While Mrs. McIntyre distributed her handbills, an official of the school district, who supported the tax proposal, advised her that the unsigned leaflets did not conform to the Ohio election laws. Undeterred, Mrs. McIntyre appeared at another meeting on the next evening and handed out more of the handbills.

The proposed school levy was defeated at the next two elections, but it finally passed on its third try in November 1988. Five months later, the same school official filed a complaint with the Ohio Elections Commission charging that Mrs. McIntyre's distribution of unsigned leaflets violated § 3599.09(A) of the Ohio Code. The Commission agreed and imposed a fine of $100.

The Franklin County Court of Common Pleas reversed. Finding that Mrs. McIntyre did not "mislead the public nor act in a surreptitious manner," the court concluded that the statute was unconstitutional as applied to her conduct. The Ohio Court of Appeals, by a divided vote, reinstated the fine. . . .

The Ohio Supreme Court affirmed by a divided vote. . . .

Mrs. McIntyre passed away during the pendency of this litigation. Even though the amount in controversy is only $100, petitioner, as the executor of her estate, has pursued her claim in this Court. . . .

II

Ohio maintains that the statute under review is a reasonable regulation of the electoral process. The State does not suggest that all anonymous publications are pernicious or that a statute totally excluding them from the marketplace of ideas would be valid. This is a wise (albeit implicit) concession, for the anonymity of an author is not ordinarily a sufficient reason to exclude her work product from the protections of the First Amendment.

"Anonymous pamphlets, leaflets, brochures and even books have played an important role in the progress of mankind." Talley v. California, 362 U.S. 60, 64 (1960). Great works of literature have frequently been produced by authors writing under assumed names. . . .[A]t least in the field of literary endeavor, the interest in having anonymous works enter the marketplace of ideas unquestionably outweighs any public interest in requiring disclosure as a condition of entry. . . .

The freedom to publish anonymously extends beyond the literary realm. In *Talley*, the Court held that the First Amendment protects the distribution of unsigned handbills urging readers to boycott certain Los Angeles merchants who were allegedly engaging in discriminatory employment practices. . . .On occasion, quite apart from any threat of persecution, an advocate may believe her ideas will be more persuasive if her readers are unaware of her identity. Anonymity thereby provides a way for a writer who may be personally unpopular to ensure that readers will not prejudge her message simply because they do not like its proponent. Thus, even in the field of political rhetoric, where "the identity of the speaker is an important component of many attempts to persuade," . . . the most effective advocates have sometimes opted for anonymity. The specific holding in *Talley* related to advocacy of an economic boycott, but the Court's reasoning embraced a respected tradition of anonymity in the advocacy of political causes. This tradition is perhaps best exemplified by the secret ballot, the hard-won right to vote one's conscience without fear of retaliation.

III

California had defended the Los Angeles ordinance at issue in *Talley* as a law "aimed at providing a way to identify those responsible for fraud, false advertising and libel." . . . We rejected that argument because nothing in the text or legislative history of the ordinance limited its application to those evils. . . . The Ohio statute likewise contains no language limiting its application to fraudulent, false, or libelous statements; to the extent, therefore, that Ohio seeks to justify § 3599.09(A) as a means to prevent the dissemination of untruths, its defense must fail for the same reason given in *Talley*. As the facts of this case demonstrate, the ordinance plainly applies even when there is no hint of falsity or libel.

Ohio's statute does, however, contain a different limitation: It applies only to unsigned documents designed to influence voters in an election. . . . We must, therefore, decide whether and to what extent the First Amendment's protection of anonymity encompasses documents intended to influence the electoral process.

Ohio places its principal reliance on cases such as Anderson v. Celebrezze, 460 U.S. 780 (1983); Storer v. Brown, 415 U.S. 724 (1974); and Burdick v. Takushi, 504 U.S.–(1992), in which we reviewed election code provisions governing the voting process itself. . . . In those cases we refused to adopt "any 'litmus-paper test' that will separate valid from invalid restrictions." . . . Instead, we pursued an analytical process comparable to that used by courts "in ordinary litigation": we considered the relative interests of the State and the injured voters, and we evaluated the extent to which the State's interests necessitated the contested restrictions. . . .

The "ordinary litigation" test does not apply here. Unlike the statutory provisions challenged in *Storer* and *Anderson*, § 3599.09(A) of the Ohio Code does not control the mechanics of the electoral process. It is a regulation of pure speech. Moreover, even though this provision applies evenhandedly to advocates of differing viewpoints, it is a direct regulation of the content of speech. . . . [O]nly those publications containing speech designed to influence the voters in an election need bear the required markings. . . .

Indeed, as we have explained on many prior occasions, the category of speech regulated by the Ohio statute occupies the core of the protection afforded by the First Amendment . . .

Of course, core political speech need not center on a candidate for office. The principles . . . extend equally to issue-based elections such as the school-tax referendum that Mrs. McIntyre sought to influence through her handbills. . . . Indeed, the speech in which Mrs. McIntyre engaged—handing out leaflets in the advocacy of a politically controversial viewpoint—is the essence of First Amendment expression. . . . That this advocacy occurred in the heat of a controversial referendum vote only strengthens the protection afforded to Ms. McIntyre's expression . . .

When a law burdens core political speech, we apply "exacting scrutiny," . . . Our precedents thus make abundantly clear that the Ohio Supreme Court applied a significantly more lenient standard than is appropriate in a case of this kind.

IV

Nevertheless, the State argues that even under the strictest standard of review, the disclosure requirement in § 3599.09(A) is justified by two important and legitimate state interests. Ohio judges its interest in preventing fraudulent and libelous statements and its interest in providing the electorate with relevant information to be sufficiently compelling to justify the anonymous speech ban. These two interests necessarily overlap to some extent, but it is useful to discuss them separately.

Insofar as the interest in informing the electorate means nothing more than the provision of additional information that may either buttress or undermine the argument in a document, we think the identity of the speaker is no different from other components of the document's content that the author is free to include or exclude. . . . The simple interest in providing voters with additional relevant information does not justify a state requirement that a writer make statements or disclosures she would otherwise omit. Moreover, in the case of a handbill written by a private citizen who is not known to the recipient, the name and address of the author adds little, if anything, to the reader's ability to evaluate the document's message. Thus, Ohio's informational interest is plainly insufficient to support the constitutionality of its disclosure requirement.

The state interest in preventing fraud and libel stands on a different footing. We agree with Ohio's submission that this interest carries special weight during election campaigns when false statements, if credited, may have serious adverse consequences for the public at large. Ohio does not, however, rely solely on § 3599.09(A) to protect that interest. Its Election Code includes detailed and specific prohibitions against making or disseminating false statements during political campaigns. . . . These regulations apply both to candidate elections and to issue-driven ballot measures. Thus, Ohio's prohibition of anonymous leaflets plainly is not its principal weapon against fraud. Rather, it serves as an aid to enforcement of the specific prohibitions and as a deterrent to the making of false statements by unscrupulous prevaricators. Although these ancillary benefits are assuredly legitimate, we are not persuaded that they justify § 3599.09(A)'s extremely broad prohibition.

As this case demonstrates, the prohibition encompasses documents that are not even arguably false or misleading. It applies not only to the activities of candidates and their organized supporters, but also to individuals acting independently and using only their own modest resources. It applies not only to elections of public officers, but also to ballot issues that present neither a substantial risk of libel nor any potential appearance of corrupt advantage. It applies not only to leaflets distributed on the eve of an election, when the opportunity for reply is limited, but also to those distributed months in advance. It applies no matter what the character or strength of the author's interest in anonymity. Moreover, as this case also demonstrates, the absence of the author's name on a document does not necessarily protect either that person or a distributor of a forbidden document from being held responsible for compliance with the election code. Nor has the State explained why it can more easily enforce the direct bans on disseminating false documents against anonymous authors and distributors than against wrongdoers who might use false names and addresses in an attempt to avoid detection. We recognize that a State's enforcement interest might justify a more limited identification requirement, but Ohio has shown scant cause for inhibiting the leafleting at issue here.

V

Finally, Ohio vigorously argues that our opinions in First Nat. Bank of Boston v. Bellotti, 435 U.S. 765 (1978), and Buckley v. Valeo, 424 U.S. 1 (1976), amply support the constitutionality of its disclosure requirement. Neither case is controlling: the former concerned the scope of First Amendment protection afforded to corporations; the relevant portion of the latter concerned mandatory disclosure of campaign-related expenditures. Neither case involved a prohibition of anonymous campaign literature.

. . .

Not only is the Ohio statute's infringement on speech more intrusive than the *Buckley* disclosure requirement, but it rests on different and less powerful state interests. The Federal Election Campaign Act of 1971, at issue in *Buckley*, regulates only candidate elections, not referenda or other issue-based ballot measures; and we construed "independent expenditures" to mean only those expenditures that "expressly advocate the election or defeat of a clearly identified candidate." . . . In candidate elections, the Government can identify a compelling state interest in avoiding the corruption that might result from campaign expenditures. Disclosure of expenditures lessens the risk that individuals will spend money to support a candidate as a quid pro quo for special treatment after the candidate is in office. . . . In short, although *Buckley* may permit a more narrowly drawn statute, it surely is not authority for upholding Ohio's open-ended provision.

VI

Under our Constitution, anonymous pamphleteering is not a pernicious, fraudulent practice, but an honorable tradition of advocacy and of dissent. . . . Ohio has not shown that its interest in preventing the misuse of anonymous election-related speech justifies a prohibition of all uses of that speech. . . . One would be hard pressed to think of a better example of the pitfalls of Ohio's blunderbuss approach than the facts of the case before us.

The judgment of the Ohio Supreme Court is reversed.

It is so ordered.

Justice Ginsburg, concurring.

. . .

In for a calf is not always in for a cow. The Court's decision finds unnecessary, overintrusive, and inconsistent with American ideals the State's imposition of a fine on an individual leafleteer who, within her local community, spoke her mind, but sometimes not her name. We do not thereby hold that the State may not in other, larger circumstances, require the speaker to disclose its interest by disclosing its identity. Appropriately leaving open matters not presented by McIntyre's handbills, the Court recognizes that a State's interest in protecting an election process "might justify a more limited identification requirement." . . .

Justice Thomas, concurring in the judgment.

I agree with the majority's conclusion that Ohio's election law, Ohio Rev.Code Ann. § 3599.09(A), is inconsistent with the First Amendment. I would apply, however, a different methodology to this case. Instead of asking whether "an honorable tradition" of anonymous speech has existed throughout American history, or what the "value" of anonymous speech might be, we should determine whether the phrase "freedom of speech, or of the press," as originally understood, protected anonymous political leafletting. I believe that it did.

. . .

III

The historical record is not as complete or as full as I would desire. For example, there is no evidence that, after the adoption of the First Amendment, the Federal Government attempted to require writers to attach their names to political documents. Nor do we have any indication that the federal courts of the early Republic would have squashed such an effort as a violation of the First Amendment. . . . [T]he Framers' universal practice of publishing anonymous articles and pamphlets, indicates that the Framers shared the belief that such activity was firmly part of the freedom of the press. It is only an innovation of modern times that has permitted the regulation of anonymous speech.

. . .

IV

This evidence leads me to agree with the majority's result, but not its reasoning. . . .

While, like Justice Scalia, I am loath to overturn a century of practice shared by almost all of the States, I believe the historical evidence from the framing outweighs recent tradition. . . . Because the majority has adopted an analysis that is largely unconnected to the Constitution's text and history, I concur only in the judgment.

Justice Scalia, with whom The Chief Justice joins, dissenting.

. . . [T]he Court invalidates a species of protection for the election process that exists, in a variety of forms, in every State except California, and that has a pedigree dating back to the end of the 19th century. . . . I dissent from this imposition of free-speech imperatives that are demonstrably not those of the American people today, and that there is inadequate reason to believe were those of the society that begat the First Amendment or the Fourteenth.

I

The question posed by the present case is not the easiest sort to answer for those who adhere to the Court's (and the society's) traditional view that the Constitution bears its original meaning and is unchanging. . . . That technique is simple of application when government conduct that is claimed to violate the Bill of Rights or the Fourteenth Amendment is shown, upon investigation, to have been engaged in without objection at the very time the Bill of Rights or the Fourteenth Amendment was adopted. There is no doubt, for example, that laws against libel and obscenity do not violate "the freedom of speech" to which the First Amendment refers; they existed and were universally approved in 1791. Application of the principle of an unchanging Constitution is also simple enough at the other extreme, where the government conduct at issue was not engaged in at the time of adoption, and there is ample evidence that the reason it was not engaged in is that it was thought to violate the right embodied in the constitutional guarantee. Racks and thumbscrews, well known instruments for inflicting pain, were not in use because they were regarded as cruel punishments.

The present case lies between those two extremes. Anonymous electioneering was not prohibited by law in 1791 or in 1868. In fact, it was widely practiced at the earlier date, an understandable legacy of the revolutionary era in which political dissent could produce governmental reprisal. . . .

But to prove that anonymous electioneering was used frequently is not to establish that it is a constitutional right. . . .

Evidence that anonymous electioneering was regarded as a constitutional right is sparse, and as far as I am aware evidence that it was generally regarded as such is nonexistent. . . .

. . .

What we have, then, is the most difficult case for determining the meaning of the Constitution. No accepted existence of governmental restrictions of the sort at issue here demonstrates their constitutionality, but neither can their nonexistence clearly be attributed to constitutional objections. . . . In the present case, absent other indication I would be inclined to agree with the concurrence that a society which used anonymous political debate so regularly would not regard as constitutional even moderate restrictions made to improve the election process. . . .

But there is other indication, of the most weighty sort: the widespread and longstanding traditions of our people. Principles of liberty fundamental enough to have been embodied within constitutional guarantees are not readily erased from the Nation's consciousness. A governmental practice that has become general throughout the United States, and particularly one that has the validation of long, accepted usage, bears a strong presumption of constitutionality. And that is what we have before us here. Section 3599.09(A) was enacted by the General Assembly of the State of Ohio almost 80 years ago. . . . Even at the time of its adoption, there was nothing unique or extraordinary about it. The earliest statute of this sort was adopted by Massachusetts in 1890, little more than 20 years after the Fourteenth Amendment was ratified. No less than 24 States had similar laws by the end of World War I, and today every State of the Union except California has one, as does the District of Columbia, see D.C.Code Ann. § 1–1420 (1992), and as does the Federal Government where advertising relating to candidates for federal office is concerned, see 2 U.S.C. § 441d(a). Such a universal and long established American legislative practice must be given precedence, I think, over historical and academic speculation regarding a restriction that assuredly does not go to the heart of free speech.

It can be said that we ignored a tradition as old, and almost as widespread, in Texas v. Johnson, 491 U.S. 397 (1989), where we held unconstitutional a state law prohibiting desecration of the United States flag. See also United States v. Eichman, 496 U.S. 310 (1990). But those cases merely stand for the proposition that post-adoption tradition cannot alter the core meaning of a constitutional guarantee. . . .

II

. . . Even if I were to close my eyes to practice, . . . and were to be guided exclusively by deductive analysis from our case law, I would reach the same result.

. . . Our cases plainly . . . suggest that no justification for regulation is more compelling than protection of the electoral process. . . .

. . .

The Court's unprecedented protection for anonymous speech does not even have the virtue of establishing a clear (albeit erroneous) rule of law. For after having announced that this statute, because it "burdens core political speech," requires "exacting scrutiny" . . . (ordinarily the kiss of death), the opinion goes on to proclaim soothingly (and unhelpfully) that "a State's enforcement interest might justify a more limited identification requirement." . . . Perhaps, then, not all the State statutes I have alluded to are invalid, but just some of them; or indeed maybe all of them remain valid in "larger circumstances"! . . . Must a parade permit, for example, be issued to a group that refuses to provide its identity, or that agrees to do so only under assurance that the identity will not be made public? Must a municipally owned theater that is leased for private productions book anonymously sponsored presentations? Must a government periodical that has a "letters to the editor" column disavow the policy that most newspapers have against the publication of anonymous letters? Must a public university that makes its facilities available for a speech by Louis Farrakhan or David Duke refuse to disclose the on-campus or off-campus group that has sponsored or paid for the speech? Must a municipal "public-access" cable channel permit anonymous (and masked) performers? . . .

. . .

I respectfully dissent.

SECTION 5. SPEECH AND ASSOCIATION RIGHTS OF GOVERNMENT EMPLOYEES

Connick v. Myers
461 U.S. 138, 103 S.Ct. 1684, 75 L.Ed.2d 708 (1983).

Justice White delivered the opinion of the Court.

In Pickering v. Board of Education, 391 U.S. 563 (1968), we stated that a public employee does not relinquish First Amendment rights to comment on matters of public interest by virtue of government employment. We also recognized that the State's interests as an employer in regulating the speech of its employees "differ significantly from those it possesses in connection with regulation of the speech of the citizenry in general." . . . The problem, we thought, was arriving "at a balance between the interests of the [employee], as a citizen, in commenting upon matters of public concern and the interest of the State, as an employer, in promoting the efficiency of the public services it performs through its employees." . . . We return to this problem today and consider whether the First and Fourteenth Amendments prevent the discharge of a state employee for circulating a questionnaire concerning internal office affairs.

I

The respondent, Sheila Myers, was employed as an Assistant District Attorney in New Orleans for five and a half years. She served at the pleasure of petitioner Harry Connick, the District Attorney for Orleans Parish. During this period Myers competently performed her responsibilities of trying criminal cases.

In the early part of October 1980, Myers was informed that she would be transferred to prosecute cases in a different section of the criminal court. Myers was strongly opposed to the proposed transfer and expressed her view to several of her supervisors, including Connick. Despite her objections, on October 6 Myers was notified that she was being transferred. Myers again spoke with Dennis Waldron, one of the First Assistant District Attorneys, expressing her reluctance to accept the transfer. A number of other office matters were discussed and Myers later testified that, in response to Waldron's suggestion that her concerns were not shared by others in the office, she informed him that she would do some research on the matter.

That night Myers prepared a questionnaire soliciting the views of her fellow staff members concerning office transfer policy, office morale, the need for a grievance committee, the level of confidence in supervisors, and whether employees felt pressured to work in political campaigns. Early the following morning, Myers typed and copied the questionnaire. She also met with Connick who urged her to accept the transfer. She said she would "consider" it. Connick then left the office. Myers then distributed the questionnaire to 15 Assistant District Attorneys. Shortly after noon, Dennis Waldron learned that Myers was distributing the survey. He immediately phoned Connick and informed him that Myers was creating a "mini-insurrection" within the office. Connick returned to the office and told Myers that she was being terminated because of her refusal to accept the transfer. She was also told that her distribution of the questionnaire was considered an act of insubordination. Connick particularly objected to the question which inquired whether employees "had confidence in and would rely on the word" of various superiors in the office, and to a question concerning pressure to work in political campaigns which he felt would be damaging if discovered by the press.

Myers filed suit under 42 U.S.C. § 1983, . . . contending that her employment was wrongfully terminated because she had exercised her constitutionally-protected right of free speech. The District Court agreed, ordered Myers reinstated, and awarded backpay, damages, and attorney's fees. . . .

. . . [T]he United States Court of Appeals for the Fifth Circuit . . . affirmed. . . .

II

For at least 15 years, it has been settled that a State cannot condition public employment on a basis that infringes the employee's constitutionally protected interest in freedom of expression. Keyishian v. Board of Regents, 385 U.S. 589, 605–606 (1967); Pickering v. Board of Education, 391 U.S. 563 (1968); Perry v. Sindermann, 408 U.S. 593, 597 (1972); Branti v. Finkel, 445 U.S. 507, 515–516 (1980). Our task, as we defined it in *Pickering,* is to seek "a balance between the interests of the [employee], as a citizen, in commenting upon matters of public concern and the interest of the State, as an employer, in promoting the efficiency of the public services it performs through its employees." . . . The District Court, and thus the Court of Appeals as well, misapplied our decision in *Pickering* and consequently, in our view, erred in striking the balance for respondent.

A

The District Court got off on the wrong foot in this case by initially finding that, "[t]aken as a whole, the issues presented in the questionnaire relate to the effective functioning of the District Attorney's Office and are matters of public importance and concern." Connick contends at the outset that no balancing of interests is required in this case because Myers' questionnaire concerned only internal office matters and that such speech is not upon a matter of "public concern," as the term was used in *Pickering*. Although we do not agree that Myers' communication in this case was wholly without First Amendment protection, there is much force to Connick's submission. The repeated emphasis in *Pickering* on the right of a public employee "as a citizen, in commenting upon matters of public concern," was not accidental. This language, reiterated in all of *Pickering*'s progeny, reflects both the historical evolvement of the rights of public employees, and the common-sense realization that government offices could not function if every employment decision became a constitutional matter.

For most of this century, the unchallenged dogma was that a public employee had no right to object to conditions placed upon the terms of employment—including those which restricted the exercise of constitutional rights. The classic formulation of this position was Justice Holmes, who, when sitting on the Supreme Judicial Court of Massachusetts, observed: "[A policeman] may have a constitutional right to talk politics, but he has no constitutional right to be a policeman." McAuliffe v. Mayor of New Bedford, 155 Mass. 216, 220, 29 N.E. 517, 517 (1892). For many years, Holmes' epigram expressed this Court's law. Adler v. Board of Education, 342 U.S. 485 (1952); Garner v. Los Angeles Bd. of Public Works, 341 U.S. 716 (1951); Public Workers v. Mitchell, 330 U.S. 75 (1947); United States v. Wurzbach, 280 U.S. 396 (1930); Ex parte Curtis, 106 U.S. 371 (1882).

The Court cast new light on the matter in a series of cases arising from the widespread efforts in the 1950s and early 1960s to require public employees, particularly teachers, to swear oaths of loyalty to the state and reveal the groups with which they associated. In Wieman v. Updegraff, 344 U.S. 183 (1952), the Court held that a State could not require its employees to establish their loyalty by extracting an oath denying past affiliation with Communists. In Cafeteria Workers v. McElroy, 367 U.S. 886 (1961), the Court recognized that the government could not deny employment because of previous membership in a particular party. See also Shelton v. Tucker, 364 U.S. 479, 490 (1960); Torcaso v. Watkins, 367 U.S. 488 (1961); Cramp v. Board of Public Instruction, 368 U.S. 278 (1961). By the time Sherbert v. Verner, 374 U.S. 398 (1963), was decided, it was already "too late in the day to doubt that the liberties of religion and expression may be infringed by the denial of or placing of conditions upon a benefit or privilege." Id., at 404. It was therefore no surprise when in Keyishian v. Board of Regents, [385 U.S. 589 (1967)], the Court invalidated New York statutes barring employment on the basis of membership in "subversive" organizations, observing that the theory that public employment which may be denied altogether may be subjected to any conditions, regardless of how unreasonable, had been uniformly rejected. Id., at 605–606.

In all of these cases, the precedents in which *Pickering* is rooted, the invalidated statutes and actions sought to suppress the rights of public employees to participate in public affairs. The issue was whether government employees could be prevented or "chilled" by the fear of discharge from joining political parties and other associations that certain public officials might find "subversive." . . .

Pickering v. Board of Education, supra, followed from this understanding of the First Amendment. In *Pickering,* the Court held impermissible under the First Amendment the dismissal of a high school teacher for openly criticizing the Board of Education on its allocation of school funds between athletics and education and its methods of informing taxpayers about the need for additional revenue. Pickering's subject was "a matter of legitimate public concern" upon which "free and open debate is vital to informed decision-making by the electorate." . . .

Our cases following *Pickering* also involved safeguarding speech on matters of public concern. The controversy in Perry v. Sindermann, 408 U.S. 593

(1972), arose from the failure to rehire a teacher in the state college system who had testified before committees of the Texas Legislature and had become involved in public disagreement over whether the college should be elevated to 4–year status—a change opposed by the Regents. In Mt. Healthy City Board of Ed. v. Doyle, 429 U.S. 274 (1977), a public school teacher was not rehired because, allegedly, he had relayed to a radio station the substance of a memorandum relating to teacher dress and appearance that the school principal had circulated to various teachers. The memorandum was apparently prompted by the view of some in the administration that there was a relationship between teacher appearance and public support for bond issues, and indeed, the radio station promptly announced the adoption of the dress code as a news item. Most recently, in Givhan v. Western Line Consolidated School District, 439 U.S. 410 (1979), we held that First Amendment protection applies when a public employee arranges to communicate privately with his employer rather than to express his views publicly. Although the subject-matter of Mrs. Givhan's statements were not the issue before the Court, it is clear that her statements concerning the school district's allegedly racially discriminatory policies involved a matter of public concern.

Pickering, its antecedents and progeny, lead us to conclude that if Myer's questionnaire cannot be fairly characterized as constituting speech on a matter of public concern, it is unnecessary for us to scrutinize the reasons for her discharge. When employee expression cannot be fairly considered as relating to any matter of political, social, or other concern to the community, government officials should enjoy wide latitude in managing their offices, without intrusive oversight by the judiciary in the name of the First Amendment. Perhaps the government employer's dismissal of the worker may not be fair, but ordinary dismissals from government service which violate no fixed tenure or applicable statute or regulation are not subject to judicial review even if the reasons for the dismissal are alleged to be mistaken or unreasonable. Board of Regents v. Roth, 408 U.S. 564 (1972); Perry v. Sindermann, [408 U.S. 593 (1972)]; Bishop v. Wood, 426 U.S. 341, 349–350 (1976).

We do not suggest, however, that Myers' speech, even if not touching upon a matter of public concern, is totally beyond the protection of the First Amendment. . . . For example, an employee's false criticism of his employer on grounds not of public concern may be cause for his discharge but would be entitled to the same protection in a libel action accorded an identical statement made by a man on the street. We hold only that when a public employee speaks not as a citizen upon matters of public concern, but instead as an employee upon matters only of personal interest, absent the most unusual circumstances, a federal court is not the appropriate forum in which to review the wisdom of a personnel decision taken by a public agency allegedly in reaction to the employee's behavior. Cf. Bishop v. Wood, [426 U.S. 341], 349–350, [(1976)]. Our responsibility is to ensure that citizens are not deprived of fundamental rights by virtue of working for the government; this does not require a grant of immunity for employee grievances not afforded by the First Amendment to those who do not work for the State.

Whether an employee's speech addresses a matter of public concern must be determined by the content, form, and context of a given statement, as revealed by the whole record. In this case, with but one exception, the questions posed by Myers to her co-workers do not fall under the rubric of matters of "public concern." We view the questions pertaining to the confidence and trust that Myers' coworkers possess in various supervisors, the level of office morale, and the need for a grievance committee as mere extensions of Myers' dispute over her transfer to another section of the criminal court.

Unlike the dissent, we do not believe these questions are of public import in evaluating the performance of the District Attorney as an elected official. Myers did not seek to inform the public that the District Attorney's Office was not discharging its governmental responsibilities in the investigation and prosecution of criminal cases. Nor did Myers seek to bring to light actual or potential wrongdoing or breach of public trust on the part of Connick and others. Indeed, the questionnaire, if released to the public, would convey no information at all other than the fact that a single employee is upset with the status quo. While discipline and morale in the workplace are related to an agency's efficient performance of its duties, the focus of Myers' questions is not to evaluate the performance of the office but rather to gather ammunition for another round of controversy with her superiors. These questions reflect one employee's dissatisfaction with a transfer and an attempt to turn that displeasure into a cause célèbre.[8]

To presume that all matters which transpire within a government office are of public concern would mean that virtually every remark—and certainly every criticism directed at a public official—would plant the seed of a constitutional case. While as a matter of good judgment, public officials should be receptive to constructive criticism offered by their employees, the First Amendment does not require a public office to be run as a roundtable for employee complaints over internal office affairs.

One question in Myers' questionnaire, however, does touch upon a matter of public concern. Question 11 inquires if assistant district attorneys "ever feel pressured to work in political campaigns on behalf of office supported candidates." We have recently noted that official pressure upon employees to work for political candidates not of the worker's own choice constitutes a coercion of belief in violation of fundamental constitutional rights. Branti v. Finkel, 445 U.S. [507], 515–516 [(1980)]; Elrod v. Burns, 427 U.S. 347 (1976). In addition, there is a demonstrated interest in this country that government service should depend upon meritorious performance rather than political service. CSC v. Letter Carriers, 413 U.S. 548 (1973); Public Workers v. Mitchell, 330 U.S. 75 (1947). Given this history, we believe it apparent that the issue of whether assistant district attorneys are pressured to work in political campaigns is a matter of interest to the community upon which it is essential that public employees be able to speak out freely without fear of retaliatory dismissal.

B

Because one of the questions in Myers' survey touched upon a matter of public concern and contributed to her discharge, we must determine whether Connick was justified in discharging Myers. Here the District Court again erred in imposing an unduly onerous burden on the State to justify Myers' discharge. The District Court viewed the issue of whether Myers' speech was upon a matter of "public concern" as a threshold inquiry, after which it became the government's burden to "clearly demonstrate" that the speech involved "substantially interfered" with official responsibilities. Yet *Pickering* unmistakably states, and respondent agrees, that the State's burden in justifying a particular discharge varies depending upon the nature of the employee's expression.

---

[8] This is not a case like *Givhan,* supra, where an employee speaks out as a citizen on a matter of general concern, not tied to a personal employment dispute, but arranges to do so privately. Mrs. Givhan's right to protest racial discrimination—a matter inherently of public concern—is not forfeited by her choice of a private forum.... Here, however, a questionnaire not otherwise of public concern does not attain that status because its subject matter could, in different circumstances, have been the topic of a communication to the public that might be of general interest....

Although such particularized balancing is difficult, the courts must reach the most appropriate possible balance of the competing interests.

C

The *Pickering* balance requires full consideration of the government's interest in the effective and efficient fulfillment of its responsibilities to the public. . . .

We agree with the District Court that there is no demonstration here that the questionnaire impeded Myers' ability to perform her responsibilities. The District Court was also correct to recognize that "it is important to the efficient and successful operation of the District Attorney's office for Assistants to maintain close working relationships with their superiors." . . . Connick's judgment, and apparently also that of his first assistant Dennis Waldron, who characterized Myers' actions as causing a "mini-insurrection," was that Myers' questionnaire was an act of insubordination which interfered with working relationships. When close working relationships are essential to fulfilling public responsibilities, a wide degree of deference to the employer's judgment is appropriate. Furthermore, we do not see the necessity for an employer to allow events to unfold to the extent that the disruption of the office and the destruction of working relationships is manifest before taking action. We caution that a stronger showing may be necessary if the employee's speech more substantially involved matters of public concern.

. . .

Also relevant is the manner, time, and place in which the questionnaire was distributed. As noted in *Givhan v. Western Line Consolidated School District,* . . . "Private expression . . . may in some situations bring additional factors to the *Pickering* calculus. When a government employee personally confronts his immediate superior, the employing agency's institutional efficiency may be threatened not only by the content of the employee's message but also by the manner, time, and place in which it is delivered." Here the questionnaire was prepared and distributed at the office; the manner of distribution required not only Myers to leave her work but for others to do the same in order that the questionnaire be completed. Although some latitude in when official work is performed is to be allowed when professional employees are involved, and Myers did not violate announced office policy, the fact that Myers, unlike Pickering, exercised her rights to speech at the office supports Connick's fears that the functioning of his office was endangered.

Finally, the context in which the dispute arose is also significant. This is not a case where an employee, out of purely academic interest, circulated a questionnaire so as to obtain useful research. Myers acknowledges that it is no coincidence that the questionnaire followed upon the heels of the transfer notice. When employee speech concerning office policy arises from an employment dispute concerning the very application of that policy to the speaker, additional weight must be given to the supervisor's view that the employee has threatened the authority of the employer to run the office. Although we accept the District Court's factual finding that Myers' reluctance to accede to the transfer order was not a sufficient cause in itself for her dismissal, and thus does not constitute a sufficient defense under Mt. Healthy City Board of Ed. v. Doyle, 429 U.S. 274 (1977), this does not render irrelevant the fact that the questionnaire emerged after a persistent dispute between Myers and Connick and his deputies over office transfer policy.

III

Myers' questionnaire touched upon matters of public concern in only a most limited sense; her survey, in our view, is most accurately characterized as an employee grievance concerning internal office policy. The limited First Amendment interest involved here does not require that Connick tolerate action which he reasonably believed would disrupt the office, undermine his authority, and destroy close working relationships. Myers' discharge therefore did not offend the First Amendment. We reiterate, however, the caveat we expressed in *Pickering,* . . . : "Because of the enormous variety of fact situations in which critical statements by . . . public employees may be thought by their superiors . . . to furnish grounds for dismissal, we do not deem it either appropriate or feasible to lay down a general standard against which all such statements may be judged."

Our holding today is grounded in our longstanding recognition that the First Amendment's primary aim is the full protection of speech upon issues of public concern, as well as the practical realities involved in the administration of a government office. Although today the balance is struck for the government, this is no defeat for the First Amendment. For it would indeed be a Pyrrhic victory for the great principles of free expression if the Amendment's safeguarding of a public employee's right, as a citizen, to participate in discussions concerning public affairs were confused with the attempt to constitutionalize the employee grievance that we see presented here. The judgment of the Court of Appeals is

Reversed.

Justice Brennan, with whom Justice Marshall, Justice Blackmun, and Justice Stevens join, dissenting.

. . . It is hornbook law . . . that speech about "the manner in which government is operated or should be operated" is an essential part of the communications necessary for self-governance the protection of which was a central purpose of the First Amendment. Mills v. Alabama, 384 U.S. 214, 218 (1966). Because the questionnaire addressed such matters and its distribution did not adversely affect the operations of the District Attorney's Office or interfere with Myers' working relationship with her fellow employees, I dissent.

I

. . .

The Court's decision today is flawed in three respects. First, the Court distorts the balancing analysis required under *Pickering* by suggesting that one factor, the context in which a statement is made, is to be weighed *twice*—first in determining whether an employee's speech addresses a matter of public concern and then in deciding whether the statement adversely affected the government's interest as an employer. Second, in concluding that the effect of respondent's personnel policies on employee morale and the work performance of the District Attorney's Office is not a matter of public concern, the Court impermissibly narrows the class of subjects on which public employees may speak out without fear of retaliatory dismissal. Third, the Court misapplies the *Pickering* balancing test in holding that Myers could constitutionally be dismissed for circulating a questionnaire addressed to at least one subject that *was* "a matter of interest to the community," in the absence of evidence that her conduct disrupted the efficient functioning of the District Attorney's Office.

II

. . .

The Court seeks to distinguish *Givhan* on the ground that speech protesting racial discrimination is "inherently of public concern." Ante, n. 8. In so doing, it suggests that there are two classes of speech of public concern: statements "of public import" because of their content, form and context, and statements that, by virtue of their subject matter, are "inherently of public concern." In my view, however, whether a particular statement by a public employee is addressed to a subject of public concern does not depend on where it was said or why. The First Amendment affords special protection to speech that may inform public debate about how our society is to be governed—regardless of whether it actually becomes the subject of a public controversy.

III

Although the Court finds most of Myers' questionnaire unrelated to matters of public interest, it does hold that one question . . . addressed a matter of public importance and concern. . . .the Court misapplies the *Pickering* test and holds—against our previous authorities—that a public employer's mere apprehension that speech will be disruptive justifies suppression of that speech when all the objective evidence suggests that those fears are essentially unfounded.

. . .

Such extreme deference to the employer's judgment is not appropriate when public employees voice critical views concerning the operations of the agency for which they work. . . . In order to protect public employees' First Amendment right to voice critical views on issues of public importance, the courts must make their own appraisal of the effects of the speech in question.

IV

The Court's decision today inevitably will deter public employees from making critical statements about the manner in which government agencies are operated for fear that doing so will provoke their dismissal. As a result, the public will be deprived of valuable information with which to evaluate the performance of elected officials. Because protecting the dissemination of such information is an essential function of the First Amendment, I dissent.

RANKIN v. MCPHERSON, 483 U.S. 378 (1987). McPherson was a clerical employee in a county constable's office. On hearing a radio report of the attempted assassination of President Reagan in March, 1981, she said to a fellow employee: "If they go for him again, I hope they get him." The Court held that McPherson's discharge violated the First Amendment. The statement was speech on a matter of public concern, and did not constitute a threat to kill the President. Asserted state interests did not outweigh McPherson's first amendment rights. Her duties were clerical, and discharge was not based on an assessment that the remark demonstrated a character trait that made her unfit to perform that work. The remark did not disrupt the operation of the office, nor was there danger that it had discredited the office. Justice Marshall's opinion for the court concluded:

> "We cannot believe that every employee in Constable Rankin's office, whether computer operator, electrician, or file clerk, is equally required, on pain of discharge, to avoid any statement susceptible of being interpreted by the Constable as an indication that the employee may be unworthy of

employment in his law enforcement agency. At some point, such concerns are so removed from the effective functioning of the public employer that they cannot prevail over the free speech rights of the public employee."

Justice Powell's concurrence remarked that in the case of private speech in the workplace on matters of public concern "it will be an unusual case" where discharge can be justified.

"The risk that a single, offhand comment directed to only one other worker will lower morale, disrupt the work force, or otherwise undermine the mission of the office borders on the fanciful."

Justice Scalia, joined by Chief Justice Rehnquist and Justices White and O'Connor, dissented. The question was whether McPherson could "ride with the cops and cheer for the robbers." Although the first amendment would prohibit criminal punishment for a statement expressing approval of a serious and violent crime, such a statement is not speech on a matter of public concern. Even if the statement was speech on a matter of public concern, the discharge was justified by interests in maintaining an esprit de corps and a proper public image for a law enforcement office.

United States Civil Service Commission v. National Association of Letter Carriers AFL–CIO

413 U.S. 548, 93 S.Ct. 2880, 37 L.Ed.2d 796 (1973).

Mr. Justice White delivered the opinion of the Court.

... [Section] 9(a) of the Hatch Act, now codified in 5 U.S.C. § 7324(a)(2), [prohibits] federal employees taking "an active part in political management or in political campaigns," ... A divided three-judge court sitting in the District of Columbia had held the section unconstitutional. We reverse the judgment of the District Court.

I

The case began when the National Association of Letter Carriers, six individual federal employees and certain local Democratic and Republican political committees filed a complaint, asserting on behalf of themselves and all federal employees that 5 U.S.C. § 7324(a)(2) was unconstitutional on its face and seeking an injunction against its enforcement.

. . .

II

As the District Court recognized, the constitutionality of the Hatch Act's ban on taking an active part in political management or political campaigns has been here before. This very prohibition was attacked in [United Public Workers v. Mitchell, 330 U.S. 75 (1947)] . . .

. . .

We unhesitatingly reaffirm the *Mitchell* holding that Congress had, and has, the power to prevent Mr. Poole and others like him from holding a party office, working at the polls, and acting as party paymaster for other party workers. An Act of Congress going no farther would in our view unquestionably be valid. So would it be if, in plain and understandable language, the statute forbade activities such as organizing a political party or club; actively participating in fund-raising activities for a partisan candidate or political party;

becoming a partisan candidate for, or campaigning for, an elective public office; actively managing the campaign of a partisan candidate for public office; initiating or circulating a partisan nominating petition or soliciting votes for a partisan candidate for public office; or serving as a delegate, alternate or proxy to a political party convention. Our judgment is that neither the First Amendment nor any other provision of the Constitution invalidates a law barring this kind of partisan political conduct by federal employees.

. . .

Until now, the judgment of Congress, the Executive, and the country appears to have been that partisan political activities by federal employees must be limited if the Government is to operate effectively and fairly, elections are to play their proper part in representative government, and employees themselves are to be sufficiently free from improper influences. E.g., 84 Cong.Rec. 9598, 9603; 86 Cong.Rec. 2360, 2621, 2864, 9376. The restrictions so far imposed on federal employees are not aimed at particular parties, groups, or points of view, but apply equally to all partisan activities of the type described. They discriminate against no racial, ethnic or religious minorities. Nor do they seek to control political opinions or beliefs, or to interfere with or influence anyone's vote at the polls.

But as the Court held in Pickering v. Board of Education, 391 U.S. 563, 568 (1968), the government has an interest in regulating the conduct and "the speech of its employees that differ[s] significantly from those it possesses in connection with regulation of the speech of the citizenry in general. The problem in any case is to arrive at a balance between the interest of the [employee], as a citizen, in commenting upon matters of public concern and the interest of the [government], as an employer, in promoting the efficiency of the public services it performs through its employees." Although Congress is free to strike a different balance than it has, if it so chooses, we think the balance it has so far struck is sustainable by the obviously important interests sought to be served by the limitations on partisan political activities now contained in the Hatch Act.

. . .

. . . We agree with the basic holding of *Mitchell* that plainly identifiable acts of political management and political campaigning on the part of federal employees may constitutionally be prohibited. Until now this has been the judgment of the lower federal courts, and we do not understand the District Court in this case to have questioned the constitutionality of a law that was specifically limited to prohibiting the conduct in which Mr. Poole in the *Mitchell* case admittedly engaged.

III

But however constitutional the proscription of identifiable partisan conduct in understandable language may be, the District Court's judgment was that § 7324(a)(2) was both unconstitutionally vague and fatally overbroad. Appellees make the same contentions here, but we cannot agree that the section is unconstitutional on its face for either reason. . . .

. . . [J]udgment . . . reversed.

United States v. National Treasury Employees Union

513 U.S. 454, 115 S.Ct. 1003, 130 L.Ed.2d 964 (1995).

Justice Stevens delivered the opinion of the Court.

In 1989 Congress enacted a law that broadly prohibits federal employees from accepting any compensation for making speeches or writing articles. The prohibition applies even when neither the subject of the speech or article nor the person or group paying for it has any connection with the employee's official duties. We must decide whether that statutory prohibition comports with the Constitution's command that "Congress shall make no law ... abridging the freedom of speech." We hold that it does not.

I

In 1967 Congress authorized the appointment every four years of a special Commission on Executive, Legislative, and Judicial Salaries, whose principal function would be to recommend appropriate levels of compensation for the top positions in all three branches of the Federal Government. Each of the first five quadrennial commissions recommended significant salary increases, but those recommendations went largely ignored. The Report of the 1989 Quadrennial Commission, however, was instrumental in leading to the enactment of the Ethics Reform Act of 1989, which contains the provision challenged in this case.

The 1989 Quadrennial Commission's report noted that inflation had decreased the salary levels for senior Government officials, measured in constant dollars, by approximately 35% since 1969. The report "also found that because their salaries are so inadequate, many members of Congress are supplementing their official compensation by accepting substantial amounts of 'honoraria' for meeting with interest groups which desire to influence their votes. Albeit to a less troubling extent, the practice of accepting honoraria also extends to top officials of the Executive and Judicial branches." ... Accordingly, the Commission recommended that "salary levels for top officials be set at approximately the same amount in constant dollars" as those in effect in 1969 and further that "Congress enact legislation abolishing the practice of accepting honoraria in all three branches." ...

The President's Commission on Federal Ethics Law Reform subsequently issued a report that endorsed the Quadrennial Commission's views. ...

Although not adopted in their entirety, the two Commissions' recommendations echo prominently in the Ethics Reform Act of 1989. Section 703 of that Act provided a 25% pay increase to Members of Congress, federal judges, and Executive Branch employees above the salary grade GS–15. ...Another section—the one at issue here—amended § 501(b) of the Ethics in Government Act of 1978 to create an "Honoraria Prohibition," which reads: "An individual may not receive any honorarium while that individual is a Member, officer or employee."

Section 505 of the Ethics Reform Act defined "officer or employee" to include nearly all employees of the Federal Government and "Member" to include any Representative, Delegate, or Resident Commissioner to Congress. The Congressional Operations Appropriations Act, 1992, extended both the salary increase and the prohibition against honoraria to the Senate. The 1989 Act defined "honorarium" to encompass any compensation paid to a Government employee for "an appearance, speech or article." The 1992 Appropriations Act amended that definition to exclude any series of appearances, speeches, or articles unrelated to the employee's official duties or status. The definition now reads as follows:

"(3) The term 'honorarium' means a payment of money or any thing of value for an appearance, speech or article (including a series of appearances, speeches, or articles if the subject matter is directly related to the individual's official duties or the payment is made because of the individual's status with the Government) by a Member, officer or employee, excluding any actual and necessary travel expenses incurred by such individual (and one relative) to the extent that such expenses are paid or reimbursed by any other person, and the amount otherwise determined shall be reduced by the amount of any such expenses to the extent that such expenses are not paid or reimbursed." ...

. . .

II

Two unions and several career civil servants employed full-time by various Executive departments and agencies filed suit in the United States District Court for the District of Columbia to challenge the constitutionality of the honoraria ban ...

. . .

The District Court granted respondents' motion for summary judgment, held the statute "unconstitutional insofar as it applies to Executive Branch employees of the United States government," and enjoined the Government from enforcing the statute against any Executive Branch employee. ...

The Court of Appeals affirmed. ...

. . .

III

Federal employees who write for publication in their spare time have made significant contributions to the marketplace of ideas. They include literary giants like Nathaniel Hawthorne and Herman Melville, who were employed by the Customs Service; Walt Whitman, who worked for the Departments of Justice and Interior; and Bret Harte, an employee of the Mint. Respondents have yet to make comparable contributions to American culture, but they share with these great artists important characteristics that are relevant to the issue we confront.

Even though respondents work for the Government, they have not relinquished "the First Amendment rights they would otherwise enjoy as citizens to comment on matters of public interest." Pickering v. Board of Ed. of Township High School Dist., 391 U.S. 563, 568 (1968). They seek compensation for their expressive activities in their capacity as citizens, not as Government employees. They claim their employment status has no more bearing on the quality or market value of their literary output than it did on that of Hawthorne or Melville. With few exceptions, the content of respondents' messages has nothing to do with their jobs and does not even arguably have any adverse impact on the efficiency of the offices in which they work. They do not address audiences composed of co-workers or supervisors; instead, they write or speak for segments of the general public. Neither the character of the authors, the subject matter of their expression, the effect of the content of their expression on their official duties, nor the kind of audiences they address has any relevance to their employment.

In *Pickering* and a number of other cases we have recognized that Congress may impose restraints on the job-related speech of public employees that would be plainly unconstitutional if applied to the public at large. ... When a court is required to determine the validity of such a restraint, it must "arrive at a balance between the interests of the [employee], as a citizen, in commenting upon matters of public concern and the interest of the State, as an employer, in promoting the efficiency of the public services it performs through its employees." *Pickering*, 391 U.S., at 568.

... Respondents' expressive activities in this case fall within the protected category of citizen comment on matters of public concern rather than employee comment on matters related to personal status in the workplace. The speeches and articles for which they received compensation in the past were addressed to a public audience, were made outside the workplace, and involved content largely unrelated to their government employment.

The sweep of § 501(b) makes the Government's burden heavy. Unlike *Pickering* and its progeny, this case does not involve a post hoc analysis of one employee's speech and its impact on that employee's public responsibilities. ...Rather, the Government asks us to apply *Pickering* to Congress' wholesale deterrent to a broad category of expression by a massive number of potential speakers. In Civil Service Comm'n v. Letter Carriers, 413 U.S. 548 (1973), we established that the Government must be able to satisfy a balancing test of the *Pickering* form to maintain a statutory restriction on employee speech. Because the discussion in that case essentially restated in balancing terms our approval of the Hatch Act in Public Workers v. Mitchell, 330 U.S. 75 (1947), we did not determine how the components of the *Pickering* balance should be analyzed in the context of a sweeping statutory impediment to speech.

We normally accord a stronger presumption of validity to a congressional judgment than to an individual executive's disciplinary action. ...The widespread impact of the honoraria ban, however, gives rise to far more serious concerns than could any single supervisory decision. In addition, unlike an adverse action taken in response to actual speech, this ban chills potential speech before it happens. Cf. Near v. Minnesota ex rel. Olson, 283 U.S. 697 (1931). For these reasons, the Government's burden is greater with respect to this statutory restriction on expression than with respect to an isolated disciplinary action. The Government must show that the interests of both potential audiences and a vast group of present and future employees in a broad range of present and future expression are outweighed by that expression's "necessary impact on the actual operation" of the Government. *Pickering*, 391 U.S., at 571.

Although § 501(b) neither prohibits any speech nor discriminates among speakers based on the content or viewpoint of their messages, its prohibition on compensation unquestionably imposes a significant burden on expressive activity. ...Publishers compensate authors because compensation provides a significant incentive toward more expression. By denying respondents that incentive, the honoraria ban induces them to curtail their expression if they wish to continue working for the Government.

The ban imposes a far more significant burden on respondents than on the relatively small group of lawmakers whose past receipt of honoraria motivated its enactment. The absorbing and time-consuming responsibilities of legislators and policymaking executives leave them little opportunity for research or creative expression on subjects unrelated to their official responsibilities. Such officials often receive invitations to appear and talk about subjects related to their work because of their official identities. In contrast, invitations to rank-and-file employees usually depend only on the market value of their messages. The honoraria ban is unlikely to reduce significantly the number of appearances by high-ranking officials as long as travel expense reimbursement for the speaker and one relative is available as an alternative form of remuneration. In contrast, the denial of compensation for lower-paid, nonpolicymaking employees will inevitably diminish their expressive output.

The large-scale disincentive to Government employees' expression also imposes a significant burden on the public's right to read and hear what the employees would otherwise have written and said. ...We have no way to measure the true cost of that burden, but we cannot ignore the risk that it might deprive us of the work of a future Melville or Hawthorne. The honoraria ban imposes the kind of burden that abridges speech under the First Amendment.

IV

Because the vast majority of the speech at issue in this case does not involve the subject matter of government employment and takes place outside the workplace, the Government is unable to justify § 501(b) on the grounds of immediate workplace disruption asserted in *Pickering* and the cases that followed it. Instead, the Government submits that the ban comports with the First Amendment because the prohibited honoraria were "reasonably deemed by Congress to interfere with the efficiency of the public service." United Public Workers v. Mitchell, 330 U.S. 75, 101 (1947).

In *Mitchell* we upheld the prohibition of the Hatch Act, 5 U.S.C. § 7324(a)(2), on partisan political activity by all classified federal employees, including, for example, a skilled mechanic at the Mint named Poole who had no policymaking authority. We explained that "[t]here are hundreds of thousands of United States employees with positions no more influential upon policy determination than that of Mr. Poole. Evidently what Congress feared was the cumulative effect on employee morale of political activity by all employees who could be induced to participate actively." 330 U.S., at 101. In Civil Service Commn. v. Letter Carriers, 413 U.S. 548 (1973), we noted that enactment of the Hatch Act in 1939 reflected "the conviction that the rapidly expanding Government work force should not be employed to build a powerful, invincible, and perhaps corrupt political machine." ... An equally important concern was "to further serve the goal that employment and advancement in the Government service not depend on political performance, and at the same time to make sure that Government employees would be free from pressure and from express or tacit invitation to vote in a certain way or perform political chores in order to curry favor with their superiors rather than to act out their own beliefs." ...

Thus, the Hatch Act aimed to protect employees' rights, notably their right to free expression, rather than to restrict those rights. Like the Hatch Act, the honoraria ban affects hundreds of thousands of federal employees. Unlike partisan political activity, however, honoraria hardly appear to threaten employees' morale or liberty. Moreover, Congress effectively designed the Hatch Act to combat demonstrated ill effects of Government employees' partisan political activities. In contrast, the Government has failed to show how it serves the interests it asserts by applying the honoraria ban to respondents.

The Government's underlying concern is that federal officers not misuse or appear to misuse power by accepting compensation for their unofficial and nonpolitical writing and speaking activities. This interest is undeniably powerful, but the Government cites no evidence of misconduct related to honoraria in the vast rank and file of federal employees below grade GS–16. ...[T]he Government relies here on limited evidence of actual or apparent impropriety by legislators and high-level executives, together with the purported administrative costs of avoiding or detecting lower-level employees' violations of established policies.

... [T]he Government has based its defense of the ban on abuses of honoraria by Members of Congress. Congress reasonably could assume that payments of honoraria to judges or high-ranking officials in the Executive Branch might generate a similar appearance of improper influence. Congress could not, however, reasonably extend that assumption to all federal employees below Grade GS–16, an immense class of workers with negligible power to confer favors on those who might pay to hear them speak or to read their articles. A federal employee, such as a supervisor of mechanics at the Mint, might impair efficiency and morale by using political criteria to judge the performance of his or her staff. But one can envision scant harm, or appearance of harm, resulting from the same employee's accepting pay to lecture on the Quaker religion or to write dance reviews.

Although operational efficiency is undoubtedly a vital governmental interest, ... several features of the honoraria ban's text cast serious doubt on the Government's submission that Congress perceived honoraria as so threatening to the efficiency of the entire federal service as to render the ban a reasonable response to the threat. ...The first is the rather strange parenthetical reference to "a series of appearances, speeches, or articles" that the 1991 amendment inserted in the definition of the term "honorarium." The amended definition excludes such a series from the prohibited category unless "the subject matter is directly related to the individual's official duties or the payment is made because of the individual's status with the Government." In other words, accepting pay for a series of articles is prohibited if and only if a nexus exists between the author's employment and either the subject matter of the expression or the identity of the payor. For an individual article or speech, in contrast, pay is taboo even if neither the subject matter nor the payor bears any relationship at all to the author's duties.

Congress' decision to provide a total exemption for all unrelated series of speeches undermines application of the ban to individual speeches and articles with no nexus to Government employment. Absent such a nexus, no corrupt bargain or even appearance of impropriety appears likely. The Government's only argument against a general nexus limitation is that a wholesale prophylactic rule is easier to enforce than one that requires individual nexus determinations. The nexus limitation for series, however, unambiguously reflects a congressional judgment that agency ethics officials and the OGE can enforce the statute when it includes a nexus test. A blanket burden on the speech of nearly 1.7 million federal employees requires a much stronger justification than the Government's dubious claim of administrative convenience.

The definition's limitation of "honoraria" to expressive activities also undermines the Government's submission that the breadth of § 501 is reasonably necessary to protect the efficiency of the public service. Both Commissions that recommended the ban stressed the importance of defining honoraria in a way that would close "potential loopholes such as receipt of consulting, professional or similar fees; payments for serving on boards; travel; sport, or other entertainment expenses not reasonably necessary for the appearance involved; or any other benefit that is the substantial equivalent of an honorarium." Those recommendations reflected a considered judgment that compensation for "an appearance, speech or article" poses no greater danger than compensation for other services that a Government employee might perform in his or her spare time. Congress, however, chose to restrict only expressive activities. One might reasonably argue that expressive activities, because they occupy a favored position in the constitutional firmament, should be exempt from even a comprehensive ban on outside income. Imposing a greater burden on speech than on other off-duty activities assumed to pose the same threat to the efficiency of the federal service is, at best, anomalous.

The fact that § 501 singles out expressive activity for special regulation heightens the Government's burden of justification. . . . The Government has not persuaded us that § 501(b) is a reasonable response to the posited harms.

We also attach significance to the OGE regulations that limit the coverage of the statutory terms "appearance, speech or article." 5 CFR § 2636.203 (1994). The regulations exclude a wide variety of performances and writings that would normally appear to have no nexus with an employee's job, such as sermons, fictional writings, and athletic competitions, countermanding the Commissions' recommendation that an even more inclusive honoraria ban would be appropriate. The exclusions, of course, make the task of the OGE and agency ethics officials somewhat easier, but they "diminish the credibility of the government's rationale" that paying lower-level employees for speech entirely unrelated to their work jeopardizes the efficiency of the entire federal service. We recognize our obligation to defer to considered congressional judgments about matters such as appearances of impropriety, but on the record of this case we must attach greater weight to the powerful and realistic presumption that the federal work force consists of dedicated and honorable civil servants. The exclusions in the OGE regulations are more consistent with that presumption than with the honoraria ban's dubious application not merely to policymakers, whose loss of honoraria was offset by a salary increase, but to all Executive Branch employees below Grade GS–16 as well.

These anomalies in the text of the statute and regulations underscore our conclusion: the speculative benefits the honoraria ban may provide the Government are not sufficient to justify this crudely crafted burden on respondents' freedom to engage in expressive activities. Section 501(b) violates the First Amendment.

V

After holding § 501(b) invalid because it was not as carefully tailored as it should have been, the Court of Appeals approved a remedy that is itself arguably overinclusive. The relief granted by the District Court and upheld by the Court of Appeals enjoined enforcement of the entire honoraria ban as applied to the entire Executive Branch of the Government. That injunction provides relief to senior executives who are not parties to this case. It also prohibits enforcement of the statute even when an obvious nexus exists between the employee's job and either the subject matter of his or her expression or the interest of the person paying for it. As an alternative to its request for outright reversal, the Government asks us to modify the judgment by upholding the statute as it applies, first, to employees not party to this action and, second, to situations in which a nexus is present.

For three reasons, we agree with the Government's first suggestion—that the relief should be limited to the parties before the Court. First, although the occasional case requires us to entertain a facial challenge in order to vindicate a party's right not to be bound by an unconstitutional statute, . . . we neither want nor need to provide relief to nonparties when a narrower remedy will fully protect the litigants. . . . In this case, granting full relief to . . . Executive Branch employees below Grade GS–16 does not require passing on the applicability of § 501(b) to the senior executives who received a 25 percent salary increase that offsets the honoraria ban's disincentive to speak and write. Second, the Government conceivably might advance a different justification for an honoraria ban limited to more senior officials, thus presenting a different constitutional question than the one we decide today. Third, as the Court of Appeals recognized, its remedy required it to tamper with the text of the statute, a practice we strive to avoid.

Our obligation to avoid judicial legislation also persuades us to reject the Government's second suggestion—that we modify the remedy by crafting a nexus requirement for the honoraria ban. We cannot be sure that our attempt to redraft the statute to limit its coverage to cases involving an undesirable nexus between the speaker's official duties and either the subject matter of the speaker's expression or the identity of the payor would correctly identify the nexus Congress would have adopted in a more limited honoraria ban. We cannot know whether Congress accurately reflected its sense of an appropriate nexus in the terse, 33–word parenthetical statement with which it exempted series of speeches and articles from the definition of honoraria in the 1991 amendment; in an elaborate, nearly 600–word provision with which it later exempted Department of Defense military school faculty and students from the ban; or in neither. The process of drawing a proper nexus, even more than the defense of the statute's application to senior employees, would likely raise independent constitutional concerns whose adjudication is unnecessary to decide this case. We believe the Court of Appeals properly left to Congress the task of drafting a narrower statute.

Insofar as the judgment of the Court of Appeals affirms the injunction against enforcement of § 501(b) against respondents, it is affirmed; insofar as it grants relief to parties not before the Court, it is reversed. The case is remanded for further proceedings consistent with this opinion.

It is so ordered.

Justice O'Connor, concurring in the judgment in part and dissenting in part.

Although I agree that aspects of the honoraria ban run afoul of the First Amendment, I write separately for two reasons. First, I wish to emphasize my understanding of how our precedents ... direct the Court's conclusion. Second, I write to express my disagreement with the Court's remedy, which in my view paints with too broad a brush.

I

. . .

The Government, when it acts as employer, possesses substantial leeway; in appropriate circumstances, it may restrain speech that the Constitution would otherwise protect. ...In this case, however, the Government has exceeded the limits of its latitude. The bare assertion of interest in a wide-ranging prophylactic ban here, without any showing that Congress considered empirical or anecdotal data pertaining to abuses by lower-echelon executive employees, cannot suffice to outweigh the substantial burden on the 1.7 million affected employees. I agree with the Court that § 501 is unconstitutional to the extent that it bars this class of employees from receiving honoraria for expressive activities that bear no nexus to government employment.

II

The class before us is defined by pay scale, not by its members' propensity to write articles without nexus to government employment. As to any member of the class, the honoraria ban may have unconstitutional applications. But the ban may be susceptible of constitutional application to every member of the class, as well. We do not decide the question—a far harder case for respondents, in my view—whether it is constitutional to apply the honoraria ban to speech by this class that bears a relationship to government employment. I believe that the Court overlooks this nuance when it enjoins all enforcement of § 501 against the class, any one of whose members may, in the future, receive honoraria for work-related activities. I would give respondents relief tailored to what they request: invalidation of the statute insofar as it applies to honoraria they receive for speech without nexus to government employment. . . .

. . .

The Court assumes that it would venture into judicial legislation were it to invalidate the provision as it applies to no-nexus speech. But it is equally if not more inconsistent with congressional intent to strike a greater portion of the statute than is necessary to remedy the problem at hand. . . .

. . .

In sum, I agree with the Court that § 501 is unconstitutional insofar as it bars the respondent class of Executive Branch employees from receiving honoraria for nonwork-related speeches, appearances, and articles. In contrast to the Court, I would hold § 501 invalid only to that extent.

Chief Justice Rehnquist, with whom Justice Scalia and Justice Thomas join, dissenting.

I believe that the Court's opinion is seriously flawed in two respects. First, its application of the First Amendment understates the weight which should be accorded to the governmental justifications for the honoraria ban and over-states the amount of speech which actually will be deterred. Second, its discussion of the impact of the statute which it strikes down is carefully limited to only a handful of the most appealing individual situations, but when it deals with the remedy it suddenly shifts gears and strikes down the statute as applied to the entire class of Executive Branch employees below grade GS–16. I therefore dissent.

I

. . .

. . . I cannot say that the balance that Congress has struck between its interests and the interests of its employees to receive compensation for their First Amendment expression is unreasonable. . . .

The Court largely ignores the Government's foremost interest—prevention of impropriety and the appearance of impropriety—by focusing solely on the burdens of the statute as applied to several carefully selected Executive Branch employees whose situations present the application of the statute where the Government's interests are at their lowest ebb . . .

. . .

. . . The theory underlying the Court's distinction—that federal employees below grade GS–16 have negligible power to confer favors on those who might pay to hear them speak or to read their articles—is seriously flawed. Tax examiners, bank examiners, enforcement officials, or any number of federal employees have substantial power to confer favors even though their compensation level is below Grade GS–16.

Furthermore, we rejected the same distinction in Public Workers v. Mitchell . . .

The Court dismisses the Hatch Act experience as irrelevant, because it aimed to protect employees' rights, notably their right to free expression, rather than to restrict those rights. This is, indeed, a strange characterization of § 9(a) of the Hatch Act. ...[I]t can hardly be said that the Act protected the rights of workers who wished to engage in partisan political activity. ...

The Government's related concern regarding the difficulties that would attach in administering a case-by-case analysis of the propriety of particular honoraria also supports the honoraria ban's validity. ...

. . .

Unlike our prototypical application of *Pickering* which normally involves a response to the content of employee speech, the honoraria ban prohibits no speech and is unrelated to the message or the viewpoint expressed by the government employee. ...Furthermore, the honoraria ban exempts from its prohibition travel and other expenses related to employee speech. ...Because there is only a limited burden on respondents' First Amendment rights, Congress reasonably could have determined that its paramount interests in preventing impropriety and the appearance of impropriety in its work force justified the honoraria ban. ...

. . .

II

... Even if I agreed that application of the honoraria ban to expressive activity unrelated to an employee's Government employment violated the First Amendment, I could not agree with the Court's remedy.

. . .

... I would affirm the Court of Appeals only insofar as its judgment affirmed the injunction against the enforcement of § 501(b) as applied to Executive Branch employees below grade GS–16 who seek honoraria that are unrelated to their Government employment.

Rutan v. Republican Party of Illinois

497 U.S. 62, 110 S.Ct. 2729, 111 L.Ed.2d 52 (1990).

Justice Brennan delivered the opinion of the Court.

To the victor belong only those spoils that may be constitutionally obtained. Elrod v. Burns, 427 U.S. 347 (1976), and Branti v. Finkel, 445 U.S. 507 (1980), decided that the First Amendment forbids government officials to discharge or threaten to discharge public employees solely for not being supporters of the political party in power, unless party affiliation is an appropriate requirement for the position involved. Today we are asked to decide the constitutionality of several related political patronage practices—whether promotion, transfer, recall, and hiring decisions involving low-level public employees may be constitutionally based on party affiliation and support. We hold that they may not.

I

The petition and cross-petition before us arise from a lawsuit protesting certain employment policies and practices instituted by Governor James Thompson of Illinois. On November 12, 1980, the Governor issued an executive order proclaiming a hiring freeze for every agency, bureau, board, or commission subject to his control. The order prohibits state officials from hiring any employee, filling any vacancy, creating any new position, or taking any similar action ... without the Governor's "express permission after submission of appropriate requests to [his] office." ...

Requests for the Governor's "express permission" have allegedly become routine. Permission has been granted or withheld through an agency expressly created for this purpose, the Governor's Office of Personnel (Governor's Office). ...

By means of the freeze, according to petitioners, the Governor has been using the Governor's Office to operate a political patronage system to limit state employment and beneficial employment-related decisions to those who are supported by the Republican Party. In reviewing an agency's request that a particular applicant be approved for a particular position, the Governor's Office has looked at whether the applicant voted in Republican primaries in past election years, whether the applicant has provided financial or other support to the Republican Party and its candidates, whether the applicant has promised to join and work for the Republican Party in the future, and whether the applicant has the support of Republican Party officials at state or local levels.

Five people (including the three petitioners) brought suit against various Illinois and Republican Party officials in the United States District Court for the Central District of Illinois. ... Cynthia B. Rutan has been working for the State since 1974 as a rehabilitation counselor. She claims that since 1981 she has been repeatedly denied promotions to supervisory positions for which she was qualified because she had not worked for or supported the Republican Party. Franklin Taylor, who operates road equipment for the Illinois Department of Transportation, claims that he was denied a promotion in 1983 because he did not have the support of the local Republican Party. Taylor also maintains that he was denied a transfer to an office nearer to his home because of opposition from the Republican Party chairmen in the counties in which he worked and to which he requested a transfer. James W. Moore claims that he has been repeatedly denied state employment as a prison guard because he did not have the support of Republican Party officials.

The two other plaintiffs, before the Court as cross-respondents, allege that they were not recalled after layoffs because they lacked Republican credentials. Ricky Standefer was a state garage worker who claims that he was not recalled, although his fellow employees were, because he had voted in a Democratic primary and did not have the support of the Republican Party. Dan O'Brien, formerly a dietary manager with the mental health department, contends that he was not recalled after a layoff because of his party affiliation and that he later obtained a lower paying position with the corrections department only after receiving support from the chairman of the local Republican Party.

The District Court dismissed the complaint ... Noting that this Court had previously determined that the patronage practice of discharging public employees on the basis of their political affiliation violates the First Amendment, the Court of Appeals held that other patronage practices violate the First Amendment only when they are the "substantial equivalent of a dismissal." ...

. . .

II

A

In *Elrod*, supra, we decided that a newly elected Democratic sheriff could not constitutionally engage in the patronage practice of replacing certain office staff with members of his own party "when the existing employees lack or fail to obtain requisite support from, or fail to affiliate with, that party." ... The plurality explained that conditioning public employment on the provision of support for the favored political party "unquestionably inhibits protected belief and association." ... It reasoned that conditioning employment on political activity pressures employees to pledge political allegiance to a party with which they prefer not to associate, to work for the election of political candidates they do not support, and to contribute money to be used to further policies with which they do not agree. The latter, the plurality noted, had been recognized by this Court as "tantamount to coerced belief." ... At the same time, employees are constrained from joining, working for or contributing to the political party and candidates of their own choice.... "[P]olitical belief and association constitute the core of those activities protected by the First Amendment," the plurality emphasized. Both the plurality and the concurrence drew support from Perry v. Sindermann, 408 U.S. 593 (1972), in which this Court held that the State's refusal to renew a teacher's contract because he had been publicly critical of its policies imposed an unconstitutional condition on the receipt of a public benefit....

The Court then decided that the government interests generally asserted in support of patronage fail to justify this burden on First Amendment rights because patronage dismissals are not the least restrictive means for fostering those interests.... The plurality acknowledged that a government has a significant interest in ensuring that it has effective and efficient employees. It expressed doubt, however, that "mere difference of political persuasion motivates poor performance" and concluded that, in any case, the government can ensure employee effectiveness and efficiency through the less drastic means of discharging staff members whose work is inadequate.... The plurality also found that a government can meet its need for politically loyal employees to implement its policies by the less intrusive measure of dismissing, on political grounds, only those employees in policymaking positions.... Finally, although the plurality recognized that preservation of the democratic process "may in some instances justify limitations on First Amendment freedoms," it concluded that the "process functions as well without the practice, perhaps even better." Patronage, it explained, "can result in the entrenchment of one or a few parties to the exclusion of others" and "is a very effective impediment to the associational and speech freedoms which are essential to a meaningful system of democratic government." ...

Four years later, in *Branti,* supra, we decided that the First Amendment prohibited a newly appointed public defender, who was a Democrat, from discharging assistant public defenders because they did not have the support of the Democratic Party. The Court rejected an attempt to distinguish the case from *Elrod,* deciding that it was immaterial whether the public defender had attempted to coerce employees to change political parties or had only dismissed them on the basis of their private political beliefs. We explained that conditioning continued public employment on an employee's having obtained support from a particular political party violates the First Amendment because of "the coercion of belief that necessarily flows from the knowledge that one must have a sponsor in the dominant party in order to retain one's job." ... "In sum," we said, "there is no requirement that dismissed employees prove that they, or other employees, have been coerced into changing, either actually or ostensibly, their political allegiance." ... To prevail, we concluded, public employees need show only that they were discharged because they were not affiliated with or sponsored by the Democratic Party.... [5]

B

We first address the claims of the four current or former employees. Respondents urge us to view *Elrod* and *Branti* as inapplicable because the patronage dismissals at issue in those cases are different in kind from failure to promote, failure to transfer, and failure to recall after layoff. Respondents initially contend that the employee petitioners' First Amendment rights have not been infringed because they have no entitlement to promotion, transfer, or rehire. We rejected just such an argument in *Elrod* ... and *Branti*.... In *Perry,* ... we held explicitly that the plaintiff teacher's lack of a contractual or tenure right to re-employment was immaterial to his First Amendment claim....

. . .

Respondents next argue that the employment decisions at issue here do not violate the First Amendment because the decisions are not punitive, do not in any way adversely affect the terms of employment, and therefore do not chill the exercise of protected belief and association by public employees. This is not credible. Employees who find themselves in dead-end positions due to their political backgrounds are adversely affected. They will feel a significant obligation to support political positions held by their superiors, and to refrain from acting on the political views they actually hold, in order to progress up the career ladder. Employees denied transfers to workplaces reasonably close to their homes until they join and work for the Republican Party will feel a daily pressure from their long commutes to do so. And employees who have been laid off may well feel compelled to engage in whatever political activity is necessary to regain regular paychecks and positions corresponding to their skill and experience.

The same First Amendment concerns that underlay our decisions in *Elrod,* supra, and *Branti,* supra, are implicated here. Employees who do not compromise their beliefs stand to lose the considerable increases in pay and job satisfaction attendant to promotions, the hours and maintenance expenses that are consumed by long daily commutes, and even their jobs if they are not rehired after a "temporary" layoff. These are significant penalties and are imposed for the exercise of rights guaranteed by the First Amendment. Unless these patronage practices are narrowly tailored to further vital government interests, we must conclude that they impermissibly encroach on First Amendment freedoms....

We find, however, that our conclusions in *Elrod,* supra, and *Branti,* supra, are equally applicable to the patronage practices at issue here. A government's interest in securing effective employees can be met by discharging, demoting or transferring staffmembers whose work is deficient. A government's interest in securing employees who will loyally implement its policies can be adequately served by choosing or dismissing certain high-level employees on the basis of their political views.... Likewise, the "preservation of the democratic process"

---

[5] Branti v. Finkel ... also refined the exception created by Elrod v. Burns ... for certain employees. In *Elrod,* we suggested that policymaking and confidential employees probably could be dismissed on the basis of their political views.... In *Branti,* we said that a State demonstrates a compelling interest in infringing First Amendment rights only when it can show that "party affiliation is an appropriate requirement for the effective performance of the public office involved." ... The scope of this exception does not concern us here as respondents concede that the five employees who brought this suit are not within it.

is no more furthered by the patronage promotions, transfers, and rehires at issue here than it is by patronage dismissals. First, "political parties are nurtured by other, less intrusive and equally effective methods." ... Political parties have already survived the substantial decline in patronage employment practices in this century.... Second, patronage decidedly impairs the elective process by discouraging free political expression by public employees.... Respondents, who include the Governor of Illinois and other state officials, do not suggest any other overriding government interest in favoring Republican Party supporters for promotion, transfer, and rehire.

We therefore determine that promotions, transfers, and recalls after layoffs based on political affiliation or support are an impermissible infringement on the First Amendment rights of public employees. In doing so, we reject the Seventh Circuit's view ... that only those employment decisions that are the "substantial equivalent of a dismissal" violate a public employee's rights under the First Amendment. We find this test unduly restrictive because it fails to recognize that there are deprivations less harsh than dismissal that nevertheless press state employees and applicants to conform their beliefs and associations to some state-selected orthodoxy.... The First Amendment prevents the government, except in the most compelling circumstances, from wielding its power to interfere with its employees' freedom to believe and associate, or to not believe and not associate.

. . .

C

Petitioner James W. Moore presents the closely related question whether patronage hiring violates the First Amendment. Patronage hiring places burdens on free speech and association similar to those imposed by the patronage practices discussed above. A state job is valuable. Like most employment, it provides regular paychecks, health insurance, and other benefits. In addition, there may be openings with the State when business in the private sector is slow. There are also occupations for which the government is a major (or the only) source of employment, such as social workers, elementary school teachers, and prison guards. Thus, denial of a state job is a serious privation.

Nonetheless, respondents contend that the burden imposed is not of constitutional magnitude. Decades of decisions by this Court belie such a claim. We premised Torcaso v. Watkins, 367 U.S. 488 (1961), on our understanding that loss of a job opportunity for failure to compromise one's convictions states a constitutional claim. We held that Maryland could not refuse an appointee a commission for the position of notary public on the ground that he refused to declare his belief in God ... In Keyishian v. Board of Regents of Univ. of New York, 385 U.S. 589, 609–610 (1967), we held a law affecting appointment and retention of teachers invalid because it premised employment on an unconstitutional restriction of political belief and association. In Elfbrandt v. Russell, 384 U.S. 11, 19 (1966), we struck down a loyalty oath which was a prerequisite for public employment.

... Under our sustained precedent, conditioning hiring decisions on political belief and association plainly constitutes an unconstitutional condition, unless the government has a vital interest in doing so.... See also Sherbert v. Verner, 374 U.S. 398 (1963) (unemployment benefits); Speiser v. Randall, [357 U.S. 513 (1958)](tax exemption). We find no such government interest here, for the same reasons that we found the government lacks justification for patronage promotions, transfers or recalls.

The court below, having decided that the appropriate inquiry in patronage cases is whether the employment decision at issue is the substantial equivalent of a dismissal ... reasoned that "rejecting an employment application does not impose a hardship upon an employee comparable to the loss of [a] job." Just as we reject the Seventh Circuit's proffered test, we [reject its distinction between hiring and dismissal.] ...

... It is unnecessary here to consider whether not being hired is less burdensome than being discharged because the government is not pressed to do either on the basis of political affiliation. The question in the patronage context is not which penalty is more acute but whether the government, without sufficient justification, is pressuring employees to discontinue the free exercise of their First Amendment rights.

If Moore's employment application was set aside because he chose not to support the Republican Party, as he asserts, then Moore's First Amendment rights have been violated. Therefore, we find that Moore's complaint was improperly dismissed.

III

We hold that the rule of *Elrod* and *Branti* extends to promotion, transfer, recall, and hiring decisions based on party affiliation and support and that all of the petitioners and cross-respondents have stated claims upon which relief may be granted....

... [a]

Justice Scalia, with whom the Chief Justice and Justice Kennedy join, and with whom Justice O'Connor joins as to Parts II and III, dissenting.

Today the Court establishes the constitutional principle that party membership is not a permissible factor in the dispensation of government jobs, except those jobs for the performance of which party affiliation is an "appropriate requirement." It is hard to say precisely (or even generally) what that exception means, but if there is any category of jobs for whose performance party affiliation is not an appropriate requirement, it is the job of being a judge, where partisanship is not only unneeded but positively undesirable. It is, however, rare that a federal administration of one party will appoint a judge from another party. And it has always been rare. See Marbury v. Madison, 5 U.S. (1 Cranch) 137 (1803). Thus, the new principle that the Court today announces will be enforced by a corps of judges (the Members of this Court included) who overwhelmingly owe their office to its violation. Something must be wrong here, and I suggest it is the Court.

The merit principle for government employment is probably the most favored in modern America, having been widely adopted by civil-service legislation at both the state and federal levels. But there is another point of view, described in characteristically Jacksonian fashion by an eminent practitioner of the patronage system, George Washington Plunkitt of Tammany Hall:

"I ain't up on syllygisms, but I can give you some arguments that nobody can answer.

"First, this great and glorious country was built up by political parties; second, parties can't hold together if their workers don't get offices when they win; third, if the parties go to pieces, the government they built up

---

[a] A concurring opinion by Justice Stevens is omitted.

must go to pieces, too; fourth, then there'll be hell to pay." W. Riordon, Plunkitt of Tammany Hall 13 (1963).

It may well be that the Good Government Leagues of America were right, and that Plunkitt, James Michael Curley and their ilk were wrong; but that is not entirely certain. As the merit principle has been extended and its effects increasingly felt; as the Boss Tweeds, the Tammany Halls, the Pendergast Machines, the Byrd Machines and the Daley Machines have faded into history; we find that political leaders at all levels increasingly complain of the helplessness of elected government, unprotected by "party discipline," before the demands of small and cohesive interest-groups.

The choice between patronage and the merit principle—or, to be more realistic about it, the choice between the desirable mix of merit and patronage principles in widely varying federal, state, and local political contexts—is not so clear that I would be prepared, as an original matter, to chisel a single, inflexible prescription into the Constitution. Fourteen years ago, in Elrod v. Burns, 427 U.S. 347 (1976), the Court did that.

Elrod was limited however, as was the later decision of Branti v. Finkel, 445 U.S. 507 (1980), to patronage firings, leaving it to state and federal legislatures to determine when and where political affiliation could be taken into account in hirings and promotions. Today the Court makes its constitutional civil-service reform absolute, extending to all decisions regarding government employment. Because the First Amendment has never been thought to require this disposition, which may well have disastrous consequences for our political system, I dissent.

I

The restrictions that the Constitution places upon the government in its capacity as lawmaker, i.e., as the regulator of private conduct, are not the same as the restrictions that it places upon the government in its capacity as employer. We have recognized this in many contexts, with respect to many different constitutional guarantees. Private citizens perhaps cannot be prevented from wearing long hair, but policemen can. Kelley v. Johnson, 425 U.S. 238, 247 (1976). Private citizens cannot have their property searched without probable cause, but in many circumstances government employees can. O'Connor v. Ortega, 480 U.S. 709, 723 (1987). . . . Private citizens cannot be punished for refusing to provide the government information that may incriminate them, but government employees can be dismissed when the incriminating information that they refuse to provide relates to the performance of their job. Gardner v. Broderick, 392 U.S. 273, 277–278 (1968). With regard to freedom of speech in particular: Private citizens cannot be punished for speech of merely private concern, but government employees can be fired for that reason. Connick v. Myers, 461 U.S. 138, 147 (1983). Private citizens cannot be punished for partisan political activity, but federal and state employees can be dismissed and otherwise punished for that reason. Public Workers v. Mitchell, 330 U.S. 75, 101 (1947); CSC v. Letter Carriers, 413 U.S. 548, 556 (1973); Broadrick v. Oklahoma, 413 U.S. 601, 616–617 (1973).

Once it is acknowledged that the Constitution's prohibition against laws "abridging the freedom of speech" does not apply to laws enacted in the government's capacity as employer the same way it does to laws enacted in the government's capacity as regulator of private conduct, it may sometimes be difficult to assess what employment practices are permissible and what are not. That seems to me not a difficult question, however, in the present context. The provisions of the Bill of Rights were designed to restrain transient majorities from impairing long-recognized personal liberties. They did not create by implication novel individual rights overturning accepted political norms. Thus, when a practice not expressly prohibited by the text of the Bill of Rights bears the endorsement of a long tradition of open, widespread, and unchallenged use that dates back to the beginning of the Republic, we have no proper basis for striking it down. Such a venerable and accepted tradition is not to be laid on the examining table and scrutinized for its conformity to some abstract principle of First Amendment adjudication devised by this Court. To the contrary, such traditions are themselves the stuff out of which the Court's principles are to be formed. They are, in these uncertain areas, the very points of reference by which the legitimacy or illegitimacy of other practices are to be figured out. When it appears that the latest "rule," or "three-part test," or "balancing test" devised by the Court has placed us on a collision course with such a landmark practice, it is the former that must be recalculated by us, and not the latter that must be abandoned by our citizens. I know of no other way to formulate a constitutional jurisprudence that reflects, as it should, the principles adhered to, over time, by the American people, rather than those favored by the personal (and necessarily shifting) philosophical dispositions of a majority of this Court.

... [P]atronage was, without any thought that it could be unconstitutional, a basis for government employment from the earliest days of the Republic until *Elrod*—and has continued unabated since *Elrod*, to the extent still permitted by that unfortunate decision. ... Given that unbroken tradition regarding the application of an ambiguous constitutional text, there was in my view no basis for holding that patronage-based dismissals violated the First Amendment— much less for holding, as the Court does today, that even patronage hiring does so.

II

Even accepting the Court's own mode of analysis, however, and engaging in "balancing" a tradition that ought to be part of the scales, *Elrod, Branti,* and today's extension of them seem to me wrong.

. . .

B

. . .

... [E]ven laying tradition entirely aside, it seems to me our balancing test is amply met....

The whole point of my dissent is that the desirability of patronage is a policy question to be decided by the people's representatives; I do not mean, therefore, to endorse that system. But in order to demonstrate that a legislature could reasonably determine that its benefits outweigh its "coercive" effects, I must describe those benefits as the proponents of patronage see them: As Justice Powell discussed at length in his *Elrod* dissent, patronage stabilizes political parties and prevents excessive political fragmentation—both of which are results in which States have a strong governmental interest. Party strength requires the efforts of the rank-and-file, especially in "the dull periods between elections," to perform such tasks as organizing precincts, registering new voters, and providing constituent services....

. . .

It is self-evident that eliminating patronage will significantly undermine party discipline; and that as party discipline wanes, so will the strength of the two-party system. . . .

The patronage system does not, of course, merely foster political parties in general; it fosters the two-party system in particular. When getting a job, as opposed to effectuating a particular substantive policy, is an available incentive for party-workers, those attracted by that incentive are likely to work for the party that has the best chance of displacing the "ins," rather than for some splinter group that has a more attractive political philosophy but little hope of success. . . .

Equally apparent is the relatively destabilizing nature of a system in which candidates cannot rely upon patronage-based party loyalty for their campaign support, but must attract workers and raise funds by appealing to various interest-groups. . . . There is little doubt that our decisions in *Elrod* and *Branti,* by contributing to the decline of party strength, have also contributed to the growth of interest-group politics in the last decade. . . .

Patronage, moreover, has been a powerful means of achieving the social and political integration of excluded groups. . . . By supporting and ultimately dominating a particular party "machine," racial and ethnic minorities have— on the basis of their politics rather than their race or ethnicity—acquired the patronage awards the machine had power to confer. . . . The abolition of patronage, however, prevents groups that have only recently obtained political power, especially blacks, from following this path to economic and social advancement.

. . .

While the patronage system has the benefits argued for above, it also has undoubted disadvantages. It facilitates financial corruption, such as salary kickbacks and partisan political activity on government-paid time. It reduces the efficiency of government, because it creates incentives to hire more and less-qualified workers and because highly qualified workers are reluctant to accept jobs that may only last until the next election. And, of course, it applies some greater or lesser inducement for individuals to join and work for the party in power.

. . . I do not deny that the patronage system influences or redirects, perhaps to a substantial degree, individual political expression and political association. But like the many generations of Americans that have preceded us, I do not consider that a significant impairment of free speech or free association.

. . . To oppose our *Elrod–Branti* jurisprudence, one need not believe that the patronage system is necessarily desirable; nor even that it is always and everywhere arguably desirable; but merely that it is a political arrangement that may sometimes be a reasonable choice, and should therefore be left to the judgment of the people's elected representatives. . . .

C

. . . Even in the field of constitutional adjudication, where the pull of stare decisis is at its weakest . . . one is reluctant to depart from precedent. But when that precedent is not only wrong, not only recent, not only contradicted by a long prior tradition, but also has proved unworkable in practice, then all reluctance ought to disappear. In my view that is the situation here. . . .

. . .

... [T]he "tests" devised to implement *Branti* have produced inconsistent and unpredictable results. That uncertainty undermines the purpose of both the nonpatronage rule and the exception. ...

This uncertainty and confusion are not the result of the fact that *Elrod,* and then *Branti,* chose the wrong "line." My point is that there is no right line—or at least no right line that can be nationally applied and that is known by judges. ...The appropriate "mix" of party-based employment is a political question if there ever was one, and we should give it back to the voters of the various political units to decide, through civil-service legislation crafted to suit the time and place, which mix is best.

III

Even were I not convinced that *Elrod* and *Branti* were wrongly decided, I would hold that they should not be extended beyond their facts, viz., actual discharge of employees for their political affiliation....

. . .

SPEECH AND ASSOCIATION RIGHTS OF GOVERNMENT CONTRACTORS

In Board of County Commissioners v. Umbehr, ___ U.S. ___, 116 S.Ct. 2342 (1996), the Court extended Pickering v. Board of Education to the case of a government contractor whose trash hauling contract was terminated after he publicly criticized the county's governing board. On the same day, in O'Hare v. City of Northlake, ___ U.S. ___, 116 S.Ct. 2353(1996), the Court extended Elrod v. Burns and Branti v. Finkel to a person whose towing service was removed from a city list of available towing companies after he refused to contribute to the mayor's re-election campaign and instead supported the mayor's opponent. In *Umbehr,* Justice O'Connor's opinion for the Court reserved the question whether the First Amendment would be implicated by government's speech-motivated refusal to contract in the first instance. The opinion further stated that once the plaintiff had proved that termination was motivated by speech on a matter of public concern, the defendant might still prevail even if it failed to prove that it would have terminated the contract regardless of the speech. An additional defense would be that government's legitimate interests as a contractor outweighed the plaintiff's free speech interests. That additional defense would not be available in *O'Hare.* Justice Kennedy's opinion for the Court in *O'Hare* explained that where a contract was terminated because of the plaintiff's political affiliation, the reasonableness inquiry was confined to the question whether political affiliation was an appropriate requirement for the effective performance of the contracted work. Justices Scalia and Thomas dissented in both cases.

CHAPTER 16

FREEDOM OF THE PRESS

Introduction. The materials pulled together in this chapter relate to the first amendment protections as applied to the print and electronic media. Many of the issues that have arisen in the three previous chapters are involved in these cases.

It has been suggested that the power of government to regulate the press is limited by the first amendment under three general principles. (1) The government may not impose special burdens on the press—at least where it appears that the purpose is to curb the press. (2) The government may not impose even nondiscriminatory burdens on the press where they are so heavy as to impair significantly the institutional viability of the press. (3) The government may not interfere with editorial control and judgment. Barrett, *Freedom of the Press, American Style,* in American Bar Association, *Legal Institutions Today; English and American Approaches Compared,* 214, 225–227 (H. Jones ed. 1977); DeVore & Nelson, *Commercial Speech and Paid Access to the Press,* 26 Hast.L.J. 745 (1975).

In examining the materials that follow the student should ask whether the cases support these limiting principles.

SECTION 1. INTRODUCTION

A. RELATIONSHIP BETWEEN THE SPEECH AND PRESS CLAUSES

The first amendment protects against "abridging the freedom of speech, or of the press." Does the latter phrase confer upon the press any freedom not otherwise conferred by the "freedom of speech" clause?

Justice Stewart argued in a speech that the free press clause does add to the protections accorded by the free speech clause. He said, in part:

"[T]he Free Press guarantee is, in essence, a *structural* provision of the Constitution. Most of the other provisions in the Bill of Rights protect specific liberties or specific rights of individuals: freedom of speech, freedom of worship, the right to counsel, the privilege against compulsory self-incrimination, to name a few. In contrast, the Free Press Clause extends protection to an institution. The publishing business is, in short, the only organized private business that is given explicit constitutional protection.

"This basic understanding is essential, I think, to avoid an elementary error of constitutional law. It is tempting to suggest that freedom of the press means only that newspaper publishers are guaranteed freedom of expression. They *are* guaranteed that freedom, to be sure, but so are we all, because of the Free Speech Clause. If the Free Press guarantee meant no more than freedom of expression, it would be a constitutional redundancy. Between 1776 and the drafting of our Constitution, many of the state constitutions contained clauses protecting freedom of the press while at the same time recognizing no general freedom of speech. By including both guarantees in the First Amendment, the Founders quite clearly recognized the distinction between the two.

"It is also a mistake to suppose that the only purpose of the constitutional guarantee of a free press is to insure that a newspaper will serve as a neutral forum for debate, a 'market place for ideas,' a kind of Hyde Park corner for the community. A related theory sees the press as a neutral conduit of information between the people and their elected leaders. These theories, in my view, again give insufficient weight to the institutional autonomy of the press that it was the purpose of the Constitution to guarantee."[1]

In a concurring opinion in a case concerned with other issues,[2] Chief Justice Burger expressed disagreement with Justice Stewart's position. He said:

"I perceive two fundamental difficulties with a narrow reading of the Press Clause. First, although certainty on this point is not possible, the history of the Clause does not suggest that the authors contemplated a 'special' or 'institutional' privilege. See Lange, The Speech and Press Clauses, 23 UCLA L.Rev. 77, 88–99 (1975)....

"...

"Those interpreting the Press Clause as extending protection only to, or creating a special role for, the 'institutional press' must either (a) assert such an intention on the part of the Framers for which no supporting evidence is available, ... (b) argue that events after 1791 somehow operated to 'constitutionalize' this interpretation, see Benzanson, [The New Free Press Guarantee, 63 Va.L.Rev. 731, 788 (1977)]; or (c) candidly acknowledging the absence of historical support, suggest that the intent of the Framers is not important today. See Nimmer, [Is Freedom of the Press a Redundancy: What Does It Add To Freedom of Speech?, 26 Hastings L.J. 639, 640–641 (1975)].

"To conclude that the Framers did not intend to limit the freedom of the press to one select group is not necessarily to suggest that the Press Clause is redundant. The Speech Clause standing alone may be viewed as a protection of the liberty to express ideas and beliefs, while the Press Clause focuses specifically on the liberty to disseminate expression broadly and 'comprehends every sort of publication which affords a vehicle of information and opinion.' ... Yet there is no fundamental distinction between expression and dissemination. The liberty encompassed by the Press Clause, although complementary to and a natural extension of Speech Clause liberty, merited special mention simply because it had been more often the object of official restraints....

"The second fundamental difficulty with interpreting the Press Clause as conferring special status on a limited group is one of definition.... The very task of including some entities within the 'institutional press' while excluding others, whether undertaken by legislature, court or administrative agency, is reminiscent of the abhorred licensing system of Tudor and Stuart England—a system the First Amendment was intended to ban from this country.... Further, the officials undertaking that task would be required to distinguish the protected from the unprotected on the basis of such variables as content of expression, frequency or fervor of expression, or ownership of the technological means of dissemination. Yet nothing in this Court's opinions supports such a confining approach to the scope of Press Clause protection....

---

[1] "*Or of the Press,*" a speech given at Yale Law School, Nov. 2, 1974, as reprinted in 26 Hast.L.J. 631, 633–634 (1975).

[2] First Nat'l Bank of Boston v. Bellotti, 435 U.S. 765, 798–802 (1978).

"Because the First Amendment was meant to guarantee freedom to express and communicate ideas, I can see no difference between the right of those who seek to disseminate ideas by way of a newspaper and those who give lectures or speeches and seek to enlarge the audience by publication and wide dissemination."

B.   REGULATION OF THE BUSINESS OF PUBLISHING

Minneapolis Star and Tribune Co. v. Minnesota Commissioner of Revenue

460 U.S. 575, 103 S.Ct. 1365, 75 L.Ed.2d 295 (1983).

Justice O'Connor delivered the opinion of the Court.

This case presents the question of a State's power to impose a special tax on the press and, by enacting exemptions, to limit its effect to only a few newspapers.

I

Since 1967, Minnesota has imposed a sales tax on most sales of goods for a price in excess of a nominal sum.... In general, the tax applies only to retail sales.... An exemption for industrial and agricultural users shields from the tax sales of components to be used in the production of goods that will themselves be sold at retail.... As part of this general system of taxation and in support of the sales tax,.... Minnesota also enacted a tax on the "privilege of using, storing or consuming in Minnesota tangible personal property." This use tax applies to any nonexempt tangible personal property unless the sales tax was paid on the sales price.... Like the classic use tax, this use tax protects the State's sales tax by eliminating the residents' incentive to travel to States with lower sales taxes to buy goods rather than buying them in Minnesota....

The appellant, Minneapolis Star and Tribune Company, "Star Tribune", is the publisher of a morning newspaper and an evening newspaper in Minneapolis. From 1967 until 1971, it enjoyed an exemption from the sales and use tax provided by Minnesota for periodic publications. ...In 1971, however, while leaving the exemption from the sales tax in place, the legislature amended the scheme to impose a "use tax" on the cost of paper and ink products consumed in the production of a publication. ...Ink and paper used in publications became the only items subject to the use tax that were components of goods to be sold at retail. In 1974, the legislature again amended the statute, this time to exempt the first $100,000 worth of ink and paper consumed by a publication in any calendar year, in effect giving each publication an annual tax credit of $4,000. ...Publications remained exempt from the sales tax ...

After the enactment of the $100,000 exemption, 11 publishers, producing 14 of the 388 paid circulation newspapers in the State, incurred a tax liability in 1974. Star Tribune was one of the 11, and, of the $893,355 collected, it paid $608,634, or roughly two-thirds of the total revenue raised by the tax. ...In 1975, 13 publishers, producing 16 out of 374 paid circulation papers, paid a tax. That year, Star Tribune again bore roughly two-thirds of the total receipts from the use tax on ink and paper. ...

Star Tribune instituted this action to seek a refund of the use taxes it paid from January 1, 1974 to May 31, 1975. It challenged the imposition of the use tax on ink and paper used in publications as a violation of the guarantees of freedom of the press and equal protection in the First and Fourteenth Amendments. The Minnesota Supreme Court upheld the tax against the federal constitutional challenge. . . . We . . . reverse.

II

Star Tribune argues that we must strike this tax on the authority of Grosjean v. American Press Co., Inc., 297 U.S. 233 (1936). Although there are similarities between the two cases, we agree with the State that *Grosjean* is not controlling.

In *Grosjean,* the State of Louisiana imposed a license tax of 2% of the gross receipts from the sale of advertising on all newspapers with a weekly circulation above 20,000. Out of at least 124 publishers in the State, only 13 were subject to the tax. After noting that the tax was "single in kind" and that keying the tax to circulation curtailed the flow of information, . . . this Court held the tax invalid as an abridgment of the freedom of the press. Both the brief and the argument of the publishers in this Court emphasized the events leading up to the tax and the contemporary political climate in Louisiana. . . . All but one of the large papers subject to the tax had "ganged up" on Senator Huey Long, and a circular distributed by Long and the governor to each member of the state legislature described "lying newspapers" as conducting "a vicious campaign" and the tax as "a tax on lying . . ." . . . Although the Court's opinion did not describe this history, it stated, "[The tax] is bad because, in the light of its history and of its present setting, it is seen to be a deliberate and calculated device in the guise of a tax to limit the circulation of information," . . . an explanation that suggests that the motivation of the legislature may have been significant.

. . . We think that the result in *Grosjean* may have been attributable in part to the perception on the part of the Court that the state imposed the tax with an intent to penalize a selected group of newspapers. In the case currently before us, however, there is no legislative history and no indication, apart from the structure of the tax itself, of any impermissible or censorial motive on the part of the legislature. We cannot resolve the case by simple citation to *Grosjean*. Instead, we must analyze the problem anew under the general principles of the First Amendment.

III

Clearly, the First Amendment does not prohibit all regulation of the press. It is beyond dispute that the States and the Federal Government can subject newspapers to generally applicable economic regulations without creating constitutional problems. See, e.g., Citizen Publishing Co. v. United States, 394 U.S. 131, 139 (1969) (antitrust laws); Lorain Journal Co. v. United States, 342 U.S. 143, 155–156 (1951) (same); Breard v. Alexandria, 341 U.S. 622 (1951) (prohibition of door-to-door solicitation); Oklahoma Press Publishing Co. v. Walling, 327 U.S. 186, 192–193 (1946) (Fair Labor Standards Act); Mabee v. White Plains Publishing Co., 327 U.S. 178 (1946) (same); Associated Press v. United States, 326 U.S. 1, 6–7, 19–20 (1945) (antitrust laws); Associated Press v. NLRB, 301 U.S. 103, 132–133 (1937) (NLRA); see also Branzburg v. Hayes, 408 U.S. 665 (1972) (enforcement of subpoenas). Minnesota, however, has not chosen to apply its general sales and use tax to newspapers. Instead, it has created a special tax that applies only to certain publications protected by the First Amendment. Although the State argues now that the tax on paper and ink is part of the general scheme of taxation, the use tax provision . . . is facially discriminatory, singling out publications for treatment that is, to our knowledge, unique in Minnesota tax law.

Minnesota's treatment of publications differs from that of other enterprises in at least two important respects: it imposes a use tax that does not serve the function of protecting the sales tax, and it taxes an intermediate transaction rather than the ultimate retail sale. A use tax ordinarily serves to complement the sales tax by eliminating the incentive to make major purchases in States with lower sales taxes; it requires the resident who shops out-of-state to pay a use tax equal to the sales tax savings. . . . But the use tax on ink and paper serves no such complementary function; it applies to all uses, whether or not the taxpayer purchased the ink and paper in-state, and it applies to items exempt from the sales tax.

Further, the ordinary rule in Minnesota, as discussed above, is to tax only the ultimate, or retail, sale rather than the use of components like ink and paper. . . . Publishers, however, are taxed on their purchase of components, even though they will eventually sell their publications at retail.

By creating this special use tax, which, to our knowledge, is without parallel in the State's tax scheme, Minnesota has singled out the press for special treatment. We then must determine whether the First Amendment permits such special taxation. . . . The cases approving . . . economic regulation, . . . emphasized the general applicability of the challenged regulation to all businesses, . . . suggesting that a regulation that singled out the press might place a heavier burden of justification on the State, and we now conclude that the special problems created by differential treatment do indeed impose such a burden.

. . .

. . . A power to tax differentially, as opposed to a power to tax generally, gives a government a powerful weapon against the taxpayer selected. When the State imposes a generally applicable tax, there is little cause for concern. We need not fear that a government will destroy a selected group of taxpayers by burdensome taxation if it must impose the same burden on the rest of its constituency. See Railway Express Agency v. New York, 336 U.S. 106, 112–113 (1949) (Jackson, J., concurring). When the State singles out the press, though, the political constraints that prevent a legislature from passing crippling taxes of general applicability are weakened, and the threat of burdensome taxes becomes acute. That threat can operate as effectively as a censor to check critical comment by the press, undercutting the basic assumption of our political system that the press will often serve as an important restraint on government. . . .

. . .

IV

. . .

. . . Minnesota invites us to look beyond the form of the tax to its substance. The tax is, according to the State, merely a substitute for the sales tax, which, as a generally applicable tax, would be constitutional as applied to the press.[9] There are two fatal flaws in this reasoning. First, the State has

---

[9] Star Tribune insists that the premise of the State's argument—that a generally applicable sales tax would be constitutional—is incorrect . . . We think that Breard v. Alexandria, 341 U.S. 622 (1951) . . . rebuts Star Tribune's argument. There, we upheld an

offered no explanation of why it chose to use a substitute for the sales tax rather than the sales tax itself. The court below speculated that the State might have been concerned that collection of a tax on such small transactions would be impractical.... That suggestion is unpersuasive, for sales of other low-priced goods are not exempt. If the real goal of this tax is to duplicate the sales tax, it is difficult to see why the State did not achieve that goal by the obvious and effective expedient of applying the sales tax.

Further, even assuming that the legislature did have valid reasons for substituting another tax for the sales tax, we are not persuaded that this tax does serve as a substitute. The State asserts that this scheme actually *favors* the press over other businesses, because the same rate of tax is applied, but, for the press, the rate applies to the cost of components rather than to the sales price. We would be hesitant to fashion a rule that automatically allowed the State to single out the press for a different method of taxation as long as the effective burden was no different from that on other taxpayers or the burden on the press was lighter than that on other businesses. One reason for this reluctance is that the very selection of the press for special treatment threatens the press not only with the current *differential* treatment, but with the possibility of subsequent differentially *more burdensome* treatment....

A second reason to avoid the proposed rule is that courts as institutions are poorly equipped to evaluate with precision the relative burdens of various methods of taxation. The complexities of factual economic proof always present a certain potential for error, and courts have little familiarity with the process of evaluating the relative economic burden of taxes. In sum, the possibility of error inherent in the proposed rule poses too great a threat to concerns at the heart of the First Amendment, and we cannot tolerate that possibility. Minnesota, therefore, has offered no adequate justification for the special treatment of newspapers.

V

Minnesota's ink and paper tax violates the First Amendment not only because it singles out the press, but also because it targets a small group of newspapers. The effect of the $100,000 exemption enacted in 1974 is that only a handful of publishers pay any tax at all, and even fewer pay any significant amount of tax. The State explains this exemption as part of a policy favoring an "equitable" tax system, although there are no comparable exemptions for small enterprises outside the press. Again, there is no legislative history supporting the State's view of the purpose of the amendment. Whatever the motive of the legislature in this case, we think that recognizing a power in the State not only to single out the press but also to tailor the tax so that it singles out a few members of the press presents such a potential for abuse that no interest suggested by Minnesota can justify the scheme. It has asserted no interest other than its desire to have an "equitable" tax system. The current system, it explains, promotes equity because it places the burden on large publications that impose more social costs than do smaller publications and that are more likely to be able to bear the burden of the tax. Even if we were willing to accept the premise that large businesses are more profitable and therefore better able to bear the burden of the tax, the State's commitment to this "equity" is

ordinance prohibiting door-to-door solicitation, even though it applied to prevent the door-to-door sale of subscriptions to magazines, an activity covered by the First Amendment. Although Martin v. Struthers, 319 U.S. 141 (1943), had struck down a similar ordinance as applied to the distribution of free religious literature, the *Breard* Court explained that case as emphasizing that the information distributed was religious in nature and that the distribution was noncommercial. 341 U.S., at 642–643....

questionable, for the concern has not led the State to grant benefits to small businesses in general. And when the exemption selects such a narrowly defined group to bear the full burden of the tax, the tax begins to resemble more a penalty for a few of the largest newspapers than an attempt to favor struggling smaller enterprises.

VI

We need not and do not impugn the motives of the Minnesota legislature in passing the ink and paper tax.... Since Minnesota has offered no satisfactory justification for its tax on the use of ink and paper, the tax violates the First Amendment, and the judgment below is

Reversed.

Justice White, concurring in part and dissenting in part.

This case is not difficult. The exemption for the first $100,000 of paper and ink limits the burden of the Minnesota tax to only a few papers. This feature alone is sufficient reason to invalidate the Minnesota tax and reverse the judgment of the Minnesota Supreme Court. The Court recognizes that Minnesota's tax violates the First Amendment for this reason, and I subscribe to Part V of the Court's opinion and concur in the judgment.

. . .

There may be cases, I recognize, where the Court cannot confidently ascertain whether a differential method of taxation imposes a greater burden upon the press than a generally applicable tax. In these circumstances, I too may be unwilling to entrust freedom of the press to uncertain economic proof. But, as Justice Rehnquist clearly shows, this is not such a case....

Justice Rehnquist, dissenting.

. . .

... We need no expert testimony from modern day Euclids or Einsteins to determine that the $1,224,747 paid in use taxes is significantly less burdensome than the $3,685,092 that could have been levied by a sales tax. *A fortiori,* the Minnesota taxing scheme which singles out newspapers for "differential treatment" has benefited, not burdened, the "freedom of speech, [and] of the press."

. . .

The Court finds in very summary fashion that the exemption newspapers receive for the first $100,000 of ink and paper used also violates the First Amendment because the result is that only a few of the newspapers actually pay a use tax. I cannot agree. As explained by the Minnesota Supreme Court, the exemption is in effect a $4,000 credit which benefits all newspapers.... *Minneapolis Star & Tribune* was benefited to the amount of $16,000 in the two years in question; $4,000 each year for its morning paper and $4,000 each year for its evening paper.... Absent any improper motive on the part of the Minnesota legislature in drawing the limits of this exemption, it cannot be construed as violating the First Amendment....

To collect from newspapers their fair share of taxes under the sales and use tax scheme and at the same time avoid abridging the freedoms of speech and press, the Court holds today that Minnesota must subject newspapers to millions of additional dollars in sales tax liability. Certainly this is a hollow victory for the newspapers and I seriously doubt the Court's conclusion that this result would have been intended by the "Framers of the First Amendment."

For the reasons set forth above, I would affirm the judgment of the Minnesota Supreme Court.

SELECTIVE TAXATION AND REGULATION OF THE PRESS: CONTENT–BASED AND CONTENT–NEUTRAL SELECTIVITY

In Arkansas Writers' Project, Inc. v. Ragland, 481 U.S. 221 (1987), the Court invalidated a sales tax exemption for magazines that were "religious, professional, trade and sports journals," noting that selective taxation based on media content involved "a more disturbing use of selective taxation than *Minneapolis Star*." The Court did not decide whether another provision of the challenged Arkansas statute—an exemption for all newspapers—was invalid. Differential taxation of different media was at issue in Leathers v. Medlock, 499 U.S. 439 (1991), where another Arkansas tax was upheld. Cable television operators complained of a law extending the general sales tax to cable television. The Court concluded that different taxation of different media was not constitutionally suspect if the tax did not single out the media, did not purposely interfere with first amendment activities, and was not content-based.

The Court relied on this analysis in Simon & Schuster, Inc. v. Members of New York State Crime Victims Board, 502 U.S. 105 (1991), holding New York's "Son of Sam" law unconstitutional. If the work disclosed commission of a crime by the author, the law required the author's publisher to deposit funds payable to the author in an escrow account to compensate victims of that crime. The Court concluded that the statute was presumptively unconstitutional because it imposed a financial burden on speakers because of the content of their speech. The state's compelling interest in compensating victims from the fruits of crime could not justify a law that was limited to compensation from the proceeds of speech about that crime.

SECTION 2. RESTRAINTS ON EDITORIAL JUDGMENT

Pittsburgh Press Co. v. Pittsburgh Commission on Human Relations

413 U.S. 376, 93 S.Ct. 2553, 37 L.Ed.2d 669 (1973).

Mr. Justice Powell delivered the opinion of the Court.

The Human Relations Ordinance of the City of Pittsburgh (the Ordinance) has been construed below by the courts of Pennsylvania as forbidding newspapers to carry "help-wanted" advertisements in sex-designated columns except where the employer or advertiser is free to make hiring or employment referral decisions on the basis of sex. We are called upon to decide whether the Ordinance as so construed violates the freedoms of speech and of the press guaranteed by the First and Fourteenth Amendments. . . .

. . .

Respondents rely principally on the argument that this regulation is permissible because the speech is commercial speech unprotected by the First Amendment. . . .

But Pittsburgh Press contends that . . . the focus in this case must be upon the exercise of editorial judgment by the newspaper as to where to place the advertisement rather than upon its commercial content. . . .

. . .

. . . [W]e are not persuaded that either the decision to accept a commercial advertisement which the advertiser directs to be placed in a sex-designated column or the actual placement there lifts the newspaper's actions from the category of commercial speech. By implication at least, an advertiser whose want-ad appears in the "Jobs—Male Interest" column is likely to discriminate against women in his hiring decisions. Nothing in a sex-designated column heading sufficiently disassociates the designation from the want ads placed beneath it to make the placement severable for First Amendment purposes from the want-ads themselves. The combination, which conveys essentially the same message as an overtly discriminatory want ad, is in practical effect an integrated commercial statement.

Pittsburgh Press goes on to argue that if this package of advertisement and placement is commercial speech, then commercial speech should be accorded a higher level of protection . . . Insisting that the exchange of information is as important in the commercial realm as in any other, the newspaper here would have us abrogate the distinction between commercial and other speech.

Whatever the merits of this contention may be in other contexts, it is unpersuasive in this case. Discrimination in employment is not only commercial activity, it is *illegal* commercial activity under the Ordinance. We have no doubt that a newspaper constitutionally could be forbidden to publish a want ad proposing a sale of narcotics or soliciting prostitutes. Nor would the result be different if the nature of the transaction were indicated by placement under columns captioned "Narcotics for Sale" and "Prostitutes Wanted" rather than stated within the four corners of the advertisement.

. . .

We emphasize that nothing in our holding allows government at any level to forbid *Pittsburgh Press* to publish and distribute advertisements commenting on the Ordinance, the enforcement practices of the Commission, or the propriety of sex preferences in employment. Nor, *a fortiori,* does our decision authorize any restriction whatever, whether of content or layout, on stories or commentary originated by Pittsburgh Press, its columnists, or its contributors. On the contrary, we reaffirm unequivocally the protection afforded to editorial judgment and to the free expression of views on these and other issues, however controversial. We hold only that the Commission's modified order, narrowly drawn to prohibit placement in sex-designated columns of advertisements for nonexempt job opportunities, does not infringe the First Amendment rights of Pittsburgh Press.

Affirmed.[a]

---

[a] Dissenting opinions by Chief Justice Burger, Justice Douglas, and Justice Blackmun, are omitted.

Mr. Justice Stewart, with whom Mr. Justice Douglas joins, dissenting.

. . .

So far as I know, this is the first case in this or any other American court that permits a government agency to enter a composing room of a newspaper and dictate to the publisher the layout and makeup of the newspaper's pages. This is the first such case, but I fear it may not be the last. The camel's nose is in the tent. . . .

So long as Members of this Court view the First Amendment as no more than a set of "values" to be balanced against other "values," that Amendment will remain in grave jeopardy. . . .

Those who think the First Amendment can and should be subordinated to other socially desirable interests will hail today's decision. But I find it frightening. For I believe the constitutional guarantee of a free press is more than precatory. I believe it is a clear command that government must never be allowed to lay its heavy editorial hand on any newspaper in this country.

Miami Herald Publishing Co. v. Tornillo

418 U.S. 241, 94 S.Ct. 2831, 41 L.Ed.2d 730 (1974).

Mr. Chief Justice Burger delivered the opinion of the Court.

The issue in this case is whether a state statute granting a political candidate a right to equal space to reply to criticism and attacks on his record by a newspaper, violates the guarantees of a free press.

I

In the fall of 1972, appellee, Executive Director of the Classroom Teachers Association, apparently a teachers' collective-bargaining agent, was a candidate for the Florida House of Representatives. On September 20, 1972, and again on September 29, 1972, appellant printed editorials critical of appellee's candidacy. In response to these editorials appellee demanded that appellant print verbatim his replies, defending the role of the Classroom Teachers Association and the organization's accomplishments for the citizens of Dade County. Appellant declined to print the appellee's replies, and appellee brought suit in Circuit Court, Dade County, seeking declaratory and injunctive relief and actual and punitive damages in excess of $5,000. The action was premised on Florida Statute § 104.38 (1973), a "right of reply" statute which provides that if a candidate for nomination or election is assailed regarding his personal character or official record by any newspaper, the candidate has the right to demand that the newspaper print, free of cost to the candidate, any reply the candidate may make to the newspaper's charges. The reply must appear in as conspicuous a place and in the same kind of type as the charges which prompted the reply, provided it does not take up more space than the charges. Failure to comply with the statute constitutes a first-degree misdemeanor.

Appellant sought a declaration that § 104.38 was unconstitutional. . . .

. . . [T]he Florida Supreme Court [held] that § 104.38 did not violate constitutional guarantees. . . .

. . .

III

A

. . .

Appellant contends the statute is void on its face because it purports to regulate the content of a newspaper in violation of the First Amendment. Alternatively it is urged that the statute is void for vagueness since no editor could know exactly what words would call the statute into operation. It is also contended that the statute fails to distinguish between critical comment which is and which is not defamatory.

B

The appellee and supporting advocates of an enforceable right of access to the press vigorously argue that government has an obligation to ensure that a wide variety of views reach the public. The contentions of access proponents will be set out in some detail. It is urged that at the time the First Amendment to the Constitution was ratified in 1791 as part of our Bill of Rights the press was broadly representative of the people it was serving. While many of the newspapers were intensely partisan and narrow in their views, the press collectively presented a broad range of opinions to readers. Entry into publishing was inexpensive; pamphlets and books provided meaningful alternatives to the organized press for the expression of unpopular ideas and often treated events and expressed views not covered by conventional newspapers. A true marketplace of ideas existed in which there was relatively easy access to the channels of communication.

Access advocates submit that although newspapers of the present are superficially similar to those of 1791 the press of today is in reality very different from that known in the early years of our national existence. In the past half century a communications revolution has seen the introduction of radio and television into our lives, the promise of a global community through the use of communications satellites, and the specter of a "wired" nation by means of an expanding cable television network with two-way capabilities. The printed press, it is said, has not escaped the effects of this revolution. Newspapers have become big business and there are far fewer of them to serve a larger literate population. Chains of newspapers, national newspapers, national wire and news services, and one-newspaper towns, are the dominant features of a press that has become noncompetitive and enormously powerful and influential in its capacity to manipulate popular opinion and change the course of events. Major metropolitan newspapers have collaborated to establish news services national in scope. Such national news organizations provide syndicated "interpretive reporting" as well as syndicated features and commentary, all of which can serve as part of the new school of "advocacy journalism."

The elimination of competing newspapers in most of our large cities, and the concentration of control of media that results from the only newspaper's being owned by the same interests which own a television station and a radio station, are important components of this trend toward concentration of control of outlets to inform the public.

The result of these vast changes has been to place in a few hands the power to inform the American people and shape public opinion. Much of the editorial opinion and commentary that is printed is that of syndicated columnists distributed nationwide and, as a result, we are told, on national and world issues there tends to be a homogeneity of editorial opinion, commentary, and interpretative analysis. The abuses of bias and manipulative reportage are, likewise, said to be the result of the vast accumulations of unreviewable power in the modern media empires. In effect, it is claimed, the public has lost any ability to respond or to contribute in a meaningful way to the debate on issues. The monopoly of the means of communication allows for little or no critical analysis of the media except in professional journals of very limited readership. . . .

The obvious solution, which was available to dissidents at an earlier time when entry into publishing was relatively inexpensive, today would be to have additional newspapers. But the same economic factors which have caused the disappearance of vast numbers of metropolitan newspapers, have made entry into the marketplace of ideas served by the print media almost impossible. It is urged that the claim of newspapers to be "surrogates for the public" carries with it a concomitant fiduciary obligation to account for that stewardship. From this premise it is reasoned that the only effective way to insure fairness and accuracy and to provide for some accountability is for government to take affirmative action. The First Amendment interest of the public in being informed is said to be in peril because the "marketplace of ideas" is today a monopoly controlled by the owners of the market.

.   .   .

IV

However much validity may be found in these arguments, at each point the implementation of a remedy such as an enforceable right of access necessarily calls for some mechanism, either governmental or consensual. If it is governmental coercion, this at once brings about a confrontation with the express provisions of the First Amendment and the judicial gloss on that Amendment developed over the years.

.   .   .

Appellee's argument that the Florida statute does not amount to a restriction of appellant's right to speak because "the statute in question here has not prevented the *Miami Herald* from saying anything it wished" begs the core question. Compelling editors or publishers to publish that which "'reason' tells them should not be published" is what is at issue in this case. The Florida statute operates as a command in the same sense as a statute or regulation forbidding appellant to publish specified matter. . . . The Florida statute exacts a penalty on the basis of the content of a newspaper. The first phase of the penalty resulting from the compelled printing of a reply is exacted in terms of the cost in printing and composing time and materials and in taking up space that could be devoted to other material the newspaper may have preferred to print. It is correct, as appellee contends, that a newspaper is not subject to the finite technological limitations of time that confront a broadcaster but it is not correct to say that, as an economic reality, a newspaper can proceed to infinite expansion of its column space to accommodate the replies that a government agency determines or a statute commands the readers should have available.

Faced with the penalties that would accrue to any newspaper that published news or commentary arguably within the reach of the right-of-access statute, editors might well conclude that the safe course is to avoid controversy. Therefore, under the operation of the Florida statute, political and electoral coverage would be blunted or reduced. . . .

Even if a newspaper would face no additional costs to comply with a compulsory access law and would not be forced to forgo publication of news or opinion by the inclusion of a reply, the Florida statute fails to clear the barriers of the First Amendment because of its intrusion into the function of editors. A newspaper is more than a passive receptacle or conduit for news, comment, and advertising. The choice of material to go into a newspaper, and the decisions made as to limitations on the size and content of the paper, and treatment of public issues and public officials—whether fair or unfair—constitute the exercise of editorial control and judgment. It has yet to be demonstrated how governmental regulation of this crucial process can be exercised consistent with First Amendment guarantees of a free press as they have evolved to this time. Accordingly, the judgment of the Supreme Court of Florida is reversed.

It is so ordered.[a]

Mr. Justice Brennan, with whom Mr. Justice Rehnquist joins, concurring.

I join the Court's opinion which, as I understand it, addresses only "right of reply" statutes and implies no view upon the constitutionality of "retraction" statutes affording plaintiffs able to prove defamatory falsehoods a statutory action to require publication of a retraction. See generally Note, *Vindication of the Reputation of a Public Official*, 80 Harv.L.Rev. 1730, 1739–1747 (1967).[b]

SECTION 3. PROHIBITION OF PUBLICATION OF GOVERNMENT INFORMATION

New York Times Co. v. United States [the Cases of the Pentagon Papers.]

403 U.S. 713, 91 S.Ct. 2140, 29 L.Ed.2d 822 (1971).

Per Curiam.

We granted certiorari in these cases in which the United States seeks to enjoin the *New York Times* and the *Washington Post* from publishing the contents of a classified study entitled "History of U.S. Decision–Making Process on Viet Nam Policy." [Commonly referred to as the "Pentagon Papers."]

"Any system of prior restraints of expression comes to this Court bearing a heavy presumption against its constitutional validity." Bantam Books, Inc. v. Sullivan, 372 U.S. 58, 70 (1963); see also Near v. Minnesota, 283 U.S. 697 (1931). The Government "thus carries a heavy burden of showing justification for the imposition of such a restraint." Organization for a Better Austin v. Keefe, 402 U.S. 415, 419 (1971). The District Court for the Southern District of New York in the *New York Times* case and the District Court for the District of Columbia and the Court of Appeals for the District of Columbia Circuit in the *Washington Post* case held that the Government had not met that burden. We agree.

The judgment of the Court of Appeals for the District of Columbia Circuit is therefore affirmed. The order of the Court of Appeals for the Second Circuit is reversed and the case is remanded with directions to enter a judgment affirming the judgment of the District Court for the Southern District of New York. . . .

Mr. Justice Black, with whom Mr. Justice Douglas joins, concurring.

I adhere to the view that the Government's case against the Washington Post should have been dismissed and that the injunction against the New York Times should have been vacated without oral argument when the cases were

---

[a] A concurring opinion by Justice White is omitted.

[b] A good, in-depth analysis is contained in Powe, *Tornillo,* 1988 Sup.Ct.Rev. 345.

first presented to this Court. I believe that every moment's continuance of the injunctions against these newspapers amounts to a flagrant, indefensible, and continuing violation of the First Amendment.... In my view it is unfortunate that some of my Brethren are apparently willing to hold that the publication of news may sometimes be enjoined. Such a holding would make a shambles of the First Amendment....

... In my view, far from deserving condemnation for their courageous reporting, the New York Times, the Washington Post, and other newspapers should be commended for serving the purpose that the Founding Fathers saw so clearly. In revealing the workings of government that led to the Vietnam war, the newspapers nobly did precisely that which the Founders hoped and trusted they would do.

... The Government argues in its brief that in spite of the First Amendment, "[t]he authority of the Executive Department to protect the nation against publication of information whose disclosure would endanger the national security stems from two interrelated sources: the constitutional power of the President over the conduct of foreign affairs and his authority as Commander-in-Chief."

... To find that the President has "inherent power" to halt the publication of news by resort to the courts would wipe out the First Amendment and destroy the fundamental liberty and security of the very people the Government hopes to make "secure." No one can read the history of the adoption of the First Amendment without being convinced beyond any doubt that it was injunctions like those sought here that Madison and his collaborators intended to outlaw in this Nation for all time.

. . .

Mr. Justice Douglas, with whom Mr. Justice Black joins, concurring.

. . .

... [T]he First Amendment provides that "Congress shall make no law ... abridging the freedom of speech or of the press." That leaves, in my view, no room for governmental restraint on the press.

There is, moreover, no statute barring the publication by the press of the material which the Times and the Post seek to use. ...

. . .

The stays in these cases that have been in effect for more than a week constitute a flouting of the principles of the First Amendment as interpreted in Near v. Minnesota.

Mr. Justice Brennan, concurring.

I

I write separately in these cases only to emphasize what should be apparent: that our judgments in the present cases may not be taken to indicate the propriety, in the future, of issuing temporary stays and restraining orders to block the publication of material sought to be suppressed by the Government. So far as I can determine, never before has the United States sought to enjoin a newspaper from publishing information in its possession....

II

The error that has pervaded these cases from the outset was the granting of any injunctive relief whatsoever, interim or otherwise. The entire thrust of the Government's claim throughout these cases has been that publication of the material sought to be enjoined "could," or "might," or "may," prejudice the national interest in various ways. But the First Amendment tolerates absolutely no prior judicial restraints of the press predicated upon surmise or conjecture that untoward consequences may result.* Our cases, it is true, have indicated that there is a single, extremely narrow class of cases in which the First Amendment's ban on prior judicial restraint may be overridden. Our cases have thus far indicated that such cases may arise only when the Nation "is at war," Schenck v. United States, 249 U.S. 47, 52 (1919), during which times "[n]o one would question but that a Government might prevent actual obstruction to its recruiting service or the publication of the sailing dates of transports or the number and location of troops." Near v. Minnesota, 283 U.S. 697, 716 (1931). Even if the present world situation were assumed to be tantamount to a time of war, or if the power of presently available armaments would justify even in peacetime the suppression of information that would set in motion a nuclear holocaust, in neither of these actions has the Government presented or even alleged that publication of items from or based upon the material at issue would cause the happening of an event of that nature. "[T]he chief purpose of [the First Amendment's] guaranty [is] to prevent previous restraints upon publication." Near v. Minnesota, supra, at 713. Thus, only governmental allegation and proof that publication must inevitably, directly and immediately cause the occurrence of an event kindred to imperiling the safety of a transport already at sea can support even the issuance of an interim restraining order. In no event may mere conclusions be sufficient: for if the Executive Branch seeks judicial aid in preventing publication, it must inevitably submit the basis upon which that aid is sought to scrutiny by the judiciary. And therefore, every restraint issued in this case, whatever its form, has violated the First Amendment—and not less so because that restraint was justified as necessary to afford the courts an opportunity to examine the claim more thoroughly. Unless and until the Government has clearly made out its case, the First Amendment commands that no injunction may issue.

Mr. Justice Stewart, with whom Mr. Justice White joins, concurring.

In the governmental structure created by our Constitution, the Executive is endowed with enormous power in the two related areas of national defense and international relations. This power, largely unchecked by the Legislative and Judicial branches, has been pressed to the very hilt since the advent of the nuclear missile age. For better or for worse, the simple fact is that a President of the United States possesses vastly greater constitutional independence in these two vital areas of power than does, say, a prime minister of a country with a parliamentary form of government.

---

* Freedman v. Maryland, 380 U.S. 51 (1965), and similar cases regarding temporary restraints of allegedly obscene materials are not in point. For those cases rest upon the proposition that "obscenity is not protected by the freedoms of speech and press." Roth v. United States, 354 U.S. 476, 481 (1957). Here there is no question but that the material sought to be suppressed is within the protection of the First Amendment; the only question is whether, notwithstanding that fact, its publication may be enjoined for a time because of the presence of an overwhelming national interest. Similarly, copyright cases have no pertinence here: the Government is not asserting an interest in the particular form of words chosen in the documents, but is seeking to suppress the ideas expressed therein. And the copyright laws, of course, protect only the form of expression and not the ideas expressed.

In the absence of the governmental checks and balances present in other areas of our national life, the only effective restraint upon executive policy and power in the areas of national defense and international affairs may lie in an enlightened citizenry—in an informed and critical public opinion which alone can here protect the values of democratic government. For this reason, it is perhaps here that a press that is alert, aware, and free most vitally serves the basic purpose of the First Amendment. For without an informed and free press there cannot be an enlightened people.

Yet it is elementary that the successful conduct of international diplomacy and the maintenance of an effective national defense require both confidentiality and secrecy. Other nations can hardly deal with this Nation in an atmosphere of mutual trust unless they can be assured that their confidences will be kept. And within our own executive departments, the development of considered and intelligent international policies would be impossible if those charged with their formulation could not communicate with each other freely, frankly, and in confidence. In the area of basic national defense the frequent need for absolute secrecy is, of course, self-evident.

I think there can be but one answer to this dilemma, if dilemma it be. The responsibility must be where the power is. If the Constitution gives the Executive a large degree of unshared power in the conduct of foreign affairs and the maintenance of our national defense, then under the Constitution the Executive must have the largely unshared duty to determine and preserve the degree of internal security necessary to exercise that power successfully.... [I]t is the constitutional duty of the Executive—as a matter of sovereign prerogative and not as a matter of law as the courts know law—through the promulgation and enforcement of executive regulations, to protect the confidentiality necessary to carry out its responsibilities in the fields of international relations and national defense.

This is not to say that Congress and the courts have no role to play. Undoubtedly Congress has the power to enact specific and appropriate criminal laws to protect government property and preserve government secrets. Congress has passed such laws, and several of them are of very colorable relevance to the apparent circumstances of these cases. And if a criminal prosecution is instituted, it will be the responsibility of the courts to decide the applicability of the criminal law under which the charge is brought. Moreover, if Congress should pass a specific law authorizing civil proceedings in this field, the courts would likewise have the duty to decide the constitutionality of such a law as well as its applicability to the facts proved.

But in the cases before us we are asked neither to construe specific regulations nor to apply specific laws. We are asked, instead, to perform a function that the Constitution gave to the Executive, not the Judiciary. We are asked, quite simply, to prevent the publication by two newspapers of material that the Executive Branch insists should not, in the national interest, be published. I am convinced that the Executive is correct with respect to some of the documents involved. But I cannot say that disclosure of any of them will surely result in direct, immediate, and irreparable damage to our Nation or its people. That being so, there can under the First Amendment be but one judicial resolution of the issues before us. I join the judgments of the Court.

Mr. Justice White, with whom Mr. Justice Stewart joins, concurring.

I concur in today's judgments, but only because of the concededly extraordinary protection against prior restraints enjoyed by the press under our constitutional system.... [T]he United States has not satisfied the very heavy burden that it must meet to warrant an injunction against publication in these cases, at least in the absence of express and appropriately limited congressional authorization for prior restraints in circumstances such as these.

. . .

. . . [T]erminating the ban on publication of the relatively few sensitive documents the Government now seeks to suppress does not mean that the law either requires or invites newspapers or others to publish them or that they will be immune from criminal action if they do. Prior restraints require an unusually heavy justification under the First Amendment; but failure by the Government to justify prior restraints does not measure its constitutional entitlement to a conviction for criminal publication. That the Government mistakenly chose to proceed by injunction does not mean that it could not successfully proceed in another way.

. . .

The Criminal Code contains numerous provisions potentially relevant to these cases. . . .

. . .

It is thus clear that Congress has addressed itself to the problems of protecting the security of the country and the national defense from unauthorized disclosure of potentially damaging information. . . . It has not, however, authorized the injunctive remedy against threatened publication. It has apparently been satisfied to rely on criminal sanctions and their deterrent effect on the responsible as well as the irresponsible press. I am not, of course, saying that either of these newspapers has yet committed a crime or that either would commit a crime if it published all the material now in its possession. That matter must await resolution in the context of a criminal proceeding if one is instituted by the United States. In that event, the issue of guilt or innocence would be determined by procedures and standards quite different from those that have purported to govern these injunctive proceedings.

Mr. Justice Marshall, concurring.

. . .

The problem here is whether in these particular cases the Executive Branch has authority to invoke the equity jurisdiction of the courts to protect what it believes to be the national interest. . . .

It would . . . be utterly inconsistent with the concept of separation of powers for this Court, to use its power of contempt to prevent behavior that Congress has specifically declined to prohibit. There would be a similar damage to the basic concept of these co-equal branches of Government if when the Executive Branch has adequate authority granted by Congress to protect "national security" it can choose instead to invoke the contempt power of a court to enjoin the threatened conduct. . . .

. . .

Mr. Chief Justice Burger, dissenting.

. . .

. . . [W]e have been forced to deal with litigation concerning rights of great magnitude without an adequate record, and surely without time for adequate treatment either in the prior proceedings or in this Court. . . . I agree generally with Mr. Justice Harlan and Mr. Justice Blackmun but I am not prepared to reach the merits.

. . .

Mr. Justice Harlan, with whom The Chief Justice and Mr. Justice Blackmun join, dissenting.

. . . With all respect, I consider that the Court has been almost irresponsibly feverish in dealing with these cases.

. . .

Forced as I am to reach the merits of these cases, I dissent from the opinion and judgments of the Court. Within the severe limitations imposed by the time constraints under which I have been required to operate, I can only state my reasons in telescoped form. . . .

. . .

. . . It is plain to me that the scope of the judicial function in passing upon the activities of the Executive Branch of the Government in the field of foreign affairs is very narrowly restricted. This view is, I think, dictated by the concept of separation of powers upon which our constitutional system rests.

. . .

. . . I agree that, in performance of its duty to protect the values of the First Amendment against political pressures, the judiciary must review the initial Executive determination to the point of satisfying itself that the subject matter of the dispute does lie within the proper compass of the President's foreign relations power. Constitutional considerations forbid "a complete abandonment of judicial control." . . . Moreover, the judiciary may properly insist that the determination that disclosure of the subject matter would irreparably impair the national security be made by the head of the Executive Department concerned—here the Secretary of State or the Secretary of Defense—after actual personal consideration by that officer. . . .

But in my judgment the judiciary may not properly go beyond these two inquiries and redetermine for itself the probable impact of disclosure on the national security. . . .

Even if there is some room for the judiciary to override the executive determination, it is plain that the scope of review must be exceedingly narrow. I can see no indication in the opinions of either the District Court or the Court of Appeals in the *Post* litigation that the conclusions of the Executive were given even the deference owing to an administrative agency, much less that owing to a co-equal branch of the Government operating within the field of its constitutional prerogative. . . .

Pending further hearings in each case conducted under the appropriate ground rules, I would continue the restraints on publication. I cannot believe that the doctrine prohibiting prior restraints reaches to the point of preventing courts from maintaining the *status quo* long enough to act responsibly in matters of such national importance as those involved here.

Mr. Justice Blackmun, dissenting.

I join Mr. Justice Harlan in his dissent. I also am in substantial accord with much that Mr. Justice White says, by way of admonition, in the latter part of his opinion.

. . .

PROTECTION OF THE COURTS AGAINST CRITICISM

The early history of the use of the contempt power to punish the press for criticism of judges and judicial action was recounted in section 1 of Chapter 13. In 1941 the Court reinterpreted the federal statute restricting the use of contempt as preventing the federal courts from punishing acts outside the geographical environs of the courthouse. Nye v. United States, 313 U.S. 33 (1941). Shortly thereafter the Court substantially eliminated the power of the state and federal courts to punish the press for publications alleged to interfere with judicial impartiality by holding that under the first amendment only publications that create an imminent and serious threat to the ability of the court fairly to decide issues before it can be punished. Bridges v. California, 314 U.S. 252 (1941); Pennekamp v. Florida, 328 U.S. 331 (1946); Craig v. Harney, 331 U.S. 367 (1947).

Nebraska Press Association v. Stuart

427 U.S. 539, 96 S.Ct. 2791, 49 L.Ed.2d 683 (1976).

Mr. Chief Justice Burger delivered the opinion of the Court.

The respondent State District Judge entered an order restraining the petitioners from publishing or broadcasting accounts of confessions or admissions made by the accused or facts "strongly implicative" of the accused in a widely reported murder of six persons. We granted certiorari to decide whether the entry of such an order on the showing made before the state court violated the constitutional guarantee of freedom of the press.

On the evening of October 18, 1975, local police found the six members of the Henry Kellie family murdered in their home in Sutherland, Neb., a town of about 850 people. Police released the description of a suspect, Erwin Charles Simants, to the reporters who had hastened to the scene of the crime. Simants was arrested and arraigned in Lincoln County Court the following morning, ending a tense night for this small rural community.

The crime immediately attracted widespread news coverage, by local, regional, and national newspapers, radio and television stations. Three days after the crime, the County Attorney and Simants' attorney joined in asking the County Court to enter a restrictive order relating to "matters that may or may not be publicly reported or disclosed to the public," because of the "mass coverage by news media" and the "reasonable likelihood of prejudicial news which would make difficult, if not impossible, the impaneling of an impartial jury and tend to prevent a fair trial." The County Court heard oral argument but took no evidence; no attorney for members of the press appeared at this stage. The County Court granted the prosecutor's motion for a restrictive order and entered it the next day, October 22. The order prohibited everyone in attendance from "releas[ing] or authoriz[ing] the release for public dissemination in any form or manner whatsoever any testimony given or evidence adduced"; . . .

. . .

The Nebraska Supreme Court . . . modified the District Court's order to accommodate the defendant's right to a fair trial and the petitioners' interest in reporting pretrial events. The order as modified prohibited reporting of only three matters: (a) the existence and nature of any confessions or admissions made by the defendant to law enforcement officers, (b) any confessions or admissions made to any third parties, except members of the press, and © other facts "strongly implicative" of the accused....

. . .

III

. . .

... The trial of Bruno Hauptmann in a small New Jersey community for the abduction and murder of the Charles Lindberghs' infant child, probably was the most widely covered trial up to that time, and the nature of the coverage produced widespread public reaction....

The excesses of press and radio and lack of responsibility of those in authority in the Hauptmann case and others of that era led to efforts to develop voluntary guidelines for courts, lawyers, press and broadcasters. See generally J. Lofton, Justice and the Press 117–130 (1966). The effort was renewed in 1965 when the American Bar Association embarked on a project to develop standards for all aspects of criminal justice, including guidelines to accommodate the right to a fair trial and the rights of a free press. See Powell, The Right to a Fair Trial, 51 ABA J. 534 (1965). The resulting standards, approved by the Association in 1968, received support from most of the legal profession. American Bar Association Project on Standards for Criminal Justice, Fair Trial and Free Press (Approved Draft, 1968)....

In practice, of course, even the most ideal guidelines are subjected to powerful strains when a case such as Simants' arises, with reporters from many parts of the country on the scene. Reporters from distant places are unlikely to consider themselves bound by local standards. They report to editors outside the area covered by the guidelines, and their editors are likely to be guided only by their own standards. To contemplate how a state court can control acts of a newspaper or broadcaster outside its jurisdiction, even though the newspapers and broadcasts reach the very community from which jurors are to be selected, suggests something of the practical difficulties of managing such guidelines.

. . .

IV

. . .

In Sheppard v. Maxwell, 384 U.S. 333 (1966), the Court focused sharply on the impact of pretrial publicity and a trial court's duty to protect the defendant's constitutional right to a fair trial. ...[T]he Court ordered a new trial for the petitioner, even though the first trial had occurred 12 years before. Beyond doubt the press had shown no responsible concern for the constitutional guarantee of a fair trial; the community from which the jury was drawn had been inundated by publicity hostile to the defendant. But the trial judge "did not fulfill his duty to protect [the defendant] from the inherently prejudicial publicity which saturated the community and to control disruptive influences in the courtroom." ... The Court noted that "unfair and prejudicial news comment on pending trials has become increasingly prevalent," ... and issued a strong warning:

> "Due process requires that the accused receive a trial by an impartial jury free from outside influences. Given the pervasiveness of modern communications and the difficulty of effacing prejudicial publicity from the minds of the jurors, *the trial courts must take strong measures to ensure that the balance is never weighed against the accused....* Of course, there is

nothing that proscribes the press from reporting events that transpire in the courtroom. But where there is a reasonable likelihood that prejudicial news prior to trial will prevent a fair trial, the judge should *continue the case* until the threat abates, *or transfer it* to another county not so permeated with publicity. In addition, *sequestration of the jury* was something the judge should have raised sua sponte with counsel. If publicity during the proceedings threatens the fairness of the trial, a new trial should be ordered. But we must remember that reversals are but palliatives; the cure lies in those remedial measures that will prevent the prejudice at its inception. The courts must take such steps by rule and regulation that will protect their processes from prejudicial outside interferences. *Neither prosecutors, counsel for defense, the accused, witnesses, court staff nor enforcement officers coming under the jurisdiction of the court should be permitted to frustrate its function.* Collaboration between counsel and the press as to information affecting the fairness of a criminal trial is not only subject to regulation, but is highly censurable and worthy of disciplinary measures." Id., at 362–363 (emphasis added).

Because the trial court had failed to use even minimal efforts to insulate the trial and the jurors from the "deluge of publicity," ... the Court vacated the judgment of conviction and a new trial followed, in which the accused was acquitted.

Cases such as these are relatively rare, and we have held in other cases that trials have been fair in spite of widespread publicity. In Stroble v. California, 343 U.S. 181 (1952), for example, the Court affirmed a conviction and death sentence challenged on the ground that pretrial news accounts, including the prosecutor's release of the defendant's recorded confession, were allegedly so inflammatory as to amount to a denial of due process. The Court disapproved of the prosecutor's conduct, but noted that the publicity had receded some six weeks before trial, that the defendant had not moved for a change of venue, and that the confession had been found voluntary and admitted in evidence at trial. The Court also noted the thorough examination of jurors on *voir dire* and the careful review of the facts by the state courts, and held that petitioner had failed to demonstrate a denial of due process. See also Murphy v. Florida, 421 U.S. 794 (1975); Beck v. Washington, 369 U.S. 541 (1962).

Taken together, these cases demonstrate that pretrial publicity—even pervasive, adverse publicity—does not inevitably lead to an unfair trial. The capacity of the jury eventually impaneled to decide the case fairly is influenced by the tone and extent of the publicity, which is in part, and often in large part, shaped by what attorneys, police, and other officials do to precipitate news coverage. The trial judge has a major responsibility. What the judge says about a case, in or out of the courtroom, is likely to appear in newspapers and broadcasts. More important, the measures a judge takes or fails to take to mitigate the effects of pretrial publicity—the measures described in *Sheppard*—may well determine whether the defendant receives a trial consistent with the requirements of due process. That this responsibility has not always been properly discharged is apparent from the decisions just reviewed.

.   .   .

V

... None of our decided cases on prior restraint involved restrictive orders entered to protect a defendant's right to a fair and impartial jury, but the opinions on prior restraint have a common thread relevant to this case.

.   .   .

A prior restraint, ... has an immediate and irreversible sanction. If it can be said that a threat of criminal or civil sanctions after publication "chills" speech, prior restraint "freezes" it at least for the time.

. . .

VI

We turn now to the record in this case to determine whether, as Learned Hand put it, "the gravity of the 'evil,' discounted by its improbability, justifies such invasion of free speech as is necessary to avoid the danger." United States v. Dennis, 183 F.2d 201, 212 (C.A.2 1950), aff'd, 341 U.S. 494 (1951) ... To do so, we must examine the evidence before the trial judge when the order was entered to determine (a) the nature and extent of pretrial news coverage; (b) whether other measures would be likely to mitigate the effects of unrestrained pretrial publicity; and © how effectively a restraining order would operate to prevent the threatened danger. The precise terms of the restraining order are also important. We must then consider whether the record supports the entry of a prior restraint on publication, one of the most extraordinary remedies known to our jurisprudence.

. . .

We have ... examined this record to determine the probable efficacy of the measures short of prior restraint on the press and speech. There is no finding that alternative measures would not have protected Simants' rights, and the Nebraska Supreme Court did no more than imply that such measures might not be adequate. Moreover, the record is lacking in evidence to support such a finding.

. . .

To the extent that this order prohibited the reporting of evidence adduced at the open preliminary hearing, it plainly violated settled principles: "[t]here is nothing that proscribes the press from reporting events that transpire in the courtroom." Sheppard v. Maxwell, 384 U.S. at 362–363. . . .

The third prohibition of the order was defective in another respect as well. As part of a final order, entered after plenary review, this prohibition regarding "implicative" information is too vague and too broad to survive the scrutiny we have given to restraints on First Amendment rights. . . .

. . .

Of necessity our holding is confined to the record before us. But our conclusion is not simply a result of assessing the adequacy of the showing made in this case; it results in part from the problems inherent in meeting the heavy burden of demonstrating, in advance of trial, that without prior restraint a fair trial will be denied. The practical problems of managing and enforcing restrictive orders will always be present. In this sense, the record now before us is illustrative rather than exceptional. It is significant that when this Court has reversed a state conviction because of prejudicial publicity, it has carefully noted that some course of action short of prior restraint would have made a critical difference. . . . However difficult it may be, we need not rule out the possibility of showing the kind of threat to fair trial rights that would possess the requisite degree of certainty to justify restraint. This Court has frequently denied that First Amendment rights are absolute and has consistently rejected the proposition that a prior restraint can never be employed. . . .

. . .

Mr. Justice Brennan, with whom Mr. Justice Stewart and Mr. Justice Marshall join, concurring in the judgment.

The question presented in this case is whether, consistently with the First Amendment, a court may enjoin the press, in advance of publication, from reporting or commenting on information acquired from public court proceedings, public court records, or other sources about pending judicial proceedings.... The right to a fair trial by a jury of one's peers is unquestionably one of the most precious and sacred safeguards enshrined in the Bill of Rights. I would hold, however, that resort to prior restraints on the freedom of the press is a constitutionally impermissible method for enforcing that right; judges have at their disposal a broad spectrum of devices for ensuring that fundamental fairness is accorded the accused without necessitating so drastic an incursion on the equally fundamental and salutary constitutional mandate that discussion of public affairs in a free society cannot depend on the preliminary grace of judicial censors.

. . .

There is, beyond peradventure, a clear and substantial damage to freedom of the press whenever even a temporary restraint is imposed on reporting of material concerning the operations of the criminal justice system, an institution of such pervasive influence in our constitutional scheme. And the necessary impact of reporting even confessions can never be so direct, immediate and irreparable that I would give credence to any notion that prior restraints may be imposed on that rationale. It may be that such incriminating material would be of such slight news value or so inflammatory in particular cases that responsible organs of the media, in an exercise of self-restraint, would choose not to publicize that material, and not make the judicial task of safeguarding precious rights of criminal defendants more difficult. Voluntary codes such as the Nebraska Bar–Press Guidelines are a commendable acknowledgment by the media that constitutional prerogatives bring enormous responsibilities, and I would encourage continuation of such voluntary cooperative efforts between the bar and the media. However, the press may be arrogant, tyrannical, abusive, and sensationalist, just as it may be incisive, probing, and informative. But at least in the context of prior restraints on publication, the decision of what, when, and how to publish is for editors, not judges.... Every restrictive order imposed on the press in this case was accordingly an unconstitutional prior restraint on the freedom of the press, and I would therefore reverse the judgment of the Nebraska Supreme Court and remand for further proceedings not inconsistent with this opinion.

Mr. Justice White, concurring.

Technically there is no need to go farther than the Court does to dispose of this case, and I join the Court's opinion. I should add, however, that for the reasons which the Court itself canvasses there is grave doubt in my mind whether orders with respect to the press such as were entered in this case would ever be justifiable. It may be the better part of discretion, however, not to announce such a rule in the first case in which the issue has been squarely presented here. Perhaps we should go no farther than absolutely necessary until the federal courts, and ourselves, have been exposed to a broader spectrum of cases presenting similar issues. If the recurring result, however, in case after case is to be similar to our judgment today, we should at some point announce a more general rule and avoid the interminable litigation that our failure to do so would necessarily entail.

Mr. Justice Powell, concurring.

Although I join the opinion of the Court, in view of the importance of the case I write to emphasize the unique burden that rests upon the party, whether it be the State or a defendant, who undertakes to show the necessity for prior restraint on pretrial publicity.

In my judgment a prior restraint properly may issue only when it is shown to be necessary to prevent the dissemination of prejudicial publicity that otherwise poses a high likelihood of preventing, directly and irreparably, the impaneling of a jury meeting the Sixth Amendment requirement of impartiality. This requires a showing that (I) there is a clear threat to the fairness of trial, (ii) such a threat is posed by the actual publicity to be restrained, and (III) no less restrictive alternatives are available. Notwithstanding such a showing, a restraint may not issue unless it also is shown that previous publicity or publicity from unrestrained sources will not render the restraint inefficacious. The threat to the fairness of the trial is to be evaluated in the context of Sixth Amendment law on impartiality, and any restraint must comply with the standards of specificity always required in the First Amendment context.

I believe these factors are sufficiently addressed in the Court's opinion to demonstrate beyond question that the prior restraint here was impermissible.

Mr. Justice Stevens, concurring in the judgment.

For the reasons eloquently stated by Mr. Justice Brennan, I agree that the judiciary is capable of protecting the defendant's right to a fair trial without enjoining the press from publishing information in the public domain, and that it may not do so. Whether the same absolute protection would apply no matter how shabby or illegal the means by which the information is obtained, no matter how serious an intrusion on privacy might be involved, no matter how demonstrably false the information might be, no matter how prejudicial it might be to the interests of innocent persons, and no matter how perverse the motivation for publishing it, is a question I would not answer without further argument. ...I do, however, subscribe to most of what Mr. Justice Brennan says and, if ever required to face the issue squarely, may well accept his ultimate conclusion.

The Florida Star v. B.J.F.

491 U.S. 524, 109 S.Ct. 2603, 105 L.Ed.2d 443 (1989).

[The report in this case appears, supra at p. 1266.]

SECTION 4. GOVERNMENT DEMANDS FOR CONFIDENTIAL PRESS INFORMATION

Branzburg v. Hayes

408 U.S. 665, 92 S.Ct. 2646, 33 L.Ed.2d 626 (1972).

Opinion of the Court by Mr. Justice White, announced by The Chief Justice.

[Branzburg was a Louisville Courier–Journal reporter who observed two persons synthesizing hashish from marihuana, a violation of local law. After making his observations the basis of a news article, he was called before a grand jury and refused to identify the persons involved. Pappas, a television-reporter-photographer, was sent to New Bedford, Massachusetts, to cover a Black Panther conference and gained entrance to the Panther headquarters. He was called before a grand jury investigating civil disorders and refused to testify as to anything he heard while within the Panther headquarters. Caldwell was a New York Times reporter assigned to cover the Black Panthers and other black militant groups. He wrote several articles and was called to testify and bring his records before a federal grand jury investigating possible threats and conspiracies to assassinate the President. He refused to appear. All three cases raised the issue whether requiring reporters to appear and testify before state or federal grand juries was consistent with the First Amendment.]

Petitioners Branzburg and Pappas and respondent Caldwell press First Amendment claims that may be simply put: that to gather news it is often necessary to agree either not to identify the source of information published or to publish only part of the facts revealed, or both; that if the reporter is nevertheless forced to reveal these confidences to a grand jury, the source so identified and other confidential sources of other reporters will be measurably deterred from furnishing publishable information, all to the detriment of the free flow of information protected by the First Amendment. Although the newsmen in these cases do not claim an absolute privilege against official interrogation in all circumstances, they assert that the reporter should not be forced either to appear or to testify before a grand jury or at trial until and unless sufficient grounds are shown for believing that the reporter possesses information relevant to a crime the grand jury is investigating, that the information the reporter has is unavailable from other sources, and that the need for the information is sufficiently compelling to override the claimed invasion of First Amendment interests occasioned by the disclosure. . . .

. . . [W]ithout some protection for seeking out the news, freedom of the press could be eviscerated. But these cases involve no intrusions upon speech or assembly, no prior restraint or restriction on what the press may publish, and no express or implied command that the press publish what it prefers to withhold. . . .

The sole issue before us is the obligation of reporters to respond to grand jury subpoenas as other citizens do and to answer questions relevant to an investigation into the commission of crime. . . .

. . .

Despite the fact that news gathering may be hampered, the press is regularly excluded from grand jury proceedings, our own conferences, the meetings of other official bodies gathered in executive session, and the meetings of private organizations. Newsmen have no constitutional right of access to the scenes of crime or disaster when the general public is excluded, and they may be prohibited from attending or publishing information about trials if such restrictions are necessary to assure a defendant a fair trial before an impartial tribunal. . . .

It is thus not surprising that the great weight of authority is that newsmen are not exempt from the normal duty of appearing before a grand jury and answering questions relevant to a criminal investigation. At common law, courts consistently refused to recognize the existence of any privilege authorizing a newsman to refuse to reveal confidential information to a grand jury. . . .

. . .

A number of States have provided newsmen a statutory privilege of varying breadth, but the majority have not done so, and none has been provided by federal statute. Until now the only testimonial privilege for unofficial witnesses that is rooted in the Federal Constitution is the Fifth Amendment privilege against compelled self-incrimination. We are asked to create another by interpreting the First Amendment to grant newsmen a testimonial privilege that other citizens do not enjoy. This we decline to do. . . .

This conclusion itself involves no restraint on what newspapers may publish or on the type or quality of information reporters may seek to acquire, nor does it threaten the vast bulk of confidential relationships between reporters and their sources. Grand juries address themselves to the issues of whether crimes have been committed and who committed them. Only where news sources themselves are implicated in crime or possess information relevant to the grand jury's task need they or the reporter be concerned about grand jury subpoenas. Nothing before us indicates that a large number or percentage of *all* confidential news sources falls into either category and would in any way be deterred by our holding that the Constitution does not, as it never has, exempt the newsman from performing the citizen's normal duty of appearing and furnishing information relevant to the grand jury's task.

. . .

The argument that the flow of news will be diminished by compelling reporters to aid the grand jury in a criminal investigation is not irrational, nor are the records before us silent on the matter. But we remain unclear how often and to what extent informers are actually deterred from furnishing information when newsmen are forced to testify before a grand jury. The available data indicates that some newsmen rely a great deal on confidential sources and that some informants are particularly sensitive to the threat of exposure and may be silenced if it is held by this Court that, ordinarily, newsmen must testify pursuant to subpoenas, but the evidence fails to demonstrate that there would be a significant constriction of the flow of news to the public if this Court reaffirms the prior common law and constitutional rule regarding the testimonial obligations of newsmen. Estimates of the inhibiting effect of such subpoenas on the willingness of informants to make disclosures to newsmen are widely divergent and to a great extent speculative. . . .

Accepting the fact, however, that an undetermined number of informants not themselves implicated in crime will nevertheless, for whatever reason, refuse to talk to newsmen if they fear identification by a reporter in an official investigation, we cannot accept the argument that the public interest in possible future news about crime from undisclosed, unverified sources must take precedence over the public interest in pursuing and prosecuting those crimes reported to the press by informants and in thus deterring the commission of such crimes in the future.

. . .

The privilege claimed here is conditional, not absolute; given the suggested preliminary showings and compelling need, the reporter would be required to testify. Presumably, such a rule would reduce the instances in which reporters could be required to appear, but predicting in advance when and in what circumstances they could be compelled to do so would be difficult. . . .

We are unwilling to embark the judiciary on a long and difficult journey to such an uncertain destination. The administration of a constitutional newsman's privilege would present practical and conceptual difficulties of a high order. Sooner or later, it would be necessary to define those categories of newsmen who qualified for the privilege, a questionable procedure in light of the traditional doctrine that liberty of the press is the right of the lonely pamphleteer who uses carbon paper or a mimeograph just as much as of the large metropolitan publisher who utilizes the latest photocomposition methods. . . .

In each instance where a reporter is subpoenaed to testify, the courts would also be embroiled in preliminary factual and legal determinations with respect to whether the proper predicate had been laid for the reporters' appearance: Is there probable cause to believe a crime has been committed? Is it likely that the reporter has useful information gained in confidence? Could the grand jury obtain the information elsewhere? Is the official interest sufficient to outweigh the claimed privilege?

Thus, in the end, by considering whether enforcement of a particular law served a "compelling" governmental interest, the courts would be inextricably involved in distinguishing between the value of enforcing different criminal laws. By requiring testimony from a reporter in investigations involving some crimes but not in others, they would be making a value judgment that a legislature had declined to make, since in each case the criminal law involved would represent a considered legislative judgment, not constitutionally suspect, of what conduct is liable to criminal prosecution. The task of judges, like other officials outside the legislative branch is not to make the law but to uphold it in accordance with their oaths.

At the federal level, Congress has freedom to determine whether a statutory newsman's privilege is necessary and desirable and to fashion standards and rules as narrow or broad as deemed necessary to deal with the evil discerned and, equally important, to refashion those rules as experience from time to time may dictate. There is also merit in leaving state legislatures free, within First Amendment limits, to fashion their own standards in light of the conditions and problems with respect to the relations between law enforcement officials and press in their own areas. It goes without saying, of course, that we are powerless to bar state courts responding in their own way and construing their own constitutions so as to recognize a newsman's privilege, either qualified or absolute.

. . .

Finally, as we have earlier indicated, news gathering is not without its First Amendment protections, and grand jury investigations if instituted or conducted other than in good faith, would pose wholly different issues for resolution under the First Amendment. Official harassment of the press undertaken not for purposes of law enforcement but to disrupt a reporter's relationship with his news sources would have no justification. Grand juries are subject to judicial control and subpoenas to motions to quash. We do not expect courts will forget that grand juries must operate within the limits of the First Amendment as well as the Fifth.

. . .

[The Court ruled on the three cases as follows: (1) Caldwell had no constitutional privilege not to appear before the grand jury; (2) Branzburg was obligated to answer questions regarding the commission of crimes he had observed; and (3) in Pappas the decision of the Massachusetts Court was affirmed, holding that "petitioner must appear before the grand jury to answer the questions put to him, subject, of course, to the supervision of the presiding judge as to the propriety, purposes and scope of the grand jury inquiry and the pertinence of the probable testimony."]

Mr. Justice Powell, concurring.

I add this brief statement to emphasize what seems to me to be the limited nature of the Court's holding. The Court does not hold that newsmen, subpoenaed to testify before a grand jury, are without constitutional rights with respect to the gathering of news or in safeguarding their sources. Certainly, we do not hold, as suggested in Mr. Justice Stewart's dissenting opinion, that state and federal authorities are free to "annex" the news media as "an investigative arm of government." The solicitude repeatedly shown by this Court for First Amendment freedoms should be sufficient assurance against any such effort, even if one seriously believed that the media—properly free and untrammeled in the fullest sense of these terms—were not able to protect themselves.

As indicated in the concluding portion of the opinion, the Court states that no harassment of newsmen will be tolerated. If a newsman believes that the grand jury investigation is not being conducted in good faith he is not without remedy. Indeed, if the newsman is called upon to give information bearing only a remote and tenuous relationship to the subject of the investigation, or if he has some other reason to believe that his testimony implicates confidential source relationships without a legitimate need of law enforcement, he will have access to the Court on a motion to quash and an appropriate protective order may be entered. The asserted claim to privilege should be judged on its facts by the striking of a proper balance between freedom of the press and the obligation of all citizens to give relevant testimony with respect to criminal conduct. The balance of these vital constitutional and societal interests on a case-by-case basis accords with the tried and traditional way of adjudicating such questions.

In short, the courts will be available to newsmen under circumstances where legitimate First Amendment interests require protection.

Mr. Justice Douglas, dissenting....

. . .

It is my view that there is no "compelling need" that can be shown which qualifies the reporter's immunity from appearing or testifying before a grand jury, unless the reporter himself is implicated in a crime. His immunity in my view is therefore quite complete, for, absent his involvement in a crime, the First Amendment protects him against an appearance before a grand jury and if he is involved in a crime, the Fifth Amendment stands as a barrier. Since in my view there is no area of inquiry not protected by a privilege, the reporter need not appear for the futile purpose of invoking one to each question. And, since in my view a newsman has an absolute right not to appear before a grand jury it follows for me that a journalist who voluntarily appears before that body may invoke his First Amendment privilege to specific questions....

. . .

Mr. Justice Stewart, with whom Mr. Justice Brennan and Mr. Justice Marshall join, dissenting.

The Court's crabbed view of the First Amendment reflects a disturbing insensitivity to the critical role of an independent press in our society. The question whether a reporter has a constitutional right to a confidential relationship with his source is of first impression here, but the principles that should guide our decision are as basic as any to be found in the Constitution. While Mr. Justice Powell's enigmatic concurring opinion gives some hope of a more flexible view in the future, the Court in these cases holds that a newsman has no First Amendment right to protect his sources when called before a grand jury. The Court thus invites state and federal authorities to undermine the historic independence of the press by attempting to annex the journalistic profession as an investigative arm of government. Not only will this decision impair performance of the press' constitutionally protected functions, but it will, I am convinced, in the long run, harm rather than help the administration of justice.

. . .

... [W]hen a reporter is asked to appear before a grand jury and reveal confidences, I would hold that the government must (1) show that there is probable cause to believe that the newsman has information that is clearly relevant to a specific probable violation of law; (2) demonstrate that the information sought cannot be obtained by alternative means less destructive of First Amendment rights; and (3) demonstrate a compelling and overriding interest in the information.

This is not to say that a grand jury could not issue a subpoena until such a showing were made, and it is not to say that a newsman would be in any way privileged to ignore any subpoena that was issued. Obviously, before the government's burden to make such a showing were triggered, the reporter would have to move to quash the subpoena, asserting the basis on which he considered the particular relationship a confidential one.

. . .

ZURCHER v. STANFORD DAILY, 436 U.S. 547 (1978). The Court held that the first and fourth amendments did not preclude issuance of a search warrant for search of a newsroom. On the first amendment issue, Justice White's opinion for the Court concluded that the first amendment did not immunize the media from search warrants issued on probable cause. Justice Powell, who supplied the controlling fifth vote, joined the Court's opinion but also wrote a concurring opinion, in which he asserted that "a warrant which would be sufficient to support the search of an apartment or automobile would [not necessarily] be reasonable in supporting the search of a newspaper office." He concluded that, while there was no justification for a separate procedure for searches of the press, first amendment values should be taken into account in making the "reasonableness" and "particularity" judgments under the fourth amendment.[1]

HERBERT v. LANDO, 441 U.S. 153 (1979). Herbert, a retired Army officer, brought a diversity suit in federal court, claiming that a CBS television documentary on Vietnamese war atrocities defamed him. In pretrial deposition, the program's producer was asked questions about his opinions with respect to the material gathered by him and about his conversations with editorial colleagues. The Court held that the First Amendment gave the producer no privilege to refuse to answer the questions. It was conceded that the libel plaintiff was a public figure who could not recover without proof of malice in the sense of knowing falsity or reckless disregard of the truth. New York Times Co. v. Sullivan, 376 U.S. 254 (1964); Curtis Pub. Co. v. Butts, 388 U.S. 130 (1967). Since that standard required plaintiff to prove the state of the defendant's mind, erecting a First Amendment privilege against disclosure of the editorial process "would constitute a substantial interference with the ability of a defamation plaintiff to establish the ingredients of malice as required by *New*

---

[1] The Privacy Protection Act of 1980, 42 U.S.C. § 2000aa, requires state and federal law enforcement officers to use subpoena procedures to obtain documents from persons engaged in the communications industry. Search warrants are permitted in exceptional circumstances, such as when it is believed that the desired documents would be destroyed.

York Times." Justice White's opinion for the Court did, however, indicate that editorial discussions may have some constitutional protection from "casual inquiry."

> "There is no law that subjects the editorial process to private or official examination merely to satisfy curiosity or to serve some general end such as the public interest; and if there were, it would not survive constitutional scrutiny as the First Amendment is presently construed. No such problem exists here, however, where there is a specific claim of injury arising from a publication that is alleged to have been knowingly or recklessly false."

Justices Brennan, Marshall and Stewart dissented in part.

SECTION 5. PRESS ACCESS TO GOVERNMENT INFORMATION

PRESS ACCESS DECISIONS PRIOR TO 1980

No Supreme Court decision, prior to 1980, sustained a press claim that the First Amendment provided the press with a special right of access to information controlled by the government. The settled proposition, as explained by Justice Stewart for the Court in Pell v. Procunier, 417 U.S. 817 (1974), was that the "Constitution does not ... require government to accord the press special access to information not shared by members of the public generally." In *Pell,* the Court sustained a California policy placing limits on interviews with individual prisoners. In Houchins v. KQED, Inc., 438 U.S. 1 (1978), the Court sustained a county jail policy limiting reporters' access to jail facilities. Both decisions were by a closely divided Court, with the dissenters arguing that a First Amendment right of press access was necessary to allow the media to play its societal function in the discussion of public affairs.

In Gannett Co., Inc. v. DePasquale, 443 U.S. 368 (1979), the five-Justice majority rejected an alternative constitutional source of press access. In a murder case, pre-trial hearings to suppress evidence had been closed to the public and the press on motion of the criminal defendants. The Court held that the sixth amendment's guarantee of a public trial was only for the benefit of the accused, and did not give the public or the press any right of access to criminal trials. Significantly, one member of the majority, Justice Powell, wrote a concurrence arguing that there was a First Amendment right of press access to criminal proceedings distinct from the general public's right of access.

Richmond Newspapers, Inc. v. Virginia

448 U.S. 555, 100 S.Ct. 2814, 65 L.Ed.2d 973 (1980).

Mr. Chief Justice Burger announced the judgment of the Court and delivered an opinion, in which Mr. Justice White and Mr. Justice Stevens joined.

The narrow question presented in this case is whether the right of the public and press to attend criminal trials is guaranteed under the United States Constitution.

I

In March 1976, one Stevenson was indicted for the murder of a hotel manager who had been found stabbed to death on December 2, 1975. Tried promptly in July 1976, Stevenson was convicted of second-degree murder in the Circuit Court of Hanover County, Va. The Virginia Supreme Court reversed the conviction in October 1977, holding that a bloodstained shirt purportedly belonging to Stevenson had been improperly admitted into evidence. . . .

Stevenson was retried in the same court. This second trial ended in a mistrial on May 30, 1978, when a juror asked to be excused after trial had begun and no alternate was available.

A third trial, which began in the same court on June 6, 1978, also ended in a mistrial. It appears that the mistrial may have been declared because a prospective juror had read about Stevenson's previous trials in a newspaper and had told other prospective jurors about the case before the retrial began.

Stevenson was tried in the same court for a fourth time beginning on September 11, 1978. Present in the courtroom when the case was called were appellants Wheeler and McCarthy, reporters for appellant Richmond Newspapers, Inc. Before the trial began, counsel for the defendant moved that it be closed to the public . . .

The trial judge, who had presided over two of the three previous trials, asked if the prosecution had any objection to clearing the courtroom. The prosecutor stated he had no objection and would leave it to the discretion of the court. . . . [The trial judge] ordered "that the Courtroom be kept clear of all parties except the witnesses when they testify." The record does not show that any objections to the closure order were made by anyone present at the time, including appellants Wheeler and McCarthy.

Later that same day, however, appellants sought a hearing on a motion to vacate the closure order. The trial judge granted the request and scheduled a hearing to follow the close of the day's proceedings. When the hearing began, the court ruled that the hearing was to be treated as part of the trial; accordingly, he again ordered the reporters to leave the courtroom, and they complied.

. . . .

. . . The court denied the motion to vacate and ordered the trial to continue the following morning "with the press and public excluded."

What transpired when the closed trial resumed the next day was disclosed in the following manner by an order of the court entered September 12, 1978:

> "[I]n the absence of the jury, the defendant by counsel made a Motion that a mis-trial be declared, which motion was taken under advisement. At the conclusion of the Commonwealth's evidence, the attorney for the defendant moved the Court to strike the Commonwealth's evidence on grounds stated to the record, which Motion was sustained by the Court. And the jury having been excused, the Court doth find the accused NOT GUILTY of Murder, as charged in the Indictment, and he was allowed to depart."

On September 27, 1978 the trial court granted appellants' motion to intervene *nunc pro tunc* in the *Stevenson* case. Appellants then petitioned the Virginia Supreme Court for writs of mandamus and prohibition and filed an appeal from the trial court's closure order. On July 9, 1979, the Virginia Supreme Court dismissed the mandamus and prohibition petitions and, finding no reversible error, denied the petition for appeal.

Appellants then sought review in this Court, . . .

The criminal trial which appellants sought to attend has long since ended, and there is thus some suggestion that the case is moot. . . . If the underlying dispute is "capable of repetition, yet evading review," . . . it is not moot.

Since the Virginia Supreme Court declined plenary review, it is reasonably foreseeable that other trials may be closed by other judges without any more showing of need than is presented on this record. More often than not, criminal trials will be of sufficiently short duration that a closure order "will evade review, or at least considered plenary review in this Court." . . . Accordingly, we turn to the merits.

II

We begin consideration of this case by noting that the precise issue presented here has not previously been before this Court for decision. In Gannett Co., Inc. v. DePasquale, . . . the Court was not required to decide whether a right of access to *trials,* as distinguished from hearings on *pre*trial motions, was constitutionally guaranteed. The Court held that the Sixth Amendment's guarantee to the accused of a public trial gave neither the public nor the press an enforceable right of access to a *pre*trial suppression hearing. One concurring opinion specifically emphasized that "a hearing on a motion before trial to suppress evidence is not a *trial.* . . ." . . . Moreover, the Court did not decide whether the First and Fourteenth Amendments guarantee a right of the public to attend trials . . .; nor did the dissenting opinion reach this issue. . . .

. . .

A

The origins of the proceeding which has become the modern criminal trial in Anglo–American justice can be traced back beyond reliable historical records. We need not here review all details of its development, but a summary of that history is instructive. What is significant for present purposes is that throughout its evolution, the trial has been open to all who cared to observe.

. . .

B

. . . [T]he historical evidence demonstrates conclusively that at the time when our organic laws were adopted, criminal trials both here and in England had long been presumptively open. This is no quirk of history; rather, it has long been recognized as an indispensable attribute of an Anglo–American trial. Both Hale in the 17th century and Blackstone in the 18th saw the importance of openness to the proper functioning of a trial; it gave assurance that the proceedings were conducted fairly to all concerned, and it discouraged perjury, the misconduct of participants, and decisions based on secret bias or partiality. . . .

. . .

People in an open society do not demand infallibility from their institutions, but it is difficult for them to accept what they are prohibited from observing. When a criminal trial is conducted in the open, there is at least an opportunity both for understanding the system in general and its workings in a particular case: . . .

. . .

C

From this unbroken, uncontradicted history, supported by reasons as valid today as in centuries past, we are bound to conclude that a presumption of openness inheres in the very nature of a criminal trial under our system of justice. . . .

Despite the history of criminal trials being presumptively open since long before the Constitution, the State presses its contention that neither the Constitution nor the Bill of Rights contains any provision which by its terms guarantees to the public the right to attend criminal trials. Standing alone, this is correct, but there remains the question whether, absent an explicit provision, the Constitution affords protection against exclusion of the public from criminal trials.

III

A

The First Amendment, in conjunction with the Fourteenth, prohibits governments from "abridging the freedom of speech, or of the press; or the right of the people peaceably to assemble, and to petition the Government for a redress of grievances." These expressly guaranteed freedoms share a common core purpose of assuring freedom of communication on matters relating to the functioning of government. Plainly it would be difficult to single out any aspect of government of higher concern and importance to the people than the manner in which criminal trials are conducted; as we have shown, recognition of this pervades the centuries-old history of open trials and the opinions of this Court.

. . . [T]he First Amendment guarantees of speech and press, standing alone, prohibit government from summarily closing courtroom doors which had long been open to the public at the time that Amendment was adopted. . . .

It is not crucial whether we describe this right to attend criminal trials to hear, see, and communicate observations concerning them as a "right of access," cf. *Gannett,* supra, at 397 (Powell, J., concurring); Saxbe v. Washington Post Co., 417 U.S. 843 (1974); Pell v. Procunier, 417 U.S. 817 (1974),[11] or a "right to gather information," for we have recognized that "without some protection for seeking out the news, freedom of the press could be eviscerated." Branzburg v. Hayes, 408 U.S. 665, 681 (1972). The explicit, guaranteed rights to speak and to publish concerning what takes place at a trial would lose much meaning if access to observe the trial could, as it was here, be foreclosed arbitrarily.

B

The right of access to places traditionally open to the public, as criminal trials have long been, may be seen as assured by the amalgam of the First Amendment guarantees of speech and press; and their affinity to the right of assembly is not without relevance. From the outset, the right of assembly was regarded not only as an independent right but also as a catalyst to augment the free exercise of the other First Amendment rights with which it was deliberately linked by the draftsmen. . . . [A] trial courtroom . . . is a public place where the people generally—and representatives of the media—have a right to be present, and where their presence historically has been thought to enhance the integrity and quality of what takes place.

---

[11] *Procunier* and *Saxbe* are distinguishable in the sense that they were concerned with penal institutions which, by definition, are not "open" or public places. . . .

C

. . .

We hold that the right to attend criminal trials[17] is implicit in the guarantees of the First Amendment; . . .

D

Having concluded there was a guaranteed right of the public under the First and Fourteenth Amendments to attend the trial of Stevenson's case, we return to the closure order challenged by appellants. The Court in *Gannett,* supra, made clear that although the Sixth Amendment guarantees the accused a right to a public trial, it does not give a right to a private trial. 443 U.S., at 382. Despite the fact that this was the fourth trial of the accused, the trial judge made no findings to support closure; no inquiry was made as to whether alternative solutions would have met the need to ensure fairness; there was no recognition of any right under the Constitution for the public or press to attend the trial. In contrast to the pretrial proceeding dealt with in *Gannett,* there exist in the context of the trial itself various tested alternatives to satisfy the constitutional demands of fairness. See, e.g., Nebraska Press Ass'n v. Stuart, 427 U.S., at 563–565; Sheppard v. Maxwell, 384 U.S., at 357–362. There was no suggestion that any problems with witnesses could not have been dealt with by their exclusion from the courtroom or their sequestration during the trial. . . . Nor is there anything to indicate that sequestration of the jurors would not have guarded against their being subjected to any improper information. All of the alternatives admittedly present difficulties for trial courts, but none of the factors relied on here was beyond the realm of the manageable. Absent an overriding interest articulated in findings, the trial of a criminal case must be open to the public. Accordingly, the judgment under review is

Reversed.

Mr. Justice Powell took no part in the consideration or decision of this case.

Mr. Justice White, concurring.

This case would have been unnecessary had Gannett Co. v. DePasquale, 443 U.S. 368 (1979), construed the Sixth Amendment to forbid excluding the public from criminal proceedings except in narrowly defined circumstances. But the Court there rejected the submission of four of us to this effect, thus requiring that the First Amendment issue involved here be addressed. On this issue, I concur in the opinion of The Chief Justice.

Mr. Justice Stevens, concurring.

This is a watershed case. Until today the Court has accorded virtually absolute protection to the dissemination of information or ideas, but never before has it squarely held that the acquisition of newsworthy matter is entitled to any constitutional protection whatsoever. An additional word of emphasis is therefore appropriate.

Twice before, the Court has implied that any governmental restriction on access to information, no matter how severe and no matter how unjustified, would be constitutionally acceptable so long as it did not single out the press for special disabilities not applicable to the public at large. In a dissent joined

---

[17] Whether the public has a right to attend trials of civil cases is a question not raised by this case, but we note that histori- cally both civil and criminal trials have been presumptively open.

by Mr. Justice Brennan and Mr. Justice Marshall in Saxbe v. Washington Post Co., 417 U.S. 843, 850, Mr. Justice Powell unequivocally rejected the conclusion that "*any* governmental restriction on press access to information, so long as it is nondiscriminatory, falls outside the purview of First Amendment concern." ... And in Houchins v. KQED, Inc., 438 U.S. 1, 19–40, I explained at length why Mr. Justice Brennan, Mr. Justice Powell, and I were convinced that "[a]n official prison policy of concealing ... knowledge from the public by arbitrarily cutting off the flow of information at its source abridges the freedom of speech and of the press protected by the First and Fourteenth Amendments to the Constitution." ... Since Mr. Justice Marshall and Mr. Justice Blackmun were unable to participate in that case, a majority of the Court neither accepted nor rejected that conclusion or the contrary conclusion expressed in the prevailing opinions. Today, however, for the first time, the Court unequivocally holds that an arbitrary interference with access to important information is an abridgment of the freedoms of speech and of the press protected by the First Amendment.

It is somewhat ironic that the Court should find more reason to recognize a right of access today than it did in *Houchins*. For *Houchins* involved the plight of a segment of society least able to protect itself, an attack on a long-standing policy of concealment, and an absence of any legitimate justification for abridging public access to information about how government operates. In this case we are protecting the interests of the most powerful voices in the community, we are concerned with an almost unique exception to an established tradition of openness in the conduct of criminal trials, and it is likely that the closure order was motivated by the judge's desire to protect the individual defendant from the burden of a fourth criminal trial.[2]

In any event, for the reasons stated in Part II of my *Houchins* opinion, ... as well as those stated by The Chief Justice today, I agree that the First Amendment protects the public and the press from abridgment of their rights of access to information about the operation of their government, including the Judicial Branch; given the total absence of any record justification for the closure order entered in this case, that order violated the First Amendment.

Mr. Justice Brennan, with whom Mr. Justice Marshall joins, concurring in the judgment.

Gannett Co. v. DePasquale, 443 U.S. 368 (1979), held that the Sixth Amendment right to a public trial was personal to the accused, conferring no right of access to pretrial proceedings that is separately enforceable by the public or the press. The instant case raises the question whether the First Amendment, of its own force and as applied to the States through the Fourteenth Amendment, secures the public an independent right of access to trial proceedings. Because I believe that the First Amendment—of itself and as applied to the States through the Fourteenth Amendment—secures such a public right of access, I agree with those of my Brethren who hold that, without more, agreement of the trial judge and the parties cannot constitutionally close a trial to the public.

I

... [T]he Court has not ruled out a public access component to the First Amendment in every circumstance. Read with care and in context, our deci-

---

[2] ...The absence of any articulated reason for the closure order is a sufficient basis for distinguishing this case from Gannett v. DePasquale, 443 U.S. 368. The decision today is in no way inconsistent with the perfectly unambiguous holding in *Gannett* that the rights guaranteed by the Sixth Amendment are rights that may be asserted by the accused rather than members of the general public. . . .

sions must therefore be understood as holding only that any privilege of access to governmental information is subject to a degree of restraint dictated by the nature of the information and countervailing interests in security or confidentiality. . . .

The Court's approach in right of access cases simply reflects the special nature of a claim of First Amendment right to gather information. Customarily, First Amendment guarantees are interposed to protect communication between speaker and listener. When so employed against prior restraints, free speech protections are almost insurmountable. . . . But the First Amendment embodies more than a commitment to free expression and communicative interchange for their own sakes; it has a *structural* role to play in securing and fostering our republican system of self-government. . . . Implicit in this structural role is . . . the antecedent assumption that valuable public debate—as well as other civic behavior—must be informed. The structural model links the First Amendment to that process of communication necessary for a democracy to survive, and thus entails solicitude not only for communication itself, but also for the indispensable conditions of meaningful communication.

However, because "the stretch of this protection is theoretically endless," . . . it must be invoked with discrimination and temperance. . . . An assertion of the prerogative to gather information must . . . be assayed by considering the information sought and the opposing interests invaded.

This judicial task is as much a matter of sensitivity to practical necessities as it is of abstract reasoning. But at least two helpful principles may be sketched. First, the case for a right of access has special force when drawn from an enduring and vital tradition of public entree to particular proceedings or information. . . . Such a tradition commands respect in part because the Constitution carries the gloss of history. More importantly, a tradition of accessibility implies the favorable judgment of experience. Second, the value of access must be measured in specifics. Analysis is not advanced by rhetorical statements that all information bears upon public issues; what is crucial in individual cases is whether access to a particular government process is important in terms of that very process.

To resolve the case before us, therefore, we must consult historical and current practice with respect to open trials, and weigh the importance of public access to the trial process itself.

II

. . .

Tradition, contemporaneous state practice, and this Court's own decisions manifest a common understanding that "[a] trial is a public event. What transpires in the court room is public property." . . .

III

. . .

Popular attendance at trials, in sum, substantially furthers the particular public purposes of that critical judicial proceeding. In that sense, public access is an indispensable element of the trial process itself. . . .

IV

As previously noted, resolution of First Amendment public access claims in individual cases must be strongly influenced by the weight of historical practice and by an assessment of the specific structural value of public access in the circumstances. With regard to the case at hand, our ingrained tradition of public trials and the importance of public access to the broader purposes of the trial process, tip the balance strongly toward the rule that trials be open. What countervailing interests might be sufficiently compelling to reverse this presumption of openness need not concern us now,[24] ...

Mr. Justice Stewart, concurring in the judgment.

. . .

... [A] trial courtroom is a place where representatives of the press and of the public are not only free to be, but where their presence serves to assure the integrity of what goes on.

But this does not mean that the First Amendment right of members of the public and representatives of the press to attend civil and criminal trials is absolute. Just as a legislature may impose reasonable time, place and manner restrictions upon the exercise of First Amendment freedoms, so may a trial judge impose reasonable limitations upon the unrestricted occupation of a courtroom by representatives of the press and members of the public.... [A] trial courtroom must be a quiet and orderly place. ...Moreover, every courtroom has a finite physical capacity, and there may be occasions when not all who wish to attend a trial may do so.[3] And while there exist many alternative ways to satisfy the constitutional demands of a fair trial, those demands may also sometimes justify limitations upon the unrestricted presence of spectators in the courtroom.[5]

Since in the present case the trial judge appears to have given no recognition to the right of representatives of the press and members of the public to be present at the Virginia murder trial over which he was presiding, the judgment under review must be reversed.

It is upon the basis of these principles that I concur in the judgment.

Mr. Justice Blackmun, concurring in the judgment.

My opinion and vote in partial dissent last Term in Gannett Co. v. DePasquale, 443 U.S. 368, 406 (1979), compels my vote to reverse the judgment of the Supreme Court of Virginia.

. . .

II

... I remain convinced that the right to a public trial is to be found where the Constitution explicitly placed it—in the Sixth Amendment.

The Court, however, has eschewed the Sixth Amendment route. The plurality turns to other possible constitutional sources and invokes a veritable potpourri of them—the Speech Clause of the First Amendment, the Press

---

[24] For example, national security concerns about confidentiality may sometimes warrant closures during sensitive portions of trial proceedings, such as testimony about state secrets. Cf. United States v. Nixon, 418 U.S. 683, 714–716 (1974).

[3] In such situations, representatives of the press must be assured access. Houchins v. KQED, Inc., 438 U.S. 1, 16 (opinion concurring in the judgment).

[5] This is not to say that only constitutional considerations can justify such restrictions. The preservation of trade secrets, for example, might justify the exclusion of the public from at least some segments of a civil trial. And the sensibilities of a youthful prosecution witness, for example, might justify similar exclusion in a criminal trial for rape, so long as the defendant's Sixth Amendment right to a public trial were not impaired....

Clause, the Assembly Clause, the Ninth Amendment, and a cluster of penumbral guarantees recognized in past decisions. . . .

. . . [W]ith the Sixth Amendment set to one side in this case, I am driven to conclude, as a secondary position, that the First Amendment must provide some measure of protection for public access to the trial. . . .

. . .

Mr. Justice Rehnquist, dissenting.

. . .

For the reasons stated in my separate concurrence in Gannett Co. v. DePasquale, 443 U.S. 368, 403 (1979), I do not believe that either the First or Sixth Amendment, as made applicable to the States by the Fourteenth, require that a State's reasons for denying public access to a trial, where both the prosecuting attorney and the defendant have consented to an order of closure approved by the judge, are subject to any additional constitutional review at our hands. . . .

. . .

The issue here is not whether the "right" to freedom of the press conferred by the First Amendment to the Constitution overrides the defendant's "right" to a fair trial conferred by other Amendments to the Constitution; it is instead whether any provision in the Constitution may fairly be read to prohibit what the trial judge in the Virginia state court system did in this case. Being unable to find any such prohibition in the First, Sixth, Ninth, or any other Amendments to the United States Constitution, or in the Constitution itself, I dissent.

PRESS ACCESS DECISIONS SINCE RICHMOND NEWSPAPERS, INC. v. VIRGINIA

In Globe Newspaper Co. v. Superior Court, 457 U.S. 596 (1982), Justice Brennan's opinion for the Court read the *Richmond Newspapers* case simply as establishing a right of access to criminal trials embodied in the First Amendment. The Court held unconstitutional on its face a unique Massachusetts statute requiring exclusion of the press and public during testimony of the victim at trials for specified sexual offenses against persons under the age of 18. The Court conceded that the First Amendment might not preclude restrictions on public and press access in individual cases based on "particularized determinations."

In Press–Enterprise Co. v. Superior Court, 464 U.S. 501 (1984), the Court held that a state court's decision closing the six weeks of *voir dire* examination of jurors in a criminal trial violated the Constitution. Chief Justice Burger's opinion for the Court stated that the "presumption of openness" of criminal trials "may be overcome only by an overriding interest based on findings that closure is essential to preserve higher values and is narrowly tailored to serve that interest."

In Press–Enterprise Co. v. Superior Court (Press–Enterprise II), 478 U.S. 1 (1986), the Court held that a California statute, requiring that preliminary hearings in criminal cases be closed on a finding of "reasonable likelihood of substantial prejudice," violated the first amendment. Citing the preliminary hearing conducted by Chief Justice Marshall in 1807 in the trial of Aaron Burr, Chief Justice Burger's opinion for the Court concluded that "there has been a tradition of accessibility to preliminary hearings of the type conducted in California." California preliminary hearings were also "sufficiently like a trial" to justify the same right of access as to the trial. Thus, the preliminary hearing could only be closed to the public under the standards announced in *Richmond Newspapers* and *Press–Enterprise I*. Justice Stevens' dissent, joined by Justice Rehnquist, argued that a finding of "reasonable probability of prejudice" established interests in protecting a fair trial and the reputation of the accused that justified denying access to the preliminary hearing and its transcript "for at least the short time before trial."

SECTION 6. SPECIAL PROBLEMS OF THE ELECTRONIC MEDIA

Columbia Broadcasting System, Inc. v. Democratic National Committee

412 U.S. 94, 93 S.Ct. 2080, 36 L.Ed.2d 772 (1973).

Mr. Chief Justice Burger delivered the opinion of the Court (Parts I, II, and IV) together with an opinion (Part III), in which Mr. Justice Stewart and Mr. Justice Rehnquist joined.

We granted the writs of certiorari in these cases to consider whether a broadcast licensee's general policy of not selling advertising time to individuals or groups wishing to speak out on issues they consider important violates the Federal Communications Act of 1934, 47 U.S.C. § 151 et seq., or the First Amendment.

. . .

The complainants in these actions are the Democratic National Committee (DNC) and the Business Executives' Move for Vietnam Peace (BEM), a national organization of businessmen opposed to United States involvement in the Vietnam conflict. In January 1970, BEM filed a complaint with the Commission charging that radio station WTOP in Washington, D.C., had refused to sell it time to broadcast a series of one-minute spot announcements expressing BEM views on Vietnam. WTOP, in common with many, but not all, broadcasters, followed a policy of refusing to sell time for spot announcements to individuals and groups who wished to expound their views on controversial issues. WTOP took the position that since it presented full and fair coverage of important public questions, including the Vietnam conflict, it was justified in refusing to accept editorial advertisements. WTOP also submitted evidence showing that the station had aired the views of critics of our Vietnam policy on numerous occasions. BEM challenged the fairness of WTOP's coverage of criticism of that policy, but it presented no evidence in support of that claim.

Four months later, in May 1970, DNC filed with the Commission a request for a declaratory ruling:

"That under the First Amendment to the Constitution and the Communications Act, a broadcaster may not, as a general policy, refuse to sell time to responsible entities, such as the DNC, for the solicitation of funds and for comment on public issues."

DNC claimed that it intended to purchase time from radio and television stations and from the national networks in order to present the views of the Democratic Party and to solicit funds. Unlike BEM, DNC did not object to the policies of any particular broadcaster but claimed that its prior "experiences in this area make it clear that it will encounter considerable difficulty—if not total frustration of its efforts—in carrying out its plans in the event the Commission should decline to issue a ruling as requested." DNC cited Red Lion Broadcasting Co. v. FCC, 395 U.S. 367 (1969), as establishing a limited constitutional right of access to the airwaves.

In two separate opinions, the Commission rejected respondents' claim that "responsible" individuals and groups have a right to purchase advertising time to comment on public issues without regard to whether the broadcaster has complied with the Fairness Doctrine....

. . .

A majority of the Court of Appeals reversed the Commission,....

. . .

I

Mr. Justice White's opinion for the Court in Red Lion Broadcasting Co. v. FCC, 395 U.S. 367 (1969), makes clear that the broadcast media pose unique and special problems not present in the traditional free speech case. Unlike other media, broadcasting is subject to an inherent physical limitation. Broadcast frequencies are a scarce resource; they must be portioned out among applicants. All who possess the financial resources and the desire to communicate by television or radio cannot be satisfactorily accommodated. The Court spoke to this reality when, in *Red Lion,* we said "it is idle to post an unabridgeable First Amendment right to broadcast comparable to the right of every individual to speak, write, or publish." Id., at 388.

Because the broadcast media utilize a valuable and limited public resource, there is also present an unusual order of First Amendment values. *Red Lion* discussed at length the application of the First Amendment to the broadcast media. In analyzing the broadcasters' claim that the Fairness Doctrine and two of its component rules violated their freedom of expression, we held that "[n]o one has a First Amendment right to a license or to monopolize a radio frequency; to deny a station license because 'the public interest' requires it 'is not a denial of free speech.'" Id., at 389. Although the broadcaster is not without protection under the First Amendment, United States v. Paramount Pictures, Inc., 334 U.S. 131, 166 (1948), "[i]t is the right of the viewers and listeners, not the right of the broadcasters, which is paramount.... It is the right of the public to receive suitable access to social, political, esthetic, moral and other ideas and experiences which is crucial here. That right may not constitutionally be abridged either by Congress or by the FCC." *Red Lion,* [395 U.S.], at 390.

Balancing the various First Amendment interests involved in the broadcast media and determining what best serves the public's right to be informed is a task of a great delicacy and difficulty. The process must necessarily be undertaken within the framework of the regulatory scheme that has evolved over the course of the past half-century. For during that time, Congress and its chosen regulatory agency have established a delicately balanced system of regulation intended to serve the interests of all concerned. The problems of regulation are rendered more difficult because the broadcast industry is dynamic in terms of technological change; solutions adequate a decade ago are not necessarily so now, and those acceptable today may well be outmoded 10 years hence.... Thus, before confronting the specific legal issues in these cases, we turn to an examination of the legislative and administrative development of our broadcast system over the last half century.

II

This Court has on numerous occasions recounted the origins of our modern system of broadcast regulation. See, e.g., *Red Lion,* [395 U.S.] at 375–386; National Broadcasting Co. v. United States, 319 U.S. 190, 210–217 (1943); . . . .

. . .

The legislative history of the Radio Act of 1927, the model for our present statutory scheme, see FCC v. Pottsville Broadcasting Co., [309 U.S. 134], 137 [(1940)], reveals that in the area of discussion of public issues Congress chose to leave broad journalistic discretion with the licensee. Congress specifically dealt with—and firmly rejected—the argument that the broadcast facilities should be open on a nonselective basis to all persons wishing to talk about public issues. . . .

. . . Congress after prolonged consideration adopted § 3(h), which specifically provides that "a person engaged in radio broadcasting shall not, insofar as such person is so engaged, be deemed a common carrier."

Other provisions of the 1934 Act also evince a legislative desire to preserve values of private journalism under a regulatory scheme which would insure fulfillment of certain public obligations. Although the Commission was given the authority to issue renewable three-year licenses to broadcasters and to promulgate rules and regulations governing the use of those licenses, both consistent with the "public convenience, interest, or necessity," § 326 of the Act specifically provides that:

> "Nothing in this chapter shall be understood or construed to give the Commission the power of censorship over the radio communications or signals transmitted by any radio station, and no regulation or condition shall be promulgated or fixed by the Commission which shall interfere with the right of free speech by means of radio communication." 47 U.S.C. § 326.

From these provisions it seems clear that Congress intended to permit private broadcasting to develop with the widest journalistic freedom consistent with its public obligations. . . .

Subsequent developments in broadcast regulation illustrate how this regulatory scheme has evolved. Of particular importance, in light of Congress' flat refusal to impose a "common carrier" right of access for all persons wishing to speak out on public issues, is the Commission's "Fairness Doctrine," which evolved gradually over the years spanning federal regulation of the broadcast media. Formulated under the Commission's power to issue regulations consistent with the "public interest," the doctrine imposes two affirmative responsibilities on the broadcaster: coverage of issues of public importance must be adequate and must fairly reflect differing viewpoints. See Red Lion, 395 U.S., at 377. In fulfilling the Fairness Doctrine obligations, the broadcaster must provide free time for the presentation of opposing views if a paid sponsor is unavailable, . . . and it must initiate programming on public issues if no one else seeks to do so. . . .

. . .

With this background in mind, we next proceed to consider whether a broadcaster's refusal to accept editorial advertisements is governmental action violative of the First Amendment.

III

That "Congress shall make no law ... abridging the freedom of speech, or of the press" is a restraint on government action, not that of private persons. Public Utilities Comm'n v. Pollak, 343 U.S. 451, 461 (1952). The Court has not previously considered whether the action of a broadcast licensee such as that challenged here is "governmental action" for purposes of the First Amendment. The holding under review thus presents a novel question, and one with far-reaching implications. ...

The Court of Appeals held that broadcasters are instrumentalities of the Government for First Amendment purposes, relying on the thesis, familiar in other contexts, that broadcast licensees are granted use of part of the public domain and are regulated as "proxies" or "'fiduciaries' of the people." These characterizations are not without validity for some purposes, but they do not resolve the sensitive constitutional issues inherent in deciding whether a particular licensee action is subject to First Amendment restraints.

In dealing with the broadcast media, as in other contexts, the line between private conduct and governmental action cannot be defined by reference to any general formula unrelated to particular exercises of governmental authority....

In deciding whether the First Amendment encompasses the conduct challenged here, it must be kept in mind that we are dealing with a vital part of our system of communication. The electronic media have swiftly become a major factor in the dissemination of ideas and information. More than 7,000 licensed broadcast stations undertake to perform this important function. To a large extent they share with the printed media the role of keeping people informed.

As we have seen, with the advent of radio a half century ago, Congress was faced with a fundamental choice between total Government ownership and control of the new medium—the choice of most other countries—or some other alternative. Long before the impact and potential of the medium was realized, Congress opted for a system of private broadcasters licensed and regulated by Government. The legislative history suggests that this choice was influenced not only by traditional attitudes toward private enterprise, but by a desire to maintain for licensees, so far as consistent with necessary regulation, a traditional journalistic role. The historic aversion to censorship led Congress to enact § 326 of the Act, which explicitly prohibits the Commission from interfering with the exercise of free speech over the broadcast frequencies. Congress pointedly refrained from divesting broadcasters of their control over the selection of voices; § 3(h) of the Act stands as a firm congressional statement that broadcast licensees are not to be treated as common carriers, obliged to accept whatever is tendered by members of the public. Both these provisions clearly manifest the intention of Congress to maintain a substantial measure of journalistic independence for the broadcast licensee.

The regulatory scheme evolved slowly, but very early the licensee's role developed in terms of a "public trustee" charged with the duty of fairly and impartially informing the public audience. In this structure the Commission acts in essence as an "overseer," but the initial and primary responsibility for fairness, balance, and objectivity rests with the licensee. This role of the Government as an "overseer" and ultimate arbiter and guardian of the public interest and the role of the licensee as a journalistic "free agent" call for a delicate balancing of competing interests. The maintenance of this balance for more than 40 years has called on both the regulators and the licensees to walk a "tightrope" to preserve the First Amendment values written into the Radio Act and its successor, the Communications Act.

The tensions inherent in such a regulatory structure emerge more clearly when we compare a private newspaper with a broadcast licensee. The power of a privately owned newspaper to advance its own political, social, and economic views is bounded by only two factors: first, the acceptance of a sufficient number of readers—and hence advertisers—to assure financial success; and, second, the journalistic integrity of its editors and publishers. A broadcast licensee has a large measure of journalistic freedom but not as large as that exercised by a newspaper. A licensee must balance what it might prefer to do as a private entrepreneur with what it is required to do as a "public trustee." To perform its statutory duties, the Commission must oversee without censoring. . . .

. . . The licensee's policy against accepting editorial advertising cannot be examined as an abstract proposition, but must be viewed in the context of its journalistic role. It does not help to press on us the idea that editorial ads are "like" commercial ads, for the licensee's policy against editorial spot ads is expressly based on a journalistic judgment that 10–to–60 second spot announcements are ill suited to intelligible and intelligent treatment of public issues; the broadcaster has chosen to provide a balanced treatment of controversial questions in a more comprehensive form. Obviously the licensee's evaluation is based on its own journalistic judgment of priorities and newsworthiness.

Moreover, the Commission has not fostered the licensee policy challenged here; it has simply declined to command particular action because it fell within the area of journalistic discretion. The Commission explicitly emphasized that "there is of course no Commission policy thwarting the sale of time to comment on public issues." . . .

Thus, it cannot be said that the Government is a "partner" to the action of the broadcast licensee complained of here, nor is it engaged in a "symbiotic relationship" with the licensee, profiting from the invidious discrimination of its proxy. Compare Moose Lodge No. 107 v. Irvis, 407 U.S. 163, 174–177 (1972), with Burton v. Wilmington Parking Authority, 365 U.S. at 723–724. The First Amendment does not reach acts of private parties in every instance where the Congress or the Commission has merely permitted or failed to prohibit such acts.

. . .

Were we to read the First Amendment to spell out governmental action in the circumstances presented here, few licensee decisions on the content of broadcasts or the processes of editorial evaluation would escape constitutional scrutiny. . . . Congress, and the Commission as its agent, must remain in a posture of flexibility to chart a workable "middle course" in its quest to preserve a balance between the essential public accountability and the desired private control of the media.

More profoundly, it would be anomalous for us to hold, in the name of promoting the constitutional guarantees of free expression, that the day-to-day editorial decisions of broadcast licensees are subject to the kind of restraints urged by respondents. To do so in the name of the First Amendment would be a contradiction. Journalistic discretion would in many ways be lost to the rigid limitations that the First Amendment imposes on Government. Application of such standards to broadcast licensees would be antithetical to the very ideal of vigorous, challenging debate on issues of public interest. Every licensee is already held accountable for the totality of its performance of public interest obligations.

The concept of private, independent broadcast journalism, regulated by Government to assure protection of the public interest, has evolved slowly and cautiously over more than 40 years and has been nurtured by processes of adjudication. That concept of journalistic independence could not co-exist with a reading of the challenged conduct of the licensee as governmental action. Nor could it exist without administrative flexibility to meet changing needs and swift technological developments. We therefore conclude that the policies complained of do not constitute governmental action violative of the First Amendment. . . .

IV

There remains for consideration the question whether the "public interest" standard of the Communications Act requires broadcasters to accept editorial advertisements or, whether, assuming governmental action, broadcasters are required to do so by reason of the First Amendment.

. . .

The Commission was justified in concluding that the public interest in providing access to the marketplace of "ideas and experiences" would scarcely be served by a system so heavily weighted in favor of the financially affluent, or those with access to wealth. Cf. *Red Lion,* supra, 395 U.S., at 392, 89 S.Ct., at 1807. Even under a first-come-first-served system, proposed by the dissenting Commissioner in these cases, the views of the affluent could well prevail over those of others, since they would have it within their power to purchase time more frequently. Moreover, there is the substantial danger, as the Court of Appeals acknowledged, that the time allotted for editorial advertising could be monopolized by those of one political persuasion.

. . .

By minimizing the difficult problems involved in implementing . . . a right of access, the Court of Appeals failed to come to grips with another problem of critical importance to broadcast regulation and the First Amendment—the risk of an enlargement of Government control over the content of broadcast discussion of public issues. . . . This risk is inherent in the Court of Appeals' remand requiring regulations and procedures to sort out requests to be heard— a process involving the very editing that licensees now perform as to regular programming. . . .

Under a constitutionally commanded and Government supervised right-of-access system urged by respondents and mandated by the Court of Appeals, the Commission would be required to oversee far more of the day-to-day operations of broadcasters' conduct, deciding such questions as whether a particular individual or group has had sufficient opportunity to present its viewpoint and whether a particular viewpoint has already been sufficiently aired. Regimenting broadcasters is too radical a therapy for the ailment respondents complain of.

. . .

Conceivably at some future date Congress or the Commission—or the broadcasters—may devise some kind of limited right of access that is both practicable and desirable. Indeed, the Commission noted in these proceedings that the advent of cable television will afford increased opportunities for the discussion of public issues. . . .

. . .

Reversed.

Mr. Justice Stewart, concurring.

While I join [Parts I, II, and III of the Court's opinion], my views closely approach those expressed by Mr. Justice Douglas concurring in the judgment.

The First Amendment prohibits the Government from imposing controls upon the press. Private broadcasters are surely part of the press. ...Yet here the Court of Appeals held, and the dissenters today agree, that the First Amendment *requires* the Government to impose controls upon private broadcasters—in order to preserve First Amendment "values." The appellate court accomplished this strange convolution by the simple device of holding that private broadcasters *are* Government. This is a step along a path that could eventually lead to the proposition that private *newspapers* "are" Government. Freedom of the press would then be gone. In its place we would have such governmental controls upon the press as a majority of this Court at any particular moment might consider First Amendment "values" to require. It is a frightening specter.

I

. . .

The First Amendment protects the press *from* governmental interference; it confers no analogous protection *on* the Government. ...If, as the dissent today would have it, the proper analogy is to public forums—that is, if broadcasters are Government for First Amendment purposes—then broadcasters are inevitably drawn to the position of common carriers. For this is precisely the status of Government with respect to public forums—a status mandated by the First Amendment.

To hold that broadcaster action is governmental action would thus produce a result wholly inimical to the broadcasters' own First Amendment rights ...

II

Part IV of the Court's opinion, as I understand it, seems primarily to deal with the respondents' statutory argument—that the obligation of broadcasters to operate in the "public interest" supports the judgment of the Court of Appeals. Yet two of my concurring Brethren understand Part IV as a discussion of the First Amendment issue that would exist in these cases were the action of broadcasters to be equated with governmental action. So, according to my Brother Blackmun, "the governmental action issue does not affect the outcome of this case." ...

I find this reasoning quite wrong and wholly disagree with it, for the simple reason that the First Amendment and the public interest standard of the statute are not coextensive ... For example, the Fairness Doctrine is an aspect of the "public interest" regulation of broadcasters that would not be compelled or even permitted by the First Amendment itself if broadcasters were the Government.

If the "public interest" language of the statute were intended to enact the substance of the First Amendment, a discussion of whether broadcasters action is governmental action would indeed be superfluous. For anything that Government could not do because of the First Amendment, the broadcasters could not do under the statute. But this theory proves far too much, since it would make the statutory scheme, with its emphasis on broadcaster discretion and its proscription on interference with "the right of free speech by means of radio communication," a nullity....

   . . .

Mr. Justice White, concurring.

I join Parts I, II, and IV of the Court's opinion and its judgment. I do not, however, concur in the Part III opinion.

   . . .

... I am not ready to conclude, as is done in the opinion in Part III, that the First Amendment may be put aside for lack of official action necessary to invoke its proscriptions. But, assuming *arguendo,* as the Court does in Part IV of its opinion, that Congress or the Commission is sufficiently involved in the denial of access to the broadcasting media to require review under the First Amendment, I would reverse the judgment of the Court of Appeals. Given the constitutionality of the Fairness Doctrine, and accepting Part IV of the Court's opinion, I have little difficulty in concluding that statutory and regulatory recognition of broadcaster freedom and discretion to make up their own programs and to choose their method of compliance with the Fairness Doctrine is consistent with the First Amendment.

Mr. Justice Blackmun, with whom Mr. Justice Powell joins, concurring.

... The Court's conclusion that the First Amendment does not compel the result reached by the Court of Appeals demonstrates that the governmental action issue does not affect the outcome of this case. I therefore refrain from deciding it.

Mr. Justice Douglas, concurring in the judgment.

While I join the Court in reversing the judgment below, I do so for quite different reasons.

My conclusion is that the TV and radio stand in the same protected position under the First Amendment as do newspapers and magazines. The philosophy of the First Amendment requires that result, for the fear that Madison and Jefferson had of government intrusion is perhaps even more relevant to TV and radio than it is to newspapers and other like publications....

   . . .

If a broadcast licensee is not engaged in governmental action for purposes of the First Amendment, I fail to see how constitutionally we can treat TV and radio differently than we treat newspapers....

   . . .

... [T]he prospect of putting Government in a position of control over publishers is to me an appalling one, even to the extent of the Fairness Doctrine. ...

It is said, of course, that Government can control the broadcasters because their channels are in the public domain in the sense that they use the airspace that is the common heritage of all the people. But parks are also in the public domain. Yet people who speak there do not come under Government censorship. ...It is the tradition of Hyde Park, not the tradition of the censor, that is reflected in the First Amendment. TV and radio broadcasters are a vital part of the press; and since the First Amendment allows no Government control over it, I would leave this segment of the press to its devices.

Licenses are, of course, restricted in time and while, in my view, Congress has the power to make each license limited to a fixed term and nonreviewable, there is no power to deny renewals for editorial or ideological reasons. The reason is that the First Amendment gives no preference to one school of thought over others.

The Court in today's decision by endorsing the Fairness Doctrine sanctions a federal saddle on broadcast licensees that is agreeable to the traditions of nations that never have known freedom of press and that is tolerable in countries that do not have a written constitution containing prohibitions as absolute as those in the First Amendment. . . .

. . .

Mr. Justice Brennan, with whom Mr. Justice Marshall concurs, dissenting.

. . .

[W]e have explicitly recognized that, in light of the unique nature of the electronic media, the public have strong First Amendment interests in the reception of a full spectrum of views—presented in a vigorous and uninhibited manner—on controversial issues of public importance. And, as we have seen, it has traditionally been thought that the most effective way to insure this "uninhibited, robust, and wide-open" debate is by fostering a "free trade in ideas" by making our forums of communication readily available to all persons wishing to express their views. Although apparently conceding the legitimacy of these principles, the Court nevertheless upholds the absolute ban on editorial advertising because, in its view, the Commission's Fairness Doctrine, in and of itself, is sufficient to satisfy the First Amendment interests of the public. I cannot agree.

. . . [T]he Fairness Doctrine does not in any sense require broadcasters to allow "non-broadcaster" speakers to use the airwaves to express their own views on controversial issues of public importance. On the contrary, broadcasters may meet their fairness responsibilities through presentation of carefully edited news programs, panel discussions, interviews, and documentaries. As a result, broadcasters retain almost exclusive control over the selection of issues and viewpoints to be covered, the manner of presentation and, perhaps most important, who shall speak. Given this doctrinal framework, I can only conclude that the Fairness Doctrine, standing alone, is insufficient—in theory as well as in practice—to provide the kind of "uninhibited, robust, and wide-open" exchange of views to which the public is constitutionally entitled.

. . .

Our legal system reflects a belief that truth is best illuminated by a collision of genuine advocates. Under the Fairness Doctrine, however, accompanied by an absolute ban on editorial advertising, the public is compelled to rely *exclusively* on the "journalistic discretion" of broadcasters, who serve in theory as surrogate spokesmen for all sides of all issues. . . .

. . .

. . . [T]he *absolute* ban on editorial advertising seems particularly offensive because, although broadcasters refuse to sell any air time whatever to groups or individuals wishing to speak out on controversial issues of public importance, they make such air time readily available to those "commercial" advertisers who seek to peddle their goods and services to the public. Thus, as the system now operates, any person wishing to market a particular brand of beer, soap, toothpaste, or deodorant has direct, personal, and instantaneous access to the electronic media. He can present his own message, in his own words, in any format he selects and at a time of his own choosing. Yet a similar individual seeking to discuss war, peace, pollution, or the suffering of the poor is denied this right to speak. Instead, he is compelled to rely on the beneficence of a corporate "trustee" appointed by the Government to argue his case for him.

It has been long recognized, however, that although access to public forums may be subjected to reasonable "time, place, and manner" regulations, "[s]elective exclusions from a public forum may not be based on *content* alone. . . ." Police Dept. of Chicago v. Mosley, supra, 408 U.S. at 96 (emphasis added). . . . Here, of course, the differential treatment accorded "commercial" and "controversial" speech clearly violates that principle. Moreover, and not without some irony, the favored treatment given "commercial" speech under the existing scheme clearly reverses traditional First Amendment priorities. For it has generally been understood that "commercial" speech enjoys *less* First Amendment protection than speech directed at the discussion of controversial issues of public importance. . . .

. . .

CBS, INC. v. FEDERAL COMMUNICATIONS COMMISSION, 453 U.S. 367 (1981). The Carter–Mondale Presidential Committee requested each of the three major networks to sell time for a 30–minute program during the December 4–7, 1979 period for a program in connection with President Carter's formal announcement of his candidacy. Each of the networks declined, giving as a principal reason that it was too early to begin selling time for the 1980 Presidential campaign. The Carter–Mondale committee filed a complaint with the Federal Communications Commission charging that the networks had violated their statutory obligation (under 47 U.S.C. § 312(a)(7)) "to allow reasonable access to or to permit purchase of reasonable amounts of time for the use of a broadcasting station by a legally qualified candidate for Federal elective office on behalf of his candidacy." The Commission upheld the challenge. It held that under the statute it had the power to determine whether a campaign has begun and the statutory obligations have attached. It also held that the broadcasters must evaluate and respond to access requests on an individualized basis and offer reasons for denial which could be evaluated by the Commission. The Supreme Court, in an opinion by Chief Justice Burger, upheld the Commission in its determination as to the meaning of the statute and its application in this case. Responding to the argument by the network that as so construed the statute was in violation of the First Amendment the Court said:

"A licensed broadcaster is 'granted the free and exclusive use of a limited and valuable part of the public domain; when he accepts that franchise it is burdened by enforceable public obligations.' . . . This Court has noted the limits on a broadcast license:

'A license permits broadcasting, but the licensee has no constitutional right to be the one who holds the license or to monopolize a . . . frequency to the exclusion of his fellow citizens. There is nothing in the First Amendment which prevents the Government from requiring a licensee to share his frequency with others. . . .' Red Lion Broadcasting Co. v. FCC, 395 U.S., at 389. . . .

" ... Section 312(a)(7) ... makes a significant contribution to freedom of expression by enhancing the ability of candidates to present, and the public to receive, information necessary for the effective operation of the democratic process.

. . .

"Section 312(a)(7) represents an effort by Congress to assure that an important resource—the airwaves—will be used in the public interest. We hold that the statutory right of access, as defined by the Commission and applied in these cases, properly balances the First Amendment rights of federal candidates, the public, and broadcasters."

Denver Area Educational Telecommunications Consortium, Inc. v. Federal Communications Commission

__ U.S. __, 116 S.Ct. 2374, 135 L.Ed.2d 888 (1996).

[The report in this case appears supra, page 1293.]

CHAPTER 17

RELIGION AND THE CONSTITUTION

Introduction. This chapter deals with the first amendment's prohibitions of laws "respecting an establishment of religion" and of laws "prohibiting the free exercise thereof." As Justice Rutledge stated in his dissenting opinion in Everson v. Board of Educ., 330 U.S. 1, 40 (1947): " 'establishment' and 'free exercise' were correlative and coextensive ideas, representing only different facets of the single great and fundamental freedom." A single ideal of government neutrality in matters of religion forbids both government aid to and government burdens on religious groups, religious activities, and individual religious beliefs.

Despite their common purpose, there has been an uneasy tension between applications of the free exercise and establishment clauses, caused by potential conflict between the two constitutional commands. Consider a common example. Suppose a state university permits a wide range of speakers on political or social issues to use a particular university facility without charge. If speakers engaged in religious conversion, worship, or advocacy are singled out and denied permission to speak, does this constitute discrimination against religion in violation of the free exercise clause? If religious speakers are permitted, is the state subsidizing religious worship in violation of the establishment clause?

A question, then, that runs throughout this chapter is whether there is any single, reconciling interpretation of the establishment and free exercise clauses. A prominent attempt at reconciliation is Kurland, *Of Church and State and the Supreme Court,* 29 U.Chi.L.Rev. 1 (1961), *Selected Essays* 699 (1963). Professor Kurland's hypothesis is criticized in Pfeffer, *Religion–Blind Government,* 15 Stan.L.Rev. 389 (1963).

SECTION 1. THE ESTABLISHMENT CLAUSE

A. INTRODUCTION

Everson v. Board of Education

330 U.S. 1, 67 S.Ct. 504, 91 L.Ed. 711 (1947).

Mr. Justice Black delivered the opinion of the Court.

A New Jersey statute authorizes its local school districts to make rules and contracts for the transportation of children to and from schools. The appellee, a township board of education, acting pursuant to this statute authorized reimbursement to parents of money expended by them for the bus transportation of their children on regular busses operated by the public transportation system. Part of this money was for the payment of transportation of some children in the community to Catholic parochial schools. These church schools give their students, in addition to secular education, regular religious instruction conforming to the religious tenets and modes of worship of the Catholic Faith. The superintendent of these schools is a Catholic priest.

The appellant, in his capacity as a district taxpayer, filed suit in a state court challenging the right of the Board to reimburse parents of parochial school students.... The New Jersey Court of Errors and Appeals [held] that neither the statute nor the resolution passed pursuant to it was in conflict with the State constitution or the provisions of the Federal Constitution in issue....

The only contention here is that the state statute and the resolution, in so far as they authorized reimbursement to parents of children attending parochial schools, violate the Federal Constitution in these two respects, which to some extent, overlap. *First.* They authorize the State to take by taxation the private property of some and bestow it upon others, to be used for their own private purposes. This, it is alleged, violates the due process clause of the Fourteenth Amendment. *Second.* The statute and the resolution forced inhabitants to pay taxes to help support and maintain schools which are dedicated to, and which regularly teach, the Catholic Faith. This is alleged to be a use of state power to support church schools contrary to the prohibition of the First Amendment which the Fourteenth Amendment made applicable to the states.

First. ... It is much too late to argue that legislation intended to facilitate the opportunity of children to get a secular education serves no public purpose. Cochran v. Louisiana State Board of Education, 281 U.S. 370.... The same thing is no less true of legislation to reimburse needy parents, or all parents, for payment of the fares of their children so that they can ride in public busses to and from schools rather than run the risk of traffic and other hazards incident to walking or "hitchhiking." ...

. . .

Second. The New Jersey statute is challenged as a "law respecting an establishment of religion." The First Amendment, as made applicable to the states by the Fourteenth, ... commands that a state "shall make no law respecting an establishment of religion, or prohibiting the free exercise thereof." ... Whether this New Jersey law is one respecting ... "establishment of religion" requires an understanding of the meaning of that language, particularly with respect to the imposition of taxes. Once again, therefore, it is not inappropriate briefly to review the background and environment of the period in which that constitutional language was fashioned and adopted.

A large proportion of the early settlers of this country came here from Europe to escape the bondage of laws which compelled them to support and attend government favored churches....

These practices of the old world were transplanted to and began to thrive in the soil of the new America. The very charters granted by the English Crown to the individuals and companies designated to make the laws which would control the destinies of the colonials authorized these individuals and companies to erect religious establishments which all, whether believers or nonbelievers, would be required to support and attend. An exercise of this authority was accompanied by a repetition of many of the old-world practices and persecutions....

These practices became so commonplace as to shock the freedom-loving colonials into a feeling of abhorrence. The imposition of taxes to pay ministers' salaries and to build and maintain churches and church property aroused their indignation. It was these feelings which found expression in the First Amendment. No one locality and no one group throughout the Colonies can rightly be given entire credit for having aroused the sentiment that culminated in adoption of the Bill of Rights' provisions embracing religious liberty. But Virginia, where the established church had achieved a dominant influence in political affairs and where many excesses attracted wide public attention, provided a great stimulus and able leadership for the movement. The people there, as elsewhere, reached the conviction that individual religious liberty could be achieved best under a government which was stripped of all power to tax, to support, or otherwise to assist any or all religions, or to interfere with the beliefs of any religious individual or group.

The movement toward this end reached its dramatic climax in Virginia in 1785–86 when the Virginia legislative body was about to renew Virginia's tax levy for the support of the established church. Thomas Jefferson and James Madison led the fight against this tax. Madison wrote his great Memorial and Remonstrance against the law. In it, he eloquently argued that a true religion did not need the support of law; that no person, either believer or non-believer, should be taxed to support a religious institution of any kind; that the best interest of a society required that the minds of men always be wholly free; and that cruel persecutions were the inevitable result of government-established religions. Madison's Remonstrance received strong support throughout Virginia, and the Assembly postponed consideration of the proposed tax measure until its next session. When the proposal came up for consideration at that session, it not only died in committee, but the Assembly enacted the famous "Virginia Bill for Religious Liberty" originally written by Thomas Jefferson. The preamble to that Bill stated among other things that

> "Almighty God hath created the mind free; that all attempts to influence it by temporal punishments, or burthens, or by civil incapacitations, tend only to beget habits of hypocrisy and meanness, and are a departure from the plan of the Holy author of our religion who being Lord both of body and mind, yet chose not to propagate it by coercions on either ...; that to compel a man to furnish contributions of money for the propagation of opinions which he disbelieves, is sinful and tyrannical; that even the forcing him to support this or that teacher of his own religious persuasion, is depriving him of the comfortable liberty of giving his contributions to the particular pastor, whose morals he would make his pattern...."

And the statute itself enacted

> "That no man shall be compelled to frequent or support any religious worship, place, or ministry whatsoever, nor shall be enforced, restrained, molested, or burthened, in his body or goods, nor shall otherwise suffer on account of his religious opinions or belief...."

This Court has previously recognized that the provisions of the First Amendment, in the drafting and adoption of which Madison and Jefferson played such leading roles, had the same objective and were intended to provide the same protection against governmental intrusion on religious liberty as the Virginia statute.[a] ... Prior to the adoption of the Fourteenth Amendment, the First Amendment did not apply as a restraint against the states. Most of them did soon provide similar constitutional protections for religious liberty. But some states persisted for about half a century in imposing restraints upon the

---

[a] For a very different reading of the historical record, see Howe, *Religion and the Free Society: The Constitutional Question, Selected Essays* 780 (1963). Professor Howe, stressing that the Bill of Rights did not in its inception limit the states, argues that the prohibition on establishment was a "non-libertarian" limitation on national power. Compare Pfeffer, *Church, State, and Freedom* 134–143 (rev. ed. 1967).

free exercise of religion and in discriminating against particular religious groups.... ·

The meaning and scope of the First Amendment, preventing establishment of religion or prohibiting the free exercise thereof, in the light of its history and the evils it was designed forever to suppress, have been several times elaborated by the decisions of this Court prior to the application of the First Amendment to the states by the Fourteenth. The broad meaning given the Amendment by these earlier cases has been accepted by this Court in its decisions concerning an individual's religious freedom rendered since the Fourteenth Amendment was interpreted to make the prohibitions of the First applicable to state action abridging religious freedom. There is every reason to give the same application and broad interpretation to the "establishment of religion" clause....

The "establishment of religion" clause of the First Amendment means at least this: Neither a state nor the Federal Government can set up a church. Neither can pass laws which aid one religion, aid all religions, or prefer one religion over another. Neither can force nor influence a person to go to or to remain away from church against his will or force him to profess a belief or disbelief in any religion. No person can be punished for entertaining or professing religious beliefs or disbeliefs, for church attendance or non-attendance. No tax in any amount, large or small, can be levied to support any religious activities or institutions, whatever they may be called, or whatever form they may adopt to teach or practice religion. Neither a state nor the Federal Government can, openly or secretly, participate in the affairs of any religious organizations or groups and vice versa. In the words of Jefferson, the clause against establishment of religion by law was intended to erect "a wall of separation between church and State." Reynolds v. United States, [98 U.S.] at 164.

We must consider the New Jersey statute in accordance with the foregoing limitations imposed by the First Amendment. But we must not strike that state statute down if it is within the State's constitutional power even though it approaches the verge of that power.... New Jersey cannot consistently with the "establishment of religion" clause of the First Amendment contribute tax-raised funds to the support of an institution which teaches the tenets and faith of any church. On the other hand, other language of the amendment commands that New Jersey cannot hamper its citizens in the free exercise of their own religion. Consequently, it cannot exclude individual Catholics, Lutherans, Mohammedans, Baptists, Jews, Methodists, Non-believers, Presbyterians, or the members of any other faith, *because of their faith, or lack of it,* from receiving the benefits of public welfare legislation. While we do not mean to intimate that a state could not provide transportation only to children attending public schools, we must be careful, in protecting the citizens of New Jersey against state-established churches, to be sure that we do not inadvertently prohibit New Jersey from extending its general state law benefits to all its citizens without regard to their religious belief.

Measured by these standards, we cannot say that the First Amendment prohibits New Jersey from spending tax-raised funds to pay the bus fares of parochial school pupils as a part of a general program under which it pays the fares of pupils attending public and other schools. It is undoubtedly true that children are helped to get to church schools. There is even a possibility that some of the children might not be sent to the church schools if the parents were compelled to pay their children's bus fares out of their own pockets when transportation to a public school would have been paid for by the State. The same possibility exists where the state requires a local transit company to provide reduced fares to school children including those attending parochial schools, or where a municipally owned transportation system undertakes to carry all school children free of charge. Moreover, state-paid policemen, detailed to protect children going to and from church schools from the very real hazards of traffic, would serve much the same purpose and accomplish much the same result as state provisions intended to guarantee free transportation of a kind which the state deems to be best for the school children's welfare. And parents might refuse to risk their children to the serious danger of traffic accidents going to and from parochial schools, the approaches to which were not protected by policemen. Similarly, parents might be reluctant to permit their children to attend schools which the state had cut off from such general government services as ordinary police and fire protection, connections for sewage disposal, public highways and sidewalks. Of course, cutting off church schools from these services, so separate and so indisputably marked off from the religious function, would make it far more difficult for the schools to operate. But such is obviously not the purpose of the First Amendment. That Amendment requires the state to be a neutral in its relations with groups of religious believers and non-believers; it does not require the state to be their adversary. State power is no more to be used so as to handicap religions, than it is to favor them.

This Court has said that parents may, in the discharge of their duty under state compulsory education laws, send their children to a religious rather than a public school if the school meets the secular educational requirements which the state has power to impose. See Pierce v. Society of Sisters, 268 U.S. 510. It appears that these parochial schools meet New Jersey's requirements. The State contributes no money to the schools. It does not support them. Its legislation, as applied, does no more than provide a general program to help parents get their children, regardless of their religion, safely and expeditiously to and from accredited schools.

The First Amendment has erected a wall between church and state. That wall must be kept high and impregnable. We could not approve the slightest breach. New Jersey has not breached it here.

Affirmed.

Mr. Justice Jackson [with whom Mr. Justice Frankfurter joined], dissenting.

. . . The Court's opinion marshals every argument in favor of state aid and puts the case in its most favorable light, but much of its reasoning confirms my conclusions that there are no good grounds upon which to support the present legislation. In fact, the undertones of the opinion, advocating complete and uncompromising separation of Church from State, seem utterly discordant with its conclusion yielding support to their commingling in educational matters. The case which irresistibly comes to mind as the most fitting precedent is that of Julia who, according to Byron's reports, "whispering 'I will ne'er consent,'— consented."

. . .

Mr. Justice Rutledge, with whom Mr. Justice Frankfurter, Mr. Justice Jackson and Mr. Justice Burton agree, dissenting.

. . .

Two great drives are constantly in motion to abridge, in the name of education, the complete division of religion and civil authority which our forefathers made. One is to introduce religious education and observances into the public schools. The other, to obtain public funds for the aid and support of various private religious schools. See Johnson, The Legal Status of Church–State Relationships in the United States (1934); Thayer, Religion in Public Education (1947); Note (1941) 50 Yale L.J. 917. In my opinion both avenues were closed by the Constitution. Neither should be opened by this Court. The matter is not one of quantity, to be measured by the amount of money expended. Now as in Madison's day it is one of principle, to keep separate the separate spheres as the First Amendment drew them; to prevent the first experiment upon our liberties; and to keep the question from becoming entangled in corrosive precedents. We should not be less strict to keep strong and untarnished the one side of the shield of religious freedom than we have been of the other.

The judgment should be reversed.

DENOMINATIONAL PREFERENCES

The Court was unanimous in *Everson* in the conclusion that the establishment clause forbids aid to all religions as well as aid to one religion. Still, in Larson v. Valente, 456 U.S. 228 (1982), the Court referred to the proposition that "one religious denomination cannot be officially preferred over another" as "the clearest command of the Establishment Clause." (The Court invalidated a charitable contribution statute that exempted from its requirements religious organizations that solicit less than 50 percent of their funds from nonmembers.)

THE "THREE–PART *LEMON* TEST"

In cases decided after 1971, it is common to begin opinions concerning the establishment clause by reciting standards summarized in Chief Justice Burger's opinion for the Court in Lemon v. Kurtzman, 403 U.S. 602, 612–613 (1971). To be valid against attack under the establishment clause:

> "First, the statute must have a secular legislative purpose; second, its principal or primary effect must be one that neither advances nor inhibits religion ...; finally, the statute must not foster 'an excessive government entanglement with religion.'"

> Despite their apparent simplicity, the three *"Lemon* standards"—which will be examined time and again in the cases to follow—have substantial ambiguities and remain controversial.

LAMB'S CHAPEL v. CENTER MORICHES UNION FREE SCHOOL DISTRICT, 508 U.S. 384 (1993). The School District permitted the use of school property for "social, civic and recreational meetings" but did not allow student bible clubs to meet on school property. The Court concluded that precluding use of school property by bible clubs was a violation of the Free Speech Clause. The Court answered an argument, that allowing use of school property for bible study would be an establishment, by stating that "this would not have been an establishment of religion under the three-part test articulated in Lemon v. Kurtzman." In a concurrence, Justice Scalia objected to the Court's use of the *Lemon* test, arguing that it was

> "[l]ike some ghoul in a late-night horror movie that repeatedly sits up in its grave and shuffles abroad, after being repeatedly killed and buried, *Lemon* stalks our Establishment Clause jurisprudence once again, frightening the little children and school attorneys of Center Moriches Union Free School District ...

" . . .

" . . . It is there to scare us (and our audience) when we wish it to do so, but we can command it to return to the tomb at will. . . . When we wish to strike down a practice it forbids, we invoke it . . .; when we wish to uphold a practice it forbids, we ignore it entirely . . . Such a docile and useful monster is worth keeping around, at least in a somnolent state; one never knows when one might need him."

Justice White's opinion for the Court responded to Justice Scalia in a footnote.

"While we are somewhat diverted by Justice Scalia's evening at the cinema, we return to the reality that there is a proper way to inter an established decision and *Lemon*, however frightening it might be to some, has not been overruled."

B. GOVERNMENT RELIGIOUS EXERCISES, CEREMONIES, DISPLAYS, AND PRACTICES

1. PUBLIC SCHOOLS

Zorach v. Clauson

343 U.S. 306, 72 S.Ct. 679, 96 L.Ed. 954 (1952).

Mr. Justice Douglas delivered the opinion of the Court.

New York City has a program which permits its public schools to release students during the school day so that they may leave the school buildings and school grounds and go to religious centers for religious instruction or devotional exercises. A student is released on written request of his parents. Those not released stay in the classrooms. The churches make weekly reports to the schools, sending a list of children who have been released from public school but who have not reported for religious instruction.

This "released time" program involves neither religious instruction in public school classrooms nor the expenditure of public funds. All costs, including the application blanks, are paid by the religious organizations. The case is therefore unlike McCollum v. Board of Education, 333 U.S. 203, which involved a "released time" program from Illinois. In that case the classrooms were turned over to religious instructors. We accordingly held that the program violated the First Amendment which (by reason of the Fourteenth Amendment) prohibits the states from establishing religion or prohibiting its free exercise.

Appellants, who are taxpayers and residents of New York City and whose children attend its public schools, challenge the present law, contending it is in essence not different from the one involved in the *McCollum* case. Their argument, stated elaborately in various ways, reduces itself to this: the weight and influence of the school is put behind a program for religious instruction; public school teachers police it, keeping tab on students who are released; the classroom activities come to a halt while the students who are released for religious instruction are on leave; the school is a crutch on which the churches are leaning for support in their religious training; without the cooperation of the schools this "released time" program, like the one in the *McCollum* case, would be futile and ineffective. The New York Court of Appeals sustained the law against this claim of unconstitutionality.

The briefs and arguments are replete with data bearing on the merits of this type of "released time" program. . . . Those matters are of no concern here, since our problem reduces itself to whether New York by this system has either prohibited the "free exercise" of religion or has made a law "respecting an establishment of religion" within the meaning of the First Amendment.

It takes obtuse reasoning to inject any issue of the "free exercise" of religion into the present case. No one is forced to go to the religious classroom and no religious exercise or instruction is brought to the classrooms of the public schools. A student need not take religious instruction. He is left to his own desires as to the manner or time of his religious devotions, if any.

There is a suggestion that the system involves the use of coercion to get public school students into religious classrooms. There is no evidence in the record before us that supports that conclusion.[6] The present record indeed tells us that the school authorities are neutral in this regard and do no more than release students whose parents so request. If in fact coercion were used, if it were established that any one or more teachers were using their office to persuade or force students to take the religious instruction, a wholly different case would be presented.[7] Hence we put aside that claim of coercion both as respects the "free exercise" of religion and "an establishment of religion" within the meaning of the First Amendment.

Moreover, apart from that claim of coercion, we do not see how New York by this type of "released time" program has made a law respecting an establishment of religion within the meaning of the First Amendment. . . . There cannot be the slightest doubt that the First Amendment reflects the philosophy that Church and State should be separated. And so far as interference with the "free exercise" of religion and an "establishment" of religion are concerned, the separation must be complete and unequivocal. The First Amendment within the scope of its coverage permits no exception; the prohibition is absolute. The First Amendment, however, does not say that in every and all respects there shall be a separation of Church and State. Rather, it studiously defines the manner, the specific ways, in which there shall be no concert or union or dependency one on the other. That is the common sense of the matter. Otherwise the state and religion would be aliens to each other—hostile, suspicious, and even unfriendly. Churches could not be required to pay even property taxes. Municipalities would not be permitted to render police or fire protection to religious groups. Policemen who helped parishioners into their places of worship would violate the Constitution. Prayers in our legislative halls; the appeals to the Almighty in the messages of the Chief Executive; the proclamations making Thanksgiving Day a holiday; "so help me God" in our courtroom oaths—these and all other references to the Almighty that run through our laws, our public rituals, our ceremonies would be flouting the First Amendment. A fastidious atheist or agnostic could even object to the supplica-

---

[6] Nor is there any indication that the public schools enforce attendance at religious schools by punishing absentees from the released time programs for truancy.

[7] Appellants contend that they should have been allowed to prove that the system is in fact administered in a coercive manner. The New York Court of Appeals declined to grant a trial on this issue, noting, *inter alia,* that appellants had not properly raised their claim in the manner required by state practice. 303 N.Y. 161, 174, 100 N.E.2d 463, 469. This independent state ground for decision precludes appellants from raising the issue of maladministration in this proceeding. . . .

The only allegation in the complaint that bears on the issue is that the operation of the program "has resulted and inevitably results in the exercise of pressure and coercion upon parents and children to secure attendance by the children for religious instruction." But this charge does not even implicate the school authorities. The New York Court of Appeals was therefore generous in labeling it a "conclusory" allegation. . . .

tion with which the Court opens each session: "God save the United States and this Honorable Court."

We would have to press the concept of separation of Church and State to these extremes to condemn the present law on constitutional grounds. The nullification of this law would have wide and profound effects. A Catholic student applies to his teacher for permission to leave the school during hours on a Holy Day of Obligation to attend a mass. A Jewish student asks his teacher for permission to be excused for Yom Kippur. A Protestant wants the afternoon off for a family baptismal ceremony. In each case the teacher requires parental consent in writing. In each case the teacher, in order to make sure the student is not a truant, goes further and requires a report from the priest, the rabbi, or the minister. The teacher in other words cooperates in a religious program to the extent of making it possible for her students to participate in it. Whether she does it occasionally for a few students, regularly for one, or pursuant to a systematized program designed to further the religious needs of all the students does not alter the character of the act.

We are a religious people whose institutions presuppose a Supreme Being. We guarantee the freedom to worship as one chooses. We make room for as wide a variety of beliefs and creeds as the spiritual needs of man deem necessary. We sponsor an attitude on the part of government that shows no partiality to any one group and that lets each flourish according to the zeal of its adherents and the appeal of its dogma. When the state encourages religious instruction or cooperates with religious authorities by adjusting the schedule of public events to sectarian needs, it follows the best of our traditions. For it then respects the religious nature of our people and accommodates the public service to their spiritual needs. To hold that it may not would be to find in the Constitution a requirement that the government show a callous indifference to religious groups. That would be preferring those who believe in no religion over those who do believe. Government may not finance religious groups nor undertake religious instruction nor blend secular and sectarian education nor use secular institutions to force one or some religion on any person. But we find no constitutional requirement which makes it necessary for government to be hostile to religion and to throw its weight against efforts to widen the effective scope of religious influence. The government must be neutral when it comes to competition between sects. It may not thrust any sect on any person. It may not make a religious observance compulsory. It may not coerce anyone to attend church, to observe a religious holiday, or to take religious instruction. But it can close its doors or suspend its operations as to those who want to repair to their religious sanctuary for worship or instruction. No more than that is undertaken here.

. . .

In the *McCollum* case the classrooms were used for religious instruction and the force of the public school was used to promote that instruction. Here, as we have said, the public schools do no more than accommodate their schedules to a program of outside religious instruction. We follow the *McCollum* case. But we cannot expand it to cover the present released time program unless separation of Church and State means that public institutions can make no adjustments of their schedules to accommodate the religious needs of the people. We cannot read into the Bill of Rights such a philosophy of hostility to religion.

Affirmed.

Mr. Justice Black, dissenting.

. . .

... In considering whether a state has entered this forbidden field the question is not whether it has entered too far but whether it has entered at all. New York is manipulating its compulsory education laws to help religious sects get pupils. This is not separation but combination of Church and State. ...

. . .

Mr. Justice Frankfurter, dissenting.

By way of emphasizing my agreement with Mr. Justice Jackson's dissent, I add a few words.

. . .

... Of course, a State may provide that the classes in its schools shall be dismissed, for any reason, or no reason, on fixed days, or for special occasions. The essence of this case is that the school system did not "close its doors" and did not "suspend its operations." ...

The pith of the case is that formalized religious instruction is substituted for other school activity which those who do not participate in the released-time program are compelled to attend. The school system is very much in operation during this kind of released time. . . .

. . .

Mr. Justice Jackson, dissenting.

. . .

A number of Justices just short of a majority of the majority that promulgates today's passionate dialectics joined in answering them in McCollum v. Board of Education, 333 U.S. 203. The distinction attempted between that case and this is trivial, almost to the point of cynicism, magnifying its nonessential details and disparaging compulsion which was the underlying reason for invalidity. A reading of the Court's opinion in that case along with its opinion in this case will show such difference of overtones and undertones as to make clear that the *McCollum* case has passed like a storm in a teacup. The wall which the Court was professing to erect between Church and State has become even more warped and twisted than I expected. Today's judgment will be more interesting to students of psychology and of the judicial processes than to students of constitutional law.

Lee v. Weisman

505 U.S. 577, 112 S.Ct. 2649, 120 L.Ed.2d 467 (1992).

Justice Kennedy delivered the opinion of the Court.

School principals in the public school system of the city of Providence, Rhode Island, are permitted to invite members of the clergy to offer invocation and benediction prayers as part of the formal graduation ceremonies for middle schools and for high schools. The question before us is whether including clerical members who offer prayers as part of the official school graduation ceremony is consistent with the Religion Clauses of the First Amendment, provisions the Fourteenth Amendment makes applicable with full force to the States and their school districts.

I

A

Deborah Weisman graduated from Nathan Bishop Middle School, a public school in Providence, at a formal ceremony in June 1989. She was about 14 years old. For many years it has been the policy of the Providence School Committee and the Superintendent of Schools to permit principals to invite members of the clergy to give invocations and benedictions at middle school and high school graduations. Many, but not all, of the principals elected to include prayers as part of the graduation ceremonies. Acting for himself and his daughter, Deborah's father, Daniel Weisman, objected to any prayers at Deborah's middle school graduation, but to no avail. The school principal, petitioner Robert E. Lee, invited a rabbi to deliver prayers at the graduation exercises for Deborah's class. Rabbi Leslie Gutterman, of the Temple Beth El in Providence, accepted.

It has been the custom of Providence school officials to provide invited clergy with a pamphlet entitled "Guidelines for Civic Occasions," prepared by the National Conference of Christians and Jews. The Guidelines recommended that public prayers at nonsectarian civic ceremonies be composed with "inclusiveness and sensitivity," though they acknowledge that "[p]rayer of any kind may be inappropriate on some civic occasions." The principal gave Rabbi Gutterman the pamphlet before the graduation and advised him the invocation and benediction should be nonsectarian.

Rabbi Gutterman's prayers were as follows:

"Invocation

"God of the Free, Hope of the Brave:

"For the legacy of America where diversity is celebrated and the rights of minorities are protected, we thank You. May these young men and women grow up to enrich it.

"For the liberty of America, we thank You. May these new graduates grow up to guard it.

"For the political process of America in which all its citizens may participate, for its court system where all may seek justice we thank You. May those we honor this morning always turn to it in trust.

"For the destiny of America we thank You. May the graduates of Nathan Bishop Middle School so live that they might help to share it.

"May our aspirations for our country and for these young people, who are our hope for the future, be richly fulfilled. AMEN"

"Benediction

"O God, we are grateful to You for having endowed us with the capacity for learning which we have celebrated on this joyous commencement.

"Happy families give thanks for seeing their children achieve an important milestone. Send Your blessings upon the teachers and administrators who helped prepare them.

"The graduates now need strength and guidance for the future, help them to understand that we are not complete with academic knowledge alone. We must each strive to fulfill what You require of us all: To do justly, to love mercy, to walk humbly.

"We give thanks to You, Lord, for keeping us alive, sustaining us and allowing us to reach this special, happy occasion. AMEN"

The record in this case is sparse in many respects, and we are unfamiliar with any fixed custom or practice at middle school graduations, referred to by the school district as "promotional exercises." We are not so constrained with reference to high schools, however. High school graduations are such an integral part of American cultural life that we can with confidence describe their customary features, confirmed by aspects of the record and by the parties' representations at oral argument. In the Providence school system, most high school graduation ceremonies are conducted away from the school, while most middle school ceremonies are held on school premises. Classical High School, which Deborah now attends, has conducted its graduation ceremonies on school premises. The parties stipulate that attendance at graduation ceremonies is voluntary. The graduating students enter as a group in a processional, subject to the direction of teachers and school officials, and sit together, apart from their families. We assume the clergy's participation in any high school graduation exercise would be about what it was at Deborah's middle school ceremony. There the students stood for the Pledge of Allegiance and remained standing during the Rabbi's prayers. Even on the assumption that there was a respectful moment of silence both before and after the prayers, the Rabbi's two presentations must not have extended much beyond a minute each, if that. We do not know whether he remained on stage during the whole ceremony, or whether the students received individual diplomas on stage, or if he helped to congratulate them.

The school board (and the United States, which supports it as amicus curiae) argued that these short prayers and others like them at graduation exercises are of profound meaning to many students and parents throughout this country who consider that due respect and acknowledgment for divine guidance and for the deepest spiritual aspirations of our people ought to be expressed at an event as important in life as a graduation. We assume this to be so in addressing the difficult case now before us, for the significance of the prayers lies also at the heart of Daniel and Deborah Weisman's case.

B

Deborah's graduation was held on the premises of Nathan Bishop Middle School on June 29, 1989. Four days before the ceremony, Daniel Weisman, in his individual capacity as a Providence taxpayer and as next friend of Deborah, sought a temporary restraining order in the United States District Court for the District of Rhode Island to prohibit school officials from including an invocation or benediction in the graduation ceremony. The court denied the motion for lack of adequate time to consider it. Deborah and her family attended the graduation, where the prayers were recited. In July 1989, Daniel Weisman filed an amended complaint seeking a permanent injunction barring petitioners, various officials of the Providence public schools, from inviting the clergy to deliver invocations and benedictions at future graduations. We find it unnecessary to address Daniel Weisman's taxpayer standing, for a live and justiciable controversy is before us. Deborah Weisman is enrolled as a student at Classical High School in Providence and from the record it appears likely, if not certain, that an invocation and benediction will be conducted at her high school graduation.

. . . The District Court held that petitioners' practice of including invocations and benedictions in public school graduations violated the Establishment Clause of the First Amendment, and it enjoined petitioners from continuing the practice. The court applied the three-part Establishment Clause test set forth in Lemon v. Kurtzman, 403 U.S. 602 (1971). . . .

On appeal, the United States Court of Appeals for the First Circuit affirmed. The majority opinion . . . adopted the opinion of the district Court. . . . We . . . affirm.

II

These dominant facts mark and control the confines of our decision: State officials direct the performance of a formal religious exercise at promotional and graduation ceremonies for secondary schools. Even for those students who object to the religious exercise, their attendance and participation in the state-sponsored religious activity are in a fair and real sense obligatory, though the school district does not require attendance as a condition for receipt of the diploma.

. . . We can decide the case without reconsidering the general constitutional framework by which public schools' efforts to accommodate religion are measured. Thus we do not accept the invitation of petitioners and amicus the United States to reconsider our decision in Lemon v. Kurtzman, supra. The government involvement with religious activity in this case is pervasive, to the point of creating a state-sponsored and state-directed religious exercise in a public school. Conducting this formal religious observance conflicts with settled rules pertaining to prayer exercises for students, and that suffices to determine the question before us.

The principle that government may accommodate the free exercise of religion does not supersede the fundamental limitations imposed by the Establishment Clause. It is beyond dispute that, at a minimum, the Constitution guarantees that government may not coerce anyone to support or participate in religion or its exercise, or otherwise act in a way which "establishes a [state] religion or religious faith, or tends to do so." Lynch, supra, at 678 . . . The State's involvement in the school prayers challenged today violates these central principles.

That involvement is as troubling as it is undenied. A school official, the principal, decided that an invocation and a benediction should be given; this is a choice attributable to the State, and from a constitutional perspective it is as if a state statute decreed that the prayers must occur. The principal chose the religious participant, here a rabbi, and that choice is also attributable to the State. The reason for the choice of a rabbi is not disclosed by the record, but the potential for divisiveness over the choice of a particular member of the clergy to conduct the ceremony is apparent.

Divisiveness, of course, can attend any state decision respecting religions, and neither its existence nor its potential necessarily invalidates the State's attempts to accommodate religion in all cases. The potential for divisiveness is of particular relevance here though, because it centers around an overt religious exercise in a secondary school environment where, as we discuss below, subtle coercive pressures exist and where the student had no real alternative which would have allowed her to avoid the fact or appearance of participation.

The State's role did not end with the decision to include a prayer and with the choice of clergyman. Principal Lee provided Rabbi Gutterman with a copy of the "Guidelines for Civic Occasions," and advised him that his prayers should be nonsectarian. Through these means the principal directed and controlled the content of the prayer. . . . It is a cornerstone principle of our Establishment Clause jurisprudence that "it is no part of the business of government to compose official prayers for any group of the American people to recite as a part of a religious program carried on by government," Engel v. Vitale, 370 U.S. 421, 425 (1962), and that is what the school officials attempted to do.

Petitioners argue, and we find nothing in the case to refute it, that the directions for the content of the prayers were a good-faith attempt by the school to ensure that the sectarianism which is so often the flashpoint for religious animosity be removed from the graduation ceremony. . . . The school's explanation, however, does not resolve the dilemma caused by its participation. . . .

We are asked to recognize the existence of a practice of nonsectarian prayer, prayer within the embrace of what is known as the Judeo–Christian tradition . . . But though the First Amendment does not allow the government to stifle prayers which aspire to these ends, neither does it permit the government to undertake that task for itself.

The First Amendment's Religion Clauses mean that religious beliefs and religious expression are too precious to be either proscribed or prescribed by the State. The design of the Constitution is that preservation and transmission of religious beliefs and worship is a responsibility and a choice committed to the private sphere, which itself is promised freedom to pursue that mission. It must not be forgotten then, that while concern must be given to define the protection granted to an objector or a dissenting non-believer, these same Clauses exist to protect religion from government interference. . . .

These concerns have particular application in the case of school officials, whose effort to monitor prayer will be perceived by the students as inducing a participation they might otherwise reject. . . .

The degree of school involvement here made it clear that the graduation prayers bore the imprint of the State and thus put school-age children who objected in an untenable position. We turn our attention now to consider the position of the students, both those who desired the prayer and she who did not.

. . . [S]tudents may consider it an odd measure of justice to be subjected during the course of their educations to ideas deemed offensive and irreligious, but to be denied a brief, formal prayer ceremony that the school offers in return. This argument cannot prevail, however. It overlooks a fundamental dynamic of the Constitution.

The First Amendment protects speech and religion by quite different mechanisms. Speech is protected by insuring its full expression even when the government participates, for the very object of some of our most important speech is to persuade the government to adopt an idea as its own. . . . The method for protecting freedom of worship and freedom of conscience in religious matters is quite the reverse. In religious debate or expression the government is not a prime participant, for the Framers deemed religious establishment antithetical to the freedom of all. The Free Exercise Clause embraces a freedom of conscience and worship that has close parallels in the speech provisions of the First Amendment, but the Establishment Clause is a specific prohibition on forms of state intervention in religious affairs with no precise counterpart in the speech provisions. Buckley v. Valeo, 424 U.S. 1, 92–93, and n. 127 (1976) (per curiam). . . . [I]n the hands of government what might begin as a tolerant expression of religious views may end in a policy to indoctrinate and coerce. A state-created orthodoxy puts at grave risk that freedom of belief and conscience which are the sole assurance that religious faith is real, not imposed.

    . . .

As we have observed before, there are heightened concerns with protecting freedom of conscience from subtle coercive pressure in the elementary and secondary public schools. See, e.g., Abington School District, 307 (1963) . . . Our decisions in Engel v. Vitale, 370 U.S. 421 (1962), and Abington School District [v. Schempp, 374 U.S. 203 (1963)], recognize, among other things, that prayer exercises in public schools carry a particular risk of indirect coercion. The concern may not be limited to the context of schools, but it is most pronounced there. . . . What to most believers may seem nothing more than a reasonable request that the nonbeliever respect their religious practices, in a school context may appear to the nonbeliever or dissenter to be an attempt to employ the machinery of the State to enforce a religious orthodoxy.

We need not look beyond the circumstances of this case to see the phenomenon at work. The undeniable fact is that the school district's supervision and control of a high school graduation ceremony places public pressure, as well as peer pressure, on attending students to stand as a group or, at least, maintain respectful silence during the Invocation and Benediction. This pressure, though subtle and indirect, can be as real as any overt compulsion. Of course, in our culture standing or remaining silent can signify adherence to a view or simple respect for the views of others. And no doubt some persons who have no desire to join a prayer have little objection to standing as a sign of respect for those who do. But for the dissenter of high school age, who has a reasonable perception that she is being forced by the State to pray in a manner her conscience will not allow, the injury is no less real. There can be no doubt that for many, if not most, of the students at the graduation, the act of standing or remaining silent was an expression of participation in the Rabbi's prayer. That was the very point of the religious exercise. It is of little comfort to a dissenter, then, to be told that for her the act of standing or remaining in silence signifies mere respect, rather than participation. What matters is that, given our social conventions, a reasonable dissenter in this milieu could believe that the group exercise signified her own participation or approval of it.

Finding no violation under these circumstances would place objectors in the dilemma of participating, with all that implies, or protesting. We do not address whether that choice is acceptable if the affected citizens are mature adults, but we think the State may not, consistent with the Establishment Clause, place primary and secondary school children in this position. Research in psychology supports the common assumption that adolescents are often susceptible to pressure from their peers towards conformity, and that the influence is strongest in matters of social convention. Brittain, Adolescent Choices and Parent–Peer Cross–Pressures, 28 Am. Sociological Rev. 385 (June 1963); Clasen & Brown, The Multidimensionality of Peer Pressure, Peer Conformity Dispositions, and Self–Reported Behavior Among Adolescents, 22 Developmental Psychology 521 (July 1986). To recognize that the choice imposed by the State constitutes an unacceptable constraint only acknowledges that the government may no more use social pressure to enforce orthodoxy than it may use more direct means.

The injury caused by the government's action, and the reason why Daniel and Deborah Weisman object to it, is that the State, in a school setting, in effect required participation in a religious exercise. It is, we concede, a brief exercise during which the individual can concentrate on joining its message, meditate on her own religion, or let her mind wander. But the embarrassment and the intrusion of the religious exercise cannot be refuted by arguing that these prayers, and similar ones to be said in the future, are of a de minimis character. To do so would be an affront to the Rabbi who offered them and to all those for whom the prayers were an essential and profound recognition of divine authority. And for the same reason, we think that the intrusion is greater than the two minutes or so of time consumed for prayers like these. Assuming, as we must, that the prayers were offensive to the student and the parent who now object, the intrusion was both real and, in the context of a secondary school, a violation of the objectors' rights. That the intrusion was in the course of promulgating religion that sought to be civic or nonsectarian rather than pertaining to one sect does not lessen the offense or isolation to the objectors. At best it narrows their number, at worst increases their sense of isolation and affront.

There was a stipulation in the District Court that attendance at graduation and promotional ceremonies is voluntary. Petitioners and the United States, as amicus, made this a center point of the case, arguing that the option of not attending the graduation excuses any inducement or coercion in the ceremony itself. The argument lacks all persuasion. Law reaches past formalism. And to say a teenage student has a real choice not to attend her high school graduation is formalistic in the extreme. . . .

. . .

The Government's argument gives insufficient recognition to the real conflict of conscience faced by the young student. The essence of the Government's position is that with regard to a civic, social occasion of this importance it is the objector, not the majority, who must take unilateral and private action to avoid compromising religious scruples, here by electing to miss the graduation exercise. This turns conventional First Amendment analysis on its head. It is a tenet of the First Amendment that the State cannot require one of its citizens to forfeit his or her rights and benefits as the price of resisting conformance to state-sponsored religious practice. To say that a student must remain apart from the ceremony at the opening invocation and closing benediction is to risk compelling conformity in an environment analogous to the classroom setting, where we have said the risk of compulsion is especially high. Just as in *Engel v. Vitale,* . . . and *Abington School District v. Schempp,* . . . we found that provisions within the challenged legislation permitting a student to be voluntarily excused from attendance or participation in the daily prayers did not shield those practices from invalidation, the fact that attendance at the graduation ceremonies is voluntary in a legal sense does not save the religious exercise.

Inherent differences between the public school system and a session of a State Legislature distinguish this case from Marsh v. Chambers, 463 U.S. 783 (1983). The considerations we have raised in objection to the invocation and benediction are in many respects similar to the arguments we considered in *Marsh.* But there are also obvious differences. The atmosphere at the opening of a session of a state legislature where adults are free to enter and leave with little comment and for any number of reasons cannot compare with the constraining potential of the one school event most important for the student to attend. The influence and force of a formal exercise in a school graduation are far greater than the prayer exercise we condoned in *Marsh.* . . .

We do not hold that every state action implicating religion is invalid if one or a few citizens find it offensive. People may take offense at all manner of religious as well as nonreligious messages, but offense alone does not in every case show a violation. We know too that sometimes to endure social isolation or even anger may be the price of conscience or nonconformity. But, by any reading of our cases, the conformity required of the student in this case was too high an exaction to withstand the test of the Establishment Clause. The prayer exercises in this case are especially improper because the State has in every practical sense compelled attendance and participation in an explicit religious exercise at an event of singular importance to every student, one the objecting student had no real alternative to avoid.

Our jurisprudence in this area is of necessity one of line-drawing, of determining at what point a dissenter's rights of religious freedom are infringed by the State. . . .

. . . No holding by this Court suggests that a school can persuade or compel a student to participate in a religious exercise. That is being done here, and it is forbidden by the Establishment Clause of the First Amendment.

For the reasons we have stated, the judgment of the Court of Appeals is

Affirmed.

Justice Blackmun, with whom Justice Stevens and Justice O'Connor join, concurring.

.   .   .

II

I join the Court's opinion today because I find nothing in it inconsistent with the essential precepts of the Establishment Clause developed in our precedents. . . . Government pressure to participate in a religious activity is an obvious indication that the government is endorsing or promoting religion.

.   .   .

Justice Souter, with whom Justice Stevens and Justice O'Connor join, concurring.

I join the whole of the Court's opinion, and fully agree that prayers at public school graduation ceremonies indirectly coerce religious observance. I write separately nonetheless on two issues of Establishment Clause analysis that underlie my independent resolution of this case: whether the Clause applies to governmental practices that do not favor one religion or denomination over others, and whether state coercion of religious conformity, over and above state endorsement of religious exercise or belief, is a necessary element of an Establishment Clause violation.

I

.   .   .

A

Since *Everson,* we have consistently held the Clause applicable no less to governmental acts favoring religion generally than to acts favoring one religion over others.

.   .   .

Such is the settled law. Here, as elsewhere, we should stick to it absent some compelling reason to discard it . . . .

.   .   .

II

Petitioners rest most of their argument on a theory that, whether or not the Establishment Clause permits extensive nonsectarian support for religion, it does not forbid the state to sponsor affirmations of religious belief that coerce neither support for religion nor participation in religious observance. I appreciate the force of some of the arguments supporting a "coercion" analysis of the Clause. See generally *Allegheny County*, supra, at 655–679 (opinion of Kennedy, J.) ... But we could not adopt that reading without abandoning our settled law, a course that, in my view, the text of the Clause would not readily permit. Nor does the extratextual evidence of original meaning stand so unequivocally at odds with the textual premise inherent in existing precedent that we should fundamentally reconsider our course.

A

. . .

Our precedents may not always have drawn perfectly straight lines. They simply cannot, however, support the position that a showing of coercion is necessary to a successful Establishment Clause claim.

B

Like the provisions about "due" process and "unreasonable" searches and seizures, the constitutional language forbidding laws "respecting an establishment of religion" is not pellucid. But virtually everyone acknowledges that the Clause bans more than formal establishments of religion in the traditional sense, that is, massive state support for religion through, among other means, comprehensive schemes of taxation. ...

While some argue that the Framers added the word "respecting" simply to foreclose federal interference with State establishments of religion, ... the language sweeps more broadly than that.... While petitioners insist that the prohibition extends only to the "coercive" features and incidents of establishment, they cannot easily square that claim with the constitutional text. The First Amendment forbids not just laws "respecting an establishment of religion," but also those "prohibiting the free exercise thereof." Yet laws that coerce nonadherents to "support or participate in any religion or its exercise," ... would virtually by definition violate their right to religious free exercise.... Thus, a literal application of the coercion test would render the Establishment Clause a virtual nullity ...

. . .

C

. . .

While we may be unable to know for certain what the Framers meant by the Clause, we do know that, around the time of its ratification, a respectable body of opinion supported a considerably broader reading than petitioners urge upon us. This consistency with the textual considerations is enough to preclude fundamentally reexamining our settled law, and I am accordingly left with the task of considering whether the state practice at issue here violates our traditional understanding of the Clause's proscriptions.

III

While the Establishment Clause's concept of neutrality is not self-revealing, our recent cases have invested it with specific content: the state may not favor or endorse either religion generally over nonreligion or one religion over others. . . . cf. Lemon v. Kurtzman, 403 U.S. 602, 612–613 (1971). This principle against favoritism and endorsement has become the foundation of Establishment Clause jurisprudence, ensuring that religious belief is irrelevant to every citizen's standing in the political community, . . . and protecting religion from the demeaning effects of any governmental embrace . . .

. . .

Petitioners [argue] that graduation prayers are no different from presidential religious proclamations and similar official "acknowledgments" of religion in public life. But religious invocations in Thanksgiving Day addresses and the like, rarely noticed, ignored without effort, conveyed over an impersonal medium, and directed at no one in particular, inhabit a pallid zone worlds apart from official prayers delivered to a captive audience of public school students and their families. . . . When public school officials, armed with the State's authority, convey an endorsement of religion to their students, they strike near the core of the Establishment Clause. However "ceremonial" their messages may be, they are flatly unconstitutional.

Justice Scalia with whom The Chief Justice, Justice White, and Justice Thomas join, dissenting.

. . .

. . . In holding that the Establishment Clause prohibits invocations and benedictions at public-school graduation ceremonies, the Court . . . lays waste a tradition that is as old as public-school graduation ceremonies themselves, and that is a component of an even more longstanding American tradition of nonsectarian prayer to God at public celebrations generally. As its instrument of destruction, the bulldozer of its social engineering, the Court invents a boundless, and boundlessly manipulable, test of psychological coercion . . .

I

. . .

The history and tradition of our Nation are replete with public ceremonies featuring prayers of thanksgiving and petition. . . .

In addition to this general tradition of prayer at public ceremonies, there exists a more specific tradition of invocations and benedictions at public-school graduation exercises. . . .

II

The Court presumably would separate graduation invocations and benedictions from other instances of public "preservation and transmission of religious beliefs" on the ground that they involve "psychological coercion." . . . [T]he Court has gone beyond the realm where judges know what they are doing. The Court's argument that state officials have "coerced" students to take part in the invocation and benediction at graduation ceremonies is, not to put too fine a point on it, incoherent.

. . .

III

The deeper flaw in the Court's opinion does not lie in its wrong answer to the question whether there was state-induced "peer-pressure" coercion; it lies, rather, in the Court's making violation of the Establishment Clause hinge on such a precious question. . . .

.   .   .

. . . [W]hile I have no quarrel with the Court's general proposition that the Establishment Clause "guarantees that government may not coerce anyone to support or participate in religion or its exercise," I see no warrant for expanding the concept of coercion beyond acts backed by threat of penalty—a brand of coercion that, happily, is readily discernible . . .

.   .   .

The Court relies on our "school prayer" cases . . . But whatever the merit of those cases, they do not support, much less compel, the Court's psycho-journey. . . .[T]he classroom is inherently an instructional setting, and daily prayer there—where parents are not present . . .—might be thought to raise special concerns regarding state interference with the liberty of parents to direct the religious upbringing of their children . . . Voluntary prayer at graduation—a one-time ceremony at which parents, friends and relatives are present—can hardly be thought to raise the same concerns.

IV

.   .   .

. . . Given the odd basis for the Court's decision, invocations and benedictions will be able to be given at public-school graduations next June, as they have for the past century and a half, so long as school authorities make clear that anyone who abstains from screaming in protest does not necessarily participate in the prayers. All that is seemingly needed is an announcement, or perhaps a written insertion at the beginning of the graduation Program, to the effect that, while all are asked to rise for the invocation and benediction, none is compelled to join in them, nor will be assumed, by rising, to have done so. That obvious fact recited, the graduates and their parents may proceed to thank God, as Americans have always done, for the blessings He has generously bestowed on them and on their country.

.   .   .

Edwards v. Aguillard

482 U.S. 578, 107 S.Ct. 2573, 96 L.Ed.2d 510 (1987).

Justice Brennan delivered the opinion of the Court.

The question for decision is whether Louisiana's "Balanced Treatment for Creation–Science and Evolution–Science in Public School Instruction" Act (Creationism Act), La.Rev.Stat.Ann. §§ 17:286.1–17:286.7 (West 1982), is facially invalid as violative of the Establishment Clause of the First Amendment.

I

The Creationism Act forbids the teaching of the theory of evolution in public schools unless accompanied by instruction in "creation science." § 17:286.4A. No school is required to teach evolution or creation science. If either is taught, however, the other must also be taught. Ibid. The theories of evolution and creation science are statutorily defined as "the scientific evidences for [creation or evolution] and inferences from those scientific evidences." §§ 17:286.3(2) and (3).

Appellees, who include parents of children attending Louisiana public schools, Louisiana teachers, and religious leaders, challenged the constitutionality of the Act in District Court, seeking an injunction and declaratory relief. Appellants, Louisiana officials charged with implementing the Act, defended on the ground that the purpose of the Act is to protect a legitimate secular interest, namely, academic freedom. Appellees attacked the Act as facially invalid because it violated the Establishment Clause and made a motion for summary judgment. The District Court granted the motion. . . .

The Court of Appeals affirmed. . . . We . . . affirm.

II

The Establishment Clause forbids the enactment of any law "respecting an establishment of religion." The Court has applied a three-pronged test to determine whether legislation comports with the Establishment Clause. First, the legislature must have adopted the law with a secular purpose. Second, the statute's principal or primary effect must be one that neither advances nor inhibits religion. Third, the statute must not result in an excessive entanglement of government with religion. Lemon v. Kurtzman, 403 U.S. 602, 612–613 (1971).[4] State action violates the Establishment Clause if it fails to satisfy any of these prongs.

. . .

The Court has been particularly vigilant in monitoring compliance with the Establishment Clause in elementary and secondary schools. Families entrust public schools with the education of their children, but condition their trust on the understanding that the classroom will not purposely be used to advance religious views that may conflict with the private beliefs of the student and his or her family. Students in such institutions are impressionable and their attendance is involuntary. . . . The State exerts great authority and coercive power through mandatory attendance requirements, and because of the students' emulation of teachers as role models and the children's susceptibility to peer pressure.[5] . . .

. . .

[4] The *Lemon* test has been applied in all cases since its adoption in 1971, except in Marsh v. Chambers, 463 U.S. 783 (1983), where the Court held that th[e] [Ne]braska Legislature's practice of opening a session with a prayer by a chaplain paid by the State did not violate the Establishment Clause. The Court based its conclusion in that case on the historical acceptance of the practice. Such a historical approach is not useful in determining the proper roles of church and state in public schools, since free public education was virtually nonexistent at the time the Constitution was adopted. See Wallace v. Jaffree, 472 U.S. 38, 80 (1985) (O'Connor, J., concurring in judgment) (citing Abington School Dist. v. Schempp, 374 U.S. 203, 238, and n. 7 (1963) (Brennan, J., concurring)).

[5] The potential for undue influence is far less significant with regard to college students who voluntarily enroll in courses. "This distinction warrants a difference in constitutional results." Abington School Dist. v. Schempp, supra, at 253 (Brennan, J., concurring). Thus, for instance, the Court has not questioned the authority of state colleges and universities to offer courses on religion or theology. See Widmar v. Vincent, 454 U.S. 263, 271 (1981) (Powell, J.); id., at 281 (Stevens, J., concurring in judgment).

III

Lemon 's first prong focuses on the purpose that animated adoption of the Act.... If the law was enacted for the purpose of endorsing religion, "no consideration of the second or third criteria [of *Lemon*]is necessary." Wallace v. Jaffree, supra, at 56. In this case, appellants have identified no clear secular purpose for the Louisiana Act.

True, the Act's stated purpose is to protect academic freedom. ...This phrase might, in common parlance, be understood as referring to enhancing the freedom of teachers to teach what they will. The Court of Appeals, however, correctly concluded that the Act was not designed to further that goal. We find no merit in the State's argument that the "legislature may not [have] use[d] the terms 'academic freedom' in the correct legal sense. They might have [had] in mind, instead, a basic concept of fairness; teaching all of the evidence." Even if "academic freedom" is read to mean "teaching all of the evidence" with respect to the origin of human beings, the Act does not further this purpose. The goal of providing a more comprehensive science curriculum is not furthered either by outlawing the teaching of evolution or by requiring the teaching of creation science.

A

While the Court is normally deferential to a State's articulation of a secular purpose, it is required that the statement of such purpose be sincere and not a sham. ...

It is clear from the legislative history that the purpose of the legislative sponsor, Senator Bill Keith, was to narrow the science curriculum. During the legislative hearings, Senator Keith stated: "My preference would be that neither [creationism nor evolution] be taught." Such a ban on teaching does not promote—indeed, it undermines—the provision of a comprehensive scientific education.

It is equally clear that requiring schools to teach creation science with evolution does not advance academic freedom. The Act does not grant teachers a flexibility that they did not already possess to supplant the present science curriculum with the presentation of theories, besides evolution, about the origin of life. Indeed, the Court of Appeals found that no law prohibited Louisiana public school teachers from teaching any scientific theory....

. . .

Furthermore, the goal of basic "fairness" is hardly furthered by the Act's discriminatory preference for the teaching of creation science and against the teaching of evolution. While requiring that curriculum guides be developed for creation science, the Act says nothing of comparable guides for evolution.... Similarly, research services are supplied for creation science but not for evolution.... Only "creation scientists" can serve on the panel that supplies the resource services.... The Act forbids school boards to discriminate against anyone who "chooses to be a creation-scientist" or to teach "creationism," but fails to protect those who choose to teach evolution or any other noncreation science theory, or who refuse to teach creation science....

If the Louisiana Legislature's purpose was solely to maximize the comprehensiveness and effectiveness of science instruction, it would have encouraged the teaching of all scientific theories about the origins of humankind. But under the Act's requirements, teachers who were once free to teach any and all facets of this subject are now unable to do so. Moreover, the Act fails even to ensure that creation science will be taught, but instead requires the teaching of this theory only when the theory of evolution is taught. Thus we agree with the Court of Appeals' conclusion that the Act does not serve to protect academic freedom, but has the distinctly different purpose of discrediting "evolution by counterbalancing its teaching at every turn with the teaching of creationism...."

B

. . .

As in *Stone* and *Abington,* we need not be blind in this case to the legislature's preeminent religious purpose in enacting this statute. There is a historic and contemporaneous link between the teachings of certain religious denominations and the teaching of evolution. It was this link that concerned the Court in Epperson v. Arkansas, 393 U.S. 97 (1968), which also involved a facial challenge to a statute regulating the teaching of evolution. In that case, the Court reviewed an Arkansas statute that made it unlawful for an instructor to teach evolution or to use a textbook that referred to this scientific theory. Although the Arkansas anti-evolution law did not explicitly state its predominate religious purpose, the Court could not ignore that "[t]he statute was a product of the upsurge of 'fundamentalist' religious fervor" that has long viewed this particular scientific theory as contradicting the literal interpretation of the Bible. Id., at 98, 106–107. After reviewing the history of anti-evolution statutes, the Court determined that "there can be no doubt that the motivation for the [Arkansas] law was the same [as other anti-evolution statutes]: to suppress the teaching of a theory which, it was thought, 'denied' the divine creation of man." Id., at 109. The Court found that there can be no legitimate state interest in protecting particular religions from scientific views "distasteful to them," id., at 107 (citation omitted), and concluded "that the First Amendment does not permit the State to require that teaching and learning must be tailored to the principles or prohibitions of any religious sect or dogma," id., at 106.

These same historic and contemporaneous antagonisms between the teachings of certain religious denominations and the teaching of evolution are present in this case. The preeminent purpose of the Louisiana Legislature was clearly to advance the religious viewpoint that a supernatural being created humankind. The term "creation science" was defined as embracing this particular religious doctrine by those responsible for the passage of the Creationism Act. Senator Keith's leading expert on creation science, Edward Boudreaux, testified at the legislative hearings that the theory of creation science included belief in the existence of a supernatural creator. Senator Keith also cited testimony from other experts to support the creation-science view that "a creator [was] responsible for the universe and everything in it." The legislative history therefore reveals that the term "creation science," as contemplated by the legislature that adopted this Act, embodies the religious belief that a supernatural creator was responsible for the creation of humankind.

Furthermore, it is not happenstance that the legislature required the teaching of a theory that coincided with this religious view. The legislative history documents that the Act's primary purpose was to change the science curriculum of public schools in order to provide persuasive advantage to a particular religious doctrine that rejects the factual basis of evolution in its entirety. . . .

In this case, the purpose of the Creationism Act was to restructure the science curriculum to conform with a particular religious viewpoint. Out of many possible science subjects taught in the public schools, the legislature chose to affect the teaching of the one scientific theory that historically has been opposed by certain religious sects. As in *Epperson,* the legislature passed the Act to give preference to those religious groups which have as one of their tenets the creation of humankind by a divine creator. The "overriding fact" that confronted the Court in *Epperson* was "that Arkansas' law selects from the body of knowledge a particular segment which it proscribes for the sole reason that it is deemed to conflict with ... a particular interpretation of the Book of Genesis by a particular religious group." ...

We do not imply that a legislature could never require that scientific critiques of prevailing scientific theories be taught. Indeed, the Court acknowledged in *Stone* that its decision forbidding the posting of the Ten Commandments did not mean that no use could ever be made of the Ten Commandments, or that the Ten Commandments played an exclusively religious role in the history of Western Civilization. 449 U.S., at 42. In a similar way, teaching a variety of scientific theories about the origins of humankind to schoolchildren might be validly done with the clear secular intent of enhancing the effectiveness of science instruction. But because the primary purpose of the Creationism Act is to endorse a particular religious doctrine, the Act furthers religion in violation of the Establishment Clause.

. . .

V

The Louisiana Creationism Act advances a religious doctrine by requiring either the banishment of the theory of evolution from public school classrooms or the presentation of a religious viewpoint that rejects evolution in its entirety. The Act violates the Establishment Clause of the First Amendment because it seeks to employ the symbolic and financial support of government to achieve a religious purpose. The judgment of the Court of Appeals therefore is

Affirmed.

Justice Powell, with whom Justice O'Connor joins, concurring.

. . .

... The Establishment Clause is properly understood to prohibit the use of the Bible and other religious documents in public school education only when the purpose of the use is to advance a particular religious belief.

. . .

Justice White, concurring in the judgment.

As it comes to us, this is not a difficult case....

. . .

Here, the District Judge, relying on the terms of the Act, discerned its purpose to be the furtherance of a religious belief, and a panel of the Court of Appeals agreed. Of those four judges, two are Louisianians. I would accept this view of the statute. Even if as an original matter I might have arrived at a different conclusion based on a reading of the statute and the record before us, I cannot say that the two courts below are so plainly wrong that they should be reversed....

. . .

Justice Scalia, with whom The Chief Justice joins, dissenting.

Even if I agreed with the questionable premise that legislation can be invalidated under the Establishment Clause on the basis of its motivation alone, without regard to its effects, I would still find no justification for today's decision. . . . [T]he question of its constitutionality cannot rightly be disposed of on the gallop, by impugning the motives of its supporters.

I

. . . [T]he parties are sharply divided over what creation science consists of. Appellants insist that it is a collection of educationally valuable scientific data that has been censored from classrooms by an embarrassed scientific establishment. Appellees insist it is not science at all but thinly veiled religious doctrine. Both interpretations of the intended meaning of that phrase find considerable support in the legislative history.

· · ·

II

· · ·

B

· · ·

In sum, even if one concedes, for the sake of argument, that a majority of the Louisiana Legislature voted for the Balanced Treatment Act partly in order to foster (rather than merely eliminate discrimination against) Christian fundamentalist beliefs, our cases establish that that alone would not suffice to invalidate the Act, so long as there was a genuine secular purpose as well. We have, moreover, no adequate basis for disbelieving the secular purpose set forth in the Act itself, or for concluding that it is a sham enacted to conceal the legislators' violation of their oaths of office. I am astonished by the Court's unprecedented readiness to reach such a conclusion, which I can only attribute to an intellectual predisposition created by the facts and the legend of Scopes v. State, 154 Tenn. 105, 289 S.W. 363 (1927)—an instinctive reaction that any governmentally imposed requirements bearing upon the teaching of evolution must be a manifestation of Christian fundamentalist repression. In this case, however, it seems to me the Court's position is the repressive one. The people of Louisiana, including those who are Christian fundamentalists, are quite entitled, as a secular matter, to have whatever scientific evidence there may be against evolution presented in their schools, just as Mr. Scopes was entitled to present whatever scientific evidence there was for it. . . .

· · ·

Because I believe that the Balanced Treatment Act had a secular purpose, which is all the first component of the *Lemon* test requires, I would reverse the judgment of the Court of Appeals and remand for further consideration.

III

I have to this point assumed the validity of the *Lemon* "purpose" test. In fact, however, I think the pessimistic evaluation that The Chief Justice made of the totality of *Lemon* is particularly applicable to the "purpose" prong: it is "a constitutional theory [that] has no basis in the history of the amendment it seeks to interpret, is difficult to apply and yields unprincipled results. . . ." Wallace v. Jaffree, 472 U.S., at 112 (Rehnquist, J., dissenting).

· · ·

Given the many hazards involved in assessing the subjective intent of governmental decisionmakers, the first prong of *Lemon* is defensible, I think, only if the text of the Establishment Clause demands it. That is surely not the case.... It is, in short, far from an inevitable reading of the Establishment Clause that it forbids all governmental action intended to advance religion; and if not inevitable, any reading with such untoward consequences must be wrong.

. . .

2.   RELIGIOUS SPEECH AND DISPLAYS ON PUBLIC PROPERTY

County of Allegheny v. American Civil Liberties Union
492 U.S. 573, 109 S.Ct. 3086, 106 L.Ed.2d 472 (1989).

Justice Blackmun announced the judgment of the Court and delivered the opinion of the Court with respect to Parts III–A, IV, and V, an opinion with respect to Parts I and II, in which Justice O'Connor and Justice Stevens join, an opinion with respect to Part III–B, in which Justice Stevens joins, and an opinion with respect to Part VI.

This litigation concerns the constitutionality of two recurring holiday displays located on public property in downtown Pittsburgh. The first is a creche placed on the Grand Staircase of the Allegheny County Courthouse. The second is a Chanukah menorah placed just outside the City–County Building, next to a Christmas tree and a sign saluting liberty. The Court of Appeals for the Third Circuit ruled that each display violates the Establishment Clause of the First Amendment because each has the impermissible effect of endorsing religion.... We agree that the creche display has that unconstitutional effect but reverse the Court of Appeals' judgment regarding the menorah display.

I

A

. . .

Since 1981, the county has permitted the Holy Name Society, a Roman Catholic group, to display a creche in the County Courthouse during the Christmas holiday season....

... The ... wooden representation of a manger, ... has at its crest an angel bearing a banner that proclaims "Gloria in Excelsis Deo!"

During the 1986–1987 holiday season, the creche was on display on the Grand Staircase from November 26 to January 9. It had a wooden fence on three sides and bore a plaque stating: "This Display Donated by the Holy Name Society." ... No figures of Santa Claus or other decorations appeared on the Grand Staircase. Cf. Lynch v. Donnelly, 465 U.S. 668, 671 (1984)....

. . .

B

The City–County Building is separate and a block removed from the County Courthouse ...

For a number of years, the city has had a large Christmas tree under the middle arch outside the Grant Street entrance. Following this practice, city employees on November 17, 1986, erected a 45–foot tree under the middle arch and decorated it with lights and ornaments. A few days later, the city placed at the foot of the tree a sign bearing the Mayor's name and entitled "Salute to Liberty." Beneath the title, the sign stated:

"During this holiday season, the City of Pittsburgh salutes liberty. Let these festive lights remind us that we are the keepers of the flame of liberty and our legacy of freedom."

At least since 1982, the city has expanded its Grant Street holiday display to include a symbolic representation of Chanukah, an 8–day Jewish holiday ...

. . .

Chanukah, like Christmas, is a cultural event as well as a religious holiday....

. . .

On December 22 of the 1986 holiday season, the city placed at the Grant Street entrance to the City–County Building an 18–foot Chanukah menorah of an abstract tree-and-branch design. The menorah was placed next to the city's 45–foot Christmas tree, against one of the columns that supports the arch into which the tree was set. The menorah is owned by Chabad, a Jewish group, but is stored, erected, and removed each year by the city. The tree, the sign, and the menorah were all removed on January 13....

II

This litigation began on December 10, 1986, when respondents, the Greater Pittsburgh Chapter of the American Civil Liberties Union and seven local residents, filed suit against the county and the city, seeking permanently to enjoin the county from displaying the creche in the County Courthouse and the city from displaying the menorah in front of the City–County Building.... Chabad was permitted to intervene to defend the display of its menorah.

... [T]he District Court denied respondent's request for a permanent injunction....

... [T]he Court of Appeals reversed....

. . .

III

A

. . .

... [T]his Court has come to understand the Establishment Clause to mean that government may not promote or affiliate itself with any religious doctrine or organization, may not discriminate among persons on the basis of their religious beliefs and practices, may not delegate a governmental power to a religious institution, and may not involve itself too deeply in such an institution's affairs....

. . .

... [W]e have paid particularly close attention to whether the challenged governmental practice either has the purpose or effect of "endorsing" religion, a concern that has long had a place in our Establishment Clause jurisprudence....

... [T]he prohibition against governmental endorsement of religion "preclude[s] government from conveying or attempting to convey a message that religion or a particular religious belief is *favored* or *preferred*." Wallace v.

Jaffree, 472 U.S., at 70 (O'Connor, J., concurring in judgment) (emphasis added)....

... The Establishment Clause, at the very least, prohibits government from appearing to take a position on questions of religious belief or from "making adherence to a religion relevant in any way to a person's standing in the political community." Lynch v. Donnelly, 465 U.S., at 687 (O'Connor, J., concurring).

B

We have had occasion in the past to apply Establishment Clause principles to the government's display of objects with religious significance. In Stone v. Graham, 449 U.S. 39 (1980), we held that the display of a copy of the Ten Commandments on the walls of public classrooms violates the Establishment Clause. Closer to the facts of this litigation is Lynch v. Donnelly, supra, in which we considered whether the city of Pawtucket, R.I., had violated the Establishment Clause by including a creche in its annual Christmas display, located in a private park within the downtown shopping district. By a 5–4 decision in that difficult case, the Court upheld inclusion of the creche in the Pawtucket display, holding, inter alia, that the inclusion of the creche did not have the impermissible effect of advancing or promoting religion.

The rationale of the majority opinion in *Lynch* is none too clear: the opinion contains two strands, neither of which provides guidance for decision in subsequent cases. First, the opinion states that the inclusion of the creche in the display was "no more an advancement or endorsement of religion" than other "endorsements" this Court has approved in the past, 465 U.S., at 683— but the opinion offers no discernible measure for distinguishing between permissible and impermissible endorsements. Second, the opinion observes that any benefit the government's display of the creche gave to religion was no more than "indirect, remote, and incidental," ibid.—without saying how or why.

Although Justice O'Connor joined the majority opinion in *Lynch,* she wrote a concurrence that differs in significant respects from the majority opinion. The main difference is that the concurrence provides a sound analytical framework for evaluating governmental use of religious symbols.

First and foremost, the concurrence squarely rejects any notion that this Court will tolerate some government endorsement of religion. Rather, the concurrence recognizes any endorsement of religion as "invalid," id., at 690, because it "sends a message to nonadherents that they are outsiders, not full members of the political community, and an accompanying message to adherents that they are insiders, favored members of the political community." Id., at 688.

Second, the concurrence articulates a method for determining whether the government's use of an object with religious meaning has the effect of endorsing religion. The effect of the display depends upon the message that the government's practice communicates: the question is "what viewers may fairly understand to be the purpose of the display." Id., at 692. That inquiry, of necessity, turns upon the context in which the contested object appears: "a typical museum setting, though not neutralizing the religious content of a religious painting, negates any message of endorsement of that content." Ibid. The concurrence thus emphasizes that the constitutionality of the creche in that case depended upon its "particular physical setting," ibid., and further observes: "Every government practice must be judged in its unique circumstances to determine whether it [endorses] religion." Id., at 694.

The concurrence applied this mode of analysis to the Pawtucket creche, seen in the context of that city's holiday celebration as a whole. In addition to the creche, the city's display contained: a Santa Claus House with a live Santa distributing candy; reindeer pulling Santa's sleigh; a live 40–foot Christmas tree strung with lights; statues of carolers in old-fashioned dress; candy-striped poles; a "talking" wishing well; a large banner proclaiming "SEASONS GREETINGS"; a miniature "Village" with several houses and a church; and various "cut-out" figures, including those of a clown, a dancing elephant, a robot, and a teddy bear. See 525 F.Supp. 1150, 1155 (D.R.I. 1981). The concurrence concluded that both because the creche is "a traditional symbol" of Christmas, a holiday with strong secular elements, and because the creche was "displayed along with purely secular symbols," the creche's setting "changes what viewers may fairly understand to be the purpose of the display" and "negates any message of endorsement" of "the Christian belief represented by the creche." 465 U.S., at 692.

The four *Lynch* dissenters agreed with the concurrence that the controlling question was "whether Pawtucket ha[d] run afoul of the Establishment Clause by endorsing religion through its display of the creche." Id., at 698, n. 3 (Brennan, J., dissenting). The dissenters also agreed with the general proposition that the context in which the government uses a religious symbol is relevant for determining the answer to that question. Id., at 705–706. They simply reached a different answer: the dissenters concluded that the other elements of the Pawtucket display did not negate the endorsement of Christian faith caused by the presence of the creche....

Thus, despite divergence at the bottom line, the five Justices in concurrence and dissent in *Lynch* agreed upon the relevant constitutional principles: the government's use of religious symbolism is unconstitutional if it has the effect of endorsing religious belief, and the effect of the government's use of religious symbolism depends upon its context.... Accordingly, our present task is to determine whether the display of the creche and the menorah, in their respective "particular physical settings," has the effect of endorsing or disapproving religious beliefs....

IV

. . .

Under the Court's holding in *Lynch,* the effect of a creche display turns on its setting. Here, unlike in *Lynch,* nothing in the context of the display detracts from the creche's religious message.... Here, in contrast, the creche stands alone: it is the single element of the display on the Grand Staircase.

. . .

... Thus, by permitting the "display of the creche in this particular physical setting," *Lynch,* 465 U.S., at 692, (O'Connor, J., concurring), the county sends an unmistakable message that it supports and promotes the Christian praise to God that is the creche's religious message.

The fact that the creche bears a sign disclosing its ownership by a Roman Catholic organization does not alter this conclusion. On the contrary, the sign simply demonstrates that the government is endorsing the religious message of that organization, rather than communicating a message of its own. ...

Finally, the county argues that it is sufficient to validate the display of the creche on the Grand Staircase that the display celebrates Christmas, and Christmas is a national holiday. ...The government may acknowledge Christmas as a cultural phenomenon, but under the First Amendment it may not observe it as a Christian holy day by suggesting that people praise God for the birth of Jesus.

In sum, *Lynch* teaches that government may celebrate Christmas in some manner and form, but not in a way that endorses Christian doctrine. Here, Allegheny County has transgressed this line. . . .

V

. . .

Justice Kennedy's reasons for permitting the creche on the Grand Staircase and his condemnation of the Court's reasons for deciding otherwise are so far-reaching in their implications that they require a response in some depth:

A

In *Marsh,* the Court relied specifically on the fact that Congress authorized legislative prayer at the same time that it produced the Bill of Rights. Justice Kennedy, however, argues that *Marsh* legitimates all "practices with no greater potential for an establishment of religion" than those "accepted traditions dating back to the Founding."

. . .

Justice Kennedy's reading of *Marsh* would gut the core of the Establishment Clause, as this Court understands it. The history of this Nation, it is perhaps sad to say, contains numerous examples of official acts that endorsed Christianity specifically. . . . Some of these examples date back to the Founding of the Republic, but this heritage of official discrimination against non-Christians has no place in the jurisprudence of the Establishment Clause. Whatever else the Establishment Clause may mean (and we have held it to mean no official preference even for religion over nonreligion . . .), it certainly means at the very least that government may not demonstrate a preference for one particular sect or creed (including a preference for Christianity over other religions). "The clearest command of the Establishment Clause is that one religious denomination cannot be officially preferred over another." Larson v. Valente, 456 U.S. 228, 244 (1982). There have been breaches of this command throughout this Nation's history, but they cannot diminish in any way the force of the command. . . .

B

. . .

. . . In order to define precisely what government could and could not do under Justice Kennedy's "proselytization" test, the Court would have to decide a series of cases with particular fact patterns that fall along the spectrum of government references to religion (from the permanent display of a cross atop city hall to a passing reference to divine Providence in an official address). . . . Justice Kennedy's formulation of this essential Establishment Clause inquiry is no less fact-intensive than the "endorsement" formulation adopted by the Court. . . .

. . . [W]hen all is said and done, Justice Kennedy's effort to abandon the "endorsement" inquiry in favor of his "proselytization" test seems nothing more than an attempt to lower considerably the level of scrutiny in Establishment Clause cases. We choose, however, to adhere to the vigilance the Court has managed to maintain thus far, and to the endorsement inquiry that reflects our vigilance.

C

Of course, not all religious celebrations of Christmas located on government property violate the Establishment Clause. It obviously is not unconstitutional, for example, for a group of parishioners from a local church to go caroling through a city park on any Sunday in Advent or for a Christian club at a public university to sing carols during their Christmas meeting. Cf. Widmar v. Vincent, 454 U.S. 263 (1981). The reason is that activities of this nature do not demonstrate the government's allegiance to, or endorsement of, the Christian faith.

Equally obvious, however, is the proposition that not all proclamations of Christian faith located on government property are permitted by the Establishment Clause just because they occur during the Christmas holiday season, as the example of a Mass in the courthouse surely illustrates. . . .

VI

The display of the Chanukah menorah in front of the City–County Building may well present a closer constitutional question. The menorah, one must recognize, is a religious symbol: it serves to commemorate the miracle of the oil as described in the Talmud. But the menorah's message is not exclusively religious. The menorah is the primary visual symbol for a holiday that, like Christmas, has both religious and secular dimensions.

. . .

. . . If the city celebrates both Christmas and Chanukah as religious holidays, then it violates the Establishment Clause. The simultaneous endorsement of Judaism and Christianity is no less constitutionally infirm than the endorsement of Christianity alone.

Conversely, if the city celebrates both Christmas and Chanukah as secular holidays, then its conduct is beyond the reach of the Establishment Clause. . . .

. . .

. . . [T]he combination of the tree and the menorah communicates, not a simultaneous endorsement of both Christian and Jewish faith, but instead, a secular celebration of Christmas coupled with an acknowledgment of Chanukah as a contemporaneous alternative tradition.

. . .

The Mayor's sign further diminishes the possibility that the tree and the menorah will be interpreted as a dual endorsement of Christianity and Judaism.

. . .

The conclusion here that, in this particular context, the menorah's display does not have an effect of endorsing religious faith does not foreclose the possibility that the display of the menorah might violate either the "purpose" or "entanglement" prong of the *Lemon* analysis. These issues were not addressed by the Court of Appeals and may be considered by that court on remand.

VII

Lynch v. Donnelly confirms, and in no way repudiates, the long-standing constitutional principle that government may not engage in a practice that has the effect of promoting or endorsing religious beliefs. The display of the creche in the County Courthouse has this unconstitutional effect. The display of the menorah in front of the City–County Building, however, does not have this effect, given its "particular physical setting."

The judgment of the Court of Appeals is affirmed in part and reversed in part, and the cases are remanded for further proceedings.

. . .

Justice O'Connor, with whom Justice Brennan and Justice Stevens join as to Part II, concurring in part and concurring in the judgment.

I

. . .

The constitutionality of the two displays at issue in this case turns on how we interpret and apply the holding in Lynch v. Donnelly, 465 U.S. 668 (1984) . . .

. . .

I joined the majority opinion in *Lynch* because, as I read that opinion, it was consistent with the analysis set forth in my separate concurrence . . .

. . .

In *Lynch,* I concluded that the city's display of a creche in its larger holiday exhibit in a private park in the commercial district had neither the purpose nor the effect of conveying a message of government endorsement of Christianity or disapproval of other religions. . . . Nor, in my view, did Pawtucket's display of the creche along with secular symbols of the Christmas holiday objectively convey a message of endorsement of Christianity.

For the reasons stated in Part IV of the Court's opinion in this case, I agree that the creche displayed on the Grand Staircase of the Allegheny County Courthouse, the seat of county government, conveys a message to nonadherents of Christianity that they are not full members of the political community, and a corresponding message to Christians that they are favored members of the political community. . . .

II

. . .

Justice Kennedy submits that the endorsement test is inconsistent with our precedents and traditions because, in his words, if it were "applied without artificial exceptions for historical practice," it would invalidate many traditional practices recognizing the role of religion in our society. . . . [E]xamples of ceremonial deism do not survive Establishment Clause scrutiny simply by virtue of their historical longevity alone. Historical acceptance of a practice does not in itself validate that practice under the Establishment Clause if the practice violates the values protected by that Clause, just as historical acceptance of racial or gender based discrimination does not immunize such practices from scrutiny under the 14th Amendment.

Under the endorsement test, the "history and ubiquity" of a practice is relevant ... because it provides part of the context in which a reasonable observer evaluates whether a challenged governmental practice conveys a message of endorsement of religion. It is the combination of the longstanding existence of practices such as opening legislative sessions with legislative prayers or opening Court sessions with "God save the United States and this honorable Court," as well as their nonsectarian nature, that lead me to the conclusion that those particular practices, despite their religious roots, do not convey a message of endorsement of particular religious beliefs.... The question under endorsement analysis, in short, is whether a reasonable observer would view such longstanding practices as a disapproval of their particular religious choices, in light of the fact that they serve a secular purpose rather than a sectarian one and have largely lost their religious significance over time....

. . .

III

For reasons which differ somewhat from those set forth in Part VI of Justice Blackmun's opinion, I also conclude that the city of Pittsburgh's combined holiday display of a Chanukah menorah, a Christmas tree, and a sign saluting liberty does not have the effect of conveying an endorsement of religion.... Although Justice Blackmun's opinion acknowledges that a Christmas tree alone conveys no endorsement of Christian beliefs, it formulates the question posed by Pittsburgh's combined display of the tree and the menorah as whether the display "has the effect of endorsing *both* Christian and Jewish faiths, or rather simply recognizes that both Christmas and Chanukah are part of the same winter-holiday season, which has attained a secular status in our society." (emphasis added).

That formulation of the question disregards the fact that the Christmas tree is a predominantly secular symbol and, more significantly, obscures the religious nature of the menorah and the holiday of Chanukah.... In my view, the relevant question for Establishment Clause purposes is whether the city of Pittsburgh's display of the menorah, the religious symbol of a religious holiday, next to a Christmas tree and a sign saluting liberty sends a message of government endorsement of Judaism or whether it sends a message of pluralism and freedom to choose one's own beliefs.

... One need not characterize Chanukah as a "secular holiday" or strain to argue that the menorah has a "secular dimension," in order to conclude that the city of Pittsburgh's combined display does not convey a message of endorsement of Judaism or of religion in general.

. . .

In sum, I conclude that the city of Pittsburgh's combined holiday display had neither the purpose nor the effect of endorsing religion, but that Allegheny County's creche display had such an effect. Accordingly, I join Parts I, II, III–A, IV, V, and VII of the Court's opinion and concur in the judgment.

Justice Brennan, with whom Justice Marshall and Justice Stevens join, concurring in part and dissenting in part.

... I continue to believe that the display of an object that "retains a specifically Christian [or other] religious meaning," ... is incompatible with the separation of church and state demanded by our Constitution. I therefore agree with the Court that Allegheny County's display of a creche at the county courthouse signals an endorsement of the Christian faith in violation of the

Establishment Clause, and join Parts III–A, IV, and V of the Court's opinion. I cannot agree, however, that the city's display of a 45–foot Christmas tree and an 18–foot Chanukah menorah at the entrance to the building housing the Mayor's office shows no favoritism towards Christianity, Judaism, or both. Indeed, I should have thought that the answer as to the first display supplied the answer to the second.

. . .

Justice Stevens, with whom Justice Brennan and Justice Marshall join, concurring in part and dissenting in part.

. . .

In my opinion the Establishment Clause should be construed to create a strong presumption against the display of religious symbols on public property. There is always a risk that such symbols will offend nonmembers of the faith being advertised as well as adherents who consider the particular advertisement disrespectful. . . .

. . .

Justice Kennedy, with whom the Chief Justice, Justice White and Justice Scalia join, concurring in the judgment in part and dissenting in part.

The majority holds that the County of Allegheny violated the Establishment Clause by displaying a creche in the county courthouse, because the "principal or primary effect" of the display is to advance religion within the meaning of Lemon v. Kurtzman, 403 U.S. 602, 612–613 (1971). This view of the Establishment Clause reflects an unjustified hostility toward religion, a hostility inconsistent with our history and our precedents, and I dissent from this holding. The creche display is constitutional, and, for the same reasons, the display of a menorah by the city of Pittsburgh is permissible as well. On this latter point, I concur in the result, but not the reasoning, of Part VI of Justice Blackmun's opinion.

I

In keeping with the usual fashion of recent years, the majority applies the Lemon test to judge the constitutionality of the holiday displays here in question. I am content for present purposes to remain within the Lemon framework, but do not wish to be seen as advocating, let alone adopting, that test as our primary guide in this difficult area. . . .

The only Lemon factor implicated in this case directs us to inquire whether the "principal or primary effect" of the challenged government practice is "one that neither advances nor inhibits religion." 403 U.S., at 612. The requirement of neutrality inherent in that formulation has sometimes been stated in categorical terms. For example, in Everson v. Board of Education, 330 U.S. 1 (1947), the first case in our modern Establishment Clause jurisprudence, Justice Black wrote that the Clause forbids laws "which aid one religion, aid all religions, or prefer one religion over another." . . .

These statements must not give the impression of a formalism that does not exist. Taken to its logical extreme, some of the language quoted above would require a relentless extirpation of all contact between government and religion. But that is not the history or the purpose of the Establishment Clause. Government policies of accommodation, acknowledgment, and support for religion are an accepted part of our political and cultural heritage. . . .

Rather than requiring government to avoid any action that acknowledges or aids religion, the Establishment Clause permits government some latitude in recognizing and accommodating the central role religion plays in our society. . . .

. . .

The ability of the organized community to recognize and accommodate religion in a society with a pervasive public sector requires diligent observance of the border between accommodation and establishment. Our cases disclose two limiting principles: government may not coerce anyone to support or participate in any religion or its exercise; and it may not, in the guise of avoiding hostility or callous indifference, give direct benefits to religion in such a degree that it in fact "establishes a [state] religion or religious faith, or tends to do so." Lynch v. Donnelly, supra, at 678. These two principles, while distinct, are not unrelated, for it would be difficult indeed to establish a religion without some measure of more or less subtle coercion, be it in the form of taxation to supply the substantial benefits that would sustain a state-established faith, direct compulsion to observance, or governmental exhortation to religiosity that amounts in fact to proselytizing.

It is no surprise that without exception we have invalidated actions that further the interests of religion through the coercive power of government. Forbidden involvements include compelling or coercing participation or attendance at a religious activity, see Engel v. Vitale, 370 U.S. 421 (1962); McGowan v. Maryland, supra, at 452 (discussing *McCollum v. Board of Education,* supra), requiring religious oaths to obtain government office or benefits, Torcaso v. Watkins, 367 U.S. 488 (1961), or delegating government power to religious groups, Larkin v. Grendel's Den, Inc., 459 U.S. 116 (1982). The freedom to worship as one pleases without government interference or oppression is the great object of both the Establishment and the Free Exercise Clauses. Barring all attempts to aid religion through government coercion goes far toward attainment of this object. . . .

As Justice Blackmun observes, some of our recent cases reject the view that coercion is the sole touchstone of an Establishment Clause violation. See Engel v. Vitale, supra, at 430 (dictum) (rejecting, without citation of authority, proposition that coercion is required to demonstrate an Establishment Clause violation) . . . That may be true if by "coercion" is meant *direct* coercion in the classic sense of an establishment of religion that the Framers knew. But coercion need not be a direct tax in aid of religion or a test oath. Symbolic recognition or accommodation of religious faith may violate the Clause in an extreme case. I doubt not, for example, that the Clause forbids a city to permit the permanent erection of a large Latin cross on the roof of city hall. This is not because government speech about religion is per se suspect, as the majority would have it, but because such an obtrusive year-round religious display would place the government's weight behind an obvious effort to proselytize on behalf of a particular religion.

. . .

In determining whether there exists an establishment, or a tendency toward one, we refer to the other types of church-state contacts that have existed unchallenged throughout our history, or that have been found permissible in our caselaw. . . .[I]n *Marsh v. Chambers,* we found that Nebraska's practice of employing a legislative chaplain did not violate the Establishment Clause, because "legislative prayer presents no more potential for establishment than the provision of school transportation, beneficial grants for higher education, or tax exemptions for religious organizations." ... Noncoercive government action within the realm of flexible accommodation or passive acknowledgment of existing symbols does not violate the Establishment Clause unless it benefits religion in a way more direct and more substantial than practices that are accepted in our national heritage.

II

These principles are not difficult to apply to the facts of the case before us. In permitting the displays on government property of the menorah and the creche, the city and county sought to do no more than "celebrate the season," and to acknowledge, along with many of their citizens, the historical background and the religious as well as secular nature of the Chanukah and Christmas holidays. This interest falls well within the tradition of government accommodation and acknowledgment of religion that has marked our history from the beginning. . . .

If government is to participate in its citizens' celebration of a holiday that contains both a secular and a religious component, enforced recognition of only the secular aspect would signify the callous indifference toward religious faith that our cases and traditions do not require . . .

. . .

Our cases do not suggest, moreover, that the use of public property necessarily converts otherwise permissible government conduct into an Establishment Clause violation. To the contrary, in some circumstances the First Amendment may *require* that government property be available for use by religious groups, see Widmar v. Vincent, 454 U.S. 263 (1981); Fowler v. Rhode Island, 345 U.S. 67 (1953); Niemotko v. Maryland, 340 U.S. 268 (1951). . . .

Nor can I comprehend why it should be that placement of a government-owned creche on private land is lawful while placement of a privately owned creche on public land is not. If anything, I should have thought government ownership of a religious symbol presented the more difficult question under the Establishment Clause, but as *Lynch* resolved that question to sustain the government action, the sponsorship here ought to be all the easier to sustain. In short, nothing about the religious displays here distinguishes them in any meaningful way from the creche we permitted in *Lynch*.

. . . On the same reasoning, I agree that the menorah display is constitutional.

III

The majority invalidates display of the creche, not because it disagrees with the interpretation of *Lynch* applied above, but because it chooses to discard the reasoning of the *Lynch* majority opinion in favor of Justice O'Connor's concurring opinion in that case. It has never been my understanding that a concurring opinion . . . could take precedence over an opinion joined in its entirety by five Members of the Court. . . .

. . .

A

. . .

. . . *Marsh* stands for the proposition, not that specific practices com 1791 are an exception to the otherwise broad sweep of the Establi: Clause, but rather that the meaning of the Clause is to be determi reference to historical practices and understandings. Whatever test we choose to apply must permit not only legitimate practices two centuries old but also any other practices with no greater potential for an establishment of religion. . . .

If the endorsement test, applied without artificial exceptions for historical practice, reached results consistent with history, my objections to it would have less force. But, as I understand that test, the touchstone of an Establishment Clause violation is whether nonadherents would be made to feel like "outsiders" by government recognition or accommodation of religion. Few of our traditional practices recognizing the part religion plays in our society can withstand scrutiny under a faithful application of this formula.

B

. . .

. . . This test could provide workable guidance to the lower courts, if ever, only after this Court has decided a long series of holiday display cases, using little more than intuition and a tape measure. Deciding cases on the basis of such an unguided examination of marginalia is irreconcilable with the imperative of applying neutral principles in constitutional adjudication. . . .

. . .

IV

. . .

A further contradiction arises from the majority's approach, for the Court also assumes the difficult and inappropriate task of saying what every religious symbol means. . . . This Court is ill equipped to sit as a national theology board, and I question both the wisdom and the constitutionality of its doing so. Indeed, were I required to choose between the approach taken by the majority and a strict separationist view, I would have to respect the consistency of the latter.

. . .

. . . I might have voted against installation of these particular displays were I a local legislative official. But we have no jurisdiction over matters of taste within the realm of constitutionally permissible discretion. Our role is enforcement of a written Constitution. In my view, the principles of the Establishment Clause and our Nation's historic traditions of diversity and pluralism allow communities to make reasonable judgments respecting the accommodation or acknowledgment of holidays with both cultural and religious aspects. No constitutional violation occurs when they do so by displaying a symbol of the holiday's religious origins.

I dissent.

Capitol Square Review and Advisory Board v. Pinette
___ U.S. ___, 115 S.Ct. 2440, 132 L.Ed.2d 650 (1995).

Justice Scalia announced the judgment of the Court and delivered the opinion of the Court with respect to Parts I, II, and III, and an opinion with respect to Part IV, in which the Chief Justice, Justice Kennedy and Justice Thomas join.

. . . The question in this case is whether a State violates the Establishment Clause when, pursuant to a religiously neutral state policy, it permits a private party to display an unattended religious symbol in a traditional public forum located next to its seat of government.

I

Capitol Square is a 10–acre, state-owned plaza surrounding the Statehouse in Columbus, Ohio. For over a century the square has been used for public speeches, gatherings, and festivals advocating and celebrating a variety of causes, both secular and religious. . . .

It has been the Board's policy "to allow a broad range of speakers and other gatherings of people to conduct events on the Capitol Square." . . . The Board has also permitted a variety of unattended displays on Capitol Square: a State-sponsored lighted tree during the Christmas season, a privately-sponsored menorah during Chanukah, a display showing the progress of a United Way fundraising campaign, and booths and exhibits during an arts festival. . . .

In November 1993, after reversing an initial decision to ban unattended holiday displays from the square during December 1993, the Board authorized the State to put up its annual Christmas tree. On November 29, 1993, the Board granted a rabbi's application to erect a menorah. That same day, the Board received an application from respondent Donnie Carr, an officer of the Ohio Ku Klux Klan, to place a cross on the square from December 8, 1993, to December 24, 1993. The Board denied that application on December 3, inform-ing the Klan by letter that the decision to deny "was made upon the advice of counsel, in a good faith attempt to comply with the Ohio and United States Constitutions, as they have been interpreted in relevant decisions by the Federal and State Courts."

. . . [T]he Ohio Klan . . . filed the present suit in the United States District Court for the Southern District of Ohio, seeking an injunction requiring the Board to issue the requested permit. The Board defended on the ground that the permit would violate the Establishment Clause. The District Court issued the injunction and . . . the Board permitted the Klan to erect its cross. The Board then received, and granted, several additional applications to erect crosses on Capitol Square during December 1993 and January 1994.

On appeal by the Board, the United States Court of Appeals for the Sixth Circuit affirmed the District Court's judgment. . . .

II

First, a preliminary matter: Respondents contend that we should treat this as a case in which freedom of speech (the Klan's right to present the message of the cross display) was denied because of the State's disagreement with that message's political content, rather than because of the State's desire to distance itself from sectarian religion. . . . The record facts before us and the opinions below address only the Establishment Clause issue; that is the question upon which we granted certiorari; and that is the sole question before us to decide.

. . .

III

There is no doubt that compliance with the Establishment Clause is a state interest sufficiently compelling to justify content-based restrictions on speech. . . .Whether that interest is implicated here, however, is a different question. And we do not write on a blank slate in answering it. We have twice previously addressed the combination of private religious expression, a forum available for public use, content-based regulation, and a State's interest in complying with the Establishment Clause. Both times, we have struck down the restriction on religious content. . . .

In *Lamb's Chapel*, a school district allowed private groups to use school facilities during off-hours for a variety of civic, social and recreational purposes, excluding, however, religious purposes. We held that . . . the school district violated an applicant's free-speech rights by denying it use of the facilities solely because of the religious viewpoint of the program it wished to present. . . .

Lamb's Chapel followed naturally from our decision in Widmar [v. Vincent, 454 U.S. 263 (1981)], in which we examined a public university's exclusion of student religious groups from facilities available to other student groups. There also we addressed official discrimination against groups who wished to use a "generally open forum" for religious speech. . . .

Quite obviously, the factors that we considered determinative in *Lamb's Chapel* and *Widmar* exist here as well. The State did not sponsor respondents' expression, the expression was made on government property that had been opened to the public for speech, and permission was requested through the same application process and on the same terms required of other private groups.

IV

Petitioners argue that one feature of the present case distinguishes it from *Lamb's Chapel* and *Widmar*: the forum's proximity to the seat of government, which, they contend, may produce the perception that the cross bears the State's approval. They urge us to apply the so-called "endorsement test," see, e.g., Allegheny County v. American Civil Liberties Union, Greater Pittsburgh Chapter, 492 U.S. 573 (1989); Lynch v. Donnelly, 465 U.S. 668 (1984), and to find that, because an observer might mistake private expression for officially endorsed religious expression, the State's content-based restriction is constitutional.

We must note, to begin with, that it is not really an "endorsement test" of any sort, much less the "endorsement test" which appears in our more recent Establishment Clause jurisprudence, that petitioners urge upon us. "Endorsement" connotes an expression or demonstration of approval or support. . . . Our cases have accordingly equated "endorsement" with "promotion" or "favoritism." . . . We find it peculiar to say that government "promotes" or "favors" a religious display by giving it the same access to a public forum that all other displays enjoy. . . . Where we have tested for endorsement of religion, the subject of the test was either expression by the government itself, *Lynch*, supra, or else government action alleged to discriminate in favor of private religious expression or activity, Board of Ed. of Kiryas Joel Village School Dist. v. Grumet, 512 U.S. 687 (1994), *Allegheny County*, supra. The test petitioners propose, which would attribute to a neutrally behaving government private religious expression, has no antecedent in our jurisprudence, and would better be called a "transferred endorsement" test.

Petitioners rely heavily on *Allegheny County* and *Lynch*, but each is easily distinguished. In *Allegheny County* we held that the display of a privately-sponsored creche on the "Grand Staircase" of the Allegheny County Courthouse violated the Establishment Clause. That staircase was not, however, open to all on an equal basis, so the County was favoring sectarian religious expression. . . . In *Lynch* we held that a city's display of a creche did not violate the Establishment Clause because, in context, the display did not endorse religion. ... The opinion does assume, as petitioners contend, that the government's use of religious symbols is unconstitutional if it effectively endorses sectarian religious belief. But the case neither holds nor even remotely assumes that the government's neutral treatment of private religious expression can be unconstitutional.

Petitioners argue that absence of perceived endorsement was material in *Lamb's Chapel* and *Widmar*. We did state in *Lamb's Chapel* that there was "no realistic danger that the community would think that the District was endorsing religion or any particular creed,". ... But that conclusion was not the result of empirical investigation; it followed directly, we thought, from the fact that the forum was open and the religious activity privately sponsored. ... [W]e in effect said, given an open forum and private sponsorship, erroneous conclusions do not count. So also in *Widmar*. Once we determined that the benefit to religious groups from the public forum was incidental and shared by other groups, we categorically rejected the State's Establishment Clause defense. ...

What distinguishes *Allegheny County* and the dictum in *Lynch* from *Widmar* and *Lamb's Chapel* is the difference between government speech and private speech. ... Petitioners assert ... that the distinction disappears whenever private speech can be mistaken for government speech. That proposition cannot be accepted, at least where, as here, the government has not fostered or encouraged the mistake.

Of course, giving sectarian religious speech preferential access to a forum close to the seat of government (or anywhere else for that matter) would violate the Establishment Clause (as well as the Free Speech Clause, since it would involve content discrimination). And one can conceive of a case in which a governmental entity manipulates its administration of a public forum close to the seat of government (or within a government building) in such a manner that only certain religious groups take advantage of it, creating an impression of endorsement that is in fact accurate. But those situations, which involve governmental favoritism, do not exist here. ...

The contrary view, most strongly espoused by Justice Stevens, but endorsed by Justice Souter and Justice O'Connor as well, exiles private religious speech to a realm of less-protected expression heretofore inhabited only by sexually explicit displays and commercial speech. ... [I]t is outright perverse when one considers that private religious expression receives preferential treatment under the Free Exercise Clause. It is no answer to say that the Establishment Clause tempers religious speech. By its terms that Clause applies only to the words and acts of government. It was never meant, and has never been read by this Court, to serve as an impediment to purely private religious speech connected to the State only through its occurrence in a public forum.

Since petitioners' "transferred endorsement" principle cannot possibly be restricted to squares in front of state capitols, the Establishment Clause regime that it would usher in is most unappealing. ... Policy makers would find themselves in a vise between the Establishment Clause on one side and the Free Speech and Free Exercise Clauses on the other. Every proposed act of private, religious expression in a public forum would force officials to weigh a host of imponderables. How close to government is too close? What kind of building, and in what context, symbolizes state authority? If the State guessed wrong in one direction, it would be guilty of an Establishment Clause violation; if in the other, it would be liable for suppressing free exercise or free speech (a risk not run when the State restrains only its own expression).

... It has radical implications for our public policy to suggest that neutral laws are invalid whenever hypothetical observers may—even reasonably—confuse an incidental benefit to religion with state endorsement.

If Ohio is concerned about misperceptions, nothing prevents it from requiring all private displays in the Square to be identified as such. That would be a content-neutral "manner" restriction which is assuredly constitutional. ...But the State may not, on the claim of misperception of official endorsement, ban all private religious speech from the public square, or discriminate against it by requiring religious speech alone to disclaim public sponsorship.

* * *

Religious expression cannot violate the Establishment Clause where it (1) is purely private and (2) occurs in a traditional or designated public forum, publicly announced and open to all on equal terms. Those conditions are satisfied here, and therefore the State may not bar respondents' cross from Capitol Square.

The judgment of the Court of Appeals is

affirmed.[a]

Justice O'Connor, with whom Justice Souter and Justice Breyer join, concurring in part and concurring in the judgment.

I join Parts I, II, and III of the Court's opinion and concur in the judgment. ...I see no necessity to carve out, as the plurality opinion would today, an exception to the endorsement test for the public forum context.

For the reasons given by Justice Souter, whose opinion I also join, I conclude on the facts of this case that there is "no realistic danger that the community would think that the [State] was endorsing religion or any particular creed," ... I write separately, however, to emphasize that ... the endorsement test necessarily focuses upon the perception of a reasonable, informed observer.

I

. . .

While the plurality would limit application of the endorsement test ..., I believe that an impermissible message of endorsement can be sent in a variety of contexts, not all of which involve direct government speech or outright favoritism. It is true that neither *Allegheny* nor *Lynch*, our two prior religious display cases, involved the same combination of private religious speech and a public forum that we have before us today. Nonetheless, as Justice Souter aptly demonstrates, we have on several occasions employed an endorsement perspective in Establishment Clause cases where private religious conduct has intersected with a neutral governmental policy providing some benefit in a manner that parallels the instant case. Thus, while I join the discussion of *Lamb's Chapel* and Widmar v. Vincent, ... in Part III of the Court's opinion, I do so with full recognition that the factors the Court properly identifies ultimately led in each case to the conclusion that there was no endorsement of religion by the State. ...

. . .

[a] A concurring opinion by Justice Thomas is omitted.

None of this is to suggest that I would be likely to come to a different result from the plurality where truly private speech is allowed on equal terms in a vigorous public forum that the government has administered properly. ...

To the plurality's consideration of the open nature of the forum and the private ownership of the display, however, I would add the presence of a sign disclaiming government sponsorship or endorsement on the Klan cross, which would make the State's role clear to the community. ...

... I part company with the plurality on a fundamental point: I disagree that "[i]t has radical implications for our public policy to suggest that neutral laws are invalid whenever hypothetical observers may—even reasonably—confuse an incidental benefit to religion with State endorsement." On the contrary, when the reasonable observer would view a government practice as endorsing religion, I believe that it is our duty to hold the practice invalid. ...

. . .

In the end, I would recognize that the Establishment Clause inquiry cannot be distilled into a fixed, per se rule. ...

II

Today, Justice Stevens reaches a different conclusion regarding whether the Board's decision to allow respondents' display on Capitol Square constituted an impermissible endorsement of the cross' religious message. Yet I believe it is important to note that we have not simply arrived at divergent results after conducting the same analysis. Our fundamental point of departure, it appears, concerns the knowledge that is properly attributed to the test's "reasonable observer [who] evaluates whether a challenged governmental practice conveys a message of endorsement of religion." In my view, proper application of the endorsement test requires that the reasonable observer be deemed more informed than the casual passerby postulated by the dissent.

. . .

I therefore disagree that the endorsement test should focus on the actual perception of individual observers, who naturally have differing degrees of knowledge. ...In my view, ... the endorsement test creates a more collective standard ... In this respect, the applicable observer is similar to the "reasonable person" in tort law ... A State has not made religion relevant to standing in the political community simply because a particular viewer of a display might feel uncomfortable.

. . .

The dissent's property-based argument fails to give sufficient weight to the fact that the cross at issue here was displayed in a forum traditionally open to the public. ...The reasonable observer would recognize the distinction between speech the government supports and speech that it merely allows in a place that traditionally has been open to a range of private speakers accompanied, if necessary, by an appropriate disclaimer.

In this case, I believe, the reasonable observer would view the Klan's cross display fully aware that Capitol Square is a public space in which a multiplicity of groups, both secular and religious, engage in expressive conduct. ...On the facts of this case, therefore, I conclude that the reasonable observer would not interpret the State's tolerance of the Klan's private religious display in Capitol Square as an endorsement of religion.

. . .

Justice Souter, with whom Justice O'Connor and Justice Breyer join, concurring in part and concurring in the judgment.

I concur in Parts I, II, and III of the Court's opinion. . . .

. . . [M]y analysis of the Establishment Clause issue differs from Justice Scalia's, and I vote to affirm in large part because of the possibility of affixing a sign to the cross adequately disclaiming any government sponsorship or endorsement of it.

The plurality's opinion declines to apply the endorsement test to the Board's action, in favor of a per se rule . . . This per se rule would be an exception to the endorsement test, not previously recognized and out of square with our precedents.

I

. . . [I]n some circumstances an intelligent observer may mistake private, unattended religious displays in a public forum for government speech endorsing religion. . . .

. . . Given the domination of the square by the government's own displays, one would not be a dimwit as a matter of law to think that an unattended religious display there was endorsed by the government, even though the square has also been the site of three privately sponsored, unattended displays over the years . . . When an individual speaks in a public forum, it is reasonable for an observer to attribute the speech, first and foremost, to the speaker, while an unattended display (and any message it conveys) can naturally be viewed as belonging to the owner of the land on which it stands.

In sum, I do not understand that I am at odds with the plurality when I assume that in some circumstances an intelligent observer would reasonably perceive private religious expression in a public forum to imply the government's endorsement of religion. My disagreement with the plurality is simply that I would attribute these perceptions of the intelligent observer to the reasonable observer of Establishment Clause analysis under our precedents, where I believe that such reasonable perceptions matter.

II

. . .

Allegheny County's endorsement test cannot be dismissed, as Justice Scalia suggests, as applying only to situations in which there is an allegation that the Establishment Clause has been violated through "expression by the government itself" or "government action . . . discriminat[ing] in favor of private religious expression." . . . Unless we are to retreat entirely to government intent and abandon consideration of effects, it makes no sense to recognize a public perception of endorsement as a harm only in that subclass of cases in which the government owns the display. . . .

. . .

III

As for the specifics of this case, one must admit that a number of facts known to the Board, or reasonably anticipated, weighed in favor of upholding its denial of the permit. For example, the Latin cross the Klan sought to erect is the principal symbol of Christianity around the world, and display of the cross alone could not reasonably be taken to have any secular point. It was displayed immediately in front of the Ohio Statehouse, with the government's flags flying nearby, and the government's statues close at hand. For much of the time the cross was supposed to stand on the square, it would have been the only private display on the public plot (the menorah's permit expired several days before the cross actually went up). There was nothing else on the Statehouse lawn that would have suggested a forum open to any and all private, unattended religious displays.

Based on these and other factors, the Board was understandably concerned about a possible Establishment Clause violation if it had granted the permit. But a flat denial of the Klan's application was not the Board's only option to protect against an appearance of endorsement, and the Board was required to find its most "narrowly drawn" alternative. . . . The Board, . . . could have granted the application subject to the condition that the Klan attach a disclaimer . . . In the alternative, the Board could have instituted a policy of restricting all private, unattended displays to one area of the square, with a permanent sign marking the area as a forum for private speech carrying no endorsement from the State.

With such alternatives available, the Board cannot claim that its flat denial was a narrowly tailored response to the Klan's permit application and thus cannot rely on that denial as necessary to ensure that the State did not "appea[r] to take a position on questions of religious belief." . . . For these reasons, I concur in the judgment.

Justice Stevens, dissenting.

The Establishment Clause should be construed to create a strong presumption against the installation of unattended religious symbols on public property. Although the State of Ohio has allowed Capitol Square, the area around the seat of its government, to be used as a public forum, and although it has occasionally allowed private groups to erect other sectarian displays there, neither fact provides a sufficient basis for rebutting that presumption. On the contrary, the sequence of sectarian displays disclosed by the record in this case illustrates the importance of rebuilding the "wall of separation between church and State" that Jefferson envisioned.

. . .

II

. . .

In determining whether the State's maintenance of the Klan's cross in front of the Statehouse conveyed a forbidden message of endorsement, we should be mindful of the power of a symbol standing alone and unexplained. Even on private property, signs and symbols are generally understood to express the owner's views. The location of the sign is a significant component of the message it conveys.

. . .

III

. . .

. . . For a religious display to violate the Establishment Clause, I think it is enough that some reasonable observers would attribute a religious message to the State.

The plurality appears to rely on the history of this particular public forum—specifically, it emphasizes that Ohio has in the past allowed three other private unattended displays. Even if the State could not reasonably have been understood to endorse the prior displays, I would not find this argument convincing, because it assumes that all reasonable viewers know all about the history of Capitol Square-a highly unlikely supposition. But the plurality's argument fails on its own terms, because each of the three previous displays conveyed the same message of approval and endorsement that this one does.

. . .

Justice Ginsburg, dissenting.

We confront here ... a large Latin cross that stood alone and unattended in close proximity to Ohio's Statehouse....Near the stationary cross were the government's flags and the government's statues. No human speaker was present to disassociate the religious symbol from the State. No other private display was in sight. No plainly visible sign informed the public that the cross belonged to the Klan and that Ohio's government did not endorse the display's message.

If the aim of the Establishment Clause is genuinely to uncouple government from church, ... a State may not permit, and a court may not order, a display of this character... .Justice Souter, in the final paragraphs of his opinion, suggests two arrangements that might have distanced the State ... : a sufficiently large and clear disclaimer,; or an area reserved for unattended displays carrying no endorsement from the State, a space plainly and permanently so marked. Neither arrangement is even arguably present in this case. The District Court's order did not mandate a disclaimer. And the disclaimer the Klan appended to the foot of the cross was unsturdy: it did not identify the Klan as sponsor; it failed to state unequivocally that Ohio did not endorse the display's message; and it was not shown to be legible from a distance. The relief ordered by the District Court thus violated the Establishment Clause.

Whether a court order allowing display of a cross, but demanding a sturdier disclaimer, could withstand Establishment Clause analysis is a question more difficult than the one this case poses. I would reserve that question for another day and case. But I would not let the prospect of what might have been permissible control today's decision on the constitutionality of the display the District Court's order in fact authorized.

C.   FINANCIAL AID TO CHURCH-RELATED SCHOOLS AND CHURCH-RELATED INSTRUCTION

1.   ELEMENTARY AND SECONDARY SCHOOLS

AID TO PUPILS AND THEIR PARENTS

In *Everson* the Court upheld the provision of transportation of students to religious schools. In Board of Educ. v. Allen, 392 U.S. 236 (1968), the Court by a vote of 6 to 3 upheld a New York law providing for the loaning of text books free of charge to students in all private schools, including church schools. The Court decided that the state statute was valid because "no funds or books are furnished to parochial schools, and the financial benefit is to parents and children, not to schools. Perhaps free books make it more likely that some children choose to attend a sectarian school, but that was true of the state-paid bus fares in *Everson* and does not alone demonstrate an unconstitutional degree of support for a religious institution." Justice Black, who had written the *Everson* opinion, was one of the dissenters. He said: "[I]t is not difficult to distinguish books, which are the heart of any school, from bus fares, which provide a convenient and helpful general public transportation service."

PAYMENTS TO RELIGIOUS SCHOOLS

The *Allen* decision added fuel to the controversy whether direct government payments to religious elementary and secondary schools violated the establishment clause. In Lemon v. Kurtzman, 403 U.S. 602 (1971), however, the Court struck down a Pennsylvania statute authorizing reimbursement of nonpublic schools for part of the expenses of teachers' salaries, textbooks and instructional materials. A possible simple distinction between aid to religious schools and aid to parents and children, for expenses of attending religious schools, did not survive the next round of cases. In 1973, the Court concluded that direct grants to parents, to reimburse the costs of their children's attendance at nonpublic schools, were also invalid. Committee for Public Education and Religious Liberty v. Nyquist, 413 U.S. 756 (1973); Sloan v. Lemon, 413 U.S. 825 (1973).

TAX EXEMPTIONS, DEDUCTIONS AND CREDITS

In Walz v. Tax Commission of New York, 397 U.S. 664 (1970), the Court sustained the universal practice of exempting church property used for religious worship from the payment of real estate taxes. The Court concluded that the "unbroken practice" of according tax exemptions to churches had not led to an established church and had "operated affirmatively to help guarantee the free exercise of all forms of religious beliefs."

Two cases concerning tax treatment of parents' payments for the cost of religious education are in some tension. In Committee for Public Education & Religious Liberty v. Nyquist, 413 U.S. 756 (1973), the Court struck down a state law giving tax credits, whose amounts were determined by parental income, for each child attending a nonpublic school. The Court concluded that the tax credits were indistinguishable from direct tuition grants to parents—a practice also held invalid in *Nyquist*. In Mueller v. Allen, 463 U.S. 388 (1983), however, the Court sustained state income tax deductions for amounts spent on tuition, textbook, and transportation expenses of children attending elementary or secondary schools. The Court noted that the deduction was applicable to expenses for schooling of all children, including those attending public schools (although the most substantial benefit would flow to parents whose children attended schools charging tuition). Moreover, the tax benefit took the form of a deduction, rather than a fixed dollar credit.

The Court distinguished both Walz v. Tax Commission and Mueller v. Allen in Texas Monthly v. Bullock, 489 U.S. 1 (1989). The Court held that it was unconstitutional to exempt from a sales tax applicable to periodicals generally, sales of periodicals "published or distributed by a religious faith and that consist wholly of writings promulgating the teachings of the faith and books that consist wholly of writings sacred to a religious faith." Here, the exemption was equivalent to a subsidy amounting to state sponsorship of religious belief. In *Walz*, the tax exemption was within a broad class of charitable tax exemptions, and in *Mueller* the exemption was equally available to parents sending their children to nonsectarian schools.

Grand Rapids School District v. Ball

473 U.S. 373, 105 S.Ct. 3216, 87 L.Ed.2d 267 (1985).

Justice Brennan delivered the opinion of the Court.

The School District of Grand Rapids, Michigan, adopted two programs in which classes for nonpublic school students are financed by the public school system, taught by teachers hired by the public school system, and conducted in "leased" classrooms in the nonpublic schools. Most of the nonpublic schools involved in the programs are sectarian religious schools. This case raises the question whether these programs impermissibly involve the government in the support of sectarian religious activities and thus violate the Establishment Clause of the First Amendment.

I

A

At issue in this case are the Community Education and Shared Time programs offered in the nonpublic schools of Grand Rapids, Michigan. These programs, first instituted in the 1976–1977 school year, provide classes to nonpublic school students at public expense in classrooms located in and leased from the local nonpublic schools.

The Shared Time program offers classes during the regular school day that are intended to be supplementary to the "core curriculum" courses that the State of Michigan requires as a part of an accredited school program. Among the subjects offered are "remedial" and "enrichment" mathematics, "remedial" and "enrichment" reading, art, music, and physical education. A typical nonpublic school student attends these classes for one or two class periods per week; approximately "ten percent of any given nonpublic school student's time during the academic year would consist of Shared Time instruction." Although Shared Time itself is a program offered only in the nonpublic schools, there was testimony that the courses included in that program are offered, albeit perhaps in a somewhat different form, in the public schools as well. All of the classes that are the subject of this case are taught in elementary schools, with the exception of Math Topics, a remedial mathematics course taught in the secondary schools.

The Shared Time teachers are full-time employees of the public schools, who often move from classroom to classroom during the course of the school day. A "significant portion" of the teachers (approximately 10%) "previously taught in nonpublic schools, and many of those had been assigned to the same nonpublic school where they were previously employed." The School District of Grand Rapids hires Shared Time teachers in accordance with its ordinary hiring procedures. The public school system apparently provides all of the supplies, materials, and equipment used in connection with Shared Time instruction.

The Community Education program is offered throughout the Grand Rapids community in schools and on other sites, for children as well as adults. The classes at issue here are taught in the nonpublic elementary schools and commence at the conclusion of the regular schoolday. Among the courses offered are Arts and Crafts, Home Economics, Spanish, Gymnastics, Yearbook Production, Christmas Arts and Crafts, Drama, Newspaper, Humanities, Chess, Model Building, and Nature Appreciation. The District Court found that "[a]lthough certain Community Education courses offered at nonpublic school sites are not offered at the public schools on a Community Education basis, all Community Education programs are otherwise available at the public schools, usually as a part of their more extensive regular curriculum."

Community Education teachers are part-time public school employees. Community Education courses are completely voluntary and are offered only if 12 or more students enroll. Because a well-known teacher is necessary to attract the requisite number of students, the School District accords a preference in hiring to instructors already teaching within the school. Thus, "virtually every Community Education course conducted on facilities leased from nonpublic schools has an instructor otherwise employed full time by the same nonpublic school."

Both programs are administered similarly. The Director of the program, a public school employee, sends packets of course listings to the participating nonpublic schools before the school year begins. The nonpublic school administrators then decide which courses they want to offer. The Director works out an academic schedule for each school, taking into account, *inter alia,* the varying religious holidays celebrated by the schools of different denominations.

Nonpublic school administrators decide which classrooms will be used for the programs, and the Director then inspects the facilities and consults with Shared Time teachers to make sure the facilities are satisfactory. The public school system pays the nonpublic schools for the use of the necessary classroom space by entering into "leases" at the rate of $6 per classroom per week. The "leases," however, contain no mention of the particular room, space, or facility leased and teachers' rooms, libraries, lavatories, and similar facilities are made available at no additional charge. Each room used in the programs has to be free of any crucifix, religious symbol, or artifact, although such religious symbols can be present in the adjoining hallways, corridors, and other facilities used in connection with the program. During the time that a given classroom is being used in the programs, the teacher is required to post a sign stating that it is a "public school classroom." However, there are no signs posted outside the school buildings indicating that public school courses are conducted inside or that the facilities are being used as a public school annex.

Although petitioners label the Shared Time and Community Education students as "part-time public school students," the students attending Shared Time and Community Education courses in facilities leased from a nonpublic school are the same students who attend that particular school otherwise. There is no evidence that any public school student has ever attended a Shared Time or Community Education class in a nonpublic school. The District Court found that "[t]hough Defendants claim the Shared Time program is available to all students, the record is abundantly clear that only nonpublic school students wearing the cloak of a 'public school student' can enroll in it." The District Court noted that "[w]hereas public school students are assembled at the public facility nearest to their residence, students in religious schools are assembled on the basis of religion without any consideration of residence or school district boundaries." Thus, "beneficiaries are wholly designated on the basis of religion," and these "public school" classes, in contrast to ordinary public school classes which are largely neighborhood based, are as segregated by religion as are the schools at which they are offered.

Forty of the forty-one schools at which the programs operate are sectarian in character. The schools of course vary from one another, but substantial evidence suggests that they share deep religious purposes. For instance, the Parent Handbook of one Catholic school states the goals of Catholic education as "[a] God oriented environment which *permeates* the total educational program," "[a] Christian atmosphere which guides and encourages participation in the church's commitment to social justice," and "[a] continuous development of knowledge of the Catholic faith, its traditions, teachings and theology." A policy statement of the Christian schools similarly proclaims that "it is not sufficient that the teachings of Christianity be a separate subject in the curriculum, but *the Word of God must be an all-pervading force in the educational program.*" These Christian schools require all parents seeking to enroll their children either to subscribe to a particular doctrinal statement or to agree to have their children taught according to the doctrinal statement. The District Court found that the schools are "pervasively sectarian," and concluded "without hesitation that the purposes of these schools is to advance their particular religions," and that "a substantial portion of their functions are subsumed in the religious mission."

B

Respondents are six taxpayers who filed suit against the School District of Grand Rapids and a number of state officials.... After an 8–day bench trial, the District Court entered a judgment on the merits on behalf of respondents and enjoined further operation of the programs.

... A divided panel of the Court of Appeals affirmed. We ... affirm.

II

A

. . .

We have noted that the three-part test first articulated in Lemon v. Kurtzman, at 612–613, guides "[t]he general nature of our inquiry in this area," Mueller v. Allen, 463 U.S. 388, 394 (1983).... We have particularly relied on *Lemon* in every case involving the sensitive relationship between government and religion in the education of our children. The government's activities in this area can have a magnified impact on impressionable young minds, and the occasional rivalry of parallel public and private school systems offers an all-too-ready opportunity for divisive rifts along religious lines in the body politic....

As has often been true in school aid cases, there is no dispute as to the first test. Both the District Court and the Court of Appeals found that the purpose of the Community Education and Shared Time programs was "manifestly secular." We find no reason to disagree with this holding, and therefore go on to consider whether the primary or principal effect of the challenged programs is to advance or inhibit religion.

B

. . .

Given that 40 of the 41 schools in this case are ... "pervasively sectarian," the challenged public school programs operating in the religious schools may impermissibly advance religion in three different ways. First, the teachers participating in the programs may become involved in intentionally or inadvertently inculcating particular religious tenets or beliefs. Second, the programs may provide a crucial symbolic link between government and religion, thereby enlisting—at least in the eyes of impressionable youngsters—the powers of government to the support of the religious denomination operating the school. Third, the programs may have the effect of directly promoting religion by impermissibly providing a subsidy to the primary religious mission of the institutions affected.

(1)

Although Establishment Clause jurisprudence is characterized by few absolutes, the Clause does absolutely prohibit government-financed or government-sponsored indoctrination into the beliefs of a particular religious faith....

In Meek v. Pittenger, 421 U.S. 349 (1975), the Court invalidated a statute providing for the loan of state-paid professional staff—including teachers—to nonpublic schools to provide remedial and accelerated instruction, guidance counseling and testing, and other services on the premises of the nonpublic schools ... The program in *Meek,* if not sufficiently monitored, would simply have entailed too great a risk of state-sponsored indoctrination.

The programs before us today share the defect that we identified in *Meek.* With respect to the Community Education Program, the District Court found that "virtually every Community Education course conducted on facilities leased from nonpublic schools has an instructor otherwise employed full time by the same nonpublic school." These instructors, many of whom no doubt teach in the religious schools precisely because they are adherents of the controlling denomination and want to serve their religious community zealously, are expected during the regular school day to inculcate their students with the tenets and beliefs of their particular religious faiths. Yet the premise of the program is that those instructors can put aside their religious convictions and engage in entirely secular Community Education instruction as soon as the school day is over. Moreover, they are expected to do so before the same religious school students and in the same religious-school classrooms that they employed to advance religious purposes during the "official" school day. Nonetheless, as petitioners themselves asserted, Community Education classes are not specifically monitored for religious content.

. . .

The Shared Time program, though structured somewhat differently, nonetheless also poses a substantial risk of state-sponsored indoctrination. The most important difference between the programs is that most of the instructors in the Shared Time program are full-time teachers hired by the public schools. Moreover, although "virtually every" Community Education instructor is a full-time religious school teacher, only "[a] significant portion" of the Shared Time instructors previously worked in the religious schools. Nonetheless, as with the Community Education program, no attempt is made to monitor the Shared Time courses for religious content.

Thus, despite these differences between the two programs, our holding in *Meek* controls the inquiry with respect to Shared Time, as well as Community Education. Shared Time instructors are teaching academic subjects in religious schools in courses virtually indistinguishable from the other courses offered during the regular religious-school day. The teachers in this program, even more than their Community Education colleagues, are "performing important educational services in schools in which education is an integral part of the dominant sectarian mission and in which an atmosphere dedicated to the advancement of religious belief is constantly maintained." Meek v. Pittenger, 421 U.S., at 371. Teachers in such an atmosphere may well subtly (or overtly) conform their instruction to the environment in which they teach, while students will perceive the instruction provided in the context of the dominantly religious message of the institution, thus reinforcing the indoctrinating effect. As we stated in *Meek,* "[w]hether the subject is 'remedial reading,' 'advanced reading,' or simply 'reading,' a teacher remains a teacher, and the danger that religious doctrine will become intertwined with secular instruction persists." Id., at 370. Unlike types of aid that the Court has upheld, such as state-created standardized tests, Committee for Public Education ... v. Regan, 444 U.S. 646 (1980), or diagnostic services, Wolman v. Walter, [433 U.S.,] at 241–244, there is a "substantial risk" that programs operating in this environment would "be used for religious educational purposes." Committee for Public Education . . . v. Regan, supra, at 656.

The Court of Appeals of course recognized that respondents adduced no evidence of specific incidents of religious indoctrination in this case. But the absence of proof of specific incidents is not dispositive. When conducting a supposedly secular class in the pervasively sectarian environment of a religious school, a teacher may knowingly or unwillingly tailor the content of the course to fit the school's announced goals. If so, there is no reason to believe that this kind of ideological influence would be detected or reported by students, by their parents, or by the school system itself. The students are presumably attending religious schools precisely in order to receive religious instruction. After spending the balance of their school day in classes heavily influenced by a religious perspective, they would have little motivation or ability to discern improper ideological content that may creep into a Shared Time or Community Education course. Neither their parents nor the parochial schools would have cause to complain if the effect of the publicly supported instruction were to advance the schools' sectarian mission. And the public school system itself has no incentive to detect or report any specific incidents of improper state-sponsored indoctrination. Thus, the lack of evidence of specific incidents of indoctrination is of little significance.

(2)

Our cases have recognized that the Establishment Clause guards against more than direct, state-funded efforts to indoctrinate youngsters in specific religious beliefs. Government promotes religion as effectively when it fosters a close identification of its powers and responsibilities with those of any—or all— religious denominations as when it attempts to inculcate specific religious doctrines. If this identification conveys a message of government endorsement or disapproval of religion, a core purpose of the Establishment Clause is violated. See Lynch v. Donnelly, 465 U.S. 668, 688 (1984) (O'Connor, J., concurring); . . .

. . . .

Our school-aid cases have recognized a sensitivity to the symbolic impact of the union of church and state. Grappling with problems in many ways parallel to those we face today, McCollum v. Board of Education, 333 U.S. 203 (1948), held that a public school may not permit part-time religious instruction on its premises as a part of the school program, even if participation in that instruction is entirely voluntary and even if the instruction itself is conducted only by nonpublic school personnel. Yet in Zorach v. Clauson, 343 U.S. 306 (1952), the Court held that a similar program conducted off the premises of the public school passed constitutional muster. The difference in symbolic impact helps to explain the difference between the cases. The symbolic connection of church and state in the *McCollum* program presented the students with a graphic symbol of the "concert or union or dependency" of church and state, see *Zorach,* supra, at 312. This very symbolic union was conspicuously absent in the *Zorach* program.

In the programs challenged in this case, the religious school students spend their typical school day moving between religious school and "public-school" classes. Both types of classes take place in the same religious school building and both are largely composed of students who are adherents of the same denomination. In this environment, the students would be unlikely to discern the crucial difference between the religious school classes and the "public school" classes, even if the latter were successfully kept free of religious indoctrination.... Consequently, even the student who notices the "public school" sign temporarily posted would have before him a powerful symbol of state endorsement and encouragement of the religious beliefs taught in the same class at some other time during the day.

... This effect—the symbolic union of government and religion in one sectarian enterprise—is an impermissible effect under the Establishment Clause.

(3)

. . .

... [T]he Court has never accepted the mere possibility of subsidization ... as sufficient to invalidate an aid program. On the other hand, this effect is not wholly unimportant for Establishment Clause purposes. If it were, the public schools could gradually take on themselves the entire responsibility for teaching secular subjects on religious school premises. The question in each case must be whether the effect of the proffered aid is "direct and substantial," Committee for Public Education ... v. Nyquist, supra, at 784–785, n. 39, or indirect and incidental. "The problem, like many problems in constitutional law, is one of degree." Zorach v. Clauson, 343 U.S., at 314.

We have noted in the past that the religious school has dual functions, providing its students with a secular education while it promotes a particular religious perspective. See Mueller v. Allen, 463 U.S., at 401–402; Board of Education v. Allen, supra. In *Meek* and *Wolman,* we held unconstitutional state programs providing for loans of instructional equipment and materials to religious schools, on the ground that the programs advanced the "primary, religion-oriented educational function of the sectarian school." ... Cf. Wolman, supra, at 243 (upholding provision of diagnostic services, which were "'general welfare services for children that may be provided by the State regardless of the incidental benefit that accrues to church-related schools,' ") ... The programs challenged here, which provide teachers in addition to the instructional equipment and materials, have a similar—and forbidden—effect of advancing religion. This kind of direct aid to the educational function of the religious school is indistinguishable from the provision of a direct cash subsidy to the religious school that is most clearly prohibited under the Establishment Clause.

Petitioners claim that the aid here, like the textbooks in *Allen,* flows primarily to the students, not to the religious schools. Of course, all aid to religious schools ultimately "flows to" the students, and petitioners' argument if accepted would validate all forms of nonideological aid to religious schools, including those explicitly rejected in our prior cases. Yet in *Meek,* we held unconstitutional the loan of instructional materials to religious schools and in *Wolman,* we rejected the fiction that a similar program could be saved by masking it as aid to individual students. ...It follows *a fortiori* that the aid here, which includes not only instructional materials but also the provision of instructional services by teachers in the parochial school building, "inescapably [has] the primary effect of providing a direct and substantial advancement of the sectarian enterprise." ... Where, as here, no meaningful distinction can be made between aid to the student and aid to the school, "the concept of a loan to individuals is a transparent fiction." ...

Petitioners also argue that this "subsidy" effect is not significant in this case, because the Community Education and Shared Time programs supplemented the curriculum with courses not previously offered in the religious schools and not required by school rule or state regulation. Of course, this fails to distinguish the programs here from those found unconstitutional in *Meek*. See 421 U.S., at 368. As in *Meek,* we do not find that this feature of the program is controlling. First, there is no way of knowing whether the religious schools would have offered some or all of these courses if the public school system had not offered them first. The distinction between courses that "supplement" and those that "supplant" the regular curriculum is therefore not nearly as clear as petitioners allege. Second, although the precise courses offered in these programs may have been new to the participating religious schools, their general subject matter—reading, mathematics, etc.—was surely a part of the curriculum in the past, and the concerns of the Establishment Clause may thus be triggered despite the "supplemental" nature of the courses. Cf. Meek v. Pittenger, 421 U.S., at 370–371. Third, and most important, petitioners' argument would permit the public schools gradually to take over the entire secular curriculum of the religious school, for the latter could surely discontinue existing courses so that they might be replaced a year or two later by a Community Education or Shared Time course with the same content. The average religious school student, for instance, now spends 10% of the schoolday in Shared Time classes. But there is no principled basis on which this Court can impose a limit on the percentage of the religious schoolday that can be subsidized by the public school. To let the genie out of the bottle in this case would be to permit ever larger segments of the religious school curriculum to be turned over to the public school system, thus violating the cardinal principle that the State may not in effect become the prime supporter of the religious school system. See Lemon v. Kurtzman, 403 U.S., at 624–625.

III

We conclude that the challenged programs have the effect of promoting religion in three ways. The state-paid instructors, influenced by the pervasively sectarian nature of the religious schools in which they work, may subtly or overtly indoctrinate the students in particular religious tenets at public expense. The symbolic union of church and state inherent in the provision of secular, state-provided instruction in the religious school buildings threatens to convey a message of state support for religion to students and to the general public. Finally, the programs in effect subsidize the religious functions of the parochial schools by taking over a substantial portion of their responsibility for teaching secular subjects. For these reasons, the conclusion is inescapable that the Community Education and Shared Time programs have the "primary or principal" effect of advancing religion, and therefore violate the dictates of the Establishment Clause of the First Amendment.

. . . Because "the controlling constitutional standards have become firmly rooted and the broad contours of our inquiry are now well defined," Committee for Public Education . . . v. Nyquist, 413 U.S., at 761, the position of those lines has by now become quite clear and requires affirmance of the Court of Appeals.

It is so ordered.

Chief Justice Burger, concurring in the judgment in part and dissenting in part.

I agree with the Court that, under our decisions in Lemon v. Kurtzman, 403 U.S. 602 (1971), and Earley v. DiCenso, 403 U.S. 602 (1971), the Grand Rapids Community Education program violates the Establishment Clause. As to the Shared Time program, I dissent for the reasons stated in my dissenting opinion in Aguilar v. Felton, 473 U.S. 402 (1985).

Justice O'Connor, concurring in the judgment in part and dissenting in part.

For the reasons stated in my dissenting opinion in Aguilar v. Felton, 473 U.S. 402 (1985), I dissent from the Court's holding that the Grand Rapids Shared Time program impermissibly advances religion....

. . .

I agree with the Court, however, that the Community Education program violates the Establishment Clause.... When full-time parochial school teachers receive public funds to teach secular courses to their parochial school students under parochial school supervision, I agree that the program has the perceived and actual effect of advancing the religious aims of the church-related schools. This is particularly the case where, as here, religion pervades the curriculum and the teachers are accustomed to bring religion to play in everything they teach. I concur in the judgment of the Court that the Community Education program violates the Establishment Clause.

Justice White, dissenting.

As evidenced by my dissenting opinions in Lemon v. Kurtzman, 403 U.S. 602, 661 (1971) and Committee for Public Education v. Nyquist, 413 U.S. 756, 813 (1973), I have long disagreed with the Court's interpretation and application of the Establishment Clause in the context of state aid to private schools. For the reasons stated in those dissents, I am firmly of the belief that the Court's decisions in these cases, like its decisions in *Lemon* and *Nyquist,* are "not required by the First Amendment and [are] contrary to the long-range interests of the country." 413 U.S., at 820. For those same reasons, I am satisfied that what the States have sought to do in these cases is well within their authority and is not forbidden by the Establishment Clause. Hence, I dissent and would reverse the judgment in each of these cases.

Justice Rehnquist, dissenting.

I dissent for the reasons stated in my dissenting opinion in Wallace v. Jaffree....

. . .

Aguilar v. Felton

473 U.S. 402, 105 S.Ct. 3232, 87 L.Ed.2d 290 (1985).

Justice Brennan delivered the opinion of the Court.

The City of New York uses federal funds to pay the salaries of public employees who teach in parochial schools. In this companion case to *School District of Grand Rapids v. Ball,* we determine whether this practice violates the Establishment Clause of the First Amendment.

I

A

The program at issue in this case, originally enacted as Title I of the Elementary and Secondary Education Act of 1965, authorizes the Secretary of Education to distribute financial assistance to local educational institutions to meet the needs of educationally deprived children from low-income families. The funds are to be appropriated in accordance with programs proposed by local educational agencies and approved by state educational agencies. 20 U.S.C. § 3805(a). "To the extent consistent with the number of educationally deprived children in the school district of the local educational agency who are enrolled in private elementary and secondary schools, such agency shall make provisions for including special educational services and arrangements ... in which such children can participate." § 3806(a). The proposed programs must also meet the following statutory requirements: the children involved in the program must be educationally deprived, § 3804(a), the children must reside in areas comprising a high concentration of low-income families, § 3805(b), and the programs must supplement, not supplant, programs that would exist absent funding under Title I. § 3807(b).

Since 1966, the City of New York has provided instructional services funded by Title I to parochial school students on the premises of parochial schools. Of those students eligible to receive funds in 1981–1982, 13.2% were enrolled in private schools. Of that group, 84% were enrolled in schools affiliated with the Roman Catholic Archdiocese of New York and the Diocese of Brooklyn and 8% were enrolled in Hebrew day schools. With respect to the religious atmosphere of these schools, the Court of Appeals concluded that "the picture that emerges is of a system in which religious considerations play a key role in the selection of students and teachers, and which has as its substantial purpose the inculcation of religious values."

The programs conducted at these schools include remedial reading, reading skills, remedial mathematics, English as a second language, and guidance services. These programs are carried out by regular employees of the public schools (teachers, guidance counselors, psychologists, psychiatrists and social workers) who have volunteered to teach in the parochial schools. The amount of time that each professional spends in the parochial school is determined by the number of students in the particular program and the needs of these students.

The City's Bureau of Nonpublic School Reimbursement makes teacher assignments, and the instructors are supervised by field personnel, who attempt to pay at least one unannounced visit per month. The field supervisors, in turn, report to program coordinators, who also pay occasional unannounced supervisory visits to monitor Title I classes in the parochial schools. The professionals involved in the program are directed to avoid involvement with religious activities that are conducted within the private schools and to bar religious materials in their classrooms. All material and equipment used in the programs funded under Title I are supplied by the Government and are used only in those programs. The professional personnel are solely responsible for the selection of the students. Additionally, the professionals are informed that contact with private school personnel should be kept to a minimum. Finally, the administrators of the parochial schools are required to clear the classrooms used by the public school personnel of all religious symbols.

B

In 1978, six taxpayers commenced this action in the District Court for the Eastern District of New York, alleging that the Title I program administered by the City of New York violates the Establishment Clause.... The District Court granted the appellants' motion for summary judgment....

A unanimous panel of the Court of Appeals for the Second Circuit reversed ... [W]e affirm the judgment below.

II

... The New York programs challenged in this case are very similar to the programs we examined in *Ball*. ...

The appellants attempt to distinguish this case on the ground that the City of New York, unlike the Grand Rapids Public School District, has adopted a system for monitoring the religious content of publicly funded Title I classes in the religious schools. At best, the supervision in this case would assist in preventing the Title I program from being used, intentionally or unwittingly, to inculcate the religious beliefs of the surrounding parochial school. But appellants' argument fails in any event, because the supervisory system established by the City of New York inevitably results in the excessive entanglement of church and state, an Establishment Clause concern distinct from that addressed by the effects doctrine. Even where state aid to parochial institutions does not have the primary effect of advancing religion, the provision of such aid may nonetheless violate the Establishment Clause owing to the nature of the interaction of church and state in the administration of that aid.

. . .

The critical elements of the entanglement proscribed in *Lemon* and *Meek* are thus present in this case. First, . . . the aid is provided in a pervasively sectarian environment. Second, because assistance is provided in the form of teachers, ongoing inspection is required to ensure the absence of a religious message. . . . In short, the scope and duration of New York's Title I program would require a permanent and pervasive State presence in the sectarian schools receiving aid.

This pervasive monitoring by public authorities in the sectarian schools infringes precisely those Establishment Clause values at the root of the prohibition of excessive entanglement. Agents of the State must visit and inspect the religious school regularly, alert for the subtle or overt presence of religious matter in Title I classes. . . . In addition, the religious school must obey these same agents when they make determinations as to what is and what is not a "religious symbol" and thus off limits in a Title I classroom. In short, the religious school, which has as a primary purpose the advancement and preservation of a particular religion must endure the ongoing presence of state personnel whose primary purpose is to monitor teachers and students in an attempt to guard against the infiltration of religious thought.

The administrative cooperation that is required to maintain the educational program at issue here entangles Church and State in still another way that infringes interests at the heart of the Establishment Clause. Administrative personnel of the public and parochial school systems must work together in resolving matters related to schedules, classroom assignments, problems that arise in the implementation of the program, requests for additional services, and the dissemination of information regarding the program. Furthermore, the program necessitates "frequent contacts between the regular and the remedial teachers (or other professionals), in which each side reports on individual student needs, problems encountered, and results achieved."

. . .

III

Despite the well-intentioned efforts taken by the City of New York, the program remains constitutionally flawed owing to the nature of the aid, to the institution receiving the aid, and to the constitutional principles that they implicate—that neither the State nor Federal Government shall promote or hinder a particular faith or faith generally through the advancement of benefits or through the excessive entanglement of church and state in the administration of those benefits.

Affirmed.[a]

Justice Powell, concurring.

. . .

. . . The constitutional defect in the Title I program . . . is that it provides a direct financial subsidy to be administered in significant part by public school teachers within parochial schools—resulting in both the advancement of religion and forbidden entanglement. If, for example, Congress could fashion a program of evenhanded financial assistance to both public and private schools that could be administered, without governmental supervision in the private schools, so as to prevent the diversion of the aid from secular purposes, we would be presented with a different question.

I join the opinions and judgments of the Court.

Chief Justice Burger, dissenting.

. . .

On the merits of this case, I dissent for the reasons stated in my separate opinion in Meek v. Pittenger, 421 U.S. 349 (1975)....

. . .

Justice Rehnquist, dissenting.

I dissent for the reasons stated in my dissenting opinion in Wallace v. Jaffree . . . [T]he Court takes advantage of the "Catch-22" paradox of its own creation, . . . whereby aid must be supervised to ensure no entanglement but the supervision itself is held to cause an entanglement. The Court in *Aguilar* strikes down nondiscriminatory nonsectarian aid to educationally deprived children from low-income families. The Establishment Clause does not prohibit such sorely needed assistance; we have indeed traveled far afield from the concerns which prompted the adoption of the First Amendment when we rely on gossamer abstractions to invalidate a law which obviously meets an entirely secular need. I would reverse.

Justice O'Connor, with whom Justice Rehnquist joins as to Parts II and III, dissenting.

Today the Court affirms the holding of the Court of Appeals that public schoolteachers can offer remedial instruction to disadvantaged students who attend religious schools "only if such instruction . . . [is] afforded at a neutral site off the premises of the religious school." This holding rests on the theory, enunciated in Part V of the Court's opinion in Meek v. Pittenger, 421 U.S. 349, 367–373 (1975), that public schoolteachers who set foot on parochial school premises are likely to bring religion into their classes, and that the supervision necessary to prevent religious teaching would unduly entangle church and state. Even if this theory were valid in the abstract, it cannot validly be applied to New York City's 19–year–old Title I program. The Court greatly exaggerates the degree of supervision necessary to prevent public school teachers from inculcating religion, and thereby demonstrates the flaws of a test that condemns benign cooperation between church and state. I would uphold Congress' efforts to afford remedial instruction to disadvantaged schoolchildren in both public and parochial schools.

---

[a] A dissenting opinion by Justice White   is omitted.

I

. . .

The Court's discussion of the effect of the New York City Title I program is even more perfunctory than its analysis of the program's purpose. . . . While addressing the effect of the Grand Rapids program at such length, the Court overlooks the effect of Title I in New York City.

One need not delve too deeply in the record to understand why the Court does not belabor the effect of the Title I program. The abstract theories explaining why on-premises instruction might possibly advance religion dissolve in the face of experience in New York. . . . Indeed, in 19 years there has never been a single incident in which a Title I instructor "subtly or overtly" attempted to "indoctrinate the students in particular religious tenets at public expense."

Common sense suggests a plausible explanation for this unblemished record. New York City's public Title I instructors are professional educators who can and do follow instructions not to inculcate religion in their classes. . . .

The only type of impermissible effect that arguably could carry over from the *Grand Rapids* decision to this litigation, then, is the effect of subsidizing "the religious functions of the parochial schools by taking over a substantial portion of their responsibility for teaching secular subjects." That effect is tenuous, however, in light of the statutory directive that Title I funds may be used only to provide services that otherwise would not be available to the participating students. 20 U.S.C. § 3807(b). The Secretary of Education has vigorously enforced the requirement that Title I funds supplement rather than supplant the services of local education agencies. . . .

Even if we were to assume that Title I remedial classes in New York may have duplicated to some extent instruction parochial schools would have offered in the absence of Title I, the Court's delineation of this third type of effect proscribed by the Establishment Clause would be seriously flawed. Our Establishment Clause decisions have not barred remedial assistance to parochial school children, but rather remedial assistance *on the premises of the parochial school.* Under Wolman v. Walter, 433 U.S. 229, 244–248 (1977), the New York City classes prohibited by the Court today would have survived Establishment Clause scrutiny if they had been offered in a neutral setting off the property of the private school. Yet it is difficult to understand why a remedial reading class offered on parochial school premises is any more likely to supplant the secular course offerings of the parochial school than the same class offered in a portable classroom next door to the school. Unless *Wolman* was wrongly decided, the defect in the Title I program cannot lie in the risk that it will supplant secular course offerings.

II

. . .

. . . [E]xperience has demonstrated that the analysis in Part V of the *Meek* opinion is flawed. At the time *Meek* was decided, thoughtful dissents pointed out the absence of any record support for the notion that public school teachers would attempt to inculcate religion simply because they temporarily occupied a parochial school classroom, or that such instruction would produce political divisiveness. 421 U.S., at 385 (opinion of Burger, C.J.); *Id.,* at 387 (opinion of Rehnquist, J.). Experience has given greater force to the arguments of the dissenting opinions in *Meek*. It is not intuitively obvious that a dedicated public school teacher will tend to disobey instructions and commence proselytizing students at public expense merely because the classroom is within a parochial school. *Meek* is correct in asserting that a teacher of remedial reading "remains a teacher," but surely it is significant that the teacher involved is a professional, full-time public school employee who is unaccustomed to bringing religion into the classroom. Given that not a single incident of religious indoctrination has been identified as occurring in the thousands of classes offered in Grand Rapids and New York over the past two decades, it is time to acknowledge that the risk identified in *Meek* was greatly exaggerated.

. . .

The Court's reliance on the potential for political divisiveness as evidence of undue entanglement is also unpersuasive. There is little record support for the proposition that New York's admirable Title I program has ignited any controversy other than this litigation. . . .

I adhere to the doubts about the entanglement test that were expressed in *Lynch*. It is curious indeed to base our interpretation of the Constitution on speculation as to the likelihood of a phenomenon which the parties may create merely by prosecuting a lawsuit. My reservations about the entanglement test, however, have come to encompass its institutional aspects as well. . . .

. . .

Board of Education of Kiryas Joel Village School District v. Grumet

512 U.S. 687, 114 S.Ct. 2481, 129 L.Ed.2d 546 (1994).

Justice Souter delivered the opinion of the Court.

The Village of Kiryas Joel in Orange County, New York, is a religious enclave of Satmar Hasidim, practitioners of a strict form of Judaism. The village fell within the Monroe–Woodbury Central School District until a special state statute passed in 1989 carved out a separate district, following village lines, to serve this distinctive population. . . .The question is whether the Act creating the separate school district violates the Establishment Clause of the First Amendment, binding on the States through the Fourteenth Amendment. Because this unusual act is tantamount to an allocation of political power on a religious criterion and neither presupposes nor requires governmental impartiality toward religion, we hold that it violates the prohibition against establishment.

I

The Satmar Hasidic sect takes its name from the town near the Hungarian and Romanian border where, in the early years of this century, Grand Rebbe Joel Teitelbaum molded the group into a distinct community. After World War II and the destruction of much of European Jewry, the Grand Rebbe and most of his surviving followers moved to the Williamsburg section of Brooklyn, New York. Then, 20 years ago, the Satmars purchased an approved but undeveloped subdivision in the town of Monroe and began assembling the community that has since become the Village of Kiryas Joel. When a zoning dispute arose in the course of settlement, the Satmars presented the Town Board of Monroe with a petition to form a new village within the town, a right that New York's Village Law gives almost any group of residents who satisfy certain procedural niceties. . . .Neighbors who did not wish to secede with the Satmars objected strenuously, and after arduous negotiations the proposed boundaries of the Village of Kiryas Joel were drawn to include just the 320 acres owned and inhabited entirely by Satmars. The village, incorporated in 1977, has a population of about 8,500 today. Rabbi Aaron Teitelbaum, eldest son of the current Grand Rebbe, serves as the village rov (chief rabbi) and rosh yeshivah (chief authority in the parochial schools).

The residents of Kiryas Joel are vigorously religious people who make few concessions to the modern world and go to great lengths to avoid assimilation into it. They interpret the Torah strictly; segregate the sexes outside the home; speak Yiddish as their primary language; eschew television, radio, and English-language publications; and dress in distinctive ways that include headcoverings and special garments for boys and modest dresses for girls. Children are educated in private religious schools, most boys at the United Talmudic Academy where they receive a thorough grounding in the Torah and limited exposure to secular subjects, and most girls at Bais Rochel, an affiliated school with a curriculum designed to prepare girls for their roles as wives and mothers. . . .

These schools do not, however, offer any distinctive services to handicapped children, who are entitled under state and federal law to special education services even when enrolled in private schools. . . . Starting in 1984 the Monroe–Woodbury Central School District provided such services for the children of Kiryas Joel at an annex to Bais Rochel, but a year later ended that arrangement in response to our decisions in Aguilar v. Felton, 473 U. S. 402 (1985), and School Dist. of Grand Rapids v. Ball, 473 U. S. 373 (1985). Children from Kiryas Joel who needed special education (including the deaf, the mentally retarded, and others suffering from a range of physical, mental, or emotional disorders) were then forced to attend public schools outside the village, which their families found highly unsatisfactory. Parents of most of these children withdrew them from the Monroe–Woodbury secular schools, citing "the panic, fear and trauma [the children] suffered in leaving their own community and being with people whose ways were so different," . . .

. . .

By 1989, only one child from Kiryas Joel was attending Monroe–Woodbury's public schools; the village's other handicapped children received privately funded special services or went without. It was then that the New York Legislature passed the statute at issue in this litigation, which provided that the Village of Kiryas Joel "is constituted a separate school district, . . . and shall have and enjoy all the powers and duties of a union free school district. . . ." 1989 N. Y. Laws, ch. 748. The statute thus empowered a locally elected board of education to take such action as opening schools and closing them, hiring teachers, prescribing textbooks, establishing disciplinary rules, and raising property taxes to fund operations. . . .

Although it enjoys plenary legal authority over the elementary and secondary education of all school-aged children in the village, . . . the Kiryas Joel Village School District currently runs only a special education program for handicapped children. The other village children have stayed in their parochial schools, relying on the new school district only for transportation, remedial education, and health and welfare services. If any child without handicap in Kiryas Joel were to seek a public-school education, the district would pay tuition to send the child into Monroe–Woodbury or another school district nearby. Under like arrangements, several of the neighboring districts send their handicapped Hasidic children into Kiryas Joel, so that two thirds of the full-time students in the village's public school come from outside. In all, the new district serves just over 40 full-time students, and two or three times that many parochial school students on a part-time basis.

Several months before the new district began operations, the New York State School Boards Association and respondents Grumet and Hawk brought this action . . . , challenging Chapter 748 under the national and state constitutions as an unconstitutional establishment of religion. . . . [T]he trial court ruled for the plaintiffs (respondents here), finding that the statute failed all three prongs of the test in Lemon v. Kurtzman, 403 U. S. 602 (1971) . . .

A divided Appellate Division affirmed on the ground that Chapter 748 had the primary effect of advancing religion . . .

. . . .

II

"A proper respect for both the Free Exercise and the Establishment Clauses compels the State to pursue a course of 'neutrality' toward religion," Committee for Public Ed. & Religious Liberty v. Nyquist, 413 U. S. 756, 792–793 (1973), favoring neither one religion over others nor religious adherents collectively over nonadherents. . . . Chapter 748, the statute creating the Kiryas Joel Village School District, departs from this constitutional command by delegating the State's discretionary authority over public schools to a group defined by its character as a religious community, in a legal and historical context that gives no assurance that governmental power has been or will be exercised neutrally.

Larkin v. Grendel's Den, Inc., 459 U. S. 116 (1982), provides an instructive comparison with the litigation before us. There, the Court was requested to strike down a Massachusetts statute granting religious bodies veto power over applications for liquor licenses. Under the statute, the governing body of any church, synagogue, or school located within 500 feet of an applicant's premises could, simply by submitting written objection, prevent the Alcohol Beverage Control Commission from issuing a license. . . . [T]he Court found that in two respects the statute violated "the wholesome 'neutrality' of which this Court's cases speak . . . The Act brought about a 'fusion of governmental and religious functions' . . . by delegating 'important, discretionary governmental powers' to religious bodies, thus impermissibly entangling government and religion. . . . And it lacked 'any effective means of guaranteeing' that the delegated power '[would] be used exclusively for secular, neutral, and nonideological purposes,' . . .; this, along with the 'significant symbolic benefit to religion' associated with 'the mere appearance of a joint exercise of legislative authority by Church and State,' led the Court to conclude that the statute had a 'primary' and 'principal' effect of advancing religion," . . . Comparable constitutional problems inhere in the statute before us.

A

Larkin presented an example of united civic and religious authority, an establishment rarely found in such straightforward form in modern America . . .

The Establishment Clause problem presented by Chapter 748 is more subtle, but it resembles the issue raised in *Larkin* to the extent that the earlier case teaches that a State may not delegate its civic authority to a group chosen according to a religious criterion. . . . What makes this litigation different from *Larkin* is the delegation here of civic power to the "qualified voters of the village of Kiryas Joel," . . . as distinct from a religious leader such as the village rov, or an institution of religious government like the formally constituted parish council in *Larkin*. In light of the circumstances of this case, however, this distinction turns out to lack constitutional significance.

... If New York were to delegate civic authority to "the Grand Rebbe," *Larkin* would obviously require invalidation ... , and the same is true if New York delegates political authority by reference to religious belief. ...

Of course, Chapter 748 delegates power not by express reference to the religious belief of the Satmar community, but to residents of the "territory of the village of Kiryas Joel." ... But our analysis does not end with the text of the statute at issue, ... and the context here persuades us that Chapter 748 effectively identifies these recipients of governmental authority by reference to doctrinal adherence, even though it does not do so expressly. ...

It is undisputed that those who negotiated the village boundaries when applying the general village incorporation statute drew them so as to exclude all but Satmars, and that the New York Legislature was well aware that the village remained exclusively Satmar in 1989 when it adopted Chapter 748. ...

The origin of the district in a special act of the legislature, rather than the State's general laws governing school district reorganization, is likewise anomalous. ...[T]he Kiryas Joel Village School District is exceptional to the point of singularity, as the only district coming to our notice that the legislature carved from a single existing district to serve local residents. ...

Because the district's creation ran uniquely counter to state practice, following the lines of a religious community where the customary and neutral principles would not have dictated the same result, we have good reasons to treat this district as the reflection of a religious criterion for identifying the recipients of civil authority. ...

B

The fact that this school district was created by a special and unusual Act of the legislature also gives reason for concern whether the benefit received by the Satmar community is one that the legislature will provide equally to other religious (and nonreligious) groups. ...

The fundamental source of constitutional concern here is that the legislature itself may fail to exercise governmental authority in a religiously neutral way. The anomalously case-specific nature of the legislature's exercise of state authority in creating this district for a religious community leaves the Court without any direct way to review such state action for the purpose of safeguarding a principle at the heart of the Establishment Clause, that government should not prefer one religion to another, or religion to irreligion ..... Because the religious community of Kiryas Joel did not receive its new governmental authority simply as one of many communities eligible for equal treatment under a general law, we have no assurance that the next similarly situated group seeking a school district of its own will receive one ... Here the benefit flows only to a single sect, but aiding this single, small religious group causes no less a constitutional problem than would follow from aiding a sect with more members or religion as a whole, ... and we are forced to conclude that the State of New York has violated the Establishment Clause.

C

. . .

... [T]here are several alternatives here for providing bilingual and bicultural special education to Satmar children. Such services can perfectly well be offered to village children through the Monroe–Woodbury Central School District. Since the Satmars do not claim that separatism is religiously mandated, their children may receive bilingual and bicultural instruction at a public school already run by the Monroe–Woodbury district. Or if the educationally appropriate offering by Monroe–Woodbury should turn out to be a separate program of bilingual and bicultural education at a neutral site near one of the village's parochial schools, ... no Establishment Clause difficulty would inhere in such a scheme, administered in accordance with neutral principles that would not necessarily confine special treatment to Satmars. ...

. . .

III

Justice Cardozo once cast the dissenter as "the gladiator making a last stand against the lions." B. Cardozo, Law and Literature 34 (1931). Justice Scalia's dissent is certainly the work of a gladiator, but he thrusts at lions of his own imagining. We do not disable a religiously homogeneous group from exercising political power conferred on it without regard to religion. Unlike the states of Utah and New Mexico (which were laid out according to traditional political methodologies taking account of lines of latitude and longitude and topographical features ...), the reference line chosen for the Kiryas Joel Village School District was one purposely drawn to separate Satmars from non-Satmars. ...The dissent protests it is novel to insist "up front" that a statute not tailor its benefits to apply only to one religious group ... [U]nder the dissent's theory, if New York were to pass a law providing school buses only for children attending Christian day schools, we would be constrained to uphold the statute against Establishment Clause attack until faced by a request from a non-Christian family for equal treatment under the patently unequal law. ...And to end on the point with which Justice Scalia begins, the license he takes in suggesting that the Court holds the Satmar sect to be New York's established church, is only one symptom of his inability to accept the fact that this Court has long held that the First Amendment reaches more than classic, 18th century establishments. ...

. . .

Affirmed.

Justice Blackmun, concurring.

For the reasons stated by Justice Souter and Justice Stevens, whose opinions I join, I agree that the New York statute under review violates the Establishment Clause of the First Amendment. I write separately only to note my disagreement with any suggestion that today's decision signals a departure from the principles described in Lemon v. Kurtzman, 403 U. S. 602 (1971). ...

. . .

Justice Stevens with whom Justice Blackmun and Justice Ginsburg join, concurring.

... [T]he State could have taken steps to alleviate the children's fear by teaching their schoolmates to be tolerant and respectful of Satmar customs. Action of that kind would raise no constitutional concerns and would further the strong public interest in promoting diversity and understanding in the public schools.

Instead, the State responded with a solution that affirmatively supports a religious sect's interest in segregating itself and preventing its children from associating with their neighbors. . . .

Affirmative state action in aid of segregation of this character is unlike the evenhanded distribution of a public benefit or service, a "release time" program for public school students involving no public premises or funds, or a decision to grant an exemption from a burdensome general rule. It is, I believe, fairly characterized as establishing, rather than merely accommodating, religion. . . .

Justice O'Connor, concurring in part and concurring in the judgment.

I

The question at the heart of this case is: What may the government do, consistently with the Establishment Clause, to accommodate people's religious beliefs? . . .

. . .

II

. . . Religious needs can be accommodated through laws that are neutral with regard to religion. . . .

We have time and again held that the government generally may not treat people differently based on the God or gods they worship, or don't worship. . . .

This emphasis on equal treatment is, I think, an eminently sound approach. . . .

That the government is acting to accommodate religion should generally not change this analysis. What makes accommodation permissible, even praiseworthy, is not that the government is making life easier for some particular religious group as such. Rather, it is that the government is accommodating a deeply held belief. Accommodations may thus justify treating those who share this belief differently from those who do not; but they do not justify discriminations based on sect. A state law prohibiting the consumption of alcohol may exempt sacramental wines, but it may not exempt sacramental wine use by Catholics but not by Jews. A draft law may exempt conscientious objectors, but it may not exempt conscientious objectors whose objections are based on theistic belief (such as Quakers) as opposed to nontheistic belief (such as Buddhists) or atheistic belief. . . . The Constitution permits "nondiscriminatory religious-practice exemption[s]," . . . not sectarian ones.

III

I join Parts I, II–B, II–C, and III of the Court's opinion because I think this law, rather than being a general accommodation, singles out a particular religious group for favorable treatment. . . .

. . .

Our invalidation of this statute in no way means that the Satmars' needs cannot be accommodated. There is nothing improper about a legislative intention to accommodate a religious group, so long as it is implemented through generally applicable legislation. New York may, for instance, allow all villages to operate their own school districts. If it does not want to act so broadly, it may set forth neutral criteria that a village must meet to have a school district of its own; these criteria can then be applied by a state agency, and the decision would then be reviewable by the judiciary. A district created under a generally applicable scheme would be acceptable even though it coincides with a village which was consciously created by its voters as an enclave for their religious group. I do not think the Court's opinion holds the contrary.

I also think there is one other accommodation that would be entirely permissible: the 1984 scheme, which was discontinued because of our decision in *Aguilar*. . . . If the government provides this education on-site at public schools and at nonsectarian private schools, it is only fair that it provide it on-site at sectarian schools as well.

I thought this to be true in *Aguilar*, . . . and I still believe it today. . . . It is the Court's insistence on disfavoring religion in *Aguilar* that led New York to favor it here. The court should, in a proper case, be prepared to reconsider *Aguilar*, in order to bring our Establishment Clause jurisprudence back to what I think is the proper track-government impartiality, not animosity, towards religion.

IV

One aspect of the Court's opinion in this case is worth noting: Like the opinions in two recent cases, Lee v. Weisman, 505 U. S. (1992); Zobrest v. Catalina Foothills School Dist., 509 U. S. (1993), and the case I think is most relevant to this one, Larson v. Valente, 456 U. S. 228 (1982), the Court's opinion does not focus on the Establishment Clause test we set forth in Lemon v. Kurtzman, 403 U. S. 602 (1971).

. . .

. . . I think it is more useful to recognize the relevant concerns in each case on their own terms, rather than trying to squeeze them into language that does not really apply to them.

. . .

Experience proves that the Establishment Clause, like the Free Speech Clause, cannot easily be reduced to a single test. There are different categories of Establishment Clause cases, which may call for different approaches. . . .

. . .

As the Court's opinion today shows, the slide away from *Lemon*'s unitary approach is well under way. . . . [A]bandoning the *Lemon* framework need not mean abandoning some of the insights that the test reflected, nor the insights of the cases that applied it.

. . .

Justice Kennedy, concurring in the judgment.

The Court's ruling that the Kiryas Joel Village School District violates the Establishment Clause is in my view correct, but my reservations about what the Court's reasoning implies for religious accommodations in general are sufficient to require a separate writing. As the Court recognizes, a legislative accommodation that discriminates among religions may become an establishment of religion. But the Court's opinion can be interpreted to say that an accommodation for a particular religious group is invalid because of the risk that the legislature will not grant the same accommodation to another religious group suffering some similar burden. This rationale seems to me without grounding in our precedents and a needless restriction upon the legislature's ability to respond to the unique problems of a particular religious group. The real vice of the school district, in my estimation, is that New York created it by drawing political boundaries on the basis of religion. I would decide the issue we confront upon this narrower theory . . .

I

This is not a case in which the government has granted a benefit to a general class of recipients of which religious groups are just one part. . . . But for the forbidden manner in which the New York Legislature sought to go about it, the State's attempt to accommodate the special needs of the handicapped Satmar children would have been valid.

. . .

II

. . .

. . . I agree with the Court insofar as it invalidates the school district for being drawn along religious lines. . . . This explicit religious gerrymandering violates the First Amendment Establishment Clause.

. . .

III

. . .

Before 1985, the handicapped Satmar children of Kiryas Joel attended the private religious schools within the village that the other Satmar children attended. Because their handicaps were in some cases acute (ranging from mental retardation and deafness to spina bifida and cerebral palsy), the State of New York provided public funds for special education of these children at annexes to the religious schools. Then came the companion cases of School Dist. of Grand Rapids v. Ball, 473 U. S. 373 (1985), and Aguilar v. Felton, 473 U. S. 402 (1985). In *Grand Rapids*, the Court invalidated a program in which public school teachers would offer supplemental classes at private schools, including religious schools, at the end of the regular school day. And in *Aguilar*, the Court invalidated New York City's use of Title I funding to pay the salaries of public school teachers who taught educationally deprived children of low-income families at parochial schools in the city. After these cases, the Monroe–Woodbury School District suspended its special education program at the Kiryas Joel religious schools . . .

The decisions in *Grand Rapids* and *Aguilar* may have been erroneous. In light of the case before us, and in the interest of sound elaboration of constitutional doctrine, it may be necessary for us to reconsider them at a later date. . . .

One misjudgment is no excuse, however, for compounding it with another. We must confront this case as it comes before us, without bending rules to free the Satmars from a predicament into which we put them. The Establishment Clause forbids the government to draw political boundaries on the basis of religious faith. For this reason, I concur in the judgment of the Court.

Justice Scalia, with whom The Chief Justice and Justice Thomas join, dissenting.

. . . [T]he Founding Fathers would be astonished to find that the Establishment Clause . . . has been employed to prohibit characteristically and admirably

American accommodation of the religious practices (or more precisely, cultural peculiarities) of a tiny minority sect. . . .

I

Unlike most of our Establishment Clause cases involving education, these cases involve no public funding, however slight or indirect, to private religious schools. They do not involve private schools at all. The school under scrutiny is a public school . . . The only thing distinctive about the school is that all the students share the same religion.

None of our cases has ever suggested that there is anything wrong with that. . . . There is no danger in educating religious students in a public school.

For these very good reasons, Justice Souter's opinion does not focus upon the school, but rather upon the school district and the New York Legislature that created it. His arguments . . . are two: that reposing governmental power in the Kiryas Joel School District is the same as reposing governmental power in a religious group; and that in enacting the statute creating the district, the New York State Legislature was discriminating on the basis of religion, i.e., favoring the Satmar Hasidim over others. . . .

II

. . .

. . . If the conferral of governmental power upon a religious institution as such (rather than upon American citizens who belong to the religious institution) is not the test of *Grendel's Den* invalidity, there is no reason why giving power to a body that is overwhelmingly dominated by the members of one sect would not suffice to invoke the Establishment Clause. That might have made the entire States of Utah and New Mexico unconstitutional at the time of their admission to the Union, and would undoubtedly make many units of local government unconstitutional today.

. . .

III

. . .

. . . What happened in the creation of the village is in fact precisely what happened in the creation of the school district, so that the former cannot possibly infect the latter . . . Entirely secular reasons (zoning for the village, cultural alienation of students for the school district) produced a political unit whose members happened to share the same religion. There is no evidence (indeed, no plausible suspicion) of the legislature's desire to favor the Satmar religion, as opposed to meeting distinctive secular needs or desires of citizens who happened to be Satmars. . . .

IV

But even if Chapter 748 were intended to create a special arrangement for the Satmars because of their religion . . . , it would be a permissible accommodation. . . .

. . .

Contrary to the Court's suggestion, I do not think that the Establishment Clause prohibits formally established "state" churches and nothing more. I have always believed, and all my opinions are consistent with the view, that the

Establishment Clause prohibits the favoring of one religion over others. In this respect, it is the Court that attacks lions of straw. What I attack is the Court's imposition of novel "up front" procedural requirements on state legislatures. . . .

. . .

2.   HIGHER EDUCATION

TILTON v. RICHARDSON, 403 U.S. 672 (1971). The Higher Education Facilities Act of 1963 provided for federal grants to institutions of higher education for the construction of academic facilities. The Act provided that only facilities used for non-sectarian instruction would be financed and that the restriction to non-sectarian use would have to be observed for 20 years. The Court by a vote of 5 to 4, but without an opinion of the Court, sustained the application of the statute to grants made for buildings at four church-related colleges. The Court held invalid the portion of the Act that would have permitted religious uses of the buildings after 20 years.

HUNT v. McNAIR, 413 U.S. 734 (1973). South Carolina established an educational facilities authority to assist through the issuance of revenue bonds higher educational institutions in constructing and financing buildings, facilities and site preparation, but not including any facility for sectarian instruction or religious worship. The act was challenged here as applied to the issuance of bonds to finance the construction of dining hall facilities at a Baptist college. The court upheld the statute, relying on Tilton v. Richardson. It said: "Aid normally may be thought to have a primary effect of advancing religion when it flows to an institution in which religion is so pervasive that a substantial portion of its functions are subsumed in the religious mission or when it funds a specifically religious activity in an otherwise substantially secular setting." In this case the court relied on the fact that the college had no religious test for faculty or student body and that the Baptist percentage of the student body (60%) was about the same as the percentage of Baptists in the surrounding community.

Roemer v. Board of Public Works

426 U.S. 736, 96 S.Ct. 2337, 49 L.Ed.2d 179 (1976).

Mr. Justice Blackmun announced the judgment of the Court and delivered an opinion in which The Chief Justice and Mr. Justice Powell joined.

We are asked once again to police the constitutional boundary between church and state. Maryland, this time, is the alleged trespasser. It has enacted a statute which, as amended, provides for annual noncategorical grants to private colleges, among them religiously affiliated institutions, subject only to the restrictions that the funds not be used for "sectarian purposes." A three-judge District Court, by a divided vote, refused to enjoin the operation of the statute, 387 F.Supp. 1282 (D.Md.1974), and a direct appeal has been taken to this Court. . . .

Plaintiffs in this suit, appellants here, are four individual Maryland citizens and taxpayers. Their complaint sought a declaration of the statute's invalidity, an order enjoining payments under it to church-affiliated institutions, and a declaration that the State was entitled to recover from such institutions any amounts already disbursed. In addition to the responsible state officials, plaintiff-appellants joined as defendants the five institutions they claimed were constitutionally ineligible for this form of aid: Western Maryland College, College of Notre Dame, Mount Saint Mary's College, Saint Joseph College, and Loyola College. Of these, the last four are affiliated with the Roman Catholic Church; Western Maryland was a Methodist affiliate. The District Court ruled with respect to all five. Western Maryland, however, has since been dismissed as a defendant-appellee. We are concerned, therefore, only with the four Roman Catholic affiliates.

After carefully assessing the role that the Catholic Church plays in the lives of these institutions, a matter to which we return in greater detail below, and applying the three-part requirement of *Lemon I,* 403 U.S., at 612–613, that state aid such as this have a secular purpose, a primary effect other than the advancement of religion, and no tendency to entangle the State excessively in church affairs, the District Court ruled that the amended statute was constitutional and was not to be enjoined. . . .

II.

A system of government that makes itself felt as pervasively as ours could hardly be expected never to cross paths with the church. In fact, our State and Federal Governments impose certain burdens upon, and impart certain benefits to, virtually all our activities, and religious activity is not an exception. The Court has enforced a scrupulous neutrality by the State, as among religions, and also as between religious and other activities, but a hermetic separation of the two is an impossibility it has never required. It long has been established, for example, that the State may send a cleric, indeed even a clerical order, to perform a wholly secular task. In Bradfield v. Roberts, 175 U.S. 291 (1899), the Court upheld the extension of public aid to a corporation which, although composed entirely of members of a Roman Catholic sisterhood acting "under the auspices of said church," id., at 297, was limited by its corporate charter to the secular purpose of operating a charitable hospital.

And religious institutions need not be quarantined from public benefits that are neutrally available to all. The Court has permitted the State to supply transportation for children to and from church-related as well as public schools. Everson v. Board of Education, 330 U.S. 1 (1947). It has done the same with respect to secular textbooks loaned by the State on equal terms to students attending both public and church-related elementary schools. Board of Education v. Allen, 392 U.S. 236 (1968). Since it had not been shown in *Allen* that the secular textbooks would be put to other than secular purposes, the Court concluded that, as in *Everson,* the State was merely "extending the benefits of state laws to all citizens." Id., at 242. Just as *Bradfield* dispels any notion that a religious person can never be in the State's pay for a secular purpose,[13] *Everson* and *Allen* put to rest any argument that the State may never act in such a way that has the incidental effect of facilitating religious activity. The Court has not been blind to the fact that in aiding a religious institution to perform a secular task, the State frees the institution's resources to be put to sectarian ends.[14] If this were impermissible, however, a church could not be protected by the police and fire departments, or have its public sidewalk kept in

---

[13] It could scarcely be otherwise, or individuals would be discriminated against for their religion, and the Nation would have to abandon its accepted practice of allowing members of religious orders to serve in the Congress and in other public offices.

[14] See Hunt v. McNair, 413 U.S. 734, 743 (1973) ("the Court has not accepted the recurrent argument that all aid is forbidden because aid in one aspect of an institution frees it to spend its resources on religious ends"). . . .

repair. The Court never has held that religious activities must be discriminated against in this way.

Neutrality is what is required. The State must confine itself to secular objectives, and neither advance nor impede religious activity. Of course, that principle is more easily stated than applied. The Court has taken the view that a secular purpose and a facial neutrality may not be enough, if in fact the State is lending direct support to a religious activity. The State may not, for example, pay for what is actually a religious education, even though it purports to be paying for a secular one, and even though it makes its aid available to secular and religious institutions alike. The Court also has taken the view that the State's efforts to perform a secular task, and at the same time avoid aiding in the performance of a religious one, may not lead it into such an intimate relationship with religious authority that it appears either to be sponsoring or to be excessively interfering with that authority.[15] . . .

. . .

[The opinion next discussed in detail *Lemon I,* Tilton v. Richardson, Hunt v. McNair, *Nyquist, Levitt,* and Meek v. Pittenger.]

So the slate we write on is anything but clean. Instead, there is little room for further refinement of the principles governing public aid to church-affiliated private schools. Our purpose is not to unsettle those principles, so recently reaffirmed, see Meek v. Pittenger, supra, or to expand upon them substantially, but merely to insure that they are faithfully applied in this case.

III.

The first part of *Lemon I* 's three-part test is not in issue; appellants do not challenge the District Court's finding that the purpose of Maryland's aid program is the secular one of supporting private higher education generally, as an economic alternative to a wholly public system. The focus of the debate is on the second and third parts, those concerning the primary effect of advancing religion, and excessive church-state entanglement. We consider them in the same order.

A.

While entanglement is essentially a procedural problem, the primary effect question is the substantive one of what private educational activities, by whatever procedure, may be supported by state funds. *Hunt* requires (1) that no state aid at all go to institutions that are so "pervasively sectarian" that secular activities cannot be separated from sectarian ones, and (2) that if secular activities *can* be separated out, they alone may be funded.

(1) The District Court's finding in this case was that the appellee colleges are not "pervasively sectarian." 387 F.Supp., at 1293. This conclusion it supported with a number of subsidiary findings concerning the role of religion on these campuses:

. . .

We cannot say that the foregoing findings as to the role of religion in particular aspects of the colleges are clearly erroneous. . . . The general picture

---

[15] The importance of avoiding persistent and potentially frictional contact between governmental and religious authorities is such that it has been held to justify the *extension,* rather than the withholding, of certain benefits to religious organizations. The Court upheld the exemption of such organizations from property taxation partly on this ground. Walz v. Tax Commission, 397 U.S. 664, 674–675 (1970).

that the District Court has painted of the appellee institutions is similar in almost all respects to that of the church-affiliated colleges considered in *Tilton* and *Hunt*. We find no constitutionally significant distinction between them, at least for purposes of the "pervasive sectarianism" test.

(2) Having found that the appellee institutions are not "so permeated by religion that the secular side cannot be separated from the sectarian," 387 F.Supp., at 1293, the District Court proceeded to the next question posed by *Hunt*: whether aid in fact was extended only to "the secular side." This requirement the court regarded as satisfied by the statutory prohibition against sectarian use, and by the administrative enforcement of that prohibition through the Council for Higher Education. We agree.... We must assume that the colleges, and the Council, will exercise their delegated control over use of the funds in compliance with the statutory, and therefore the constitutional, mandate. It is to be expected that they will give a wide berth to "specifically religious activity," and thus minimize constitutional questions. Should such questions arise, the courts will consider them. It has not been the Court's practice, in considering facial challenges to statutes of this kind, to strike them down in anticipation that particular applications may result in unconstitutional use of funds. See e.g., Hunt v. McNair, 413 U.S., at 744; Tilton v. Richardson, 403 U.S., at 682 (plurality opinion).

B.

If the foregoing answer to the "primary effect" question seems easy, it serves to make the "excessive entanglement" problem more difficult. The statute itself clearly denies the use of public funds for "sectarian purposes." It seeks to avert such use, however, through a process of annual interchange—proposal and approval, expenditure and review—between the colleges and the Council. In answering the question whether this will be an "excessively entangling" relationship, we must consider the several relevant factors identified in prior decisions:

(1) First is the character of the aided institutions. This has been fully described above. As the District Court found, the colleges perform "essentially secular educational functions," 387 F.Supp., at 1288, that are distinct and separable from religious activity. This finding, which is a prerequisite under the "pervasive sectarianism" test to any state aid at all, is also important for purposes of the entanglement test because it means that secular activities, for the most, can be taken at face value. There is no danger, or at least only a substantially reduced danger, that an ostensibly secular activity—the study of biology, the learning of a foreign language, an athletic event—will actually be infused with religious content or significance. The need for close surveillance of purportedly secular activities is correspondingly reduced....

(2) As for the form of aid, we have already noted that no particular use of state funds is before us in this case. The *process* by which aid is disbursed, and a use for it chosen, are before us. We address this as a matter of the "resulting relationship" of secular and religious authority.

(3) As noted, the funding process is an annual one....

We agree with the District Court that "excessive entanglement" does not necessarily result from the fact that the subsidy is an annual one. It is true that the Court favored the "one-time, single-purpose" construction grants in *Tilton* because they entailed "no continuing financial relationships or dependencies, no annual audits, and no government analysis of an institution's expenditures." 403 U.S., at 688 (plurality opinion). The present aid program cannot claim these aspects. But if the question is whether this case is more like *Lemon*

I or more like *Tilton*—and surely that is the fundamental question before us—the answer must be that it is more like *Tilton*.

Tilton is distinguishable only by the form of aid. . . .

While the form-of-aid distinctions of *Tilton* are thus of questionable importance, the character-of-institution distinctions of *Lemon I* are most impressive. To reiterate a few of the relevant points: the elementary and secondary schooling in *Lemon* came at an impressionable age; the aided schools were "under the general supervision" of the Roman Catholic diocese; each had a local Catholic parish that assumed "ultimate financial responsibility" for it; the principals of the schools were usually appointed by church authorities; religion "pervade[d] the school system"; teachers were specifically instructed by the "Handbook of School Regulations" that "[r]eligious formation is not confined to formal courses; nor is it restricted to a single subject area." 403 U.S. at 617–618. These things made impossible what is crucial to a nonentangling aid program: the ability of the State to identify and subsidize separate secular functions carried out at the school, without on-the-site inspections being necessary to prevent diversion of the funds to sectarian purposes. The District Court gave primary importance to this consideration, and we cannot say it erred.

(4) As for political divisiveness, the District Court recognized that the annual nature of the subsidy, along with its promise of an increasing demand for state funds as the colleges' dependency grew, aggravated the danger of "[p]olitical fragmentation . . . on religious lines." *Lemon I*, 403 U.S., at 623. Nonetheless, the District Court found that the program "does not create a substantial danger of political entanglement." 387 F.Supp., at 1291. Several reasons were given. As was stated in *Tilton*, the danger of political divisiveness is "substantially less" when the aided institution is not an elementary or secondary school, but a college, "whose student constituency is not local but diverse and widely dispersed." 403 U.S., at 688–689. Furthermore, political divisiveness is diminished by the fact that the aid is extended to private colleges generally, more than two thirds of which have no religious affiliation; this is in sharp contrast to *Nyquist*, for example, where 95% of the aided schools were Roman Catholic parochial schools. Finally, the substantial autonomy of the colleges was thought to mitigate political divisiveness, in that controversies surrounding the aid program are not likely to involve the Catholic Church itself, or even the religious character of the schools, but only their "fiscal responsibility and educational requirements." 387 F.Supp., at 1290–1291.

The District Court's reasoning seems to us entirely sound. . . .

There is no exact science in gauging the entanglement of church and state. The wording of the test, which speaks of "*excessive* entanglement," itself makes that clear. The relevant factors we have identified are to be considered "cumulatively" in judging the degree of entanglement. Tilton v. Richardson, 403 U.S., at 688. They may cut different ways, as certainly they do here. In reaching the conclusion that it did, the District Court gave dominant importance to the character of the aided institutions and to its finding that they are capable of separating secular and religious functions. For the reasons stated above, we cannot say that the emphasis was misplaced, or the finding erroneous.

The judgment of the District Court is affirmed.

It is so ordered.

Mr. Justice White, with whom Mr. Justice Rehnquist joins, concurring in the judgment.

While I join in the judgment of the Court, I am unable to concur in the plurality opinion substantially for the reasons set forth in my opinions in Lemon v. Kurtzman, 403 U.S. 602 (1971) (*Lemon I*), and Committee for Public Education v. Nyquist, 413 U.S. 756 (1973). I am no more reconciled now to *Lemon I* than I was when it was decided. See *Nyquist,* supra, at 820 (White, J. dissenting). The threefold test of *Lemon I* imposes unnecessary, and, as I believe today's plurality opinion demonstrates, superfluous tests for establishing "when the State's involvement with religion passes the peril point" for First Amendment purposes. Id., at 822.

"It is enough for me that the [State is] financing a separable secular function of overriding importance in order to sustain the legislation here challenged." Lemon I, supra, at 664 (opinion of White, J.). As long as there is a secular legislative purpose, and as long as the primary effect of the legislation is neither to advance nor inhibit religion, I see no reason—particularly in light of the "sparse language of the Establishment Clause," Committee for Public Education v. Nyquist, supra, at 820—to take the constitutional inquiry further. See *Lemon I,* supra, at 661 (opinion of White, J.); *Nyquist,* supra, at 813 (opinion of White, J.). However, since 1970, the Court has added a third element to the inquiry: whether there is "an excessive government entanglement with religion." Walz v. Tax Comm'n, 397 U.S. 664, 674. I have never understood the constitutional foundation for this added element; it is at once both insolubly paradoxical, see Lemon I, supra, at 668, and—as the Court has conceded from the outset—a "blurred, indistinct and variable barrier." *Lemon I,* 403 U.S., at 614. It is not clear that the "weight and contours of entanglement as a separate constitutional criterion," *Nyquist,* supra, at 822, are any more settled now than when they first surfaced. Today's plurality opinion leaves the impression that the criterion really may not be "separate" at all. In affirming the District Court's conclusion that the legislation here does not create an "excessive entanglement" of church and state the plurality emphasizes with approval that "the District Court gave dominant importance to the character of the aided institutions and to its finding that they are capable of separating secular and religious functions." Yet these are the same factors upon which the plurality focus in concluding that the Maryland legislation satisfies the first part of the *Lemon I* test: that on the record the "appellee colleges are not 'pervasively sectarian,' "and that the aid at issue was capable of, and is in fact, extended only to "the secular side" of the appellee colleges' operations. It is unclear to me how the first and third parts of the *Lemon I* test are substantially different. The "excessive entanglement" test appears no less "curious and mystifying" than when it was first announced. *Lemon I,* supra, at 666.

I see no reason to indulge in the redundant exercise of evaluating the same facts and findings under a different label. No one in this case challenges the District Court's finding that the purpose of the legislation here is secular. And I do not disagree with the plurality that the primary effect of the aid program is not advancement of religion. That is enough in my view to sustain the aid programs against constitutional challenge, and I would say no more.

Mr. Justice Brennan, with whom Mr. Justice Marshall joins, dissenting.

I agree with Judge Bryan, dissenting from the judgment under review, that the Maryland Act *"in these instances* does in truth offend the Constitution by its provisions of funds, in that it exposes State money for use in advancing religion, no matter the vigilance to avoid it." 387 F.Supp., at 1298 (emphasis in original). Each of the institutions is a church-affiliated or church-related body.

The subsidiary findings concerning the role of religion on each of the campuses, summarized by the plurality opinion, conclusively establish that fact. In that circumstance, I agree with Judge Bryan that "[o]f telling decisiveness here is the payment of the grants directly to the colleges unmarked in purpose. . . . Presently the Act is simply a blunderbuss discharge of public funds to a church-affiliated or church-related college." Id., at 1298–1299. In other words, the Act provides for payment of general subsidies to religious institutions from public funds and I have heretofore expressed my view that "[g]eneral subsidies of religious activities would, of course, constitute impermissible state involvement with religion." Walz v. Tax Commission, 397 U.S. 664, 690 (1970) (concurring opinion). This is because general subsidies "tend to promote that type of interdependence between religion and state which the First Amendment was designed to prevent." Abington School Dist. v. Schempp, 374 U.S. 203, 236 (1963) (Brennan, J., concurring). "What the Framers meant to foreclose, and what our decisions under the Establishment Clause have forbidden, are those involvements of religions with secular institutions which . . . serve the essentially religious activities of religious institutions." Id., at 294–295. . . .

The discrete interests of government and religion are mutually best served when each avoids too close a proximity to the other. . . .

. . .

Mr. Justice Stewart, dissenting.

In my view, the decisive differences between this case and Tilton v. Richardson, 403 U.S. 672, lie in the nature of the theology courses that are a compulsory part of the curriculum at each of the appellee institutions and the type of governmental assistance provided to these church-affiliated colleges. In *Tilton* the Court emphasized that the theology courses were taught as academic subjects. . . .

. . . Here, by contrast, the District Court was unable to find that the compulsory religion courses were taught as an academic discipline. . . .

In the light of these findings, I cannot agree with the Court's assertion that there is "no constitutionally significant distinction" between the colleges in *Tilton* and those in the present case. The findings in *Tilton* clearly established that the federal building construction grants benefited academic institutions that made no attempt to inculcate the religious beliefs of the affiliated church. In the present case, by contrast, the compulsory theology courses may be "devoted to deepening religious experiences in the particular faith rather than to teaching theology as an academic discipline." 387 F.Supp., at 1288. In view of this salient characteristic of the appellee institutions and the noncategorical grants provided to them by the State of Maryland, I agree with the conclusion of the dissenting member of the three-judge court that the challenged Act "*in these instances* does in truth offend the Constitution by its provisions of funds, in that it exposes State money for use in advancing religion, no matter the vigilance to avoid it." Id., at 1298 (emphasis in the original).

For the reasons stated, and those expressed by Mr. Justice Brennan and Mr. Justice Stevens, I dissent from the judgment and opinion of the Court.

Mr. Justice Stevens, dissenting.

My views are substantially those expressed by Mr. Justice Brennan. However, I would add emphasis to the pernicious tendency of a state subsidy to tempt religious schools to compromise their religious mission without wholly abandoning it. The disease of entanglement may infect a law discouraging wholesome religious activity as well as a law encouraging the propagation of a given faith.

Rosenberger v. Rector and Visitors of the University of Virginia

___ U.S. ___, 115 S.Ct. 2510, 132 L.Ed.2d 700 (1995).

Justice Kennedy delivered the opinion of the Court.

The University of Virginia, [a state university] ... , authorizes the payment of outside contractors for the printing costs of a variety of student publications. It withheld any authorization for payments on behalf of petitioners for the sole reason that their student paper "primarily promotes or manifests a particular belie[f] in or about a deity or an ultimate reality." That the paper did promote or manifest views within the defined exclusion seems plain enough. The challenge is to the University's regulation and its denial of authorization, the case raising issues under the Speech and Establishment Clauses of the First Amendment.

I

. . .

Before a student group is eligible to submit bills from its outside contractors for payment by the fund described below, it must become a "Contracted Independent Organization" (CIO). CIO status is available to any group the majority of whose members are students, whose managing officers are fulltime students, and that complies with certain procedural requirements. . . .

All CIOs may exist and operate at the University, but some are also entitled to apply for funds from the Student Activities Fund (SAF). ... The SAF receives its money from a mandatory fee of $14 per semester assessed to each full-time student. . . .

Some, but not all, CIOs may submit disbursement requests to the SAF. ...The Guidelines ... specify ... that the costs of certain activities of CIOs that are otherwise eligible for funding will not be reimbursed by the SAF. The student activities which are excluded from SAF support are religious activities, philanthropic contributions and activities, political activities, activities that would jeopardize the University's tax exempt status, those which involve payment of honoraria or similar fees, or social entertainment or related expenses. The prohibition on "political activities" is defined so that it is limited to electioneering and lobbying. The Guidelines provide that "[t]hese restrictions on funding political activities are not intended to preclude funding of any otherwise eligible student organization which ... espouses particular positions or ideological viewpoints, including those that may be unpopular or are not generally accepted." A "religious activity," by contrast, is defined as any activity that "primarily promotes or manifests a particular belie[f] in or about a deity or an ultimate reality."

. . .

Petitioners' organization, Wide Awake Productions (WAP), qualified as a CIO. Formed by petitioner Ronald Rosenberger and other undergraduates in 1990, WAP was established "[t]o publish a magazine of philosophical and religious expression," "[t]o facilitate discussion which fosters an atmosphere of sensitivity to and tolerance of Christian viewpoints," and "[t]o provide a unifying focus for Christians of multicultural backgrounds." WAP publishes Wide Awake: A Christian Perspective at the University of Virginia. The paper's Christian viewpoint was evident from the first issue, in which its editors wrote that the journal "offers a Christian perspective on both personal and community issues, especially those relevant to college students at the University of Virginia." The editors committed the paper to a two-fold mission: "to challenge Christians to live, in word and deed, according to the faith they proclaim and to encourage students to consider what a personal relationship with Jesus Christ means." The first issue had articles about racism, crisis pregnancy, stress, prayer, C.S. Lewis' ideas about evil and free will, and reviews of religious music. In the next two issues, Wide Awake featured stories about homosexuality, Christian missionary work, and eating disorders, as well as music reviews and interviews with University professors. Each page of Wide Awake, and the end of each article or review, is marked by a cross. The advertisements carried in Wide Awake also reveal the Christian perspective of the journal. For the most part, the advertisers are churches, centers for Christian study, or Christian bookstores. By June 1992, WAP had distributed about 5,000 copies of Wide Awake to University students, free of charge.

WAP had acquired CIO status soon after it was organized. This is an important consideration in this case, for had it been a "religious organization," WAP would not have been accorded CIO status. As defined by the Guidelines, a "religious organization" is "an organization whose purpose is to practice a devotion to an acknowledged ultimate reality or deity." At no stage in this controversy has the University contended that WAP is such an organization.

A few months after being given CIO status, WAP requested the SAF to pay its printer $5,862 for the costs of printing its newspaper. The Appropriations Committee of the Student Council denied WAP's request on the ground that Wide Awake was a "religious activity" within the meaning of the Guidelines, i.e., that the newspaper "promote[d] or manifest[ed] a particular belie[f] in or about a deity or an ultimate reality." ...

... WAP, Wide Awake, and three of its editors and members filed suit in the United States District Court for the Western District of Virginia ... They alleged that refusal to authorize payment of the printing costs of the publication, solely on the basis of its religious editorial viewpoint, violated their rights to freedom of speech and press, to the free exercise of religion, and to equal protection of the law. ... The suit sought damages for the costs of printing the paper, injunctive and declaratory relief, and attorney's fees.

On cross-motions for summary judgment, the District Court ruled for the University ...

The United States Court of Appeals for the Fourth Circuit ... affirmed ..., concluding that the discrimination by the University was justified by the "compelling interest in maintaining strict separation of church and state."

II

It is axiomatic that the government may not regulate speech based on its substantive content or the message it conveys. ...

... [T]he State [is forbidden] from exercising viewpoint discrimination, even when the limited public forum is one of its own creation. In a case involving a school district's provision of school facilities for private uses, we declared that "[t]here is no question that the District, like the private owner of property, may legally preserve the property under its control for the use to which it is dedicated." Lamb's Chapel v. Center Moriches Union Free School

Dist., 508 U.S. 384, ___ (1993). The necessities of confining a forum to the limited and legitimate purposes for which it was created may justify the State in reserving it for certain groups or for the discussion of certain topics. . . . Once it has opened a limited forum, however, the State must respect the lawful boundaries it has itself set. . . . Thus, in determining whether the State is acting to preserve the limits of the forum it has created so that the exclusion of a class of speech is legitimate, we have observed a distinction between, on the one hand, content discrimination, which may be permissible if it preserves the purposes of that limited forum, and, on the other hand, viewpoint discrimination, which is presumed impermissible when directed against speech otherwise within the forum's limitations. . . .

The SAF is a forum more in a metaphysical than in a spatial or geographic sense, but the same principles are applicable. . . . The most recent and most apposite case is our decision in *Lamb's Chapel*, supra. There, a school district had opened school facilities for use after school hours by community groups for a wide variety of social, civic, and recreational purposes. The district, however, had enacted a formal policy against opening facilities to groups for religious purposes. . . . Our conclusion was unanimous: "[I]t discriminates on the basis of viewpoint to permit school property to be used for the presentation of all views about family issues and child-rearing except those dealing with the subject matter from a religious standpoint." . . .

The University does acknowledge (as it must in light of our precedents) that "ideologically driven attempts to suppress a particular point of view are presumptively unconstitutional in funding, as in other contexts," but insists that this case does not present that issue because the Guidelines draw lines based on content, not viewpoint. As we have noted, discrimination against one set of views or ideas is but a subset or particular instance of the more general phenomenon of content discrimination. . . . And, it must be acknowledged, the distinction is not a precise one. It is, in a sense, something of an understatement to speak of religious thought and discussion as just a viewpoint, as distinct from a comprehensive body of thought. The nature of our origins and destiny and their dependence upon the existence of a divine being have been subjects of philosophic inquiry throughout human history. We conclude, nonetheless, that here, as in *Lamb's Chapel*, viewpoint discrimination is the proper way to interpret the University's objections to Wide Awake. By the very terms of the SAF prohibition, the University does not exclude religion as a subject matter but selects for disfavored treatment those student journalistic efforts with religious editorial viewpoints. Religion may be a vast area of inquiry, but it also provides, as it did here, a specific premise, a perspective, a standpoint from which a variety of subjects may be discussed and considered. The prohibited perspective, not the general subject matter, resulted in the refusal to make third-party payments, for the subjects discussed were otherwise within the approved category of publications.

The dissent's assertion that no viewpoint discrimination occurs because the Guidelines discriminate against an entire class of viewpoints reflects an insupportable assumption that all debate is bipolar and that anti-religious speech is the only response to religious speech. Our understanding of the complex and multifaceted nature of public discourse has not embraced such a contrived description of the marketplace of ideas. If the topic of debate is, for example, racism, then exclusion of several views on that problem is just as offensive to the First Amendment as exclusion of only one. It is as objectionable to exclude both a theistic and an atheistic perspective on the debate as it is to exclude one, the other, or yet another political, economic, or social viewpoint. The dissent's declaration that debate is not skewed so long as multiple voices are silenced is simply wrong; the debate is skewed in multiple ways.

The University's denial of WAP's request for third-party payments in the present case is based upon viewpoint discrimination not unlike the discrimination the school district relied upon in Lamb's Chapel and that we found invalid. . . .

The University tries to escape the consequences of our holding in *Lamb's Chapel* by urging that this case involves the provision of funds rather than access to facilities. . . . Were the reasoning of Lamb's Chapel to apply to funding decisions as well as to those involving access to facilities, it is urged, its holding "would become a judicial juggernaut, constitutionalizing the ubiquitous content-based decisions that schools, colleges, and other government entities routinely make in the allocation of public funds."

To this end the University relies on our assurance in Widmar v. Vincent, [454 U.S. 263 (1981).] There, in the course of striking down a public university's exclusion of religious groups from use of school facilities made available to all other student groups, we stated: "Nor do we question the right of the University to make academic judgments as to how best to allocate scarce resources." 454 U. S., at 276. The quoted language in *Widmar* was but a proper recognition of the principle that when the State is the speaker, it may make content-based choices. When the University determines the content of the education it provides, it is the University speaking, and we have permitted the government to regulate the content of what is or is not expressed when it is the speaker or when it enlists private entities to convey its own message. . . . When the government disburses public funds to private entities to convey a governmental message, it may take legitimate and appropriate steps to ensure that its message is neither garbled nor distorted by the grantee. . . .

It does not follow, however, and we did not suggest in *Widmar*, that viewpoint-based restrictions are proper when the University does not itself speak or subsidize transmittal of a message it favors but instead expends funds to encourage a diversity of views from private speakers. A holding that the University may not discriminate based on the viewpoint of private persons whose speech it facilitates does not restrict the University's own speech, which is controlled by different principles. . . .

. . .

The University urges that, from a constitutional standpoint, funding of speech differs from provision of access to facilities because money is scarce and physical facilities are not. Beyond the fact that in any given case this proposition might not be true as an empirical matter, the underlying premise that the University could discriminate based on viewpoint if demand for space exceeded its availability is wrong as well. The government cannot justify viewpoint discrimination among private speakers on the economic fact of scarcity. Had the meeting rooms in Lamb's Chapel been scarce, had the demand been greater than the supply, our decision would have been no different. It would have been incumbent on the State, of course, to ration or allocate the scarce resources on some acceptable neutral principle; but nothing in our decision indicated that scarcity would give the State the right to exercise viewpoint discrimination that is otherwise impermissible.

. . .

III

Before its brief on the merits in this Court, the University had argued at all stages of the litigation that inclusion of WAP's contractors in SAF funding authorization would violate the Establishment Clause. Indeed, that is the ground on which the University prevailed in the Court of Appeals. We granted certiorari on this question: "Whether the Establishment Clause compels a state university to exclude an otherwise eligible student publication from participation in the student activities fund, solely on the basis of its religious viewpoint, where such exclusion would violate the Speech and Press Clauses if the viewpoint of the publication were nonreligious." The University now seems to have abandoned this position ... That the University itself no longer presses the Establishment Clause claim is some indication that it lacks force; but as the Court of Appeals rested its judgment on the point and our dissenting colleagues would find it determinative, it must be addressed.

. . .

A central lesson of our decisions is that a significant factor in upholding governmental programs in the face of Establishment Clause attack is their neutrality towards religion. We have decided a series of cases addressing the receipt of government benefits where religion or religious views are implicated in some degree. ...More than once have we rejected the position that the Establishment Clause even justifies, much less requires, a refusal to extend free speech rights to religious speakers who participate in broad-reaching government programs neutral in design. See *Lamb's Chapel*, 508 U. S., at ___ ...

The governmental program here is neutral toward religion. There is no suggestion that the University created it to advance religion or adopted some ingenious device with the purpose of aiding a religious cause. The object of the SAF is to open a forum for speech and to support various student enterprises, including the publication of newspapers, in recognition of the diversity and creativity of student life. ...WAP did not seek a subsidy because of its Christian editorial viewpoint; it sought funding as a student journal, which it was.

The neutrality of the program distinguishes the student fees from a tax levied for the direct support of a church or group of churches. A tax of that sort, of course, would run contrary to Establishment Clause concerns dating from the earliest days of the Republic. The apprehensions of our predecessors involved the levying of taxes upon the public for the sole and exclusive purpose of establishing and supporting specific sects. The exaction here, by contrast, is a student activity fee designed to reflect the reality that student life in its many dimensions includes the necessity of wide-ranging speech and inquiry and that student expression is an integral part of the University's educational mission. ...[T]he $14 paid each semester by the students is not a general tax designed to raise revenue for the University. ...The SAF cannot be used for unlimited purposes, much less the illegitimate purpose of supporting one religion. Much like the arrangement in *Widmar*, the money goes to a special fund from which any group of students with CIO status can draw for purposes consistent with the University's educational mission; and to the extent the student is interested in speech, withdrawal is permitted to cover the whole spectrum of speech, whether it manifests a religious view, an antireligious view, or neither. Our decision, then, cannot be read as addressing an expenditure from a general tax fund. Here, the disbursements from the fund go to private contractors for the cost of printing that which is protected under the Speech Clause of the First Amendment. This is a far cry from a general public assessment designed and effected to provide financial support for a church.

Government neutrality is apparent in the State's overall scheme in a further meaningful respect. The program respects the critical difference "between government speech endorsing religion, which the Establishment Clause forbids, and private speech endorsing religion, which the Free Speech and Free Exercise Clauses protect." ... The University has taken pains to disassociate itself from the private speech involved in this case. The Court of Appeals' apparent concern that Wide Awake's religious orientation would be attributed to the University is not a plausible fear, and there is no real likelihood that the speech in question is being either endorsed or coerced by the State ...

The Court of Appeals (and the dissent) are correct to extract from our decisions the principle that we have recognized special Establishment Clause dangers where the government makes direct money payments to sectarian institutions ... The error is not in identifying the principle but in believing that it controls this case. Even assuming that WAP is no different from a church and that its speech is the same as the religious exercises conducted in *Widmar* (two points much in doubt), the Court of Appeals decided a case that was, in essence, not before it, and the dissent would have us do the same. We do not confront a case where, even under a neutral program that includes nonsectarian recipients, the government is making direct money payments to an institution or group that is engaged in religious activity. Neither the Court of Appeals nor the dissent, we believe, takes sufficient cognizance of the undisputed fact that no public funds flow directly to WAP's coffers.

It does not violate the Establishment Clause for a public university to grant access to its facilities on a religion-neutral basis to a wide spectrum of student groups, including groups which use meeting rooms for sectarian activities, accompanied by some devotional exercises. ... This is so even where the upkeep, maintenance, and repair of the facilities attributed to those uses is paid from a student activities fund to which students are required to contribute. *Widmar*, supra, at 265. The government usually acts by spending money. Even the provision of a meeting room, as in ... *Widmar*, involved governmental expenditure, if only in the form of electricity and heating or cooling costs. The error made by the Court of Appeals, as well as by the dissent, lies in focusing on the money that is undoubtedly expended by the government, rather than on the nature of the benefit received by the recipient. ... If a religious student organization obtained access on that religion-neutral basis and used a computer to compose or a printer or copy machine to print speech with a religious content or viewpoint, the State's action in providing the group with access would no more violate the Establishment Clause than would giving those groups access to an assembly hall. ... Any benefit to religion is incidental to the government's provision of secular services for secular purposes on a religion-neutral basis. Printing is a routine, secular, and recurring attribute of student life.

By paying outside printers, the University in fact attains a further degree of separation from the student publication, for it avoids the duties of supervision, escapes the costs of upkeep, repair, and replacement attributable to student use, and has a clear record of costs. ...

Were the dissent's view to become law, it would require the University, in order to avoid a constitutional violation, to scrutinize the content of student speech, lest the expression in question-speech otherwise protected by the Constitution-contain too great a religious content. The dissent, in fact, anticipates such censorship as "crucial" in distinguishing between "works characterized by the evangelism of Wide Awake and writing that merely happens to express views that a given religion might approve." That eventuality raises the specter of governmental censorship, to ensure that all student writings and publications meet some baseline standard of secular orthodoxy. To impose that standard on student speech at a university is to imperil the very sources of free speech and expression. As we recognized in *Widmar*, official censorship would be far more inconsistent with the Establishment Clause's dictates than would governmental provision of secular printing services on a religion-blind basis. ...Merely to draw the distinction would require the university—and ultimately the courts—to inquire into the significance of words and practices to different religious faiths, and in varying circumstances by the same faith. Such inquiries would tend inevitably to entangle the State with religion in a manner forbidden by our cases. ...

* * *

... The viewpoint discrimination inherent in the University's regulation required public officials to scan and interpret student publications to discern their underlying philosophic assumptions respecting religious theory and belief. That course of action was a denial of the right of free speech and would risk fostering a pervasive bias or hostility to religion, which could undermine the very neutrality the Establishment Clause requires. There is no Establishment Clause violation in the University's honoring its duties under the Free Speech Clause.

The judgment of the Court of Appeals must be, and is, reversed. It is so ordered.

Justice O'Connor, concurring.

. . .

This case lies at the intersection of the principle of government neutrality and the prohibition on state funding of religious activities. ...Not to finance Wide Awake, according to petitioners, violates the principle of neutrality by sending a message of hostility toward religion. To finance Wide Awake, argues the University, violates the prohibition on direct state funding of religious activities.

When two bedrock principles so conflict, understandably neither can provide the definitive answer. Reliance on categorical platitudes is unavailing. Resolution instead depends on the hard task of judging-sifting through the details and determining whether the challenged program offends the Establishment Clause. Such judgment requires courts to draw lines, sometimes quite fine, based on the particular facts of each case. ...

. . .

So it is in this case. The nature of the dispute does not admit of categorical answers, nor should any be inferred from the Court's decision today. Instead, certain considerations specific to the program at issue lead me to conclude that by providing the same assistance to Wide Awake that it does to other publications, the University would not be endorsing the magazine's religious perspective.

First, the student organizations, at the University's insistence, remain strictly independent of the University. ...Any reader of Wide Awake would be on notice of the publication's independence from the University. ...

Second, financial assistance is distributed in a manner that ensures its use only for permissible purposes. A student organization seeking assistance must submit disbursement requests; if approved, the funds are paid directly to the third-party vendor and do not pass through the organization's coffers. This ...

ensures that the funds are used only to further the University's purpose in maintaining a free and robust marketplace of ideas, from whatever perspective. This feature also makes this case analogous to a school providing equal access to a generally available printing press (or other physical facilities), and unlike a block grant to religious organizations.

Third, assistance is provided to the religious publication in a context that makes improbable any perception of government endorsement of the religious message. . . .

Finally, . . . Unlike monies dispensed from state or federal treasuries, the Student Activities Fund is collected from students who themselves administer the fund and select qualifying recipients only from among those who originally paid the fee. The government neither pays into nor draws from this common pool . . . The Student Activities Fund, then, represents not government resources, whether derived from tax revenue, sales of assets, or otherwise, but a fund that simply belongs to the students.

The Court's decision today therefore neither trumpets the supremacy of the neutrality principle nor signals the demise of the funding prohibition in Establishment Clause jurisprudence. . . . [P]articular features of the University's program—such as the explicit disclaimer, the disbursement of funds directly to third-party vendors, the vigorous nature of the forum at issue, and the possibility for objecting students to opt out—convince me that providing such assistance in this case would not carry the danger of impermissible use of public funds to endorse Wide Awake's religious message.

Subject to these comments, I join the opinion of the Court.

Justice Thomas, concurring.

I agree with the Court's opinion and join it in full, but I write separately to express my disagreement with the historical analysis put forward by the dissent. . . .

. . .

Legal commentators have disagreed about the historical lesson to take from the Assessment Controversy. For some, the experience in Virginia is consistent with the view that the Framers saw the Establishment Clause simply as a prohibition on governmental preferences for some religious faiths over others. See R. Cord, Separation of Church and State: Historical Fact and Current Fiction 20–23 (1982); Smith, Getting Off on the Wrong Foot and Back on Again: A Reexamination of the History of the Framing of the Religion Clauses of the First Amendment and a Critique of the Reynolds and Everson Decisions, 20 Wake Forest L. Rev. 569, 590–591 (1984). Other commentators have rejected this view, concluding that the Establishment Clause forbids not only government preferences for some religious sects over others, but also government preferences for religion over irreligion. See, e.g., Laycock, "Nonpreferential" Aid to Religion: A False Claim About Original Intent, 27 Wm. & Mary L. Rev. 875, 875 (1986).

I find much to commend the former view. . . .

But resolution of this debate is not necessary to decide this case. Under any understanding of the Assessment Controversy, the history cited by the dissent cannot support the conclusion that the Establishment Clause "categorically condemn[s] state programs directly aiding religious activity" when that aid is part of a neutral program available to a wide array of beneficiaries. . Even if Madison believed that the principle of nonestablishment of religion precluded government financial support for religion per se (in the sense of government benefits specifically targeting religion), there is no indication that at the time of the framing he took the dissent's extreme view that the government must discriminate against religious adherents by excluding them from more generally available financial subsidies.

. . .

Justice Souter, with whom Justice Stevens, Justice Ginsburg, and Justice Breyer join, dissenting.

The Court today, for the first time, approves direct funding of core religious activities by an arm of the State. It does so, however, only after erroneous treatment of some familiar principles of law implementing the First Amendment's Establishment and Speech Clauses, and by viewing the very funds in question as beyond the reach of the Establishment Clause's funding restrictions as such. Because there is no warrant for distinguishing among public funding sources for purposes of applying the First Amendment's prohibition of religious establishment, I would hold that the University's refusal to support petitioners' religious activities is compelled by the Establishment Clause. I would therefore affirm.

I

. . .

A

. . .

Using public funds for the direct subsidization of preaching the word is categorically forbidden under the Establishment Clause, and if the Clause was meant to accomplish nothing else, it was meant to bar this use of public money. Evidence on the subject antedates even the Bill of Rights itself, as may be seen in the writings of Madison . . . Four years before the First Congress proposed the First Amendment, Madison gave his opinion on the legitimacy of using public funds for religious purposes, in the Memorial and Remonstrance Against Religious Assessments, which played the central role in ensuring the defeat of the Virginia tax assessment bill in 1786 and framed the debate upon which the Religion Clauses stand . . .

Madison wrote against a background in which nearly every Colony had exacted a tax for church support . . . Madison's Remonstrance captured the colonists' "conviction that individual religious liberty could be achieved best under a government which was stripped of all power to tax, to support, or otherwise to assist any or all religions, or to interfere with the beliefs of any religious individual or group." . . . Their sentiment as expressed by Madison in Virginia, led not only to the defeat of Virginia's tax assessment bill, but also directly to passage of the Virginia Bill for Establishing Religious Freedom, written by Thomas Jefferson. That bill's preamble declared that "to compel a man to furnish contributions of money for the propagation of opinions which he disbelieves, is sinful and tyrannical," . . . and its text provided "[t]hat no man shall be compelled to frequent or support any religious worship, place, or ministry whatsoever . . . ," . . .

The principle against direct funding with public money is patently violated by the contested use of today's student activity fee. . . The University exercises the power of the State to compel a student to pay it, . . . and the use of any part of it for the direct support of religious activity thus strikes at what we have repeatedly held to be the heart of the prohibition on establishment. . . .

The Court, accordingly, has never before upheld direct state funding of the sort of proselytizing published in Wide Awake and, in fact, has categorically condemned state programs directly aiding religious activity . . .

. . .

B

. . .

. . . In the doubtful cases (those not involving direct public funding), where there is initially room for argument about a law's effect, evenhandedness serves to weed out those laws that impermissibly advance religion by channeling aid to it exclusively. Evenhandedness is therefore a prerequisite to further enquiry into the constitutionality of a doubtful law, but evenhandedness goes no further. It does not guarantee success under Establishment Clause scrutiny.

. . .

C

. . .

. . . The common factual thread running through *Widmar* and *Lamb's Chapel*, is that a governmental institution created a limited forum for the use of students in a school or college, or for the public at large, but sought to exclude speakers with religious messages. . . . [E]ach case drew ultimately on unexceptionable Speech Clause doctrine treating the evangelist, the Salvation Army, the millennialist or the Hare Krishna like any other speaker in a public forum. It was the preservation of free speech on the model of the street corner that supplied the justification going beyond the requirement of evenhandedness.

. . . The analogy breaks down entirely, however, if the cases are read more broadly than the Court wrote them, to cover more than forums for literal speaking. There is no traditional street corner printing provided by the government on equal terms to all comers, and the forum cases cannot be lifted to a higher plane of generalization without admitting that new economic benefits are being extended directly to religion in clear violation of the principle barring direct aid. The argument from economic equivalence thus breaks down on recognizing that the direct state aid it would support is not mitigated by the street corner analogy in the service of free speech. Absent that, the rule against direct aid stands as a bar to printing services as well as printers.

. . .

II

Given the dispositive effect of the Establishment Clause's bar to funding the magazine, there should be no need to decide whether in the absence of this bar the University would violate the Free Speech Clause by limiting funding as it has done. . . . But the Court's speech analysis may have independent application, and its flaws should not pass unremarked.

. . .

. . . Other things being equal, viewpoint discrimination occurs when government allows one message while prohibiting the messages of those who can reasonably be expected to respond. . . . It is precisely this element of taking sides in a public debate that identifies viewpoint discrimination and makes it the most pernicious of all distinctions based on content. Thus, if government assists those espousing one point of view, neutrality requires it to assist those espousing opposing points of view, as well.

There is no viewpoint discrimination in the University's application of its Guidelines to deny funding to Wide Awake. Under those Guidelines, a "religious activit[y]," which is not eligible for funding, is "an activity which primarily promotes or manifests a particular belief(s) in or about a deity or an ultimate reality." It is clear that this is the basis on which Wide Awake Productions was denied funding. . . .

If the Guidelines were written or applied so as to limit only such Christian advocacy and no other evangelical efforts that might compete with it, the discrimination would be based on viewpoint. But that is not what the regulation authorizes; it applies to Muslim and Jewish and Buddhist advocacy as well as to Christian. And since it limits funding to activities promoting or manifesting a particular belief not only "in" but "about" a deity or ultimate reality, it applies to agnostics and atheists as well as it does to deists and theists. . . The Guidelines, and their application to Wide Awake, thus do not skew debate by funding one position but not its competitors. As understood by their application to Wide Awake, they simply deny funding for hortatory speech that "primarily promotes or manifests" any view on the merits of religion; they deny funding for the entire subject matter of religious apologetics.

. . .

The Guidelines are thus substantially different from the access restriction considered in *Lamb's Chapel* . . .

. . . [I]n *Lamb's Chapel* we unanimously determined that the access restriction, as applied to a speaker wishing to discuss family values from a Christian perspective, impermissibly distinguished between speakers on the basis of viewpoint. . . . Equally obvious is the distinction between that case and this one, where the regulation is being applied, not to deny funding for those who discuss issues in general from a religious viewpoint, but to those engaged in promoting or opposing religious conversion and religious observances as such. If this amounts to viewpoint discrimination, the Court has all but eviscerated the line between viewpoint and content.

. . .

III

Since I cannot see the future I cannot tell whether today's decision portends much more than making a shambles out of student activity fees in public colleges. Still, my apprehension is whetted by Chief Justice Burger's warning in Lemon v. Kurtzman, 403 U.S. 602, 624 (1971): "in constitutional adjudication some steps, which when taken were thought to approach 'the verge,' have become the platform for yet further steps. A certain momentum develops in constitutional theory and it can be a 'downhill thrust' easily set in motion but difficult to retard or stop."

I respectfully dissent.

WITTERS v. WASHINGTON DEPARTMENT OF SERVICES FOR THE BLIND, 474 U.S. 481 (1986). Witters was a blind person studying at a private Christian college, preparing for a career as a pastor, missionary, or church youth director. He applied for a grant under a Washington statute providing funds for education and training of the visually handicapped. The Washington Supreme Court concluded that the establishment clause required denial of the aid request, because providing financial assistance would have the principal effect of aiding religion. The Supreme Court reversed. Justice Marshall's opinion for the Court concluded that providing aid to Witters to finance his education did not "advance religion in a manner inconsistent with the" establishment clause. The Court relied on three factors: the aid was paid directly to the student, and ultimately flowed to the religious institution only as a result of the recipient's choice; funding did not create financial incentives for students to seek sectarian education, but was made available for all forms of education and training; and, "importantly," no significant portion of aid under the program went to religious institutions. The Court did not rely upon Mueller v. Allen, 463 U.S. 388 (1983) p. 1643, supra. Justice Powell's concurrence, joined by Chief Justice Burger and Justice Rehnquist, and Justice O'Connor's concurrence, emphasized that *Mueller* was controlling so long as aid was provided to students without reference to what college the student chose or whether the student sought training for a religious career. Justice White, who joined the Court's opinion, stated that he agreed "with most of Justice Powell's concurring opinion with respect to the relevance of *Mueller*."

ZOBREST v. CATALINA FOOTHILLS SCHOOL DISTRICT, 509 U.S. 1 (1993). The Court held that it did not violate the Establishment Clause to provide a government-paid sign-language interpreter for a deaf student in a Roman Catholic high school. Justice Rehnquist's opinion for the Court held that *Witters* controlled. "The service at issue in this case is part of a general government program that distributes benefits neutrally to any child qualifying as 'handicapped' ... without regard to the 'sectarian-nonsectarian, or public-nonpublic nature' of the school the child attends. By according parents freedom to select a school of their choice, the statute ensures that a government-paid interpreter will be present in a sectarian school only as a result of the private decision of individual parents." Justice Blackmun's dissent, joined by Justice Souter,[a] noted that the Court had never before "authorized a public employee to participate directly in religious indoctrination." In *Witters*, "governmental involvement ended with the disbursement of funds."

SECTION 2. THE FREE EXERCISE OF RELIGION

PROTECTION OF RELIGIOUS EXPRESSION AS FREE SPEECH

Many of the cases in the preceding chapters on freedom of speech involved religious expression. The flag salute cases provide a graphic example of the manner in which the constitutional protection of freedom of speech can protect religious expression and belief. In Minersville School District v. Gobitis, 310 U.S. 586 (1940), the Court sustained a requirement that pupils participate in a compulsory flag salute at the beginning of the school day. Justice Frankfurter's opinion treated the issue as a problem under the free exercise clause—involving constitutional protection for conduct compelled by religious belief. Three years later, in West Virginia Board of Education v. Barnette, 319 U.S. 624 (1943), the case was overruled. Justice Jackson's opinion found that it was not necessary to confront Justice Frankfurter's conclusion that the free exercise clause did not relieve religious dissenters from the legal obligation to obey an otherwise-valid law. The issue, instead, was whether the speech clause of the first amendment prohibited government compulsion requiring an individual to profess a belief. The Court concluded that the free speech clause prohibited compulsory flag

---

[a] Justices Stevens & O'Connor joined Justices Blackmun and Souter in arguing that the case should be remanded without reaching the constitutional issue.

salutes, whether an individual's objection was religious or not. (The free speech analysis, of the *Barnette* case, and the later decision in Wooley v. Maynard, 430 U.S. 705 (1977), is summarized, supra, at pp. 1455–1457.)

Sherbert v. Verner

374 U.S. 398, 83 S.Ct. 1790, 10 L.Ed.2d 965 (1963).

Mr. Justice Brennan delivered the opinion of the Court.

Appellant, a member of the Seventh-day Adventist Church was discharged by her South Carolina employer because she would not work on Saturday, the Sabbath Day of her faith. When she was unable to obtain other employment because from conscientious scruples she would not take Saturday work, she filed a claim for unemployment compensation benefits under the South Carolina Unemployment Compensation Act.... The appellee Employment Security Commission, in administrative proceedings under the statute, found that appellant's restriction upon her availability for Saturday work brought her within the provision disqualifying for benefits insured workers who fail, without good cause, to accept "suitable work when offered ... by the employment office or the employer...." The Commission's finding was sustained ... by the South Carolina Supreme Court,....[4]....

II.

. . .

Significantly South Carolina expressly saves the Sunday worshiper from having to make the kind of choice which we were hold infringes the Sabbatarian's religious liberty. When in times of "national emergency" the textile plants are authorized by the State Commission of Labor to operate on Sunday, "no employee shall be required to work on Sunday ... who is conscientiously opposed to Sunday work...." The unconstitutionality of the disqualification of the Sabbatarian is thus compounded by the religious discrimination which South Carolina's general statutory scheme necessarily effects.

III.

We must next consider whether some compelling state interest enforced in the eligibility provisions of the South Carolina statute justifies the substantial

---

[4] It has been suggested that appellant is not within the class entitled to benefits under the South Carolina statute because her unemployment did not result from discharge or layoff due to lack of work. It is true that unavailability for work for some personal reasons not having to do with matters of conscience or religion has been held to be a basis of disqualification for benefits. But appellant claims that the Free Exercise Clause prevents the State from basing the denial of benefits upon the "personal reason" she gives for not working on Saturday. Where the consequence of disqualification so directly affects First Amendment rights, surely we should not conclude that every "personal reason" is a basis for disqualification in the absence of explicit language to that effect in the statute or decisions of the South Carolina Supreme Court. Nothing we have found in the statute or in

the cited decisions, and certainly nothing in the South Carolina Court's opinion in this case so construes the statute. Indeed, the contrary seems to have been that court's basic assumption, for if the eligibility provisions were thus limited, it would have been unnecessary for the court to have decided appellant's constitutional challenge to the application of the statute under the Free Exercise Clause.

Likewise, the decision of the State Supreme Court does not rest upon a finding that appellant was disqualified for benefits because she had been "discharged for misconduct"—by reason of her Saturday absences—within the meaning of § 68–114(2). That ground was not adopted by the South Carolina Supreme Court, and the appellees do not urge in this Court that the disqualification rests upon that ground.

infringement of appellant's First Amendment right. It is basic that no showing merely of a rational relationship to some colorable state interest would suffice; in this highly sensitive constitutional area, "[o]nly the gravest abuses, endangering paramount interests, give occasion for permissible limitation," Thomas v. Collins, 323 U.S. 516, 530. No such abuse or danger has been advanced in the present case. The appellees suggest no more than a possibility that the filing of fraudulent claims by unscrupulous claimants feigning religious objections to Saturday work might not only dilute the unemployment compensation fund but also hinder the scheduling by employers of necessary Saturday work. But that possibility is not apposite here because no such objection appears to have been made before the South Carolina Supreme Court, and we are unwilling to assess the importance of an asserted state interest without the views of the state court. Nor, if the contention had been made below, would the record appear to sustain it; there is no proof whatever to warrant such fears of malingering or deceit as those which the respondents now advance. Even if consideration of such evidence is not foreclosed by the prohibition against judicial inquiry into the truth or falsity of religious beliefs, United States v. Ballard, 322 U.S. 78—a question as to which we intimate no view since it is not before us—it is highly doubtful whether such evidence would be sufficient to warrant a substantial infringement of religious liberties. For even if the possibility of spurious claims did threaten to dilute the fund and disrupt the scheduling of work, it would plainly be incumbent upon the appellees to demonstrate that no alternative forms of regulation would combat such abuses without infringing First Amendment rights.

In these respects, then, the state interest asserted in the present case is wholly dissimilar to the interests which were found to justify the less direct burden upon religious practices in Braunfeld v. Brown, [366 U.S. 599 (1961)]. The Court recognized that the Sunday closing law which that decision sustained undoubtedly served "to make the practice of [the Orthodox Jewish merchants'] ... religious beliefs more expensive," 366 U.S., at 605. But the statute was nevertheless saved by a countervailing factor which finds no equivalent in the instant case—a strong state interest in providing one uniform day of rest for all workers. That secular objective could be achieved, the Court found, only by declaring Sunday to be that day of rest. Requiring exemptions for Sabbatarians, while theoretically possible, appeared to present an administrative problem of such magnitude, or to afford the exempted class so great a competitive advantage, that such a requirement would have rendered the entire statutory scheme unworkable. In the present case no such justifications underlie the determination of the state court that appellant's religion makes her ineligible to receive benefits.

IV.

... [We do not] declare the existence of a constitutional right to unemployment benefits on the part of all persons whose religious convictions are the cause of their unemployment. This is not a case in which an employee's religious convictions serve to make him a nonproductive member of society. Finally, nothing we say today constrains the States to adopt any particular form or scheme of unemployment compensation. Our holding today is only that South Carolina may not constitutionally apply the eligibility provisions so as to constrain a worker to abandon his religious convictions respecting the day of rest....

. . .

The judgment of the South Carolina Supreme Court is reversed and the case is remanded for further proceedings not inconsistent with this opinion.[a]

Mr. Justice Stewart, concurring in the result.

. . .

... I cannot agree that today's decision can stand consistently with Braunfeld v. Brown, supra. The Court says that there was a "less direct burden upon religious practices" in that case than in this. With all respect, I think the Court is mistaken, simply as a matter of fact. The *Braunfeld* case involved a state *criminal* statute....

The impact upon the appellant's religious freedom in the present case is considerably less onerous. We deal here not with a criminal statute, but with the particularized administration of South Carolina's Unemployment Compensation Act. Even upon the unlikely assumption that the appellant could not find suitable non-Saturday employment, the appellant at the worst would be denied a maximum of 22 weeks of compensation payments. I agree with the Court that the possibility of that denial is enough to infringe upon the appellant's constitutional right to the free exercise of her religion. But it is clear to me that in order to reach this conclusion the Court must explicitly reject the reasoning of *Braunfeld v. Brown.* I think the *Braunfeld* case was wrongly decided and should be overruled, and accordingly I concur in the result reached by the Court in the case before us.

Mr. Justice Harlan, whom Mr. Justice White joins, dissenting.

. . .

South Carolina's Unemployment Compensation Law was enacted in 1936 in response to the grave social and economic problems that arose during the depression of that period.... Thus the purpose of the legislature was to tide people over, and to avoid social and economic chaos, during periods when *work was unavailable....*

The South Carolina Supreme Court has uniformly applied this law in conformity with its clearly expressed purpose. It has consistently held that one is not "available for work" if his unemployment has resulted not from the inability of industry to provide a job but rather from personal circumstances, no matter how compelling. The reference to "involuntary unemployment" in the legislative statement of policy, whatever a sociologist, philosopher, or theologian might say, has been interpreted not to embrace such personal circumstances.... Thus in no proper sense can it be said that the State discriminated against the appellant on the basis of her religious beliefs or that she was denied benefits *because* she was a Seventh-day Adventist. She was denied benefits just as any other claimant would be denied benefits who was not "available for work" for personal reasons.[1]

---

[a] A concurring opinion by Justice Douglas is omitted.

[1] I am completely at a loss to understand note 4 of the Court's opinion. Certainly the Court is not basing today's decision on the unsupported supposition that *some* day, the South Carolina Supreme Court may conclude that there is *some personal* reason for unemployment that may not disqualify a claimant for relief. In any event, I submit it is perfectly clear that South Carolina would not compensate persons who became unemployed for *any* personal reason, as distinguished from layoffs or lack of work, since the State Supreme Court's decisions make it plain that such persons would not be regarded as "available for work" within the manifest meaning of the eligibility requirements. Nor can I understand what this Court means when it says that "if the eligibility provisions were thus limited, it would have been unnecessary for the [South Carolina] court to have decided appellant's constitutional challenge...."

... What the Court is holding is that if the State chooses to condition unemployment compensation on the applicant's availability for work, it is constitutionally compelled to *carve out an exception*—and to provide benefits— for those whose unavailability is due to their religious convictions.[2]

. . .

THOMAS v. REVIEW BOARD OF THE INDIANA EMPLOYMENT SECURITY DIVISION, 450 U.S. 707 (1981). Thomas, a Jehovah's Witness, quit his job because of religious opposition to participating in the production of armaments, when his employer transferred him to a department making turrets for military tanks. He was denied unemployment compensation. The Indiana Supreme Court upheld the denial, because the unemployment compensation statute denied compensation to employees "who quit work voluntarily for personal reasons" that were not objectively job-related. Relying on Sherbert v. Verner, the Supreme Court reversed.

The sole dissenter, Justice Rehnquist, contended that Sherbert v. Verner should be overruled. In a footnote, he argued that *Sherbert* was distinguishable from *Thomas* because the Indiana statute had been construed to make *every* personal subjective reason for refusing employment a basis for disqualification.

Wisconsin v. Yoder

406 U.S. 205, 92 S.Ct. 1526, 32 L.Ed.2d 15 (1972).

[Respondents Yoder, Yutzy and Miller were members of the Amish religious sect and residents of Wisconsin where it was required that children attend school until the age of 16. Because of their religion's tenets, they refused to send their children (ages 14 and 15) to school after completing the eighth grade. They believe that by sending their children to high school they would not only expose themselves to possible censure of their church community, but also endanger their own salvation and that of their children. It was agreed that respondents' religious beliefs were sincere. Those beliefs required members of the community to make their living by farming or closely related activities. High school, and higher education generally, was objected to because the values taught were in marked contrast with Amish values and way of life. Respondents were convicted of violating the Wisconsin compulsory attendance law; the Supreme Court of Wisconsin reversed the conviction, sustaining respondents' claim under the free exercise clause of the first amendment.]

Mr. Chief Justice Burger delivered the opinion of the Court.

. . .

The essence of all that has been said and written on the subject is that only those interests of the highest order and those not otherwise served can overbalance legitimate claims to the free exercise of religion. We can accept it as settled, therefore, that however strong the State's interest in universal

---

[2] The Court does suggest, in a rather startling disclaimer, that its holding is limited in applicability to those whose religious convictions do not make them "nonproductive" members of society, noting that most of the Seventh-day Adventists in the Spartanburg area are employed. But surely this disclaimer cannot be taken seriously, for the Court cannot mean that the case would have come out differently if none of the Seventh-day Adventists in Spartanburg had been gainfully employed, or if the appellant's religion had prevented her from working on Tuesdays instead of Saturdays. Nor can the Court be suggesting that it will make a value judgment in each case as to whether a particular individual's religious convictions prevent him from being "productive." I can think of no more inappropriate function for this Court to perform.

compulsory education, it is by no means absolute to the exclusion or subordination of all other interests....

.   .   .

So long as compulsory education laws were confined to eight grades of elementary basic education imparted in a nearby rural schoolhouse, with a large proportion of students of the Amish faith, the Old Order Amish had little basis to fear that school attendance would expose their children to the worldly influence they reject. But modern compulsory secondary education in rural areas is now largely carried on in a consolidated school, often remote from the student's home and alien to his daily home life.... The conclusion is inescapable that secondary schooling, by exposing Amish children to worldly influences in terms of attitudes, goals and values contrary to beliefs, and by substantially interfering with the religious development of the Amish child and his integration into the way of life of the Amish faith community at the crucial adolescent state of development, contravenes the basic religious tenets and practice of the Amish faith, both as to the parent and the child....

In sum, the unchallenged testimony of acknowledged experts in education and religious history, almost 300 years of consistent practice, and strong evidence of a sustained faith pervading and regulating respondents' entire mode of life support the claim that enforcement of the State's requirement of compulsory formal education after the eighth grade would gravely endanger if not destroy the free exercise of respondents' religious beliefs.

.   .   .

The State advances two primary arguments in support of its system of compulsory education. It notes, as Thomas Jefferson pointed out early in our history, that some degree of education is necessary to prepare citizens to participate effectively and intelligently in our open political system if we are to preserve freedom and independence. Further, education prepares individuals to be self-reliant and self-sufficient participants in society. We accept these propositions.

However, the evidence adduced by the Amish in this case is persuasively to the effect that an additional one or two years of formal high school for Amish children in place of their long established program of informal vocational education would do little to serve those interests. Respondents' experts testified at trial, without challenge, that the value of all education must be assessed in terms of its capacity to prepare the child for life. It is one thing to say that compulsory education for a year or two beyond the eighth grade may be necessary when its goal is the preparation of the child for life in modern society as the majority live, but it is quite another if the goal of education be viewed as the preparation of the child for life in the separated agrarian community that is the keystone of the Amish faith. See Meyer v. Nebraska, 262 U.S., at 400....

Whatever their idiosyncrasies as seen by the majority, this record strongly shows that the Amish community has been a highly successful social unit within our society even if apart from the conventional "mainstream." Its members are productive and very law-abiding members of society; they reject public welfare in any of its usual modern forms. The Congress itself recognized their self-sufficiency by authorizing exemption of such groups as the Amish from the obligation to pay social security taxes.

It is neither fair nor correct to suggest that the Amish are opposed to education beyond the eighth grade level. What this record shows is that they are opposed to conventional formal education of the type provided by a certified high school because it comes at the child's crucial adolescent period of religious development....

The State, however, supports its interest in providing an additional one or two years of compulsory high school education to Amish children because of the possibility that some such children will choose to leave the Amish community, and that if this occurs they will be ill-equipped for life. The State argues that if Amish children leave their church they should not be in the position of making their way in the world without the education available in the one or two additional years the State requires. However, on this record, that argument is highly speculative. There is no specific evidence of the loss of Amish adherents by attrition, nor is there any showing that upon leaving the Amish community Amish children, with their practical agricultural training and habits of industry and self-reliance would become burdens on society because of educational shortcomings....

In these terms, Wisconsin's interest in compelling the school attendance of Amish children to age 16 emerges as somewhat less substantial than requiring such attendance for children generally. For, while agricultural employment is not totally outside the legitimate concerns of the child labor laws, employment of children under parental guidance and on the family farm from age 14 to age 16 is an ancient tradition which lies at the periphery of the objectives of such laws. There is no intimation that the Amish employment of their children on family farms is in any way deleterious to their health or that Amish parents exploit children at tender years. Any such inference would be contrary to the record before us. Moreover, employment of Amish children on the family farm does not present the undesirable economic aspects of eliminating jobs which might otherwise be held by adults....

Contrary to the suggestion of the dissenting opinion of Mr. Justice Douglas, our holding today in no degree depends on the assertion of the religious interest of the child as contrasted with that of the parents. It is the parents who are subject to prosecution here for failing to cause their children to attend school, and it is their right of free exercise, not that of their children, that must determine Wisconsin's power to impose criminal penalties on the parent....

Our holding in no way determines the proper resolution of possible competing interests of parents, children, and the State in an appropriate state court proceeding in which the power of the State is asserted on the theory that Amish parents are preventing their minor children from attending high school despite their expressed desires to the contrary. Recognition of the claim of the State in such a proceeding would, of course, call into question traditional concepts of parental control over the religious upbringing and education of their minor children recognized in this Court's past decisions. It is clear that such an intrusion by a State into family decisions in the area of religious training would give rise to grave questions of religious freedom comparable to those raised here and those presented in Pierce v. Society of Sisters. On this record we neither reach nor decide those issues....

For the reasons stated we hold, with the Supreme Court of Wisconsin, that the First and Fourteenth Amendments prevent the State from compelling respondents to cause their children to attend formal high school to age 16. Our disposition of this case, however, in no way alters our recognition of the obvious fact that courts are not school boards or legislatures, and are ill-equipped to determine the "necessity" of discrete aspects of a State's program of compulsory education....

Nothing we hold is intended to undermine the general applicability of the State's compulsory school attendance statutes or to limit the power of the State to promulgate reasonable standards that, while not impairing the free exercise of religion, provide for continuing agricultural vocational education under parental and church guidance by the Old Order Amish or others similarly situated. The States have had a long history of amicable and effective relationships with church-sponsored schools, and there is no basis for assuming that, in this related context, reasonable standards cannot be established concerning the content of the continuing vocational education of Amish children under parental guidance, provided always that state regulations are not inconsistent with what we have said in this opinion.

Affirmed.

Mr. Justice Powell and Mr. Justice Rehnquist took no part in the consideration or decision of this case.

Mr. Justice Stewart, with whom Mr. Justice Brennan joins, concurring.

. . .

This case in no way involves any questions regarding the right of the children of Amish parents to attend public high schools, or any other institutions of learning, if they wish to do so. As the Court points out, there is no suggestion whatever in the record that the religious beliefs of the children here concerned differ in any way from those of their parents. . . .

Mr. Justice White, with whom Mr. Justice Brennan and Mr. Justice Stewart, join, concurring.

Cases such as this one inevitably call for a delicate balancing of important but conflicting interests. I join the opinion and judgment of the Court because I cannot say that the State's interest in requiring two more years of compulsory education in the ninth and tenth grades outweighs the importance of the concededly sincere Amish religious practice to the survival of that sect.

. . .

I join the Court because the sincerity of the Amish religious policy here is uncontested, because the potential adverse impact of the state requirement is great and because the State's valid interest in education has already been largely satisfied by the eight years the children have already spent in school.

Mr. Justice Douglas, dissenting in part.

I agree with the Court that the religious scruples of the Amish are opposed to the education of their children beyond the grade schools, yet I disagree with the Court's conclusion that the matter is within the dispensation of parents alone. The Court's analysis assumes that the only interests at stake in the case are those of the Amish parents on the one hand, and those of the State on the other. The difficulty with this approach is that, despite the Court's claim, the parents are seeking to vindicate not only their own free exercise claims, but also those of their high-school-age children.

. . .

. . . Frieda Yoder has in fact testified that her own religious views are opposed to high-school education. I therefore join the judgment of the Court as to respondent Jonas Yoder. But Frieda Yoder's views may not be those of Vernon Yutzy or Barbara Miller. I must dissent, therefore, as to respondents Adin Yutzy and Wallace Miller as their motion to dismiss also raised the question of their children's religious liberty.

This issue has never been squarely presented before today. Our opinions are full of talk about the power of the parents over the child's education. See Pierce v. Society of Sisters, 268 U.S. 510; Meyer v. Nebraska, 262 U.S. 390. And we have in the past analyzed similar conflicts between parent and State with little regard for the views of the child. See Prince v. Massachusetts, 321 U.S. 158. Recent cases, however, have clearly held that the children themselves have constitutionally protectible interests. . . .

. . .

The views of the two children in question were not canvassed by the Wisconsin courts. The matter should be explicitly reserved so that new hearings can be held on remand of the case. . . .

Employment Division, Department of Human Resources of Oregon v. Smith

494 U.S. 872, 110 S.Ct. 1595, 108 L.Ed.2d 876 (1990).

Justice Scalia delivered the opinion of the Court.

This case requires us to decide whether the Free Exercise Clause of the First Amendment permits the State of Oregon to include religiously inspired peyote use within the reach of its general criminal prohibition on use of that drug, and thus permits the State to deny unemployment benefits to persons dismissed from their jobs because of such religiously inspired use.

I

Oregon law prohibits the knowing or intentional possession of a "controlled substance" . . . [including] the drug peyote, a hallucinogen derived from the plant Lophophpra williamsii Lemaire. . . .

Respondents Alfred Smith and Galen Black were fired from their jobs with a private drug rehabilitation organization because they ingested peyote for sacramental purposes at a ceremony of the Native American Church, of which both are members. When respondents applied to petitioner Employment Division for unemployment compensation, they were determined to be ineligible for benefits because they had been discharged for work-related "misconduct". . . .

. . . The Oregon Supreme Court reasoned . . . that the criminality of respondents' peyote use was irrelevant to resolution of their constitutional claim—since the purpose of the "misconduct" provision under which respondents had been disqualified was not to enforce the State's criminal laws but to preserve the financial integrity of the compensation fund, and since that purpose was inadequate to justify the burden that disqualification imposed on respondents' religious practice. . . .

Before this Court in 1987, petitioner continued to maintain that the illegality of respondents' peyote consumption was relevant to their constitutional claim. We agreed, concluding that "if a State has prohibited through its criminal laws certain kinds of religiously motivated conduct without violating the First Amendment, it certainly follows that it may impose the lesser burden of denying unemployment compensation benefits to persons who engage in that conduct." Employment Div., Dept. of Human Resources of Oregon v. Smith, 485 U.S. 660, 670 (1988) (*Smith I*). We noted, however, that the Oregon Supreme Court had not decided whether respondents' sacramental use of peyote was in fact proscribed by Oregon's controlled substance law, and that this issue was a matter of dispute between the parties. . . . [W]e vacated the judgment of the Oregon Supreme Court and remanded for further proceedings. . . .

On remand, the Oregon Supreme Court held that respondents' religiously inspired use of peyote fell within the prohibition of the Oregon statute ... It then considered whether that prohibition was valid under the Free Exercise Clause, and concluded that it was not. The court therefore reaffirmed its previous ruling that the State could not deny unemployment benefits to respondents for having engaged in that practice.

. . .

II

Respondents' claim for relief rests on our decisions in Sherbert v. Verner, supra, Thomas v. Review Board, Indiana Employment Security Div., supra, and Hobbie v. Unemployment Appeals Comm'n of Florida, 480 U.S. 136 (1987) ... As we observed in *Smith I,* however, the conduct at issue in those cases was not prohibited by law. We held that distinction to be critical, for "if Oregon does prohibit the religious use of peyote, and if that prohibition is consistent with the Federal Constitution, there is no federal right to engage in that conduct in Oregon," and "the State is free to withhold unemployment compensation from respondents for engaging in work-related misconduct, despite its religious motivation." 485 U.S., at 672. Now that the Oregon Supreme Court has confirmed that Oregon does prohibit the religious use of peyote, we proceed to consider whether that prohibition is permissible under the Free Exercise Clause.

A

... The free exercise of religion means, first and foremost, the right to believe and profess whatever religious doctrine one desires. Thus, the First Amendment obviously excludes all "governmental regulation of religious *beliefs* as such." ... The government may not compel affirmation of religious belief, see Torcaso v. Watkins, 367 U.S. 488 (1961), punish the expression of religious doctrines it believes to be false, United States v. Ballard, 322 U.S. 78, 86–88 (1944), impose special disabilities on the basis of religious views or religious status, see McDaniel v. Paty, 435 U.S. 618 (1978); ... or lend its power to one or the other side in controversies over religious authority or dogma, see Presbyterian Church v. Hull Church, 393 U.S. 440, 445–452 (1969); Kedroff v. St. Nicholas Cathedral, 344 U.S. 94, 95–119 (1952); Serbian Eastern Orthodox Diocese v. Milivojevich, 426 U.S. 696, 708–725 (1976).

But the "exercise of religion" often involves not only belief and profession but the performance of (or abstention from) physical acts: assembling with others for a worship service, participating in sacramental use of bread and wine, proselytizing, abstaining from certain foods or certain modes of transportation. It would be true, we think (though no case of ours has involved the point), that a state would be "prohibiting the free exercise [of religion]" if it sought to ban such acts or abstentions only when they are engaged in for religious reasons, or only because of the religious belief that they display. It would doubtless be unconstitutional, for example, to ban the casting of "statutes that are to be used for worship purposes," or to prohibit bowing down before a golden calf.

Respondents in the present case, however, seek to carry the meaning of "prohibiting the free exercise [of religion]" one large step further. They contend that their religious motivation for using peyote places them beyond the reach of a criminal law that is not specifically directed at their religious practice, and that is concededly constitutional as applied to those who use the drug for other reasons. They assert, in other words, that "prohibiting the free exercise [of religion]" includes requiring any individual to observe a generally applicable law that requires (or forbids) the performance of an act that his religious belief forbids (or requires). As a textual matter, we do not think the words must be given that meaning. It is no more necessary to regard the collection of a general tax, for example, as "prohibiting the free exercise [of religion]" by those citizens who believe support of organized government to be sinful, than it is to regard the same tax as "abridging the freedom . . . of the press" of those publishing companies that must pay the tax as a condition of staying in business. . . .

. . . We have never held that an individual's religious beliefs excuse him from compliance with an otherwise valid law prohibiting conduct that the State is free to regulate. On the contrary, the record of more than a century of our free exercise jurisprudence contradicts that proposition. As described succinctly by Justice Frankfurter in Minersville School Dist. Bd. of Educ. v. Gobitis, 310 U.S. 586, 594–595 (1940):

> "Conscientious scruples have not, in the course of the long struggle for religious toleration, relieved the individual from obedience to a general law not aimed at the promotion or restriction of religious beliefs. The mere possession of religious convictions which contradict the relevant concerns of a political society does not relieve the citizen from the discharge of political responsibilities (footnote omitted)."

We first had occasion to assert that principle in Reynolds v. United States, 98 U.S. 145 (1879), where we rejected the claim that criminal laws against polygamy could not be constitutionally applied to those whose religion commanded the practice. "Laws," we said, "are made for the government of actions, and while they cannot interfere with mere religious belief and opinions, they may with practices. . . . Can a man excuse his practices to the contrary because of his religious belief? To permit this would be to make the professed doctrines of religious belief superior to the law of the land, and in effect to permit every citizen to become a law unto himself." Id., at 166–167.

Subsequent decisions have consistently held that the right of free exercise does not relieve an individual of the obligation to comply with a "valid and neutral law of general applicability on the ground that the law proscribes (or prescribes) conduct that his religion prescribes (or proscribes)." United States v. Lee, 455 U.S. 252, 263, n. 3 (1982) (Stevens, J., concurring in judgment); see Minersville School Dist. Bd. of Educ. v. Gobitis, supra, at 595 (collecting cases). In Prince v. Massachusetts, 321 U.S. 158 (1944), we held that a mother could be prosecuted under the child labor laws for using her children to dispense literature in the streets, her religious motivation notwithstanding. We found no constitutional infirmity in "excluding [these children] from doing there what no other children may do." Id., at 171. In Braunfeld v. Brown, 366 U.S. 599 (1961) (plurality opinion), we upheld Sunday-closing laws against the claim that they burdened the religious practices of persons whose religions compelled them to refrain from work on other days. In Gillette v. United States, 401 U.S. 437, 461 (1971), we sustained the military selective service system against the claim that it violated free exercise by conscripting persons who opposed a particular war on religious grounds.

Our most recent decision involving a neutral, generally applicable regulatory law that compelled activity forbidden by an individual's religion was United States v. Lee, 455 U.S. at 258–261. There, an Amish employer, on behalf of himself and his employees, sought exemption from collection and payment of

Social Security taxes on the ground that the Amish faith prohibited participation in governmental support programs. We rejected the claim that an exemption was constitutionally required. There would be no way, we observed, to distinguish the Amish believer's objection to Social Security taxes from the religious objections that others might have to the collection or use of other taxes. "If, for example, a religious adherent believes war is a sin, and if a certain percentage of the federal budget can be identified as devoted to war-related activities, such individuals would have a similarly valid claim to be exempt from paying that percentage of the income tax. The tax system could not function if denominations were allowed to challenge the tax system because tax payments were spent in a manner that violates their religious belief." Id., at 260. . . .

The only decisions in which we have held that the First Amendment bars application of a neutral, generally applicable law to religiously motivated action have involved not the Free Exercise Clause alone, but the Free Exercise Clause in conjunction with other constitutional protections, such as freedom of speech and of the press, see Cantwell v. Connecticut, 310 U.S. at 304–307 (invalidating a licensing system for religious and charitable solicitations under which the administrator had discretion to deny a license to any cause he deemed nonreligious); Murdock v. Pennsylvania, 319 U.S. 105 (1943) (invalidating a flat tax on solicitation as applied to the dissemination of religious ideas); Follett v. McCormick, 321 U.S. 573 (1944) (same), or the right of parents, acknowledged in Pierce v. Society of Sisters, 268 U.S. 510 (1925), to direct the education of their children, see Wisconsin v. Yoder, 406 U.S. 205 (1972) (invalidating compulsory school-attendance laws as applied to Amish parents who refused on religious grounds to send their children to school).[1] Some of our cases prohibiting compelled expression, decided exclusively upon free speech grounds, have also involved freedom of religion, cf. Wooley v. Maynard, 430 U.S. 705 (1977) (invalidating compelled display of a license plate slogan that offended individual religious beliefs); West Virginia Board of Education v. Barnette, 319 U.S. 624 (1943) (invalidating compulsory flag salute statute challenged by religious objectors). And it is easy to envision a case in which a challenge on freedom of association grounds would likewise be reinforced by Free Exercise Clause concerns. Cf. Roberts v. United States Jaycees, 468 U.S. 609, 622 (1984) ("An individual's freedom to speak, to worship, and to petition the government for the redress of grievances could not be vigorously protected from interference by the State [if] a correlative freedom to engage in group effort toward those ends were not also guaranteed.").

The present case does not present such a hybrid situation, but a free exercise claim unconnected with any communicative activity or parental right. Respondents urge us to hold, quite simply, that when otherwise prohibitable conduct is accompanied by religious convictions, not only the convictions but the conduct itself must be free from governmental regulation. We have never held that, and decline to do so now. There being no contention that Oregon's drug law represents an attempt to regulate religious beliefs, the communication of religious beliefs, or the raising of one's children in those beliefs, the rule to which we have adhered ever since *Reynolds* plainly controls. . . .

---

[1] Both lines of cases have specifically adverted to the non-free exercise principle involved. . . . *Yoder* said that "the Court's holding in *Pierce* stands as a charter of the rights of parents to direct the religious upbringing of their children. And, when the interests of parenthood are combined with a free exercise claim of the nature revealed by this record, more than merely a 'reasonable relation to some purpose within the competency of the State is required to sustain the validity of the State's requirement under the First Amendment.'"406 U.S., at 233.

B

Respondents argue that even though exemption from generally applicable criminal laws need not automatically be extended to religiously motivated actors, at least the claim for a religious exemption must be evaluated under the balancing test set forth in Sherbert v. Verner, 374 U.S. 398 (1963).... We have never invalidated any governmental action on the basis of the *Sherbert* test except the denial of unemployment compensation. Although we have sometimes purported to apply the *Sherbert* test in contexts other than that, we have always found the test satisfied, see United States v. Lee, 455 U.S. 252 (1982); Gillette v. United States, 401 U.S. 437 (1971). In recent years we have abstained from applying the *Sherbert* test (outside the unemployment compensation field) at all. In Bowen v. Roy, 476 U.S. 693 (1986), we declined to apply *Sherbert* analysis to a federal statutory scheme that required benefit applicants and recipients to provide their Social Security numbers. The plaintiffs in that case asserted that it would violate their religious beliefs to obtain and provide a Social Security number for their daughter. We held the statute's application to the plaintiffs valid regardless of whether it was necessary to effectuate a compelling interest. See id., at 699–701. In Lyng v. Northwest Indian Cemetery Protective Assn., 485 U.S. 439 (1988), we declined to apply *Sherbert* analysis to the Government's logging and road construction activities on lands used for religious purposes by several Native American Tribes, even though it was undisputed that the activities "could have devastating effects on traditional Indian religious practices," 485 U.S., at 451. In Goldman v. Weinberger, 475 U.S. 503 (1986), we rejected application of the *Sherbert* test to military dress regulations that forbade the wearing of yarmulkes. In O'Lone v. Estate of Shabazz, 482 U.S. 342 (1987), we sustained, without mentioning the *Sherbert* test, a prison's refusal to excuse inmates from work requirements to attend worship services.

Even if we were inclined to breathe into *Sherbert* some life beyond the unemployment compensation field, we would not apply it to require exemptions from a generally applicable criminal law. The *Sherbert* test, it must be recalled, was developed in a context that lent itself to individualized governmental assessment of the reasons for the relevant conduct. As a plurality of the Court noted in *Roy*, a distinctive feature of unemployment compensation programs is that their eligibility criteria invite consideration of the particular circumstances behind an applicant's unemployment ... As the plurality pointed out in *Roy*, our decisions in the unemployment cases stand for the proposition that where the State has in place a system of individual exemptions, it may not refuse to extend that system to cases of "religious hardship" without compelling reason. Bowen v. Roy, supra, at 708.

Whether or not the decisions are that limited, they at least have nothing to do with an across-the-board criminal prohibition on a particular form of conduct. Although, as noted earlier, we have sometimes used the *Sherbert* test to analyze free exercise challenges to such laws, ... we have never applied the test to invalidate one. We conclude today that the sounder approach, and the approach in accord with the vast majority of our precedents, is to hold the test inapplicable to such challenges. The government's ability to enforce generally applicable prohibitions of socially harmful conduct, like its ability to carry out other aspects of public policy, "cannot depend on measuring the effects of a governmental action on a religious objector's spiritual development." *Lyng*, supra, at 451. To make an individual's obligation to obey such a law contingent upon the law's coincidence with his religious beliefs, except where the State's interest is "compelling"—permitting him, by virtue of his beliefs, "to become a law unto himself," Reynolds v. United States, 98 U.S., at 167—contradicts both constitutional tradition and common sense.[2]

The "compelling government interest" requirement seems benign, because it is familiar from other fields. But using it as the standard that must be met before the government may accord different treatment on the basis of race, see, e.g., Palmore v. Sidoti, 466 U.S. 429, 432 (1984), or before the government may regulate the content of speech, see, e.g., Sable Communications of California v. FCC, 492 U.S. 115, 126 (1989), is not remotely comparable to using it for the purpose asserted here. What it produces in those other fields—equality of treatment, and an unrestricted flow of contending speech—are constitutional norms; what it would produce here—a private right to ignore generally applicable laws—is a constitutional anomaly.

Nor is it possible to limit the impact of respondents' proposal by requiring a "compelling state interest" only when the conduct prohibited is "central" to the individual's religion.... It is no more appropriate for judges to determine the "centrality" of religious beliefs before applying a "compelling interest" test in the free exercise field, than it would be for them to determine the "importance" of ideas before applying the "compelling interest" test in the free speech field.... Repeatedly and in many different contexts, we have warned that courts must not presume to determine the place of a particular belief in a religion or the plausibility of a religious claim.... [4]

If the "compelling interest" test is to be applied at all, then, it must be applied across the board, to all actions thought to be religiously commanded. Moreover, if "compelling interest" really means what it says (and watering it down here would subvert its rigor in the other fields where it is applied), many laws will not meet the test. Any society adopting such a system would be courting anarchy, but that danger increases in direct proportion to the society's diversity of religious beliefs, and its determination to coerce or suppress none of them.... The rule respondents favor would open the prospect of constitutionally required religious exemptions from civic obligations of almost every conceivable kind—ranging from compulsory military service, see, e.g., Gillette v. United States, 401 U.S. 437 (1971), to the payment of taxes, see, e.g., United States v. Lee, supra; to health and safety regulation such as manslaughter and child neglect laws, see, e.g., Funkhouser v. State, 763 P.2d 695 (Okla.Crim.App. 1988), compulsory vaccination laws, see, e.g., Cude v. State, 237 Ark. 927, 377 S.W.2d 816 (1964), drug laws, see, e.g., Olsen v. Drug Enforcement Administration, 279 U.S.App.D.C. 1, 878 F.2d 1458 (1989), and traffic laws, see Cox v. New Hampshire, 312 U.S. 569 (1941); to social welfare legislation such as minimum wage laws, see Susan and Tony Alamo Foundation v. Secretary of Labor, 471

---

[2] Justice O'Connor seeks to distinguish Lyng v. Northwest Indian Cemetery Protective Assn., supra, and Bowen v. Roy, supra, on the ground that those cases involved the government's conduct of "its own internal affairs," ... [I]t is hard to see any reason in principle or practicality why the government should have to tailor its health and safety laws to conform to the diversity of religious belief, but should not have to tailor its management of public lands, Lyng, supra, or its administration of welfare programs, Roy, supra.

[4] ...Justice O'Connor ... agrees that "our determination ... cannot, and should not, turn on the centrality of the particular religious practice at issue." ... Earlier in her opinion, however, Justice O'Connor appears to contradict this, saying that the proper approach is "to determine whether the burden on the specific plaintiffs before us is constitutionally significant and whether the particular criminal interest asserted by the State before us is compelling." "Constitutionally significant burden" would seem to be "centrality" under another name.... There is no way out of the difficulty that, if general laws are to be subjected to a "religious practice" exception, both the importance of the law at issue and the centrality of the practice at issue must reasonably be considered....

U.S. 290 (1985), child labor laws, see Prince v. Massachusetts, 321 U.S. 158 (1944), animal cruelty laws, see, e.g., Church of the Lukumi Babalu Aye Inc. v. City of Hialeah, 723 F.Supp. 1467 (S.D.Fla.1989), cf. State v. Massey, 229 N.C. 734, 51 S.E.2d 179, appeal dism'd, 336 U.S. 942 (1949), environmental protection laws, see United States v. Little, 638 F.Supp. 337 (D.Mont.1986), and laws providing for equality of opportunity for the races, see, e.g., Bob Jones University v. United States, 461 U.S. 574, 603–604 (1983). The First Amendment's protection of religious liberty does not require this.

Values that are protected against government interference through enshrinement in the Bill of Rights are not thereby banished from the political process.... [A] society that believes in the negative protection accorded to religious belief can be expected to be solicitous of that value in its legislation.... It is therefore not surprising that a number of States have made an exception to their drug laws for sacramental peyote use. But to say that a nondiscriminatory religious-practice exemption is permitted, or even that it is desirable, is not to say that it is constitutionally required, and that the appropriate occasions for its creation can be discerned by the courts. It may fairly be said that leaving accommodation to the political process will place at a relative disadvantage those religious practices that are not widely engaged in; but that unavoidable consequence of democratic government must be preferred to a system in which each conscience is a law unto itself or in which judges weigh the social importance of all laws against the centrality of all religious beliefs.

Because respondents' ingestion of peyote was prohibited under Oregon law, and because that prohibition is constitutional, Oregon may, consistent with the Free Exercise Clause, deny respondents unemployment compensation when their dismissal results from use of the drug. The decision of the Oregon Supreme Court is accordingly reversed.

It is so ordered.

Justice O'Connor, with whom Justice Brennan, Justice Marshall, and Justice Blackmun join as to Parts I and II, concurring in the judgment.*

Although I agree with the result the Court reaches in this case, I cannot join its opinion. In my view, today's holding dramatically departs from well-settled First Amendment jurisprudence, appears unnecessary to resolve the question presented, and is incompatible with our Nation's fundamental commitment to individual religious liberty.

. . .

II

The Court today extracts from our long history of free exercise precedents the single categorical rule that "if prohibiting the exercise of religion ... is ... merely the incidental effect of a generally applicable and otherwise valid provision, the First Amendment has not been offended." Indeed, the Court holds that where the law is a generally applicable criminal prohibition, our usual free exercise jurisprudence does not even apply. To reach this sweeping result, however, the Court must not only give a strained reading of the First Amendment but must also disregard our consistent application of free exercise doctrine to cases involving generally applicable regulations that burden religious conduct.

---

* Although Justice Brennan, Justice Marshall, and Justice Blackmun join Parts I and II of the opinion, they do not concur in the judgment.

A

. . . Because the First Amendment does not distinguish between religious belief and religious conduct, conduct motivated by sincere religious belief, like the belief itself, must therefore be at least presumptively protected by the Free Exercise Clause.

The Court today, however, interprets the Clause to permit the government to prohibit, without justification, conduct mandated by an individual's religious beliefs, so long as that prohibition is generally applicable. But a law that prohibits certain conduct—conduct that happens to be an act of worship for someone—manifestly does prohibit that person's free exercise of his religion. A person who is barred from engaging in religiously motivated conduct is barred from freely exercising his religion. Moreover, that person is barred from freely exercising his religion regardless of whether the law prohibits the conduct only when engaged in for religious reasons, only by members of that religion, or by all persons. It is difficult to deny that a law that prohibits religiously motivated conduct, even if the law is generally applicable, does not at least implicate First Amendment concerns.

. . .

To say that a person's right to free exercise has been burdened, of course, does not mean that he has an absolute right to engage in the conduct. . . . [W]e have respected both the First Amendment's express textual mandate and the governmental interest in regulation of conduct by requiring the Government to justify any substantial burden on religiously motivated conduct by a compelling state interest and by means narrowly tailored to achieve that interest. . . .

The Court attempts to support its narrow reading of the Clause by claiming that "[w]e have never held that an individual's religious beliefs excuse him from compliance with an otherwise valid law prohibiting conduct that the State is free to regulate." But as the Court later notes, as it must, in cases such as *Cantwell* and *Yoder* we have in fact interpreted the Free Exercise Clause to forbid application of a generally applicable prohibition to religiously motivated conduct. . . .

The Court endeavors to escape from our decisions in *Cantwell* and *Yoder* by labeling them "hybrid" decisions, but there is no denying that both cases expressly relied on the Free Exercise Clause, . . . and that we have consistently regarded those cases as part of the mainstream of our free exercise jurisprudence. Moreover, in each of the other cases cited by the Court to support its categorical rule, we rejected the particular constitutional claims before us only after carefully weighing the competing interests. . . . That we rejected the free exercise claims in those cases hardly calls into question the applicability of First Amendment doctrine in the first place. Indeed, it is surely unusual to judge the vitality of a constitutional doctrine by looking to the win-loss record of the plaintiffs who happen to come before us.

B

. . .

In my view, . . . the essence of a free exercise claim is relief from a burden imposed by government on religious practices or beliefs, whether the burden is imposed directly through laws that prohibit or compel specific religious practices, or indirectly through laws that, in effect, make abandonment of one's own religion or conformity to the religious beliefs of others the price of an equal place in the civil community. . . .

Indeed, we have never distinguished between cases in which a State conditions receipt of a benefit on conduct prohibited by religious beliefs and cases in which a State affirmatively prohibits such conduct. The *Sherbert* compelling interest test applies in both kinds of cases....

... Even if, as an empirical matter, a government's criminal laws might usually serve a compelling interest in health, safety, or public order, the First Amendment at least requires a case-by-case determination of the question, sensitive to the facts of each particular claim.... Given the range of conduct that a State might legitimately make criminal, we cannot assume, merely because a law carries criminal sanctions and is generally applicable, that the First Amendment never requires the State to grant a limited exemption for religiously motivated conduct.

. . .

Finally, the Court today suggests that the disfavoring of minority religions is an "unavoidable consequence" under our system of government and that accommodation of such religions must be left to the political process. In my view, however, the First Amendment was enacted precisely to protect the rights of those whose religious practices are not shared by the majority and may be viewed with hostility. The history of our free exercise doctrine amply demonstrates the harsh impact majoritarian rule has had on unpopular or emerging religious groups such as the Jehovah's Witnesses and the Amish....

III

The Court's holding today not only misreads settled First Amendment precedent; it appears to be unnecessary to this case. I would reach the same result applying our established free exercise jurisprudence.

. . .

... [T]he critical question in this case is whether exempting respondents from the State's general criminal prohibition "will unduly interfere with fulfillment of the governmental interest." ... Although the question is close, I would conclude that uniform application of Oregon's criminal prohibition is "essential to accomplish" its overriding interest in preventing the physical harm caused by the use of a ... controlled substance. Oregon's criminal prohibition represents that State's judgment that the possession and use of controlled substances, even by only one person, is inherently harmful and dangerous. Because the health effects caused by the use of controlled substances exist regardless of the motivation of the user, the use of such substances, even for religious purposes, violates the very purpose of the laws that prohibit them.... Moreover, in view of the societal interest in preventing trafficking in controlled substances, uniform application of the criminal prohibition at issue is essential to the effectiveness of Oregon's stated interest in preventing any possession of peyote....

For these reasons, I believe that granting a selective exemption in this case would seriously impair Oregon's compelling interest in prohibiting possession of peyote by its citizens. Under such circumstances, the Free Exercise Clause does not require the State to accommodate respondents' religiously motivated conduct....

Respondents contend that any incompatibility is belied by the fact that the Federal Government and several States provide exemptions for the religious use of peyote ... But other governments may surely choose to grant an exemption without Oregon, with its specific asserted interest in uniform application of its drug laws, being *required* to do so by the First Amendment. Respondents also note that the sacramental use of peyote is central to the tenets of the Native American Church, but I agree with the Court that ... our determination of the constitutionality of Oregon's general criminal prohibition cannot, and should not, turn on the centrality of the particular religious practice at issue. This does not mean, of course, that courts may not make factual findings as to whether a claimant holds a sincerely held religious belief that conflicts with, and thus is burdened by, the challenged law. The distinction between questions of centrality and questions of sincerity and burden is admittedly fine, but it is one that is an established part of our free exercise doctrine ...

I would therefore adhere to our established free exercise jurisprudence and hold that the State in this case has a compelling interest in regulating peyote use by its citizens and that accommodating respondents' religiously motivated conduct "will unduly interfere with fulfillment of the governmental interest." *Lee,* 455 U.S., at 259. Accordingly, I concur in the judgment of the Court.

Justice Blackmun, with whom Justice Brennan and Justice Marshall join, dissenting.

This Court over the years painstakingly has developed a consistent and exacting standard to test the constitutionality of a state statute that burdens the free exercise of religion. Such a statute may stand only if the law in general, and the State's refusal to allow a religious exemption in particular, are justified by a compelling interest that cannot be served by less restrictive means.

Until today, I thought this was a settled and inviolate principle of this Court's First Amendment jurisprudence....

. . .

... I agree with Justice O'Connor's analysis of the applicable free exercise doctrine, and I join parts I and II of her opinion. As she points out, "the critical question in this case is whether exempting respondents from the State's general criminal prohibition 'will unduly interfere with fulfillment of the governmental interest.' " I do disagree, however, with her specific answer to that question.

. . .

... The State's asserted interest ... amounts only to the symbolic preservation of an unenforced prohibition....

. . .

The State proclaims an interest in protecting the health and safety of its citizens from the dangers of unlawful drugs. It offers, however, no evidence that the religious use of peyote has ever harmed anyone. The factual findings of other courts cast doubt on the State's assumption that religious use of peyote is harmful....

The carefully circumscribed ritual context in which respondents used peyote is far removed from the irresponsible and unrestricted recreational use of unlawful drugs. The Native American Church's internal restrictions on, and supervision of, its members' use of peyote substantially obviate the State's health and safety concerns....

. . .

Finally, the State argues that granting an exception for religious peyote use would erode its interest in the uniform, fair, and certain enforcement of its drug laws. The State fears that, if it grants an exemption for religious peyote use, a flood of other claims to religious exemptions will follow. It would then be placed in a dilemma, it says, between allowing a patchwork of exemptions that would hinder its law enforcement efforts, and risking a violation of the Establishment Clause by arbitrarily limiting its religious exemptions. This argument, however, could be made in almost any free exercise case. . . .

The State's apprehension of a flood of other religious claims is purely speculative. Almost half the States, and the Federal Government, have maintained an exemption for religious peyote use for many years, and apparently have not found themselves overwhelmed by claims to other religious exemptions. . . .

Finally, although I agree with Justice O'Connor that courts should refrain from delving into questions of whether, as a matter of religious doctrine, a particular practice is "central" to the religion, I do not think this means that the courts must turn a blind eye to the severe impact of a State's restrictions on the adherents of a minority religion. . . .

Respondents believe, and their sincerity has never been at issue, that the peyote plant embodies their deity, and eating it is an act of worship and communion. Without peyote, they could not enact the essential ritual of their religion. . . .

If Oregon can constitutionally prosecute them for this act of worship, they, like the Amish, may be "forced to migrate to some other and more tolerant region." *Yoder*, 406 U.S., at 218. This potentially devastating impact must be viewed in light of the federal policy—reached in reaction to many years of religious persecution and intolerance—of protecting the religious freedom of Native Americans. See American Indian Religious Freedom Act, 92 Stat. 469, 42 U.S.C. § 1996 ("it shall be the policy of the United States to protect and preserve for American Indians their inherent right of freedom to believe, express, and exercise the traditional religions . . ., including but not limited to access to sites, use and possession of sacred objects, and the freedom to worship through ceremonials and traditional rites"). Congress recognized that certain substances, such as peyote, "have religious significance because they are sacred, they have power, they heal, they are necessary to the exercise of the rites of the religion, they are necessary to the cultural integrity of the tribe, and, therefore, religious survival." H.R.Rep. No. 95–1308, p. 2 (1978).

The American Indian Religious Freedom Act, in itself, may not create rights enforceable against government action restricting religious freedom, but this Court must scrupulously apply its free exercise analysis to the religious claims of Native Americans, however unorthodox they may be. Otherwise, both the First Amendment and the stated policy of Congress will offer to Native Americans merely an unfulfilled and hollow promise.

. . .

For these reasons, I conclude that Oregon's interest in enforcing its drug laws against religious use of peyote is not sufficiently compelling to outweigh respondents' right to the free exercise of their religion. Since the State could not constitutionally enforce its criminal prohibition against respondents, the interests underlying the State's drug laws cannot justify its denial of unemployment benefits. . . .

I dissent.

CHURCH OF THE LUKUMI BABALU AYE, INC. v. CITY OF HIALEAH, 508 U.S. 520 (1993). The church practices the Santeria religion, whose services include animal sacrifices. When the church proposed to build a house of worship in Hialeah, the city enacted ordinances that targeted the practice of animal sacrifice by the church. One ordinance provided that "[i]t shall be unlawful for any person, persons, corporations or associations to sacrifice any animal within the corporate limits of the City of Hialeah, Florida." "Sacrifice" was defined as "to unnecessarily kill, torment, torture, or mutilate an animal in a public or private ritual or ceremony not for the primary purpose of food consumption." The ordinance contained an exemption for slaughtering by "licensed establishment[s]" of animals "specifically raised for food purposes." The Court held that the ordinances violated the free exercise clause since they were neither "neutral" nor "of general applicability." The ordinances were drafted so that "almost the only conduct subject to [them] is the religious exercise of Santeria church members." All of the asserted governmental purposes (protecting public health and preventing cruelty to animals) were only pursued in the context of Santeria religious practices. "A law that targets religious conduct for distinctive treatment or advances legitimate governmental interests only against conduct with a religious motivation will survive strict scrutiny only in rare cases."

THE RELIGIOUS FREEDOM RESTORATION ACT

The Religious Freedom Restoration Act (PL 103–141; 42 U.S.C. § 2000bb), enacted in 1993, provides, in relevant part:

SEC. 2. CONGRESSIONAL FINDINGS AND DECLARATION OF PURPOSES.

(a) FINDINGS.—The Congress finds that—

(1) the framers of the Constitution, recognizing free exercise of religion as an unalienable right, secured its protection in the First Amendment to the Constitution;

(2) laws "neutral" toward religion may burden religious exercise as surely as laws intended to interfere with religious exercise;

(3) governments should not substantially burden religious exercise without compelling justification;

(4) in Employment Division v. Smith, 494 U.S. 872 (1990) the Supreme Court virtually eliminated the requirement that the government justify burdens on religious exercise imposed by laws neutral toward religion; and

(5) the compelling interest test as set forth in prior Federal court rulings is a workable test for striking sensible balances between religious liberty and competing prior governmental interests.

(b) PURPOSES.—The purposes of this Act are—

(1) to restore the compelling interest test as set forth in Sherbert v. Verner, 374 U.S. 398 (1963) and Wisconsin v. Yoder, 406 U.S. 205 (1972) and to guarantee its application in all cases where free exercise of religion is substantially burdened; and

(2) to provide a claim or defense to persons whose religious exercise is substantially burdened by government.

SEC. 3. FREE EXERCISE OF RELIGION PROTECTED.

(a) IN GENERAL.—Government shall not substantially burden a person's exercise of religion even if the burden results from a rule of general applicability, except as provided in subsection (b).

(b) EXCEPTION.—Government may substantially burden a person's exercise of religion only if it demonstrates that application of the burden to the person—

(1) is in furtherance of a compelling governmental interest; and

(2) is the least restrictive means of furthering that compelling governmental interest.

(c) JUDICIAL RELIEF.—A person whose religious exercise has been burdened in violation of this section may assert that violation as a claim or defense in a judicial proceeding and obtain appropriate relief against a government. Standing to assert a claim or defense under this section shall be governed by the general rules of standing under article III of the Constitution.

SEC. 5. DEFINITIONS.

As used in this Act—

(1) the term "government" includes a branch, department, agency, instrumentality, and official (or other person acting under color of law) of the United States, a State, or a subdivision of a State;

(2) the term "State" includes the District of Columbia, the Commonwealth of Puerto Rico, and each territory and possession of the United States;

(3) the term "demonstrates" means meets the burdens of going forward with the evidence and of persuasion; and

(4) the term "exercise of religion" means the exercise of religion under the First Amendment to the Constitution.

SEC. 6. APPLICABILITY.

(a) IN GENERAL.—This Act applies to all Federal and State law, and the implementation of that law, whether statutory or otherwise, and whether adopted before or after the enactment of this Act.

(b) RULE OF CONSTRUCTION.—Federal statutory law adopted after the date of the enactment of this Act is subject to this Act unless such law explicitly excludes such application by reference to this Act.

(c) RELIGIOUS BELIEF UNAFFECTED.—Nothing in this Act shall be construed to authorize any government to burden any religious belief.

*

THE UNITED STATES SUPREME COURT

A Chart

1789–1993*

The following chart is designed to provide a means of identifying the composition of the Court at any specified date, and thereby to help the student follow the relationship between changes in the personnel and doctrines of the Court.

If the student is concerned with a decision bearing a date which approximates a change in the Court's personnel it will be necessary to consult the footnotes. These notes show, following the dates of birth and death, political affiliation, and home state at the time of appointment, each justice's dates of commission and termination of service. Of course, members do not always participate in decisions rendered during their term of service; the fact of participation must be independently verified. Large X's indicate vacancies.

The information reflected in the chart and footnotes has been gathered primarily from the Dictionary of American Biography,[1] Warren, The Supreme Court in United States History[2] and for dates of commission and termination of service, the Senate Manual, and the Official Reports of the Supreme Court.

* This chart was originally prepared by Paul Gay, and has been updated by the editors.

1. New York, Scribner, 1928–37. 20 v. Supplement one, 1944; Supplement two, 1959.

2. Boston, Little Brown, 1922. 3 v.

Washington 1789–1797		Adams 1797–1801	Jefferson 1801–1809	Madison 1809–1817

Jay[1] 1789–	–1795	2 Ells-worth[10] 1796–1800	Marshall[13] 1801–		
Rut-ledge 2	John-son 7	Paterson[8] 1793–	–1806	Livingston[15] 1806–	
Cushing[3] 1789–				–1810	Story[17] 1811–
Wilson[4] 1789–		–1798	Washington[11] 1798–		
Blair[5] 1789–		–1796	Chase[9] 1796–	–1811	Duvall[18] 1811–
	Iredell[6] 1790–		–1799	Moore[12] 1799–	–1804	Johnson[14] 1804–
						Todd[16] 1807–

1.   John Jay, 1745–1829. Fed., N. Y. 9–26–1789 to 6–29–1795.

2.   John Rutledge, 1739–1800. Fed., S. C. 9–26–1789 to 3–5–1791. Comm. C.J. 7–1–1795 (recess appoint.) pres. August term 1795, rejected by Senate 12–15–1795.

3.   William Cushing, 1732–1810. Fed., Mass. 9–27–1789 to 9–13–1810.

4.   James Wilson, 1742–1798. Fed., Pa. 9–29–1789 to 8–21–1798.

5.   John Blair, 1732–1800. Fed., Va. 9–30–1789 to 1–27–1796.

6.   James Iredell, 1751–1799. Fed., N. C. 2–10–1790 to 10–20–1799.

7.   Thomas Johnson, 1732–1819. Fed., Md. 11–7–1791 to 2–1–1793.

8.   William Paterson, 1745–1806. Fed., N. J. 3–4–1793 to 9–9–1806.

9.   Samuel Chase, 1741–1811. Fed., Md. 1–27–1796 to 6–19–1811.

10.   Oliver Ellsworth, 1745–1807. Fed., Conn. 3–4–1796 to 12–15–1800.

11.   Bushrod Washington, 1762–1829. Fed., Va. 12–20–1798 to 11–26–1829.

12.   Alfred Moore, 1755–1810. Fed., N. C. 12–10–1799 to 1–26–1804.

13.   John Marshall, 1755–1835. Fed., Va. 1–31–1801 to 7–6–1835.

14.   William Johnson, 1771–1834. Rep., S. C. 3–26–1804 to 8–4–1834.

15.   [Henry] Brockholst Livingston, 1757–1823. Rep., N. Y. 11–10–1806 to 3–18–1823.

16.   Thomas Todd, 1765–1826. Rep., Ky. 3–3–1807 to 2–7–1826. Post created by Congress by Act February 24, 1807.

17.   Joseph Story, 1779–1845. Rep., Mass. 11–18–1811 to 9–10–1845.

18.   Gabriel Duval[l], 1752–1844. Rep., Md. 11–18–1811 to 1–14–1835.

Monroe 1817–1825	J. Q. Adams 1825–1829	Jackson 1829–1837	Van Buren 1837–1841	Harrison 3/4–4/4 Tyler 1841–1845
Marshall		–1835	**Taney**[24] 1836–	
Livingston –1823	**Thompson**[19] 1823–		–1843	N[29]
Story				
Washington –1829		**Baldwin**[22] 1830–		–1844
Duvall		–1835	**Barbour**[25] 1836– –1841	**Daniel**[23] 1841–
Johnson		–1834	**Wayne**[23] 1835–	
Todd –1826	**Trim-ble**[20] '26–8	**McLean**[21] 1829–		
			Catron[26] 1837–	
			McKinley[27] 1837–	

19. Smith Thompson, 1768–1843. Rep., N. Y. 12–9–1823 to 12–18–1843.

20. Robert Trimble, 1777–1828. Rep., Ky. 5–9–1826 to 8–25–1828.

21. John McLean, 1785–1861. Dem./Rep., Ohio 3–7–1829 to 4–4–1861.

22. Henry Baldwin, 1780–1844. Dem., Pa. 1–6–1830 to 4–21–1844.

23. James Moore Wayne, 1790–1867. Dem., Ga. 1–9–1835 to 7–5–1867.

24. Roger Brooke Taney, 1777–1864. Dem., Md. 3–15–1836 to 10–12–1864.

25. Philip Pendleton Barbour, 1783–1841. Dem., Va. 3–15–1836 to 2–25–1841.

26. John Catron, ca. (1778–86) 1865. Dem., Tenn. 3–8–1837 to 5–30–1865. Post created by Congress by Act of March 3, 1837 and abolished by Congress by Act of July 23, 1866.

27. John McKinley, 1780–1852. Dem., Ky./Ala. 9–25–1837 to 7–19–1852. Post created by Congress by Act of March 3, 1837.

28. Peter Vivian Daniel, 1784–1860. Dem., Va. 3–3–1841 to 5–31–1860.

29. Samuel Nelson, 1792–1873. Dem., N. Y. 2–13–1845 to 11–28–1872.

Polk 1845–1849	Taylor 1849–1850 Fillmore 1850–1853	Pierce 1853–1857	Buchanan 1857–1861	Lincoln 1861– 4/15/65	Johnson 1865–1869	Grant 1869–

| Taney | | | | −1864 | Chase[39] 1864– | −1873 |

| Nelson[29] | | | | | | −1872 |

| S Woodbury[30] 1845–   −1851 | Curtis[32] 1851–   −1857 | Clifford[34] 1858– | | | | |

| X Grier[31] 1846– | | | | | −1870 | S[40] 1870– |

| Daniel | | | −1860 | X Miller[36] 1862– | | |

| Wayne | | | | | −1867 | X B[41] 1870– |

| McLean | | | −1861 | Swayne[35] 1862– | | |

| Catron | | | | −1865* X | | |

| McKinley   −1852 | X Campbell 1853–   −1861 | X Davis[37] 1862– | | | | |

| Field[38] 1863– | | | | | | |

30. Levi Woodbury, 1789–1851. Dem., N. H. 9–20–1845 to 9–4–1851.

31. Robert Cooper Grier, 1794–1870. Dem., Pa. 8–4–1846 to 1–31–1870.

32. Benjamin Robbins Curtis, 1809–1874. Whig, Mass. 12–20–1851 to 9–30–1857.

33. John Archibald Campbell, 1811–1889. Dem., Ala. 3–22–1853 to 4–30–1861.

34. Nathan Clifford, 1803–1881. Dem., Me. 1–12–1858 to 7–25–1881.

35. Noah Haynes Swayne, 1804–1884. Rep., Ohio 1–24–1862 to 1–24–1881.

36. Samuel Freeman Miller, 1816–1890. Rep., Iowa 7–16–1862 to 10–13–1890.

37. David Davis, 1815–1886. Rep./Dem., Ill. 12–8–1862 to 3–4–1877.

38. Stephen Johnson Field, 1816–1899. Dem., Cal. 3–10–1863 to 12–1–1897. Post created by Congress by Act of March 3, 1863.

39. Salmon Portland Chase, 1808–1873. Rep., Ohio 12–6–1864 to 5–7–1873.

40. William Strong, 1808–1895. Dem./Rep., Pa. 2–18–1870 to 12–14–1880.

41. Joseph P. Bradley, 1813–1892. Whig/Rep., N. J. 3–21–1870 to 1–22–1892.

* Post abolished by Congress by Act of July 23, 1866.

Grant −1877	Hayes 1877–1881	Garfield 3/4–9/19 **Arthur** 1881–1885	Cleve- land 1885–1889	Harrison 1889–1893	Cleve- land 1893–1897	McKinley 1897– 9/14/1901
Waite[43] 1874–			−1888	**Fuller**[50] 1888–		
Hunt[42] 1872–		−1882	**Blatchford**[48] 1882–	−1893	**White**[55] 1894–	
Clifford	−1881	**Gray**[47] 1881–				
Strong	−1880	**Woods**[45] 1880–	−1887	**Lamar**[49] 1888– −1893	**Jack- son**[54] 1893–5	**Peckham**[56] 1895–
Miller				−1890	**Brown**[52] 1890–	
Bradley				−1892	**Shiras**[53] 1892–	
Swayne	−1881	**Matthews**[46] 1881–	−1889	**Brewer**[51] 1889–		
Davis −1877	**Harlan**[44] 1877–					
Field					−1897	**McKen- na**[57] 1898–

42. Ward Hunt, 1810–1886. Rep., N. Y. 12–11–1872 to 1–27–1882.

43. Morrison Remick Waite, 1816–1888. Rep., Ohio 1–21–1874 to 3–23–1888.

44. John Marshall Harlan, 1833–1911. Rep., Ky. 11–29–1877 to 10–14–1911.

45. William Burnham Woods, 1824–1887. Rep., Ga. 12–21–1880 to 5–14–1887.

46. [Thomas] Stanley Matthews, 1824–1889. Rep., Ohio 5–12–1881 to 3–22–1889.

47. Horace Gray, 1828–1902. Rep., Mass. 12–20–1881 to 9–15–1902.

48. Samuel Blatchford, 1820–1893. Rep., N. Y. 3–22–1882 to 7–7–1893.

49. Lucius Quintus Cincinnatus Lamar, 1825–1893. Dem., Miss. 1–16–1888 to 1–23–1893.

50. Melville Weston Fuller, 1833–1910. Dem., Ill. 7–20–1888 to 7–4–1910.

51. David Josiah Brewer, 1837–1910. Rep., Kan. 12–18–1889 to 3–28–1910.

52. Henry Billings Brown, 1836–1913. Rep., Mich. 12–29–1890 to 5–28–1906.

53. George Shiras, 1832–1924. Rep., Pa. 7–26–1892 to 2–23–1903.

54. Howell Edmunds Jackson, 1832–1895. Whig/Dem., Tenn. 2–18–1893 to 8–8–1895.

55. Edward Douglass White, 1845–1921. Dem., La. Asso. Just. 2–19–1894 to 12–18–1910; C. J. 12–12–1910 to 5–19–1921.

56. Rufus Wheeler Peckham, 1838–1909. Dem., N. Y. 12–9–1895 to 10–24–1909.

57. Joseph McKenna, 1843–1926. Rep., Cal. 1–21–1898 to 1–5–1925.

T. Roosevelt 1901–1909	Taft 1909–1913	Wilson 1913–1921	Harding 1921–8/2/23	Coolidge 1923–1929
Fuller –1910	White[55] 1910–	–1921	Taft[69] 1921–	–1930
White –1910	Van Devanter[63] 1910–			
Gray –1902	Holmes[58] 1902–			
Peckham –1909	Lurton[61] 1909– –1914	McReynolds[66] 1914–		
Brown –1906	Moody[60] 1906– –1910	Lamar[64] 1910– –1916	Brandeis[67] 1916–	
Shiras –1903	Day[59] 1903–		–1922	Butler[71] 1922–
Brewer –1910	Hughes[62] 1910– –1916	Clark[68] 1916– –1922	Sutherland[70] 1922–	
Harlan –1911	Pitney[65] 1912–		–1922	Sanford[72] 1923–
McKenna			–1925	Stone[73] 1925–

55. Edward Douglass White, 1845–1921. Dem., La. Asso. Just. 2–19–1894 to 12–18–1910; C. J. 12–12–1910 to 5–19–1921.

58. Oliver Wendell Holmes, 1841–1935. Rep., Mass. 12–4–1902 to 1–12–1932.

59. William Rufus Day, 1849–1923. Rep., Ohio 2–23–1903 to 11–13–1922.

60. William Henry Moody, 1853–1917. Rep., Mass. 12–12–1906 to 11–20–1910.

61. Horace Harmon Lurton, 1844–1914. Dem., Tenn. 12–20–1909 to 7–12–1914.

62. Charles Evans Hughes, 1862–1948. Rep., N. Y. Asso. Just. 5–2–1910 to 6–10–1916; C. J. 2–13–1930 to 6–30–1941.

63. Willis Van Devanter, 1859–1941. Rep., Wyo. 12–16–1910 to 6–2–1937.

64. Joseph Rucker Lamar, 1857–1916. Dem., Ga. 12–17–1910 to 1–2–1916.

65. Mahlon Pitney, 1858–1924. Rep., N. J. 3–13–1912 to 12–31–1922.

66. James Clark McReynolds, 1862–1946. Dem., Tenn. 8–29–1914 to 1–31–1941.

67. Louis Dembitz Brandeis, 1856–1941. Dem., Mass. 6–1–1916 to 2–13–1939.

68. John Hessin Clarke, 1857–1945. Dem., Ohio 7–24–1916 to 9–18–1922.

69. William Howard Taft, 1857–1930. Rep., Conn. 6–30–1921 to 2–3–1930.

70. George Sutherland, 1862–1942. Rep., Utah 9–5–1922 to 1–17–1938.

71. Pierce Butler, 1866–1939. Dem., Minn. 12–21–1922 to 11–16–1939.

72. Edward Terry Sanford, 1865–1930. Rep., Tenn. 1–29–1923 to 3–8–1930.

73. Harlan Fiske Stone, 1872–1946. Rep., N. Y. Asso. Just. 2–5–1925 to 7–2–1941; C. J. 7–3–1941 to 4–22–1946.

Hoover 1929–1933	F. D. Roosevelt 1933–4/12/1945		Truman 1945–1953
T. '30 **Hughes**[62] 1930–	–1941	**Stone**[73] 1941– –1946	**Vinson**[85] 1946– –1953
Van Devanter –1937	**Black**[76] 1937–		
Holmes –1932 **Cardozo**[75] 1932– –1938	**Frankfurter**[78] 1939–		
McReynolds –1941	**B.**[81] '41–2 **Rutledge**[83] 1943– –1949		**Minton**[87] 1949–
Brandeis –1939	**Douglas**[79] 1939–		
Butler –1939	**Murphy**[80] 1940– –1949		**Clark**[86] 1949–
Sutherland –1938	**Reed**[77] 1938–		
S. '30 **Roberts**[74] 1930–	–1945	**Burton**[84] 1945–	
Stone (To C. J.) –1941	**Jackson**[82] 1941–		

62. Charles Evans Hughes, 1862–1948. Rep., N. Y. Asso. Just. 5–2–1910 to 6–10–1916; C. J. 2–13–1930 to 6–30–1941.

73. Harlan Fiske Stone, 1872–1946. Rep., N. Y. Asso. Just. 2–5–1925 to 7–2–1941; C. J. 7–3–1941 to 4–22–1946.

74. Owen Josephus Roberts, 1875–1955. Rep., Pa. 5–20–1930 to 7–31–1945.

75. Benjamin Nathan Cardozo, 1870–1938. Dem., N. Y. 3–2–1932 to 7–9–1938.

76. Hugo Lafayette Black, 1886–1971. Dem., Ala. 8–18–1937 to 9–17–1971.

77. Stanley Forman Reed, 1884–1980. Dem., Ky. 1–27–1938 to 2–25–1957.

78. Felix Frankfurter, 1882–1965. Ind., Mass. 1–20–1939 to 8–28–1962.

79. William Orville Douglas, 1898–1980. Dem., Conn. 4–15–1939 to 11–12–1975.

80. Frank Murphy, 1890–1949. Dem., Mich. 1–18–1940 to 7–19–1949.

81. James Francis Byrnes, 1879–1972. Dem., S. C. 6–25–1941 to 10–3–1942.

82. Robert Hougwout Jackson, 1892–1954. Dem., N. Y. 7–11–1941 to 10–9–1954.

83. Wiley Blount Rutledge, 1894–1949. Dem., Iowa 2–11–1943 to 9–10–1949.

84. Harold Hitz Burton, 1888–1964. Rep., Ohio 9–22–1945 to 10–13–1958.

85. Frederick Moore Vinson, 1890–1953. Dem., Ky. 6–21–1946 to 9–8–1953.

86. Thomas Campbell Clark, 1899–1977. Dem., Texas 8–19–1949 to 6–12–1967.

87. Sherman Minton, 1890–1965. Dem., Ind. 10–5–1949 to 10–15–1956.

Eisenhower 1953–1961	Kennedy 1961–1963	Johnson 1963–1969

Warren[88]
1953–

Black

Frankfurter	−1962	Goldberg[94] 1962–	−1965	Fortas[95] 1965–

Minton −1956	Brennan[90] 1956–

Douglas

Clark	−1967	Marshall[96] 1967–

Reed −1957	Whittaker[91] 1957– −1962	White[93] 1962–

Burton −1958	Stewart[92] 1958–

J. '54	Harlan[89] 1954–

88. Earl Warren, 1891–1974, Rep., Cal. 10–2–1953 to 6–23–1969.
89. John Marshall Harlan, 1899–1971. Rep., N. Y. 3–17–1955 to 9–23–1971.
90. William Joseph Brennan, 1906– . Dem., N. J. 10–15–1956 to 7–20–1990.
91. Charles Evans Whittaker, 1901–1973. Rep., Mo. 3–19–1957 to 4–1–1962.
92. Potter Stewart, 1915–1985. Rep., Ohio 10–13–1958 to 7–7–1981.
93. Byron R. White, 1917– . Dem., Colo. 4–16–1962 to 6–28–1993.
94. Arthur Joseph Goldberg, 1908–1990. Dem., Ill. 10–1–1962 to 7–26–1965.
95. Abe Fortas, 1910–1982. Dem., Tenn. 10–4–1965 to 5–15–1969.
96. Thurgood Marshall, 1908–1993. Dem., N. Y. 10–2–1967 to 10–7–1991.

Nixon 1969–1974	Ford 1974–1977	Carter 1977–1981	Reagan 1981–1989

Warren −1969	**Burger**[97] 1969–	−1986	**Rehnquist**[100] 1986–*
Black −1971	**Powell**[99] 1971–	−1987	**Kennedy**[104] 1988–*
Fortas −1969	**Blackmun**[98] 1970–		
Brennan			
Douglas −1975	**Stevens**[101] 1975–*		
Marshall			
White			
Stewart −1981	**O'Connor**[102] 1981–*		
Harlan −1971	**Rehnquist**[100] 1971–	(To C. J.) −1986	**Scalia**[103] 1986–*

97. Warren Earl Burger, 1907–1995. Rep., Va. 6–23–1969 to 9–26–1986.

98. Harry Andrew Blackmun, 1908– . Rep., Minn. 5–14–1970 to 6–30–1994.

99. Lewis Franklin Powell, Jr., 1907– . Dem., Va. 12–19–1971 to 6–26–1987.

100. William Hubbs Rehnquist, 1924– . Rep., Ariz. Asso. Just. 12–15–1971 to 9–26–1986; C.J. 9–26–1986 to –.

101. John Paul Stevens, 1920– . Rep., Ill. 12–19–1975 to –.

102. Sandra Day O'Connor, 1930– . Rep., Ariz. 9–25–1981 to –.

103. Antonin Scalia, 1936– . Rep., Washington, D.C. 9–26–1986 to –.

104. Anthony M. Kennedy, 1936– . Rep., Cal. 2–18–1988 to –.

Bush 1989–1993	Clinton 1993–*	

Rehnquist

Kennedy

Blackmun	−1994	Breyer[108] 1994–*

Brennan −1990	Souter[105] 1990–*

Stevens

Marshall	−1991	Thomas[106] 1991–*

White	−1993	Ginsburg[107] 1993–*

O'Connor

Scalia

105. David H. Souter, 1939– . Rep., N.H. 10–19–1990 to –.

106. Clarence Thomas, 1945– . Rep., Washington, D.C. 10–23–1991 to –.

107. Ruth B. Ginsburg, 1933– . Dem., Washington, D.C. 8–10–1993 to –.

108. Stephen G. Breyer, 1938– . Dem., Mass. 8–14–1994 to –.

* This table represents the composition of the Court to January 20, 1997.

INDEX

References are to Pages

†

1–56662–529–7

90000

9 781566 625296